Webster's ATLAS

and zip code directory

A Merriam-Webster®

G. & C. MERRIAM COMPANY
Springfield, Massachusetts, U.S.A.

Hammond Publications Advisory Board

PRINTED IN THE UNITED STATES OF AMERICA

Library of Congress Cataloging in Publication Data
Main entry under title:
Webster's atlas and zip code directory.
"A Merriam-Webster."
Maps by Hammond Incorporated.
Includes indexes.
1. Atlases. 2. Zip codes — United States — Maps.
I. Hammond Incorporated.
G1019.W35 1976 912 75-45358
ISBN 0-87779-088-4

Contents

GAZETTEER-INDEX OF THE WORLD IV
INTRODUCTION TO MAPS AND INDEXES VI
GLOSSARY OF ABBREVIATIONS VIII

World and Polar Regions

World 1
Arctic Ocean 4
Antarctica 5

Europe

Europe 6
United Kingdom and Ireland 10
Norway, Sweden, Finland, Denmark and Iceland 18
Germany 22
Netherlands, Belgium and Luxembourg 25
France 28
Spain and Portugal 31
Italy 34
Switzerland and Liechtenstein 37
Austria, Czechoslovakia and Hungary 40
Balkan States 43
Poland 46
Union of Soviet Socialist Republics 48

Asia

Asia 54
Near and Middle East 58
Turkey, Syria, Lebanon and Cyprus 61
Israel and Jordan 64
Iran and Iraq 66
Indian Subcontinent and Afghanistan 68
Burma, Thailand, Indochina and Malaya 72
China and Mongolia 75
Japan and Korea 79
Philippines 82
Southeast Asia 84

Pacific Ocean and Australia

Pacific Ocean 86
Australia 88
Western Australia 92
Northern Territory 93
South Australia 94
Queensland 95
New South Wales and Victoria 96
Tasmania 99
New Zealand 100

Africa

Africa 102
Western Africa 106
Northeastern Africa 110
Central Africa 113
Southern Africa 117

South America

South America 120
Venezuela 124
Colombia 126
Peru and Ecuador 128
Guianas 131
Brazil 132
Bolivia 136
Chile 138
Argentina 141
Paraguay and Uruguay 144

North America

North America 146
Mexico 150
Central America 153
West Indies 156

Canada

Canada 162
Newfoundland 166
Nova Scotia and Prince Edward Island 168
New Brunswick 170
Quebec 172
Ontario 175
Manitoba 178
Saskatchewan 180
Alberta 182
British Columbia 184
Yukon and Northwest Territories 186

United States

United States 188
Alabama 193
Alaska 196
Arizona 198
Arkansas 201
California 204
Colorado 207
Connecticut 210
Florida 212
Georgia 215
Hawaii 218
Idaho 220
Illinois 222
Indiana 225
Iowa 228
Kansas 231
Kentucky and Tennessee 234
Louisiana 238
Maine 241
Maryland and Delaware 244
Massachusetts and Rhode Island 247
Michigan 250
Minnesota 253
Mississippi 256
Missouri 259
Montana 262
Nebraska 264
Nevada 266
New Hampshire and Vermont 268
New Jersey 271
New Mexico 274
New York 276
North Carolina 279
North Dakota 282
Ohio 284
Oklahoma 287
Oregon 290
Pennsylvania 293
South Carolina 296
South Dakota 298
Texas 301
Utah 304
Virginia 306
Washington 309
West Virginia 312
Wisconsin 315
Wyoming 318
The Fifty States 320
ZIP CODE DIRECTORY 320A

World Index 321

GEOGRAPHICAL TERMS 345
AIRLINE DISTANCE TABLES 346
WORLD STATISTICS 348
MAP PROJECTIONS 350

Gazetteer-Index of the World

This alphabetical list of grand divisions, countries, states, colonial possessions, etc., gives area, population, capital or chief town, and index references and page numbers on which they are shown on the largest scale. The index reference shows the square on the respective map in which the name of the entry may be located.

Country	Area (Sq. Miles)	Population	Capital or Chief Town	Index Ref.	Plate No.
Afars and Issas, Terr.	8,498	125,050	Djibouti	H 5	111
*Afghanistan	250,000	17,078,263	Kabul	A 2	68
Africa	11,682,000	345,000,000	....	......	102
Alabama, U.S.A.	51,609	3,444,165	Montgomery	......	194
Alaska, U.S.A.	586,412	302,173	Juneau	......	196
*Albania	11,100	2,126,000	Tiranë	E 5	45
Alberta, Canada	255,285	1,627,874	Edmonton	......	182
*Algeria	919,515	13,547,000	Algiers	D 3	106
American Samoa	76	27,159	Pago Pago	J 7	87
Andorra	175	19,000	Andorra la Vella	G 1	33
Angola	481,351	5,430,000	Luanda	C 6	115
Antarctica	5,500,000	....	....	......	5
Antigua	171	63,000	St. Johns	E11	161
*Argentina	1,072,162	23,983,000	Buenos Aires	......	143
Arizona, U.S.A.	113,909	1,772,482	Phoenix	......	198
Arkansas, U.S.A.	53,104	1,923,295	Little Rock	......	202
Ascension	34	1,486	Georgetown	A 5	102
Asia	17,032,000	2,043,997,000	....	......	54
*Australia	2,967,741	12,630,000	Canberra	......	88
*Austria	32,374	7,419,341	Vienna	......	41
Bahama Islands	4,404	168,838	Nassau	C 1	156
*Bahrain	231	207,000	Manama	F 4	59
Bangladesh	55,126	70,000,000	Dacca	G 4	68
*Barbados	166	253,620	Bridgetown	B 8	161
*Belgium	11,779	9,660,154	Brussels	......	27
Bermuda	20	52,000	Hamilton	H 3	156
*Bhutan	18,000	1,034,774	Thimphu	G 3	68
*Bolivia	424,163	4,804,000	La Paz, Sucre	......	136
*Botswana	219,815	629,000	Gaborone	C 4	118
*Brazil	3,284,426	90,840,000	Brasília	......	132
British Columbia, Canada	366,255	2,184,621	Victoria	......	184
British Honduras	8,867	122,000	Belmopan	C 2	154
British Indian Ocean Terr.	30	2,000	Victoria (Seychelles)	L10	54
Brunei	2,226	130,000	Bandar Seri Begawan	E 4	85
*Bulgaria	42,829	8,501,000	Sofia	F 4	45
*Burma	261,789	27,000,000	Rangoon	B 2	72
*Burundi	10,747	3,475,000	Bujumbura	E 4	115
California, U.S.A.	158,693	19,953,134	Sacramento	......	204
*Cambodia	70,898	6,701,000	Phnom Penh	E 4	72
*Cameroon	183,568	5,836,000	Yaoundé	B 2	115
*Canada	3,851,809	21,568,311	Ottawa	......	162
Canal Zone	647	44,198	Balboa Heights	G 6	154
Cape Verde Islands	1,557	250,000	Praia	B 8	106
Cayman Islands	100	10,652	Georgetown	B 3	156
*Central African Republic	240,534	1,518,000	Bangui	C 2	115
Central America	196,928	16,090,000	....	......	154
*Ceylon (Sri Lanka)	25,332	12,300,000	Colombo	E 7	68
*Chad	495,753	3,510,000	Fort-Lamy	C 4	111
Channel Islands	75	117,000	St. Helier	E 7	13
*Chile	292,257	8,834,820	Santiago	......	138
*China (mainland)	3,691,506	740,000,000	Peking	......	77
China (Taiwan)	13,948	14,577,000	Taipei	K 7	77
*Colombia	439,513	21,117,000	Bogotá	......	126
Colorado, U.S.A.	102,247	2,207,259	Denver	......	208
Comoro Is.	838	270,000	Moroni	G 2	118
*Congo, Rep. of	132,046	915,000	Brazzaville	B 4	115
Connecticut, U.S.A.	5,009	3,032,217	Hartford	......	210
Cook Islands	93	20,000	Avarua	K 7	87
*Costa Rica	19,575	1,800,000	San José	E 5	154
*Cuba	44,206	8,553,395	Havana	......	158
*Cyprus	3,473	649,000	Nicosia	E 5	63
*Czechoslovakia	49,370	14,497,000	Prague	......	41
*Dahomey	44,290	2,640,000	Porto-Novo	E 7	106
Delaware, U.S.A.	2,057	548,104	Dover	......	245
*Denmark	16,625	4,912,865	Copenhagen	......	21
District of Columbia, U.S.A.	67	756,510	Washington	F 5	245
Dominica	290	70,302	Roseau	E 7	161
*Dominican Republic	18,704	4,011,589	Santo Domingo	......	158
*Ecuador	109,483	6,144,000	Quito	......	128
*Egypt	386,100	33,329,000	Cairo	E 2	111
*El Salvador	8,260	3,418,455	San Salvador	C 4	154
England, U.K.	50,327	46,102,300	London	......	13
*Equatorial Guinea	10,832	286,000	Santa Isabel	A 3	115
*Ethiopia	471,776	24,764,000	Addis Ababa	G 5	111
Europe	4,063,000	652,000,000	....	......	7
Faerøe Islands, Den.	540	38,000	Tórshavn	B 2	21
Falkland Islands	4,618	2,000	Stanley	E 8	120
*Fiji	7,015	519,000	Suva	H 8	87
*Finland	130,128	4,706,000	Helsinki	......	18
Florida, U.S.A.	58,560	6,789,443	Tallahassee	......	212
*France	212,841	50,770,000	Paris	......	28
French Guiana	35,135	48,000	Cayenne	E 3	131
French Polynesia	1,544	109,000	Papeete	L 8	87
*Gabon	103,346	500,000	Libreville	B 4	115
*Gambia	4,003	357,000	Bathurst	A 6	106
Georgia, U.S.A.	58,876	4,589,575	Atlanta	......	216
Germany, East (German Democratic Republic)	41,814	17,117.000	Berlin	......	22
Germany, West (Federal Republic of)	95,959	61,194,600	Bonn	......	22
*Ghana	91,843	8,545,561	Accra	D 7	106
Gibraltar	2	27,000	Gibraltar	D 4	33
Gilbert and Ellice Is.	369	55,185	Bairiki	J 6	87
*Great Britain and Northern Ireland (United Kingdom)	94,214	55,534,000	London	......	10
*Greece	50,548	8,838,000	Athens	F 6	45
Greenland	840,000	47,000	Godthåb	B12	4
Grenada	133	105,000	St. George's	D 9	161
Guadeloupe & Dependencies	687	324,000	Basse-Terre	A 5	161
Guam	209	84,996	Agaña	F 4	87
*Guatemala	42,042	5,200,000	Guatemala	B 3	154
*Guinea	94,925	3,890,000	Conakry	B 6	106
*Guyana	83,000	763,000	Georgetown	B 3	131
*Haiti	10,694	4,867,190	Port-au-Prince	......	158
Hawaii, U.S.A.	6,450	769,913	Honolulu	......	218
*Holland (Netherlands)	13,958	13,077,000	Amsterdam, The Hague	......	27
*Honduras	43,277	2,495,000	Tegucigalpa	D 3	154
Hong Kong	398	4,089,000	Victoria	H 7	77
*Hungary	35,915	10,315,597	Budapest	......	41
*Iceland	39,768	204,578	Reykjavík	B 1	21
Idaho, U.S.A.	83,557	713,008	Boise	......	220
Illinois, U.S.A.	56,400	11,113,976	Springfield	......	222
*India	1,261,483	546,955,945	New Delhi	......	68
Indiana, U.S.A.	36,291	5,193,669	Indianapolis	......	227
*Indonesia	763,264	119,572,000	Djakarta	......	85
Iowa, U.S.A.	56,290	2,825,041	Des Moines	......	229
*Iran	636,293	28,448,000	Tehran	......	66
*Iraq	167,924	9,431,000	Baghdad	......	66
*Ireland	26,600	2,944,000	Dublin	......	17
Ireland, Northern, U.K.	5,459	1,512,500	Belfast	......	17
Isle of Man, U.K.	227	50,000	Douglas	C 3	13
*Israel	7,993	2,911,000	Jerusalem	......	65
*Italy	116,303	54,504,000	Rome	......	34
*Ivory Coast	124,503	4,800,000	Abidjan	C 7	106
*Jamaica	4,411	1,972,000	Kingston	......	158
*Japan	143,622	104,665,171	Tokyo	......	81
*Jordan	37,297	2,300,000	Amman	......	65
Kansas, U.S.A.	82,264	2,249,071	Topeka	......	232
Kentucky, U.S.A.	40,395	3,219,311	Frankfort	......	237
*Kenya	224,902	10,880,200	Nairobi	G 3	115
Korea, North	46,540	13,300,000	P'yŏngyang	......	81
Korea, South	38,452	31,683,000	Seoul	......	81
*Kuwait	6,177	733,196	Al Kuwait	E 4	59
*Laos	90,428	2,900,000	Vientiane	D 3	72
*Lebanon	4,015	2,800,000	Beirut	F 6	63
*Lesotho	11,716	930,000	Maseru	D 5	118
*Liberia	43,000	1,200,000	Monrovia	C 7	106
*Libya	679,359	1,900,000	Tripoli	C 2	111
Liechtenstein	61	21,000	Vaduz	J 2	39
Louisiana, U.S.A.	48,523	3,643,180	Baton Rouge	......	238
*Luxembourg	999	339,000	Luxembourg	J 9	27

*Members of the United Nations

GAZETTEER-INDEX OF THE WORLD

Country	Area (Sq. Miles)	Population	Capital or Chief Town	Index Ref.	Plate No.
Macao	6.2	292,000	Macao	H 7	77
Maine, U.S.A.	33,215	993,663	Augusta	......	242
*Malagasy Republic	226,657	7,011,563	Tananarive	H 3	118
*Malawi	45,483	4,530,000	Zomba	F 6	115
Malaya, Malaysia	50,670	9,000,000	Kuala Lumpur	D 6	72
*Malaysia	128,308	10,583,000	Kuala Lumpur	......	72,85
*Maldives	115	110,770	Malé	L 9	54
*Mali	463,948	4,929,000	Bamako	C 6	106
*Malta	122	321,000	Valletta	E 7	34
Manitoba, Canada	251,000	988,247	Winnipeg	......	179
Martinique	425	332,000	Fort-de-France	D 5	161
Maryland, U.S.A.	10,577	3,922,399	Annapolis	......	245
Massachusetts, U.S.A.	8,257	5,689,170	Boston	......	249
*Mauritania	397,954	1,140,000	Nouakchott	B 5	106
*Mauritius	787	823,000	Port Louis	G 5	118
*Mexico	761,601	48,313,438	Mexico City	......	150
Michigan, U.S.A.	58,216	8,875,083	Lansing	......	250
Midway Islands	2	2,220	....	J 3	87
Minnesota, U.S.A.	84,068	3,805,069	St. Paul	......	254
Mississippi, U.S.A.	47,716	2,216,912	Jackson	......	256
Missouri, U.S.A.	69,686	4,677,399	Jefferson City	......	261
Monaco	368 acres	23,035	Monaco	G 6	28
*Mongolia	604,090	1,300,000	Ulan Bator	......	77
Montana, U.S.A.	147,138	694,409	Helena	......	262
Montserrat	38	12,300	Plymouth	F 3	156
*Morocco	172,413	15,577,000	Rabat	C 2	106
Mozambique	302,328	7,376,000	Lourenço Marques	E 4	118
Nauru	8.2	7,000	Uaboe dist.	G 6	87
Nebraska, U.S.A.	77,227	1,483,791	Lincoln	......	264
*Nepal	54,362	10,845,000	Kathmandu	E 3	68
*Netherlands	13,958	13,077,000	Amsterdam, The Hague	......	27
Netnerlands Antilles	390	220,000	Willemstad	E 4	156
Nevada, U.S.A.	110,540	488,738	Carson City	......	266
New Brunswick, Canada	28,354	634,557	Fredericton	......	170
New Caledonia	7,335	100,579	Nouméa	G 8	87
Newfoundland, Canada	156,185	522,104	St. John's	......	166
New Guinea, Terr. of (Aust. Trust.)	92,160	1,722,572	Port Moresby	......	85,87
New Hampshire, U.S.A.	9,304	737,681	Concord	......	268
New Hebrides	5,700	80,000	Vila	G 7	87
New Jersey, U.S.A.	7,836	7,168,164	Trenton	......	273
New Mexico, U.S.A.	121,666	1,016,000	Santa Fe	......	274
New York, U.S.A.	49,576	18,241,266	Albany	......	276
*New Zealand	103,736	2,815,000	Wellington	......	100
*Nicaragua	45,698	1,984,000	Managua	D 4	154
*Niger	489,189	4,016,000	Niamey	F 5	106
*Nigeria	356,669	66,174,000	Lagos	F 6	106
Niue	100	5,323	Alofi	K 7	87
North America	9,363,000	314,000,000	....	......	146
North Carolina, U.S.A.	52,586	5,082,059	Raleigh	......	281
North Dakota, U.S.A.	70,665	617,761	Bismarck	......	282
Northern Ireland, U.K.	5,459	1,512,500	Belfast	......	17
Northwest Territories, Canada	1,304,903	34,807	Yellowknife	......	187
*Norway	125,181	3,893,000	Oslo	......	18
Nova Scotia, Canada	21,425	788,960	Halifax	......	168
Ohio, U.S.A.	41,222	10,652,017	Columbus	......	284
Oklahoma, U.S.A.	69,919	2,559,253	Oklahoma City	......	288
*Oman	82,000	565,000	Muscat	G 5	59
Ontario, Canada	412,582	7,703,106	Toronto	......	175,177
Oregon, U.S.A.	96,981	2,091,385	Salem	......	291
Pacific Islands, U.S. Trust Terr. of the	687	94,900	Garapan	F 5	87
*Pakistan	310,403	60,000,000	Islamabad	......	68
*Panama	29,209	1,425,343	Panamá	G 6	154
Papua, Australia	86,100	648,000	Port Moresby	......	85,87
*Paraguay	157,047	2,314,000	Asunción	......	144
Pennsylvania, U.S.A.	45,333	11,793,909	Harrisburg	......	294
*Persia (Iran)	636,293	28,448,000	Tehran	......	66
*Peru	496,222	13,586,300	Lima	......	128
*Philippines	115,707	39,079,000	Quezon City	......	82
Pitcairn Islands	18	74	Adamstown	O 8	87
*Poland	120,664	32,889,000	Warsaw	......	47
*Portugal	35,510	9,560,000	Lisbon	......	33
Portuguese Guinea	13,948	530,000	Bissau	A 6	106
Portuguese Timor	5,762	590,000	Dili	H 7	85
Prince Edward Island, Canada	2,184	111,641	Charlottetown	E 2	168
Puerto Rico	3,435	2,712,033	San Juan	......	161
*Qatar	8,500	100,000	Doha	F 4	59
Québec, Canada	594,860	6,027,764	Québec	......	172,174
Réunion	970	436,000	St-Denis	F 5	118
Rhode Island, U.S.A.	1,214	949,723	Providence	......	249
Rhodesia	150,332	5,310,000	Salisbury	D 3	118
*Rumania	91,699	20,394,000	Bucharest	F 3	45

Country	Area (Sq. Miles)	Population	Capital or Chief Town	Index Ref.	Plate No.
*Rwanda	10,169	3,500,000	Kigali	E 4	115
Sabah, Malaysia	29,388	633,000	Kota Kinabalu	F 4	85
St. Christopher-Nevis-Anguilla	138	56,000	Basseterre	......	156,161
St. Helena	47	4,707	Jamestown	B 6	102
St. Lucia	238	110,000	Castries	G 6	161
St-Pierre and Miquelon	93.5	5,235	St-Pierre	C 4	166
St. Vincent	150	89,129	Kingstown	A 8	161
San Marino	23.4	19,000	San Marino	D 3	34
São Tomé e Príncipe	372	66,000	São Tomé	F 8	106
Sarawak, Malaysia	48,250	950,000	Kuching	E 5	85
Saskatchewan, Canada	251,700	926,242	Regina	......	181
*Saudi Arabia	920,000	7,200,000	Riyadh, Mecca	D 4	59
Scotland, U.K.	30,411	5,194,000	Edinburgh	......	15
*Senegal	75,750	3,780,000	Dakar	A 5	106
Seychelles	91	51,396	Victoria	H 5	118
*Siam (Thailand)	198,456	35,448,000	Bangkok	D 3	72
*Sierra Leone	27,925	2,512,000	Freetown	B 7	106
*Singapore	226	2,034,000	Singapore	F 6	72
Solomon Islands Prot.	10,983	161,525	Honiara	F 6	87
*Somalia	246,200	2,730,000	Mogadishu	H 3	115
*South Africa	471,663	21,282,000	Cape Town, Pretoria	C 5	118
South America	6,875,000	186,000,000	....	......	120
South Carolina, U.S.A.	31,055	2,590,516	Columbia	......	296
South Dakota, U.S.A.	77,047	666,257	Pierre	......	298
South-West Africa	317,838	615,000	Windhoek	B 3	118
*Spain	194,896	33,290,000	Madrid	......	33
Spanish Sahara, Spain	102,702	63,000	El Aaiún	B 4	106
*Sri Lanka (Ceylon)	25,332	12,300,000	Colombo	E 7	68
*Sudan	967,495	15,312,000	Khartoum	E 4	111
Surinam	55,144	389,000	Paramaribo	C 3	131
*Swaziland	6,704	411,879	Mbabane	E 5	118
*Sweden	173,665	7,978,000	Stockholm	......	18
Switzerland	15,941	6,230,000	Bern	......	39
*Syria	71,498	5,866,000	Damascus	G 5	63
*Tanzania	362,819	12,896,000	Dar es Salaam	F 5	115
Tennessee, U.S.A.	42,244	3,924,164	Nashville	......	237
Texas, U.S.A.	267,339	11,196,730	Austin	......	302
*Thailand	198,456	35,448,000	Bangkok	D 3	72
*Togo	21,853	2,004,711	Lomé	E 7	106
Tokelau Islands	3.9	2,000	Fakaofo	J 6	87
Tonga	270	83,000	Nuku'alofa	J 8	87
*Trinidad and Tobago	1,980	1,040,000	Port of Spain	A10	161
Tristan da Cunha	40	269	Edinburgh	G10	2
*Tunisia	63,378	5,027,000	Tunis	F 2	106
*Turkey	301,381	34,375,000	Ankara	......	63
Turks and Caicos Is.	166	6,000	Cockburn Town	D 2	156
*Uganda	92,674	9,764,000	Kampala	F 3	115
*Ukrainian S.S.R., U.S.S.R.	232,046	47,126,517	Kiev	D 5	52
*Union of Soviet Socialist Republics	8,649,498	241,748,000	Moscow	......	48,52
*United Arab Emirates	32,278	179,126	Abu Dhabi	F 5	58
*United Kingdom	94,214	55,534,000	London	......	10
*United States of America, land land and water	3,554,609 3,615,123	203,235,298	Washington, D.C.	......	188
*Upper Volta	105,841	5,330,000	Ouagadougou	D 6	106
*Uruguay	72,172	2,900,000	Montevideo	......	145
Utah, U.S.A.	84,916	1,059,273	Salt Lake City	......	304
Vatican City	109 acres	1,000	....	B 6	34
*Venezuela	352,143	10,398,907	Caracas	......	124
Vermont, U.S.A.	9,609	444,732	Montpelier	......	268
Vietnam, North	61,293	21,340,000	Hanoi	E 3	72
Vietnam, South	66,897	16,543,434	Saigon	F 4	72
Virginia, U.S.A.	40,817	4,648,494	Richmond	......	307
Virgin Islands, British	59	10,484	Road Town	H 1	156
Virgin Islands, U.S.A.	133	62,468	Charlotte Amalie	......	161
Wake Island, U.S.A.	2.5	1,647	....	G 4	87
Wales, U.K.	8,017	2,724,540	Cardiff	......	13
Washington, U.S.A.	68,192	3,409,169	Olympia	......	310
Western Samoa	1,133	139,810	Apia	J 7	87
West Virginia, U.S.A.	24,181	1,744,237	Charleston	......	312
*White Russian S.S.R. (Byelorussian S.S.R.), U.S.S.R.	80,154	9,002,338	Minsk	C 4	52
Wisconsin, U.S.A.	56,154	4,417,933	Madison	......	317
World	57,491,000	3,632,000,000	....	......	1,2
Wyoming, U.S.A.	97,914	332,416	Cheyenne	......	319
*Yemen Arab Republic	75,000	5,000,000	San'a	D 7	59
*Yemen, Peoples Dem. Rep. of	111,075	1,220,000	Aden	E 7	59
*Yugoslavia	98,766	20,586,000	Belgrade	C 3	45
Yukon Territory, Canada	207,076	18,388	Whitehorse	E 3	187
*Zaire	905,563	21,637,876	Kinshasa	D 4	115
*Zambia	290,586	4,056,995	Lusaka	E 7	115

Introduction to the Maps and Indexes

The following notes have been added to aid the reader in making the best use of this atlas. Though he may be familiar with maps and map indexes, the publisher believes that a quick review of the material below will add to his enjoyment of this reference work.

Arrangement — The Plan of the Atlas. The atlas has been designed with maximum convenience for the user as its objective. All geographically related information pertaining to a country or region appears on adjacent pages, eliminating the task of searching throughout the entire volume for data on a given area. Thus, the reader will find, conveniently assembled, political, topographic, economic and special maps of a political area or region, accompanied by detailed map indexes, statistical data, and illustrations of the national flags of the area.

The sequence of country units in this American-designed atlas is international in arrangement. Units on the world as a whole are followed by a section on the polar regions which, in turn, is followed by pages devoted to Europe and its countries. Every continent map is accompanied by special population distribution, climatic and vegetation maps of that continent. Following the maps of the European continent and its countries, the geographic sequence plan proceeds as follows: Asia, the Pacific and Australia, Africa, South America, North America, and ends with detailed coverage on the United States.

Political Maps — The Primary Reference Tool. The most detailed maps in each country unit are the *political maps.* It is our feeling that the reader is likely to refer to these maps more often than to any other in the book when confronted by such questions as — Where? How big? What is it near? Answering these common queries is the function of the political maps. Each political map stresses *political* phenomena — countries, internal political divisions, boundaries, cities and towns. The major political unit or units, shown on the map, are banded in distinctive colors for easy identification and delineation. First-order political subdivisions (states, provinces, counties on the state maps) are shown, scale permitting.

The reader is advised to make use of the *legend* appearing under the title on each political map. Map *symbols,* the special "language" of maps, are explained in the legend. Each variety of dot, circle, star or interrupted line has a special meaning which should be clearly understood by the user so that he may interpret the map data correctly.

Each country has been portrayed at a *scale* commensurate with its political, areal, economic or tourist importance. In certain cases, a whole map unit may be devoted to a single nation if that nation is considered to be of prime interest to most atlas users. In other cases, several nations will be shown on a single map if, as separate entities, they are of lesser relative importance. Areas of dense settlement and important significance within a country have been enlarged and portrayed in inset maps inserted on the margins of the main map. The reader is advised to refer to the linear or "bar" scale appearing on each map or map inset in order to ascertain the basic scale of the map or to determine the distance between points.

The *projection* system used for each map is noted near the title of the map. Map projections are the special graphic systems used by cartographers to render the curved three-dimensional surface of the globe on a flat surface. Optimum map projections determined by the attributes of the area have been used by the publishers for each map in the atlas.

A word here as to the choice of place names on the maps. Throughout the atlas names appear, with a few exceptions, in their local official spellings. However, conventional Anglicized spellings are used for major geographical divisions and for towns and topographic features for which English forms exist; i.e., "Spain" instead of "España" or "Munich" instead of "München." Names of this type are normally followed by the local official spelling in parentheses. As an aid to the user the indexes are cross-referenced for all current and most former spellings of such names.

Names of cities and towns in the United States follow the forms listed in the *Directory of Post Offices* of the United States Postal Service. Domestic physical names follow the decisions of the Board on Geographic Names, U.S. Department of the Interior, and of various state geographic name boards.

It is the belief of the publishers that the boundaries shown in a general reference atlas should reflect current geographic and political realities. This policy has been followed consistently in the atlas. The presentation of *de facto* boundaries in cases of territorial dispute between various nations does not imply the political endorsement of such boundaries by the publisher, but simply the honest representation of boundaries as they exist at the time of the printing of the atlas maps.

Indexes — Pinpointing a Location. Each political map is accompanied by a comprehensive index of the place names appearing on the map. If you are unfamiliar with the location of a particular geographical place and wish to find its position within the confines of the subject area of the map, consult the map index as your first step. The name of the feature sought will be found in its proper alphabetical sequence with a key reference letter-number combination corresponding to its location on the map. After noting the key reference letter-number combination for the place name, turn to the map. The place name will be found within the square formed by the two lines of latitude and the two lines of longitude which enclose the co-ordinates — i.e., the marginal letters and numbers. The diagram below illustrates the system of indexing.

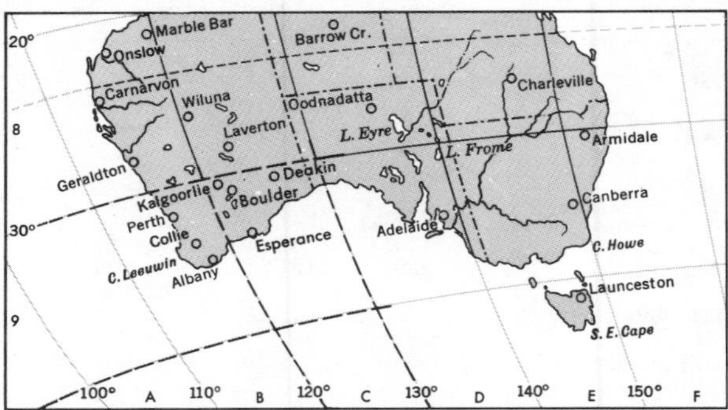

In the case of maps consisting entirely of insets, the place name is found near the intersection point of the imaginary lines connecting the co-ordinates at right angles. See below.

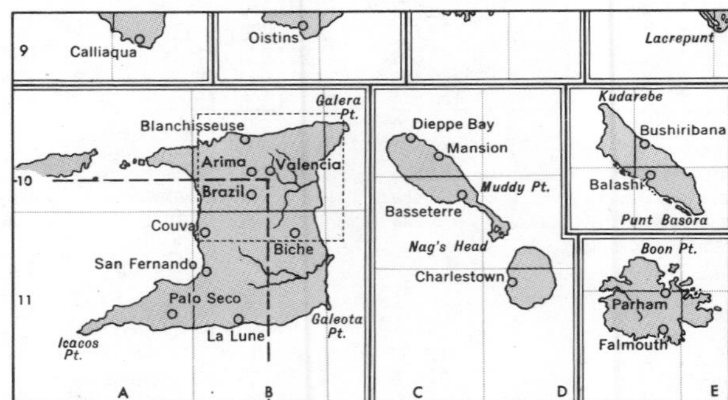

Where space on the map has not permitted giving the complete form of the place name, the complete form is shown in the index. Where a place is known by more than one name or by various spellings of the same name, the different forms have been included in the index. Physical features are listed under their proper names and not according to their generic terms; that is to say, Rio Negro will be found under Negro and not under Rio Negro. On the other hand, Rio Grande will be found under Rio Grande. Accompanying most index entries for cities and towns, and for other political units, are *population figures* for the particular entries. The large number of population figures in the atlas makes this work one of the most comprehensive statistical sources available to the public today. The population figures have been taken from the latest official censuses and estimates of the various nations.

Population and area figures for countries and major political units are listed in bold type *fact lists* on the margins of the indexes. In addition, the capital, largest city, highest point, monetary unit, principal languages and the prevailing religions of the country concerned are also listed. The Gazetteer-Index of the World on the preceding pages provides a quick reference index for countries and other important areas. Though population and area figures for each major unit area also found in the map section, the Gazetteer-Index provides a conveniently arranged statistical comparison contained in two pages.

All index entries for cities and towns in the United States are preceded by a five-digit postal ZIP code number applying to the community. This useful feature permits the reader to address his mail so that it will be routed and delivered more efficiently and quickly by the U.S. Postal Service. A dagger (†) designates those places that do not possess a post office. The ZIP code number listed in such cases refers to that of the nearest post office. An asterisk (*) marks those larger cities which are divided into multiple ZIP code areas. Using the single ZIP code number listed in such cases will direct your letter to the proper city with dispatch. However, if the precise ZIP code number of the address within the city is needed, it is suggested that the reader refer to the latest National ZIP Code Directory at his local post office. This detailed guide lists every street in a multiple ZIP code city with the proper ZIP code for the street.

Relief Maps. Accompanying each political map is a relief map of the area. The purpose of the relief map is to illustrate the surface configuration (TOPOGRAPHY) of the region. A shading technique in color simulates the relative ruggedness of the terrain — plains, plateaus, valleys, hills and mountains. Graded colors, ranging from greens for lowlands, yellows for intermediate elevations to browns in the highlands, indicate the height above sea level of each part of the land. A vertical scale at the margin of the map shows the approximate height in meters and feet represented by each color.

Economic Maps — Agriculture, Industry and Resources. One of the most interesting features that will be found in each country unit is the economic map. From this map one can determine the basic activities of a nation as expressed through its economy. A perusal of the map yields a full understanding of the area's economic geography and natural resources.

The agricultural economy is manifested in two ways: color bands and commodity names. The color bands express broad categories of *dominant land use*, such as, cereal belts, forest lands, livestock range lands, nonagricultural wastes. The red commodity names, on the other hand, pinpoint the areas of production of *specific* crops; i.e., wheat, cotton, sugar beets, etc.

Major mineral occurrences are denoted by standard letter symbols appearing in blue. The relative size of the letter symbols signifies the relative importance of the deposit.

The manufacturing sector of the economy is presented by means of diagonal line patterns expressing the various *industrial areas* of consequence within a country. The products of each major industrial area are listed in boxes at the margin of the map.

The fishing industry is represented by names of commercial fish species appearing offshore in blue letters. Major waterpower sites are designated by blue symbols.

The publishers have tried to make this work the most comprehensive and useful atlas available, and it is hoped that it will prove a valuable reference work. Any constructive suggestions from the reader will be welcomed.

Sources and Acknowledgments

A multitude of sources goes into the making of a large-scale reference work such as this. To list them all would take many pages and would consume space better devoted to the maps and reference materials themselves. However, certain general sources were very useful in preparing this work and are listed below.

STATISTICAL OFFICE OF THE UNITED NATIONS.
Demographic Yearbook. New York. Issued annually.

STATISTICAL OFFICE OF THE UNITED NATIONS.
Statistical Yearbook. New York. Issued annually.

THE GEOGRAPHER, U.S. DEPARTMENT OF STATE.
International Boundary Study papers. Washington. Various dates.

THE GEOGRAPHER, U.S. DEPARTMENT OF STATE.
Geographic Notes. Washington. Various dates.

UNITED STATES BOARD ON GEOGRAPHIC NAMES.
Decisions on Geographic Names in the United States. Washington. Various dates.

UNITED STATES BOARD ON GEOGRAPHIC NAMES.
Official Standard Names Gazetteers. Washington. Various dates.

CANADIAN PERMANENT COMMITTEE ON GEOGRAPHICAL NAMES.
Gazetteer of Canada series. Ottawa. Various dates.

UNITED STATES POSTAL SERVICE.
Directory of Post Offices. Washington. 1970.

UNITED STATES POSTAL SERVICE.
National Zip Code Directory. Washington. 1970-1971.

UNITED STATES POSTAL SERVICE.
Postal Bulletin. Washington. Issued weekly.

UNITED STATES DEPARTMENT OF THE INTERIOR. BUREAU OF MINES.
Minerals Yearbook. 4 vols. Washington. Various dates.

UNITED STATES GEOLOGICAL SURVEY.
Elevations and distances in the United States. Washington. 1969.

UNITED STATES DEPARTMENT OF COMMERCE. JOINT PUBLICATIONS RESEARCH SERVICE.
JPRS reports dealing with foreign geography. Washington. Various dates.

CARTACTUAL.
Cartactual — Topical Map Service. Budapest. Issued bi-monthly.

AMERICAN GEOGRAPHICAL SOCIETY.
Focus. New York. Issued ten times a year.

A sample list of sources used for specific countries follows:

Algeria
COMMISSARIAT NATIONAL AU RECENSEMENT DE LA POPULATION.
Résultats Préliminaires du Recensement Général de la Population Effectué en 1966. Oran.

Barbados
BARBADOS STATISTICAL SERVICE.
1970 Census. St. Michael.

Chile
INSTITUTO NACIONAL DE ESTADÍSTICAS.
XIV Censo Nacional de Población y III de Vivienda. 1970. Santiago.

Dominican Republic
OFICINA NACIONAL DE ESTADÍSTICA.
Censo Nacional de Población y Habitación. 9 y 10 Enero de 1970. Santo Domingo.

France
INSTITUT NATIONAL DE LA STATISTIQUE ET DES ÉTUDES ÉCONOMIQUES.
Recensement de 1968. Population de la France. Paris.

Ghana
CENSUS OFFICE.
1970 Population Census of Ghana. Accra.

Iran
IRANIAN STATISTICAL CENTER.
National Census of Population and Housing, 1966. Tehran.

Ireland
THE CENTRAL STATISTICS OFFICE.
Census of Population of Ireland 1966. Dublin.

Kenya
MINISTRY OF ECONOMIC PLANNING AND DEVELOPMENT. STATISTICS DIVISION.
Provisional Results of the 1969 Population Census. Nairobi.

Kuwait
MINISTRY OF GUIDANCE & INFORMATION.
Population Census 1970. Kuwait.

Mexico
DIRECCIÓN GENERAL DE ESTADÍSTICA.
IX Censo General de Población 1970. México, D.F.

New Caledonia
INSTITUT NATIONAL DE LA STATISTIQUE ET DES ÉTUDES ÉCONOMIQUES (France).
Recensement de 1969. Paris.

Panama
DIRECCIÓN DE ESTADÍSTICA Y CENSO.
Censos Nacionales de 1970. Panamá.

Rhodesia
CENTRAL STATISTICAL OFFICE.
1969 Population Censuses. Salisbury.

Tanzania
CENTRAL STATISTICAL BUREAU.
1967 Population Census. Dar es Salaam.

Togo
DIRECTION DE LA STATISTIQUE.
Résultats Provisoires du Recensement Général de la Population 1970. Lomé.

U.S.S.R.
CENTRAL STATISTICAL ADMINISTRATION.
Preliminary Results of the All-Union Census of Population 1970. Moscow.

United States
BUREAU OF THE CENSUS.
1970 Census of Population. Washington.

CORPS OF ENGINEERS.
Reservoir status lists and maps. Various districts.

Zaire
MINISTÈRE DE L'INTÉRIEUR ET DES AFFAIRES COUTUMIÈRES.
Recensement Général de la Population 1970. Kinshasa.

Zambia
CENTRAL STATISTICAL OFFICE.
Population and Housing Census — 1969. Lusaka.

Glossary of Abbreviations

A

A. A. F. — Army Air Field
Acad. — Academy
A. C. T. — Australian Capital Territory
adm. — administration; administrative
adm. city-co. — administrative city-county
A. F. B. — Air Force Base
Afgh., Afghan. — Afghanistan
Afr. — Africa
A. & I. — Terr. of the Afars and Issas
Ala. — Alabama
Alb. — Albania
Alg. — Algeria
Alta. — Alberta
Amer. — American
Amer. Samoa — American Samoa
And. — Andorra
Ant. — Antarctica
Ar. — Arabia
arch. — archipelago
Arg. — Argentina
Ariz. — Arizona
Ark. — Arkansas
A. S. S. R. — Autonomous Soviet Socialist Republic
Austr., Austral. — Australian, Australia
aut. — autonomous
Aut. Obl. — Autonomous Oblast
aut. prov. — autonomous province

B

B. — bay
Bah. Is. — Bahama Islands
Barb. — Barbados
Battlef. — Battlefield
Bch. — Beach
Belg. — Belgium
Berm. — Bermuda
Bol. — Bolivia
Bots. — Botswana
Br. — Branch
Br. — British
Braz. — Brazil
Br. Col. — British Columbia
Br. Ind. Oc. Terr. — British Indian Ocean Territory
Bulg. — Bulgaria

C

C. — cape
Calif. — California
can. — canal
cap. — capital
Cent. Afr. Rep. — Central African Republic
Cent. Amer. — Central America
C. G. Sta. — Coast Guard Station
C. H. — Court House
chan. — channel
Chan. Is. — Channel Islands
Chem. Ctr. — Chemical Center
co. — county
C. of G. H. — Cape of Good Hope
Col. — Colombia
Colo. — Colorado
comm. — commissary
Conn. — Connecticut
cont. — continent
cord. — cordillera (mountain range)
C. Rica — Costa Rica
C. S. — County Seat
C. Verde Is. — Cape Verde Islands
Cy. — City
C. Z. — Canal Zone
Czech. — Czechoslovakia

D

D. C. — District of Columbia
Del. — Delaware
Dem. — Democratic
Den. — Denmark
depr. — depression
dept. — department
des. — desert
dist., dist's — district, districts
div. — division
Dom. Rep. — Dominican Republic
dry riv. — dry river

E

E. — East
Ec., Ecua. — Ecuador
E. Ger. — East Germany
elec. div. — electoral division
El Salv. — El Salvador
Eng. — England
Eq. Guin. — Equatorial Guinea
escarp. — escarpment
est. — estuary
Eth. — Ethiopia

F

Falk. Is. — Falkland Islands
Fin. — Finland
Fk., Fks. — Fork, Forks
Fla. — Florida
for. — forest
Fr. — France, French
Fr. Gui. — French Guiana
Fr. Poly. — French Polynesia
Ft. — Fort

G

G. — gulf
Ga. — Georgia
Game Res. — Game Reserve
Ger. — Germany
geys. — geyser
Gibr. — Gibraltar
Gilb. & Ell. Is. — Gilbert and Ellice Islands
glac. — glacier
gov. — governorate
Gr. — Group
Greenl. — Greenland
Gt. Brit. — Great Britain
Guad. — Guadeloupe
Guat. — Guatemala
Guy. — Guyana

H

har., harb., hbr. — harbor
hd. — head
highl. — highland, highlands
Hist. — Historic, Historical
Hond. — Honduras
Hts. — Heights
Hung. — Hungary

I

i., isl., — island, isle
Ice., Icel. — Iceland
Ida. — Idaho
Ill. — Illinois
Ind. — Indiana
ind. city — independent city
Indon. — Indonesia
Ind. Res. — Indian Reservation
int. div. — internal division
inten. — intendency
interm. str. — intermittent stream
Int'l — International
Ire. — Ireland
is., isls. — islands
Isr. — Israel
isth. — isthmus

J

Jam. — Jamaica
Jct. — Junction

K

Kans. — Kansas
Ky. — Kentucky

L

L. — Lake, Loch, Lough
La. — Louisiana
Lab. — Laboratory
lag. — lagoon
Ld. — Land
Leb. — Lebanon
Les. — Lesotho
Liecht. — Liechtenstein
Lux. — Luxembourg

M

Malag. Rep. — Malagasy Republic
Man. — Manitoba
Mart. — Martinique
Mass. — Massachusetts
Maur. — Mauritania
Md. — Maryland
met. area — metropolitan area
Mex. — Mexico
Mich. — Michigan
Minn. — Minnesota
Miss. — Mississippi
Mo. — Missouri
Mon. — Monument
Mong. — Mongolia
Mont. — Montana
Mor. — Morocco
Moz., Mozamb. — Mozambique
mt. — mount
mtn. — mountain

N

N., No. — North, Northern
N. Amer. — North America
N. A. S. — Naval Air Station
Nat'l — National
Nat'l Cem. — National Cemetery
Nat'l Mem. Park — National Memorial Park
Nat'l Mil. Park — National Military Park
Nat'l Pkwy. — National Parkway
Nav. Base — Naval Base
Nav. Sta. — Naval Station
N. B., N. Br. — New Brunswick
N. C. — North Carolina
N. Dak. — North Dakota
Nebr. — Nebraska
Neth. — Netherlands
Neth. Ant. — Netherlands Antilles
Nev. — Nevada
New Cal. — New Caledonia
Newf. — Newfoundland
New Hebr. — New Hebrides
N. H. — New Hampshire
Nic. — Nicaragua
N. Ire. — Northern Ireland
N. J. — New Jersey
N. Mex. — New Mexico
Nor. — Norway, Norwegian
No. Terr. — Northern Territory (Australia)
N. S. — Nova Scotia
N. S. W. — New South Wales
N. W. T. — Northwest Territories (Canada)
N. Y. — New York
N. Z. — New Zealand

O

Obl. — Oblast
O. F. S. — Orange Free State
Okla. — Oklahoma
Okr. — Okrug
Ont. — Ontario
Ord. Depot — Ordnance Depot
Oreg. — Oregon

P

Pa. — Pennsylvania
Pac. — Pacific
Pac. Is. — Pacific Islands, Territory of the
Pak. — Pakistan
Pan. — Panama
Par. — Paraguay
par. — parish
passg. — passage
P.D.R. Yemen — Peoples Democratic Republic of Yemen
P. E. I. — Prince Edward Island
pen. — peninsula
Phil., Phil. Is. — Philippines
Pk. — Park
pk. — peak
plat. — plateau
Port. — Portugal, Portuguese
P. Rico — Puerto Rico
pref. — prefecture
prom. — promontory
prov. — province, provincial
prov. dist. — provincial district
pt. — point

Q

Que. — Québec
Queens. — Queensland

R

R. — River
ra. — range
Rec., Recr. — Recreation, Recreational
reg. — region
Rep. — Republic
Rep. of Congo — Republic of Congo
res. — reservoir
Res. — Reservation, Reserve
Rhod. — Rhodesia
R. I. — Rhode Island
riv. — river
Rum. — Rumania

S

S. — South
Sa. — Sierra, Serra
S. Afr., S. Africa — South Africa
salt dep. — salt deposit
salt des. — salt desert
S. Amer. — South America
São T. & Pr. — São Tomé and Príncipe
Sask. — Saskatchewan
Saudi Ar. — Saudi Arabia
S. Aust., S. Austral. — South Australia
S. C. — South Carolina
Scot. — Scotland
Sd. — Sound
S. Dak. — South Dakota
Sen. — Senegal
sen. dist. — senatorial district
Seych. — Seychelles
S. F. S. R. — Soviet Federated Socialist Republic
Sing. — Singapore
S. Leone — Sierra Leone
S. Marino — San Marino
Sol. Is. Prot. — Solomon Islands Protectorate, British
Sp. — Spanish
Spr., Sprs. — Spring, Springs
S. S. R. — Soviet Socialist Republic
St., Ste. — Saint, Sainte
Sta. — Station
St. Chr.-N.-A. — Saint Christopher-Nevis-Anguilla
St. P. & M. — Saint Pierre and Miquelon
str., strs. — strait, straits
Sur. — Surinam
S. W. Afr. — South-West Africa
Swaz. — Swaziland
Switz. — Switzerland

T

Tanz. — Tanzania
Tas. — Tasmania
Tenn. — Tennessee
terr., terrs. — territory, territories
Terr. N. G. — New Guinea, Territory of
Tex. — Texas
Thai. — Thailand
Trin. & Tob. — Trinidad and Tobago
Tun. — Tunisia
twp. — township

U

U.A.E. — Union of (United) Arab Emirates
U. K. — United Kingdom
Upp. Volta — Upper Volta
urb. area — urban area
Urug. — Uruguay
U. S. — United States
U. S. S. R. — Union of Soviet Socialist Republics

V

Va. — Virginia
Vall. — Valley
Ven., Venez. — Venezuela
V. I. (Br.) — Virgin Islands (British)
V. I. (U. S.) — Virgin Islands (U. S.)
Vic. — Victoria
Vill. — Village
vol. — volcano
Vt. — Vermont

W

W. — West, Western
Wash. — Washington
W. Aust., W. Austral. — Western Australia
W. Ger. — West Germany
Wis. — Wisconsin
W. Samoa — Western Samoa
W. Va. — West Virginia
Wyo. — Wyoming

Y

Yugo. — Yugoslavia
Yukon — Yukon Territory

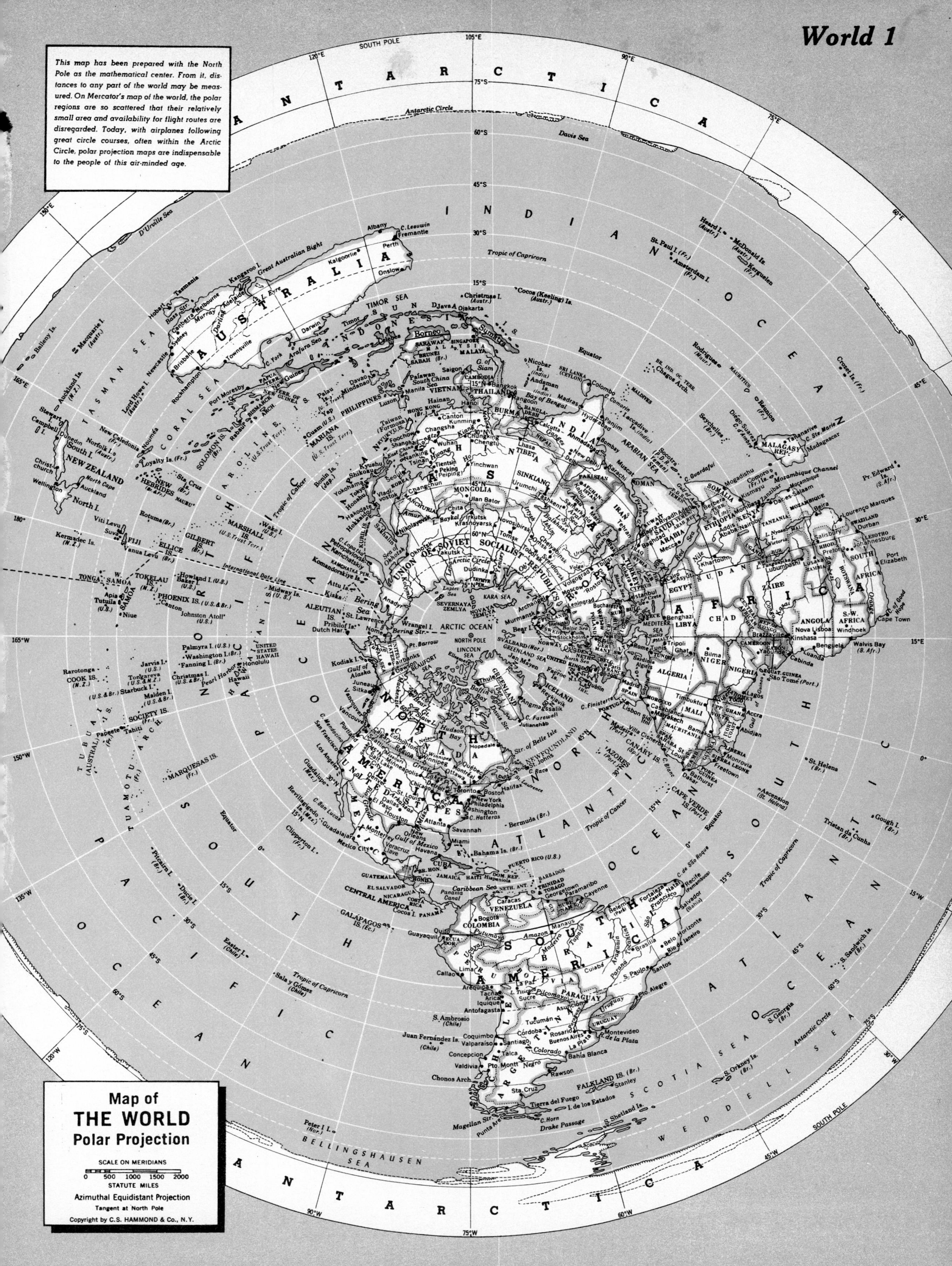

This map has been prepared with the North Pole as the mathematical center. From it, distances to any part of the world may be measured. On Mercator's map of the world, the polar regions are so scattered that their relatively small area and availability for flight routes are disregarded. Today, with airplanes following great circle courses, often within the Arctic Circle, polar projection maps are indispensable to the people of this air-minded age.
Map of
THE WORLD
Polar Projection
SCALE ON MERIDIANS
0 500 1000 1500 2000
STATUTE MILES
Azimuthal Equidistant Projection
Tangent at North Pole
Copyright by C.S. HAMMOND & Co., N.Y.
SOUTH POLE
ANTARCTICA
Antarctic Circle
INDIAN OCEAN
AUSTRALIA
NEW ZEALAND
ASIA
UNION OF SOVIET SOCIALIST REPUBLICS
CHINA
INDIA
EUROPE
AFRICA
ARCTIC OCEAN
NORTH POLE
NORTH AMERICA
UNITED STATES
CANADA
SOUTH AMERICA
NORTH PACIFIC OCEAN
SOUTH PACIFIC OCEAN
NORTH ATLANTIC OCEAN
SOUTH ATLANTIC OCEAN
Tropic of Capricorn
Tropic of Cancer
Equator
Arctic Circle
International Date Line
SCOTIA SEA
WEDDELL SEA
BELLINGSHAUSEN SEA
Davis Sea
D'Urville Sea
TASMAN SEA
CORAL SEA
ARABIAN SEA
Bay of Bengal
Caribbean Sea
Gulf of Mexico

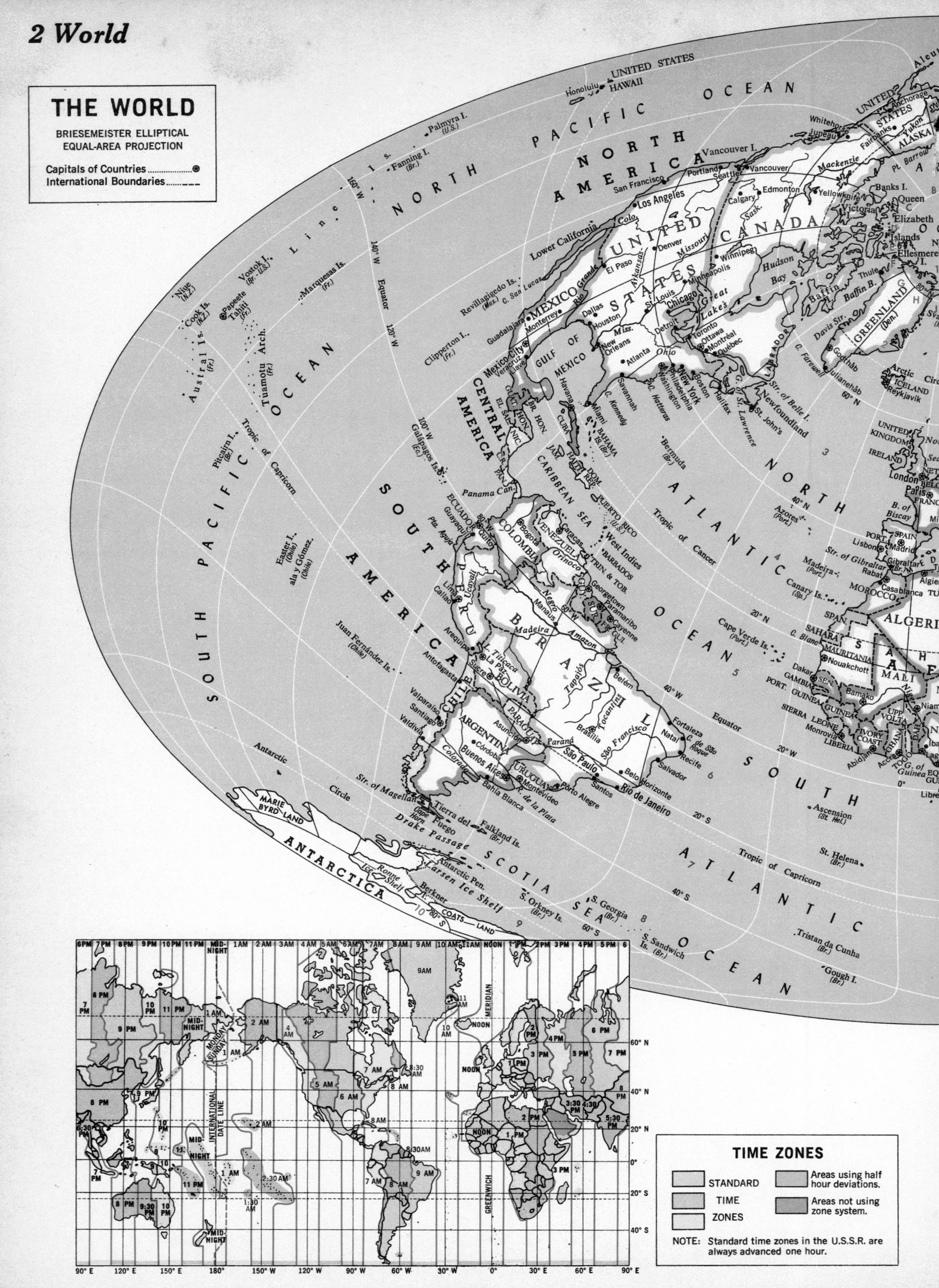
THE WORLD
BRIESEMEISTER ELLIPTICAL EQUAL-AREA PROJECTION
Capitals of Countries
International Boundaries
NORTH PACIFIC OCEAN
SOUTH PACIFIC OCEAN
NORTH ATLANTIC OCEAN
SOUTH ATLANTIC OCEAN
NORTH AMERICA
SOUTH AMERICA
CENTRAL AMERICA
UNITED STATES
CANADA
MEXICO
GREENLAND (Den.)
BRAZIL
ARGENTINA
CHILE
PERU
BOLIVIA
PARAGUAY
URUGUAY
COLOMBIA
VENEZUELA
ECUADOR
ALGERIA
MOROCCO
MAURITANIA
MALI
SAHARA
ICELAND
UNITED KINGDOM
IRELAND
ANTARCTICA
MARIE BYRD LAND
COATS LAND
GULF OF MEXICO
CARIBBEAN SEA
SCOTIA SEA
Drake Passage
Hudson Bay
Baffin Bay
Tropic of Cancer
Tropic of Capricorn
Equator
Antarctic Circle
Arctic Circle
Honolulu
HAWAII
Los Angeles
San Francisco
Vancouver
Seattle
Portland
Denver
El Paso
Dallas
Houston
New Orleans
Atlanta
St. Louis
Chicago
Detroit
Minneapolis
Winnipeg
Calgary
Edmonton
Toronto
Ottawa
Montréal
Québec
Boston
New York
Philadelphia
Washington
Halifax
St. John's
Savannah
Miami
Havana
Mexico City
Monterrey
Guadalajara
Veracruz
Panama Can.
Bogotá
Caracas
Quito
Guayaquil
Lima
Callao
La Paz
Sucre
Arequipa
Antofagasta
Valparaíso
Santiago
Valdivia
Córdoba
Buenos Aires
Montevideo
Bahía Blanca
Asunción
São Paulo
Rio de Janeiro
Belo Horizonte
Brasília
Salvador
Recife
Natal
Fortaleza
Belém
Manaus
Georgetown
Paramaribo
Cayenne
Amazon
Orinoco
London
Paris
Lisbon
Madrid
Rabat
Casablanca
Algiers
Dakar
Nouakchott
Bamako
Monrovia
Abidjan
Accra
Reykjavik
Godthåb
Julianehåb
Anchorage
Fairbanks
Juneau
Whitehorse
Bermuda (Br.)
Azores (Port.)
Madeira (Port.)
Canary Is. (Sp.)
Cape Verde Is. (Port.)
Ascension (St. Hel.)
St. Helena (Br.)
Tristan da Cunha (Br.)
Gough I. (Br.)
Falkland Is. (Br.)
S. Georgia (Br.)
S. Orkney Is. (Br.)
S. Sandwich Is. (Br.)
Easter I. (Chile)
Sala y Gómez (Chile)
Juan Fernández Is. (Chile)
Galápagos Is. (Ec.)
Pitcairn I. (Br.)
Tahiti (Fr.)
Papeete
Cook Is. (N.Z.)
Niue (N.Z.)
Austral Is. (Fr.)
Tuamotu Arch. (Fr.)
Marquesas Is. (Fr.)
Vostok I. (Br.-U.S.)
Palmyra I. (U.S.)
Fanning I. (Br.)
Clipperton I. (Fr.)
Revillagigedo Is. (Mex.)
Line Is.
Str. of Magellan
Tierra del Fuego
Cape Horn
Antarctic Pen.
Larsen Ice Shelf
Ronne Ice Shelf
Berkner I.
TIME ZONES
STANDARD TIME ZONES
Areas using half hour deviations.
Areas not using zone system.
NOTE: Standard time zones in the U.S.S.R. are always advanced one hour.
6PM 7PM 8PM 9PM 10PM 11PM MID-NIGHT 1AM 2AM 3AM 4AM 5AM 6AM 7AM 8AM 9AM 10AM 11AM NOON 1PM 2PM 3PM 4PM 5PM 6
INTERNATIONAL DATE LINE
MONDAY
SUNDAY
GREENWICH MERIDIAN
60° N
40° N
20° N
0°
20° S
40° S
90° E 120° E 150° E 180° 150° W 120° W 90° W 60° W 30° W 0° 30° E 60° E 90° E

WORLD
LAND AREA 57,491,000 sq. mi.
WATER AREA 139,459,000 sq. mi.
TOTAL SURFACE AREA 196,950,000 sq. mi.
POPULATION 3,782,000,000

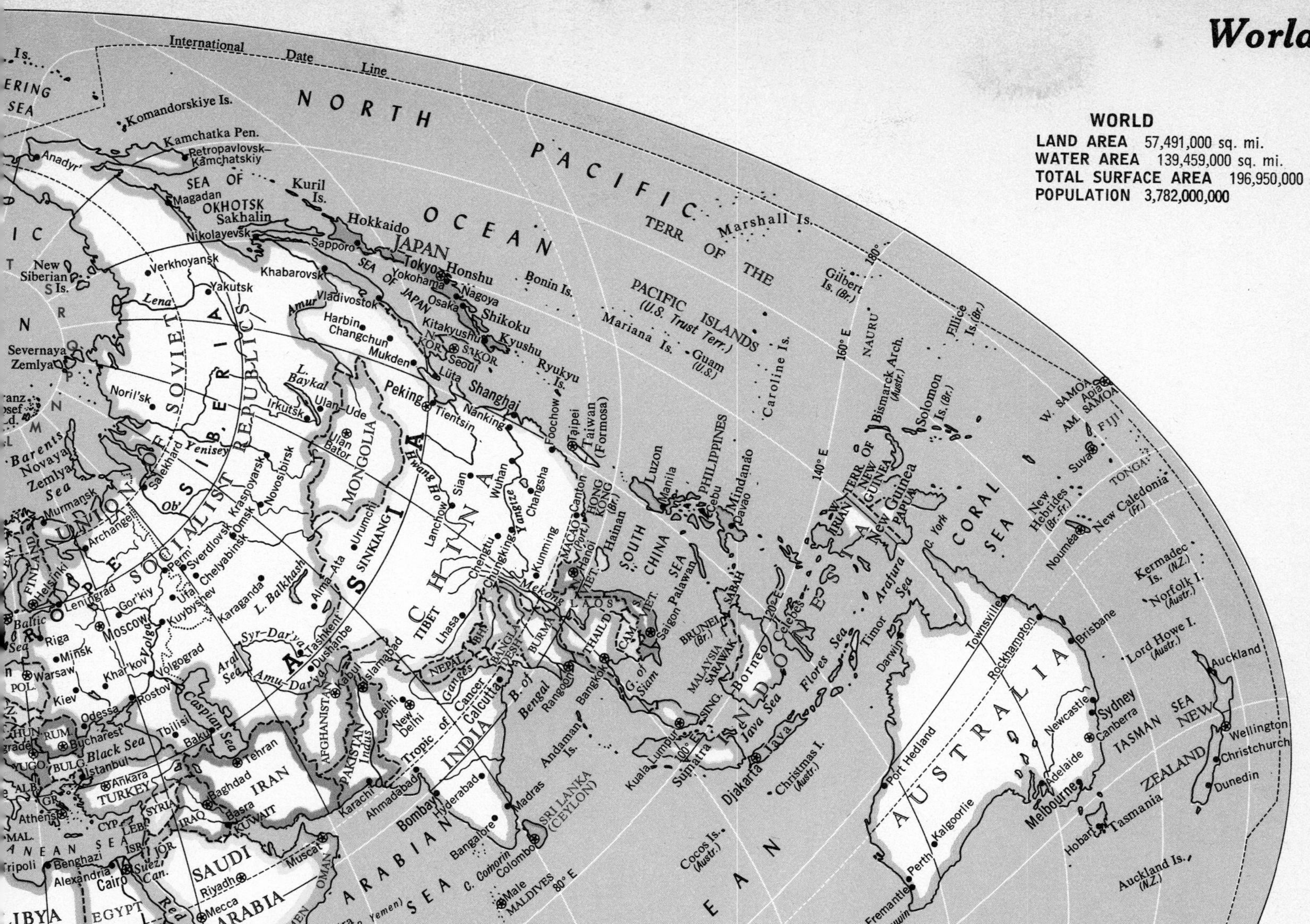

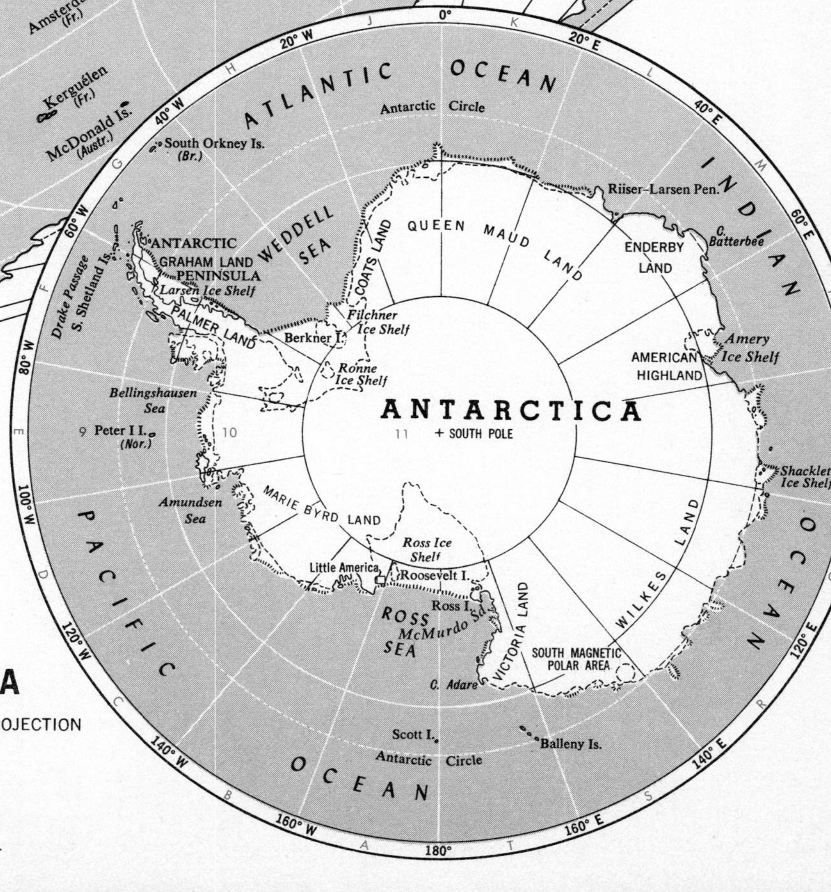

ANTARCTICA

AZIMUTHAL EQUIDISTANT PROJECTION

4 Arctic Ocean

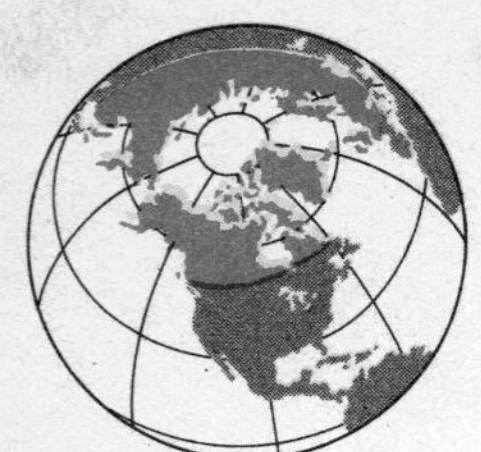

Aklavik, Canada C16
Akureyri, Iceland ....C 1
Alaska (gulf), U.S.A. D17
Alaska (mts.), U.S.A. C17
Alaska (pen.), U.S.A. D18
Alaska (state), U.S.A. C17
Alert, Canada A12
Aleutian (isls.), U.S.A. D18
Alexander (arch.), U.S.A. D16
Alexandra Land (isl.), U.S.S.R. ....A 8
Ambarchik, U.S.S.R. ....B 1
Amundsen (gulf), Canada B16
Anadyr', U.S.S.R. ....C 1
Anadyr' (gulf), U.S.S.R. C18
Anadyr' (river), U.S.S.R. ....C 1
Angmagssalik, Greenland C11
Archangel, U.S.S.R. ....C 7
Anchorage, U.S.A. D17
Arctic Bay, Canada B14
Arctic Ocean A15
Atlantic Ocean D11
Attu (isl.), U.S.A. ....D 1
Axel Heiberg (isl.), Canada A14
Baffin (bay) B13
Baffin (isl.), Canada C13
Banks (isl.), Canada B16
Barents (sea) ....B 8
Barrow, U.S.A. B17
Barrow (point), U.S.A. B18
Bathurst (isl.), Canada B15
Bathurst Inlet, Canada C15
Bear (isl.), Norway ....B 9
Bear (isls.), U.S.S.R. ....B 1
Beaufort (sea) B16
Belush'ya Guba, U.S.S.R. ....B 7
Belyy (isl.), U.S.S.R. ....B 6
Bering (strait) C18
Bol'shevik (isl.), U.S.S.R. ....A 4
Boothia (gulf), Canada B14
Boothia (pen.), Canada B14
Borden (isl.), Canada B15
Boris Vil'kitskiy (strait), U.S.S.R. ....B 4
Bristol (bay), U.S.A. D18
Brodeur (pen.), Canada B14
Brooks (range), U.S.A. C17
Bulun, U.S.S.R. ....B 3
Cambridge Bay, Canada B15
Canada C14
Chelyuskin (cape), U.S.S.R. ......B 4
Chokurdakh, U.S.S.R. ....B 2
Chukchi (pen.), U.S.S.R. C18
Chukchi (sea) C18
Clyde, Canada B13
Columbia (cape), Canada A13
Cook (inlet), U.S.A. D17
Coppermine, Canada C15
Cordova, U.S.A. C17
Craig Harbour, Canada B13
Cumberland (sound), Canada......C13
Daneborg, Greenland B10
Danmarkshavn, Greenland B10
Davis (strait) C12
Dawson, Canada C16
Denmark (strait) C11
Devon (isl.), Canada B14
Dezhnev (cape), U.S.S.R. C18
Dikson, U.S.S.R. ....B 5
Disko (isl.), Greenland C12
Dmitriy Laptev (str.), U.S.S.R., ...B 2
Dudinka, U.S.S.R. ....B 5
Dundas Harbour, Canada B14
Dvina, Northern (river), U.S.S.R. ....C 7
East (Dezhnev) (cape), U.S.S.R. C18
East Siberian (sea), U.S.S.R. ....B 1
Edge (isl.), Norway ....B 8
Ellef Ringnes (isl.), Canada B15
Ellesmere (isl.), Canada B14
Eureka, Canada A14
Faddeyevskiy (isl.), U.S.S.R. ....B 2
Fairbanks, U.S.A. C17
Farewell (cape), Greenland D12
Finland ....C 8
Fort Simpson, Canada C15

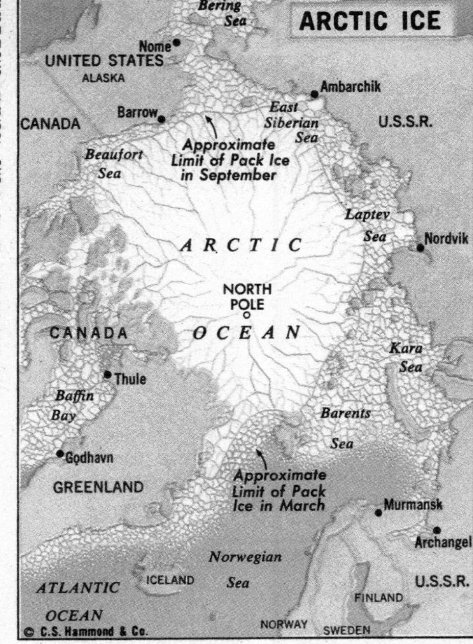

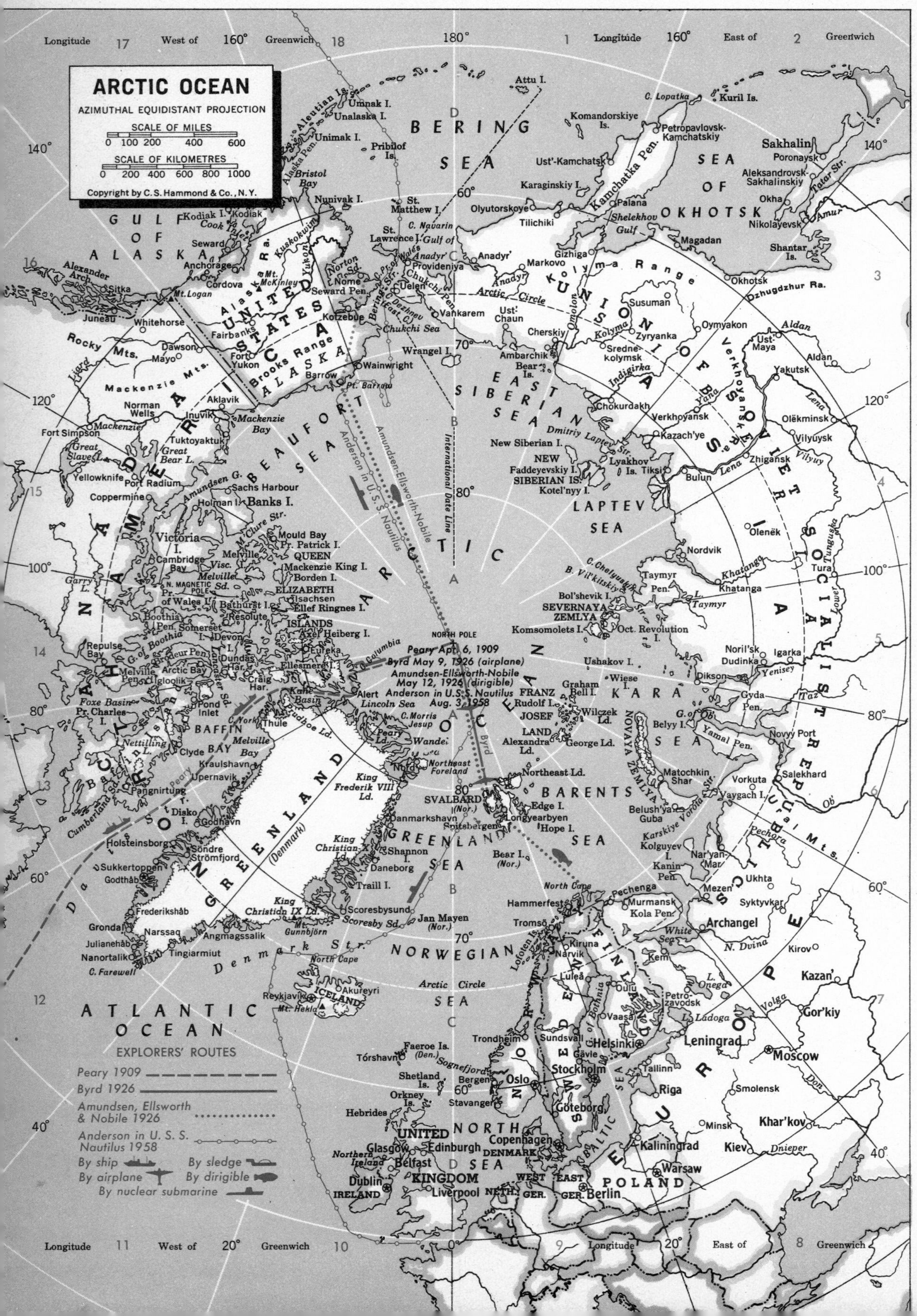

Fort Yukon, U.S.A. C17
Foxe (basin), Canada C13
Franz Josef Land (isls.), U.S.S.R. ....A 7
Frederikshåb, Greenland C12
Garry (lake), Canada C14
George Land (isl.), U.S.S.R. ....B 7
Godhavn, Greenland C12
Godthåb (cap.), Greenland C12
Graham Bell (isl.), U.S.S.R. ......A 6
Great Bear (lake), Canada..........C16
Great Slave (lake), Canada C15
Greenland B12
Greenland (sea) B10
Grondal, Greenland C12
Gunnbjørn (mt.), Greenland C11
Gyda (pen.), U.S.S.R. ....C 6
Hammerfest, Norway ....B 9
Hekla (mt.), Iceland C11
Holman Island, Canada B15
Holsteinsborg, Greenland............C12
Hope (isl.), Norway ....B 8
Iceland C10
Igarka, U.S.S.R. ....C 5
Igloolik, Canada B14
Indigirka (river), U.S.S.R. ....C 2
Inuvik, Canada C16
Isachsen, Canada B15
Jan Mayen (isl.), Norway B10
Julianehåb, Greenland D12
Juneau, U.S.A. D16
Kane (basin) B13
Kanin (pen.), U.S.S.R. ....C 7
Kara (sea), U.S.S.R. ....B 6
Karskiye Vorota (strait), U.S.S.R. ....B 7
Kazach'ye, U.S.S.R. ....C 3
Kem', U.S.S.R. ....C 8
Khatanga, U.S.S.R. ....B 4
Khatanga (river), U.S.S.R. ....B 4
King Christian IX Land (reg.), Greenland C11
King Christian X Land (reg.), Greenland B11
King Frederik VIII Land (reg.), Greenland B11
Kiruna, Sweden ....C 8
Kodiak, U.S.A. D17
Kodiak (isl.), U.S.A. D17
Kola (pen.), U.S.S.R. ....C 8
Kolguyev (isl.), U.S.S.R. ....B 7
Kolyma (range), U.S.S.R. ....C 1
Kolyma (river), U.S.S.R. ....C 2
Komsomolets (isl.), U.S.S.R. ....A 5
Kotel'nyy (isl.), U.S.S.R. ....B 2
Kotzebue, U.S.A. C18
Kraulshavn, Greenland B13
Kuskokwim (river), U.S.A. C17
Lancaster (sound), Canada B14
Laptev (sea), U.S.S.R. ....B 3
Lena (river), U.S.S.R. ....C 3
Lincoln (sea) A12
Lofoten (isls.), Norway ....C 9
Logan (mt.), Canada C17
Longyearbyen, Norway ....B 8
Lyakhov (isls.), U.S.S.R. ....B 3
Mackenzie (bay), Canada B16
Mackenzie (mts.), Canada C16
Mackenzie (river), Canada C16
Mackenzie King (isl.), Canada...B15
M'Clure (strait), Canada B15
Markovo, U.S.S.R. ....C 1
Matochkin Shar, U.S.S.R. ....B 7
Mayo, Canada C16
McKinley (mt.), U.S.A. C17
Melville (bay), Greenland B13
Melville (isl.), Canada B15
Melville (pen.), Canada C14
Mezen', U.S.S.R. ....C 7
Morris Jesup (cape), Greenland A11
Mould Bay, Canada B16
Murmansk, U.S.S.R. ....C 8
Nanortalik, Greenland D12
Narssaq, Greenland C12
Narvik, Norway ....C 9
Nar'yan-Mar, U.S.S.R. ....C 7
Navarin (cape), U.S.S.R. C18
Nettilling (lake), Canada C13
New Siberian (isl.), U.S.S.R. ....B 2
New Siberian (isls.), U.S.S.R. ...B 2
Nizhniye Kresty, U.S.S.R. ....C 1
Nome, U.S.A. C18
Nord, Greenland A10
Nordvik, U.S.S.R. ....B 4
Noril'sk, U.S.S.R. ....B 5
Norman Wells, Canada C16
North (cape), Iceland C11
North (cape), Norway ....B 8
Northeast Foreland (pen.), Greenland A10
Northeast Land (isl.), Norway...B 8
North Magnetic Pole, Canada.....B15
North Pole ....A 1
Norton (sound), U.S.A. C18
Norway ....C 9
Norwegian (sea) C10
Novaya Zemlya (isls.), U.S.S.R. ....B 7
Novyy Port, U.S.S.R. ....C 6
Nunivak (isl.), U.S.A. D18
Ob' (gulf), U.S.S.R. ....B 6
Ob' (river), U.S.S.R. ....C 6
October Revolution (isl.), U.S.S.R. ....B 5
Olenek, U.S.S.R. ....C 4
Omolon (river), U.S.S.R. ....C 1
Oymyakon, U.S.S.R. ....C 2
Pangnirtung, Canada C13
Peary Land (reg.), Greenland....A11
Pechenga, U.S.S.R. ....C 8
Pechora (river), U.S.S.R. ....C 7
Pond Inlet, Canada B13
Port Radium, Canada C15
Pribilof (isls.), U.S.A. D18
Prince Charles (isl.), Canada......C13
Prince of Wales (cape), U.S.A. ..C18
Prince of Wales (isl.), Canada....B14
Prince Patrick (isl.), Canada.....B16
Provideniya, U.S.S.R. C18
Prudhoe Land (reg.), Greenland B13
Queen Elizabeth (isls.), Canada B15
Repulse Bay, Canada C14
Resolute, Canada B14
Reykjavík (cap.), Iceland............C11
Rocky (mts.), Canada D16
Rudolf (isl.), U.S.S.R. ....A 7
Sachs Harbour, Canada B16
Saint Lawrence (isl.), U.S.A. ...C18
Saint Matthew (isl.), U.S.A. C18
Scoresby (sound), Greenland......B10
Scoresbysund, Greenland B10
Severnaya Zemlya (isls.), U.S.S.R. ....A 4
Seward, U.S.A. D17
Seward (pen.), U.S.A. C18
Shannon (isl.), Greenland B10
Siberia (reg.), U.S.S.R. ....C 2
Sitka, U.S.A. D16
Somerset (isl.), Canada B14
Søndre Strømfjord, Greenland C12
Spitsbergen (isl.), Norway ....B 9
Srednekolymsk, U.S.S.R. ....C 2
Sukkertoppen, Greenland C12
Susuman, U.S.S.R. ....C 2
Svalbard (isls.), Norway ....B 9
Sweden ....D 9
Taymyr (lake), U.S.S.R. ....B 5
Taymyr (pen.), U.S.S.R. ....B 4
Taz (river), U.S.S.R. ....C 5
Thule, Greenland B13
Tiksi, U.S.S.R. ....B 3
Tingiarmiut, Greenland C12
Traill (isl.), Greenland B10
Tromsø, Norway ....B 9
Tuktoyaktuk, Canada C16
Uelen, U.S.S.R. C18
Umnak (isl.), U.S.A. D18
Unalaska (isl.), U.S.A. D18
Unimak (isl.), U.S.A. D18
Union of Soviet Socialist Republics ....C 2
United States C17
Upernavik, Greenland B12
Ural (mts.), U.S.S.R. ....C 6
Ushakov (isl.), U.S.S.R. ....B 5
Ust'-Chaun, U.S.S.R. ....C 1
Vankarem, U.S.S.R. ....C 1
Vaygach (isl.), U.S.S.R. ....C 6
Verkhoyansk, U.S.S.R. ....C 3
Verkhoyansk (range), U.S.S.R. ....C 3
Victoria (isl.), Canada B15
Viscount Melville (sound), Canada B15
Vorkuta, U.S.S.R. ....C 6
Wainwright, U.S.A. B18
Wandel (sea), Greenland A10
White (sea), U.S.S.R. ....C 8
Whitehorse, Canada C16
Wiese (isl.), U.S.S.R. ....B 6
Wilczek Land (isl.), U.S.S.R. ....B 6
Wrangel (isl.), U.S.S.R. B18
Yamal (pen.), U.S.S.R. ....B 6
Yana (river), U.S.S.R. ....C 3
Yellowknife, Canada C15
Yenisey (river), U.S.S.R. ....C 5
York (cape), Greenland B13
Yukon (river) C17
Zhigansk, U.S.S.R. ....C 3
Zyryanka, U.S.S.R. ....C 2

ARCTIC OCEAN

AZIMUTHAL EQUIDISTANT PROJECTION

SCALE OF MILES: 0 100 200 400 600

SCALE OF KILOMETRES: 0 200 400 600 800 1000

EXPLORERS' ROUTES

Peary 1909

Byrd 1926

Amundsen, Ellsworth & Nobile 1926

Anderson in U. S. S. Nautilus 1958

By ship — By sledge — By airplane — By dirigible — By nuclear submarine

Peary Apr. 6, 1909
Byrd May 9, 1926 (airplane)
Amundsen-Ellsworth-Nobile May 12, 1926 (dirigible)
Anderson in U.S.S. Nautilus Aug. 3, 1958

ANTARCTICA

AZIMUTHAL EQUIDISTANT PROJECTION

SCALE OF MILES: 0 200 400 600 800

SCALE OF KILOMETRES: 0 200 400 600 800 1000

EXPLORERS' ROUTES

- Palmer 1820
- Amundsen 1910-12
- Scott 1910-13
- Byrd 1928-30
- Fuchs 1957-58
- By ship
- By sledge
- By airplane
- By snow tractor

Amundsen Dec. 14, 1911
Scott Jan. 17, 1912
Byrd Nov. 29, 1929 (airplane)
Fuchs Jan. 20, 1958

Adare (cape) ....B 9
Adelaide (isl.) C15
Adélie Coast (region) ....C 7
Alexander (isl.) B15
American Highland ....B 4
Amery Ice Shelf ....C 4
Amundsen (bay) ....C 3
Amundsen (sea) B13
Antarctic (pen.) C15
Balleny (isls.) ....C 9
Banzare Coast (region) ....C 7
Barr Smith (mt.) ....C 5
Batterbee (cape) ....C 3
Beardmore (glacier) ....A 8
Bellingshausen (sea) C14
Berkner (isl.) B16
Biscoe (isls.) C15
Bouvet (isl.) ....D 1
Bransfield (strait) C16
Budd Coast (region) ....C 6
Byrd Station A12
Caird Coast (region) B17
Charcot (isl.) C15
Clarie Coast (region) ....C 7
Coats Land (region) B18
Colbeck (cape) B10
Coronation (isl.) C16
Daly (cape) ....C 4
Darnley (cape) ....C 4
Dart (cape) B12
Davis (sea) ....C 5
Davis (sta.) ....C 4
Drake (passage) C15
Dumont d'Urville (sta.) ....C 7
Edith Ronne Ice Shelf B16
Edward VII (pen.) B11
Eights Coast (region) B14
Elephant (isl.) C16
Ellsworth Land (reg.) A14
Enderby Land (region) B14
English Coast (reg.) B15
Executive Committee (range) B12
Farr (bay) ....C 5
Filchner Ice Shelf B16
Ford (ranges) B11
Gaussberg (mt.) ....C 5
George V Coast (region) ....C 8
Getz Ice Shelf B12
Goodenough (cape) ....C 7
Graham Land (region) C15
Grytviken D17
Hilton Inlet (bay) B16
Hobbs Coast (region) B12
Hollick-Kenyon (plateau) B13
Hope (bay) C15
Joinville (isl.) C16
Kainan (bay) B10
Keltie (cape) ....C 7
Kemp Coast (region) ....C 3
King George (isl.) C16
Kirkpatrick (mt.) ....A 8
Knox Coast (region) ....C 6
Larsen Ice Shelf C16
Lazarev (sta.) ....C 1
Levick (mt.) ....B 8
Lister (mt.) ....B 8
Little America B10
Luitpold Coast (region) B17
Lützow-Holm (bay) ....C 3
Mackenzie (bay) ....C 4
Mac-Robertson Land (region) ....C 4
Marguerite (bay) C15
Marie Byrd Land (region) B12
Markham (mt.) ....A 8
Mawson ....C 4
McMurdo (sound) ....B 9
Mertz (glacier) ....C 8
Mirnyy ....C 5
New Schwabenland (region) ....B 1
Ninnis (glacier) ....C 8
Norvegia (cape) B18
Oates Coast (region) ....B 8
Palmer (arch.) C15
Palmer Land (region) B15
Palmer Station C15
Peter I (isl.) C14
Prince Edward (isls.) ....E 2
Prince Olav Coast (region) ....C 3
Princess Astrid Coast (region) ....B 1
Princess Martha Coast (region) B18
Princess Ragnhild Coast (region) ....B 2
Prydz (bay) ....C 4
Queen Mary Cqast (region) ....C 5
Queen Maud Land (region) ....B 1
Riiser-Larsen (pen.) ....C 2
Ronne Entrance (bay) B15
Roosevelt (isl.) A10
Ross (isl.) ....B 9
Ross (sea) B10
Ross Ice Shelf A10
Sabine (mt.) ....B 9
Sabrina Coast (region) ....C 6
Sanae (sta.) B18
Scotia (sea) D16
Scott (isl.) C10
Shackleton Ice Shelf ....C 5
Sidley (mt.) B12
Siple (mt.) B12
South Georgia (isl.) D17
South Magnetic Polar Area ....C 8
South Orkney (isls.) C16
South Polar (plateau) ....A 1
South Pole ....A 4
South Sandwich (isls.) D17
South Shetland (isls.) C15
Sulzberger (bay) B11
Thurston (isl.) C14
Transantarctic (mts.) A11
Victoria Land (region) ....B 8
Vincennes (bay) ....C 6
Vinson Massif (mt.) B14
Walgreen Coast (region) B13
Weddell (sea) C17
West Ice Shelf ....C 5
Wilhelm II Coast (region) ....C 5
Wilkes Land (region) ....C 7

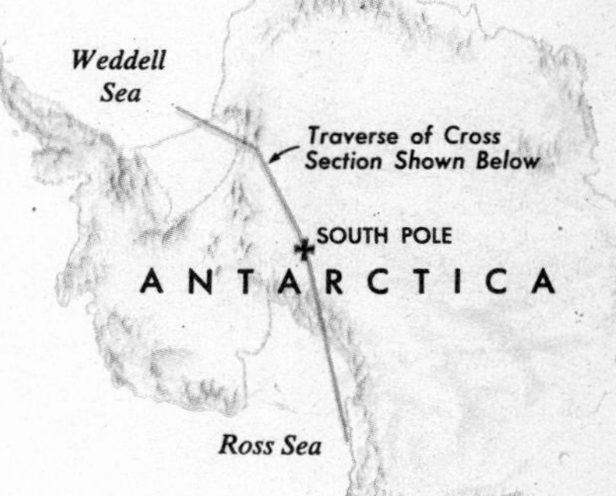

ANTARCTIC CROSS SECTION: WEDDELL SEA TO ROSS SEA

Meters: 3000, 2000, 1000, Sea Level, –1000, –2000

Weddell Sea · Filchner Ice Shelf · Whichaway Nunataks · Recovery Glacier · ICE · SOUTH POLE · Beardmore Glacier · Queen Alexandra Range · Ross Ice Shelf · Ross Island · Ross Sea · ROCK · ROCK

VERTICAL EXAGGERATION 95 TIMES

Information Based on American Geographical Society's "Antarctic Map Folio Series"

Aachen, W. Germany ..... E 3
Aberdeen, Scotland ..... D 3
Adriatic (sea) ..... F 4
Aegean (sea) ..... G 5
Albania ..... G 4
Ålborg, Denmark ..... E 3
Alps (mts.) ..... F 4
Amsterdam (cap.), Neth. ..... E 3
Andorra ..... E 4
Antwerp, Belg. ..... E 3
Arad, Rumania ..... G 4
Araks (river) ..... J 5
Archangel, U.S.S.R. ..... J 2
Århus, Denmark ..... E 3
Armenian S.S.R., U.S.S.R. ..... J 4
Astrakhan', U.S.S.R. ..... J 4
Athens (cap.), Greece ..... G 5
Atlantic Ocean ..... C 4
Austria ..... F 4
Azerbaidzhan S.S.R., U.S.S.R. ..... J 4
Azov (sea), U.S.S.R. ..... H 4
Baku, U.S.S.R. ..... K 5
Balaton (lake), Hungary ..... F 4
Balearic (isls.), Spain ..... E 5
Balkans (mts.) ..... G 4
Baltic (sea) ..... F 3
Barcelona, Spain ..... E 4
Barents (sea) ..... H 1
Bari, Italy ..... F 4
Basel, Switzerland ..... E 4
Belfast (cap.), No. Ireland ..... D 3
Belgium ..... E 3
Belgrade (cap.), Yugoslavia ..... G 4
Bergen, Norway ..... E 2
Berlin (cap.), E. Germany ..... F 3
Bern (cap.), Switzerland ..... E 4
Bilbao, Spain ..... D 4

Birmingham, England ..... D 3
Biscay (bay) ..... D 4
Black (sea) ..... H 4
Bologna, Italy ..... F 4
Bonn (cap.), W. Germany ..... E 3
Bordeaux, France ..... D 4
Bornholm (isl.), Denmark ..... F 3
Bosporus (strait), Turkey ..... G 4
Bothnia (gulf) ..... G 2
Braşov, Rumania ..... G 4
Bratislava, Czechoslovakia ..... F 4
Bremen, W. Germany ..... E 3
Brest, France ..... D 4
Bristol, England ..... D 3
British Isles ..... D 3
Brno, Czechoslovakia ..... F 4
Brussels (cap.), Belgium ..... E 3
Bucharest (cap.), Rumania ..... G 4
Budapest (cap.), Hungary ..... G 4
Bug (river) ..... G 3
Bulgaria ..... G 4
Burgas, Bulgaria ..... G 4
Burgos, Spain ..... D 4
Calais, France ..... E 3
Cardiff, Wales ..... D 3
Carpathians (mts.) ..... G 4
Cartagena, Spain ..... D 5
Caspian (sea) ..... J 4
Caucasus (mts.), U.S.S.R. ..... J 4
Channel (isls.) ..... D 4
Cologne, W. Germany ..... E 3
Constance (lake) ..... F 4
Constanţa, Rumania ..... G 4
Copenhagen (cap.), Denmark ..... E 3
Córdoba, Spain ..... D 5
Cork, Ireland ..... D 3
Corsica (Corse) (isl.), France ..... E 4

Cracow, Poland ..... G 3
Crete (isl.), Greece ..... G 5
Crimea (pen.), U.S.S.R. ..... H 4
Czechoslovakia ..... F 4
Danube (river) ..... G 4
Dardanelles (strait), Turkey ..... G 5
Debrecen, Hungary ..... G 4
Denmark ..... E 3
Dnepropetrovsk, U.S.S.R. ..... H 4
Dnieper (river), U.S.S.R. ..... H 4
Dniester (river), U.S.S.R. ..... G 4
Don (river), U.S.S.R. ..... J 4
Donets (river) ..... H 4
Douro (Duero) (river) ..... D 4
Drava (river) ..... F 4
Dresden, E. Germany ..... F 3
Dublin (cap.), Ireland ..... D 3
East Germany ..... F 3
Ebro (river), Spain ..... D 4
Edinburgh (cap.), Scotland ..... D 3
Edirne, Turkey ..... G 4
Elbe (river) ..... F 3
El'brus (mt.), U.S.S.R. ..... J 4
England ..... D 3
English (channel) ..... D 3
Essen, W. Germany ..... E 3
Estonian S.S.R., U.S.S.R. ..... G 3
Etna (mt.), Italy ..... F 5
Faerøe (isls.), Denmark ..... D 2
Finisterre (cape), Spain ..... C 4
Finland ..... G 2
Florence, Italy ..... F 4
France ..... E 4
Frankfurt, W. Germany ..... E 3
Garonne (river), France ..... E 4
Gdańsk, Poland ..... F 3
Geneva, Switz. ..... E 4

Geneva (lake) ..... E 4
Genoa, Italy ..... E 4
Georgian S.S.R., U.S.S.R. ..... J 4
Germany ..... F 3
Ghent, Belgium ..... E 3
Gibraltar ..... D 5
Gibraltar (strait) ..... D 5
Glasgow, Scotland ..... D 3
Gor'kiy, U.S.S.R. ..... J 3
Göteborg, Sweden ..... F 3
Granada, Spain ..... D 5
Graz, Austria ..... F 4
Greece ..... G 5
Guadalquivir (river), Spain ..... D 5
Guadiana (river) ..... D 5
Hague, The (cap.), Neth. ..... E 3
Hamburg, W. Germany ..... F 3
Hammerfest, Norway ..... G 1
Helsinki (Helsingfors) (cap.), Finland ..... G 2
Hungary ..... F 4
Iceland ..... C 2
Ionian (sea) ..... F 5
Ireland ..... C 3
Irish (sea) ..... D 3
Iron Gate (gorge) ..... G 4
İstanbul, Turkey ..... G 4
Italy ..... F 4
Jan Mayen (isl.), Norway ..... D 1
Jönköping, Sweden ..... F 3
Kalinin, U.S.S.R. ..... H 3
Kaliningrad, U.S.S.R. ..... G 3
Kaluga, U.S.S.R. ..... H 3
Kama (river), U.S.S.R. ..... K 2
Karachayevsk, U.S.S.R. ..... J 4
Karl-Marx-Stadt, East Germany ..... F 3

Karlskrona, Sweden ..... F 3
Karlsruhe, W. Germany ..... E 4
Karlstad, Sweden ..... F 3
Kassel, W. Germany ..... E 3
Katowice, Poland ..... F 3
Kattegat (strait) ..... F 3
Kaunas, U.S.S.R. ..... G 3
Kavalla, Greece ..... G 4
Kazan', U.S.S.R. ..... J 3
Kecskemét, Hungary ..... G 4
Khar'kov, U.S.S.R. ..... H 3
Kherson, U.S.S.R. ..... H 4
Kiel, W. Germany ..... F 3
Kielce, Poland ..... G 4
Kiev, U.S.S.R. ..... H 3
Kirov, U.S.S.R. ..... J 3
Kirovograd, U.S.S.R. ..... H 4
Kishinev, U.S.S.R. ..... G 4
Kjölen (mts.) ..... F 2
Kola (pen.), U.S.S.R. ..... H 2
Krasnodar, U.S.S.R. ..... H 4
Kristiansand, Norway ..... E 3
Kristiansund, Norway ..... E 2
Krivoy Rog, U.S.S.R. ..... H 4
Kuopio, Finland ..... G 2
Kursk, U.S.S.R. ..... H 3
Kuybyshev, U.S.S.R. ..... J 3
La Coruña, Spain ..... D 4
Ladoga (lake), U.S.S.R. ..... H 2
Land's End (prom.), Eng. ..... D 3
Latvian S.S.R., U.S.S.R. ..... G 3
Lausanne, Switzerland ..... E 4
Leeds, England ..... D 3
Leghorn, Italy ..... E 4
Le Havre, France ..... D 4
Leipzig, E. Germany ..... F 3
Leningrad, U.S.S.R. ..... H 3

León, Spain ..... D 4
Liechtenstein ..... F 4
Liège, Belgium ..... E 3
Lille, France ..... E 3
Limerick, Ireland ..... D 3
Linköping, Sweden ..... F 3
Linz, Austria ..... F 4
Lions (gulf) ..... E 4
Lisbon (Lisboa) (cap.), Port. ..... C 5
Lithuanian S.S.R., U.S.S.R. ..... G 3
Liverpool, England ..... D 3
Ljubljana, Yugoslavia ..... F 4
Łódź, Poland ..... F 3
Lofoten (isls.), Norway ..... F 2
Loire (river), France ..... E 4
London (cap.), England ..... D 3
Luxembourg ..... E 4
Lyon, France ..... E 4
Madrid (cap.), Spain ..... D 4
Majorca (Mallorca) (isl.), Spain ..... E 5
Málaga, Spain ..... D 5
Malta ..... F 5
Man (isl.) ..... D 3
Manchester, England ..... D 3
Marmara (sea), Turkey ..... G 4
Marseille, France ..... E 4
Mediterranean (sea) ..... F 5
Minsk, U.S.S.R. ..... G 3
Moldavian S.S.R., U.S.S.R. ..... G 4
Monaco ..... E 4
Morava (river) ..... G 4
Moscow (Moskva) (cap.), U.S.S.R. ..... H 3
Munich, W. Germany ..... F 4
Murcia, Spain ..... D 5
Murmansk, U.S.S.R. ..... H 2

Nantes, France ..... D 4
Naples (Napoli), Italy ..... F 4
Netherlands ..... E 3
Nice, France ..... E 4
North (cape), Norway ..... G 1
North (sea) ..... E 3
Northern Dvina (river), U.S.S.R. ..... J 2
Northern Ireland ..... D 3
Norway ..... F 2
Norwegian (sea) ..... D 2
Nuremberg, W. Germany ..... F 4
Odense, Denmark ..... E 3
Oder (river) ..... F 3
Odessa, U.S.S.R. ..... H 4
Onega (lake), U.S.S.R. ..... H 2
Oporto, Portugal ..... D 4
Orenburg, U.S.S.R. ..... K 3
Orkney (isls.), Scotland ..... D 3
Orléans, France ..... E 4
Oslo (cap.), Norway ..... E 2
Palermo, Italy ..... F 5
Palma Spain ..... E 5
Paris (cap.), France ..... E 4
Pentland (firth), Scotland ..... D 3
Perm', U.S.S.R. ..... K 3
Piraeus, Greece ..... G 5
Ploieşti, Rumania ..... G 4
Plovdiv, Bulgaria ..... G 4
Plymouth, England ..... D 3
Po (river), Italy ..... F 4
Poland ..... G 3
Portugal ..... D 5
Poznań, Poland ..... F 3
Prague (Praha) (cap.), Czechoslovakia ..... F 3
Pyrenees (mts.) ..... D 4

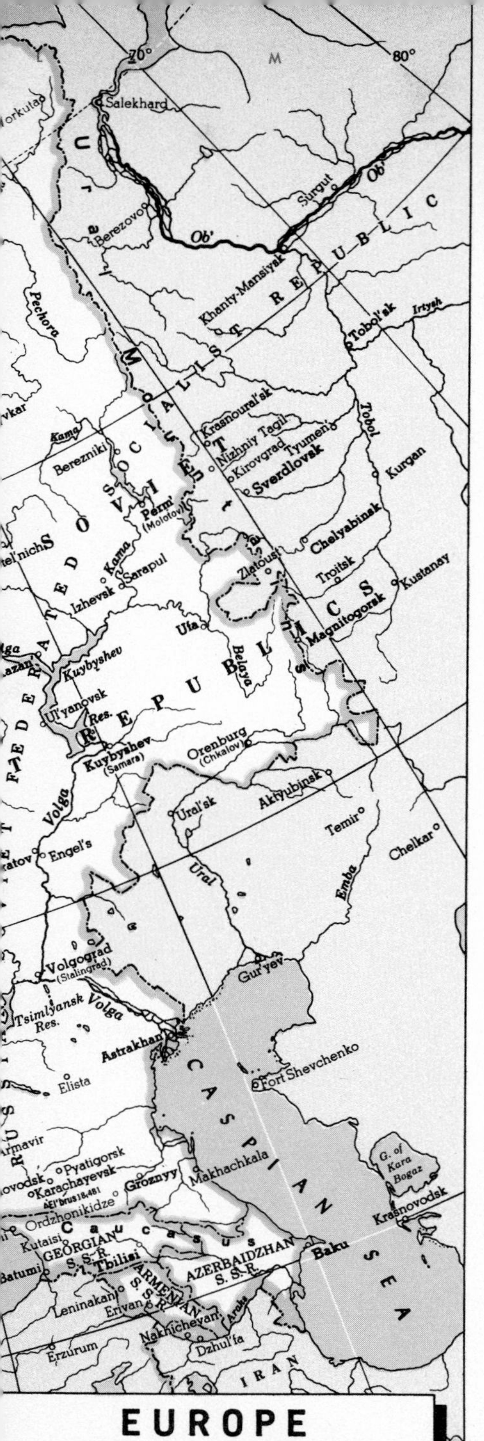

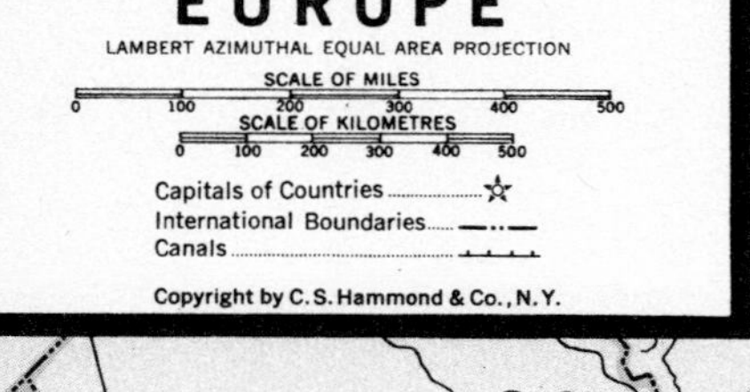

AREA 4,063,000 sq. mi.
POPULATION 652,000,000
LARGEST CITY London
HIGHEST POINT El'brus 18,481 ft.
LOWEST POINT Caspian Sea -92 ft.

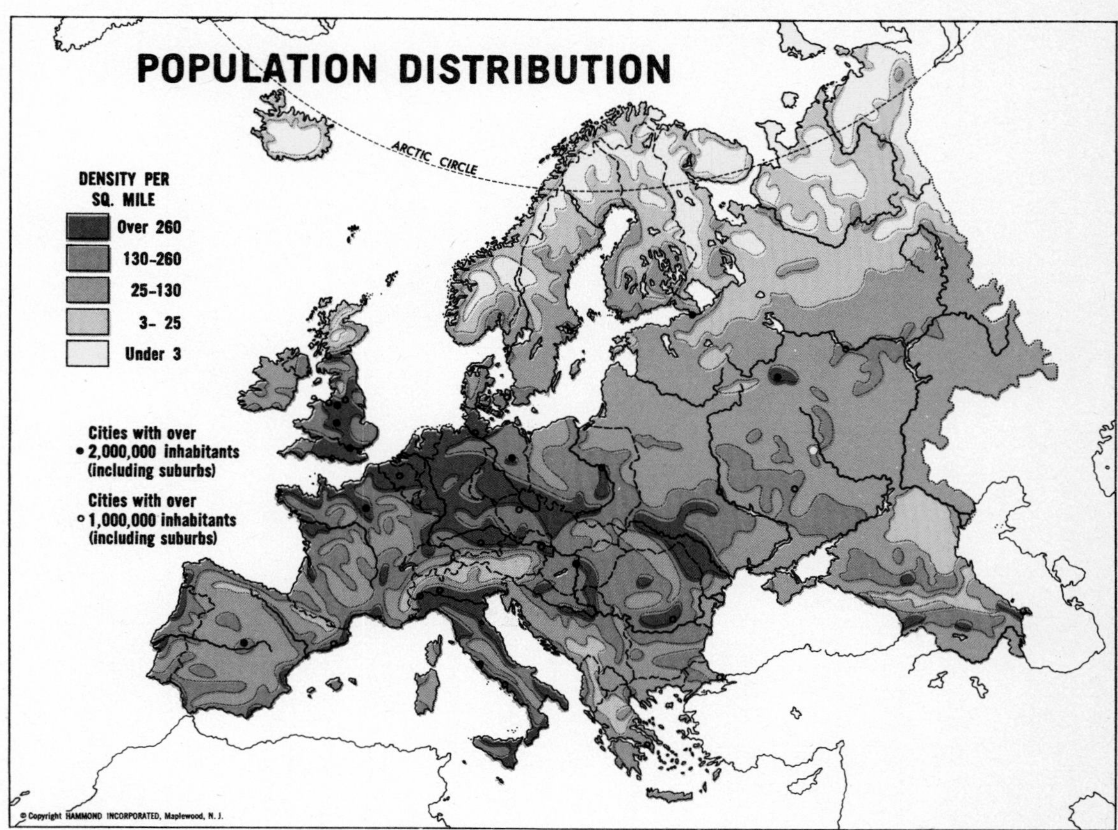

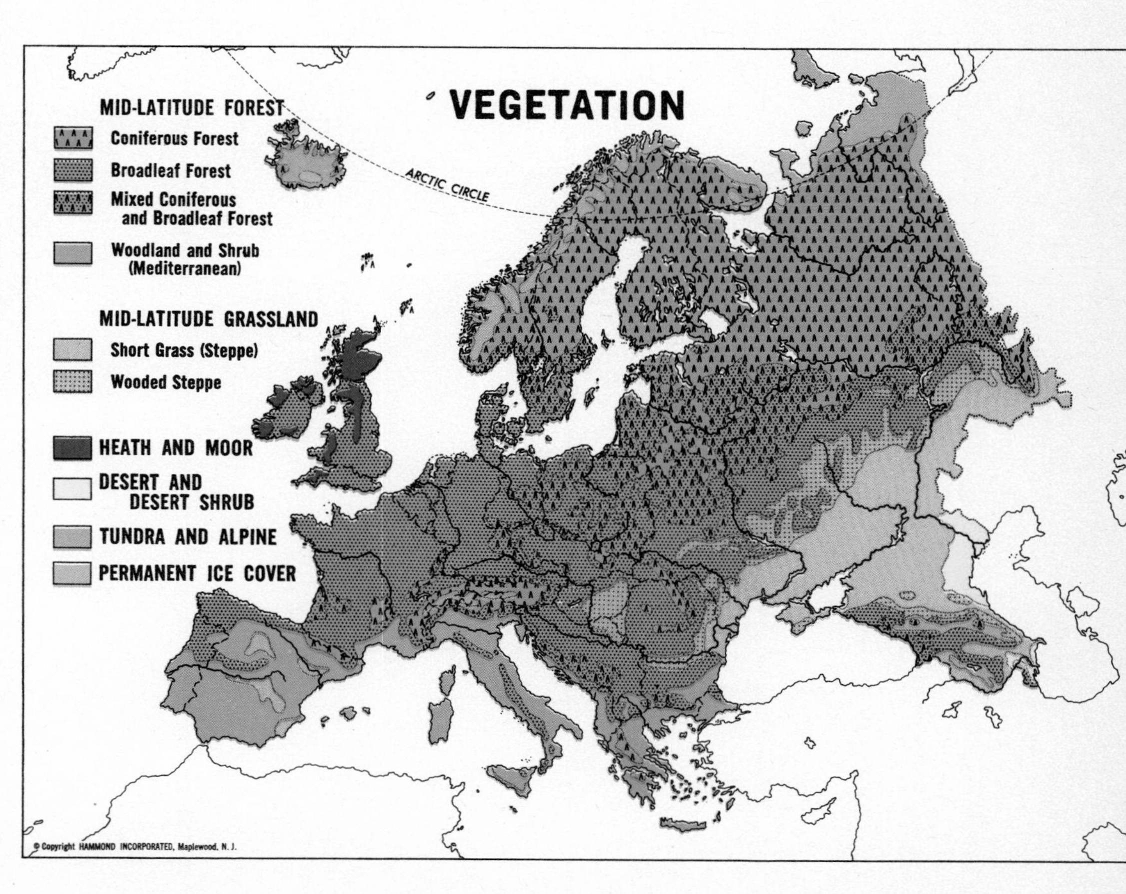

Reykjavík (cap.), Iceland .... B 2
Rhine (river) .... E 4
Rhodope (mts.) .... G 4
Rhône (river) .... E 4
Riga, U.S.S.R. .... G 3
Rome (cap.), Italy .... F 4
Rostov, U.S.S.R. .... J 4
Rotterdam, Neth. .... E 3
Rumania .... G 4
Russian S.F.S.R., U.S.S.R. .... J 4
Saint George's (chan.) .... D 3
Salonika, Greece .... G 4
Salzburg, Austria .... F 4
San Marino .... F 4
Saragossa, Spain .... D 4
Sarajevo, Yugoslavia .... F 4
Saratov, U.S.S.R. .... J 3
Sardinia (Sardegna) (isl.), Italy .... E 5
Sava (river) .... F 4
Scotland .... D 3
Seine (river), France .... E 4
Seville, Spain .... D 5
Shetland (isls.), Scotland .... D 2
Sicily (Sicilia) (isl.), Italy .... F 5
Skagerrak (strait) .... E 3
Sofia (cap.), Bulgaria .... G 4
Sognefjord (fjord), Norway .... E 2
Southampton, England .... D 3
Spain .... D 4
Stockholm (cap.), Sweden .... G 3
Strasbourg, France .... E 4
Stuttgart, W. Germany .... E 4
Sweden .... F 2
Switzerland .... E 4
Szeged, Hungary .... F 4
Tagus (Tajo, Tejo) (riv.) .... D 5
Tampere, Finland .... G 2
Taranto (gulf), Italy .... F 5
Tbilisi, U.S.S.R. .... J 4
Tiber (riv.), Italy .... F 4
Tiranë (cap.), Albania .... F 4
Trieste, Italy .... F 4
Trondheim, Norway .... F 2
Turin (Torino), Italy .... E 4
Turku, Finland .... G 2
Tyrrhenian (sea) .... F 5
Ufa, U.S.S.R. .... K 3
Ukranian, S.S.R., U.S.S.R. .... H 4
Union of Soviet Socialist Republics .... H 3
United Kingdom .... D 3
Ural (mts.), U.S.S.R. .... L 2
Ural (river), U.S.S.R. .... K 4
Valencia, Spain .... E 5
Varna, Bulgaria .... G 4
Vatican City .... F 4
Venice (Venezia), Italy .... F 4
Vesuvius (mt.), Italy .... F 4
Vienna (cap.), Austria .... F 4
Vistula (riv.), Poland .... F 3
Volga (river), U.S.S.R. .... J 4
Volgograd, U.S.S.R. .... J 4
Wales .... D 3
Warsaw (cap.), Poland .... G 3
Weser (river), Germany .... E 3
West Germany .... E 3
White (sea), U.S.S.R. .... H 2
White Russian S.S.R., U.S.S.R. .... G 3
Wrocław, Poland .... F 3
Yugoslavia .... F 4
Zagreb, Yugoslavia .... F 4
Zürich, Switzerland .... E 4

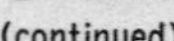

8 Europe
(continued)

30° 20° 10° 0° 10° 20° 30° 40° 50° 60°

ICELAND Reykjavík Horn Fontur Arctic Circle NORWEGIAN SEA Faeroe Is. (Den.) Shetland Is. Orkney Is. Hebrides Moray Firth Aberdeen Ben Nevis UNITED KINGDOM Glasgow Belfast U.K. IRELAND Dublin IRISH SEA Liverpool Birmingham London C. Clear St. Georges Chan. Land's End English Channel Channel Is. (U.K.) NORTH SEA Lindesnes Skagerrak Hardangerfjord

Nordkapp Sørøy Hammerfest Vesterålen Lofoten Is. Vestfjord Kiruna Tromsø BARENTS SEA Kolguyev I. Kanin Pen. Cheshskaya Bay Murmansk Kola Pen. WHITE SEA Archangel Northern Dvina Oulu Gulf of Bothnia FINLAND Tampere Helsinki Lake Ladoga Lake Onega Leningrad Gulf of Finland Trondheim Glittertind Sundsvall Bergen Oslo Åland Is. Västerås Stockholm Vänern Hiiumaa Saaremaa Gotland NORWAY SWEDEN Göteborg Kattegat DENMARK Copenhagen BALTIC SEA Bornholm Rügen Riga Gdańsk Western Dvina Minsk Moscow Volga Gor'kiy UNION OF SOVIET SOCIALIST REPUBLICS

Frisian Is. NETHERLANDS Amsterdam Hamburg Elbe EAST GERMANY Berlin POLAND Vistula Warsaw Łódź Bug Kiev Khar'kov Don Dnieper Donetsk WEST GERMANY Weser BELGIUM Brussels Cologne Bonn Leipzig Oder Prague CZECHOSLOVAKIA Cracow L'vov Brno Le Havre Seine Paris LUX. Stuttgart Danube Carpathians Prut Odessa SEA OF AZOV Crimea Krasnodar Nantes Loire FRANCE Rhine Munich Vienna AUSTRIA Budapest HUNGARY Cluj RUMANIA Bay of Biscay Bordeaux Dordogne Garonne Lyon Rhône Bern SWITZ. LIECH. Graz Zagreb Sava Belgrade Bucharest YUGOSLAVIA Danube Balkan Mts. BLACK SEA C. Finisterre Bilbao Pyrenees Oporto Douro Ebro SPAIN Saragossa Madrid Tagus Lisbon PORTUGAL Guadiana Valencia Barcelona Gulf of Lions Marseille MONACO Genoa Milan Turin Venice SAN MARINO ADRIATIC SEA Apennines Corsica VATICAN CITY Rome Naples Sardinia ITALY Sofia BULGARIA Skopje Tiranë ALBANIA Istanbul Bosporus Sea of Marmara Thessaloniki Ankara TURKEY C. de São Vicente Balearic Is. Minorca Majorca Ibiza Cádiz Málaga Str. of Gibraltar GIBRALTAR (U.K.) Tangier TYRRHENIAN SEA C. Teulada MEDITERRANEAN SEA IONIAN SEA GREECE Lésvos Évvoia AEGEAN SEA Athens Izmir Rabat Casablanca MOROCCO Oran Algiers Constantine ALGERIA C. Bon Tunis TUNISIA Palermo Sicily Etna 11,053 C. Passero MALTA Valletta C. Taínaron Crete Rhodes CYPRUS Nicosia LEBANON Beirut AFRICA

Longitude West of Greenwich 0° Longitude East of Greenwich 10° 20° 30°

VEGETATION/RELIEF

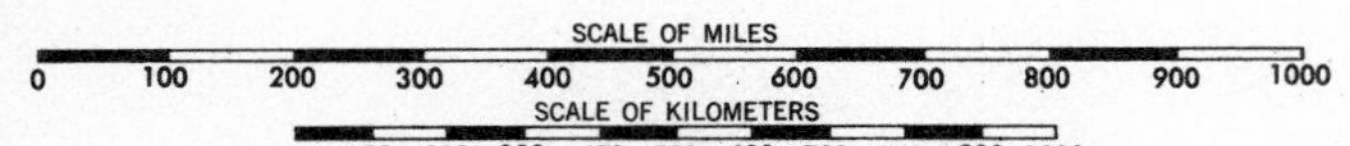

Capitals of Countries
International Boundaries
Canals
Elevations in Feet
Depths in Fathoms

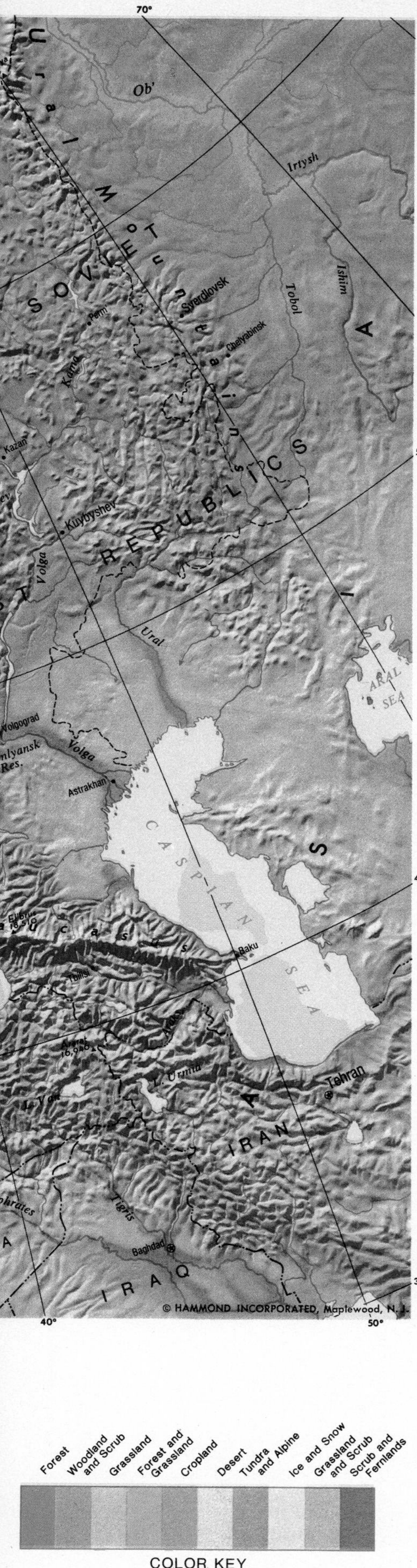
Ob'
Irtysh
Tobol
Ishim
Sverdlovsk
Chelyabinsk
Perm
Kama
Kazan
Kuybyshev
Volga
Ural
Volgograd
Astrakhan
ARAL SEA
CASPIAN SEA
Baku
Tbilisi
Tehran
IRAN
IRAQ
Baghdad
Tigris
Urmia
SOVIET SOCIALIST REPUBLICS
© HAMMOND INCORPORATED, Maplewood, N.J.
Forest
Woodland and Scrub
Grassland
Forest and Grassland
Cropland
Desert
Tundra and Alpine
Ice and Snow
Grassland and Scrub
Scrub and Fernlands
COLOR KEY

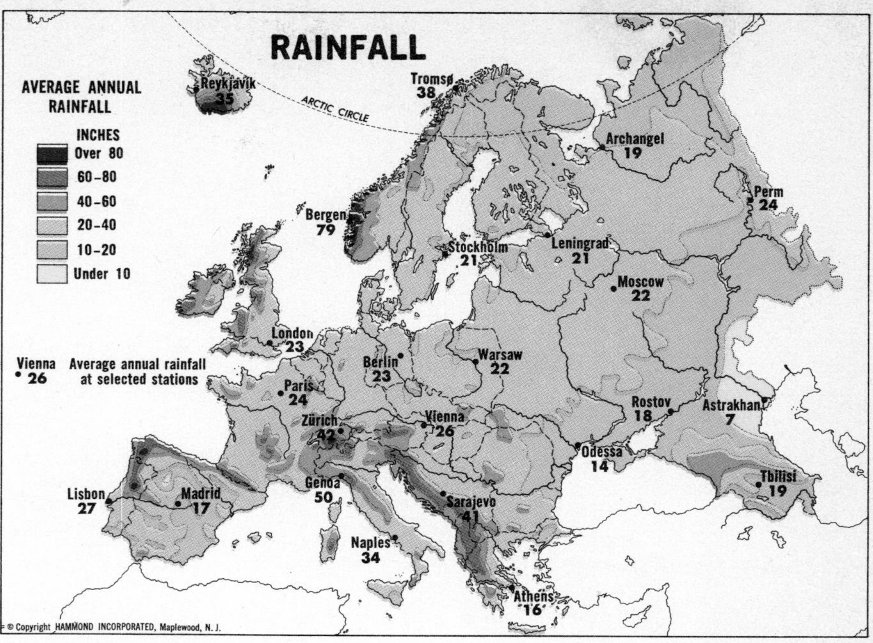
RAINFALL
AVERAGE ANNUAL RAINFALL
INCHES
Over 80
60-80
40-60
20-40
10-20
Under 10
Vienna 26 Average annual rainfall at selected stations
ARCTIC CIRCLE
Reykjavík 35
Tromsø 38
Archangel 19
Perm 24
Bergen 79
Stockholm 21
Leningrad 21
Moscow 22
London 23
Warsaw 22
Berlin 23
Paris 24
Rostov 18
Astrakhan 7
Zürich 42
Vienna 26
Odessa 14
Tbilisi 19
Lisbon 27
Madrid 17
Genoa 50
Sarajevo 41
Naples 34
Athens 16
© Copyright HAMMOND INCORPORATED, Maplewood, N. J.

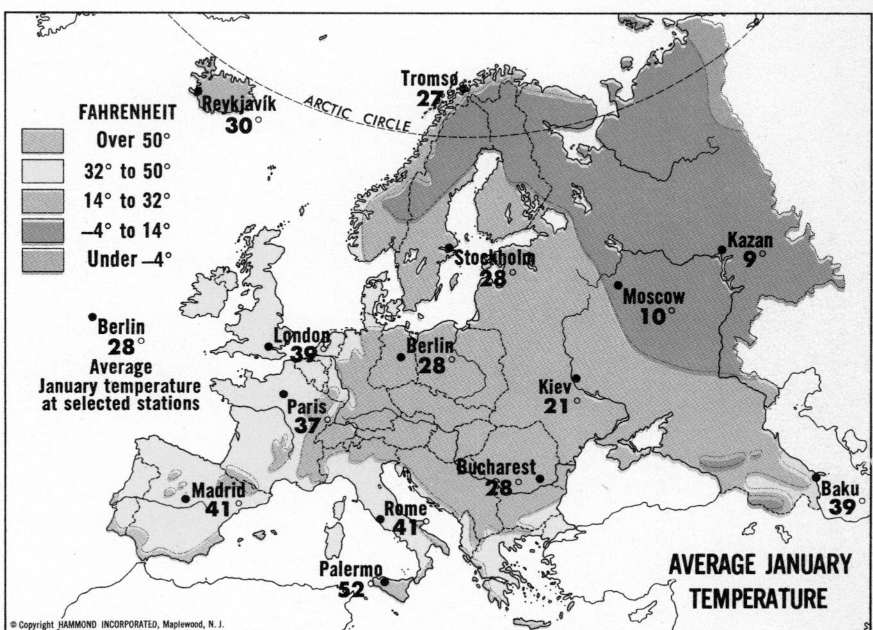
FAHRENHEIT
Over 50°
32° to 50°
14° to 32°
–4° to 14°
Under –4°
Berlin 28° Average January temperature at selected stations
ARCTIC CIRCLE
Reykjavík 30°
Tromsø 27°
Kazan 9°
Stockholm 28°
Moscow 10°
London 39°
Berlin 28°
Kiev 21°
Paris 37°
Bucharest 28°
Baku 39°
Madrid 41°
Rome 41°
Palermo 52°
AVERAGE JANUARY TEMPERATURE
© Copyright HAMMOND INCORPORATED, Maplewood, N. J.

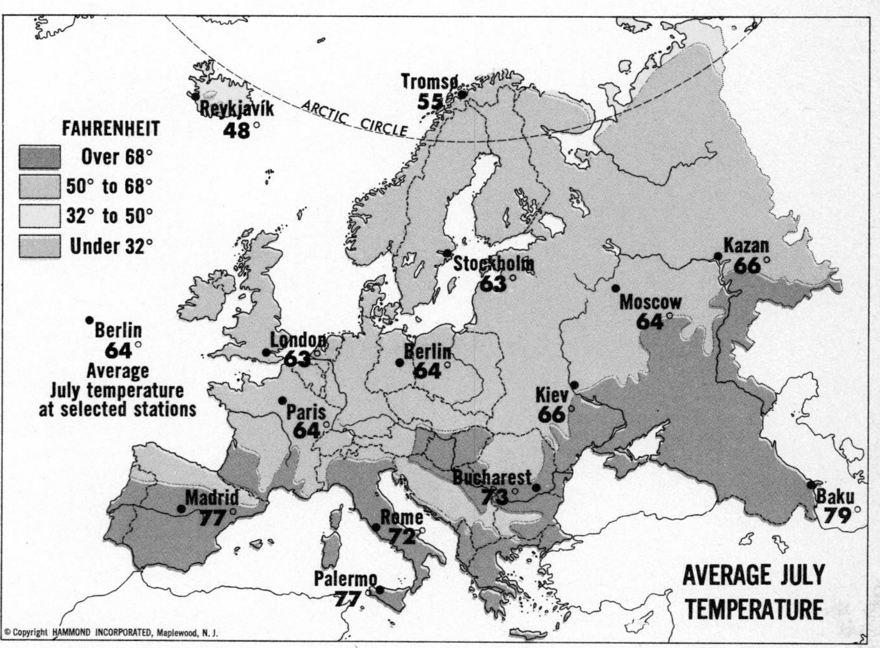
FAHRENHEIT
Over 68°
50° to 68°
32° to 50°
Under 32°
Berlin 64° Average July temperature at selected stations
ARCTIC CIRCLE
Reykjavík 48°
Tromsø 55°
Kazan 66°
Stockholm 63°
Moscow 64°
London 63°
Berlin 64°
Kiev 66°
Paris 64°
Bucharest 73°
Madrid 77°
Rome 72°
Baku 79°
Palermo 77°
AVERAGE JULY TEMPERATURE
© Copyright HAMMOND INCORPORATED, Maplewood, N. J.

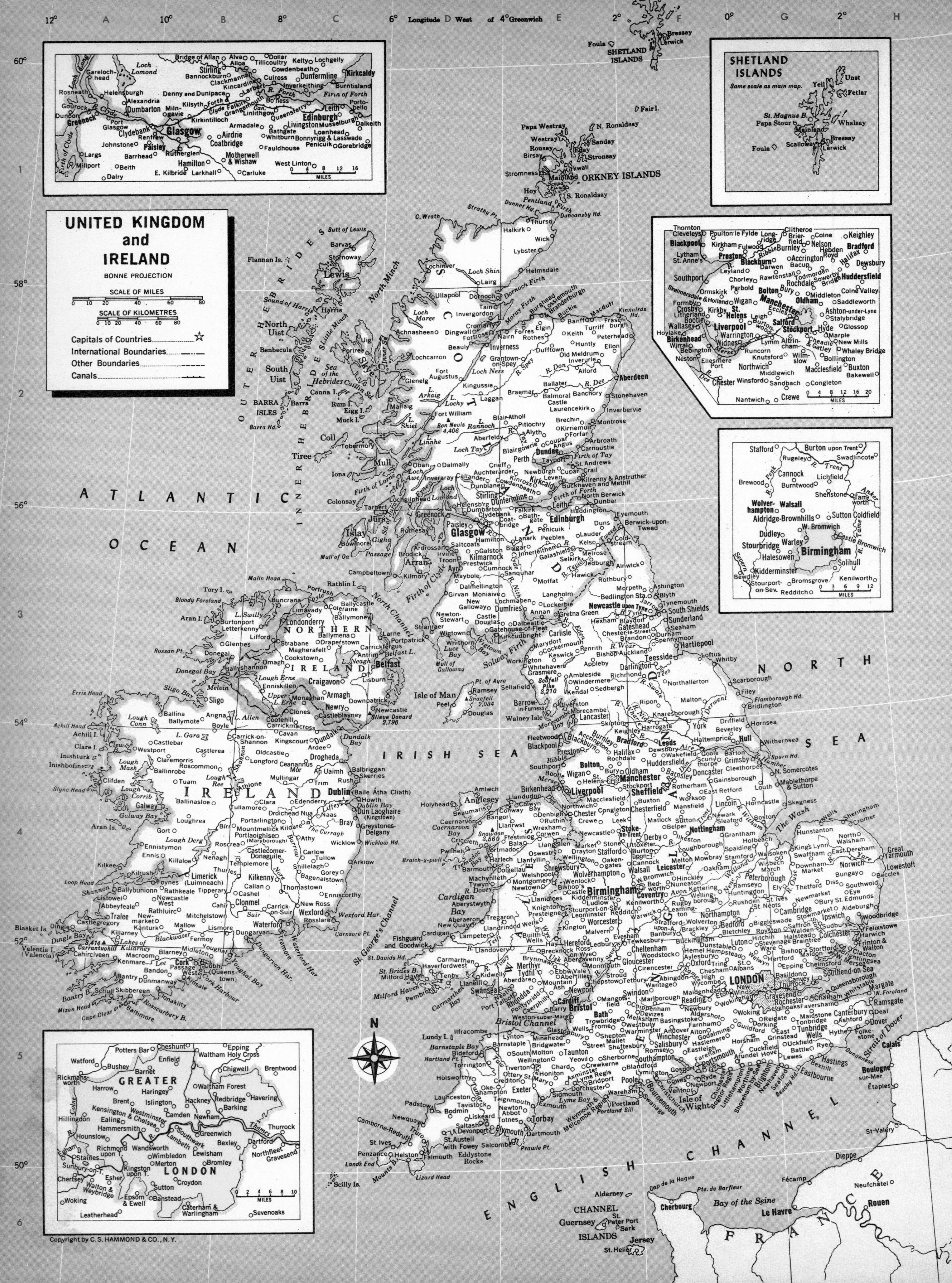

UNITED KINGDOM
and
IRELAND
BONNE PROJECTION
SCALE OF MILES
0 10 20 40 60 80
SCALE OF KILOMETRES
0 10 20 40 60 80
Capitals of Countries
International Boundaries
Other Boundaries
Canals
Longitude West of 4° Greenwich
SHETLAND ISLANDS
Same scale as main map.
ORKNEY ISLANDS
OUTER HEBRIDES
INNER HEBRIDES
SCOTLAND
ENGLAND
WALES
NORTHERN IRELAND
IRELAND
ATLANTIC OCEAN
NORTH SEA
IRISH SEA
ENGLISH CHANNEL
North Channel
St. George's Channel
Bristol Channel
Strait of Dover
CHANNEL ISLANDS
FRANCE
Bay of the Seine
GREATER LONDON
Edinburgh
Glasgow
Belfast
Dublin (Baile Átha Cliath)
Cardiff
LONDON
Birmingham
Manchester
Liverpool
Copyright by C. S. HAMMOND & CO., N.Y.

UNITED KINGDOM

AREA 94,214 sq. mi.
POPULATION 55,534,000
CAPITAL London
LARGEST CITY London
HIGHEST POINT Ben Nevis 4,406 ft.
MONETARY UNIT pound sterling
MAJOR LANGUAGES English, Gaelic, Welsh
MAJOR RELIGIONS Protestantism, Roman Catholicism

IRELAND

AREA 26,600 sq. mi.
POPULATION 2,944,000
CAPITAL Dublin
LARGEST CITY Dublin
HIGHEST POINT Carrantuohill 3,414 ft.
MONETARY UNIT Irish pound
MAJOR LANGUAGES English, Gaelic
MAJOR RELIGION Roman Catholicism

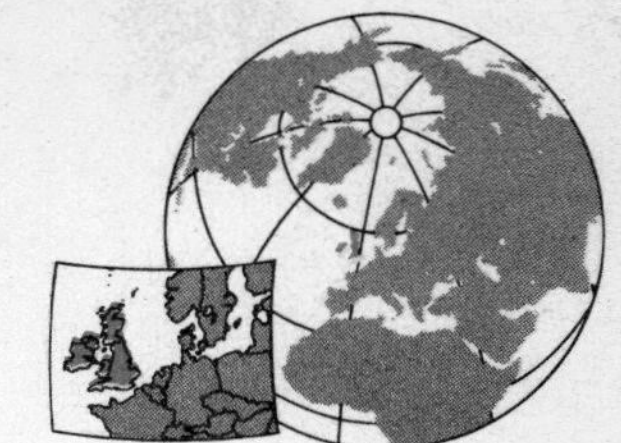

UNITED KINGDOM

IRELAND

ENGLAND

AREA 50,327 sq. mi.
POPULATION 46,102,300
CAPITAL London
LARGEST CITY London
HIGHEST POINT Scafell Pike 3,210 ft.

WALES

AREA 8,017 sq. mi.
POPULATION 2,724,540
LARGEST CITY Cardiff
HIGHEST POINT Snowdon 3,560 ft.

SCOTLAND

AREA 30,411 sq. mi.
POPULATION 5,194,700
CAPITAL Edinburgh
LARGEST CITY Glasgow
HIGHEST POINT Ben Nevis 4,406 ft.

NORTHERN IRELAND

AREA 5,459 sq. mi.
POPULATION 1,512,500
CAPITAL Belfast
LARGEST CITY Belfast
HIGHEST POINT Slieve Donard 2,796 ft.

UNITED KINGDOM

Index .... Page
GREATER LONDON 11
BIRMINGHAM AREA 11
LIVERPOOL-MANCHESTER AREA 11
ENGLAND 11,12
WALES 12
ISLE OF MAN 12
CHANNEL ISLANDS 12
SCOTLAND 12,14
NORTHERN IRELAND 16

IRELAND

Index .... Page 16

GREATER LONDON

CITIES and TOWNS

Banstead, 44,790 .... B 6
Barking, 167,960 .... C 5
Barnet, 314,530 .... B 5
Bexley, 215,610 .... C 5
Brent, 281,530 .... B 5
Brentwood, 58,250 .... C 5
Bromley, 303,550 .... B 5
Bushey, 25,290 .... B 5
Camden, 228,080 .... B 5
Caterham and Warlingham, 37,760 .... B 6
Chertsey, 45,250 .... B 6
Cheshunt, 43,890 .... B 5
Chigwell, 56,030 .... C 5
Croydon, 327,130 .... B 6
Dartford, 46,280 .... C 5
Ealing, 297,910 .... B 5
Egham, 30,800 .... B 5
Enfield, 265,600 .... B 5
Epping, 11,380 .... C 5
Epsom and Ewell, 72,190 .... B 6
Esher, 63,190 .... B 6
Gravesend, 55,310 .... C 5
Greenwich, 228,030 .... C 5
Hackney, 238,530 .... B 5
Hammersmith, 192,810 .... B 5
Haringey, 242,300 .... B 5
Harrow, 207,700 .... B 5
Havering, 252,860 .... C 5
Hillingdon, 237,050 .... B 5
Hounslow, 205,060 .... B 5
Islington, 235,990 .... B 5
Kensington and Chelsea, 208,480 .... B 5
Kingston-upon-Thames, 143,670 .... B 6
Lambeth, 325,070 .... B 5
Leatherhead, 39,200 .... B 6
Lewisham, 282,080 .... B 5
London (cap.), 7,703,410 .... B 5
London, ‡12,956,440 .... B 5
Merton, 183,570 .... B 5
Newham, 252,090 .... B 5
Northfleet, 25,450 .... C 5
Potters Bar, 25,240 .... B 5
Redbridge, 244,800 .... C 5
Richmond-upon-Thames, 176,600 .... B 5
Rickmansworth, 30,360 .... A 5
Sevenoaks, 18,150 .... C 6
Southwark, 290,530 .... B 5
Staines, 56,610 .... B 5
Sunbury-on-Thames, 40,120 .... B 6
Sutton, 166,430 .... B 6
Thurrock, 124,830 .... C 5
Waltham Forest, 235,880 .... B 5
Waltham Holy Cross, 13,670 .... B 5
Walton and Weybridge, 52,530 .... B 6
Wandsworth, 319,190 .... B 5
Watford, 76,700 .... B 5
Westminster, 240,360 .... B 5
Wimbledon, 57,312 .... B 5
Woking, 78,180 .... B 6

OTHER FEATURES

Colne (river) .... A 5
Thames (river) .... C 5

BIRMINGHAM AREA

CITIES and TOWNS

Aldridge-Brownhills, 87,530 .... G 3
Bewdley, 6,400 .... F 3
Birmingham, 1,086,400 .... G 3
Birmingham, *2,440,540 .... G 3
Brewood, 5,751 .... F 2
Bromsgrove, 39,440 .... G 3
Burntwood, †12,085 .... G 2
Burton-on-Trent, 50,850 .... G 2
Cannock, 54,540 .... G 2
Castle Bromwich, 9,205 .... G 3
Dudley, 181,380 .... G 3
Halesowen, 51,930 .... G 3
Kenilworth, 21,000 .... G 3
Kidderminster, 46,740 .... G 3
Lichfield, 22,930 .... G 2
Redditch, 37,910 .... G 3
Rugeley, 19,320 .... G 2
Shenstone, 5,174 .... G 3
Solihull, 110,350 .... G 3
Stafford, 54,200 .... G 2
Stourbridge, 52,290 .... G 3
Stourport-on-Severn, 16,090 .... G 3
Sutton Coldfield, 82,220 .... G 3
Swadlincote, 20,130 .... G 2
Tamworth, 37,360 .... G 3
Walsall, 184,260 .... G 3
Warley, 167,810 .... G 3
West Bromwich, 171,850 .... G 3
Wolverhampton, 264,520 .... G 3

OTHER FEATURES

Anker (river) .... G 3
Penk (river) .... G 2
Severn (river) .... F 3
Tame (river) .... G 3
Trent (river) .... G 2

LIVERPOOL-MANCHESTER AREA

CITIES and TOWNS

Accrington, 36,340 .... G 1
Altrincham, 41,000 .... G 2
Ashton-under-Lyne, 48,180 .... G 2
Bacup, 16,270 .... G 1
Bakewell, 4,170 .... G 2
Bebington, 57,060 .... F 2
Birkenhead, 141,950 .... F 2
Blackburn, 100,010 .... G 1
Blackpool, 146,700 .... F 1
Bollington, 6,150 .... G 2
Bolton, 152,500 .... G 2
Bootle, 79,950 .... F 2
Bradford, 293,210 .... H 1
Brierfield, 7,290 .... G 1
Burnley, 76,610 .... G 1
Burtonwood, †2,766 .... G 2
Bury, 67,070 .... G 2
Buxton, 20,100 .... G 2
Cheadle and Gatley, 57,290 .... G 2
Chester, 60,880 .... F 2
Chorley, 30,990 .... G 2
Clitheroe, 12,910 .... G 1
Colne, 18,890 .... G 1
Colne Valley, 21,000 .... G 2
Congleton, 19,610 .... G 2
Crewe, 51,960 .... G 2
Crosby, 58,580 .... F 2
Darwen, 28,500 .... G 1
Dewsbury, 51,560 .... H 2
Eccles, 39,830 .... G 2
Ellesmere Port, 56,750 .... F 2
Formby, 21,730 .... F 2
Fulwood, 19,880 .... G 1
Glossop, 21,830 .... G 2
Halifax, 93,570 .... G 1
Hebden Royd, 8,800 .... G 1
Hoylake, 32,190 .... F 2
Huddersfield, 130,600 .... G 2
Hyde, 38,710 .... G 2
Keighley, 55,400 .... H 1
Kirkby, 65,260 .... F 2
Kirkham, 6,380 .... F 1
Knutsford, 11,900 .... G 2
Leigh, 46,200 .... G 2
Leyland, 23,100 .... F 1
Litherland, 24,540 .... F 2
Liverpool, 677,450 .... F 2
Liverpool, *1,341,660 .... F 2
Longridge, 6,170 .... G 1
Lymm, 9,380 .... G 2
Lytham Saint Anne's, 37,000 .... F 1
Macclesfield, 41,870 .... G 2
Manchester, 593,770 .... G 2
Manchester, *2,433,370 .... G 2
Marple, 24,100 .... G 2
Middleton, 57,510 .... G 2
Middlewich, 8,000 .... G 2
Nantwich, 11,200 .... G 2
Nelson, 31,230 .... G 1
Neston, 16,940 .... F 2
New Mills, 8,880 .... G 2
Northwich, 18,940 .... G 2
Oldham, 108,280 .... G 2
Ormskirk, 25,900 .... F 2
Parbold, †976 .... G 2
Poulton le Fylde, 16,150 .... F 1
Preston, 102,100 .... F 1
Rawtenstall, 21,640 .... G 2
Rochdale, 86,600 .... G 2
Runcorn, 31,560 .... G 2
Saddleworth, 19,620 .... G 2
Saint Helens, 102,770 .... F 2
Salford, 137,750 .... G 2
Sandbach, 12,160 .... G 2
Skelmersdale and Holland, 23,640 .... F 2
Southport, 79,430 .... F 2
Sowerby Bridge, 16,610 .... G 2
Stalybridge, 21,620 .... G 2
Stockport, 140,030 .... G 2
Thornton Cleveleys, 26,250 .... F 1
Todmorden, 15,430 .... G 2
Wallasey, 101,360 .... F 2
Warrington, 70,870 .... F 2
Whaley Bridge, 5,390 .... G 2
Widnes, 55,120 .... F 2
Wigan, 79,780 .... G 2
Wilmslow, 28,790 .... G 2
Winsford, 22,040 .... G 2
Wirral, 26,000 .... F 2

OTHER FEATURES

Dee (river) .... F 2
Irish (sea) .... F 2
Mersey (river) .... F 2
Ribble (river) .... G 1

ENGLAND

(map on page 13)

COUNTIES

Bedfordshire, 443,960 .... G 5
Berkshire, 623,540 .... F 6
Buckinghamshire, 578,210 .... G 6
Cambridgeshire and Isle of Ely, 302,560 .... H 5
Cheshire, 1,512,820 .... E 4
Cornwall, 362,180 .... C 7
Cumberland, 295,530 .... D 3
Derbyshire, 891,570 .... F 4
Devon, 881,590 .... D 7
Dorset, 348,840 .... E 7
Durham, 1,433,990 .... F 3
Essex, 1,314,680 .... H 6
Gloucestershire, 1,078,050 .... E 6
Hampshire (Hants), 1,551,900 .... F 6
Herefordshire, 142,060 .... E 5
Hertfordshire, 903,390 .... G 6
Huntingdon and Peterborough, 196,670 .... G 5
Isle of Wight, 102,100 .... F 7
Kent, 1,388,820 .... H 6
Lancashire, 5,182,380 .... E 4
Leicestershire, 740,170 .... F 5
Lincolnshire-Holland, 105,170 .... G 5
Lincolnshire-Kesteven, 233,040 .... G 5
Lincolnshire-Lindsey, 464,350 .... G 4
London (greater), 7,703,410 .... G 6
Norfolk, 609,930 .... H 5
Northamptonshire, 453,920 .... G 5
Northumberland, 823,030 .... E 2
Nottinghamshire, 969,730 .... F 4
Oxfordshire, 374,610 .... F 6
Rutland, 29,860 .... G 5
Shropshire (Salop), 332,330 .... E 5
Somerset, 664,690 .... E 6
Southampton (Hampshire), 1,551,900 .... F 6
Staffordshire, 1,846,970 .... E 5
Suffolk, East, 384,210 .... J 5
Suffolk, West, 163,760 .... G 7
Surrey, 1,002,140 .... G 6
Sussex, East, 736,050 .... H 7
Sussex, West, 469,900 .... G 7
Warwickshire, 2,139,640 .... F 5
Westmorland, 71,710 .... E 3
Wight, Isle of, 102,100 .... F 7
Wiltshire, 496,930 .... F 6
Worcestershire, 683,820 .... E 5
Yorkshire-East Riding, 545,430 .... G 4
Yorkshire-North Riding, 721,870 .... F 3
Yorkshire-West Riding, 3,800,750 .... F 4

CITIES and TOWNS

Abingdon, 17,820 .... F 6
Accrington, 36,340 .... E 4
Aldershot, 38,120 .... G 6
Alfreton, 22,440 .... F 4
Andover, 24,780 .... F 6
Arnold, 31,780 .... G 4
Ashford, 35,360 .... H 6
Ashington, 25,830 .... F 2
Aylesbury, 36,730 .... G 6
Banbury, 27,900 .... F 5
Barnet, 314,530 .... G 6
Barnsley, 74,880 .... F 4
Barnstaple, 16,850 .... C 6
Barrow-in-Furness, 63,460 .... D 3
Basildon, 122,760 .... H 6
Basingstoke, 43,570 .... F 6
Bath, 84,760 .... E 6
Batley, 40,276 .... F 4
Bedford, 68,650 .... G 5
Bedlington Station (Bedlingtonshire), 30,040 .... F 2
Bedworth, 40,700 .... F 5
Beeston and Stapleford, 63,600 .... F 5
Belper, 16,360 .... F 4
Benfleet, 46,270 .... H 6
Berwick-upon-Tweed, 11,530 .... F 2
Beverley, 17,320 .... G 4
Bexhill, 33,470 .... H 7
Bideford, 11,240 .... C 6
Birkenhead, 141,950 .... D 4
Birmingham, 1,086,400 .... F 5
Birmingham, *2,440,540 .... F 5
Bishop Auckland, 34,480 .... F 3
Bishop's Stortford, 21,270 .... H 6
Blackburn, 100,010 .... E 4
Blackpool, 146,700 .... D 4
Blaydon, 32,000 .... F 3
Bletchley, 28,300 .... G 5
Blyth, 35,130 .... F 2
Bognor Regis, 31,710 .... G 7
Bolsover, 11,770 .... F 4
Bolton, 152,500 .... E 4
Bootle, 79,950 .... D 4
Boston, 25,260 .... H 5
Bournemouth, 149,820 .... F 7
Bracknell, 20,378 .... G 6
Bradford, 293,210 .... F 4
Braintree and Bocking, 23,380 .... H 6
Brandon and Byshottles, 18,490 .... F 3
Brentwood, 58,250 .... H 6
Bridgwater, 26,800 .... D 6
Bridlington, 26,430 .... G 3
Brighouse, 33,130 .... F 4
Brighton, 163,600 .... G 7
Bristol, 427,230 .... E 6
Broadstairs and St. Peter's, 20,900 .... J 6
Bromsgrove, 39,440 .... E 5
Burgess Hill, 17,980 .... G 7
Burnham-on-Sea, 11,530 .... D 6
Burnley, 76,610 .... E 4
Burton-upon-Trent, 50,850 .... F 5
Bury, 67,070 .... E 4
Bury Saint Edmunds, 25,140 .... H 5
Buxton, 20,100 .... F 4
Camborne-Redruth, 38,380 .... B 7
Cambridge, 100,200 .... H 5
Cannock, 54,540 .... E 5
Canterbury, 33,140 .... J 6
Carlisle, 71,090 .... D 3
Carlton, 42,640 .... G 5
Castleford, 39,160 .... F 4

(continued on following page)

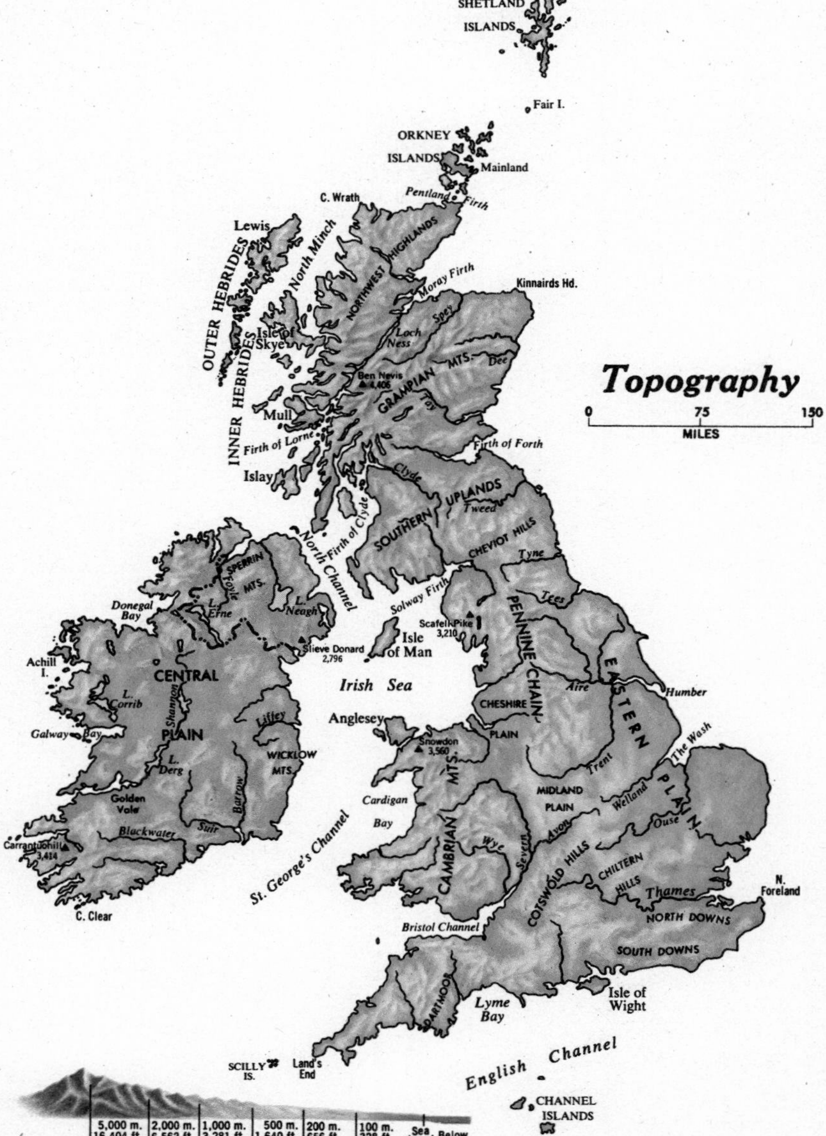

12 United Kingdom and Ireland

(continued)

ENGLAND (continued)

Caterham and Warlingham, 37,760 G 6
Chatham, 55,460 H 6
Cheadle and Gatley, 57,290 F 5
Chelmsford, 56,900 H 6
Cheltenham, 76,000 E 6
Chesham, 20,750 G 6
Cheshunt, 43,890 G 6
Chester, 60,880 E 4
Chesterfield, 70,420 F 4
Chester-le-Street, 20,800 F 3
Chichester, 20,740 G 7
Chippenham, 18,970 E 6
Chorley, 30,990 E 4
Christchurch, 31,780 F 7
Cirencester, 13,080 F 6
Clacton, 35,730 J 6
Cleethorpes, 35,370 H 4
Clevedon, 13,980 E 6
Clitheroe, 12,910 E 4
Coalville, 28,470 F 5
Colchester, 75,210 H 6
Colne, 18,890 E 4
Congleton, 19,610 E 4
Consett, 37,010 F 3
Corby, 49,210 G 5
Coventry, 335,650 F 5
Cowes, 18,000 F 7
Crawley, 64,520 G 6
Crewe, 51,960 E 4
Crook and Willington, 23,050 F 3
Croydon, 327,130 G 6
Cuckfield, 24,640 G 6
Dalton-in-Furness, 11,000 D 3
Darlington, 84,700 F 3
Dawley, 24,240 E 5
Deal, 27,130 J 6
Derby, 221,240 F 5
Dewsbury, 51,560 F 4
Doncaster, 84,050 G 4
Dorchester, 13,660 E 7
Dorking, 22,850 G 6
Dover, 35,640 J 6
Dunstable, 29,780 G 6
Durham, 25,780 F 3
Ealing, 297,910 G 6
East Grinstead, 8,390 G 6
East Retford, 18,860 G 4
Eastbourne, 69,290 H 7
Eastleigh, 45,100 F 7
Ellesmere Port, 56,750 E 4
Ely, 10,020 H 5
Epping, 11,380 H 6
Evesham, 13,170 F 5
Exeter, 92,880 D 7
Exmouth, 23,630 D 7
Falmouth, 17,350 B 7
Fareham, 79,740 F 7
Farnborough, 42,060 G 6
Farnham, 30,150 G 6
Faversham, 14,610 J 6
Felixstowe, 19,310 J 6
Fleet, 21,900 G 6
Fleetwood, 28,970 D 4
Folkestone, 45,270 J 6
Frinton and Walton, 12,060 J 6
Frome, 12,600 E 6
Gainsborough, 17,680 G 4
Gateshead, 100,060 F 3
Gillingham, 90,840 H 6
Glossop, 21,830 F 4
Gloucester, 90,530 E 6
Godalming, 18,230 G 6
Goole, 18,430 G 4
Gosport, 76,160 F 7
Grantham, 26,630 G 5
Gravesend, 55,310 H 6
Great Yarmouth, 50,760 J 5
Greenwich, 228,030 H 6
Grimsby, 96,500 H 4
Guildford, 55,890 G 6
Guisborough, 13,000 G 3
Halifax, 93,570 F 4
Haltemprice, 51,790 G 4
Harlow, 76,240 H 6
Harrogate, 62,680 F 4
Hartlepool, 98,710 F 3
Harwich, 14,870 J 6
Haslemere, 13,560 G 6
Haslingden, 14,280 E 4
Hastings, 69,020 H 7
Heanor, 24,470 F 4
Hemel Hempstead, 66,200 G 6
Hereford, 47,170 E 5
Herne Bay, 24,510 J 6
Hertford, 19,180 G 6
Hetton, 17,250 F 3
Heysham (Morecambe and Heysham), 40,880 D 3
High Wycombe, 57,360 G 6
Hinckley, 45,070 F 5
Hitchin, 27,410 G 6
Horsham, 26,360 G 6
Hove, 71,190 G 7
Hoylake, 32,190 D 4
Hucknall, 26,440 F 4
Huddersfield, 130,600 F 4
Hull (Kingston-upon-Hull), 292,600 G 4
Huntingdon and Godmanchester, 15,650 G 5
Hythe, 11,700 H 6
Ilkeston, 35,400 F 5
Ilkley, 19,820 F 4
Ipswich, 122,050 J 5
Jarrow, 29,370 F 3
Keighley, 55,400 F 4
Kendal, 20,160 E 3
Kenilworth, 21,000 F 5
Kettering, 40,040 G 5
Keynsham, 18,670 E 6
Kidderminster, 46,740 E 5
King's Lynn, 30,650 H 5
Kingston-upon-Hull (Hull), 292,600 G 4
Kingston-upon-Thames, 143,670 G 6
Kingswood, 29,340 E 6
Kirkby-in-Ashfield, 22,610 F 4
Knottingley, 17,010 F 4
Knutsford, 11,900 E 4
Lancaster, 48,170 E 3
Leamington (Royal Leamington Spa), 45,090 F 5
Leatherhead, 39,200 G 6
Leeds, 503,720 F 4
Leeds, *1,727,300 F 4
Leek, 19,180 E 4
Leicester, 278,470 G 5
Leigh, 46,200 E 4
Leighton-Linslade, 19,370 G 6
Letchworth, 29,870 G 6
Lewes, 14,030 H 7
Leyland, 23,100 E 4
Lichfield, 22,930 F 5
Lincoln, 75,570 G 4
Littlehampton, 18,200 G 7
Liverpool, 677,450 D 4
Liverpool, *1,341,660 D 4
London (cap.), 7,703,410 G 6
London, ‡12,956,440 G 6
Long Eaton, 33,170 F 5
Loughborough, 40,190 F 5
Louth, 11,480 H 4
Lowestoft, 50,730 J 5
Luton, 156,690 G 6
Lymington, 33,510 F 7
Lytham Saint Anne's, 37,000 D 4
Macclesfield, 41,870 F 4
Maidenhead, 46,050 G 6
Maidstone, 67,400 H 6
Maldon, 12,920 H 6
Malvern, 29,810 E 5
Manchester, 593,770 E 4
Manchester, *2,433,370 E 4
Mangotsfield, 23,530 E 6
Mansfield, 56,210 F 4
March, 14,080 H 5
Margate, 49,080 J 6
Maryport, 12,000 D 3
Matlock, 20,240 F 4
Melton Mowbray, 18,440 G 5
Morecambe and Heysham, 40,880 E 3
Morley, 44,120 F 4
Morpeth, 14,620 F 2
Nantwich, 11,200 E 4
Nelson, 31,230 E 4
New Windsor, 31,270 G 6
Newark, 24,580 G 4
Newbury, 22,170 F 6
Newcastle (Newcastle-under-Lyme), 76,570 E 5
Newcastle upon Tyne, 240,340 F 2
Newcastle upon Tyne, *839,910 F 2
Newham, 252,090 H 6
Newmarket, 12,190 H 5
Newport, 21,440 F 7
Newquay, 12,420 B 7
Newton Abbot, 18,660 D 7
Northampton, 123,800 G 5
Northfleet, 25,450 H 6
Northwich, 18,940 E 4
Norton-Radstock, 14,540 E 6
Norwich, 118,800 J 5
Nottingham, 303,090 F 5
Nuneaton, 64,650 F 5
Oakengates, 15,770 E 5
Old Fletton, 13,330 G 5
Oldham, 108,280 E 4
Ormskirk, 25,900 E 4
Otley, 13,090 F 4
Oxford, 109,720 F 6
Penrith, 11,170 E 3
Penzance, 18,790 B 7
Peterborough, 66,800 G 5
Plymouth, 248,470 D 7
Pontefract, 30,820 F 4
Poole, 101,930 F 7
Portland, 12,780 E 7
Portslade-by-Sea, 18,420 G 7
Portsmouth, 214,800 G 7
Preston, 102,100 E 4
Prudhoe, 10,930 F 3
Queensborough-in-Sheppey, 28,790 G 5
Ramsgate, 39,140 J 6
Rawmarsh, 19,740 F 4
Reading, 127,530 F 6
Redditch, 37,910 F 5
Reigate, 57,830 G 6
Ripley, 17,910 F 4
Ripon, 11,840 F 3
Rochdale, 86,600 E 4
Rochester, 55,810 H 6
Rotherham, 86,450 F 4
Rugby, 57,700 F 5
Rugeley, 19,320 F 5
Runcorn, 31,560 E 4
Rushden, 18,130 G 5
Ryde, 22,290 F 7
Saint Albans, 52,680 G 6
Saint Austell with Fowey, 29,900 C 7
Saint Helens, 102,770 E 4
Salisbury, 36,440 F 6
Saltburn and Marske-by-the-Sea, 17,820 G 3
Sandbach, 12,160 E 4
Sandown-Shanklin, 14,030 F 7
Scarborough, 42,500 G 3
Scunthorpe, 69,720 G 4
Seaford, 15,600 H 7
Seaham, 24,800 F 3
Selby, 11,340 F 4
Sevenoaks, 18,150 H 6
Sheffield, 528,860 F 4
Shildon, 13,660 F 3
Shipley, 29,010 F 4
Shoreham-by-Sea, 18,050 G 7
Shrewsbury, 54,190 E 5
Sidmouth, 12,180 D 7
Sittingbourne and Milton, 30,820 H 6
Skegness, 12,680 H 4
Skelton and Brotton, 14,270 G 3
Skipton, 12,940 E 3
Slough, 92,750 G 6
South Shields, 106,150 F 3
Southampton, 210,000 F 7
Southend-on-Sea, 164,700 H 6
Southport, 79,430 D 4
Southwick, 11,360 G 7
Spalding, 16,300 G 5
Spennymoor, 18,400 F 3
Stafford, 54,200 E 5
Stalybridge, 21,620 F 4
Stamford, 14,000 G 5
Stockport, 140,030 E 4
Stoke-on-Trent, 272,260 E 4
Stourbridge, 52,290 E 5
Stourport-on-Severn, 16,090 E 5
Stratford-upon-Avon, 19,110 F 5
Stretford, 58,820 E 4
Stroud, 18,970 E 6
Sunderland, 218,970 F 3
Sutton-in-Ashfield, 40,570 F 4
Swindon, 98,290 F 6
Tamworth, 37,360 F 5
Taunton, 37,420 D 6
Teesside, 393,810 F 3
Teignmouth, 12,260 D 7
Thurrock, 124,830 H 6
Tiverton, 14,810 D 7
Tonbridge, 28,970 H 6
Torbay, 100,820 D 7
Trowbridge, 17,940 E 6
Truro, 14,590 C 7
Tunbridge Wells (Royal Tunbridge Wells), 44,930 H 6
Tynemouth, 72,390 F 2
Ulverston, 10,850 D 3
Wakefield, 59,630 F 4
Wallasey, 101,360 D 4
Wallsend, 47,120 F 2
Walsall, 184,260 F 5
Ware, 14,240 H 6
Warminster, 12,710 E 6
Warrington, 70,870 E 4
Warwick, 18,720 F 5
Watford, 76,700 G 6
Wellingborough, 35,680 G 5
Wellington, 16,890 E 5
Welwyn (Welwyn Garden City), 41,230 G 6
West Bromwich, 171,850 F 5
Weston-super-Mare, 47,960 E 6
Weymouth and Melcombe Regis, 42,120 E 7
Whitby, 12,130 G 3
Whitehaven, 26,760 D 3
Whitley Bay, 38,040 F 2
Whitstable, 23,780 J 6
Widnes, 55,120 E 4
Wigan, 79,780 E 4
Wigston, 28,130 G 5
Wilmslow, 28,790 E 4
Winchester, 31,070 F 6
Windsor (New Windsor), 31,270 G 6
Winsford, 22,050 E 4
Wisbech, 17,510 H 5
Witham, 13,080 H 6
Woking, 78,180 G 6
Wokingham, 19,580 F 6
Wolverhampton, 264,520 E 5
Wolverton, 13,600 G 5
Wombwell, 18,970 F 4
Worcester, 71,540 E 5
Workington, 29,710 D 3
Worksop, 35,660 F 4
Worthing, 83,100 G 7
Yeovil, 25,740 E 7
York, 107,940 F 4

OTHER FEATURES

Aire (river) F 4
Avon (river) F 5
Avon (river) F 6
Axe Edge (mt.) F 4
Beachy (head) H 7
Bigbury (bay) C 7
Blackwater (river) J 6
Bridlington (bay) G 3
Bristol (channel) C 6
Brown Willy (mt.) C 7
Carter Fell (mt.) E 2
Cheviot (hills) E 2
Cornish Heights (hills) B 7
Cotswold (hills) E 6
Cross Fell (mt.) E 3
Cumbrian (mts.) D 3
Dartmoor (forest) C 7
Dee (river) D 4
Derwent (river) G 4
Don (river) F 4
Dorset Heights (hills) E 7
Dover (strait) J 6
Dukeries, The (dist.) F 4
Dungeness (prom.) J 7
East Anglian Heights (hills) H 5
Eddystone (rocks) C 7
Eden (river) E 3
English (channel) D 8
Esk (river) D 2
Exmoor (forest) D 6
Flamborough (head) H 3
Formby (head) D 4
Foulness (isl.), 316 J 6
Hartland (point) C 6
High Willhays (mt.) C 7
Holy (Lindisfarne) (isl.), 190 F 2
Humber (river) H 4
Isle of Purbeck (pen.) F 7
Land's End (prom.) B 7
Liddel Water (river) E 2
Lincoln Wolds (hills) G 4
Lindisfarne (Holy) (isl.), 190 F 2
Little Ouse (river) H 5
Lizard (head) B 8
Lundy (isl.), 32 C 6
Lune (river) E 3
Lyme (bay) E 7
Manacles, The (rocks) C 7
Mendip (hills) E 6
Mersea (isl.), 3,840 J 6
Morte (point) C 6
Mounts (bay) B 8
Naze, The (prom.) J 6
Nene (river) H 5
New Forest (dist.) F 7
Nidd (river) F 3
North Foreland (prom.) J 6
North Tyne (river) E 2
Orfordness (prom.) J 5
Ouse (river) F 3
Ouse (river) H 5
Parrett (river) E 6
Peak, The (mt.) F 4
Peel Fell (mt.) E 2
Pennine (range) E 3
Portland (pen.) E 7
Prawle (point) D 7
Ribble (river) E 4
Saint Austell (bay) C 7
Saint Bees (head) D 3
Saint Mary's (isl.), 1,736 A 8
Scafell Pike (mt.) D 3
Scilly (isls.), 1,980 A 8
Selsey Bill (point) G 7
Severn (river) E 6
Sheppey (isl.), 28,790 H 6
Skiddaw (mt.) D 3
Solent (channel) F 7
Solway (firth) D 3
South Downs (hills) G 7
South Tyne (river) E 3
Spithead (channel) F 7
Spurn (head) H 4
Swale (river) F 3
Tamar (river) C 7
Tees (river) F 3
Thames (river) H 6
Till (river) E 2
Trent (river) G 4
Tresco (isl.), 283 A 7
Trevose (head) B 7
Tweed (river) E 2
Tyne (river) F 3
Ure (river) F 3
Walney (isl.), 9,811 D 3
Wash, The (bay) H 4
Waveney (river) J 5
Wear (river) F 3
Wharfe (river) F 4
Widemouth (bay) C 7
Wight (isl.), 102,100 F 7
Witham (river) G 4
Wye (river) D 5
Yare (river) J 5

WALES

COUNTIES

Anglesey, 58,210 C 4
Breconshire, 54,940 D 6
Caernarvonshire, 120,620 C 5
Cardiganshire, 53,500 C 5
Carmarthenshire, 163,600 C 6
Denbighshire, 182,050 D 4
Flintshire, 169,210 D 4
Glamorganshire, 1,258,450 D 6
Merionethshire, 37,700 D 5
Monmouthshire, 463,990 E 6
Montgomeryshire, 42,870 D 5
Pembrokeshire, 101,150 C 6
Radnorshire, 18,250 D 5

CITIES and TOWNS

Aberaeron, 1,220 C 5
Aberdare, 38,210 D 6
Abergavenny, 9,600 E 6
Abergele, 11,520 D 4
Abertillery, 22,610 E 6
Aberystwyth, 10,420 C 5
Amlwch, 3,890 C 4
Ammanford, 5,940 C 6
Bala, 1,600 D 5
Bangor, 14,930 C 4
Barmouth, 2,210 C 5
Barry, 42,500 D 6
Beaumaris, 2,060 C 4
Bethesda, 4,210 C 4
Betws-y-Coed, 800 C 4
Brecknock, 6,380 D 6
Bridgend, 15,260 D 6
Brynmawr, 6,530 D 6
Builth Wells, 1,560 D 5
Burry Port, 5,900 C 6
Caerleon, 6,030 E 6
Caernarvon, 9,130 C 4
Caerphilly, 39,890 D 6
Cardiff, 285,860 E 6
Cardigan, 3,830 C 5
Carmarthen, 12,820 C 6
Chepstow, 7,840 E 6
Colwyn Bay, 25,060 D 4
Conway, 11,910 D 4
Cowbridge, 1,430 D 6
Criccieth, 1,580 C 5
Cwmamman, 4,050 D 6
Denbigh, 8,600 D 4
Dolgellau, 2,670 D 5
Ebbw Vale, 26,470 D 6
Ffestiniog, 6,350 D 5
Fishguard and Goodwick, 4,940 B 6
Flint, 14,650 D 4
Haverfordwest, 10,490 C 6
Hay, 1,340 D 5
Holyhead, 10,970 C 4
Holywell, 8,750 D 4
Kidwelly, 2,950 C 6
Knighton, 2,120 D 5
Lampeter, 2,120 C 5
Llandeilo, 1,880 C 6
Llandovery, 2,090 D 6
Llandrindod Wells, 3,240 D 5
Llandudno, 16,610 D 4
Llanelli, 27,570 C 6
Llanfairfechan, 3,230 C 4
Llanfyllin, 1,110 D 5
Llangefni, 3,580 C 4
Llangollen, 3,030 D 5
Llanidloes, 2,320 D 5
Llanrwst, 2,590 D 4
Llwchwr, 26,030 D 6
Machynlleth, 1,760 D 5
Menai Bridge, 2,390 C 4
Merthyr Tydfil, 56,360 D 6
Milford Haven, 13,670 B 6
Mold, 8,040 D 4
Monmouth, 6,280 E 6
Montgomery, 1,000 D 5
Mountain Ash, 28,130 D 6
Narberth, 1,040 C 6
Neath, 29,690 D 6
New Quay, 870 C 5
Newcastle Emlyn, 670 C 6
Newport, 112,000 E 6
Newtown, 5,590 D 5
Neyland, 2,410 C 6
Pembroke, 14,200 B 6
Penarth, 23,120 D 6
Penmaenmawr, 3,970 C 4
Pontypool, 36,600 E 6
Pontypridd, 35,010 D 6
Port Talbot, 50,970 D 6
Porthcawl, 13,410 D 6
Portmadoc, 3,840 C 5
Prestatyn, 13,670 D 4
Presteigne, 1,300 D 5
Pwllheli, 3,790 C 5
Rhondda, 94,300 D 6
Rhyl, 21,510 D 4
Risca, 16,030 D 6
Ruthin, 4,180 D 4
Swansea, 171,320 C 6
Tenby, 4,580 C 6
Tywyn, 4,440 C 5
Welshpool, 6,820 D 5
Wrexham, 37,620 E 4

OTHER FEATURES

Bardsey (isl.), 17 C 5
Berwyn (mts.) D 5
Braich-y-Pwll (prom.) C 5
Bristol (channel) E 5
Cader Idris (mts.) D 5
Caldy (isl.), 61 C 6
Cambrian (mts.) D 5
Cardigan (bay) C 5
Carmel (head) C 4
Clwyd (river) D 4
Dee (river) D 4
Gower (pen.), 16,100 C 6
Great Ormes (head) C 4
Holyhead (Holy) (isl.), 12,550 C 4
Lleyn (pen.), 19,840 C 5
Menai (strait) C 4
Pencilan (head) C 5
Plynlimon (mt.) D 5
Ramsey (isl.) B 6
Saint Brides (bay) B 6
Saint David's (head) B 6
Saint George's (channel) B 5
Saint Gowans (head) B 6
Severn (river) D 5
Skerries (isls.) C 4
Skomer (isl.) B 6
Snowdon (mt.) D 4
Snowdonia Nat'l Park D 5
Swansea (bay) D 6
Teifi (river) C 5
Towy (river) D 6
Tremadoc (bay) C 5
Usk (river) D 6
Wye (river) D 5

ISLE OF MAN

Total Population 50,000

CITIES and TOWNS

Douglas (cap.), 19,517 C 3
Michael, 353 C 3
Onchan, 3,609 C 3
Peel, 2,739 C 3
Ramsey, 3,880 C 3

OTHER FEATURES

Ayre (point) C 3
Calf of Man (isl.) B 3
Langness (prom.) C 3
Snaefell (mt.) C 3
Spanish (head) C 4

CHANNEL ISLANDS

Total Population 117,000

CITIES and TOWNS

Saint Anne, Alderney, †1,472 E 8
Saint Helier (cap.), Jersey, 19,661 E 8
Saint Peter Port (cap.), Guernsey, 15,804 E 8
Saint Sampson's, Guernsey, †5,916 E 8

OTHER FEATURES

Alderney (isl.), 1,472 E 8
Guernsey (isl.), 48,000 E 8
Herm (isl.), 90 E 8
Jersey (isl.), 68,000 E 8
Sark (isl.), 550 E 8

*City and suburbs.
†Population of parish.
‡Population of conurbation.

SCOTLAND

(map on page 15)

COUNTIES

Aberdeen, 317,803 L 5
Angus, 277,279 K 6
Argyll, 58,360 F 7
Ayr, 354,005 H 9
Banff, 43,753 K 5
Berwick, 20,499 L 8
Bute, 12,465 F 8
Caithness, 28,202 J 3
Clackmannan, 44,084 J 7
Dumfries, 87,276 J 9
Dunbarton, 277,635 G 7
East Lothian, 55,070 L 8
Fife, 325,139 K 7
Forfar (Angus), 277,279 K 6
Inverness, 84,786 G 5
Kincardine, 25,694 M 6
Kinross, 6,347 K 7
Kirkcudbright, 27,899 H 9
Lanark, 1,541,455 J 8
Midlothian, 595,590 K 8
Moray, 52,241 K 5
Nairn, 7,991 J 5
Orkney, 17,264 K 1
Peebles, 13,339 K 8
Perth, 124,199 H 7
Renfrew, 359,090 G 8
Ross and Cromarty, 56,641 F 4
Roxburgh, 42,619 L 9
Selkirk, 20,273 K 9
Stirling, 203,977 H 7
Sutherland, 12,995 G 3
West Lothian, 106,030 J 8
Wigtown, 27,611 G10
Zetland, 17,089 M 3

CITIES and TOWNS

Abbotsford, 15 L 8
Aberchirder, 838 L 4
Aberdeen, 181,089 N 5
Aberfeldy, 1,542 J 6
Aberfoyle, 853 H 7
Aberlour, 801 K 5
Abernethy, 772 K 7
Aboyne, 1,012 L 5
Acharacle, 93 E 6
Achiltibuie, 49 E 3
Achmore, 158 C 3
Achnasheen, 50 F 4
Airdrie, 36,188 D 2
Alexandria, 8,229 B 2
Alford, 758 L 5
Alloa, 14,205 E 1
Alness, 1,177 H 4
Alva, 4,180 J 7
Alyth, 1,705 K 6
Annan, 6,019 K10
Applecross, 25 E 5
Arbroath, 21,632 L 6
Ardcharnich, 16 F 4
Ardgour, 21 F 6
Ardrishaig, 1,047 F 8
Ardrossan, 9,946 G 8
Arinagour, 54 C 6
Arisaig, 174 E 6
Armadale, 6,384 E 2
Arrochar, 100 G 7
Auchinleck, 5,694 H 9
Auchterarder, 2,343 J 7
Auchtermuchty, 1,331 K 7
Auldearn, 359 J 4
Aultbea, 99 E 4
Aviemore, 635 J 5
Avoch, 899 H 4
Ayr, 47,635 G 9
Ayton, 425 M 8
Badachro, 35 E 4
Badcall, 17 F 3
Ballachulish, 381 F 6
Ballantrae, 420 F 9
Ballater, 1,076 K 5
Balmaha, 40 C 1
Balmoral Castle, 66 K 5
Balquhidder, 38 H 7
Baltasound, 240 M 2
Banavie, 167 F 6
Banchory, 2,066 M 5
Banff, 3,492 L 4
Bannockburn, 3,887 D 1
Barr, 224 G 9
Barrhead, 17,560 C 2
Barvas, 378 D 3
Bathgate, 14,763 J 8
Bearsden, 23,143 C 2
Beauly, 1,386 G 5
Beith, 4,993 B 2
Bellshill, 16,527 D 2
Berriedale, 30 K 3
Bettyhill, 99 H 3
Biggar, 1,668 J 8
Bishopbriggs, 19,779 D 2
Blair-Atholl, 509 J 6
Blairgowrie and Rattray, 5,071 J 6
Blantyre, 16,288 D 2
Boddam, 854 N 5
Bonar Bridge, 437 H 4
Bo'ness, 13,493 J 7
Bonhill, 4,024 B 2
Bonnybridge, 5,742 D 2
Bonnyrigg and Lasswade, 7,017 K 8
Bowmore, 840 D 8
Bracadale, 246 D 5
Braemar, 468 K 5
Brechin, 6,775 L 6
Bridge of Allan, 4,285 D 1
Broadford, 293 E 5
Brodick, 647 F 8
Brora, 1,256 J 3
Buckhaven and Methil, 18,815 L 7
Buckie, 7,697 L 4
Bunessan, 107 D 7
Burghead, 1,368 J 4
Burntisland, 5,451 K 7
Burravoe, 136 N 2
Cairnryan, 167 G10
Callander, 1,777 H 7
Cambuslang, 18,868 D 2
Campbeltown, 6,285 E 9
Cannich, 197 G 5
Canonbie, 194 K 9
Carbost, 118 C 5
Cargill, 21 K 7
Carloway, 232 C 3
Carluke, 8,110 E 2
Carnoustie, 5,663 L 6
Carnwath, 1,072 J 8
Carsphairn, 61 H 9
Carstairs Jct., 1,353 J 8
Castlebay, 122 B 6
Castle Douglas, 3,264 H10
Cawdor, 136 J 5
Ceres, 609 L 7
Chirnside, 821 M 8
Clackmannan, 2,476 J 7
Closeburn, 218 J 9
Clydebank, 49,997 C 2
Coatbridge, 52,804 D 2
Cockburnspath, 261 M 8
Cockenzie and Port Seton, 3,565 L 8
Coldingham, 392 M 8
Coldstream, 1,267 M 8
Colmonell, 231 G 9
Corpach, 376 F 6
Coupar Angus, 1,978 K 6
Cove and Kilcreggan, 1,292 B 1
Cowdenbeath, 10,480 K 7
Coylton, 233 H 9
Craignure, 43 E 7
Crail, 968 L 7
Crawford, 417 J 9
Creetown, 829 H10
Crieff, 5,569 J 7
Crinan, 34 E 7
Cromarty, 587 J 4
Cruden Bay, 489 N 5
Cullen, 1,253 L 4
Cults, 2,448 M 5
Cumbernauld, 26,678 D 2
Cumnock and Holmhead, 5,920 H 9
Cupar, 6,559 K 7
Dalbeattie, 3,229 J10
Dalkeith, 9,368 K 8
Dalmally, 155 G 7
Dalmellington, 2,130 H 9
Dalry, Ayr, 5,623 B 2
Dalry, Kirkcudbright, 448 H 9
Dalwhinnie, 132 H 6
Darvel, 3,165 H 8
Daviot, 38 H 5
Denny and Dunipace, 8,587 D 1
Dervaig, 82 D 6
Dingwall, 3,912 H 4
Dores, 143 H 5
Dornie, 102 F 5
Dornoch, 930 H 4
Douglas, 2,075 J 8
Doune, 758 H 7
Drummore, 390 G10
Dufftown, 1,536 K 5
Dumbarton, 25,510 B 2
Dumfries, 28,149 J 9
Dunbar, 2,931 M 8
Dunbeath, 159 K 3
Dunblane, 3,884 D 1
Dundee, 181,950 K 7
Dundonald, 1,293 H 8
Dunfermline, 50,305 J 7
Dunkeld, 279 J 6
Dunnet, 72 K 2
Dunoon, 9,431 A 2
Duns, 1,885 M 8
Dunscore, 169 J 9
Dunvegan, 157 D 5
Durness, 97 G 2
Dyce, 1,530 M 5
Earlston, 1,367 L 8
East Kilbride, 62,243 C 2
East Linton, 912 L 7
Ecclefechan, 834 K 9
Eddleston, 181 K 8
Edinbain, 149 D 5
Edinburgh (cap.), 465,421 K 8
Edzell, 644 L 6
Elderslie, 4,616 C 2
Elgin, 16,416 K 4
Elie and Earlsferry, 802 L 7
Ellon, 1,877 M 5
Elvanfoot, 85 J 9
Eriboll, 24 G 3
Errol, 744 K 7
Ettrick, 38 K 9
Evanton, 484 H 4
Ewes, 20 K 9
Eyemouth, 2,257 M 8
Falkirk, 38,625 E 1
Fearn, 210 J 4
Fetteresso, 20 M 6
Findhorn, 629 K 4
Findochty, 1,207 K 4
Findon, 77 M 5
Fochabers, 1,054 K 4
Ford, 50 F 7
Fordoun, 126 M 6
Forfar, 9,870 L 6
Forres, 4,711 K 4
Fort Augustus, 372 G 5
Fort William, 4,006 F 6
Fortingall, 33 H 6
Fortrose, 1,027 H 4
Fraserburgh, 10,898 N 4
Gairloch, 104 E 4
Galashiels, 12,073 L 8
Galston, 4,058 H 8
Gardenstown, 906 M 4
Garelochhead, 1,042 A 1
Gatehouse-of-Fleet, 797 H10
Girvan, 6,868 G 9
Glamis, 205 L 6
Glasgow, 927,948 D 2
Glasgow, *1,746,313 D 2
Glenbarr, 56 E 8
Glenelg, 290 E 5
Glenisla, 25 K 6
Glenluce, 706 G10
Glenrothes, 26,700 K 7
Golspie, 1,167 H 4
Gourock, 10,618 B 2
Grangemouth, 22,701 J 8
Grantown-on-Spey, 1,600 J 5
Greenlaw, 544 M 8
Greenock, 70,267 A 2
Gretna Green, 86 K 9
Haddington, 4,070 L 8
Halkirk, 608 K 3
Hamilton, 46,397 D 2
Harris (Tarbert), 416 C 4
Hawick, 16,685 L 9
Helensburgh, 13,594 B 1
Helmsdale, 768 K 3
Hillswick, 64 M 2
Hobkirk, 25 L 9
Hopeman, 1,146 K 4
Howmore, 38 A 5
Huntly, 3,878 L 5
Hurlford, 4,152 H 8
Hutton, 78 K 9
Innerleithen, 2,275 K 8
Insch, 917 L 5
Insh, 26 J 5
Inveraray, 468 F 7
Inverbervie, 885 M 6
Invergordon, 2,074 M 4
Inverie, 36 E 5
Inverkeilor, 224 M 6
Inverkeithing, 5,367 K 7
Inverness, 32,058 H 5
Inverurie, 5,351 M 5
Irvine, 21,382 G 8
Jamestown, 1,193 C 1
Jedburgh, 3,874 M 9
John O'Groats, 184 K 2
Johnshaven, 625 M 6
Johnstone, 22,633 B 2
Keiss, 364 K 2
Keith, 4,091 L 4
Kelso, 4,411 M 8
Kentallen, 91 F 6
Kilbarchan, 2,330 B 2
Kilbirnie, 8,158 B 2
Kildonan, 22 J 3
Kildrummy, 273 L 5
Kilfinan, 30 F 8
Killin, 583 H 7
Kilmacolm, 2,902 B 2
Kilmarnock, 47,631 G 8
Kilmelford, 69 F 7
Kilmore, 78 F 7
Kilmory, 81 F 9
Kilmuir, 87 D 5
Kilrenny and Anstruther, 2,814 L 7
Kilsyth, 9,659 D 2
Kincardine, 26 H 4
Kincardine O'Neil, 166 L 5
Kingussie, 1,013 H 5
Kinloch Rannoch, 236 H 6
Kinlochbervie, 117 G 3
Kinlochleven, 1,515 G 6
Kinross, 2,361 K 7
Kintore, 783 M 5
Kirkcaldy, 52,097 K 7
Kirkcolm, 318 F10
Kirkcowan, 401 G10
Kirkcudbright, 2,730 H10
Kirkintilloch, 24,801 C 2
Kirkoswald, 296 G 9
Kirkpatrick Fleming, 231 K 9
Kirkwall, 4,688 K 2
Kirriemuir, 4,107 L 6
Kyle of Lochalsh, 606 E 5
Laggan, 43 H 5
Lairg, 538 H 3
Lamlash, 528 F 8
Lanark, 8,407 J 8
Langholm, 2,393 K 9
Larbert, 4,167 D 1
Largs, 8,908 B 2
Larkhall, 13,931 D 2
Latheron, 51 K 3
Lauder, 564 L 8
Laurencekirk, 1,365 M 6
Leith, 51,378 K 8
Lennoxtown, 3,155 C 2
Lerwick, 5,919 N 3
Leslie, 3,229 K 7
Lesmahagow, 3,558 H 8
Leuchars, 1,332 L 7
Leven, 8,987 L 7
Leverburgh, 175 C 4
Linlithgow, 5,191 K 8
Livingston, 8,100 C 1
Lochaline, 200 E 6
Lochboisdale, 316 B 5
Lochcarron, 210 E 5
Lochgelly, 8,021 K 7
Lochgilphead, 1,253 F 7
Lochinver, 240 F 3
Lochmaben, 1,265 J 9
Lochmaddy, 353 B 4
Lochranza, 95 F 8
Lochwinnoch, 2,066 B 2
Lockerbie, 2,878 K 9
Logierait, 104 J 6
Lossiemouth and Branderburgh, 6,419 K 4
Lothbeg, 9 J 3
Luss, 140 B 1
Lybster, 534 K 3
Macduff, 3,502 M 4
Mallaig, 849 E 5
Markinch, 2,349 K 7
Marykirk, 126 M 6
Mauchline, 3,538 H 8
Maybole, 4,548 G 9
Meigle, 347 K 6
Melrose, 2,242 L 8
Melvaig, 36 E 4
Melvich, 130 H 2
Methlick, 299 M 5
Methven, 796 J 7
Mid Yell, 166 N 2
Millport, 1,159 A 2
Milngavie, 9,955 C 2
Moffat, 1,866 K 9
Moniaive, 409 J 9
Monifieth, 5,170 L 7
Montrose, 10,269 M 6
Motherwell and Wishaw, 75,022 D 2
Muirkirk, 3,409 H 9
Musselburgh, 17,244 L 8
Muthill, 726 J 7
Nairn, 4,986 J 4
Neilston, 3,795 C 2
New Abbey, 352 J10
New Aberdour, 739 M 4
Newarthill, 6,840 D 2
Newburgh, Aberdeen, 458 N 5
Newburgh, Fife, 2,107 K 7
New Cumnock, 5,508 H 9
New Deer, 619 M 5
New Galloway, 339 H 9
Newmilns and Greenholm, 3,506 H 8
Newport-on-Tay, 3,427 L 7
Newton-Stewart, 1,810 G10
Nigg, 33 J 4

(continued)

ENGLAND and WALES
CONIC PROJECTION
SCALE OF MILES
0 10 20 40 60 80
SCALE OF KILOMETRES
0 10 20 40 60 80
Capitals of Countries
Other Capitals
Administrative Centers
County Boundaries
Canals
Copyright by C. S. HAMMOND & CO., N.Y.
Longitude 1° West of Greenwich 0° Longitude East of 1° Greenwich
56°
55°
54°
53°
52°
51°
50°
NORTH SEA
IRISH SEA
ENGLISH CHANNEL
ST. GEORGE'S CHANNEL
NORTH CHANNEL
Bristol Channel
SCOTLAND
NORTHERN IRELAND
IRELAND
FRANCE
ISLE OF MAN
CHANNEL ISLANDS
SCILLY ISLES
ISLE OF WIGHT
NORTHUMBERLAND
CUMBERLAND
DURHAM
WESTMORLAND
YORK
NORTH RIDING
EAST RIDING
WEST RIDING
LANCASHIRE
CHESHIRE
DERBY
NOTTINGHAM
LINCOLN
LINDSEY
KESTEVEN
HOLLAND
NORFOLK
WEST SUFFOLK
EAST SUFFOLK
CAMBS. & ELY
HUNTS. & Huntingdon
NORTHAMPTON
LEICESTER
RUTLAND
STAFFORD
SHROPSHIRE
WORCESTER
WARWICK
HEREFORD
GLOUCESTER
OXFORD
BUCKINGHAM
BEDFORD
HERTFORD
ESSEX
LONDON
BERKS
WILTS
SOMERSET
DORSET
DEVON
CORNWALL
HAMPSHIRE
SURREY
KENT
EAST SUSSEX
WEST SUSSEX
ANGLESEY
CAERNARVON
DENBIGH
FLINT
MERIONETH
MONTGOMERY
CARDIGAN
RADNOR
BRECONSHIRE
PEMBROKE
CARMARTHEN
GLAMORGAN
MONMOUTH
SNOWDONIA NAT'L PARK
GLASGOW
Edinburgh
Belfast
Dublin (Baile Átha Cliath)
Newcastle upon Tyne
Carlisle
Teesside
Leeds
Bradford
Manchester
Liverpool
Sheffield
Hull
Nottingham
Birmingham
Wolverhampton
Coventry
Leicester
Cambridge
Norwich
Oxford
Bristol
Cardiff
Swansea
Plymouth
Exeter
Southampton
Portsmouth
Brighton
Reading
Dover
Calais
Boulogne sur-Mer
Le Havre
Rouen
Cherbourg
Caen
Guernsey
Jersey
Alderney
Sark
Bay of the Seine
Cardigan Bay
Liverpool Bay
Morecambe Bay
The Wash
Solway Firth
Firth of Forth
Firth of Clyde
Strait of Dover
Lizard Head
Land's End

14 United Kingdom and Ireland

(continued)

SCOTLAND (continued)

North Berwick, 4,534 ... L 7
Oban, 6,743 ... F 7
Old Meldrum, 1,126 ... M 5
Oykel Bridge, 45 ... G 4
Paisley, 95,182 ... C 2
Peebles, 5,598 ... K 8
Penicuik, 81,293 ... K 8
Perth, 41,654 ... J 7
Peterhead, 13,332 ... N 4
Pierowall, 108 ... K 1
Pitlochry, 2,482 ... J 6
Pittenweem, 1,445 ... L 7
Plockton, 254 ... E 5
Poolewe, 81 ... E 4
Port Appin, 96 ... F 6
Portaskaig, 30 ... D 8
Port Ellen, 721 ... D 8
Port Glasgow, 21,985 ... B 2
Portknockie, 1,122 ... L 4
Portlethen, 75 ... M 5
Portmahomack, 207 ... J 4
Portobello, 27,141 ... K 8
Port of Ness, 93 ... D 3
Portpatrick, 681 ... F10
Portree, 1,356 ... D 5
Portsoy, 1,698 ... L 4
Port William, 528 ... G10
Prestonpans, 6,816 ... L 8
Prestwick, 13,741 ... G 9
Queensferry, 4,256 ... K 8
Quendale, 11 ... M 3
Rackwick, 12 ... K 2
Reay, 187 ... J 2
Renfrew, 19,114 ... C 2
Renton, 3,898 ... B 2
Rhynie, 363 ... L 5
Rosehearty, 1,144 ... M 4
Rosneath, 222 ... A 1
Rothes, 1,099 ... K 4
Rothesay, 6,329 ... F 8
Rothiemay, 24 ... L 4
Rutherglen, 25,213 ... C 2
Ruthwell, 96 ... K 9
Saddell, 44 ... E 8
Saint Andrews, 10,890 ... L 7
Saint Boswells, 1,007 ... L 8
Saint Combs, 713 ... N 4
Saint Cyrus, 347 ... M 6
Saint Margaret's Hope, 205 ... L 2
Saint Mary's, 151 ... L 2
Salen, 171 ... E 7
Saltcoats, 14,170 ... G 8
Sandness, 27 ... M 3
Sandwick, 43 ... N 3
Sanquhar, 2,066 ... J 9
Scalasaig, 45 ... D 7
Scalloway, 878 ... M 3
Scarinish, 103 ... C 7
Scone, 3,047 ... K 7
Scourie, 71 ... F 3
Scrabster, 129 ... J 2
Selkirk, 5,527 ... L 8
Shieldaig, 68 ... E 5
Shotts, 10,304 ... E 2
Skipness, 69 ... F 8
Spean Bridge, 229 ... G 6
Stevenston, 11,281 ... G 8
Stewarton, 4,156 ... H 8
Stirling, 28,786 ... D 1
Stonehaven, 4,573 ... M 6
Stonehouse, 3,686 ... M 8
Stoneykirk, 196 ... G10
Stornoway, 5,352 ... C 3
Stow, 453 ... L 8
Strachur, 36 ... F 7
Stranraer, 9,401 ... G10
Strathaven, 4,321 ... H 8
Strichen, 967 ... M 4
Stromness, 1,556 ... K 2
Strontian, 39 ... E 6
Tain, 1,719 ... H 4
Tarbert, Argyll, 1,236 ... F 8
Tarbert, Inverness, 416 ... C 4
Tarland, 396 ... L 5
Tayport, 2,916 ... L 7
Thornhill, 1,482 ... J 9
Thurso, 9,167 ... K 2
Tillicoultry, 4,125 ... J 7
Tobermory, 616 ... D 6
Tomintoul, 278 ... K 5
Tongue, 108 ... H 3
Torridon, 13 ... F 5
Tranent, 6,988 ... L 8
Traquair, 55 ... K 8
Troon, 10,906 ... G 8
Turriff, 2,784 ... M 4
Tweedsmuir, 30 ... J 9
Uig, Inverness, 107 ... D 4
Uig, Ross and Cromarty, 166 ... B 3
Ullapool, 676 ... F 4
Voe, 147 ... M 3
Walls, 132 ... M 3
Watten, 251 ... K 2
West Calder, 1,535 ... K 8
West Kilbride, 3,042 ... G 8
West Linton, 667 ... K 8
Whitburn, 9,596 ... E 2
Whithorn, 998 ... H10
Wick, 7,346 ... K 3
Wigtown, 1,149 ... H10
Yarrow, 30 ... K 8
Yetholm, 426 ... M 8

OTHER FEATURES

Abbey (head) ... J10
A'Chralaig (mt.) ... F 5
Affric (lake) ... G 5
Ailsa Craig (isl.), 10 ... F 9
Aird (pt.) ... D 4
Almond (riv.) ... J 7
Alness (riv.) ... H 4
Alsh (inlet) ... E 5
Annan (riv.) ... K 9
Appin (dist.), 429 ... F 6
Ardgour (dist.), 299 ... F 6
Ardivachar (pt.) ... A 5
Ardle (riv.) ... K 6
Ardnamurchan (dist.), 772 ... D 6
Ardnamurchan (pt.) ... D 6
Argyll (dist.), 4,435 ... F 7
Arisaig (dist.), 682 ... E 6
Arkaig (lake) ... F 6
Arran (isl.), 3,700 ... F 8
Askival (mt.) ... D 6
Assynt (dist.), 831 ... F 3
Assynt (lake) ... G 3
Athol (dist.), 1,458 ... H 6
Auskerry (isl.), 3 ... M 1
Avon (riv.) ... K 5
Awe (lake) ... F 7
Ayr (riv.) ... H 9
Badenoch (dist.), 6,473 ... H 6
Baleshare (isl.), 59 ... A 4
Barra (head) ... A 6
Barra (isl.), 1,369 ... A 5
Barra (isls.), 1,469 ... B 6
Barra (passg.) ... B 6
Battock (mt.) ... L 6
Beauly (firth) ... H 5
Beinn Bheigeir (mt.) ... D 8
Bell Rock (isl.), 3 ... M 7
Ben Alder (mt.) ... G 6
Ben Avon (mt.) ... K 5
Benbecula (isl.), 1,358 ... A 5
Benbecula (sound) ... A 5
Ben Dearg (mt.) ... G 4
Benderloch (dist.) ... F 7
Beneveian (lake) ... G 5
Ben Griam More (mt.) ... H 3
Ben Hee (mt.) ... G 3
Ben Hope (mt.) ... G 3
Ben Klibreck (mt.) ... H 3
Ben Lawers (mt.) ... H 6
Ben Macdhui (mt.) ... J 5
Ben Mhor (mt.) ... B 5
Ben More (mt.), Argyll ... E 7
Ben More (mt.), Perth ... G 7
Ben More Assynt (mt.) ... G 3
Ben Nevis (mt.) ... F 6
Ben Vorlich (mt.) ... H 7
Ben Wyvis (mt.) ... G 4
Bernera (isl.), 317 ... C 3
Berneray (isl.), 3 ... A 6
Berneray (isl.), 201 ... B 4
Black Isle (dist.), 5,673 ... H 4
Blackwater (res.) ... G 6
Boisdale (inlet) ... B 5
Boreray (isl.), 5 ... B 4
Bracadale (inlet) ... C 5
Braemar (dist.), 5,091 ... K 5
Bran (falls) ... J 6
Breadalbane (dist.), 3,877 ... H 7
Bressay (isl.), 269 ... N 3
Brims Ness (prom.) ... J 2
Broad (bay) ... D 3
Broad Law (mt.) ... K 9
Broom (inlet) ... F 4
Brora (riv.) ... H 3
Brough (head) ... K 1
Brough Ness (prom.) ... L 2
Buchan (dist.), 53,172 ... M 4
Buchan Ness (prom.) ... N 5
Buddon Ness (prom.) ... L 7
Burrow (head) ... H10
Bute (isl.), 9,793 ... F 8
Bute (sound) ... F 8
Butt of Lewis (prom.) ... D 3
Cairn Gorm (mt.) ... J 5
Cairngorm (mts.) ... J 5
Cairn Mor (mt.) ... K 5
Cairnsmore (mt.) ... H 9
Cairn Toul (mt.) ... J 5
Caledonian (canal) ... G 5
Canna (isl.), 24 ... C 5
Canna (sound) ... C 6
Caolisport (inlet) ... E 8
Carn Eige (mt.) ... F 5
Carrick (dist.), 21,867 ... G 9
Carron (inlet) ... E 5
Carron (river) ... G 4
Cellar (head) ... D 3
Cheviot (hills) ... L 9
Clar Nan (lake) ... J 3
Clisham (mt.) ... C 4
Clyde (falls) ... J 8
Clyde (firth) ... F 9
Clyde (river) ... G 8
Cnoc Moy (mt.) ... E 9
Coire (lake) ... H 3
Coll (isl.), 147 ... C 6
Colonsay (isl.), 164 ... C 7
Conon (river) ... H 4
Copinsay (isl.), 3 ... L 2
Corryvreckan (gulf) ... E 7
Corsewall (pt.) ... F 9
Cowal (dist.), 16,247 ... F 7
Creag Meagaidh (mt.) ... G 6
Cree (river) ... G 9
Creran (inlet) ... F 7
Cromarty (firth) ... H 4
Cuillin (hills) ... D 5
Cumbraes (isls.), 1,646 ... A 2
Dee (riv.) ... H 9
Dee (riv.) ... M 5
Dennis (head) ... M 1
Deveron (riv.) ... L 5
Dhuheartach (isl.), 3 ... C 7
Don (riv.) ... L 5
Doon (lake) ... G 9
Dornoch (firth) ... J 4
Duich (inlet) ... F 5
Duirinish (dist.), 1,268 ... C 5
Dulnain (riv.) ... J 5
Duncansby (head) ... L 2
Dunnet (head) ... J 2
Dunvegan (head) ... C 4
Durness, Kyle of (inlet) ... G 2
Earn (lake) ... H 7
Earn (riv.) ... J 7
East Loch Tarbert (inlet) ... C 4
Eck (lake) ... F 7
Eday (isl.), 198 ... L 1
Eddrachillis (bay) ... F 3
Eden (riv.) ... L 7
Egilsay (isl.), 54 ... L 1
Eigg (isl.), 74 ... D 6
Eil (inlet) ... F 6
Eishort (inlet) ... D 5
Enard (bay) ... F 3
Eport (inlet) ... B 4
Eriboll (inlet) ... G 2
Ericht (lake) ... H 6
Eriskay (isl.), 231 ... B 5
Erisort (inlet) ... D 3
Esk (riv.) ... L 9
Etive (inlet) ... F 7
Ettrick Pen (mt.) ... K 9
Eye (pen.) ... D 3
Eynhallow (sound) ... K 1
Eynort (inlet) ... B 5
Fair (isl.), 64 ... L 3
Fannich (lake) ... F 4
Farrar (riv.) ... G 5
Fetlar (isl.), 127 ... N 2
Fife Ness (prom.) ... L 7
Findhorn (riv.) ... J 5
Fionn (lake) ... F 4
Flannan (isls.), 3 ... A 3
Fleet (inlet) ... J 4
Foinaven (mt.) ... G 3
Formartine (dist.), 15,010 ... M 5
Forth (firth) ... L 7
Forth (riv.) ... H 7
Forth and Clyde (canal) ... H 8
Foula (isl.), 54 ... L 3
Foyers (falls) ... H 5
Fyne (inlet) ... F 8
Gair (inlet) ... E 4
Gairloch (dist.), 1,788 ... E 4
Gallan (head) ... B 3
Galloway (dist.), 57,994 ... H10
Galloway, Mull of (prom.) ... G10
Garioch (dist.), 7,950 ... L 5
Garry (lake) ... G 5
Garry (riv.) ... J 6
Gigha (isl.), 163 ... E 8
Gigha (sound) ... E 8
Girdle Ness (prom.) ... N 5
Glas Maol (mt.) ... K 6
Glass (lake) ... G 4
Glass (riv.) ... G 5
Glenelg (dist.), 1,549 ... E 5
Goat Fell (mt.) ... F 8
Grampian (mts.) ... G 6
Greenstone (pt.) ... E 4
Grimsay (isl.), 239 ... B 5
Gruinard (bay) ... E 4
Gruinard (dist.) ... F 4
Gruinart (inlet) ... D 8
Gulvain (mt.) ... F 6
Gunna (sound) ... C 6
Halladale (riv.) ... J 3
Harris (dist.), 2,493 ... C 4
Harris (sound) ... B 4
Hebrides (isls.), 43,676 ... A 5
Hebrides, Inner (isls.), 13,964 ... D 5
Hebrides, Outer (isls.), 29,712 ... A 5
Hebrides (sea) ... C 5
Helmsdale (riv.) ... J 3
Herma Ness (prom.) ... M 2
Holm (sound) ... L 2
Holy (isl.), 7 ... F 9
Holy Loch (inlet) ... A 2
Hope (lake) ... G 3
Hourn (inlet) ... F 5
Hoy (isl.), 511 ... K 2
Hynish (bay) ... C 7
Hyskier (isl.), 3 ... C 6
Inchard (inlet) ... F 3
Inchcape (Bell) Rock (isl.), 3 ... M 7
Inchkeith (isl.), 3 ... K 7
Indaal (inlet) ... D 8
Inner (sound) ... E 5
Inner Hebrides (isls.), 13,964 ... D 5
Inver (inlet) ... F 3
Iona (isl.), 130 ... D 7
Isla (riv.) ... K 6
Islay (isl.), 3,860 ... D 8
Jura (isl.), 249 ... E 7
Katrine (lake) ... G 7
Keal, Na (inlet) ... D 7
Kebock (head) ... D 3
Kilbrennan (sound) ... F 9
Kinnairds (head) ... N 4
Kintyre (dist.), 9,914 ... E 9
Kintyre, Mull of (prom.) ... E 9
Knapdale (dist.), 2,711 ... E 8
Knoydart (dist.), 1,234 ... E 5
Kyle (dist.) ... H 9
Laggan (bay) ... D 8
Lammermuir (hills) ... L 8
Langavat (lake) ... C 3
Laxford (inlet) ... F 3
Lennox (hills) ... C 1
Leven (inlet) ... F 6
Leven (lake) ... K 7
Lewis (dist.), 21,614 ... C 3
Lewis, Butt of (prom.) ... D 3
Liddel Water (riv.) ... L 9
Linnhe (inlet) ... F 6
Lismore (isl.), 155 ... F 7
Little Minch (sound) ... C 4
Lochaber (dist.), 7,591 ... F 6
Lochalsh (dist.), 1,651 ... E 5
Lochnager (mt.) ... K 6
Lochy (lake) ... G 6
Lomond (lake) ... G 7
Long (inlet) ... B 1
Lorne (dist.), 12,656 ... F 7
Lorne (firth) ... E 7
Lothians (dist.) ... K 8
Loyal (lake) ... H 3
Lubnaig (lake) ... H 7
Luce (bay) ... G10
Lyon (riv.) ... H 6
Maddy (inlet) ... B 4
Mainland (isl.), 13,282 ... N 3
Mainland (isl.), 13,495 ... K 1
Mam Soul (mt.) ... F 5
Mar (dist.), 16,918 ... E 4
Maree (lake) ... F 4
May (isl.), 7 ... M 7
Merrick (mt.) ... H 9
Mhor (lake) ... H 5
Minginish (dist.), 578 ... D 5
Moidart (dist.), 247 ... E 6
Monach (isls.) ... A 4
Monach (sound) ... A 4
Monadhliath (mts.) ... H 5
Monar (lake) ... F 5
Morar (dist.), 1,106 ... E 6
Morar (lake) ... E 6
Moray (firth) ... J 4
More (lake) ... G 3
Moriston (riv.) ... G 5
Morven (dist.), 422 ... E 6
Morven (mt.) ... J 3
Muck (isl.), 29 ... D 6
Muirnag (hill) ... D 3
Mull (head) ... L 1
Mull (head) ... L 2
Mull (isl.), 2,149 ... E 7
Mull (sound) ... E 7
Nairn (riv.) ... J 5
Na Keal (inlet) ... D 7
Nan Clar (lake) ... J 3
Naver (lake) ... H 3
Naver (riv.) ... H 3
Neist (pt.) ... C 5
Ness (lake) ... H 5
Ness (riv.) ... H 5
Nevis (inlet) ... E 5
Nith (riv.) ... J 9
North (chan.) ... E 9
North (sound) ... L 1
North Esk (riv.) ... L 6
North Minch (sound) ... E 3
North Ronaldsay (firth) ... M 1
North Ronaldsay (isl.), 161 ... M 1
North Uist (isl.), 1,620 ... A 4
Noss (head) ... L 3
Noup (head) ... K 1
Oa, Mull of (prom.) ... D 8
Ochil (hills) ... J 7
Oich (riv.) ... G 5
Orchy (riv.) ... G 7
Orkney (isls.), 17,264 ... J 1
Oronsay (isl.), 2 ... D 7
Oronsay (passg.) ... D 7
Orrin (riv.) ... G 5
Outer Hebrides (isls.), 29,712 ... A 5
Oykell (riv.) ... G 4
Pabbay (isl.), 2 ... B 4
Papa Stour (isl.), 55 ... L 3
Papa Westray (isl.), 139 ... L 1
Paps of Jura (peaks) ... E 8
Park (dist.), 797 ... C 3
Peel Fell (mt.) ... L 9
Pentland (firth) ... K 2
Pladda (isl.), 6 ... F 9
Queensberry (mt.) ... J 9
Quoich (lake) ... F 5
Raasay (isl.), 211 ... D 5
Raasay (sound) ... D 5
Rannoch (dist.), 832 ... H 6
Rannoch (lake) ... H 6
Rattray (head) ... N 4
Renish (pt.) ... C 4
Resort (inlet) ... B 3
Rhinns (pt.) ... C 8
Rhu Coigach (cape) ... E 3
Roag (inlet) ... C 3
Rona (isl.), 49 ... D 4
Ross of Mull (pen.), 471 ... D 7
Rousay (isl.), 237 ... K 1
Rudha Hunish (cape) ... D 4
Rudh Re (cape) ... E 4
Rum (isl.), 40 ... D 6
Rum (sound) ... D 6
Ryan (inlet) ... F 9
Saint Abb's (head) ... M 8
Saint Andrews (bay) ... L 7
Saint Kilda (isl.), 65 ... B 8
Saint Magnus (bay) ... M 3
Saint Mary's Loch (lake) ... K 9
Sanda (isl.), 7 ... E 9
Sanday (isl.), Inverness ... D 5
Sanday (isl.), Orkney, 670 ... M 1
Sanday (sound) ... L 1
Scalpay (isl.), 470 ... C 4
Scalpay (isl.), 2 ... E 5
Scapa Flow (chan.) ... K 2
Scarba (isl.), 5 ... E 7
Scarp (isl.), 46 ... B 3
Scavaig (inlet) ... D 5
Scradain (inlet) ... D 7
Scurdie Ness (prom.) ... M 6
Seaforth (inlet) ... C 4
Sgurr a Choir Ghlais (mt.) ... G 5
Sgurr Mhor (mt.) ... F 4
Sgurr Na Ciche (mt.) ... F 5
Sgurr Na Lapaich (mt.) ... F 5
Shapinsay (isl.), 416 ... L 1
Shee Water (riv.) ... J 6
Shell (inlet) ... D 4
Shetland (isls.), 17,089 ... M 3
Shiel (lake) ... E 6
Shin (falls) ... H 4
Shin (lake) ... G 3
Shona (isl.), 11 ... E 6
Sidlaw (hills) ... K 6
Sinclair's (bay) ... K 2
Skeir Graitich (isl.) ... D 4
Skerryvore (isl.), 3 ... B 7
Skye (isl.), 7,478 ... D 5
Sleat (dist.), 524 ... E 5
Sleat (pt.) ... D 5
Sleat (sound) ... E 5
Small (isls.), 143 ... C 6
Snizort (inlet) ... D 4
Soay (isl.), 11 ... D 5
Solway (firth) ... J10
South Esk (riv.) ... K 6
South Ronaldsay (isl.), 980 ... L 2
South Uist (isl.), 2,376 ... A 5
Spean (riv.) ... G 6
Spey (riv.) ... K 4
Staffin (bay) ... D 4
Start (pt.) ... M 1
Stinchar (riv.) ... G 9
Stoer (pt.) ... F 3
Stornoway (harb.) ... D 3
Storr, The (mt.) ... D 4
Strathbogie (dist.), 9,152 ... L 5
Strathmore (dist.) ... J 7
Strathy (pt.) ... H 2
Stroma (isl.), 12 ... K 2
Stronsay (firth) ... L 1
Stronsay (isl.), 497 ... M 1
Sumburgh (head) ... M 3
Sunart (inlet) ... E 6
Swona (isl.), 3 ... K 2
Taransay (isl.), 5 ... B 4
Tarbat Ness (prom.) ... J 4
Tarbert (inlet) ... D 8
Tay (firth) ... L 7
Tay (lake) ... H 7
Tay (riv.) ... K 7
Teith (riv.) ... H 7
Teviot (riv.) ... L 9
Thurso (riv.) ... J 3
Tilt (riv.) ... J 6
Tiree (isl.), 993 ... C 6
Tirry (riv.) ... H 3
Tiumpan (head) ... D 3
Toe (head) ... B 4
Tolsta (head) ... D 3
Ton Mhor (pt.) ... C 8
Tongue, Kyle of (inlet) ... G 2
Tor Ness (prom.) ... K 2
Torridon (inlet) ... E 4
Treig (lake) ... G 6
Trossachs, The (valley) ... H 7
Trotternish (dist.), 389 ... D 4
Troup (head) ... M 4
Tuath (inlet) ... D 7
Tummel (falls) ... J 6
Tummel (river) ... J 6
Turnberry (pt.) ... G 9
Tweed (riv.) ... M 8
Tyne (riv.) ... M 7
Ugie (riv.) ... N 4
Ulva (isl.), 28 ... D 7
Unst (isl.), 1,148 ... N 2
Vaternish (dist.), 198 ... C 4
Vaternish (pt.) ... C 4
Vatersay (isl.), 95 ... A 6
Voil (lake) ... G 7
Watten (lake) ... K 3
West Burra (isl.), 561 ... M 3
West Loch Tarbert (inlet) ... B 4
Westray (firth) ... K 1
Westray (isl.), 872 ... K 1
Whalsay (isl.), 764 ... N 3
Whiten (head) ... G 2
Wide (firth) ... L 1
Wigtown (bay) ... H10
Wrath (cape) ... F 2
Yarrow Water (riv.) ... L 8
Yell (isl.), 1,155 ... M 2
Yell (sound) ... M 2
Ythan (riv.) ... M 5

*City and suburbs.

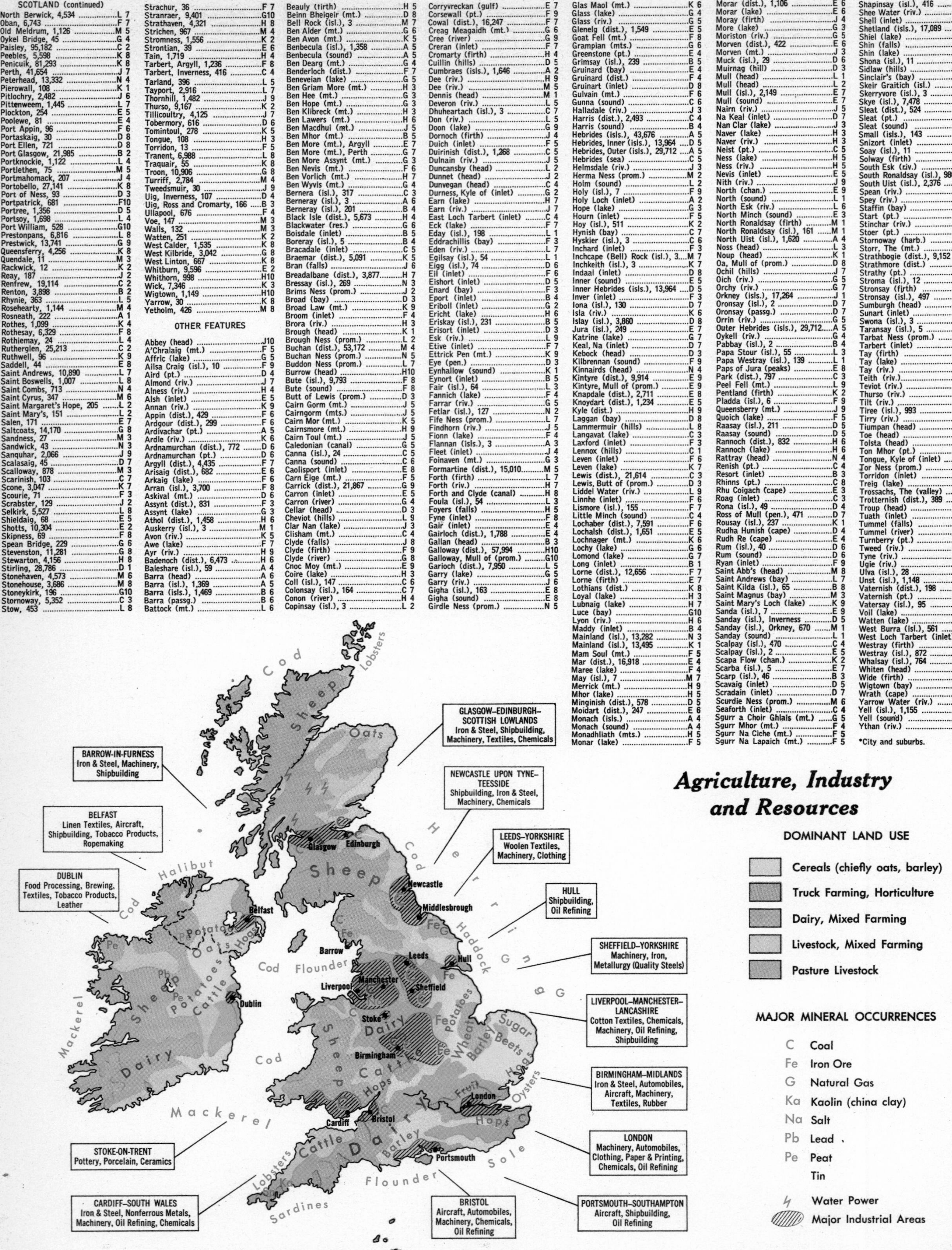

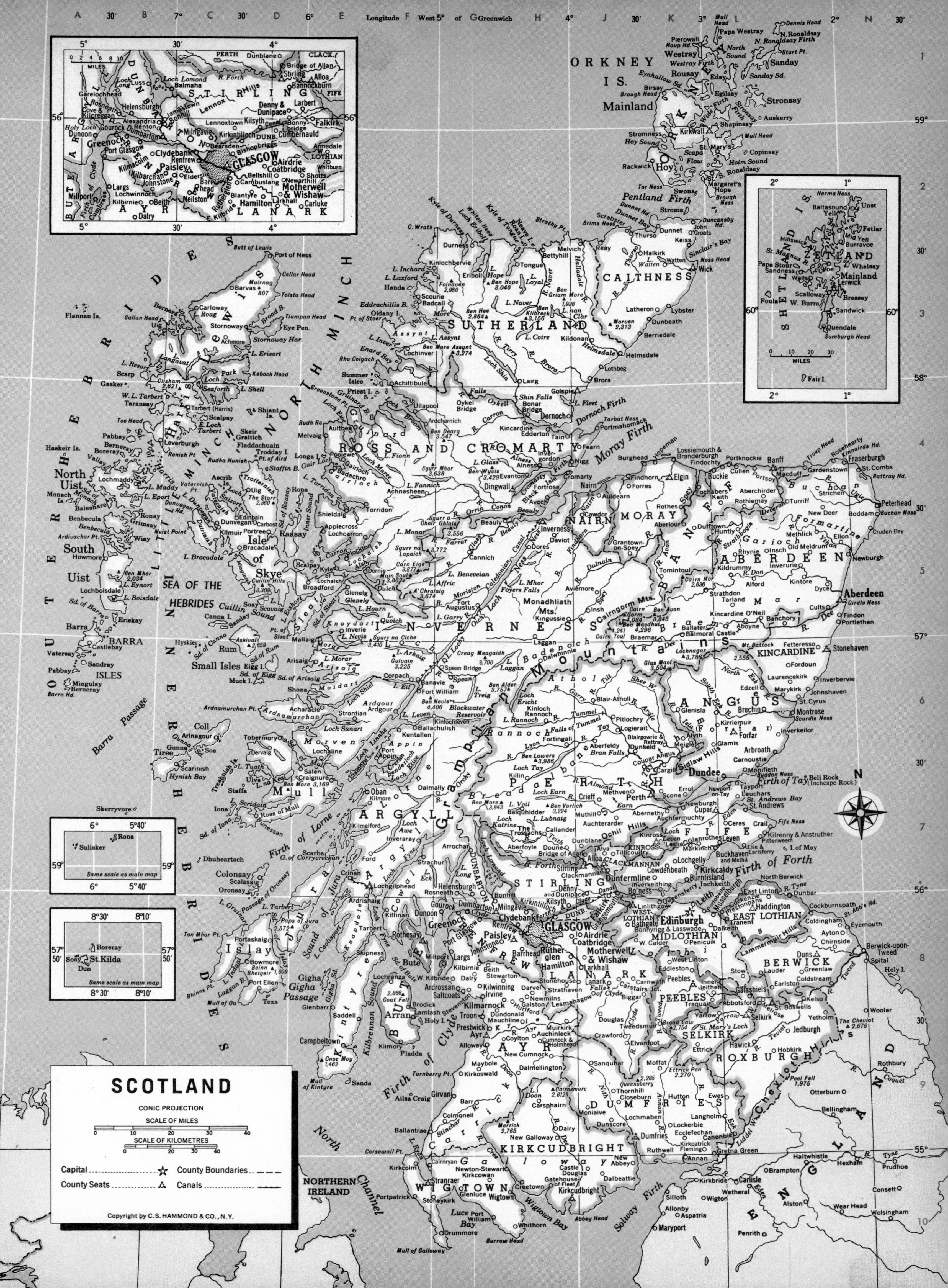

SCOTLAND
CONIC PROJECTION
SCALE OF MILES
0 10 20 30 40
SCALE OF KILOMETRES
0 20 30 40
Capital
County Seats
County Boundaries
Canals
Copyright by C. S. HAMMOND & CO., N.Y.
Longitude West 5° of Greenwich
ORKNEY IS.
Mainland
Westray
Rousay
Sanday
Stronsay
Hoy
Pentland Firth
SHETLAND IS.
ZETLAND
Unst
Yell
Fetlar
Lerwick
Fair I.
Foula
CAITHNESS
Wick
Thurso
SUTHERLAND
Dornoch
ROSS AND CROMARTY
Dingwall
Moray Firth
NAIRN
MORAY
Elgin
BANFF
ABERDEEN
Aberdeen
Peterhead
Fraserburgh
INVERNESS
Inverness
Grampian Mountains
Cairngorm Mts.
Monadhliath Mts.
Ben Nevis 4,406
KINCARDINE
Stonehaven
ANGUS
Forfar
Dundee
Firth of Tay
PERTH
Perth
FIFE
Cupar
KINROSS
CLACKMANNAN
Alloa
Firth of Forth
STIRLING
Stirling
DUNBARTON
ARGYLL
Inveraray
Mull
Islay
Jura
Firth of Lorne
BUTE
Arran
Firth of Clyde
RENFREW
Paisley
GLASGOW
LANARK
Hamilton
Edinburgh
WEST LOTHIAN
MIDLOTHIAN
EAST LOTHIAN
Haddington
BERWICK
Duns
PEEBLES
SELKIRK
ROXBURGH
Jedburgh
AYR
Ayr
DUMFRIES
Dumfries
KIRKCUDBRIGHT
WIGTOWN
Wigtown
Solway Firth
North Channel
NORTHERN IRELAND
ENGLAND
Cheviot Hills
OUTER HEBRIDES
Lewis
Harris
North Uist
Benbecula
South Uist
Barra
Stornoway
The Minch
Little Minch
North Minch
Sea of the Hebrides
Isle of Skye
Portree
Rum
Eigg
Coll
Tiree
Colonsay
Sulisker
Rona
Boreray
St. Kilda
Same scale as main map

16 United Kingdom and Ireland

(continued)

IRELAND

COUNTIES

Carlow, 33,342 H 6
Cavan, 56,594 G 4
Clare, 73,702 D 6
Cork, 330,443 D 7
Galway, 149,887 D 5
Donegal, 113,842 F 2
Dublin, 718,332 J 5
Kerry, 116,458 B 7
Kildare, 64,402 H 5
Kilkenny, 61,668 G 6
Laoighis, 45,069 G 6
Leitrim, 33,470 E 3
Leix (Laoighis), 45,069 G 6
Limerick, 133,339 D 7
Longford, 30,643 F 4
Louth, 67,378 J 4
Mayo, 123,330 C 4
Meath, 65,122 H 4
Monaghan, 47,088 H 3
Offaly, 51,533 F 5
Roscommon, 59,217 E 4
Sligo, 53,561 D 3
Tipperary, 123,822 F 6
Waterford, 71,439 F 7
Westmeath, 52,861 G 5
Wexford, 83,308 H 7
Wicklow, 58,473 J 5

CITIES and TOWNS

Abbeydorney, 164 B 7
Abbeyfeale, 1,272 C 7
Abbeylara, 113 F 4
Abbeyleix, 1,085 G 6
Achill Sound, 277 B 4
Aclare, 117 D 3
Adare, 590 D 6
Aghadoe, †371 C 7
Aghagower, †558 C 4
Ahascragh, 234 E 5
Annagassan, 194 J 4
Annascaul, 212 B 7
An Uaimh, 3,998 H 4
Ardagh, Limerick, 122 C 7
Ardagh, Longford, 102 F 4
Ardara, 547 E 2
Ardee, 2,710 H 4
Ardfinnan, 428 F 7
Ardmore, 290 F 8
Arklow, 5,390 J 6
Arthurstown, 136 H 7
Arva, 512 F 4
Ashford, 309 J 5
Askeaton, 706 D 6
Athboy, 680 H 4
Athea, 299 C 7
Athenry, 1,266 D 5
Athleague, 132 E 4
Athlone, 9,624 F 5
Athy, 3,842 H 6
Aughrim, 528 J 6
Avoca, 248 J 6
Bagenalstown (Muinebeag), 2,071 H 6
Baile Atha Cliath (Dublin) (cap.), 537,448 K 5
Bailieborough, 1,136 G 4
Balbriggan, 2,943 J 4
Balla, 324 C 4
Ballaghaderreen, 1,308 E 4
Ballina, 6,027 C 3
Ballinagh, 389 G 4
Ballinakill, 315 G 6
Ballinamore, 793 F 3
Ballinasloe, 5,711 E 5
Ballincollig, 960 D 8
Ballindine, 222 C 4
Ballingarry, Limerick, 360 D 7
Ballingarry, Tipperary, 209 F 6
Ballinlough, 252 D 4
Ballinrobe, 1,165 C 4
Ballintober, †938 E 4
Ballintra, 250 E 2
Ballisodare, 529 E 3
Ballybay, 716 G 3
Ballybofey, 1,030 F 2
Ballybunion, 1,163 B 7
Ballycanew, 168 J 6
Ballycastle, 191 C 3
Ballyconnell, 592 F 3
Ballycotton, 412 F 8
Ballydehob, 303 C 8
Ballydesmond, 178 C 7
Ballyduff, 379 B 7
Ballygar, 315 E 4
Ballyhaunis, 1,174 D 4
Ballyheigue, 417 B 7
Ballyjamesduff, 581 G 4
Ballylanders, 280 E 7
Ballylongford, 594 B 6
Ballymahon, 830 F 4
Ballymakeery-Ballyvourney, 321 C 8
Ballymore, 179 F 5
Ballymore Eustace, 348 J 5
Ballymote, 965 D 3
Ballynacargy, 288 G 4
Ballyporeen, 270 E 7
Ballyragget, 478 G 6
Ballyroan, 122 G 6
Ballyshannon, 2,322 E 3
Ballytore, 269 H 5
Ballyvaughn, 152 C 5
Balrothery, 102 J 4
Baltimore, 188 C 9
Baltinglass, 116 H 6
Banagher, 1,050 F 5
Bandon, 2,308 D 8
Bannow, †820 H 7
Bantry, 2,234 C 8
Barna, 143 C 5
Belmullet, 724 B 3
Belturbet, 1,093 G 3
Birr, 3,221 F 5
Blackwater, 216 J 7
Blarney, 995 D 8
Blessington, 491 J 5
Borris, 413 H 6
Borrisokane, 750 E 6
Boyle, 1,739 E 4
Bray (Brí Chualann), 11,688 K 5
Bruff, 545 D 7
Bunclody-Carrickduff, 891 H 6
Buncrana, 2,960 G 1
Bundoran, 1,326 E 3
Bunmahon, 265 G 7
Burtonport, 224 E 2
Buttevant, 981 D 7
Cahir, 1,662 F 7
Cahirciveen, 1,659 A 8
Callan, 1,346 G 7
Cappamore, 501 E 6
Cappawhite, 318 E 6
Cappoquin, 806 F 7
Carbury, †926 H 5
Carlingford, 471 J 3
Carlow, 7,708 H 6
Carndonagh, 1,016 G 1
Carnew, 551 H 6
Carrick, 153 D 2
Carrickmacross, 1,940 H 4
Carrick-on-Shannon, 1,497 F 4
Carrick-on-Suir, 4,672 F 7
Carrigaholt, 160 B 6
Carrigallen, 202 F 4
Carrigart, 196 F 1
Carrowkeel, 118 G 1
Cashel, 2,679 F 7
Castlebar, 5,482 C 4
Castlebellingham, 656 J 4
Castleblayney, 2,127 H 3
Castlebridge, 181 J 7
Castlecomer-Donaguile, 1,129 G 6
Castledermot, 551 H 6
Castlefin, 565 F 2
Castlegregory, 235 A 7
Castleisland, 1,718 B 7
Castlemaine, 171 B 7
Castlepollard, 778 G 4
Castlerea, 1,568 D 4
Castletown, 264 F 6
Castletownbere, 721 B 8
Castletownroche, 381 D 7
Castletownshend, 177 C 9
Cavan, 3,208 G 3
Ceanannus Mór, 2,193 G 4
Celbridge, 1,305 H 5
Charlestown-Bellahy, 727 D 4
Charleville (Rathluirc), 1,956 D 7
Clara, 2,477 F 5
Claregalway, 627 D 5
Claremorris, 1,519 C 4
Clashmore, 175 F 8
Clifden, 1,025 B 5
Cloghan, 399 G 6
Clogh-Chatsworth, 303 F 5
Clogheen, 576 F 7
Clogherhead, 585 J 4
Clonakilty, 2,417 D 8
Clonaslee, 275 F 5
Clondalkin, 3,434 J 5
Clones, 2,107 G 3
Clonmacnoise, †411 F 5
Clonmany, 238 G 1
Clonmel, 10,640 F 7
Clonroche, 193 H 7
Cloon, 106 F 4
Cloughjordan, 479 E 6
Cloyne, 612 E 8
Coachford, 275 D 8
Cóbh, 5,266 E 8
Coill Dubh, 645 H 5
Collooney, 553 E 3
Cong, 178 C 4
Convoy, 616 F 2
Coolaney, 124 D 3
Coole, 344 G 4
Coolgreany, 124 J 6
Cootehill, 1,296 G 3
Cork, 77,980 E 8
Corofin, 362 C 6
Courtmacsherry, 205 D 8
Courtown Harbour-Riverchapel, 396 J 6
Crookhaven, 62 B 9
Croom, 720 D 6
Crosshaven, 858 E 8
Crossmolina, 777 C 3
Culdaff, 108 G 1
Cullen, 113 C 7
Daingean, 679 G 5
Delvin, 165 G 4
Dingle, 1,460 A 7
Doaghbeg, †795 F 1
Donabate, 318 J 5
Donegal, 1,458 F 2
Doneraile, 725 D 7
Dooagh, 387 A 4
Douglas, †3,113 D 8
Drishane, †1,511 C 7
Drogheda, 17,085 J 4
Droichead Nua, 3,668 H 5
Dromahair, 229 E 3
Dromore West, 99 D 3
Drumcar, †1,205 J 4
Drumcliffe, 772 E 3
Drumconrath, 195 H 4
Drumkeerin, 136 E 3
Drumlish, 343 F 4
Drumshanbo, 565 E 3
Dublin (cap.), 537,448 K 5
Dublin, *595,288 K 5
Duleek, 379 J 4
Dunboyne, 521 H 5
Duncannon, 226 H 7
Dundalk, 19,790 H 3
Dunfanaghy, 324 F 1
Dungarvan, 5,188 F 7
Dungloe, 793 E 2
Dunkineely, 261 E 2
Dún Laoghaire, 47,792 K 5
Dunlavin, 416 H 5
Dunleen, 529 J 4
Dunmanway, 1,411 C 8
Dunmore, 500 D 4
Dunmore East, 547 G 7
Dunshaughlin, 231 H 5
Durrow, Laoighis, 439 G 6
Durrow, Westmeath, 435 F 5
Easky, 317 D 3
Edenderry, 2,691 G 5
Elphin, 494 E 4
Emyvale, 255 G 3
Ennis, 5,699 D 6
Enniscorthy, 5,754 J 7
Enniskerry, 652 J 5
Ennistymon, 1,145 C 6
Eyrecourt, 355 E 5
Fahan, 322 G 1
Feakle, 129 D 6
Fenit, 308 B 7
Ferbane, 896 F 5
Fermoy, 3,241 E 7
Ferns, 557 J 6
Fethard, Tipperary, 962 F 7
Fethard, Wexford, 218 H 7
Fiddown, 152 G 7
Foxford, 876 C 4
Foynes, 686 C 6
Frankford (Kilcormac), 1,018 F 5
Frenchpark, 155 E 4
Freshford, 656 G 6
Galbally, 266 E 7
Galway, 22,028 C 5
Geashill, 170 G 5
Glandore, 151 C 8
Glencolumbkille, 95 D 2
Glencullen, 161 J 5
Glengarriff, 392 C 8
Glenties, 828 E 2
Glenville, 146 E 7
Glin, 763 C 6
Golden, 153 F 7
Gorey, 2,671 J 6
Gort, 1,044 D 5
Gowran, 365 G 6
Granard, 1,044 F 4
Greencastle, 233 H 1
Greenore, 142 J 4
Greystones-Delgany, 3,551 K 5
Hacketstown, 509 H 6
Holycross, 921 F 6
Hospital, 572 E 7
Inchigeela, 157 C 8
Inniscrone, 533 C 3
Johnstown, 326 G 6
Kanturk, 1,985 D 7
Keel, 459 A 4
Kells, 128 G 7
Kells (Ceanannus Mór), 2,193 G 4
Kenmare, 1,046 B 8
Kilbeggan, 799 G 5
Kilbehenny, 86 E 7
Kilcar, 229 D 2
Kilcock, 739 H 5
Kilconnell, 113 E 5
Kilcoole, 549 K 5
Kilcormac, 1,018 F 5
Kilcullen, 637 H 5
Kildare, 2,551 H 5
Kildysart, 295 C 6
Kilfenora, 135 C 6
Kilfinane, 565 D 7
Kilgarvan, 183 B 8
Kilkee, 1,392 B 6
Kilkelly, 257 D 4
Kilkenny, 10,159 G 6
Killala, 337 C 3
Killaloe, 835 D 6
Killarney, 6,825 C 7
Killavullen, 167 D 7
Killenaule, 531 F 6
Killeshandra, 397 F 3
Killimor, 195 E 5
Killorglin, 1,100 B 7
Killucan-Rathwire, 314 G 4
Killybegs, 1,065 E 2
Kilmacrennan, 251 F 1
Kilmacthomas, 446 G 7
Kilmallock, 1,159 D 7
Kilmeaden, 77 G 7
Kilmihill, 264 C 6
Kilnaleck, 279 G 4
Kilronan, 231 B 5
Kilrush, 2,861 C 6
Kilsheelan, 172 F 7
Kiltimagh, 980 C 4
Kilworth, 334 E 7
Kingscourt, 793 H 4
Kingstown (Dún Laoghaire), 47,792 K 5
Kinlough, 203 E 3
Kinnegad, 351 G 5
Kinnitty, 275 F 5
Kinsale, 1,587 D 8
Kinvara, 338 D 5
Knightstown, 337 A 8
Knock, 218 D 4
Knocklong, 289 D 7
Knocktopher, 127 G 7
Labasheeda, 142 C 6
Laghey, 184 E 2
Lahinch, 389 C 6
Lanesborough-Ballyleague, 720 E 4
Laracor, 386 H 4
Laytown-Bettystown, 766 J 4
Leenane, 123 B 4
Leighlinbridge, 457 H 6
Leitrim, 111 F 3
Leixlip, 915 H 5
Letterkenny, 4,329 F 2
Lifford, 864 F 2
Limerick, 50,786 D 6
Liscarroll, 228 D 7
Lisdoonvarna, 625 C 5
Lismore, 810 F 7
Listowel, 7,859 C 7
Littleton, 274 F 6
Longford, 3,558 F 4
Lorrha, 84 E 5
Loughrea, 2,784 E 5
Louisburgh, 346 B 4
Louth, 207 J 4
Lucan-Doddsborough, 1,657 J 5
Luimneach (Limerick), 50,786 D 6
Lusk, 495 J 4
Macroom, 2,169 C 8
Malahide, 2,534 J 5
Malin, 164 G 1
Mallow, 5,545 D 7
Manorhamilton, 920 E 3
Manulla, †774 C 4
Maryborough (Portlaoighise), 3,133 G 5
Maynooth, 1,753 H 5
Meathas Truim, 624 G 4
Midleton, 2,772 E 8
Milford, 611 F 1
Millstreet, 1,283 D 7
Miltown Malbay, 700 C 6
Mitchelstown, 2,655 E 7
Moate, 1,261 F 5
Mohill, 905 F 4
Monaghan, 4,013 G 3
Monasterevan, 1,273 H 5
Moneygall, 284 F 6
Monivea, 222 D 5
Mooncoin, 507 G 7
Mount Bellew, 306 D 5
Mountcharles, 400 E 2
Mountmellick, 2,436 G 5
Mountrath, 1,051 F 5
Moville, 1,097 G 1
Moycullen, 127 C 5
Moynalty, 128 H 4
Muff, 219 G 1
Muinebeag, 2,071 H 6
Mullagh, 213 H 4
Mullaghmore, 137 D 3
Mullinahone, 322 F 7
Mullinavat, 339 G 7
Mullingar, 5,834 G 4
Naas, 4,023 H 5
Navan (An Uaimh), 3,998 H 4
Nenagh, 4,317 E 6
Newbliss, 192 G 3
Newbridge (Droichead Nua), 3,668 H 5
Newcastle, 2,527 D 7
New Inn, 164 F 7
Newmarket, 791 C 7
Newmarket-on-Fergus, 807 D 6
New Pallas, 171 E 6
Newport, Mayo, 459 C 4
Newport, Tipperary, 581 E 6
New Ross, 4,494 H 7
Newtownforbes, 318 F 4
Newtownmountkennedy-Killadreenan, 935 J 5
Newtownsandes, 304 C 6
O'Briensbridge-Montpelier, 232 D 6
Oola, 314 E 6
Oranmore, 346 D 5
Oughterard, 618 C 5
Passage East, 494 G 7
Passage West, 2,561 E 8
Patrickswell, 305 D 6
Pettigo, 313 F 2
Portarlington, 2,846 G 5
Portlaoighise, 3,133 G 5
Portlaw, 1,113 G 7
Portmarnock, 669 J 5
Portumna, 836 E 5
Queenstown (Cóbh), 5,266 E 8
Quilty, 190 C 6
Rahan, †635 F 5
Ramelton, 759 F 1
Raphoe, 818 F 2
Rathangan, 569 G 5
Rathcormac, 267 E 7
Rathdowney, 896 F 6
Rathdrum, 1,128 J 6
Rathkeale, 1,459 D 7
Rathluirc, 1,956 D 7
Rathmore, 417 J 5
Rathmullen, 491 F 1
Rathnew-Merrymeeting, 861 J 6
Rathowen, 119 F 4
Rathvilly, 293 H 6
Ratoath, 289 J 5
Riverstown, 203 E 3
Rockcorry, 190 H 3
Rosapenna, †905 F 1
Roscommon, 1,600 E 4
Roscrea, 3,372 F 6
Rosscarbery, 380 C 8
Rosslare, 529 J 7
Roundstone, 250 A 5
Rush, 2,118 J 4
Saggart, 426 F 2
Saint Johnstown, 458 F 2
Sallybrook-Riverstown, 563 E 8
Scariff-Tuamgraney, 600 E 6
Schull, 419 B 8
Scotstown, 199 H 3
Shannon Airport, 234 D 6
Shercock, 254 G 4
Shillelagh, 202 J 6
Shinrone, 402 F 5
Shrule, 250 C 4
Silvermines, 222 E 6
Sixmilebridge, 448 D 6
Skerries, 2,721 J 4
Skibbereen, 2,028 C 8
Slane, 421 H 4
Sligo, 13,145 E 3
Smithborough, 94 G 3
Sneem, 282 B 8
Spiddal, 134 C 5
Stradbally, Laoighis, 792 G 5
Stradbally, Waterford, 213 F 7
Stranorlar, 848 F 2
Strokestown, 707 E 4
Swanlinbar, 306 F 3
Swinford, 1,115 C 4
Swords, 1,816 J 5
Taghmon, 347 H 7
Tallow, 819 F 7
Tarbert, 455 C 6
Teltown, †684 H 4
Templemore, 1,779 F 6
Templetouhy, 156 F 6
Termonfeckin, 300 J 4
Thomastown, 1,209 G 7
Thurles, 6,421 F 6
Timoleague, 291 D 8
Tinahely, 417 H 6
Tipperary, 4,684 E 7
Toomevara, 231 E 6
Tralee, 10,723 B 7
Tramore, 2,882 G 7
Trim, 1,371 H 4
Tuam, 3,500 D 4
Tubbercurry, 878 D 3
Tulla, 389 D 6
Tullamore, 6,243 G 5
Tullaroan, 118 G 6
Tullow, 1,725 H 6
Tyrellspass, 259 G 5
Urlingford, 562 F 6
Virginia, 515 G 4
Waterford, 28,216 G 7
Waterville-Spunkane, 702 A 8
Westport, 2,882 C 4
Wexford, 11,328 H 7
Whitegate, 397 E 8
Wicklow, 3,125 K 6
Woodford, 264 E 5
Youghal, 5,043 F 8

OTHER FEATURES

Achill (isl.), 4,220 A 4
Aherlow (riv.) E 7
Allen (lake) E 3
Allen, Bog of (marsh) H 5
Allow (riv.) D 7
Annalee (riv.) G 3
Anner (riv.) F 7
Aran (isl.), 948 D 2
Aran (isls.), 1,651 B 5
Arrow (lake) E 3
Awbeg (riv.) D 7
Ballinskelligs (bay) A 8
Ballyhoura (hills) E 7
Ballynakill (harb.) A 4
Ballysadare (bay) D 3
Ballyteige (bay) H 7
Bandon (riv.) D 8
Bann (riv.) J 6
Bantry (bay) B 8
Barrow (riv.) H 7
Baurtregaum (mt.) A 7
Bear (isl.), 382 B 8
Beltra (lake) C 4
Ben Dash (hill) C 6
Benwee (head) B 3
Bertraghboy (bay) A 5
Black (head) C 5
Blacksod (bay) A 3
Blackstairs (mt.) H 6
Blackwater (riv.) D 7
Blackwater (riv.) H 4
Blasket (isls.) A 7
Bloody Foreland (prom.) E 1
Blue Stack (mts.) E 2
Boderg (lake) E 4
Boggeragh (mts.) D 7
Bolus (head) A 8
Bonet (riv.) E 3
Boyne (riv.) J 4
Brandon (bay) A 7
Brandon (mt.) A 7
Brannock (isls.) A 5
Bray (head) A 8
Bride (riv.) E 7
Broad Haven (harb.) B 3
Brosna (riv.) F 5
Bull, The (isl.) A 8
Caha (mts.) B 8
Cahore (pt.) J 6
Cark (mt.) F 2
Carlingford (inlet) J 3
Carnsore (pt.) J 7
Carra (lake) C 4
Carrantuohill (mt.) B 7
Carrigan (head) D 2
Carrowmore (lake) B 3
Clare (riv.) D 5
Clare with Inishturk (isls.), 313 A 4
Clear (cape) B 9
Clear (isl.) C 9
Clew (bay) B 4
Comeragh (mts.) F 7
Conn (lake) C 3
Connacht (prov.), 419,465 C 4
Connemara (dist.), 23,841 B 5
Corrib (lake) C 5
Courtmacsherry (bay) D 8
Croagh Patrick (mt.) C 4
Crossfarnoge (pt.) J 7
Cuilcagh (mt.) F 3
Cullin (lake) C 4
Curragh, The H 5
Cutra (lake) D 5
Dee (riv.) H 4
Deel (riv.) C 3
Deel (riv.) D 7
Deel (riv.) F 2
Derg (lake) E 6
Derg (lake) F 2
Derravaragh (lake) G 4
Derryveagh (mts.) E 2
Devilsbit (mt.) F 6
Dingle (bay) A 7
Donegal (bay) D 3
Donegal (pt.) B 6
Doulus (head) A 8
Downpatrick (head) C 3
Drum (hills) F 7
Dublin (bay) J 5
Dunaff (head) F 1
Dunany (pt.) J 4
Dundalk (bay) J 4
Dunkellin (riv.) D 5
Dunmanus (bay) B 8
Dursey (isl.) A 8
Eask (lake) E 2
Ennell (lake) G 5
Erkina (riv.) G 6
Erne (riv.) E 3
Erris (head) A 3
Errigal (mt.) E 1
Fanad (head) F 1
Fastnet Rock (isl.) B 9
Feale (riv.) C 7
Feeagh (lake) B 4
Fergus (riv.) D 6
Finn (riv.) F 2
Finn (riv.) G 3
Flesk (riv.) C 7
Foul (sound) B 5
Foyle (inlet) G 1
Foyle (riv.) G 2
Galley (head) D 9
Galtee (mts.) E 7
Galtymore (mt.) E 7
Galway (bay) C 5
Gara (lake) D 4
Garadice (lake) F 3
Gartan (lake) F 2
Garvan (isls.) G 1
Gill (lake) E 3
Glen (lake) F 1
Glyde (riv.) H 4
Gola (isl.) E 1
Golden Vale (plain) E 7
Gorumna (isl.), †1,730 B 5
Gowna (lake) G 4
Grand (canal) G 5
Great Blasket (isl.) A 7
Greenore (pt.) J 7
Gregory's (sound) B 5
Gweebarra (bay) D 2
Gweebarra (riv.) E 2
Hags (head) B 6
Helvick (head) G 7
High (isl.) A 4
Hook (head) H 7
Horn (head) E 1
Iar Connaught (dist.), 4,051 C 5
Inishbofin (isl.), 248 A 4
Inishbofin (isl.) E 1
Inisheer (isl.), 358 B 5
Inishmaan (isl.), 357 C 5
Inishmore (isl.), 936 B 5
Inishmurray (isl.) D 3
Inishowen (head) H 1
Inishowen (pen.) G 1
Inishshark (isl.) A 4
Inishtrahull (isl.) G 1
Inishturk with Clare (isls.), 313 A 4
Inny (riv.) A 8
Inny (riv.) F 4
Inver (bay) E 2
Ireland's Eye (isl.) K 5
Irish (sea) K 4
Joyce's Country (dist.), 2,425 B 4
Keeper (hill) E 6
Kenmare (riv.) A 8
Kerry (head) A 7
Key (lake) E 3
Kilkieran (bay) B 5
Killary (harb.) A 4
Kinsale, Old Head of (head) E 8
Kippure (mt.) J 5
Knockadoon (head) F 8
Knockanefune (mt.) C 7
Knockboy (mt.) B 8
Knockmealdown (mts.) F 7
Lady's Island Lake (inlet) J 7
Lambay (isl.) K 5
Lamb's (head) A 8
Laune (riv.) B 7
Leane (lake) B 7
Leane (lake) G 4
Lee (riv.) D 8
Leinster (mt.) H 6
Leinster (prov.), 1,332,149 G 5
Lettermullen (isl.) B 5
Liffey (riv.) H 5
Liscannor (bay) B 6
Little Brosna (riv.) E 5
Long Island (bay) B 9
Loop (head) A 6
Loughros More (bay) D 2
Lugnaquillia (mt.) J 5
Lung (riv.) D 4
Macgillicuddy's Reeks (mts.) B 7
Macnean (lake) F 3
Maigue (riv.) D 6
Maine (riv.) C 7
Malin (head) F 1
Mangerton (mt.) C 8
Mask (lake) C 4
Maumakeogh (mt.) C 3
Maumturk (mts.) B 5
Melvin (lake) E 3
Mine (head) F 8
Mizen (head) B 9
Mizen (head) K 6
Moher (cliffs) B 6
Monavullagh (mts.) F 7
Moy (riv.) C 3
Muckish (mt.) E 1
Muckno (lake) H 3
Mulkear (riv.) E 6
Mullaghareirk (mts.) C 7
Mulroy (bay) F 1
Munster (prov.), 849,203 D 7
Mutton (isl.) B 6
Mweelrea (mt.) B 4
Mweenish (isl.) B 5
Nagles (mts.) E 7
Nephin (mt.) C 3
Nephin Beg (mt.) B 3
Nore (riv.) G 7
North (sound) B 5
North Inishkea (isl.) A 3
Omey (isl.) A 5
Oughter (lake) G 3
Ovoca (riv.) J 6
Owell (lake) G 4
Owenmore (riv.) B 3
Owenmore (riv.) D 3
Owey (isl.) D 1
Ox (Slieve Gamph) (mts.) D 3
Paps, The (mt.) C 7
Partry (mts.) C 4
Pollaphuca (res.) J 5
Puffin (isl.) A 8
Punchestown H 5
Ramor (lake) G 4
Rathlin O'Birne (isl.) C 2
Ree (lake) F 5
Rinn (lake) F 4
Roaringwater (bay) B 9
Rosses (bay) D 1
Rosskeeragh (pt.) D 3
Rosslare (bay) J 7
Royal (canal) G 4
Saint Finan's (bay) A 8
Saint George's (chan.) K 7
Saint John's (pt.) D 2
Saltee (isls.) H 7
Scarriff (isl.) A 8
Seven (heads) D 8
Seven Hogs, The (isls.) A 7
Shannon (riv.) E 6
Shannon, Mouth of the (est.) B 6
Sheeffry (hills) B 4
Sheep Haven (harb.) F 1
Sheeps (head) B 8
Shehy (mts.) C 8
Sherkin (isl.) C 9
Silvermine (mts.) E 6
Slaney (riv.) H 7
Slieve Anierin (mt.) F 3
Slieve Aughty (mts.) D 5
Slieve Bernagh (mt.) D 6
Slieve Bloom (mts.) F 5
Slieve Callan (mt.) C 6
Slievecar (mt.) B 3
Slieve Elva (mt.) C 5
Slievefelim (mts.) E 6
Slieve Gamph (mts.) D 3
Slieve League (mt.) D 2
Slieve Mishkish (mts.) B 8
Slievenaman (mt.) F 7
Slyne (head) A 5
Smerwick (harb.) A 7
South (sound) C 5
Stacks (mts.) B 7
Suck (riv.) E 5
Sugarloaf (mt.) B 8
Suir (riv.) G 7
Swilly (inlet) F 1
Tara (hill) H 4
Tawin (isl.) C 5
Toe (head) C 9
Tory (isl.) E 1
Tralee (bay) B 7
Tramore (bay) G 7
Trawbreaga (bay) F 1
Truskmore (mt.) E 3
Twelve Pins (mt.) B 4
Ulster (prov.), 217,524 G 2
Valentia (Valencia) (isl.), 926 A 8
Veagh (lake) F 1
Wexford (bay) J 7
Wicklow (mts.) J 6
Wicklow (head) K 6
Youghal (bay) F 8

NORTHERN IRELAND

COUNTIES

Antrim, 333,800 J 2
Armagh, 128,200 H 3
Belfast (city), 385,900 K 2
Down, 300,800 J 3
Fermanagh, 49,900 F 3
Londonderry, 177,300 H 2
Tyrone, 136,600 G 2

CITIES and TOWNS

Aghadowey, †679 H 1
Ahoghill, 885 J 2
Annalong, 553 K 3
Antrim, 33,980 J 2
Ardglass, 737 K 3
Armagh, 11,920 H 3
Armoy, 383 J 1
Augher, 222 G 3
Aughnacloy, 805 H 3
Ballycastle, 2,960 J 1
Ballyclare, 4,690 J 2
Ballygally, 276 K 2
Ballygawley, 427 G 3
Ballykelly, 367 G 1
Ballymena, 16,730 J 2
Ballymoney, 3,700 J 1
Ballynahinch, 2,042 J 3
Ballynure, 291 K 2
Ballywalter, 789 K 2
Banbridge, 6,620 J 3
Bangor, 30,030 K 2
Belfast (cap.), 385,900 J 2
Belfast, *528,700 J 2
Bellaghy, 663 H 2
Belleek, 162 E 3
Beragh, 349 G 2
Bessbrook, 3,199 J 3
Brookeborough, 294 G 3
Broughshane, 716 J 2
Bushmills, 936 J 1
Caledon, 350 H 3
Carnlough, 586 J 2
Carrickfergus, 13,130 K 2
Carrowdore, 297 K 2
Castledawson, 906 H 2
Castlederg, 1,367 F 2
Castlewellan, 1,241 K 3
Claudy, 286 G 2
Clogher, 197 G 3
Coalisland, 1,351 H 2
Coleraine, 14,090 H 1
Comber, 3,987 K 2
Cookstown, 6,190 H 2
Craigavon, 11,140 J 3
Crossgar, 842 K 3
Crossmaglen, 932 H 3
Crumlin, 394 J 2
Cullybackey, 758 J 2
Cushendall, 618 J 1
Derrygonnelly, 296 F 3
Dervock, 558 J 1
Doagh, 486 J 2
Donaghdee, 3,730 K 2
Downpatrick, 5,290 K 3
Draperstown, 592 H 2
Dromara, 280 J 3
Dromore, Down, 1,980 J 3
Dromore, Tyrone, 503 G 3
Drumquin, 307 F 2
Dunbarton, 905 J 3
Dundrum, 641 K 3
Dungannon, 7,590 H 3
Dungiven, 1,102 H 2
Dunnamanagh, 352 G 2
Ederny, 227 F 2
Enniskillen, 7,020 F 3
Feeny, 206 H 2
Fintona, 990 G 3
Fivemiletown, 77 G 3
Garvagh, 550 H 2
Gilford, 780 J 3
Glenarm, 673 J 2
Glenavy, 1,306 J 2
Glynn, 389 K 2
Gortin, 261 G 2
Greyabbey, 611 K 2
Hillsborough, 806 J 3
Hilltown, 309 J 3
Holywood, 7,930 K 2
Irvinestown, 934 F 3
Jonesborough, 274 J 3
Keady, 1,960 H 3
Kells, 495 J 2
Kesh, †689 F 3
Kilkeel, 2,570 K 3
Killeter, †442 F 2
Killough, 504 K 3
Killyleagh, 1,876 K 3
Kilrea, 952 H 2
Kircubbin, 843 K 3
Lack, †571 F 2
Larne, 17,840 K 2
Limavady, 5,230 H 1
Lisburn, 24,870 J 2
Lisnaskea, 977 G 3
Londonderry, 55,000 G 2
Loughbrickland, 300 J 3
Loughgall, †1,086 H 3
Maghera, 1,607 H 2
Magherafelt, 2,459 H 2
Maguire's Bridge, 339 G 3
Markethill, 813 H 3
Middletown, 161 H 3
Millisle, 386 K 2
Moira, 501 J 3
Moneymore, 807 H 2
Moy, 751 H 3
Moygashel, 1,146 H 3
Newcastle, 4,450 J 3
Newry, 11,960 J 3
Newtownabbey, 53,450 K 2
Newtownards, 14,180 K 2
Newtownbutler, 358 G 3
Newtownhamilton, 589 H 3
Newtownstewart, 1,125 G 2
Omagh, 10,710 G 2
Pettigoe, 76 F 2
Pomeroy, 349 H 2
Portaferry, 1,406 K 3
Portavogie, 1,071 K 3
Portglenone, 613 H 2
Portrush, 4,420 H 1
Portstewart, 4,660 H 1
Randalstown, 1,579 J 2
Rasharkin, 799 J 2
Rathfriland, 1,558 J 3
Rostrevor, 1,265 J 3
Saintfield, 702 K 3
Sion Mills, 1,616 G 2
Sixmilecross, 245 H 2
Stewartstown, 621 H 2
Strabane, 9,040 G 2
Strangford, 413 K 3
Tandragee, 1,570 H 3
Templepatrick, †775 J 2
Tempo, 269 G 3
Trillick, 220 G 3
Tynan, †805 H 3
Warrenpoint, 3,750 J 3
Whitehead, 2,760 K 2

OTHER FEATURES

Arney (riv.) F 3
Bann (riv.) H 2
Beg (lake) J 2
Belfast (inlet) K 2
Binevenagh (mt.) H 1
Blackwater (riv.) H 3
Bush (riv.) H 1
Copeland (isl.) K 2
Derg (riv.) F 2
Erne (lake) F 3
Fair (head) J 1
Foyle (inlet) G 1
Foyle (riv.) G 2
Garron (pt.) K 1
Giant's Causeway H 1
Knocklayd (mt.) J 1
Lagan (riv.) K 2
Larne (inlet) K 2
Macnean (lake) F 3
Magee, Island (pen.) K 2
Magilligan (pt.) H 1
Maidens, The (isls.) K 2
Main (riv.) J 2
Mourne (mts.) J 3
Mourne (riv.) G 2
Neagh (lake) J 2
North (chan.) K 1
Owenkillew (riv.) G 2
Rathlin (isl.), 159 J 1
Red (bay) K 1
Roe (riv.) H 1
Saint John's (pt.) K 3
Slemish (mt.) J 2
Slieve Beagh (mt.) G 3
Slieve Donard (mt.) K 3
Slieve Gullion (mt.) J 3
Sperrin (mts.) G 2
Strangford (inlet) K 3
Torr (head) K 1
Trostan (mt.) J 1
Ulster (prov.), 1,512,500 G 2
Upper Lough Erne (lake) F 3

*City and suburbs.
†Population of district.

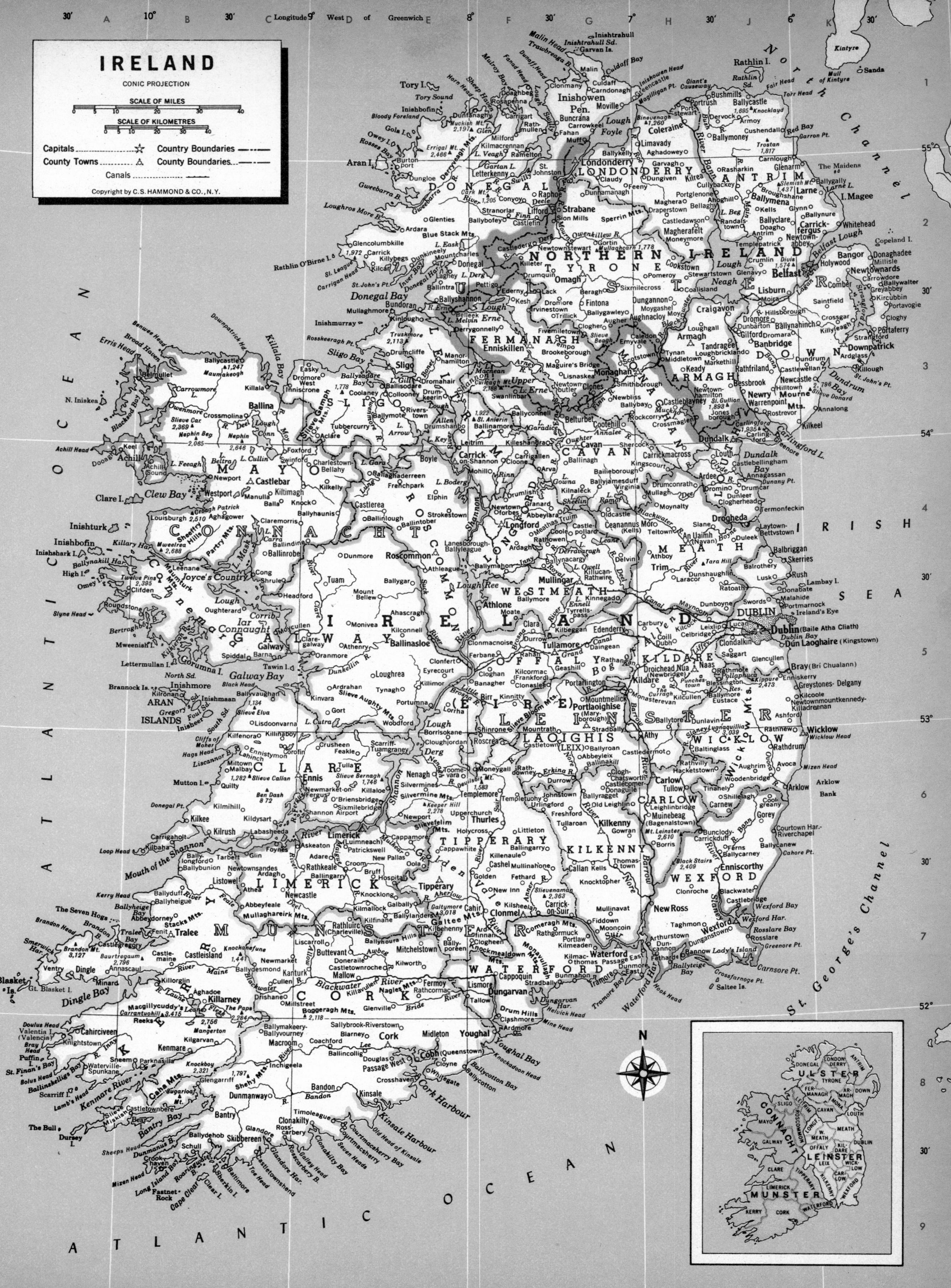
IRELAND
CONIC PROJECTION
SCALE OF MILES
SCALE OF KILOMETRES
Capitals
County Towns
Canals
Country Boundaries
County Boundaries
Copyright by C.S. HAMMOND & CO., N.Y.
Longitude West of Greenwich
NORTHERN IRELAND
IRELAND (EIRE)
ULSTER
CONNACHT
LEINSTER
MUNSTER
ATLANTIC OCEAN
IRISH SEA
North Channel
St. George's Channel
DONEGAL
LONDONDERRY
ANTRIM
TYRONE
FERMANAGH
ARMAGH
DOWN
MONAGHAN
CAVAN
LEITRIM
SLIGO
MAYO
GALWAY
ROSCOMMON
LONGFORD
WESTMEATH
MEATH
LOUTH
DUBLIN
KILDARE
OFFALY
LAOIGHIS
WICKLOW
CARLOW
KILKENNY
WEXFORD
TIPPERARY
WATERFORD
CLARE
LIMERICK
KERRY
CORK
Belfast
Dublin (Baile Atha Cliath)
Dun Laoghaire (Kingstown)
Londonderry
Armagh
Omagh
Enniskillen
Downpatrick
Monaghan
Cavan
Sligo
Castlebar
Galway
Roscommon
Longford
Mullingar
Trim
Naas
Tullamore
Portlaoighise
Wicklow
Carlow
Kilkenny
Wexford
Clonmel
Waterford
Dungarvan
Ennis
Limerick
Tralee
Cork
Lifford
Carrick-on-Shannon
Dundalk
Drogheda
Athlone
Killarney
Shannon
Lough Neagh
Lough Ree
Lough Derg
Lough Corrib
Galway Bay
Donegal Bay
Clew Bay
Dingle Bay
Bantry Bay
Mouth of the Shannon
ARAN ISLANDS
Achill
Rathlin I.
Tory I.
Cape Clear
Mizen Head
Malin Head
Carnsore Pt.
Kintyre
N

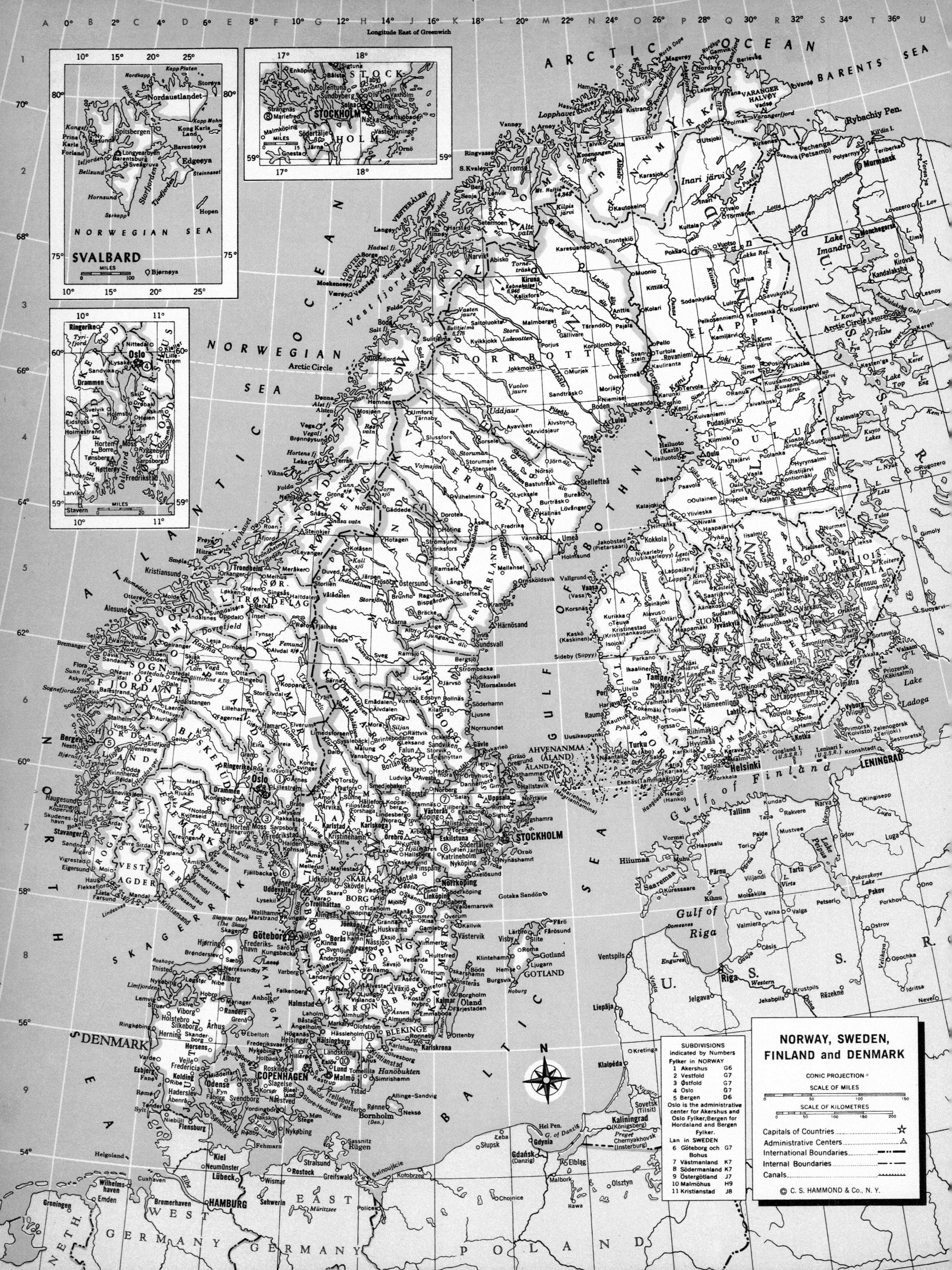
NORWAY, SWEDEN, FINLAND and DENMARK
CONIC PROJECTION
SCALE OF MILES
SCALE OF KILOMETRES
Capitals of Countries
Administrative Centers
International Boundaries
Internal Boundaries
Canals
© C. S. HAMMOND & Co., N. Y.
SUBDIVISIONS indicated by Numbers
Fylker in NORWAY
1 Akershus G6
2 Vestfold G7
3 Østfold G7
4 Oslo G7
5 Bergen D6
Oslo is the administrative center for Akershus and Oslo Fylker; Bergen for Hordaland and Bergen Fylker.
Lan in SWEDEN
6 Göteborg och Bohus G7
7 Västmanland K7
8 Södermanland K7
9 Östergötland J7
10 Malmöhus H9
11 Kristianstad J8
Longitude East of Greenwich
SVALBARD
NORWEGIAN SEA
ARCTIC OCEAN
BARENTS SEA
ATLANTIC OCEAN
NORTH SEA
SKAGERRAK
KATTEGAT
GULF OF BOTHNIA
BALTIC SEA
Gulf of Finland
Gulf of Riga
Arctic Circle
DENMARK
WEST GERMANY
EAST GERMANY
POLAND
U. S. S. R.
NETH.
STOCKHOLM
Oslo
COPENHAGEN
Helsinki
LENINGRAD
HAMBURG

NORWAY

AREA 125,181 sq. mi.
POPULATION 3,893,000
CAPITAL Oslo
LARGEST CITY Oslo
HIGHEST POINT Glittertind 8,110 ft.
MONETARY UNIT krone (crown)
MAJOR LANGUAGE Norwegian
MAJOR RELIGION Protestantism

SWEDEN

AREA 173,665 sq. mi.
POPULATION 7,978,000
CAPITAL Stockholm
LARGEST CITY Stockholm
HIGHEST POINT Kebnekaise 6,946 ft.
MONETARY UNIT krona (crown)
MAJOR LANGUAGE Swedish
MAJOR RELIGION Protestantism

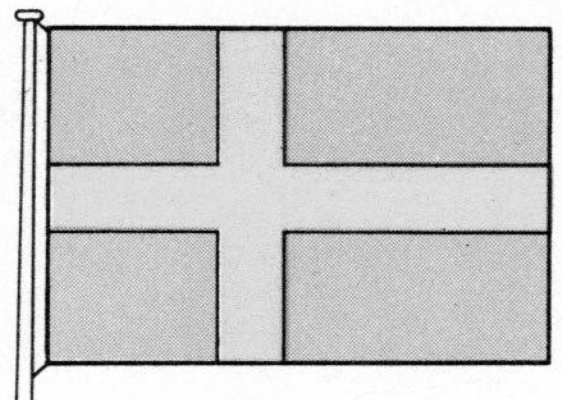

FINLAND

AREA 130,128 sq. mi.
POPULATION 4,706,000
CAPITAL Helsinki
LARGEST CITY Helsinki
HIGHEST POINT Mt. Haltia 4,343 ft.
MONETARY UNIT Markka (Mark)
MAJOR LANGUAGES Finnish, Swedish
MAJOR RELIGION Protestantism

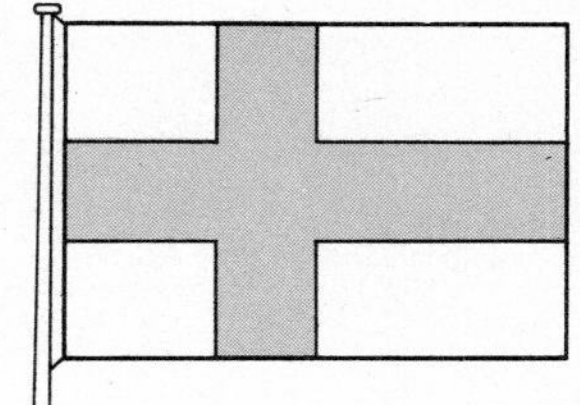

FINLAND

PROVINCES

Ahvenanmaa, 21,584 ....L 6
Häme, 623,756 ....O 6
Keski-Suomi, 248,599 ....O 5
Kuopio, 265,434 ....P 5
Kymi, 348,989 ....Q 6
Lappi, 220,755 ....P 3
Mikkeli, 225,685 ....P 6
Oulu, 422,828 ....P 4
Pohjois-Karjala, 193,199 ....Q 5
Turku-Pori, 680,713 ....N 6
Uusimaa, 999,053 ....O 6
Vaasa, 447,785 ....N 5

CITIES and TOWNS

Äänekoski, 10,977 ....O 5
Åbo (Turku), 155,000 ....N 6
Alavus (Alavo), †11,139 ....N 5
Björneborg (Pori), 71,972 ....M 6
Borgå (Porvoo), 15,738 ....O 6
Brahestad (Raahe), 7,637 ....O 4
Ekenäs (Tammisaari), 6,401 ....N 6
Espoo (Esbo), 88,086 ....O 6
Forssa, 15,260 ....N 6
Fredrikshamn (Hamina), 10,872 ....P 6
Gamlakarleby (Kokkola), 20,715 ....N 5
Haapajärvi, 8,943 ....O 5
Haapamäki, 2,200 ....O 5
Hämeenlinna (Tavastehus), 37,333 ....O 6
Hamina, 10,872 ....P 6
Hangö (Hanko), 9,668 ....N 7
Harjavalta, 8,191 ....N 6
Heinola, 13,696 ....P 6
Helsinki (Helsingfors) (cap.), 531,286 ....O 6
Helsinki, *700,000 ....O 6
Himanka, †3,260 ....N 5
Hyrynsalmi, †5,629 ....Q 4
Hyvinkää (Hyvinge), 33,062 ....O 6
Iisalmi, 7,551 ....P 5
Ilomantsi, †12,050 ....R 5
Imatra, 35,054 ....Q 6
Ivalo ....P 2
Jakobstad (Pietarsaari), 19,114 ....N 5
Joensuu, 35,385 ....R 5
Juuka, †9,925 ....Q 5
Jyväskylä, 56,824 ....O 5
Kajaani, 19,131 ....P 4
Kalajoki, †7,314 ....N 4
Karis (Karjaa), 7,940 ....N 6
Karkkila, 8,504 ....N 6
Kaskö (Kaskinen), 1,436 ....M 5
Kauttua ....M 6
Kemi, 30,199 ....O 4
Kemijärvi, 6,546 ....P 3
Kerava (Kervo), 13,322 ....O 6
Kittilä, †8,347 ....O 3
Kokemäki, †10,922 ....N 6
Kokkola (Gamlakarleby), 20,715 ....N 5
Kotka, 33,953 ....P 6
Kouvola, 25,275 ....P 6
Kristiinankaupunki (Kristinestad), 2,726 ....N 5
Kuhmo, †14,847 ....Q 4
Kuopio, 63,800 ....Q 5
Kurikka, 11,373 ....M 5
Kuusamo, †20,324 ....Q 4
Lahti, 87,237 ....O 6
Lappeenranta, 50,543 ....P 6
Lieksa, 4,703 ....R 5
Loimaa, 6,366 ....N 6
Lovisa (Loviisa), 6,695 ....P 6
Maarianhamina (Mariehamn), 8,512 ....M 7
Mänttä, 7,277 ....O 6
Mariehamn (Maarianhamina), 8,512 ....M 7
Mikkeli (Sankt Michel), 24,962 ....P 6
Muonio, †3,226 ....O 3
Naantali (Nådendal), 6,784 ....M 6
Nivala, †10,784 ....O 5
Nokia, 19,200 ....N 6
Nurmes, 2,329 ....Q 5
Nykarleby (Uusikaarlepyy), 1,289 ....N 5
Nyslott (Savonlinna), 17,618 ....Q 6
Nystad (Uusikaupunki), 6,845....M 6
Oulainen, 7,898 ....O 4
Oulu (Uleåborg), 85,094 ....O 4
Outokumpu, 10,862 ....Q 5
Parikkala, †7,052 ....Q 6
Parkano, †8,587 ....N 6
Pello, †7,139 ....O 3
Pieksämäki, 12,821 ....P 5
Pietarsaari (Jakobstad), 19,114 ....N 5
Pori (Björneborg), 71,972 ....M 6
Porvoo (Borgå), 15,738 ....O 6
Posio, †7,454 ....Q 3
Pudasjärvi, †15,622 ....P 4
Raahe (Brahestad), 7,637 ....O 4
Rauma (Raumo), 25,218 ....M 6
Riihimäki, 22,442 ....O 6
Rovaniemi, 28,680 ....O 3
Saarijärvi, †11,586 ....O 5
Salo, 16,715 ....N 6
Sankt Michel (Mikkeli), 24,962..P 6
Savonlinna, 17,618 ....Q 6
Savukoski, †2,392 ....Q 3
Seinäjoki, 19,836 ....N 5
Sodankylä, †11,745 ....P 3
Sotkamo, †14,127 ....Q 4
Suolahti, 5,563 ....O 5
Suomussalmi, †15,507 ....Q 4
Suonenjoki, 10,012 ....P 5
Tammerfors (Tampere), 156,100 ....N 6
Tammisaari (Ekenäs), 6,401 ....N 6
Tampere (Tammerfors), 156,000 ....N 6
Tapiola ....O 6
Tavastehus (Hämeenlinna), 37,333 ....O 6
Teuva, †8,280 ....N 5
Toijala, 7,505 ....N 6
Tornio (Torneå), 7,325 ....O 4
Turku (Åbo), 155,000 ....N 6
Uleåborg (Oulu), 85,094 ....O 4
Ulvila (Ulvsby), †7,800 ....N 6
Utsjoki, †1,436 ....P 2
Uusikaarlepyy (Nykarleby), 1,289 ....N 5
Uusikaupunki (Nystad), 6,845...M 6
Vaala, †6,675 ....P 4
Vaasa (Vasa), 49,109 ....M 5
Valkeakoski, 15,949 ....N 6
Vammala, 5,605 ....N 6
Varkaus, 24,619 ....Q 5
Vasa (Vaasa), 48,262 ....M 5

OTHER FEATURES

Ahvenanmaa (Åland) (isls.), 21,584 ....L 6
Finland (gulf) ....P 7
Haltia (mt.) ....M 2
Hangöudd (prom.) ....N 7
Hauki (lake) ....Q 5
Ii (river) ....O 4
Inari (lake) ....P 2
Juo (lake) ....Q 5
Kala (river) ....O 4
Kalla (lake) ....P 5
Keitele (lake) ....O 5
Kemi (lake) ....Q 3
Kemi (river) ....O 3
Kianta (lake) ....Q 4
Kilpis (lake) ....M 2
Kitinen (river) ....P 3
Kivi (lake) ....O 5
Koitere (lake) ....R 5
Kuusamo (lake) ....Q 4
Längelmä (lake) ....O 6
Lapland (reg.) ....O 2
Lapuan (river) ....N 5
Lesti (lake) ....O 5
Lokka (res.) ....P 3
Muo (lake) ....R 4
Muonio (river) ....M 2
Nasi (lake) ....O 6
Onkivesi (lake) ....P 5
Orihvesi (lake) ....Q 5
Oulu (river) ....O 4
Ounas (river) ....O 3
Päijänne (lake) ....O 6
Pasvik (river) ....Q 2
Pielinen (lake) ....Q 5
Puru (lake) ....Q 6
Puula (lake) ....P 5
Pyhä (lake) ....M 6
Pyhä (lake) ....O 5
Saimaa (lake) ....Q 6
Siika (river) ....O 4
Simo (lake) ....P 3
Simo (river) ....O 4
Tana (Teno) (river) ....P 2
Tornio (river) ....O 3
Vallgrund (isl.), 2,063 ....M 5
Ylikitka (lake) ....Q 3

NORWAY

COUNTIES

Akershus, 282,928 ....D 4
Aust-Agder, 78,184 ....E 7
Bergen, 117,465 ....D 6
Buskerud, 191,789 ....F 6
Finnmark, 75,553 ....O 2
Hedmark, 177,300 ....G 6
Hordaland, 243,545 ....E 6
Møre og Romsdal, 219,384 ....E 5
Nord-Trøndelag, 117,376 ....H 4
Nordland, 244,165 ....J 3
Oppland, 168,819 ....F 6
Oslo (city), 485,200 ....D 3
Østfold, 212,450 ....D 4
Rogaland, 256,501 ....E 7
Sogn og Fjordane, 100,711 ....E 6
Sør-Trøndelag, 224,654 ....G 5
Telemark, 155,834 ....F 7
Troms, 132,407 ....L 2
Vest-Agder, 117,226 ....E 7
Vestfold, 167,778 ....D 4

CITIES and TOWNS

Åfjord, †4,105 ....G 5
Ål, †4,377 ....F 6
Ålesund, 18,558 ....D 5
Åndalsnes, 2,202 ....F 5
Arendal, 11,579 ....F 7
Askim, †9,673 ....E 4
Bamble, †8,338 ....F 7
Barentsburg ....C 2
Bergen, 117,465 ....D 6
Bergen, *270,000 ....D 6
Bodø, 14,048 ....J 3
Borre, 6,636 ....D 4
Drammen, 47,261 ....C 4
Drammen, *48,700 ....C 4
Drøbak, 2,683 ....D 4
Eigersund, 9,730 ....D 7
Elverum, †13,604 ....G 6
Farsund, 7,697 ....E 7
Flekkefjord, 8,616 ....E 7
Flora, 7,836 ....D 6
Fredrikstad, 30,006 ....D 4
Gjøvik, 24,256 ....G 6
Grimstad, 2,610 ....F 7
Gulen, †3,212 ....D 6
Halden, 10,006 ....G 7
Hamar, 14,712 ....G 6
Hammerfest, 6,806 ....N 1
Harstad, 18,892 ....K 2
Haugesund, 27,569 ....D 7
Holmestrand, 6,857 ....C 4
Honningsvåg, 2,813 ....O 1
Horten, 13,387 ....D 4
Kirkenes, 4,433 ....Q 2
Kongsberg, 17,578 ....F 7
Kongsvinger, 13,080 ....H 6
Kragerø, †10,067 ....F 7
Kristiansand, 52,542 ....F 8
Kristiansand, *54,900 ....F 8
Kristiansund, 18,466 ....E 5
Kvinnherad, †9,848 ....E 6
Larvik, 10,728 ....C 4
Lenvik, †10,209 ....L 2
Lesja, †2,755 ....F 5
Lillehammer, 19,808 ....F 6
Lillesand, †4,975 ....F 7
Lillestrøm, 10,547 ....E 3
Løkken, †5,054 ....F 5
Longyearbyen ....D 2
Lysaker, 5,393 ....D 3
Mandal, 10,622 ....E 7
Mo, 8,348 ....J 3
Molde, 17,862 ....E 5
Moss, 23,198 ....D 4
Mysen, 2,500 ....G 7
Namsos, 10,998 ....G 4
Narvik, 13,543 ....K 2
Nesttun, 3,827 ....D 6
Notodden, 13,680 ....F 7
Odda, †10,444 ....E 6
Orkanger, 2,874 ....F 5
Oslo (cap.), 483,196 ....D 3
Oslo, *635,700 ....D 3
Porsgrunn, 28,167 ....G 7
Ringerike, 28,577 ....C 3
Risør, 6,110 ....F 7
Rjukan, 6,308 ....F 7
Røros, †5,259 ....G 5
Sandefjord, 6,085 ....C 4
Sandnes, 28,534 ....D 7
Sandvika, 3,751 ....C 3
Sarpsborg, 13,185 ....D 4
Ski, †12,337 ....D 4
Skien, 47,302 ....F 7
Skjåk, †2,692 ....F 6
Stavanger, 79,700 ....D 7
Stavanger, *80,800 ....D 7
Stavern, 2,148 ....D 4
Steinkjer, 19,874 ....G 4
Stor-Elvdal, †4,151 ....G 6
Sulitjelma, 2,129 ....K 3
Sunndalsøra, 2,376 ....F 5
Svolvaer, 3,812 ....J 2
Tana, †3,286 ....Q 1
Telemark ....C 4
Tønsberg, 11,566 ....D 4
Tromsø, 34,600 ....L 2
Trondheim, 118,703 ....F 5
Trondheim, *123,600 ....F 5
Ullensvang, †4,940 ....E 6
Vadsø, 5,320 ....Q 1
Vardø, 4,185 ....R 1
Volda, 2,647 ....E 5
Voss, †13,473 ....E 6

OTHER FEATURES

Alst (fjord) ....G 3
Alsten (isl.), 4,348 ....H 4
Alta (river) ....N 2
Alte (lake) ....L 2
Ands (fjord) ....K 2
Bardu (river) ....L 2
Barentsöya (isl.) ....D 2
Bellsund (bay) ....C 2
Bjørna (fjord) ....D 6
Bjørnøya (isl.) ....D 3
Bokn (fjord) ....D 7
Bremanger (isl.), 2,028 ....D 6
Dønna (isl.), 1,978 ....H 3
Dovrefjeld (mts.) ....F 5
Edgeøya (isl.) ....E 2
Femund (lake) ....G 5
Folda (fjord) ....G 4
Folda (fjord) ....J 3
Frohavet (bay) ....F 5
Frøya (isl.), 4,034 ....F 5
Glittertind (mt.) ....F 6
Glomma (river) ....G 6
Hadsel (fjord) ....J 2
Hardanger (fjord) ....D 7
Hardanger (mts.) ....E 6
Hinlopen (strait) ....C 1
Hinnøy (isl.), 27,599 ....K 2
Hitra (isl.), 3,134 ....F 5
Hopen (isl.) ....E 2
Hornsund (bay) ....C 2
Hortens (fjord) ....G 4
Is (fjord) ....B 2
Jostedals (glacier) ....E 6
Karmøy (isl.), 19,234 ....D 7
Kob (fjord) ....O 1
Kong Karls Land (isls.) ....E 1
Kvaløy (isl.), 6,869 ....O 1
Lagen (river) ....G 6
Lakse (fjord) ....P 1
Langøy (isl.), 16,500 ....J 2
Lapland (reg.) ....K 2
Lindesnes (cape) ....E 8
Lista (pen.), 7,702 ....E 7
Lofoten (isls.), 28,980 ....H 2
Lopphavet (bay) ....M 1
Magerøy (isl.), 5,545 ....P 1
Mohn (cape) ....E 1
Moskenesøy (isl.), 2,318 ....H 3
Namsen (river) ....H 4
Nord (fjord) ....E 6
Nordaustlandet (isl.) ....D 1
Nordkyn (cape) ....Q 1
North (cape) ....P 1
Norwegian (sea) ....F 3
Ofot (fjord) ....K 2
Otter (river) ....E 7
Pasvik (river) ....Q 2
Platen (cape) ....D 1
Porsanger (fjord) ....O 1
Rana (river) ....J 3
Ran (fjord) ....H 3
Rauma (river) ....F 5
Reisa (river) ....M 2
Ringvassøy (isl.), 1,472 ....L 2
Romsdals (fjord) ....E 5
Salt (fjord) ....J 3
Seiland (isl.), 769 ....N 1
Senja (isl.), 10,541 ....K 2
Skagerrak (strait) ....E 8
Smøla (isl.), 2,840 ....E 5
Snåsa (lake) ....H 4
Sogne (fjord) ....D 6
Sørkapp (cape) ....C 2
Sørøy (isl.), 2,350 ....N 1
South Kvaløy (isl.), 3,444 ....K 2
Spitsbergen (isl.) ....C 2
Steinneset (cape) ....E 2
Stor (fjord) ....D 2
Sunn (fjord) ....D 6
Tana (river) ....P 1
Tjuv (fjord) ....D 2
Tunn (lake) ....H 4
Tyri (fjord) ....C 3
Vågå (lake) ....F 6
Vannøy (isl.), 1,112 ....L 1
Varanger (fjord) ....Q 1
Vega (isl.) ....G 4
Vest (fjord) ....H 3

(continued on following page)

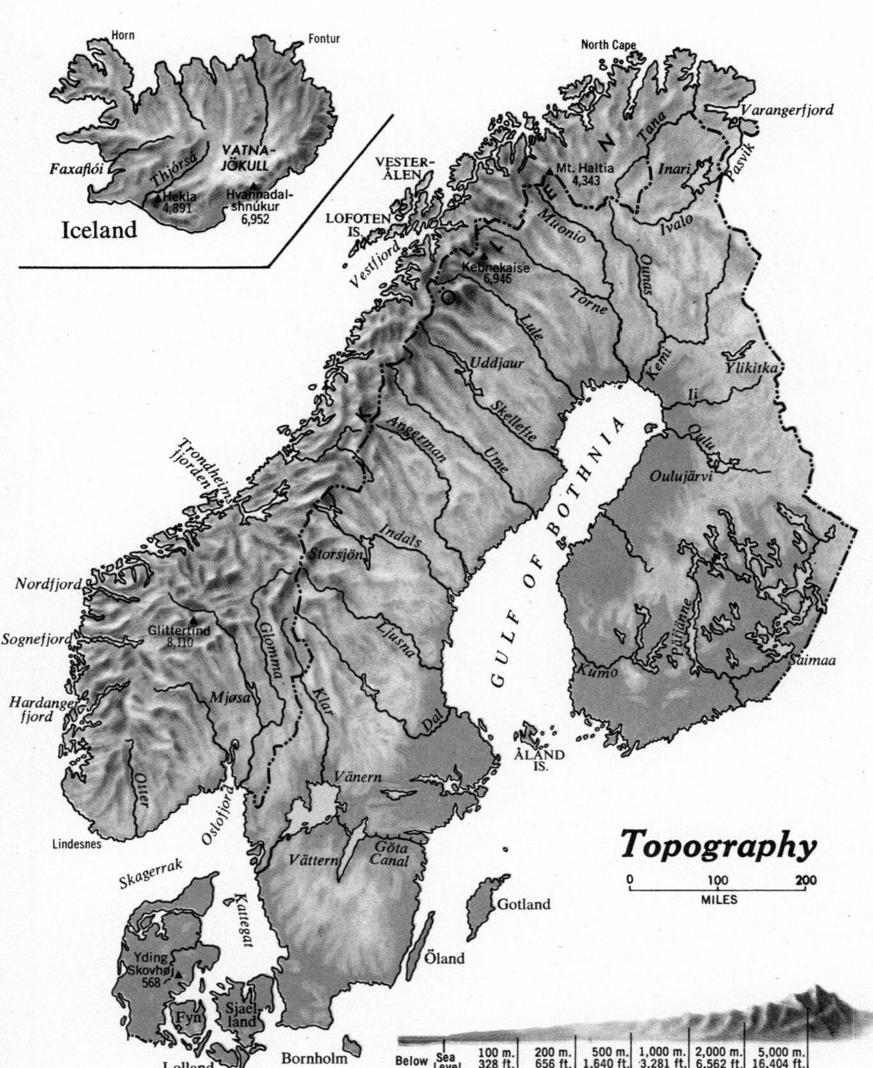

20 Norway, Sweden, Finland, Denmark and Iceland
(continued)

NORWAY (continued)

Vesterålen (isls.), 34,385 ... J 2
Vestvågøy (isl.), 11,749 ... H 3
Vikna (isl.), 3,411 ... G 4

SWEDEN

COUNTIES

Älvsborg, 391,851 ... H 7
Blekinge, 150,901 ... J 8
Gävleborg, 294,916 ... K 6
Göteborg och Bohus, 685,449 ... G 7
Gotland, 50,438 ... L 8
Halland, 185,810 ... H 8
Jämtland, 121,552 ... J 5
Jönköping, 292,303 ... H 8
Kalmar, 234,175 ... K 8
Kopparberg, 270,971 ... J 6
Kristianstad, 258,295 ... J 8
Kronoberg, 164,309 ... J 8
Malmöhus, 683,752 ... H 9
Norrbotten, 261,410 ... L 3
örebro, 259,794 ... J 7
östergötland, 369,374 ... J 7
Skaraborg, 248,970 ... H 7
Södermanland, 239,451 ... K 7
Stockholm, 1,406,580 ... L 7
Uppsala, 191,821 ... K 6
Värmland, 273,139 ... H 7
Västerbotten, 235,307 ... K 4
Västernorrland, 277,715 ... K 5
Västmanland, 255,142 ... K 7

CITIES and TOWNS

Åhus, 4,758 ... J 9
Alingsås, 19,810 ... H 7
Älmhult, 6,023 ... H 8
Alvesta, 8,957 ... J 8
Älvsbyn, 4,343 ... M 4
Åmål, 9,397 ... H 7
Anderstorp, 3,960 ... H 8
Ånge, 4,000 ... J 5
Ängelholm, 13,985 ... H 8
Arboga, 12,266 ... J 7
Årjäng, 2,893 ... H 7
Arvidsjaur, 7,767 ... L 4
Arvika, 15,901 ... H 7
Åseda, 3,629 ... J 8
Åsele, 4,727 ... K 4
Åtvidaberg, 9,010 ... K 7
Avesta, 29,232 ... J 6
Båstad, 2,202 ... H 8
Bengtsfors, 3,411 ... H 7
Boden, 24,912 ... M 4
Bollnäs, 17,123 ... K 6
Borås, 70,238 ... H 8
Borlänge, 29,097 ... J 6
Bräcke, 2,658 ... J 5
Brunflo, 2,700 ... J 5
Bureå, 4,583 ... M 4
Burträsk, 6,747 ... M 4
Charlottenberg, 3,112 ... H 6
Danderyd, 15,657 ... H 1
Djursholm, 7,681 ... H 1
Dorotea, 3,964 ... K 4
Edsbyn, 7,132 ... J 6
Eksjö, 9,897 ... J 8
Emmaboda, 3,697 ... J 8
Enköping, 17,684 ... G 1
Eskilstuna, 65,580 ... K 7
Eslöv, 14,737 ... H 9
Fagersta, 16,609 ... J 6
Falkenberg, 12,920 ... H 8
Falköping, 16,032 ... H 7
Falun, 33,840 ... J 6
Filipstad, 7,559 ... H 7
Finspång, 17,616 ... J 7
Flen, 9,112 ... K 7
Forshaga, 4,655 ... H 7
Frösö, 9,520 ... J 5
Frövi, 3,082 ... J 7
Gällivare, 9,718 ... M 3
Gamleby, 3,949 ... K 8
Gävle, 60,868 ... K 6
Gnesta, 3,275 ... G 2
Göteborg, 444,131 ... G 8
Göteborg, *647,122 ... G 8
Gränna, 3,195 ... J 8
Hagfors, 8,964 ... H 6
Hällefors, 12,011 ... J 7
Hallsberg, 12,121 ... J 7
Hallstahammar, 14,099 ... K 7
Halmstad, 46,655 ... H 8
Hälsingborg, 80,801 ... H 8
Haparanda, 9,429 ... N 4
Härnösand, 16,637 ... L 5
Hässleholm, 16,031 ... H 8
Hedemora, 17,744 ... K 6
Hjo, 4,783 ... J 7
Höganäs, 13,846 ... H 8
Holmsund, 5,778 ... M 5
Hudiksvall, 16,057 ... K 6
Hultsfred, 4,979 ... K 8
Huskvarna, 18,198 ... J 8
Järna, 4,591 ... G 2
Järpen, 2,962 ... H 5
Järvsö, 4,850 ... K 6
Jokkmokk, 4,869 ... L 3
Jönköping, 53,774 ... H 8
Jörn, 4,275 ... M 4
Kalmar, 37,938 ... K 8
Karlshamn, 12,351 ... J 8
Karlskoga, 38,284 ... J 7
Karlskrona, 37,358 ... K 8
Karlstad, 54,321 ... H 7
Katrineholm, 21,660 ... K 7
Kinna, 6,386 ... H 8
Kiruna, 29,210 ... L 3
Kisa, 4,353 ... J 8
Köping, 20,807 ... J 7
Kopparberg, 7,985 ... J 7
Kramfors, 11,729 ... K 5
Kristianstad, 27,527 ... J 9
Kristinehamn, 21,925 ... H 7
Kumla, 15,039 ... J 7
Kungälv, 11,213 ... G 8
Kungsbacka, 7,205 ... G 8
Laholm, 3,853 ... H 8
Landskrona, 32,079 ... H 9
Långsele, 4,640 ... K 5
Långshyttan, 3,124 ... K 6
Laxå, 9,498 ... J 7
Leksand, 8,608 ... J 6
Lidingö, 35,400 ... H 1
Lidköping, 19,700 ... H 7
Lindesberg, 6,863 ... J 7
Linköping, 77,881 ... K 7
Ljungby, 11,930 ... J 8
Ljusdal, 10,630 ... J 6
Ljusne, 4,808 ... K 6
Ludvika, 21,989 ... J 6
Luleå, 36,428 ... N 4
Lund, 50,494 ... H 9
Lycksele, 6,333 ... L 4
Lysekil, 8,000 ... G 7
Malmberget, 12,384 ... M 3
Malmköping, 3,450 ... F 1
Malmö, 256,064 ... H 9
Malmö, *428,338 ... H 9
Markaryd, 5,980 ... H 8
Mariefred, 2,502 ... G 1
Mariestad, 15,700 ... H 7
Mellerud, 4,317 ... H 7
Mjölby, 12,790 ... J 7
Mölndal, 31,072 ... H 8
Mönsterås, 6,687 ... K 8
Mora, 13,307 ... J 6
Motala, 27,907 ... J 7
Nacka, 25,798 ... H 1
Nässjö, 20,000 ... J 8
Nora, 9,215 ... J 7
Norberg, 6,160 ... K 6
Norrköping, 94,296 ... K 7
Norrsundet, 4,575 ... K 6
Norrtälje, 11,803 ... L 7
Norsjö, 5,171 ... L 4
Nybro, 10,956 ... J 8
Nyköping, 31,195 ... K 7
Nynäshamn, 10,676 ... L 7
Ockelbo, 5,819 ... K 6
Olofström, 16,218 ... J 8
örbyhus, 2,266 ... K 6
örebro, 86,977 ... J 7
öregrund, 2,026 ... L 6
örnsköldsvik, 16,539 ... L 5
Oskarshamn, 24,873 ... K 8
östersund, 26,600 ... J 5
östhammar, 8,858 ... L 6
övertorneå, 3,589 ... N 3
överum, 2,533 ... K 7
Oxelösund, 14,835 ... K 7
Pajala, 3,871 ... N 3
Piteå, 8,476 ... M 4
Ramnäs, 4,092 ... J 7
Ramsele, 4,547 ... K 5
Rättvik, 7,551 ... J 6
Rimbo, 3,426 ... L 7
Ronneby, 10,125 ... J 8
Ryd, 4,100 ... J 8
Säffle, 12,599 ... H 7
Sala, 11,800 ... K 7
Saltsjöbaden, 6,507 ... J 1
Sandviken, 25,476 ... K 6
Säter, 4,629 ... J 6
Sävsjö, 5,547 ... J 8
Sigtuna, 3,970 ... H 1
Simrishamn, 7,966 ... J 9
Skänninge, 4,482 ... J 7
Skara, 10,376 ... H 7
Skellefteå, 61,880 ... M 4
Skövde, 27,976 ... H 7
Smedjebacken, 10,504 ... J 6
Söderhamn, 13,778 ... K 6
Söderköping, 5,954 ... K 7
Södertälje, 52,601 ... G 1
Sollefteå, 9,715 ... K 5
Sollentuna, 35,038 ... H 1
Solna, 57,707 ... H 1
Sölvesborg, 6,782 ... J 9
Sorsele, 3,550 ... K 4
Stockholm (cap.), 756,697 ... G 1
Stockholm, *1,288,769 ... G 1
Storvik, 2,432 ... K 6
Strängnäs, 9,506 ... F 1
Strömstad, 9,817 ... G 7
Strömsund, 6,058 ... K 5
Sundbyberg, 28,773 ... G 1
Sundsvall, 62,222 ... K 5
Sunne, 11,018 ... H 7
Sveg, 4,975 ... J 5
Svenljunga, 2,925 ... H 8
Täby, 33,694 ... H 1
Tidaholm, 7,250 ... J 7
Tierp, 4,303 ... K 6
Tillberga, 270 ... K 7
Timrå, 12,800 ... K 5
Tomelilla, 6,349 ... J 9
Torsby, 6,796 ... H 6
Torshälla, 7,939 ... K 7
Tranås, 18,845 ... J 7
Trelleborg, 35,249 ... H 9
Trollhättan, 40,945 ... H 7
Uddevalla, 36,510 ... G 7
Ulricehamn, 8,504 ... H 8
Umeå, 51,955 ... M 5
Uppsala, 97,315 ... L 7
Vadstena, 6,893 ... J 7
Vaggeryd, 4,840 ... J 8
Valdemarsvik, 3,590 ... K 7
Vänersborg, 19,975 ... H 7
Vännäs, 4,045 ... L 5
Vansbro, 2,941 ... H 6
Vara, 11,056 ... H 7
Varberg, 18,451 ... G 8
Värnamo, 15,939 ... J 8
Västerås, 110,539 ... J 7
Västerhaninge, 9,814 ... H 1
Västervik, 23,014 ... K 8
Vaxholm, 4,322 ... J 1
Vaxjö, 32,760 ... J 8
Vetlanda, 10,780 ... J 8
Vilhelmina, 9,426 ... K 4
Vimmerby, 7,257 ... J 8
Virserum, 4,650 ... J 8
Visby, 18,338 ... L 8
Vislanda, 2,594 ... H 8
Wallhamn ... G 7
Ystad, 14,002 ... H 9

OTHER FEATURES

Angerman (river) ... K 5
Asnen (lake) ... J 8
Bothnia (gulf) ... M 5
Byske (river) ... L 4
Fårö (isl.), 790 ... L 8
Göta (river) ... H 7
Gotland (isl.), 50,438 ... L 8
Hornslandet (pen.) ... K 6
Kalix (river) ... N 3
Kalmarsund (sound) ... K 8
Kattegat (strait) ... G 8
Kebnekaise (mt.) ... L 3
Lainio (river) ... N 3
Lapland (dist.) ... K 2
Lule (river) ... M 3
Muonio (river) ... M 2
öland (isl.), 20,416 ... K 8
Ornö (isl.), 224 ... J 1
österdal (river) ... H 6
Pite (river) ... M 4
Skellefte (river) ... L 4
Stora Lulevatten (lake) ... L 3
Storuman (lake) ... K 4
Sulitjelma (mt.) ... K 3
Torne (river) ... M 3
Torneträsk (lake) ... L 2
Uddjaur (lake) ... L 4
Ume (river) ... L 4
Vänern (lake) ... H 7
Vättern (lake) ... J 7
Vesterdal (river) ... H 6
Vindel (river) ... L 4
Vojmsjön (lakes) ... J 4

*City and suburbs.
†Population of parish or commune.

DENMARK

INTERNAL DIVISIONS

Århus (county), 525,167 ... D 5
Bornholm (county), 47,405 ... F 9
Copenhagen (commune), 634,500 ... F 6
Færøe Islands, 38,000 ... B 2
Frederiksberg (commune), 102,751 ... F 6
Frederiksborg (county), 252,557 ... F 5
Fyn (county), 430,958 ... D 7
København (Copenhagen) (commune), 634,500 ... F 6
København (county), 609,469 ... F 6
Nordjylland (county), 455,062 ... D 4
Ribe (county), 196,894 ... B 6
Ringkøbing (county), 240,014 ... B 5
Roskilde (county), 147,434 ... E 6
Sønderjylland (county), 237,270 ... C 7
Storstrøm (county), 251,815 ... E 7
Vejle (county), 304,358 ... C 6
Vestsjælland (county), 256,997 ... E 6
Viborg (county), 220,214 ... B 4

CITIES and TOWNS

Åbenrå, 15,156 ... C 7
Åbybro, 6,309 ... C 3
Ærøskøbing, 1,228 ... D 8
Agerbæk, 804, ... B 6
Åkirkeby, 1,549 ... F 9
Ålborg, 82,346 ... D 4
Ålborg, *153,307 ... D 4
Ålestrup, 5,228 ... C 4
Allingåbro, 1,352 ... D 5
Allinge-Sandvig, 2,023 ... F 8
Ansager, 1,123 ... B 6
Arden, 1,353 ... C 4
Århus, 109,498 ... D 5
Århus, *232,173 ... D 5
Års, 5,075 ... C 4
Årup, †5,033 ... D 7
Aså, 1,348 ... D 3
Askov, 725 ... C 7
Asnæs, 2,493 ... E 6
Assens, Århus, 1,266 ... D 4
Assens, Fyn, †10,777 ... D 7
Augustenborg, 3,537 ... D 8
Auning, 1,367 ... D 5
Avlum, 3,694 ... B 5
Bælum, 1,922 ... D 4
Bagenkop, 774 ... D 8
Ballerup, †50,128 ... F 6
Bandholm, 1,248 ... E 8
Bested, 1,886 ... B 4
Birkerød, †20,835 ... F 6
Bjerringbro, 6,469 ... C 5
Bogense, †6,450 ... D 6
Bolderslev, 729 ... C 8
Børkop, †9,053 ... C 6
Borup, 2,344 ... E 7
Brabrand, 12,514 ... C 5
Brædstrup, 3,925 ... C 6
Bramminge, 5,937 ... B 7
Brande, 6,814 ... B 6
Bredebro, †3,747 ... B 7
Broager, †5,387 ... C 8
Brønderslev, 10,274 ... C 3
Brøns, 867 ... B 7
Brørup, 4,066 ... C 7
Brovst, †8,086 ... C 3
Christiansfeld, 958 ... C 7
Copenhagen (cap.), 634,500 ... F 6
Copenhagen, *1,346,720 ... F 6
Dronninglund, 9,179 ... D 3
Dybvad, 793 ... D 3
Ebeltoft, 3,168 ... D 5
Egernsund, 1,360 ... C 8
Egtved, 2,857 ... C 6
Ejby, 3,265 ... D 7
Esbjerg, 62,483 ... B 7
Fåborg, 5,630 ... D 7
Fakse, 7,268 ... F 7
Fakse Ladeplads, 1,639 ... F 7
Farsø, 4,126 ... C 4
Farum, †9,583 ... F 6
Fjerritslev, 2,686 ... C 3
Fredensborg, 3,977 ... F 6
Fredericia, 34,464 ... C 6
Frederiksberg, 102,751 ... F 6
Frederikshavn, 24,640 ... D 3
Frederikssund, 7,835 ... E 6
Frederiksværk, 4,385 ... E 6
Fuglebjerg, 5,082 ... E 7
Gedser, 1,195 ... F 8
Gedsted, 1,924 ... C 4
Gelsted, 2,461 ... C 7
Gentofte, †78,641 ... F 6
Gilleleje, 4,300 ... F 5
Give, 8,573 ... C 6
Gjerlev, 1,209 ... D 4
Glamsbjerg, †5,677 ... D 7
Glostrup, †28,169 ... F 6
Glumsø, 819 ... E 7
Glyngøre, 1,047 ... C 4
Gørding, 2,422 ... B 7
Gørlev, 2,437 ... E 6
Græsted, 2,899 ... F 5
Gram, 3,935 ... C 7
Gråsten, †6,336 ... C 8
Grenå, 13,277 ... D 5
Grindsted, 9,345 ... B 6
Gylling, 990 ... D 6
Haderslev, 20,291 ... C 7
Hadsten, 6,919 ... C 5
Hadsund, 6,862 ... D 4
Hals, 3,016 ... D 3
Hammel, 7,456 ... C 5
Hammerum, 2,415 ... C 5
Hanstholm, 3,358 ... B 3
Harboør, 2,224 ... A 4
Hårby, †4,671 ... D 7
Hårlev, 980 ... F 7
Hasle, 1,542 ... F 8
Haslev, 10,173 ... E 7
Havdrup, 5,163 ... F 6
Hedensted, 4,791 ... C 6
Hellebæk, 2,240 ... F 5
Helsinge, 4,707 ... F 6
Helsingør, 30,211 ... F 6
Herning, 32,512 ... B 5
Hillerød, 23,500 ... F 6
Hinnerup, †5,614 ... D 5
Hirtshals, 8,598 ... C 2
Hjallerup, 1,385 ... C 3
Hjerm, 1,421 ... B 5
Hjørring, 15,699 ... C 3
Hobro, 8,845 ... C 4
Højer, 1,407 ... B 8
Højslev, 2,863 ... C 4
Holbæk, 17,892 ... E 6
Holeby, 4,359 ... E 8
Holstebro, 24,009 ... B 5
Holsted, 2,773 ... B 6
Høng, †7,355 ... E 7
Hornslet, 3,371 ... D 5
Horsens, 35,621 ... C 6
Hørsholm, 18,060 ... F 6
Hørve, 2,829 ... E 6
Hov, 607 ... D 6
Humlum, 2,357 ... B 4
Hundested, †6,301 ... E 6
Hurup, 2,560 ... B 4
Hvidbjerg, 2,361 ... B 4
Hvide Sande, 1,775 ... A 6
Hviding, 750 ... B 7
Ikast, 11,110 ... C 5
Jelling, 4,780 ... C 6
Jerslev, 2,672 ... D 3
Juelsminde, 7,245 ... D 6
Jyderup, 3,246 ... E 6
Kalundborg, 11,762 ... D 6
Karby, 2,302 ... B 4
Karise, 1,733 ... F 7
Karup, 1,891 ... C 5
Kastrup ... F 6
Kerteminde, †10,296 ... D 7
Kibæk, 1,179 ... B 5
Kjellerup, 3,506 ... C 5
Klaksvík, Færøe Is., 3,894 ... B 2
København (Copenhagen), (cap.), 634,500 ... F 6
Køge, 17,360 ... F 7
Kolding, 39,609 ... C 7
Kolind, 2,590 ... D 5
Kørsør, 15,550 ... E 7
Kværndrup, 1,963 ... D 7
Langå, 2,801 ... C 5
Lem, 1,060 ... B 5
Lemvig, 6,766 ... B 4
Løgstør, 3,666 ... C 4
Løgumkloster, 2,089 ... B 7
Lohals, 634 ... D 7
Løjt Kirkeby, 2,724 ... C 7
Løkken, 1,388 ... C 3
Løsning, 2,418 ... C 6
Lundby, 2,392 ... E 7
Lunderskov, †4,402 ... C 7
Lyngby, †61,245 ... F 6
Malling, 4,332 ... D 5
Mariager, 3,733 ... D 4
Maribo, 5,235 ... E 8
Marstal, 4,095 ... D 8
Middelfart, 9,015 ... C 7
Møgeltønder, 1,181 ... B 8
Næstved, 24,831 ... E 7
Nakskov, 15,994 ... E 8
Neksø, 3,499 ... F 9
Nibe, 2,786 ... C 4
Nordborg, 3,016 ... C 7
Nordby, 2,353 ... B 7
Nørre Åby, †5,195 ... C 7
Nørre Alslev, 1,939 ... E 8
Nørre Broby, 858 ... D 7
Nørre Nebel, 867 ... B 6
Nørre Snede, 3,019 ... C 6
Nørresundby, 23,848 ... D 3
Nørre Vorupør, 632 ... B 4
Nyborg, 11,698 ... D 7
Nykøbing, Storstrøm, 17,364 ... E 8
Nykøbing, Vestsjælland, 4,905 ... E 6
Nykøbing, Viborg, 8,710 ... B 4
Nysted, 1,211 ... E 8
Odder, 8,144 ... D 6
Odense, 102,698 ... D 7
Odense, *163,593 ... D 7
Ølgod, 7,091 ... B 6
Ørsted, 1,925 ... D 5
Øster Vrå, 931 ... D 3
Otterup, †10,462 ... D 7
Ovtrup, 549 ... B 6
Pandrup, 1,383 ... C 3
Pedersborg, 1,560 ... E 7

Agriculture, Industry and Resources

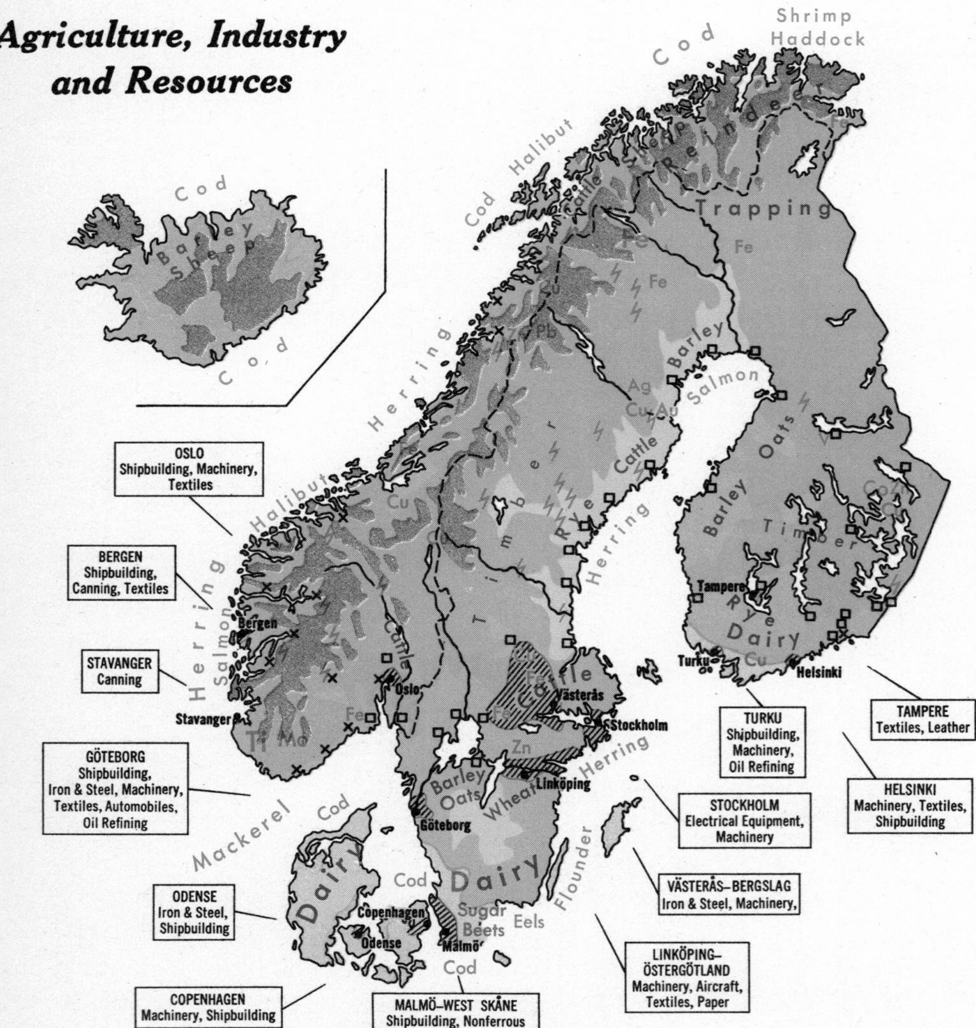

DOMINANT LAND USE

- Cash Cereals, Dairy
- Dairy, Cattle, Hogs
- Dairy, General Farming
- General Farming (chiefly cereals)
- Nomadic Sheep Herding
- Forests, Limited Mixed Farming
- Nonagricultural Land

MAJOR MINERAL OCCURRENCES

Ag Silver
Au Gold
Co Cobalt
Cu Copper
Fe Iron Ore
Mo Molybdenum
Pb Lead
Ti Titanium
V Vanadium
Zn Zinc

Water Power
Major Industrial Areas
× Electrochemical & Electrometallurgical Centers
□ Paper, Pulp & Sawmilling Centers

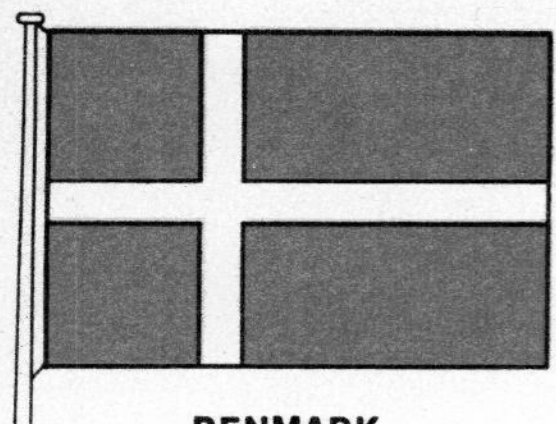

DENMARK

ICELAND

DENMARK

AREA 16,614 sq. mi.
POPULATION 4,912,865
CAPITAL Copenhagen
LARGEST CITY Copenhagen
HIGHEST POINT Yding Skovhøj 568 ft.
MONETARY UNIT krone (crown)
MAJOR LANGUAGE Danish
MAJOR RELIGION Protestantism

ICELAND

AREA 39,768 sq. mi.
POPULATION 204,578
CAPITAL Reykjavík
LARGEST CITY Reykjavík
HIGHEST POINT Hvannadalshnúkur 6,952 ft.
MONETARY UNIT króna (crown)
MAJOR LANGUAGE Icelandic
MAJOR RELIGION Protestantism

Præstø, 4,926 ....E 7
Ramme, 1,560 ....B 4
Randers, 41,253 ....C 5
Ranum, 2,320 ....C 4
Ribe, 8,224 ....B 7
Ringe, 6,907 ....D 7
Ringkøbing, 6,536 ....B 5
Ringsted, 12,499 ....E 7
Rødby, 4,751 ....E 8
Rødding, 2,826 ....B 7
Rødekro, †7,874 ....C 7
Rødkærsbro, 992 ....C 5
Rødvig Ladeplads, 1,068 ....F 7
Rømø, 817 ....B 7
Rønde, 4,487 ....D 5
Rønne, 12,440 ....F 9
Rørby, 1,081 ....E 6
Roskilde, 39,984 ....E 6
Roslev, 1,260 ....B 4
Rudkøbing, †7,069 ....D 8
Ruds Vedby, 954 ....E 6
Ry, 5,945 ....C 5
Ryomgård, 947 ....D 5
Sæby, 4,378 ....D 3
Sakskøbing, 2,523 ....E 8
Silkeborg, 26,129 ....C 5
Sindal, †8,695 ....D 3
Skælskør, 8,776 ....E 7
Skærbæk, 3,016 ....B 7
Skagen, 11,699 ....D 2
Skals, 1,968 ....C 4
Skanderborg, 11,227 ....D 5
Skårup, 2,215 ....D 7
Skibby, †4,585 ....E 6
Skive, 17,980 ....B 4
Skjern, 6,058 ....B 6
Skodborg, 1,728 ....C 7
Skørping, 2,347 ....C 4
Slagelse, 23,169 ....E 7
Slangerup, 2,701 ....E 6
Snedsted, 2,571 ....B 4
Søllested, 857 ....E 8
Sønderborg, 23,069 ....C 8
Sønderho, 352 ....B 7
Sønder Nissum, 1,236 ....A 5
Sønder Omme, 2,449 ....B 6
Søndersø, †9,479 ....D 7
Sorø, 5,591 ....E 7
Stege, 3,872 ....F 8
Stenlille, 1,617 ....E 6
Stenstrup, 1,993 ....D 7
Stoholm, 1,178 ....C 5
Store Heddinge, 2,245 ....F 7
Støvring, 1,980 ....C 4
Strandby, 1,752 ....D 3
Struer, 9,263 ....B 5
Stubbekøbing, 2,061 ....E 8
Sulsted, 5,006 ....C 3
Svaneke, 1,164 ....F 8
Svendborg, 23,149 ....D 7
Svenstrup, 3,530 ....C 4
Svinninge, †5,681 ....E 6
Tarm, 2,702 ....B 6
Tårnby, †45,868 ....F 6
Tåstrup, †29,154 ....F 6
Them, 2,419 ....C 5
Thisted, 8,730 ....B 4
Thyborøn, 2,404 ....B 4
Thyregod, 2,442 ....C 6
Tim, 1,175 ....B 5
Tinglev, 2,695 ....C 8
Tistrup, 653 ....B 6
Toftlund, 3,311 ....B 7
Tølløse, †8,036 ....E 6
Tommerup, †6,076 ....D 7
Tønder, 7,489 ....B 8
Tørring, 2,039 ....C 6
Tórshavn (cap.), Færøe Is., 9,738 ....A 3
Tranebjerg, 701 ....D 6
Troense, 631 ....D 7
Trustrup, 801 ....D 5
Tversted, 1,973 ....D 2
Uldum, 1,182 ....C 6
Ulfborg, 2,053 ....B 5
Vamdrup, 4,760 ....C 7
Varde, 11,456 ....B 6
Vejen, 7,470 ....C 7
Vejle, 31,763 ....C 6
Vemb, 1,937 ....B 5
Vester Skerninge, 503 ....D 7
Vestervig, 2,513 ....B 4
Viborg, 25,468 ....C 5
Viby, 1,038 ....F 7
Videbæk, †10,368 ....B 5
Vig, 2,678 ....E 6
Vildbjerg, 2,698 ....B 5
Vinderup, †7,857 ....B 5
Vodskov, 2,327 ....D 3
Vojens, 6,975 ....C 7
Vorbasse, 1,952 ....B 6
Vordingborg, 11,640 ....E 7
Vrå, 4,371 ....C 3

OTHER FEATURES

Ærø (isl.), 9,295 ....D 8
Ålborg (bay) ....D 4
Als (isl.), 50,518 ....C 8
Amager (isl.), 177,818 ....F 6
Anholt (isl.), 196 ....E 4
Årø (isl.), 259 ....C 7
Bågø (isl.), 113 ....C 7
Blåvands Huk (point) ....A 6
Bornholm (isl.), 47,405 ....F 9
Dovns Klint (prom.) ....D 8
Endelave (isl.), 257 ....D 6
Eysturoy (isl.), Færøe Is., 7,714 ....B 3
Færøe (isls.), 38,000 ....B 2
Fakse (bay) ....F 7
Falster (isl.), 49,405 ....F 8
Fanø (isl.), 2,705 ....B 7
Fehmarn (strait) ....E 8
Fejø (isl.), 933 ....E 8
Femø (isl.), 381 ....E 8
Frisian, North (isls.), 3,653 ....B 7
Fyn (isl.), 397,234 ....D 7
Fyns Hoved (prom.) ....D 6
Gedser Odde (point) ....E 8
Gelså (river) ....C 7
Gilbjerg Hoved (prom.) ....F 5
Gjerrild Klint (prom.) ....D 5
Gudenå (river) ....C 5
Horsens (fjord) ....D 6
Isefjord (fjord) ....E 6
Jammerbugt (bay) ....C 3
Jutland (Jylland) (pen.) 2,088,642 ....C 5
Jyske Ås (hills) ....D 3
Kattegat (strait) ....E 4
Knøsen (mt.) ....D 3
Knudshoved (prom.) ....D 7
Køge (bay) ....F 7
Læsø (isl.), 2,722 ....D 3
Langeland (isl.), 17,132 ....D 8
Langelands Bælt (channel) ....D 8
Lille Bælt (channel) ....C 7
Lilleå (river) ....B 5
Limfjorden (fjord) ....A, D 4
Løgstør Bredning (fjord) ....C 4
Lolland (isl.), 74,819 ....E 8
Mariager (fjord) ....D 4
Mollebjerg (mt.) ....C 6
Møn (isl.), 12,436 ....F 8
Møns Klint (prom.) ....F 8
Mors (isl.), 25,026 ....B 4
Nissum (fjord) ....A 5
North Frisian (isls.), 3,653 ....B 7
Odense (fjord) ....D 7
Omme (river) ....B 6
Omø (isl.), 241 ....E 7
Øresund (sound) ....F 6
Ringkøbing (fjord) ....B 6
Rømø (isl.), 817 ....B 7
Røsnaes (prom.) ....D 6
Samsø (isl.), 5,192 ....D 6
Samsø Bælt (channel) ....D 6
Sandoy (isl.), Færøe Is., 1,684 ....B 3
Sejerø (isl.), 561 ....E 6
Sjælland (isl.), 2,116,294 ....E 6
Sjællands Odde (point) ....E 5
Skagens Odde (The Skaw) (point) ....D 2
Skagerrak (strait) ....C 2
Skive (river) ....C 5
Stevns Klint (prom.) ....F 7
Storå (river) ....B 5
Store Bælt (channel) ....D 6
Streymoy (isl.), Færøe Is., 14,078 ....A 2
Sudhuroy (isl.), Færøe Is., 5,734 ....B 3
Suså (river) ....E 7
Tannis (bay) ....D 2
Tranebjerg (mt.) ....C 6
Varde (river) ....B 6
Vejle (fjord) ....C 6
Vigsø (bay) ....B 3
Vorgod (river) ....B 6
Yding Skovhøj (mt.) ....C 6

ICELAND

CITIES and TOWNS

Akranes, 4,253 ....B 1
Akureyri, 10,755 ....C 1
Hafnarfjördhur, 9,696 ....B 1
Húsavík, 1,993 ....C 1
Ísafjördhur, 2,680 ....B 1
Keflavík, 5,663 ....B 1
Neskaupstadhur (Nes), 1,552 ....D 1
Olafsfjördhur, 1,086 ....C 1
Reykjavík (capital), 81,693 ....B 1
Reykjavík, *98,521 ....B 1
Saudhárkrókur, 1,600 ....B 1
Seydhisfjördhur, 884 ....D 1
Siglufjördhur, 2,161 ....C 1
Vestmannæyjar, 5,186 ....B 2

OTHER FEATURES

Bjargtangur (point) ....A 1
Breidhafjördhur (fjord) ....B 1
Faxaflói (bay) ....B 1
Fontur (prom.) ....D 1
Gerpir (cape) ....D 1
Grímsey (isl.), 79 ....C 1
Hekla (volcano) ....B 1
Hofsjökull (glacier) ....C 1
Horn (cape) ....B 1
Hornafjördhur (fjord) ....D 1
Húnaflói (bay) ....B 1
Hvannadalshnúkur (mt.) ....C 1
Hvítá (river) ....B 1
Ísafjördhur (fjord) ....B 1
Jökulsá (river) ....C 1
Lagarfljót (stream) ....C 1
Langjökull (glacier) ....B 1
North (Horn) (cape) ....B 1
öndverdharnes (mt.) ....A 1
Reykjanestá (cape) ....A 2
Rifstangi (cape) ....C 1
Skagata (cape) ....B 1
Skjálfandafljót (river) ....C 1
Surtsey (isl.) ....B 2
Thjórsá (river) ....C 1
Vatnajökull (glacier) ....C 1
Vopnafjörd (fjord) ....D 1

*City and suburbs.

†Population of rural municipality.

DENMARK and ICELAND

CONIC PROJECTION

SCALE OF MILES

0 10 20 30 40 50

SCALE OF KILOMETERS

0 10 20 30 40 50

Capitals of Countries
Capitals of Counties (amter)
International Boundaries
Internal Boundaries

Denmark is divided into fourteen counties plus Copenhagen and Frederiksberg communes.

GERMANY
CONIC PROJECTION
SCALE OF MILES
0 20 40 60 80
SCALE OF KILOMETERS
0 20 40 60 80
Capitals of Countries
State and District Capitals
International Boundaries
State and District Boundaries
Canals
East Germany is divided into districts bearing the same name as their respective capitals.
Longitude East 10° of Greenwich
DENMARK
BALTIC SEA
NORTH SEA
NORTH FRISIAN ISLANDS
EAST FRISIAN ISLANDS
WEST FRISIAN ISLANDS
SCHLESWIG-HOLSTEIN
MECKLENBURG
Pomerania
BRANDENBURG
EAST GERMANY
LOWER SAXONY
NORTH RHINE-WESTPHALIA
HESSE
THURINGIA
SAXONY
RHINELAND-PALATINATE
SAARLAND
BADEN-WÜRTTEMBERG
BAVARIA
NETHERLANDS
BELGIUM
LUXEMBOURG
FRANCE
SWITZERLAND
AUSTRIA
CZECHOSLOVAKIA
POLAND
HAMBURG
BREMEN
BERLIN
Hannover
Cologne (Köln)
Bonn
Frankfurt
Stuttgart
MUNICH (München)
Nuremberg (Nürnberg)
Leipzig
Dresden
Magdeburg
Rostock
Kiel
Erfurt
Karl-Marx-Stadt (Chemnitz)
Potsdam
Schwerin
Halle
Wiesbaden
Mainz
Düsseldorf
Saarbrücken
Black Forest (Schwarzwald)
Swabian Jura
Franconian Jura
Bohemian Forest
Bavarian Forest
Erzgebirge
Thuringian Wald
Harz
Lüneburger Heide
Rhine
Elbe
Danube
Main
Weser
Oder
Mosel
BERLIN
WEST
EAST
MILES 0 5
© Copyright by C.S. HAMMOND & Co., Maplewood, N.J.

WEST GERMANY

AREA 95,959 sq. mi.
POPULATION 61,194,600
CAPITAL Bonn
LARGEST CITY Berlin (West)
HIGHEST POINT Zugspitze 9,718 ft.
MONETARY UNIT West German Deutsch mark
MAJOR LANGUAGE German
MAJOR RELIGIONS Protestantism, Roman Catholicism

EAST GERMANY

AREA 41,814 sq. mi.
POPULATION 17,117,000
CAPITAL Berlin (East)
LARGEST CITY Berlin (East)
HIGHEST POINT Fichtelberg 3,983 ft.
MONETARY UNIT East German Deutsch mark
MAJOR LANGUAGE German
MAJOR RELIGIONS Protestantism, Roman Catholicism

Topography

0 50 100 MILES

Below Sea Level | 100 m. 328 ft. | 200 m. 656 ft. | 500 m. 1,640 ft. | 1,000 m. 3,281 ft. | 2,000 m. 6,562 ft. | 5,000 m. 16,404 ft.

EAST GERMANY

DISTRICTS

Berlin (East), 1,084,000 .... F 4
Cottbus, 839,133 .... F 3
Dresden, 1,887,739 .... E 3
Erfurt, 1,249,540 .... D 3
Frankfurt, 660,666 .... F 2
Gera, 735,175 .... D 3
Halle, 1,932,733 .... E 3
Karl-Marx-Stadt, 2,082,927 .... E 3
Leipzig, 1,510,773 .... E 3
Magdeburg, 1,323,644 .... D 2
Neubrandenburg, 633,209 .... E 2
Potsdam, 1,127,498 .... E 2
Rostock, 842,743 .... D 1
Schwerin, 594,786 .... D 2
Suhl, 549,398 .... D 3

CITIES and TOWNS

Aken, 12,126 .... D 3
Altenburg, 47,462 .... E 3
Angermünde, 12,200 .... E 2
Anklam, 19,436 .... E 2
Annaberg-Buchholz, 28,663 .... E 3
Apolda, 29,735 .... D 3
Arnstadt, 27,674 .... D 3
Aschersleben, 36,777 .... D 3
Aue, 31,723 .... E 3
Auerbach, 19,673 .... E 3
Bad Doberan, 13,197 .... D 1
Bad Dürrenberg, 16,500 .... D 3
Bad Freienwalde, 11,845 .... F 2
Bad Langensalza, 16,952 .... D 3
Bad Salzungen, 12,722 .... C 3
Barth, 12,688 .... E 1
Bautzen, 44,041 .... F 3
Bergen, 10,979 .... E 1
Berlin (East) (capital), 1,084,000 .... F 4
Bernau, 14,078 .... E 2
Bernburg, 45,885 .... D 3
Bischofswerda, 11,345 .... F 3
Bitterfeld, 30,916 .... E 3
Blankenburg, 19,595 .... D 3
Boizenburg, 11,370 .... D 2
Borna, 20,669 .... E 3
Brandenburg, 90,753 .... E 2
Burg, 29,906 .... D 2
Calbe, 16,464 .... D 3
Chemnitz (Karl-Marx-Stadt), 295,443 .... D 3
Coswig, 18,600 .... E 3
Cottbus, 75,541 .... F 3
Crimmitschau, 30,752 .... E 3
Delitzsch, 23,480 .... E 3
Demmin, 16,755 .... E 2
Dessau, 95,682 .... E 3
Döbeln, 28,430 .... E 3
Dresden, 499,848 .... E 3
Ebersbach, 11,293 .... F 3
Eberswalde, 33,680 .... E 2
Eilenburg, 21,366 .... E 3
Eisenach, 50,234 .... D 3
Eisenberg, 13,858 .... D 3
Eisenhüttenstadt, 38,138 .... F 2
Eisleben, 32,402 .... D 3
Erfurt, 193,745 .... D 3
Falkensee, 29,884 .... E 3
Falkenstein, 15,269 .... E 3
Finsterwalde, 22,441 .... E 3
Forst, 29,823 .... F 3
Frankfurt-an-der-Oder, 58,866 .... F 2
Freiberg, 49,122 .... E 3
Freital, 42,675 .... E 3
Fürstenwalde, 30,527 .... F 2
Gardelegen, 13,218 .... D 2
Genthin, 15,619 .... E 2
Gera, 109,989 .... E 3
Glauchau, 33,103 .... E 3
Görlitz, 88,632 .... F 3
Gotha, 57,692 .... D 3
Greifswald, 47,402 .... E 1
Greiz, 39,313 .... E 3
Grevesmühlen, 10,914 .... D 2
Grimma, 16,509 .... E 3
Grimmen, 12,943 .... E 1
Grossenhain, 19,848 .... E 3
Grossräschen, 12,737 .... E 3
Guben (Wilhelm-Pieck-Stadt), 26,586 .... F 3
Güstrow, 38,185 .... E 2
Hagenow, 10,434 .... D 2
Halberstadt, 46,071 .... D 3
Haldensleben, 20,547 .... D 2
Halle, 263,928 .... D 3
Heidenau, 20,161 .... E 3
Heiligenstadt, 12,627 .... D 3
Hennigsdorf, 21,398 .... E 3
Hettstedt, 19,218 .... D 3
Hoyerswerda, 43,922 .... F 3
Ilmenau, 19,852 .... D 3
Jena, 85,032 .... D 3
Johanngeorgenstadt, 10,801 .... E 3
Jüterbog, 14,416 .... E 3
Kamenz, 16,236 .... F 3
Karl-Marx-Stadt, 295,443 .... E 3
Kleinmachnow, 13,919 .... E 4
Klingenthal, 14,748 .... E 3
Köpenick, 52,294 .... F 4
Köthen, 38,154 .... E 3
Kottbus (Cottbus), 75,541 .... F 3
Lauchhammer, 28,680 .... E 3
Leipzig, 590,291 .... E 3
Lichtenberg, 62,841 .... F 4
Limbach-Oberfrohna, 26,053 .... E 3
Löbau, 17,068 .... F 3
Lübben, 12,742 .... E 3
Lübbenau, 16,976 .... F 3
Luckenwalde, 29,282 .... E 2
Ludwigslust, 11,512 .... D 2
Magdeburg, 268,269 .... D 2
Markkleeberg, 21,854 .... E 3
Meerane, 24,262 .... E 3
Meiningen, 25,025 .... D 3
Meissen, 47,166 .... E 3
Merseburg, 55,562 .... D 3
Meuselwitz, 10,582 .... E 3
Mittweida, 20,440 .... E 3
Mücheln, 10,842 .... D 3
Mühlhausen, 46,155 .... D 3
Nauen, 12,017 .... E 2
Naumburg, 37,990 .... D 3
Neubrandenburg, 38,740 .... E 2
Neuenhagen, 13,116 .... F 4
Neugersdorf, 11,889 .... F 3
Neuruppin, 22,424 .... E 2
Neustadt, 10,085 .... D 3
Neustrelitz, 27,624 .... E 2
Nordhausen, 42,279 .... D 3
Oelsnitz, 15,954 .... E 3
Oelsnitz im Erzgebirge, 18,377 .... E 3
Olbernhau, 14,240 .... E 3
Oranienburg, 20,401 .... E 2
Oschatz, 15,582 .... E 3
Oschersleben, 18,078 .... D 2
Pankow, 68,785 .... F 3
Parchim, 19,226 .... D 2
Pasewalk, 14,086 .... F 2
Perleberg, 13,707 .... D 2
Pirna, 42,562 .... E 3
Plauen, 81,739 .... E 3
Pössneck, 19,468 .... D 3
Potsdam, 110,671 .... E 2
Prenzlau, 20,276 .... F 2
Quedlinburg, 30,840 .... D 3
Radeberg, 17,410 .... E 3
Radebeul, 41,437 .... E 3
Rathenow, 28,979 .... E 2
Reichenbach, 29,372 .... E 3
Ribnitz-Damgarten, 15,301 .... E 1
Riesa, 43,322 .... E 3
Rosslau, 16,256 .... E 3
Rosswein, 10,649 .... E 3
Rostock, 190,275 .... E 1
Rüdersdorf, 11,837 .... E 2
Rudolstadt, 30,433 .... D 3
Saalfeld, 32,145 .... D 3
Salzwedel, 19,534 .... D 2
Sangerhausen, 29,373 .... D 3
Sassnitz, 13,253 .... E 1
Schkeuditz, 17,131 .... E 3
Schmalkalden, 14,569 .... D 3
Schmölln, 13,992 .... E 3
Schneeberg, 21,225 .... E 3
Schönebeck, 44,551 .... D 2
Schöneiche, 10,101 .... E 2
Schwedt, 23,359 .... F 2
Schwerin, 92,356 .... D 2
Sebnitz, 14,655 .... F 3
Senftenberg, 24,532 .... F 3
Sömmerda, 16,061 .... D 3
Sondershausen, 22,456 .... D 3
Sonneberg, 29,804 .... D 3
Spremberg, 23,367 .... F 3
Stassfurt, 25,622 .... D 3
Stendal, 36,193 .... D 2
Stralsund, 68,925 .... E 1
Strausberg, 17,985 .... F 2
Suhl, 28,698 .... D 3
Tangermünde, 12,992 .... D 2
Teltow, 13,735 .... E 4
Templin, 11,203 .... E 2
Teterow, 11,039 .... E 2
Thale, 17,273 .... D 3
Torgau, 20,941 .... E 3
Torgelow, 13,584 .... F 2
Treptow, 22,302 .... F 4
Ueckermünde, 11,614 .... F 2
Zwickau, 127,688 .... E 3
Waltershausen, 14,250 .... D 3
Waren, 20,008 .... E 2
Weida, 11,950 .... D 3
Weimar, 64,300 .... D 3
Weissenfels, 47,704 .... D 3
Weissensee, 50,691 .... F 3
Weisswasser, 16,016 .... F 3
Werdau, 23,783 .... E 3
Wernigerode, 32,579 .... D 3
Wilhelm-Pieck-Stadt, 26,586 .... F 3
Wismar, 55,235 .... D 2
Wittenberg, 46,816 .... E 3
Wittenberge, 32,621 .... D 2
Wittstock, 10,358 .... E 2
Wolgast, 14,955 .... E 1
Wurzen, 24,349 .... E 3
Zehdenick, 12,306 .... E 2
Zeitz, 46,393 .... E 3
Zella-Mehlis, 17,121 .... D 3
Zerbst, 19,527 .... E 3
Zeulenroda, 18,534 .... D 3
Zittau, 43,259 .... F 3
Zwickau, 127,688 .... E 3

OTHER FEATURES

Altmark (reg.), 288,928 .... D 2
Arkona (cape) .... E 1
Baltic (sea) .... F 1
Black Elster (riv.) .... E 3
Brandenburg (region), 3,726,413 .... E 2
Brocken (mt.) .... D 3
Darsser Ort (point) .... E 1
Elbe (riv.) .... D 2
Elster (riv.) .... E 3
Erzgebirge (mts.) .... E 3
Fichtelberg (mt.) .... E 3
Havel (riv.) .... E 2
Kummerowersee (lake) .... E 2
Lusatia (reg.) .... F 3
Malchinersee (lake) .... E 2
Mecklenburg (reg.), 1,226,685 .... E 2
Mecklenburg (bay) .... D 1
Mulde (riv.) .... E 3
Müritzee (lake) .... E 2
Neisse (riv.) .... F 3
Oder (riv.) .... F 2
Penne (riv.) .... E 2
Plauersee (lake) .... E 2
Pomerania (region), 711,075 .... E 2
Pomeranian (bay) .... F 1
Rhön (mts.) .... D 3
Rügen (isl.), 92,348 .... E 1
Saale (riv.) .... D 3
Saxony (region), 5,318,661 .... E 3
Schaalsee (lake) .... D 2
Schwerinersee (lake) .... D 2
Spree (riv.) .... F 3
Spreewald (forest) .... F 3
Stettin (bay) .... F 2
Stubbenkammer (point) .... E 1
Thüringer Wald (forest) .... D 3
Thuringia (Thüringen) (reg.), 2,017,924 .... D 3
Tollensee (lake) .... E 2
Ücker (riv.) .... E 2
Unstrut (riv.) .... D 3
Usedom (isl.) .... F 1
Warnow (riv.) .... D 2
Werra (riv.) .... D 3
White Elster (riv.) .... E 3

WEST GERMANY

STATES

Baden-Württemberg, 8,909,700 .... C 4
Bavaria, 10,568,900 .... D 4
Berlin (West) (free city), 2,134,256 .... E 4
Bremen, 755,977 .... C 2
Hamburg, 1,817,122 .... D 2
Hesse, 5,422,600 .... C 3
Lower Saxony, 7,100,400 .... C 2
North Rhine-Westphalia, 17,129,800 .... B 3
Rhineland-Palatinate, 3,671,300 .... B 4
Saarland, 1,127,400 .... B 4
Schleswig-Holstein, 2,557,200 .... C 1

CITIES and TOWNS

Aachen, 177,642 .... B 3
Aalen, 35,102 .... D 4
Ahlen, 50,411 .... B 3
Ahrensburg, 25,829 .... D 2
Alfeld, 13,726 .... C 2
Alsdorf, 31,726 .... B 3
Altena, 31,164 .... B 3
Altona .... C 2
Alzey, 12,749 .... C 4
Amberg, 42,141 .... E 4
Andernach, 22,367 .... B 3
Ansbach, 30,083 .... D 4
Arnsberg, 22,577 .... C 3
Aschaffenburg, 56,236 .... C 4
Augsburg, 214,376 .... D 4
Aurich, 12,299 .... B 2
Backnang, 28,086 .... C 4
Bad Dürkheim, 15,792 .... C 4
Baden-Baden, 38,852 .... C 4
Bad Harzburg, 11,356 .... D 3
Bad Hersfeld, 23,494 .... C 3
Bad Homburg vor der Höhe, 41,236 .... C 3
Bad Honnef am Rhein, 20,649 .... B 3
Bad Kissingen, 12,672 .... D 3
Bad Kreuznach, 42,707 .... B 4
Bad Mergentheim, 12,552 .... D 4
Bad Nauheim, 15,222 .... C 3
Bad Oeynhausen, 14,127 .... C 2
Bad Oldesloe, 18,915 .... D 2
Bad Pyrmont, 16,527 .... C 2
Bad Reichenhall, 14,894 .... E 5
Bad Salzuflen, 49,030 .... C 2
Bad Schwartau, 16,909 .... D 2
Bad Segeberg, 12,494 .... D 2
Bad Tölz, 12,468 .... D 5
Bad Vilbel, 18,315 .... C 3
Bad Wildungen, 12,189 .... C 3
Balingen, 13,693 .... C 4
Bamberg, 68,713 .... D 4
Bayreuth, 63,387 .... D 4
Bendorf, 14,361 .... B 3
Bensheim, 27,495 .... C 4
Berchtesgaden, 4,074 .... E 5
Bergisch Gladbach, 50,095 .... B 3
Berlin (West), 2,134,256 .... E 4
Betzdorf, 10,388 .... B 3
Biberach an der Riss, 25,597 .... C 4
Bielefeld, 169,347 .... C 2
Bietigheim, 22,488 .... C 4
Bingen, 24,452 .... B 4
Böblingen, 36,644 .... C 4
Bocholt, 48,134 .... B 3
Bochum, 346,886 .... B 3
Bonn (cap.), 299,376 .... B 3
Borghorst, 17,072 .... B 2
Borken, 30,614 .... B 3
Bottrop, 108,161 .... B 3
Brackwede, 40,254 .... C 3
Brake, 19,388 .... C 2
Bramsche, 10,733 .... B 2
Braunschweig (Brunswick), 225,168 .... D 2
Bremen, 607,184 .... C 2
Bremerhaven, 148,793 .... C 2
Brilon, 15,301 .... C 3
Bruchsal, 27,103 .... C 4
Brühl, 41,782 .... B 3
Brunswick, 225,168 .... D 2
Bückeburg, 13,396 .... C 2
Burghausen, 16,630 .... E 4
Burgsteinfurt, 12,554 .... B 2
Buxtehude, 23,140 .... C 2
Celle, 56,335 .... D 2
Charlottenburg .... F 4
Clausthal-Zellerfeld, 15,744 .... D 3
Cloppenburg, 18,162 .... B 2
Coburg, 41,369 .... D 3
Coesfeld, 26,565 .... B 3
Cologne, 866,308 .... B 3
Crailsheim, 16,687 .... D 4
Cuxhaven, 45,218 .... C 2
Dachau, 33,093 .... D 4
Darmstadt, 141,075 .... C 4
Deggendorf, 18,601 .... E 4
Delmenhorst, 63,685 .... C 2
Detmold, 64,473 .... C 3
Diepholz, 11,639 .... C 2
Dillenburg, 10,236 .... C 3
Dillingen an der Donau, 11,606 .... D 4
Dingolfing, 10,747 .... E 4
Donaueschingen, 11,643 .... C 5
Donauwörth, 11,266 .... D 4
Dorsten, 39,393 .... B 3
Dortmund, 648,883 .... B 3
Duderstadt, 10,421 .... D 3
Dudweiler, 30,078 .... B 4
Duisburg, 457,891 .... B 3
Dülmen, 21,094 .... B 3
Düren, 54,867 .... B 3
Düsseldorf, 680,806 .... B 3
Eberbach, 14,369 .... C 4
Ebingen, 22,004 .... C 4
Eckernförde, 21,971 .... D 1
Ehingen, 12,957 .... C 4
Eichstätt, 10,040 .... D 4
Einbeck, 18,618 .... C 3
Eiserfeld, 22,490 .... B 1
Ellwangen, 13,128 .... D 4
Elmshorn, 41,353 .... C 2
Emden, 48,313 .... B 2
Emmendingen, 15,986 .... B 4
Emmerich, 24,512 .... B 3
Erkelenz, 12,275 .... B 3
Erlangen, 85,727 .... D 4
Eschwege, 22,219 .... D 3
Eschweiler, 39,622 .... B 3
Espelkamp, 12,309 .... C 2
Essen, 704,769 .... B 3
Esslingen am Neckar, 86,497 .... C 4
Ettlingen, 21,342 .... C 4
Euskirchen, 41,965 .... B 3
Eutin, 18,177 .... D 1
Fellbach, 29,343 .... C 4
Flensburg, 96,778 .... C 1
Forchheim, 21,582 .... D 4
Frankenthal, 40,505 .... C 4
Frankfurt am Main, 660,410 .... C 3
Frechen, 30,786 .... B 3
Freiburg im Breisgau, 165,960 .... B 5
Freising, 30,264 .... D 4
Freudenstadt, 14,356 .... C 4
Friedberg, 17,401 .... C 3
Friedrichshafen, 42,483 .... C 5
Fulda, 44,262 .... C 3
Fürstenfeldbruck, 22,495 .... D 4
Fürth, 94,310 .... D 4
Füssen, 10,891 .... D 5
Gaggenau, 14,773 .... C 4
Garmisch-Partenkirchen, 27,313 .... D 5
Geesthacht, 23,594 .... D 2
Geislingen an der Steige, 27,209 .... C 4
Geldern, 22,602 .... B 3
Gelsenkirchen, 348,620 .... B 3
Giessen, 74,731 .... C 3
Gifhorn, 23,001 .... D 2
Glückstadt, 16,199 .... C 2
Goch, 27,721 .... B 3
Göggingen, 15,840 .... D 4
Göppingen, 46,899 .... C 4
Goslar, 41,653 .... D 3
Göttingen, 115,227 .... D 3
Grevenbroich, 28,197 .... B 3
Griesheim, 16,392 .... C 4
Gronau, 26,596 .... B 2
Gummersbach, 45,026 .... B 3
Günzburg, 13,449 .... D 4
Gütersloh, 76,343 .... C 3
Haar, 12,388 .... D 4
Hagen, 203,048 .... B 3
Haltern, 15,264 .... B 3
Hamburg, 1,817,122 .... D 2
Hameln, 47,114 .... C 2
Hamm, 84,302 .... B 3
Hanau, 55,674 .... C 3
Hannover, 517,783 .... C 2
Harburg-Wilhelmsburg .... C 2
Hassloch, 17,852 .... C 4
Haunstetten, 22,205 .... D 4
Heide, 23,419 .... C 1
Heidelberg, 121,929 .... C 4
Heidenheim an der Brenz, 50,170 .... D 4
Heilbronn, 99,440 .... C 4
Helmstedt, 27,161 .... D 2
Hennef, 26,589 .... B 3
Herborn, 10,395 .... C 3
Herford, 67,267 .... C 2
Herne, 100,798 .... B 3
Hildesheim, 95,926 .... D 2
Hockenheim, 15,615 .... C 4
Hof, 54,805 .... D 3
Holzminden, 22,273 .... C 3
Homburg, 32,258 .... B 4
Höxter, 32,823 .... C 3
Hürth, 52,011 .... B 3
Husum, 25,037 .... C 1
Hüttental, 40,287 .... C 3
Ibbenbüren, 17,780 .... B 2
Idar-Oberstein, 32,590 .... B 4
Immenstadt, 10,775 .... D 5
Ingolstadt, 71,954 .... D 4
Iserlohn, 57,792 .... B 3
Itzehoe, 35,678 .... C 2
Jülich, 20,152 .... B 3
Kaiserslautern, 99,859 .... B 4
Karlsruhe, 257,144 .... C 4
Kassel, 213,494 .... C 3
Kaufbeuren, 39,940 .... D 5
Kehl, 15,958 .... B 4
Kelheim, 11,701 .... D 4
Kempten, 44,617 .... D 5
Kevelaer, 20,257 .... B 3
Kiel, 276,600 .... C 1
Kirchheim unter Teck, 28,878 .... C 4
Kitzingen, 18,308 .... D 4
Kleve, 44,150 .... B 3
Koblenz, 106,189 .... B 3
Köln (Cologne), 866,308 .... B 3
Konstanz, 61,617 .... C 5
Korbach, 17,324 .... C 3
Kornwestheim, 28,574 .... C 4
Krefeld, 228,726 .... B 3
Kulmbach, 22,768 .... D 3
Lage, 30,949 .... C 3
Lahr, 25,028 .... B 4
Lampertheim, 24,053 .... C 4
Landau in der Pfalz, 32,318 .... C 4
Landsberg am Lech, 14,378 .... D 4
Landshut, 51,393 .... E 4
Langen, 30,230 .... C 4
Langenhagen, 37,077 .... C 2
Lauenburg, 11,445 .... D 2
Lauf an der Pegnitz, 15,771 .... D 4
Leer, 29,919 .... B 2
Lehrte, 21,792 .... D 2
Lemgo, 38,526 .... C 2
Lengerich, 21,451 .... B 2
Leverkusen, 111,588 .... B 3
Lichtenfels, 11,218 .... D 3
Limburg an der Lahn, 14,889 .... C 3
Lindau, 26,260 .... C 5
Lingen, 25,810 .... B 2
Lippstadt, 42,299 .... C 3
Lohr am Main, 11,291 .... C 4
Lörrach, 32,939 .... B 5
Lübbecke, 11,433 .... C 2
Lübeck, 242,191 .... D 2
Lüdenscheid, 80,096 .... B 3
Ludwigsburg, 79,538 .... C 4
Ludwigshafen am Rhein, 174,698 .... C 4
Lüneburg, 59,944 .... D 2
Lünen, 72,195 .... B 3

(continued on following page)

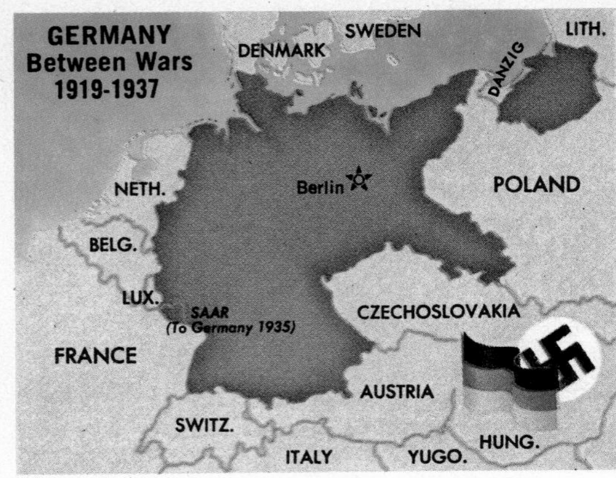

WEST GERMANY (continued)

Place	Key
Mainz, 176,720	C 4
Mannheim, 330,920	C 4
Marburg an der Lahn, 51,382	C 3
Marktredwitz, 15,605	E 3
Marl, 75,779	B 3
Mayen, 18,485	B 3
Memmingen, 35,454	D 5
Meppen, 17,892	B 2
Merzig, 12,443	B 4
Meschede, 16,222	C 3
Metzingen, 14,093	C 4
Minden, 51,527	C 2
Mittenwald, 10,026	D 5
Mölln, 15,307	D 2
Mönchengladbach, 152,172	B 3
Moosburg an der Isar, 11,730	D 4
Mosbach, 13,876	C 4
Mühldorf am Inn, 10,998	E 4
Mülheim an der Ruhr, 191,080	B 3
Münden, 19,111	C 3
Munich (München), 1,326,331	D 4
Münster, 204,571	B 3
Neckarsulm, 18,523	C 4
Neheim-Hüsten, 36,864	C 3
Neuburg an der Donau, 18,530	D 4
Neu-Isenburg, 36,014	C 3
Neumarkt in der Oberpfalz, 18,930	D 4
Neumünster, 84,636	C 1
Neunkirchen, 44,326	B 4
Neuss, 117,599	B 3
Neustadt an der Weinstrasse, 51,058	B 4
Neustadt bei Coburg, 12,496	D 3
Neustadt in Holstein, 16,222	D 1
Neu-Ulm, 27,710	D 4
Neuwied, 31,359	B 3
Nienburg, 22,467	C 2
Norden, 16,355	B 2
Nordenham, 27,368	C 2
Nordhorn, 42,895	B 2
Nördlingen, 14,238	D 4
Northeim, 19,150	C 3
Nuremberg (Nürnberg), 477,108	D 4
Nürtingen, 21,284	C 4
Oberammergau, 4,641	D 5
Oberhausen, 249,045	B 3
Oberlahnstein, 20,131	B 3
Oberursel, 24,933	C 3
Ochtrup, 15,823	B 2
Offenbach am Main, 118,754	C 3
Offenburg, 32,628	B 4
Oldenburg, 131,434	C 2
Opladen, 43,531	B 3
Osnabrück, 141,000	C 2
Osterholz-Scharmbeck, 15,211	C 2
Osterode am Harz, 16,757	D 3
Paderborn, 68,735	C 3
Papenburg, 16,714	B 2
Passau, 31,574	E 4
Peine, 30,882	D 2
Penzberg, 10,784	D 5
Pforzheim, 90,780	C 4
Pfullingen, 15,967	C 4
Pinneberg, 36,439	C 2
Pirmasens, 56,172	B 4
Plettenberg, 30,233	C 3
Plön, 11,142	D 1
Porz am Rhein, 78,076	B 3
Preetz, 14,653	D 1
Radolfzell, 15,512	C 5
Rastatt, 29,102	C 4
Rastede, 16,851	C 2
Ratingen, 43,420	B 3
Ratzeburg, 12,335	D 2
Ravensburg, 31,819	C 5
Recklinghausen, 125,535	B 3
Regensburg, 128,083	E 4
Rehau, 10,565	D 3
Remscheid, 137,374	B 3
Rendsburg, 35,453	C 1
Reutlingen, 77,853	C 4
Rheine, 51,167	B 2
Rheinfelden, 16,547	B 5
Rheinhausen, 71,698	B 3
Rheydt, 100,633	B 3
Rosenheim, 36,376	D 5
Rotenburg, 16,664	C 2
Roth bei Nürnberg, 11,550	D 4
Rothenburg ob der Tauber, 12,002	D 4
Rottenburg am Neckar, 13,495	C 4
Rottweil, 19,881	C 4
Rüsselsheim, 57,308	C 4
Saarbrücken, 130,765	B 4
Saarlouis (Saarlautern), 36,251	B 4
Säckingen, 12,614	C 5
Salzgitter, 118,020	D 2
Sankt Ingbert, 28,774	B 4
Sankt Wendel, 10,138	B 4
Schleswig, 33,317	C 1
Schöneberg	E 4
Schöningen, 14,551	D 2
Schramberg, 19,050	C 4
Schwabach, 25,774	D 4
Schwäbisch Gmünd, 44,628	C 4
Schwäbisch Hall, 23,765	C 4
Schwandorf in Bayern, 15,995	E 4
Schweinfurt, 59,293	D 3
Schwelm, 34,199	B 3
Schwenningen am Neckar, 35,487	C 4
Schwetzingen, 16,613	C 4
Seesen, 13,027	D 3
Selb, 18,498	E 3
Sennestadt, 20,518	C 3
Siegburg, 34,586	B 3
Siegen, 57,996	C 3
Sindelfingen, 41,029	C 4
Singen, 39,719	C 5
Soest, 40,580	C 3
Solingen, 175,895	B 3
Soltau, 14,981	C 2
Sonthofen, 16,504	D 5
Spandau	E 3
Speyer, 42,323	C 4
Springe, 12,698	C 2
Stade, 31,637	C 2
Stadthagen, 16,876	C 2
Starnberg, 10,622	D 4
Stolberg, 39,589	B 3
Straubing, 36,943	E 4
Stuttgart, 628,412	C 4
Sulzbach-Rosenberg, 18,691	D 4
Tailfingen, 16,787	C 4
Tempelhof	F 4
Traunstein, 14,117	E 5
Trier, 103,412	B 4
Tübingen, 56,008	C 4
Tuttlingen, 26,587	C 5
Überlingen, 12,837	C 5
Uelzen, 23,775	D 2
Uetersen, 16,734	C 2
Ulm, 92,486	C 4
Varel, 12,759	C 2
Vechta, 16,326	C 2
Verden, 16,741	C 2
Viersen, 83,988	B 3
Villingen im Schwarzwald, 37,652	C 4
Völklingen, 39,763	B 4
Waldshut, 10,621	C 5
Walsrode, 13,904	C 2
Wangen im Allgäu, 14,159	C 5
Wanne-Eickel, 99,923	B 3
Warendorf, 18,969	B 3
Wedel, 31,134	C 2
Weiden in der Oberpfalz, 43,097	D 4
Weilheim in Oberbayern, 14,433	D 5
Weingarten, 18,420	C 5
Weinheim, 29,544	C 4
Weissenburg in Bayern, 13,718	D 4
Wertheim, 12,035	C 4
Wesel, 44,710	B 3
Westerstede, 16,387	B 2
Wetzlar, 37,230	C 3
Wiesbaden, 260,614	B 3
Wilhelmshaven, 103,150	B 2
Witten, 97,807	B 3
Wolfenbüttel, 41,225	D 2
Wolfsburg, 89,442	D 2
Worms, 78,004	C 4
Wunstorf, 17,589	C 2
Wuppertal, 414,722	B 3
Würzburg, 120,317	C 4
Zirndorf, 15,363	D 4
Zweibrücken, 32,883	B 4
Zwischenahn, 19,906	B 2

OTHER FEATURES

Aller (riv.)	C 2
Allgäu (reg.), 249,600	D 5
Alz (riv.)	E 4
Ammersee (lake)	D 4
Amrum (isl.), 2,155	C 1
Baltrum (isl.), 924	B 2
Bavarian (forest)	E 4
Bavarian Alps (mts.)	D 5
Black (forest)	C 4
Bodensee (Constance) (lake)	C 5
Bohemian (forest)	E 4
Borkum (isl.), 5,348	B 2
Breisgau (reg.), 675,500	B 5
Chiemsee (lake)	E 5
Constance (lake)	C 5
Danube (Donau) (riv.)	C 4
Dümmer (lake)	C 2
East Friesland (region), 599,700	B 2
East Frisian (isls.), 20,962	B 2
Eder (res.)	C 3
Eider (riv.)	C 1
Eifel (mts.)	B 3
Elbe (riv.)	C 2
Ems (riv.)	B 2
Fehmarn (isl.), 12,586	D 1
Feldberg (mt.)	B 5
Fichtelgebirge (mts.)	D 3
Föhr (isl.), 8,585	C 1
Franconian Jura (mts.)	D 4
Frankenwald (forest)	D 3
Fulda (riv.)	C 3
Grosser Arber (mt.)	E 4
Halligen, The (isls.), 5,112	C 1
Hardt (mts.)	C 4
Harz (mts.)	D 3
Hegau (reg.), 189,900	C 5
Helgoland (isl.), 3,184	B 1
Hunsrück (mts.)	B 4
Iller (riv.)	D 4
Inn (riv.)	E 4
Isar (riv.)	E 4
Jade (bay)	C 2
Juist (isl.), 2,147	B 2
Kaiserstuhl (mt.)	B 4
Kiel (canal)	C 1
Königssee (lake)	E 5
Lahn (riv.)	C 3
Langeoog (isl.), 2,611	B 2
Lech (riv.)	D 4
Leine (riv.)	C 2
Lippe (riv.)	C 3
Lüneburger Heide (dist.)	C 2
Main (riv.)	C 4
Mecklenburg (bay)	D 1
Mosel (riv.)	B 3
Neckar (riv.)	C 4
Nord-Ostsee (Kiel) (canal)	C 1
Norderney (isl.), 8,983	B 2
Nordstrand (isl.), 3,079	C 1
North (sea)	A 1
North Friesland (reg.), 163,800	C 1
North Frisian (islands), 36,259	B 1
Oberpfälzer Wald (forest)	E 4
Odenwald (forest)	C 4
Pellworm (isl.), 2,033	C 1
Regen (riv.)	E 4
Regnitz (riv.)	D 4
Rhine (Rhein) (riv.)	B 3
Rhön (mts.)	D 3
Ruhr (riv.)	B 3
Saar (riv.)	B 4
Salzach (riv.)	E 5
Sauer (riv.)	B 4
Sauerland (reg.)	B 3
Schwarzwald (Black) (forest)	C 4
Spessart (range)	C 4
Spiekeroog (isl.), 823	B 2
Starnbergersee (lake)	D 5
Steigerwald (forest)	D 4
Steinhuder (lake)	C 2
Swabian Jura (mts.)	C 4
Sylt (isl.), 20,407	C 1
Tauber (riv.)	C 4
Taunus (range)	C 3
Tegernsee (lake)	D 5
Teutoburger Wald (forest)	C 2
Vechte (riv.)	B 2
Vogelsberg (mt.)	C 3
Walchensee (lake)	D 5
Wangerooge (isl.), 2,126	B 2
Wasserkuppe (mt.)	C 3
Watzmann (mt.)	E 5
Werra (riv.)	D 3
Weser (riv.)	C 2
Westerwald (forest)	C 3
Wurmsee (Starnbergersee) (lake)	D 5
Zugspitze (mt.)	D 5

Agriculture, Industry and Resources

DOMINANT LAND USE

- Wheat, Sugar Beets
- Cereals (chiefly rye, oats, barley)
- Potatoes, Rye
- Dairy, Livestock
- Mixed Cereals, Dairy
- Truck Farming
- Grapes, Fruit
- Forests

MAJOR MINERAL OCCURRENCES

Ag	Silver	Lg	Lignite
Ba	Barite	Mg	Magnesium
C	Coal	Na	Salt
Cu	Copper	O	Petroleum
Fe	Iron Ore	Pb	Lead
G	Natural Gas	U	Uranium
Gr	Graphite	Zn	Zinc
K	Potash		

Water Power

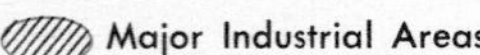
Major Industrial Areas

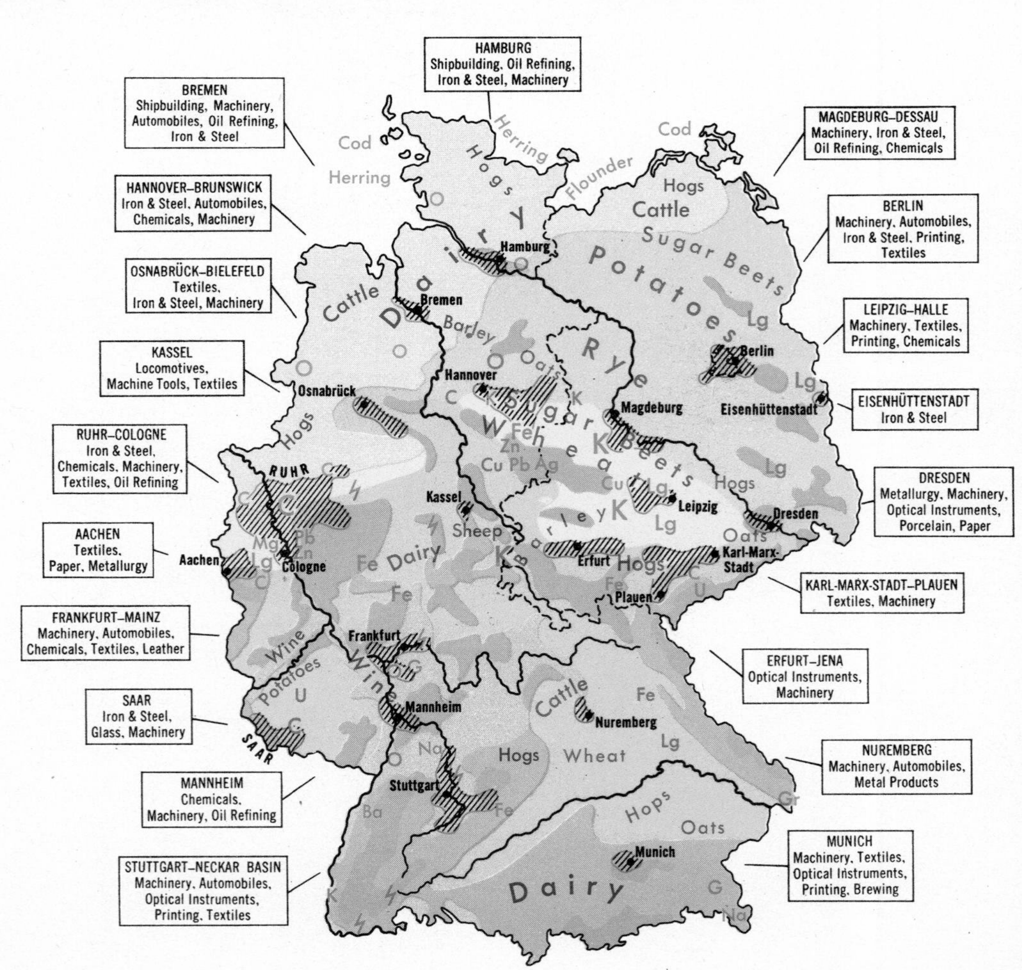

NETHERLANDS

AREA 13,958 sq. mi.
POPULATION 13,077,000
CAPITALS The Hague, Amsterdam
LARGEST CITY Amsterdam
HIGHEST POINT Vaalserberg, 1,056 ft.
MONETARY UNIT guilder
MAJOR LANGUAGE Dutch
MAJOR RELIGIONS Protestantism, Roman Catholicism

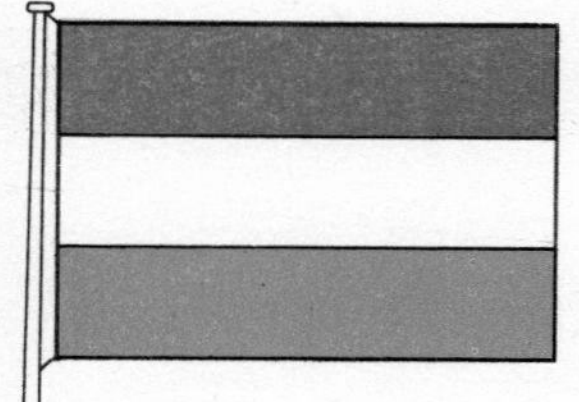

BELGIUM

AREA 11,779 sq. mi.
POPULATION 9,660,154
CAPITAL Brussels
LARGEST CITY Brussels (greater)
HIGHEST POINT Botrange 2,277 ft.
MONETARY UNIT Belgian franc
MAJOR LANGUAGES French (Walloon), Flemish
MAJOR RELIGION Roman Catholicism

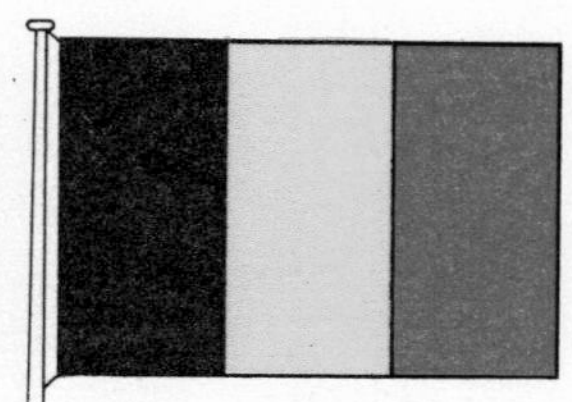

LUXEMBOURG

AREA 999 sq. mi.
POPULATION 339,000
CAPITAL Luxembourg
LARGEST CITY Luxembourg
HIGHEST POINT Ardennes Plateau, 1,825 ft.
MONETARY UNIT Luxembourg franc
MAJOR LANGUAGES Luxembourgeois (German dialect), French, German
MAJOR RELIGION Roman Catholicism

BELGIUM

PROVINCES

Antwerp, 1,529,826 ....F 6
Brabant, 2,166,372 ....F 7
East Flanders, 1,310,638 ....D 7
Hainault, 1,331,810 ....D 7
Liège, 1,016,131 ....H 7
Limburg, 650,338 ....G 7
Luxembourg, 219,369 ....G 9
Namur, 383,618 ....F 8
West Flanders, 1,052,052 ....B 7

CITIES and TOWNS†

Aalst, 45,900 ....D 7
Aalter, 8,569 ....C 6
Aarlen (Arlon), 14,191 ....H 9
Aarschot, 12,329 ....F 7
Aat (Ath), 11,094 ....D 7
Adinkerke, 2,713 ....A 6
Alken, 8,054 ....G 7
Alost (Aalst), 45,900 ....D 7
Amay, 7,561 ....G 7
Andenne, 8,068 ....G 8
Anderlecht, 103,832 ....B 9
Anderlues, 12,930 ....E 8
Antoing, 3,435 ....C 7
Antwerp (Antwerpen), 234,099 ....E 6
Antwerp, *673,259 ....E 6
Ardooie, 7,163 ....C 7
Arendonk, 9,516 ....G 6
Arlon, 14,191 ....H 9
As, 4,087 ....H 6
Asse, 12,631 ....E 7
Assebroek, 15,195 ....C 6
Assesse, 1,138 ....G 8
Ath, 11,094 ....D 7
Athus, 7,185 ....H 9
Audenarde (Oudenaarde), 21,980 ....D 7
Auderghem, 32,782 ....C 9
Autelbas, 1,606 ....H 9
Auvelais, 8,412 ....F 8
Aywaille, 3,813 ....H 8
Baerle-Duc, 2,171 ....F 6
Balen, 14,719 ....G 6
Barvaux, 1,727 ....H 8
Basècles, 4,245 ....D 7
Bastogne (Bastenaken), 6,476 ....H 9
Beaumont, 1,762 ....E 8
Beauraing, 2,703 ....F 8
Berchem, 49,880 ....F 6
Berchem-Sainte-Agathe, 17,689 ....B 9
Bergen (Mons), 27,042 ....E 8
Bertrix, 4,481 ....G 9
Beveren, 15,350 ....E 6
Bilzen, 7,000 ....G 7
Binche, 10,340 ....E 8
Blankenberge, 10,400 ....C 6
Bocholt, 5,582 ....H 6
Boom, 17,280 ....E 6
Borgerhout, 50,226 ....E 6
Borgloon, 3,543 ....G 7
Borgworm (Waremme), 7,623 ....G 7
Bouillon, 3,089 ....G 9
Bourg-Leopold (Leopoldsburg), 9,621 ....G 6
Boussu, 11,626 ....D 8
Bovigny, 1,015 ....H 8
Braine-l'Alleud, 16,028 ....E 7
Braine-le-Comte, 11,343 ....D 7
Bredene, 9,381 ....B 6
Bree, 10,462 ....H 6
Bruges (Brugge), 52,249 ....C 6
Bruges, *112,611 ....C 6
Brussels (Bruxelles) (cap.), *1,073,111 ....C 9
Charleroi, 24,895 ....E 8
Charleroi, *218,089 ....E 8
Châtelet, 15,314 ....F 8
Châtelineau, 20,293 ....F 8
Chièvres, 3,154 ....D 7
Chimay, 3,309 ....E 8
Ciney, 7,431 ....G 8
Comblain-au-Pont, 3,538 ....G 8
Comines, 8,219 ....B 7
Couillet, 15,055 ....E 8
Courcelles, 17,157 ....E 8
Courtrai, 45,310 ....C 7
Couvin, 4,192 ....F 8
Cul-des-Sarts, 993 ....E 9
Deinze, 6,214 ....D 7
Denderleeuw, 9,699 ....E 7
Dendermonde, 9,663 ....E 6
De Panne, 6,792 ....A 6
Dessel, 7,170 ....G 6
Deurne, 75,819 ....F 6
Diegem, 4,760 ....C 9
Diest, 9,587 ....F 7
Diksmuide, 6,557 ....B 6
Dilbeek, 13,620 ....B 9
Dinant, 9,700 ....G 8
Dison, 8,809 ....H 7
Dixmude (Diksmuide), 6,557 ....B 6
Doel, 1,395 ....E 6
Doornik (Tournai), 33,309 ....C 7
Dour, 10,407 ....D 8
Drogenbos, 4,648 ....B 9
Drongen, 8,312 ....D 6
Dudzele, 2,112 ....C 6
Duffel, 13,560 ....F 6
Ecaussinnes d'Enghien, 6,696 ....E 7
Edingen (Enghien), 4,279 ....D 7
Eeklo, 19,007 ....D 6
Eernegem, 5,865 ....B 6
Eigenbrakel (Braine-l'Alleud), 16,028 ....E 7
Ekeren, 24,535 ....E 6
Ellezelles, 3,676 ....D 7
Enghien, 4,279 ....D 7
Ensival, 5,515 ....H 7
Erquelinnes, 4,812 ....E 8
Esneux, 5,923 ....H 7
Essen, 10,515 ....F 6
Étalle, 1,179 ....H 9
Etterbeek, 52,299 ....C 9
Eupen, 14,856 ....J 7
Evere, 24,289 ....C 9
Evergem, 12,329 ....D 6
Flémalle-Haute, 7,800 ....G 7
Fleurus, 8,475 ....F 8
Florennes, 4,070 ....F 8
Florenville, 2,526 ....G 9
Forest, 55,799 ....B 9
Fosses-la-Ville, 3,887 ....F 8
Frameries, 11,624 ....D 8
Frasnes-lez-Buissenal, 2,672 ....D 7
Furnes (Veurne), 7,475 ....B 6
Ganshoren, 19,154 ....B 9
Gaurain-Ramecroix, 3,599 ....D 7
Gedinne, 1,021 ....F 9
Geel, 28,484 ....F 6
Geldenaken (Jodoigne), 4,194 ..F 7
Gembloux, 11,030 ....F 7
Gemmenich, 2,608 ....H 7
Genk, 55,596 ....H 7
Gent (Ghent), 153,301 ....D 6
Gentbrugge, 22,986 ....D 6
Geraardsbergen, 9,201 ....D 7
Ghent, 153,301 ....D 6
Ghent, *229,687 ....D 6
Gilly, 24,155 ....E 8
Gosselies, 10,970 ....E 8
Grammont (Geraardsbergen), 9,201 ....D 7
Haacht, 4,372 ....F 7
Hal (Halle), 20,071 ....E 7
Halen, 5,321 ....G 7
Halle, 20,071 ....E 7
Hamme, 17,083 ....E 6
Hamont, 6,626 ....H 6
Hannut (Hannuit), 3,069 ....G 7
Harelbeke, 17,981 ....C 7
Hasselt, 38,773 ....G 7
Havelange, 1,495 ....G 8
Heer, 578 ....F 8
Heist, 9,289 ....C 6
Heist-op-den-Berg, 13,206 ....F 6
Herbeumont, 590 ....G 9
Herentals, 18,377 ....F 6
Herselt, 7,318 ....F 6
Herstal, 29,602 ....H 7
Herve, 4,357 ....H 7
Hoboken, 31,815 ....E 6
Hoei (Huy), 13,398 ....G 8
Hoeselt, 5,570 ....H 7
Hoogstraten, 4,376 ....F 6
Hornu, 10,905 ....D 8
Houffalize, 1,297 ....H 8
Huy, 13,398 ....G 8
Ieper, 18,461 ....B 7
Ingelmunster, 9,973 ....C 7
Ixelles, 92,532 ....C 9
Izegem, 22,729 ....C 7
Jambes, 14,924 ....F 8
Jemappes, 12,906 ....D 8
Jemeppe, 12,232 ....G 7
Jette, 37,354 ....B 9
Jodoigne, 4,194 ....F 7
Jumet, 28,811 ....E 8
Kain, 4,900 ....C 7
Kalmthout, 12,122 ....F 6
Kapellen, 12,297 ....F 6
Kessel-Lo, 21,351 ....F 7
Knokke, 14,268 ....C 6
Koekelare, 6,423 ....B 6
Koekelberg, 17,348 ....B 9
Koersel, 10,756 ....G 6
Kontich, 13,193 ....E 6
Kortemark, 5,839 ....C 6
Kortrijk (Courtrai), 45,310 ....C 7
Kraainem, 10,560 ....C 9
La Louvière, 23,447 ....E 8
La Louvière, *113,795 ....E 8
La Roche-en-Ardenne, 1,894 ....G 8
Lanaken, 8,216 ....H 7
Landen, 5,247 ....G 7
Langemark, 4,787 ....B 7
Lede, 10,229 ....D 7
Ledeberg, 11,056 ....D 7
Lens, 1,790 ....D 7
Leopoldsburg, 9,621 ....G 6
Lessines (Lessen), 9,047 ....D 7
Leuven (Louvain), 32,125 ....F 7
Leuze, 7,128 ....D 7
Libramont, 2,774 ....G 9
Lichtervelde, 7,372 ....C 6
Liedekerke, 10,273 ....D 7
Liège, 150,127 ....H 7
Liège, *446,990 ....H 7
Lier (Lierre), 28,557 ....F 6
Lierneux, 2,847 ....H 8
Limbourg (Limburg), 3,973 ....J 7
Linkebeek, 4,096 ....C10
Lokeren, 26,654 ....D 6
Lommel, 20,567 ....G 6
Looz (Borgloon), 3,543 ....G 7
Louvain, 32,125 ....F 7
Luik (Liège), 150,127 ....H 7
Maaseik, 8,383 ....H 6
Machelen, 7,331 ....C 9
Maldegem, 14,182 ....C 6
Malines (Mechelen), 65,728 ....F 6
Malmédy, 6,482 ....J 8
Marche-en-Famenne, 4,423 ....G 8
Marchin, 4,361 ....G 8
Marcinelle, 25,992 ....E 8
Mariembourg, 1,776 ....E 8
Martelange, 1,594 ....H 9
Mechelen, 65,728 ....F 6
Meerhout, 8,359 ....G 6
Meerle, 2,809 ....F 6
Melsbroek, 2,034 ....D 9
Menen (Menin), 22,458 ....C 7
Merchtem, 8,772 ....E 7
Merelbeke, 13,755 ....D 7
Merksem, 39,011 ....E 6
Merksplas, 4,950 ....F 6
Messancy, 3,064 ....H 9
Mettet, 3,366 ....F 8
Meulebeke, 10,619 ....C 7
Moeskron (Mouscron), 37,624 ....C 7
Mol, 27,320 ....G 6
Molenbeek-Saint-Jean, 67,271 ....B 9
Mons, 27,042 ....E 8
Montegnée, 11,882 ....G 7
Montignies-sur-Sambre, 24,048 ....F 8
Mortsel, 27,999 ....E 6
Mouscron, 37,624 ....C 7
Namur (Namen), 32,621 ....F 8
Neerlinter, 1,431 ....G 7
Neerpelt, 8,273 ....G 6
Neufchâteau, 2,739 ....G 9
Nieuwpoort (Nieuport), 7,165 ....B 6
Ninove, 12,087 ....D 7
Nivelles (Nijvel), 15,384 ....E 7
Oostende (Ostend), 57,749 ....B 6
Oostkamp, 8,560 ....C 6
Ophoven, 2,487 ....H 6
Opwijk, 9,622 ....E 7
Ostend, 57,749 ....B 6
Oud-Turnhout, 8,219 ....F 6
Oudenaarde, 21,980 ....D 7
Ougrée, 21,152 ....H 7
Overijse, 14,119 ....F 7
Overpelt, 10,002 ....G 6
Peer, 5,882 ....G 6
Péruwelz, 7,814 ....D 8
Perwez (Perwijs), 2,858 ....F 7
Philippeville, 1,822 ....E 8
Poperinge, 12,619 ....B 7
Poppel, 2,246 ....G 6
Putte, 6,856 ....F 6
Quaregnon, 18,289 ....D 8
Quiévrain, 5,685 ....D 8
Raeren, 3,490 ....J 7
Rance, 1,443 ....E 8
Rebecq-Rognon, 3,831 ....E 7
Renaix (Ronse), 25,371 ....D 7
Retie, 6,339 ....G 6
Rièzes, 307 ....E 9
Rochefort, 4,242 ....G 8
Roeselare, 40,077 ....C 7
Roeulx, 2,605 ....E 8
Ronse, 25,371 ....D 7
Roulers (Roeselare), 40,077 ....C 7
Ruisbroek, 5,685 ....B 9
's Gravenbrakel (Braine-le-Comte), 11,343 ....D 7
Saint-Georges, 6,085 ....G 7
Saint-Gérard, 1,626 ....F 8
Saint-Gilles, 57,238 ....B 9
Saint-Hubert, 3,104 ....G 8
Saint-Josse-ten-Noode, 24,335 ....C 9
Saint-Léger, 1,600 ....H 9
Saint-Vith (Sankt-Vith), 2,935 ....J 8
Schaerbeek, 120,650 ....C 9
Schoten, 28,543 ....F 6
Seraing, 40,937 ....G 7
Sint-Amandsberg, 24,778 ....D 6
Sint-Andries, 15,062 ....C 6
Sint-Lenaarts, 4,464 ....F 6
Sint-Niklaas, 48,851 ....E 6
Sint-Pieters-Leeuw, 15,978 ....B 9
Sint-Truiden (Saint-Trond), 21,131 ....G 7
Sivry, 1,384 ....E 8
Soignies, 11,320 ....D 7
Spa, 9,683 ....H 8
Staden, 5,581 ....B 7
Stavelot, 4,661 ....H 8
Steenokkerzeel, 3,877 ....C 9
Stene, 9,304 ....B 6
Stokkem, 3,380 ....H 6
Strombeek-Bever, 10,027 ....C 9
Tamines, 8,139 ....F 8
Tamise (Temse), 14,559 ....E 6
Templeuve, 3,737 ....C 7
Temse, 14,559 ....E 6
Termonde (Dendermonde), 9,663 ....E 6
Tessenderlo, 10,665 ....G 6
Theux, 5,491 ....H 8
Thuin, 5,877 ....E 8
Tielt, Brabant, 3,813 ....F 7
Tielt, West Flanders, 13,887 ....C 7
Tienen (Tirlemont), 22,660 ....F 7
Tongeren (Tongres), 16,880 ....G 7
Torhout, 14,301 ....C 6
Tournai, 33,309 ....C 7
Tronchiennes (Drongen), 8,312 ....D 6
Tubize (Tubeke), 10,269 ....E 7
Turnhout, 37,828 ....F 6
Uccle (Ukkel), 76,579 ....B 9
Verviers, 35,730 ....H 7

(continued on following page)

Agriculture, Industry and Resources

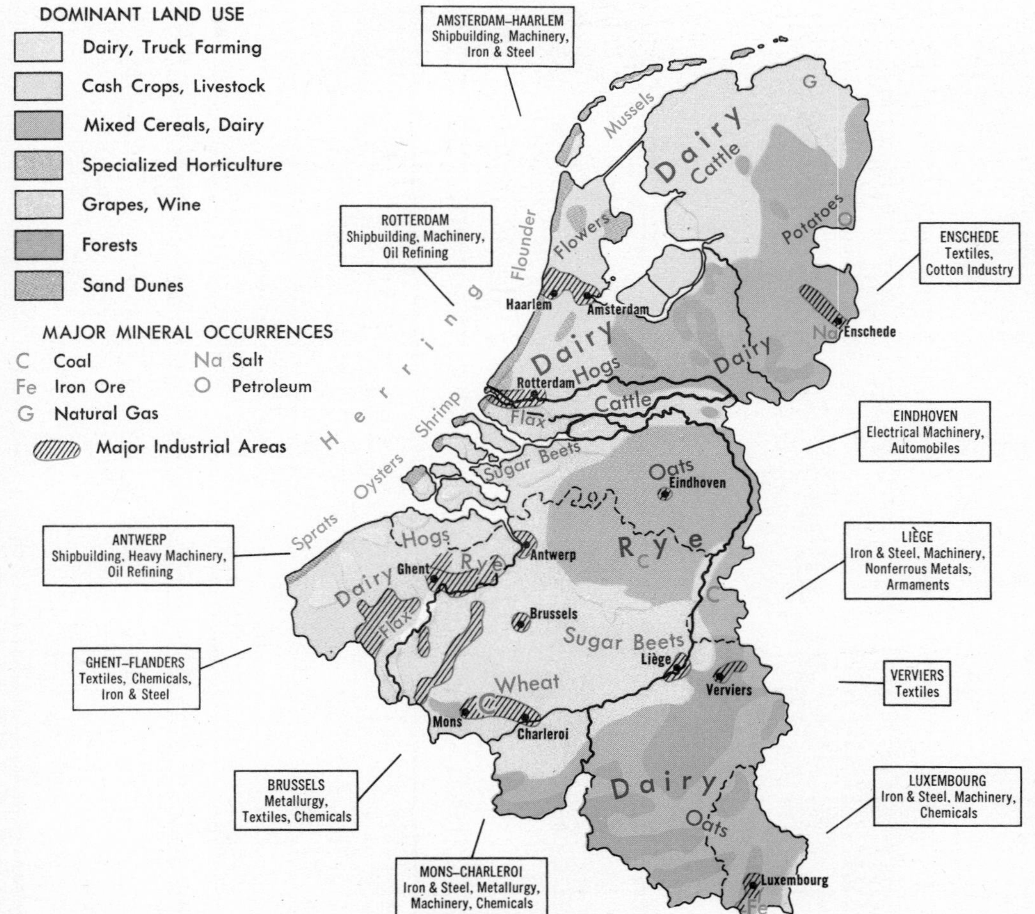

26 Netherlands, Belgium and Luxembourg

(continued)

BELGIUM (continued)

Veurne, 7,475 ... B 6
Vielsalm, 3,702 ... J 8
Villers-devant-Orval, 777 ... G 9
Vilvoorde (Vilvorde), 34,040 ... F 7
Virton, 3,956 ... H 9
Visé, 6,595 ... H 7
Vorst (Forest), 55,799 ... B 9
Waarschoot, 7,852 ... D 6
Waasten (Warneton), 3,215 ... B 7
Waha, 2,664 ... G 8
Waimes, 2,787 ... J 8
Walcourt, 2,077 ... F 8
Wandre, 6,833 ... H 7
Waregem, 16,928 ... C 7
Waremme, 7,623 ... G 7
Warneton, 3,215 ... B 7
Wasmes, 13,933 ... D 7
Waterloo, 14,615 ... E 7
Watermael-Boitsfort, 24,730 ... C 9
Watervliet, 1,812 ... D 6
Wavre (Waver), 11,007 ... F 7
Weismes (Waimes), 2,787 ... J 8
Wemmel, 11,404 ... B 9
Wenduine, 1,756 ... C 6
Wervik, 12,728 ... B 7
Westende, 2,746 ... B 6
Westerlo, 7,630 ... F 6
Wetteren, 20,775 ... D 7
Wezembeek-Oppem, 10,536 ... D 9
Wezet (Visé), 6,595 ... H 7
Willebroek, 15,650 ... E 6
Wilrijk, 42,109 ... E 6
Wingene, 7,178 ... C 6
Woluwe-Saint-Lambert, 44,102 ... C 9
Woluwe-Saint-Pierre, 37,314 ... C 9
Wolvertem, 5,326 ... E 7
Ypres (Ieper), 18,461 ... B 7
Yvoir, 2,837 ... F 8
Zaventem, 9,941 ... C 9
Zeebrugge ... C 6
Zele, 18,386 ... E 6
Zellik, 5,165 ... B 9
Zelzate, 11,751 ... D 6
Zinnik (Soignies), 11,320 ... D 7
Zonhoven, 12,910 ... G 6
Zottegem, 6,905 ... D 7

OTHER FEATURES

Albert (canal) ... F 6
Ardennes (plateau) ... F 9
Botrange (mt.) ... J 8
Dender (river) ... D 7
Dyle (river) ... F 7
Hohe Venn (plateau) ... H 8
Lesse (river) ... F 8
Mark (river) ... F 6
Meuse (river) ... F 8
Nethe (river) ... F 6
Ourthe (river) ... H 8
Rupel (river) ... F 7
Scheldt (Schelde) (river) ... C 7
Schnee Eifel (plateau) ... J 8
Semois (river) ... G 9
Senne (river) ... E 7
Vesdre (river) ... H 7
Weisserstein (mt.) ... J 8
Yser (river) ... B 7
Zitterwald (plateau) ... J 8

LUXEMBOURG

CITIES and TOWNS

Clervaux, 933 ... J 8
Diekirch, 4,899 ... J 9
Differdange, 9,808 ... H 9
Dudelange, 14,849 ... J10
Echternach, 3,472 ... J 9
Esch-sur-Alzette, 27,921 ... J 9
Esch-sur-Sauer, 265 ... H 9
Ettelbrück, 5,557 ... J 9
Grevenmacher, 2,850 ... J 9
Luxembourg (cap.), 77,458 ... J 9
Mersch, 1,682 ... J 9
Pétange, 6,251 ... H 9
Redange, 990 ... H 9
Remich, 1,958 ... J 9
Troisvierges, 928 ... J 8
Vianden, 1,381 ... J 9
Wasserbillig, 2,047 ... J 9
Wiltz, 1,538 ... H 9

OTHER FEATURES

Alzette (river) ... J 9
Clerf (river) ... J 8
Eisling (mts.) ... H 9
Mosel (river) ... J 9
Our (river) ... J 9
Sauer (river) ... J 9

NETHERLANDS

PROVINCES

Drenthe, 366,590 ... K 3
Friesland, 521,751 ... H 2
Gelderland, 1,505,760 ... H 4
Groningen, 517,305 ... K 2
Limburg, 998,570 ... H 6
North Brabant, 1,787,783 ... F 5
North Holland, 2,244,456 ... F 3
Overijssel, 920,882 ... J 4
South Holland, 2,968,670 ... E 5
Utrecht, 801,285 ... G 4
Zeeland, 305,754 ... D 6

CITIES and TOWNS

Aalsmeer, †18,166 ... F 4
Aalst, 4,423 ... G 6
Aalten, †16,295 ... K 5
Aardenburg, †3,853 ... C 6
Akkrum, 2,296 ... H 2
Alkmaar, †52,091 ... F 3
Almelo, †58,941 ... K 4
Amersfoort, †78,189 ... G 4
Amstelveen, †69,167 ... B 5
Amsterdam (cap.), 831,463 ... B 4
Amsterdam, *918,676 ... B 4
Andijk, †4,602 ... G 3
Anjum, 939 ... J 2
Apeldoorn, 123,628 ... H 4
Apeldoorn, *214,974 ... H 4
Appelscha, 1,622 ... J 3
Appingedam, †10,987 ... K 2
Arnhem, 132,531 ... H 4
Arnhem, *232,860 ... H 4
Assen, †38,956 ... K 3
Asten, †11,209 ... H 6
Axel, †8,904 ... D 6
Baarle-Nassau, †4,948 ... F 6
Baarn, †24,106 ... G 4
Badhoevedorp, 8,699 ... B 5
Balkbrug, 2,468 ... J 3
Barneveld, †30,046 ... H 4
Bath, 128 ... E 6
Beilen, †12,289 ... K 3
Bergeijk (Hof), †7,816 ... G 6
Bergen, †13,060 ... F 3
Bergen op Zoom, †39,051 ... E 5
Bergum, †4,252 ... H 2
Berkel, †5,936 ... F 5
Berkhout, †3,941 ... F 3
Beverwijk, †41,357 ... F 4
Blerick, 14,593 ... J 6
Bloemendaal, †19,253 ... E 4
Blokzijl, †1,375 ... H 3
Bodegraven, †14,083 ... F 4
Bolsward, †9,247 ... H 2
Borculo, †8,510 ... J 4
Borger, †10,972 ... K 3
Borne, †15,423 ... K 4
Boskoop, †11,600 ... F 4
Boxmeer, †10,850 ... H 5
Boxtel, †19,080 ... G 5
Breda, 121,209 ... F 5
Breda, *233,704 ... F 5
Breezand, 1,962 ... F 3
Breskens, †3,857 ... C 6
Brielle, †8,314 ... E 5
Broek, †2,260 ... C 4
Brouwershaven, †3,256 ... D 5
Brummen, †18,077 ... J 4
Buiksloot, 23,738 ... B 4
Bussum, †41,787 ... G 4
Callantsoog, †1,698 ... F 3
Coevorden, †12,481 ... K 3
Colijnsplaat, 1,477 ... D 5
Culemborg, 11,083 ... G 5
Cuyk, †12,144 ... H 5
Dalen, †4,630 ... K 3
De Bilt, †29,153 ... G 4
Dedemsvaart, 6,384 ... J 3
De Koog, 701 ... F 2
Delft, 83,698 ... E 4
Delfzijl, †21,990 ... K 2
Den Burg, 3,579 ... F 2
Den Helder, †60,612 ... F 3
Denekamp, †10,919 ... L 4
Deurne, †23,949 ... H 6
Deventer, †65,319 ... J 4
De Wijk, †4,120 ... J 3
Diemen, †9,558 ... C 5
Dieren, 8,612 ... J 4
Diever, †3,180 ... J 3
Dinxperlo, †6,248 ... K 5
Dirksland, †6,092 ... E 5
Doesburg, †9,451 ... J 4
Doetinchem, †31,097 ... J 5
Dokkum, †9,886 ... H 2
Domburg, †3,154 ... C 5
Dongen, †16,231 ... F 5
Doorn, †10,084 ... G 4
Doornspijk, †10,463 ... H 4
Dordrecht, †88,699 ... F 5
Dordrecht, *99,284 ... F 5
Drachten, 16,529 ... J 2
Driebergen, †15,828 ... G 4
Druten, †9,761 ... H 5
Duivendrecht, 2,656 ... C 5
Durgerdam, 640 ... C 4
Echt, †15,795 ... H 6
Edam, †18,184 ... G 4
Ede, †71,952 ... H 4
Eefde, 2,396 ... J 4
Egmond aan Zee, †5,554 ... E 3
Eindhoven, 188,631 ... G 6
Eindhoven, *301,049 ... G 6
Elburg, †5,135 ... H 4
Elst, †15,182 ... H 5
Emmeloord, 7,251 ... H 3
Emmen, †79,707 ... K 3
Enkhuizen, †11,502 ... G 3
Enschede, 139,245 ... K 4
Epe, †27,515 ... H 4
Erica, 3,026 ... K 3
Ermelo, †37,198 ... H 4
Etten, †19,698 ... F 5
Flushing, †40,197 ... C 6
Franeker, †9,575 ... H 2
Geertruidenberg, †5,575 ... F 5
Geldermalsen, †7,946 ... G 5
Geldrop, †26,909 ... H 6
Geleen, †36,121 ... H 7
Gemert, †14,329 ... H 5
Gendringen, †18,028 ... J 5
Genemuiden, †5,524 ... H 3
Gennep, †6,922 ... H 5
Giessendam, †13,588 ... F 5
Giethoorn, †2,486 ... J 3
Goes, †25,822 ... D 6
Goirle, †11,428 ... G 5
Goor, †9,702 ... K 4
Gorinchem, †26,380 ... G 5
Gorredijk, 3,006 ... J 2
Gouda, †45,990 ... F 4
Gouda, *84,695 ... F 4
Graauw, †1,277 ... E 6
Gramsbergen, †5,431 ... K 3
Grave, †7,405 ... H 5
Groenlo, †7,888 ... K 4
Groesbeek, †17,308 ... H 5
Groningen, 168,843 ... K 2
Groningen, *185,757 ... K 2
Grouw, 3,191 ... H 2
Haamstede, 1,179 ... D 5
Haarlem, 172,235 ... F 4
Haarlemmermeer (Hoofddorp), 4,949 ... F 4
Hague, The (cap.), 550,613 ... E 4
Hague, The, *702,296 ... E 4
Halfweg, 2,171 ... A 4
Hallum, 1,424 ... H 2
Hardenberg, †26,011 ... J 3
Harderwijk, 14,054 ... H 4
Hardinxveld, †13,588 ... G 5
Harlingen, †12,552 ... G 2
Hasselt, †5,005 ... J 3
Hattem, †9,034 ... H 4
Heemstede, †26,507 ... F 4
Heer, †12,217 ... H 7
Heerde, †15,341 ... H 4
Heerenveen, †31,434 ... H 3
Heerlen, †75,147 ... J 7
Heiloo, †17,736 ... F 3
Hellendoorn, †29,410 ... J 4
Hellevoetsluis, †9,653 ... E 5
Helmond, †57,889 ... H 6
Helmond, *79,164 ... H 6
Hengelo, Gelderland, †7,360 ... J 4
Hengelo, Overijssel, †69,618 ... K 4
Heusden, †4,587 ... G 5
Hillegom, †16,963 ... E 4
Hilvarenbeek, †7,358 ... G 6
Hilversum, 99,792 ... G 4
Hindeloopen, †881 ... G 3
Hippolytushoef, 3,035 ... G 3
Hoek, †2,817 ... D 6
Hoek van Holland (Hook of Holland), 5,114 ... D 5
Hoensbroek, †22,703 ... H 7
Hof, †7,816 ... G 6
Holijsloot, 344 ... C 4
Hollum, 890 ... H 2
Holwerd, 1,691 ... H 2
Hoofddorp, 4,949 ... F 4
Hoogeveen, †37,485 ... J 3
Hoogezand, †30,189 ... K 2
Hoogkarspel, †3,681 ... G 3
Hook of Holland, 5,114 ... D 5
Hoorn, †18,574 ... G 3
Horst, †15,310 ... H 6
Huissen, †9,101 ... J 5
Huizen, †20,554 ... G 4
Hulst, †6,699 ... E 6
IJlst, †1,932 ... H 2
IJmuiden, 3,587 ... E 4
IJsselstein, †9,633 ... F 4
IJzendijke, †2,492 ... D 6
Ilpendam, †2,955 ... C 4
Joure, 5,509 ... H 3
Kampen, †28,902 ... H 3
Katwijk aan Zee, †36,236 ... E 4
Kerkbuurt en Thij, †8,244 ... J 3
Kerkdriel, 3,122 ... G 5
Kerkrade, †48,150 ... J 7
Kesteren, †7,290 ... G 5
Kloosterveen, †7,296 ... K 3
Kollum, 2,543 ... J 2
Koog aan de Zaan, †6,114 ... A 4
Krimpen aan den IJssel, †17,801 ... F 5
Landsmeer, †6,511 ... C 4
Laren, †6,528 ... G 4
Leek, †11,628 ... J 2
Leerdam, †13,282 ... F 5
Leeuwarden, 100,006 ... H 2
Leiden, 101,221 ... E 4
Lelystad, 716 ... H 4
Lemmer, 4,399 ... H 3
Lent, 2,032 ... H 5
Lisse, †17,049 ... F 4
Lith, †4,698 ... G 5
Lochem, †9,452 ... J 4
Lonneker, 1,599 ... L 4
Loon op Zand, †16,437 ... G 5
Losser, 18,713 ... L 4
Maarssen, †14,734 ... F 4
Maasbree, †7,676 ... H 6
Maassluis, †25,878 ... E 5
Maastricht, †93,927 ... H 7
Makkum, 2,416 ... G 2
Margraten, †2,844 ... H 7
Medemblik, †5,192 ... G 3
Meerssen, †8,800 ... H 7
Meppel, †19,364 ... J 3
Middelburg, †30,211 ... C 6
Middelharnis, †12,488 ... E 5
Middenmeer, 1,775 ... F 3
Millingen aan den Rijn, †4,764 ... J 5
Moerdijk, 601 ... F 5
Monnikendam, †6,014 ... C 4
Montfoort, †2,392 ... G 4
Muiden, †5,724 ... G 4
Muntendam, †3,695 ... K 2
Naaldwijk, †22,306 ... E 4
Naarden, †17,447 ... G 4
Nagele, 766 ... H 3
Neede, †9,739 ... K 4
Nes, 894 ... H 2
Nieuw-Buinen, 3,966 ... K 3
Nieuw-Schoonebeek, 1,602 ... L 3
Nieuwe Pekela, †5,163 ... L 2
Nieuwendam, 15,679 ... C 4
Nieuweschans, †1,846 ... L 2
Nieuwkoop, †7,835 ... F 4
Nijkerk, †17,718 ... H 4
Nijmegen, 148,790 ... H 5
Nijmegen, *210,865 ... H 5
Nijverdal, 11,986 ... J 4
Noordwijk, †20,925 ... E 4
Norg, †5,386 ... J 2
Numansdorp, †5,169 ... E 5
Nunspeet, 7,103 ... H 4
Odoorn, †11,730 ... K 3
Oisterwijk, †13,797 ... G 5
Oldenzaal, †22,604 ... K 4
Olst, †8,325 ... J 4
Ommen, †14,712 ... J 3
Onstwedde, 1,867 ... K 2
Oostburg, †4,044 ... C 6
Oosterend, 118 ... G 2
Oosterhout, †31,826 ... F 5
Oostmahorn, 131 ... J 2
Oost-Vlieland, 695 ... F 2
Oostzaan, †4,869 ... C 4
Ootmarsum, †3,339 ... K 4
Oss, †40,085 ... H 5
Otterlo, 984 ... H 4
Oud-Beijerland, †10,114 ... E 5
Ouddorp, †4,226 ... D 5
Oude-Pekela, †8,085 ... K 2
Oude-Tonge, 2,459 ... E 5
Oudenbosch, †9,346 ... E 5
Oudeschild, 939 ... F 2
Oudewater, †4,466 ... F 4
Overloon, 1,007 ... H 5
Purmerend, †23,288 ... F 4
Putten, †15,726 ... H 4
Raalte, †19,885 ... J 4
Renkum, †33,619 ... H 5
Reusel, †6,144 ... G 6
Rheden, †48,713 ... J 4
Rhenen, †14,860 ... H 5
Ridderkerk, †41,899 ... F 5
Rijnsburg, †8,600 ... F 4
Rijssen, †17,360 ... J 4
Rijswijk, †50,172 ... E 4
Roden, †12,444 ... J 2
Roermond, †35,850 ... J 6
Roosendaal, †45,935 ... F 5
Rotterdam, 686,586 ... E 5
Rotterdam, *1,052,871 ... E 5
Rutten, 491 ... H 3
Ruurlo, †6,829 ... J 4
's Gravendeel, †5,830 ... E 5
's Gravenhage (The Hague) (cap.), 550,613 ... E 4
's Gravenhage, *702,296 ... E 4
's Gravenzande, †12,907 ... E 4
's Heerenberg, 5,196 ... J 5
's Hertogenbosch, †81,574 ... G 5
's Hertogenbosch, *193,356 ... G 5
Sappemeer, †30,189 ... K 2
Schagen, †6,772 ... F 3
Scheveningen, 80,015 ... E 4
Schiedam, †83,049 ... E 5
Schiermonnikoog, †814 ... J 1
Schijndel, †16,362 ... H 5
Schiphol, 3,368 ... B 5
Schoonebeek, †7,426 ... L 3
Schoonhoven, †7,565 ... F 5
Sint Annaland, †2,826 ... E 5
Sint Jacobiparochie, 1,246 ... H 2
Sittard, †33,887 ... H 6
Sliedrecht, †19,868 ... F 5
Slochteren, †12,901 ... K 2
Sloten, Friesland, †751 ... H 3
Sloten, North Holland, 1,332 ... B 5
Sloterdijk, 1,215 ... B 4
Sluis, †2,810 ... C 6
Smilde (Kloosterveen), †7,296 ... K 3
Sneek, †26,244 ... H 2
Soest, †35,713 ... G 4
Soesterberg, 4,627 ... G 4
Stadskanaal, †32,829 ... L 3
Staphorst, †10,498 ... J 3
Staveren, †934 ... G 3
Steenbergen, †12,512 ... E 5
Steenwijk, †12,226 ... J 3
Steenwijkerwold (Kerkbuurt en Thij), †8,244 ... J 3
Stiens, 2,008 ... H 2
Tegelen, †18,168 ... J 6
Ter Apel, 2,508 ... L 3
Termunten, †4,721 ... K 2
Terneuzen, †22,014 ... D 6
Tholen, †3,798 ... E 5
Tiel, †21,789 ... G 5
Tilburg, 152,589 ... G 5
Tilburg, *268,395 ... G 5
Twello, 5,929 ... J 4
Uden, †23,311 ... H 5
Uitgeest, †7,151 ... F 3
Uithoorn, †17,492 ... F 4
Uithuizen, †4,939 ... K 2
Ulrum, †3,631 ... J 2
Urk, 8,027 ... H 3
Utrecht, 278,966 ... G 4
Utrecht, *401,981 ... G 4
Vaals, †10,338 ... H 7
Valkenswaard, †23,238 ... H 6
Van Ewijcksluis, 231 ... F 3
Veendam, †23,709 ... K 2
Veenendaal, †29,637 ... G 4
Veenhuizen, †4,097 ... J 2
Veere, †3,822 ... D 5
Veghel, †18,374 ... H 5
Velp, †9,488 ... J 5
Velsen, †67,580 ... F 4
Venlo, †62,694 ... J 6
Venlo, *95,516 ... J 6
Venraij, †26,056 ... H 6
Vianen, †8,173 ... G 5
Vlaardingen, †79,085 ... E 5
Vlagtwedde, †16,622 ... L 3
Vlijmen, †12,314 ... G 5
Vlissingen (Flushing), †40,197 ... C 6
Volendam, 10,123 ... G 4
Voorburg, †45,011 ... E 4
Voorst, †21,379 ... J 4
Vorden, †6,893 ... J 4
Vreeswijk, †5,393 ... G 4
Vrieseveen, †14,658 ... K 4
Vught, †22,633 ... G 5
Waalwijk, †23,304 ... F 5
Wageningen, †26,572 ... H 5
Wamel, †8,217 ... H 5
Weert, †35,190 ... H 6
Weesp, †17,261 ... C 5
West-Terschelling, †4,294 ... G 2
Westkapelle, †2,478 ... C 5
Westzaan, †4,502 ... A 4
Wierden, †17,653 ... K 4
Wierum, 628 ... H 2
Wijhe, †6,225 ... J 4
Wijk aan Zee, 2,414 ... E 4
Wijk bij Duurstede, †5,342 ... G 5
Wijk en Aalburg, †3,583 ... G 5
Wildervank, 5,280 ... K 2
Willemstad, †2,306 ... F 5
Winkel, †2,450 ... F 3
Winschoten, †18,043 ... L 2
Winsum, †3,631 ... K 2
Winterswijk, †26,230 ... K 5
Woensdrecht, †7,892 ... E 6
Woerden, †18,448 ... F 4
Wolvega, 6,620 ... J 3
Workum, †4,019 ... G 3
Wormerveer, †14,804 ... F 4
Yerseke, 4,799 ... E 6
Zaandam, †63,535 ... B 4
Zaandijk, †5,696 ... B 4
Zaltbommel, †7,004 ... G 5
Zandvoort, †15,451 ... E 4
Zeist, †55,619 ... G 4
Zevenbergen, †10,270 ... E 5
Zierikzee, †7,842 ... D 5
Zoutkamp, 1,083 ... J 2
Zundert, †12,124 ... F 6
Zutphen, †27,610 ... J 4
Zwanenburg, 6,999 ... B 4
Zwartsluis, †4,091 ... H 3
Zwijndrecht, †31,761 ... F 5
Zwolle, †76,167 ... J 3

OTHER FEATURES

Alkmaardermeer (lake) ... F 3
Ameland (isl.), †2,899 ... H 2
Bergumeer (lake) ... J 2
Beulaker Wijde (lake) ... H 3
Borndiep (channel) ... H 2
De Fluessen (lake) ... G 3
De Honte (bay) ... D 6
De Peel (region), 69,356 ... H 6
De Twente (reg.), 491,403 ... K 4
De Zaan (river) ... B 4
Dollart (bay) ... L 2
Dommel (river) ... H 6
Duiveland (isl.), 13,317 ... D 5
East Flevoland Polder, 863 ... H 4
Eastern Scheldt (estuary) ... D 5
Eijerlandsche Gat (strait) ... F 2
Friesche Gat (channel) ... J 2
Galgenberg (hill) ... H 4
Goeree (isl.) ... D 5
Grevelingen (strait) ... E 5
Griend (isl.) ... G 2
Groninger Wad (sound) ... J 2
Groote IJ Polder, 20 ... B 4
Haarlemmermeer Polder, 58,966 ... B 5
Haringvliet (strait) ... E 5
Het IJ (estuary) ... C 4
Hoek van Holland (cape) ... D 5
Hondsrug (hills) ... K 3
Houtrak Polder, 339 ... A 4
Hunse (river) ... K 3
IJmeer (bay) ... C 4
IJssel (river) ... J 4
IJsselmeer (lake) ... G 3
Lauwers (channel) ... J 1
Lauwers Zee (bay) ... J 2
Lek (river) ... F 5
Lemelerberg (hill) ... J 4
Linde (river) ... J 3
Lower Rhine (river) ... H 5
Maas (river) ... G 5
Mark (river) ... F 6
Marken (isl.), 1,865 ... G 4
Markerwaard Polder ... G 3
Marsdiep (channel) ... F 3
Noordergat (channel) ... F 2
North (sea) ... E 3
North Beveland (isl.), 6,777 ... D 5
North East Polder, 31,929 ... H 3
North Holland (canal) ... C 4
North Sea (canal) ... F 4
Old Rhine (river) ... E 4
Ooster Eems (channel) ... K 1
Oostzaan Polder, 4,869 ... B 4
Orange (canal) ... K 3
Overflakkee (isl.), 27,814 ... E 5
Pinkegat (channel) ... H 2
Regge (river) ... K 4
Roer (river) ... J 6
Rottumeroog (isl.), 3 ... J 1
Schiermonnikoog (isl.), 814 ... J 1
Schouwen (isl.), 9,731 ... D 5
Simonszand (isl.) ... J 1
Slotermeer (lake) ... H 3
Sneekermeer (lake) ... H 2
South Beveland (isl.), 61,968 ... D 6
South Flevoland Polder, 14,925 ... G 4
Terschelling (isl.), 4,294 ... G 2
Texel (isl.), 11,394 ... F 2
Tjeukemeer (lake) ... H 3
Vaalserberg (mt.) ... J 7
Vecht (river) ... J 4
Vechte (river) ... J 3
Veeregat (channel) ... D 5
Veluwe (region), 457,834 ... H 4
Vlie Stroom (strait) ... G 2
Vlieland (isl.), 933 ... F 2
Voorne (isl.), 22,742 ... D 5
Waal (river) ... G 5
Waddenzee (sound) ... G 2
Walcheren (isl.), 89,793 ... C 5
West Frisian (isls.), 18,336 ... F 2
Wester Eems (channel) ... K 1
Western Scheldt (De Honte) (bay) ... D 6
Westgat (channel) ... F 3
Wieringermeer Polder, 16,562 ... G 3
Wilhelmina (canal) ... G 6
Willems (canal) ... G 5

*City and suburbs.
†Population of commune.

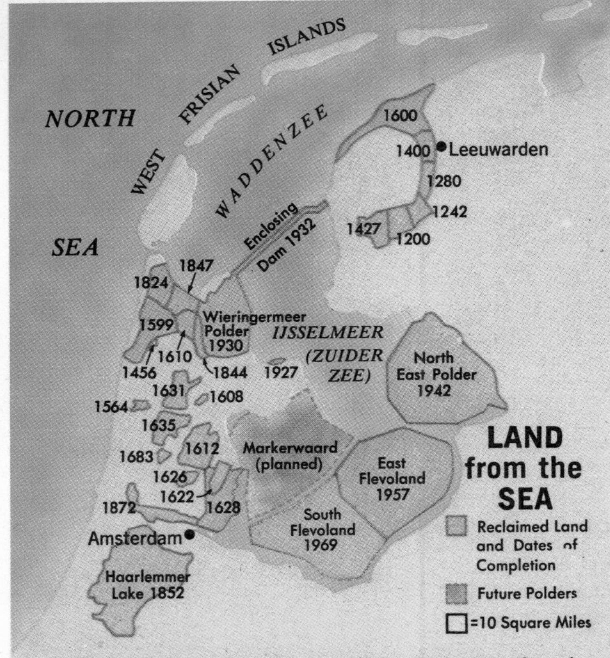

For centuries the Dutch have been renowned for the drainage of marshes and the construction of polders, i.e., arable land reclaimed from the sea. Future projects will convert much of the present IJsselmeer to agricultural land.

NETHERLANDS, BELGIUM and LUXEMBOURG
CONIC PROJECTION
SCALE OF MILES
0 5 10 20 30 40
SCALE OF KILOMETRES
0 5 10 20 30 40 50
Capitals of Countries
Provincial Capitals
International Boundaries
Provincial Boundaries
Canals
Copyright by C. S. Hammond & Co., N.Y.
Longitude 5° East of Greenwich
A 30′ B 3° C 30′ D 4° E 30′ F G 30′ H 6° J 30′ K 7°
NORTH SEA
WEST FRISIAN ISLANDS
WADDEN ZEE
IJSSELMEER
MARKERWAARD
NORTH EAST POLDER
EAST FLEVOLAND
SOUTH FLEVOLAND
NETHERLANDS
GRONINGEN
FRIESLAND
DRENTHE
OVERIJSSEL
GELDERLAND
UTRECHT
NORTH HOLLAND
SOUTH HOLLAND
ZEELAND
NORTH BRABANT
LIMBURG
BELGIUM
WEST FLANDERS
EAST FLANDERS
ANTWERP
BRABANT
HAINAUT
NAMUR
LIÈGE
LUXEMBOURG
FRANCE
GERMANY
AMSTERDAM
BRUSSELS
Luxembourg
The Hague
Rotterdam
Utrecht
Haarlem
Leeuwarden
Groningen
Assen
Zwolle
Arnhem
's Hertogenbosch
Maastricht
Middelburg
Antwerp (Antwerpen)
Ghent (Gent)
Bruges (Brugge)
Hasselt
Liège (Luik)
Namur (Namen)
Mons (Bergen)
Arlon (Aarlen)
Eindhoven
Tilburg
Breda
Nijmegen
Aachen
Cologne (Köln)
Düsseldorf
Essen
Lille
Dunkirk (Dunkerque)
Trier
Bonn
Groote IJ Polder
AMSTERDAM
MILES 0 1 2 4 6
Wemmel
Schaerbeek
BRUSSELS
Anderlecht
Woluwe-St.-Lambert
Uccle (Ukkel)
MILES 0 1 2 3 4 5

FRANCE
CONIC PROJECTION
SCALE OF MILES
0 20 40 60 80 100
SCALE OF KILOMETRES
0 20 40 60 80 100
Capitals of Countries
Capitals of Departments
International Boundaries
Department Boundaries
Canals
© C.S. HAMMOND & Co., N.Y.
Longitude 2° West of Greenwich 0° Longitude East of 2° Greenwich
PARIS and ENVIRONS
MILES
CORSICA
Same Scale as Main Map
UNITED KINGDOM
ENGLAND
LONDON
NETHERLANDS
BELGIUM
GERMANY
LUXEMBOURG
SWITZERLAND
ITALY
SPAIN
ANDORRA
MONACO
ENGLISH CHANNEL
(La Manche)
CHANNEL ISLANDS
NORTH SEA
BAY OF BISCAY
MEDITERRANEAN SEA
Gulf of Lions
Strait of Dover
PARIS
Amsterdam
Brussels
Bern
Barcelona
Saragossa
Lyon
Marseille
Bordeaux
Toulouse
Nantes
Strasbourg
Lille
Nice
Montpellier
Orléans
Dijon
Limoges
Clermont-Ferrand
Grenoble
Reims
Le Havre
Brest
Rennes
Tours
Cherbourg
Ajaccio
Bastia

DEPARTMENTS

Ain, 339,262 ... F 4
Aisne, 526,346 ... E 3
Allier, 386,533 ... E 4
Alpes-de-Haute-Provence, 104,813 ... G 5
Alpes-Maritimes, 722,070 ... G 6
Ardèche, 256,927 ... F 5
Ardennes, 309,380 ... F 3
Ariège, 138,478 ... D 6
Aube, 270,325 ... E 3
Aude, 278,323 ... E 6
Aveyron, 281,568 ... E 5
Bas-Rhin, 827,367 ... G 3
Belfort (terr.), 118,450 ... G 4
Bouches-du-Rhône, 1,470,271 ... F 6
Calvados, 519,695 ... C 3
Cantal, 169,330 ... E 5
Charente, 331,016 ... D 5
Charente-Maritime, 483,622 ... C 5
Cher, 304,601 ... E 4
Corrèze, 237,858 ... D 5
Corsica (Corse), 269,831 ... B 6
Côte-d'Or, 421,192 ... F 4
Côtes-du-Nord, 506,102 ... B 3
Creuse, 156,876 ... D 4
Deux-Sèvres, 326,462 ... C 4
Dordogne, 374,073 ... D 5
Doubs, 426,363 ... G 4
Drôme, 342,891 ... F 5
Essonne, 674,157 ... E 3
Eure, 383,385 ... D 3
Eure-et-Loir, 302,207 ... D 3
Finistère, 768,929 ... A 3
Gard, 478,544 ... F 6
Gers, 181,577 ... D 6
Gironde, 1,009,390 ... C 5
Haut-Rhin, 585,018 ... G 4
Haute-Garonne, 690,712 ... D 6
Haute-Loire, 208,337 ... E 5
Haute-Marne, 214,336 ... F 3
Haute-Saône, 214,176 ... G 4
Haute-Savoie, 378,550 ... G 5
Haute-Vienne, 341,589 ... D 5
Hautes-Alpes, 91,790 ... G 5
Hautes-Pyrénées, 225.730 ... D 6
Hauts-de-Seine, 1,461,619 ... A 2
Hérault, 591,397 ... E 6
Ille-et-Vilaine, 652,722 ... C 3
Indre, 247,178 ... D 4
Indre-et-Loire, 437,870 ... D 4
Isère, 768,450 ... F 5
Jura, 233,547 ... F 4
Landes, 277,381 ... C 5
Loir-et-Cher, 267,896 ... D 4
Loire, 722,383 ... F 5
Loire-Atlantique, 861,452 ... C 4
Loiret, 430,629 ... E 4
Lot, 151,198 ... D 5
Lot-et-Garonne, 290,592 ... D 5
Lozère, 77,258 ... E 5
Maine-et-Loire, 584,709 ... C 4
Manche, 451,939 ... C 3
Marne, 485,388 ... F 3
Mayenne, 252,762 ... C 3
Meurthe-et-Moselle, 705,413 ... G 3
Meuse, 209,513 ... F 3
Morbihan, 540,474 ... B 4
Moselle, 971,314 ... G 3
Nièvre, 247,702 ... E 4
Nord, 2,417,899 ... E 2
Oise, 540,988 ... E 3
Orne, 288,524 ... C 3
Paris, 2,590,771 ... B 2
Pas-de-Calais, 1,397,159 ... E 2
Puy-de-Dôme, 547,743 ... E 5
Pyrénées-Atlantiques, 508,734 ... C 6
Pyrénées-Orientales, 281,976 ... E 6
Rhône, 1,325,611 ... F 5
Saône-et-Loire, 550,362 ... F 4
Sarthe, 461,839 ... D 3
Savoie, 288,921 ... G 5
Seine-et-Marne, 604,340 ... E 3
Seine-Maritime, 1,113,977 ... D 3
Seine-Saint-Denis, 1,251,792 ... B 1
Somme, 512,113 ... E 3
Tarn, 332,011 ... E 6
Tarn-et-Garonne, 183,572 ... D 5
Val-de-Marne, 1,121,340 ... B 2
Val-d'Oise, 693,269 ... E 3
Var, 555,926 ... G 6
Vaucluse, 353,966 ... F 6
Vendée, 421,250 ... C 4
Vienne, 340,256 ... D 4
Vosges, 388,201 ... G 3
Yonne, 283,376 ... E 4
Yvelines, 853,386 ... D 3

CITIES and TOWNS

Abbeville, 23,770 ... D 2
Agde, 8,812 ... E 6
Agen, 34,592 ... D 5
Aix-en-Provence, 74,948 ... F 6
Aix-les-Bains, 20,594 ... G 5
Ajaccio, 38,776 ... B 7
Albert, 10,937 ... E 2
Albertville, 15,422 ... G 5
Albi, 38,867 ... E 6
Alençon, 30,368 ... D 3
Aléria, 1,000 ... B 6
Alès, 31,948 ... E 5
Ambérieu-en-Bugey, 8,570 ... F 5
Amboise, 8,408 ... D 4
Amiens, 116,107 ... D 3
Angers, 127,415 ... C 4
Angoulême, 46,584 ... D 5
Annecy, 53,361 ... G 5
Annonay, 19,591 ... F 5
Antibes, 47,393 ... G 6
Antony, 56,556 ... B 2
Apt, 8,502 ... F 6
Arcachon, 14,852 ... C 5
Argentan, 14,418 ... D 3
Argenteuil, 87,106 ... A 1
Arles, 33,575 ... F 6
Armentières, 24,460 ... E 2
Arras, 48,494 ... E 2
Asnières, 79,942 ... A 1
Aubagne, 17,055 ... F 6
Aubenas, 10,480 ... F 5
Aubervilliers, 73,559 ... B 1
Aubusson, 5,641 ... E 4
Auch, 18,072 ... D 6
Audincourt, 13,487 ... G 4
Aulnay-sous-Bois, 61,384 ... B 1
Auray, 8,180 ... B 4
Aurignac, 783 ... D 6
Aurillac, 26,776 ... E 5
Autun, 17,194 ... F 4
Auxerre, 33,700 ... E 4
Avallon, 6,615 ... E 4
Avesnes-sur-Helpe, 6,253 ... F 2
Avignon, 78,871 ... F 6
Avion, 22,390 ... E 2
Avranches, 9,751 ... C 3
Bagnères-de-Bigorre, 9,139 ... D 6
Bagnères-de-Luchon, 4,079 ... D 6
Bagnolet, 33,607 ... B 2
Bagnols-sur-Cèze, 15,336 ... F 5
Bar-le-Duc, 18,874 ... F 3
Bar-sur-Seine, 2,642 ... F 3
Barfleur, 825 ... C 3
Bastia, 48,800 ... B 6
Bayeux, 11,190 ... C 3
Bayonne, 39.761 ... C 6
Beaucaire, 8,820 ... F 6
Beaune, 16,441 ... F 4
Beauvais, 46,284 ... E 3
Bédarieux, 6,929 ... E 6
Belfort, 53,001 ... G 4
Belley, 5,958 ... F 5
Berck, 13,658 ... D 2
Bergerac, 24,184 ... D 5
Bernay, 9,298 ... D 3
Besançon, 107,939 ... G 4
Bessèges, 5,421 ... F 5
Béthune, 26,144 ... E 2
Béziers, 74,517 ... E 6
Biarritz, 26,628 ... C 6
Blois, 39,279 ... D 4
Bobigny, 39,321 ... B 1
Bolbec, 12,517 ... D 3
Bondy, 51,555 ... B 1
Bordeaux, 263,808 ... C 5
Bordeaux, †648,000 ... C 5
Boulogne-Billancourt, 108,846 ... A 2
Boulogne-sur-Mer, 49,064 ... D 2
Bourg-en-Bresse, 35,064 ... F 4

Bourges, 67,137 ... E 4
Bressuire, 8,010 ... C 4
Brest, 150,696 ... A 3
Briançon, 7,551 ... G 5
Briare, 4,725 ... E 4
Brignoles, 8,010 ... G 6
Brive-la-Gaillarde, 45,314 ... D 5
Bruay-en-Artois, 38,608 ... E 2
Caen, 106,790 ... C 3
Cahors, 17,775 ... D 5
Calais, 70,153 ... D 2
Caluire-et-Cuire, 37,541 ... F 5
Calvi, 2,523 ... B 6
Cambrai, 37,290 ... E 2
Cannes, 66,590 ... G 6
Carcassonne, 40,580 ... D 6
Carentan, 5,207 ... C 3
Carmaux, 13,423 ... E 5
Carpentras, 18,092 ... F 5
Castelnaudary, 8,550 ... E 6
Castelsarrasin, 7,912 ... D 6
Castres, 35,975 ... E 6
Cavaillon, 14,815 ... F 6
Cayeux-sur-Mer, 2,489 ... D 2
Chalon-sur-Saône, 47,004 ... F 4
Châlons-sur-Marne, 48,558 ... F 3
Chambéry, 49,858 ... F 5
Chambord, 200 ... D 4
Chamonix-Mont Blanc, 5,907 ... G 5
Champigny-sur-Marne, 70,353 ... C 2
Chantilly, 10,156 ... E 3
Charenton-le-Pont, 22,220 ... B 2
Charleville-Mézières, 55,230 ... F 3
Chartres, 34,128 ... D 3
Château-du-Loir, 5,239 ... D 4
Château-Gontier, 7,881 ... C 4
Château-Renault, 5,082 ... D 4
Château-Thierry, 10,858 ... E 3
Châteaubriant, 11,196 ... C 4
Châteaudun, 13,715 ... D 3
Châteauneuf-sur-Loire, 4,603 ... E 4
Châteauroux, 48,867 ... D 4
Châtellerault, 33,491 ... D 4
Châtillon, 24,468 ... B 2
Châtillon-sur-Seine, 6,128 ... F 4
Chatou, 22,495 ... A 1
Chaumont, 25,602 ... F 3
Chauny, 13,714 ... E 3
Chelles, 22,111 ... C 1
Cherbourg, 37,933 ... C 3
Chinon, 5,435 ... D 4
Choisy-le-Roi, 41,080 ... B 2
Cholet, 40,224 ... C 4
Clamart, 54,866 ... A 2
Clermont, 7,119 ... E 3
Clermont-Ferrand, 145,856 ... E 5
Clichy, 52,398 ... B 1
Cluny, 3,552 ... F 4
Cluses, 12,391 ... G 4
Cognac, 21,137 ... C 5
Colmar, 58,623 ... G 3
Colombes, 80,224 ... A 1
Commentry, 8,129 ... E 4
Commercy, 7,043 ... F 3
Compiègne, 28,881 ... E 3
Concarneau, 16,458 ... A 4
Cosne-sur-Loire, 8,931 ... E 4
Coudekerque-Branche, 22,972 ... E 2
Coulommiers, 11.182 ... E 3

AREA 212,841 sq. mi.
POPULATION 50,770,000
CAPITAL Paris
LARGEST CITY Paris
HIGHEST POINT Mont Blanc 15,771 ft.
MONETARY UNIT franc
MAJOR LANGUAGE French
MAJOR RELIGION Roman Catholicism

Topography

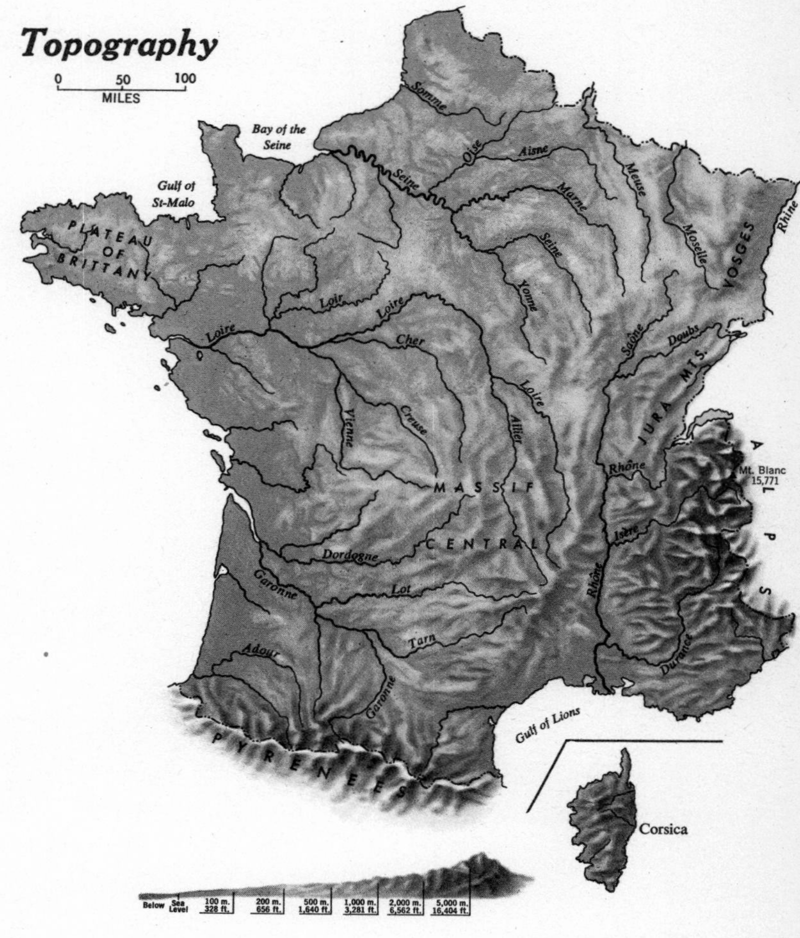

HISTORIC PROVINCES

A resident of the city of Caen thinks of himself as a Norman rather than as a citizen of the modern department of Calvados. In spite of the passing of nearly two centuries, the historic provinces which existed before 1790 command the local patriotism of most Frenchmen.

Courbevoie, 57,998 ... A 1
Coutances, 8,599 ... C 3
Coutras, 4,251 ... C 5
Creil, 31,792 ... E 3
Crépy-en-Valois, 8,506 ... E 3
Créteil, 48,757 ... B 2
Cusset, 12,286 ... E 4
Dax, 18,185 ... C 6
Deauville, 5,103 ... C 3
Decazeville, 9,581 ... E 5
Denain, 27,840 ... E 2
Dieppe, 29,829 ... D 3
Digne, 11,973 ... G 5
Digoin, 9,585 ... F 4
Dijon, 143,120 ... F 4
Dinan, 12,999 ... B 3
Dinard, 9,042 ... B 3
Dôle, 25,620 ... F 4
Domrémy-la-Pucelle, 184 ... F 3
Douai, 47,347 ... E 2
Douarnenez, 18,442 ... A 3
Draguignan, 16,139 ... G 6
Drancy, 69,226 ... B 1
Dreux, 28,156 ... D 3
Dunkirk (Dunkerque), 26,038 ... E 2
Elbeuf, 19,110 ... D 3
Embrun, 3,986 ... G 5
Épernay, 26,094 ... E 3
Épinal, 36,219 ... G 3
Épinay-sur-Seine, 41,538 ... B 1
Étampes, 15,542 ... E 3
Étaples, 9,092 ... D 2
Eu, 7,866 ... D 3
Évreux, 41,004 ... D 3
Évry, 7,047 ... E 3
Falaise, 6,977 ... C 3
Fécamp, 21,098 ... D 3
Figeac, 8,462 ... D 5
Firminy, 24,545 ... F 5
Flers, 16,677 ... C 3
Foix, 9,061 ... D 6
Fontainebleau, 17,565 ... E 3
Fontenay-le-Comte, 10,884 ... C 4
Fontenay-sous-Bois, 38,737 ... C 2
Forbach, 23,062 ... G 3
Fougères, 25,745 ... C 3
Fourmies, 14,895 ... F 2
Fréjus, 22,567 ... G 6
Gagny, 35,745 ... C 1
Gap, 22,027 ... G 5
Gardanne, 12,601 ... F 6
Gennevilliers, 45,925 ... B 1
Gentilly, 18,638 ... B 2
Gex, 3,078 ... G 4
Gien, 11,655 ... E 4
Gisors, 7,024 ... D 3
Givet, 7,697 ... F 2
Givors, 17,545 ... F 5
Granville, 12,315 ... C 3
Grasse, 24,398 ... G 6
Graulhet, 10,318 ... E 6
Gray, 7,782 ... F 4
Grenoble, 161,230 ... F 5
Guebwiller, 10,684 ... G 4
Guéret, 12,441 ... D 4
Guingamp, 9,091 ... B 3
Guise, 6,732 ... E 3
Haguenau, 22,335 ... G 3
Ham, 5,565 ... E 3
Harfleur, 15,503 ... D 3
Hautmont, 17,818 ... F 2
Hayange, 10,218 ... F 3
Hazebrouck, 16,768 ... E 2
Hendaye, 7,536 ... C 6
Hénin-Liétard, 25,067 ... E 2
Hennebont, 7,605 ... B 4
Héricourt, 7,376 ... G 4
Hirson, 11,764 ... F 3
Honfleur, 9,017 ... D 3
Hyères, 27,600 ... G 6
Issoire, 11,745 ... E 5
Issoudun, 14,559 ... D 4
Issy-les-Moulineaux, 50,260 ... A 2
Istres, 8,713 ... F 6
Ivry-sur-Seine, 60,342 ... B 2
Joigny, 9,609 ... E 3
La Baule-Escoublac, 11,962 ... B 4
La Ciotat, 19,485 ... F 6
La Courneuve, 42,812 ... B 1
La Flèche, 9,536 ... C 4
La Grand-Combe, 8,608 ... E 5
La Roche-sur-Yon, 32,279 ... C 4
La Rochelle, 72,075 ... C 4
La Seyne-sur-Mer, 42,958 ... F 6
La Tour-du-Pin, 5,649 ... F 5
L'Aigle, 7,478 ... D 3
Landerneau, 12,356 ... B 3
Langeac, 4,584 ... E 5
Langres, 8,945 ... F 4
Lannion, 10,066 ... B 3
Laon, 25,623 ... E 3
Laval, 45,051 ... C 3
Lavelanet, 8,512 ... E 6
Le Blanc-Mesnil, 48,212 ... B 1
Le Bourget, 9,625 ... B 1
Le Cateau, 8,922 ... E 2
Le Chesnay, 13,586 ... A 2
Le Creusot, 33,581 ... F 4
Le Croisic, 4,092 ... B 4
Le Havre, 198,021 ... C 3
Le Mans, 140,520 ... C 3
Le Puy, 24,816 ... F 5
Le Teil, 7,872 ... F 5
Le Tourquet-Paris-Plage, 4,403 ... D 2
Le Tréport, 6,194 ... D 2
Lens, 41,800 ... E 2
Les Andelys, 6,292 ... D 3
Les Sables-d'Olonne, 17,856 ... B 4
Levallois-Perret, 58,890 ... B 1
Lézignan-Corbières, 7,101 ... E 6
Libourne, 19,981 ... C 5
Liévin, 35,733 ... E 2
Lille, 189,697 ... E 2
Lille, †1,042,000 ... E 2
Limoges, 127,605 ... D 5
Limoux, 9,150 ... E 6
Lisieux, 23,337 ... D 3
Livry-Gargan, 32,015 ... C 1
Lodève, 6,899 ... E 6
Longwy, 21,052 ... F 3
Lons-le-Saunier, 18,649 ... F 4
Lorient, 66,023 ... B 4
Loudun, 6,118 ... D 4
Lourdes, 17,627 ... C 6
Louviers, 15,159 ... D 3
Lunel, 10,178 ... E 6
Lunéville, 22,961 ... G 3
Luxeuil-les-Bains, 9,203 ... G 4
Lyon, 524,500 ... F 5
Lyon, †1,305,000 ... F 5
Mâcon, 33,266 ... F 4
Maisons-Alfort, 53,118 ... B 2
Maisons-Laffitte, 24,041 ... A 1
Malakoff, 36,198 ... B 2
Manosque, 13,352 ... G 6
Mantes-la-Jolie, 25,842 ... D 3
Marmande, 12,145 ... C 5
Marseille, 880,527 ... F 6
Marseille, †1,015,000 ... F 6
Martigues, 17,771 ... F 6
Maubeuge, 31,992 ... F 2
Mayenne, 10,010 ... C 3
Mazamet, 14,650 ... E 6
Meaux, 29,966 ... E 3
Melun, 33,345 ... E 3
Mende, 9,424 ... E 5
Menton, 23,401 ... G 6
Metz, 105,533 ... G 3
Meudon, 30,735 ... A 2
Millau, 21,420 ... E 5
Moissac, 7,694 ... D 5
Mont-de-Marsan, 22,771 ... C 6
Mont-Dore, 2,045 ... E 5
Mont-Saint-Michel, 72 ... C 3
Montargis, 18,087 ... E 3
Montauban, 33,945 ... D 5
Montbéliard, 23,402 ... G 4
Montbrison, 8,733 ... E 5
Montceau-les-Mines, 18,621 ... F 4
Montdidier, 5,785 ... E 3
Montélimar, 23,831 ... F 5
Montfort, 2,563 ... C 3
Montigny-les-Metz, 24,417 ... G 3
Montluçon, 57,638 ... E 4
Montpellier, 152,105 ... E 6
Montreuil, 95,420 ... B 2
Montrouge, 44,788 ... B 2
Morlaix, 16,750 ... B 3
Moulins, 25,778 ... E 4
Moûtiers, 4,066 ... G 5
Moyeuvre-Grande, 14,559 ... G 3
Mulhouse, 115,632 ... G 4
Muret, 10,515 ... D 6
Nancy, 121,910 ... G 3
Nanterre, 90,124 ... A 1
Nantes, 253,105 ... C 4
Narbonne, 35,236 ... E 6
Nemours, 8,081 ... E 3
Neufchâteau, 7,656 ... F 3
Neufchâtel-en-Bray, 5,734 ... D 3
Neuilly-sur-Seine, 70,787 ... B 1
Nevers, 42,092 ... E 4
Nice, 301,400 ... G 6
Nîmes, 115,561 ... F 6
Niort, 46,749 ... C 4
Nogent-le-Rotrou, 11,040 ... D 3
Nogent-sur-Seine, 4,271 ... E 3
Noisy-le-Sec, 34,058 ... B 1
Noyon, 11,567 ... E 3
Nyons, 4,311 ... F 5
Oloron-Sainte-Marie, 12,597 ... C 6
Orange, 17,582 ... F 5
Orléans, 94,382 ... D 3
Orly, 30,151 ... B 2
Orthez, 8,778 ... C 6
Oullins, 26,520 ... F 5
Oyonnax, 19,571 ... F 4
Pamiers, 13,183 ... D 6
Pantin, 47,580 ... B 1
Paray-le-Monial, 10,324 ... F 4
Paris (cap.), 2,580,010 ... B 2
Paris, *7,953,065 ... B 2
Paris, †9,283,000 ... B 2
Parthenay, 11,177 ... C 4
Pau, 71,865 ... C 6
Périgueux, 36,991 ... D 5
Perpignan, 100,086 ... E 6
Pessac, 35,343 ... C 5
Ploërmel, 3,720 ... B 4
Poitiers, 68,082 ... D 4
Pont-à-Mousson, 13,283 ... G 3
Pont-l'Abbé, 6,227 ... A 4
Pont-l'Évêque, 2,823 ... D 3
Pontarlier, 16,250 ... G 4
Pontivy, 9,674 ... B 3
Pontoise, 16,633 ... E 3
Port-de-Bouc, 13,447 ... F 6
Port-Louis, 3,921 ... B 4

(continued on following page)

Port-St-Louis-du-Rhône, 7,194 ....F 6
Port-Vendres, 5,358 ....E 6
Porto-Vecchio, 3,324 ....B 7
Privas, 8,113 ....F 5
Provins, 11,205 ....E 3
Puteaux, 37,801 ....A 2
Quiberon, 4,305 ....B 4
Quimper, 47,811 ....A 4
Quimperlé, 9,701 ....B 4
Rambouillet, 14,043 ....D 3
Redon, 8,767 ....C 4
Reims, 151,988 ....E 3
Remiremont, 9,018 ....G 3
Rennes, 176,024 ....C 3
Rethel, 7,737 ....F 3
Révin, 11,978 ....F 3
Rezé, 31,113 ....C 4
Rive-de-Gier, 15,483 ....F 5
Roanne, 53,178 ....E 4
Rochefort, 28,223 ....C 4
Rodez, 23,041 ....E 5
Romans-sur-Isère, 29,430 ....F 5
Romilly-sur-Seine, 16,867 ....F 3
Romorantin-Lanthenay, 13,516 ...D 4
Roubaix, 114,239 ....E 2
Rouen, 118,323 ....D 3
Royan, 17,187 ....C 5
Rueil-Malmaison, 60,130 ....A 2
Sablé-sur-Sarthe, 8,194 ....C 4
Saint-Affrique, 6,443 ....E 6
Saint-Amand-Mont-Rond, 11,035..E 4
Saint-Brieuc, 49,305 ....B 3
Saint-Céré, 3,682 ....D 5
Saint-Chamond, 35,362 ....F 5
Saint-Claude, 12,344 ....F 4
Saint-Cloud, 28,016 ....A 2
Saint-Denis, 99,027 ....B 1
Saint-Dié, 24,652 ....G 3
Saint-Dizier, 35,742 ....F 3
Saint-Étienne, 212,843 ....F 5
Saint-Florent-sur-Cher, 6,261....E 4
Saint-Flour, 5,582 ....E 5
Saint-Gaudens, 9,776 ....D 6
Saint-Germain-en-Laye, 36,251....D 3
Saint-Girons, 7,462 ....D 6
Saint-Jean-d'Angély, 8,883 ....C 4
Saint-Jean-de-Luz, 10,206 ....C 6
Saint-Jean-de-Maurienne, 8,407...G 5
Saint-Jean-Pied-de-Port, 1,677 ...C 6
Saint-Junien, 8,624 ....D 5
Saint-Lô, 17,347 ....C 3
Saint-Malo, 40,252 ....B 3
Saint-Mandé, 22,998 ....B 2
Saint-Maur-des-Fossés, 77,122 ....B 2
Saint-Mihiel, 5,262 ....F 3
Saint-Nazaire, 60,696 ....B 4
Saint-Omer, 17,647 ....E 2
Saint-Ouen, 48,304 ....B 1
Saint-Quentin, 63,932 ....E 3
Saint-Raphaël, 16,117 ....G 6
Saint-Tropez, 5,138 ....G 6
Saint-Vallier, 4,863 ....F 5
Saint-Yrieix-la-Perche 4,655 ....D 5
Sainte-Mère-Église, 889 ....C 3
Sainte-Savine, 11,616 ....E 3
Saintes, 24,594 ....C 4
Salins-les-Bains, 4,084 ....F 4
Salon-de-Provence, 24,803 ....F 6
Sarrebourg, 11,104 ....G 3
Sarreguemines, 23,074 ....G 3
Sartène, 4,117 ....B 7
Sartrouville, 39,722 ....A 1
Saumur, 21,354 ....D 4
Saverne, 9,432 ....G 3
Sceaux, 19,837 ....A 2
Sedan, 22,998 ....F 3
Sélestat, 14,558 ....G 3
Senlis, 10,111 ....E 3
Sens, 22,658 ....E 3
Sète, 40,220 ....E 6
Sèvres, 20,025 ....A 2
Soissons, 25,409 ....E 3
Sotteville-lès-Rouen, 33,503 ....D 3
Stiring-Wendel, 13,757 ....G 3
Strasbourg, 247,526 ....H 3
Suresnes, 40,393 ....A 2
Tarare, 12,116 ....F 5
Tarascon, 8,848 ....F 6
Tarbes, 55,200 ....D 6
Thann, 8,108 ....G 4
Thiers, 14,430 ....E 5
Thionville, 35,747 ....G 3
Thonon-les-Bains, 20,095 ....G 4
Thouars, 11,526 ....C 4
Tonnerre, 5,562 ....E 4
Toulon, 169,593 ....F 6
Toulouse, 331,751 ....D 6
Tourcoing, 93,675 ....E 2
Tours, 126,414 ....D 4
Trouville-sur-Mer, 5,718 ....C 3
Troyes, 74,409 ....F 3
Tulle, 17,640 ....D 5
Uckange, 10,326....G 3
Uzès, 6,201 ....F 5
Valence, 60,662 ....F 5
Valenciennes, 46,237 ....E 2
Valognes, 5,218 ....C 3
Vannes, 36,380 ....B 4
Vence, 6,450 ....G 6
Vendôme, 15,854 ....D 4
Vénissieux, 47,460 ....F 5
Verdun-sur-Meuse, 21,308 ....F 3
Vernon, 16,983 ....D 3
Versailles, 89,035 ....A 2
Vesoul, 16,079 ....F 4
Vichy, 33,458 ....E 4
Vienne, 26,512 ....F 5
Vierzon, 32,429 ....D 4
Villefranche, 6,619 ....G 6
Villefranche-de-Rouergue, 9,382...E 5
Villefranche-sur-Saône, 25,995.....F 4
Villejuif, 48,737 ....B 2
Villemomble, 28,731 ....C 1
Villeneuve-St-Georges, 30,229 ....E 3
Villeneuve-sur-Lot, 18,612 ....D 5
Villeurbanne, 119,420 ....F 5
Vincennes, 49,116 ....B 2
Vire, 10,819 ....C 3
Vitré, 10,125 ....C 3
Vitry-le-François, 16,409 ....F 3
Vitry-sur-Seine, 77,616 ....B 2
Vittel, 6,343 ....F 3
Voiron, 15,693 ....F 5
Wissembourg, 5,341 ....G 3
Yvetot, 9,208 ....D 3

OTHER FEATURES

Adour (river) ....C 6
Ain (river) ....F 4
Aisne (river) ....E 3
Ajaccio (gulf) ....B 7
Allier (river) ....E 5
Aube (river) ....F 3
Auvergne (mts.) ....E 5
Belle-Île (isl.), 4,442 ....B 4
Biscay (bay) ....B 5
Blanc (mt.) ....G 5
Bonifacio (strait) ....B 7
Calais (strait) ....D 2
Causses (region) ....E 5
Cévennes (mts.) ....E 5
Charente (river) ....C 5
Cher (river) ....D 4
Corse (cape) ....B 6
Corsica (isl.), 269,831 ....B 6
Côte-d'Or (mts.) ....F 4
Cotentin (pen.) ....C 3
Cottian Alps (range) ....G 5
Creuse (river) ....D 4
Dordogne (river) ....D 5
Dore (mts.) ....E 5
Doubs (river) ....G 4
Drôme (river) ....F 5
Dronne (river) ....D 5
Durance (river) ....F 6
English (channel) ....B 3
Eure (river) ....D 3
Forez (mts.) ....E 5
Fréjus (pass) ....G 5
Gard (river) ....F 5
Gave de Pau (river) ....C 6
Garonne (river) ....C 5
Geneva (lake) ....G 4
Gers (river) ....D 6
Gironde (river) ....C 5
Graian Alps (range) ....G 5
Gris-Nez (cape) ....D 2
Groix (isl.), 3,161 ....B 4
Hague (cape) ....C 3
Hérault (river) ....E 6
Hyères (isls.) ....G 6
Indre (river) ....D 4
Isère (river) ....F 5
Isle (river) ....D 5
Jura (mts.) ....F 4
Langres (plateau) ....F 4
Limousin (region) ....D 5
Lions (gulf) ....F 6
Little Saint Bernard (pass) ....G 5
Loir (river) ....D 4
Loire (river) ....C 4
Lot (river) ....D 5
Manche, La (English) (chan.)....B 3
Maritime Alps (range) ....G 5
Marne (river) ....C 2
Mayenne (river) ....C 4
Mediterranean (sea) ....E 7
Médoc (reg.) ....C 5
Meuse (river) ....F 3
Mont Cenis (tunnel) ....G 5
Morvan (plateau) ....E 4
Moselle (river) ....G 3
Noirmoutier (isl.), 8,091 ....B 4
North (sea) ....E 1
Oise (river) ....E 3
Oléron, d' (isl.), 16,355 ....C 5
Omaha (beach) ....C 3
Orb (river) ....E 6
Orne (river) ....C 3
Ouessant (isl.), 1,817 ....A 3
Penmarch (point) ....A 4
Perche (reg.) ....D 3
Puy-de-Dôme (mt.) ....E 5
Pyrenees (range) ....C 6
Ré (isl.), 9,967 ....C 4
Rhine (river) ....G 3
Rhône (river) ....F 5
Risle (river) ....D 3
Riviera (region) ....G 6
Saint-Florent (gulf) ....B 6
Saint-Malo (gulf) ....B 3
Saône (river) ....F 4
Sarthe (river) ....D 4
Sein (isl.), 835 ....A 3
Seine (bay) ....C 3
Seine (river) ....D 3
Sologne (reg.) ....E 4
Somme (river) ....D 2
Tarn (river) ....E 6
Ushant (Ouessant) (isl.), 1,817..A 3
Utah (beach) ....C 3
Vaccarès (lagoon) ....F 6
Vienne (river) ....D 4
Vilaine (river) ....C 4
Vosges (mts.) ....G 3
Yeu, d' (isl.), 4,786 ....B 4
Yonne (river) ....E 3

*City and suburbs.
†Population of metropolitan area.

MONACO

CITIES and TOWNS

Monte Carlo, 9,948 ....G 6

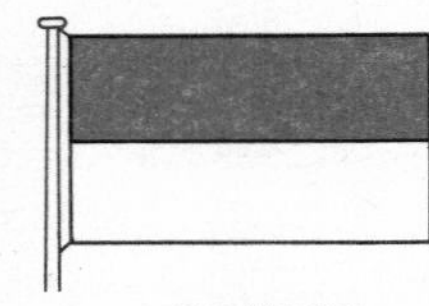

MONACO

AREA 368 acres
POPULATION 23,035

WINE
REGIONS
Reims
Caen
CALVADOS
(distilled from cider)
CHAMPAGNE
ALSACE
Colmar
Chablis
BURGUNDY
Côte-d'Or
Anjou
Touraine
Angers
POUILLY
SANCERRE
Tours
LOIRE VALLEY
QUINCY
REUILLY
Beaune
Mâconnais
JURA
Mâcon
Beaujolais
COGNAC
Cognac
Médoc
BORDEAUX
Bordeaux
Bergerac
Valence
CÔTES DE DURAS
Graves
Sauternes
CÔTES
DU
RHÔNE
GAILLAC
ARMAGNAC
Auch
LANGUEDOC
Avignon
PROVENCE
Pau
JURANÇON
LIMOUX
ROUSSILLON
Béziers
Toulon

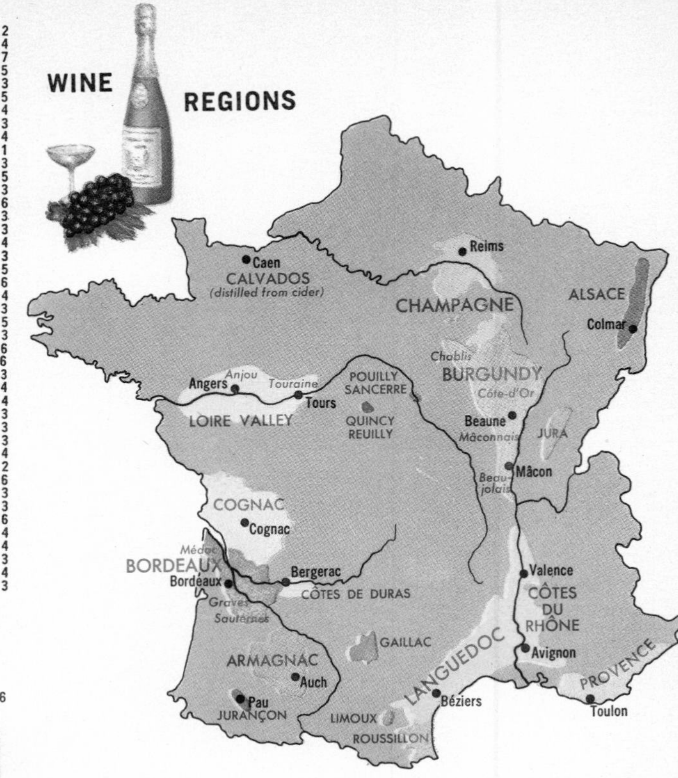

Climate, soil and variety of grape planted determine the quality of wine. Long, hot and fairly dry summers with cool, humid nights constitute an ideal climate. The nature of the soil is such a determining influence that identical grapes planted in Bordeaux, Burgundy and Champagne, will yield wines of widely different types.

Agriculture, Industry and Resources

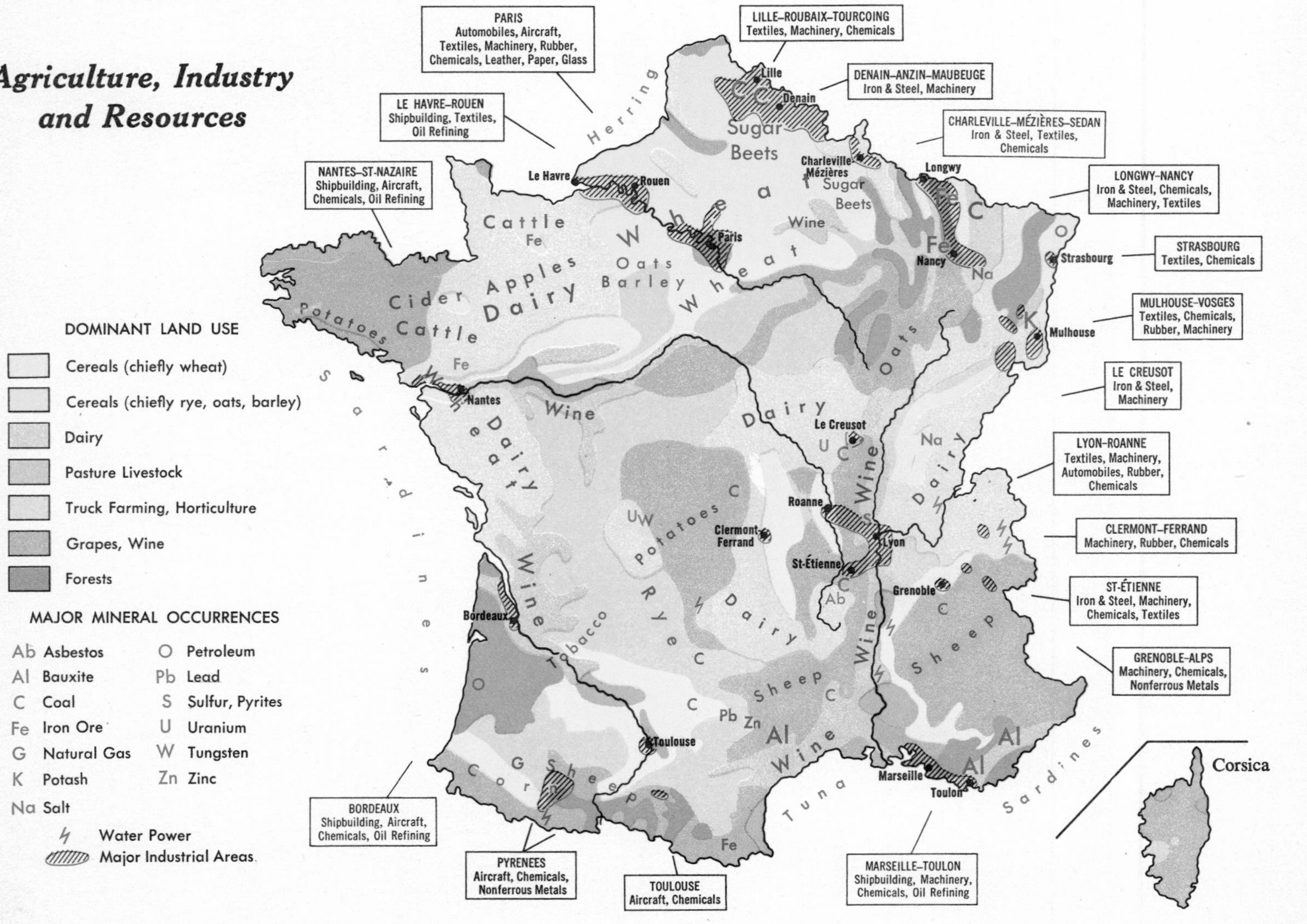

PARIS
Automobiles, Aircraft, Textiles, Machinery, Rubber, Chemicals, Leather, Paper, Glass
LILLE–ROUBAIX–TOURCOING
Textiles, Machinery, Chemicals
DENAIN–ANZIN–MAUBEUGE
Iron & Steel, Machinery
LE HAVRE–ROUEN
Shipbuilding, Textiles, Oil Refining
CHARLEVILLE–MÉZIÈRES–SEDAN
Iron & Steel, Textiles, Chemicals
NANTES–ST-NAZAIRE
Shipbuilding, Aircraft, Chemicals, Oil Refining
LONGWY–NANCY
Iron & Steel, Chemicals, Machinery, Textiles
STRASBOURG
Textiles, Chemicals
MULHOUSE–VOSGES
Textiles, Chemicals, Rubber, Machinery
LE CREUSOT
Iron & Steel, Machinery
LYON–ROANNE
Textiles, Machinery, Automobiles, Rubber, Chemicals
CLERMONT–FERRAND
Machinery, Rubber, Chemicals
ST-ÉTIENNE
Iron & Steel, Machinery, Chemicals, Textiles
GRENOBLE–ALPS
Machinery, Chemicals, Nonferrous Metals
BORDEAUX
Shipbuilding, Aircraft, Chemicals, Oil Refining
PYRENEES
Aircraft, Chemicals, Nonferrous Metals
TOULOUSE
Aircraft, Chemicals
MARSEILLE–TOULON
Shipbuilding, Machinery, Chemicals, Oil Refining
Herring
Lille
Denain
Sugar Beets
Charleville
Mézières
Longwy
Le Havre
Rouen
Paris
Nancy
Strasbourg
Mulhouse
Cattle
Cider Apples
Dairy
Potatoes
Oats
Barley
Wheat
Wine
Nantes
Le Creusot
Roanne
Clermont-Ferrand
Lyon
St-Étienne
Grenoble
Bordeaux
Tobacco
Rye
Sheep
Toulouse
Marseille
Toulon
Corn
Tuna
Sardines
Corsica
DOMINANT LAND USE
Cereals (chiefly wheat)
Cereals (chiefly rye, oats, barley)
Dairy
Pasture Livestock
Truck Farming, Horticulture
Grapes, Wine
Forests
MAJOR MINERAL OCCURRENCES
Ab Asbestos
Al Bauxite
C Coal
Fe Iron Ore
G Natural Gas
K Potash
Na Salt
O Petroleum
Pb Lead
S Sulfur, Pyrites
U Uranium
W Tungsten
Zn Zinc
Water Power
Major Industrial Areas

ANDORRA

CITIES and TOWNS

Andorra la Vella (cap.), 2,250....G 1

GIBRALTAR

PHYSICAL FEATURES

Europa (point) ....D 4

PORTUGAL

PROVINCES

Algarve, 315,300 ....B 4
Alto Alentejo, 410,200 ....C 3
Baixo Alentejo, 275,000 ....B 3
Beira Alta, 761,500 ....C 2
Beira Baixa, 321,100 ....C 3
Beira Litoral, 1,448,800 ....B 2
Douro Litoral, 1,352,600 ....B 2
Estremadura, 1,998,600 ....B 3
Madeira, 268,700 ....A 2
Minho, 944,800 ....B 2
Ribatejo, 479,400 ....B 3
Trás-os-Montes e Alto Douro, 586,500 ....C 2

CITIES and TOWNS

Águeda, 8,345 ....B 2
Alcácer do Sal, 14,733 ....B 3
Alcântara, 30,625 ....A 1
Alcobaça, 5,166 ....B 3
Aldeia Nova, 7,678 ....C 4
Algés, 14,517 ....A 1
Alhos Vedros, 19,606 ....B 3
Aljezur, 5,333 ....B 4
Aljustrel, 9,913 ....B 4
Almada, 30,688 ....A 1
Almeirim, 8,902 ....B 3
Alpiarça, 7,856 ....B 3
Amadora, 36,331 ....A 1
Amareleja, 4,816 ....C 3
Aveiro, 16,011 ....B 2
Baixa da Banheira, 12,525.............B 3
Barcelos, 5,420 ....B 2
Batalha, 7,053 ....B 3
Beja, 15,702 ....C 3
Belas, 7,509 ....A 1
Belém, 20,416 ....A 1
Benfica, 23,161 ....A 1
Braga, 40,977 ....B 2
Bragança, 8,075 ....C 2
Caldas da Rainha, 10,635 ....B 3
Calheta, 5,404 ....A 2
Campo Maior, 8,807 ....C 3
Cantanhede, 6,630 ....B 2
Caparica, 10,363 ....A 1
Carnaxide, 28,301 ....A 1
Cartaxo, 6,665 ....B 3
Cascais, 10,861 ....B 3
Castelo Branco, 14,838 ....C 3
Castro Marim, 5,347 ....C 4
Chaves, 13,156 ....C 2
Coimbra, 46,313 ....B 2
Cova da Piedade, 15,720 ....A 1
Covilhã, 23,091 ....C 2
Elvas, 11,742 ....C 3
Espinho, 13,503 ....B 2
Estoril, 11,193 ....B 3
Estremoz, 10,122 ....C 3
Évora, 24,144 ....C 3
Fafe, 7,126 ....B 2
Faro, 18,909 ....B 4
Fátima, 5,852 ....B 3
Ferreira do Alentejo, 8,108.............B 3
Figueira da Foz, 10,855 ....B 2
Funchal, 43,301 ....A 2
Gondomar, 11,182 ....B 2
Guarda, 9,094 ....C 2
Guimarães, 23,229 ....B 2
Ilhavo, 12,646 ....B 2
Lagos, 10,008 ....B 4
Lamego, 10,236 ....C 2
Lavos, 5,744 ....B 2
Leiria, 7,477 ....B 3
Lisbon (Lisboa) (cap.), 828,000..A 1
Loulé, 16,152 ....B 4
Louriçal, 5,608 ....B 3
Lourinhã, 8,677 ....B 3
Lousã, 8,191 ....B 2
Machico, 11,608 ....A 2
Marinha Grande, 15,699 ....B 3
Matosinhos, 37,694 ....B 2
Mértola, 5,682 ....C 4
Miranda do Corvo, 5,103 ....B 2
Montargil, 6,357 ....B 3
Montemor-o-Novo, 13,115 ....B 3
Montijo, 17,751 ....B 3
Moscavide, 22,065 ....A 1
Mourão, 12,126 ....C 3
Muge, 5,546 ....B 3
Nazaré, 9,189 ....B 3
Nisa, 5,262 ....C 3
Óbidos, 4,599 ....B 3
Odivelas, 27,423 ....A 1
Oeiras, 6,857 ....B 3
Olhão, 16,017 ....C 4
Olivais, 11,896 ....A 1
Oporto, 324,400 ....B 2
Ovar, 14,128 ....B 2
Peniche, 11,357 ....B 3
Pombal, 9,973 ....B 3
Ponta do Sol, 7,426 ....A 2
Ponte de Sor, 13,010 ....B 3
Portalegre, 11,017 ....C 3
Portimão, 12,129 ....B 4
Porto (Oporto), 324,400 ....B 2
Povoa de Varzim, 17,696 ....B 2
Proença-a-Nova, 6,060 ....B 3
Queluz, 14,703 ....A 1
Ribeira Brava, 8,726 ....A 2
Sacavém, 10,624 ....A 1
Santa Cruz, 9,858 ....A 2
Santarém, 16,449 ....B 3
Santiago do Cacém, 6,939 ....B 3
São Brás de Alportel, 9,058.................C 4
São João da Madeira, 11,921 ....B 2
São Teotónio, 8,183 ....B 4
Serpa, 10,967 ....C 4
Sertã, 6,909 ....B 3
Sesimbra, 16,837 ....B 3
Setúbal, 44,435 ....B 3
Sines, 8,866 ....B 4
Sintra, 19,930 ....B 3
Soure, 9,655 ....B 2
Tavira, 12,046 ....C 4
Tomar, 12,974 ....B 3
Tôrres Novas, 11,974 ....B 3
Tôrres Vedras, 13,091 ....B 3
Vagos, 8,281 ....B 2
Vendas Novas, 9,675 ....B 3
Viana do Castelo, 14,371 ....B 2
Vila do Conde, 12,771 ....B 2
Vila Franca de Xira, 13,404....................B 3
Vila Nova de Gaia, 45,739......................B 2

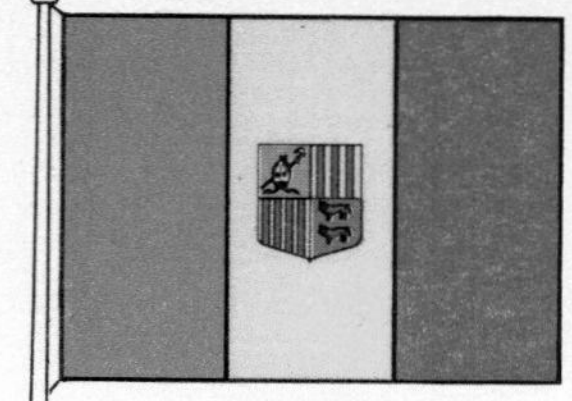

ANDORRA

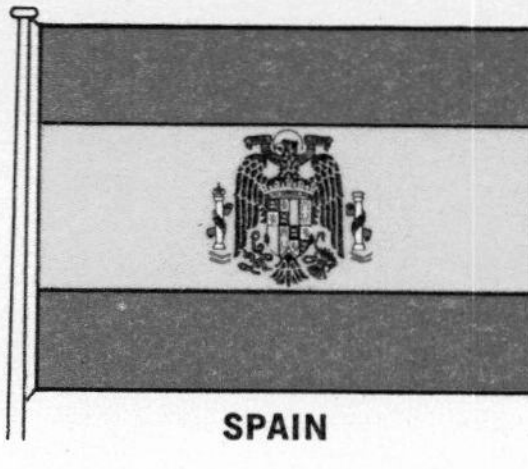

SPAIN

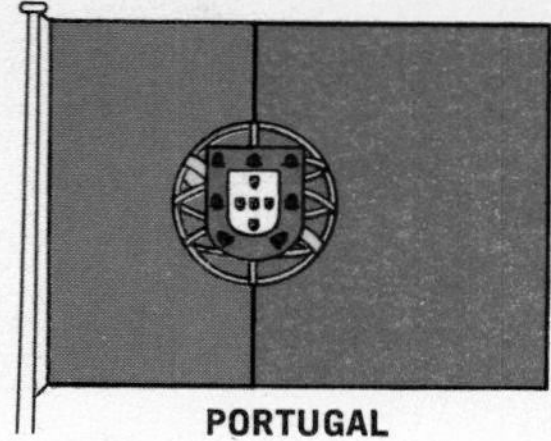

PORTUGAL

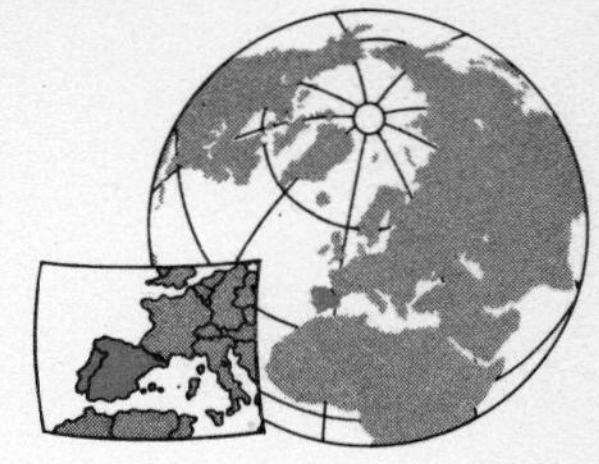

SPAIN

AREA 194,896 sq. mi.
POPULATION 33,290,000
CAPITAL Madrid
LARGEST CITY Madrid
HIGHEST POINT Pico de Teide 12,172 ft. (Canary Is.); Mulhacén 11,411 ft. (mainland)
MONETARY UNIT peseta
MAJOR LANGUAGES Spanish, Catalan, Basque
MAJOR RELIGION Roman Catholicism

ANDORRA

AREA 175 sq. mi.
POPULATION 19,000
CAPITAL Andorra la Vella
MONETARY UNIT French franc, Spanish peseta
MAJOR LANGUAGE Catalan
MAJOR RELIGION Roman Catholicism

PORTUGAL

AREA 35,510 sq. mi.
POPULATION 9,560,000
CAPITAL Lisbon
LARGEST CITY Lisbon
HIGHEST POINT Malhão da Estrêla 6,532 ft.
MONETARY UNIT escudo
MAJOR LANGUAGE Portuguese
MAJOR RELIGION Roman Catholicism

GIBRALTAR

AREA 2 sq. mi.
POPULATION 27,000
CAPITAL Gibraltar
MONETARY UNIT pound sterling
MAJOR LANGUAGES English, Spanish
MAJOR RELIGION Roman Catholicism

Vila Real, 10,263 ....C 2
Vila Real de Sto. António, 11,096 ....C 4
Viseu, 16,961 ....C 2

OTHER FEATURES

Carvoeiro (cape) ....B 3
Desertas (isls.) ....A 2
Douro (river) ....C 2
Estrela, Serra da (mts.) ....C 2
Foia (mt.) ....B 4
Guadiana (river) ....C 4
Lima (river) ....B 2
Madeira (isl.), 265,432 ....A 2
Minho (river) ....B 2
Mira (river) ....B 4
Monchique (mts.) ....B 4
Mondego (cape) ....B 3
Mondego (river) ....C 2
Monsanto (hill) ....A 1
Ossa (mts.) ....C 3
Palha, Mar da (bay) ....A 1
Roca (cape) ....B 3
Sado (river) ....B 3
Saint Vincent (cape) ....B 4
Santa María (cape) ....C 4
Setúbal (bay) ....B 3
Tagus (river) ....B 3
Tâmega (river) ....C 2
Tejo (Tagus) (river) ....B 3
Xarrama (river) ....B 3

SPAIN

PROVINCES

Álava, 148,899 ....E 1
Albacete, 358,290 ....E 3
Alicante, 746,917 ....F 3
Almería, 360,798 ....E 4
Ávila, 231,916 ....D 2
Badajoz, 839,363 ....C 3
Baleares (Balearic Is.), 451,343..H 3
Barcelona, 3,213,212 ....G 2
Burgos, 372,138 ....E 1
Cáceres, 540,060 ....C 3
Cádiz, 874,837 ....D 4
Castellón, 344,350 ....G 2
Ciudad Real, 589,262 ....D 3
Córdoba, 802,633 ....D 3
Cuenca, 305,432 ....E 2
Gerona, 361,250 ....H 1
Granada, 760,210 ....E 4
Guadalajara, 174,572 ....E 2
Guipúzcoa, 532,095 ....E 1
Huelva, 413,459 ....C 4
Huesca, 231,376 ....F 1
Jaén, 720,559 ....E 4
La Coruña, 1,004,149 ....B 1
Las Palmas, 492,466 ....C 4
León, 600,935 ....C 1
Lérida, 336,818 ....G 2
Logroño, 228,922 ....E 1
Lugo, 464,922 ....C 1
Madrid, 2,973,619 ....E 2
Málaga, 783,436 ....D 4
Murcia, 817,545 ....F 4
Navarra, 409,239 ....F 1
Orense, 442,420 ....C 1
Oviedo, 1,034,244 ....C 1
Palencia, 230,426 ....D 1
Pontevedra, 681,295 ....B 1
Salamanca, 401,276 ....C 2
Santa Cruz de Tenerife, 525,095 ....B 5
Santander, 443,113 ....D 1
Saragossa, 670,357 ....F 2
Segovia, 192,229 ....D 2
Seville, 1,295,094 ....D 4
Soria, 140,517 ....E 2
Tarragona, 363,830 ....G 2
Teruel, 205,565 ....F 2
Toledo, 516,870 ....D 3
Valencia, 1,462,005 ....F 3
Valladolid, 368,685 ....D 2
Vizcaya, 852,768 ....E 1
Zamora, 293,489 ....D 2

CITIES and TOWNS

Adra, 10,211 ....E 4
Aguilar, 13,760 ....D 4
Aguilas, 11,970 ....F 4
Alagón, 5,270 ....F 2
Alayor, 4,988 ....J 3
Albacete, 61,635 ....F 3
Albox, 4,036 ....E 4
Alburqerque, 9,540 ....C 3
Alcalá de Chivert, 4,049 ....G 2
Alcalá de Guadaira. 27,378 ....D 4
Alcalá de Henares, 20,572 ....G 4
Alcalá de los Gazules, 7,015 ....D 4
Alcalá la Real, 8,351 ....E 4
Alcanar, 6,332 ....G 2
Alcañiz, 9,489 ....F 2
Alcántara, 3,564 ....C 3
Alcantarilla, 15,748 ....F 4
Alcaudete, 9,280 ....E 4
Alcázar de San Juan, 23,788..........E 3
Alcira, 22,417 ....F 3
Alcoy, 48,712 ....F 3
Alfaro, 8,570 ....F 1
Algeciras, 51,096 ....D 4
Algemesí, 16,683 ....F 3
Alhama de Granada, 6,989 ....E 4
Alhama de Murcia, 7,175 ....F 4
Alicante, 103,289 ....F 3
Almadén, 13,206 ....D 3
Almagro, 9,232 ....E 3
Almansa, 15,391 ....F 3
Almendralejo, 20,867 ....C 3
Almería, 76,643 ....E 4
Almodóvar del Campo, 8,115..........D 3
Almonte, 9,444 ....C 4
Almuñécar, 5,644 ....E 4
Álora, 6,459 ....D 4
Amposta, 11,026 ....G 2
Andújar, 23,897 ....D 3
Antequera, 28,400 ....D 4
Aracena, 5,605 ....C 4
Aranda de Duero, 12,623 ....E 2
Aranjuez, 25,988 ....E 2
Archena, 5,802 ....F 3
Archidona. 7.262 ....D 4

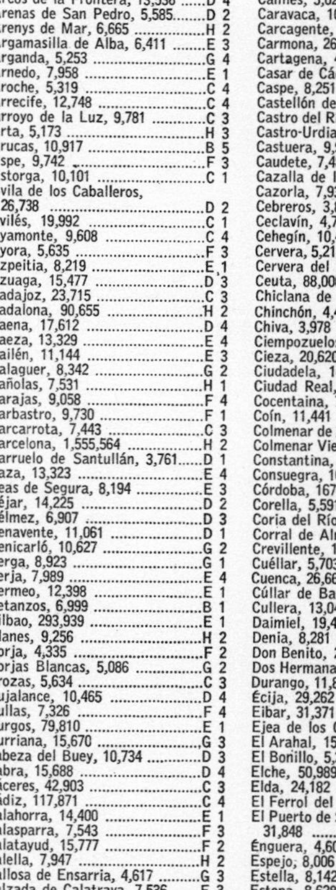

Arcos de la Frontera, 13,536 ......D 4
Arenas de San Pedro, 5,585........D 2
Arenys de Mar, 6,665 ....H 2
Argamasilla de Alba, 6,411 ....E 3
Arganda, 5,253 ....G 4
Arnedo, 7,958 ....E 1
Aroche, 5,319 ....C 4
Arrecife, 12,748 ....C 4
Arroyo de la Luz, 9,781 ....C 3
Arta, 5,173 ....H 3
Arucas, 10,917 ....B 5
Aspe, 9,742 ....F 3
Astorga, 10,101 ....C 1
Ávila de los Caballeros, 26,738 ....D 2
Avilés, 19,992 ....C 1
Ayamonte, 9,608 ....C 4
Ayora, 5,635 ....F 3
Azpeitia, 8,219 ....E 1
Azuaga, 15,477 ....D 3
Badajoz, 23,715 ....C 3
Badalona, 90,655 ....H 2
Baena, 17,612 ....D 4
Baeza, 13,329 ....E 4
Bailén, 11,144 ....E 3
Balaguer, 8,342 ....G 2
Bañolas, 7,531 ....H 1
Barajas, 9,058 ....F 4
Barbastro, 9,730 ....F 1
Barcarrota, 7,443 ....C 3
Barcelona, 1,555,564 ....H 2
Barruelo de Santullán, 3,761......D 1
Baza, 13,323 ....E 4
Beas de Segura, 8,194 ....E 3
Béjar, 14,225 ....D 2
Bélmez, 6,907 ....D 3
Benavente, 11,061 ....D 1
Benicarló, 10,627 ....G 2
Berga, 8,923 ....G 1
Berja, 7,989 ....E 4
Bermeo, 12,398 ....E 1
Betanzos, 6,999 ....B 1
Bilbao, 293,939 ....E 1
Blanes, 9,256 ....H 2
Borja, 4,335 ....F 2
Borjas Blancas, 5,086 ....G 2
Brozas, 5,634 ....C 3
Bujalance, 10,465 ....D 4
Bullas, 7,326 ....F 4
Burgos, 79,810 ....E 1
Burriana, 15,670 ....G 3
Cabeza del Buey, 10,734 ....D 3
Cabra, 15,688 ....D 4
Cáceres, 42,903 ....C 3
Cádiz, 117,871 ....C 4
Calahorra, 14,400 ....E 1
Calasparra, 7,543 ....F 3
Calatayud, 15,777 ....F 2
Calella, 7,947 ....H 2
Callosa de Ensarria, 4,617 ....G 3
Calzada de Calatrava, 7,536............E 3
Campanario, 8,910 ....D 3
Campillos, 8,791 ....D 4
Campo de Criptana, 13,616..............E 3
Candeleda, 6,507 ....D 2
Cangas, 4,059 ....B 1
Caniles, 5,026 ....E 4
Caravaca, 10,016 ....E 3
Carcagente, 15,791 ....F 3
Carmona, 26,368 ....D 4
Cartagena, 42,424 ....F 4
Casar de Cáceres, 4,560 ....C 3
Caspe, 8,251 ....G 2
Castellón de la Plana, 52,868..........G 3
Castro del Río, 11,200 ....D 4
Castro-Urdiales, 7,128 ....E 1
Castuera, 9,905 ....D 3
Caudete, 7,481 ....F 3
Cazalla de la Sierra, 9,414................D 4
Cazorla, 7,932 ....E 4
Cebreros, 3,898 ....D 2
Ceclavín, 4,778 ....C 3
Cehegín, 10,467 ....F 3
Cervera, 5,215 ....G 2
Cervera del Río Alhama, 3,648....E 1
Ceuta, 88,000 ....D 5
Chiclana de la Frontera, 19,155..C 4
Chinchón, 4,432 ....G 5
Chiva, 3,978 ....F 3
Ciempozuelos, 9,042 ....F 5
Cieza, 20,620 ....F 3
Ciudadela, 10,872 ....H 2
Ciudad Real, 35,015 ....D 3
Cocentaina, 7,405 ....F 3
Coín, 11,441 ....D 4
Colmenar de Oreja, 5,119 ....G 5
Colmenar Viejo, 8,133 ....F 4
Constantina, 12,015 ....D 4
Consuegra, 10,572 ....E 3
Córdoba, 167,808 ....D 4
Corella, 5,591 ....F 1
Coria del Río, 13,781 ....C 4
Corral de Almaguer, 8,621 ....E 3
Crevillente, 12,025 ....F 3
Cuéllar, 5,703 ....D 2
Cuenca, 26,663 ....E 2
Cúllar de Baza, 3,769 ....E 4
Cullera, 13,040 ....F 3
Daimiel, 19,485 ....E 3
Denia, 8,281 ....G 3
Don Benito, 22,642 ....C 3
Dos Hermanas, 21,517 ....D 4
Durango, 11,882 ....E 1
Écija, 29,262 ....D 4
Eibar, 31,371 ....E 1
Ejea de los Caballeros, 9,000..........F 1
El Arahal, 15,107 ....D 4
El Bonillo, 5,215 ....E 3
Elche, 50,989 ....F 3
Elda, 24,182 ....F 3
El Ferrol del Caudillo, 62,010..........B 1
El Puerto de Santa María, 31,848 ....C 4
Énguera, 4,606 ....F 3
Espejo, 8,006 ....D 4
Estella, 8,142 ....E 1
Estepa, 8,628 ....D 4
Estepona, 11,309 ....D 4
Felanitx, 7,860 ....H 3
Fermoselle, 3,885 ....C 2
Figueras, 16,460 ....H 1
Fraga, 8,264 ....G 2

Agriculture, Industry and Resources

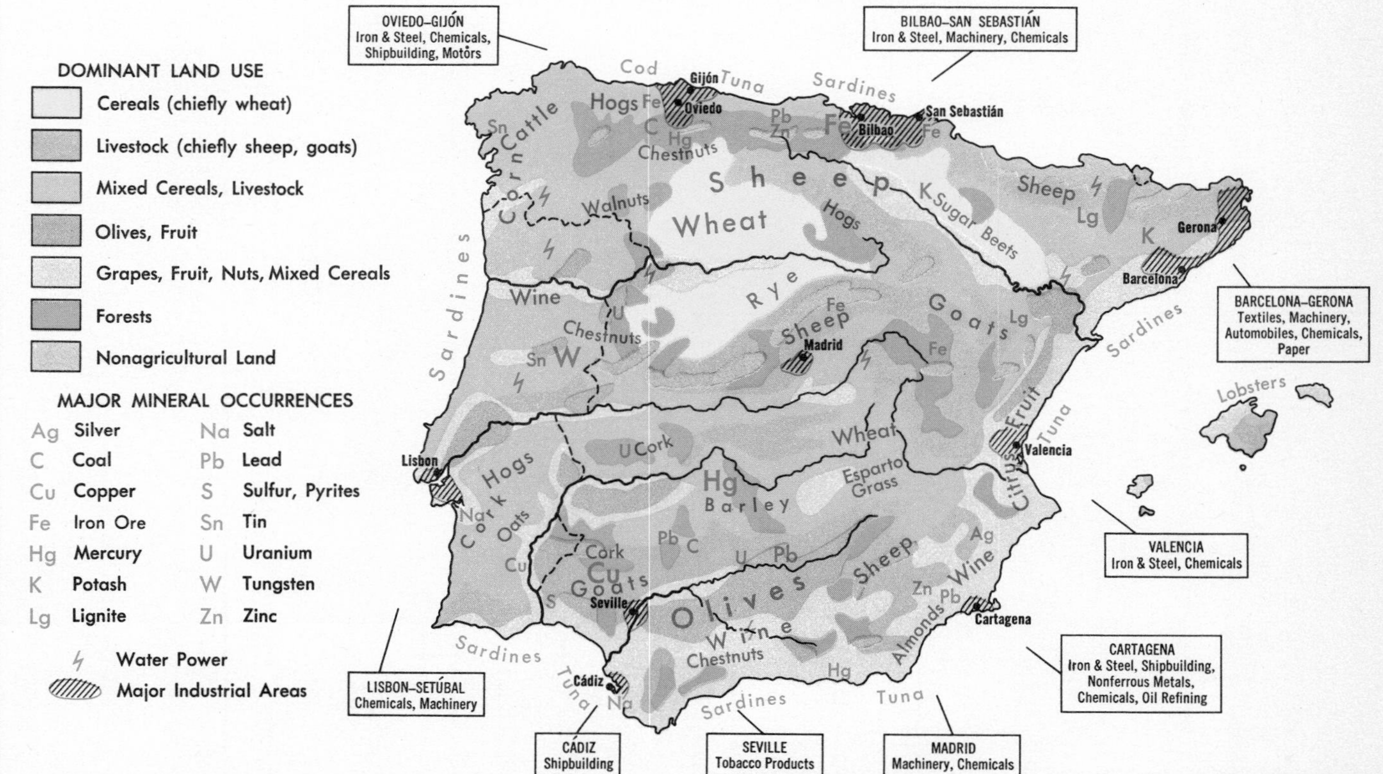

(continued on following page)

32 Spain and Portugal
(continued)

SPAIN (continued)

Fregenal de la Sierra, 9,506........C 3
Fuengirola, 5,622 ....D 4
Fuensalida, 4,697 ....D 2
Fuente de Cantos, 8,484 ....C 3
Fuente-Obejuna, 5,353 ....D 3
Fuentes de Andalucía, 8,357.......D 4
Gálvez, 3,828 ....D 3
Gándara, 400 ....C 1
Gandía, 15,940 ....F 3
Garrovillas, 5,665 ....C 3
Gerona, 28,134 ....H 2
Getafe, 21,066 ....F 4
Gijón, 92,020 ....D 1
Granada, 150,186 ....E 4
Granollers, 18,810 ....H 2
Guadalajara, 20,135 ....E 2
Guadalcanal, 5,483 ....D 3
Guadix, 15,897 ....E 4
Guareña, 8.438 ....C 3
Guernica y Luno, 4,855 ....E 1
Haro, 8,375 ....E 1
Hellín, 17,071 ....F 3
Herencia, 8,606 ....E 3
Herrera del Duque, 5,404 ....D 3
Hinojosa del Duque, 14,074.........D 3
Hortaleza, 8,552 ....G 4
Hospitalet, 122,813 ....H 2
Huelma, 5,468 ....E 4
Huelva, 56,548 ....C 4
Huércal-Overa, 4,406 ....F 4
Huesca, 24,338 ....F 1
Huéscar, 5,097 ....E 4
Ibiza, 11,259 ....G 3
Igualada, 19,866 ....G 2
Illora, 5,586 ....E 4
Inca, 13,816 ....H 3
Iniesta, 4,292 ....F 3
Irún, 20,212 ....F 1
Isla Cristina, 9,616 ....C 4
Jaca, 9,821 ....F 1
Jaén, 59,699 ....E 4
Jaraiz, 8,130 ....D 2
Jativa, 19,195 ....F 3
Jávea, 4,929 ....G 3
Jerez de la Frontera, 96,209 ....C 4
Jerez de los Caballeros, 12,349 ....C 3
Jijona, 5,147 ....F 3
Jimena de la Frontera, 3,620......D 4
Jódar, 14,289 ....E 4
Jumilla, 15,703 ....F 3
La Bañeza, 7,869 ....C 1
La Bisbal, 5,194 ....H 1
La Carolina, 10,915 ....E 3
La Coruña, 161,260 ....B 1
La Gineta, 3,237 ....E 3
La Línea, 58,169 ....D 4
La Orotava, 8,019 ....B 4
La Palma del Condado, 8,526......C 4
La Puebla, 9,931 ....H 3
La Puebla de Montalbán, 7,286..D 3
La Rambla, 8,057 ....D 4
Laredo, 6,382 ....E 1
La Roda, 11,739 ....E 3
La Solana, 14,948 ....E 3
Las Palmas, 166,236 ....B 4
Las Pedroñeras, 6,418 ....E 3
La Unión, 9,357 ....F 4
Lavadores, 9,708 ....B 1
Lebrija, 13,663 ....D 4
Ledesma, 2,527 ....C 2
Leganés, 8,064 ....F 4
Lena, Pola de, 3,966 ....D 1
León, 73,483 ....D 1
Lérida, 50,047 ....G 2
Linares, 50,527 ....E 3
Liria, 9,723 ....F 3
Llerena, 7,854 ....C 3
Lluchmayor, 9,827 ....H 3
Logroño, 58,545 ....E 1
Logrosán, 6,595 ....D 3
Loja, 11,441 ....D 4
Lora del Río, 15,086 ....D 4
Lorca, 19,854 ....F 4
Los Navalmorales, 4,686 ....D 3
Los Navalucillos, 4,823 ....D 3
Los Santos de Maimona, 8,910....C 3
Los Yébenes, 6,596 ....E 3
Luarca, 4,070 ....C 1
Lucena, 19,975 ....D 4
Lugo, 45,497 ....C 1
Madrid (cap.), 2,850,631 ....F 4
Madridejos, 9,795 ....E 3
Madroñera, 5,256 ....D 3
Mahón, 14,836 ....J 3
Málaga, 259,245 ....D 4
Malagón, 9,246 ....E 3
Malpartida de Cáceres, 5,751.......C 3
Malpartida de Plasencia, 6,757....C 2
Manacor, 17,544 ....H 3
Mancha Real, 7,587 ....E 4
Manlleu, 8,489 ....H 1
Manresa, 46,105 ....G 2
Manzanares, 16,639 ....E 3
Marbella, 7,302 ....D 4
Marchena, 15,879 ....D 4
Marín, 8,838 ....B 1
Martos, 16,442 ....E 4
Mataró, 29,937 ....H 2
Mazarrón, 3,379 ....F 4
Medina del Campo, 13,640 ....D 2
Medina de Ríoseco, 4,897 ....D 2
Medina-Sidonia, 6,869 ....D 4
Menasalbas, 4,407 ....D 3
Mérida, 28,791 ....C 3
Miajadas, 8,632 ....D 3
Mieres, 19,308 ....D 1
Miranda de Ebro, 22,836 ....E 1
Moguer, 6,776 ....C 4
Monasterio, 7,559 ....C 3
Monforte, 13,737 ....C 1
Monóvar, 7,972 ....F 3
Montánchez, 4,190 ....D 3
Montefrío, 4,917 ....D 4
Montehermoso, 6,006 ....C 2
Montellano, 8,694 ....D 4
Montijo, 12,519 ....C 3
Montilla, 19,830 ....D 4
Montoro, 11,243 ....D 3
Monzón 9,020 ....G 2
Mora, 10,613 ....E 3
Moratalla, 5,675 ....E 3
Morón de la Frontera, 29,096......D 4
Mota del Cuervo, 5,403 ....E 3
Motril, 18,624 ....E 4
Mula, 9,912 ....F 3
Munera, 5,931 ....E 3
Murcia, 83,190 ....F 4
Nava del Rey, 3,815 ....D 2
Navalcarnero, 4,681 ....F 4
Navalmoral de la Mata, 8,978.....D 3
Navalucillos, Los, 4,823...................D 3
Nerja, 5,767 ....E 4
Nerva, 11,974 ....C 4
Novelda, 11,003 ....F 3
Nules, 7,626 ....F 3
Ocaña, 6,592 ....E 3
Oliva, 13,342 ....F 3
Oliva de la Frontera, 11,141.......C 3
Olivenza, 8,304 ....C 3
Olot, 13,099 ....H 1
Olvera, 9,088 ....D 4
Onda, 10,666 ....F 3
Onteniente, 18,787 ....F 3
Orellana la Vieja, 6,925 ....D 3
Orense, 42,371 ....C 1
Orihuela, 15,873 ....F 3
Osuna, 17,671 ....D 4
Oviedo, 91,550 ....C 1
Padul, 6,868 ....E 4
Palafrugell, 7,476 ....H 2
Palamós, 5,481 ....H 2
Palencia, 48,144 ....D 2
Palma, 136,431 ....H 3
Palma del Río, 14,053 ....D 4
Pamplona, 59,227 ....F 1
Paredes de Nava, 4,065 ....D 1
Pego, 8,291 ....F 3
Peñafiel, 5,333 ....E 2
Peñaranda de Bracamonte, 5.943 D 2
Peñarroya-Pueblonuevo, 17,449....D 3
Piedrabuena, 5,453 ....D 3
Pinos-Puente, 8,311 ....E 4
Plasencia, 21,297 ....C 2
Pollensa, 7,370 ....H 3
Ponferrada, 17,042 ....C 1
Pontevedra, 19,739 ....B 1
Porcuna, 9,671 ....D 4
Portugalete, 20,514 ....E 1
Posadas, 8,440 ....D 4
Pozoblanco, 14,728 ....D 3
Priego de Córdoba, 13,469 ....D 4
Puebla de Don Fadrique, 3,771....E 4
Puebla de Montalbán, La, 7,286..D 3
Puente-Genil, 24,836 ....D 4
Puertollano, 48,528 ....D 3
Puerto Real, 12,717 ....D 4
Quesada, 6,503 ....E 4
Quintana de la Serena, 7,160......D 3
Quintanar de la Orden, 9,483......E 3
Reinosa, 10,044 ....D 1
Requena, 8,278 ....F 3
Reus, 32,037 ....G 2
Ripoll, 7,821 ....H 1
Ronda, 17,703 ....D 4
Rota, 14,236 ....C 4
Rute, 8,945 ....D 4
Sabadell, 98,049 ....H 2
Sagunto, 15,210 ....F 3
Salamanca, 90,388 ....D 2
Sallent, 7,462 ....H 2
Sama, 7,149 ....D 1
San Carlos de la Rápita, 6,844....G 2
San Clemente, 6,411 ....E 3
San Felíu de Guixols, 9,077.........H 2
San Fernando, 51,406 ....C 4
San Lorenzo de El Escorial,7,455 E 2
Sanlucar de Barrameda, 32,580....C 4
Sanlúcar la Mayor, 6,094 ....C 4
San Sebastián, 98,603 ....E 1
Santa Cruz de la Palma, 9,928....B 4
Santa Cruz de la Mudela, 8,724...E 3
Santa Cruz de la Zarza, 5,588.....E 3
Santa Cruz de Tenerife, 82,620....B 4
Santa Eugenia, 5,336 ....B 1
Santafe, 8,212 ....E 4
Santander, 98,784 ....D 1
Santiago, 37,916 ....B 1
Santoña, 7,535 ....E 1
San Vicente de Alcántara, 8,059..C 3
Saragossa, 295,080 ....F 2
Segorbe, 7,136 ....F 3
Segovia, 33,360 ....D 2
Sestao, 24,992 ....E 1
Seville (Sevilla), 423,762............D 4
Sitges, 6,796 ....G 2
Socuéllamos, 14,742 ....E 3
Sóller, 6,011 ....H 3
Sonseca, 5,994 ....D 3
Soria, 18,872 ....E 2
Sueca, 19,005 ....F 3
Tabernes de Valldigna, 12,890.....G 3
Tafalla, 7,320 ....F 1
Talavera de la Reina, 28,107.......D 2
Tarancón, 7,678 ....E 3
Tarazona de Aragón, 11,004.........F 2
Tarazona de la Mancha, 6,850.....F 3
Tarifa, 9,147 ....D 4
Tarragona, 35,689 ....G 2
Tarrasa, 89,128 ....G 2
Tárrega, 7,317 ....G 2
Tauste, 6,544 ....F 2
Telde, 11,761 ....B 5
Teruel, 18,304 ....F 2
Tobarra, 7,029 ....F 3
Toledo, 29,367 ....D 3
Tolosa, 10,980 ....F 1
Tomelloso, 27,715 ....E 3
Toro, 9,123 ....D 2
Torredonjimeno, 12,848 ....D 4

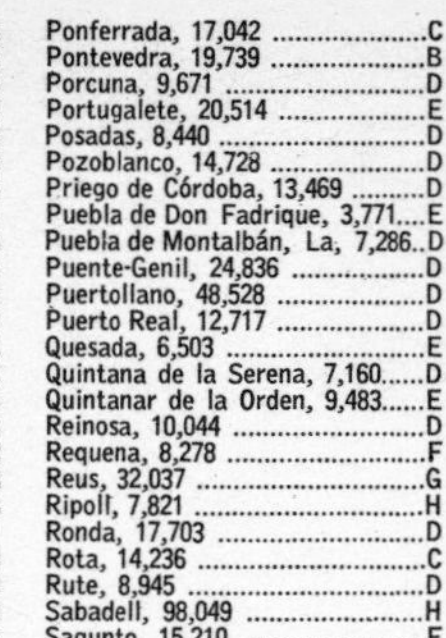

Topography

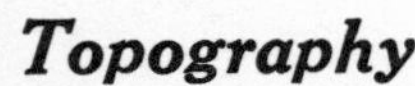
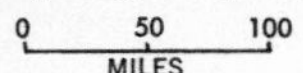

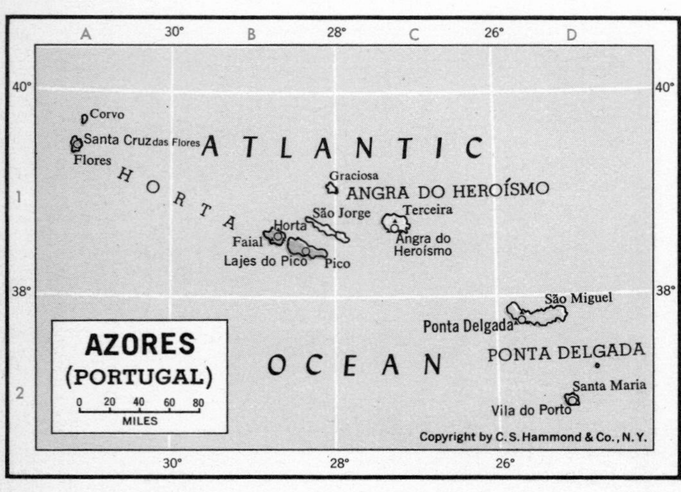

AZORES

DISTRICTS

Angra do Heroísmo, 103,800........C 1
Horta, 44,900 ....A 1
Ponta Delgada, 185,600 ....D 2

CITIES and TOWNS

Angra do Heroísmo, 13,502 ....C 1
Horta, 7,109 ....B 1
Lajes do Pico, 2,508 ....B 1
Ponta Delgada, 22,316 ....C 2
Santa Cruz das Flores, 1,898......A 1
Vila do Porto, 5,373 ....D 2

OTHER FEATURES

Corvo (isl.), 681 ....A 1
Faial (isl.), 20,281 ....B 1
Flores (isl.), 6,583 ....A 1
Graciosa (isl.), 8,669 ....C 1
Pico (isl.), 21,831..........................C 1
Santa Maria (isl.), 13,233 ....D 2
São Jorge (isl.), 15,895 ....B 1
São Miguel (isl.), 168,691 ....D 2
Terceira (isl.), 71,610...................C 1

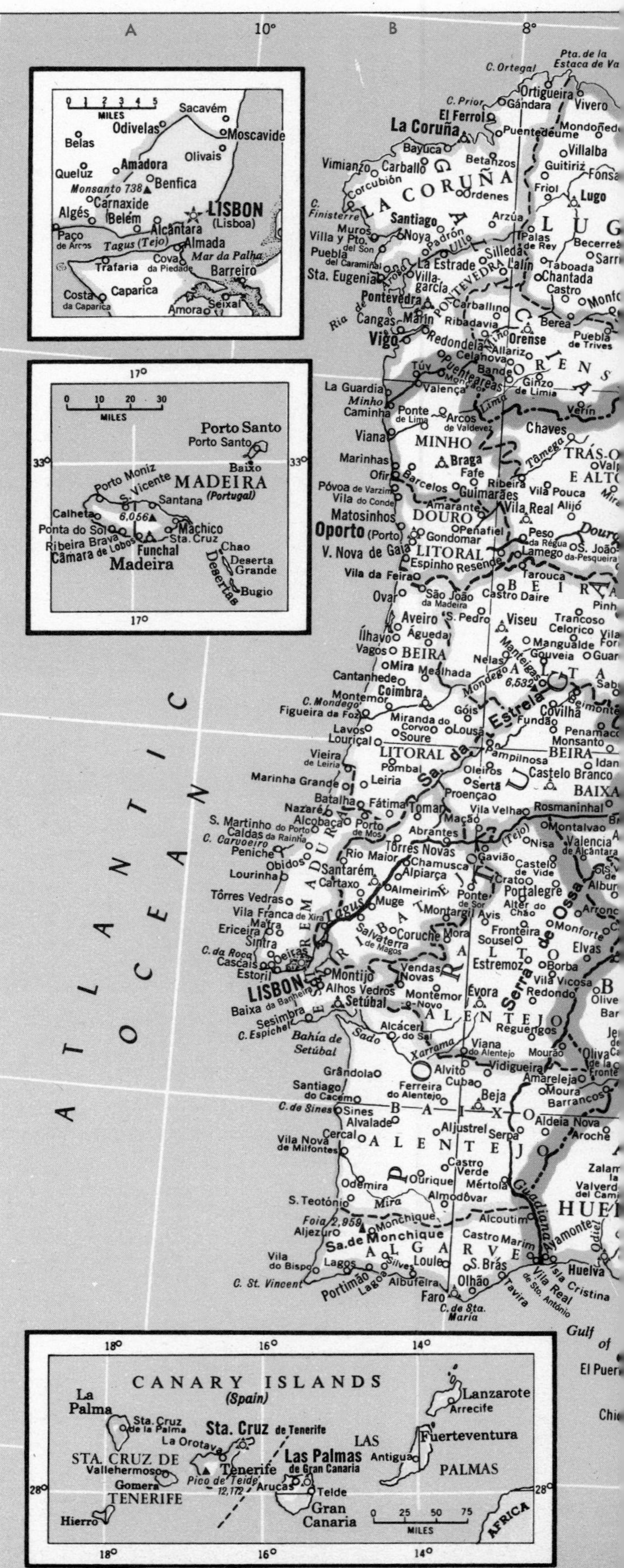

Torrejoncillo, 5,499 ....C 3
Torrelavega, 13,612 ....D 1
Torremolinos, 7,980 ....D 4
Torrente, 23,432 ....F 3
Torrevieja, 8,961 ....F 4
Torrox, 5,211 ....E 4
Tortosa, 18,674 ....G 2
Totana, 10,156 ....F 4
Trigueros, 6,151 ....C 4
Trujillo, 13,326 ....D 3
Tudela, 16,422 ....F 1
Úbeda, 26,930 ....E 3
Ubrique, 8,915 ....D 4
Urda, 5,479 ....E 3
Utiel, 9,720 ....F 3
Utrera, 25,935 ....D 4
Valdepeñas, 24,462 ....E 3
Valdeverdeja, 3,607 ....D 3
Valencia, 466,577 ....F 3
Valencia de Alcántara, 13,159....C 3
Valladolid, 133,486 ....D 2
Vall de Uxó, 18,577 ....F 3
Vallehermoso, 887 ....A 5
Valls, 10,890 ....G 2
Valverde del Camino, 10,843....C 4
Vejer de la Frontera, 11,853....C 4
Vélez-Málaga, 14,348 ....D 4
Vélez Rubio, 4,113 ....E 4
Vich, 18,184 ....H 2
Vigo, 69,429 ....B 1
Villacañas, 10,113 ....E 3
Villacarrillo, 10,970 ....E 3
Villafranca de los Barros, 14,591..C 3
Villafranca del Panadés, 11,306...G 2
Villagarcía, 4,391 ....B 1
Villahermosa, 5,496 ....E 3
Villajoyosa, 7,508 ....F 3
Villanueva de Córdoba, 15,719....D 3
Villanueva del Arzobispo, 9,307...E 3
Villanueva de la Serena, 17,647....D 3
Villanueva de los Infantes, 9,909..E 3
Villanueva y Geltrú, 25,669 ....G 2
Villar del Arzobispo, 3,876 ....F 3
Villarreal de los Infantes, 20,025 ....G 3
Villarrobledo, 19,585 ....E 3
Villarrubia de los Ojos, 9,043....E 3
Villena, 18,333 ....F 3
Vinaroz, 10,968 ....G 2
Vitoria, 65,946 ....E 1
Yecla, 17,955 ....F 3
Zafra, 9,950 ....C 3
Zalamea de la Serena, 8,543....D 3
Zamora, 41,319 ....D 2
Zaragoza (Saragossa), 295,080....F 2
Zarza la Mayor, 3,728....C 3
Zorita, 5,718 ....D 3

OTHER FEATURES

Alagón (river) ....C 2
Alborán (isl.) ....E 5
Alcudia (bay) ....H 3
Almanzor (mt.) ....D 2
Almanzora (river) ....F 4
Andalusia (reg.), 6,011,026....D 4
Aneto (mt.) ....G 1
Aragón (reg.), 1,107,298 ....F 2
Aragón (river) ....F 1
Asturias (reg.), 1,034,244 ....D 1
Autza (mt.) ....F 1
Balearic (isls.), 451,343 ....H 3
Bañuelo (mt.) ....D 3
Barbate (river) ....D 4
Biscay (bay) ....E 1
Cádiz (gulf) ....C 4
Canary (isls.), 1,017,361 ....B 4
Cantabrian (mts.) ....D 1
Castile, New (reg.), 4,559,755....E 3
Castile, Old (reg.), 2,207,946....D 2
Catalonia (reg.), 4,275,110 ....G 2
Cinca (river) ....G 2
Columbretes (isls.) ....G 3
Costa Brava (reg.) ....H 2
Costa del Sol (reg.) ....D 4
Creus (cape) ....H 1
Cuenca (mts.) ....F 3
Demanda (mts.) ....E 1
Douro (Duero) (river) ....C 2
Duratón (river) ....E 2
Ebro (river) ....G 2
Eresma (river) ....D 2
Esla (river) ....D 2
Estremadura (region), 1,379,423..C 3
Finisterre (cape) ....B 1
Formentor (cape) ....H 2
Fuerteventura (isl.), 18,138....C 4
Galicia (reg.), 2,592,786 ....B 1
Gata (cape) ....E 4
Gata (mts.) ....C 2
Genil (river) ....D 4
Gibraltar (strait) ....D 5
Gomera (isl.), 27,790 ....B 5
Gran Canaria (isl.), 400,837....B 5
Gredos (mts.) ....D 2
Guadalimar (river) ....E 3
Guadalquivir (river) ....C 4
Guadarrama (mts.) ....E 2
Guadarrama (river) ....F 4
Guadiana (river) ....D 3
Gúdar, Sierra da (mts.) ....F 2
Henares (river) ....G 4
Hierro (isl.), 7,957 ....A 5
Huelva (river) ....C 4
Ibiza (Iviza) (isl.), 34,495....G 3
Jalón (river) ....E 2
Jarama (river) ....E 2
Júcar (river) ....F 3
Lanzarote (isl.), 34,805 ....C 4
León (reg.), 1,295,700 ....D 1
Lima (river) ....B 2
Llobregat (river) ....H 2
Majorca (isl.), 363,199 ....H 3
Mallorca (Majorca) (isl.), 363,199 ....H 3
Mancha, La (dist.) ....E 3
Manzanares (river) ....F 4
Marismas, Las (marsh)....C 4
Menor, Mar (lagoon) ....F 4
Menorca (Minorca) (isl.), 42,954 ....J 2
Miño (river) ....B 1
Minorca (isl.), 42,954 ....J 2
Moncayo (mt.) ....F 2
Montserrat (mt.) ....G 2
Morena, Sierra (range) ....E 3
Mulhacén (mt.) ....E 4
Murcia (reg.), 1,175,835 ....F 3
Nao (cape) ....G 3
Navia (river) ....C 1
Nevada, Sierra (range) ....E 4
Orbigo (river) ....D 1
Ortegal (cape) ....B 1
Palma, La (isl.), 67,141....A 4
Peñalara (mt.) ....E 2
Penibética (mts.) ....E 4
Peñarroya (mt.) ....F 2
Perales (river) ....F 4
Perdido (mt.) ....G 1
Puigmal (mt.) ....H 1
Pyrenees (mts.) ....G 1
Rosas (gulf) ....H 1
Rouge (mt.) ....G 1
San Jorge (gulf) ....G 2
San Pedro (mts.) ....C 3
Sebollera (mt.) ....E 2
Segre (river) ....G 2
Segura (river) ....F 3
Sil (river) ....C 1
Tagus (Tajo) (river) ....D 3
Teide (peak) ....B 5
Tenerife (isl.), 387,767 ....B 5
Ter (river) ....H 1
Tinto (river) ....C 4
Toledo (mts.) ....E 3
Torote (river) ....G 4
Trafalgar (cape) ....C 4
Turia (river) ....F 3
Ulla (river) ....B 1
Urgel (plain) ....G 2
Valencia (gulf) ....G 3
Valencia (lagoon) ....G 3
Valencia (reg.), 2,553,272 ....F 3
Vascongadas (reg.), 1,533,762....E 1

*City and suburbs.

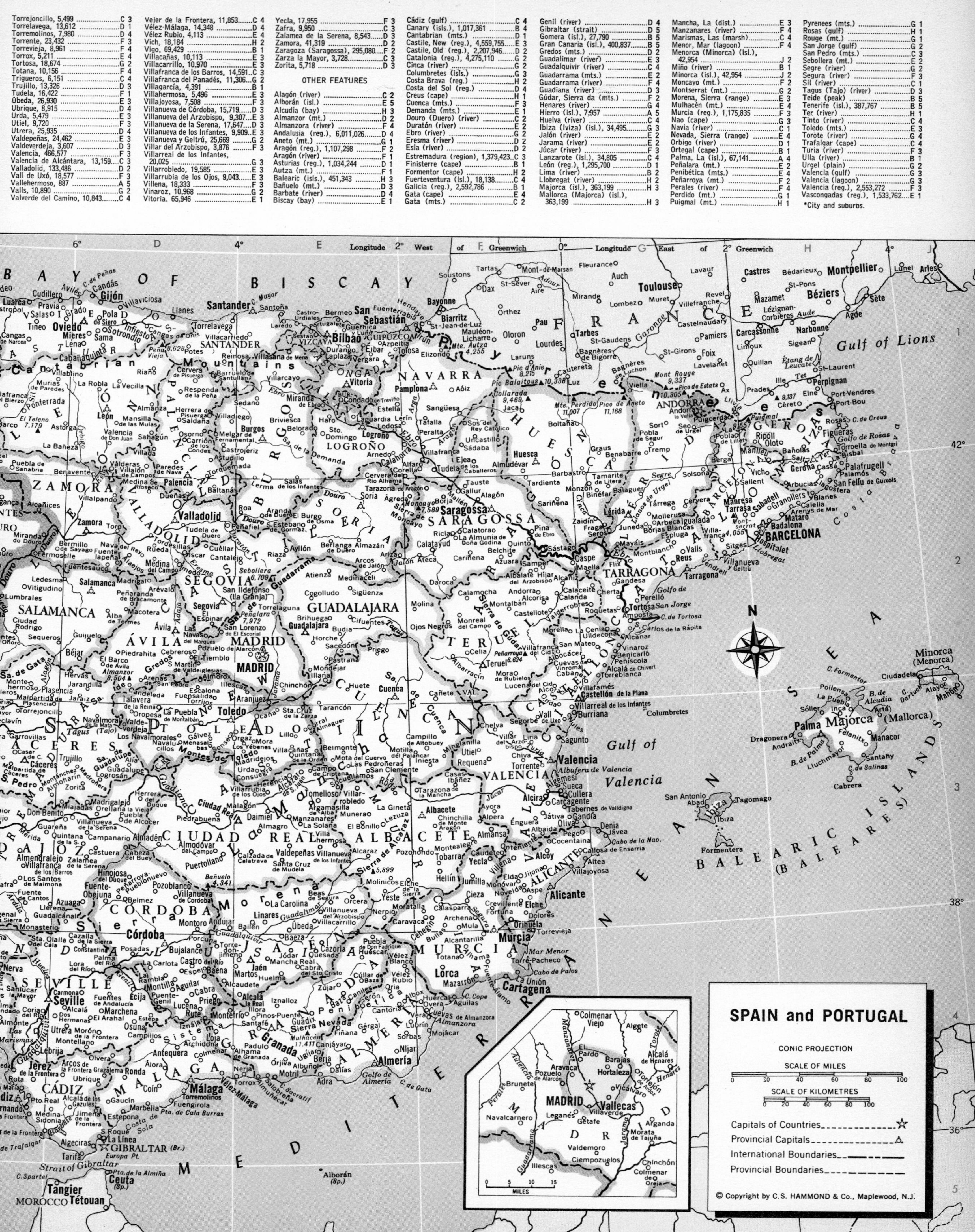

ITALY
CONIC PROJECTION
SCALE OF MILES
0 20 40 60 80 100
SCALE OF KILOMETERS
0 20 40 60 80 100
Capitals of Countries
Regional Capitals
Provincial Capitals
International Boundaries
Regional Boundaries
ITALY is divided for administrative purposes into 20 regions, shown on the map in separate colors. The regions are subdivided into provinces bearing the same names as their respective capitals, except:
PROVINCE
CAPITAL
MASSA-CARRARA
Massa
PESARO-URBINO
Pesaro
Copyright by C.S. HAMMOND & Co., N.Y.
SWITZERLAND
AUSTRIA
HUNGARY
YUGOSLAVIA
FRANCE
CORSICA
SARDINIA
SICILY
TUNISIA
MALTA
LIGURIAN SEA
TYRRHENIAN SEA
ADRIATIC SEA
IONIAN SEA
MEDITERRANEAN SEA
Gulf of Venice
Gulf of Genoa
Gulf of Taranto
Gulf of Gaeta
Gulf of Salerno
Gulf of Manfredonia
Gulf of Squillace
Gulf of Sant'Eufemia
Gulf of Tunis
Gulf of Hammamet
Strait of Sicily
Strait of Messina
Str. of Bonifacio
Malta Channel
TUSCAN ARCH.
LIPARI ISLANDS
EGADI ISLANDS
PONTINE ISLANDS
PELAGIE ISLANDS
Bern
Rome
Milan
Turin
Genoa
Venice
Trieste
Bologna
Florence
Naples
Bari
Palermo
Messina
Catania
Cagliari
Valletta
Tunis
VATICAN CITY
ROME and ENVIRONS

VATICAN CITY
AREA 109 acres
POPULATION 1,000

SAN MARINO
AREA 23.4 sq. mi.
POPULATION 19,000

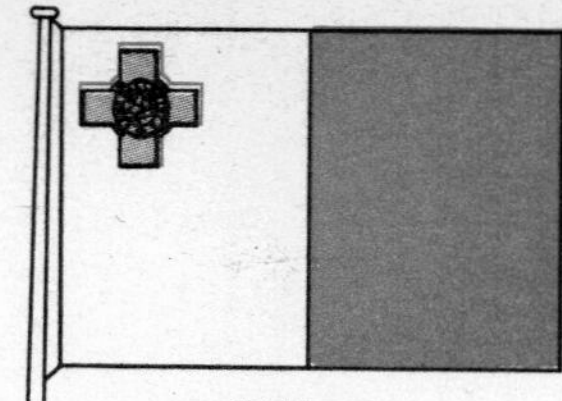

MALTA

AREA 122 sq. mi.
POPULATION 321,000
CAPITAL Valletta
LARGEST CITY Sliema
HIGHEST POINT 787 ft.
MONETARY UNIT Maltese pound
MAJOR LANGUAGES Maltese, English
MAJOR RELIGION Roman Catholicism

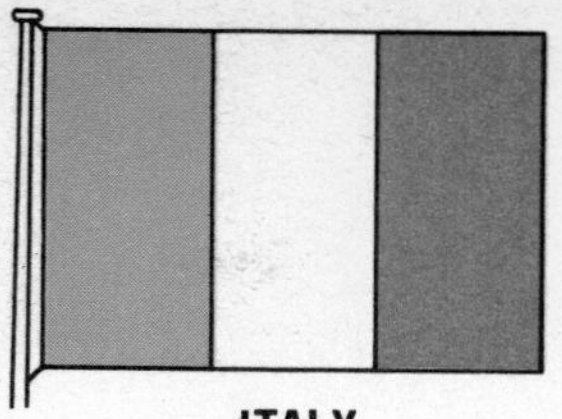

ITALY

AREA 116,303 sq. mi.
POPULATION 54,504,000
CAPITAL Rome
LARGEST CITY Rome
HIGHEST POINT Dufourspitze (Mte. Rosa) 15,203 ft.
MONETARY UNIT lira
MAJOR LANGUAGE Italian
MAJOR RELIGION Roman Catholicism

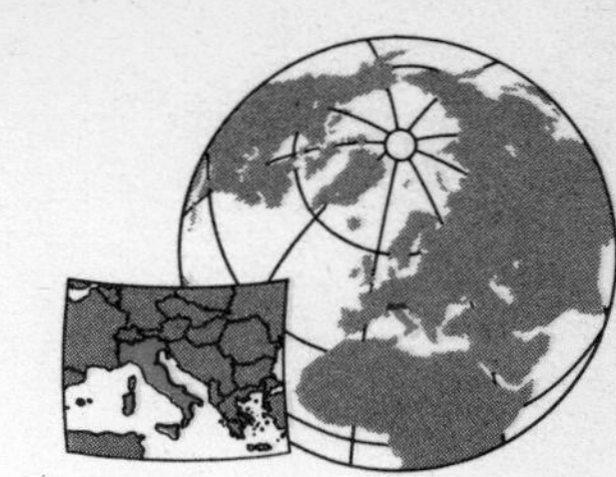

ITALY

REGIONS

Abruzzi, 1,206,266 ....D 3
Aosta, 100,959 ....A 2
Apulia, 3,421,217 ....F 4
Basilicata, 644,297 ....F 4
Calabria, 2,045,047 ....F 5
Campania, 4,760,759 ....E 4
Emilia-Romagna, 3,666,680 ....C 2
Friuli-Venezia Giulia, 1,204,298...D 1
Latium, 3,958,957 ....D 4
Liguria, 1,735,349 ....B 2
Lombardy, 7,406,152 ....B 2
Marche, 1,347,489 ....D 3
Molise, 358,052 ....E 4
Piedmont, 3,914,250 ....A 2
Puglia (Apulia), 3,421,217 ....F 4
Sardinia, 1,419,362 ....B 4
Sicily, 4,721,001 ....E 6
Trentino-Alto Adige, 785,967 ....C 1
Tuscany, 3,286,160 ....C 3
Umbria, 794,745 ....D 3
Venetia, 3,846,562 ....C 2

PROVINCES

Agrigento, 472,945 ....D 6
Alessandria, 478,613 ....B 2
Ancona, 405,709 ....D 3
Aosta, 100,959 ....A 2
Arezzo, 308,964 ....C 3
Ascoli Piceno, 335,627 ....D 3
Asti, 214,604 ....B 2
Avellino, 464,904 ....E 4
Bari, 1,263,245 ....F 4
Belluno, 234,921 ....D 1
Benevento, 313,020 ....E 4
Bergamo, 744,670 ....B 2
Bologna, 841,474 ....C 2
Bolzano, 373,863 ....C 1
Brescia, 882,949 ....C 2
Brindisi, 345,635 ....G 4
Cagliari, 754,965 ....B 5
Caltanissetta, 302,513 ....D 6
Campobasso, 358,052 ....E 4
Caserta, 649,327 ....E 4
Catania, 893,542 ....E 6
Catanzaro, 741,509 ....F 5
Chieti, 373,632 ....E 3
Como, 622,132 ....B 2
Cosenza, 694,398 ....F 5
Cremona, 351,160 ....B 2
Cuneo, 536,356 ....A 2
Enna, 229,126 ....E 6
Ferrara, 403,218 ....C 2
Florence, 1,012,703 ....C 3
Foggia, 665,286 ....E 4
Forlì, 521,128 ....D 2
Frosinone, 438,254 ....D 4
Genoa, 1,031,091 ....B 2
Gorizia, 137,745 ....D 2
Grosseto, 220.305 ....C 3
Imperia, 202,160 ....B 3
L'Aquila, 328,989 ....D 3
La Spezia, 239,256 ....B 2
Latina, 319,056 ....D 4
Lecce, 678,338 ....G 4
Leghorn, 310,210 ....C 3
Lucca, 365,540 ....C 3
Macerata, 291,412 ....D 3
Mantua, 387,255 ....C 2
Massa-Carrara, 202,981 ....C 2
Matera, 200,131 ....F 4
Messina, 685,260 ....E 5
Milan, 3,156,815 ....B 2
Modena, 511,355 ....C 2
Naples, 2,421,243 ....E 4
Novara, 460,190 ....B 2
Nuoro, 283,206 ....B 4
Padua, 694,017 ....C 2
Palermo, 1,111,397 ....D 5
Parma, 389,199 ....C 2
Pavia, 518,193 ....B 2
Perugia, 570,149 ....D 3
Pesaro e Urbino, 314,741 ....D 3
Pescara, 242,958 ....E 3
Piacenza, 291,059 ....B 2
Pisa, 362,396 ....C 3
Pistoia, 232,999 ....C 2
Pordenone, 241,724 ....D 2
Potenza, 444,166 ....E 4
Ragusa, 252,769 ....E 6
Ravenna, 329,559 ....D 2
Reggio di Calabria, 609,140....E 5
Reggio nell'Emilia, 379,688 ....C 2
Rieti, 162,405 ....D 3
Rome, 2,775,380 ....F 6
Rovigo, 277,811 ....C 2
Salerno, 912,265 ....E 4
Sassari, 381,191 ....B 4
Savona, 262,842 ....B 2
Siena, 270,062 ....C 3
Sondrio, 161,450 ....B 1
Syracuse, 345,777 ....E 6
Taranto, 468,713 ....F 4
Teramo, 260,687 ....D 3
Terni, 224,596 ....D 3
Trapani, 427,672 ....D 5
Trento, 412,104 ....C 1
Treviso, 607,616 ....D 2
Trieste, 298,645 ....E 2
Turin, 1,824,254 ....A 2
Udine, 526,184 ....D 1
Varese, 581,528 ....B 2
Venice, 749,173 ....D 2
Vercelli, 400,233 ....B 2
Verona, 667,517 ....C 2
Vicenza, 615,507 ....C 2
Viterbo, 263,862 ....C 3

CITIES and TOWNS

Acireale, 26,744 ....E 6
Acqui Terme, 14,070 ....B 2
Acri, 7,660 ....F 5
Adrano, 31,411 ....E 6
Adria, 11,456 ....D 2
Agira, 13,157 ....E 6
Agrigento, 46,947 ....D 6
Agropoli, 7,200 ....E 4
Alassio, 10,492 ....A 2
Alatri, 5,311 ....D 4
Alba, 16,396 ....B 2
Albano Laziale, 13,007 ....F 7
Albenga, 9,429 ....B 3
Albino, 6,875 ....B 2
Alcamo, 42,974 ....D 6
Alessandria, 65,908 ....B 2
Alghero, 22,139 ....B 4
Altamura, 41,528 ....F 4
Amalfi, 5,183 ....E 4
Amantea, 5,910 ....E 5
Ancona, 77,748 ....D 3
Andria, 69,499 ....F 4
Anzio, 12,102 ....D 4
Aosta, 28,637 ....A 2
Aprilia, 8,784 ....D 4
Aragona, 12,119 ....D 6
Arezzo, 43,868 ....C 3
Ariano Irpino, 11,302 ....E 4
Ascoli Piceno, 33,825 ....D 3
Assisi, 5,302 ....D 3
Asti, 44,455 ....B 2
Augusta, 25,774 ....E 6
Avellino, 31,744 ....E 4
Aversa, 40,245 ....E 4
Avezzano, 24,120 ....D 3
Avigliano, 5,119 ....E 4
Avola, 27,197 ....E 6
Bagheria, 31,435 ....D 5
Barcellona Pozzo di Gotto, 32,147 ....D 5
Bari, 293,963 ....F 4
Barletta, 67,419 ....F 4
Bassano del Grappa, 24,077....C 2
Belluno, 15,400 ....D 1
Benevento, 41,467 ....E 4
Bergamo, 110,666 ....B 2
Biancavilla, 19,858 ....E 6
Biella, 42,994 ....B 2
Bisceglie, 40,520 ....F 4
Bitonto, 34,160 ....F 4
Bitti, 5,623 ....B 4
Bologna, 443,178 ....C 2
Bolzano, 84,685 ....C 1
Bondeno, 6,413 ....C 2
Bonorva, 6,192 ....B 4
Bordighera, 9,045 ....A 3
Borgomanero, 11,843 ....B 2
Borgo San Lorenzo, 6,135 ....C 2
Bosa, 7,890 ....B 4
Bra, 14,472 ....A 2
Bracciano, 6,460 ....C 3
Brescia, 140,518 ....C 2
Bressanone, 10,095 ....C 1
Brindisi, 63,480 ....G 4
Bronte, 19,418 ....E 6
Busto Arsizio, 58,483 ....B 2
Cagliari, 172,925 ....B 5
Caltagirone, 37,634 ....E 6
Caltanissetta, 51,699 ....D 6
Camaiore, 7,130 ....C 3
Campobasso, 27,568 ....E 4
Campo Tures, 1,162 ....C 1
Canicatti, 29,613 ....E 6
Canosa di Puglia, 32,908 ....E 4
Cantù, 17,298 ....B 2
Capua, 13,334 ....E 4
Caravaggio, 9,938 ....B 2
Carbonia, 26,227 ....B 5
Carini, 15,486 ....D 5
Carloforte, 7,153 ....B 5
Carmagnola, 6,583 ....A 2
Carpi, 27,647 ....C 2
Carrara, 37,386 ....C 2
Casale Monferrato, 31,226 ....B 2
Casalmaggiore, 5,995 ....C 2
Cascina-Navacchio, 23,739 ....C 3
Caserta, 36,337 ....E 4
Cassano allo Ionio, 9,250 ....F 5
Cassino, 11,369 ....E 4
Castelfranco Veneto, 9,978 ....D 2
Castel Gandolfo, 2,861 ....F 7
Castellammare del Golfo, 16,581 ....D 5
Castellammare di Stabia, 49,064 ....E 4
Castel San Pietro Terme, 4,824..C 2
Castelvetrano, 30,009 ....D 6
Castrovillari, 13,063 ....F 5
Catania, 358,700 ....E 6
Catanzaro, 44,198 ....F 5
Cava de'Tirreni, 19,883 ....E 4
Cavarzere, 6,109 ....D 2
Cecina, 13,749 ....C 3
Cefalù, 10,360 ....E 5
Ceglie Messapico, 17,891 ....F 4
Celano, 9,743 ....D 3
Cerignola, 43,345 ....E 4
Cernobbio, 6,857 ....B 2
Cesena, 31,153 ....D 2
Cesenatico, 7,684 ....D 2
Chiari, 9,552 ....C 2
Chiavari, 22,835 ....B 2
Chieri, 15,358 ....A 2
Chieti, 31,374 ....E 3
Chioggia, 25,058 ....D 2
Chivasso, 11,806 ....A 2
Ciampino, 10,012 ....F 7
Cittadella, 5,698 ....C 2
Città di Castello, 15,564 ....D 3
Cittanova, 11,567 ....F 5
Cividale del Friuli, 7,698 ....D 1
Civitavecchia, 34,996 ....C 3
Clusone, 5,729 ....C 2
Codriopo, 5,064 ....D 2
Colle di Val d'Elsa, 7,329 ....C 3
Comacchio, 9,743 ....D 2
Comiso, 24,016 ....E 6
Como, 64,301 ....B 2
Conegliano, 16,910 ....D 2
Conversano, 15,543 ....F 4
Corato, 38,774 ....F 4
Cori, 6,930 ....F 7
Corigliano Calabro, 13,526 ....F 5
Corleone, 14,185 ....D 6
Correggio, 8,146 ....C 2
Cortina d'Ampezzo, 4,291 ....D 1
Cosenza, 70,201 ....F 5
Courmayeur, 1,013 ....A 2
Crema, 20,679 ....B 2
Cremona, 64,775 ....B 2
Crotone, 36,516 ....F 5
Cuneo, 32,978 ....A 2
Desenzano del Garda, 8,017 ....C 2
Domodossola, 15,097 ....B 1
Dorgali, 6,976 ....B 4
Eboli, 19,550 ....E 4
Empoli, 22,484 ....C 3
Enna, 26,206 ....E 6
Este, 11,007 ....C 2
Fabriano, 15,127 ....D 3
Faenza, 40,425 ....D 2
Fano, 24,591 ....D 3
Fasano, 17,990 ....F 4
Favara, 27,523 ....D 6
Feltre, 9,446 ....C 1
Fermo, 14,453 ....D 3
Ferrandina, 8,381 ....F 4
Ferrara, 90,419 ....C 2
Fidenza, 13,567 ....B 2
Finale Emilia, 6,711 ....C 2
Finale Ligure, 9,789 ....B 2
Firenze (Florence), 413,455....C 3
Fiumicino, 9,489 ....F 7
Florence, 413,455 ....C 3
Floridia, 16,104 ....E 6
Foggia, 108,682 ....E 4
Foligno, 23,094 ....D 3
Fondi, 14,991 ....D 4
Forlì, 65,376 ....D 2
Formia, 15,048 ....D 4
Fossano, 12,563 ....A 2
Francavilla Fontana, 27,629....F 4
Frascati, 12,602 ....F 6
Frosinone, 20,998 ....D 4
Gaeta, 20,436 ....D 4
Galatina, 19,654 ....G 4
Galatone, 13,487 ....F 4
Gallarate, 34,870 ....B 2
Gallipoli, 15,958 ....F 4
Gela, 54,526 ....E 6
Gemona, 7,698 ....D 1
Genoa (Genova), 747,794....B 2
Genzano di Roma, 11,666 ....F 7
Giarre, 11,859 ....E 6
Gioia del Colle, 23,734 ....F 4
Giovinazzo, 14,189 ....F 4
Giulianova, 11,220 ....E 3
Gorizia, 35,307 ....D 2
Gravina in Puglia, 30,615 ....F 4
Grosseto, 36,558 ....C 3
Grottaferrata, 5,356 ....F 7
Grottaglie, 22,218 ....F 4
Guastalla, 7,511 ....C 2
Gubbio, 9,730 ....D 3
Iesi, 26,018 ....D 3
Iglesias, 20,518 ....B 5
Imola, 32,148 ....C 2
Imperia, 30,522 ....B 3
Isernia, 9,689 ....E 4
Ivrea, 19,344 ....B 2
La Maddalena, 10,414 ....B 4
Lanciano, 15,182 ....E 3
Lanusei, 5,208 ....B 5
L'Aquila, 29,462 ....D 3
La Spezia, 111,768 ....B 2
Latina, 26,171 ....D 4
Lavello, 12,857 ....E 4
Lecce, 68,385 ....G 4
Lecco, 47,468 ....B 2
Leghorn, 152,517 ....C 3
Legnago, 10,126 ....C 2
Lendinara, 6,475 ....C 2
Lentini, 31,788 ....E 6
Leonforte, 17,690 ....E 6
Licata, 38,222 ....D 6
Lido di Ostia, 25,662 ....F 7
Lido di Venezia, 16,581 ....D 2
Lipari, 3,852 ....E 5
Livorno (Leghorn), 152,517....C 3
Lodi, 34,281 ....B 2
Lonigo, 5,774 ....C 2
Lucca, 45,398 ....C 3
Lucera, 24,399 ....E 4
Lugo, 16,550 ....D 2
Macerata, 27,054 ....D 3
Macomer, 7,782 ....B 4
Maglie, 12,205 ....G 4
Manduria, 23,971 ....F 4
Manfredonia, 34,583 ....F 4
Mantua, 55,806 ....C 2
Marino, 9,798 ....F 7
Marsala, 34,294 ....D 6
Martina Franca, 27,588 ....F 4
Massa, 46,992 ....C 2
Massafra, 18.884 ....F 4
Massa Marittima, 6,804 ....C 3
Matera, 36,727 ....F 4
Mazara del Vallo, 35,356 ....D 6
Mazzarino, 17,195 ....E 6
Melfi, 15,122 ....E 4
Menfi, 12,335 ....D 6
Merano, 29,196 ....C 1
Mesagne, 25,042 ....G 4
Messina, 202,095 ....E 5
Mestre, 138,822 ....D 2
Milan, 1,573,009 ....B 2
Milazzo, 14,034 ....E 5
Mirandola, 9,272 ....C 2
Mira Taglio, 8,380 ....D 2
Mistretta, 9,979 ....E 6
Modena, 107,814 ....C 2
Modica, 28,998 ....E 6
Mola di Bari, 22,397 ....F 4
Molfetta, 61,226 ....F 4
Moncalieri, 14,339 ....A 2
Mondovì Breo, 9,893 ....A 2
Monfalcone, 26,708 ....D 2
Monopoli, 25,161 ....F 4
Monreale, 18,881 ....D 5
Monselice, 7,766 ....C 2
Montebelluna, 6,088 ....D 2
Montefiascone, 6,428 ....D 3
Monterotondo, 9,616 ....F 6
Monte Sant'Angelo, 20,512 ....F 4
Montevarchi, 12,413 ....C 3
Monza, 79,715 ....B 2
Mortara, 12,243 ....B 2
Naples, 1,119,392 ....E 4
Nardò, 23,006 ....F 4
Narni, 5,551 ....D 3
Naro, 14,295 ....D 6
Nettuno, 16,187 ....D 4
Nicastro, 21,240 ....F 5
Nicosia, 16,624 ....E 6
Niscemi, 24,468 ....E 6
Nizza Monferrato, 6,229 ....B 2
Nocera Inferiore, 38,690 ....E 4
Noto, 21,586 ....E 6
Novara, 79,188 ....B 2
Novi Ligure, 23,349 ....B 2
Nuoro, 22,559 ....B 4
Olbia, 13,795 ....B 4
Oliena, 6,974 ....B 4
Orbetello, 6,800 ....C 3
Oristano, 16,305 ....B 5
Ortona, 11,315 ....E 3
Orvieto, 9,617 ....D 3
Osimo, 9,406 ....D 3
Ostuni, 25,190 ....F 4
Otranto, 3,510 ....G 4
Ozieri, 10,194 ....B 4
Pachino, 20,645 ....E 6
Padua, 169,298 ....C 2
Palazzolo Acreide, 10,802 ....E 6
Palermo, 531,306 ....D 5
Palestrina, 7,897 ....F 7
Palma di Montechiaro, 20,425....D 6
Palmi, 14,576 ....E 5
Pantelleria, 3,100 ....C 6
Paola, 9,701 ....E 5
Parma, 118,602 ....C 2
Partanna, 12,931 ....D 6
Partinico, 25,924 ....D 6
Paterno, 39,912 ....E 6
Patti, 6,748 ....E 5
Pavia, 69,581 ....B 2
Penne, 5,709 ....D 3
Pergine Valsugana, 4,877 ....C 1
Perugia, 52,534 ....D 3
Pesaro, 47,185 ....D 3
Pescara, 81,697 ....E 3
Pescia, 8,737 ....C 3
Piacenza, 78,985 ....B 2
Piazza Armerina, 23,915 ....E 6
Pietrasanta, 6,785 ....B 3
Pinerolo, 25,262 ....A 2
Piombino, 30,843 ....C 3
Piove di Sacco, 6,230 ....C 2
Pisa, 76,846 ....C 3
Pisticci, 11,469 ....F 4
Pistoia, 41,058 ....C 2
Poggibonsi, 12,932 ....C 3
Pont-Canavese, 4,071 ....A 2
Pontecorvo, 5,845 ....D 4
Pontremoli, 4,839 ....C 2
Popoli, 6,749 ....E 3
Pordenone, 29,461 ....D 2
Porto Civitanova, 18,288 ....D 3
Porto Empedocle, 16,110 ....D 6
Portoferraio, 6,318 ....C 3
Portofino, 735 ....B 2
Portogruaro, 8,913 ....D 2
Portomaggiore, 5,532 ....C 2
Porto Recanati, 4,986 ....D 3
Porto Torres, 10,108 ....B 4
Potenza, 34,216 ....F 4
Pozzallo, 11,862 ....E 6
Pozzuoli, 44,038 ....D 4
Prato, 75,402 ....C 3
Prima Porta, 9,978 ....F 6
Priverno, 9,154 ....D 4
Putignano, 15,976 ....F 4
Quartu Sant'Elena, 22,271 ....B 5
Ragusa, 50,718 ....E 6
Rapallo, 16,628 ....B 2
Ràvenna, 56,815 ....D 2
Recanati, 7,242 ....D 3
Reggio di Calabria, 93,964....E 5
Reggio nell'Emilia, 83,073 ....C 2
Rho, 27,586 ....B 2
Riesi, 17,899 ....E 6
Rieti, 21,278 ....D 3
Rimini, 72,720 ....D 2
Rionero in Vulture, 13,567 ....E 4
Riva, 7,626 ....C 2
Rome (cap.), 2,043,055 ....F 6
Rome, *2,656,104 ....F 6
Ronciglione, 5,772 ....C 3
Rossano, 13,323 ....F 5
Rovereto, 20,505 ....C 2
Rovigo, 22,804 ....C 2
Ruvo di Puglia, 23,216 ....F 4
Sala Consilina, 6,742 ....E 4
Salemi, 12,237 ....D 6
Salerno, 103,778 ....E 4
Salsomaggiore Terme, 10,376 ....B 2
Saluzzo, 11,991 ....A 2
Sambiase, 11,551 ....F 5
San Bartolomeo in Galdo, 8,745..E 4
San Benedetto del Tronto, 28,053 ....E 3
San Cataldo, 21,778 ....D 6
San Giovanni in Fiore, 16,528 ....F 5
San Giovanni in Persiceto, 8,692 ....C 2
San Marco in Lamis, 17,933 ....E 4
Sannicandro Garganico, 17,238 ....E 4
San Remo, 40,068 ....A 3
Sansepolcro, 10,063 ....D 3
San Severino Marche, 5,582 ....D 3
San Severo, 47,897 ....E 4
Santa Maria Capua Vetere, 29,925 ....E 4
Santeramo in Colle, 19,587....F 4
San Vito al Tagliamento, 5,278 D 2

(continued on following page)

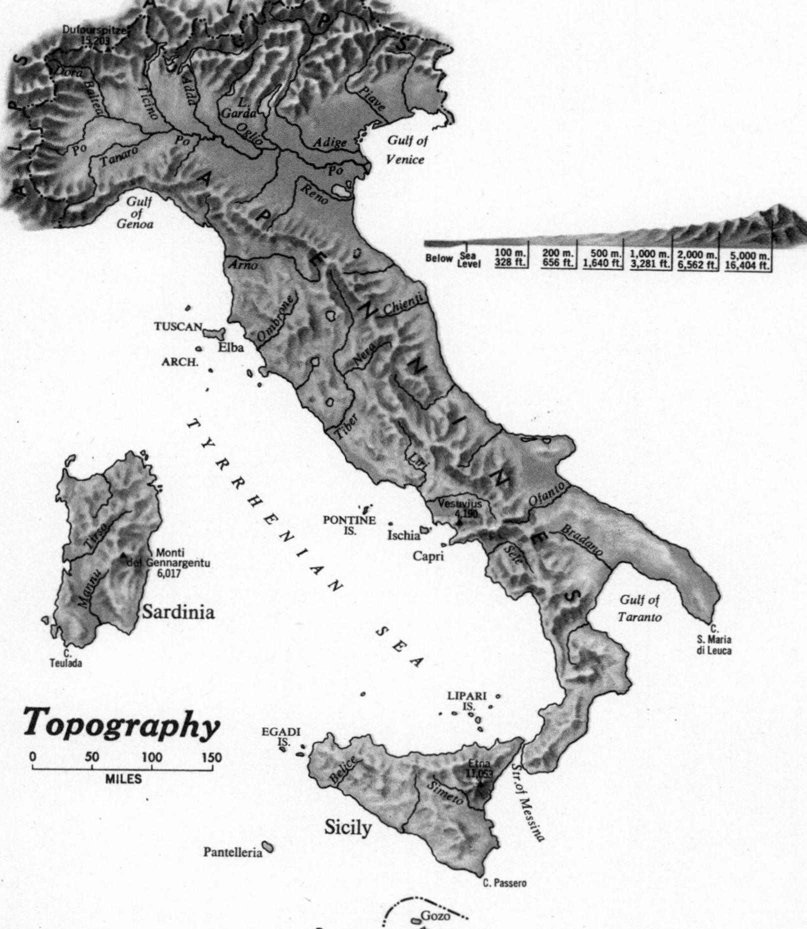

Topography

San Vito dei Normanni, 17,703..F 4
Saronno, 24,881 ....B 2
Sarroch, 2,439 ....B 5
Sassari, 76,322 ....B 4
Sassuolo, 19,429 ....C 2
Savigliano, 11,758 ....A 2
Savona, 64,480 ....B 2
Schio, 21,290 ....C 2
Sciacca, 27.668 ....D 6
Scicli, 18,727 ....E 6
Segni, 7,660 ....F 7
Senigallia, 21,194 ....D 3
Sesto Fiorentino, 20,148 ....C 3
Sestri Levante, 11,576 ....B 2
Settebagni, 1,601 ....F 6
Sezze, 7,368 ....D 4
Siderno, 7,251 ....F 5
Siena, 49,415 ....C 3
Siniscola, 6,018 ....B 4
Sinnai, 7,441 ....B 5
Siracusa (Syracuse), 74,783........E 6
Sondrio, 15,503 ....B 1
Sora, 10,160 ....D 4
Soresina, 8,866 ....C 2
Sorrento, 8,560 ....E 4
Sorso, 9,345 ....B 4
Spoleto, 17,005 ....D 3
Squinzano, 13,255 ....G 4
Stresa, 3,281 ....B 2
Sulmona, 18,286 ....E 3
Suzzara, 8,813 ....C 2
Syracuse, 74,783 ....E 6
Taormina, 5,530 ....E 6
Taranto, 175,803 ....F 4
Tarquinia, 8,965 ....C 3
Taurianova, 13,060 ....E 5
Tempio Pausania, 9,319 ....B 4
Teramo, 25,061 ....D 3
Termini Imerese, 23,375 ....D 6
Termoli, 9,324 ....E 3
Terni, 65,194 ....D 3
Terracina, 20,013 ....D 4
Terralba, 8,049 ....B 5
Tirano, 6,251 ....C 1
Tivoli, 25,129 ....F 6
Tolentino, 8,385 ....D 3
Torino (Turin), 1,032,555 ....A 2
Torre Annunziata, 59,370 ....E 4
Torre del Greco, 58,245 ....E 4
Torremaggiore, 16,872 ....E 4
Tortona, 18,790 ....B 2
Trani, 37,313 ....F 4
Trapani, 66,805 ....D 5
Trento, 50,174 ....C 1
Treviglio, 18,189 ....B 2
Treviso, 75,208 ....D 2
Tricase, 9,046 ....G 5
Trieste, 254,086 ....E 2
Trino, 7,753 ....B 2
Turin, 1,032,555 ....A 2
Udine, 78,963 ....D 1
Urbino, 7,405 ....D 3
Valdagno, 17,058 ....C 2
Valenza, 15,304 ....B 2
Varazze, 9,748 ....B 2
Varese, 47,896 ....B 2
Vasto, 13,080 ....E 3
Velletri, 20,153 ....F 7
Venice (Venezia), 137,566 ....D 2
Venosa, 12,183 ....E 4
Ventimiglia, 15,433 ....A 3
Verbania, 21,911 ....B 2
Vercelli, 48,954 ....B 2
Verona, 175,581 ....C 2
Viadana, 5,906 ....C 2
Viareggio, 41,021 ....C 3
Vibo Valentia, 13,854 ....F 5
Vicenza, 78,921 ....C 2
Vigevano, 51,551 ....B 2
Villacidro, 11,231 ....B 5
Villafranca, 8,529 ....C 2
Viterbo, 32,742 ....C 3
Vittoria, 42,088 ....E 6
Vittorio Veneto, 19,175 ....D 1
Vizzini, 10,630 ....E 6
Voghera, 30,267 ....B 2
Volterra, 11,460 ....C 3

OTHER FEATURES

Adda (river) ....B 2
Adige (river) ....C 2
Adriatic (sea) ....E 3
Albano (lake) ....F 7
Alicudi (isl.), 230 ....E 5
Aniene (river) ....F 6
Apennines (range) ....D 3
Apennines, Central (range) ....D 3
Apennines, Northern (range)........B 2
Apennines, Southern (range)........E 4
Arno (river) ....C 3
Asinara (isl.), 709 ....B 4
Bernina (mt.) ....B 1
Bernina (pass) ....C 1
Blanc (mt.) ....A 2
Bolsena (lake) ....C 3
Bonifacio (strait) ....B 4
Bracciano (lake) ....D 3
Brenner (pass) ....C 1
Cagliari (gulf) ....B 5
Capraia (isl.), 467 ....B 3
Capri (isl.), 10,845 ....E 4
Carbonara (cape) ....B 5
Carnic Alps (range) ....D 1
Castellammare (gulf) ....D 5
Chienti (river) ....D 3
Cimone (mt.) ....C 2
Circeo (cape) ....D 4
Coghinas (river) ....B 4
Como (lake) ....B 1
Cottian Alps (range) ....A 2
Crati (river) ....F 5
Dolomite Alps (range) ....C 1
Dora Baltea (river) ....A 2
Dora Riparia (river) ....A 2
Egadi (isls.), 6,133 ....C 6
Elba (isl.), 27,577 ....C 3
Etna (volcano) ....E 6
Favignana (isl.), 4,726 ....D 6
Filicudi (isl.), 447 ....E 5
Gaeta (gulf) ....D 4
Garda (lake) ....C 2
Gennargentu (mts.) ....B 5
Genoa (gulf) ....B 2
Giannutri (isl.), 3 ....C 3
Giglio (isl.), 2,256 ....C 3
Gorgona (isl.), 292 ....B 3
Graian Alps (range) ....A 2
Gran Paradiso (mt.) ....A 2
Great Saint Bernard (pass)........A 2
Ionian (sea) ....F 6
Ischia (isl.), 34,213 ....D 4
Iseo (lake) ....C 2
Julian Alps (range) ....D 1
Lampedusa (isl.), 4,387 ....D 7
Lepontine Alps (range)........B 1
Levanzo (isl.), 307 ....D 5
Ligurian (sea) ....B 3
Linosa (isl.), 424 ....D 7
Lipari (isl.), 8,844 ....E 5
Lipari (isls.), 13,774 ....E 5
Liri (river) ....D 4
Maggiore (lake) ....B 1
Malta (channel) ....E 6
Manfredonia (gulf) ....F 4
Mannu (river) ....B 5
Marettimo (isl.), 1,100 ....C 6
Maritime Alps (range) ....A 2
Marmolada (mt.) ....C 1
Mediterranean (sea) ....C 6
Messina (strait) ....E 6
Metauro (river) ....D 3
Mincio (river) ....C 2
Mont Cenis (tunnel) ....A 2
Montecristo (isl.), 8 ....C 3
Nera (river) ....D 3
Ofanto (river) ....E 4
Ombrone (river) ....C 3
Oristano (gulf) ....B 5
Orosei (gulf) ....B 4
Ortles (range) ....C 1
Otranto (strait) ....G 5
Ötztal Alps (range) ....C 1
Palmarola (isl.) ....D 4
Panarea (isl.), 272 ....E 5
Panaro (river) ....C 2
Pantelleria (isl.), 9,601 ....D 6
Parma (river) ....C 2
Pelagie (isls.), 4,811 ....D 7
Pennine Alps (range) ....A 2
Pescara (river) ....D 3
Pianosa (isl.), 878 ....C 3
Piave (river) ....D 2
Po (river) ....C 2
Policastro (gulf) ....E 5
Pompeii (ruins) ....E 4
Pontine (isls.), 5,732 ....D 4
Ponza (isl.), 4,660 ....D 4
Rosa (mt.) ....A 1
Salerno (gulf) ....E 4
Salina (isl.), 2,737 ....E 5
Salso (river) ....D 6
Sangro (river) ....E 4
San Pietro (isl.), 7,275 ....B 5
Santa Maria di Leuca (cape).....G 5
Sant'Antioco (isl.), 10,993 ....B 5
Sant'Eufemia (gulf) ....F 5
San Vito (cape) ....D 5
Sardinia (island), 1,400,103 ....B 4
Sele (river) ....E 4
Sicily (island), 4,683,076 ....E 6
Sicily (strait) ....D 6
Simeto (river) ....E 6
Spartivento (cape) ....B 5
Spartivento (cape) ....F 6
Squillace (gulf) ....F 5
Stromboli (isl.), 469 ....E 5
Stura (river) ....A 2
Tagliamento (river) ....D 1
Tanaro (river) ....B 2
Taranto (gulf) ....F 5
Testa del Gargano (cape) ....F 4
Teulada (cape) ....B 5
Tiber (river) ....D 3
Trasimeno (lake) ....D 3
Trebbia (river) ....B 2
Tremiti (isls.), 349 ....E 3
Trieste (gulf) ....D 2
Tuscan (arch.), 31,481 ....B 3
Tyrrhenian (sea) ....C 4
Ustica (isl.), 1,262 ....D 5
Varano (lake) ....F 3
Vaticano (cape) ....E 5
Venice (gulf) ....D 2
Ventotene (isl.), 811 ....D 4
Vesuvius (volcano) ....E 4
Volturno (river) ....E 4
Vulcano (isl.), 356 ....E 5

MALTA

CITIES and TOWNS

Sliema, 21,000 ....E 7
Valletta (cap.), 15,432 ....E 7
Victoria, 5,456 ....E 6

OTHER FEATURES

Gozo and Comino (isls.), 29,975..E 6
Malta (isl.), 288,200 ....E 7

SAN MARINO

CITIES and TOWNS

San Marino (cap.), 2,621 ....D 3
San Marino *3,817 ....D 3

VATICAN CITY

Vatican City, 1,000 ....B 6

*City and suburbs.

Agriculture, Industry and Resources

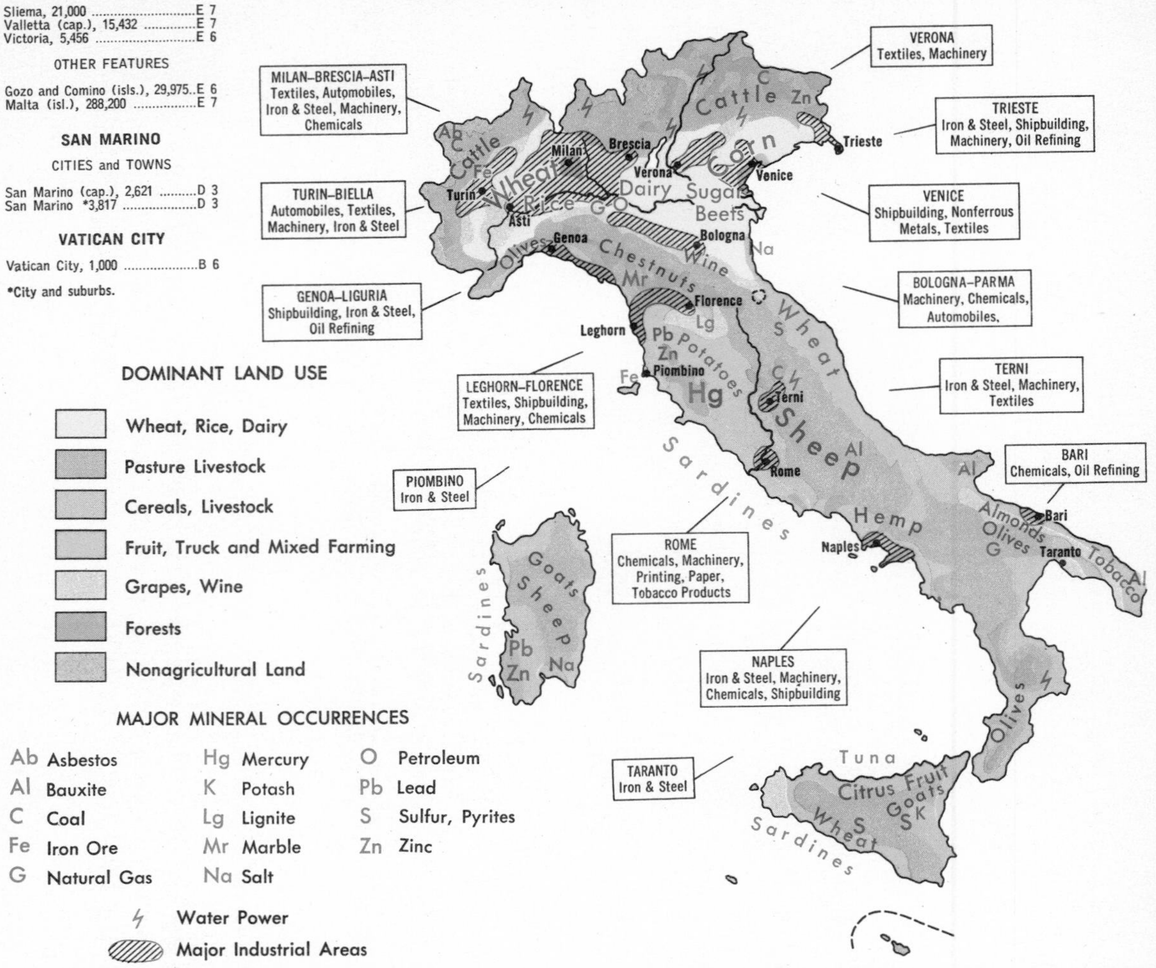

VERONA
Textiles, Machinery
MILAN–BRESCIA–ASTI
Textiles, Automobiles, Iron & Steel, Machinery, Chemicals
TRIESTE
Iron & Steel, Shipbuilding, Machinery, Oil Refining
TURIN–BIELLA
Automobiles, Textiles, Machinery, Iron & Steel
VENICE
Shipbuilding, Nonferrous Metals, Textiles
GENOA–LIGURIA
Shipbuilding, Iron & Steel, Oil Refining
BOLOGNA–PARMA
Machinery, Chemicals, Automobiles.
LEGHORN–FLORENCE
Textiles, Shipbuilding, Machinery, Chemicals
TERNI
Iron & Steel, Machinery, Textiles
PIOMBINO
Iron & Steel
BARI
Chemicals, Oil Refining
ROME
Chemicals, Machinery, Printing, Paper, Tobacco Products
NAPLES
Iron & Steel, Machinery, Chemicals, Shipbuilding
TARANTO
Iron & Steel
Milan
Brescia
Verona
Venice
Trieste
Turin
Asti
Genoa
Bologna
Florence
Leghorn
Piombino
Terni
Rome
Naples
Bari
Taranto
Cattle
Wheat
Rice
Corn
Dairy
Sugar Beets
Olives
Chestnuts
Wine
Potatoes
Sheep
Hemp
Almonds
Tobacco
Goats
Sardines
Tuna
Citrus Fruit
DOMINANT LAND USE
Wheat, Rice, Dairy
Pasture Livestock
Cereals, Livestock
Fruit, Truck and Mixed Farming
Grapes, Wine
Forests
Nonagricultural Land
MAJOR MINERAL OCCURRENCES
Ab Asbestos
Al Bauxite
C Coal
Fe Iron Ore
G Natural Gas
Hg Mercury
K Potash
Lg Lignite
Mr Marble
Na Salt
O Petroleum
Pb Lead
S Sulfur, Pyrites
Zn Zinc
Water Power
Major Industrial Areas

THE MEDITERRANEAN
SCALE OF MILES
SCALE OF KILOMETRES
Capitals of Countries
Canals
© C. S. HAMMOND & Co., Maplewood, N. J.
ATLANTIC OCEAN
Bay of Biscay
MEDITERRANEAN SEA
BLACK SEA
TYRRHENIAN SEA
IONIAN SEA
AEGEAN SEA
ADRIATIC SEA
PARIS
MADRID
ROME
Milan
Turin
Genoa
Naples
Palermo
Barcelona
Marseille
Lisbon
Algiers
Tunis
Tripoli
Benghazi
Alexandria
CAIRO
Athens
Istanbul
Ankara
Budapest
Belgrade
Bucharest
Sofia
Beirut
Casablanca
MOROCCO
ALGERIA
LIBYA
EGYPT
TURKEY
SPAIN
FRANCE
PORTUGAL
ITALY
Longitude West of Greenwich
Longitude East of Greenwich
Tropic of Cancer

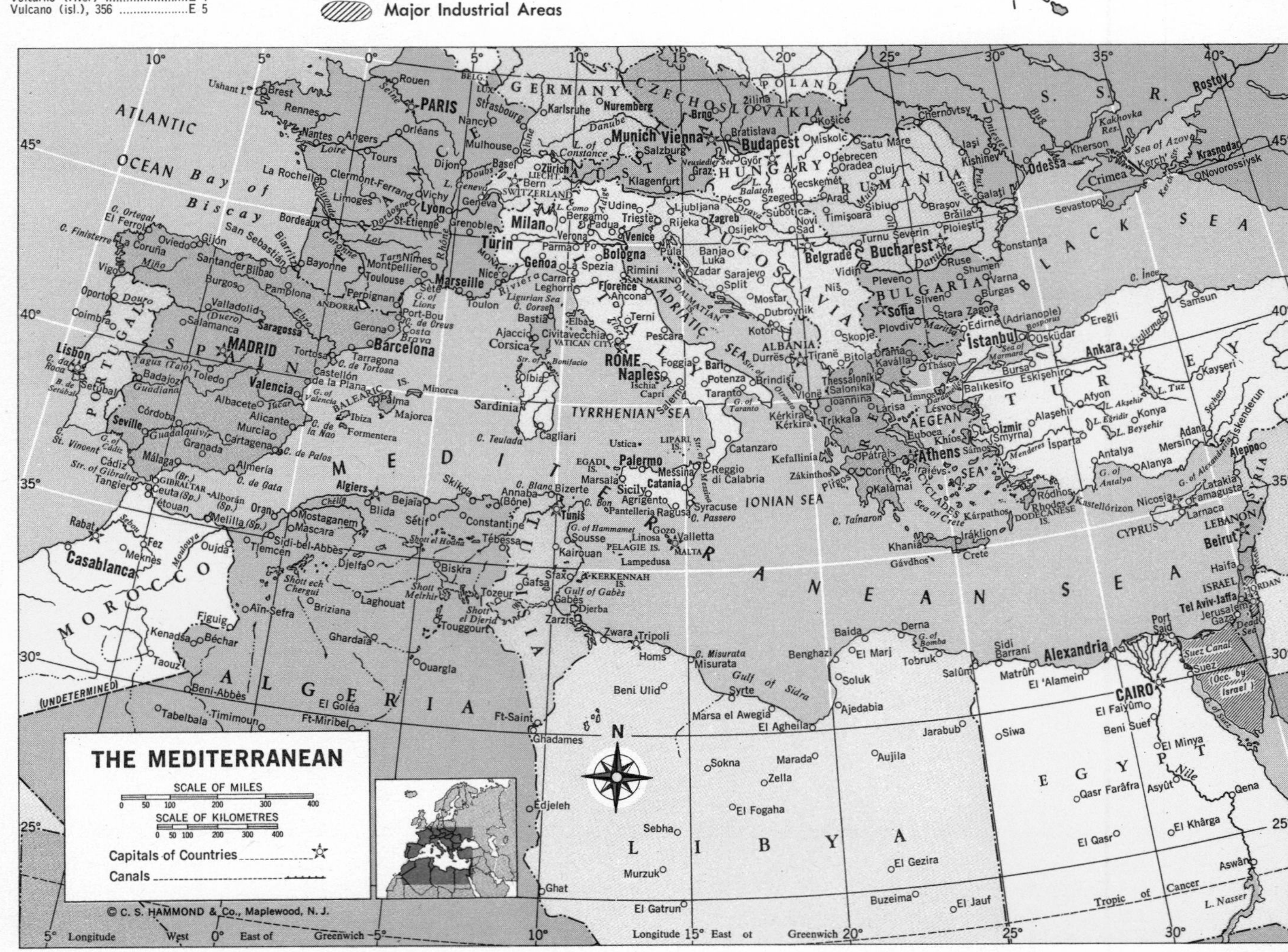

SWITZERLAND

AREA 15,941 sq. mi.
POPULATION 6,230,000
CAPITAL Bern
LARGEST CITY Zürich
HIGHEST POINT Dufourspitze (Mte. Rosa) 15,203 ft.
MONETARY UNIT Swiss franc
MAJOR LANGUAGES German, French, Italian, Romansch
MAJOR RELIGIONS Protestantism, Roman Catholicism

LIECHTENSTEIN

AREA 61 sq. mi.
POPULATION 21,000
CAPITAL Vaduz
LARGEST CITY Vaduz
HIGHEST POINT Naafkopf 8,445 ft.
MONETARY UNIT Swiss franc
MAJOR LANGUAGE German
MAJOR RELIGION Roman Catholicism

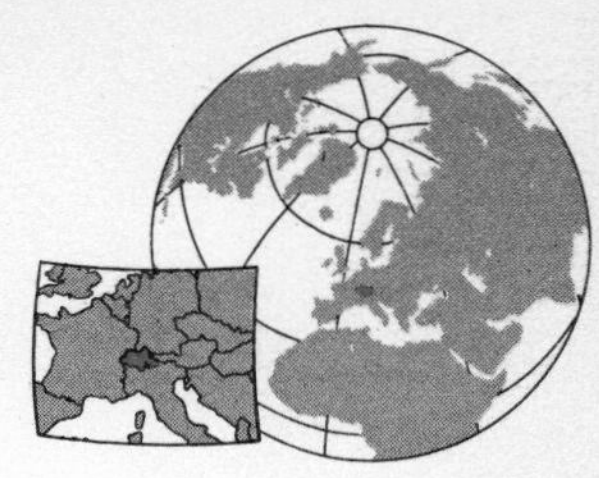

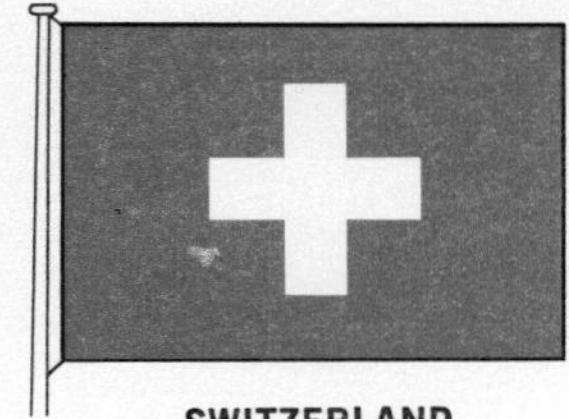

SWITZERLAND

LIECHTENSTEIN

LANGUAGES

Basel
Zürich
St. Gallen
Biel
Lucerne
Bern
Chur
Fribourg
Lausanne
St. Moritz
Geneva
Sion
Bellinzona

German
French
Italian
Romansch

Switzerland is a multilingual nation with four official languages. 70% of the people speak German, 19% French, 10% Italian and 1% Romansch.

SWITZERLAND

CANTONS

Aargau, 397,000 ....F 2
Appenzell, Ausser-Rhoden, (canton), 50,000 ....H 2
Appenzell, Inner-Rhoden, (canton), 13,500 ....H 2
Baselland (canton), 177,900 ....E 2
Baselstadt (canton), 237,300 ....E 1
Bern, 958,000 ....D 2
Fribourg, 163,000 ....D 3
Geneva, 304,400 ....B 4
Glarus, 42,000 ....H 3
Graubünden (Grisons), 155,000 ....J 3
Luzern (Lucerne), 274,000 ....F 2
Neuchâtel, 161,000 ....C 3
Nidwalden, 25,000 ....F 3
Obwalden, 25,000 ....F 3
Sankt Gallen, 363,000 ....H 2
Schaffhausen, 72,000 ....G 1
Schwyz, 84,800 ....G 2
Solothurn (Soleure), 220,000 ....E 2
Thurgau, 183,000 ....H 1
Ticino, 220,000 ....G 4
Uri, 33,000 ....G 3
Valais, 191,000 ....E 4
Vaud, 486,000 ....C 3
Zug, 61,000 ....G 2
Zürich, 1,048,000 ....G 2

CITIES and TOWNS

Aadorf, 2,258 ....G 2
Aarau, 17,400 ....F 2
Aarau, *47,800 ....F 2
Aarberg, 2,355 ....D 2
Aarburg, 5,302 ....E 2
Adelboden, 2,881 ....E 3
Aeschi bei Spiez, 1,319 ....E 3
Affoltern am Albis, 4,904 ....F 2
Affoltern im Emmental, 1,206....E 2
Aigle, 4,381 ....C 4
Airolo, 2,023 ....G 3
Alle, 1,471 ....D 2
Allschwil, 15,500 ....D 1
Alpnach, 3,211 ....F 3
Altdorf, 7,477 ....G 3
Altstätten, 8,751 ....J 2
Amriswil, 6,752 ....H 1
Andermatt, 1,523 ....G 3
Appenzell, 5,082 ....H 2
Arbedo-Castione, 1,467 ....G 4
Arbon, 13,100 ....H 1
Ardon, 1,432 ....D 4
Arlesheim, 5,219 ....E 2
Arosa, 2,600 ....J 3
Arth, 6,321 ....F 2
Ascona, 3,053 ....G 4
Attalens, 1,023 ....C 3
Aubonne, 1,766 ....B 4
Avenches, 1,776 ....D 3
Baar, 9,114 ....F 2
Baden, 14,900 ....F 2
Baden, *54,500 ....F 2
Bad Ragaz, 2,699 ....H 2
Balerna, 3,040 ....G 5
Balsthal, 5,735 ....E 2
Bäretswil, 2,577 ....G 2
Basel, 213,200 ....E 1
Basel, *364,800 ....E 1
Bassecourt, 2,284 ....D 2
Bätterkinden, 1,916 ....E 2
Bauma, 3,214 ....G 2
Beatenberg, 1,303 ....E 3
Beckenried, 2,042 ....G 3
Beinwil am See, 2,346 ....F 2
Bellinzona, 14,900 ....H 4
Bellinzona, *25,700 ....H 4
Belp, 4,922 ....D 3
Bergün-Bravuogn, 551 ....J 3
Bern (cap.), 166,800 ....D 3
Bern, *258,000 ....D 3
Beromünster, 1,443 ....F 2
Bex, 4,667 ....D 4
Biasca, 3,349 ....H 4
Biberist, 7,188 ....D 2
Biel (Bienne), 67,800 ....D 2
Biel, *87,000 ....D 2
Bière, 1,166 ....B 3
Binningen, 13,800 ....D 1
Bischofszell, 3,811 ....H 1
Blumenstein, 1,121 ....E 3
Bodio, 1,276 ....G 4
Bolligen, 19,400 ....E 3
Boltigen, 1,691 ....D 3
Boncourt, 1,493 ....C 2
Bönigen, 1,883 ....E 3
Boswil; 1,663 ....F 2
Boudry, 3,086 ....C 3
Bourg-Saint-Pierre, 524 ....D 5
Breil-Brigels, 1,272 ....H 3
Breitenbach, 1,851 ....E 2
Bremgarten, 4,555 ....F 2
Brienz, 2,864 ....F 3
Brig, 4,647 ....E 4
Brissago, 1,845 ....G 4
Brittnau, 3,070 ....E 2
Brugg, 6,683 ....F 2
Brusio, 1,445 ....K 4
Bubendorf, 1,690 ....E 2
Bubikon, 2,612 ....G 2
Buchs, 6,345 ....H 2
Bülach, 8,188 ....G 1
Bulle, 5,983 ....D 3
Buochs, 2,733 ....F 3
Büren an der Aare, 2,432....D 2
Burgdorf, 15,600 ....E 2
Bürglen, 3,175 ....G 3
Bürglen, 1,899 ....H 1
Bussigny-près-Lausanne, 2,381....B 3
Bütschwil, 3,414 ....H 2
Carouge, 15,600 ....B 4
Castagnola, 3,775 ....G 4
Cazis, 1,553 ....H 3
Cernier, 1,545 ....C 2
Chalais, 1,597 ....E 4
Cham, 6,483 ....F 2
Chamoson, 2,088 ....D 4
Charmey, 1,144 ....D 3
Châteaux-d'Oex, 3,378 ....D 4
Châtel-Saint-Denis, 2,666 ....C 3
Chavornay, 1,414 ....C 3
Chexbres, 1,449 ....C 3
Chiasso, 7,377 ....G 5
Chur, 29,100 ....J 3
Churwalden, 877 ....J 3
Coire (Chur), 29,100 ....J 3
Conthey, 3,563 ....D 4
Coppet, 774 ....B 4
Corcelles-près-Payerne, 1,253 ....C 3
Corgémont, 1,414 ....D 2
Cossonay, 1,284 ....C 3
Courgenay, 1,666 ....D 2
Courroux, 1,667 ....D 2
Court, 1,493 ....D 2
Courtelary, 1,330 ....C 2
Courtételle, 1,618 ....D 2
Couvet, 3,450 ....C 3
Cully, 1,375 ....C 4
Därstetten, 900 ....D 3
Davos (Dorf and Platz), 9,588 ..J 3
Degersheim, 3,221 ....H 2
Delémont, 9,542 ....D 2
Derendingen, 4,463 ....E 2
Diemtigen, 1,934 ....D 3
Diessenhofen, 2,222 ....G 1
Dietikon, 20,600 ....F 2
Disentis-Mustèr, 2,376 ....G 3
Dombresson, 1,040 ....C 2
Dornach, 4,260 ....E 2
Dübendorf, 17,100 ....G 2
Düdingen, 4,248 ....D 3
Dürnten, 4,271 ....G 2
Dürrenroth, 1,221 ....E 2
Ebnat-Kappel, 4,979 ....H 2
Echallens, 1,428 ....C 3
Egg, 3,018 ....G 2
Eggiwil, 2,591 ....E 3
Eglisau, 1,911 ....G 1
Egnach, 3,483 ....H 1
Einsiedeln, 8,792 ....G 2
Elgg, 2,643 ....G 2
Emmem, 21,400 ....F 2
Engelberg, 2,646 ....F 3
Engi, 1,064 ....H 3
Ennenda, 3,076 ....H 2
Entlebuch, 3,318 ....F 3
Erlenbach im Simmental, 1,471..E 3
Ermatingen, 1,857 ....H 1
Erstfeld, 4,126 ....G 3
Eschenbach, 2,866 ....G 2
Escholzmatt, 3,257 ....E 3
Estavayer-le-Lac, 2,583 ....C 3
Evolène, 1,786 ....D 4
Faido, 1,441 ....G 4

(continued on following page)

Agriculture, Industry and Resources

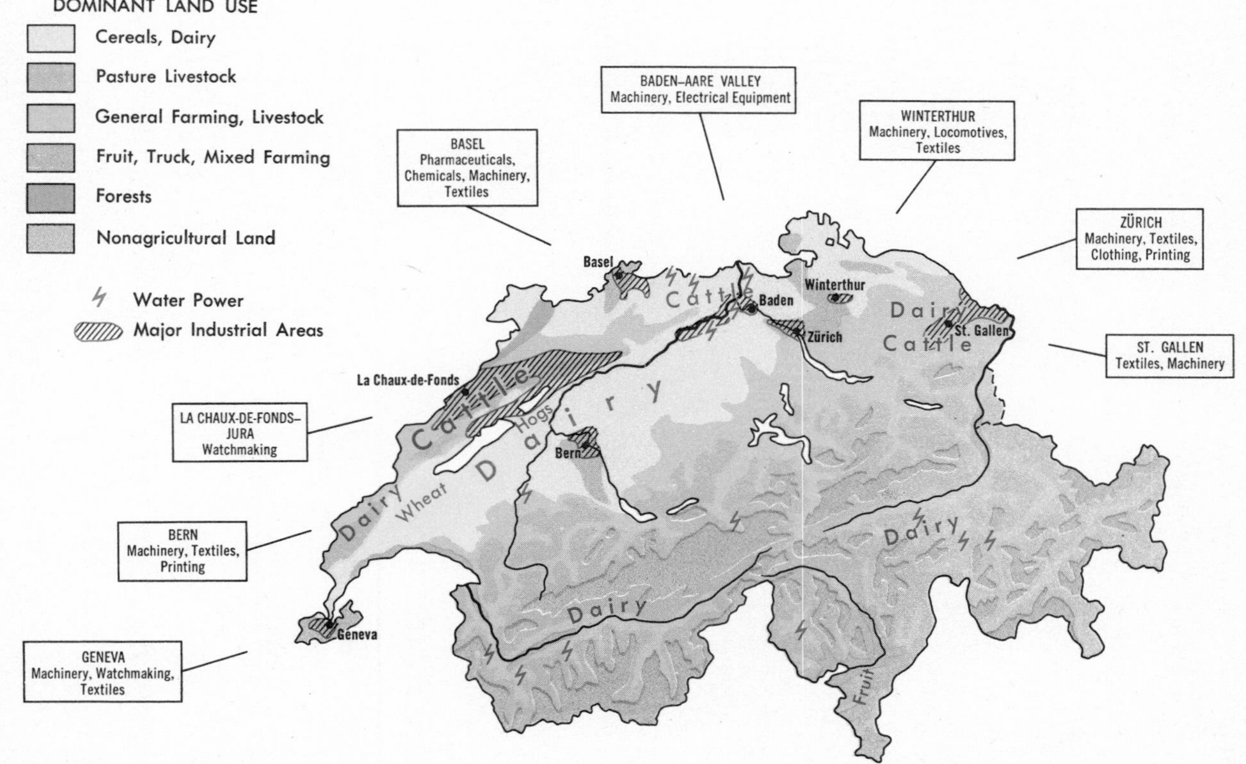

38 Switzerland and Liechtenstein

(continued)

Topography

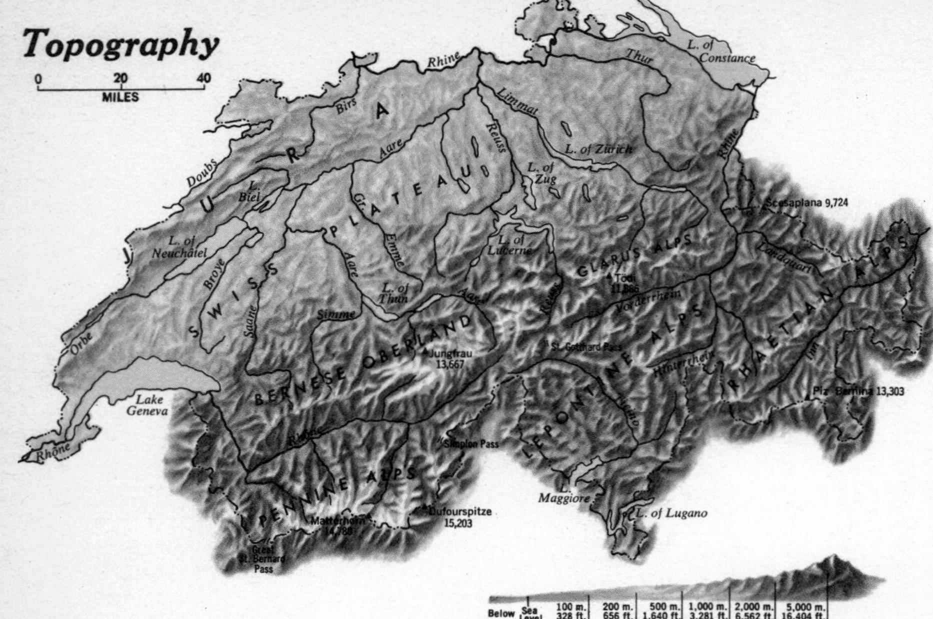

SWITZERLAND (continued)

Flawil, 7,256 ... H 2
Fleurier, 3,814 ... C 3
Flims, 1,444 ... H 3
Flüelen, 1,717 ... G 3
Flums, 4,462 ... H 2
Frauenfeld, 16,800 ... G 1
Fribourg, 38,500 ... D 3
Fribourg, *47,300 ... D 3
Frick, 2,123 ... E 1
Frutigen, 5,565 ... E 3
Fully, 3,419 ... D 4
Gais, 2,488 ... H 2
Gelterkinden, 3,870 ... E 2
Geneva (Genève), 169,500 ... B 4
Geneva, *307,500 ... B 4
Gersau, 1,754 ... G 2
Gimel, 1,091 ... B 3
Giornico, 1,063 ... G 4
Giswil, 2,656 ... F 3
Giubiasco, 4,281 ... H 4
Gland, 1,545 ... B 4
Glarus, 5,852 ... H 2
Glattfelden, 2,426 ... F 1
Gordola, 1,794 ... G 4
Göschenen, 1,284 ... G 3
Gossau, 9,731 ... H 2
Grabs, 4,218 ... H 2
Grandson, 2,091 ... C 3
Gränichen, 4,411 ... F 2
Grenchen, 19,800 ... D 2
Grenchen, *23,400 ... D 2
Grindelwald, 3,244 ... E 3
Grossandelfingen, 1,102 ... G 1
Grosswangen, 2,373 ... F 2
Gruyères, 1,349 ... D 3
Gsteig, 937 ... D 4
Guggisberg, 2,021 ... D 3
Gurtnellen, 1,048 ... G 3
Hallau, 1,966 ... F 1
Heiden, 3,158 ... H 2
Heimberg, 2,125 ... E 3
Hemberg, 1,011 ... H 2
Henau (Uzwil), 7,828 ... H 2
Hérémence, 1,868 ... D 4
Herisau, 15,500 ... H 2
Hermance, 512 ... B 4
Herzogenbuchsee, 4,641 ... E 2
Hinwil, 4,811 ... G 2
Hochdorf, 4,452 ... F 2
Horgen, 15,300 ... G 2
Hospental, 289 ... F 3
Huttwil, 4,664 ... E 2
Igis, 3,902 ... J 3
Ilanz, 1,843 ... H 3
Illnau, 6,160 ... G 2
Ingenbohl, 5,046 ... G 2
Innertkirchen, 1,230 ... F 3
Ins, 2,486 ... D 2
Interlaken, 4,738 ... E 3
Jegenstorf, 1,397 ... D 2
Jenaz, 1,143 ... J 3
Jona, 5,686 ... G 2
Jungfraujoch ... E 3
Kaltbrunn, 2,527 ... H 2
Kandersteg, 937 ... E 4
Kerns, 3,553 ... F 3
Kerzers, 2,228 ... D 3
Kilchberg, 6,784 ... F 2
Kirchberg, 3,304 ... E 2
Kirchberg, 5,554 ... G 2
Kleinlützel, 1,269 ... D 2
Klingnau, 2,192 ... F 1
Klosters, 3,181 ... J 3
Kloten, 8,446 ... G 2
Koblenz, 1,114 ... F 1
Kölliken, 3,007 ... F 2
Köniz, 30,600 ... D 3
Kreuzlingen, 14,900 ... H 1
Kriens, 17,200 ... F 2
Küsnacht, 12,800 ... G 2
Küssnacht, 12,400 ... F 2
Küttigen, 3,457 ... F 2
L'Abbaye, 1,124 ... B 3
La Chaux-de-Fonds, 42,800 ... C 2
Lachen, 3,913 ... G 2
La Neuveville, 3,216 ... D 2
Langenthal, 12,400 ... E 2
Langnau, 9,201 ... E 3
Langnau am Albis, 2,850 ... G 2
La Roche, 1,043 ... D 3
La Sarraz, 1,026 ... C 3
La Tour-de-Peilz, 6,820 ... C 4
Läufelfingen, 1,176 ... E 2
Laufen, 3,955 ... D 2
Laufenburg, 1,850 ... F 1
Laupen, 1,607 ... D 3
Lauperswil, 2,652 ... E 3
Lausanne, 138,300 ... C 3
Lausanne, *214,900 ... C 3
Lauterbrunnen, 3,216 ... E 3
Le Brassus (Le Chenit), 5,242 ... B 3
Le Châble, 4,237 ... D 4
Le Lieu, 970 ... B 3
Le Locle, 15,100 ... C 2
Le Mont, 1,719 ... C 3
Lengnau, 3,524 ... D 2
Lenk, 1,900 ... D 4
Le Noirmont, 1,559 ... C 2
Lens, 1,743 ... D 4
Lenzburg, 6,378 ... F 2
Les Bois, 1,098 ... C 2
Les Ponts-de-Martel, 1,429 ... C 2
Les Verrières, 1,084 ... B 3
Leuk, 2,546 ... E 4
Leukerbad, 619 ... E 4
Leysin, 2,241 ... C 4
Liestal, 11,300 ... E 2
Linthal, 2,645 ... H 3
Littau, 8,715 ... F 2
Locarno, 12,200 ... G 4
Locarno, *21,000 ... G 4
Lucens, 1,620 ... C 3
Lucerne, 73,000 ... F 2
Lucerne, *148,500 ... F 2
Lugano, 21,100 ... G 4
Lugano, *50,000 ... G 4
Lungern, 1,794 ... F 3
Luthern, 1,801 ... E 2
Lutry, 3,481 ... C 3
Lützelflüh, 3,960 ... E 3
Luzein, 1,013 ... J 3
Luzern (Lucerne), 73,000 ... F 2
Lyss, 5,616 ... D 2
Maienfeld, 1,488 ... J 2
Malans, 1,358 ... J 3
Malters, 4,579 ... F 2
Malvaglia, 1,120 ... H 4
Männedorf, 6,182 ... G 2
Marbach, 1,347 ... E 3
Martigny, 7,593 ... C 4
Meilen, 8,203 ... G 2
Meiringen, 3,749 ... F 3
Melchnau, 1,511 ... E 2
Melide, 1,046 ... G 5
Mellingen, 1,941 ... F 2
Mels, 5,254 ... H 2
Mendrisio, 5,100 ... G 5
Menzingen, 3,340 ... G 2
Menznau, 2,275 ... E 2
Mesocco, 1,324 ... H 4
Minusio, 3,663 ... G 4
Möhlin, 4,681 ... E 1
Mollis, 2,303 ... H 2
Montana-Vermala, 1,543 ... E 4
Monthey, 6,834 ... C 4
Montreux-Le Châtelard, 20,100 ... C 4
Morges, 8,420 ... B 3
Moudon, 2,806 ... C 3
Moutier, 7,472 ... D 2
Müllheim, 1,475 ... G 1
Mümliswil-Ramiswil, 2,714 ... E 2
Münchenbuchsee, 3,652 ... E 2
Münsingen, 6,051 ... E 3
Muotathal, 2,592 ... G 3
Muri, 3,957 ... F 2
Muri bei Bern, 7,855 ... E 3
Murten, 3,330 ... D 3
Müstair, 717 ... K 3
Muttenz, 14,000 ... E 1
Näfels, 3,617 ... H 2
Naters, 3,797 ... E 4
Nebikon, 1,206 ... F 2
Nesslau, 2,002 ... H 2
Netstal, 2,925 ... H 2
Neuchâtel, 36,300 ... C 3
Neuchâtel, *52,600 ... C 3
Neuenegg, 2,921 ... D 3
Neuhausen am Rheinfall, 11,800 ... G 1
Neunkirch, 1,208 ... F 1
Niederbipp, 3,141 ... E 2
Niederurnen, 3,347 ... G 2
Niederweningen, 1,027 ... F 1
Nunningen, 1,372 ... E 2
Nyon, 7,643 ... B 4
Oberägeri, 2,656 ... G 2
Oberburg, 3,030 ... E 2
Oberdiessbach, 1,927 ... E 3
Oberdorf, 1,132 ... E 2
Oberriet, 5,498 ... J 2
Obersaxen, 710 ... H 3
Oberuzwil, 4,394 ... H 2
Oensingen, 2,907 ... E 2
Ollon, 4,126 ... D 4
Olten, 21,900 ... E 2
Olten, *47,100 ... E 2
Orbe, 3,824 ... C 3
Ormont-Dessous, 996 ... D 4
Orsières, 2,281 ... D 4
Payerne, 6,024 ... C 3
Peseux, 4,933 ... C 3
Pfäffikon, 5,735 ... G 2
Pfaffnau, 2,575 ... E 2
Pieterlen, 2,978 ... D 2
Pontresina, 1,067 ... J 3
Porrentruy, 7,095 ... C 2
Poschiavo, 3,743 ... J 4
Pratteln, 9,492 ... E 1
Pully, 15,900 ... C 4
Quinto, 1,365 ... G 3
Rafz, 1,925 ... G 1
Ramsen, 1,181 ... G 1
Rapperswil, 7,585 ... G 2
Raron, 1,077 ... E 4
Rechthalten, 1,015 ... D 3
Regensdorf, 4,997 ... F 2
Reichenbach, 2,829 ... E 3
Reiden, 2,795 ... F 2
Reigoldswil, 1,192 ... E 2
Reinach, 5,174 ... F 2
Renens, 15,200 ... C 3
Rheinau, 2,363 ... G 1
Rheineck, 3,047 ... J 2
Rheinfelden, 5,197 ... E 1
Richterswil, 5,842 ... G 2
Riehen, 20,100 ... E 1
Riggisberg, 1,949 ... E 3
Riva San Vitale, 1,358 ... G 5
Rivera, 950 ... G 4
Roggwil, 3,420 ... E 2
Rohrbach, 1,534 ... E 2
Rolle, 2,942 ... B 4
Romanshorn, 7,755 ... H 1
Romont, 2,982 ... C 3
Rorschach, 13,400 ... H 2
Rorschach, *24,500 ... H 2
Rosenlaui ... F 3
Rothrist, 5,048 ... E 2
Rougemont, 860 ... D 4
Roveredo, 1,878 ... H 4
Rüeggisberg, 2,035 ... E 3
Rüschegg, 1,628 ... D 3
Ruswil, 4,657 ... F 2
Rüthi, 1,521 ... J 2
Rüti, Glarus, 738 ... H 3
Rüti, Zürich, 8,282 ... G 2
Saanen, 5,649 ... D 4
Saas-Fee, 739 ... E 4
Sachseln, 2,721 ... F 3
Saignelégier, 1,636 ... D 2
Saint-Blaise, 2,412 ... D 2
Sainte-Croix, 6,925 ... B 3
Saint-Imier, 6,704 ... D 2
Saint-Martin, 1,155 ... E 4
Saint-Maurice, 3,196 ... C 4
Saint Moritz, 3,751 ... J 3
Saint Niklaus, 2,071 ... E 4
Saint-Prex, 1,897 ... B 4
Saint-Stephan, 1,227 ... D 3
Saint-Ursanne, 1,304 ... D 2
Samedan, 2,106 ... J 3
Sankt Gallen, 78,900 ... H 2
Sargans, 2,571 ... H 2
Sarnen, 6,554 ... F 3
Satigny, 1,594 ... A 4
Savièse, 3,203 ... D 4
Savognin, 632 ... J 3
Saxon, 2,305 ... D 4
Schaffhausen, 37,400 ... G 1
Schaffhausen, *56,900 ... G 1
Schangnau, 1,031 ... E 3
Schänis, 2,328 ... H 2
Schiers, 2,363 ... J 3
Schinznach-Dorf, 1,081 ... F 2
Schlarigna-Celerina, 868 ... J 3
Schleitheim, 1,494 ... G 1
Schlieren, 11,600 ... F 2
Schönenwerd, 4,561 ... E 2
Schüpfheim, 3,771 ... F 3
Schwanden, 3,020 ... H 2
Schwyz, 12,200 ... G 2
Scuol-Schuls, 1,429 ... K 3
Sedrun, 1,855 ... G 3
Seewis, 969 ... J 3
Sembrancher, 710 ... D 4
Sempach, 1,345 ... F 2
Semsales, 762 ... C 3
Seon, 3,006 ... F 2
Sevelen, 2,370 ... H 2
Sierre, 8,690 ... D 4
Siggenthal, 7,376 ... F 1
Signau, 2,555 ... E 3
Sigriswil, 3,739 ... E 3
Silenen, 2,261 ... G 3
Sils im Domleschg, 737 ... H 3
Silvaplana, 346 ... J 4
Sins, 2,195 ... F 2
Sion, 18,900 ... D 4
Sirnach, 3,075 ... G 2
Sissach, 4,574 ... E 2
Solothurn (Soleure), 18,900 ... E 2
Solothurn, *36,400 ... E 2
Sonvico, 1,005 ... G 4
Spiez, 8,168 ... E 3
Stäfa, 6,947 ... G 2
Stalden, 1,007 ... E 4
Stammheim, 1,460 ... G 1
Stans, 4,337 ... F 3
Steckborn, 3,514 ... G 1
Steffisburg, 12,100 ... E 3
Stein, 1,060 ... E 1
Stein am Rhein, 2,588 ... G 1
Sulgen, 1,252 ... H 1
Sulz, 1,022 ... F 1
Sumiswald, 5,525 ... E 2
Sursee, 5,324 ... F 2
Tafers, 1,621 ... D 3
Täuffelen, 1,500 ... D 2
Tavannes, 3,939 ... D 2
Thalwil, 13,200 ... G 2
Thayngen, 3,013 ... G 1
Therwil, 1,946 ... E 1
Thun, 33,700 ... E 3
Thun, *56,700 ... E 3
Thusis, 1,998 ... H 3
Trachselwald, 1,269 ... E 2
Tramelan, 5,567 ... D 2
Trogen, 2,101 ... H 2
Trub, 1,981 ... E 3
Trun, 1,583 ... G 3
Turbenthal, 2,685 ... G 2
Turgi, 1,860 ... F 1
Ueberstorf, 1,536 ... D 3
Uetendorf, 2,810 ... E 3
Unterägeri, 3,832 ... G 2
Unterkulm, 2,149 ... F 2
Unterseen, 3,783 ... E 3
Untervaz, 1,142 ... H 3
Urnäsch, 2,330 ... H 2
Uster, 20,800 ... G 2
Utzenstorf, 2,821 ... E 2
Uznach, 3,173 ... H 2
Uzwil, 7,828 ... H 2
Vallorbe, 3,990 ... B 3
Vals, 968 ... H 3
Vaz-Obervaz, 1,568 ... J 3
Vechigen, 3,153 ... E 3
Vernayaz, 1,188 ... D 4
Versoix, 3,426 ... B 4
Vevey, 18,000 ... C 4
Vevey, *29,600 ... C 4
Veyrier, 2,705 ... B 4
Villeneuve, 2,366 ... C 4
Visp, 3,658 ... E 4
Vouvry, 1,368 ... C 4
Wädenswil, 14,300 ... G 2
Wahlern, 4,723 ... D 3
Wald, 7,778 ... G 2
Waldenburg, 1,284 ... E 2
Waldkirch, 2,487 ... H 2
Wallenstadt, 3,296 ... H 2
Walzenhausen, 2,345 ... J 2
Wangen an der Aare, 1,936 ... E 2
Wängi, 1,681 ... H 1
Wartau, 3,284 ... H 2
Wattwil, 7,480 ... H 2
Weesen, 1,280 ... H 2
Weggis, 2,243 ... F 2
Weinfelden, 6,954 ... H 1
Wettingen, 19,700 ... F 2
Wetzikon, 12,600 ... G 2
Wil, 12,900 ... H 2
Wilchingen, 1,061 ... F 1
Wilderswil, 1,701 ... E 3
Wildhaus, 1,179 ... H 2
Willisau, 2,508 ... F 2
Wimmis, 1,756 ... E 3
Windisch, 5,377 ... F 1
Winterthur, 92,500 ... G 1
Winterthur, *104,600 ... G 1
Wohlen, 8,636 ... F 2
Wohlen bei Bern, 2,985 ... D 3
Wolfenschiessen, 1,647 ... F 3
Wolhusen, 3,446 ... F 2
Wollerau, 2,415 ... G 2
Worb, 5,885 ... E 3
Wynigen, 2,221 ... E 2
Yverdon, 19,200 ... C 3
Yvonand, 1,290 ... C 3
Zäziwil, 1,265 ... E 3
Zell, Luzern, 1,582 ... E 2
Zell, Zürich, 3,347 ... G 2
Zermatt, 2,731 ... E 4
Zizers, 1,290 ... J 3
Zofingen, 1,290 ... F 2
Zollikofen, 6,237 ... E 3
Zollikon, 12,100 ... G 2
Zug, 22,300 ... G 2
Zuoz, 1,001 ... J 3
Zürich, 432,400 ... F 2
Zürich, *671,500 ... F 2
Zurzach, 2,694 ... F 1
Zweisimmen, 2,676 ... D 3

OTHER FEATURES

Aa (river) ... F 3
Aare (river) ... E 3
Ägerisee (lake) ... G 2
Albristhorn (mt.) ... D 4
Aletschhorn (mt.) ... F 4
Allaine (river) ... D 2
Areuse (river) ... C 3
Ault (peak) ... H 3
Baldeggersee (lake) ... F 2
Balmhorn (mt.) ... E 4
Bärenhorn (mt.) ... H 3
Basodino (mt.) ... G 4
Bernese Oberland (region) ... E 3
Bernina, Piz (mt.) ... J 4
Bernina (pass) ... K 4
Bernina (river) ... J 4
Beverin (mt.) ... H 3
Biel (lake) ... D 2
Birs (river) ... D 2
Blindenhorn (mt.) ... F 4
Blümlisalp (mt.) ... E 3
Bodensee (Constance) (lake) ... H 1
Borgne (river) ... D 4
Breithorn (mt.) ... E 5
Breithorn (mt.) ... E 4
Brienz (lake) ... F 3
Brienzer Rothorn (mt.) ... F 3
Broye (river) ... C 3
Brulé (mt.) ... D 4
Buchegg (mts.) ... D 2
Bürkelkopf (mt.) ... K 3
Bütschelegg (mt.) ... D 3
Calancasca (river) ... H 4
Campo Tencia (peak) ... G 4
Ceneri (mt.) ... G 4
Cheville (pass) ... D 4
Churfirsten (mt.) ... H 2
Claridenstock (mt.) ... G 3
Collon (mt.) ... D 5
Constance (lake) ... H 1
Dammastock (mt.) ... F 3
Davos (valley) ... J 3
Dent Blanche (mt.) ... E 4
Dent de Lys (mt.) ... D 4
Dent de Ruth (mt.) ... D 3
Dent d'Hérens (mt.) ... E 5
Dents du Midi (mt.) ... C 4
Diablerets (mt.) ... D 4
Doldenhorn (mt.) ... E 4
Dolent (mt.) ... C 5
Dom (mt.) ... E 4
Doubs (river) ... C 2
Drance (river) ... D 4
Dufourspitze (mt.) ... E 5
Emmental (valley) ... E 3
Engadine (valley) ... J-K 3-4
Err (mt.) ... J 3
Finsteraarhorn (mt.) ... F 3
Finstermünz (pass) ... K 3
Fletschhorn (mt.) ... F 4
Flüela (pass) ... J 3
Fluhberg (mt.) ... G 2
Fort (mt.) ... D 4
Furka (pass) ... F 3
Generoso (mt.) ... H 5
Geneva (lake) ... C 4
Giacomo (pass) ... G 4
Gibloux (mt.) ... D 3
Glâne (river) ... C 3
Glärnisch (mt.) ... H 2

Glarus Alps (mts.) ..... H 3
Glatt (river) ..... G 2
Goms (valley) ..... F 4
Grand Combin (mt.) ..... D 5
Grande Dixence (dam) ..... D 4
Grauehörner (mts.) ..... H 3
Great Saint Bernard (mt.) ..... D 5
Greifensee (lake) ..... G 2
Greina (pass) ..... G 3
Gridone (mt.) ..... G 4
Grimsel (pass) ..... F 3
Gross Emme (river) ..... E 2
Gross Litzner (mt.) ..... K 3
Hallwilersee (lake) ..... F 2
Hausstock (mt.) ..... H 3
Hinterrhein (river) ..... H 3
Hochwang (mt.) ..... J 3
Hohenstollen (mt.) ..... F 3
Honegg (mt.) ..... E 3
Hörnli (mt.) ..... G 2
Ilfis (river) ..... E 3
Inn (river) ..... K 3
Joch (pass) ..... F 3
Jorat (mt.) ..... C 3
Joux (lake) ..... B 3
Julia (river) ..... J 3
Jungfrau (mt.) ..... E 3
Jura (mts.) ..... B 3
Kaiseregg (mt.) ..... D 3
Kesch (mt.) ..... J 3
Kisten (pass) ..... H 3
Klausen (pass) ..... G 3
Kleine Emme (river) ..... F 3
La Berra (mt.) ..... D 3
La Dôle (mt.) ..... B 4
Landquart (river) ..... J 3
Le Gros Crêt (mt.) ..... B 3
Léman (Geneva) (lake) ..... C 4
Leone (mt.) ..... F 4
Lepontine Alps (range) ..... G 4
Le Raimeux (mt.) ..... D 2
Limmat (river) ..... F 2
Linard (mt.) ..... K 3
Linden (mts.) ..... F 2
Linth (river) ..... G 3
Lorze (river) ..... F 2
Lötschberg (tunnel) ..... E 4
Lower Engadine (valley) ..... K 3
Lucerne (Luzern) (lake) ..... F 3
Lugano (lake) ..... H 5
Madrisahorn (mt.) ..... J 3
Maggia (river) ..... G 4
Maggiore (lake) ..... G 5
Männlifluh (mt.) ..... E 3
Marmontana (mt.) ..... H 4
Matterhorn (mt.) ..... E 5
Mauvoisin (dam) ..... D 4
Moësa (river) ..... H 4
Molare (mt.) ..... G 3
Montoz (mt.) ..... D 2
Morat (lake) ..... D 3
Moro (mt.) ..... E 5
Moron (mt.) ..... D 2
Muota (river) ..... G 3
Muretto (pass) ..... J 4
Murg (river) ..... G 1
Murtaröl (mt.) ..... K 3
Muttler (mt.) ..... K 3
Napf (mt.) ..... E 3
National Park ..... K 3
Neuchâtel (lake) ..... C 3
Noirmont (mt.) ..... B 4
Oberalp (pass) ..... G 3
Oberalpstock (mt.) ..... G 3
Ochsen (mt.) ..... D 3
Ofen (pass) ..... K 3
Ofenhorn (mt.) ..... F 4
Orbe (river) ..... B 3
Pennine Alps (range) ..... E 5
Pilatus (mt.) ..... F 3
Plessur (river) ..... J 3
Poschiavo (river) ..... K 4
Poschiavo (valley) ..... K 4
Pragel (pass) ..... G 2
Quatervals (mt.) ..... K 3
Reuss (river) ..... F 2
Rhaetian Alps (range) ..... J 3
Rhätikon (mts.) ..... J 2
Rheinwaldhorn (mt.) ..... G 4
Rhine (river) ..... E 1, J 2
Rhône (river) ..... D 4
Rigi (mt.) ..... F 2
Rimpfischhorn (mt.) ..... E 4
Ringelspitz (mt.) ..... H 3
Risoux (mt.) ..... B 3
Rosa (mt.) ..... E 5
Rosstock (mt.) ..... G 3
Rothorn (mt.) ..... D 4
Saane (Sarine) (river) ..... D 3
Saint Gotthard (pass) ..... G 3
Saint Gotthard (tunnel) ..... G 3
San Bernardino (pass) ..... H 3
Säntis (mt.) ..... H 2
Sarine (Saane) (river) ..... D 3
Sarnen (lake) ..... F 3
Sasseneire (mt.) ..... E 4
Scaletta (pass) ..... J 3
Schesaplana (mt.) ..... J 2
Schreckhorn (mt.) ..... F 3
Schwarzhorn (mt.) ..... E 4
Schwarzhorn (mt.) ..... F 3
Scopi (mt.) ..... G 3
Seez (river) ..... H 2
Segnes (pass) ..... H 3
Sempach (lake) ..... F 2
Sense (river) ..... D 3
Septimer (pass) ..... J 4
Sesvenna (mt.) ..... K 3
Sihlsee (lake) ..... G 2
Silvretta (mts.) ..... K 3
Simme (river) ..... D 3
Simplon (pass) ..... F 4
Simplon (tunnel) ..... F 4
Sol (mt.) ..... H 3
Sonnenhorn (mt.) ..... F 4
Splügen (pass) ..... H 3
Stockhorn (mt.) ..... E 3
Sulzflüh (mt.) ..... J 2
Susten (pass) ..... G 3
Sustenhorn (mt.) ..... G 3
Tamaro (mt.) ..... G 4
Tamina (river) ..... H 3
Tendre (peak) ..... B 3
Terri (mt.) ..... D 2
Terri (mt.) ..... H 3
Thièle (river) ..... C 3
Thun (lake) ..... E 3
Thur (river) ..... G 1
Ticino (river) ..... G 4
Tödi (mt.) ..... G 3
Toggenburg (dist.) ..... H 2
Töss (river) ..... G 1
Tour d'Ai (mt.) ..... C 4
Turnen (mt.) ..... D 3
Umbrail (mt.) ..... K 3
Untersee (lake) ..... H 1
Unterwalden (reg.), 50,000 ..... F 3
Upper Engadine (valley) ..... J 4
Uri-Rotstock (mt.) ..... G 3
Vadret (mt.) ..... J 3
Valserrhein (river) ..... H 3
Vélan (mt.) ..... D 5
Visp (river) ..... E 4
Vorab (mt.) ..... H 3
Vorderrhein (river) ..... G 3
Wallenstadt (lake) ..... H 2
Wandfluhhorn (mt.) ..... G 4
Weissenstein (mts.) ..... D 2
Weisshorn (mt.) ..... E 4
Weisshorn (mt.) ..... J 3
Wetterhorn (mt.) ..... F 3
Wildhorn (mt.) ..... D 4
Wildstrubel (mt.) ..... E 4
Zellersee (lake) ..... G 1
Zucchero (mt.) ..... G 4
Zug (lake) ..... F 2
Zürich (lake) ..... G 2

*City and suburbs.

LIECHTENSTEIN

CITIES and TOWNS

Schaan, 3,022 ..... H 2
Triesen, 1,789 ..... H 2
Vaduz (cap.), 3,514 ..... H 2

OTHER FEATURES

Naafkopf (mt.) ..... J 2
Ochsenkopf (mt.) ..... J 2
Rhätikon (mts.) ..... J 2
Rhine (river) ..... J 2

40 Austria, Czechoslovakia and Hungary

AUSTRIA

PROVINCES

Burgenland, 271,001 ....D 3
Carinthia, 495,226 ....B 3
Lower Austria, 1,374,012 ....C 2
Salzburg, 347,292 ....B 3
Styria, 1,137,865 ....C 3
Tirol, 462,899 ....A 3
Upper Austria 1,131,623 ....B 2
Vienna (city), 1,631,423 ....D 2
Vorarlberg, 226,323 ....A 3

CITIES and TOWNS

Admont, 3,057 ....C 3
Aigen, 1,941 ....B 2
Alt Aussee, 2,026 ....B 3
Altheim, 4,271 ....B 2
Althofen, 3,221 ....C 3
Amstetten, 12,086 ....C 2
Andau, 3,011 ....D 3
Arnoldstein, 6,229 ....B 3
Aspang, 2,359 ....D 3
Attnang-Puchheim, 7,525 ....B 2
Bad Aussee, 5,144 ....B 3
Bad Goisern, 6,028 ....B 3
Bad Hofgastein, 4,700 ....B 3
Bad Ischl, 12,703 ....B 3
Bad Sankt Leonhard, 1,939 ....C 3
Baden, 22,484 ....D 2
Badgastein, 5,742 ....B 3
Berndorf, 8,992 ....C 3
Bischofshofen, 8,287 ....B 3
Bludenz, 11,127 ....A 3
Bramberg, 2,620 ....B 3
Braunau, 14,449 ....B 2
Bregenz, 21,428 ....A 3
Bruck an der Leitha, 6,791 ....D 2
Bruck an der Mur, 16,087 ....C 3
Deutsch Feistritz, 3,427 ....C 3
Deutsch Landsberg, 5,227 ....C 3
Deutsch Wagram, 4,207 ....D 2
Deutschkreutz, 3,901 ....D 3
Dornbirn, 28,075 ....A 3
Ebenfurth, 2,342 ....D 3
Ebensee, 9,602 ....B 3
Eferding, 3,151 ....B 2
Eggenburg, 3,338 ....C 2
Eisenerz, 12,435 ....C 3
Horn, 4,705 ....C 2
Hüttenberg, 2,257 ....C 3
Imst, 5,057 ....A 3
Innsbruck, 113,468 ....A 3
Jenbach, 5,479 ....A 3
Judenburg, 9,869 ....C 3
Kapfenberg, 23,859 ....C 3
Kappl, 1,970 ....A 3
Kaprun, 2,164 ....B 3
Kindberg, 5,766 ....C 3
Kirchdorf an der Krems, 2,964 ..C 3
Kitzbühel, 7,744 ....B 3
Klagenfurt, 69,218 ....C 3
Klosterneuburg, 22,787 ....D 2
Knittelfeld, 14,259 ....C 3
Köflach, 12,367 ....C 3
Königswiesen, 2,707 ....C 2
Korneuburg, 8,276 ....D 2
Kössen, 2,361 ....B 3
Kötschach-Mauthen, 2,763 ....B 3
Krems, 21,046 ....C 2
Kufstein, 11,215 ....B 3
Kundl, 2,508 ....A 3
Laa an der Thaya, 4,925 ....D 2
Laakirchen, 6,722 ....B 3
Lambach, 3,019 ....C 2
Landeck, 6,514 ....A 3
Landskron, 9,058 ....B 3
Längenfeld, 2,314 ....A 3
Langenlois, 4,655 ....C 2
Langenwang, 3,734 ....C 3
Lavamünd, 2,506 ....C 3
Leibnitz, 6,356 ....C 3
Lenzing, 5,372 ....B 3
Leoben, 36,257 ....C 3
Leonfelden, 2,546 ....C 2
Lienz, 11,132 ....B 3
Liezen, 5,444 ....C 3
Lilienfeld, 3,307 ....C 3
Linz, 205,762 ....C 2
Lustenau, 12,582 ....A 3
Mannersdorf, 3,909 ....D 3
Marchegg, 2,159 ....D 2
Mariazell, 2,191 ....C 3
Matrei, 3,430 ....B 3
Mattersburg, 4,270 ....D 3
Mattighofen, 3,919 ....B 2
Mauerkirchen, 2,175 ....B 2
Mautern, 2,365 ....C 3
Mauthausen, 3,836 ....C 2
Mauthen-Kötschach, 2,763 ....B 3
Mayrhofen, 2,523 ....A 3
Schärding, 5,710 ....B 2
Scheibbs, 3,231 ....C 2
Schladming, 3,249 ....B 3
Schrems, 3,080 ....C 2
Schruns, 3,304 ....A 3
Schwarzach, 3,186 ....B 3
Schwaz, 9,455 ....A 3
Schwertberg, 3,369 ....C 2
Sierning, 7,527 ....C 2
Sillian, 1,948 ....B 3
Solbad Hall, 10,750 ....A 3
Spital, 2,421 ....C 3
Spittal, 10,045 ....B 3
Steinach, 2,155 ....A 3
Steyr, 38,306 ....C 2
Stockerau, 11,853 ....D 2
Strassburg, 2,972 ....C 3
Tamweg, 4,431 ....B 3
Telfs, 5,438 ....A 3
Ternitz, 9,032 ....D 3
Traiskirchen, 7,026 ....D 2
Traun, 16,026 ....C 2
Trieben, 4,023 ....C 3
Trofaiach, 6,909 ....C 3
Tulln, 6,306 ....D 2
Velden, 2,039 ....C 3
Vienna (capital), 1,642,072 ....D 2
Villach, 32,971 ....B 3
Vöcklabruck, 9,353 ....B 2
Voitsberg, 6,353 ....C 3
Völkermarkt, 3,678 ....C 3
Vordernberg, 2,896 ....C 3
Waidhofen an der Thaya,
3,748 ....C 2
Waidhofen an der Ybbs,
5,586 ....C 3
Weitensfeld, 2,998 ....B 3
Weiz, 8,146 ....C 3
Wels, 41,060 ....C 2
Weyer, 2,367 ....C 3
Wiener Neustadt, 33,845 ....D 3
Wildon, 2,020 ....C 3
Wilhelmsburg, 6,196 ....C 2
Wolfsberg, 9,470 ....C 3
Wörgl, 6,828 ....A 3
Ybbs, 5,324 ....C 2
Zams, 2,782 ....A 3
Zell am See, 6,455 ....B 3
Zeltweg, 7,340 ....C 3
Zirl, 3,165 ....A 3
Zistersdorf, 3,011 ....D 2
Zwettl, 3,836 ....C 2
Eisenstadt, 7,167 ....D 3
Enns, 8,919 ....C 2
Feldbach, 3,687 ....C 3
Feldkirch, 17,343 ....A 3
Feldkirchen in Kärnten, 3,181 ....B 3
Ferlach, 5,672 ....C 3
Fieberbrunn, 3,010 ....B 3
Fohnsdorf, 11,571 ....C 3
Frankenmarkt, 2,565 ....B 3
Frauenkirchen, 2,812 ....D 3
Friesach, 3,388 ....C 3
Freistadt, 5,375 ....C 2
Frohnleiten, 4,969 ....C 3
Fulpmes, 2,282 ....A 3
Fürstenfeld, 6,415 ....C 3
Gaming, 4,218 ....C 3
Gänserndorf, 3,378 ....D 2
Gleisdorf, 4,385 ....C 3
Gloggnitz, 7,228 ....D 3
Gmünd, Carinthia, 2,195 ....B 3
Gmünd, Lower Austria, 6,522 ....C 2
Gmunden, 12,518 ....B 3
Golling an der Salzach,
2,845 ....B 3
Götzis, 7,034 ....A 3
Gratwein, 2,515 ....C 3
Graz, 253,000 ....C 3
Grein, 2,518 ....C 2
Grieskirchen, 4,137 ....B 2
Gross Sieghearts, 2,599 ....C 2
Grünburg, 3,609 ....C 3
Güssing, 2,715 ....D 3
Haag, 4,671 ....C 2
Hainburg, 6,437 ....D 2
Hainfeld, 3,883 ....C 2
Hallein, 13,329 ....B 3
Hallstatt, 1,373 ....B 3
Hartberg, 3,629 ....C 3
Haslach an der Mühl, 2,565 ....C 2
Heidenreichstein, 3,653 ....C 2
Heiligenblut, 1,195 ....B 3
Hermagor, 2,778 ....B 3
Herzogenburg, 5,166 ....C 2
Hieflau, 2,003 ....C 3
Hohenau an der March, 3,907 ....D 2
Hohenberg, 2,093 ....C 3
Hohenems, 9,188 ....A 3
Hollabrunn, 5,832 ....D 2
Hopfgarten in Nordtirol, 4,163 ....B 3
Melk, 3,534 ....C 2
Mistelbach an der Zaya, 5,434 ....D 2
Mittersill, 3,502 ....B 3
Mödling, 17,274 ....D 2
Mondsee, 2,050 ....B 3
Murau, 2,755 ....C 3
Mürzzuschlag, 11,586 ....C 3
Nassereith, 1,744 ....A 3
Neuberg an der Mürz, 2,411 ....C 3
Neumarkt, Styria, 1,880 ....C 3
Neumarkt am Wallersee, 2,877 ....B 3
Neunkirchen, 10,027 ....C 3
Neusiedl am See, 3,826 ....D 3
Neustift im Stubaital, 2,195 ....A 3
Ober Grafendorf, 3,825 ....C 2
Oberndorf bei Salzburg, 3,084 ....B 3
Obervellach, 2,371 ....B 3
Oberwart, 4,740 ....D 3
Paternion, 5,581 ....B 3
Perg, 4,106 ....C 2
Peuerbach, 2,105 ....B 2
Pinkafeld, 3,826 ....C 3
Pöchlarn, 2,921 ....C 2
Pörtschach, 2,449 ....C 3
Poysdorf, 2,738 ....D 2
Pregarten, 2,818 ....C 2
Radenthein, 5,651 ....B 3
Radstadt, 3,311 ....B 3
Rankweil, 6,451 ....A 3
Rechnitz, 3,374 ....D 3
Reichenau an der Rax, 4,441 ....C 3
Retz, 2,941 ....D 2
Reutte, 4,285 ....A 3
Ried im Innkreis, 9,471 ....B 2
Rottenmann, 4,139 ....C 3
Saalfelden, 8,901 ....B 3
Salzburg, 120,204 ....B 3
Sankt Aegyd am Neuwalde,
3,206 ....C 3
Sankt Anton am Arlberg, 1,741 ....A 3
Sankt Johann, 4,713 ....B 3
Sankt Michael, 3,433 ....C 3
Sankt Michael im Lungau,
2,422 ....B 3
Sankt Paul, 1,808 ....C 3
Sankt Pölten, 40,112 ....C 2
Sankt Valentin, 7,750 ....C 2
Sankt Veit an der Glan, 10,950 ....C 3
Sankt Wolfgang, 2,234 ....B 3

OTHER FEATURES

Allgäu Alps (mts.) ....A 3
Atter (lake) ....B 3
Bavarian Alps (mts.) ....A 3
Bodensee (Constance) (lake) ....A 3
Brenner (pass) ....A 3
Carnic Alps (mts.) ....B 3
Coglians (Hohe Warte) (peak)...B 3
Constance (lake) ....A 3
Danube (river) ....C 2
Donau (Danube) (river) ....D 2
Drau (river) ....C 3
Enns (river) ....C 3
Fertő tó (Neusiedler) (lake)......D 3
Greiner (forest) ....C 2
Grossglockner (mt.) ....B 3
Gross Höllkogel (mt.) ....B 3
Gross Peilstein (mt.) ....C 2
Hochgolling (mt.) ....B 3
Hohe Tauern (range) ....B 3
Hohe Warte (peak) ....B 3
Inn (river) ....B 2
Kamp (river) ....C 2
Karawanken (mts.) ....C 3
Laufnitz (river) ....D 3
March (river) ....D 2
Mühlviertel (region),
196,037 ....C 2
Mur (river) ....C 3
Mürz (river) ....C 3
Neusiedler (lake) ....D 3
Niedere Tauern (range) ....B 3
Olsa (river) ....C 3
Ötztal Alps (mts.) ....A 3
Parseierspitze (mt.) ....A 3
Raab (river) ....C 3
Rhine (river) ....A 3
Salzach (river) ....B 2
Salzkammergut (region) ....B 3
Semmering (pass) ....C 3
Thaya (river) ....C 2
Traun (lake) ....B 3
Traun (river) ....C 2
Wildspitze (mt.) ....A 3
Zugspitze (mt.) ....A 3

CZECHOSLOVAKIA

REPUBLICS

Czech Soc. Rep., 9,778,000 ....B 1
Slovak Soc. Rep., 4,421,000 ....E 2

REGIONS

Jihočeský, 659,000 ....C 2
Jihomoravský, 1,941,000 ....D 2
Prague (city), 1,025,000 ....C 1
Severočeský, 1,122,000 ....C 1
Severomoravský, 1,695,000 ....C 1
Středočeský, 1,271,000 ....C 2
Středoslovenský, 1,379,000 ....E 2
Východočeský, 1,213,000 ....C 1
Východoslovenský, 1,199,000 ....F 2
Západočeský, 852,000 ....B 2
Západoslovenský, 1,843,000 ....D 2

CITIES and TOWNS

As, 10,000 ....B 1
Austerlitz (Slavkov), 4,869 ....D 2
Bánovce, 3,563 ....E 2
Banská Bystrica, 29,000 ....E 2
Banská Štiavnica, 10,381 ....E 2
Bardejov, 11,000 ....F 2
Bechyně, 2,398 ....C 2
Benešov, 10,000 ....C 2
Beroun, 17,000 ....B 2
Bílina, 12,000 ....B 1
Blansko, 11,000 ....D 2
Blatná, 3,596 ....B 2
Blovice, 2,629 ....B 2
Bojkovice, 2,902 ....D 2
Bor, 2,257 ....B 2
Boskovice, 6,396 ....D 2
Brandýs nad Labem-Stará
Boleslav, 13,161 ....C 1
Bratislava, 278,835 ....D 2
Břeclav, 13,000 ....D 2
Březnice, 2,634 ....B 2
Brezno, 11,000 ....E 2
Brno, 333,831 ....D 2
Broumov, 6,370 ....D 1
Brtnice, 2,176 ....C 2
Bruntál, 9,000 ....D 2
Bučovice, 3,381 ....D 2
Budišov, 3,677 ....D 2
Bystřice nad Pernštejnem,
2,653 ....D 2
Bystřice pod Hostýnem, 4,973 ....D 2
Bytča, 4,528 ....E 2
Čadca, 13,000 ....E 2
Čalovo, 4,536 ....D 3
Čáslav, 10,000 ....C 2
Česká Kamenice, 6,084 ....C 1
Česká Lípa, 15,000 ....C 1
Česká Třebová, 14,000 ....D 2
České Budějovice, 70,000 ....C 2
Český Brod, 5,754 ....C 1
Český Krumlov, 10,000 ....C 2
Český Těšín, 16,000 ....E 2
Cheb, 24,000 ....B 1
Chlumec, 4,345 ....C 1
Choceň, 6,789 ....D 1
Chodov, 5,383 ....B 1
Chomutov, 37,000 ....B 1
Chotěboř, 4,846 ....C 2
Chrastava, 3,618 ....C 1
Chrudim, 17,000 ....C 2
Čierny Balog, 5,978 ....E 2
Cukmantl, 2,362 ....D 1
Dačice, 2,810 ....C 2
Děčín, 42,000 ....C 1
Detva, 7,786 ....E 2
Dobřany, 4,905 ....B 2
Dobříš, 4,390 ....C 2
Dobruška, 4,093 ....D 1
Dobšiná, 3,957 ....F 2
Doksy, 3,061 ....C 1
Dolný Kubín, 5,000 ....E 2
Domažlice, 8,000 ....B 2
Dubnica nad Váhom, 11,250 ....E 2
Duchcov, 8,229 ....B 1
Dunajská Streda, 9,000 ....D 3
Dvory, 5,475 ....E 3
Dvůr Králové nad Labem. 16,000 ....C 1
Falknov (Sokolov), 20,000 ....B 1
Fil'akovo, 5,950 ....E 2
Františkovy Lázně, 5,212 ....B 1
Frýdek-Místek, 32,000 ....E 2
Frýdlant nad Ostravicí, 4,178 ....E 2
Frýdlant v čechách, 5,460 ....C 1
Fulnek, 2,765 ....D 2
Galanta, 8,000 ....D 2
Gelnica, 3,240 ....F 2
Golčův Jeníkov, 1,920 ....C 2
Gottwaldov, 63,000 ....D 2
Handlová, 16,000 ....E 2
Havířov, 72,000 ....E 2
Havlíčkův, Brod, 16,000 ....C 2
Hlinsko, 5,189 ....D 2
Hlohovec, 14,000 ....D 2
Hlučín, 11,000 ....E 2
Hodonín, 19,000 ....D 2

(continued)

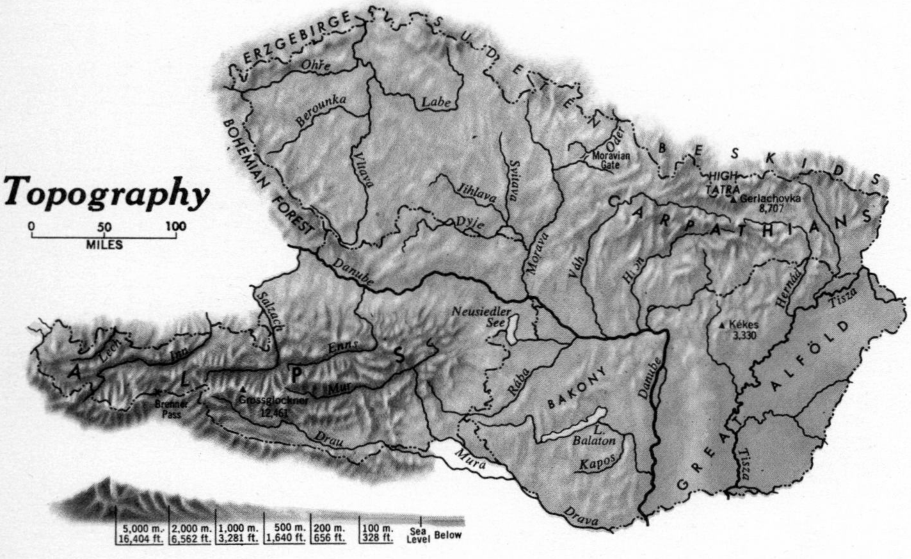

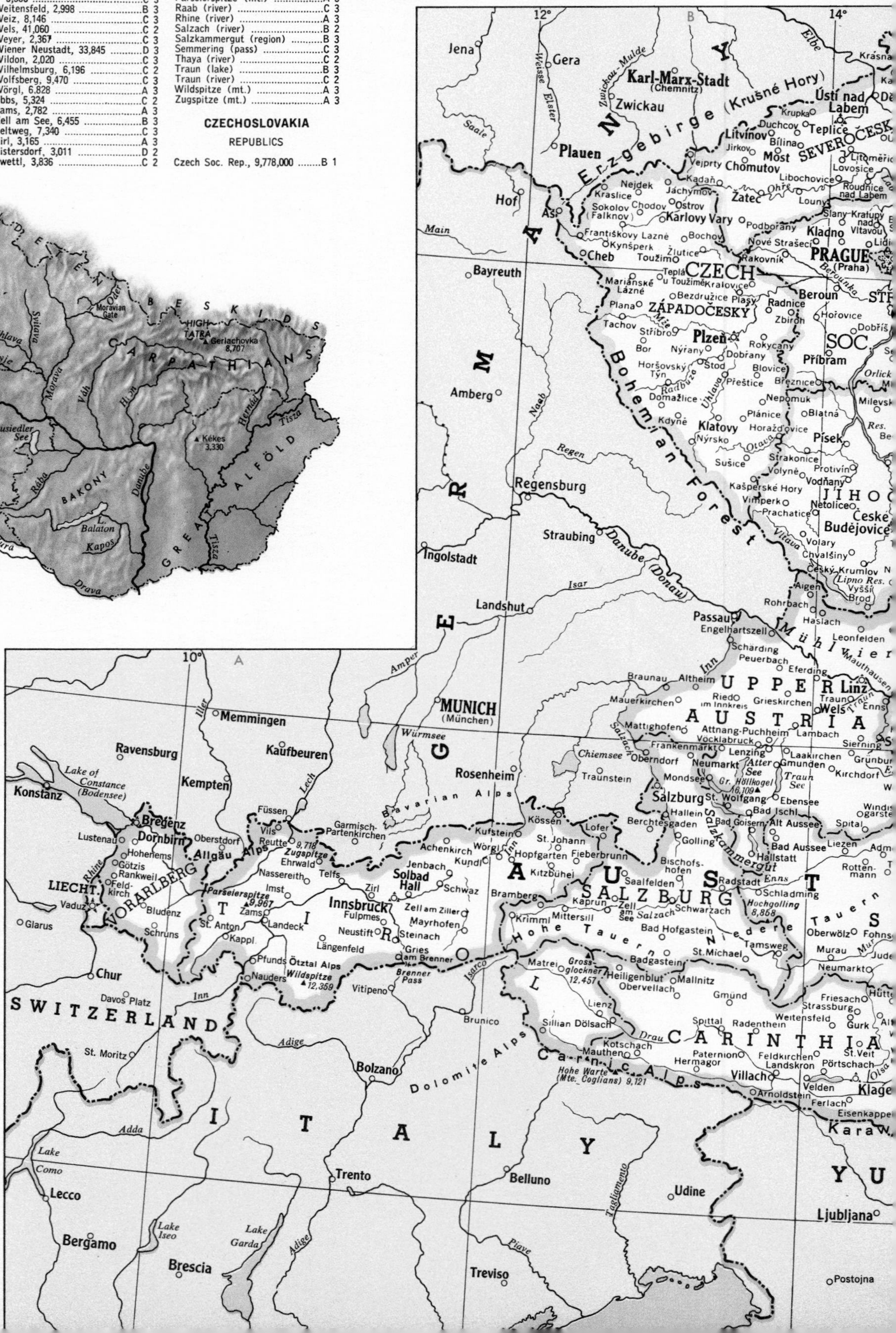

AUSTRIA
AREA 32,374 sq. mi.
POPULATION 7,419,341
CAPITAL Vienna
LARGEST CITY Vienna
HIGHEST POINT Grossglockner 12,457 ft.
MONETARY UNIT schilling
MAJOR LANGUAGE German
MAJOR RELIGION Roman Catholicism

CZECHOSLOVAKIA
AREA 49,370 sq. mi.
POPULATION 14,497,000
CAPITAL Prague
LARGEST CITY Prague
HIGHEST POINT Gerlachovka 8,707 ft.
MONETARY UNIT koruna (crown)
MAJOR LANGUAGES Czech, Slovak
MAJOR RELIGIONS Roman Catholicism, Protestantism

HUNGARY
AREA 35,915 sq. mi.
POPULATION 10,315,597
CAPITAL Budapest
LARGEST CITY Budapest
HIGHEST POINT Kékes 3,330 ft.
MONETARY UNIT forint
MAJOR LANGUAGE Hungarian
MAJOR RELIGIONS Roman Catholicism, Protestantism

AUSTRIA

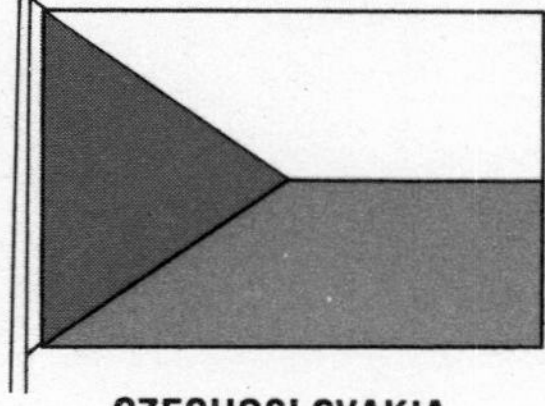
CZECHOSLOVAKIA

HUNGARY

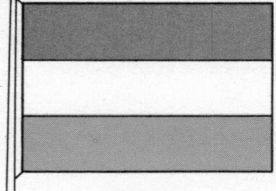

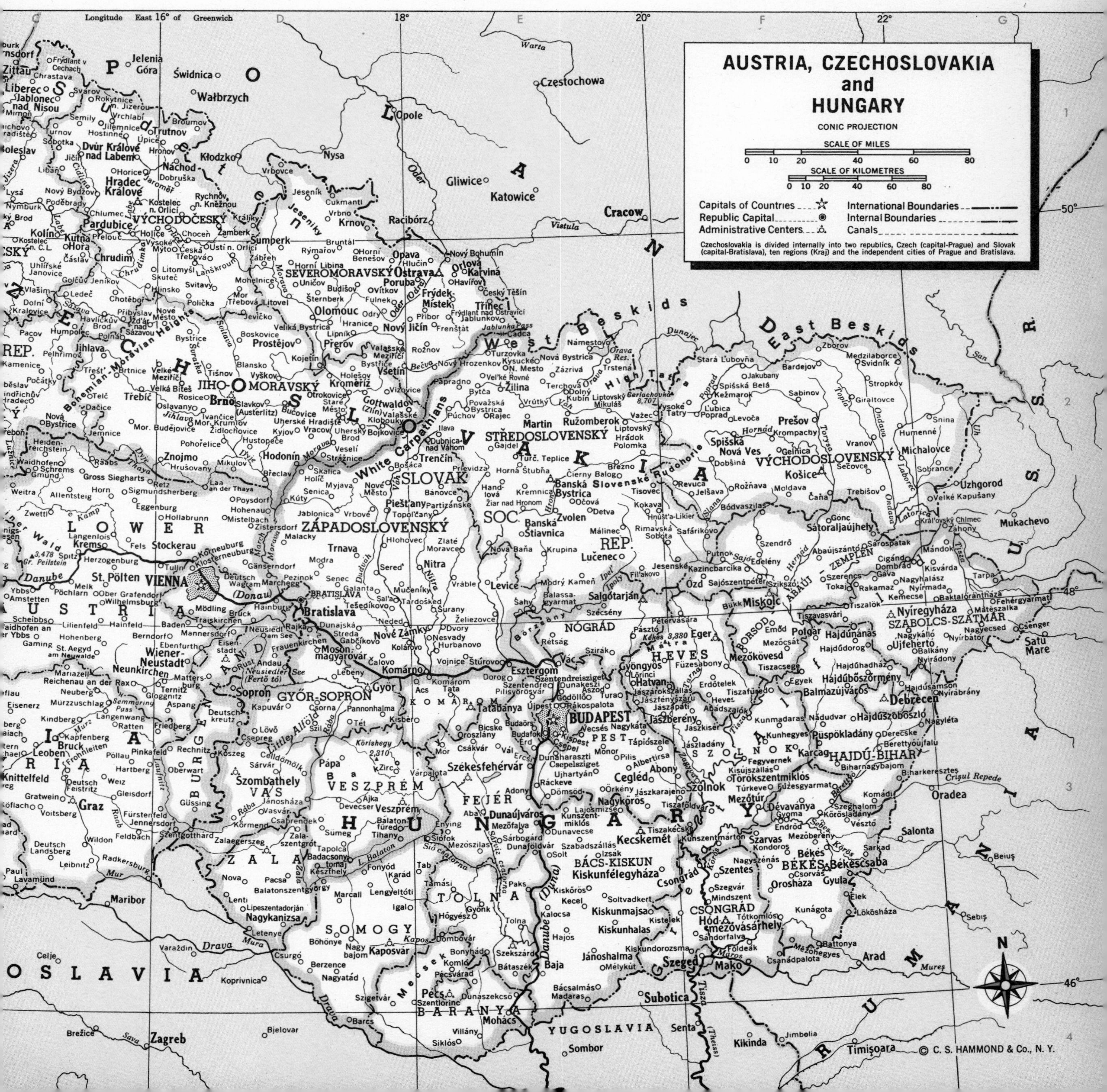

AUSTRIA, CZECHOSLOVAKIA and HUNGARY

CONIC PROJECTION

SCALE OF MILES: 0 10 20 40 60 80
SCALE OF KILOMETRES: 0 10 20 40 60 80

Capitals of Countries ☆ — International Boundaries
Republic Capital ◉ — Internal Boundaries
Administrative Centers △ — Canals

Czechoslovakia is divided internally into two republics, Czech (capital-Prague) and Slovak (capital-Bratislava), ten regions (Kraj) and the independent cities of Prague and Bratislava.

Longitude East 16° of Greenwich

42 Austria, Czechoslovakia and Hungary

(continued)

CZECHOSLOVAKIA (continued)

Holešov, 6,599 ....D 2
Holíč, 5,881 ....D 2
Holice, 5,695 ....D 1
Horaždovice, 3,098 ....B 2
Hořice, 7,133 ....C 1
Horní Benešov, 3,181 ....D 2
Horní Libina, 4,583 ....D 2
Hořovice, 4,697 ....C 2
Horšovský Týn, 3,475 ....B 2
Hostinné, 4,412 ....C 1
Hradec Králové, 62,000 ....C 1
Hranice, 12,000 ....D 2
Hronov, 11,000 ....D 1
Hrušovany, 3,128 ....D 2
Humenné, 14,000 ....G 2
Humpolec, 5,083 ....C 2
Hurbanovo, 3,578 ....E 3
Hustopeče, 2,698 ....D 2
Ilava, 2,043 ....E 2
Ivančice, 4,742 ....D 2
Jablonec nad Nisou, 33,000 ....C 1
Jablunkov, 4,467 ....E 2
Jáchymov, 6,806 ....B 1
Jaroměř, 12,000 ....C 1
Jelšava, 2,456 ....F 2
Jemnice, 3,383 ....C 2
Jeseník, 5,873 ....D 1
Jesenské, 1,567 ....F 2
Jevičko, 2.881 ....D 2
Jičín, 13,000 ....C 1
Jihlava, 37,000 ....C 2
Jilemnice, 3,362 ....C 1
Jindřichův Hradec, 12,000 ....C 2
Jirkov, 12.000 ....B 1
Kadaň, 5,062 ....B 1
Kamenice, 2,692 ....C 2
Kaplice, 1,931 ....C 2
Karlovy Vary, 45,000 ....B 1
Karviná, 70.000 ....E 2
Kašperské Hory, 2,814 ....B 2
Kdyně, 2,609 ....B 2
Kežmarok, 7,372 ....F 2
Kladno, 55,000 ....B 1
Klatovy, 16,000 ....B 2
Kojetín, 5,292 ....D 2
Kokava, 5,398 ....E 2
Kolárovo, 11,000 ....D 3
Kolín, 25,000 ....C 1
Komárno, 26,000 ....D 3
Košice, 115,332 ....F 2
Kostelec nad Černými, Lesy, 3,616 ....C 2
Kostelec nad Orlicí, 5,539 ....D 1
Králíky, 3,895 ....D 1
Kralovice, 2,268 ....B 2
Král'ovský Chlmec, 3,410 ....G 2
Kralupy nad Vltavou, 14,000 ....C 1
Kraslice, 6,294 ....B 1
Krásna Lípa, 5,041 ....C 1
Kremnica, 4,979 ....E 2
Krnov, 22,000 ....D 1
Kroměříž, 22,000 ....D 2
Krompachy, 3,340 ....F 2
Krupina, 5,418 ....E 2
Krupka, 10,000 ....B 1
Kutná Hora, 17,000 ....C 2
Kúty, 3,348 ....D 2
Kyjov, 5,620 ....D 2
Kynšperk, 5,398 ....B 1
Kysucké Nové Mesto, 2,318 ....E 2
Lanškroun, 6,558 ....D 2
Ledeč, 2,625 ....C 2
Levice, 15,000 ....E 2
Levoča, 7,584 ....F 2
Libáň, 2,261 ....C 1
Liberec, 71,000 ....C 1
Libochovice, 2,879 ....B 1
Lidice, 478 ....C 1
Lipník, 6,887 ....D 2
Liptovský Mikuláš, 14,000 ....E 2
Lišov, 2,691 ....C 2
Litoměřice, 18,000 ....C 1
Litomyšl, 6,384 ....D 2
Litovel, 4,496 ....D 2
Litvínov, 22,000 ....B 1
Lomnice, 2,228 ....C 2
Louny, 13,000 ....B 1
Lovosice, 4,962 ....C 1
L'ubica, 3,335 ....F 2
Lučenec, 18,000 ....E 2
Lysá, 6,500 ....C 1
Malacky, 11,000 ....D 2
Mariánské Lázně, 13,000 ....B 2
Martin, 29.000 ....E 2
Mělník, 15,000 ....C 1
Michalovce, 18,000 ....G 2
Mikulov, 5,220 ....D 2
Milevsko, 3,754 ....C 2
Mimoň, 5,349 ....C 1
Mladá Boleslav, 27,000 ....C 1
Mladá Vožice, 1,732 ....C 2
Mnichovo Hradiště, 4,647 ....C 1
Modra, 6,239 ....D 2
Modrý Kameň, 1,836 ....E 2
Mohelnice, 4,949 ....D 2
Moldava, 2,241 ....F 2
Moravská Třebová, 5,844 ....D 2
Moravské Budějovice, 4,348 ....D 2
Moravský Krumlov, 2,897 ....D 2
Most, 56,000 ....B 1
Mučeníky, 5,207 ....D 2
Myjava, 9,935 ....D 2
Náchod, 18,000 ....D 1
Neded, 4,553 ....D 2
Nejdek, 5,748 ....B 1
Nepomuk, 1,860 ....B 2
Nesvady, 5,070 ....E 3
Netolice, 2.503 ....C 2
Nitra, 39,000 ....E 2
Nová Baňa, 5,113 ....E 2
Nová Bystřice, 2,418 ....C 2
Nové Město na Moravě, 3,250 ....D 2
Nové Město nad Váhom, 14,000 ....D 2
Nové Strašecí, 3,288 ....B 1
Nové Zamky, 24,000 ....D 3
Nový Bohumín, 12,000 ....E 2
Nový Bor, 5,994 ....C 1
Nový Bydžov, 6,120 ....C 1
Nový Hrozenkov, 5,302 ....E 2
Nový Jičín, 17,000 ....E 2
Nymburk, 13,000 ....C 1
Nýřany, 4,420 ....B 2
Nýrsko, 4,124 ....B 2
Odry, 5,340 ....D 2
Olomouc, 77,000 ....D 2
Opava, 46,000 ....E 2
Orlová, 22,000 ....E 2
Oslavany, 3,606 ....D 2
Ostrava, 271,905 ....E 2
Ostrov, 19,000 ....B 1
Otrokovice-Kvítkovice, 11,000 ....D 2
Pacov, 2,775 ....C 2
Pardubice, 65,000 ....C 1
Partizánske, 3,171 ....E 2
Pelhřimov, 8,000 ....C 2
Pezinok, 12,000 ....D 2
Piešt'any, 21,000 ....D 2
Písek, 22,000 ....C 2
Planá, 5,216 ....B 2
Plánice, 1,718 ....B 2
Plasy, 1,472 ....B 2
Plzeň, 143,945 ....B 2
Počatky, 2,141 ....C 2
Podbořany, 3,893 ....B 1
Poděbrady, 13,000 ....C 1
Pohořelice, 3,068 ....D 2
Polička, 5,600 ....D 2
Polná, 4,005 ....C 2
Poprad, 18,000 ....F 2
Poruba, 21,179 ....D 2
Považská Bystrica, 13,000 ....E 2
Prachatice, 6,000 ....B 2
Prague (Praha) (capital), 1,031,870 ....C 1
Přelouč, 4,228 ....C 1
Přerov, 35,000 ....D 2
Prešov, 39,000 ....F 2
Přeštice, 4,616 ....B 2
Příbor, 5,491 ....E 2
Příbram, 29,000 ....B 2
Přibyslav, 2,556 ....C 2
Prievidza, 24,000 ....E 2
Prostějov, 35,000 ....D 2
Protivín, 3,217 ....C 2
Púchov, 4,316 ....E 2
Radnice, 2,342 ....B 2
Rajec, 2,753 ....E 2
Rakovník, 12,000 ....B 1
Ríčany, 6,376 ....C 2
Rimavská Sobota, 12,000 ....E 2
Rokycany, 13,000 ....B 2
Rokytnice nad Jizerou, 3,893 ....C 1
Rosice, 4,900 ....D 2
Roudnice nad Labem, 11,000 ....C 1
Rožňava, 11,000 ....F 2
Rožnov, 3,989 ....E 2
Rumburk, 6,759 ....C 1
Ružomberok, 20,000 ....E 2
Rychnov nad Kněžnou, 6.000 ....D 1
Rýmařov, 4,328 ....D 2
Sabinov, 3,909 ....F 2
Šafaríkovo, 3,180 ....F 2
Šahy, 4,019 ....E 2
Šal'a, 4,397 ....D 2
Sečovce, 3,354 ....F 2
Sedlčany, 2,083 ....C 2
Semily, 6,549 ....C 1
Senec, 6,184 ....D 2
Senica, 8,000 ....D 2
Sered', 6,208 ....D 2
Skalica, 5,440 ....D 2
Skuteč, 3,348 ....D 2
Slaný, 12,000 ....C 1
Slavkov, 4,869 ....D 2
Snina, 5,002 ....G 2
Soběslav, 4,643 ....C 2
Sobotka, 2,147 ....C 1
Sokolov, 20.000 ....B 1
Spišská Belá, 3,072 ....F 2
Spišská Nová Ves, 20,000 ....F 2
Stará L'ubovňa, 1,989 ....F 2
Staré Mešto, 6.350 ....D 2
Šternberk, 12,000 ....D 2
Stod, 2,502 ....B 2
Strakonice, 16,000 ....B 2
Strážnice, 5,147 ....D 2
Stříbro, 4,659 ....B 2
Stropkov, 2,506 ....F 2
Štúrovo, 4,082 ....E 3
Šumperk, 22,000 ....D 1
Šurany, 5,381 ....E 2
Sušice, 6,793 ....B 2
Svárov, 3,381 ....C 1
Svitavy, 14,000 ....D 2
Tábor, 21,000 ....C 2
Tachov, 8,000 ....B 2
Tardošked, 6,689 ....E 2
Telč, 4,381 ....C 2
Teplá u Toužimě, 2,500 ....B 2
Teplice, 52,000 ....B 1
Terchová, 4,400 ....E 2
Tišnov, 4,885 ....D 2
Tisovec, 3,988 ....E 2
Topol'čany, 12,000 ....E 2
Třebíč, 21,000 ....C 2
Trebišov, 10,000 ....F 2
Třeboň, 4,663 ....C 2
Trenčin, 26,000 ....E 2
Třešt', 4,900 ....C 2
Trhové Sviny, 2,953 ....C 2
Třinec, 27,000 ....E 2
Trnava, 35,000 ....D 2
Trstená, 2,468 ....E 2
Trutnov, 24,000 ....D 1
Turnov, 12,000 ....C 1
Turzovka, 9,823 ....E 2
Týn, 4,135 ....C 2
Uherské Hradiště, 15,000 ....D 2
Uherský Brod, 6,457 ....D 2
Uhlířské Janovice, 1,979 ....C 2
Uničov, 3,325 ....D 2
Úpice, 5,498 ....C 1
Ústí nad Labem, 72,000 ....C 1
Ústí nad Orlicí, 11,000 ....D 2
Valašské Klobouky, 2,525 ....D 2
Valašské Meziříčí, 15,000 ....D 2
Varnsdorf, 14,000 ....C 1
Važec, 2,747 ....E 2
Vejprty, 5,476 ....B 1
Velká Bíteš, 1,714 ....D 2
Velká Bystřice, 4,459 ....D 2
Vel'ké Kapušany, 2,371 ....G 2
Velké Meziříčí, 6,217 ....D 2
Veselí nad Lužnicí, 4,382 ....C 2
Veselí nad Moravou, 4,636 ....D 2
Vítkov, 2,685 ....D 2
Vizovice, 3,583 ....D 2
Vlašim, 5,066 ....C 2
Vodňany, 5,374 ....C 2
Volary, 5,034 ....B 2
Volyně, 3,019 ....B 2
Votice, 2,191 ....C 2
Vráble, 3,148 ....E 2
Vracov, 4,171 ....D 2
Vranov, 3,964 ....F 2
Vrchlabí, 11,000 ....C 1
Vrútky, 5,927 ....E 2
Vsetín, 20,000 ....D 2
Vyškov, 13,000 ....D 2
Vysoké Mýto, 7,983 ....D 2
Vysoké Tatry, 14,445 ....F 2
Vyšší Brod, 1,905 ....C 2
Zábřeh, 5,847 ....D 2
Žamberk, 4,278 ....D 1
Žatec, 16,000 ....B 1
Zbiroh, 1,718 ....B 2
Zborov, 1,551 ....F 2
Žd'ár nad Sázavou, 12,000 ....C 2
Želiezovce, 3,748 ....E 2
Žiar nad Hronom, 11,000 ....E 2
Zidlochovice, 2,696 ....D 2
Žilina, 38,000 ....E 2
Zlaté Moravce, 4,003 ....E 2
Zlín (Gottwaldov), 63,000 ....D 2
Žlutice, 2,114 ....B 1
Znojmo, 25.000 ....D 2
Zvolen, 23,000 ....E 2

OTHER FEATURES

Berounka (river) ....C 2
Beskids, East (mts.) ....F 1
Beskids, West (mts.) ....E 2
Bohemia (region), 6,142,000 ....C 2
Bohemian (forest) ....B 2
Bohemian-Moravian Heights ....C 2
Dudváh (river) ....D 2
Dunajec (river) ....F 2
Dyje (river) ....D 2
Erzgebirge (mts.) ....B 1
Gerlachovka (mt.) ....E 2
Hornád (river) ....F 2
Hron (river) ....E 2
Ipel' (river) ....E 2
Jablunka (pass) ....E 2
Jeseniky (mts.) ....D 1
Jihlava (river) ....D 2
Kamýcká (res.) ....C 2
Krušné Hory (Erzgebirge) (mts.) ....B 1
Labe (river) ....C 1
Laborec (river) ....F 2
Lipno (res.) ....C 2
Lužnice (river) ....C 2
Moldau (Vltava) (river) ....C 2
Morava (river) ....D 2
Moravia (region), 3,636,000 ....D 2
Nitra (river) ....E 2
Oder (Odra) (river) ....D 2
Ohře (river) ....B 1
Orava (res.) ....E 2
Orava (river) ....E 2
Orlice (river) ....C 1
Orlická (res.) ....C 2
Otava (river) ....B 2
Poprad (river) ....F 2
Slana (river) ....F 2
Slapská (res.) ....C 2
Slovakia (region), 4,421,000 ....E 2
Slovenske Rudohorie (mts.) ....E 2
Štěchovická (res.) ....C 2
Sudeten (mts.) ....C 1
Tatra, High (mts.) ....E 2
Uh (river) ....G 2
Váh (river) ....D 2
Vltava (river) ....C 2
White Carpathians (mts.) ....E 2

HUNGARY

COUNTIES

Bács-Kiskun, 560,000 ....E 3
Baranya, 280,000 ....E 4
Békés, 440,000 ....F 3
Borsod-Abaúj-Zemplén, 600,000 ....F 2
Budapest (city), 1,990,000 ....E 3
Csongrád, 320,000 ....F 3
Fejér, 390,000 ....E 3
Győr-Sopron, 400,000 ....D 3
Hajdú-Bihar, 360,000 ....F 3
Heves, 340,000 ....F 3
Komárom, 300,000 ....E 3
Nógrád, 240,000 ....E 3
Pest, 870,000 ....E 3
Somogy, 360,000 ....D 3
Szabolcs-Szatmár, 540,000 ....G 3
Szolnok, 440,000 ....F 3
Tolna, 260,000 ....E 3
Vas, 280,000 ....D 3
Veszprém, 420,000 ....D 3
Zala, 260,000 ....D 3

CITIES and TOWNS

Aba, 4.369 ....E 3
Abádszalók, 7,257 ....F 3
Abaújszántó, 4,586 ....F 2
Abony, 16,048 ....E 3
Ács, 8,507 ....E 3
Adony, 4,211 ....E 3
Ajka, 21,000 ....D 3
Albertirsa, 11,490 ....E 3
Aszód, 5,361 ....E 3
Bácsalmás, 9,514 ....E 3
Baja, 34,000 ....E 3
Balassagyarmat, 13,000 ....E 2
Balatonfüred, 7,561 ....D 3
Balkány, 8,224 ....G 3
Balmazújváros, 18,645 ....F 3
Barcs, 7,245 ....D 4
Bátaszék, 7,378 ....E 3
Battonya, 11,019 ....F 3
Békés, 21,296 ....F 3
Békéscsaba, 53,000 ....F 3
Berettyóújfalu, 11,577 ....F 3
Berzence, 3,651 ....D 3
Bicske, 9,106 ....E 3
Biharkeresztes, 4,844 ....F 3
Biharnagybajom, 4,762 ....F 3
Böhönye, 3,809 ....D 3
Bonyhád, 9,354 ....E 3
Budafok, 39,870 ....E 3
Budaörs, 12,682 ....E 3
Budapest (capital), 1,990,000 ....E 3
Cegléd, 37,000 ....S 3
Celldömölk, 9,762 ....D 3
Cigánd, 5,220 ....F 2
Csákvár, 5,135 ....E 3
Csanádpalota, 5,264 ....F 3
Csenger, 4,835 ....G 3
Csepel, 86,287 ....E 3
Csepreg, 4,348 ....D 3
Csongrád, 20,000 ....E 3
Csorna, 9,192 ....D 3
Csorvás, 7,622 ....F 3
Csurgó, 5,400 ....D 3
Debrecen, 160,000 ....F 3
Derecske, 9,980 ....F 3
Dévaványa, 12,137 ....F 3
Devecser, 5,741 ....D 3
Dombóvár, 15,605 ....E 3
Dombrád, 6,868 ....F 2
Dömsöd, 6,532 ....E 3
Dorog, 9,994 ....E 3
Dunaföldvár, 11,039 ....E 3
Dunaharaszti, 13,655 ....E 3
Dunakeszi, 15,636 ....E 3
Dunaújváros, 45,000 ....E 3
Dunavecse, 4,908 ....E 3
Edelény, 6,851 ....F 2
Eger, 45,000 ....F 3
Egyek, 8,678 ....F 3
Elek, 6,325 ....F 3
Emőd, 5,233 ....F 3
Endrőd, 9,263 ....F 3
Enying, 6,406 ....E 3
Ercsi, 7,850 ....E 3
Érd, 25,900 ....E 3
Erdőtelek, 4,634 ....F 3
Esztergom, 26,000 ....E 3
Fegyvernek, 7,835 ....F 3
Fehérgyarmat, 6,024 ....G 3
Földeák, 4,275 ....F 3
Füzesabony, 7,125 ....F 3
Füzesgyarmat, 7,807 ....F 3
Gödöllő, 22,000 ....E 3
Gönc, 3,093 ....F 2
Gyoma, 10,921 ....F 3
Gyöngyös, 32,000 ....E 3
Győnk, 2,684 ....E 3
Győr, 81,000 ....D 3
Gyula, 25,000 ....F 3
Hajdúböszörmény, 30,000 ....F 3
Hajdúdorog, 10,559 ....F 3
Hajdúhadház, 13,030 ....F 3
Hajdúnánás, 17,000 ....F 3
Hajdúsámson, 7,784 ....F 3
Hajdúszoboszló, 22,000 ....F 3
Hajós, 5,584 ....E 3
Hatvan, 21,000 ....E 3
Heves, 11,349 ....F 3
Hogyesz, 3,501 ....E 3
Hódmezővásárhely, 53,000 ....F 3
Izsák, 8,609 ....E 3
Jánoshalma, 12,897 ....E 3
Jánosháza, 3,468 ....D 3
Jászapáti, 10,495 ....E 3
Jászárokszállás, 10,745 ....E 3
Jászberény, 30,000 ....E 3
Jászfényszaru, 7,542 ....E 3
Jászkarajenő, 4,955 ....E 3
Jászkisér, 7,280 ....F 3
Jászladány, 8.841 ....F 3
Kalocsa, 15.000 ....E 3
Kaposvár, 52,000 ....D 3
Kapuvár, 10,748 ....D 3
Karád, 3,438 ....D 3
Karcag, 24,000 ....F 3
Kazincbarcika, 29,000 ....F 2
Kecel, 10,193 ....E 3
Kecskemét, 76,000 ....E 3
Kemecse, 4,681 ....F 2
Keszthely, 17,000 ....D 3
Kisbér, 4,567 ....D 3
Kiskőrös, 12,954 ....E 3
Kiskundorozsma, 8,679 ....E 3
Kiskunfélegyháza, 33,000 ....E 3
Kiskunhalas, 28,000 ....E 3
Kiskunmajsa, 12,311 ....E 3
Kispest, 66,547 ....E 3
Kistelek, 8,925 ....E 3
Kisújszállás, 13,000 ....F 3
Kisvárda, 13,050 ....G 2
Komádi, 9,850 ....F 3
Komárom, 11,000 ....E 3
Komló, 28,000 ....E 3
Kondoros, 7,462 ....F 3
Körmend, 7,548 ....D 3
Körösladány, 7,302 ....F 3
Kőszeg, 10,000 ....D 3
Kunágota, 5,547 ....F 3
Kunhegyes, 10,792 ....F 3
Kunmadaras, 8,463 ....F 3
Kunszentmárton, 13,383 ....F 3
Kunszentmiklós, 8,198 ....E 3
Lajosmizse, 12,617 ....E 3
Lébény, 3,588 ....D 3
Lengyeltóti, 3,392 ....D 3
Letenye, 4,507 ....D 3
Lökösháza, 2,511 ....F 3
Lőrinci, 11,142 ....E 3
Madaras, 5,177 ....E 3
Makó, 29,000 ....F 3
Mándok, 4,828 ....G 2
Marcali, 7,877 ....D 3
Mátészalka, 11,496 ....G 3
Mélykút, 8,168 ....E 3
Mezőberény, 12,830 ....F 3
Mezőcsát, 6,583 ....F 3
Mezőfalva, 4,951 ....E 3
Mezőhegyes, 9,137 ....F 3
Mezőkövesd, 18,160 ....F 3
Mezőszilas, 3,434 ....E 3
Mezőtúr, 22,000 ....F 3
Mindszent, 9,179 ....F 3
Miskolc, 180,000 ....F 2
Mohács, 18,000 ....E 4
Monor, 15,360 ....E 3
Mór, 11,622 ....E 3
Mosonmagyaróvár, 25,000 ....D 3
Nádudvar, 10,006 ....F 3
Nagyatád, 8,791 ....D 3
Nagybajom, 4,972 ....D 3
Nagyecsed, 8,348 ....G 3
Nagyhalász, 6,650 ....F 2
Nagykálló, 11,329 ....F 3
Nagykanizsa, 38,000 ....D 3
Nagykáta, 11,924 ....E 3
Nagykőrös, 26,000 ....E 3
Nagyléta, 6,902 ....G 3
Nagyszénás, 7,439 ....F 3
Nyírábrány, 4,517 ....G 3
Nyírádony, 7,325 ....G 3
Nyírbátor, 10,167 ....G 3
Nyíregyháza, 65,000 ....F 3
Nyírmada, 4,826 ....F 2
Örkény, 5,001 ....E 3
Orosháza, 33,000 ....F 3
Oroszlány, 20,000 ....E 3
Ózd, 40,000 ....F 2
Paks, 11,919 ....E 3
Pannonhalma, 3,529 ....D 3
Pápa, 27,000 ....D 3
Pásztó, 8,091 ....E 3
Pécs, 140,000 ....E 3
Pécsvárad, 3,199 ....E 3
Pétervására, 2,727 ....F 3
Pilis, 8,458 ....E 3
Pilisvörösvár, 9,627 ....E 3
Polgár, 9,353 ....F 3
Püspökladány, 15,488 ....F 3
Putnok, 6,440 ....F 2
Ráckeve, 7,456 ....E 3
Rakamaz, 5,381 ....F 2
Rákospalota, 63,344 ....E 3
Sajószentpéter, 12,846 ....F 2
Salgótarján, 37,000 ....E 2
Sándorfalva, 5,815 ....F 3
Sárbogárd, 6,853 ....E 3
Sarkad, 12,169 ....F 3
Sárospatak, 12,799 ....F 2
Sárvár, 11,247 ....D 3
Sátoraljaújhely, 17,000 ....F 2
Siklós, 5,897 ....E 4
Siófok, 10,322 ....E 3
Solt, 7,199 ....E 3
Soltvadkert, 8,244 ....E 3
Sopron, 45,000 ....D 3
Sümeg, 5,925 ....D 3
Szabadszállás, 8,799 ....E 3
Szarvas, 19,000 ....F 3
Szécsény, 4,410 ....E 2
Szeged, 120,000 ....E 3
Szeghalom, 10,093 ....F 3
Szegvár, 6,970 ....F 3
Székesfehérvár, 71,000 ....E 3
Szekszárd, 23,000 ....E 3
Szendrő, 3,773 ....F 2
Szentendre, 12,000 ....E 3
Szentes, 32,000 ....F 3
Szentgotthárd, 5,421 ....D 3
Szerencs, 7,789 ....F 2
Szigetvár, 10,000 ....D 3
Szikszó, 6,110 ....F 2
Szolnok, 61,000 ....F 3
Szombathely, 62,000 ....D 3
Tab, 4,265 ....E 3
Tamási, 7,689 ....E 3
Tápiószele, 5,632 ....E 3
Tapolca, 10,000 ....D 3
Tarpa, 3,966 ....G 2
Tata, 19,000 ....E 3
Tatabánya, 64,000 ....E 3
Tét, 4,861 ....D 3
Tiszacsege, 7,002 ....F 3
Tiszaföldvár, 12,377 ....F 3
Tiszafüred, 11,214 ....F 3
Tiszakécske, 12,834 ....E 3
Tiszalök, 6,125 ....F 2
Tiszavasvári, 12,201 ....F 3
Tokaj, 5,031 ....F 2
Tolna, 8,741 ....E 3
Törökszentmiklós, 24,000 ....F 3
Tótkomlós, 9,368 ....F 3
Tura, 8,169 ....E 3
Túrkeve, 11,000 ....F 3
Újfehértó, 14,386 ....F 3
Újpest, 79,961 ....E 3
Vác, 29,000 ....E 3
Várpalota, 27,000 ....E 3
Vasvár, 4,293 ....D 3
Vecsés, 16,411 ....E 3
Veszprém, 33,000 ....D 3
Vésztő, 10,463 ....F 3
Villány, 2,769 ....E 4
Zahony, 2,117 ....G 2
Zalaegerszeg, 33,000 ....D 3
Zalaszentgrót, 4,470 ....D 3
Zirc, 5,427 ....D 3

OTHER FEATURES

Bakony (mts.) ....D 3
Balaton (lake) ....D 3
Berettyó (river) ....F 3
Börsöny (mts.) ....E 3
Bükk (mts.) ....F 2
Csepelsziget (isl.) ....E 3
Danube (river) ....E 3
Dráva (river) ....D 3
Duna (Danube) (river) ....E 3
Fertö tó (Neusiedler) (lake) ....D 3
Great Alföld (plain) ....F 3
Hernád (river) ....F 2
Ipoly (river) ....E 2
Kapos (river) ....E 3
Kékes (mt.) ....E 3
Kőrishegy (mt.) ....D 3
Körös (river) ....F 3
Little Alföld (plain) ....D 3
Maros (river) ....F 3
Matra (mts.) ....E 3
Mecsek (mts.) ....D 3
Neusiedler (lake) ....D 3
Rába (river) ....D 3
Sajo (river) ....F 2
Sebes Körös (river) ....F 3
Sió (canal) ....E 3
Szentendreisziget (isl.) ....E 3
Tarna (river) ....F 3
Tisza (river) ....F 3
Zala (river) ....D 3

Agriculture, Industry and Resources

ÚSTÍ–ORE MTS.
Iron & Steel, Chemicals, Machinery

LIBEREC–SUDETEN
Textiles, Machinery

PARDUBICE
Machinery, Chemicals

OLOMOUC
Machinery, Textiles

OSTRAVA
Iron & Steel, Machinery, Chemicals

PLZEŇ
Automobiles, Iron & Steel, Machinery, Brewing, Armaments

PRAGUE–KLADNO
Machinery, Iron & Steel, Automobiles, Chemicals

GOTTWALDOV
Machinery, Rubber, Shoes

KOŠICE
Iron & Steel

BRNO
Machinery, Automobiles, Chemicals, Textiles

MISKOLC
Iron & Steel, Machinery

LINZ–STEYR
Iron & Steel, Chemicals, Automobiles

GRAZ–MÜRZ VALLEY
Iron & Steel, Machinery, Chemicals, Paper

VIENNA
Machinery, Electrical Equipment, Textiles, Chemicals

BUDAPEST
Machinery, Iron & Steel, Chemicals

DOMINANT LAND USE

- Cereals (chiefly wheat, corn)
- Other Cereals, Livestock, Dairy
- General Farming, Livestock
- General Farming, Truck Farming
- Pasture Livestock
- Grapes, Wine
- Forests
- Nonagricultural Land

MAJOR MINERAL OCCURRENCES

Ag Silver
Al Bauxite
C Coal
Fe Iron Ore
G Natural Gas
Gr Graphite
Hg Mercury
Lg Lignite
Mg Magnesium
Mn Manganese
Na Salt
O Petroleum
Sb Antimony
U Uranium

Water Power

Major Industrial Areas

YUGOSLAVIA
AREA 98,766 sq. mi.
POPULATION 20,586,000
CAPITAL Belgrade
LARGEST CITY Belgrade
HIGHEST POINT Triglav 9,393 ft.
MONETARY UNIT Yugoslav dinar
MAJOR LANGUAGES Serbo-Croatian, Slovenian, Macedonian, Albanian
MAJOR RELIGIONS Eastern Orthodoxy, Roman Catholicism, Islam

ALBANIA
AREA 11,100 sq. mi.
POPULATION 2,126,000
CAPITAL Tiranë
LARGEST CITY Tiranë
HIGHEST POINT Korab 9,026 ft.
MONETARY UNIT lek
MAJOR LANGUAGE Albanian
MAJOR RELIGIONS Islam, Eastern Orthodoxy, Roman Catholicism

RUMANIA
AREA 91,699 sq. mi.
POPULATION 20,394,000
CAPITAL Bucharest
LARGEST CITY Bucharest
HIGHEST POINT Moldoveanul 8,343 ft.
MONETARY UNIT leu
MAJOR LANGUAGES Rumanian, Hungarian
MAJOR RELIGION Eastern Orthodoxy

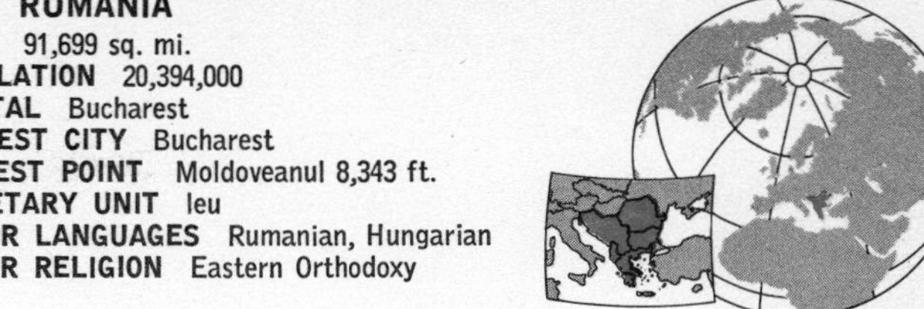

BULGARIA
AREA 42,829 sq. mi.
POPULATION 8,501,000
CAPITAL Sofia
LARGEST CITY Sofia
HIGHEST POINT Musala 9,597 ft.
MONETARY UNIT lev
MAJOR LANGUAGE Bulgarian
MAJOR RELIGION Eastern Orthodoxy

GREECE
AREA 50,548 sq. mi.
POPULATION 8,838,000
CAPITAL Athens
LARGEST CITY Athens
HIGHEST POINT Olympus 9,570 ft.
MONETARY UNIT drachma
MAJOR LANGUAGE Greek
MAJOR RELIGION Eastern (Greek) Orthodoxy

BULGARIA

GREECE

YUGOSLAVIA

ALBANIA

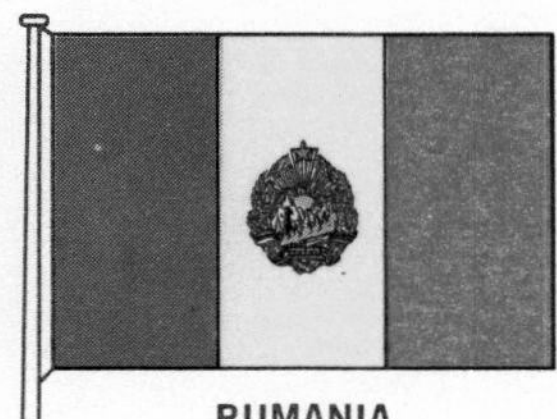
RUMANIA

Agriculture, Industry and Resources

DOMINANT LAND USE

- Cereals (chiefly wheat, corn)
- Mixed Farming, Horticulture
- Pasture Livestock
- Tobacco, Cotton
- Grapes, Wine
- Forests
- Nonagricultural Land

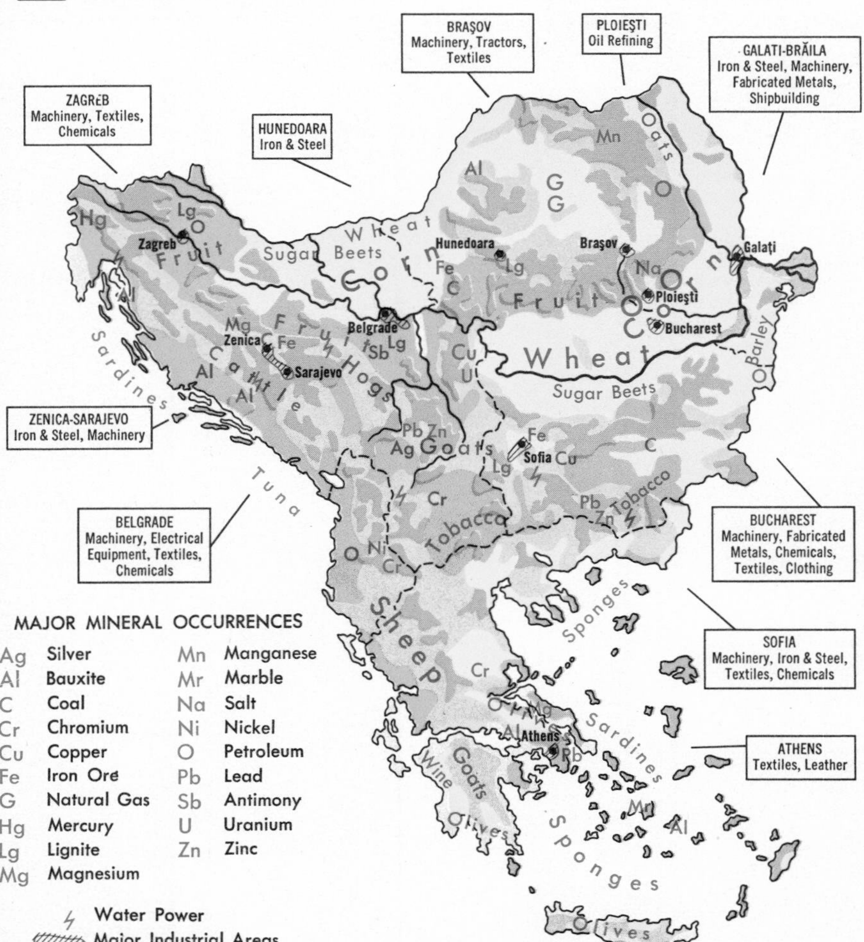

ALBANIA

CITIES and TOWNS

Berat, 22,000 ....D 5
Bajram Cur, 1,795 ....D 4
Burrel, 3,150 ....D 5
Çorovodë, 1,790 ....E 5
Delvinë, 5,700 ....D 6
Durrës, 47,900 ....D 5
Elbasan, 35,300 ....E 5
Ersekë, 2,150 ....E 5
Fier, 17,900 ....D 5
Gjirokastër, 15,000 ....D 5
Kavajë, 17,700 ....D 5
Korcë, 43,700 ....E 5
Kruë, 6,700 ....D 5
Kucovë (Stalin), 12,300 ....D 5
Kukës, 3,900 ....E 4
Leskovik, 1,625 ....E 5
Lezh, 3,000 ....D 5
Lushnje, 16,000 ....D 5
Peqin, 3,800 ....D 5
Përmet, 4,000 ....E 5
Peshkopi, 5,500 ....E 5
Pogradec, 8,900 ....E 5
Pukë, 1,700 ....E 4
Sarandë, 7,700 ....E 6
Shijak, 5,100 ....D 5
Shkodër, 47,000 ....D 5
Stalin, 12,300 ....D 5
Tepelenë, 2,500 ....D 5
Tiranë (Tirana) (cap.), 170,000 ....E 5
Vlorë, 46,900 ....D 5

OTHER FEATURES

Adriatic (sea) ....B 4
Drin (riv.) ....E 4
Korab (mt.) ....E 5
Ohrid (lake) ....E 5
Otranto (str.) ....D 5
Prespa (lake) ....E 5
Sazan (isl.) ....D 5
Scutari (lake) ....D 4
Tomor (mt.) ....E 5
Vijosë (riv.) ....D 5

BULGARIA

CITIES and TOWNS

Alfatar, 3,650 ....H 4
Akhtopol, 1,058 ....H 4
Alfatar, 4,042 ....H 4
Ardino, 2,558 ....G 5
Asenovgrad, 37,411 ....G 5
Aytos, 17,769 ....H 4
Balchik, 8,714 ....H 4
Bansko, 7,851 ....F 5
Belogradchik, 5,174 ....F 4
Berkovitsa, 11,553 ....F 4
Blagoyevgrad, 32,744 ....F 5
Botevgrad, 12,051 ....F 4
Bregovo, 4,725 ....F 3
Breznik, 4,093 ....F 4
Burgas, 122,212 ....H 4
Byala, 9,347 ....G 4
Byala Slatina, 14,942 ....F 4
Chirpan, 17,857 ....G 4
Devin, 4,475 ....G 5
Dimitrovgrad, 41,787 ....G 4
Dobrich (Tolbukhin), 55,111 ....H 4
Dryanovo, 8,187 ....G 4
Elena, 4,071 ....G 4
Elin Pelin, 8,074 ....F 4
Elkhovo, 11,315 ....H 4
Gabrovo, 57,758 ....G 4
General Toshevo, 8,251 ....H 4
Godech, 4,074 ....F 4
Gorna Dzhumaya (Blagoyevgrad), 32,744 ....F 5
Gorna Oryakhovitsa, 26,290 ....G 4
Gotse Delchev, 14,457 ....F 5
Grudovo, 9,177 ....F 4
Ikhtiman, 10,325 ....F 4
Isperikh, 8,445 ....H 4
Ivaylovgrad, 2,907 ....H 5
Karapelit, 2,033 ....H 4
Karlovo (Levskigrad), 20,287 ..G 4
Karnobat (Polyanovgrad), 18,727 ....H 4
Kavarna, 8,291 ....J 4
Kazanlŭk, 44,418 ....G 4
Kharmanlii, 15,478 ....H 5
Khaskovo, 57,682 ....G 5
Kolarovgrad (Shumen), 59.362 ....H 4
Kotel, 7,209 ....H 4
Krumovgrad, 2,230 ....G 5
Kubrat, 7,531 ....H 4
Kula, 6,474 ....F 4
Kŭrdzhali, 33,319 ....G 5
Kyustendil, 38,199 ....F 4
Levskigrad, 20,287 ....G 4
Lom, 28,189 ....F 4
Lovech, 30,843 ....G 4
Lukovit, 9,716 ....G 4
Mallco Tŭrnovo, 3,744 ....H 4
Maritsa, 8,532 ....H 4
Michurin, 2,783 ....H 4
Mikhaylovgrad, 27,240 ....F 4
Momchilgrad, 6,084 ....G 5
Nesebŭr, 2,333 ....H 4
Nikopol, 5,763 ....G 4
Nova Zagora, 19,257 ....H 4
Novi Pazar, 12,476 ....H 4
Omurtag, 8,148 ....H 4
Oryakhovo, 7,498 ....F 4
Panagyurishte, 18,298 ....F 4
Pazardzhik, 55,410 ....G 4
Pernik, 75,844 ....F 4
Peshtera, 14,606 ....G 4
Petrich, 20,653 ....F 5
Pirdop, 8,252 ....G 4
Pleven, 79,234 ....G 4
Plovdiv, 234,547 ....G 4
Polyanovgrad, 18,727 ....H 4
Pomorie, 9,567 ....H 4
Popina, 2,699 ....H 3
Popovo, 15,609 ....H 4
Provadiya, 13,837 ....H 4
Radomir, 8,458 ....F 4
Razgrad, 26,297 ....H 4
Razlog, 10,425 ....F 5
Rositsa, 1,505 ....H 4
Ruse, 142,894 ....H 4
Samokov, 21,585 ....F 4
Sandanski, 14,590 ....F 5
Sevlievo, 20,396 ....G 4
Shabla, 3,788 ....J 4
Shumen, 59,362 ....H 4
Silistra, 32,996 ....H 3
Simeonovgrad (Maritsa), 8,532 ....H 4
Sliven, 68,331 ....H 4
Smolyan, 17,479 ....G 5
Smyadovo, 5,349 ....H 4
Sofia (cap.), 840,113 ....F 4
Sofia, *923,400 ....F 4
Sozopol, 3,257 ....H 4
Stanke Dimitrov, 35,813 ....F 4
Stara Zagora, 100,565 ....G 4
Sveti Vrach (Sandanski), 14,590 ....F 5
Svilengrad, 12,438 ....G 5
Svishtov, 21,522 ....G 4
Teteven, 9,807 ....G 4
Tolbukhin, 55,111 ....H 4
Topolovgrad, 6,633 ....H 4
Troyan, 18,982 ....G 4
Trŭn, 2,922 ....F 4
Tŭrgovishte, 25,528 ....H 4
Tutrakan, 9,909 ....H 4
Varna, 200,827 ....J 4
Veliko Tŭrnovo, 37,269 ....G 4
Vidin, 36,820 ....F 4
Vratsa, 39,052 ....F 4
Yambol, 58,405 ....H 4
Zlatograd, 6,508 ....G 5

OTHER FEATURES

Balkan (mts.) ....G 4
Black (sea) ....J 4
Danube (Dunav) (riv.) ....H 4
Emine (cape) ....J 4
Iskŭr (riv.) ....G 4
Kaliakra (cape) ....J 4
Lom (riv.) ....H 4
Maritsa (riv.) ....G 4
Mesta (riv.) ....F 5
Musala (mt.) ....F 4
Osŭm (riv.) ....G 4
Rhodope (mts.) ....G 5
Ruen (mt.) ....F 4
Struma (riv.) ....F 5
Timok (riv.) ....F 3
Tundzha (riv.) ....G 4
Vit (riv.) ....G 4

GREECE

REGIONS

Aegean Islands, 477,476 ....G 6
Áyion Óros (aut. dist.), 2,687 ....G 5
Central Greece and Euboea, 2,823,658 ....F 6
Crete, 483,258 ....G 8
Epirus, 352,604 ....E 6
Greater Athens, 1,852,709 ....F 7
Ionian Islands, 212,573 ....D 6
Macedonia, 1,890,654 ....F 5
Pelopónnisos, 1,096,390 ....F 7
Thessalía, 695,385 ....F 6
Thrace, 356,555 ....G 5

CITIES and TOWNS

Agrínion, 24,763 ....E 6
Aíyina, 4,989 ....F 7
Aíyion, 17,762 ....F 6
Alexandroúpolis, 18,712 ....H 5
Alivérion, 3,523 ....G 6
Almirós, 6,010 ....F 6
Amaliás, 15,468 ....E 7
Amfilokhía, 5,408 ....E 6
Ámfissa, 6,076 ....F 6
Ándissa, 2,530 ....H 6
Andravídha, 3,155 ....E 6
Ándros, 2,032 ....G 7
Áno Viánnos, 1,820 ....G 8
Anóyia, 2,461 ....G 8
Ardhéa, 3,222 ....F 5
Argalastí, 1,864 ....F 6
Árgos, 16,712 ....F 7
Argostólion, 7,322 ....E 6
Arkhángelos, 2,918 ....J 7
Arnaía, 2,612 ....F 5
Árta, 16,899 ....E 6
Astipálaia, 1,205 ....H 7
Atalándi, 4,552 ....F 6
Athens (cap.), 627,564 ....F 7
Athens, *2,347,000 ....F 7
Áyios Matthaíos, 1,892 ....D 6
Áyios Nikólaos, 3,709 ....G 8
Candia (Iráklion), 63,458 ....G 8
Canea (Khaniá), 38,467 ....G 8
Chalcis (Khalkís), 24,745 ....F 6
Corinth, 15,892 ....F 7
Delvinákion, 1,076 ....E 6
Dhidhimótikhon, 7,287 ....H 5
Dhíkaia, 1,181 ....H 5
Dhimitsána, 1,300 ....F 7
Dhomokós, 2,017 ....F 6
Dráma, 32,195 ....F 5
Édhessa, 15,534 ....F 5
Elassón, 6,501 ....F 6
Elevtheroúpolis, 5,448 ....G 5
Ermoúpolis, 14,402 ....G 7
Fársala, 6,356 ....F 6
Filiátes, 3,065 ....E 6
Filiatrá, 6,753 ....E 7
Flórina, 11,933 ....E 5
Gargaliánoi, 6,637 ....E 7
Grevená, 6,892 ....E 5
Ídhra, 2,546 ....F 7
Ierápetra, 6,488 ....G 8
Igoumenítsa, 3,235 ....E 6
Ioánnina, 34,997 ....E 6
Iráklion, 63,458 ....G 8
Istiaía, 3,882 ....F 6
Itháki, 2,632 ....E 6
Kalámai, 38,211 ....F 7
Kalampáka, 4,640 ....E 6
Kalávrita, 2,039 ....F 6
Kálimnos, 10,211 ....H 7
Kardhítsa, 23,708 ....E 6
Kariá, 1,739 ....E 6
Kariaí, 429 ....G 5
Káristos, 3,335 ....G 6
Karpenísion, 3,523 ....E 6
Kastéllion, 2,071 ....F 8
Kastéllion, 1,351 ....G 8
Kastoría, 10,162 ....E 5
Kateríni, 28,046 ....F 5
Kaválla, 44,517 ....G 5
Kéa, 1,788 ....G 7
Kérkira, 26,991 ....D 6
Khalkís, 24,745 ....F 6
Khaniá, 38,467 ....G 8
Khíos, 24,053 ....G 6
Kiáton, 6,069 ....F 6
Kilkís, 10,963 ....F 5
Kími, 3,252 ....F 6
Kiparissía, 4,602 ....E 7
Kíthira, 469 ....F 7
Komotiní, 28,355 ....G 5
Kónitsa, 3,485 ....E 5
Koropí, 7,862 ....G 7
Kos, 8,138 ....H 7

(continued on following page)

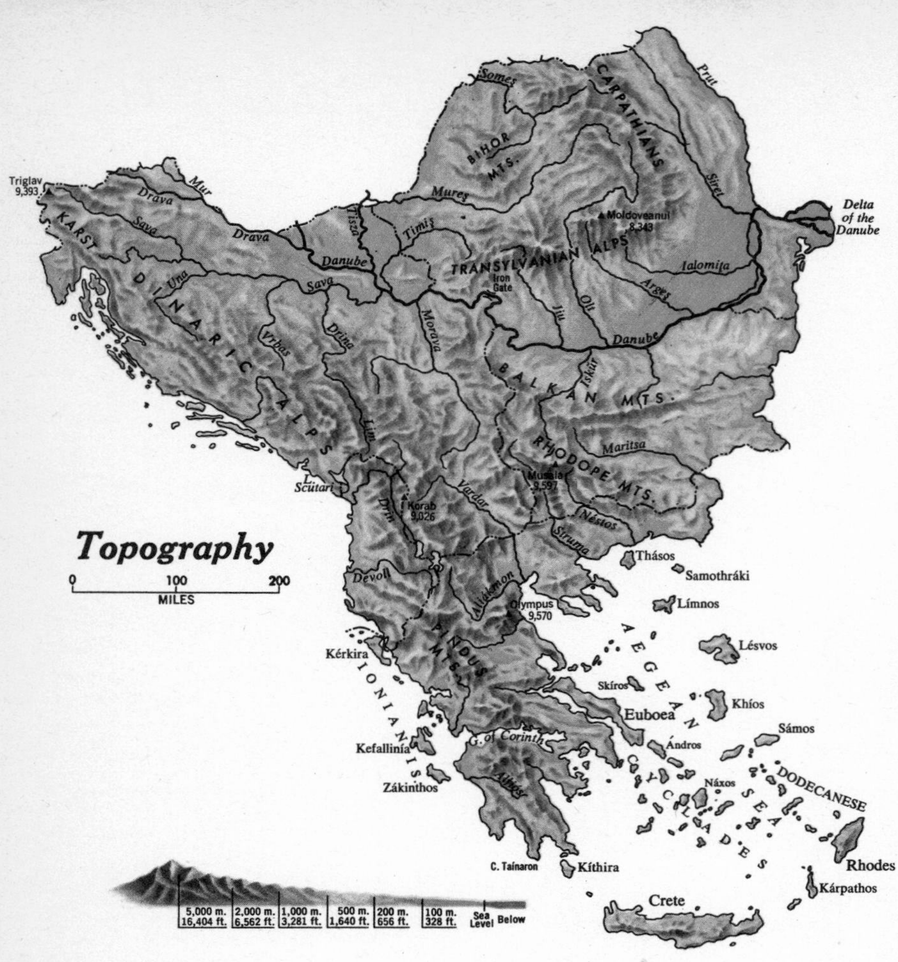

GREECE (continued)

Kozáni, 21,537 F 5
Kranídhion, 3,942 F 7
Lamía, 21,509 F 6
Langadhás, 6,739 F 5
Lárisa, 55,391 F 6
Lávrion, 6,553 G 7
Leonídhion, 3,297 F 7
Levádhia, 12,609 F 6
Levkás, 6,552 E 6
Limenária, 1,999 G 5
Limín Vathéos,
5,469 H 7
Límni, 2,394 F 6
Litókhoron, 5,032 F 5
Lixoúrion, 3,977 E 6
Loutrá Aidhipsoú,
1,859 F 6
Marathón, 2,167 G 6
Megalópolis, 2,235 F 7
Mégara, 15,450 F 6
Meligalá, 1,960 F 7
Mesolóngion, 11,266 E 6
Messíni, 8,249 F 7
Métsovon, 2,976 E 6
Mikínai, 361 F 7
Mílos, 944 G 7
Mírina, 3,460 G 6
Missolonghi (Mesolóngion),
11,266 E 6
Míthimna, 1,828 G 6
Mitilíni, 25,758 H 6
Moláoi, 2,526 F 7
Monólithos, 496 H 7
Moúdhros, 1,236 G 6
Náousa, 15,492 F 5
Návpaktos, 7,080 F 6
Návplion, 8,918 F 7
Náxos, 2,458 G 7
Néa Filippiás, 3,001 E 6
Neápolis, 2,464 F 7
Neméa, 4,720 F 7
Néon Karlóvasi,
5,308 H 7
Nigríta, 9,979 F 5
Olimbía, 771 E 7
Orestiás, 10,281 H 5
Paramithiá, 2,827 E 6
Pátrai, 95,364 E 6
Péta, 2,522 E 6
Pigádhia, 1,281 H 8
Pílos, 2,434 E 7
Piraiévs (Piraeus),
183,877 F 7
Pírgos, 20,558 E 7
Pirgí, 1,914 G 6
Píthion, 1,535 H 5
Plomárion, 5,172 H 6
Políkastron, 3,821 F 5
Políkhnitos, 5,131 G 6
Políyiros, 3,541 F 5
Póros, 4,392 F 7
Préveza, 11,172 E 6
Psakhná, 4,433 F 6
Ptolemaís, 12,747 E 5
Réthimnon, 14,999 G 8
Ródhos (Rhodes),
27,393 J 7
Salamís, 11,161 F 6
Salonika (Thessaloníki),
448,000 F 5
Sámi, 1,065 E 6
Samothráki, 1,555 G 5
Sápai, 2,589 G 5
Sérrai, 40,063 F 5
Sérvia, 4,132 F 5
Siátista, 4,737 E 5
Sidhirókastron, 8,177 F 5
Símí, 2,982 H 7
Sitía, 5,327 H 8
Skíros, 2,411 G 6
Skópelos, 2,955 F 6
Souflíon, 6,693 H 5
Sparta, 10,412 F 7
Spétsai, 3,314 F 7
Stilís, 4,673 F 6
Thebes (Thívai),
15,779 F 6
Thessaloníki, 448,000 F 5
Thásos, 1,875 G 5
Thíra, 1,481 G 7
Thívai, 15,779 F 6
Timbákion, 2,816 G 8
Tínos, 2,888 G 7
Tírnavos, 10,805 F 6
Tríkkala, 27,876 E 6
Trípolis, 18,500 F 7
Vartholomión, 3,244 E 7
Vathí, 3,161 H 7
Velvendós, 4,158 F 5
Véroia, 25,765 F 5
Vólos, 49,221 F 6
Vólos, *67,424 F 6
Vónitsa, 2,996 E 6
Vrondádhes, 4,685 G 6
Xánthi, 26,377 G 5
Yiannitsá, 19,693 F 5
Yíthion, 4,992 F 7
Zákinthos, 9,506 E 7
Zante (Zákinthos),
9,506 E 7

OTHER FEATURES

Aegean (sea) G 6
Akrítas (cape) E 7
Aktí (pen.) G 5
Amorgós (isl.), 2,396 G 7
Anáfi (isl.), 471 G 7
Andikíthira (isl.), 178 F 8
Ándros (isl.), 12,928 G 7
Arda (riv.) G 5
Argolís (gulf) F 7
Astipálaia (isl.),
1,539 H 7
Áthos (mt.) G 5
Áyios Evstrátios (isl.),
1,061 G 6
Áyios Yeóryios
(cape) G 5
Cephalonia (Kefallinía) (isl.),
39,793 E 6
Chios (Khíos) (isl.),
60,061 G 6
Corfu (Kérkira) (isl.),
99,092 D 6
Corinth (gulf) F 6
Crete (isl.), 483,075 G 8
Crete (sea) G 7
Cyclades (isls.),
99,959 G 7
Dhrépanon (cape) G 6
Dodecanese (isls.),
123,021 H 8
Euboea (isl.),
163,215 G 6
Évros (riv.) H 5
Gávdhos (isl.), 172 F 8
Ikaría (isl.), 9,577 G 7
Ionian (sea) D 7
Íos (isl.), 1,343 G 7
Itháki (Ithaca) (isl.),
5,210 E 6
Kálimnos (isl.),
10,211 H 7
Kafirévs (cape) G 6
6,689 H 8
Kárpathos (isl.), 6,689 H 8
Kásos (isl.), 1,422 H 8
Kassándra (pen.) F 6
Kéa (isl.), 2,361 G 7
Kefallinía (isl.),
39,793 E 6
Kérkira (isl.),
99,092 D 6
Khálki (isl.), 501 H 7
Khaní, (gulf) G 8
Khíos (isl.), 60,061 G 6
Kiparissía (gulf) E 7
Kíthira (isl.), 5,340 F 7
Kíthnos (isl.), 2,064 G 7
Kos (isl.), 18,187 H 7
Kriós (cape) F 8
Lakonía (gulf) F 7
Léros (isl.), 6,611 H 7
Lésvos (isl.),
117,371 G 6
Levítha (isl.), 7 H 7
Levkás (isl.), 2,697 E 6
Límnos (isl.),
21,808 G 6
Maléa (cape) F 7
Matapan (Taínaron)
(cape) F 7
Merabéllou (gulf) H 8
Mesará (gulf) G 8
Messíni (gulf) E 7
Míkonos (isl.),
3,633 G 7
Mílos (isl.), 4,910 G 7
Mirtóön (sea) F 7
Náxos (isl.), 16,703 G 7
Néstos (riv.) G 5
Nísiros (isl.), 1,788 H 7
Northern Sporades (isls.),
9,810 F 6
Olympus (mt.) F 5
Óssa (mt.) F 6
Parnassus (mt.) F 6
Páros (isl.), 7,830 G 7
Pátmos (isl.),
2,564 H 7
Paxoí (isl.), 2,678 D 6
Pindus (mts.) E 6
Piniós (riv.) E 6
Prespa (lake) E 5
Psará (isl.), 576 G 6
Rhodes (isl.),
63,951 H 7
Rhodope (mts.) G 5
Salonika (Thermaic)
(gulf) F 6
Sámos (isl.),
41,124 H 7
Samothráki (isl.),
3,830 G 5
Saría (isl.), 18 H 8
Saronic (gulf) F 7
Sérifos (isl.),
1,878 G 7
Sídheros (cape) H 8
Sífnos (isl.), 2,258 G 7
Sími (isl.), 3,123 H 7
Síros (isl.), 19,570 G 7
Sithoniá (pen.) F 5
Skíros (isl.), 2,882 G 6
Spátha (cape) F 8
Strimón (gulf) F 5
Strofádhes (isls.),
10 E 7
Taínaron (cape) F 7
Thásos (isl.),
15,916 G 5
Thermaic (gulf) F 6
Thíra (isl.), 7,751 G 7
Tílos (isl.), 789 H 7
Tínos (isl.), 9,273 G 7
Toronaic (gulf) F 5
Vardar (riv.) E 5
Voïviïs (lake) F 6
Vólvi (lake) F 5
Voúxa (cape) F 8
Zákinthos (Zante) (isl.),
35,499 E 7

RUMANIA

CITIES and TOWNS

Aiud, 11,886 F 2
Alba Iulia, 22,225 F 2
Alexandria, 21,907 G 3
Anina, 11,837 E 3
Arad, 132,757 E 2
Arad, *137,444 E 2
Babadag, 5,549 J 3
Bacău, 73,481 H 2
Bacău, *87,465 H 2
Baia Mare, 62,769 F 2
Baia Mare,
*108,709 F 2
Băilești, 15,932 F 3
Balș, 6,956 G 3
Beiuș, 6,467 F 2
Bîrlad, 41,061 H 2
Bîrlad, *52,497 H 2
Bistrița, 25,534 G 2
Blaj, 8,731 F 2
Botoșani, 35,185 H 2
Botoșani, *50,204 H 2
Brad, 9,963 F 2
Brăila, 147,495 H 3
Brașov, 175,264 G 3
Brașov, *264,537 G 3
Bucharest (București) (cap.),
1,431,993 G 3
Bucharest, *1,518,725 G 3
Buhuș, 12,382 H 2
Buzău, 56,380 H 3
Buzău, *82,454 H 3
Buziaș, 5,140 E 3
Călafat, 8,069 F 3
Călărași, 35,698 H 3
Caracal, 22,715 G 3
Caransebeș, 15,195 F 3
Carei, 16,780 F 2
Cernavodă, 8,802 J 3
Cîmpia Turzii,
11,514 F 2
Cîmpina, 22,862 H 3
Cîmpulung, 24,891 G 3
Cîmpulung Moldovenesc,
13,627 G 2
Cisnădie, 12,246 F 3
Cluj, 193,375 F 2
Cluj, *223,519 F 2
Comanești, 12,392 H 2
Constanța, 165,245 J 3
Constanța, *202,024 J 3
Corabia, 11,502 G 4
Craiova, 166,249 F 3
Craiova, *174,669 F 3
Curtea de Argeș,
10,764 G 3
Dej, 26,968 F 2
Deva, 26,952 F 3
Deva, *45,836 F 3
Dorohoi, 14,771 H 2
Drăgășani, 9,963 F 3
Făgăraș, 22,941 G 3
Fălticeni, 13,305 H 2
Fetești, 21,425 H 3
Focșani, 35,075 H 3
Focșani, *40,701 H 3
Găești, 7,179 G 3
Galați, 160,097 H 3
Gheorgheni, 11,969 G 2
Gherla, 7,617 G 2
Giurgiu, 39,225 G 3
Giurgiu, *55,471 G 3
Hațeg, 3,853 F 3
Hîrșova, 4,761 J 3
Hunedoara, 68,303 F 3
Hunedoara, *100,953 F 3
Huși, 20,703 J 2
Iași, 173,569 H 2
Iași, *196,167 H 2
Isaccea, 5,203 J 3
Jimbolia, 11,281 E 3
Lipova, 10,064 E 2
Lugoj, 35,388 F 3
Lupeni, 29,377 F 3
Mangalia, 4,792 J 4
Medgidia, 27,989 J 3
Mediaș, 46,396 G 2
Miercurea Ciuc,
11,996 G 2
Mizil, 7,460 H 3
Moinești, 12,934 H 2
Moldova Nouă,
3,582 E 3
Moreni, 11,687 G 3
Năsăud, 5,725 G 2
Ocna Mureș, 10,701 G 2
Odobești, 4,977 H 3
Odorhei, 14,162 G 2
Oltenița, 14,111 H 3
Oradea, 132,266 E 2
Oradea, *136,375 E 2
Orăștie, 10,488 F 3
Orașul Gheorghe Georghiu-Dej,
35,689 H 2
Oravița, 8,175 E 3
Orșova, 6,527 F 3
Panciu, 7,679 H 3
Pașcani, 15,008 H 2
Petrila, 24,804 F 3
Petroșeni, 35,237 F 3
Petroșeni, *130,111 F 3
Piatra Neamț, 45,925 G 2
Piatra Neamț,
*58,397 G 2
Pitești, 60,094 G 3
Pitești, *78,784 G 3
Ploiești, 156,382 H 3
Ploiești, *191,663 H 3
Pucioasa, 9,259 G 3
Rădăuți, 15,949 G 2
Reghin, 23,317 G 2
Reșița, 58,683 E 3
Reșița, *121,458 E 3
Rîmnicu Sărat,
22,325 H 3
Rîmnicu Vîlcea,
23,880 F 3
Roman, 38,990 H 2
Roman, *49,496 H 2
Roșiori de Vede,
21,707 G 3
Săcele, 22,822 G 3
Salonta, 16,276 E 2
Satu Mare, 68,257 F 2
Sebeș, 11,628 F 3
Sfîntu Gheorge,
20,759 G 3
Sibiu, 117,020 G 3
Sighetul-Marmației,
29,768 F 2
Sighișoara, 25,100 G 2
Șimleu Silvaniei, 8,560 F 2
Sinaia, 9,006 G 3
Sînnicolau Mare,
9,956 E 2
Siret, 5,664 G 1
Slănic, 6,842 G 3
Slatina, 13,381 G 3
Slobozia, 9,632 H 3
Solca, 2,384 G 2
Strehaia, 8,545 F 3
Suceava, 37,715 G 2
Suceava, *76,327 G 2
Sulina, 3,622 J 3
Techirghiol, 2,705 J 3
Tecuci, 28,458 H 3
Timișoara, 184,797 E 3
Timișoara, *194,159 E 3
Tîrgoviște, 29,754 G 3
Tîrgoviște, *48,005 G 3
Tîrgu Jiu, 30,837 F 3
Tîrgu Jiu, *33,019 F 3
Tîrgu Mureș, 86,458 G 2
Tîrgu Mureș,
*104,922 G 2
Tîrgu Neamț, 10,373 G 2
Tîrgu Ocna, 11,227 H 2
Tîrgu Secuiesc,
7,500 H 2
Tîrnăveni, 20,354 F 2
Toplița, 8,944 G 2
Tulcea, 35,552 J 3
Turda, 42,318 G 2
Turda, *69,768 G 2
Turnu Măgurele,
26,409 G 4
Turnu Severin,
45,394 F 3
Turnu Severin,
*52,497 F 3
Urlați, 8,658 H 3
Urziceni, 6,061 H 3
Vasile Roaită,
3,286 J 3
Vaslui, 14,850 H 2
Vatra Dornei,
10,822 G 2
Vișeu de Sus,
13,956 F 2
Zalău, 13,378 F 2
Zărnești, 6,673 G 3
Zimnicea, 12,445 G 4

OTHER FEATURES

Argeș (riv.) G 3
Buzău (riv.) H 3
Carpathian (mts.) G 2
Crișul Alb (riv.) F 2
Crișul Repede (riv.) F 2
Danube (river) H 4
Ialomița (marshes) J 3
Jiu (riv.) F 3
Moldoveanul (mt.) G 3
Mureș (riv.) E 2
Negoiul (mt.) G 3
Olt (riv.) G 3
Pietrosul (mt.) G 2
Prut (riv.) J 2
Siret (riv.) H 2
Someș (riv.) F 2
Timiș (riv.) E 3
Transylvanian Alps (mts.) G 3

YUGOSLAVIA

INTERNAL DIVISIONS

Bosnia and Hercegovina (rep.),
3,594,000 C 3
Croatia (rep.),
4,281,000 C 3
Kosovo-Mitohiyan (aut. prov.),
1,089,000 E 4
Macedonia (rep.),
1,506,000 E 5
Montenegro (rep.),
471,894 D 4
Serbia (rep.),
7,637,800 E 3
Slovenia (rep.),
1,624,900 B 2
Voyvodina (aut. prov.),
1,880,000 D 3

CITIES and TOWNS

Aleksinac, 8,828 E 4
Apatin, 17,000 D 3
Bačka Topola,
14,000 D 3
Bakar B 3
Banja Luka, 55,000 C 3
Bar, 2,184 D 4
Bečej, 22,000 E 3
Bela Crkva, 11,000 E 3
Belgrade (Beograd) (cap.),
745,000 E 3
Belgrade, *1,050,000 E 3
Bihać, 17,000 B 3
Bijeljina, 19,000 D 3
Bijelo Polje, 5,856 D 4
Bileća, 2,491 D 4
Biograd, 2,418 B 4
Bitola (Bitolj),
52,000 E 5
Bjelovar, 16,000 C 3
Bled, 4,156 A 2
Bor, 19,000 E 3
Bosanska Dubica,
6,259 C 3
Bosanska Gradiška,
6,363 C 3
Bosanska Kostajnica,
2,034 B 3
Bosanska Krupa,
6,191 C 3
Bosanski Brod, 7,350 D 3
Bosanski Novi, 7,023 C 3
Bosanski Petrovac,
3,473 C 3
Bosanski Šamac,
3,654 D 3
Brčko, 20,000 D 3
Brežice, 2,641 B 3
Brod, 30,000 D 3
Bugojno, 5,453 C 3
Buje, 1,955 A 3
Čačak, 30,000 F 4
Čapljina, 3,275 C 4
Caribrod (Dimitrovgrad)
3,665 F 4
Celje, 28,000 B 2
Cetinje, 9,359 D 4
Ćuprija, 12,000 E 4
Debar, 6,323 E 5
Derventa, 9,843 C 3
Dimitrovgrad, 3,665 F 4
Djakovica, 22,000 E 4
Djakovo, 13,000 D 3
Donji Vakuf, 3,764 C 3
Drvar, 3,646 C 3
Dubrovnik, 24,000 C 4
Fiume (Rijeka),
108,000 B 3
Foča, 6,763 D 4
Fojnica, 1,549 C 4
Gacko, 1,368 D 4
Gevgelija, 7,332 F 5
Glamoč, 1,626 C 3
Gnjilane, 14,000 E 4
Gornji Vafuf, 1,860 C 4
Gospić, 6,767 B 3
Gostivar, 14,000 E 5
Gračac, 2,183 B 3
Gračanica, 7,656 D 3
Gradačac, 5,878 D 3
Grubišno Polje, 2,655 C 3
Gusinje, 2,756 D 4
Hercegnovi, 3,797 D 4
Ivangrad, 6,969 E 4
Jajce, 6,853 C 3
Jesenice, 16,000 A 2
Kamnik, 5,062 B 2
Kanjiža, 10,000 D 2
Kardeljevo, 3,267 C 4
Karlovac, 35,000 B 3
Kavadarci, 13,000 E 5
Kičevo, 11,000 E 5
Kikinda, 32,000 E 3
Kladanj, 2,825 D 3
Ključ, 2,320 C 3
Knin, 5,116 C 3
Knjaževac, 7,448 F 4
Kočevje, 5,819 B 3
Konjic, 5,927 D 4
Koper, 12,000 A 3
Koprivnica, 12,000 C 2
Korčula, 2,458 C 4
Kosovska Mitrovica,
29,000 E 4
Kostajnica, 2,080 C 3
Kotor, 4,764 D 4
Kragujevac, 56,000 E 3
Kraljevo (Rankovićevo), 26,000 E 4
Kranj, 23,000 B 2
Križevci, 6,642 C 2
Krk, 1,280 B 3
Krško, 3,518 B 3
Kruševac, 31,000 E 4
Kumanovo, 33,000 E 4
Leskovac, 37,000 E 4
Livno, 5,181 C 4
Ljubljana, 183,000 B 2
Ljubuški, 2,168 C 4
Loznica, 12,000 D 3
Maglaj, 4,556 D 3
Makarska, 3,634 C 4
Maribor, 89,000 B 2
Mladenovac, 12,000 E 3
Modriča, 5,053 D 3
Mostar, 53,000 D 4
Našice, 4,187 C 3
Negotin, 8,635 F 3
Nevesinje, 2,349 D 4
Nikšić, 25,000 D 4
Niš, 92,000 E 4
Nova Gradiška, 9,229 C 3
Novi, 2,075 B 3
Novi Pazar, 23,000 E 4
Novi Sad, 119,000 D 3
Novo Mesto, 6,885 B 3
Novska, 3,844 C 3
Ogulin, 3,522 B 3
Ohrid, 18,000 E 5
Omiš, 2,171 C 4
Opatija, 7,974 A 3
Osijek, 78,000 D 3
Pag, 2,431 B 3
Pančevo, 49,000 E 3
Paraćin, 17,000 E 4
Peć, 30,000 E 4
Petrinja, 7,366 C 3
Piran, 5,474 B 3
Pirot, 20,000 F 4
Plav, 2,535 D 4
Pljevlja, 12,000 D 4
Podgorica (Titograd),
37,000 D 4
Pola (Pula), 40,000 A 3
Poreč, 3,006 A 3
Postojna, 4,857 B 3
Požarevac, 23,000 E 3
Požega, 14,000 C 3
Preševo, 5,680 E 4
Priboj, 5,490 D 4
Prijedor, 13,000 C 3
Prijepolje, 4,566 D 4
Prilep, 40,000 E 5
Priština, 43,000 E 4
Prizren, 29,000 E 4
Prokuplje, 15,000 E 4
Prozor, 1,052 C 4
Ptuj, 7,392 C 2
Pula, 40,000 A 3
Rab, 1,548 B 3
Rača, 1,351 E 3
Radeče, 1,500 B 2
Radoviš, 6,246 F 5
Ragusa (Dubrovnik),
24,000 C 4
Rankovićevo, 26,000 E 4
Raška, 2,278 E 4
Rijeka, 108,000 B 3
Rogatica, 3,040 D 4
Rovinj, 7,155 A 3
Ruma, 21,000 D 3
Šabac, 30,000 D 3
Sanski Most, 5,096 C 3
Sarajevo, 223,000 D 4
Senj, 3,903 B 3
Senta, 22,000 D 3
Šibenik, 27,000 C 4
Sisak, 29,000 C 3
Sinj, 4,134 C 4
Škofja Loka, 3,429 A 2
Skopje, 230,000 E 5
Skradin, 1,118 C 4
Smederevo, 29,000 E 3
Sombor, 31,000 D 3
Split, 106,000 C 4
Srebrenica, 1,859 D 3
Sremska Mitrovica,
22,000 D 3
Sremski Karlovci, 6,390 D 3
Stari Majdan, 1,445 C 3
Štip, 22,000 F 5
Stolac, 2,970 D 4
Struga, 6,857 E 5
Strumica, 17,000 F 5
Subotica, 76,000 D 2
Surdulica, 5,007 F 4
Svetozarevo, 22,000 E 4
Svilajnac, 5,895 E 3
Tešanj, 3,148 C 3
Tetovo, 27,000 E 5
Titograd, 37,000 D 4
Titovo Užice, 26,000 D 4
Titov Veles, 29,000 E 5
Travnik, 12,000 C 3
Trbovlje, 16,000 B 2
Trebinje, 4,073 D 4
Trogir, 5,003 C 4
Tržič, 4,881 B 2
Tuzla, 55,000 D 3
Ulcinj, 5,705 D 5
Valjevo, 27,000 D 3
Varaždin, 28,000 B 2
Vareš, 7,647 D 3
Veliki Bečkerek (Zrenjanin),
56,000 E 3
Vinkovci, 24,000 D 3
Virovitica, 10,000 C 3
Višegrad, 3,309 D 4
Vranje, 18,000 E 4
Vrbas, 18,000 D 3
Vršac, 32,000 E 3
Vukovar, 25,000 D 3
Žabari, 1,984 E 3
Zadar, 28,000 B 3
Zagreb, 503,000 C 3
Zaječar, 18,000 E 4
Zara (Zadar), 28,000 B 3
Zenica, 50,000 C 3
Žepče, 2,709 C 3
Zrenjanin, 56,000 E 3
Zvornik, 5,444 D 3

OTHER FEATURES

Adriatic (sea) B 4
Bobotov Kuk (mt.) D 4
Bosna (riv.) D 3
Brač (isl.), 14,227 C 4
Čazma (riv.) C 3
Cres (isl.), 4,949 B 3
Danube (riv.) E 3
Dinaric Alps (mts.) B 3
Drava (riv.) C 3
Drina (riv.) D 3
Dugi Otok (isl.), 4,873 B 3
Hvar (isl.), 12,147 C 4
Ibar (riv.) E 4
Kamenjak (cape) A 3
Korab (mt.) E 5
Korčula (isl.), 10,245 C 4
Kornat (isl.), 6 B 4
Krk (isl.), 14,548 B 3
Kvarner (gulf) B 3
Lastovo (Lagosta) (isl.),
1,449 C 4
Lim (riv.) D 4
Lošinj (isl.), 5,068 B 3
Mljet (isl.), 1,963 C 4
Morava (riv.) E 3
Mur (riv.) B 2
Neretva (riv.) C 4
Ohrid (lake) E 5
Pag (isl.), 8,017 B 3
Pelagruž (Pelagosa)
(isl.) C 4
Prespa (lake) E 5
Rab (isl.), 8,400 B 3
Ruen (mt.) F 4
Sava (riv.) C 3
Scutari (lake) D 4
Solta (isl.), 2,735 C 4
Tara (riv.) D 4
Timok (riv.) F 3
Tisza (riv.) E 3
Triglav (mt.) A 2
Una (riv.) C 3
Vardar (riv.) E 5
Vis (isl.), 7,004 C 4
Vrbas (riv.) C 3
Žirje (isl.), 506 B 4

*City and suburbs.

THE BALKAN STATES
CONIC PROJECTION
SCALE OF MILES
0 25 50 75 100 125 150 175
SCALE OF KILOMETRES
0 25 50 75 100 125 150 175
Capitals of Countries
Administrative Centers
International Boundaries
Major Internal Boundaries
Minor Internal Boundaries
Canals
BULGARIA and GREECE are divided into counties and departments, respectively. Because of the scale no attempt has been made to delimit and name these subdivisions; their administrative centers have, however, been designated.
The larger divisions named in Greece are well-known geographical regions, without administrative function.
RUMANIA consists of thirty-nine counties and three cities of regional status, Bucharest, Constanţa and Petroşeni. Scale does not permit delimiting these counties.
ALBANIA is divided into twenty-seven districts. Scale does not permit the delimitation of these divisions.
YUGOSLAVIA is a federation of six republics. The Serbian republic includes an autonomous province (Voyvodina), and an autonomous region (Kosovo-Mitohiyan).
20° Longitude East of 22° Greenwich
CZECHOSLOVAKIA
AUSTRIA
HUNGARY
RUMANIA
YUGOSLAVIA
BULGARIA
ALBANIA
GREECE
TURKEY
U.S.S.R.
ITALY
GERMANY
VIENNA
BUDAPEST
BUCHAREST
Belgrade
Sofia
Tiranë
ISTANBUL
Athens
ADRIATIC SEA
BLACK SEA
AEGEAN SEA
IONIAN SEA
TYRRHENIAN SEA
MEDITERRANEAN SEA
SEA OF MARMARA
SEA OF CRETE
Crete
Transylvanian Alps
Carpathian Mountains
Balkan Mts.
Rhodope Mts.
Dinaric Alps
Pindus Mts.
Danube
N
© C. S. HAMMOND & Co., N. Y.

Topography

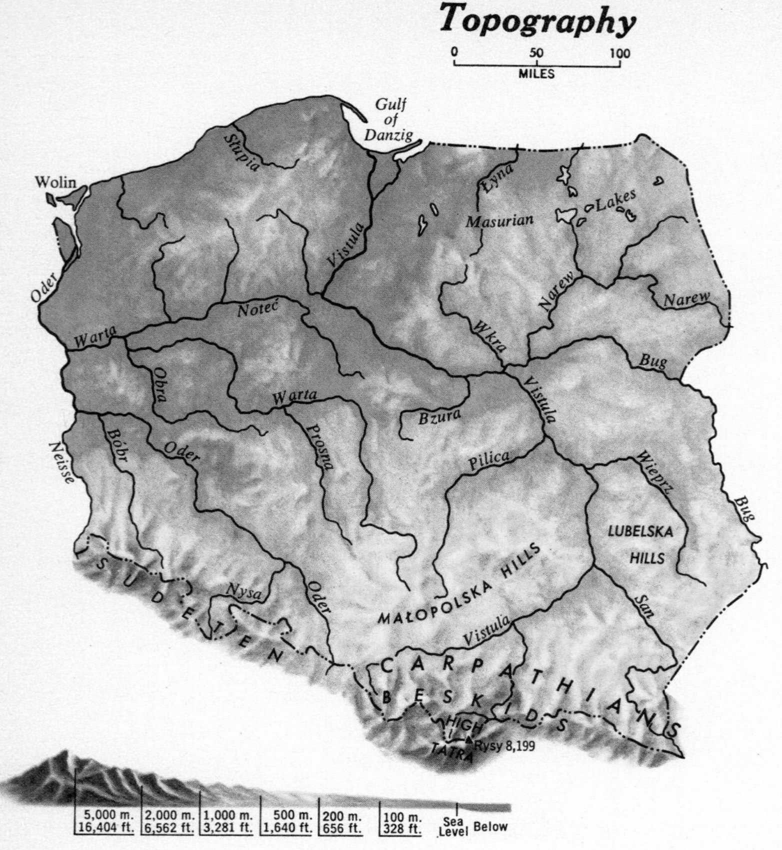

PROVINCES

Białystok, 1,177,000 ....F 2
Bydgoszcz, 1,871,000 ....D 2
Cracow (Kraków),
 2,159,000 ....D 4
Cracow (Kraków) (city),
 540,200 ....D 4
Gdańsk, 1,393,000 ....C 1
Katowice, 3,585,000 ....D 3
Kielce, 1,910,000 ....E 3
Koszalin, 774,000 ....C 2
Łódź, 1,675,000 ....D 3
Łódź (city),
 750,400 ....D 3
Lublin, 1,920,000 ....F 3
Olsztyn, 973,000 ....E 2
Opole, 1,027,000 ....C 3
Poznań, 2,159,000 ....C 2
Poznań (city),
 446,700 ....C 2
Rzeszów, 1,720,000 ....E 4
Szczecin, 872,000 ....B 2
Warsaw, 2,483,000 ....E 2
Warsaw (city),
 1,282,600 ....E 2
Wrocław, 1,994,000 ....C 3
Wrocław (city),
 487,000 ....C 3
Zielona Góra, 866,000 ....B 2

CITIES and TOWNS

Aleksandrów Łódzki,
 13,800 ....D 3
Allenstein (Olsztyn),
 80,700 ....E 2
Augustów, 18,400 ....F 2
Auschwitz (Oświęcim),
 36,900 ....D 3
Będzin, 41,800 ....C 4
Belgard (Białogard),
 20,100 ....B 2
Beuthen (Bytom),
 191,000 ....B 4
Biała Podlaska,
 23,500 ....F 2
Białogard, 20,100 ....B 2
Białystok, 149,000 ....F 2
Bielawa, 31,500 ....C 3
Bielsk Podlaski,
 13,000 ....F 2
Bielsko-Biała, 86,300 ....D 4
Bochnia, 13,600 ....E 4
Bogatynia,. 12,800 ....B 3
Bolesławiec, 28,400 ....B 3
Breslau (Wrocław),
 487,000 ....C 3
Brieg (Brzeg), 28,600 ....C 3
Brodnica, 16,300 ....D 2
Bromberg (Bydgoszcz),
 264,400 ....D 2
Brzeg, 28,600 ....C 3
Bydgoszcz,
 264,400 ....D 2
Bytom, 191,000 ....B 4
Chełm, 35,300 ....F 3
Chełmno, 17,800 ....D 2
Chełmza, 14,800 ....D 2
Chodziez, 13,100 ....C 2
Chojnice, 23,100 ....C 2
Chojnów, 10,900 ....B 3
Chorzów, 153,100 ....B 4
Chrzanów, 24,800 ....D 3
Ciechanów, 21,500 ....E 2
Cieplice Śląskie-Zdrój,
 15,700 ....B 3
Cieszyn, 24,700 ....D 4
Cracow (Kraków),
 540,200 ....E 3

Agriculture, Industry and Resources

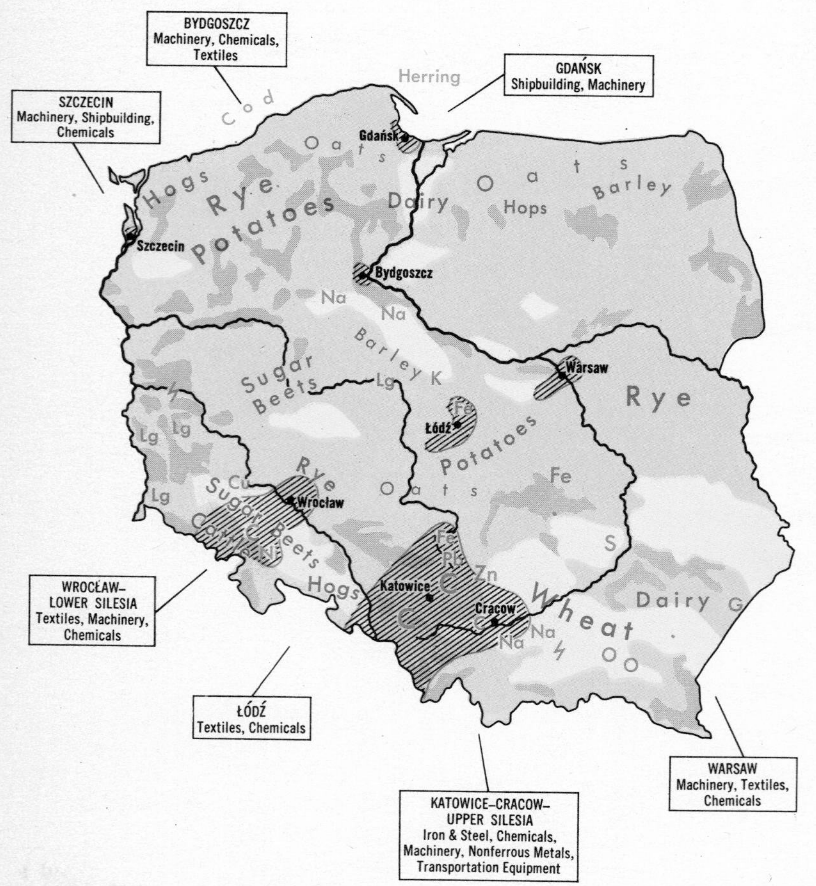

DOMINANT LAND USE

- Cereals (chiefly wheat)
- Rye, Oats, Barley, Potatoes
- General Farming, Livestock
- Forests

MAJOR MINERAL OCCURRENCES

C	Coal	Na	Salt
Cu	Copper	Ni	Nickel
Fe	Iron Ore	O	Petroleum
G	Natural Gas	Pb	Lead
K	Potash	S	Sulfur
Lg	Lignite	Zn	Zinc

ϟ Water Power

Major Industrial Areas

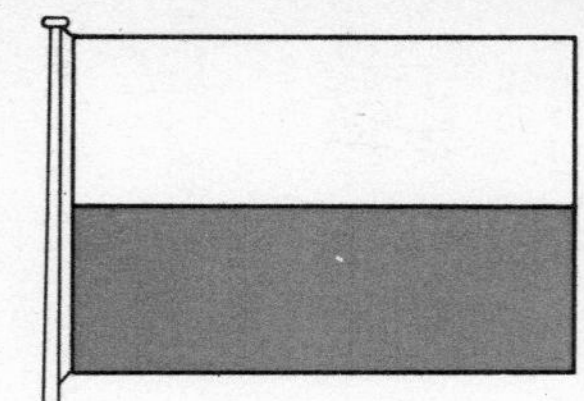

AREA 120,664 sq. mi.
POPULATION 32,889,000
CAPITAL Warsaw
LARGEST CITY Warsaw
HIGHEST POINT Rysy 8,199 ft.
MONETARY UNIT zloty
MAJOR LANGUAGE Polish
MAJOR RELIGION Roman Catholicism

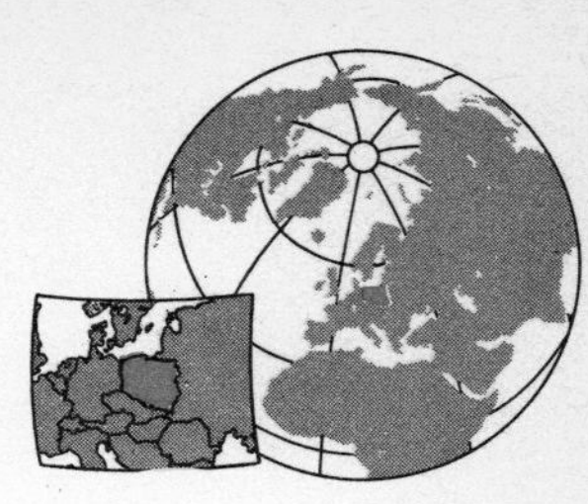

Czechowice-Dziedzice, 24,600 .... D 4
Czeladź, 31,400 .... B 4
Częstochowa, 179,400 .... D 3
Dąbrowa Górnicza, 60,100 .... C 4
Danzig (Gdańsk), 333,500 .... D 1
Dębica, 20,900 .... E 3
Dęblin, 11,700 .... E 3
Dębno, 10,200 .... B 2
Dirschau (Tczew), 38,000 .... D 1
Dzierżoniów, 31,900 .... C 3
Elbląg (Elbing), 86,700 .... D 1
Ełk, 25,300 .... F 2
Frankenstein (Ząbkowice Śląskie), 13,000 .... C 3
Gdańsk, 333,500 .... D 1
Gdynia, 171,900 .... D 1
Giżycko, 16,600 .... E 1
Glatz (Kłodzko), 25,600 .... C 3
Gliwice (Gleiwitz), 164,900 .... A 4
Głowno, 12,700 .... D 3
Głuchołazy, 14,000 .... C 3
Gniezno (Gnesen), 48,000 .... C 2
Gorlice, 14,000 .... E 4
Görlitz (Zgorzelec), 26,400 .... B 3
Gorzów Wielkopolski, 69,700 .... B 2
Gostyń, 12,200 .... C 3
Gostynin, 10,900 .... D 2
Graudenz (Grudziądz), 73,700 .... D 2
Grodziec, 10,500 .... B 3
Grodzisk Mazowiecki, 19,200 .... E 2
Grodzisk Wielkopolski, 8,300 .... C 2
Grudziądz, 73,700 .... D 2
Grünberg (Zielona Góra), 66,200 .... B 3
Gryfice, 12,500 .... B 2
Hajnówka, 14,400 .... F 2
Haynau (Chojnów), 10,900 .... B 3
Hindenburg (Zabrze), 197,600 .... A 4
Hirschberg (Jelenia Góra), 54,900 .... B 3
Hohensalza (Inowrocław), 52,000 .... C 2
Hrubieszów, 13,400 .... F 3
Inowrocław, 52,000 .... C 2
Jarocin, 17,700 .... C 3
Jarosław, 27,300 .... F 3
Jawor (Jauer), 15,300 .... C 3
Jaworzno, 63,000 .... D 3
Jędrzejów, 13,700 .... E 3
Jelenia Góra, 54,900 .... B 3
Kalisz, 77,500 .... D 3
Kamienna Góra, 21,100 .... C 3
Katowice, 291,600 .... B 4
Kędzierzyn, 27,900 .... D 3
Kętrzyn, 17,400 .... E 1
Kielce, 113,200 .... E 3
Kłobuck, 11,500 .... D 3
Kłodzko, 25,600 .... C 3
Kluczbork, 16,300 .... D 3
Knurów, 23,500 .... A 4
Koło, 12,100 .... D 2
Kołobrzeg, 23,000 .... B 1
Königshütte (Chorzów), 153,100 .... B 4
Konin, 29,300 .... D 2
Końskie, 11,700 .... E 3
Konstantynów, 12,500 .... D 3
Kościan, 17,300 .... C 2
Kościerzyna, 13,500 .... C 1
Koszalin, 56,800 .... C 1
Kraków (Cracow), 540,200 .... E 3
Kraśnik, 13,700 .... F 3
Krasnystaw, 11,800 .... F 3
Krosno, 24,600 .... E 4
Krotoszyn, 20,900 .... C 3
Krynica, 9,300 .... E 4
Kutno, 28,100 .... D 2
Kwidzyń, 22,800 .... D 2
Łańcut, 11,300 .... F 3
Landeshut (Kamienna Góra), 21,100 .... C 3
Landsberg (Gorzów Wielkopolski), 69,700 .... B 2
Langenbielau (Bielawa), 31,500 .... C 3
Lauban (Lubań), 16,800 .... B 3
Lębork (Lauenburg), 24,100 .... C 1
Łęczyca, 13,700 .... D 2
Lędziny, 13,600 .... B 4
Legionowo, 20,100 .... E 2
Legnica, 73,400 .... C 3
Leszno, 32,500 .... C 3
Lidzbark Warminski, 12,200 .... E 1
Liegnitz (Legnica), 73,400 .... C 3
Lipno, 11,200 .... D 2
Łódź, 750,400 .... D 3
Łomża, 23,700 .... F 2
Łowicz, 18,800 .... E 2
Lubań, 16,800 .... B 3
Lublin, 211,900 .... F 3
Lubliniec, 18,500 .... D 3
Luboń, 16,100 .... C 2
Łuków, 13,400 .... F 3
Lyck (Ełk), 25,300 .... F 2
Malbork, 29,500 .... D 2
Marienburg (Malbork), 29,500 .... D 2
Marienwerder (Kwidzyń), 22,800 .... D 2
Międzyrzec Podlaski, 12,900 .... F 3
Międzyrzecz, 12,200 .... B 2
Mielec, 26,000 .... E 3
Mikołow, 20,000 .... B 4
Mińsk Mazowiecki, 21,700 .... E 2
Mława, 17,900 .... E 2
Mrągowo, 12,600 .... E 2
Mysłowice (Myslowitz), 44,200 .... B 4
Nakło nad Notecią, 16,000 .... C 2
Neisse (Nysa), 29,000 .... C 3
Neusalz (Nowa Sól), 30,700 .... B 3
Neustadt (Prudnik), 19,200 .... C 3
Neustettin (Szczecinek), 27,000 .... C 2
Nowa Ruda, 18,900 .... C 3
Nowa Sól, 30,700 .... B 3
Nowy Dwór, 14,900 .... E 3
Nowy Sącz, 38,600 .... E 4
Nowy Targ, 20,600 .... E 4
Nysa, 29,000 .... C 3
Oels (Oleśnica), 24,700 .... C 3
Oława (Ohlau), 15,300 .... C 3
Oleśnica, 24,700 .... C 3
Olkusz, 14,500 .... D 3
Olsztyn, 80,700 .... E 2
Opoczno, 11,600 .... E 3
Opole (Oppeln), 78,800 .... C 3
Ostróda (Osterode), 20,000 .... D 2
Ostrołęka, 18,600 .... E 2
Ostrów Mazowiecka, 14,300 .... E 2
Ostrów Wielkopolski, 47,100 .... C 3
Ostrowiec Świętokrzyski, 45,600 .... E 3
Oświęcim, 37,300 .... D 3
Otwock, 38,200 .... E 2
Ozorków, 17,400 .... D 2
Pabianice, 60,100 .... D 3
Piekary Śląskie, 36,000 .... B 4
Piła, 40,700 .... C 2
Pionki, 13,600 .... E 3
Piotrków Trybunalski, 58,200 .... D 3
Pleszew, 12,200 .... C 3
Płock, 60,300 .... D 2
Płońsk 10,900 .... E 2
Poznań (Posen), 446,700 .... C 2
Prudnik, 19,200 .... C 3
Pruszków, 39,400 .... E 2
Przemyśl, 51,000 .... F 4
Pszczyna, 17,400 .... D 4
Puławy, 26,100 .... F 3
Pułtusk, 11,900 .... E 2
Pyskowice, 22,900 .... A 4
Racibórz, 37,800 .... C 3
Radom, 148,400 .... E 3
Radomsko, 29,900 .... D 3
Ratibor (Racibórz), 37,800 .... C 3
Rawicz, 13,600 .... C 3
Ruda Śląska, 142,800 .... B 4
Rumia, 21,500 .... D 1
Rybnik, 39,500 .... D 3
Rzeszów, 72,200 .... E 3
Sandomierz, 15,600 .... E 3
Sanok, 19,300 .... F 4
Schneidemühl (Piła), 40,700 .... C 2
Schweidnitz (Świdnica), 46,700 .... C 3
Siedlce, 36,500 .... F 2
Siemianowice Śląskie, 67,000 .... B 4
Sieradz, 16,300 .... D 3
Sierpc, 12,200 .... D 2
Skarżysko-Kamienna, 38,200 .... E 3
Skierniewice, 24,900 .... D 2
Słupsk, 61,800 .... C 1
Sochaczew, 18,300 .... E 2
Sopot, 44,900 .... D 1
Sorau (Żary), 28,400 .... B 3
Sosnowiec, 143,300 .... B 4
Śrem, 12,400 .... C 2
Środa Wielkopolska, 13,900 .... C 2
Stalowa Wola, 27,300 .... E 3
Starachowice, 40,600 .... E 3
Stargard Szczeciński, 40,600 .... B 2
Starogard Gdański, 30,600 .... D 2
Stettin (Szczecin), 322,000 .... B 2
Stolp (Słupsk), 61,800 .... C 1
Strzegom, 14,000 .... C 3
Strzelce Opolskie, 14,000 .... D 3
Suwałki, 22,900 .... F 1
Świdnica, 46,700 .... C 3
Świdnik, 19,300 .... F 3
Świdwin, 11,500 .... B 2
Świebodzin, 14,000 .... B 2
Świecie, 15,700 .... D 2
Świetochłowice, 58,300 .... B 4
Świnoujście (Swinemünde), 24,100 .... B 2
Szamotuły, 12,700 .... C 2
Szczecin, 322,000 .... B 2
Szczecinek, 27,000 .... C 2
Szczytno, 15,600 .... E 2
Tarnów, 81,000 .... E 3
Tarnowskie Góry, 32,600 .... D 3
Tczew, 38,000 .... D 1
Teschen (Cieszyn), 24,700 .... D 4
Thorn (Toruń), 117,800 .... D 2
Tomaszów Mazowiecki, 53,200 .... E 3
Toruń (Thorn), 117,800 .... D 2
Turek, 17,500 .... D 2
Tychy, 66,200 .... B 4
Wąbrzeźno, 12,100 .... D 2
Wągrowiec, 14,400 .... C 2
Wałbrzych, 126,600 .... C 3
Wałcz, 18,000 .... C 2
Waldenburg (Wałbrzych), 126,600 .... C 3
Warsaw (capital), 1,282,600 .... E 2
Warszawa (Warsaw) (cap.), 1,282,600 .... E 2
Wejherowo, 30,600 .... D 1
Wieliczka, 12,800 .... E 3
Wieluń, 12,900 .... D 3
Włocławek, 70,200 .... D 2
Wołomin, 22,800 .... E 2
Wrocław, 487,000 .... C 3
Września, 16,100 .... C 2
Ząbkowice Śląskie 13,000 .... C 3
Zabrze, 197,600 .... A 4
Żagań, 21,100 .... B 3
Zakopane, 26,100 .... D 4
Zambrów, 13,200 .... F 2
Zamość, 31,500 .... F 3
Żary, 28,400 .... B 3
Zawiercie, 37,700 .... D 3
Zduńska Wola, 28,000 .... D 3
Zgierz, 40,900 .... D 3
Zgorzelec, 26,400 .... B 3
Zielona Góra, 66,200 .... B 3
Złotoryja, 13,700 .... B 3
Złocieniec, 10,100 .... C 2
Żoppot (Sopot) 44,900 .... D 1
Żyrardów, 31,500 .... E 2
Żywiec, 21,700 .... D 4

OTHER FEATURES

Alle (Łyna) (river) .... E 1
Baltic (sea) .... B 1
Beskids (mts.) .... E 4
Brda (river) .... C 2
Bug (river) .... F 2
Bzura (river) .... D 2
Danzig (Gdańsk) (gulf) .... D 1
Drawa (river) .... B 2
Drwęca (river) .... D 2
Dukla (pass) .... E 4
Dunajec (river) .... E 4
Gdańsk (Danzig) (gulf) .... D 1
Gwda (river) .... C 2
Hel (pen.) .... D 1
High Tatra (mts.) .... D 4
Kłodnica (river) .... B 4
Łyna (river) .... E 1
Mamry (Mauer) (lake) .... E 1
Mauer (Mamry) (lake) .... E 1
Narew (river) .... E 2
Neisse (Nysa Łużycka) (river) .... B 3
Nitze (Noteć) (river) .... B 2
Noteć (Nitze) (river) .... B 2
Nysa Kłodzka (river) .... C 3
Nysa Łużycka (Neisse) (river) .... B 3
Oder (Odra) (river) .... B 2
Odra (Oder) (river) .... B 2
Orava (res.) .... D 4
Pilica (river) .... E 3
Pomeranian (bay) .... B 1
Prosna (river) .... C 2
Rysy (mt.) .... E 4
San (river) .... F 3
Śniardwy (Spirding) (lake) .... E 2
Sołokija (river) .... F 3
Spirding (Śniardwy) (lake) .... E 2
Sudeten (range) .... C 3
Uznam (Usedom) (isl.), 20,100 .... B 1
Vistula (Wisła) (river) .... D 2
Warta (Warthe) (river) .... C 2
Wieprz (river) .... F 3
Wisła (Vistula) (river) .... D 2
Wkra (river) .... E 2
Wolin (Wollin) (isl.), 38,400 .... B 2

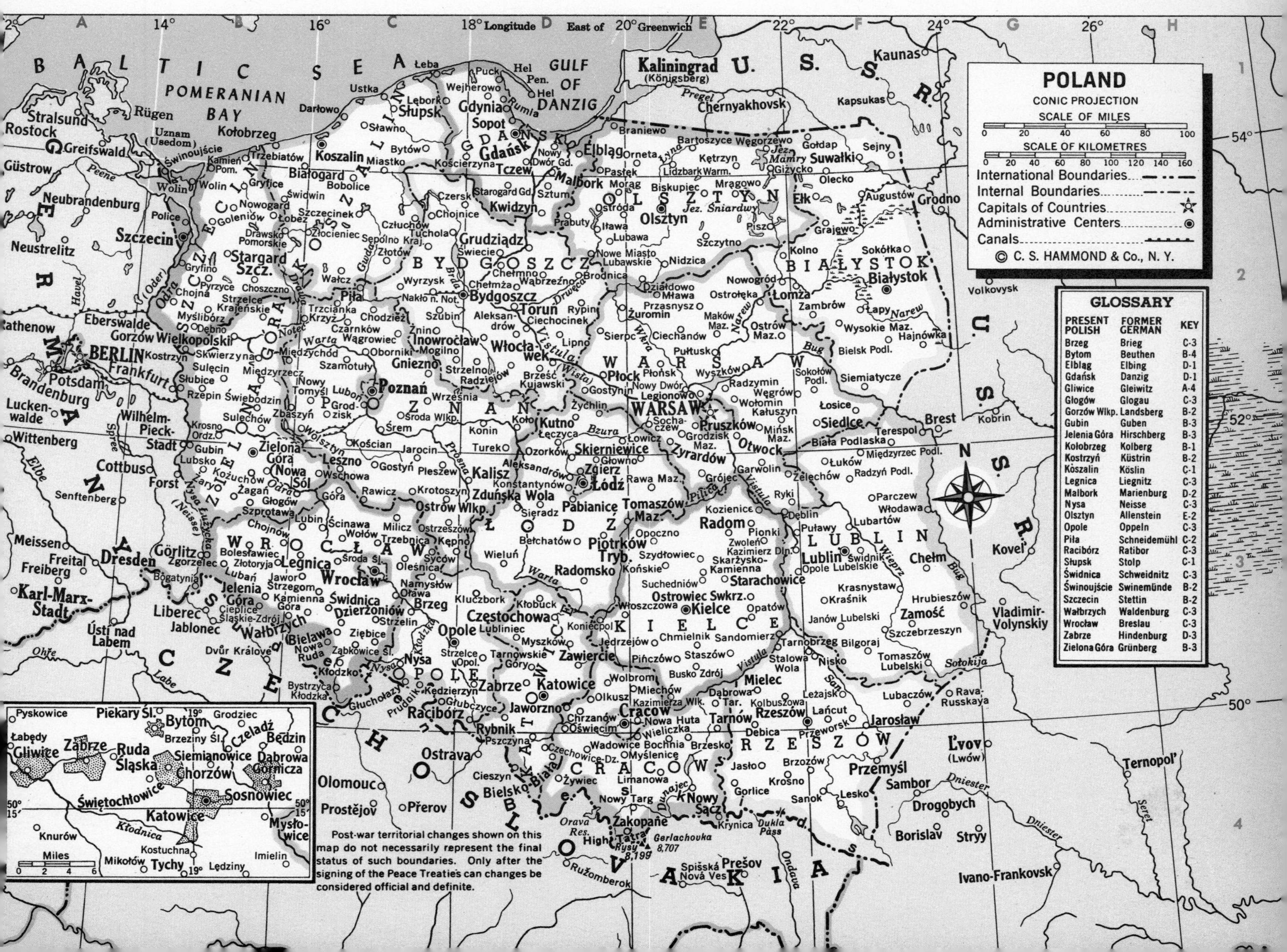

POLAND
CONIC PROJECTION
SCALE OF MILES
0 20 40 60 80 100
SCALE OF KILOMETRES
0 20 40 60 80 100 120 140 160
International Boundaries
Internal Boundaries
Capitals of Countries
Administrative Centers
Canals
© C. S. HAMMOND & Co., N. Y.
GLOSSARY
PRESENT POLISH | FORMER GERMAN | KEY
Brzeg | Brieg | C-3
Bytom | Beuthen | B-4
Elbląg | Elbing | D-1
Gdańsk | Danzig | D-1
Gliwice | Gleiwitz | A-4
Głogów | Glogau | C-3
Gorzów Wlkp. | Landsberg | B-2
Gubin | Guben | B-3
Jelenia Góra | Hirschberg | B-3
Kołobrzeg | Kolberg | B-1
Kostrzyń | Küstrin | B-2
Koszalin | Köslin | C-1
Legnica | Liegnitz | C-3
Malbork | Marienburg | D-2
Nysa | Neisse | C-3
Olsztyn | Allenstein | E-2
Opole | Oppeln | C-3
Piła | Schneidemühl | C-2
Racibórz | Ratibor | C-3
Słupsk | Stolp | C-1
Świdnica | Schweidnitz | C-3
Świnoujście | Swinemünde | B-2
Szczecin | Stettin | B-2
Wałbrzych | Waldenburg | C-3
Wrocław | Breslau | C-3
Zabrze | Hindenburg | D-3
Zielona Góra | Grünberg | B-3
Post-war territorial changes shown on this map do not necessarily represent the final status of such boundaries. Only after the signing of the Peace Treaties can changes be considered official and definite.
18° Longitude East of 20° Greenwich
BALTIC SEA
POMERANIAN BAY
GULF OF DANZIG
WARSAW
Kaliningrad (Königsberg)
Gdańsk
Szczecin
Poznań
Wrocław
Łódź
Cracow
Lublin
Białystok
Katowice
BERLIN
Dresden
Ľvov (Lwów)

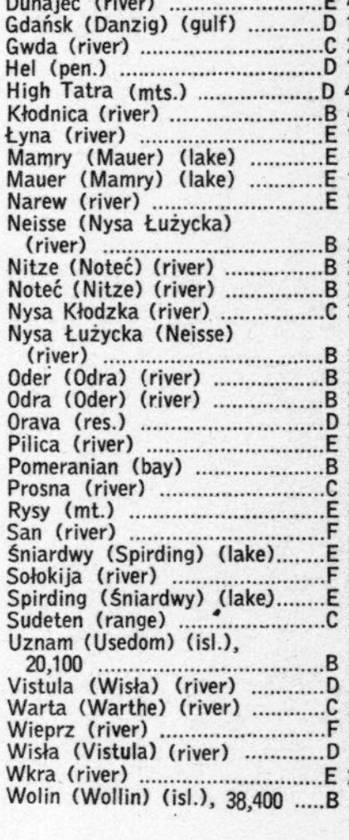

Union of Soviet Socialist Republics

UNION REPUBLICS

Armenian S.S.R., 2,491,900 ....E 6
Azerbaidzhan S.S.R., 5,117,100 ....E 5
Estonian S.S.R., 1,356,100 ....C 4
Georgian S.S.R., 4,686,000 ....D 5
Kazakh S.S.R., 12,849,000 ....G 5
Kirgiz S.S.R., 2,932,800 ....H 5
Latvian S.S.R., 2,364,100 ....C 4
Lithuanian S.S.R., 3,128,000 ....C 4
Moldavian S.S.R., 3,568,900 ....C 5
Russian S.F.S.R., 130,079,210 ....D 4
Tadzhik S.S.R., 2,900,000 ....H 6
Turkmen S.S.R., 2,158,880 ....F 6
Ukrainian S.S.R., 47,126,517 ....C 5
Uzbek S.S.R., 11,960,000 ....G 5
White Russian S.S.R., 9,002,338 ....C 4

INTERNAL DIVISIONS

Abkhaz A.S.S.R., 487,000 ....E 5
Adygey Aut. Oblast, 385,000 ....D 5
Adzhar A.S.S.R., 310,000 ....E 5
Aginsk-Buryat Nat'l Okrug, 66,000 ....M 4
Bashkir A.S.S.R., 3,818,000 ....F 4
Buryat A.S.S.R., 812,000 ....M 4
Chechen-Ingush A.S.S.R., 1,065,000 ....E 5
Chukchi Nat'l Okrug, 101,000 ....R 3
Chuvash A.S.S.R., 1,224,000 ....E 4
Dagestan A.S.S.R., 1,429,000 ....E 5
Evenki Nat'l Okrug, 13,000 ....K 3
Gorno-Altay Aut. Oblast, 168,000 ....J 4
Gorno-Badakhshan Aut. Oblast, 98,000 ....H 6
Jewish Aut. Oblast, 172,000 ....O 5
Kabardin-Balkar A.S.S.R., 588,000 ....E 5
Kalmuck A.S.S.R., 268,000 ....E 5
Karachay-Cherkess Aut. Oblast, 345,000 ....E 5
Karakalpak A.S.S.R., 702,000 ....G 5
Karelian A.S.S.R., 713,000 ....D 3
Khakass Aut. Oblast, 446,000 ....J 4
Khanty-Mansi Nat'l Okrug, 271,000 ....H 3
Komi A.S.S.R., 965,000 ....F 3
Komi-Permyak Nat'l Okrug, 212,000 ....F 4
Koryak Nat'l Okrug, 31,000 ....R 3
Mari A.S.S.R., 685,000 ....E 4
Mordvinian A.S.S.R., 1,029,000 ....E 4
Nagorno-Karabakh Aut. Oblast, 150,000 ....E 5
Nakhichevan' A.S.S.R., 202,000 ....E 6
Nenets Nat'l Okrug, 39,000 ....F 3
North Ossetian A.S.S.R., 552,000 ....E 5
South Ossetian Aut. Oblast, 99,000 ....E 5
Tatar A.S.S.R., 3,131,000 ....F 4
Taymyr Nat'l Okrug, 38,000 ....K 2
Tuvinian A.S.S.R., 231,000 ....K 4
Udmurt A.S.S.R., 1,418,000 ....F 4
Ust'-Ordynsk-Buryat Nat'l Okrug, 146,000 ....L 4
Yakut A.S.S.R., 664,000 ....N 3
Yamal-Nenets Nat'l Okrug, 80,000 ....H 3

CITIES and TOWNS

Abakan, 90,000 ....J 4
Achinsk, 97,000 ....K 4
Adimi ....O 5
Aginskoye, 9,000 ....M 4
Akmolinsk (Tselinograd), 180,000 ....H 4
Aktyubinsk, 150,000 ....F 4
Aldan, 19,000 ....N 4
Aleksandrovsk-Sakhalinskiy, 22,000 ....P 5
Aleysk, 32,000 ....J 4
Alga, 17,000 ....F 5
Allakh-Yun' ....O 3
Alma-Ata, 730,000 ....H 5
Ambarchik ....R 3
Amderma ....F 3
Amursk, 15,000 ....O 4
Anadyr', 8,000 ....S 3
Andizhan, 188,000 ....H 5
Angarsk, 203,000 ....L 4
Anzhero-Sudzhensk, 106,000 ....J 4
Aral'sk, 26,000 ....G 5
Archangel, 343,000 ....E 3
Arkalyk, 15,000 ....G 4
Armavir, 145,000 ....E 5
Artem, 61,000 ....O 5
Artemovskiy ....M 4
Arzamas, 67,000 ....E 4
Ashkhabad, 253,000 ....F 6
Ashkhabad, *256,000 ....F 6
Asino, 30,000 ....J 4
Astrakhan', 410,000 ....E 5
Atbasar, 41,000 ....G 4
Atka ....Q 3
Ayaguz, 40,000 ....J 5
Ayan ....O 4
Aykhal ....M 3
Bagdarin ....M 4
Baku, 852,000 ....F 5
Baku, *1,266,000 ....F 5
Balashov, 83,000 ....E 4
Balkhash, 76,000 ....H 5
Balturino, 10,000 ....K 4
Barabinsk, 40,000 ....H 4
Baranovichi, 101,000 ....C 4
Barnaul, 439.000 ....J 4
Batumi, 101,000 ....E 5
Baykit ....K 3
Baykonur ....G 5
Bayram-Ali, 33,000 ....G 6
Belgorod, 151,000 ....D 4
Belogorsk, 57,000 ....N 4
Belomorsk, 18,000 ....D 3
Beloretsk, 67,000 ....F 4
Belovo, 108,000 ....J 4
Berdichev, 71,000 ....C 5
Berdsk, 53,000 ....J 4
Berezniki, 146,000 ....F 4
Berezovo, 6,000 ....G 3
Beringovskiy ....T 3
Bilibino, 13,000 ....R 3
Birobidzhan, 56,000 ....O 5
Biysk, 186,000 ....J 4
Blagoveshchensk, 128,000 ....N 4
Bobruysk, 138,000 ....C 4
Bodaybo, 19,000 ....M 4
Borisoglebsk, 64,000 ....E 4
Borzya, 28,000 ....M 4
Boshchakul' ....H 4
Bratsk, 155,000 ....L 4
Brest, 122,000 ....C 4
Bryansk, 318,000 ....D 4
Bugul'ma, 72,000 ....F 4
Bukhara, 112,000 ....G 5
Bulun ....N 2
Buzuluk, 67,000 ....F 4
Chagda ....O 4
Chapayevo ....F 4
Chapayevsk, 86,000 ....F 4
Chardzhou, 96,000 ....G 6
Cheboksary, 216,000 ....E 4
Chelkar, 25,000 ....F 5
Chelyabinsk, 875,000 ....G 4
Cheremkhovo, 99,000 ....L 4
Cherepovets, 188,000 ....D 4
Cherkessk, 67,000 ....E 5
Chernigov, 159,000 ....D 4
Chernovtsv, 187,000 ....C 5
Chernyshevsk, 10,000 ....M 4
Chernyshevskiy, 10,000 ....M 3
Cherskiy ....Q 3
Chimbay, 20,000 ....F 5
Chimkent, 247,000 ....G 5
Chirchik, 107,000 ....H 5
Chita, 241,000 ....M 4
Chokurdakh ....P 2
Chul'man ....N 4
Chumikan ....O 4
Dalnegorsk, 33,500 ....O 5
Dalnerechensk, 30,000 ....O 5
Daugavpils, 100,400 ....C 4
Dikson ....J 2
Dimitrovgrad, 81,000 ....F 4
Dnepropetrovsk, 862,000 ....D 5
Dolinsk, 18,000 ....P 5
Donetsk, 879,000 ....D 5
Drogobych, 56,000 ....C 5
Druzhina ....P 3
Dudinka, 22,000 ....J 3
Dushanbe, 376,000 ....G 6
Dzerzhinsk, 221,000 ....E 4
Dzhalal-Abad, 44,000 ....H 5
Dzhalinda ....N 4
Dzhambul, 187,000 ....H 5
Dzhetygara, 39,000 ....G 4
Dzhezkazgan, 62,000 ....G 5
Ekibastuz, 46,000 ....H 4
Ekimchan ....O 4
El'dikan ....O 3
Elista, 50,000 ....E 5
Engel's, 130,000 ....E 4
Erivan, 767,000 ....E 6
Evensk ....Q 3
Fergana, 111,000 ....H 5
Fort-Shevchenko, 12,000 ....F 5
Frolovo, 30,000 ....E 5
Frunze, 430,600 ....H 5
Gasan-Kuli ....F 6
Gizhiga ....R 3
Gol'chikha ....J 2
Gomel', 272,000 ....D 4
Gor'kiy, 1,170,000 ....E 4
Gorno-Altaysk, 34,000 ....J 5
Grodno, 132,000 ....C 4
Groznyy, 341,000 ....E 5
Gubakha, 40,000 ....F 4
Gulistan, 31,000 ....G 5
Gur'yev, 114,000 ....F 5
Gusinoözersk, 10,000 ....L 4
Gydy ....H 2
Igarka, 22,000 ....J 3
Ilanskiy, 24,000 ....K 4
Iliysk, 17,000 ....H 5
Indiga ....E 3
Inta, 50,000 ....G 3
Iolotan', 10,000 ....G 6
Irkutsk, 451,000 ....L 4
Ishim, 56,000 ....H 4
Ishimbay, 54,000 ....F 4
Isil'-Kul', 26,000 ....H 4
Ivano-Frankovsk, 105,000 ....C 5

ADMINISTRATIVE DIVISIONS NOT NAMED ON MAP

Division	Ref.	Division	Ref.
1. Abkhaz A.S.S.R.	E5	13. Khakass Aut. Oblast	J4
2. Adygey Aut. Oblast	D5	14. Komi-Permyak Nat'l Okrug	F4
3. Adzhar A.S.S.R.	E5	15. Mari A.S.S.R.	E4
4. Aginsk-Buryat Nat'l Okrug	M4	16. Mordivian A.S.S.R.	E4
5. Chechen-Ingush A.S.S.R.	E5	17. Nagorno-Karabakh Aut. Oblast	E5
6. Chuvash A.S.S.R.	E4	18. Nakhichevan' A.S.S.R.	E6
7. Gorno-Altay Aut. Oblast	J4	19. North Ossetian A.S.S.R.	E5
8. Gorno-Badakhshan Aut. Oblast	H6	20. South Ossetian Aut. Oblast	E5
9. Jewish Aut. Oblast	O5	21. Tatar A.S.S.R.	F4
10. Kabardin-Balkar A.S.S.R.	E5	22. Tuvinian A.S.S.R.	K4
11. Karachay-Cherkess Aut. Oblast	E5	23. Udmurt A.S.S.R.	F4
12. Karakalpak A.S.S.R.	G5	24. Ust'-Ordynsk-Buryat Nat'l Okrug	L4

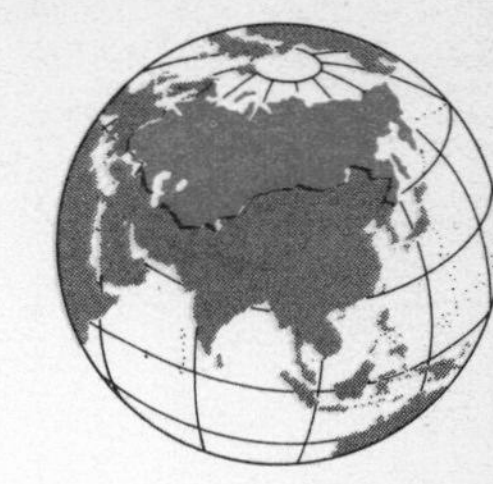

AREA 8,649,498 sq. mi.
POPULATION 241,748,000
CAPITAL Moscow
LARGEST CITY Moscow
HIGHEST POINT Communism Peak 24,590 ft.
MONETARY UNIT ruble
MAJOR LANGUAGES Russian, Ukrainian, White Russian, Uzbek, Azerbaidzhani, Tatar, Georgian, Lithuanian, Armenian, Yiddish, Latvian, Mordvinian, Kirghiz, Tadzhik, Estonian, Kazakh, Moldavian, German, Chuvash, Turkmenian, Bashkir
MAJOR RELIGIONS Eastern (Russian) Orthodoxy, Islam, Judaism, Protestantism (Baltic States)

Place	Key
Ivanovo, 420,000	E 4
Izhevsk, 422,000	F 4
Izmail, 70,000	C 5
Kachug	L 4
Kalachinsk, 24,000	H 4
Kalakan	M 4
Kalinin, 345,000	D 4
Kaliningrad, 297,000	B 4
Kalmykovo	F 5
Kaluga, 211,000	D 4
Kamenskoye	R 3
Kamensk-Ural'skiy, 169,000	G 4
Kamyshin, 97,000	E 4
Kamyshlov, 34,000	G 4
Kansk, 95,000	K 4
Karabekaul	G 6
Karaganda, 523,000	H 5
Karasuk, 26,000	H 4
Karazhal, 18,000	H 5
Karkaralinsk, 9,000	H 5
Karshi, 71,000	G 6
Kaunas, 306,200	C 4
Kazach'ye	O 2
Kazalinsk, 22,000	G 5
Kazan', 869,000	F 4
Kazandzhik	F 6
Kem, 23,000	D 3
Kemerovo, 385,000	J 4
Kentau, 55,000	G 5
Kerki, 23,000	G 6
Kezhma	K 4
Khabarovsk, 436,000	O 5
Khandyga	O 3
Khanty-Mansiysk, 25,000	H 3
Khar'kov, 1,223,000	D 4
Kharovsk, 10,000	D 3

UNION REPUBLICS

	AREA (sq. mi.)	POPULATION	CAPITAL and LARGEST CITY
RUSSIAN S.F.S.R.	6,592,819	130,079,210	Moscow 6,942,000
KAZAKH S.S.R.	1,048,301	12,849,000	Alma-Ata 730,000
UKRAINIAN S.S.R.	232,046	47,126,517	Kiev 1,632,000
TURKMEN S.S.R.	188,456	2,158,880	Ashkhabad 253,000
UZBEK S.S.R.	173,591	11,960,000	Tashkent 1,385,000
WHITE RUSSIAN S.S.R.	80,154	9,002,338	Minsk 907,000
KIRGIZ S.S.R.	76,641	2,932,800	Frunze 430,600
TADZHIK S.S.R.	55,251	2,900,000	Dushanbe 376,000
AZERBAIDZHAN S.S.R.	33,436	5,117,100	Baku 852,000
GEORGIAN S.S.R.	26,911	4,686,000	Tbilisi 889,000
LITHUANIAN S.S.R.	25,174	3,128,000	Vilna 371,700
LATVIAN S.S.R.	24,595	2,364,100	Riga 731,800
ESTONIAN S.S.R.	17,413	1,356,100	Tallinn 362,706
MOLDAVIAN S.S.R.	13,012	3,568,900	Kishinev 356,900
ARMENIAN S.S.R.	11,500	2,491,900	Erivan 767,000

Place	Key
Khatanga	L 2
Kherson, 261,000	D 5
Khilok, 17,000	M 4
Khiva, 25,000	F 5
Khodzheyli, 36,000	F 5
Kholmsk, 42,000	P 5
Khorog, 12,300	H 6
Kiev, 1,632,000	D 4
Kirensk, 10,000	L 4
Kirov, 333,000	E 4
Kirovabad, 189,800	E 5
Kirovograd, 189,000	D 5
Kiselevsk, 127,000	J 4
Kishinev, 356,900	C 5
Kizel, 49,000	F 4
Kizyl-Arvat, 24,000	F 6
Klaipeda, 139,900	B 4
Kokand, 133,000	H 5
Kokchetav, 81,000	H 4
Kolomna, 135,900	D 4
Kolpashevo, 27,000	J 4
Komsomol'sk, 218,000	O 4
Kondopoga, 25,000	D 3
Kopeysk, 156,000	G 4
Korf	R 3
Korsakov, 35,000	P 5
Koslan	E 3
Kostroma, 223,000	E 4
Kotlas, 56,000	E 3
Kovel', 35,000	C 4
Kovrov, 123,000	E 4
Kozhevnikovo	L 2
Krasino	F 2
Krasnodar, 464,000	E 5
Krasnokamsk, 55,000	F 4
Krasnotur'insk, 59,000	G 3
Krasnoural'sk, 42,000	G 4
Krasnovishersk, 16,000	F 3
Krasnovodsk, 49,000	F 5
Krasnoyarsk, 648,000	K 4
Kremenchug, 148,000	D 5
Krivoy Rog, 573,000	D 5
Kudymkar, 20,000	F 4
Kul'sary, 14,000	F 5
Kungur, 74,000	F 4
Kupino, 24,000	H 4
Kurgan, 244,000	G 4
Kurgan-Tyube, 34,600	G 6
Kuril'sk, 2,000	P 5
Kursk, 284,000	D 4
Kushka	G 6
Kustanay, 124,000	G 4
Kutaisi, 161,000	E 5
Kuybyshev, 1,045,000	F 4
Kyakhta	L 4
Kyusyur	N 2
Kyzyl, 52,000	K 4
Kzyl-Orda, 122,000	G 5
Labytnangi	G 3
Leninabad, 103,200	G 5
Leninakan, 165,000	E 5
Leningrad, 3,513,000	D 4
Leningrad, *3,950,000	D 4
Leninogorsk, 72,000	J 5
Leninsk-Kuznetskiy, 128,000	J 4
Leninskoye	O 5
Lenkoran', 35,500	E 6
Lensk, 21,000	M 3
Lesozavodsk, 37,000	O 5
Liepāja. 92,800	B 4
Lipetsk, 289,000	E 4
Luga, 30,000	D 4
Lutsk, 94,000	C 4
Luza, 10,000	E 3
L'vov, 553,000	C 4
Lys'va, 73,000	F 4
Magadan, 92,000	P 4
Magdagachi, 10,000	N 4
Magnitogorsk, 364,000	G 4
Makhachkala, 186,000	E 5
Makinsk, 28,000	G 4
Maklakovo, 20,000	K 4
Mama	M 4
Markovo	S 3
Mary, 62,000	G 6
Maykop, 110,000	D 5
Mednogorsk, 41,000	F 4
Medvezh'yegorsk, 18,000	D 3
Megion	H 3
Mezen'	E 3
Miass, 131,000	G 4
Michurinsk, 94,000	E 4
Millerovo, 38,000	E 5
Minsk, 907,000	C 4
Minsk, *917,000	C 4
Minusinsk, 47,000	K 4
Mirnyy, 24,000	M 3
Mogilev, 202,000	D 4
Mogocha, 10,000	N 4
Molodechno, 50,000	C 4
Monchegorsk, 49,000	C 3
Moscow (capital), 6,942,000	D 4
Moscow, *7,061,000	D 4
Motygino, 10,000	K 4
Mozyr', 49,000	C 4
Murgab	H 6
Murmansk, 309,000	D 3
Muvnak, 12,000	F 5
Nadym	H 3
Nagornyy	N 4
Nakhichevan', 33,200	E 6
Nakhodka, 104,000	O 5
Nal'chik, 146,000	E 5
Namangan, 175,000	H 5
Naminga, 5,000	M 4
Napas	J 4
Nar'yan-Mar, 15,000	F 3
Naryn, 21,000	H 5
Navoi, 61,000	G 6
Nebit-Dag, 56,000	F 6
Nel'kan	O 4
Nepa	L 4
Nerchinsk, 10,000	M 4
Nikolayev, 331,000	D 5
Nikolayevsk, 34,000	P 4
Nikol'skoye	R 4
Nimnyrskiy	N 4
Nizhne-Angarsk	M 4
Nizhneudinsk, 39,000	K 4
Nizhniy Tagil, 378,000	G 4
Nordvik	M 2
Noril'sk, 135,000	J 3
Novaya Kazanka	F 5
Novgorod, 128,000	D 4
Novokuznetsk, 499,000	J 4
Novomoskovsk, 134,000	E 4

Topography

(continued on following page)

Union of Soviet Socialist Republics
(continued)

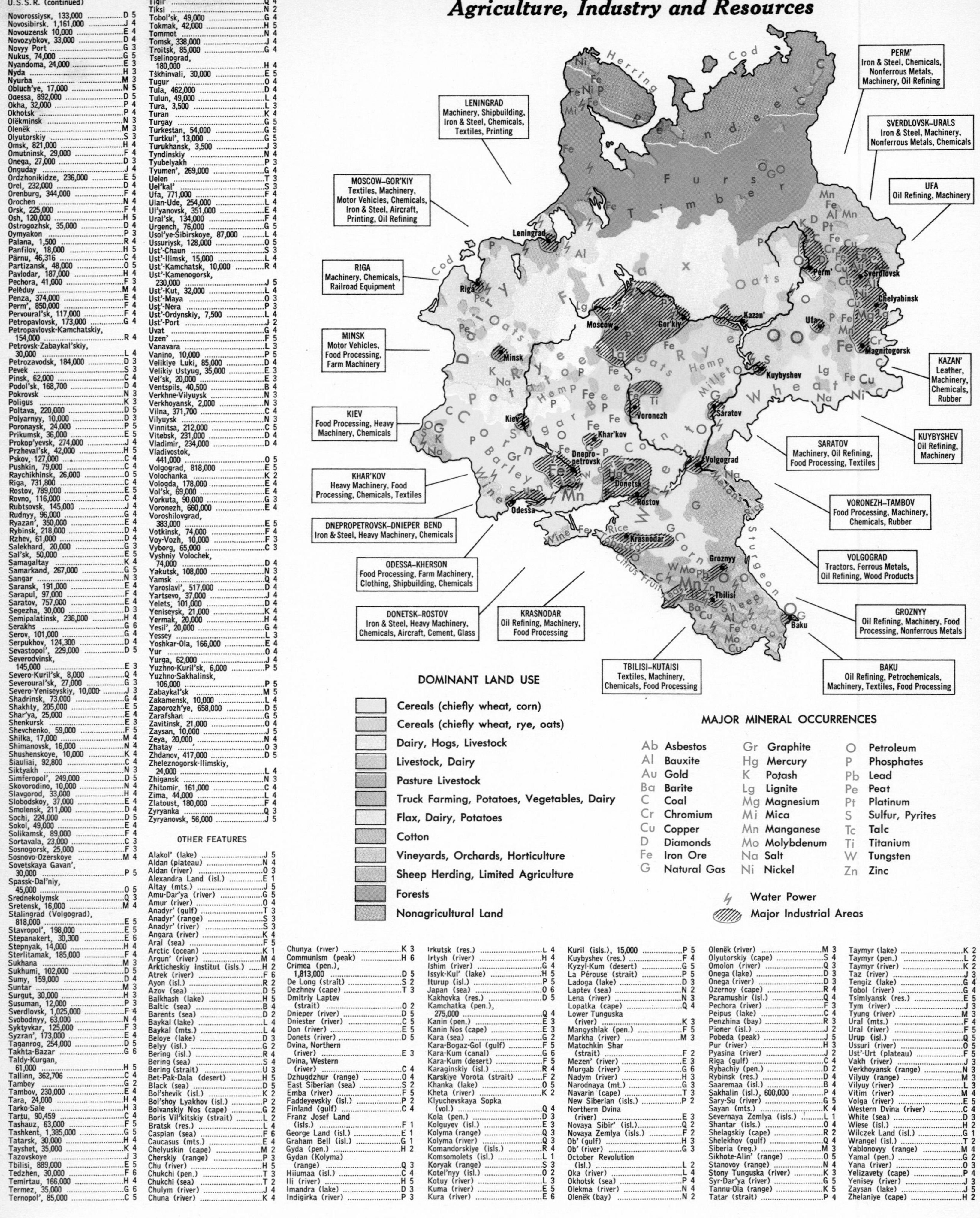

U.S.S.R. (continued)

Novorossiysk, 133,000 D 5
Novosibirsk, 1,161,000 J 4
Novouzensk 10,000 E 4
Novozybkov, 33,000 D 4
Novyy Port G 3
Nukus, 74,000 G 5
Nyandoma, 24,000 E 3
Nyda H 3
Nyurba M 3
Obluch'ye, 17,000 N 5
Odessa, 892,000 D 5
Okha, 32,000 P 4
Okhotsk P 4
Olëkminsk N 3
Olenëk M 3
Olyutorskiy S 3
Omsk, 821,000 H 4
Omutninsk, 29,000 F 4
Onega, 27,000 D 3
Onguday J 4
Ordzhonikidze, 236,000 E 5
Orel, 232,000 D 4
Orenburg, 344,000 F 4
Orochen N 4
Orsk, 225,000 F 4
Osh, 120,000 H 5
Ostrogozhsk, 35,000 D 4
Oymyakon P 3
Palana, 1,500 R 4
Panfilov, 18,000 H 5
Pärnu, 46,316 C 4
Partizansk, 48,000 O 5
Pavlodar, 187,000 H 4
Pechora, 41,000 F 3
Pelëduy M 4
Penza, 374,000 E 4
Perm', 850,000 F 4
Pervoural'sk, 117,000 F 4
Petropavlovsk, 173,000 G 4
Petropavlovsk-Kamchatskiy, 154,000 R 4
Petrovsk-Zabaykal'skiy, 30,000 L 4
Petrozavodsk, 184,000 D 3
Pevek S 3
Pinsk, 62,000 C 4
Podol'sk, 168,700 D 4
Pokrovsk N 3
Poligus K 3
Poltava, 220,000 D 5
Polyarnyy, 10,000 D 3
Poronaysk, 24,000 P 5
Prikumsk, 36,000 E 5
Prokop'yevsk, 274,000 J 4
Przheval'sk, 42,000 H 5
Pskov, 127,000 C 4
Pushkin, 79,000 C 4
Raychikhinsk, 26,000 O 5
Riga, 731,800 C 4
Rostov, 789,000 E 5
Rovno, 116,000 C 4
Rubtsovsk, 145,000 J 4
Rudnyy, 96,000 G 4
Ryazan', 350,000 E 4
Rybinsk, 218,000 D 4
Rzhev, 61,000 D 4
Salekhard, 20,000 G 3
Sal'sk, 50,000 E 5
Samagaltay K 4
Samarkand, 267,000 G 5
Sangar N 3
Saransk, 191,000 E 4
Sarapul, 97,000 F 4
Saratov, 757,000 E 4
Segezha, 30,000 D 3
Semipalatinsk, 236,000 H 4
Serakhs G 6
Serov, 101,000 G 4
Serpukhov, 124,300 D 4
Sevastopol', 229,000 D 5
Severodvinsk, 145,000 E 3
Severo-Kuril'sk, 8,000 Q 4
Severoural'sk, 27,000 G 3
Severo-Yeniseyskiy, 10,000 J 3
Shadrinsk, 73,000 G 4
Shakhty, 205,000 E 5
Shar'ya, 25,000 E 4
Shenkursk E 3
Shevchenko, 59,000 F 5
Shilka, 17,000 M 4
Shimanovsk, 16,000 N 4
Shushenskoye, 10,000 K 4
Siauliai, 92,800 C 4
Siktyakh N 3
Simferopol', 249,000 D 5
Skovorodino, 10,000 N 4
Slavgorod, 33,000 H 4
Slobodskoy, 37,000 E 4
Smolensk, 211,000 D 4
Sochi, 224,000 D 5
Sokol, 49,000 E 4
Solikamsk, 89,000 F 4
Sortavala, 23,000 C 3
Sosnogorsk, 25,000 F 3
Sosnovo-Ozerskoye M 4
Sovetskaya Gavan', 30,000 P 5
Spassk-Dal'niy, 45,000 O 5
Srednekolymsk Q 3
Sretensk, 16,000 M 4
Stalingrad (Volgograd), 818,000 E 5
Stavropol', 198,000 E 5
Stepanakert, 30,300 E 6
Stepnyak, 14,000 H 4
Sterlitamak, 185,000 F 4
Sukhana M 3
Sukhumi, 102,000 D 5
Sumy, 159,000 D 4
Suntar M 3
Surgut, 30,000 H 3
Susuman, 12,000 P 3
Sverdlovsk, 1,025,000 F 4
Svobodnyy, 63,000 N 4
Syktyvkar, 125,000 F 3
Syzran', 173,000 E 4
Taganrog, 254,000 D 5
Takhta-Bazar G 6
Taldy-Kurgan, 61,000 H 5
Tallinn, 362,706 C 4
Tambey G 2
Tambov, 230,000 E 4
Tara, 24,000 H 4
Tarko-Sale H 3
Tartu, 90,459 C 4
Tashauz, 63,000 F 5
Tashkent, 1,385,000 G 5
Tatarsk, 30,000 H 4
Tayshet, 35,000 K 4
Tazovskoye J 3
Tbilisi, 889,000 E 5
Tedzhen, 30,000 F 6
Temirtau, 166,000 H 4
Termez, 35,000 G 6
Ternopol', 85,000 C 5
Tigil' Q 4
Tiksi N 2
Tobol'sk, 49,000 G 4
Tokmak, 42,000 H 5
Tommot N 4
Tomsk, 338,000 J 4
Troitsk, 85,000 G 4
Tselinograd, 180,000 H 4
Tskhinvali, 30,000 E 5
Tugur O 4
Tula, 462,000 D 4
Tulun, 49,000 L 4
Tura, 3,500 L 3
Turan K 4
Turgay G 5
Turkestan, 54,000 G 5
Turtkul', 13,000 G 5
Turukhansk, 3,500 J 3
Tyndinskiy N 4
Tyubelyakh P 3
Tyumen', 269,000 G 4
Uelen T 3
Uel'kal' S 3
Ufa, 771,000 F 4
Ulan-Ude, 254,000 L 4
Ul'yanovsk, 351,000 E 4
Ural'sk, 134,000 F 4
Urgench, 76,000 G 5
Usol'ye-Sibirskoye, 87,000 L 4
Ussuriysk, 128,000 O 5
Ust'-Chaun S 3
Ust'-Ilimsk, 15,000 L 4
Ust'-Kamchatsk, 10,000 R 4
Ust'-Kamenogorsk, 230,000 J 5
Ust'-Kut, 32,000 L 4
Ust'-Maya O 3
Ust'-Nera P 3
Ust'-Ordynskiy, 7,500 L 4
Ust'-Port J 2
Uvat G 4
Uzen' F 5
Vanavara L 3
Vanino, 10,000 P 5
Velikiye Luki, 85,000 D 4
Velikiy Ustyug, 35,000 E 3
Vel'sk, 20,000 E 3
Ventspils, 40,500 B 4
Verkhne-Vilyuysk N 3
Verkhoyansk, 2,000 N 3
Vilna, 371,700 C 4
Vilyuysk N 3
Vinnitsa, 212,000 C 5
Vitebsk, 231,000 D 4
Vladimir, 234,000 D 4
Vladivostok, 441,000 O 5
Volgograd, 818,000 E 5
Volochanka K 2
Vologda, 178,000 E 4
Vol'sk, 69,000 E 4
Vorkuta, 90,000 G 3
Voronezh, 660,000 E 4
Voroshilovgrad, 383,000 E 5
Votkinsk, 74,000 F 4
Voy-Vozh, 10,000 F 3
Vyborg, 65,000 C 3
Vyshniy Volochek, 74,000 D 4
Yakutsk, 108,000 N 3
Yamsk Q 4
Yaroslavl', 517,000 D 4
Yartsevo, 37,000 J 4
Yelets, 101,000 D 4
Yeniseysk, 21,000 K 4
Yermak, 20,000 H 4
Yesil', 20,000 G 4
Yessey L 3
Yoshkar-Ola, 166,000 E 4
Yur O 4
Yurga, 62,000 J 4
Yuzhno-Kuril'sk, 6,000 P 5
Yuzhno-Sakhalinsk, 106,000 P 5
Zabaykal'sk M 5
Zakamensk, 10,000 L 4
Zaporozh'ye, 658,000 D 5
Zarafshan G 5
Zavitinsk, 21,000 O 4
Zaysan, 10,000 J 5
Zeya, 20,000 N 4
Zhatay O 3
Zhdanov, 417,000 D 5
Zheleznogorsk-Ilimskiy, 24,000 L 4
Zhigansk N 3
Zhitomir, 161,000 C 4
Zima, 44,000 L 4
Zlatoust, 180,000 F 4
Zyryanka Q 3
Zyryanovsk, 56,000 J 5

OTHER FEATURES

Alakol' (lake) J 5
Aldan (plateau) N 4
Aldan (river) O 3
Alexandra Land (isl.) E 1
Altay (mts.) J 5
Amu-Dar'ya (river) G 5
Amur (river) O 4
Anadyr' (gulf) T 3
Anadyr' (range) S 3
Anadyr' (river) S 3
Angara (river) K 4
Aral (sea) F 5
Arctic (ocean) K 1
Argun' (river) M 4
Arkticheskiy Institut (isls.) H 2
Atrek (river) F 6
Ayon (isl.) R 2
Azov (sea) D 5
Balkhash (lake) H 5
Baltic (sea) B 4
Barents (sea) D 2
Baykal (lake) L 4
Baykal (mts.) L 4
Beloye (lake) D 3
Belyy (isl.) G 2
Bering (isl.) R 4
Bering (sea) S 4
Bering (strait) U 3
Bet-Pak-Dala (desert) H 5
Black (sea) D 5
Bol'shevik (isl.) K 2
Bol'shoy Lyakhov (isl.) P 2
Bolvanskiy Nos (cape) G 2
Boris Vil'kitskiy (strait) L 2
Bratsk (res.) L 4
Caspian (sea) F 6
Caucasus (mts.) E 5
Chelyuskin (cape) M 2
Cherskiy (range) P 3
Chu (river) H 5
Chukchi (pen.) T 3
Chukchi (sea) T 2
Chulym (river) J 4
Chuna (river) K 4
Chunya (river) K 3
Communism (peak) H 6
Crimea (pen.), 1,813,000 D 5
De Long (strait) S 2
Dezhnev (cape) T 3
Dmitriy Laptev (strait) O 2
Dnieper (river) D 5
Dniester (river) C 5
Don (river) E 5
Donets (river) D 5
Dvina, Northern (river) E 3
Dvina, Western (river) C 4
Dzhugdzhur (range) O 4
East Siberian (sea) S 2
Emba (river) F 5
Faddeyevskiy (isl.) P 2
Finland (gulf) C 4
Franz Josef Land (isls.) F 1
George Land (isl.) E 1
Graham Bell (isl.) G 1
Gyda (pen.) H 2
Gydan (Kolyma) (range) Q 3
Hiiumaa (isl.) C 4
Ili (river) H 5
Imandra (lake) D 3
Indigirka (river) P 3
Irkutsk (res.) L 4
Irtysh (river) H 4
Ishim (river) G 4
Issyk-Kul' (lake) H 5
Iturup (isl.) P 5
Japan (sea) O 6
Kakhovka (res.) D 5
Kamchatka (pen.), 275,000 Q 4
Kanin (pen.) E 3
Kanin Nos (cape) E 3
Kara (sea) G 2
Kara-Bogaz-Gol (gulf) F 5
Kara-Kum (canal) G 6
Kara-Kum (desert) F 5
Karaginskiy (isl.) R 4
Karskiye Vorota (strait) F 2
Khanka (lake) O 5
Kheta (river) K 2
Klyuchevskaya Sopka (vol.) Q 4
Kola (pen.) D 3
Kolguyev (isl.) E 3
Kolyma (range) Q 3
Kolyma (river) Q 3
Komandorskiye (isls.) R 4
Komsomolets (isl.) K 1
Koryak (range) S 3
Kotel'nyy (isl.) O 2
Kotuy (river) L 3
Kuma (river) E 5
Kura (river) E 6
Kuril (isls.), 15,000 P 5
Kuybyshev (res.) E 4
Kyzyl-Kum (desert) G 5
La Pérouse (strait) P 5
Ladoga (lake) D 3
Laptev (sea) N 2
Lena (river) N 3
Lopatka (cape) Q 4
Lower Tunguska (river) K 3
Mangyshlak (pen.) F 5
Markha (river) M 3
Matochkin Shar (strait) F 2
Mezen' (river) E 3
Murgab (river) G 6
Nadym (river) H 3
Narodnaya (mt.) F 3
Navarin (cape) T 3
New Siberian (isls.) P 2
Northern Dvina (river) E 3
Novaya Sibir' (isl.) Q 2
Novaya Zemlya (isls.) F 2
Ob' (gulf) H 3
Ob' (river) G 3
October Revolution (isl.) L 2
Oka (river) L 4
Okhotsk (sea) P 4
Olekma (river) N 4
Olenëk (bay) N 2
Olenëk (river) M 3
Olyutorskiy (cape) S 4
Omolon (river) Q 3
Onega (lake) D 3
Onega (river) D 3
Ozernoy (cape) R 3
Paramushir (isl.) Q 4
Pechora (river) F 3
Peipus (lake) C 4
Penzhina (bay) R 3
Pioner (isl.) J 2
Pobeda (peak) Q 3
Pur (river) H 3
Pyasina (river) J 2
Riga (gulf) C 4
Rybachiy (pen.) D 2
Rybinsk (res.) D 4
Saaremaa (isl.) B 4
Sakhalin (isl.), 600,000 P 4
Sary-Su (river) G 5
Sayan (mts.) K 4
Severnaya Zemlya (isls.) L 1
Shantar (isls.) O 4
Shelagskiy (cape) R 2
Shelekhov (gulf) Q 4
Siberia (reg.) M 3
Sikhote-Alin' (range) O 5
Stanovoy (range) N 4
Stony Tunguska (river) K 3
Syr-Dar'ya (river) G 5
Tannu-Ola (range) K 5
Tatar (strait) P 4
Taymyr (lake) K 2
Taymyr (pen.) L 2
Taymyr (river) K 2
Taz (river) J 3
Tengiz (lake) G 4
Tobol (river) G 4
Tsimlyansk (res.) E 5
Tym (river) J 3
Tyung (river) M 3
Ural (mts.) F 4
Ural (river) F 5
Urup (isl.) Q 5
Ussuri (river) O 5
Ust'-Urt (plateau) F 5
Vakh (river) J 3
Verkhoyansk (range) N 3
Vilyuy (range) M 3
Vilyuy (river) L 3
Vitim (river) M 4
Volga (river) E 5
Western Dvina (river) C 4
White (sea) D 3
Wiese (isl.) H 2
Wilczek Land (isl.) G 1
Wrangel (isl.) T 2
Yablonovyy (range) M 4
Yamal (pen.) G 2
Yana (river) O 3
Yelizavety (cape) P 4
Yenisey (river) J 3
Zaysan (lake) J 5
Zhelaniye (cape) H 2

Agriculture, Industry and Resources

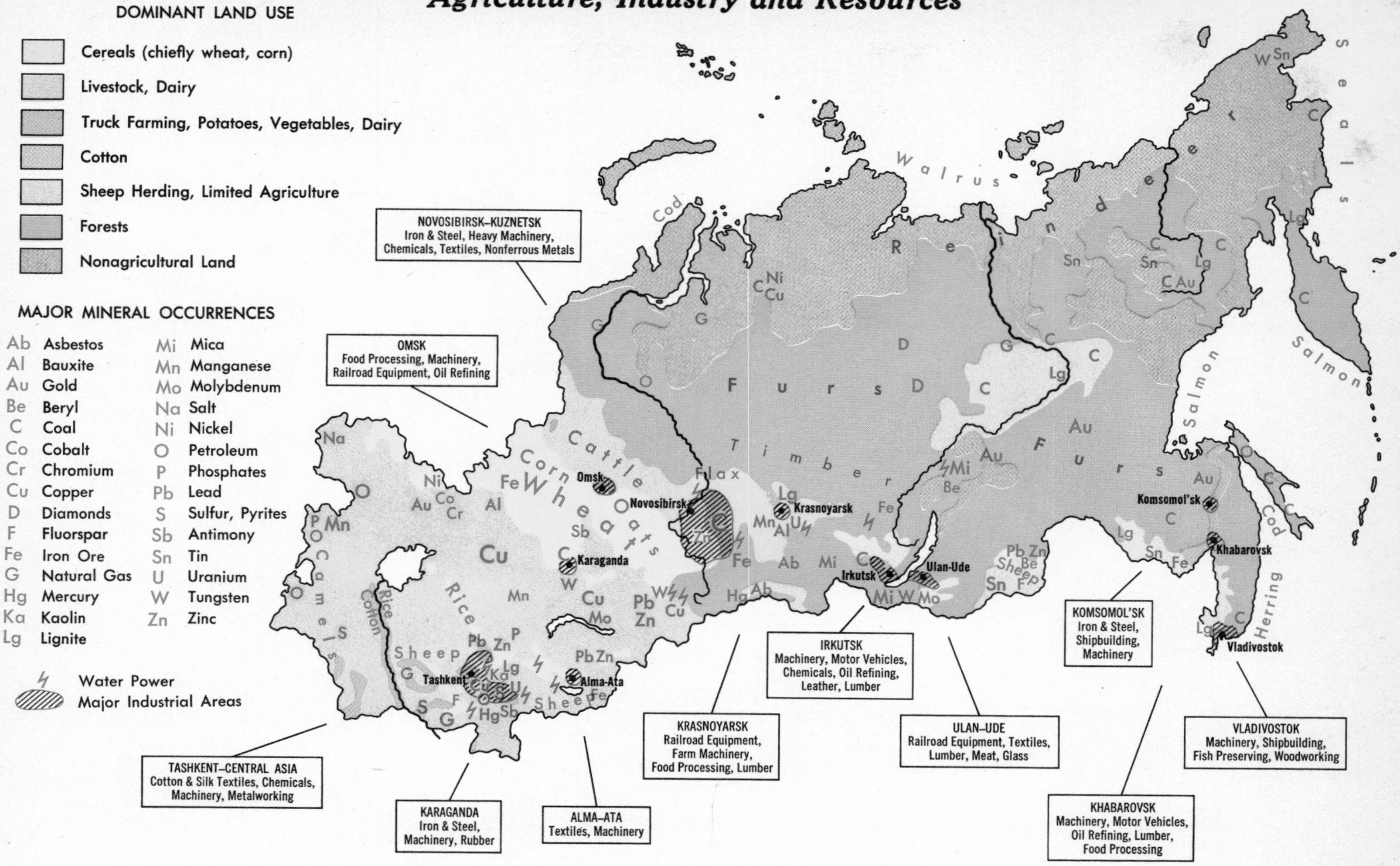
DOMINANT LAND USE
Cereals (chiefly wheat, corn)
Livestock, Dairy
Truck Farming, Potatoes, Vegetables, Dairy
Cotton
Sheep Herding, Limited Agriculture
Forests
Nonagricultural Land
MAJOR MINERAL OCCURRENCES
Ab Asbestos
Al Bauxite
Au Gold
Be Beryl
C Coal
Co Cobalt
Cr Chromium
Cu Copper
D Diamonds
F Fluorspar
Fe Iron Ore
G Natural Gas
Hg Mercury
Ka Kaolin
Lg Lignite
Mi Mica
Mn Manganese
Mo Molybdenum
Na Salt
Ni Nickel
O Petroleum
P Phosphates
Pb Lead
S Sulfur, Pyrites
Sb Antimony
Sn Tin
U Uranium
W Tungsten
Zn Zinc
Water Power
Major Industrial Areas
NOVOSIBIRSK–KUZNETSK Iron & Steel, Heavy Machinery, Chemicals, Textiles, Nonferrous Metals
OMSK Food Processing, Machinery, Railroad Equipment, Oil Refining
TASHKENT–CENTRAL ASIA Cotton & Silk Textiles, Chemicals, Machinery, Metalworking
KARAGANDA Iron & Steel, Machinery, Rubber
ALMA–ATA Textiles, Machinery
KRASNOYARSK Railroad Equipment, Farm Machinery, Food Processing, Lumber
IRKUTSK Machinery, Motor Vehicles, Chemicals, Oil Refining, Leather, Lumber
ULAN–UDE Railroad Equipment, Textiles, Lumber, Meat, Glass
KOMSOMOL'SK Iron & Steel, Shipbuilding, Machinery
KHABAROVSK Machinery, Motor Vehicles, Oil Refining, Lumber, Food Processing
VLADIVOSTOK Machinery, Shipbuilding, Fish Preserving, Woodworking
Walrus
Cod
Reindeer
Seals
Salmon
Furs
Timber
Flax
Cattle
Corn
Oats
Wheat
Rice
Cotton
Sheep
Camels
Herring
Omsk
Novosibirsk
Karaganda
Tashkent
Alma-Ata
Krasnoyarsk
Irkutsk
Ulan-Ude
Komsomol'sk
Khabarovsk
Vladivostok

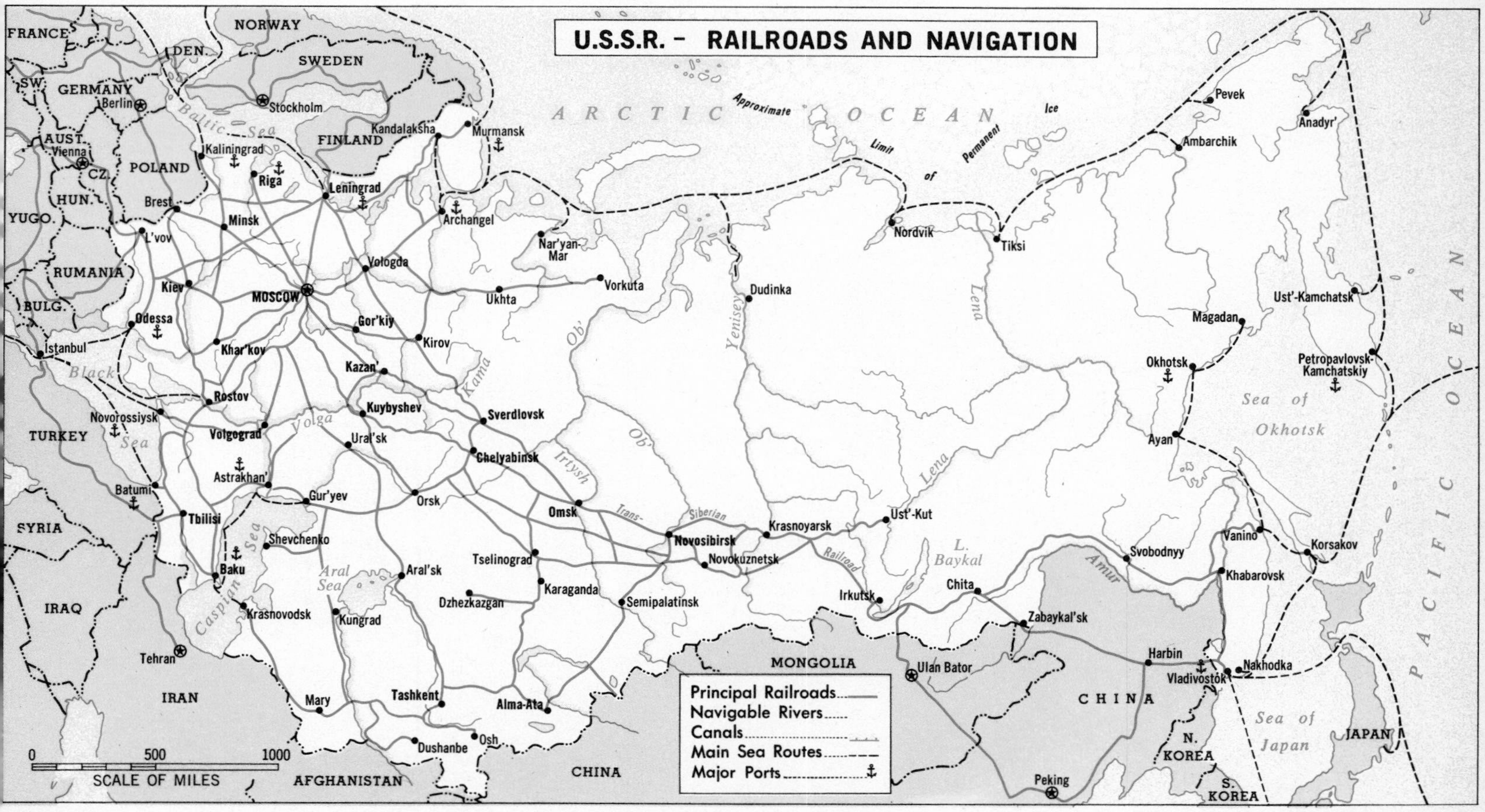
U.S.S.R. - RAILROADS AND NAVIGATION
Principal Railroads
Navigable Rivers
Canals
Main Sea Routes
Major Ports
0 500 1000
SCALE OF MILES
ARCTIC OCEAN
Approximate Limit of Permanent Ice
PACIFIC OCEAN
Sea of Okhotsk
Sea of Japan
Black Sea
Baltic Sea
Caspian Sea
Aral Sea
L. Baykal
Trans-Siberian Railroad
Volga
Kama
Ob'
Irtysh
Yenisey
Lena
Amur
FRANCE
NORWAY
SWEDEN
DEN.
SW.
GERMANY
AUST.
CZ.
POLAND
HUN.
FINLAND
YUGO.
RUMANIA
BULG.
TURKEY
SYRIA
IRAQ
IRAN
AFGHANISTAN
CHINA
MONGOLIA
N. KOREA
S. KOREA
JAPAN
Berlin
Vienna
Stockholm
Kaliningrad
Riga
Leningrad
Kandalaksha
Murmansk
Archangel
Brest
Minsk
L'vov
Kiev
MOSCOW
Vologda
Odessa
Istanbul
Khar'kov
Gor'kiy
Kirov
Kazan'
Rostov
Novorossiysk
Volgograd
Kuybyshev
Astrakhan'
Ural'sk
Sverdlovsk
Chelyabinsk
Batumi
Tbilisi
Gur'yev
Shevchenko
Baku
Krasnovodsk
Kungrad
Aral'sk
Orsk
Omsk
Tselinograd
Karaganda
Dzhezkazgan
Semipalatinsk
Novosibirsk
Novokuznetsk
Krasnoyarsk
Irkutsk
Ust'-Kut
Tehran
Mary
Tashkent
Alma-Ata
Dushanbe
Osh
Nar'yan-Mar
Vorkuta
Ukhta
Dudinka
Nordvik
Tiksi
Pevek
Ambarchik
Anadyr'
Ust'-Kamchatsk
Magadan
Okhotsk
Petropavlovsk-Kamchatskiy
Ayan
Chita
Ulan Bator
Zabaykal'sk
Svobodnyy
Khabarovsk
Vanino
Korsakov
Harbin
Vladivostok
Nakhodka
Peking

(continued on following page)

Administrative Divisions bear same names as their respective Capitals or Centers, except:

Abkhaz A.S.S.R.	Sukhumi	F6
Adygey Aut. Oblast	Maykop	F6
Adzhar A.S.S.R.	Batumi	F6
Bashkir A.S.S.R.	Ufa	J4
Chechen-Ingush A.S.S.R.	Groznyy	G6
Chuvash A.S.S.R.	Cheboksary	G3
Crimean Oblast	Simferopol'	D6
Dagestan A.S.S.R.	Makhachkala	G6
Kabardin-Balkar A.S.S.R.	Nal'chik	F6
Kalmuck A.S.S.R.	Elista	F5
Karachay-Cherkess Aut. Obl.	Cherkessk	F6
Karelian A.S.S.R.	Petrozavodsk	D2
Komi A.S.S.R.	Syktyvkar	H2
Komi-Permyak Nat'l Okrug	Kudymkar	H3
Mari A.S.S.R.	Yoshkar-Ola	G3
Mordvinian A.S.S.R.	Saransk	G4
Nagorno-Karabakh Aut. Obl.	Stepanakert	G7
Nenets Nat'l Okrug	Nar'yan-Mar	H1
North Ossetian A.S.S.R.	Ordzhonikidze	F6
South Ossetian Aut. Obl.	Tskhinvali	F6
Tatar A.S.S.R.	Kazan'	G3
Trans-Carpathian Oblast	Uzhgorod	B5
Udmurt A.S.S.R.	Izhevsk	H3
Volyn Oblast	Lutsk	C4

U.S.S.R. - EUROPEAN

UNION REPUBLICS

Armenian S.S.R., 2,491,900 .... F 6
Azerbaidzhan S.S.R., 5,117,100 .. G 6
Estonian S.S.R., 1,356,100 .... C 3
Georgian S.S.R., 4,686,000 .... F 6
Latvian S.S.R., 2,364,100 .... B 3
Lithuanian S.S.R., 3,128,000 .... B 3
Moldavian S.S.R., 3,568,900 .... C 5
Russian S.F.S.R., 130,079,210 .... F 3
Ukrainian S.S.R., 47,126,517 .... D 5
White Russian S.S.R., 9,002,338 .. C 4

INTERNAL DIVISIONS

Abkhaz A.S.S.R., 487,000 .... F 6
Adygey Aut. Oblast, 385,000 .... F 6
Adzhar A.S.S.R., 310,000 .... F 6
Bashkir A.S.S.R., 3,818,000 .... J 4
Chechen-Ingush A.S.S.R., 1,065,000 .... G 6
Chuvash A.S.S.R., 1,224,000 .... G 3
Crimean Oblast, 1,813,000 .... D 6
Dagestan A.S.S.R., 1,429,000 .... G 6
Kabardin-Balkar A.S.S.R., 588,000 .... F 6
Kalmuck A.S.S.R., 268,000 .... F 5
Karachay-Cherkess Aut. Oblast, 345,000 .... F 6
Karelian A.S.S.R., 713,000 .... D 2
Komi A.S.S.R., 965,000 .... H 2
Komi-Permyak Nat'l Okrug, 212,000 .... H 3
Mari A.S.S.R., 685,000 .... G 3
Mordvinian A.S.S.R., 1,029,000 .. G 4
Nagorno-Karabakh Aut. Oblast, 150,000 .... G 7
Nakhichevan' A.S.S.R., 202,000 .. F 7
Nenets Nat'l Okrug, 39,000 .... H 1
North Ossetian A.S.S.R., 552,000 F 6
South Ossetian Aut. Oblast, 99,000 .... F 6
Tatar A.S.S.R., 3,131,000 .... G 3
Trans-Carpathian Oblast, 1,057,000 .... B 5
Udmurt A.S.S.R., 1,418,000 .... H 3
Volyn Oblast, 974,000 .... C 4

CITIES and TOWNS

Abdulino, 27,000 .... H 4
Agdam, 21,300 .... G 6
Agryz, 21,000 .... H 3
Akhaltsikhe, 20,000 .... F 6
Akhtubinsk, 33,000 .... G 5
Akhtyrka, 42,000 .... E 4
Alagir, 18,000 .... F 6
Alatyr', 47,000 .... G 4
Aleksandriya, 69,000 .... D 5
Alekseyevka, 24,000 .... E 4
Aleksin, 61,000 .... E 4
Ali-Bayramly, 33,900 .... G 7
Al'met'yevsk, 87,000 .... H 3
Alushta, 21,000 .... D 6
Anapa, 25,000 .... E 6
Apatity, 40,000 .... D 1
Apsheronsk, 36,000 .... F 6
Archangel (Arkhangel'sk), 343,000 .... F 2
Armavir, 145,000 .... F 5
Arzamas, 67,000 .... F 3
Astrakhan', 410,000 .... G 5
Atkarsk, 30,000 .... G 4
Azov, 59,000 .... E 5
Bakhchisaray, 12,000 .... D 6
Bakhmach, 14,000 .... D 4
Baku, 852,000 .... H 6
Baku, *1,266,000 .... H 6
Balakhna, 36,000 .... F 3
Balaklava, 5,000 .... D 6
Balakovo, 103,000 .... G 4
Balashov, 83,000 .... F 4
Baltiysk, 18,000 .... A 4
Baranovichi, 101,000 .... C 4
Barysh, 21,000 .... G 4
Bataysk, 85,000 .... E 5
Batumi, 101,000 .... F 6
Belaya Tserkov', 109,000 .... C 5
Belebey, 35,000 .... H 4
Belev, 18,000 .... E 4
Belgorod, 151,000 .... E 4
Belgorod-Dnestrovskiy, 30,000 .... D 5
Belomorsk, 18,000 .... D 2
Beloretsk, 67,000 .... J 4
Bel'tsy, 101,800 .... C 5
Bendery, 72,300 .... C 5
Berdichev, 71,000 .... C 5
Berdyansk, 100,000 .... E 5
Beregovo, 30,000 .... B 5
Berezniki, 146,000 .... J 3
Beslan, 28,000 .... F 6
Bezhetsk, 31,000 .... E 3
Birsk, 36,000 .... J 3
Blagoveshchensk, 15,000 .... J 4
Bobruysk, 138,000 .... C 4
Bologoye, 32,000 .... D 3
Bor, 55,000 .... F 3
Borislav, 36,000 .... B 5
Borisoglebsk, 64,000 .... F 4
Borisov, 84,000 .... C 4
Borovichi, 55,000 .... D 3
Borzhomi, 17,000 .... F 6
Brest, 122,000 .... B 4
Bryansk, 318,000 .... D 4
Bugul'ma, 72,000 .... H 4
Buguruslan, 49,000 .... H 4
Buy, 25,000 .... F 3
Buynaksk, 41,000 .... G 6
Buzuluk, 67,000 .... H 4
Bykhov, 16,000 .... C 4
Cēsis, 17,700 .... C 3
Chadyr-Lunga, 20,200 .... C 5
Chapayevsk, 86,000 .... G 4
Chaykovskiy, 48,000 .... H 3
Cheboksary, 216,000 .... G 3
Cherepovets, 188,000 .... E 3
Cherkassy, 158,000 .... D 5
Cherkessk, 67,000 .... F 6
Chernigov, 159,000 .... D 4
Chernovtsy, 187,000 .... C 5
Chervonograd, 41,000 .... B 4
Chiatura, 30,000 .... F 6
Chistopol', 60,000 .... H 3
Chkalov (Orenburg), 344,000 .... J 4
Chortkov, 21,000 .... B 5
Chusovoy, 58,000 .... J 3
Danilov, 17,000 .... E 3
Daugavpils, 100,400 .... C 3
Davlekanovo, 22,000 .... H 4
Derbent, 57,000 .... G 6
Dimitrovgrad, 81,000 .... G 4
Dneprodzerzhinsk, 227,000 .... D 5
Dnepropetrovsk, 862,000 .... D 5
Dobrush, 17,000 .... D 4
Donetsk, 879,000 .... E 5
Drogobych, 56,000 .... B 5
Dubna, 43,700 .... E 3
Dubna, 8,000 .... E 4
Dvinsk (Daugavpils), 100,400 .... C 3
Dzerzhinsk, 221,000 .... F 3
Dzhankoy, 42,000 .... D 5
Elektrostal', 123,100 .... E 3
Elista, 50,000 .... F 5
Engel's, 130,000 .... G 4
Erivan, 767,000 .... F 6
Ertil', 20,000 .... F 4
Fastov, 42,000 .... C 4
Feodosiya, 65,000 .... D 5
Frolovo, 30,000 .... F 5
Furmanov, 44,000 .... F 3
Gagarin, 15,000 .... D 3
Gagra, 23,000 .... E 6
Galich, 20,000 .... F 3
Gandzha (Kirovabad), 189,800 .... G 6
Gatchina, 63,000 .... D 3
Gay, 35,000 .... J 4
Gaysin, 23,000 .... C 5
Gelendzhik, 24,000 .... E 6
Genichesk, 19,000 .... E 5
Georgiu-Dezh, 48,000 .... E 4
Glazov, 68,000 .... H 3
Glukhov, 30,000 .... D 4
Gomel', 272,000 .... D 4
Gori, 45,000 .... F 6
Gorki, 24,000 .... D 4
Gor'kiy, 1,170,000 .... F 3
Gorlovka, 335,000 .... E 5
Gornyatskiy, 30,000 .... K 1
Gorodets, 34,000 .... F 3
Gremyachinsk, 34,000 .... J 3
Grodno, 132,000 .... B 4
Groznyy, 341,000 .... G 6
Gryazi, 40,000 .... F 4
Gubakha, 40,000 .... J 3
Gubkin, 54,000 .... E 4
Gudauta, 14,000 .... F 6
Gukovo, 65,000 .... F 5
Gus'-Khrustal'nyy, 65,000 .... F 3
Ichnya, 14,000 .... D 4
Inta, 50,000 .... K 1
Inza, 20,000 .... G 4
Ishimbay, 54,000 .... J 4
Ivano-Frankovsk, 105,000 .... B 5
Ivanovo, 420,000 .... E 3
Izhevsk, 422,000 .... H 3
Izmail, 70,000 .... C 5
Izyum, 52,000 .... E 5
Jelgava, 55,300 .... B 3
Kadiyevka, 137,000 .... E 5
Kagul, 26,000 .... C 5
Kakhovka, 25,000 .... D 5
Kalach, 23,000 .... F 5
Kalinin, 345,000 .... E 3
Kaliningrad, 297,000 .... B 4
Kaliningrad, 105,900 .... E 3
Kalinkovichi, 22,000 .... C 4
Kaluga, 211,000 .... E 4
Kamenets-Podol'skiy, 57,000 .... C 5
Kamenka, 30,000 .... F 4
Kamensk-Shakhtinskiy, 68,000 .... F 5
Kamyshin, 97,000 .... F 4
Kanash, 45,000 .... G 3
Kandalaksha, 42,000 .... D 1
Kapsukas, 28,700 .... B 4
Kashin, 19,000 .... E 3
Kasimov, 37,000 .... F 4
Kaspiysk, 39,000 .... G 6
Kaunas, 306,200 .... B 4
Kazan', 869,000 .... G 3
Kazatin, 28,000 .... C 5
Kem', 21,000 .... D 2
Kerch', 128,000 .... E 5
Khachmas, 22,300 .... G 6
Khar'kov, 1,223,000 .... E 5
Khasavyurt, 54,000 .... G 6
Kherson, 261,000 .... D 5
Khmel'nitskiy, 113,000 .... C 5
Khorol, 13,000 .... D 5
Khvalynsk, 19,000 .... G 4
Kiev, 1,632,000 .... D 4
Kiliya, 26,000 .... C 5
Kimovsk, 44,000 .... E 4
Kimry, 53,000 .... E 3
Kinel', 38,000 .... H 4
Kineshma, 96,000 .... F 3
Kirov, 30,000 .... D 4
Kirov, 333,000 .... G 3
Kirovabad, 189,800 .... G 6
Kirovakan, 107,000 .... G 6
Kirovo-Chepetsk, 51,000 .... H 3
Kirovograd, 189,000 .... D 5
Kirovsk, 48,000 .... D 1
Kirsanov, 24,000 .... F 4
Kishinev, 356,900 .... C 5
Kislovodsk, 90,000 .... F 6
Kizel, 49,000 .... J 3
Kizlyar, 30,000 .... G 6
Klaipėda, 139,900 .... B 3
Klimovichi, 13,000 .... D 4
Klintsy, 58,000 .... D 4
Kobrin, 25,000 .... B 4
Kobuleti, 18,000 .... F 6
Kohtla-Järve, 68,318 .... C 3
Kolomna, 135,900 .... E 4
Kolpino, 70,000 .... D 3
Kommunarsk, 123,000 .... E 5
Komrat, 21,400 .... C 5
Kondopoga, 25,000 .... D 2
Königsberg (Kaliningrad), 297,000 .... B 4
Konotop, 68.000 .... D 4
Konstantinovka, 105,000 .... E 5
Korosten', 56,000 .... C 4
Kostroma, 223,000 .... F 3
Kotel'nich, 30,000 .... G 3
Kotel'nikovo, 21,000 .... F 5
Kotlas, 56,000 .... G 2
Kotovo, 20,000 .... G 4
Kotovsk, 38,000 .... C 5
Kotovsk, 32,000 .... F 4
Kovel', 35,000 .... C 4
Kovrov, 123,000 .... F 3
Kramatorsk, 150,000 .... E 5
Krasnoarmeysk, 21,000 .... G 4
Krasnodar, 464,000 .... E 6
Krasnograd, 18,000 .... E 5
Krasnokamsk, 55,000 .... H 3
Krasnovishersk, 16,000 .... J 2
Krasnyy Kut, 17,000 .... G 4
Krasnyy Luch, 103,000 .... E 5
Kremenchug, 148,000 .... D 5
Krichev, 26,000 .... D 4
Krivoy Rog, 573,000 .... D 5
Krolevets, 18,000 .... D 4
Kropotkin, 68,000 .... F 5
Krymsk, 44,000 .... E 6
Kuba, 18,900 .... G 6
Kudymkar, 20,000 .... H 3
Kulebaki, 48,000 .... F 3
Kumertau, 42,000 .... J 4
Kungur, 74,000 .... J 3
Kupyansk, 28,000 .... E 5
Kursk, 284,000 .... E 4
Kutaisi, 161,000 .... F 6

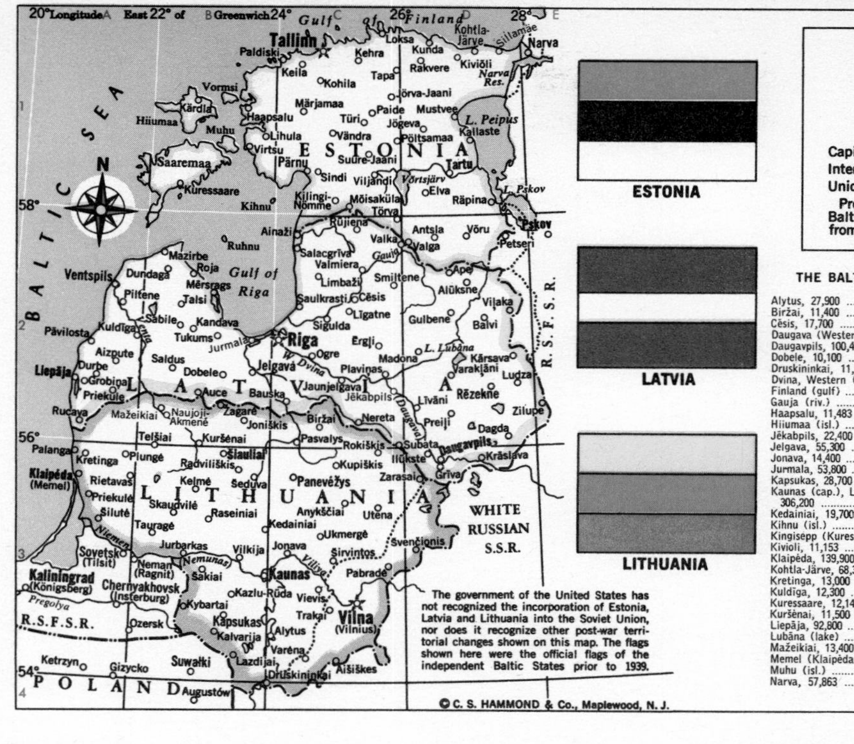

BALTIC SEA
Gulf of Finland
Gulf of Riga
ESTONIA
LATVIA
LITHUANIA
WHITE RUSSIAN S.S.R.
R.S.F.S.R.
POLAND
Tallinn
Riga
Kaunas
Vilna (Vilnius)
Kaliningrad (Königsberg)
The government of the United States has not recognized the incorporation of Estonia, Latvia and Lithuania into the Soviet Union, nor does it recognize other post-war territorial changes shown on this map. The flags shown here were the official flags of the independent Baltic States prior to 1939.
© C. S. HAMMOND & Co., Maplewood, N. J.

THE BALTIC STATES

SCALE OF MILES: 0 25 50 75 100
SCALE OF KILOMETRES: 0 30 60 90 120 150 180
Capitals .... ☆
International Boundaries .... —·—
Union Republic Boundaries .... —·—
Prewar boundaries of the Baltic States where divergent from present boundaries ....

THE BALTIC STATES

Alytus, 27,900 .... C 3
Biržai, 11,400 .... C 2
Cēsis, 17,700 .... C 2
Daugava (Western Dvina) (riv.) .. C 2
Daugavpils, 100,400 .... D 3
Dobele, 10,100 .... B 2
Druskininkai, 11,200 .... C 3
Dvina, Western (river) .... C 2
Finland (gulf) .... D 1
Gauja (riv.) .... C 2
Haapsalu, 11,483 .... B 1
Hiiumaa (isl.) .... B 1
Jēkabpils, 22,400 .... C 2
Jelgava, 55,300 .... B 2
Jonava, 14,400 .... C 3
Jurmala, 53,800 .... B 2
Kapsukas, 28,700 .... B 3
Kaunas (cap.), Lithuania, 306,200 .... C 3
Kedainiai, 19,700 .... C 3
Kihnu (isl.) .... B 1
Kingisepp (Kuressaare), 12,140 .. B 1
Kivioli, 11,153 .... D 1
Klaipėda, 139,900 .... A 3
Kohtla-Järve, 68,318 .... D 1
Kretinga, 13,000 .... A 3
Kuldīga, 12,300 .... A 2
Kuressaare, 12,140 .... B 1
Kuršėnai, 11,500 .... B 2
Liepāja, 92,800 .... A 2
Lubāna (lake) .... D 2
Mažeikiai, 13,400 .... A 2
Memel (Klaipėda), 139,900 .... A 3
Muhu (isl.) .... B 1
Narva, 57,863 .... E 1
Naujoji-Akmene, 10,200 .... B 2
Niemen (Nemunas) (riv.) .... A 3
Ogre, 15,700 .... C 2
Panevėžys, 73,500 .... C 3
Pärnu, 46,316 .... C 1
Peipus (lake) .... D 1
Plungė, 13,600 .... B 3
Radviliškis, 16,900 .... B 3
Rakvere, 17,891 .... D 1
Rēzekne, 30,800 .... D 2
Riga (cap.), Latvia, 731,800 .... C 2
Riga (gulf) .... B 2
Saaremaa (isl.) .... B 1
Saldus, 10,000 .... B 2
Šiauliai, 92,800 .... B 3
Sillamäe, 13,505 .... D 1
Silutė, 12,400 .... A 3
Tallinn (cap.), Estonia, 362,706 .... C 1
Tapa, 10,037 .... C 1
Tartu, 90,459 .... D 1
Tauragė, 19,500 .... B 3
Telšiai, 20,200 .... B 2
Tukums, 14,800 .... B 2
Ukmergė, 21,600 .... C 3
Utena, 13,300 .... C 3
Valga, 16,795 .... D 2
Valmiera, 20,300 .... C 2
Venta (riv.) .... B 2
Ventspils, 40,500 .... A 2
Viliya (riv.) .... C 3
Viljandi, 20,814 .... C 1
Vilna (Vilnius), 371,700 .... C 3
Vormsi (isl.) .... B 1
Võrtsjärv (lake) .... D 1
Voru, 15,398 .... D 2
Western Dvina (riv.) .... C 2

Kuvandyk, 24,000 .... J 4
Kuybyshev, 1,045,000 .... H 4
Kuznetsk, 84,000 .... G 4
Labinsk, 50,000 .... F 6
Lebedin, 29,000 .... D 4
Leninakan, 165,000 .... F 6
Leningrad, 3,513,000 .... C 3
Leningrad, *3,950,000 .... C 3
Leninogorsk, 45,000 .... H 4
Lenkoran', 35,500 .... G 7
L'gov, 28,000 .... E 4
Lida, 48,000 .... C 4
Liepāja, 92,800 .... B 3
Lipetsk, 289,000 .... E 4
Lisichansk, 118,000 .... E 5
Livny, 37,000 .... E 4
Lodeynoye Pole, 20,000 .... D 2
Lozovaya, 34,000 .... E 5
Lubny, 39,000 .... D 4
Luga, 30,000 .... C 3
Lutsk, 94,000 .... B 4
L'vov (Lwów), 553,000 .... B 5
Lys'va, 73,000 .... J 3
Lyubertsy, 139,400 .... E 3
Lyubotin, 38,000 .... E 4
Lyudinovo, 33,000 .... D 4
Makeyevka, 392,000 .... E 5
Makhachkala, 186,000 .... G 6
Makharadze, 24,000 .... F 6
Manturovo, 21,000 .... F 3
Marganets, 47,000 .... E 5
Mariupol' (Zhdanov), 417,000 .... E 5
Marks, 18,000 .... G 4
Maykop, 110,000 .... F 6
Mednogorsk, 41,000 .... J 4
Medvezh'yegorsk, 18,000 .... D 2
Melenki, 19,000 .... F 3
Meleuz, 28,000 .... J 4
Melitopol', 137,000 .... D 5
Memel (Klaipėda), 139,900 .... B 3
Merefa, 32,000 .... E 5
Michurinsk, 94,000 .... F 4
Mikhaylovka, 50,000 .... F 4
Millerovo, 38,000 .... F 5
Mineralnye Vody, 55,000 .... F 6
Mingechaur, 43,100 .... G 6
Minsk, 907,000 .... C 4
Minsk, *917,000 .... C 4
Mirgorod, 28,000 .... D 5
Mogilev, 202,000 .... C 4
Mogilev-Podol'skiy, 27,000 .... C 5
Molodechno, 50,000 .... C 4
Molotov (Perm'), 850,000 .... J 3
Monchegorsk, 49,000 .... D 1
Morshansk, 45,000 .... F 4
Moscow (Moskva) (cap.), 6,942,000 .... E 3
Moscow, *7,061,000 .... E 3
Mozhaysk, 20,300 .... E 3
Mozhga, 34,000 .... H 3
Mozyr', 49,000 .... C 4
Mtsensk, 24,000 .... E 4
Mukachevo, 57,000 .... B 5
Murmansk, 309,000 .... D 1
Murom, 99,000 .... F 3
Mytishchi, 118,700 .... E 3
Naberezhnye Chelny, 38,000 .... H 3
Nakhichevan', 33,200 .... F 7
Nal'chik, 146,000 .... F 6
Narva, 57,863 .... C 3
Nar'yan-Mar, 15,000 .... H 1
Neftekamsk, 35,000 .... J 3
Nelidovo, 30,000 .... D 3
Nerekhta, 28,000 .... F 3
Nevinnomyssk, 85,000 .... F 6
Nezhin, 56,000 .... D 4
Nikel', 17,000 .... C 1
Nikolayev, 331,000 .... D 5
Nikopol', 125,000 .... D 5
Nizhnekamsk, 49,000 .... H 3
Nizhniy Lomov, 19,000 .... F 4
Nosovka, 23,000 .... D 4
Novaya Kakhovka, 40,000 .... D 5
Novgorod, 128,000 .... D 3
Novoanninskiy, 21,000 .... F 4
Novocherkassk, 162,000 .... F 5
Novograd-Volynskiy, 36,000 .... C 4
Novogrudok, 20,000 .... C 4
Novokuybyshevsk, 104,000 .... G 4
Novomoskovsk, 134,000 .... E 4
Novopolotsk, 40,000 .... C 3
Novorossiysk, 133,000 .... E 6
Novoshakhtinsk, 102,000 .... E 5
Novotroitsk, 83,000 .... J 4
Novoukrainka, 22,000 .... D 5
Novovolynsk, 40,000 .... B 4
Novozybkov, 33,000 .... D 4
Nyandoma, 24,000 .... F 2
Obninsk, 49,000 .... E 3
Ochamchire, 20,000 .... F 6
Odessa, 892,000 .... D 5
Oktyabr'sk, 36,000 .... G 4
Oktyabr'skiy, 77,000 .... H 4
Olenegorsk, 21,000 .... D 1
Omutninsk, 29,000 .... H 3
Onega, 27,000 .... E 2
Ordzhonikidze, 236,000 .... F 6
Orel, 232,000 .... E 4
Orenburg, 344,000 .... J 4
Orgeyev, 25,800 .... C 5
Orsha, 101,000 .... C 4
Orsk, 225,000 .... J 4
Osipenko (Berdyansk), 100,000 .... E 5
Osipovichi, 19,000 .... C 4
Ostashkov, 22,000 .... D 3
Ostrogozhsk, 35,000 .... E 4
Ostrov, 19,000 .... C 3
Otradnyy, 46,000 .... H 4
Panevėžys, 73,500 .... B 3
Pärnu, 46,316 .... C 3
Pavlovo, 63,000 .... F 3
Pechora, 41,000 .... J 1
Penza, 374,000 .... F 4
Perm', 850,000 .... J 3
Pervomaysk, 59,000 .... D 5
Pervomayskiy, 18,000 .... F 2
Petrovsk, 32,000 .... G 4
Petrozavodsk, 184,000 .... D 2
Pinsk, 62,000 .... C 4
Piryatin, 18,000 .... D 4
Pochep, 16,000 .... D 4
Podol'sk, 168,700 .... E 3
Polonnoye, 23,000 .... C 4
Polotsk, 64,000 .... C 3
Poltava, 220,000 .... D 5
Postavy, 13,000 .... C 3
Poti, 48,000 .... F 6
Povorino, 22,000 .... F 4
Prikumsk, 36,000 .... F 6
Priluki, 57,000 .... D 4
Primorsko-Akhtarsk, 30,000 .... E 5
Priyutovo, 20,000 .... H 4
Promyshlennyy, 22,000 .... K 1
Pskov, 127,000 .... C 3
Pugachev, 38,000 .... G 4
Pushkin, 79,000 .... C 3
Pyatigorsk, 93,000 .... F 6
Pyatikhatki, 20,000 .... D 5
Radomyshl', 12,000 .... C 4
Rakhov, 11,000 .... B 5
Rakvere, 17,891 .... C 3
Rasskazovo, 40,000 .... F 4
Rechitsa, 48,000 .... C 4
Revel (Tallinn), 362,706 .... B 3
Rēzekne, 30,800 .... C 3
Riga, 731,800 .... B 3
Rogachev, 12,000 .... D 4
Romny, 48,000 .... D 4
Roslavl', 48,000 .... D 4
Rossosh', 36,000 .... E 4
Rostov, 32,000 .... E 3
Rostov, 789,000 .... F 5
Rovno, 116,000 .... C 4
Rtishchevo, 40,000 .... F 4
Rubezhnoye, 58,000 .... E 5
Rustavi, 98,000 .... G 6
Ruzayevka, 38,000 .... F 4
Ryazan', 350,000 .... E 4
Rybinsk, 218,000 .... E 3
Rybnitsa, 32,400 .... C 5
Rzhev, 61,000 .... D 3
Safonovo, 44,000 .... D 3
Saki, 23,000 .... D 5
Salavat, 114,000 .... H 4
Sal'sk, 50,000 .... F 5
Sal'yany, 24,200 .... G 7
Samara (Kuybyshev), 1,045,000 .. H 4
Saransk, 191,000 .... G 4
Sarapul, 97,000 .... H 3
Saratov, 757,000 .... G 4
Sarny, 10,000 .... C 4
Sasovo, 28,000 .... F 4
Segezha, 30,000 .... D 2
Semenov, 25,000 .... F 3
Serdobel (Sortavala), 23,000 .... D 2
Serdobsk, 33,000 .... F 4
Serpukhov, 124,300 .... E 4
Sevastopol', 229,000 .... D 6
Severodonetsk, 90,000 .... E 5
Severodvinsk, 145,000 .... E 2
Severomorsk, 45,000 .... D 1
Shakhty, 205,000 .... F 5
Shakhun'ya, 22,000 .... G 3
Shar'ya, 25,000 .... G 3
Shchekino, 61,000 .... E 4
Shcherbakov (Rybinsk), 218,000 .. E 3
Sheki, 43,200 .... G 6
Shemakha, 17,900 .... G 6
Shepetovka, 39,000 .... C 4
Shostka, 64,000 .... D 4
Shumerlya, 33,000 .... G 3
Shuya, 69,000 .... F 3
Šiauliai, 92,800 .... B 3
Sibay, 42,000 .... J 4
Simferopol', 249,000 .... D 6
Skopin, 23,000 .... F 4
Slantsy, 40,000 .... C 3
Slavuta, 24,000 .... C 4
Slavyansk, 124,000 .... E 5
Slavyansk-na-Kubani, 52,000 .... E 5
Slobodskoy, 37,000 .... H 3
Slonim, 30,000 .... B 4
Slutsk, 36,000 .... C 4
Smela, 55,000 .... D 5
Smolensk, 211,000 .... D 4
Sochi, 224,000 .... E 6
Sokol, 49,000 .... F 3
Solikamsk, 89,000 .... J 3
Sol'-Iletsk, 25,000 .... J 4
Sorochinsk, 25,000 .... H 4
Soroki, 21,700 .... C 5
Sortavala, 23,000 .... D 2
Sosnogorsk, 25,000 .... H 2
Sovetsk, 38,000 .... B 4
Sovetsk, 19,000 .... G 3
Stalingrad (Volgograd), 818,000 .... F 5
Staraya Russa, 34,000 .... D 3
Staryy Oskol, 52,000 .... E 4
Stavropol', 198,000 .... F 5
Stepanakert, 30,300 .... G 7
Stepnoy (Elista), 50,000 .... G 5
Sterlitamak, 185,000 .... J 4
Stupino, 59,300 .... E 4
Sukhumi, 102,000 .... F 6
Sumgait, 124,400 .... G 6
Sumy, 159,000 .... E 4
Svetlogorsk, 40,000 .... C 4
Svetlograd, 30,000 .... F 5
Syktyvkar, 125,000 .... H 2
Syzran', 173,000 .... G 4
Taganrog, 254,000 .... E 5
Tallinn, 362,706 .... B 3
Tambov, 230,000 .... F 4
Tartu, 90,459 .... C 3
Tauragė, 19,500 .... B 3
Tbilisi, 889,000 .... F 6
Telavi, 23,000 .... G 6
Telšiai, 20,200 .... B 3
Temryuk, 28,000 .... E 5
Ternopol', 85,000 .... C 5
Teykovo, 34,000 .... E 3
Tiflis (Tbilisi), 889,000 .... F 6
Tighina (Bendery), 72,300 .... C 5
Tikhoretsk, 60,000 .... F 5
Tikhvin, 29,000 .... D 3
Timashevsk, 35,000 .... E 5
Tiraspol', 105,700 .... D 5
Togliatti, 251,000 .... G 4
Tokmak, 39,000 .... E 5
Torzhok, 47,000 .... D 3
Tskhinvali, 30,000 .... F 6
Tuapse, 51,000 .... E 6
Tula, 462,000 .... E 4
Tul'chin, 14,000 .... C 5
Tuymazy, 35,000 .... H 4
Tyrnyauz, 19,000 .... F 6
Uchaly, 18,000 .... J 4
Ufa, 771,000 .... J 4
Uglich, 36,000 .... E 3
Ukhta, 63,000 .... H 2
Ukmergė, 21,600 .... C 3
Ul'yanovsk, 351,000 .... G 4
Uman', 63,000 .... D 5
Uryupinsk, 37,000 .... F 4
Usman', 19,000 .... E 4
Uzhgorod, 65,000 .... B 5
Uzlovaya, 62,000 .... E 4
Valga, 16,795 .... C 3
Valmiera, 20,300 .... C 3
Valuyki, 29,000 .... E 4
Vasil'kov, 27,000 .... D 4
Velikiye Luki, 85,000 .... D 3
Velikiy Ustyug, 35,000 .... F 2
Vel'sk, 20,000 .... F 2
Ventspils, 40,500 .... B 3
Vichuga, 53,000 .... F 3
Viipuri (Vyborg), 65,000 .... C 2
Vilna (Vilnius), 371,700 .... C 4
Vinnitsa, 212,000 .... C 5
Vitebsk, 231,000 .... C 3
Vladimir, 234,000 .... F 3
Volgodonsk, 25,000 .... F 5
Volgograd, 818,000 .... F 5
Volkhov, 46,000 .... D 3
Volkovysk, 22,000 .... B 4
Vologda, 178,000 .... F 3
Vol'sk, 69,000 .... G 4
Volzhsk, 44,000 .... G 3
Volzhskiy, 142,000 .... G 5
Vorkuta, 90,000 .... K 1
Voronezh, 660,000 .... E 4
Voroshilovgrad, 383,000 .... F 5
Voskresensk, 66,900 .... E 3
Votkinsk, 74,000 .... H 3
Voznesensk, 36,000 .... D 5
Vyatskiye Polyany, 33,000 .... H 3
Vyaz'ma, 42,000 .... D 3
Vyborg, 65,000 .... C 2
Vyksa, 46,000 .... F 3
Vyshniy Volochek, 74,000 .... D 3
Yalta, 62,000 .... D 6
Yanaul, 18,000 .... J 3
Yaroslavl', 517,000 .... E 3
Yartsevo, 37,000 .... D 3
Yefremov, 47,000 .... E 4
Yelabuga, 36,000 .... H 3
Yelets, 101,000 .... E 4
Yenakiyevo, 92,000 .... E 5
Yershov, 20,000 .... G 4
Yessentuki, 65,000 .... F 6
Yevpatoria, 79,000 .... D 5
Yeysk, 64,000 .... E 5
Yoshkar-Ola, 166,000 .... G 3
Yur'yevets, 23,000 .... F 3
Zagorsk, 92,400 .... E 3
Zaporozh'ye, 658,000 .... E 5
Zelenodol'sk, 77,000 .... G 3
Zhdanov, 417,000 .... E 5
Zherdevka, 20,000 .... F 4
Zhigulevsk, 52,000 .... G 4
Zhitomir, 161,000 .... C 4
Zhlobin, 25,000 .... D 4
Zhmerinka, 34,000 .... C 5
Zhodino, 17,000 .... C 4
Znamenka, 30,000 .... D 5
Zolotonosha, 27,000 .... D 5
Zugdidi, 39,000 .... F 6
Zvenigorodka, 21,000 .... D 5

OTHER FEATURES

Apsheron (pen.) .... H 6
Araks (river) .... G 7
Azov (sea) .... E 5
Baltic (sea) .... B 3
Barents (sea) .... E 1
Belaya (river) .... H 3
Beloye (lake) .... E 2
Berezina (river) .... C 4
Black (sea) .... D 6
Bug (river) .... B 4
Bug (river) .... D 5
Caspian (sea) .... G 6
Caucasus (mts.) .... F 6
Central Ural (mts.) .... J 2
Chir (river) .... F 5
Crimea (pen.), 1,813,000 .... D 5
Dagö (Hiiumaa) (isl.) .... B 3
Denezhkin Kamen' (mt.) .... K 2
Desna (river) .... D 4
Dnieper (river) .... D 5
Dniester (river) .... C 5
Don (river) .... F 5
Donets (river) .... E 5
Dvina (bay) .... E 2
Dvina, Northern (river) .... F 2
Dvina, Western (river) .... C 3
Dykh-Tau (mt.) .... F 6
El'brus (mt.) .... F 6
Finland (gulf) .... C 3
Goryn' (river) .... C 4
Hiiumaa (isl.) .... B 3
Ilek (river) .... J 4
Il'men (lake) .... D 3
Izhma (river) .... H 2
Kakhovka (res.) .... D 5
Kama (river) .... H 3
Kandalaksha (gulf) .... D 1
Kanin (pen.) .... G 1
Kapydzhik (mt.) .... G 7
Kara (sea) .... K 1
Kazbek (mt.) .... F 6
Khoper (river) .... F 4
Kil'din (isl.) .... D 1
Kinel' (river) .... H 4
Kola (pen.) .... E 1
Kolguyev (isl.) .... G 1
Kolva (river) .... J 1
Kuban' (river) .... E 5
Kubeno (lake) .... E 3
Kura (river) .... G 6
Kuyto (lake) .... D 2
Ladoga (lake) .... D 2
Lapland (reg.) .... C 1
Lovat' (river) .... D 3
Mansel'ka (mts.) .... C 1
Manych-Gudilo (lake) .... F 5
Matveyev (isl.) .... J 1
Medveditsa (river) .... F 4
Mezen' (river) .... G 1
Mezhdusharskiy (isl.) .... G 1
Moksha (river) .... F 4
Moskva (river) .... E 3
Msta (river) .... D 3
Niemen (river) .... B 4
North Ural (mts.) .... K 1
Northern Dvina (river) .... F 2
Novaya Zemlya (isls.) .... H 1
Oka (river) .... F 4
Onega (bay) .... E 2
Onega (lake) .... E 2
Ösel (Saaremaa) (isl.) .... B 3
Pay-Yer (mt.) .... K 1
Pechora (river) .... H 1
Pechora (sea) .... H 1
Peipus (lake) .... C 3
Pinega (river) .... G 2
Ponoy (river) .... E 1
Pripet (marsh) .... C 4
Pripyat' (river) .... C 4
Prut (river) .... C 5
Psel (river) .... D 4
Riga (gulf) .... B 3
Russkiy Zavorot (cape) .... H 1
Rybachiy (pen.) .... D 1
Saaremaa (isl.) .... B 3
Samara (river) .... H 4
Seg (lake) .... D 2
Sevan (lake) .... G 6
Seym (river) .... D 4
Solovetskiye (isls.) .... E 1
South Ural (mts.) .... J 4
Suda (river) .... E 3
Sukhona (river) .... F 2
Sura (river) .... G 4
Svir' (river) .... D 2
Sysola (river) .... H 2
Tel'pos-Iz (mt.) .... K 2
Timan Ridge (mts.) .... H 1
Top (lake) .... D 1
Tuloma (river) .... D 1
Ufa (river) .... J 3
Undzha (river) .... F 3
Ural (mts.) .... J 2
Ural (river) .... J 4
Usa (river) .... K 1
Vaga (river) .... F 2
Valday (hills) .... D 3
Vaygach (isl.) .... K 1
Velikaya (river) .... C 3
Vetluga (river) .... G 3
Vodl (lake) .... E 2
Volga (river) .... G 5
Volga-Don (canal) .... F 5
Volkhov (river) .... D 3
Vorona (river) .... F 4
Vorskla (river) .... E 4
Vozhe (lake) .... F 2
Vyatka (river) .... H 3
Vychegda (river) .... G 2
Vyg (lake) .... E 2
Vym' (river) .... H 2
Western Dvina (river) .... C 3
White (sea) .... E 1
Yamantau (mt.) .... J 4
Yug (river) .... G 2
Yugorskiy (pen.) .... K 1

*City and suburbs.

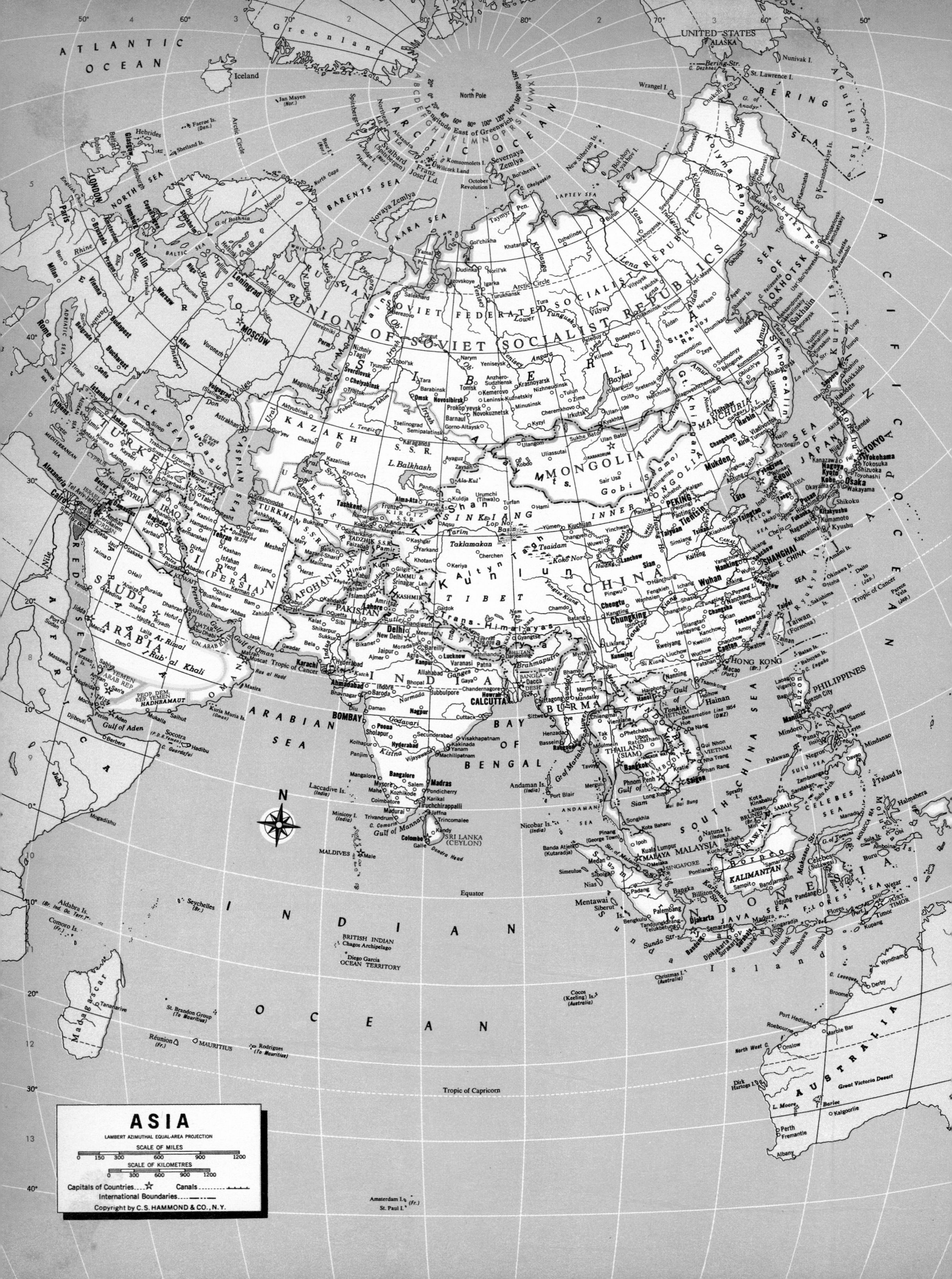

ASIA
LAMBERT AZIMUTHAL EQUAL-AREA PROJECTION
SCALE OF MILES
0 150 300 600 900 1200
SCALE OF KILOMETRES
0 300 600 900 1200
Capitals of Countries
Canals
International Boundaries
Copyright by C.S. HAMMOND & CO., N.Y.
ATLANTIC OCEAN
ARCTIC OCEAN
North Pole
Longitude East of Greenwich
Greenland
Iceland
NORTH SEA
BARENTS SEA
KARA SEA
LAPTEV SEA
BERING SEA
SEA OF OKHOTSK
PACIFIC OCEAN
UNION OF SOVIET SOCIALIST REPUBLICS
SOVIET FEDERATED SOCIALIST REPUBLICS
SIBERIA
EUROPE
MOSCOW
BLACK SEA
CASPIAN SEA
MEDITERRANEAN SEA
TURKEY
SYRIA
IRAQ
IRAN (PERSIA)
SAUDI ARABIA
AFGHANISTAN
PAKISTAN
INDIA
KAZAKH S.S.R.
MONGOLIA
INNER MONGOLIA
MANCHURIA
SINKIANG
TIBET
CHINA
KOREA
JAPAN
SEA OF JAPAN
PEKING
SHANGHAI
TOKYO
BURMA
THAILAND (SIAM)
CAMBODIA
VIETNAM
PHILIPPINES
SOUTH CHINA SEA
MALAYSIA
INDONESIA
KALIMANTAN
ARABIAN SEA
BAY OF BENGAL
BOMBAY
CALCUTTA
SRI LANKA (CEYLON)
MALDIVES
INDIAN OCEAN
AFRICA
RED SEA
Madagascar
AUSTRALIA
Tropic of Cancer
Equator
Tropic of Capricorn
Arctic Circle

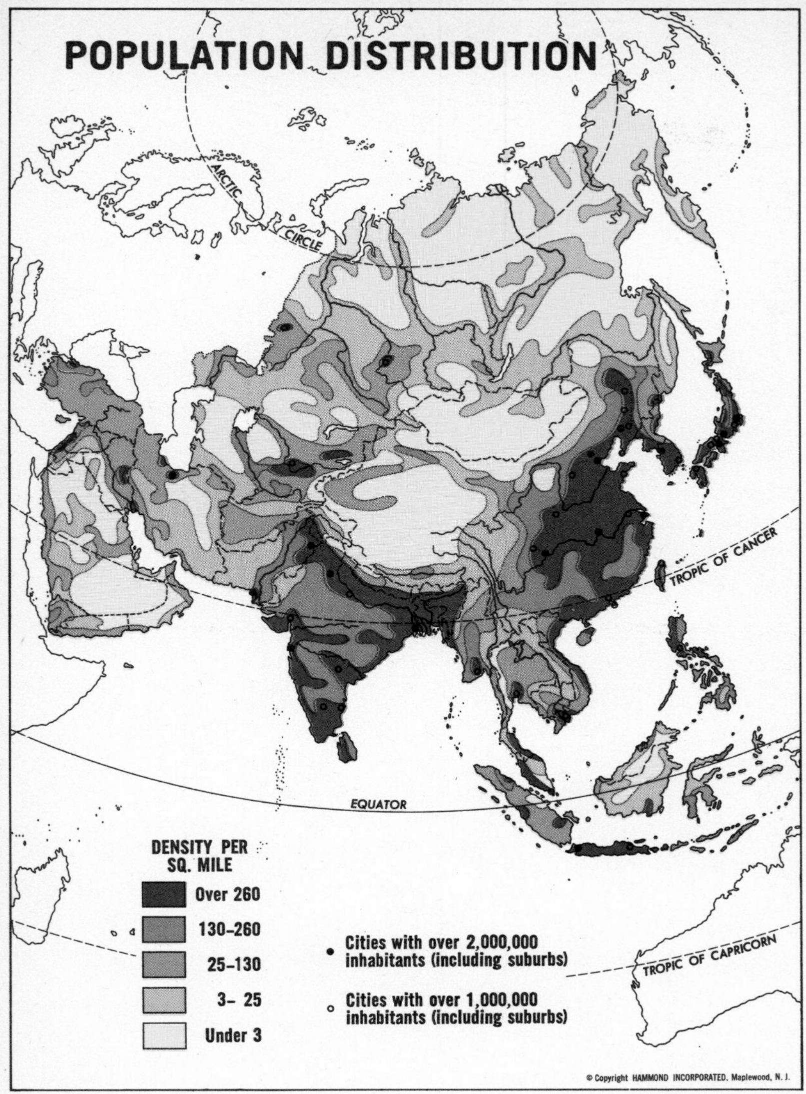

AREA 17,032,000 sq. mi.
POPULATION 2,043,997,000
LARGEST CITY Tokyo
HIGHEST POINT Mt. Everest 29,028 ft.
LOWEST POINT Dead Sea -1,290 ft.

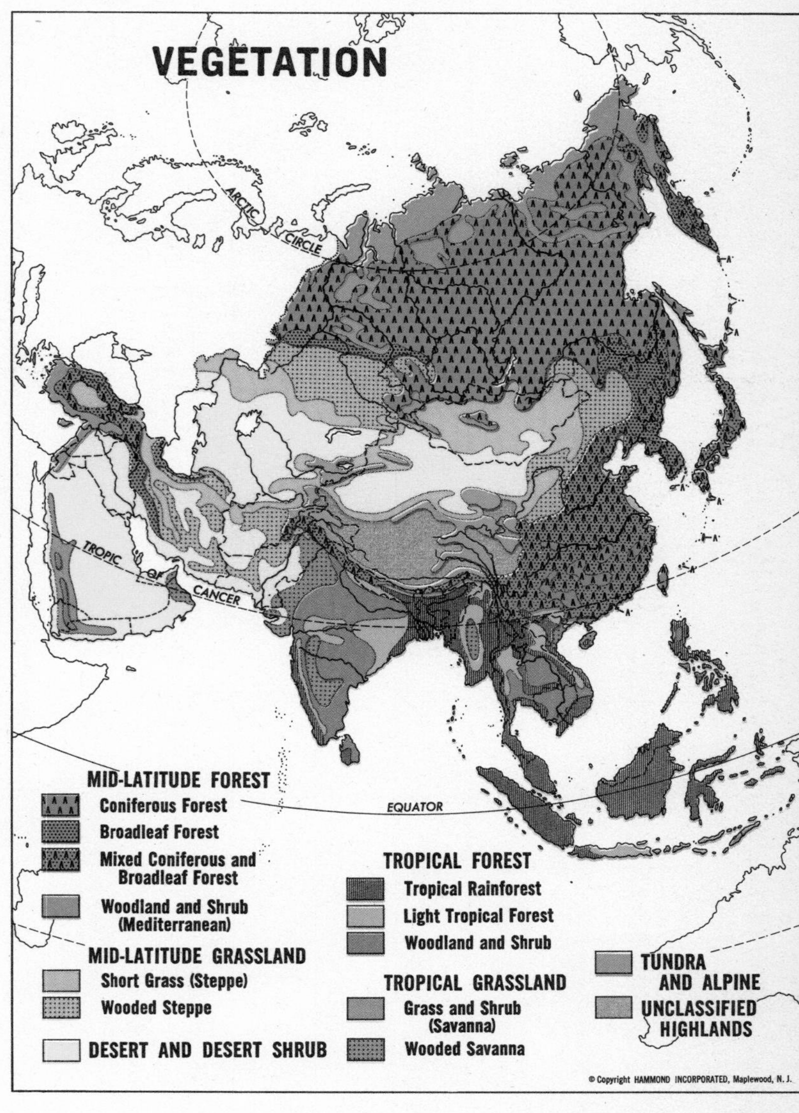

Aden (cap.), P.D.R. Yemen .... H 8
Aden (gulf) .... H 8
Afghanistan .... K 6
Agra, India .... L 7
Ahmadabad, India .... K 7
Aleppo, Syria .... G 6
Allahabad, India .... L 7
Alma-Ata, U.S.S.R. .... L 5
Altay (mts.) .... M 5
Amman (cap.), Jordan .... G 6
Amoy, China .... P 7
Amritsar, India .... L 6
Amsterdam (isl.) L13
Amu-Dar'ya (river), U.S.S.R. .... K 5
Amur (river) .... S 4
Anadyr' (river), U.S.S.R. .... W 3
Andaman (sea) .... N 9
Angara (river), U.S.S.R. .... N 4
Angkor Wat (ruins), Cambodia .... O 8
Ankara (cap.), Turkey .... G 5
'Aqaba, Jordan .... G 7
Arabia (peninsula) .... H 7
Arabian (sea) .... K 8
Aral (sea), U.S.S.R. .... J 5
Ararat (mt.), Turkey .... H 6
Arctic Ocean .... E 1
Argun' (river) .... P 5
Ashkhabad, U.S.S.R. .... J 6
Baghdad (cap.), Iraq .... H 6
Bahrain .... J 7
Bali (island), Indonesia P10
Balkh, Afghanistan .... K 6
Balkhash (lake), U.S.S.R. .... L 5
Bandar 'Abbas, Iran .... J 7
Bandjarmasin, Indonesia P10
Bandung, Indonesia O10
Bangalore, India .... L 8
Bangkok (cap.), Thailand .... N 8
Bangladesh .... N 7
Barnaul, U.S.S.R. .... M 4
Basra, Iraq .... H 7
Baykal (lake), U.S.S.R. .... P 4
Beirut (cap.), Lebanon .... G 6
Bengal (bay) .... M 8
Bering (sea) .... X 4
Bering (strait) .... Y 3
Bhutan .... M 7
Black (sea) .... G 5
Blagoveshchensk, U.S.S.R. .... R 4
Bombay, India .... L 8
Borneo (isl.) .... P 9
Brahmaputra (river) .... N 7
British Indian Ocean Terr. L10
Brunei .... P 9
Bukhara, U.S.S.R. .... K 6
Burma .... N 7
Bursa, Turkey .... F 6
Calcutta, India .... M 7
Cambodia .... O 8
Canton, China .... P 7
Caspian (sea) .... H 5
Cebu, Philippines .... R 9
Celebes (Sulawesi) (island), Indonesia R10
Celebes (sea) .... R 9
Ceylon (Sri Lanka) .... M 9
Chefoo, China .... P 6
Chelyabinsk, U.S.S.R. .... K 4
Chelyuskin (cape), U.S.S.R. .... P 2
Chengtu, China .... O 6
Chiangmai, Thailand .... N 8
China .... O 6
Chita, U.S.S.R. .... P 4
Chittagong, Bangladesh .... N 7
Christmas (island), Australia O11
Chukchi (pen.), U.S.S.R. .... X 3
Chungking, China .... O 7
Cocos (isls.), Australia N11
Colombo (cap.), Ceylon .... L 9
Comorin (cape), India .... L 9
Cuttack, India .... M 8
Cyprus .... G 6
Dacca (cap.), Bangladesh .... N 7
Daito (islands), Japan .... S 7
Damascus (cap.), Syria .... G 6
Delhi, India .... L 7
Dezhnev (cape), U.S.S.R. .... X 3
Dhahran, Saudi Arabia .... H 7
Dili (cap.), Portuguese Timor R10
Djakarta (cap.), Indonesia O10
Djokjakarta, Indonesia O10
East China (sea) .... R 6
Euphrates (river) .... H 6
Everest (mt.) .... M 7
Flores (sea), Indonesia R10
Foochow, China .... P 7
Formosa (Taiwan) (island), China .... R 7
Frunze, U.S.S.R. .... L 5
Fuji (mt.), Japan .... S 6
Fukuoka, Japan .... R 6
Ganges (river), India .... M 7
Gobi (desert) .... O 5
Godavari (river), India .... L 8
Grand (canal), China .... P 6
Great Wall (ruins), China .... O 6
Hadhramaut (region), P.D.R. Yemen .... H 8
Hainan (island), China .... P 8
Haiphong, North Vietnam .... O 7
Hakodate, Japan .... T 5
Halmahera (island), Indonesia .... R 9
Hangchow, China .... R 7
Hanoi (capital), North Vietnam .... O 7
Harbin, China .... R 5
Helmand (river), Afghanistan .... K 6
Herat, Afghanistan .... K 6
Himalaya (mts.) .... L 6
Hindu Kush (mts.) .... K 6
Hiroshima, Japan .... S 6
Hokkaido (island), Japan .... T 5
Hong Kong .... P 7
Honshu (island), Japan .... T 6
Hue, South Vietnam .... O 8
Hwang Ho (river), China .... P 6
Hyderabad, India .... L 8
Hyderabad, Pakistan .... L 7
Inch'ŏn, South Korea .... R 6
India .... L 7
Indian Ocean L10
Indigirka (river), U.S.S.R. .... T 3
Indochina (region) .... O 8
Indonesia P10
Indus (river) .... K 7
Inner Mongolia (region), China .... P 5
Iran .... J 6
Iraq .... H 6
Irkutsk, U.S.S.R. .... O 4
Irrawaddy (river), Burma .... N 7
Irtysh (river), U.S.S.R. .... K 4
Isfahan, Iran .... J 6
Islamabad (cap.), Pakistan .... L 6
Israel .... G 6
Izmir, Turkey .... F 6
Japan .... S 6
Java (island), Indonesia O10
Jerusalem (cap.), Israel .... G 6
Jidda, Saudi Arabia .... G 7
Jordan .... G 6
Kabul (capital), Afghanistan .... L 6
Kalimantan (region), Indonesia P10
Kamchatka (peninsula), U.S.S.R. .... U 4
Kandahar, Afghanistan .... K 6
Kanpur, India .... L 7
Kara (sea), U.S.S.R. .... K 2
Karachi, Pakistan .... K 7
Karakorum (ruins), Mongolia .... O 5
Kathmandu (cap.), Nepal .... M 7
Kazakh S.S.R., U.S.S.R. .... J 5
Kerulen (river) .... P 5
Khabarovsk, U.S.S.R. .... S 5
Khyber (pass), Pakistan .... K 6
Kirgiz S.S.R., U.S.S.R. .... L 5
Kirin, China .... R 5
Kirkuk, Iraq .... H 6
Kitakyushu, Japan .... S 6
Kobe, Japan .... S 6
Koko Nor (lake), China .... N 6
Kolyma (range), U.S.S.R. .... V 3
Korea, North .... R 6
Korea, South .... R 6
Krasnoyarsk, U.S.S.R. .... N 4
Kuala Lumpur (cap.), Malaysia .... O 9
Kunlun (range), China .... M 6
Kunming, China .... O 7
Kure, Japan .... S 6
Kuril (islands), U.S.S.R. .... T 5
Kuwait .... H 7
Kyoto, Japan .... S 6
Kyushu (island), Japan .... S 6
Lahore, Pakistan .... L 6
Lanchow, China .... O 6
Laos .... O 8
La Pérouse (strait) .... T 5
Laptev (sea), U.S.S.R. .... R 2
Lebanon .... G 6
Lena (river), U.S.S.R. .... R 3
Lhasa, China .... N 6
Lopatka (cape), U.S.S.R. .... V 4
Lop Nor (basin), China .... M 5
Lucknow, India .... M 7
Lüta, China .... R 6
Luzon (island), Philippines .... R 8
Macao .... P 7
Madras, India .... M 8
Magnitogorsk, U.S.S.R. .... J 4
Malacca (strait) .... O 9
Malaya (region), Malaysia .... O 9
Malaysia .... O 9
Maldives .... L 9
Male (cap.), Maldives .... L 9
Manchuria (region), China .... R 5
Mandalay, Burma .... N 7
Manila, Philippines .... P 8
Mannar (gulf) .... L 9
Mecca (capital), Saudi Arabia .... H 7
Medan, Indonesia .... N 9
Medina, Saudi Arabia .... H 7
Mediterranean (sea) .... F 6
Mekong (river) .... O 8
Meshed, Iran .... J 6
Mindanao (island), Philippines .... R 9
Molucca (islands), Indonesia .... R 9
Mongolia .... O 5
Mosul, Iraq .... H 6
Moulmein, Burma .... N 8
Mukden, China .... R 5
Muscat (cap.), Oman .... J 7
Mysore, India .... L 8
Nagasaki, Japan .... R 6
Nagoya, Japan .... S 6
Naha, Japan .... R 7
Nanking, China .... P 6
Nepal .... M 7
New Delhi (cap.), India .... L 7
New Siberian (islands), U.S.S.R. .... T 2
Nicosia (cap.), Cyprus .... G 6
Ningpo, China .... R 7
Novosibirsk, U.S.S.R. .... L 4
Ob' (river), U.S.S.R. .... K 3
Okhotsk (sea) .... T 4
Okinawa (islands), Japan .... R 7
Oman .... J 7
Oman (gulf) .... J 7
Omsk, U.S.S.R. .... L 4
Osaka, Japan .... S 6
Pacific Ocean .... V 5
Pakistan .... L 6
Pamir (plateau) .... L 6
Peking (cap.), China (mainland) .... P 5
Persian (gulf) .... J 7
Philippines .... R 8
Phnom Penh (capital), Cambodia .... O 8
Pinang, Malaysia .... N 9
Poona, India .... L 8
Portuguese, Timor R10
Pusan, South Korea .... S 6
P'yŏngyang (capital), North Korea .... R 5
Qatar .... J 7
Quezon City (cap.), Philippines .... R 8
Rangoon (cap.), Burma .... N 8
Red (sea) .... G 7
Riyadh (capital), Saudi Arabia .... H 7
Russian Soviet Federated Socialist Rep., U.S.S.R. .... M 3
Ryukyu (isls.), Japan .... R 7
Sabah (region), Malaysia .... P 9
Saigon (cap.), S. Vietnam .... O 8
Saint Paul (isl.) L13
Sakhalin (isl.), U.S.S.R. .... T 4
Salween (river) .... N 8
Samarkand, U.S.S.R. .... K 6
San'a (cap.), Yemen Arab Rep. .... H 8
Sapporo, Japan .... T 5
Sarawak (region), Malaysia .... P 9
Saudi Arabia .... H 7
Seoul (cap.), South Korea .... R 6
Severnaya Zemlya (islands), U.S.S.R. .... O 1
Shanghai, China .... R 6
Shikoku (island), Japan .... S 6
Siam (gulf) .... O 9
Sian, China .... O 6
Siberia (region), U.S.S.R. .... N 4
Sikkim (state), India .... M 7
Singapore .... O 9
Sinkiang (region), China .... M 5
Socotra (isl.), P.D.R. Yemen .... J 8
South China (sea) .... P 8
Sri Lanka .... M 9
Stanovoy (range), U.S.S.R. .... S 4
Sulawesi (Celebes) (island), Indonesia R10
Sulu (sea) .... P 9
Sumatra (island), Indonesia O10
Sunda (strait), Indonesia O10
Surabaja, Indonesia P10
Sutlej (river) .... L 6
Sverdlovsk, U.S.S.R. .... K 4
Syr-Dar'ya (riv.), U.S.S.R. .... K 5
Syria .... G 6
Tabriz, Iran .... H 6
Tadzhik S.S.R., U.S.S.R. .... L 6
Taipei (cap.), China (Taiwan) .... R 7
Taiwan (island), China .... R 7
Ta'izz, Yemen Arab Rep. .... H 8
Taymyr (pen.), U.S.S.R. .... N 2
Taklamakan (desert), China .... M 6
Tarim (river), China .... M 6
Tashkent, U.S.S.R. .... K 5
Tatar (strait), U.S.S.R. .... T 4
Taymyr (pen.), U.S.S.R. .... N 2
Tehran (cap.), Iran .... G 6
Tel Aviv-Jaffa, Israel .... G 6
Thailand .... O 8
Tibet (region), China .... M 6
Tien Shan (range) .... L 5
Tientsin, China .... P 6
Tigris (river) .... H 6
Timor (island) R10
Tokyo (cap.), Japan .... T 6
Tomsk, U.S.S.R. .... M 4
Tonkin (gulf) .... O 8
Trans-Himalayas (range), China .... M 6
Tsaidam (swamp), China .... N 6
Tsingtao, China .... R 6
Tsitsihar, China .... R 5
Tunguska, Lower (river), U.S.S.R. .... O 3
Turkey .... G 6
Turkmen S.S.R., U.S.S.R. .... J 6
Udjung Pandang, Indon. P10
Ulan Bator (cap.), Mongolia .... O 5
Ulan-Ude, U.S.S.R. .... O 4
Uliassutai, Mongolia .... N 5
Union of Arab Emirates .... J 7
Union of Soviet Socialist Republics .... N 3
Ural (mts.), U.S.S.R. .... J 4
Ural (river), U.S.S.R. .... J 5
Urmia (lake), (Iran) .... H 6
Urumchi, China .... M 5
Ussuri (river) .... S 5
Uzbek S.S.R., U.S.S.R. .... J 5
Van (lake), Turkey .... H 6
Varanasi, India .... M 7
Verkhoyansk, U.S.S.R. .... S 3
Vientiane (cap.), Laos .... O 8
Vietnam, North .... O 8
Vietnam, South .... O 8
Vijayawada, India .... L 8
Vladivostok, U.S.S.R. .... S 5
Wakayama, Japan .... S 6
Wenchow, China .... R 7
Wŏnsan, North Korea .... R 6
Wrangel (island), U.S.S.R. .... X 2
Wuhan (Hankow, Hanyang and Wuchang), China .... P 6
Yakutsk, U.S.S.R. .... R 3
Yalu (river) .... R 5
Yana (river), U.S.S.R. .... S 3
Yanam, India .... M 8
Yangtze Kiang (river), China .... O 7
Yarkand, China .... L 6
Yellow (sea) .... R 6
Yemen Arab Rep. .... H 8
Yemen, Peoples Demorcratic Rep. of .... H 8
Yenisey (river), U.S.S.R. .... M 3
Yezd, Iran .... J 6
Yokohama, Japan .... T 6
Yokosuka, Japan .... T 6
Yümen, China .... N 5
Zamboanga, Philippines .... P 9
Zlatoust, U.S.S.R. .... J 4

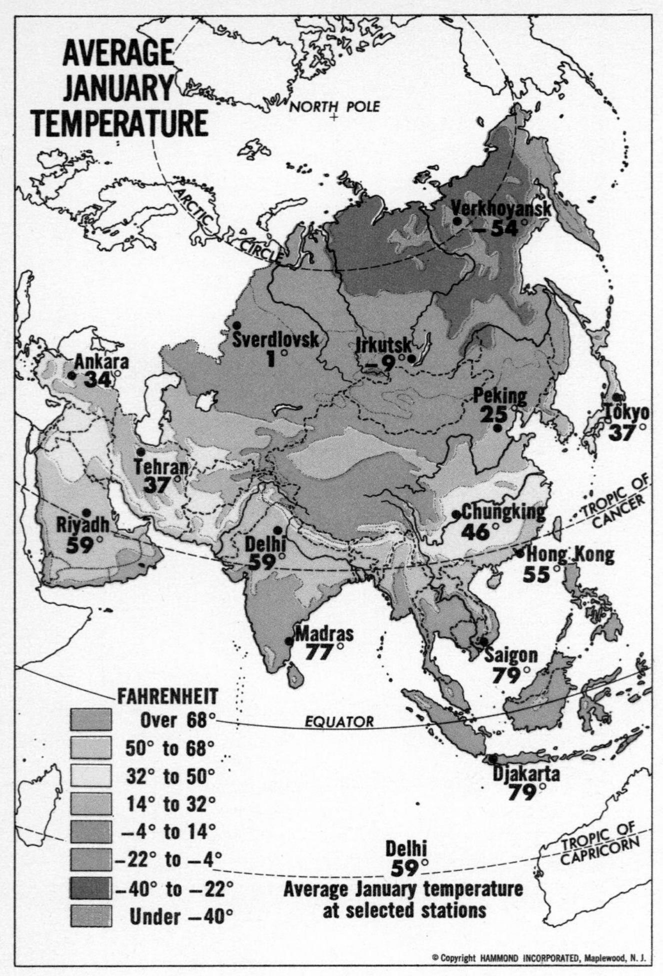
AVERAGE JANUARY TEMPERATURE
NORTH POLE
ARCTIC CIRCLE
Verkhoyansk -54°
Sverdlovsk 1°
Irkutsk -9°
Ankara 34°
Peking 25°
Tokyo 37°
Tehran 37°
Riyadh 59°
Delhi 59°
Chungking 46°
TROPIC OF CANCER
Hong Kong 55°
Madras 77°
Saigon 79°
EQUATOR
Djakarta 79°
FAHRENHEIT
Over 68°
50° to 68°
32° to 50°
14° to 32°
-4° to 14°
-22° to -4°
-40° to -22°
Under -40°
Delhi 59°
Average January temperature at selected stations
TROPIC OF CAPRICORN
© Copyright HAMMOND INCORPORATED, Maplewood, N. J.

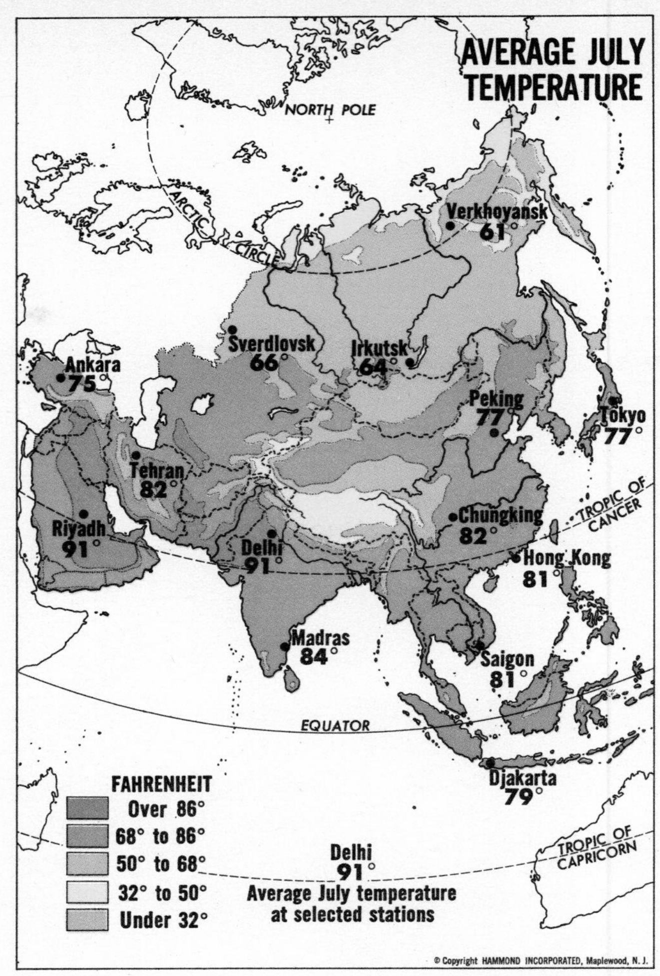
AVERAGE JULY TEMPERATURE
NORTH POLE
ARCTIC CIRCLE
Verkhoyansk 61°
Sverdlovsk 66°
Irkutsk 64°
Ankara 75°
Peking 77°
Tokyo 77°
Tehran 82°
Riyadh 91°
Delhi 91°
Chungking 82°
TROPIC OF CANCER
Hong Kong 81°
Madras 84°
Saigon 81°
EQUATOR
Djakarta 79°
FAHRENHEIT
Over 86°
68° to 86°
50° to 68°
32° to 50°
Under 32°
Delhi 91°
Average July temperature at selected stations
TROPIC OF CAPRICORN
© Copyright HAMMOND INCORPORATED, Maplewood, N. J.

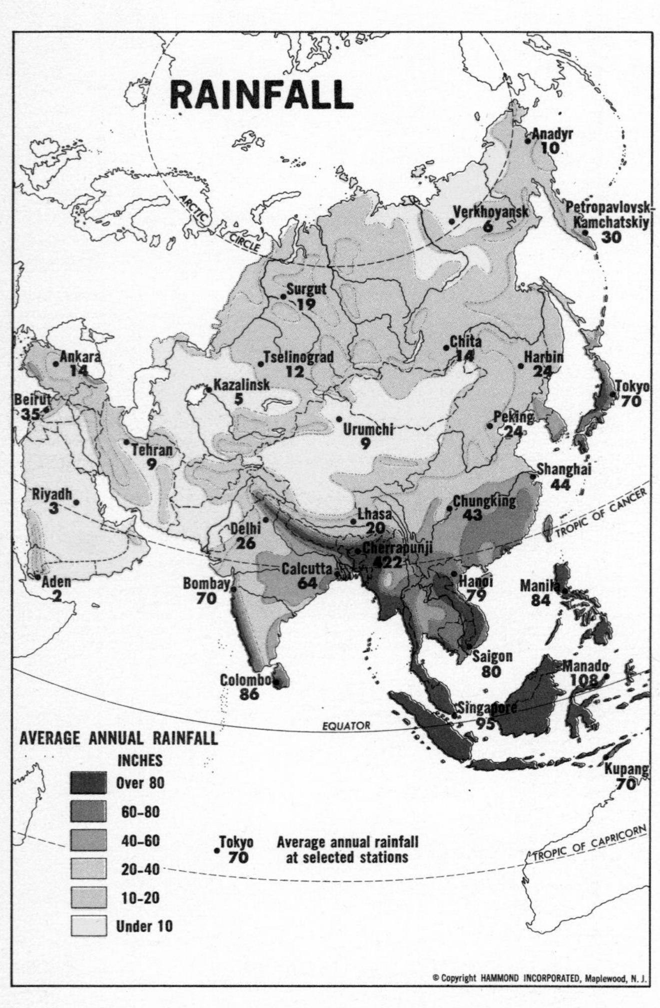
RAINFALL
Anadyr 10
Verkhoyansk 6
Petropavlovsk-Kamchatskiy 30
Surgut 19
Ankara 14
Tselinograd 12
Chita 14
Harbin 24
Kazalinsk 5
Beirut 35
Tokyo 70
Urumchi 9
Peking 24
Tehran 9
Shanghai 44
Riyadh 3
Lhasa 20
Chungking 43
TROPIC OF CANCER
Delhi 26
Cherrapunji 422
Calcutta 64
Aden 2
Bombay 70
Hanoi 79
Manila 84
Saigon 80
Colombo 86
Manado 108
Singapore 95
EQUATOR
AVERAGE ANNUAL RAINFALL
INCHES
Over 80
60-80
40-60
20-40
10-20
Under 10
Tokyo 70
Average annual rainfall at selected stations
Kupang 70
TROPIC OF CAPRICORN
© Copyright HAMMOND INCORPORATED, Maplewood, N. J.

VEGETATION/RELIEF

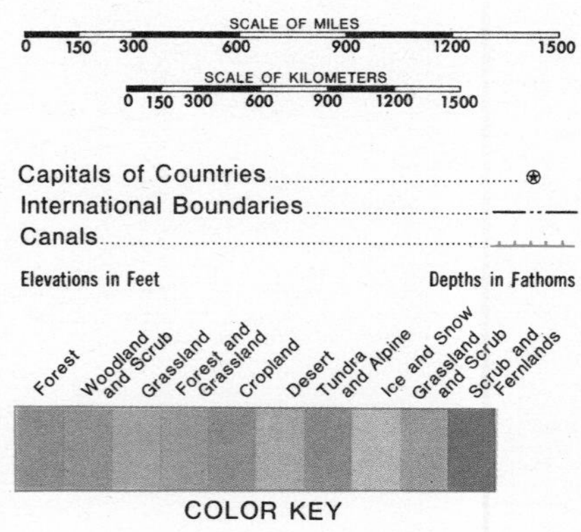
SCALE OF MILES
0 150 300 600 900 1200 1500
SCALE OF KILOMETERS
0 150 300 600 900 1200 1500
Capitals of Countries
International Boundaries
Canals
Elevations in Feet
Depths in Fathoms
Forest
Woodland and Scrub
Grassland
Forest and Grassland
Cropland
Desert
Tundra and Alpine
Ice and Snow
Grassland and Scrub
Scrub and Fernlands
COLOR KEY

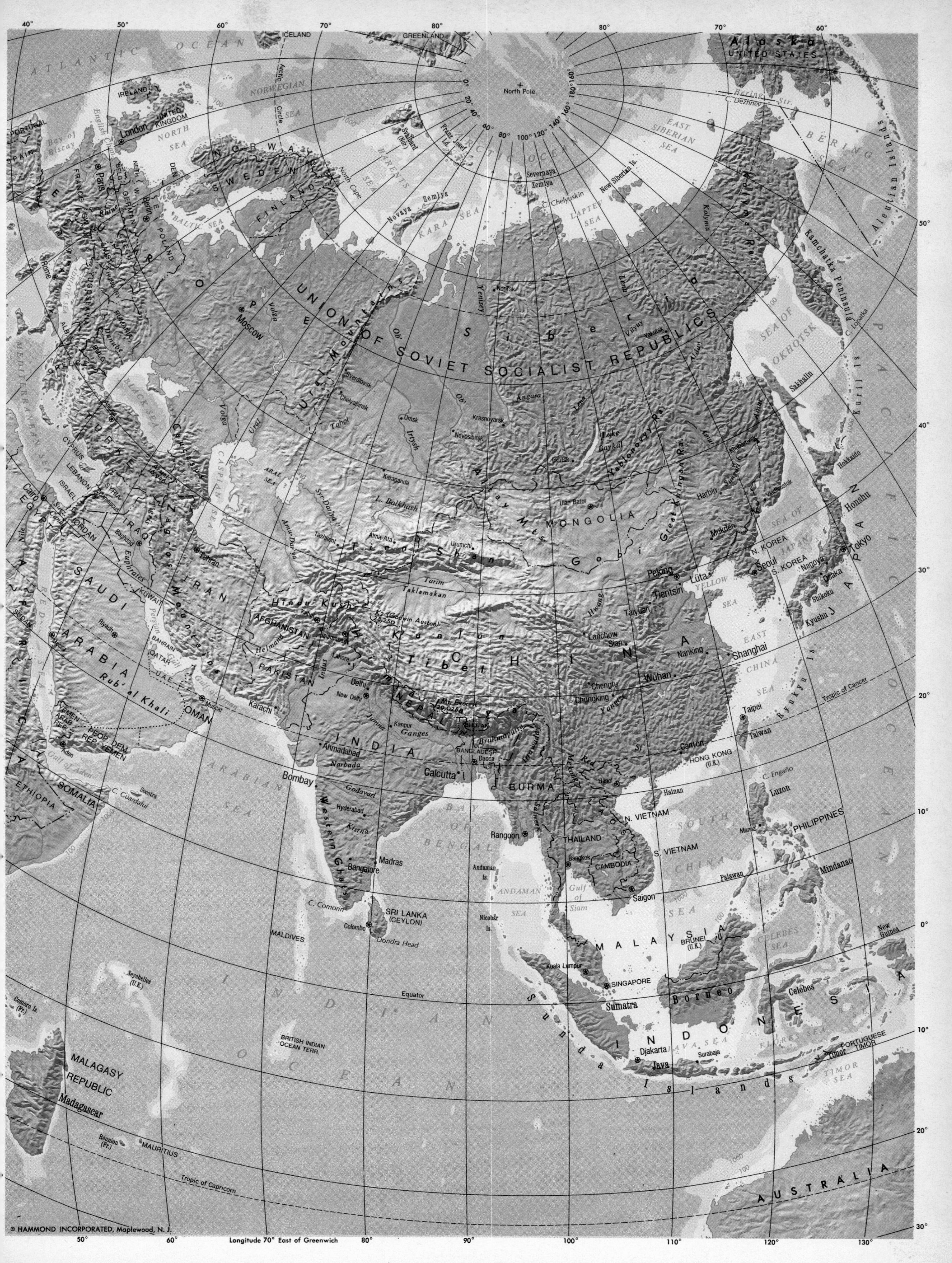

ATLANTIC OCEAN
ICELAND
GREENLAND
Alaska
UNITED STATES
North Pole
NORWEGIAN SEA
Arctic Circle
IRELAND
UNITED KINGDOM
London
NORTH SEA
English Channel
PORTUGAL
SPAIN
Bay of Biscay
FRANCE
Paris
BELG.
NETH.
W. GERMANY
E. GER.
Berlin
DEN.
POLAND
Rhine
Rome
NORWAY
SWEDEN
FINLAND
BALTIC SEA
North Cape
Svalbard (Nor.)
Franz Josef Ld.
BARENTS SEA
Novaya Zemlya
KARA SEA
ARCTIC OCEAN
Severnaya Zemlya
C. Chelyuskin
LAPTEV SEA
New Siberian Is.
EAST SIBERIAN SEA
C. Dezhnev
Bering Str.
BERING SEA
Aleutian Islands
Kolyma
Kamchatka Peninsula
SEA OF OKHOTSK
C. Lopatka
Sakhalin
Kuril Is.
PACIFIC OCEAN
EUROPE
Moscow
Volga
Danube
GREECE
BULG.
ALB.
YUGOSLAVIA
MEDITERRANEAN SEA
BLACK SEA
Ural Mountains
Ural
Ob'
Yenisey
Norilsk
Lena
Vilyuy
Yakutsk
Aldan
UNION OF SOVIET SOCIALIST REPUBLICS
Siberia
Sverdlovsk
Chelyabinsk
Tobol
Omsk
Irtysh
Novosibirsk
Krasnoyarsk
Angara
Irkutsk
Lake Baykal
Yablonovyy Ra.
Amur
Khabarovsk
Hokkaido
Vladivostok
CASPIAN SEA
ARAL SEA
Caucasus
TURKEY
CYPRUS
LEBANON
SYRIA
Damascus
ISRAEL
JORDAN
Cairo
EGYPT
Nile
Suez Canal
IRAQ
Baghdad
Euphrates
Zagros Mts.
Tehran
IRAN
KUWAIT
SAUDI ARABIA
Riyadh
Mecca
BAHRAIN
QATAR
U.A.E.
Persian Gulf
Rub' al Khali
Gulf of Oman
Muscat
OMAN
YEMEN ARAB REP.
PEOP. DEM. REP. YEMEN
Aden
Gulf of Aden
RED SEA
SUDAN
ETHIOPIA
SOMALIA
C. Guardafui
Socotra
AFRICA
Karaganda
L. Balkhash
Syr Darya
Amu Darya
Tashkent
Alma-Ata
Tien Shan
Urumchi
Altay Mts.
Ulan Bator
MONGOLIA
Gobi
Great Khingan Ra.
Harbin
Mukden
SEA OF JAPAN
N. KOREA
S. KOREA
Seoul
JAPAN
Honshu
Tokyo
Nagoya
Osaka
Shikoku
Kyushu
Peking
Lüta
Tientsin
YELLOW SEA
Taiyuan
Hwang
Tarim
Taklamakan
Hindu Kush
Kabul
AFGHANISTAN
Islamabad
Helmand
PAKISTAN
Lahore
Indus
K2 (Godwin Austen) 28,250
Kunlun
Tibet
CHINA
Lanchow
Sian
Nanking
Shanghai
EAST CHINA SEA
Wuhan
Chengtu
Chungking
Yangtze
Taipei
Taiwan
Ryukyu Is.
Tropic of Cancer
Karachi
Delhi
New Delhi
Himalaya
NEPAL
Mt. Everest 29,028
BHUTAN
Kanpur
Jumna
Ganges
Brahmaputra
INDIA
Ahmadabad
Narbada
BANGLADESH
Dacca
Calcutta
Irrawaddy
Mekong
Red
Si
Canton
HONG KONG (U.K.)
Hanoi
Hainan
BURMA
Bombay
Godavari
Hyderabad
Kistna
Western Ghats
Madras
Bangalore
ARABIAN SEA
BAY OF BENGAL
Rangoon
Salween
THAILAND
N. VIETNAM
S. VIETNAM
Bangkok
CAMBODIA
Saigon
Gulf of Siam
LAOS
Andaman Is.
ANDAMAN SEA
Nicobar Is.
C. Comorin
SRI LANKA (CEYLON)
Colombo
Dondra Head
MALDIVES
C. Engaño
Luzon
PHILIPPINES
Manila
SOUTH CHINA SEA
Palawan
SULU SEA
Mindanao
MALAYSIA
BRUNEI (U.K.)
CELEBES SEA
New Guinea
Kuala Lumpur
SINGAPORE
Borneo
Celebes
Sumatra
INDONESIA
BANDA SEA
Djakarta
JAVA SEA
FLORES SEA
Surabaja
Java
Timor
PORTUGUESE TIMOR
TIMOR SEA
Sunda Islands
Seychelles (U.K.)
Comoro Is. (Fr.)
Equator
INDIAN OCEAN
BRITISH INDIAN OCEAN TERR.
MALAGASY REPUBLIC
Madagascar
Réunion (Fr.)
MAURITIUS
Tropic of Capricorn
AUSTRALIA
Longitude 70° East of Greenwich

SAUDI ARABIA | KUWAIT | YEMEN ARAB REPUBLIC | BAHRAIN | QATAR | OMAN | PEOPLES DEM. REP. OF YEMEN

AFGHANISTAN

CITIES and TOWNS

Andkhui, 30,000 ....J 2
Baghlan, 92,000 ....J 2
Bala Murghab, 10,000 ....H 2
Balkh, 15,000 ....J 2
Bamian, 25,000 ....J 3
Chahar Burjak. 500 ....H 3
Charikar, 83,700 ....J 2
Daulatabad, 15,000 ....H 3
Daulat Yar, 2,000 ....J 3
Doshi, 5,000 ....J 2
Faizabad, 57,000 ....K 2
Farah, 26,400 ....H 3
Gardez, 33,000 ....J 3
Ghazni, 39,900 ....J 3
Ghurian, 10,000 ....H 3
Girishk, 10,000 ....H 3
Haibak, 35,200 ....J 2
Herat, 71,563 ....H 3
Jalalabad, 48,919 ....K 3
Jurm, 10,000 ....K 2
Juwain, 2,000 ....H 3
Kabul (capital), 472,313 ....J 3
Kabul, *600,000 ....J 3
Kala Bist, 26,100 ....H 3
Kalat-i-Ghilzai, 40,500 ....J 3
Kandahar, 127,036 ....J 3
Kandahar, *142,000 ....J 3
Khanabad, 30,000 ....J 2
Kushk, 10,000 ....H 3
Landi Muhammad Amin Khan, 1,000 ....H 3
Maimana, 48,750 ....H 2
Matun, 15,000 ....J 3
Mazar-i-Sharif, 43,197 ....J 2
Mukur, 10,000 ....J 3
Obeh, 5,000 ....H 3
Panjao, 3,000 ....J 3
Qala Panja, 1,000 ....K 2
Qaleh-i-Kang, 15,600 ....H 3
Rudbar, 1,000 ....H 3
Rustak, 10,000 ....J 2
Sabzawar, 5,000 ....H 3
Sar-i-Pul, 5,000 ....J 2
Shahjui, 5,000 ....J 3
Shibarghan, 50,440 ....H 2
Shindand (Sabzawar), 5,000 ....H 3
Taiwara, 5,000 ....H 3
Tashkurghan, 30,000 ....J 2
Zebak, 3,000 ....K 2

OTHER FEATURES

Chagai (hills) ....H 4
Farah Rud (river) ....H 3
Gaud-i-Zirreh (marsh) ....H 4
Hari Rud (river) ....H 3
Helmand (river) ....J 3
Hindu Kush (mts.) ....J 2
Jam (mt.) ....H 3
Kabul (river) ....K 3
Kunar (river) ....K 2
Kunduz (river) ....J 2
Lora (river) ....J 3
Margo, Dasht-i (desert) ....H 3

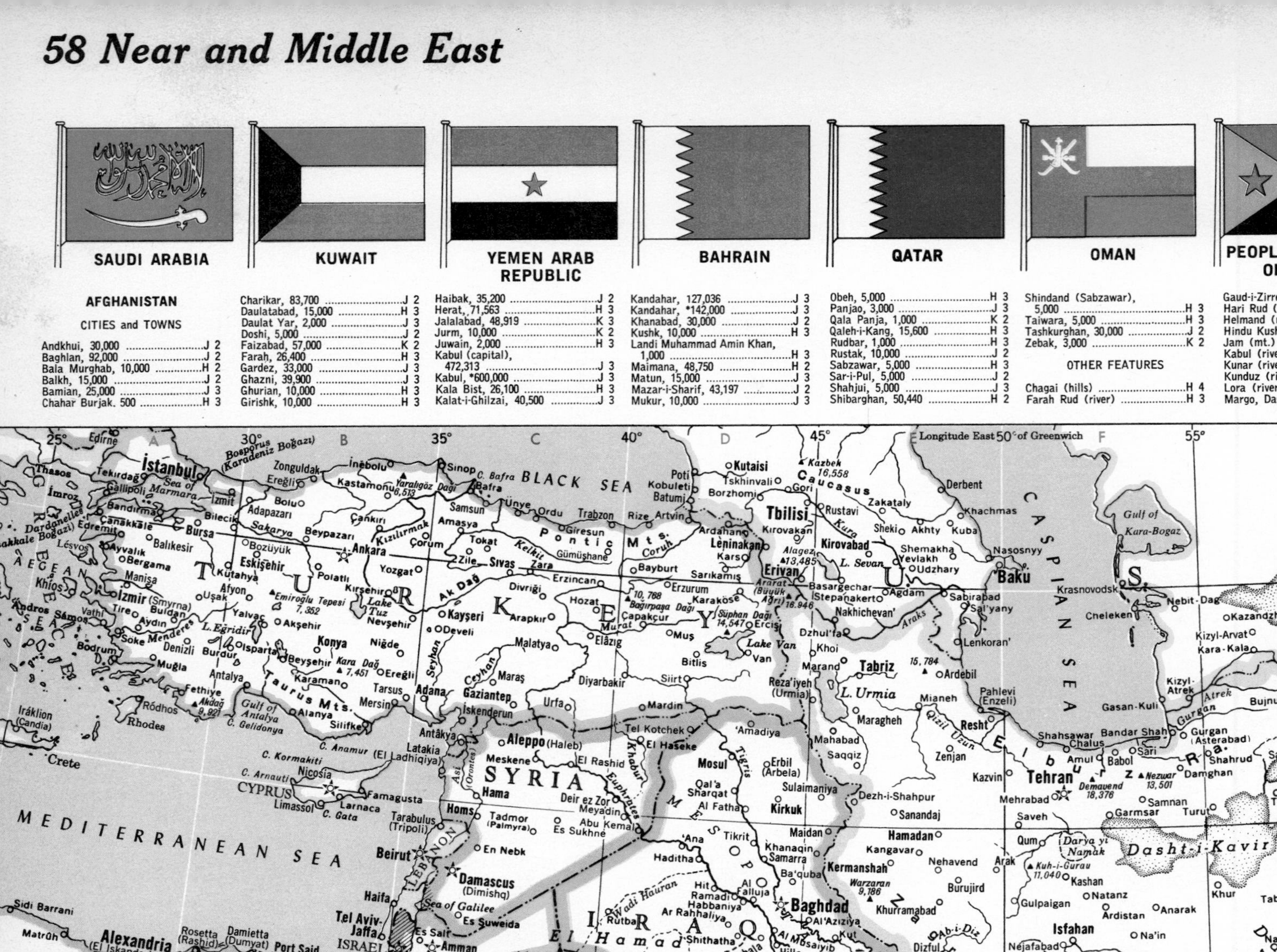

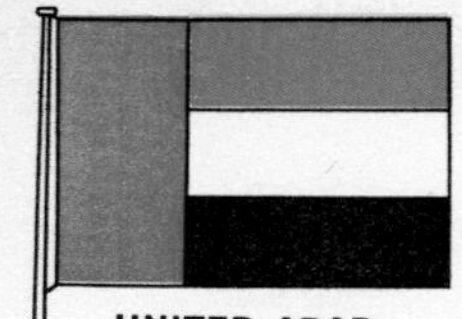

UNITED ARAB EMIRATES

Murghab (river) ....H 2
Namaksar (salt lake) ....H 3
Paropamisus (range) ....H 3
Pyandzh (river) ....K 2
Registan (desert) ....H 3

BAHRAIN

CITIES and TOWNS

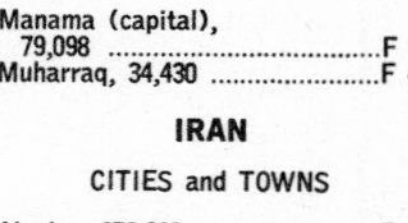

Manama (capital), 79,098 ....F 4
Muharraq, 34,430 ....F 4

IRAN

CITIES and TOWNS

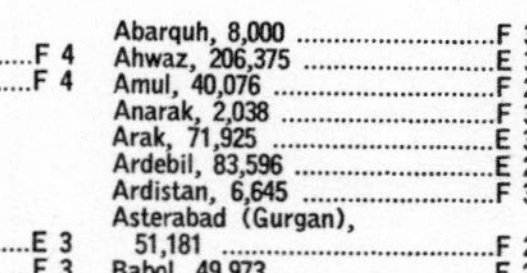

Abadan, 272,962 ....E 3
Abadeh, 16,000 ....F 3
Abarquh, 8,000 ....F 3
Ahwaz, 206,375 ....E 3
Amul, 40,076 ....F 2
Anarak, 2,038 ....F 3
Arak, 71,925 ....E 3
Ardebil, 83,596 ....E 2
Ardistan, 6,645 ....F 3
Asterabad (Gurgan), 51,181 ....F 2
Babol, 49,973 ....F 2
Bafq, 5,000 ....G 3
Baft, 6,000 ....G 4
Bahramabad, 21,000 ....G 3
Bam, 22,000 ....G 4
Bandar ʻAbbas, 34,627 ....G 4
Bandar Shah, 13,000 ....F 2
Bandar Shahpur, 6,000 ....E 3
Barfrush (Babol), 49,973 ....F 2
Birjand, 25,854 ....G 3
Borazjun, 20,000 ....F 4
Bujnurd, 31,248 ....G 2
Burujird, 71,476 ....E 3
Bushire, 26,032 ....F 4
Chalus, 15,000 ....F 2
Damghan, 13,000 ....F 2
Darab, 13,000 ....G 4
Dizful, 84,499 ....E 3
Duzdab (Zahidan), 40,000 ....H 4

(continued on following page)

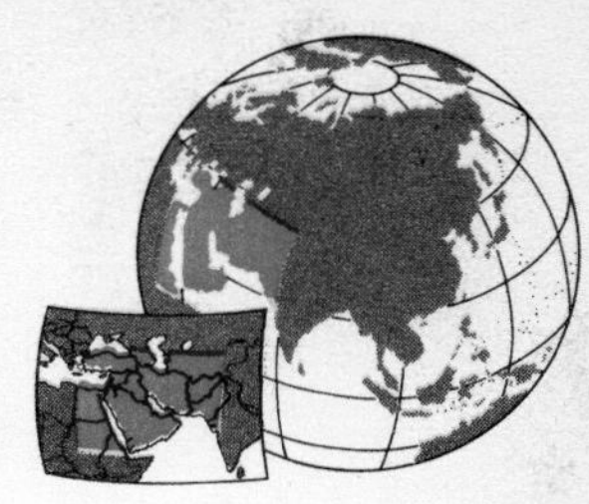

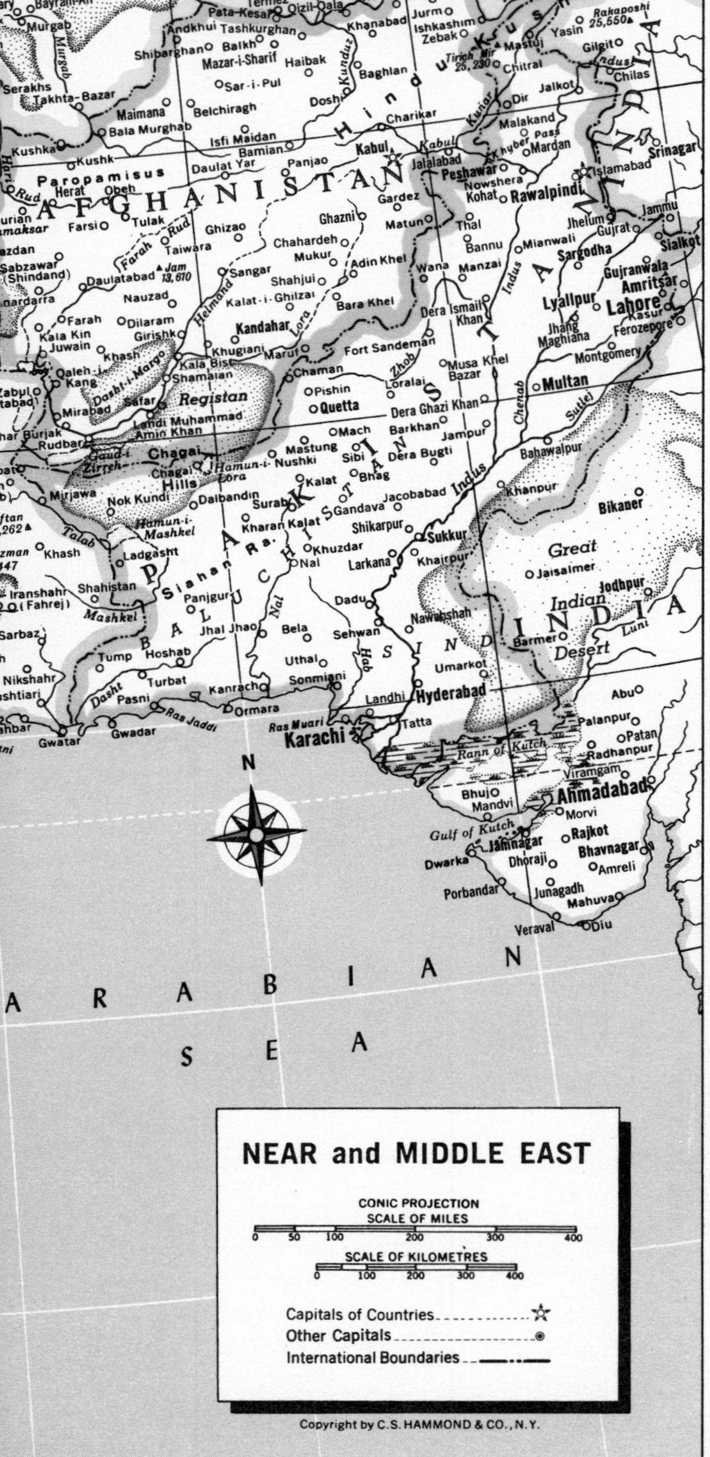

SAUDI ARABIA

AREA 920,000 sq. mi.
POPULATION 7,200,000
CAPITALS Riyadh, Mecca
MONETARY UNIT riyal
MAJOR LANGUAGE Arabic
MAJOR RELIGION Islam

KUWAIT

AREA 8,000 sq. mi.
POPULATION 733,196
CAPITAL Al Kuwait
MONETARY UNIT Kuwaiti dinar
MAJOR LANGUAGE Arabic
MAJOR RELIGION Islam

YEMEN ARAB REPUBLIC

AREA 75,000 sq. mi.
POPULATION 5,000,000
CAPITAL Sanʻa
MONETARY UNIT bakcha
MAJOR LANGUAGE Arabic
MAJOR RELIGION Islam

PEOPLES DEMOCRATIC REPUBLIC OF YEMEN

AREA 111,075 sq. mi.
POPULATION 1,220,000
CAPITAL Aden
MONETARY UNIT East African shilling
MAJOR LANGUAGE Arabic
MAJOR RELIGION Islam

BAHRAIN

AREA 231 sq. mi.
POPULATION 207,000
CAPITAL Manama
MONETARY UNIT Bahrain dinar
MAJOR LANGUAGE Arabic
MAJOR RELIGION Islam

QATAR

AREA 8,500 sq. mi.
POPULATION 100,000
CAPITAL Doha
MONETARY UNIT Qatar-Dubai riyal
MAJOR LANGUAGE Arabic
MAJOR RELIGION Islam

UNITED ARAB EMIRATES

AREA 31,628 sq. mi.
POPULATION 155,881
CAPITAL Abu Dhabi
MONETARY UNIT rupee, Bahrain dinar, Qatar-Dubai riyal
MAJOR LANGUAGE Arabic
MAJOR RELIGION Islam

OMAN

AREA 82,000 sq. mi.
POPULATION 565,000
CAPITAL Muscat
MONETARY UNIT rial saidi
MAJOR LANGUAGE Arabic
MAJOR RELIGION Islam

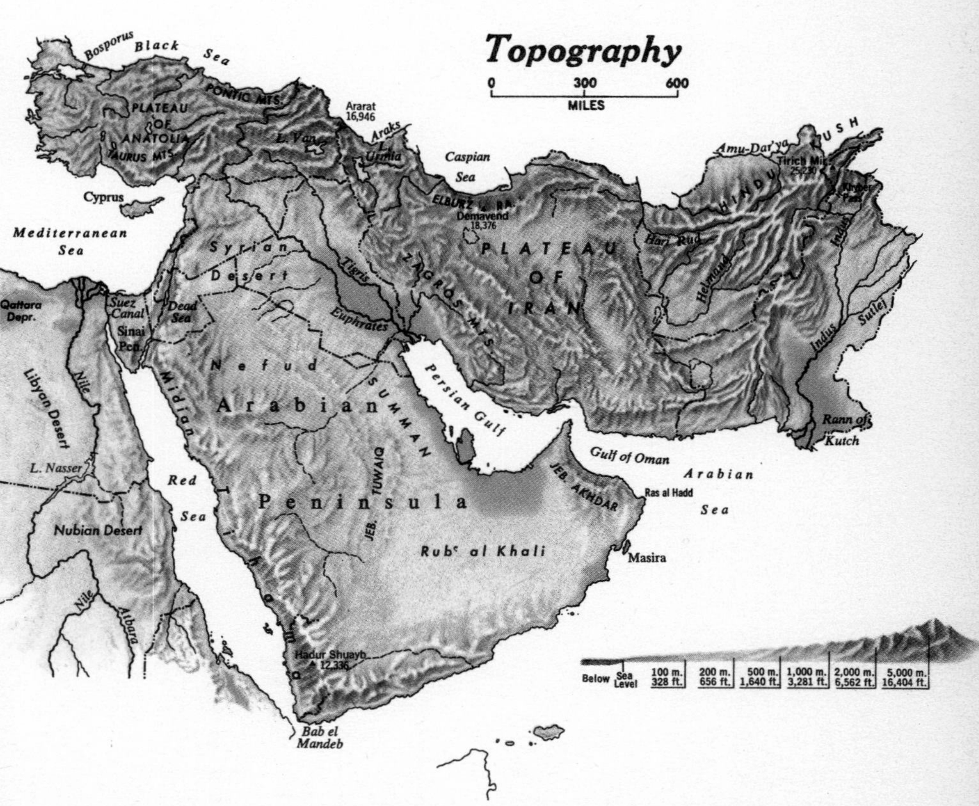

(continued)

IRAN (continued)

Enzeli (Pahlevi), 41,785 E 2
Estahbanat, 18,187 F 4
Fahrej (Iranshahr), 5,000 H 4
Fasa, 19,000 F 4
Firdaus, 11,000 G 3
Gach Saran F 3
Garmsar, 4,723 F 2
Gulpaigan, 20,515 F 3
Gunabad, 8,000 G 3
Gurgan, 51,181 F 2
Hamadan, 124,167 E 3
Iranshahr, 5,000 H 4
Isfahan, 424,045 F 3
Jahrum, 38,236 F 4
Juimand (Gunabad), 8,000 G 3
Kangavar, 9,414 E 3
Kashan, 58,468 F 3
Kashmar, 17,000 G 2
Kazerun, 39,758 F 4
Kazvin, 88,106 E 2
Kerman, 85,404 G 3
Kermanshah, 187,930 E 3
Khaf, 5,000 H 3
Khoi, 47,648 E 2
Khorramshahr, 88,536 E 3
Khur, 2,912 G 3
Khurramabad, 59,578 E 3
Lar, 22,000 F 4
Mahabad, 28,610 E 2
Maragheh, 54,106 E 2
Marand, 24,000 E 2
Meshed, 409,616 H 2
Mianeh, 28,447 E 2
Mirjawa, 11,000 H 4
Na'in, 5,925 F 3
Naishapur (Nishapur), 33,482 G 2
Nasratabad (Zabul), 20,000 H 3
Natanz, 4,370 F 3
Nehavend, 24,000 E 3
Nejafabad, 43,384 F 3
Nishapur, 33,482 G 2
Pahlevi, 41,785 E 2
Qain, 6,000 G 3
Quchan, 29,133 G 2
Qum, 134,292 F 3
Ravar, 7,000 G 3
Resht, 143,557 E 2
Reza'iyeh, 110,749 D 2
Sabzawar, 42,415 G 2
Sabzawaran, 7,000 G 4
Samnan, 31,058 F 2
Sanandaj, 54,578 E 2
Saqqiz, 17,000 E 2
Sari, 44,547 F 2
Saveh, 17,565 F 2
Shahr-i-Tajan (Sari), 44,547 F 2
Shahriza, 34,220 F 3
Shahrud, 30,767 G 2
Shahsawar, 12,000 F 2
Shiraz, 269,865 F 4
Shirvan, 11,000 G 2
Shushtar, 24,000 E 3
Sirjan, 12,160 G 4
Sultanabad (Arak), 71,925 E 3
Sultanabad (Kashmar), 17,000 G 2
Susangird, 21,000 E 3
Tabas (Tabas-Masina), 10,000 H 3
Tabriz, 403,413 E 2
Tehran (capital), 2,719,730 F 2
Tun (Firdaus), 11,000 G 3
Turbat-i-Haidari, 30,106 G 2
Turbat-i-Shaikh Jam, 13,000 H 2
Turshiz (Kashmar), 17,000 G 2
Turun G 2
Urmia (Reza'iyeh), 110,749 D 2
Yezd, 93,241 F 3
Zabul, 20,000 H 3
Zahidan, 39,732 H 4
Zarand, 5,000 G 3
Zenjan, 58,714 E 2

OTHER FEATURES

Araks (river) E 2
Atrek (river) G 2
Bazman, Kuh-i-(mt.) H 4
Demavend (mt.) F 2
Diz, Ab-i- (river) E 3
Elburz (mts.) F 2
Galvkhaneh (lake) F 3
Gurgan (river) F 2
Haliri (river) G 4
Jaz Murian, Hamun-i- (marsh) G 4
Karun (river) E 3
Kavir, Dasht-i- (salt desert) G 3
Kavir-i-Namak (salt desert) G 3
Lut, Dasht-i- (desert) G 3
Maidani, Ras (cape) G 4
Mand Rud (river) F 4
Mashkel (river) H 4
Mehran (river) F 4
Namak, Darya-i- (salt lake) F 3
Namaksar (salt lake) H 3
Namakzar (marsh) G 3
Nezwar (mt.) F 2
Oman (gulf) G 5
Persian (gulf) F 4
Qais (isl.) F 4
Qishm (isl.) G 4
Qizil Uzun (river) E 2
Safidar, Kuh-i- (mt.) F 4
Shaikh Shu'aib (isl.) F 4
Shir (mt.) F 3
Taftan (mt.) H 4
Talab (river) H 4
Tashk (lake) F 4
Urmia (lake) E 2
Zagros (mts.) E 3

IRAQ

CITIES and TOWNS

Al 'Aziziya, 7,450 E 3
Al Falluja, 38,072 D 3
Al Musaiyib, 15,955 D 3
Al Qurna, 5,638 E 3
'Amadiya, 2,578 D 2
'Amara, 64,847 E 3
An Najaf, 128,096 D 3
An Nasiriya, 60,405 E 3
'Ana, 6,884 D 3
Ar Rahhaliya D 3
Arbela (Erbil), 90,320 D 2
As Salman, 1,789 E 3
Baghdad (capital), 502,503 E 3
Baghdad, *1,745,328 E 3
Ba'quba, 34,575 D 3
Basra, 313,327 E 3
Erbil, 90,320 D 2
Habbaniya, 14,405 D 3
Haditha, 6,870 D 3
Hai, 16,988 E 3
Hilla, 84,717 D 3
Hit, 9,131 D 3
Karbala', 83,301 D 3
Khanaqin, 23,522 D 3
Kirkuk, 167,413 D 2
Kut, 42,116 E 3
Maidan, 354 E 3
Mosul, 315,157 D 2
Qal'a Sharqat, 2,434 D 2
Ramadi, 28,723 D 3
Rutba, 5,091 D 3
Samarra, 24,746 D 3
Samawa, 33,473 D 3
Shithatha, 2,326 D 3
Sulaimaniya, 86,822 E 2
Tikrit, 9,921 D 3

OTHER FEATURES

Al Batin, Wadi (river) E 4
'Aneiza, Jebel (mt.) C 3
'Ar'ar, Wadi (dry river) D 3
El Hamad (desert) D 3
Euphrates (river) E 3
Hauran, Wadi (dry river) D 3
Mesopotamia (reg.) D 3
Tigris (river) E 3

KUWAIT

CITIES and TOWNS

Al Kuwait (capital), 80,008 E 4
Al Kuwait, *217,364 E 4
Mina al-Ahmadi E 4

OTHER FEATURES

Bubiyan (isl.) E 4
Persian (gulf) F 4

OMAN

CITIES and TOWNS

Adam G 5
Buraimi G 5
Dhank G 5
Ibra G 5
'Ibri G 5
Juwara G 6
Kamil G 5
Khaluf G 5
Khasab G 4
Manah G 5
Matrah, 15,000 G 5
Mina al Fahal G 5
Murbat G 6
Muscat (capital), 7,500 G 5
Nizwa G 5
Quryat G 5
Risut F 6
Salala, 4,000 F 6
Sarur G 5
Shinas G 5
Sohar G 5
Sur G 5
Suwaiq G 5

OTHER FEATURES

Akhdar, Jebel (range) G 5
Arabian (sea) H 5
Batina (reg.) G 5
Dhofar (reg.), 120,000 F 6
Hadd, Ras al (cape) G 5
Hallaniya (isl.), 78 G 6
Jibsh, Ras (cape) G 5
Kuria Muria (isls.), 78 G 6
Madraka, Ras (cape) G 6
Masira (gulf) G 6
Masira (isl.) G 5
Musandam, Ras (cape) G 4
Nus, Ras (cape) G 6
Oman (gulf) G 5
Oman (reg.) G 5
Ruus al Jibal (dist.) G 4
Sauqira (bay) G 6
Sauqira, Ras (cape) G 6
Sham, Jebel (mt.) G 5
Sharbatat, Ras (cape) G 6

QATAR

CITIES and TOWNS

Doha (capital), 45,000 F 4
Dukhan, 2,500 F 4
Umm Sa'id, 3,500 F 5

OTHER FEATURES

Persian (gulf) F 4
Rakan, Ras (cape) F 4

SAUDI ARABIA

PROVINCES

'Asir, 900,000 D 6
Eastern, 2,250,000 E 4
Hejaz, 1,250,000 C 4
Nejd, 1,500,000 D 4

CITIES and TOWNS

Abha D 6
Abqaiq E 4
Abu 'Arish D 6
Abu Hadriya E 4
'Ain al Mubarrak C 5
Al 'Ain C 4
Al 'Ala C 4
Al 'Auda E 4
Al Lith C 5
Al Muadhdham C 4
Al Qahm D 6
'Anaiza D 4
Artawiya E 4
Badr C 5
Buraida D 4
Buraimi G 5
Dam D 5
Dammam, 3,000 F 4
Dar al Hamra C 4
Dhaba C 4
Dhahran, 12,500 E 4
Dharma E 5
Dilam E 5
Doqa D 6
Duwadami D 4
Er Ras D 4
Faid D 4
Haddar E 5
Hadiya C 4
Hafar al Batin E 4
Hail, 20,000 D 4
Halli D 6
Hamar E 5
Hanakiya D 5
Haql C 4
Haradh E 5
Haraja D 6
Hariq E 5
Hauta E 5
Hofuf, 83,000 E 4
Jabrin E 5
Jauf, 5,000 C 4
Jidda, 194,000 C 5
Jubail F 4
Jubba D 4
Junaina D 5
Kaf C 3
Khaibar D 4
Khamis Mushait D 6
Khurma D 5
Khurs D 5
Laila E 5
Majma'a D 4
Maqna C 4
Mastaba C 5
Mastura C 5
Mecca (capital), 185,000 C 5
Medain Salih C 4
Medina, 72,000 C 5
Mendak D 5
Mina Sa'ud E 4
Mubarraz E 4
Mudhnib D 4
Muwailih C 4
Najran D 6
Nisab D 4
Oqair E 4
Qadhima C 5
Qafar D 4
Qasr al Haiyanya D 4
Qatif E 4
Qizan D 6
Qunfidha D 6
Qusaiba D 4
Rabigh C 5
Ras Tanura F 4
Riyadh (capital), 225,000 E 5
Rumaihiya E 4
Sabya D 6
Sakaka D 4
Salwa F 5
Shaqra D 4
Shuqaiq D 6
Sufeina D 5
Sulaiyil E 5
Taif, 54,000 D 5
Taima C 4
Tamra D 5
Tebuk C 4
Truba D 5
Turaba D 5
Umm Lajj C 4
Wejh C 4
Yamama E 5
Yenbo C 5
Zilfi E 4

OTHER FEATURES

Abu-mad (cape) C 5
'Ar'ar, Wadi (dry river) D 3
Al Ahqaf (Bahr es Safi) (desert) E 6
'Aneiza, Jebel (mt.) C 3
'Aqaba (gulf) C 4
Arafat, Jebel (mt.) D 5
Ar'ar, Wadi (dry river) D 3
Arma (plateau) E 4
Aswad, Ras al (cape) C 5
Bahr es Safi (desert) E 6
Barida, Ras (cape) C 5
Bisha, Wadi (dry river) D 5
Dahana (desert) E 4
Dawasir, Wadi (dry river) E 5
Dawasir, Hadb (range) D 6
Farasan (isls.) D 6
Hasa (reg.) E 4
Hatiba, Ras (cape) C 5
Jafura (desert) F 5
Mashabi (isl.) C 4
Midian (district) C 4
Misha'ab, Ras (cape) E 4
Nefud (desert) D 4
Nefud Dahi (desert) D 5
Persian (gulf) F 4
Ranya, Wadi (dry river) D 5
Red (Nefud) (desert) D 4
Red (sea) C 5
Rima, Wadi (river) D 4
Rimal, Ar (desert) F 5
Rub' al Khali (desert) F 5
Safaniya, Ras (cape) E 4
Salma, Jebel (mts.) D 4
Shaibara (isl.) C 4
Shammar, Jebel (plateau) D 4
Sirhan, Wadi (dry river) C 3
Subh, Jebel (mt.) C 5
Summan (plateau) E 4
Tihama (reg.) C 5
Tiran (isl.) B 4
Tiran (str.) B 4
Tuwaiq, Jebel (range) E 5

UNITED ARAB EMIRATES

CITIES and TOWNS

Abu Dhabi (capital), 22,000 F 5
Abu Dhabi, *35,000 F 5
'Ajman, 3,725 G 4
'Arada F 5
Buraimi G 5
Dubai, 13,092 F 4
Dubai, *57,400 F 4
Fujairah, 761 G 4
Jebel Dhauna F 5
Ras al Khaimah, 5,244 F 4
Sharjah, 19,198 F 4
Sharjah, *20,621 F 4
Umm al Qaiwain, 2,928 F 4

OTHER FEATURES

Das (isl.) F 4
Persian (gulf) F 4
Yas (isl.) F 5
Zirko (isl.) F 5

YEMEN ARAB REP.

CITIES and TOWNS

'Amran D 6
Bait al Faqih D 7
Dhamar D 7
Harib E 6
Hodeida, 40,000 D 7
Huth D 6
Ibb D 7
Luhaiya (Loheia) D 6
Maida, 2,500 D 6
Manakha D 6
Marib D 6
Mocha D 7
Sa'ada D 6
Safir E 6
San'a (capital), 100,000 D 6
Sheikh Sa'id D 7
Ta'izz, 80,000 D 7
Yarim, 5,000 D 7
Zabid, 8,000 D 7

OTHER FEATURES

Hanish (isls.) D 7
Manar, Jebel (mt.) D 7
Red (sea) C 5
Sabir, Jebel (mt.) D 7
Tihama (reg.) C 5
Zuqar (isl.) D 7

YEMEN, PEOPLES DEM. REPUBLIC OF

CITIES and TOWNS

Aden (capital), 150,000 E 7
Aden, *225,000 E 7
Ahwar E 7
Al Qatn E 6
Balhaf E 7
Bir 'Ali E 7
Damqut F 6
'Einat E 6
Ghaida F 6
Hadibu F 7
Hajarain E 6
Haura E 7
Hureidha E 6
'Irqa E 7
Lahej E 7
Leijun E 6
Lodar E 7
Madinat ash Sha'b, 29,897 E 7
Maqatin E 7
Meifa E 7
Mukalla, 30,000 E 7
Nisab E 7
Nuqub E 6
Qishn F 6
Riyan E 7
Saihut, 10,000 F 6
Seiyun E 6
Shabwa E 6
Shibam, 6,000 E 6
Shihr E 7
Shuqra E 7
Taburkum E 6
Tarim E 6
Yeshbum E 7
Zinjibar E 7

OTHER FEATURES

Fartak, Ras (cape) F 6
Hadhramaut (dist.), 350,000 E 7
Hadhramaut, Wadi (dry river) F 7
Kamaran (island), 2,200 D 6
Mandeb, Bab el (strait) D 7
Perim (isl.), 381 D 7
Socotra (island), 14,000 F 7

*City and suburbs.

Agriculture, Industry and Resources

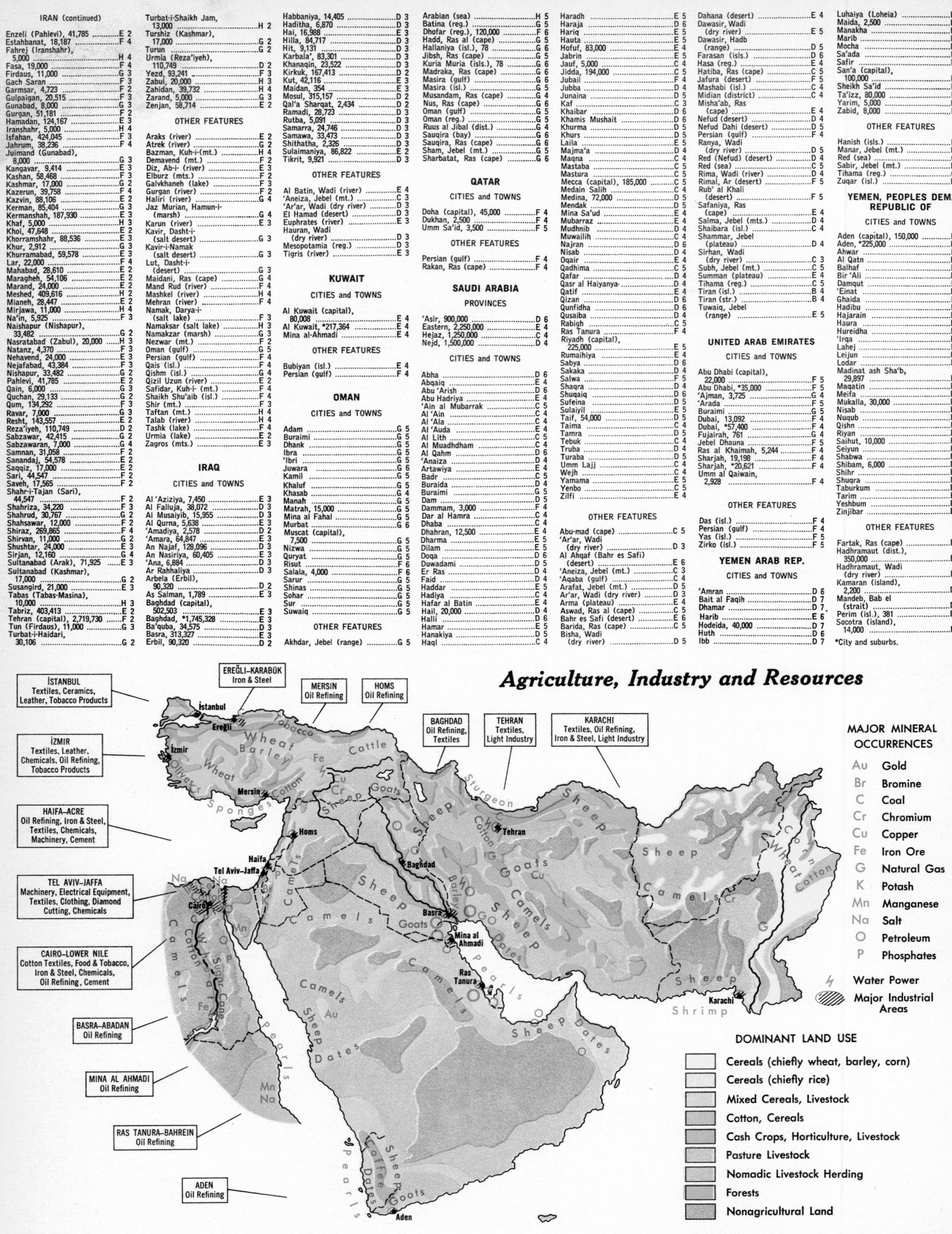

TURKEY

SYRIA

LEBANON

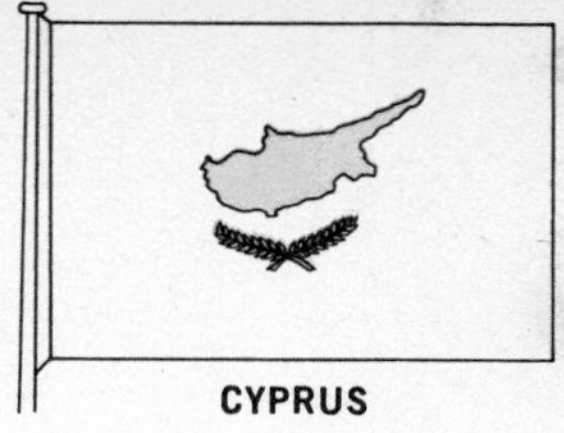
CYPRUS

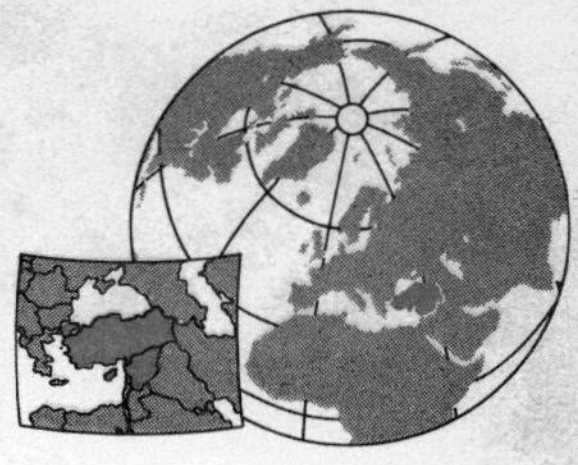

TURKEY

AREA 301,381 sq. mi.
POPULATION 34,375,000
CAPITAL Ankara
LARGEST CITY İstanbul (greater)
HIGHEST POINT Ararat 16,914 ft.
MONETARY UNIT Turkish pound (lira)
MAJOR LANGUAGE Turkish
MAJOR RELIGION Islam

SYRIA

AREA 71,498 sq. mi.
POPULATION 5,866,000
CAPITAL Damascus
LARGEST CITY Damascus
HIGHEST POINT Hermon 9,232 ft.
MONETARY UNIT Syrian pound
MAJOR LANGUAGES Arabic, Kurdish, Armenian
MAJOR RELIGIONS Islam, Christianity

LEBANON

AREA 4,015 sq. mi.
POPULATION 2,800,000
CAPITAL Beirut
LARGEST CITY Beirut
HIGHEST POINT Qurnet es Sauda 10,131 ft.
MONETARY UNIT Lebanese pound
MAJOR LANGUAGE Arabic
MAJOR RELIGIONS Christianity, Islam

CYPRUS

AREA 3,473 sq. mi.
POPULATION 649,000
CAPITAL Nicosia
LARGEST CITY Nicosia
HIGHEST POINT Troodos 6,406 ft.
MONETARY UNIT Cypriot pound
MAJOR LANGUAGES Greek, Turkish
MAJOR RELIGIONS Eastern (Greek) Orthodoxy, Islam

CYPRUS

CITIES and TOWNS

Famagusta, 38,000 ..... F 5
Famagusta, *41,000 ..... F 5
Kyrenia, 3,500 ..... E 5
Kyrenia, *4,500 ..... E 5
Larnaca, 20,000 ..... E 5
Larnaca, *21,000 ..... E 5
Lefka, 3,673 ..... E 5
Lefkara, 2,075 ..... E 5
Limassol, 46,500 ..... E 5
Limassol, *50,000 ..... E 5
Morphou, 6,642 ..... E 5
Nicosia (capital), 47,000 ..... E 5
Nicosia, *112,000 ..... E 5
Paphos, 10,000 ..... E 5
Paphos, *11,500 ..... E 5
Yialousa, 2,541 ..... F 5

OTHER FEATURES

Andreas (cape) ..... F 5
Arnauti (cape) ..... E 5
Famagusta (bay) ..... F 5
Gata (cape) ..... E 5
Greco (cape) ..... F 5
Klides (isls.) ..... F 5
Kormakiti (cape) ..... E 5
Larnaca (bay) ..... E 5
Morphou (bay) ..... E 5
Sovereign Base Area, 3,602 ..... E 5
Troodos (mt.) ..... E 5

LEBANON

CITIES and TOWNS

'Aleih, 18,630 ..... F 6
Amyun, 7,926 ..... F 5
Ba'albek, 15,560 ..... G 5
Batrun, 5,976 ..... F 5
Beirut (capital), 700,000 ..... F 6
Beirut, *840,000 ..... F 6
En Naqura, 967 ..... F 6
Hermil, 2,652 ..... G 5
Merj 'Uyun, 9,318 ..... F 6
Rasheiya, 6,731 ..... F 6
Rayak, 1,480 ..... G 6
Saida, 32,200 ..... F 6
Sidon (Saida), 32,200 ..... F 6
Sur, 16,483 ..... F 6
Tarabulus (Tripoli), 127,611 ..... F 5
Tyre (Sur), 16,483 ..... F 6
Zahle, 53,121 ..... F 6
Zegharta, 18,210 ..... G 5

OTHER FEATURES

Hermon (mt.) ..... F 6
Lebanon (range) ..... F 6
Litani (Leontes) (river) ..... F 6
Sauda, Qurnet es (mt.) ..... G 5

SYRIA

GOVERNORATES

Aleppo, 1,131,854 ..... G 4
Damascus, 1,060,484 ..... G 6
Damascus (municipality), 630,063 ..... G 6
Deir es Zor, 286,010 ..... H 5
Der'a, 221,275 ..... G 6
El Quneitra, 6,396 ..... F 6
Es Suweida, 151,500 ..... G 6
Hama, 390,084 ..... G 5
Haseke, 309,279 ..... J 4
Homs, 504,098 ..... G 5
Idlib, 374,751 ..... G 5
Latakia, 625,473 ..... G 5
Rashid, 124,876 ..... H 5

CITIES and TOWNS

Abu Kemal, 6,907 ..... J 5
Aleppo, 566,770 ..... G 4
A'zaz, 13,923 ..... G 4
Baniyas, 8,537 ..... F 5
Damascus (cap.), 789,840 ..... G 6
Deir ez Zor, 60,335 ..... H 5
Der'a, 20,465 ..... G 6
Dimishq (Damascus) (capital), 789,840 ..... G 6
Duma, 30,050 ..... G 6
El Bab, 27,366 ..... G 4
El Haseke, 23,074 ..... J 4
El Ladhiqiya (Latakia), 72,378 ..... F 5
El Quneitra, 206 ..... F 6
El Rashid, 11,998 ..... H 5
En Nebk, 16,334 ..... G 5
Es Suweida, 17,592 ..... G 6
Haleb (Aleppo), 566,770 ..... G 4
Hama, 196,224 ..... G 5
Harim, 6,837 ..... G 4
Homs, 231,877 ..... G 5
Idlib, 37,501 ..... G 5
Jeble, 15,715 ..... F 5
Jerablus, 8,610 ..... G 4
Jisr esh Shughur, 13,131 ..... G 5
Latakia, 72,378 ..... F 5
Masyaf, 7,058 ..... G 5
Membij, 13,796 ..... G 4
Meyadin, 12,515 ..... J 5
Palmyra (Tadmor), 10,670 ..... H 5
Qamishliye, 31,448 ..... J 4
Quteife, 4,993 ..... G 6
Raqqa (El Rashid), 11,998 ..... H 5
Safita, 9,650 ..... G 5
Selemiya, 25,728 ..... G 5
Tadmor, 10,670 ..... H 5
Tartus, 19,137 ..... F 5
Zebdani, 10,010 ..... G 6

OTHER FEATURES

'Abdul 'Aziz, Jebel (mts.) ..... J 4
Abu Rujmein, Jebel (mts.) ..... H 5
'Asi (river) ..... G 5
Druz, Jebel ed (mts.) ..... G 6
Euphrates (El Furat) (river) ..... J 5
Furat, El (river) ..... H 4
Hermon (mt.) ..... F 6
Khabur (river) ..... J 5
Orontes ('Asi) (river) ..... G 5
Ruad (island) ..... F 5
Sharqi, Jebel esh (range) ..... G 5
Tigris (river) ..... K 4

TURKEY

PROVINCES

Adana, 902,712 ..... F 4
Adıyaman, 267,288 ..... H 4
Afyon-Karahisar, 502,248 ..... D 3
Ağrı, 246,961 ..... K 3
Amasya, 285,729 ..... G 2
Ankara, 1,644,302 ..... E 3
Antalya, 486,910 ..... D 4
Artvin, 210,065 ..... J 2
Aydın, 524,918 ..... B 4
Balıkesir, 708,342 ..... B 3
Bilecik, 139,041 ..... D 2
Bingöl, 150,521 ..... J 3
Bitlis, 154,069 ..... J 3
Bolu, 383,939 ..... D 2
Burdur, 194,950 ..... D 4
Bursa, 755,504 ..... C 2
Çanakkale, 350,317 ..... B 2
Çankırı, 250,706 ..... E 2
Çorum, 485,567 ..... F 2
Denizli, 463,369 ..... C 4
Diyarbakır, 475,916 ..... H 4
Edirne, 303,234 ..... B 2
Elâzığ, 322,727 ..... H 3
Erzincan, 258,586 ..... H 3
Erzurum, 628,001 ..... J 3
Eskişehir, 415,101 ..... D 3
Gaziantep, 511,026 ..... G 4
Giresun, 428,015 ..... H 2
Gümüşhane, 262,731 ..... H 2
Hakkâri, 83,937 ..... K 4
Hatay, 506,154 ..... G 4
İçel, 511,273 ..... F 4
Isparta, 266,240 ..... D 4
İstanbul, 2,293,823 ..... C 2
İzmir, 1,234,667 ..... B 3
Kars, 606,313 ..... K 2
Kastamonu, 441,638 ..... E 2
Kayseri, 536,206 ..... F 3
Kırklareli, 258,386 ..... B 2
Kırşehir, 196,836 ..... F 3
Kocaeli, 335,518 ..... D 2
Konya, 1,122,622 ..... E 4
Kütahya, 398,081 ..... C 3
Malatya, 452,624 ..... H 3
Manisa, 748,545 ..... B 3
Maraş, 438,423 ..... G 4
Mardin, 397,880 ..... J 4
Muğla, 334,973 ..... C 4
Muş, 198,716 ..... J 3
Nevşehir, 203,316 ..... F 3
Niğde, 362,044 ..... F 4
Ordu, 543,863 ..... G 2
Rize, 281,099 ..... J 2
Sakarya, 404,078 ..... D 2
Samsun, 755,946 ..... F 2
Siirt, 264,832 ..... J 4
Sinop, 266,069 ..... F 2
Sivas, 705,186 ..... G 3
Tekirdağ, 287,381 ..... B 2
Tokat, 495,352 ..... G 2
Trabzon, 595,782 ..... H 2
Tunceli, 154,175 ..... H 3
Urfa, 450,798 ..... H 4
Uşak, 190,536 ..... C 3
Van, 266,840 ..... K 3
Yozgat, 437,883 ..... F 3
Zonguldak, 650,191 ..... D 2

CITIES and TOWNS

Abana, 2,455 ..... F 1
Acıgol, 3,265 ..... F 3
Acıpayam, 4,118 ..... C 4
Adalia (Antalya), 71,833 ..... D 4
Adana, 289,919 ..... F 4
Adapazarı, 86,124 ..... D 2
Adilcevaz, 6,148 ..... K 3
Adıyaman, 22,153 ..... H 4
Afşin, 8,069 ..... G 3
Afyon, 44,026 ..... D 3
Ağlasun, 3,730 ..... D 4
Ağlı, 3,425 ..... E 2
Ağrı (Karaköse), 24,168 ..... K 3
Ahlat, 5,879 ..... K 3
Akçaabat, 7,600 ..... H 2
Akçadağ, 5,995 ..... G 3
Akçakale, 4,526 ..... H 4
Akçakoca, 7,179 ..... D 2
Akdağmadeni, 4,321 ..... F 3
Akhisar, 46,167 ..... B 3
Aksaray, 24,414 ..... F 3
Akşehir, 25,269 ..... D 3
Akseki, 2,505 ..... D 4
Akviran, 3,786 ..... E 4
Akyazi, 9,090 ..... D 2
Alaca, 8,288 ..... F 2
Alaçam, 7,833 ..... F 2
Alanya, 12,436 ..... D 4
Alaşehir, 16,012 ..... C 3
Alexandretta (Iskenderun), 69,382 ..... G 4
Aliağa, 3,087 ..... B 3
Alibeyköyü, 15,199 ..... D 6
Almus, 4,110 ..... G 2
Alpu, 2,709 ..... D 3
Altindağ, 89,838 ..... E 2
Altınova, 6,368 ..... B 3
Altıntaş, 2,361 ..... C 3
Amasya, 34,168 ..... G 2
Anadoluhisari, 13,959 ..... D 6
Anamur, 11,246 ..... E 4
Andırın, 3,695 ..... G 4
Ankara (capital), 905,660 ..... E 3
Antâkya, 57,855 ..... G 4
Antalya, 71,833 ..... D 4
Araç, 2,820 ..... E 2
Aralık, 2,879 ..... L 3
Arapkir, 7,056 ..... H 3
Ardahan, 9,117 ..... K 2
Ardeşen, 5,488 ..... J 2
Arhavi, 4,510 ..... J 2
Arnavutköy, 22,468 ..... D 6
Arsin, 4,028 ..... H 2
Artova, 2,863 ..... G 2
Artvin, 9,847 ..... J 2
Aşkale, 6,943 ..... J 3
Aslanköy, 3,656 ..... F 4
Avanos, 5,675 ..... F 3
Ayancık, 5,320 ..... F 2
Ayas, 3,873 ..... E 2
Aybastı, 7,450 ..... G 2
Aydın, 43,483 ..... B 4
Ayvacık, 2,277 ..... B 3
Ayvalık, 16,283 ..... B 3
Babadağ, 5,511 ..... C 4
Babaeski, 13,879 ..... B 2
Bafra, 26,239 ..... F 2
Bahçe, 2,264 ..... G 4
Bakırköy, 65,285 ..... D 6
Baklan, 2,680 ..... C 4
Balâ, 3,646 ..... E 3
Balıkesir, 69,341 ..... B 3
Banaz, 3,495 ..... C 3
Bandırma, 33,116 ..... B 2
Barak, 3,117 ..... G 4
Bartın, 14,259 ..... E 2
Başkale, 4,007 ..... K 3
Başmakçı, 5,093 ..... D 4
Batman, 24,990 ..... J 4
Bayburt, 15,184 ..... H 2
Bayındır, 11,273 ..... B 3
Bayramiç, 4,607 ..... B 3
Bergama, 24,121 ..... B 3
Beşiktaş, 58,814 ..... D 6
Besni, 11,625 ..... G 4
Beykoz, 37,730 ..... D 5
Beylerbeyl, 21,741 ..... D 6
Beyoğlu, 39,984 ..... D 6
Beypazarı, 9,860 ..... D 2
Beyşehir, 7,456 ..... D 4
Biga, 12,063 ..... B 2
Bigadiç, 4,820 ..... C 3
Bilecik, 9,722 ..... D 2
Bingöl (Çapakçur), 11,727 ..... J 3
Birecik, 15,317 ..... H 4
Bismil, 4,444 ..... J 4
Bitlis, 18,725 ..... J 3
Bodrum, 5,136 ..... B 4
Boğazlıyan, 7,925 ..... F 3
Bolu, 21,700 ..... D 2
Bolvadin, 20,139 ..... D 3
Bor, 14,309 ..... F 4
Borçka, 3,763 ..... J 2
Bornova, 30,445 ..... B 3
Boyabat, 9,418 ..... F 2
Bozdoğan, 6,739 ..... C 4
Bozkır, 3,112 ..... E 4
Bozkurt, 2,954 ..... F 2
Bozova, 3,425 ..... H 4
Bozüyük, 10,842 ..... D 3
Bucak, 10,094 ..... D 4
Bulancak, 9,343 ..... G 2
Bulanık, 6,186 ..... K 3
Buldan, 9,813 ..... C 3
Bünyan, 8,467 ..... G 3
Burdur, 29,268 ..... D 4
Burhaniye, 12,597 ..... B 3

(continued on following page)

Agriculture, Industry and Resources

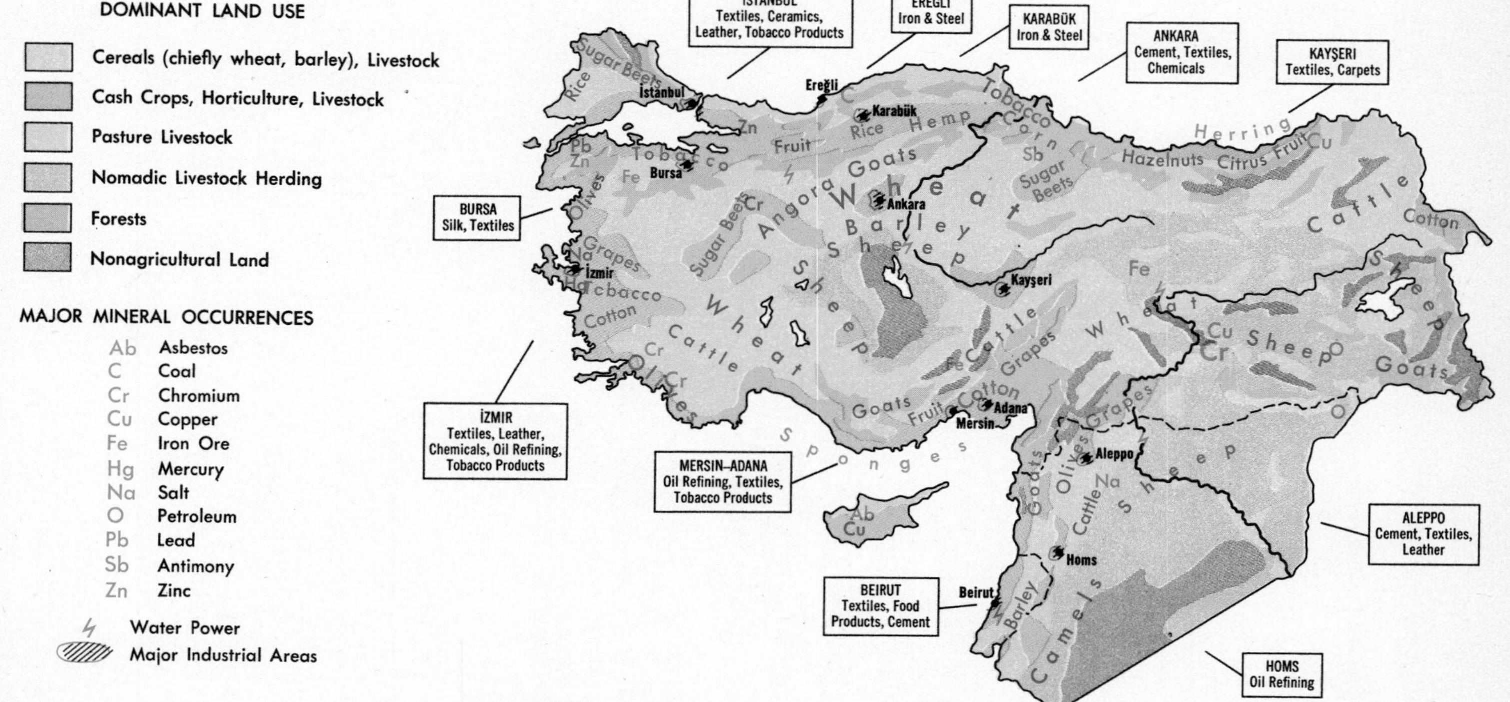

Turkey, Syria, Lebanon and Cyprus

(continued)

TURKEY (continued)

Bursa, 211,644 ....C 2
Büyükada, 5,261 ....D 6
Büyükdere ....D 5
Çal, 2,925 ....C 3
Çalköy, 2,232 ....C 3
Çamlıdere, 3,132 ....E 2
Çan, 5,826 ....B 2
Çanakkale, 22,789 ....B 6
Çandır, 4,619 ....F 3
Çankaya, 161,804 ....E 3
Çankırı, 21,450 ....E 2
Çapakçur, 11,727 ....J 3
Çardak, 2,410 ....C 6
Çarşamba, 18,003 ....G 2
Çatalca, 5,811 ....C 2
Çay, 9,761 ....D 3
Çayeli, 11,496 ....J 2
Çayırıralan, 4,357 ....F 3
Cebeci, 204,592 ....E 3
Çekerek, 3,286 ....F 2
Çelikhan, 3,305 ....H 4
Çemişkezek, 2,235 ....H 3
Çerkeş, 2,865 ....E 2
Çerkezköy, 5,355 ....C 2
Çermik, 5,420 ....H 3
Çeşme, 4,068 ....B 3
Çetinkaya, 2,525 ....G 3
Cevizli, 2,580 ....D 4
Ceyhan, 41,124 ....F 4
Ceylanpınar, 12,508 ....H 4
Cide, 2,130 ....E 2
Çifteler, 5,901 ....D 3
Cihanbeyli, 6,739 ....E 3
Çıldır, 2,040 ....K 2
Cimin, 4,405 ....H 3
Çine, 8,271 ....B 4
Çivril, 5,780 ....C 3
Cizre, 8,662 ....K 4
Çölemerik, 6,129 ....K 4
Çorlu, 27,187 ....B 2
Çorum, 41,574 ....F 2
Çubuk, 8,857 ....E 2
Çukur, 4,045 ....F 3
Çumra, 10,299 ....E 4
Darende, 7,643 ....G 3
Demirci, 10,050 ....C 3
Demirkent, 3,855 ....E 4
Demirköy, 3,309 ....C 2
Denizli, 64,331 ....C 4
Derik, 6,684 ....J 4
Derinkuyu, 4,056 ....F 3
Develi, 13,411 ....F 3
Devrek, 5,058 ....D 2
Dicle, 3,577 ....J 3
Dikili, 5,805 ....B 3
Dinar, 11,298 ....D 3
Dirmil, 2,736 ....C 4
Divriği, 9,160 ....H 3
Diyadin, 2,934 ....K 3
Diyarbakır, 102,653 ....H 4
Doğanbey, 3,058 ....D 4
Doğanhisar, 5,966 ....D 3
Doğanşehir, 4,944 ....G 3
Döger, 2,913 ....D 3
Doğubeyazıt, 8,523 ....K 3
Dörtyol, 11,595 ....F 4
Dumlu, 3,416 ....J 2
Dursunbey, 6,533 ....C 3
Düzce, 22,274 ....D 2
Eceabat, 2,842 ....B 6
Edirne, 46,091 ....B 2
Edremit, 25,003 ....B 3
Eğridir, 8,912 ....D 4
Elâzığ, 78,605 ....H 3
Elbistan, 13,492 ....G 3
Eldivan, 3,344 ....E 2
Eleşkirt, 6,019 ....K 3
Elmalı, 8,482 ....C 4
Emet, 4,815 ....C 3
Emirdağ, 10,914 ....D 3
Emirgazi, 3,509 ....E 4
Enez, 1,808 ....B 2
Erbaa, 13,168 ....G 2
Erciş, 14,072 ....K 3
Erdek, 7,813 ....B 2
Erdemli, 10,304 ....F 4
Ereğli, 38,362 ....F 4
Ereğli, 18,978 ....D 2
Erenköy, 35,980 ....D 6
Ergani, 10,528 ....H 3
Erkilet, 3,223 ....F 3
Ermenak, 8,017 ....E 4
Eruh, 3,298 ....K 4
Erzin, 10,257 ....G 4
Erzincan, 45,197 ....H 3
Erzurum, 105,317 ....J 3
Eskimalatya, 4,244 ....H 3
Eskişehir, 173,882 ....D 3
Eşme, 5,035 ....C 3
Espiye, 5,318 ....H 2
Eynesil, 5,210 ....H 2
Eyüp, 58,244 ....D 6
Ezbider, 3,185 ....H 2
Ezine, 7,819 ....B 3
Fakılı, 3,377 ....F 3
Fatih, 71,965 ....D 6
Fatsa, 9,738 ....G 2
Feke, 3,030 ....F 4
Fethiye, 8,386 ....C 4
Fevzipaşa, 3,917 ....G 4
Fındıklı, 3,928 ....J 2
Finike, 4,352 ....D 4
Foça, 2,953 ....B 3
Gallipoli, 12,945 ....C 6
Gaziantep, 160,152 ....G 4
Gazipaşa, 3,524 ....E 4
Gebze, 9,269 ....C 2
Gediz, 7,486 ....C 3
Gelibolu (Gallipoli), 12,945 ....C 6
Gemerek, 4,660 ....G 3
Gemlik, 15,716 ....C 2
Genç, 3,114 ....J 3
Genezin, 4,691 ....F 3
Gercüş, 2,593 ....J 4
Gerede, 6,677 ....E 2
Germencik, 7,344 ....B 4
Gerze, 5,387 ....E 2
Gevaş, 4,019 ....K 3
Geyve, 5,001 ....D 2
Giresun, 25,331 ....H 2
Göksun, 4,511 ....G 3
Gölbaşı, 5,044 ....G 4
Gölcük, 21,544 ....C 2
Göle, 3,826 ....K 2
Gölhisar, 5,562 ....C 4
Gölköy, 5,852 ....G 2
Gölmarmara, 8,301 ....C 3
Gölpazarı, 3,960 ....D 2
Gönen, 11,666 ....B 2
Gördes, 5,665 ....C 3
Görele, 5,687 ....H 2
Göynük, 2,084 ....D 2
Güdül, 4,385 ....E 2
Gülnar, 4,983 ....E 4
Gülşehir, 3,549 ....F 3
Gümüş, 2,949 ....F 2
Gümüşhacıköy, 10,199 ....F 2
Gümüşhane, 8,092 ....H 2
Güney, 7,416 ....C 3
Gürün, 6,374 ....G 3
Hacıbektaş, 3,739 ....F 3
Hacılar, 10,149 ....F 3
Hadım, 7,176 ....E 4
Hafik, 2,634 ....G 3
Hakkâri (Çölemerik), 6,129 ....K 4
Halfeti, 2,622 ....H 4
Hani, 4,802 ....J 3
Harput, 2,205 ....H 3
Haruniye, 5,198 ....G 4
Hatay (Antâkya), 57,855 ....G 4
Havran, 7,205 ....B 3
Havza, 10,338 ....F 2
Haymana, 5,396 ....E 3
Hayrabolu, 9,444 ....B 2
Hazro, 3,483 ....J 3
Hekimhan, 4,288 ....H 3
Helete, 3,636 ....G 4
Hendek, 10,788 ....D 2
Hilvan, 3,390 ....H 4
Hınıs, 5,263 ....J 3
Hisarönü, 3,730 ....E 2
Hopa, 5,703 ....J 2
Horasan, 5,236 ....K 2
Hozat, 4,540 ....H 3
İçel (Mersin), 86,692 ....F 4
İçme, 2,680 ....J 3
İdil, 2,109 ....J 4
Iğdır, 15,701 ....K 3
Ilgaz, 2,924 ....E 2
Ilgın, 10,196 ....D 3

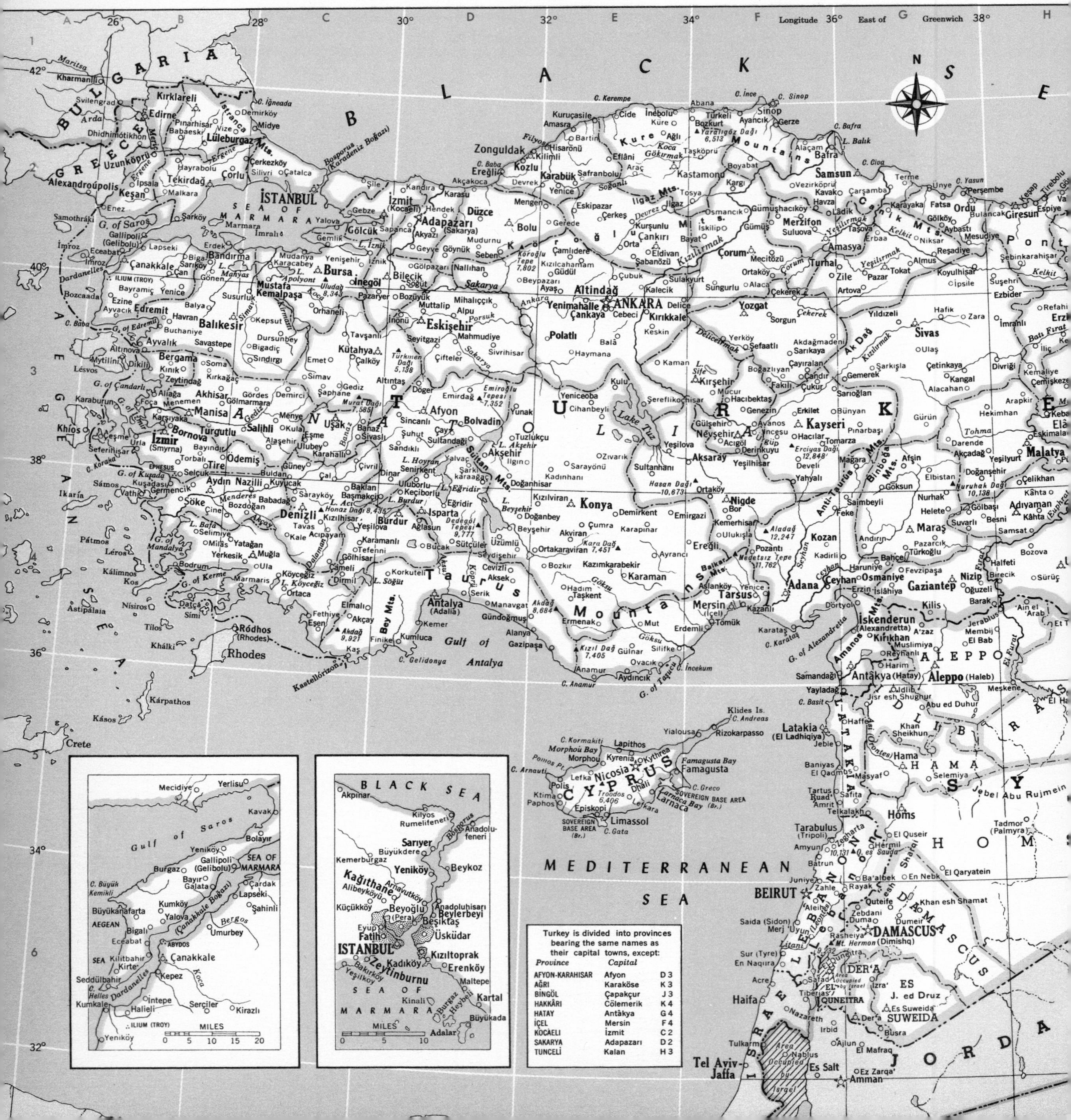

Turkey is divided into provinces bearing the same names as their capital towns, except:

Province	Capital	
AFYON-KARAHISAR	Afyon	D 3
AĞRI	Karaköse	K 3
BİNGÖL	Çapakçur	J 3
HAKKÂRI	Cölemerik	K 4
HATAY	Antâkya	G 4
İÇEL	Mersin	F 4
KOCAELİ	İzmit	C 2
SAKARYA	Adapazarı	D 2
TUNCELİ	Kalan	H 3

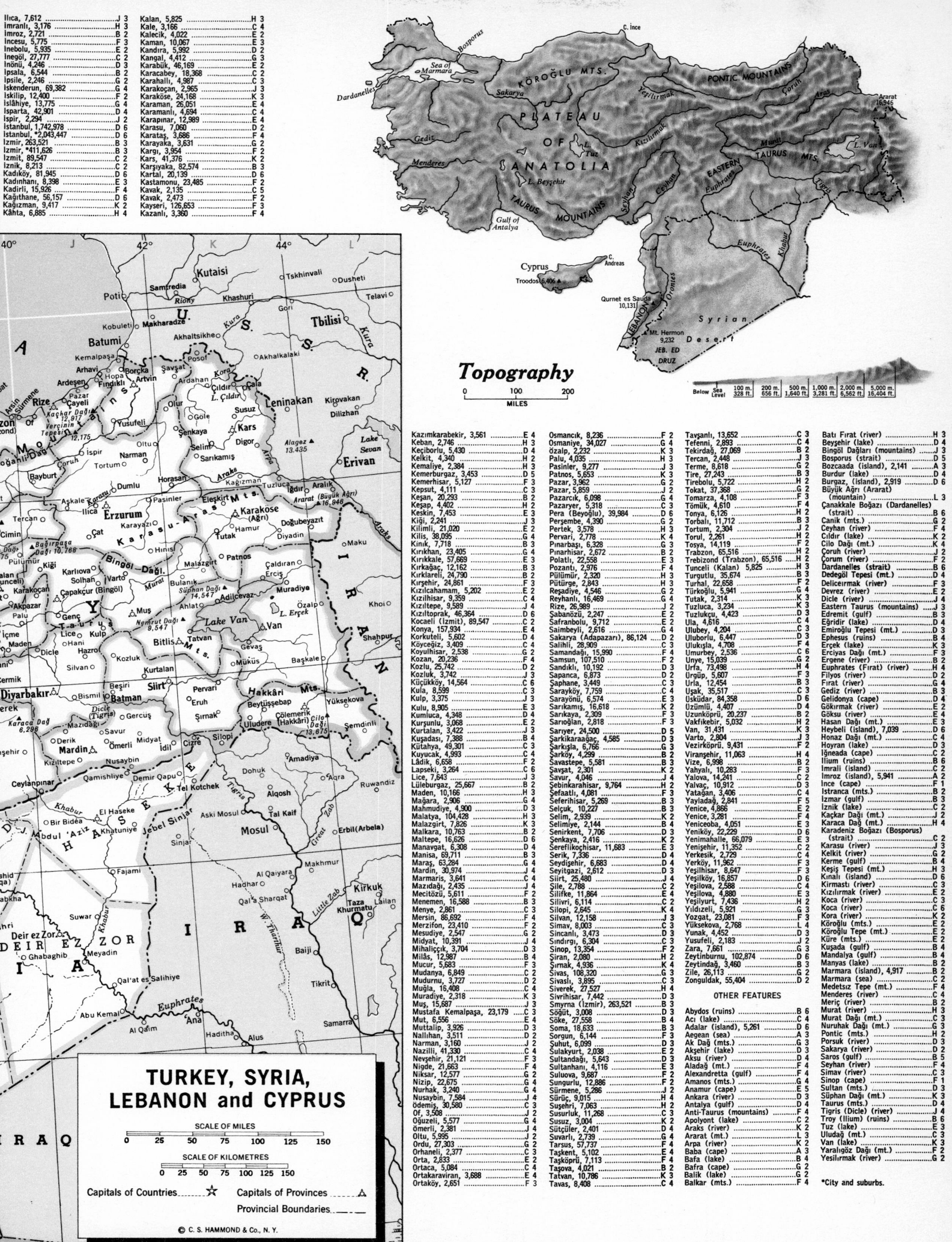

Ilıca, 7,612 .... J 3
İmranlı, 3,176 .... H 3
İmroz, 2,721 .... B 2
İncesu, 5,775 .... F 3
İnebolu, 5,935 .... E 2
İnegöl, 27,777 .... C 2
İnönü, 4,246 .... D 3
İpsala, 6,544 .... B 2
İpsile, 2,246 .... G 2
İskenderun, 69,382 .... G 4
İskilip, 12,400 .... F 2
İslâhiye, 13,775 .... G 4
İsparta, 42,901 .... D 4
İspir, 2,294 .... J 2
İstanbul, 1,742,978 .... D 6
İstanbul, *2,043,447 .... D 6
İzmir, 263,521 .... B 3
İzmir, *411,626 .... B 3
İzmit, 89,547 .... C 2
İznik, 8,213 .... C 2
Kadıköy, 81,945 .... D 6
Kadınhanı, 8,398 .... E 3
Kadirli, 15,926 .... F 4
Kağıthane, 56,157 .... D 6
Kağızman, 9,417 .... K 2
Kâhta, 6,885 .... H 4
Kalan, 5,825 .... H 3
Kale, 3,166 .... C 4
Kalecik, 4,022 .... E 2
Kaman, 10,067 .... E 3
Kandıra, 5,992 .... D 2
Kangal, 4,412 .... G 3
Karabük, 46,169 .... E 2
Karacabey, 18,368 .... C 2
Karahallı, 4,987 .... C 3
Karakoçan, 2,965 .... J 3
Karaköse, 24,168 .... K 3
Karaman, 26,051 .... E 4
Karamanlı, 4,694 .... C 4
Karapınar, 12,989 .... E 4
Karasu, 7,060 .... D 2
Karataş, 3,686 .... F 4
Karayaka, 3,631 .... G 2
Kargı, 3,954 .... F 2
Kars, 41,376 .... K 2
Karşıyaka, 82,574 .... B 3
Kartal, 20,139 .... D 6
Kastamonu, 23,485 .... F 2
Kavak, 2,135 .... C 5
Kavak, 2,473 .... F 2
Kayseri, 126,653 .... F 3
Kazanlı, 3,360 .... F 4
Kazımkarabekir, 3,561 .... E 4
Keban, 2,746 .... H 3
Keçiborlu, 5,430 .... D 4
Kelkit, 4,340 .... H 2
Kemaliye, 2,384 .... H 3
Kemerburgaz, 3,453 .... D 5
Kemerhisar, 5,127 .... F 3
Kepsut, 4,111 .... C 3
Keşan, 20,293 .... B 2
Keşap, 4,402 .... H 2
Keskin, 7,453 .... E 3
Kiğı, 2,241 .... J 3
Kilimli, 21,020 .... E 2
Kilis, 38,095 .... G 4
Kınık, 7,718 .... B 3
Kırıkhan, 23,405 .... G 4
Kırıkkale, 57,669 .... E 3
Kırkağaç, 12,162 .... B 3
Kırklareli, 24,790 .... B 2
Kırşehir, 24,861 .... F 3
Kızılcahamam, 5,202 .... E 2
Kızilhisar, 9,359 .... C 4
Kızıltepe, 9,589 .... J 4
Kızıltoprak, 46,364 .... D 6
Kocaeli (İzmit), 89,547 .... C 2
Konya, 157,934 .... E 4
Korkuteli, 5,602 .... D 4
Köyceğiz, 3,409 .... C 4
Koyulhisar, 2,538 .... G 2
Kozan, 20,236 .... F 4
Kozlu, 25,742 .... D 2
Kozluk, 3,742 .... J 3
Küçükköy, 14,564 .... C 6
Kula, 8,599 .... C 3
Kulp, 3,375 .... J 3
Kulu, 8,905 .... E 3
Kumluca, 4,348 .... D 4
Kurşunlu, 3,068 .... E 2
Kurtalan, 3,422 .... J 3
Kuşadası, 7,388 .... B 4
Kütahya, 49,301 .... C 3
Kuyucak, 4,993 .... C 4
Lâdik, 6,658 .... F 2
Lapseki, 3,264 .... C 6
Lice, 7,643 .... J 3
Lüleburgaz, 25,667 .... B 2
Maden, 10,166 .... H 3
Mağara, 2,906 .... G 4
Mahmudiye, 4,900 .... D 3
Malatya, 104,428 .... H 3
Malazgirt, 7,826 .... K 3
Malkara, 10,763 .... B 2
Maltepe, 16,626 .... D 6
Manavgat, 6,308 .... D 4
Manisa, 69,711 .... B 3
Maraş, 63,284 .... G 4
Mardin, 30,974 .... J 4
Marmaris, 3,641 .... C 4
Mazıdağı, 2,435 .... J 4
Mecitözü, 5,611 .... F 2
Menemen, 16,588 .... B 3
Menye, 2,861 .... C 3
Mersin, 86,692 .... F 4
Merzifon, 23,410 .... F 2
Mesudiye, 2,547 .... G 2
Midyat, 10,391 .... J 4
Mihaliççık, 3,704 .... D 3
Milâs, 12,987 .... B 4
Mucur, 5,683 .... F 3
Mudanya, 6,849 .... C 2
Mudurnu, 3,727 .... D 2
Muğla, 16,408 .... C 4
Muradiye, 2,318 .... K 3
Muş, 15,687 .... J 3
Mustafa Kemalpaşa, 23,179 .... C 3
Mut, 6,556 .... E 4
Muttalip, 3,926 .... D 3
Nallıhan, 3,511 .... D 2
Narman, 3,160 .... J 2
Nazilli, 41,330 .... C 4
Nevşehir, 21,121 .... F 3
Nigde, 21,663 .... F 4
Niksar, 12,577 .... G 2
Nizip, 22,675 .... G 4
Nurhak, 3,240 .... G 4
Nusaybin, 7,584 .... J 4
Ödemiş, 30,580 .... C 3
Of, 3,508 .... J 2
Oğuzeli, 5,577 .... G 4
Ömerli, 2,381 .... J 4
Oltu, 5,995 .... J 2
Ordu, 27,303 .... G 2
Orhaneli, 2,377 .... C 3
Orta, 2,833 .... E 2
Ortaca, 5,084 .... C 4
Ortakaraviran, 3,688 .... E 4
Ortaköy, 2,651 .... F 3
Osmancık, 8,236 .... F 2
Osmaniye, 34,027 .... G 4
Özalp, 2,232 .... K 3
Palu, 4,035 .... H 3
Pasinler, 9,277 .... J 3
Patnos, 5,653 .... K 3
Pazar, 3,962 .... G 2
Pazar, 5,859 .... J 2
Pazarcık, 6,098 .... G 4
Pazaryer, 5,318 .... C 3
Pera (Beyoğlu), 39,984 .... D 6
Perşembe, 4,390 .... G 2
Pertek, 3,578 .... H 3
Pervari, 2,778 .... K 4
Pınarbaşı, 6,328 .... G 3
Pınarhisar, 2,672 .... B 2
Polatlı, 22,558 .... E 3
Pozantı, 2,976 .... F 4
Pülümür, 2,320 .... H 3
Pütürge, 2,843 .... H 3
Reşadiye, 4,546 .... G 2
Reyhanlı, 16,469 .... G 4
Rize, 26,989 .... J 2
Şabanözü, 2,247 .... E 2
Safranbolu, 9,712 .... E 2
Saimbeyli, 2,616 .... G 4
Sakarya (Adapazarı), 86,124 .... D 2
Salihli, 28,909 .... C 3
Samandağı, 15,990 .... F 4
Samsun, 107,510 .... F 2
Sandıklı, 10,192 .... D 3
Sapanca, 6,873 .... D 2
Şaphane, 3,449 .... C 3
Sarayköy, 7,759 .... C 4
Sarayönü, 6,574 .... E 3
Sarıkamış, 16,618 .... K 2
Sarıkaya, 2,309 .... F 3
Sarıoğlan, 2,818 .... F 3
Sarıyer, 24,500 .... D 5
Şarkikaraağaç, 4,585 .... D 3
Şarkışla, 6,766 .... G 3
Şarköy, 4,299 .... B 2
Savastepe, 5,581 .... B 3
Şavşat, 2,301 .... K 2
Savur, 4,046 .... J 4
Şebinkarahisar, 9,764 .... H 2
Şefaatlı, 4,081 .... F 3
Seferihisar, 5,269 .... B 3
Selçuk, 10,227 .... B 3
Selim, 2,939 .... K 2
Selimiye, 2,144 .... B 4
Senirkent, 7,706 .... D 3
Şenkaya, 2,416 .... K 2
Şereflikoçhisar, 11,683 .... E 3
Serik, 7,336 .... D 4
Seydişehir, 6,683 .... D 4
Seyitgazi, 2,612 .... D 3
Siirt, 25,480 .... J 4
Şile, 2,788 .... C 2
Silifke, 11,864 .... E 4
Silivri, 6,114 .... C 2
Silopi, 2,645 .... K 4
Silvan, 12,158 .... J 3
Simav, 8,003 .... C 3
Sincanlı, 3,473 .... D 3
Sındırgı, 6,304 .... C 3
Sinop, 13,354 .... F 2
Şiran, 2,080 .... H 2
Şırnak, 4,936 .... K 4
Sivas, 108,320 .... G 3
Sivaslı, 3,895 .... C 3
Siverek, 27,527 .... H 4
Sivrihisar, 7,442 .... D 3
Smyrna (İzmir), 263,521 .... B 3
Söğüt, 3,008 .... D 3
Söke, 27,558 .... B 4
Soma, 18,633 .... B 3
Sorgun, 6,144 .... F 3
Şuhut, 6,099 .... D 3
Sulakyurt, 2,038 .... E 2
Sultandağı, 5,643 .... D 3
Sultanhanı, 4,116 .... E 3
Suluova, 9,687 .... F 2
Sungurlu, 12,886 .... F 2
Sürmene, 5,286 .... J 2
Sürüç, 9,015 .... H 4
Suşehri, 7,063 .... H 2
Susurluk, 11,268 .... C 3
Susuz, 3,004 .... K 2
Sütçüler, 2,401 .... D 4
Suvarlı, 2,739 .... G 4
Tarsus, 57,737 .... F 4
Taşkent, 5,102 .... E 4
Taşköprü, 7,113 .... F 4
Taşova, 4,021 .... B 2
Tatvan, 10,786 .... K 3
Tavas, 8,408 .... C 4
Tavşanlı, 13,652 .... C 3
Tefenni, 2,893 .... C 4
Tekirdağ, 27,069 .... B 2
Tercan, 2,448 .... J 3
Terme, 8,618 .... G 2
Tire, 27,243 .... B 3
Tirebolu, 5,722 .... H 2
Tokat, 37,368 .... G 2
Tomarza, 4,108 .... F 3
Tömük, 4,610 .... F 4
Tonya, 6,126 .... H 2
Torbalı, 11,712 .... B 3
Tortum, 2,304 .... J 2
Torul, 2,261 .... H 2
Tosya, 14,119 .... F 2
Trabzon, 65,516 .... H 2
Trebizond (Trabzon), 65,516 .... H 2
Tunceli (Kalan) 5,825 .... H 3
Turgutlu, 35,674 .... B 3
Turhal, 22,658 .... F 2
Türkoğlu, 5,941 .... G 4
Tutak, 2,314 .... K 3
Tuzluca, 3,234 .... K 3
Tuzlukçu, 4,423 .... D 3
Ula, 4,616 .... C 4
Ulubey, 4,204 .... C 3
Uluborlu, 6,447 .... D 3
Ulukışla, 4,708 .... F 4
Umurbey, 2,536 .... C 6
Unye, 15,039 .... G 2
Urfa, 73,498 .... H 4
Ürgüp, 5,607 .... F 3
Urla, 12,454 .... B 3
Uşak, 35,517 .... C 3
Üsküdar, 84,358 .... D 6
Üzümlü, 4,407 .... D 4
Uzunköprü, 20,237 .... B 2
Vakfikebir, 5,032 .... H 2
Van, 31,431 .... K 3
Varto, 2,804 .... J 3
Vezirköprü, 9,431 .... F 2
Viranşehir, 11,063 .... H 4
Vize, 6,998 .... B 2
Yahyalı, 10,283 .... F 3
Yalova, 14,241 .... C 2
Yalvaç, 10,912 .... D 3
Yatağan, 3,406 .... C 4
Yayladağ, 2,841 .... F 5
Yenice, 4,866 .... E 2
Yenice, 3,281 .... F 4
Yeniceoba, 4,051 .... E 3
Yeniköy, 22,229 .... D 6
Yenimahalle, 66,079 .... E 3
Yenişehir, 11,352 .... C 2
Yerkesik, 2,729 .... C 4
Yerköy, 11,962 .... F 3
Yeşilhisar, 8,647 .... F 3
Yeşilköy, 16,857 .... D 6
Yeşilova, 2,588 .... C 4
Yeşilova, 4,880 .... E 3
Yeşilyurt, 7,436 .... H 2
Yıldızeli, 5,921 .... G 3
Yozgat, 23,081 .... F 3
Yüksekova, 2,768 .... L 4
Yunak, 4,452 .... D 3
Yusufeli, 2,183 .... J 2
Zara, 7,661 .... G 3
Zeytinburnu, 102,874 .... D 6
Zeytindağ, 3,460 .... B 3
Zile, 26,113 .... G 2
Zonguldak, 55,404 .... D 2

OTHER FEATURES

Abydos (ruins) .... B 6
Acı (lake) .... C 4
Adalar (island), 5,261 .... D 6
Aegean (sea) .... A 3
Ak Dağ (mts.) .... G 3
Akşehir (lake) .... D 3
Aksu (river) .... D 4
Aladağ (mt.) .... F 4
Alexandretta (gulf) .... F 4
Amanos (mts.) .... G 4
Anamur (cape) .... E 5
Ankara (river) .... D 3
Antalya (gulf) .... D 4
Anti-Taurus (mountains) .... F 4
Apolyont (lake) .... C 2
Araks (river) .... K 2
Ararat (mt.) .... L 3
Arpa (river) .... K 2
Baba (cape) .... A 3
Bafa (lake) .... B 4
Bafra (cape) .... G 2
Balik (lake) .... G 2
Balkar (mts.) .... F 4
Batı Fırat (river) .... H 3
Beyşehir (lake) .... D 4
Bingöl Dağları (mountains) .... J 3
Bosporus (strait) .... D 5
Bozcaada (island), 2,141 .... A 3
Burdur (lake) .... D 4
Burgaz, (island), 2,919 .... D 6
Büyük Ağrı (Ararat) (mountain) .... L 3
Çanakkale Boğazı (Dardanelles) (strait) .... B 6
Canik (mts.) .... G 2
Ceyhan (river) .... F 4
Cıldır (lake) .... K 2
Cilo Dağı (mt.) .... K 4
Çoruh (river) .... J 2
Çorum (river) .... F 2
Dardanelles (strait) .... B 6
Dedegöl Tepesi (mt.) .... D 4
Deliceırmak (river) .... F 3
Devrez (river) .... E 2
Dicle (river) .... J 4
Eastern Taurus (mountains) .... J 3
Edremit (gulf) .... B 3
Eğridir (lake) .... D 4
Emiroğlu Tepesi (mt.) .... D 3
Ephesus (ruins) .... B 4
Erçek (lake) .... K 3
Erciyas Dağı (mt.) .... F 3
Ergene (river) .... B 2
Euphrates (Fırat) (river) .... H 4
Filyos (river) .... D 2
Fırat (river) .... G 4
Gediz (river) .... B 3
Gelidonya (cape) .... D 4
Gökırmak (river) .... E 2
Göksu (river) .... E 4
Hasan Dağı (mt.) .... E 3
Heybeli (island), 7,039 .... D 6
Honaz Dağı (mt.) .... C 4
Hoyran (lake) .... D 3
İğneada (cape) .... C 2
Ilium (ruins) .... B 6
İmrali (island) .... C 2
İmroz (island), 5,941 .... A 2
İnce (cape) .... F 1
İstranca (mts.) .... B 2
İzmar (gulf) .... B 3
İznik (lake) .... C 2
Kaçkar Dağı (mt.) .... J 2
Karaca Dağ (mt.) .... H 4
Karadeniz Boğazı (Bosporus) (strait) .... C 2
Karasu (river) .... J 3
Kelkit (river) .... G 2
Kerme (gulf) .... B 4
Keşiş Tepesi (mt.) .... H 3
Kınalı (island) .... D 6
Kirmastı (river) .... C 3
Kızılırmak (river) .... E 2
Koca (river) .... C 3
Koca (river) .... C 6
Kora (river) .... K 2
Köroğlu (mts.) .... E 2
Köroğlu Tepe (mt.) .... E 2
Küre (mts.) .... E 2
Kuşada (gulf) .... B 4
Mandalya (gulf) .... B 4
Manyas (lake) .... B 2
Marmara (island), 4,917 .... B 2
Marmara (sea) .... C 2
Medetsız Tepe (mt.) .... F 4
Menderes (river) .... C 4
Meriç (river) .... B 2
Murat (river) .... H 3
Murat Dağı (mt.) .... C 3
Nuruhak Dağı (mt.) .... G 3
Pontic (mts.) .... H 2
Porsuk (river) .... D 3
Sakarya (river) .... D 2
Saros (gulf) .... B 5
Seyhan (river) .... F 4
Simav (river) .... C 3
Sinop (cape) .... F 1
Sultan (mts.) .... D 3
Süphan Dağı (mt.) .... K 3
Taurus (mts.) .... D 4
Tigris (Dicle) (river) .... J 4
Troy (Ilium) (ruins) .... B 6
Tuz (lake) .... E 3
Uludağ (mt.) .... C 3
Van (lake) .... K 3
Yaralıgöz Dağı (mt.) .... F 2
Yesilırmak (river) .... G 2

*City and suburbs.

64 Israel and Jordan

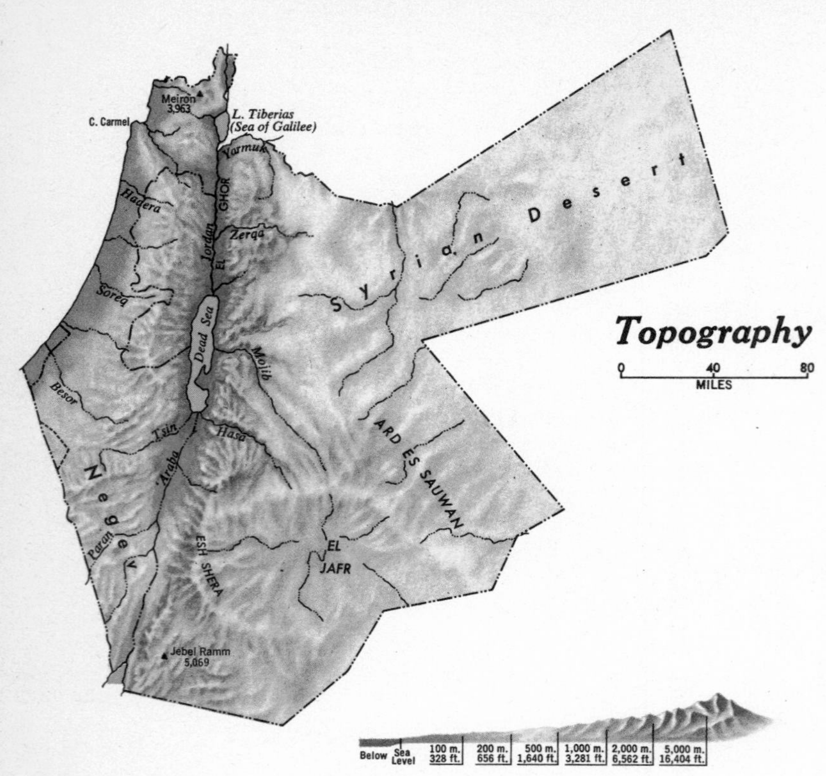

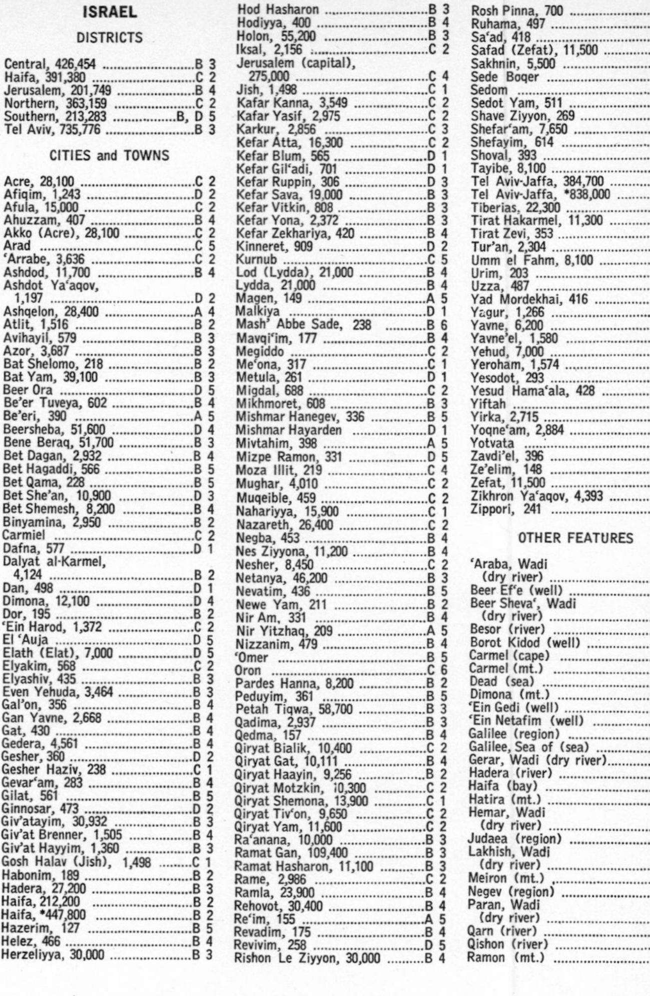

ISRAEL

DISTRICTS

Central, 426,454	B 3
Haifa, 391,380	C 2
Jerusalem, 201,749	B 4
Northern, 363,159	C 2
Southern, 213,283	B, D 5
Tel Aviv, 735,776	B 3

CITIES and TOWNS

Acre, 28,100	C 2
Afiqim, 1,243	D 2
Afula, 15,000	C 2
Ahuzzam, 407	B 4
Akko (Acre), 28,100	C 2
Arad	C 5
'Arrabe, 3,636	C 2
Ashdod, 11,700	B 4
Ashdot Ya'aqov, 1,197	D 2
Ashqelon, 28,400	A 4
Atlit, 1,516	B 2
Avihayil, 579	B 3
Azor, 3,687	B 3
Bat Shelomo, 218	B 2
Bat Yam, 39,100	B 3
Beer Ora	D 5
Be'er Tuveya, 602	B 4
Be'eri, 390	A 5
Beersheba, 51,600	D 4
Bene Beraq, 51,700	B 3
Bet Dagan, 2,932	B 4
Bet Hagaddi, 566	B 5
Bet Qama, 228	B 5
Bet She'an, 10,900	D 3
Bet Shemesh, 8,200	B 4
Binyamina, 2,950	B 2
Carmiel	C 2
Dafna, 577	D 1
Dalyat al-Karmel, 4,124	B 2
Dan, 498	D 1
Dimona, 12,100	D 4
Dor, 195	B 2
'Ein Harod, 1,372	C 2
El 'Auja	D 5
Elath (Elat), 7,000	D 5
Elyakim, 568	C 2
Elyashiv, 435	B 3
Even Yehuda, 3,464	B 3
Gal'on, 356	B 4
Gan Yavne, 2,668	B 4
Gat, 430	B 4
Gedera, 4,561	B 4
Gesher, 360	D 2
Gesher Haziv, 238	C 1
Gevar'am, 283	B 4
Gilat, 561	B 5
Ginnosar, 473	D 2
Giv'atayim, 30,932	B 3
Giv'at Brenner, 1,505	B 4
Giv'at Hayyim, 1,360	B 3
Gosh Halav (Jish), 1,498	C 1
Habonim, 189	B 2
Hadera, 27,200	B 3
Haifa, 212,200	B 2
Haifa, *447,800	B 2
Hazerim, 127	B 5
Helez, 466	B 4
Herzeliyya, 30,000	B 3
Hod Hasharon	B 3
Hodiyya, 400	B 4
Holon, 55,200	B 3
Iksal, 2,156	C 2
Jerusalem (capital), 275,000	C 4
Jish, 1,498	C 1
Kafar Kanna, 3,549	C 2
Kafar Yasif, 2,975	C 2
Karkur, 2,856	C 3
Kefar Atta, 16,300	C 2
Kefar Blum, 565	D 1
Kefar Gil'adi, 701	D 1
Kefar Ruppin, 306	D 3
Kefar Sava, 19,000	B 3
Kefar Vitkin, 808	B 3
Kefar Yona, 2,372	B 3
Kefar Zekhariya, 420	B 4
Kinneret, 909	D 2
Kurnub	C 5
Lod (Lydda), 21,000	B 4
Lydda, 21,000	B 4
Magen, 149	A 5
Malkiya	D 1
Mash' Abbe Sade, 238	B 6
Mavqi'im, 177	B 4
Megiddo	C 2
Me'ona, 317	C 1
Metula, 261	D 1
Migdal, 688	C 2
Mikhmoret, 608	B 3
Mishmar Hanegev, 336	B 5
Mishmar Hayarden	D 1
Mivtahim, 398	A 5
Mizpe Ramon, 331	D 5
Moza Illit, 219	C 4
Mughar, 4,010	C 2
Muqeible, 459	C 2
Nahariyya, 15,900	C 1
Nazareth, 26,400	C 2
Negba, 453	B 4
Nes Ziyyona, 11,200	B 4
Nesher, 8,450	C 2
Netanya, 46,200	B 3
Nevatim, 436	B 5
Newe Yam, 211	B 2
Nir Am, 331	B 4
Nir Yitzhaq, 209	A 5
Nizzanim, 479	B 4
'Omer	B 5
Oron	C 6
Pardes Hanna, 8,200	B 2
Peduyim, 361	B 5
Petah Tiqwa, 58,700	B 3
Qadima, 2,937	B 3
Qedma, 157	B 4
Qiryat Bialik, 10,400	C 2
Qiryat Gat, 10,111	B 4
Qiryat Haayin, 9,256	B 2
Qiryat Motzkin, 10,300	C 2
Qiryat Shemona, 13,900	C 1
Qiryat Tiv'on, 9,650	C 2
Qiryat Yam, 11,600	C 2
Ra'anana, 10,000	B 3
Ramat Gan, 109,400	B 3
Ramat Hasharon, 11,100	B 3
Rame, 2,986	C 2
Ramla, 23,900	B 4
Rehovot, 30,400	B 4
Re'im, 155	A 5
Revadim, 175	B 4
Revivim, 258	D 5
Rishon Le Ziyyon, 30,000	B 4
Rosh Pinna, 700	D 2
Ruhama, 497	B 4
Sa'ad, 418	B 5
Safad (Zefat), 11,500	C 2
Sakhnin, 5,500	C 2
Sede Boqer	D 5
Sedom	D 5
Sedot Yam, 511	B 3
Shave Ziyyon, 269	B 2
Shefar'am, 7,650	C 2
Shefayim, 614	B 3
Shoval, 393	B 5
Tayibe, 8,100	C 3
Tel Aviv-Jaffa, 384,700	B 3
Tel Aviv-Jaffa, *838,000	B 3
Tiberias, 22,300	C 2
Tirat Hakarmel, 11,300	B 2
Tirat Zevi, 353	D 3
Tur'an, 2,304	C 2
Umm el Fahm, 8,100	C 2
Urim, 203	B 5
Uzza, 487	B 4
Yad Mordekhai, 416	A 1
Yagur, 1,266	C 2
Yavne, 6,200	B 4
Yavne'el, 1,580	C 2
Yehud, 7,000	B 3
Yeroham, 1,574	B 6
Yesodot, 293	B 4
Yesud Hama'ala, 428	D 1
Yiftah	D 1
Yirka, 2,715	C 2
Yoqne'am, 2,884	C 2
Yotvata	D 5
Zavdi'el, 396	B 4
Ze'elim, 148	A 5
Zefat, 11,500	C 2
Zikhron Ya'aqov, 4,393	B 2
Zippori, 241	C 2

OTHER FEATURES

'Araba, Wadi (dry river)	D 5
Beer Ef'e (well)	C 5
Beer Sheva', Wadi (dry river)	B 4
Besor (river)	B 5
Borot Kidod (well)	C 5
Carmel (cape)	B 2
Carmel (mt.)	C 2
Dead (sea)	C 4
Dimona (mt.)	C 5
'Ein Gedi (well)	C 5
'Ein Netafim (well)	D 5
Galilee (region)	C 2
Galilee, Sea of (sea)	D 2
Gerar, Wadi (dry river)	B 5
Hadera (river)	B 3
Haifa (bay)	C 2
Hatira (mt.)	B 6
Hemar, Wadi (dry river)	C 5
Judaea (region)	B 5
Lakhish, Wadi (dry river)	B 4
Meiron (mt.)	C 1
Negev (region)	D 5
Paran, Wadi (dry river)	D 5
Qarn (river)	C 1
Qishon (river)	C 2
Ramon (mt.)	D 5

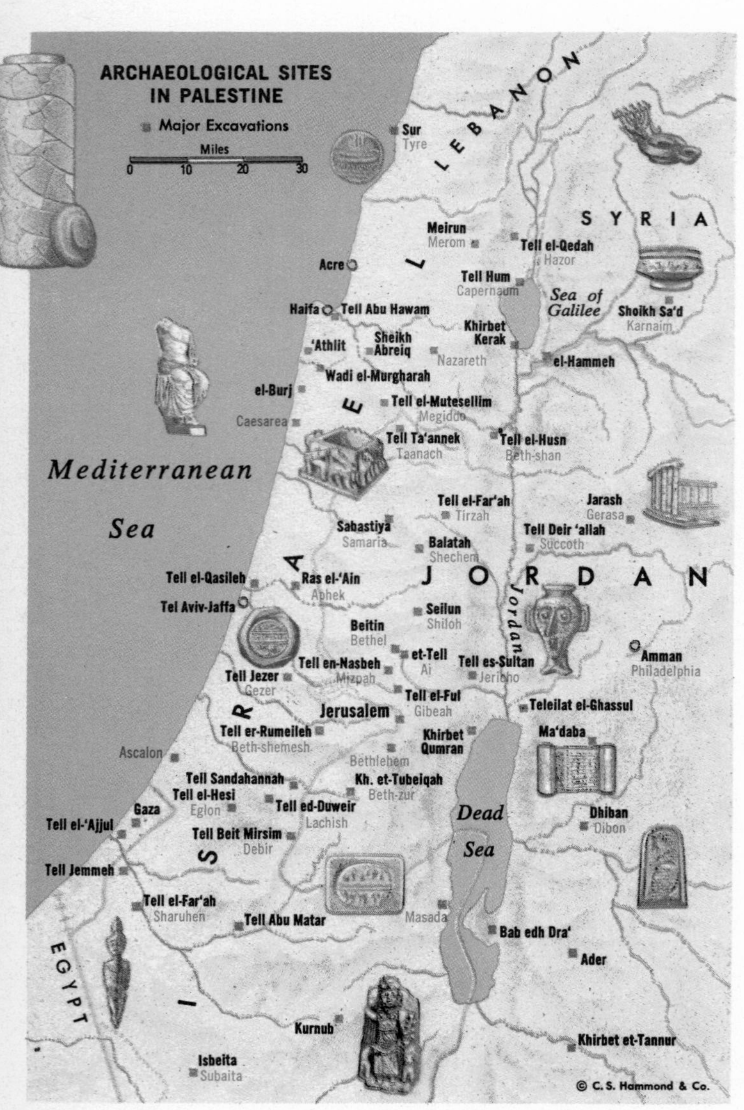

Agriculture, Industry and Resources

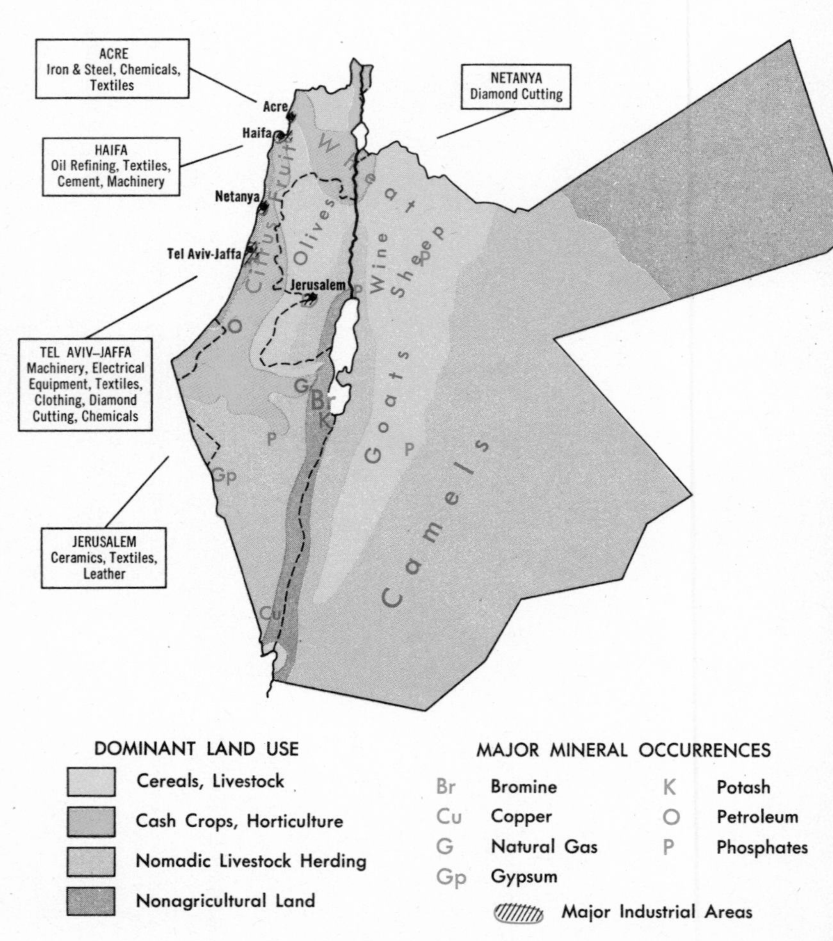

ISRAEL

JORDAN

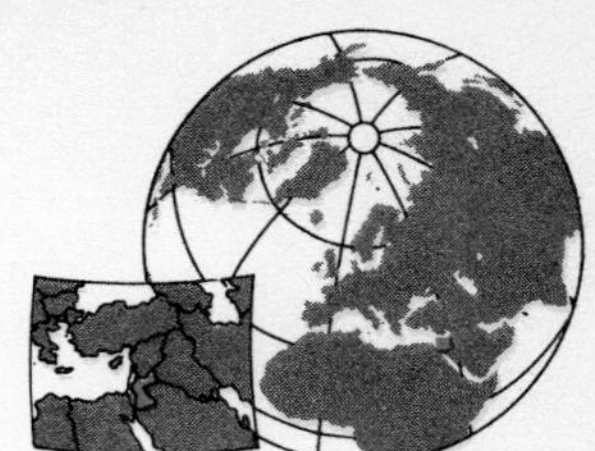

ISRAEL	
AREA	7,993 sq. mi.
POPULATION	2,911,000
CAPITAL	Jerusalem
LARGEST CITY	Tel Aviv-Jaffa
HIGHEST POINT	Meiron 3,963 ft.
MONETARY UNIT	Israeli pound
MAJOR LANGUAGES	Hebrew, Arabic
MAJOR RELIGIONS	Judaism, Islam, Christianity

JORDAN	
AREA	37,297 sq. mi.
POPULATION	2,300,000
CAPITAL	Amman
LARGEST CITY	Amman
HIGHEST POINT	Jeb. Ramm 5,069 ft.
MONETARY UNIT	Jordanian dinar
MAJOR LANGUAGE	Arabic
MAJOR RELIGION	Islam

Rubin, Wadi (dry river) ....B 4
Shiqma (river) ....B 4
Tabor (mt.) ....C 2
Tiberias (Galilee) (sea) ....D 2
Tseelim, Wadi (dry river) ....C 5
Tsin, Wadi (dry river) ....D 5
Yarmuk (river) ....D 2
Yarqon (river) ....B 3

JORDAN

DISTRICTS

'Ajlun, 334,000 ....D 3
Amman, 526,000 ....D 4
El Balqa, 95,000 ....D 4
El Karak, 81,000 ....E 5
Hebron, 145,000 ....C 5
Jerusalem, 418,000 ....C 4
Ma'an, 58,000 ....D 5
Nablus, 414,000 ....C 3

CITIES and TOWNS

'Ajja, 1,322 ....C 3
'Ajlun, 5,390 ....D 3
Amman (capital), 330,220 ....D 4
'Anabta, 4,018 ....C 3
Anin, 914 ....C 2
'Anjara, 3,163 ....D 3
'Anza, 807 ....C 3
'Aqaba, 8,908 ....D 6
'Aqraba, 2,501 ....C 3
Ariha (Jericho), 5,312 ....C 4
'Arraba, 4,231 ....C 3
'Arura, 849 ....C 3
'Attil, 3,808 ....C 3
Bal'ama, 769 ....E 3
Baqura, 3,042 ....D 2
Beit Fajjar, 2,474 ....C 4
Beit Hanina, 3,067 ....C 4
Beit Jala, 6,041 ....C 4
Beit Lahm (Bethlehem), 14,439 ....C 4
Beit Nuba, 1,350 ....B 4
Beit Sahur, 5,380 ....C 4
Bethlehem, 14,439 ....C 4
Biddu, 1,259 ....C 4
Bir Zeit, 2,311 ....C 4
Birqin, 2,036 ....C 3
Burqa, 2,477 ....C 3
Damiya, 483 ....D 3
Dana, 844 ....E 5
Deir Abu Sa'id, 1,927 ....D 3
Deir Ballut, 1,058 ....C 3
Deir Sharaf, 973 ....C 3
Dhahiriya, 4,875 ....B 5
Dhira', 214 ....C 5
Duma, 524 ....C 3
Dura, 4,954 ....C 4
El 'Al, 492 ....D 4
El Bira, 9,674 ....C 4
El Husn, 3,728 ....D 3
El Karak, 7,422 ....E 4
El Khalil (Hebron), 38,309 ....C 4
El Kitta, 987 ....D 3
El Madwar, 164 ....E 3
El Mafraq, 9,499 ....E 3
El Majdal, 259 ....D 3
El Quweira, 268 ....E 5
El Yaduda, 251 ....D 4
Er Rafid, 787 ....D 2
Er Ramtha, 10,791 ....E 2
Er Rihiya, 555 ....C 5
Er Rumman, 293 ....D 3
Er Ruseifa, 6,200 ....E 3
Es Sahab, 2,580 ....E 4
Es Salt, 16,176 ....D 3
Es Sukhna, 649 ....E 3
Esh Shaubak ....D 5
Et Tafila, 4,506 ....E 5
Et Taiyiba, 2,606 ....D 2
Ez Zababida, 1,474 ....C 3
Ez Zarqa', 121,303 ....E 3
Falama, 162 ....C 3
Halhul, 6,041 ....C 4
Harima, 635 ....D 2
Haris, 641 ....C 3
Hawara, 2,342 ....D 2
Hebron, 38,309 ....C 4
Hisban, 718 ....D 4
'Ibbin, 1,364 ....D 3
Idna, 3,713 ....B 4
'Imwas, 1,955 ....C 4
Irbid, 44,685 ....D 2
Jaba', 2,817 ....C 3
Jabir, 135 ....E 2
Jalama, 784 ....C 3
Jalbun, 914 ....C 3
Jalud, 221 ....C 3
Jarash, 3,796 ....D 3
Jenin, 8,346 ....C 3
Jericho, 5,312 ....C 4
Jerusalem (old city), 60,488 ....C 4
Jifna, 655 ....C 4
Kharas, 1,364 ....C 4
Kitim, 1,026 ....D 3
Kuraiyima ....D 3
Ma'ad, 125 ....D 2
Ma'an, 6,643 ....E 5
Ma'daba, 11,224 ....D 4
Ma'in, 1,271 ....D 4
Manja, 353 ....D 4
Mazra', 1,194 ....C 5
Nablus, 41,709 ....C 3
Nabulus (Nablus). 41,709 ....C 3
Nahhalin, 1,109 ....C 4
Na'ur, 2,382 ....D 4
Ni'lin, 1,227 ....C 4
Nitil, 348 ....D 4
Qabalan, 1,970 ....C 3
Qabatiya, 6,005 ....C 3
Qaffin, 2,480 ....C 3
Qalqiliya, 8,926 ....C 3
Qibya, 926 ....C 4
Qumeim, 955 ....D 2
Rafidiya, 1,123 ....C 3
Ramallah, 12,134 ....C 4
Rammun, 1,198 ....C 4
Rantis, 897 ....C 3
Ra's en Naqb, 225 ....E 5
Safi, 3,468 ....E 5
Safut, 421 ....D 3
Salfit, 3,201 ....C 3
Samar, 716 ....D 2
Samu, 3,784 ....C 5
Sarih, 3,390 ....D 2
Shu'fat, 2,732 ....C 4
Shunat Nimrin, 109 ....D 4
Shuweika, 2,332 ....C 3
Silat Dhahr, 3,566 ....C 3
Sinjil, 1,823 ....C 3
Siris, 1,285 ....C 3
Subeihi, 514 ....D 3
Suf, 3,259 ....D 3
Suweilih, 3,457 ....D 3
Suweima, 315 ....D 4
Tammun, 2,952 ....C 4
Tarqumiya, 2,412 ....C 4
Tubas, 5,262 ....C 3
Tulkarm, 10,255 ....C 3
Tur, 4,289 ....C 4
Um Jauza, 582 ....D 3
Wadi es Sir, 4,455 ....D 4
Wadi Musa, 654 ....E 5
Waqqas, 2,321 ....D 2
Ya'bad, 4,857 ....C 3
Yabrud, 277 ....C 4
Yamun, 4,173 ....C 3
Yatta, 7,281 ....C 5
Zububa, 633 ....C 2
Zuweiza, 126 ....D 4

OTHER FEATURES

'Ajlun (range) ....D 3
Anabta (mt.) ....C 3
'Aqaba (gulf) ....D 6
'Araba, Wadi (dry river) ....D 5
Dead (sea) ....C 4
Ebal (mt.) ....C 3
El Ghor (reg.) ....C 5
El Lisan (pen.) ....C 5
Hasa, Wadi (dry river) ....E 5
Hebron (mt.) ....C 4
Jordan (river) ....D 3
Judaea (region) ....C 4
Khirbet Qumran (site) ....D 4
Kufrinja (mt.) ....D 3
Kufrinja, Wadi (dry river) ....D 3
Mashash, Wadi (dry river) ....C 4
Nebo (mt.) ....D 4
Petra (ruins) ....D 5
Samaria (region) ....C 3
Shallala, Wadi (dry river) ....D 2
Shu'eib, Wadi (dry river) ....D 4
Tell 'Asur (mt.) ....C 4
Tur (mt.) ....C 4
Yabis, Wadi (dry river) ....D 3
Yamun (mt.) ....C 3
Zarqa' (river) ....D 3

GAZA STRIP

Total Population, 480,000

CITIES and TOWNS

'Abasan, 1,481 ....A 5
Bani Suheila, 7,561 ....A 5
Beit Hanun, 4,756 ....A 4
Deir el Balah, 10,854 ....A 5
Gaza, 87,793 ....A 5
Gaza, *118,272 ....A 5
Jabaliya, 10,508 ....A 4
Khan Yunis, 29,522 ....A 5
Rafah, 10,812 ....A 5

*City and suburbs.

ISRAEL and JORDAN

CYLINDRICAL PROJECTION

SCALE OF MILES

SCALE OF KILOMETRES

Capitals of Countries
District Capitals
International Boundaries
District Boundaries
Demilitarized Zone Boundaries
Neutral Zone Boundaries

66 Iran and Iraq

IRAN

INTERNAL DIVISIONS

- Bakhtiari (governorate), 298,448 .... F 4
- Boyer Ahmedi and Kahkiluye (governorate) .... G 5
- Central (province), 4,979,081 .... G 3
- East Azerbaijan (province), 2,596,439 .... E 1
- Fars (province), 1,429,804 .... H 6
- Gilan (province), 1,752,504 .... F 2
- Hamadan (governorate), 889,888 .... F 3
- Ilam (governorate) .... E 4
- Isfahan (province), 1,703,701 .... H 4
- Kerman (province), 761,851 .... K 6
- Kermanshah (prov.), 924,717 .... E 3
- Khurasan (prov.), 2,497,381 .... K 3
- Khuzistan (prov.), 1,578,079 .... F 5
- Kurdistan (prov.), 619,573 .... E 3
- Luristan (governorate), 686,307 .... F 4
- Mazanderan (province), 1,841,637 .... H 2
- Ports and Islands (province), 346,410 .... H 7
- Samnan (governorate), 207,786 .... J 3
- Seistan and Baluchistan (prov.), 454,996 .... M 6
- Southern Coast (province), 251,921 .... G 6
- West Azerbaijan (province), 1,087,182 .... D 1
- Yezd (governorate) .... J 5
- Zenjan (governorate) .... F 2

CITIES and TOWNS

- Abadan, 272,962 .... F 5
- Abadeh, 16,000 .... H 5
- Abarquh, 8,000 .... H 5
- Abhar, 11,000 .... F 2
- Ahar, 24,000 .... E 1
- Ahwaz, 206,375 .... F 5
- Amul, 40,076 .... H 2
- Anarak, 2,038 .... H 4
- Andimeshk, 16,000 .... F 4
- Aradan, †8,978 .... H 3
- Arak, 71,925 .... F 3
- Ardebil, 83,596 .... F 1
- Ardistan, 6,645 .... H 4
- Asadabad, 7,000 .... F 3
- Asterabad (Gurgan), 51,181 .... J 2
- Azarshahr, 6,000 .... D 2
- Azna, 5,000 .... F 4
- Babol, 49,973 .... H 2
- Babulsar, 12,000 .... H 2
- Bafq, 5,000 .... J 5
- Baft, 6,000 .... K 6
- Bahramabad, 21,000 .... K 5
- Bam, 22,000 .... L 6
- Bandar ʻAbbas, 34,627 .... J 7
- Bandar Maʻshur, 17,000 .... F 5
- Bandar Shah, 13,000 .... H 2
- Bandar Shahpur, 6,000 .... F 5
- Behbehan, 39,874 .... G 5
- Behshahr, 26,032 .... H 2
- Bijar, 12,000 .... E 3
- Birjand, 25,854 .... L 4
- Borazjun, 20,000 .... G 6
- Bujnurd, 31,248 .... K 2
- Bukan, 9,000 .... D 2
- Burujird, 71,476 .... F 4
- Bushire, 26,032 .... G 6
- Chalus, 15,000 .... G 2
- Dalijan, 6,000 .... G 4
- Damghan, 13,000 .... J 2
- Darab, 13,000 .... J 6
- Daran, 4,609 .... G 4
- Darreh Gaz, 11,000 .... L 2
- Daulatabad (Malayer), 28,434 .... F 3
- Deh Haqq, 4,115 .... G 4
- Demavend, 5,391 .... H 3
- Dizful, 84,499 .... F 4
- Duzdab (Zahidan), 40,000 .... M 6
- Enzeli (Pahlevi), 41,785 .... F 2
- Estahbanat, 18,187 .... H 6
- Fahrej (Iranshahr), 5,000 .... M 7
- Fariman, 8,000 .... L 3
- Farrashband, 3,532 .... G 6
- Fasa, 19,000 .... H 6
- Firdaus, 11,000 .... K 3
- Firuzabad, 8,718 .... H 6
- Firuzkuh, 4,684 .... H 3
- Fumen, 9,000 .... F 2
- Gach Saran .... G 5
- Ganaveh, 9,000 .... G 6
- Garmsar, 4,723 .... H 3
- Golshan (Tabas), 10,000 .... K 4
- Gulpaigan, 20,515 .... G 4
- Gumishan, 6,000 .... J 2
- Gunabad, 8,000 .... L 3
- Gunbad-i-Qabus, 40,667 .... K 3
- Gurgan, 51,181 .... J 2
- Haft Kel, 10,000 .... F 5
- Hamadan, 124,167 .... F 3
- Hashtpar, 5,000 .... F 2
- Homayunshahr, 46,836 .... G 4
- Ilam, 15,000 .... E 4
- Iranshahr, 5,000 .... M 7
- Isfahan, 424,045 .... G 4
- Jahrum, 38,236 .... H 6
- Kangavar, 9,414 .... F 3
- Karaj, 44,243 .... G 3
- Kashan, 58,468 .... G 3
- Kashmar, 17,000 .... L 3
- Kazerun, 39,758 .... G 6
- Kazvin, 88,106 .... F 2
- Kerman, 85,404 .... K 5
- Kermanshah, 187,930 .... E 3
- Khaf, 5,000 .... L 3
- Khoi, 47,648 .... D 1
- Khorramshahr, 88,536 .... F 5
- Khunsar, 10,947 .... G 4
- Khur, 2,912 .... J 4
- Khurramabad, 59,578 .... F 4
- Lahijan, 25,725 .... E 2
- Lar, 22,000 .... J 7
- Mahabad, 28,610 .... D 2
- Mahallat, 12,000 .... G 4
- Mahan, 8,000 .... K 5
- Maibud, 15,000 .... J 4
- Maku, 7,000 .... D 1
- Malayer, 28,434 .... F 3
- Maragheh, 54,106 .... E 2
- Marand, 24,000 .... D 1
- Marvdasht, 25,498 .... H 6
- Masjid-i-Sulaiman, 64,488 .... F 5
- Meshed, 409,616 .... L 2
- Meshed-i-Sar (Babulsar), 12,000 .... H 2
- Meshkinshahr, 9,000 .... F 1
- Mianeh, 28,447 .... E 2
- Mirjawa, 11,000 .... M 6
- Miyanduab, 19,000 .... E 2
- Naft-i-Shah, 3,043 .... D 4
- Na'in, 5,925 .... H 4
- Nasratabad (Zabul), 20,000 .... M 5
- Natanz, 4,370 .... H 4
- Naushahr, 8,000 .... G 2
- Nehavend, 24,000 .... F 3
- Nejafabad, 43,384 .... G 4
- Niriz, 16,114 .... J 6
- Nishapur, 33,482 .... L 2
- Pahlevi (Enzeli), 41,785 .... F 2
- Qain, 6,000 .... L 4
- Qasr-i-Shirin, 15,904 .... E 3
- Quchan, 29,133 .... L 2
- Qum, 134,292 .... G 3
- Rafsenjan (Bahramabad), 21,000 .... K 5
- Rai, 102,825 .... G 3
- Ram Hormuz, 9,000 .... F 5
- Ramsar, 12,000 .... G 2
- Ravar, 7,000 .... K 5
- Resht, 143,557 .... F 2
- Reza'iyeh, 110,749 .... D 2
- Sabzawar, 42,415 .... K 2
- Sabzawaran, 7,000 .... K 6
- Saidabad (Sirjan), 20,000 .... J 6
- Samnan, 31,058 .... H 3
- Sanandaj, 54,578 .... E 3
- Sang-i-Sar, 9,000 .... H 3
- Saqqiz, 17,000 .... E 2
- Sarab, 16,000 .... E 2
- Sardasht, 6,000 .... D 2
- Sari, 44,547 .... H 2
- Savanat (Estahbanat), 18,187 .... H 6
- Saveh, 17,565 .... G 3
- Shahabad, 12,000 .... E 3
- Shahdegan, 6,000 .... F 5
- Shahi, 38,898 .... H 2
- Shahpur, 22,000 .... D 1
- Shahr-i-Kurd, 24,000 .... G 4
- Shahriza, 34,220 .... H 4
- Shahrud, 30,767 .... J 2
- Shahsawar, 12,000 .... G 2
- Shiraz, 269,865 .... H 6
- Shirvan, 11,000 .... K 2
- Shushtar, 24,000 .... F 4
- Sinneh (Sanandaj), 54,578 .... E 3
- Sirjan, 20,000 .... J 6
- Sultanabad (Kashmar), 17,000 .... L 3
- Sunqur, 10,433 .... E 3
- Susangird, 21,000 .... F 5
- Tabas, 10,000 .... K 4
- Tabriz, 403,413 .... D 2
- Taft, 7,000 .... J 5
- Tajrish, 157,486 .... G 3
- Takistan, 13,485 .... F 2
- Tehran (capital), 2,719,730 .... G 3
- Tuiserkan, 12,000 .... F 3
- Tun (Firdaus), 11,000 .... K 3
- Turbat-i-Haidari, 30,106 .... L 3
- Turbat-i-Shaikh Jam, 13,000 .... M 3
- Urmia (Reza'iyeh), 110,749 .... D 2
- Ushnuiyeh, 5,000 .... D 2
- Veramin, 11,183 .... G 3
- Yezd, 93,241 .... J 5
- Zabul, 20,000 .... M 5
- Zahidan, 39,732 .... M 6
- Zarand, 5,000 .... K 5
- Zarghan, 7,000 .... H 6
- Zenjan, 58,714 .... F 2

OTHER FEATURES

- Ab-i-Diz (river) .... F 4
- Aji Chai (river) .... E 1
- Arabi (isl.) .... G 7
- Aras (Araks) (river) .... D 1
- Atrek (river) .... J 2
- Bakhtegan (lake) .... J 6
- Baluchistan (region) .... M 7
- Bampur (river) .... M 7
- Behistun (ruins) .... E 3
- Caspian (sea) .... F 1
- Darya-yi-Namak (salt lake) .... G 3
- Dasht-i-Kavir (salt desert) .... H 3
- Dasht-i-Lut (desert) .... K 5
- Demavend (mt.) .... G 3
- Dez (Ab-i-Diz) (river) .... F 4
- Elburz (range) .... G 2
- Farsi (isl.) .... G 7
- Gurgan (river) .... J 2
- Hamun-i-Helmand (marsh) .... M 5
- Hamun-i-Jaz-Murian (marsh) .... L 7
- Hamun-i-Sabari (lake) .... M 5
- Hanjam (isl.) .... J 7
- Hari Rud (river) .... M 3
- Hashtadan (reg.) .... M 3
- Hormuz (strait) .... K 7
- Kalar, Kuh-i- (mt.) .... F 3
- Karkheh (river) .... E 4
- Karun (river) .... F 5
- Kashaf Rud (river) .... M 2
- Kharg (isl.), 647 .... F 6
- Kuh, Ras el (cape) .... K 8
- Kuh-i-Aladagh (mts.) .... K 2
- Kuh-i-Bagraband (mts.) .... M 8
- Kuh-i-Bazqush (mts.) .... E 2
- Kuh-i-Dinar (mts.) .... G 5
- Kuh-i-Gugird (mts.) .... H 3
- Kuh-i-Jagatai (mts.) .... K 2
- Kuh-i-Shah Jehan (mts.) .... L 2
- Kur Rud (river) .... H 6
- Kurang (river) .... G 4
- Laristan (region) .... J 7
- Maidani (cape) .... L 8
- Makran (region) .... M 8
- Mand Rud (river) .... G 6
- Mashkel (river) .... M 8
- Mehran (river) .... J 7
- Mura, Qalʻeh-i- (river) .... J 3
- Namaksar (lake) .... M 4

Namakzar (dry lake) ....L 4
Nezwar (mt.) ....H 3
Nihing (river) ....N 7
Oman (gulf) ....M 8
Pasargadae (ruins) ....H 5
Persepolis (ruins) ....H 6
Persian (gulf) ....F 6
Pusht-i-Kuh (mts.) ....E 4
Qais (isl.) ....J 7
Qarajeh Dagh (mts.) ....E 1
Qara Su (river) ....E 1
Qara Su (river) ....G 3
Qaranqu (river) ....E 2
Qishm (isl.) ....J 7
Qizil Uzun (river) ....F 2
Sefid Rud (river) ....F 2
Shaikh Shu'aib (island) ....H 7
Shelagh (river) ....M 5
Shirvan (river) ....E 3
Shur (river) ....J 7
Siah Kuh (mts.) ....L 3
Silop (river) ....M 8
Susa (ruins) ....F 4
Talab (river) ....N 6
Tashk (lake) ....J 6
Urmia (lake) ....D 2
Yezd (region) ....J 5
Zagros (mts.) ....E 4
Zaindeh Rud (river) ....H 4
Zarineh (river) ....E 2
Zilbir Chai (river) ....D 1
Zuhreh Rud (river) ....F 5

IRAQ

PROVINCES

Anbar, 319,289 ....C 4
Babil, 448,023 ....D 4
Baghdad, 2,124,323 ....C 3
Basra, 673,623 ....E 5
Dhi Qar, 346,663 ....E 5
Diyala, 400,049 ....D 4
Dohuk ....C 2
Erbil, 360,285 ....D 2
Karbala', 339,692 ....C 4
Kirkuk, 462,027 ....D 3
Maysan ....C 5
Muthanna ....D 5
Ninawa ....C 2
Qadisiya, 500,033 ....E 5
Sulaimaniya, 408,220 ....D 3
Wasit, 335,495 ....D 4

CITIES and TOWNS

Ad Diwaniya, 60,553 ....D 5
'Afaq, 5,390 ....D 4
Al 'Azair, 2,255 ....E 5
Al 'Aziziya, 7,450 ....D 4
Al Falluja, 38,072 ....C 4
Al Kufa, 30,862 ....D 4
Al Kumait, 2,225 ....E 4
Al Musaiyib, 15,955 ....D 4
Al Qa'im, 3,372 ....B 3
Al Qaiyara, 3,060 ....C 3
Al Qosh, 3,863 ....C 2
Al Qurna, 5,638 ....E 5
'Ali Gharbi, 5,735 ....E 4
'Ali Sharqi, 1,980 ....E 4
'Amadiya, 2,578 ....C 2
'Amara, 64,847 ....E 5
An Najaf, 128,096 ....D 5
An Nasiriya, 60,405 ....D 5
'Ana, 6,884 ....B 3
'Aqra, 8,659 ....D 2
Ar Rahhaliya ....C 4
Arbela (Erbil), 90,320 ....D 2

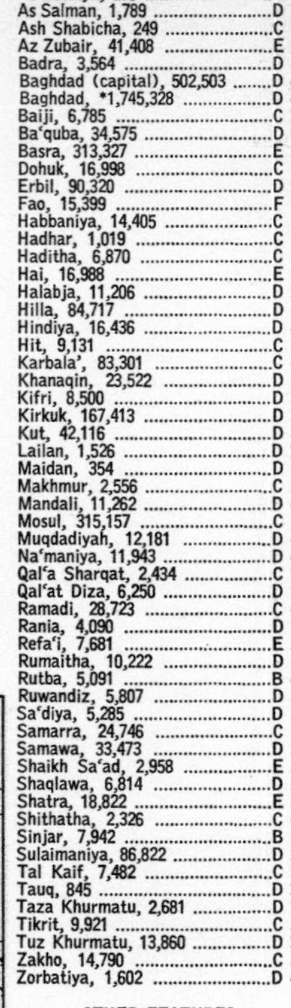
As Busaiya, 295 ....E 5
As Salman, 1,789 ....D 5
Ash Shabicha, 249 ....C 5
Az Zubair, 41,408 ....E 5
Badra, 3,564 ....D 4
Baghdad (capital), 502,503 ....D 4
Baghdad, *1,745,328 ....D 4
Baiji, 6,785 ....C 3
Ba'quba, 34,575 ....D 4
Basra, 313,327 ....E 5
Dohuk, 16,998 ....C 2
Erbil, 90,320 ....D 2
Fao, 15,399 ....F 6
Habbaniya, 14,405 ....C 4
Hadhar, 1,019 ....C 3
Haditha, 6,870 ....C 3
Hai, 16,988 ....E 4
Halabja, 11,206 ....D 3
Hilla, 84,717 ....D 4
Hindiya, 16,436 ....D 4
Hit, 9,131 ....C 4
Karbala', 83,301 ....C 4
Khanaqin, 23,522 ....D 3
Kifri, 8,500 ....D 3
Kirkuk, 167,413 ....D 3
Kut, 42,116 ....D 4
Lailan, 1,526 ....D 3
Maidan, 354 ....D 3
Makhmur, 2,556 ....C 3
Mandali, 11,262 ....D 4
Mosul, 315,157 ....C 2
Muqdadiyah, 12,181 ....D 4
Na'maniya, 11,943 ....D 4
Qal'a Sharqat, 2,434 ....C 3
Qal'at Diza, 6,250 ....D 2
Ramadi, 28,723 ....C 4
Rania, 4,090 ....D 2
Refa'i, 7,681 ....E 5
Rumaitha, 10,222 ....D 5
Rutba, 5,091 ....B 4
Ruwandiz, 5,807 ....D 2
Sa'diya, 5,285 ....D 3
Samarra, 24,746 ....C 3
Samawa, 33,473 ....D 5
Shaikh Sa'ad, 2,958 ....E 4
Shaqlawa, 6,814 ....D 2
Shatra, 18,822 ....E 5
Shithatha, 2,326 ....C 4
Sinjar, 7,942 ....B 2
Sulaimaniya, 86,822 ....D 3
Tal Kaif, 7,482 ....C 2
Tauq, 845 ....D 3
Taza Khurmatu, 2,681 ....D 3
Tikrit, 9,921 ....C 3
Tuz Khurmatu, 13,860 ....D 3
Zakho, 14,790 ....C 2
Zorbatiya, 1,602 ....D 4

OTHER FEATURES

Adhaim (river) ....D 3
Al Hajara (plain) ....D 5
'Aneiza, Jebel (mt.) ....A 4
'Arab, Shatt-al- (river) ....F 5
'Ar'ar, Wadi (dry river) ....B 5
Babylon (ruins) ....D 4
Bahr al Milh (lake) ....C 4
Batin, Wadi al (dry river) ....E 6
Ctesiphon (ruins) ....D 4
Darbandikhan (dam) ....D 3
Euphrates (river) ....D 4
Great Zab (river) ....C 2
Hajara, Al (plain) ....D 5
Haji Ibrahim (mt.) ....D 2
Hammar, Hor al (lake) ....E 5
Hauran, Wadi (dry river) ....B 4
Ibrahim, Haji (mt.) ....D 2
Little Zab (river) ....C 3
Mesopotamia (region) ....B 3
Nineveh (ruins) ....C 2
Sa'diya, Hor (lake) ....E 4
Saniya, Hor (lake) ....E 5
Sha'ib Hisb, Wadi (dry river) ....C 5
Shatt-al-'Arab (river) ....F 5
Sinjar, Jebel (mts.) ....B 2
Siyah Kuh (mt.) ....D 2
Syrian (desert) ....B 4
Tigris (river) ....C 2
Ubaiyidh, Wadi (dry river) ....B 5
Ur (ruins) ....D 5

*City and suburbs.
†Population of sub-district.

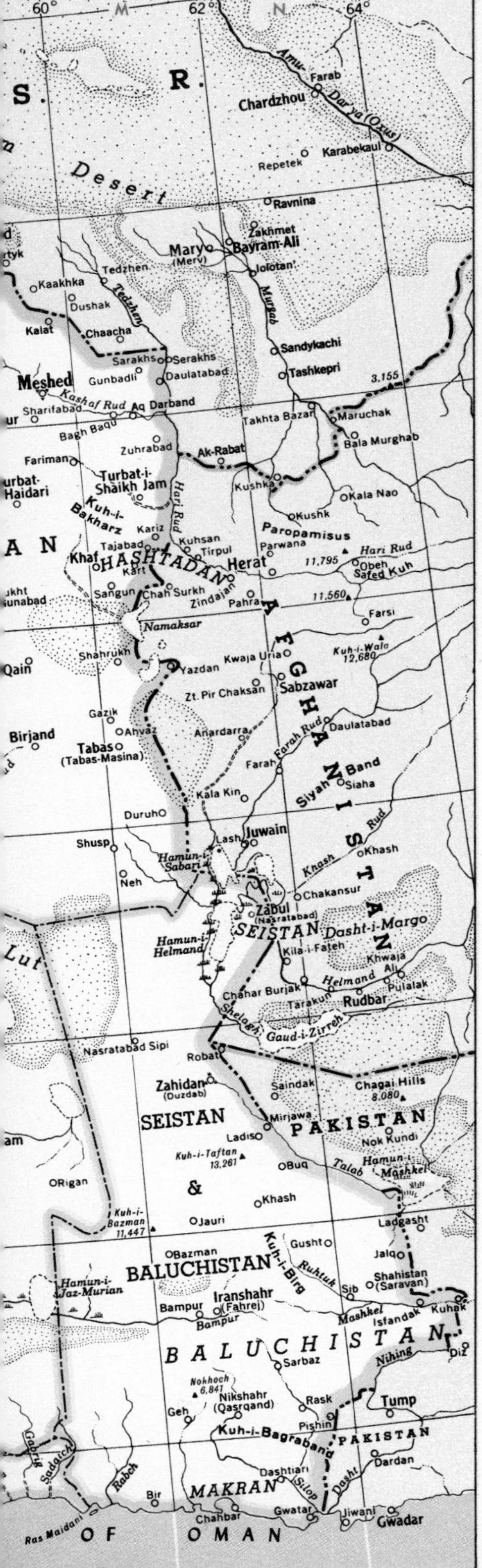

IRAN

IRAQ

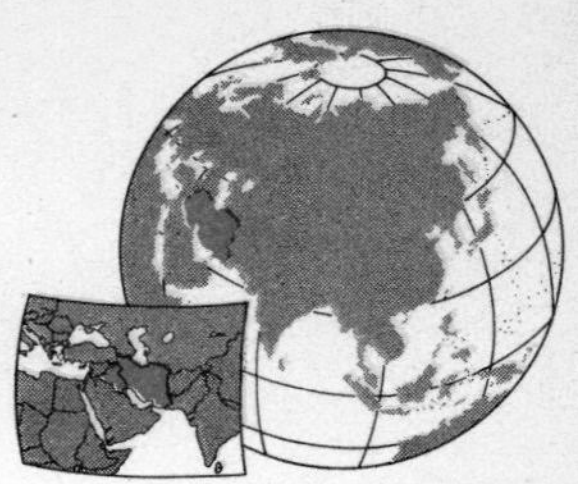

IRAN

AREA 636,293 sq. mi.
POPULATION 28,448,000
CAPITAL Tehran
LARGEST CITY Tehran
HIGHEST POINT Demavend 18,376 ft.
MONETARY UNIT rial
MAJOR LANGUAGES Persian, Azerbaijani, Kurdish
MAJOR RELIGIONS Islam, Zoroastrianism

IRAQ

AREA 167,924 sq. mi.
POPULATION 9,431,000
CAPITAL Baghdad
LARGEST CITY Baghdad
HIGHEST POINT Haji Ibrahim 11,811 ft.
MONETARY UNIT Iraqi dinar
MAJOR LANGUAGES Arabic, Kurdish
MAJOR RELIGION Islam

Topography

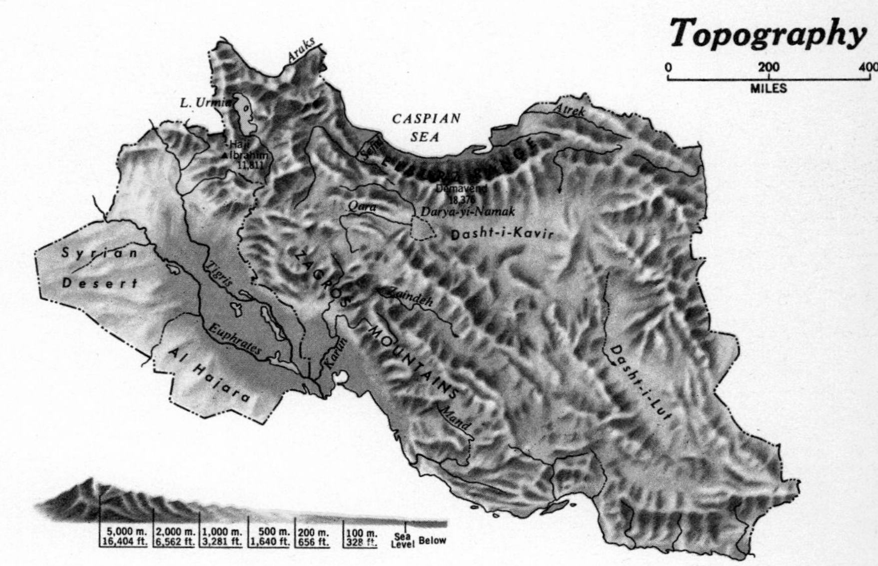

Agriculture, Industry and Resources

DOMINANT LAND USE

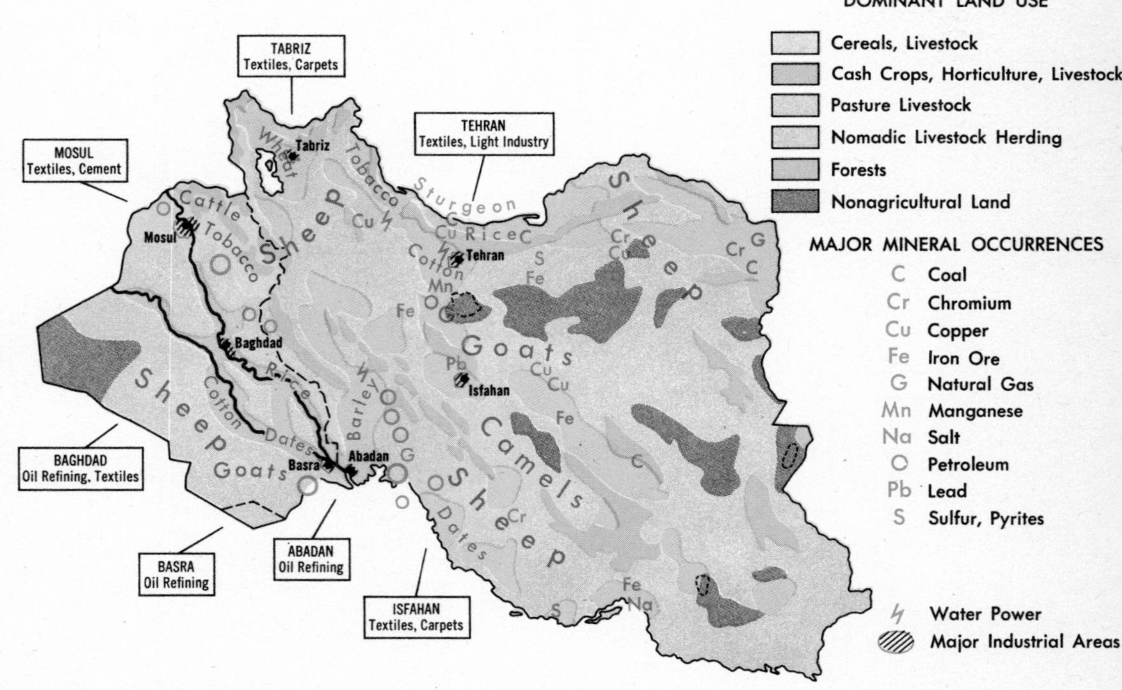

INDIAN
SUBCONTINENT
and AFGHANISTAN
CONIC PROJECTION
SCALE OF MILES
0 50 100 200 300
SCALE OF KILOMETRES
0 50 100 200 300
Capitals of Countries
Provincial and State Capitals
International Boundaries
Provincial and State Boundaries
Canals
Copyright by C. S. HAMMOND & CO., N. Y.
Longitude East of Greenwich
U. S. S. R.
AFGHANISTAN
IRAN
SINKIANG
NEPAL
BHUTAN
SIKKIM
BANGLADESH
SRI LANKA (CEYLON)
JAMMU AND KASHMIR
RAJASTHAN
UTTAR PRADESH
MADHYA PRADESH
MAHARASHTRA
ANDHRA PRADESH
MYSORE
KERALA
TAMIL NADU
GUJARAT
BIHAR
ORISSA
ASSAM
MEGHALAYA
W. BENGAL
PUNJAB
HARYANA
HIMACHAL PRADESH
NORTH-WEST FRONTIER PROV.
BALUCHISTAN
SIND
ARABIAN SEA
BAY OF BENGAL
INDIAN OCEAN
MALDIVES
LACCADIVE MINICOY AND AMINDIVI IS. (India)
ANDAMAN AND NICOBAR IS. (India)
Tropic of Cancer
Himalaya
Hindu Kush
Karakoram
Kunlun
Pamir
Taklamakan
Great Indian Desert
Vindhya Ra.
Satpura Ra.
Malabar Coast
Coromandel Coast
Mt. Everest 29,028
K2 (Godwin Austen) 28,250
KARACHI
BOMBAY
CALCUTTA
MADRAS
DELHI
New Delhi
Kabul
Hyderabad
Bangalore
Colombo
N
MILES
0 2 4 6
Howrah
Hooghly
Bombay Har.
Salsette I.
Trombay
Elephanta

INDIA

AREA 1,261,483 sq. mi.
POPULATION 546,955,945
CAPITAL New Delhi
LARGEST CITY Calcutta (greater)
HIGHEST POINT K2 (Godwin Austen) 28,250 ft.
MONETARY UNIT Indian rupee
MAJOR LANGUAGES Hindi, English, Bihari, Telugu, Marathi, Bengali, Tamil, Gujarati, Rajasthani, Kanarese, Malayalam, Oriya, Punjabi, Assamese, Kashmiri
MAJOR RELIGIONS Hinduism, Islam, Christianity, Sikhism, Buddhism, Jainism, Zoroastrianism, Animism

PAKISTAN

AREA 310,403 sq. mi.
POPULATION 60,000,000
CAPITAL Islamabad
LARGEST CITY Karachi
HIGHEST POINT Tirich Mir 25,230 ft.
MONETARY UNIT Pakistani rupee
MAJOR LANGUAGES Urdu, English, Punjabi, Pushtu, Sindhi, Baluchi
MAJOR RELIGIONS Islam, Hinduism, Sikhism, Christianity

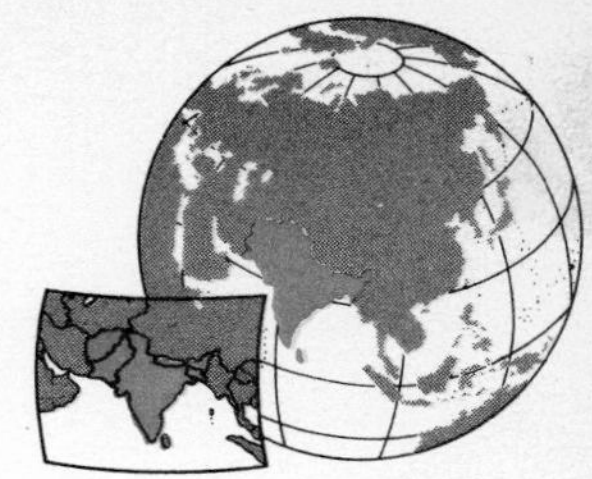

SRI LANKA (CEYLON)

AREA 25,332 sq. mi.
POPULATION 12,300,000
CAPITAL Colombo
LARGEST CITY Colombo
HIGHEST POINT Pidurutalagala 8,281 ft.
MONETARY UNIT Ceylonese rupee
MAJOR LANGUAGES Singhalese, Tamil, English
MAJOR RELIGIONS Buddhism, Hinduism, Christianity

AFGHANISTAN

AREA 250,000 sq. mi.
POPULATION 17,078,263
CAPITAL Kabul
LARGEST CITY Kabul
HIGHEST POINT Hindu Kush 24,556 ft.
MONETARY UNIT afghani
MAJOR LANGUAGES Pushtu, Dari, Uzbek
MAJOR RELIGION Islam

NEPAL

AREA 54,362 sq. mi.
POPULATION 10,845,000
CAPITAL Kathmandu
LARGEST CITY Kathmandu
HIGHEST POINT Mt. Everest 29,028 ft.
MONETARY UNIT Nepalese rupee
MAJOR LANGUAGES Nepali, Maithili, Tamang, Newari, Tharu
MAJOR RELIGIONS Hinduism, Buddhism

MALDIVES

AREA 115 sq. mi.
POPULATION 110,770
CAPITAL Male
LARGEST CITY Male
HIGHEST POINT 20 ft.
MONETARY UNIT Indian & Ceylonese rupee
MAJOR LANGUAGE Divehi
MAJOR RELIGION Islam

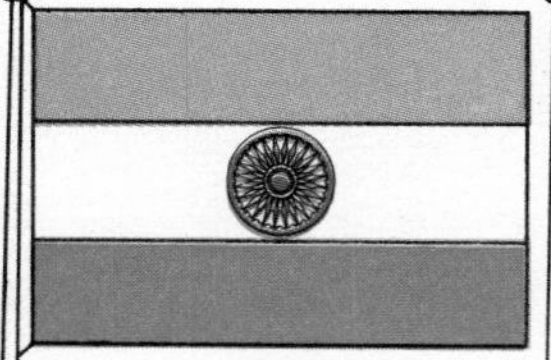

INDIA

PAKISTAN

SRI LANKA (CEYLON)

BHUTAN

BHUTAN

AREA 18,000 sq. mi.
POPULATION 1,034,774
CAPITAL Thimphu
LARGEST CITY Thimphu
HIGHEST POINT Chomo Lhari 23,997 ft.
MONETARY UNIT Indian rupee
MAJOR LANGUAGES Tibetan dialects, Nepali
MAJOR RELIGIONS Buddhism, Hinduism

AFGHANISTAN

MALDIVES

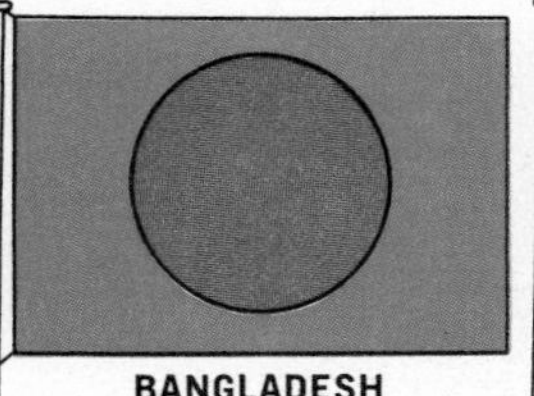

BANGLADESH

NEPAL

BANGLADESH

AREA 55,126 sq. mi.
POPULATION 70,000,000
CAPITAL Dacca
LARGEST CITY Dacca
HIGHEST POINT Mowdok Mual 3,292 ft.
MONETARY UNIT taka
MAJOR LANGUAGES Bengali, English
MAJOR RELIGIONS Islam, Hinduism, Christianity

AFGHANISTAN

CITIES and TOWNS

Andkhui, 30,000 .... B 1
Baghlan, 92,000 .... B 1
Bala Murghab, 10,000 .... A 1
Balkh, 15,000 .... B 1
Bamian, 25,000 .... B 2
Chahar Burjak, 500 .... A 2
Charikar, 83,700 .... B 1
Daulatabad, 15,000 .... A 2
Daulat Yar, 2,000 .... B 2
Faizabad, 57,000 .... C 1
Farah, 26,400 .... A 2
Gardez, 33,000 .... B 2
Ghazni, 39,900 .... B 2
Ghurian, 10,000 .... A 2
Girishk, 10,000 .... A 2
Haibak, 35,200 .... B 1
Herat, 71,563 .... A 2
Jalalabad, 48,919 .... B 2
Jurm, 10,000 .... C 1
Juwain, 2,000 .... A 2
Kabul (cap.), 472,313 .... B 2
Kabul, *600,000 .... B 2
Kala Bist, 26,100 .... A 2
Kalat-i-Ghilzai, 40,500 .... B 2
Kandahar, 127,036 .... B 2
Kandahar, *142,000 .... B 2
Khanabad, 30,000 .... B 1
Kushk, 10,000 .... A 1
Landi Muhammad Amin Khan, 1,000 .... A 2
Maimana, 48,750 .... A 1
Matun, 15,000 .... B 2
Mazar-i-Sharif, 43,197 .... B 1
Mukur, 10,000 .... B 2
Obeh, 5,000 .... A 2
Panjao, 3,000 .... B 2
Qala Panja, 1,000 .... C 1
Qaleh-i-Kang, 15,600 .... A 2
Rudbar, 1,000 .... A 2
Rustak, 10,000 .... B 1
Sabzawar, 5,000 .... A 2
Sar-i-Pul, 5,000 .... B 1
Shahjui, 5,000 .... B 2
Shibarghan, 50,440 .... B 1
Shindand (Sabzawar), 5,000 .... A 2
Taiwara, 5,000 .... A 2
Tashkurghan, 30,000 .... B 1
Zebak, 3,000 .... C 1

OTHER FEATURES

Baroghil (pass) .... C 1
Chagai (hills) .... A 3
Farah Rud (river) .... A 2
Hari Rud (river) .... A 1
Helmand (river) .... B 2
Hindu Kush (mts.) .... B 1
Jam (mt.) .... A 2
Kabul (river) .... C 2
Kunar (river) .... C 1
Kunduz (river) .... B 1
Lora (river) .... B 2
Margo, Dasht-i- (des.) .... A 2
Namaksar (salt lake) .... A 2
Paropamisus (range) .... A 2
Registan (desert) .... B 2
Tarnak (river) .... B 2
Zirreh, Gaud-i- (marsh) .... A 3

BANGLADESH

CITIES and TOWNS

Barisal, 69,936 .... G 4
Bogra, 33,784 .... F 4
Chittagong, 364,205 .... G 4
Chittagong, *437,000 .... G 4
Comilla, 54,504 .... G 4
Dacca (cap.), 556,712 .... G 4
Dacca, *829,000 .... G 4
Dinajpur, 37,711 .... F 3
Faridpur, 28,333 .... F 4
Jessore, 46,366 .... F 4
Khulna, 127,970 .... F 4
Khulna, *320,000 .... F 4
Mymensingh, 53,256 .... G 4
Narayanganj, 162,054 .... G 4
Narayanganj, *327,000 .... G 4
Noakhali, 19,874 .... G 4
Pabna, 40,792 .... F 4
Rajshahi, 56,885 .... F 4
Rangamati, 6,416 .... G 4
Rangpur, 40,634 .... F 3
Sylhet, 37,740 .... G 4

OTHER FEATURES

Bengal (bay) .... F 5
Brahamputra (riv.) .... G 3
Ganges (river) .... F 3
Sundarbans (swamp) .... F 4

BHUTAN

CITIES and TOWNS

Bumthang, 10,000 .... G 3
Paro Dzong, 35,000 .... F 3
Punakha, 12,000 .... G 3
Taga Dzong, 18,000 .... G 3
Thimphu (cap.), 50,000 .... G 3
Tongsa Dzong .... G 3

OTHER FEATURES

Chomo Lhari (mt.) .... F 3
Kula Kangri (mt.) .... G 3

INDIA

INTERNAL DIVISIONS

Andaman and Nicobar Islands (terr.), 115,092 .... G 6
Andhra Pradesh (state), 43,394,951 .... D 5
Arunachal Pradesh (terr.), 381,000 .... G 3
Assam (state), 14,630,422 .... G 3
Bihar (state), 56,387,296 .... F 4
Chandigarh (terr.), 150,000 .... D 2
Dadra and Nagar Haveli (terr.), 69,000 .... C 4
Delhi (terr.), 4,044,281 .... D 3
Goa, Daman and Diu (terr.), 675,000 .... C 4
Gujarat (state), 25,189,000 .... C 4
Haryana (state), 9,914,145 .... D 3
Himachal Pradesh (state), 3,432,000 .... D 2
Jammu and Kashmir (state), 4,615,025 .... D 2

(continued on following page)

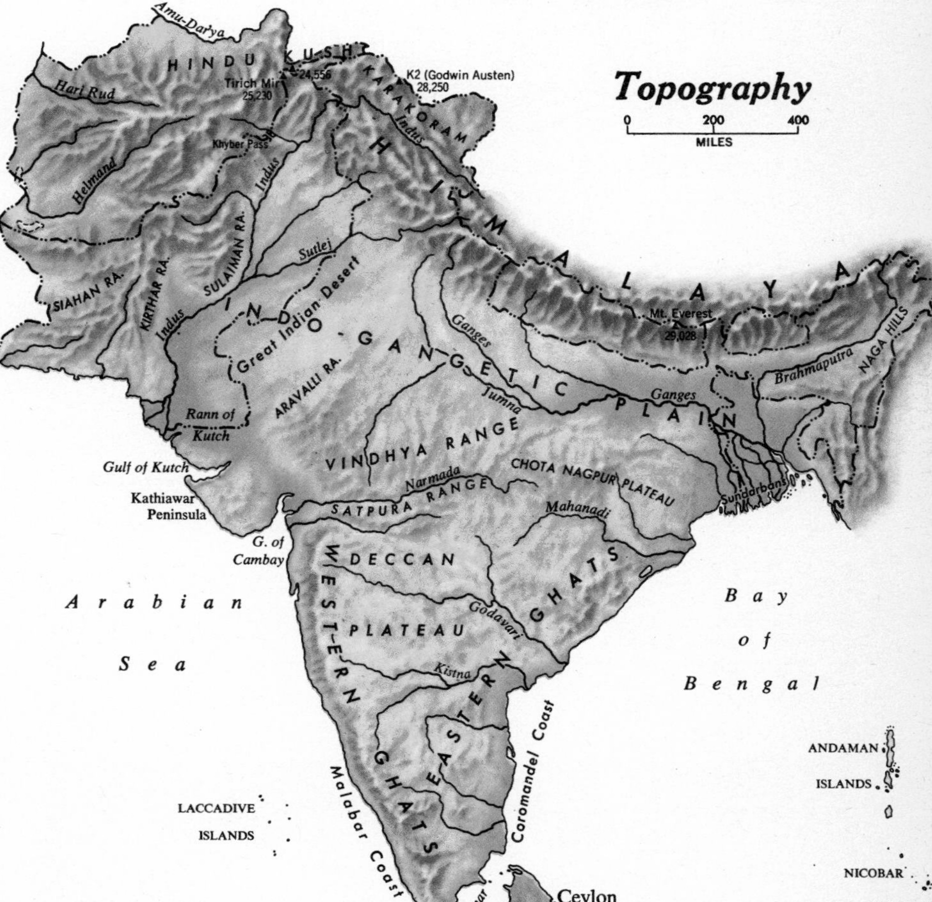

INDIA (continued)

Kerala (state), 20,296,000 ......D 6
Laccadive, Minicoy and Amindivi Islands (terr.), 27,000 ......C 6
Madhya Pradesh (state), 41,449,729 ......D 4
Maharashtra (state), 50,295,081..C 5
Manipur (state), 1,035,000 ......G 4
Meghalaya (state), 983,336 ......G 3
Mizoram (terr.), 321,686 ......G 4
Mysore (state), 27,985,000 ......D 6
Nagaland (state), 515,551 ......G 3
Orissa (state), 20,674,000 ......E 5
Pondicherry (terr.), 430,000 ......E 6
Punjab (state), 13,935,000 ......D 2
Rajasthan (state), 25,724,595 ....C 3
Sikkim (state), 191,000 ......F 3
Tamil Nadu (state), 33,686,953 ......D 6
Tripura (state), 1,424,000 ......G 4
Uttar Pradesh (state), 88,299,453 ......D 3
West Bengal (state), 44,440,095 ......F 4

CITIES and TOWNS

Abu Road, 17,728 ......C 4
Achalpur, 36,538 ......D 4
Achalpur, *54,028 ......D 4
Adilabad, 20,970 ......D 5
Adoni, 69,951 ......D 5
Agartala, 54,878 ......G 4
Agra, 610,328 ......D 3
Agra, *658,781 ......D 3
Ahmadabad, 1,507,921 ......C 4
Ahmadabad, *1,746,111 ......C 4
Ahmadnagar, 131,973 ......C 5
Aijal, 31,436 ......G 4
Ajanta ......D 4
Ajmer, 265,156 ......C 3
Akola, 143,919 ......D 4
Aligarh, 232,278 ......D 3
Allahabad, 521,568 ......E 3
Allahabad, *537,047 ......E 3
Alleppey, 161,279 ......D 7
Almora, 16,004 ......D 3
Almora, *16,602 ......D 3
Alwar, 72,707 ......D 3
Amalner, 46,963 ......C 4
Ambala, 87,750 ......D 2
Ambala, *200,576 ......D 2
Amravati, 177,066 ......D 4
Amreli, 34,699 ......C 4
Amritsar, 424,961 ......C 2
Amritsar, *459,179 ......C 2
Anakapalle, 46,402 ......E 5
Anantapur, 52,280 ......D 6
Anantnag, 21,087 ......D 2
Andheri, 122,401 ......B 7
Arcot, 25,029 ......D 6
Arrah, 76,766 ......E 3
Aruppukkottai, 50,200 ......D 7
Aruppukkottai, *55,977 ......D 7
Arvi, 21,478 ......D 4
Asansol, 134,050 ......F 4
Asansol, *278,350 ......F 4
Aurangabad, Bihar, 14,154 ......E 4
Aurangabad, Maharashtra, 87,579 ......D 5
Aurangabad, *97,701 ......D 5
Azamgarh, 32,391 ......E 3
Badagara, 43,908 ......D 6
Bagalkot, 39,934 ......D 5
Bahraich, 56,033 ......E 3
Baidyabati, 44,312 ......F 1
Balasore, 33,931 ......F 4
Ballia, 38,216 ......E 3
Bally, 247,844 ......F 1
Balrampur, 31,776 ......E 3
Banda, 37,744 ......D 3
Bandra, 38,099 ......B 7
Bangalore, 1,027,327 ......D 6
Bangalore, *1,648,232 ......D 6
Bankura, 62,833 ......F 4
Bansberia, 45,463 ......F 1
Baramati, 21,118 ......C 5
Barasat, 29,281 ......F 1
Barasat, *61,621 ......F 1
Bareilly, 325,560 ......D 3
Bareilly, *343,559 ......D 3
Baripada, 20,301 ......F 4
Barmer, 27,600 ......C 3
Barnagore, 143,621 ......F 1
Baroda, 400,725 ......C 4
Barpeta, 22,207 ......G 3
Barrackpore, 63,778 ......F 1
Barrackpore, *158,244 ......F 1
Barsi, 50,389 ......D 5
Basirhat, 53,943 ......F 4
Bassein, 22,598 ......C 5
Bassein, *28,238 ......C 5
Batala, 51,300 ......D 2
Beawar, 53,931 ......C 3
Belgaum, 156,105 ......C 5
Belgaum, *176,857 ......C 5
Bellary, 85,673 ......D 5
Belur, 29,737 ......F 1
Benares (Varanasi), 619,822 ......E 3
Berhampore, 62,317 ......F 4
Berhampur, 76,931 ......F 5
Bettiah, 39,990 ......E 3
Bhadrak, 25,285 ......F 4
Bhadravati, 24,495 ......D 6
Bhadravati, *65,776 ......D 6
Bhadreswar, 35,489 ......F 1
Bhagalpur, 174,538 ......F 4
Bhandara, 27,710 ......E 4
Bhandup, 33,020 ......B 7
Bharatpur, 49,776 ......D 3
Bhatinda, 52,253 ......C 2
Bhatpara, 159,219 ......F 1
Bhavnagar, 217,533 ......C 4
Bhilai, 86,116 ......E 4
Bhilwara, 43,499 ......C 3
Bhimavaram, 43,281 ......E 5
Bhir (Bir), 33,066 ......D 5
Bhiwandi, 47,630 ......C 5
Bhiwani, 58,194 ......D 3
Bhopal, 310,733 ......D 4
Bhopal, *441,939 ......D 4
Bhubaneswar, 38,211 ......F 4
Bhuj, 38,953 ......B 4
Bhuj, *40,180 ......B 4
Bhusawal, 73,994 ......D 4
Bhusawal, *79,121 ......D 4
Bidar, 32,420 ......D 5
Bihar, 78,581 ......F 3
Bijapur, 78,854 ......D 5
Bijnor, 33,821 ......D 3
Bikaner, 186,560 ......C 3
Bilaspur, 86,706 ......E 4
Bina, 27,476 ......D 4
Bir, 33,066 ......D 5
Birmitrapur, 20,301 ......E 4
Bobbili, 25,592 ......E 5
Bodhan, 30,929 ......D 5
Bodinayakkanur, 44,914 ......D 6
Bombay, *5,931,989 ......B 7
Broach, 73,639 ......C 4
Budaun, 58,770 ......D 3
Budge-Budge, 39,824 ......F 2
Bulsar, 35,028 ......C 4
Bulsar, *37,586 ......C 4
Bundi, 26,478 ......D 3
Burdwan, 147,528 ......F 4
Burhanpur, 82,090 ......D 4
Calcutta, 7,040,345 ......F 2
Calicut (Kozhikode), 315,786 ......D 6
Cambay, 51,291 ......C 4
Cannanore, 46,101 ......C 6
Cannanore, *48,960 ......B 6
Cawnpore (Kanpur), 1,163,524 ..E 3
Chaibasa, 22,019 ......F 4
Champdani, 42,129 ......F 1
Chanda, 51,484 ......D 5
Chandernagore, 67,105 ......F 1
Chandigarh, 89,321 ......D 2
Chandigarh, *110,614 ......D 2
Chapra, 75,580 ......F 3
Chembur, 85,582 ......B 7
Chhatarpur, 22,146 ......D 4
Chhindwara, 37,244 ......D 4
Chidambaram, 40,694 ......E 6
Chik Ballapur, 23,025 ......D 6
Chikmagalur, 30,253 ......D 6
Chingleput, 25,977 ......E 6
Chiplun, 17,355 ......C 5
Chiplun, *22,760 ......C 5
Chirala, 45,410 ......E 5
Chitradurga, 33,336 ......D 6
Chittoor, 47,876 ......D 6
Churu, 41,727 ......C 3
Cocanada (Kakinada), 146,332 ..E 5
Cochin, 35,076 ......D 6
Coimbatore, 393,145 ......D 6
Cooch Behar, 41,922 ......F 3
Cuddalore, 79,168 ......E 6
Cuddapah, 49,027 ......D 6
Cuttack, 198,405 ......F 4
Dabhoi, 30,841 ......C 4
Daltonganj, 25,270 ......E 4
Damoh, 46,656 ......D 4
Darbhanga, 121,438 ......F 3
Darjeeling, 40,651 ......F 3
Datia, 29,430 ......D 3
Davangere, 78,124 ......D 6
Dehra Dun, 136,469 ......D 2
Dehra Dun, *167,297 ......D 2
Delhi, *3,629,842 ......D 3
Deoghar, 35,105 ......F 4
Deolali, 37,264 ......C 5
Deoria, 28,407 ......E 3
Dewas, 34,577 ......D 4
Dhamtari, 31,552 ......E 4
Dhanbad, 57,400 ......F 4
Dhar, 28,325 ......C 4
Dharwar, 77,163 ......C 5
Dholpur, 27,412 ......D 3
Dhond, 12,912 ......C 5
Dhond, *27,168 ......C 5
Dhoraji, 48,951 ......C 4
Dhubri, 28,355 ......G 3
Dhulia, 98,893 ......C 4
Dibrugarh, 58,480 ......G 3
Dindigul, 92,947 ......D 6
Dohad, 35,483 ......C 4
Dohad, *50,434 ......C 4
Domjor, 8,670 ......F 1
Domjor, *30,843 ......F 1
Dum Dum, 20,041 ......F 1
Dum Dum, *174,177 ......F 1
Durg, 64,132 ......E 4
Durg, *204,784 ......E 4
Durgapur, *41,696 ......F 4
Dwarka, 11,912 ......B 4
Dwarka, *14,314 ......B 4
Eluru, 130,166 ......E 5
Ernakulam, 203,493 ......D 6
Ernakulam, *474,187 ......D 6
Erode, 73,762 ......D 6
Erode, *96,528 ......D 6
Etawah, 69,681 ......D 3
Faizabad, 83,717 ......E 3
Faizabad, *88,296 ......E 3
Fatehgarh, 87,793 ......D 3
Fatehgarh, *94,591 ......D 3
Fatehpur, 27,039 ......C 3
Fatehpur, 28,323 ......E 3
Ferozepore, 47,060 ......C 2
Ferozepore, *97,932 ......C 2
Firozabad, 98,611 ......D 3
Gadag, 76,614 ......D 5
Gandhinagar, 24,049 ......C 4
Ganganagar, 63,854 ......C 3
Gangtok, 6,848 ......F 3
Garden Reach, 152,347 ......F 2
Garulia, 29,041 ......F 1
Gauhati, 210,561 ......G 3
Gaya, 167,500 ......F 4
Ghat Kopar, 34,256 ......B 7
Ghaziabad, 63,190 ......D 3
Ghaziabad, *70,438 ......D 3
Ghazipur, 37,147 ......E 3
Goalpara, 13,692 ......G 3
Godhra, 52,167 ......C 4
Gonda, 43,496 ......E 3
Gondal, 45,069 ......C 4
Gopalpur, 3,536 ......F 5
Gorakhpur, 234,497 ......E 3
Gudur, 25,618 ......D 6
Gulbarga, 97,069 ......D 5
Guna, 31,031 ......D 4
Guntakal, 48,083 ......D 5
Guntur, 264,138 ......D 5
Gwalior, 361,780 ......D 3
Haflong, 3,265 ......G 3
Harda, 22,279 ......D 4
Hardoi, 36,725 ......E 3
Hardwar, 58,513 ......D 2
Hardwar, *59,960 ......D 2
Hassan, 32,172 ......D 6
Hathras, 64,045 ......D 3
Hazaribagh, 40,958 ......F 4
Hindupur, 32,445 ......D 6
Hinganghat, 36,890 ......D 4
Hingoli, 23,407 ......D 5
Hissar, 60,222 ......D 3
Honavar, 10,453 ......C 6
Hooghly-Chinsura, 83,104 ......F 1
Hoshangabad, 19,284 ......D 4
Hospet, 53,242 ......D 5
Howrah, 590,385 ......F 2
Hubli, 217,284 ......C 5
Hubli, *303,696 ......C 5
Hunza (Baltit) ......C 1
Hyderabad, 1,294,800 ......D 5
Hyderabad, *1,798,910 ......D 5
Ichchapuram, 12,961 ......F 5
Ichhapur, 12,382 ......F 1
Imphal, 67,717 ......G 4
Indore, 483,969 ......D 4
Itarsi, 33,611 ......D 4
Jabalpur, 406,214 ......D 4
Jabalpur, *497,946 ......D 4
Jagdalpur, 20,412 ......E 5
Jagtial, 20,941 ......D 5
Jaipur, 533,151 ......D 3
Jaisalmer, 8,362 ......C 3
Jajpur, 13,802 ......F 4
Jalgaon, 80,351 ......D 4
Jalna, 67,158 ......D 4
Jalor, 12,882 ......C 3
Jalpaiguri, 48,738 ......F 3
Jamalpur, 57,039 ......F 3
Jammu, 102,738 ......D 2
Jammu, *108,257 ......D 2
Jamnagar, 200,918 ......B 4
Jamshedpur, 402,462 ......F 4
Jamshedpur, *465,740 ......F 4
Jaora, 31,140 ......D 4
Jaunpur, 61,851 ......E 3
Jeypore, 25,291 ......E 5
Jhalawar, 14,643 ......D 4
Jhansi, 177,456 ......D 3
Jhansi, *216,736 ......D 3
Jhunjhunu, 24,962 ......D 3
Jind, 24,216 ......D 3
Jodhpur, 270,404 ......C 3
Jorhat, 24,953 ......G 3
Jubbulpore (Jabalpur), 406,214..D 4
Juhu, 9,990 ......B 7
Jullundur, 281,623 ......D 2
Jullundur, *333,938 ......D 2
Junagadh, 74,298 ......B 4
Kadayanallur, 41,249 ......D 7
Kadiri, 24,307 ......D 6
Kakinada, 146,332 ......E 5
Kalyan, 73,482 ......C 5
Kalyan, *194,334 ......C 5
Kamarhati, 190,695 ......F 1
Kamptee, 40,859 ......D 4
Kamptee, *46,643 ......D 4
Kanchipuram, 92,714 ......E 6
Kandla, 9,617 ......C 4
Kandukur, 12,436 ......E 5
Kangra, 5,775 ......D 2
Kanker, 6,487 ......E 4
Kannauj, 24,646 ......D 3
Kanpur, 1,163,524 ......E 3
Kanpur, *1,273,042 ......E 3
Karad, 33,772 ......C 5
Karaikudi, 43,698 ......D 7
Karanja, 26,440 ......D 4
Karauli, 23,696 ......D 3
Kargil ......D 2
Karikal, 22,252 ......E 6
Karkal, 15,535 ......C 6
Karnal, 72,109 ......D 3
Karur, 50,564 ......D 6
Karwar, 23,906 ......C 6
Kasaragod, 27,635 ......C 6
Kasganj, 37,559 ......D 3
Katarnian Ghat ......E 3
Katihar, 46,837 ......F 3
Katihar, *59,344 ......F 3
Katni (Murwara), 46,169 ......E 4
Kavali, 20,544 ......E 6
Kavaratti, 2,828 ......C 6
Kawardha, 10,117 ......E 4
Kendrapara, 15,830 ......F 4
Keonjhar, 12,624 ......F 4
Khamgaon, 44,432 ......D 4
Khamman, 35,888 ......D 5
Khandwa, 63,505 ......D 4
Kharagpur, 163,929 ......F 4
Khardah, 28,362 ......F 1
Khurda, 12,497 ......F 4
Kirkee, 58,496 ......C 5
Kishangarh, 25,244 ......D 3
Kishtwar, 4,140 ......D 2
Kohima, 7,246 ......G 3
Kolar, 32,587 ......D 6
Kolar Gold Fields, 167,610 ......D 6
Kolhapur, 245,206 ......C 5
Kolhapur, *259,482 ......C 5
Konnagar, 29,443 ......F 1
Koppal, 19,530 ......D 5
Koraput, 7,461 ......E 5
Kota, 205,429 ......D 3
Kotrung, 31,031 ......F 1
Kottayam, 52,685 ......D 7
Kotturu, 11,493 ......D 6
Kovur, 14,580 ......E 6
Kozhikode, 315,786 ......D 6
Kozhikode, *381,096 ......D 6
Krishnanagar, 70,440 ......F 4
Kulu, 4,886 ......D 2
Kumbakonam, 92,581 ......D 6
Kumbakonam, *96,746 ......D 6
Kumta, 16,223 ......C 6
Kurla, 98,018 ......B 7
Kurnool, 157,448 ......D 5
Lansdowne, 6,381 ......D 3
Latur, 40,913 ......D 5
Ledo ......H 3
Leh, 3,720 ......D 2
Lohardaga, 13,203 ......E 4
Lucknow, 763,604 ......E 3
Lucknow, *830,298 ......E 3
Ludhiana, 363,403 ......D 2
Lumding, 23,186 ......G 3
Machilipatnam, 126,855 ......E 5
Madh, 3,307 ......B 7
Madhubani, 28,229 ......F 3
Madras, 2,047,735 ......E 6
Madras, *2,470,288 ......E 6
Madugula, 7,688 ......E 5
Madurai, 486,480 ......D 7
Mahabaleshwar, 6,029 ......C 5
Mahbubnagar, 35,588 ......D 5
Mahe, 7,951 ......D 6
Mahoba, 24,878 ......D 3
Mahuva, 31,668 ......C 4
Mahuva, *32,732 ......C 4
Malad, 88,287 ......B 6
Malakanagiri, 2,510 ......E 5
Malegaon, 243,474 ......C 4
Maler-Kotla, 39,543 ......D 2
Malkapur, 29,687 ......D 4
Malvan, 17,828 ......C 5
Mandi, 13,034 ......D 2
Mandla, 19,416 ......E 4
Mandsaur, 41,876 ......C 4
Mandvi, 26,609 ......B 4
Mangalore, 168,646 ......C 6
Mangalore, *234,680 ......C 6
Mangrol, 21,089 ......B 4
Manmad, 23,570 ......C 4
Manmad, *31,551 ......C 4
Mannargudi, 33,558 ......E 6
Manori, 2,492 ......B 6
Marmagao, 14,140 ......C 5
Mathura, 135,166 ......D 3
Mathura, *144,485 ......D 3
Mattancheri, 83,896 ......D 7
Mau, 48,785 ......E 3
Mayuram, 51,393 ......D 6
Meerut, 244,824 ......D 3
Meerut, *335,565 ......D 3
Mehsana, 32,577 ......C 4
Mercara, 14,453 ......D 6
Mhow, 48,032 ......D 4
Midnapore, 59,532 ......F 4
Miraj, 53,345 ......D 5
Mirzapur, 113,177 ......E 4
Modasa, 16,084 ......C 4
Mominabad, 17,443 ......D 5
Monghyr, 89,768 ......F 3
Moradabad, 205,509 ......D 3
Moradabad, *221,433 ......D 3
Morvi, 50,192 ......C 4
Mulund, 56,430 ......B 6
Murud, 10,055 ......C 5
Murwara, 46,169 ......E 4
Murwara, *60,472 ......E 4
Muzaffarabad ......B 2
Muzaffarnagar, 87,622 ......D 3
Muzaffarpur, 152,831 ......E 3
Mysore, 262,136 ......D 6
Nadiad, 78,952 ......C 4
Nagapattinam, 59,063 ......E 6
Nagapattinam, *61,305 ......E 6
Nagaur, 24,296 ......C 3
Nagercoil, 136,264 ......D 7
Nagina, 30,247 ......D 3
Nagpur, 876,020 ......D 4
Nagpur, *933,344 ......D 4
Nahan, 12,439 ......D 2
Naihati, 58,457 ......F 1
Naini Tal, 14,995 ......D 3
Naini Tal, *16,080 ......D 3
Nainpur, 13,728 ......E 4
Nalgonda, 24,383 ......D 5
Nander, 81,087 ......D 5
Nandurbar, 41,055 ......C 4
Nandyal, 42,927 ......D 5
Narayanpet, 20,504 ......D 5
Narnaul, 23,959 ......D 3
Narsinghgarh, 11,558 ......D 4
Narsinghpur, 17,940 ......D 4
Nasik, 169,451 ......C 4
Nasik, *282,782 ......C 4
Nasirabad, 24,148 ......C 3
Navsari, 51,300 ......C 4
Navsari, *53,600 ......C 4
Nellore, 134,404 ......E 6
New Delhi (cap.), 324,283 ......D 3
Nimach, 36,287 ......D 4
Nirmal, 19,896 ......D 5
Nizamabad, 79,093 ......D 5
North Lakhimpur, 6,576 ......G 3
Nova Goa (Panjim), †79,437 ......C 5
Nowgong, 8,604 ......G 3
Nowgong, *38,600 ......G 3
Okha Port, 8,909 ......B 4
Okha Port, *9,630 ......B 4
Ongole, 35,804 ......E 5
Ootacamund, 50,140 ......D 6
Orai, 29,587 ......D 3
Osmanabad, 18,868 ......D 5
Pachmarhi, 653 ......D 4
Pachmarhi, *6,142 ......D 4
Palanpur, 29,139 ......C 4
Palayankottai, 51,002 ......D 7
Palghat, 77,620 ......D 6
Pali, 33,303 ......C 3
Palni, 39,832 ......D 6
Palni, *56,909 ......D 6
Panchur, 25,131 ......F 2
Pandharpur, 45,421 ......C 5
Panihati, 93,749 ......F 1
Panipat, 67,026 ......D 3
Panjim, 179,437 ......C 5
Panna, 16,737 ......E 4
Panruti, 18,754 ......D 6
Parbhani, 36,795 ......D 5
Parlakhemundi, 22,708 ......E 5
Partapgarh, 14,573 ......C 4
Parvatipuram, 25,281 ......E 5
Patan, 50,264 ......C 4
Patiala, 154,414 ......D 2
Patna, 449,471 ......F 3
Patna, *451,520 ......F 3
Phalodi, 15,722 ......C 3
Pilibhit, 57,527 ......D 3
Point Calimere ......E 6
Pondicherry, 40,421 ......E 6
Ponnani, 22,977 ......D 6
Poona, 718,220 ......C 5
Poona, *1,123,399 ......C 5
Porbandar, 74,476 ......B 4
Porbandar, *75,081 ......B 4
Port Blair, 14,075 ......G 6
Porto Novo, 15,139 ......E 6
Proddatur, 50,616 ......D 6
Pudukkottai, 50,488 ......D 6
Punch, 10,196 ......C 2
Puri, 60,815 ......F 5
Purnea, 40,602 ......F 3
Purulia, 48,134 ......F 4
Puttur, 12,498 ......D 6
Quilon, 91,018 ......D 7
Radhanpur, 15,058 ......C 4
Raichur, 63,329 ......D 5
Raigarh, 36,933 ......E 4
Raipur, 204,632 ......E 4
Rairakhol, 2,441 ......E 4
Rajahmundry, 155,450 ......E 5
Rajapalaiyam, 71,203 ......D 7
Rajapur, 8,270 ......C 5
Rajgarh, 9,095 ......D 4
Rajkot, 270,186 ......C 4
Rajnandgaon, 44,678 ......E 4
Rajpipla, 21,426 ......C 4
Rajpur, 24,812 ......F 2
Rajpura, 11,211 ......D 2
Rajpura, *27,925 ......D 2
Rameswaram, 6,801 ......D 7
Rampur, 136,349 ......D 3
Rampur, 2,079 ......D 2
Ranchi, 137,280 ......F 4
Ranchi, *176,789 ......F 4
Ratangarh, 26,631 ......C 3
Ratlam, 87,472 ......C 4
Ratnagiri, 31,091 ......C 5
Raurkela, 90,287 ......F 4
Raxaul, 9,699 ......E 3
Rayagada, 14,537 ......E 5
Renigunta, 5,942 ......E 6
Rewa, 43,065 ......E 4
Rewari, 36,994 ......D 3
Rishra, 38,535 ......F 1
Robertsganj, 6,584 ......E 4
Sadiya ......H 3
Sagar, 97,556 ......D 4
Sagar, *120,262 ......D 4
Saharanpur, 223,459 ......D 3
Salem, 297,168 ......D 6
Samalkot, 31,924 ......E 5
Sambalpur, 38,915 ......E 4
Sambhal, 68,940 ......D 3
Sangamner, 21,729 ......C 5
Sangli, 88,753 ......C 5
Sangli, *150,407 ......C 5
Santa Cruz, 101,232 ......B 7
Santipur, 51,190 ......F 4
Sardarshahr, 32,072 ......C 3
Sarnath ......E 3
Sasaram, 37,782 ......E 4
Satara, 44,353 ......C 5
Satara, *48,709 ......C 5
Satna, 38,046 ......E 4
Savantvadi, 15,120 ......C 5
Savanur, 16,930 ......D 6
Secunderabad, 187,471 ......D 5
Sehore, 28,489 ......D 4
Seoni, 30,274 ......D 4
Serampore, 91,521 ......F 1
Seringapatam, 11,423 ......D 6
Shahdol, 22,196 ......E 4
Shahjahanpur, 121,107 ......E 3
Shahjahanpur, *129,737 ......E 3
Shajapur, 17,317 ......D 4
Sheo, 156,033 ......C 3
Sheopur, 14,591 ......D 3
Shillong, Assam, 14,089 ......G 3
Shillong, Meghalaya, 73,529 ......G 3
Shillong, *130,195 ......G 3
Shimoga, 63,764 ......D 6
Shivpuri, 28,681 ......D 3
Sholapur, 398,996 ......D 5
Shorapur, 17,689 ......D 5
Sibsagar, 15,106 ......H 3
Sidhi, 5,021 ......E 4
Sidhpur, 33,850 ......C 4
Sikar, 50,636 ......D 3
Silchar, 41,062 ......G 4
Siliguri, 65,471 ......F 3
Silvassa ......B 4
Simla, 42,597 ......D 2
Singur, 7,915 ......F 1

BRITISH INDIA

British India. *The provinces of British India were directly administered by Britain. A few areas were leased from the Indian princes.*

Indian States. *The Indian States, sometimes referred to as the "Native" or "Princely States," were under the nominal control of maharajas or other hereditary princes.*

Possessions of Other Countries in India

State or Provincial Boundaries

Other Internal Boundaries

Sirohi, 14,451 ....C 4
Sironj, 17,288 ....D 4
Sirsa, 33,363 ....D 3
Sirsi, 21,240 ....D 6
Sitapur, 53,884 ....E 3
Skardu ....D 1
Sonepur, 7,108 ....E 4
South Suburban, 307,471 ....F 2
South Suburban, *513,337 ....F 2
Srikakulam, 35,071 ....E 5
Srinagar, 285,257 ....D 2
Sundargarh, 11,329 ....E 4
Surada, 8,703 ....E 5
Surat, 368,917 ....C 4
Suratgarh, 8,330 ....C 3
Surendranagar, 48,602 ....C 4
Tanda, 32,687 ....E 3
Tehri, 4,508 ....D 2
Tellicherry, 44,763 ....C 6
Tenali, 78,525 ....E 5
Tezpur, 24,159 ....G 3
Thana, 154,770 ....B 6
Thana, *164,896 ....B 6
Thanjavur, 120,681 ....D 6
Tinsukia, 28,468 ....H 3
Tiruchendur, 15,182 ....D 7
Tiruchendur, *22,752 ....D 7
Tiruchchirappalli, 279,283 ....D 6
Tirunelveli, 87,988 ....D 7
Tirupati, 35,845 ....D 6
Tiruppattur, 30,799 ....D 6
Tiruvannamalai, 46,441 ....D 6
Titagarh, 76,429 ....F 1
Titlagarh, 7,433 ....E 4
Tollygunge ....F 2
Tonk, 43,413 ....D 3
Tranquebar, 14,754 ....E 6
Trichur, 73,038 ....D 6
Trivandrum, 336,757 ....D 7
Trivandrum, *435,566 ....D 7
Trombay, 17,258 ....B 7
Tuensang ....G 3
Tumkur, 47,277 ....D 6
Tuni, 22,452 ....E 5
Tura, 8,888 ....G 3
Tuticorin, 150,784 ....D 7
Tuticorin, *157,943 ....D 7
Udaipur, 133,368 ....C 4
Udhampur, 10,263 ....D 2
Udipi, 24,610 ....C 6
Ujjain, 157,435 ....D 4
Ulhasnagar, 137,636 ....C 5
Umrer, 22,682 ....D 4
Unnao, 29,780 ....E 3
Uran, 10,229 ....B 7
Uttarpara, 21,132 ....F 1
Vaniyambadi, 42,048 ....D 6
Vaniyambadi, *47,918 ....D 6
Varanasi, 619,822 ....E 3
Varanasi, *643,720 ....E 3
Vellore, 120,643 ....D 6
Vellore, *138,914 ....D 6
Vengurla, 12,061 ....C 5
Venkatagiri, 17,114 ....D 6
Veraval, 46,637 ....C 4
Veraval, *60,857 ....C 4
Vesava, 14,580 ....B 7
Vidisha, 27,718 ....D 4
Vijayawada, 312,822 ....D 5
Villupuram, 43,496 ....D 6
Vinukonda, 11,374 ....D 5
Virajpet, 8,138 ....D 6
Viramgam, 38,955 ....C 4
Visakhapatnam, 285,837 ....E 5
Visnagar, 25,982 ....C 4
Vizagapatam (Visakhapatnam), 285,837 ....E 5
Vizianagaram, 76,808 ....E 5
Waltair ....E 5
Warangal, 178,559 ....D 5
Wardha, 49,113 ....D 4
Wun, 18,176 ....D 5
Yanam, 7,032 ....E 5
Yellamanchili, 13,556 ....E 5
Yellandlapad ....E 5
Yeola, 21,039 ....C 4
Yeotmal, 45,587 ....D 4
Ziro ....G 3

OTHER FEATURES

Abor (hills) ....G 3
Adam's Bridge (shoals) ....D 7
Agatti (isl.), 2,411 ....C 6
Amindivi (isls.), 7,854 ....C 6
Amini (isl.), 3,530 ....C 6
Anai Mudi (mt.) ....D 6
Andaman (isls.) ....G 6
Andaman (sea) ....G 6
Androth (isl.), 4,183 ....C 6
Arabian (sea) ....B 5
Back (bay) ....B 7
Baltistan (region) ....D 1
Banas (river) ....D 3
Bengal (bay) ....F 5
Berar (region), 4,580,302 ....D 4
Betwa (river) ....D 4
Bhima (river) ....D 5
Bidyadhari (river) ....F 2
Bombay (harb.) ....B 7
Brahmaputra (river) ....G 3
Cambay (gulf) ....C 4
Camorta (isl.) ....G 7
Car Nicobar (isl.) ....G 7
Chambal (river) ....D 3
Chenab (river) ....D 2
Cherial (river) ....F 2
Chetlat (isl.), 953 ....C 6
Chilka (lake) ....F 5
Coco (channel) ....G 6
Colaba (pt.) ....B 7
Colair (lake) ....E 5
Comorin (cape) ....D 7
Coromandel Coast (reg.) ....E 6
Daman (dist.), 22,390 ....C 4
Damodar (river) ....F 4
Deccan (plateau) ....D 6
Diu (dist.), 14,280 ....C 4
Duncan (passage) ....G 6
Eastern Ghats (mts.) ....D 6
Elephanta (isl.) ....B 7
False (pt.) ....F 4
False Divi (pt.) ....E 5
Ganges (mouths) ....F 4
Ganges (Ganga) (river) ....F 3
Ghaghara (river) ....E 3
Ghea (river) ....F 1
Goa (dist.), 589,997 ....C 5
Godavari (river) ....D 5
Godwin Austen (K2) (mt.) ....D 1
Golconda (ruins) ....D 5
Great (channel) ....G 7
Great Indian (des.) ....C 3
Great Nicobar (isl.) ....G 7
Hagari (river) ....D 6
Himalaya (mts.) ....D 2
Hooghly (river) ....F 2
Indravati (river) ....E 5
Indus (river) ....D 2
Interview (isl.) ....G 6
Jhelum (river) ....C 2
Jumna (river) ....E 3
K2 (mt.) ....D 1
Kadmat (isl.), 1,851 ....C 6
Kalpeni (isl.), 2,613 ....C 7
Kamet (mt.) ....D 2
Kanchenjunga (mt.) ....F 3
Karakoram (mts.) ....D 1
Kaveri (riv.) ....D 6
Khasi (hills) ....G 3
Kiltan (isl.), 1,520 ....C 6
Kistna (Krishna) (river) ....D 5
Kunlun (range) ....D 1
Kutch (gulf) ....B 4
Kutch, Rann of (salt marsh) ....B 4
Laccadive (isls.), 12,115 ....C 6
Ladakh (region), 88,651 ....D 2
Landfall (isl.) ....G 6
Little Andaman (isl.) ....G 6
Little Nicobar (isl.) ....G 7
Luni (river) ....C 3
Lushai (hills) ....G 4
Mahanadi (river) ....E 4
Mahim (bay) ....B 7
Malabar (hill) ....B 7
Malabar (pt.) ....B 7
Malabar Coast (reg.) ....C 6
Malad (creek) ....B 7
Mannar (gulf) ....D 7
Manori (creek) ....B 7
Middle Andaman (isl.) ....G 6
Minicoy (isl.), 4,139 ....C 7
Miri (hills) ....G 3
Mishmi (hills) ....H 3
Nancowry (isl.) ....G 7
Nanda Devi (mt.) ....D 2
Nanga Parbat (mt.) ....D 1
Narcondam (isl.) ....G 6
Narmada (river) ....D 4
Nicobar (isls.) ....G 7
Nine Degree (chan.) ....C 7
North Andaman (isl.) ....G 6
North Sentinel (isl.) ....G 6
Palk (strait) ....D 7
Palmyras (pt.) ....F 4
Pangong Tso (lake) ....D 2
Penganga (river) ....D 5
Penner (river) ....D 6
Periyar (lake) ....D 7
Pitti (isl.), 80 ....C 6
Pulicat (lake) ....E 6
Rakaposhi (mt.) ....C 1
Ritchies (arch.) ....G 6
Rutland (isl.) ....G 6
Salsette (isl.), 1,566,572 ....B 7
Sambhar (lake) ....C 3
Saraswati (river) ....F 1
Sarsati (river) ....F 1
Satpura (range) ....D 4
Shipki (pass) ....D 2
Soda (plains) ....D 1
Sombrero (channel) ....G 7
Son (river) ....E 3
South Andaman (isl.) ....G 6
Suheli Par (isl.) ....C 6
Sundarbans (swamp) ....F 4
Sutlej (river) ....C 3
Tapti (river) ....D 4
Tel (river) ....E 4
Ten Degree (chan.) ....G 7
Thana (creek) ....B 7
Tillanchong (isl.) ....G 7
Tolly's Nullah (river) ....F 2
Towers of Silence ....B 7
Travancore (region) ....D 7
Tulsi (lake) ....B 6
Tungabhadra (river) ....D 5
Vehar (lake) ....B 7
Vindhya (range) ....D 4
Wardha (river) ....D 4
Western Ghats (mts.) ....C 5
Yamuna (Jumna) (river) ....E 3
Zaskar (mts.) ....D 2

MALDIVES

Maldives, 110,770 ....C 7

NEPAL

CITIES and TOWNS

Bhaktapur, 33,877 ....F 3
Bhojpur ....F 3
Biratnagar, 35,355 ....F 3
Birganj, 10,769 ....F 3
Dailekh ....E 3
Dhangarhi ....E 3
Dhankuta ....F 3
Doti ....E 3
Ilam ....F 3
Jaleswar ....F 3
Janakpur, 8,928 ....F 3
Kathmandu (capital), 121,019 ....E 3
Lalitpur, 47,713 ....E 3
Mukhtinath ....E 3
Mustang ....E 3
Nepalganj, 15,817 ....E 3
Palpa ....E 3
Pokhara, 5,413 ....E 3
Pyuthan ....E 3
Ramechhap ....F 3
Sallyana ....E 3
Simikot ....E 3

OTHER FEATURES

Annapurna (mt.) ....E 3
Bheri (river) ....E 3
Dhaulagiri (mt.) ....E 3
Everest (mt.) ....F 3
Himalaya (mts.) ....F 3
Kanchenjunga (mt.) ....F 3

PAKISTAN

PROVINCES

Baluchistan, 1,400,000 ....B 3
Capital Territory, 50,000 ....C 2
North-West Frontier, 9,500,000 ....C 2
Punjab, 36,290,000 ....C 2
Sind, 11,900,000 ....B 3

CITIES and TOWNS

Abbottabad, 31,036 ....C 2
Ahmadpur East, 20,423 ....C 3
Attock ....C 2
Bahawalnagar, 36,290 ....C 2
Bahawalpur, 84,377 ....C 3
Bahawalpur, *147,000 ....C 3
Bannu, 31,623 ....C 2
Bela, 3,139 ....B 3
Campbellpore, 19,041 ....C 2
Chagai, ‡41,263 ....A 3
Chitral ....C 1
Dadu, 19,142 ....B 3
Dera Bugti ....B 3
Dera Ghazi Khan, 47,105 ....C 3
Dera Ismail Khan, 46,140 ....C 2
Dir ....C 1
Fort Sandeman 8,058 ....B 2
Gujranwala, 196,154 ....C 2
Gujranwala, *289,000 ....C 2
Gujrat, 59,608 ....C 2
Gwadar ....A 4
Hyderabad, 434,537 ....B 3
Hyderabad, *698,000 ....B 3
Islamabad (capital), 50,000 ....C 2
Jacobabad, 35,278 ....B 3
Jhang-Maghiana, 94,971 ....C 2
Jhang-Maghiana, *118,000 ....C 2
Jhelum, 52,585 ....C 2
Kalat, 5,321 ....B 3
Karachi, 1,912,598 ....B 4
Karachi, *3,060,000 ....B 4
Khairpur, 34,144 ....B 3
Kharan Kalat, 2,692 ....A 3
Kohat, 49,854 ....C 2
Ladgasht ....A 3
Lahore, 1,296,477 ....C 2
Lahore, *1,823,000 ....C 2
Larkana, 48,008 ....B 3
Loralai, 5,519 ....B 2
Lyallpur, 425,248 ....C 2
Lyallpur, *854,000 ....C 2
Malakand ....C 2
Mardan, 77,932 ....C 2
Mardan, *113,000 ....C 2
Mastung ....B 3
Mianwali, 31,398 ....C 2
Miram Shah ....C 2
Mirpur Khas, 60,861 ....B 3
Montgomery, 15,180 ....C 2
Multan, 358,201 ....C 2
Multan, *597,000 ....C 2
Murree ....C 2
Nawabshah, 45,651 ....B 3
Nowshera ....C 2
Nushki, 3,153 ....B 3
Parachinar, 22,953 ....B 2
Peshawar, 218,691 ....C 2
Peshawar, *296,000 ....C 2
Quetta, 106,633 ....B 2
Quetta, *130,000 ....B 2
Rahimyar Khan, 43,548 ....C 3
Rahimyar Khan, *130,000 ....C 3
Rawalpindi, 340,175 ....C 2
Rawalpindi, *445,000 ....C 2
Rohri ....B 3
Saidu, 15,920 ....C 2
Sargodha, 129,291 ....C 2
Sargodha, *194,000 ....C 2
Sehwan ....B 3
Shahbandar ....B 4
Shikarpur ....B 3
Sialkot, 164,346 ....C 2
Sialkot, *167,000 ....C 2
Sibi, 13,327 ....B 3
Sukkur, 103,216 ....B 3
Sukkur, *131,000 ....B 3
Tando Adam ....B 3
Tatta, 12,786 ....B 4
Tump ....A 3
Turbat, 4,578 ....A 3
Uch ....B 3
Umarkot ....B 3
Wana ....C 2

OTHER FEATURES

Arabian (sea) ....B 5
Baroghil (pass) ....C 1
Beji (river) ....B 3
Bolan (pass) ....B 3
Chagai (hills) ....A 3
Chenab (river) ....C 2
Dasht (river) ....A 3
Hab (river) ....B 3
Hindu Kush (mts.) ....C 1
Indus (mouths) ....B 4
Indus (river) ....B 3
Jaddi, Ras (cape) ....A 4
Jhelum (river) ....C 2
Kabul (river) ....C 2
Khyber (pass) ....C 2
Kunar (river) ....C 1
Kutch, Rann of (salt marsh) ....B 4
Lora, Hamuni-i- (swamp) ....A 3
Mashkel, Hamun-i (swamp) ....A 3
Mohenjo Daro (ruins) ....B 3
Muari, Ras (cape) ....B 4
Nal (river) ....B 3
Ravi (river) ....C 2
Siahan (range) ....A 3
Sulaiman (range) ....C 3
Sutlej (river) ....C 3
Talab (river) ....A 3
Taxila (ruins) ....C 2
Tirich Mir (mt.) ....C 1
Zhob (river) ....B 2

SRI LANKA (CEYLON)

CITIES and TOWNS

Anuradhapura, 29,397 ....E 7
Badulla, 27,088 ....E 7
Batticaloa, 22,957 ....E 7
Colombo (cap.), 551,200 ....D 7
Galle, 64,942 ....D 7
Hambantota, 5,387 ....E 7
Jaffna, 94,248 ....E 7
Kalmunai, 16,488 ....E 7
Kalutara, 25,286 ....D 7
Kandy, 67,768 ....E 7
Kurunegala, 21,293 ....E 7
Mannar, 8,988 ....E 7
Matara, 32,284 ....E 7
Moratuwa, 77,632 ....D 7
Mullaittivu, 4,025 ....E 7
Negombo, 47,026 ....D 7
Nuwara Eliya, 19,988 ....E 7
Polgahawela, 5,293 ....D 7
Polonnaruwa, 5,921 ....E 7
Puttalam, 13,250 ....E 7
Ratnapura, 21,582 ....D 7
Tangalla, 7,920 ....E 7
Trincomalee, 34,872 ....E 7
Vavuniya, 7,176 ....E 7

OTHER FEATURES

Adam's (peak) ....E 7
Adam's Bridge (shoals) ....D 7
Dondra (head) ....E 7
Kirigalpota (mt.) ....E 7
Mannar (gulf) ....D 7
Palk (strait) ....D 7
Pidurutalagala (mt.) ....E 7

*City and suburbs.
†Population of sub-division.
‡Population of district.

Agriculture, Industry and Resources

DOMINANT LAND USE

Cereals (chiefly wheat, barley, corn)
Cereals (chiefly millet, sorghum)
Cereals (chiefly rice)
Cotton, Cereals
Pasture Livestock
Nomadic Livestock Herding
Forests
Nonagricultural Land

MAJOR MINERAL OCCURRENCES

Ab Asbestos
Al Bauxite
Au Gold
Be Beryl
C Coal
Cr Chromium
Cu Copper
Fe Iron Ore
G Natural Gas
Gp Gypsum
Gr Graphite
Lg Lignite
Mg Magnesium
Mi Mica
Mn Manganese
Na Salt
O Petroleum
Ti Titanium
U Uranium

Water Power
Major Industrial Areas

LAHORE–SIALKOT
Textiles, Light Industry

ASANSOL–DAMODAR VALLEY
Iron & Steel, Locomotives, Chemicals

KARACHI
Textiles, Oil Refining, Iron & Steel, Light Industry

DACCA
Textiles, Chemicals

AHMADABAD
Cotton Textiles, Chemicals

CALCUTTA
Jute & Cotton Textiles, Machinery, Chemicals, Aluminum

BOMBAY-POONA
Cotton Textiles, Machinery, Chemicals, Automobiles, Electrical Equipment, Oil Refining

JAMSHEDPUR
Iron & Steel, Metal Products, Agricultural Equipment, Nonferrous Metals

BURMA, THAILAND, INDOCHINA and MALAYA
CONIC PROJECTION
SCALE OF MILES
SCALE OF KILOMETRES
International Boundaries
Division and State Boundaries
Capitals of Countries
Division and State Capitals
Longitude East of Greenwich
Tropic of Cancer
INDIA
CHINA
BURMA
THAILAND (SIAM)
CAMBODIA
LAOS
NORTH VIETNAM
SOUTH VIETNAM
MALAYA
MALAYSIA
SINGAPORE
INDONESIA
SUMATRA
BHUTAN
BANGLADESH
KACHIN STATE
SHAN STATE
SAGAING
MANDALAY
KAYAH STATE
KAWTHOOLEI STATE
IRRAWADDY
ARAKAN
TENASSERIM
CHIN HILLS SPECIAL DIVISION
BAY OF BENGAL
ANDAMAN SEA
ANDAMAN IS. (India)
NICOBAR IS. (India)
GULF OF SIAM
GULF OF TONKIN
SOUTH CHINA SEA
HAINAN
Strait of Malacca
RANGOON
BANGKOK (Krung Thep)
Vientiane
Hanoi
Haiphong
Phnom Penh
SAIGON
Kuala Lumpur
Singapore
Mandalay
Kunming
Da Nang
Hue
Chiengmai
Moulmein
Penang (George Town)
JOHOR
Copyright by C.S. HAMMOND & Co., N.Y.

BURMA

BURMA

AREA 261,789 sq. mi.
POPULATION 27,000,000
CAPITAL Rangoon
LARGEST CITY Rangoon
HIGHEST POINT Hkakabo Razi 19,296 ft.
MONETARY UNIT kyat
MAJOR LANGUAGES Burmese, Karen, Shan
MAJOR RELIGIONS Buddhism, Tribal religions

THAILAND

AREA 198,456 sq. mi.
POPULATION 35,448,000
CAPITAL Bangkok
LARGEST CITY Bangkok
HIGHEST POINT Doi Inthanon 8,452 ft.
MONETARY UNIT baht
MAJOR LANGUAGES Thai, Lao, Chinese
MAJOR RELIGIONS Buddhism, Tribal religions

THAILAND

LAOS

AREA 91,459 sq. mi.
POPULATION 2,900,000
CAPITAL Vientiane
LARGEST CITY Vientiane
HIGHEST POINT Phu Bia 9,252 ft.
MONETARY UNIT kip
MAJOR LANGUAGES Lao, French
MAJOR RELIGION Buddhism

CAMBODIA

AREA 69,898 sq. mi.
POPULATION 6,701,000
CAPITAL Phnom Penh
LARGEST CITY Phnom Penh
HIGHEST POINT 5,948 ft.
MONETARY UNIT riel
MAJOR LANGUAGES Khmer (Cambodian), French
MAJOR RELIGION Buddhism

NORTH VIETNAM

AREA 61,293 sq. mi.
POPULATION 21,340,000
CAPITAL Hanoi
LARGEST CITY Hanoi
HIGHEST POINT Fan Si Pan 10,308 ft.
MONETARY UNIT dong
MAJOR LANGUAGES Vietnamese, Thai, Muong, Meo, Yao
MAJOR RELIGIONS Buddhism, Taoism, Confucianism

LAOS

SOUTH VIETNAM

AREA 66,263 sq. mi.
POPULATION 16,543,434
CAPITAL Saigon
LARGEST CITY Saigon
HIGHEST POINT Ngoc Linh 8,524 ft.
MONETARY UNIT piaster
MAJOR LANGUAGES Vietnamese, Chinese, Khmer, Jarai, French
MAJOR RELIGIONS Buddhism, Taoism, Confucianism, Roman Catholicism, Cao-Dai

MALAYSIA

AREA 128,308 sq. mi.
POPULATION 10,583,000
CAPITAL Kuala Lumpur
LARGEST CITY Kuala Lumpur
HIGHEST POINT Mt. Kinabalu 13,455 ft.
MONETARY UNIT Malayan dollar
MAJOR LANGUAGES Malay, Chinese, English, Tamil, Dayak, Kadazan
MAJOR RELIGIONS Islam, Confucianism, Buddhism, Tribal religions, Hinduism, Taoism

SINGAPORE

AREA 226 sq. mi.
POPULATION 2,034,000
CAPITAL Singapore
LARGEST CITY Singapore
HIGHEST POINT Bukit Timah 581 ft.
MONETARY UNIT Malayan dollar
MAJOR LANGUAGES Chinese, Malay, Tamil, English
MAJOR RELIGIONS Confucianism, Buddhism, Taoism, Hinduism, Islam, Christianity

CAMBODIA

NORTH VIETNAM

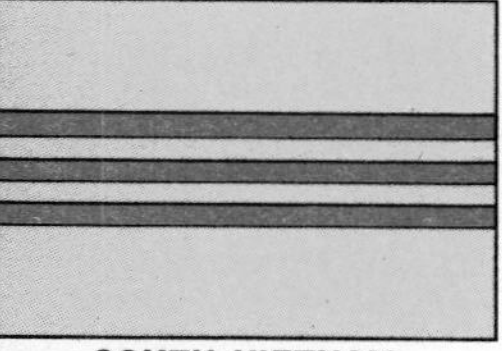

SOUTH VIETNAM

MALAYSIA

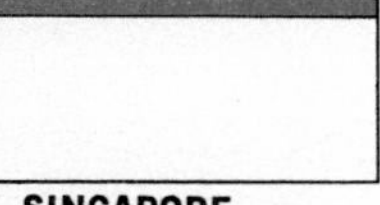

SINGAPORE

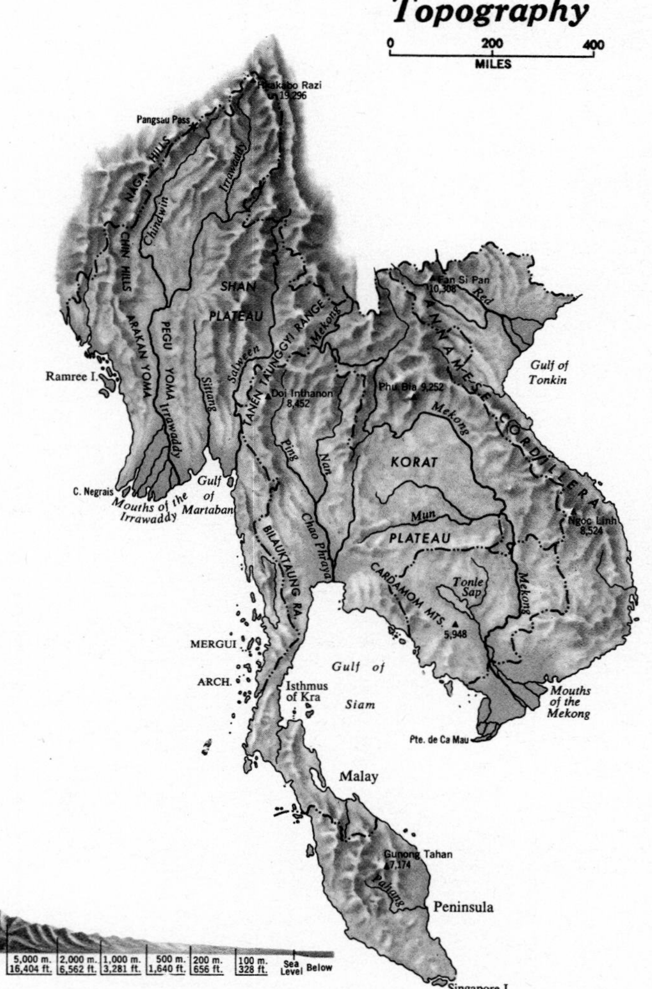

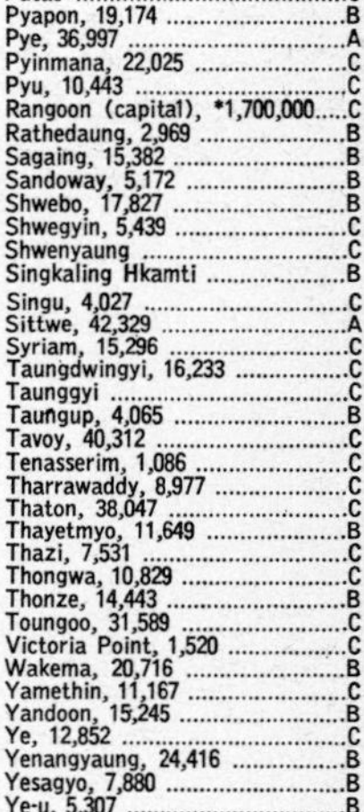

BURMA

INTERNAL DIVISIONS

Arakan (div.) ....B 3
Chin Hills (special div.) ....B 2
Irrawaddy (div.) ....B 3
Kachin (state) ....C 1
Kawthoolei (state) ....C 3
Kayah (state) ....C 3
Magwe (div.) ....B 2
Mandalay (div.) ....B 2
Pegu (div.) ....C 3
Sagaing (div.) ....B 1
Shan (state) ....C 2
Tenasserim (div.) ....C 4

CITIES and TOWNS

Allanmyo, 15,580 ....B 3
Amarapura, 11,268 ....B 2
Amherst, 6,000 ....C 3
Athok, 4,819 ....B 3
Bassein, ‡105,000 ....B 3
Bhamo, 9,821 ....C 1
Bilin, 5,248 ....C 3
Chauk, 24,464 ....B 2
Danubyu, 9,833 ....B 3
Falam ....B 3
Fort Hertz (Putao) ....C 1
Gangaw, 3,800 ....B 2
Gyobingauk, 9,922 ....C 3
Henzada, ‡100,000 ....B 3
Insein, 27,030 ....C 3
Kalemyo, 3,158 ....B 2
Kalewa, 2,230 ....B 2
Kama, 3,523 ....B 3
Kamayut, 23,032 ....C 3
Kanbalu, 3,281 ....B 2
Kani, 2,600 ....B 2
Katha, 7,648 ....C 1
Kawlin, 3,735 ....B 2
Kyaikto, 13,154 ....C 3
Kyangin, 6,073 ....B 3
Kyaukpadaung, 5,480 ....B 2
Kyaukpyu, 7,335 ....B 3
Kyaukse, 8,659 ....C 2
Kywebwe, 3,150 ....C 3
Labutta, 12,982 ....B 3
Lashio ....C 2
Letpadan, 15,896 ....C 3
Loi-kaw ....C 3
Madauk, 4,618 ....C 3
Magwe, 13,270 ....B 2
Mahlaing, 6,543 ....B 2
Mandalay, ‡300,000 ....C 2
Martaban, 5,661 ....C 3
Ma-ubin, 23,362 ....B 3
Maungdaw, 3,772 ....B 2
Mawlaik, 2,993 ....B 2
Maymyo, 22,287 ....C 2
Meiktila, 19,474 ....B 2
Mergui, 33,697 ....C 4
Minbu, 9,096 ....B 2
Minbya, 5,783 ....B 2
Minhla, 6,470 ....B 3
Mogaung, 2,920 ....C 1
Mogok, 8,334 ....C 2
Monywa, 26,297 ....B 2
Moulmein, ‡175,000 ....C 3
Mudon, 20,136 ....C 3
Myanaung, 11,155 ....B 3
Myaungmya, 24,532 ....B 3
Myebon, 3,499 ....B 2
Myingyan, 36,439 ....B 2
Myitkyina, 12,382 ....C 1
Myitnge, 3,888 ....C 2
Myohaung, 6,534 ....B 2
Nyaunglebin, 12,155 ....C 3
Pa-an, 4,139 ....C 3
Pagan, 2,824 ....B 2
Pakokku, 30,943 ....B 2
Palaw, 5,596 ....C 4
Papun ....C 3
Paungde, 17,286 ....B 3
Pegu, 47,378 ....C 3
Putao ....C 1
Pyapon, 19,174 ....B 3
Pye, 36,997 ....A 3
Pyinmana, 22,025 ....C 3
Pyu, 10,443 ....C 3
Rangoon (capital), *1,700,000 ....C 3
Rathedaung, 2,969 ....B 2
Sagaing, 15,382 ....B 2
Sandoway, 5,172 ....B 3
Shwebo, 17,827 ....B 2
Shwegyin, 5,439 ....C 3
Shwenyaung ....C 2
Singkaling Hkamti ....B 1
Singu, 4,027 ....C 2
Sittwe, 42,329 ....A 3
Syriam, 15,296 ....C 3
Taungdwingyi, 16,233 ....C 2
Taunggyi ....C 2
Taungup, 4,065 ....B 3
Tavoy, 40,312 ....C 4
Tenasserim, 1,086 ....C 5
Tharrawaddy, 8,977 ....C 3
Thaton, 38,047 ....C 3
Thayetmyo, 11,649 ....B 3
Thazi, 7,531 ....C 2
Thongwa, 10,829 ....C 3
Thonze, 14,443 ....B 3
Toungoo, 31,589 ....C 3
Victoria Point, 1,520 ....C 5
Wakema, 20,716 ....B 3
Yamethin, 11,167 ....C 2
Yandoon, 15,245 ....B 3
Ye, 12,852 ....C 4
Yenangyaung, 24,416 ....B 2
Yesagyo, 7,880 ....B 2
Ye-u, 5,307 ....B 2

OTHER FEATURES

Amya (pass) ....C 4
Andaman (sea) ....B 4
Arakan Yoma (mts.) ....B 3
Bengal (bay) ....B 3
Bilauktaung (range) ....C 4
Chaukan (pass) ....C 1
Cheduba (isl.), 2,621 ....B 3
Chin (hills) ....B 2
Chindwin (river) ....B 2
Coco (chan.) ....B 4
Combermere (bay) ....B 3
Dawna (range) ....C 3
Great Coco (isl.) ....B 4
Great Tenasserim (river) ....C 4
Hkakabo Razi (mt.) ....C 1
Indawgyi (lake) ....C 1
Inle (lake) ....C 2
Irrawaddy (river) ....B 3
Irrawaddy, Mouths of the (delta) ....B 4
Kaladan (river) ....B 2
Khao Luang (mt.) ....C 5
Loi Leng (mt.) ....C 2
Manipur (river) ....B 2
Martaban (gulf) ....C 4
Mekong (river) ....D 2
Mergui (arch.) ....C 5
Mon (river) ....B 2
Mu (river) ....B 2
Nam Hka (river) ....C 2
Nam Pawn (river) ....C 2
Nam Teng (river) ....C 2
Negrais (cape) ....B 3
Pakchan (river) ....C 5
Pangsau (pass) ....B 1
Pegu Yoma (mts.) ....B 3
Preparis (isl.) ....B 4
Ramree (isl.), 11,133 ....B 3
Salween (river) ....C 3
Shan (plateau) ....C 2
Sittang (river) ....C 3
Taungthonton (mt.) ....B 1
Tavoy (point) ....C 4
Tenasserim (isl.) ....C 4
Three Pagodas (pass) ....C 4
Victoria (mt.) ....B 2

(continued on following page)

(continued)

CAMBODIA

CITIES and TOWNS

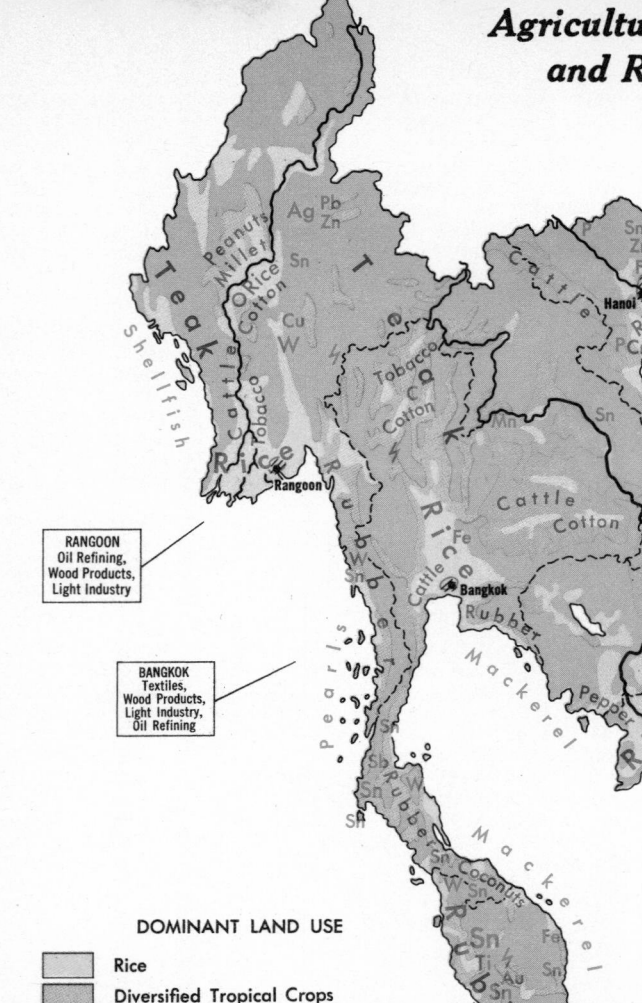

Banam, †87,048 E 5
Battambang, 38,846 D 4
Cheom Ksan E 4
Chhlong, †46,108 E 4
Chong Kal, †16,918 D 4
Kampot, 12,558 E 5
Kep, 7,565 E 5
Khemarak Phouinville D 5
Kohnieh E 4
Kompong Cham, 28,534 E 4
Kompong Chhnang, 12,847 D 4
Kompong Kleang E 4
Kompong Som, 6,578 D 5
Kompong Speu, 7,453 E 5
Kompong Thom, 9,682 E 4
Kompong Trabek, †108,227 E 5
Koulen E 4
Kratie, 11,908 E 4
Krauchmar, †63,262 E 4
Moung, †88,321 D 4
Pailin, †15,536 D 4
Phnom Penh (capital), *500,000 E 5
Phsar Babau D 4
Phsar Oudong, †50,456 E 5
Phum Rovieng, †21,151 E 4
Phum Troun E 4
Poipet D 4
Prek Po E 5
Prey Veng, 8,792 E 5
Pursat, 14,329 D 4
Ream D 5
Sambor, †11,213 E 4
Siem Pang, †8,959 E 4
Siem Reap, 10,230 D 4
Sisophon, †29,581 D 4
Sre Khtum E 4
Stung Treng, 3,369 E 4
Suong E 5
Svay Rieng, 11,184 E 5
Takeo, 11,312 E 5
Virachei, †16,912 E 4

OTHER FEATURES

Angkor Wat (ruins) E 4
Dang Raek, Phanom (mts.) D 4
Joncs (plain) E 5
Kas Kong (isl.) D 5
Kas Tang (isl.) D 5
Kong, Kas (isl.) D 5
Mekong (river) E 4
Phanom Dang Raek (mts.) D 4
Preapatang (rapids) E 4
Rong, Koh (isl.) D 5
Samit (point) D 5
Se Khong (river) E 4
Se San (river) E 4
Siam (gulf) D 5
Srepok (river) E 4
Stung Sen (river) E 4
Tang, Kas (isl.) D 5
Tonle Sap (lake) D 4

LAOS

CITIES and TOWNS

Attopeu, 2,750 E 4
Ban Bung Sai E 4
Borikhane D 3
Botene D 2
Boun Neua, 2,500 D 2
Boun Tai, †11,681 D 2
Champassak, 3,500 E 4
Houei Sai, 1,500 D 2
Hua Muong D 2
Keng Kok, 2,000 E 3
Kham Keut, †31,206 E 3
Khone E 4
Khong, 1,750 E 4
Khong Sédone, 2,000 E 4
Luang Prabang, 7,596 D 3
Mahaxay, 2,000 E 3
Muong Beng, †2,305 D 2
Muong Bo D 3
Muong Hai, †476 D 2
Muong Hôm D 3
Muong Lan, †836 D 3
Muong May E 4
Muong Phalane E 3
Muong Phine E 3
Muong Phong D 3
Muong Sai, 2,000 D 2
Muong Sing, 1,091 D 2
Muong Son D 2
Muong Song Khone, 2,000 E 3
Muong Wapi E 4
Muong Yo D 2
Nam Tha, 1,459 D 2
Napé E 3
Nong Het D 3
Ou Neua, †4,300 D 2
Pak Beng, 12,964 D 3
Pak Hin Boun, 1,750 E 3
Pak Sane, 2,500 D 3
Paklay, 2,000 D 3
Pakse, 8,000 E 4
Phiafay, †17,216 E 4
Phon Tiou E 3
Phong Saly, 2,500 D 2
Sam Neua, 3,000 D 2
Saravane, 2,350 E 4
Savannakhet, 8,500 E 3
Sayaboury, 2,500 D 3
Tchepone, 1,250 E 3
Tha-deua D 3
Thakhek, 5,500 E 3
Tourakom D 3
Vang Vieng, 1,250 D 3
Vien Phou Kha D 2
Vientiane (capital), 132,253 D 3
Vientiane, *162,297 D 3
Xieng Khouang, 3,500 D 3

OTHER FEATURES

Bolovens (plateau) E 4
Hou, Nam (river) D 2
Jars (plain) D 3
Mekong (river) D 3
Nam Hou (river) D 2
Nam Tha (river) D 2
Phu Bia (mt.) D 3
Phu Co Pi (mt.) E 3
Phu Loi (mt.) D 2
Rao Co (mt.) E 3
Se Khong (river) E 4
Tha, Nam (river) D 2
Tran Ninh (plateau) D 3

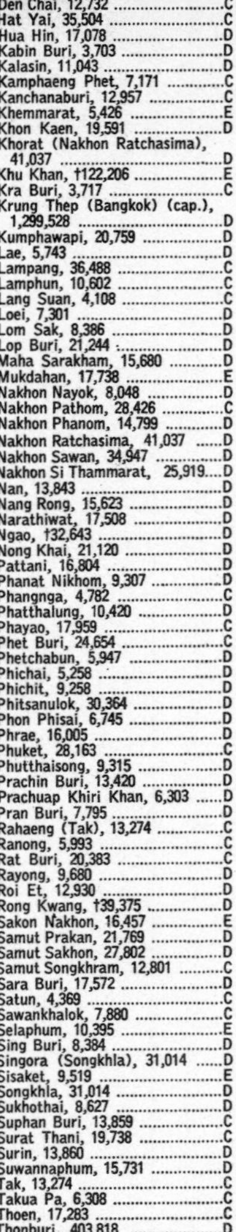

MALAYSIA★

STATES

Johor, 1,236,412 D 7
Kedah, 885,775 D 6
Kelantan, 645,200 D 6
Melaka, 391,003 D 7
Negeri Sembilan, 488,318 D 7
Pahang, 405,156 D 7
Perak, 1,568,024 D 6
Perlis, 113,350 D 6
Pinang, 724,169 D 6
Selangor, 1,339,142 D 7
Terengganu, 360,388 D 6

CITIES and TOWNS

Alor Gajah, 2,135 D 7
Alor Setar, 52,915 D 6
Baling, 4,121 D 6
Bandar Maharani, 39,046 D 7
Bandar Penggaram, 39,294 D 7
Batu Gajah, 10,143 D 6
Bentong, 18,845 D 7
Butterworth, 42,504 D 6
Cameron Highlands D 6
Chukai, 10,803 D 6
Gemas, 4,873 D 7
George Town (Pinang), 234,903 C 6
Ipoh, 125,770 D 6
Johor Baharu, 74,909 F 5
Kajang, 9,630 D 7
Kampar, 24,602 D 6
Kangar, 6,064 D 6
Kelang, 75,649 D 7
Keluang, 31,181 D 7
Kota Baharu, 38,103 D 6
Kota Tinggi, 7,475 F 5
Kuala Dungun, 12,515 D 6
Kuala Lipis, 8,753 D 6
Kuala Lumpur (cap.), 325,000 D 7
Kuala Pilah, 12,024 D 7
Kuala Selangor, 2,285 D 7
Kuala Terengganu, 29,446 D 6
Kuantan, 23,034 D 7
Kulai, 7,759 F 5
Lumut, 2,947 D 6
Melaka (Malacca), 69,848 D 7
Mersing, 7,228 E 7
Pekan, 2,070 D 7
Pekan Nanas, 7,129 F 5
Pinang, 234,903 C 6
Pontian Kechil, 8,459 E 5
Port Dickson, 4,416 D 7
Port Swettenham, 16,925 D 7
Port Weld, 2,260 D 6
Raub, 15,363 D 6
Segamat, 18,445 D 7
Sematan D 6
Seremban, 52,091 D 7
Sungei Petani, 22,916 C 6
Taiping, 48,206 D 6
Tanah Merah, 775 D 6
Telok Anson, 37,042 D 6
Tumpat, 8,946 D 6

OTHER FEATURES

Aur, Pulau (isl.), 415 E 7
Belumut, Gunong (mt.) D 7
Gelang, Tanjong (point) D 6
Johor (river) F 5
Johore (str.) E 6
Kelantan (river) D 6
Langkawi, Palau (isl.), 16,535 C 6
Ledang, Gunong (mt.) D 7
Lima, Pulau (isl.) F 6
Malacca (str.) D 7
Malaya (region), 9,000,000 E 6
Pahang (river) D 7
Pangkor, Pulau (isl.), 2,580 D 6
Perak, Gunong (mt.) D 6
Perhentian (isls.), 447 D 6
Pulai (river) E 5
Pinang, Pulau (isl.), 338,898 C 6
Ramunia, Tanjong (point) F 6
Redang, Pulau (isl.), 470 D 6
Sedili Kechil, Tanjong (point) F 5
Tahan, Gunong (mt.) D 6
Temiang, Bukit (mt.) D 6
Tenggol, Pulau (isl.), 2,386 D 6
Tinggi, Pulau (isl.), 440 E 7

SINGAPORE

CITIES and TOWNS

Jurong E 6
Nee Soon, 6,043 F 6
Paya Lebar, 45,440 F 6
Serangoon, 3,798 F 6
Singapore (cap.), *1,987,900 F 6
Woodlands, 737 F 6

OTHER FEATURES

Johore (str.) E 6
Keppel (harb.) F 6
Main (str.) F 6
Singapore (str.) F 6
Tekong Besar, Pulau (isl.), 4,074 F 6

THAILAND (SIAM)

CITIES and TOWNS

Amnat, 11,335 E 4
Ang Thong, 6,458 C 4
Ayutthaya, 24,597 C 4
Ban Aranyaprathet, 11,112 D 4
Ban Kantang, 5,076 C 6
Ban Khlong Yai, 3,815 D 5
Ban Pak Phanang, 11,963 D 5
Ban Pua, 12,317 D 3
Ban Sattahip, 22,942 D 4
Ban Tha Uthen, 7,297 D 3
Bang Lamung, 9,087 D 4
Bang Saphan, 6,959 C 5
Bangkok (capital), 1,299,528 D 4
Bangkok, *2,000,000 D 4
Banphot Phisai, 6,036 C 3
Buriram, 12,579 D 4
Chachoengsao, 19,809 G 4
Chai Badan, 6,158 D 4
Chai Buri, †31,135 D 3
Chainat, 4,652 D 4
Chaiya, 3,607 C 5
Chaiyaphum, 9,633 D 4
Chang Khoeng, 6,037 D 4
Chanthaburi, 10,780 D 4
Chiang Dao, 8,017 C 3
Chiang Khan, 5,810 D 3
Chiang Rai, 11,663 C 3
Chiang Saen, 5,443 C 2
Chiengmai, 65,600 C 3
Chon Buri, 32,496 D 4
Chumphon, 9,342 C 5
Dan Sai, 6,710 D 3
Den Chai, 12,732 C 3
Hat Yai, 35,504 C 6
Hua Hin, 17,078 D 4
Kabin Buri, 3,703 D 4
Kalasin, 11,043 D 3
Kamphaeng Phet, 7,171 C 3
Kanchanaburi, 12,957 C 4
Khemmarat, 5,426 E 4
Khon Kaen, 19,591 D 3
Khorat (Nakhon Ratchasima), 41,037 D 4
Khu Khan, †122,206 E 4
Kra Buri, 3,717 C 5
Krung Thep (Bangkok) (cap.), 1,299,528 D 4
Kumphawapi, 20,759 D 3
Lae, 5,743 D 3
Lampang, 36,488 C 3
Lamphun, 10,602 C 3
Lang Suan, 4,108 C 5
Loei, 7,301 D 3
Lom Sak, 8,386 D 3
Lop Buri, 21,244 D 4
Maha Sarakham, 15,680 D 3
Mukdahan, 17,738 E 3
Nakhon Nayok, 8,048 D 4
Nakhon Pathom, 28,426 C 4
Nakhon Phanom, 14,799 D 3
Nakhon Ratchasima, 41,037 D 4
Nakhon Sawan, 34,947 D 4
Nakhon Si Thammarat, 25,919 D 5
Nan, 13,843 D 3
Nang Rong, 15,623 D 4
Narathiwat, 17,508 D 6
Ngao, †32,643 D 3
Nong Khai, 21,120 D 3
Pattani, 16,804 D 6
Phanat Nikhom, 9,307 D 4
Phangnga, 4,782 C 5
Phatthalung, 10,420 D 6
Phayao, 17,959 C 3
Phet Buri, 24,654 C 4
Phetchabun, 5,947 D 3
Phichai, 5,258 D 3
Phichit, 9,258 D 3
Phitsanulok, 30,364 D 3
Phon Phisai, 6,745 D 3
Phrae, 16,005 D 3
Phuket, 28,163 C 6
Phutthaisong, 9,315 D 4
Prachin Buri, 13,420 D 4
Prachuap Khiri Khan, 6,303 D 5
Pran Buri, 7,795 D 4
Rahaeng (Tak), 13,274 C 3
Ranong, 5,993 C 5
Rat Buri, 20,383 C 4
Rayong, 9,680 D 4
Roi Et, 12,930 D 4
Rong Kwang, †39,375 D 3
Sakon Nakhon, 16,457 E 3
Samut Prakan, 21,769 D 4
Samut Sakhon, 27,802 D 4
Samut Songkhram, 12,801 C 4
Sara Buri, 17,572 D 4
Satun, 4,369 C 6
Sawankhalok, 7,880 C 3
Selaphum, 10,395 E 3
Sing Buri, 8,384 D 4
Singora (Songkhla), 31,014 D 6
Sisaket, 9,519 E 4
Songkhla, 31,014 D 6
Sukhothai, 8,627 D 3
Suphan Buri, 13,859 C 4
Surat Thani, 19,738 C 5
Surin, 13,860 D 4
Suwannaphum, 15,731 D 4
Tak, 13,274 C 3
Takua Pa, 6,308 C 5
Thoen, 17,283 C 3
Thonburi, 403,818 D 4
Thonburi, *460,000 D 4
Trang, 17,158 C 6
Trat, 3,813 D 4
Ubon, 27,092 E 4
Udon Thani, 29,965 D 3
Uthai Thani, 10,729 C 4
Uttaradit, 9,120 D 3
Warin Chamrap, 7,067 E 4
Yala, 18,083 D 6
Yasothon, 9,717 D 4

OTHER FEATURES

Amya (pass) C 4
Bilauktaung (range) C 4
Chao Phraya, Mae Nam (river) D 4
Chi, Mae Nam (river) D 3
Chong Pak Phra (cape) C 5
Dang Raek, Phanom (mts.) D 4
Doi Inthanon (mt.) C 3
Doi Pha Hom Pok (mt.) C 2
Doi Pia Fai (mt.) D 4
Kao Prawa (mt.) C 3
Khao Luang (mt.) C 5
Khwae Noi, Mae Nam (river) C 4
Ko Chang (isl.) D 4
Ko Kut (isl.) D 5
Ko Lanta (isl.), 9,486 C 6
Ko Phangan (isl.) C 5
Ko Phuket (isl.), 75,652 C 5
Ko Samui (isl.), 30,818 D 5
Ko Tao (isl.) C 5
Ko Terutao (isl.) C 6
Ko Thalu (isls.) C 5
Kra (isthmus) C 5
Laem Pho (cape) D 6
Laem Talumphuk (cape) D 5
Luang (mt.) C 5
Mae Klong, Mae Nam (river) C 4
Mekong (river) E 3
Mulayit Taung (mt.) C 3
Mun, Mae Nam (river) D 4
Nan, Mae Nam (river) D 3
Nong Lahan (lake) D 3
Pa Sak, Mae Nam (river) D 4
Pakchan (river) C 5
Phanom Dang Raek (mts.) D 4
Ping, Mae Nam (river) C 3
Samui (str.) D 5
Siam (gulf) D 5
Tapi, Mae Nam (river) C 5
Tha Chin, Mae Nam (river) C 4
Thale Luang (lagoon) D 6
Three Pagodas (pass) C 4
Wang, Mae Nam (river) C 3

VIETNAM (NORTH)

CITIES and TOWNS

Ba Don E 3
Bac Can E 2
Bac Ninh, 22,560 E 2
Bai Thuong E 3
Bao Ha D 2
Bao Lac E 2
Cao Bang E 2
Co Lieu E 3
Con Cuong E 3
Cua Rao E 3
Dien Bien Phu D 2
Dong Hoi E 3
Ha Giang E 2
Ha Tinh E 3
Haiphong, 182,496 E 2
Haiphong, ‡*600,000 E 2
Hanoi (capital), 414,620 E 2
Hanoi, ‡*1,400,000 E 2
Hoa Binh E 2
Hoi Xuan E 2
Hon Gay, ‡100,000 E 2
Huong Khe E 3
Ke Bao E 2
Lai Chau D 2
Lang Mo E 3
Lang Son, 15,071 E 2
Lao Cai D 2
Loc Chou E 3
Luc An Chau E 2
Mon Cay E 2
Muong Khuong E 2
Nam Dinh, ‡125,000 E 2
Nghia Lo E 2
Ninh Binh E 2
Phuc Loi E 3
Phu Dien E 3
Phu Lang Thuong E 2
Phuly E 2
Phu Qui E 3
Phu Tho, 10,888 E 2
Quang Khe E 3
Quang Yen E 2
Ron E 3
Son La D 2
Son Tay, 19,213 E 2
Thai Binh, 14,739 E 2
Thai Nguyen, ‡110,000 E 2
Thanh Hoa, 31,211 E 3
That Khe E 2
Tien Yen E 2
Trung Khanh Phu E 2
Tuyen Quang E 2
Van Hoa E 2
Van Yen E 2
Vinh, 43,954 E 3
Vinh Yen E 2
Vu Liet E 3
Yen Bai E 2
Yen Minh E 2

OTHER FEATURES

Bach Long Vi, Dao (isl.) F 2
Black (river) D 2
Cat Ba, Dao (isl.) E 2
Dao Bach Long Vi (isl.) F 2
Demilitarized Zone E 3
Fan Si Pan (mt.) D 2
Lay (cape) E 3
Mui Duong (cape) E 3
Nightingale (Bach Long Vi) (isl.) F 2
Rao Co (mt.) E 3
Red (river) E 2
Sip Song Chau Thai (mts.) D 2
Song Bo (Black) (river) D 2
Song Ca (river) E 3
Song Coi (Red) (river) E 2
Tigre (isl.) E 3
Tonkin (gulf) E 3

VIETNAM (SOUTH)

CITIES and TOWNS

An Khe F 4
An Loc, 15,276 E 5
Bac Lieu (Vinh Loi), 53,841 E 5
Ban Me Thuot, 68,771 F 4
Bien Hoa, 87,135 E 5
Binh Dinh F 4
Binh Son F 4
Bong Son F 4
Bu Dop E 4
Cam Ranh, 84,281 F 5
Can Tho, 92,132 E 5
Cao Lanh, 16,482 E 5
Cap Saint-Jacques (Vung Tau), 79,270 E 5
Chau Phu, 37,175 E 5
Cheo Reo F 4
Chu Lai F 4
Da Lat, 83,992 F 5
Da Nang, 363,343 E 3
Dak Bla F 4
Dam Doi E 5
Di Linh F 5
Duong Dong D 5
Go Cong, 33,191 E 5
Go Quao E 5
Ha Tien E 5
Ham Tan, 19,323 F 5
Hoa Da F 5
Hoi An, 45,059 F 4
Hon Chong E 5
Hue, 170,884 E 3
Khanh Hoa F 4
Khanh Hung, 59,015 E 5
Kontum, 33,554 F 4
Loc Ninh E 5
Long Xuyen, 72,658 E 5
Mo Duc F 4
Moc Hoa, 3,191 E 5
My Tho, 109,967 E 5
Nha Trang, 103,184 F 4
Phan Rang, 33,377 F 5
Phan Ri F 5
Phan Thiet, 80,122 F 5
Phoc Tuy, 16,419 E 5
Phu Cuong, 28,267 E 5
Phu Loc E 3
Phu My F 4
Phu Rieng E 5
Phu Vinh (Tra Vinh), 48,485 E 5
Pleiku, 23,720 E 4
Pleime E 4
Quan Long, 59,331 E 5
Quang Nam E 4
Quang Ngai, 14,119 F 4
Quang Tri, 15,874 E 3
Qui Nhon, 116,821 F 4
Rach Gia, 66,745 E 5
Sa Dec, 51,867 E 5
Saigon (capital), 1,706,869 E 5
Song Cau F 4
Son Ha F 4
Tam Ky, 38,532 F 4
Tam Quan F 4
Tan An, 38,082 E 5
Tay Ninh, 22,957 E 5
Tra Vinh, 48,485 E 5
Truc Giang, 68,629 E 5
Tuy Hoa, 63,552 F 4
Van Gia F 4
Vinh Loi, 53,841 E 5
Vinh Long, 30,667 E 5
Vo Dat E 5
Vung Tau, 79,270 E 5

OTHER FEATURES

Batangan (cape) F 4
Bên Gôi (bay) F 4
Ca Mau (Mui Bai Bung) (pt.) E 5
Cam Ranh (bay) F 5
Chon May (bay) E 3
Chu Yang Sin (mt.) F 4
Con Son (isls.), 3,147 E 5
Cu Lao Hon (isls.) F 5
Dama, Poulo (isls.) D 5
Dao Phu Quoc (isl.) D 5
Darlac (plateau) F 4
Demilitarized Zone E 3
Dent du Tigre (mt.) E 3
Deux Frères, Les (isls.) E 5
Hon Khoai (isl.) E 5
Hon Panjang (isl.) D 5
Ia Drang (riv.) E 4
Joncs (plain) E 5
Ke Ga (point) F 5
Kontum (plateau) E 4
Lang Bian (mts.) F 4
Mekong, Mouths of the (delta) E 5
Mui Bai Bung (pt.) E 5
Mui Dinh (cape) F 5
Nam Tram (cape) F 4
Nui Ba Den (mt.) E 5
Phu Quoc, Dao (isl.) D 5
Poulo Dāma (isls.) D 5
Poulo Way (isls.) D 5
Se San (river) E 4
Siam (gulf) D 5
Song Ba (river) F 4
Song Cai (river) F 4
South China (sea) F 4
Varella (cape) F 4
Way, Poulo (isls.) D 5

★See page 84 for other Malaysian entries.
*City and suburbs.
†Population of sub-division.

‡City populations courtesy of Kingsley Davis, Office of Int'l Pop. & Urban Research, Inst. of Int'l Studies, Univ. of California.

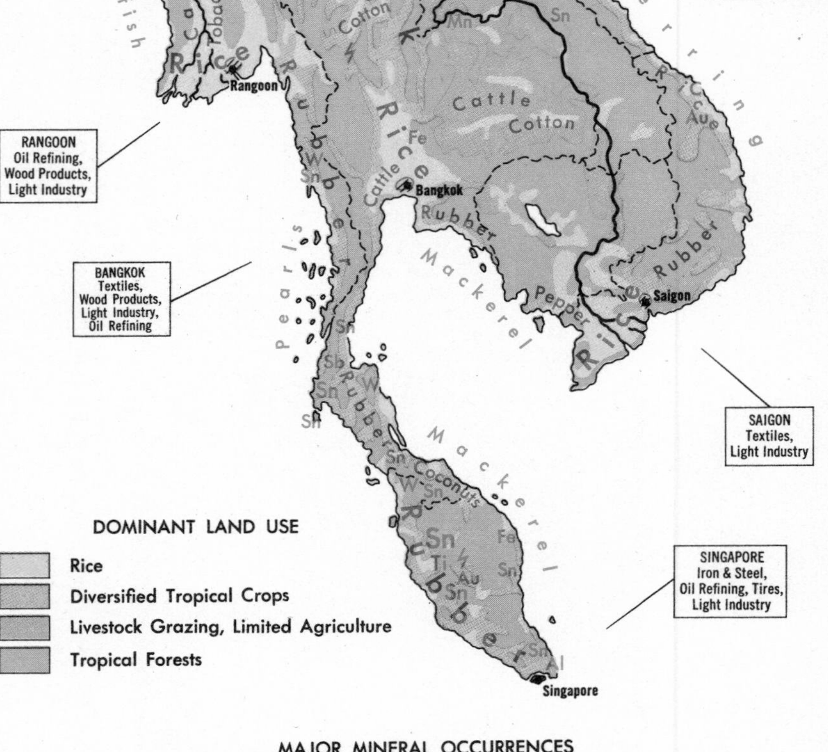

CHINA (MAINLAND)

AREA 3,691,506 sq. mi.
POPULATION 740,000,000
CAPITAL Peking
LARGEST CITY Shanghai
HIGHEST POINT Mt. Everest 29,028 ft.
MONETARY UNIT yüan
MAJOR LANGUAGES Chinese, Chuang, Uigur, Yi, Tibetan, Miao, Mongol
MAJOR RELIGIONS Confucianism, Buddhism, Taoism, Islam

CHINA (TAIWAN)

AREA 13,948 sq. mi.
POPULATION 14,577,000
CAPITAL Taipei
LARGEST CITY Taipei
HIGHEST POINT Hsinkao Shan 12,959 ft.
MONETARY UNIT new Taiwan dollar
MAJOR LANGUAGES Chinese, Formosan
MAJOR RELIGIONS Confucianism, Buddhism, Taoism, Christianity, Tribal religions

MONGOLIA

AREA 604,247 sq. mi.
POPULATION 1,300,000
CAPITAL Ulan Bator
LARGEST CITY Ulan Bator
HIGHEST POINT Tabun Bogdo 15,266 ft.
MONETARY UNIT tugrik
MAJOR LANGUAGES Mongolian, Kazakh
MAJOR RELIGION Buddhism

HONG KONG

AREA 398 sq. mi.
POPULATION 4,089,000
CAPITAL Victoria
MONETARY UNIT Hong Kong dollar
MAJOR LANGUAGES Chinese, English
MAJOR RELIGIONS Confucianism, Buddhism, Christianity

MACAO

AREA 6.2 sq. mi.
POPULATION 292,000
CAPITAL Macao
MONETARY UNIT pataca
MAJOR LANGUAGES Chinese, Portuguese
MAJOR RELIGIONS Confucianism, Buddhism, Taoism, Christianity

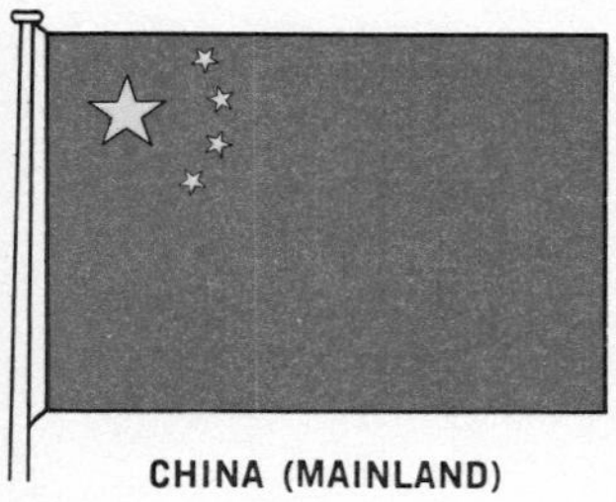

CHINA (MAINLAND) 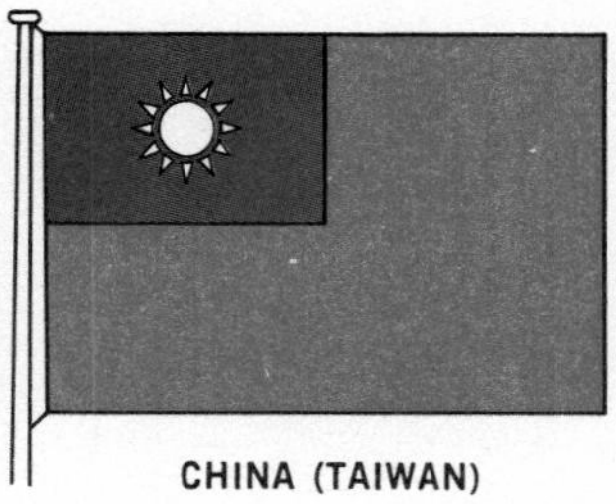 | CHINA (TAIWAN)  | MONGOLIA

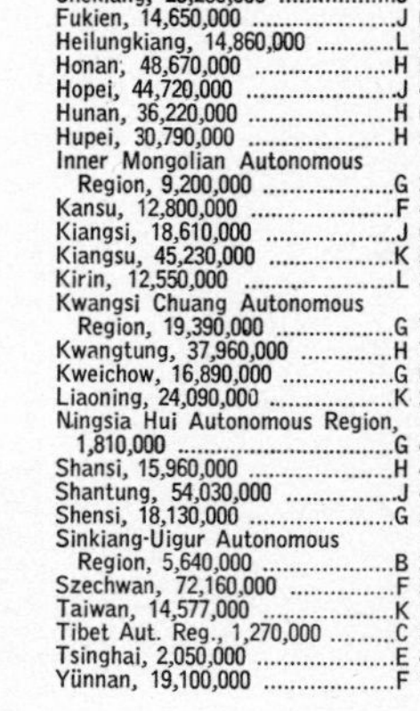

CHINA AND MONGOLIA TRANSPORTATION

SCALE OF MILES: 0 – 500 – 1000

- Railroads
- Under Construction
- Connecting Roads
- Under Construction
- Navigable Rivers
- Canals
- Major Seaports

CHINA

PROVINCES

Anhwei, 33,560,000	J 5
Chekiang, 25,280,000	J 6
Fukien, 14,650,000	J 6
Heilungkiang, 14,860,000	L 2
Honan, 48,670,000	H 5
Hopei, 44,720,000	J 4
Hunan, 36,220,000	H 6
Hupei, 30,790,000	H 5
Inner Mongolian Autonomous Region, 9,200,000	G 3
Kansu, 12,800,000	F 4
Kiangsi, 18,610,000	J 6
Kiangsu, 45,230,000	K 5
Kirin, 12,550,000	L 3
Kwangsi Chuang Autonomous Region, 19,390,000	G 7
Kwangtung, 37,960,000	H 7
Kweichow, 16,890,000	G 6
Liaoning, 24,090,000	K 3
Ningsia Hui Autonomous Region, 1,810,000	G 4
Shansi, 15,960,000	H 4
Shantung, 54,030,000	J 4
Shensi, 18,130,000	G 5
Sinkiang-Uigur Autonomous Region, 5,640,000	B 3
Szechwan, 72,160,000	F 5
Taiwan, 14,577,000	K 7
Tibet Aut. Reg., 1,270,000	C 5
Tsinghai, 2,050,000	E 4
Yünnan, 19,100,000	F 7

CITIES and TOWNS†

Ahpa	F 5
Aicheng	G 8
Aigun	L 1
Aihui (Aigun)	L 1
Aliho	K 1
Altai	C 2
Amoy, 400,000	J 7
Ankang	G 5
Anking, 160,000	J 5
Anshan, 1,500,000	K 3
Anshun, 40,000	G 6
Ansi	E 3
Anta, 110,000	L 2
Antung (Tantung), 450,000	K 3
Anyang, 225,000	H 4
Aqsu	B 3
Atushi, 5,000	A 4
Awati	B 3
Baba Hatim	B 4
Bai	B 3
Barkha	B 5
Barkhatu	B 4
Barkol	D 3
Batang	E 6
Bayinhot	F 4
Canton, 2,300,000	H 7
Chalainor	J 2
Chamdo	E 5
Changchih, 300,000	H 4
Changchow, 400,000	J 5
Changchow, 81,200	J 7
Changchun, 1,500,000	K 3
Changki	C 3
Changpeh	H 3
Changsha, 850,000	H 6
Changteh, 225,000	H 6
Changting	J 6
Changyeh, 45,000	E 4
Chankiang, 220,000	H 7
Chaoan (Chaochow), 101,000	J 7
Chaochow, 101,000	J 7
Chaotung, 50,000	F 6
Chaoyang, 30,000	J 3
Charkhliq	C 4
Chefoo, 180,000	K 4
Chendo	E 5
Chengan	G 6
Chengchow, 1,500,000	H 5
Chengteh, 200,000	J 3
Chengtu, 2,000,000	F 5
Chenhsien, 50,000	H 6
Chenpa	G 5
Chenyüan	G 6
Chenyüeh	F 7
Cherchen	C 4
Chiai, 221,817	K 7
Chiehmo (Cherchen)	C 4
Chihfeng, 49,000	J 3
Chihshui	G 6
Chihtan	G 4
Chimunai	C 2
Chinchow	G 7
Chinchow, 750,000	J 3
Chinkiang, 250,000	K 5
Chinsi, 45,000	K 3
Chinwangtao, 400,000	K 4
Chira	B 4
Chomo Dzong	D 6
Chüanchow, 130,000	J 7
Chucheng	J 4
Chuchow, 350,000	H 6
Chuguchak	B 2
Chühsien	J 6
Chumatien, 45,000	H 5
Chunghsin	K 7
Chungking, 3,500,000	G 6
Chungning	G 4
Chungshan, 135,000	H 7
Chungtien	E 6
Chushul	D 6
Dairen (in Lüta)	K 4
Denchin	E 5
Draya	E 5
Drepung	D 6
Durbuljin	B 2
Ed Dzong	D 5
Enshih	G 5
Erhlien	H 3
Fatshan, 120,000	H 7
Fengfeng, 45,000	H 4
Fenghsien	G 5
Fengkieh	G 5
Fengning	J 3
Fenyang, 25,000	H 4
Foochow, 900,000	J 6
Fowyang, 75,000	J 5
Fuchin	M 2
Fuhai	C 2
Fushun, 1,700,000	K 3
Fusin, 350,000	K 3
Fusingchen, 20,000	F 7
Fuyü, 62,969	L 2
Fuyüan	M 2
Gartok	B 5
Giamda Dzong (Taichao)	D 5
Golmo, 40,000	D 4
Gulo Gomba	B 5
Guma	A 4
Gyangtse	C 6
Gyatsa Dzong	D 6
Haikow (Hoihow), 500,000	H 7
Hailar, 60,000	J 2
Hailun	L 2
Hailung, 20,000	L 3
Hami	D 3
Hanchung, 120,000	G 5
Hangchow, 1,100,000	J 5
Hankow (in Wuhan)	H 5
Hantan, 500,000	H 4
Hanyang (in Wuhan)	H 5
Harbin, 2,750,000	L 2
Hengshui	J 4
Hengyang, 310,000	H 6
Hingi	G 6
Hochih	G 7
Hochwan, 75,000	G 5
Hofei, 400,000	J 5
Hofeng	C 2
Hoihow, 500,000	H 7
Hokang, 350,000	M 2
Hoppo, 80,000	G 7
Hotien (Khotan)	A 4
Hotso	F 5
Hsüchang, 58,000	H 5

(continued on following page)

CHINA (continued)

Hsünkow L 2
Huhehot, 700,000 H 3
Huma L 1
Hunchun, 13,246 M 3
Hunkiang L 3
Huocheng B 3
Hwainan, 350,000 J 5
Hwaiteh, 60,000 K 3
Hwangchung F 4
Hwangling G 4
Hwangshih, 200,000 J 5
Hwangyüan F 4
Hweili F 6
Hwohsien H 4
Ichang, 150,000 H 5
Ichun, 200,000 L 2
Ierhsieh J 2
Iliang F 7
Ining (Kuldja), 160,000 B 3
Ipin, 275,000 F 6
Ishan G 7
Jechiang (Charkhliq) C 4
Jyekundo E 5
Kaifeng, 330,000 J 5
Kailu K 3
Kalgan, 1,000,000 J 3
Kanchow, 135,000 H 6
Kangting F 6
Kantse F 5
Kaohsiung, 719,899 J 7
Karamai, 43,000 B 2
Kashgar, 175,000 A 4
Kashing, 132,000 K 5
Keelung, 304,740 K 6
Kelpin (Koping) A 3
Kenho K 1
Keriya B 4
Khabakhe C 2
Khana Abasa H 3
Khetinsiring D 5
Khobuk-Saur (Hofeng) C 2
Khotan A 4
Kiamusze, 275,000 L 2
Kian, 100,000 J 6
Kiangling H 5
Kiaoho L 3
Kiaohsien K 4
Kiayükwan E 4
Kienko G 5
Kienow J 6
Kienshui F 7
Kienyang, 50,000 H 6
Kinghung E 7
Kingku F 7
Kingpeng J 3
Kingtehchen, 300,000 J 6
Kingyang G 4
Kinhwa, 46,200 J 6
Kinta E 3
Kirin, 1,200,000 L 3
Kishow G 6
Kisi, 350,000 M 2
Kitai C 3
Kiuchüan, 50,000 E 4
Kiukiang, 120,000 J 6
Kiungshan H 8
Kokiu, 250,000 F 7
Kongmoon, 150,000 H 7
Koping A 3
Kucha B 3
Kueitun C 3
Kulang F 4
Kuldja, 160,000 B 3
Kungliu B 3
Kunming, 1,700,000 F 6
Kurla C 3
Kütsing F 6
Kuyang G 3
Kuyüan G 4
Kwanghwa H 5
Kwangnan G 7
Kweilin, 225,000 G 6
Kweiping H 7
Kweisui (Huhehot), 700,000 H 3
Kweiyang, 1,500,000 G 6
Kweiyang H 6
Laiyang K 4
Lanchow, 1,500,000 F 4
Lantsang E 7
Leiyang H 6
Lhakang Dzong D 6
Lhasa, 175,000 D 6
Lhatse Dzong C 6
Lhuntse Dzong D 6
Liangtang G 5
Liaoyang, 250,000 K 3
Liaoyüan, 300,000 L 3
Lienyünkang, 300,000 J 5
Lihsien H 6
Likiang F 6
Linchwan, 45,000 J 6
Linfen H 4
Lingling H 6
Linhai K 6
Linho G 3
Linhsien H 7
Linkow M 2
Linping H 7
Linsi J 3
Linsia, 75,000 F 4
Lintsang E 7
Lintsing, 45,000 J 4
Liping G 6
Lishui K 6
Litang F 6
Liuchow, 250,000 G 7
Loho, 55,000 H 5
Loshan, 250,000 F 6
Loyang, 750,000 H 5
Luchow, 225,000 F 6
Luhsi E 7
Lukchun D 3
Lungchen, 14,000 L 2
Lungyen J 6
Lupeh K 3
Lüshun (Port Arthur) (in Lüta) K 4
Lüta, ‡4,000,000 K 4
Maerhkang F 5
Mahai D 4
Manass C 3
Manchouli, 30,000 J 2
Mangyai D 4
Mani C 5
Manning (Wanning) H 8
Maralbashi A 4
Markham Dzong E 6
Mato E 4
Meihsien J 7
Mendong Gomba C 5
Menyüan F 4
Merket A 4
Mienning F 6
Mienyang G 5
Minhsien F 5
Mintsin F 4
Mishan M 2
Moho K 1
Mowming, 15,000 H 7
Moyü (Qara Qash) B 4
Mukden, 3,750,000 K 3
Muli F 6
Mutankiang, 400,000 M 3
Nachü D 5
Nanchang, 900,000 H 6
Nancheng, 50,000 J 6
Nanchung, 275,000 G 5
Nangtsien E 5
Nanhsiung H 6
Nanking, 2,000,000 J 5
Nanning, 375,000 G 7
Nanping, 53,445 J 6
Nanyang, 75,000 H 5
Neikiang, 240,000 F 6
Nenkiang L 2
Ningan L 3
Ningpo, 350,000 K 6
Ningsia (Yinchwan), 175,000 F 4
Ningsiang H 6
Ningteh J 6
Ningtu J 6
Ningwu H 4
Noh B 5
Noho K 2
Omin (Durbuljin) B 2
Owpu L 1
Pachen D 5
Pachu (Maralbashi) A 4
Pachung G 5
Paicheng (Bai) B 3
Paicheng, 75,000 K 2
Pailingmiao H 3
Paiyin, 50,000 F 4
Paiyü E 5
Pakhoi, 175,000 G 7
Pangkiang H 3
Paochang H 3
Paoki, 275,000 G 5
Paoshan E 7
Paoting, 350,000 J 4
Paotow, 800,000 G 3
Pehan, 130,000 L 2
Peihai (Pakhoi), 175,000 G 7
Peiping (Peking) (cap.), ‡8,000,000 J 3
Peking (cap.), ‡8,000,000 J 3
Penglai K 4
Pengpu, 400,000 J 5
Penki, 750,000 K 3
Phongdo Dzong D 5
Pichieh G 6
Pikiang E 6
Pingchüan J 3
Pingliang, 60,000 G 4
Pinglo H 7
Pingsiang, 7,000 G 7
Pingsiang, 210,000 H 6
Pingtung, 153,953 K 7
Pingwu F 5
Pingyao H 4
Pinyang G 7
Pishan (Guma) A 4
Pohsien, 75,000 J 5
Pokotu K 2
Poli M 2
Port Arthur (in Lüta) K 4
Poseh G 7
Pucheng J 6
Puerh F 7
Putien J 6
Qara Qash B 4
Qara Shahr C 3
Qaraqum C 3
Qarghaliq A 4
Rima E 6
Rudok B 5
Rungmar Thok B 5
Saka C 6
Sanga Cho Dzong E 6
Sanho K 1
Sanming J 6
Santai F 5
Shahyar B 3
Shangchih L 3
Shanghai, ‡8,500,000 K 5
Shanghang J 7
Shanghsien H 5
Shangjao, 100,000 J 6
Shangkiu, 250,000 J 5
Shangnan H 5
Shangshui, 100,000 J 5
Shanhaikwan K 3
Shanshan D 3
Shantan F 4
Shaohing, 225,000 K 6
Shaoyang, 275,000 H 6
Sharasume (Altai) C 2
Shasi, 125,000 H 5
Shentsa Dzong C 5
Shenyang (Mukden), 3,750,000 K 3
Shigatse, 26,000 C 6
Shihchü E 5
Shihchüan G 5
Shihhotzu, 70,000 C 3
Shihkiachwang, 1,500,000 J 4
Shihtsuishan, 60,000 G 4
Shiukwan, 125,000 H 7
Shobando E 5
Shwangcheng L 2
Shwangliao K 3
Shwangyashan, 150,000 M 2
Siaho F 4
Siakwan, 26,200 F 6
Sian, 1,900,000 G 5
Siangfan, 150,000 H 5
Siangtan, 300,000 H 6
Siangyin H 6
Sichang F 6
Sienyang, 120,000 G 5
Silin G 7
Silinhot, 20,000 J 3
Sinchu, 188,062 K 7
Singi Obo C 5
Singsingsia D 3
Singtai, 75,000 H 4
Sinhailien (Lienyünkang), 300,000 J 5
Sinhsien H 4
Sinhwa H 6
Sining, 250,000 F 4
Sinsiang, 300,000 H 4
Sinyang, 125,000 H 5
Siushui J 6
Soche (Yarkand), 80,000 A 4
Solun K 2
Soochow, 1,300,000 K 5
Süchow, 1,500,000 J 5
Suhsien J 5
Suihsien H 5
Suihwa, 36,000 L 2
Suining, 75,000 F 5
Suiteh G 4
Sungpan F 5
Sutsien J 5
Süyung F 6
Swatow, 400,000 J 7
Szeping, 180,000 K 3
Tahcheng (Chuguchak) B 2
Tahsien G 5
Taian, 20,000 J 4
Taichao D 5
Taichung, 407,054 J 7
Tainan, 441,556 J 7
Taipei (cap.), 1,604,543 K 7
Taitung, 69,984 K 7
Taiyüan, 2,725,000 H 4
Taklakhar B 5
Talai, 20,000 K 2
Tali E 6
Tangshan, 1,200,000 J 4
Tanhsien G 8
Tantung, 450,000 K 3
Taoan, 75,000 K 2
Taocheng F 6
Taofu F 5
Tapanshang J 3
Tardin D 4
Tash Qurghan A 4
Tashigong A 5
Tatsaitan E 4
Tatung, 300,000 H 3
Tayü H 6
Tehchow, 45,000 J 4
Tehko E 5
Tehtsin E 6
Telingha E 4
Tengchung E 7
Tengkow G 4
Tepao G 7
Thok Daurakpa C 5
Thok Jalung B 5
Tiehling, 52,945 K 3
Tienshui, 100,000 F 5
Tientsin, ‡4,500,000 J 4
Tinghai K 5
Tingri Dzong C 6

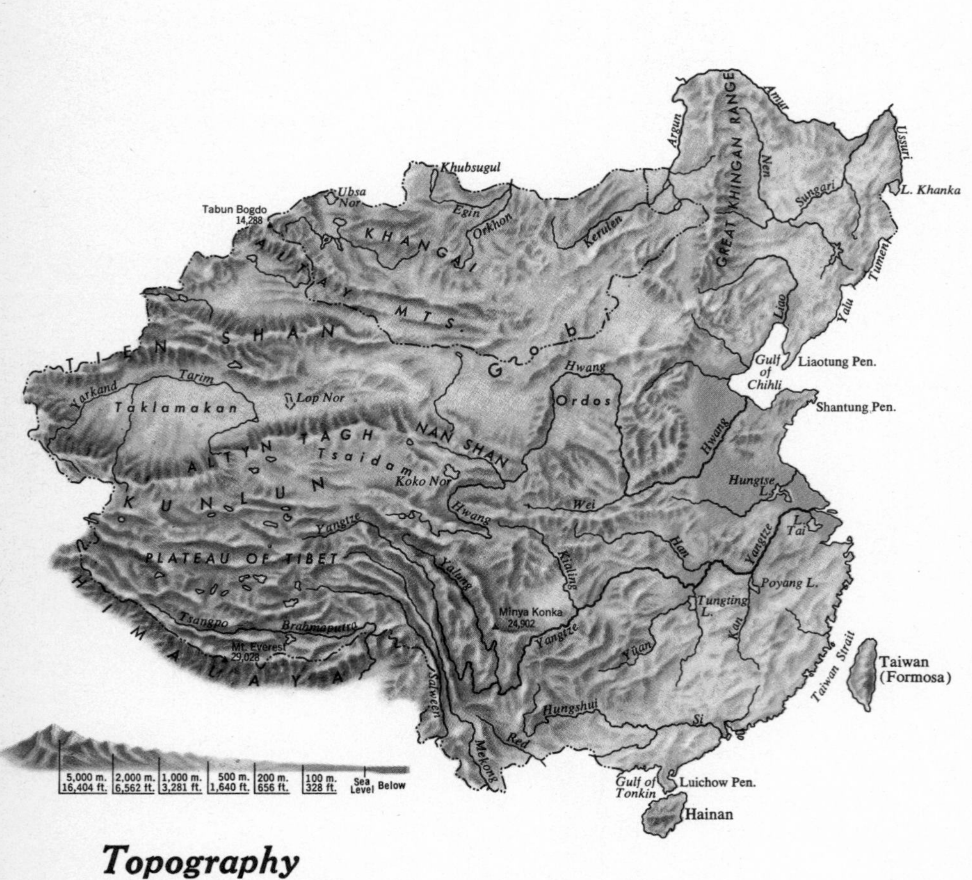

Topography

0 300 600
MILES

Tingsi ....G 5
Tingsin ....E 3
Tokoto ....H 3
Töling ....B 5
Tolun ....J 3
Toqsun ....C 3
Tradom ....B 6
Tsagan Usu ....E 4
Tsoachwang ....J 4
Tsangchow, 75,000 ....J 4
Tsaochwang ....J 4
Tselo (Chira) ....B 4
Tsiaotso, 300,000 ....H 4
Tsinan, 1,500,000 ....J 4
Tsingkiang, 110,000 ....J 5
Tsingkiang ....J 6
Tsingshih, 100,000 ....H 6
Tsingtao, 1,900,000 ....K 4
Tsining, 160,000 ....H 3
Tsining, 86,200 ....J 4
Tsitsihar, 1,500,000 ....K 2
Tsunyi, 275,000 ....G 6
Tsuyung ....F 6
Tuhshan ....G 6
Tulan ....E 4
Tumen ....M 3
Tungchwan ....F 6
Tungchwan, 45,000 ....G 4
Tungfang ....G 8
Tungho ....L 2
Tunghwa, 275,000 ....L 3
Tungjen ....F 4
Tungjen ....G 6
Tungkiang, 96,652 ....M 2
Tungkwan ....H 5
Tungliao, 40,000 ....K 3
Tungü ....K 2
Tunhwa, 80,000 ....L 3
Tunhwang ....D 3
Tunki, 75,000 ....J 6
Tushantze ....B 3
Turfan ....C 3
Tuyün, 60,000 ....G 6
Tzekung, 350,000 ....G 6
Tzekwei ....H 5
Tzepo, 1,750,000 ....J 4
Uch Turfan ....A 3
Ulanhot, 100,000 ....K 2
Ulughchat ....A 4
Uniket ....J 2
Urumchi, 500,000 ....C 3
Wanhsien, 175,000 ....G 5
Wanning ....H 8
Weifang, 260,000 ....J 4
Weihai, 50,000 ....K 4
Weining ....F 6
Weisi ....E 6
Wenchow, 250,000 ....J 6
Wenhsien ....F 5
Wenshan ....F 7
Wompo ....C 5
Wuchang (in Wuhan) ....H 5
Wuchang ....L 3
Wuchow, 150,000 ....H 7
Wuchung, 45,000 ....G 4
Wuchwan ....H 3
Wuhan, ‡4,250,000 ....H 5
Wuhing, 160,000 ....J 5
Wuhu, 300,000 ....J 5
Wusih, 900,000 ....K 5
Wusu ....B 3
Wuta ....G 3
Wutu ....F 5
Wuwei ....F 4
Wuyüan ....G 3
Yaan, 100,000 ....F 6
Yangchow, 210,000 ....K 5
Yangchüan, 350,000 ....H 4
Yangi Hissar ....A 4
Yarkand, 80,000 ....A 4
Yatung ....C 6
Yehsien ....K 4
Yenan ....G 4
Yenki (Qara Shahr) ....C 3
Yenki, 130,000 ....L 3
Yenyüan ....F 6
Yinchwan, 175,000 ....F 4
Yingkow, 215,000 ....K 3
Yingtak ....H 7
Yiyang, 75,000 ....H 6
Yüanling ....H 6
Yüchi ....F 7
Yüehsi ....F 6
Yühsien ....H 4
Yülin ....G 4
Yülin ....G 8
Yülin ....H 7
Yümen ....E 3
Yümen, 325,000 ....E 4
Yungan ....J 6
Yungkia (Wenchow), 250,0000....J 6
Yungteng ....F 4
Yünhsien ....H 5
Yüshashan ....D 4
Yüshu (Jyekundo) ....E 5
Yütien (Keriya) ....B 4
Yütze, 100,000 ....H 4

OTHER FEATURES

Achchik Kol (lake) ....C 4
Alashan (desert) ....F 4
Altay (mts.) ....C 2
Altyn Tagh (range) ....C 4
Amne Machin (mts.) ....F 5
Amur (river) ....L 2
Argun (river) ....J 1
Bagrach Kol (lake) ....C 3
Bam Tso (lake) ....D 5
Bashi (channel) ....K 7
Bayan Kara Shan (range) ....E 5
Black (river) ....F 7
Bogdo Ula (mts.) ....C 3
Bor Nor (lake) ....J 2
Chang Tang (plat.) ....B 5
Cherchen (river) ....C 4
Chihli (gulf) ....K 4
Chushan (arch.) ....K 5
Dre Chu (river) ....E 5
Dza Chu (river) ....E 5
Dzungaria (region) ....C 3
East China (sea) ....L 6
Ebi Nor (lake) ....B 2
Erh Hai (lake) ....F 6
Everest (mt.) ....C 6
Fen Ho (river) ....H 4
Formosa (Taiwan) (isl.), 12,888,478 ....K 7
Formosa (Taiwan) (str.) ....J 7
Gashun Nor (lake) ....E 3
Genghis Khan Wall (ruins) ....H 2
Gobi (desert) ....G 3
Grand (canal) ....J 4
Great Khingan (range) ....K 2
Great Wall (ruins) ....G 4
Gurla Mandhata (mt.) ....B 5
Hainan (isl.) ....G 8
Han Kiang (river) ....H 5
Hangchow (bay) ....K 5
Himalaya (mts.) ....B-D 6
Hulun Nor (lake) ....J 2
Hungtow (isl.), 2,465 ....K 7
Hwang Ho (river) ....H 5
Indus (river) ....A 5
Inner Mongolia (reg.) ....H 3
Jiggitai Tso (lake) ....C 4
Kailas (mt.) ....B 5
Kaopao (lake) ....J 5
Kara Nor (lake) ....E 4
Karakhoto (ruins) ....F 3
Karakoram (mts.) ....A 4
Kashum Tso (lake) ....C 5
Kerulen (river) ....H 2
Khanka (lake) ....M 3
Khotan (river) ....B 4
Kialing Kiang (river) ....G 5
Kiungchow (str.) ....G 7
Koko Nor (lake) ....E 4
Kumara (river) ....K 1
Kunlun (mts.) ....C 4
Kyaring Tso (lake) ....C 5
Kyaring Tso (lake) ....E 4
Liao Ho (river) ....J 3
Liaotung (pen.) ....K 4
Lighten Tso (lake) ....B 5
Lop Nor (dry lake) ....D 3
Luichow (pen.) ....G 7
Manasarowar (lake) ....B 5
Manass (river) ....C 3
Manchuria (reg.), 51,500,000 ....K 2
Matsu (isl.) ....K 6
Mekong (river) ....F 7
Min Kiang (river) ....F 5
Min Kiang (river) ....J 6
Min Shan (range) ....F 5
Minya Konka (mt.) ....F 6
Montcalm (lake) ....C 5
Muztagh (mt.) ....B 4
Muztagh Ata (mt.) ....A 4

(continued on following page)

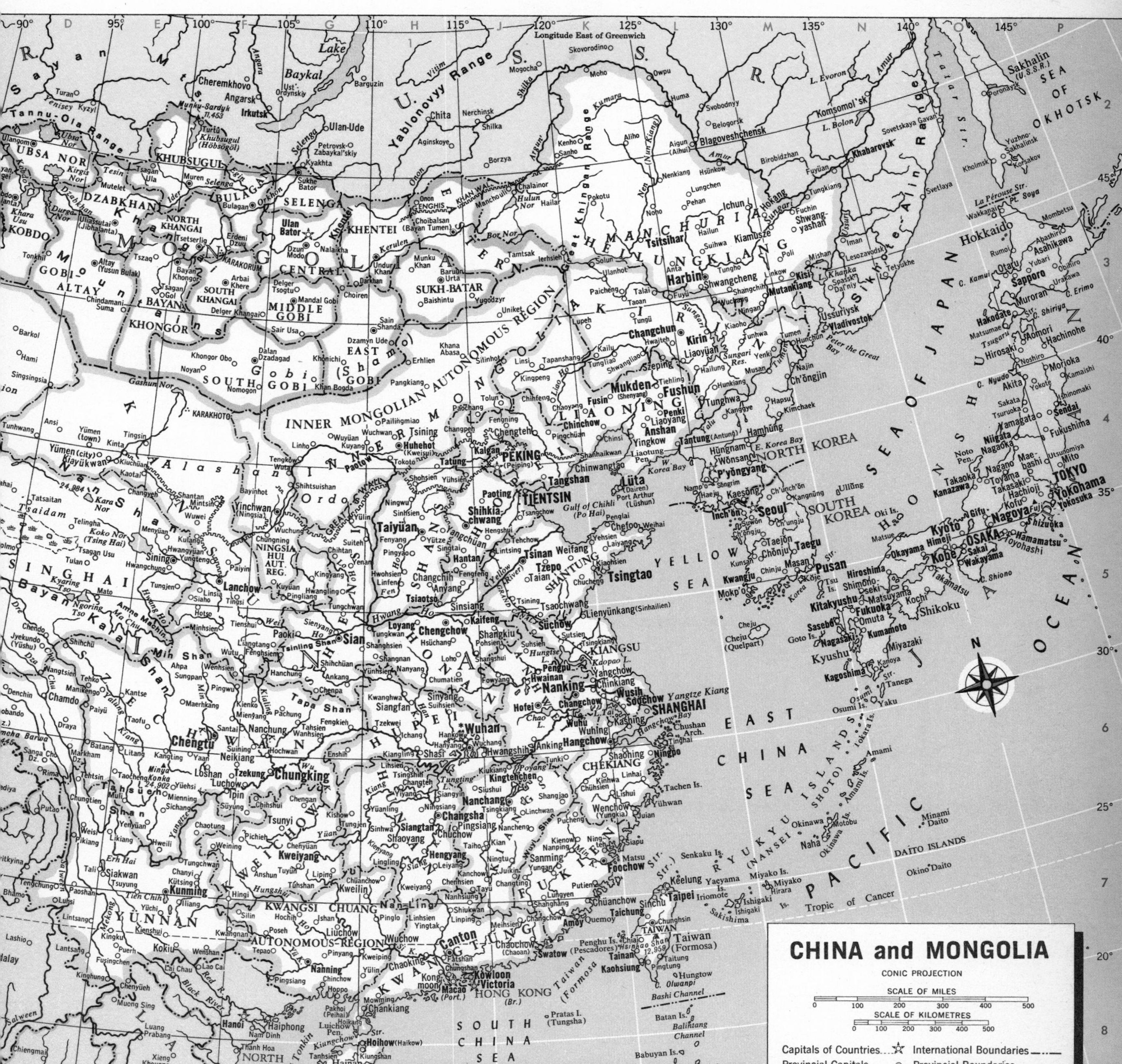

(continued)

CHINA (continued)

Nam Tso (lake) .... D 5
Namcha Barwa (mt.) .... E 6
Nan Shan (range) .... E 4
Nen (river) .... K 2
Nganglaring Tso (lake) .... B 5
Ngangtse Tso (lake) .... C 5
Ngoring Tso (lake) .... E 5
Nyenchen Tanglha (range) .... C 6
Olwanpi (cape) .... K 7
Ordos (desert) .... G 4
Pangong Tso (lake) .... A 5
Penghu (isls.), 113,503 .... J 7
Pescadores (Penghu) (isls.), 113,503 .... J 7
Pobeda (peak) .... B 3
Po Hai (Chihli) (gulf) .... K 4
Poyang (lake) .... J 6
Pratas (isl.) .... J 7
Quemoy (isl.), 60,000 .... J 7
Red (river) .... F 7
Salween (river) .... E 6
Shamo (Gobi) (des.) .... G 3
Si Kiang (river) .... H 7
Siang Kiang (river) .... H 6
Sinkao Shan (mt.) .... K 7
South China (sea) .... H 7
Sungari (river) .... M 2
Sutlej (river) .... A 5
Tachen (isls.) .... K 6
Tahsüeh Shan (range) .... F 6
Tai (lake) .... J 5
Taiwan (isl.), 12,888,478 .... K 7
Taiwan (str.) .... J 7
Taklamakan (desert) .... B 4
Tanglha (range) .... C 5
Tangra Tso (lake) .... C 5
Tapa Shan (range) .... G 5
Tarbagatay (range) .... B 2
Tarim (river) .... C 3
Tarok Tso (lake) .... B 5
Tien Chih (lake) .... F 7
Tien Shan (range) .... B 3
Tonkin (gulf) .... G 8
Trans-Himalayas (range) .... C 5
Tsaidam (swamp) .... E 4
Tsangpo (river) .... C 6
Tsing Hai (Koko Nor) (lake) .... E 4
Tsinling Shan (range) .... G 5
Tungsha (Pratas) (isl.) .... J 7
Tungting (lake) .... H 6
Turfan (depr.) .... C 3
Ulan Muren (river) .... D 5
Ulugh Muztagh (mt.) .... C 4
Ulyungur Nor (lake) .... C 2
Urungu (river) .... C 2
Ussuri (river) .... M 2
Wei Ho (river) .... G 5
West Korea (bay) .... K 4
Wu Kiang (river) .... G 6
Wuyi Shan (range) .... J 6
Yalu (river) .... L 3
Yalung Kiang (river) .... E 5
Yamdrok Tso (lake) .... D 6
Yangtze Kiang (river) .... K 5
Yarkand (river) .... A 4
Yellow (Hwang Ho) (river) .... J 4
Yellow (sea) .... K 4
Yü Kiang (river) .... G 7
Yüan Kiang (river) .... G 6
Zilling Tso (lake) .... C 5

HONG KONG

CITIES and TOWNS

Kowloon, 692,800 .... H 7
Victoria (cap.), 694,500 .... H 7
Victoria, *1,034,000 .... H 7

MACAO

CITIES and TOWNS

Macao (cap.), 262,000 .... H 7

MONGOLIA

PROVINCES

Bayan Khongor, 43,600 .... E 2
Bayan Ulegei, 45,100 .... C 2
Bulagan, 31,200 .... F 2
Central, 50,400 .... G 2
Dzabkhan, 56,800 .... E 2
Eastern, 34,300 .... H 2
East Gobi, 26,300 .... G 3
Gobi-Altay, 40,500 .... D 2
Khentei, 35,400 .... G 2
Khubsugul, 61,100 .... E 1
Kobdo, 44,800 .... D 2
Middle Gobi, 27,500 .... G 2
North Khangai, 60,300 .... F 2
Selenga, 43,300 .... G 2
South Gobi, 21,900 .... F 3
South Khangai, 53,800 .... F 2
Sukh-Batar, 30,400 .... H 2
Ubsa Nor, 49,000 .... D 2

CITIES and TOWNS

Arbai Khere, 6,000 .... F 2
Altay, 7,000 .... E 2
Baishintu .... H 2
Baruun Urta, 6,000 .... H 2
Bayan Khongor, 4,400 .... F 2
Bayan Tumen (Choibalsan), 14,000 .... H 2
Bayan Ulegei, 8,000 .... D 2
Bulagan, 8,000 .... F 2
Chindamani Suma .... E 2
Choibalsan, 14,000 .... H 2
Dalan Dzadagad, 4,000 .... G 3
Darkhan, 30,000 .... G 2
Delger Khangai .... F 2
Delger Tsogtu .... G 2
Dzamyn Ude .... G 3
Dzun Modo, 6,000 .... G 2
Erdeni Dzuu .... F 2
Jibhalanta (Uliassutai), 7,000 .... E 2
Jirgalanta (Kobdo), 11,000 .... D 2
Khan Bogda .... G 3
Khongor Obo .... F 3
Khonichi .... G 3
Kobdo, 11,000 .... D 2
Mandal Gobi, 5,000 .... G 2
Munku Khan .... H 2
Muren, 9,000 .... F 2
Nalaikha, 14,000 .... G 2
Nomogon .... F 3
Noyan .... F 3
Onon .... H 2
Sain Shanda, 7,000 .... H 3
Sair Usa .... G 3
Sukhe Bator, 9,000 .... G 2
Suok .... C 2
Tamtsak .... J 2
Tsagan Ula .... E 2
Tsetserlig, 14,000 .... F 2
Tszaq .... E 2
Ulan Bator (cap.), 268,800 .... G 2
Ulangom, 10,000 .... D 2
Uliassutai, 7,000 .... E 2
Undur Khan, 7,000 .... H 2
Yugodzyr .... J 2
Yusun Bulak (Altay), 7,000 .... E 2

OTHER FEATURES

Altay (mts.) .... C 2
Bor Nor (lake) .... J 2
Durga Nor (lake) .... D 2
Dzabkhan (river) .... D 2
Egin (river) .... F 2
Genghis Khan Wall (ruins) .... H 2
Gobi (desert) .... G 3
Höbsögöl (Khubsugul) (lake) .... F 1
Ider (river) .... E 2
Karakorum (ruins) .... F 2
Kerulen (river) .... H 2
Khangai (mts.) .... E 2
Khara Usu (lake) .... D 2
Khentei (mts.) .... G 2
Khubsugul (lake) .... F 1
Kirgis Nor (lake) .... D 2
Kobdo (river) .... D 2
Munku-Sardyk (mt.) .... F 1
Onon (river) .... H 2
Orkhon (river) .... F 2
Selenga (river) .... F 2
Shamo (Gobi) (des.) .... G 3
Tabun Bogdo (mt.) .... C 2
Tannu-Ola (range) .... D 1
Tesin (river) .... E 2
Ubsa Nor (lake) .... D 1

*City and suburbs.
‡Popuation of municipality.

†Populations of mainland cities over 100,000 courtesy of Kingsley Davis, Office of Int'l Pop. & Urban Research, Inst. of Int'l Studies, Univ. of California.

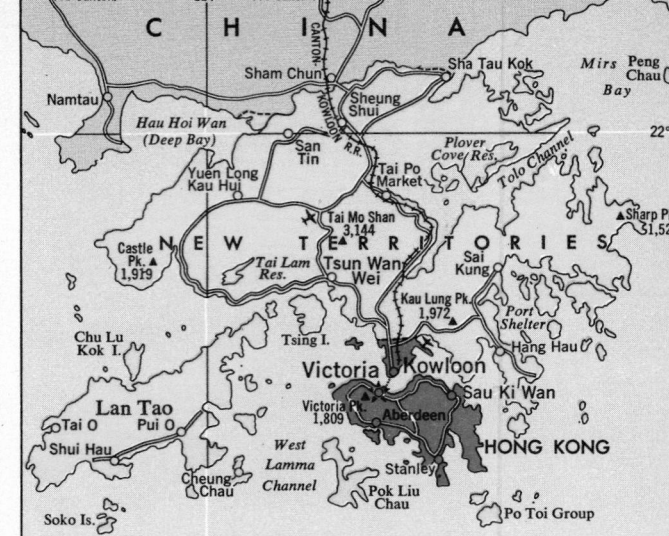

HONG KONG and the NEW TERRITORIES

SCALE OF MILES

Agriculture, Industry and Resources

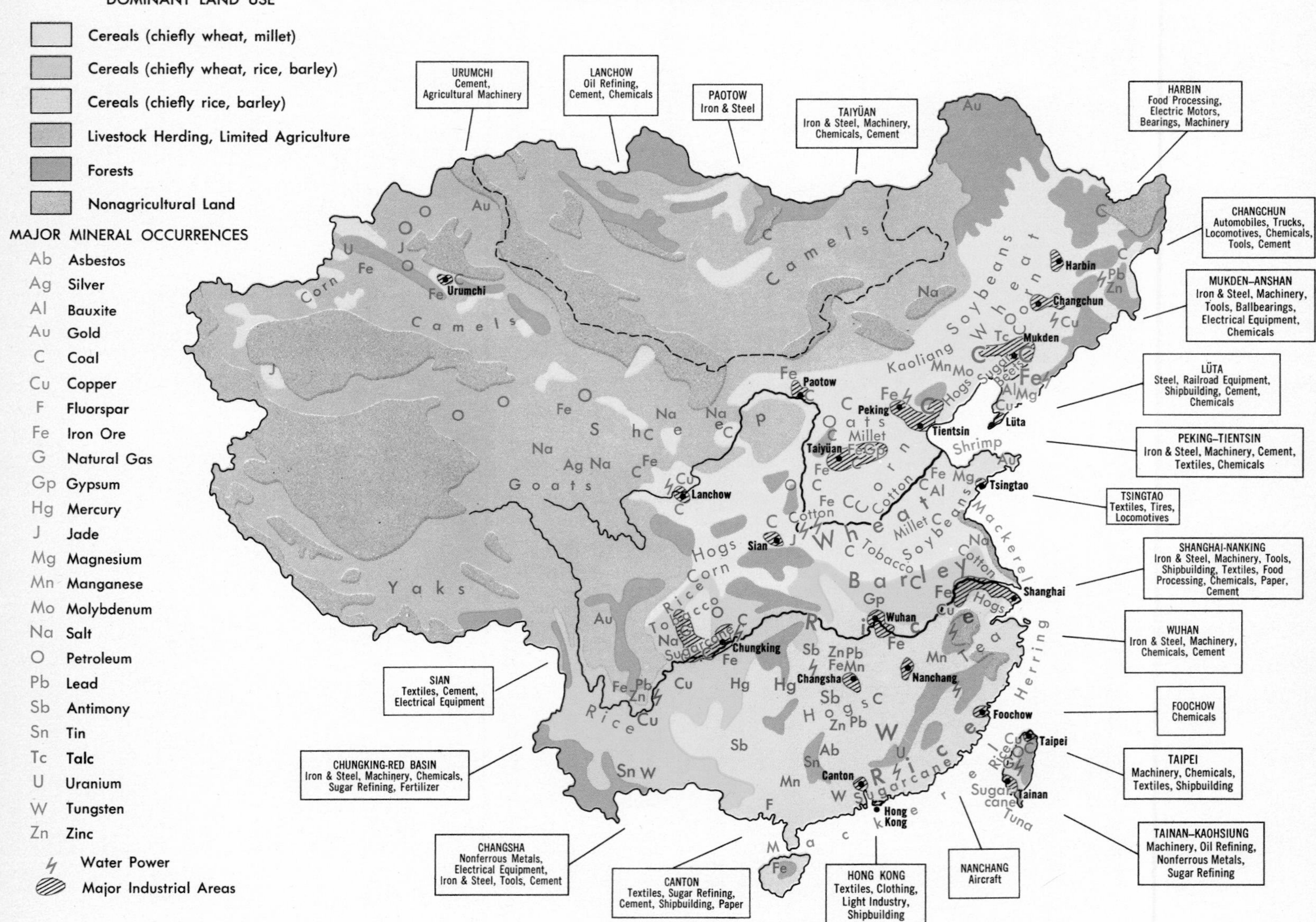

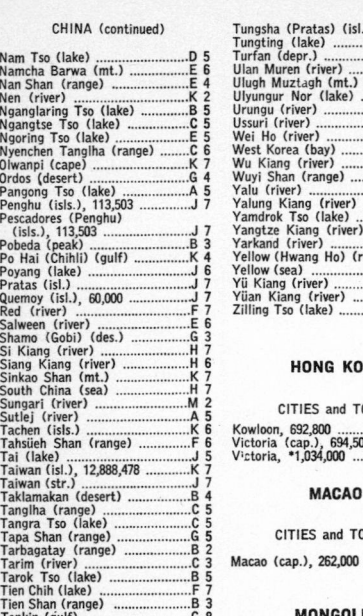

JAPAN

AREA 143,622 sq. mi.
POPULATION 104,665,171
CAPITAL Tokyo
LARGEST CITY Tokyo
HIGHEST POINT Fuji 12,389 ft.
MONETARY UNIT yen
MAJOR LANGUAGE Japanese
MAJOR RELIGIONS Buddhism, Shintoism

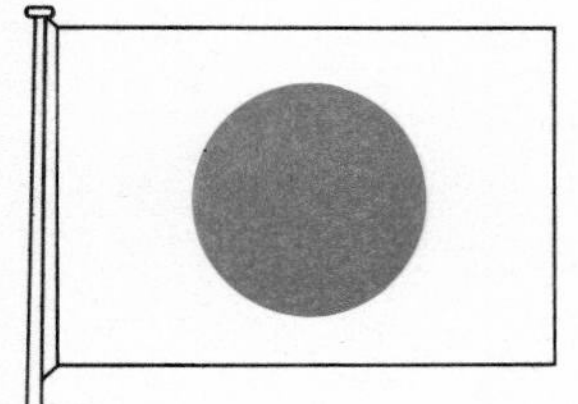

NORTH KOREA

AREA 46,540 sq. mi.
POPULATION 13,300,000
CAPITAL P'yŏngyang
LARGEST CITY P'yŏngyang
HIGHEST POINT Paektu 9,003 ft.
MONETARY UNIT won
MAJOR LANGUAGE Korean
MAJOR RELIGIONS Confucianism, Buddhism, Christianity

SOUTH KOREA

AREA 38,452 sq. mi.
POPULATION 31,683,000
CAPITAL Seoul
LARGEST CITY Seoul
HIGHEST POINT Halla 6,398 ft.
MONETARY UNIT won
MAJOR LANGUAGE Korean
MAJOR RELIGIONS Confucianism, Buddhism, Chondogyo, Christianity

JAPAN

PREFECTURES

Aichi, 4,798,653	H 6
Akita, 1,279,835	J 4
Aomori, 1,416,591	K 3
Chiba, 2,701,770	P 2
Ehime, 1,446,384	F 7
Fukui, 750,557	G 5
Fukuoka, 3,964,611	D 7
Fukushima, 1,983,754	K 5
Gifu, 1,700,365	H 6
Gumma, 1,605,584	J 5
Hiroshima, 2,281,146	E 6
Hokkaido, 5,171,800	K 2
Hyogo, 4,309,944	H 7
Ibaraki, 2,056,154	K 5
Ishikawa, 980,499	H 5
Iwate, 1,411,118	K 4
Kagawa, 900,845	G 6
Kagoshima, 1,853,541	E 8
Kanagawa, 4,430,743	O 2
Kochi, 812,714	F 7
Kumamoto, 1,770,736	E 7
Kyoto, 2,102,808	J 7
Mie, 1,514,467	H 6
Miyagi, 1,753,126	F 4
Miyazaki, 1,080,692	E 8
Nagano, 1,958,007	J 5
Nagasaki, 1,641,245	D 7
Nara, 825,965	J 8
Niigata, 2,398,931	J 5
Oita, 1,187,480	E 7
Okayama, 1,645,135	F 6
Okinawa, 1,108,271	N 6
Osaka, 6,657,189	J 8
Saga, 871,885	E 7
Saitama, 3,014,983	O 2
Shiga, 853,385	J 7
Shimane, 821,620	F 6
Shizuoka, 2,912,521	H 6
Tochigi, 1,521,656	K 5
Tokushima, 815,115	G 7
Tokyo, 10,869,244	O 2
Tottori, 579,853	G 6
Toyama, 1,025,465	H 5
Wakayama, 1,026,975	G 6
Yamagata, 1,263,103	K 4
Yamaguchi, 1,543,573	E 6
Yamanashi, 763,194	J 6

CITIES and TOWNS

Abashiri, 44,195	M 1
Ageo, 54,776	O 2
Aizuwakamatsu, 104,000	J 5
Ajigasawa, 20,504	J 3
Akabira, 46,646	K 2
Akashi, 187,000	H 8
Aki, 26,605	F 7
Akita, 233,000	J 4
Akkeshi, 19,039	M 2
Akune, 36,026	E 7
Amagasaki, 532,000	H 8
Amagi, 44,060	E 7
Amaha, 18,062	O 3
Anan, 59,105	G 7
Aomori, 252,000	K 3
Asahi, 31,063	K 6
Asahikawa, 293,000	L 2
Ashibetsu, 52,123	L 2
Ashikaga, 153,000	J 5
Ashiya, 63,195	H 8
Atami, 54,540	J 6
Atsugi, 61,383	O 2
Awaji, 9,972	H 8
Ayabe, 48,339	G 6
Beppu, 144,000	E 7
Bibai, 63,051	L 2
Biratori, 12,930	L 2
Chiba, 407,000	P 2
Chichibu, 60,330	J 6
Chigasaki, 119,000	O 3
Chitose, 51,243	K 2
Chofu, 145,000	O 2
Choshi, 91,492	K 6
Daito, 57,107	J 8
Ebetsu, 44,510	K 2
Esashi, Hokkaido, 15,380	J 3
Esashi, Hokkaido, 11,401	L 1
Esashi, Iwate, 42,666	K 4
Fuchu, Hiroshima, 45,341	F 6
Fuchu, Tokyo, 148,000	O 2
Fuji, 173,000	J 6
Fujieda, 70,789	J 6
Fujisawa, 211,000	O 3
Fukuchiyama, 58,223	G 6
Fukue, 36,876	D 7
Fukui, 193,000	G 5
Fukuoka, 812,000	D 7
Fukushima, 225,000	K 5
Fukuyama, 233,000	F 6
Funabashi, 281,000	P 2
Furukawa, 52,853	K 4
Futtsu, 16,445	O 3
Gifu, 398,000	H 6
Gobo, 30,040	G 7
Gose, 35,788	J 8
Gosen, 38,113	J 5
Goshogawara, 47,433	K 3
Gotsu, 30,209	F 6
Habikino, 50,333	J 8
Haboro, 30,266	K 1
Hachinohe, 209,000	K 3
Hachioji, 229,000	O 2
Hagi, 53,905	E 6
Hakodate, 249,000	K 3
Hakui, 29,090	H 5
Hamada, 44,439	E 6
Hamamatsu, 420,000	H 6
Hanamaki, 62,710	K 4
Hanawa, 20,507	K 3
Hanno, 47,825	O 2
Haramachi, 40,643	K 5
Hayama, 17,617	O 3
Higashiosaka, 454,000	J 8
Hikone, 62,740	H 6
Himeji, 403,000	G 6
Himi, 62,452	H 5
Hirakata, 164,000	J 7
Hirara, 32,591	L 7
Hirata, 33,128	F 6
Hiratsuka, 151,000	O 3
Hiroo, 13,598	L 2
Hirosaki, 162,000	K 3
Hiroshima, 542,000	E 6
Hitachi, 184,000	K 5
Hitachiota, 36,974	K 5
Hitoyoshi, 44,831	E 7
Hofu, 94,342	E 6
Hondo, 39,790	E 7
Honjo, 38,361	J 4
Hyuga, 43,678	E 7
Ibaraki, 143,000	J 7
Ibusuki, 32,386	E 8
Ichihara, 134,000	P 2
Ichikawa, 236,000	P 2
Ichinohe, 25,165	K 3
Ichinomiya, 210,000	H 6
Ichinoseki, 57,238	K 4
Ide, 8,199	J 7
Iida, 79,145	H 6
Iizuka, 82,033	E 7
Ikeda, Hokkaido, 15,529	L 2
Ikeda, Osaka, 82,478	H 7
Ikuno, 9,466	G 6
Imabari, 109,000	F 6
Imari, 67,316	D 7
Imazu, 11,245	G 6
Ina, 51,944	H 6
Isahaya, 63,886	D 7
Ise, 104,000	H 6
Ishigaki, 41,315	L 7
Ishige, 18,481	P 2
Ishinomaki, 106,000	K 4
Ishioka, 36,789	K 5
Itami, 141,000	H 7
Ito, 59,404	J 6
Itoigawa, 39,332	H 5
Itoman, 34,065	N 6
Iwaizumi, 24,846	K 4
Iwaki, 337,000	K 5
Iwakuni, 106,000	E 6
Iwami, 18,004	G 6
Iwamisawa, 65,508	L 2
Iwanai, 25,405	K 2
Iwasaki, 5,432	J 3
Iwata, 58,940	H 6
Iwatsuki, 41,946	O 2
Iyo, 28,611	F 7
Izuhara, 21,989	D 6
Izumi, 84,771	J 8
Izumiotsu, 53,312	J 8
Izumisano, 66,521	G 6
Izumo, 68,765	F 6
Joyo, 20,038	J 7
Kadoma, 121,000	J 7
Kaga, 54,860	H 5
Kagoshima, 406,000	E 8
Kaizuka, 69,365	H 8
Kakogawa, 115,000	G 6
Kamaishi, 82,104	L 4
Kamakura, 136,000	O 3
Kameoka, 43,335	J 7
Kaminoyama, 38,679	J 4
Kamiyaku, 12,458	E 8
Kamo, 9,034	J 7
Kanazawa, 344,000	H 5
Kanonji, 44,200	F 6
Kanoya, 70,519	E 8
Kanuma, 77,240	J 5
Karatsu, 73,999	D 7
Kaseda, 28,565	D 8
Kashihara, 57,065	J 8
Kashiwa, 133,000	P 2
Kashiwazaki, 71,465	J 5
Kasugai, 141,000	H 6
Kasukabe, 42,460	O 2
Katsuta, 52,625	K 5
Katsuura, 29,133	K 6
Kawachi, 91,853	J 8
Kawachinagano, 40,109	J 8
Kawagoe, 148,000	O 2
Kawaguchi, 284,000	O 2
Kawanishi, 61,282	H 7
Kawasaki, 910,000	J 6
Kazusa, 12,787	P 3
Kembuchi, 8,013	L 1
Kesennuma, 59,884	K 4
Kikonai, 11,353	K 3
Kiryu, 132,000	J 5
Kisarazu, 54,928	P 3
Kishiwada, 156,000	J 8
Kitaibaraki, 55,334	K 5
Kitakata, 40,424	J 5
Kitakyushu, 1,042,319	E 6
Kitami, 74,841	L 2
Kizu, 10,814	J 7
Kobayashi, 41,922	E 8
Kobe, 1,288,754	H 7
Kochi, 242,000	F 7
Kodaira, 125,000	O 2
Kofu, 185,000	J 6
Kokubu, 31,249	E 8
Komagane, 28,327	H 6
Komatsu, 91,163	H 5
Koriyama, 240,000	K 5
Koshigaya, 112,000	P 2
Koza, 55,923	N 6
Kuji, 38,374	K 3
Kuki, 26,773	O 2
Kumagaya, 119,000	J 5
Kumamoto, 432,000	E 7
Kumaño, 30,041	H 7
Kumiyama, 7,231	J 7
Kurashiki, 332,000	F 6
Kurayoshi, 50,114	F 6
Kure, 237,000	F 6
Kurume, 188,000	E 7
Kushikino, 31,781	E 8
Kushima, 36,425	E 8
Kushimoto, 20,252	G 7
Kushiro, 195,000	M 2
Kutchan, 19,738	K 2
Kyonan, 13,980	O 3
Kyoto, 1,418,933	J 7
Machida, 154,000	O 2
Maebashi, 225,000	J 5
Maibara, 13,415	G 6
Maizuru, 96,641	G 6
Mashike, 13,063	K 2
Masuda, 52,729	E 6
Matsubara, 71,406	H 8
Matsudo, 206,000	P 2
Matsue, 115,000	F 6
Matsumae, 19,111	J 3
Matsumoto, 159,000	H 5
Matsunaga, 34,610	F 6
Matsusaka, 104,000	H 6
Matsuto, 29,649	H 5
Matsuyama, 310,000	F 7
Mihara, 82,175	F 6
Miki, 38,542	H 7
Mikuni, 22,135	G 5
Minamata, 45,577	E 7
Minobu, 12,250	J 6
Minoo, 43,851	J 7
Misawa, 36,326	K 3
Mishima, 43,479	J 7
Mitaka, 146,000	O 2
Mito, 167,000	K 5
Mitsukaido, 36,584	P 2
Miura, 42,601	O 3
Miyako, 56,575	L 4
Miyakonojo, 121,000	E 8
Miyazaki, 212,000	E 8
Miyazu, 33,285	G 6
Miyoshi, 37,871	F 6
Mizusawa, 45,985	K 4
Mobara, 42,486	K 6
Mombetsu, 40,389	L 1
Mooka, 38,117	K 5
Mori, 18,330	K 2
Moriguchi, 164,000	J 7
Morioka, 191,000	K 4
Motobu, 15,068	N 6
Muko, 20,730	J 7
Murakami, 32,651	J 4
Muroran, 181,000	K 2
Muroto, 28,746	G 7
Musashino, 135,000	O 2
Mutsu, 39,282	K 3
Nachikatsuura, 24,889	H 7
Nagahama, Ehime, 16,193	F 7
Nagahama, Shiga, 49,871	H 6
Nagano, 280,000	J 5
Nagaoka, 27,522	J 7
Nagaoka, 159,000	J 5
Nagasaki, 422,000	D 7
Nagato, 29,246	E 6
Nago, 19,601	N 6
Nagoya, 2,036,022	H 6
Naha, 284,000	N 6
Nakaminato, 33,620	K 5
Nakamura, 35,717	F 7
Nakasato, 15,898	K 3
Nakatsu, 58,371	E 7
Nakoso, 46,731	K 5
Nanao, 48,715	H 5
Nankoku, 41,237	F 7
Naoetsu, 45,650	H 5
Nara, 191,000	J 8
Narashino, 64,897	P 2
Nayoro, 36,106	L 1
Naze, 44,111	O 5
Nemuro, 45,149	M 2
Neyagawa, 174,000	J 7
Nichinan, 57,612	E 8
Niigata, 379,000	J 5
Niihama, 130,000	F 6
Niimi, 34,063	F 6
Niitsu, 56,594	J 5
Nikko, 32,031	J 5
Nishinomiya, 357,000	H 8
Nishinoomote, 30,490	E 8
Nobeoka, 134,000	E 7
Noboribetsu, 39,101	K 2
Noda, 59,799	P 2
Nogata, 57,839	E 7
Nose, 9,906	J 7
Noshiro, 61,921	J 3
Noto, 17,719	H 5
Numata, 44,347	J 5
Numazu, 186,000	J 6
Obama, 35,160	G 6
Obihiro, 129,000	L 2
Oda, 42,322	F 6
Odate, 59,662	K 3
Odawara, 151,000	J 6
Ofunato, 38,347	K 4
Oga, 43,333	J 4
Ogaki, 134,000	H 6

(continued on following page)

Agriculture, Industry and Resources

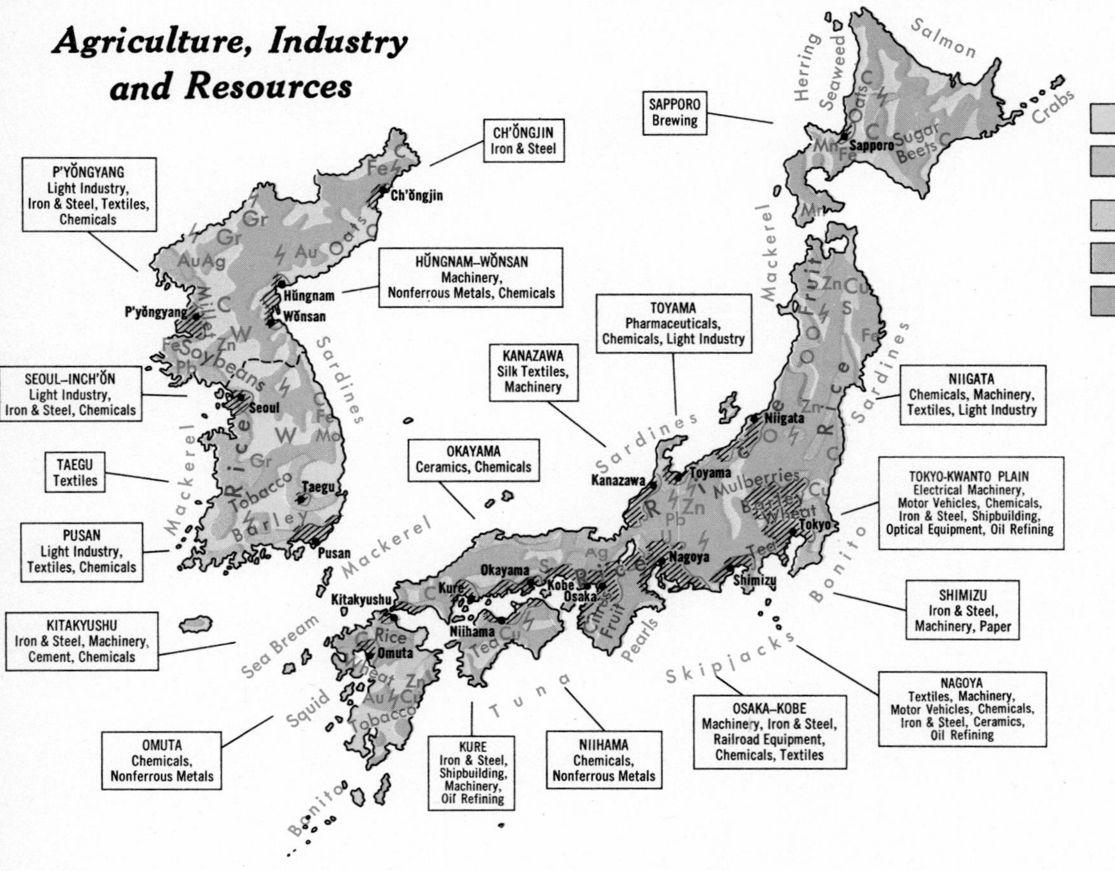

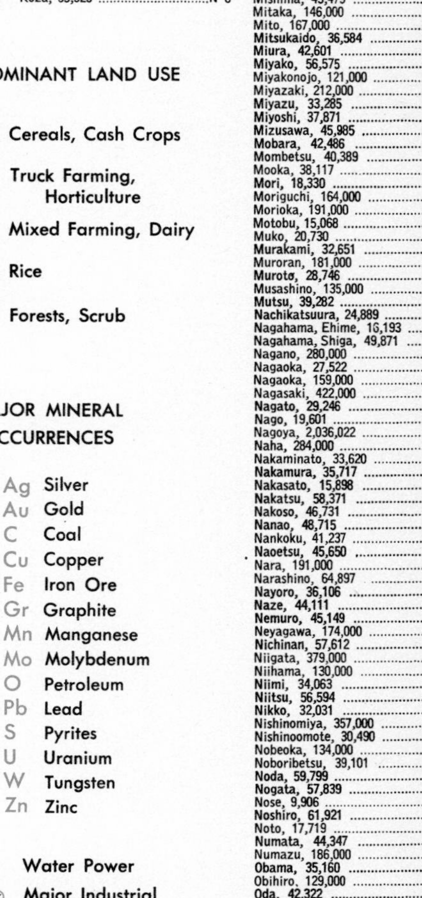

Japan and Korea
(continued)

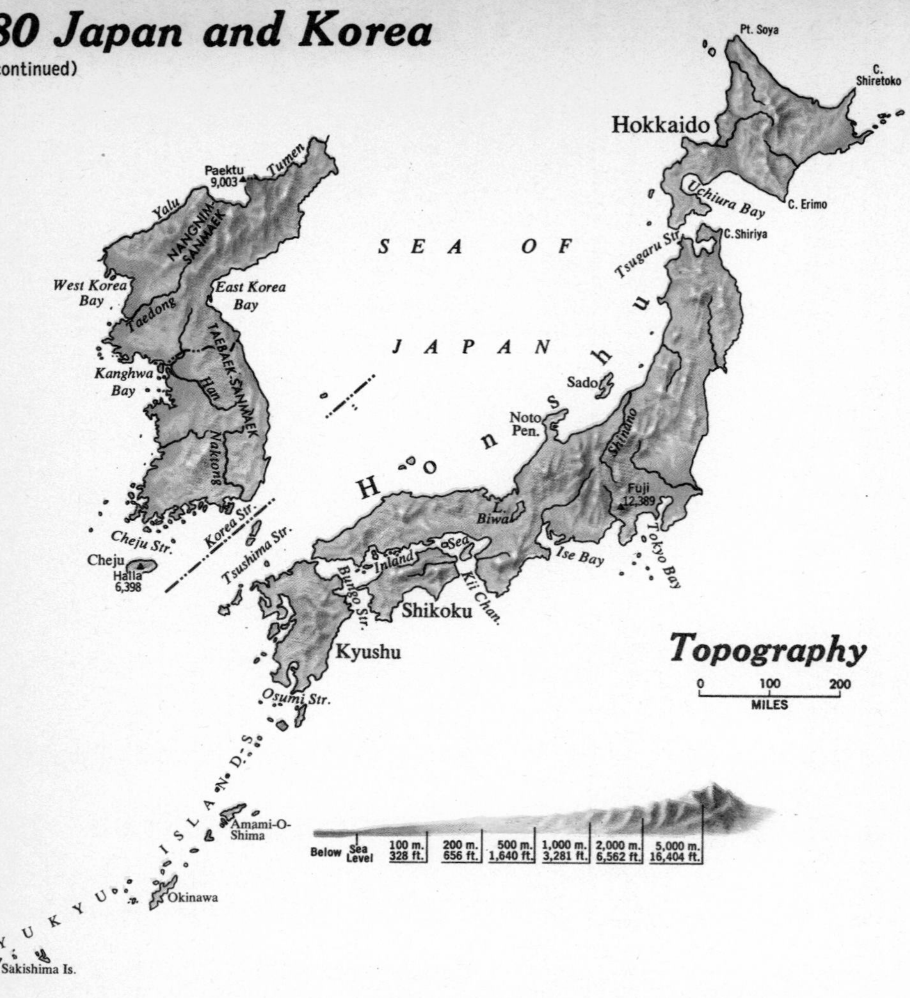

JAPAN (continued)

Ogi, 5,500 ..... J 5
Ohata, 13,015 ..... K 3
Oita, 243,000 ..... E 7
Ojiya, 47,376 ..... J 5
Okawa, 51,197 ..... E 7
Okaya, 56,986 ..... H 5
Okayama, 322,000 ..... F 6
Okazaki, 200,000 ..... H 6
Omagari, 39,900 ..... K 4
Omiya, 248,000 ..... O 2
Omu, 9,494 ..... L 1
Omura, Bonin Islands, 203 ..... M 3
Omura, Nagasaki, 56,425 ..... E 7
Omuta, 206,000 ..... E 7
Onagawa, 18,080 ..... K 4
Ono, 43,747 ..... H 6
Onoda, 43,584 ..... E 6
Onomichi, 90,740 ..... F 6
Osaka, 2,980,409 ..... J 8
Ota, 87,898 ..... J 5
Otaru, 205,000 ..... K 2
Otawara, 41,026 ..... K 5
Otsu, 164,000 ..... J 7
Owase, 34,019 ..... H 6
Oyabe, 35,646 ..... H 5
Oyama, 90,632 ..... J 5
Ozu, 40,165 ..... F 7
Rausu, 8,931 ..... M 1
Rikuzentakata, 31,040 ..... K 4
Rumoi, 40,231 ..... K 2
Ryotsu, 26,494 ..... J 4
Ryugasaki, 34,917 ..... P 2
Sabae, 50,114 ..... H 5
Saga, 153,000 ..... E 7
Sagamihara, 224,000 ..... O 2
Saigo, 16,569 ..... F 5
Saiki, 51,145 ..... E 7
Saito, 42,543 ..... E 7
Sakado, 24,854 ..... O 2
Sakai, Ibaraki, 21,689 ..... P 1
Sakai, Osaka, 544,000 ..... J 8
Sakaide, 61,284 ..... G 6
Sakaiminato, 32,846 ..... F 6
Sakata, 95,982 ..... J 4
Saku, 55,149 ..... J 5
Sakurai, 49,939 ..... J 8
Sanda, 32,265 ..... H 7
Sanjo, 74,080 ..... J 5
Sapporo, 1,010,122 ..... K 2
Sarufutsu, 7,450 ..... L 1
Sasebo, 268,000 ..... D 7
Satte, 25,169 ..... O 1
Sawara, 47,561 ..... K 6
Sayama, 40,183 ..... O 2
Sendai, Kagoshima, 67,142 ..... E 8
Sendai, Miyagi, 515,000 ..... K 4
Seta, 20,327 ..... J 7
Shari, 18,015 ..... M 2
Shibata, 73,992 ..... J 5
Shibetsu, 36,502* ..... M 2
Shimabara, 44,175 ..... E 7
Shimizu, 230,000 ..... J 6
Shimoda, 28,645 ..... J 6
Shimonoseki, 276,000 ..... E 6
Shingu, 40,051 ..... H 7
Shinjo, 43,037 ..... K 4
Shiogama, 58,363 ..... K 4
Shiroishi, 41,928 ..... K 4
Shizunai, 26,533 ..... L 2
Shizuoka, 392,000 ..... H 6
Shobara, 26,515 ..... F 6
Shuri, 28,282 ..... N 6
Soka, 102,000 ..... O 2
Soma, 38,430 ..... K 5
Sonobe, 15,241 ..... J 7
Suita, 239,000 ..... J 7
Sukagawa, 46.999 ..... K 5
Sukumo, 26,992 ..... F 7
Sumoto, 46,313 ..... G 6
Sunagawa, 30,205 ..... K 2
Susaki, 32,020 ..... F 7
Suttsu, 8,043 ..... J 2
Suwa, 46,276 ..... H 6
Suzu, 32,122 ..... H 5
Suzuka, 115,000 ..... H 6
Tachikawa, 115,000 ..... O 2
Tajimi, 60,175 ..... H 6
Takada, 73,668 ..... J 5
Takaishi, 45,679 ..... H 7
Takamatsu, 271,000 ..... G 6
Takaoka, 158,000 ..... H 5
Takarazuka, 109,000 ..... H 7
Takasaki, 184,000 ..... J 5
Takatsuki, 178,000 ..... J 7
Takawa, 74,063 ..... E 7
Takayama, 53,399 ..... H 5
Takefu, 62,588 ..... G 6
Tanabe, Kyoto, 17,333 ..... J 7
Tanabe, Wakayama, 62,276 ..... G 7
Tateyama, 55,866 ..... K 6
Tendo, 43,903 ..... J 4
Tenri, 54,169 ..... J 8
Teshio, 9,493 ..... K 1
Toba, 30,098 ..... H 6
Tobetsu, 19,406 ..... K 2
Togane, 31,922 ..... K 6
Tojo, 16,866 ..... F 6
Tokushima, 225,000 ..... G 7
Tokuyama, 100,000 ..... F 6
Tokyo (capital), 8,832,647 ..... O 2
Tokyo, *11,350,000 ..... O 2
Tomakomai, 81,812 ..... K 2
Tomiyama, 7,863 ..... O 3
Tondabayashi, 47,985 ..... J 8
Tosa, 30,772 ..... F 7
Tosashimizu, 26,725 ..... F 7
Tosu, 44,419 ..... E 7
Tottori, 117,000 ..... G 6
Towada, 46,713 ..... K 3
Toyama, 264,000 ..... H 5
Toyohashi, 253,000 ..... H 6
Toyonaka, 334,000 ..... J 7
Toyooka, 43,259 ..... G 6
Toyota, 161,000 ..... H 6
Tsu, 123,000 ..... H 6
Tsubame, 40,134 ..... J 5
Tsuchiura, 78,971 ..... J 5
Tsuruga, 54,508 ..... G 6
Tsuruoka, 95,615 ..... J 4
Tsuyama, 76,007 ..... F 6
Ube, 149,000 ..... E 6
Uchinoura, 10,036 ..... E 8
Ueda, 73,940 ..... J 5
Ugo, 25,661 ..... K 4
Uji, 68,934 ..... J 7
Uozu, 46,854 ..... H 5
Urakawa, 21,552 ..... L 2
Urawa, 250,000 ..... O 2
Ushibuka, 30,995 ..... D 7
Usuki, 42,731 ..... E 7
Utsunomiya, 283,000 ..... K 5
Uwajima, 66,484 ..... F 7
Wajima, 35,798 ..... H 5
Wakasa, 8,455 ..... G 8
Wakayama, 353,000 ..... G 6
Wakkanai, 51,539 ..... K 1
Warabi, 69,715 ..... O 2
Yaizu, 77,008 ..... J 6
Yakumo, 22,487 ..... J 2
Yamagata, 201,000 ..... K 4
Yamaguchi, 103,000 ..... E 6
Yamato, 64,991 ..... O 2
Yamatokoriyama, 45,765 ..... J 8
Yamatotakada, 47,371 ..... J 8
Yao, 197,000 ..... J 8
Yatabe, 20,093 ..... P 2
Yatsushiro, 105,000 ..... E 7
Yawata, 19,204 ..... J 7
Yawatahania, 50,005 ..... F 7
Yoichi, 26,154 ..... K 2
Yokawa, 8,146 ..... H 7
Yokkaichi, 230,000 ..... H 6
Yokohama, 2,237,513 ..... O 3
Yokosuka, 340,000 ..... O 3
Yokote, 44,331 ..... K 4
Yonago, 108,000 ..... F 6
Yonezawa, 94,435 ..... K 5
Yono, 51,746 ..... O 2
Yotsukura, 20,226 ..... K 5
Yubari, 85,141 ..... L 2
Yubetsu, 9,720 ..... L 1
Yukuhashi, 47,495 ..... E 7
Yuzawa, 39,879 ..... K 4
Zushi, 43,211 ..... O 3

OTHER FEATURES

Abashiri (river) ..... M 1
Abukuma (river) ..... K 4
Agano (river) ..... J 4
Akan Nat'l Park ..... M 2
Amakusa (isls.), 233,465 ..... D 7
Amami (isls.), 186,193 ..... N 5
Amami-O-Shima (isl.), 94,348 ..... N 5
Ara (river) ..... O 2
Asahi (mt.) ..... J 4
Asama (mt.) ..... J 5
Ashizuri (cape) ..... F 7
Aso (mt.) ..... E 7
Aso Nat'l Park ..... E 7
Atsumi (bay) ..... H 6
Awa (isl.), 771 ..... J 4
Awaji (isl.), 185,473 ..... H 8
Bandai (mt.) ..... K 5
Bandai-Asahi Nat'l Park ..... J 4
Biwa (lake) ..... H 6
Bonin (isls.), 203 ..... M 3
Boso (pen.) ..... K 6
Bungo (strait) ..... F 7
Chichi (isl.), 203 ..... M 3
Chichibu-Tama Nat'l Park ..... J 6
Chokai (mt.) ..... J 4
Chubu Sangaku Nat'l Park ..... H 5
Dai (mt.) ..... F 6
Daimanji (mt.) ..... F 5
Daio (cape) ..... H 6
Daisen-Oki National Park ..... F 6
Daisetsu (mt.) ..... L 2
Daisetsu-Zan Nat'l Park ..... L 2
Dogo (isl.), 23,669 ..... F 5
Dozen (isl.), 12,516 ..... F 5
East China (sea) ..... C 8
Edo (river) ..... P 2
Erabu (isl.), 22,049 ..... N 5
Erimo (cape) ..... L 3
Esan (point) ..... K 3
Fuji (mt.) ..... J 6
Fuji (river) ..... J 6
Fuji-Hakone-Izu Nat'l Park ..... H 6
Gassan (mt.) ..... J 4
Goto (isls.), 159,190 ..... D 7
Habomai (isls.) ..... N 2
Hachiro (lagoon) ..... J 3
Haha (isl.) ..... M 3
Hakken (mt.) ..... H 6
Haku (mt.) ..... H 5
Hukusan Nat'l Park ..... H 5
Harima (sea) ..... G 6
Hida (river) ..... H 6
Hodaka (mt.) ..... H 5
Hokkaido (isl.), 5,171,800 ..... L 2
Honshu (isl.) 76,757,913 ..... J 5
Ie (isl.), 7,059 ..... N 6
Iheya (isl.), 3,083 ..... N 6
Iki (isl.), 45,654 ..... D 7
Ina (river) ..... H 7
Inawashiro (lake) ..... K 5
Inubo (cape) ..... K 6
Iriomote (isl.), 7,026 ..... K 7
Iro (cape) ..... J 6
Ise (bay) ..... H 6
Ise-Shima Nat'l Park ..... H 6
Ishigaki (isl.), 41,315 ..... L 7
Ishikari (bay) ..... K 2
Ishikari (river) ..... L 2
Ishizuchi (mt.) ..... F 7
Iwaki (mt.) ..... K 3
Iwate (mt.) ..... K 4
Iwo (isl.) ..... M 4
Iyo (sea) ..... E 7
Izu (isls.), 35,592 ..... J 6
Izu (pen.) ..... J 6
Japan (sea) ..... G 4
Joshinetsu-Kogen Nat'l Park ..... J 5
Kagoshima (bay) ..... E 8
Kamui (cape) ..... K 2
Kariba (mt.) ..... K 2
Kasumiga (lagoon) ..... K 5
Kazan-Retto (Volcano) (isls.) ..... M 4
Kerama (isls.), 2,467 ..... M 6
Kii (channel) ..... G 7
Kikai (isl.), 14,231 ..... O 5
Kino (river) ..... G 6
Kirishima-Yaku Nat'l Park ..... E 8
Kita Iwo (isl.) ..... M 4
Kitakami (river) ..... K 4
Koma (mt.) ..... K 2
Koshiki (isls.), 16,301 ..... D 8
Kuchino (isl.) ..... O 4
Kuju (mt.) ..... E 7
Kume (isl.), 5,922 ..... M 6
Kutcharo (lake) ..... M 2
Kyushu (isl.), 12,370,190 ..... E 7
Meakan (mt.) ..... L 2
Minami Iwo (isl.) ..... L 5
Miura (pen.) ..... O 3
Miyako (isl.), 47,150 ..... L 7
Miyako (isls.), 69,825 ..... L 7
Mogami (river) ..... K 4
Motsuta (cape) ..... J 2
Muko (river) ..... H 7
Muroto (point) ..... G 7
Mutsu (bay) ..... K 3
Naka (river) ..... K 5
Nampo-Shoto (isls.), 203 ..... M 3
Nii (isl.), 3,913 ..... J 6
Nikko Nat'l Park ..... J 5
Nojima (cape) ..... K 6
Noshappu (point) ..... N 2
Noto (pen.) ..... H 5
Nyudo (cape) ..... J 4
Oani (river) ..... K 3
Obitsu (river) ..... P 3
Oga (pen.) ..... J 4
Ogasawara-Gunto (Bonin) (isls.), 203 ..... M 3
Okhotsk (sea) ..... M 1
Oki (isls.), 36,185 ..... F 5
Okinawa (isl.), 782,267 ..... N 6
Okinawa (isls.), 812,339 ..... N 6
Okushiri (isl.), 7,142 ..... J 2
Oma (cape) ..... K 3
Omono (river) ..... J 4
Ono (river) ..... E 7
Ontake (mt.) ..... H 6
Osaka (bay) ..... H 8
Oshima (isl.), 11,840 ..... J 6
Osumi (isls.), 82,372 ..... E 8
Osumi (pen.) ..... E 8
Osumi (str.) ..... E 8
Otakine (mt.) ..... K 5
Rebun (isl.), 8,374 ..... K 1
Rikuchu-Kaigan Nat'l Park ..... L 4
Rishiri (isl.), 17,663 ..... K 1
Ryukyu (isls.), 1,108,271 ..... L 7
Sado (isl.), 102,925 ..... J 4
Sagami (bay) ..... O 3
Sagami (river) ..... O 2
Sagami (sea) ..... J 6
Saikai Nat'l Park ..... D 7
Sakishima (isls.), 121,837 ..... K 7
San'in Kaigan Nat'l Park ..... G 6
Sata (cape) ..... E 8
Setonaikai Nat'l Park ..... H 7
Shikoku (isl.), 3,975,058 ..... F 7
Shikotan (isl.) ..... N 2
Shikotsu (lake) ..... K 2
Shikotsu-Toya Nat'l Park ..... K 2
Shimane (pen.) ..... F 6
Shimokita (pen.) ..... K 3
Shinano (river) ..... J 5
Shiono (cape) ..... H 7
Shiragami (cape) ..... J 3
Shirane (mt.) ..... J 5
Shirane (mt.) ..... H 6
Shiretoko (cape) ..... M 1
Shiriya (cape) ..... K 3
Soya (point) ..... L 1
Suo (sea) ..... E 7
Suruga (bay) ..... J 6
Suwanose (isl.) ..... O 4
Suzu (point) ..... H 5
Takeshima (isls.) ..... F 5
Tama (river) ..... O 2
Tanega (isl.), 60,130 ..... E 8
Tarama (isl.), 2,603 ..... L 7
Tazawa (lake) ..... K 4
Teshio (mt.) ..... L 1
Teshio (river) ..... L 1
Tobi (isl.) ..... J 4
Tokachi (mt.) ..... L 2
Tokachi (river) ..... L 2
Tokara (arch), 2,722 ..... O 5
Tokuno (isl.), 18,920 ..... O 5
Tokyo (bay) ..... O 2
Tone (river) ..... J 5
Tosa (bay) ..... F 7
Towada (lake) ..... K 3
Towada-Hachimantai Nat'l Park ..... K 3
Toya (lake) ..... K 2
Toyama (bay) ..... H 5
Tsu (isls.), 65,304 ..... D 6
Tsugaru (strait) ..... K 3
Tsurugi (mt.) ..... G 7
Tsushima (isls.), 65,304 ..... D 6
Tsushima (strait) ..... D 7
Unzen (mt.) ..... D 7
Unzen-Amakusa Nat'l Park ..... D 7
Volcano (isls.) ..... M 4
Wakasa (bay) ..... G 6
Yaeyama (isls.), 52,012 ..... K 7
Yaku (isl.), 22,242 ..... E 8
Yonaguni (isl.), 3,671 ..... K 7
Yoron (isl.), 7,181 ..... N 6
Yoshino (river) ..... G 6
Yoshino-Kumano Nat'l Park ..... H 7
Zao (mt.) ..... K 5

KOREA (NORTH)

CITIES and TOWNS

Anju ..... B 4

Changjon ....D 4
Chasŏng ....C 3
Ch'ŏngjin, †250,000 ....E 3
Chŏngju ....B 4
Chŭngson ....B 4
Haeju, †140,000 ....B 4
Hamhŭng-Hŭngnam, †200,000 ....C 4
Hoeryŏng ....D 2
Hongwŏn ....C 3
Hŭngnam-Hamhŭng, †200,000....C 4
Hyesan ....D 3
Iwŏn ....D 3
Kaesŏng, †175,000 ....C 4
Kanggye ....C 3
Kapsan ....C 3
Kilchu ....D 3
Kimchaek, †100,000 ....D 3
Kosŏng ....D 4
Kusŏng ....B 4
Manp'o ....C 3
Musan ....D 2
Najin ....E 2
Namp'o, †140,000 ....B 4
Nanam ....D 3
Ongjin ....B 5
Pak'chŏn ....B 4
P'anmunjŏm ....C 5
Pukch'ŏng ....C 3
P'yŏnggang ....C 4
P'yŏngyang (cap.), †800,000 ....C 4
P'yŏngyang, *1,221,300 ....C 4
Sariwŏn ....B 4
Sinp'o ....D 4
Sinŭiju, †300,000 ....B 3
Sŏnch'ŏn ....B 4
Sunch'ŏn ....B 4
Tanch'ŏn ....D 3
Ŭiju ....B 3
Unggi ....E 2
Unsan ....C 4
Wŏnsan, †275,000 ....C 4
Yangdŏk ....C 4
Yongamp'o ....B 4

OTHER FEATURES

Baktu (mt.) ....C 3
Chang Pai Shan (range)....D 2
Changjin (res.) ....C 3
East Korea (bay) ....D 4
Kŏmdŏk (mt.) ....D 3
Kumgang (mt.) ....D 4
Nangnim-sanmaek (range) ....C 3
Paektu (Baktu) (mt.) ....C 3
Puksubaek (mt.)....C 3
Supong (res.) ....B 3
Taedong (river) ....C 4
Tumen (river) ....D 2
Tuun (mt.) ....C 3
West Korea (bay) ....B 4
Yalu (river) ....C 3

KOREA (SOUTH)

CITIES and TOWNS

Andong, 63,816 ....D 5
Ansŏng, 23,698 ....C 5
Changhŭng, 30,166 ....C 6
Changsŏng, 26,816 ....C 6
Chech'ŏn, 49,883 ....D 5
Cheju, 87,569 ....C 7
Chinhae, 80,804 ....D 6
Chinju, 107,126 ....D 6
Choch'iwŏn, 25,423 ....C 5
Ch'ŏnan, 71,315 ....C 5
Ch'ŏngju, 123,736 ....C 5
Chŏngŭp, 47,036 ....C 6
Chŏnju, 220,654 ....C 6
Ch'unch'ŏn, 100,043 ....D 5
Ch'ungju, 80,212 ....C 5
Hongch'ŏn, 23,473 ....D 5
Hongsŏng, 21,912 ....C 5
Inch'ŏn, 525,072 ....C 5
Iri, 78,448 ....C 6
Kanggyŏng, 26,430 ....C 5
Kangnŭng, 65,422 ....D 5
Kimch'ŏn, 56,981 ....D 5
Koch'ang, 34,707 ....C 6
Kongju, 30,320 ....C 5
Kunsan, 102,343 ....C 6
Kwangju, 403,737 ....C 6
Kyŏngju, 85,895 ....D 6
Masan, 154,856 ....D 6
Miryang, 40,288 ....D 6
Mokp'o, 162,322 ....C 6
Muju, 18,174 ....C 6
Namwŏn, 44,193 ....C 6
P'anmunjŏm ....C 5
P'ohang, 66,190 ....D 5
Posŏng, 22,247 ....C 6
Pusan, 1,425,703 ....D 6
Samch'ŏk, 35,117 ....D 5
Samnangjin, 21,936 ....D 6
Sangju, 47,558 ....D 5
Seoul (cap.), 4,100,000 ....C 5
Sŏsan, 30,416 ....C 5
Sunch'ŏn, 79,313 ....C 6
Suwŏn, 127,752 ....C 5
Taegu, 845,073 ....D 6
Taejŏn, 315,094 ....C 5
Tamyang, 14,856 ....C 6
Ŭisŏng, 21,306 ....D 5
Ulchin, 27,579 ....D 5
Ulsan, 112,858 ....D 6
Wŏnju, 103,852 ....D 5
Yangyang, 10,832 ....D 4
Yŏngch'ŏn, 44,305 ....D 6
Yŏngdŏk, 19,220 ....D 5
Yŏngju, 46,338 ....D 5
Yŏsu, 102,011 ....C 6

OTHER FEATURES

Cheju (isl.), 336,694 ....C 7
Cheju (strait) ....C 7
Dagelet (Ullŭng) (isl.), 27,032 ....E 5
Halla (mt.) ....C 7
Han (river) ....C 5
Kŏje (isl.), 117,906 ....D 6
Korea (strait) ....D 6
Kŭm (river) ....C 5
Naktong (river) ....D 6
Port Hamilton (So) (isl.) ....C 6
Quelpart (Cheju) (isl.), 336,694..C 7
So (isl.) ....C 6
Taebaek (mt.) ....D 5
Ullŭng (isl.), 22,032 ....E 5

*City and suburbs.

JAPAN is divided into prefectures bearing the same names as their capitals except:

Prefecture	Capital	Ref.
AICHI	NAGOYA	H 6
EHIME	MATSUYAMA	F 7
GUMMA	MAEBASHI	J 5
HOKKAIDO	SAPPORO	K 2
HYOGO	KOBE	H 7
IBARAKI	MITO	K 5
ISHIKAWA	KANAZAWA	H 5
IWATE	MORIOKA	K 4
KAGAWA	TAKAMATSU	G 6
KANAGAWA	YOKOHAMA	O 3
MIE	TSU	H 6
MIYAGI	SENDAI	K 4
OKINAWA	NAHA	N 6
SAITAMA	URAWA	O 2
SHIGA	OTSU	J 7
SHIMANE	MATSUE	F 6
TOCHIGI	UTSUNOMIYA	K 5
YAMANASHI	KOFU	J 6

†Populations courtesy of Kingsley Davis, Office of Int'l Pop. & Urban Research, Inst. of Int'l Studies, Univ. of California.

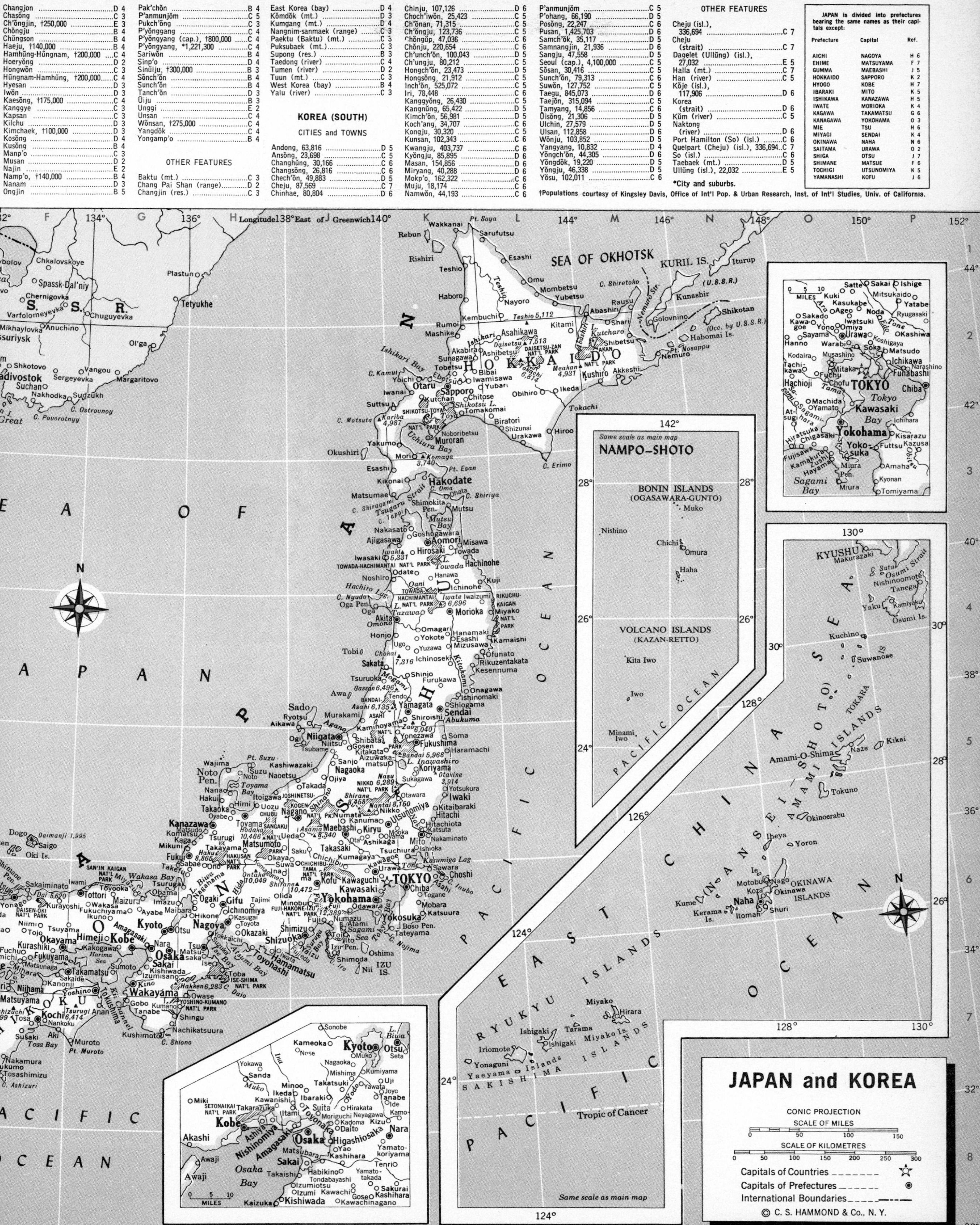

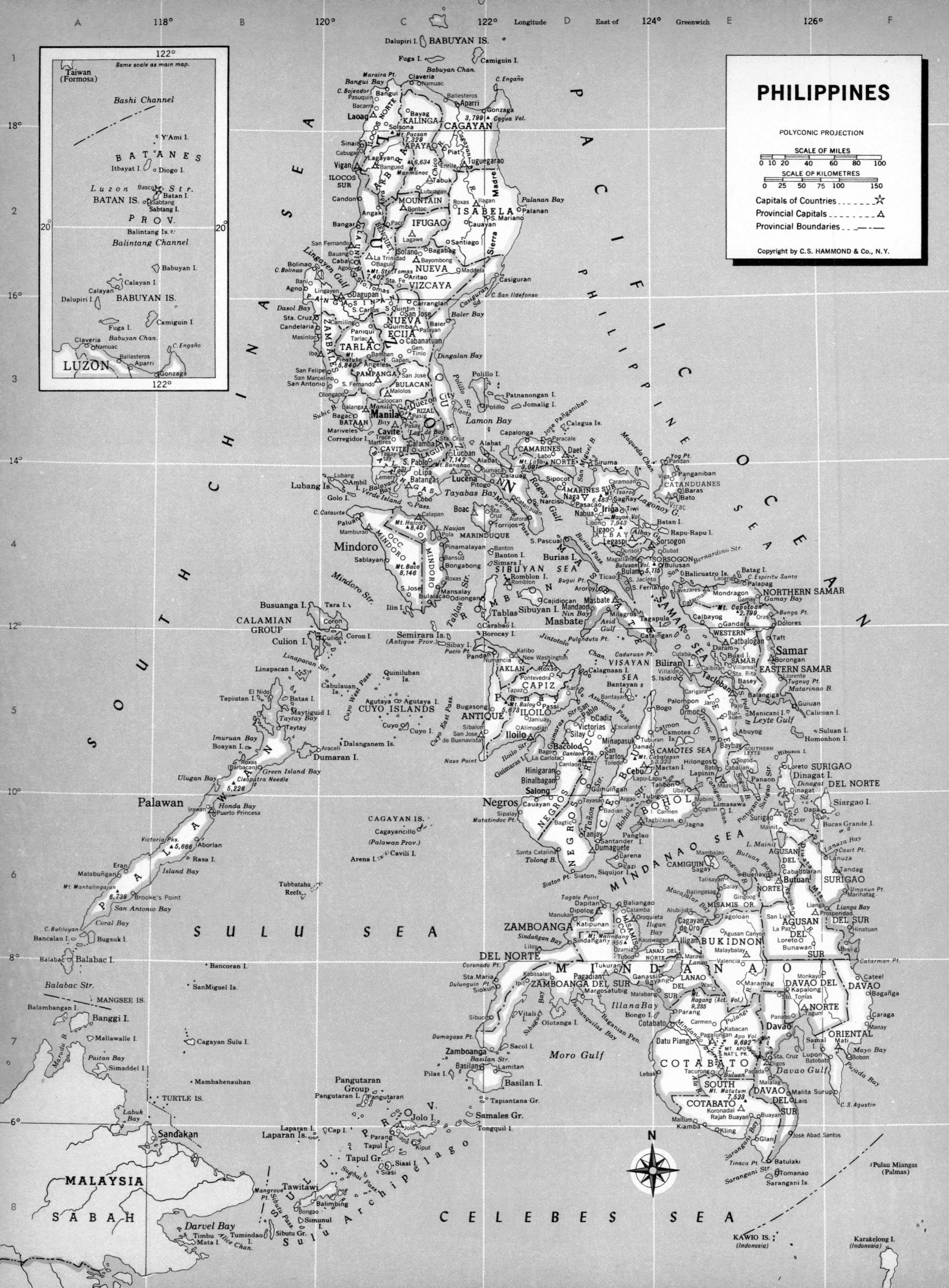

PHILIPPINES
POLYCONIC PROJECTION
SCALE OF MILES
0 10 20 40 60 80 100
SCALE OF KILOMETRES
0 25 50 75 100 150
Capitals of Countries
Provincial Capitals
Provincial Boundaries
Copyright by C.S. HAMMOND & Co., N.Y.
Longitude East of Greenwich
118° 120° 122° 124° 126°
18° 16° 14° 12° 10° 8° 6°
Same scale as main map.
Taiwan (Formosa)
Bashi Channel
Y'Ami I.
BATANES
Itbayat I.
Diogo I.
Luzon Str.
Basco
Batan I.
BATAN IS.
Sabtang
Sabtang I.
PROV.
Balintang Is.
Balintang Channel
Babuyan I.
Calayan I.
Calayan
Dalupiri I.
BABUYAN IS.
Camiguin I
Fuga I.
Babuyan Chan.
Claveria
Namuac
C. Engaño
Ballesteros
Aparri
Gonzaga
LUZON
PACIFIC OCEAN
PHILIPPINE SEA
SOUTH CHINA SEA
SULU SEA
CELEBES SEA
MINDANAO SEA
VISAYAN SEA
SIBUYAN SEA
CAMOTES SEA
SAMAR SEA
Moro Gulf
Davao Gulf
Lamon Bay
Tayabas Bay
Lingayen Gulf
Leyte Gulf
Manila
Quezon City
Mindoro
Palawan
Negros
Samar
Masbate
Cebu
BOHOL
Panay
CAPIZ
ILOILO
ANTIQUE
AKLAN
MINDANAO
ZAMBOANGA DEL NORTE
ZAMBOANGA DEL SUR
BUKIDNON
COTABATO
SOUTH COTABATO
DAVAO DEL NORTE
DAVAO ORIENTAL
DAVAO DEL SUR
AGUSAN DEL NORTE
AGUSAN DEL SUR
SURIGAO DEL NORTE
SURIGAO DEL SUR
MISAMIS OR.
NORTHERN SAMAR
EASTERN SAMAR
WESTERN SAMAR
CATANDUANES
SORSOGON
ALBAY
CAMARINES NORTE
CAMARINES SUR
MARINDUQUE
ROMBLON
CAGAYAN
ISABELA
IFUGAO
MOUNTAIN
KALINGA-APAYAO
ILOCOS NORTE
ILOCOS SUR
NUEVA VIZCAYA
NUEVA ECIJA
TARLAC
PAMPANGA
BULACAN
BATAAN
RIZAL
CAVITE
LAGUNA
BATANGAS
QUEZON
CALAMIAN GROUP
CUYO ISLANDS
CAGAYAN IS.
SULU ARCHIPELAGO
SULU PROV.
Jolo I.
Basilan I.
Tawitawi
MALAYSIA
SABAH
Sandakan
TURTLE IS.
MANGSEE IS.
Balabac I.
Balabac Str.
Banggi I.
KAWIO IS. (Indonesia)
Karakelong I. (Indonesia)
Pulau Miangas (Palmas)
Pulau Marore
N

AREA 115,707 sq. mi.
POPULATION 39,079,000
CAPITAL Quezon City
LARGEST CITY Manila
HIGHEST POINT Apo 9,692 ft.
MONETARY UNIT Philippine peso
MAJOR LANGUAGES Pilipino (Tagalog), English, Spanish, Bisayan, Ilocano, Bikol
MAJOR RELIGIONS Roman Catholicism, Islam, Tribal religions

PROVINCES

Abra, 115,193 ....C 2
Agusan del Norte, 174,758 ....E 6
Agusan del Sur, 96,252 ....E 6
Aklan, 226,232 ....D 5
Albay, 514,980 ....D 4
Antique, 238,405 ....D 5
Bataan, 145,323 ....C 3
Batanes, 10,309 ....A 2
Batangas, 681,414 ....C 4
Benguet, 183,657 ....C 2
Bohol, 592,194 ....E 6
Bukidnon, 194,368 ....E 6
Bulacan, 555,819 ....C 3
Cagayan, 445,289 ....C 1
Camarines Norte, 188,091 ....D 3
Camarines Sur, 819,565 ....D 4
Camiguin, 44,717 ....E 6
Capiz, 315,079 ....D 5
Catanduanes, 156,329 ....E 4
Cavite, 378,138 ....C 3
Cebu, 1,332,847 ....D 5
Cotabato, 766,583 ....E 7
Davao del Norte, 226,728 ....E 7
Davao del Sur, 533,702 ....E 7
Davao Oriental, 132,593 ....F 7
Eastern Samar, 237,747 ....E 4
Ifugao, 76,788 ....C 2
Ilocos Norte, 287,333 ....C 1
Ilocos Sur, 338,058 ....C 2
Iloilo, 966,266 ....D 5
Isabela, 442,062 ....C 2
Kalinga-Apayao, 80,393 ....C 2
Laguna, 472,064 ....C 3
Lanao del Norte, 270,603 ....E 6
Lanao del Sur, 378,327 ....E 7
La Union, 293,330 ....C 2
Leyte, 963,364 ....E 5
Manila (city), 1,499,000 ....C 3
Marinduque, 114,586 ....C 4
Masbate, 335,971 ....D 4
Misamis Occidental, 248,371 ....D 6
Misamis Oriental, 343,898 ....E 6
Mountain, 95,001 ....C 2
Negros Occidental, 1,332,323 ....D 6
Negros Oriental, 597,761 ....D 6
Northern Samar, 261,424 ....E 4
Nueva Ecija, 608,362 ....C 3
Nueva Vizcaya, 138,090 ....C 2
Occidental Mindoro, 84,316 ....C 4
Oriental Mindoro, 228,998 ....C 4
Palawan, 162,669 ....B 6
Pampanga, 617,259 ....C 3
Pangasinan, 1,124,144 ....C 3
Quezon, 653,426 ....C 3
Rizal, 1,456,362 ....C 3
Romblon, 131,658 ....D 4
Sorsogon, 347,771 ....E 4
South Cotabato, 262,536 ....E 7
Southern Leyte, 209,608 ....E 5
Sulu, 326,898 ....B 8
Surigao del Norte, 194,981 ....F 5
Surigao del Sur, 165,016 ....F 6
Tarlac, 426,647 ....C 3
Western Samar, 368,823 ....E 4
Zambales, 213,442 ....C 3
Zamboanga del Norte, 281,429 ....D 6
Zamboanga del Sur, 742,204 ....D 7

CITIES and TOWNS

Abuyog, 7,018 ....E 5
Agoo, 6,511 ....C 2
Alimodian, 6,732 ....D 5
Alubijid, 5,105 ....E 6
Angeles, †102,400 ....C 3
Aparri, 13,167 ....C 1
Bacarra, 7,268 ....C 1
Bacolod, †156,900 ....D 5
Bago, †58,834 ....D 5
Bagtic, 6,932 ....D 6
Baguio, †58,000 ....C 2
Balangiga, 5,343 ....E 5
Balingasag, 5,502 ....E 6
Bangued, 7,602 ....C 2
Bantayan, 7,920 ....D 5
Basey, 6,240 ....E 5
Basilan, †209,100 ....C 7
Batangas, †102,100 ....C 4
Baybay, 10,021 ....E 5
Bayombong, 8,312 ....C 2
Binalbagan, 13,545 ....D 5
Bogo, 6,786 ....E 5
Bontoc, 5,472 ....C 2
Buenavista, 5,770 ....E 6
Bulan, 16,042 ....D 4
Bulusan, 5,394 ....E 4
Burauen, 8,677 ....E 5
Butuan, †110,100 ....E 6
Cabadbaran, 5,954 ....E 6
Cabanatuan, †80,000 ....C 3
Cadiz, †118,200 ....D 5
Cagayan de Oro, †78,000 ....E 6
Caibiran, 7,213 ....E 5
Calamba, 12,142 ....C 3
Calbayog, †103,100 ....E 4
Caloocan, †194,600 ....C 3
Camiling, 9,799 ....C 3
Canlaon, †26,000 ....D 5
Carigara, 8,299 ....E 5
Catarman, 8,248 ....E 4
Catbalogan, 14,274 ....E 5
Cavite, †63,000 ....C 3
Cebu, †332,100 ....D 5
Cotabato, †43,000 ....D 7
Daet, 19,726 ....D 3
Dagupan, †73,000 ....C 2
Danao, †37,000 ....D 5
Dapitan, †31,000 ....D 6
Datu Piang, 21,951 ....E 7
Davao, †337,000 ....E 7
Digos, 8,725 ....E 7
Dipolog, 15,102 ....D 6
Donsol, 5,509 ....D 4
Dumaguete, †40,000 ....D 6
Enrile, 5,570 ....C 2
Escalante, 5,304 ....D 5
Gapan, 6,741 ....C 3
General Tinio, 9,772 ....C 3
Gingoog, †60,000 ....E 6
Gubat, 8,392 ....E 4
Guihulñgan, 6,401 ....D 5
Guimba, 8,280 ....C 3
Guiuan, 5,865 ....E 5
Gumaca, 9,175 ....D 4
Hinigaran, 10,231 ....D 5
Ilagan, 6,375 ....C 2
Iligan, †67,000 ....E 6
Iloilo, †201,000 ....D 5
Iriga, †101,000 ....D 4
Janiuay, 5,840 ....D 5
Jaro, 7,243 ....E 5
Jose Pañganiban, 5,291 ....D 3
Kalibo, 6,025 ....D 5
Koronadal, 3,677 ....E 7
La Carlota, †56,722 ....D 5
Lagawe, 3,019 ....C 2
Lais, 7,752 ....E 7
Laoag, †50,198 ....C 1
Laoang, 8,557 ....E 4
Lapu-Lapu, †56,000 ....D 5
La Trinidad, 3,334 ....C 2
Lebak, 5,626 ....D 7
Legaspi, †69,000 ....D 4
Lemery, 8,617 ....C 4
Lianga, 5,772 ....E 6
Ligao, 10,547 ....D 4
Lingayen, 8,221 ....C 2
Lipa, †79,000 ....C 4
Lucban, 14,292 ....C 3
Lucena, †56,000 ....C 4
Maasin, 7,968 ....E 5
Magallanes, 6,002 ....D 4
Malabang, 7,884 ....D 7
Malalag, 5,242 ....E 7
Malaybalay, 7,624 ....E 6
Malita, 5,947 ....E 7
Malolos, 2,240 ....C 3
Mambajao, 3,880 ....E 6
Mandaon, 11,419 ....D 4
Manila, †1,499,000 ....C 3
Manila, *2,369,000 ....C 3
Marawi, †31,000 ....E 6
Masbate, 11,647 ....D 4
Mati, 7,870 ....F 7
Minapasuk, 10,497 ....D 5
Nabua, 14,146 ....D 4
Naga, †63,000 ....D 4
Olongapo, †45,330 ....C 3
Ormoc, †72,000 ....E 5
Oroquieta, 5,331 ....D 6
Ozamiz, †50,000 ....D 6
Paco, 5,475 ....C 2
Pagadian, 17,865 ....D 7
Pagalungan, 770 ....E 7
Palanan, 5,599 ....D 2
Palayan, †20,854 ....C 3
Palo, 8,916 ....E 5
Palompon, 6,399 ....E 5
Panabo, 5,539 ....E 7
Paniqui, 6,492 ....C 3
Parang, 5,894 ....E 7
Pasay, †174,100 ....C 3
Pinamalayan, 6,236 ....C 4
Prosperidad, 3,478 ....E 6
Puerto Princesa, 7,551 ....B 6
Quezon City (cap.), †545,500 ....C 3
Rajah Buayan, †114,000 ....E 7
Roxas, Capiz, †57,000 ....D 5
Roxas, Isabela, 5,612 ....C 2
Salong, 28,743 ....D 5
San Antonio, 8,717 ....B 3
San Carlos, Negros Occ., †165,200 ....D 5
San Carlos, Pangasinan, †73,900 ....C 3
San Felipe, 5,900 ....B 3
San Jacinto, 5,120 ....D 4
San Jose, Bulacan, 5,326 ....C 3
San Jose, Nueva Ecija, 13,444 ....C 3
San Jose de Buenavista, 6,364 ....C 5
San Marcelino, 6,841 ....B 3
San Pablo, Laguna, †81,000 ....C 3
San Pablo, Negros Occ., 13,725 ....D 5
Santa Cruz, Davao, 6,456 ....E 7
Santa Cruz, Laguna, 5,248 ....C 3
Santo Tomas, 9,450 ....E 7
Silay, †69,000 ....D 5
Sindañgan, 5,867 ....D 6
Sipocot, 5,914 ....D 4
Tabuk, 3,378 ....C 2
Tacloban, †61,000 ....E 5
Tacurong, 6,413 ....E 7
Tagaytay, †8,000 ....C 3
Tagbilaran, †20,250 ....E 6
Tagum, 5,263 ....E 7
Tanjay, 12,355 ....D 6
Tarlac, †121,400 ....C 3
Toledo, †73,000 ....D 5
Trece Martires, †5,000 ....C 3
Tuguegarao, 10,497 ....C 2
Victorias, 12,446 ....D 5
Vigan, 10,498 ....C 2
Villalon, 7,003 ....E 5
Virac, 9,143 ....E 4
Wao, 6,131 ....E 7
Zamboanga, †176,800 ....C 7

OTHER FEATURES

Abra (riv.) ....C 2
Agusan (riv.) ....E 6
Agutáya (isl.), 2,541 ....C 5
Alabat (isl.), 21,365 ....D 3
Albay (gulf) ....D 4
Alice (chan.) ....B 8
Ambil (isl.), 296 ....C 4
Apo (vol.) ....E 7
Asid (gulf) ....D 4
Asuncion (passage) ....D 5
Babuyan (chan.) ....C 1
Babuyan (isls.), 5,388 ....A 2
Baganian (pen.) ....D 7
Balabac (isl.), 2,870 ....A 7
Balayan (bay) ....C 4
Balicuatro (isls.), 8,044 ....E 4
Balintang (chan.) ....A 2
Bancalan (isl.), 231 ....A 6
Bantayan (isl.), 46,593 ....D 5
Banton (isl.), 6,155 ....D 4
Bashi (chan.) ....A 1
Basilan (isl.), 134,435 ....D 7
Batag (isl.), 4,561 ....E 4
Batan (isl.), Albay, 10,000 ....E 4
Batan (isl.), Batanes, 6,178 ....B 2
Batan (isls.), 10,309 ....A 2
Batas (isl.), 147 ....B 5
Bay (lag.) ....C 3
Biliran (isl.), 78,707 ....E 5
Bohol (isl.), 531,707 ....E 6
Bohol (str.) ....D 6
Bojeador (cape) ....C 1
Bolinao (cape) ....B 2
Bongo (isl.), 2,446 ....D 7
Borocay (isl.), 2,378 ....D 5
Buad (isl.), 11,549 ....E 5
Bucas Grande (isl.), 4,883 ....F 6
Bugsuk (isl.), 482 ....A 6
Buluan (lake) ....E 7
Bulusan (vol.) ....D 4
Burias (isl.), 15,494 ....D 4
Busuanga (isl.), 13,190 ....B 4
Butuan (bay) ....E 6
Cabalasan (mt.) ....E 5
Cabulauan (isls.), 469 ....C 5
Cagayan (isls.), 3,880 ....C 6
Cagayan (riv.) ....C 2
Cagayan Sulu (isl.), 10,789 ....B 7
Cagua (vol.) ....D 1
Calagnaan (isl.), 2,197 ....D 5
Calagua (isls.), 1,509 ....D 3
Calamian Group (isls.), 21,975 ....B 4
Calayan (isl.), 3,409 ....A 2
Calicoan (isl.), 2,557 ....E 5
Camiguin (isl.), 1,177 ....B 3
Camotes (isls.), 50,826 ....E 5
Camotes (sea) ....E 5
Capotoan (mt.) ....E 4
Carabao (isl.), 2,697 ....D 4
Casiguran (sound) ....C 2
Catanduanes (isl.), 154,698 ....E 4
Cebu (isl.), 1,163,756 ....D 6
Cleopatra Needle (mt.) ....B 5
Coral (bay) ....A 6
Coron (isl.), 409 ....C 5
Corregidor (isl.), 65 ....C 3
Culion (isl.), 4,785 ....B 5
Cuyo (isl.), 15,541 ....C 5
Cuyo (isls.), 24,728 ....C 5
Cuyo East (passage) ....C 5
Cuyo West (passage) ....C 5
Dalanganem (isls.), 499 ....C 5
Daram (isl.), 23,310 ....E 5
Davao (gulf) ....E 7
Dinagat (isl.), 19,543 ....E 5
Dingalan (bay) ....C 3
Diuata (mts.) ....E 6
Dumaran (isl.), 4,453 ....C 5
Engaño (cape) ....D 1
Espiritu Santo (cape) ....E 4
Fuga (isl.), 802 ....C 1
Golo (isl.), 1,191 ....C 4
Green Island (bay) ....B 5
Guimaras (isl.), 56,137 ....D 5
Hibuson (isl.), 880 ....E 5
Homonhon (isl.), 2,315 ....E 5
Ilin (isl.), 5,379 ....C 4
Illana (bay) ....D 7
Iloilo (str.) ....D 5
Island (bay) ....B 6
Itbayat (isl.), 2,365 ....A 2
Jintotolo (chan.) ....D 5
Jolo (isl.), 165,607 ....C 7
Jomalig (isl.), 1,284 ....D 3
Lagonoy (gulf) ....E 4
Lamon (bay) ....C 3
Lanao (lake) ....E 7
Lapinin (isl.), 9,618 ....E 5
Leyte (gulf) ....E 5
Leyte (isl.), 1,053,782 ....E 5
Limasawa (isl.), 1,874 ....E 6
Linapacan (isl.), 922 ....B 5
Lingayen (gulf) ....C 2
Lubang (isls.), 16,748 ....B 4
Luzon (isl.), 12,702,731 ....C 3
Luzon (str.) ....A 2
Macajalar (bay) ....E 6
Mactan (isl.), 50,014 ....E 5
Mainit (lake) ....E 6
Mangsee (isls.), 143 ....A 7
Manicani (isl.), 1,341 ....E 5
Manila (bay) ....C 3
Mantalingajan (mt.) ....A 6
Maqueda (chan.) ....D 3
Marinduque (isl.), 112,048 ....C 4
Masbate (isl.), 264,273 ....D 4
Mayon (vol.) ....D 4
Maytiguid (isl.), 456 ....B 5
Mindanao (isl.), 4,699,475 ....D 7
Mindanao (riv.) ....E 7
Mindanao (sea) ....D 6
Mindoro (isl.), 290,394 ....C 4
Mindoro (str.) ....C 4
Mompog (passage) ....D 4
Moro (gulf) ....D 7
Mount Apo Nat'l Park ....E 7
Naujan (lake) ....C 4
Negros (isl.), 1,862,115 ....D 6
Olutanga (isl.), 16,616 ....D 7
Palawan (isl.), 100,664 ....B 6
Panaon (isl.), 28,933 ....E 5
Panay (isl.), 1,659,832 ....D 5
Panglao (isl.), 24,631 ....D 6
Pangutaran (isl.), 8,153 ....C 7
Pangutaran Group (isls.), 10,235 ....C 7
Patnanongan (isl.), 2,760 ....D 3
Philippine (sea) ....D 3
Pilas (isl.), 7,882 ....C 7
Polillo (isl.), 18,766 ....C 3
Quiniluban (isls.), 673 ....C 5
Ragang (vol.) ....E 7
Ragay (gulf) ....D 4
Rapu-Rapu (isl.), 6,799 ....E 4
Romblon (isl.), 15,178 ....D 4
Sabtang (isl.), 1,766 ....B 2
Sacol (isl.), 4,385 ....D 7
Samal (isl.), 33,103 ....E 7
Samales Group (isls.), 5,816 ....D 7
Samar (isl.), 733,809 ....E 4
Samar (sea) ....E 4
San Agustin (cape) ....F 7
San Bernardino (str.) ....E 4
Sarangani (isls.), 4,701 ....E 8
Semirara (isls.), 5,993 ....C 5
Siargao (isl.), 38,388 ....F 6
Siasi (isl.), 18,353 ....C 8
Sibay (isl.), 1,167 ....C 5
Sibutu (passage) ....B 8
Sibutu Group (isls.), 10,624 ....B 8
Sibuyan (isl.), 25,161 ....D 4
Sibuyan (sea) ....D 4
Sierra Madre (range) ....D 2
Simara (isl.), 6,510 ....D 4
Simunul (isl.), 6,040 ....B 8
Siquijor (isl.), 59,555 ....D 6
Subic (bay) ....C 3
Sulu (arch.), 315,573 ....B 8
Sulu (sea) ....B 6
Suluan (isl.), 834 ....F 5
Taal (lake) ....C 4
Tablas (isl.), 71,429 ....D 4
Tagapula (isl.), 4,592 ....E 4
Tapiantana Group (isls.), 6,081 ....D 7
Tapul (isl.), 7,927 ....C 8
Tapul Group (isls.), 57,856 ....C 8
Tara (isl.), 385 ....C 4
Tawitawi (isl.), 8,257 ....B 8
Ticao (isl.), 47,403 ....D 4
Tinaca (pt.) ....E 8
Tongquil (isl.), 1,662 ....D 8
Tubbataha (reefs) ....B 6
Tumindao (isl.), 1,847 ....B 8
Turtle (isls.), 536 ....B 7
Ulugan (bay) ....B 5
Umanun (pt.) ....F 6
Verde Island (passage) ....C 4
Victoria (peaks) ....B 6
Visayan (sea) ....D 5
Vitali (isl.), 3,297 ....D 7
Yog (pt.) ....E 3

*City and suburbs.
†Population of municipality.

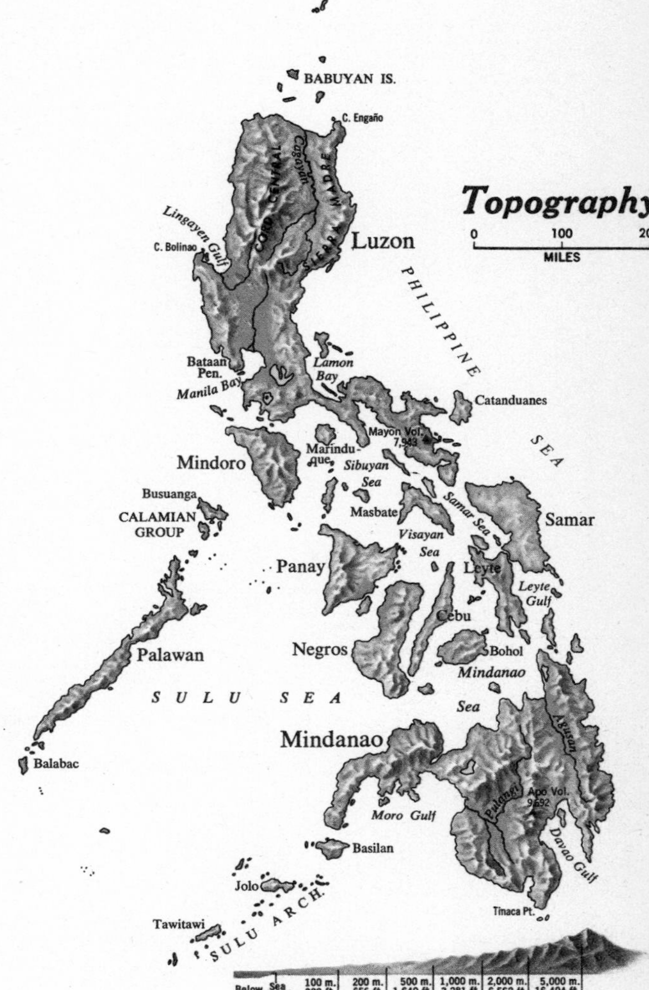

Agriculture, Industry and Resources

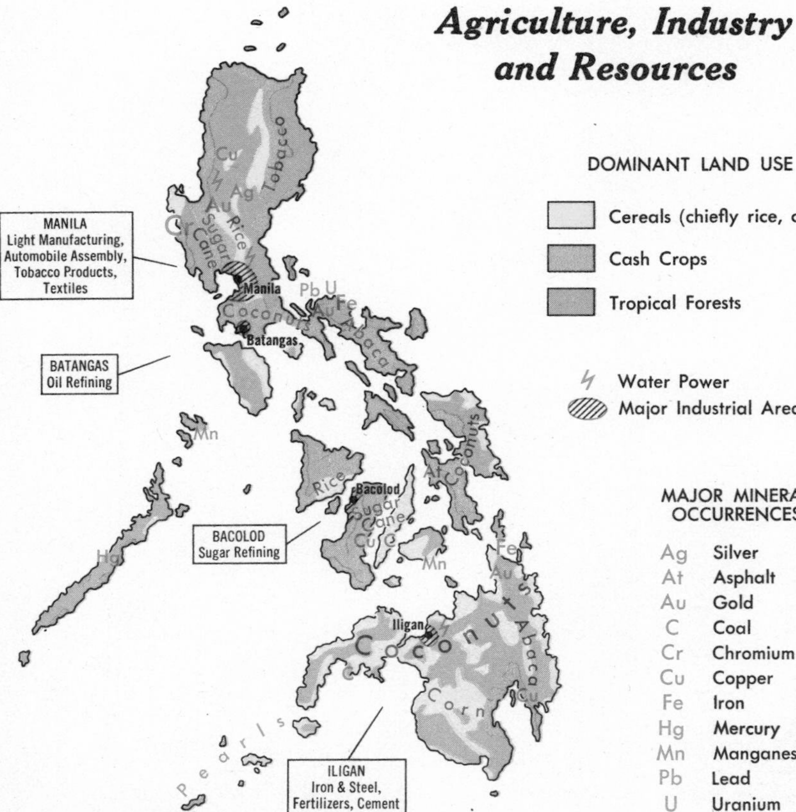

BRUNEI

CITIES and TOWNS

Bandar Seri Begawan (cap.), 37,000 ... E 4

INDONESIA

CITIES and TOWNS

Agats, 300 ... K 7
Amahai, †8,017 ... H 6
Amboina, 70,000 ... H 6
Ambon (Amboina), 70,000 ... H 6
Balikpapan, 113,000 ... F 6
Banda Atjeh, 49,000 ... A 4
Bandanaira, 13,686 ... H 6
Bandjarmasin, 264,000 ... E 6
Bandung, 1,006,000 ... H 2
Bangil, 34,112 ... K 2
Bangkalan, †29,536 ... K 2
Banjuwangi, 53,576 ... L 2
Bantul, 30,572 ... J 2
Barabai, 9,366 ... F 6
Barus, †35,716 ... B 5
Batang, 57,561 ... J 2
Batavia (Djakarta) (cap.), 3,429,000 ... H 1
Baturadja, †26,706 ... C 6
Batusangkar, 10,437 ... C 6
Bekasi, 32,012 ... H 2
Bengkajang, †17,029 ... E 5
Bengkalis, †36,433 ... C 5
Bengkulu, 31,000 ... C 6
Benteng, 7,035 ... F 7
Bindjai, 56,000 ... B 5
Bitung, 15,249 ... H 5
Blitar, 78,000 ... K 2
Blora, 49,296 ... K 2
Bodjonegoro, †61,749 ... J 2
Bogor, 172,000 ... H 2
Bondowoso, †44,215 ... L 2
Bonthain, †40,289 ... F 7
Brebes, †72,971 ... H 2
Bukittinggi, 62,000 ... B 6
Bula, 3,116 ... J 6
Bulukumba, 14,137 ... G 7
Bumiaju, †52,790 ... H 2
Buntok, 3.884 ... F 6
Demak, †42,915 ... J 2
Denpasar, †52,000 ... E 7
Djailolo, †10,170 ... H 5
Djajapura, 14,462 ... K 6
Djakarta (cap.), 3,429,000 ... H 1
Djakarta, *5,692,000 ... H 1
Djambi (Telanaipura) 139,000 ... C 6
Djeneponto, 10,350 ... F 7
Djepara, †54,025 ... J 2
Djokjakarta, 385,000 ... J 2
Djombang, †57,370 ... K 2
Dompu, 8,886 ... F 7
Fakfak, 2,430 ... J 6
Galela, †7,384 ... H 5
Garut, †67,542 ... H 2
Gorontalo, 88,000 ... G 5
Gresik, 36,790 ... K 2
Hollandia (Djajapura), 14,462 ... K 6
Indramaju, †56,117 ... H 2
Isimu, 4,304 ... G 5
Kaimana, 1,128 ... J 6
Kajuagung, 15,000 ... D 6
Kalianda, †31,073 ... D 7
Kampung Baru (Tolitoli), 8,333 ... G 5
Karangasem, 16,022 ... F 7
Kau, †7,497 ... H 5
Kebumen, †64,874 ... J 2
Kediri, 196,000 ... K 2
Kendal, 23,129 ... J 2
Kendari, †91,065 ... G 6
Kendawangan, 6,845 ... D 6
Klaten, 33,400 ... J 2
Kolaka, †18,671 ... G 6
Kotaagung, †25,314 ... C 7
Kragan, 23,786 ... K 2
Krawang, 49,867 ... H 2
Kualakurun, †11,489 ... E 6
Kudus, 62,130 ... J 2
Kumai, 8,835 ... E 6
Kuningan, †77,181 ... H 2
Kupang, †7,171 ... G 8
Kutaradja (Banda Atjeh), 49,000 ... A 4
Kutoardjo, 44,962 ... J 2
Labuan, †22,259 ... G 2
Lahat, †25,781 ... C 6
Lamongan, †34,825 ... K 2
Langsa, †47,044 ... B 5
Lawang, †40,239 ... K 2
Longiram, 7,776 ... F 5
Longnawan, †16,234 ... F 5
Lubuklinggau, 14,890 ... C 6
Lubuksikaping, 11,778 ... B 5
Lumadjang, 55,700 ... K 2
Madiun, 152,000 ... K 2
Madjalengka, †47,055 ... H 2
Madjene, †37,727 ... F 6
Magelang, 119,000 ... J 2
Magetan, †54,159 ... K 2
Makassar (Udjung Pandang), 473,000 ... F 7
Malang, 419,000 ... K 2
Malili, 5,735 ... G 6
Malinau, 9,677 ... F 5
Mamudju, †47,309 ... F 6
Manado, 160,000 ... G 5
Manokwari, 10,461 ... J 6
Marabahan, 8,893 ... E 6
Martapura, †53,216 ... F 6
Masamba, †15,152 ... G 6
Medan, 590,000 ... B 5
Menggala, 20,343 ... D 6
Meulaboh, 6,544 ... B 5
Merak, †36,293 ... G 1
Merauke, 5,989 ... K 7
Mindiptana, 1,577 ... L 7
Modjokerto, 64,000 ... K 2
Muarabungo, 10,706 ... C 6
Muarateweh, 6,135 ... F 6
Muntok, †25,883 ... D 6
Namlea, 16,018 ... H 6
Nangapinoh, †24,836 ... E 6
Nangatajap, †8,285 ... E 6
Negara, 10,161 ... E 7
Ngabang, †24,516 ... D 5
Ngawi, 29,220 ... K 2
Padang, 178,000 ... B 6
Padangpandjang, 32,000 ... B 6
Padangsidimpuan, †71,704 ... B 5
Painan, 12,060 ... C 6
Pajakumbuh, †74,393 ... C 6
Pakanbaru, 87,000 ... C 5
Palangkaraja, 9,000 ... E 6
Paleleh, 5,466 ... G 5
Palembang, 585,000 ... D 6
Pamangkat, †51,871 ... D 5
Pamekasan, †42,650 ... L 2
Pameungpeuk, †24,662 ... H 2
Panarukan, 6,846 ... K 2
Pandeglang, †24,823 ... G 1
Pangkalanberandan, †23,806 ... B 5
Pangkalpinang, 74,000 ... D 6
Pare, †85,528 ... K 2
Parepare, 84,000 ... F 6
Pariaman, †45,812 ... B 6
Pasuruan, 78,000 ... K 2
Pati, †56,749 ... J 2
Patjitan, 44,383 ... J 2
Pekalongan, 125,000 ... J 2
Pemalang, †93,608 ... J 2
Pematangsiantar, 142,000 ... B 5
Perahbumulih, 41,951 ... C 6
Pinrang, 23,818 ... F 6
Piru, †23,633 ... H 6
Ponorogo, 49,993 ... J 2
Pontianak, 185,000 ... D 6
Poso, †41,292 ... G 6
Praja, 26,729 ... F 7
Prapat, 5,552 ... B 5
Probolinggo, 85,000 ... K 2
Purbolinggo, 31,719 ... J 2
Purwakarta, †88,680 ... H 2
Purwodadi, †54,648 ... J 2
Purwokerto, 22,623 ... H 2
Purworedjo, 23,209 ... J 2
Putussibau, †8,357 ... E 5
Rangkasbitung, †51,176 ... G 2
Rantauprapat, 25,707 ... C 5
Rembang, 39,939 ... K 2
Rengat, †22,982 ... C 6
Ruteng, 15,814 ... G 7
Sabang, 6,747 ... B 4
Salatiga, 72,000 ... J 2
Samarinda, 87,000 ... F 6
Sambas, †53,290 ... D 5
Sampang, 47,596 ... K 2
Sanana, 23,388 ... H 6
Sanggau, †28,039 ... E 5
Sangkulirang, 6,108 ... F 5
Saparua, 53,390 ... H 6
Saumlaki, †22,732 ... J 7
Sawahlunto, 15,000 ... C 6
Semarang, 619,000 ... J 2
Semitau, †9,255 ... E 5
Sengkang, †17,948 ... F 6
Serang, †43,661 ... G 1
Serui, 2,743 ... K 6
Sibolga, 48,000 ... B 5
Sidoardjo, †40,591 ... K 2
Sigli, 4,050 ... B 4
Sindjai, 18,390 ... G 7
Singaradja ... F 7
Singkawang, †61,107 ... D 5
Sintang, †25,067 ... E 5
Situbondo, 30,000 ... L 2
Sorong, 9,151 ... J 6
Sragen, 32,310 ... J 2
Subang, †22,825 ... H 2
Sukabumi, 90,000 ... H 2
Sukadana, 6,899 ... E 6
Sumbawa Besar, †22,308 ... F 7
Sumedang, †74,062 ... H 2
Sumenep, 33,628 ... L 2
Surabaja, 1,241,000 ... K 2
Surakarta, 453,000 ... J 2
Tandjungbalai, 36,000 ... C 5
Tandjungkarang-Telukbetung, 164,000 ... D 7
Tandjungpandan, †39,253 ... D 6
Tandjungpriok, †140,573 ... H 1
Tandjungpura, †20,726 ... B 5
Tangerang, †81,042 ... G 1
Tapaktuan, 9,650 ... B 5
Tarakan, 24,807 ... F 5
Tarutung, †41,041 ... B 5
Tasikmalaja, †101,466 ... H 2
Tebingtinggi, 32,000 ... B 5
Tegal, 110,000 ... J 2
Telanaipura, 139,000 ... C 6
Temanggung, 8,107 ... J 2
Tenggarong, †15,516 ... F 6
Ternate, 23,500 ... H 5
Tjiamis, †80,018 ... H 2
Tjiandjur, †77,927 ... H 2
Tjidulang, †32,475 ... H 2
Tjilatjap, 78,619 ... H 2
Tjimahi, †90,718 ... H 2
Tjirebon, 176,000 ... H 2
Tjurup, 14,480 ... C 6
Tobelo, †14,430 ... H 5
Tolitoli, 8,333 ... G 5
Tondano, †29,584 ... H 5
Trenggalek, †37,762 ... K 2
Tuban, 48,123 ... K 2
Tulungagung, 43,115 ... K 2
Turen, †57,711 ... K 2
Udjung Pandang, 473,000 ... F 7
Wahai, †8,781 ... H 6
Wonogiri, †45,704 ... J 2
Wonosobo, 33,917 ... J 2

OTHER FEATURES

Alas (str.) ... F 7
Anambas (isls.), 15,700 ... D 5
Arafura (sea) ... J 8
Aru (isls.), 27,006 ... K 7
Asahan (river) ... B 5
Babar (isls.), 14,133 ... H 7
Bali (isl.), 2,196,000 ... F 7
Bali (sea) ... F 7
Banda (sea) ... H 7
Banggai (arch.), 144,747 ... G 6
Bangka (isl.), 384,000 ... D 6
Banjak (isls.), 1,696 ... B 5
Barisan (mts.) ... C 6
Barito (river) ... E 6
Batjan (isls.), 21,861 ... H 6
Batu (isls.), 60,806 ... B 6
Bawean (isl.), 47,589 ... K 1
Belitung (Billiton) (isl.), 126,000 ... D 6
Bengalen (passage) ... A 4
Berau (bay) ... J 6
Biak (isl.), 31,139 ... K 6
Billiton (isl.), 126,000 ... D 6
Binongko (isl.), 10,580 ... G 7
Bintan (isl.), 65,301 ... C 5
Bone (gulf) ... G 7
Borneo (isl.) ... E 5
Borneo (Kalimantan) (reg.), 4,243,000 ... E 5
Bosch, van den (cape) ... J 6
Bunguran (Natuna) (isls.), 15,261 ... D 5
Buru (isl.), 16,018 ... H 6
Butung (isl.), 311,000 ... G 6
Celebes (isl.), 7,665,000 ... G 6
Celebes (sea) ... G 5
Ceram (isl.), 73,453 ... H 6
Damar (isls.) ... H 7
Dampier (str.) ... J 6
Diamond (point) ... B 4
Digul (river) ... K 7
Djaja (mt.) ... K 6
Djajawidjaja (range) ... K 6
Djemadja (isl.), 3,874 ... D 5
Doberai (pen.) ... J 6
Dolak (isl.) ... K 7
Enggano (isl.), 686 ... C 7
Ewab (isls.), 76,606 ... J 7
Flores (isl.), 1,108,000 ... G 7
Flores (sea) ... F 7
Frederik Hendrik (Dolak) (isl.) ... K 7
Gebe (isl.), 5,410 ... H 6
Geelvink (Sarera) (bay) ... K 6
Good Hope (cape) ... J 5
Gorong (isls.), 33,241 ... J 6
Halmahera (isl.), 97,133 ... H 5
Idenburg (river) ... K 6
Japen (isl.), 23,701 ... K 6
Java (head) ... C 7
Java (isl.), 69,323,000 ... J 2
Java (sea) ... D 6
Kabaena (isl.), 14,380 ... G 7
Kabia (Salajar) (isl.), 107,000 ... G 7
Kai (Ewab) (isls.), 76,606 ... J 7
Kalao (isl.), 670 ... G 7
Kalaotoa (isl.), 2,031 ... G 7
Kalimantan (reg.), 4,243,000 ... E 5
Kangean (isls.), 52,893 ... F 7
Kapuas (river) ... D 6
Karakelong (isl.), 15,276 ... H 5
Karimata (arch.), 1,623 ... D 6
Karimundjawa (isls.), 1,611 ... J 1
Kerintji (mt.) ... C 6
Kisar (isl.), 16,569 ... H 7
Komodo (isl.) ... F 7
Krakatau (Rakata) (isl.) ... C 7
Laut (isl.), 42,099 ... F 6
Leuser (mt.) ... B 5
Lingga (arch.), 39,307 ... D 5
Lingga (isl.), 14,309 ... D 6
Lombok (isl.), 1,602,000 ... F 7
Madura (isl.), 2,650,000 ... K 2
Mahakam (river) ... F 6
Makassar (str.) ... F 6
Malacca (str.) ... C 5
Mamberamo (river) ... K 6
Maoke (mts.) ... K 6
Mapia (isls.) ... J 5
Mentawai (isls.), 23,649 ... B 6
Misool (isl.), 3,022 ... J 6
Molucca (sea) ... H 6
Moluccas (isls.), 973,000 ... H 6
Morotai (isl.), 19,523 ... H 5
Muli (str.) ... K 7
Müller (mts.) ... E 5
Muna (isl.), 139,000 ... G 7
Musi (river) ... C 6
Natuna (isls.), 15,261 ... D 5
Ngundju (cape) ... F 8
Nias (isl.), 388,000 ... B 5
Obi (isls.), 6,358 ... H 6
Ombai (str.) ... H 7
Perkam (cape) ... K 6
Puting (cape), Borneo ... E 6
Puting (cape), Sumatra ... C 7
Radja Ampat Group (isls.), 17,158 ... H 6
Raja (mt.) ... E 6
Rakata (isl.) ... C 7
Rantekombola (mt.) ... F 6
Riau (arch.), 342,000 ... C 5
Rokan (river) ... C 5
Roti (isl.), 68,330 ... G 8
Rouffaer (river) ... K 6
Salajar (isl.), 107,000 ... G 7
Salawati (isl.), 5,125 ... J 6
Sandalwood (Sumba) (isl.), 311,000 ... F 7
Sangihe (isl.), 83,585 ... H 5
Sangihe (isls.), 126,931 ... G 5
Sarera (bay) ... K 6
Sawu (isls.), 78,785 ... G 8
Sawu (sea) ... G 7
Schouten (isls.), 41,647 ... K 6
Schwaner (mts.) ... E 6
Seaflower (channel) ... B 6
Sebuko (bay) ... F 5
Selatan (cape) ... E 6
Semeru (mt.) ... K 2
Siau (isl.), 29,762 ... H 5
Siberut (str.) ... B 6
Simeulue (isl.), 25,951 ... A 5
Singkep (isl.), 17,712 ... D 6
Sipora (isl.), 5,671 ... B 6
Slamet (mt.) ... J 2
Sorik Merapi (mt.) ... B 5
South Natuna (isls.), 3,318 ... D 5
Sudirman (range) ... K 6
Sula (isls.), 30,779 ... H 6
Sulawesi (Celebes) (isl.), 7,665,000 ... G 6
Sumatra (isl.), 17.345,000 ... B 5
Sumba (isl.), 311,000 ... F 7
Sumba (str.) ... F 7
Sumbawa (isl.), 625,000 ... F 7
Sunda (str.) ... C 7
Tahulandang (isl.), 13,584 ... H 5
Talaud (isls.), 28,738 ... H 5
Taliabu (isl.), 7,391 ... G 6
Tambelan (isls.), 3,551 ... D 5
Tanimbar (isls.), 41,233 ... J 7
Tidore (isl.), 24,064 ... H 5
Timor (sea) ... H 7
Timor, Indonesian (reg.), 866,000 H 7
Toba (lake) ... B 5
Tolo (gulf) ... G 6
Tomini (gulf) ... G 6
Tukangbesi (isls.), 59,775 ... G 7
Vals (cape) ... K 7
Vogelkop (Deberai) (pen.) ... J 6
Waigeo (isl.), 9,011 ... J 5
Wangiwangi (isl.), 19,719 ... G 7
Weh (isl.) ... B 4
West Irian (reg.), 933,000 ... K 6
Wetar (isl.), 11,383 ... H 7

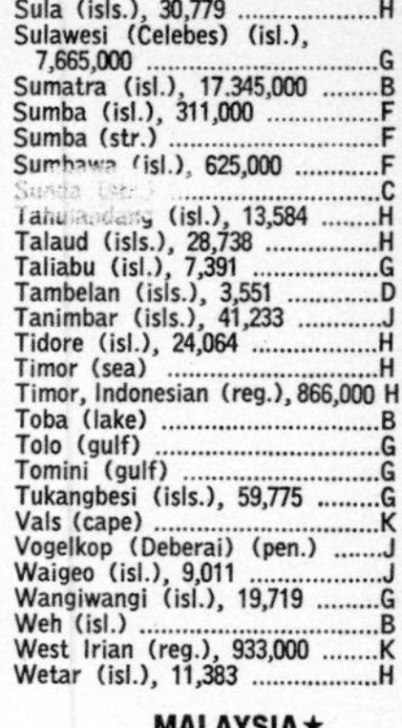

MALAYSIA★

STATES

Sabah, 633,000 ... F 4
Sarawak, 950,000 ... E 5

CITIES and TOWNS

Beaufort, †25.408 ... F 4

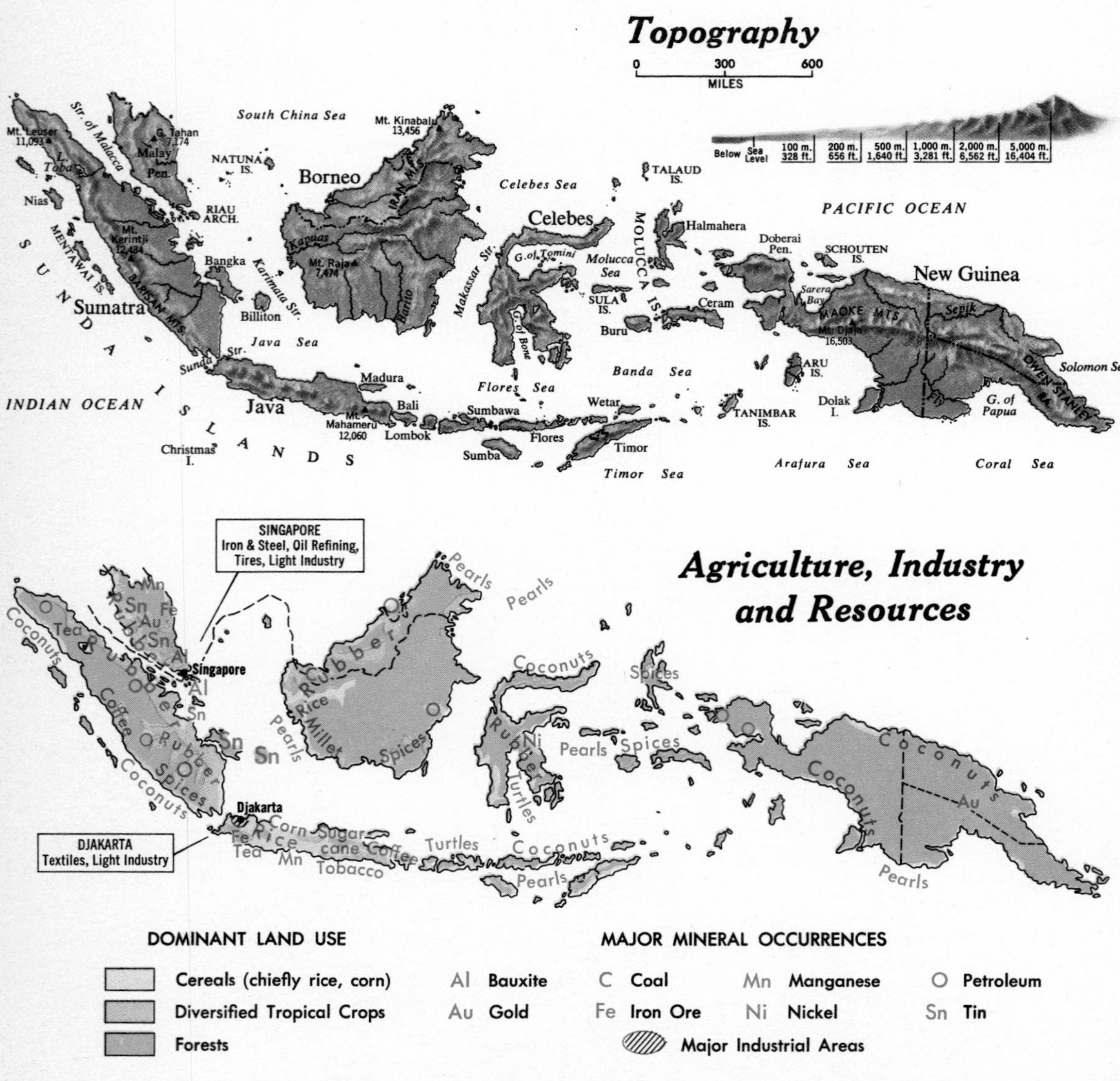

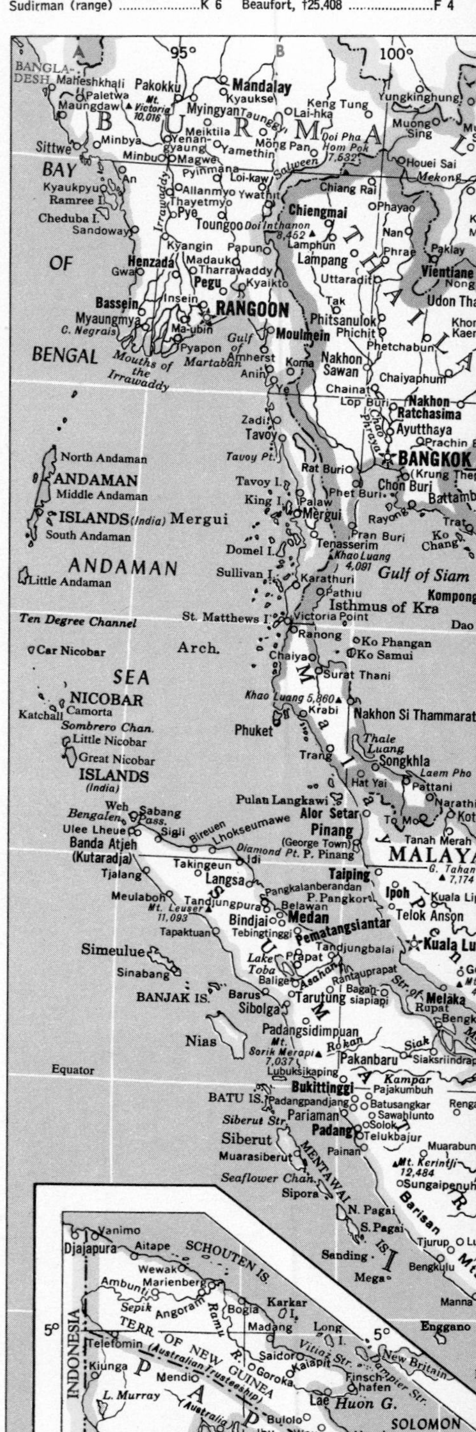

Bintulu, 5,307 ....E 5
Keningau, †14,645 ....F 4
Kota Kinabalu, 21,704 ....F 4
Kuching, 56,000 ....E 5
Kudat, 3,660 ....F 4
Lahad Datu, †19,534 ....F 5
Marudi, 2,663 ....E 5
Miri, 20,000 ....E 5
Papar, †28,210 ....F 4
Ranau, †17,033 ....F 4
Sandakan, 28,805 ....F 4
Sematan ....D 5
Semporna, †16,895 ....F 5
Sibu, 29,630 ....E 5
Simanggang, 5,648 ....E 5
Tawau, 10,276 ....F 5
Victoria, 3,213 ....E 4

OTHER FEATURES

Balambangan (isl.) ....F 4
Banggi (isl.) ....F 4
Iran (mts.) ....E 5
Kinabalu (mt.) ....F 4
Labuan (isl.), 14,904 ....E 4
Labuk (bay) ....F 4
Rajang (river) ....E 5
Sirik (cape) ....E 5

TERRITORY OF NEW GUINEA

CITIES and TOWNS

Aitape, 540 ....B 6
Ambunti, ‡697 ....B 6
Angoram, 1,822 ....B 6
Bogia, 639 ....B 6
Bulolo, 2,724 ....B 7
Finschhafen, 436 ....C 7
Goroka, 4,826 ....B 7
Lae, 12,392 ....B 7
Madang, 6,601 ....B 7
Morobe, 12,132 ....C 7
Saidor ....B 7
Telefomin, ‡395 ....B 7
Vanimo, 512 ....B 6
Wau, 1,072 ....B 7
Wewak, 5,090 ....B 6

OTHER FEATURES

Dampier (str.) ....C 7
Huon (gulf) ....C 7
Karkar (isl.), 14,966 ....B 6
Long (isl.), 7,044 ....B 7
New Britain (isl.), 138,689 ....C 7
Ramu (river) ....B 7
Schouten (isls.), 6,633 ....B 6
Sepik (river) ....B 6
Solomon (sea) ....C 7
Torres (str.) ....A 7

PAPUA

CITIES and TOWNS

Abau, ‡3,024 ....C 7
Baniara, ‡1,110 ....C 7
Buna, 307 ....C 7
Daru, 3,663 ....B 7
Ioma, ‡3,552 ....C 7
Kairuku, ‡4,582 ....B 7
Kerema, 820 ....B 7
Kiunga, ‡918 ....B 7
Kokoda, ‡1,615 ....C 7
Mendi, 1,687 ....B 7
Popondetta, 2,139 ....C 7
Port Moresby (cap.), 56,206 ....B 7
Rigo, ‡1,184 ....C 7
Samarai, 2,201 ....C 8
Tufi, ‡462 ....C 7

OTHER FEATURES

D'Entrecasteaux (isls.), 32,288....C 7
Fly (river) ....A 7
Kiriwina (isl.), 8,990 ....C 7
Louisiade (arch.), 11,451 ....D 8
Milne (bay) ....C 8
Misima (isl.), 5,247 ....C 8
Papua (gulf) ....B 7
Rossel (isl.), 1,933 ....D 8
Tagula (isl.), 1,654 ....C 8
Trobriand (isls.), 10,199 ....C 7
Woodlark (isl.), 1,848 ....C 7

PORTUGUESE TIMOR

CITIES and TOWNS

Dili (cap.), 9,753 ....H 7
Vila Salazar, 1,598 ....H 7
Viqueque, 240 ....H 7

OTHER FEATURES

Oe-Cusse (reg.), 21,398....G 7

★See page 74 for other Malaysian entries.
*City and suburbs.
†Population of sub-division.
‡Population of district.

INDONESIA

AREA 735,264 sq. mi.
POPULATION 119,572,000
CAPITAL Djakarta
LARGEST CITY Djakarta
HIGHEST POINT Mt. Djaja 16,503 ft.
MONETARY UNIT rupiah
MAJOR LANGUAGES Bahasa Indonesian, local Indonesian languages, Papuan languages
MAJOR RELIGIONS Islam, Tribal religions, Christianity, Hinduism

PORTUGUESE TIMOR

AREA 5,762 sq. mi.
POPULATION 590,000
CAPITAL Dili

BRUNEI

AREA 2,226 sq. mi.
POPULATION 130,000
CAPITAL Bandar Seri Begawan

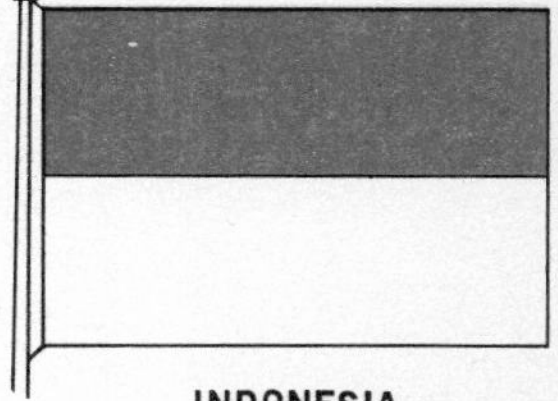

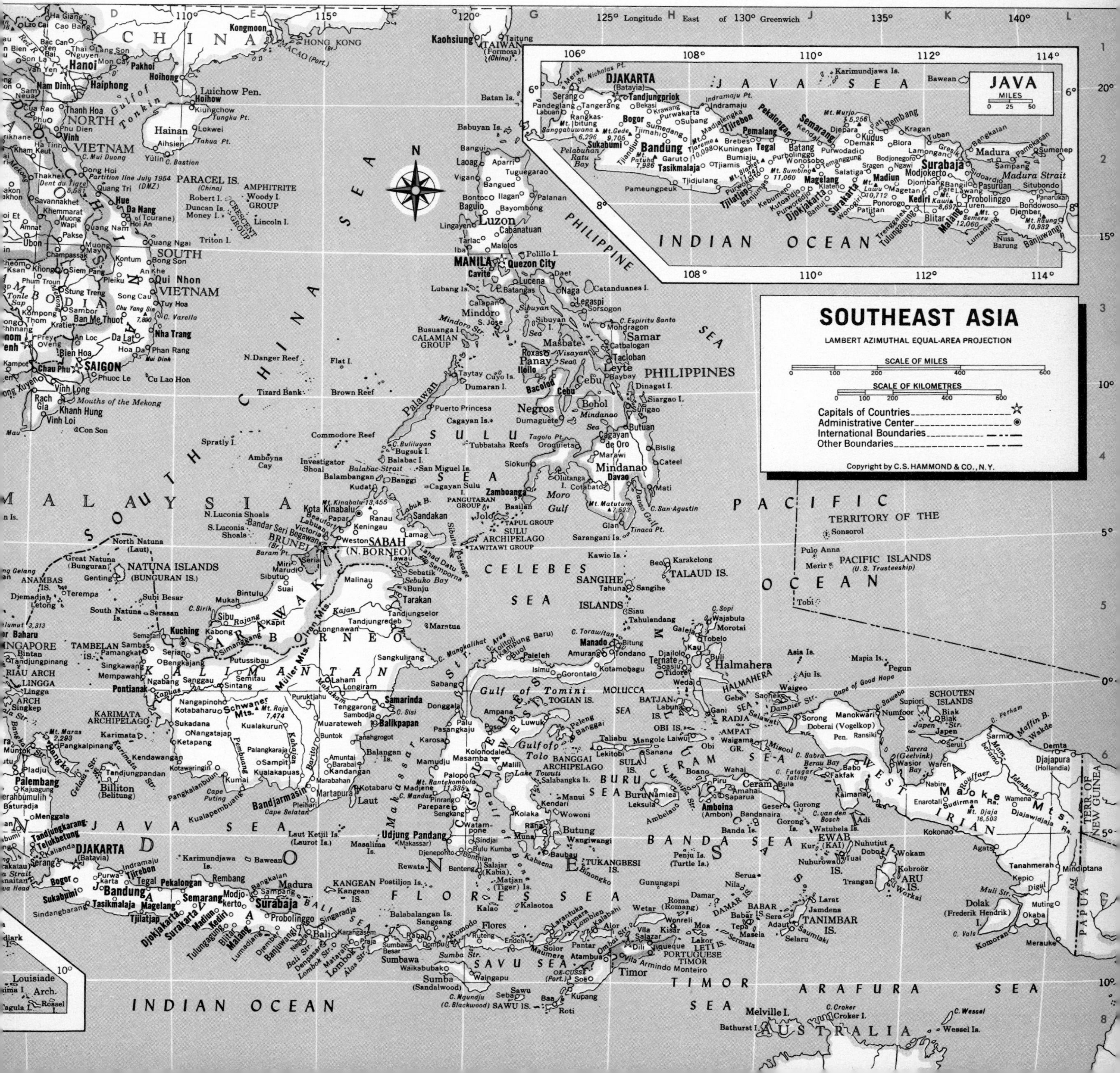

INDONESIA

SOUTHEAST ASIA

LAMBERT AZIMUTHAL EQUAL-AREA PROJECTION

SCALE OF MILES
0 100 200 400 600

SCALE OF KILOMETRES
0 100 200 400 600

Capitals of Countries ★
Administrative Center ◉
International Boundaries
Other Boundaries

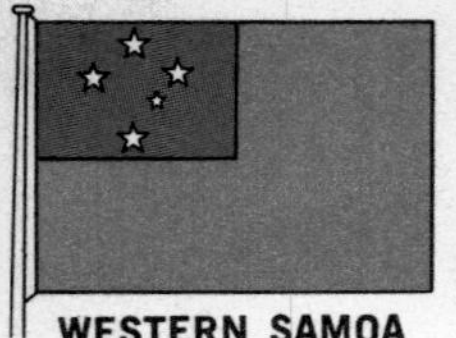

WESTERN SAMOA

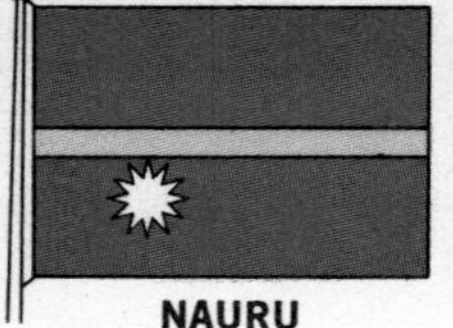

NAURU

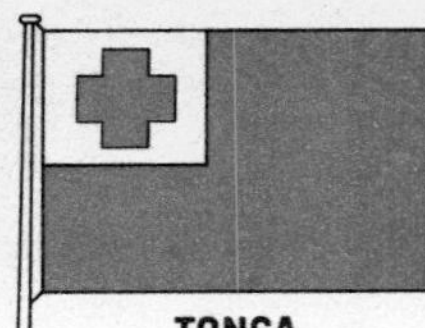

TONGA

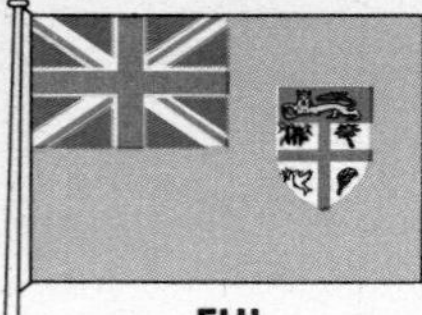

FIJI

WESTERN SAMOA

AREA 1,097 sq. mi.
POPULATION 139,810
CAPITAL Apia
LARGEST CITY Apia
HIGHEST POINT Mt. Silisili 6,094 ft.
MONETARY UNIT West Samoan pound
MAJOR LANGUAGES Samoan, English
MAJOR RELIGIONS Protestantism, Roman Catholicism

NAURU

AREA 8.2 sq. mi.
POPULATION 7,000
MONETARY UNIT Australian dollar

TONGA

AREA 270 sq. mi.
POPULATION 83,000
CAPITAL Nukuʻalofa
LARGEST CITY Nukuʻalofa
HIGHEST POINT 3,389 ft.
MONETARY UNIT Tongan pound
MAJOR LANGUAGES Tongan, English
MAJOR RELIGION Protestantism

FIJI

AREA 7,015 sq. mi.
POPULATION 519,000
CAPITAL Suva
LARGEST CITY Suva
HIGHEST POINT Tomaniivi (Mt. Victoria) 4,341 ft.
MONETARY UNIT Fijian pound
MAJOR LANGUAGES Fijian, Hindi, English
MAJOR RELIGIONS Protestantism, Hinduism

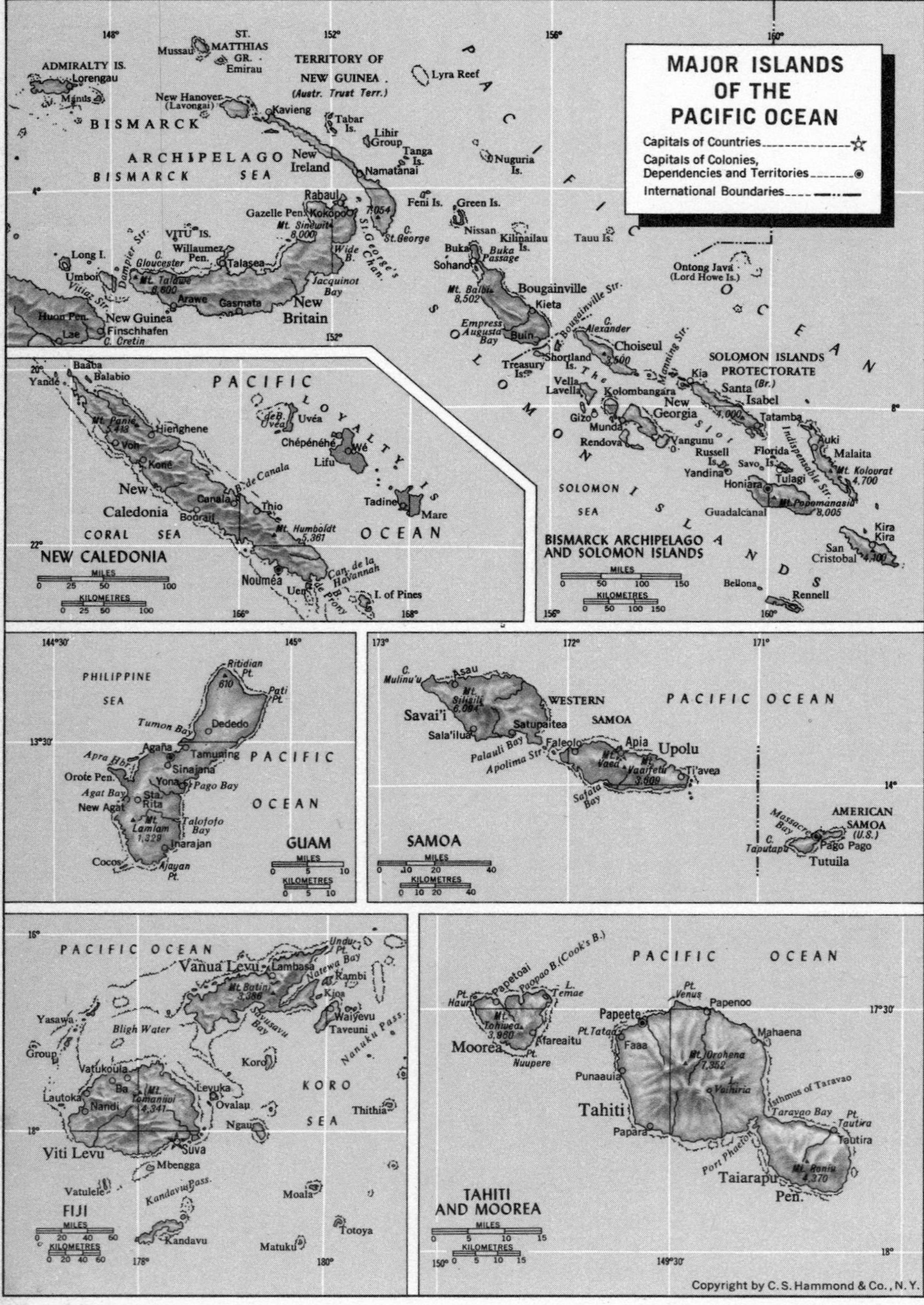

Abaing (atoll), 3,271 ....H 5
Abemama (atoll), 2,126 ....H 5
Adamstown, 74 ....N 8
Adelaide, †727,916 ....D 9
Admiralty (isls.), 21,588 ....E 6
Agaña, 2,131 ....E 4
Agrihan (isl.), 64 ....E 4
Ahau, 414 ....H 7
Ailinglapalap (atoll), 1,281 ....G 5
Ailuk (atoll), 371 ....H 4
Aitutaki (atoll), 2,579 ....K 7
Alamagan (isl.), 48 ....E 4
Albany, 11,419 ....B 9
Albury, 25,112 ....E 9
Alice Springs, 6,037 ....D 8
Alofi, 1,117 ....K 7
Amanu (atoll), 117 ....N 7
Ambrym (isl.), 4,200 ....G 7
American Samoa, 27,159 ....J 7
Anaa (atoll), 360 ....M 7
Anatahan (isl.), 23 ....E 4
Aneityum (isl.) 300 ....H 9
Angaur (isl.), 533 ....D 5
Apataki (atoll), 108 ....M 7
Apia, 27,000 ....J 7
Armidale, 14,984 ....F 9
Arnhem Land (reg.) ....D 7
Arno (atoll), 1,198 ....H 5
Arorae (atoll), 1,830 ....H 6
Atafu (atoll), 615 ....J 6
Atiu (isl.), 1,327 ....L 8
Atuona, 663 ....M 7
Auckland, 152,200 ....H 9
Auki, 600 ....G 6
Austral (isls.), 5,053 ....L 8
Australia, 12,630,600 ....C 8
Australian Cap. Terr., 136,300....F 9
Avarua, 4,100 ....L 8
Babelthuap (isl.), 5,222 ....D 5
Bairiki, 1,300 ....H 6
Baker (isl.) ....J 5
Ballarat, *56,290 ....E 9
Banks (isls.), 3,250 ....G 7
Belep (isls.), 551 ....G 7
Bendigo, *42,208 ....E 9
Beru (atoll), 2,412 ....H 6
Bikini (atoll) ....G 4
Bismarck (arch.), 209,051 ....E 6
Blackall, 2,004 ....E 8
Blue Mountains, 30,731 ....E 9
Bora-Bora (isl.), 2,071....L 7
Bougainville (isl.), 72,661 ....F 6
Boulder, 5,234 ....C 9
Bourail, 672 ....G 8
Bowen, 5,144 ....E 7
Brisbane, †718,822 ....F 8
Broken Hill, 30,014 ....E 9
Broome, 1,570 ....C 7
Bunbury, 15,459 ....B 9
Bundaberg, 25,402 ....E 8
Butaritari (atoll), 2,714....H 5
Cairns, 29,326 ....E 7
Canberra, *136,300 ....F 9
Canton (isl.), 421 ....J 6
Carnarvon, 2,956 ....B 8
Caroline (isls.), 54,563 ....E 5
Charleville, 4,871 ....E 8
Charters Towers, 7,602 ....E 7
Chatham (isls.), 520 ....J10
Chichi (isl.), 203 ....E 3
Choiseul (isl.), 6,600 ....F 6
Christchurch, 165,000 ....H10
Christmas (isl.), 367 ....L 5
Cloncurry, 2,149 ....E 8
Collie, 7,628 ....B 9
Cook (isls.), 20,000 ....K 7
Coral (sea) ....F 7
Cunnamulla, 1,980 ....E 8
Daito (isls.), 3,896 ....D 3
Daly Waters, ‡265 ....D 7
Danger (Pukapuka) (atoll), 684 ....K 7
Daru, 3,663 ....E 6
Darwin, 18,042 ....D 7
D'Entrecasteaux (isls.), 32,288....F 6
Derby, 1,424 ....C 7
Devonport, 14,874 ....E10
Dunedin, 77,800 ....H10
Easter (isls.), 1,598 ....Q 8
Eauripik (atoll), 158 ....E 5
Ebon (atoll), 731 ....G 5
Efate (isl.), 10,000 ....G 7
Elato (atoll), 35 ....E 5
Ellice (isls.), 5,780 ....H 6
Enderbury (isl.) ....J 6
Eniwetok (atoll) ....G 4
Erromanga (isl.), 600 ....H 7
Esperance, 2,677 ....C 9
Espiritu Santo (isl.), 10,000....G 7
Fais (isl.), 230 ....E 5
Fakaofo (isl.), 740 ....J 6
Fakarava (atoll), 230 ....M 7
Fanning (isl.), 376 ....L 5
Faraulep (atoll), 178 ....E 5
Fatuhiva (isl.), 459 ....N 7
Fiji, 519,000 ....H 8
Fly (riv.) ....E 6
Fremantle, 25,284 ....B 9
French Polynesia, 109,000 ....L 8
Funafuti (atoll), 826 ....H 6
Furneaux Group (isls.), 1,234 ....E 9
Gambier (isls.), 516....N 8
Garapan, 4,100 ....E 4
Gardner (isl.), 230 ....J 6
Geelong, *105,059 ....E 9
Geraldton, 12,125 ....B 8
Gilbert (isls.), 44,205 ....H 6
Gilbert & Ellice Islands, 55,185 ....J 6
Gisborne, 25,600 ....H 9
Grafton, 15,951 ....F 8
Great Barrier (reef) ....E 7
Greenwich (Kapingamarangi) (atoll), 411 ....F 5
Greymouth, 8,590 ....H10
Guadalcanal (isl.), 23,922 ....F 7
Guam (isl.), 84,996....E 4
Gympie, 11,279 ....F 8
Haʻapai Group (isls.), 10,591....J 8
Halls Creek, ‡577 ....C 7
Hamilton, 67,700 ....H 9
Hao (atoll), 448 ....N 7
Hastings, 28,100 ....H 9
Hawaii (isl.), 63,468 ....L 3
Hawaii (state), 769,913 ....K 4
Hawaiian (isls.), 772,133 ....J 3
Hikueru (atoll), 115 ....M 7
Hilo, 26,353 ....L 4
Hivaoa (isl.), 1,027 ....N 6
Hobart, 53,257 ....E10
Honiara, 11,389 ....F 6
Honolulu, 324,871 ....L 3
Honolulu, *630,528 ....L 3
Hoorn (isls.), 3,000 ....J 7
Howland (isl.) ....J 5
Huahine (isl.), 2,814 ....L 7
Hughenden, 2,033 ....E 8
Hull (isl.), 583 ....J 6
Ifalik (atoll), 321 ....E 5
Invercargill, 45,300 ....H10
Ipswich, 54,531 ....F 8
Iwo (isl.) ....E 3
Jaluit (atoll), 932 ....G 5
Jarvis (isl.) ....K 6
Johnston (atoll), 1,007 ....L 4
Kalgoorlie, *19,908 ....B 9
Kandavu (isl.), 6,600 ....H 7
Kangaroo (isl.), 3,375 ....D 9
Kapingamarangi (atoll), 411....F 5
Katherine, 1,302 ....D 7
Kauai (isl.), 29,524 ....L 3
Kavieng, 2,142 ....E 6
Kermadec (isls.), 9 ....J 9
Kieta, 755 ....F 6
Kili (atoll), 320 ....G 5
King (isl.), 2,462 ....E10
Kingman Reef (isl.) ....K 5
Koror, 5,541 ....D 5
Kusaie (isl.), 3,648 ....G 5
Kwajalein (atoll), 3,841 ....G 5
Lae, 12,392 ....E 6
Lamotrek (atoll), 203 ....E 5
Lanai (isl.), 2,204 ....L 3
Lau Group (isls.), 15,988 ....J 7
Launceston, 37,217 ....E10
Laverton, ‡206 ....C 8
Lavongai (isl.), 7,829 ....F 6
Levuka, 1,685 ....H 7
Lifu (isl.), 6,837 ....G 8
Line (isls.), 1,180 ....K 5
Lismore, 19,734 ....F 8
Lithgow, 13,165 ....F 9
Little Makin (isl.), 1,387 ....H 5
Longreach, 3,871 ....E 8
Lord Howe (isl.), 267 ....G 9
Lord Howe (Ontong Java) (isl.), 900 ....G 6
Louisiade (archipelago), 11,451..F 7
Loyalty (isls.), 12,248 ....G 8
Luganville, 3,500 ....G 7
Mackay, 24,578 ....F 8
Madang, 6,601 ....E 6
Maitland, 28,428 ....F 9
Majuro (atoll), 5,957 ....H 5
Makatea (isl.), 55 ....L 7
Makin (Butaritari) (atoll), 2,714 ....H 5
Malaita (isl.), 54,000 ....G 6
Malekula (isl.), 11,200 ....G 7
Maloelap (atoll), 494 ....H 5
Mangaia (isl.), 2,002 ....L 8
Mangareva (isl.), 516 ....N 8
Manihiki (atoll), 584 ....K 7
Manra (Sydney), (isl.) ....J 6
Manua (isls.), 2,112 ....K 7
Manuae (atoll), 15 ....K 7
Manus (isl.), 11,088 ....E 6
Marble Bar, ‡567 ....C 8
Marcus (isl.) ....F 3
Maré (isl.), 3,410 ....G 8
Mariana (isls.), 11,827 ....E 4
Mariana Trench ....E 4
Marquesas (isls.), 5,174 ....N 6
Marshall (isls.), 19,328 ....G 4
Marutea (atoll) ....N 8
Maryborough, 20,393 ....F 8
Matautu ....J 7
Maui (isl.), 38,691 ....L 3
Mauke (isl.), 671 ....L 8
Meekatharra, ‡1,011 ....B 8
Mehetia (isl.) ....M 7
Melanesia (reg.) ....E 5
Melbourne, †2,110,168 ....E 9
Micronesia (reg.) ....E 4
Midway (isls.), 2,220....J 3
Mili (atoll), 360 ....F 5

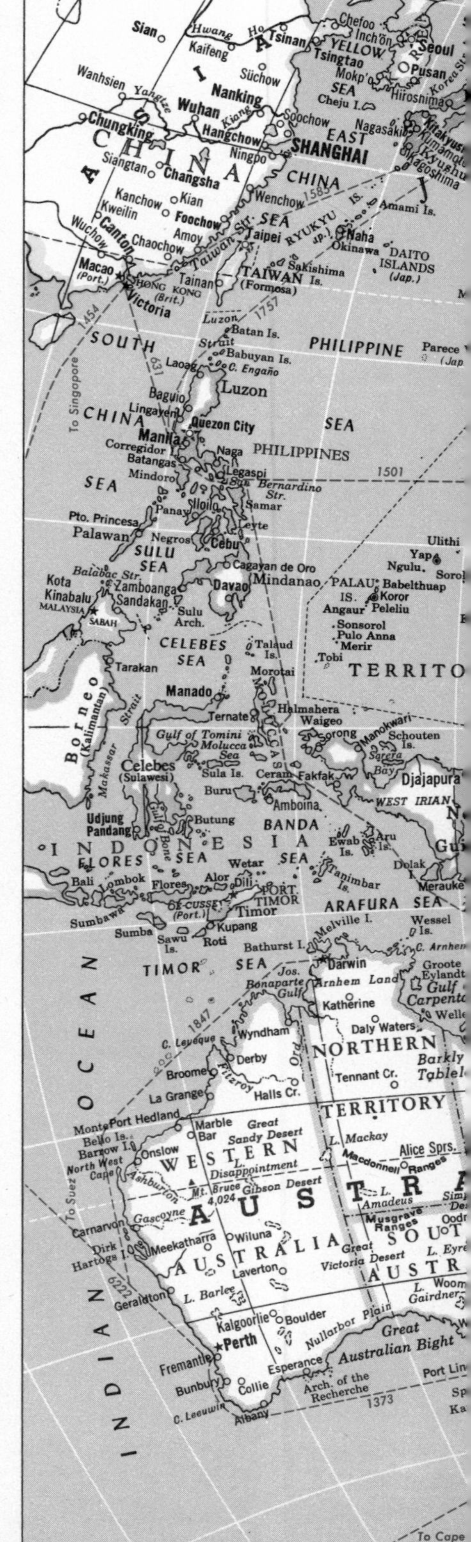

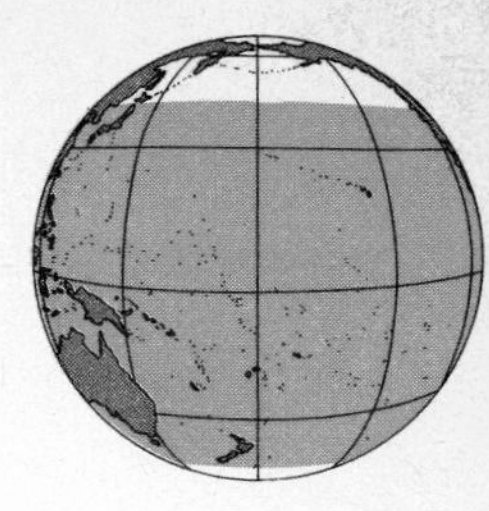

Mitiaro (isl.), 293 ....L 7
Moen (isl.), 4,966 ....F 5
Moerai, 684 ....L 8
Mokil (atoll), 393 ....G 5
Molokai (isl.), 5,089 ....L 3
Moorea (isl.), 4,370 ....L 7
Morobe, 12,132 ....E 6
Mount Gambier, 17,251 ....D 9
Mururoa (isl.) ....M 8
Namatanai, ‡2,221 ....F 6
Namonuito (atoll) ....E 5
Namorik (atoll), 490 ....G 5
Nandi, 2,542 ....H 7
Nanumea (atoll), 1,076 ....H 6
Napier, 36,700 ....H 9
Nassau (isl.), 167 ....K 7
Nauru, 7,000 ....G 6
Ndeni (isl.) ....G 7
Neiafu, 3,593 ....J 7
Nelson, 27,900 ....H10
New Britain (isl.), 138,689 ....F 6
New Caledonia (isl.), 86,802 ....G 8
Newcastle, *233,936 ....F 9
New Georgia (isl.) ....F 6
New Georgia (isl.) ....F 6
New Guinea (isl.) ....E 6
New Guinea, Terr. of, 1,722,572 ....F 6
New Hebrides (isls.), 80,000 ....G 7
New Ireland (isl.), 48,774 ....F 6
New South Wales (state), 4,595,400 ....E 9
New Zealand, 2,815,000 ....G 9
Ngatik (atoll), 442 ....F 5
Ngulu (isl.), 43 ....D 5
Niihau (isl.), 237 ....K 3
Nikumaroro (Gardner) (isl.), 230 ....J 6
Ninigo Group (isls.), 1,051 ....E 6
Niuafo'ou (isl.), 599 ....J 7
Niuatoputapu (isl.), 1,294 ....J 7
Niue (isl.), 5,323 ....K 7
Niutao (atoll), 796 ....H 6
Niutao (atoll), 796 ....H 6
Norfolk (isl.), 1,147 ....G 8
North (isl.), 1,956,411 ....H 9
North East New Guinea (reg.), 1,420,568 ....E 6
Northern Territory (terr.), 73,000 ....D 7
Nouméa, 41,853 ....G 8
Nouméa, *47,966 ....G 8
Nui (atoll), 569 ....H 6
Nuku'alofa, 15,685 ....J 8
Nukuhiva (isl.), 1,351 ....M 6
Nukulaelae (atoll), 354 ....H 6
Nukumanu (atoll), 675 ....F 6
Nukunono (atoll), 528 ....J 6
Nukuoro (atoll), 408 ....F 5
Oahu (isl.), 629,145 ....L 3
Ocean (isl.), 2,192 ....G 6
Oeno (isl.) ....O 8
Onotoa (atoll), 1,960 ....H 6
Ontong Java (isl.), 900 ....G 6
Orange, 22,196 ....E 9
Orona (Hull) (isl.), 583 ....J 6
Pacific Islands, Terr. of, 98,009 ....F 5
Pagan (isl.), 62 ....E 4
Pago Pago, 2,451 ....J 7
Palau (isls.), 12,291 ....D 5
Palmerston (atoll), 86 ....K 7
Palmerston North, 49,200 ....H10
Palmyra (isl.) ....K 5
Pangai, 1,670 ....J 7
Papeete, 22,278 ....M 7
Papeete, *37,485 ....M 7
Papua, 648,000 ....E 6
Peleliu (isl.), 810 ....D 5
Penrhyn (Tongareva) (atoll), 545 ....L 6
Perth, †499,969 ....B 9
Phoenix (isls.), 1,018 ....H 6
Pines, Isle of (isl.), 978 ....G 8
Pingelap (atoll), 815 ....G 5
Pitcairn (isl.), 74 ....O 8
Polynesia (reg.) ....K 7
Ponape (isl.), 13,976 ....F 5
Port Augusta, 10,103 ....D 9
Port Hedland, 1,778 ....B 8
Port Lincoln, 8,888 ....D 9
Port Moresby, 56,206 ....E 6
Port Pirie, 15,566 ....D 9
Puka-Puka (atoll), 98 ....N 7
Pukapuka (atoll), 684 ....K 7
Pulap (atoll), 302 ....E 5
Pulo Anna (isl.), 13 ....D 5
Pulusuk (atoll), 305 ....E 5
Puluwat (atoll), 412 ....E 5
Queensland (state), 1,810,000 ....E 8
Rabaul, 8,737 ....F 6
Raiatea (isl.), 6,187 ....L 7
Raivavae (isl.), 999 ....M 8
Rakahanga (atoll), 323 ....K 7
Ralik Chain (isls.), 9,268 ....G 5
Rangiroa (atoll), 868 ....M 7
Rapa (isl.), 363 ....M 8
Rapa Nui (Easter) (isl.), 1,598 ....Q 8
Raroia (atoll), 52 ....M 7
Rarotonga (isl.), 9,971 ....K 8
Ratak Chain (isls.), 10,060 ....G 5
Reao (atoll), 255 ....N 7
Rennell (isl.), 900 ....F 7
Rimatara (isl.), 747 ....L 8
Rockhampton, 46,083 ....F 8
Roma, 5,996 ....E 8
Rongelap (atoll), 107 ....G 4
Rota (isl.), 1,344 ....E 4
Rotuma (isl.), 3,365 ....H 7
Rurutu (isl.), 1,546 ....L 8
Saipan (isl.), 9,590 ....E 4
Sala y Gómez (isl.) ....P 8
Samarai 2,201 ....E 7
Samoa (isls.), 170,159 ....J 7
San Cristobal (isl.), 8,500 ....G 7
Santa Cruz (isls.), 2,800 ....G 6
Santa Isabel (isl.), 8,548 ....G 6
Satawal (isl.), 345 ....E 5
Savai'i (isl.), 36,159 ....J 7
Senyavin (isls.) ....F 5
Society (isls.), 81,487 ....L 7
Sohano, 877 ....F 6
Solomon (isls.), 234,186 ....F 6
Solomon (sea) ....F 6
Solomon Islands Prot., 161,525 ....F 6
Sonsorol (isl.), 92 ....D 5
Sorol (atoll), 15 ....D 5
South (isl.), 798,681 ....G10
South Australia (state), 1,169,600 ....D 8
Starbuck (isl.) ....L 6
Stewart (isl.), 332 ....G10
Suva, 54,157 ....H 7
Suva, *80,248 ....H 7
Suwarrow (Suvarov) (atoll) ....K 7
Swains (isl.), 74 ....K 7
Sydney, †2,446,345 ....F 9
Sydney (isl.) ....J 6
Tabiteuea (atoll), 4,419 ....H 6
Tahaa (isl.), 3,567 ....L 7
Tahiti (isl.), 61,519 ....L 7
Takaroa (atoll), 161 ....M 7
Tamworth, 21,680 ....E 9
Tanna (isl.), 10,500 ....H 7
Taongi (atoll) ....G 4
Tarawa (atoll), 12,642 ....H 5
Tasman (sea) ....G 9
Tasmania (state), 393,700 ....E10
Taveuni (isl.), 6,351 ....H 7
Tennant Creek, 1,001 ....D 7
Tikopia (isl.), 1,400 ....G 7
Timaru, 27,800 ....H10
Tinian (isl.), 696 ....E 4
Tobi (isl.), 80 ....D 5
Tokelau (isls.), 2,000 ....J 6
Tonga, 83,000 ....J 8
Tongareva (atoll), 545 ....L 6
Tongatapu (isl.), 47,606 ....J 8
Toowoomba, 55,799 ....F 8
Torres (isls.) 200 ....G 7
Townsville, 58,847 ....E 7
Trobriand (isls.), 10,199 ....F 6
Truk (isls.), 18,792 ....F 5
Tuamotu (archipelago), 6,148 ....M 7
Tubuai (isl.), 1,398 ....M 8
Tubuai (Austral) (isls.), 5,053 ....L 8
Tureia (atoll), 40 ....N 8
Tutuila (isl.), 24,973 ....J 7
Uahuka (isl.), 359 ....N 6
Uapou (isl.), 1,414 ....M 6
Ujelang (atoll), 281 ....F 5
Ulithi (atoll), 523 ....D 5
Upolu (isl.), 94,691 ....J 7
Uturoa, 2,394 ....L 7
Uvéa (isl.), 2,001 ....G 7
Vahitahi (atoll), 109 ....N 7
Vaitupu (atoll), 876 ....H 6
Vanua Levu (isl.), 71,933 ....H 7
Vava'u Group (isls.), 13,533 ....J 7
Victoria (state), 3,461,400 ....E 9
Vila, 7,000 ....G 7
Viti Levu (isl.), 341,784 ....H 7

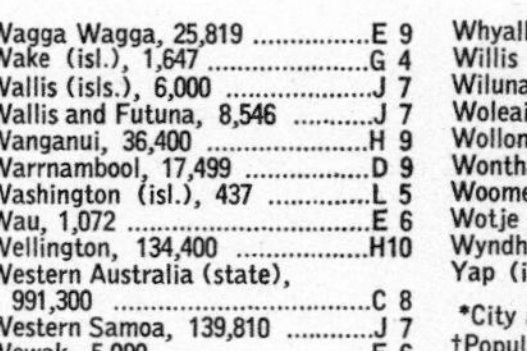

Wagga Wagga, 25,819 ....E 9
Wake (isl.), 1,647 ....G 4
Wallis (isls.), 6,000 ....J 7
Wallis and Futuna, 8,546 ....J 7
Wanganui, 36,400 ....H 9
Warrnambool, 17,499 ....D 9
Washington (isl.), 437 ....L 5
Wau, 1,072 ....E 6
Wellington, 134,400 ....H10
Western Australia (state), 991,300 ....C 8
Western Samoa, 139,810 ....J 7
Wewak, 5,090 ....E 6
Whangarei, 29,600 ....H 9
Whyalla, 22,121 ....D 9
Willis (islets), 3 ....F 7
Wiluna, ‡219 ....C 8
Woleai (atoll), 586 ....E 5
Wollongong, *162,153 ....F 9
Wonthaggi, 4,026 ....E 9
Woomera, 4,745 ....D 9
Wotje (atoll), 376 ....H 5
Wyndham, 1,156 ....C 7
Yap (isl.), 4,380 ....D 5

*City and suburbs.
†Population of metropolitan area.
‡Population of sub-district.

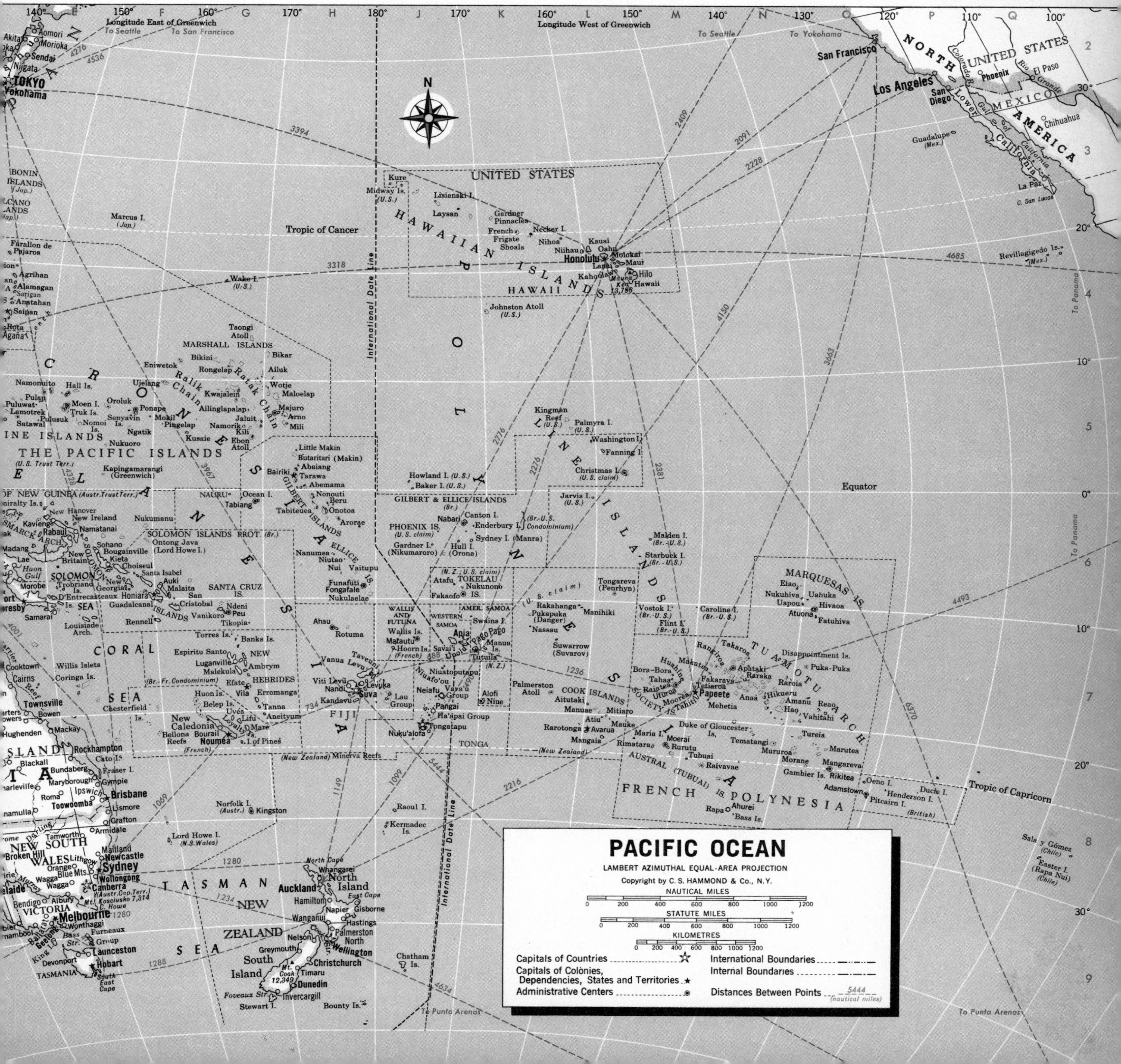

PACIFIC OCEAN

LAMBERT AZIMUTHAL EQUAL-AREA PROJECTION

NAUTICAL MILES 0 200 400 600 800 1000 1200
STATUTE MILES 0 200 400 600 800 1000 1200
KILOMETRES 0 200 400 600 800 1000 1200

Capitals of Countries ☆
Capitals of Colonies, Dependencies, States and Territories ★
Administrative Centers ◉
International Boundaries
Internal Boundaries
Distances Between Points 5444 (nautical miles)

AUSTRALIAN CAPITAL TERRITORY

CITIES and TOWNS

Canberra (capital), 92,308 .... H 7
Canberra, *136,300 .... H 7

CORAL SEA ISLANDS TERRITORY

Total Population, 3

Bougainville (reef) .... H 3
Cato (isl.) .... K 4
Coral (sea) .... H 2
Coringa (islets) .... H 3
Great Barrier (reef) .... H 3
Holmes (reef) .... H 3
Lihou (reef and cays) .... J 3
Magdelaine (cays) .... J 3
Saumarez (reef) .... J 4
Willis (islets), 3 .... H 3

NEW SOUTH WALES

CITIES and TOWNS

Albury, 25,112 .... H 7
Armidale, 14,984 .... J 6
Auburn, 48,691 .... L 3
Bankstown, 159,981 .... L 3
Bathurst, 17,222 .... H 6
Blacktown, 111,488 .... K 3
Blue Mountains, 30,731 .... J 6
Botany, 31,871 .... L 3
Campbelltown, 25,695 .... L 3
Cessnock, 15,331 .... J 6
Cessnock, *34,515 .... J 6
Dubbo, 15,561 .... H 6
Goulburn, 20,871 .... J 7
Grafton, 15,951 .... J 5
Hurstville, 64,851 .... L 3
Kogarah, 47,654 .... L 3
Lismore, 19,734 .... J 5
Lithgow, 13,165 .... J 6
Liverpool, 68,959 .... L 3
Maitland, 28,428 .... J 6
Manly, 38,141 .... L 3
Newcastle, *233,936 .... J 6
Orange, 22,196 .... H 6
Parramatta, 106,996 .... K 3
Penrith, 46,357 .... K 3
Randwick, 113,634 .... L 3
Rockdale, 81,463 .... L 3
Ryde, 81,291 .... L 3
Strathfield, 26,704 .... L 3
Sutherland, 131,739 .... L 3
Sydney (capital), †2,446,345 .... L 3
Tamworth, 21,680 .... J 6
Taree, 10,560 .... J 6
Wagga Wagga, 25,819 .... H 7
Waverley, 63,607 .... L 3
Willoughby, 54,576 .... L 3
Wollongong, *149,506 .... K 4

OTHER FEATURES

Australian Alps (mts.) .... H 7
Botany (bay) .... L 3
Byron (cape) .... J 5
Darling (river) .... G 6
Great Dividing (range) .... J 6
Kosciusko (mt.) .... H 7
Lord Howe (isl.), 267 .... K 6
Murray (river) .... G 6
Murrumbidgee (river) .... H 6

NORFOLK ISLANDS

Total Population, 1,147

CITIES and TOWNS

Cascade .... L 5
Kingston .... L 5

OTHER FEATURES

Anson (bay) .... L 5
Ball (bay) .... M 5
Cable Station .... L 5
Pitt (mt.) .... L 5

NORTHERN TERRITORY

CITIES and TOWNS

Adelaide River, ‡300 .... E 2
Alice Springs, 6,037 .... E 4
Anthony Lagoon, ‡162 .... F 3
Daly Waters, ‡265 .... E 3
Darwin (capital), 18,042 .... E 2
Harts Range, ‡95 .... E 4
Hatches Creek, ‡74 .... F 7
Katherine, 1,302 .... E 2
Kulgera, ‡229 .... E 5
Larrimah, ‡88 .... E 3
Mataranka, ‡114 .... E 2
Pine Creek, ‡577 .... E 2
Tennant Creek, 1,001 .... E 3
Wave Hill, ‡289 .... E 3

OTHER FEATURES

Arafura (sea) .... E 1
Arnhem Land (region) .... E 2
Ayers Rock (mt.) .... E 5
Barkly Tableland .... F 3
Bathurst (isl.) .... D 2
Carpentaria (gulf) .... F 2
Cobourg (pen.) .... E 2
Daly (river) .... E 2
Groote Eylandt (isl.) .... F 2
Macdonnell (ranges) .... E 4
Melville (isl.) .... E 2
Simpson (desert) .... F 5
Timor (sea) .... D 2

QUEENSLAND

CITIES and TOWNS

Ayr, 8,674 .... H 3
Brisbane (capital), 656,222 .... K 2
Brisbane, †718,822 .... K 2
Bundaberg, 25,402 .... J 4
Cairns, 29,326 .... H 3
Charters Towers, 7,602 .... H 4
Corinda, 12,643 .... K 2
Dalby, 8,860 .... J 5
Gladstone, 12,426 .... J 4
Gold Coast, 49,481 .... J 5
Gympie, 11,279 .... J 5
Ingham, 5,354 .... H 3
Innisfail, 7,432 .... H 3
Ipswich, 54,531 .... K 2
Kingaroy, 5,080 .... J 5
Mackay, 24,578 .... H 4
Maryborough, 20,393 .... J 5
Moorooka, 16,801 .... K 2
Mount Isa, 16,877 .... F 4
Redcliffe. 27,327 .... K 1
Rockhampton, 46,083 .... J 4
Sandgate, 22,621 .... K 2
Thursday Island, 2,551 .... G 2
Toowoomba, 55,799 .... J 5
Townsville, 58,847 .... H 3
Warwick, 10,065 .... J 5
Wynnum, 23,191 .... K 2

OTHER FEATURES

Barwon (river) .... H 5
Bulloo (river) .... G 5
Burdekin (river) .... H 3
Cape York (pen.) .... G 2
Carpentaria (gulf) .... F 2
Diamantina (river) .... G 4
Fitzroy (river) .... J 4
Flattery (cape) .... H 2
Flinders (river) .... G 3
Fraser (isl.) .... J 5
Georgina (river) .... F 4
Great Barrier (reef) .... H 3
Great Dividing (range) .... G 3
Great Sandy (Fraser) (isl.) .... J 5
Moreton (isl.) .... L 1
Norman (river) .... G 3
Sturt (desert) .... G 5
Thomson (river) .... G 4
Torres (strait) .... G 2
York (cape) .... G 2

SOUTH AUSTRALIA

CITIES and TOWNS

Adelaide (capital), †727,916 .... D 7
Elizabeth, 32,949 .... D 7
Hindmarsh, 11,352 .... D 7
Kensington and Norwood, 11,928 .... D 7
Maralinga and Woomera, 4,745 .... E 6
Marion, 66,950 .... D 8
Mitcham, 49,470 .... D 8
Mount Gambier, 17,251 .... F 7
Port Adelaide, 39,823 .... D 7
Port Augusta, 10,103 .... F 6
Port Pirie, 15,566 .... F 6
Reynella-Port Noarlunga, 11,818 .... D 8
Salisbury, 35,762 .... D 7
Unley, 39,727 .... D 8
West Torrens, 46,222 .... D 7
Whyalla, 22,121 .... F 6
Woodville, 73,878 .... D 7
Woomera and Maralinga, 4,745 .... F 6

OTHER FEATURES

Eyre (lake) .... F 5
Eyre (peninsula) .... F 6
Flinders (range) .... F 6
Frome (lake) .... G 6
Great Australian (bight) .... D 6
Investigator (strait) .... F 7
Kangaroo (isl.), 3,375 .... F 7
Murray (river) .... G 6
Musgrave (range) .... E 5
Nullarbor (plain) .... D 6
Saint Vincent (gulf) .... D 7
Simpson (desert) .... F 5
Spencer (gulf) .... F 6
Torrens (lake) .... F 6
Yorke (peninsula) .... F 7

TASMANIA

CITIES and TOWNS

Burnie, 15,806 .... H 8
Deloraine, 1,793 .... H 8
Devonport, 14,874 .... H 8
Hobart (capital), 53,257 .... H 8
Hobart, †119,469 .... H 8
Launceston, 37,217 .... H 8
New Norfolk, 5,770 .... H 8
Queenstown, 4,295 .... G 8
Saint Mary's .... H 8
Ulverstone, 6,842 .... H 8
Waratah, ‡698 .... G 8
Wynyard, 3,355 .... H 8
Zeehan, 1,017 .... G 8

OTHER FEATURES

Bass (strait) .... H 7
Furneaux Group (isls.), 1,234 .... H 8
King (isl.), 2,462 .... G 7
Ossa (mt.) .... H 8
Tasman (pen.) .... H 8

VICTORIA

CITIES and TOWNS

Ararat, 8,233 .... G 7
Ballarat, 41,639 .... G 7
Ballarat, *56,290 .... G 7
Bendigo, 30,806 .... G 7
Bendigo, *42,208 .... G 7
Brighton, 40,617 .... M 7
Camberwell, 99,908 .... M 7
Caulfield, 76,119 .... M 7
Chelsea, 24,789 .... M 7
Coburg, 68,568 .... M 6
Dandenong, 31,698 .... M 7
Essendon, 58,258 .... L 6
Footscray, 58,823 .... L 7
Frankston, 38,718 .... M 7
Geelong, 18,129 .... L 7
Geelong, *105,059 .... L 7
Hamilton, 10,054 .... G 7
Heidelberg, 63,929 .... M 6
Horsham, 10,562 .... G 7

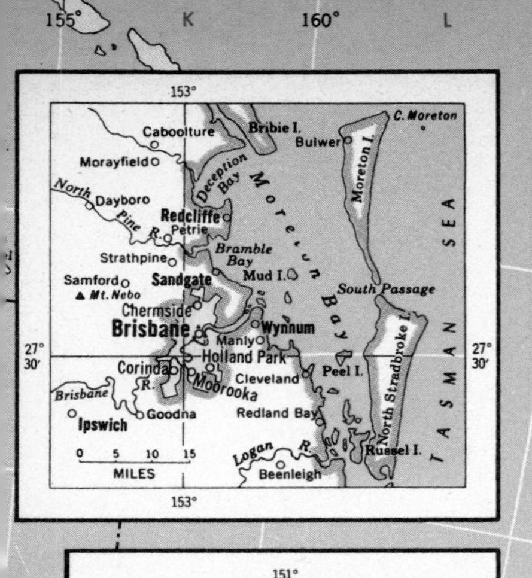

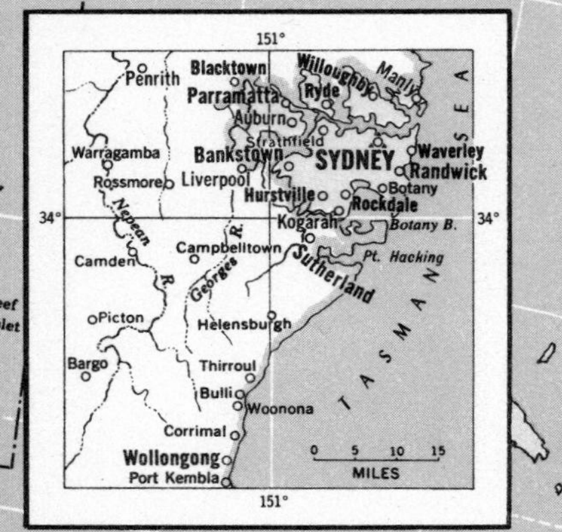

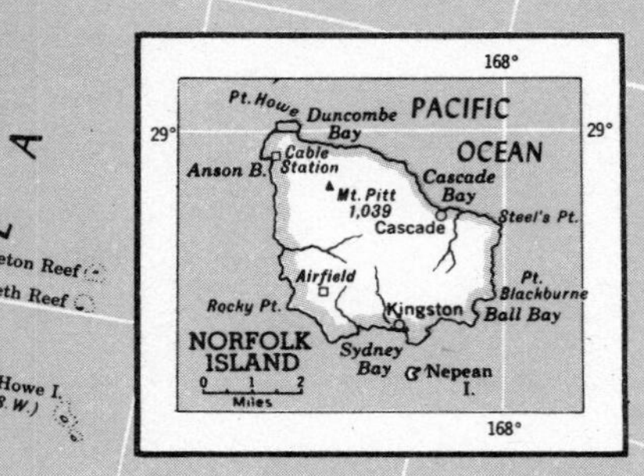

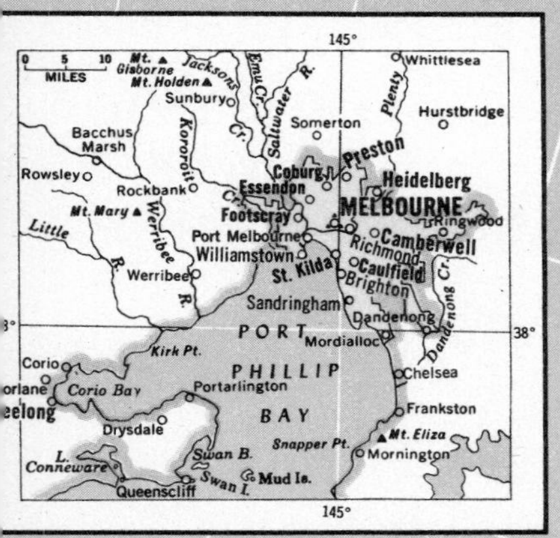

AREA 2,967,741 sq. mi.
POPULATION 12,630,000
CAPITAL Canberra
LARGEST CITY Sydney (greater)
HIGHEST POINT Mt. Kosciusko 7,316 ft.
LOWEST POINT Lake Eyre -39 ft.
MONETARY UNIT Australian dollar
MAJOR LANGUAGE English
MAJOR RELIGIONS Protestantism, Roman Catholicism

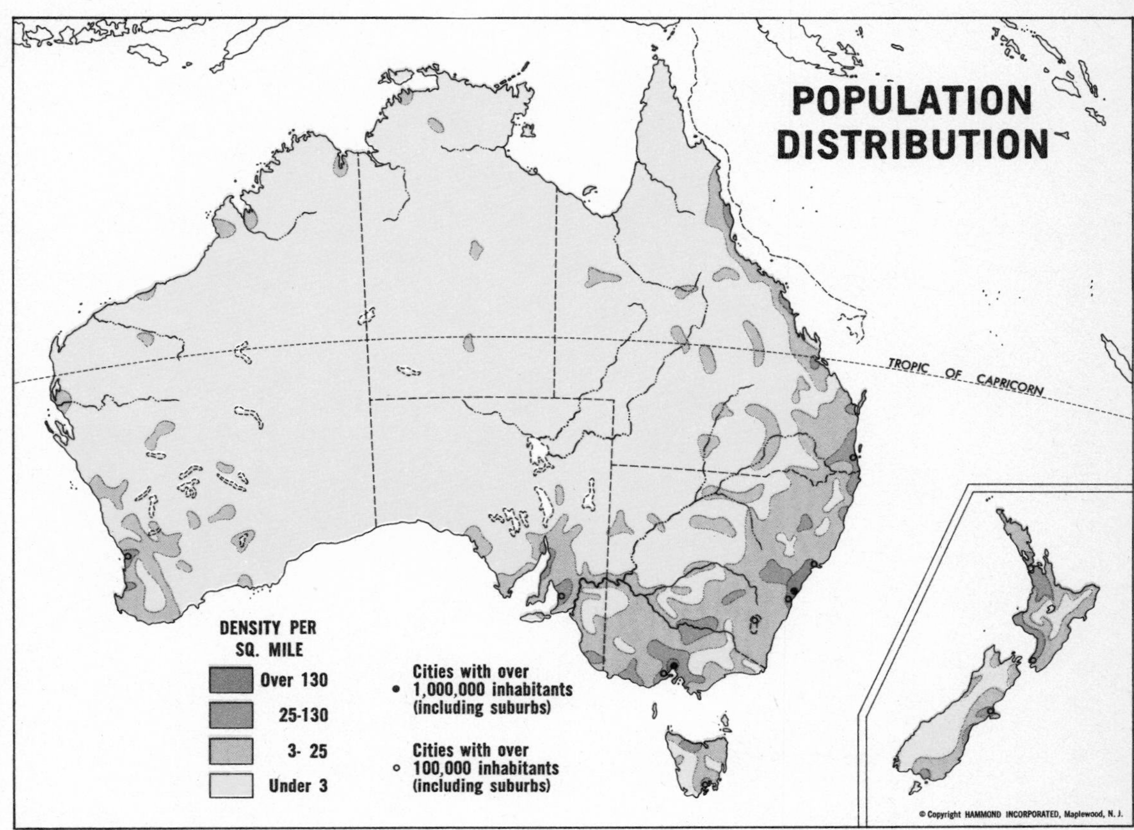

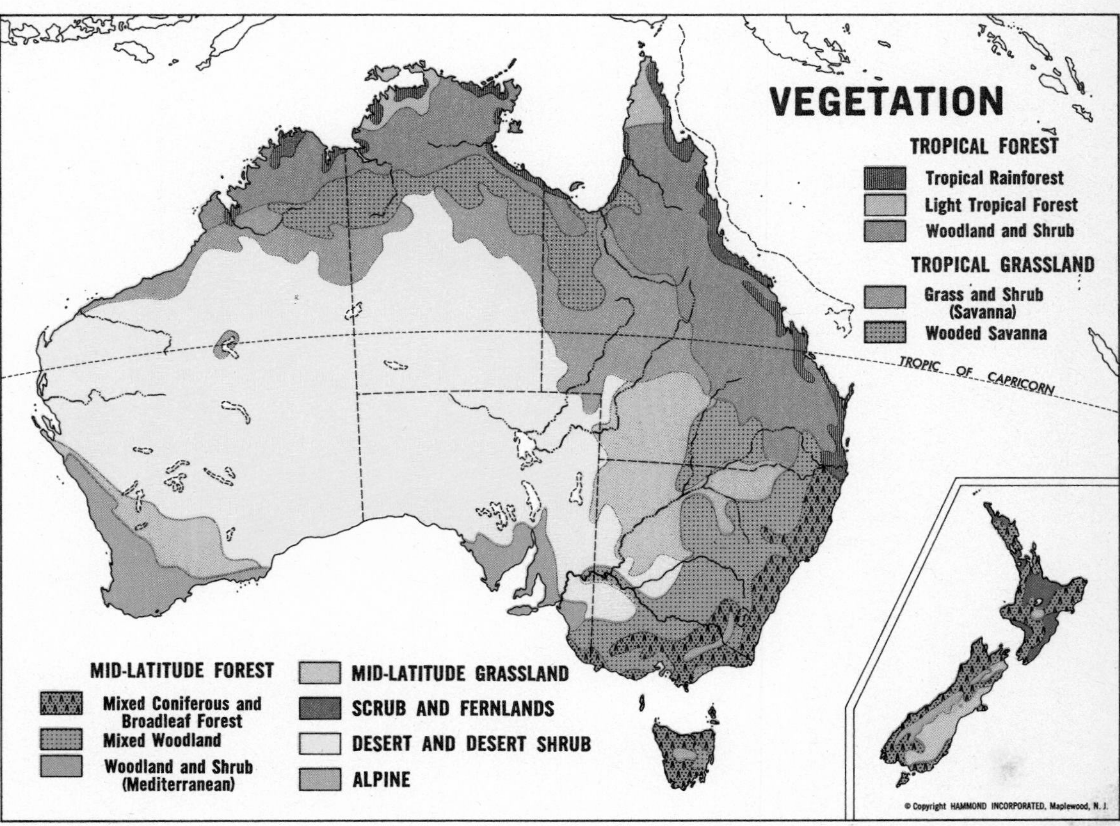

Melbourne (capital), †2,110,168 ....H 7
Mildura, 12,931 ....G 6
Mordialloc, 28,076 ....M 7
Port Melbourne, 12,591 ....L 7
Preston, 89,767 ....M 6
Richmond, 32,530 ....M 7
Ringwood, 29,141 ....M 6
Saint Kilda, 58,129 ....M 7
Sale, 8,640 ....H 7
Sandringham, 36,671 ....M 7
Wangaratta, 15,175 ....H 7
Warrnambool, 17,499 ....G 7
Werribee, 8,228 ....L 7
Williamstown, 30,449 ....L 7

OTHER FEATURES

Australian Alps (mts.) ....H 7
Bass (strait) ....H 7
Murray (river) ....G 6
Port Phillip (bay) ....M 7
Tasman (sea) ....J 7
Wilsons (promontory) ....H 7

WESTERN AUSTRALIA

CITIES and TOWNS

Albany, 11,419 ....B 6
Armadale, 3,463 ....B 2
Boulder, 5,234 ....C 6
Bunbury, 15,459 ....A 6
Collie, 7,628 ....B 6
Fremantle, 25,284 ....B 2
Geraldton, 12,125 ....A 5
Kalgoorlie, 9,174 ....C 6
Kalgoorlie, *19,908 ....C 6
Midland, 9,335 ....B 2
Narrogin, 4,861 ....B 6
Nedlands, 23,320 ....B 2
Northam, 7,400 ....B 2
Perth (capital), †499,969 ....B 2
Rockingham, 3,767 ....B 2
Subiaco, 16,621 ....B 2
Wittenoom Gorge ....B 4

OTHER FEATURES

Ashburton (river) ....B 4
Avon (river) ....B 2
Bruce (mt.) ....B 4
Dampier Land (region) ....C 3
Exmouth (gulf) ....A 4
Fitzroy (river) ....C 3
Gascoyne (river) ....B 5
Geographe (bay) ....A 6
Gibson (desert) ....C 4
Great Australian (bight) ....D 6
Great Sandy (desert) ....C 4
Great Victoria (desert) ....D 5
Hamersley (range) ....B 4
Joseph Bonaparte (gulf) ....D 2
Kimberley (plateau) ....D 3
Leeuwin (cape) ....A 6
Lévêque (cape) ....C 3
Murchison (river) ....B 5
Nullarbor (plain) ....D 6
Ord (river) ....D 3
Shark (bay) ....A 5
Swan (river) ....B 2
Timor (sea) ....D 2
Yule (river) ....B 4

*City and suburbs.
†Population of metropolitan area.
‡Population of district.

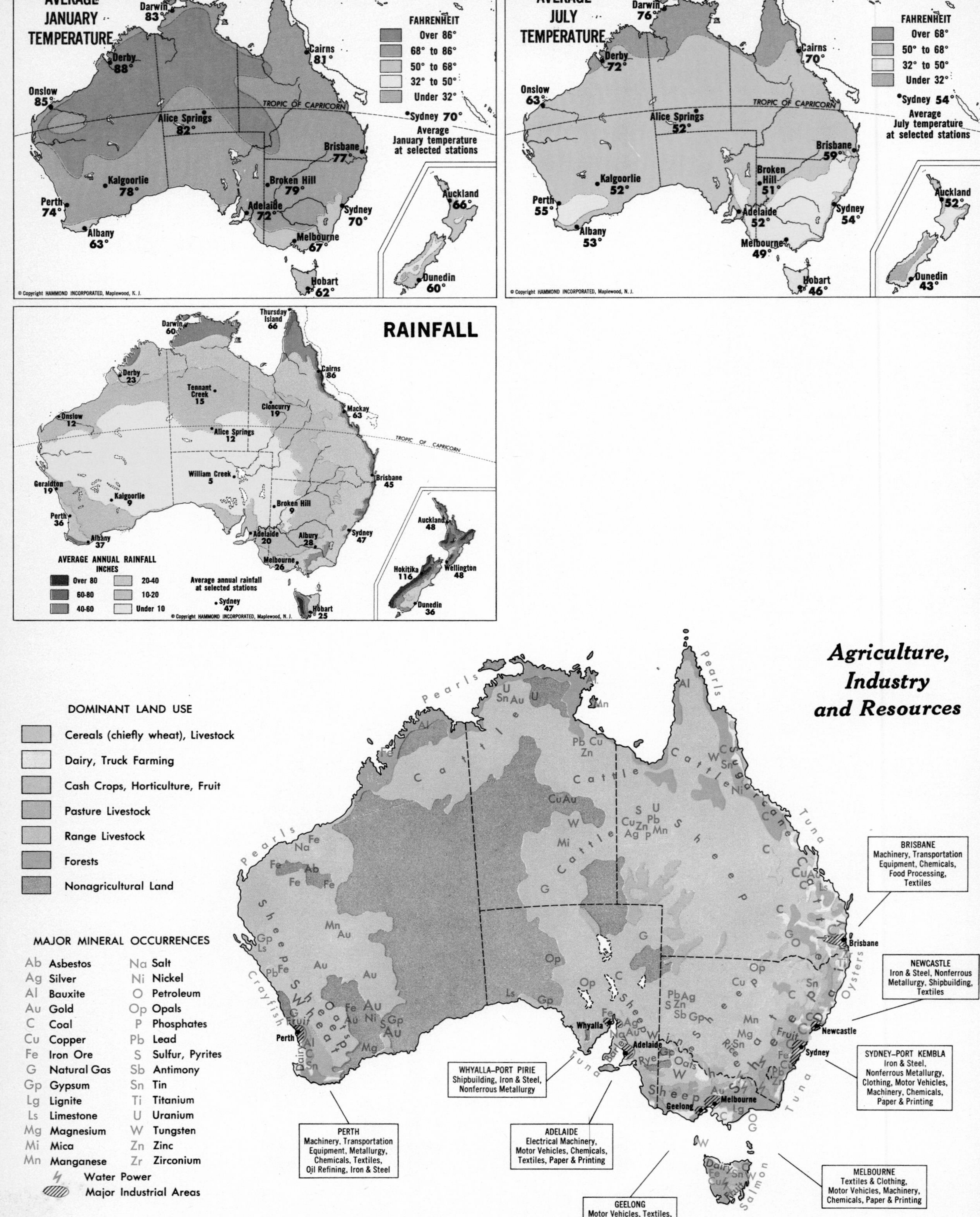
AVERAGE JANUARY TEMPERATURE
FAHRENHEIT
Over 86°
68° to 86°
50° to 68°
32° to 50°
Under 32°
•Sydney 70°
Average January temperature at selected stations
Darwin 83°
Derby 88°
Onslow 85°
Alice Springs 82°
Cairns 81°
Brisbane 77°
Kalgoorlie 78°
Broken Hill 79°
Perth 74°
Adelaide 72°
Sydney 70°
Albany 63°
Melbourne 67°
Hobart 62°
Auckland 66°
Dunedin 60°
TROPIC OF CAPRICORN
© Copyright HAMMOND INCORPORATED, Maplewood, N. J.
AVERAGE JULY TEMPERATURE
FAHRENHEIT
Over 68°
50° to 68°
32° to 50°
Under 32°
•Sydney 54°
Average July temperature at selected stations
Darwin 76°
Derby 72°
Onslow 63°
Alice Springs 52°
Cairns 70°
Brisbane 59°
Kalgoorlie 52°
Broken Hill 51°
Perth 55°
Adelaide 52°
Sydney 54°
Albany 53°
Melbourne 49°
Hobart 46°
Auckland 52°
Dunedin 43°
TROPIC OF CAPRICORN
© Copyright HAMMOND INCORPORATED, Maplewood, N. J.
RAINFALL
Darwin 60
Thursday Island 66
Derby 23
Cairns 86
Tennant Creek 15
Cloncurry 19
Mackay 63
Onslow 12
Alice Springs 12
TROPIC OF CAPRICORN
William Creek 5
Brisbane 45
Geraldton 19
Kalgoorlie 9
Broken Hill 9
Auckland 48
Perth 36
Albany 37
Adelaide 20
Albury 28
Sydney 47
Melbourne 26
Wellington 48
Hokitika 116
Hobart 25
Dunedin 36
AVERAGE ANNUAL RAINFALL INCHES
Over 80
60-80
40-60
20-40
10-20
Under 10
Average annual rainfall at selected stations
•Sydney 47
© Copyright HAMMOND INCORPORATED, Maplewood, N. J.
Agriculture, Industry and Resources
DOMINANT LAND USE
Cereals (chiefly wheat), Livestock
Dairy, Truck Farming
Cash Crops, Horticulture, Fruit
Pasture Livestock
Range Livestock
Forests
Nonagricultural Land
MAJOR MINERAL OCCURRENCES
Ab Asbestos
Ag Silver
Al Bauxite
Au Gold
C Coal
Cu Copper
Fe Iron Ore
G Natural Gas
Gp Gypsum
Lg Lignite
Ls Limestone
Mg Magnesium
Mi Mica
Mn Manganese
Na Salt
Ni Nickel
O Petroleum
Op Opals
P Phosphates
Pb Lead
S Sulfur, Pyrites
Sb Antimony
Sn Tin
Ti Titanium
U Uranium
W Tungsten
Zn Zinc
Zr Zirconium
Water Power
Major Industrial Areas
Pearls
Cattle
Sheep
Sugarcane
Tuna
Oysters
Crayfish
Salmon
Oats
Wheat
Barley
Rye
Rice
Fruit
Dairy
Perth
Whyalla
Adelaide
Geelong
Melbourne
Sydney
Newcastle
Brisbane
BRISBANE
Machinery, Transportation Equipment, Chemicals, Food Processing, Textiles
NEWCASTLE
Iron & Steel, Nonferrous Metallurgy, Shipbuilding, Textiles
SYDNEY–PORT KEMBLA
Iron & Steel, Nonferrous Metallurgy, Clothing, Motor Vehicles, Machinery, Chemicals, Paper & Printing
WHYALLA–PORT PIRIE
Shipbuilding, Iron & Steel, Nonferrous Metallurgy
PERTH
Machinery, Transportation Equipment, Metallurgy, Chemicals, Textiles, Oil Refining, Iron & Steel
ADELAIDE
Electrical Machinery, Motor Vehicles, Chemicals, Textiles, Paper & Printing
GEELONG
Motor Vehicles, Textiles, Machinery, Oil Refining
MELBOURNE
Textiles & Clothing, Motor Vehicles, Machinery, Chemicals, Paper & Printing

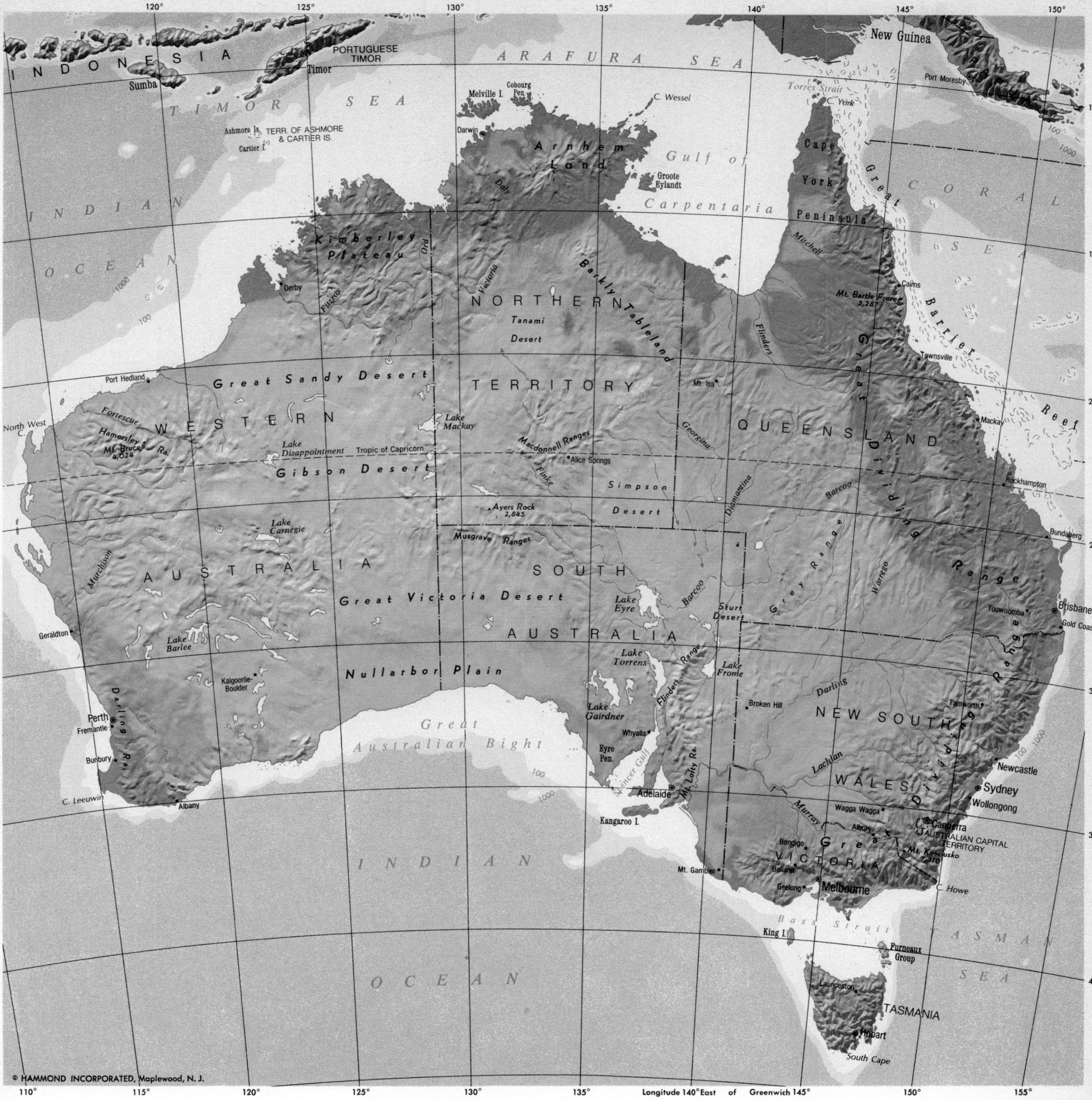

INDONESIA
Sumba
Timor
PORTUGUESE TIMOR
ARAFURA SEA
New Guinea
Port Moresby
TIMOR SEA
Ashmore Is.
Cartier I.
TERR. OF ASHMORE & CARTIER IS.
Melville I.
Cobourg Pen.
Darwin
C. Wessel
Torres Strait
C. York
Arnhem Land
Gulf of Carpentaria
Groote Eylandt
Cape York Peninsula
CORAL SEA
Great Barrier Reef
INDIAN OCEAN
Kimberley Plateau
Derby
NORTHERN TERRITORY
Tanami Desert
Barkly Tableland
Mt. Bartle Frere 5,287
Cairns
Townsville
Port Hedland
Great Sandy Desert
Mt. Isa
North West C.
WESTERN AUSTRALIA
Hamersley Ra.
Mt. Bruce 4,024
Lake Disappointment
Tropic of Capricorn
Lake Mackay
Macdonnell Ranges
Alice Springs
QUEENSLAND
Mackay
Gibson Desert
Simpson Desert
Rockhampton
Ayers Rock 2,845
Lake Carnegie
Musgrave Ranges
Bundaberg
Great Dividing Range
SOUTH AUSTRALIA
Great Victoria Desert
Lake Eyre
Sturt Desert
Brisbane
Toowoomba
Gold Coast
Geraldton
Lake Barlee
Lake Torrens
Lake Frome
Kalgoorlie-Boulder
Nullarbor Plain
Flinders Range
Broken Hill
Tamworth
NEW SOUTH WALES
Perth
Fremantle
Darling Ra.
Lake Gairdner
Whyalla
Great Australian Bight
Eyre Pen.
Spencer Gulf
Mt. Lofty Ra.
Newcastle
Sydney
Wollongong
Bunbury
C. Leeuwin
Albany
Adelaide
Kangaroo I.
Wagga Wagga
Canberra
AUSTRALIAN CAPITAL TERRITORY
Albury
Bendigo
Ballarat
VICTORIA
Mt. Kosciusko 7,316
Mt. Gambier
Geelong
Melbourne
C. Howe
Bass Strait
King I.
TASMAN SEA
Furneaux Group
Launceston
TASMANIA
Hobart
South Cape

Longitude 140° East of Greenwich

VEGETATION/RELIEF

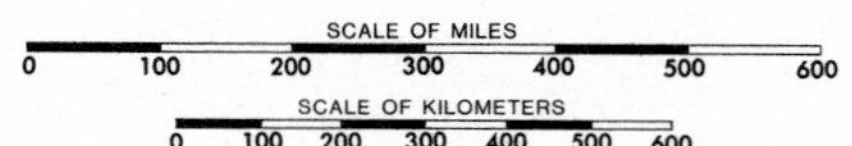

Capital of Country
State and Territorial Capitals
International Boundaries
State and Territorial Boundaries

Elevations in Feet
Depths in Fathoms

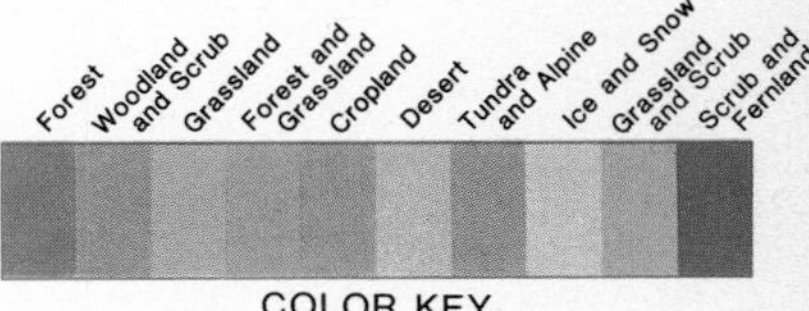

AREA 975,920 sq. mi.
POPULATION 991,300
CAPITAL Perth
LARGEST CITY Perth
HIGHEST POINT Mt. Bruce 4,024 ft.

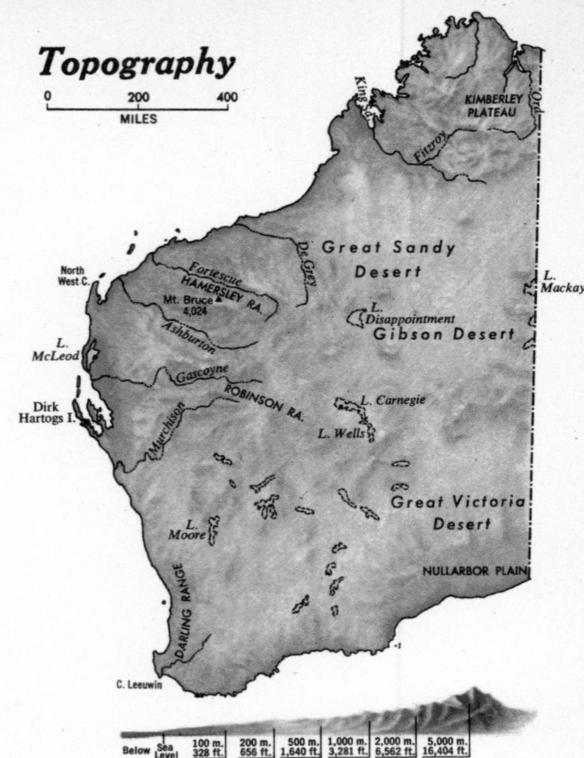

CITIES and TOWNS

Albany, 11,419 .... B 6
Armadale, 3,463 .... A 1
Augusta, ⊙3,238 .... A 6
Beverley, ⊙1,773 .... B 1
Boddington, ⊙761 .... B 2
Boulder, 5,234 .... C 5
Bridgetown, 1,569 .... B 6
Brookton, ⊙1,341 .... B 2
Broome, 1,570 .... C 2
Bruce Rock, ⊙2,142 .... B 5
Bunbury, 15,459 .... A 2
Busselton, 4,278 .... A 6
Capel, ⊙2,132 .... A 2
Carnamah, ⊙996 .... A 5
Carnarvon, 2,956 .... A 4
Collie, 7,628 .... B 2
Coolgardie, ⊙762 .... C 5
Coorow, ⊙808 .... B 5
Corrigin, ⊙2,099 .... B 6
Cranbrook, ⊙1,419 .... B 6
Cuballing, ⊙732 .... B 2
Cue, ⊙430 .... B 4
Cunderdin, ⊙2,114 .... B 5
Dalwallinu, ⊙2,425 .... B 5
Dampier, 1,080 .... B 3
Dandaragan, ⊙619 .... A 5
Denmark, ⊙1,775 .... B 6
Derby, 1,424 .... C 2
Donnybrook, 981 .... A 2
Esperance, 2,677 .... C 6
Exmouth Gulf, ⊙2,248 .... A 3
Fremantle, 25,284 .... A 1
Geraldton, 12,125 .... A 5
Gingin, ⊙1,021 .... A 1
Gnowangerup, 981 .... B 6
Goomalling, ⊙1,567 .... B 1
Gosnells, 7,135 .... A 1
Halls Creek, ⊙577 .... D 2
Harvey, 2,066 .... A 2
Jarrahdale, ⊙1,728 .... B 2
Kalamunda-Gooseberry Hill, 3,068 .... B 1
Kalgoorlie, 9,174 .... C 5
Kalgoorlie, □19,908 .... C 5
Katanning, 3,506 .... B 6
Kellerberrin, 1,343 .... B 5
Kojonup, ⊙2,711 .... B 6
Kwinana, 1,272 .... A 1
Lake Grace, ⊙1,986 .... B 6
Learmonth, ... A 3
Leonora, ⊙623 .... C 5
Mandurah, 2,730 .... A 2
Manjimup, 3,186 .... B 6
Marble Bar, ⊙567 .... C 3
Meekatharra, ⊙1,011 .... B 4
Menzies, ⊙404 .... C 5
Merredin, 3,599 .... B 5
Midland, 9,335 .... A 1
Mingenew, ⊙978 .... A 5
Moora, 1,185 .... B 5
Morawa, ⊙1,718 .... B 5
Mount Barker, 1,594 .... B 6
Mount Magnet, ⊙1,016 .... B 5
Mukinbudin, ⊙869 .... B 5
Mullewa, ⊙1,825 .... A 5
Nannup, ⊙1,272 .... B 6
Narrogin, 4,861 .... B 2
Nedlands, 23,320 .... A 1
Norseman, 1,863 .... C 6
Northam, 7,400 .... B 1
Northampton, ⊙2,021 .... A 5
Nullagine, ⊙211 .... C 3
Nungarin, ⊙539 .... B 5
Onslow, ... A 3
Pardoo, ... B 3
Pemberton, 930 .... A 6
Perenjori, ⊙1,311 .... B 5
Perth (cap.), ‡499,969 .... A 1
Pingelly, ⊙1,453 .... B 2
Port Hedland, 1,778 .... B 3
Quairading, ⊙1,687 .... B 1
Ravensthorpe, ⊙782 .... B 6
Rockingham, 3,767 .... A 2
Roebourne, ⊙702 .... B 3
South Perth, 32,042 .... A 1
Subiaco, 16,621 .... A 1
Tableland, ⊙1,815 .... D 2
Three Springs, ⊙1,038 .... A 5
Toodyay, ⊙1,388 .... B 1
Wagin, 1,750 .... B 2
Wandering, ⊙611 .... B 2
Wanneroo, 612 .... A 1
Waroona, 1,013 .... A 2
Wickepin, ⊙1,380 .... B 2
Williams, ⊙1,193 .... B 2
Wiluna, ⊙219 .... C 4
Wundowie, 1,040 .... B 1
Wyalkatchem, ⊙1,252 .... B 5
Wyndham, 1,156 .... E 1
Yalgoo, ⊙392 .... B 5
Yampi Sound, ... C 2
York, 1,421 .... B 1

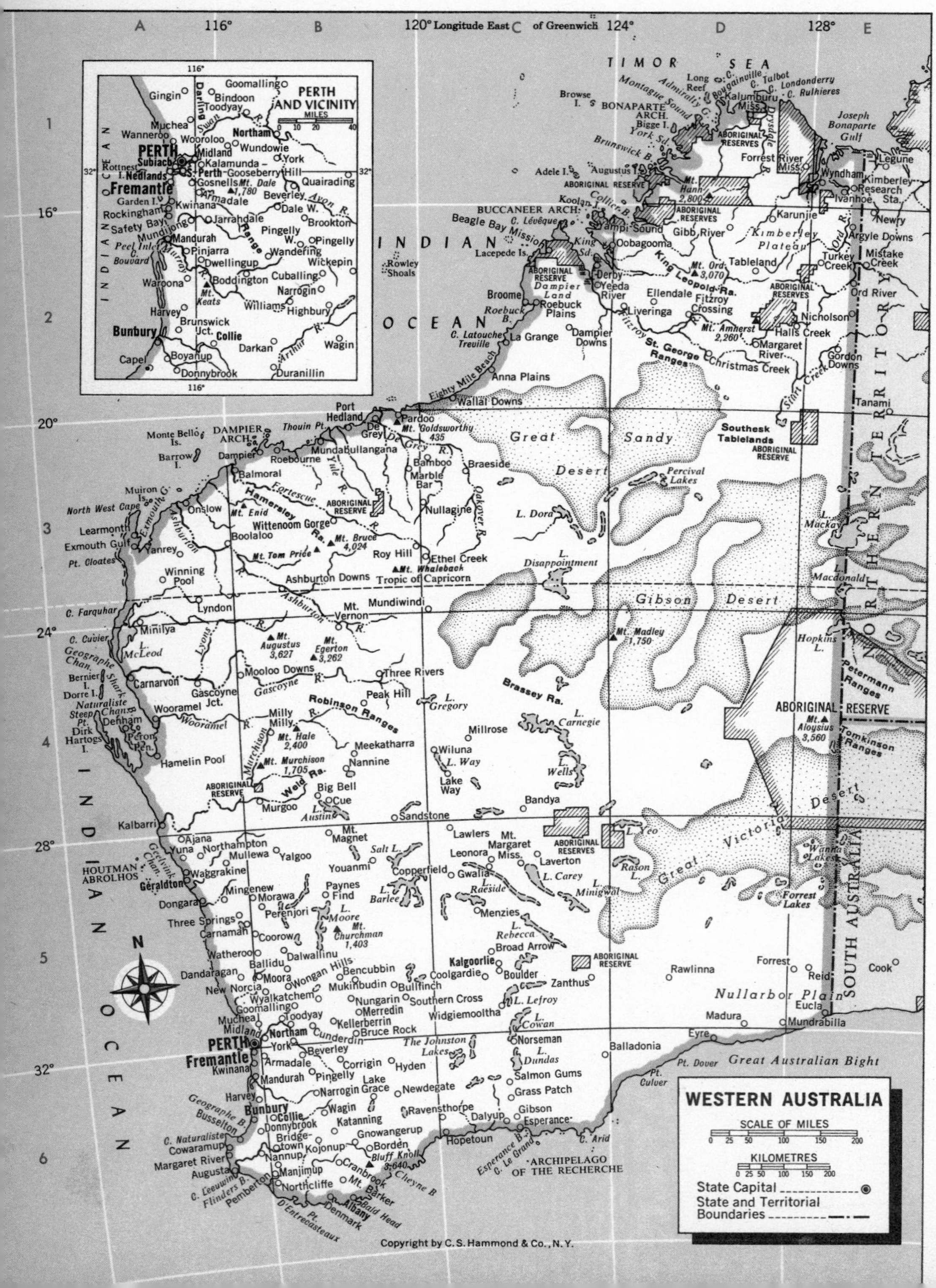

OTHER FEATURES

Adele (isl.) .... C 1
Admiralty (gulf) .... D 1
Aloysius (mt.) .... E 4
Amherst (mt.) .... D 2
Arid (cape) .... C 6
Arthur (riv.) .... B 2
Ashburton (riv.) .... A 3
Augustus (isl.) .... D 1
Augustus (mt.) .... B 4
Austin (lake) .... B 4
Avon (riv.) .... A 1
Bald (head) .... B 6
Barlee (lake) .... B 5
Barrow (isl.) .... A 3
Bernier (isl.) .... A 4
Bigge (isl.) .... D 1
Bluff Knoll (mt.) .... B 6
Bonaparte (arch.) .... D 1
Bougainville (cape) .... D 1
Bouvard (cape) .... A 2
Brassey (range) .... C 4
Browse (isl.) .... C 1
Bruce (mt.) .... B 3
Brunswick (bay) .... D 1
Buccaneer (arch.) .... C 2
Carey (lake) .... C 5
Carnegie (lake) .... C 4
Cheyne (bay) .... B 6
Churchman (mt.) .... B 5
Cloates (pt.) .... A 3
Collier (bay) .... C 1
Cowan (lake) .... C 5
Culver (pt.) .... D 6
Cuvier (cape) .... A 4
Dale (mt.) .... B 1
Dampier (arch.) .... B 3
Dampier Land (reg.) .... C 2
Darling (range) .... A 1
De Grey (riv.) .... B 3
D'Entrecasteaux (pt.) .... B 6
Dirk Hartogs (isl.) .... A 4
Disappointment (lake) .... C 3
Dora (lake) .... C 3
Dorre (isl.) .... A 4
Dover (pt.) .... D 6
Drysdale (riv.) .... D 1
Dundas (lake) .... C 6
Egerton (mt.) .... B 4
Eighty Mile (beach) .... C 2
Enid (mt.) .... B 3
Esperance (bay) .... C 6
Exmouth (gulf) .... A 3
Farquhar (cape) .... A 3
Fitzroy (riv.) .... D 2
Flinders (bay) .... A 6
Fortescue (riv.) .... B 3
Garden (isl.) .... A 1
Gascoyne (riv.) .... B 4
Geelvink (chan.) .... A 5
Geographe (bay) .... A 6
Geographe (chan.) .... A 4
Gibson (des.) .... D 3
Goldsworthy (mt.) .... C 3
Great Australian (bight) .... E 6
Great Sandy (des.) .... C 3
Great Victoria (des.) .... D 5
Gregory (lake) .... C 4
Hale (mt.) .... B 4
Hamersley (range) .... B 3
Hann (mt.) .... D 1
Hopkins (lake) .... E 4
Houtman Abrolhos (isls.) .... A 5
Indian Ocean .... A 5
Johnston, The (lakes) .... C 6
Joseph Bonaparte (gulf) .... E 1
Keats (mt.) .... A 2
Kimberley (plat.) .... D 2
King (sound) .... C 2
King Leopold (range) .... D 2
Koolan (isl.) .... C 1
Lacepede (isls.) .... C 2
Latouche Treville (cape) .... C 2
Leeuwin (cape) .... A 6
Lefroy (lake) .... C 5
Le Grand (cape) .... C 6
Lévêque (cape) .... C 2
Londonderry (cape) .... D 1
Long (reef) .... D 1
Lyons (riv.) .... A 4
Macdonald (lake) .... E 3
Mackay (lake) .... E 3
Madley (mt.) .... D 4
McLeod (lake) .... A 4
Minigwal (lake) .... C 5
Montague (sound) .... D 1
Monte Bello (isls.) .... A 3
Moore (lake) .... B 5
Muiron (isls.) .... A 3
Murchison (mt.) .... B 4
Murchison (riv.) .... B 4
Murray (riv.) .... A 2
Naturaliste (cape) .... A 6
Naturaliste (chan.) .... A 4
North West (cape) .... A 3
Nullarbor (plain) .... D 5
Oakover (riv.) .... C 3
Ord (mt.) .... D 2
Ord (riv.) .... E 2
Peel (inlet) .... A 2
Percival (lakes) .... D 3
Peron (pen.) .... A 4
Petermann (ranges) .... E 4
Raeside (lake) .... C 5
Rason (lake) .... D 5
Rebecca (lake) .... C 5
Recherche (arch.) .... C 6
Robinson (ranges) .... B 4
Roebuck (bay) .... C 2
Rottnest (isl.) .... A 1
Rowley (shoals) .... B 2
Rulhieres (cape) .... D 1
Saint George (ranges) .... D 2
Salt (lake) .... B 5
Shark (bay) .... A 4
Southesk Tablelands .... D 3
Steep (pt.) .... A 4
Sturt (creek) .... D 2
Swan (riv.) .... A 1
Talbot (cape) .... D 1
Thouin (pt.) .... B 3
Timor (sea) .... D 1
Tomkinson (ranges) .... E 4
Tom Price (mt.) .... B 3
Wanna (lakes) .... E 5
Way (lake) .... C 4
Weld (range) .... B 4
Wells (lake) .... C 4
Whaleback (mt.) .... B 3
Wooramel (riv.) .... A 4
Yeo (lake) .... D 5
York (sound) .... D 1
Yule (riv.) .... B 3

⊙ Population of district.
‡ Population of met. area.
□ Population of urban area.

WESTERN AUSTRALIA
SCALE OF MILES
KILOMETRES
State Capital
State and Territorial Boundaries

AREA 520,280 sq. mi.
POPULATION 73,000
CAPITAL Darwin
LARGEST CITY Darwin
HIGHEST POINT Mt. Ziel 4,955 ft.

CITIES and TOWNS

Adelaide River, ⊙300 .... B 2
Aileron, ... C 7
Alexandria, ... E 5
Alice Springs, 6,037 .... D 7
Alroy Downs, ... E 5
Andado, ... D 8
Angas Downs, ... C 8
Anthony Lagoon, ⊙162 .... D 4
Areyonga, ... C 8
Argadargada, ... E 6
Arltunga, ... D 7
Auvergne, ... B 3
Avon Downs, ⊙231 .... E 5
Banka Banka, ... C 5
Barrow Creek, ... D 6
Batchelor, ⊙551 .... B 2
Bathurst Island Mission, ... B 1
Birdum, ... C 3
Birrimbah, ... C 3
Birrindudu, ... A 5
Bundooma, ... D 8
Burramurra, ... E 6
Calvert Hills, ... E 4
Charlotte Waters, ... D 8
Claravale, ... B 3
Coniston, ... C 7
Coolibah, ... B 3
Creswell Downs, ... E 4
Daly River, ⊙237 .... B 2
Daly Waters, ⊙265 .... C 4
Darwin (cap.), 18,042 .... B 2
Douglas, ... B 2
Elliott, ⊙234 .... C 4
Epenarra, ... D 6
Erldunda, ... C 8
Eva Downs, ... D 5
Ewaninga, ... D 8
Fitzroy, ... B 4
Frewena, ... D 5
Harts Range, ⊙95 .... D 7
Hatches Creek, ⊙74 .... D 6
Helen Springs, ... C 5
Henbury, ... C 8
Humpty Doo, ... B 2
Inverway, ... A 4
Katherine, 1,302 .... B 3
Kildurk, ... A 4
Killarney, ... B 4
Koolpinyah, ... B 2
Kulgera, ⊙229 .... C 8
Kurundi, ... D 6
Lake Nash, ⊙113 .... E 6
Larrimah, ⊙88 .... C 3
Legune, ... A 3
Limbunya, ... B 4
Litchfield, ... B 2
Lucy Creek, ... E 7
Mainoru, ... C 3
Mataranka, ⊙114 .... C 3
Mistake Creek, ... A 4
Montejinni, ... C 4
Mount Cavanagh, ... C 8
Mount Doreen, ... B 7
Murray Downs, ... D 6
Napperby, ... C 7
Newcastle Waters, ... C 4
Newry, ... A 3
Nutwood Downs, ... D 3
O.T. Downs, ... D 4
Pine Creek, ⊙577 .... C 2
Plenty River Mine, ... D 7
Powell Creek, ... C 5
Rankine Store, ... E 5
Ringwood, ... D 7
Robinson River, ... E 4
Rockhamoton Downs, ... D 5
Rodinga, ... D 8
Roper River Mission, ⊙357 .... D 3
Roper Valley, ... D 3
Rosewood, ... A 4
Rum Jungle, ... B 2
Soudan, ... E 6
Stirling, ... C 6
Tanami, ... A 5
Tarlton Downs, ... E 7
Tea Tree Well Store, ... C 7
Tempe Downs, ... C 8
Tennant Creek, 1,001 .... C 5
The Granites, ... B 6
Top Springs, ... C 4
Ucharonidge, ... D 4
Umbeara, ... C 8
Urapunga, ... D 3
Utopia, ... D 7
Victoria River Downs, ... B 4
Waterloo, ... A 4
Wave Hill, ⊙289 .... B 4
White Quartz Hill, ... D 7
Willeroo, ... B 3
Willowra, ... C 6
Wollogorang, ⊙87 .... F 4
Yambah, ... C 7

OTHER FEATURES

Amadeus (lake) .... B 8
Arafura (sea) .... D 1
Arnhem (cape) .... E 2
Arnhem Land (reg.) .... D 2
Arnold (riv.) .... D 3
Barkly Tableland .... D 4
Bathurst (isl.) .... A 1
Beagle (gulf) .... A 2
Beatrice (cape) .... E 3
Bennett (lake) .... B 7
Bickerton (isl.) .... E 2
Blaze (pt.) .... A 2
Boucaut (bay) .... D 1
Carpentaria (gulf) .... E 3
Central Wedge (mt.) .... C 7
Clarence (str.) .... B 2
Cobourg (pen.) .... C 1
Conner (mt.) .... B 8
Croker (cape) .... C 1
Daly (riv.) .... B 2
Davenport (mt.) .... B 7
Dobbie (mt.) .... E 7
Drummond (mt.) .... E 5
Dry (riv.) .... C 3
Dundas (str.) .... B 1
East Alligator (riv.) .... C 2
Ehrenberg (range) .... B 7
Elcho (isl.) .... D 1
Ewing (mt.) .... E 7
Finke (riv.) .... C 8
Fitzmaurice (riv.) .... B 3
Flora (riv.) .... B 3
Ford (cape) .... A 2
Georgina (riv.) .... E 6
Goulburn (isls.) .... C 1
Goyder (riv.) .... D 2
Grey (cape) .... E 2
Groote Eylandt (isl.) .... E 2
Hale (riv.) .... D 8
Hanson (riv.) .... C 6
Hay (cape) .... A 3
Hay (dry riv.) .... E 7
Hogarth (mt.) .... E 6
Hopkins (lake) .... A 8
Joseph Bonaparte (gulf) .... A 3
Katherine (riv.) .... C 3
Lander (riv.) .... C 6
Leisler (mt.) .... A 7
Limmen (bight) .... D 3
Limmen Bight (riv.) .... D 4
Macdonald (lake) .... B 7
Macdonnell (ranges) .... C 7
MacKay (lake) .... A 7
Mann (riv.) .... D 2
Marshall (riv.) .... D 7
Melville (bay) .... E 2
Melville (isl.) .... B 1
Murchison (range) .... D 6
Napier (mt.) .... A 4
Neale (lake) .... A 8
Newcastle (creek) .... C 4
Nicholson (riv.) .... E 5
Old Marsh Bed .... B 6
Olga (mt.) .... B 8
Peron (isls.) .... A 2
Petermann (ranges) .... A 8
Port Darwin (inlet) .... B 2
Ranken (riv.) .... E 6
Robinson (riv.) .... E 4
Roper (riv.) .... C 3
Rose (riv.) .... D 2
Sandover (riv.) .... D 6
Simpson (des.) .... E 8
Singleton (mt.) .... B 6
Sir Edward Pellew Group (isls.) .... E 3
South Alligator (riv.) .... C 2
Stanley (mt.) .... B 7
Stewart (cape) .... D 1
Stirling (creek) .... A 4
Sturt (plain) .... C 4
Sylvester (lake) .... D 5
Tanami (des.) .... C 5
Timor (sea) .... A 2
Todd (riv.) .... D 8
Vanderlin (isl.) .... E 3
Van Diemen (cape) .... A 1
Van Diemen (gulf) .... B 1
Victoria (riv.) .... B 3
Warwick (chan.) .... E 3
Wessel (cape) .... E 1
Wessel (isls.) .... E 1
West Baines (riv.) .... A 4
White (lake) .... A 6
Winnecke (creek) .... B 5
Woods (lake) .... C 4
Young (mt.) .... D 3
Ziel (mt.) .... C 7

⊙ Population of district.

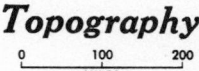

Topography

0 100 200
MILES

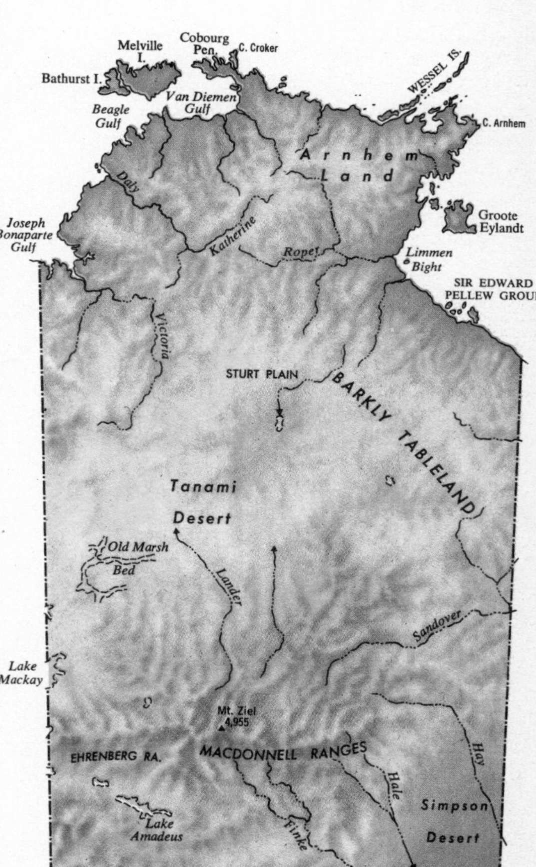

94 South Australia

AREA 380,070 sq. mi.
POPULATION 1,169,600
CAPITAL Adelaide
LARGEST CITY Adelaide
HIGHEST POINT Mt. Woodroffe 4,970 ft.

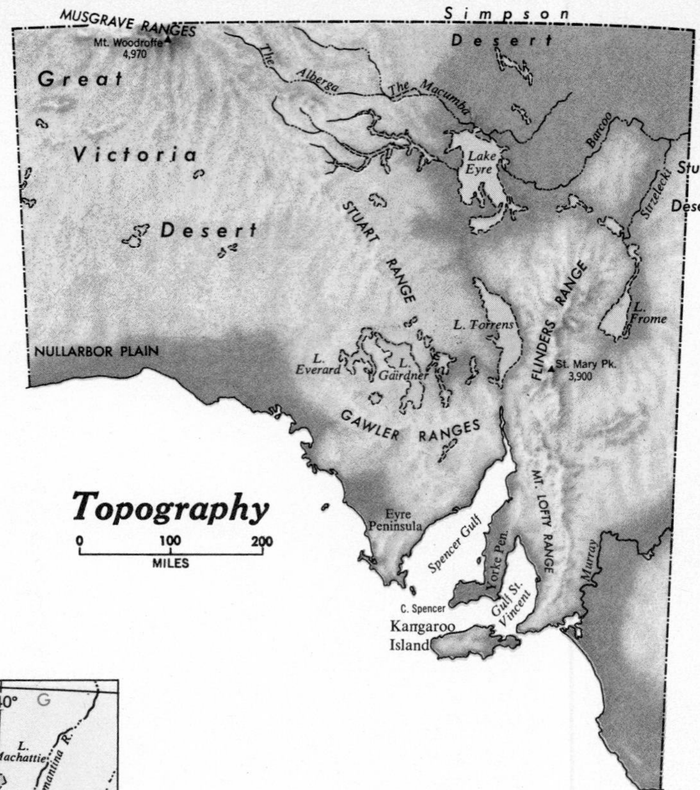

Topography

0 100 200
MILES

CITIES and TOWNS

Adelaide (cap.), ‡727,916 .. B 6
Angaston, 1,887 .... F 6
Balaklava, 1,199 .... F 6
Barmera, 1,484 .... G 6
Beachport, ⊙1,903 .... F 7
Berri, 2,232 .... G 6
Bordertown, 1,758 .... G 7
Brighton, 22,620 .... A 8
Burnside, 38,758 .... B 8
Burra, 1,342 .... F 5
Campbelltown, 32,083 .... B 7
Ceduna, 1,406 .... D 5
Clare, 1,579 .... F 5
Cleve, ⊙2,817 .... E 5
Colonel Light Gardens,
 3,404 .... A 8
Coober Pedy, ... D 3
Crystal Brook, 1,235 .... E 5
Elizabeth, 32,949 .... B 7
Elliston, ⊙1,424 .... D 5
Enfield, 80,261 .... B 7
Gawler, 6,645 .... B 6
Gladstone, 1,035 .... F 5
Glenelg, 14,762 .... A 8
Gumeracha, ⊙2,654 .... C 7
Hindmarsh, 11,352 .... A 7
Hope Valley-Tea Tree
 Gully, ⊙21,314 .... B 7
Jamestown, 1,282 .... F 5
Kadina, 3,022 .... F 5
Kapunda, 1,119 .... F 6
Keith, 1,097 .... G 7
Kensington and Norwood,
 11,928 .... B 8
Kimba, ⊙1,703 .... E 5
Kingscote, 1,071 .... E 6
Kingston, 1,065 .... G 7
Lameroo, ⊙1,947 .... G 6
Leigh Creek, 1,014 .... F 4
Lobethal, 1,098 .... C 7
Loxton, 2,418 .... G 6
Maitland, 1,017 .... E 6
Mannum, 2,034 .... F 6
Maralinga and Woomera,
 4,745 .... B 3
Marion, 66,950 .... A 8
Meadows, ⊙2,824 .... B 8
Meningie, ⊙4,104 .... F 6
Millicent, 4,533 .... F 7
Minlaton, ⊙2,504 .... E 6
Mitcham, 49,470 .... B 8
Moonta, 1,122 .... E 5
Mount Barker, 1,934 .... C 8
Mount Gambier, 17,251 .... G 7
Murray Bridge, 5,957 .... F 6
Nangwarry, 977 .... G 7
Naracoorte, 4,378 .... G 7
Nuriootpa, 2,041 .... F 6
Orroroo, ⊙1,228 .... F 5
Payneham, 16,844 .... B 7
Penola, 1,383 .... G 7
Peterborough, 3,117 .... F 5
Pinnaroo, ⊙1,717 .... G 6
Port Adelaide, 39,823 .... A 7
Port Augusta, 10,103 .... E 5
Port Lincoln, 8,888 .... E 6
Port Pirie, 15,566 .... E 5
Prospect, 21,411 .... B 7
Radium Hill, ... G 5
Renmark, 6,275 .... G 5
Reynella-Port Noarlunga,
 11,818 .... A 8
Robe, ⊙941 .... F 7
Salisbury, 35,762 .... B 7
Snowtown, ⊙1,694 .... E 5
Stirling-Bridgewater,
 4,487 .... B 8
Strathalbyn, 1,449 .... F 6
Streaky Bay, ⊙2,134 .... D 5
Tailem Bend, 1,947 .... F 6
Tanunda, 1,986 .... C 6
Thebarton, 12,296 .... A 7
Tumby Bay, ⊙2,793 .... E 6
Unley, 39,727 .... B 8
Victor Harbor, 3,128 .... F 6
Waikerie, ⊙3,818 .... F 6
Wallaroo, 2,094 .... E 5
West Torrens, 46,222 .... A 8
Whyalla, 22,121 .... E 5
Willunga, ⊙2,190 .... F 6
Wilmington, ⊙828 .... F 6
Woodville, 73,878 .... A 7
Woomera and Maralinga,
 4,745 .... E 4
Yorketown, ⊙2,734 .... E 6

OTHER FEATURES

Acraman (lake) .... D 5
Alberga, The (riv.) .... D 2
Alexandrina (lake) .... F 6
Anxious (bay) .... D 5
Arckaringa (creek) .... D 2
Barcoo (creek) .... F 3
Barossa (res.) .... C 6
Birksgate (range) .... A 2
Blanche (lake) .... F 3
Brady (mt.) .... D 3
Cadibarrawirracanna
 (lake) .... D 3
Callabonna (lake) .... F 3
Catastrophe (cape) .... D 6
Coffin (bay) .... D 6
Coffin Bay (pen.) .... D 6
Coopers (Barcoo) (creek) ... F 3
Coorong, The (lag.) .... F 6
Dey Dey (lake) .... B 3
Encounter (bay) .... F 6
Everard (lake) .... D 4
Everard (ranges) .... C 2
Eyre (pen.) .... D 5
Eyre North (lake) .... E 3
Eyre South (lake) .... E 3
Finke (riv.) .... C 1
Flinders (range) .... F 4
Frome (lake) .... G 4
Gairdner (lake) .... D 4
Gawler (ranges) .... E 5
Gawler (riv.) .... B 6
Gilles (lake) .... E 5
Goyders (lag.) .... F 2
Great Australian (bight) ..... A 5
Great Victoria (des.) .... B 3
Gregory (lake) .... F 3
Hack (mt.) .... F 4
Hamilton, The (riv.) .... D 2
Harris (lake) .... D 4
Head of Bight (bay) .... B 4
Indian Ocean .... E 7
Investigator (str.) .... E 6
Investigator Group (isls.) .... D 5
Island (lag.) .... E 4
Jaffa (cape) .... F 7
Kangaroo (isl.), 3,375 .... E 7
Lacepede (bay) .... F 7
Little Para (riv.) .... B 7
Lofty (mt.) .... B 8
Macfarlane (lake) .... E 5
Macumba, The (riv.) .... E 2
Maurice (lake) .... B 3
Meramangye (lake) .... C 3
Morris (mt.) .... B 2
Mount Bold (res.) .... B 8
Murray (riv.) .... F 6
Musgrave (ranges) .... B 2
Neales, The (riv.) .... E 3
Neptune (isls.) .... D 6
Northumberland (cape) ...... F 8
Nukey Bluff (mt.) .... D 5
Nullarbor (plain) .... A 4
Nurrari (lakes) .... B 3
Nuyts (arch.) .... C 5
Nuyts (cape) .... C 5
Onkaparinga (riv.) .... B 8
Peera Peera Poolanna
 (lake) .... F 2
Saint Mary (peak) .... F 4
Saint Vincent (gulf) .... F 6
Serpentine (lakes) .... A 3
Simpson (des.) .... E 1
Sir Joseph Banks Group
 (isls.) .... E 6
South Para (riv.) .... C 7
Spencer (cape) .... E 6
Spencer (gulf) .... E 6
Stevenson, The (riv.) .... D 2
Streaky (bay) .... C 5
Strzelecki (creek) .... G 3
Stuart (range) .... D 3
Sturt (des.) .... G 3
Sturt (riv.) .... B 8
The Alberga (riv.) .... D 2
The Coorong (lag.) .... F 6
The Hamilton (riv.) .... D 2
The Macumba (riv.) .... E 2
The Neales (riv.) .... E 3
The Stevenson (riv.) .... D 2
The Warburton (riv.) .... F 2
Thistle (isl.) .... E 6
Torrens (lake) .... E 4
Torrens (riv.) .... C 7
Warburton, The (riv.) .... F 2
Warren (res.) .... C 7
Whidbey (isls.) .... D 6
Wilkinson (lakes) .... C 3
Wilson Bluff (prom.) .... A 4
Woodroffe (mt.) .... B 2
Wright (lake) .... A 2
Yarle (lakes) .... B 4
Yorke (pen.) .... E 6

⊙ Population of district.
‡ Population of met. area.

SOUTH AUSTRALIA

SCALE OF MILES
0 25 50 100 150
KILOMETRES
0 25 50 100 150

State Capital ⊙
State and Territorial Boundaries

ADELAIDE AND VICINITY

CORAL SEA ISLANDS TERR.
Total Population
3

PHYSICAL FEATURES

Bougainville (reef) ....C 2
Flinders (reefs) ....D 3
Great Barrier (reef) ....C 2
Heralds (cays) ....D 3
Holmes (reef) ....C 3
Marion (reef) ....E 3
Osprey (reef) ....C 2
Saumarez (reef) ....E 4

QUEENSLAND

CITIES and TOWNS

Ascot, 16,450 ....E 2
Ayr, 8,674 ....C 3
Balmoral, 15,758 ....E 2
Biloela, 3,537 ....D 5
Bowen, 5,144 ....D 3
Brisbane (cap.), 656,222 .....D 2
Brisbane, ‡718,822 ....D 2
Bundaberg, 25,402 ....D 5
Cairns, 29,326 ....C 3
Caloundra, 3,657 ....E 5
Camp Hill, 12,392 ....E 3
Cardwell, ⊙5,640 ....C 3
Charleville, 4,871 ....C 5
Charters Towers, 7,602 ....C 4
Chermside, 26,189 ....D 2
Camp Hill, 12,392 ....E 3
Coopers Plains, 16,817 ....D 3
Corinda, 12,643 ....D 3
Dalby, 8,860 ....D 5
East Brisbane, 10,780 ....E 3
Ekibin, 13,224 ....D 3
Esk, ⊙6,120 ....E 5
Geebung, 17,850 ....E 2
Gladstone, 12,426 ....D 4
Gold Coast, 49,481 ....E 6
Goondiwindi, 3,529 ....D 6
Greenslopes, 13,351 ....E 3
Gympie, 11,279 ....E 5
Holland Park, 22,645 ....E 3
Home Hill, 3,507 ....C 3
Inala, 18,705 ....D 3
Indooroopilly, 15,321 ....D 3
Ingham, 5,354 ....C 3
Innisfail, 7,432 ....C 3
Ipswich, 54,531 ....E 5
Kingaroy, 5,080 ....D 5
Longreach, 3,871 ....B 4
Mackay, 24,578 ....D 4
Mareeba, 4,799 ....C 3
Maryborough, 20,393 ....E 5
Mary Kathleen, ...A 4
Mirani, ⊙5,379 ....D 4
Mitchelton, 13,998 ....D 2
Moorooka, 16,801 ....D 3
Mount Isa, 16,877 ....A 4
Mount Morgan, 4,055 ....D 4
Nambour, 6,219 ....E 5
Newmarket, 12,212 ....D 2
Nundah, 15,609 ....E 2
Redcliffe, 27,327 ....E 5
Rockhampton, 46,083 ....D 4
Roma, 5,996 ....D 5
Sandgate, 22,621 ....D 2
Stafford, 17,692 ....D 2
Stanthorpe, 3,641 ....D 6
Taroom, ⊙3,367 ....D 5
Toowoomba, 52,139 ....D 5
Townsville, 58,847 ....C 3
Warwick, 10,065 ....D 6
Weipa, ...B 2
Windsor, 14,023 ....D 2
Wynnum, 23,191 ....E 5
Yeppoon, 3,418 ....D 4
Yeronga, 11,769 ....D 3

OTHER FEATURES

Albatross (bay) ....B 2
Alice (riv.) ....C 4
Archer (riv.) ....B 2
Balonne (riv.) ....D 6
Banks (isl.) ....B 1
Barcoo (creek) ....B 5
Barkly Tableland ....A 4
Bartle Frere (mt.) ....C 3
Beal (range) ....B 5
Belyando (riv.) ....C 4
Bentinck (isl.) ....A 3
Bigge (range) ....D 5
Bowling Green (cape) ....C 3
Bramble (bay) ....E 2
Brisbane (riv.) ....D 2
Brisbane Airport ....E 2
Broad (sound) ....D 4
Bulimba (creek) ....E 3
Bulloo (lake) ....B 6
Bulloo (riv.) ....B 6
Bunker Group (isls.) ....E 4
Burdekin (riv.) ....C 3
Cabbage Tree (creek) ....D 2
Cape York (pen.) ....B 2
Capricorn (chan.) ....D 4
Capricorn Group (isls.) ....E 4
Carnarvon (range) ....D 5
Carpentaria (gulf) ....A 2
Caryapundy (swamp) ....B 6
Clarke (range) ....C 4
Cloncurry (riv.) ....B 4
Coleman (riv.) ....B 2
Comet (riv.) ....D 5
Condamine (riv.) ....D 5
Coopers (Barcoo) (creek) ....B 5
Coral (sea) ....C 1
Culgoa (riv.) ....C 6
Cumberland (isls.) ....D 4
Curtis (isl.) ....D 4
Darling Downs ....D 5
Dawson (riv.) ....D 5
Diamantina (riv.) ....B 4
Direction (cape) ....B 2
Downfall (creek) ....D 2
Drummond (range) ....C 5
Duifken (pt.) ....B 2
Endeavour (str.) ....B 1
Enoggera (creek) ....D 2
Fitzroy (riv.) ....D 4
Flattery (cape) ....C 2
Flinders (riv.) ....B 3
Fraser (isl.) ....E 5
Galilee (lake) ....C 4
Georgina (riv.) ....A 4

AREA 667,000 sq. mi.
POPULATION 1,810,000
CAPITAL Brisbane
LARGEST CITY Brisbane
HIGHEST POINT Mt. Bartle Frere 5,287 ft.

Topography

Gilbert (riv.) ....B 3
Great Dividing (range) ....C 4
Great Sandy (Fraser) (isl.) ....E 5
Gregory (range) ....B 3
Gregory (riv.) ....A 3
Grenville (cape) ....B 1
Grey (range) ....B 5
Halifax (bay) ....C 3
Hamilton (riv.) ....B 4
Hervey (bay) ....E 5
Hinchinbrook (isl.) ....C 3
Holroyd (riv.) ....B 2
Hook (isl.) ....D 4
Isaacs (riv.) ....D 4
Kedron (brook) ....D 2
Keerweer (cape) ....B 2
Leichhardt (range) ....C 4
Leichhardt (riv.) ....A 3
Machattie (lake) ....B 5
Macintyre (riv.) ....D 6
Manifold (cape) ....D 4
Maranoa (riv.) ....C 5
Mary (riv.) ....E 5
McIlwraith (range) ....B 2
Melville (cape) ....C 2
Mitchell (riv.) ....B 2
Moonah (creek) ....A 4
Moreton (bay) ....E 5
Moreton (isl.) ....E 5
Mornington (isl.) ....A 3
Nicholson (riv.) ....A 3
Nogoa (riv.) ....C 5
Norman (creek) ....D 3
Norman (riv.) ....B 3
Normandy (riv.) ....C 2
Northumberland (isls.) ....D 4
Oxley (creek) ....D 3
Palmer (riv.) ....B 2
Paroo (riv.) ....C 6
Peak (range) ....C 4
Pera (head) ....B 2
Prince of Wales (isl.) ....B 1
Princess Charlotte (bay) ....C 2
Sandy (cape) ....E 5
Selwyn (range) ....B 4
Sidmouth (cape) ....C 2
Simpson (des.) ....A 5
Staaten (riv.) ....B 3
Sturt (des.) ....B 3
Suttor (riv.) ....C 4
Swain (reefs) ....E 4
Thompson (riv.) ....B 5
Torres (str.) ....B 1
Trinity (bay) ....C 3
Tully (falls) ....C 3
Warrego (range) ....C 5
Warrego (riv.) ....C 5
Wellesley (isls.) ....A 3
Whitsunday (isl.) ....D 4
Wide (bay) ....E 5
Willies (range) ....C 6
Wilson (riv.) ....B 5
Yamma Yamma (lake) ....B 5
York (cape) ....B 1

⊙ Population of district.
‡ Population of met. area.

New South Wales and Victoria

AUSTRALIAN CAPITAL TERRITORY
Total Population
136,300

CITIES and TOWNS

Canberra (cap.),
  Australia, 92,308 .... E 4
Canberra, ‡136,300 .... E 4
Jervis Bay, ... F 4

OTHER FEATURES

Saint George (head) .... F 4

NEW SOUTH WALES

CITIES and TOWNS

Aberdeen, 1,127 .... F 3
Abermain, ... F 3
Adaminaby, ... E 5
Adelong, ... D 4
Albert, ... D 3
Albury, 25,112 .... D 5
Alstonville, ... G 1
Ardlethan, ... D 4
Ariah Park, ... D 4
Armidale, 14,984 .... F 2
Ashfield, 41,933 .... J 3
Ashford, ⊙2,930 .... F 1
Ashley, ... E 1
Attunga, ... F 2
Auburn, 48,691 .... J 3
Baan Baa, ... E 2
Ballina, 4,931 .... G 1
Balpunga, ... A 3
Balranald, 1,490 .... B 4
Bangalow, ... G 1
Bankstown, 159,981 .... J 3
Baradine, ... E 2
Barellan, ... D 4
Bargo, ... F 4
Barham, 1,139 .... C 4
Barmedman, ... D 4
Barooga, ... C 4
Barraba, 1,425 .... F 2
Barringun, ... C 1
Baryulgil, ... G 1
Batemans Bay-
  Batehaven, 1,445 .... F 4
Bathurst, 17,222 .... E 3
Batlow, 1,448 .... E 4
Baulkham Hills, 24,873 .... H 3
Bega, 3,925 .... E 5
Bellata, ... E 1
Bellbird-Cessnock,
  15,331 .... F 3
Bellingen, 1,390 .... G 2
Belmont, ... F 3
Belmore, ... J 3
Bemboka, ... E 5
Benanee, ... B 4
Bendemeer, ... F 2
Bermagui, ... F 5
Berrigan, ⊙6,641 .... C 4
Berry, ... F 4
Bibbenluke, ⊙2,220 .... E 5
Bigga, ... E 4
Binda, ... E 4
Bingara, 1,504 .... F 1
Binnalong, ... E 4
Binnaway, ... E 2
Birriwa, ... E 3
Blacktown, 111,488 .... H 3
Blayney, 1,909 .... E 3
Blue Mountains, 30,731 .... F 3
Bobadah, ... D 3
Bodalla, ... F 5
Bogan Gate, ... D 3
Boggabilla, ... F 1
Boggabri, 1,199 .... F 2
Bomaderry-Nowra, 9,633 .... F 4
Bombala, 1,495 .... E 5
Bonalbo, ... G 1
Bondi, ... K 3
Bonnyrigg, ... H 3
Booligal, ... C 3
Boomi, ⊙2,654 .... E 1
Booroorban, ... C 4
Boorowa, 1,181 .... E 4
Boree Creek, ... D 4
Botany, 31,871 .... J 4
Bourke, 3,262 .... D 2
Bowral, 5,210 .... F 4
Bowraville, 883 .... G 2
Braidwood, ... E 4
Branxton-Greta, 2,539 .... F 3
Bredbo, ... E 4
Brewarrina, 1,255 .... D 1
Bribbaree, ... D 3
Broken Hill, 30,036 .... A 3
Browning, ... E 4
Brunswick Heads, 1,068 .... G 1
Bugaldie, ... E 2

Bulahdelah, ... G 3
Bundanoon, 696 .... F 4
Bundarra, ... F 2
Bungendore, ... E 4
Burcher, ... D 3
Burns, ... A 3
Burraboi, ... C 4
Burren Junction, ... E 2
Burta, ... A 3
Burwood, 31,843 .... J 3
Byrock, ... D 2
Byron Bay, 2,314 .... G 1
Camden, 8,661 .... F 4
Campbelltown, 25,695 .... F 4
Canbelego, ... D 2
Canowindra, 1,717 .... E 3
Canterbury, 115,802 .... J 3
Captains Flat, 598 .... E 4
Caragabal, ... D 3
Carinda, ... D 2
Carrathool, ⊙4,057 .... C 4
Carroll, ... F 2
Casino, 8,502 .... G 1
Cassilis, ... E 3
Central Tilba, ... F 5
Cessnock, *34,515 .... F 3
Cessnock-Bellbird, 15,331 .... F 3
Clare, ... B 3
Cobar, 2,348 .... C 2
Cobargo, ... E 5
Cobbadah, ... F 2
Coffs Harbour, 7,667 .... G 2
Collarenebri, ... E 1
Collie, ... E 2
Comboyne, ... G 2
Come-by-Chance, ... E 2
Conargo, ⊙2,033 .... C 4
Concord, 27,037 .... J 3
Condoblin, 3,571 .... D 3
Coogee, ... K 3
Coolah, ⊙4,646 .... E 2
Coolamon, 1,031 .... D 4
Cooma, 9,103 .... E 5
Coonabarabran, 2,738 .... E 2

NEW SOUTH WALES		VICTORIA	
AREA	309,433 sq. mi.	AREA	87,884 sq. mi.
POPULATION	4,595,400	POPULATION	3,461,400
CAPITAL	Sydney	CAPITAL	Melbourne
LARGEST CITY	Sydney	LARGEST CITY	Melbourne
HIGHEST POINT	Mt. Kosciusko 7,316 ft.	HIGHEST POINT	Mt. Bogong 6,508 ft.

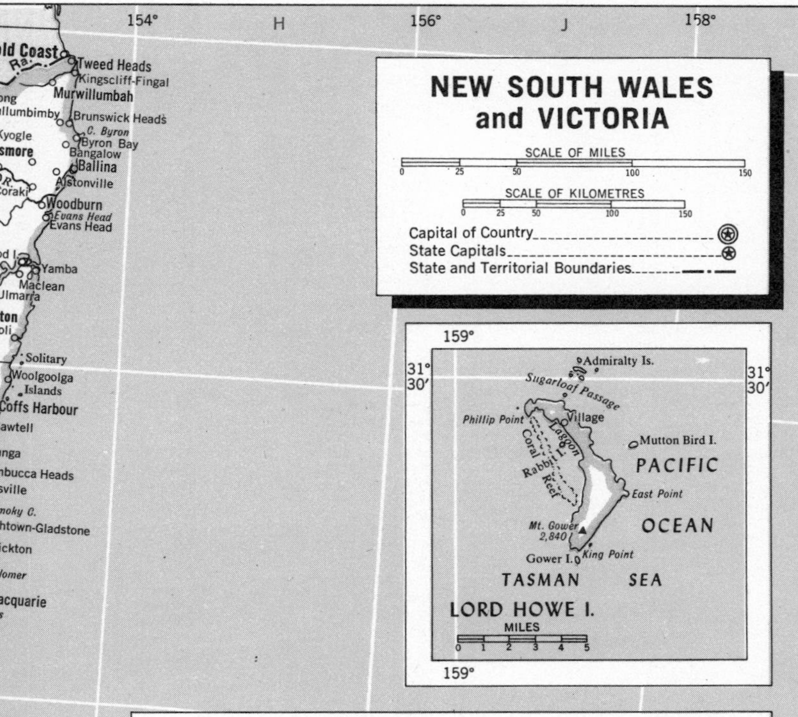

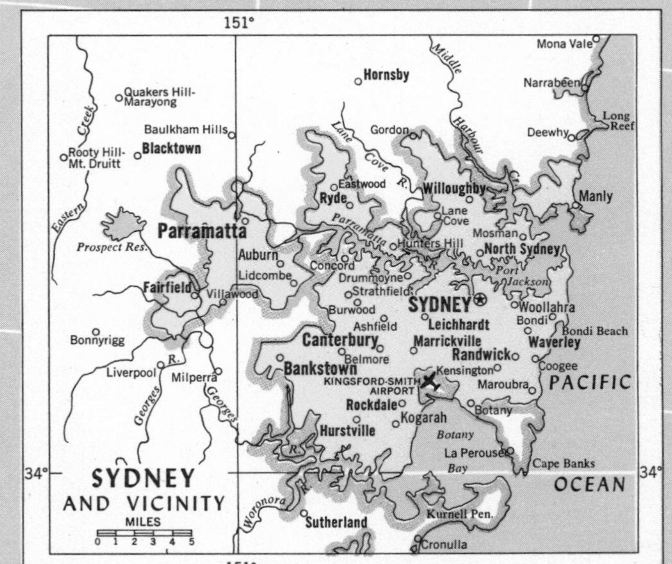

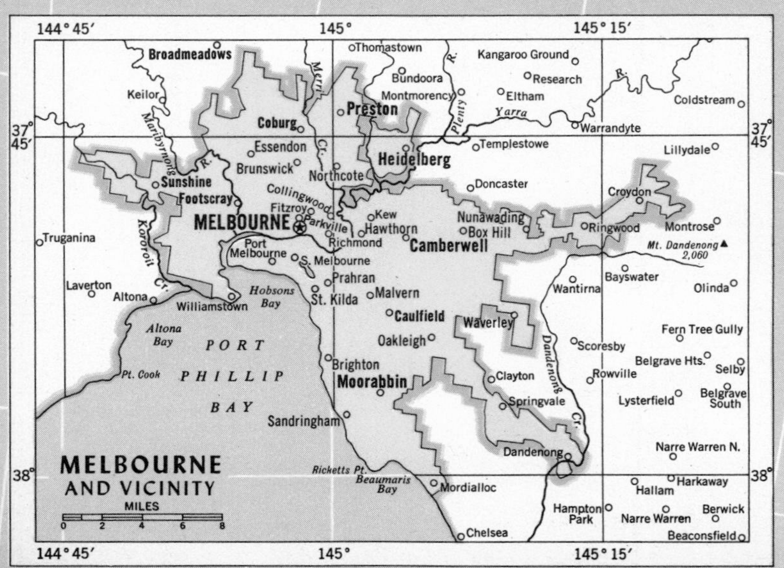

Topography

0 100 200 MILES

MAIN BARRIER RANGE, Paroo, Warrego, Macintyre, Dumaresq, Clarence, Gwydir, Barwon, Namoi, Bogan, Macquarie, Darling, GREAT DIVIDING RANGE, Hunter, Sugarloaf Pt., BLUE MTS., Lachlan, Wollondilly, Murrumbidgee, Lake Tyrrell, Moulamein, Murray, L. George, L. Hume, L. Eucumbene, Loddon, Mt. Bogong 6,508, Mt. Kosciusko 7,316, ALPS, Glenelg, Eildon, GREAT AUSTRALIAN, Snowy, C. Howe, Port Phillip Bay, Yarra, L. Wellington, Portland Bay, C. Otway, Wilsons Promontory

Below Sea Level | 100 m. 328 ft. | 200 m. 656 ft. | 500 m. 1,640 ft. | 1,000 m. 3,281 ft. | 2,000 m. 6,562 ft. | 5,000 m. 16,404 ft.

Coonamble, 3,396 .... E 2
Cootamundra, 6,219 .... D 4
Copmanhurst, ⊙2,400 .... G 1
Corowa, 2,709 .... D 4
Cowra, 7,076 .... E 3
Cronulla, ... J 4
Crookwell, 2,267 .... E 4
Culcairn, 1,019 .... D 4
Deewhy, ... K 3
Deniliquin, 6,239 .... C 4
Dorrigo, 1,102 .... G 2
Drummoyne, 30,630 .... J 3
Dubbo, 15,561 .... E 3
Dungalear Station, ... D 1
Dungog, 2,099 .... F 3
Eden, 1,416 .... E 5
Ermeran Station, ... D 3
Evans Head, 1,083 .... G 1
Fairfield, 101,226 .... H 3
Finley, 1,783 .... C 4
Forbes, 7,369 .... E 3
Forster, 1,831 .... G 3
Gilgandra, 2,414 .... E 2
Gilgunnia, ... C 3
Glen Innes, 5,737 .... F 1
Gloucester, 2,032 .... F 2
Goombalie, ... C 1
Gordon, ... J 3
Gosford, 11,310 .... F 3
Goulburn, 20,871 .... E 4
Grafton, 15,951 .... G 1
Grenfell, 2,377 .... E 3
Greta-Branxton, 2,539 .... F 3
Griffith, 9,537 .... C 4
Gulgong, 1,441 .... E 3
Gundagai, 2,116 .... D 4
Gunnedah, 7,507 .... F 2
Gunning, ⊙2,094 .... E 4
Guyra, 1,664 .... F 2
Hatfield, ... B 3
Hay, 2,952 .... C 4
Hillston, 1,034 .... C 3
Holbrook, 1,135 .... D 4
Hornsby, 72,462 .... J 3
Hunters Hill, 14,233 .... J 3
Hurstville, 64,851 .... J 4
Huskisson, 641 .... F 4
Illabo, ⊙1,979 .... D 4
Inverell, 8,413 .... F 1
Jerilderie, 1,037 .... C 4
Jindalee, ⊙2,124 .... E 4
Junee, 3,904 .... D 4
Kandos, 2,051 .... F 3
Karpakora, ... B 3
Keewong, ... C 3
Kempsey, 8,181 .... G 2
Kiama, 5,865 .... F 4
Kiandra, ... E 4
Kinalung, ... B 3
Kingscliff-Fingal, 1,798 .... G 1
Kogarah, 47,654 .... J 4
Kurri Kurri-Weston, 11,567 .... F 3
Kyogle, 2,846 .... G 1
Lake Cargelligo, 1,128 .... D 3
Lane Cove, 25,109 .... J 3
Leeton, 5,817 .... D 4
Leichhardt, 59,325 .... J 3
Lette, ... B 4
Lidcombe, ... J 3
Lismore, 19,734 .... G 1
Lithgow, 13,165 .... F 3
Liverpool, 68,959 .... H 4
Lockhart, 1,023 .... D 4
Lyndhurst, ⊙5,722 .... E 3
Macksville, 2,129 .... G 2
Maclean, 2,224 .... G 1
Maitland, 28,428 .... F 3
Manilla, 1,761 .... F 2
Manly, 38,141 .... K 3
Marfield, ... C 3
Maroubra, ... K 3
Marrickville, 76,763 .... J 3
Marsden, ... D 3
Melrose, ... D 3
Merimbula, 841 .... F 5
Merriwa, 923 .... F 3
Milpa, ... B 2
Milperra, ... H 4
Mittagong, 2,837 .... F 4
Moama, 967 .... C 5
Mogil Mogil, ... E 1
Molong, 1,430 .... E 3
Mona Vale, ... K 2
Moree, 8,031 .... E 1
Moruya, 1,449 .... F 4
Mosman, 28,136 .... J 3
Moss Vale, 3,144 .... F 4
Mossgiel, ... C 4
Mount Arrowsmith, ... A 2
Mount Drysdale, ... C 2
Mudgee, 5,372 .... E 3
Mullumbimby, 1,981 .... G 1
Murrumburrah, 2,435 .... E 4
Murrurundi, 969 .... F 2
Murwillumbah, 7,311 .... G 1
Muswellbrook, 6,312 .... F 3
Nambucca Heads, 2,332 .... G 2
Narooma, 1,295 .... F 5
Narrabeen, ... K 3
Narrabri, 5,953 .... E 2
Narrandera, 4,905 .... D 4
Narromine, 2,465 .... E 3
New Angledool, ... E 1
Newcastle, 143,025 .... F 3
Newcastle, *233,936 .... F 3
Newport, ... F 3
North Sydney, 51,754 .... J 3
Nowra-Bomaderry, 9,633 .... F 4
Nundle, ⊙1,346 .... F 2
Nymboida, ⊙1,469 .... G 1
Nyngan, 2,584 .... D 2
Oberon, 1,773 .... E 3
Orange, 22,196 .... E 3
Para Station, ... B 3
Parkes, 8,438 .... E 3
Parramatta, 106,996 .... H 3
Peak Hill, 1,379 .... E 3
Penrith, 46,357 .... F 3
Picton, 1,327 .... F 4
Popilta, ... A 3
Portland, 2,221 .... E 3
Port Macquarie, 7,063 .... G 2
Queanbeyan, 12,515 .... E 4
Quirindi, 2,730 .... F 2
Randwick, 113,634 .... J 3
Raymond Terrace, 4,953 .... F 3
Rockdale, 81,463 .... J 4
Ryde, 81,291 .... J 3
Rylstone, ⊙4,743 .... E 3
Salisbury Downs, ... B 1
Sawtell, 1,558 .... G 2
Scone, 2,915 .... F 3
Shellharbour, 22,061 .... F 4
Singleton, 6,188 .... F 3
Smithtown-Gladstone, 1,101 .... G 2
Stephens Creek, ... A 2
Strathfield, 26,704 .... J 3
Stroud, ⊙6,751 .... G 3
Sutherland, 131,739 .... J 4
Swansea, ... F 3
Sydney (cap.), ‡2,446,345 .... J 3
Tamworth, 21,680 .... F 2
Taree, 10,560 .... G 2
Temora, 4,536 .... D 4
Tenterfield, 3,270 .... G 1

(continued on following page)

(continued)

NEW SOUTH WALES
(continued)

Terrigal-Avoca, 2,492 F 3
The Entrance-Long Jetty, 9,131 F 3
Thurloo Downs, B 1
Tibbita, C 4
Tiltagara, C 2
Tocumwal, 1,262 C 4
Tongo, B 2
Torrowangee, A 2
Tumbarumba, 1,443 D 4
Tumut, 4,277 E 4
Tuncurry, 1,022 G 3
Tweed Heads, 3,829 G 1
Ulladulla, 1,661 F 4
Ulmarra, ⊙2,800 G 1
Uralla, 1,614 F 2
Urana, ⊙2,430 D 4
Urunga, 924 G 2
Village, J 2
Villawood, H 3
Wagga Wagga, 25,819 D 4
Wakool, ⊙5,431 C 4
Walcha, 1,544 F 2
Walgett, 1,985 E 2
Wallerawang, 1,580 F 3
Warialda, 1,324 F 1
Warragamba, 1,697 F 3
Warren, 1,678 D 2
Wauchope, 3,169 G 2
Waverley, 63,607 K 3
Waverley Downs, B 1
Wee Waa, 1,488 E 2
Wellington, 5,825 E 3
Wentworth, 1,083 B 4
Werris Creek, 2,118 F 2
West Wyalong, 2,858 D 3
Wetuppa, B 4
Whyjonta, B 1
Willoughby, 54,576 J 3
Windsor-Richmond, 13,299 F 3
Wingham, 2,827 G 2
Wollongong, 149,506 F 4
Wollongong, *162,153 F 4
Woodburn, ⊙4,083 G 1
Woolgoolga, 1,199 G 2
Woollahra, 47,326 K 3
Woy Woy-Ettalong, 16,287 F 3
Wyong, 1,937 F 3
Yallock, C 3
Yalpunga, A 1
Yamba, 950 G 1
Yancannia, B 2
Yantara, B 1
Yass, 4,098 E 4
Young, 5,754 E 4

OTHER FEATURES

Admiralty (isls.) J 1
Ana Branch, Darling (riv.) A 3
Australian Alps (mts.) D 5
Bancannia (lake) A 2
Banks (cape) K 4
Baradine (creek) E 2
Barrington Tops (mt.) F 2
Barwon (riv.) D 2
Birrie (riv.) D 1
Blue (mts.) F 3
Bogan (riv.) D 2
Bokhara (riv.) D 1
Bondi (beach) K 3
Botany (bay) J 4
Brewster (lake) D 3
Broken (bay) F 3
Burrinjuck (res.) E 4
Byron (cape) G 1
Capertee (riv.) F 3
Caryapundi (swamp) B 1
Castlereagh (riv.) E 2
Cawndilla (lake) A 3
Clarence (riv.) G 1
Colo (riv.) F 3
Cowal (lake) D 3
Crowdy (head) G 2
Crowl (creek) C 2
Culgoa (riv.) D 1
Cuttaburra (creek) C 1
Darling (riv.) B 3
Dumaresq (riv.) F 1
East (pt.) J 2
Eastern (creek) H 3
Eucumbene (lake) E 5
Evans (head) G 1
George (lake) E 4
Georges (riv.) H 4
Gower (isl.) J 2
Gower (mt.) J 2
Great Dividing (range) E 3
Green (cape) F 5
Gunderbooka (ranges) C 2
Gwydir (riv.) E 1
Horton (riv.) F 2
Howe (cape) F 5
Hume (res.) D 4
Hunter (riv.) F 3
Innes (lake) G 2
Irrara (creek) C 1
Jindabyne (res.) E 5
King (pt.) J 2
Kingsford-Smith Airport J 4
Kosciusko (mt.) E 5
Kulkyne (creek) C 1
Kurnell (pen.) J 4
Lachlan (range) C 3
Lachlan (riv.) C 3
Lane Cove (riv.) J 3
Liverpool (range) F 2
Long Reef (pt.) K 3
Lord Howe (isl.), 267 J 2
Macintyre (riv.) E 1
Macquarie (lake) F 3
Macquarie (riv.) D 2
Main Barrier (range) A 2
Manning (riv.) F 2
Marra (creek) D 2
Marrowie (creek) C 3
Marthaguy (creek) D 2
McPherson (range) G 1
Medgun (creek) E 1
Menindee (lake) B 3
Middle Harbour (creek) J 3
Monaro (range) E 5
Moomin (creek) E 1
Moonie (riv.) E 1
Moulamein (creek) C 4
Mount Royal (range) F 2
Murray (riv.) A 4
Murrumbidgee (riv.) C 4
Mutton Bird (isl.) J 2
Myall (lake) G 3
Namoi (riv.) E 2
Narran (lake) D 1
Narran (riv.) D 1
Nedgera (creek) E 2
New England (range) F 1
Nymboida (riv.) G 1
Ottleys (creek) F 1
Paroo (chan.) B 2
Paroo (riv.) C 1
Parramatta (riv.) J 3
Peery (lake) B 2
Phillip (pt.) J 2
Pian (creek) E 1
Pitarpunga (lake) B 4
Plomer (pt.) G 2
Poopeloe (lake) C 2
Popilta (lake) A 3
Port Jackson (inlet) J 3
Port Stephens (inlet) G 3
Prospect (res.) H 3
Rabbit (isl.) J 2
Richmond (range) G 1
Richmond (riv.) G 1
Riverina (reg.) C 4
Robe (mt.) A 2
Round, The (mt.) G 2
Salt, The (lake) B 2
Severn (riv.) F 1
Shoalhaven (riv.) E 4
Smoky (cape) G 2
Snowy (mts.) E 5
Snowy (riv.) E 5
Solitary (isls.) G 1
Stony (ranges) B 2
Sturt (mt.) A 1
Sugarloaf (passg.) J 1
Sugarloaf (pt.) G 3
Talyawalka (creek) B 2
Talyawalka Ana Branch, Darling (riv.) B 3
Tandou (lake) A 3
Tasman (sea) F 5
The Round (mt.) G 2
The Salt (lake) B 2
Timbarra (riv.) G 1
Tongo (lake) B 2
Travellers (lake) B 3
Tuggerah (lake) F 3
Tumut (res.) E 4
Twofold (bay) F 5
Urana (lake) D 4
Victoria (lake) A 3
Wallis (lake) G 3
Warrego (riv.) C 1
Whalan (creek) E 1
Willandra Billabong (creek) C 3
Wollondilly (riv.) F 4
Wongallarra (lake) C 2
Woronora (riv.) J 4
Wyangala (res.) E 3
Yanko (creek) C 4
Yantara (lake) B 1

VICTORIA

CITIES and TOWNS

Alexandra, 2,014 C 5
Altona, 25,020 H 5
Apollo Bay, 957 B 6
Ararat, 8,233 B 5
Avoca, 1,016 B 5
Bacchus Marsh, 3,707 C 5
Bairnsdale, 7,785 D 5
Ballarat, 41,639 C 5
Ballarat, □56,290 C 5
Bayswater, K 5
Beaufort, 1,264 B 5
Beechworth, 3,554 D 5
Belgrave Heights, J 5
Belgrave South, K 5
Benalla, 8,224 D 5
Bendigo, 30,806 C 5
Bendigo, □42,208 C 5
Berwick, 1,720 K 6
Birchip, 1,147 B 4
Box Hill, 54,529 J 5
Bright, 747 D 5
Brighton, 40,617 J 5
Broadford, 1,605 C 5
Broadmeadows, 88,065 H 4
Brunswick, 52,012 H 5
Bundoora, J 4
Camberwell, 99,908 J 5
Camperdown, 3,540 C 6
Casterton, 2,492 A 5
Castlemaine, 7,103 C 5
Caulfield, 76,119 J 5
Charlton, 1,603 B 5
Chelsea, 24,789 J 6
Clunes, ⊙1,514 B 5
Cobden, 1,233 B 6
Cobram, 2,888 C 4
Coburg, 68,568 H 5
Cohuna, 2,061 C 4
Colac, 9,498 B 6
Coldstream, K 4
Coleraine, 1,518 A 5
Collingwood, 22,459 J 5
Corryong, 1,665 D 5
Creswick, 1,658 B 5
Croydon, 21,353 K 5
Dandenong, 31,698 K 5
Darby, D 6
Daylesford, 2,664 C 5
Dimboola, 1,872 B 5
Donald, 1,626 B 5
Doncaster and Templestowe, 33,382 J 5
Drouin, 2,655 C 6
Eaglehawk, 5,230 C 5
Echuca, 7,043 C 5
Eltham, 15,216 J 4
Essendon, 58,258 H 5
Euroa, 2,789 C 5
Fitzroy, 27,219 H 5
Footscray, 58,823 H 5
Geelong, 18,129 C 6
Geelong, □105,059 C 6
Geelong West, 17,538 C 6
Hallam, K 5
Hamilton, 10,054 B 5
Harkaway, K 5
Hawthorn, 36,728 J 5
Healesville, 2,676 C 5
Heathcote, 1,187 C 5
Heidelberg, 63,929 J 5
Heyfield, 1,893 D 6
Heywood, 1,011 A 6
Hopetoun, 1,024 B 4
Horsham, 10,562 B 5
Kaniva, ⊙2,371 A 5
Keilor, 43,398 H 5
Kerang, 4,164 B 4
Kew, 32,816 J 5
Kilmore, 1,096 C 5
Koondrook, 604 B 4
Koroit, 1,416 B 6
Korumburra, 2,991 D 6
Kyabram, 4,645 C 5
Kyneton, 3,446 C 5
Lakes Entrance, 1,837 E 5
Laverton, 6,128 H 5
Leongatha, 3,246 C 6
Lillydale, 14,066 J 4
Lysterfield, K 5
Maffra, 3,569 D 5
Maldon, 1,065 C 5
Malvern, 50,059 J 5
Mansfield, 2,019 D 5
Maryborough, 7,707 B 5
Melbourne (cap.), ‡2,110,168 H 5
Merbein, 1,684 A 4
Mildura, 12,931 A 4
Moe, 16,531 D 6
Montmorency, J 4
Montrose, K 5
Moorabbin, 103,787 J 5
Mooroopna, 2,568 C 5
Mordialloc, 28,076 J 6
Morea, A 5
Mornington, 7,349 C 6
Mortlake, 1,248 B 6
Morwell, 16,610 D 5
Mount Beauty, 1,568 D 5
Murtoa, 1,109 B 5
Myrtleford, 2,545 D 5
Narre Warren, K 6
Narre Warren North, K 5
Nathalia, 1,369 C 5
Newtown and Chilwell, 11,700 C 6
Nhill, 2,251 A 5
Northcote, 56,200 J 5
Numurkah, 2,770 C 5
Nunawading, 74,577 J 5
Oakleigh, 52,766 J 5

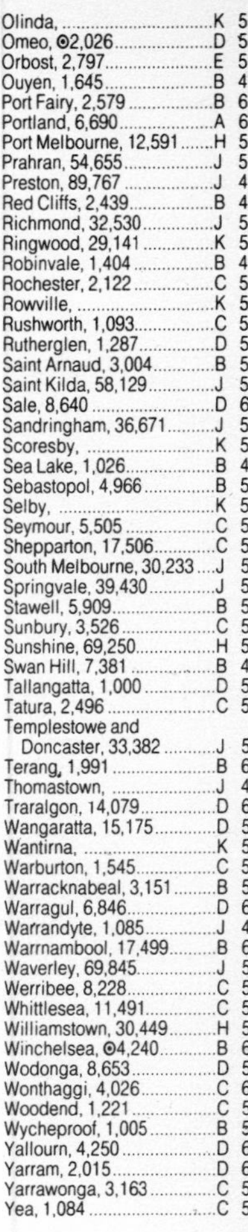

Olinda, K 5
Omeo, ⊙2,026 D 5
Orbost, 2,797 E 5
Ouyen, 1,645 B 4
Port Fairy, 2,579 B 6
Portland, 6,690 A 6
Port Melbourne, 12,591 H 5
Prahran, 54,655 J 5
Preston, 89,767 J 4
Red Cliffs, 2,439 B 4
Richmond, 32,530 J 5
Ringwood, 29,141 K 5
Robinvale, 1,404 B 4
Rochester, 2,122 C 5
Rowville, K 5
Rushworth, 1,093 C 5
Rutherglen, 1,287 D 5
Saint Arnaud, 3,004 B 5
Saint Kilda, 58,129 J 5
Sale, 8,640 D 6
Sandringham, 36,671 J 5
Scoresby, K 5
Sea Lake, 1,026 B 4
Sebastopol, 4,966 B 5
Selby, K 5
Seymour, 5,505 C 5
Shepparton, 17,506 C 5
South Melbourne, 30,233 J 5
Springvale, 39,430 J 5
Stawell, 5,909 B 5
Sunbury, 3,526 C 5
Sunshine, 69,250 H 5
Swan Hill, 7,381 B 4
Tallangatta, 1,000 D 5
Tatura, 2,496 C 5
Templestowe and Doncaster, 33,382 J 5
Terang, 1,991 B 6
Thomastown, J 4
Traralgon, 14,079 D 6
Wangaratta, 15,175 D 5
Wantirna, K 5
Warburton, 1,545 C 5
Warracknabeal, 3,151 B 5
Warragul, 6,846 D 6
Warrandyte, 1,085 J 4
Warrnambool, 17,499 B 6
Waverley, 69,845 J 5
Werribee, 8,228 C 5
Whittlesea, 11,491 C 5
Williamstown, 30,449 H 5
Winchelsea, ⊙4,240 B 6
Wodonga, 8,653 D 5
Wonthaggi, 4,026 C 6
Woodend, 1,221 C 5
Wycheproof, 1,005 B 5
Yallourn, 4,250 D 6
Yarram, 2,015 D 6
Yarrawonga, 3,163 C 5
Yea, 1,084 C 5

OTHER FEATURES

Altona (bay) H 5
Australian Alps (mts.) D 5
Avoca (riv.) B 5
Barry (mts.) D 5
Beaumaris (bay) J 6
Bogong (mt.) D 5
Bridgewater (cape) A 6
Buller (mt.) D 5
Campaspe (riv.) C 5
Cook (pt.) H 5
Corangamite (lake) B 6
Corner (inlet) D 6
Dandenong (creek) K 5
Dandenong (mt.) K 5
Difficult (mt.) B 5
Discovery (bay) A 6
Eildon (lake) C 5
French (isl.), 210 C 6
Gippsland (reg.) D 6
Glenelg (riv.) A 5
Goulburn (riv.) C 5
Hindmarsh (lake) A 5
Hobsons (bay) H 5
Hopkins (riv.) B 5
Hume (lake) D 4
Indian Ocean B 6
Kororoit (creek) H 5
Loddon (riv.) B 5
Maribyrnong (riv.) H 5
Mitchell (riv.) D 5
Mitta Mitta (riv.) D 5
Mornington (pen.) C 6
Mount Emu (creek) B 5
Murray (riv.) A 4
Nelson (cape) A 6
Ninety Mile (beach) D 6
Otway (cape) B 6
Ovens (riv.) D 5
Phillip (isl.), 1,407 C 6
Plenty (riv.) J 4
Portland (bay) A 6
Port Phillip (bay) C 6
Ricketts (pt.) J 6
Rocklands (res.) B 5
Snake (isl.) D 6
South East (pt.) D 6
Tamboritha (mt.) D 5
Tasman (sea) F 5
Tyrrell (lake) B 4
Venus (bay) C 6
Waranga (res.) C 5
Waratah (bay) C 6
Wellington (lake) D 6
Western Port (inlet) C 6
Wilsons (prom.) D 6
Wimmera (riv.) A 5
Yarra (riv.) C 5

* City and suburbs.
⊙ Population of district.
‡ Population of met. area.
□ Population of urban area.

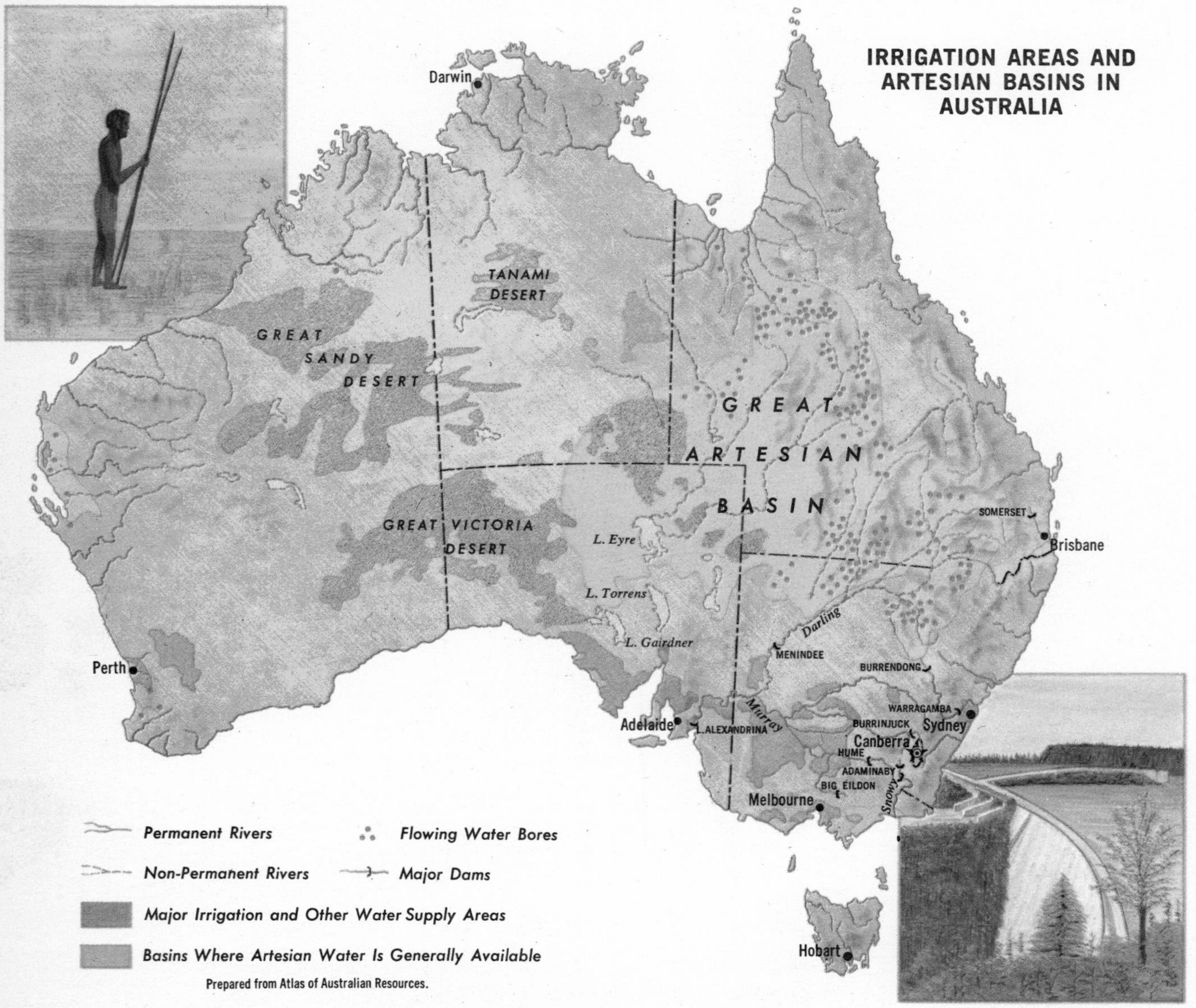

IRRIGATION AREAS AND ARTESIAN BASINS IN AUSTRALIA

Permanent Rivers
Non-Permanent Rivers
Flowing Water Bores
Major Dams
Major Irrigation and Other Water Supply Areas
Basins Where Artesian Water Is Generally Available

Prepared from Atlas of Australian Resources.

AREA 26,215 sq. mi.
POPULATION 393,700
CAPITAL Hobart
LARGEST CITY Hobart
HIGHEST POINT Mt. Ossa, 5,305 ft.

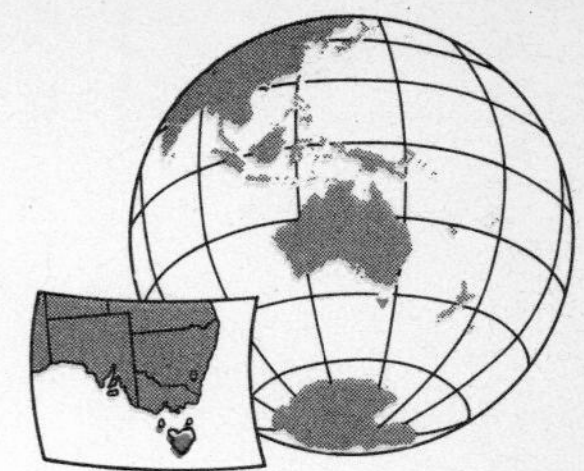

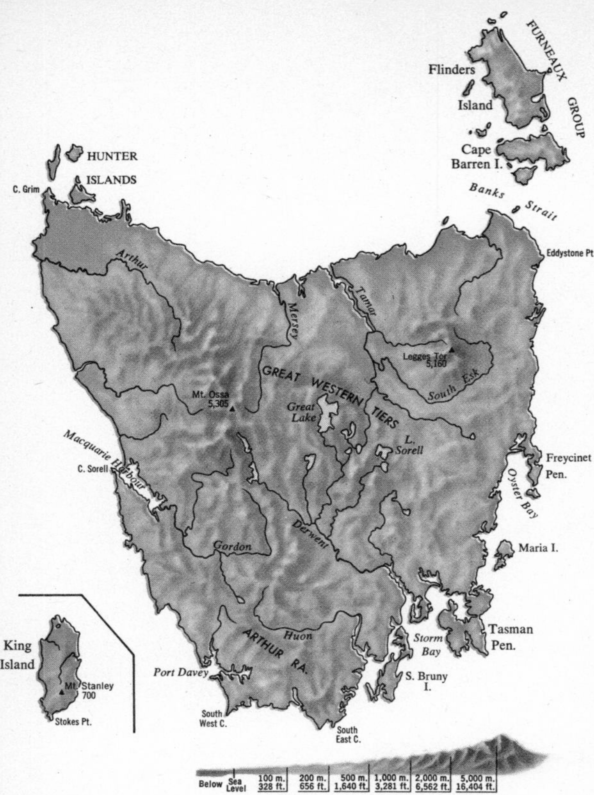

Topography

0 30 60
MILES

Gordon (riv.) ....B 4
Great (lake) ....C 3
Great Western Tiers (mts.) ..C 3
Grim (cape) ....A 2
Hartz (mt.) ....C 5
Hibbs (pt.) ....B 4
High Rocky (pt.) ....B 4
Hogan Group (isls.) ....D 1
Hummock (isl.) ....D 2
Hunter (isl.) ....A 2
Hunter (isls.) ....B 2
Huon (riv.) ....C 5
Indian Ocean ....A 4
Kent Group (isls.) ....D 1
King (isl.), 2,462 ....A 1
King (riv.) ....B 4
King William (lake) ....C 4
Lake (riv.) ....D 3
Legges Tor (mt.) ....D 3
Leven (riv.) ....B 3
Lodi (cape) ....E 3
Lofty (range) ....B 3
Long (pt.) ....E 3
Low Rocky (pt.) ....B 4
Lyell (mt.) ....B 4
Maatsuyker (isls.) ....C 5
Macquarie (harb.) ....B 4
Macquarie (riv.) ....D 3
Maria (isl.) ....E 4
Marion (bay) ....E 4
Mersey (riv.) ....C 3
Munro (mt.) ....E 2
Naturaliste (cape) ....E 2
Nive (riv.) ....C 4
Norfolk (bay) ....D 4
North (pt.) ....E 1
North Bruny (isl.) ....D 5
North Esk (riv.) ....D 3
Ossa (mt.) ....C 3
Ouse (riv.) ....C 4
Oyster (bay) ....E 4
Peron (cape) ....E 4
Phoques (bay) ....A 1
Picton (mt.) ....C 5
Pieman (riv.) ....B 3
Pillar (cape) ....E 5
Port Davey (inlet) ....B 5
Portland (cape) ....D 2
Ramsey (mt.) ....B 3
Raoul (cape) ....D 5
Reid (rocks) ....B 1
Ringarooma (bay) ....D 2
Robbins (isl.) ....B 2
Rocky (cape) ....B 2
Saint Clair (lake) ....C 4
Saint Helens (pt.) ....E 3
Saint Vincent (cape) ....B 5
Sandy (cape) ....A 3
Schouten (isl.) ....E 4
Sorell (cape) ....B 4
Sorell (lake) ....D 4
South (cape) ....C 5
South Bruny (isl.) ....D 5
South East (cape) ....C 5
South Esk (riv.) ....D 3
South West (cape) ....B 5
Stanley (mt.) ....A 1
Stokes (pt.) ....A 1
Stony (head) ....C 2
Storm (bay) ....D 5
Strzelecki (mt.) ....D 2
Swan (isl.) ....E 2
Tamar (riv.) ....D 3
Tasman (head) ....D 5
Tasman (pen.) ....E 5
Tasman (sea) ....E 4
Three Hummock (isl.) ....B 2
Tooms (lake) ....D 4
Vansittart (isl.) ....E 2
Walker (isl.) ....B 2
Waterhouse (isl.) ....D 2
West (pt.) ....A 2
West Sister (isl.) ....D 1
Wickham (cape) ....A 1

⊙ Population of district.
‡ Population of met. area.

CITIES and TOWNS

Adventure Bay, ...D 5
Avoca, ...D 3
Bagdad, ...D 4
Barrington, ...C 3
Beaconsfield, 1,028 ....C 3
Bell Bay, ...C 3
Bicheno, ...E 3
Boat Harbour, ...B 2
Bothwell, ⊙1,008 ....C 4
Bracknell, ...C 3
Branxholm, ...D 3
Bridgewater, ...D 4
Bridport, ...D 3
Brighton, 1,150 ....D 4
Burnie, 15,806 ....B 3
Bushy Park, ...C 4
Cambridge, ...D 4
Campbell Town, ⊙1,753 ....D 3
Chudleigh, ...C 3
Colebrook, ...D 4
Conara Junction, ...D 3
Cornwall, ...E 3
Cranbrook, ...D 4
Cressy, ...C 3
Currie, ...A 1
Cygnet, ...C 5
Deloraine, 1,793 ....C 3
Derby, ...D 3
Derwent Bridge, ...C 4
Devonport, 14,874 ....C 3
Dover, ...C 5
Dunalley, ...D 4
Egg Lagoon, ...A 1
Ellendale, ...C 4
Elliott, ...B 3
Emita, ...D 2
Evandale, ⊙1,554 ....D 3
Fingal, ⊙3,791 ....E 3
Flowerdale, ...B 2
Forest, ...B 2
Forth, ...C 3
Franklin, ...C 5
George Town, 4,086 ....C 3
Glenorchy, 37,770 ....D 4
Gormanston, ⊙540 ....B 4
Hamilton, ⊙4,329 ....C 4
Hobart (cap.), 53,257 ....D 4
Hobart, ‡119,469 ....D 4
Latrobe, 2,241 ....C 3
Lauderdale, 916 ....D 4
Launceston, 37,217 ....C 3
Launceston, ‡60,456 ....C 3
Lillydale, ⊙7,841 ....D 3
Longford, 1,688 ....C 3
New Norfolk, 5,770 ....C 4
Oatlands, ⊙2,501 ....D 4
Penguin, 2,149 ....C 3
Perth, 1,002 ....D 3
Queenstown, 4,295 ....B 4
Richmond, ⊙1,658 ....D 4
Ringarooma, ⊙2,866 ....D 3
Rosebery, 1,774 ....B 3
Ross, ⊙617 ....D 4
Saint Leonards, ⊙13,660 ....D 3
Scottsdale, 1,698 ....D 3
Smithton, 2,698 ....A 2
Somerset, 2,236 ....B 3
Sorell, 1,652 ....D 4
Strahan, ⊙470 ....B 4
Temma, ...A 3
Ulverstone, 6,842 ....C 3
Waratah, ⊙698 ....B 3
Westbury, ⊙4,964 ....C 3
Wynyard, 3,355 ....B 3
Zeehan, 1,017 ....B 3

OTHER FEATURES

Anderson (bay) ....D 2
Anne (mt.) ....C 4
Anser Group (isls.) ....C 1
Arthur (lake) ....D 4
Arthur (range) ....C 5
Arthur (riv.) ....B 3
Babel (isls.) ....E 1
Banks (str.) ....D 2
Barn Bluff (mt.) ....B 3
Barren (cape) ....E 2
Bass (str.) ....C 1
Bathurst (harb.) ....C 5
Cape Barren (isl.) ....E 2
Chappell (isls.) ....D 2
Circular (head) ....B 2
Clarke (isl.) ....E 2
Clyde (riv.) ....D 4
Cox (bight) ....C 5
Cradle (mt.) ....B 3
Crescent (lake) ....D 4
Curtis Group (isls.) ....C 1
D'Aguilar (range) ....B 4
Davey (riv.) ....B 4
Deal (isl.) ....D 1
Dee (riv.) ....C 4
Denison (range) ....C 4
D'Entrecasteaux (chan.) ....D 5
Derwent (riv.) ....C 4
Donaldson (riv.) ....B 3
East Sister (isl.) ....E 1
Echo (lake) ....C 4
Eddystone (pt.) ....E 2
Elliott (bay) ....B 5
Fires (bay) ....E 3
Florence (riv.) ....C 4
Forestier (cape) ....E 4
Forestier (pen.) ....E 4
Forth (riv.) ....C 3
Frankland (cape) ....D 1
Frankland (range) ....B 4
Franklin (riv.) ....B 4
Frenchmans Cap (mt.) ....B 4
Freycinet (pen.) ....E 4
Furneaux Group (isls.), 1,234 ....E 1

TASMANIA

MILES 0 10 20 30
KILOMETRES 0 10 20 30
State Capital ⊙
State Boundaries

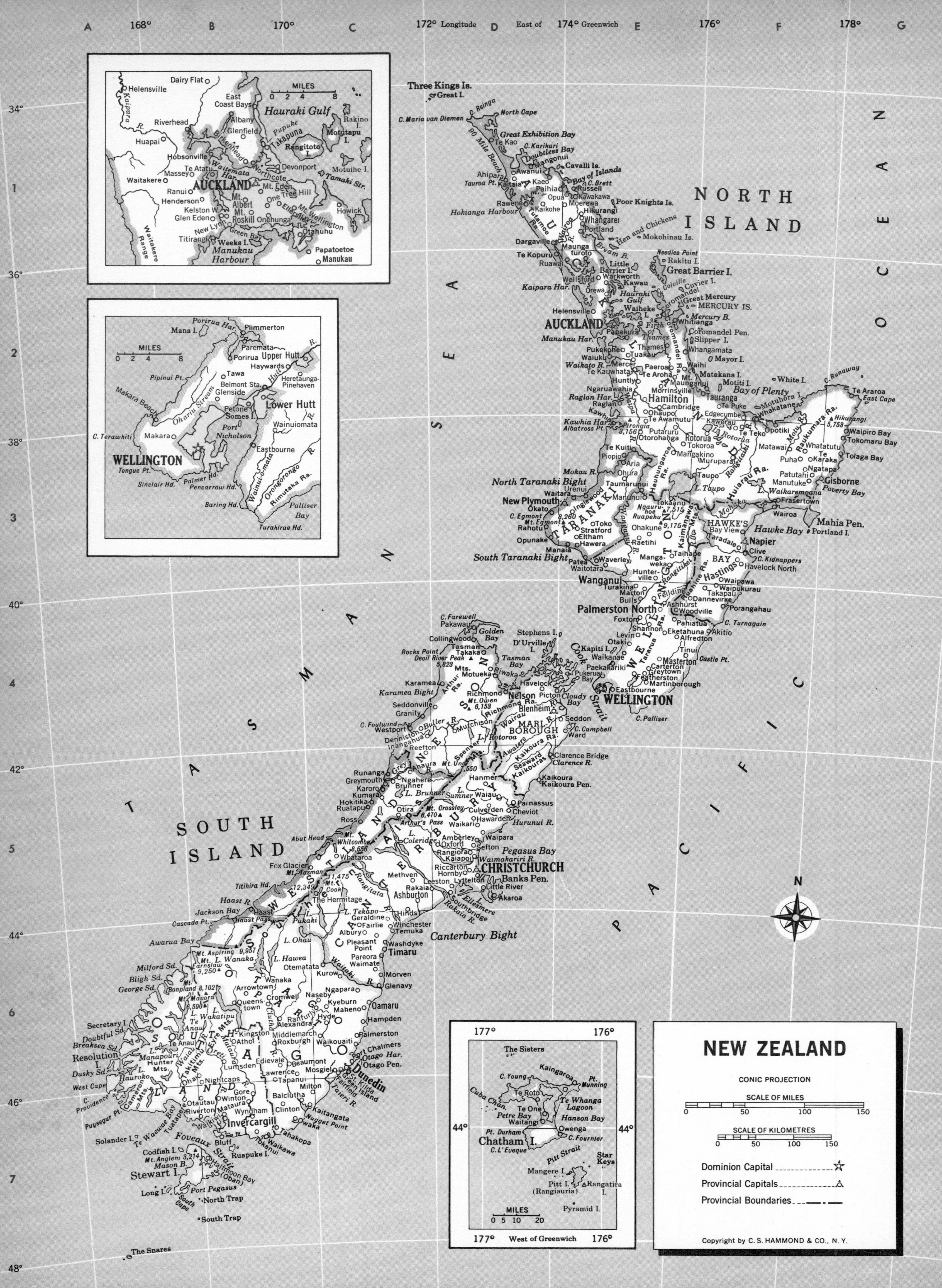

NEW ZEALAND
CONIC PROJECTION
SCALE OF MILES
0 50 100 150
SCALE OF KILOMETRES
0 50 100 150
Dominion Capital
Provincial Capitals
Provincial Boundaries
Copyright by C. S. HAMMOND & CO., N. Y.
172° Longitude East of 174° Greenwich
A 168° B 170° C D E 176° F 178° G
34° 36° 38° 40° 42° 44° 46° 48°
1 2 3 4 5 6 7
NORTH ISLAND
SOUTH ISLAND
TASMAN SEA
PACIFIC OCEAN
AUCKLAND
WELLINGTON
CHRISTCHURCH
Dunedin
Invercargill
Hamilton
Napier
Gisborne
New Plymouth
Wanganui
Palmerston North
Nelson
Timaru
Oamaru
Three Kings Is.
North Cape
Bay of Islands
Bay of Plenty
Hawke Bay
Cook Strait
Foveaux Strait
Stewart I.
Canterbury Bight
Pegasus Bay
Banks Pen.
North Taranaki Bight
South Taranaki Bight
Great Barrier I.
Mahia Pen.
The Snares
N
MILES
0 2 4 8
Hauraki Gulf
Manukau Harbour
Rangitoto I.
Porirua Har.
Lower Hutt
Upper Hutt
Palliser Bay
177° 176°
The Sisters
Chatham I.
Pitt Strait
Pitt I. (Rangiauria)
Pyramid I.
MILES
0 5 10 20
177° West of Greenwich 176°
44° 44°

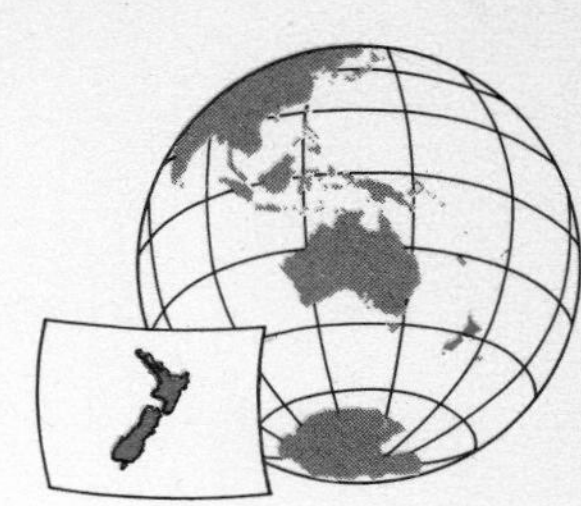

AREA 103,736 sq. mi.
POPULATION 2,815,000
CAPITAL Wellington
LARGEST CITY Auckland
HIGHEST POINT Mt. Cook 12,349 ft.
MONETARY UNIT New Zealand dollar
MAJOR LANGUAGES English, Maori
MAJOR RELIGION Protestantism

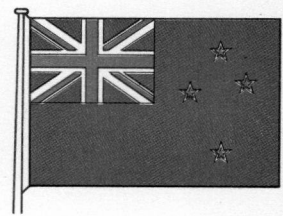

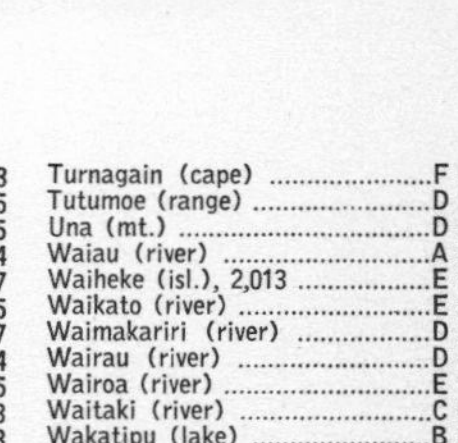

Topography

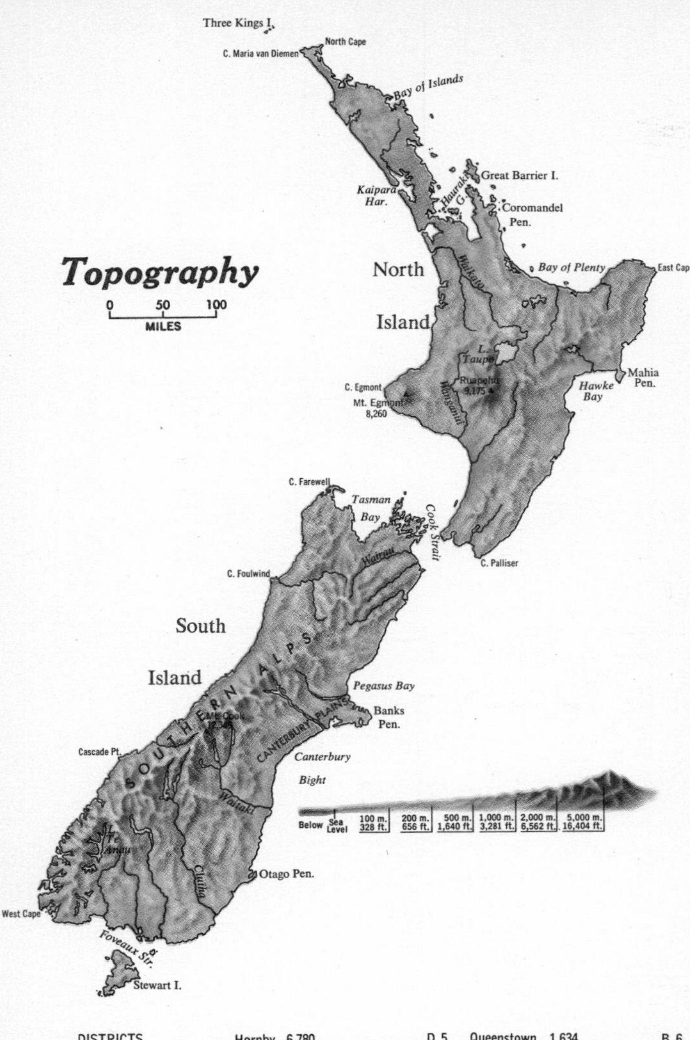

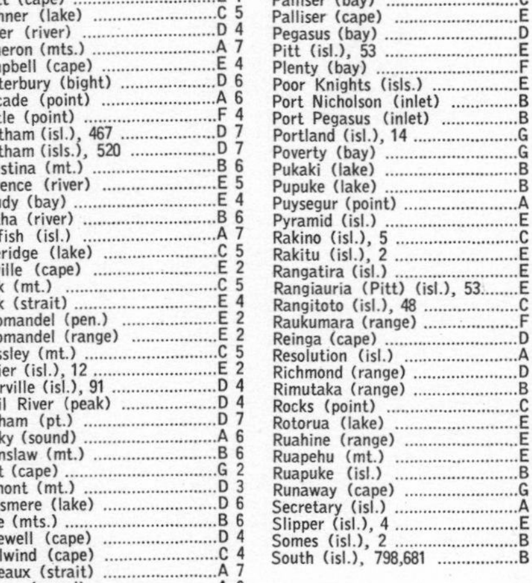

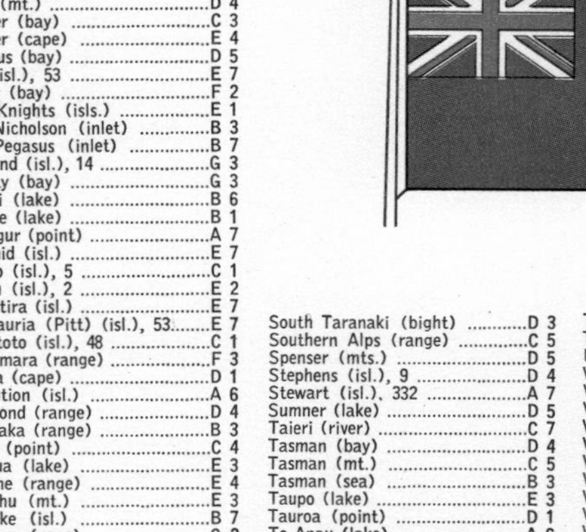

DISTRICTS

Auckland (prov. dist.), 1,189,811 ....E 2
Canterbury (prov. dist.), 385,981 ....C 5
Hawke's Bay (prov. dist.), 128,300 ....F 3
Marlborough (prov. dist.), 30,200 ....D 4
Nelson (prov. dist.), 68,300 ....D 4
Otago (prov. dist.), 290,100 ....A 6
Otago (land dist.), 183,200 ....B 6
Southland (land dist.), 106,900....A 6
Taranaki (prov. dist.), 101,200 ..E 3
Wellington (prov. dist.), 537,100 ....E 4
Westland (prov. dist.), 24,100....C 5

CITIES and TOWNS

Alexandra, 3,160 ....B 6
Ashburton, 12,950 ....C 5
Ashhurst, 922 ....E 4
Auckland, 152,200 ....B 1
Auckland, †588,400 ....B 1
Balclutha, 4,570 ....B 7
Bay View, 945 ....F 3
Belmont Hill, 1,119 ....B 2
Birkenhead, 12,800 ....B 1
Blenheim, 13,950 ....D 4
Bluff, 3,300 ....B 7
Bulls, 1,803 ....E 4
Cambridge, 6,060 ....E 2
Carterton, 3,640 ....E 4
Christchurch, 165,000 ....D 5
Christchurch, †256,300 ....D 5
Clive, 1,017 ....F 3
Cromwell, 1,062 ....B 6
Dannevirke, 5,780 ....F 4
Dargaville, 3,910 ....D 1
Devonport, 11,100 ....C 1
Dunedin, 77,800 ....C 6
Dunedin, †109,800 ....C 6
Eastbourne, 4,610 ....B 3
East Coast Bays, 13,150 ....B 1
Edgecumbe, 1,277 ....F 2
Ellerslie, 4,260 ....B 1
Eltham, 2,319 ....E 3
Fairfield, 1,106 ....C 6
Featherston, 1,857 ....E 4
Feilding, 9,360 ....E 4
Foxton, 2,830 ....E 4
Geraldine, 1,876 ....C 6
Gisborne, 25,600 ....G 3
Gisborne, †28,500 ....G 3
Glen Eden, 6,230 ....B 1
Glenfield, 16,450 ....B 1
Gore, 8,380 ....B 7
Green Bay, 2,022 ....B 1
Green Island, 5,990 ....C 7
Greymouth, 8,590 ....C 5
Greytown, 1,715 ....E 4
Hamilton, 67,700 ....E 2
Hamilton, †68,000 ....E 2
Hastings, 28,100 ....F 3
Hastings, †39,200 ....F 3
Havelock North, 5,950 ....F 3
Hawera, 8,210 ....E 3
Helensville, 1,305 ....B 1
Henderson, 5,780 ....B 1
Heretaunga-Pinehaven, 4,990....C 2
Hikurangi, 1,091 ....E 1
Hobsonville. 1,612 ....B 1
Hokitika, 3,310 ....C 5
Hornby, 6,780 ....D 5
Howick, 9,890 ....C 1
Huntly, 5,420 ....E 2
Hutt, †118,400 ....B, C 2
Inglewood, 2,003 ....E 3
Invercargill, 45.300 ....B 7
Invercargill, †47,800 ....B 7
Kaiapoi, 3,610 ....D 5
Kaikohe, 3,120 ....D 1
Kaikoura, 1,571 ....D 5
Kaitaia, 3,110 ....D 1
Kaitangata, 1,208 ....C 7
Kawakawa, 1,032 ....E 1
Kawerau, 6,010 ....F 3
Kelston West, 5,490 ....B 1
Levin, 11,950 ....E 4
Lower Hutt, 58,700 ....C 2
Lyttelton, 3,510 ....D 5
Mangakino, 1,466 ....E 3
Manukau, 84,700 ....C 1
Martinborough, 1,462 ....E 4
Marton, 4,780 ....E 4
Massey ....B 1
Masterton, 17,950 ....E 4
Mataura, 2,720 ....B 7
Milton, 1,861 ....C 7
Moerewa, 1,090 ....E 1
Morrinsville, 4,530 ....E 2
Mosgiel, 8,100 ....C 6
Motueka, 3,840 ....D 4
Mount Albert, 25,700 ....B 1
Mount Eden, 18,400 ....B 1
Mount Maunganui, 7,210 ....F 2
Mount Roskill, 34,400 ....B 1
Mount Wellington, 19,650 ....C 1
Murupara, 2,670 ....F 3
Napier, 36,700 ....F 3
Napier, †39,900 ....F 3
Nelson, 27,900 ....D 4
Nelson, †28,400 ....D 4
New Lynn, 10,150 ....B 1
New Plymouth, 32,300 ....D 3
New Plymouth, †35,800 ....D 3
Ngaruawahia, 3,790 ....E 2
Northcote, 8,640 ....B 1
Oamaru, 13,350 ....C 6
Ohai, 939 ....A 6
Ohakune, 1,458 ....E 3
One Tree Hill, 12,900 ....B 1
Onehunga, 16,050 ....B 1
Opotiki, 2,560 ....F 3
Opua, 151 ....D 1
Orewa, 1,357 ....E 2
Otahuhu, 10,000 ....C 1
Otaki, 3,660 ....E 4
Otematata, 3,890 ....B 6
Otorohanga, 1,951 ....E 3
Paekakariki, 1,934 ....E 4
Pahiatua, 2,590 ....E 4
Palmerston North, 49,200 ....E 4
Palmerston North, †50,900 ....E 4
Papakura, 12,950 ....E 2
Papatoetoe, 21,400 ....C 1
Patea, 2,013 ....E 3
Petone, 10,200 ....B 2
Picton, 2,610 ....D 4
Pinehaven (Heretaunga-Pinehaven), 4,990 ....C 2
Plimmerton-Paremata, 3,910 ....B 2
Porirua, 24,900 ....B 2
Port Chalmers, 3,040 ....C 6
Pukekohe, 6,800 ....E 2
Pukerua Bay, 1,220 ....E 4
Putaruru, 4,500 ....E 3
Queenstown, 1,634 ....B 6
Raetihi, 1,376 ....E 3
Raglan, 1,019 ....E 2
Ranfurly, 946 ....B 6
Rangiora, 4,270 ....D 5
Ranui, 1,897 ....B 1
Reefton, 1,730 ....C 5
Riccarton, 7,220 ....D 5
Richmond, 4,870 ....D 4
Riverton, 1,258 ....A 7
Riwaka, 993 ....D 4
Rotorua, 27,600 ....F 3
Rotorua, †35,300 ....F 3
Runanga, 1,683 ....C 5
Saint Kilda, 6,720 ....C 7
Shannon, 1,544 ....E 4
Stratford, 5,470 ....E 3
Taihape, 2,880 ....E 3
Takapuna, 23,800 ....B 1
Taradale ....F 3
Taumarunui, 6,080 ....E 3
Taupo, 8,530 ....F 3
Tauranga, 25,500 ....F 2
Tauranga, †33,500 ....F 2
Tawa, 10,200 ....B 2
Te Anau, 951 ....A 6
Te Aroha, 3,220 ....E 2
Te Atatu ....B 1
Te Awamutu, 6,780 ....E 3
Te Karaka, 637 ....F 3
Te Kuiti, 4,830 ....E 3
Temuka, 3,190 ....C 6
Te Puke, 3,090 ....F 2
Thames, 5,680 ....E 2
The Hermitage, 306 ....C 5
Timaru, 27,800 ....C 6
Timaru, †28,400 ....C 6
Titirangi, 5,740 ....B 1
Tokoroa, 12,450 ....F 3
Tuakau, 1,677 ....E 2
Tuatapere, 954 ....A 7
Upper Hutt, 19,750 ....B 2
Waihi, 3,170 ....F 2
Waikanae, 1,570 ....E 4
Waimate, 3,300 ....C 6
Wainuiomata, 15,000 ....B 3
Waipawa, 1,848 ....F 3
Waipukurau, 3,670 ....F 4
Wairoa, 5,190 ....F 3
Waitangi, 179 ....D 7
Waitara, 4,870 ....E 3
Waiuku, 1,759 ....E 2
Wanganui, 36,400 ....E 3
Wanganui, †38,500 ....E 3
Warkworth, 1,200 ....E 2
Waverley, 1,062 ....E 3
Wellington (capital), 134,400 ....A 3
Wellington, †175,500 ....A 3
Wellsford, 1,431 ....E 2
Westport, 5,230 ....C 4
Whakatane, 9,080 ....F 2
Whangarei, 29,600 ....E 1
Whangarei, †31,600 ....E 1
Winton, 1,740 ....B 7
Woodville, 1,529 ....F 4

OTHER FEATURES

Abut (head) ....B 5
Arthur (range) ....D 4
Arthur's (pass) ....C 5
Aspiring (mt.) ....B 6
Awarua (bay) ....A 6
Banks (pen.) ....D 5
Bligh (sound) ....A 6
Breaksea (sound) ....A 6
Bream (bay) ....E 1
Brett (cape) ....E 1
Brunner (lake) ....C 5
Buller (river) ....D 4
Cameron (mts.) ....A 7
Campbell (cape) ....E 4
Canterbury (bight) ....D 6
Cascade (point) ....A 6
Castle (point) ....F 4
Chatham (isl.), 467 ....D 7
Chatham (isls.), 520 ....D 7
Christina (mt.) ....B 6
Clarence (river) ....E 5
Cloudy (bay) ....E 4
Clutha (river) ....B 6
Codfish (isl.) ....A 7
Coleridge (lake) ....C 5
Colville (cape) ....E 2
Cook (mt.) ....C 5
Cook (strait) ....E 4
Coromandel (pen.) ....E 2
Coromandel (range) ....E 2
Crossley (mt.) ....C 5
Cuvier (isl.), 12 ....E 2
D'Urville (isl.), 91 ....D 4
Devil River (peak) ....D 4
Durham (pt.) ....D 7
Dusky (sound) ....A 6
Earnslaw (mt.) ....B 6
East (cape) ....G 2
Egmont (mt.) ....D 3
Ellesmere (lake) ....D 6
Eyre (mts.) ....B 6
Farewell (cape) ....D 4
Foulwind (cape) ....C 4
Foveaux (strait) ....A 7
George (sound) ....A 6
Golden (bay) ....D 4
Great Barrier (isl.), 272 ....F 2
Great Mercury (isl.), 7 ....E 2
Grey (river) ....C 5
Hauhangaroa (range) ....E 3
Hauraki (gulf) ....E 2
Hawea (lake) ....B 6
Hawke's (bay) ....F 3
Hen and Chickens (isls.) ....E 1
Hikurangi (mt.) ....G 2
Hokianga (harb.) ....D 1
Hunter (mts.) ....A 6
Hurunui (river) ....D 5
Hutt (river) ....C 2
Islands, Bay of (bay) ....E 1
Jackson (bay) ....B 5
Kaikoura (pen.) ....D 5
Kaikoura (range) ....D 4
Kaimanawa (mts.) ....E 3
Kaipara (harb.) ....D 2
Kapiti (isl.), 2 ....E 4
Karamea (bight) ....C 4
Karikari (cape) ....D 1
Kawau (isl.), 103 ....E 2
Kawhia (harb.) ....E 3
Kidnappers (cape) ....F 3
Little Barrier (isl.), 4 ....E 2
Mahia (pen.) ....G 3
Mana (isl.), 5 ....B 2
Manapouri (lake) ....A 6
Manukau (harb.) ....D 2
Maria van Diemen (cape) ....D 1
Mason (bay) ....A 7
Matakana (isl.), 396 ....F 2
Mataura (river) ....B 6
Mayor (isl.), 47 ....F 2
Mercury (bay) ....F 2
Mercury (isls.), 7 ....F 2
Milford (sound) ....A 6
Mokau (river) ....E 3
Mokohinau (isls.), 7 ....E 1
Motiti (isl.), 7 ....F 2
Motuhora (isl.) ....F 2
Motuihe (isl.), 6 ....C 1
Motutapu (isl.), 27 ....C 1
Munning (point) ....E 7
Needles (point) ....E 2
Ninety-Mile (beach) ....D 1
North (isl.), 1,956,411 ....F 1
North Taranaki (bight) ....D 3
Nugget (point) ....C 7
Ohariu (stream) ....B 2
Otago (pen.), ...C 6
Owen (mt.) ....D 4
Palliser (bay) ....C 3
Palliser (cape) ....E 4
Pegasus (bay) ....D 5
Pitt (isl.), 53 ....E 7
Plenty (bay) ....F 2
Poor Knights (isls.) ....E 1
Port Nicholson (inlet) ....B 3
Port Pegasus (inlet) ....B 7
Portland (isl.), 14 ....G 3
Poverty (bay) ....G 3
Pukaki (lake) ....B 6
Pupuke (lake) ....B 1
Puysegur (point) ....A 7
Pyramid (isl.) ....E 7
Rakino (isl.), 5 ....C 1
Rakitu (isl.), 2 ....E 2
Rangatira (isl.) ....E 7
Rangiauria (Pitt) (isl.), 53....E 7
Rangitoto (isl.), 48 ....C 1
Raukumara (range) ....F 3
Reinga (cape) ....D 1
Resolution (isl.) ....A 6
Richmond (range) ....D 4
Rimutaka (range) ....B 3
Rocks (point) ....C 4
Rotorua (lake) ....E 3
Ruahine (range) ....E 4
Ruapehu (mt.) ....E 3
Ruapuke (isl.) ....B 7
Runaway (cape) ....G 2
Secretary (isl.) ....A 6
Slipper (isl.), 4 ....E 2
Somes (isl.), 2 ....B 2
South (isl.), 798,681 ....B 5
South Taranaki (bight) ....D 3
Southern Alps (range) ....C 5
Spenser (mts.) ....D 5
Stephens (isl.), 9 ....D 4
Stewart (isl.), 332 ....A 7
Sumner (lake) ....D 5
Taieri (river) ....C 7
Tasman (bay) ....D 4
Tasman (mt.) ....C 5
Tasman (sea) ....B 3
Taupo (lake) ....E 3
Tauroa (point) ....D 1
Te Anau (lake) ....A 6
Tekapo (lake) ....C 5
Three Kings (isls.) ....C 1
Titihiri (head) ....B 5
Tongue (point) ....A 3
Turnagain (cape) ....F 4
Tutumoe (range) ....D 1
Una (mt.) ....D 5
Waiau (river) ....A 6
Waiheke (isl.), 2,013 ....E 2
Waikato (river) ....E 2
Waimakariri (river) ....D 5
Wairau (river) ....D 4
Wairoa (river) ....E 1
Waitaki (river) ....C 6
Wakatipu (lake) ....B 6
Wanaka (lake) ....B 6
Wanganui (river) ....E 3
West (cape) ....A 6
Whitcombe (mt.) ....C 5
White (isl.) ....F 2

†Population of urban area.

Agriculture, Industry and Resources

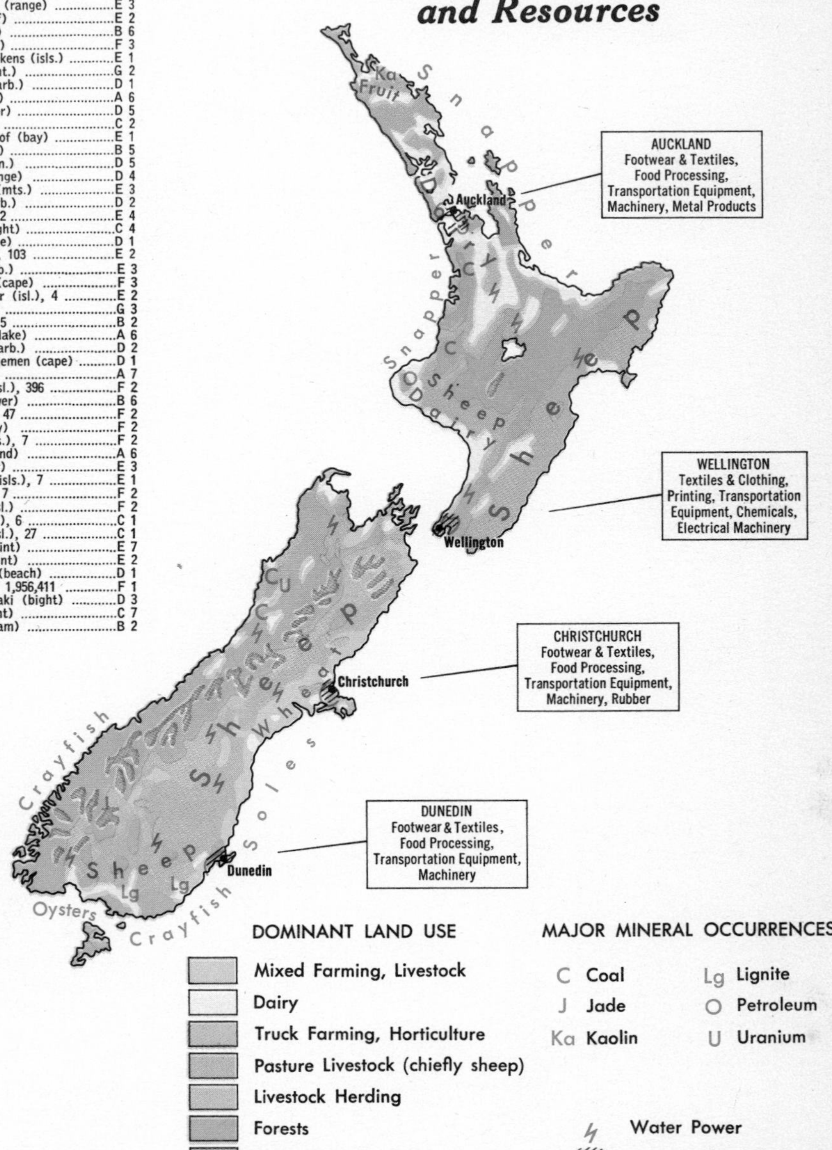

AFRICA
LAMBERT AZIMUTHAL EQUAL-AREA PROJECTION
SCALE OF MILES
0 100 200 400 600 800
SCALE OF KILOMETRES
0 200 400 600 800
Capitals
Canals
International Boundaries
Mountain Peaks
Copyright by C. S. Hammond & Co., N.Y.
AFRICA 1939
British
French
Italian
Portuguese
Spanish
Belgian
Mandates
MOROCCO
TUNISIA
IFNI
ALGERIA
LIBYA
EGYPT
RIO DE ORO
FRENCH WEST AFRICA
GAMBIA
PORT. GUINEA
ANGLO-EGYPTIAN SUDAN
FR. SOM.
SOM. PROT.
SIERRA LEONE
LIBERIA
GOLD COAST
TOGO
NIGERIA
ITALIAN EAST AFRICA
CAMEROONS
RIO MUNI
FRENCH EQUATORIAL AFRICA
UGANDA
KENYA
BELGIAN CONGO
R.-U.
TANGANYIKA
ANGOLA
NO. RHODESIA
NYASALAND
SO. RHODESIA
MOZAMBIQUE
MADAGASCAR
SOUTH-WEST AFRICA
BECH. PROT.
UNION OF SOUTH AFRICA
SWAZILAND
BASUTOLAND
CAPE VERDE IS.
(ILHAS DO CABO VERDE)
MILES
0 20 40 60
Santo Antão
São Vicente
Santa Luzia
São Nicolau
Sal
Boa Vista
Maio
São Tiago
Fogo
Brava
Praia
20° Longitude West of 10° Greenwich
Longitude East of Greenwich
EUROPE
ASIA
ATLANTIC OCEAN
INDIAN OCEAN
MEDITERRANEAN SEA
BLACK SEA
CASPIAN SEA
RED SEA
Gulf of Guinea
Gulf of Aden
Mozambique Channel
Persian Gulf
Equator
Tropic of Cancer
Tropic of Capricorn
FRANCE
SPAIN
PORTUGAL
ITALY
YUGOSLAVIA
RUMANIA
BULGARIA
ALBANIA
GREECE
TURKEY
U.S.S.R.
IRAN
IRAQ
SYRIA
LEBANON
ISRAEL
JORDAN
CYPRUS
KUWAIT
SAUDI ARABIA
YEMEN ARAB REP.
PEOP. DEM. REP. YEMEN
MOROCCO
ALGERIA
TUNISIA
LIBYA
EGYPT
SPANISH SAHARA
MAURITANIA
MALI
NIGER
CHAD
SUDAN
SENEGAL
GAMBIA
PORT. GUINEA
GUINEA
SIERRA LEONE
LIBERIA
IVORY COAST
UPPER VOLTA
GHANA
TOGO
DAHOMEY
NIGERIA
CAMEROON
CENTRAL AFRICAN REPUBLIC
EQUATORIAL GUINEA
GABON
REP. OF CONGO
ZAIRE
UGANDA
KENYA
RWANDA
BURUNDI
TANZANIA
ETHIOPIA
TERR. OF THE AFARS & ISSAS (Fr.)
SOMALIA
ANGOLA
ZAMBIA
MALAWI
MOZAMBIQUE
RHODESIA
BOTSWANA
SOUTH-WEST AFRICA
SOUTH AFRICA
CAPE OF GOOD HOPE
TRANSVAAL
ORANGE FREE STATE
NATAL
TRANSKEI
LESOTHO
SWAZI.
MALAGASY REP.
Madagascar
Madeira (Port.)
Canary Is. (Sp.)
Ascension (St. Helena)
St. Helena (Br.)
Annobón (Equatorial Guinea)
São Tomé (Port.)
Príncipe (Port.)
Comoro Is. (Fr.)
Aldabra Is. (Br. Ind. Oc. Terr.)
Europa (Réunion)
Madrid
Lisbon
Rome
Athens
Ankara
Istanbul
Tehran
Baghdad
Damascus
Beirut
Riyadh
Mecca
Rabat
Algiers
Tunis
Tripoli
Benghazi
Cairo
Alexandria
Port Said
Suez
Khartoum
Omdurman
Addis Ababa
Asmara
Massawa
Djibouti
Mogadishu
Nairobi
Mombasa
Dar es Salaam
Kampala
Kigali
Bujumbura
Kinshasa (Léopoldville)
Brazzaville
Libreville
Yaoundé
Douala
Bangui
Ft.-Lamy
Niamey
Bamako
Dakar
Nouakchott
Conakry
Freetown
Monrovia
Abidjan
Accra
Lomé
Porto-Novo
Lagos
Ibadan
Kano
Ouagadougou
Timbuktu
Luanda
Lusaka
Zomba
Salisbury
Bulawayo
Gaborone
Windhoek
Pretoria
Johannesburg
Mbabane
Maseru
Lourenço Marques
Durban
Bloemfontein
Kimberley
Cape Town
Port Elizabeth
East London
Tananarive
Atlas Mountains
Ahaggar
Tahat 9,850
Tibesti
Emi Koussi 11,204
Jebel 'Uweinat 6,255
Cameroon 13,350
Ras Dashan 15,157
Kenya 17,058
Kilimanjaro 19,340
Elgon 14,178
Ruwenzori
Mlanje 9,843
Tsiafajavona 8,669
Libyan Desert
Nubian Desert
Kalahari Desert
Namib
L. Chad
L. Victoria
L. Tanganyika
L. Nyasa (L. Malawi)
L. Albert
L. Edward
L. Kivu
L. Rudolf
L. Tana
L. Volta
Lake Nasser
Victoria Falls (Mosi-Ao-Tunya)
Congo
Zaire
Nile
Niger
Zambezi
Limpopo
Orange
Benue
Ubangi
Kasai
Okovango
Cubango
Blue Nile
White Nile
C. Bon
C. Blanc
C. Verde
C. Palmas
C. Lopez
C. Fria
C. Guardafui
C. Delgado
C. Amber
C. Ste-Marie
C. of Good Hope
C. Agulhas

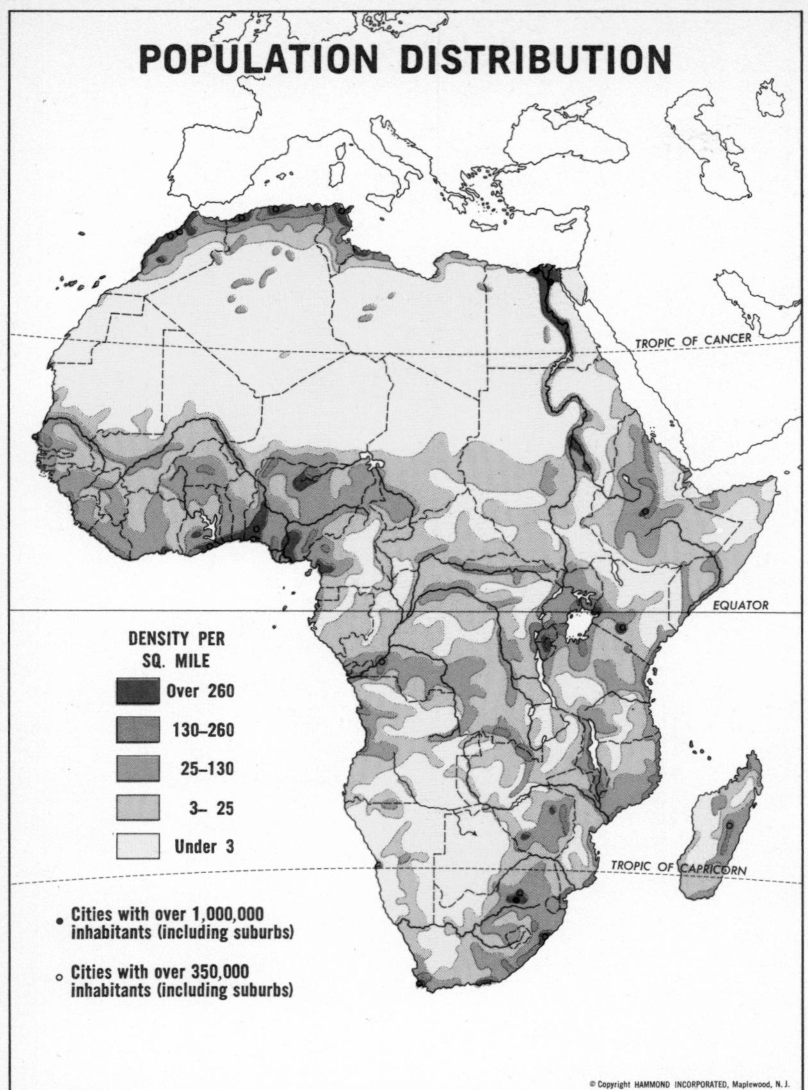

AREA 11,682,000 sq. mi.
POPULATION 345,000,000
LARGEST CITY Cairo
HIGHEST POINT Kilimanjaro 19,340 ft.
LOWEST POINT Qattara Depression -436 ft.

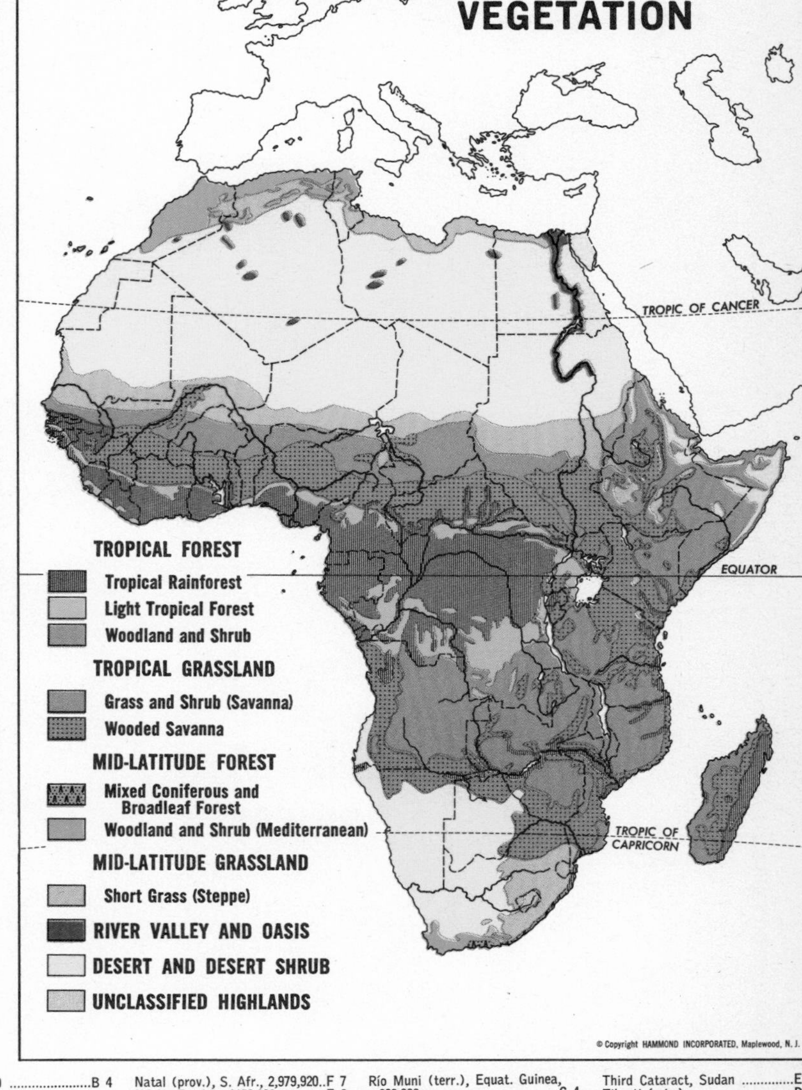

Abécher, Chad, 19,650 ....E 3
Abéokuta, Nigeria, 217,201 ....C 4
Abidjan (cap.), Ivory Coast, *425,000 ....B 4
Accra (capital), Ghana, *848,825 ....B 4
Addis Ababa (cap.), Ethiopia, 644,120 ....F 4
Aden (gulf) ....G 3
Adwa, Ethiopia ....F 3
Afars and Issas, Terr. of the 125,050 ....G 3
Agulhas (cape), S. Africa ....D 8
Ahaggar (mts.), Algeria ....C 2
Albert (lake) ....F 4
Alexandria, Egypt, 1,803,900....E 1
Algeria, 13,547,000 ....C 1
Algiers (cap.), Algeria, *1,800,000 ....C 1
Angola, 5,430,000 ....D 6
Annaba, Algeria, *223,000 ....C 1
Annobón (isl.), Equat. Guinea, 1,408 ....C 5
Antsirabe, Malag. Rep., 29,914....G 6
Ascension (isl.), St. Helena, 1,486 ....A 5
Asmara, Ethiopia, 190,500 ....F 3
Aswân, Egypt, 127,700 ....F 2
Asyût, Egypt, 154,100 ....F 2
Atbara, Sudan, 36,000 ....F 3
Atlas (mts.) ....B 1
Bamako (capital), Mali, *182,000 ....B 3
Bangui (cap.), Central African Rep., *240,000 ....D 4
Bata, Equat. Guinea, 27,024....D 4
Bathurst (cap.), Gambia, *48,333 ....A 3
Beira, Mozambique, †58,235 ....F 6
Benghazi, Libya, 137,295....D 1
Benguela, Angola, 23,256....D 6
Beni Suef, Egypt, 78,829 ....F 2
Benin City, Nigeria, 116,774....C 4
Biskra, Algeria, 59,275....C 1
Bissau (cap.), Port. Guinea, 20,000 ....A 3
Bizerte, Tunisia, 51,700....C 1
Blanc (cape) ....A 2
Blantyre, Malawi, 109,461 ....F 6
Bloemfontein (cap.), O.F.S., S. Africa, ‡147,000 ....E 7
Blue Nile (riv.) ....F 3
Bobo-Dioulasso, Upper Volta, 56,100 ....B 3
Boma, Zaire, 33,143 ....D 5
Bon (cape), Tunisia ....D 1
Bône (Annaba), Algeria, *223,000 ....C 1
Botswana, 629,000 ....E 7
Bouaké, Ivory Coast, 100,000....B 4
Brazzaville (cap.), Rep. of Congo, *200,000 ....D 5
British Indian Ocean Territory, 2,000 ....G 5
Broken Hill, Zambia, ‡67,200....E 6
Bujumbura (cap.), Burundi, 90 000 ....F 5
Bukavu, Zaire, 134,861 ....E 5
Bulawayo, Rhodesia, ‡270,000....E 7
Burundi, 3,475,000 ....F 5
Cairo (capital), Egypt, 4,219,853 ....E 2
Calvinia, S. Afr., 6,700 ....D 8
Cameroon, 5,836,000 ....D 4
Canary (isls.), Spain, 944,448....A 2
Cape Coast, Ghana, 41,230....B 4
Cape of Good Hope (prov.), South Africa, 3,936,306....E 8
Cape Town (cap.), South Africa, ‡817,000 ....D 8
Cape Verde (isls.), 250,000....G 8
Casablanca, Morocco, 1,320,000 ....B 1
Central African Republic, 1,518,000 ....D 4
Ceuta, Spain, 88,000 ....B 1
Chad, 3,510,000 ....D 3
Chad (lake) ....D 3
Comoro (isls.), 270,000 ....G 6
Conakry (cap.), Guinea, *197,267 ....A 4
Congo, Rep. of, 915,000 ....D 5
Congo (riv.) ....E 4
Constantine, Algeria, 243,558 ....C 1
Cotonou, Dahomey, 120,000....C 4
Cyrenaica (region), Libya, 450,954 ....E 1
Dahomey, 2,640,000 ....C 4
Dakar (cap.), Senegal, *661,000 ....A 3
Damietta, Egypt, 71,780 ....F 1
Dar es Salaam (cap.), Tanzania, 272,821 ....F 5
Diégo-Suarez, Malag. Rep., 40,237 ....G 6
Dire Dawa, Ethiopia, 40,000 ....G 4
Djibouti (cap.), Terr. of the Afars & Issas, *61,500....G 3
Douala, Cameroon, 230,000....D 4
Durban, S. Africa, ‡690,000 ....F 8
East London, S. Africa, 134,100..E 8
Ebolowa, Cameroon, 16,000....D 4
Edward (lake) ....E 5
Egypt, 33,329,000 ....E 2
El Aaiún (cap.), Sp. Sahara, 10,000 ....A 2
El Faiyûm, Egypt, 133,800....E 2
El Fasher, Sudan, 26,161....E 3
El Jadida, Morocco, 40,302....B 1
El Minya, Egypt, 112,800 ....E 2
El Obeid, Sudan, 53,000....E 3
Elgon (mt.) ....F 4
Entebbe, Uganda, 10,941....F 5
Enugu, Nigeria, 160,567....C 4
Equatorial Guinea, 286,000 ....C 4
Eritrea (reg.), Eth., 1,757,912....F 3
Essaouira, Morocco, 26,392....A 1
Ethiopia, 24,769,000....F 4
Etosha Pan (salt dep.), S. W. Africa ....D 6
Fernando Po (isl.), Equat. Guinea, 78,000 ....C 4
Fez, Morocco, 280,000 ....B 1
Fezzan (reg.), Libya, 79,326....D 2
Fianarantsoa, Malag. Rep., 45,790 ....G 7
Fifth Cataract, Sudan ....F 3
Fort-Archambault, Chad, 35,000..E 4
Fort Hall, Kenya, 5,389 ....F 5
Fort-Lamy (cap.), Chad, 132,500 ....D 3
Fourth Cataract, Sudan ....F 3
Freetown (cap.), Sierra Leone, 170,600 ....A 4
Fria (cape), S.W. Africa ....D 6
Funchal (cap.), Madeira, Port., 43,301 ....A 1
Gaborone (cap.), Botswana, 18,000 ....E 7
Gabès, Tunisia, 32,300 ....D 1
Gabon, 500,000 ....D 5
Gambia, 357,000 ....A 3
Garoua, Cameroon, 30,000 ....D 4
Germiston, S. Africa, ‡222,000....E 7
Ghana, 8,545,561 ....B 4
Gondar, Ethiopia, 24,673 ....F 3
Good Hope (cape), S. Africa....D 8
Grahamstown, S. Africa, 37,600..E 8
Guardafui (cape), Somalia....H 3
Guinea, 3,890,000 ....A 3
Guinea (gulf) ....C 4
Gwelo, Rhodesia, ‡50,000....E 6
Harar, Ethiopia, 40,499 ....G 4
Harghessa, Somalia, †40,254....G 4
Ibadan, Nigeria, 727,565....C 4
Ilorin, Nigeria, 241,849 ....C 4
Impfondo, Rep. of Congo, 2,000..D 4
Ivory Coast, 4,800,000 ....B 4
Jinja, Uganda, 29,741 ....F 4
Johannesburg, South Africa, *1,305,000 ....E 7
Kaduna, Nigeria, 173,849 ....C 3
Kalahari (des.) ....E 7
Kampala (cap.), Uganda, 330,000 ....F 4
Kananga, Zaire, 428,960 ....E 5
Kankan, Guinea, 50,000 ....B 3
Kano, Nigeria, 342,610....C 3
Kaolack, Senegal, 70,000 ....A 3
Kariba (lake) ....E 6
Kasai (riv.) ....E 5
Katanga (reg.), Zaire, 2,753,714 ....E 5
Kayes, Mali, 23,600 ....A 3
Kénitra, Morocco, 125,000 ....B 1
Kenya, 10,880,200 ....F 4
Kenya (mt.), Kenya ....F 5
Khartoum (cap.), Sudan, 194,000 ....F 3
Kigali (capital), Rwanda, 24,000 ....E 5
Kilimanjaro (mt.), Tanzania....F 5
Kimberley, S. Africa, 95,200....E 7
Kinshasa (cap.), Zaire, 1,323,039 ....D 5
Kioga (lake), Uganda ....F 4
Kisangani, Zaire, 229,596....E 4
Kivu (lake) ....E 5
Kumasi, Ghana, *540,200 ....B 4
Lagos (capital), Nigeria, 841,749 ....C 4
Las Palmas (cap.), Canary Is., Spain, 166,236 ....A 2
Lesotho, 930,000 ....E 7
Liberia, 1,200,000 ....B 4
Libreville (cap.), Gabon, *57,000 ....C 4
Libya, 1,900,000 ....D 2
Libyan (des.) ....E 2
Likasi, Zaire, 146,394 ....E 6
Limpopo (riv.) ....E 7
Livingstone, Zambia, ‡33,440 ....E 6
Lobito, Angola, 50,164 ....D 6
Lokoja, Nigeria, 13,103 ....C 4
Lomé (cap.), Togo, *149,879....C 4
Lourenço Marques (cap.), Mozambique, *177,929 ....F 7
Luanda (cap.), Angola, 400,000..D 5
Lubumbashi, Zaire, 318,000 ....E 6
Lusaka (cap.), Zambia, ‡238,200 ....E 6
Madagascar (isl.) ....G 7
Madeira (isls.), Port., 268,700....A 1
Maiduguri, Nigeria, 162,316....D 3
Majunga, Malag. Rep., 47,654....G 6
Malagasy Republic, 7,011,563 ....G 6
Malawi, 4,530,000 ....F 6
Mali, 4,929,000 ....B 3
Marrakech, Morocco, 295,000....A 1
Maseru (cap.), Lesotho, 18,797..E 8
Matadi, Zaire, 110,436 ....D 5
Maun, Botswana, 4,591 ....E 6
Mauritania, 1,140,000 ....A 3
Mbabane (cap.), Swaziland, 13,803 ....F 7
Mbandaka, Zaire, 107,910 ....E 4
Meknès, Morocco, 235,000 ....B 1
Melilla, Spain, 77,000 ....B 1
Merowe, Sudan, 1,620 ....F 3
Mogadishu (Mogadiscio) (cap.), Somalia, 172,677 ....G 4
Mombasa, Kenya, 234,400 ....G 5
Monrovia (cap.), Liberia, *100,000 ....A 4
Morocco, 15,577,000 ....B 1
Moroni (cap.), Comoro Is., 11,515 ....G 6
Mostaganem, Algeria, 75,332 ....B 1
Mozambique, 7,376,000 ....F 6
Mozambique (channel) ....G 6
Nairobi (cap.), Kenya, 477,600..F 5
Nasser (lake) ....F 2
Natal (prov.), S. Afr., 2,979,920..F 7
Ndola, Zambia, ‡150,800 ....E 6
N'Gaoundéré, Cam., 15,000 ....D 4
Niamey (cap.), Niger, *122,672..C 3
Niger, 4,016,000 ....C, D 3
Niger (river) ....C 3
Nigeria, 66,174,000 ....C 4
Nile (river) ....F 2
Nouakchott (cap.), Mauritania, 14,500 ....A 3
Nova Lisboa, Angola, 109,000 ....D 6
Nubian (des.), Sudan ....F 2
Nyasa (lake) ....F 6
Omdurman, Sudan, 206,000....F 3
Oran, Algeria, *393,000 ....B 1
Orange (river) ....D 7
Orange Free State (prov.), South Africa, 1,386,547....E 7
Ouagadougou (cap.), Upper Volta, *100,000 ....B 3
Oujda, Morocco, 150,000....B 1
Oyo, Nigeria, 130,290 ....C 4
Palmas (cape) ....B 4
Pemba (isl.), Tanzania, 164,321 ....G 5
Pietermaritzburg (cap.), Natal, S. Africa, ‡128,598 ....F 7
Pointe-Noire, Rep. of Congo, 100.000 ....D 5
Port Elizabeth, S. Africa, ‡448,000 ....E 8
Port Harcourt, Nigeria, 208,237..C 4
Port Said, Egypt, 283,400 ....F 1
Port Sudan, Sudan, 110,000....F 3
Porto-Novo (cap.), Dahomey, 80,000 ....C 4
Portuguese Guinea, 530,000....A 3
Praia (cap.), Cape Verde Is., 3,628 ....G 8
Pretoria (cap.), S. Africa, 479,700 ....E 7
Qena, Egypt, 57,417 ....F 2
Quelimane, Moz., †62,717 ....F 6
Rabat (cap.), Morocco, *435,000 ....B 1
Red (sea) ....F 2
Rhodesia, 5,310,000 ....E 6
Río de Oro (reg.), Sp. Sahara...A 2
Río Muni (terr.), Equat. Guinea, 203,000 ....C 4
Rudolf (lake), Kenya ....F 4
Rufisque, Senegal, 50,000 ....A 3
Rwanda, 3,500,000 ....F 5
Ruwenzori (range) ....E 4
Sahara (desert) ....C 2
Saint Helena (isl.), 4,707 ....B 6
Saint-Louis, Senegal, 50,000....A 3
Salisbury (cap.), Rhodesia, ‡423,000 ....F 6
Santa Cruz (cap.), Canary Is., Spain, 82,620 ....A 2
Santa Isabel (cap.), Equat. Guinea, 37,237 ....C 4
Sekondi-Takoradi, Ghana, *209,400 ....B 4
Senegal, 3,780,000 ....A 3
Serowe, Botswana, 35,000 ....E 7
Sétif, Algeria, 98,337 ....C 1
Sfax, Tunisia, 65,000 ....D 1
Sidi-bel-Abbès, Algeria, 91,527....C 1
Sierra Leone, 2,512,000 ....A 4
Sinai (pen.), Egypt, 49,769 ....F 2
Sixth Cataract, Sudan ....F 3
Skikda, Algeria, 72,742 ....C 1
Sohâg, Egypt, 61,944 ....F 2
Somalia, 2,730,000 ....G 4
Sousse, Tunisia, 48,200 ....D 1
South Africa, 21,282,000 ....E 7
South-West Africa, 615,000 ....D 7
Spanish Sahara (prov.), Spain, 63,000 ....A 2
Stanley (falls), Zaire ....E 4
Sudan, 15,312,000 ....E 3
Suez, Egypt, 264,500 ....F 2
Suez (canal), Egypt ....F 1
Swaziland, 411,879 ....F 7
Tamale, Ghana, 40,443....B 4
Tamatave, Malag. Rep., 53,173...G 6
Tana (lake), Ethiopia....F 3
Tananarive (cap.), Malag. Rep., *447,016 ....G 6
Tanga, Tanzania, 61,058 ....F 5
Tanganyika (lake) ....F 5
Tangier, Morocco, 160,000....B 1
Tanzania, 12,896,000 ....F 5
Taouz, Morocco, 641 ....B 1
Thiès, Senegal, 70,000 ....A 3
Third Cataract, Sudan ....E 3
Tibesti (mts.) ....D 2
Timbuktu, Mali, 14,900 ....B 3
Tlemcen, Algeria, 87,210....B 1
Togo, 2,004,711 ....C 4
Transkei (prov.), S. Africa, 1,439,195 ....E 8
Transvaal (prov.), S. Africa, 6,273,477 ....E 7
Tripoli (cap.), Libya, 247,365....D 1
Tripolitania (reg.), Libya, 1,034,089 ....D 1
Tuléar, Malag. Rep., 33,842....G 7
Tunis (cap.), Tunisia, *800,000....D 1
Tunisia, 5,027,000 ....C 1
Ubangi (river) ....E 3
Uganda, 9,764,000 ....F 4
Uitenhage, S. Africa, 63,400....E 8
Umtali, Rhodesia, ‡50,000 ....F 6
Umtata (cap.), Transkei, South Africa, 17,200....E 8
Upper Volta, 5,330,000 ....B 3
Vaal (riv.), S. Africa ....E 7
Verde (cape), Senegal ....A 3
Victoria (falls) ....E 6
Victoria (lake) ....F 5
Volta (lake), Ghana ....B 4
Volta (river) ....C 4
Wad Medani, Sudan, 48,000 ....F 3
Walvis Bay, S. Africa, 12,234....D 7
White Nile (river)....F 4
Windhoek (cap.), S.W. Africa, 36,050 ....D 7
Yaoundé (cap.), Cameroon, 130,000 ....D 4
Zaire, 21,637,876 ....E 5
Zaire (Congo) (riv.) ....E 4
Zambezi (river) ....E 6
Zambia, 4,056,995 ....E 6
Zanzibar, Tanzania, *95,047 ....G 5
Zanzibar (isl.), Tanzania, 190,494 ....G 5
Zomba (cap.), Malawi, 19,666....F 6

*City and suburbs.
†Population of sub-district.
‡Population of urban or met. area.

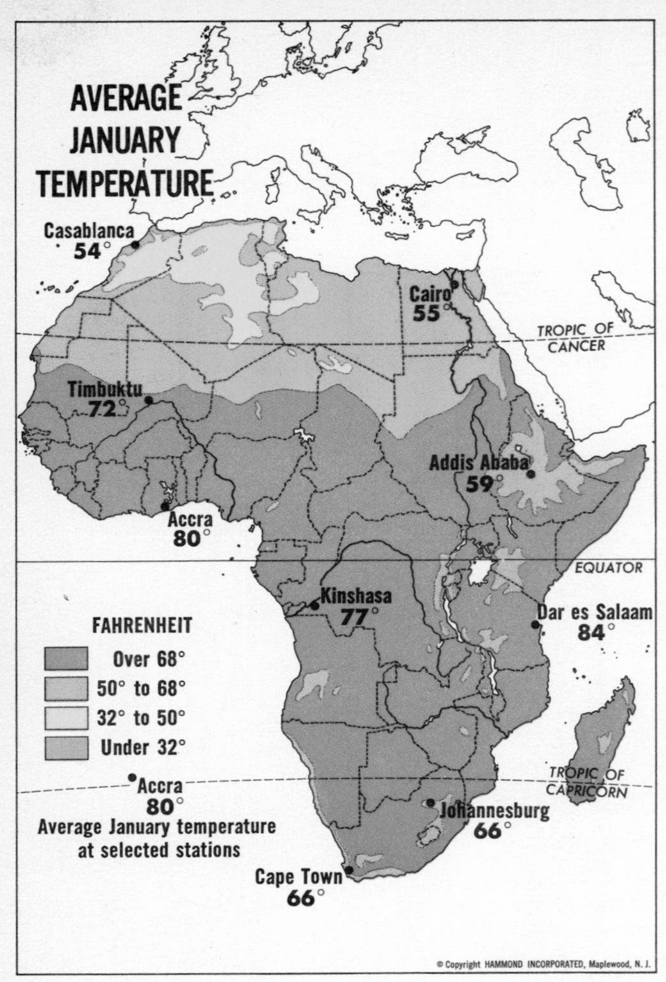

AVERAGE JANUARY TEMPERATURE
Casablanca 54°
Cairo 55°
TROPIC OF CANCER
Timbuktu 72°
Addis Ababa 59°
Accra 80°
EQUATOR
Kinshasa 77°
Dar es Salaam 84°
FAHRENHEIT
Over 68°
50° to 68°
32° to 50°
Under 32°
Accra 80°
Average January temperature at selected stations
TROPIC OF CAPRICORN
Johannesburg 66°
Cape Town 66°
© Copyright HAMMOND INCORPORATED, Maplewood, N. J.

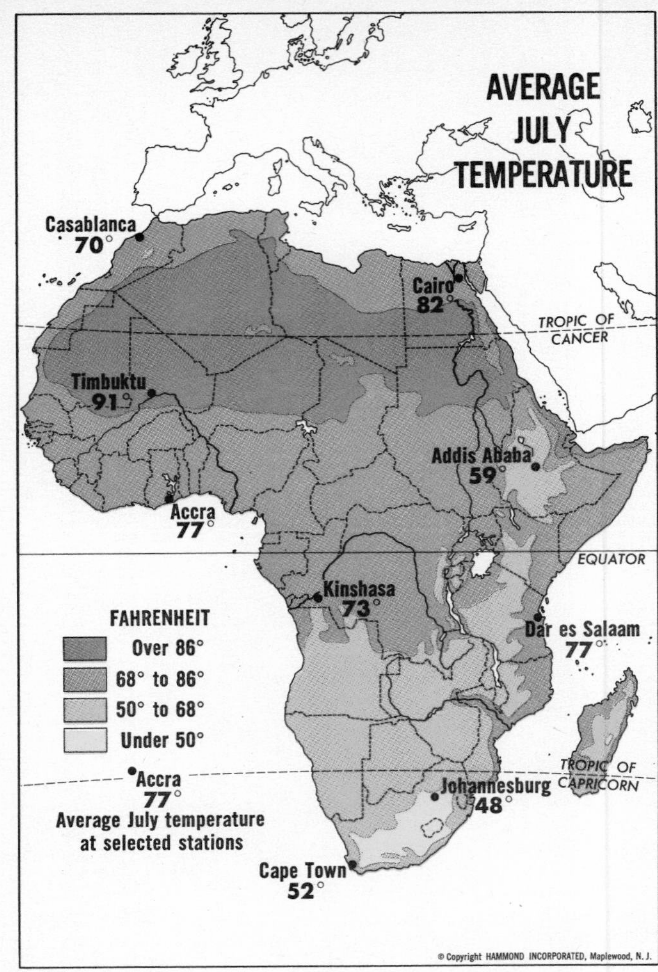

AVERAGE JULY TEMPERATURE
Casablanca 70°
Cairo 82°
TROPIC OF CANCER
Timbuktu 91°
Addis Ababa 59°
Accra 77°
EQUATOR
Kinshasa 73°
Dar es Salaam 77°
FAHRENHEIT
Over 86°
68° to 86°
50° to 68°
Under 50°
Accra 77°
Average July temperature at selected stations
TROPIC OF CAPRICORN
Johannesburg 48°
Cape Town 52°
© Copyright HAMMOND INCORPORATED, Maplewood, N. J.

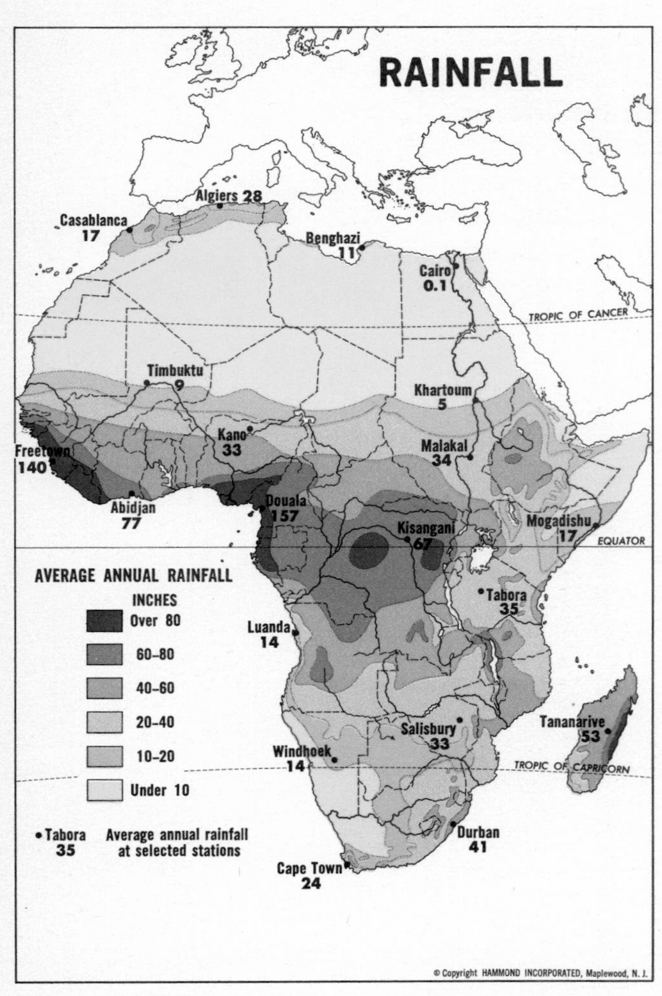

RAINFALL
Algiers 28
Casablanca 17
Benghazi 11
Cairo 0.1
TROPIC OF CANCER
Timbuktu 9
Khartoum 5
Kano 33
Malakal 34
Freetown 140
Abidjan 77
Douala 157
Kisangani 67
Mogadishu 17
EQUATOR
AVERAGE ANNUAL RAINFALL
INCHES
Over 80
60–80
40–60
20–40
10–20
Under 10
Tabora 35
Luanda 14
Salisbury 33
Tananarive 53
Windhoek 14
TROPIC OF CAPRICORN
Tabora 35
Average annual rainfall at selected stations
Durban 41
Cape Town 24
© Copyright HAMMOND INCORPORATED, Maplewood, N. J.

VEGETATION/RELIEF

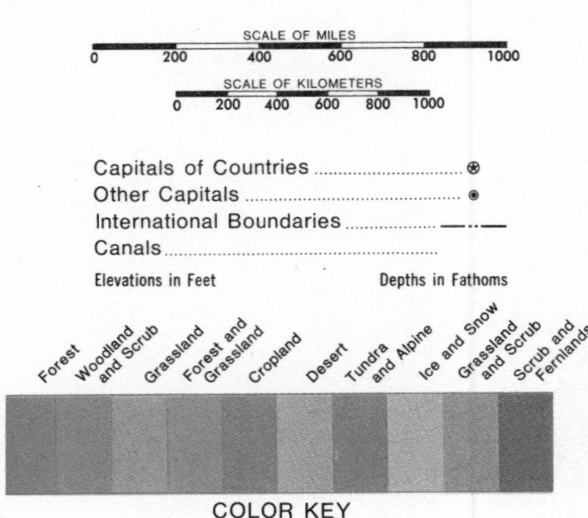

SCALE OF MILES
0 200 400 600 800 1000
SCALE OF KILOMETERS
0 200 400 600 800 1000
Capitals of Countries
Other Capitals
International Boundaries
Canals
Elevations in Feet
Depths in Fathoms
Forest
Woodland and Scrub
Grassland
Forest and Grassland
Cropland
Desert
Tundra and Alpine
Ice and Snow
Grassland and Scrub
Scrub and Fernlands
COLOR KEY

Paris
WEST GERMANY
CZECH.
FRANCE
SW.
AUST.
HUNGARY
E U R O P E
U. S. S. R.
Volga
ARAL SEA
Bay of Biscay
RUMANIA
Caucasus
ATLANTIC
OCEAN
YUGOSLAVIA
ADRIATIC SEA
Danube
BLACK SEA
CASPIAN SEA
Corsica
BULGARIA
Madrid
Rome
ITALY
İstanbul
PORTUGAL
SPAIN
Balearic Is.
Sardinia
ALB.
GREECE
AEGEAN SEA
T U R K E Y
MEDITERRANEAN SEA
Str. of Gibraltar
Algiers
Annaba
Sicily
Tehran
Tangier
Oran
C. Bon
Tunis
Crete
CYPRUS
SYRIA
Tigris
Madeira (Port.)
Rabat
Casablanca
TUNISIA
MALTA
LEBANON
IRAQ
IRAN
MOROCCO
Sfax
ISRAEL
Toubkal 13,665
Atlas Mountains
Tripoli
Benghazi
Alexandria
Port Said
Suez Canal
JORDAN
Euphrates
A S I A
Canary Is. (Sp.)
Gulf of Sidra
Cairo
Sinai Pen.
KUWAIT
Las Palmas
Wadi Draa
ALGERIA
Libyan Desert
Persian Gulf
El Aaiún
Asyût
SAUDI
SPANISH SAHARA
LIBYA
EGYPT
Nile
QATAR
U.A.E.
Tanezrouft
Ahaggar
Aswân
Tropic of Cancer
RED SEA
C. Blanc
S a h a r a
Lake Nasser
ARABIA
Tamanrasset
Tibesti
Nubian Desert
MAURITANIA
Rub' al Khali
Port Sudan
Nouakchott
MALI
Timbuktu
NIGER
Bodélé Depression
YEMEN
C. Verde
Senegal
Niger
Khartoum
Asmara
ARAB REP.
PEOP. DEM. REP. YEMEN
Dakar
SENEGAL
CHAD
SUDAN
GAMBIA
L. Chad
El Fasher
El Obeid
Ras Dashan 15,157
Banjul
Bamako
Niamey
Blue Nile
TERR. OF AFARS & ISSAS
Gulf of Aden
C. Guardafui
PORT. GUINEA
Bissau
UPPER VOLTA
Ouagadougou
Kano
N'Djamena
White Nile
Djibouti
GUINEA
Ethiopian Highlands
Conakry
GHANA
TOGO
DAHOMEY
NIGERIA
Addis Ababa
Freetown
IVORY COAST
Benue
Sarh
ETHIOPIA
SIERRA LEONE
Bouaké
L. Volta
Ibadan
Sudd
Monrovia
Kumasi
Porto Novo
Lagos
CENTRAL AFRICAN REPUBLIC
Wabi Shebelle
LIBERIA
Abidjan
Accra
Lomé
CAMEROON
Bangui
Ubangi
Bomu
Juba
C. Palmas
Malabo
Cameroon 13,350
Yaoundé
Uele
L. Rudolf
SOMALIA
Macias Nguema I.
Gulf of Guinea
EQUAT. GUINEA
Congo
Lake Albert
UGANDA
KENYA
Mogadishu
Principe (Port.)
Libreville
Kisangani
Stanley Falls
Margherita 16,795
Kampala
Kenya 17,058
Equator
São Tomé (Port.)
C. Lopez
GABON
Mbandaka
L. Victoria
Nairobi
Pagalu (Equat. Guinea)
CONGO
ZAIRE
RWANDA
Kigali
Bukavu
BURUNDI
Bujumbura
Kilimanjaro 19,340
Lualaba
Brazzaville
Kinshasa
Mombasa
Pemba
TANZANIA
CABINDA (Angola)
Kananga
Lake Tanganyika
Zanzibar
Dar es Salaam
Cuanza
Kasai
Ascension (St. Helena)
Luanda
Malange
Katanga
Lake Mweru
C. Delgado
COMORO ISLANDS (Fr.)
C. Amber
ATLANTIC
Lubumbashi
Ruvuma
ANGOLA
Nova Lisboa
Kitwe
MALAWI
Lake Nyasa
ZAMBIA
Cubango
Cunene
Lusaka
Zambezi
Zomba
Mozambique Channel
MALAGASY REP.
St. Helena (U.K.)
Nampula
C. Fria
Livingstone
Kariba Lake
Salisbury
Victoria Falls
MOZAMBIQUE (Port.)
Etosha Pan
RHODESIA
Tamatave
Namib Desert
Bulawayo
Beira
Tananarive
Makgadikgadi Salt Pan
SOUTH-WEST AFRICA
Madagascar
Windhoek
BOTSWANA
OCEAN
Walvis Bay (S. Afr.)
Kalahari Desert
Limpopo
Tropic of Capricorn
Gaborone
Pretoria
Lourenço Marques
C. Ste-Marie
Johannesburg
Mbabane
SWAZILAND
Vaal
SOUTH AFRICA
Orange
LESOTHO
Maseru
Drakensberg
Durban
INDIAN OCEAN
Great Karoo
East London
Cape Town
C. of Good Hope
C. Agulhas
Port Elizabeth
© HAMMOND INCORPORATED, Maplewood, N.J.
Longitude 10° West of Greenwich
Longitude 10° East of Greenwich

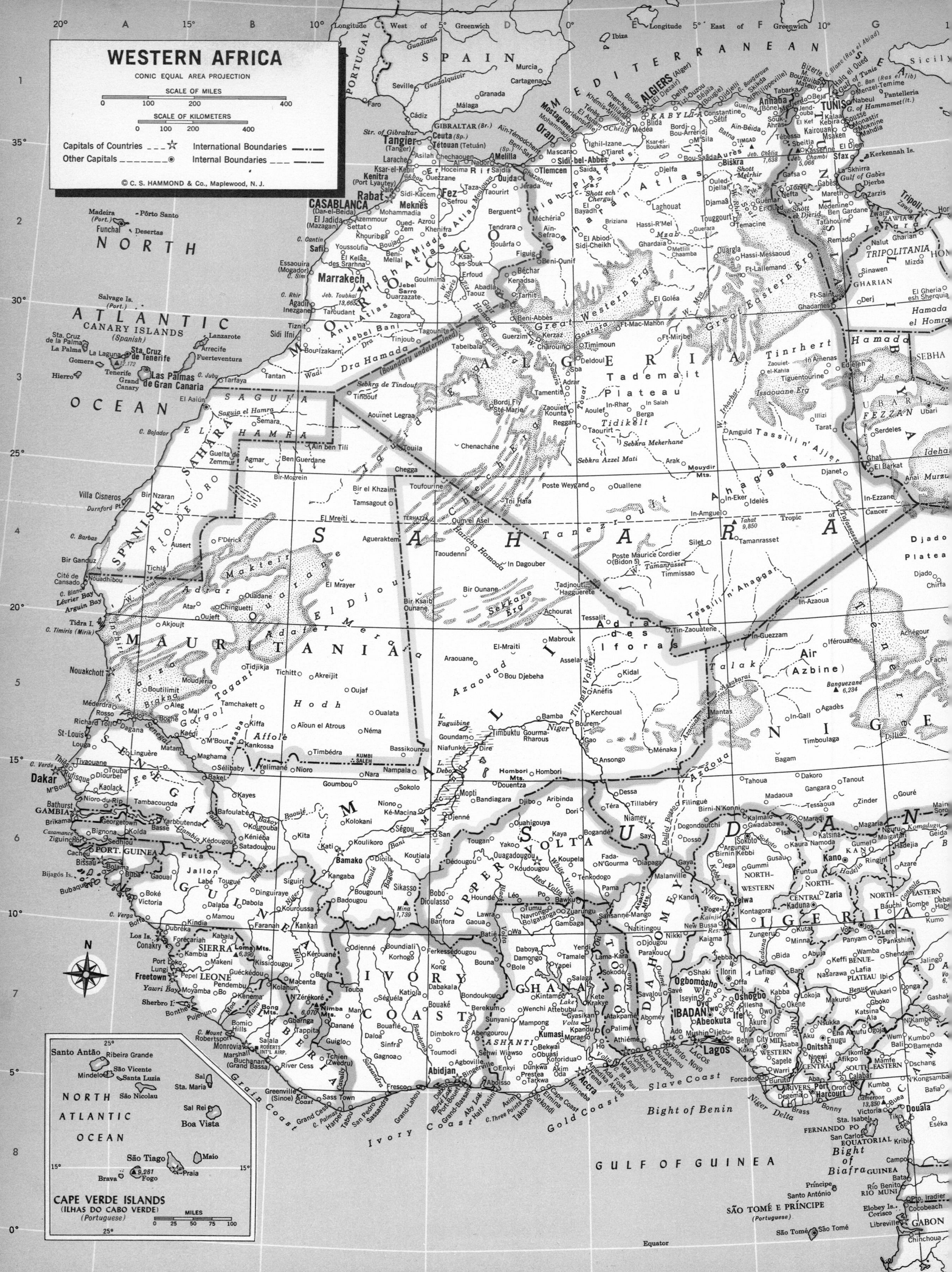

WESTERN AFRICA
CONIC EQUAL AREA PROJECTION
SCALE OF MILES
0 100 200 400
SCALE OF KILOMETERS
0 100 200 400
Capitals of Countries
Other Capitals
International Boundaries
Internal Boundaries
© C. S. HAMMOND & Co., Maplewood, N. J.
Longitude West of Greenwich
Longitude East of Greenwich
MEDITERRANEAN
SPAIN
PORTUGAL
NORTH ATLANTIC OCEAN
MOROCCO
ALGERIA
SAHARA
SPANISH SAHARA
MAURITANIA
MALI
NIGER
SENEGAL
GAMBIA
PORT. GUINEA
GUINEA
SIERRA LEONE
LIBERIA
IVORY COAST
UPPER VOLTA
GHANA
TOGO
DAHOMEY
NIGERIA
TUNISIA
LIBYA
TRIPOLITANIA
FEZZAN
CANARY ISLANDS (Spanish)
Madeira (Port.)
GULF OF GUINEA
Bight of Benin
Bight of Biafra
Gold Coast
Ivory Coast
Slave Coast
Grain Coast
Niger Delta
Tropic of Cancer
Equator
FERNANDO PO
EQUATORIAL GUINEA
RIO MUNI
GABON
SÃO TOMÉ E PRÍNCIPE (Portuguese)
CAPE VERDE ISLANDS (ILHAS DO CABO VERDE) (Portuguese)
Santo Antão
Ribeira Grande
São Vicente
Mindelo
Santa Luzia
São Nicolau
Sal
Sta. Maria
Sal Rei
Boa Vista
São Tiago
Maio
Praia
Fogo
Brava
NORTH ATLANTIC OCEAN
MILES
0 25 50 75 100
Algiers
Tunis
Tripoli
Rabat
Casablanca
Marrakech
Fez
Tangier
Oran
Dakar
Bathurst
Conakry
Freetown
Monrovia
Abidjan
Accra
Lomé
Porto-Novo
Lagos
Ibadan
Kano
Niamey
Ouagadougou
Bamako
Timbuktu
Nouakchott
Douala
Libreville

ALGERIA
AREA 919,595 sq. mi.
POPULATION 13,547,000
CAPITAL Algiers
LARGEST CITY Algiers
HIGHEST POINT Tahat 9,850 ft.
MONETARY UNIT Algerian franc
MAJOR LANGUAGES Arabic, Berber, French
MAJOR RELIGION Islam

DAHOMEY
AREA 44,290 sq. mi.
POPULATION 2,640,000
CAPITAL Porto-Novo
LARGEST CITY Cotonou
HIGHEST POINT Atakora Mts. 2,083 ft.
MONETARY UNIT CFA franc
MAJOR LANGUAGES Fon, Somba, Yoruba, Bariba, French
MAJOR RELIGIONS Tribal religions, Islam, Roman Catholicism

GAMBIA
AREA 4,003 sq. mi.
POPULATION 357,000
CAPITAL Bathurst
LARGEST CITY Bathurst
HIGHEST POINT 100 ft.
MONETARY UNIT West African pound
MAJOR LANGUAGES Mandingo, Fulani, Wolof, English
MAJOR RELIGIONS Islam, Tribal religions, Christianity

GHANA
AREA 91,843 sq. mi.
POPULATION 8,545,561
CAPITAL Accra
LARGEST CITY Accra
HIGHEST POINT Togo Hills 2,900 ft.
MONETARY UNIT cedi
MAJOR LANGUAGES Twi, Fante, Dagomba, Ewe, Ga, English
MAJOR RELIGIONS Tribal religions, Christianity

GUINEA
AREA 94,925 sq. mi.
POPULATION 3,890,000
CAPITAL Conakry
LARGEST CITY Conakry
HIGHEST POINT Nimba Mts. 6,070 ft.
MONETARY UNIT Guinean franc
MAJOR LANGUAGES Fulani, Mandingo, Susu, French
MAJOR RELIGIONS Islam, Tribal religions

IVORY COAST
AREA 124,503 sq. mi.
POPULATION 4,800,000
CAPITAL Abidjan
LARGEST CITY Abidjan
HIGHEST POINT Nimba Mts. 5,745 ft.
MONETARY UNIT CFA franc
MAJOR LANGUAGES Bale, Bete, Senufu, French
MAJOR RELIGIONS Tribal religions, Islam

LIBERIA
AREA 43,000 sq. mi.
POPULATION 1,200,000
CAPITAL Monrovia
LARGEST CITY Monrovia
HIGHEST POINT Wutivi 5,584 ft.
MONETARY UNIT Liberian dollar
MAJOR LANGUAGES Kru, Kpelle, Bassa, Vai, English
MAJOR RELIGIONS Christianity, Tribal religions

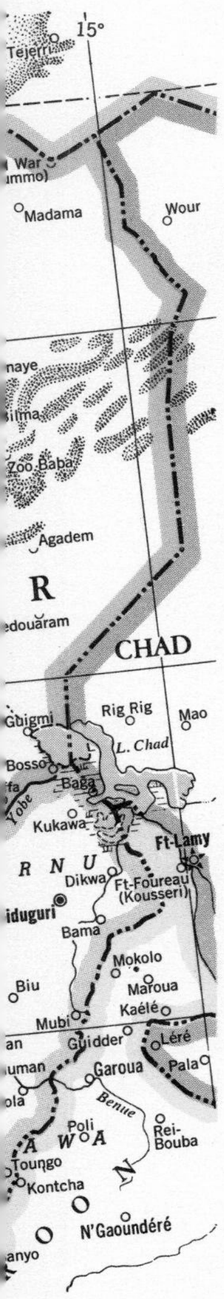

MALI
AREA 463,948 sq. mi.
POPULATION 4,929,000
CAPITAL Bamako
LARGEST CITY Bamako
HIGHEST POINT Hombori Mts. 3,789 ft.
MONETARY UNIT Malian franc
MAJOR LANGUAGES Bambara, Senufu, Fulani, Soninke, French
MAJOR RELIGIONS Islam, Tribal religions

MAURITANIA
AREA 397,954 sq. mi.
POPULATION 1,140,000
CAPITAL Nouakchott
LARGEST CITY Nouakchott
HIGHEST POINT 2,972 ft.
MONETARY UNIT CFA franc
MAJOR LANGUAGES Arabic, French, Wolof
MAJOR RELIGION Islam

MOROCCO
AREA 172,413 sq. mi.
POPULATION 15,577,000
CAPITAL Rabat
LARGEST CITY Casablanca
HIGHEST POINT Jeb. Toubkal 13,665 ft.
MONETARY UNIT dirham
MAJOR LANGUAGES Arabic, Berber, French
MAJOR RELIGIONS Islam, Judaism

NIGER
AREA 489,189 sq. mi
POPULATION 4,016,000
CAPITAL Niamey
LARGEST CITY Niamey
HIGHEST POINT Banguezane 6,234 ft.
MONETARY UNIT CFA franc
MAJOR LANGUAGES Hausa, Songhai, Fulani, French
MAJOR RELIGIONS Islam, Tribal religions

NIGERIA
AREA 356,669 sq. mi.
POPULATION 66,174,000
CAPITAL Lagos
LARGEST CITY Lagos
HIGHEST POINT Vogel 6,700 ft.
MONETARY UNIT naira
MAJOR LANGUAGES Hausa, Yoruba, Ibo, Fulani, Tiv, Kanuri, Ibibio, English
MAJOR RELIGIONS Islam, Christianity

PORTUGUESE GUINEA
AREA 13,948 sq. mi.
POPULATION 530,000
CAPITAL Bissau
LARGEST CITY Bissau
HIGHEST POINT 689 ft.
MONETARY UNIT Portuguese escudo
MAJOR LANGUAGES Balante, Fulani, Mandjako, Mandingo, Portuguese
MAJOR RELIGIONS Islam, Tribal religions, Roman Catholicism

SENEGAL
AREA 75,750 sq. mi.
POPULATION 3,780,000
CAPITAL Dakar
LARGEST CITY Dakar
HIGHEST POINT Futa Jallon 1,640 ft.
MONETARY UNIT CFA franc
MAJOR LANGUAGES Wolof, Fulani, Serer, French
MAJOR RELIGIONS Islam, Tribal religions, Roman Catholicism

SIERRA LEONE
AREA 27,925 sq. mi.
POPULATION 2,512,000
CAPITAL Freetown
LARGEST CITY Freetown
HIGHEST POINT Loma Mts. 6,390 ft.
MONETARY UNIT leone
MAJOR LANGUAGES Mende, Temne, Vai, English
MAJOR RELIGIONS Tribal religions, Islam, Christianity

SPANISH SAHARA
AREA 102,702 sq. mi.
POPULATION 63,000
CAPITAL El Aaiún
LARGEST CITY El Aaiún
HIGHEST POINT 2,700 ft.
MONETARY UNIT Spanish peseta
MAJOR LANGUAGES Arabic, Spanish
MAJOR RELIGION Islam

TOGO
AREA 21,853 sq. mi.
POPULATION 2,004,711
CAPITAL Lomé
LARGEST CITY Lomé
HIGHEST POINT Agou 3,445 ft.
MONETARY UNIT CFA franc
MAJOR LANGUAGES Ewe, Kabre, Gurma, French
MAJOR RELIGIONS Tribal religions, Roman Catholicism, Islam

TUNISIA
AREA 63,378 sq. mi.
POPULATION 5,027,000
CAPITAL Tunis
LARGEST CITY Tunis
HIGHEST POINT Jeb. Chambi 5,066 ft.
MONETARY UNIT Tunisian dinar
MAJOR LANGUAGES Arabic, French
MAJOR RELIGION Islam

UPPER VOLTA
AREA 105,841 sq. mi.
POPULATION 5,330,000
CAPITAL Ouagadougou
LARGEST CITY Ouagadougou
HIGHEST POINT 2,352 ft.
MONETARY UNIT CFA franc
MAJOR LANGUAGES Mossi, Lobi, Fulani, Bobo, French
MAJOR RELIGIONS Islam, Tribal religions, Roman Catholicism

CAPE VERDE ISLANDS
AREA 1,557 sq. mi.
POPULATION 250,000
CAPITAL Praia

SÃO TOMÉ E PRÍNCIPE
AREA 372 sq. mi.
POPULATION 66,000
CAPITAL São Tomé

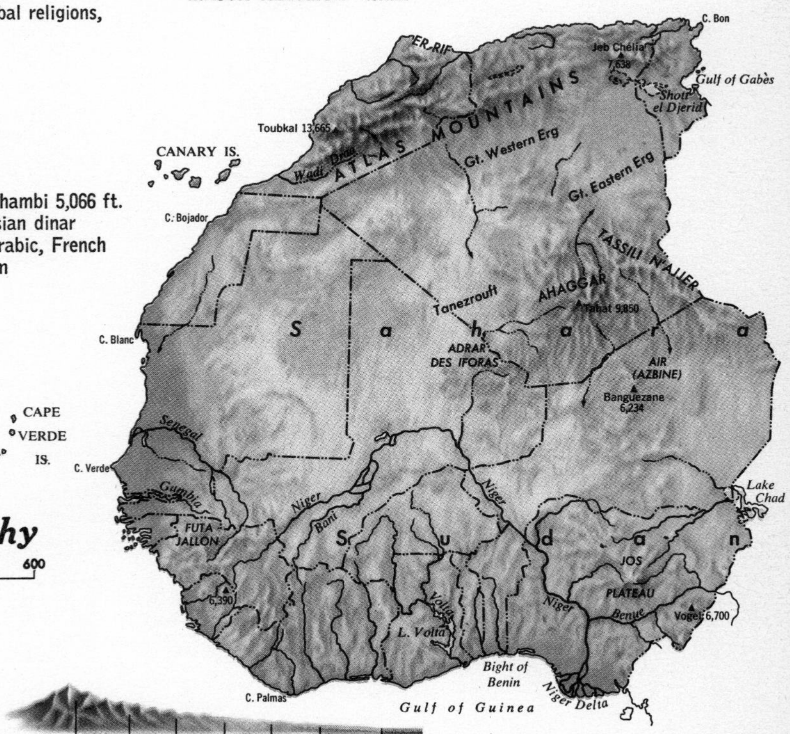

Topography

0 200 400 600 MILES

(continued on following page)

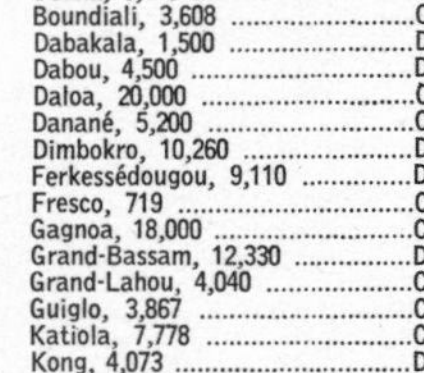

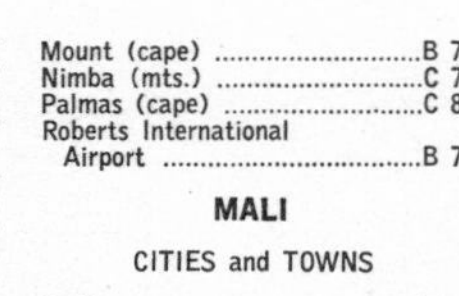

ALGERIA DAHOMEY GAMBIA GHANA

GUINEA IVORY COAST LIBERIA MALI

MAURITANIA MOROCCO NIGER

NIGERIA SENEGAL SIERRA LEONE

TOGO TUNISIA UPPER VOLTA

ALGERIA

CITIES and TOWNS

Abadla, 7,288 ..... D 2
Adrar, 13,332 ..... D 3
Aïn-Béïda, 30,757 ..... F 1
Aïn-Sefra, 16,818 ..... D 2
Aïn-Témouchent, 33,481 ..... D 1
Algiers (cap.), 943,142 ..... E 1
Algiers, *1,800,000 ..... E 1
Amguid ..... F 3
Annaba, 152,006 ..... F 1
Annaba, *223,000 ..... F 1
Aoulef, 11,285 ..... E 3
Arak ..... E 3
Batna, 69,090 ..... F 1
Béchar, 46,505 ..... D 2
Béjaïa, 64,876 ..... F 1
Beni-Abbès, 3,943 ..... D 2
Beni-Ounif, 5,271 ..... D 2
Beni-Saf, 23,368 ..... D 1
Berga ..... E 3
Bidon 5 (Poste Maurice Cordier) ..... E 4
Biskra, 59,275 ..... F 2
Blida, 99,238 ..... E 1
Bordj-Bou-Arréridj, 43,494 ..... E 1
Bordj Fly Sainte-Marie ..... D 3
Boufarik, 33,881 ..... E 1
Bougie (Béjaïa), 64,876 ..... F 1
Bou-Saâda, 26,262 ..... E 1
Briziana, 7,498 ..... E 2
Charouïn ..... D 3
Cherchell, 27,464 ..... E 1
Constantine, 243,558 ..... F 1
Deldoul ..... F 3
Dellys, 23,718 ..... E 1
Djamaâ, 25,925 ..... F 2
Djanet ..... F 4
Djelfa, 30,304 ..... E 2
Djidjelli, 35,371 ..... F 1
Edjeleh ..... F 3
El Abiod-Sidi-Cheikh, 10,512 ..... E 2
El Asnam, 69,745 ..... E 1
El Bayadh, 24,770 ..... E 2
El Djezair (Algiers) (cap.), 943,142 ..... E 1
El Goléa, 16,679 ..... E 2
El Oued, 43,547 ..... F 2
Fort-Lallemand ..... F 2
Fort-Mac-Mahon ..... E 3
Fort-Miribel ..... E 3
Ghardaïa, 46,609 ..... E 2
Ghazaouet, 20,785 ..... D 2
Guelma, 39,817 ..... F 1
Guémar, 20,394 ..... F 2
Guerara, 14,173 ..... E 2
Guerzim ..... D 3
Hassi-Messaoud ..... F 2
Hassi-R'Mel ..... E 2
Idelès ..... F 4
Ighil-Izane, 43,547 ..... E 1
Igli, 2,912 ..... D 2
Illizi, 4,000 ..... F 3
In-Amenas ..... F 3
In-Amguel ..... E 4
In-Eker ..... F 4
In-Rhar ..... E 3
In Salah, 12,645 ..... E 3
Kenadsa, 7,258 ..... D 2
Kerzaz, 2,492 ..... D 3
Khémis-Miliana, 36,530 ..... E 1
Ksar-el-Boukhari, 30,338 ..... E 1
Laghouat, 38,166 ..... E 2
Mascara, 43,108 ..... D 1
Méchéria, 12,151 ..... D 2
Médéa, 53,567 ..... E 1
Metlili Chaamba, 17,999 ..... E 2
Miliana, 28,410 ..... E 1
Mohammadia, 38,441 ..... D 1
Mostaganem, 75,332 ..... D 1
M'Sila, 36,930 ..... E 1
Oran, 327,493 ..... D 1
Oran, *393,000 ..... D 1
Ouallene ..... E 4
Ouargla, 48,323 ..... F 2
Ouled-Djellal, 14,597 ..... F 2
Philippeville (Skikda), 72,742 ..... F 1
Poste Maurice Cordier ..... E 4
Poste Weygand ..... D 4
Reggan, 11,075 ..... D 3
Saïda, 38,348 ..... E 2
Sba ..... D 3
Sétif, 98,337 ..... F 1
Sidi-bel-Abbès, 91,527 ..... D 1
Silet ..... E 4
Skikda, 72,742 ..... F 1
Souk-Ahras, 42,680 ..... F 1
Tabelbala, 1,972 ..... D 3
Tamanrasset, 16,298 ..... F 4
Tamentit ..... D 3
Taourirt ..... E 3
Tarat ..... F 3
Tarhit ..... D 2
Tébessa, 46,148 ..... F 1
Temacine ..... F 2
Ténès, 22,881 ..... E 1
Tiaret, 40,934 ..... E 1
Tiguentourine ..... F 3
Timimoun, 15,349 ..... E 3
Tindouf, 3,414 ..... C 3
Tizi-Ouzou, 53,546 ..... E 1
Tlemcen, 87,210 ..... D 2
Touggourt, 50,159 ..... F 2
Zaouiet-el-Kahla, 1,080 ..... F 3
Zaouïet-Kounta, 11,455 ..... D 3

OTHER FEATURES

Adrar des Iforas (plat.) ..... E 4
Ahaggar (range) ..... F 4
Aouïnet Legraa (well) ..... C 3
Atlas (mts.) ..... E 2
Aurés (mts.) ..... F 1
Azzel Mati, Sebkra (lake) ..... E 3
Bougaroun (cape) ..... F 1
Chech Erg (des.) ..... D 3
Chélia (mt.) ..... F 1
Chéliff (riv.) ..... E 1
Chenachane (well) ..... D 3
Chergui, Shott Ech (salt lake) ..... E 2
Gourara (oasis), 28,893 ..... E 3
Great Eastern Erg (des.) ..... F 2
Great Western Erg (des.) ..... E 2
High Plateaus (ranges) ..... D 2
Iguidi Erg (des.) ..... C 3
In-Ezzane (well) ..... G 4
In-Guezzam (well) ..... F 5
Irharhar, Wadi (dry riv.) ..... F 3
Issaouane Erg (des.) ..... F 3
Kabylia (reg.) ..... E 1
Medjerda (riv.) ..... F 1
Mekerhane, Sebkra (salt lake) ..... E 3
Melrhir, Shott (salt lake) ..... F 2
Mouydir (mts.) ..... E 3
Mya, Wadi (dry riv.) ..... E 2
Mzab (oasis), 52,500 ..... E 2
Raoui Erg (des.) ..... D 3
Rhir, Wadi (dry riv.) ..... F 2
Sahara (des.) ..... E 4
Saharan Atlas (mts.) ..... E 2
Saoura, Wadi (dry riv.) ..... D 3
Souf (oasis), 92,014 ..... F 2
Tademait (plat.) ..... E 3
Tahat (mt.) ..... F 4
Tamanrasset, Wadi (dry river) ..... E 4
Tanezrouft (des.) ..... E 4
Tassili n'Ahaggar (plat.) ..... E 4
Tassili n'Ajjer (plat.) ..... F 3
Tidikelt (oasis), 17,280 ..... E 3
Timgad (ruins) ..... F 1
Timmissao (well) ..... E 4
Tindouf, Sebkra de (salt lake) ..... C 3
Tinrhert Hamada (des.) ..... F 3
Tni Haïa (well) ..... D 4
Touat (oasis), 35,537 ..... E 3
Touila (well) ..... C 3

CAPE VERDE ISLANDS

CITIES and TOWNS

Mindelo, 7,312 ..... A 7
Praia (cap.), 3,628 ..... B 8
Ribeira Grande, †17,573 ..... B 7
Sal Rei, †3,309 ..... B 8
Santa Maria, †2,626 ..... B 8

OTHER FEATURES

Boa Vista (isl.), 3,309 ..... B 8
Brava (isl.), 8,646 ..... B 8
Fogo (isl.), 25,457 ..... B 8
Maio (isl.), 2,718 ..... B 8
Sal (isl.), 2,626 ..... B 7
Santa Luzia (isl.) ..... B 8
Santo Antão (island), 36,703 ..... A 7
São Nicolau (island), 13,894 ..... B 8
São Tiago (island), 86,835 ..... B 8
São Vicente (island), 21,361 ..... B 7

DAHOMEY

CITIES and TOWNS

Abomey, 19,000 ..... E 7
Athiémé, 1,782 ..... E 7
Cotonou, 120,000 ..... E 7
Djougou, 7,000 ..... E 7
Grand-Popo, 2,545 ..... E 7
Kandi, 5,100 ..... E 6
Malanville, 1,900 ..... E 6
Natitingou, 2,260 ..... E 6
Nikki ..... E 7
Ouidah, 18,915 ..... E 7
Parakou, 10,600 ..... E 7
Porto-Novo (cap.), 80,000 ..... E 7
Savalou, 5,000 ..... E 7
Savé, 6,262 ..... E 7

OTHER FEATURES

Atakora (mts.) ..... E 6
Benin (bight) ..... E 8
Guinea (gulf) ..... E 8
Ouémé (riv.) ..... E 7
Slave Coast (reg.) ..... E 7

GAMBIA

CITIES and TOWNS

Basse, 1,639 ..... B 6
Bathurst (cap.), 31,800 ..... A 6
Bathurst, *48,333 ..... A 6
Brikama, 4,195 ..... A 6
Georgetown, 1,592 ..... A 6

GHANA

CITIES and TOWNS

Accra (cap.), 337,828 ..... D 7
Accra, *848,825 ..... D 7
Ada Foah, 3,332 ..... E 7
Akim Oda, 19,666 ..... D 7
Amedika Akuse, 3,638 ..... E 7
Attebubu, 4,216 ..... D 7
Axim, 5,619 ..... D 8
Bawku, 12,719 ..... D 6
Bekwai, 9,093 ..... D 7
Berekum, 11,148 ..... D 7
Bole, 3,118 ..... D 7
Bolgatanga, 5,515 ..... D 6
Cape Coast, 41,230 ..... D 7
Daboya, 1,579 ..... D 7
Damongo, 6,575 ..... D 7
Dunkwa, 12,689 ..... D 7
Elmina, 8,534 ..... D 8
Enkyi, 4,007 ..... D 7
Gambaga, 2,936 ..... D 6
Gyasikan, 4,989 ..... D 7
Half Assini, 4,575 ..... D 8
Ho, 14,519 ..... E 7
Keta, 16,719 ..... E 7
Kete Krakye, 3,928 ..... E 7
Kintampo, 4,678 ..... D 7
Koforidua, 34,856 ..... D 7
Kpandu, 8,070 ..... D 7
Kumasi, 281,600 ..... D 7
Kumasi, *340,200 ..... D 7
Lawra, 3,237 ..... D 6
Mampong, 7,943 ..... D 7
Mpraeso, 5,193 ..... D 7
Navrongo, 5,274 ..... D 6
Obuasi, 22,818 ..... D 7
Prestea, 13,246 ..... D 7
Salaga, 4,199 ..... D 7
Sehwi Wiawso, 4,430 ..... D 7
Sekondi, 34,513 ..... D 8
Sekondi-Takoradi, 128,200 ..... D 8
Sekondi-Takoradi, *209,400 ..... D 8
Sunyani, 12,160 ..... D 7
Takoradi, 40,937 ..... D 8
Tamale, 40,443 ..... D 7
Tarkwa, 13,545 ..... D 7
Tema, 14,937 ..... E 7
Tumu, 2,773 ..... D 6
Wa, 14,342 ..... D 6
Wenchi, 10,672 ..... D 7
Winneba, 25,376 ..... D 7
Yapei, 515 ..... D 7
Yendi, 16,096 ..... D 7
Zuarungu, 1,278 ..... D 6

OTHER FEATURES

Ashanti (region), 1,109,133 ..... D 7
Black Volta (riv.) ..... D 6
Gold Coast (reg.) ..... D 8
Guinea (gulf) ..... E 8
Oti (riv.) ..... E 7
Saint Paul (cape) ..... E 7
Three Points (cape) ..... D 8
Volta (lake) ..... D 7
Volta (riv.) ..... E 7
White Volta (riv.) ..... D 6

GUINEA

CITIES and TOWNS

Beyla, 6,035 ..... C 7
Boffa, 1,014 ..... B 6
Boké, 6,000 ..... B 6
Conakry (capital), 43,000 ..... B 7
Conakry, *197,267 ..... B 7
Dabola, 5,600 ..... B 6
Dalaba, 5,450 ..... B 6
Dinguiraye, 2,600 ..... B 6
Dubréka, 740 ..... B 7
Faranah, 4,000 ..... B 6
Forécariah, 5,250 ..... B 7
Gaoual, 3,208 ..... B 6
Guéckédou, 1,421 ..... B 7
Kankan, 50,000 ..... C 6
Kérouané ..... C 7
Kindia, 25,000 ..... B 6
Kissidougou, 12,000 ..... B 7
Kouroussa, 6,100 ..... C 6
Labé, 11,609 ..... B 6
Macenta, 22,500 ..... C 7
Mamou, 9,000 ..... B 6
N'Zérékoré, 11,000 ..... C 7
Siguiri, 12,000 ..... C 6
Tougué, 9,810 ..... B 6
Victoria, 1,913 ..... B 6

OTHER FEATURES

Bafing (riv.) ..... B 6
Futa Jallon (mts.) ..... B 6
Los (isls.) ..... B 7
Milo (riv.) ..... C 7
Niger (riv.) ..... C 6
Nimba (mts.) ..... C 7
Verga (cape) ..... B 6

IVORY COAST

CITIES and TOWNS

Abengourou, 18,000 ..... D 7
Abidjan (capital), 180,000 ..... D 7
Abidjan, *425,000 ..... D 7
Aboisso, 3,310 ..... D 7
Agboville, 15,475 ..... D 7
Bingerville, 2,500 ..... D 7
Bondoukou, 5,216 ..... D 7
Bouaflé, 5,000 ..... C 7
Bouaké, 100,000 ..... D 7
Bouna, 3,410 ..... D 7
Boundiali, 3,608 ..... C 7
Dabakala, 1,500 ..... D 7
Dabou, 4,500 ..... D 7
Daloa, 20,000 ..... C 7
Danané, 5,200 ..... C 7
Dimbokro, 10,260 ..... D 7
Ferkessédougou, 9,110 ..... D 7
Fresco, 719 ..... C 7
Gagnoa, 18,000 ..... C 7
Grand-Bassam, 12,330 ..... D 7
Grand-Lahou, 4,040 ..... C 8
Guiglo, 3,867 ..... C 7
Katiola, 7,778 ..... C 7
Kong, 4,073 ..... D 7
Korhogo, 25,000 ..... C 7
Man, 24,000 ..... C 7
Odienné, 6,000 ..... C 7
Port-Bouet ..... D 7
San Pedro, 21 ..... C 8
Sassandra, 5,300 ..... D 7
Séguéla, 7,598 ..... C 7
Sinfra, 5,965 ..... C 7
Tabou, 3,030 ..... C 8
Touba, 1,217 ..... C 7
Toumodi, 3,000 ..... D 7

OTHER FEATURES

Aby (lag.) ..... D 8
Bandama (riv.) ..... C 7
Cavally (riv.) ..... C 7
Comoé (riv.) ..... D 7
Ebrié (lag.) ..... D 8
Ivory Coast (reg.) ..... C 8
Sassandra (riv.) ..... C 7

LIBERIA

CITIES and TOWNS

Bomi Hills, 2,441 ..... B 7
Buchanan, 11,909 ..... B 7
Gbarnga, 2,810 ..... C 7
Grand Bassa (Buchanan), 11,909 ..... B 7
Grand Cess ..... C 8
Greenville, 3,962 ..... C 8
Harper, 6,095 ..... C 8
Kolahun ..... C 7
Marshall ..... B 7
Monrovia (capital), 85,000 ..... B 7
Monrovia, *100,000 ..... B 7
River Cess ..... C 7
Robertsport, 2,417 ..... B 7
Salala ..... B 7
Sass Town ..... C 8
Sinoe (Greenville), 3,962 ..... C 8
Tappita ..... C 7
Tchien, 945 ..... C 7
Zwedru (Tchien), 945 ..... C 7

OTHER FEATURES

Bong (mts.) ..... B 7
Cavally (riv.) ..... C 7
Grain Coast (reg.) ..... B 8
Kru Coast (reg.), 21,280 ..... C 8
Mano (riv.) ..... B 7
Mount (cape) ..... B 7
Nimba (mts.) ..... C 7
Palmas (cape) ..... C 8
Roberts International Airport ..... B 7

MALI

CITIES and TOWNS

Anéfis ..... E 5
Ansongo, 1,200 ..... E 5
Araouane ..... D 5
Badougou ..... C 6
Bafoulabé, 1,300 ..... B 6
Bamako (cap.), 88,500 ..... C 6
Bamako, *182,000 ..... C 6
Bamba ..... D 5
Bandiagara, 6,700 ..... D 6
Bou Djebeha ..... D 5
Bougouni, 5,500 ..... C 6
Bourem, 2,700 ..... E 5
Dioila, 1,900 ..... C 6
Dire, 3,300 ..... D 5
Djenné, 8,200 ..... D 6
Douentza, 7,100 ..... D 6
Gao, 15,400 ..... E 5
Goumbou, 5,000 ..... C 6
Goundam, 10,000 ..... D 5
Gourma-Rharous, 2,700 ..... D 5
Hombori, 3,600 ..... D 5
Kangaba, 6,200 ..... C 6
Kati, 5,900 ..... C 6
Kayes, 23,600 ..... B 6
Ké-Macina, 3,100 ..... C 6
Kéniéba, 800 ..... B 6
Kerchoual ..... E 5
Kidal, 1,200 ..... E 5
Kita, 8,600 ..... C 6
Kolokani, 7,300 ..... C 6
Koulikoro, 10,000 ..... C 6
Kourouba, 807 ..... B 6
Koutiala, 11,300 ..... C 6
Mabrouk ..... D 5
Ménaka, 1,400 ..... E 5
Mopti, 32,000 ..... D 6
Nampala ..... C 5
Nara, 2,500 ..... C 5
Niafunké, 5,100 ..... D 5
Niono, 4,000 ..... C 6
Nioro, 11,000 ..... C 5
San, 14,900 ..... D 6
Satadougou, 180 ..... B 6
Ségou, 27,200 ..... C 6
Sikasso, 21,800 ..... C 6
Sokolo, 3,457 ..... C 6
Taoudenni ..... D 4
Tessalit ..... E 4
Timbuktu, 14,900 ..... D 5
Tin-Zaouatene ..... E 5
Yelimané, 1,700 ..... B 5

OTHER FEATURES

Achourat (well) ..... D 4
Adrar des Iforas (plat.) ..... E 4
Asselar (well) ..... D 5
Azaouad (reg.) ..... D 5
Azaouak (dry riv.) ..... E 5
Bafing (riv.) ..... B 6
Bagoé (riv.) ..... C 6
Bakoy (riv.) ..... B 6
Bani (riv.) ..... C 6
Baoulé (riv.) ..... C 6
Bir Ounane (well) ..... D 4
Chech Erg (des.) ..... D 3
Debo (lake) ..... D 5
El-Mraiti (well) ..... D 5
Faguibine (lake) ..... D 5
Falémé (riv.) ..... B 6
Haricha Hamada (des.) ..... D 4
Hombori (mts.) ..... D 5
In Dagouber (well) ..... D 4
Macina (depr.) ..... D 6
Mina (mt.) ..... C 6
Niger (riv.) ..... D 5
Oum el Asel (well) ..... D 4
Sahara (des.) ..... D 4
Sekkane (des.) ..... D 4
Tadjnout Hagguerete (well) ..... D 4
Terhazza (ruins) ..... C 4
Tilemsi (valley) ..... E 5
Toufourine (well) ..... C 4

MAURITANIA

CITIES and TOWNS

Aïoun el Atrous, 3,054 ..... C 5
Akjoujt, 2,500 ..... B 5
Akreïjit ..... C 5
Aleg, 1,000 ..... B 5
Atar, 7,120 ..... B 4
Bassikounou ..... C 5
Bir Mogrein, 1,052 ..... B 4
Boghé, 2,316 ..... B 5
Boutilimit, 3,000 ..... B 5
Chinguetti, 600 ..... B 4
Cité de Cansado ..... A 4
F'Dérick, †900 ..... B 4
Kaédi, 11,000 ..... B 5
Kankossa, †13,000 ..... B 5
Kiffa, 2,600 ..... B 5
Maghama, 3,157 ..... B 5
Mal ..... B 5
M'Bout, 1,400 ..... B 5
Méderdra, 1,473 ..... A 5
Moudjéria, 753 ..... B 5
Néma, 2,946 ..... C 5
Nouadhibou, 11,250 ..... A 4
Nouakchott (capital), 14,500 ..... A 5
Ouadane ..... B 4
Oualata, 1,285 ..... C 5
Oujaf ..... C 5
Oujeft ..... B 4
Rosso, 3,923 ..... A 5
Sélibaby, 2,600 ..... B 5
Tamchakett, 641 ..... B 5
Tamsagout ..... C 4
Tazadit ..... A 4
Tichitt, 1.000 ..... C 5
Tidjikja, 5,900 ..... B 5
Timbédra, 1,200 ..... C 5

OTHER FEATURES

Adafer (reg.) ..... B 5
Adrar (reg.), 50,920 ..... B 4
Affolé (reg.) ..... B 5
Agmar (well) ..... B 3
Agueraktem (well) ..... C 4
Aïn ben Tili (well) ..... C 3
Arguin (bay) ..... A 4
Assaba (reg.), 100,000 ..... B 5
Atoui, Wadi (dry riv.) ..... B 4
Ben Guerdane (well) ..... B 3
Bir el Khzaim (well) ..... C 4
Blanc (cape) ..... A 4
Brakna (reg.), 82,020 ..... B 5
Chegga (well) ..... C 3
Djouf, El (des.) ..... C 4
El Mrayer (well) ..... C 4
El Mreïti (well) ..... C 4
Gorgol (reg.), 54,037 ..... B 5
Hodh (reg.), 183,945 ..... C 5
Iguidi Erg (des.) ..... C 3
Inchiri (reg.), 15,443 ..... A 5
Kumbi Saleh (ruins) ..... C 5
Lévrier (bay) ..... A 4
Makteïr (des.) ..... B 4
Meraia (reg.) ..... C 5
Mirik (Timiris) (cape) ..... A 5
Ouarane (reg.) ..... B 4
Sahara (des.) ..... C 4
Senegal (riv.) ..... B 5
Tagant (reg.), 52,703 ..... B 5
Tidra (isl.) ..... A 5
Timiris (cape) ..... A 5
Touila (well) ..... C 3
Trarza (reg.), 105,737 ..... A 5

MOROCCO

CITIES and TOWNS

Agadir, 16,695 ..... C 2
Al Hoceima, 11,262 ..... D 1
Asilah, 10,839 ..... C 1
Azemmour, 12,449 ..... C 2
Azrou, 14,143 ..... C 2
Beni-Mellal, 28,933 ..... C 2
Berguent, 2,607 ..... D 2
Bouârfa, 8,775 ..... D 2
Bou-Izakarn, 661 ..... C 3
Boujad, 14,728 ..... C 2
Casablanca, 1,320,000 ..... C 2
Chechaouen, 13,712 ..... D 1
Dar-el-Beida (Casablanca), 1,320,000 ..... C 2
El Jadida, 40,302 ..... C 2
El Kelâa des Srarhna, 10,187 ..... C 2
Erfoud, 4,491 ..... D 2
Essaouira, 26,392 ..... B 2
Fédala (Mohammedia), 35,010 ..... C 2
Fez, 280,000 ..... D 2
Figuig, 12,108 ..... D 2
Goulmima, 1,804 ..... C 2
Inezgane, 6,917 ..... C 2
Jerada, 18,872 ..... D 2
Kénitra, 125,000 ..... C 2
Khenifra, 18,503 ..... C 2
Khouribga, 40,838 ..... C 2
Ksar-el-Kebir, 34,035 ..... C 2
Ksar-es-Souk, 6,554 ..... D 2
Larache, 30,763 ..... C 1

Marrakech, 295,000 C 2
Mazagan (El Jadida), 40,302 C 2
Meknès, 235,000 C 2
Mogador (Essaouira), 26,392 B 2
Mohammedia, 35,010 C 2
Nador, 17,583 D 1
Ouarzazate, 4,200 C 2
Oued-Zem, 18,640 C 2
Ouezzane, 26,203 C 2
Oujda, 150,000 D 2
Petitjean (Sidi-Kacem), 19,478 C 2
Port-Lyautey (Kénitra), 125,000 C 2
Rabat (capital), 227,445 C 2
Rabat, *435,000 C 2
Safi, 125,000 C 2
Saïdia, 1,102 D 2
Salé, 75,799 C 2
Sefrou, 21,478 D 2
Settat, 29,617 C 2
Sidi Ifni, 12,751 B 3
Sidi-Kacem, 19,478 C 2
Tagounite, 354 C 3
Tangier (Tanger), 160,000 C 1
Tantan, 2,153 B 3
Taourirt, 7,343 D 2
Taouz, 641 D 2
Tarfaya, 1,521 B 3
Taroudant, 17,141 C 2
Taza, 31,667 D 2
Tendrara, 1,563 D 2
Tétouan (Tetuán), 120,000 C 1
Tinjoub C 3
Tiznit, 7,694 B 3
Youssoufia, 8,302 C 2
Zagora, 2,200 C 2

OTHER FEATURES

Anti-Atlas (ranges) C 3
Atlas (mts.) C 2
Bani, Jebel (mts.) C 3
Cantin (cape) C 2
Dra Hamada (des.) C 3
Dra, Wadi (dry riv.) C 3
Er Rif (range) D 2
Gibraltar (str.) C 1
High Atlas (ranges) C 2
Juby (cape) B 3
Middle Atlas (ranges) C 2
Moulouya (riv.) D 2
Rhéris, Wadi (dry riv.) D 2
Rhir (cape) B 2
Rif, Er (range) D 2
Sarro, Jebel (mts.) C 2
Sebou (riv.) C 2
Sim (cape) B 2
Toubkal, Jebel (mt.) C 2
Ziz, Wadi (dry riv.) D 2

NIGER

CITIES and TOWNS

Agadès, 7,100 F 5
Bilma, 1,500 G 5
Birni-N'Konni, 7,900 E 6
Bosso, 509 G 6
Chirfa G 4
Dakoro, 2,400 F 6
Dessa E 6
Diffa, 477 G 6
Djado G 4
Dogondoutchi, 7,700 E 6
Dosso, 3,500 E 6
Fachi, 1,060 G 5
Filingué, 6,000 E 6
Gangara F 6
Gaya, 4,200 E 6
Gouré, 2,100 G 6
Iférouane F 5
In-Gall, 1,555 F 5
Madama G 4
Madaoua, 2,800 F 6
Magaria, 4,000 F 6
Mainé-Soroa, 1,500 G 6
Maradi, 22,400 F 6
N'Guigmi, 4,000 G 6
Niamey (cap.), 42,000 E 6
Niamey, *122,672 E 6
Say, 2,700 E 6
Tahoua, 18,100 F 6
Tanout, 1,600 F 6
Téra, 6,600 E 6
Tessaoua, 6,700 F 6
Tillabéry, 1,600 E 6
Zinder, 24,000 F 6

OTHER FEATURES

Achégour (well) G 5
Agadem (well) G 5
Aïr (mts.) F 5
Anaye (well) G 5
Assakarai (dry riv.) F 5
Azaoua (reg.) E 5
Azbine (Aïr) (mts.) F 5
Bagam (well) F 5
Banguezane (mt.) F 5
Bedouaram (well) G 5
Chad (lake) G 6
Dallol Bosso (dry riv.) E 6
Dillia (dry riv.) G 5
Djado (plat.) G 4
El War (well) G 4
In-Azaoua (well) F 4
Mantas (well) E 6
Niger (riv.) E 6
Sudan (reg.) E 6
Talak (reg.) E 5
Ténéré (des.) G 5
Timboulaga (well) F 5
Tummo (El War) (well) G 4
Zoo Baba (well) G 5

NIGERIA

STATES

Benue-Plateau, 4,009,408 F 7
East-Central, 6,223,831 F 7
Kano, 5,774,842 F 6
Kwara, 2,406,265 E 7
Lagos, 1,443,567 E 7
Mid-Western, 2,535,839 F 7
North-Central, 4,098,305 F 6
North-Eastern, 7,815,443 G 6
North-Western, 5,733,296 E 6
Rivers, 1,544,314 F 8
South-Eastern, 4,626,317 F 7
Western, 9,487,576 E 7

CITIES and TOWNS

Aba, 151,923 F 7
Abeokuta, 217,201 E 7
Abuja F 7
Ado, 182,673 E 7
Afikpo F 7
Aku, 20,809 F 7
Akure, 38,853 F 7
Argungu E 6
Asaba, 17,387 F 7
Azare G 6
Baga G 6
Bama G 6
Baro F 7
Bauchi F 6
Benin City, 116,774 F 7
Bida F 7
Birnin Kebbi E 6
Biu G 6
Bonny F 8
Brass F 8
Burutu, 6,784 F 7
Calabar, 46,705 F 7
Deba Habe G 6
Degema F 8
Dikwa G 6
Donga G 7
Ede, 156,036 E 7
Eha Amufu, 29,434 F 7
Enugu, 160,567 F 7
Forcados E 7
Funtua F 6
Gashaka G 7
Gboko F 7
Geidam G 6
Gombe G 6
Gumel F 6
Gummi E 6
Gusau, 40,202 F 6
Gwadabawa F 6
Hadejia G 6
Ibadan, 727,565 E 7
Ibi F 7
Ife, 150,818 E 7
Ijebu-Ode, 27,558 E 7
Ikom F 7
Ilesha, 192,302 E 7
Ilorin, 241,849 E 7
Isa F 6
Iseyin, 49,680 E 7
Iwo, 183,907 E 7
Jalingo G 7
Jebba E 7
Jega E 6
Jos, 38,527 F 7
Kabba, 7,305 F 7
Kaduna, 173,849 F 6
Kaiama E 7
Kalmalo F 6
Kano, 342,610 F 6
Katsina, 52,672 F 6
Katsina Ala F 7
Kaura Namoda F 6
Keffi F 7
Koko E 7
Kontagora F 6
Kukawa G 6
Kumo G 7
Kuta F 7
Lafia F 7
Lafiagi F 7
Lagos (cap.), 841,749 E 7
Lere F 7
Lokoja, 13,103 F 7
Maiduguri, 162,316 G 6
Maigatari F 6
Makurdi F 7
Minna F 7
Mubi G 6
Mushin, 169,287 E 7
Nasarawa F 7
New Bussa, 10,000 E 6
Nguru, 23,084 G 6
Nnewi, 28,777 F 7
Nsukka F 7
Numan G 7
Offa, 20,668 E 7
Ogbomosho, 370,963 E 7
Ogoja F 7
Okene, 32,602 F 7
Ondo, 36,233 E 7
Onitsha, 189,067 F 7
Oron F 8
Oshogbo, 242,336 E 7
Owo, 30,662 F 7
Oyo, 130,290 E 7
Pankshin F 7
Panyam F 7
Port Harcourt, 208,237 F 8
Ringim F 6
Sapele, 33,638 F 7
Shaki, 22,983 E 7
Shendam F 7
Sokoto, 47,643 F 6
Toungo G 7
Uromi, 22,339 F 7
Vom F 7
Wamba F 7
Warri, 19,526 F 7
Wukari F 7
Yan G 7
Yelwa F 6
Yola G 7
Zaria, 192,706 F 6
Zungeru F 7

OTHER FEATURES

Adamawa (reg.) G 7
Benin (bight) E 8
Benue (riv.) F 7
Biafra (bight) F 8
Bornu (reg.) G 6
Chad (lake) G 6
Cross (riv.) F 7
Donga (riv.) G 7
Foge (isl.) E 6
Gongola (riv.) G 6
Guinea (gulf) E 8
Hadejia (riv.) F 6
Kaduna (riv.) F 7
Kainji (res.) E 6
Kebbi (riv.) E 6
Komadugu Yobe (riv.) G 6
Niger (delta) F 8
Niger (riv.) F 7
Osse (riv.) E 7
Slave Coast (reg.) E 7
Sokoto (riv.) F 6
Sudan (reg.) F 6
Vogel (peak) G 7

PORTUGAL—Madeira

CITIES and TOWNS

Funchal, 43,301 A 2

OTHER FEATURES

Desertas (isls.) A 2
Madeira (island), 265,432 A 2
Madeira (islands), 268,700 A 2
Pôrto Santo (island), 3,505 A 2
Salvage (isls.) A 2

PORTUGUESE GUINEA

CITIES and TOWNS

Bissau (capital), 20,000 A 6
Bolama, †4,642 A 6
Buba B 6
Bubaque A 6
Cacheu, †70,233 A 6

OTHER FEATURES

Bijagós (isls.), 9,332 A 6

SÃO TOMÉ E PRÍNCIPE

CITIES and TOWNS

Santo António, †4,605 F 8
São Tomé (capital), 7,364 F 8

OTHER FEATURES

Príncipe (isl.), 4,605 F 8
São Tomé (isl.), 58,880 F 8

SENEGAL

CITIES and TOWNS

Bakel, 2,500 B 6
Bignona, 5,432 A 6
Dagana, 4,000 A 5
Dakar (cap.), 550,000 A 6
Dakar, *661,000 A 6
Diourbel, 30,000 A 6
Kaolack, 70,000 A 6
Kédougou, 1,938 B 6
Louga, 15,000 A 5
Matam, 5,000 B 5
M'Bour, 15,000 A 6
Nioro-du-Rip, 2,788 A 6
Podor, 5,000 B 5
Richard Toll, 894 A 5
Rufisque, 50,000 A 6
Saint-Louis, 50,000 A 5
Sedhiou, 2,419 A 6
Tambacounda, 10,027 B 6
Thiès, 70,000 A 5
Tivaouane, 8,000 A 5
Touba, 2,575 A 6
Yarboutenda B 6
Ziguinchor, 30,000 A 6

OTHER FEATURES

Casamance (riv.) A 6
Falémé (riv.) B 6
Ferlo (reg.) B 6
Gambia (riv.) B 6
Senegal (riv.) B 5
Verde (cape) A 6

SIERRA LEONE

CITIES and TOWNS

Bo, 26,613 B 7
Bonthe, 6,230 B 7
Freetown (capital), 170,600 B 7
Kabala, 4,610 B 7
Kambia, 3,700 B 7
Kenema, 13,246 B 7
Lungi, 2,170 B 7
Makeni, 12,304 B 7
Moyamba, 4,564 B 7
Pendembu, 2,696 B 7
Pepel B 7
Port Loko, 5,809 B 7
Pujehun, 2,034 B 7

OTHER FEATURES

Loma (mts.) B 7
Moa (riv.) B 7
Sherbro (isl.), 6,894 B 7
Yawri (bay) B 7

SPAIN—Canary Islands, Ceuta and Melilla

CITIES and TOWNS

Arrecife, 12,748 B 3
Ceuta, 88,000 C 1
La Laguna, 15,899 A 3
Las Palmas de Gran Canaria, 166,236 B 3
Melilla, 77,000 D 1
Santa Cruz de la Palma, 9,928 A 3
Santa Cruz de Tenerife, 82,620 A 3

OTHER FEATURES

Canary (isls.), 944,448 A 3
Fuerteventura (island), 18,138 B 3
Gomera (isl.), 27,790 A 3
Grand Canary (island), 400,837 A 3
Hierro (isl.), 7,957 A 3
Lanzarote (isl.), 34,805 B 3
La Palma (isl.), 67,141 A 3
Tenerife (isl.), 387,767 A 3

SPANISH SAHARA

CITIES and TOWNS

El Aaiún (cap.), 10,000 B 3
Semara, 1,000 B 3
Villa Cisneros, 4,000 A 4

OTHER FEATURES

Atoui, Wadi (dry riv.) B 4
Ausert (well) B 4
Barbas (cape) A 4
Bir Ganduz (well) A 4
Bir Nzaran (well) B 4
Blanc (cape) A 4
Bojador (cape) B 3
Durnford (pt.) A 4
Guelta de Zemmur (well) B 3
Río de Oro (reg.) B 4
Saguia el Hamra (dry riv.) B 3
Saguia el Hamra (region) B 3
Tichlá (well) B 4

TOGO

CITIES and TOWNS

Anécho, ‡11,040 E 7
Atakpamé, ‡18,008 E 7
Kpémé, 2,229 E 7
Lama-Kara E 7
Lomé (cap.), 90,600 E 7
Lomé, *149,879 E 7
Palimé, ‡20,331 E 7
Sansanné-Mango E 6
Sokodé, ‡30,271 E 7

OTHER FEATURES

Guinea (gulf) E 8
Mono (riv.) E 7
Oti (riv.) E 7
Slave Coast (reg.) E 7

TUNISIA

CITIES and TOWNS

Beja, 28,100 F 1
Ben Gardane, 2,138 G 2
Bizerte, 51,700 F 1
El Djem, 6,800 G 1
El Kef, 23,200 F 1
Fort-Saint F 2
Gabès, 32,300 F 2
Gafsa, 32,400 F 2
Halq el Oued, 27,500 G 1
Jendouba, 14,800 F 1
Kairouan, 46,200 F 1
Kalaa-Kebira, 16,800 F 1
Kasserine, 9,800 F 1
La Skhirra, 1,500 G 2
Mahdia, 10,900 G 1
Mareth, 153 F 2
Mateur, 15,600 F 1
Médenine, 8,000 F 2
Menzel Bourguiba, 36,700 F 1
Menzel-Temime, 12,500 G 1
Moknine, 18,500 G 1
Monastir, 16,500 G 1
Msaken, 27,500 G 1
Nabeul, 34,100 G 1
Nefta, 15,000 F 2
Remada, 1,866 F 2
Sbeitla, 4,000 F 1
Sfax, 65,000 G 2
Sousse, 48,200 G 1
Tabarka, 356 F 1
Tatahouine, 3,100 G 2
Tozeur, 11,820 F 2
Tunis (cap.), 662,000 G 1
Tunis, *800,000 G 1
Zarzis, 30,080 G 2

OTHER FEATURES

Abiad, Ras el (Blanc) (cape) G 1
Blanc (cape) G 1
Bon (cape) G 1
Chambi, Jebel (mt.) F 2
Djerba (isl.), 62,445 G 2
Djerid, Shott el (salt lake) F 2
Gabès (gulf) G 2
Hammamet (gulf) G 1
Jefara (reg.) G 2
Kerkennah (isls.), 13,704 G 2
Merjerda (riv.) F 1
Tib, Ras el (Bon) (cape) G 1
Tunis (gulf) G 1

UPPER VOLTA

CITIES and TOWNS

Aribinda, 3,150 D 6
Banfora, 4,511 D 6
Batié, 1,335 D 6
Bobo-Dioulasso, 56,100 D 6
Bogandé, 3,125 E 6
Dédougou, 3,680 D 6
Diapaga, 3,050 E 6
Djibo D 6
Dori, 3,500 D 6
Fada-N'Gourma, 4,867 E 6
Gaoua, 5,907 D 6
Houndé, 1,153 D 6
Kaya, 10,304 D 6
Koudougou, 7,940 D 6
Koupela, 3,800 D 6
Léo, 2,139 D 6
Ouagadougou (capital), 77,500 D 6
Ouagadougou, *100,000 D 6
Ouahigouya, 12,960 D 6
Pama, 1,411 E 6
Po, 4,000 D 6
Tenkodogo, 6,561 E 6
Tougan, 5,000 D 6
Yako, 5,110 D 6

OTHER FEATURES

Black Volta (riv.) D 6
Red Volta (riv.) D 6
Sudan (reg.) E 6
White Volta (riv.) D 6

*City and suburbs.
†Population of sub-district or division.
‡Population of commune

Agriculture, Industry and Resources

DOMINANT LAND USE

- Cereals, Horticulture, Livestock
- Market Gardening, Diversified Tropical Crops
- Plantation Agriculture
- Oases
- Pasture Livestock
- Nomadic Livestock Herding
- Forests
- Nonagricultural Land

MAJOR MINERAL OCCURRENCES

Al	Bauxite	Gp	Gypsum
Au	Gold	Mn	Manganese
C	Coal	Na	Salt
Co	Cobalt	O	Petroleum
Cr	Chromium	P	Phosphates
Cu	Copper	Pb	Lead
D	Diamonds	Sb	Antimony
Fe	Iron Ore	Sn	Tin
G	Natural Gas	Ti	Titanium
Gn	Granite	Zn	Zinc

Water Power
Major Industrial Areas

CASABLANCA
Textiles, Food & Tobacco, Iron & Steel, Machinery, Chemicals, Oil Refining

ALGIERS
Food & Tobacco, Iron & Steel, Machinery, Chemicals, Rubber, Oil Refining

TUNIS
Machinery, Chemicals, Canning, Consumer Products

DAKAR
Chemicals, Food Processing, Textiles, Shoes

KANO
Textiles, Chemicals, Shoes, Light Industry

IBADAN
Food Processing, Chemicals, Rubber

ABIDJAN
Consumer Products, Vehicle Assembly, Oil Refining

ACCRA–TEMA
Vehicle Assembly, Food Processing, Oil Refining, Chemicals

LAGOS
Machinery, Chemicals, Brewing

PORT HARCOURT
Chemicals, Tobacco, Light Industry, Oil Refining, Tires

LIBYA
EGYPT
CHAD
MEDITERRANEAN SEA
Longitude East of Greenwich
Crete (Greece)
CYPRUS
SOVEREIGN BASE AREA (British)
SYRIA
Damascus
Beirut
LEBANON
Haifa
ISRAEL
Tel Aviv-Jaffa
Jerusalem
Amman
JORDAN
Syrian Desert
Dead Sea
TUNISIA
Gabès
Djerba
Zarzis
Médenine
Tripoli
Homs
Misurata
TRIPOLITANIA
GHARIAN
HOMS
MISURATA
Gulf of Sidra
BAIDA
Benghazi
Derna
Tobruk
G. of Bomba
CYRENAICA
DERNA
Bir Hakeim
El Bardi
G. of Salûm
Salûm
Sidi Barrani
Matrûh
ALEXANDRIA (El Iskandarîya)
Rosetta (Rashîd)
Damietta (Dumyât)
Port Said (Bur Sa'îd)
Suez Canal
Ismailia
Suez (Occ. by Israel)
Tanta
Giza
CAIRO (El Qâhira)
Sinai Pen.
Gulf of Aqaba
Aqaba
Hamada el Homra
Libyan Plateau
Qattara Depression
Great Sand Sea
Calansho Sand Sea
SEBHA
FEZZAN
LIBYA
BENGHAZI
Serir Calansho
Jalo Oasis
Siwa Oasis
Bahariya Oasis
Farâfra Oasis
EGYPT
Dakhla Oasis
Khârga Oasis
Kufra Oasis
Rebiana Sand Sea
Gilf Kebir Plat.
Arabian (Eastern) Desert
El Faiyûm
Beni Suef
El Minya
Asyût
Sohâg
Qena
Luxor
Aswân
ASWÂN HIGH DAM
Lake Nasser
RED SEA
Hurghada
Port Safâga
El Quseir
Medina
Yenbo
Jidda
Ras Banâs
Foul Bay
Berenice
Halaib
Ras Hadarba
Marsa Oseif
Dungunab
Port Sudan
Suakin
Tokar
SAHARA
Serir Tibesti
Djado Plateau
NIGER
Ténéré
Bilma
Tibesti
Emi Koussi 11,204
Bette Pk. 7,500
Jebel Uweinat 6,255
Selima Oasis
NORTHERN
Nubian Desert
Jef Jef Plateau
BORKU
Largeau (Faya)
Bodélé Depression
Mourdi Depression
Ennedi
CHAD
KANEM
L. Chad
BORNU
Maiduguri
Ft-Lamy
WADAI
Abécher
BAGUIRMI
SUDAN
DAR FUR
El Fasher
Jebel Marra 10,073
KORDOFAN
El Obeid
Nuba Mts.
3rd Cataract
4th Cataract
5th Cataract
6th Cataract
Dongola
Atbara
Berber
Shendi
Omdurman
Khartoum
Khartoum North
Kassala
Wad Medani
Gezira
BLUE NILE
White Nile
Blue Nile
UPPER NILE
BAHR EL GHAZAL
EQUATORIA
Wau
Malakal
Juba
Sudd
ETHIOPIA
Asmara
GOJJAM
BEGEMDIR & SIMEN
WALLAGA
ILUBABOR
KAFFA
GAMU GOFA
SHOA
CAMEROON
NIGERIA NORTH-EASTERN
ADAMAWA
CENTRAL AFRICAN REPUBLIC
Bangui
Ft-Archambault
Moundou
HAUT-ZAIRE
ZAIRE
REP. OF CONGO
EQUATEUR
UGANDA
GARAMBA NAT'L PARK
KENYA
L. Rudolf

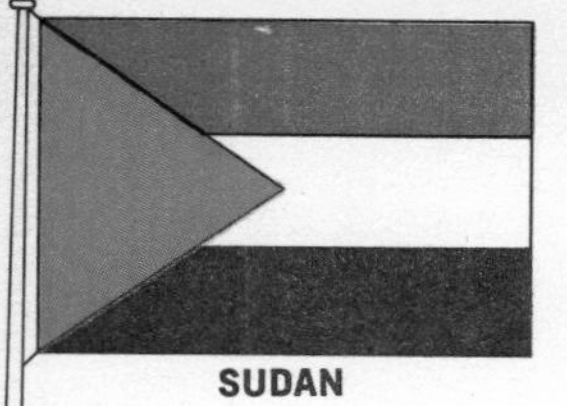

SUDAN

ETHIOPIA

LIBYA

AREA 679,359 sq. mi.
POPULATION 1,900,000
CAPITAL Tripoli
LARGEST CITY Tripoli
HIGHEST POINT Bette Pk. 7,500 ft.
MONETARY UNIT Libyan dinar
MAJOR LANGUAGES Arabic, Berber
MAJOR RELIGION Islam

TERRITORY OF THE AFARS AND ISSAS

AREA 8,498 sq. mi.
POPULATION 125,050
CAPITAL Djibouti

EGYPT

AREA 386,100 sq. mi.
POPULATION 33,329,000
CAPITAL Cairo
LARGEST CITY Cairo
HIGHEST POINT Jeb. Katherina 8,651 ft.
MONETARY UNIT Egyptian pound
MAJOR LANGUAGE Arabic
MAJOR RELIGIONS Islam, Christianity

CHAD

AREA 495,753 sq. mi.
POPULATION 3,510,000
CAPITAL Fort-Lamy
LARGEST CITY Fort-Lamy
HIGHEST POINT Emi Koussi 11,204 ft.
MONETARY UNIT CFA franc
MAJOR LANGUAGES Arabic, Bagirmi, French
MAJOR RELIGIONS Islam, Tribal religions

SUDAN

AREA 967,495 sq. mi.
POPULATION 15,312,000
CAPITAL Khartoum
LARGEST CITY Omdurman
HIGHEST POINT Jeb. Marra 10,073 ft.
MONETARY UNIT Sudanese pound
MAJOR LANGUAGES Arabic, Dinka, Nubian, Beja, Nuer
MAJOR RELIGIONS Islam, Tribal religions

ETHIOPIA

AREA 471,776 sq. mi.
POPULATION 24,764,000
CAPITAL Addis Ababa
LARGEST CITY Addis Ababa
HIGHEST POINT Ras Dashan 15,157 ft.
MONETARY UNIT Ethiopian dollar
MAJOR LANGUAGES Amharic, Galla, Tigrinya, Somali, Sidamo
MAJOR RELIGIONS Coptic Christianity, Islam

AFARS & ISSAS, TERR.

CITIES and TOWNS

Ali Sabieh, 2,000 ....H 5
Dikhil, 1,000 ....H 5
Djibouti (capital), 41,200 ....H 5
Djibouti, *61,500 ....H 5
Obock, 582 ....H 5
Tadjoura, 2,000 ....H 5

OTHER FEATURES

Abbe (lake) ....H 5
Aden (gulf) ....J 5
Bab el Mandeb (str.) ....H 5

CHAD

CITIES and TOWNS

Abécher, 19,650 ....D 5
Abou Deia, 1,100 ....C 5
Adré ....D 5
Ain-Galakka ....C 4
Am-Dam, 1,002 ....D 5
Am-Timan, 1,500 ....D 5
Aozi ....C 3
Aozou ....C 3
Arada ....D 4
Ati, 6,000 ....C 5
Baibokoum, 3,138 ....C 6
Bardaı, 800 ....C 3
Biltine, 4,000 ....D 5
Bokoro, 4,700 ....C 5
Bol, 1,500 ....B 5
Bongor, 11,000 ....C 5
Bousso, 1,800 ....C 5
Doba, 7,375 ....C 6
Fada, 1,500 ....D 4
Faya (Largeau), 5,200 ....C 4
Fianga, 923 ....C 6
Fort-Archambault, 35,000 ....C 6
Fort-Lamy (capital), 132,500 ....C 5
Fort-Lamy, *91,688 ....C 5
Goré ....C 6
Gouro ....C 4
Ham ....C 5
Kélo, 6,067 ....C 6
Koro Toro ....C 4
Koumra, 6,351 ....C 6
Kouno ....C 6
Kyabé, 3,000 ....C 6
Lai, 8,000 ....C 6
Largeau, 5,200 ....C 4
Léré, 3,500 ....B 6
Madadi ....D 4
Mangueigne, 1,700 ....D 5
Mao ....C 5
Massakori, 2,000 ....C 5
Massénya, 1,700 ....C 5
Melfi, 3,000 ....C 5
Mogororo ....D 5
Moissala, 3,000 ....C 6
Mongo, 7,000 ....C 5
Moundou, 34,100 ....C 6
Moussoro ....C 5
Oum Chalouba ....D 4
Oum Hadjer, 4,500 ....D 5
Ounianga-Kébir ....D 4
Pala, 4,200 ....B 6
Rig Rig, 286 ....B 5
Wour ....C 3
Yarda ....C 4
Ziguei ....C 5
Zouar ....C 3

OTHER FEATURES

Baguirmi (region), 81,666 ....C 5
Bahr el'Ghazaı (dry riv.) ....C 5
Batha (riv.) ....C 5
Bodélé (depr.) ....C 4
Borku (region), 21,962 ....C 4
Chad (lake) ....C 5
Domar (dry riv.) ....C 4
Emi Koussi (mt.) ....C 4
Ennedi (plat.) ....D 4
Fittri (lake) ....C 5
Haouach, Wadi (dry riv.) ....C 4
Jef Jef (plat.) ....D 3
Kanem (region), 261,108 ....C 5
Logone (riv.) ....C 5
Maro (dry riv.) ....C 4
Mbéré (riv.) ....C 6
Mourdi (depr.) ....D 4
Pendé (riv.) ....C 6
Sahara (des.) ....C 3
Salamat (riv.) ....C 6
Sara (riv.) ....C 6
Shari (riv.) ....C 5
Sudan (reg.) ....C 5
Tibesti (mts.) ....C 3
Wadai (region), 314,775 ....D 5

EGYPT

CITIES and TOWNS

Abnûb, 27,751 ....J 4
Abu Qurqâs, 19,318 ....J 4
Akhmin, 41,580 ....F 2
Alexandria, 1,803,900 ....J 2
Aswân, 127,700 ....F 3
Asyût, 154,100 ....J 4
Bâris, 1,347 ....F 3
Benha, 52,686 ....J 3
Beni Mazar, 30,583 ....J 4
Beni Suef, 78,829 ....J 3
Biba, 20,773 ....J 4
Bûlaq, 928 ....F 2
Bur Sa'id (Port Said), 283,400 ....K 3
Cairo (cap.), 4,219,853 ....J 3
Dairût, 24,364 ....J 4
Damanhur, 146,300 ....J 3
Damietta, 71,780 ....J 3
Disûq, 39,473 ....J 3
Dumyât (Damietta), 71,780 ....J 3
Dûsh, 794 ....F 3
El 'Alamein, 593 ....E 1
El 'Arish, 29,973 ....F 1
El Bawiti, 2,478 ....E 2
El Faiyûm, 133,800 ....J 3
El Fashn, 25,961 ....J 4

Topography

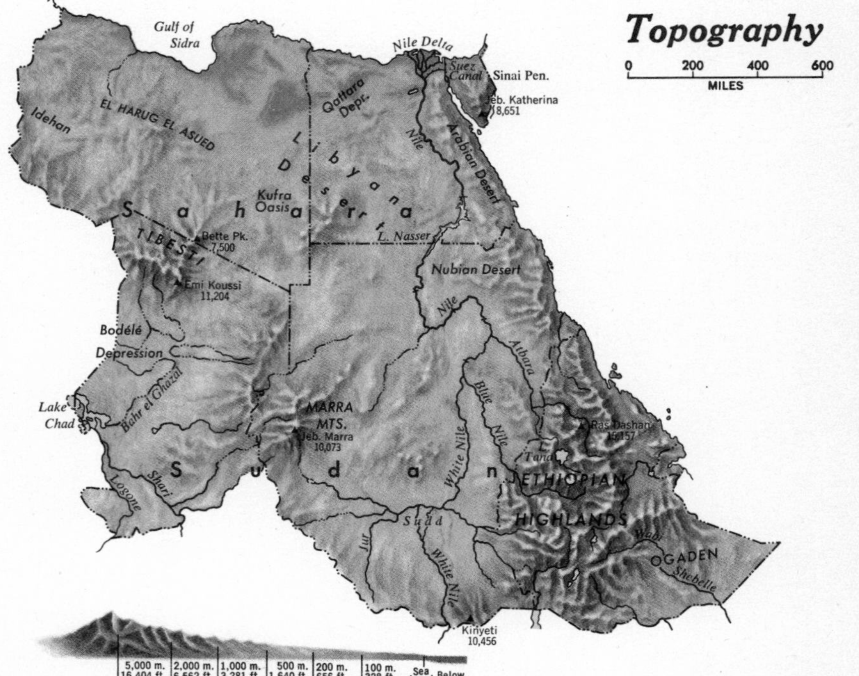

(continued on following page)

(continued)

EGYPT (continued)

El Hammam, 3,664 .... E 1
El Iskandariya (Alexandria), 1,803,900 .... J 2
El Karnak, 14,121 .... F 2
El Khârga, 9,277 .... F 2
El Mahalla el Kubra, 225,700 .... J 3
El Mansûra, 191,700 .... K 3
El Minya, 112,800 .... J 4
El Qâhira (Cairo) (cap.), 4,219,853 .... J 3
El Qantara, 11,201 .... K 3
El Qasr, 1,789 .... E 2
El Quseir, 4,336 .... F 2
El Tûr, 418 .... F 2
El Wasta, 11,283 .... J 3
Gaza, 87,793 .... F 1
Gaza, *118,272 .... F 1
Gemsa, 225 .... F 2
Girga, 42,017 .... F 2
Giza, 571,249 .... J 3
Heliopolis, 124,774 .... J 3
Helwân, 94,385 .... J 3
Hurghada, 2,012 .... F 2
Idfu, 25,105 .... F 3
Imbâba, 226,300 .... J 3
Ismailia, 156,500 .... K 3
Isna, 25,342 .... F 2
Kôm Ombo, 21,783 .... F 3
Luxor, 35,074 .... F 2
Maghâgha, 28,650 .... J 4
Mallawi, 52,614 .... J 4
Manfalût, 28,540 .... J 4
Matrûh, 9,254 .... E 1
Minûf, 41,914 .... J 3
Mût, 3,496 .... E 2
Port Fuad, 12,881 .... K 3
Port Safâga, 1,448 .... F 2
Port Said, 283,400 .... K 3
Port Taufiq, 26,075 .... K 3
Qalyub, 43,202 .... J 3
Qasr Farâfra, 747 .... E 2
Qena, 57,417 .... F 2
Ras Ghârib, 5,857 .... F 2
Rashid (Rosetta), 32,368 .... J 2
Rosetta, 32,368 .... J 2
Rudeis .... F 2
Salûm, 1,348 .... E 1
Samalût, 17,368 .... J 4
Shibin el Kom, 54,910 .... J 3
Sidi Barrani, 1,583 .... E 1
Sinnûris, 31,831 .... J 3
Siwa, 3,839 .... E 2
Sohâg, 61,944 .... F 2
Suez, 264,500 .... K 3
Tahta, 36,165 .... F 2
Tanta, 230,400 .... J 3
Zagazig, 151,300 .... J 3
Zifta, 31,421 .... J 3

OTHER FEATURES

Abu Qir (bay) .... J 2
Abydos (ruins) .... F 2
'Allaqi, Wadi (dry riv.) .... F 3
'Aqaba (gulf) .... G 2
Arabian (des.) .... F 2
Aswân (dam) .... F 3
Aswân High (dam) .... F 3
Bahariya (oasis), 6,779 .... E 2
Bahr Yusef (stream) .... J 4
Bânâs, Ras (cape) .... G 3
Berenice (ruins) .... F 3
Birket Qârûn (lake) .... J 3
Bir Taba (well) .... F 2
Bitter (lakes) .... K 3
Dakhla (oasis), 21,586 .... E 2
Eastern (Arabian) (des.) .... F 2
Farâfra (oasis), 747 .... E 2
Foul (bay) .... G 3
Ghard Abu Muharik (des.) .... J 4
Gilf Kebir (plat.) .... E 3
Great Sand Sea (des.) .... E 2
Katherina, Jebel (mt.) .... F 2
Khârga (oasis), 12,346 .... F 2
Libyan (des.) .... E 2
Libyan (plat.) .... E 1
Mediterranean (sea) .... E 1
Memphis (ruins) .... J 3
Muhammad, Ras (cape) .... F 2
Nasser (lake) .... F 3
Nile (riv.) .... F 2
Pyramids (ruins) .... J 3
Qattâra (depr.) .... E 2
Red (sea) .... G 3
Sahara (des.) .... E 3
Salûm (gulf) .... E 1
Sinai (mt.) .... F 2
Sinai (pen.), 49,769 .... F 2
Siwa (oasis), 3,839 .... E 2
Suez (canal) .... K 3
Suez (gulf) .... F 2
Tiran (str.) .... F 2
'Uweinat, Jebel (mt.) .... E 3

ETHIOPIA

GOVERNORATES

Arusi, 1,092,565 .... G 6
Begemdir and Simen, 2,125,069 .... G 5
Eritrea, 1,757,912 .... G 4
Gamu-Gofa, 563,749 .... G 6
Gojjam, 1,414,944 .... G 5
Harar, 1,540,211 .... H 6
Ilubabor, 1,061,208 .... F 6
Kaffa, 876,836 .... G 6
Mendebo, 353,736 .... H 6
Shoa, 2,614,689 .... G 6
Sidamo, 2,242,515 .... G 7
Tigre, 3,104,451 .... H 5
Wallaga, 2,386,218 .... G 6
Wallo, 2,946,924 .... H 5

CITIES and TOWNS

Addis Ababa (capital), 644,120 .... G 6
Addis Alam, 7,789 .... G 6
Adigrat .... G 5
Adi Ugri .... G 5
Adola .... G 6
Adwa .... G 5
Agordat .... G 4
Aksum, 11,596 .... G 5
Ankober, 12,871 .... H 6
Arba Mench .... G 6
Asmara, 190,500 .... G 4
Asosa .... F 5
Assab .... H 5
Asselle, 9,523 .... G 6
Awareh .... H 6
Awash .... H 6
Bako .... G 6
Bedessa .... H 6
Beica .... F 6
Burei .... G 6
Burye, 18,139 .... G 5
Callafo .... H 6
Chilga .... G 5
Dagabur .... H 6
Dallol .... G 5
Dangila, 2,351 .... G 5
Debra Birhan .... G 6
Debra Markos, 20,096 .... G 5
Debra Tabor .... G 5
Dembidollo .... F 6
Dessye, 40,000 .... G 5
Dilla .... G 6
Dire Dawa, 40,000 .... H 6
Dolo .... H 7
Domo .... J 6
Edd .... H 5
El Carre .... H 6
El Der .... H 6
Filtu .... H 6
Gabredarre .... H 6
Galadi .... J 6
Gambela, 9,955 .... F 6
Gardula .... G 6
Gedo .... G 6
Gerlogubi .... H 6
Ginir .... H 6
Goba, 6,389 .... H 6
Gondar, 24,673 .... G 5
Gore .... G 6
Gorrahei .... H 6
Hadama, 7,293 .... G 6
Harar, 40,499 .... H 6
Harkiko .... G 4
Hosseina, 5,803 .... G 6
Imi .... H 6
Jijiga .... H 6
Jimma, 39,559 .... G 6
Jiran .... G 6
Karkabat .... G 4
Keren .... G 4
Koma .... G 6
Lalibela .... G 5
Magdala .... G 5
Maji .... G 6
Makale, 16,873 .... G 5
Massawa, 25,000 .... G 4
Masslo .... G 6
Mega .... G 7
Mendi .... G 6
Mersa Fatma .... H 5
Metamma .... G 5
Miesso, 32,960 .... H 6
Murle .... G 6
Mustahil .... H 6
Nakamti, 5,889 .... G 6
Nakfa .... G 4
Negelli .... G 6
Nejo .... G 6
Saio (Dembidollo) .... F 6
Soddu, 5,595 .... G 6
Sokota .... G 5
Tessenei .... G 4
Thio .... H 5
Tori .... F 6
Umm Hajar .... G 5
Waka .... G 6
Waldia .... G 5
Wardere .... J 6
Wota .... G 6
Yaballo .... G 6
Yirga Alam .... G 6
Zula .... G 4

OTHER FEATURES

Abaya (lake) .... G 6
Abbai (riv.) .... G 5
Abbe (lake) .... H 5
Akobo (riv.) .... F 6
Amhara (reg.) .... G 5
Assale (lake) .... H 5
Awash (riv.) .... H 5
Bale (mt.) .... G 6
Baraka (dry riv.) .... G 4
Baro (riv.) .... G 6
Billate (riv.) .... G 6
Blue Nile (Abbai) (riv.) .... G 5
Buri (pen.) .... H 4
Chamo (lake) .... G 6
Dahlak (arch.) .... H 4
Dahlak (isl.) .... H 4
Danakil (reg.) .... H 5
Dawa (riv.) .... H 7
Fafan (riv.) .... H 6
Ganale Dorya (riv.) .... H 6
Gughe (mt.) .... G 6
Haud (reg.) .... J 6
Kasar, Ras (cape) .... G 4
Ogaden (reg.) .... H 6
Omo (riv.) .... G 6
Ras Dashan (mt.) .... G 5
Red (sea) .... G 3
Rudolf (lake) .... G 7
Simen (mts.) .... G 5
Stefanie (lake) .... G 7
Takkaze (riv.) .... G 5
Tana (lake) .... G 5
Wabi (riv.) .... H 6
Wabi Shebelle (riv.) .... H 6
Zwai (lake) .... G 6

LIBYA

PROVINCES

Baida, 88,016 .... D 1
Benghazi, 278,826 .... D 2
Derna, 84,112 .... D 1
Gharian, 180,883 .... B 1
Homs, 136,679 .... B 1
Misurata, 145,894 .... C 1
Sebha, 47,436 .... B 2
Tripoli, 379,925 .... B 1
Ubari, 31,890 .... B 2
Zawia, 190,708 .... B 1

CITIES and TOWNS

Ajedabia, †15,430 .... D 1
Aujila, †2,993 .... D 2
Baida, 12,799 .... D 1
Barce (El Marj), 10,645 .... D 1
Benghazi, 137,295 .... C 1
Beni Ulid, †4,293 .... B 1
Berken, †3,114 .... B 2
Bir Hakeim .... D 1
Brak, †7,042 .... B 2
Bu Ngem .... C 1
Buzeima .... D 3
Cyrene (Shahat), †6,266 .... D 1
Derj, †2,272 .... B 1
Derna, 21,432 .... D 1
Edri, †4,271 .... B 2
El Abiar, †14,260 .... D 1
El Agheila, †852 .... C 1
El Azizia, †18,753 .... B 1
El Bardi, †3,755 .... D 1
El Barkat, †1,476 .... B 3
El Ergh .... D 2
El Fogaha, †607 .... C 2
El Gatrun, †1,660 .... B 3
El Gezira .... D 2
El Gheria esh Sherqia .... B 1
El Jauf, †4,330 .... D 3
El Marj, 10,645 .... D 1
Ez Zuetina, †2,430 .... D 1
Ghadames, †2,636 .... A 2
Gharian, †10,807 .... B 1
Ghat, †1,639 .... B 3
Homs, †13,864 .... B 1
Hon, †3,435 .... C 2
Jaghbub (Jarabub), †1,101 .... D 2
Jarabub, †1,101 .... D 2
Marada, †2,172 .... C 2
Marsa el Awegia .... C 1
Marsa el Brega, †2,797 .... D 1
Marsa el Hariga .... D 1
Marsa Susa, †2,062 .... D 1
Mekili, †703 .... D 1
Misurata, †36,850 .... C 1
Mizda, †2,508 .... B 1
Murzuk, †3,863 .... B 2
Nalut, †9,010 .... B 1
Ras Lanuf .... C 1
Sebha, †9,804 .... B 2
Serdeles .... B 2
Shahat, †6,266 .... D 1
Sinawen, †715 .... B 1
Sokna, †1,873 .... C 2
Soluk, †12,395 .... D 1
Suk el Juma, †81,123 .... B 1
Syrte, 7,093 .... C 1
Tagrifet .... C 2
Tarhuna, †25,502 .... B 1
Tejerri .... B 3
Tesawa .... B 2
Tmessa, 4,806 .... C 2
Tobruk, 15,867 .... D 1
Tokra, †5,900 .... D 1
Traghen, †2,952 .... B 2
Tripoli (capital), 247,365 .... B 1
Ubari, †1,711 .... B 2
Umm el Abid .... C 2
Waddan, †3,519 .... C 2
Wau el Kebir .... C 2
Zawia, †28,349 .... B 1
Zella, †2,560 .... C 2
Zliten, †17,950 .... C 1
Zuila, †1,839 .... C 2
Zwara, †14,578 .... B 1

OTHER FEATURES

Ain Dawa (well) .... D 3
Akhdar, Jebel (mts.) .... D 1
'Amir, Ras (cape) .... D 1
Anai (well), †1,795 .... B 3
Ben Ghnema, Jebel (mts.) .... C 2
Bette (peak) .... C 3
Bey el Kebir, Wadi (dry riv.) .... B 1
Bishiara (well) .... D 3
Bomba (gulf) .... D 1
Calansho, Serir (des.) .... D 2
Calansho Sand Sea (desert) .... D 2
Cyrenaica (region), 450,954 .... D 1
Fezzan (region), 79,326 .... B 2
Great Sand Sea (des.) .... D 2
Harug el Asued, El (mts.) .... C 2
Homra, Hamada el (desert) .... B 2
Hosenofu (well) .... D 3
Idehan (des.) .... B 2
Idehan Murzuk (des.) .... B 2
Jalo (oasis), 3,910 .... D 2
Jefara (reg.) .... B 1
Jofra (oasis), 8,827 .... C 2
Kufra (oasis), 5,509 .... D 3
Leptis Magna (ruins) .... B 1
Libyan (des.) .... D 2
Libyan (plat.) .... D 1
Mediterranean (sea) .... C 1
Nefusa, Jebel (mts.) .... B 1
Rebiana (oasis), †666 .... D 3
Rebiana Sand Sea (des.) .... D 3
Sabratha (ruins) .... B 1
Sahara (des.) .... D 3
Sarra (well) .... D 3
Shati, Wadi esh (dry riv.) .... B 2
Sidra (gulf) .... C 1
Soda, Jebel es (mts.) .... C 2
Tazerbo (oasis), †1,307 .... D 2
Tibesti, Serir (des.) .... C 3
Tinrhert Hamada (des.) .... B 2
Tripolitania (region), 1,034,089 .... B 1
'Uweinat, Jebel (mt.) .... E 3
Wau en Namus (well) .... C 3
Zelten, Jebel (mts.) .... D 2

SUDAN

PROVINCES

Bahr el Ghazal, 1,238,779 .... E 6
Blue Nile, 2,724,968 .... F 5
Darfur, 1,467,688 .... D 5
Equatoria, 1,129,388 .... E 6
Kassala, 1,413,069 .... G 4
Khartoum, 749,932 .... F 4
Kordofan, 2,022,201 .... E 5
Northern, 982,046 .... E 3
Upper Nile, 1,110,769 .... F 6

CITIES and TOWNS

Abu Hamed .... F 4
Abu Matariq .... E 5
Abu Zabad .... E 5
Abwong .... F 6
Abyei .... E 6
Adarama .... G 4
Adok .... F 6
Akobo .... F 6
Amadi .... F 6
'Aqiq .... G 4
Argo, 2,329 .... F 4
Aroma, 3,451 .... G 4
Atbara, 36,000 .... F 4
Aweil, 2,438 .... E 6
Ayod .... F 6
Babanusa .... E 5
Bara, 4,885 .... F 5
Bentiu .... E 6
Berber, 10,977 .... F 4
Bor .... F 6
Bo River Post .... E 6
Buram .... E 5
Deim Zubeir .... E 6
Delgo .... F 3
Derudeb .... G 4
Dilling, 5,596 .... E 5
Dongola, 3,350 .... F 4
Dungunab .... G 3
Ed Da'ein .... E 5
Ed Damer, 5,458 .... F 4
Ed Debba .... F 4
Ed Dueim, 12,319 .... F 5
El Abbasiya, 2,846 .... F 5
El Fasher, 26,161 .... E 5
El Fifi .... D 5
El Geteina .... F 5
El Hilla .... E 5
El Khandaq .... E 4
El Obeid, 53,000 .... E 5
El Odaiya .... E 5
En Nahud, 16,499 .... E 5
Er Rahad, 6,706 .... F 5
Er Roseires, 3,927 .... F 5
Famaka .... F 5
Fangak .... F 6
Fashoda (Kodok), 9,100 .... F 6
Gabras .... E 5
Gallabat .... G 5
Gebeit Mine .... G 3
Gedaref, 17,537 .... G 5
Geneina, 11,817 .... D 5
Gogrial .... E 6
Goz Regeb .... G 4
Haiya Junction .... G 4
Halaib .... G 3
Heiban .... F 5
Juba, 10,660 .... F 7
Kadugli, 4,716 .... E 5
Kafia Kingi .... D 6
Kajok .... E 6
Kaka .... F 5
Kapoeta .... F 7
Karima, 5,989 .... F 4
Karora .... G 4
Kassala, 40,000 .... G 4
Kerma .... F 4
Khartoum (capital), 194,000 .... F 4
Khartoum North, 40,000 .... F 4
Khashm el Girba .... G 5
Kodok, 9,100 .... F 6
Kongor .... F 6
Korti .... F 4
Kosti, 22,688 .... F 5
Kubbum .... D 5
Kurmuk, 1,647 .... F 5
Kutum .... D 5
Lado .... F 6
Loka .... F 7
Malakal, 9,680 .... F 6
Maridi, 839 .... E 7
Marsa Oseif .... G 3
Melut, 334 .... F 5
Merowe, 1,620 .... F 4
Meshra' er Req .... E 6
Mongalla .... F 6
Muglad, 3,735 .... E 5
Muhammad Qol .... G 3
Musmar .... G 4
Nagishot .... F 7
Nasir .... F 6
Nimule .... F 7
Nyala, 12,278 .... E 5
Nyamlell .... E 6
Nyerol .... F 6
Omdurman, 206,000 .... F 4
Opari .... F 7
Pibor Post .... F 6
Port Sudan, 110,000 .... G 4
Raga .... E 6
Rashad, 1,683 .... F 5
Rejaf .... F 7
Renk .... F 5
Rufa'a, 9,137 .... F 5
Rumbek, 2,944 .... E 6
Sennar, 8,093 .... F 5
Shambe .... F 6
Shendi, 11,031 .... F 4
Shereik .... F 4
Showak, 2,171 .... G 5
Singa, 9,436 .... F 5
Sinkat, 5,175 .... G 4
Sodiri, 1,804 .... E 5
Suakin, 4,228 .... G 4
Suki, 7,388 .... F 5
Tali Post .... F 6
Talodi, 2,736 .... F 5
Tambura .... E 6
Tendelti, 7,555 .... F 5
Tokar, 16,802 .... G 4
Tombe .... F 6
Tonga .... F 6
Tonj, 2,071 .... E 6
Torit, 2,353 .... F 7
Towot .... F 6
Trinkitat .... G 4
Umm Keddada, 2,410 .... E 5
Umm Ruwaba, 7,805 .... F 5
Wad Medani, 48,000 .... F 5
Wankai .... E 6
Wau, 8,009 .... E 6
Yambio, 3,890 .... E 7
Yei, 739 .... F 7
Yirol, 1,895 .... F 6
Zalingei, 3,314 .... D 5

OTHER FEATURES

Abu Dara, Ras (cape) .... G 3
Abu Habl, Wadi (dry riv.) .... F 5
Abu Shagara, Ras (cape) .... G 3
Abu Tabari (well) .... E 4
Adda (riv.) .... D 6
Akobo (riv.) .... F 6
'Amur, Wadi (dry riv.) .... G 4
Asoteriba, Jebel (mt.) .... G 3
Atbara (riv.) .... G 4
Bahr Azoum (riv.) .... D 5
Bahr el 'Arab (riv.) .... E 6
Bahr ez Zeraf (riv.) .... F 6
Baraka (dry riv.) .... G 4
Blue Nile (riv.) .... F 5
Dar Hamid (region) .... F 5
Dar Masalit (reg.), 323,616 .... D 5
Dinder (riv.) .... G 5
El 'Atrun (oasis) .... E 4
Fifth Cataract .... F 4
Fourth Cataract .... F 4
Gabgaba, Wadi (dry riv.) .... F 3
Gezira, El (reg.) .... F 5
Ghalla, Wadi el (dry riv.) .... E 5
Hadarba, Ras (cape) .... G 3
Howar, Wadi (dry riv.) .... E 4
Ibra, Wadi (dry riv.) .... D 5
Jebel Abyad (plat.) .... E 4
Jebel Aulia (dam) .... F 4
Jur (riv.) .... E 6
Kasar, Ras (cape) .... G 4
Kinyeti (mt.) .... F 7
Laqiya 'Umran (well) .... E 3
Libyan (desert) .... E 3
Lol (dry riv.) .... E 6
Lotagipi (swamp) .... F 6
Marra, Jebel (mt.) .... D 5
Meroe (ruins) .... F 4
Milk, Wadi el (dry riv.) .... E 4
Muqaddam, Wadi (dry riv.) .... F 4
Napata (ruins) .... F 4
Naqa (ruins) .... F 4
Nasser (lake) .... F 3
Nile (riv.) .... F 4
Nuba (mts.) .... E 5
Nubian (des.) .... E 5
Nukheila (oasis) .... E 4
Nuri (ruins) .... F 4
Oda, Jebel (mt.) .... G 3
Pibor (riv.) .... F 6
Red (sea) .... G 3
Sahara (des.) .... E 3
Second Cataract .... F 3
Selima (oasis) .... E 3
Sennar (dam) .... F 5
Setit (riv.) .... G 5
Sixth Cataract .... F 4
Sobat (riv.) .... F 6
Suakin (arch.) .... G 4
Sudan (reg.) .... E 5
Sudd (swamp) .... F 6
Sue (riv.) .... E 6
Third Cataract .... E 4
'Uweinat, Jebel (mt.) .... E 3
White Nile (riv.) .... F 5

*City and suburbs.
†Population of sub-district or division.

Agriculture, Industry and Resources

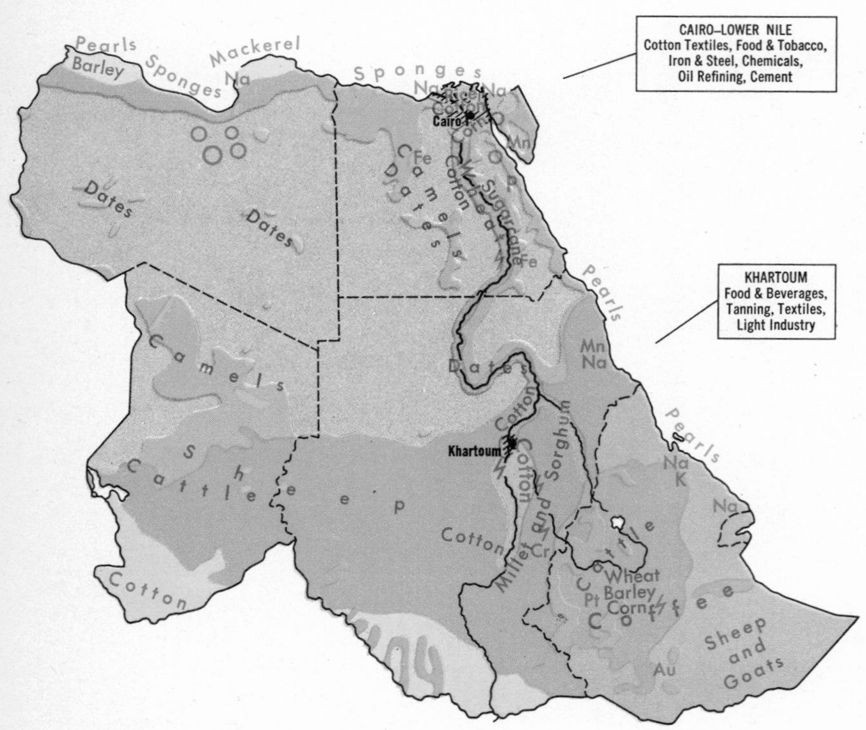

DOMINANT LAND USE

Cereals, Horticulture, Livestock
Cash Crops, Mixed Cereals
Cotton, Cereals
Market Gardening, Diversified Tropical Crops
Plantation Agriculture
Oases
Pasture Livestock
Nomadic Livestock Herding
Forests
Nonagricultural Land

MAJOR MINERAL OCCURRENCES

Au Gold
Cr Chromium
Fe Iron Ore
K Potash
Mn Manganese
Na Salt
O Petroleum
P Phosphates
Pt Platinum

Water Power
Major Industrial Areas

ANGOLA

AREA 481,351 sq. mi.
POPULATION 5,430,000
CAPITAL Luanda
LARGEST CITY Luanda
HIGHEST POINT Mt. Moco 8,593 ft.
MONETARY UNIT Portuguese escudo
MAJOR LANGUAGES Mbundu, Kongo, Lunda, Portuguese
MAJOR RELIGIONS Tribal religions, Roman Catholicism

BURUNDI

AREA 10,747 sq. mi.
POPULATION 3,475,000
CAPITAL Bujumbura
LARGEST CITY Bujumbura
HIGHEST POINT 8,858 ft.
MONETARY UNIT Rwanda-Burundi franc
MAJOR LANGUAGES Kirundi, French
MAJOR RELIGIONS Tribal religions, Roman Catholicism

CAMEROON

AREA 183,568 sq.mi.
POPULATION 5,836,000
CAPITAL Yaoundé
LARGEST CITY Douala
HIGHEST POINT Cameroon 13,350 ft.
MONETARY UNIT CFA franc
MAJOR LANGUAGES Fang, Bamileke, Fulani, Duala, French, English
MAJOR RELIGIONS Tribal religions, Christianity, Islam

CENTRAL AFRICAN REPUBLIC

AREA 240,534 sq. mi.
POPULATION 1,518,000
CAPITAL Bangui
LARGEST CITY Bangui
HIGHEST POINT Gao 4,659 ft.
MONETARY UNIT CFA franc
MAJOR LANGUAGES Banda, Gbaya, Sango, French
MAJOR RELIGIONS Tribal religions, Christianity, Islam

REPUBLIC OF CONGO

AREA 175,676 sq. mi.
POPULATION 915,000
CAPITAL Brazzaville
LARGEST CITY Brazzaville
HIGHEST POINT Leketi Mts. 3,412 ft.
MONETARY UNIT CFA franc
MAJOR LANGUAGES Kongo, Bateke, Lingala, French
MAJOR RELIGIONS Christianity, Tribal religions

EQUATORIAL GUINEA

AREA 10,832 sq. mi.
POPULATION 286,000
CAPITAL Santa Isabel
LARGEST CITY Santa Isabel
HIGHEST POINT 9,868 ft.
MONETARY UNIT peseta
MAJOR LANGUAGES Fang, Bubi, Spanish
MAJOR RELIGIONS Tribal religions, Christianity

GABON

AREA 103,346 sq. mi.
POPULATION 500,000
CAPITAL Libreville
LARGEST CITY Libreville
HIGHEST POINT Ibounzi 5,165 ft.
MONETARY UNIT CFA franc
MAJOR LANGUAGES Fang and other Bantu languages, French
MAJOR RELIGIONS Tribal religions, Christianity

KENYA

AREA 224,960 sq. mi.
POPULATION 10,880,200
CAPITAL Nairobi
LARGEST CITY Nairobi
HIGHEST POINT Kenya 17,058 ft.
MONETARY UNIT East African shilling
MAJOR LANGUAGES Kikuyu, Luo, Kavirondo, Kamba, Swahili, English
MAJOR RELIGIONS Tribal religions, Christianity

MALAWI

AREA 45,483 sq. mi.
POPULATION 4,530,000
CAPITAL Zomba
LARGEST CITY Blantyre
HIGHEST POINT Mlanje 9,843 ft.
MONETARY UNIT Malawi pound
MAJOR LANGUAGES Chichewa, Yao, English
MAJOR RELIGIONS Tribal religions, Islam

RWANDA

AREA 10,169 sq. mi.
POPULATION 3,500,000
CAPITAL Kigali
LARGEST CITY Kigali
HIGHEST POINT Karisimbi 14,780 ft.
MONETARY UNIT Rwanda-Burundi franc
MAJOR LANGUAGES Kinyarwanda, French
MAJOR RELIGIONS Tribal religions, Roman Catholicism

SOMALIA

AREA 246,200 sq. mi.
POPULATION 2,730,000
CAPITAL Mogadishu
LARGEST CITY Mogadishu
HIGHEST POINT Surud Ad 7,900 ft.
MONETARY UNIT somalo
MAJOR LANGUAGES Somali, Arabic; Italian, English
MAJOR RELIGIONS Islam, Roman Catholicism

TANZANIA

AREA 362,819 sq. mi.
POPULATION 12,896,000
CAPITAL Dar es Salaam
LARGEST CITY Dar es Salaam
HIGHEST POINT Kilimanjaro 19,340 ft.
MONETARY UNIT East African shilling
MAJOR LANGUAGES Nyamwezi-Sukuma, Swahili, English
MAJOR RELIGIONS Tribal religions, Christianity, Islam

UGANDA

AREA 92,674 sq. mi.
POPULATION 9,764,000
CAPITAL Kampala
LARGEST CITY Kampala
HIGHEST POINT Margherita 16,795 ft.
MONETARY UNIT East African shilling
MAJOR LANGUAGES Ganda, Acholi, Teso, Nyoro, Soga, Nkole, English
MAJOR RELIGIONS Tribal religions, Christianity

ZAIRE

AREA 905,563 sq. mi.
POPULATION 21,637,876
CAPITAL Kinshasa
LARGEST CITY Kinshasa
HIGHEST POINT Margherita 16,795 ft.
MONETARY UNIT zaire
MAJOR LANGUAGES Luba, Mongo, Kongo, Kinyarwanda, Zande, Lingala, Swahili, French
MAJOR RELIGIONS Tribal religions, Christianity

ZAMBIA

AREA 290,586 sq. mi.
POPULATION 4,056,995
CAPITAL Lusaka
LARGEST CITY Lusaka
HIGHEST POINT Sunzu 6,782 ft.
MONETARY UNIT kwacha
MAJOR LANGUAGES Bemba, Tonga, Lozi, Luvale, Nyanje, English
MAJOR RELIGIONS Tribal religions

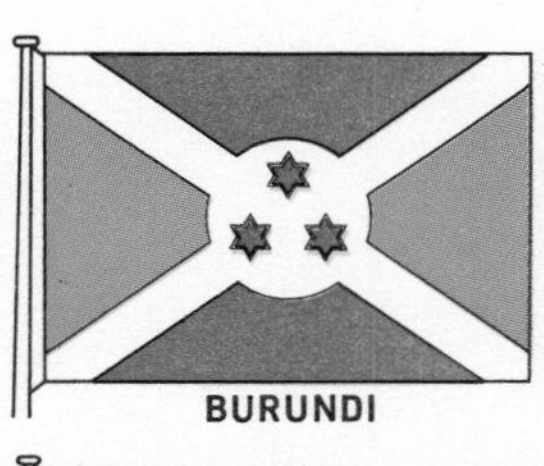
BURUNDI

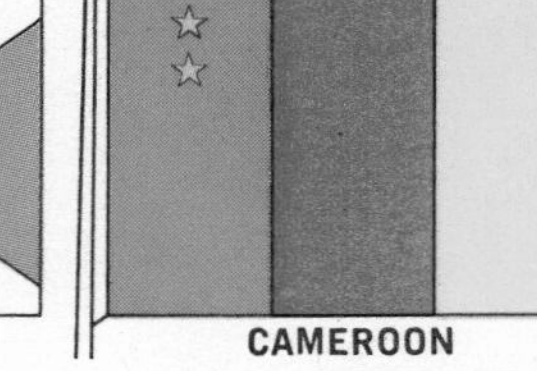
CAMEROON

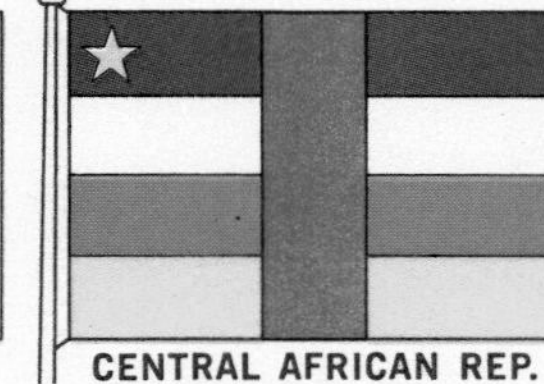
CENTRAL AFRICAN REP.

REPUBLIC OF CONGO

EQUATORIAL GUINEA

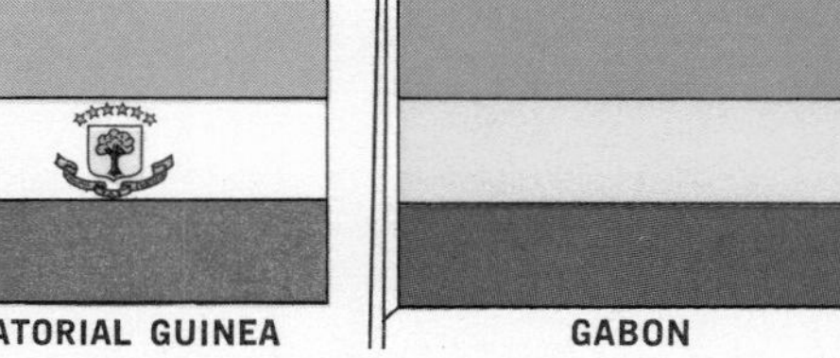
GABON

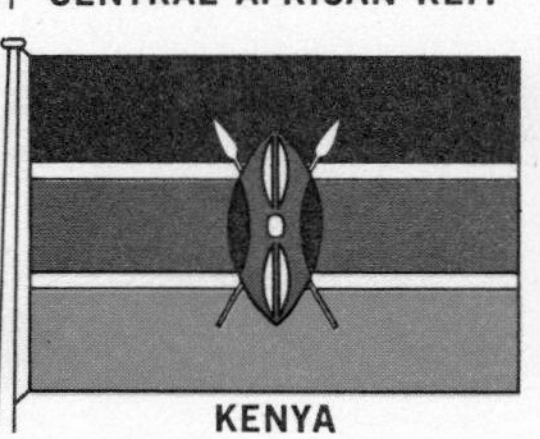
KENYA

MALAWI

RWANDA

SOMALIA

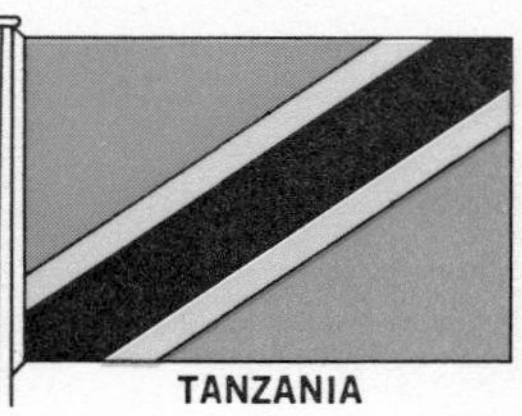
TANZANIA

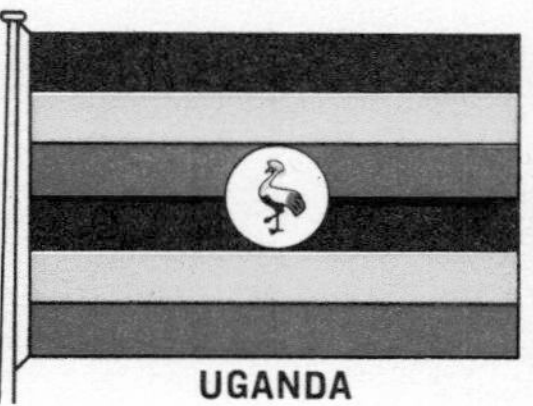
UGANDA

ZAIRE

ZAMBIA

ANGOLA

DISTRICTS

Benguela, 453,834 ....B 6
Bié, 445,127 ....C 6
Cabinda, 55,919 ....B 5
Cuando Cubango, 112,622 ....C 7
Cuanza-Norte, 252,560 ....B 5
Cuanza-Sul, 389,174 ....B 6
Huambo, 571,299 ....C 6
Huila, 571,198 ....B 7
Luanda, 273,732 ....B 5
Lunda, 244,940 ....C 5
Malange, 442,900 ....C 6
Moçâmedes, 34,468 ....B 7
Moxico, 261,749 ....D 6
Uige, 392,063 ....C 5
Zaire, 102,777 ....B 5

CITIES and TOWNS

Alto Chicapa ....C 6
Alto Cuale, 16,872 ....C 5
Ambriz ....B 5
Ambrizete ....B 5
Andulo, 14,492 ....C 6
Baía dos Tigres ....B 7
Baía Farta, 3,353 ....B 6
Bela Vista ....C 6
Bembe ....B 5
Benguela, 23,256 ....B 6
Cabinda, 4,635 ....B 5
Caconda, 5,331 ....B 6
Cacuso ....C 5
Caiundo, 9,366 ....C 7
Calulo ....C 6
Caluquembe, 40,589 ....B 6
Camanongue, 9,798 ....D 6
Cambo, 22,951 ....C 5
Cambulo, 19,248 ....D 5
Cangamba ....C 6
Capenda-Capulemba, 10,851 ....C 5
Carmona, 6,251 ....C 5
Cassai ....D 6
Cassamba ....D 6
Cassinga ....C 7
Catete ....B 5
Catumbela, 11,149 ....B 6
Caúngula ....C 5
Cazombo ....D 6
Chiange ....B 7
Chinguar, 4,009 ....C 6
Chipindo, 37,885 ....C 6
Chitado ....B 7
Chitembo ....C 6
Cuchi, 25,683 ....C 5
Cuilo ....C 5
Cuito-Cuanavale ....C 7
Cuma ....B 6
Damba ....B 5
Dirico ....D 7
Dombe Grande ....B 6
Dondo, 6,234 ....B 5
Duque de Bragança ....C 5
Folgares, 4,133 ....C 6
Forte República, 21,004 ....C 5
Foz do Cunene ....B 7
Gabela, 4,846 ....B 6
Golungo Alto, 2,250........B 5
Henrique de Carvalho, 3,092........D 5
Iona ....B 7
Lobito, 50,164 ....B 7
Lóvua ....D 5
Luanda (capital), 400,000 ....B 5
Lucira ....B 6
Luiana, 7,867 ....D 7
Luso, 3,777 ....C 6
Macondo ....D 6
Malange, 127,000 ....C 5
Maquela do Zombo ....C 5
Massango (Forte República), 21,004 ....C 5
Mavinga ....D 7
Moçâmedes, 7,963 ....B 7
Mucope, 6,715 ....B 7
Mucusso ....D 7
Munhango ....C 6
Muxima ....B 5
Negage, 25,269 ....C 5
Nharêa, 34,486 ....C 6
Nóqui ....B 5
Nova Chaves ....D 6
Nova Gaia ....C 5
Nova Lisboa, 109,000 ....C 6
Novo Redondo, 12,324 ....B 6
Oncócua ....B 7
Porto Alexandre, 5,943 ....B 7
Porto Amboim, 10,711 ....B 6
Portugália ....D 5
Quela ....C 5
Quibala ....C 6
Quibaxe ....B 5
Quinzau ....B 5
Robert Williams ....C 6
Sá da Bandeira, 15,086 ....B 6
Salazar, 5,571 ....B 5
Santa Comba ....C 6
Santo Antônio do Zaire ....B 5
São Salvador do Congo, 3,525........B 5
São Nicolau ....B 6
Serpa Pinto ....C 6
Silva Porto, 5,606 ....C 6
Songo, 15,721 ....B 5
Vila da Ponte ....C 6
Vila Gago Coutinho ....D 6
Vila General Machado, 4,241 ....C 6
Vila Guilherme Capelo ....B 5
Vila Mariano Machado, 8,021 ....B 6
Vila Norton de Matos ....B 6
Vila Paiva Couceiro ....B 6
Vila Pereira de Eça ....C 7
Vila Roçadas ....B 7
Vila Teixeira da Silva ....C 6
Vila Teixeira de Sousa ....D 6

OTHER FEATURES

Bero (riv.) ....B 7
Cambo (riv.) ....C 5
Chicapa (riv.) ....D 5
Coporolo (riv.) ....B 6
Cuango (riv.) ....C 6
Cuanza (riv.) ....C 5
Cubango (riv.) ....C 7
Cuito (riv.) ....C 7
Cunene (riv.) ....B 7
Cuvo (riv.) ....B 6
Loge (riv.) ....B 5
Lungwebungu (riv.) ....D 6
M'Bridge (riv.) ....B 5
Moco (mt.) ....C 6
Negro (cape) ....B 7
Palmeirinhas (pt.) ....B 5
Santa Maria (cape) ....B 6
Zambezi (riv.) ....D 6

BURUNDI

CITIES and TOWNS

Bujumbura (capital), 90,000 ....E 4
Bururi ....F 4
Gitega, 3,579 ....F 4

OTHER FEATURES

Ruzizi (riv.) ....E 4
Tanganyika (lake) ....E 5

CAMEROON

CITIES and TOWNS

Abong-Mbang, 2,037 ....B 3
Bafia ....B 3
Bafoussam, 8,000 ....B 3
Bamenda, 1,455 ....B 2
Batouri, 5,120 ....B 3
Bertoua, 2,500 ....B 3
Bétaré-Oya, 1,400 ....B 2
Bonabéri ....A 3
Buea, 3,000 ....A 3
Campo, 2,159 ....B 3
Djoum ....B 3
Douala, 230,000 ....B 3
Dschang, 6,000 ....A 2
Ebolowa, 16,000 ....B 3
Edéa, 12,000 ....B 3
Fort-Foureau, 8,216 ....B 1
Foumban, 20,000 ....B 2
Garoua, 30,000 ....B 2
Guidder, 6,488 ....B 2
Kaélé, 5,000 ....B 2

(continued on following page)

(continued)

CAMEROON (continued)

Place	Key
Kontcha	B 2
Kousseri, 2,000	B 1
Kribi, 7,000	B 3
Kumba, 10,000	A 3
Kumbo	B 2
Lomié, 10,127	B 3
Mamfé, 10,000	A 2
Maroua, 24,979	B 1
M'Balmayo, 5,500	B 3
Meiganga, 2,000	B 2
Mokolo, 5,145	B 1
Moloundou, 8,575	C 3
N'Gaoundéré, 15,000	B 2
N'Kambe, 4,000	B 2
N'Kongsamba, 39,800	B 3
Poli, 700	B 2
Rei-Bouba, 3,500	B 2
Sangmélima, 4,800	B 3
Tibati, 4,000	B 2
Tiko, 15,000	A 3
Victoria, 15,000	A 3
Wum, 9,710	A 2
Yabassi	B 3
Yaoundé (cap.), 130,000	B 3
Yokadouma	B 3
Yoko	B 2

OTHER FEATURES

Place	Key
Adamawa (reg.)	B 2
Benue (riv.)	A 2
Biafra (bight)	A 3
Cameroon (mt.)	A 3
Cross (riv.)	A 2
Dja (riv.)	B 3
Donga (riv.)	B 2
Logone (riv.)	C 2
Lom (riv.)	B 2
Mbéré (riv.)	B 2
Sanaga (riv.)	B 3

CENTRAL AFRICAN REPUBLIC

CITIES and TOWNS

Place	Key
Baboua, 2,000	C 2
Bakala, 1,000	D 2
Bambari, 32,000	D 2
Bangassou, 28,000	D 3
Bangui (capital), 111,266	C 3
Bangui, *240,000	C 3
Bania	C 3
Batangafo, 7,500	C 2
Berbérati, 40,000	C 3
Birao	D 2
Bocaranga, 4,000	C 2
Boda	C 3
Bossangoa, 36,000	C 2
Bossembele, 1,700	C 2
Bouali	C 3
Bouar, 29,000	C 2
Bouca, 3,000	C 2
Bozoum, 4,700	C 2
Bria, 25,000	D 2
Carnot, 4,000	C 3
Damara, 800	C 2
Djéma	E 2
Fort-Crampel, 5,000	C 2
Fort-de-Possel, 500	C 2
Fort-Sibut, 526	C 2
Gaza	C 3
Goubéré	E 2
Grimari, 1,400	C 2
Hyrra Banda	D 2
Ippy, 6,000	D 2
Kaka	E 2
Kembé	D 3
Kouango	D 2
Kouki	C 2
Koundé	B 2
Makounda	C 2
M'Baiki, 18,000	C 3
M'Bres, 7,000	D 2
Mobaye	D 3
Mouka	D 2
Ndélé, 4,013	D 2
Ngourou	D 2
Nola, 500	C 3
Obo, 3,000	E 2
Ouadda	D 2
Ouanda-Djalé	D 2
Ouango, 2,000	D 3
Paoua, 3,500	C 2
Rafai, 8,891	D 2
Yalinga, 1,500	D 2
Zako	D 2

Zémio, 1,500	D 2
Zemongo	E 2

OTHER FEATURES

Bamingui (riv.)	C 2
Dar Rounga (region), 25,000	D 2
Gao (mt.)	C 2
Kadei (riv.)	C 3
Kotto (riv.)	D 2
Lobaye (riv.)	C 2
Pendé (riv.)	C 2
Sara (riv.)	C 2
Shari (riv.)	C 2
Shinko (riv.)	D 2
Ubangi (riv.)	C 3

CONGO, REPUBLIC OF

CITIES and TOWNS

Boko, 800	B 4
Brazzaville (capital), 94,000	C 4
Brazzaville, *200,000	C 4
Djambala, 2,000	B 4
Dolisie, 20,000	B 4
Dongou, 2,190	C 3
Epéna, 8,446	C 3
Ewo, 700	B 4
Fort-Rousset, 5,082	C 4
Gamboma, 1,700	C 4
Ikelemba, 400	C 3
Impfondo, 2,000	C 3
Kayes, 1,500	B 4
Kellé, 1,282	B 4
Kibangou, 1,000	B 4
Kinkala, 1,000	B 4
Komono, 750	B 4
Loudima, 400	B 4
Madingo, 2,500	B 4
Makoua, 2,000	C 3
Mindouli, 1,600	B 4
Mossaka, 2,128	C 4
Mossendjo, 3,000	B 4
M'Pouya	C 4
M'Vouti	B 4
Okoyo	C 4
Ouesso, 4,464	C 3
Pangala	B 4
Pointe-Noire, 100,000	B 4
Sembé	B 3
Sibiti, 1,000	B 4
Souanké, 280	B 3
Zanaga, 800	B 4

OTHER FEATURES

Alima (riv.)	B 4
Congo (riv.)	C 4
Crystal (mts.)	B 4
Kouilou (riv.)	B 4
Niari (riv.)	B 4
Sanga (riv.)	C 3
Ubangi (riv.)	C 3

EQUATORIAL GUINEA

TERRITORIES

Fernando Po, 78,000	A 3
Río Muni, 203,000	B 3

CITIES and TOWNS

Bata, 27,024	B 3
Puerto Iradier	A 3
Río Benito, 14,503	A 3
San Carlos, 19,933	A 3
Santa Isabel (capital), 37,237	A 3

OTHER FEATURES

Corisco (isl.)	A 3
Elobey (isls.)	A 3
Fernando Po (island), 78,000	A 3

GABON

CITIES and TOWNS

Bitam, 2,080	B 3
Booué, 114	B 3
Cocobeach, 100	B 3
Franceville, 2,000	B 4
Kango, 300	B 3
Koula-Moutou, 3,170	B 4
Lalara, 1,333	B 3
Lambaréné, 7,000	B 4
Lastoursville, 2,000	B 4
Lekoni, 3,020	B 4
Libreville (capital), *57,000	A 3
Makokou, 1,150	B 3
Mayumba, 1,000	A 4
M'Bigou, 1,500	B 4
Mekambo, 800	B 3
Mimongo, 350	B 4
Minvoul, 200	B 3
Mitzic, 1,180	B 3
Moanda, 2,700	B 4
Mouila, 1,800	B 4
N'Dendé, 1,560	B 4
N'Djolé, 500	B 4
Okondja, 1,600	B 4
Oyem, 3,050	B 3
Port-Gentil, 30,000	A 4
Setté-Cama, 1,609	A 4
Tchibanga, 2,080	B 4

OTHER FEATURES

Crystal (mts.)	B 4
Ibounzi (mt.)	B 4
Ivindo (riv.)	B 3
Lopez (cape)	A 4
N'Dogo (lag.)	B 4
N'Gounié (riv.)	B 4
N'Komi (lag.)	A 4
Ogooué (riv.)	A 4
Onangué (lake)	A 4
Pongara (pt.)	A 3

KENYA

PROVINCES

Central, 1,664,000	G 4
Coast, 924,800	G 4
Eastern, 1,899,200	G 4
Nairobi (city district), 477,600	G 4
North Eastern, 244,200	G 3
Nyanza, 2,115,900	F 4
Rift Valley, 2,219,400	G 3
Western, 1,335,100	G 3

CITIES and TOWNS

Baragoi	G 3
Eldoret, 16,900	G 3
El Wak	H 3
Embu, 5,213	G 4
Fort Hall, 5,389	G 4
Garissa	G 4
Garsen	G 4
Gazi, 6,452	G 4
Gilgil	G 4
Hadu	G 4
Isiolo, 5,445	G 3
Kajiado	G 4
Kakamega	F 3
Karungu	F 4
Kericho, 10,900	F 4
Kiambu	G 4
Kibwezi	G 4
Kipini	H 4
Kisii	F 4
Kisumu, 30,700	F 4
Kitale, 11,500	G 3
Kitui	G 4
Konza	G 4
Kwale	G 4
Laisamis	G 3
Lamu, 5,828	H 4
Lodwar	G 3
Lokitaung	G 3
Lolgorien	G 4
Machakos	G 4
Magadi	G 4
Malindi, 5,818	H 4
Marsabit	G 3
Meru	G 3
Mombasa, 234,400	G 4
Moyale	G 3
Nairobi (capital), 477,600	G 4
Naivasha	G 4
Nakuru, 47,800	G 4
Namanga	G 4
Nanyuki, 11,200	G 3
Ngong	G 4
North Horr	G 3
Nyeri, 9,900	G 4
Port Victoria	F 3
Rumuruti	G 3
South Horr	G 3
Thika, 18,100	G 4
Thomson's Falls, 5,316	G 3
Todenyang	G 3
Tsavo	G 4
Vanga	G 4
Voi	G 4
Wajir	H 3
Witu	H 4

OTHER FEATURES

Dawa (riv.)	H 3
Elgon (mt.)	F 3
Formosa (bay)	H 4
Galana (riv.)	G 4
Gedi (ruins)	G 4
Kavirondo (gulf)	F 4
Kenya (mt.)	G 4
Lorian (swamp)	G 3
Lotagipi (swamp)	F 2
Nyira (mt.)	G 3
Patta (isl.)	H 4
Royal Tsavo Nat'l Park	G 4
Rudolf (lake)	G 3
Tana (riv.)	G 4
Victoria (lake)	F 4

MALAWI

CITIES and TOWNS

Bandawe	F 6
Blantyre, 109,461	F 7
Chilumbe	F 6
Chipoka	F 6
Chiromo	F 7
Chitipa, 1,429	F 5
Cholo, 1,394	F 7
Dedza, 2,318	F 6
Dowa, 750	F 6
Fort Johnston, 1,467	G 6
Karonga, 1,128	F 5
Kasungu, 1,628	F 6
Lilongwe, 19,425	F 6
Livingstonia	F 6
Mchinji, 831	F 6
Mzimba, 4,156	F 6
Ncheu, 1,118	F 6
Nkhata Bay, 1,188	F 6
Nkhota Kota, 1,117	F 6
Nsanje, 1,373	G 7
Salima, 2,307	F 6
Zomba (cap.), 19,666	G 7

OTHER FEATURES

Chilwa (lake)	G 7
Malawi (Nyasa) (lake)	F 6
Mlanje (mt.)	G 7
Nyasa (lake)	F 6
Shire (riv.)	G 7

RWANDA

CITIES and TOWNS

Butare, 3,714	E 4
Cyangugu, 284	E 4
Gisenyi, 3,956	E 4
Kigali (cap.), 24,000	F 4
Nyabisindu, 1,010	F 4

OTHER FEATURES

Kagera Nat'l Park	F 4
Karisimbi (mt.)	E 4
Kivu (lake)	E 4
Ruzizi (riv.)	E 4

SOMALIA

PROVINCES

Benadir, 392,189	H 3
Hiran, 176,603	J 3
Lower Juba, 113,774	H 3
Mijirtein, 82,710	J 2
Mudugh, 141,197	J 2
North-East	J 1
North-West	H 1
Upper Juba, 362,397	H 3

CITIES and TOWNS

Adadle	H 2
Afgoi, ◉16,575	J 3
Afmadu, ◉2,580	H 3
Alula, ◉6,063	K 1
Ankhor	J 1
Audegle, ◉8,865	J 3
Baduen	J 2
Baidoa, ◉14,962	H 3
Balad, ◉1,936	J 3
Barawa (Brava), ◉6,168	H 3
Bardera, ◉7,874	H 3
Bargal, ◉2,222	K 1
Belet Uen, ◉11,426	J 3
Bender Beila, ◉6,084	K 2
Bender Kasim (Bosaso), ◉7,560	J 1
Berbera, ◉12,219	J 2
Bereda, ◉9,323	K 1
Birikao (Bur Gavo)	H 4
Bohotleh	J 2
Borama, ◉3,244	H 2
Bosaso, ◉7,560	J 1
Brava, ◉6,168	H 3
Bulhar	H 2
Bulo Burti, ◉5,247	J 3
Bur Acaba, ◉10,924	H 3
Burao, ◉12,617	J 2
Bur Gavo	H 4
Candala, ◉3,213	J 1
Coriolei, ◉4,341	H 3
Dante (Hafun)	K 1
Dif	H 3
Dinsor, ◉4,301	H 3
Dusa Mareb, ◉3,125	J 2
Eil, ◉2,234	J 2
El Athale (Itala), ◉900	J 3
El Bur, ◉3,224	J 3
El Dere, ◉10,924	J 3
El Hamurre	J 2
Erigavo, ◉4,279	J 1
Ferfer	J 2
Galkayu, ◉9,477	J 2
Garad	J 2
Gardo, ◉4,076	J 2
Garoe, ◉5,672	J 2
Gobwen	H 4
Hafun	K 1
Harardera, ◉824	J 3
Harghessa, ◉40,254	H 2
Hodur, ◉3,137	H 3
Hordio	K 1
Iddan	J 2

(continued on following page)

(continued)

SOMALIA (cantinued)

Iet, ◉1,370 .... H 3
Itala, ◉900 .... J 3
Jamama, ◉22,030 .... H 3
Jelib, ◉3,232 .... H 3
Johar, ◉13,156 .... H 3
Kismayu, ◉17,872 .... H 4
Las Anod, ◉2,441 .... J 2
Las Dureh .... J 1
Las Khoreh, ◉2,245 .... J 1
Lugh, ◉3,768 .... H 3
Marek .... J 3
Margherita (Jamama), ◉22,030 .... H 3
Merka, ◉56,385 .... H 3
Mogadishu, 172,677 .... J 3
Obbia, ◉2,106 .... J 2
Odweina, ◉1,422 .... J 2
Skushuban, ◉1,384 .... J 1
Taleh .... J 2
Tijeglo, ◉5,459 .... H 3
Uanle Uen, ◉9,650 .... H 3
Upper Sheikh .... J 2
Villabruzzi (Johar), ◉13,156 .... J 3
Vittorio d'Africa .... H 3
Zeila, ◉1,226 .... H 1

OTHER FEATURES

Aden (gulf) .... J 1
Chiamboni, Ras (cape) .... H 4
Guardafui (cape) .... K 1
Guban (reg.) .... H 1
Hafun, Ras (cape) .... K 1
Haud (plat.) .... J 2
Juba (riv.) .... H 3
Negro (bay) .... J 2
Nogal (reg.) .... J 2
Surud Ad (mt.) .... J 1
Wabi Shebelle (riv.) .... H 3

TANZANIA

PROVINCES

Arusha, 610,474 .... G 4
Coast, 511,506 .... G 5
Dar es Salaam (city), 272,821 .... G 5
Dodoma, 709,380 .... G 5
Iringa, 689,905 .... G 5
Kigoma, 473,443 .... F 4
Kilimanjaro, 652,722 .... G 4
Mara, 544,125 .... F 4
Mbeya, 969,053 .... F 5
Morogoro, 685,104 .... G 5
Mtwara, 1,041,146 .... G 5
Mwanza, 1,055,883 .... F 4
Pemba, 164,321 .... H 5
Ruvuma, 393,043 .... G 6
Shinyanga, 899,468 .... F 4
Singida, 457,938 .... F 5
Tabora, 562,871 .... F 5
Tanga, 771,060 .... G 5
West Lake, 658,712 .... F 4
Zanzibar (city), 95,047 .... F 4
Zanzibar (rural), 95,447 .... G 5

CITIES and TOWNS

Arusha, 32,452 .... G 4
Bagamoyo, 5,112 .... G 5
Biharamulo, 1,011 .... F 4
Bukene, 2,288 .... F 4
Bukoba, 8,141 .... F 4
Chake Chake, 4,862 .... G 5
Chunya, 2,398 .... F 5
Dar es Salaam (capital), 272,821 .... G 5
Dodoma, 23,559 .... G 5
Geita, 3,066 .... F 4
Handeni .... G 5
Ifakara, †21,101 .... G 5
Iringa, 21,746 .... G 5
Itigi, †6,633 .... F 5
Kahama, 3,211 .... F 4
Kaliua, †13,071 .... F 5
Karema, †3,171 .... F 5
Kasanga, †10,462 .... F 5
Kasulu .... F 4
Kibara, †18,827 .... F 4
Kibaya, †4,422 .... G 5
Kibondo .... F 4
Kigoma-Ujiji, 21,369 .... E 4
Kilosa, 4,458 .... G 5
Kilwa Kivinje, 2,790 .... G 5
Kilwa Masoko .... G 5
Kinyangiri, †14,111 .... G 4
Kipili, †2,964 .... F 5
Kisiju, †26,298 .... G 5
Kitunda, †2,491 .... F 5
Kizimkazi, 992 .... G 5
Koani, 1,102 .... G 5
Kondoa, 4,514 .... G 4
Kongwa, †27,411 .... G 5
Korogwe, 6,675 .... G 5
Lindi, 13,352 .... G 5
Liwale, †22,205 .... G 5
Longido, †1,998 .... G 4
Lushoto, 1,803 .... G 4
Mahenge, †32,047 .... G 5
Makumbako .... G 5
Manyoni, †4,362 .... G 5
Masasi .... G 6
Mbamba Bay, †10,936 .... G 6
Mbeya, 12,479 .... F 5
Mbulu, †7,004 .... G 4
Mchinga, †5,778 .... H 5
Mohoro-Kikobo, †6,112 .... G 5
Mombo, †29,782 .... G 4
Morogoro, 25,262 .... G 5
Moshi, 26,864 .... G 4
Mpanda, †4,220 .... F 5
Mpwapwa, 2,429 .... G 5
Mtwara-Mikindani, 20,413 .... H 6
Murongo, †20,118 .... F 4
Musoma, 15,412 .... F 4
Muwale .... F 5
Mwadui, 7,383 .... F 4
Mwanza, 34,861 .... F 4
Mwaya, †15,940 .... F 5
Mwesi, †803 .... F 5
Nachingwea, 3,751 .... G 6
Newala, †7,458 .... G 6
Ngara .... F 4
Njombe .... F 5
Nzega, 2,386 .... F 4
Pangani, 2,955 .... G 5
Rungwa, †903 .... F 5
Sadani, †760 .... G 5
Same, †8,105 .... G 4
Sekenke .... F 4
Shinyanga, 5,135 .... F 4
Singida, 9,478 .... F 4
Songea, 5,430 .... G 6
Sumbawanga, †34,106 .... F 5
Tabora, 21,012 .... F 5
Tanga, 61,058 .... G 4
Tukuyu, 4,089 .... F 5
Tunduru .... G 6
Urambo, †16,625 .... F 4
Utete, †5,642 .... G 5
Uvinza, †12,812 .... F 5
Wete, 8,469 .... G 4
Zanzibar, 68,490 .... G 5
Zanzibar, *95,047 .... G 5

OTHER FEATURES

Eyasi (lake) .... F 4
Gombe (riv.) .... F 4
Great Ruaha (riv.) .... G 5
Juani (isl.), 696 .... G 5
Kalambo (falls) .... F 5
Kanzi (cape) .... G 5
Kilimanjaro (mt.) .... G 4
Kilombero (riv.) .... G 5
Kungwe (mt.) .... F 5
Mafia (isl.), 15,459 .... H 5
Manyara (lake) .... G 4
Masai (steppe) .... G 4
Mbarangandu (riv.) .... G 5
Mbemkuru (riv.) .... G 5
Meru (mt.) .... G 4
Natron (lake) .... G 4
Ngorongoro (crater) .... F 4
Njombe (riv.) .... F 5
Nyasa (lake) .... F 6
Olduvai Gorge (canyon) .... G 4
Pangani (riv.) .... G 4
Pemba (isl.), 164,321 .... H 5
Rufiji (riv.) .... G 5
Rukwa (lake) .... F 5
Rungwa (riv.) .... F 5
Rungwe (mt.) .... F 5
Ruvuma (riv.) .... G 4
Serengeti Nat'l Park .... F 4
Tanganyika (lake) .... E 5
Victoria (lake) .... F 4
Wami (riv.) .... G 5
Wembere (riv.) .... F 4
Zanzibar (isl.), 190,494 .... G 5

UGANDA

CITIES and TOWNS

Arua, 4,645 .... F 3
Atura, 119 .... F 3
Butiaba, 1,216 .... F 3
Entebbe, 10,941 .... F 4
Fort Portal, 8,317 .... F 3
Gulu, 4,770 .... F 3
Hoima, 1,056 .... F 3
Jinja, 29,741 .... F 3
Kaabong .... F 3
Kabale, 10,919 .... E 4
Kampala (capital), 330,000 .... F 3
Kasese, 1,564 .... F 3
Katwe, 2,057 .... F 4
Kilembe .... F 3
Kitgum, 3,454 .... F 3
Lira, 2,929 .... F 3
Masaka, 4,785 .... F 4
Masindi, 1,571 .... F 3
Mbale, 23,539 .... F 3
Mbarara, 3,844 .... F 4
Moroto, 2,082 .... F 3
Moyo, 2,009 .... F 3
Mubende, 1,878 .... F 3
Namasagali .... F 3
Pakwach, 1,467 .... F 3
Rhino Camp, 3,478 .... F 3
Soroti, 6,645 .... F 3
Tororo, 6,365 .... F 3
Yumbe, 949 .... F 3

OTHER FEATURES

Albert (lake) .... F 3
Edward (lake) .... E 4
Elgon (mt.) .... F 3
George (lake) .... F 4
Kioga (lake) .... F 3
Margherita (mt.) .... E 3
Murchison (falls) .... F 3
Owen Falls (dam) .... F 3
Queen Elizabeth Nat'l Park .... F 4
Ruwenzori (range) .... E 3
Sese (isls.) .... F 4
Victoria (lake) .... F 4

ZAIRE

PROVINCES

Bandundu, 2,600,556 .... C 4
Bas-Zaïre, 1,504,361 .... B 4
Equateur, 2,431,812 .... D 3
Haut-Zaïre, 3,356,419 .... E 3
Kasai-Occidental, 2,433,861 .... D 4
Kasai-Oriental, 1,872,231 .... D 5
Katanga, 2,753,714 .... E 5
Kinshasa (city), 1,323,039 .... C 4
Kivu, 3,361,883 .... E 4

CITIES and TOWNS

Aba .... F 3
Abumombazi, †5,773 .... D 3
Aketi, 15,339 .... D 3
Ango .... E 3
Avakubi .... E 3
Bagata .... C 4
Balangala .... D 3
Bambesa .... E 3
Bambili .... E 3
Banana .... B 5
Bandundu, 74,467 .... C 4
Banzyville, 6,608 .... D 3
Baraka .... E 4
Basankusu, 5,613 .... C 3
Basoko .... D 3
Basongo .... D 4
Batama .... E 3
Baudouinville .... E 5
Befale, 3,407 .... D 3
Bena-Dibele .... D 4
Beni .... E 3
Bikoro, 6,491 .... C 4
Boende, 391 .... D 4
Bokungu, 4,952 .... D 4
Bolobo .... C 4
Bolomba, 5,636 .... C 3
Boma, 33,143 .... B 5
Bomboma, 1,319 .... C 3
Bomongo, 4,827 .... C 3
Bondo, 453 .... D 3
Bongandanga, 4,476 .... D 3
Bosobolo, 2,809 .... D 3
Budjala, 415 .... C 3
Bukama .... E 5
Bukavu, 134,861 .... E 4
Bumba, 5,182 .... D 3
Bunia, 12,410 .... E 3
Bunkeya .... E 6
Busanga, †2,792 .... D 6
Businga, 2,827 .... D 3
Busu-Djanoa, †5,520 .... D 3
Buta, 10,845 .... D 3
Butembo, 9,980 .... E 3
Dekese .... D 4
Demba .... D 5
Dibaya .... D 5
Dibaya-Lubue .... C 4
Dilolo .... D 6
Dimbelenge .... D 5
Djolu, 2,516 .... D 3
Djugu .... F 3
Djuma .... C 4
Dongo, 559 .... C 3
Doruma .... E 3
Dungu .... E 3
Elila .... E 4
Equateur .... C 3
Etoile .... E 6
Faradje .... E 3
Feshi .... C 5
Fizi .... E 4
Gandajika .... D 5
Gemena, 8,135 .... D 3
Goma, 14,115 .... E 4
Gombari .... E 3
Gumba-Mobeka, †7,023 .... C 3
Idiofa .... C 4
Ikela, 3,166 .... D 4
Imese, 115 .... C 3
Ingende, 6,730 .... C 4
Inongo .... C 4
Irumu .... E 3
Isangi .... D 3
Isangila .... B 5
Isiro, 17,430 .... E 3
Kabalo .... E 5
Kabare .... E 4
Kabinda .... D 5
Kabongo .... E 5
Kabunda .... E 6
Kahemba .... C 5
Kalehe .... E 4
Kalemie, 29,934 .... E 5
Kalima .... E 4
Kaloko .... E 5
Kama .... E 4
Kambove (with Shinkolobwe), 14,517 .... E 6
Kamina, 20,915 .... D 5
Kanda Kanda .... D 5
Kaniama .... D 5
Kapanga .... D 5
Kasaji .... D 6
Kasangulu .... C 4
Kasenyi .... E 3
Kasese .... E 4
Kasongo .... E 4
Kasongo-Lunda .... C 5
Katako-Kombe .... D 4
Katana .... E 4
Katenga .... E 5
Kazumba .... D 5
Kenge .... C 4
Kibombo .... E 4
Kikwit, 111,960 .... C 5
Kilo .... E 3
Kilwa .... E 5
Kindu-Port Empain, 19,385 .... E 4
Kiniama .... E 6
Kinshasa (capital), 1,323,039 .... C 4
Kipushi, 22,602 .... E 6
Kirundu .... E 4
Kisangani, 229,596 .... E 3
Kolwezi, 45,192 .... E 6
Komba .... D 3
Kongolo, 10,434 .... E 5
Kungu, 7,912 .... C 3
Kutu, †2,072 .... C 4
Kwamouth .... C 4
Libenge, 2,632 .... C 3
Lienartville .... E 3
Likasi, 146,394 .... E 6
Likati .... D 3
Lisala, 574 .... D 3
Lodja, 7,227 .... D 4
Lokolama .... D 4
Lomela, †7,757 .... D 4
Loto .... D 4
Lotumbe .... C 4
Luashi .... D 6
Lubefu .... D 4
Lubudi, 5,915 .... E 5
Lubumbashi, 318,000 .... E 6
Lubutu .... E 4
Luebo .... D 5
Luena .... E 5
Luishia .... E 6
Lukula .... B 4
Luluabourg, 428,960 .... D 5
Lunyama .... E 5
Luofu .... E 4
Luozi .... B 5
Luputa .... D 5
Lusambo, 9,395 .... D 4
Lusangi .... E 4
Madimba .... C 5
Malonga .... D 6
Mambasa .... E 3
Manono, 12,234 .... E 5
Masi-Manimba .... C 4
Masisi .... E 4
Matadi, 110,436 .... B 5
Mbandaka, 107,910 .... C 3
Mbuji-Mayi, 256,154 .... D 5
Moanda .... B 5
Moba .... E 5
Moliro .... E 5
Monga .... D 3
Monkoto, 5,209 .... D 4
Monveda .... D 3
Mungbere .... E 3
Mushie, 12,118 .... C 4
Mutshatsha .... D 6
Muyumba .... E 5
Mwadingusha .... E 6
Mwanza .... E 5
Mwene Ditu .... D 5
Mwenga .... E 4
Niangara .... E 3
Niemba .... E 5
Nouvelle-Anvers, †4,330 .... C 3
Nyunzu .... E 5
Oshwe .... C 4
Panda .... E 6
Pangi .... E 4
Penge .... D 5
Piana-Mwanga .... E 5
Poie .... D 4
Poko .... E 3
Ponthierville .... D 4
Port-Francqui .... D 4
Punia .... E 4
Pweto .... E 5
Rutshuru .... E 4
Sakania .... E 6
Sampwe .... E 5
Sandoa .... D 5
Shabunda .... E 4
Shinkolobwe (with Kambove), 14,517 .... E 6
Songololo .... B 5
Thysville, 16,369 .... C 5
Titule .... E 3
Tolo .... C 4
Tondo .... C 4
Tshela .... B 4
Tshikapa .... D 5
Tshofa .... D 5
Uvira .... E 4
Vanga .... C 4
Wafania, 584 .... D
Waka, 264 .... D
Wamba .... E
Watsa, 6,077 .... E
Yakoma, †5,685 .... D
Yangambi, 18,849 .... D
Zongo, †4,128 C

OTHER FEATURES

Albert (lake) .... F
Albert Nat'l Park .... E
Aruwimi (riv.) .... E
Bomu (riv.) .... D
Congo (riv.) C
Edward (lake) .... E
Elila (riv.) .... E
Fimi (riv.) C
Garamba Nat'l Park .... E
Giri (riv.) C
Itimbiri (riv.) .... D
Ituri (for.) .... E
Karisimbi (mt.) .... E
Kasai (riv.) C
Kivu (lake) .... E
Kwa (riv.) C
Kwango (riv.) C
Kwilu (riv.) C
Léopold II (lake) C
Lindi (riv.) .... E
Livingstone (falls) .... B
Loange (riv.) C
Lokoro (riv.) C
Lomami (riv.) .... D
Lomela (riv.) .... D
Lowa (riv.) .... E
Lua (riv.) C
Lualaba (riv.) .... E
Luapula (riv.) .... E
Lubilash (riv.) .... D
Lufira (riv.) .... E
Luilaka (riv.) .... D
Lukenie (riv.) .... D
Lukuga (riv.) .... E
Lulua (riv.) .... D
Luvua (riv.) .... E
Margherita (mt.) .... E
Mweru (lake) .... E
Marungu (mts.) .... E
Ruwenzori (range) .... E
Ruzizi (riv.) .... E
Sankuru (riv.) .... D
Stanley (falls) .... E
Stanley Pool (lake) C
Tanganyika (lake) .... E
Tshuapa (riv.) .... D
Tumba (lake) C
Ubangi (riv.) C
Uele (riv.) .... E
Ulindi (riv.) .... E
Upemba (lake) .... E
Upemba Nat'l Park .... E
Virunga (range) .... E
Zaire (Congo) (riv.) C

ZAMBIA

CITIES and TOWNS

Abercorn (Mbala), ‡5,200 .... F
Balovale, 2,260 .... D
Bancroft (Chililabombwe), ‡39,900 .... E
Broken Hill (Kabwe), ‡67,200 .... E
Chilanga, 2,510 .... E
Chililabombwe, ‡39,900 .... E
Chingola, ‡92,800 .... E
Chinsali, 1,110 .... F
Chipata, ‡13,300 .... F
Chisamba, 790 .... E
Choma, ‡11,300 .... E
Feira, 310 .... E
Fort Rosebery (Mansa), ‡5,700 .... E
Isoka, 1,370 .... F
Kabompo, 990 .... D
Kabwe, ‡67,200 .... E
Kafue, 2,490 .... E
Kalabo, 2,420 .... D
Kalomo, 2,560 .... E
Kapiri Mposhi, 440 .... E
Kasama, ‡8,900 .... F
Kasempa, 670 .... E
Kawambwa, 1,430 .... E
Kitwe, ‡179,300 .... E
Lealui .... D
Livingstone, ‡43,000 .... E
Luanshya, ‡90,400 .... E
Lukulu .... D
Lundazi, 1,750 .... F
Lusaka (capital), ‡238,200 .... E
Luwingu, 850 .... E
Mankoya, 1,600 .... D
Mansa, ‡5,700 .... E
Mazabuka, ‡9,400 .... E
Mbala, ‡5,200 .... F
Mongu, ‡10,700 .... D
Monze, ‡4,300 .... E
Mpika, 660 .... F
Mporokoso, 790 .... F
Mpulungu, 1,830 .... F
Mufulira, ‡101,200 .... E
Mumbwa, 1,400 .... E
Mwinilunga, 700 .... D
Nakonde .... F
Namwala, 880 .... E
Nchanga, 35,030 .... E
Ndola, ‡150,800 .... E
Nkana, 54,500 .... E
Petauke, 1,640 .... F
Roan Antelope, 36,300 .... E
Senanga, 1,500 .... D
Serenje, 1,650 .... F
Sesheke, 910 .... D
Solwezi, 1,930 .... E

OTHER FEATURES

Bangweulu (lake) .... F
Barotseland (reg.), 417,000 .... D
Chambeshi (riv.) .... F
Dongwe (riv.) .... D
Kabampo (riv.) .... D
Kafue (riv.) .... E
Kariba (dam) .... E
Kariba (lake) .... E
Kwando (riv.) .... D
Luangwa (riv.) .... F
Mosi-Ao-Tunya (Victoria) (falls) .... E
Mulungushi (dam) .... E
Mweru (lake) .... E
Sunzu (mt.) .... F
Tanganyika (lake) .... E
Victoria (falls) .... E
Zambezi (riv.) .... D

*City and suburbs.
†Population of sub-district or divisio
‡Population of urban area.
◉Population of municipality.

Agriculture, Industry and Resources

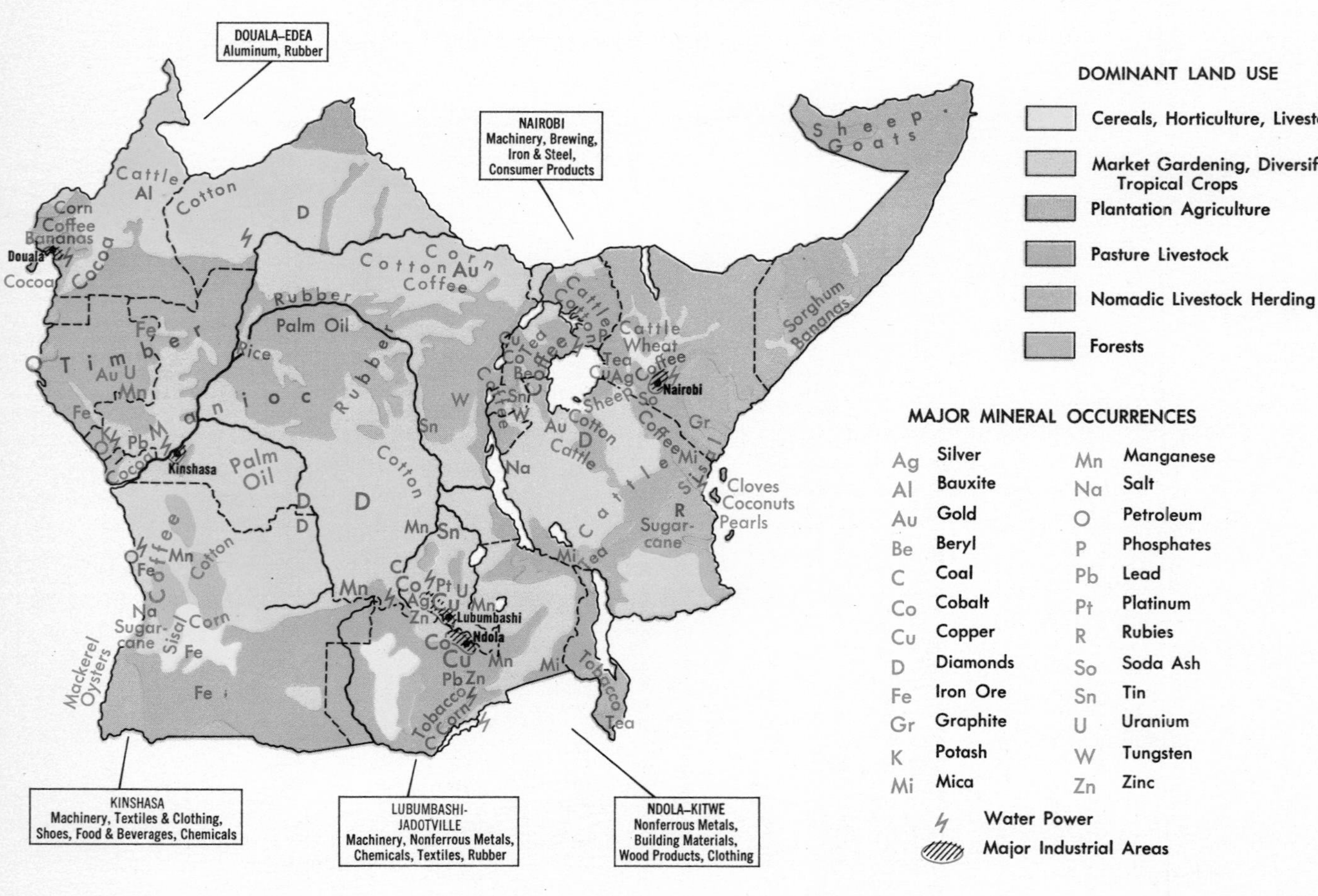

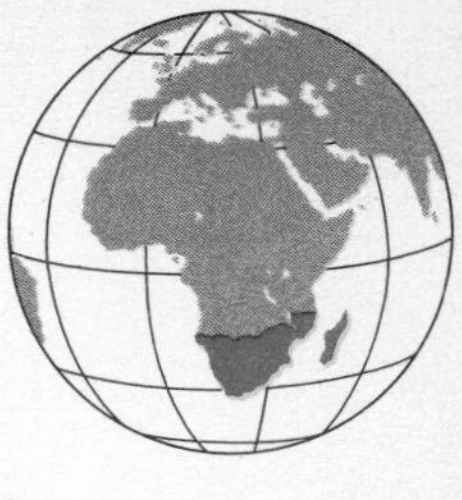

SOUTH-WEST AFRICA
AREA 317,838 sq. mi.
POPULATION 615,000
CAPITAL Windhoek
LARGEST CITY Windhoek
HIGHEST POINT Brandberg 8,550 ft.
MONETARY UNIT rand
MAJOR LANGUAGES Ovambo, Hottentot, Herero, Afrikaans, English
MAJOR RELIGIONS Tribal religions, Protestantism

BOTSWANA
AREA 219,815 sq. mi.
POPULATION 629,000
CAPITAL Gaborone
LARGEST CITIES Serowe and Kanye
HIGHEST POINT Tsodilo Hill 5,922 ft.
MONETARY UNIT pound sterling
MAJOR LANGUAGES Setswana, Shona, Bushman, English
MAJOR RELIGIONS Tribal religions, Protestantism

RHODESIA
AREA 150,332 sq. mi.
POPULATION 5,310,000
CAPITAL Salisbury
LARGEST CITY Salisbury
HIGHEST POINT Mt. Inyangani 8,517 ft.
MONETARY UNIT Rhodesian pound
MAJOR LANGUAGES English, Shona, Ndabele
MAJOR RELIGIONS Tribal religions, Protestantism

SOUTH AFRICA
AREA 471,663 sq. mi.
POPULATION 21,282,000
CAPITALS Cape Town, Pretoria
LARGEST CITY Johannesburg
HIGHEST POINT Injasuti 11,182 ft.
MONETARY UNIT rand
MAJOR LANGUAGES Afrikaans, English, Xhosa, Zulu, Sesotho, Pedi
MAJOR RELIGIONS Protestantism, Roman Catholicism, Islam, Hinduism

MOZAMBIQUE
AREA 302,328 sq. mi.
POPULATION 7,376,000
CAPITAL Lourenço Marques
LARGEST CITY Lourenço Marques
HIGHEST POINT Mt. Binga 7,992 ft.
MONETARY UNIT Portuguese escudo
MAJOR LANGUAGES Makua, Thonga, Shona, Portuguese
MAJOR RELIGIONS Tribal religions, Roman Catholicism

MALAGASY REPUBLIC
AREA 226,657 sq. mi.
POPULATION 7,011,563
CAPITAL Tananarive
LARGEST CITY Tananarive
HIGHEST POINT Maromokotro 9,436 ft.
MONETARY UNIT CFA franc
MAJOR LANGUAGES Malagasy, French
MAJOR RELIGIONS Tribal religions, Roman Catholicism, Protestantism

MAURITIUS
AREA 709 sq. mi.
POPULATION 823,000
CAPITAL Port Louis
LARGEST CITY Port Louis
HIGHEST POINT 2,711 ft.
MONETARY UNIT Mauritius rupee
MAJOR LANGUAGES English, French, French Creole, Hindi
MAJOR RELIGIONS Hinduism, Christianity

LESOTHO
AREA 11,716 sq. mi.
POPULATION 930,000
CAPITAL Maseru
LARGEST CITY Maseru
HIGHEST POINT 11,425 ft.
MONETARY UNIT rand
MAJOR LANGUAGES Sesotho, English
MAJOR RELIGIONS Tribal religions, Christianity

SWAZILAND
AREA 6,704 sq. mi.
POPULATION 411,879
CAPITAL Mbabane
LARGEST CITY Mbabane
HIGHEST POINT Emlembe 6,109 ft.
MONETARY UNIT rand
MAJOR LANGUAGES Swazi, English
MAJOR RELIGIONS Tribal religions, Christianity

RÉUNION
AREA 969 sq. mi.
POPULATION 436,000
CAPITAL St-Denis

SEYCHELLES
AREA 109 sq. mi.
POPULATION 51,396
CAPITAL Victoria

COMORO ISLANDS
AREA 838 sq. mi.
POPULATION 270,000
CAPITAL Moroni

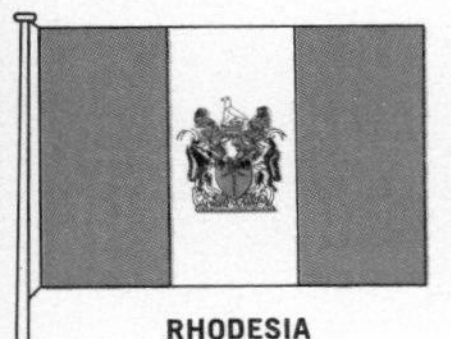
RHODESIA

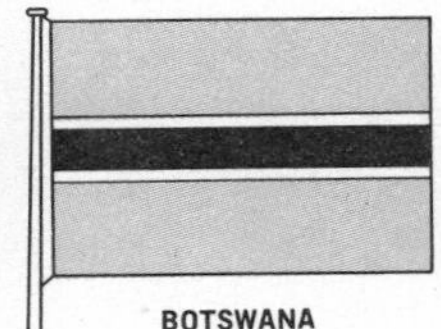
BOTSWANA

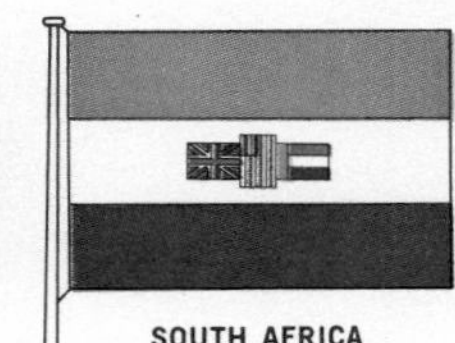
SOUTH AFRICA

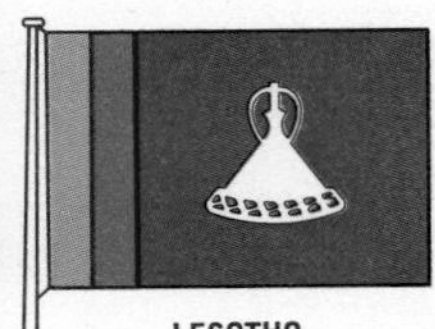
LESOTHO

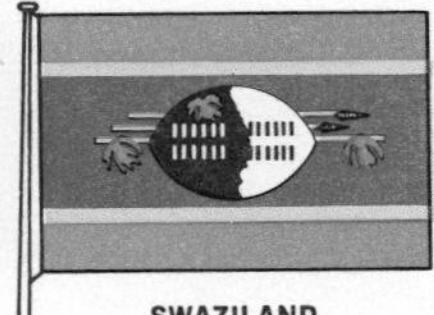
SWAZILAND

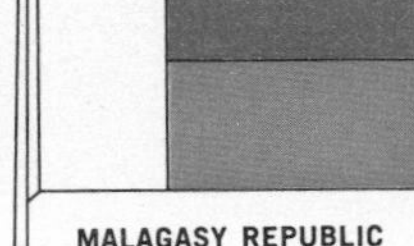
MALAGASY REPUBLIC

MAURITIUS

Agriculture, Industry and Resources

DOMINANT LAND USE

- Cereals, Horticulture, Livestock
- Market Gardening, Diversified Tropical Crops
- Plantation Agriculture
- Pasture Livestock
- Nomadic Livestock Herding
- Forests
- Nonagricultural Land

MAJOR MINERAL OCCURRENCES

Ab	Asbestos	Mn	Manganese
Ag	Silver	Na	Salt
Au	Gold	Ni	Nickel
Be	Beryl	P	Phosphates
C	Coal	Pb	Lead
Cr	Chromium	Pt	Platinum
Cu	Copper	Sb	Antimony
D	Diamonds	Sn	Tin
Fe	Iron Ore	U	Uranium
Gr	Graphite	V	Vanadium
Lt	Lithium	W	Tungsten
Mg	Magnesium	Zn	Zinc
Mi	Mica		

Water Power
Major Industrial Areas

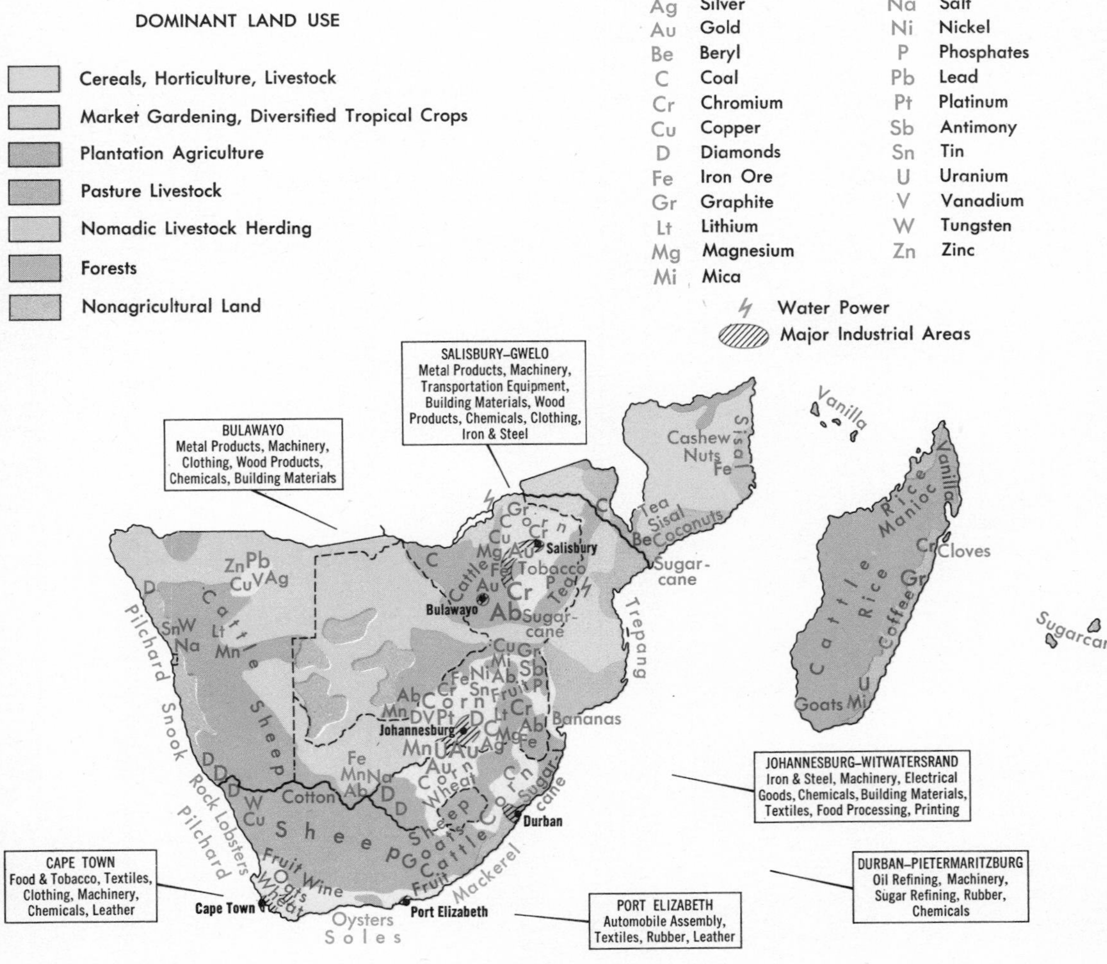

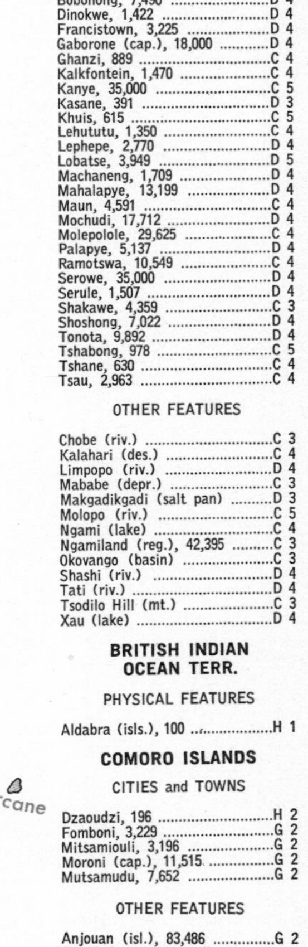
BOTSWANA

CITIES and TOWNS

Bobonong, 7,490 ....D 4
Dinokwe, 1,422 ....D 4
Francistown, 3,225 ....D 4
Gaborone (cap.), 18,000 ....D 4
Ghanzi, 889 ....C 4
Kalkfontein, 1,470 ....C 4
Kanye, 35,000 ....C 5
Kasane, 391 ....D 3
Khuis, 615 ....C 5
Lehututu, 1,350 ....C 4
Lephepe, 2,770 ....D 4
Lobatse, 3,949 ....D 5
Machaneng, 1,709 ....D 4
Mahalapye, 13,199 ....D 4
Maun, 4,591 ....C 4
Mochudi, 17,712 ....D 4
Molepolole, 29,625 ....C 4
Palapye, 5,137 ....D 4
Ramotswa, 10,549 ....C 4
Serowe, 35,000 ....D 4
Serule, 1,507 ....D 4
Shakawe, 4,359 ....C 3
Shoshong, 7,022 ....D 4
Tonota, 9,892 ....D 4
Tshabong, 978 ....C 5
Tshane, 630 ....C 4
Tsau, 2,963 ....C 4

OTHER FEATURES

Chobe (riv.) ....C 3
Kalahari (des.) ....C 4
Limpopo (riv.) ....D 4
Mababe (depr.) ....C 3
Makgadikgadi (salt pan) ....D 3
Molopo (riv.) ....C 5
Ngami (lake) ....C 4
Ngamiland (reg.), 42,395 ....C 3
Okovango (basin) ....C 3
Shashi (riv.) ....D 4
Tati (riv.) ....D 4
Tsodilo Hill (mt.) ....C 3
Xau (lake) ....D 4

BRITISH INDIAN OCEAN TERR.

PHYSICAL FEATURES

Aldabra (isls.), 100 ....H 1

COMORO ISLANDS

CITIES and TOWNS

Dzaoudzi, 196 ....H 2
Fomboni, 3,229 ....G 2
Mitsamiouli, 3,196 ....G 2
Moroni (cap.), 11,515 ....G 2
Mutsamudu, 7,652 ....G 2

OTHER FEATURES

Anjouan (isl.), 83,486 ....G 2
Grand Comoro (island), 118,443 ....G 2
Mayotte (isl.), 32,494 ....G 2
Mohéli (isl.), 9,525 ....G 2

LESOTHO

CITIES and TOWNS

Leribe, 3,799 ....D 5
Mafeteng, 5,050 ....D 5
Maseru (cap.), 18,797 ....D 5
Mohaleshoek, 3,753 ....D 6

MALAGASY REPUBLIC

PROVINCES

Diégo Suarez, 575,424 ....H 2
Fianarantsoa, 1,720,922 ....H 3
Majunga, 839,654 ....H 3
Tamatave, 1,096,235 ....H 3
Tananarive, 1,692,607 ....H 3
Tuléar, 1,086,721 ....G 4

CITIES and TOWNS

Ambalavao, 6,045 ....H 4
Ambanja, 5,198 ....H 2
Ambato Boina, 3,108 ....H 3
Ambatofinandrahana, 2,039 ....H 4
Ambatolampy, 10,504 ....H 3
Ambatondrazaka, 14,297 ....H 3
Ambilobe, 7,877 ....H 2
Amboasary, 2,260 ....H 4
Ambodifototra, 1,080 ....J 3
Ambohimahasoa, 5,114 ....H 4
Ambositra, 15,131 ....H 4
Ambovombe, 3,161 ....H 5
Ampanihy, 2,078 ....G 4
Analalava, 3,061 ....H 2
Andapa, 8,296 ....H 2
Andilamena, 2,767 ....H 3
Ankazoabo, 1,528 ....G 4
Anororoa, 2,445 ....H 3
Antalaha, 18,083 ....J 2
Antsalova, 1,867 ....G 3
Antsirabe, 29,914 ....H 3
Antsohihy, 7,618 ....H 2
Arivonimamo, 7,011 ....H 3
Bealanana, 2,820 ....H 2
Befandriana, 2,714 ....H 3
Bekily, 1,556 ....G 4
Belo-sur-Tsiribihina, 4,391 ....G 3
Beroroha, 1,549 ....G 4
Besalampy, 2,519 ....G 3
Betioky, 2,256 ....G 4
Betroka, 4,071 ....H 4
Brickaville, 1,750 ....H 3
Diégo-Suarez, 40,237 ....H 2
Fandriana, 3,406 ....H 4
Farafangana, 10,753 ....H 4
Fénérive, 7,080 ....H 3
Fianarantsoa, 45,790 ....H 4
Fort-Dauphin, 12,677 ....H 5
Hell-Ville, 9,481 ....H 2
Ifanadiana, 1,090 ....H 4
Ihosy, 6,578 ....H 4
Ivohibe, 1,150 ....H 4
Maevatanana, 5,147 ....H 3
Mahabo, 2,821 ....G 4
Mahanoro, 4,930 ....H 3
Maintirano, 4,594 ....G 3
Majunga, 47,654 ....H 3
Manakara, 17,567 ....H 4
Mananara, 3,163 ....J 3
Mananjary, 13,019 ....H 4
Mandritsara, 6,025 ....H 3
Manja, 4,671 ....G 4
Maroantsetra, 7,184 ....J 3
Marolambo, 953 ....H 4
Marovoay, 18,074 ....H 3
Miandrivazo, 2,485 ....G 3
Midongy Sud, 959 ....H 4
Mitsinjo, 1,204 ....H 3
Morafenobe, 725 ....G 3
Moramanga, 10,706 ....H 3
Morombe, 6,684 ....G 4
Morondava, 15,032 ....G 4
Nosy-Varika, 938 ....H 4
Port-Bergé, 3,345 ....H 3
Sambava, 6,198 ....J 2
Soalala, 774 ....H 3
Soanierana-Ivongo, 2,592 ....H 3
Tamatave, 53,173 ....H 3

(continued on following page)

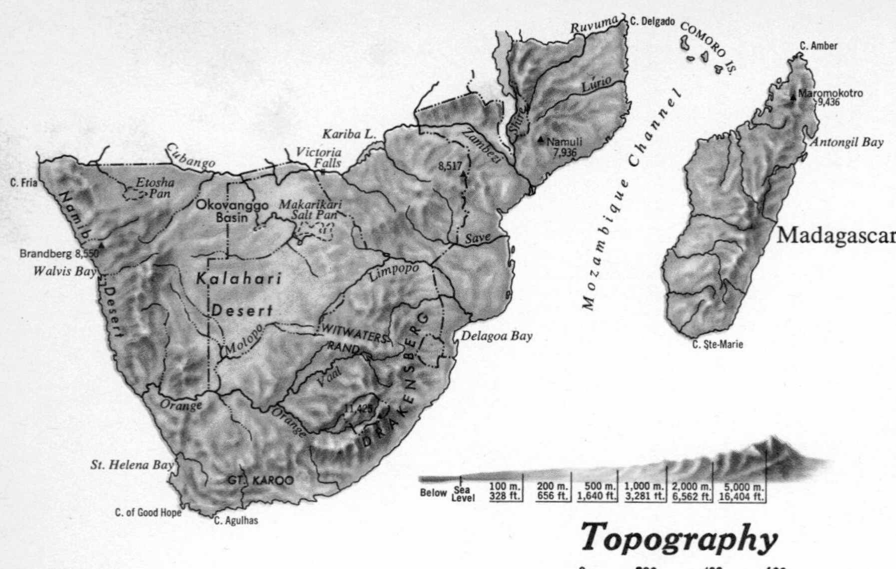

Topography

0 200 400 600
MILES

MALAGASY REPUBLIC (continued)

Tananarive (capital), 332,885 ....H 3
Tananarive, *447,016 ....H 3
Tsiroanomandidy, 9,956 ....H 3
Tuléar, 33,842 ....G 4
Vangaindrano, 2,665 ....H 4
Vatomandry, 3,739 ....H 3
Vohémar, 3,622 ....J 2
Vohipeno ....H 4

OTHER FEATURES

Alaotra (lake) ....H 3
Amber (cape) ....H 2
Antongil (bay) ....J 3
Barren (isls.) ....G 3
Betsiboka (riv.) ....H 3
Boby, Pic (mt.) ....H 4
Chesterfield (isl.) ....G 3
Ikopa (riv.) ....H 3
Itasy (lake) ....H 3
Madagascar (isl.) ....G 4
Mahajamba (bay) ....H 2
Mananara (riv.) ....H 4
Mananbao (riv.) ....G 3
Mangoky (riv.) ....G 4
Mangoro (riv.) ....H 3
Maromokotro (mt.) ....H 2
Masoala (pen.) ....J 3
Menarandra (riv.) ....H 4
Mozambique (chan.) ....G 3
Nossi-Bé (isl.), 26,462 ....H 2
Onilahy (riv.) ....G 4
Radama (isls.) ....H 2
Saint-André (cape) ....G 3
Sainte-Marie (cape) ....G 5
Sainte-Marie (isl.), 9,090 ....J 3
Saint-Sébastien (cape) ....H 2
Sofia (riv.) ....H 3
Tsiafajavona (mt.) ....H 3
Tsiribihina (riv.) ....G 3

MAURITIUS

CITIES and TOWNS

Curepipe, 49,000 ....G 5
Mahébourg, 13,005 ....G 5
Port Louis (capital), 131,000 ....G 5
Poudre d'Or, 1,208 ....G 5
Quatre Bornes, 28,389 ....G 5
Souillac, 2,606 ....G 5

MOZAMBIQUE

DISTRICTS

Cabo Delgado, 542,165 ....F 2
Gaza, 675,150 ....E 4
Inhambane, 583,772 ....E 4
Lourenço Marques, 436,897 ....E 5
Manica e Sofala, 781,070 ....E 3
Moçambique, 1,444,555 ....F 2
Niassa, 276,810 ....F 2
Tete, 470,100 ....E 3
Zambézia, 1,363,619 ....F 3

CITIES and TOWNS

Alto Molócuè, †50,093 ....F 3
António Enes, †33,245 ....G 3
Bartolomeu Dias ....F 4
Beira, †58,235 ....F 3
Bela Vista, 206 ....E 5
Caniçado, †30,647 ....E 4
Chemba, †28,317 ....E 3
Chibuto, †122,989 ....E 4
Chicoa, †11,852 ....E 3
Cóbuè, †6,305 ....F 2
Dona Ana, †10,894 ....F 3
Entre-Rios, †28,475 ....F 2
Errego, †80,886 ....F 3
Espungabera, †37,353 ....E 4
Fíngoè, †14,926 ....E 2
Furancungo, †18,185 ....E 2
Homoíne, †57,959 ....E 4
Ibo, †4,394 ....G 2
Inhambane, †22,016 ....F 4
Inhaminga, †21,280 ....F 3
Inharrime, †40,721 ....F 4
João Belo, †48,959 ....E 5
Lourenço Marques (cap.), 65,716 ....E 5
Lourenço Marques, *177,929 ....E 5
Lumbo, †14,357 ....G 3
Lúrio, †9,932 ....G 2
Macia, †83,412 ....E 4
Macomia, †12,913 ....F 2
Magude, †44,183 ....E 5
Máguè, †10,695 ....E 3
Malvérnia, †11,373 ....E 4
Mandimba ....F 2
Manhiça, †6,267 ....E 5
Maniamba, †11,708 ....F 2
Manjacaze, †63,626 ....E 5
Marromeu, †33,096 ....F 3
Marrupa, †15,540 ....F 2
Massinga, †80,526 ....F 4
Maúa, †29,346 ....F 2
Meconta, †28,187 ....F 3
Mecúfi, †26,290 ....G 2
Mecula, †5,203 ....F 2
Memba, †51,703 ....G 2
Milange, †76,466 ....F 3
Moamba, 993 ....E 5
Moatize, †30,885 ....E 3
Mocambique, †12,166 ....G 3
Mocímboa da Praia, †28,335 ....G 2
Mocuba, †43,484 ....F 3
Mogincual, †21,786 ....G 3
Moma, †64,685 ....F 3
Montepuez, †46,667 ....F 2
Mopeia, †28,683 ....F 3
Morrumbala, †56,457 ....F 3
Morrumbene, †68,094 ....F 4
Mossuril, †25,494 ....G 2
Muecate, †35,068 ....F 2
Mueda, †51,229 ....F 2
Nacala, †43,439 ....G 2
Namacurra, †38,037 ....F 3
Namarrói, †55,925 ....F 3
Nampula, †104,648 ....F 3
Nova Mambone, †12,498 ....F 4
Nova Freixo, †146,186 ....F 2
Nova Luzitânia, †68,678 ....E 3
Nova Sofala, †16,468 ....F 4
Pafúri, †1,883 ....E 4
Palma, †15,451 ....G 2
Panda, †35,462 ....E 4
Pebane, †18,826 ....F 3
Porto Amélia, †21,005 ....G 2
Quelimane, †62,717 ....F 3
Quionga, †2,486 ....G 2
Quissanga, †11,463 ....G 2
Quissico, †69,940 ....F 4
Ribáuè, †29,689 ....F 3
Tete, †38,196 ....E 3
Vila Cabral, †28,701 ....F 2
Vila Coutinho, †41,193 ....E 2
Vila de Maganja, †52,722 ....F 3
Vila de Manica, †14,151 ....E 3
Vila de Sena, †46,616 ....E 3
Vila do Chinde, †25,617 ....F 3
Vila do Dondo, †39,683 ....F 3
Vila Fontes, †29,434 ....E 3
Vila Gouveia, †18,449 ....E 3
Vila Luísa, 294 ....E 5
Vilanculos, †67,041 ....E 4
Vila Paiva de Andrada †44,692 ....E 3
Vila Pery, †36,406 ....E 3
Zumbo, †9,978 ....E 3

OTHER FEATURES

Angoche (isl.) ....G 3
Bazaruto (isl.) ....F 4
Binga (mt.) ....E 3
Caça Nat'l Park ....E 3
Changane (riv.) ....E 4
Chilwa (lake) ....F 3
Delagoa (bay) ....E 5
Delgado (cape) ....G 2
Ligonha (riv.) ....F 3
Lugenda (riv.) ....F 2
Lúrio (riv.) ....F 2
Mazoe (riv.) ....E 3
Mozambique (chan.) ....G 3
Namuli (mt.) ....F 3
Nyasa (lake) ....E 2
Ruvuma (riv.) ....F 2
São Sebastião (cape) ....F 4
Save (riv.) ....E 4
Shire (riv.) ....E 3
Zambezi (riv.) ....E 3

RÉUNION

CITIES and TOWNS

Le Port, 13,281 ....F 5
Saint-André, 1,501 ....G 5
Saint-Benoît, 4,095 ....G 5
Saint-Denis (capital), 37,047 ....F 5
Saint-Denis, *65,614 ....F 5
Saint-Joseph, 5,969 ....G 6
Saint-Louis, 7,753 ....F 5
Saint-Pierre, 8,752 ....F 6

OTHER FEATURES

Bassas da India (isl.) ....F 4
Europa (isl.) ....G 4
Glorioso (isls.) ....H 2
Juan de Nova (isl.) ....G 3
Piton des Neiges (mt.) ....G 5

RHODESIA

CITIES and TOWNS

Beitbridge, 760 ....E 4
Bindura, 5,530 ....E 3
Bulawayo, 245,590 ....D 3
Bulawayo, ‡270,000 ....D 3
Chipinga, 1,730 ....E 4
Dett, 2,180 ....D 3
Eiffel Flats, 4,230 ....E 3
Enkeldoorn, 1,600 ....E 3
Fort Victoria, 11,350 ....E 4
Fort Victoria, ‡12,000 ....E 4
Gatooma, 20,960 ....D 3
Gatooma, ‡23,000 ....D 3
Gwaai, †2,160 ....D 3
Gwanda, 5,880 ....D 4
Gwelo, 46,230 ....D 3
Gwelo, ‡50,000 ....D 3
Hartley, 7,170 ....E 3
Inyanga, 310 ....E 3
Kariba, 5,950 ....D 3
Marandellas, 10,980 ....E 3
Marandellas, ‡11,000 ....E 3
Matetsi, 220 ....D 3
Matopos, †9,390 ....D 4
Mazoe, 410 ....E 3
Melsetter, 680 ....E 3
Mount Darwin, 1,250 ....E 3
Plumtree, 1,690 ....D 4
Que Que, 32,860 ....D 3
Que Que, ‡37,000 ....D 3
Rusape, 3,960 ....E 3
Salisbury (capital), 385,530 ....E 3
Salisbury, ‡423,000 ....E 3
Selukwe, 3,030 ....E 3
Shabani, 15,810 ....E 4
Shabani, ‡17,000 ....E 4
Shamva, 750 ....E 3
Sinoia, 13,250 ....D 3
Sinoia, ‡14,000 ....D 3
Tuli, †1,580 ....D 4
Umtali, 45,510 ....E 3
Umtali, ‡50,000 ....E 3
Umvuma, 1,750 ....D 3
Wankie, 20,190 ....D 3
Wankie, ‡21,000 ....D 3
West Nicholson, 2,640 ....D 4

OTHER FEATURES

Inyanga National Park, 580 ....E 3
Kariba (lake) ....D 3
Lundi (riv.) ....E 4
Mashonaland (reg.), 1,445,070 ....E 3
Matabeleland (reg.), 894,100 ....D 3
Mazoe (riv.) ....E 3
Mosi-Ao-Tunya (Victoria falls) ....C 3
Mushandike National Park ....D 4
Sabi (riv.) ....E 3
Sanyati (riv.) ....D 3
Shangani (riv.) ....D 3
Shashi (riv.) ....D 4
Umvukwe (range) ....E 3
Victoria (falls) ....C 3
Zambezi (riv.) ....E 3
Zimbabwe Nat'l Park ....E 4

SEYCHELLES

CITIES and TOWNS

Anse Boileau, ◉2,399 ....H 5
Anse Royale, ◉2,373 ....H 5
Cascade, ◉1,583 ....H 5
Victoria (cap.), 14,000 ....H 5

OTHER FEATURES

Assumption (isl.), 31 ....H 1
Astove (isl.), 50 ....H 2
Cerf (isl.), 34 ....H 5
Cosmoledo (isls.), 57 ....H 1
Curieuse (isl.) ....H 5
Felicité (isl.) ....J 5
Frigate (isl.), 94 ....J 5
La Digue (isl.), 1,842 ....J 5
Mahé (isl.), 33,478 ....H 5
Morne Seychellois (mt.) ....H 5
North (isl.), 53 ....H 5
Praslin (isl.), 3,886 ....H 5
Sainte Anne (isl.), 32 ....H 5
Silhouette (isl.), 780 ....H 5

SOUTH AFRICA

PROVINCES

Cape of Good Hope, 3,936,306 ....C 6
Natal, 2,979,920 ....E 5
Orange Free State, 1,386,547 ....D 4
Transkei, 1,439,195 ....D 6
Transvaal, 6,273,477 ....D 4

CITIES and TOWNS

Aberdeen, 5,100 ....C 6
Adelaide, 7,000 ....D 6
Alberton, 44,800 ....H 6
Alexander Bay, 2,073 ....B 5
Aliwal North, 10,700 ....D 6
Barberton, 13,200 ....E 5
Barkly East, 3,650 ....D 6
Beaufort West, 16,300 ....C 6
Bellville, 42,500 ....F 6
Benoni, 126,700 ....J 6
Bethal, 16,600 ....D 5
Bethlehem, 31,400 ....D 5
Bloemfontein, 146,200 ....C 5
Bloemfontein, ‡147,000 ....C 5
Bloubergstrand, 230 ....E 6
Boksburg, 83,300 ....J 6
Botrivier, 937 ....F 7
Brakpan, 84,400 ....J 6
Brandvlei, 1,419 ....B 6
Brits, 11,800 ....D 5
Britstown, 2,834 ....C 6
Burgersdorp, 10,000 ....D 6
Butterworth, 2,367 ....D 6
Caledon, 4,300 ....G 7
Calvinia, 6,700 ....B 6
Cape Town (capital), 625,000 ....E 6
Cape Town, ‡817,000 ....E 6
Carnarvon, 4,800 ....C 6
Ceres, 6,200 ....B 6
Christiana, 6,800 ....D 5
Clanwilliam, 2,216 ....B 6
Colesberg, 6,800 ....D 6
Cradock, 21,300 ....D 6
Daleside, 1,103 ....H 7
De Aar, 16,600 ....C 6
Dibeng, 911 ....C 5
Douglas, 5,200 ....C 5
Dundee, 16,600 ....E 5
Durban, 662,900 ....E 5
Durban, ‡690,000 ....E 5
Durbanville, 3,057 ....F 6
East London, 134,100 ....D 6
Edenburg, 3,118 ....D 5
Edenvale, 30,200 ....H 6
Eersterivier, 1,826 ....F 6
Elliot, 3,517 ....D 6
Eloff, 970 ....J 6
Empangeni, 9,900 ....E 5
Ermelo, 22,800 ....E 5
Eshowe, 4,800 ....E 5
Estcourt, 12,900 ....D 5
Ficksburg, 10,300 ....D 5
Fort Beaufort, 9,900 ....D 6
Franschhoek, 1,534 ....F 6
Garies, 1,103 ....B 6
George, 19,600 ....C 6
Germiston, 189,600 ....H 6
Germiston, ‡222,000 ....H 6
Glencoe, 10,000 ....E 5
Goodwood, 82,600 ....F 6
Gordon's Bay, 900 ....F 7
Graaff-Reinet, 17,700 ....C 6
Grabouw, 5,200 ....F 7
Grahamstown, 37,600 ....D 6
Grasmere, 3,338 ....H 7
Greytown, 9,800 ....E 5
Griquatown, 2,526 ....C 5
Harrismith, 16,200 ....D 5
Hawston, 1,211 ....G 7
Heidelberg, 12,200 ....J 7
Heilbron, 7,900 ....D 5
Henley on Klip, 717 ....H 7
Hermanus, 5,200 ....G 7
Hopetown, 2,631 ....C 5
Howick, 4,900 ....E 5
Humansdorp, 3,128 ....C 6
Ingwavuma, 655 ....E 5
Irene, 1,284 ....H 6
Jagersfontein, 3,893 ....D 6
Jameson Park, 447 ....J 7
Johannesburg, 595,083 ....H 6
Johannesburg, *1,305,000 ....H 6
Keimoes, 2,997 ....C 5
Kempton Park, 56,200 ....J 6
Kenhardt, 2,833 ....C 5
Kimberley, 95,200 ....C 5
King William's Town, 15,000 ....D 6
Kirkwood, 7,400 ....D 6
Kleinmond, 639 ....F 7
Klerksdorp, 60,400 ....D 5
Knysna, 13,900 ....C 6
Koffiefontein, 2,987 ....D 5
Kokstad, 10,000 ....D 6
Kommetjie, 280 ....E 7
Kraaifontein, 4,800 ....F 6
Kroonstad, 50,700 ....D 5
Krugersdorp, 100,500 ....H 6
Kuilsrivier, 7,200 ....F 6
Kuruman, 7,000 ....C 5
Ladybrand, 8,000 ....D 5
Ladysmith, 27,900 ....D 5
Lambert's Bay, 3,211 ....B 6
Louis Trichardt, 14,800 ....E 4
Lydenburg, 8,000 ....E 4
Maclear, 3,550 ....D 6
Mafeking, 6,200 ....C 5
Malmesbury, 8,800 ....B 6
Margate, 2,915 ....E 6
Matatiele, 3,251 ....D 6
Messina, 12,500 ....D 4
Meyerton, 17,100 ....H 7
Middelburg, C. of Good Hope, 11,700 ....D 6
Middelburg, Transvaal, 25,100 ....D 5
Molteno, 4,600 ....D 6
Montagu, 5,800 ....C 6
Moorreesburg, 4,000 ....B 6
Moroka, 2,673 ....H 6
Mossel Bay, 15,600 ....C 6
Nelspruit, 31,700 ....E 5
Newcastle, 16,900 ....E 5
Nigel, 38,400 ....J 7
Noupoort, 7,200 ....C 6
Nylstroom, 6,700 ....D 4
Odendaalsrus, 17,500 ....D 5
Okiep, 2,973 ....B 5
Onrusrivier, 398 ....G 7
Oudtshoorn, 25,800 ....C 6
Paarl, 48,800 ....F 6
Parow, 48,100 ....F 6
Parys, 15,400 ....D 5
Pietermaritzburg, 111,000 ....E 5
Pietermaritzburg, ‡128,598 ....E 5
Pietersburg, 35,700 ....D 4
Piet Retief, 8,100 ....D 5
Piketberg, 4,500 ....B 6
Pinelands, 14,100 ....F 6
Pinetown, 21,100 ....E 5
Pniel, 1,309 ....F 6
Port Alfred, 6,600 ....D 6
Port Elizabeth, 374,100 ....D 6
Port Elizabeth, ‡448,000 ....D 6
Port Nolloth, 2,624 ....B 5
Port Saint Johns, 1,172 ....D 6
Port Shepstone, 4,200 ....E 6
Postmasburg, 10,000 ....C 5
Potchefstroom, 51,800 ....D 5
Potgietersrus, 12,700 ....D 4
Pretoria (capital), 479,700 ....D 5
Prieska, 7,600 ....C 5
Prince Albert, 4,500 ....C 6
Queenstown, 42,200 ....D 6
Randfontein, 45,400 ....G 6
Reitz, 7,000 ....D 5
Richmond, 2,692 ....C 6
Riversdale, 1,386 ....H 7
Riversdale, 5,100 ....C 6
Robertson, 8,200 ....C 6
Roodeport-Maraisburg, 115,600 ....H 6
Rustenburg, 32,500 ....D 5
Saldanha, 2,243 ....B 6
Senekal, 7,400 ....D 5
Simonstown, 8,900 ....E 7
Somerset East, 9,800 ....D 6
Somerset West, 9,500 ....F 6
Springbok, 4,100 ....B 5
Springfontein, 2,860 ....C 6
Springs, 142,300 ....J 6
Standerton, 22,500 ....D 5
Stanger, 11,200 ....E 5
Stellenbosch, 29,900 ....F 6
Strand, 21,200 ....F 7
Stutterheim, 10,600 ....D 6
Swellendam, 4,900 ....C 6
Taung, 860 ....C 5
Thabazimbi, 8,800 ....D 4

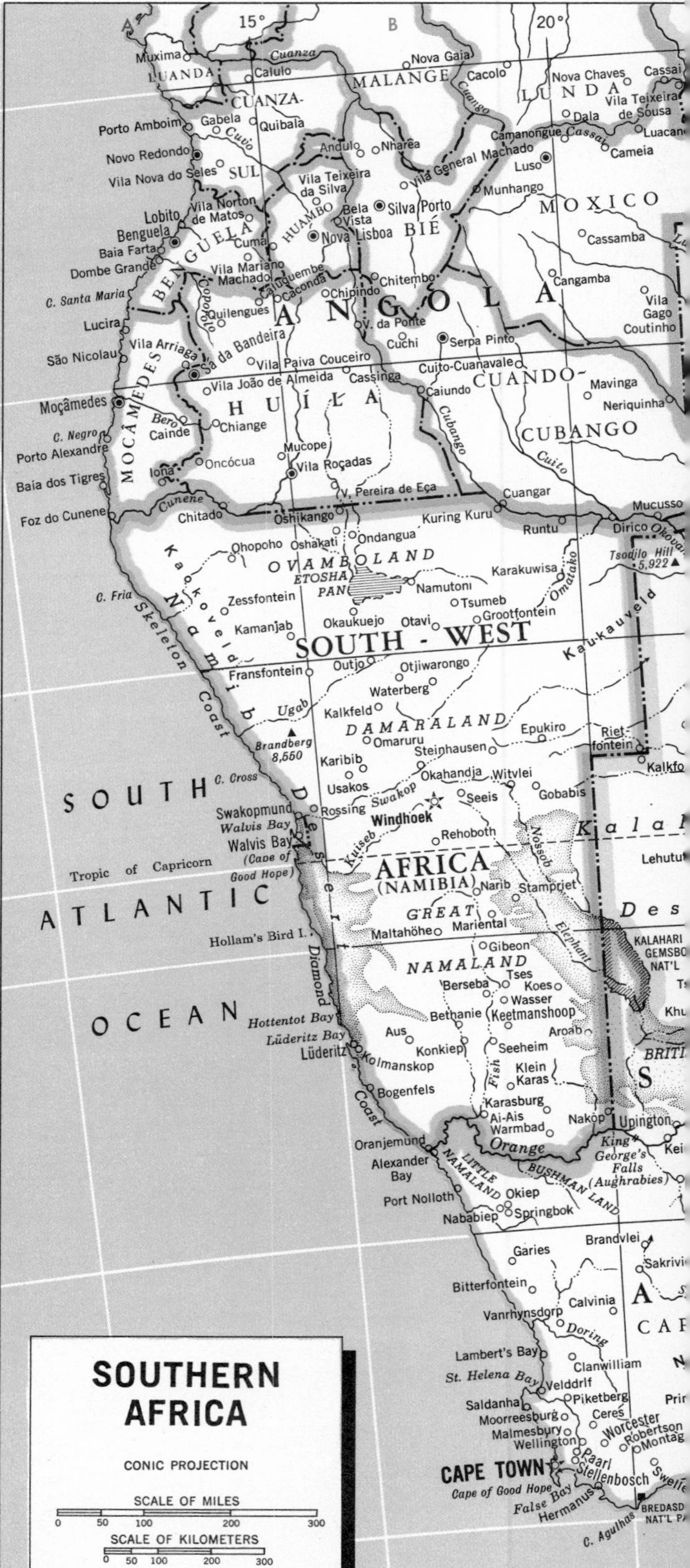

Tzaneen, 8,900 ... E 4
Uitenhage, 63,400 ... C 6
Umtata, 17,200 ... D 6
Umzinto, 6,000 ... E 6
Upington, 28,000 ... C 5
Vanrhynsdorp, 2,133 ... B 6
Velddrif, 2,945 ... B 6
Vereeniging, 94,500 ... D 5
Victoria West, 4,100 ... C 6
Villiersdorp, 1,590 ... G 6
Vishoek, 7,500 ... E 7
Volksrust, 9,800 ... D 5
Vrede, 7,300 ... D 5
Vryburg, 17,100 ... C 5
Vryheid, 14,300 ... E 5
Walvis Bay, 12,234 ... A 4
Warmbad, 6,700 ... D 5
Warrenton, 8,600 ... C 5
Welkom, 137,400 ... D 5
Wellington, 13,200 ... B 6
Westonaria, 35,400 ... H 7
Willowmore, 4,200 ... C 6
Winburg, 5,000 ... D 5
Witbank, 37,800 ... D 5
Wolmaransstad, 6,200 ... D 5
Worcester, 37,000 ... B 6
Zastron, 4,800 ... D 6
Zeerust, 9,300 ... D 5
Zwelitsha, 6,232 ... D 6

OTHER FEATURES

Addo Nat'l Park ... D 6
Agulhas (cape) ... B 6
Algoa (bay) ... D 6
Aughrabies (King George's) (falls) ... B 5
Blesbok (riv.) ... J 7
Bot (riv.) ... G 7
Bredasdorp Nat'l Park ... C 6
British Bechuanaland (reg.), 271,517 ... C 5
Bushman Land (reg.), 11,096 ... B 5
Cape (pen.) ... E 7
Cape (pt.) ... F 7
Crocodile (riv.) ... H 6
Diep (riv.) ... F 6
Doring (riv.) ... B 6
Drakensberg (range) ... D 6
Duiker (pt.) ... E 6
False (bay) ... F 7
Good Hope (cape) ... E 7
Great Fish (riv.) ... D 6
Great Karoo (reg.) ... C 6
Great Kei (riv.) ... D 6
Griqualand West (reg.), 266,483 ... C 5
Groote (riv.) ... C 6
Hangklip (cape) ... F 7
Hartbees (riv.) ... C 5
Hout (bay) ... E 6
Jukskei (riv.) ... H 6
Kalahari Gemsbok Nat'l Park ... C 5
King George's (falls) ... B 5
Klip (riv.) ... H 6
Kruger Nat'l Park ... C 6
Kruis (riv.) ... F 6
Limpopo (riv.) ... D 4
Little Namaland (reg.) ... B 5
Maclear (cape) ... F 7
Molopo (riv.) ... C 5
Mountain Zebra Nat'l Park ... C 6
Nieuwveld (range) ... C 6
Olifants (riv.) ... D 4
Orange (riv.) ... B 5
Palmiet (riv.) ... F 7
Plettenberg (bay) ... C 6
Pondoland (reg.), 414,217 ... D 6
Robben (isl.) ... E 6
Royal Natal Nat'l Park ... D 5
Saint Francis (bay) ... D 6
Saint Helena (bay) ... B 6
Saint Lucia (cape) ... E 5
Saint Lucia (lake) ... E 5
Sak (riv.) ... C 6
Sand (riv.) ... D 4
Sandown (bay) ... F 7
Seal (isl.) ... F 7
Slangkop (pt.) ... E 7
Sneeuwkop (mt.) ... F 6
Stettyn (mt.) ... F 6
Table (bay) ... E 6
Table (mt.) ... E 6
Vaal (riv.) ... D 5
Walvis (bay) ... A 4
Witwatersberg (range) ... G 6
Witwatersrand (reg.), 2,186,814 ... H 7
Zonderend (riv.) ... G 6
Zululand (reg.), 570,160 ... E 5
Zwart (riv.) ... G 7

SOUTH-WEST AFRICA

CITIES and TOWNS

Aroab, 820 ... B 5
Aus, 693 ... B 5
Berseba ... B 5
Bethanie, 1,142 ... B 5
Gibeon, 489 ... B 5
Gobabis, 4,326 ... B 4
Grootfontein, 1,919 ... B 3
Kalkfeld, 926 ... B 4
Kamanjab, 193 ... A 3
Karasburg, 2,234 ... B 5
Karibib, 1,398 ... B 4
Katima Mulilo ... C 3
Keetmanshoop, 8,064 ... B 5
Koes, 422 ... B 5
Lüderitz, 3,633 ... A 5
Maltahöhe, 1,048 ... B 4
Mariental, 3,498 ... B 4
Okahandja, 2,977 ... B 4
Omaruru, 2,698 ... B 4
Ondangua ... B 3
Oranjemund, 3,125 ... B 5
Oshakati ... B 3
Otavi, 1,303 ... B 3
Otjiwarongo, 6,368 ... B 4
Outjo, 2,963 ... B 4
Rehoboth, 2,973 ... B 4
Seeheim ... B 5
Stampriet, 432 ... B 4
Swakopmund, 4,701 ... A 4
Tsumeb, 7,823 ... B 3
Usakos, 4,278 ... B 4
Warmbad, 177 ... B 5
Windhoek (capital), 36,050 ... B 4
Witvlei, 362 ... B 4
Zessfontein ... A 3

OTHER FEATURES

Brandberg (mt.) ... A 4
Caprivi Strip (reg.), 15,871 ... C 3
Cross (cape) ... A 4
Cubango (riv.) ... B 3
Damaraland (reg.) ... B 4
Diamond Coast (reg.) ... A 5
Elephant (riv.) ... B 5
Etosha (salt pan) ... B 3
Fish (riv.) ... B 5
Fria (cape) ... A 3
Great Namaland (reg.) ... B 4
Hollam's Bird (isl.) ... A 4
Hottentot (bay) ... A 5
Kalahari (des.) ... C 4
Kaokoveld (mts.) ... A 3
Kaukauveld (mts.) ... C 3
Kuiseb (riv.) ... B 4
Lüderitz (bay) ... A 5
Namib (des.) ... A 3
Nossob (riv.) ... B 4
Okovango (riv.) ... C 3
Omatako (riv.) ... B 3
Orange (riv.) ... B 5
Ovamboland (reg.), 203,862 ... B 3
Skeleton Coast (reg.) ... A 3
Swakop (riv.) ... B 4
Ugab (riv.) ... A 4
Zambezi (riv.) ... E 3

SWAZILAND

CITIES and TOWNS

Manzini, 6,081 ... E 5
Mbabane (cap.), 13,803 ... E 5
Stegi, 1,457 ... E 5

*City and suburbs.
◉Population of parish.
‡Population of urban area.
†Population of sub-district or division.

SOUTH AMERICA
LAMBERT AZIMUTHAL EQUAL-AREA PROJECTION
SCALE OF MILES
0 100 200 400 600
SCALE OF KILOMETRES
0 100 200 400 600
Capitals of Countries
International Boundaries
Canals
© C.S. HAMMOND & Co., N.Y.
Longitude 70° West of Greenwich
80° 70° 60° 50° 40°
B C D E F G
10° 0° 10° 20° 30° 40° 50°
2 3 4 5 6 7 8
GALAPAGOS ISLANDS
(ARCHIPIELAGO DE COLON)
(ECUADOR)
SCALE OF MILES
0 50 100 150
92° 90°
PACIFIC OCEAN
Equator
I. Pinta
I. Marchena
I. Santiago
I. Chaves
I. Fernandina
Isla Isabela
I. San Cristóbal
I. Floreana
I. Española
CARIBBEAN SEA
ATLANTIC OCEAN
PACIFIC OCEAN
WEST INDIES
NETH. ANTILLES
BARBADOS
TRINIDAD & TOBAGO
Port of Spain
Trinidad
Tobago
Grenada (Br.)
St. Vincent (Br.)
St. Lucia (Br.)
Aruba
Curaçao
Bonaire
Willemstad
Pta. Gallinas
GUAJIRA PEN.
Sta. Marta
Barranquilla
Cartagena
Ciénaga
L. Maracaibo
Maracaibo
Coro
Pto. Cabello
La Guaira
Caracas
Valencia
Barquisimeto
Trujillo
Valera
Mérida
San Fernando
Barcelona
Cumaná
Carúpano
I. de Margarita
G. of Paria
Ciudad Bolívar
Orinoco
VENEZUELA
Mompós
Turbo
Cúcuta
Pamplona
Bucaramanga
Arauca
Alto Ritacuva 18,022
Chiquinquirá
Tunja
Medellín
Manizales
Tolima 17,110
Ibagué
Bogotá
COLOMBIA
Neiva
Cali
Huila 18,865
Popayán
Pasto
Buenaventura
C. Corrientes
Malpelo I. (Col.)
Tumaco
Esmeraldas
Ibarra
Quito
Cotopaxi 19,347
Chimborazo 20,561
Riobamba
ECUADOR
Manta
Guayaquil
Gulf of Guayaquil
Cuenca
Loja
Equator
Napo
Putumayo
Caquetá
Apaporis
Vaupés
Guaviare
Vichada
Meta
Pto. Carreño
Puerto Ayacucho
Sa. Pacaraima
Roraima 9,094
Boa Vista
Pico da Neblina 9,889
Sa. Tapirapecó
São Felipe
Taracuá
Barcelos
Moura
Rio Negro
Rio Branco
Japurá
Pto. Córdoba
Içá
Leticia
Loreto
Iquitos
Tigre
Marañón
Requena
Benjamin Constant
Eirunepé
Javari
Juruá
Purus
Xingu
Lábrea
Humaitá
Manicoré
Borba
Manaus
Tefé
Amazon
(Rio Amazonas)
Madeira
Parintins
Santarém
Belterra
Itaituba
Fordlândia
Óbidos
Prainha
Jamundá
Mapuera
Trombetas
Jari
Macapá
Canal do Norte
I. Caviana
Canal do Sul
I. de Marajó
Rio Pará
Belém
Bragança
Cametá
São Luís
Camocim
Parnaíba
Fortaleza (Ceará)
Aracati
Rocas
I. Fernando de Noronha
C. de São Roque
Areia Branca
Natal
João Pessoa (Paraíba)
Recife (Pernambuco)
Maceió
Aracaju
Salvador (Bahia)
Ilhéus
Belmonte
Caravelas
Vitória
Campos
C. de São Tomé
Cabo Frio
Niterói
RIO DE JANEIRO
Angra dos Reis
I. S. Sebastião
Santos
SÃO PAULO
Paranaguá
Joinville
Florianópolis
I. de Santa Catarina
Laguna
Pôrto Alegre
L. dos Patos
Pelotas
Rio Grande
L. Mirim
Morawhanna
Demerara
Georgetown
New Amsterdam
Nieuw-Nickerie
Coronie
Paramaribo
Rockstone
GUYANA
SURINAM (DUTCH GUIANA)
FR. GUIANA
Cayenne
Devils Island
Mana
Sinnamary
St. Georges
Oyapock
Maroni
Essequibo
Cuyuni
Sa. Acaraí
I. de Maracá
Dam
Codó
Caxias
Teresina
Crateús
Iguatu
Cajazeiras
Juàzeiro do Norte
Paulistana
Petrolina
Juàzeiro
Remanso
Propriá
Senhor do Bonfim
Alagoinhas
Cachoeira
França
Brumado
Jequié
Tocantinópolis
Carolina
Alto Parnaíba
Pôrto Nacional
Conceição do Araguaia
Marabá
Alcobaça
Bacabal
Tocantins
Gurupi
Sa. da Desordem
Sa. do Estrondo
Serra do Estrondo
Araguaia
Xingu
Iriri
Tapajós
Jamanxim
São Manuel
Juruena
Arinos
Roosevelt
Aripuanã
Roncador
Serra do Roncador
Rio das Mortes
I. do Bananal
BRAZIL
CAATINGAS
CAMPOS
Paraná
Carinhanha
Palma
São Francisco
Pardo
FEDERAL DISTRICT
Brasília
Goiás
Goiânia
Anápolis
Pirapora
Montes Claros
Minas Novas
Diamantina
Paranaíba
Araguarí
Uberaba
Belo Horizonte
Ouro Prêto
Barbacena
Juiz de Fora
Petrópolis
São João
Araraquara
Campinas
Ribeirão Prêto
Rio Grande
Tietê
Londrina
Sorocaba
Juguiá
Curitiba
Castro
Pto. Mendes
Iguaçu
Pto. Tibiriça
Campo Grande
Porto Esperanca
Corumbá
Cuiabá
Planalto de Mato Grosso
Diamantino
Mato Grosso
Serra dos Parecis
Guaporé
Pôrto Velho
Alto Madeira
Rio Branco
Abunã
Villa Bella
Guajará Mirim
Riberalta
Beni
Mamoré
Sta. Ana
Trinidad
San Ignacio
Grande
L. Concepción
Pto. Quijarro
Pto. Suárez
BOLIVIA
La Paz
Illampu 21,276
L. Titicaca
Cochabamba
Santa Cruz
Oruro
Sajama 21,391
L. Poopó
Sucre
Potosí
Río Mulato
Uyuni
Tupiza
Tarija
Villa Montes
Mariscal Estigarribia
CHACO
PARAGUAY
La Quiaca
Yacuiba
Orán
Embarcación
Pilcomayo
Bermejo
Asunción
Villarrica
Encarnación
Posadas
Concepción
Pto. Casado
Yaco
Cocama
Cerro de Pasco
La Oroya
Huacho
Callao
Lima
Pisco
Pta. Huacas
Ica
Ayacucho
Cuzco
Sta. Ana
Pto. Maldonado
Urubamba
Apurimac
Huascaran 22,205
Huaráz
Chimbote
Trujillo
Pacasmayo
Chiclayo
Cajamarca
Jaén
Piura
Paita
Pta. Aguja
Lobitos
Ucayali
PERU
Vilcanota 17,999
Juliaca
Puno
Arequipa
El Misti 19,199
Matarani
Mollendo
Moquegua
Ilo
Tacna
Arica
Lomas
Pisagua
Iquique
Ollagüe
Tocopilla
Calama
Antofagasta
Vol. Llullaillaco 22,057
Taltal
Chañaral
Caldera
Copiapó
Huasco
Vallenar
La Serena
Coquimbo
Ovalle
Los Vilos
Viña del Mar
Valparaíso
Santiago
Maipo 17,464
Talca
Constitución
Talcahuano
Concepción
Arauco
Chillán
Temuco
Villarrica
Valdivia
Pto. Montt
Ancud
Castro
Isla de Chiloé
G. del Corcovado
ARCHIPIÉLAGO de los CHONOS
PEN. TAITAO
C. Tres Montes
G. de Penas
I. Campana
I. Wellington
I. Madre de Dios
I. Hanover
Pto. Natales
Strait of Magellan
I. Desolación
I. Sta. Inés
I. Clarence
I. Hoste
Cape Horn (Cabo de Hornos)
Bahía Nassau
Ushuaia
Tierra del Fuego
Punta Arenas
Turbio
I. de los Estados (Staten I.)
C. San Diego
CHILE
Tropic of Capricorn
I. de San Félix (Chile)
I. San Ambrosio (Chile)
I. Alejandro Selkirk
I. Robinson Crusoe
JUAN FERNÁNDEZ IS. (Chile)
S. Antonio
Jujuy
Salta
Rosario
Salado
Tucumán
22,572
Ojos del Salado
Santiago del Estero
Tinogasta
Catamarca
Chilecito
La Rioja
Jachal
Mar Chiquita
San Juan
Mercedario 22,211
Aconcagua 22,831
Mendoza
San Luis
San Rafael
Córdoba
Villa María
Río Cuarto
Santa Fe
Rosario
Reconquista
Resistencia
Formosa
Corrientes
Concordia
Paraná
Uruguay
Pergamino
Mercedes
BUENOS AIRES
Chivilcoy
La Plata
Avellaneda
Río de la Plata
General Alvear
Victorica
Sta. Rosa
Dolores
Tandil
C. San Antonio
Mar del Plata
Quequén
Gral. Acha
Bahía Blanca
Colorado
Neuquén
Zapala
Negro
Viedma
San Carlos de Bariloche
Ñorquincó
Golfo San Matías
Pen. Valdés
Puerto Madryn
Rawson
Salina Grande
Chubut
Las Plumas
Camarones
Comodoro Rivadavia
Golfo San Jorge
Colonia Las Heras
C. Tres Puntas
Puerto Deseado
Deseado
Buenos Aires
L. San Martín
Chico
San Julián
L. Viedma
L. Argentino
Santa Cruz
Bahía Grande
Río Gallegos
ARGENTINA
GRAN CHACO
PAMPAS
PATAGONIA
URUGUAY
Rivera
Santana do Livramento
Bagé
Salto
Paysandú
Melo
Mercedes
Florida
Rocha
Montevideo
Uruguaiana
Cruz Alta
Caxias do Sul
Sa. do Mar
FALKLAND ISLANDS (Br.)
West Falkland
East Falkland
Stanley
Cordillera de los Andes
N

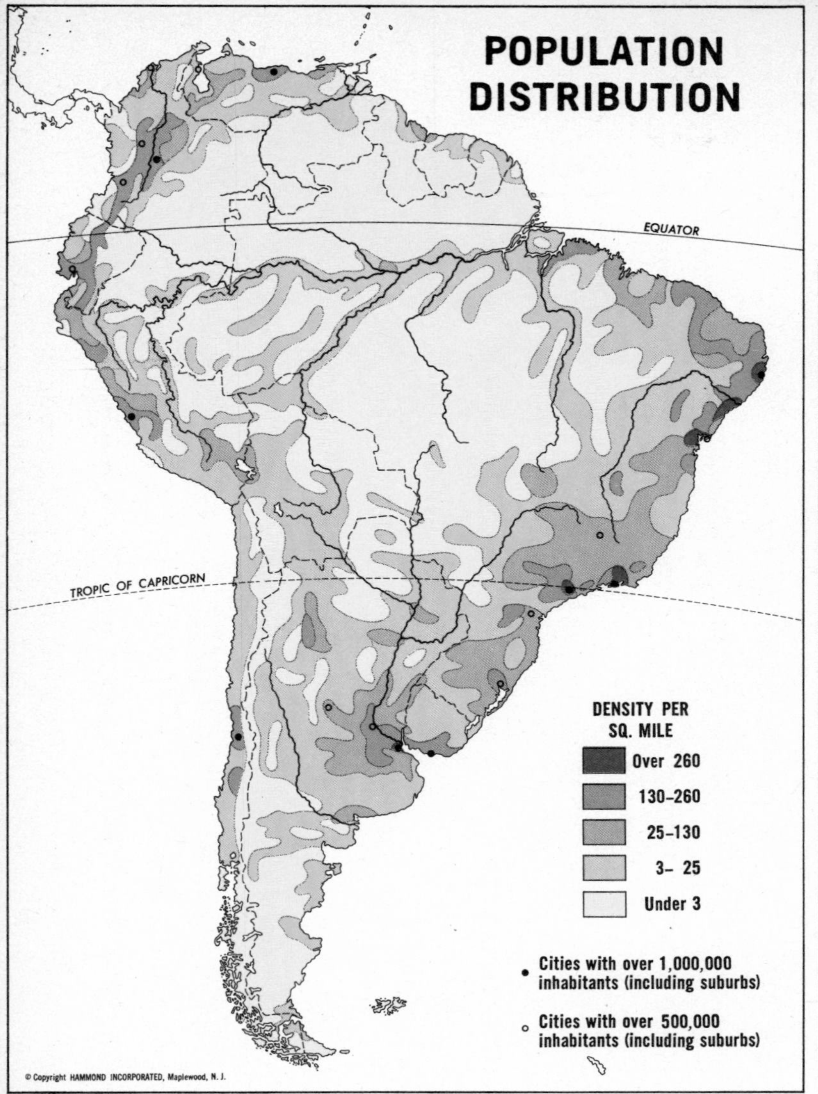

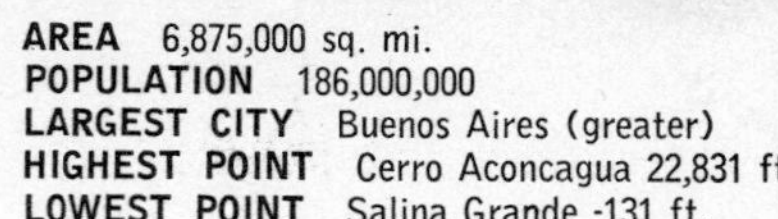

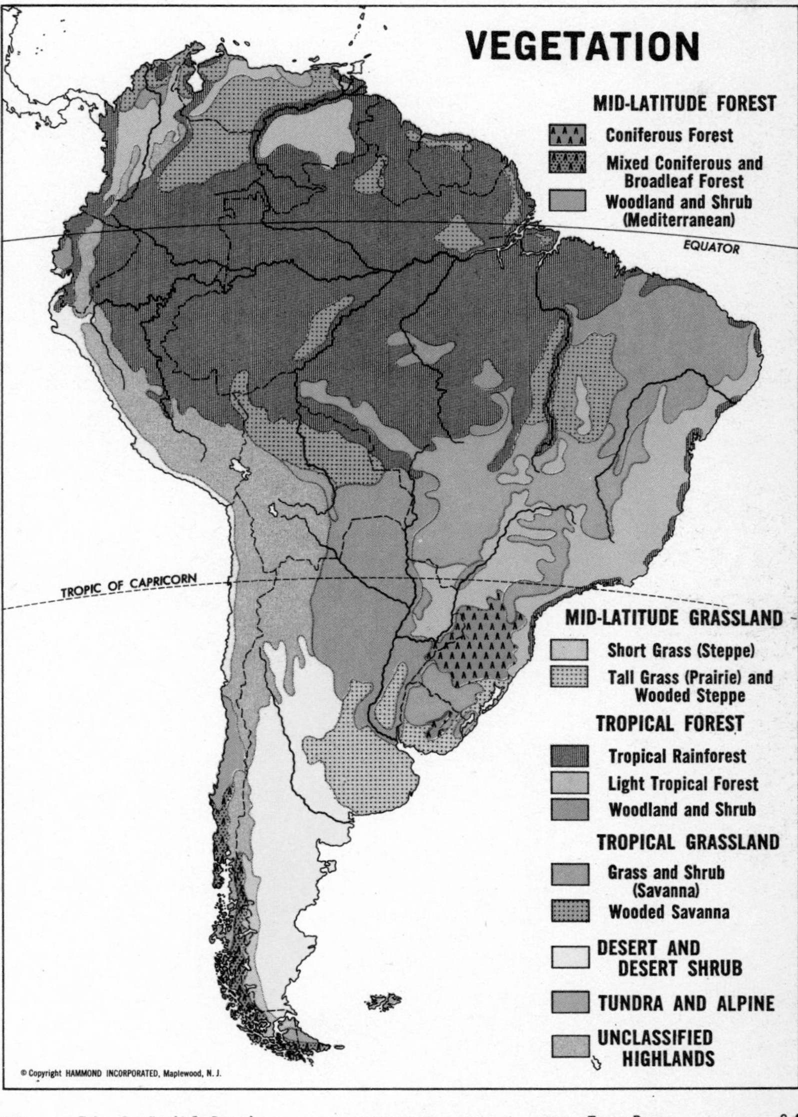

Abunã (river) ....D 4
Acaraí (range) ....E 2
Aconcagua (mt.) ....D 6
Aguja (pt.), Peru ....B 3
Alagoinhas, Brazil ....G 4
Alejandro Selkirk (isl.), Chile ....C 6
Amazon (river) ....D, E 3
Anápolis, Brazil ....F 4
Andes (mts.) ....C 2-6
Antofagasta, Chile ....C 5
Apaporis (river), Colombia ....C 3
Apurímac (river), Peru ....C 4
Aracaju, Brazil ....G 4
Araguaia (river), Brazil ....F 3
Araguari, Brazil ....F 4
Araraquara, Brazil ....F 5
Arauca (river) ....D 2
Arequipa, Peru ....C 4
Argentina ....D 6
Arica, Chile ....C 4
Arinos (river), Brazil ....E 4
Aripuanã (river), Brazil ....E 3
Asunción (capital), Paraguay ....E 5
Avellaneda, Argentina ....E 6
Ayacucho, Peru ....C 4
Bagé, Brazil ....E 6
Bahia (Salvador), Brazil ....G 4
Bahía Blanca, Argentina ....D 6
Barbacena, Brazil ....F 5
Barcelona, Venezuela ....D 2
Barquisimeto, Venezuela ....D 2
Barranquilla, Colombia ....C 1
Belém, Brazil ....F 3
Belo Horizonte, Brazil ....F 4
Blanca (bay), Argentina ....E 6
Bogotá (capital), Colombia ....C 2
Bolivia ....D 4
Brasília (capital), Brazil ....F 4
Brazil ....E 4
Bucaramanga, Colombia ....C 2
Buenaventura, Colombia ....C 2
Buenos Aires (capital), Argentina ....D 6
Buenos Aires (lake) ....C 7
Caatingas (region), Brazil ....F 3
Cajamarca, Peru ....C 3
Calama, Chile ....D 5
Cali, Colombia ....C 2
Callao, Peru ....C 4
Campinas, Brazil ....F 5
Campo Grande, Brazil ....E 5
Campos, Brazil ....F 5
Campos (region), Brazil ....F 4
Caquetá (river), Colombia ....C 3
Caracas (capital), Venezuela ....D 2
Cartagena, Colombia ....C 1
Carúpano, Venezuela ....D 1
Catamarca, Argentina ....D 5
Caxias do Sul, Brazil ....E 5
Cayenne (capital), French Guiana ....E 2
Ceará (Fortaleza), Brazil ....G 3
Cerro de Pasco, Peru ....C 4
Chaco, Gran (region) ....D 5
Chiclayo, Peru ....B 3
Chile ....C 6
Chillán, Chile ....C 6
Chiloé (isl.), Chile ....C 7
Chimborazo (mt.), Ecuador ....B 3
Chimbote, Peru ....B 3
Chiquinquirá, Colombia ....C 2
Chiquita (lake), Argentina ....D 6
Chivilcoy, Argentina ....D 6
Chonos (arch.), Chile ....C 7
Chubut (river), Argentina ....D 7
Ciénaga, Colombia ....C 1
Ciudad Bolívar, Venezuela ....D 2
Cochabamba, Bolivia ....D 4
Colombia ....C 2
Colorado (river), Argentina ....D 6
Comodoro Rivadavia, Argentina ....D 7
Concepción, Chile ....C 6
Concepción, Paraguay ....E 5
Concordia, Argentina ....E 6
Copiapó, Chile ....C 5
Coquimbo, Chile ....C 6
Corcovado (gulf), Chile ....C 7
Córdoba, Argentina ....D 6
Coro, Venezuela ....D 1
Corrientes, Argentina ....E 5
Corrientes (cape), Colombia ....C 2
Corumbá, Brazil ....E 4
Cotopaxi (mt.), Ecuador ....C 3
Courantyne (river) ....E 2
Cruz Alta, Brazil ....E 5
Cúcuta, Colombia ....C 2
Cuenca, Ecuador ....C 3
Cuiabá, Brazil ....E 4
Cumaná, Venezuela ....D 2
Curaçao (isl.), Netherlands Antilles ....D 1
Curitiba, Brazil ....F 5
Cuzco, Peru ....C 4
Deseado (river), Argentina ....D 7
Devils (isl.), Fr. Guiana ....E 2
Ecuador, 5,084,000 ....C 3
Encarnación, Paraguay ....E 5
Esmeraldas, Ecuador ....B 2
Essequibo (river), Guyana ....E 2
Estados, Los (Staten) (isl.), Argentina ....D 8
Falkland (isls.) ....E 8
Florianópolis, Brazil ....F 5
Fortaleza, Brazil ....G 3
Franca, Brazil ....F 4
French Guiana ....E 2
Frio (cape), Brazil ....F 5
Georgetown (capital), Guyana ....E 2
Goiânia, Brazil ....E 4
Gran Chaco (region) ....D 5
Grande (bay), Argentina ....D 8
Grande (river), Brazil ....F 5
Guajira (pen.) ....C 1
Guaporé (river) ....D 4
Guaviare (river), Colombia ....C 2
Guayaquil, Ecuador ....B 3
Guyana ....E 2
Hanover (isl.), Chile ....C 8
Horn (cape), Chile ....D 8
Hoste (isl.), Chile ....D 8
Huacho, Peru ....C 4
Huaráz, Peru ....C 3
Huascarán (mt.), Peru ....C 3
Huila (mt.), Colombia ....C 2
Ibagué, Colombia ....C 2
Ibarra, Ecuador ....C 2
Ica, Peru ....C 4
Iguacú (river) ....E 5
Ilhéus, Brazil ....G 4
Illampu (mt.), Bolivia ....D 4
Imeri (mts.) ....D 2
Iquique, Chile ....C 5
Iquitos, Peru ....C 3
Jaguaribe (river), Brazil ....G 3
Japurá (river), Brazil ....D 3
Javarí (river) ....C 3
Jequié, Brazil ....F 4
João Pessoa, Brazil ....G 3
Joinville, Brazil ....E 5
Juan Fernández (isls.), Chile ....C 6
Juàzeiro, Brazil ....G 3
Juiz de Fora, Brazil ....F 5
Jujuy, Argentina ....D 5
Juliaca, Peru ....C 4
Juruá (river), Brazil ....D 3
Juruena (river), Brazil ....E 4
La Guaira, Venezuela ....D 1
La Oroya, Peru ....C 4
La Paz (capital), Bolivia ....D 4
La Plata, Argentina ....E 6
La Plata (estuary) ....E 6
La Rioja, Argentina ....D 5
La Serena, Chile ....C 5
Lima (capital), Peru ....C 4
Llanos del Orinoco (plain) ....D 2
Llullaillaco (vol.) ....D 5
Loja, Ecuador ....C 3
Londrina, Brazil ....E 5
Macapá, Brazil ....E 2
Maceió, Brazil ....G 3
Madeira (river), Brazil ....D 3
Madre de Dios (isl.), Chile ....C 8
Magdalena (river), Colombia ....C 2
Magellan (str.) ....D 8
Maipo (vol.) ....D 6
Malpelo (isl.), Colombia ....B 2
Mamoré (river), Bolivia ....D 4
Manaus, Brazil ....E 3
Manizales, Colombia ....C 2
Manta, Ecuador ....B 3
Mar (mts.), Brazil ....F 5
Mar del Plata, Argentina ....F 6
Maracaibo, Venezuela ....C 1
Maracaibo (lake), Venezuela ....C 1
Marajó (isl.), Brazil ....F 3
Marañón (river), Peru ....C 3
Margarita (isl.), Venezuela ....D 1
Maroni (river) ....E 2
Mato Grosso (plat.), Brazil ....E 4
Medellín, Colombia ....C 2
Melo, Uruguay ....E 6
Mendoza, Argentina ....D 6
Mercedes, Argentina ....D 6
Mercedes, Uruguay ....E 6
Mérida, Venezuela ....C 2
Meta (river) ....D 2
Mirim (lagoon) ....E 6
Misti, El (mt.), Peru ....C 4
Mollendo, Peru ....C 4
Montes Claros, Brazil ....F 4
Montevideo (capital), Uruguay ....E 6
Moquegua, Peru ....C 4
Nassau (bay) ....D 8
Natal, Brazil ....G 3
Negro (river), Argentina ....D 6
Negro (river), Brazil ....D 3
Neiva, Colombia ....C 2
Netherlands Antilles ....D 1
New Amsterdam, Guyana ....E 2
Niterói, Brazil ....F 5
Ojos del Salado (mt.), Chile ....D 5
Orinoco (river) ....D 2
Oruro, Bolivia ....D 4
Ovalle, Chile ....C 6
Oyapock (river) ....E 2
Pacaraima (mts.) ....D 2
Pacasmayo, Peru ....B 3
Paita, Peru ....B 3
Pampas (plain), Argentina ....D 6
Pará (estuary), Brazil ....F 2
Paraguay ....E 5
Paraguay (river) ....E 4
Paraíba (João Pessoa), Brazil ....G 3
Paramaribo (capital), Surinam ....E 2
Paraná, Argentina ....E 6
Paraná (river) ....E 5
Paranaíba (river), Brazil ....F 4
Parecis (mts.), Brazil ....D 4
Parima (mts.) ....D 2
Parnaíba, Brazil ....F 3
Parnaíba (river), Brazil ....F 3
Pasto, Colombia ....C 2
Patagonia (region), Argentina ....D 7
Paysandú, Uruguay ....E 6
Pelotas, Brazil ....E 6
Penas (gulf), Chile ....C 7
Pergamino, Argentina ....D 6
Pernambuco (Recife), Brazil ....G 3
Peru ....C 4
Petrópolis, Brazil ....F 5
Pilcomayo (river) ....D 5
Pisco, Peru ....C 4
Piura, Peru ....B 3
Poopó (lake), Bolivia ....D 4
Popayán, Colombia ....C 2
Pôrto Alegre, Brazil ....E 5
Posadas, Argentina ....E 5
Potosí, Bolivia ....D 4
Puerto Cabello, Venezuela ....D 1
Puerto Montt, Chile ....C 7
Puno, Peru ....C 4
Punta Arenas, Chile ....D 8
Purus (river) ....D 3
Putumayo (river) ....C 3
Quito (capital), Ecuador ....C 3
Recife, Brazil ....G 3
Resistencia, Argentina ....D 5
Ribeirão Prêto, Brazil ....F 5
Río Cuarto, Argentina ....D 6
Rio de Janeiro, Brazil ....F 5
Rio Grande, Brazil ....E 6
Riobamba, Ecuador ....C 3
Rivera, Uruguay ....E 6
Robinson Crusoe (isl.), Chile ....B 6
Roraima (mt.) ....D 2
Rosario, Argentina ....D 6
Sajama (mt.) ....D 4
Salado (river), Argentina ....D 5
Salta, Argentina ....D 5
Salto, Uruguay ....E 6
Salvador, Brazil ....G 4
San Ambrosio (isl.), Chile ....C 5
San Antonio (cape), Argentina ....E 6
San Carlos de Bariloche, Argentina ....D 7
San Félix (isl.), Chile ....B 5
San Fernando, Venezuela ....D 2
San Jorge (gulf), Argentina ....D 7
San Juan, Argentina ....D 6
San Luis, Argentina ....D 6
San Martín (lake) ....C 7
San Rafael, Argentina ....D 6
Santa Catarina (isl.), Brazil ....F 5
Santa Cruz, Bolivia ....D 4
Santa Fe, Argentina ....D 6
Santa Marta, Colombia ....C 1
Santarém, Brazil ....E 3
Santiago (capital), Chile ....D 6
Santiago del Estero, Argentina ....D 5
Santos, Brazil ....F 5
São Francisco (river), Brazil ....F 4
São João da Boa Vista, Brazil ....F 5
São Luís, Brazil ....F 3
São Manuel (river), Brazil ....E 3
São Paulo, Brazil ....F 5
São Roque (cape), Brazil ....G 3
Selvas (forest), Brazil ....D 3
Sorocaba, Brazil ....F 5
Stanley (capital), Falkland Islands ....E 8
Staten (isl.), Argentina ....D 8
Sucre (capital), Bolivia ....D 4
Surinam ....E 2
Tacna, Peru ....C 4
Taitao (pen.), Chile ....C 7
Talca, Chile ....C 6
Talcahuano, Chile ....C 6
Tandil, Argentina ....D 6
Tapajós (river), Brazil ....E 3
Taracuá, Brazil ....D 3
Tarija, Bolivia ....D 5
Temuco, Chile ....C 6
Teresina, Brazil ....F 3
Tierra del Fuego (isl.) ....D 8
Titicaca (lake) ....D 4
Tocopilla, Chile ....C 5
Tolima (mt.), Colombia ....C 2
Tres Montes (cape), Chile ....C 7
Tres Puntas (cape), Argentina ....D 7
Trinidad, Bolivia ....D 4
Trujillo, Peru ....B 3
Tucumán, Argentina ....D 5
Tunja, Colombia ....C 2
Uberaba, Brazil ....F 4
Ucayali (river), Peru ....C 3
Urabá (gulf), Colombia ....C 2
Urubamba (river), Peru ....C 4
Uruguaiana, Brazil ....E 5
Uruguay ....E 6
Uruguay (river) ....E 5
Ushuaia, Argentina ....D 8
Valdés (pen.), Argentina ....D 7
Valdivia, Chile ....C 6
Valencia, Venezuela ....D 2
Valera, Venezuela ....C 2
Valparaíso, Chile ....C 6
Vaupés (river), Colombia ....C 2
Venezuela ....D 2
Venezuela (gulf), Venezuela ....C 1
Viedma (lake), Argentina ....C 7
Vilcanota (mt.), Peru ....C 4
Villa María, Argentina ....D 6
Villarrica, Paraguay ....E 5
Viña del Mar, Chile ....C 6
Vitória, Brazil ....G 5
Willemstad (capital), Netherlands Antilles ....D 1
Xingu (river), Brazil ....E 3

(continued)

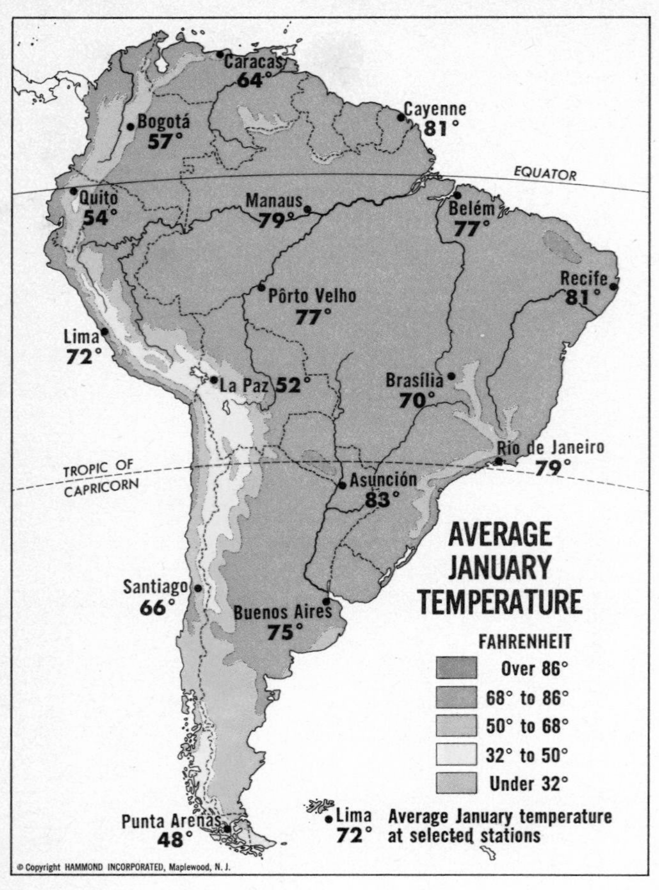

Caracas 64°
Bogotá 57°
Cayenne 81°
EQUATOR
Quito 54°
Manaus 79°
Belém 77°
Pôrto Velho 77°
Recife 81°
Lima 72°
La Paz 52°
Brasília 70°
TROPIC OF CAPRICORN
Rio de Janeiro 79°
Asunción 83°
AVERAGE JANUARY TEMPERATURE
Santiago 66°
Buenos Aires 75°
FAHRENHEIT
Over 86°
68° to 86°
50° to 68°
32° to 50°
Under 32°
Punta Arenas 48°
Lima 72° Average January temperature at selected stations
© Copyright HAMMOND INCORPORATED, Maplewood, N. J.

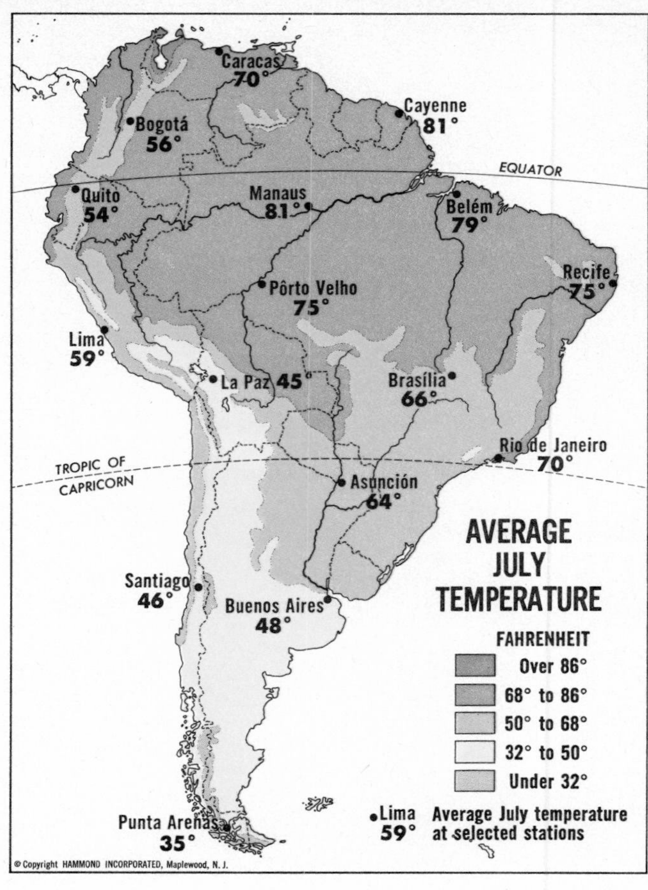

Caracas 70°
Bogotá 56°
Cayenne 81°
EQUATOR
Quito 54°
Manaus 81°
Belém 79°
Pôrto Velho 75°
Recife 75°
Lima 59°
La Paz 45°
Brasília 66°
TROPIC OF CAPRICORN
Rio de Janeiro 70°
Asunción 64°
AVERAGE JULY TEMPERATURE
Santiago 46°
Buenos Aires 48°
FAHRENHEIT
Over 86°
68° to 86°
50° to 68°
32° to 50°
Under 32°
Punta Arenas 35°
Lima 59° Average July temperature at selected stations
© Copyright HAMMOND INCORPORATED, Maplewood, N. J.

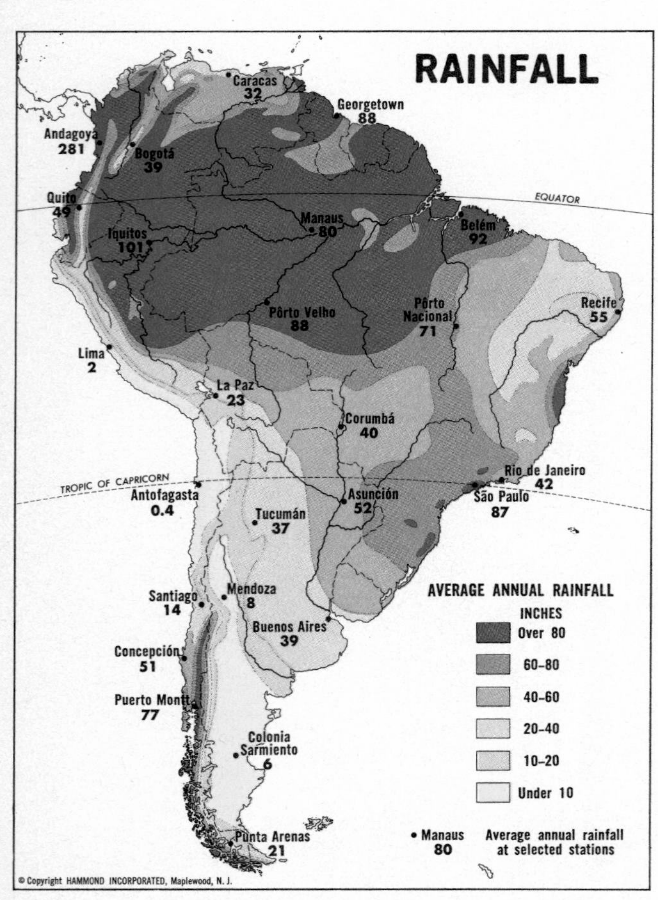

RAINFALL
Caracas 32
Georgetown 88
Andagoya 281
Bogotá 39
EQUATOR
Quito 49
Manaus 80
Iquitos 101
Belém 92
Pôrto Velho 88
Pôrto Nacional 71
Recife 55
Lima 2
La Paz 23
Corumbá 40
TROPIC OF CAPRICORN
Rio de Janeiro 42
Antofagasta 0.4
Asunción 52
São Paulo 87
Tucumán 37
Santiago 14
Mendoza 8
AVERAGE ANNUAL RAINFALL
INCHES
Over 80
60-80
40-60
20-40
10-20
Under 10
Buenos Aires 39
Concepción 51
Puerto Montt 77
Colonia Sarmiento 6
Punta Arenas 21
Manaus 80 Average annual rainfall at selected stations
© Copyright HAMMOND INCORPORATED, Maplewood, N. J.

VEGETATION/RELIEF

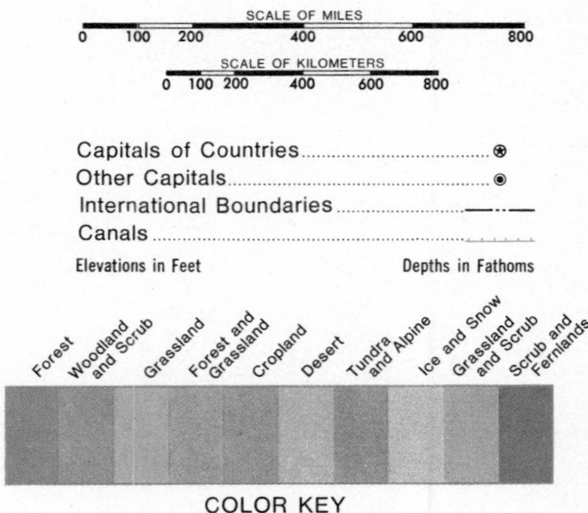

SCALE OF MILES
0 100 200 400 600 800
SCALE OF KILOMETERS
0 100 200 400 600 800
Capitals of Countries
Other Capitals
International Boundaries
Canals
Elevations in Feet
Depths in Fathoms
Forest
Woodland and Scrub
Grassland
Forest and Grassland
Cropland
Desert
Tundra and Alpine
Ice and Snow
Grassland and Scrub
Scrub and Fernlands
COLOR KEY

CARIBBEAN SEA
G. of Venezuela
Pta. Gallinas
Aruba
NETH. ANTILLES
Curaçao
Bonaire
Willemstad
GRENADA
BARBADOS
West Indies
Tobago
TRINIDAD & TOBAGO
Port of Spain
Trinidad
Barranquilla
Maracaibo
Caracas
L. Maracaibo
CANAL ZONE
Panamá
G. of Panamá
PANAMA
Pico Bolívar 16,427
Ciudad Guyana
Orinoco
VENEZUELA
Guri Res.
Bucaramanga
Arauca
Medellín
Angel Fall
Roraima 9,095
Georgetown
GUYANA
Paramaribo
Cayenne
SURINAM (Neth.)
FRENCH GUIANA
Bogotá
Meta
Caroni
Cauca
Magdalena
Cali
COLOMBIA
Orinoco
Essequibo
Courantyne
Maroni
Pico da Neblina 9,889
Vaupés
Caquetá
Jari
Quito
Putumayo
Equator
I. de Marajó
B. de Marajó
Amazon
Chimborazo 20,561
ECUADOR
Japurá
Negro
Içá
Manaus
Belém
São Luís
Guayaquil
Gulf of Guayaquil
Iquitos
Amazon
Amazon
Tocantins
Xingu
Tapajós
Fortaleza
Teresina
Selvas
Yavari
Juruá
Purus
Madeira
Pta. Aguja
Cabo de São Roque
Natal
Parnaíba
Caatingas
Ucayali
Marañón
Aripuanã
Teles Pires
Araguaia
Trujillo
Recife
Huascarán 22,205
Maceió
BRAZIL
Tocantins
Callao
Lima
Guaporé
Mamoré
Juruena
Planalto de Brazilian
Paraguaçu
Salvador
Beni
BOLIVIA
Cuzco
Mato Grosso
Brasília
Goiânia
São Francisco
Lake Titicaca
Ancohuma 21,489
Arequipa
La Paz
Cochabamba
Grande
Jequitinhonha
Highlands
Arica
Lake Poopó
Sucre
Chaco
Paraguai
Campo Grande
Belo Horizonte
Grande
Pico da Bandeira 9,482
Paraná
PARAGUAY
Tietê
Paraíba
C. de São Tomé
C. Frio
Tropic of Capricorn
Antofagasta
Volcán Llullaillaco 22,057
Pilcomayo
Asunción
São Paulo
Rio de Janeiro
Santos
Bermejo
Iguassú Falls
Curitiba
Iguaçu
Gran Chaco
Tucumán
Salado del Norte
Ojos del Salado 22,572
I. de San Félix (Chile)
I. San Ambrosio (Chile)
CHILE
I. de Santa Catarina
Paraná
Uruguay
Córdoba
Porto Alegre
Lagoa dos Patos
Santa Fé
Rosario
Negro
Lagoa Mirim
Aconcagua 22,831
Valparaíso
Mendoza
URUGUAY
Santiago
Buenos Aires
Montevideo
I. Robinson Crusoe
I. Alejandro Selkirk
Juan Fernandez Is. (Chile)
La Plata
Río de la Plata
C. San Antonio
Salado
Pampas
Concepción
Colorado
Bahía Blanca
Limay
Negro
ARGENTINA
Golfo San Matías
Puerto Montt
Pen. Valdés
Isla de Chiloé
Chubut
Archipiélago de los Chonos
Golfo San Jorge
C. Tres Puntas
Pen. Taitao
Deseado
G. de Penas
Patagonia
Bahía Grande
Falkland Islands (U.K.)
Stanley
Archipiélago Reina Adelaida
Str. of Magellan
Str. of Magellan
Tierra del Fuego
Punta Arenas
Cape Horn
ATLANTIC OCEAN
ATLANTIC OCEAN
PACIFIC OCEAN
© HAMMOND INCORPORATED, Maplewood, N. J.
Longitude West of Greenwich

INTERNAL DIVISIONS

Amazonas (terr.), 12,831 ... E 5
Anzoátegui (state), 501,384 ... F 3
Apure (state), 158,487 ... D 4
Aragua (state), 429,344 ... E 3
Barinas (state), 193,914 ... D 3
Bolívar (state), 383,315 ... F 4
Carabobo (state), 512,173 ... D 2
Cojedes (state), 95,177 ... D 3
Delta Amacuro (terr.), 34,278 ... H 3
Dependencias Federales (terr.), 1,000 ... E 2
Distrito Federal, 2,009,561 ... E 2
Falcón (state), 408,051 ... D 2
Guárico (state), 330,147 ... E 3
Lara (state), 611,192 ... C 2
Mérida (state), 335,428 ... C 3
Miranda (state), 702,603 ... E 2
Monagas (state), 316,732 ... G 3
Nueva Esparta (state), 112,611 ... G 2
Portuguesa (state), 284,523 ... D 3
Sucre (state), 493,840 ... G 2
Táchira (state), 525,840 ... B 3
Trujillo (state), 382,441 ... C 3
Yaracuy (state), 222,041 ... D 2
Zulia (state), 1,342,994 ... B 2

CITIES and TOWNS

Acarigua, 30,683 ... D 3
Achaguas, 1,934 ... D 4
Adícora, 563 ... D 2
Aguada Grande, 1,601 ... D 2
Agua Fría, 539 ... D 2
Agua Linda, 25 ... E 5
Aguasay, 1,458 ... G 3
Altagracia, 7,362 ... C 2
Altagracia de Orituco, 13,013 ... E 3
Amuay, 998 ... C 2
Anaco, 23,105 ... F 3
Aparurén ... G 5
Apurito, 739 ... D 4
Arabopó ... H 5
Aragua de Barcelona, 8,241 ... F 3
Aragua de Maturín, 2,643 ... G 3
Araure, 12,316 ... D 3
Aricagua, 230 ... C 3
Arichuna, 983 ... E 4
Aripao, 400 ... F 4
Arismendi, 1,243 ... D 3
Aroa, 6,356 ... D 2
Atapirire, 203 ... F 3
Bachaquero, 14,490 ... C 3
Baragua, 831 ... D 2
Barbaçoas, 1,579 ... E 3
Barcelona, 42,379 ... F 2
Barinas, 25,748 ... C 3
Barinitas, 7,208 ... C 3
Barquisimeto, 280,086 ... D 2
Barrancas, Barinas, 3,154 ... C 3
Barrancas, Monagas, 4,189 ... G 3
Betijoque, 3,915 ... C 3
Biruaca, 631 ... E 4
Biscucuy, 3,900 ... D 3
Bobare, 970 ... D 2
Bobures, 2,159 ... C 3
Boca de Aroa, 1,674 ... D 2
Boca del Mangle, 1,075 ... D 2
Boca del Pao, 283 ... F 3
Boconó, 10,430 ... C 3
Borbón, 373 ... F 4
Borojó, 367 ... C 2
Bruzual, 556 ... D 4
Buena Vista, Anzoátegui, 2,335 ... F 3
Buena Vista, Apure, 64 ... D 4
Buena Vista, Falcón, 786 ... D 2
Cabimas, 141,314 ... C 2
Cabruta, 813 ... E 4
Cabudare, 4,480 ... D 3
Cabure, 1,440 ... D 2
Cachipo, 1,091 ... G 3
Cacuri, 45 ... F 5
Cagua, 16,233 ... E 2
Caicara, 4,776 ... G 3
Caicara de Orinoco, 3,281 ... E 4
Calabozo, 15,739 ... E 3
Calderas, 857 ... C 3
Camaguán, 1,917 ... E 3
Camatagua, 1,419 ... E 3
Campo Claro, 1,620 ... G 2
Candelaria, 158 ... F 4
Cantaura, 14,068 ... F 3
Capatárida, 1,278 ... C 2
Capure, 459 ... G 2
Carabobo, Bolívar ... H 4
Carabobo, Carabobo, 2,319 ... D 3
Caracas (cap.), 786,710 ... E 2
Caracas, *2,064,033 ... E 2
Carache, 2,635 ... C 3
Carapa, 115 ... G 3
Cariaco, 4,281 ... G 2
Caribén, 25 ... E 4
Caripe, 3,583 ... G 2
Caripito, 21,598 ... G 2
Carirubana, 3,421 ... C 2
Carmelo, 1,944 ... C 2
Carora, 23,227 ... C 2
Carrasquero, 1,353 ... B 2
Carúpano, 38,197 ... G 2
Casanay, 3,561 ... G 2
Casigua, Falcón, 406 ... C 2
Casigua, Zulia, 5,320 ... B 3
Caucagua, 4,705 ... E 2
Cazorla, 657 ... E 3
Chaguaramas, 1,363 ... E 3
Chichiriviche, 2,512 ... D 2
Chivacoa, 12,871 ... D 2
Choroní, 352 ... E 2
Churuguara, 4,458 ... D 2
Ciudad Bolívar, 63,266 ... G 3
Ciudad Bolivia, 2,080 ... C 3
Ciudad de Nutrias, 541 ... D 3
Ciudad Guayana, 127,681 ... G 3
Ciudad Ojeda, 53,745 ... C 2
Ciudad Piar, 4,598 ... G 4
Clarines, 2,018 ... F 3
Cojoro, 156 ... C 2
Colón, 169 ... E 6
Comunidad, 44 ... E 6
Coporito, 659 ... H 3
Coro, 45,506 ... D 2
Corozo Pando, 286 ... E 3
Cúa, 5,567 ... E 2
Cubiro, 1,742 ... D 3
Cuchivero, 122 ... F 4
Cumaná, 69,937 ... F 2
Cumanacoa, 7,354 ... F 2
Cunaviche, 596 ... E 4
Curiapo, 375 ... H 3
Dabajuro, 3,927 ... C 2
Delicias, 1,398 ... B 4
Democracia, 12 ... E 6
Dolores, 1,122 ... D 3
Duaca, 5,771 ... D 2
Ejido, 5,457 ... C 3
El Almacén, 31 ... G 4
El Amparo de Apure, 1,087 ... C 4
El Baúl, 1,550 ... D 3
El Callao, 5,039 ... G 4
El Calvario, 567 ... E 3
El Carmen ... E 7
El Chaparro, 1,703 ... F 3
El Cristo, 328 ... G 4
El Dorado, 2,094 ... H 4
El Empedrado, 1,739 ... C 3
El Guapo, 842 ... F 2
El Manteco, 999 ... G 4
El Miamo, 269 ... H 4
Elorza, 2,121 ... D 4
El Palmar, 1,986 ... G 4
El Pao, Anzoátegui, 586 ... F 3
El Pao, Bolívar, 2,115 ... G 3
El Pao, Cojedes, 1,081 ... D 3
El Perú, 1,487 ... H 4
El Pilar, 3,326 ... G 2
El Rastro, 748 ... E 3
El Roque, 348 ... E 2
El Samán de Apure, 1,099 ... D 4
El Socorro, 3,153 ... F 3
El Sombrero, 5,712 ... E 3
El Tigre, 41,961 ... F 3
El Tocuyo, 14,560 ... C 3
El Toro, 199 ... H 3
El Vigía, 8,874 ... C 3
El Vínculo, 1,224 ... D 1
El Yagual, 435 ... D 4
Encontrados, 2,991 ... B 3
Esperanza, 15 ... E 6
Espino, 470 ... F 3
Garcitas, 1,224 ... C 3
Guacara, 11,353 ... D 2
Guachara, 462 ... D 4
Guadarrama, 461 ... D 3
Guaina ... G 5
Guana, 87 ... G 5
Guanare, 18,452 ... D 3
Guanarito, 1,048 ... D 3
Guanoco, 437 ... G 2
Guanta, 8,048 ... F 2
Guardatinajas, 704 ... E 3
Guarero, 646 ... B 2
Guarico, 3,653 ... D 3
Guariquén, 633 ... G 2
Guasdualito, 4,586 ... C 4
Guasimal, 303 ... D 4
Guasipati, 3,446 ... H 4
Guayabal, 40 ... E 6
Guayabal, 841 ... E 3
Güiria, 11,061 ... G 2
Guri, 158 ... G 4
Guzmán Blanco, 151 ... E 6
Higuerote, 3,852 ... F 2
Icabarú, 475 ... H 5
Independencia, 3,658 ... B 4
Irapa, 4,532 ... G 2
Juangriego, 4,505 ... G 2
Judibana, 4,375 ... C 2
Jusepin, 2,471 ... G 3
Kavanayen, 401 ... H 5
La Aduana, 106 ... D 3
La Asunción, 5,517 ... G 2
La Canoa, 256 ... G 3
La Ceiba, Apure, 13 ... C 4
La Ceiba, Trujillo, 199 ... C 3
La Concepción, 18,015 ... B 2
La Concepción, 9,488 ... B 2
La Esmeralda, 30 ... F 6
La Esperanza ... H 3
La Fría, 4,771 ... B 3
La Grita, 7,866 ... C 3
La Guaira, 20,497 ... E 2
Lagunetas, 522 ... C 3
La Horqueta, 330 ... G 3
La Inglesa, 100 ... G 3
La Leona, 327 ... G 3
La Luz, 414 ... D 3
La Margarita ... H 3
La Paragua, 833 ... G 4
Las Bonitas, 306 ... F 4
Las Lajitas ... F 4

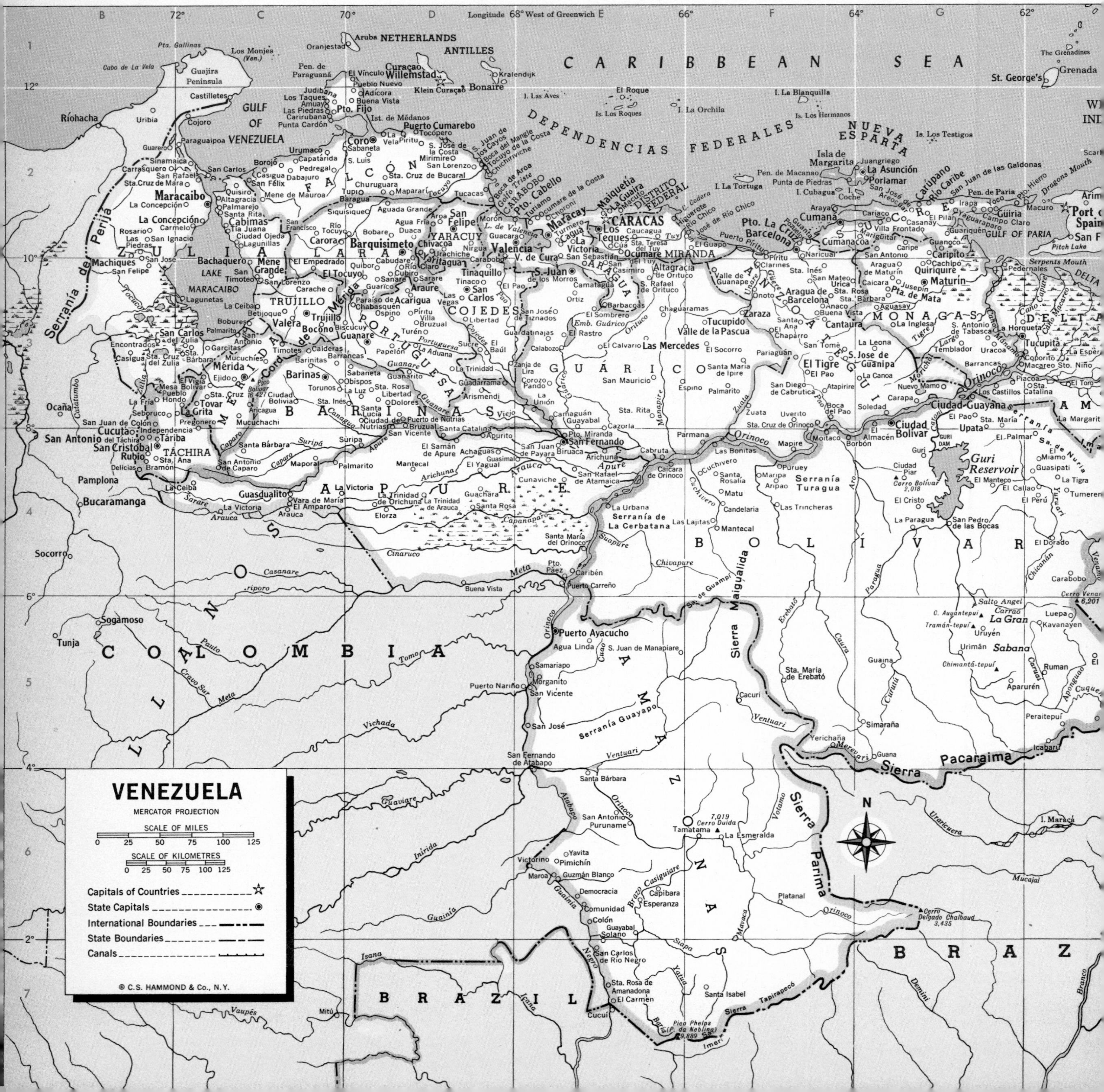

VENEZUELA

MERCATOR PROJECTION

SCALE OF MILES: 0 25 50 75 100 125

SCALE OF KILOMETRES: 0 25 50 75 100 125

Capitals of Countries ☆
State Capitals ◉
International Boundaries
State Boundaries
Canals

AREA 352,143 sq. mi.
POPULATION 10,398,907
CAPITAL Caracas
LARGEST CITY Caracas
HIGHEST POINT Pico Bolívar 16,427 ft.
MONETARY UNIT bolívar
MAJOR LANGUAGE Spanish
MAJOR RELIGION Roman Catholicism

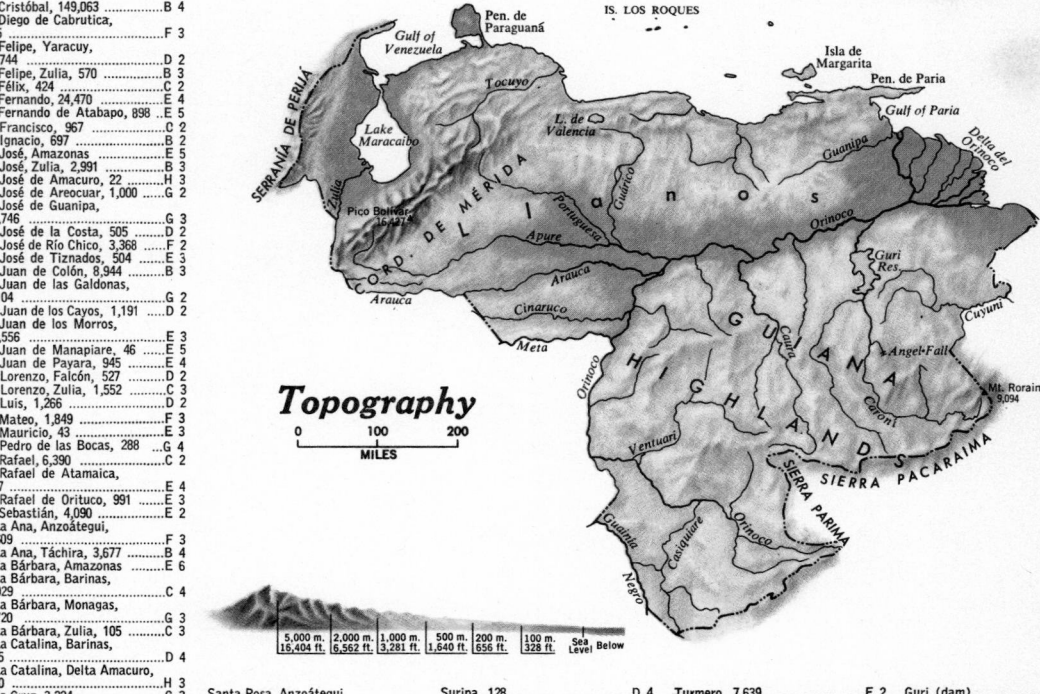

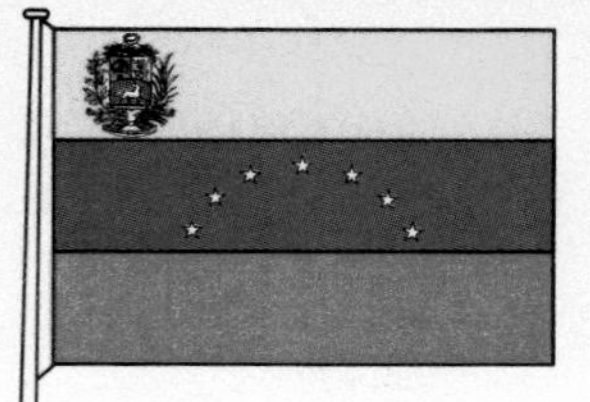

Las Mercedes, 5,410 ....E 3
Las Piedras, Falcón, 2,068 ....C 2
Las Piedras, Zulia, 2,069 ....B 2
Las Trincheras, 157 ....F 4
Las Vegas, 1,190 ....D 3
La Tigra, 234 ....H 4
La Trinidad, 141 ....D 4
La Trinidad de Arauca, 68 ....D 3
La Trinidad de Orichuna, 820 ....D 4
La Unión, 1,068 ....E 3
La Urbana, 444 ....E 4
La Vela de Coro, 4,963 ....D 2
La Victoria, Apure, 109 ....D 4
La Victoria, Aragua, 22,293 ....E 2
Libertad, Barinas, 1,218 ....D 3
Libertad, Cojedes, 1,000 ....D 3
Los Castillos, 92 ....G 3
Los Taques, 2,097 ....C 2
Los Teques, 36,073 ....E 2
Macareo Santo Niño, 376 ....H 3
Machiques, 11,115 ....B 3
Macuro, 899 ....H 2
Macuto, 7,041 ....E 2
Maiquetía, 75,687 ....E 2
Mantecal, Apure, 987 ....D 4
Mantecal, Bolívar, 21 ....F 4
Mapararí, 1,330 ....D 2
Mapire, 658 ....F 4
Maporal, 224 ....C 4
Maracaibo, 625,101 ....C 2
Maracaibo, *655,000 ....C 2
Maracay, 185,655 ....E 2

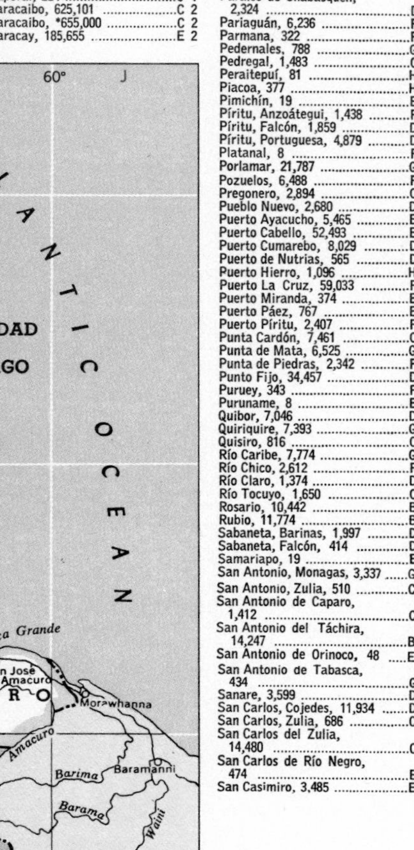

Marigüitar, 3,075 ....G 2
Maripa, 802 ....F 4
Maroa, 417 ....E 6
Matu, 87 ....F 4
Maturín, 54,362 ....G 3
Mene de Mauroa, 3,597 ....C 2
Mene Grande, 11,673 ....C 3
Mérida, 46,339 ....C 3
Mesa Bolívar, 1,227 ....C 3
Mirimire, 1,473 ....D 2
Moitaco, 364 ....F 4
Morganito, 103 ....E 5
Morón, 7,079 ....D 2
Mucuchachí, 391 ....C 3
Mucuchíes, 1,034 ....C 3
Naricual, 656 ....F 2
Nirgua, 7,371 ....D 2
Nuevo Mamo, 284 ....G 3
Obispos, 651 ....D 3
Ocumare de la Costa, 1,332 ....E 2
Ocumare del Tuy, 15,006 ....E 2
Onoto, 1,090 ....F 3
Ortiz, 1,309 ....E 3
Ospino, 1,590 ....D 3
Palmarejo, 943 ....C 2
Palmarito, Apure, 1,176 ....D 4
Palmarito, Guárico, 74 ....F 3
Palmarito, Mérida, 903 ....C 3
Papelón, 414 ....D 3
Paraguaipoa, 1,443 ....C 2
Paraíso de Chabasquén, 2,324 ....D 3
Pariaguán, 6,236 ....F 3
Parmana, 322 ....F 4
Pedernales, 788 ....G 3
Pedregal, 1,483 ....C 2
Peraitepuí, 81 ....H 5
Piacoa, 377 ....H 3
Pimichín, 19 ....E 6
Píritu, Anzoátegui, 1,438 ....F 2
Píritu, Falcón, 1,859 ....D 2
Píritu, Portuguesa, 4,879 ....D 3
Platanal, 8 ....F 6
Porlamar, 21,787 ....G 2
Pozuelos, 6,488 ....F 2
Pregonero, 2,894 ....C 3
Pueblo Nuevo, 2,680 ....D 1
Puerto Ayacucho, 5,465 ....E 5
Puerto Cabello, 52,493 ....E 2
Puerto Cumarebo, 8,029 ....D 2
Puerto de Nutrias, 565 ....D 3
Puerto Hierro, 1,096 ....H 2
Puerto La Cruz, 59,033 ....F 2
Puerto Miranda, 374 ....E 4
Puerto Páez, 767 ....E 4
Puerto Píritu, 2,407 ....F 2
Punta Cardón, 7,461 ....C 2
Punta de Mata, 6,525 ....G 3
Punta de Piedras, 2,342 ....F 2
Punto Fijo, 34,457 ....D 2
Puruey, 343 ....F 4
Puruname, 8 ....E 6
Quibor, 7,046 ....D 3
Quiriquire, 7,393 ....G 3
Quisiro, 816 ....C 2
Río Caribe, 7,774 ....G 2
Río Chico, 2,612 ....F 2
Río Claro, 1,374 ....D 3
Río Tocuyo, 1,650 ....C 2
Rosario, 10,442 ....B 2
Rubio, 11,774 ....B 4
Sabaneta, Barinas, 1,997 ....D 3
Sabaneta, Falcón, 414 ....D 2
Samariapo, 19 ....E 5
San Antonio, Monagas, 3,337 ....G 2
San Antonio, Zulia, 510 ....C 3
San Antonio de Caparo, 1,412 ....C 4
San Antonio del Táchira, 14,247 ....B 4
San Antonio de Orinoco, 48 ....E 6
San Antonio de Tabasca, 434 ....G 3
Sanare, 3,599 ....D 3
San Carlos, Cojedes, 11,934 ....D 3
San Carlos, Zulia, 686 ....C 2
San Carlos del Zulia, 14,480 ....C 3
San Carlos de Río Negro, 474 ....E 7
San Casimiro, 3,485 ....E 3

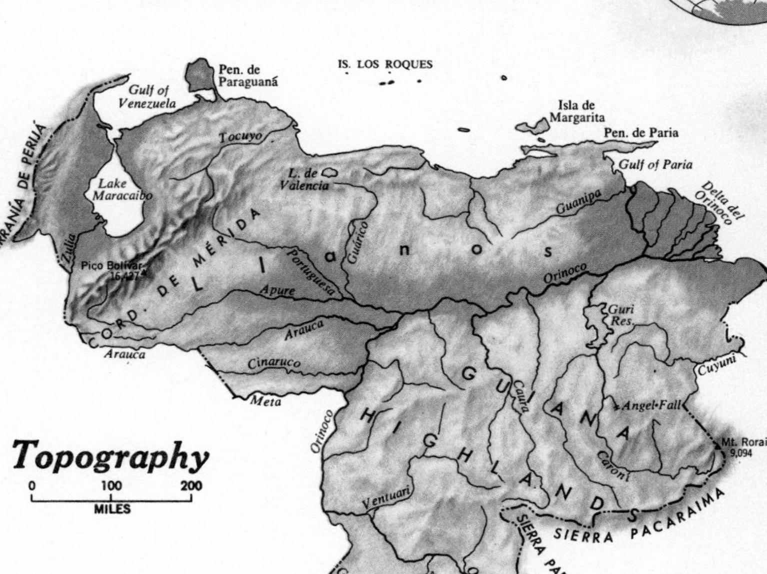

5,000 m. 16,404 ft. | 2,000 m. 6,562 ft. | 1,000 m. 3,281 ft. | 500 m. 1,640 ft. | 200 m. 656 ft. | 100 m. 328 ft. | Sea Level | Below

San Cristóbal, 149,063 ....B 4
San Diego de Cabrutica, 455 ....F 3
San Felipe, Yaracuy, 28,744 ....D 2
San Felipe, Zulia, 570 ....B 3
San Félix, 424 ....C 2
San Fernando, 24,470 ....E 4
San Fernando de Atabapo, 898 ..E 5
San Francisco, 967 ....C 2
San Ignacio, 697 ....B 2
San José, Amazonas ....E 5
San José, Zulia, 2,991 ....B 3
San José de Amacuro, 22 ....H 3
San José de Areocuar, 1,000 ....G 2
San José de Guanipa, 20,746 ....G 3
San José de la Costa, 505 ....D 2
San José de Río Chico, 3,368 ....F 2
San José de Tiznados, 504 ....E 3
San Juan de Colón, 8,944 ....B 3
San Juan de las Galdonas, 1,104 ....G 2
San Juan de los Cayos, 1,191 ....D 2
San Juan de los Morros, 28,556 ....E 3
San Juan de Manapiare, 46 ....E 5
San Juan de Payara, 945 ....E 4
San Lorenzo, Falcón, 527 ....D 2
San Lorenzo, Zulia, 1,552 ....C 3
San Luis, 1,266 ....D 2
San Mateo, 1,849 ....F 3
San Mauricio, 43 ....E 3
San Pedro de las Bocas, 288 ...G 4
San Rafael, 6,390 ....C 2
San Rafael de Atamaica, 597 ....E 4
San Rafael de Orituco, 991 ....E 3
San Sebastián, 4,090 ....E 2
Santa Ana, Anzoátegui, 3,609 ....F 3
Santa Ana, Táchira, 3,677 ....B 4
Santa Bárbara, Amazonas ....E 6
Santa Bárbara, Barinas, 2,029 ....C 4
Santa Bárbara, Monagas, 1,720 ....G 3
Santa Bárbara, Zulia, 105 ....C 3
Santa Catalina, Barinas, 425 ....D 4
Santa Catalina, Delta Amacuro, 440 ....H 3
Santa Cruz, 3,224 ....C 3
Santa Cruz de Bucaral, 1,829 ....D 2
Santa Cruz del Zulia, 2,041 ....B 3
Santa Cruz de Mara, 1,919 ....C 2
Santa Cruz de Orinoco, 419 ....F 3
Santa Elena, 752 ....H 5
Santa Inés, Anzoátegui, 917 ....F 3
Santa Inés, Barinas, 257 ....C 3
Santa Isabel ....F 7
Santa Lucía, 563 ....D 3
Santa María, Bolívar, 468 ....G 3
Santa Mariá de Erebató, 468 ....F 5
Santa María de Ipire, 3,167 ....F 3
Santa María del Orinoco, 57 ....E 4
Santa Rita, Guárico, 306 ....E 3
Santa Rita, Zulia, 5,342 ....C 2

Santa Rosa, Anzoátegui, 1,036 ....F 3
Santa Rosa, Apure, 27 ....D 4
Santa Rosa, Barinas, 957 ....D 3
Santa Rosa de Amanadona, 163 ....E 7
Santa Rosalía, 239 ....F 4
Santa Teresa del Tuy, 6,958 ....E 2
San Timoteo, 2,823 ....C 3
San Tomé, 5,625 ....F 3
San Vicente, Amazonas, 14 .....E 5
San Vicente, Apure, 252 ....D 4
Sarare, 2,664 ....D 3
Seboruco, 2,440 ....B 3
Simaraña ....G 5
Sinamaica, 1,345 ....B 2
Siquisique, 2,579 ....D 2
Solano ....E 6
Soledad, 5,653 ....G 3
Sucre, 65 ....D 3

Suripa, 128 ....D 4
Tamatama, 35 ....F 6
Táriba, 9,835 ....B 4
Temblador, 2,041 ....G 3
Tia Juana, 5,846 ....C 2
Timotes, 2,548 ....C 3
Tinaco, 4,485 ....D 3
Tinaquillo, 8,142 ....D 3
Tocópero, 721 ....D 2
Tocuyo de la Costa, 3,351 ....D 2
Torunos, 676 ....C 3
Tovar, 9,614 ....C 3
Trujillo, 18,957 ....C 3
Tucacas, 3,853 ....D 2
Tucupido, 7,016 ....F 3
Tucupita, 9,922 ....H 3
Tumeremo, 3,926 ....H 4
Tupí, 91 ....D 2
Turén, 341 ....D 3
Turiamo, 31 ....E 2

Turmero, 7,639 ....E 2
Upata, 12,717 ....G 3
Urachiche, 3,630 ....D 2
Uracoa, 858 ....G 3
Urica, 1,577 ....F 3
Urimán, 237 ....G 5
Urumaco, 941 ....C 2
Uruyén ....G 5
Uverito, 336 ....F 3
Valencia, 177,199 ....E 2
Valencia, *224,552 ....E 2
Valera, 46,643 ....C 3
Valle de Guanape, 3,254 ....F 3
Valle de la Pascua, 24,308 ....F 3
Villa Bruzual, 10,278 ....D 3
Villa de Cura, 19,945 ....E 2
Villa Frontado, 1,597 ....G 2
Yaguaraparo, 2,673 ....G 2
Yaritagua, 14,740 ....D 2
Yavita, 49 ....E 6
Yerichaña ....F 5
Yoco, 2,181 ....G 2
Zanja de Lira, 58 ....E 3
Zaraza, 10,084 ....F 3
Zuata, 783 ....F 3

OTHER FEATURES

Amacuro (river) ....H 4
Angel (Salto Angel) (fall) ....G 5
Apongua (river) ....H 5
Apure (river) ....E 4
Arauca (river) ....E 4
Arichuna (river) ....D 4
Aro (river) ....F 4
Atabapo (river) ....E 6
Auyantepui (mt.) ....G 5
Baria (river) ....E 7
Blanquilla, La (isl.), 46 ....F 2
Bolívar (mt.) ....C 3
Bolívar (mt.) ....G 4
Canagua (river) ....C 3
Caño Capure (river) ....H 3
Caño Macareo (river) ....H 3
Caño Mánamo (river) ....G 3
Capanaparo (river) ....E 4
Caparo (river) ....C 4
Caroní (river) ....G 4
Carrao (river) ....G 5
Caruai (river) ....H 5
Casiquiare, Brazo (river) ....E 6
Catatumbo (river) ....B 3
Caura (river) ....F 5
Cerbatana, La (mts.) ....E 4
Chicanán (river) ....H 4
Chimantá–tepuí (mt.) ....G 5
Chivapure (river) ....E 4
Cinaruco (river) ....D 4
Coche (isl.) ....F 2
Codera (cape) ....F 2
Cojedes (river) ....D 3
Cuao (river) ....E 5
Cubagua (isl.) ....F 2
Cuchivero (river) ....F 4
Cuquenán (river) ....H 5
Curutú (river) ....G 5
Cuyuni (river) ....H 4
Delgado Chalbaud (mt.) ....G 6
Dragons Mouth (strait) ....H 2
Duida (mt.) ....F 6
Erebato (river) ....F 5
Gran Sabana, La (plain) ....G 5
Guainía (river) ....E 6
Guampí (mts.) ....F 4
Guanare (river) ....D 3
Guanare Viejo (river) ....D 3
Guanipa (river) ....G 3
Guárico (res.) ....E 3
Guárico (river) ....E 3
Guayapo (mts.) ....E 5
Güere (river) ....F 3
Guri (dam) ....G 4
Guri (res.) ....G 4
Hermanos, Los (isls.) ....F 2
Icabaru (river) ....G 5
Imataca (mts.) ....H 4
Imeri (mts.) ....F 7
La Blanquilla (isl.), 46 ....F 2
La Grand Sabana (plain) ....G 5
La Orchila (isl.), 35 ....F 2
Las Aves (isl.), 6 ....E 2
La Tortuga (isl.), 25 ....F 2
Los Hermanos (isls.) ....F 2
Los Monjes (isls.) ....C 1
Los Roques (isls.), 537 ....E 2
Los Testigos (isls.), 59 ....G 2
Macanao (pen.) ....F 2
Maigualida (mts.) ....F 4
Manapire (river) ....E 3
Maracaibo (lake) ....C 3
Margarita (isl.), 85,296 ....F 2
Mavaca (river) ....F 6
Médanos (isthmus) ....D 2
Merevari (river) ....E 4
Mérida (mts.) ....C 3
Meta (river) ....E 4
Monjes, Los (isls.) ....C 1
Morichal Largo (river) ....G 3
Neblina (Phelps) (pk.) ....E 7
Negro (river) ....E 7
Nuria (mts.) ....H 4
Ocamo (river) ....F 6
Orchila, La (isl.), 35 ....F 2
Orinoco (delta) ....H 3
Orinoco (river) ....G 3
Orituco (river) ....E 3
Pacaraima (mts.) ....G 5
Pao (river) ....D 3
Pao (river) ....F 3
Paragua (river) ....G 4
Paraguaná (peninsula), 104,535 ....C 1
Paria (gulf) ....H 2
Paria (pen.) ....G 2
Parida, La (Bolívar) (mt.) ....G 4
Parima (mts.) ....F 6
Perijá (mts.) ....B 2
Phelps (pk.) ....E 7
Portuguesa (river) ....D 3
Roques, Los (isls.), 537 ....E 2
Roraima (mt.) ....H 5
Salto Angel (fall) ....G 5
Sarare (river) ....C 4
Serpents Mouth (strait) ....H 3
Siapa (river) ....E 7
Sipapo (river) ....E 5
Suapure (river) ....E 4
Suripá (river) ....C 4
Tapirapecó (mts.) ....F 7
Testigos, Los (isls.), 59 ....G 2
Tigre (river) ....G 3
Tocuco (river) ....B 3
Tocuyo (river) ....D 2
Tortuga, La (isl.), 25 ....F 2
Tramán–tepuí (mt.) ....G 5
Triste (gulf) ....D 2
Turagua (mts.) ....F 4
Tuy (river) ....E 2
Unare (river) ....F 3
Valencia (lake) ....E 2
Venamo (mt.) ....H 4
Venamo (river) ....H 4
Venezuela (gulf) ....C 2
Ventuari (river) ....E 5
Votamo (river) ....F 6
Yatua (river) ....E 7
Yuruari (river) ....H 4
Zuata (river) ....F 3
Zulia (river) ....B 3

*City and suburbs.

Agriculture, Industry and Resources

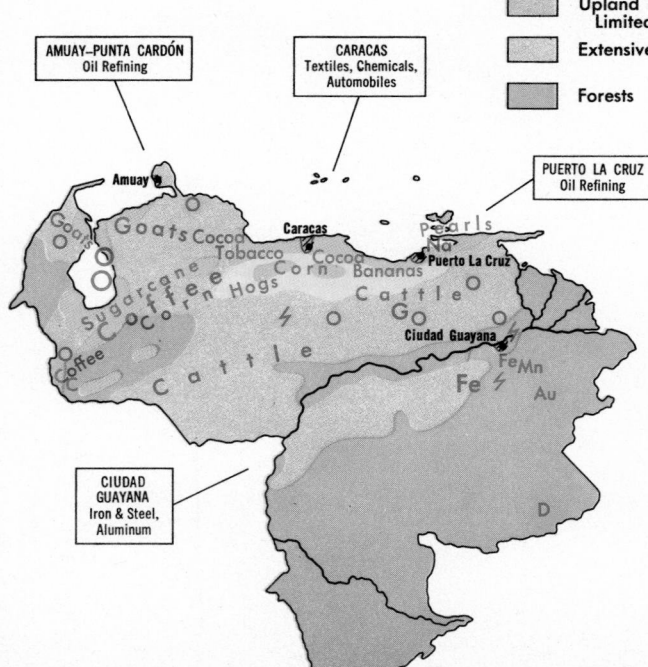

DOMINANT LAND USE

- Diversified Tropical Crops (chiefly plantation agriculture)
- Upland Cultivated Areas
- Upland Livestock Grazing, Limited Agriculture
- Extensive Livestock Ranching
- Forests

AMUAY–PUNTA CARDÓN
Oil Refining

CARACAS
Textiles, Chemicals, Automobiles

PUERTO LA CRUZ
Oil Refining

CIUDAD GUAYANA
Iron & Steel, Aluminum

Amuay
Goats
Cocoa
Tobacco
Caracas
Pearls
Na
Puerto La Cruz
Sugarcane
Coffee
Corn
Hogs
Bananas
Cattle
Ciudad Guayana
Fe
Mn
Au
D

MAJOR MINERAL OCCURRENCES

Au Gold
C Coal
D Diamonds
Fe Iron Ore
G Natural Gas
Mn Manganese
Na Salt
O Petroleum

Water Power
Major Industrial Areas

COLOMBIA
MERCATOR PROJECTION
SCALE OF MILES
0 25 50 75 100 125 150
SCALE OF KILOMETRES
0 25 50 75 100 125 150
Capitals of Countries
Other Capitals
International Boundaries
Other Boundaries
Canals
Copyright by C.S. HAMMOND & Co., N.Y
Longitude 74° West of Greenwich 72°
78° 76° 70° 68°
12° 10° 8° 6° 4° 2° 0° 2° 4°
A B C D E F G
1 2 3 4 5 6 7 8 9 10
CARIBBEAN SEA
PACIFIC OCEAN
PANAMA
Panamá
Gulf of
ARCH. DE LAS PERLAS
VENEZUELA
Gulf of Venezuela
Lake Maracaibo
Maracaibo
Cabimas
Guajira Peninsula
Paraguana Peninsula
Coro
Aruba
NETH. ANTILLES
Curaçao
Bonaire
Willemstad
ISLAS LOS ROQUES (Ven.)
Los Monjes (Ven.)
Golfo Triste
Puerto Cabello
CARACAS
Maracay
Lago de Valencia
Valencia
Barquisimeto
Trujillo
Mérida
Barinas
San Cristóbal
San Fernando de Apure
Apure
Arauca
Orinoco
Meta
Puerto Carreño
Puerto Ayacucho
Samariapo
San Fernando de Atabapo
Ventuari
Guaviare
Inírida
Guainía
LA GUAJIRA
Riohacha
MAGDALENA
Santa Marta
Barranquilla
ATLÁNTICO
Cartagena
BOLÍVAR
CESAR
Valledupar
SUCRE
Sincelejo
CÓRDOBA
Montería
NORTE DE SANTANDER
Cúcuta
Pamplona
Ocaña
ANTIOQUIA
Medellín
SANTANDER
Bucaramanga
Barrancabermeja
CHOCÓ
Quibdó
CALDAS
Manizales
RISARALDA
Pereira
QUINDÍO
Armenia
BOYACÁ
Tunja
Sogamoso
CUNDINAMARCA
BOGOTÁ
DISTRITO ESPECIAL
TOLIMA
Ibagué
VALLE DEL CAUCA
Cali
Buenaventura
Palmira
Buga
Tuluá
CAUCA
Popayán
HUILA
Neiva
NARIÑO
Pasto
Tumaco
Ipiales
PUTUMAYO
Mocoa
CAQUETÁ
Florencia
META
Villavicencio
ARAUCA
CASANARE
VICHADA
GUAINÍA
VAUPÉS
Mitú
AMAZONAS
Leticia
Serranía de la Macarena
Cordillera Occidental
Cordillera Central
Cordillera Oriental
Serranía de Perijá
Serranía de Baudó
Nevado del Huila 18,865
Nevado del Tolima 17,110
Pico Cristóbal Colón 19,029
ECUADOR
Quito
Ibarra
Tulcán
PERU
Iquitos
BRAZIL
Amazon
Putumayo
Caquetá
Japurá
Negro
Equator
Benjamin Constant
INTENDENCIA DE SAN ANDRÉS Y PROVIDENCIA
Same scale as main map
CARIBBEAN SEA
80°
15°
Banco de Serranilla
Banco Alicia
Bajo Nuevo
Roca que Vela
Banco de Quitasueño
Banco de Serrana
Cayos de Roncador
I. Sta. Catalina
Sta. Isabel
Isla de Providencia
San Andrés
Isla de San Andrés
Vigía
Cayos del E.S.E. (Courtown Cays)
Cayos de Albuquerque

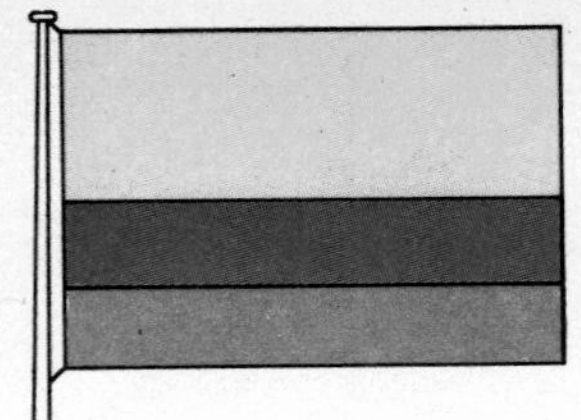

AREA 439,513 sq. mi.
POPULATION 21,117,000
CAPITAL Bogotá
LARGEST CITY Bogotá
HIGHEST POINT Pico Cristóbal Colón 19,029 ft.
MONETARY UNIT Colombian peso
MAJOR LANGUAGE Spanish
MAJOR RELIGION Roman Catholicism

INTERNAL DIVISIONS

Amazonas (intendency), 16,000...D 8
Antioquia (dept.), 3,031,000........C 4
Arauca (commissary), 32,000......E 4
Atlántico (dept.), 903,000 ....C 2
Bolívar (dept.), 849,000 ....C 3
Boyacá (dept.), 1,194,000 ....D 5
Caldas (dept.), 810,000 ....C 5
Caquetá (intendency), 157,000....C 7
Cauca (dept.), 696,000 ....B 6
Cesar (dept.), 357,000 ....D 3
Chocó (dept.), 210,000 ....B 4
Córdoba (dept.), 760,000 ....C 3
Cundinamarca (dept.), 1,187,000 ....C 5
Distrito Especial, 2,416,000 ....C 5
Guainía (comm.), 5,000 ....F 6
Guajira, La (dept.), 173,000 ....D 2
Huila (dept.), 485,000 ....C 6
La Guajira (dept.), 173,000 ....D 2
Magdalena (dept.), 683,000 ......D 3
Meta (dept.), 248,000 ....D 6
Nariño (dept.), 787,000 ....B 7
Norte de Santander (dept.), 615,000 ....D 4
Putumayo (comm.), 77,000 ....C 7
Quindío (dept.), 346,000 ....C 5
Risaralda (dept.), 512,000..........C 5
San Andrés y Providencia (intendency), 27,000 ....B10
Santander (dept.), 1,137,000 ....D 4
Sucre (dept.), 361,000 ....C 3
Tolima (dept.), 902,000 ....C 5
Valle del Cauca (dept.), 2,114,000 ....B 6
Vaupés (commissary), 18,000 ....E 7
Vichada (commissary), 9,000 ....F 5

CITIES and TOWNS

Acacías, 6,508 ....D 6
Acandí, 1,686 ....B 3
Agrado, 2,751 ....C 6
Agua de Dios, 7,401 ....C 5
Aguachica, 8,556 ....D 3
Aguadas, 10,822 ....C 5
Agustín Codazzi, 11,673 ....D 3
Aipe, 3,404 ....C 6
Algeciras, 3,778 ....C 6
Almaguer, 1,251 ....B 7
Amalfi, 4,667 ....C 4
Amanavén, †1,164 ....G 6
Andes, 11,135 ....C 5
Anserma, 14,129 ....B 5
Antioquia, 6,002 ....B 4
Anza, 680 ....C 4
Aracataca, 5,304 ....D 2
Araracuara ....E 8
Arauca, 4,280 ....E 4
Arauquita, 413 ....E 4
Arjona, 16,510 ....C 2
Armenia, 162,837 ....B 5
Armero, 17,495 ....C 5
Ayapel, 5,610 ....C 3
Bagado, 865 ....B 5
Baranoa, 14,064 ....C 2
Baraya, 2,696 ....C 6
Barbacoas, 4,011 ....A 7
Barbosa, 6,018 ....D 5
Barichara, 2,798 ....D 4
Barrancabermeja, 59,625 ....D 4
Barrancas, 2,010 ....D 2
Barranco de Loba, 1,648 ....C 3
Barranquilla, 816,706 ....C 2
Belén de los Andaquíes, 1,420....C 7
Bello, 127,377 ....C 4
Boca del Pepé, 566 ....B 5
Bogotá (cap.), 2,037,904 ....D 5
Bogotá, *2,416,000 ....D 5
Bolívar, Antioquia, 9,532 ....C 5
Bolívar, Cauca, 3,641 ....B 7
Bucaramanga, 279,703 ....D 4
Buenaventura, 113,301 ....B 6
Buesaco, 2,278 ....B 7
Buga, 65,535 ....B 6
Caicedonia, 16,327 ....C 5
Calamar, Bolívar, 6,055 ....C 2
Calamar, Vaupés ....D 7
Calarcá, 30,342 ....C 5
Cali, 820,809 ....B 6
Camoruco ....E 4
Campo de la Cruz, 10,044 ....C 2
Campoalegre, 9,768 ....C 6
Cañasgordas, 4,464 ....B 4
Cartagena, 229,040 ....C 2
Cartago, 55,682 ....B 5
Carurú, 277 ....E 7
Casuarito, †75 ....G 4
Caucasia, 5,616 ....C 4
Cereté, 11,849 ....C 3
Cerro de San Antonio, 3,397 ....C 2
Chaparral, 13,261 ....C 6
Chimichagua, 5,093 ....D 3
Chinácota, 4,081 ....D 4
Chinchiná, 15,944 ....C 5
Chinú, 7,552 ....C 3
Chiquinquirá, 16,926 ....C 5
Chiriguaná, 6,516 ....D 3
Ciénaga, 142,893 ....C 2
Ciénaga de Oro, 8,047 ....C 3
Cisneros, 7,554 ....C 4
Colombia, 1,599 ....C 6
Colón, 1,133 ....B 7
Condoto, 4,094 ....B 5
Contratación, 3,117 ....D 4
Convención, 7,371 ....D 3
Corinto, 5,008 ....B 6
Corozal, 14,000 ....C 3
Cravo Norte, 566 ....F 4
Cúcuta, 207,091 ....D 4
Cumbal, 2,549 ....B 7
Cuñare ....D 7
Dabeiba, 4,218 ....B 4
Dagua, 4,635 ....B 6
Dibulla ....D 2
Duitama, 31,865 ....D 5
El Banco, 14,889 ....D 3
El Carmen, Chocó, 1,689 ....B 5
El Carmen, Norte de Santander, 2,737 ....D 3
El Carmen de Bolívar, 19,196....C 3
El Cerrito, 12,200 ....B 6
El Cocuy, 2,869 ....D 4
El Tambo, 4,003 ....B 6
Envigado, 40,686 ....C 4
Espinal, 22,791 ....C 5
Facatativá, 20,742 ....C 5
Florencia, 17,709 ....C 7
Fonseca, 5,190 ....D 2
Fontibón ....C 5
Fresno, 7,058 ....C 5
Fundación, 14,128 ....D 2
Fusagasugá, 18,755 ....C 5
Gachalá, 1,253 ....D 5
Gamarra, 4,664 ....D 3
Garzón, 11,999 ....C 6
Gigante, 4,594 ....C 6
Girardot, 66,584 ....C 5
Gramalote, 3,098 ....D 4
Guacamaya ....C 6
Guamal, Magdalena, 4,695 ....C 3
Guamal, Meta, 2,113 ....D 6
Guape ....D 6
Guapí, 3,066 ....B 6
Guateque, 4,646 ....D 5
Honda, 19,945 ....C 5
Ibagué, 178,821 ....C 5
Ipiales, 23,320 ....B 7
Iscuandé, 1,777 ....A 6
Istmina, 3,996 ....B 5
Itagüí, 101,066 ....C 4
Ituango, 3,466 ....C 4
Jurado, 708 ....B 4
La Cruz, 4,014 ....B 7
La Dorada, 26,168 ....C 5
La Gloria, 2,915 ....D 3
La Palma, 4,594 ....C 5
La Plata, 5,863 ....C 6
La Unión, 3,875 ....B 7
Leticia, 4,013 ....F10
Líbano, 18,640 ....C 5
Lorica, 12,880 ....C 3
Los Andes, 1,392 ....B 7
Macaranaima ....E 7
Magangué, 27,354 ....C 3
Maicao, 9,347 ....D 2
Maipures ....F 5
Majagual, 2,197 ....C 3
Málaga, 9,674 ....D 4
Manare ....E 4
Maní, 586 ....D 5
Manizales, 267,543 ....C 5
Matanza, 1,264 ....D 4
Medellín, 967,825 ....C 4
Medina, 893 ....D 5
Mercaderes, 2,376 ....B 7
Micay ....B 6
Miraflores, Boyacá, 3,257 ....D 5
Miraflores, Vaupés, 245 ....E 7
Miranda, 5,527 ....B 6
Mitú, 1,623 ....E 7
Mituas ....F 6
Mocoa, 2,571 ....B 7
Mompós, 10,965 ....C 3
Moniquirá, 4,882 ....D 5
Montería, 167,446 ....B 3
Morichal, 12,512 ....E 6
Mosquera, 766 ....A 6
Murindó, 319 ....B 4
Muzo, 792 ....D 5
Natagaima, 8,372 ....C 6
Naya ....B 6
Neiva, 111,727 ....C 6
Nóvita, 883 ....B 5
Nueva Antioquia, 1236 ....F 5
Nunchía, 461 ....D 5
Nuquí, 1,500 ....B 5
Obando ....G 6
Ocaña, 28,028 ....D 3
Orocué, 1,600 ....E 5
Ortega, 4,450 ....C 6
Pacho, 7,192 ....C 5
Pacoa, 1960 ....G 6
Páez, 1,570 ....C 6
Paipa, 3,105 ....D 5
Palmira, 164,394 ....B 6
Pamplona, 25,502 ....D 4
Pasto, 123,153 ....B 7
Patía, 3,045 ....B 6
Paz de Ariporo, 1,216 ....E 5
Paz de Río, 2,748 ....D 4
Pedraza, 1,757 ....C 2
Pereira, 224,421 ....C 5
Piedecuesta, 12,278 ....D 4
Pitalito, 10,818 ....B 7
Pivijay, 8,200 ....C 2
Planeta Rica, 5,959 ....C 3
Plato, 13,364 ....C 3
Popayán, 58,500 ....B 6
Pore, 193 ....D 5
Potosí, 1,149 ....C 7
Pradera, 11,223 ....B 6
Puente Nacional, 2,913 ....D 5
Puerto Asís, 2,902 ....B 7
Puerto Berrío, 15,812 ....C 4
Puerto Carreño, 1,115 ....G 4
Puerto Colombia, 7,143 ....C 2
Puerto Escondido, 1,543 ....B 3
Puerto Leguízamo, 3,014 ....C 8
Puerto López, La Guajira ....E 2
Puerto López, Meta, 3,586 ....D 5
Puerto Murillo, †1,014 ....G 4
Puerto Nariño, 1926 ....F 5
Puerto Rico, Caquetá, †10,328 ....C 7
Puerto Rico, Meta ....C 6
Puerto Rondón, 951 ....E 4
Puerto Salgar, 6,398 ....C 5
Puerto Tejada, 14,863 ....B 6
Puerto Wilches, 4,635 ....D 4
Pupiales, 2,432 ....B 7
Purificación, 7,044 ....C 6
Quibdó, 19,989 ....B 5
Remedios, 2,090 ....C 4
Remolino, 3,373 ....C 2
Restrepo, 2,603 ....D 5
Ricaurte, 866 ....A 7
Río de Oro, 2,482 ....D 3
Riohacha, 11,708 ....D 2
Rionegro, Antioquia, 2,708 ....D 4
Rionegro, Santander, 12,541 ....C 4
Riosucio, Caldas, 11,274 ....C 5
Riosucio, Chocó, 1,817 ....B 4
Roberto Payán, 402 ....A 7
Robles, 4,278 ....D 2
Rovira, 4,582 ....C 5
Sabanalarga, 20,254 ....C 2
Sácama, 54 ....D 4
Sahagún, 11,560 ....C 3
Salamina, 14,263 ....C 5
Salazar, 3,020 ....D 4
Samaniego, 3,181 ....B 7
San Agustín, 3,250 ....B 7
San Andrés, Antioquia, 1,773 ....C 4
San Andrés, San Andrés y Providencia, 9,040 ....A10
San Antero, 6,596 ....C 3
San Felipe, 187 ....G 7
San Francisco, 1,248 ....B 7
San Gil, 18,518 ....D 4
San Jacinto, 10,210 ....C 3
San José del Guaviare, 215 ....D 6
San José del Ocuné, 105 ....E 5
San Juan del César, 9,347 ....D 2
San Marcos, 7,083 ....C 3
San Martín, 6,739 ....D 6
San Onofre, 10,737 ....C 3
San Pablo, 4,103 ....B 7
San Roque, 3,272 ....C 4
San Vicente del Caguán, 1,764....C 6
Sandoná, 6,776 ....B 7
Santa Bárbara, 7,779 ....C 5
Santa Isabel, 468 ....B 9
Santa Marta, 137,474 ....D 2
Santa Rosa de Cabal, 31,646 ....C 5
Santa Rosa de Osos, 6,860 ....C 4
Santander, 11,426 ....B 6
Santiago, 929 ....B 7
Sardinata, 2,964 ....D 3
Segovia, 9,234 ....C 4
Sevilla, 26,757 ....C 5
Sibundoy-Las Casas, 1,999 ....B 7
Silvia, 3,180 ....B 6
Simití, 2,825 ....C 4
Sincé, 10,631 ....C 3
Sincelejo, 44,001 ....C 3
Sipí, 155 ....B 5
Sitionuevo, 5,969 ....C 2
Soatá, 4,361 ....D 4
Socorro, 13,716 ....D 4
Sogamoso, 32,274 ....D 5
Soledad, 37,617 ....C 2
Sonsón, 16,955 ....C 5
Sopetrán, 3,646 ....C 4
Sucre, Bolívar, 3,035 ....C 3
Sucre, Caquetá ....C 7
Tadó, 1,947 ....B 5
Támara, 1,034 ....D 5
Tame, 3,063 ....E 4
Tibaná, 924 ....D 5
Tierralta, 4,415 ....C 3
Timaná, 2,999 ....C 7
Timbío, 4,145 ....B 6
Timbiquí, 1,406 ....B 6
Toledo, 2,314 ....D 4
Tolú, 7,954 ....C 3
Trinidad, 572 ....E 5
Tuluá, 56,539 ....B 5
Tumaco, 25,145 ....A 7
Tunja, 40,451 ....D 5
Túquerres, 10,698 ....B 7
Turbaco, 14,255 ....C 2
Turbo, 7,375 ....B 3
Ubaté, 6,261 ....D 5
Uribia, 1,763 ....D 2
Urrao, 7,712 ....B 4
Valdivia, 2,264 ....C 4
Valledupar, 120,009 ....D 2
Vélez, 7,033 ....D 4
Venadillo, 6,931 ....C 5
Villanueva, 8,288 ....D 2
Villa Amazónica, 1,344 ....B 7
Villa Rosario, 5,184 ....D 4
Villavicencio, 45,277 ....D 5
Villeta, 5,280 ....C 5
Yarumal, 16,823 ....C 4
Yavaraté, †1,963 ....F 7
Yopal, 2,878 ....D 5
Yumbo, 15,276 ....B 6
Zapatoca, 7,305 ....D 4
Zaragoza, 2,134 ....C 4
Zarzal, 17,768 ....B 5
Zipaquirá, 22,648 ....D 5

OTHER FEATURES

Abibe (mts.) ....B 4
Aguja (cape) ....C 2
Albuquerque (cays) A10
Alicia (bank) ....B 8
Alto Ritacuva (mt.) ....D 4
Amazon (Amazonas) (river) ......E 9
Ancón de Sardinas (bay) ....A 7
Angostura (falls) ....E 6
Apaporis (river) ....F 8
Araracuara (mts.) ....E 7
Arauca (river) ....E 4
Ariari (river) ....D 6
Ariguaní (river) ....D 3
Ariporo (river) ....E 4
Atabapo (river) ....G 6
Atrato (river) ....B 4
Augusta (cape) ....C 2
Ayapel (mts.) ....C 4
Bajo Nuevo (shoal) ....C 8
Baudó (mts.) ....B 5
Baudó (river) ....B 5
Bita (river) ....F 5
Caguán (river) ....C 7
Cahuinarí (river) ....E 8
Caquetá (river) ....E 8
Caraparaná (river) ....D 8
Casanare (river) ....E 4
Cauca (river) ....C 4
Cazueleja (mt.) ....C 6
Central (mts.) ....C 5
César (river) ....D 2
Chaira (lagoon) ....C 7
Chamusa (mts.) ....C 8
Charambirá (point) ....B 5
Chiribiquete (mts.) ....D 7
Chocó (bay) ....B 6
Cocha (lake) ....D 7
Cocuy (mts.) ....D 4
Coredó (Humboldt) (bay) ....B 4
Corrientes (cape) ....B 5
Courtown (Este Sudeste) (cays) A10
Cravo Norte (river) ....E 4
Cravo Sur (river) ....E 5
Cristóbal Colón (mt.) ....D 2
Cuemaní (river) ....D 7
Cupica (gulf) ....B 4
Cuquiarí (river) ....E 7
Cusiana (river) ....D 5
Este Sudeste (cays) A10
Gallinas (point) ....E 1
Grande (isl.) ....B 4
Guainía (river) ....F 6
Guajira (pen.) ....E 1
Guapí (bay) ....A 6
Guaviare (river) ....F 6
Guayabero (river) ....D 6
Huila (mt.) ....C 6
Humboldt (Coredó) (bay) ....B 4
Igara-Paraná (river) ....D 8
Inírida (river) ....F 6
Isana (river) ....F 7
Lebrija (river) ....D 4
Llanos (plains) ....D 5
Losada (river) ....C 6
Macarena (mts.) ....D 6
Magdalena (river) ....C 3
Manacacías (river) ....D 6
Mapiripán (lake) ....E 6
Marzo (cape) ....B 4
Mesai (river) ....D 7
Meta (river) ....E 5
Metica (river) ....D 6
Miritiparaná (river) ....E 8
Morrosquillo (gulf) ....C 3
Muco (river) ....E 5
Naipo (isl.) ....F 6
Nechí (river) ....C 4
Occidental, Cordillera (mts.) ....B 5
Oriental, Cordillera (mts.) ....D 5
Orinoco (river) ....G 5
Orteguaza (river) ....C 7
Papunáua (river) ....E 6
Patía (river) ....B 6
Pauto (river) ....E 5
Perijá (mts.) ....D 2
Providencia (isl.), 2,318 ....B 9
Pupurí (river) ....F 7
Puracé (volcano) ....B 6
Putumayo (river) ....E 9
Quitasueño (bank) ....A 8
Riosucio (river) ....C 5
Roncador (cays) ....B 9
Saldaña (river) ....C 6
Salto Grande (falls) ....D 8
San Andrés (isl.), 14,413 ....A10
San Jorge (river) ....C 3
San Juan (river) ....B 5
Santa Marta, Nev. de (range)...D 2
Serrana (bank) ....B 9
Serranilla (bank) ....B 8
Sinú (river) ....B 3
Sogamoso (river) ....D 4
Solano (point) ....B 4
Suárez (river) ....D 4
Taraira (river) ....F 8
Tequendama (falls) ....C 5
Tibugá (gulf) ....B 5
Tolima (mt.) ....C 5
Tomo (river) ....F 5
Tortugas (gulf) ....B 6
Truandó (river) ....B 4
Tumaco (inlet) ....A 6
Tunahí (mts.) ....E 7
Upía (river) ....D 5
Urabá (gulf) ....B 3
Uva (lake) ....E 6
Uva (river) ....E 6
Vaupés (river) ....E 7
Vela (cape) ....D 1
Vela, Roca que (cay) ....B 8
Vichada (river) ....F 5
Yarí (river) ....D 8
Zapatosa (swamp) ....D 3

*City and suburbs.

Agriculture, Industry and Resources

DOMINANT LAND USE

- Diversified Tropical Crops (chiefly plantation agriculture)
- Upland Cultivated Areas
- Upland Livestock Grazing, Limited Agriculture
- Extensive Livestock Ranching
- Forests
- Nonagricultural Land

MAJOR MINERAL OCCURRENCES

Ag	Silver	G	Natural Gas
Au	Gold	Na	Salt
C	Coal	O	Petroleum
Em	Emeralds	Pt	Platinum
Fe	Iron Ore	S	Sulfur
		U	Uranium

Water Power

Major Industrial Areas

PAZ DEL RÍO
Iron & Steel

CALI
Textiles, Paper, Drugs

MEDELLÍN
Textiles, Clothing, Leather Goods

BOGOTÁ
Textiles, Leather Goods, Cement, Electrical Equipment

Bonito
Tobacco
Coffee
Bananas
Rice
Cattle
Hogs
Cocoa
Wheat
Corn
Sheep
Sugar-cane
Cinchona
Wild Rubber
Medellín
Paz del Río
Bogotá
Cali

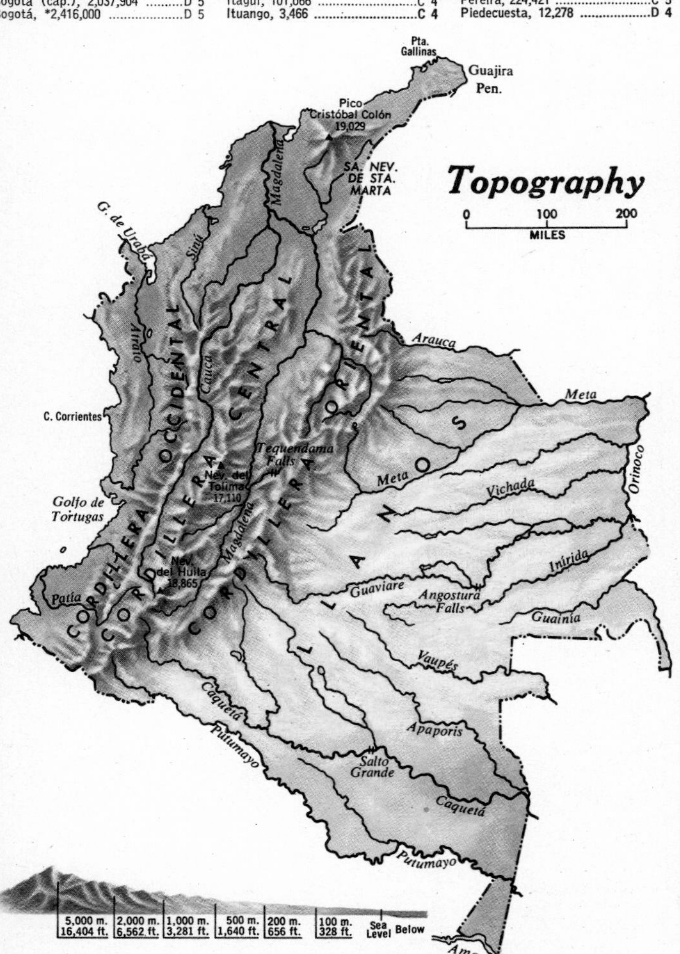

PERU and ECUADOR
BIPOLAR OBLIQUE CONIC CONFORMAL PROJECTION
SCALE OF MILES
0 50 100 150 200
SCALE OF KILOMETRES
0 50 100 150 200
Capitals of Countries
Other Capitals
International Boundaries
Other Boundaries
Copyright by C. S. Hammond & Co., N. Y.
PROVINCES OF ECUADOR
INDICATED BY NUMBERS
1 Imbabura C-2
2 Cotopaxi C-3
3 Tungurahua C-3
4 Los Ríos C-3
5 Bolívar C-3
6 Chimborazo C-3
7 Cañar C-4
8 El Oro C-4
GALÁPAGOS ISLANDS
(ARCHIPIÉLAGO DE COLÓN)
(Ecuador)
Same scale as main map
PACIFIC OCEAN
Longitude 76° West of Greenwich
C O L O M B I A
E C U A D O R
P E R U
B R A Z I L
B O L I V I A
CHILE
P A C I F I C O C E A N
Equator

PERU

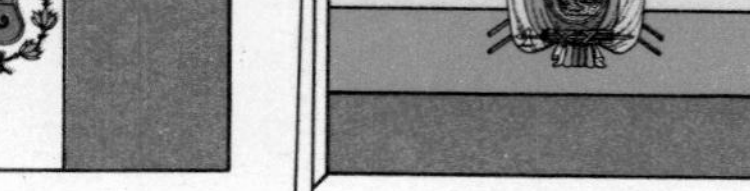

ECUADOR

PERU

AREA 496,222 sq. mi.
POPULATION 13,586,300
CAPITAL Lima
LARGEST CITY Lima
HIGHEST POINT Huascarán 22,205 ft.
MONETARY UNIT sol
MAJOR LANGUAGES Spanish, Quechua, Aymara
MAJOR RELIGION Roman Catholicism

ECUADOR

AREA 109,483 sq. mi.
POPULATION 6,144,000
CAPITAL Quito
LARGEST CITY Guayaquil
HIGHEST POINT Chimborazo 20,561 ft.
MONETARY UNIT sucre
MAJOR LANGUAGES Spanish, Quechua
MAJOR RELIGION Roman Catholicism

PERU

DEPARTMENTS

Amazonas, 171,100 .... C 5
Ancash, 744,700 .... D 7
Apurímac, 330,400 .... F10
Arequipa, 518,300 .... F10
Ayacucho, 474,100 .... E 9
Cajamarca, 1,007,600 .... C 6
Callao (province), 335,400 .... D 9
Cuzco, 756,100 .... F 9
Huancavelica, 367,100 .... E 9
Huánuco, 430,100 .... D 7
Ica, 362.700 .... E10
Junín, 699,100 .... E 8
La Libertad, 784,900 .... C 6
Lambayeque, 485,500 .... B 6
Lima, 3,155,800 .... D 8
Loreto, 504,600 .... E 5
Madre de Dios, 24,200 .... G 8
Moquegua, 68,800 .... G11
Pasco, 188,000 .... E 8
Piura, 922,300 .... B 5
Puno, 848,200 .... G10
San Martín, 229,400 .... D 6
Tacna, 93,900 .... G11
Tumbes, 84,000 .... B 4

CITIES and TOWNS

Abancay, 9,053 .... F 9
Acarí, 1,428 .... E10
Acobamba, 2,167 .... E 9
Acolla, 4,415 .... E 8
Acomayo, Cuzco, 1,874 .... G 9
Acomayo, Huánuco, 1,198 .... E 7
Acora, 941 .... H11
Acuracay, 96 .... F 5
Aija, 1,710 .... D 7
Alca, 539 .... F10
Ambo, 1,606 .... D 8
Ancón, 3,760 .... D 8
Andahuaylas, 4,674 .... F 9
Andamarca, 339 .... E 8
Anta, 2,574 .... F 9
Antabamba, 2,294 .... F10
Aplao, 1,316 .... F11
Aquia, 897 .... D 8
Arequipa, 194,700 .... G11
Ascope, 3,845 .... C 6
Astillero .... H 9
Atalaya, 816 .... E 8
Atico, 297 .... F11
Ayabaca, 3,415 .... C 5
Ayacucho, 28,500 .... F 9
Ayavirí, 7,553 .... G10
Azángaro, 4,771 .... H10
Bagua, 2,343 .... C 5
Balsapuerto, 203 .... D 5
Bambamarca, 4,281 .... C 6
Barranca, Lima, 11,320 .... C 8
Barranca, Loreto, 184 .... D 5
Bartra Antiguo .... E 4
Bartra Nuevo .... E 4
Bayóvar .... B 5
Bellavista, 2,129 .... C 5
Bolívar, 1,057 .... D 6
Bolognesi .... F 6
Bolognesi, 516 .... F 8
Borja, 300 .... D 5
Bretaña, 766 .... E 5
Buldibuyo, 616 .... D 7
Caballococha, 1,197 .... G 4
Cabana, 1,910 .... C 7
Cabo Blanco .... B 5
Cahuapanas, 125 .... D 5
Cailloma, 607 .... G10
Cajabamba, 5,253 .... C 6
Cajacay, 809 .... D 8
Cajamarca, 28,200 .... C 6
Cajatambo, 2,257 .... D 8
Calca, 3,489 .... G 9
Callalli, 133 .... G10
Callao, 335,400 .... D 9
Camaná, 5,120 .... F11
Candarave, 859 .... G11
Cangallo, 1,578 .... E 9
Canta, 2,491 .... D 8
Capachica, 193 .... H10
Carás, 4,033 .... D 7
Caravelí, 1,954 .... F10
Carhuás, 2,175 .... D 7
Carumás, 727 .... G11
Cascas, 2,403 .... C 6
Casma, 4,975 .... C 7
Castilla, 29,541 .... B 5
Castrovirreyna, 784 .... E 9
Catacaos, 12,135 .... B 5
Celendín, 5,646 .... D 6
Cerro Azul, 1,571 .... D 9
Cerro de Pasco, 23,400 .... D 8
Chachapoyas, 6,860 .... D 6
Chala, 1,054 .... E10
Chalhuanca, 2,840 .... F10
Chancay, 6,145 .... D 8
Chao .... C 7
Chepén, 16,119 .... C 6
Chicama, 1,362 .... C 6
Chiclayo, 140,800 .... C 6
Chilca (Pucusana), 1,331 .... D 9
Chilete, 1,105 .... C 6
Chimbote, 102,800 .... C 7
Chincha Alta, 26,500 .... D 9
Chiquián, 3,354 .... D 8
Chirinos, 490 .... C 5
Chivay, 2,320 .... G10
Chorrillós, 31,703 .... D 9
Chosica .... D 8
Chota, 4,961 .... C 6
Chulucanas, 19,714 .... B 5
Chupaca, 2,180 .... E 9
Chuquibamba, 2,983 .... F10
Chuquibambilla, 1,423 .... F 9
Churín, 610 .... D 8
Cocachacra, 2,869 .... G11
Cocama .... G 8
Cojata, 763 .... H10
Colasay, 466 .... C 5
Colcamar, 1,370 .... D 6
Conaica, 1,408 .... E 9
Concepción, 4,184 .... E 8
Concordia, 66 .... E 5
Contamana, 4,708 .... E 6
Contumazá, 2,532 .... C 6
Coracora, 4,116 .... F10
Córdova, 620 .... E10
Corongo, 2,241 .... D 7
Cotahuasi, 1,618 .... F10
Culebras .... C 7
Cumaría .... F 7
Cutervo, 4,702 .... C 6
Cuyocuyo, 708 .... H10
Cuzco, 108,900 .... F 9
Desaguadero, 948 .... H11
Deustua, 416 .... G10
Dos de Mayo, 970 .... E 6
Echarate, 374 .... F 9
El Portugués .... C 7
Esperanza, 261 .... G 7
Ferreñafe, 12,112 .... C 6
Fitzcarrald .... G 8
Francisco de Orellana, 306 .... F 4
Guadalupe, 2,896 .... E 9
Güeppi .... E 3
Huacho, 29,400 .... D 8
Huacrachuco, 757 .... D 7
Hualgayoc, 1,223 .... C 6
Hualla, 2,586 .... F 9
Huallanca, Ancash, 491 .... D 7
Huallanca, Huánuco, 1,202 .... D 7
Huamachuco, 5,730 .... D 6
Huancabamba, 3,215 .... C 5
Huancané, 4,053 .... H10
Huancapi, 2,415 .... E 9
Huancavelica, 11,039 .... E 9
Huancayo, 95,000 .... E 9
Huanchaco, 1,006 .... C 7
Huanta, 5,728 .... E 9
Huánuco, 34,500 .... E 7
Huaral, 11,481 .... D 8
Huaráz, 20,345 .... D 7
Huari, 2,467 .... D 7
Huariaca, 1,534 .... E 8
Huarmey, 5,232 .... C 8
Huarochirí, 2,125 .... D 9
Huarocondo, 2,921 .... F 9
Huaura, 1,442 .... D 8
Huaylas, 1,258 .... C 7
Iberia, 526 .... F 5
Ica, 72,300 .... E10
Ichuña, 183 .... G11
Ilave, 4,278 .... H11
Ilo, 9,986 .... G11
Imperial, 6,345 .... D 9
Inambari, 9 .... H 9
Iñapari, 159 .... H 8
Intutu, 344 .... E 4
Iparia, 171 .... E 7
Iquitos, 76,100 .... F 4
Jaén, 4,420 .... C 5
Jauja, 12,751 .... E 8
Jayanca, 4,240 .... B 6
Jeberos, 1,842 .... D 5
Juanjuí, 5,105 .... D 6
Juli, 3,874 .... H11
Juliaca, 35,000 .... G10
Jumbilla, 876 .... C 5
Junín, 5,004 .... E 8
Lagunas, 3,637 .... E 5
La Huaca, 1,863 .... B 5
La Jalca, 1,401 .... D 6
La Joya, 1,305 .... G11
Lamas, 7,139 .... D 6
Lambayeque, 10,629 .... B 6
Lampa, 3,123 .... G10
Lamud, 2,609 .... C 6
Lanlacuni Bajo, 229 .... G 9
La Oroya, 32,600 .... D 8
Las Piedras, 13 .... H 9
Las Yaras, 367 .... G11
La Tina .... B 5
La Unión, 2,013 .... D 7
Leimebamba, 1,026 .... D 6
Lima (capital), *2,541,300 .... D 8
Limbani, 903 .... H10
Lircay, 2,077 .... E 9
Llata, 2,255 .... D 7
Lobitos, 3,071 .... B 5
Locumba, 349 .... G11
Lomas, 111 .... E10
Lucerna .... H 9
Lurín, 2,741 .... D 9
Machupicchu, 1,026 .... F 9
Macusani, 1,601 .... G10
Madre de Dios, †802 .... G 9
Máncora, 7,943 .... B 5
Manú, †686 .... G 9
Marcapata, 334 .... G 9
Marcona, 6,744 .... E10
Margos, 1,195 .... D 8
Masisea, 1,520 .... E 7
Matarani F11
Matucana, 2,883 .... D 8
Mavila .... H 8
Mazán, 411 .... F 4
Mazocruz, 156 .... H11
Mendoza, 1,002 .... D 6
Miraflores, 52,142 .... G11
Mishagua .... F 8
Moho, 1,377 .... H10
Mollendo, 12,483 .... F11
Monsefú, 11,141 .... C 6
Moquegua, 7,795 .... G11
Morales, 2,430 .... D 6
Morococha, 6,519 .... D 8
Morropón, 4,730 .... C 5
Motupe, 1,286 .... C 6
Moyobamba, 8,373 .... D 6
Nauta, 1,905 .... F 5
Nazca, 13,587 .... E10
Negritos, 14,810 .... B 5
Nueva Alejandría, †264 .... F 5
Nuñoa, 2,137 .... G10
Ocoña, 1,207 .... F11
Ocros, 1,204 .... D 8
Ollachea, 903 .... G 9
Ollantaytambo, 1,632 .... F 9
Olmos, 3,628 .... C 5
Omaguas .... F 4
Omas, 217 .... D 9
Omate, 856 .... G11
Orcotuna, 2,716 .... E 8
Orellana, 1,596 .... E 6
Otuzco, 4,311 .... C 6
Oxapampa, 2,535 .... E 8
Oyón, 2,171 .... D 8
Pacasmayo, 11,956 .... C 6
Pachiza, 1,307 .... D 6
Paijan, 5,815 .... C 6
Paita, 9,615 .... B 5
Palpa, 2,615 .... E10
Pampachiri, 448 .... F10
Pampacolca, 1,876 .... F10
Pampas, 2,495 .... E 9
Panao, 1,262 .... E 7
Pantoja, 528 .... E 3
Parinari, 126 .... E 5
Paruro, 1,905 .... F 9
Pataz, 324 .... D 6
Pativilca, 15,325 .... D 8
Paucarbamba, 715 .... E 9
Paucartambo, Cuzco, 1,928 .... E 8
Paucartambo, Pasco, 1,717 .... G 9
Pevas, 696 .... G 4
Picota, 2,014 .... D 6
Pimentel, 6,252 .... B 6
Pinquén .... G 9
Pisac, 1,230 .... G 9
Pisco, 27,300 .... D 9
Piura, 111,400 .... B 5
Pizacoma, 86 .... H11
Pomabamba, 2,522 .... D 7
Porvenir .... E 5
Poto, 161 .... H10
Pozuzo, 121 .... E 8
Puca Barranca .... F 4
Pucallpa, 45,600 .... E 7
Pucará, 1,119 .... G10
Pucaurco, 12 .... G 4
Pucusana, 1,331 .... D 9
Puerto Alianza .... D 5
Puerto América, 150 .... D 5
Puerto Arturo .... F 3
Puerto Bermúdez, 230 .... E 8
Puerto Caballas E10
Puerto Chicama, 3,002 .... C 6
Puerto Eten, 2,192 .... B 6
Puerto José Pardo .... D 4
Puerto Leguía, Loreto .... D 4
Puerto Leguía, Puno .... G 9
Puerto Maldonado, 3,518 .... H 9
Puerto Morín .... C 7
Puerto Ocopa, 1,304 .... E 8
Puerto Pardo .... F 7
Puerto Pizarro .... B 4
Puerto Portillo, 49 .... F 7
Puerto Prado, 419 .... E 8
Puerto Samanco, 1,733 .... C 7
Puerto Tahuantinsuyo .... G 9
Puerto Victoria .... E 7
Puno, 32,100 .... G10
Punta de Bombón, 3,943 .... F11
Punta Moreno .... C 6
Puquina, 1,030 .... G11
Puquio, 8,144 .... F10
Putina, 3,512 .... H10
Querecotillo, 6,205 .... B 5
Quicacha, 299 .... F10
Quilca, 171 .... F11
Quillabamba, 8,644 .... F 9
Quince Mil .... G 9
Ramón Castilla, †8,106 .... G 5
Recuay, 1,755 .... D 7
Requena, 3,931 .... F 5
Reventazón .... B 6
Rioja, 4,361 .... D 6
Salaverry, 4,605 .... C 7
San José, 2,612 .... B 6
San José de Sisa, 4,190 .... D 6
San Juan, 717 .... E10
San Lorenzo, 84 .... H 8
San Martín .... E 3
San Miguel, Ayacucho, 1,271 .... F 9
San Miguel, Cajamarca, 1,871 .... C 6
San Pedro de Lloc, 7,497 .... C 6
San Ramón, 3,016 .... E 8
San Vicente de Cañete, 7,184 .... D 9
Saña, 18,421 .... C 6
Sandia, 3,026 .... H10
Santa, 2,966 .... C 7
Santa Clotilde, 824 .... E 4
Santa Cruz, Cajamarca, 1,729 .... C 6
Santa Cruz, Loreto, 739 .... E 5
Santa Elena, 271 .... F 5
Santa Isabel de Sihuas, 118 .... F11
Santa María de Nanay, 123 .... F 4
Santiago, 1,613 .... E10
Santiago de Cao, 1,033 .... C 6
Santiago de-Chocorvos, 344 .... E 9
Santiago de Chuco, 4,649 .... C 7
Santo Tomás, Amazonas, 1,097 .... C 6

Topography

0 100 200
MILES

5,000 m. 16,404 ft.	2,000 m. 6,562 ft.	1,000 m. 3,281 ft.	500 m. 1,640 ft.	200 m. 656 ft.	100 m. 328 ft.	Sea Level	Below

Santo Tomás, Cuzco, 1,659 .... G10
Santo Tomás de Andoas, 65 .... D 4
Saposoa, 4,456 .... D 6
Saquena, 688 .... F 5
Satipo, 2,499 .... E 8
Sauce, 1,761 .... D 6
Sayán, 1,764 .... D 8
Sechura, 5,157 .... B 5
Sicuani, 10,664 .... G10
Sihuas, 1,404 .... D 7
Sullana, 43,500 .... B 5
Sumbay G10
Sumbilca, 1,365 .... D 8
Supe, 2,499 .... D 8
Tacna, 41,200 .... G11
Tahuamanu, †4,011 .... H 8
Talara, 39,600 .... B 5
Tambo de Mora, 1,128 .... D 9
Tambo Grande, 4,404 .... B 5
Tamshiyacu, 1,623 .... F 5
Tarapoto, 13,907 .... D 6
Tarata, 2,673 .... H11
Tarma, 15,452 .... E 8
Tarqui .... E 3
Tayabamba, 1,519 .... D 7
Ticaco, 1,206 .... H11
Tingo María, 5,208 .... D 7
Tiruntán, 847 .... E 6
Tocache, 1,607 .... D 7
Tonegrama .... D 4
Topara, 1,437 .... D 9
Toquepala G11
Torata, 669 .... G11
Tournavista .... E 7
Trujillo, 156,200 .... C 7
Tumbes, 30,000 .... B 4
Ubinas, 348 .... G11
Uchiza, 1,006 .... D 7
Unini .... F 8
Urcos, 2,733 .... G 9
Urubamba, 3,325 .... F 9
Vinchos, 473 .... E 9
Virú, 2,647 .... C 7
Vitor, 117 .... G11
Yambrasbamba, 306 .... D 5
Yanahuanca, 962 .... D 8
Yanaoca, 1,146 .... G10
Yauca, 2,364 .... E10
Yauli, 1,696 .... D 8
Yauri, 2,834 .... G10
Yauyos, 1,456 .... E 9
Yunguyo, 2,506 .... H11
Yurimaguas, 11,655 .... E 5
Zarumilla, 3,499 .... B 4
Zorritos, 2,862 .... B 4

OTHER FEATURES

Acarí (river) E10
Aguaytía (river) .... E 7
Aguja (point) .... B 5
Amazon (river) .... F 4
Andes, Cordillera de los (mts.) F10
Apurímac (river) .... F 9
Azángaro (river) G10
Azul, Cordillera (mts.) .... E 7
Blanca, Cordillera (mts.) .... D 7
Blanco (cape) .... B 5
Blanco (river) .... F 6
Boquerón, El (pass) .... E 7
Cañete (river) .... D 9
Casma (river) .... C 7
Chimbote (bay) .... C 7
Chincha (isls.) .... D 9
Chira (river) .... B 5
Coles (point) G11
Cóndor, Cordillera del (mts.) .... C 5
Coropuna, Nudo (mt.) F10
Corrientes (river) .... E 4
El Boquerón (pass) .... E 7
El Misti (mt.) G11
Ene (river) .... E 8
Ferrol (pen.) .... C 7
Grande (river) E10
Guañape (isls.) .... C 7
Heath (river) .... H 9
Huallaga (river) .... D 5
Huasaga (river) .... D 4
Huascarán (mt.) .... D 7
Huayabamba (river) .... D 6
Ica (river) E10
Inambari (river) .... H 9
Independencia (bay) D10
Junín (lake) .... E 8
La Montaña (reg.) .... F 8
Lachay (Salinas) (point) .... D 8
Las Piedras (river) .... G 8
Las Viejas (isl.) D10
Lobos de Afuera (isls.) .... B 6
Lobos de Tierra (isl.) .... B 6
Locumba (river) G11
Madre de Dios (river) .... G 9
Majes (river) F11
Mantaro (river) .... E 8
Manú (river) .... G 8
Marañón (river) .... E 5
Mayo (river) .... D 6
Misti, El (mt.) G11
Montaña, La (reg.) .... F 8
Morona (river) .... D 5
Nanay (river) .... E 4
Napo (river) .... F 4
Negra, Cordillera (mts.) .... D 7
Negra (point) .... B 6
Ñermete (point) .... B 5
Nudo Coropuna (mt.) F10
Occidental, Cordillera (mts.) F10
Ocoña (river) F11
Oriental, Cordillera (mts.) H10
Pachitea (river) .... E 7
Paita (bay) .... B 5
Pampas (river) .... E 9
Paracas (pen.), †727 .... D 9
Parinacochas (lake) F10
Pariñas (point) .... B 5
Pastaza (river) .... D 5
Pativilca (river) .... D 8
Perené (river) .... E 8
Pichis (river) .... E 8
Piedras, Las (river) .... G 8
Pisco (bay) .... D 9
Pisco (river) .... D 9
Pirua (river) .... B 5
Puinagua, Canal de (river) .... E 5
Purus (river) .... G 8
Putumayo (river) .... G 4
Rímac (river) .... D 9
Salinas (Lachay) (point) .... D 8
Sama (river) G11

(continued on following page)

PERU (continued)

San Gallán (isl.) ....D 9
San Lorenzo (isl.) ....D 9
San Nicolás (bay) E10
Santa (river) ....C 7
Santiago (river) ....D 4
Sechura (bay) ....B 5
Tahuamanu (river) ....H 8
Tambo (river) G11
Tambopata (river) ....H 9
Tapiche (river) ....E 6
Tigre (river) ....E 4
Titicaca (lake) H10
Tumbes (river) ....B 4
Ucayali (river) ....F 5
Urituyacu (river) ....D 5
Urubamba (river) ....F 8
Viejas, Las (isl.) D10
Vilcabamba, Cordillera (mts.) ..F 9
Vilcanota (mt.) G10
Vitor (river) F11
Yaguas (river) ....G 4
Yavarí (river) ....G 5
Yavero (river) ....F 9

ECUADOR

PROVINCES

Azuay, 274,642 ....C 4
Bolívar, 131,651 ....C 3
Cañar, 112,733 ....C 4
Carchi, 94,649 ....C 2
Chimborazo, 276,668 ....C 3
Colón, Archipiélago de (terr.), 2,391 ....C 8
Cotopaxi, 154,971 ....C 3
El Oro, 160,650 ....C 4
Esmeraldas, 124,881 ....C 2
Guayas, 979,223 ....B 4
Imbabura, 174,039 ....C 2
Loja, 285,448 ....C 4
Los Ríos, 250,062 ....C 3
Manabí, 612,542 ....B 3
Morona-Santiago, 25,503 ....C 4
Napo, 24,253 ....D 3
Pastaza, 13,693 ....D 3
Pichincha, 587,835 ....C 3
Tungurahua, 178,709 ....C 3
Zamora-Chinchipe, 11,464 ....C 5

CITIES and TOWNS

Alausí, 6,676 ....C 4
Ambato, 53,372 ....C 3
Andoas Nuevo ....D 4
Arapicos ....D 3
Archidona ....D 3
Arenillas, 3,925 ....B 4
Atuntaqui, 8,759 ....C 2
Azogues, 8,075 ....C 4
Baba, 693 ....C 3
Babahoyo, 16,444 ....C 3
Baeza, 213 ....D 3
Bahía de Carâquez, 8,845 ....B 3
Balao, 1,415 ....C 4
Balzar, 6,588 ....C 3
Bolívar, 410 ....C 2
Cajabamba, 2,094 ....C 3
Calceta 4,946 ....C 3
Cañar, 4,935 ....C 4
Canelos ....D 3
Cariamanga, 5,381 ....C 5
Carondelet, 318 ....C 2
Catacocha, 3,796 ....C 5
Catamayo, 4,097 ....C 4
Catarama, 2,424 ....C 3
Cayambe, 8,101 ....D 3
Celica, 3,467 ....B 4
Chone, 12,832 ....B 3
Chunchi, 2,388 ....C 4
Coca ....D 3
Cojimíes, 1,538 ....B 2
Cononaco ....E 3
Cuenca, 60,402 ....C 4
Cuyabeno ....E 3
Daule, 7,428 ....B 3
Edén ....E 3
El Ángel, 4,009 ....C 2
El Corazón, 1,118 ....C 3
El Progreso ....C 9
El Pun, 612 ....D 2
Esmeraldas, 33,403 ....B 2
Farfán ....D 2
Floreana B10
Girón, 1,914 ....C 4
Gualaceo, 3,065 ....C 4
Gualaquiza, 635 ....C 4
Guale ....B 3
Guamote, 2,640 ....C 4
Guano, 4,455 ....C 3
Guaranda, 9,900 ....C 3
Guayaquil, 738,591 ....B 4
Ibarra, 25,835 ....D 2
Jama, 1,743 ....B 3
Jipijapa, 13,367 ....B 3
La Libertad, 13,565 ....B 4
La Tola, 650 ....C 2
Latacunga, 14,856 ....C 3
Loja, 26,785 ....C 4
Loreto ....D 3
Macará, 5,027 ....C 5
Macas, 1,355 ....D 4
Machachi, 3,951 ....C 3
Machala, 29,036 ....B 4
Machalilla, 615 ....B 3
Manglaralto, 799 ....B 3
Manta, 33,622 ....B 3
Méndez, 527 ....C 4
Mera ....C 3
Miazal ....D 4
Milagro, 28,148 ....C 4
Montecristi, 4,540 ....B 3
Morona ....D 4
Mulaló, 427 ....C 3
Napo ....D 3
Nuevo Rocafuerte, 435 ....E 3
Otavalo, 8,630 ....C 2
Paján, 1,818 ....B 3
Palanda ....C 5
Papallacta ....D 3
Pasaje, 13,215 ....C 4
Paute, 1,511 ....C 4
Pedernales, 610 ....B 2
Pelileo, 2,545 ....C 3
Píllaro, 2,714 ....C 3
Piñas, 3,344 ....C 4
Playas, 5,067 ....B 4
Portoviejo, 32,228 ....B 3
Posorja, 2,086 ....B 4
Puerto Baquerizo Moreno ....C 9
Puerto de Cayo, 713 ....B 3
Pujilí, 2,534 ....C 3
Putumayo ....E 3
Puyo, 2,290 ....D 3
Quevedo, 20,602 ....C 3
Quito (capital), 496,410 ....C 3
Río Tigre ....D 4
Riobamba, 41,625 ....C 3
Rocafuerte, 4,349 ....B 3
Rosa Zárate, 1,662 ....C 2
Salinas, 5,460 ....B 4
San Gabriel, 6,803 ....D 2
San Lorenzo, 575 ....C 2
San Miguel, 2,410 ....C 3
San Miguel de Salcedo, 3,442 ....C 3
Sangolquí, 5,501 ....C 3
Santa Ana, 3,940 ....B 3
Santa Cruz ....B 9
Santa Elena, 4,241 ....B 4
Santa Isabel, 1,602 ....C 4
Santa Rosa, 8,935 ....C 4
Santa Rosa de Sucumbíos, 132 ....D 2
Santo Domingo de los Colorados, 6,951 ....C 3
Saraguro, 1,562 ....C 4
Sarayacu ....D 3
Sigsig, 1,228 ....C 4
Sigüe ....D 2
Sucre, 2,578 ....B 3
Sucúa, 1,153 ....C 4
Tabacundo, 2,009 ....C 2
Tachina ....C 2
Tena, 1,029 ....D 3
Tulcán, 16,448 ....D 2
Valdez, 3,358 ....C 2
Viche, 230 ....C 2
Villamil ....B 9
Vinces, 5,901 ....C 3
Yacuambí, 405 ....C 4
Yaguachi, 2,996 ....C 4
Yaupi ....D 4
Zamora, 1,030 ....C 5
Zapotillo, 460 ....B 5
Zaruma, 9,000 ....C 4
Zumba, 450 ....C 5

OTHER FEATURES

Aguarico (river) ....D 3
Albemarle (point) ....B 9
Ancón de Sardinas (bay) ....C 2
Antisana (mt.) ....D 3
Baltra (isl.) ....B 9
Banks (bay) ....B 9
Bobonaza (river) ....D 3
Cayambe (mt.) ....D 2
Chaves (Santa Cruz) (isl.), 626 ....C 9
Chimborazo (mt.) ....C 3
Cotopaxi (mt.) ....C 3
Cristóbal (point) ....B 9
Culpepper (isl.) ....B 8
Curaray (river) ....D 3
Darwin (Culpepper) (isl.) ....B 8
Esmeraldas (river) ....C 2
Española (isl.) C10
Fernandina (isl.) ....B 9
Floreana (Santa María) (isl.), 46 ....B10
Galápagos (isls.), 2,391 ....C 8
Galera (point) ....B 2
Genovesa (isl.) ....C 9
Guayaquil (gulf) ....B 4
Guayas (river) ....C 4
Isabel (bay) ....B 9
Isabela (isl.), 336 ....B 9
La Puntilla (cape) ....B 4
Manta (bay) ....B 3
Marchena (isl.) ....B 9
Mira (river) ....C 2
Napo (river) ....D 3
Naranjal (river) ....C 4
Pasado (cape) ....B 3
Pastaza (river) ....D 4
Pindo (river) ....D 3
Pinta (isl.) ....B 9
Pinzón (isl.) ....B 9
Puná (isl.), 5,459 ....B 4
Puntilla, La (cape) ....B 4
Putumayo (river) ....E 2
Rosa (cape) B10
San Cristóbal (isl.), 1,404 ....C 9
San Francisco (cape) ....B 2
Sangay (mt.) ....C 4
San Lorenzo (cape) ....B 3
San Miguel (river) ....D 2
San Salvador (isl.) ....B 9
Santa Cruz (isl.), 626 ....C 9
Santa Elena (bay) ....B 3
Santa Fé (isl.) ....C 9
Santa María (isl.), 46 ....B10
Santiago (San Salvador) (isl.) ....C 9
Tumbes (river) ....B 4
Wenman (isl.) ....B 8
Wolf (Wenman) (isl.) ....B 8
Zamora (river) ....B 4

*City and suburbs.
†Population of district.

FRENCH GUIANA

DISTRICTS

Cayenne, 36,187 ....E 3
St-Laurent-du-Maroni, 8,205 ....E 4

CITIES and TOWNS

Camopi, †276 ....E 4
Cayenne (cap.), 19,668 ....E 3
Cayenne, *24,581 ....E 3
Counamama ....E 3
Edmond ....E 3
Grand-Santi, 60 ....D 3
Guisambourg ....F 3
Inini ....E 4
Iracoubo, 504 ....E 3
Kaw, 258 ....E 3
Kourou, 868 ....E 3
Macouria (Tonate), 301........E 3
Mana, 568 ....E 3
Maripa ....E 4
Maripasoula, 166 ....D 4
Montsinéry, 107 ....E 3
Organobo ....E 3
Oscar ....E 4
Ouanary, 79 ....F 3
Ouaqui ....D 4
P. I. (Paul Isnard), †47 ....E 3
Paul Isnard, †47 ....E 3
Régina ....E 3
Rémire, 650 ....E 3
Roura, 84 ....E 3
Saint-Élie, 78 ....E 3
Saint-Georges-de-l'Oyapoc, 502....F 4
Saint-Jean ....D 3
Saint-Laurent-du-Maroni, 3,486...E 3
Saül, 81 ....E 4
Saut-Tigre ....E 3
Sinnamary, 1,355 ....E 3
Tonate, 301 ....E 3

OTHER FEATURES

Approuague (river) ....E 4
Béhague (point) ....F 3
Camopi (river) ....E 4
Chaîne Granitique (range) ....E 4
Comté (river) ....E 3
Connétable (isls.) ....F 3
Devil's (isl.) ....E 3
Granitique, Chaîne (range) ....E 4
Inini (river) ....E 4
Itany (river) ....D 4
Mana (river) ....E 3
Maroni (river) ....D 3
Marouini (river) ....D 4
Oyapock (river) ....E 4
Rémire (isls.) ....F 3
Salut (isls.) ....F 3
Sinnamary (river) ....E 3
Tampoc (river) ....E 4

GUYANA

DISTRICTS

East Berbice, 115,511 ....C 3
East Demerara, 256,908 ....B 2
Essequibo, 29,729 ....B 2
Essequibo Islands, 15,728 ....B 2
Mazaruni-Potaro, 12,029 ....A 2
North West, 12,809 ....A 2
Rupununi, 10,031 ....B 4
West Berbice, 26,524 ....C 2
West Demerara, 81,061 ....B 3

CITIES and TOWNS

Adventure, 507 ....B 2
Anna Regina, 848 ....B 2
Apoteri ....B 3
Arakaka ....B 2
Atkinson Field ....B 2
Aurora ....B 2
Baramanni ....B 2
Baramita ....A 2
Bartica, 2,352 ....B 2
Charity, 838 ....B 2
Christianburg-Wismar-Mackenzie, 5,843 ....B 2
Dadanawa ....B 4
Danielstown, 478 ....B 2
Enmore ....C 2
Enterprise ....B 2
Epira ....C 3
Five Stars ....A 2
Fort Wellington ....C 2
Georgetown (cap.), 97,190 ....C 2
Georgetown, *102,688 ....C 2
Imbaimadai ....A 3
Ituni ....B 3
Kamakusa ....A 3
Kamarang, 510 ....A 3
Kurupukari ....B 3
Lethem ....B 4
Lumid Pau ....B 4
Mabaruma, 343 ....B 1
Mahaica, 8,646 ....C 2
Mahaicony, 8,272 ....C 2
Morawhanna, 305 ....B 1
Mount Everard ....B 2
New Amsterdam, 14,300 ....C 2
Orealla ....C 3
Paradise ....C 3
Parika, 577 ....B 2
Pickersgill, 334 ....B 2
Port Kaituma ....B 2
Queenstown, 1,067 ....B 2
Rockstone ....B 2
Rosignol, 1,204 ....C 2
Skeldon, 4,367 ....C 3
Springlands, 181 ....C 2
Suddie, 512 ....B 2
Takama ....C 3
Tumatumari ....B 3
Tumereng ....B 2
Vreed-en-Hoop, 3,156 ....B 2
Yupukari ....B 4

OTHER FEATURES

Akarai (mts.) ....B 5
Amakara (river) ....A 2
Amuku (mts.) ....B 4
Barama (river) ....A 2
Barima (river) ....B 2
Berbice (river) ....B 3
Canje (river) ....C 2
Courantyne (river) ....C 3
Cuyuni (river) ....B 2
Demerara (river) ....B 3
Enwarak (mt.) ....B 3
Essequibo (river) ....B 3
Great (fall) ....B 3
Ireng (river) ....B 3
Kaieteur (fall) ....B 3
Kamaria (falls) ....B 2
Kanuku (mts.) ....B 4
Kurungiku (mts.) ....B 3

Agriculture, Industry and Resources

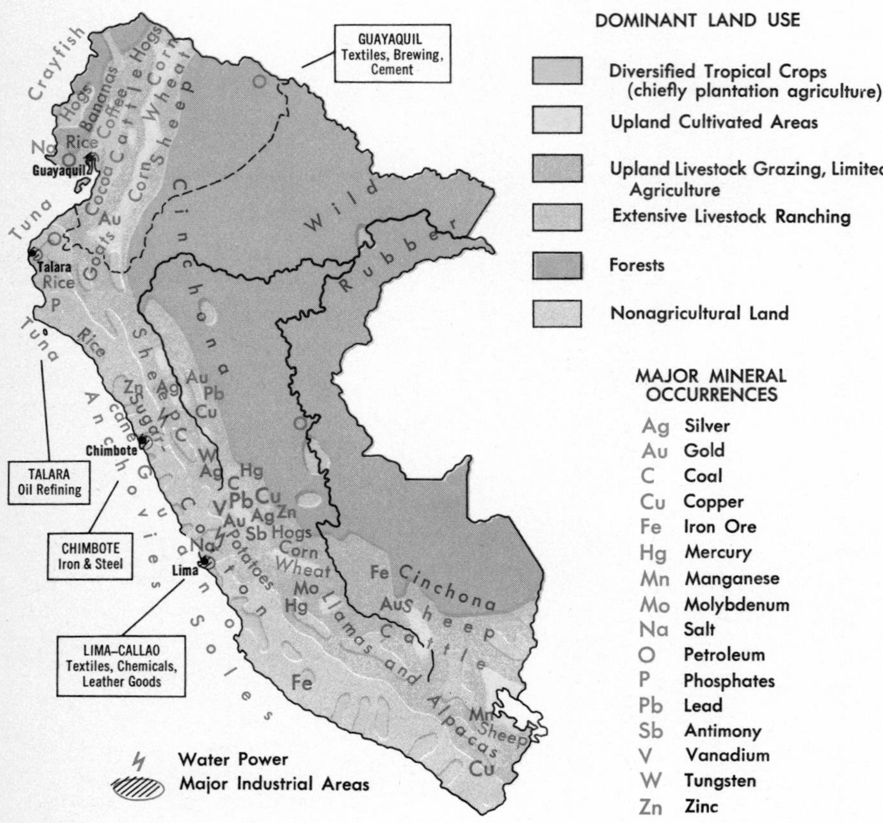

Agriculture, Industry and Resources

DOMINANT LAND USE

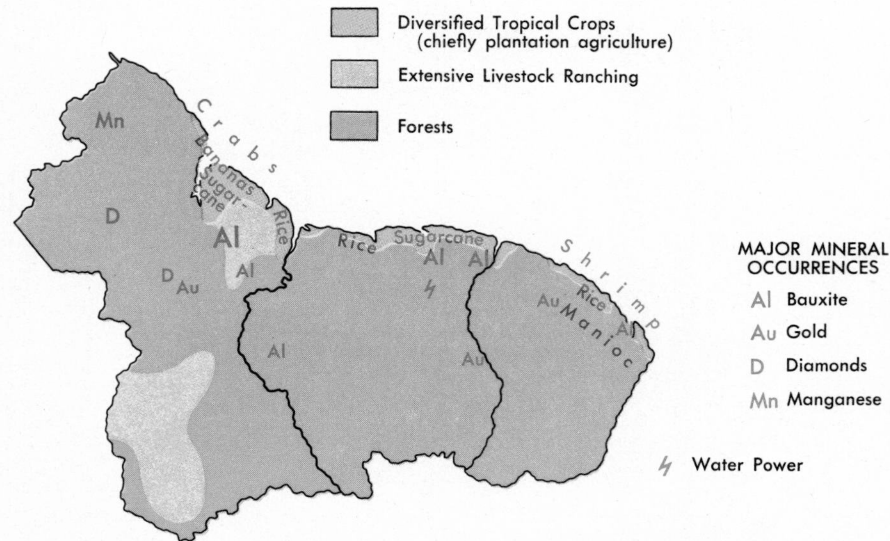

GUYANA

AREA 83,000 sq. mi.
POPULATION 763,000
CAPITAL Georgetown
LARGEST CITY Georgetown
HIGHEST POINT Mt. Roraima 9,094 ft.
MONETARY UNIT Guyana dollar
MAJOR LANGUAGES English, Hindi
MAJOR RELIGIONS Christianity, Hinduism, Islam

SURINAM

AREA 55,144 sq. mi.
POPULATION 389,000
CAPITAL Paramaribo
LARGEST CITY Paramaribo
HIGHEST POINT Julianatop 4,200 ft.
MONETARY UNIT Surinam guilder
MAJOR LANGUAGES Dutch, Hindi, Indonesian
MAJOR RELIGIONS Christianity, Islam, Hinduism

FRENCH GUIANA

AREA 35,135 sq. mi.
POPULATION 48,000
CAPITAL Cayenne
LARGEST CITY Cayenne
HIGHEST POINT 2,723 ft.
MONETARY UNIT French franc
MAJOR LANGUAGE French
MAJOR RELIGIONS Roman Catholicism, Protestantism

Kuyuwini (river) .... B 4
Kwitaro (river) .... B 4
Leguan (isl.), 6,567 .... B 2
Marudi (mts.) .... B 5
Mazaruni (river) .... A 2
Moruka (river) .... B 2
New (river) .... C 4
Pakaraima (mts.) .... A 3
Playa (point) .... B 1
Pomeroon (river) .... B 2
Potaro (river) .... B 3
Puruni (river) .... B 2
Roraima (mt.) .... A 3
Rupununi (river) .... B 4
Sororieng (mt.) .... B 2
Surwakwima (fall) .... A 2
Takutu (river) .... B 4
Venamo (mt.) .... A 3
Waini (river) .... B 2
Wenamu (river) .... A 2

SURINAM

DISTRICTS

Brokopondo, 1,376 .... D 4
Commewijne, 18,796 .... D 3
Coronie, 4,069 .... C 3
Marowijne, 10,074 .... D 4
Nickerie, 24,730 .... C 3
Para .... D 3
Paramaribo, 122,634 .... D 2
Saramacca, 10,979 .... C 3
Suriname, 80,870 .... D 3

CITIES and TOWNS

Ajoewa .... C 4
Alalapadu .... C 4
Albina, 1,000 .... D 3
Asidonhoppo .... D 4
Berg-en-Dal .... D 3
Bitagron .... C 3
Brokopondo .... D 3
Burnside .... C 2
Calcutta, 1,100 .... D 3
Cottica .... D 4
Domburg, 1,200 .... D 3
Groningen, 600 .... D 3
Huwelijkszorg .... D 3
Kwakoegron .... D 3
Kwatta .... D 2
Lelydorp, 300 .... D 3
Magalie .... D 4
Marienburg, 3,500 .... D 2
Moengo, 2,100 .... D 3
Nieuw-Amsterdam, 1,400 .... D 2
Nieuw-Nickerie, 7,400 .... C 2
Paramaribo (cap.), 110,867 .... D 2
Paramaribo, *182,100 .... D 2
Paranam .... D 3
Saramaccapolder .... D 2
Totness, 1,300 .... C 3
Wageningen, 800 .... C 3
Zanderij .... D 3

OTHER FEATURES

Bakhuys (mts.) .... C 3
Coeroeni (river) .... C 4
Commewijne (river) .... D 3
Coppename (river) .... C 3
Corantijn (river) .... C 3
Cottica (river) .... D 3
Eilerts-de-Haan (mts.) .... C 4
Frederik Willem IV (falls) .... C 4
Julianatop (mt.) .... C 4
Kayser (mts.) .... C 4
Lely (mts.) .... D 3
Litani (river) .... D 4
Marowijne (river) .... D 3
Nickerie (river) .... C 3
Orange (mts.) .... D 4
Saramacca (river) .... D 3
Sipaliwini (river) .... C 4
Suriname (river) .... D 3
Tapanahoni (river) .... D 4
Toekomstig (res.) .... C 3
Van Blommestein (lake) .... D 3
Wilhelmina (mts.) .... C 4

*City and suburbs.
†Population of municipality.

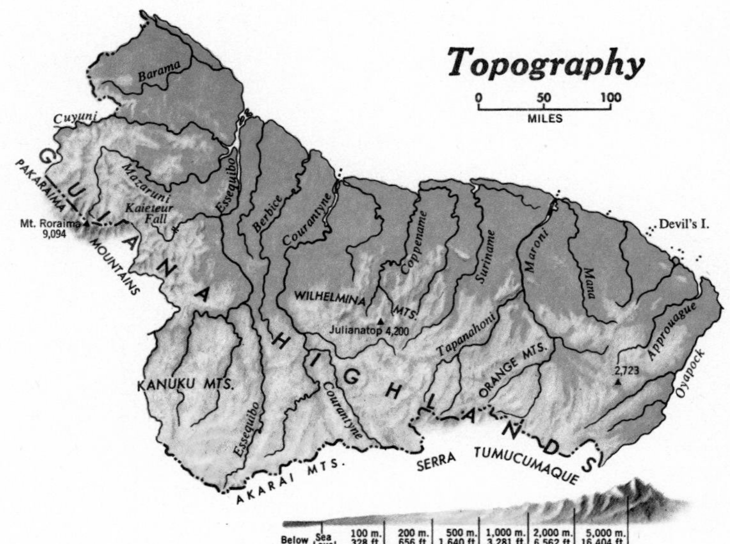

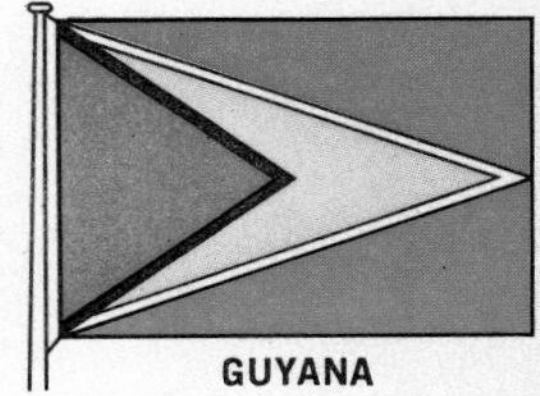
GUYANA

SURINAM

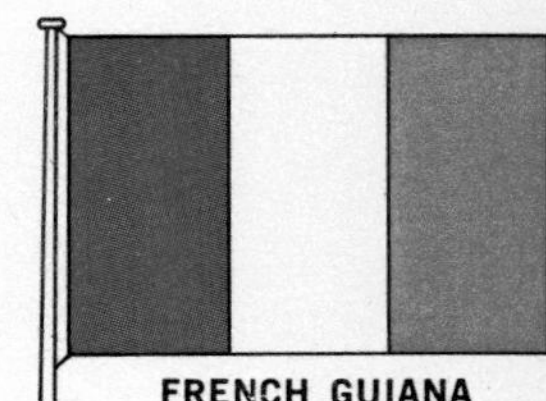
FRENCH GUIANA

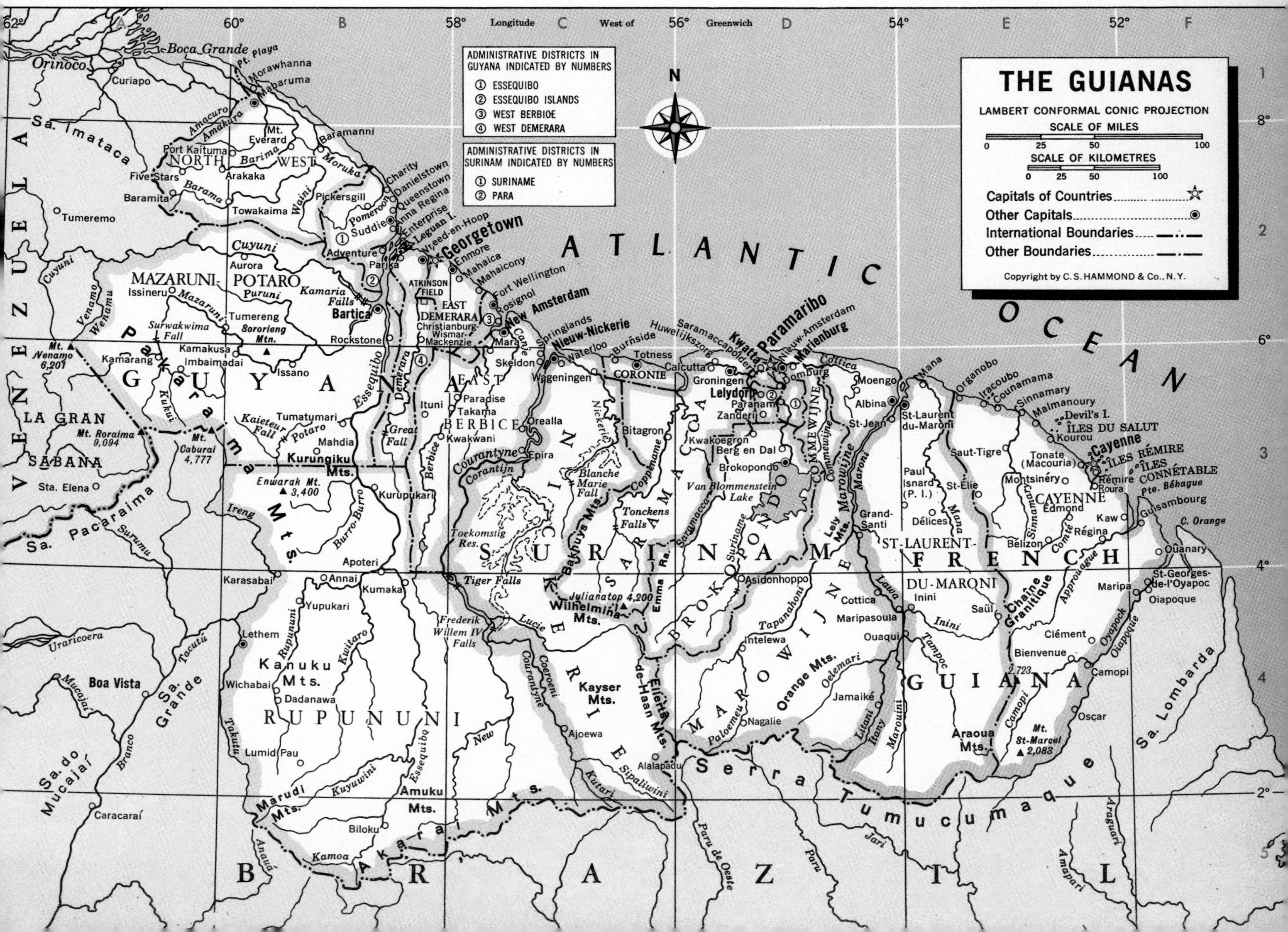

ADMINISTRATIVE DISTRICTS IN GUYANA INDICATED BY NUMBERS
① ESSEQUIBO
② ESSEQUIBO ISLANDS
③ WEST BERBICE
④ WEST DEMERARA

ADMINISTRATIVE DISTRICTS IN SURINAM INDICATED BY NUMBERS
① SURINAME
② PARA

THE GUIANAS

LAMBERT CONFORMAL CONIC PROJECTION
SCALE OF MILES
0 25 50 100
SCALE OF KILOMETRES
0 25 50 100

Capitals of Countries
Other Capitals
International Boundaries
Other Boundaries

BRAZIL
BIPOLAR OBLIQUE CONIC CONFORMAL PROJECTION
SCALE OF MILES
0 50 100 200 300
SCALE OF KILOMETRES
0 50 100 200 300
Capitals of Countries
State Capitals
International Boundaries
State Boundaries
Copyright by C.S. HAMMOND & CO., N.Y.
Longitude 48° West of Greenwich 44°
GUYANA
SURINAM
FR. GUIANA
AMAPÁ
RORAIMA
AMAZONAS
PARÁ
MARANHÃO
PIAUÍ
CEARÁ
RIO GRANDE DO NORTE
PARAÍBA
PERNAMBUCO
ALAGOAS
SERGIPE
BAHIA
GOIÁS
FEDERAL DISTRICT
Brasília
MATO GROSSO
MINAS GERAIS
ESPÍRITO SANTO
RIO DE JANEIRO
GUANABARA
SÃO PAULO
PARANÁ
SANTA CATARINA
RIO GRANDE DO SUL
RONDÔNIA
BOLIVIA
PARAGUAY
ARGENTINA
URUGUAY
ATLANTIC OCEAN
Tropic of Capricorn
Equator
Amazon
Manaus
Belém
São Luís
Fortaleza
Natal
João Pessoa
Recife
Maceió
Aracaju
Salvador (Bahia)
Vitória
Belo Horizonte
Niterói
Goiânia
Cuiabá
Curitiba
Florianópolis
Pôrto Alegre
Teresina
Asunción
BRAZIL
WESTERN PART
COLOMBIA
PERU
VENEZUELA
AMAZONAS
ACRE
RONDÔNIA (GUAPORÉ)

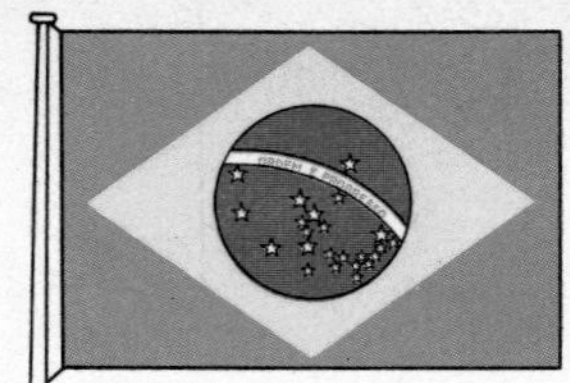

AREA 3,284,426 sq. mi.
POPULATION 90,840,000
CAPITAL Brasília
LARGEST CITY São Paulo (greater)
HIGHEST POINT Pico da Neblina 9,889 ft.
MONETARY UNIT cruzeiro
MAJOR LANGUAGE Portuguese
MAJOR RELIGION Roman Catholicism

Topography

SA. PACARAIMA
SA. TUMUCUMAQUE
Mouths of the Amazon
I. de Marajó
Pico da Neblina 9,889
Amazon
S e l v a s
C a a t i n g a s
C. de São Roque
São Francisco
SERRA DOS PARECIS
PLANALTO DE MATO GROSSO
BRAZILIAN HIGHLANDS
C a m p o s
SERRA DO ESPINHACO
SA. DOS AIMORÉS
Pico da Bandeira 9,482
SA. DA MANTIQUEIRA
C. Frio
SERRA DO MAR
Iguaçu Falls
L. dos Patos
L. Mirim

5,000 m. 16,404 ft. | 2,000 m. 6,562 ft. | 1,000 m. 3,281 ft. | 500 m. 1,640 ft. | 200 m. 656 ft. | 100 m. 328 ft. | Sea Level | Below

0 200 400 MILES

STATES and TERRITORIES

Acre, 196,000 ... G10
Alagoas, 1,381,000 ... G 5
Amapá (terr.), 100,000 ... D 2
Amazonas, 875,000 ... G 9
Bahia, 6,778,000 ... F 6
Ceará, 3,764,000 ... G 4
Espírito Santo, 1,446,000 ... F 7
Federal District, 348,000 ... E 6
Goiás, 2,950,000 ... D 6
Guanabara, 4,007,000 ... F 8, †E 3
Guaporé (Rondônia) (terr.), 97,000 ... H10
Maranhão, 3,314,000 ... E 4
Mato Grosso, 1,293,000 ... B 6
Minas Gerais, 11,230,000 ... E 7, †D 2
Pará, 1,872,000 ... C 4
Paraíba, 2,219,000 ... G 4
Paraná, 6,743,000 ... D 9, †B 4
Pernambuco, 4,645,000 ... G 5
Piauí, 1,391,000 ... F 4
Rio de Janeiro, 4,340,000 ... F 8, †E 3
Rio Grande do Norte, 1,271,000 ... G 4
Rio Grande do Sul, 6,397,000 ... C10
Rondônia (terr.), 107,000 ... H10
Roraima (terr.), 40,000 ... H 8
Santa Catarina, 2,624,000 ... D 9
São Paulo, 16,081,000 ... D 8, †B 2
Sergipe, 838,000 ... G 5

CITIES and TOWNS

Abaeté, 7,988 ... E 7
Abaetetuba, 11,196 ... D 3
Acaraú, 3,042 ... F 3
Acopiara, 3,953 ... G 4
Acorizal, 892 ... C 6
Açu, 8,158 ... G 4
Afuá, 600 ... D 3
Agudos, 6,564 ... †B 3
Alagoa Grande, 12,115 ... H 4
Alagoinhas, 38,246 ... G 6
Alcobaça, 1,812 ... G 7
Alegre, 7,487 ... †F 2
Alegrete, 33,735 ... B10
Além Paraíba, 18,399 ... †E 2
Alenquer, 7,027 ... C 3
Alfenas, 16,051 ... †C 2
Alfredo Chaves, 1,209 ... F 8
Altamira, 2,939 ... C 3
Alto Araguaia, 2,077 ... C 7
Alto Longa, 784 ... F 4
Alto Parnaiba, 1,300 ... E 5
Altos, 5,056 ... F 4
Amambaí, 2,601 ... C 8
Amarante, 3,199 ... F 4
Amargosa, 6,059 ... F 6
Americana, 32,000 ... †C 3
Amparo, 14,348 ... †C 3
Anápolis, 48,847 ... D 7
Andaraí, 2,510 ... F 6
Angra dos Reis, 10,634 ... †D 3
Anicuns, 3,642 ... D 7
Andrelândia, 4,617 ... †D 2
Antonina, 8,520 ... †B 4
Aparecida, 15,290 ... †D 3
Apiaí, 2,728 ... †B 4
Aquidauana, 11,997 ... C 8
Aracaju, *156,243 ... G 5
Aracati, 11,016 ... G 4
Araçatuba, 53,563 ... †A 2
Araçuaí, 6,763 ... F 7
Araguacema, 1,745 ... D 5
Araguaiana, 568 ... C 6
Araguari, 35,520 ... D 7
Araioses, 1,487 ... F 3
Araranguá, 7,775 ... D10
Araraquara, 58,076 ... †B 2
Araras, 23,898 ... †C 3
Arari, 4,004 ... E 3
Araxá, 24,041 ... E 7
Arcoverde, 18,008 ... G 5
Areia Branca, 8.904 ... G 4
Aripuanã, 178 ... B 5
Arraias, 1,446 ... E 6
Assis, 30,207 ... †A 3
Aurora, 3,622 ... G 4
Avaré, 20,334 ... †B 3
Bacabal, *19,753 ... E 4
Bagé, 47,930 ... C10
Bahia (Salvador), *892,392 ... G 6
Baião, 2,265 ... D 3
Baixo Guandu, 6,975 ... F 7
Balsas, 1,946 ... E 4
Bambuí, 8,148 ... †C 2
Barão de Cocais, 7,223 ... †E 1
Barbacena, 41,931 ... †E 2
Barcelos, 1,904 ... H 9
Bariri, 8,403 ... †B 3
Barra, 7,237 ... F 5
Barra-do-Bugres, 658 ... B 6
Barra-do-Corda, 3,723 ... E 4
Barra do Piraí, 29,398 ... †E 3
Barra Mansa, 47,398 ... †D 3
Barras, 3,388 ... F 4
Barreiras, 7,175 ... E 6
Barreirinha, 701 ... B 3
Barreirinhas, 2,184 ... F 3
Barreiros, 10,402 ... H 5
Barretos, 39,950 ... †B 2
Batalha, 15,559 ... F 3
Batatais, 15,266 ... †C 2
Baturité, 7,198 ... G 4
Bauru, *110,961 ... †B 3
Bebedouro, 18,249 ... †B 2
Bela Vista, 8,878 ... C 8
Bela Vista de Goiás, 2,687 ... D 7
Belém, *563,996 ... E 3
Belmonte, 7,897 ... G 6
Belo Horizonte, *1,167,026 ... †D 1
Belo Horizonte, ‡1,300,000 ... †D 1
Beneditinos, 828 ... F 4
Benjamin Constant, 3,224 ... G 9
Bento Gonçalves, 13,662 ... C10
Bertolínia, 714 ... F 4
Betim, 8,963 ... †D 2
Bicas, 7,469 ... †E 2
Birigui, 18,721 ... †A 2
Blumenau, 46,591 ... D 9
Boa Esperança, 9,263 ... †D 2
Boa Vista, 10,180 ... H 8
Bôca do Acre, 2,994 ... G10
Bocaiúva, 5,952 ... E 7
Boiaçu, 180 ... H 8
Bom Conselho, 6,840 ... G 5
Bom Despacho, 13,568 ... †D 1
Bom Jesus, 1,431 ... E 5
Bom Jesus da Lapa, 6,107 ... F 6
Bom Retiro, 1,601 ... D10
Bom Sucesso, 6,173 ... †D 2
Borba, 1,304 ... H 9
Botucatu, 33,878 ... †B 3
Bragança, 12,848 ... E 3
Bragança Paulista, 27,328 ... †C 3
Brasiléia, 1,902 ... G10
Brasília (capital), 130,968 ... D 6
Brasília, ‡379,699 ... D 6
Brasília, 3,182 ... F 7
Brumado, 7,054 ... F 6
Brusque, 16,127 ... D 9
Buri, 2,666 ... †B 3
Buriti, 1,951 ... F 3
Buriti Alegre, 5,042 ... D 7
Buriti dos Lopes, 1,812 ... F 3
Cabedelo, 10,738 ... H 4
Cabo Frio, 13,117 ... †F 3
Caçador, 10,480 ... D 9
Caçapava, 7,987 ... †D 3
Caçapava do Sul, 6,712 ... C10
Cáceres, 8,246 ... B 7
Cachoeira, 11,415 ... G 6
Cachoeira do Arari, 2,532 ... D 3
Cachoeira do Sul, 38,661 ... C10
Cachoeiro de Itapemirim, *110,301 ... G 8
Caeté, 10,840 ... †E 1
Caetıte, 4,823 ... F 6
Cafelândia, 6,573 ... †B 2
Caiapônia, 2,476 ... C 7
Caicó, 15,826 ... G 4
Cajàzeiras, 15,884 ... G 4
Cajuru, 4,971 ... †C 2
Camaquã, 9,732 ... C10
Cambará, 6,028 ... †A 3
Cametá, 5,695 ... D 3
Camocim, 10,788 ... F 3
Campanha, 6,178 ... †D 2
Campina Grande, *157,149 ... G 4
Campinas, *252,145 ... †C 3
Campina Verde, 4,464 ... D 7
Campo Belo, 15,742 ... †D 2
Campo Florido, 1,307 ... †B 1
Campo Formoso, 3,925 ... F 5
Campo Grande, *111,205 ... C 8
Campo Largo, 7,915 ... †B 4
Campo Maior, 13,939 ... F 4
Campos, *389,045 ... †F 2
Campos Altos, 5,243 ... †C 1
Cananéia, 1,948 ... †C 4
Canavieiras, 10,264 ... G 6
Cândido Mendes, 819 ... E 3
Canguaretama, 4,261 ... H 4
Canindé, 5,854 ... G 4
Canoas, *122,040 ... D10
Canoinhas, 9,252 ... D 9
Cantagalo, 3,479 ... †E 3
Canto do Buriti, 1,636 ... F 5
Canutama, 977 ... G 9
Capanema, 9,678 ... E 3
Capão Bonito, 6,829 ... †B 4
Capela, 5,172 ... G 5
Caraguatatuba, 4,655 ... †D 3
Carandaí, 2,792 ... †E 2
Carangola, 11,896 ... †E 2
Caratinga, *123,344 ... †E 1
Caraúbas, 3,066 ... G 4
Caravelas, 3,096 ... G 7
Carinhanha, 2,163 ... E 6
Carolina, 8,137 ... E 4
Caruaru, *115,414 ... G 5
Carutapera, 2,477 ... E 3
Casa Branca, 8,980 ... †C 2
Casa Nova, 1,525 ... F 5
Cascatinha, 19,497 ... †E 3
Cascavel, 3,336 ... G 4
Cássia, 7,034 ... †C 2
Castanhal, 9,528 ... E 3
Castelo, 5,729 ... F 8
Castelo do Piauí, 1,185 ... F 4
Castro, 9,249 ... †B 4
Castro Alves, 7,388 ... G 6
Cataguases, 21,476 ... †E 2
Catalão, 11,471 ... D 7
Catanduva, 37,307 ... †B 2
Catolé do Rocha, 5,217 ... G 4
Cavalcante, 660 ... D 6
Caxambu, 10,491 ... †D 2
Caxias, *124,403 ... F 4
Caxias do Sul, *110,241 ... D10
Ceará (Fortaleza), *846,069 ... G 3
Ceará-Mirim, 8,290 ... H 4
Ceres, 6,895 ... D 7
Cêrro Azul, 1,460 ... †B 4
Chaves, 428 ... D 3
Cicero Dantas, 2,972 ... G 5
Coari, 5,908 ... H 9
Codajás, 1,505 ... H 9
Codó, *100,933 ... E 4
Colatina, *140,729 ... F 7
Colinas, 2,972 ... F 4
Conceição da Barra, 2,229 ... G 7
Conceição do Araguaia, 2,332 ... D 5
Concórdia, 5,864 ... D 9
Conde, 4,190 ... G 5
Conselheiro Lafaiete, 29,208 ... †E 2
Corinto, 12,247 ... E 7
Cornélio Procópio, 17,524 ... D 8
Coroatá, 7,720 ... F 3
Coromandel, 5,148 ... E 7
Corrente, 2,214 ... E 5
Correntina, 2,636 ... E 6
Corumbá, 36,744 ... B 7
Coxim, 1,371 ... C 7
Crateús, 14,572 ... F 4
Crato, 27,649 ... G 4
Criciúma, 25,331 ... D10
Cristalina, 3,810 ... E 7
Cruz Alta, 33,190 ... C10
Cruzeiro, 27,005 ... †D 3
Cruzeiro do Sul, 2,826 ... G10
Cubatão, 18,885 ... †C 3
Cuiabá, 43,112 ... C 6
Curaça, 1,264 ... G 5
Curitiba, *616,548 ... †B 4
Currais Novos, 7,782 ... G 4
Curuçá, 3,871 ... E 3
Cururupu, 4,822 ... E 3
Curvelo, 21,772 ... E 7
Diamantina, 14,252 ... F 7
Diamantino, 645 ... B 6
Dianópolis, 2,145 ... E 5
Divinópolis, 41,544 ... †D 2
Dois Córregos, 7,272 ... †B 3
Dom Pedrito, 15,429 ... C10
Dores do Indaiá, 10,354 ... E 7
Dourados, 10,757 ... C 8
Duque de Caxias, *324,261 ... †E 3
Eirunepé, 3,023 ... G10
Eldorado, 1,524 ... †B 4
Erechim, 24,941 ... C 9
Erval, 1,404 ... C11
Escada, 13,761 ... H 5
Esperança, 9,105 ... G 4
Esplanada, 3,792 ... G 5
Estância, 16,106 ... G 5
Exu, 2,549 ... G 4
Faro, 1,434 ... B 3
Feira de Santana, *136,000 ... G 5
Fernandópolis, 14,375 ... †A 2
Ferreira Gomes, 439 ... D 2
Ferros, 2,456 ... F 7
Flores, 2,102 ... G 4
Floriano, 16,063 ... F 4
Florianópolis, *130,012 ... E 9
Formiga, 18,763 ... †D 2
Formosa, 9,449 ... E 6
Fortaleza, *846,069 ... G 3
Foz do Iguaçu, 7,407 ... C 9
Franca, 47,244 ... †C 2
Fronteiras, 1,320 ... F 4
Frutal, 8,252 ... †B 2
Garanhuns, 34,050 ... G 5
Garça, 18,155 ... †B 3
Gilbués, 588 ... E 5
Goiana, 19,026 ... H 4
Goiandira, 3,169 ... E 7
Goiânia, *345,085 ... D 7
Goiás, 7,121 ... D 6
Governador Valadares, *124,606 ... F 7
Grajaú, 2,539 ... E 4
Granja, 5,074 ... F 3
Guacuí, 7,724 ... †F 2
Guajará-Mirim, 7,115 ... H10
Guamá, 2,470 ... E 3
Guarabira, 15,848 ... H 4
Guarapuava, *126,080 ... C 9
Guaratinguetá, 38,293 ... †D 3
Guarujá, 6,506 ... †C 4
Guarulhos, *119,572 ... †C 3
Guarus, 21,492 ... †F 2
Guaxupé, 14,168 ... †C 2
Guimarães, 1,512 ... E 3
Guiratinga, 4,203 ... C 7
Gurupá, 912 ... D 3
Gurupi, 4,148 ... D 5
Humaitá, 1,192 ... H10
Ibaiti, 3,628 ... †A 3
Ibiá, 6,999 ... E 7
Ibipetuba, 2,298 ... F 5
Ibitinga, 8,881 ... †B 2
Icó, 5,586 ... G 4
Icoraci, 11,512 ... D 3
Igarapava, 9,083 ... †C 2
Igarapé-Miri, 2,591 ... D 3
Iguape, 5,465 ... †C 4
Iguatu, 16,540 ... G 4
Ijuí, 19,671 ... C10
Ilhéus, *100,687 ... G 6
Imbituba, 6,638 ... D10
Imbituva, 3,290 ... †A 4
Imperatriz, 9,004 ... E 4
Inhumas, 8,298 ... D 7
Ipameri, 8,987 ... E 7
Ipiaú, 13,164 ... G 6
Ipu, 7,724 ... F 4
Irati, 12,764 ... †A 4
Itabaiana, Paraíba, 11,847 ... H 4
Itabaiana, Sergipe, 11,050 ... G 5
Itaberaba, 8,555 ... F 6
Itabira, 15,539 ... F 7
Itabirito, 10,511 ... †E 2
Itabuna, 54,268 ... G 6
Itacoatiara, 8,818 ... B 3
Itaguatins, 1,596 ... D 4
Itaí, 1,601 ... †B 3
Itajaí, 38,889 ... D 9
Itajubá, 31,262 ... †D 3
Itamarandiba, 2,404 ... F 7
Itanhaém, 5,376 ... †C 4
Itapecerica, 7,696 ... †D 2
Itapecuru-Mirim, 3,385 ... F 3
Itapemirim, 4,095 ... F 8
Itaperuna, 18,095 ... †F 2
Itapetininga, 29,468 ... †B 3
Itapeva, 13,510 ... †B 3
Itapicuru, 900 ... G 5
Itapipoca, 7,186 ... G 3
Itapira, 16,859 ... †C 3
Itapiranga, 477 ... B 3
Itápolis, 7,430 ... †B 2
Itaporanga, 5,328 ... G 4
Itaqui, 13,223 ... B10
Itararé, 12,812 ... †B 4
Itariri, 1,318 ... †C 4
Itatiba, 12,336 ... †C 3
Itaúna, 22,319 ... †D 2
Itu, 23,435 ... †C 3
Ituaçu, 1,431 ... F 6
Ituberá, 4,097 ... G 6
Ituiutaba, 29,724 ... D 7
Itumbiara, 12,575 ... D 7
Iturama, 1,518 ... †A 1
Ituverava, 11,890 ... †C 2
Jaboticabal, 20,231 ... †B 2
Jacareí, 28,131 ... †D 3
Jacarèzinho, 14,813 ... †A 3
Jacobina, 12,373 ... F 5
Jacupiranga, 2,144 ... †B 4
Jaguaquara, 5,363 ... F 6
Jaguarão, 12,336 ... C11
Jaguariaíva, 6,465 ... †B 4
Jaicós, 1,308 ... F 4
Januária, 9,741 ... E 6
Jaraguá, 3,813 ... D 6
Jardim, 3,104 ... G 4
Jataí, 14,022 ... D 7
Jaú, 31,229 ... †B 3
Jequié, 40,158 ... F 6
Jequitinhonha, 5,410 ... F 7
Jeremoabo, 3,177 ... G 5
Joaçaba, 7,921 ... D 9
João Pessoa, *189,096 ... H 4
João Pinheiro, 3,433 ... E 7
Joaquim Tavora, 3,574 ... †B 3
Joinville, 44,255 ... D 9
Juàzeiro, 21,196 ... G 5
Juàzeiro do Norte, 53,421 ... F 4
Juiz de Fora, *194,135 ... †E 2
Jundiaí, *124,368 ... †C 3
Lábrea, 2,080 ... G10
Laguna, 17,451 ... D10
Lajes, 35,112 ... D 9
Lambari, 6,825 ... †D 2
Lapa, 7,167 ... D 9
Laranjeiras, 4,296 ... G 5
Laranjeiras do Sul, 3,802 ... C 9
Lavras, 23,793 ... †D 2
Leme, 11,785 ... †C 3
Lençóis, 2,483 ... F 6
Leopoldina, 17,726 ... †E 2
Lima Duarte, 3,554 ... †E 2
Limeira, 45,256 ... †C 3
Limoeiro, 21,252 ... H 4
Limoeiro do Norte, 5,705 ... G 4
Linhares, 5,751 ... F 7
Lins, 32,204 ... †B 2
Londrina, *226,332 ... D 8
Lorena, 26,068 ... †D 3
Luís Correia, 1,523 ... F 3
Luz, 5,633 ... †D 1
Luziânia, 4,849 ... E 7
Luzilândia, 3,434 ... F 3
Macaé, 19,830 ... †F 3
Macapá, 27,585 ... D 2
Macau, 11,876 ... G 4
Macaúbas, 2,504 ... F 6
Maceió, *221,250 ... H 5
Machado, 8,373 ... †C 2
Mafra, 12,981 ... D 9
Magé, 10,712 ... †E 3
Mallet, 1,816 ... D 9
Manacapuru, 2,584 ... H 9
Manaus, *249,797 ... H 9
Manga, 2,000 ... E 6
Manhuaçu, 10,546 ... †E 2
Manhumirim, 9,477 ... †E 2
Manicoré, 2,268 ... H 9
Marabá, 8,533 ... D 4
Maragogipe, 12,575 ... G 6
Maranguape, 8,715 ... G 3
Marapanim, 3,542 ... E 3
Marechal-Deodoro, 5,269 ... H 5
Mariana, 6,378 ... †E 2
Marília, *107,305 ... †A 3
Marques de Valença, 18,935 ... †D 3
Massapê, 4,760 ... G 3
Mata de São João, 8,117 ... G 6
Mato Grosso, 520 ... B 6
Maués, 4,161 ... B 3
Mazagão, 919 ... B 3
Miguel Alves, 4,537 ... F 4
Mimoso do Sul, 5,278 ... †F 2
Minas Novas, 1,708 ... F 7
Mineiros, 5,105 ... C 7
Miracema, 9,810 ... †E 2
Mirador, 818 ... B 4
Miranda, 2,075 ... C 8
Mirassol, 13,674 ... †B 2
Mocajuba, 1,352 ... D 3
Mococa, 14,306 ... †C 2
Mogi das Cruzes, *111,554 ... †C 3
Mogi-Mirim, 18,345 ... †C 3
Monte Alegre, 3,911 ... C 3
Monte Alegre de Minas, 4,464 ... D 7
Monte Aprazível, 7,235 ... †A 2
Monte Azul, 4,860 ... F 6
Monteiro, 6,028 ... G 4
Montenegro, 14,491 ... D10
Monte Santo, 1,607 ... G 5
Montes Claros, *121,428 ... E 7
Morrinhos, 9,879 ... D 7
Morro do Chapéu, 2,039 ... F 5
Mossoró, 38,833 ... G 4
Mucugê, 723 ... F 6
Mucuri, 603 ... G 7
Mundo Novo, 3,237 ... F 5
Muqui, 4,262 ... F 8
Muriaé, 22,571 ... †E 2
Muzambinho, 18,073 ... †C 2
Natal, *239,590 ... H 4

(continued on following page)

(continued)

Nazaré, 14,644 .... G 6
Neópolis, 7,356 .... G 5
Neves, 85,741 .... †E 3
Nioaque, 2,578 .... C 8
Niquelândia, 1,262 .... D 6
Niterói, *303,575 .... †E 3
Nossa Senhora do Livramento, 980 .... B 6
Nova Cruz, 6,780 .... H 4
Nova Era, 7,326 .... †E 1
Nova Friburgo, 49,901 .... †E 3
Nova Granada, 5,134 .... †B 2
Nova Iguaçu, *478,319 .... †E 3
Nova Iorque, 797 .... E 4
Nova Lima, 21,135 .... †E 2
Nova Russas, 4,666 .... F 4
Novo Hamburgo, 25,610 .... D10
Novo Horizonte, 8,581 .... †B 2
Óbidos, 5,901 .... C 3
Oeiras, 6,098 .... F 4
Olímpia, 14,629 .... †B 2
Olinda, *119,458 .... H 4
Oliveira, 12,919 .... †D 2
Oriximiná, 3,974 .... C 3
Orlândia, 6,898 .... †C 2
Orleães, 3,070 .... D10
Ourinhos, 25,717 .... †B 3
Ouro Fino, 8,044 .... †C 3
Ouro Prêto, 14,722 .... †E 2
Palmares, 17,327 .... H 5
Palmas, 5,540 .... C 9
Palmeira, 5,916 .... †B 4
Palmeira das Missoes, 8,017 .... C 9
Palmeiras, 2,040 .... F 6
Palmeiras de Goiás, 2,378 .... D 7
Pará (Belém), *563,996 .... E 3
Pará de Minas, 15,858 .... †D 1
Paracatu, 10,677 .... E 7
Paraguaçu Paulista, 11,391 .... D 8
Paraíba do Sul, 7,675 .... †E 3
Paranã, 970 .... E 6
Paranaguá, 27,728 .... †B 4
Paranaíba, 3,853 .... D 7
Parati, 3,046 .... †D 3
Paratinga, 2,403 .... F 6
Parintins, 9,068 .... B 3
Parnaguá, 508 .... E 5
Parnaíba, 39,951 .... F 3
Parnamirim, 1,589 .... F 4
Passagem Franca, 1,703 .... E 4
Passo Fundo, 47,299 .... D10
Passos, 28,555 .... †C 2
Patos, 27,275 .... G 4
Patos de Minas, 31,471 .... E 7
Patrocínio, 13,933 .... E 7
Pau dos Ferros, 4,298 .... G 4
Paulo de Faria, 2,722 .... †B 2
Peçanha, 3,602 .... F 7
Pederneiras, 8,053 .... †B 3
Pedra Azul, 8,238 .... F 6
Pedreiras, 10,189 .... E 4
Pedro Afonso, 3,175 .... E 5
Pedro Segundo, 3,160 .... F 4
Peixe, 822 .... D 6
Pelotas, *208,672 .... C10
Penalva, 5,339 .... E 3
Penápolis, 14,400 .... †A 2
Penedo, 17,084 .... G 5
Pernambuco (Recife), *1,100,464 .... H 5
Petrolina, 14,652 .... G 5
Petrópolis, *200,052 .... †E 3
Piaçabuçu, 4,864 .... H 5
Picos, 8,176 .... F 4
Piedade, 4,812 .... †C 3
Pilão Arcado, 1,457 .... F 5
Pilar, 7,201 .... H 5
Pindamonhangaba, 19,144 .... †D 3
Pinhal, 14,260 .... †C 3
Pinheiro, 6,537 .... E 3
Piquete, 10,543 .... †D 3
Piracanjuba, 3,869 .... D 7
Piracicaba, *137,184 .... †C 3
Piracuruca, 4,320 .... F 3
Piraí do Sul, 4,842 .... †B 4
Piraju, 10,658 .... †B 3
Pirajuí, 6,465 .... †B 2
Pirapora, 13,772 .... E 7
Pirassununga, 16,784 .... †C 3
Pirenópolis, 3,088 .... D 6
Pires do Rio, 8,390 .... D 7
Piripiri, 9,635 .... F 4
Pitangui, 7,421 .... †D 1
Piuí, 9,164 .... †D 2
Poções, 6,115 .... F 6
Poconé, 4,702 .... B 7
Poços de Caldas, 32,291 .... †C 2
Pompéia, 7,462 .... †A 3
Ponta de Pedras, 1,907 .... D 3
Ponta Grossa, *152,581 .... †B 4
Ponta Porã, 9,610 .... C 8
Ponte Nova, 22,536 .... †E 2
Porangatu, 2,886 .... D 5
Porciúncula, 4,868 .... †E 2
Portel, 1,821 .... D 3
Pôrto Alegre, *932,801 .... D10
Pôrto de Moz, 879 .... D 3
Pôrto Esperança, 486 .... B 7
Pôrto Feliz, 11,786 .... † C 3
Pôrto Franco, 1,750 .... E 4
Pôrto Murtinho, 4,476 .... B 8
Pôrto Nacional, 4,926 .... E 5
Pôrto Seguro, 2,697 .... G 7
Pôrto União, 9,954 .... D 9
Pôrto Velho, 19,387 .... H10
Posse, 1,953 .... E 6
Pouso Alegre, 18,852 .... †D 3
Poxoréu, 3,315 .... C 6
Prainha, 778 .... C 3
Prata, 4,725 .... D 7
Presidente Dutra, 3,349 .... E 4
Presidente Prudente, 54,055 .... D 8
Presidente Venceslau, 13,140 .... D 8
Promissão, 9,683 .... †B 2
Propriá, 15,947 .... G 5
Prudentópolis, 4,524 .... D 9
Quaraí, 10,575 .... C10
Queimadas, 3,553 .... F 5
Quipapá, 3,421 .... G 5
Quixadá, 8,747 .... G 4
Quixeramobim, 6,384 .... F 4
Raposos, 7,631 .... †E 2
Raul Soares, 6,194 .... †E 2
Recife, *1,100,464 .... H 5
Recife, ‡1,200,000 .... H 5
Registro, 4,913 .... †C 4
Remanso, 5,125 .... F 5
Resende, 13,544 .... †D 3
Riachão, 1,907 .... E 4
Ribeira, 603 .... †B 4
Ribeirão Prêto, *169,845 .... †C 2
Rio Bonito, 11,916 .... †E 3
Rio Branco, 17,245 .... G10
Rio Brilhante, 876 .... C 8
Rio Claro, 48,548 .... †C 3
Rio de Janeiro, *4,207,322 .... †E 3
Rio de Janeiro, ‡4,400,000 .... †E 3
Rio do Sul, 13,433 .... D 9
Rio Grande, *117,500 .... D11
Rio Negro, 10,225 .... D 9
Rio Pardo, 14,412 .... C10
Rio Pomba, 6,083 .... †E 2
Rio Real, 3,171 .... G 5
Rio Tinto, 16,811 .... H 4
Rio Verde, 11,268 .... D 7
Rolândia, 10,023 .... D 8
Rondônia, 1,293 .... H10
Rosário, 6,999 .... F 3
Rosário-do-Sul, 15,786 .... C10
Rosário-Oeste, 2,607 .... C 6
Russas, 7,102 .... G 4
Sabará, 10,004 .... †E 1
Sabinópolis, 4,101 .... F 7
Sacramento, 5,872 .... †C 1
Salgueiro, 8,936 .... G 5
Salinas, 5,186 .... F 7
Salinópolis, 4,101 .... E 3
Salto, 12,643 .... †C 3
Salvador, *892,392 .... G 6
Salvador, ‡892,392 .... G 6
Santa Cruz, 5,286 .... G 4
Santa Cruz do Rio Pardo, 13,889 .... †B 3
Santa Cruz do Sul, 18,898 .... C10
Santa Filomena, 652 .... E 5
Santa Maria, *141,610 .... C10
Santa Maria da Vitória, 3,208 .... F 6
Santana, 4,357 .... E 6
Santana do Ipanema, 8,139 .... G 5
Santana do Livramento, 37,666 .... C10
Santarém, *111,706 .... C 3
Santa Rita do Sapucaí, 8,464 .... †D 3
Santa Vitória do Palmar, 8,224 .... C11
Santiago, 15,140 .... C10
Santo Amaro, 17,226 .... G 6
Santo André, *289,442 .... †C 3

HIGHWAYS OF SOUTHEASTERN BRAZIL
SCALE OF MILES
0 50 100 150 200
SCALE OF KILOMETRES
0 50 100 150 200
Major Roads
Under Construction
Other Roads
© C. S. HAMMOND & Co.
Belo Horizonte
RIO DE JANEIRO
SÃO PAULO
Curitiba
ATLANTIC OCEAN

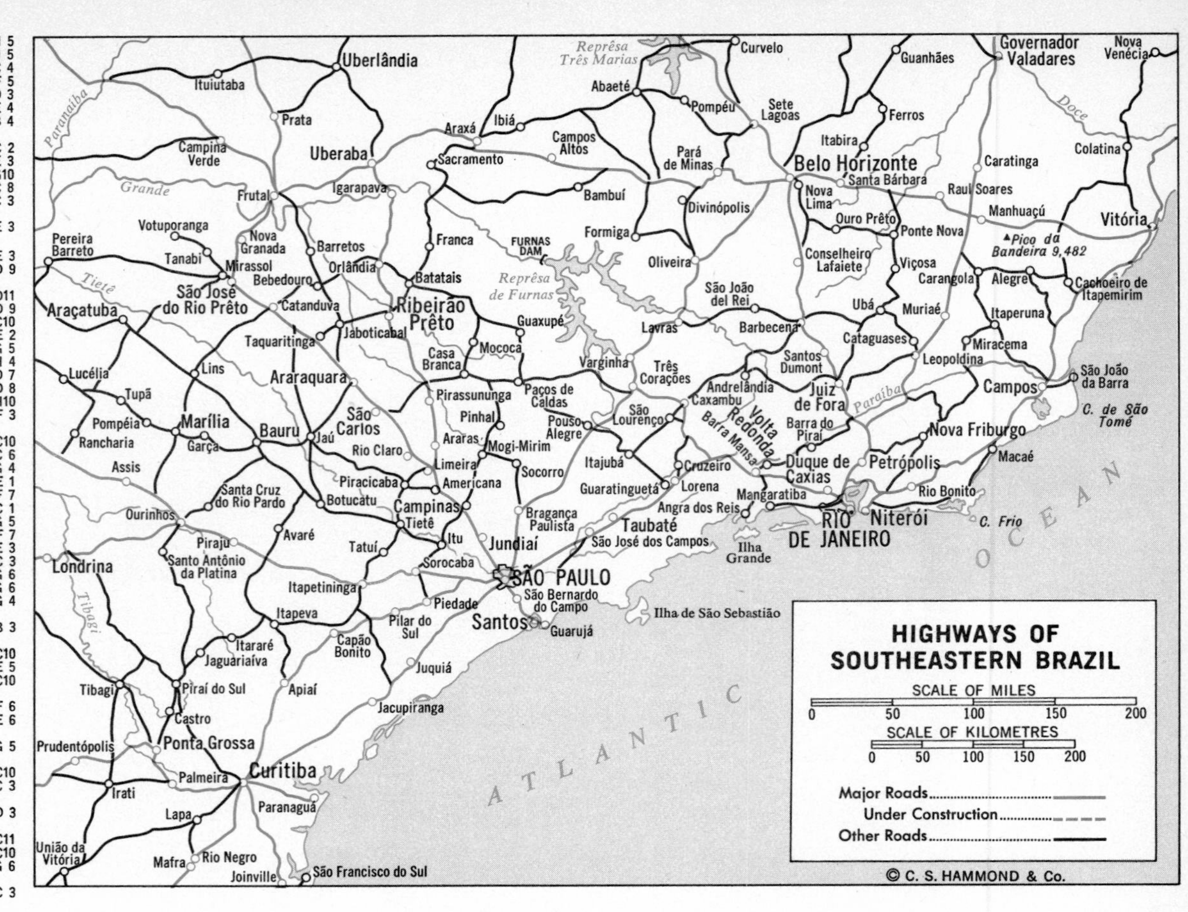

Agriculture, Industry and Resources

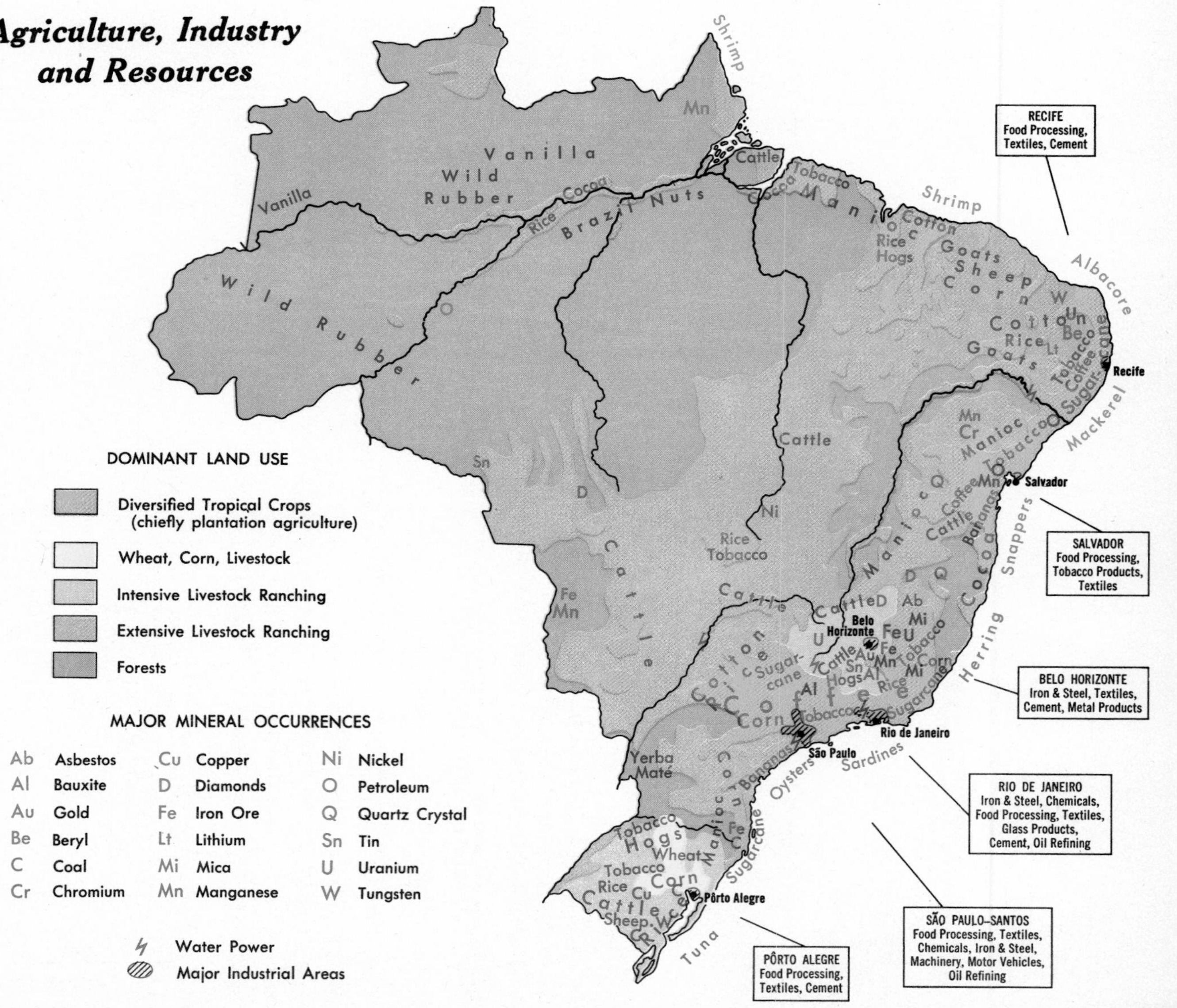

DOMINANT LAND USE
Diversified Tropical Crops (chiefly plantation agriculture)
Wheat, Corn, Livestock
Intensive Livestock Ranching
Extensive Livestock Ranching
Forests
MAJOR MINERAL OCCURRENCES
Ab Asbestos
Al Bauxite
Au Gold
Be Beryl
C Coal
Cr Chromium
Cu Copper
D Diamonds
Fe Iron Ore
Lt Lithium
Mi Mica
Mn Manganese
Ni Nickel
O Petroleum
Q Quartz Crystal
Sn Tin
U Uranium
W Tungsten
Water Power
Major Industrial Areas
RECIFE
Food Processing, Textiles, Cement
SALVADOR
Food Processing, Tobacco Products, Textiles
BELO HORIZONTE
Iron & Steel, Textiles, Cement, Metal Products
RIO DE JANEIRO
Iron & Steel, Chemicals, Food Processing, Textiles, Glass Products, Cement, Oil Refining
SÃO PAULO–SANTOS
Food Processing, Textiles, Chemicals, Iron & Steel, Machinery, Motor Vehicles, Oil Refining
PÔRTO ALEGRE
Food Processing, Textiles, Cement

Santo Ângelo, 25,415 ... C10
Santo Antônio da Platina, 9,378 ... †A 3
Santo Antonio do Leverger, 2,028 ... C 6
Santos, *313,771 ... †C 3
Santos Dumont, 20,414 ... †E 2
São Bento, 7,094 ... E 3
São Bernardo do Campo, 61,645 ... †C 3
São Borja, 20,339 ... C10
São Caetano do Sul, *135,095 ... †C 3
São Carlos, 50,010 ... †C 3
São Cristóvão, 7,624 ... G 5
São Domingos, 907 ... E 6
São Félix, 5,993 ... G 6
São Fidélis, 6,145 ... †F 2
São Francisco, 4,074 ... E 6
São Francisco do Sul, 11,593 ... E 9
São Gabriel, 22,967 ... C10
São João da Boa Vista, 25,226 ... †C 2
São João del Rei, 34,654 ... †D 2
São João do Piauí, 2,688 ... F 5
São João dos Patos, 2,590 ... F 4
São João Nepomuceno, 9,436 ... †E 2
São Joaquim da Barra, 13,853 ... †C 2
São José, 3,295 ... D 9
São José da Laje, 5,822 ... H 5
São José de Mipibu, 5,179 ... H 4
São José do Rio Pardo, 14,186 ... †C 2
São José do Rio Prêto, 66,476 ... †B 2
São José dos Campos, 55,349 ... †D 3
São José dos Pinhais, 7,574 ... D 9
São Leopoldo, 41,023 ... D10
São Lourenço, 14,680 ... †D 3
São Lourenço do Sul, 6,877 ... C10
São Luís, *218,783 ... F 3
São Luís Gonzaga, 12,926 ... C10
São Manuel, 10,009 ... †B 3
São Mateus, 6,075 ... G 7
São Miguel Arcanjo, 3,633 ... †C 3
São Miguel dos Campos, 6,511 ... G 5
São Miguel Paulista, 39,644 ... †C 3
São Paulo, *5,684,706 ... †C 3
São Paulo, ‡6,300,000 ... †C 3
São Pedro, 4,474 ... †C 3
São Pedro do Piauí, 2,139 ... F 4
São Raimundo Nonato, 3,751 ... F 5
São Roque, 12,409 ... †C 3
São Sebastião, 3,490 ... †D 3
São Sebastião do Paraíso, 14,451 ... †C 2
São Simão, 5,742 ... †C 2
São Vicente, 73,578 ... †C 4
Senador Pompeu, 8,210 ... G 4
Sena Madureira, 1,962 ... G10
Senhor do Bonfim, 13,958 ... F 5
Serra do Navio, 9 ... C 2
Serra Talhada, 12,164 ... G 4
Serrinha, 10,284 ... G 5
Sertânia, 7,556 ... G 5
Sertanópolis, 6,469 ... D 8
Sete Lagoas, 36,302 ... E 7
Sitio da Abadia, 482 ... E 6
Silvânia, 2,920 ... D 7
Sobral, 32,281 ... G 3
Socorro, 6,402 ... †C 3
Sorocaba, *142,835 ... †C 3
Soure, 6,666 ... D 3
Taquaritinga, 11,624 ... †B 2
Tarauacá, 2,292 ... G10
Tatuí, 22,550 ... †C 3
Taubaté, 64,863 ... E 8
Tefé, 2,781 ... G 9
Teófilo-Otoni, *134,476 ... F 7
Teresina, *184,836 ... F 4
Teresópolis, 29,540 ... †E 3
Tibagi, 1,746 ... †A 4
Tietê, 8,729 ... †C 3
Tijucas, 4,420 ... D 9
Tocantínia, 1,414 ... D 5
Tocantinópolis, 4,927 ... D 4
Três Corações, 17,498 ... †D 2
Três Lagoas, 14,520 ... C 8
Três Pontas, 11,534 ... †D 2
Três Rios, 22,246 ... †E 3
Tubarão, 20,615 ... D10
Tucano, 4,007 ... G 5
Tupã, 28,723 ... †A 2
Tupanciretã, 8,659 ... C10
Tutóia, 3,337 ... F 3
Uaupés, 571 ... G 9
Ubá, 21,767 ... †E 2
Ubaíra, 2,352 ... G 6
Ubaitaba, 3,581 ... G 6
Ubatuba, 3,748 ... †D 3
Uberaba, *100,634 ... †C 1
Uberlândia, *101,149 ... E 7
Unaí, 4,214 ... E 7
União, 4,296 ... F 4
União da Vitória, 15,822 ... D 9
União dos Palmares, 10,406 ... H 5
Uruaçu, 4,392 ... D 5
Uruçuí, 2,233 ... E 4
Urucurituba, 520 ... B 3
Uruguaiana, 48,358 ... B10
Valença, 17,137 ... G 6
Valença do Piauí, 3,046 ... F 4
Valparaíso, 7,974 ... D 8
Varginha, 24,944 ... †D 2
Vera Cruz, 5,535 ... †B 3
Viana, 5,385 ... E 3
Viçosa, Alagoas, 7,285 ... G 5
Viçosa, Minas Gerais, 9,342 ... †E 2
Vigia, 7,246 ... E 3
Visconde do Rio Branco, 12,363 ... †E 2
Viseu, 1,606 ... E 3
Vitória, *121,843 ... G 8
Vitória da Conquista, 46,778 ... F 6
Vitória de Santo Antão, 27,053 ... G 4
Volta Redonda, *118,114 ... †D 3
Votuporanga, 18,722 ... †B 2
Xapecó, 8,465 ... C 9
Xapuri, 2,000 ... G10
Xique-Xique, 5,467 ... F 5

OTHER FEATURES

Abacaxis (river) ... B 4
Abunã (river) ... G10
Acaraí (range) ... B 2
Acre (river) ... G10
Amambaí (range) ... C 7
Amaparí (river) ... C 2
Amazon (river) ... C 3
Anauá (river) ... B 2
Aporé (river) ... D 7
Araguaia (river) ... D 6
Araguarí (river) ... D 2
Araruama (lagoon) ... †E 3
Arinos (river) ... B 5
Aripuanã (river) ... A 4
Balsas (river) ... E 5
Bananal (isl.) ... D 5
Bandeira, Pico da (mt.) ... F 8
Branco (river) ... H 8
Buzios (cape) ... †F 3
Canumã (river) ... B 4
Capim (river) ... D 3
Carajás (range) ... D 4
Cardoso (isl.) ... †C 4
Cassiporé (cape) ... D 2
Caviana (isl.) ... D 2
Chavantes (range) ... D 5
Claro (river) ... D 7
Coluene (river) ... C 6
Comprida (isl.) ... †C 4
Cuiabá (river) ... B 7
Doce (river) ... F 7
Dois Irmãos (range) ... F 5
Erepecuru (river) ... B 3
Espigão Mestre (Geral) (range) ... E 6
Espinhaço (range) ... F 7
Estrondo (range) ... D 4
Feia (lake) ... †F 3
Feio (river) ... †B 2
Formosa (range) ... C 5
Frio (cape) ... †F 3
Furnas (dam) ... †C 2
Furnas (res.) ... †C 2
Geral (range) ... D 9
Geral de Goiás (range) ... E 6
Gi-Paraná (river) ... H10
Gradaús (range) ... D 4
Grajaú (river) ... E 4
Grande (isl.) ... †D 3
Grande (river) ... †B 1, D 8
Guanabara (bay) ... †E 3
Guaporé (river) ... H10
Guariba (river) ... B 5
Gurguéia (river) ... E 5
Gurupi (range) ... E 4
Gurupi (river) ... E 3
Ibicuí (river) ... C10
Içá (river) ... G 9
Iguaçu (river) ... C 9
Iguazú (falls) ... C 9
Ilha Grande (bay) ... †D 3
Iriri (river) ... C 4
Itapecuru (river) ... F 4
Itararé (river) ... †B 3
Ivaí (river) ... C 8
Jacuipe (river) ... F 5
Jaguaribe (river) ... G 4
Japurá (river) ... G 9
Jari (river) ... C 3
Javarí (river) ... F 9
Jequitinhonha (river) ... F 7
Juruá (river) ... G10
Juruena (river) ... B 5
Madeira (river) ... A 4
Manso (river) ... C 6
Mantiqueira (range) ... †D 3
Mar (range) ... †C 4, E 9
Maracá (isl.) ... D 2
Marajó (isl.) ... D 3
Mato Grosso (plateau) ... B 6
Mirim (lagoon) ... C11
Moji Guaçu (river) ... †C 2
Mortes (Manso) (river) ... D 6
Neblina, Pico da (mt.) ... G 8
Negro (river) ... H 9
Nhamundá (river) ... B 3
Norte (range) ... B 5
Orange (cape) ... D 1
Orgãos (range) ... †E 3
Oyapock (river) ... C 2
Pacajá Grande (river) ... D 4
Pacaraima (range) ... H 8
Papagaio (river) ... B 6
Pará (river) ... D 3
Paracatu (river) ... E 7
Paraguaçu (river) ... F 6
Paraguai (river) ... B 8
Paraíba (river) ... †E 2
Paranã (river) ... E 6
Paraná (river) ... C 8
Paranapanema (river) ... †B 3, C 8
Paranapiacaba (range) ... †B 4
Paranatinga (river) ... C 6
Pardo (river) ... †B 2, D 8
Pardo (river) ... F 6
Parecis (range) ... B 6
Parnaíba (river) ... E 5
Paru (river) ... C 3
Patos (lagoon) ... D10
Peixoto (dam) ... †C 2
Penitente (range) ... E 5
Piauí (range) ... F 5
Piauí (river) ... F 3
Piracambu (range) ... E 3
Purus (river) ... H 9
Ribeira (river) ... †B 4
Roncador (range) ... D 5
Roosevelt (river) ... A 5
Santa Catarina (isl.), 98,520 ... E 9
São Francisco (river) ... F 5
São Lourenço (river) ... C 7
São Marcos (bay) ... F 3
São Roque (cape) ... H 4
São Sebastião (isl.), 1,823 ... †D 3
São Tomé (cape) ... G 8
Sapucaí (river) ... †D 2
Sepetiba (bay) ... †D 3
Sete Quedas (falls) ... C 9
Tacutú (river) ... B 2
Tapajós (river) ... B 4
Taquarí (river) ... C 7
Teles Pires (river) ... B 5
Tibagi (river) ... †A 4
Tietê (river) ... †B 2, D 8
Tocantins (river) ... D 4
Tombador (range) ... B 6
Trombetas (river) ... B 3
Tumucumaque (range) ... C 2
Turvo (river) ... †B 2
Uaupés (river) ... G 9
Uraricuera (river) ... H 8
Urucún, Morro do (mt.) ... B 7
Uruguai (river) ... C 9
Verde (river) ... C 7
Xingu (river) ... C 3

‡Population of metropolitan area.
*Population of municipality.
†Keys refer to map on page 135.

DEPARTMENTS

Beni, 181,000 .... C 3
Chuquisaca, 427,400 .... C 6
Cochabamba, 741,100 .... C 5
La Paz, 1,433,000 .... A 4
Oruro, 317,700 .... A 6
Pando, 29,900 .... B 2
Potosí, 807,400 .... B 7
Santa Cruz, 432,300 .... E 5
Tarija, 191,600 .... D 7

CITIES and TOWNS

Abapó, 466 .... D 6
Acchilla, 208 .... C 7
Achacachi, 3,621 .... A 5
Aiquile, 3,465 .... C 6
Alcalá, 236 .... C 6
Alejandría .... C 3
Alto Seco .... D 6
Amarete, 992 .... A 4
Amboró .... D 6
Ananea, 302 .... A 4
Ancoraimes, 769 .... A 4
Andamarca .... B 6
Añimbo, 443 .... C 7
Anzaldo, 1,056 .... C 5
Apolo, 1,043 .... A 4
Aquío .... D 6
Araca .... B 5
Arampampa, 829 .... B 5
Arani, 2,200 .... C 5
Arcopongo .... B 5
Aroma .... B 6
Arque, 1,254 .... B 5
Arroyo Grande .... A 2
Ascención, 2,097 .... D 4
Asunción .... B 2
Asunta, 45 .... B 5
Atén, 199 .... A 4
Atocha .... B 7
Ayacucho, 729 .... D 5
Ayata, 479 .... A 4
Azurduy, 1,234 .... C 6
Barrera .... B 3
Baures, 592 .... D 3
Bella Flor .... A 2
Bella Vista .... E 3
Berenguela .... A 5
Bermejo .... C 8
Betanzos, 1,097 .... C 6
Bolívar .... B 3
Bolpebra .... A 2
Boyuibe, 537 .... D 7
Buena Hora .... E 4
Buena Vista .... B 2
Buena Vista, 435 .... D 5
Cabezas, 298 .... D 6
Cachuela Esperanza, 1,073 .... C 2
Caiza, 838 .... C 7
Cajuata, 447 .... B 5
Calacoto, 415 .... A 5
Calamarca, 802 .... A 5
Calcha .... B 7
Calcha .... C 7
Callapa, 636 .... A 5
Camacho .... C 7
Camargo, 1,609 .... C 7
Camatindi .... D 7
Camiri, 4,969 .... D 7
Cañas .... C 8
Candelaria .... F 5
Canquella, 148 .... A 7
Capinota, 1,734 .... B 5
Capirenda .... D 7
Caquiaviri, 760 .... A 5
Carabuco, 626 .... A 4
Caracollo, 909 .... B 5
Caranavi .... B 4
Carandaití, 1,403 .... D 7
Carangas .... A 6
Caraparí, 351 .... D 7
Carmen .... B 2
Carrizal .... C 7
Cataricahua, 3,240 .... B 6
Cavari, 249 .... B 5
Cavinas .... B 3
Chachacomani, 159 .... A 6
Chaguaya, 643 .... C 7
Challacollo, 284 .... B 6
Challacota .... B 6
Challana .... A 4
Challapata, 2,529 .... B 6
Chapacura .... A 2
Chaquí, 291 .... C 6
Charagua, 1,185 .... D 6
Charaña, 794 .... A 5
Chayanta, 1,272 .... B 6
Chiguana, 154 .... A 7
Chiñijo, 27 .... A 4
Chivé .... A 3
Chocaya, 444 .... B 7
Choquecota .... A 6
Chorrillos .... B 2
Chulumani, 2,362 .... B 5
Chuma, 931 .... A 4
Chuquichambi .... B 5
Chuquichuqui .... C 6
Cliza, 3,121 .... C 5
Cobija, 2,537 .... A 2
Cocani .... B 7
Cocapata .... B 5
Cochabamba, 157,000 .... C 5
Cohoni, 890 .... B 5
Coipasa .... A 6
Collpa, 481 .... C 6
Colquechaca, 1,070 .... B 6
Colquiri, 806 .... B 5

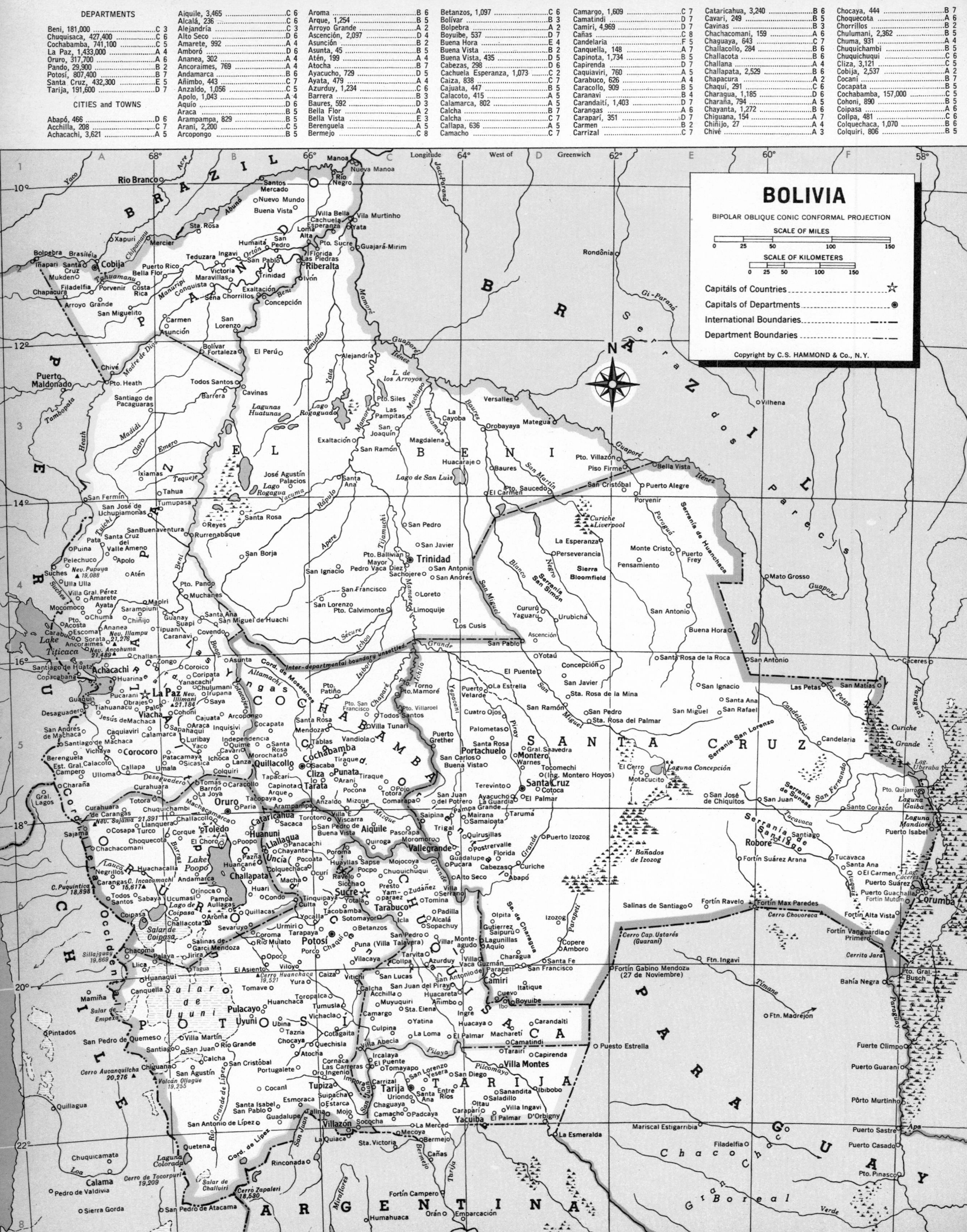

Comarapa, 1,096 C 5
Concepción B 2
Concepción, 1,056 D 5
Condo B 6
Conquista B 2
Copacabana, 1,981 A 5
Copere D 6
Coripata, 1,647 B 5
Cornaca, 264 C 7
Corocoro, 4,431 A 5
Coroico, 2,235 B 5
Coroma B 6
Corque, 423 B 6
Cosapa, 297 A 6
Costa Rica A 2
Cotagaita, 1,353 C 7
Cotoca, 915 D 5
Covendo, 71 B 4
Cuatro Ojos D 5
Cuevo, 902 D 7
Culpina, 981 C 7
Culta B 6
Curahuara, 510 A 5
Curahuara de Carangas, 235 A 5
Curiche, 257 D 6
Cururú D 4
Desaguadero, 201 A 5
D'Orbigny D 7
El Asiento B 6
El Carmen, 232 D 3
El Carmen F 6
El Cerro, 117 E 5
El Choro, 224 B 6
El Palmer D 7
El Palmar, 437 D 5
El Palmar, 832 D 7
El Perú B 3
El Puente C 7
El Puente D 5
Entre Ríos, 1,011 C 7
Escoma, 220 A 4
Esmoraca B 7
Estación General Campero A 5
Estarca C 7
Exaltación B 2
Exaltación, 405 C 3
Filadelfia A 2
Florida C 2
Florida, 128 D 6
Fortaleza B 3
Fortín Alta Vista F 6
Fortín Campero C 8
Fortín Max Paredes F 6
Fortín Mutum F 6
Fortín Ravelo E 6
Fortín Suárez Arana F 6
Fortín Vanguardia Primero F 6
General Saavedra, 1,006 D 5
Guadalupe, 71 B 7
Guadalupe, 2,355 C 6
Guanay, 574 B 4
Guaqui, 2,266 A 5
Gutiérrez, 770 D 6
Huacaraje, 673 D 3
Huacareta, 239 C 7
Huacaya, 229 D 7
Huachacalla, 801 A 6
Huanaqui, 359 A 7
Huancané, 148 B 6
Huanchaca B 7
Huanuni, 5,696 B 6
Huari, 1,070 B 6
Huarina, 1,151 A 5
Huayllas, 206 C 6
Humaitá B 2
Ibibobo D 7
Ibo, 425 D 7
Ichoca, 591 B 5
Icla, 196 C 6
Impora, 274 C 7
Independencia, 1,742 B 5
Ingavi B 2
Ingeniero Montero Hoyos (Tocomechi), 575 D 5
Ingre, 162 D 7
Inquisivi, 530 B 5
Ipitá, 441 D 6
Ircalaya C 7
Irupana, 1,937 B 5
Itatique D 7
Itaú, 102 D 7
Ivón C 2
Ixiamas, 292 A 3
Izozog D 6
Jesús de Machaca, 529 A 5
Jirira B 6
José Agustín Palacios B 3
La Cayoba C 3
La Esmeralda D 8
La Esperanza D 4
La Estrella D 5
La Guardia, 470 D 5
La Joya, 401 B 5
La Loma C 7
La Merced C 8
La Paz (cap.), 525,000 B 5
Lagunillas, 840 D 6
Lanza, 526 B 5
Las Carreras, 155 C 7
Las Pampitas C 3
Las Petas F 5
Las Piedras C 2
Limoquije C 4
Llallagua, 6,719 B 6
Llanquera, 613 A 6
Llica, 560 A 6
Loma Alta B 2
Loreto, 589 C 4
Los Cusis D 4
Luribay, 392 B 5
Macha, 1,050 B 6
Machacamarca, 1,746 B 5
Machareti D 7
Magdalena, 1,724 C 3
Mairana, 508 D 6
Manoa C 1
Mapiri, 289 B 4
Maravillas B 2
Mategua, 38 D 3
Mayor Pedro Vaca Diez, 358 C 4
Mecoya C 8
Mendoza C 5
Mercier B 2
Mizque, 870 C 5
Mocomoco, 977 A 4
Mojo, 469 C 7
Mojocoya, 498 C 6
Monte Cristo E 4
Monteagudo, 971 D 6
Montero, 2,713 D 5
Morochata, 461 B 5
Moromoro, 556 C 6
Motacucito E 5
Muchanes B 4
Mukden A 2
Muyuquiri C 7
Negrillos, 85 A 6
Nueva Manoa C 1
Nuevo Mundo B 2
Obrajes A 5
Ocurí, 1,531 C 6
Opoco B 6
Orinoca B 6
Oro Ingenio C 7
Orobayaya D 3
Oruro, 86,985 B 5
Padcaya, 324 C 7
Padilla, 2,462 C 6
Palaya, 300 A 6
Palca, 887 A 5
Palometas D 5
Pampa Aullagas B 6
Pampa Grande, 727 D 5
Panacachi, 952 B 6
Paria, 335 B 5
Pasorapa, 1,016 C 6
Pata, 122 A 4
Patacamaya, 1,278 B 5
Pazña, 671 B 6
Pelechuco, 873 A 4
Pensamiento E 4
Perseverancia D 4
Piso Firme D 3
Pocoata, 859 B 6
Pocona, 518 C 5
Pocpo C 6
Pojo, 1,047 C 5
Poopó, 736 B 6
Porco, 817 B 6
Poroma, 171 C 6
Portachuelo, 2,456 D 5
Portugalete B 7
Porvenir A 2
Porvenir E 4
Postrervalle, 750 D 6
Potosí, 55,233 C 6
Presto, 725 C 6
Pucara, 762 C 6
Pucarani, 1,041 A 5
Puerto Acosta, 1,302 A 4
Puerto Alegre E 3
Puerto Ballivián C 4
Puerto Calvimonte C 4
Puerto Frey E 4
Puerto General Busch G 7
Puerto Grether C 5
Puerto Guachalla F 6
Puerto Heath A 3
Puerto Isabel G 6
Puerto Izozog D 6
Puerto Mamoré C 5
Puerto Pando B 4
Puerto Patiño C 5
Puerto Quijarro, 1,006 G 5

AREA 424, 163 sq. mi.
POPULATION 4,804,000
CAPITALS La Paz, Sucre
LARGEST CITY La Paz
HIGHEST POINT Nevada Ancohuma 21,489 ft.
MONETARY UNIT Bolivian peso
MAJOR LANGUAGES Spanish, Quechua, Aymara
MAJOR RELIGION Roman Catholicism

Puerto Rico B 2
Puerto San Francisco C 5
Puerto Saucedo D 3
Puerto Siles, 357 C 3
Puerto Suárez, 1,159 F 6
Puerto Sucre, 1,470 C 2
Puerto Torno C 5
Puerto Velarde D 5
Puerto Villaroel C 5
Puerto Villazón D 3
Puina A 4
Pulacayo, 7,984 B 7
Puna, 852 C 6
Punata, 5,014 C 5
Quechisla, 171 C 7
Quetena, 183 B 8
Quillacas, 1,170 B 6
Quillacollo, 9,123 B 5
Quime, 1,256 B 5
Quiroga C 6
Quirusillas, 433 D 6
Ravelo, 907 C 6
Reyes, 1,404 B 4
Riberalta, 6,549 C 2
Río Grande, 281 B 7
Río Mulato, 381 B 6
Río Negro C 1
Roboré, 3,715 F 6
Rurrenabaque, 1,225 B 4
Sabaya, 649 A 6
Sacaba, 2,752 C 5
Sacaca, 1,778 B 6
Sachojere, 401 C 4
Saipina, 573 C 6
Saipurú D 6
Sajama, 231 A 6
Saladillo D 7
Salinas de Garci Mendoza, 335 B 6
Salinas de Santiago E 6
Samaipata, 1,656 D 6
San Agustín B 7
San Andrés, 399 C 4
San Andrés de Machaca, 101 A 5
San Antonio, 436 C 4
San Antonio E 4
San Antonio de Lípez B 7
San Antonio del Parapetí, 497 D 7
San Borja, 708 B 4
San Buenaventura, 307 A 4
San Carlos, 570 D 5
San Cristóbal B 7
San Cristóbal E 3
San Diego D 7
San Fermín A 3
San Francisco, 185 C 4
San Francisco D 7
San Ignacio, 1,757 C 4
San Ignacio, 1,819 E 5
San Javier, 233 C 4
San Javier, 564 D 5
San Joaquín, 1,959 C 3
San José de Chiquitos, 1,933 E 5
San José de Uchupiamonas, 277 A 4
San Juan, 131 B 7
San Juan F 5
San Juan del Piray, 541 C 7
San Juan del Potrero, 263 C 5
San Lorenzo B 2
San Lorenzo, 496 C 4
San Lorenzo, 785 C 7
San Lucas, 925 C 7
San Matías, 887 F 5
San Miguel, 502 E 5
San Miguel de Huachi, 25 B 4
San Miguelito A 2
San Pablo B 2
San Pablo, 11 B 7
San Pablo D 4
San Pedro B 2
San Pedro, 262 C 4
San Pedro, 182 C 6
San Pedro, 80 D 5
San Pedro de Buena Vista, 1,094 C 6
San Pedro de Quemes A 7
San Rafael E 5
San Ramón, 1,161 C 3
San Ramón, 379 D 5
Sanandita, 379 D 7
Santa Ana, 171 B 4
Santa Ana, 2,225 C 3
Santa Ana C 7
Santa Ana, 275 E 5
Santa Ana, 663 F 6
Santa Cruz A 2
Santa Cruz, 108,720 D 5
Santa Cruz del Valle Ameno, 442 A 4
Santa Elena C 7
Santa Fe D 6
Santa Isabel B 7
Santa Rosa B 2
Santa Rosa, 765 B 4
Santa Rosa, 491 B 5
Santa Rosa C 5
Santa Rosa, 995 D 5
Santa Rosa de la Mina, 99 D 5
Santa Rosa de la Roca, 101 E 5
Santa Roso del Palmar, 441 E 5
Santiago, 172 A 7
Santiago, 765 F 6
Santiago de Huata, 948 A 5
Santiago de Machaca, 218 A 5
Santiago de Pacaguaras A 3
Santo Corazón F 5
Santos Mercado B 2
Sapahaqui, 55 B 5
Sapse C 6
Sarampiuni, 138 A 4
Saya, 339 B 5
Sena B 2
Sevaruyo, 475 B 6
Sicasica, 1,486 B 5
Siccha C 6
Sococha C 7
Sopachuy, 713 C 6
Sorata, 2,087 A 4
Sotomayor, 510 C 6
Suapi B 4
Suches A 4
Sucre (capital), 58,359 C 6
Suipacha C 7
Tablas C 5
Tacobamba C 6
Tacopaya, 795 B 5
Tagua B 6
Tahua, 114 B 3
Talina, 122 B 7
Tapacarí, 980 B 5
Tarabuco, 2,833 C 6
Tarairí D 7
Tarapaya, 357 B 6
Tarata, 3,016 C 5
Tarija, 20,851 C 7
Tarumá D 6
Tarvita, 404 C 6
Tazna B 7
Teduzara B 2
Terevinto D 5
Tiahuanacu, 1,227 A 5
Tinquipaya, 766 C 6
Tipuani B 4
Tiraque, 1,390 C 5
Tiraque, 234 C 5
Tocomechi (Ingeniero Montero Hoyos), 575 D 5
Todos Santos, 68 A 6
Todos Santos B 3
Todos Santos, 408 C 5
Toledo, 3,273 B 6
Tomás Barrón, 1,852 B 5
Tomave, 201 B 7
Tomayapo C 7

Topography

0 100 200
MILES

Below Sea Level | 100 m. 328 ft. | 200 m. 656 ft. | 500 m. 1,640 ft. | 1,000 m. 3,281 ft. | 2,000 m. 6,562 ft. | 5,000 m. 16,404 ft.

Tomina, 708 C 6
Toropalca B 7
Torotoro, 1,233 C 6
Totora, 210 A 5
Totora, 2,290 C 5
Trigal, 749 C 6
Trinidad B 2
Trinidad, 14,505 C 4
Tucavaca F 6
Tumupasa, 349 B 4
Tumusla C 7
Tupiza, 8,248 C 7
Turco, 131 A 6
Ubina B 7
Ucumasi B 6
Ulla Ulla, 52 A 4
Ulloma, 116 A 5
Umala, 481 B 5
Uncía, 4,507 B 6
Uriondo, 860 C 7
Urmiri B 6
Urubichá, 1,369 D 4
Uyuni, 6,968 B 7
Vallegrande, 5,094 C 6
Vandiola C 5
Versalles, 83 D 3
Viacha, 6,607 A 5
Vichacla, 317 C 7
Vichaya, 422 A 5
Victoria B 2
Vilacaya, 200 C 6
Villa Abecia, 539 C 7
Villa Bella, 88 C 2
Villa E. Viscarra, 658 C 6
Villa General Pérez, 802 A 4
Villa Ingavi, 122 D 7
Villa Martín, 543 B 7
Villa Montes, 3,105 D 7
Villa Serrano, 1,570 C 6
Villa Talavera (Puna), 852 C 6
Villa Tunari, 510 C 5
Villa Vaca Guzmán, 699 D 6
Villar, 322 C 6
Villazón, 6,261 C 7
Viloyo B 6
Vitichi, 1,515 C 7
Warnes, 1,571 D 5
Yaco, 835 B 5
Yacuiba, 5,027 D 7
Yaguarú D 4
Yamparáez, 725 C 6
Yanacachi B 5
Yata C 2
Yatina C 7
Yesera C 7
Yocalla B 6
Yotala, 1,554 C 6
Yotaú D 5
Yura, 136 B 7
Zongo, 141 B 5
Zudáñez, 1,868 C 6

OTHER FEATURES

Altamachi (river) B 5
Ancohuma, Nevada (mt.) A 4
Andes (mts.) A 3
Apere (river) C 4
Arroyas, Los (lake) C 3
Barras (river) B 6
Baures (river) D 3
Beni (river) B 2
Bermejo (river) C 8
Blanco (river) D 4
Bloomfield, Sierra (mts.) D 4
Boopi (river) B 4
Cáceres (lagoon) F 6
Candelaria (river) F 5
Capitán Ustarés, Cerro (mt.) E 6
Central, Cordillera (mts.) C 6
Challviri (salt depr.) B 8
Chaparé (river) C 5
Charagua (mts.) D 6
Chipamanu (river) A 2
Coipasa (lake) B 6
Coipasa (salt depr.) A 6
Colorada (lagoon) A 8
Concepción (lagoon) E 5
Cotacajes (river) B 5
Desaguadero (river) B 5
Empexa (salt depr.) A 7
Gaiba (lagoon) G 5
Grande (marsh) F 5
Grande (river) C 4
Grande (river) C 6
Grande de Lípez (river) B 7
Guaporé (river) C 3
Guaraní (Capitán Ustarés) (mt.) E 6
Heath (river) A 3
Huanchaca, Cerro (mt.) B 7
Huanchaca, Serranía de (mts.) E 4
Ichilo (river) C 5
Illampu, Nevada (mt.) A 4
Illimani, Nevada (mt.) B 5
Incacamachi, Cerro (mt.) A 6
Isiboro (river) C 5
Iténez (Guaporé) (river) C 3
Itonamas (river) C 3
Izozog (swamp) E 6
Las Petas (river) F 5
Las Yungas (region) B 5
Lauca (river) A 6
Lípez, Cordillera de (mts.) B 8
Liverpool (swamp) D 4
Machupo (river) C 3
Madidi (river) A 3
Madre de Dios (river) A 3
Mamoré (river) C 2
Mandioré (lagoon) G 6
Manuripi (river) B 2
Mizque (river) C 6
Mosetenes, Cordillera de (mts.) B 5
Negro (river) D 4
Occidental, Cordillera (mts.) A 6
Ollagüe (volcano) A 7
Oriental, Cordillera (mts.) C 5
Ortón (river) B 2
Otuquis (river) F 6
Paraguá (river) E 4
Paraguay (river) F 7
Parapetí (river) D 6
Petas, Las (river) F 5
Pilaya (river) C 7
Pilcomayo (river) D 7
Piray (river) D 5
Poopó (lake) B 6
Pupuya, Nevada (mt.) A 4
Puquintica, Cerro (mt.) A 6
Rápulo (river) C 4
Real, Cordillera (mts.) A 5
Rogagua (lake) B 3
Rogaguado (lake) C 3
Sajama, Nevada (mt.) A 6
San Fernando (river) F 5
San Juan (river) C 7
San Luis (lake) C 3
San Martín (river) D 3
San Miguel (river) D 4
San Simón, Serranía (mts.) D 4
Santiago, Serranía de (mts.) F 6
Sillajguay (mt.) A 6
Suches (river) A 4
Tahuamanu (river) A 2
Tarija (river) C 8
Titicaca (lake) A 4
Tocorpuri, Cerros de (mt.) A 8
Tucavaca (river) F 6
Tuichi (river) A 4
Uberaba (lagoon) F 5
Uyuni (salt depr.) B 7
Yacuma (river) B 3
Yapacani (river) C 5
Yata (river) C 3
Yungas, Las (region) B 5
Zapaleri, Cerro (mt.) B 8

Agriculture, Industry and Resources

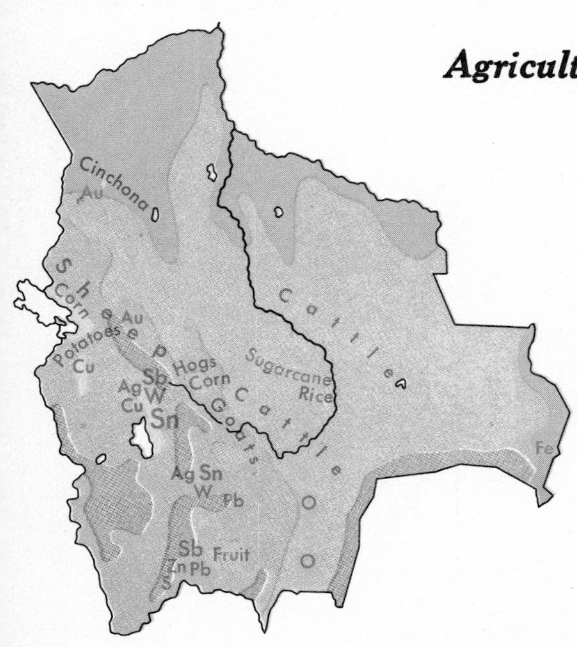

DOMINANT LAND USE

- Diversified Tropical Crops (chiefly plantation agriculture)
- Upland Cultivated Areas
- Upland Livestock Grazing, Limited Agriculture
- Extensive Livestock Ranching
- Forests
- Nonagricultural Land

MAJOR MINERAL OCCURRENCES

Ag	Silver	O	Petroleum	Sn	Tin
Au	Gold	Pb	Lead	W	Tungsten
Cu	Copper	S	Sulfur	Zn	Zinc
Fe	Iron Ore	Sb	Antimony		

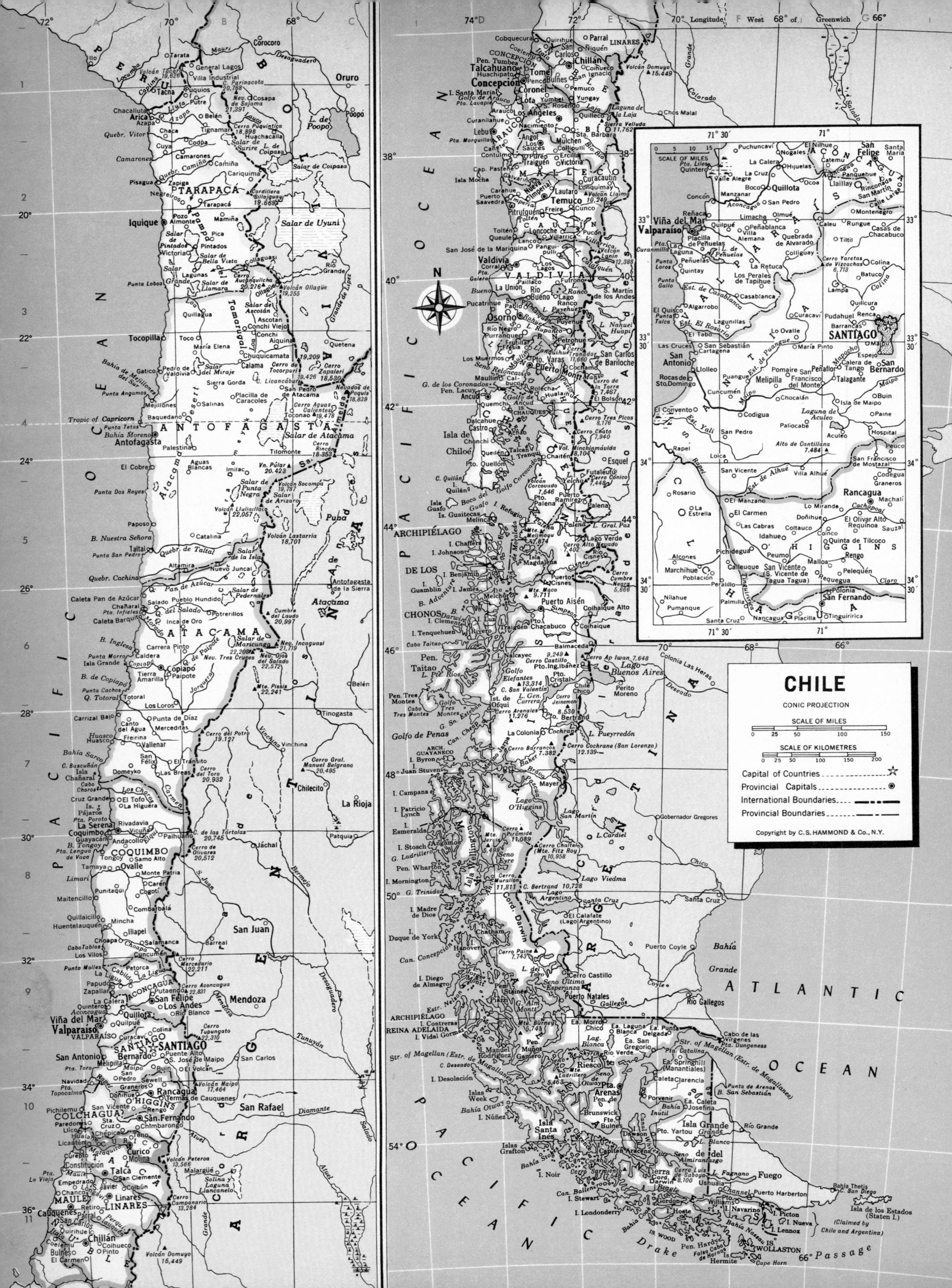
CHILE
CONIC PROJECTION
SCALE OF MILES
0 25 50 100 150
SCALE OF KILOMETRES
0 25 50 100 150 200
Capital of Countries
Provincial Capitals
International Boundaries
Provincial Boundaries
Copyright by C.S. HAMMOND & Co., N.Y.
PACIFIC OCEAN
ATLANTIC OCEAN
SANTIAGO
Valparaíso
Viña del Mar
Antofagasta
Concepción
Iquique
Arica
Tacna
Oruro
La Serena
Coquimbo
Talca
Chillán
Temuco
Valdivia
Osorno
Puerto Montt
Ancud
Puerto Aisén
Punta Arenas
Tierra del Fuego
Str. of Magellan
Drake Passage
Cape Horn
Isla Grande de Tierra del Fuego
Mendoza
San Juan
San Rafael
La Rioja
Tropic of Capricorn
TARAPACÁ
ANTOFAGASTA
ATACAMA
COQUIMBO
ACONCAGUA
VALPARAÍSO
SANTIAGO
O'HIGGINS
COLCHAGUA
CURICÓ
TALCA
MAULE
LINARES
CONCEPCIÓN
BÍO-BÍO
ARAUCO
MALLECO
CAUTÍN
VALDIVIA
OSORNO
LLANQUIHUE
CHILOÉ
AISÉN
MAGALLANES
ARGENTINA
BOLIVIA
PERU
Salar de Uyuni
Salar de Atacama
Atacama Desert
Chos Malal
Lago Buenos Aires
Lago Argentino
Lago Viedma
Río Gallegos
Santa Cruz
Ushuaia
Isla de los Estados (Staten I.)
(Claimed by Chile and Argentina)
Longitude West of Greenwich

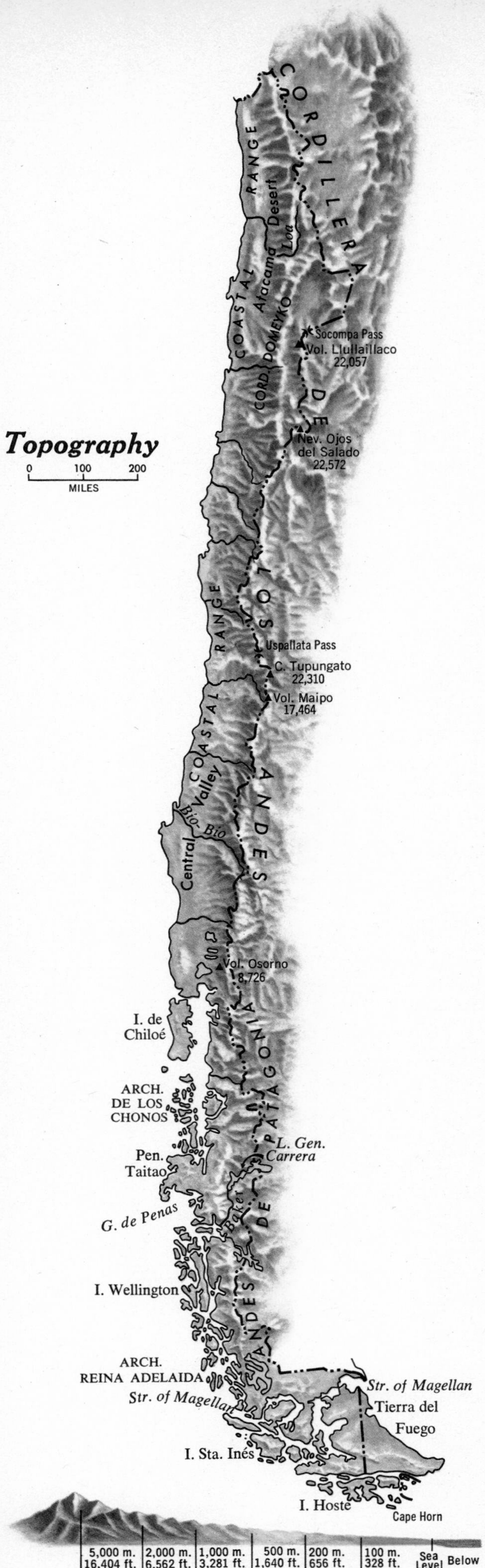

AREA 292,257 sq. mi.
POPULATION 8,834,820
CAPITAL Santiago
LARGEST CITY Santiago
HIGHEST POINT Ojos del Salado 22,572 ft.
MONETARY UNIT Chilean escudo
MAJOR LANGUAGE Spanish
MAJOR RELIGION Roman Catholicism

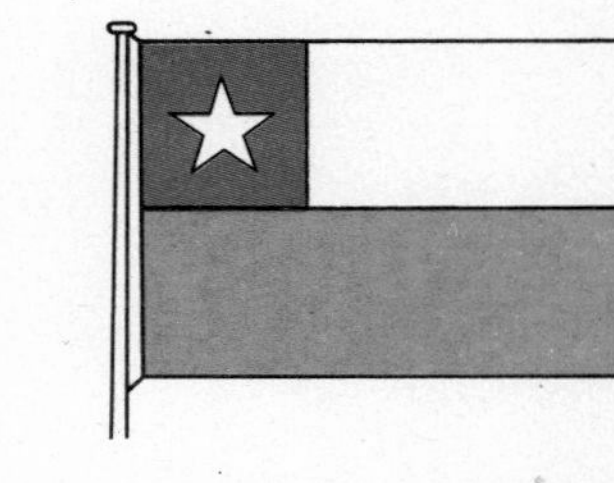

PROVINCES

Aconcagua, 160,821 .... A 9
Aisén, 51,022 .... D 6
Antofagasta, 250,665 .... B 4
Arauco, 98,810 .... D 1
Atacama, 152,326 .... B 6
Bío-Bío, 193,002 .... D 1
Cautín, 420,682 .... E 2
Chiloé, 110,728 .... D 4
Colchagua, 167,899 .... A10
Concepción, 638,118 .... D 1
Coquimbo, 336,821 .... A 8
Curicó, 113,710 .... A10
Linares, 189,010 .... A11
Llanquihue, 197,986 .... D 3
Magallanes, 88,706 .... E10
Malleco, 176,060 .... E 2
Maule, 82,339 .... A11
Ñuble, 314,738 .... E 1
O'Higgins, 306,739 .... A10
Osorno, 158,673 .... D 3
Santiago, 3,217,870 .... A 9
Talca, 231,088 .... A11
Tarapacá, 174,730 .... B 2
Valdivia, 275,404 .... D 3
Valparaíso, 726,953 .... A 9

CITIES and TOWNS

Achao, †11,501 .... D 4
Aculeo, 20 .... G 4
Aguas Blancas, †203 .... B 4
Aiquina, 105 .... B 3
Alcones, 682 .... F 5
Algarrobo, †3,941 .... F 3
Altamira, 93 .... B 5
Ancud, †22,127 .... D 4
Andacollo, †9,987 .... A 8
Angol, †35,995 .... D 1
Antofagasta, †126,252 .... A 4
Arauco, †20,018 .... D 1
Arica, †92,394 .... A 1
Ascotán, 23 .... B 3
Azapa, 225 .... A 1
Balmaceda, 735 .... E 6
Baquedano, 1,412 .... A 4
Barrancas, †184,241 .... G 3
Batuco, 1,125 .... G 3
Belén, †925 .... B 1
Boco, 1,655 .... F 2
Buin, †31,233 .... G 4
Bulnes, †16,107 .... E 1
Cabildo, †13,018 .... A 9
Calama, †71,983 .... B 3
Calbuco, †21,673 .... D 4
Caldera, †3,268 .... A 6
Calera de Tango, †6,198 .... G 4
Caleta Barquito, 932 .... A 6
Caleta Clarencia, 60 .... E10
Caleta Pan de Azúcar, 8 .... A 6
Caleu, 187 .... G 2
Calle Larga, †7,172 .... G 2
Calleuque .... F 5
Camarones, 259 .... B 2
Camiña, 234 .... B 2
Cañete, †15,179 .... D 2
Canto del Agua, 269 .... A 7
Capitán Pastene, 1,669 .... D 2
Carahue, †12,733 .... D 2
Carén, 225 .... A 8
Cariquima, 20 .... B 2
Carrera Pinto, 68 .... B 6
Carrizal Bajo, 207 .... A 7
Cartagena, †7,124 .... F 3
Casablanca, †12,292 .... F 3
Castro, †22,682 .... D 4
Catalina, †1,637 .... B 5
Catemu, †8,728 .... G 2
Cauquenes, †38,476 .... A11
Cerro Castillo, †537 .... E 9
Chaca, 37 .... B 1
Chacalluta, 75 .... A 1
Chaitén, †4,067 .... E 4
Chañaral, †36,949 .... A 6
Chanco, †12,433 .... A11
Chépica, †11,199 .... A10
Chile Chico, 1,926 .... E 6
Chillán, †102,361 .... A11
Chimbarongo, †17,592 .... A10
Choapa, 258 .... A 9
Chocalán, 187 .... F 4
Chonchi, †8,911 .... D 4
Chuquicamata, 24,798 .... B 3
Cobquecura, †6,298 .... D 1
Cochamó, †5,042 .... E 3
Codegua, †6,757 .... G 4
Codigua, 530 .... F 4
Codpa, †950 .... B 1
Coelemu, †11,967 .... D 1
Cogotí, 212 .... A 8
Coihaique, †24,032 .... E 6
Coihaique Alto, 24 .... E 6
Coihueco, †17,276 .... A11
Coinco, †4,942 .... G 5
Colbún, †12,924 .... A11
Colina, †18,058 .... G 3
Collaguasi, 8 .... B 3
Colliguay, 102 .... F 3
Collipulli, †15,058 .... E 2
Coltauco, †11,857 .... F 5
Combarbalá, †17,332 .... A 8
Concepción, †189,929 .... D 1
Conchi, 9 .... B 3
Conchi Viejo, 17 .... B 3
Concón, 5,381 .... F 2
Constitución, †23,543 .... A11
Contulmo, †13,987 .... D 2
Copiapó, †51,809 .... B 6
Coquimbo, †55,360 .... A 8
Coronel, †73,568 .... D 1
Corral, †5,533 .... D 3
Cruz Grande, 478 .... A 7
Cunco, †18,836 .... E 2
Cuncumén, Coquimbo, 1,052 .... A 9
Cuncumén, Santiago .... F 4
Curacautín, †15,862 .... E 2
Curacaví, †11,481 .... G 3
Curanilahue, †21,207 .... D 1
Curepto, †13,020 .... A10
Curicó, †59,621 .... A10
Cuya, 86 .... B 2
Dalcahue, †7,084 .... D 4
Domeyko, 1,814 .... A 7
Doñihue, †8,837 .... G 5
El Carmen, Ñuble, †13,226 .... A11
El Carmen, O'Higgins, 625 .... F 5
El Cobre, 7 .... A 4
El Convento, 733 .... F 4
El Manzano, 1,073 .... F 5
El Ñilhue, 341 .... G 1
El Olivar Alto, †5,414 .... G 5
El Quisco, †2,152 .... E 3
El Tabo, †2,180 .... F 3
El Tofo, 1,175 .... A 7
El Tránsito, 235 .... B 7
El Volcán, 250 .... B10
Empedrado, †7,887 .... A11
Ercilla, †8,061 .... E 2
Espejo, 3,481 .... G 3
Estancia Caleta Josefina, †1,042 .... F10
Estancia Laguna Blanca, 119 .... E 9
Estancia Morro Chico, †785 .... E 9
Estancia Punta Delgada, 233 .... E 9
Estancia San Gregorio, †1,156 .... E 9
Estancia Springhill (Manantiales), 291 .... F10
Freire, †23,313 .... E 2
Freirina, †5,523 .... A 7
Fresia, †15,359 .... D 3
Frutillar, †12,721 .... D 3
Fuerte Bulnes, 18 .... E10
Futaleufú, †2,366 .... E 4
Futrono, †7,109 .... E 3
Galvarino, †9,495 .... D 2
Gatico, 16 .... A 4
General Lagos, †810 .... B 1
Graneros, †13,523 .... G 5
Guayacán, 1,514 .... A 8
Hijuelas, †7,128 .... F 2
Hospital, 460 .... G 4
Huachipato, †16,336 .... D 1
Hualaihué, 391 .... E 4
Hualañé, †6,912 .... A10
Huara, †1,934 .... B 2
Huasco, †4,971 .... A 7
Huentelauquén, 355 .... A 8
Idahue, 1,832 .... F 5
Illapel, †20,660 .... A 8
Imalac, 27 .... B 4
Inca de Oro, 1,406 .... B 6
Iquique, †64,900 .... A 2
Isla de Maipo, †12,903 .... G 4
La Calera, †28,728 .... F 2
La Colonia, 41 .... D 7
La Cruz, †8,907 .... F 2
La Estrella, †3,707 .... F 5
La Higuera, †6,991 .... A 7
La Laguna, 316 .... F 2
La Ligua, †15,719 .... A 9
La Retuca, 173 .... F 3
La Serena, †71,898 .... A 8
La Unión, †32,010 .... D 3
Lago Ranco, †12,767 .... D 3
Lago Verde, 193 .... E 5
Lagunas, †5,653 .... B 3
Lagunillas, 468 .... F 3
Lampa, †10,220 .... G 3
Lanco, †14,479 .... D 2
Las Breas, 14 .... B 7
Las Cabras †12,119 .... F 5
Las Cruces, 612 .... F 3
Lautaro, †26,011 .... E 2
Lebu, †16,946 .... D 1
Licantén, †6,354 .... A10
Limache, †22,472 .... F 2
Linares, †61,011 .... A11
Llaillay, †14,074 .... G 2
Llico, 330 .... A10
Llolleo, 9,846 .... F 4
Lo Miranda, 2,270 .... G 5
Lo Ovalle, 129 .... F 3
Loica, 446 .... F 4
Loncoche, †17,539 .... D 2
Longaví, †15,909 .... A11
Lonquimay, †9,524 .... E 2
Los Andes, †30,408 .... B 9
Los Ángeles, †89,810 .... D 1
Los Lagos, †14,934 .... D 3
Los Loros, 269 .... A 6
Los Muermos, †9,296 .... D 3
Los Perales de Tapihue, 176 .... F 3
Los Sauces, †7,613 .... D 2
Los Vilos, †10,453 .... A 9
Lota, †51,548 .... D 1
Machalí, †28,415 .... G 5
Maipú, †117,872 .... G 3
Maitencillo, 31 .... A 8
Malloa, †9,742 .... G 5
Mamiña, 341 .... B 2
Manantiales, 291 .... F10
Manzanar, 248 .... F 2
Marchihue, †4,451 .... F 5
María Elena, 9,572 .... B 3
María Pinto, †5,980 .... G 3
Maullín, †14,544 .... D 4
Mayer, 29 .... E 7
Mejillones, †3,333 .... A 4
Melinca, 166 .... D 5
Melipilla, †49,306 .... F 4
Merceditas, 33 .... B 7
Mincha, †11,329 .... A 8
Molina, †30,398 .... A10
Montenegro, 327 .... G 2
Monte Patria, †18,927 .... A 8
Mulchén, †23,379 .... E 1
Nacimiento, †17,651 .... D 1
Nancagua, †11,076 .... F 6
Navidad, †6,618 .... A10
Negreiros, †1,144 .... B 2
Nilahue, 428 .... E 6
Ñiquén, †13,640 .... E 1
Nogales, †18,529 .... F 2
Nueva Imperial, †30,286 .... D 2
Nuevo Juncal, 2 .... B 5
Ocoa, 871 .... G 2
Ollagüe, 333 .... B 3
Olmué, †8,804 .... F 2
Osorno, †105,793 .... D 3
Ovalle, †53,433 .... A 8
Paihuano, †6,048 .... B 8
Paillaco, †13,612 .... D 3
Paine, †21,876 .... G 4
Paipote, 2,278 .... B 6
Palena, †2,508 .... E 5
Palestina, 7 .... B 4
Paliocabe, 77 .... F 4
Palmilla, †12,429 .... F 6
Panguipulli, †32,834 .... E 2
Panquehue, †4,230 .... G 2
Paposo, 87 .... A 5
Papudo, †2,594 .... A 9
Paredones, †7,404 .... A10
Parral, †30,427 .... A11
Pedro de Valdivia, 11,028 .... B 4
Pelequen, 1,068 .... G 5
Pemuco, †7,577 .... E 1
Peñablanca, 5,586 .... F 2
Peñaflor, †37,788 .... G 4
Penco, †33,962 .... D 1
Peñuelas, 359 .... F 3
Peralillo, †7,965 .... F 5
Petorca, †8,343 .... A 9
Petrohué, 40 .... E 3
Peuco, 211 .... G 4
Peumo, †11,308 .... F 5
Pica, †1,487 .... B 2
Pichidegua, †13,550 .... F 5
Pichilemu, †8,042 .... A10
Pintados, 144 .... B 2
Pinto, †8,687 .... A11
Pisagua, †1,880 .... A 2
Pitrufquén, †16,797 .... D 2
Placilla, †6,411 .... F 6
Placilla de Caracoles, 2 .... B 4
Placilla de Peñuelas, 1,495 .... F 2
Población, 1,026 .... F 5
Polonia .... G 6
Pomaire, 1,366 .... F 4
Porvenir, †3,600 .... E10
Potrerillos, 6,168 .... B 6
Pozo Almonte, †1,798 .... B 2
Puangue .... F 4
Pucatrihue, 60 .... D 3
Puchuncaví, †7,542 .... F 2
Pucón, †16,872 .... E 2
Pudahuel, 172 .... G 3
Pueblo Hundido, 2,123 .... B 6
Puente Alto, †81,031 .... B10
Puerto Aisén, †15,000 .... E 6
Puerto Bertrand, 52 .... E 7
Puerto Chacabuco, 130 .... D 6
Puerto Cisnes, †2,800 .... E 5
Puerto Cristal, 698 .... E 6
Puerto Ingeniero Ibáñez, †1,900 .... E 6
Puerto Montt, †86,750 .... E 4
Puerto Natales, †13,577 .... E 9
Puerto Palena, 105 .... D 5
Puerto Quellón, †7,734 .... D 4
Puerto Ramírez, 82 .... E 5
Puerto Saavedra, 805 .... D 2
Puerto Varas, †21,003 .... E 3
Puerto Williams, †949 .... F11
Puerto Yartou, 14 .... E10
Pumanque, †3,137 .... F 6
Punitaqui, †16,167 .... A 8
Punta Arenas, †64,958 .... E10
Punta de Díaz, 11 .... B 7
Puquios, 105 .... B 1
Purén, †11,604 .... D 2
Purranque, †18,201 .... D 3
Putaendo, †12,806 .... A 9
Putre, †855 .... B 1
Puyehue, 39 .... E 3
Quebrada de Alvarado, 429 .... F 2
Queilén, †6,055 .... D 4
Quemchi, †6,707 .... D 4
Queule, 235 .... D 2
Quilicura, †22,644 .... G 3
Quillagua, 288 .... B 3
Quillaicillo, 195 .... A 8
Quilleco, †16,043 .... E 1
Quillota, †49,202 .... F 2
Quilpué, †56,399 .... F 2
Quinta de Tilcoco, †6,513 .... G 5
Quintay, 166 .... F 3
Quintero, †11,847 .... F 2
Quirihue, †11,178 .... E 1
Rancagua, †95,030 .... G 5
Rapel, 699 .... F 4
Reñaca, 1,267 .... F 2
Renca, †67,168 .... G 3
Rengo, †28,230 .... G 5
Requegua, 1,699 .... G 5
Requíhoa, †10,730 .... G 5
Retiro, †15,146 .... A11
Rinconada San Martín, †4,118 .... G 2
Río Blanco, 456 .... B 9
Río Bueno, †28,469 .... D 3
Río Cisnes, 244 .... E 5
Río Negro, †15,582 .... D 3
Río Verde, †554 .... E10
Rivadavia, 443 .... A 7
Rocas de Santo Domingo, †4,114 .... F 4
Rolecha, 573 .... D 4
Rosario, †3,383 .... F 5
Rungue, 312 .... G 2
Salado, 1,375 .... A 6
Salamanca, †18,741 .... A 9
Salinas, 7 .... B 4
Samo Alto, †5,689 .... A 8
San Antonio, †53,100 .... F 3
San Bernardo, †117,766 .... G 4
San Carlos, †30,651 .... E 1
San Clemente, †23,273 .... A11
San Felipe, †34,292 .... G 2
San Félix, 495 .... A 7
San Fernando, †44,160 .... G 6
San Francisco de Mostazal, †11,439 .... G 4
San Francisco del Monte, †14,897 .... G 4
San Ignacio, †13,523 .... E 1
San Javier, †27,592 .... A11
San José de la Mariquina, 2,878 .... D 2
San José de Maipo, †9,601 .... B10
San Pablo, †7,978 .... D 3
San Pedro, Santiago, †8,255 .... F 4
San Pedro, Valparaíso, 1,420 .... F 2
San Pedro de Atacama, 515 .... C 4
San Rosendo, †14,337 .... E 1
San Sebastián, 494 .... F 3
San Vicente, 230 .... F 4
San Vicente (San Vicente de Tagua Tagua), †28,333 .... F 5
Santa Bárbara, †14,345 .... E 1
Santa Cruz, †19,338 .... F 6
Santa María, †8,162 .... G 2
Santiago (capital), 2,596,929 .... G 3
Sewell, 10,866 .... A10
Sierra Gorda, †8,805 .... B 4
Talagante, †23,619 .... G 4
Talca, †102,522 .... A11
Talcahuano, †150,011 .... D 1
Taltal, †7,417 .... A 5
Tamaya, 248 .... A 8
Tarapacá, 130 .... B 2
Temuco, †146,039 .... E 2
Teno, †17,675 .... A10
Termas de Cauquenes, 210 .... B10
Tierra Amarilla, †6,842 .... A 6
Tignamar, 226 .... B 1
Tilomonte, 3 .... B 4
Tiltil, †9,198 .... G 2
Tinguiririca, 1,012 .... G 6
Toco, †8,734 .... B 3
Toconao, 452 .... C 4
Tocopilla, †22,301 .... A 3
Toltén, †16,265 .... D 2
Tomé, †44,480 .... D 1
Tongoy, 935 .... A 8
Totoral, 109 .... A 6
Traiguén, †21,084 .... D 2
Valdivia, †90,942 .... D 3
Valle Alegre, 241 .... F 2
Vallenar, †41,907 .... A 7
Valparaíso, †251,459 .... E 2
Victoria, Malleco, †28,382 .... E 2
Victoria, Tarapacá, 4,943 .... B 3
Vicuña, †13,806 .... A 8
Villa Alemana, †37,547 .... F 2
Villa Alhué, †5,078 .... G 4
Villa Industrial, 28 .... B 1
Villarrica, †23,924 .... E 2
Viña del Mar, †184,332 .... F 2
Yumbel, †21,858 .... E 1
Yungay, †10,725 .... E 1
Zapallar, †2,894 .... A 9

OTHER FEATURES

Aconcagua (river) .... F 2
Aculeo (lagoon) .... G 4
Adventure (bay) .... D 5
Aguas Calientes (mt.) .... C 4
Alhué (river) .... F 4
Almirantazgo (bay) F11
Almeida (mts.) .... C 4
Almirante Montt (gulf) .... D 9
Alto Nevado (mt.) .... E 5
Ancho (channel) .... D 8
Ancud (gulf) .... D 4
Angamos (isl.) .... D 8
Angamos (point) .... A 4
Ap Iwan (mt.) .... E 6
Arauco (gulf) .... D 1
Arenales (mt.) .... D 7
Ascotán (salt deposit) .... B 3
Atacama (desert) .... B 4
Atacama (salt deposit) .... C 4
Aucanquilcha (mt.) .... B 3
Azapa (river) .... B 1
Baker (river) .... D 7
Ballenero (channel) E11
Barrancos (mt.) .... D 7
Bascuñán (cape) .... A 7
Beagle (channel) E11
Bella Vista (salt deposit) .... B 3
Benjamín (isl.), 16 .... D 5
Bertrand (mt.) .... D 8
Bío-Bío (river) .... E 2
Blanca (lagoon) E10
Blanco (lake) F10
Bravo (river) .... D 7
Brunswick (pen.) E10

(continued on following page)

140 Chile

(continued)

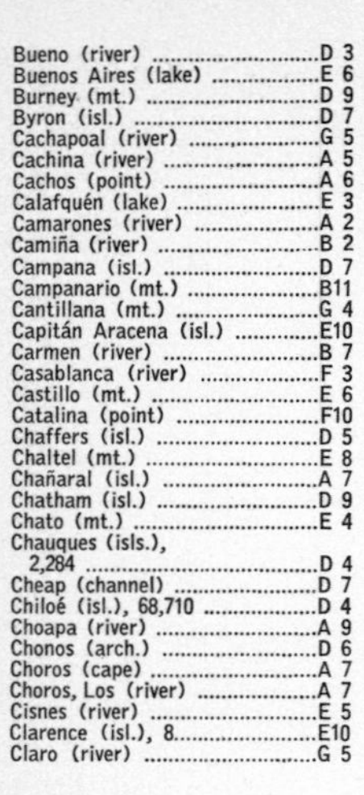

Bueno (river) D 3
Buenos Aires (lake) E 6
Burney (mt.) D 9
Byron (isl.) D 7
Cachapoal (river) G 5
Cachina (river) A 5
Cachos (point) A 6
Calafquén (lake) E 3
Camarones (river) A 2
Camiña (river) B 2
Campana (isl.) D 7
Campanario (mt.) B11
Cantillana (mt.) G 4
Capitán Aracena (isl.) E10
Carmen (river) B 7
Casablanca (river) F 3
Castillo (mt.) E 6
Catalina (point) F10
Chaffers (isl.) D 5
Chaltel (mt.) E 8
Chañaral (isl.) A 7
Chatham (isl.) D 9
Chato (mt.) E 4
Chauques (isls.), 2,284 D 4
Cheap (channel) D 7
Chiloé (isl.), 68,710 D 4
Choapa (river) A 9
Chonos (arch.) D 6
Choros (cape) A 7
Choros, Los (river) A 7
Cisnes (river) E 5
Clarence (isl.), 8 E10
Claro (river) G 5
Clemente (isl.) D 6
Cochrane (lake) E 7
Cochrane (mt.) E 7
Cockburn (channel) E11
Colina (river) G 3
Concepción (channel) D 9
Cónico (mt.) E 4
Contreras (isl.) D 9
Cook (bay) E11
Copiapó (river) A 6
Corcovado (gulf) D 4
Corcovado (vol.) D 5
Coronados (gulf) D 4
Cumbre Negra (mt.) E 5
Curanmilla (point) E 2
Darwin (bay) D 6
Darwin (mts.) E11
Darwin (mts.) D 8
Dawson (isl.), 147 E10
Deseado (cape) D10
Desolación (isl.) D10
Diego de Almagro (isl) D 9
Domeyko (mts.) B 4
Dos Reyes (point) A 5
Drake (passage) E11
Duque de York (isl.) C 9
Dungeness (point) F10
Elefantes (gulf) D 6
Elqui (river) A 8
Esmeralda (isl.) C 8
Eyre (bay) D 8
Fagnano (lake) F11
Fitz Roy (Chaltel) (mt.) E 8
Galera (point) D 3
Gallo (point) E 3
General Paz (lake) E 5
Gordon (isl.) E11
Grafton (isls.) D10
Grande (isl.), 2 A 6
Grande (river) F10
Grande (salt deposit) B 3
Grande de Tierra del Fuego (isl.), 5,467 E11
Guafo (gulf) D 5
Guafo (isl.) D 5
Guaitecas (isls.), 8 D 5
Guamblin (isl.), 851 D 5
Guayaneco (arch.) D 7
Hanover (isl.) D 9
Hardy (pen.) F11
Hermite (isls.) F11
Horn (cape) F11
Hornos, Falso (cape) F11
Hoste (isl.), 20 F11
Huasco (river) A 7
Imperial (river) D 2
Incaguasi (mt.) C 6
Inglesa (bay) A 6
Inútil (bay) E10
Isla (salt deposit) B 5
Itata (river) A11
James (isl.) D 5
Jeinemeni (mt.) E 6
Jervis (mt.) D 8
Johnson (isl.) D 5
Jorge Montt (isl.) D 9
Jorquera (river) B 6
Juan Stuven (isl.) D 7

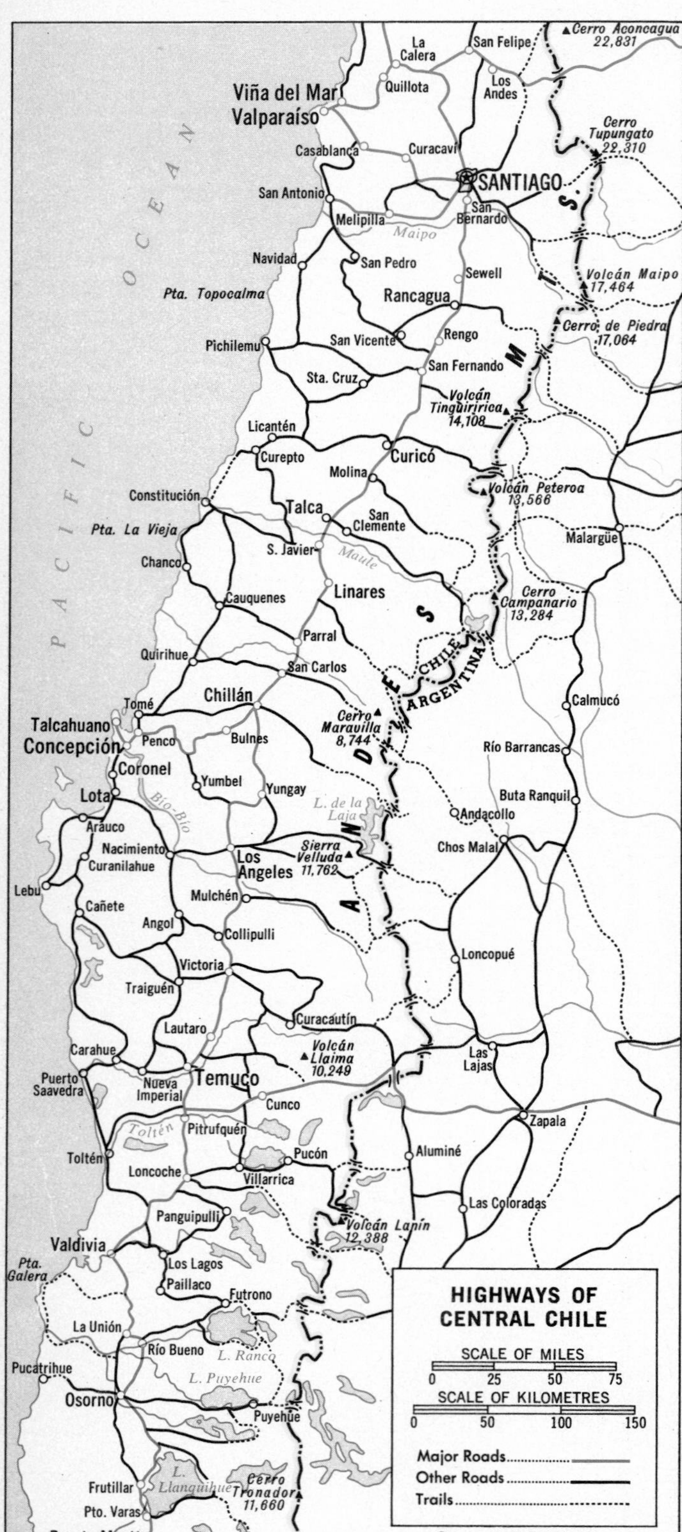

Agriculture, Industry and Resources

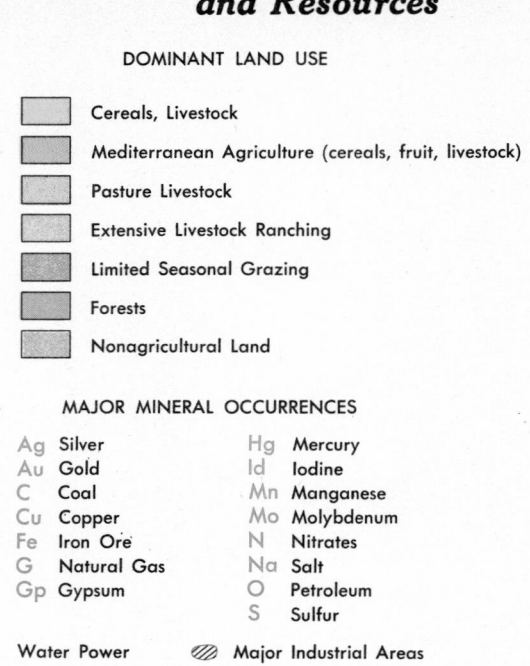

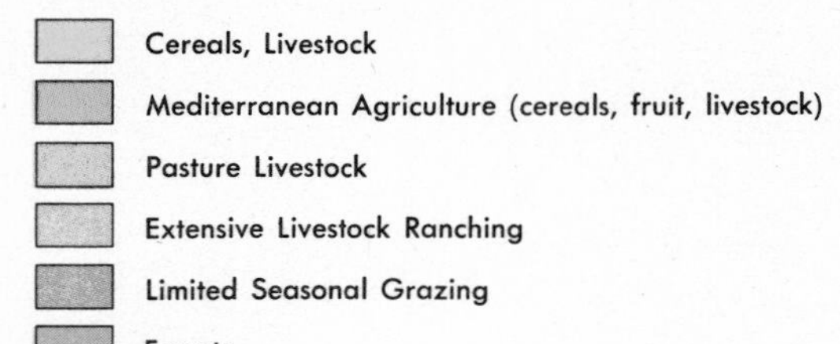

MAJOR MINERAL OCCURRENCES

Ag Silver
Au Gold
C Coal
Cu Copper
Fe Iron Ore
G Natural Gas
Gp Gypsum
Hg Mercury
Id Iodine
Mn Manganese
Mo Molybdenum
N Nitrates
Na Salt
O Petroleum
S Sulfur

Water Power
Major Industrial Areas

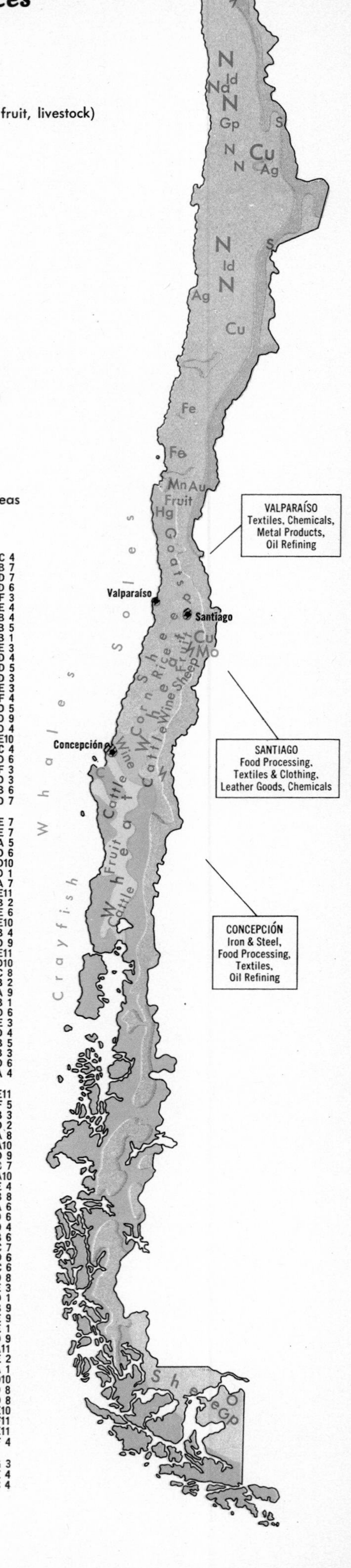

La Ligua (river) A 9
Lacuy (pen.) D 4
Ladrillero (gulf) C 8
Ladrillero (mt.) E10
Laja (lagoon) E 1
Laja (river) E 1
Lanín (vol.) E 2
Lastarria (vol.) B 5
Lauca (river) B 1
Lavapié (point) D 1
Lengua de Vaca (point) A 8
Lennox (isl.) F11
Licancábur (mt.) B 4
Liles (point) F 2
Limarí (river) A 8
Llaima (vol.) E 2
Llamara (salt deposit) B 3
Llanquihue (lake) E 3
Llullaillaco (vol.) B 5
Lluta (river) B 1
Loa (river) B 3
Lobos (point) A 3
Lóndonderry (isl.) E11
Loros (point) E 3
Luis de Saboya (mt.) F11
Luz (isl.), 23 D 6
Macá (mt.) D 5
Madre de Dios (isl.) D 8
Magdalena (isl.) D 5
Magellan (Magallanes) (strait) D10
Maipo (river) F 4
Maipo (vol.) B10
Manso (river) E 4
Manuel Rodríguez (isl.) D10
Mapocho (river) G 3
Maricunga (salt deposit) B 6
Mataquito (river) A10
Maule (river) A11
Maullín (river) D 3
Mejillones del Sur (bay) A 4
Melchor (isl.), 12 D 6
Melimoyu (mt.) D 5
Merino Jarpa (isl.) D 7
Minchinmávida (vol.) E 4
Miraje (salt deposit) B 3
Mocha (isl.), 689 D 2
Molles (point) A 9
Morado (river) A 6
Moraleda (channel) D 5
Moreno (bay) A 4
Morguilla (point) D 1
Mornington (isl.) D 8
Morro (point) A 6
Muñoz Gamero (pen.) D10
Murallón (mt.) D 8
Nalcayec (isl.) D 6
Nassau (bay) F11
Navarino (isl.), 436 F11
Nelson (strait) D 9
Nevados de Poquis (mt.) C 4
Noir (isl.) E11
Nuestra Señora (bay) A 5
Nueva (isl.) F11
Núñez (isl.) D10
O'Higgins (lake) D 7
Ofqui (isthmus) D 6
Ojos del Salado (mt.) B 6
Olivares (mt.) B 8
Ollagüe (vol.) C 3
Otway (bay) D10
Otway (sound) E10
Paine (mt.) D 9
Paipote (river) B 6
Pájaros (isls.) A 7
Palena (lake) E 5
Palena (river) D 5
Pan de Azúcar (river) B 5
Parinacota (mt.) B 1
Pascua (river) D 7
Patricio Lynch (isl.) D 7
Pedernales (salt deposit) B 5
Penas (gulf) D 7
Peñuelas (lake) F 2
Perquilauquén (river) A11
Peteroa (vol.) B10
Piazzí (isl.) D 9
Picton (isl.) F11
Pilmaiquén (river) D 3
Pintados (salt deposit) B 2
Pirámide (mt.) D 8
Poquis, Nevados de (mt.) C 4
Potro (mt.) B 7
Prat (isl.) D 7
Presidente Ríos (lake) D 6
Puangue (river) F 3
Puelo (river) E 4
Púlar (mt.) B 4
Punta Negra (salt deposit) B 5
Puquintica (mt.) B 1
Puyehue (lake) E 3
Quilán (cape) D 4
Quilán (isl.) D 5
Rahue (river) D 3
Ranco (lake) E 3
Rapel (river) F 4
Refugio (isl.) D 5
Reina Adelaida (arch.) D 9
Reloncaví (bay) D 4
Riesco (isl.), 264 E10
Rincón (mt.) C 4
Rivero (isl.) D 6
Rosario (river) F 3
Rupanco (lake) D 3
Salado (river) B 6
San Esteban (gulf) D 7
San Lorenzo (Cochrane) (mt.) E 7
San Martín (lake) E 7
San Pedro (point) A 5
San Valentín (mt.) D 6
Santa Inés (isl.) D10
Santa María (isl.), 74 D 1
Sarco (bay) A 7
Sarmiento (mt.) E11
Sillajguay (mt.) B 2
Simpson (river) E 6
Skyring (bay) E10
Socompa (vol.) B 4
Staines (pen.) D 9
Stewart (isl.) E11
Stokes (bay) D10
Stosch (isl.) C 8
Surire (salt deposit) B 2
Tablas (cape) A 9
Tacora (vol.) B 1
Taitao (pen.) D 6
Talca (point) E 3
Talcán (isl.) D 4
Taltal (river) B 5
Tamarugal (plain) B 3
Tenquehuen (isl.) D 6
Tetas (point) A 4
Tierra del Fuego, Grande de (isl.), 5,467 E11
Tinquiririca (river) F 5
Tocorpuri (mt.) B 3
Toltén (river) D 2
Tongoy (bay) A 8
Topocalma (point) A10
Toro (lake) D 9
Toro (mt.) E 7
Toro (point) A10
Torre, La (mt.) E 4
Tortolas (mt.) B 8
Totoral (river) A 6
Traiguén (isl.), 23 D 6
Tranqui (isl.) D 4
Tres Cruces (mt.) B 6
Tres Montes (cape) C 7
Tres Montes (gulf) D 6
Tres Montes (pen.) C 6
Trinidad (gulf) D 8
Tronador (mt.) E 3
Tumbes (pen.) D 1
Tupungato (mt.) B 9
Última Esperanza (sound) E 9
Velluda (mt.) E 1
Vidal Gormaz (isl.) D 9
Vieja, La (point) A11
Villarrica (lake) E 2
Vitor (river) A 1
Week (isls.) D10
Wellington (isl.), 47 D 8
Wharton (pen.) D 8
Whiteside (channel) E10
Wollaston (isls.) F11
Wood (isls.) E11
Yali (river) F 4
Yaretas de Vizcachas (mt.) G 3
Yelcho (lake) E 4
Zapaleri (mt.) C 4

†Population of commune.

PROVINCES

Buenos Aires, 6,734,548 ....D 4
Catamarca, 172,407 ....C 2
Chaco, 535,443 ....D 2
Chubut, 142,195 ....C 5
Córdoba, 1,759,997 ....D 3
Corrientes, 543,226 ....E 2
Distrito Federal (fed. dist.), 2,966,816 ....H 7
Entre Ríos, 803,505 ....E 3
Formosa, 178,458 ....D 1
Jujuy, 239,783 ....C 1
La Pampa, 158,489 ....C 4
La Rioja, 128,270 ....C 2
Mendoza, 825,535 ....C 4
Misiones, 391,094 ....F 2
Neuquén, 111,008 ....C 4
Río Negro, 192,595 ....C 5
Salta, 412,652 ....D 1
San Juan, 352,461 ....C 3
San Luis, 174,251 ....C 3
Santa Cruz, 52,853 ....C 6
Santa Fe, 1,865,537 ....D 3
Santiago del Estero, 477,156 ....D 2
Tierra del Fuego, Antártida e Islas del Atlántico Sur (terr.), 13,452 ....C 7
Tucumán, 780,348 ....C 2

CITIES and TOWNS

Abra Pampa, 1,391 ....C 1
Acebal, 2,026 ....F 6
Acevedo. 1,057 ....F 6
Acuña, 805 ....G 5
Adolfo Alsina, 5,836 ....D 4
Aguilares, 9,816 ....C 2
Aimogasta, 2,721 ....C 2
Alberti, 4,447 ....G 7
Alcaraz, 376 ....G 5
Alcorta, 3,781 ....F 6
Alejandra, 881 ....F 5
Allen, 11,389 ....C 4
Alpachiri, 733 ....D 4
Alta Gracia, 11,570 ....D 3
Aluminé, 744 ....B 4
Alvear, 4,252 ....E 2
Ameghino, 2,770 ....D 3
Aminga, 480 ....C 2
Añatuya, 11,753 ....D 2
Anchorena, 862 ....C 4
Andacollo, 587 ....B 4
Andalgalá, 3,260 ....C 2
Angélica, 434 ....E 5
Anguil, 734 ....D 4
Antofagasta de la Sierra, 462 ....C 2
Apóstoles, 6,507 ....E 2
Arrecifes, 7,635 ....F 6
Arribeños, 1,739 ....F 7
Arroyo Seco, 5,193 ....F 6
Ascensión, 1,775 ....F 7
Astra, 1,019 ....C 6
Avellaneda, †329,626 ....G 7
Ayacucho, 9,220 ....E 4
Azul, 28,609 ....E 4
Bahía Blanca, †150,354 ....D 4
Bahía Thetis, †438 ....C 7
Baibiene, 380 ....G 4
Baigorrita, 1,206 ....F 7
Balcarce, 15,210 ....E 4
Balnearia, 4,306 ....D 3
Bañado de Ovanta, 198 ....C 2
Bandera, 2,035 ....D 2
Baradero, 10,194 ....G 6
Barrancas, 1,953 ....F 6
Barranqueras, 19,779 ....E 2
Barreal, 1,790 ....C 3
Basavilbaso, 6,614 ....G 6
Batavia, 457 ....C 3
Beazley, 1,070 ....C 3
Belén, 5,469 ....C 2
Bella Vista, Corrientes, 8,334 ....E 2
Bella Vista, Tucumán, 6,816 ......D 2
Bell Ville, 15,796 ....D 3
Bernardo de Irigoyen, 1,400........F 2
Bolívar, 14,010 ....D 4
Bovril, 1,955 ....G 5
Bragado, 16,104 ....F 7
Buenos Aires (capital), 3,549,000 ....H 7
Buenos Aires, *9,070,000 ....H 7
Bustinza, 918 ....F 6
Cachi, 491 ....C 2
Cafayate, 2,407 ....C 2
Calchaqui, 2,782 ....F 5
Caleta Olivia, 3,639 ....C 6
Caleufú, 1,197 ....D 4
Camarones, 501 ....D 5
Campana, 14,452 ....G 6
Campo Gallo, 2,336 ....D 2
Cañada de Gómez, 12,354 ....F 6
Cañada Honda, 345 ....C 3
Canals, 5,359 ....D 3
Cañuelas, 5,614 ....G 7
Carabelas, 3,476 ....F 6
Carcaraña, 4,516 ....F 6
Carlos Casares, 7,558 ....F 7
Carlos Tejedor, 2,897 ....D 4
Carmen de Areco, 4,411 ....F 7
Carmen de Patagones, 5,423 ....D 5
Caseros, 4,975 ....D 4
Casilda, 11,023 ....F 6
Castelli, Buenos Aires, 3,263 .....H 7
Castelli, Chaco, 4,131 ....D 2
Catamarca, 45,929 ....C 2
Catriló, 1,794 ....D 4
Cayasta, 592 ....F 5
Cayastacito, 483 ....F 5
Cereales, 367 ....D 4
Ceres, 6,525 ....D 2
Chabas, 2,937 ....F 6
Chacabuco, 12,530 ....F 7
Chajarí, 9,075 ....G 5
Chamical, 3,756 ....C 3
Charadai, 1,872 ....D 2
Charata, 8,953 ....D 2
Chascomús, 9,105 ....H 7
Chepes, 2,941 ....C 3
Chicoana, 1,093 ....C 2
Chilecito, 9,809 ....C 2
Chivilcoy, 23,386 ....F 7
Choele-Choel, 3,079 ....C 4
Chos Malal, 2,874 ....C 4
Chumbicha, 2,188 ....C 2
Cinco Saltos, 10,196 ....C 4
Cipolletti, 19,862 ....C 4
Clarke, 506 ....F 6
Clodomira, 4,685 ....D 2
Clorinda, 10,043 ....E 2
Colón, Buenos Aires, 5,628 ....F 6

AREA 1,072,070
POPULATION 23,983,000
CAPITAL Buenos Aires
LARGEST CITY Buenos Aires
HIGHEST POINT Cerro Aconcagua 22,831 ft.
MONETARY UNIT Argentine peso
MAJOR LANGUAGE Spanish
MAJOR RELIGION Roman Catholicism

Agriculture, Industry and Resources

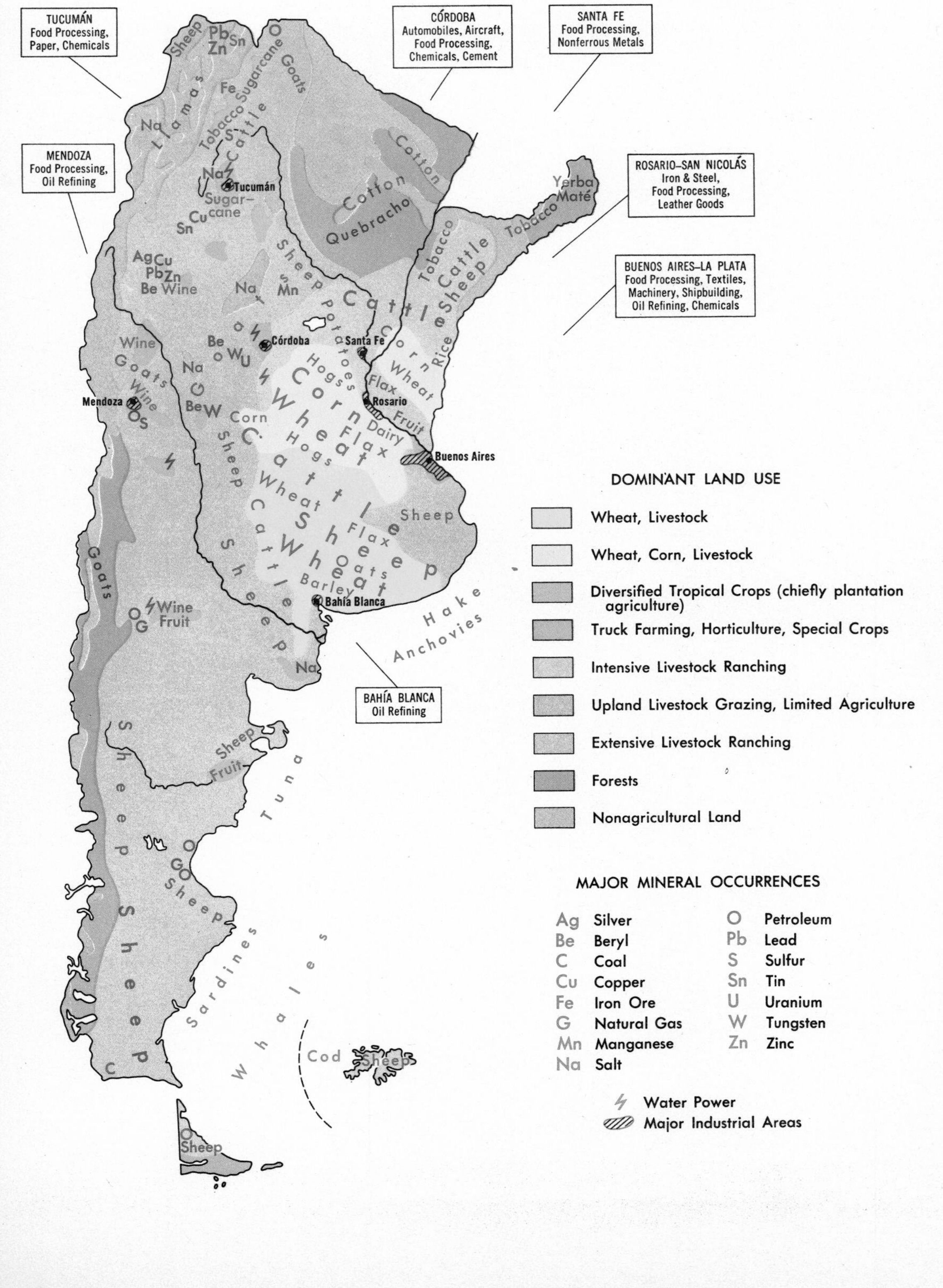

TUCUMÁN
Food Processing, Paper, Chemicals

CÓRDOBA
Automobiles, Aircraft, Food Processing, Chemicals, Cement

SANTA FE
Food Processing, Nonferrous Metals

MENDOZA
Food Processing, Oil Refining

ROSARIO–SAN NICOLÁS
Iron & Steel, Food Processing, Leather Goods

BUENOS AIRES–LA PLATA
Food Processing, Textiles, Machinery, Shipbuilding, Oil Refining, Chemicals

BAHÍA BLANCA
Oil Refining

DOMINANT LAND USE

- Wheat, Livestock
- Wheat, Corn, Livestock
- Diversified Tropical Crops (chiefly plantation agriculture)
- Truck Farming, Horticulture, Special Crops
- Intensive Livestock Ranching
- Upland Livestock Grazing, Limited Agriculture
- Extensive Livestock Ranching
- Forests
- Nonagricultural Land

MAJOR MINERAL OCCURRENCES

Ag	Silver	O	Petroleum
Be	Beryl	Pb	Lead
C	Coal	S	Sulfur
Cu	Copper	Sn	Tin
Fe	Iron Ore	U	Uranium
G	Natural Gas	W	Tungsten
Mn	Manganese	Zn	Zinc
Na	Salt		

Water Power
Major Industrial Areas

Colón, Entre Ríos, 6,813 ....G 6
Colonia Elisa, 1,338 ....E 2
Colonia Las Heras, 1,880 ....C 6
Comandante Fontana, 1,686 ....D 2
Comandante Luis Piedrabuena, 1,441 ....C 6
Comodoro Rivadavia, 35,966 ......C 6
Concepción, Corrientes, 2,593 ....E 2
Concepción, Tucumán, 15,832 .....C 2
Concepción del Uruguay, 36,486 ....G 6
Concordia, 56,654 ....G 5
Copacabana, 957 ....C 2
Córdoba, †589,153 ....D 3
Coronda, 4,656 ....F 6
Coronel Bogado, 1,264 ....F 6
Coronel Brandsen, 3,803 ....H 7
Coronel Dorrego, 7,245 ....D 4
Coronel Moldes, 1,695 ....C 2
Coronel Pringles, 12,844 ....D 4
Coronel Suárez, 11,133 ....D 4
Corral de Bustos, 3,900 ....D 3
Corrientes, 97,507 ....E 2
Cosquín, 7,746 ....D 3
Crespo, 5,706 ....F 6
Cruz del Eje, 15,563 ....C 3
Cuadro Nacional, 1,879 ....C 3
Curuzú Cuatiá, 16,567 ....G 5
Cutral-Có, 11,292 ....C 4
Deán Funes, 13,840 ....D 3
Del Carril, 475 ....G 7
Diamante, 10,948 ....F 6
Díaz, 1,288 ....F 6
Doblas, 902 ....D 4
Dolavón, 1,277 ....C 5
Dolores, 14,438 ....E 4
Dudignac, 1,503 ....F 7
Eduardo Castex, 4,020 ....D 4
El Bolsón, 2,607 ....B 5
El Calafate, 567 ....B 7
El Chorro, 377 ....D 1
Eldorado, 2,778 ....F 2
El Huecu, 298 ....B 4
Elisa, 579 ....F 5
El Maitén, 2,382 ....B 5
Elortondo, 3,514 ....F 6
El Pintado, 388 ....D 1
El Quebrachal, 1,212 ....D 2
Embarcación, 6,371 ....D 1
Emilio Ayarza, 1,357 ....F 7
Empedrado, 3,735 ....E 2
Enrique Carbó, 956 ....G 6
Ensenada, †35,030 ....H 7
Escobar, 3,693 ....G 7
Esperanza, 10,035 ....F 5
Esquel, 9,900 ....B 5
Esquina, 7,619 ....G 5
Famatina, 1,330 ....C 2
Federación, 4,247 ....G 5
Fernández, 3,115 ....D 2
Fiambalá, 1,450 ....C 2
Firmat, 4,051 ....F 6
Fives Lille, 667 ....F 5
Formosa, 36,499 ....E 2
French, 4,007 ....F 7
Frías, 11,862 ....D 2
Gaiman, 1,286 ....C 5
Gálvez, 2,475 ....F 6
Gálvez, 7,891 ....F 6
Gan Gan, 281 ....C 5
General Acha, 4,709 ....C 4
General Alvarado, 3,537 ....E 4
General Alvear, Buenos Aires, 2,548 ....F 7
General Alvear, Mendoza, 12,325 ....C 3
General Arenales, 2,182 ....F 7
General Belgrano, 3,789 ....G 7
General Campos, 1,400 ....G 5
General Conesa, 716 ....C 5
General Galarza, 2,435 ....G 6
General Juan Madariaga, 7,073 ....E 4
General José de San Martín, 5,390 ....E 2
General La Madrid, 3,572 ....D 4
General Las Heras, 3,820 ....G 7
General Lavalle, 1,663 ....E 4
Gral. M. M. de Güemes, 8,748....D 1
General O'Brien, 2,988 ....F 7
General Paz, 1,689 ....E 2
General Pico, 11,121 ....D 4
General Roca, 21,969 ....C 4
General San Martín, 2,501 ....D 4
General Villegas, 4,738 ....D 4
Gobernador Crespo, 6,000 ....F 5
Gobernador Gregores, 772 ....C 6
Gobernador Mansilla, 947 ....G 6
Godoy Cruz, 80,024 ....C 3
Goya, 30,011 ....G 4
Gualeguay, 16,542 ....G 6
Gualeguaychú, 29,863 ....G 6
Guandacol, 1,255 ....C 2
Guardia Mitre, 746 ....D 5
Guatrache, 1,259 ....D 4
Guaymallén, 85,718 ....C 3
Hasenkamp, 1,789 ....F 5
Helvecia, 3,390 ....F 5
Hernández, 283 ....F 6
Hernando, 4,869 ....D 3
Herradura, 1,679 ....E 2
Herrera, 1,685 ....D 2
Huinca Renancó, 4,391 ....D 3
Humahuaca, 2,530 ....C 1
Humberto, 3,434 ....F 5
Ibarreta, 4,366 ....D 2
Ibicuy, 3,356 ....G 6
Icaño, Catamarca, 1,114 ....C 2
Icaño, Santiago del Estero, 1,926 ....D 2
Iglesia, 575 ....C 3
Ingeniero Huergo, 3,083 ....C 4
Ingeniero Jacobacci, 2,656 ....C 5
Ingeniero Luiggi, 1,665 ....D 4
Intendente Alvear, 2,760 ....D 4
Irigoyen, 3,500 ....F 6
Itacaruaré, 422 ....F 2
Jáchal, 6,886 ....C 3
Jaramillo, 437 ....C 6
Jesús María, 6,284 ....D 3
Joaquín V. González, 3,274 ....D 2
Jobson, 7,667 ....F 5
José de San Martín, 1,143 ....B 5
José M. Micheo, 1,165 ....G 7
Juan B. Arruabarrena, 1,997 ....G 5
Juan B. Molino, 1,483 ....F 6
Juan Ortíz, 6,240 ....F 6
Juan Pujol, 625 ....G 5
Juárez, 7,602 ....D 4
Jujuy, 44,188 ....C 1
Juncal, 943 ....F 6
Junín, 36,149 ....F 7
Junín de los Andes, 1,183 ....B 4
La Banda, 23,772 ....D 2
Labougle, 503 ....G 5
Laboulaye, 9,032 ....D 3
La Clarita, 389 ....G 5
La Cumbre, 3,961 ....C 3
La Esmeralda, 348 ....G 5
La Falda, 2,847 ....D 3
La Gallareta, 3,736 ....F 5
Lago Argentino (El Calafate), 567 ....B 7
Laguna Paiva, 7,196 ....F 5
Lanús, 381,561 ....H 7
La Paz, Entre Ríos, 11,028 ....G 5
La Paz, Mendoza, 2,502 ....C 3
La Plata, †330,310 ....H 7
La Quiaca, 6,290 ....C 1
La Rioja, 35,431 ....C 2
Las Flores, 9,287 ....E 4
Las Lajas, 1,805 ....B 4
Las Lomitas, 1,650 ....D 1
Las Palmas, 3,590 ....E 2
Las Parejas, 1,973 ....F 6
Las Plumas, 182 ....C 5
Las Rosas, 6,153 ....F 6
Las Varillas, 5,950 ....D 3
La Toma, 2,352 ....C 3
Lavalle, 1,571 ....G 4
Leleque, 401 ....B 5
Lezama, 1,962 ....H 7
Libertador General San Martín, Jujuy, 5,051 ....D 1
Libertador General San Martín, Misiones, 2,267 ....E 2
Lincoln, 12,695 ....F 7
Lobería, 7,916 ....E 4
Lobos, 8,372 ....G 7
Lomas de Zamora, †275,219 ....G 7
Loncopué, 856 ....B 4
Los Antiguos, 709 ....B 6
Los Menucos, 1,749 ....C 5
Los Toldos, 5,342 ....F 7
Lucas González, 1,145 ....G 6
Luján, 19,176 ....G 7
Lules, 4,828 ....C 2
Macachín, 1,793 ....D 4
Maciel, 1,832 ....F 6
Magdalena, 4,114 ....H 7
Maipú, 5,469 ....E 4
Makallé, 1,462 ....E 2
Malabrigo, 1,532 ....F 4
Malargüe, 4,523 ....C 4
Manucho, 2,800 ....F 5
Maquinchao, 1,851 ....C 5
Mar del Plata, 141,886 ....E 4
Marcos Juárez, 9,556 ....D 3
Marcos Paz, 4,115 ....G 7
Margarita, 1,461 ....F 5
María Grande, 2,819 ....F 5
Mburucuyá, 2,555 ....E 2
Médanos, Buenos Aires, 2,229 ....D 4
Médanos, Entre Ríos, 647 ....G 6
Mencué, 208 ....C 5
Mendoza, 109,122 ....C 3
Mercedes, Buenos Aires, 16,932 ....G 7

(continued on following page)

(continued)

Mercedes, Corrientes, 13,368 ..... G 4
Mercedes, San Luis, 35,449 ..... C 3
Merlo, 8,385 ..... G 7
Metán, 12,849 ..... D 2
Milagro, 1,967 ..... C 3
Miñones, 204 ..... G 5
Miramar (General Alvarado), 3,537 ..... E 4
Moisés Ville, 3,166 ..... E 5
Molinos, 174 ..... C 2
Monte, 2,491 ..... G 7
Monte Caseros, 12,930 ..... G 5
Monte Comán, 4,278 ..... C 3
Monte Quemado, 4,083 ..... D 2
Monteros, 11,938 ..... C 2
Morteros, 5,993 ..... D 3
Mosconi, 333 ..... F 7
Naré, 346 ..... F 5
Navarro, 2,547 ..... G 7
Necochea, 17,808 ..... E 4
Nelson, 866 ..... F 5
Neuquén, 16,738 ..... C 4
Niquivil, 1,301 ..... C 3
Nogoyá, 10,911 ..... F 6
Norberto de la Riestra, 2,809 ..... G 7
Ñorquincó, 602 ..... B 5
Nueve (9) de Julio, 13,678 ..... F 7
Obera, 12,322 ..... F 2
Olavarría, 24,204 ..... D 4
Oliva, 8,701 ..... D 3
Olta, 1,226 ..... C 3
Orán, 14,286 ..... D 1
Ordoqui, 402 ..... F 7
Palo Santo, 1,123 ..... E 2
Pampa del Chañar, 1,521 ..... C 2
Pampa del Infierno, 1,261 ..... D 2
Paraná, 107,551 ..... F 5
Paso de Indios, 1,067 ..... C 5
Paso de los Libres, 15,054 ..... E 2
Patquía, 839 ..... C 3
Paz, 2,495 ..... F 6
Pedernal, 250 ..... G 5
Pehuajó, 13,537 ..... D 4
Pellegrini, 2,310 ..... D 4
Pérez, 3,433 ..... F 6
Pergamino, 32,382 ..... F 6
Perito Moreno, 1,587 ..... B 6
Perugorria 1,110 ..... G 4
Pico Truncado, 1,527 ..... C 6
Pigüé, 5,869 ..... D 4
Pila, 1,009 ..... H 7
Pilar, 2,508 ..... F 5
Pipinas, 658 ..... H 7
Pirané, 5,285 ..... E 2
Plaza Huincul, 4,906 ..... B 4
Pomán, 1,100 ..... C 2
Posadas, 70,691 ..... E 2
Pozo Hondo, 872 ..... D 2
Presidencia de la Plaza, 4,568 ..... D 2
Presidencia Roque Sáenz Peña, 14,381 ..... D 2
Puán, 3,191 ..... D 4
Puerto Coyle, 251 ..... C 7
Puerto Deseado, 3,120 ..... D 6
Puerto Madryn, 5,586 ..... C 5
Puerto Pirámides, 425 ..... D 5
Punta Alta, 19,852 ..... D 4
Quebracho Coto. 271 ..... D 2
Quemú-Quemú, 2,735 ..... D 4
Quequén, 4,760 ..... E 4
Quimilí, 2,902 ..... D 2
Quines, 3,319 ..... C 3
Quiroga, 1,827 ..... F 7
Quitilipi, 5,217 ..... D 2
Rafaela, 23,665 ..... F 5
Raíces, 452 ..... G 6
Ramallo, 4,824 ..... F 6
Ranchos, 2,475 ..... H 7
Rauch, 5,274 ..... E 4
Rawson, Buenos Aires, 2,425 ..... F 7
Rawson, Chubut, 4,109 ..... D 5
Reconquista, 12,729 ..... D 2
Recreo, 2,834 ..... C 2
Resistencia, 84,036 ..... E 2
Rigby, 737 ..... F 6
Rinconada, 782 ..... C 1
Río Colorado, Río Negro, 5,892 ..... D 4
Río Cuarto, 48,706 ..... D 3
Río Gallegos, 14,439 ..... C 7
Río Grande, 5,103 ..... C 7
Río Segundo, 5,873 ..... D 3
Río Tercero, 10,683 ..... D 3
Rivadavia, Mendoza, 14,358 ..... C 3
Rivadavia, Salta, 215 ..... D 1
Rivas, 429 ..... G 7
Rojas, 6,608 ..... F 7
Roldán, 3,402 ..... F 6
Romang, 1,906 ..... F 4
Roque Pérez, 2,841 ..... G 7
Rosario, †671,852 ..... F 6
Rosario de la Frontera, 7,134 ..... D 2
Rosario de Lerma, 4,241 ..... C 1
Rosario del Tala, 7,350 ..... G 6
Rufino, 10,987 ..... D 3
Saforcada, 146 ..... F 7
Saladas, 3,883 ..... E 2
Saladillo, 7,586 ..... G 7
Salta, 117,400 ..... C 1
San Andrés de Giles, 5,392 ..... G 7
San Antonio de Areco, 7,436 ..... G 7
San Antonio de los Cobres, 1,439 ..... C 1
San Antonio Oeste, 5,278 ..... C 5
San Carlos, Corrientes, 1,858 ..... E 2
San Carlos, Mendoza, 809 ..... C 3
San Carlos, Santa Fe, 3,126 ..... F 5
San Carlos de Bariloche, 15,995 ..... B 5
San Cristóbal, 9,071 ..... F 5
San Fernando, †91,644 ..... G 7
San Francisco, Córdoba, 24,354 ..... D 3
San Francisco, San Luis, 1,864 ..... C 3
San Francisco del Chañar, 817 ..... C 2
San Genaro, 1,522 ..... F 6
San Ignacio, 2,106 ..... E 2
San Isidro, 2,271 ..... C 2
San Javier, Río Negro, 370 ..... D 5
San Javier, Santa Fe, 2,961 ..... F 5
San José, 2,188 ..... G 6
San José de Feliciano, 3,721 ..... G 5
San Juan, 106,564 ..... C 3
San Julián, 3,649 ..... C 6
San Justo, 6,571 ..... F 5
San Lorenzo, 11,109 ..... F 6
San Luis, 40,420 ..... C 3
San Martín, 20,466 ..... C 3
San Martín de los Andes, 4,567 ..... C 5
San Martín Norte, 485 ..... F 5
San Miguel, 1,300 ..... E 2
San Nicolás. 25,029 ..... G 6
San Pedro, Buenos Aires, 12,778 ..... F 6
San Pedro, Jujuy, 15,354 ..... D 1
San Rafael, 46,599 ..... C 3
San Salvador, 2,108 ..... G 5
San Sebastián, †3,154 ..... C 7
Santa Catalina, 331 ..... C 1
Santa Clara, 3,700 ..... F 6
Santa Cruz, 1,178 ..... C 7
Santa Elena, 8,174 ..... F 5
Santa Fe, †259,560 ..... F 5
Santa Lucia, Buenos Aires, 1,831 ..... F 6
Santa Lucia, Corrientes, 2,930 ..... E 2
Santa María, 2,826 ..... C 2
Santa Rosa, Córdoba, 2,999 ..... D 3
Santa Rosa, La Pampa, 14,623 ..... C 4
Santa Rosa, San Luis, 2,880 ..... C 3
Santa Victoria, 165 ..... D 1
Santiago del Estero, 80,395 ..... D 2
Santo Tomé, Corrientes, 10,121 ..... E 2
Santo Tomé Santa Fe, 4,446 ..... F 5
San Urbano, 1,721 ..... F 6
Sarmiento, 4,922 ..... B 6
Sauce, 3,448 ..... G 5
Sauce Luna, 501 ..... G 5
Seguí, 2,161 ..... G 6
Selva, 1,070 ..... D 2
Sierra Colorada, 541 ..... C 5
Sierra Grande, 512 ..... C 5
Solari, 1,636 ..... G 4
Soledad, 794 ..... F 5
Suipacha, 3,006 ..... G 7
Sunchales, 5,048 ..... F 5
Suncho Corral, 2,693 ..... D 2
Susana, 484 ..... F 5
Susques, 537 ..... C 1
Tafí Viejo, 21.197 ..... C 2
Tamberías, 1,129 ..... C 3
Tandil, 32,309 ..... E 4
Tapalquén, 3,018 ..... E 4
Tartagal, 16,740 ..... D 1
Telsen, 490 ..... C 5
Tigre, †91,824 ..... G 7
Tilcara, 1,675 ..... C 1
Tinogasta, 3,557 ..... C 2
Tintina, 1,500 ..... D 2
Toay, 2,457 ..... D 4
Tornquist, 2,782 ..... D 4
Tostado, 5,234 ..... D 2
Trelew, 11,852 ..... C 5
Trenel, 1,206 ..... D 4
Trenque Lauquen, 10,887 ..... D 4
Tres Arroyos, 29,996 ..... D 4
Tres Lomas, 3,425 ..... D 4
Trevelín, 1,642 ..... B 5
Tricao Malal, 370 ..... C 4
Tucumán, 271,546 ..... D 2
Tunuyán, 9,781 ..... C 3
Ulapes, 438 ..... C 3
Unión, 630 ..... C 3
Urdinarrain, 3,484 ..... G 6
Ushuaia, 4,950 ..... C 7
Valcheta, 1,697 ..... C 5
Valle Fértil, 1,293 ..... C 3
Vedia, 3,676 ..... F 7
Veinticinco (25) de Mayo, 9,063 ..... F 7
Venado Tuerto, 15,947 ..... D 3
Vergara, 1,077 ..... H 7
Verónica, 2,405 ..... H 7
Victoria, 15,108 ..... F 6
Victorica, 2,475 ..... C 4
Vicuña Mackenna, 3,032 ..... D 3
Viedma, 7,253 ..... D 5
Villa Ana, 5,413 ..... E 2
Villa Ángela, 18,518 ..... D 2
Villa Atamisqui, 1,122 ..... D 2
Villa Atuel, 6,072 ..... C 3
Villa Bustos, 1,314 ..... C 2
Villa Cañas, 7,099 ..... F 6
Villa Clara, 1,557 ..... G 5
Villa Constitución, 9,183 ..... F 6
Villa del Rosario, 4,461 ..... D 3
Villa Dolores, 13,835 ..... C 2
Villa Domínguez, 984 ..... G 6
Villa Elisa, 2,715 ..... G 6
Villa Federal, 5,256 ..... G 5
Villa General Ramírez, 3,203 ..... F 6
Villa General Roca, 325 ..... C 3
Villaguay, 12,463 ..... G 5
Villa Guillermina, 7,471 ..... D 2
Villa Hernandarias, 2,788 ..... F 5
Villalonga, 392 ..... D 5
Villa Larroque, 1,993 ..... G 6
Villa Mantero, 989 ..... G 6
Villa María, 30,362 ..... D 3
Villa Ocampo, 4,897 ..... D 2
Villa Ojo de Agua, 1,505 ..... D 2
Villa Regina, 11,360 ..... C 4
Villa San Martín, 3,354 ..... D 2
Villa Unión, 1,696 ..... C 2
Vinchina, 395 ..... C 2
Winifreda, 1,063 ..... D 4
Yacimiento Río Turbio, 3,506 ..... B 7
Yofré, 826 ..... G 4
Zapala, 7,497 ..... B 4
Zárate, 35,197 ..... G 6
Zavalla, 1,799 ..... F 6

OTHER FEATURES

Aconcagua (mt.) ..... C 3
Alerces, Los (park) ..... C 5
Andes (mts.) ..... C 2
Argentino (lake) ..... B 7
Arizaro (salt dep.) ..... C 2
Arrecifes (river) ..... G 6
Atacama, Puna de (reg.) ..... C 2
Atuel (river) ..... C 4
Barrancas (river) ..... G 5
Bermejo (river) ..... E 2
Blanca (bay) ..... D 4
Brazo Sur (river) ..... E 1
Buenos Aires (lake) ..... B 6
Campanario (mt.) ..... C 4
Chaco Austral (reg.) ..... D 2
Chaco Central (reg.) ..... D 1
Chato (mt.) ..... B 5
Chico (river) ..... C 5
Chico (river) ..... C 6

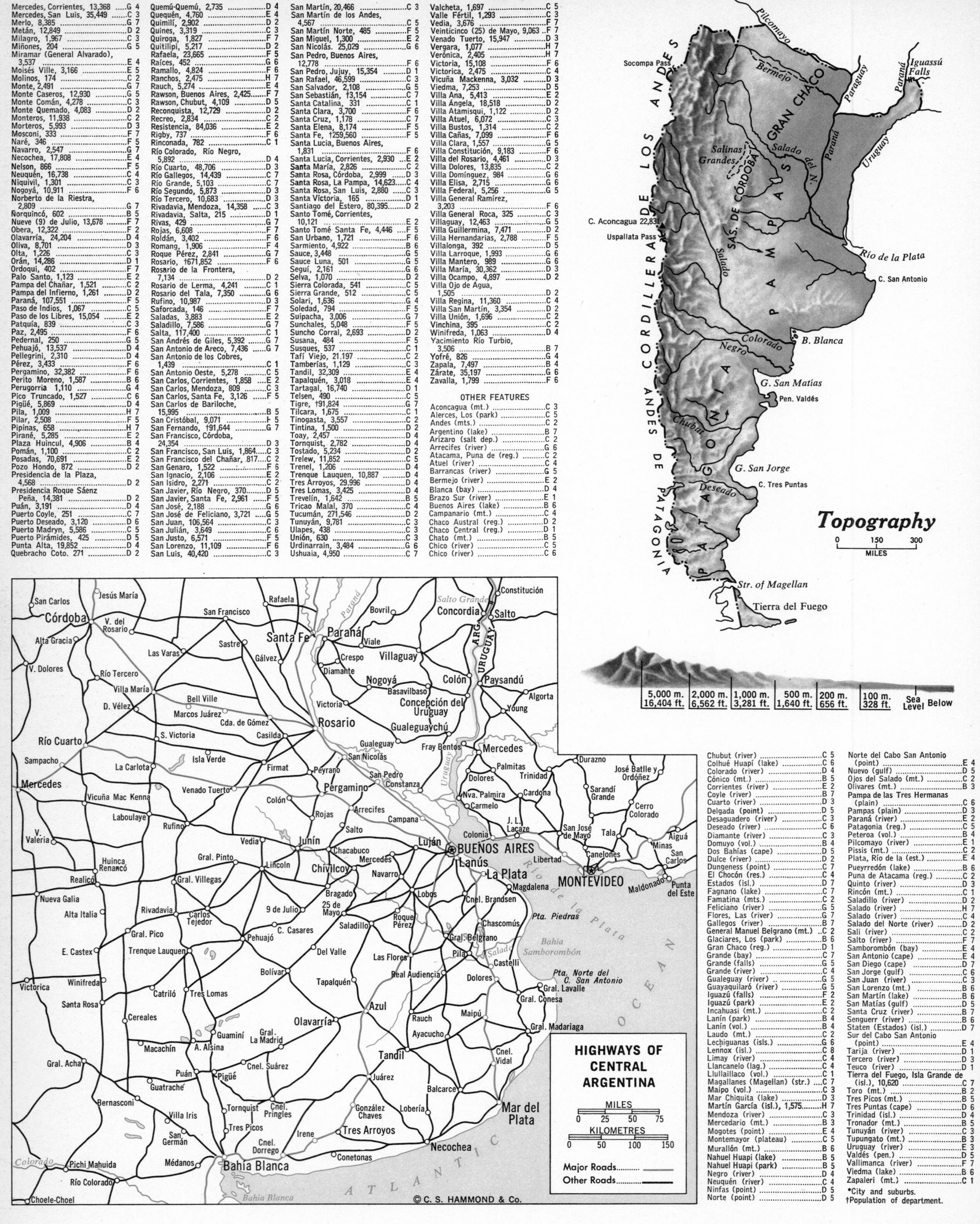

Chubut (river) ..... C 5
Colhué Huapí (lake) ..... C 6
Colorado (river) ..... D 4
Cónico (mt.) ..... B 5
Corrientes (river) ..... E 2
Coyle (river) ..... B 7
Cuarto (river) ..... D 3
Delgada (point) ..... D 5
Desaguadero (river) ..... C 3
Deseado (river) ..... C 6
Diamante (river) ..... C 3
Domuyo (vol.) ..... B 4
Dos Bahías (cape) ..... D 5
Dulce (river) ..... D 2
Dungeness (point) ..... C 7
El Chocón (res.) ..... C 4
Estados (isl.) ..... D 7
Fagnano (lake) ..... C 7
Famatina (mts.) ..... C 2
Feliciano (river) ..... G 5
Flores, Las (river) ..... G 7
Gallegos (river) ..... B 7
General Manuel Belgrano (mt.) ..... C 2
Glaciares, Los (park) ..... B 6
Gran Chaco (reg.) ..... D 1
Grande (bay) ..... C 7
Grande (falls) ..... G 5
Grande (river) ..... C 4
Gualeguay (river) ..... G 5
Guayaquilaró (river) ..... G 5
Iguazú (falls) ..... F 2
Iguazú (park) ..... E 2
Incahuasi (mt.) ..... C 2
Lanín (park) ..... B 4
Lanín (vol.) ..... B 4
Laudo (mt.) ..... C 2
Lechiguanas (isls.) ..... G 6
Lennox (isl.) ..... C 8
Limay (river) ..... C 4
Llancanelo (lag.) ..... C 4
Llullaillaco (vol.) ..... C 1
Magallanes (Magellan) (str.) ..... C 7
Maipo (vol.) ..... C 3
Mar Chiquita (lake) ..... D 3
Martín García (isl.), 1,575 ..... H 7
Mendoza (river) ..... C 3
Mercedario (mt.) ..... B 3
Mogotes (point) ..... E 4
Montemayor (plateau) ..... C 5
Murallón (mt.) ..... B 6
Nahuel Huapi (lake) ..... B 5
Nahuel Huapi (park) ..... B 5
Negro (river) ..... D 4
Neuquén (river) ..... C 4
Ninfas (point) ..... D 5
Norte (point) ..... D 5
Norte del Cabo San Antonio (point) ..... E 4
Nuevo (gulf) ..... D 5
Ojos del Salado (mt.) ..... C 2
Olivares (mt.) ..... B 3
Pampa de las Tres Hermanas (plain) ..... C 6
Pampas (plain) ..... D 3
Paraná (river) ..... E 2
Patagonia (reg.) ..... C 5
Peteroa (vol.) ..... B 4
Pilcomayo (river) ..... E 1
Pissis (mt.) ..... C 2
Plata, Río de la (est.) ..... E 4
Pueyrredón (lake) ..... B 6
Puna de Atacama (reg.) ..... C 2
Quinto (river) ..... D 3
Rincón (mt.) ..... C 1
Saladillo (river) ..... D 2
Salado (river) ..... H 7
Salado (river) ..... C 4
Salado del Norte (river) ..... D 2
Sali (river) ..... C 2
Salto (river) ..... F 7
Samborombón (bay) ..... E 4
San Antonio (cape) ..... E 4
San Diego (cape) ..... D 7
San Jorge (gulf) ..... C 6
San Juan (river) ..... C 3
San Lorenzo (mt.) ..... B 6
San Martín (lake) ..... B 6
San Matías (gulf) ..... D 5
Santa Cruz (river) ..... B 7
Senguerr (river) ..... B 6
Staten (Estados) (isl.) ..... D 7
Sur del Cabo San Antonio (point) ..... E 4
Tarija (river) ..... D 1
Tercero (river) ..... D 3
Teuco (river) ..... D 1
Tierra del Fuego, Isla Grande de (isl.), 10,620 ..... C 7
Toro (mt.) ..... B 2
Tres Picos (mt.) ..... B 5
Tres Puntas (cape) ..... D 6
Trinidad (isl.) ..... D 4
Tronador (mt.) ..... B 5
Tunuyán (river) ..... C 3
Tupungato (mt.) ..... B 3
Uruguay (river) ..... E 3
Valdés (pen.) ..... D 5
Vallimanca (river) ..... F 7
Viedma (lake) ..... B 6
Zapaleri (mt.) ..... C 1

*City and suburbs.
†Population of department.

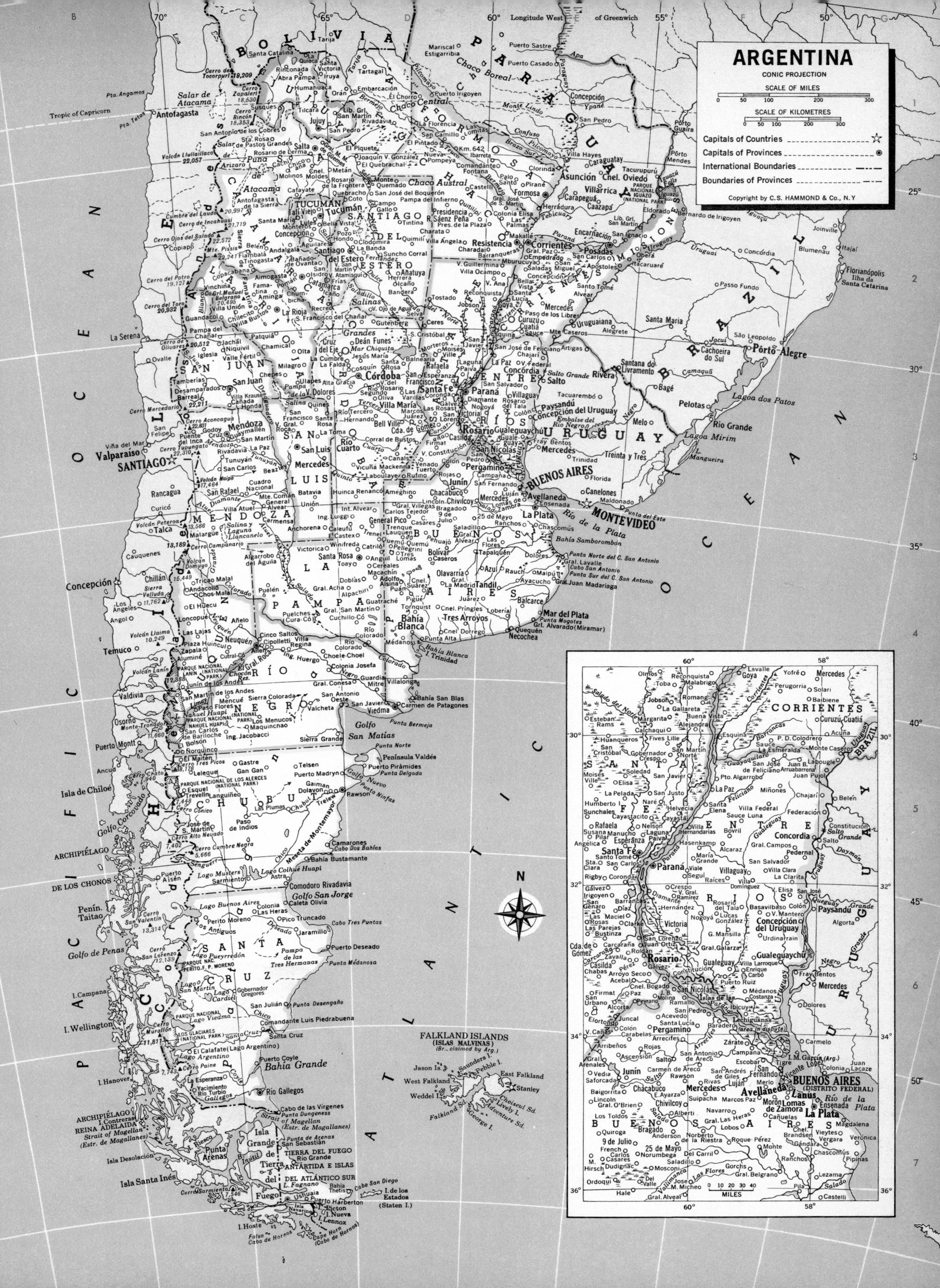

ARGENTINA
CONIC PROJECTION
SCALE OF MILES
0 50 100 200 300
SCALE OF KILOMETRES
0 50 100 200 300
Capitals of Countries
Capitals of Provinces
International Boundaries
Boundaries of Provinces
Copyright by C.S. HAMMOND & Co., N.Y
Longitude West of Greenwich
BOLIVIA
PARAGUAY
BRAZIL
URUGUAY
CHILE
PACIFIC OCEAN
ATLANTIC OCEAN
Tropic of Capricorn
JUJUY
SALTA
FORMOSA
CHACO
TUCUMÁN
SANTIAGO DEL ESTERO
CATAMARCA
LA RIOJA
SAN JUAN
CÓRDOBA
SANTA FE
MISIONES
CORRIENTES
ENTRE RÍOS
MENDOZA
SAN LUIS
LA PAMPA
BUENOS AIRES
NEUQUÉN
RÍO NEGRO
CHUBUT
SANTA CRUZ
TIERRA DEL FUEGO ANTÁRTIDA E ISLAS DEL ATLÁNTICO SUR
SANTIAGO
Asunción
MONTEVIDEO
BUENOS AIRES
Valparaíso
Antofagasta
Córdoba
Rosario
Mendoza
Tucumán
La Plata
Mar del Plata
Bahía Blanca
Golfo San Matías
Golfo San Jorge
Strait of Magellan (Estr. de Magallanes)
Isla Grande de Tierra del Fuego
Cape Horn (Cabo de Hornos)
I. de los Estados (Staten I.)
FALKLAND ISLANDS (ISLAS MALVINAS) (Br., claimed by Arg.)
West Falkland
East Falkland
Stanley
Río de la Plata
Isla de Chiloé
ARCHIPIÉLAGO DE LOS CHONOS
Penín. Taitao
Golfo de Penas
I. Wellington
ARCHIPIÉLAGO REINA ADELAIDA
Isla Desolación
Isla Santa Inés
CORRIENTES
SANTA FE
ENTRE RÍOS
BUENOS AIRES (DISTRITO FEDERAL)
Paraná
Santa Fe
Concordia
Paysandú
Concepción del Uruguay
Gualeguaychú
Avellaneda
Lanús
Lomas de Zamora
MILES
0 10 20 30 40

PARAGUAY

DEPARTMENTS

Alto Paraná, 24,067 .... E 5
Amambay, 34,505 .... E 4
Boquerón, 40,405 .... B 3
Caaguazú, 125,138 .... E 5
Caazapá, 92,401 .... D 6
Central, 229,073 .... D 5
Concepción, 85,690 .... D 4
Cordillera, 188,313 .... D 5
Distrito Federal, 288,882 .... A 6
Guairá, 114,949 .... D 5
Itapúa, 149,821 .... E 6
Misiones, 59,441 .... D 6
Ñeembucú, 57,878 .... D 6
Olimpo, 3,854 .... C 3
Paraguarí, 203,012 .... D 6
Presidente Hayes, 29,870 .... C 4
San Pedro, 91,804 .... D 5

CITIES and TOWNS

Acahay, 2,622 .... B 7
Alberdi, 1,787 .... D 6
Altos, 1,348 .... B 6
Aregúa, 3,699 .... B 6
Arroyos y Esteros, 1,447 .... B 6
Asunción (cap.), 350,000 .... A 6
Asunción, *411,500 .... A 6
Atyrá, 1,246 .... B 6
Ayolas, 321 .... D 6
Bahía Negra 415 .... C 3
Belén, 2,523 .... D 4
Bella Vista, 2,331 .... D 4
Benjamín Aceval, 3,463 .... D 5
Borja, 625 .... C 7
Buena Vista, 1,954 .... E 5
Caacupé, 6,329 .... B 6
Caaguazú, 2,291 .... E 5
Caapucú, 1,513 .... D 6
Caazapá, 3,079 .... D 6
Caballero, 1,553 .... B 6
Cañada Oruro, †442 .... A 3
Capiatá, 2,062 .... B 6
Capitán Bado, 257 .... E 4
Capitán Meza, 306 .... E 6
Caraguatay, 1,935 .... C 6
Carapeguá, 2,628 .... B 6
Carayaó, 1,376 .... C 6
Carmen del Paraná, 1,813 .... D 6
Cerrito, 801 .... D 6
Concepción, 33,500 .... D 4
Corone Bogado, 3,885 .... E 6
Coronei Martínez, 1,270 .... C 6
Coronel Oviedo, 9,468 .... C 6
Curuguaty, 497 .... E 5
Desmochados, 681 .... D 6
Emboscada, 1,040 .... B 6
Encarnación, 35,000 .... E 6
Escobar, 567 .... B 6
Eusebio Ayala, 2,532 .... B 6
Fernando de la Mora, 10,194 .... A 6
Filadelfia, †2,639 .... C 4
Fortín General Díaz, Boquerón, †508 .... B 4
Fuerte Olimpo, 2,588 .... D 3
General Aquino, 1,162 .... D 5
General Artigas, 3,450 .... E 6
Guarambaré, 3,167 .... B 6
Guazú-cuá, 153 .... D 6
Hernandarias, 1,646 .... E 5
Hohenau, 1,877 .... E 6
Horqueta, 5,095 .... D 4
Humaitá, 781 .... C 6
Irala, 295 .... E 5
Isla Pucú, 1,938 .... B 6
Isla Umbú, 202 .... C 6
Itá, 6,265 .... B 6
Itacurubí de la Cordillera, 2,137 .... C 6
Itacurubí del Rosario, 1,776 .... D 5
Itakyry, 788 .... E 5
Itapé, 1,235 .... C 6
Itauguá, 3,064 .... B 6
Iturbe, 3,274 .... C 7
Jesús, 1,814 .... E 6
Juan de Mena, 1,450 .... D 6
Lambaré, 8,300 .... B 6
Laureles, 380 .... D 6
Lima, 751 .... D 4
Limpio, 1,438 .... B 6
Loreto, 1,866 .... D 4
Luque, 11,008 .... B 6
Maciel, 400 .... D 6
Mariscal Estigarribia, 1,824 .... B 4
Mbocayaty, 701 .... C 6
Mbuyapey, 1,310 .... D 6
Ñacunday, †119 .... E 6
Natalicio Talavera, 1,020 .... D 5
Nueva Germania, 511 .... D 4
Ñumí, 346 .... D 5
Paraguarí, 4,880 .... B 6
Paso de Patria, 608 .... C 6
Pedro González, 377 .... C 6
Pedro Juan Caballero, 10,355 .... E 4
Pilar, 10,500 .... C 6
Pirayú, 2,753 .... B 6
Piribebuy, 4,038 .... B 6
Primero de Marzo, 672 .... B 6
Puerto Adela, 46 .... E 5
Puerto Antequera, 1,123 .... D 5
Puerto Casado, 1,891 .... C 4
Puerto Guaraní, 1,055 .... D 3
Puerto Mihanovich, 132 .... C 3
Puerto Pinasco, 3,872 .... C 4
Puerto Presidente Stroessner, †764 .... E 5
Puerto Sastre, 1,408 .... D 4
Quiindy, 2,851 .... B 7
Quyquyhó,, 1,168 .... D 6
Roque González, 1,436 .... B 7
Rosario, 3,313 .... D 5
San Antonio, Central, 4,247 .... A 6
San Bernardino, 570 .... B 6
San Carlos, Concepción, 870 .... D 4
San Cosme, 554 .... D 6
San Estanislao, 3,569 .... D 5
San Ignacio, 5,141 .... D 6
San Joaquín, 421 .... D 5
San José, 2,802 .... C 6
San Juan Bautista, 5,972 .... D 6
San Juan Bautista de Ñeembucú, 454 .... C 6
San Juan Nepomuceno, 3,118 .... E 6
San Lázaro, 807 .... D 4
San Lorenzo, 8,593 .... B 6
San Miguel, 1,034 .... D 6
San Pedro, 3,306 .... D 5
San Pedro del Paraná, 2,263 .... E 6
San Salvador, 1,569 .... D 4
Santa Elena, 1,364 .... C 6
Santa María, 754 .... D 6
Santa Rosa, 2,641 .... D 6
Santiago, 1,689 .... D 6
Sapucaí, 1,708 .... B 6
Tabaí, 528 .... E 6
Tacuara, 54 .... C 6
Tacuatí, 615 .... D 4
Tacurupucú (Hernandarias), 2,311 .... E 5
Tobatí, 2,520 .... B 6
Trinidad, 518 .... E 6
Unión, 806 .... D 5
Valenzuela, 994 .... B 6
Villa Florida, 1,141 .... D 6
Villa Franca, 374 .... C 6
Villa Hayes, 4,712 .... A 6
Villa Oliva, 813 .... C 5
Villarrica, 30,500 .... C 6
Villeta, 3,020 .... A 6
Yabebyry, 486 .... D 6
Yaguarón, 2,763 .... B 6
Yataity, 1,050 .... C 6
Ybycuí, 3,056 .... B 7
Ybytimí, 1,410 .... B 6
Yegros, 1,158 .... D 6
Ygatimí, 370 .... E 5
Yhú, 1,240 .... E 5
Ypacaraí, 5,281 .... B 6
Ypané, 1,469 .... A 6
Ypejhú, 64 .... E 4
Yuty, 2,573 .... D 6

OTHER FEATURES

Acaray (river) .... E 5
Aguaray-guazú (river) .... C 5
Alegre (river) .... C 3
Alto Paraná (river) .... D 6
Amambay, Cord. de (mts.) .... E 4
Apa (river) .... D 4
Aquidabán (river) .... D 4
Capitán Ustarés (hill) .... B 2
Cará (mt.) .... E 4
Chaco Boreal (reg.) .... B 4
Chovoreca (hill) .... C 2
Confuso (river) .... C 5
González (river) .... C 4
Gran Chaco (reg.) .... B 4
Guairá (falls) .... E 5
Guaraní (Cap. Ustarés) (hill) .... B 2
León (mt.) .... B 3
Mbaracayú (mts.) .... E 4
Monday (river) .... E 5
Monte Lindo (river) .... D 4
Negro (river) .... D 5
Paraguay (river) .... D 5
Pilcomayo (river) .... C 5
Siete Puntas (river) .... D 4
Tebicuary (river) .... D 6

Tímane (river) ....C 3
Verá (lagoon) ....B 7
Verde (river) ....C 4
Yacaré (river) ....C 4
Ypané (river) ....D 4
Ypoá (lake) ....B 6

URUGUAY

DEPARTMENTS

Artigas, 52,261 ....B 1
Canelones, 211,644 ....D 5
Cerro Largo, 118,880 ....E 3
Colonia, 135,185 ....B 5
Durazno, 113,797 ....C 3
Flores, 35,457 ....C 4
Florida, 104,739 ....D 4
Lavalleja, 114,090 ....D 5
Maldonado, 62,344 ....E 5
Montevideo, 1,173,114 ....B 7
Paysandú, 89,908 ....B 3
Río Negro, 49,258 ....B 3
Rivera, 86,430 ....D 2
Rocha, 84,210 ....E 4
Salto, 105,698 ....B 2
San José, 94,541 ....C 5
Soriano, 78,234 ....B 4
Tacuarembó, 119,690 ....D 3
Treinta y Tres, 81,887 ....E 4

CITIES and TOWNS

Achar, 460 ....C 3
Aiguá, 2,715 ....E 5
Algorta, 650 ....B 3
Arroyo Grande, 1,000 ....B 4
Artigas, 23,429 ....C 1
Balneario El Tesoro, 84 ....E 5
Balneario La Barra, 124 ....E 5
Balneario Solís, 225 ....D 5
Baltasar Brum, 1,764 ....B 1
Belén, 2,933 ....B 1
Bella Unión, 4,955 ....B 1
Bernabé Rivera, 683 ....B 1
Bizcocho, 117 ....B 4
Campamento, 187 ....C 1
Cañada Nieto, 407 ....B 4
Canelones, 27,000 ....B 6
Cardona, 4,110 ....B 4
Carlos Reyles, 940 ....C 4
Carmelo, 11,923 ....A 4
Carmen, 1,687 ....D 4
Castillos, 5,345 ....F 5
Casupá, 1,652 ....D 5
Cerro Chato, Treinta y Tres, 2,045 ....D 4
Clara, 1,000 ....D 3
Colonia, 9,825 ....B 5
Colonia Agraciada, 409 ....A 4
Colonia Arrué ....B 5
Colonia Artigas, 234 ....B 1
Colonia Concordia, 755 ....A 4
Colonia Itacumbú, 738 ....B 1
Colonia Lavalleja ....C 2
Colonia Palma, 94 ....B 1
Colonia Rossel y Rius ....D 4
Colonia Valdense, 1,126 ....B 5
Conchillas, 590 ....B 5
Constancia, 150 ....B 3
Constitución, 1,600 ....A 2
Corrales (J. P. Varela), 2,700 ..E 4
Cuaró ....D 2
Cufré ....B 5
Curtina ....C 3
Diego Lamas, 94 ....B 1
Dolores, 12,480 ....A 4
Durazno, 19,486 ....C 4
Egaña, 675 ....B 4
Estación Atlántida, 1,007 ....B 6
Estación Cuaró, 203 ....C 1
Estación José Ignacio, 131 ....E 5
Estación Rincón ....F 3
Estación Sosa Díaz ....C 6
Estación Villasboas ....C 4
Estanzuela ....B 5
Florida, 17,243 ....C 5
Fortaleza de Santa Teresa ....F 5
Fraile Muerto, 1,876 ....E 3
Fray Bentos, 14,625 ....A 4
Fray Marcos, 1,095 ....D 5
Garzón, 345 ....E 5
Guichón, 4,625 ....B 3
Itapeby ....B 2
Javier de Viana, 317 ....C 1
Joaquín Suárez, Canelones, 1,752 ....B 6
Joaquín Suárez, Colonia ....B 5
José Batlle y Ordóñez, 1,781 ....D 4
José Enrique Rodo, 1,319 ....B 4
José Pedro Varela (Corrales), 2,955 ....E 4
Juan D. Jackson, 163 ....C 4
Juan L. Lacaze, 9,916 ....B 5
La Bolsa, 274 ....C 1
La Cruz, 2,000 ....C 4
La Paz, Canelones, 5,214 ....B 6
La Paz, Colonia ....B 5
La Sierra, 241 ....D 5
Las Flores, 404 ....D 5
Las Piedras, 15,724 ....B 6
Lascano, 4,204 ....E 4
Libertad, 4,622 ....C 5
Mal Abrigo, 630 ....C 5
Maldonado, 15,005 ....D 6
Manga ....B 7
Mariscala, 1,305 ....E 5
Martín Chico ....A 5
Mazangano ....E 3
Melo, 28,673 ....E 3
Mercedes, 31,325 ....B 4
Merinos, 1,200 ....C 3
Migues, 1,017 ....C 6
Minas, 21,133 ....D 5
Minas de Corrales, 2,320 ....D 2
Molles (Carlos Reyles), 940 ......C 4
Montevideo (cap.), 1,154,465......B 7
Montevideo, *1,400,000 ....B 7
Nico Pérez ....D 4
Nueva Helvecia ....B 5
Nueva Palmira, 4,611 ....A 4
Nuevo Berlín, 1,531 ....B 3
Olimar, 2,499 ....E 3
Ombúes de Lavalle, 1,067 ....B 4
Palmitas, 1,288 ....B 4
Pan de Azúcar, 4,190 ....D 5
Pando, 11,623 ....B 6
Parada Esperanza, 250 ....B 3
Paso de Andrés Pérez ....B 3
Paso de León, 184 ....B 1
Paso de los Toros, 10,624 ....C 3
Paso de Ramos, 23 ....C 1
Paso del Borracho ....D 2
Paso del Parque ....B 2
Paysandú, 47,875 ....A 3
Piedras Coloradas, 200 ....B 3
Piñera, 1,000 ....C 3
Pintado, 160 ....C 1
Pirarajá, 1,000 ....E 4
Piriápolis, 4,546 ....D 5
Polanco del Yí, 300 ....D 4
Porvenir, 1,000 ....B 3
Progreso ....B 6
Puerto Amaro ....F 3
Puerto Arazatí ....C 5
Punta del Este, 5,272 ....E 6
Quebracho, 1,002 ....B 2
Río Branco, 3,345 ....F 3
Rivera, 42,623 ....D 1
Rocha, 19,895 ....E 5
Rodríguez, 1,097 ....C 5
Rosario, 6,398 ....B 5
Salto, 55,425 ....B 2
San Bautista, 1,500 ....B 6
San Carlos, 13,695 ....E 5
San Gregorio, San José ....C 4
San Gregorio, Tacuarembó 1,606 ....D 3
San José de Mayo, 21,048 ....C 5
San Ramón, 3,983 ....D 5
Sánchez ....B 3
Santa Catalina, 824 ....B 4
Santa Clara de Olimar ....D 3
Santa Lucía, 9,126 ....B 6
Santa Rosa, 1,596 ....B 6
Sarandí del Yí, 5,900 ....D 4
Sarandí de Navarro, 630 ....C 3
Sarandí Grande, 5,620 ....C 4
Sauce, Canelones, 1,570 ....B 6
Sauce, Rocha ....E 5
Sequeira, 880 ....C 1
Soca, 1,200 ....C 6
Solís, 1,531 ....D 5
Soriano, 1,036 ....A 4
Tacuarembó, 17,854 ....D 2
Tala, 1,957 ....D 5
Tambores, 1,273 ....C 2
Toledo, 1,200 ....B 6
Tomás Gomensoro, 2,144 ....B 1
Topador, 183 ....C 1
Tranqueras, 3,340 ....D 2
Treinta y Tres, 18,856 ....E 4
Tres Árboles, 400 ....C 3
Trinidad, 17,233 ....B 4
Tupambaé, 1,359 ....E 3
Veinticinco de Agosto, 1,139 ....A 6
Velázquez, 1,199 ....D 5
Vergara, 2,480 ....E 3
Villa Darwin, 445 ....B 4
Young, 6,485 ....B 3
Zapicán, 1,500 ....E 4

OTHER FEATURES

Aiguá (river) ....E 4
Alférez (river) ....E 5
Arapey Chico (river) ....B 1
Arapey Grande (river) ....B 2
Arroyo Negro (river) ....B 3
Belén (range) ....C 1
Bonete (dam) ....C 3
Brava (point) ....B 7
Cañas (range) ....C 2
Caraguatá (river) ....D 3
Castillos (lagoon) ....F 5
Cebollatí (river) ....F 4
Cordobés (river) ....D 3
Cuareim (river) ....B 1
Cuñapirú (river) ....D 2
Daymán (range) ....B 2
Daymán (river) ....B 2
Durazno (range) ....D 4
Espinillo (point) ....A 7
Este (point) ....D 6
Flores (isl.) ....D 5
Garzón (lagoon) ....E 5
Grande (range) ....D 4
Grande (river) ....B 4
Grande Inferior (range) ....C 4
Haedo (range) ....C 2
India Muerta (river) ....E 4
José Ignacio (lagoon) ....E 5
La Plata (river) ....B 5
Lobos (isl.), 11 ....E 6
Maciel (river) ....C 4
Mirador Nacional (mt.) ....D 5
Mirim (lagoon) ....F 4
Negra (lagoon) ....F 5
Negra (range) ....D 2
Negro (river) ....B 4
Negro (river) ....B 3
Olimar Grande (river) ....E 4
Pando (river) ....B 6
Parao (river) ....E 3
Plata, La (river) ....B 5
Polonio (cape) ....F 5
Queguay Chico (river) ....B 3
Queguay Grande (river) ....B 3
Río Negro (res.) ....D 3
Rocha (lagoon) ....E 5
Salto Grande (falls) ....A 2
San José (river) ....C 4
San Miguel (swamp) ....F 4
San Salvador (river) ....B 4
Santa Ana (range) ....D 2
Santa Lucía (river) ....D 5
Santa Lucía Chico (river) ....D 4
Santa María (cape) ....F 5
Sauce (lagoon) ....D 5
Sopas (river) ....C 2
Tacuarembó (river) ....D 2
Tacuarí (river) ....E 3
Tigre (isl.) ....A 7
Uruguay (river) ....A 3
Yaguarón (river) ....F 3
Yí (river) ....B 4

*City and suburbs.

†Population of district.

PARAGUAY

AREA 157,047 sq. mi.
POPULATION 2,314,000
CAPITAL Asunción
LARGEST CITY Asunción
HIGHEST POINT Amambay Range 2,264 ft.
MONETARY UNIT guaraní
MAJOR LANGUAGES Spanish, Guaraní
MAJOR RELIGION Roman Catholicism

URUGUAY

AREA 72,172 sq. mi.
POPULATION 2,900,000
CAPITAL Montevideo
LARGEST CITY Montevideo
HIGHEST POINT Mirador Nacional 1,644 ft.
MONETARY UNIT Uruguayan peso
MAJOR LANGUAGE Spanish
MAJOR RELIGION Roman Catholicism

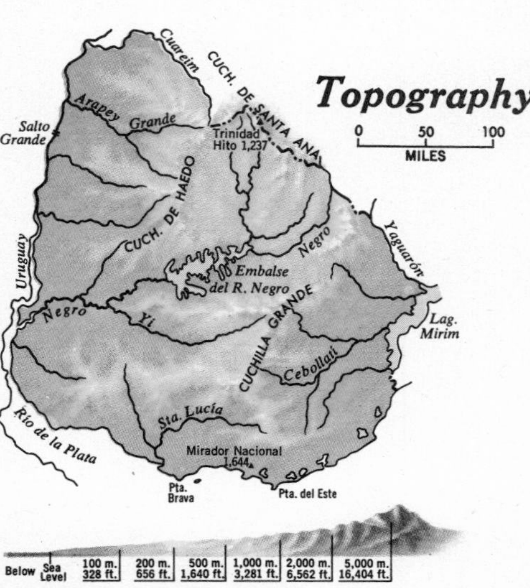

URUGUAY

CONIC PROJECTION

SCALE OF MILES 0 20 40 60

SCALE OF KILOMETRES 0 20 40 60

Capitals of Countries

Department Capitals

International Boundaries

Department Boundaries

NORTH AMERICA
LAMBERT AZIMUTHAL EQUAL-AREA PROJECTION
SCALE OF MILES
0 100 200 400 600 800
SCALE OF KILOMETRES
0 200 400 600 800
Capitals of Countries
International Boundaries
Other Boundaries
Canals
© C.S. HAMMOND & Co., N.Y.
North Pole
ARCTIC OCEAN
Longitude West of Greenwich
GREENLAND SEA
GREENLAND (Den.)
BEAUFORT SEA
Baffin Bay
Davis Strait
Hudson Bay
Hudson Strait
LABRADOR SEA
NORTHWEST TERRITORIES
CANADA
ALASKA
UNITED STATES
MEXICO
PACIFIC OCEAN
ATLANTIC OCEAN
Gulf of Mexico
CARIBBEAN SEA
WEST INDIES
GREATER ANTILLES
LESSER ANTILLES
Tropic of Cancer
Equator
SOUTH AMERICA
COLOMBIA
VENEZUELA
ECUADOR
PERU
BRAZIL
ASIA
U.S.S.R.
UNITED KINGDOM
ICELAND
BERING SEA
Bering Strait
GALÁPAGOS IS. (Ecuador)

AREA 9,363,000 sq. mi.
POPULATION 314,000,000
LARGEST CITY New York
HIGHEST POINT Mt. McKinley 20,320 ft
LOWEST POINT Death Valley -282 ft.

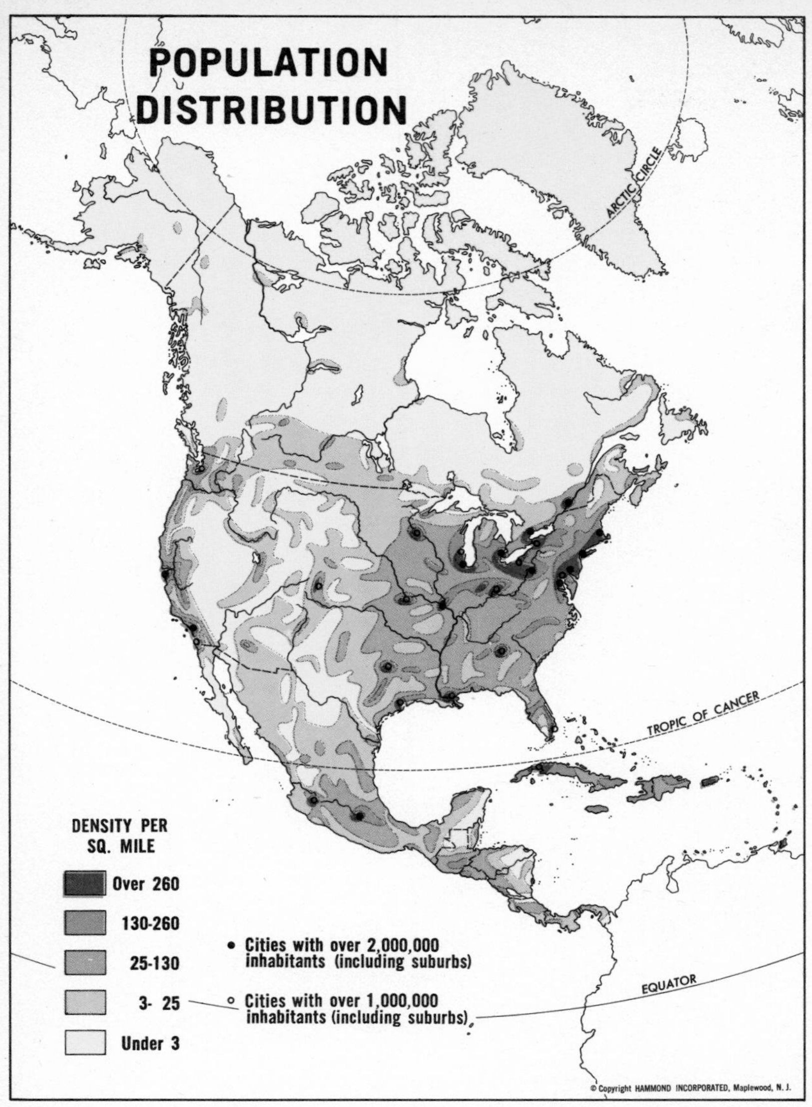

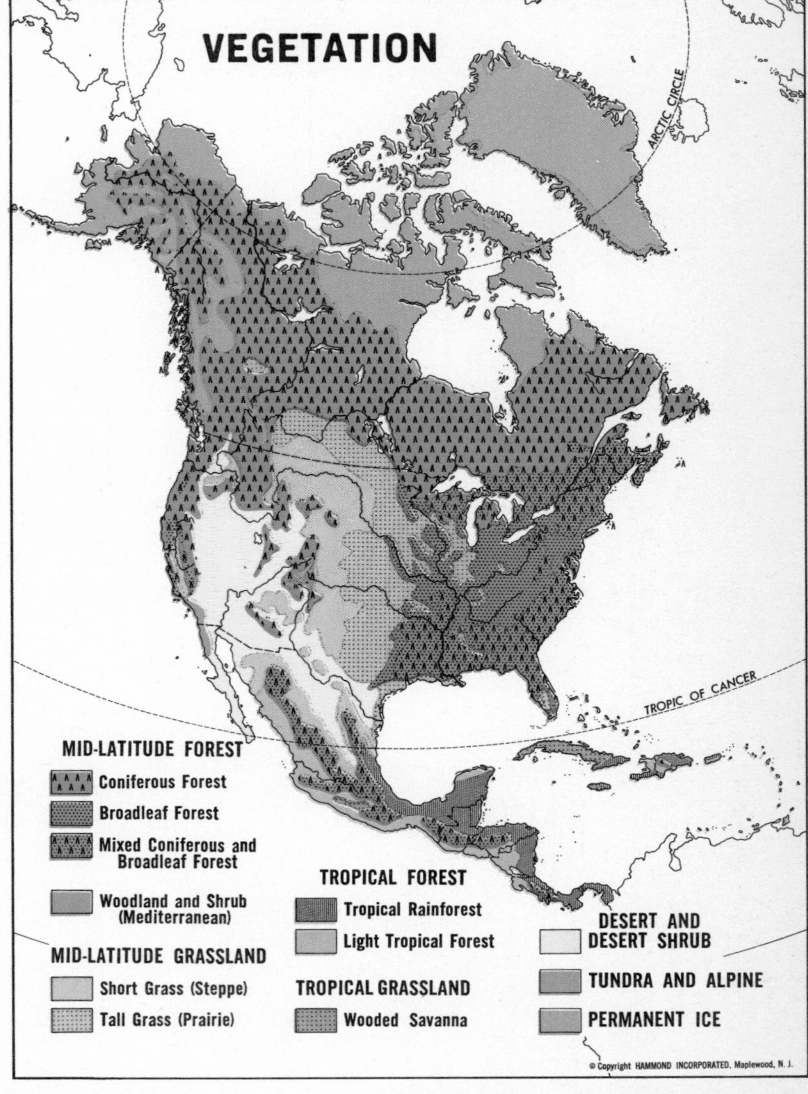

Acapulco, Mexico .... H 8
Alabama (state), U.S. .... K 6
Alabama (river), U.S. .... K 6
Alaska (state), U.S. .... C 3
Alaska (pen.), Alaska .... C 4
Albany, New York .... L 5
Alberta (prov.), Canada .... G 4
Albuquerque, N. Mexico .... H 6
Anchorage, Alaska .... C 3
Angmagssalik, Greenland .... P 3
Antigua (isl.) .... M 8
Antilles, Greater (islands) .... L 8
Antilles, Lesser (islands) .... M 8
Arctic Ocean .... B 2
Arizona (state), U.S. .... G 6
Arkansas (state), U.S. .... J 6
Arkansas (river), U.S. .... J 6
Athabasca (lake), Canada .... H 4
Atlanta, Georgia .... K 6
Augusta, Georgia .... K 6
Augusta, Maine .... M 5
Austin, Texas .... J 6
Baffin (bay) .... M 2
Baffin (island), N.W.T. .... L 2
Bahama (isls.) .... L 7
Baltimore, Maryland .... L 6
Barbados (isl.) .... M 8
Baton Rouge, Louisiana .... J 6
Belmopan (cap.), Br. Hond. .... K 8
Bering (sea) .... A 3
Bering (strait) .... B 3
Bermuda (isls.) .... M 6
Birmingham, Alabama .... K 6
Bismarck, N. Dakota .... H 5
Boise, Idaho .... G 5
Boston, Massachusetts .... L 5
British Columbia (prov.), Can. .... F 4
British Honduras .... K 8
Buffalo, New York .... L 5
Butte, Montana .... G 5
Calgary, Alberta .... G 4
California (state), U.S. .... F 6
California (gulf), Mexico .... G 7
Canada .... J 4
Canadian (river), U.S. .... J 6
Canal Zone .... L 8
Cap-Haïtien, Haiti .... L 7
Caribbean (sea) .... L 8
Carson City, Nevada .... G 6
Cascade (range), U.S. .... F 5
Charleston, S. Carolina .... L 6
Charleston, W. Virginia .... L 6
Charlotte, N. Carolina .... L 6
Charlottetown, P.E.I. .... M 5
Chattanooga, Tennessee .... K 6
Chesapeake (bay), U.S. .... L 6
Cheyenne, Wyoming .... H 5
Chicago, Illinois .... J 5
Chihuahua, Mexico .... H 7
Cincinnati, Ohio .... K 6
Cleveland, Ohio .... K 5
Clipperton (island) .... H 8
Coast (mts.), British Columbia .... F 4
Coast (ranges), U.S. .... F 5
Cocos (isl.), Costa Rica .... K 9
Cod (cape), Massachusetts .... M 5
Colón, Panama .... L 9
Colorado (state), U.S. .... H 6
Colorado (river), U.S. .... H 6
Colorado (river), U.S. .... G 6
Colorado Springs, Colorado .... H 6
Columbia, S. Carolina .... K 6
Columbia (river) .... G 5
Columbus, Georgia .... K 6
Columbus, Ohio .... K 6
Concord, New Hampshire .... L 5
Connecticut (state), U.S. .... L 5
Costa Rica .... K 8
Cuba .... L 7
Dallas, Texas .... J 6
Dayton, Ohio .... K 6
Delaware (state), U.S. .... L 6
Denmark (strait) .... R 3
Denver, Colorado .... H 5
Des Moines, Iowa .... J 5
Detroit, Michigan .... K 5
District of Columbia, U.S. .... L 6
Dominica (isl.) .... M 8
Dominican Republic .... L 8
Dover, Delaware .... L 6
Duluth, Minnesota .... J 5
Edmonton, Alberta .... G 4
El Paso, Texas .... H 6
El Salvador .... J 8
Ellesmere (island), N.W.T. .... K 2
Erie (lake) .... K 5
Fairbanks, Alaska .... D 3
Farewell (cape), Greenland .... O 4
Florida (state), U.S. .... K 7
Florida (straits) .... K 7
Fort McPherson, N.W.T. .... F 3
Fort Smith, Arkansas .... J 6
Fort Worth, Texas .... J 6
Foxe (basin), N.W.T. .... L 3
Frankfort, Kentucky .... K 6
Fraser (river), Br. Columbia .... F 4
Fredericton, New Brunswick .... M 5
Fresno, California .... F 6
Georgia (state), U.S. .... K 6
Godhavn, Greenland .... N 3
Godthåb (cap.), Greenland .... N 3
Gracias a Dios (cape), Nic. .... K 8
Grand Bahama (isl.), Bah. Is. .... L 7
Grand Rapids, Michigan .... K 5
Great Bear (lake), N.W.T. .... G 3
Great Falls, Montana .... G 5
Great Salt (lake), Utah .... G 5
Great Slave (lake), N.W.T. .... G 3
Green Bay, Wisconsin .... K 5
Greenland .... O 2
Greenland (sea) .... T 2
Grenada (isl.) .... M 8
Guadalajara, Mexico .... H 7
Guadeloupe (isl.) .... M 8
Guantánamo, Cuba .... L 7
Guatemala .... J 8
Guatemala (cap.), Guatemala .... J 8
Haiti .... L 8
Halifax, Nova Scotia .... M 5
Hamilton, Ontario .... K 5
Harrisburg, Pennsylvania .... L 5
Hartford, Connecticut .... L 5
Hatteras (cape), N. Carolina .... L 6
Havana (cap.), Cuba .... K 7
Helena, Montana .... G 5
Hispaniola (island), W. Indies .... M 7
Honduras .... K 8
Honduras (gulf), Cent. Amer. .... K 8
Houston, Texas .... J 7
Hudson (bay), Canada .... K 3
Hudson (strait), Canada .... L 3
Huron (lake) .... K 5
Idaho (state), U.S. .... G 5
Illinois (state), U.S. .... K 5
Indiana (state), U.S. .... K 6
Indianapolis, Indiana .... K 5
Inuvik, N.W.T. .... E 3
Iowa (state), U.S. .... J 5
Jackson, Mississippi .... K 6
Jacksonville, Florida .... L 6
Jamaica .... L 8
James (bay), Canada .... K 4
Jefferson City, Missouri .... J 6
Juan de Fuca (strait) .... F 5
Juneau, Alaska .... E 4
Kansas (state), U.S. .... J 6
Kansas City, Missouri .... J 6
Kennedy (cape), Florida .... L 7
Kentucky (state), U.S. .... K 6
Ketchikan, Alaska .... E 4
Key West, Florida .... K 7
Kingston (cap.), Jamaica .... L 8
Kingston, Ontario .... L 5
Knoxville, Tennessee .... K 6
Kodiak (island), Alaska .... C 4
Labrador (reg.), Newfoundland .... M 4
Lansing, Michigan .... K 5
Lexington, Kentucky .... K 6
Liard (river), Canada .... F 3
Limón, Costa Rica .... K 9
Lincoln, Nebraska .... J 5
Lincoln (sea) .... N 1
Little Rock, Arkansas .... J 6
London, Ontario .... K 5
Los Angeles, California .... G 6
Louisiana (state), U.S. .... J 6
Louisville, Kentucky .... K 6
Lower California (pen.), Mex. .... G 7
Mackenzie (river), N.W.T. .... F 3
Macon, Georgia .... K 6
Madison, Wisconsin .... K 5
Madre Occidental, Sierra (range), Mexico .... H 7
Maine (state), U.S. .... M 5
Managua (cap.), Nicaragua .... K 8
Manitoba (prov.), Canada .... J 4
Manitoba (lake), Canada .... J 4
Marquette, Michigan .... K 5
Martinique (isl.) .... M 8
Maryland (state), U.S. .... L 6
Massachusetts (state), U.S. .... L 5
Matanzas, Cuba .... K 7
Mazatlán, Mexico .... H 7
McKinley (mt.), Alaska .... C 3
Mead (lake), U.S. .... G 6
Medicine Hat, Alberta .... H 5
Memphis, Tennessee .... K 6
Mendocino (cape), California .... F 5
Mérida, Mexico .... K 7
Mexico .... H 7
Mexico (gulf) .... K 7
Mexico City (cap.), Mexico .... J 7
Miami, Florida .... K 7
Michigan (state), U.S. .... K 5
Michigan (lake), U.S. .... K 5
Milwaukee, Wisconsin .... K 5
Minneapolis, Minnesota .... J 5
Minnesota (state), U.S. .... J 5
Mississippi (state), U.S. .... K 6
Mississippi (river), U.S. .... J 6
Missouri (state), U.S. .... J 6
Missouri (river), U.S. .... J 5
Mobile, Alabama .... K 6
Montana (state), U.S. .... H 5
Monterrey, Mexico .... J 7
Montgomery, Alabama .... K 6
Montpelier, Vermont .... L 5
Montréal, Québec .... L 5
Moose Jaw, Saskatchewan .... H 4
Nares (str.) .... L 2
Nashville, Tennessee .... K 6
Nassau (cap.), Bahama Isls. .... L 7
Nebraska (state), U.S. .... H 5
Nelson (river), Manitoba .... J 4
Nevada (state), U.S. .... G 6
Nevada, Sierra (range), Calif. .... G 6
New Brunswick (prov.), Can. .... M 5
New Hampshire (state), U.S. .... L 5
New Jersey (state), U.S. .... L 5
New Mexico (state), U.S. .... H 6
New Orleans, Louisiana .... K 7
New York (state), U.S. .... L 5
New York, N.Y. .... L 5
Newfoundland (prov.), Canada .... O 5
Nicaragua .... K 8
Nicaragua (lake), Cent. Amer. .... K 8
Nome, Alaska .... B 3
Norfolk, Virginia .... L 6
North Bay, Ontario .... L 5
North Carolina (state), U.S. .... L 6
North Dakota (state), U.S. .... H 5
North Magnetic Pole .... H 2
North Saskatchewan (riv.), Can. G 4
Northwest Territories (terr.), Canada .... H 3
Nova Scotia (prov.), Canada .... M 5
Oakland, California .... F 6
Oaxaca, Mexico .... J 8
Ohio (state), U.S. .... K 5
Ohio (river), U.S. .... K 6
Oklahoma (state), U.S. .... J 6
Oklahoma City, Oklahoma .... J 6
Olympia, Washington .... F 5
Omaha, Nebraska .... J 5
Ontario (prov.), Canada .... K 4
Ontario (lake) .... L 5
Oregon (state), U.S. .... F 5
Ottawa (cap.), Canada .... L 5
Ottawa (river), Canada .... L 5
Panama .... K 8
Panamá (cap.), Panama .... L 9
Panamá (gulf), Cent. Amer. .... L 9
Parry (chan.), N.W.T. .... H-J 2
Peace (river), Canada .... G 4
Pennsylvania (state), U.S. .... L 5
Pensacola, Florida .... K 7
Philadelphia, Pennsylvania .... L 6
Phoenix, Arizona .... G 6
Pierre, S. Dakota .... H 5
Pittsburgh, Pennsylvania .... K 5
Port-au-Prince (cap.), Haiti .... L 8
Portland, Maine .... M 5
Portland, Oregon .... F 5
Prince Edward I. (prov.), Can. .... M 5
Providence, R.I. .... M 5
Prudhoe Land (reg.), Greenland .... M 2
Puebla, Mexico .... J 8
Puerto Rico .... M 8
Québec (prov.), Canada .... L 4
Québec, Québec .... L 5
Queen Charlotte (isls.), Br. Col. E 4
Queen Elizabeth (isls.), N.W.T. J 2
Raleigh, N. Carolina .... L 6
Red (river), U.S. .... J 5
Red (river), U.S. .... J 6
Regina, Saskatchewan .... H 4
Reno, Nevada .... G 6
Rhode Island (state), U.S. .... M 5
Richmond, Virginia .... L 6
Rio Grande (river) .... H 7
Rŏchester, N.Y. .... L 5
Rocky (mts.) .... F 4
Sable (cape), Nova Scotia .... M 5
Sacramento, California .... F 6
Saguenay (river), Québec .... L 5
Saint Augustine, Florida .... L 7
Saint Christopher (island) .... M 8
Saint John, New Brunswick .... M 5
Saint John's, Newfoundland .... N 5
Saint Lawrence (gulf), Canada .... M 5
Saint Larwrence (river) .... L 5
Saint Louis, Missouri .... J 6
Saint Lucia (isl.) .... M 8
Saint Paul, Minnesota .... J 5
Saint Pierre & Miquelon (isls.) .... N 5
Saint Vincent (isl.) .... M 8
Salem, Oregon .... F 5
Salt Lake City, Utah .... G 5
Saltillo, Mexico .... H 7
San Antonio, Texas .... J 7
San Diego, California .... G 6
San Francisco, California .... F 6
San José (cap.), Costa Rica .... K 9
San Juan (cap.), Puerto Rico .... M 8
San Salvador (cap.), El Sal. .... J 8
Santa Fe, N. Mexico .... H 6
Santiago de Cuba, Cuba .... L 8
Santo Domingo (cap.), Dom. Rep. .... M 8
Saskatchewan (prov.), Canada .... H 4
Saskatoon, Saskatchewan .... H 4
Sault Sainte Marie, Ontario .... K 5
Savannah, Georgia .... L 6
Seattle, Washington .... F 5
Shreveport, Louisiana .... J 6
Sierra Nevada (range), Calif. .... G 6
Sioux City, Iowa .... J 5
Sioux Falls, S. Dakota .... J 5
Sitka, Alaska .... E 4
Slave (river), Canada .... G 3
Snake (river), U.S. .... G 5
South Carolina (state), U.S. .... K 6
South Dakota (state), U.S. .... H 5
South Platte (river), U.S. .... H 5
South Saskatchewan (riv.), Can. G 4
Springfield, Illinois .... J 5
Sudbury, Ontario .... K 5
Superior (lake) .... K 5
Sverdrup (islands), N.W.T. .... J 2
Tacoma, Washington .... F 5
Tallahassee, Florida .... K 6
Tampa, Florida .... K 7
Tampico, Mexico .... J 7
Tegucigalpa (cap.), Honduras .... K 8
Tennessee (state), U.S. .... K 6
Tennessee (river), U.S. .... K 6
Texas (state), U.S. .... J 6
Thule, Greenland .... M 2
Thunder Bay, Ontario .... K 5
Toledo, Ohio .... K 5
Topeka, Kansas .... J 6
Toronto, Ontario .... K 5
Trenton, New Jersey .... L 5
Trinidad and Tobago .... M 8
Tucson, Arizona .... G 6
Tulsa, Oklahoma .... J 6
Ungava (bay), Canada .... M 4
United States .... H 6
Utah (state), U.S. .... G 6
Vancouver, British Columbia .... F 5
Vancouver (isl.), Br. Columbia .... E 5
Veracruz, Mexico .... J 8
Vermont (state), U.S. .... L 5
Victoria, British Columbia .... F 5
Victoria (island), N.W.T. .... G 2
Virgin Is. (Br.) .... M 8
Virgin Is. (U.S.) .... M 8
Virginia (state), U.S. .... L 6
Washington (state), U.S. .... F 5
Washington, D.C. (cap.), U.S. .... L 6
West Indies (islands) .... L 8
West Virginia (state), U.S. .... L 6
Whitehorse, Yukon .... E 3
Wichita, Kansas .... J 6
Winnipeg, Manitoba .... J 5
Winnipegosis (lake), Manitoba .... H 4
Wisconsin (state), U.S. .... K 5
Woods (lake) .... J 5
Wyoming (state), U.S. .... H 5
Yellowknife, N.W.T. .... G 3
Yucatán (channel) .... K 7
Yucatán (pen.), Mexico .... K 8
Yukon (river) .... C 3
Yukon Territory (terr.), Can. .... E 3

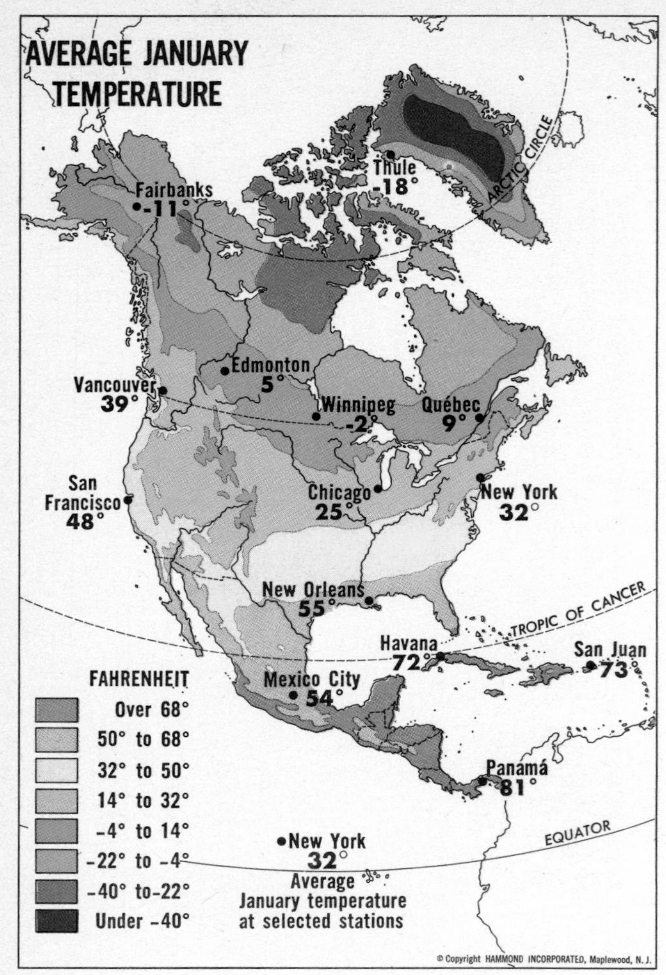
AVERAGE JANUARY TEMPERATURE
Thule -18°
Fairbanks -11°
ARCTIC CIRCLE
Edmonton 5°
Vancouver 39°
Winnipeg -2°
Québec 9°
San Francisco 48°
Chicago 25°
New York 32°
New Orleans 55°
TROPIC OF CANCER
Havana 72°
San Juan 73°
Mexico City 54°
Panamá 81°
FAHRENHEIT
Over 68°
50° to 68°
32° to 50°
14° to 32°
-4° to 14°
-22° to -4°
-40° to -22°
Under -40°
New York 32° Average January temperature at selected stations
EQUATOR
© Copyright HAMMOND INCORPORATED, Maplewood, N. J.

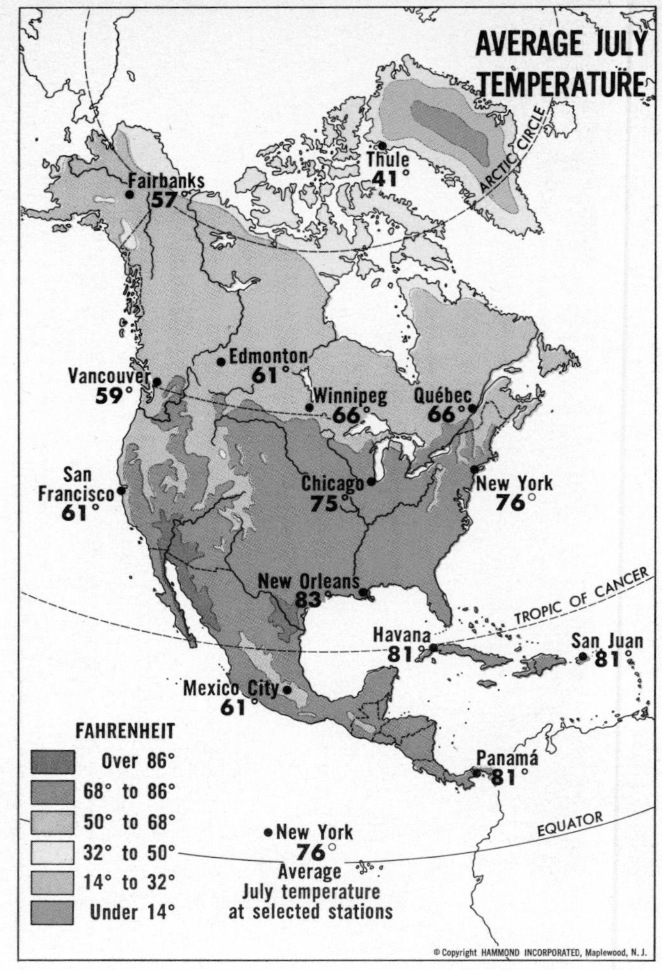
AVERAGE JULY TEMPERATURE
Thule 41°
Fairbanks 57°
ARCTIC CIRCLE
Edmonton 61°
Vancouver 59°
Winnipeg 66°
Québec 66°
San Francisco 61°
Chicago 75°
New York 76°
New Orleans 83°
TROPIC OF CANCER
Havana 81°
San Juan 81°
Mexico City 61°
Panamá 81°
FAHRENHEIT
Over 86°
68° to 86°
50° to 68°
32° to 50°
14° to 32°
Under 14°
New York 76° Average July temperature at selected stations
EQUATOR
© Copyright HAMMOND INCORPORATED, Maplewood, N. J.

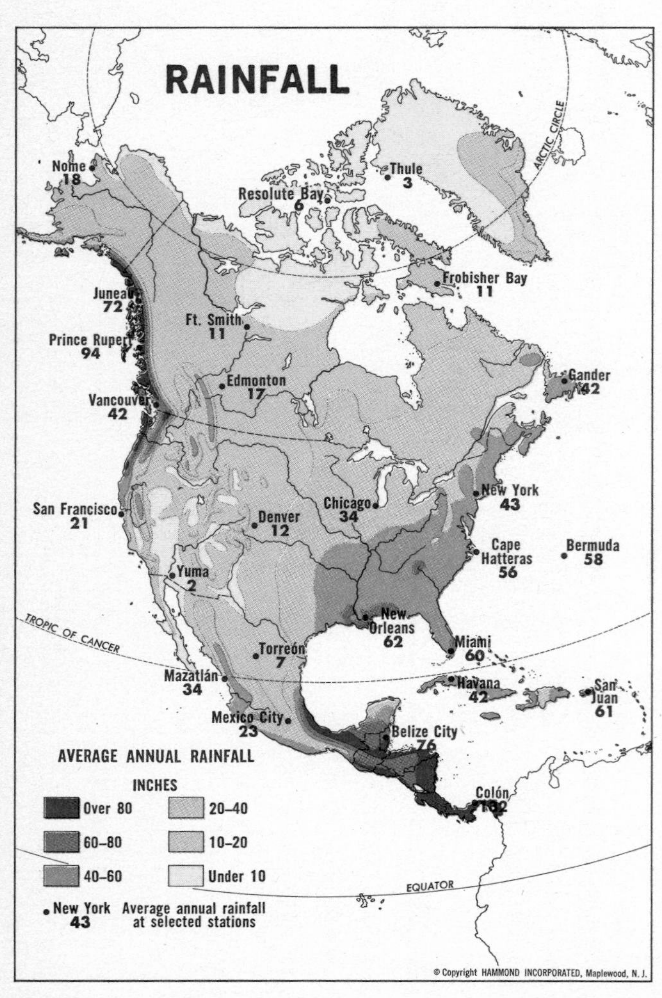
RAINFALL
Nome 18
Thule 3
Resolute Bay 6
ARCTIC CIRCLE
Frobisher Bay 11
Juneau 72
Ft. Smith 11
Prince Rupert 94
Edmonton 17
Gander 42
Vancouver 42
New York 43
San Francisco 21
Denver 12
Chicago 34
Cape Hatteras 56
Bermuda 58
Yuma 2
New Orleans 62
TROPIC OF CANCER
Miami 60
Torreón 7
Mazatlán 34
Havana 42
San Juan 61
Mexico City 23
Belize City 76
Colón 132
AVERAGE ANNUAL RAINFALL
INCHES
Over 80
60–80
40–60
20–40
10–20
Under 10
New York 43 Average annual rainfall at selected stations
EQUATOR
© Copyright HAMMOND INCORPORATED, Maplewood, N. J.

VEGETATION/RELIEF

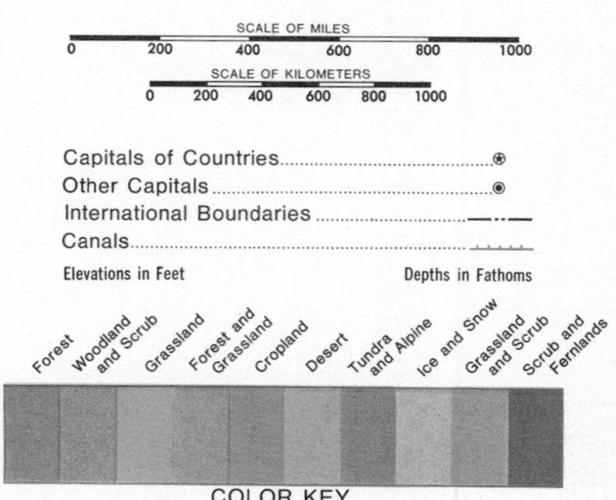
SCALE OF MILES
0 200 400 600 800 1000
SCALE OF KILOMETERS
0 200 400 600 800 1000
Capitals of Countries
Other Capitals
International Boundaries
Canals
Elevations in Feet
Depths in Fathoms
Forest
Woodland and Scrub
Grassland
Forest and Grassland
Cropland
Desert
Tundra and Alpine
Ice and Snow
Grassland and Scrub
Scrub and Fernlands
COLOR KEY

North Pole
EAST SIBERIAN SEA
ASIA
U.S.S.R.
BERING SEA
Bering Strait
St. Lawrence I.
Nome
Pt. Barrow
BEAUFORT SEA
ARCTIC OCEAN
Queen Elizabeth Islands
GREENLAND SEA
GREENLAND (Den.)
ICELAND
Reykjavík
Denmark Strait
Banks I.
Melville I.
Devon I.
Baffin Bay
Victoria I.
Arctic Circle
Davis Strait
Godthåb
C. Farewell
Alaska Pen.
Kodiak I.
Gulf of Alaska
Brooks Range
Alaska Range
Great Bear L.
Inuvik
Juneau
Alexander Arch.
Prince Rupert
Queen Charlotte Is.
Yellowknife
Great Slave L.
L. Athabasca
Peace
Athabasca
Laurentian Plateau
CANADA
Hudson Bay
Ungava Peninsula
C. Chidley
LABRADOR SEA
Labrador
Smallwood Res.
Churchill
Nelson
Newfoundland
Gander
St. John's
C. Race
Edmonton
North Saskatchewan
South Saskatchewan
Calgary
Saskatoon
Regina
Vancouver I.
Victoria
Vancouver
Columbia
Seattle
Mt. Rainier 14,410
Portland
James Bay
Eastmain
Albany
L. Winnipeg
Winnipeg
Red
Thunder Bay
Duluth
L. Superior
Sudbury
Montréal
Ottawa
Québec
St. John
Halifax
Gulf of St. Lawrence
Cape Breton I.
St. Lawrence
Rocky Mountains
Coast Mountains
Great Plains
Missouri
Minneapolis
Mississippi
L. Michigan
L. Huron
L. Ontario
L. Erie
Toronto
Buffalo
Boston
C. Cod
Milwaukee
Detroit
Cleveland
Chicago
Pittsburgh
New York
Philadelphia
Washington
Columbus
Indianapolis
Cincinnati
Ohio
C. Mendocino
Snake
Great Basin
Great Salt Lake
Salt Lake City
San Francisco
Sierra Nevada
Mt. Whitney 14,495
Las Vegas
Los Angeles
San Diego
Colorado
Phoenix
Tucson
North Platte
South Platte
Omaha
Denver
Pikes Peak 14,110
Kansas City
Arkansas
Wichita
Tulsa
Oklahoma City
St. Louis
Ozark Plateau
UNITED STATES
Nashville
Memphis
Tennessee
Mt. Mitchell 6,684
Charlotte
Norfolk
C. Hatteras
Bermuda (U.K.)
Appalachian Mts.
Birmingham
Atlanta
Albuquerque
El Paso
Ciudad Juárez
Red
Fort Worth
Dallas
Jacksonville
New Orleans
Houston
San Antonio
Rio Grande
Corpus Christi
Tampa
C. Canaveral
Miami
Nassau
BAHAMAS
Tropic of Cancer
Gulf of Mexico
Gulf of California
Lower California
C. San Lucas
Chihuahua
Culiacán
Sierra Madre Occidental
Sierra Madre Oriental
Monterrey
Tampico
MEXICO
Guadalajara
Mexico City
Popocatépetl 17,887
Veracruz
Acapulco
Bay of Campeche
Mérida
Yucatán Pen.
BELIZE
GUATEMALA
Guatemala
HONDURAS
Tegucigalpa
San Salvador
EL SALVADOR
NICARAGUA
Managua
COSTA RICA
San José
CANAL ZONE
Panamá
PANAMA
Havana
CUBA
Santiago de Cuba
HAITI
Port-au-Prince
DOMINICAN REPUBLIC
Santo Domingo
San Juan
PUERTO RICO
JAMAICA
Kingston
Turks and Caicos Is. (U.K.)
West Indies
Greater Antilles
CARIBBEAN SEA
NETHERLANDS ANTILLES
Aruba
Curaçao
Willemstad
Barranquilla
Caracas
VENEZUELA
Bogotá
COLOMBIA
SOUTH AMERICA
PACIFIC OCEAN
ATLANTIC OCEAN
1000
100
Longitude 90° West of Greenwich

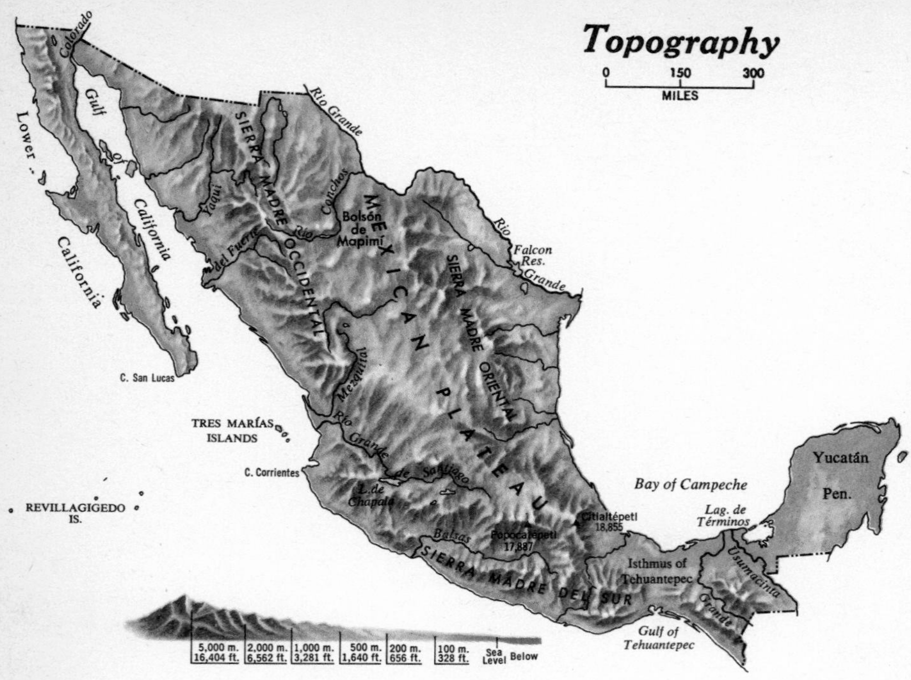

STATES and TERRITORIES

Aguascalientes, 334,936 ......H 6
Baja California, 856,773 ......B 1
Baja California (terr.), 123,786 ......C 3
Campeche, 250,391 ......O 7
Chiapas, 1,578,180 ......N 8
Chihuahua, 1,730,012 ......F 2
Coahuila, 1,140,989 ......H 3
Colima, 240,235 ......G 7
Distrito Federal, 7,005,855 ......L 1
Durango, 919,381 ......G 4
Guanajuato, 2,285,249 ......J 6
Guerrero, 1,573,098 ......J 8
Hidalgo, 1,156,177 ......K 6
Jalisco, 3,322,750 ......H 6
México, 3,797,861 ......K 7
Michoacán, 2,341,556 ......H 7
Morelos, 620,392 ......K 7
Nayarit, 547,992 ......G 6
Nuevo León, 1,653,808 ......K 4
Oaxaca, 2,011,946 ......L 8
Puebla, 2,483,770 ......L 7
Querétaro, 464,226 ......J 6
Quintana Roo (terr.), 91,044 ......P 7
San Luis Potosí, 1,257,028 ......J 5
Sinaloa, 1,273,228 ......F 4
Sonora, 1,092,458 ......D 2
Tabasco, 766,346 ......N 7
Tamaulipas, 1,438,350 ......K 4
Tlaxcala, 418,334 ......N 1
Veracruz, 3,813,613 ......L 7
Yucatán, 774,011 ......P 6
Zacatecas, 949,663 ......H 5

CITIES and TOWNS

Acámbaro, 80,259 ......J 7
Acaponeta, 29,829 ......G 5
Acapulco de Juárez, 234,866 ......J 8
Acatlán, 22,507 ......K 7
Acatzingo, 14,809 ......N 2
Acayucan, 36,352 ......M 8
Aconchi, 2,313 ......D 2
Actopan, 26,608 ......Q 1
Agualeguas, 5,536 ......J 3
Agua Prieta, 21,627 ......E 1
Aguascalientes, 222,105 ......H 6
Aguililla, 20,752 ......H 7
Ahuacatlán, 14,180 ......G 6
Ajalpan, 20,413 ......L 7
Alamos, 24,123 ......E 3
Aldama, Chihuahua, 14,117 ......G 2
Aldama, Tamaulipas, 15,336 ......L 5
Aljojuca, 5,520 ......O 1
Allende, Chihuahua, 11,039 ......G 3
Allende, Coahuila, 12,736 ......J 2
Allende, Nuevo León, 14,263 ......J 4
Almoloya del Río, 3,692 ......K 1
Altamira, 28,667 ......K 5
Altar, 3,811 ......D 1
Altotonga, 31,231 ......P 1
Alvarado, 33,152 ......M 7
Amatlán de los Reyes, 21,011 ......P 2
Amealco, 26,222 ......K 6
Ameca, 42,016 ......H 6
Amecameca de Juárez, 21,753 ......L 1
Amozoc de Mota, 13,381 ......N 2
Angostura, 29,709 ......E 4
Apan, 21,550 ......M 1
Apatzingán de la Constitución, 67,384 ......J 7
Apizaco, 20,998 ......N 1
Aquiles Serdán, 5,159 ......G 2
Aramberri, 16,051 ......J 5
Arandas, 41,958 ......H 6
Arcelia, 25,631 ......J 7
Arizpe, 4,415 ......D 1
Armeria, 16,334 ......G 7
Arriaga, 23,582 ......N 8
Arteaga, 17,455 ......H 7
Ascensión, 8,810 ......E 1
Atlixco, 72,256 ......M 2
Atotonilco, 35,297 ......H 6
Autlán de Navarro, 30,853 ......G 7
Ayutla de los Libres, 23,668 ......K 8
Azcapotzalco, 545,513 ......L 1
Azoyú, 23,554 ......K 8
Bacadéhuachi, 1,470 ......D 2
Bacerac, 2,306 ......E 1
Bácum, 17,598 ......D 3
Badiraguato, 28,995 ......F 4
Balancán, 27,241 ......O 8
Balleza, 15,122 ......F 3
Batopilas, 8,780 ......F 3
Baviácora, 4,202 ......E 2
Bavispe, 2,048 ......E 1
Benjamín Hill, 5,807 ......D 1
Boca del Río, 27,884 ......Q 1
Buenaventura, 14,629 ......F 2
Burgos, 5,529 ......K 4
Cadereyta, 28,093 ......K 6
Cadereyta Jiménez, 30,429 ......K 4
Calera, 13,030 ......H 5
Calkiní, 24,503 ......O 6
Calpulalpan, 14,633 ......M 1
Calvillo, 24,039 ......H 6
Campeche, 81,147 ......O 7
Cananea, 21,824 ......D 1
Canatlán, 63,871 ......G 4
Cancún ......Q 6
Candela, 2,202 ......J 3
Carbo, 3,242 ......D 2
Cárdenas, S. Luis Potosí, 18,091 ......K 6
Cárdenas, Tabasco, 78,477 ......N 8
Carmen, 71,240 ......N 7
Casas Grandes, 11,207 ......F 1
Catemaco, 23,671 ......M 7
Cedral, 12,426 ......J 5
Celaya, 143,703 ......J 6
Celestún, 1,535 ......O 6
Cerralvo, 6,831 ......J 3
Cerritos, 18,868 ......K 5
Chalchihuites, 11,347 ......G 5
Chalco, 41,145 ......M 1
Champotón, 27,581 ......O 7
Chapulco, 2,807 ......O 2
Charcas, 22,388 ......J 5
Chetumal, 34,237 ......Q 7
Chiapa de Corzo, 22,640 ......N 8
Chiautempan, 33,820 ......N 1
Chicoloapan de Juárez, 8,995 ......M 1
Chietla, 26,921 ......M 2
Chignahuapan, 29,556 ......N 1
Chignautla, 8,348 ......N 1
Chihuahua, 363,850 ......G 2
Chilapa, 53,263 ......K 8
Chilpancingo, 56,904 ......K 8
China, 9,018 ......K 4
Chocamán, 7,270 ......P 2
Choix, 27,515 ......E 3
Cholula, 20,913 ......M 1
Cihuatlán, 16,314 ......G 7
Cintalapa, 31,252 ......M 8
Ciudad Acuña, 32,760 ......J 2
Ciudad Camargo, Chihuahua, 29,185 ......G 3
Ciudad Camargo, Tamaulipas, 16,097 ......K 3
Ciudad Delicias, 64,385 ......G 2
Ciudad del Maíz, 35,502 ......K 5
Ciudad de Valles, 71,098 ......K 5
Ciudad Guerrero, 35,631 ......F 2
Ciudad Guzmán, 48,142 ......H 7
Ciudad Juárez, 436,054 ......F 1
Ciudad Lerdo, 53,551 ......H 4
Ciudad Madero, 89,994 ......L 5
Ciudad Mante, 79,130 ......K 5
Ciudad Miguel Alemán, 18,134 ......K 3
Ciudad Obregón, 181,972 ......E 3
Ciudad Río Bravo, 70,814 ......K 4
Ciudad Serdán, 25,288 ......O 2
Ciudad Victoria, 94,304 ......K 5
Coalcomán de Matamoros, 13,480 ......H 7
Coatepec, 34,161 ......P 1
Coatzacoalcos, 108,818 ......M 7
Cocula, 20,273 ......G 6
Colima, 72,074 ......H 7
Colón, 20,392 ......K 6
Colotlán, 14,316 ......H 5
Comala, 13,715 ......G 7
Comalcalco, 71,651 ......N 7
Comitán, 38,137 ......O 8
Comondú, 30,872 ......D 3
Compostela, 59,422 ......G 6
Concepción del Oro, 15,711 ......J 4
Concordia, 21,023 ......G 5
Córdoba, 92,870 ......P 2
Cosalá, 16,202 ......F 4
Cosamaloapan de Carpio, 75,412 ......M 7
Cosautlán de Carvajal, 8,015 ......P 1
Coscomatepec de Bravo, 19,890 ......P 2
Cosío, 7,031 ......H 5
Cosoleacaque, 20,251 ......M 7
Cotija, 17,296 ......H 7
Coyame, 3,798 ......G 2
Coyoacán, 338,850 ......L 1
Coyotepec, 8,658 ......L 1
Coyuca, 25,128 ......J 7
Coyuca de Benítez, 36,032 ......J 8
Coyutla, 12,008 ......L 6
Cozumel, 12,634 ......Q 6
Cuatrociénegas de Carranza, 9,512 ......H 3
Cuauhtémoc, 65,160 ......F 2
Cuautitlán, 40,622 ......L 1
Cuautla Morelos, 67,869 ......L 2
Cuencamé, 31,170 ......H 4
Cuernavaca, 159,909 ......L 2
Cuicatlán, 45,013 ......L 8
Cuitlahuac, 13,078 ......P 2
Culiacán, 358,812 ......F 4
Cumpas, 6,186 ......D 2
Cuna de la Independencia Nacional, 71,212 ......J 6
Cunduacán, 42,872 ......N 7
Doctor Arroyo, 45,889 ......K 5
Durango, 192,934 ......G 4
Ejutla de Crespo, 34,890 ......L 8
El Ebano, 20,571 ......K 5
El Fuerte, 62,001 ......E 3
El Oro, Durango, 18,668 ......G 4
El Oro, México, 17,086 ......K 7
El Salto, 19,604 ......G 5
Empalme, 32,541 ......D 2
Encarnación de Díaz, 29,533 ......H 6
Ensenada, 113,320 ......A 1
Escuinapa de Hidalgo, 30,763 ......G 5
Escuintla, 13,754 ......N 9
Etchojoa, 53,767 ......E 3
Fortín de las Flores, 21,370 ......P 2
Fresnillo, 101,316 ......H 5
Frontera, 43,007 ......N 7
Galeana, Chihuahua, 3,176 ......F 1
Galeana, Nuevo León, 39,143 ......J 4
García de la Cadena, 4,755 ......H 6
General Bravo, 6,063 ......K 4
General Cepeda, 13,332 ......J 4
Gómez Palacio, 135,743 ......G 4
González, 23,748 ......K 5
Guadalajara, 1,196,218 ......H 6
Guadalupe, Nvo. León, 153,454 ......J 4
Guadalupe, Zacatecas, 31,976 ......H 5
Guadalupe-Bravos, 9,649 ......F 1
Guadalupe Victoria, 27,450 ......G 4
Guadalupe y Calvo, 31,131 ......F 2
Guanacevi, 12,036 ......G 4
Guanajuato, 65,258 ......J 6
Guasave, 148,475 ......E 4
Guaymas, 84,730 ......D 3
Gutiérrez Zamora, 20,534 ......L 6
Halachó, 8,547 ......O 6
Hecelchakán, 10,974 ......O 6
Hermosillo, 206,663 ......D 2
Heroica Caborca, 29,486 ......C 1
Heroica Huamantla, 26,191 ......N 1
Heroica Nogales, 52,865 ......D 1
Hidalgo, 21,434 ......K 4
Hopelchén, 23,509 ......P 7
Huajuapan de León, 83,939 ......L 8
Huaquechula, 16,702 ......M 2
Huatabampo, 43,963 ......D 3
Huatusco de Chicuellar, 20,621 ......P 2
Huauchinango, 37,211 ......L 6
Huehuetlán, 6,962 ......M 2
Huejotzingo, 21,728 ......M 1
Huejutla de Reyes, 45,771 ......K 6
Huetamo de Núñez, 35,414 ......J 7
Hueyotlipan, 6,786 ......M 1
Huimanguillo, 70,525 ......N 8
Huitzuco, 28,159 ......K 7
Huixtla, 25,884 ......N 9
Hunucmá, 10,600 ......O 6
Ignacio de la Llave, 16,345 ......Q 2
Iguala, 60,980 ......K 7
Imuris, 5,853 ......D 1
Indé, 11,969 ......G 4
Irapuato, 175,966 ......J 6
Isla de Aguada ......O 7
Isla Mujeres, 10,469 ......Q 6
Ixmiquilpan, 35,851 ......K 6
Ixtacalco, 474,700 ......L 1
Ixtapalapa, 533,569 ......L 1
Ixtlán del Río, 16,228 ......G 6
Izamal, 16,188 ......P 6
Izúcar de Matamoros, 44,074 ......M 2
Jala, 11,174 ......G 6
Jalacingo, 15,436 ......P 1
Jalapa Enríquez, 127,081 ......P 1
Jalpa, Tabasco, 29,904 ......N 7
Jalpa, Zacatecas, 26,050 ......H 6
Jalpan, 15,319 ......K 6
Jáltipan, 19,676 ......M 8
Jaumave, 13,504 ......K 5
Jerez de Garcia Salinas, 49,202 ......H 5
Jico, 14,153 ......P 1
Jilotepec, 34,866 ......K 7
Jiménez, Chihuahua, 27,044 ......G 3
Jiménez, Coahuila, 8,019 ......J 2
Jojutla de Juárez, 31,196 ......L 2
Jonacatepec, 7,478 ......M 2
Jonuta, 14,227 ......N 7
Juan Aldama, 13,661 ......H 4
Juárez, 1,664 ......J 3
Juchipila, 14,517 ......H 6
Juchique de Ferrer, 14,094 ......Q 1
Juchitán de Zaragoza, 178,388 ......M 8
La Barca, 40,331 ......H 6
La Concordia, 15,296 ......N 9
La Cruz, Chihuahua, 3,899 ......G 3
La Cruz, Sinaloa, 19,055 ......F 5
Lagos, 66,273 ......J 6
La Paz, 49,637 ......D 5
La Piedad, 51,484 ......H 6
La Trinitaria, 28,028 ......N 9
La Yesca, 9.010 ......G 6
León, 453,976 ......J 6
Libres, 12,973 ......O 1
Linares, 49,397 ......K 4
Llera de Canales, 21,117 ......K 5
Loreto, 21,544 ......J 5
Los Mochis, 165,612 ......E 4
Los Reyes, 33,879 ......H 7
Macuspana, 75,013 ......N 8
Madera, 32,367 ......F 2
Magdalena, 13,485 ......D 1
Manuel Benavides, 5,135 ......H 2
Manzanillo, 46,170 ......G 7
Mapastepec, 16,911 ......N 9
Mapimí, 19,053 ......G 4
Martínez de la Torre, 62,707 ......L 6
Mascota, 15,260 ......G 6
Matamoros, Coahuila, 44,103 ......H 4
Matamoros, Tamaulipas, 182,887 ......L 4
Matehuala, 48,368 ......J 5
Maxcanú, 10,620 ......O 6
Mazapil, 28,656 ......J 4
Mazatán, 1,561 ......E 2
Mazatlán, 171,835 ......F 5
Melchor Múzquiz, 45,945 ......J 3
Melchor Ocampo, 4,180 ......H 4
Melchor Ocampo del Balsas, 23,248 ......H 8
Meoquí, 27,000 ......G 2
Mérida, 253,856 ......P 6
Mexicali, 390,411 ......B 1
Mexico City (México) (capital), 3,025,564 ......L 1
Mexico City, *7,157,000 ......L 1
Mezquital, 4,663 ......G 5
Miacatlán, 12,579 ......L 2
Mier, 5,916 ......K 3
Miguel Azua, 15,330 ......H 4
Minatitlán, 89,412 ......M 8
Mineral del Monte, 10,943 ......K 6
Miquihuana, 3,099 ......K 5
Misantla, 44,268 ......P 1
Mocorito, 49,957 ......F 4
Moctezuma, S. L. Potosí, 13,628 ......J 5
Moctezuma, Sonora, 3,476 ......E 2
Monclova, 80,252 ......J 3
Montemorelos, 34,067 ......K 4
Monterrey, 830,336 ......J 4
Morelia, 209,507 ......J 7
Morelos, 4,721 ......J 2
Morelos Cañada, 11,463 ......O 2
Moroleón, 33,765 ......J 6
Motozintla de Mendoza, 31,518 ......N 9
Motul, 21,087 ......P 6
Mulegé, 19,282 ......C 3
Muna, 6,147 ......P 6
Naco, 3,639 ......D 1
Nacozari de García, 3,483 ......E 1
Nadadores, 3,869 ......J 3
Nanacamilpa, 8,658 ......M 1
Naolinco de Victoria, 11,077 ......P 1
Naranjos, 21,371 ......L 6
Naucalpan, 373,605 ......L 1
Nautla, 9,425 ......L 6
Nava, 5,669 ......J 2
Navojoa, 69,792 ......E 3
Nazas, 13,189 ......G 4
Nieves, 19,938 ......H 5
Nochistlán, Oaxaca, 58,609 ......L 8
Nochistlán, Zacatecas, 28,463 ......H 6
Nogales, 19,158 ......P 2
Nombre de Dios, 17,742 ......G 5
Nonoava, 4,054 ......F 3
Nopalucan, 8,401 ......O 1
Nueva Casas Grandes, 25,333 ......F 1
Nueva Ciudad Guerrero, 4,065 ......K 3
Nuevo Laredo, 150,922 ......J 3
Nuevo Morelos, 2,245 ......K 5
Oaxaca de Juárez, 156,587 ......L 8
Ocampo, Chihuahua, 4,947 ......E 2
Ocampo, Coahuila, 10,072 ......H 3
Ocampo, Tamaulipas, 15,998 ......K 5
Ocotlán, 43,394 ......H 6
Ocotlán de Morelos, 45,752 ......L 8
Ojinaga, 23,854 ......G 2
Ojocaliente, 20,280 ......H 5
Ometepec, 23,604 ......K 8
Opódepe, 3,312 ......D 2
Oriental, 7,375 ......O 1
Orizaba, 92,728 ......P 2
Otumba de Gómez Farías, 11,960 ......M 1
Oxkutzcab, 10,295 ......P 7
Ozuluama, 22,382 ......L 6
Ozumba, 11,013 ......M 1
Pachuca, 84,543 ......K 6
Padilla, 13,643 ......K 5
Palenque, 22,684 ......O 8
Palizada, 7,445 ......O 7
Palmar de Bravo, 15,898 ......O 2
Palmillas, 2,420 ......K 5
Pánuco, 49,077 ......K 6
Papantla de Olarte, 94,623 ......L 6
Paraíso, 30,439 ......N 7
Parral, 61,729 ......G 3
Parras, 32,664 ......H 4
Pátzcuaro, 44,591 ......J 7
Pedro Montoya, 10,760 ......K 6
Pénjamo, 89,548 ......J 6
Peñón Blanco, 10,541 ......H 4
Perote, 23,556 ......P 1
Petatlán, 31,088 ......J 8
Peto, 11,986 ......P 6
Piedras Negras, 65,883 ......J 2
Pijijiapan, 20,350 ......N 9
Pitiquito, 6,100 ......D 1
Pochutla, 84,033 ......L 9
Poza Rica de Hidalgo, 121,341 ......L 6
Progreso, 22,100 ......P 6

Puebla, 521,885 ....N 2
Puente de Ixtla, 24,370 ....K 2
Puerto Juárez ....Q 6
Puerto México (Coatzacoalcos), 108,818 ....M 7
Puerto Peñasco, 12,563 ....C 1
Puerto Vallarta, 35,542 ....G 6
Purificación, 13,079 ....G 7
Puruándiro, 71,523 ....J 7
Putla, 54,874 ....L 8
Quecholac, 15,191 ....O 2
Querétaro, 140,379 ....K 6
Ramos Arizpe, 18,979 ....J 4
Rayón, San Luis Potosí, 16,041 ....K 6
Rayón, Sonora, 2,736 ....D 2
Reynosa, 143,514 ....K 3
Rincón de Romos, 18,867 ....H 5
Río Grande, 34,879 ....H 5
Ríoverde, 57,016 ....J 6
Rodeo, 14,229 ....G 4
Rosamorada, 28,568 ....G 5
Rosario, Sinaloa, 38,423 ....G 5
Rosario, Sonora, 7,524 ....E 3
Sabinas, 30,726 ....J 3
Sabinas Hidalgo, 19,223 ....K 3
Sahuaripa, 9,379 ....E 2
Sahuayo de Díaz, 42,513..............H 6
Sain Alto, 14,259 ....H 5
Salamanca, 103,740 ....J 6
Salina Cruz ....M 9
Salinas, 14,647 ....J 5
Saltillo, 191,879 ....J 4
San Andrés, Tuxtla, 77,351 ....M 7
San Antonio, 5,129 ....D 5
San Blas, Nayarit, 32,609 ....G 6
San Blas, Sonora ....E 3
San Buenaventura, 12,014 ....J 3
San Carlos, 11,349 ....K 4
San Cristóbal, 32,110 ....O 8
San Felipe, 56,021 ....J 6
San Fernando, Chiapas, 10,391 ....N 8
San Fernando, Tamaulipas, 27,656 ....L 4
San Francisco, 43,271 ....H 6
San Francisco del Oro. 16,193 ......F 3
(continued on following page)

AREA 761,601 sq. mi.
POPULATION 48,313,438
CAPITAL Mexico City
LARGEST CITY Mexico City
HIGHEST POINT Citlaltépetl 18,855 ft.
MONETARY UNIT Mexican peso
MAJOR LANGUAGE Spanish
MAJOR RELIGION Roman Catholicism

States Indicated by Numbers

1	Tlaxcala	6	Querétaro
2	Morelos	7	Guanajuato
3	Distrito Federal	8	Aguascalientes
4	México	9	Nayarit
5	Hidalgo	10	Colima

(continued)

San Gabriel Chilac, 7,303 ... K 7
San Ignacio, 22,116 ... F 5
San Javier, 390 ... D 2
San José del Cabo, 9,382 ... D 5
San Juan, Jalisco, 31,389 ... H 6
San Juan, Querétaro, 53,332 ... K 6
San Juan de Guadalupe, 8,877 ... H 4
San Juan del Río, 14,639 ... G 4
San Juan Ixtenco, 4,894 ... N 1
San Juan Xiutetelco, 11,771 ... O 1
San Luis de la Paz, 26,819 ... J 6
San Luis del Cordero, 3,155 ... H 4
San Luis Potosí, 274,320 ... J 6
San Luis Río Colorado, 63,644 ... B 1
San Marcos, 33,954 ... K 8
San Martín Texmelucan, 50,071 ... M 1
San Martín Xaltocan, 6,142 ... N 1
San Miguel, 63,937 ... J 6
San Nicolás, 1,023 ... K 4
San Nicolás Terrenate, 7,160 ... K 4
San Pedro, 70,407 ... H 4
San Pedro del Gallo, 3,843 ... G 4
Santa Ana, 10,416 ... D 1
Santa Bárbara, 20,117 ... F 3
Santa Cruz, 1,659 ... D 1
Santa Inés Zacatelco, 19,972 ... M 1
Santa María, 6,260 ... G 6
Santa María del Río, 30,072 ... J 6
Santa María del Tule ... L 8
Santander Jiménez, 5,323 ... K 4
Santa Rosalía ... C 3
Santiago, Baja California, 4,978 ... E 5
Santiago, Nayarit, 84,167 ... G 6
Santiago Jamiltepec, 104,275 ... K 8
Santiago Juxtlahuaca, 37,095 ... K 8
Santiago Papasquiaro, 35,828 ... F 4
Santiago Tuxtla, 33,471 ... M 7
Saucillo, 30,781 ... G 2
Sayula, 18,878 ... H 7
Sierra Mojada, 5,517 ... H 3
Silao, 69,866 ... J 6
Simojovel, 14,896 ... N 8
Sinaloa de Leyva, 53,639 ... E 4
Soledad de Doblado, 19,467 ... Q 2
Soledad Díez Gutiérrez, 28,337 ... J 5
Sombrerete, 48,411 ... H 5
Sotuta, 5,417 ... P 6
Soyopa, 2,314 ... E 2
Suaqui, 1,061 ... E 2
Tacámbaro de Codallos, 33,690 ... J 7
Tacotalpa, 20,912 ... N 8
Tala, 33,369 ... G 6
Talpa de Allende, 13,027 ... G 6
Tamazunchale, 60,976 ... K 6
Tamiahua, 23,689 ... L 6
Tampico, 196,147 ... L 5
Tapachula, 108,464 ... N 9
Taxco de Alarcón, 64,368 ... K 7
Teapa, 19,787 ... N 8
Tecamachalco, 21,688 ... O 2
Tecate, 17,917 ... A 1
Tecomán, 45,933 ... H 7
Tecpan de Galeana, 44,820 ... J 8
Tecuala, 41,129 ... G 5
Tehuacán, 67,520 ... L 7
Tehuantepec, 100,176 ... M 8
Tehuipango, 7,163 ... P 2
Tekax, 16,370 ... P 6
Teloloapan, 48,458 ... J 7
Temascalapa, 9,428 ... M 1
Temax, 5,821 ... P 6
Temósachic, 8,378 ... F 2
Tenabo, 3,992 ... P 6
Tenancingo, 31,808 ... K 7
Tenango de Río Blanco, 27,266 ... O 2
Tenosique de Pino Suárez, 26,954 ... O 8
Teocaltiche, 29,330 ... H 6
Teocelo, 7,441 ... P 1
Teotihuacán de Arista, 15,704 ... L 1
Teotitlán, 103,209 ... L 8
Tepatitlán, 53,683 ... H 6
Tepatlaxco de Hidalgo, 8,768 ... N 1
Tepeaca, 26,334 ... N 2
Tepeapulco, 26,254 ... M 1
Tepehuanes, 16,361 ... G 4
Tepeji, 24,107 ... K 6
Tepetlaoxtoc, 6,987 ... L 1
Tepexi de Rodríguez, 12,655 ... O 2
Tepeyahualco, 9,504 ... N 1
Tepic, 111,344 ... G 6
Tepoztlán, 12,835 ... L 1
Texcoco de Mora, 67,220 ... M 1
Teziutlán, 41,502 ... O 1
Ticul, 16,537 ... P 6
Tierra Blanca, 48,733 ... L 7
Tihuatlán, 53,447 ... L 6
Tijuana, 333,125 ... A 1
Tixtla, 19,735 ... K 8
Tizayuca, 8,717 ... L 1
Tizimín, 29,895 ... Q 6
Tlachichuca, 15,225 ... O 1
Tlacolula, 78,684 ... L 8
Tlacotalpan, 13,404 ... M 7
Tlacotepec de Mejía, 1,948 ... P 1
Tlahualilo de Zaragoza, 21,646 ... H 3
Tlalixcoyan, 28,625 ... Q 2
Tlalmanalco de Velásquez, 20,420 ... L 1
Tlalnepantla de Comonfort, 373,657 ... K 1
Tlalpan, 115,528 ... L 1
Tlaltenango, 19,145 ...
Tlaltizapán, 20,716 ... L 2
Tlapacoyan, 23,623 ... P 1
Tlapa de Comonfort, 23,261 ... K 8
Tlaquiltenango, 16,335 ... L 2
Tlaxcala, 21,424 ... M 1
Tlaxco de Morelos, 16,128 ... N 1
Tlaxiaco, 85,929 ... L 8
Tlayacapan, 5,240 ... L 1
Todos Santos, 4,506 ... D 5
Tolimán, 12,017 ... K 6
Toluca, 220,195 ... K 7
Tomatlán, 17,201 ... G 6
Tonalá, 41,562 ... N 8
Topolobampo ... E 4
Torreón, 257,045 ... H 4
Tula, 21,201 ... K 5
Tulancingo, 45,449 ... K 7
Tulcingo de Valle, 6,718 ... M 2
Tultepec, 13,693 ... L 1
Tuxpan, Jalisco, 23,569 ... H 7
Tuxpan, Nayarit, 28,345 ... G 6
Tuxpan de Rodríguez Cano, 65,211 ... L 6
Tuxtepec, 184,757 ... L 7
Tuxtla Gutiérrez, 69,326 ... N 8
Umán, 14,258 ... P 6
Ures, 10,366 ... D 2
Úrsulo Galván, 16,772 ... Q 1
Uruáchic, 7,585 ... E 3
Uruapan, 104,475 ... H 7
Valladolid, 25,367 ... P 6
Valle de Bravo, 23,591 ... J 7
Valle de Santiago, 80,504 ... J 6
Valle Hermoso, 41,546 ... L 4
Vanegas, 6,384 ... J 5
Venado, 12,147 ... J 5
Venustiano Carranza, 32,131 ... N 8
Veracruz Llave, 242,351 ... Q 1
Vicente Guerrero, Durango, 13,529 ... G 5
Vicente Guerrero, Puebla, 10,207 ... M 2
Viesca, 15,046 ... H 4
Villa de Cos, 18,012 ... H 5
Villa de Guadalupe, 12,436 ... J 5
Villa de Seris ... D 2
Villa Frontera, 31,055 ... J 3
Villa García, 9,116 ... J 5
Villagrán, 10,338 ... K 4
Villahermosa, 162,678 ... N 8
Villaldama, 4,639 ... J 3
Villa Matamoros, 5,928 ... G 3
Villanueva, 35,553 ... H 5
Villa Unión, 20,002 ... H 5
Xicoténcatl, 21,144 ... K 5
Xicotepec de Juárez, 27,372 ... K 6
Xochihuehuetlán, 6,046 ... K 8
Xochimilco, 117,083 ... L 1
Xochitlán, 8,166 ... N 2
Yajalón, 29,497 ... N 8
Yautepec, 26,182 ... L 2
Yécora, 4,898 ... E 2
Yecuatla, 10,382 ... P 1
Zaachila, 22,739 ... L 8
Zacapoaxtla, 25,479 ... O 1
Zacapu, 52,649 ... J 7
Zacatecas, 56,829 ... H 5
Zacatlán, 37,261 ... N 1
Zacoalco, 21,929 ... H 6
Zamora, 82,712 ... H 7
Zaragoza, 8,955 ... J 2
Zimatlán de Álvarez, 40,302 ... L 8
Zitácuaro, 67,173 ... J 7
Zongolica, 24,372 ... P 2
Zumpango, 35,035 ... L 1
Zumpango del Río, 21,894 ... J 8

OTHER FEATURES

Agiobampo (bay) ... E 3
Aguanaval (river) ... H 4
Amistad (res.) ... J 2
Ángel de la Guarda (island) ... C 2
Antigua (river) ... Q 1
Arena (point) ... E 5
Arenas (cay) ... O 5
Atoyac (river) ... N 2
Atoyac (river) ... Q 2
Babia (river) ... J 2
Bacalar (lake) ... P 7
Ballenas (bay) ... C 3
Balsas (river) ... J 7
Banderas (bay) ... G 6
Bavispe (river) ... E 1
Blanco (river) ... Q 2
Bravo (river) ... G 2
Burro, Sierra del (mts.) ... J 2
California (gulf) ... D 3
Campeche (bank) ... O 5
Campeche (bay) ... N 7
Candelaria (river) ... O 8
Carmen (island) ... D 3
Casas Grandes (river) ... F 1
Catoche (cape) ... Q 6
Cedros (island) ... B 2
Cerralvo (island) ... E 4
Chamela (bay) ... G 7
Chapala (lake) ... H 6
Chetumal (bay) ... P 8
Chichén-Itzá (ruins) ... P 6
Chixoy (river) ... O 8
Citlaltépetl (mt.) ... O 2
Clarión (island) ... B 7
Colorado (river) ... B 1
Conchos (river) ... G 2
Corrientes (cape) ... F 6
Coyuca (river) ... O 1
Cresciente (island) ... D 5
Cuitzeo (lake) ... J 7
Delgada (point) ... L 7
Dzibichaltún (ruins) ... P 6
El Azúcar (res.) ... K 3
Espíritu Santo (island) ... D 4
Falcón (res.) ... K 3
Falso (cape) ... D 5
Fuerte (river) ... E 3
Giganta, Sierra de la (mts.) ... D 4
Grande (river) ... N 8
Grande (river) ... G 2
Grande de Santiago (river) ... G 6
Grijalva (river) ... N 7
Guzmán (lake) ... F 1
Herrero (point) ... Q 7
Holbox (island) ... Q 6
Hondo (river) ... P 7
Jesús María, Barra (inlet) ... L 4
La Boquilla (res.) ... G 3
La Paz (bay) ... D 4
Lobos (cape) ... C 2
Lobos (point) ... D 3
Lower California (pen.), 980,559 ... B 3
Madre (lagoon) ... L 4
Madre del Sur, Sierra (mts.) ... J-L 8
Madre Occidental, Sierra (mts.) ... F 3
Madre Oriental, Sierra (mts.) ... J 4
Magdalena (bay) ... C 4
Maldonado (point) ... K 8
Mapimí, Bolsón de (depression) ... G 3
María Cleófas (island) ... F 6
María Madre (island) ... F 6
María Magdalena (island) ... F 6
Mexico (gulf) ... N 4
Mezquital (river) ... G 5
Mita (point) ... G 6
Mitla (ruins) ... M 8
Moctezuma (river) ... K 6
Monserrate (isl.) ... D 4
Montague (isl.) ... B 1
Muerto, Mar (lagoon) ... N 9
Nauhcampatépetl (mt.) ... O 1
Nayarit, Sierra (mts.) ... G 5
Nazas (river) ... G 4
Nuevo (cay) ... O 6
Orizaba (Citlaltépetl) (mt.) ... O 2
Palenque (ruins) ... O 8
Palmito de la Vírgen (isl.) ... F 5
Palmito del Verde (isl.) ... F 5
Pánuco (river) ... K 5
Parícutin (vol.) ... H 7
Pátzcuaro (lake) ... J 7
Pérez (isl.) ... P 5
Petachalco (bay) ... H 8
Popocatépetl (mt.) ... M 1
Ramos (river) ... G 4
Revillagigedo (isls.) ... C 7
Río Grande (river) ... N 8
Roca Partida (isl.) ... C 7
Sabinas (river) ... J 3
Salada (lagoon) ... A 1
San Antonio, Barra de (inlet) ... L 4
San Benedicto (isl.) ... D 7
San Benito (isl.) ... B 2
San Blas (river) ... O 8
San Jorge (bay) ... C 1
San José (isl.) ... D 4
San Lázaro (cape) ... C 4
San Lucas (cape) ... E 5
San Marcos (isl.) ... D 3
San Rafael, Barra de (inlet) ... L 4
Santa Ana, Barra de (inlet) ... N 7
Santa Catalina (isl.) ... D 4
Santa Cruz (isl.) ... D 4
Santa Eugenia (point) ... B 3
Santa Inés (bay) ... D 3
Santa Margarita (isl.) ... C 4
Santa María (lake) ... F 1
Santa María (river) ... F 1
Santiaguillo (lake) ... G 4
Sebastián Vizcaíno (bay) ... B 2
Socorro (isl.) ... D 7
Sonora (river) ... D 2
Superior (lagoon) ... M 9
Teacapán, Boca (inlet) ... F 5
Tehuantepec (gulf) ... M 9
Tehuantepec (isthmus) ... M 8
Teotihuacán (ruins) ... M 1
Términos (lagoon) ... O 7
Tiburón (isl.) ... C 2
Tres Marías (isls.) ... F 6
Triángulo Este (isl.) ... N 6
Triángulo Oeste (isl.) ... N 6
Tula (river) ... L 1
Urique (river) ... F 3
Usumacinta (river) ... O 8
Uxmal (ruins) ... P 6
Valsequillo, Presa (res.) ... N 2
Verde (river) ... F 3
Verde (river) ... L 8
Yaqui (river) ... E 2

*City and suburbs.

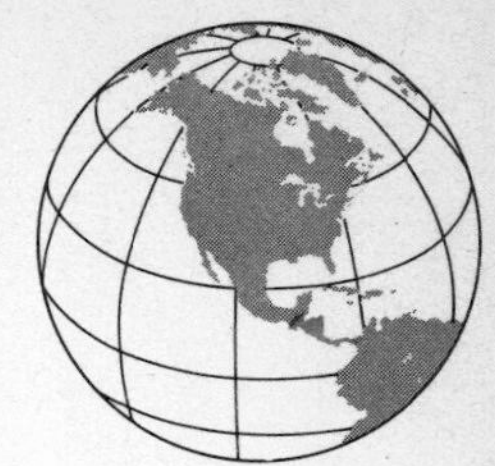

GUATEMALA
AREA 42,042 sq. mi.
POPULATION 5,200,000
CAPITAL Guatemala
LARGEST CITY Guatemala
HIGHEST POINT Tajumulco 13,845 ft.
MONETARY UNIT quetzal
MAJOR LANGUAGES Spanish, Quiché
MAJOR RELIGION Roman Catholicism

BRITISH HONDURAS
AREA 8,867 sq. mi.
POPULATION 122,000
CAPITAL Belmopan
LARGEST CITY Belize City
HIGHEST POINT Victoria Peak, 3,681 ft.
MONETARY UNIT British Honduran dollar
MAJOR LANGUAGES English, Spanish, Mayan
MAJOR RELIGIONS Protestantism, Roman Catholicism

EL SALVADOR
AREA 8,260 sq. mi.
POPULATION 3,418,455
CAPITAL San Salvador
LARGEST CITY San Salvador
HIGHEST POINT Santa Ana 7,825 ft.
MONETARY UNIT colón
MAJOR LANGUAGE Spanish
MAJOR RELIGION Roman Catholicism

HONDURAS
AREA 43,277 sq. mi.
POPULATION 2,495,000
CAPITAL Tegucigalpa
LARGEST CITY Tegucigalpa
HIGHEST POINT Las Minas 9,347 ft.
MONETARY UNIT lempira
MAJOR LANGUAGE Spanish
MAJOR RELIGION Roman Catholicism

NICARAGUA
AREA 45,698 sq. mi.
POPULATION 1,984,000
CAPITAL Managua
LARGEST CITY Managua
HIGHEST POINT Cerro Mocotón 6,913 ft.
MONETARY UNIT córdoba
MAJOR LANGUAGE Spanish
MAJOR RELIGION Roman Catholicism

COSTA RICA
AREA 19,575 sq. mi.
POPULATION 1,800,000
CAPITAL San José
LARGEST CITY San José
HIGHEST POINT Chirripó Grande 12,530 ft.
MONETARY UNIT colón
MAJOR LANGUAGE Spanish
MAJOR RELIGION Roman Catholicism

PANAMA
AREA 29,209 sq. mi.
POPULATION 1,425,343
CAPITAL Panamá
LARGEST CITY Panamá
HIGHEST POINT Vol. Chiriquí 11,401 ft.
MONETARY UNIT balboa
MAJOR LANGUAGE Spanish
MAJOR RELIGION Roman Catholicism

CANAL ZONE
AREA 647 sq. mi.
POPULATION 44,650
CAPITAL Balboa Heights

Agriculture, Industry and Resources

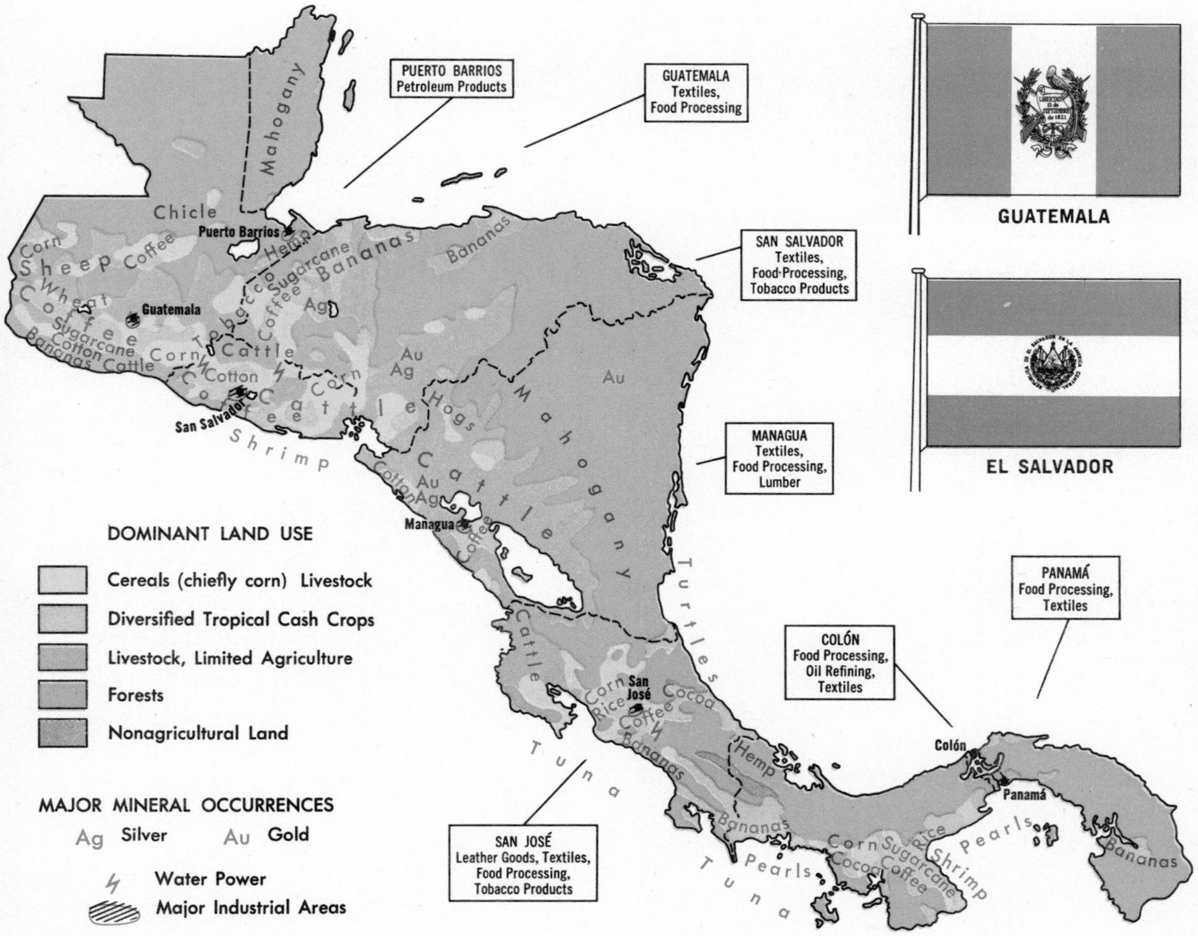

PUERTO BARRIOS
Petroleum Products
GUATEMALA
Textiles,
Food Processing
SAN SALVADOR
Textiles,
Food Processing,
Tobacco Products
MANAGUA
Textiles,
Food Processing,
Lumber
PANAMÁ
Food Processing,
Textiles
COLÓN
Food Processing,
Oil Refining,
Textiles
SAN JOSÉ
Leather Goods, Textiles,
Food Processing,
Tobacco Products
Puerto Barrios
Guatemala
San Salvador
Managua
San José
Colón
Panamá
Mahogany
Chicle
Corn
Sheep
Coffee
Wheat
Sugarcane
Cotton
Cattle
Bananas
Hemp
Tobacco
Hogs
Shrimp
Turtles
Tuna
Pearls
Rice
Cocoa
DOMINANT LAND USE
Cereals (chiefly corn) Livestock
Diversified Tropical Cash Crops
Livestock, Limited Agriculture
Forests
Nonagricultural Land
MAJOR MINERAL OCCURRENCES
Ag Silver
Au Gold
Water Power
Major Industrial Areas

GUATEMALA

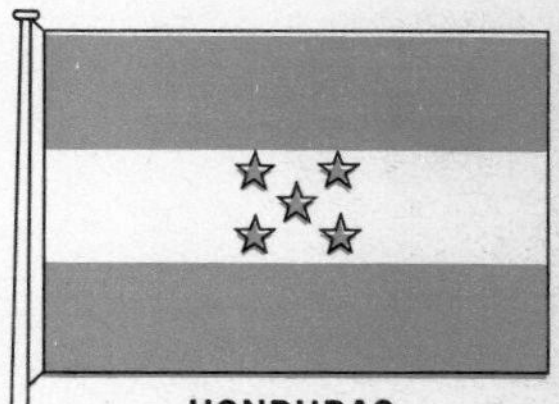

HONDURAS

EL SALVADOR

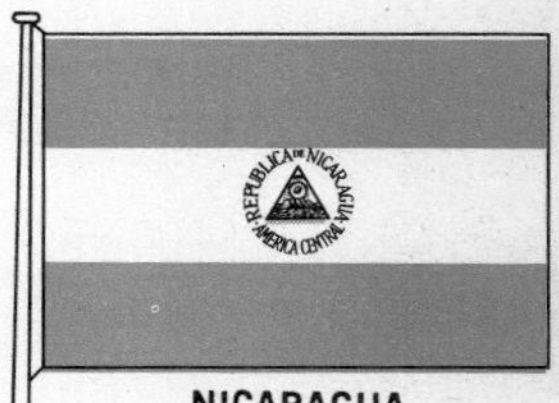

NICARAGUA

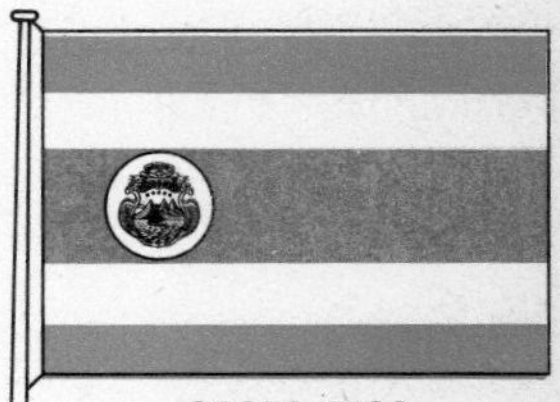

COSTA RICA

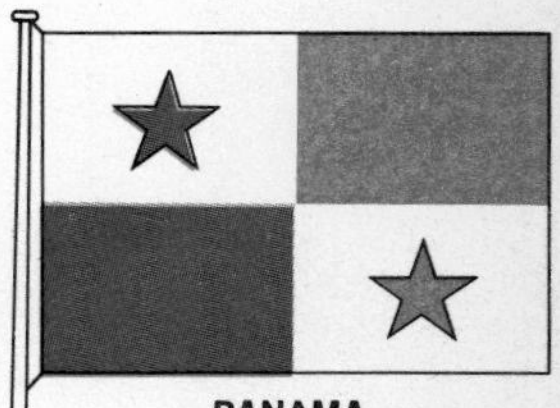

PANAMA

BRITISH HONDURAS

CITIES and TOWNS

Belize City, 37,000 ....C 2
Belize City, *48,421 ....C 2
Belmopan (capital) ....C 2
Benque Viejo, 1,607 ....C 2
Cayo, 1,890 ....C 2
Corozal Town, 3,171 ....C 1
Hill Bank, 78 ....C 2
Monkey River Town, 417 ....C 2
Orange Walk Town, 2,157 ....C 1
Punta Gorda, 1,789 ....C 2
San José, 365 ....C 2
San Pedro, 170 ....D 2
Stann Creek Town, 5,287 ....C 2

OTHER FEATURES

Ambergris (cay), †572 ....D 1
Belize (river) ....C 2
Bokel (cay) ....D 2
Cockscomb (mts.) ....C 2
Corker (cay), †360 ....D 2
Glovers (reef) ....D 2
Half Moon (cay) ....D 2
Hondo (river) ....C 1
Honduras (gulf) ....D 2
Mauger (cay) ....D 2
New (river) ....C 2
Saint Georges (cay), †34 ....D 2
Sarstún (river) ....C 3
Turneffe (isls.), 99 ....D 2

CANAL ZONE

CITIES and TOWNS

Balboa, 2,568 ....H 6
Cristóbal, 817 ....G 6

COSTA RICA

CITIES and TOWNS

Alajuela, 25,195 ....E 6
Atenas, 963 ....E 6
Atlanta ....F 6
Bagaces, 1,175 ....E 5
Beverly ....F 6
Boruca, ‡1,049 ....F 6
Buenos Aires, ‡4,624 ....F 6
Cañas, 2,991 ....E 5
Carmen ....F 5
Cartago, 19,038 ....F 6
Chomes, ‡1,991 ....E 5
Ciudad Quesada, 3,696 ....E 5
El Salvador ....F 5
Esparta, 2,860 ....E 5
Filadelfia, 1,574 ....E 5
Golfito, 6,859 ....F 6
Grecia, 4,862 ....E 5
Guácimo, 5,731 ....F 5
Guápiles, 983 ....F 5
Heredia, 20,523 ....E 5
Las Juntas, 827 ....E 5
Liberia, 11,171 ....E 5
Limón, 30,676 ....F 6
Miramar, 1,122 ....E 5
Nicoya, 3,196 ....E 5
Orotina, 1,749 ....E 6
Palmares, 1,529 ....F 6
Paquera ....E 6
Paraíso, 4,427 ....F 6
Pejivalle ....F 6
Platanilla ....F 6
Playa Bonita ....E 6
Puerto Cortés, 1,757 ....F 6
Puntarenas, 27,527 ....E 6
Quepos, 1,858 ....E 6
San Ignacio, 315 ....E 6
San José (cap.), 182,961 ....F 5
San José, *408,000 ....F 5
San Marcos, 411 ....E 6
San Ramón, 6,444 ....E 5
Santa Cruz, 3,849 ....E 5
Santa Rosa, ‡1,750 ....E 5
Santo Domingo, 3,333 ....F 6
Sibube ....F 6
Siquirres, 2,157 ....F 5
Turrialba, 8,629 ....F 6
Vesta ....F 6

OTHER FEATURES

Blanca (point) ....F 5
Blanco (cape) ....E 6
Blanco (mt.) ....F 6
Burica (point) ....F 6
Cahuita (point) ....F 6
Caño (isl.) ....F 6

(continued on following page)

(continued)

COSTA RICA (continued)

Carreta (point) ....F 6
Chirripó Grande (mt.) ....F 6
Coronada (bay) ....F 6
Cuilapa Miravalles (volcano)....E 5
Dulce (gulf) ....F 6
Góngora (mt.) ....E 5
Guionos (point) ....E 6
Irazú (mt.) ....F 6
Judas (point) ....E 6
Llerena (point) ....F 6
Matapalo (cape) ....F 6
Nicoya (gulf) ....E 6
Nicoya (pen.) ....E 6
Papagayo (gulf) ....E 5
Salinas (bay) ....D 5
San Juan (river) ....E, F 5
Santa Elena (cape) ....D 5
Talamanca (range) ....F 6
Velas (cape) ....D 5

EL SALVADOR

CITIES and TOWNS

Acajutla, 5,310 ....B 4
Ahuachapán, 16,180 ....B 4
Atiquizaya, 7,878 ....C 3
Chalatenango, 7,209 ....C 3
Chinameca, 7,020 ....C 4
Cojutepeque, 16,084 ....C 4
Estanzuelas, 2,785 ....C 4
Ilobasco, 6,432 ....C 4
Intipucá, 3,683 ....D 4
Jucuarán, 1,600 ....C 4
La Libertad, 7,015 ....C 4
La Palma, 1,992 ....C 3
La Unión, 16,459 ....D 4
Metapán, 4,896 ....C 3
Nueva San Salvador (Santa Tecla), 36,944 ....C 4
Puerto de la Concordia ....C 4
San Francisco Gotera, 4,638 ....C 4
San Miguel, 50,668 ....D 4
San Salvador (cap.), 349,725....C 4
Santa Ana, 102,301 ....C 4
Santa Rosa de Lima, 6,297 ....D 4
Santa Tecla, 36,944 ....C 4
San Vicente, 19,887 ....C 4
Sensuntepeque, 6,791 ....C 4
Sonsonate, 32,675 ....C 4
Suchitoto, 5,758 ....C 4
Texistepeque, 1,723 ....C 3
Usulután, 17,796 ....C 4
Zacatecoluca, 16,189 ....C 4

OTHER FEATURES

Fonseca (gulf) ....D 4
Güija (lake) ....C 3
Lempa (river) ....C 4
Remedios (point) ....B 4
Santa Ana (mt.) ....C 4

GUATEMALA

CITIES and TOWNS

Amatitlán, 12,225 ....B 3
Antigua, 13,576 ....B 3
Asunción Mita, 6,341 ....C 3
Cahabón, 939 ....C 3
Chahal, 323 ....C 3
Chajul, 4,187 ....B 3
Champerico, 3,823 ....A 3
Chichicastenango, 2,099 ....B 3
Chimaltenango, 9,077 ....B 3
Chinaja ....B 2
Chiquimula, 14,760 ....C 3
Chisec, 812 ....B 3
Coatepeque, 13,657 ....A 3
Cobán, 9,073 ....B 3
Comalapa, 9,202 ....B 3
Cubulco, 1,676 ....B 3
Cuilapa, 3,657 ....B 3
Cuilco, 728 ....B 3
Dolores, 630 ....C 2
El Cambio ....C 2
El Porvenir ....B 2
El Progreso, 3,458 ....B 3
Escuintla, 24,832 ....B 3
Flores, 1,503 ....C 2
Gualán, 4,425 ....C 3
Guatemala (cap.), 700,000 ....B 3
Huehuetenango, 10,185 ....B 3
Ipala, 3,190 ....C 3
Izabal ....C 3
Iztapa, 751 ....B 4
Jacaltenango, 3,873 ....B 3
Jalapa, 10,035 ....B 3
Jutiapa, 7,747 ....B 3
La Gomera, 1,397 ....B 3
La Libertad, 770 ....B 2
Livingston, 3,026 ....C 3
Los Amates, 1,131 ....C 3
Masagua, 1,100 ....B 3
Matías de Gálvez ....C 3
Mazatenango, 19,506 ....B 3
Momostenango, 3,148 ....B 3
Morales, 1,710 ....C 3
Nejapa ....B 3
Ocós, 576 ....A 3
Panzós, 1,803 ....C 3
Puerto Barrios, 22,242 ....C 3
Quezaltenango, 45,195 ....B 3
Quezaltepeque, 2,578 ....C 3
Rabinal, 4,155 ....B 3
Retalhuleu, 14,366 ....B 3
Río Hondo, 1,300 ....C 3
Sacapulas, 1,407 ....B 3
Salamá, 4,442 ....B 3
San Andrés, 939 ....B 2
San Felipe, 2,916 ....B 3
San José, 5,771 ....B 4
San Juan de Dios ....B 2
San Luis, 763 ....C 2
San Luis Jilotepeque, 5,795 ....C 3
San Marcos, 5,569 ....B 3
San Martín Jilotepeque, 2,806....B 3
San Mateo Ixtatán, 2,892 ....B 3
San Miguel ....C 2
San Pedro Carchá, 3,966 ....B 3
Santa Ana, 239 ....C 2
Santa Ana Mixtán ....B 4
Santa Cruz del Quiché, 6,472....B 3
Santa Rosa de Lima, 734....B 3
Sipacate ....B 4
Solola, 3,957 ....B 3
Tacaná, 900 ....A 3
Tejutla, 973 ....B 3
Totonicapán, 7,292 ....B 3
Yaloch ....C 2
Zacapa, 11,173 ....C 3

OTHER FEATURES

Atitlán (lake) ....B 3
Atitlán (volcano) ....B 3
Azul (river) ....C 2
Chixoy (river) ....B 2
Dulce (Izabal) (lake) ....C 3
Güija (lake) ....C 3
Honduras (gulf) ....D 2
Izabal (lake) ....C 3
Minas (mts.) ....C 3
Motagua (river) ....C 3
Pasión (river) ....B 2
Petén-Itzá (lake) ....B 2
San Pedro (river) ....B 2
Sarstun (river) ....C 3
Tacaná (volcano) ....A 3
Tajumulco (volcano) ....B 3
Tres Puntas (cape) ....C 3
Usumacinta (river) ....B 2

HONDURAS

CITIES and TOWNS

Ahuás ....E 3
Amapala, 3,491 ....D 4
Balana ....E 3
Balfate, 602 ....D 3
Belén, 201 ....C 3
Brus Laguna, 1,247 ....E 3
Caratasca ....F 3
Catacamas, 4,751 ....E 3
Cedros, 1,177 ....D 3
Chichicaste ....E 3
Choloma, 6,678 ....C 3
Choluteca, 17,350 ....D 4
Colorado ....D 3
Comayagua, 11,247 ....D 3
Comayagüela ....D 3
Concepción de María, 653 ....D 4
Concordia, 644 ....D 3
Copán, 2,190 ....C 3
Corquín, 2,817 ....C 3
Cruta ....F 3
Danlí, 8,242 ....D 3
Donel ....E 3
El Dulce Nombre, 145 ....E 3

CENTRAL AMERICA

CONIC PROJECTION

SCALE OF MILES

SCALE OF KILOMETRES

Capitals of Countries
International Boundaries
Canals

El Paraíso, Copán, 1,787 ....C 3
El Paraíso, El Paraíso, 5,758....D 4
El Porvenir, 529 ....D 3
El Progreso, 8,718 ....D 3
El Triunfo, 2,136 ....D 4
Goascorán, 1,184 ....D 4
Gracias, 2,484 ....C 3
Guaimaca, 2,620 ....D 3
Gualpatanta ....E 3
Guanaja, 1,253 ....E 2
Guarita, 599 ....C 3
Guayape, 610 ....D 3
Iriona, 119 ....E 2
Jacaleapa, 992 ....D 3
Jesús de Otoro, 2,775 ....C 3
Jutiapa, 1,711 ....D 3
Juticalpa, 7,912 ....D 3
La Ceiba, 33,934 ....D 3
La Concepción ....E 3
La Esperanza, 2,000 ....C 3
La Guata, 281 ....D 3
La Paz, 5,542 ....D 3
La Protección ....D 3
Lauterique, 272 ....D 4
Limón. 1,934 ....E 3
Manto, 943 ....D 3
Marcala, 1,968 ....C 3
Melcher ....D 3
Morazán, 3,924 ....D 3
Morocelí, 1,472 ....D 3
Nacaome, 4,376 ....D 4
Namasigüe, 1,024 ....D 4
Naranjito, 3,291 ....C 3
Nueva Armenia, 866 ....D 4
Nueva Ocotepeque, 4,608 ....C 3
Olanchito, 5,008 ....D 3
Omoa, 1,384 ....C 3
Paso Real ....E 3
Patuca ....E 3
Pespire, 1,758 ....D 4
Puerto Castilla ....D 3
Puerto Cortés, 21,600 ....D 2
Roatán, 1,883 ....D 2
Sabanagrande, 1,657 ....D 4
Salado ....D 3
San Esteban, 763 ....D 3
San Francisco, 1,122 ....D 3
San Francisco de la Paz, 1,971 ....D 3
San Juan de Flores, 1,174 ....D 3
San Luis, 2,631 ....C 3
San Marcos, 1,576 ....C 3
San Pedro Sula, 90,538 ....C 3
San Pedro Zacapa, 765 ....D 3
Santa Bárbara, 6,129 ....C 3
Santa Cruz de Yojoa, 1,833 ......D 3

Santa Rita, 3,976 ....D 3
Santa Rosa de Aguán, 1,701 ......E 2
Santa Rosa de Copán, 9,109 ......C 3
Siguatepeque, 9,462 ....D 3
Sinuapa, 882 ....C 3
Sonaguera, 1,344 ....D 3
Sulaco, 1,071 ....D 3
Tegucigalpa (cap.), 253,283 ......D 3
Tela, 14,103 ....D 3
Teupasenti, 829 ....D 3
Tocoa, 1,605 ....E 3
Trinidad, 2,817 ....C 3
Trujillo, 4,656 ....E 3
Uji ....F 3
Utila, 967 ....D 2
Villa de San Antonio, 2,287........D 3
Yocón, 269 ....D 3
Yorito, 869 ....D 3
Yoro, 4,129 ....D 3
Yuscarán, 1,854 ....D 4

OTHER FEATURES

Aguán (river) ....D 3
Bahía (isls.), 9,702 ....D 2
Bonacca (Guanaja) (isl.), 2,039 ....E 2
Brus (lagoon) ....E 2
Camarón (cape) ....E 2
Caratasca (cays) ....F 2
Caratasca (lagoon) ....F 3
Choluteca (river) ....D 4
Cisne (isls.), 28 ....F 2
Coco (river) ....E 3
Colón (mts.) ....E 3
Esperanza (mts.) ....E 3
Falso (cape) ....F 3
Fonseca (gulf) ....D 4
Gorda (cay) ....F 3
Guanaja (isl.), 2,039 ....E 2
Half Moon (reefs) ....F 3
Honduras (cape) ....E 2
Honduras (gulf) ....D 2
Patuca (point) ....E 3
Patuca (river) ....E 3
Paulaya (river) ....E 3
Pigeon (cays) ....F 3
Pija (mts.) ....D 3
Roatán (isl.), 6,552 ....D 2
San Pablo, Sierra de (mts.). ......E 3
Segovia (Coco) (river)........F 3
Sico (river) ....E 3
Sulaco (river) ....D 3
Swan (Cisne) (isls.), 28 ....F 2
Ulúa (river) ....D 3
Utila (isl.), 1,111 ....D 2
Vivario (cays) ....F 3
Wanks (Coco) (river) ....F 3
Yojoa (lake) ....D 3

NICARAGUA

CITIES and TOWNS

Acoyapa, 1,755 ....E 5
Alamikamba ....E 4
Barra de Río Grande ....F 4
Bilwaskarma ....F 3
Bluefields, 9,292 ....F 4
Boaco, 4,656 ....E 4
Bocay ....E 3
Bonanza, 2,175 ....E 4
Bragman's Bluff (Puerto Cabezas), 5,983 ....F 3
Cabo Gracias a Dios, 511........F 3
Camoapa, 2,617 ....E 4
Chichigalpa, 6,657 ....D 4
Chinandega, 22,409 ....D 4
Ciudad Darío, 3,851 ....D 4
Comalapa, 441 ....E 4
Condega, 2,229 ....D 4
Corinto, 9,177 ....D 4
Cuicuina ....E 4
Cuyu Tigni ....F 3
Diriamba, 10,499 ....D 5
El Gallo ....E 4
El Jicaral, 239 ....D 4
El Jícaro, 1,114 ....D 4
El Sauce, 2,944 ....D 4
El Viejo, 7,190 ....D 4
Esquipulas, 1,636 ....E 4
Estelí, 12,742 ....D 4
Granada, 28,507 ....E 5
Greytown (San Juan del Norte), 199 ....F 5
Jalapa, 1,868 ....E 4
Jinotega, 7,693 ....E 4
Jinotepe, 9,113 ....D 5
Juigalpa, 6,146 ....E 4
La Conquista, 364 ....D 5
La Cruz, 155 ....E 4
Laguna de Perlas ....F 4
La Libertad, 1,355 ....E 4
La Paz Central, 4,431 ....D 4
La Paz de Oriente, 828 ....E 5
La Trinidad, 2,340 ....D 4
León, 44,053 ....D 4
Managua (capital), 262,047 ....D 4
Masatepe, 4,831 ....D 5
Masaya, 23,402 ....D 5
Matagalpa, 15,030 ....E 4
Mateare, 1,254 ....D 4
Morrito, 324 ....E 5
Moyogalpa, 1,252 ....E 5
Muleculus ....E 4
Muy Muy, 691 ....E 4
Muy Muy Viejo ....E 4
Nagarote, 5,241 ....D 4
Nandaime, 5,051 ....E 5
Ocotal, 4,339 ....D 4
Ocotal ....E 4
Palsagua ....E 4
Playa Grande ....D 4
Poneloya, 995 ....D 4
Poteca ....E 4
Prinzapolka, 230 ....F 4
Puerto Cabezas, 5,983........F 3
Quilalí, 710 ....E 4
Rama (El Rama), 600 ....E 4
Rivas, 7,721 ....E 5
San Carlos, 1,547 ....E 5
Sandy Bay ....F 3
San Francisco ....E 5
San Jorge, 1,657 ....E 5
San Juan del Norte, 199 ....F 5
San Juan del Sur, 2,103 ....D 5
San Miguelito, 885 ....E 5
San Pedro ....E 4
San Rafael del Norte, 1,298........E 4
San Rafael del Sur, 2,411 ....D 5
San Ramón, 436 ....E 4
Santa Cruz ....E 4
Santo Domingo, 1,779 ....E 4
Santo Tomás, 1,530 ....E 5
Siuna, 3,743 ....E 4
Somotillo, 1,435 ....D 4
Somoto, 3,967 ....D 4
Telpaneca, 1,019 ....D 4
Terrabona, 690 ....E 4
Teustepe, 764 ....E 4
Tipitapa, 3,600 ....E 4
Tunki ....E 4
Waspán, 973 ....E 3
Yablis ....F 4

OTHER FEATURES

Alargate (reef) ....F 3
Coco (river) ....E 3
Cosegüina (point) ....D 4
Dariense (range) ....E 4
Dipilto (range) ....D 4
Escondido (river) ....F 4
Fonseca (gulf) ....D 4
Gorda (point) ....F 5
Gracias a Dios (cape) ....F 3
Grande (river) ....E 4
Great Corn (isl.), 1,896 ....F 4
Huapí (mts.) ....E 4
Isabelia (range) ....E 4
King (cays) ....F 4
Kukalaya (river) ....F 4
Little Corn (isl.) ....F 4
Managua (lake) ....E 4
Miskito (cays) ....F 3
Monkey (point) ....F 5
Mosquito Coast (reg.) ....E 4
Nicaragua (lake) ....E 5
Ometepe (isl.), 12,556 ....E 5
Pearl (cays) ....F 4
Perlas (lagoon) ....F 4
Prinzapolca (river) ....F 4
Salinas (bay) ....D 5
San Juan (river) ....E, F 5
San Juan del Norte (bay) ....F 5
Solentiname (isls.) ....E 5
Tuma (river) ....E 4
Tyra (cays) ....F 4
Waspuk (river) ....E 3
Wawa (river) ....F 3
Zapatera (isl.) ....E 5

PANAMA

CITIES and TOWNS

Aguadulce, 8,192 ....G 6
Alanje, †1,544 ....F 6
Almirante, 4,134 ....F 6
Antón, 3,022 ....G 6
Bajo Boquete, 2,625 ....F 6
Belén ....G 6
Bocas del Toro, 2,462 ....F 6
Calobre, †1,933 ....G 6
Cañazas, †5,516 ....G 6
Capira, †2,168 ....G 6
Carreto ....J 6
Chepo, †598 ....H 6
Chimán, †972 ....H 6
Chiriquí Grande, †1,517 ....F 6
Chitré, 12,575 ....G 7
Chorrera, 26,026 ....H 6
Coclé del Norte, †1,329 ....G 6
Colón, 67,641 ....H 6
David, 35,538 ....F 6
Dolega, †3,710 ....F 6
El Real ....J 6
Garachiné, †1,471 ....H 6
Guabito, †3,531 ....F 6
Gualaca, †3,125 ....F 6
Horconcitos ....F 6
La Concepción, 9,179 ....F 6
La Palma, 1,845 ....H 6
Las Palmas, †3,115 ....G 6
Las Tablas, 3,571 ....G 7
Loma Escobar (La Pintada) .....G 6
Los Santos, 3,940 ....G 7
Mandinga ....H 6
Miguel de la Borda ....G 6
Miramar, †132 ....H 6
Montijo, †3,600 ....G 6
Natá, 3,195 ....G 6
Nuevo Chagres ....G 6
Ocú, †5,267 ....G 7
Olá, †987 ....G 6
Panamá (cap.), 418,013 ....H 6
Parita, †2,320 ....G 6
Pedasí, †1,302 ....G 7
Penonomé, 5,067 ....G 6
Playón Chico ....H 6
Playón Grande ....H 6
Portobelo, †626 ....H 6
Potrerillos ....F 6
Puerto Armuelles, 12,022 ....F 6
Puerto Obaldía ....J 6
San Carlos, †1,421 ....H 6
San Cristóbal ....G 6
San Félix, †1,314 ....G 6
San Francisco, †1,576 ....G 6
Santa Fé, †1,768 ....G 6
Santiago, 14,391 ....G 6
Soná, 4,066 ....G 6
Tocumen, †5,905 ....H 6
Tolé, †4,734 ....G 6
Tonosí, †1,301 ....G 7

OTHER FEATURES

Azuero (pen.) ....G 7
Bastimentos (isl.), 574 ....G 6
Brewster (mt.) ....H 6
Burica (point) ....F 6
Cébaco (isl.) ....G 7
Chepo (river) ....H 6
Chiriquí (gulf) ....F 7
Chiriquí (lagoon) ....G 6
Chiriquí (volcano) ....F 6
Chucunaque (river) ....J 6
Coiba (isl.) ....F 7
Colón (isl.) ....G 6
Contreras (isls.) ....F 7
Darién (mts.) ....J 6
Escudo de Veraguas (isl.)........G 6
Gatun (lake) ....G 6
Gorda (point) ....H 6
Jicarón (isl.) ....F 7
Ladrones (isls.) ....F 7
Manzanillo (point) ....H 6
Montijo (gulf) ....G 7
Mosquito (gulf) ....G 6
Mulatas (arch.) ....J 6
Panamá (gulf) ....H 7
Pando (mt.) ....F 6
Parida (isl.) ....F 6
Parita (gulf) ....G 6
Perlas (arch.) ....H 6
Puercos (prom.) ....H 7
Rey (isl.) ....H 6
Rincón (point) ....G 6
San Blas (gulf) ....H 6
San Blas (range) ....H 6
San José (isl.) ....H 6
San Miguel (bay) ....H 6
Santiago (mt.) ....G 6
Secas (isls.) ....G 7
Tabasará (mts.) ....G 6
Taboga (isl.), 1,747 ....H 6
Tiburón (cape) ....J 6
Urabá (gulf) ....J 6
Valiente (pen.) ....G 6

City and suburbs.
†Population of sub-district.
‡Population of district.

CUBA

HAITI

DOMINICAN REPUBLIC

JAMAICA

TRINIDAD AND TOBAGO

BARBADOS

CUBA

AREA 44,206 sq. mi.
POPULATION 8,553,395
CAPITAL Havana
LARGEST CITY Havana
HIGHEST POINT Pico Turquino 6,561 ft.
MONETARY UNIT Cuban peso
MAJOR LANGUAGE Spanish
MAJOR RELIGION Roman Catholicism

HAITI

AREA 10,694 sq. mi.
POPULATION 4,867,190
CAPITAL Port-au-Prince
LARGEST CITY Port-au-Prince
HIGHEST POINT Pic La Selle 8,793 ft.
MONETARY UNIT gourde
MAJOR LANGUAGES Creole French, French
MAJOR RELIGION Roman Catholicism

DOMINICAN REPUBLIC

AREA 18,704 sq. mi.
POPULATION 4,011,589
CAPITAL Santo Domingo
LARGEST CITY Santo Domingo
HIGHEST POINT Pico Duarte 10,417 ft.
MONETARY UNIT Dominican peso
MAJOR LANGUAGE Spanish
MAJOR RELIGION Roman Catholicism

JAMAICA

AREA 4,411 sq. mi.
POPULATION 1,972,000
CAPITAL Kingston
LARGEST CITY Kingston
HIGHEST POINT Blue Mountain Peak, 7,402 ft.
MONETARY UNIT Jamaican pound
MAJOR LANGUAGE English
MAJOR RELIGIONS Protestantism, Roman Catholicism

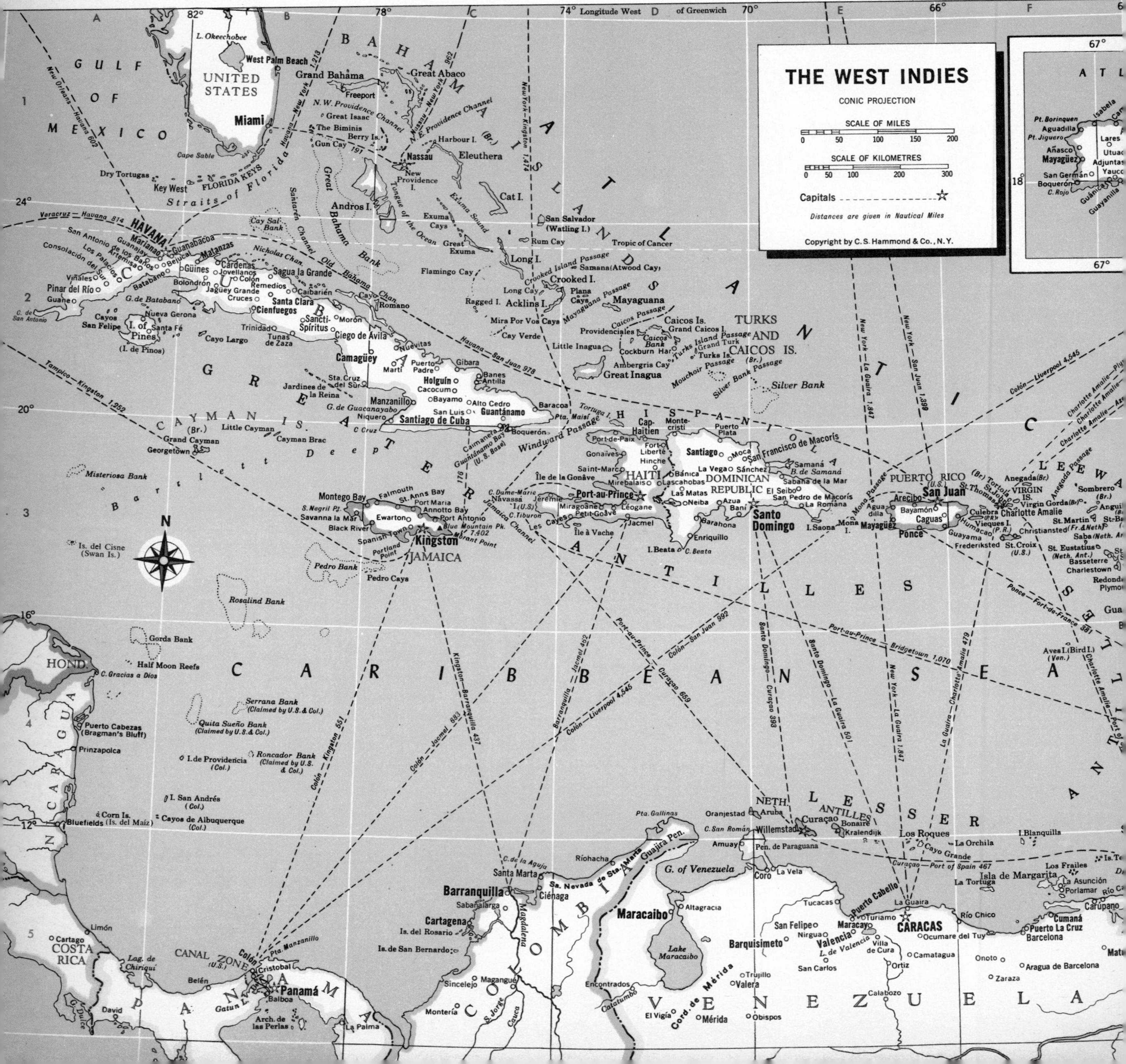

THE WEST INDIES

CONIC PROJECTION

SCALE OF MILES
0 50 100 150 200

SCALE OF KILOMETRES
0 50 100 200 300

Capitals ☆

Distances are given in Nautical Miles

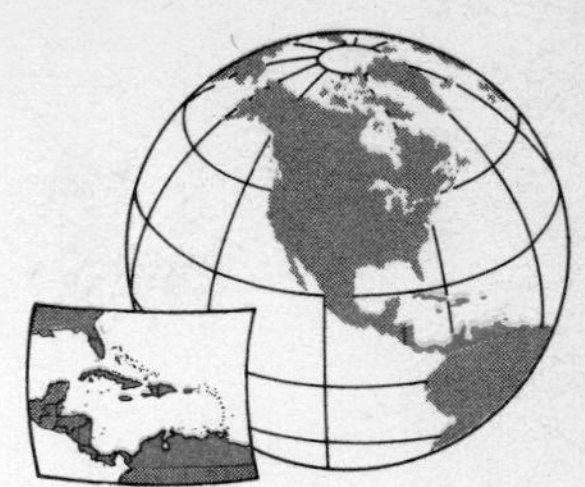

TRINIDAD AND TOBAGO

AREA 1,980 sq. mi.
POPULATION 1,040,000
CAPITAL Port of Spain
LARGEST CITY Port of Spain
HIGHEST POINT Mt. Aripo 3,084 ft.
MONETARY UNIT Trinidad and Tobago dollar
MAJOR LANGUAGES English, Hindi
MAJOR RELIGIONS Roman Catholicism, Protestantism, Hinduism, Islam

BARBADOS

AREA 166 sq. mi.
POPULATION 253,620
CAPITAL Bridgetown
LARGEST CITY Bridgetown
HIGHEST POINT Mt. Hillaby 1,104 ft.
MONETARY UNIT East Caribbean dollar
MAJOR LANGUAGE English
MAJOR RELIGION Protestantism

BAHAMA ISLANDS

AREA 4,404 sq. mi.
POPULATION 168,838
CAPITAL Nassau
MONETARY UNIT Bahaman dollar
MAJOR LANGUAGE English
MAJOR RELIGIONS Roman Catholicism, Protestantism

VIRGIN ISLANDS (U.S.)

AREA 133 sq. mi.
POPULATION 62,468
CAPITAL Charlotte Amalie
MONETARY UNIT U.S. dollar
MAJOR LANGUAGES English, Creole
MAJOR RELIGIONS Roman Catholicism, Protestantism

VIRGIN ISLANDS (BR.)

AREA 59 sq. mi.
POPULATION 10,484
CAPITAL Road Town
MONETARY UNIT British West Indian dollar
MAJOR LANGUAGES English, Creole
MAJOR RELIGION Protestantism

NETHERLANDS ANTILLES

AREA 390 sq. mi.
POPULATION 220,000
CAPITAL Willemstad
MONETARY UNIT Antilles guilder
MAJOR LANGUAGES Dutch, Papiamento, English
MAJOR RELIGIONS Roman Catholicism, Protestantism

PUERTO RICO

AREA 3,435 sq. mi.
POPULATION 2,712,033
CAPITAL San Juan
MONETARY UNIT U.S. dollar
MAJOR LANGUAGES Spanish, English
MAJOR RELIGION Roman Catholicism

BERMUDA

AREA 21 sq. mi.
POPULATION 52,000
CAPITAL Hamilton
MONETARY UNIT Bermuda dollar
MAJOR LANGUAGE English
MAJOR RELIGION Protestantism

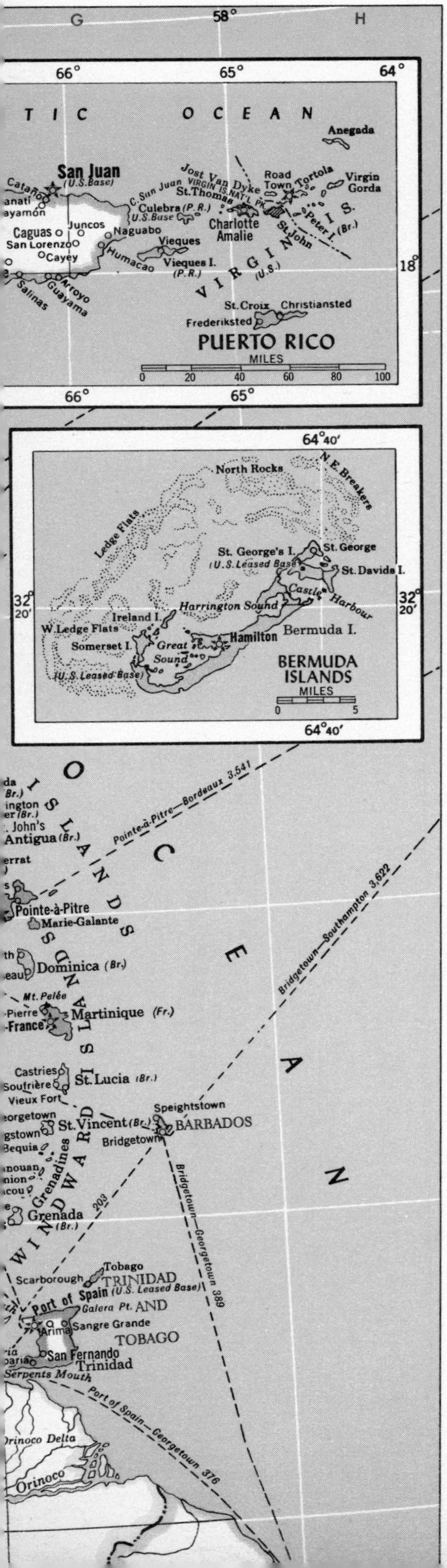

ANTIGUA

Barbuda (isl.), 1,145 ....G 3
Redonda (isl.) ....F 3
Saint John's (cap.), 24,367....G 3

BAHAMA ISLANDS

Acklins (isl.), 1,160 ....C 2
Andros (isl.), 7,460 ....B 1
Atwood (Samana) (cay), 32....D 2
Berry (isls.), 266 ....B 1
Biminis, The (isls.), 1,576....B 1
Cat (isl.), 3,131 ....C 1
Crooked (isl.), 764 ....D 2
Eleuthera (isl.), 7,247 ....C 1
Exuma (cays), 220 ....C 1
Exuma (Great Exuma) (isl.), 2,854 ....C 2
Grand Bahama (isl.), 7,847....B 1
Great Abaco (isl.), 4,746 ....C 1
Great Exuma (isl.), 2,854 ....C 2
Great Inagua (isl.), 1,240 ....D 2
Great Issac (isl.), 5 ....B 1
Gun (cay), 3 ....B 1
Harbour (isl.), 997 ....C 1
Long (cay), 22 ....C 2
Long (isl.), 4,176 ....C 2
Mayaguana (isl.), 707 ....D 2
Nassau (cap.), *100,000....C 1
New Providence (isl.), 100,000....C 1
Plana (cays), 3 ....D 2
Ragged (isl.), 371 ....C 2
Rum (cay), 77 ....C 2
Samana (cay), 32 ....D 2
San Salvador (isl.), 968 ....C 1
Tongue of the Ocean (chan.)....C 1
Watling (San Salvador) (isl.), 968 ....C 1

BARBADOS

Bridgetown (cap.), 12,430....G 4

BERMUDA

Bermuda (isl.) ....H 3
Castle (harb.) ....H 2
Great (sound) ....G 3
Hamilton (cap.), 3,000 ....H 3
Hamilton, *14,156 ....H 3
Harrington (sound) ....G 3
Ireland (isl.) ....G 3
Saint David's (isl.) ....H 2
Saint George, 1,335 ....H 2
Saint George's (isl.) ....H 2
Somerset (isl.) ....G 3

CAYMAN ISLANDS

Total Population, 10,652

Cayman Brac (isl.), 1,240 ....B 3
Georgetown (cap.), 4,106 ....B 3
Grand Cayman (isl.), 9,309 ....B 3
Little Cayman (isl.), 23 ....B 3

CUBA

Bayamo, 45,400 ....C 2
Camagüey, 178,600 ....B 2
Cárdenas, 67,400 ....B 2
Ciego de Ávila, 54,700 ....B 2
Cienfuegos, 91,800 ....B 2
Florida (straits) ....B 1
Guanabacoa, 41,000 ....B 2
Guantánamo, 135,100 ....C 2
Güines, 45,000 ....B 2
Havana (cap.), *1,577,200 ....A 2
Holguín, 100,500 ....C 2
Manzanillo, 91,200 ....C 2
Marianao, 454,700 ....A 2
Matanzas, 84,100 ....B 2
Pinar del Río, 67,600 ....A 2
Pines (Pinos) (isl.), 20,630....A 2
Sagua la Grande, 35,200 ....B 2
Sancti-Spíritus, 62,500 ....B 2
San Felipe (cay), 391 ....A 2
Santa Clara, 137,700 ....B 2
Santiago de Cuba, 259,000 ....B 2
Viñales, 1,602 ....A 2
Windward (passage) ....C 3

DOMINICA

Roseau (cap.), *16,677 ....G 4

DOMINICAN REPUBLIC

Barahona, 37,889 ....D 3
La Romana, 36,722 ....E 3
La Vega, 31,085 ....D 3
Puerto Plata, 32,181 ....D 3
San Francisco de Macorís, 43,941 ....E 3
San Pedro de Macorís, 42,473....E 3
Santiago, 155,151 ....D 3
Santo Domingo (cap.), 671,402...E 3

GRENADA

Carriacou (isl.), 6,958 ....G 4
Gouyave, 2,356 ....F 4
Grenadines (isls.), 5,612....G 4
Saint George's (cap.), *26,843....F 5

GUADELOUPE

Basse-Terre (cap.), 16,000 ....F 4
Saint-Barthélemy (isl.), 2,351....F 3
Saint-Martin (isl.), 5,062 ....F 3

HAITI

Cap-Haïtien, 30,000 ....D 3
Gonâve (isl.), 45,411 ....D 3
Jacmel, †199,598 ....D 3
Léogane, †140,607 ....D 3
Les Cayes, †95,446 ....C 3
Port-au-Prince (cap.), *352,681..D 3
Tortuga (Tortue) (isl.), 13,723..D 2

JAMAICA

Blue Mountain (peak) ....C 3
Jamaica (channel) ....C 3
Kingston (cap.), *376,520 ....C 3
Montego Bay, 23,610 ....B 3
Pedro (cays) ....C 3
Port Antonio, 7,830 ....C 3
Savanna la Mar, 9,789 ....B 3
Spanish Town, 14,706 ....C 3

MARTINIQUE

Forte-de-France (cap.), 100,000..G 4
Pelée (vol.) ....G 4

MONTSERRAT

Total Population, 12,300

Plymouth (cap.), 3,000 ....F 3

NETHERLANDS ANTILLES

Aruba (isl.), 58,868 ....E 4
Bonaire (isl.), 5,755 ....E 4
Curaçao (isl.), 196,170 ....E 4
Saba (isl.), 1,094 ....F 3
Saint Eustatius (isl.), 1,020....F 3
Sint Maarten (Saint Martin) (isl.), 4,970 ....F 3
Willemstad (cap.), *94,133....E 4

PUERTO RICO

Aguadilla, 21,031 ....F 1
Arecibo, 35,484 ....G 1
Bayamón, 147,552 ....G 1
Caguas, ‡95,661 ....G 1
Cataño, 26,459 ....G 1
Cayey, 21,562 ....G 1
Culebra (isl.), 732 ....G 1
Guayama, 20,318 ....G 1
Humacao, 12,411 ....G 1
Mayagüez, ‡85,857 ....F 1
Mona (isl.), 6 ....E 3
Ponce, ‡158,981 ....F 1
San Juan (cap.), ‡851,247 ....G 1
Vieques (isl.), 7,767 ....G 1

SAINT CHRISTOPHER-NEVIS-ANGUILLA

Anguilla (isl.), 5,605 ....F 3
Basseterre (cap.), 15,726 ....F 3
Sombrero (isl.), 5 ....F 3

SAINT LUCIA

Castries (cap.), *15,291 ....G 4

SAINT VINCENT

Bequia (isl.) ....G 4
Canouan (isl.) ....G 4
Grenadines (isls.), 6,428 ....G 4
Kingstown (cap.), *23,482 ....G 4
Union (isl.) ....G 4

TRINIDAD AND TOBAGO

Port of Spain (cap.), *250,000...G 5
Scarborough, 1,931 ....G 5
Tobago (isl.), 36,850 ....G 5
Trinidad (isl.), 973,250 ....G 5

TURKS AND CAICOS IS.

Total Population, 6,000

Caicos (isls.), 2,200 ....D 2
Cockburn Harbour, 866 ....D 2
Grand Turk (isl.), 2,339 ....D 2
Providenciales (isl.), 510 ....D 2
Turks (isls.), 3,800 ....D 2

VIRGIN ISLANDS (BRITISH)

Anegada (isl.), 290 ....H 1
Road Town (cap.), 2,183 ....H 1

VIRGIN ISLANDS (U.S.)

Charlotte Amalie (cap.), 12,220..H 1
Saint Croix (isl.), 31,779 ....H 2
Saint John (isl.), 1,729 ....H 1
Saint Thomas (isl.), 28,960 ....G 1

WEST INDIES

Antilles Gtr. (isls.), 22,094,100...D 3
Antilles, Lesser, 2,749,000 ....F 4
Hispaniola (isl.), 8,878,800 ....D 2
Leeward (isls.), 599,300 ....F 3
Navassa (isl.) ....C 3
Windward (isls.), 2,149,750....G 4

*City and suburbs.
†Population of commune.
‡Population of met. area.

(continued)

CUBA

PROVINCES

Camagüey, 889,600 ....G 2
Havana (La Habana), 2,150,300..C 1
Las Villas, 1,320,900 ....E 2
Matanzas, 483,300 ....D 1
Oriente, 2,857,200 ....H 4
Pinar del Río, 648,100 ....A 1

CITIES and TOWNS

Abreus, 1,682 ....D 2
Agramonte, 2,948 ....D 1
Aguada de Pasajeros, 9,000....D 2
Alacranes, 3,165 ....D 1
Alquízar, 9,600 ....C 1
Alto Cedro, 679 ....J 4
Alto Songo, 2,197 ....J 4
Amarillas, 1,935 ....D 2
Antilla, 7,500 ....J 3
Arcos de Canasí, 1,103 ....C 1
Artemisa, 27,300 ....C 1
Báez, 2,223 ....E 2
Bahía Honda, 5,200 ....B 1
Baire, 5,300 ....H 4
Banagüises, 1,245 ....D 1
Banes, 27,900 ....J 3
Baracoa, 13,000 ....K 4
Bartle, 1,052 ....G 3
Bauta, 16,800 ....C 1
Bayamo, 45,400 ....H 4
Bejucal, 12,900 ....C 1
Bolondrón, 3,444 ....D 1
Boquerón ....K 4
Bueycito, 1,109 ....H 4
Cabaiguán, 20,800 ....E 2
Cabañas, 2,226 ....B 1
Cacocum, 2,724 ....H 3
Caibarién, 26,400 ....H 2
Caimanera, 8,600 ....K 4
Calabazar de Sagua, 3,286 ....E 1
Calimete, 2,260 ....D 1
Camagüey, 178,600 ....G 3
Camajuani, 14,200 ....E 2
Campechuela, 7,600 ....G 4
Cañas, 1,789 ....B 1
Candelaria, 3,548 ....B 1
Caney, 2,009 ....J 4
Caonao, 3,403 ....E 2
Cárdenas, 67,400 ....D 1
Cartagena, 1,239 ....D 2
Cascajal, 1,493 ....E 1
Cascorro, 2,442 ....H 3
Casilda, 2,445 ....E 2
Cauto, 3,137 ....H 4
Cayo Mambí, 1,553 ....K 3
Central Amancia Rodríguez, 3,800 ....G 3
Central Amazonas, 1,405 ....F 2
Central América ....J 4
Central Antonio Guiteras, 8,300..H 3
Central Baraguá, 2,267 ....F 2
Central Colombia, 9,800 ....G 3
Central Jesús Menéndez, 7,400....H 3
Central Máximo Gómez, 5,100 ....F 2
Central Merceditas, 1,146 ....B 1
Central Niágara ....B 1
Central Santa Marta, 1,326 ....G 3
Central Tacaio, 1,298 ....J 3
Céspedes, 7,300 ....G 2
Chambas, 3,046 ....F 2
Cidra, 1,463 ....D 1
Ciego de Ávila, 54,700 ....F 2
Cienfuegos, 91,800 ....D 2
Cobre, 2,586 ....J 4
Cojímar, 7,400 ....C 1
Colón, 22,900 ....D 1
Consolación del Norte, 2,254 ....B 1
Consolación del Sur, 7,300 ....B 2
Contramaestre, 13.000 ....G 3
Corralillo, 1,123 ....D 1
Cristo, 6,200 ....J 4
Cruces, 15,100 ....E 2
Cueto, 8,700 ....J 3
Cumanayagua, 5,300 ....E 2
Cunagua, 1,879 ....G 2
Daiquirí ....J 4
Dos Caminos, 2,004 ....J 4
Encrucijada, 6,500 ....E 1
Esmeralda, 5,400 ....E 2
Esperanza, 7,300 ....E 2
Falla, 1,876 ....F 2
Flamenco de San Pedro ....F 3
Florida, 33,800 ....G 3
Fomento, 8,800 ....E 2
Fray Benito, 1,456 ....J 3
Garden City ....G 2
Gaspar, 1,740 ....F 2
Gibara, 8,400 ....J 3
Guadalupe, 1,098 ....F 2
Guáimaro, 4,800 ....G 3
Guamo, 2,507 ....H 3
Guanabacoa, 41,000 ....C 1
Guanajay, 13,700 ....B 1
Guane, 4,400 ....A 2
Guantánamo, 135,100 ....K 4
Guaro, 1,362 ....J 3
Guasimal, 1,752 ....E 2
Guayabal, Camagüey, 9,000 ....G 3
Guayabal, Oriente ....K 4
Guayos, 5,600 ....F 2
Güines, 45,000 ....C 1
Güira de Melena, 18,900 ....C 1
Guisa, 7,700 ....H 4
Hatuey, 1,737 ....G 3
Havana (cap.), 1,008,500 ....C 1
Havana, *1,577,200 ....C 1
Havana, ‡1,760,000 ....C 1
Holguín, 100,500 ....J 3
Imías ....K 4
Isabela de Sagua, 3,701 ....E 1
Isabel María ....A 2
Isabel Rubio, 1,394 ....A 2
Itabo ....D 1
Jagüey Grande, 6,600 ....D 2
Jamaica ....K 4
Jaruco, 6,700 ....C 1
Jatibonico, 5,700 ....F 2
Jauco ....K 4
Jíbaro ....F 2
Jiguaní, 9,000 ....H 4
Jiquí, 1,135 ....G 2
Jobabo, 3,246 ....H 3
Jovellanos, 12,400 ....D 1
Júcaro, 1,411 ....F 2
La Coloma, 1,907 ....B 2
La Fé ....A 2
La Gloria ....G 2
La Maya, 6,500 ....J 4
La Rioja, 18,180 ....H 3
Las Martinas ....A 2
Laguna Larga ....G 2
Limonar, 3,301 ....D 1
Los Arabos, 1,690 ....E 1
Los Caños ....K 4
Los Indios, 1,103 ....B 2
Los Negros ....F 2
Los Palacios, 7,000 ....B 1
Lugareño, 3,135 ....G 3
Maceo, 1,433 ....H 3
Magarabomba ....G 2
Maisí ....K 4
Majagua ....F 2
Manacas, 2,515 ....E 1
Manatí, 2,318 ....H 3
Manguito, 2,569 ....D 1
Manicaragua, 3,993 ....E 2
Mantua ....A 2
Manzanillo, 91,200 ....H 4
Marianao, 454,700 ....C 1
Mariel, 6,700 ....B 1
Martí, Camagüey ....G 3
Martí, Matanzas, 2,605 ....D 1
Matanzas, 84,100 ....C 1
Matún ....D 2
Máximo Gómez ....D 1
Mayajigua, 2,950 ....F 2
Mayarí, 7,400 ....J 3
Mayarí Arriba, 900 ....J 4
McKinley ....B 2
Media Luna ....G 4
Meneses, 1,650 ....F 2
Minas, 3,827 ....G 2
Minas de Matahambre, 5,400 ....A 1
Minas de Santa Lucía ....A 1
Miranda, 2,186 ....J 4
Morón, 26,600 ....F 2
Nicaro, 3,074 ....J 3
Niquero, 8,600 ....G 4
Nueva Gerona, 9,000 ....B 2
Nuevitas, 16,300 ....G 2
Omaja ....H 3
Orozco ....B 1
Palma Soriano, 33,700 ....J 4
Palmarito, 1,985 ....J 4
Palmira, 8,700 ....E 2
Palo Alto ....F 3
Paso Real de San Diego, 1,436....B 1
Pedro Betancourt, 8,000 ....D 1
Perico, 7,800 ....D 1
Piedrecitas, 1,619 ....F 2
Pilotos ....B 1
Pina, 3,667 ....F 2
Pinar del Río, 67,600 ....B 2
Placetas, 38,800 ....E 2
Presidio Modelo ....C 2
Preston, 3,827 ....J 3
Puerta de Golpe, 1,512 ....B 2
Puerto Esperanza, 1,867 ....A 1
Puerto Padre, 15,900 ....H 3
Puerto Samá ....J 3
Puerto Tarafa ....H 3
Puerto Vita ....J 4
Quemado de Güines, 6,500 ....E 1
Quiebra Hacha, 1,584 ....B 1
Ramón de las Yaguas ....J 4
Rancho Veloz, 2,789 ....D 1
Ranchuelo, 12,500 ....E 2
Remates ....A 2
Remedios, 12,400 ....E 2
Río Seco, 1,615 ....A 2
Rodas, 5,900 ....E 2
Sábalo ....A 2
Sabana ....K 4
Sagua de Tánamo, 10,700 ....K 3
Sagua la Grande, 35,200 ....E 1
Salado ....H 3
San Agustín ....H 3
San Andrés, 1,655 ....H 3
San Antonio, 1,300 ....K 4
San Antonio de los Baños, 23,700 C 1
San Cristóbal, 5,600 ....B 1
San Germán, 9,700 ....J 3
San José de la Plata ....H 3
San José de las Lajas, 18,000....C 1
San José de los Ramos, 1,269 ....D 1
San Juan y Martínez, 6,700 ....B 2
San Luis, Oriente, 15,700 ....J 4
San Luis, Pinar del Río, 2,735....B 2
San Manuel, 2,105 ....H 3
San Miguel ....H 3
San Nicolás, 7,000 ....C 1
San Pedro ....B 2
San Ramón, 1,037 ....H 4
Sancti-Spíritus, 62,500 ....E 2
Santa Bárbara ....B 2
Santa Clara, 137,700 ....E 2
Santa Cruz del Norte, 3,537 ....C 1
Santa Cruz del Sur, 4,200 ....G 3
Santa Fé, 11,900 ....C 2
Santa Isabel de las Lajas, 6,200..E 2
Santa Lucía, Camagüey ....H 2
Santa Lucía, Oriente ....J 3
Santa Rita, 1,655 ....H 4
Santiago de Cuba, 259,000 ....J 4
Santiago de las Vegas, 10,300....C 1
Santo, 2,210 ....E 1
Santo Domingo, 9,600 ....E 1
Senado, 1,314 ....G 2
Sibanicú, 3,378 ....G 3
Siboney ....J 4
Stewart, 1,943 ....F 2
Surgidero de Batabanó, 5,075 ....C 1
Taco-Taco ....B 1
Tánamo, 2,032 ....J 3
Tiguabos, 1,286 ....J 4
Torriente ....D 1
Trinidad, 28,000 ....E 2
Tunas de Zaza, 1,380 ....E 2
Unión de Reyes, 5,500 ....C 1
Uvero Quemado ....A 2
Varadero, 2,640 ....D 1
Veguitas, 2,014 ....H 4
Velasco, 1,444 ....H 3
Vertientes, 10,200 ....G 3
Victoria de las Tunas, 29,700 ....H 3
Viñales, 1,602 ....A 1
Vista Hermosa ....G 3
Yaguajay, 5,900 ....F 2
Yara, 3,246 ....H 4
Yuraguanal ....G 2
Zarzal, 1,421 ....H 4
Zaza del Medio, 4,252....F 2
Zulueta, 4,254 ....E 2

OTHER FEATURES

Abalos (point) ....A 2
Ana María (gulf) ....F 3
Anclitas (cay) ....F 3
Batabanó (gulf) ....C 2
Birama (point) ....G 3
Broa (inlet) ....C 1
Buena Vista (bay) ....F 2
Caballones (chan.) ....F 3

Camagüey (arch.) G 2
Cantiles (cay) C 3
Cárdenas (bay) D 1
Carraguao (point) B 2
Casilda (point) E 2
Cauto (river) H 3
Cayamas (cays) C 2
Cazones (gulf) C 2
Cienfuegos (bay) D 2
Cinco Balas (cays) E 3
Cochinos (bay) D 2
Coco (cay) G 1
Corrientes (cape) A 2
Corrientes (inlet) A 2
Cortés (inlet) B 2
Cristal, Sierra del (mts.) J 4
Cruz (cape) G 4
Diego Pérez (cay) C 2
Doce Leguas (cays) F 3
Este (point) C 3
Fragoso (cay) F 1
Francés (cape) A 2
Gorda (point) C 2
Gran Piedra (mt.) J 4
Guacanayabo (gulf) G 4
Guajaba (cay) H 2
Guanahacabibes (gulf) A 2
Guanahacabibes (pen.) A 2
Guantánamo (bay) J 4
Guantánamo Bay U.S. Naval Reserve J 4
Guarico (point) K 3
Guzmanes (cays) B 2
Hicacos (pen.) D 1
Hicacos (point) D 1
Honda (bay) B 1
Indios (chan.) B 2
Inglés (point) G 4
Jardines de la Reina (arch.) F 3
Jatibonico del Sur (river) F 3
Jigüey (bay) G 2
Laberinto de las Doce Leguas (cays) F 3
La Cañada (mt.) B 2
La Gloria (bay) G 2
Ladrillo (point) E 2
Largo (cay) D 2
Leche (lagoon) F 2
Los Barcos (point) B 2
Los Canarreos (arch.) C 2
Los Colorados (arch.) A 1
Lucrecia (cape) J 3
Macurijes (point) F 3
Maestra, Sierra (mts.) H 4
Maisí (point) K 4
Mangle (point) J 3
Masio (cay) C 2
Matanzas (bay) D 1
Matanzas (point) H 2
Mayarí (river) J 4
Nicholas (chan.) E 1
Nipe (bay) J 3
Nuevitas (bay) H 2
Ojo del Toro (mt.) G 4
Old Bahama (chan.) G 1
Pepe (cape) B 1
Perros (bay) G 2
Pigs (Cochinos) (bay) D 2
Pines (isl.), 20,630 G 3
Potrerillo (peak) E 2
Quemado (point) A 4
Romano (cay) G 2
Rosario (cay) C 2
Sabana (arch.) E 1
Sabinal (cay) H 2
Sagua la Grande (river) E 1
San Antonio (cape) A 2
San Felipe (cays) B 2
San Pedro (river) G 3
Santa Clara (bay) D 1
Santa María (cay) F 1
Siguanea (bay) B 2
Tabacal (point) H 4
Toa, Cuchillas de (mts.) K 4
Tortuguilla (point) K 4
Turquino (peak) H 4
Zapata (pen.) C 2
Zapata Occidental (swamp) D 2
Zapata Oriental (swamp) D 2

DOMINICAN REPUBLIC

PROVINCES

Azua, 91,511 D 6
Baoruco, 66,572 D 6
Barahona, 112,914 D 6
Dajabón, 50,780 D 5
Distrito Nacional, 817,467 E 6
Duarte, 200,813 E 5
El Seibo, 132,795 F 6
Espaillat, 139,579 E 5
Independencia, 32,580 D 6
La Altagracia, 87,180 F 6
La Estrelleta, 53,228 C 5
La Romana, 56,955 F 6
La Vega, 293,694 D 6
María Trinidad Sánchez, 97,043 E 5
Montecristi, 69,276 D 5
Pedernales, 12,547 D 7
Peravia, 127,587 E 6
Puerto Plata, 185,800 D 5
Salcedo, 89,773 E 5
Samaná, 53,893 E 5
San Cristóbal, 324,395 E 6
San Juan, 191,065 D 6
San Pedro de Macorís, 105,490 F 6
Sánchez Ramírez, 106,177 E 5
Santiago, 386,269 D 5
Santiago Rodríguez, 49,598 D 5
Valverde, 76,608 D 5

CITIES and TOWNS

Altamira, 1,573 D 5
Azua, 18,584 D 6
Bajos de Haina, 10,396 E 6
Baní, 23,716 E 6
Bánica, 1,303 D 5
Barahona, 37,889 D 6
Bayaguana, 2,947 E 6
Bonao E 6
Cabral, 5,575 D 6
Cabrera, 1,899 E 5
Castillo, 3,191 E 5
Cayacoa E 6
Ciudad Trujillo (Santo Domingo) (cap.), 671,402 E 6
Constanza, 4,316 D 6
Cotuí, 7,574 E 5
Dajabón, 6,027 D 5
Duvergé, 7,979 D 6
El Cercado, 3,369 D 6
El Cuey F 6
El Guayabo E 5
El Pozo E 5
El Salado F 6
El Seibo, 8,958 F 6
Elías Piña, 5,099 C 6
Enriquillo, 4,103 D 7
Esperanza, 10,684 D 5
Gaspar Hernández, 2,222 E 5
Guayubín, 1,369 D 5
Hato Mayor, 9,985 F 6
Imbert, 4,321 D 5
Jánico, 1,117 D 5
Jarabacoa, 6,329 E 5
Jaragua, 4,853 D 6
Jimaní, 2,248 C 6
La Romana, 36,722 F 6
La Vega, 31,085 D 5
Las Matas de Farfán, 7,138 D 6
Los Llanos, 1,849 F 6
Lucas E. de Peña D 5
Luperón, 1,991 D 5
Mata Palacio F 6
Miches, 4,410 F 6
Moca, 18,965 D 5
Monción, 2,007 D 5
Montecristi, 8,252 C 5
Monte Plata, 3,636 E 6
Nagua, 13,937 E 5
Najayo Abajo E 6
Neiba, 10,194 D 6
Nizao, 3,178 E 6
Oviedo, 2,117 D 7
Padre Las Casas, 2,953 D 6
Paraíso, 3,496 D 7
Pedernales, 5,919 C 7
Peña D 5
Peralta D 6
Pimentel, 5,954 E 5
Polo D 6
Puerto Plata, 32,181 D 5
Ramón Santana, 4,139 F 6
Restauración, 1,784 D 5
Río San Juan, 2,764 E 5
Sabana de la Mar, 6,841 F 5
Sabana Grande de Palenque, 1,950 E 6
Salcedo, 11,459 E 5
Salvaleón de Higüey, 21,741 F 6
Samaná, 4,435 F 5
Sánchez, 6,583 E 5
San Cristóbal, 25,829 E 6
San Francisco de Macorís, 43,941 E 5
San José de las Matas, 3,228 D 5
San José de Ocoa, 9,382 E 6
San Juan, 32,248 D 6
San Pedro de Macorís, 42,473 E 6
San Rafael del Yuma, 1,944 F 6
Santiago, 155,151 D 5
Santiago Rodríguez, 9,637 D 5
Santo Domingo (cap.), 671,402 E 6
Sosúa, 4,204 E 5
Tamayo, 4,177 D 6
Tenares, 2,663 E 5
Valverde, 27,111 D 5
Villa Altagracia, 10,300 E 6
Villa Riva 2,165 E 5
Yaguate, 1,854 E 6
Yamasá, 2,642 E 6
Yásica Abajo E 5

OTHER FEATURES

Alto Velo (chan.) C 7
Alto Velo (isl.) D 7
Balandra (point) F 5
Baoruco, Sierra de (mts.) D 6
Beata (cape) D 7
Beata (chan.) C 7
Beata (isl.) C 7
Cabrón (cape) F 5
Calderas (bay) D 6
Cana (point) F 6
Catalina (isl.) F 6
Caucedo (cape) E 6
Central, Cordillera (range) D 5
Duarte (peak) D 5
Engaño (cape) F 5
Enriquillo (lake) C 6
Escocesa (bay) E 5
Espada (point) F 6
Falso (cape) C 7
Francés Viejo (cape) E 5
Gallo (mt.) D 5
Isabela (bay) D 5
Isabela (cape) D 5
Los Frailes (isl.) C 7
Macorís (cape) E 5
Manzanillo (bay) C 5
Mona (passage) F 6
Neiba (bay) D 6
Neiba (mt.) D 6
Ocoa (bay) D 6
Oriental, Cordillera (range) F 6
Palenque (point) E 6
Palmillas (point) F 6
Rincón (bay) F 5
Rucia (point) D 5
Salinas (point) E 6
Samaná (bay) F 5
Samaná (cape) F 5
San Rafael (cape) F 5
Saona (isl.) F 6
Septentrional, Cord. (range) D 5
Tina (mt.) D 6
Yaque del Norte (river) D 5
Yaque del Sur (river) D 6
Yuma (bay) F 6
Yuna (river) E 5

HAITI

DEPARTMENTS

Artibonite, 748,357 C 5
Nord, 747,360 C 5
Nord-Ouest, 247,326 B 5
Ouest, 1,983,826 C 6
Sud, 1,041,232 A 6

CITIES and TOWNS

Abricots, †26,612 B 6
Anse-à-Pitre, †16,195 C 6
Anse-à-Veau, †41,690 B 6
Anse-d'Hainault, †18,416 A 6
Anse-Rouge, †14,657 B 5
Aquin, †95,283 B 6
Archaie, †52,221 C 6
Baie-de-Henne, †6,927 B 5
Baradères, †33,575 B 6
Bassin-Bleu, †23,623 B 5
Belladère, †35,706 C 6
Bombardopolis, †13,556 B 5
Bonbon, †8,711 A 6
Camp-Perrin, †25,398 A 6
Cap-Haïtien, 30,000 C 5
Cavaillon, †50,479 A 6
Cayes-Jacmel, †39,726 C 6
Cerca-la-Source, †20,671 C 5
Chardonnière, †15,270 A 6
Corail, †47,936 A 6
Côteaux, †28,327 A 6
Côtes-de-Fer, †122,568 B 6
Croix-des-Bouquets, †83,250 C 6
Dame-Marie, †27,430 A 2
Dessalines, †86,348 C 5
Fort-Liberté, †26,942 C 5
Gonaïves, †99,140 B 5
Grand-Goâve, †60,589 B 6
Grand-Gosier, †29,102 C 6
Grande-Rivière-du-Nord, †29,904 C 5
Grande-Saline, †30,628 B 5
Gros-Morne, †90,116 B 4
Hinche, †63,796 C 5
Jacmel, †199,598 C 6
Jean-Rabel, †55,834 B 5
Jérémie, †92,500 A 6
Kenscoff, †24,219 C 6
La Cahouane A 6
Lascahobas, †29,760 C 6
Le Borgne, †51,325 C 5
Léogane, †140,607 C 6
Les Anglais, †15,321 A 6
Les Cayes, †95,446 B 6
Limbé, †52,315 C 5
Limonade, †21,395 C 5
Maissade, †26,568 C 5
Marigot, †65,402 C 6
Miragoâne, †50,059 B 6
Mirebalais, †78,060 C 6
Môle-Saint-Nicolas, †14,352 B 5
Moron, †17,020 A 6
Ouanaminthe, †55,717 C 5
Pestel, †33,007 A 6
Pétionville, †52,221 C 6
Petit-Goâve, †123,157 B 6
Petite-Rivière-de-l'Artibonite, †65,772 B 5
Pignon, †15,512 C 5
Pilate, †40,293 C 5
Plaisance, †47,896 C 5
Pointe-à-Raquette B 6
Port-à-Piment, †14,072 A 6
Port-au-Prince (cap.), 265,000 C 6
Port-au-Prince, *352,681 C 6
Port-de-Paix, †54,016 B 5
Port-Margot, †33,043 C 5
Port-Salut, †41,055 A 6
Roseaux, †25,984 A 6
Saint-Jean-du-Sud, †18,923 B 6
Saint-Louis-du-Nord, †44,898 B 5
Saint-Louis-du-Sud, †42,807 B 6
Saint-Marc, †61,359 B 5
Saint-Michel-de-l'Atalaye, †68,813 C 5
Saint-Raphaël, †25,708 C 5
Saltrou, †57,067 C 6
Savanette, †55,505 C 6
Terre-Neuve, †15,953 B 5
Thomonde, †15,660 C 6
Tiburon, †9,860 A 6
Torbeck, †66,480 A 6
Trou-du-Nord, †29,324 C 5
Vallière, †16,089 C 5
Verrettes, †39,327 C 5

OTHER FEATURES

Artibonite (river) C 5
Baradères (bay) B 6
Cheval Blanc (point) B 5
Dame-Marie (cape) A 6
Est (point) C 4
Fantasque (point) B 6
Gonâve (gulf) B 5
Gonâve (isl.), 45,411 B 6
Grande Cayemite (isl.) B 6
Gravois (point) A 6
Irois (cape) A 6
Jean-Rabel (point) B 5
La Selle (mts.) C 6
La Selle (peak) C 6
Macaya (peak) A 6
Manzanillo (bay) C 5
Môle (cape) B 5
Noires (mts.) C 5
Ouest (point) B 4
Ouest (point) B 6
Saint-Marc (cape) B 5
Saint-Marc (chan.) B 6
Saumâtre (lake) C 6
Tortue (chan.) C 5
Tortue (isl.), 13,723 C 4
Tortuga (Tortue) (isl.), 13,723 C 4
Trois-Rivières (river) B 5
Vache (isl.) B 6
Windward (passage) A 5

JAMAICA

CITIES and TOWNS

Adelphi H 5
Albany, 1,590 J 6
Albert Town, 1,650 H 6
Alley J 7
Alligator Pond H 6
Anchovy H 5
Annotto Bay, 3,559 K 6
Balaclava, 1,153 H 6
Bath, 1,979 K 6
Bethel Town G 6
Black River, 3,077 H 6
Bluefields H 6
Bog Walk, 2,808 J 6
Brown's Town, 3,899 H 6
Buff Bay, 2,821 K 6
Cambridge H 6
Castleton J 6
Catadupa H 6
Chapelton, 4,417 J 6
Christiana, 4,404 H 6
Claremont, 1,417 J 6
Clark's Town, 1,543 H 6
Darliston H 6
Devon H 6
Discovery Bay J 5
Ewarton J 6
Falmouth, 3,727 H 5
Four Paths J 6
Frankfield, 2,123 H 6
Golden Grove K 6
Green Island G 6
Hayes J 6
Highgate, 3,313 J 6
Hope Bay K 6
Hopewell G 5
Kingston (cap.), 123,403 K 6
Kingston, *376,520 K 6
Lacovia H 6
Linstead, 3,781 J 6
Lionel Town, 2,664 J 7
Little London G 6
Lluidas Vale J 6
Lucea, 2,803 G 5
Maggotty H 6
Malvern H 6
Manchioneal K 6
Mandeville, 8,416 H 6
Maroon Town H 6
May Pen, 14,085 J 6
Moneague J 6
Montego Bay, 23,610 H 5
Moore Town K 6
Morant Bay, 5,054 K 7
Myersville H 6
Negril G 6
Ocho Rios, 4,570 J 6
Old England H 6
Old Harbour, 4,192 J 6
Oracabessa, 1,313 J 5
Petersfield G 6
Port Antonio, 7,830 K 6
Port Kaiser H 7
Port Maria, 3,998 J 6
Port Morant, 2,284 K 6
Port Rhoades J 6
Port Royal, 37,673 J 6
Porus, 2,723 H 6
Richmond J 6
Runaway Bay J 5
Saint Ann's Bay, 5,087 J 5
Saint Margaret's Bay K 6
Sandy Bay G 5
Santa Cruz, 1,426 H 6
Savanna la Mar, 9,789 G 6
Spaldings, 2,003 H 6
Spanish Town, 14,706 J 6
Stewart Town H 6
Tobolski J 6
Treasure Beach H 6
Trinityville K 6
Trout Hall J 6
Ulster Spring H 6
Williamsfield H 6
Yallahs K 6

OTHER FEATURES

Black (river) H 6
Black River (bay) G 6
Blue (mts.) K 6
Blue Mountain (peak) K 6
Galina (point) J 6
Grande (river) K 6
Great (river) H 6
Great Pedro Bluff (prom.) H 6
Long (bay) H 7
Luana (point) G 6
Minho (river) J 6
Montego (bay) G 5
Montego Bay (point) G 5
North East (point) K 6
North Negril (point) G 6
North West (point) G 5
Old Harbour (bay) J 6
Portland (point) J 7
Sir John's (peak) K 6
South East (point) K 6
South Negril (point) G 6

*City and suburbs.
†Population of commune.
‡Population of met. area.

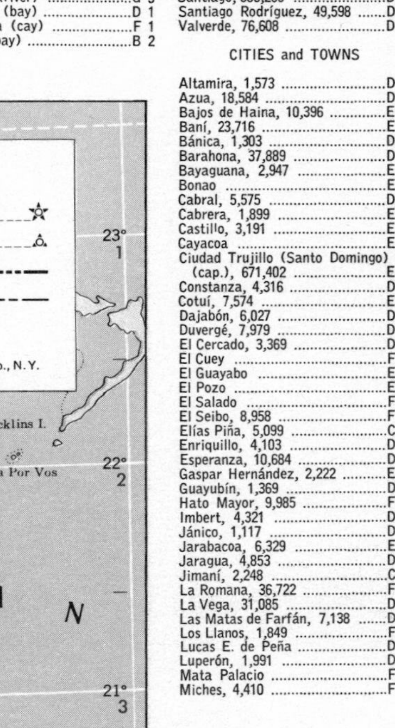

Agriculture, Industry and Resources

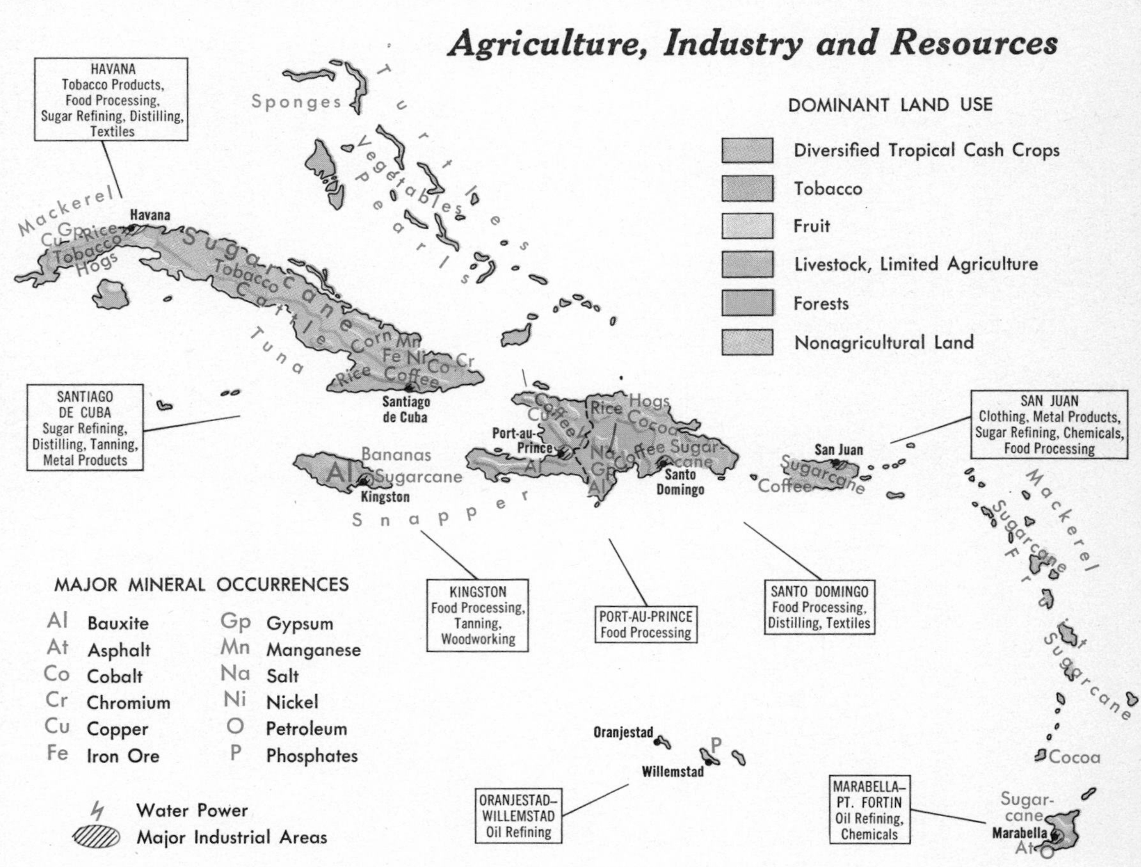

PUERTO RICO

DISTRICTS

Aguadilla, 284,983 A 1
Arecibo, 270,492 C 1
Bayamón, 359,499 D 1
Guayama, 335,305 D 2
Humacao, 283,481 F 2
Mayagüez, 267,731 B 2
Ponce, 308,988 C 2
San Juan, 601,554 E 1

CITIES and TOWNS

Adjuntas, 5,319 B 2
Aguada, 4,590 A 1
Aguadilla, 21,031 A 1
Aguas Buenas, 3,426 E 2
Aibonito, 7,582 D 2
Añasco, 4,416 A 1
Angeles, †2,817 B 2
Arecibo, 35,484 B 1
Arroyo, 5,429 E 3
Arus C 3
Bahomamey, †146 A 1
Bajadero C 1
Barceloneta, 4,515 C 1
Barranquitas, 4,508 D 2
Bayamón, 147,552 D 1
Boquerón, †2,790 A 3
Cabo Rojo, 7,181 A 2
Caguas, 63,215 E 2
Caguas, ‡95,661 E 2
Camuy, 3,892 B 1
Carolina, 94,271 E 1
Cataño, 26,459 D 1
Cayey, 21,562 D 2
Ceiba, 2,147 F 2
Central Aguirre, 1,237 D 3
Ciales, 4,046 D 1
Cidra, 6,306 D 2
Coamo, 12,077 D 2
Comerío, 6,297 D 2
Coquí, 2,643 D 3
Corozal, 5,211 D 1
Corral Viejo C 2
Coto Laurel, 1,761 C 2
Culebra, 611 G 1
Dewey (Culebra), 611 G 1
Dorado, 4,388 D 1
Ensenada, 1,268 B 3
Esperanza, †1,312 G 2
Fajardo, 18,249 F 1
Florida, 1,716 C 1
Guánica, 8,979 B 3
Guayama, 20,318 E 3
Guayanilla, 5,189 B 3
Guaynabo, 55,310 D 1
Gurabo, 6,290 E 2
Hatillo, 2,760 B 1
Hato Rey, †60,539 E 1
Hormigüeros, 6,531 A 2
Humacao, 12,411 E 2
Isabela, 9,515 A 1
Isabel Segunda, 2,378 G 2
Jayuya, 3,826 C 2
Jobos, 2,720 D 3
Juana Díaz, 8,765 C 2
Juncos, 7,985 E 2
Lajas, 3,391 A 3
Lares, 4,545 B 2
Las Marías, 474 B 2
Las Piedras, 4,636 E 2
Levittown, 17,079 D 1
Loíza, 2,707 E 1
Loíza Aldea, 3,350 E 1
Luquillo, 2,459 F 1
Manatí, 13,483 C 1
Maricao, 1,492 B 2
Maunabo, 1,829 E 3
Mayagüez, 68,872 A 2
Mayagüez, ‡85,857 A 2
Moca, 2,378 A 1
Morovis, 2,892 D 1
Naguabo, 4,169 F 2
Naranjito, 3,283 D 1
Orocovis, 3,684 C 2
Palmer, 1,456 F 1
Palo Seco, †489 D 1
Parguera, 1,028 A 3
Patillas, 2,543 E 3
Peñuelas, 3,169 B 2
Playa de Fajardo F 1
Playa de Humacao, 1,912 F 2
Playa de Ponce, †15,574 C 3
Ponce, 128,233 C 3
Ponce, ‡158,981 C 3
Puerto Nuevo, †37,644 D 1
Puerto Real, 1,502 A 2
Puerto Real (Playa de Fajardo) F 1
Punta Santiago (Playa de Humacao), 1,912 F 2
Quebradillas, 2,840 B 1
Rincón, 1,538 A 1
Río Blanco, †2,659 F 2
Río Grande, 4,164 E 1
Río Piedras, †3,761 E 1
Rosario, 640 A 2
Sabana Grande, 5,561 B 2
Sabana Seca, 5,023 D 1
Salinas, 4,461 D 3
San Antonio, 2,484 A 1
San Germán, 11,613 A 2
San Juan (capital), 452,749 E 1
San Juan, ‡851,247 E 1
San Lorenzo, 7,702 E 2
San Sebastián, 7,169 B 1
Santa Isabel, 4,495 C 3
Santurce, †128,232 E 1
Tallaboa, 1,155 B 3
Toa Alta, 3,199 D 1
Toa Baja, 2,026 D 1
Trujillo Alto, 18,477 E 1
Utuado, 11,573 B 2
Vega Alta, 8,688 D 1
Vega Baja, 17,089 C 1
Vieques (Isabel Segunda), 2,378 G 2
Villalba, 4,134 C 2
Yabucoa, 5,119 E 2
Yauco, 12,922 B 2

OTHER FEATURES

Aguadilla (bay) A 1
Algarrobo (pt.) A 2
Añasco (bay) A 1
Arenas (pt.) F 2
Bauta (river) C 2
Bayamón (river) D 1
Boquerón (bay) A 3
Borinquen (pt.) A 1
Cabullón (pt.) C 3
Caja de Muertos (isl.) C 3
Camuy (river) B 1
Candelero (pt.) F 2
Canovanas (river) E 1
Caonillas (lake) C 2
Carite (lake) E 2
Carraízo (lake) E 1
Cayey, Sierra de (mts.) D 2
Central, Cordillera (range) C 2
Cerro Gordo (pt.) D 1
Coamo (res.) D 3
Coamo (river) D 3
Culebra (isl.), 732 G 1
Culebrinas (river) A 1
Culebrita (isl.) G 2
El Toro (mt.) F 2
El Yunque (mt.) F 1
Este (pt.) G 2
Fajardo (river) F 1
Figuras (pt.) E 3
Fosforescente (bay) A 3
Grande de Añasco (river) B 2
Grande de Arecibo (river) C 1
Grande de Loíza (river) E 1
Grande de Manatí (river) C 1
Guajataca (lake) B 1
Guanajibo (pt.) A 2
Guanajibo (river) A 2
Guánica (lake) B 3
Guaniquilla (pt.) A 2
Guayabal (lake) C 2
Guayanés (pt.) F 2
Guayanés (river) E 2
Guayanilla (bay) B 3
Guayo (lake) B 2
Guilarte (mt.) B 2
Honda (bay) F 1
Humacao (river) E 2
Jacaguas (river) C 2
Jaicoa (mts.) B 1
Jiguero (pt.) A 1
Jobos (bay) D 3
La Bandera (pt.) F 1
Lima (pt.) F 2
Lobo (cay) G 1
Luquillo, Sierra de (mts.) E 2
Manglillo (pt.) B 3
Mayagüez (bay) A 2
Miquillo (pt.) F 1
Molinos (pt.) G 1
Mona (passage) A 2
Negra (pt.) G 2
Nigua (river) D 2
Ola Grande (pt.) D 3
Palmas Altas (pt.) C 1
Patillas (lake) E 3
Peñón (pt.) B 1
Petrona (pt.) D 3
Pirata (mt.) G 2
Plata (river) D 2
Puerca (pt.) F 2
Puerto Medio Mundo (bay) F 2
Puerto Nuevo (pt.) C 1
Punta, Cerro de (mt.) C 2
Ramey A.F.B., 7,507 A 1
Rincón (bay) D 3
Rojo (cape) A 3
Salinas (pt.) D 1
San José (lake) E 1
San Juan, Cabezas de (prom.) F 1
San Juan National Hist. Site D 1
Sardina (pt.) A 1
Soldado (pt.) G 2
Sucia (bay) A 3
Tanamá (river) B 1
Torrecilla (lagoon) E 1
Tortuguero (lake) D 1
Tuna (pt.) E 3
Vacía Talega (pt.) E 1
Viento (pt.) E 3
Vieques (isl.), 7,767 G 2
Vieques (passage) F 2
Vieques (sound) G 2
Yagüez (river) A 2
Yauco (lake) B 2
Yeguas (pt.) F 3

ANTIGUA

Total Population, 63,000

CITIES and TOWNS

All Saints, 2,077 D11
Cedar Grove, 899 E11
Falmouth, 239 E11
Freetown, 1,026 E11
Jennings, 850 D11
Johnsons Point, 339 D11
Liberta, 1,988 E11
Old Road, 1,178 D11
Parham, 1,123 E11
Saint John's (capital) 24,367 E11
Willikies, 1,330 E11

OTHER FEATURES

Antigua (isl.), 54,304 E11
Boggy (peak) D11
Boon (pt.) D11
Green (isl.) E11
Guiana (isl.) E11
Long (isl.) E11
Saint John's (harb.) D11
Standfast (pt.) E11
Willoughby (bay) E11

BARBADOS

CITIES and TOWNS

Bathsheba B 8
Belleplaine B 8
Bridgetown (capital), 12,430 B 9
Carlton B 8
Cave Hill B 9
Checker Hall B 8
Codrington B 8
Crab Hill B 8
Crane C 9
Drax Hall B 8
Ellerton B 9
Greenland B 8
Holetown B 8
Kendal B 8
Lodge Hill B 8
Marchfield B 8
Maxwell B 9
Maxwell Hill B 9
Mount Standfast B 8
Portland B 8
Rose Hill B 8
Rouen B 9
Saint Lawrence B 9
Saint Martins B 9
Scarboro B 9
Seawell B 9
Six Mens B 8
Speightstown, 2,415 B 8
Spring Hall B 8
Welchman Hall B 8

OTHER FEATURES

Carlisle (bay) B 9
Hillaby (mt.) B 8
Long (bay) B 9
North (pt.) B 8
Oistins (bay) B 9
Pelican (isl.) B 9
Ragged (pt.) C 8
Sam Lord's Castle C 9
South (pt.) B 9

DOMINICA

Total Population, 70,302

CITIES and TOWNS

Barroui E 6
Castle Bruce, 1,474 F 6
Coulihaut, 972 E 6
Delice, 377 F 7
Grand Bay, 2,385 F 7
Hampstead, 559 E 5
La Plaine, 746 F 6
Laudat, 364 E 6
Mahaut, 1,688 E 6
Marigot, 3,200 F 6
Petit Soufrière, 799 F 6
Portsmouth, 4,146 E 5
Rosalie, 781 F 6
Roseau (capital), 10,157 E 7
Roseau, *16,677 E 7
Saint Joseph, 2,646 E 6
Salybia, 297 F 6
Soufrière, 934 E 7
Vieille Case, 1,372 E 5
Wesley, 2,063 F 5

OTHER FEATURES

Capuchin (cape) E 5
Carib Reserve, 1,974 F 6
Clyde (river) F 6
Crampton (pt.) F 5
Diablotin, Morne (mt.) E 6
Dominica (passage) E 5
Douglas (bay) E 5
Grand (bay) F 7
Jaquet (pt.) E 5
Layou (river) E 6
Martinique (passage) E 7
Micotrin (mt.) F 6
Pagoua (bay) F 6
Prince Rupert (bay) E 5
Roseau (river) E 7
Scotts (head) E 7
Soufrière (bay) E 7
Trois Pitons, Morne (mt.) E 6

GRENADA

Total Population, 105,000

CITIES and TOWNS

Crochu D 8
Gouyave, 2,356 C 8
Grand Anse C 9
Grand Roy C 8
Grenville, 1,747 D 8
Hermitage D 8
La Taste D 8
Marquis D 8
Mount Tivoli D 8
Providence D 9
Saint George's, (capital), 9,000 C 9
Saint George's, *26,843 C 9
Sauteurs, 925 D 8
Union D 8
Victoria, 1,692 D 8
Woburn C 9
Woodford C 8

OTHER FEATURES

Bedford (pt.) D 8
David (pt.) D 8
Great Bacolet (pt.) D 8
Green (isl.) D 8
Grenville (bay) D 8
Gros (pt.) C 8
Halifax (harb.) C 8
Irvins (bay) D 8
Les Tantes (isls.) D 7
Molinière (pt.) C 9
Prickly (pt.) C 9
Ronde (isl.) D 7
Saint Catherine (mt.) D 8
Saline (pt.) C 9
Sinai (mt.) D 8
Telescope (pt.) D 8

GUADELOUPE

Total Population, 324,000

CITIES and TOWNS

Anse-Bertrand, 2,597 B 5
Baie-Mahault, 2,518 A 6
Baillif, 3,056 A 7
Baninier A 7
Basse-Terre (capital), 16,000 A 7
Bouillante, 1,993 A 6
Bourg-des-Saintes, 1,174 A 7
Capesterre, 7,000 A 7
Capesterre, 861 B 7
Deshaies, 754 A 6
Ferry A 6
Gosier, 5,000 B 6
Gourbeyre, 3,024 A 7
Goyave, 1,191 A 6
Grand-Bourg, 3,299 B 7
Grippon B 6
Lamentin, 1,457 A 6
Le Moule, 8,000 B 6
Les Abymes, 6,600 B 6
Morne-à-l'Eau, 10,000 A 6
Petit-Bourg, 3,896 A 6
Petit-Canal, 1,725 A 6
Pigeon A 6
Pointe-à-Pitre, 50,000 B 6
Pointe-Noire, 2,473 A 6
Port-Louis, 5,000 B 5
Saint-Claude, 4,800 A 7
Saint-François, 3,200 B 6
Saint-Louis, 1,500 B 7
Sainte-Anne, 3,573 B 6
Sainte-Marguerite B 6
Sainte-Marie A 6
Sainte-Rose, 3,043 A 6
Trois-Rivières, 1,743 A 7
Vieux-Fort, 1,213 B 7
Vieux-Habitants, 1,621 A 7

OTHER FEATURES

Allègre (pt.) A 6
Antigues (pt.) A 5
Basse-Terre (isl.), 134,601 A 6
Châteaux (pt.) B 6
Constant, Morne (hill) B 7
Désirade (isl.), 1,559 B 6
Fajou (isl.) A 6
Grand Cul-de-Sac Marin (bay) A 6
Grand Îlet (isl.) A 7
Grande-Terre (isl.), 150,576 B 5
Grande Vigie (pt.) B 5
Guadeloupe (isl.), 285,177 B 6
Guadeloupe (passage) A 5
Kahouanne (isl.) A 6
Marie-Galante (isl.), 15,870 B 7
Nord (pt.) B 7
Nord-Est (bay) B 6
Petit Cul-de-Sac Marin (bay) A 6
Petite-Terre (isls.) B 6
Saintes (isls.), 3,272 A 7
Saintes, Canal des (chan.) A 7
Salée (river) A 6
Sans Toucher (mt.) A 6
Soufrière (mt.) A 7
Terre-de-Bas (isl.), 1,795 A 7
Terre-de-Haut (isl.), 1,477 A 7
Vieux-Fort (pt.) A 7

MARTINIQUE

Total Population, 332,000

CITIES and TOWNS

Ajoupa-Bouillon, 1,397 C 5
Anses-d'Arlet, 1,102 C 7
Basse-Pointe, 2,324 C 5
Belle-Fontaine, 1,082 C 6
Carbet, 2,593 C 6
Case-Pilote, 1,625 C 6
Diamant, 629 D 7
Ducos, 1,976 D 6
Fond-Lahaye C 6
Fonds-Saint-Denis, 780 C 6
Fort-de-France (capital), 100,000 C 6
Fort-Desaix C 6
François, 3,195 D 6
Grande-Rivière, 1,493 C 5
Gros-Morne, 979 D 6
Lamentin, 6,721 D 6
Lorrain, 1,848 D 5
Macouba, 1,329 C 5
Marigot, 1,449 D 5
Marin, 1,789 D 7
Morne-Rouge, 2,655 C 5
Morne-Vert, 493 C 6
Prêcheur, 2,312 C 5
Rivière-Pilote, 2,039 D 7
Rivière-Salée, 1,725 D 7
Robert, 2,077 D 6
Saint-Esprit, 3,214 D 6
Saint-Joseph, 1,995 C 6
Saint-Pierre, 5,556 C 6
Sainte-Anne, 960 D 7
Sainte-Luce, 1,243 D 7
Sainte-Marie, 2,933 D 5
Schoelcher, 10,817 C 6
Trinité, 3,566 D 6
Trois-Îlets, 1,400 C 6
Vauclin, 2,908 D 6
Vert-Pré D 6

OTHER FEATURES

Cabet, Pitons du (mt.) C 6
Cabri (isl.) D 7
Caravelle (pen.) D 6
Cul-de-Sac du Marin (bay) D 7
Diable (pt.) D 5
Ferré (cape) E 7
Fort-de-France (bay) C 6
Galion (bay) D 6
Lézarde (river) D 6
Long, Îlet (isl.) D 6
Lorrain (river) D 5
Martinique (passage) C 5
Pelée (vol.) C 5
Pilote (river) D 7
Ramiers, Îlet-à- (isl.) C 6
Ramville, Îlet (isl.) D 6
Robert (harb.) D 6
Rocher du Diamant (isl.) C 7
Rose (pt.) D 6
Saint-Martin (cape) C 5
Saint-Pierre (bay) C 6
Salines (pt.) D 7
Salomon (pt.) C 7
Vauclin (mt.) D 6

NETHERLANDS ANTILLES

CITIES and TOWNS

Aresji D 9
Ascension F 8
Bacuna E 8
Balashi E10
Boven Bolivia E 8
Bubali D10
Bushiribana E10
Dokterstuin D 8
Druif D10
Emmastad G 9
Entrejo E 8
Fontein E 8
Fuik G 9
Groot Sint Joris G 9
Hato G 8
Kralendijk (capital), Bonaire, 839 E 8
Lago E10
Lagoen F 8
Montanja di Reij G 9
New Port G 9
Noord di Salinja E 8
Onima E 8
Oranjestad (capital), Aruba, 15,398 D10
Otrabanda F 9
Patrick F 8
Rincon E 8
Rooi E 8
Sabana Westpunt F 8
Santa Barbara G 9
Santa Catharina G 9
Savaneta E10
Savonet F 8
Sint Anna D10
Sint Jan D 8
Sint Kruis F 8
Sint Martha F 8
Sint Michiel F 9
Sint Nicolaas E10
Sint Willebrordus F 8
Terra Corra E 8
Westpunt D10
Willemstad (capital), 43,547 F 9
Willemstad, *94,133 F 9

OTHER FEATURES

Aruba (isl.), 58,868 E 9
Basora (pt.) E10
Bonaire (isl.), 5,755 E 9
Bullen (bay) F 8
Caracas (bay) G 9
Curaçao (isl.), 196,170 G 7
Goto (lake) D 8
Jamanota (mt.) E10
Kanon (pt.) G 9
Klein Bonaire (isl.) E 8
Kudarebe (pt.) D 9
Lac (bay) D 9
Lacre (pt.) E 9
Malmok (mt.) E 8
Noord (pt.) D 8
Noord (pt.) F 8
Paarden (bay) D10
Palm (beach) D10
Pekelmeer (lake) E 9
Piscadera (bay) F 9
Schottegat (bay) G 9
Sint Anna (bay) F 9
Sint Christoffel Berg (mt.) F 8
Sint Joris (bay) G 9
Slag (bay) D 8
Vierkant (pt.) E 8

SAINT CHRISTOPHER-NEVIS-ANGUILLA

Total Population, 56,000

CITIES and TOWNS

Basseterre (capital), 15,726 C10
Cayon, 1,524 C10
Charlestown, 2,852 C11
Cotton Ground, 747 C11
Dieppe Bay, 949 C10
Gingerland D11
Golden Rock C10
Newcastle, 361 D11
Old Road, 1,206 C10
Sadlers Village, 1,091 C10
Sandy Point, 3,608 C10
Tabernacle, 1,250 C10
Zion Hill D11

OTHER FEATURES

Brimstone (hill) C10
Dogwood (pt.) D11
Fort (pt.) C11
Great Salt (pond) D10
Heldens (pt.) C10
Horse Shoe (pt.) C11
Misery (mt.) C10
Monkey (hill) C10
Muddy (pt.) C10
Narrows, The (str.) D11
Nevis (isl.), 12,762 D11
Nevis (peak) D11
North Friars (bay) D10
Palmetto (pt.) C10
Saint Christopher (isl.), 38,291 D10
Saint Kitts (Saint Christopher) (isl.), 38,291 D10
South Friars (bay) C10

SAINT LUCIA

Total Population, 110,000

CITIES and TOWNS

Anse la Raye, 2,053 F 6
Canaries, 1,676 G 6
Castries (capital), 4,353 G 6
Castries, *15,291 G 6
Choc G 5
Choiseul, 513 F 7
Dauphin G 5
Dennery, 2,252 G 6
Gros Islet, 1,016 G 5
Laborie, 1,591 G 7
Marigot G 6
Marquis G 6
Micoud, 2,040 G 6
Praslin G 6
Soufrière, 2,682 F 6
Vieux Fort, 3,228 G 7

OTHER FEATURES

Beaumont (pt.) F 6
Canaries, Piton (mt.) G 6
Cannelles (pt.) G 7
Cannelles (river) G 6
Cap (pt.) G 5
Choc (bay) G 5
Fond d'Or (bay) G 6
Gimie (mt.) G 6
Grand Caille (pt.) F 6
Grand Cul de Sac (river) G 6
Gros Islet (bay) G 5
Gros Piton (mt.) G 6
Maria (isl.) G 7
Ministre (pt.) G 7
Moule à Chique (cape) G 7
Petit Piton (mt.) G 6
Pigeon (isl.) G 5
Port Castries (harb.) G 6
Port Praslin (bay) G 6
Roseau (river) G 6
Saint Lucia (chan.) G 5
Saint Vincent (passage) G 7
Savannes (bay) G 7
Sorcière, La (mt.) G 6
Soufrière (bay) F 6
Vierge (pt.) G 6
Vieux Fort (river) G 6

SAINT VINCENT

Total Population, 89,129

CITIES and TOWNS

Barrouallie, †2,459 A 9
Calliaqua, †3,589 A 9
Camden Park A 9
Chateaubelair, †2,173 A 8
Colonarie, †1,550 A 8
Georgetown, †2,645 A 8
Kingstown (capital), 17,258 A 9
Kingstown, *23,482 A 9
Layou, †3,060 A 9
Turema A 8
Wallibu A 8

OTHER FEATURES

Colonarie (pt.) A 9
Cumberland (bay) A 8
Dark (head) A 8
De Volet (pt.) A 8
Espagnol (pt.) A 8
Greathead (bay) A 9
Kingstown (bay) A 9
Owia (bay) A 8
Porter (pt.) A 8
Richmond (peak) A 8
Saint Andrew (mt.) A 9
Saint Vincent (passage) A 8
Soufrière (mt.) A 8
Yambu (head) A 9

TRINIDAD and TOBAGO

CITIES and TOWNS

Arima, 10,982 B10
Arouca, 4,781 B10
Basse Terre B11
Biche, 1,986 B11
Blanchisseuse, 205 B10
California A11
Carapichaima B10
Caroni, 678 B10
Cedros, 1,388 A11
Chaguanas, 3,509 A10
Chaguaramas A10
Couva, 3,567 A10
Cunapo B10
Débé, 2,189 B11
Ecclesville B11
Flanagin Town B10
Fullarton A11
Fyzabad, 1,869 A11
Gran Couva B11
Grande Rivière, 301 B10
Guaico B10
Guayaguayare, 287 B11
La Brea, 4,828 A11
La Lune, 252 B11
Marabella, 8,937 A11
Matelot, 289 B10
Matura B10
Mayaro, 1,828 B11
Moruga, 656 B11
Mucurapo, 2,851 A10
Nestor B10
Palo Seco A11
Peñal, 3,594 B11
Piarco B10
Point Fortin, 8,753 A11
Port-of-Spain (capital), 86,150 A10
Port-of-Spain, *250,000 A10
Princes Town, 6,681 B11
Redhead, 302 B10
Rio Claro, 2,174 B11
Sadhoowa B11
Saint Joseph, 4,079 B10
Saint Joseph B11
San Fernando, 39,830 A11
San Francique A11
San Juan, 19,064 A10
Sangre Grande, 5,087 B10
Sans Souci, 295 B10
Siparia, 4,174 B11
Tabaquite B11
Tableland B11
Tacarigua, 6,704 B10
Talparo B10
Toco, 979 B10
Tunapuna, 11,287 B10
Upper Manzanilla B10
Valencia, 370 B10
Waterloo A10

OTHER FEATURES

Aripo, El Cerro del (mt.) B10
Boca Grande (passage) A10
Casa Cruz (cape) B11
Chacachacare (isl.) A10
Chupara (pt.) B10
Cocos (bay) B10
Dragons Mouth (passage) A10
Erin (bay) A1
Erin (pt.) A1
Galeota (pt.) B1
Galera (pt.) C1
Guapo (bay) A1
Guatuaro (pt.) B1
Icacos (pt.) A1
Matura (bay) B1
Mayaro (bay) B1
Monos (isl.) A1
Nariva (swamp) B1
Oropuche (river) B1
Ortoire (river) B1
Paria (gulf) A1
Pitch (lake) A1
Serpents Mouth (passage) A1
Tamana (mt.) B1
Trinidad (isl.), 973,250 A
Tucuche, El (mt.) B1
U.S. Naval Base A1

VIRGIN ISLANDS (BRITISH)

CITIES and TOWNS

Road Town (capital), 2,183 D
West End, 105 D

OTHER FEATURES

Flanagan (passage) D
Frenchman (cay) C
Great Thatch (isl.) C
Great Tobago (isl.) B
Jost Van Dyke (isl.), 124 C
Little Tobago (isl.) B
Narrow, The (str.) C
Norman (isl.) D
Peter (isl.) D
Road (bay) D
Sage (mt.) D
Sir Francis Drake (chan.) D
Tortola (isl.), 8,939 D

VIRGIN ISLANDS (U. S.)

CITIES and TOWNS

Bethlehem E
Canebay E
Charlotte Amalie (capital), 12,220 B
Christiansted, 3,020 F
Cruz Bay, †1,497 C
Diamond F
East End, †26 D
Emmaus C
Fredensdal F
Frederiksted, 1,531 E
Grove Place E
Kingshill F
Longford F
Negro Bay E

OTHER FEATURES

Altona (lagoon) F
Annaly (bay) E
Baron Bluff (prom.) E
Bordeaux (mt.) C
Brass (isls.) A
Buck (isl.) G
Buck Island (chan.) F
Buck Island Reef National Mon. G
Butler (bay) E
Caneel (bay) C
Capella (isls.) B
Christiansted National Hist. Site F
Coral (bay) C
Crown (mt.) A
Dutchcap (cay) A
Eagle (mt.) E
East (pt.) G
Flanagan (passage) C
Flat (cays) B
Grass (pt.) G
Great (pond) F
Great Pond (bay) F
Green (cay) F
Hams Bluff (prom.) E
Hans Lollik (isls.) B
Hassel (isl.) B
Jersey (bay) B
Krause (lagoon) F
Leeward (passage) B
Long (pt.) E
Long (pt.) C
Lovango (cay) C
Magens (bay) B
Maho (bay) C
Narrows, The (str.) C
Nulliberg (mt.) B
Perseverance (bay) A
Picara (pt.) B
Pillsbury (sound) B
Privateer (pt.) C
Pull (pt.) F
Ram (head) C
Red (pt.) C
Reef (bay) C
Saba (isl.) A
Saint Croix (isl.), 31,779 G
Saint James (isls.) B
Saint John (isl.), 1,729 C
Saint Thomas (harb.) B
Saint Thomas (isl.), 28,960 A
Salt (cay) A
Salt (river) F
Salt River (bay) F
Sandy (pt.) D
Savana (isl.) A
Southwest (cape) E
Tague (bay) G
Thatch (cay) B
Turner Hole (bay) G
U.S. Naval Air Sta. A
Vagthus (pt.) F
Virgin (passage) A
Virgin Islands National Park C
Water (isl.) A
Westend Saltpond (lagoon) E

*City and suburbs.
†Population of municipality or sub-division.

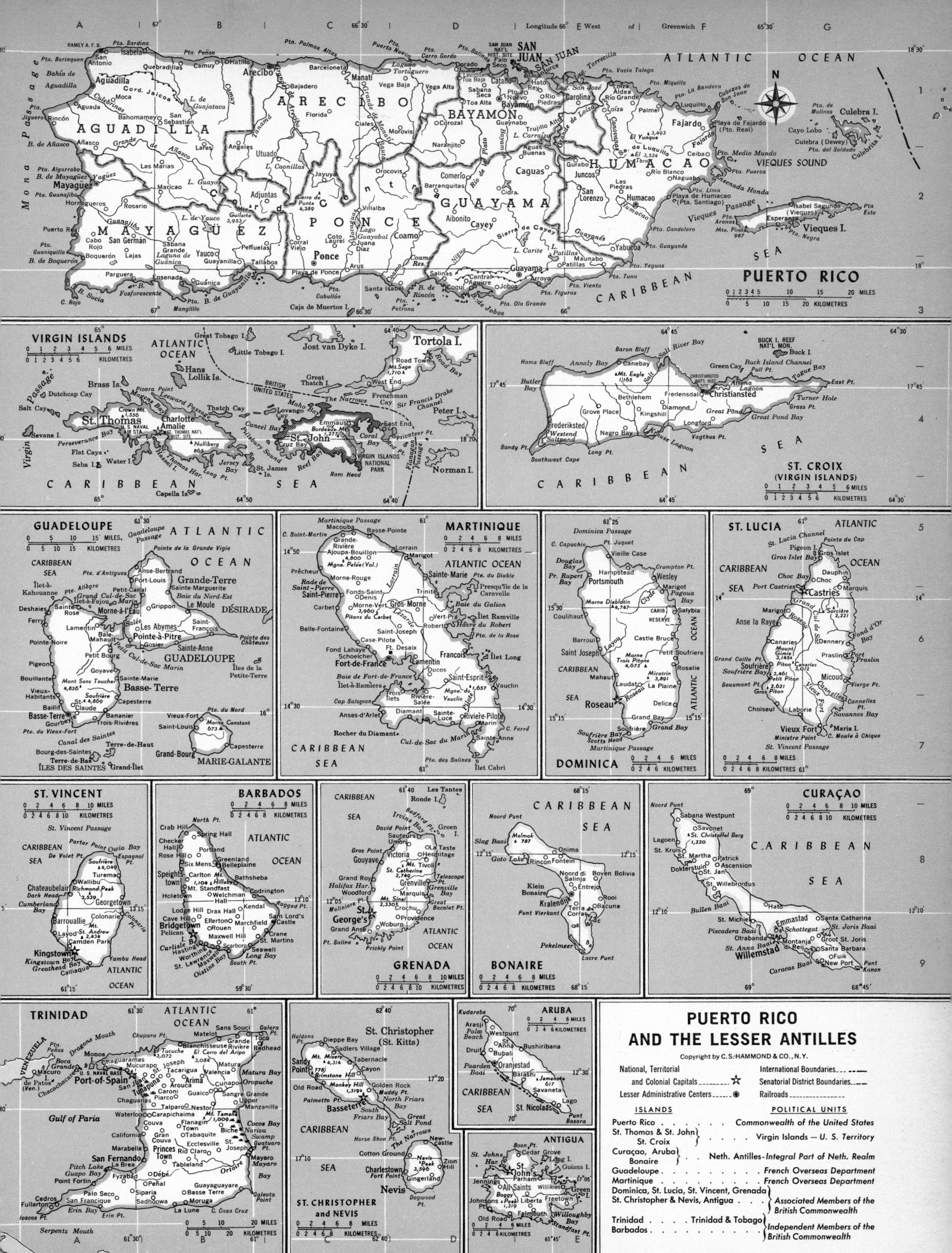
PUERTO RICO
ATLANTIC OCEAN
CARIBBEAN SEA
AGUADILLA
ARECIBO
BAYAMON
HUMACAO
MAYAGÜEZ
PONCE
GUAYAMA
San Juan
Mona Passage
Vieques Sound
Culebra I.
Vieques I.
VIRGIN ISLANDS
St. Thomas
St. John
Tortola I.
ST. CROIX (VIRGIN ISLANDS)
Christiansted
Frederiksted
GUADELOUPE
Grande-Terre
Basse-Terre
MARIE-GALANTE
ÎLES DES SAINTES
DÉSIRADE
MARTINIQUE
Fort-de-France
DOMINICA
Roseau
ST. LUCIA
Castries
ST. VINCENT
Kingstown
BARBADOS
Bridgetown
GRENADA
St. George's
BONAIRE
Kralendijk
CURAÇAO
Willemstad
TRINIDAD
Port-of-Spain
San Fernando
Gulf of Paria
ST. CHRISTOPHER and NEVIS
Basseterre
Charlestown
ARUBA
Oranjestad
ANTIGUA
St. John's
PUERTO RICO AND THE LESSER ANTILLES
Copyright by C.S. HAMMOND & CO., N.Y.
National, Territorial and Colonial Capitals
Lesser Administrative Centers
International Boundaries
Senatorial District Boundaries
Railroads
ISLANDS
POLITICAL UNITS
Puerto Rico . . . . . Commonwealth of the United States
St. Thomas & St. John, St. Croix . . . . Virgin Islands — U. S. Territory
Curaçao, Aruba, Bonaire . . Neth. Antilles-Integral Part of Neth. Realm
Guadeloupe . . . . French Overseas Department
Martinique . . . . French Overseas Department
Dominica, St. Lucia, St. Vincent, Grenada, St. Christopher & Nevis, Antigua . . . Associated Members of the British Commonwealth
Trinidad . . . . . Trinidad & Tobago, Barbados . . . . Independent Members of the British Commonwealth

Abitibi (lake), Ont. ....H 6
Aklavik, N.W.T., 677 ....C 2
Albany (river), Ont. ....H 5
Alberta (prov.), 1,627,874 ....E 5
Amherst, N.S., 9,966 ....K 6
Amos, Que., 6,984 ....J 6
Anticosti (isl.), Que., 419 ....K 6
Athabasca, Alta., 1,765 ....E 5
Athabasca (lake) ....F 4
Athabasca (river), Alta. ....E 4
Atikokan, Ont., 6,087 ....G 6
Axel Heiberg (isl.), N.W.T. ....N 3
Baffin (bay), N.W.T. ....J 1
Baffin (isl.), N.W.T. ....J 1
Baie-Saint-Paul, Que., 4,163 ....J 6
Banff, Alta., 3,219 ....E 5
Banff National Park, Alta., 3,532 ....E 5
Banks (isl.), N.W.T. ....D 1
Baskatong (res.), Que. ....J 6
Bathurst, N.B., 16,674 ....K 6
Battleford, Sask., 1,803 ....F 5
Belle Isle (strait), Newf. ....L 5
Biggar, Sask., 2,607 ....F 5
Blind River, Ont., 3,450 ....H 6
Boissevain, Man., 1,506 ....G 6
Bonavista, Newf., 4,215 ....L 6
Boothia (pen.), N.W.T. ....G 1
Bow (river), Alta. ....E 5
Brandon, Man., 31,150 ....F 6
Bridgewater, N.S., 5,231 ....K 7
British Columbia (prov.), 2,184,621 ....D 4
Burns Lake, B.C., 1,259 ....D 5
Cabot (strait) ....K 6
Calgary, Alta., †403,319 ....E 5
Callander, Ont., 1,190 ....H 6
Cambridge Bay, N.W.T., 716 ....F 2
Campbellton, N.B., 10,335 ....K 6
Camrose, Alta., 8,673 ....E 5
Cap-Chat, Que., 3,868 ....K 6
Cape Breton (isl.), N.S., 162,989 ....K 6
Cardston, Alta., 2,685 ....E 6
Carman, Man., 2,030 ....G 6
Chandler, Que., 3,843 ....K 6
Channel-Port aux Basques, Newf., 5,942 ....L 6
Chapleau, Ont., 3,389 ....H 6
Charlottetown (cap.), P.E.I., 19,133 ....K 6
Chatham, N.B., 7,833 ....K 6
Chibougamau, Que., 9,701 ....J 2
Chicoutimi, Que., 33,893 ....J 6
Chicoutimi-Jonquière, †133,703 ....J 6
Chidley (cape) ....K 3
Chilliwack, B.C., 9,135 ....D 6
Churchill, Man., 973 ....G 4
Churchill (falls), Newf. ....L 6
Coast (mts.) ....C 4
Cobalt, Ont., 2,197 ....H 6
Cochrane, Ont., 4,965 ....H 6
Coleman, Alta., 1,534 ....E 6
Columbia (river), B.C. ....D 6
Coppermine, N.W.T., 637 ....E 2
Corner Brook, Newf., 26,309 ....L 6
Cornwall, Ont., 47,116 ....J 7
Courtenay, B.C., 7,152 ....D 6
Cranbrook, B.C., 12,000 ....E 6
Cree (lake), Sask. ....F 4
Dartmouth, N.S., 64,770 ....K 7
Dauphin, Man., 8,891 ....F 5
Davis (strait), N.W.T. ....K 1
Dawson, Yukon, 762 ....C 3
Devon (isl.), N.W.T. ....M 3
Didsbury, Alta., 1,821 ....E 5
Drumheller, Alta., 5,446 ....E 5
Edmonton (cap.), Alta., †495,702 ....E 5
Edmundston, N.B., 12,365 ....K 6
Edson, Alta., 3,818 ....E 5
Ellesmere (isl.), N.W.T. ....N 3
Englehart, Ont., 1,721 ....H 6
Eskimo Point, N.W.T., 598 ....G 3
Estevan, Sask., 9,150 ....F 6
Eston, Sask., 1,418 ....F 5
Fernie, B.C., 4,422 ....E 6
Finlay (river), B.C. ....D 4
Flin Flon, Man.-Sask., 9,344 ....F 4
Fogo (isl.), Newf., 4,094 ....L 6
Fort-Chimo, Que., 693 ....K 4
Fort Frances, Ont., 9,947 ....G 6
Fort-George, Que., 1,280 ....J 5
Fort Macleod, Alta., 2,715 ....E 6
Fort McMurray, Alta., 6,847 ....E 4
Fort McPherson, N.W.T., 679 ....C 2
Fort Nelson, B.C., 2,289 ....D 4
Fort Providence, N.W.T., 587 ....E 3
Fort Resolution, N.W.T., 623 ....E 3
Fort Saskatchewan, Alta., 5,726 ..E 5
Fort Simpson, N.W.T., 747 ....D 3
Fort Smith, N.W.T., 2,364 ....E 3
Foxe (basin), N.W.T. ....J 2
Franklin (dist.), N.W.T., 7,747 ..H 1
Fraser (river), B.C. ....D 5
Fredericton (cap.), N.B., 24,254 ..K 6
Frobisher Bay, N.W.T., 2,014 ....K 3
Fundy (bay) ....K 7
Gagnon, Que., 3,787 ....K 5
Gander, Newf., 7,748 ....L 6
Gaspé, Que., 17,211 ....K 6
Georgian (bay), Ont. ....H 6
Geraldton, Ont., 3,178 ....H 6
Glace Bay, N.S., 22,440 ....L 6
Goose Bay, Newf., 496 ....K 5
Gouin (res.), Que. ....J 6
Grand Falls, Newf., 7,677 ....L 6
Grande Prairie, Alta., 13,079 ....E 4
Great Bear (lake), N.W.T. ....D 2
Great Slave (lake), N.W.T. ....E 3
Guelph, Ont., 60,087 ....H 7
Halifax (cap.), N.S., †222,637 ....K 7
Hamilton, Ont., †498,523 ....H 7
Hanna, Alta., 2,545 ....E 5
Harbour Grace, Newf., 2,771 ....L 6
Havre-Saint-Pierre, Que., 2,998 ...K 5
Hay River, N.W.T., 2,406 ....E 3
Hearst, Ont., 3,501 ....H 6
Hecate (strait), B.C. ....C 5
High River, Alta., 2,676 ....E 5
Hope, B.C., 3,153 ....D 6
Hull, Que., 63,580 ....J 6
Humboldt, Sask., 3,881 ....F 5
Indian Head, Sask., 1,810 ....F 5
Inuvik, N.W.T., 2,669 ....C 2
Inverness, N.S., 1,846 ....K 6
Iroquois Falls, Ont., 7,271 ....H 6
Jasper, Alta., 2,932 ....E 5
Jasper Nat'l Park, Alta., 3,064 ..E 5
Jonquière, Que., 28,430 ....J 6
Juan de Fuca (strait), B.C. ....D 6
Kamloops, B.C., 26,168 ....D 5
Kamsack, Sask., 2,783 ....F 5
Kane (basin), N.W.T. ....N 3
Kapuskasing, Ont., 12,834 ....H 6
Keewatin (dist.), N.W.T., 3,403 ..G 3
Kelowna, B.C., 19,412 ....E 6
Kenora, Ont., 10,952 ....G 5
Killarney, Man., 2,074 ....G 6
Kindersley, Sask., 3,451 ....F 5
Kingston, Ont., 59,047 ....J 7
Kirkland Lake, Ont., 13,599 ....H 6
Kitimat, B.C., 11,824 ....D 5
Kluane (lake), Yukon ....C 3
Kootenay (lake), B.C. ....E 5
Labrador (reg.), Newf., 28,166 ..K 4
Labrador (sea) ....L 5
Lac La Biche, Alta., 1,791 ....E 5
Lacombe, Alta., 3,436 ....E 5
Lake Louise, Alta., 165 ....E 5
Lancaster (sound), N.W.T. ....H 1
La Sarre, Que., 5,185 ....J 6
La Tuque, Que., 13,099 ....J 6
Leduc, Alta., 4,000 ....E 5
Lesser Slave (lake), Alta. ....E 4
Lethbridge, Alta., 41,217 ....E 6
Liard (river) ....D 3
Lillooet, B.C., 1,514 ....D 5
Lloydminster, Alta.-Sask., 8,691 ..E 5
Logan (mt.), Yukon ....B 3
London, Ont., †286,011 ....H 7
Lunenburg, N.S., 3,215 ....K 7
Mackenzie (dist.) N.W.T., 23,657 ....E 3
Mackenzie (river), N.W.T. ....C 2
Magdalen (isls.), Que., 13,303 ....K 6
Manicouagan (riv.), Que. ....K 5
Manitoba (prov.), 988,247 ....G 5
Manitoba (lake), Man. ....G 5
Manitoulin (isl.), Ont. ....H 6
Maple Creek, Sask., 2,268 ....F 6
Marathon, Ont., 2,456 ....H 6
Mattawa, Ont., 2,881 ....J 6
Mayo, Yukon, 381 ....C 3
M'Clintock (chan.), N.W.T. ....F 1
Medicine Hat, Alta., 26,518 ....E 5
Melfort, Sask., 4,725 ....F 5
Melville, Sask., 5,375 ....F 5
Melville (isl.), N.W.T. ....E 1
Merritt, B.C., 5,289 ....D 5
Minto (lake), Que. ....J 4
Mistassibi (river), Que. ....J 5
Mistassini (lake), Que. ....J 5
Moncton, N.B., 47,891 ....K 6
Mont-Joli, Que., 6,698 ....K 6
Mont-Laurier, Que., 8,240 ....J 6
Montréal, Que., †2,743,208 ....J 7
Moose Jaw, Sask., 31,854 ....F 5
Moosomin, Sask., 2,407 ....F 5
Moosonee, Ont., 1,793 ....H 5
Morden, Man., 3,266 ....G 6
Nanaimo, B.C., 14,948 ....D 6
Nares (strait), N.W.T. ....N 3
Nelson, B.C., 9,400 ....E 6
Nelson (river), Man. ....G 4
Newcastle, N.B., 6,460 ....K 6
New Brunswick (prov.), 634,557 ..K 6
Newfoundland (prov.), 522,104 ....L 5
Newfoundland (isl.), 493,938 ....L 6
New Liskeard, Ont., 5,488 ....H 6
New Westminster, B.C., 42,835 ..D 6
Niagara Falls, Ont., 67,163 ....J 7
Nipigon, Ont., 2,141 ....H 6
Noranda, Que., 10,741 ....J 6
North Battleford, Sask., 12,698 ..F 5
North Bay, Ont., 49,187 ....J 6
North Magnetic Pole ....F 1
North Saskatchewan (river) ....F 5
North Vancouver, B.C., 31,847 ....D 6
Northwest Territories, 34,807 ....E 2
Nottaway (river), Que. ....J 5
Nova Scotia (prov.), 788,960 ....K 7
Okanagan (lake), B.C. ....D 6
Ontario (prov.), 7,703,106 ....H 5
Ottawa (cap.), Canada, 302,341 ..J 6
Ottawa-Hull, †602,510 ....J 6
Ottawa (river) ....J 6
Owen Sound, Ont., 18,469 ....H 7
Parry (chan.), N.W.T. ....E-H 1
Parry Sound, Ont., 5,842 ....J 6
Peace (river) ....E 4
Peace River, Alta., 5,039 ....E 4
Peel (river) ....C 2
Pelly (river), Yukon ....C 3
Pembroke, Ont., 16,544 ....J 6
Péribonca (river), Que. ....J 5
Peterborough, Ont., 58,111 ....J 7
Pincher Creek, Alta., 3,227 ....E 6
Portage la Prairie, Man., 12,950 ..G 5
Port-Cartier, Que., 3,730 ....K 6
Poste-de-la-Baleine, Que., 987 ....J 4
Povungnituk, Que., 676 ....J 3
Prince Albert, Sask., 28,464 ....F 5
Prince Albert Nat'l Park, Sask., 182 ....F 5
Rocky (mts.) ....D
Rocky Mtn. House, Alta., 2,968 ..E
Rosetown, Sask., 2,614 ....F
Rossland, B.C., 3,896 ....E
Rosthern, Sask., 1,431 ....F
Rouyn, Que., 17,821 ....J
Sable (cape), N.S. ....K
Sable (isl.), N.S., 12 L
Saint Elias (mt.), Yukon C
Saint John, N.B., †106,744 ....K
Saint John's (cap.), Newf., †131,814 ....L 6
Prince Edward Island (prov.), 111,641 ....K 6
Prince George, B.C., 33,101 ....D 5
Prince Patrick (isl.), N.W.T. ....M 3
Prince Rupert, B.C., 15,747 ....C 5
Québec (prov.), 6,027,764 ....J 5
Québec (cap.), Que., †480,502 ....J 6
Queen Charlotte (isls.), B.C., 2,390 ....C 5
Queen Elizabeth (isls.), N.W.T. M 3
Quesnel, B.C., 6,252 ....C 5
Race (cape), Newf. ....L 6
Radville, Sask., 1,024 ....F 6
Rae-Edzo, N.W.T., 1,081 ....E 3
Rainy (lake), Ont. ....G 6
Rainy River, Ont., 1,196 ....G 6
Ray (cape), Newf. ....L 6
Raymond, Alta., 2,156 ....E 6
Red Deer, Alta., 27,674 ....E 5
Regina (cap.), Sask., †140,734 ....F 5
Reindeer (lake) ....F 4
Renfrew, Ont., 9,173 ....J 6
Revelstoke, B.C., 4,867 ....E 5
Riding Mtn. Nat'l Park, Man., 158 ....F 5
Rimouski, Que., 26,887 ....K 6
Rivière-du-Loup, Que., 12,760 ....K 6
Roberval, Que., 8,330 ....J 6
Robson (mt.), B.C. ....E 5

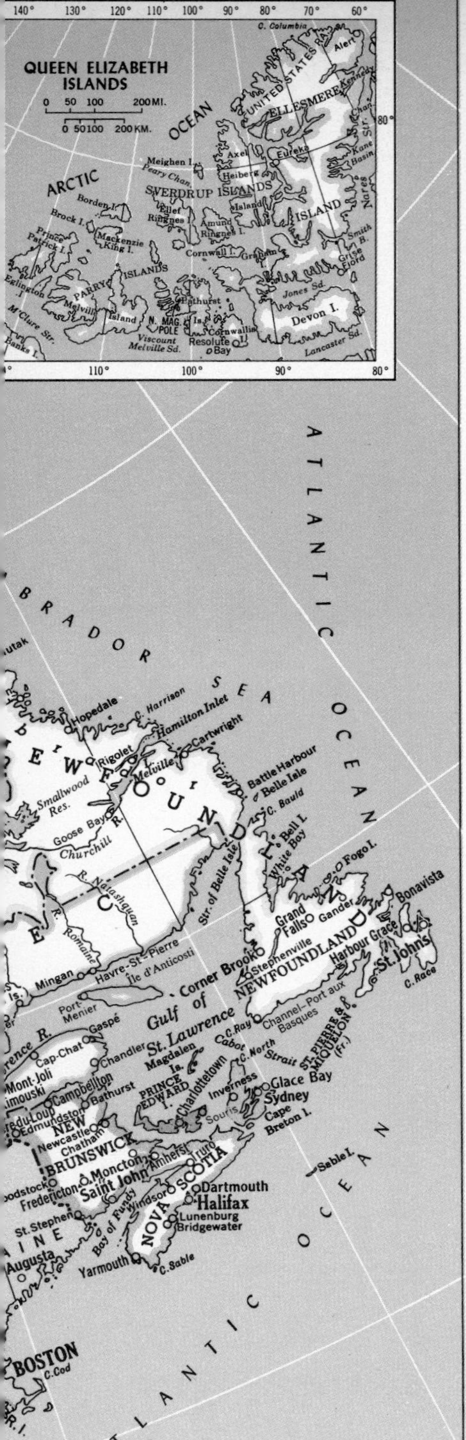

AREA 3,851,809 sq. mi.
POPULATION 21,489,000
CAPITAL Ottawa
LARGEST CITY Montréal
HIGHEST POINT Mt. Logan 19,850 ft.
MONETARY UNIT Canadian dollar
MAJOR LANGUAGES English, French
MAJOR RELIGIONS Protestantism, Roman Catholicism

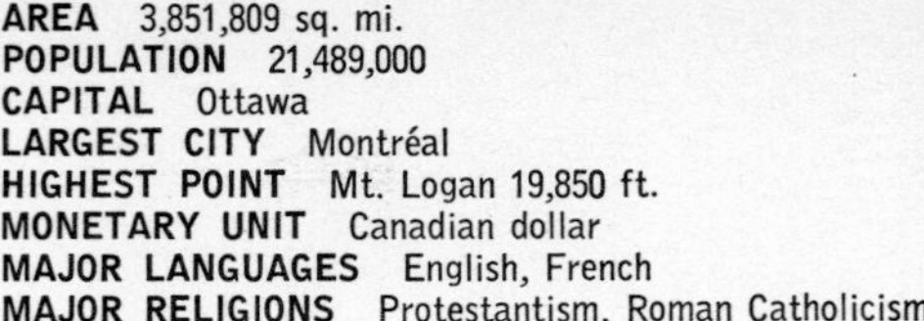

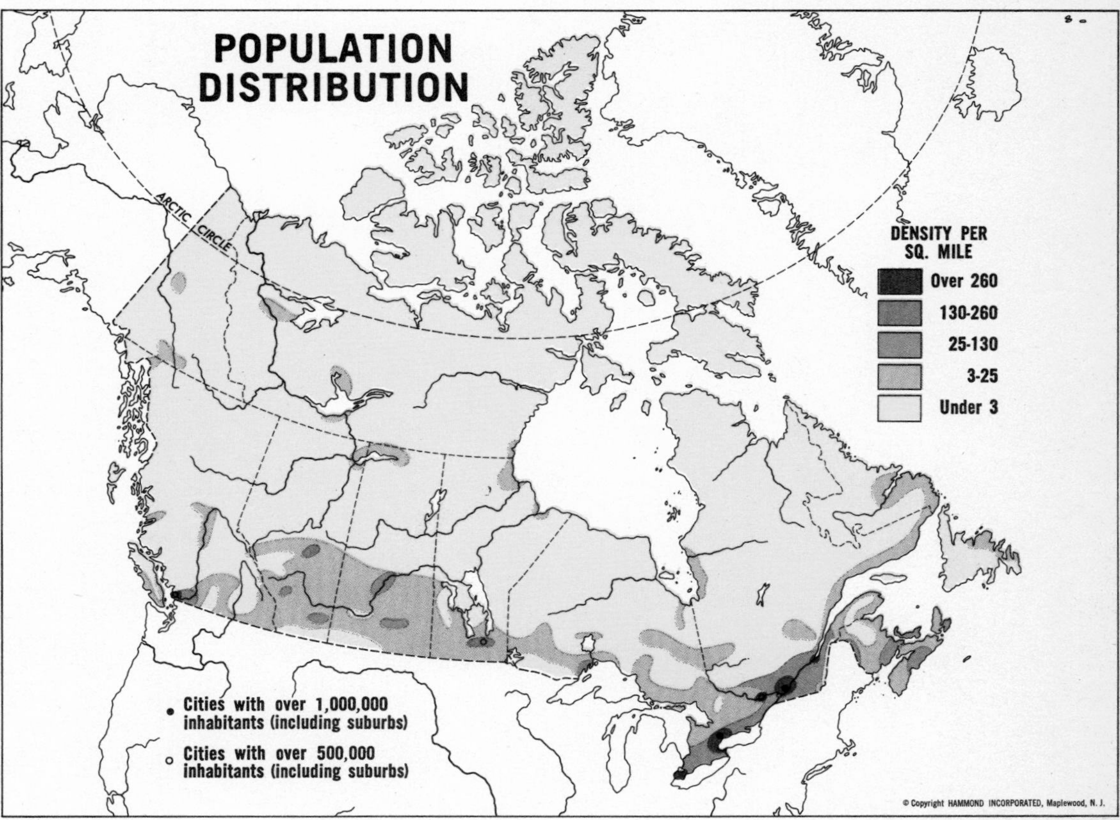

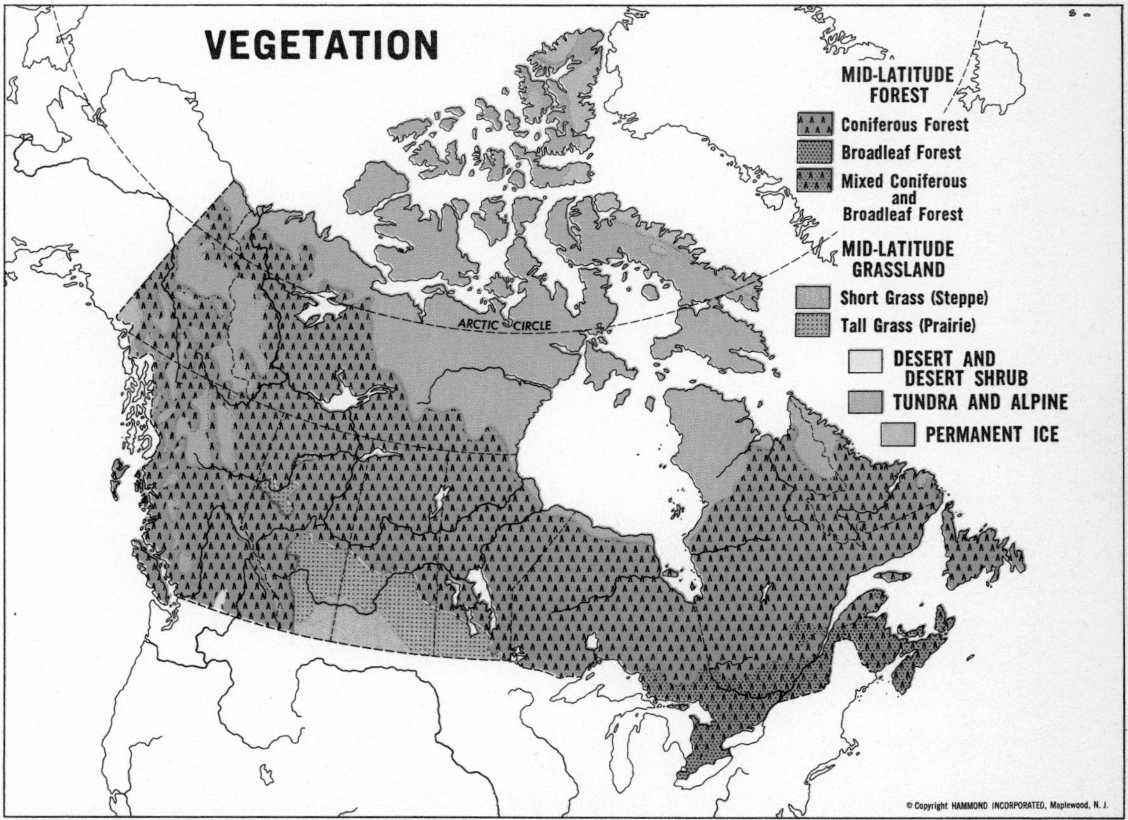

Saint Lawrence (river) ....K 6
Saint Paul, Alta., 4,161 ....E 5
Saint Pierre and Miquelon (isls.), 6,000 ....L 6
Saint Stephen, N.B., 3,409 ....K 6
Sarnia, Ont., 57,644 ....H 7
Saskatchewan (prov.), 926,242....F 5
Saskatchewan (river) ....F 5
Saskatoon, Sask., †126,449 ....F 5
Sault Ste. Marie, Ont., 80,332....H 6
Schefferville, Que., 3,271 ....K 5
Selkirk, Man., 9,331 ....G 5
Sept-Îles (Seven Is.), Que., 24,320 ....K 5
Shaunavon, Sask., 2,244 ....F 6
Shawinigan, Que., 27,792 ....J 6
Sherbrooke, Que., 80,711 ....J 7
Sioux Lookout, Ont., 2,530 ....G 5
Skeena (river), B.C. ....D 5
Slave (river) ....E 3
Smallwood (res.), Newf. ....K 5
Smithers, B.C., 3,864 ....D 5
Souris, Man., 1,674 ....F 6
Souris, P.E.I., 1,393 ....K 6
Southampton (isl.), N.W.T. ....H 3
Stettler, Alta., 4,168 ....E 5
Stewart (river), Yukon ....C 3
Stikine (river), B.C. ....C 4
Sturgeon Falls, Ont., 6,662 ....H 6
Sudbury, Ont., †155,424 ....H 6
Sverdrup (isl.), N.W.T. ....M 3
Swan River, Man., 3,522 ....E 5
Swift Current, Sask., 15,415 ....F 5
Sydney, N.S., 33,230 ....L 6
Tadoussac, Que., 1,010 ....J 6
Terrace, B.C., 7,820 ....D 5
The Pas, Man., 19,001 ....F 5
Thessalon, Ont., 1,879 ....H 6
Thompson, Man., 6,062 ....G 4
Thunder Bay, Ont., †112,093 ....J 6
Timmins, Ont., 28,542 ....H 6
Tisdale, Sask., 2,798 ....F 5
Toronto (cap.), Ont., †2,628,043..H 7
Trail, B.C., 11,149 ....E 6
Trois-Rivières, Que., 55,869 ....J 6
Truro, N.S., 13,047 ....K 6
Tuktoyaktuk, N.W.T., 596 ....C 2
Uranium City, Sask., 1,867 ....F 4
Val-d'Or, Que., 17,421 ....J 6
Vancouver, B.C., †1,082,352....D 6
Vancouver (isl.), B.C., 381,297...D 6
Vanderhoof, B.C., 1,653 ....D 5
Vegreville, Alta., 3,691 ....E 5
Vernon, B.C., 13,283 ....E 5
Victoria (cap.), B.C., †195,800...D 6
Victoria (isl.), N.W.T. ....E 1
Waterton-Glacier Int'l Peace Park, Alta., 259 ....E 6
Wetaskiwin, Alta., 6,267 ....E 5
Weyburn, Sask., 8,815 ....F 6
Whitehorse (cap.), Yukon, 11,217 ....C 3
Williams Lake, B.C., 4,072 ....D 5
Williston (lake), B.C. ....D 4
Windsor, N.S., 3,775 ....K 7
Windsor, Ont., †258,643 ....H 7
Winnipeg (cap.), Man., †540,262 ....G 6
Winnipeg (lake), Man. ....G 5
Winnipegosis (lake), Man. ....F 5
Wood Buffalo Nat'l Park, 186....E 4
Woods (lake) ....G 6
Woodstock, N.B., 4,846 ....K 6
Wynyard, Sask., 1,932 ....F 5
Yarmouth, N.S., 8,516 ....K 7
Yellowknife (cap.), N.W.T., 6,122 ....E 3
Yoho Nat'l Park, B.C. ....E 5
Yorkton, Sask., 13,430 ....F 5
Yukon Territory, 18,388 ....C 3

†Population of metropolitan area.

(continued)

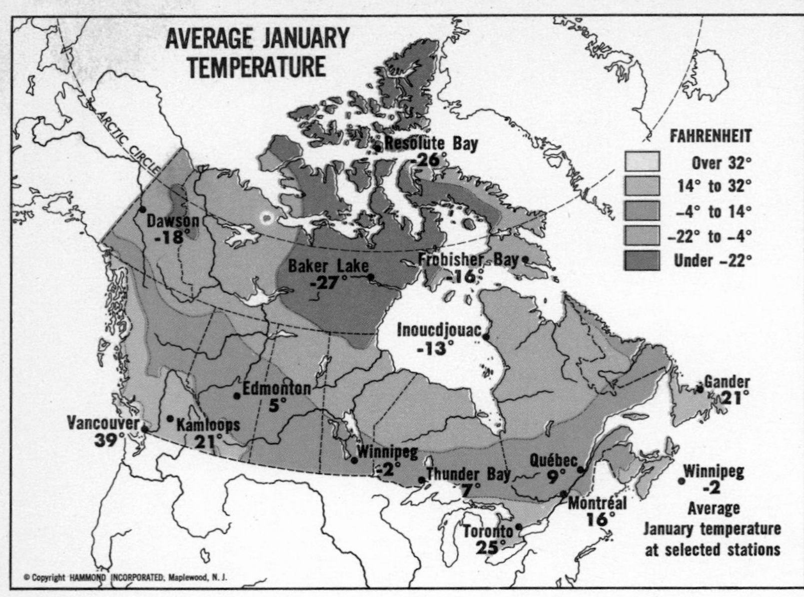

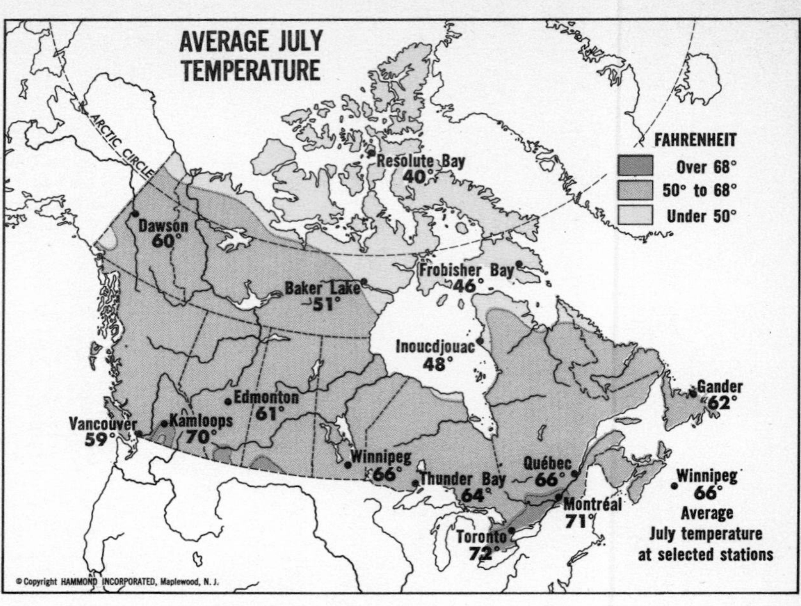

Agriculture, Industry and Resources

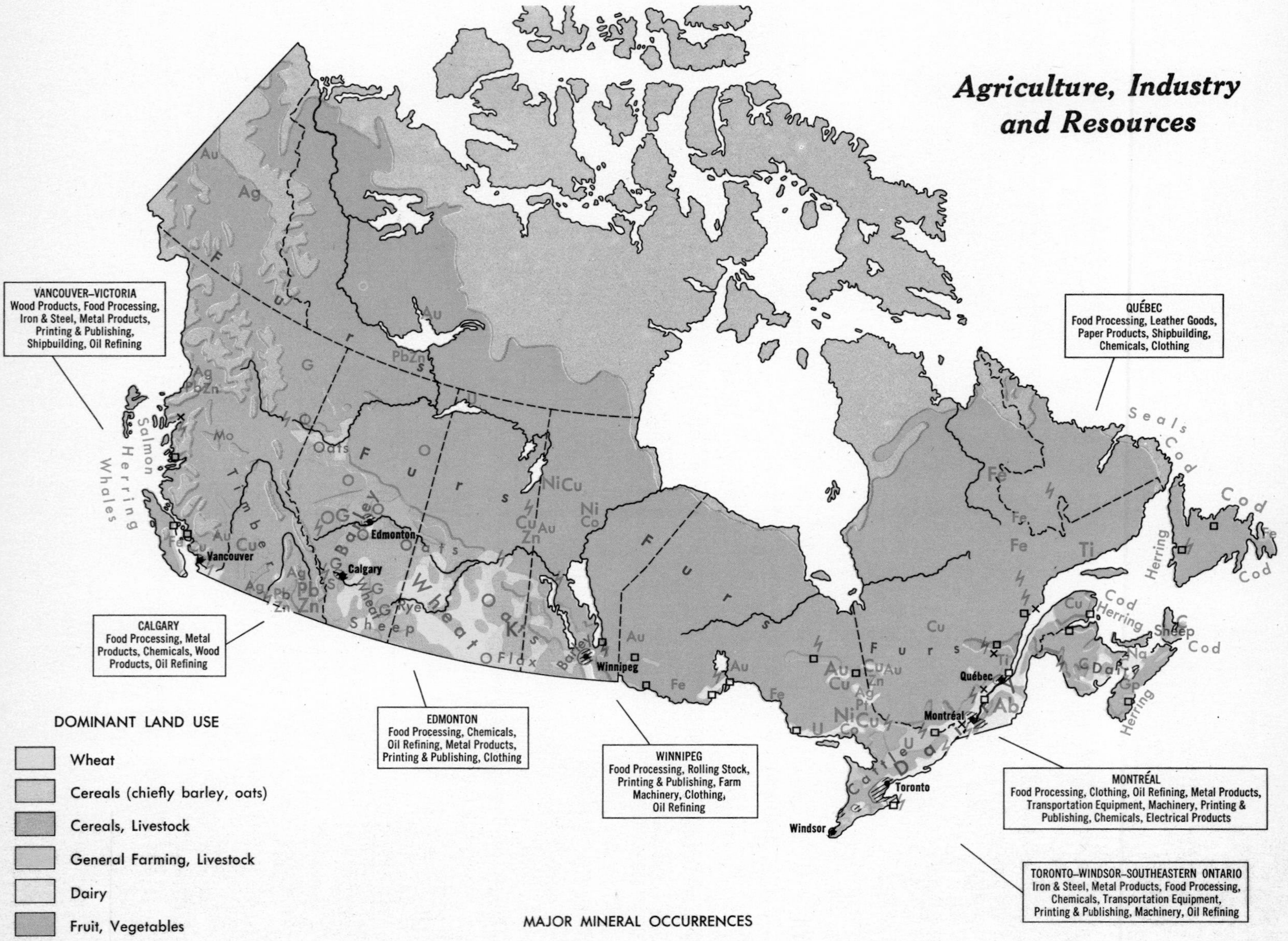

VANCOUVER–VICTORIA
Wood Products, Food Processing, Iron & Steel, Metal Products, Printing & Publishing, Shipbuilding, Oil Refining

CALGARY
Food Processing, Metal Products, Chemicals, Wood Products, Oil Refining

EDMONTON
Food Processing, Chemicals, Oil Refining, Metal Products, Printing & Publishing, Clothing

WINNIPEG
Food Processing, Rolling Stock, Printing & Publishing, Farm Machinery, Clothing, Oil Refining

QUÉBEC
Food Processing, Leather Goods, Paper Products, Shipbuilding, Chemicals, Clothing

MONTRÉAL
Food Processing, Clothing, Oil Refining, Metal Products, Transportation Equipment, Machinery, Printing & Publishing, Chemicals, Electrical Products

TORONTO–WINDSOR–SOUTHEASTERN ONTARIO
Iron & Steel, Metal Products, Food Processing, Chemicals, Transportation Equipment, Printing & Publishing, Machinery, Oil Refining

Salmon Herring Whales · Furs · Timber · Oats · Barley · Wheat · Sheep · Rye · Flax · Cattle · Seals · Cod · Herring · Vancouver · Edmonton · Calgary · Winnipeg · Québec · Montréal · Toronto · Windsor

DOMINANT LAND USE

- Wheat
- Cereals (chiefly barley, oats)
- Cereals, Livestock
- General Farming, Livestock
- Dairy
- Fruit, Vegetables
- Pasture Livestock
- Range Livestock
- Forests
- Nonagricultural Land

MAJOR MINERAL OCCURRENCES

Ab	Asbestos	Cu	Copper	Mo	Molybdenum	Pt	Platinum
Ag	Silver	Fe	Iron Ore	Na	Salt	S	Sulfur
Au	Gold	G	Natural Gas	Ni	Nickel	Ti	Titanium
C	Coal	Gp	Gypsum	O	Petroleum	U	Uranium
Co	Cobalt	K	Potash	Pb	Lead	Zn	Zinc

- Water Power
- Major Industrial Areas
- Major Pulp & Paper Mills
- Aluminum Smelters

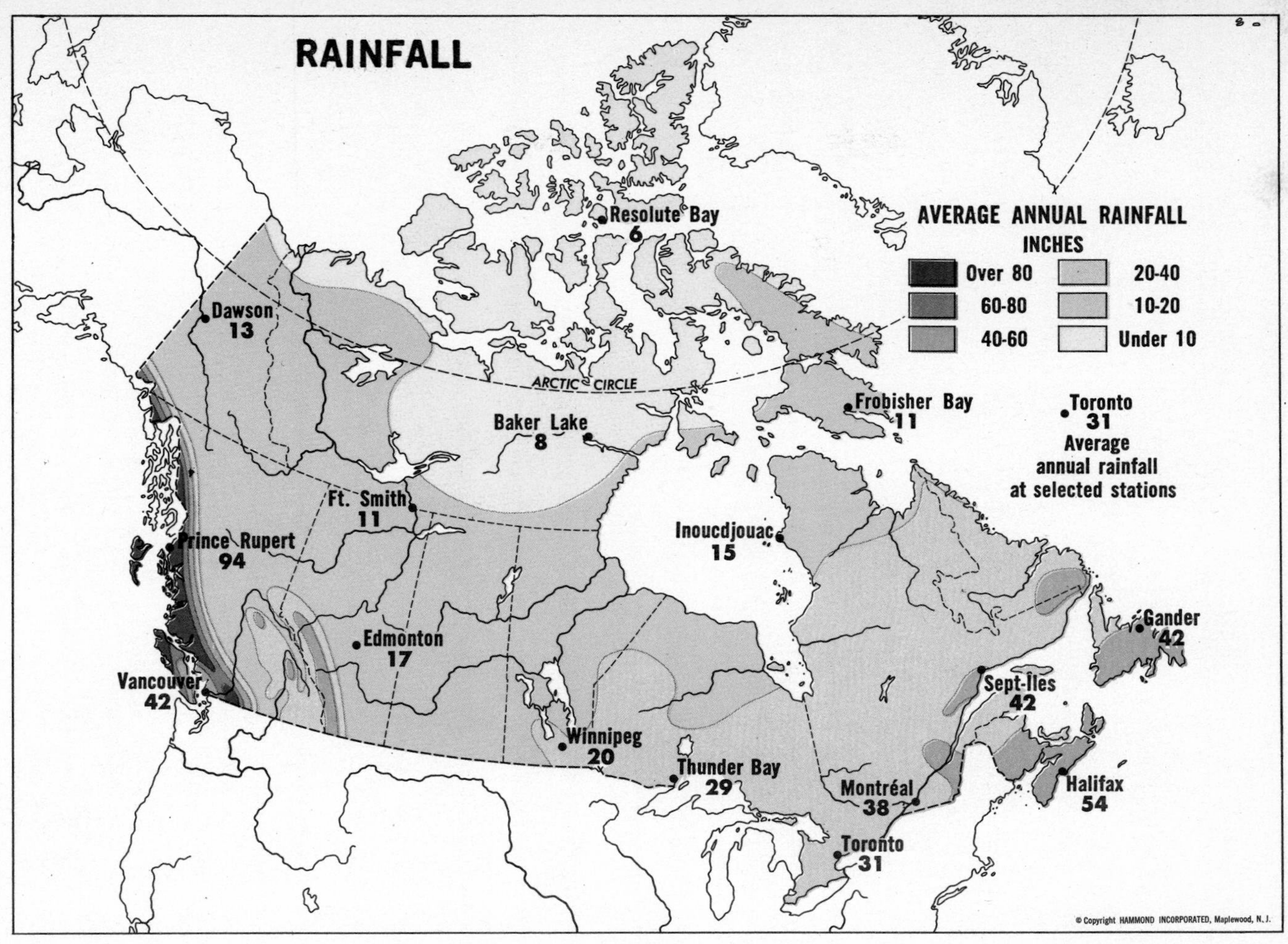

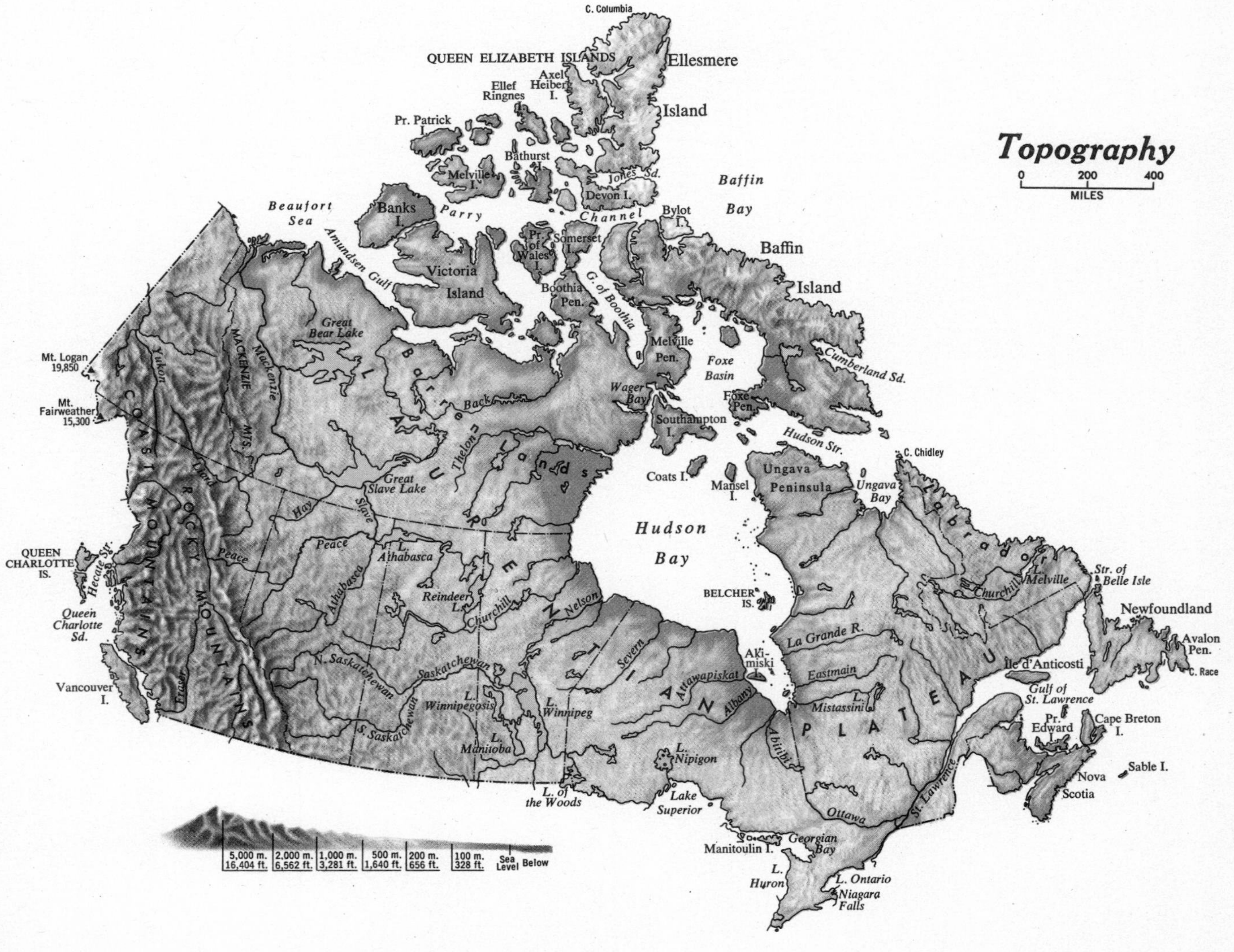

Topography

0 200 400
MILES

C. Columbia
QUEEN ELIZABETH ISLANDS
Ellesmere Island
Axel Heiberg I.
Ellef Ringnes I.
Pr. Patrick I.
Bathurst I.
Melville I.
Jones Sd.
Devon I.
Baffin Bay
Beaufort Sea
Banks I.
Parry Channel
Bylot I.
Amundsen Gulf
Pr. of Wales I.
Somerset I.
Victoria Island
Baffin Island
Boothia Pen.
G. of Boothia
Great Bear Lake
Mt. Logan 19,850
Mt. Fairweather 15,300
Yukon
MACKENZIE MTS.
Mackenzie
Barren Lands
LAURENTIAN PLATEAU
Back
Melville Pen.
Foxe Basin
Cumberland Sd.
Wager Bay
Foxe Pen.
Southampton I.
Thelon
Hudson Str.
C. Chidley
COAST MOUNTAINS
ROCKY MOUNTAINS
Dease
Great Slave Lake
Coats I.
Mansel I.
Ungava Peninsula
Ungava Bay
Labrador
Hay
Slave
Hudson Bay
QUEEN CHARLOTTE IS.
Hecate Str.
Peace
L. Athabasca
Athabasca
Reindeer L.
Churchill
Nelson
BELCHER IS.
Churchill
Melville
Str. of Belle Isle
Newfoundland
Queen Charlotte Sd.
La Grande R.
Avalon Pen.
Vancouver I.
N. Saskatchewan
Saskatchewan
Severn
Attawapiskat
Akimiski I.
Eastmain
Ile d'Anticosti
C. Race
L. Winnipegosis
L. Winnipeg
Albany
L. Mistassini
Gulf of St. Lawrence
Fraser
S. Saskatchewan
L. Manitoba
L. Nipigon
Abitibi
Pr. Edward I.
Cape Breton I.
Sable I.
Nova Scotia
L. of the Woods
Lake Superior
Ottawa
St. Lawrence
Manitoulin I.
Georgian Bay
L. Huron
L. Ontario
Niagara Falls

5,000 m. 16,404 ft. | 2,000 m. 6,562 ft. | 1,000 m. 3,281 ft. | 500 m. 1,640 ft. | 200 m. 656 ft. | 100 m. 328 ft. | Sea Level | Below

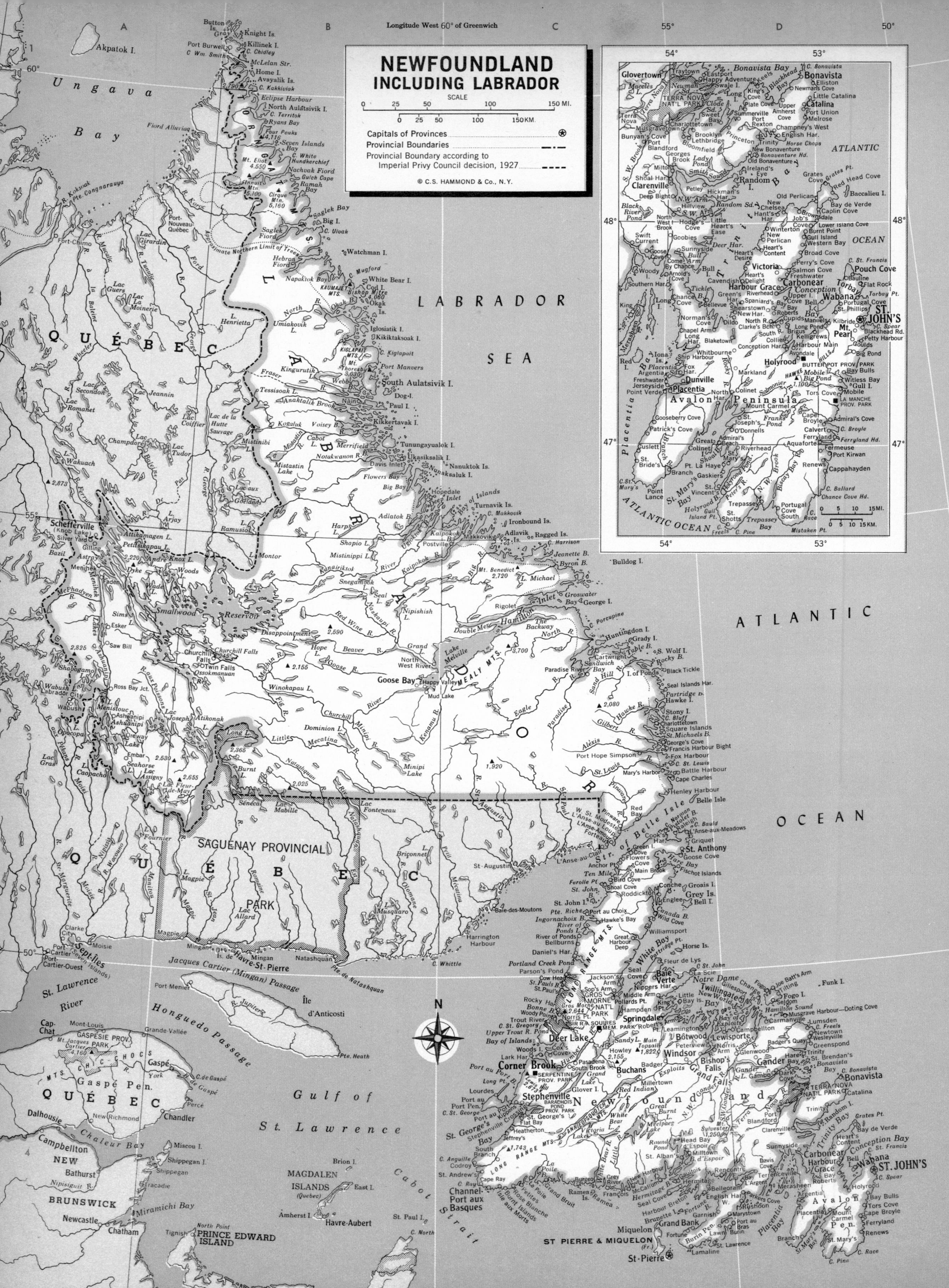
NEWFOUNDLAND
INCLUDING LABRADOR
SCALE
0 25 50 100 150 MI.
0 25 50 100 150 KM.
Capitals of Provinces
Provincial Boundaries
Provincial Boundary according to Imperial Privy Council decision, 1927
© C.S. HAMMOND & Co., N.Y.
Longitude West 60° of Greenwich
Ungava Bay
LABRADOR SEA
ATLANTIC OCEAN
QUÉBEC
SAGUENAY PROVINCIAL PARK
Gulf of St. Lawrence
Cabot Strait
Jacques Cartier (Mingan) Passage
Honguedo Passage
St. Lawrence River
Île d'Anticosti
MAGDALEN ISLANDS (Quebec)
PRINCE EDWARD ISLAND
NEW BRUNSWICK
ST PIERRE & MIQUELON
Gaspé Pen.
Akpatok I.
Button Is.
Killinek I.
Port Burwell
Fort-Chimo
Saglek Bay
Hebron Fiord
Nain
Hopedale
Makkovik
Postville
Rigolet
Cartwright
Goose Bay
Happy Valley
North West River
Lake Melville
MEALY MTS.
Churchill Falls
Twin Falls
Smallwood Reservoir
Schefferville (Knob Lake)
Wabush
Labrador City
Belle Isle
Str. of Belle Isle
St. Anthony
LONG RANGE MTS.
GROS MORNE NAT'L PARK
Deer Lake
Corner Brook
Stephenville
Channel-Port aux Basques
Baie Verte
Springdale
Grand Falls
Windsor
Botwood
Lewisporte
Gander
Buchans
TERRA NOVA NAT'L PARK
Bonavista
Trinity Bay
Conception Bay
Carbonear
Harbour Grace
Wabana
ST. JOHN'S
Avalon Pen.
Placentia Bay
Burin Pen.
Grand Bank
Fortune
St-Pierre
Miquelon
Sept-Îles
Havre-St-Pierre
Natashquan
Harrington Harbour
Gaspé
Campbellton
Bathurst
Newcastle
Chatham
Dalhousie
Chandler
Percé
Havre-Aubert
Glovertown
Clarenville
Holyrood
Placentia
Dunville
Avalon Peninsula
Mount Pearl
Trepassey
Cappahayden
Renews
Ferryland
Pouch Cove
Torbay
Bay Bulls
Whitbourne
Victoria
Catalina
Bonavista Bay
ATLANTIC OCEAN
54°
53°
48°
47°
0 5 10 15 MI.
0 5 10 15 KM.

AREA 156,185 sq. mi.
POPULATION 620,000
CAPITAL St. John's
LARGEST CITY St. John's
HIGHEST POINT Cirque Mtn. 5,160 ft.
SETTLED IN 1610
ADMITTED TO CONFEDERATION 1949
PROVINCIAL FLOWER Pitcher Plant

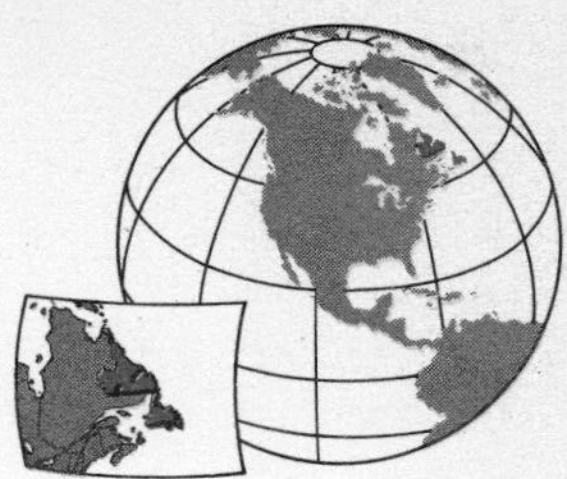

Agriculture, Industry and Resources

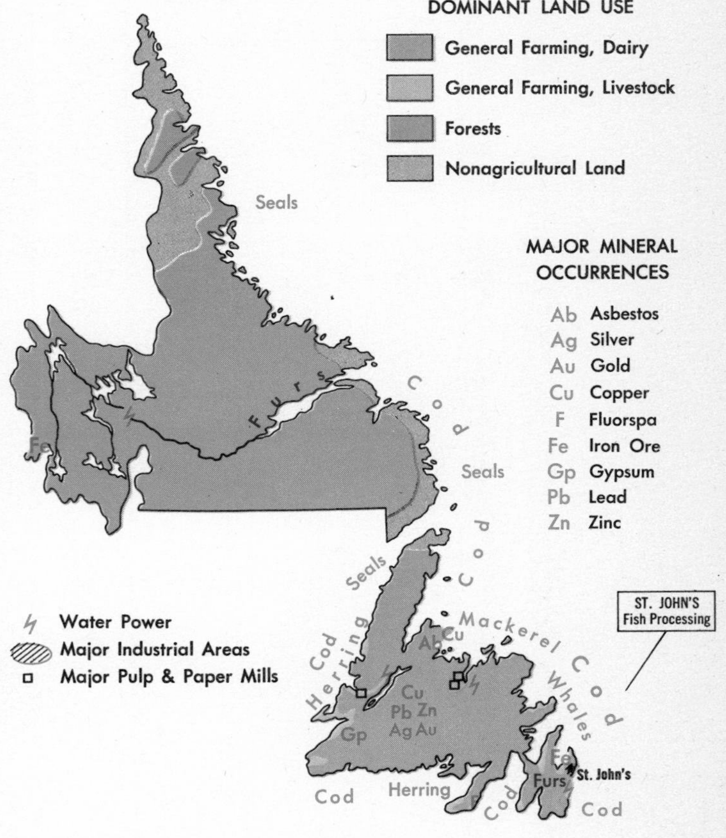

CITIES and TOWNS

ɔmiral's Beach, 402 ....D 2
ɔmiral's Cove, 121............D 2
ıchor Point, 275...............C 3
ɥuaforte, 186....................D 2
rgentia, 13........................C 2
rnold's Cove, 919..............C 2
vondale, 944......................D 2
adger, 1,187......................C 4
adger's Quay, 904.............D 4
aie Verte, 2,397.................C 4
attle Harbour, 75...............C 3
auline, 297........................D 2
ay Bulls, 1,011...................D 2
ay de Verde, 826...............D 2
ay L'Argent, 453................D 4
ay Roberts, 3,702..............D 2
ellburns, 165.....................C 3
elleoram, 530.....................C 4
ellevue, 293.......................D 2
rd Cove, 339......................C 3
shop's Falls, 4,133............C 4
ackhead Road, 1,672.......D 2
ack Tickle, 164..................C 3
aketown, 399.....................D 2
oomfield, 597.....................D 2
ɔnavista, 4,215...................D 2
ɔtwood, 4,115.....................C 4
ranch, 516..........................D 2
rigus, 746...........................D 2
road Cove, 198...................D 2
rooklyn, 167.......................D 2
rownsdale, 189...................D 2
uchans, 1,907.....................C 4
unyan's Cove, 494..............C 2
urgeo, 2,226........................C 4
urin, 2,586...........................C 4
urnt Islands, 799.................C 4
urnt Point, 257....................D 2
alvert, 470............................D 2
ampbellton, 730...................D 4
ape Broyle, 677...................D 2
ape Ray, 302........................C 4
aplin Cove, 164...................D 2
arbonear, 4,732...................D 2
armanville, 839...................D 4
artwright, 752......................C 3
atalina, 1,131.......................D 2
avendish, 286......................D 2
hampney's West, 195........D 2
hance Cove, 446.................D 2
hange Islands, 609............D 4
hannel-Port aux
Basques, 5,942.................C 4
hapel Arm, 659...................D 2
harlottetown, 309...............D 2
hurchill Falls, 2,357...........B 3
arenville, 2,193...................C 2
arke's Beach, 877..............D 2
odroy, 321............................C 4
olinet, 264............................D 2
olliers, 650...........................D 2
ome By Chance, 364..........C 2
onception Harbour, 783....D 2
onche, 505...........................C 3
ook's Harbour, 325.............C 3
orner Brook, 26,309...........C 4
ow Head, 501.......................C 4
ox's Cove, 797.....................C 4
upids, 691............................D 2
uslett, 124............................C 2

Daniel's Harbour, 415.........C 3
Dark Cove, 1,198................D 4
Davis Inlet, 193...................B 2
Deep Bight, 169...................C 2
Deer Lake, 4,421.................C 4
Dildo, 878.............................D 2
Dunville, 1,742....................D 2
Eastport, 438.......................D 1
Elliston, 551.........................D 2
Englee, 1,050.......................C 3
English Harbour West, 393..C 4
Fermeuse, 404.....................D 2
Ferryland, 716.....................D 2
Flat Bay, 357........................C 4
Flat Rock, 680......................D 2
Fleur de Lys, 672.................C 3
Flowers Cove, 372...............C 3
Fogo, 1,155..........................D 4
Forteau, 312.........................C 3
Fortune, 2,164......................C 4
Fox Harbour, 214.................C 3
Fox Harbour, 685.................D 2
François, 220.......................C 4
Freshwater, 1,562................C 2
Freshwater, 222...................D 2
Gambo, 491..........................D 4
Gander, 7,748.......................D 4
Garnish, 618.........................C 4
Gaskiers, 300.......................D 2
Gaultois, 509........................C 4
Georges Brook, 209.............D 2
Gillesport, 314......................D 4
Glenwood, 979......................D 4
Glovertown, 1,915................C 1
Goobies, 137.........................D 2
Goose Bay, 496....................B 3
Gooseberry Cove, 145.........C 2
Goose Cove, 239..................C 2
Goose Cove, 349..................C 3
Goulds, 4,695.......................D 2
Grand Bank, 3,476...............C 4
Grand Falls, 7,677................C 4
Grates Cove, 328..................D 2
Great Harbour Deep, 329....C 3
Green Island Cove, 224.......C 3
Green's Harbour, 710..........D 2
Greenspond, 449..................D 4
Grey River, 204.....................C 4
Griquet, 825..........................C 3
Gull Island, 361....................D 2
Hampden, 739......................C 4
Hant's Harbour, 522.............D 2
Happy Adventure, 364.........D 2
Happy Valley, 4,937.............B 3
Harbour Breton, 2,196.........C 4
Harbour Grace, 2,771..........D 2
Harbour Main, 652...............D 2
Hare Bay, 1,485....................D 4
Hawke's Bay, 462................C 3
Head of Bay d'Espoir, 514...C 4
Heart's Content, 599............D 2
Heart's Delight, 543.............D 2
Heart's Desire, 347..............D 2
Heatherton, 329....................C 4
Hermitage, 520.....................C 4
Hickman's Harbour, 414......D 2
Hillview, 281..........................D 2
Hodge's Cove, 391...............D 2
Holyrood, 1,282.....................D 2
Hopedale, 375.......................B 2
Howley, 409...........................C 4
Isle aux Morts, 1,158............C 4
Jackson's Arm, 491..............C 4

Jeffrey's, 280........................C 4
Jerseyside, 1,061.................B 3
Job's Cove, 182....................D 2
Joe Batt's Arm, 886..............D 4
Keels, 146.............................D 1
Kelligrews, 2,046..................D 2
Kilbride, 2,148.......................D 2
King's Cove, 271...................D 1
King's Point, 651...................C 4
Kippens, 1,383......................C 4
Labrador City, 7,622.............A 3
Lamaline, 553.......................C 4
L'Anse-au-Clair, 233.............C 3
L'Anse-au-Loup, 448.............C 3
La Poile, 173.........................C 4
Lark Harbour, 590.................C 4
La Scie, 1,255.......................C 4
Lawn, 1,000..........................C 4
Lethbridge, 657.....................D 2
Lewisporte, 3,175..................C 4
Little Bay Islands, 394..........C 4
Little Catalina, 722................D 2
Little Heart's Ease, 395........D 2
Long Harbour, 376................D 2
Long Pond, 1,758..................D 2
Lourdes, 903..........................C 4
Lower Island Cove, 406.........D 2
Lumsden, 630.........................D 4
Main Brook, 590.....................C 3
Makkovik, 292........................C 2
Manuels, 1,006.......................D 2
Markland, 311.........................D 2
Mary's Harbour, 134...............C 3
Marystown, 4,960...................D 4
McCallum, 216........................C 4
Melrose, 378...........................D 2
Middle Arm, 474......................C 4
Millertown, 316........................C 4
Milltown, 712............................C 4
Milton, 290...............................C 2
Mount Carmel, 435..................D 2
Mount Pearl, 7,211...................D 2
Musgrave Harbour-Doting
Cove, 1,238...........................D 4
Musgravetown, 586.................C 2
Nain, 708..................................B 2
New Chelsea, 215...................D 2
New Harbour, 704...................D 2
Newmans Cove, 235...............D 2
New Perlican, 308...................D 2
Newtown, 513..........................D 4
Nippers Harbour, 275..............C 4
Norman's Cove, 997................D 2
Norris Arm, 1,191.....................C 4
Norris Point, 986.......................C 4
North Harbour, 146...................D 2
North River, 256........................D 2
North West Brook, 302..............C 2
North West River, 931...............B 3
O'Donnells, 268..........................D 2
Old Perlican, 597........................D 2
Paradise River, 146...................C 3
Parkers Cove, 405......................D 4
Parson's Pond, 491.....................C 3
Pasadena, 964...........................C 4
Patrick's Cove, 170.....................C 2
Perry's Cove, 165........................D 2
Peterview, 953.............................C 4
Petley, 177...................................D 2
Petty Harbour, 940.......................D 2
Pinware, 186................................C 3
Placentia, 2,211............................C 2
Plate Cove, 517.............................D 2

Point La Haye, 320.......................D 2
Point Lance, 133...........................C 2
Point Leamington, 940..................C 4
Point Verde, 309...........................C 2
Pollards Point, 439........................C 4
Port au Bras, 393..........................D 4
Port au Choix, 861.........................C 3
Port au Port, 605............................C 4
Port Blandford, 779........................C 2
Port Hope Simpson, 232................C 3
Port Kirwan, 159.............................D 2
Port Rexton, 384.............................D 2
Portugal Cove, 1,411.......................D 2
Portugal Cove South, 371................D 2
Port Union, 578................................D 2
Pouch Cove, 1,483...........................D 2
Princeton, 180...................................D 2
Raleigh, 292.......................................C 3
Ramea, 1,208.....................................C 4
Red Bay, 296......................................C 3
Red Head Cove, 234.........................D 2
Rencontre East, 235..........................C 4
Renews, 497.......................................D 2
Rigolet, 182...C 3
Riverhead, 329....................................D 2
River of Ponds, 258............................C 3
Robert's Arm, 1,044............................C 4
Rocky Harbour, 982.............................C 4
Roddickton, 1,239................................C 3
Rose Blanche, 703...............................C 4
Rushoon, 506.......................................D 4
Saint Alban's, 1,941.............................C 4
Saint Andrew's, 257.............................C 4
Saint Anthony, 2,593............................C 3
Saint Brendan's, 276............................D 4
Saint Bride's, 598..................................C 2
Saint George's, 2,082...........................C 4
Saint John's (cap.), 88,102..................D 2
Saint John's, ‡131,814.........................D 2
Saint Joseph's, 305..............................D 2
Saint Lawrence, 2,173..........................C 4
Saint Mary's, 375..................................D 2
Saint Paul's, 347...................................C 4
Saint Phillips, 573.................................D 2
Saint Shotts, 226...................................D 2
Saint Vincent's, 593...............................D 2
Salmon Cove, 653..................................D 2
Seal Cove, 698.......................................C 3
Seal Cove, 457.......................................C 4
Seldom, 442..D 4
Ship Harbour, 255..................................D 2
Shoal Cove, 236......................................C 3
Shoal Harbour, 715.................................C 2
Sop's Arm, 382..C 4
South Branch, 339...................................C 4
South Brook, 802.....................................C 4
Southern Harbour, 679............................C 2
South River, 554.......................................D 2
Spaniard's Bay, 1,764..............................D 2
Springdale, 3,224.....................................C 4
Stephenville, 7,770...................................C 4
Stephenville Crossing,
2,129..C 4
Summerville, 374.......................................D 2
Sunnyside, 716..D 2
Sweet Bay, 192..D 2
Swift Current, 426.....................................C 2
Terrenceville, 700......................................D 4
Tilting, 406..D 4
Torbay, 2,090..D 2
Tors Cove, 325..D 2
Traytown, 344..D 1
Trepassey, 1,443...D 2
Trinity, 577..D 2
Trinity, 288..D 4
Trout River, 689..C 4
Twillingate, 1,437..C 4
Upper Island Cove, 1,819.............................D 2
Victoria, 1,601...D 2
Wabana, 5,421..D 2
Wabush, 3,387...A 3
Wesleyville, 1,142...D 4
Western Bay, 430...D 2
West Saint Modeste, 294.................................C 3
Whitbourne, 1,235..D 2
Wild Cove, 172..C 3
Windsor, 6,644..C 4
Winterton, 794...D 2
Witless Bay, 754..D 2
Woody Point, 300..C 4

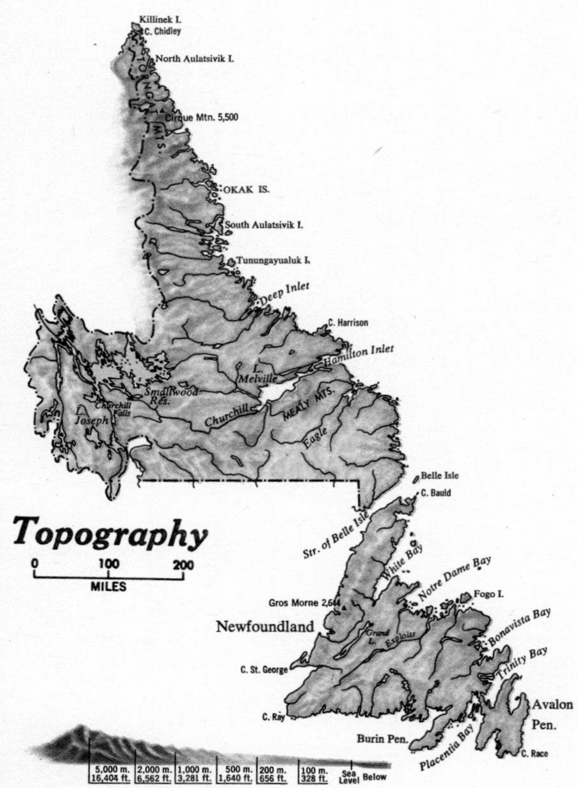

OTHER FEATURES

Alexis (riv.)..........................C 3
Anguille (cape).....................C 4
Annieopscotch (mts.)............C 4
Ashuanipi (lake)....................A 3
Ashuanipi (riv.).....................A 3
Atikonak (lake)......................B 3
Attikamagen (lake)................A 3
Avalon (pen.).........................D 2
Barachois Pond Prov.
Park...................................C 4
Bauld (cape)..........................C 3
Bell (isl.)................................C 3
Bell (isl.), 6,079.....................D 2
Belle Isle (isl.), 25.................C 3
Belle Isle (str.).......................C 3
Blackhead (bay).....................D 2
Bonavista (bay)......................D 1
Bonavista (cape)....................D 1
Bonne (bay)............................C 4
Broyle (cape)..........................D 2
Bull Arm (inlet).......................D 2
Burin (pen.).............................C 4
Butter Pot Prov. Park.............D 2
Cabot (str.)..............................B 4
Canada (bay)...........................C 3
Chidley (cape).........................B 1
Churchill (falls)........................B 3
Churchill (riv.)..........................B 3
Cirque (mt.)..............................B 2
Clode (sound)..........................D 2
Conception (bay).....................D 2
Deep (inlet)...............................B 2

Double Mer (lake)....................C 3
Dyke (lake)...............................A 3
Eagle (riv.)................................C 3
Espoir (bay)..............................C 4
Exploits (bay)............................C 4
Exploits (riv.).............................C 4
Fogo (isl.), 4,094.......................D 4
Fortune (bay).............................C 4
Freels (cape)..............................D 3
Gander (lake)..............................D 4
Gander (riv.)................................D 4
Glover (isl.)..................................C 4
Goose (riv.)..................................B 3
Grand (lake).................................B 3
Grand (lake).................................C 4
Grates (pt.)..................................D 2
Great Colinet (isl.).......................D 2
Grey (isls.)....................................C 3
Groais (isl.)...................................C 3
Gros Morne (mt.)..........................C 4
Gros Morne Nat'l Park.................C 4
Groswater (bay)............................C 3
Hamilton (inlet)..............................C 3
Hamilton (sound)...........................D 4
Hare (bay)......................................C 3
Hawke (hills)..................................D 2
Hebron (fjord)................................B 2
Hermitage (bay).............................C 4
Holyrood (bay)...............................D 2
Horse (isls.)....................................C 3
Horse Chops (head).......................D 2
Humber (riv.)...................................C 4
Ingornachoix (bay).........................C 3
Innuit (mt.).......................................B 2
Ireland's Eye (isl.)...........................D 2
Islands (bay)....................................C 4
Kaipokok (bay)..................................B 2
Kanairiktok (riv.)..............................B 3
Kaumajet (mts.)...............................B 2
Kingurutuk (lake)..............................B 2
Labrador (reg.), 28,166....................B 2
Labrador (sea)..................................C 2
La Manche Prov. Park......................D 2
La Poile (bay)....................................C 4
Little Mecatina (riv.)..........................B 3
Long (isl.)...C 2
Long (lake)...A 3
Long (pt.)...C 4
Long Range (mts.).............................C 4
Main Topsail (mt.)...............................C 4

Makkovik (cape)..................................C 2
McLelan (str.)......................................B 1
Mealy (mts.)..C 3
Meelpaeg (lake)...................................C 4
Melville (lake)......................................C 3
Menihek (lakes)...................................A 3
Merasheen (isl.)...................................C 2
Mistaken (pt.).......................................D 2
Mistastin (lake).....................................B 2
Nachvak (fjord).....................................B 2
Naskaupi (riv.).......................................B 3
Newfoundland (isl.),
493,938...C 4
Newman (sound)......................................D 2
New World (isl.), 4,563...........................C 4
Norman (cape)...C 3
North Aulatsivik (isl.)................................B 2
Notre Dame (bay).......................................C 4
Okak (bay)...B 2
Ossokmanuan (res.)....................................B 3
Petitsikapau (lake).......................................A 3
Pine (cape)...D 2
Pinware (riv.)..C 3
Pistolet (bay)..C 3
Placentia (bay)..C 2
Ponds (isl.), 164...C 3
Port au Port (bay)...C 4
Port au Port (pen.)..C 4
Port Manvers (harb.).......................................B 2
Race (cape)...D 2
Ramah (bay)...B 2
Ramea (isls.), 1,208...C 4
Random (isl.), 1,353..D 2
Random (sound)..D 2
Ray (cape)..C 4
Red (isl.)...C 2
Red Indian (lake)...C 4
Red Wine (riv.)..B 3
Rocky (riv.)...D 2
Round (pond)...C 4
Saglek (bay)...B 2
Saint Francis (cape)...D 2
Saint George (cape)...C 4
Saint George's (bay)...C 4
Saint John (bay)...C 3
Saint John (cape)...C 3
Saint Lawrence (gulf)..B 4
Saint Lewis (cape)...C 3
Saint Mary's (bay)..C 2
Saint Mary's (cape)...C 2

Saint Michaels (bay)..C 3
Salmonier (riv.)..D 2
Sandwich (bay)..C 3
Serpentine Prov. Park...C 4
Shabogamo (lake)..A 3
Shoal (bay)...D 2
Sir R.A. Squires Mem.
Park..C 4
Smallwood (res.)...B 3
Smith (sound)..D 2
South Aulatsivik (isl.)..B 2
Spear (cape)...D 2
Swale (isl.)..D 1
Sylvester (mt.)..C 4
Terra Nova (riv.)...C 2
Terra Nova Nat'l Park..D 2
Territok (cape)...B 2
Thoresby (mt.)...B 2
Tickle (bay)..D 2
Torbay (pt.)..D 2
Torngat (mts.)..B 2
Trespassey (bay)...D 2
Trinity (bay)..D 2
Tunungayualok (isl.)..B 2
Ukasiksalik (isl.), 193...B 2
Victoria (lake)..C 4
Wabush (lake)...A 3
White (bay)...C 3
White Bear (lake)..C 4
White Handkerchief
(cape)..B 2

SAINT PIERRE & MIQUELON

CITIES and TOWNS

Saint-Pierre (cap.), 4,565....C

OTHER FEATURES

Miquelon (isl.), 621.............C 4
Saint Pierre (isl.), 4,565.......C 4

‡ Population of metropolitan area.

NOVA SCOTIA

COUNTIES

Annapolis, 21,841 .... C 4
Antigonish, 16,814 .... F 3
Cape Breton, 129,075 .... H 3
Colchester, 37,735 .... E 3
Cumberland, 35,160 .... D 3
Digby, 20,349 .... C 4
Guysborough, 12,864 .... F 3
Halifax, 261,461 .... E 4
Hants, 28,935 .... D 4
Inverness, 20,375 .... G 2
Kings, 44,975 .... D 4
Lunenburg, 38,422 .... D 4
Pictou, 46,104 .... F 3
Queens, 12,950 .... C 4
Richmond, 12,734 .... H 3
Shelburne, 16,661 .... C 5
Victoria, 7,823 .... H 2
Yarmouth, 24,682 .... C 5

CITIES and TOWNS

Abercrombie, 532 .... F 3
Alder Point, 844 .... H 2
Aldershot, 1,729 .... D 3
Amherst⊙, 9,966 .... D 3
Annapolis Royal⊙, 758 .... C 4
Antigonish⊙, 5,489 .... F 3
Arcadia, 425 .... B 5
Arichat⊙, 829 .... H 3
Auburn, 519 .... D 3
Aylesford, 680 .... D 3
Baddeck⊙, 831 .... H 2
Barrington Passage, 551 .... C 5
Bear River, 733 .... C 4
Beaverbank, 958 .... E 4
Belliveau Cove, 486 .... B 4
Belmont, 663 .... E 3
Berwick, 1,412 .... D 4
Bible Hill, 3,505 .... E 3
Block House, 418 .... D 4
Blue Rock, 394 .... D 4
Bras d'Or, 655 .... H 2
Bridgetown, 1,039 .... C 4
Bridgewater, 5,231 .... D 4
Brookfield, 658 .... E 3
Brooklyn, 1,253 .... D 4
Caledonia, 459 .... C 4
Cambridge Station, 699 .... D 3
Canning, 809 .... D 3
Canso, 1,209 .... H 3
Cape North, 118 .... H 2
Centreville, 552 .... D 3
Chester, 1,031 .... D 4
Chester Basin, 588 .... D 4
Chéticamp, 1,016 .... G 2
Church Point, 258 .... B 4
Clark's Harbour, 1,082 .... C 5
Clementsport, 479 .... C 4
Comeauville, 365 .... B 4
Concession, 404 .... B 4
Conquerall Bank, 480 .... D 4
Conway, 363 .... C 4
Dartmouth, 64,770 .... E 4
Debert, 703 .... E 3
Deep Brook, 494 .... C 4
Digby⊙, 2,363 .... C 4
Dominion, 2,879 .... J 2
Donkin, 910 .... J 2
East Chester, 485 .... D 4
East Chezzetcook, 617 .... E 4
Ellershouse, 424 .... D 4
Elmsdale, 758 .... E 4
Enfield, 1,056 .... E 4
Fall River, 969 .... E 4
Falmouth, 759 .... D 3
Florence, 1,958 .... H 2
Freeport, 475 .... B 4
Glace Bay, 22,440 .... J 2
Gold River, 448 .... D 4
Granville Ferry, 445 .... C 4
Great Village, 494 .... E 3
Grosses Coques, 360 .... B 4
Guysborough⊙, 494 .... G 3
Halifax (cap.)⊙, 122,035 .... E 4
Halifax, ‡222,637 .... E 4
Hantsport, 1,447 .... D 3
Havre Boucher, 385 .... G 3
Head of Jeddore, 445 .... E 4
Head of Saint Margarets Bay, 644 .... E 4
Heatherton, 368 .... G 3
Hebron, 463 .... B 5
Herring Cove, 1,487 .... E 4
Hilden, 803 .... E 3
Hopewell, 439 .... F 3
Hubbards, 427 .... D 4
Ingonish, 338 .... H 2
Ingonish Beach, 640 .... H 2
Inverness, 1,846 .... G 2
Joggins, 777 .... D 3
Judique, 409 .... G 3
Kentville⊙, 5,198 .... D 3
Kingston, 1,429 .... D 4
Lakeside, 1,687 .... E 4
Lantz, 661 .... E 4
L'Ardoise West, 432 .... H 3
Lawrencetown, 512 .... C 4
Lequille, 526 .... C 4
Little Dover, 585 .... G 3
Liverpool⊙, 3,654 .... D 4
Lockeport, 1,208 .... C 5
Louisbourg, 1,582 .... J 3
Louisdale, 1,036 .... G 3
Lower Wedgeport, 561 .... C 5
Lower West Pubnico, 743 .... C 5
Lower Woods Harbour, 589 .... C 5
Lunenburg⊙, 3,215 .... D 4
Lyons Brook, 441 .... F 3
Mabou, 421 .... G 2
Maccan, 492 .... D 3
Mahone Bay, 1,333 .... D 4
Main-à-Dieu, 394 .... J 2
Meaghers Grant, 388 .... E 4
Melvern Square, 427 .... C 3
Meteghan, 909 .... B 4
Meteghan Centre, 368 .... B 4
Meteghan River, 414 .... B 4
Middle Musquodoboit, 638 .... E 3
Middleton, 1,870 .... C 4
Middlewood, 395 .... D 4
Milford Station, 650 .... E 3
Milton, 1,854 .... D 4
Mira Road, 1,503 .... H 2
Monastery, 418 .... G 3
Mount Uniacke, 813 .... E 4
Mulgrave, 1,196 .... G 3
Musquodoboit Harbour, 768 .... E 4
New Germany, 584 .... D 4
New Glasgow, 10,849 .... F 3
New Minas, 1,503 .... D 3
Newport, 471 .... E 3
New Road, 1,333 .... E 4
New Victoria, 1,377 .... H 2
New Waterford, 9,579 .... J 2
Nictaux, 578 .... D 4
North Sydney, 8,604 .... H 2
Oxford, 1,473 .... E 3
Parkers Cove, 395 .... C 4
Parrsboro, 1,807 .... D 3
Petit-de-Grat, 1,032 .... H 3

NOVA SCOTIA AND PRINCE EDWARD ISLAND

SCALE
0 10 20 30 40 50 MI.
0 10 20 30 40 50 KM.

Provincial Capitals .... ⊛
County Seats .... ⊙
Provincial Boundaries —·—
County Boundaries ----

Petit-Étang, 438 G 2
Pictou⊙, 4,250 F 3
Pictou Landing, 435 F 3
Pomquet, 387 G 3
Porters Lake, 840 E 4
Port Hastings, 565 G 3
Port Hawkesbury, 3,372 G 3
Port Hood⊙, 523 G 2
Port Maitland, 419 B 5
Port Morien, 470 H 3
Port Williams, 638 D 3
Pugwash, 644 E 3
Reserve Mines, 2,529 H 2
River Bourgeois, 445 H 3
River Hébert, 862 D 3
River John, 468 E 3
Riverport, 371 D 4
Sackville, 5,701 E 4
Saint Croix, 375 E 4
Saint Peters, 663 H 3
Sambro, 556 E 4
Saulnierville, 481 B 4
Sheet Harbour, 1,062 F 4
Shelburne⊙, 2,689 C 5
Shubenacadie, 633 E 3
Somerset, 371 D 3
Springhill, 5,262 E 3
Stellarton, 5,357 F 3
Stewiacke, 1,040 E 3
Sydney⊙, 33,230 H 2
Sydney Mines, 8,991 H 2
Sydney River, 2,009 H 2
Tatamagouche, 568 E 3
Terence Bay, 1,134 E 4
Thorburn, 1,019 F 3
Three Mile Plains, 1,163 D 4
Timberlea, 1,770 E 4
Trenton, 3,331 F 3
Troy, 441 G 3
Truro⊙, 13,047 E 3
Tusket, 423 C 5
Upper Musquodoboit, 362 F 3
Waterville, 552 D 3
Waverley, 1,419 E 4
Wedgeport, 840 C 5
Wellington, 411 E 4
West Arichat, 549 G 3
West Dover, 362 E 4
Western Shore, 774 D 4
Westmount, 1,790 H 2
Westport, 380 B 4
Westville, 3,898 F 3
Weymouth, 604 C 4
Whites Lake, 432 E 4
Wilmot Station, 597 D 4
Windsor⊙, 3,775 D 3
Wolfville, 2,861 D 3
Yarmouth⊙, 8,516 B 5

OTHER FEATURES

Ainslie (lake) G 2
Annapolis (basin) C 4
Annapolis (riv.) C 4
Aspy (bay) H 2
Avon (riv.) D 4
Barachois (pt.) G 4
Bedford (basin) E 4
Boularderie (isl.), 1,902 H 2
Bras d'Or (lake) H 3
Breton (cape) J 3
Brier (isl.), 380 B 4
Canso (cape) H 3
Canso (str.) G 3
Cape Breton (isl.), 162,989 J 2
Cape Breton Highlands Nat'l Park H 2
Cape Sable (isl.), 3,151 C 5
Caribou (isl.), 35 F 3
Carleton (riv.) C 4
Chebogue (harb.) B 5
Chedabucto (bay) G 3
Chéticamp (isl.), 63 G 2
Chignecto (bay) D 3
Chignecto (isth.) D 3
Cobequid (bay) E 3
Country (harb.) G 3
Craignish (hills) G 3
Cumberland (basin) D 3
Digby Gut (chan.) C 4
Digby Neck (pen.) B 4
Egmont (cape) H 2
Fourchu (cape) B 5
Fundy (bay) C 3
Gabarus (bay) H 3
Gaspereau (lake) D 4
George (cape) G 3
Georges (bay) G 3
Gold (riv.) D 4
Great Bras d'Or (chan.) H 2
Greville (bay) D 3
Guysborough (riv.) G 3
Halifax (harb.) E 4
Hébert (riv.) D 3
Ingonish North (bay) H 2
Janvrin (isl.), 162 G 3
Jeddore (harb.) F 4
John (cape) E 3
Joli (pt.) D 5
Jordan (riv.) C 5
Kejimkujik Nat'l Park C 4
Kennetcook (riv.) E 3
La Have (isl.), 7 D 4
La Have (riv.) D 4
Liscomb (isl.), 12 G 4
Lomond, Loch (lake) H 3
Long (isl.), 846 B 4
Louisbourg Nat'l Hist. Park J 3
Mabou Highlands (hills) G 2
Madame (isl.), 3,767 H 3
Mahone (bay) D 4
Malagash (pt.) E 3
McNutt (isl.), 20 C 5
Medway (riv.) C 4
Merigomish (harb.) F 3
Mersey (riv.) C 4
Minas (basin) D 3
Minas (chan.) D 3
Mira (bay) J 2
Musquodoboit (riv.) E 4
Necum Teuch (harb.) F 4
Negro (cape) C 5
North (cape) H 1
North (mt.) D 3
North Bay Ingonish (bay) H 2
North East Margaree (riv.) H 2
Northumberland (str.) E 2
Nuttby (mt.) E 3
Ohio (riv.) D 4
Panuke (lake) D 4
Pennant (pt.) E 4
Percé (cape) J 2
Petit-de-Grat (isl.), 1,032 H 3
Petpeswick (head) E 4
Pictou (harb.) F 3
Pictou (isl.), 69 F 3
Ponhook (lake) D 4
Port Hood (isl.), 39 G 2
Port Joli (harb.) D 5
Prim (pt.) C 4
Roseway (riv.) C 4
Rossignol (lake) C 4
Sable (cape) C 5
Sable (isl.), 12 J 5
Saint Andrews (chan.) H 2
Saint Ann's (bay) H 2
Saint Lawrence (bay) H 1
Saint Lawrence (cape) H 1
Saint Margarets (bay) E 4
Saint Mary's (bay) B 4
Saint Mary's (riv.) F 3
Saint Paul (isl.), 10 H 1
Saint Peters (bay) H 3
Salmon (riv.) E 3
Scatarie (isl.), 8 J 2
Scots (bay) D 3
Seal (isl.), 10 B 5
Sheet (harb.) F 4
Sherbrooke (lake) D 4
Shubenacadie (lake) E 4
Shubenacadie (riv.) E 3
Sissiboo (riv.) C 4
Sober (isl.), 113 F 4
Split (cape) D 3
Stewiacke (riv.) E 3
Sydney (harb.) H 2
Tor (bay) G 3
Tusket (riv.) C 4
Verte (bay) D 2
West (riv.) F 3
West Liscomb (riv.) F 3
Whitehaven (bay) G 3
Yarmouth (sound) B 5

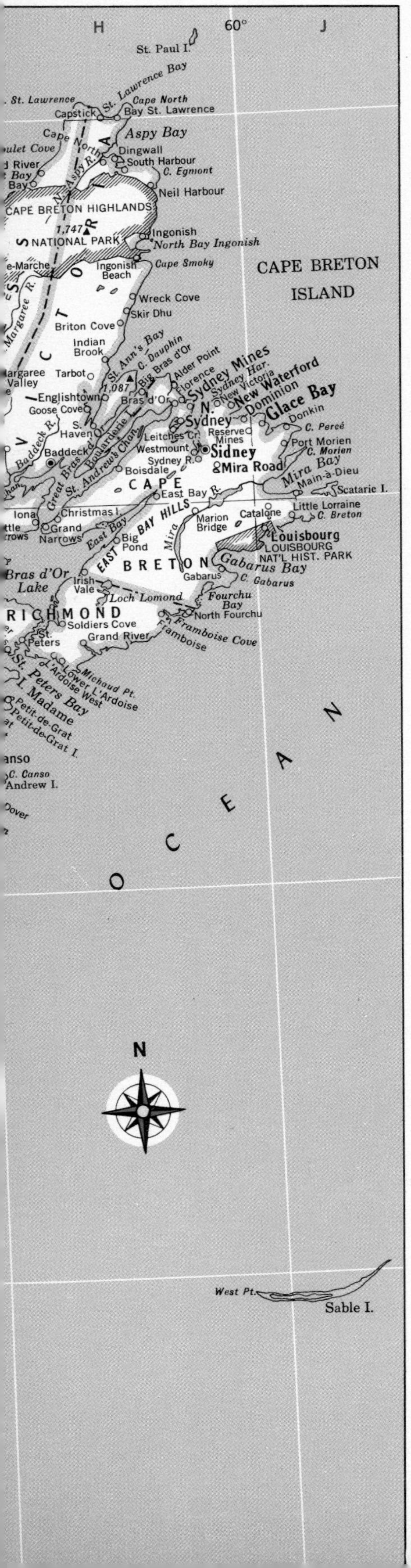

PRINCE EDWARD ISLAND

AREA 2,184 sq. mi.
POPULATION 110,000
CAPITAL Charlottetown
LARGEST CITY Charlottetown
HIGHEST POINT 465 ft.
SETTLED IN 1720
ADMITTED TO CONFEDERATION 1873
PROVINCIAL FLOWER Lady's Slipper

NOVA SCOTIA

AREA 21,425 sq. mi.
POPULATION 767,000
CAPITAL Halifax
LARGEST CITY Halifax
HIGHEST POINT Cape Breton Highlands 1,747 ft.
SETTLED IN 1605
ADMITTED TO CONFEDERATION 1867
PROVINCIAL FLOWER Trailing Arbutus or Mayflower

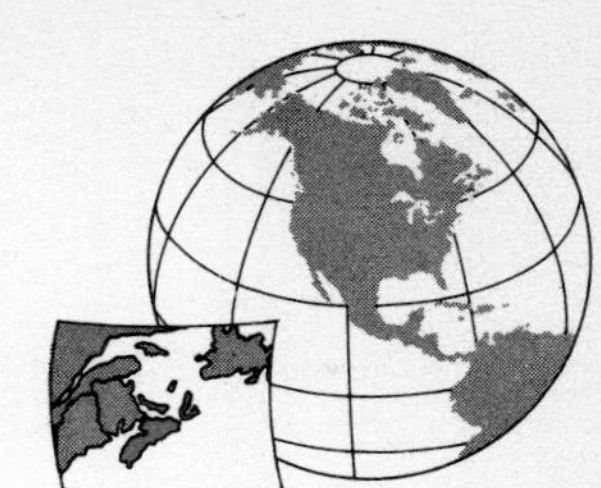

Topography

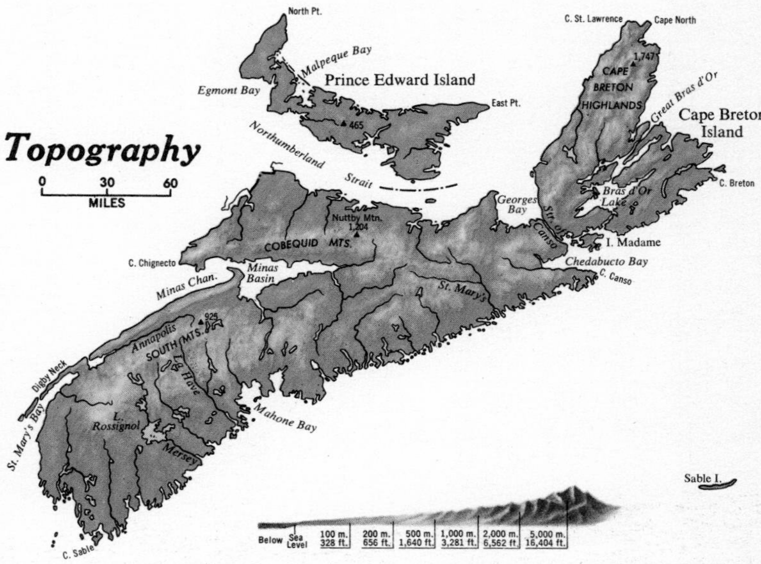

0 30 60 MILES

Below Sea Level | 100 m. 328 ft. | 200 m. 656 ft. | 500 m. 1,640 ft. | 1,000 m. 3,281 ft. | 2,000 m. 6,562 ft. | 5,000 m. 16,404 ft.

PRINCE EDWARD ISLAND

COUNTIES

Kings, 18,424 F 2
Prince, 42,082 D 2
Queens, 51,135 E 2

CITIES and TOWNS

Alberton, 973 E 2
Borden, 624 E 2
Bunbury, 527 F 2
Charlottetown (cap.)⊙, 19,133 E 2
Cornwall, 557 E 2
Elmsdale, 403 D 2
Georgetown⊙, 767 F 2
Hunter River, 362 E 2
Kensington, 1,086 E 2
Miminegash, 417 D 2
Miscouche, 750 D 2
Montague, 1,608 F 2
Morell, 387 F 2
Mount Stewart, 413 F 2
Murray Harbour, 367 F 2
Murray River, 478 F 2
North Rustico, 767 E 2
O'Leary, 795 D 2
Parkdale, 2,313 E 2
Saint Edward, 537 D 2
Saint Eleanors, 1,621 E 2
Saint Peters, 370 F 2
Sherwood, 3,807 E 2
Souris, 1,393 F 2
Stanhope, 203 E 2
Summerside⊙, 9,439 E 2
Tignish, 1,060 D 2
Victoria, 171 E 2
Wilmot, 737 E 2

OTHER FEATURES

Bedeque (bay) E 2
Cardigan (bay) F 2
Cascumpeque (bay) E 2
East (pt.) G 2
Egmont (bay) D 2
Hillsborough (bay) E 2
Malpeque (bay) E 2
North (pt.) E 1
Panmure (isl.), 45 F 2
Prince Edward Island Nat'l Park E 2
Saint Lawrence (gulf) F 2
Tracadie (bay) F 2

⊙ County seat.

‡ Population of metropolitan area.

Agriculture, Industry and Resources

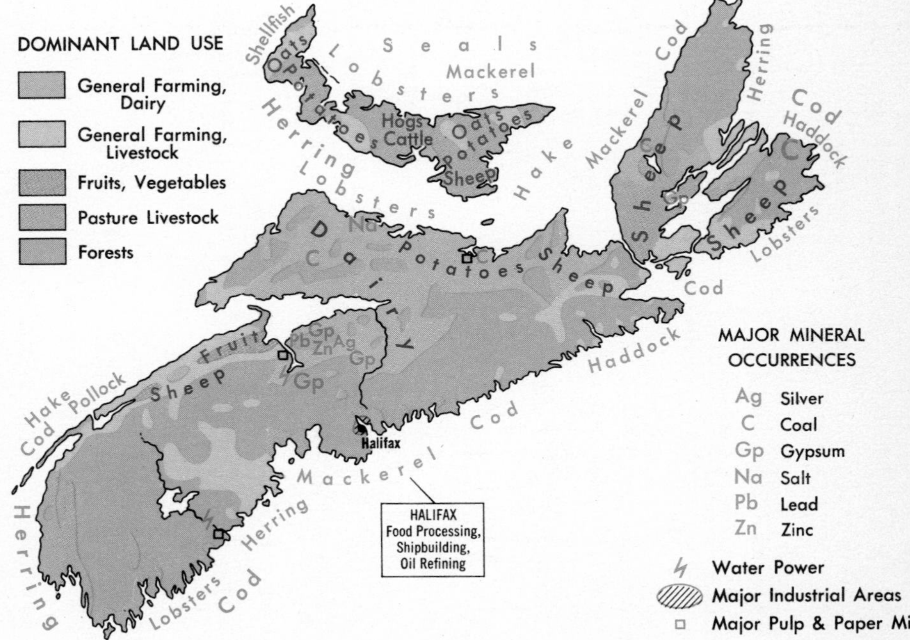

170 New Brunswick

COUNTIES

Albert, 16,307 F 3
Carleton, 24,428 C 2
Charlotte, 24,551 C 3
Gloucester, 74,752 E 1
Kent, 24,901 E 2
King's, 33,285 E 3
Madawaska, 34,976 B 1
Northumberland, 51,561 D 2
Queen's 12,486 D 3
Restigouche, 41,289 C 1
Saint John, 92,162 E 3
Sunbury, 21,268 D 3
Victoria, 19,796 C 1
Westmorland, 98,669 F 2
York, 64,126 C 3

CITIES and TOWNS

Acadie Siding, 112 E 2
Acadieville, 144 E 2
Adamsville, 119 E 2
Albert Mines, 130 F 3
Alcida, 222 E 1
Aldouane, 83 E 2
Allardville, 712 E 1
Alma, 425 F 3
Anagance, 109 E 3
Apohaqui, 352 E 3
Argyle, 63 C 2
Armstrong Brook, 321 E 1
Aroostook, 550 C 2
Arthurette, 299 C 2
Astle, 194 D 2
Atholville, 2,108 D 1
Aulac, 128 F 3
Back Bay, 567 D 3
Baie-Sainte-Anne, 735 F 1
Baie-Verte, 177 F 2
Bailey, 143 D 3
Bairdsville, 171 C 2
Baker Brook, 561 B 1
Balmoral, 896 D 1
Barker's Point, 1,882 D 3
Barnaby River, 87 E 2
Barnettville, 182 E 2
Bartibog Bridge, 163 E 1
Bas-Caraquet, 1,685 F 1
Bass River, 129 E 2
Bath, 920 C 2
Bathurst⊙, 16,674 E 1
Bathurst Mines, 45 E 1
Bayfield, 178 G 2
Bayside, 207 C 3
Beaver Brook Station, 276 E 1
Beaver Harbour, 355 D 3
Beechwood, 349 C 2
Beersville, 85 E 2
Belledune, 784 E 1
Bellefleur, 145 C 1
Bellefond, 294 E 1
Belleisle Creek, 179 E 3
Benjamin, 65 D 1
Benton, 149 C 3
Beresford, 2,325 E 1
Berry Mills, 349 E 2
Bertrand, 1,094 E 1
Berwick, 130 E 3
Black Point, 150 D 1
Black River, 91 E 3
Black River Bridge, 335 E 2
Blacks Harbour, 1,771 D 3
Blackville, 915 E 2
Blissfield, 130 D 2
Bloomfield Ridge, 218 D 2
Blue Cove, 519 E 1
Bocabec, 59 C 3
Boiestown, 332 D 2
Bonny River, 134 D 3
Bossé, 134 B 1
Bourgeois, 306 F 2
Brantville, 1,072 E 1
Breau-Village, 249 F 2
Brest, 117 E 2
Bridgedale, 416 F 3
Briggs Corner, 138 E 2
Bristol, 771 C 2
Brockway, 68 C 3
Browns Flats, 262 D 3
Buctouche, 1,964 F 2
Burnsville, 179 E 1
Burton⊙, 357 D 3
Burtts Corner, 487 D 2
Caissie-Village, 34 F 2
Cambridge-Narrows, 416 E 3
Campbellton, 10,335 D 1
Canaan Road, 130 E 2
Canaan Station, 102 E 2
Canterbury, 528 C 3
Cap-Bateau, 466 F 1
Cape Tormentine, 261 G 2
Cap Lumière, 305 F 2
Cap-Pelé, 2,081 F 2
Caraquet, 3,441 E 1
Caron Brook, 191 B 1
Carrolls Crossing, 188 D 2
Castalia, 199 D 4
Central Blissville (Bailey), 143 D 3
Centre-Acadie, 151 E 2
Centre-Saint-Simon, 517 E 1
Centreville, 566 C 2
Chance Harbour, 181 D 3
Charlo, 1,621 D 1
Chartersville, 320 F 2
Chatham, 7,833 E 1
Chatham Head, 1,440 E 2
Chipman, 1,977 E 2
Clair, 704 B 1
Clarendon, 105 D 3
Cliffordvale, 110 C 2
Clifton, 231 E 1
Cloverdale, 133 C 2
Coal Branch, 89 E 2
Coal Creek, 71 E 2
Cocagne, 234 F 2
Cocagne Cape, 258 F 2
Codys, 67 E 3
Coldstream, 160 C 2
Coles Island, 121 E 3
College Bridge, 545 F 3
Collette, 178 E 2
Connell, 107 C 2
Connors, 231 B 1
Cork Station, 70 D 3
Cornhill, 83 E 3
Cross Creek, 241 D 2
Cumberland Bay, 246 E 2
Dalhousie⊙, 6,255 D 1
Dalhousie Junction, 275 D 1
Darlington, 585 D 1
Daulnay, 539 E 1
Dawsonville, 208 C 1
Debec, 222 C 2
Dieppe, 4,277 F 2
Dipper Harbour, 109 D 3
Doaktown, 938 D 2
Dorchester⊙, 1,199 F 3
Dorchester Crossing, 574 F 2
Douglas Harbour, 46 D 3
Douglastown, 637 E 1
Drummond, 637 C 1
Duguayville, 372 E 1
Dumbarton, 59 C 3
Dumfries, 257 C 3
Dupuis Corner, 218 F 2
Durham Bridge, 182 D 2
East Shediac, 585 F 2
Edmundston⊙, 12,365 B 1
Eel River Bridge, 487 F 1
Eel River Crossing, 1,075 D 1
Elgin, 283 E 3
Elmwood, 78 C 2
Enniskillen, 77 D 3
Evandale, 33 D 3
Evangeline, 298 F 1
Fairhaven, 118 C 4
Fairisle, 444 E 1
Fairvale, 2,050 E 3
Ferry Road, 520 E 1
Fielding, 215 C 2
Five Fingers, 148 C 1
Flatlands, 280 D 1
Florenceville, 584 C 2
Fontaine, 318 F 2
Forest City, 55 C 3
Fosterville, 71 C 3
Four Falls Corner, 97 C 2
Fox Creek, 488 F 2
Fredericton (cap.)⊙, 24,254 D 3
Fredericton Junction, 615 D 3
Gagetown⊙, 609 D 3
Gardner Creek, 47 E 3
Geary, 1,023 D 3
Germantown, 71 F 3
Gillespie, 88 C 2
Glassville, 174 C 2
Glencoe, 143 D 1
Glenlivet, 231 D 1
Gloucester Junction, 167 E 1
Gondola Point, 850 D 3
Grafton, 359 C 2
Grand Bay, 1,066 D 3
Grande-Anse, 545 E 1
Grand Falls, 4,516 C 1
Grand Falls Hill, 559 C 1
Grand Harbour, 556 D 4
Gray Rapids, 307 E 2
Gunningsville, 1,669 F 2
Hammondvale, 127 E 3
Hampstead, 118 D 3
Hampton⊙, 1,748 E 3
Harcourt, 163 E 2
Hardwicke, 93 E 1
Hardwood Ridge, 222 D 2

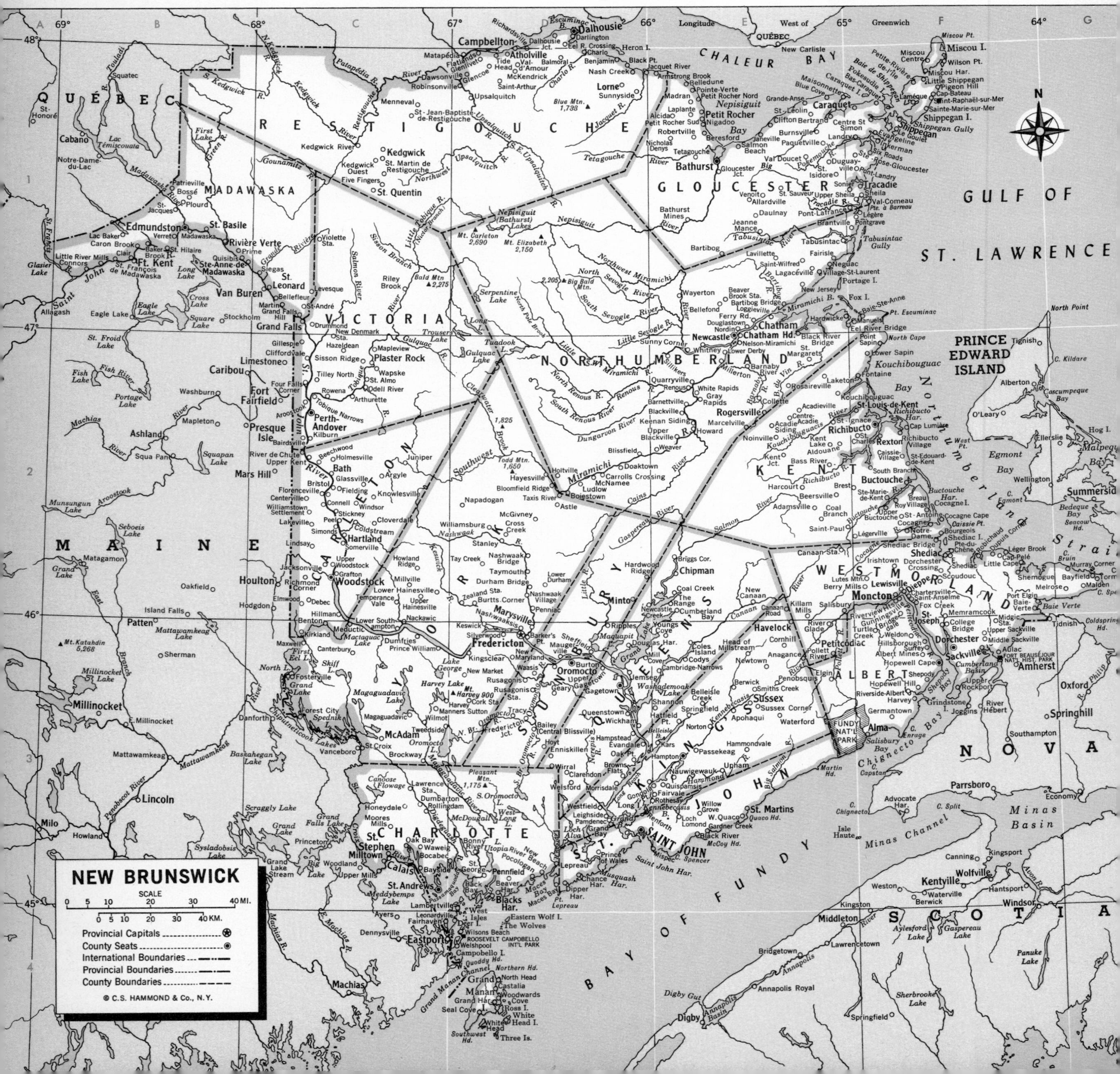

NEW BRUNSWICK

SCALE

0 5 10 20 30 40 MI.

0 5 10 20 30 40 KM.

Provincial Capitals ⊛
County Seats ⊙
International Boundaries
Provincial Boundaries
County Boundaries

Hartland, 1,009 C 2
Harvey, 54 F 3
Harvey, 383 D 3
Hatfield Point, 181 E 3
Havelock, 513 E 3
Hayesville, 120 D 2
Hazeldean, 213 C 2
Head of Millstream, 86 E 3
Hillman, 159 C 2
Hillsborough, 781 F 3
Holmesville, 251 C 2
Holtville, 300 D 2
Honeydale, 90 C 3
Hopewell Cape⊙, 162 F 3
Hopewell Hill, 164 F 3
Howard, 176 E 2
Howland Ridge, 56 C 2
Hoyt, 97 D 3
Inkerman, 500 F 1
Irishtown, 194 F 2
Jacksonville, 372 C 2
Jacquet River, 866 E 1
Janeville, 164 E 1
Jeanne Mance, 97 E 1
Jemseg, 185 D 3
Juniper, 585 C 2
Kars, 76 E 3
Kedgwick, 1,065 C 1
Kedgwick Ouest, 101 C 1
Kedgwick River, 25 C 1
Keenan Siding, 74 E 2
Kent Junction, 105 E 2
Kent Lake, 50 E 2
Keswick, 308 D 3
Kilburn, 167 C 2
Killam Mills, 60 E 2
Kingsclear, 132 D 3
Kirkland, 91 C 3
Knowlesville, 58 C 2
Kouchibouguac, 151 F 2
Lac Baker, 360 B 1
Lagacéville, 261 E 1
Laketon, 127 E 2
Lakeville, 325 C 2
Lambertville, 181 C 3
Lamèque, 933 F 1
Landry, 268 E 1
Laplante, 240 E 1
Lavillette, 500 E 1
Lawrence Station, 221 C 3
Léger Brook, 339 F 2
Légère, 514 F 1
Légerville, 199 F 2
Le Goulet, 1,155 F 1
Leighside, 597 D 3
Leonardville, 179 C 4
Lepreau, 162 D 3
Levesque, 225 C 1

Lewisville, 3,710 F 2
Lindsay, 108 C 2
Little Cape, 454 F 2
Little River Mills, 110 B 1
Little Shippegan, 100 F 1
Loch Lomond, 137 E 3
Loggieville, 877 E 1
Lorne, 999 D 1
Lower Derby, 260 E 2
Lower Durham, 115 D 2
Lower Hainesville, 119 C 2
Lower Millstream, 199 E 3
Lower Sapin, 186 F 2
Lower Southampton, 118 C 2
Ludlow, 193 D 2
Lutes Mountain, 234 E 2
Maces Bay, 133 D 3
Madran, 245 E 1
Magaguadavic, 121 C 3
Maisonnette, 620 E 1
Malden, 112 G 2
Manners Sutton, 199 D 3
Manuels, 546 F 1
Mapleview, 110 C 2
Marcelville, 78 E 2
Martin, 115 C 1
Marysville, 3,872 D 2
Maugerville, 346 D 3
Maxwell, 61 C 3
McAdam, 2,224 C 3
McGivney, 232 D 2
McKendrick, 594 D 1
McNamee, 189 D 2
Meductic, 172 C 3
Melrose, 144 F 2
Memramcook, 366 F 2
Menneval, 169 C 1
Middle Sackville, 311 F 3
Midgic Station, 211 F 3
Mill Cove, 227 D 3
Millerton, 199 E 2
Milltown, 1,893 C 3
Millville, 352 C 2
Minto, 3,880 D 2
Miscou Centre, 473 F 1
Miscou Harbour, 86 F 1
Mispec, 132 E 3
Moncton, 47,891 F 2
Moores Mills, 138 C 3
Morrisdale, 162 D 3
Murray Corner, 178 G 2
Nackawic, 1,324 C 2
Napadogan, 123 D 2
Nash Creek, 268 D 1
Nashwaak Bridge, 237 D 2
Nashwaaksis, 7,353 D 3
Nashwaak Village, 141 D 2
Nauwigewauk, 313 E 3

Neguac, 1,498 E 1
Nelson-Miramichi, 1,580 E 2
New Canaan, 44 E 2
Newcastle⊙, 6,460 E 2
Newcastle Creek, 205 D 2
New Denmark Station, 315 C 1
New Jersey, 117 E 1
New Market, 95 D 3
New Maryland, 643 D 3
New River Beach, 78 D 3
Newtown, 89 E 3
Nicholas Denys, 241 D 1
Nigadoo, 597 E 1
Noinville, 39 E 2
Nordin, 303 E 1
North Head, 649 D 4
Norton, 1,149 E 3
Notre-Dame, 362 F 2
Oak Bay, 232 C 3
Oak Point, 100 D 3
Odell River, 166 C 2
Oromocto, 11,427 D 3
Pamdenec, 422 D 3
Paquetville, 479 E 1
Passekeag, 169 E 3
Patrieville, 140 B 1
Peel, 82 C 2
Pennfield, 267 D 3
Penniac, 407 D 2
Penobsquis, 79 E 3
Perth-Andover⊙, 2,108 C 2
Petitcodiac, 1,569 E 3
Petite-Rivière-de-l'Île, 477 F 1
Petit Rocher, 1,624 E 1
Petit Rocher Nord, 414 E 1
Petit Rocher Sud, 538 E 1
Pigeon Hill, 445 F 1
Plaster Rock, 1,331 C 2
Plourd, 336 B 1
Pocologan, 108 D 3
Pointe-du-Chêne, 484 F 2
Pointe-Verte, 524 E 1
Point Sapin, 349 F 2
Pollett River, 64 E 3
Pontgrave, 202 F 1
Pont-Lafrance, 856 E 1
Pont-Landry, 562 F 1
Port Elgin, 553 F 2
Prime, 73 B 1
Prince of Wales, 131 D 3
Prince William, 236 C 3
Quarryville, 312 E 2
Queenstown, 105 D 3
Quisibis, 138 B 1
Quispamsis, 2,215 E 3
Renforth, 1,606 E 3
Renous, 211 E 2

Rexton, 755 F 2
Richardsville, 892 D 1
Richibucto⊙, 1,850 E 2
Richibucto Village, 357 F 2
Richmond Corner, 54 C 2
Riley Brook, 166 C 1
Ripples, 230 D 3
River de Chute, 57 C 2
River Glade, 242 E 3
Riverside-Albert, 509 F 3
Riverview Heights, 6,525 F 2
Rivière Verte, 1,657 B 1
Robertville, 954 E 1
Robichaud, 350 F 2
Robinsonville, 202 C 1
Rogersville, 1,077 E 2
Rollingdam, 124 C 3
Rosaireville, 87 E 2
Rothesay, 1,038 E 3
Rowena, 104 C 2
Roy, 115 F 2
Rusagonis, 182 D 3
Rusagonis Station, 76 D 3
Sackville, 3,180 F 3
Saint Almo, 53 C 2
Saint-André, 315 C 1
Saint Andrews⊙, 1,812 C 3
Saint-Anselme, 1,150 F 2
Saint-Antoine, 756 F 2
Saint-Arthur, 521 D 1
Saint Basile, 3,085 B 1
Saint-Charles, 381 F 2
Saint Croix, 50 C 3
Sainte-Anne-de-Madawaska, 1,253 B 1
Saint-Édouard-de-Kent, 207 F 2
Sainte-Marie-de-Kent, 269 F 2
Sainte-Marie-sur-Mer, 430 F 1
Sainte-Rose-Gloucester, 479 F 1
Saint François de Madawaska, 511 B 1
Saint George, 977 D 3
Saint Hilaire, 199 B 1
Saint-Ignace, 382 F 2
Saint-Isidore, 477 E 1
Saint-Jacques, 1,072 B 1
Saint-Jean-Baptiste-de-Restigouche, 293 C 1
Saint John⊙, 89,039 E 3
Saint John, ‡106,744 E 3
Saint-Joseph, 687 F 3
Saint-Léolin, 694 E 1
Saint Leonard, 1,478 C 1
Saint-Louis-de-Kent, 992 F 2
Saint Margarets, 213 E 2
Saint Martin de Restigouche, 145 C 1
Saint Martins, 484 E 3
Saint-Paul, 314 E 2
Saint Quentin, 2,093 C 1
Saint-Raphaël-sur-Mer, 588 F 1
Saint Sauveur, 626 E 1
Saint Stephen, 3,409 C 3
Saint-Wilfred, 307 E 1
Salisbury, 1,070 E 2
Salmon Beach, 382 E 1
Scoudouc, 250 F 2
Seal Cove, 613 D 4
Shannon, 72 E 3
Shediac, 2,203 F 2
Shediac Bridge, 347 F 2
Sheffield, 112 D 3
Sheila, 854 F 1
Shemogue, 189 F 2
Shepody, 88 F 3
Shippegan, 2,043 F 1
Siegas, 393 C 1
Sillikers, 275 E 2
Silverwood, 935 D 3
Simonds, 236 C 2
Sisson Ridge, 166 C 2
Six Roads, 441 F 1
Smiths Creek, 195 E 3
Somerville, 362 C 2
Sonier, 443 E 1
South Branch, 143 F 2
Springfield, 139 E 3
Stanley, 388 D 2
Stickney, 266 C 2
Sunny Corner, 572 E 2
Sunnyside, 79 D 1
Surrey, 286 F 3
Sussex, 3,942 E 3

AREA 28,354 sq. mi.
POPULATION 624,000
CAPITAL Fredericton
LARGEST CITY Saint John
HIGHEST POINT Mt. Carleton 2,690 ft.
SETTLED IN 1611
ADMITTED TO CONFEDERATION 1867
PROVINCIAL FLOWER Purple Violet

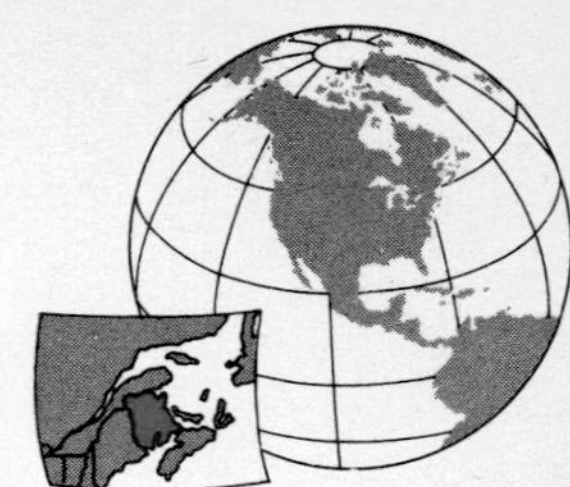

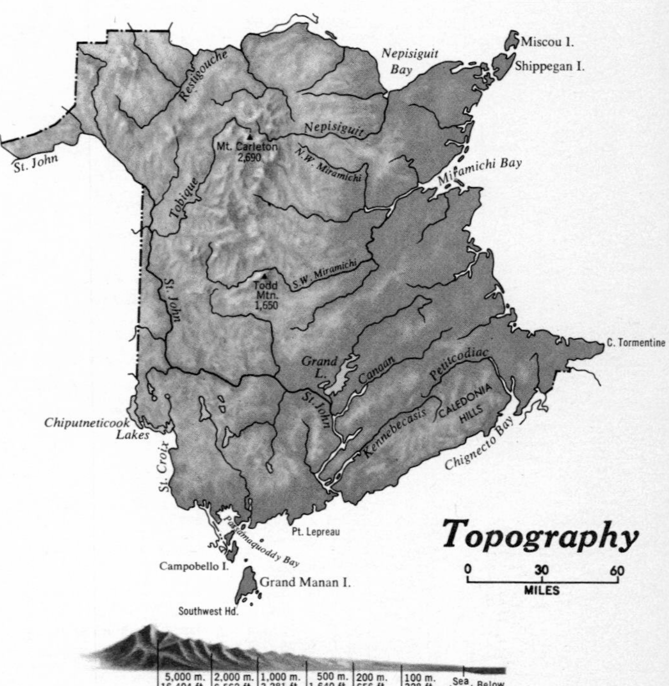

Topography

0 30 60 MILES

Agriculture, Industry and Resources

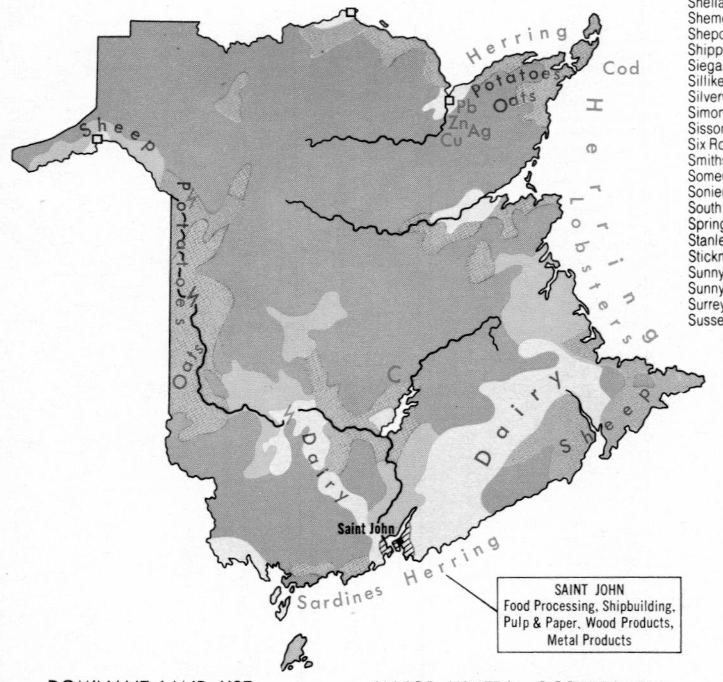

Sussex Corner, 700 E 3
Tabusintac, 253 E 1
Taxis River, 172 D 2
Tay Creek, 177 D 2
Taymouth, 280 D 2
Temperance Vale, 323 C 2
Tetagouche, 359 E 1
The Range, 88 E 2
Thibault, 231 C 1
Tide Head, 797 D 1
Tilley North, 226 C 2
Tobique Narrows, 169 C 2
Tracadie, 2,222 F 1
Tracy, 610 D 3
Turtle Creek, 200 F 3
Tweedside, 125 C 3
Upham, 132 E 3
Upper Blackville, 224 E 2
Upper Buctouche, 155 F 2
Upper Gagetown, 299 D 3
Upper Hainesville, 217 C 2
Upper Kent, 301 C 2
Upper Mills, 143 C 3
Upper Rockport, 17 F 3
Upper Sackville, 234 F 3
Upper Sheila, 748 E 1
Upper Woodstock, 336 C 2
Upsalquitch, 135 D 1
Val-Comeau, 495 F 1
Val d'Amour, 580 D 1
Val Doucet, 486 E 1
Veniot, 560 E 1
Verret, 900 B 1
Village-Saint-Laurent, 164 E 1
Violette Station, 128 C 1
Waasis, 176 D 3
Wapske, 210 C 2
Waterford, 132 E 3
Waweig, 124 C 3
Wayerton, 161 E 1
Weaver, 112 E 2
Weldon, 199 F 3
Welsford, 293 D 3
Welshpool, 172 D 4
Westfield, 461 D 3
West Quaco, 102 E 3
White Head, 178 D 4
White Rapids, 304 E 2
Whitney, 282 E 2
Wickham, 86 D 3
Williamsburg, 333 D 2
Williamstown Settlement, 197 C 2
Willow Grove, 336 E 3
Wilmot, 127 C 3
Wilson Point, 70 F 3
Wilsons Beach, 911 D 4
Windsor, 56 C 2

Wirral, 115 D 3
Woodstock⊙, 4,846 C 2
Woodwards Cove, 180 D 4
Youngs Cove, 118 E 3
Zealand Station, 442 D 2

OTHER FEATURES

Bald (mt.) C 1
Bartibog (riv.) E 1
Bay du Vin (riv.) E 2
Big Tracadie (riv.) E 1
Buctouche (harb.) F 2
Buctouche (riv.) F 2
Campobello (isl.), 1,274 D 4
Canaan (riv.) E 2
Carleton (mt.) D 1
Chaleur (bay) E 1
Chignecto (bay) F 3
Chiputneticook (lakes) C 3
Cocagne (isl.) F 2
Cumberland (basin) F 3
Deer (isl.), 730 D 4
Digdeguash (riv.) C 3
Escuminac (bay) F 1
Escuminac (pt.) F 1
Fort Beauséjour Nat'l Hist. Park F 3
Fundy (bay) E 3
Fundy Nat'l Park E 3
Gaspereau (riv.) D 2
Grand (bay) D 3
Grand (lake) C 3
Grand (lake) D 3
Grande (riv.) C 1
Grand Manan (chan.) C 4
Grand Manan (isl.), 2,547 D 4
Green (riv.) B 1
Hammond (riv.) E 3
Harvey (lake) C 3
Heron (isl.) D 1
Kedgwick (riv.) C 1
Kennebecasis (riv.) E 3
Keswick (riv.) C 2
Kouchibouguac (bay) F 2
Kouchibouguacis (riv.) E 2
Lepreau (riv.) D 3
Little (riv.) D 2
Long (isl.) D 3
Long Reach (inlet) D 3
Maces (bay) D 3
Mactaquac (lake) C 3
Madawaska (riv.) B 1
Magaguadavic (lake) C 3
Magaguadavic (riv.) C 3
Miramichi (bay) E 1

Miscou (isl.), 728 F 1
Miscou (pt.) F 1
Musquash (harb.) D 3
Nashwaak (riv.) D 2
Nepisiguit (bay) E 1
Nepisiguit (riv.) D 1
Nerepis (riv.) D 3
Northern (head) D 4
North Sevogle (riv.) D 1
Northumberland (str.) F 2
Northwest Miramichi (riv.) D 1
Oromocto (lake) C 3
Oromocto (riv.) D 3
Passamaquoddy (bay) C 3
Patapédia (riv.) C 1
Petitcodiac (riv.) F 3
Pokemouche (riv.) E 1
Pokesudie (isl.), 368 F 1
Pollett (riv.) E 3
Quaco (head) E 3
Renous (riv.) D 2
Restigouche (riv.) C 1
Richibucto (harb.) F 2
Richibucto (riv.) E 2
Roosevelt Campobello Int'l Park D 4
Saint Croix (riv.) C 3
Saint Francis (riv.) A 1
Saint John (harb.) E 3
Saint John (riv.) C 2
Saint Lawrence (gulf) F 1
Salisbury (bay) F 3
Salmon (riv.) C 1
Salmon (riv.) E 2
Shediac (isl.) F 2
Shepody (bay) F 3
Shippegan (bay) E 1
Shippegan (gully) F 1
Shippegan (isl.), 7,745 F 1
South Sevogle (riv.) D 1
Southwest (head) D 4
Southwest Miramichi (riv.) D 2
Spear (cape) G 2
Spednik (lake) C 3
Spencer (cape) E 3
Tabusintac (gully) F 1
Tabusintac (riv.) E 1
Tetagouche (riv.) D 1
Tobique (riv.) C 2
Upsalquitch (riv.) D 1
Utopia (lake) D 3
Verte (bay) G 2
Washademoak (lake) E 3
West (isls.), 974 D 4
White Head (isl.), 178 D 4

⊙ County seat.
‡ Population of metropolitan area.

Topography

0 60 120
MILES

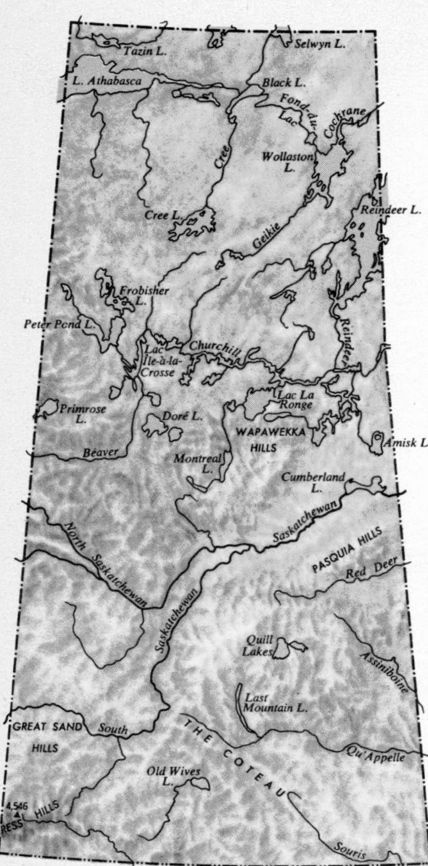

5,000 m. 16,404 ft. | 2,000 m. 6,562 ft. | 1,000 m. 3,281 ft. | 500 m. 1,640 ft. | 200 m. 656 ft. | 100 m. 328 ft. | Sea Level | Below

CITIES and TOWNS

Abbey, 246 C 5
Aberdeen, 288 E 3
Abernethy, 253 H 5
Air Ronge, 239 M 3
Alameda, 370 J 6
Alida, 230 K 6
Allan, 712 E 4
Alsask, 819 B 4
Alvena, 143 E 3
Aneroid, 163 D 6
Annaheim, 182 G 3
Antler, 115 K 6
Arborfield, 418 H 2
Archerwill, 302 H 3
Arcola, 539 J 6
Arran, 120 K 4
Asquith, 355 D 3
Assiniboia, 2,675 E 6
Avonlea, 391 G 5
Aylesbury, 88 F 5
Aylsham, 170 H 2
Balcarres, 678 H 5
Balgonie, 518 G 5
Batoche, 27 E 3
Battleford, 1,803 C 3
Beatty, 97 G 3
Beauval, 436 L 3
Beechy, 342 D 5
Bellevue, 122 F 3
Bengough, 650 F 6
Bethune, 291 F 5
Bienfait, 823 J 6
Biggar, 2,607 C 3
Big River, 836 D 2
Birch Hills, 696 F 3
Birsay, 123 D 4
Bjorkdale, 223 H 3
Black Lake, 471 M 2
Bladworth, 125 E 4
Blaine Lake, 671 D 3
Borden, 187 D 3
Bradwell, 100 E 4
Bredenbury, 472 K 5
Briercrest, 130 F 5
Broadview, 959 J 5
Brock, 205 C 4
Broderick, 115 E 4
Brownlee, 121 F 5
Bruno, 728 F 3
Buchanan, 442 J 4
Buffalo Narrows, 794 L 3
Bulyea, 109 G 5
Burstall, 507 B 5
Cabri, 737 C 5
Cadillac, 217 D 6
Calder, 186 K 4
Camsell Portage, 87 L 2
Cando, 193 C 3
Canoe Lake, 138 L 3
Canora, 2,603 J 4
Canwood, 325 E 2
Carievale, 229 K 6
Carlyle, 1,101 J 6
Carmel, 90 F 3
Carnduff, 1,075 K 6
Caron, 96 F 5
Carragana, 137 J 3
Carrot River, 953 H 2
Central Butte, 522 E 5
Ceylon, 279 G 6
Chamberlain, 161 F 5
Chaplin, 368 E 5
Chelan, 101 H 3
Chitek Lake, 131 D 2
Choiceland, 456 G 2
Christopher Lake, 143 F 2
Churchbridge, 973 J 5
Clair, 86 G 3
Climax, 341 C 6
Cochin, 163 C 2
Coderre, 161 E 5
Codette, 175 H 2
Coleville, 482 B 4
Colonsay, 526 F 4
Conquest, 261 D 4
Consul, 205 B 6
Coronach, 379 F 6
Craik, 503 F 4
Crane Valley, 84 F 6
Craven, 126 G 5
Creelman, 197 H 6
Creighton, 1,857 N 4
Crooked River, 106 H 3
Cudworth, 799 F 3
Cupar, 573 G 5
Cutbank, 217 E 4
Cut Knife, 560 B 3
Dalmeny, 417 E 3
Davidson, 1,043 E 4
Debden, 340 E 2
Delisle, 653 D 4
Delmas, 161 C 3
Denare Beach, 235 M 4
Denzil, 287 B 3
Deschambault Lake, 127 M 3
Dilke, 130 F 5
Dinsmore, 421 D 4
Dodsland, 404 C 4
Dollard, 92 C 6
Domremy, 208 F 3
Dorintosh, 87 L 4
Drake, 238 G 4
Drinkwater, 118 F 5
Dubuc, 153 J 5
Duck Lake, 584 E 3
Duff, 90 H 5
Dundurn, 354 E 4
Duval, 133 G 4
Dysart, 243 H 5
Earl Grey, 243 G 5
Eastend, 784 C 6
Eatonia, 610 B 4
Ebenezer, 140 J 4
Edam, 334 C 2
Edenwold, 129 G 5
Elbow, 361 E 4
Eldorado, 289 L 2
Elfros, 253 H 4
Elrose, 573 D 4
Elstow, 150 E 4
Endeavour, 193 J 3
Englefeld, 218 G 3
Ernfold, 100 D 5
Erwood, 94 J 3
Esterhazy, 2,896 K 5
Estevan, 9,150 J 6
Eston, 1,418 C 4
Eyebrow, 181 E 5
Fairlight, 127 K 6
Fenwood, 112 H 4
Ferland, 109 D 6
Fillmore, 396 H 6
Findlater, 96 F 5
Fiske, 85 C 4
Flaxcombe, 99 B 4
Fleming, 183 K 5
Flin Flon, 471 N 4
Foam Lake, 1,331 H 4
Fond du Lac, 328 L 2
Forget, 118 J 6
Fort Qu'Appelle, 1,606 H 5
Fosston, 119 H 3
Fox Valley, 489 B 5
Francis, 159 H 5
Frenchman Butte, 86 B 2
Frobisher, 245 J 6
Frontier, 249 C 6
Gainsborough, 375 K 6
Garrick, 120 G 2
Gerald, 174 K 5
Girvin, 86 F 4
Gladmar, 131 G 6
Glaslyn, 357 C 2
Glenavon, 340 J 5
Glen Ewen, 223 K 6
Glenside, 94 E 4
Glentworth, 126 E 6
Golden Prairie, 144 B 5
Goodeve, 169 H 4
Goodsoil, 219 L 4
Gorlitz, 94 J 4
Govan, 354 G 4
Grand Coulee, 131 G 5
Gravelbourg, 1,428 E 6
Grayson, 260 J 5
Green Lake, 450 L 4
Grenfell, 1,350 J 5
Griffin, 90 H 6
Gronlid, 138 G 2
Guernsey, 142 F 4
Gull Lake, 1,156 C 5
Hafford, 580 D 3
Hague, 431 E 3
Halbrite, 166 H 6
Hanley, 390 E 4
Harris, 254 D 4
Hawarden, 190 E 4
Hazel Dell, 105 H 4
Hazenmore, 127 D 6
Hazlet, 198 C 5
Hepburn, 305 E 3
Herbert, 1,024 D 5
Herschel, 89 C 4
Hitchcock, 91 J 6
Hodgeville, 399 E 5
Hoey, 95 F 3
Holdfast, 399 F 5
Hubbard, 119 H 4
Hudson Bay, 1,971 J 3
Humboldt, 3,881 F 3
Hyas, 215 J 4
Île-à-la-Crosse, 908 L 3
Imperial, 486 F 4
Indian Head, 1,810 H 5
Invermay, 412 J 4
Ituna, 960 H 4
Jansen, 241 G 4
Kamsack, 2,783 K 4
Kayville, 84 F 6
Kelliher, 460 H 4
Kelvington, 1,053 H 3
Kenaston, 402 E 4
Kendal, 90 H 5
Kennedy, 264 J 5
Kenosee Park, 103 J 6
Kerrobert, 1,180 C 4
Khedive, 91 G 6
Killaly, 139 J 5
Kincaid, 306 D 6
Kindersley, 3,451 B 4
Kinistino, 767 F 3
Kinoosao, 95 N 3
Kipling, 927 J 5
Kisbey, 260 J 6
Krydor, 136 D 3
Kuroki, 167 H 4
Kyle, 509 C 5
Lacadena, 84 C 5
Lac Vert, 111 G 3
Lafleche, 715 E 6
Laird, 218 E 3
Lake Alma, 173 G 6
Lake Lenore, 392 G 3
La Loche, 1,136 L 3
Lampman, 830 J 6
Lancer, 199 C 5
Landis, 297 C 3
Lang, 183 G 6
Langenburg, 1,236 K 5
Langham, 535 E 3
Lanigan, 1,430 F 4
La Ronge, 906 L 3
Lashburn, 494 B 2
Leader, 1,105 B 5
Leask, 439 E 2
Lebret, 278 H 5
Leipzig, 87 C 3
Lemberg, 409 H 5
Leoville, 399 D 2
Leross, 91 H 4
Leroy, 435 G 4
Leslie, 87 H 4
Lestock, 452 G 4
Liberty, 141 F 4
Limerick, 178 E 6
Lintlaw, 212 H 3
Lipton, 401 H 5
Livelong, 126 C 2
Lloydminster, 3,953 A 2
Lone Rock, 120 A 2
Loon Lake, 348 B 1
Loreburn, 252 E 4
Love, 133 G 2
Lucky Lake, 378 D 5
Lumsden, 900 G 5
Luseland, 728 B 3
Macdowall, 173 E 2
Macklin, 829 A 3
MacNutt, 184 K 4
Macoun, 172 H 6
Macrorie, 120 E 4
Maidstone, 691 B 2
Major, 164 B 4
Makwa, 126 C 2
Manitou Beach, 118 F 4
Mankota, 424 D 6
Manor, 409 K 6
Maple Creek, 2,268 B 6
Marcelin, 306 E 3
Marchwell, 129 K 5
Marengo, 133 B 4
Margo, 225 H 4
Marquis, 131 F 5
Marsden, 241 B 3
Marshall, 195 B 2
Martensville, 870 E 3
Maryfield, 408 K 6
Mayfair, 134 D 2
Maymont, 167 D 3
McKague, 91 G 3
McLean, 178 G 5
Meacham, 186 F 3
Meadow Lake, 3,435 C 1
Meath Park, 251 F 2
Medstead, 172 C 2
Melfort, 4,725 G 3
Melville, 5,375 J 5
Mendham, 163 B 5
Meota, 233 C 2
Mervin, 198 C 2
Meyronne, 142 E 6
Midale, 647 H 6
Middle Lake, 292 F 3
Mikado, 90 J 4
Milden, 239 D 4
Milestone, 483 G 5
Minton, 215 G 6
Mistatim, 165 H 3
Molanosa, 213 M 4
Montmartre, 510 H 5
Moose Jaw, 31,854 F 5
Moosomin, 2,407 K 5
Morse, 455 D 5
Mortlach, 310 E 5
Mossbank, 460 E 6
Mozart, 93 G 4
Muenster, 280 F 3
Naicam, 711 G 3
Neilburg, 298 B 3
Neuanlage, 107 E 3
Neudorf, 469 J 5
Neville, 154 D 6
Nipawin, 4,057 H 2
Nokomis, 533 F 4
Norquay, 513 J 4
North Battleford, 12,698 C 3
North Portal, 189 J 6
Odessa, 224 H 5
Ogema, 457 G 6
Ormiston, 173 F 6
Osler, 182 E 3
Outlook, 1,767 E 4
Oxbow, 1,380 J 6
Paddockwood, 230 F 2
Pambrun, 91 D 6
Pangman, 242 G 6
Paradise Hill, 344 B 2
Parkside, 112 E 2
Paynton, 204 B 2
Pelican Narrows, 265 N 3
Pelly, 426 K 4
Pennant, 215 C 5
Pense, 270 G 5
Perdue, 411 D 3
Piapot, 160 B 6
Pierceland, 271 K 4
Pilger, 109 F 3
Pilot Butte, 403 G 5
Pine House, 427 M 3
Pleasantdale, 153 G 3
Plenty, 208 C 4
Plunkett, 152 F 4
Ponteix, 786 D 6
Porcupine Plain, 830 H 3
Preeceville, 1,118 J 4
Prelate, 407 B 5
Prince Albert, 28,464 F 2
Prud'homme, 260 F 3
Punnichy, 451 G 4
Qu'Appelle, 451 H 5
Quill Lake, 566 G 3
Quinton, 195 G 4
Rabbit Lake, 206 D 2
Radisson, 416 D 3
Radville, 1,024 G 6
Rama, 188 H 4
Raymore, 523 G 4
Redvers, 846 K 6
Regina (cap.), 139,469 G 5
Regina, ‡140,734 G 5
Regina Beach, 334 F 5
Regway, 19 G 6
Reserve, 153 J 3
Rhein, 295 J 4
Rhineland, 84 D 5
Riceton, 112 G 5
Richmound, 208 B 5
Ridgedale, 169 H 2
Riverhurst, 264 E 5
Rocanville, 891 K 5
Roche Percée, 167 J 6
Rockglen, 550 F 6
Rosetown, 2,614 D 4
Rose Valley, 591 H 3
Rosthern, 1,431 E 3
Rouleau, 395 G 5
Rush Lake, 162 D 5
Saint Benedict, 193 F 3
Saint Brieux, 367 G 3
Saint Front, 94 G 3
Saint Gregor, 125 G 3
Saint Louis, 387 F 3
Saint Victor, 85 F 6
Saint Walburg, 656 B 2
Saltcoats, 509 J 4
Sandy Bay, 494 N 3
Saskatoon, 126,449 E 3
Saskatoon, ‡126,449 E 3
Sceptre, 234 B 5
Scott, 254 C 3
Sedley, 268 H 5
Semans, 331 G 4
Senlac, 94 B 3
Shamrock, 105 E 5
Shaunavon, 2,244 C 6
Sheho, 320 H 4
Shellbrook, 1,048 E 2
Shell Lake, 255 D 2
Simmie, 100 C 6
Simpson, 239 F 4
Sintaluta, 272 H 5
Smeaton, 315 G 2
Smiley, 124 B 4
Snowden, 87 G 2
Sonningdale, 106 D 3
Southey, 548 G 5
Sovereign, 91 D 4
Spalding, 329 G 3

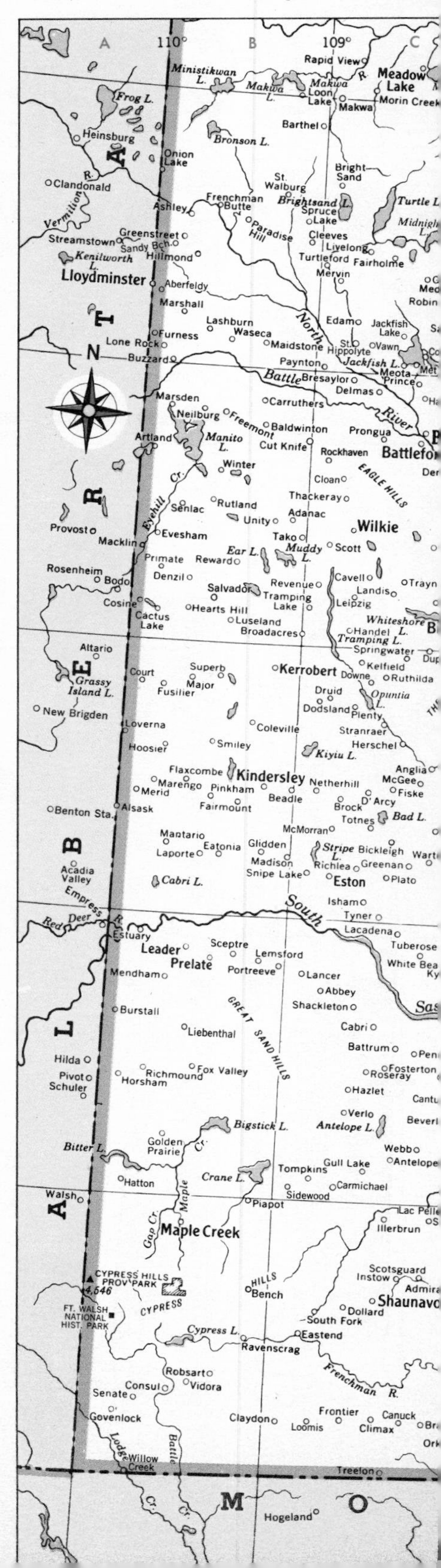

Agriculture, Industry and Resources

DOMINANT LAND USE

Wheat
Cereals (chiefly barley, oats)
Cereals, Livestock
Livestock
Forests

MAJOR MINERAL OCCURRENCES

Au Gold
Cu Copper
G Natural Gas
He Helium
K Potash
Lg Lignite
Na Salt
O Petroleum
S Sulfur
U Uranium
Zn Zinc

Water Power
Major Industrial Areas

REGINA
Food Processing, Machinery, Oil Refining

Speers, 117 .... D 3
Spiritwood, 719 .... D 2
Springside, 350 .... J 4
Springwater, 99 .... C 4
Spruce Lake, 106 .... B 2
Spy Hill, 384 .... K 5
Star City, 543 .... G 3
Stenen, 225 .... J 4
Stewart Valley, 138 .... D 5
Stockholm, 357 .... J 5
Stony Rapids, 147 .... M 2
Storthoaks, 177 .... K 6
Stoughton, 751 .... J 6
Strasbourg, 759 .... G 4
Strongfield, 110 .... E 4
Sturgis, 617 .... J 4
Success, 101 .... D 5
Swift Current, 15,415 .... D 5
Sylvania, 125 .... G 3
Tantallon, 174 .... K 5
Theodore, 434 .... J 4
Tisdale, 2,798 .... H 3
Togo, 227 .... K 4
Tompkins, 353 .... C 5
Torquay, 377 .... H 6
Tramping Lake, 241 .... B 3
Tribune, 136 .... H 6
Tugaske, 196 .... E 5
Turnor Lake, 276 .... L 3
Turtleford, 419 .... B 2
Tuxford, 153 .... F 5
Tyvan, 86 .... H 5
Unity, 2,294 .... B 3
Uranium City, 1,867 .... L 2
Val Marie, 307 .... D 6
Vanguard, 315 .... D 6
Vanscoy, 244 .... D 4
Vawn, 119 .... C 2
Veregin, 197 .... K 4
Vibank, 275 .... H 5
Viceroy, 152 .... F 6
Viscount, 395 .... F 4
Vonda, 258 .... F 3
Wadena, 1,382 .... H 4
Wakaw, 1,009 .... F 3
Waldeck, 242 .... D 5
Waldheim, 606 .... E 3
Wapella, 518 .... K 5
Warman, 781 .... E 3
Waseca, 115 .... B 2
Waskesiu Lake, 154 .... E 2
Watrous, 1,541 .... F 4
Watson, 840 .... G 3
Wawota, 536 .... J 6
Webb, 105 .... C 5
Weekes, 183 .... J 3
Weirdale, 108 .... F 2
Weldon, 254 .... F 2
Welwyn, 231 .... K 5
Weyburn, 8,815 .... H 6
White City, 129 .... G 5
White Fox, 354 .... H 2
Whitewood, 1,098 .... J 5
Wilcox, 189 .... G 5
Wilkie, 1,642 .... C 3
Willow Bunch, 482 .... F 6
Windthorst, 188 .... J 5
Wiseton, 181 .... D 4
Wishart, 269 .... H 4
Wollaston Lake, 115 .... M 2
Wolseley, 975 .... H 5
Wood Mountain, 86 .... E 6
Wroxton, 92 .... K 4
Wymark, 199 .... D 5
Wynyard, 1,932 .... G 4
Yarbo, 160 .... K 5
Yellow Creek, 163 .... F 3
Yellow Grass, 500 .... H 6
Yorkton, 13,430 .... J 4
Young, 496 .... F 4
Zealandia, 155 .... D 4
Zenon Park, 346 .... H 2

OTHER FEATURES

Allan (hills) .... E 4
Amisk (lake) .... M 4
Assiniboine (riv.) .... J 3
Athabasca (lake) .... L 2
Battle (creek) .... B 6
Battle (riv.) .... B 3
Bear (hills) .... C 4
Beaver (hills) .... H 4
Beaver (riv.) .... L 4
Beaverlodge (lake) .... L 2
Brightsand (lake) .... B 2
Candle (lake) .... F 2
Carrot (riv.) .... J 2
Churchill (riv.) .... M 3
Coteau, The (hills) .... D 4
Cowan (lake) .... D 2
Cree (lake) .... L 3
Cumberland (lake) .... J 1
Cypress (hills) .... B 6
Cypress Hills Prov. Park .... B 6
Delaronde (lake) .... E 1
Diefenbaker (lake) .... E 4
Doré (lake) .... L 3
Duck Mountain Prov. Park .... K 4
Eagle (hills) .... C 3
Eaglehill (creek) .... D 4
Fond du Lac (riv.) .... M 2
Fort Walsh Nat'l Hist. Park .... A 6
Frenchman (riv.) .... C 6
Frobisher (lake) .... L 3
Gardiner (dam) .... D 4
Good Spirit (lake) .... J 4
Goodspirit Prov. Park .... J 4
Great Sand (hills) .... B 5
Greenwater Lake Prov. Park, 13 .... H 3
Île-à-la-Crosse (lake) .... L 3
Jackfish (lake) .... C 2
Lac La Ronge Prov. Park .... M 3
La Ronge (lake) .... M 3
Last Mountain (lake) .... F 4
Lenore (lake) .... G 3
Makwa (riv.) .... B 1
Manito (lake) .... B 3
Meadow Lake Prov. Park .... G 1
Meeting (lake) .... D 2
Missouri Coteau (hills) .... F 6
Montreal (lake) .... F 1
Moose Jaw (riv.) .... G 5
Moose Mountain Prov. Park .... J 6
Nipawin Prov. Park .... G 1
North Saskatchewan (riv.) .... D 3
Old Wives (lake) .... E 5
Pasquia (hills) .... J 2
Peter Pond (lake) .... L 3
Pheasant (hills) .... J 5
Prince Albert Nat'l Park, 182 .... E 1
Qu'Appelle (riv.) .... J 5
Quill (lakes) .... G 4
Redberry (lake) .... D 3
Red Deer (riv.) .... K 3
Reindeer (lake) .... N 3
Rivers (lake) .... F 6
Saskatchewan (riv.) .... H 2
Souris (riv.) .... H 6
South Saskatchewan (riv.) .... C 5
Sturgeon (riv.) .... E 2
Swift Current (creek) .... D 5
Tazin (lake) .... L 2
Thickwood (hills) .... D 2
Tobin (lake) .... H 2
Torch (riv.) .... H 2
Touchwood (hills) .... G 4
Turtle (lake) .... C 2
Wapawekka (hills) .... M 4
Waskesiu (lake) .... E 2
Willow Bunch (lake) .... F 6
Witchekan (lake) .... D 2
Wollaston (lake) .... N 2
Wood (mt.) .... E 6
Wood (riv.) .... E 6

‡ Population of metropolitan area.

AREA 251,700 sq. mi.
POPULATION 933,000
CAPITAL Regina
LARGEST CITY Regina
HIGHEST POINT Cypress Hills 4,546 ft.
SETTLED IN 1774
ADMITTED TO CONFEDERATION 1905
PROVINCIAL FLOWER Prairie Lily

SASKATCHEWAN
NORTHERN PART

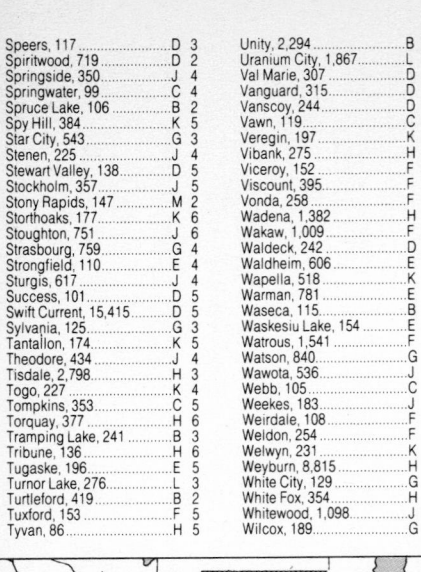

SASKATCHEWAN
SOUTHERN PART

SCALE
0 5 10 20 40 60 MI.
0 5 10 20 40 60 KM.

Provincial Capital
International Boundaries
Provincial Boundaries

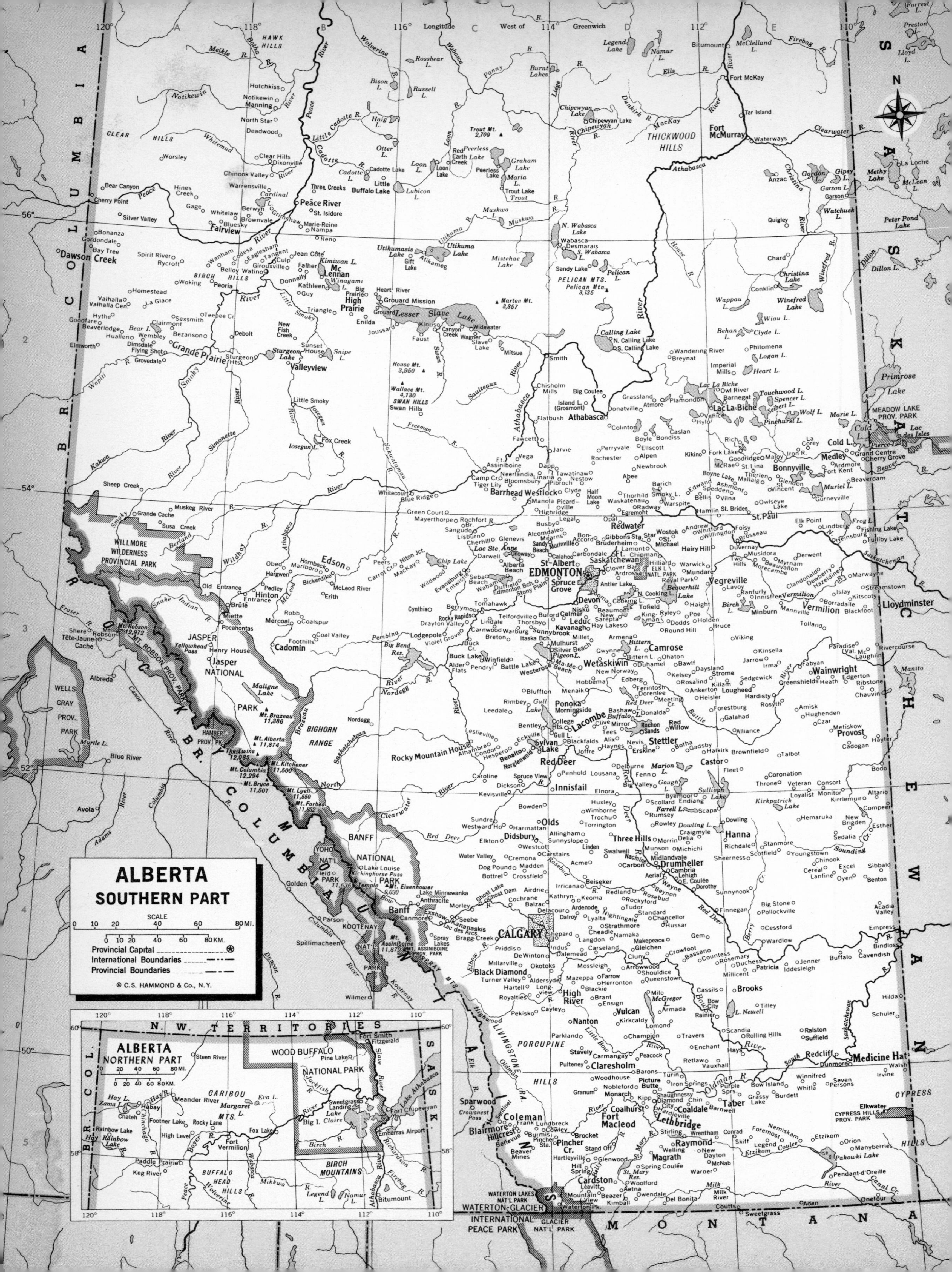
ALBERTA
SOUTHERN PART
SCALE
0 10 20 40 60 80 MI.
0 20 40 60 80 KM.
Provincial Capital
International Boundaries
Provincial Boundaries
© C.S. HAMMOND & Co., N.Y.
ALBERTA
NORTHERN PART
N.W. TERRITORIES
WOOD BUFFALO
NATIONAL PARK
CARIBOU MTS.
BUFFALO HEAD HILLS
BIRCH MOUNTAINS
Fort Smith
Fitzgerald
Fort Chipewyan
Lake Athabasca
Fort Vermilion
High Level
Steen River
Meander River
Keg River
Peace River
Hay L.
Zama L.
Rainbow Lake
Bitumount
BR. COL.
SASK.
Longitude West of Greenwich
120° 118° 116° 114° 112° 110°
56° 54° 52° 50°
BRITISH COLUMBIA
SASKATCHEWAN
MONTANA
Fort McMurray
THICKWOOD HILLS
Athabasca
Peace River
Dawson Creek
Grande Prairie
High Prairie
Lesser Slave Lake
Valleyview
Edson
Hinton
Jasper
JASPER NATIONAL PARK
BANFF NATIONAL PARK
WILLMORE WILDERNESS PROVINCIAL PARK
Mt. Robson 12,972
Mt. Columbia 12,294
Mt. Alberta 11,874
EDMONTON
St. Albert
Lac La Biche
Cold L.
Bonnyville
St. Paul
Vegreville
Vermilion
Lloydminster
Wainwright
Camrose
Wetaskiwin
Ponoka
Lacombe
Red Deer
Stettler
Rocky Mountain House
Olds
Drumheller
Hanna
CALGARY
Banff
Canmore
High River
Brooks
Medicine Hat
Lethbridge
Fort Macleod
Cardston
Taber
Coleman
Blairmore
Pincher Cr.
Claresholm
Vulcan
Nanton
PORCUPINE HILLS
LIVINGSTONE RA.
CYPRESS HILLS
Elkwater
CYPRESS HILLS PROV. PARK
WATERTON LAKES NAT'L PARK
WATERTON-GLACIER INTERNATIONAL PEACE PARK
GLACIER NAT'L PARK
Oldman R.
Bow R.
Red Deer R.
Saskatchewan R.
Athabasca R.
Smoky R.
Wapiti R.
Milk River
South Saskatchewan R.

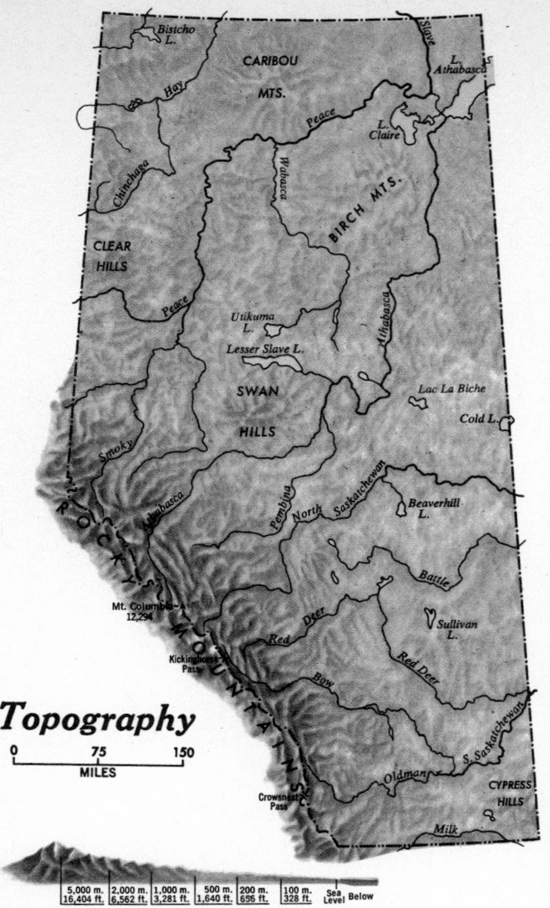

AREA 255,285 sq. mi.
POPULATION 1,614,000
CAPITAL Edmonton
LARGEST CITY Edmonton
HIGHEST POINT Mt. Columbia 12,294 ft.
SETTLED IN 1861
ADMITTED TO CONFEDERATION 1905
PROVINCIAL FLOWER Wild Rose

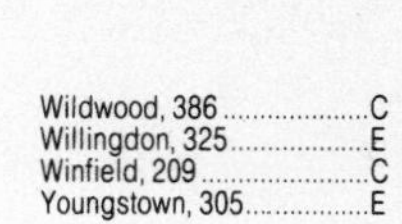

CITIES and TOWNS

Acadia Valley, 166 E 4
Acme, 300 D 4
Aerial, 151 D 4
Airdrie, 1,089 C 4
Alberta Beach, 320 C 3
Alder Flats, 133 C 3
Alix, 565 D 3
Alliance, 230 E 3
Amisk, 134 E 3
Andrew, 466 D 3
Anzac, 114 E 1
Ardmore, 230 E 2
Ardrossan, 137 D 3
Arrowwood, 166 D 4
Ashmont, 150 E 2
Athabasca, 1,765 D 2
Atikameg, 117 C 2
Banff, 3,219 C 4
Barnwell, 341 D 5
Barons, 237 D 4
Barrhead, 2,803 C 2
Bashaw, 757 D 3
Bassano, 861 D 4
Bawlf, 182 D 3
Beaumont, 337 D 3
Beaverlodge, 1,157 A 2
Beiseker, 414 D 4
Bellevue, 1,242 C 5
Bentley, 621 C 3
Berwyn, 474 B 1
Big Valley, 306 D 3
Black Diamond, 945 C 4
Blackfalds, 904 D 3
Blackfoot, 175 E 3
Blackie, 168 D 4
Blairmore, 2,037 C 5
Blue Ridge, 239 C 2
Bluesky, 124 A 1
Bon Accord, 332 D 3
Bonnyville, 2,587 E 2
Bowden, 560 C 4
Bow Island, 1,159 E 5
Boyle, 460 D 2
Bragg Creek, 203 C 4
Breton, 352 C 3
Brooks, 3,986 E 4
Brownvale, 161 B 1
Bruce, 110 E 3
Bruderheim, 350 D 3
Brûlé, 104 B 3
Buck Lake, 159 C 3
Burdett, 206 E 5
Cadomin, 109 B 3
Cadotte Lake, 192 B 1
Calgary, 403,319 C 4
Calgary, ‡403,319 C 4
Calmar, 799 D 3
Camrose, 8,673 D 3
Canmore, 1,538 C 4
Canyon Creek, 205 C 2
Carbon, 343 D 4
Carbondale, 115 D 3
Cardston, 2,685 D 5
Carmangay, 230 D 4
Caroline, 339 C 3
Carseland, 105 D 4
Carstairs, 884 D 4
Caslan, 117 D 2
Castor, 1,166 D 3
Cayley, 122 D 4
Cereal, 220 E 4
Champion, 335 D 4
Chateh, 400 A 5
Chauvin, 349 E 3
Chipewyan Lake, 118 D 1
Chipman, 181 D 3
Clairmont, 309 A 2
Clandonald, 119 E 3
Claresholm, 2,935 D 4
Clive, 247 D 3
Clyde, 233 D 2
Coaldale, 2,798 D 5
Coalhurst, 426 D 5
Cochrane, 1,046 C 4
Cold Lake, 1,309 E 2
Coleman, 1,534 C 5
Colinton, 125 D 2
College Heights, 331 D 3
Conklin, 119 E 2
Consort, 659 E 3
Cooking Lake, 196 D 3
Coronation, 877 E 3
Coutts, 407 D 5
Cowley, 201 D 5
Cremona, 186 C 4
Crossfield, 638 C 4
Czar, 196 E 3
Daysland, 593 D 3
Delburne, 383 D 3
Delia, 241 D 4
Derwent, 203 E 3
Desmarais, 258 D 2
Devon, 1,468 D 3
Dewberry, 160 E 3
Didsbury, 1,821 C 4
Dixonville, 113 B 1
Donalda, 232 D 3
Donnelly, 274 B 2
Drayton Valley, 3,900 C 3
Drumheller, 5,446 D 4
Duchess, 228 E 4
Eaglesham, 218 B 2
East Coulée, 312 D 4
Eckville, 660 C 3
Edberg, 145 D 3
Edgerton, 296 E 3
Edmonton (cap.), 438,152 D 3
Edmonton, ‡495,702 D 3
Edmonton Beach, 148 C 3
Edson, 3,818 B 3
Elk Point, 729 E 3
Elnora, 213 D 3
Empress, 266 E 4
Enilda, 201 B 2
Entwistle, 353 C 3
Erskine, 233 D 3
Evansburg, 528 C 3
Exshaw, 548 C 4
Fairview, 2,109 A 1
Falher, 918 B 2
Faust, 353 C 2
Fawcett, 141 C 2
Ferintosh, 127 D 3
Foremost, 568 E 5
Forestburg, 669 E 3
Fort Assiniboine, 173 C 2
Fort Chipewyan, 1,122 C 5
Fort Kent, 113 E 2
Fort Macleod, 2,715 D 5
Fort McKay, 200 E 1
Fort McMurray, 6,847 E 1
Fort Saskatchewan, 5,726 D 3
Fort Vermilion, 740 B 5
Fox Creek, 1,281 B 2
Frank, 224 C 5
Galahad, 179 E 3
Garden River, 134 B 5
Gibbons, 551 D 3
Gift Lake, 379 C 2
Girouxville, 347 B 2
Gleichen, 367 D 4
Glendon, 354 E 2
Glenwood, 200 D 5
Grand Centre, 2,088 E 2
Grande Cache, 2,525 A 3
Grande Prairie, 13,079 A 2
Granum, 324 D 5
Grassy Lake, 196 E 5
Grimshaw, 1,714 B 1
Grouard Mission, 277 C 2
Halkirk, 136 D 3
Hanna, 2,545 E 4
Hardieville, 473 D 5
Hardisty, 594 E 3
Hay Lakes, 211 D 3
Heisler, 199 D 3
High Level, 1,614 A 5
High Prairie, 2,354 B 2
High River, 2,676 D 4
Hillcrest, 613 C 5
Hill Spring, 213 D 5
Hines Creek, 438 A 1
Hinton, 4,911 B 3
Holden, 448 D 3
Hughenden, 267 E 3
Hussar, 170 D 4
Hythe, 487 A 2
Imperial Mills, 118 E 2
Innisfail, 2,474 D 3
Innisfree, 252 E 3
Irma, 423 E 3
Irricana, 139 D 4
Irvine, 194 E 5
Jarvie, 104 D 2
Jasper, 2,932 B 3
Joussard, 269 B 2
Kikino, 202 D 2
Killam, 851 E 3
Kinuso, 267 C 2
Kitscoty, 320 E 3
Lac La Biche, 1,791 E 2
Lacombe, 3,436 D 3
Lake Louise, 165 B 4
Lamont, 899 D 3
Langdon, 109 D 4
Lavoy, 114 E 3
Leduc, 4,000 D 3
Legal, 563 D 3
Leslieville, 159 C 3
Lethbridge, 41,217 D 5
Linden, 226 D 4
Little Buffalo Lake, 165 B 1
Lloydminster, 4,738 E 3
Lodgepole, 144 C 3
Lomond, 165 D 4
Longview, 189 C 4
Loon Lake, 135 C 1
Lougheed, 217 E 3
Lundbreck, 113 C 5
Magrath, 1,215 D 5
Mallaig, 190 E 2
Manning, 1,071 B 1
Mannville, 646 E 3
Marlboro, 156 B 3
Marwayne, 351 E 3
Mayerthorpe, 1,036 C 3
McLennan, 1,090 B 2
Meander River, 233 A 5
Medicine Hat, 26,518 E 4
Midlandvale, 392 D 4
Milk River, 775 D 5
Millet, 456 D 3
Milo, 117 D 4
Minburn, 106 E 3
Mirror, 365 D 3
Monarch, 102 D 5
Morinville, 1,475 D 3
Morrin, 197 D 4
Mulhurst, 139 D 3
Mundare, 511 D 3
Myrnam, 403 E 3
Nacmine, 350 D 4
Nampa, 283 B 1
Nanton, 991 D 4
Newbrook, 154 D 2
New Norway, 200 D 3
New Sarepta, 202 D 3
Nobleford, 401 D 5
North Calling Lake, 103 D 2
Okotoks, 1,247 C 4
Olds, 3,376 D 4
Onoway, 496 C 3
Oyen, 929 E 4
Paradise Valley, 144 E 3
Peace River, 5,039 B 1
Peerless Lake, 134 C 1
Peers, 129 B 3
Penhold, 452 D 3
Pibroch, 112 D 2
Picardville, 130 D 2
Picture Butte, 1,008 D 5
Pincher Creek, 3,227 D 5
Plamondon, 189 D 2
Pollockville, 29 E 4
Ponoka, 4,414 D 3
Provost, 1,489 E 3
Radway, 170 D 2
Rainbow Lake, 355 A 5
Ralston, 475 E 4
Ranfurly, 110 E 3
Raymond, 2,156 D 5
Redcliff, 2,255 E 4
Red Deer, 27,674 D 3
Redwater, 1,287 D 3
Rimbey, 1,450 C 3
Robb, 256 B 3
Rochester, 111 D 2
Rockyford, 286 D 4
Rocky Mountain House, 2,968 C 3
Rolling Hills, 127 E 4
Rosalind, 203 D 3
Rosemary, 208 E 4
Rycroft, 461 A 2
Ryley, 428 D 3
Saint Albert, 11,800 D 3
Saint Paul, 4,161 E 3
Sangudo, 360 C 3
Seba Beach, 165 C 3
Sedgewick, 730 E 3
Seebe, 108 C 4
Sexsmith, 559 A 2
Shaughnessy, 323 D 5
Sherwood Park, 14,282 D 3
Slave Lake, 2,052 C 2
Smith, 445 D 2
Smoky Lake, 881 D 2
Spirit River, 1,091 A 2
Spruce Grove, 3,029 D 3
Spruce View, 104 C 3
Standard, 267 D 4
Stavely, 351 D 4
Stettler, 4,168 D 3
Stirling, 436 D 5
Stony Plain, 1,770 C 3
Strathmore, 1,148 D 4
Strome, 226 E 3
Sundre, 933 C 4
Swan Hills, 1,376 C 2
Sylvan Lake, 1,597 C 3
Taber, 4,765 E 5
Thorhild, 509 D 2
Thorsby, 595 C 3
Three Hills, 1,354 D 4
Tilley, 270 E 4
Tofield, 924 D 3
Torrington, 118 D 4
Trochu, 739 D 4
Trout Lake, 162 C 1
Turin, 102 D 5
Turner Valley, 766 C 4
Two Hills, 979 E 3
Valleyview, 1,708 B 2
Vauxhall, 1,016 D 4
Vegreville, 3,691 E 3
Vermilion, 2,915 E 3
Veteran, 267 E 3
Viking, 1,178 E 3
Vilna, 303 E 2
Vulcan, 1,384 D 4
Wabamun, 336 C 3
Wabasca, 172 D 2
Wainwright, 3,872 E 3
Wanham, 268 A 2
Warburg, 464 C 3
Warner, 408 D 5
Warspite, 110 D 2
Waskatenau, 233 D 2
Waterton Park, 236 D 5
Wembley, 348 A 2
Westlock, 3,246 C 2
Westward Ho, 104 C 4
Wetaskiwin, 6,267 D 3
Whitecourt, 3,202 C 2
Whitelaw, 192 A 1
Widewater, 126 C 2
Wildwood, 386 C 3
Willingdon, 325 E 3
Winfield, 209 C 3
Youngstown, 305 E 4

OTHER FEATURES

Alberta (mt.) B 3
Assiniboine (mt.) C 4
Athabasca (lake) C 5
Athabasca (riv.) D 1
Banff Nat'l Park, 3,532 B 4
Battle (riv.) D 3
Beaverhill (lake) D 3
Belly (riv.) D 5
Berry (creek) E 4
Biche (lake) E 2
Big Bend (res.) C 3
Bighorn (range) B 3
Birch (hills) A 2
Birch (lake) E 3
Birch (mts.) B 5
Bow (riv.) D 4
Boyer (riv.) A 5
Brazeau (mt.) B 3
Brazeau (riv.) B 3
Buffalo (lake) D 3
Buffalo Head (hills) B 5
Cadotte (riv.) B 1
Calling (lake) D 2
Caribou (mts.) B 5
Chinchaga (riv.) A 5
Chip (lake) C 3
Chipewyan (riv.) D 1
Christina (riv.) E 1
Claire (lake) B 5
Clear (hills) A 1
Clearwater (riv.) C 4
Clearwater (riv.) E 1
Cold (lake) E 2
Columbia (mt.) B 3
Crowsnest (pass) C 5
Cypress (hills) E 5
Cypress Hills Prov. Park E 5
Eisenhower (mt.) C 4
Elbow (riv.) C 4
Elk Island Nat'l Park, 46 D 3
Etzikom Coulee (riv.) E 5
Firebag (riv.) E 1
Forbes (mt.) B 4
Frog (lake) E 3
Gordon (lake) E 1
Gough (lake) D 3
Graham (lake) C 1
Gull (lake) C 3
Hawk (hills) B 1
Hay (riv.) A 5
Highwood (riv.) C 4
Iosegun (lake) B 2
Jasper Nat'l Park, 3,064 A 3
Kickinghorse (pass) B 4
Kimiwan (lake) B 2
Kitchener (mt.) B 3
Lesser Slave (lake) C 2
Little Bow (riv.) D 4
Little Smoky (riv.) B 2
Livingstone (range) C 4
Lyell (mt.) B 4
Maligne (lake) B 3
McGregor (lake) D 4
McLeod (riv.) B 3
Milk (riv.) D 5
Muriel (lake) E 2
Muskwa (riv.) C 1
North Saskatchewan (riv.) E 3
North Wabasca (lake) D 1
Notikewin (riv.) A 1
Oldman (riv.) D 5
Pakowki (lake) E 5
Peace (riv.) B 1
Peerless (lake) C 1
Pelican (mts.) D 2
Pembina (riv.) C 3
Pigeon (lake) D 3
Porcupine (hills) C 4
Red Deer (riv.) D 4
Rocky (mts.) C 4
Rosebud (riv.) D 4
Sainte Anne (lake) C 3
Saint Mary (riv.) D 5
Saulteaux (riv.) C 2
Slave (riv.) C 5
Smoky (riv.) A 2
Sounding (creek) E 4
South Saskatchewan (riv.) E 4
South Wabasca (lake) D 2
Spray (mts.) C 4
Sullivan (lake) D 3
Swan (hills) C 2
Temple (mt.) B 4
The Twins (mt.) B 3
Thickwood (hills) D 1
Utikuma (lake) C 2
Vermilion (riv.) E 3
Wabasca (riv.) C 1
Waterton-Glacier Int'l Peace Park, 259 C 5
Waterton Lakes Nat'l Park, 259 C 5
Whitemud (riv.) A 1
Willmore Wilderness Prov. Park A 3
Winagami (lake) B 2
Winefred (lake) E 2
Wood Buffalo Nat'l Park, 186 B 5
Yellowhead (pass) A 3

‡ Population of metropolitan area.

Agriculture, Industry and Resources

DOMINANT LAND USE

- Wheat
- Cereals (chiefly barley, oats)
- Cereals, Livestock
- Dairy
- Pasture Livestock
- Range Livestock
- Forests
- Nonagricultural Land

MAJOR MINERAL OCCURRENCES

- C Coal
- G Natural Gas
- Na Salt
- O Petroleum
- S Sulfur

Water Power
 Major Industrial Areas

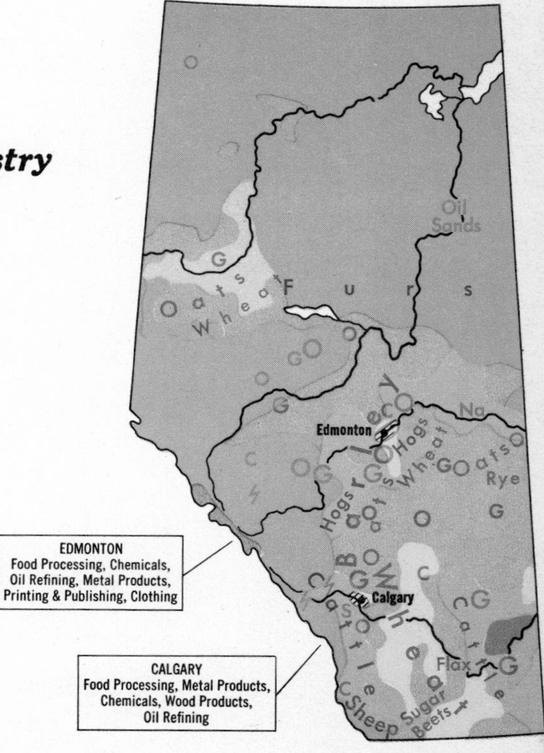

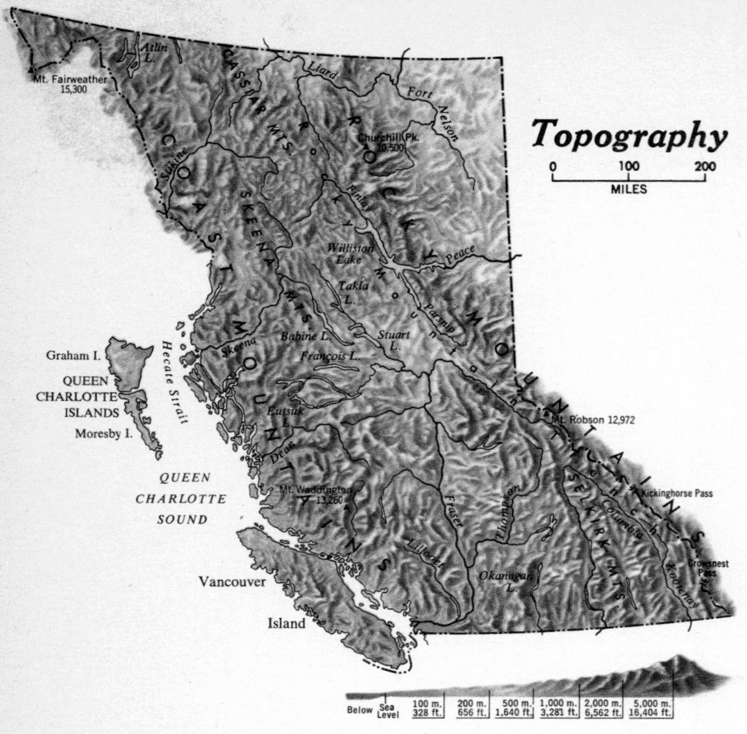

CITIES and TOWNS

Abbotsford, 706 L 3
Albert Head, 330 J 4
Alert Bay, 760 D 5
Alexandria, 168 F 4
Armstrong, 1,648 H 5
Ashcroft, 1,916 G 5
Ashton Creek, 318 H 5
Athalmer, 255 K 5
Atlin, 258 J 1
Avola, 265 H 4
Balfour, 195 J 5
Barrière, 829 H 4
Bear Lake, 302 F 3
Beaverdell, 241 H 5
Bella Coola, 273 D 4
Big Eddy, 654 H 4
Birch Island, 219 H 4
Blue River, 475 H 4
Boston Bar, 548 G 5
Bowen Island, 351 K 3
Bowser, 169 H 2
Brackendale, 692 F 5
Bralorne, 379 F 5
Britannia Beach, 738 K 2
Brouse, 446 J 5
Burnaby, •125,660 K 3
Burns Lake, 1,259 D 3
Cache Creek, 1,013 G 5
Campbell River, •10,000 E 5
Campbell River, 9,770 E 5
Canal Flats, 902 K 5
Cassiar, 1,073 K 2
Castlegar, 3,072 J 5
Cawston, 642 H 5
Caycuse, 297 J 3
Cedarside, 218 H 4
Celista, 178 H 5
Central Saanich, •5,136 K 3
Charlie Lake, 214 G 2
Chase, 1,212 H 5
Chase River, 728 J 3
Chemainus, 2,129 J 3
Cherry Creek, 449 G 5
Cherryville, 284 H 5
Chetwynd, 1,260 G 2
Chilliwack, 9,135 M 3
Chilliwhack, •23,739 M 3
Clearbrook, 3,653 L 3
Clearwater, 513 G 4
Clinton, 905 G 4
Coal Harbour, 334 D 5
Cobble Hill, 280 K 3
Coldstream, •3,602 H 5
Comox, 3,980 H 2
Coquitlam, •53,073 K 3
Courtenay, 7,152 E 5
Cranbrook, 12,000 K 5
Crawford Bay, 244 J 5
Creston, 3,204 J 5
Crofton, 972 J 3
Cultus Lake, 554 M 3
Cumberland, 1,718 E 5
Dawson Creek, 11,885 G 2
Delta, •45,860 K 3
Departure Bay, 3,744 J 3
Donald, 235 J 4
Duncan, 4,388 J 3
East Kelowna, 826 H 5
Eddontenajon, 180 K 2
Edgewater, 346 J 5
Elko, 196 K 5
Endako, 242 E 3
Enderby, 1,158 H 5
Errington, 464 J 3
Esquimalt, •12,922 K 4
Extension, 181 J 3
Falkland, 375 H 5
Fernie, 4,422 K 5
Field, 358 J 4
Flood, 295 M 3
Forest Grove, 238 G 4
Fort Fraser, 385 E 3
Fort Langley, 1,342 L 3
Fort Nelson, 2,289 M 2
Fort Saint James, 1,483 E 3
Fort Saint John, 8,264 G 2
Franklin River, 187 H 3
Fraser Lake, 1,292 E 3
Fraser Mills, •157 K 3
Fruitvale, 1,379 J 5
Gabriola Island, 655 J 3
Galiano Island, 412 K 3
Ganges, 333 K 3
Gibsons, 1,934 K 3
Gillies Bay, 543 H 2
Giscome, 416 F 3
Golden, 3,012 J 4
Gold River, 1,896 D 5
Grand Forks, 3,173 H 6
Granisle, 451 D 3
Granthams Landing, 404 J 3
Greenwood, 868 H 5
Grindrod, 283 H 5
Hagensborg, 315 D 4
Haney, 3,221 L 3
Harrison Hot Springs, 598 M 3
Hatzic, 547 L 3
Hazelton, 351 D 2
Hedley, 385 G 5
Heffley Creek, 503 G 5
Hendrix Lake, 341 G 4
Heriot Bay, 187 E 5
Hixon, 385 F 3
Holberg, 333 C 5
Honeymoon Bay, 546 J 3
Hope, 3,153 M 3
Houston, •2,232 D 3
Houston, 905 D 3
Hudson Hope, 1,116 F 2
Hudson's Hope, •1,741 F 2
Huntingdon, 202 L 3
Invermere, 1,065 J 5
Ioco, 308 K 3
Jaffray, 193 K 5
Kaleden, 640 H 5
Kamloops, 26,168 G 5
Kaslo, 755 J 5
Kelly Lake, 231 G 4
Kelowna, 19,412 H 5
Kemano, 346 D 3
Kent, •2,966 M 3
Keremeos, 605 G 5
Kimberley, 7,641 K 5
Kinnaird, 2,846 J 5
Kitimat, 11,824 C 3
Kitsault, 343 C 2
Kitwanga, 217 D 2
Kokish, 222 D 5
Lac La Hache, 417 G 4
Ladysmith, 3,664 J 3
Lake Cowichan, 2,364 J 3
Lang Bay, 285 E 5
Langley, •21,936 L 3
Langley, 4,684 L 3
Lantzville, 565 J 3
Lillooet, 1,514 G 5
Lion's Bay, 396 K 3
Lone Butte, 206 G 4
Louis Creek, 289 H 4
Lower Nicola, 361 G 5
Lower Post, 206 K 1
Lumby, 940 H 5
Lytton, 494 G 5
Mackenzie, •2,332 F 2
Mackenzie, 1,976 F 2
Madeira Park, 351 J 2
Maple Bay, 509 K 3
Maple Ridge, •24,476 L 3
Masset, 975 B 3
Matsqui, •23,554 L 3
Mayne Island, 293 K 3
McBride, 658 G 3
McConnell Creek, 233 D 2
McLure, 193 H 4
Merritt, 5,289 G 5
Merville, 227 E 5
Mesachie Lake, 266 J 3
Metchosin, 540 K 4
Mica Creek, 772 H 4
Midway, 502 H 6
Mill Bay, 347 C 2
Milnes Landing, 254 J 4
Mission, •10,220 L 3
Mission City, 3,649 L 3
Moberly, 175 J 4
Monte Lake, 176 G 5
Montrose, 1,137 J 5
Nakusp, 1,163 J 5
Nanaimo, 14,948 J 3
Naramata, 461 H 5
Nelson, 9,400 J 5
New Denver, 644 J 5
New Hazelton, 475 D 2
New Westminster, 42,835 K 3
Nicholson, 619 J 4
Nicomen Island, 527 L 3
Nootka, 2 D 5
North Bend, 424 G 5
North Cowichan, •12,170 J 3
North Pender Island, 407 K 3
North Saanich, •3,601 K 3
North Vancouver, •57,861 K 3
North Vancouver, 31,847 K 3
Nukko Lake, 182 F 3
Oak Bay, •18,426 K 4
Ocean Falls, 1,085 D 4
Okanagan Centre, 266 H 5
Okanagan Falls, 621 H 5
Okanagan Landing, 656 H 5
Okanagan Mission, 857 H 5
Old Barkerville, 3 G 3
Oliver, 1,615 H 5
One Hundred Mile House, 1,120 G 4
Osoyoos, 1,285 H 5
Oyama, 326 H 5
Parksville, 2,169 J 3
Parson, 306 J 4
Peachland, •1,446 G 5
Penticton, 18,146 H 5
Pine Valley, 264 F 2
Pitt Meadows, •2,771 L 3
Popkum, 286 M 3
Port Alberni, 20,063 H 3
Port Alice, 1,507 D 5
Port Clements, 406 B 3
Port Coquitlam, 19,560 L 3
Port Edward, 1,019 B 3
Port Hammond, 1,556 L 3
Port Hardy, •1,761 D 5
Port McNeill, 934 D 5
Port Moody, 10,778 L 3
Port Renfrew, 362 J 3
Pouce-Coupé, 595 G 2
Powell River, •13,726 E 5
Prince George, 33,101 F 3
Prince Rupert, 15,747 B 3
Princeton, 2,601 G 5
Procter, 183 J 5
Qualicum Beach, 1,245 J 3
Queen Charlotte, 665 A 3
Quesnel, 6,252 F 4
Radium Hot Springs, 393 J 5
Rayleigh, 652 G 5
Revelstoke, 4,867 J 5
Richmond, •62,121 K 3
Riondel, 572 J 5
Robson, 1,046 J 5
Rossland, 3,896 H 6
Royston, 532 H 2
Rutland, 3,279 H 5
Saanich, •65,040 K 3
Salmo, 872 J 5
Salmon Arm, •7,793 H 5
Salmon Arm, 1,981 H 5
Saltair, 1,008 J 3
Sandspit, 459 B 3
Sardis, 1,194 M 3
Saseenos, 574 J 3
Saturna Island, 174 K 3
Savona, 670 G 5
Sayward, 465 D 5
Sechelt, 590 J 2
Seventy Mile House, 225 G 4
Shawnigan Lake, 213 J 3
Shoreacres, 345 J 5
Sicamous, 814 H 5
Sidney, 4,868 K 3
Silverton, 246 J 5
Slocan, 346 J 5
Slocan Park, 360 J 5
Smithers, 3,864 D 3
Sointula, 575 D 5
Sooke, 836 J 4
Sorrento, 269 H 5
South Fort George, 1,282 F 3
South Hazelton, 483 D 2
South Slocan, 278 J 5
South Wellington, 460 J 3
Sparwood, •2,990 K 5
Sparwood, 2,154 K 5
Spences Bridge, 199 G 5
Sproat Lake, 321 H 3
Squamish, •6,121 F 5
Squamish, 1,597 F 5
Stewart, •1,357 C 2
Stoner, 182 F 3
Summerland, •5,551 G 5
Surrey, •98,601 K 3
Tahsis, 1,351 D 5
Tasu, 331 A 4
Taylor, 605 G 2
Telkwa, 712 D 3
Terrace, •9,991 C 3
Terrace, 7,820 C 3
Thrums, 365 J 5
Tofino, 461 E 5
Trail, 11,149 J 6
Ucluelet, 1,018 E 6
Union Bay, 407 H 2
Upper Fraser, 339 G 3
Valemount, 693 H 4
Valleyview, 3,787 G 5
Vananda, 497 E 5
Vancouver, 426,256 K 3
Vancouver, ‡1,082,352 K 3
Vancouver (Greater), •1,028,334 K 3
Vanderhoof, 1,653 E 3
Vavenby, 331 H 4
Vernon, 13,283 H 5
Victoria (cap.), 61,761 K 4
Victoria, ‡195,800 K 4
Warfield, 2,132 J 5
Wasa, 355 K 5
Wells, 409 G 3
Westbank, 747 H 5
West Vancouver, •36,440 K 3
Westwold, 434 G 5
White Rock, 10,349 K 3
Williams Lake, 4,072 F 4
Willow River, 422 F 3
Wilmer, 200 J 5
Wilson Creek, 408 J 2
Windermere, 421 K 5
Winfield, 875 H 5
Winlaw, 383 J 5
Woodfibre, 408 K 2
Woss Lake, 394 D 5
Wynndel, 579 J 5
Yahk, 192 J 5
Yale, 224 M 2
Yarrow, 1,039 M 3
Ymir, 292 J 5
Youbou, 1,109 J 3
Zeballos, 186 D 5

OTHER FEATURES

Adams (riv.) H 4
Alberni (inlet) H 3
Alsek (riv.) H 1

Agriculture, Industry and Resources

KITIMAT
Aluminum

VANCOUVER-VICTORIA
Wood Products, Food Processing, Iron & Steel, Metal Products, Printing & Publishing, Shipbuilding, Oil Refining

DOMINANT LAND USE

- Cereals, Livestock
- Dairy
- Fruits, Vegetables
- Pasture Livestock
- Forests
- Nonagricultural Land

MAJOR MINERAL OCCURRENCES

Ab	Asbestos	Gp	Gypsum
Ag	Silver	Mo	Molybdenum
Au	Gold	Ni	Nickel
C	Coal	O	Petroleum
Cu	Copper	Pb	Lead
Fe	Iron Ore	S	Sulfur
G	Natural Gas	Sn	Tin
		Zn	Zinc

- Water Power
- Major Industrial Areas
- Major Pulp & Paper Mills

AREA 366,255 sq. mi.
POPULATION 2,161,000
CAPITAL Victoria
LARGEST CITY Vancouver
HIGHEST POINT Mt. Fairweather 15,300 ft.
SETTLED IN 1806
ADMITTED TO CONFEDERATION 1871
PROVINCIAL FLOWER Dogwood

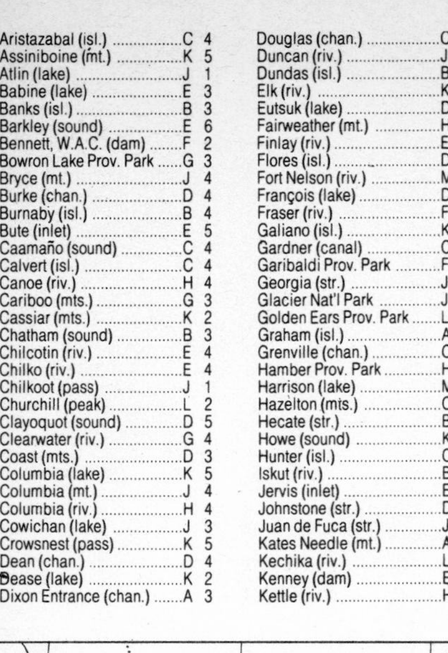

Aristazabal (isl.) ....C 4
Assiniboine (mt.) ....K 5
Atlin (lake) ....J 1
Babine (lake) ....E 3
Banks (isl.) ....B 3
Barkley (sound) ....E 6
Bennett, W.A.C. (dam) ....F 2
Bowron Lake Prov. Park ....G 3
Bryce (mt.) ....J 4
Burke (chan.) ....D 4
Burnaby (isl.) ....B 4
Bute (inlet) ....E 5
Caamaño (sound) ....C 4
Calvert (isl.) ....C 4
Canoe (riv.) ....H 4
Cariboo (mts.) ....G 3
Cassiar (mts.) ....K 2
Chatham (sound) ....B 3
Chilcotin (riv.) ....E 4
Chilko (riv.) ....E 4
Chilkoot (pass) ....J 1
Churchill (peak) ....L 2
Clayoquot (sound) ....D 5
Clearwater (riv.) ....G 4
Coast (mts.) ....D 3
Columbia (lake) ....K 5
Columbia (mt.) ....J 4
Columbia (riv.) ....H 4
Cowichan (lake) ....J 3
Crowsnest (pass) ....K 5
Dean (chan.) ....D 4
Dease (lake) ....K 2
Dixon Entrance (chan.) ....A 3
Douglas (chan.) ....C 3
Duncan (riv.) ....J 5
Dundas (isl.) ....B 3
Elk (riv.) ....K 5
Eutsuk (lake) ....D 3
Fairweather (mt.) ....H 1
Finlay (riv.) ....E 1
Flores (isl.) ....D 5
Fort Nelson (riv.) ....M 2
François (lake) ....D 3
Fraser (riv.) ....F 4
Galiano (isl.) ....K 3
Gardner (canal) ....C 3
Garibaldi Prov. Park ....F 5
Georgia (str.) ....J 3
Glacier Nat'l Park ....J 4
Golden Ears Prov. Park ....L 2
Graham (isl.) ....A 3
Grenville (chan.) ....C 3
Hamber Prov. Park ....H 4
Harrison (lake) ....M 2
Hazelton (mts.) ....C 2
Hecate (str.) ....B 3
Howe (sound) ....K 2
Hunter (isl.) ....C 4
Iskut (riv.) ....B 2
Jervis (inlet) ....E 5
Johnstone (str.) ....D 5
Juan de Fuca (str.) ....J 4
Kates Needle (mt.) ....A 1
Kechika (riv.) ....L 2
Kenney (dam) ....E 3
Kettle (riv.) ....H 5
Kickinghorse (pass) ....J 4
King (isl.) ....D 4
Klinaklini (riv.) ....E 4
Knight (inlet) ....E 5
Knox (cape) ....A 3
Kokanee Glacier Prov. Park ....J 5
Koocanusa (lake) ....K 6
Kootenay (lake) ....J 5
Kootenay (riv.) ....K 5
Kootenay Nat'l Park ....J 4
Kunghit (isl.) ....B 4
Kyuquot (sound) ....D 5
Langara (isl.) ....A 3
Liard (riv.) ....L 2
Lillooet (riv.) ....F 5
Lower Arrow (lake) ....H 5
Malaspina (str.) ....J 2
Manning Prov. Park, 23 ....G 5
Masset (inlet) ....A 3
Milbanke (sound) ....C 4
Monashee (mts.) ....H 4
Moresby (isl.) ....B 4
Morice (riv.) ....D 3
Mount Assiniboine Prov. Park ....K 5
Mount Edziza Prov. Park and Rec. Area ....B 1
Mount Revelstoke Nat'l Park ....H 4
Mount Robson Prov. Park ....H 3
Muncho Lake Prov. Park ....L 2
Muskwa (riv.) ....M 2
Nanika (dam) ....D 3
Nass (riv.) ....C 2
Nechako (riv.) ....E 3
Nootka (isl.) ....D 5
Nootka (sound) ....D 5
North Thompson (riv.) ....G 4
Observatory (inlet) ....C 2
Okanagan (lake) ....H 5
Okanogan (riv.) ....H 6
Omineca (mts.) ....E 2
Ootsa (lake) ....D 3
Pacific Rim Nat'l Park ....E 6
Parsnip (riv.) ....F 3
Peace (riv.) ....G 2
Pine (riv.) ....G 2
Pitt (isl.) ....C 3
Pitt (lake) ....L 2
Porcher (isl.) ....B 3
Portland (canal) ....B 2
Portland (inlet) ....C 3
Princess Royal (isl.) ....C 3
Principe (chan.) ....C 3
Prophet (riv.) ....M 2
Purcell (mts.) ....J 5
Quatsino (sound) ....C 5
Queen Charlotte (isls.), 2,390 ....B 3
Queen Charlotte (sound) ....C 4
Queen Charlotte (str.) ....D 5
Quesnel (lake) ....G 4
Rivers (inlet) ....D 4
Robson (mt.) ....H 3
Rocky (mts.) ....F 2
Rose (pt.) ....B 3
Saint James (cape) ....B 4
Salmon (riv.) ....F 3
Scott (cape) ....C 5
Seechelt (inlet) ....J 2
Seechelt (pen.) ....J 2
Selkirk (mts.) ....J 4
Seymour (inlet) ....D 4
Shuswap (lake) ....H 4
Sikanni Chief (riv.) ....F 1
Sir Sandford (mt.) ....H 4
Skeena (mts.) ....C 2
Skeena (riv.) ....C 3
Skidegate (inlet) ....B 3
Slocan (lake) ....J 5
Smith (sound) ....C 4
Stave (lake) ....L 3
Stikine (riv.) ....B 1
Stone Mountain Prov. Park ....L 2
Strathcona Prov. Park ....E 5
Stuart (lake) ....E 3
Tagish (lake) ....J 1
Tahtsa (lake) ....D 3
Takla (lake) ....D 2
Taku (riv.) ....J 2
Teslin (lake) ....K 1
Tetachuck (lake) ....E 3
Texada (isl.) ....J 2
Thompson (riv.) ....G 5
Tiedemann (mt.) ....E 4
Tweedsmuir Prov. Park ....D 3
Upper Arrow (lake) ....H 5
Valdes (isl.) ....K 3
Vancouver (isl.), 381,297 ....D 5
Waddington (mt.) ....E 4
Wells Gray Prov. Park ....H 4
Whitesail (lake) ....D 3
Williston (lake) ....F 2
Work (chan.) ....C 3
Yellowhead (pass) ....H 4
Yoho Nat'l Park ....J 4

‡ Population of metropolitan area.
• Population of municipality.

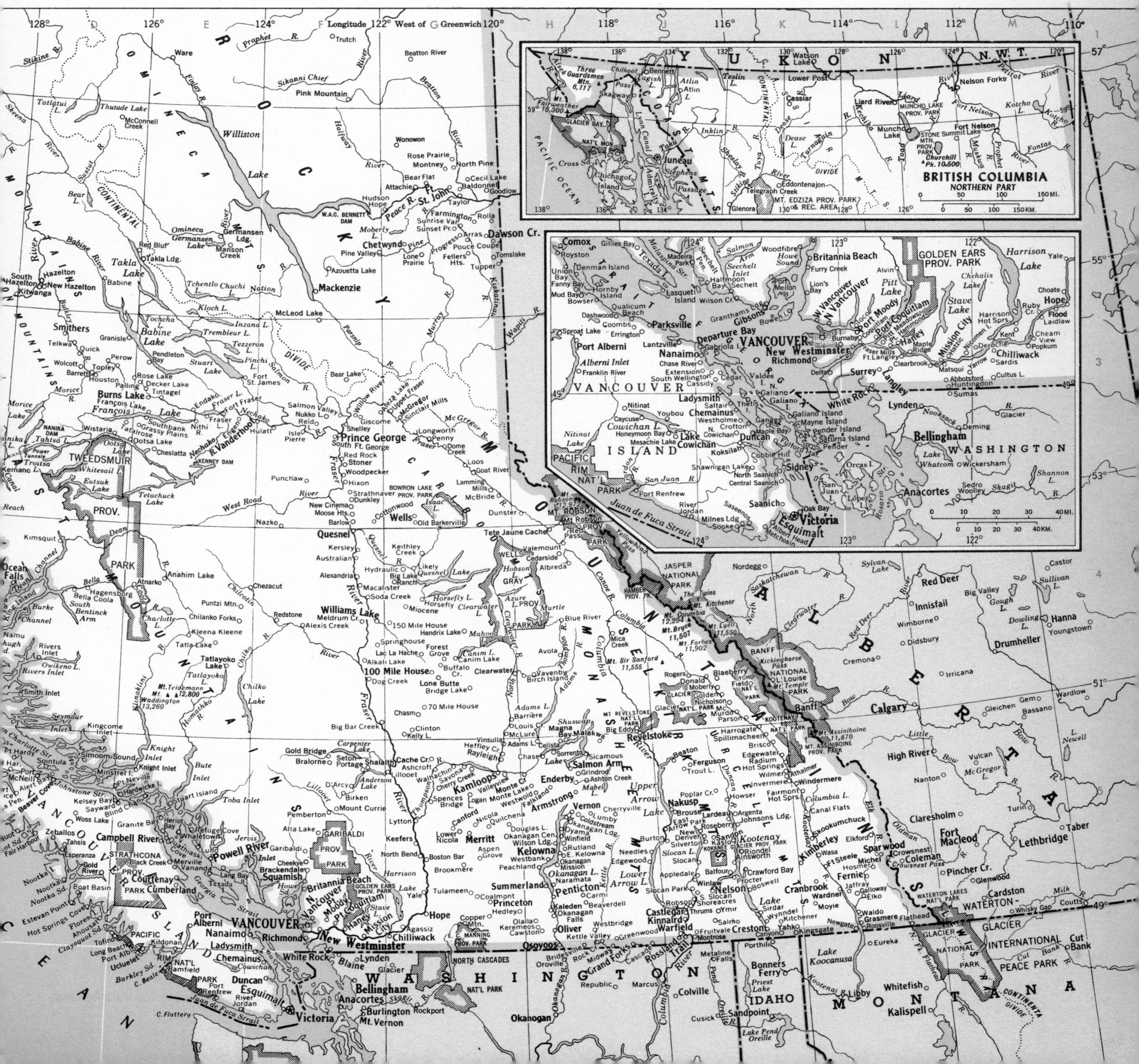

NORTHWEST TERRITORIES

DISTRICTS

Franklin, 7,747 ..... K 2
Keewatin, 3,403 ..... J 3
Mackenzie, 23,657 ..... G 3

CITIES and TOWNS

Aklavik, 677 ..... E 3
Alert, 15 ..... M 1
Amadjuak, 5 ..... L 3
Arctic Bay, 269 ..... K 2
Arctic Red River, 108 ..... E 3
Aston Bay, 8 ..... J 2
Baker Lake, 756 ..... J 3
Bell Rock, 1 ..... G 3
Broughton Island, 334 ..... M 3
Buffalo River Junction, 3 ..... G 3
Cambridge Bay, 716 ..... H 3
Cape Dorset, 597 ..... L 3
Cape Dyer, 10 ..... M 3
Cape Smith, 147 ..... L 3
Chesterfield Inlet, 258 ..... K 3
Clyde, 274 ..... M 2
Colville Lake, 65 ..... F 3
Coppermine, 637 ..... G 3
Coral Harbour, 355 ..... K 3
Dory Point, 17 ..... G 3
Enterprise, 56 ..... G 3
Eskimo Point, 598 ..... J 3
Eureka, 10 ..... K 2
Fort Franklin, 339 ..... F 3
Fort Good Hope, 327 ..... F 3
Fort Liard, 263 ..... F 3
Fort McPherson, 679 ..... E 3
Fort Norman, 248 ..... F 3
Fort Providence, 587 ..... G 3
Fort Resolution, 623 ..... G 3
Fort Simpson, 747 ..... F 3
Fort Smith, 2,364 ..... G 4
Frobisher Bay, 2,014 ..... M 3
Gjoa Haven, 276 ..... J 3
Grise Fiord, 109 ..... K 2
Hall Beach, 263 ..... K 3
Hay River, 2,406 ..... G 3
Hislop Lake, 4 ..... G 3
Holman Island, 241 ..... G 2
Igloolik, 563 ..... K 3
Inuvik, 2,669 ..... E 3
Isachsen, 2 ..... H 2
Jean-Marie River, 47 ..... F 3
Kakisa, 42 ..... G 3
Kipisa, 33 ..... M 3
Lac la Martre, 161 ..... G 3
Lake Harbour, 189 ..... L 3
Marian Lake, 29 ..... G 3
Mary River, 10 ..... L 2
Mould Bay, 6 ..... F 2
Nahanni Butte, 66 ..... F 3
Norman Wells, 301 ..... F 3
Pangnirtung, 690 ..... M 3
Paulatuk, 95 ..... F 3
Pelly Bay, 215 ..... K 3
Pine Point, 1,225 ..... G 3
Pond Inlet, 416 ..... L 2
Port Burwell, 107 ..... M 3
Port Radium, 99 ..... G 3
Rae-Edzo, 1,081 ..... G 3
Rae Lake, 73 ..... G 3
Rankin Inlet, 566 ..... J 3
Repulse Bay, 242 ..... K 3
Resolute Bay, 184 ..... J 2
Resolution Island, 8 ..... M 3
Rocher River, 4 ..... G 3
Sachs Harbour, 143 ..... F 2
Salt River, 2 ..... G 3
Sawmill Bay, 10 ..... G 3
Snare Lake, 9 ..... G 3
Snowdrift, 221 ..... G 3
Spence Bay, 209 ..... J 3
Trout Lake, 48 ..... F 3
Tuktoyaktuk, 596 ..... E 3
Tungsten, 130 ..... F 3
Twin Gorges, 5 ..... G 3
Whale Cove, 213 ..... J 3
Wrigley, 152 ..... F 3
Yellowknife (cap.), 6,122 ..... G 3

OTHER FEATURES

Adelaide (pen.) ..... J 3
Admiralty (inlet) ..... K 2
Air Force (isl.) ..... L 3
Akpatok (isl.) ..... M 3
Amadjuak (lake) ..... L 3
Amund Ringnes (isl.) ..... J 2
Amundsen (gulf) ..... F 2
Arctic Red (riv.) ..... E 3
Artillery (lake) ..... H 3
Axel Heiberg (isl.) ..... J 2
Aylmer (lake) ..... H 3
Back (riv.) ..... J 3
Baffin (bay) ..... M 2
Baffin (isl.) ..... L 2
Baffin Island Nat'l Park ..... M 3
Baker (lake) ..... J 3
Banks (isl.) ..... F 2
Barbeau (peak) ..... L 1
Barrow (str.) ..... J 2
Bathurst (cape) ..... F 2
Bathurst (inlet) ..... H 3
Bathurst (isl.) ..... H 2
Beaufort (sea) ..... D 2
Boothia (gulf) ..... K 3
Boothia (pen.) ..... J 2
Borden (isl.) ..... G 2
Borden (pen.) ..... K 2
Brodeur (pen.) ..... K 2
Bruce (mts.) ..... L 2
Buchan (gulf) ..... L 2
Burnside (riv.) ..... G 3
Byam Martin (chan.) ..... H 2
Byam Martin (isl.) ..... H 2
Bylot (isl.) ..... L 2
Camsell (riv.) ..... G 3
Challenger (mts.) ..... L 1
Chantrey (inlet) ..... J 3
Chesterfield (inlet) ..... J 3
Chidley (cape) ..... M 3
Clinton-Colden (lake) ..... H 3
Clyde (inlet) ..... M 2
Coats (isl.) ..... K 3
Coburg (isl.) ..... L 2
Columbia (cape) ..... M 1
Colville (lake) ..... F 3
Committee (bay) ..... K 3
Contwoyto (lake) ..... H 3
Coppermine (riv.) ..... G 3
Cornwall (isl.) ..... J 2
Cornwallis (isl.) ..... J 2
Coronation (gulf) ..... G 3
Croker (bay) ..... K 2
Crown Prince Frederik (isl.) ..... K 3
Cumberland (pen.) ..... M 3
Cumberland (sound) ..... M 3
Davis (str.) ..... M 3
Dease (str.) ..... H 3
Denmark (bay) ..... H 2
Devon (isl.) ..... K 2
Dolphin and Union (str.) ..... G 3
Dubawnt (lake) ..... H 3
Dubawnt (riv.) ..... H 3
Dundas (pen.) ..... G 2
Dyer (cape) ..... M 3
Eclipse (sound) ..... L 2
Eglinton (isl.) ..... F 2
Ellef Ringnes (isl.) ..... H 2
Ellesmere (isl.) ..... K 2
Ennadai (lake) ..... H 3
Eskimo (lakes) ..... E 3
Eureka (sound) ..... K 2
Evans (str.) ..... K 3
Exeter (sound) ..... M 3
Fisher (str.) ..... K 3
Fosheim (pen.) ..... K 1
Foxe (basin) ..... L 3
Foxe (chan.) ..... K 3
Foxe (pen.) ..... L 3
Franklin (bay) ..... F 2
Franklin (mts.) ..... F 3
Franklin (str.) ..... J 2
Frobisher (bay) ..... M 3
Frozen (str.) ..... K 3
Fury and Hecla (str.) ..... K 3
Gabriel (str.) ..... M 3
Garry (lake) ..... H 3
Gods Mercy (bay) ..... K 3
Great Bear (lake) ..... F 3
Great Bear (riv.) ..... F 3
Great Slave (lake) ..... G 3
Greely (fjord) ..... K 1
Grinnell (pen.) ..... J 2
Hadley (bay) ..... H 2
Hall (basin) ..... M 1
Hall (pen.) ..... M 3
Hayes (riv.) ..... J 3
Hazen (lake) ..... L 1
Hazen (str.) ..... G 2
Henik (lakes) ..... J 3
Henry Kater (cape) ..... M 3
Home (bay) ..... M 3
Hood (riv.) ..... G 3
Horn (mts.) ..... G 3
Hornaday (riv.) ..... F 3
Horton (riv.) ..... F 3
Hottah (lake) ..... G 3
Hudson (bay) ..... K 3
Hudson (str.) ..... L 3
Isachsen (cape) ..... H 2
James Ross (str.) ..... J 3
Jenny Lind (isl.) ..... H 3
Jens Munk (isl.) ..... K 3
Jones (sound) ..... K 2
Kaminuriak (lake) ..... J 3
Kane (basin) ..... L 2
Kasba (lake) ..... H 3
Kazan (riv.) ..... H 3
Keele (riv.) ..... F 3
Keith Arm (inlet) ..... F 3
Kellett (cape) ..... F 2
Kellett (str.) ..... G 2
Kennedy (chan.) ..... M 1
Kent (pen.) ..... H 3
King Christian (isl.) ..... H 2
King William (isl.) ..... J 3
Lady Ann (str.) ..... K 2
La Martre (lake) ..... G 3
Lancaster (sound) ..... K 2
Lands End (cape) ..... F 2
Larsen (sound) ..... J 2
Liard (riv.) ..... F 4
Lincoln (sea) ..... M 1
Liverpool (bay) ..... E 2
Lockhart (riv.) ..... H 3
Lougheed (isl.) ..... H 2
Lyon (inlet) ..... K 3
MacKay (lake) ..... G 3
Mackenzie (bay) ..... E 3
Mackenzie (mts.) ..... E 3
Mackenzie (riv.) ..... F 3
Mackenzie King (isl.) ..... G 2
Macmillan (pass) ..... F 3
Maguse (lake) ..... J 3
Makinson (inlet) ..... L 2
Mansel (isl.) ..... K 3
Marian (lake) ..... G 3
Markham (inlet) ..... L 1
McLeod (bay) ..... G 3
M'Clintock (chan.) ..... H 2
M'Clure (str.) ..... G 2
McTavish Arm (inlet) ..... G 3
Meighen (isl.) ..... H 1
Melville (isl.) ..... G 2
Melville (pen.) ..... K 3
Mercy (cape) ..... M 3
Mills (lake) ..... G 3
Minto (inlet) ..... G 2
Mistake (bay) ..... J 3
Nahanni Nat'l Park ..... F 3
Nansen (sound) ..... J 1
Nares (str.) ..... L 2
Navy Board (inlet) ..... K 2
Nettilling (lake) ..... L 3
Nonacho (lake) ..... H 3
North Arm (inlet) ..... G 3
North Magnetic Pole ..... H 2
Norwegian (bay) ..... J 2
Nottingham (isl.) ..... L 3
Nueltin (lake) ..... H 3
Ommanney (bay) ..... H 2
Padloping (isl.) ..... M 3
Parry (bay) ..... K 3
Parry (chan.) ..... G 2
Parry (isls.) ..... G 2
Parry (pen.) ..... F 2
Peary (chan.) ..... H 2
Peel (sound) ..... J 2
Pelly (bay) ..... J 3
Penny (str.) ..... J 2
Point (lake) ..... G 3
Pond (inlet) ..... L 2

Topography

0 200 400
MILES

QUEEN ELIZABETH ISLANDS
Barbeau Peak 8,540 ft.
Axel Heiberg I.
Ellesmere Island
Pr. Patrick I.
Melville I.
Devon I.
Banks I.
Parry Channel
Somerset I.
Baffin Island
Amundsen Gulf
Victoria I.
Pr. of Wales I.
Boothia Pen.
Gulf of Boothia
Melville Pen.
Foxe Basin
Peel
Great Bear Lake
Mackenzie
MACKENZIE MTS.
Mt. Logan 19,850
Mt. Sir James MacBrien 9,062
Great Slave Lake
Barren Grounds
Back
Thelon
Southampton I.
Hudson Bay

5,000 m. 16,404 ft.	2,000 m. 6,562 ft.	1,000 m. 3,281 ft.	500 m. 1,640 ft.	200 m. 656 ft.	100 m. 328 ft.	Sea Level	Below

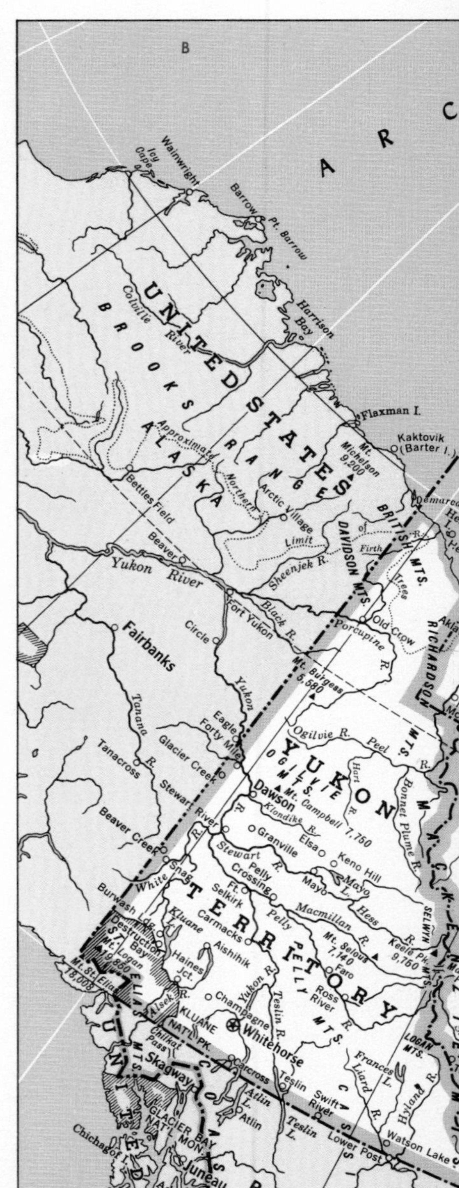

DOMINANT LAND USE

Forests

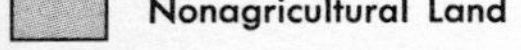
Nonagricultural Land

MAJOR MINERAL OCCURRENCES

Ab Asbestos
Ag Silver
Au Gold
C Coal
Cu Copper
Fe Iron Ore
O Petroleum
Pb Lead
Zn Zinc

Agriculture, Industry and Resources

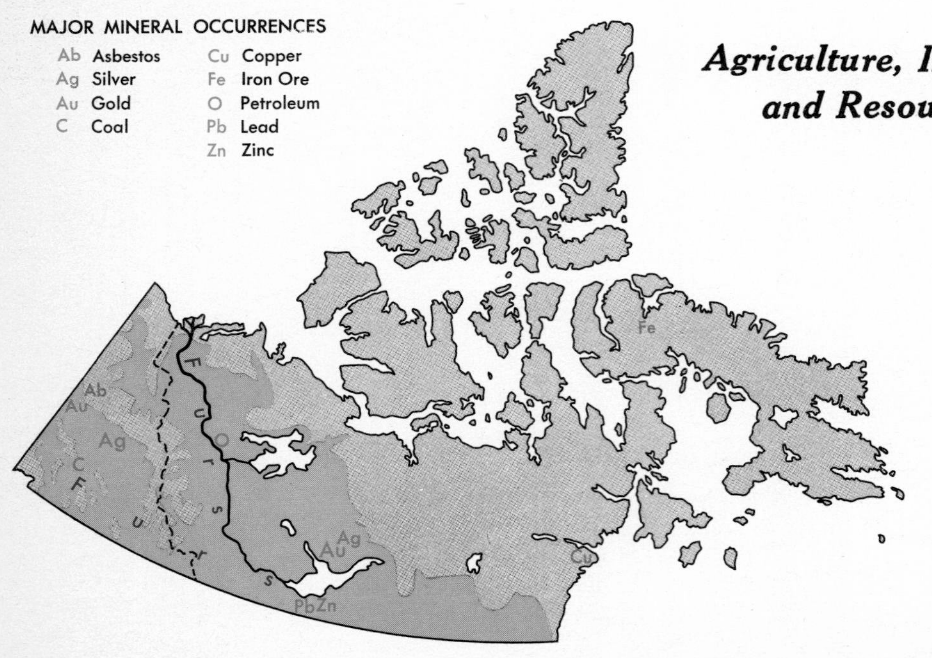

Prince Albert (pen.) ....G 2
Prince Albert (sound) ....G 2
Prince Charles (isl.) ....L 3
Prince Gustav Adolf (sea) ...H 2
Prince of Wales (isl.) ....J 2
Prince of Wales (str.) ....G 2
Prince Patrick (isl.) ....F 2
Prince Regent (inlet) ....J 2
Queen Elizabeth (isls.) ....H 1
Queen Maud (gulf) ....H 3
Queens (chan.) ....J 2
Raanes (pen.) ....K 2
Rae (isth.) ....K 3
Rae (riv.) ....G 3
Rae (str.) ....J 3
Ramparts (riv.) ....E 3
Resolution (isl.) ....M 3
Richard Collinson (inlet) ....G 2
Richards (isl.) ....E 3
Richardson (mts.) ....E 3
Robeson (chan.) ....M 1
Roes Welcome (sound) ......K 3
Royal Geographical Society (isls.) ....J 3
Russell (isl.) ....J 2
Sabine (pen.) ....H 2
Salisbury (isl.) ....L 3
Seahorse (pt.) ....L 3
Selwyn (lake) ....H 4
Sherman (inlet) ....J 3
Simpson (pen.) ....K 3
Sir James MacBrien (mt.) ...F 3
Slave (riv.) ....G 3
Smith (bay) ....L 2
Smith (cape) ....L 3
Smith (sound) ....L 2
Snare (riv.) ....G 3
Snowbird (lake) ....H 3
Somerset (isl.) ....J 2
South (bay) ....K 3
Southampton (isl.) ....K 3
South Nahanni (riv.) ....F 3
Stallworthy (cape) ....J 1
Steensby (inlet) ....L 2
Stefansson (isl.) ....H 2
Sverdrup (chan.) ....J 1
Sverdrup (isls.) ....J 2
Talbot (inlet) ....L 2
Taltson (riv.) ....G 3
Tathlina (lake) ....G 3
Tha-anne (riv.) ....J 3
Thelon (riv.) ....H 3
Thlewiaza (riv.) ....J 3
Trout (lake) ....F 3
Ungava (bay) ....M 4
Vansittart (isl.) ....K 3
Victoria (isl.) ....G 2
Victoria (str.) ....H 3
Viscount Melville (sound) ...G 2
Wager (bay) ....K 3
Wales (isl.) ....K 3
Walsingham (cape) ....M 3
Wellington (chan.) ....J 2
Wholdaia (lake) ....H 3
Winter (harb.) ....H 2
Wollaston (pen.) ....G 3
Wood Buffalo Nat'l Park ......G 3
Wynniatt (bay) ....G 2
Yathkyed (lake) ....J 3
Yellowknife (riv.) ....G 3

YUKON TERRITORY

AREA 207,076 sq. mi.
POPULATION 17,000
CAPITAL Whitehorse
LARGEST CITY Whitehorse
HIGHEST POINT Mt. Logan 19,850 ft.
SETTLED IN 1897
ADMITTED TO CONFEDERATION 1898
PROVINCIAL FLOWER Fireweed

NORTHWEST TERRITORIES

AREA 1,304,903 sq. mi.
POPULATION 34,000
CAPITAL Yellowknife
LARGEST CITY Yellowknife
HIGHEST POINT Barbeau Peak 8,540 ft.
SETTLED IN 1800
ADMITTED TO CONFEDERATION 1870
PROVINCIAL FLOWER Mountain Avens

YUKON

CITIES and TOWNS

Bear Creek, 4......................E 3
Beaver Creek, 120...............D 3
Burwash Landing, 67 ....D 3
Carcross, 188.......................E 3
Carmacks, 348......................E 3
Clinton Creek, 381...............D 3
Cowley, 11.............................E 3
Dawson, 762..........................E 3
Destruction Bay, 82..............E 3
Dominion, 12.........................E 3
Donjek, 11.............................D 3
Eagle River, 12......................E 3
Elsa, 298................................E 3
Faro, 863...............................E 3
Fort Selkirk, 3.......................E 3
Haines Junction, 179.............E 3
Herschel, 5............................E 3
Keno Hill, 79..........................E 3
Mayo, 462..............................E 3
McCabe Creek, 12 ....E 3
Old Crow, 206 ....E 3
Pelly Crossing, 141 ....E 3
Ross River, 317 ....E 3
Stewart Crossing, 43 ....E 3
Stewart River, 4 ....D 3
Swift River, 33.......................E 3
Tagish, 4................................E 3
Teslin, 340.............................E 3
Toobally Lake, 1 ....F 3
Tuchitua Lake, 17 ....E 3
Upper Liard, 219....................F 3
Watson Lake, 553..................F 3
Whitehorse (cap.), 11,217 ...E 3

OTHER FEATURES

Alsek (riv.) ....E 3
British (mts.) ....D 3
Cassiar (mts.) ....E 3
Frances (lake) ....E 3
Herschel (isl.) ....E 3
Hess (riv.) ....E 3
Hyland (riv.) ....F 3
Keele (peak) ....E 3
Klondike (riv.) ....E 3
Kluane (lake) ....E 3
Kluane Nat'l Park ....E 3
Logan (mt.) ....D 3
Mackenzie (bay) ....E 3
Mackenzie (mts.) ....E 3
Macmillan (riv.) ....E 3
Mayo (lake) ....E 3
Ogilvie (mts.) ....E 3
Peel (riv.) ....E 3
Pelly (mts.) ....E 3
Pelly (riv.) ....E 3
Porcupine (riv.) ....E 3
Richardson (mts.) ....E 3
Rocky (mts.) ....F 4
Saint Elias (mt.) ....D 3
Saint Elias (mts.) ....E 3
Selwyn (mts.) ....E 3
Stewart (riv.) ....E 3
Teslin (riv.) ....E 3
White (riv.) ....D 3
Yukon (riv.) ....E 3

YUKON AND NORTHWEST TERRITORIES

SCALE
0 50 100 200 300 MI.
0 50 100 200 300 KM.

Territorial Capitals
International Boundaries
Provincial & Territorial Boundaries
District Boundaries

All islands in Hudson and James Bays lie within the District of Keewatin.

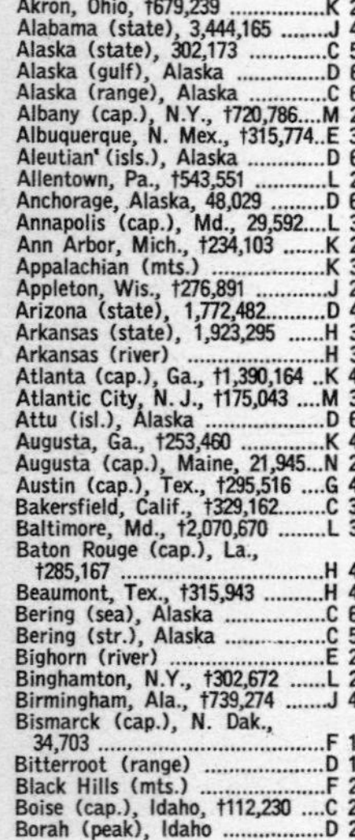

UNITED STATES

POLYCONIC PROJECTION

SCALE

0 50 100 200 300 400 MI.

0 50 100 200 300 400 KM.

Capitals of Countries ☆
State Capitals △
International Boundaries
State Boundaries

Akron, Ohio, †679,239 ... K 2
Alabama (state), 3,444,165 ... J 4
Alaska (state), 302,173 ... C 5
Alaska (gulf), Alaska ... D 6
Alaska (range), Alaska ... C 6
Albany (cap.), N.Y., †720,786 ... M 2
Albuquerque, N. Mex., †315,774 ... E 3
Aleutian (isls.), Alaska ... D 6
Allentown, Pa., †543,551 ... L 2
Anchorage, Alaska, 48,029 ... D 6
Annapolis (cap.), Md., 29,592 ... L 3
Ann Arbor, Mich., †234,103 ... K 2
Appalachian (mts.) ... K 3
Appleton, Wis., †276,891 ... J 2
Arizona (state), 1,772,482 ... D 4
Arkansas (state), 1,923,295 ... H 3
Arkansas (river) ... H 3
Atlanta (cap.), Ga., †1,390,164 ... K 4
Atlantic City, N. J., †175,043 ... M 3
Attu (isl.), Alaska ... D 6
Augusta, Ga., †253,460 ... K 4
Augusta (cap.), Maine, 21,945 ... N 2
Austin (cap.), Tex., †295,516 ... G 4
Bakersfield, Calif., †329,162 ... C 3
Baltimore, Md., †2,070,670 ... L 3
Baton Rouge (cap.), La., †285,167 ... H 4
Beaumont, Tex., †315,943 ... H 4
Bering (sea), Alaska ... C 6
Bering (str.), Alaska ... C 5
Bighorn (river) ... E 2
Binghamton, N.Y., †302,672 ... L 2
Birmingham, Ala., †739,274 ... J 4
Bismarck (cap.), N. Dak., 34,703 ... F 1
Bitterroot (range) ... D 1
Black Hills (mts.) ... F 2
Boise (cap.), Idaho, †112,230 ... C 2
Borah (peak), Idaho ... D 2
Boston (cap.), Mass., †2,753,700 M 2
Brazos (river), Tex. ... G 4
Bridgeport, Conn., †388,953 ... M 2
Brooks (range), Alaska ... C 5
Buffalo, N.Y., †1,349,211 ... L 2
California (state), 19,953,134 ... B 3
Canadian (river) ... F 3
Canaveral (Kennedy) (cape), Fla. ... L 5
Canton, Ohio, †372,210 ... K 2
Cape Fear (river), N.C. ... L 4
Carson City (cap.), Nev., 15,468 ... C 3
Cascade (range) ... B 1
Cedar Rapids, Iowa, †163,213 ... H 2
Champlain (lake) ... M 2
Charleston, S.C., †303,849 ... L 4
Charleston (cap.), W. Va., †229,515 ... K 3
Charlotte, N.C., †409,370 ... K 3
Chattahoochee (river) ... K 4
Chattanooga, Tenn., †304,927 ... J 3
Chesapeake (bay) ... L 3
Cheyenne (cap.), Wyo., 40,914 ... E 2
Cheyenne (river) ... F 2
Chicago, Ill., †6,978,947 ... J 2
Cimarron (river) ... G 3
Cincinnati, Ohio, †1,384,911 ... K 3
Cleveland, Ohio, †2,064,194 ... K 2
Coast (range) ... B 2
Cod (cape), Mass. ... N 2
Colorado (state), 2,207,259 ... E 3
Colorado (river) ... D 4
Colorado (river), Tex. ... G 4
Colorado Sprs., Colo., †235,972 ... F 3
Columbia (cap.), S.C., †322,880 ... K 4
Columbia (river) ... B 1
Columbus, Ga., †238,584 ... K 4
Columbus (cap.), Ohio, †916,228 ... K 3
Concord (cap.), N.H., 30,022 ... M 2
Connecticut (state), 3,032,217 ... M 2
Connecticut (river) ... M 2
Corpus Christi, Tex., †284,832 ... G 5
Cumberland (river) ... J 3
Dallas, Tex., †1,555,950 ... G 4
Davenport, Iowa, †362,638 ... H 2
Dayton, Ohio, †850,266 ... K 3
Death Valley (depr.), Calif. ... C 3
Delaware (state), 548,104 ... L 3
Delaware (bay) ... M 3
Denver (cap.), Colo., †1,227,529 ... F 3
Des Moines (cap.), Iowa, †286,101 ... H 2
Detroit, Mich., †4,199,931 ... K 2
District of Columbia, 756,510 ... L 3
Dover (cap.), Del., 17,488 ... L 3
Duluth, Minn., †265,350 ... H 1
Durham, N.C., †190,388 ... L 3
Elbert (mt.), Colo. ... E 3
El Paso, Tex., †359,291 ... E 4
Erie, Pa., †263,654 ... K 2
Erie (lake) ... K 2
Eugene, Oreg., †213,358 ... B 2
Evansville, Ind., †232,775 ... J 3
Everglades (swamp), Fla. ... K 5
Fayetteville, N.C., †212,042 ... L 3
Flint, Mich., †496,658 ... K 2
Florida (state), 6,789,443 ... K 5
Florida (keys), Fla. ... K 6
Ft. Smith, Ark., †160,421 ... H 3
Ft. Wayne, Ind., †280,455 ... J 2
Ft. Worth, Tex., †762,086 ... G 4
Frankfort (cap.), Ky., 21,356 ... K 3
Fresno, Calif., †413,053 ... C 3
Galveston, Tex., †169,812 ... H 5
Gary, Ind., †633,367 ... J 2
Georgia (state), 4,589,575 ... K 4
Gila (river) ... D 4
Glacier Nat'l Park, Mont. ... D 1
Golden Gate (chan.), Calif. ... B 3
Grand Canyon Nat'l Park, Ariz. ... D 3
Grand Rapids, Mich., †539,225 ... J 2
Great Salt (lake), Utah ... D 2
Greensboro, N.C., †603,895 ... K 3
Greenville, S.C., †299,502 ... K 4
Hamilton, Ohio, †226,207 ... K 3
Harrisburg (cap.), Pa., †410,626 ... L 2
Hartford (cap.), Conn., †663,891 ... M 2
Hatteras (cape), N.C. ... M 3
Havasu (lake) ... D 4
Hawaii (state), 769,913 ... F 6
Hawaii (isl.), Hawaii ... F 6
Helena (cap.), Mont., 22,730 ... D 1
Honolulu (cap.), Hawaii, †629,176 ... F 5
Houston, Tex., †1,985,031 ... G 5
Huntington, W. Va., †253,743 ... K 3
Huntsville, Ala., †228,239 ... J 4
Huron (lake), Mich. ... K 2
Idaho (state), 713,008 ... D 2
Illinois (state), 11,113,976 ... J 3
Indiana (state), 5,193,669 ... J 3
Indianapolis (cap.), Ind., †1,109,882 ... J 3
Iowa (state), 2,825,041 ... H 2
Jackson (cap.), Miss., †258,906 ... H 4
Jacksonville, Fla., †528,865 ... K 4
Jefferson City (cap.), Mo. 32,407 ... H 3
Jersey City, N. J., †609,266 ... M 2
Johnstown, Pa., †262,822 ... L 2
Juneau (cap.), Alaska, 13,556 ... E 6
Kalamazoo, Mich., †201,550 ... J 2
Kansas (state), 2,249,071 ... G 3
Kansas City, Kans.-Mo., †1,256,649 ... H 3
Kauai (isl.), Hawaii ... E 5
Kennedy (cape), Fla. ... L 5
Kentucky (state), 3,219,311 ... J 3
Kentucky (lake) ... J 3
Knoxville, Tenn., †400,337 ... K 3
Lancaster, Pa., †319,693 ... L 2
Lansing (cap.), Mich., †378,423 ... K 2
Las Vegas, Nev., †273,288 ... C 3
Lawrence, Mass., †232,395 ... M 2
Lexington, Ky., †174,323 ... K 3
Lima, Ohio, †171,472 ... K 2
Lincoln (cap.), Nebr., †167,972 ... G 2
Little Rock (cap.), Ark., †323.296 ... H 4
Long (isl.), N.Y. ... M 2
Long Beach, Calif., 358,633 ... C 4
Los Angeles, Calif., †7,032,075 ... C 4
Louisiana (state), 3,643,180 ... H 4
Louisville, Ky., †826,553 ... J 3
Lowell, Mass., †212,860 ... M 2
Lubbock, Tex., †179,295 ... F 4
Macon, Ga., †206,342 ... K 4
Madison (cap.), Wis., †290,272 ... H 2
Maine (state), 993,663 ... N 1
Maryland (state), 3,922,399 ... L 3
Massachusetts (state), 5,689,170 ... M 2
Maui (isl.), Hawaii ... F 5
Mauna Kea (mt.), Hawaii ... G 6
Mauna Loa (mt.), Hawaii ... G 6
May (cape), N. J. ... M 3
McKinley (mt.), Alaska ... D 5
Mead (lake) ... D 3
Memphis, Tenn., †770,120 ... J 3
Mendocino (cape), Calif. ... A 2
Mexico (gulf) ... J 5
Miami, Fla., †1,267,792 ... K 5
Michigan (state), 8,875,083 ... J 1
Michigan (lake) ... J 2
Milwaukee, Wis., †1,403,887 ... J 2
Minneapolis, Minn., †1,813,647 ... H 1
Minnesota (state), 3,805,069 ... H 1
Mississippi (state), 2,216,912 ... J 4
Mississippi (river) ... H 4
Missouri (state), 4,677,399 ... H 3
Missouri (river) ... H 3
Mitchell (mt.), N.C. ... K 3
Mobile, Ala., †376,690 ... J 4
Montana (state), 694,409 ... E 1
Montgomery (cap.), Ala., †201,325 ... J 4
Montpelier (cap.), Vt., 8,609 ... M 2
Nantucket (isl.), Mass. ... N 2
Nashville (cap.), Tenn., †540,982 J 3
Nebraska (state), 1,483,791 ... F 2
Nevada (state), 488,738 ... C 3
Newark, N. J., †1,856,556 ... M 2
New Hampshire (state), 737,681 ... M 2
New Haven, Conn., †355,538 ... M 2
New Jersey (state), 7,168,164 ... M 3
New Mexico (state), 1,016,000 ... E 4
New Orleans, La., †1,045,809 ... H 5
Newport News, Va., †292,159 ... L 3
New York (state), 18,190,740 ... L 2
New York, N.Y., †11,528,649 ... M 2
Norfolk, Va., †680,600 ... L 3
North Carolina (state), 5,082,059 ... L 3
North Dakota (state), 617,761 ... F 1
Oahu (isl.), Hawaii ... F 5
Oakland, Calif., 361,561 ... B 3
Ohio (state), 10,652,017 ... K 2
Ohio (river) ... J 3
Oklahoma (state), 2,559,253 ... G 3
Oklahoma City (cap.), Okla., †640,889 ... G 3
Olympia (cap.), Wash., 23,111 ... B 1
Olympic Nat'l Park, Wash. ... A 1
Omaha, Nebr., †541,453 ... G 2
Ontario (lake), N.Y. ... L 2
Oregon (state), 2,091,385 ... B 2
Orlando, Fla., †428,003 ... K 5
Ozark (mts.) ... H 3
Paterson, N. J., †1,358,794 ... M 2
Pennsylvania (state), 11,793,909 ... L 2
Pensacola, Fla., †243,075 ... J 4
Peoria, Ill., †341,979 ... J 2
Philadelphia, Pa., †4,817,914 ... M 2
Phoenix (cap.), Ariz., †968,487 ... D 4
Pierre (cap.), S. Dak., 9,699 ... F 2
Pikes (peak), Colo. ... E 3
Pittsburgh, Pa., †2,401,245 ... L 2
Platte (river), Nebr. ... G 2
Pontchartrain (lake), La. ... J 5
Portland, Maine, †141,625 ... N 2
Portland, Oreg., †1,009,129 ... B 1
Potomac (river) ... L 3
Providence (cap.), R.I., †914,110 ... M 2
Racine, Wis., †170,838 ... J 2
Rainier (mt.), Wash. ... B 1
Raleigh (cap.), N.C., †228,453 ... L 3
Reading, Pa., †296,382 ... L 2
Red (river) ... H 4
Red River of the North (river) ... G 1
Rhode Island (state), 949,723 ... M 2
Richmond (cap.), Va., †518,319 ... L 3
Rio Grande (river) ... F 5
Roanoke, Va., †181,436 ... K 3
Rochester, N.Y., †882,667 ... L 2
Rockford, Ill., †272,063 ... J 2
Rocky (mts.) ... E 3
Sacramento (cap.), Calif., †800,592 ... B 3
Saginaw, Mich., †219,743 ... K 2
Saint Clair (lake), Mich. ... K 2
Saint Lawrence (river), N.Y. ... N 1
Saint Louis, Mo., †2,363,017 ... H 3
Saint Paul (cap.), Minn., 309,980 ... H 1

AREA 3,615,123 sq. mi.
POPULATION 203,235,298
CAPITAL Washington
LARGEST CITY New York
HIGHEST POINT Mt. McKinley 20,320 ft.
MONETARY VALUE U.S. dollar
MAJOR LANGUAGE English
MAJOR RELIGIONS Protestantism, Roman Catholicism, Judaism

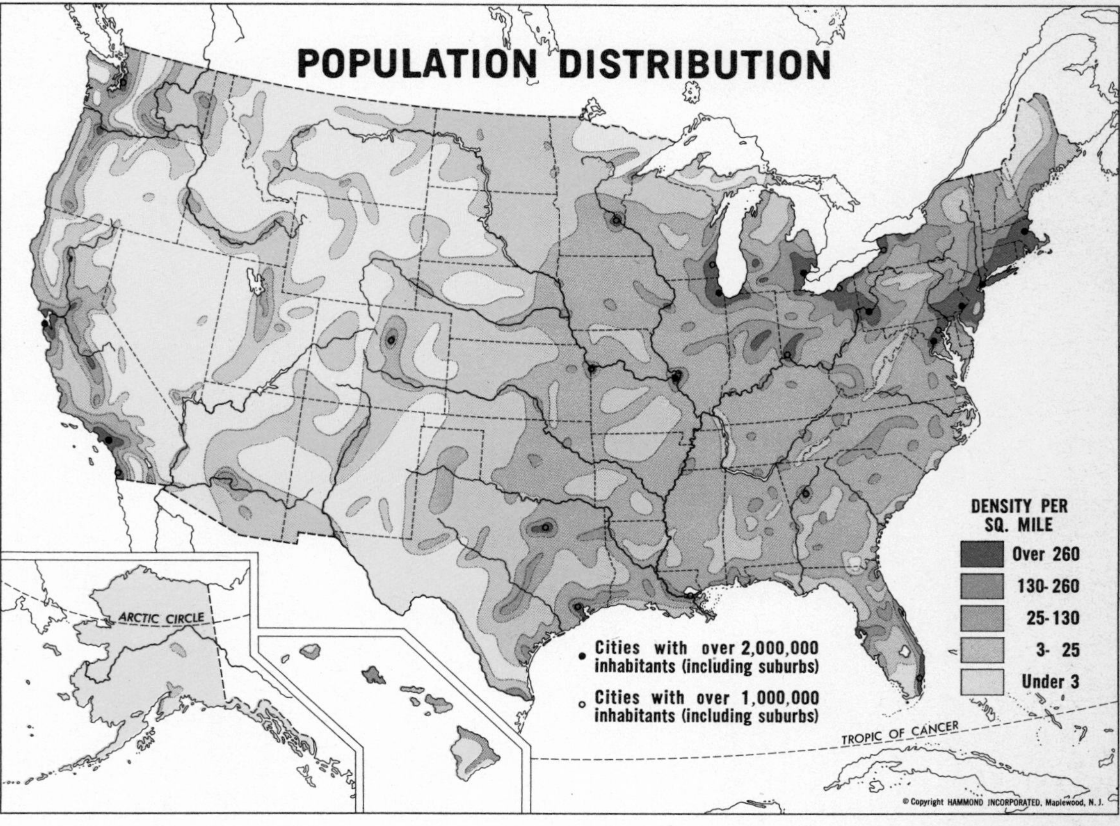

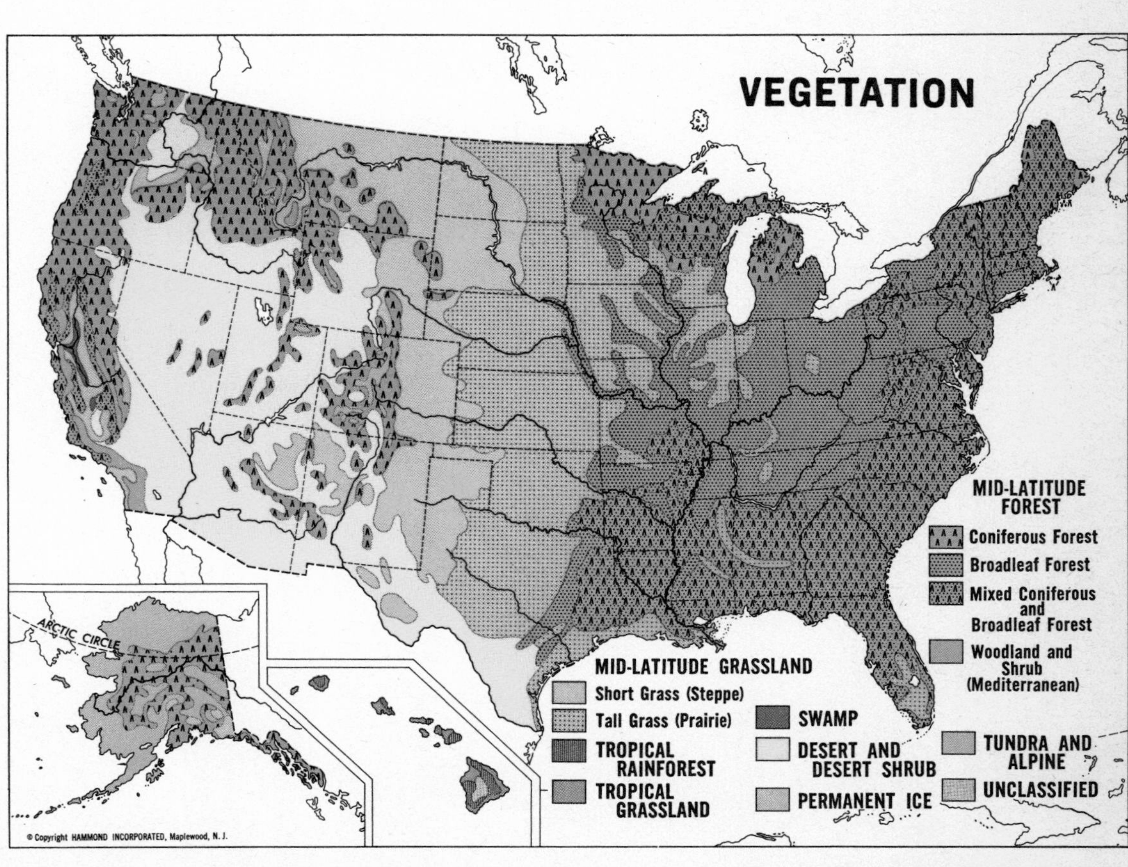

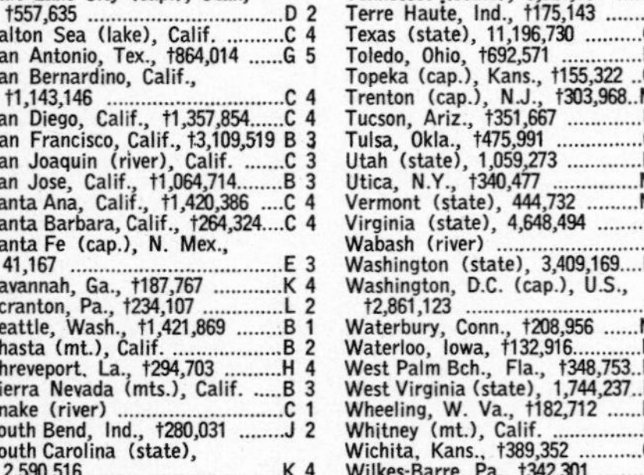

Sakakawea (lake), N. Dak. ....F 1
Salem (cap.), Oreg., 68,296........B 1
Salinas, Calif., †250,071 ....B 3
Salt Lake City (cap.), Utah, †557,635 ....D 2
Salton Sea (lake), Calif. ....C 4
San Antonio, Tex., †864,014 ......G 5
San Bernardino, Calif., †1,143,146 ....C 4
San Diego, Calif., †1,357,854......C 4
San Francisco, Calif., †3,109,519 B 3
San Joaquin (river), Calif. ....C 3
San Jose, Calif., †1,064,714........B 3
Santa Ana, Calif., †1,420,386 ....C 4
Santa Barbara, Calif., †264,324....C 4
Santa Fe (cap.), N. Mex., 41,167 ....E 3
Savannah, Ga., †187,767 ....K 4
Scranton, Pa., †234,107 ....L 2
Seattle, Wash., †1,421,869 ....B 1
Shasta (mt.), Calif. ....B 2
Shreveport, La., †294,703 ....H 4
Sierra Nevada (mts.), Calif. .....B 3
Snake (river) ....C 1
South Bend, Ind., †280,031 ....J 2
South Carolina (state), 2,590,516 ....K 4
South Dakota (state), 666,257 ....F 2
Spokane, Wash., †287,487 ....C 1
Springfield (cap.), Ill., †161,335..H 3
Springfield, Mass., †529,921 .....M 2
Springfield, Mo., †152,929 ....H 3
Springfield, Ohio, †157,115 ....K 2
Stockton, Calif., †290,208 .... B 3
Superior (lake) ....J 1
Syracuse, N.Y., †635,946 ....L 2
Tacoma, Wash., †411,027 ....B 1
Tahoe (lake) ....C 3
Tallahassee (cap.), Fla., †103,047 ....K 4
Tampa, Fla., †1,012,594 ....K 5
Tennessee (state), 3,924,164 .....J 3
Terre Haute, Ind., †175,143 ....J 3
Texas (state), 11,196,730 ....G 4
Toledo, Ohio, †692,571 ....K 2
Topeka (cap.), Kans., †155,322 ..G 3
Trenton (cap.), N.J., †303,968..M 2
Tucson, Ariz., †351,667 ....D 4
Tulsa, Okla., †475,991 ....G 3
Utah (state), 1,059,273 ....D 3
Utica, N.Y., †340,477 ....M 2
Vermont (state), 444,732 ....M 2
Virginia (state), 4,648,494 ....L 3
Wabash (river) ....J 3
Washington (state), 3,409,169....B 1
Washington, D.C. (cap.), U.S., †2,861,123 ....L 3
Waterbury, Conn., †208,956 ......M 2
Waterloo, Iowa, †132,916............H 2
West Palm Bch., Fla., †348,753..K 5
West Virginia (state), 1,744,237..K 3
Wheeling, W. Va., †182,712 ......K 2
Whitney (mt.), Calif. ....C 3
Wichita, Kans., †389,352 ....G 3
Wilkes-Barre, Pa., †342,301 ....L 2
Wilmington, Del., †498,977 ....L 3
Wisconsin (state), 4,417,933 .....H 2
Woods (lake), Minn. ....G 1
Worcester, Mass., †339,730 ....M 2
Wyoming (state), 332,416 ....E 2
Yellowstone Nat'l Park ....E 2
York, Pa., †329,540 ....L 3
Yosemite Nat'l Park, Calif. ......C 3
Youngstown, Ohio, †536,003........K 2
Yukon (river), Alaska ....C 5

†Population of metropolitan area.

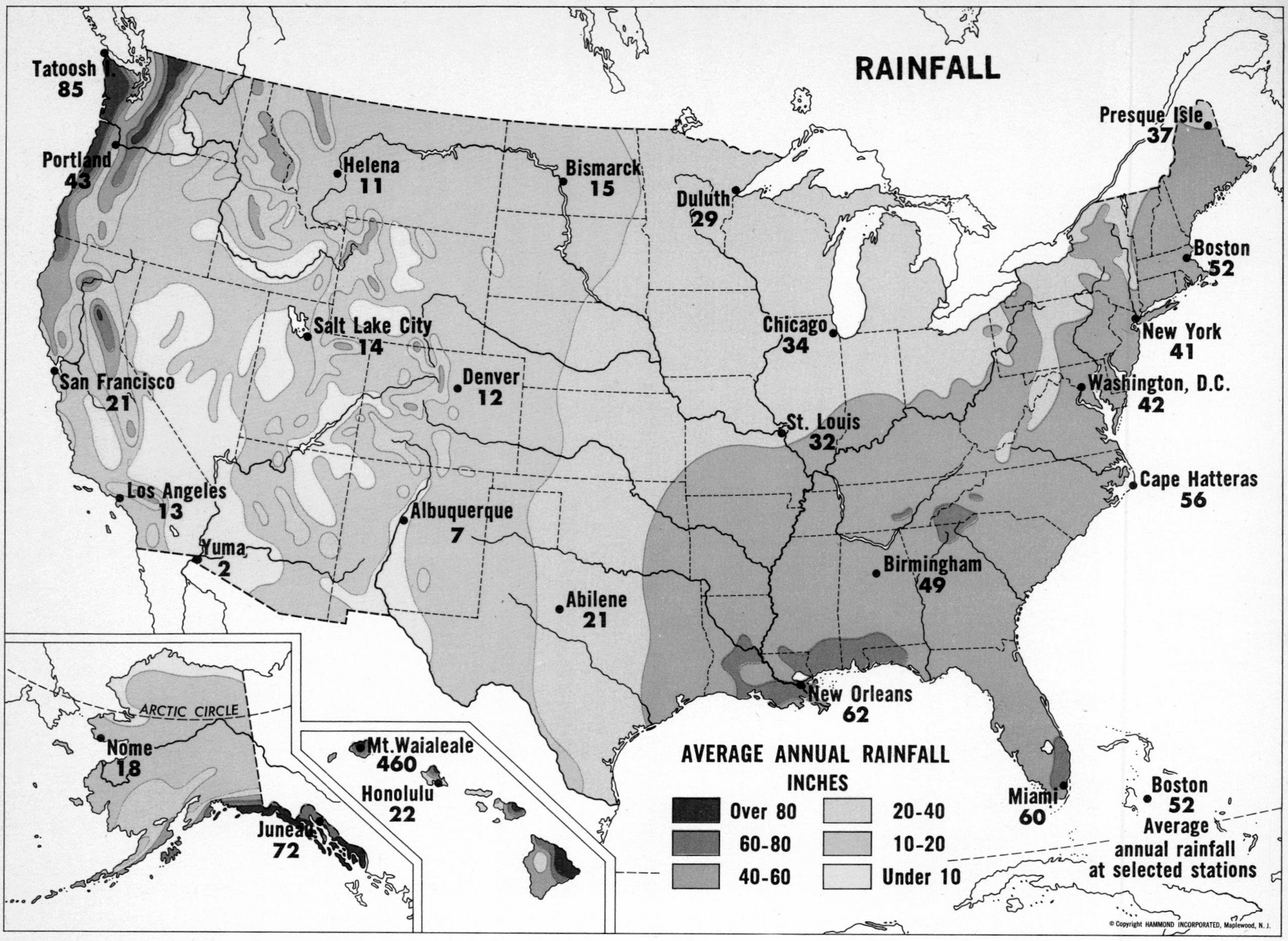

RAINFALL

Tatoosh 85
Portland 43
Helena 11
Bismarck 15
Duluth 29
Presque Isle 37
Boston 52
Salt Lake City 14
Chicago 34
New York 41
San Francisco 21
Denver 12
Washington, D.C. 42
St. Louis 32
Los Angeles 13
Cape Hatteras 56
Albuquerque 7
Yuma 2
Birmingham 49
Abilene 21
New Orleans 62
ARCTIC CIRCLE
Nome 18
Mt. Waialeale 460
Honolulu 22
Juneau 72
Miami 60

AVERAGE ANNUAL RAINFALL
INCHES

Over 80	20-40
60-80	10-20
40-60	Under 10

Boston 52
Average annual rainfall at selected stations

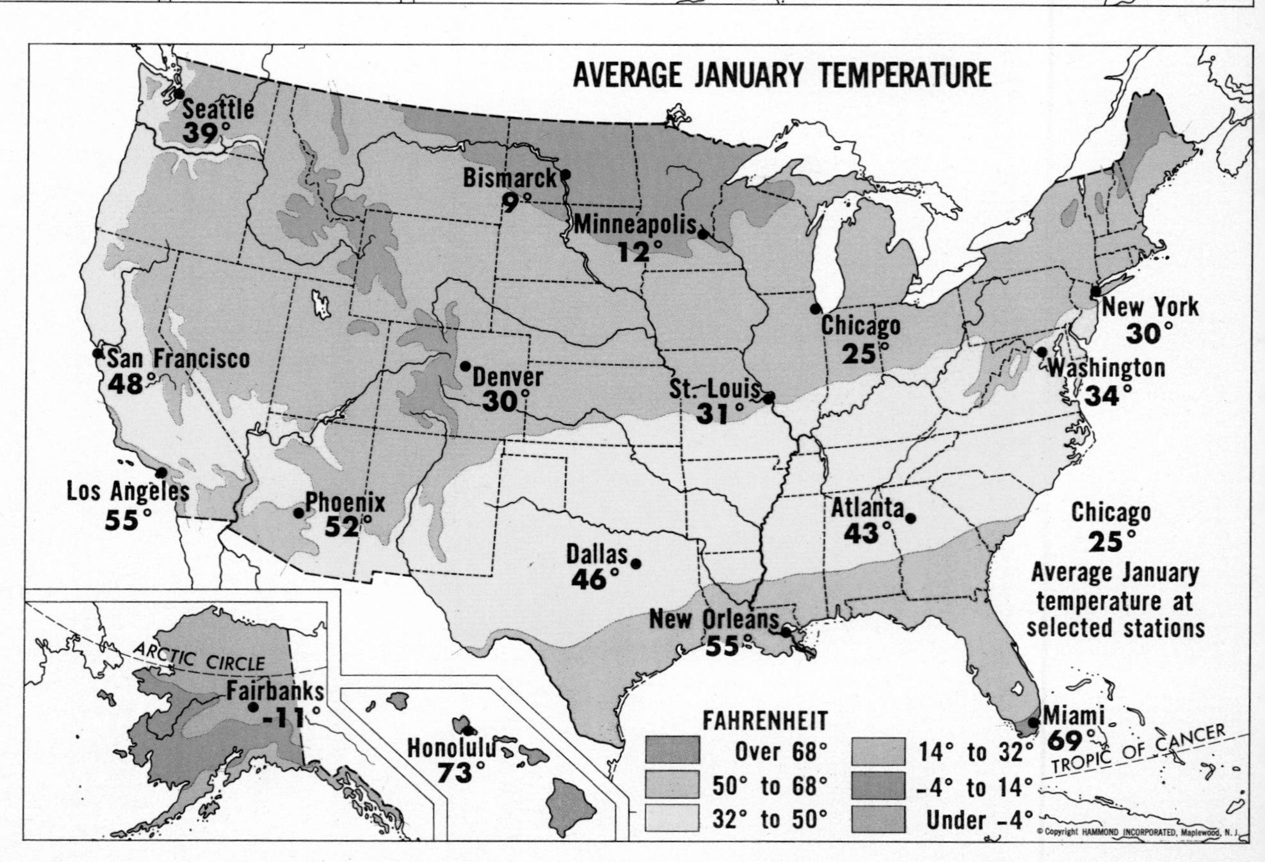

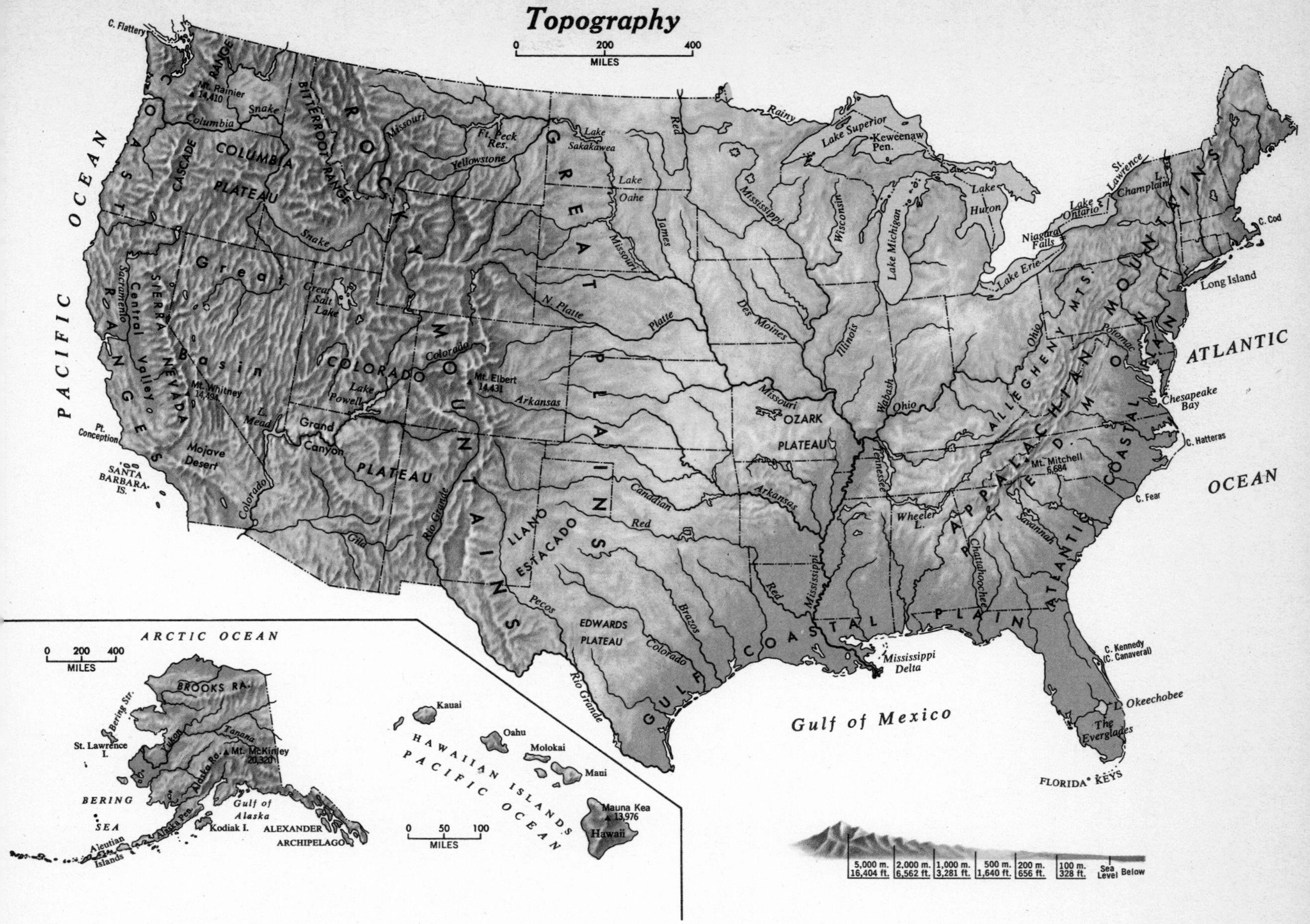

Topography
0 200 400
MILES
C. Flattery
Mt. Rainier 14,410
Snake
Columbia
COLUMBIA PLATEAU
CASCADE
BITTERROOT RANGE
ROCKY MOUNTAINS
Missouri
Ft. Peck Res.
Yellowstone
Lake Sakakawea
GREAT PLAINS
Lake Oahe
James
Red
Rainy
Lake Superior
Keweenaw Pen.
Mississippi
Wisconsin
Lake Michigan
Lake Huron
St. Lawrence
L. Champlain
Lake Ontario
Niagara Falls
Lake Erie
C. Cod
Long Island
PACIFIC OCEAN
COAST RANGES
Sacramento
Central Valley
SIERRA NEVADA
Great Basin
Great Salt Lake
Mt. Whitney 14,494
COLORADO PLATEAU
Colorado
Lake Powell
Mt. Elbert 14,431
N. Platte
Platte
Des Moines
Illinois
Wabash
Ohio
ALLEGHENY MTS.
APPALACHIAN MOUNTAINS
Potomac
ATLANTIC OCEAN
Chesapeake Bay
L. Mead
Grand Canyon
Pt. Conception
SANTA BARBARA IS.
Mojave Desert
Arkansas
Missouri
OZARK PLATEAU
Tennessee
Mt. Mitchell 6,684
PIEDMONT
COASTAL
C. Hatteras
C. Fear
Gila
Rio Grande
LLANO ESTACADO
Canadian
Red
Wheeler L.
Savannah
Chattahoochee
Pecos
EDWARDS PLATEAU
Colorado
Brazos
GULF COASTAL PLAIN
ATLANTIC
Mississippi Delta
C. Kennedy (C. Canaveral)
L. Okeechobee
The Everglades
Gulf of Mexico
FLORIDA KEYS
ARCTIC OCEAN
0 200 400
MILES
BROOKS RA.
Bering Str.
Yukon
Tanana
St. Lawrence I.
Mt. McKinley 20,320
Alaska Ra.
BERING SEA
Gulf of Alaska
Kodiak I.
ALEXANDER ARCHIPELAGO
Aleutian Islands
Kauai
Oahu
Molokai
Maui
HAWAIIAN ISLANDS
PACIFIC OCEAN
Mauna Kea 13,976
Hawaii
0 50 100
MILES
5,000 m. 16,404 ft.
2,000 m. 6,562 ft.
1,000 m. 3,281 ft.
500 m. 1,640 ft.
200 m. 656 ft.
100 m. 328 ft.
Sea Level
Below

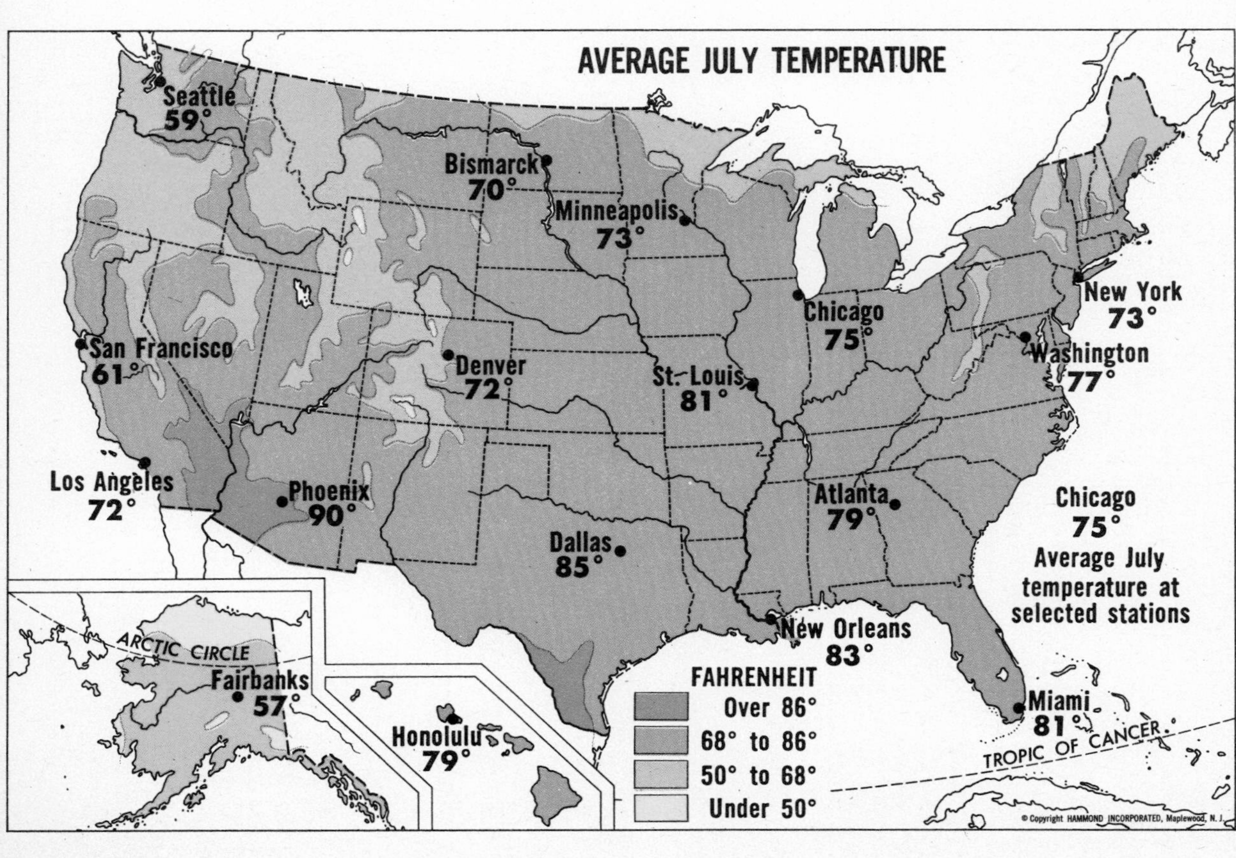

AVERAGE JULY TEMPERATURE
Seattle 59°
Bismarck 70°
Minneapolis 73°
New York 73°
Chicago 75°
San Francisco 61°
Denver 72°
St. Louis 81°
Washington 77°
Los Angeles 72°
Phoenix 90°
Atlanta 79°
Chicago 75°
Average July temperature at selected stations
Dallas 85°
New Orleans 83°
ARCTIC CIRCLE
Fairbanks 57°
Honolulu 79°
Miami 81°
TROPIC OF CANCER
FAHRENHEIT
Over 86°
68° to 86°
50° to 68°
Under 50°
© Copyright HAMMOND INCORPORATED, Maplewood, N. J.

LAND USE

PASTURE AND GRAZING LAND 42%
URBAN AREAS 7%
FOREST AND WOODLAND 22%
12% DESERTS, SWAMPS AND OTHER LAND
17% CROPLAND

EMPLOYMENT

MANUFACTURING 27%
WHOLESALE AND RETAIL TRADE 19%
GOVERNMENT 17%
SERVICES 14%
AGRICULTURE 6%
TRANSPORTATION AND PUBLIC UTILITIES 6%
CONSTRUCTION 5%
FINANCE, INSURANCE, REAL ESTATE 5%
MINING 1%

TOTAL VALUE ADDED BY MANUFACTURING

(percent by industry group)

11% Food and Related Products
5½% Printing & Publishing
8% Textiles, Clothing, Leather Goods
7% Lumber, Wood & Paper Products
3% Stone, Clay & Glass Products
13% Chemicals, Rubber, Plastics
14% Primary & Fabricated Metals
2½% Instruments and Related Products
20% Machinery & Electrical Equipment
5% Other Manufactures
11% Transportation Equipment

CROPLAND *(percent of total acreage)*

Hay 23%
Corn 22%
Wheat 16½%
Soybeans 10%
Oats 6½%
Sorghums 5%
Barley 3½%
Fruits and Nuts 1½%
Vegetables 1%
Cotton 5%
Other 6%

VALUE OF MINERAL PRODUCTION

Metals 8½%
Nonmetals 22%
Other Mineral Fuels 25½%
Petroleum 41%

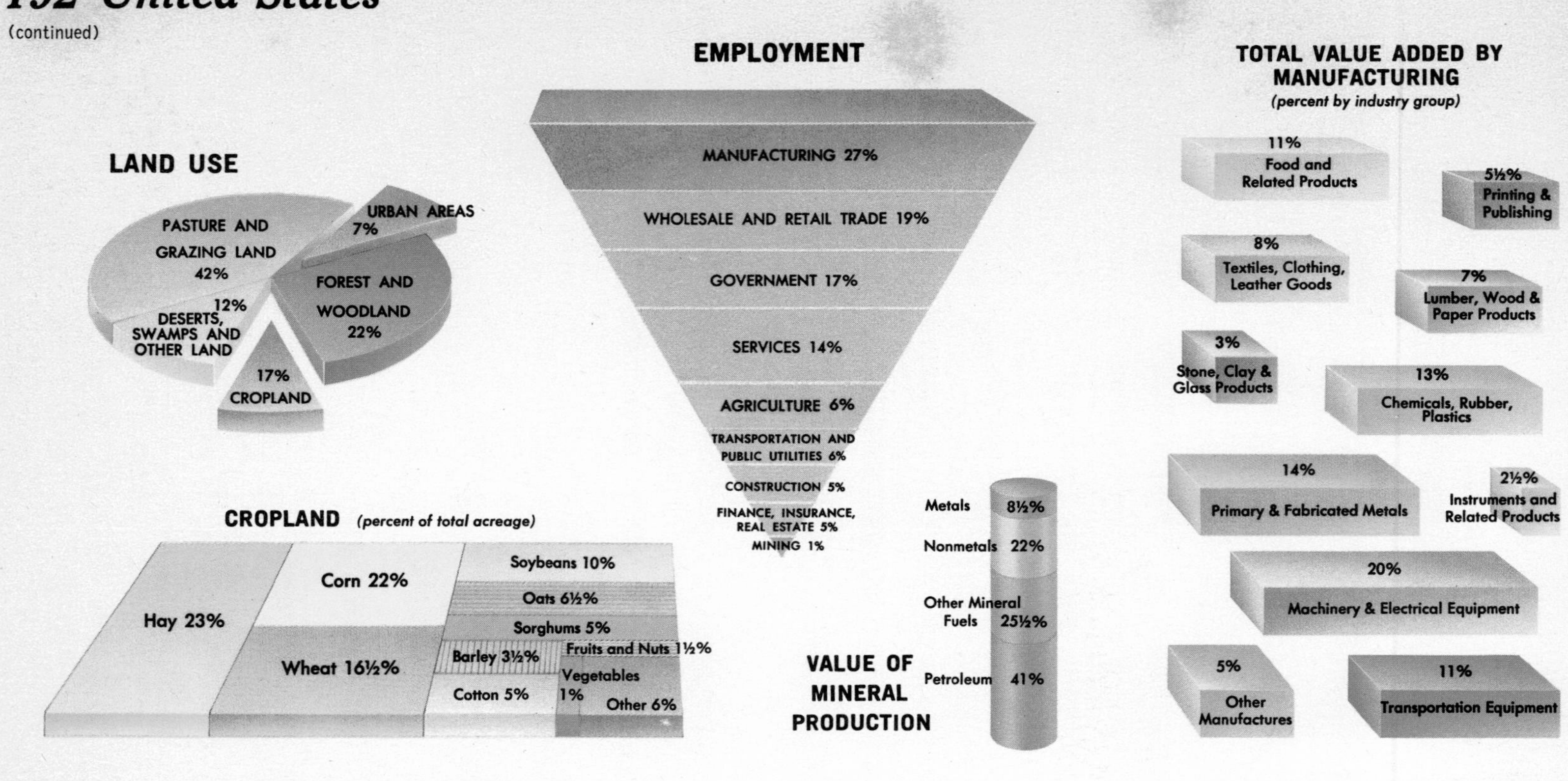

Agriculture, Industry and Resources

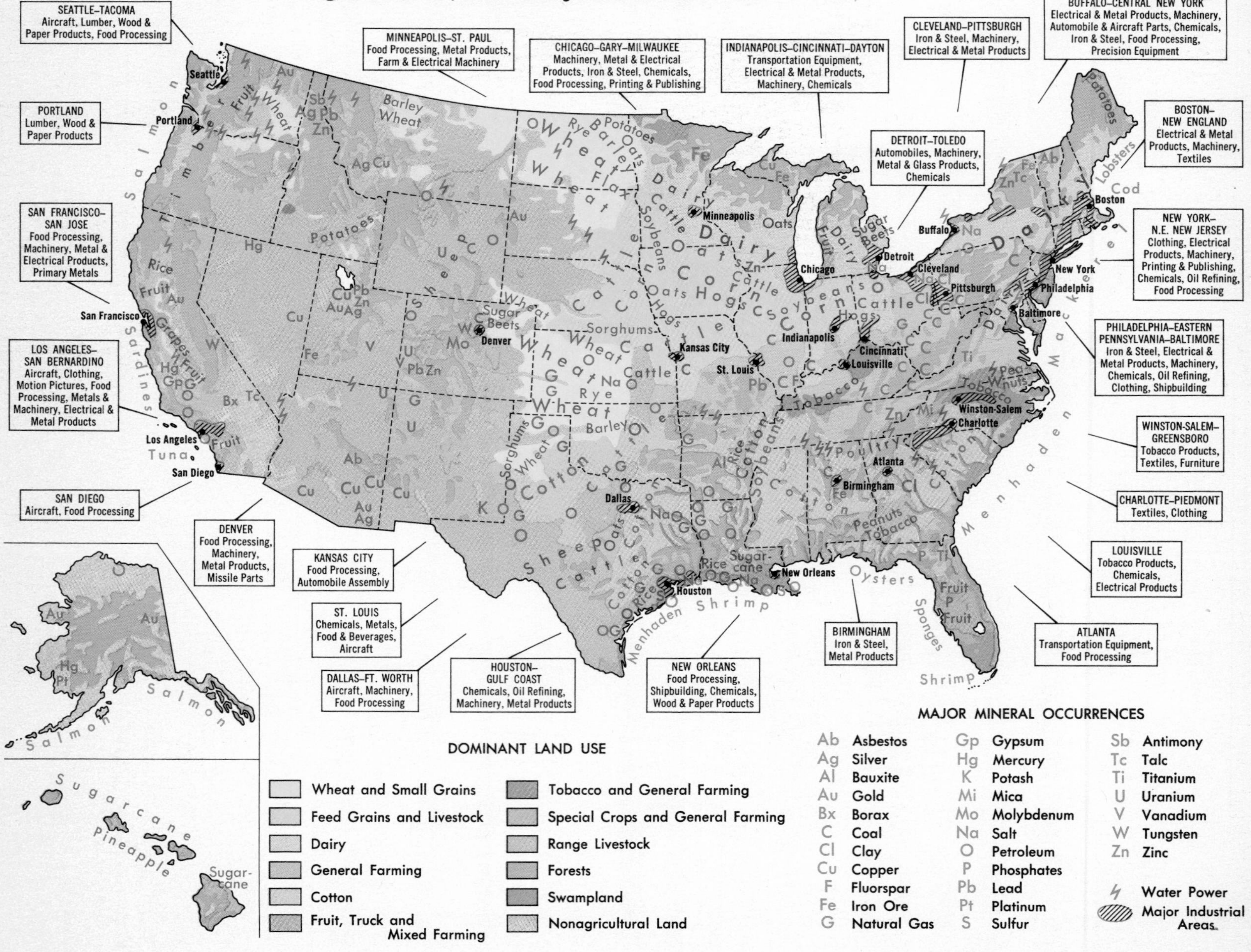

SEATTLE–TACOMA
Aircraft, Lumber, Wood & Paper Products, Food Processing
PORTLAND
Lumber, Wood & Paper Products
SAN FRANCISCO–SAN JOSE
Food Processing, Machinery, Metal & Electrical Products, Primary Metals
LOS ANGELES–SAN BERNARDINO
Aircraft, Clothing, Motion Pictures, Food Processing, Metals & Machinery, Electrical & Metal Products
SAN DIEGO
Aircraft, Food Processing
DENVER
Food Processing, Machinery, Metal Products, Missile Parts
KANSAS CITY
Food Processing, Automobile Assembly
ST. LOUIS
Chemicals, Metals, Food & Beverages, Aircraft
DALLAS–FT. WORTH
Aircraft, Machinery, Food Processing
HOUSTON–GULF COAST
Chemicals, Oil Refining, Machinery, Metal Products
NEW ORLEANS
Food Processing, Shipbuilding, Chemicals, Wood & Paper Products
BIRMINGHAM
Iron & Steel, Metal Products
MINNEAPOLIS–ST. PAUL
Food Processing, Metal Products, Farm & Electrical Machinery
CHICAGO–GARY–MILWAUKEE
Machinery, Metal & Electrical Products, Iron & Steel, Chemicals, Food Processing, Printing & Publishing
INDIANAPOLIS–CINCINNATI–DAYTON
Transportation Equipment, Electrical & Metal Products, Machinery, Chemicals
CLEVELAND–PITTSBURGH
Iron & Steel, Machinery, Electrical & Metal Products
DETROIT–TOLEDO
Automobiles, Machinery, Metal & Glass Products, Chemicals
BUFFALO–CENTRAL NEW YORK
Electrical & Metal Products, Machinery, Automobile & Aircraft Parts, Chemicals, Iron & Steel, Food Processing, Precision Equipment
BOSTON–NEW ENGLAND
Electrical & Metal Products, Machinery, Textiles
NEW YORK–N.E. NEW JERSEY
Clothing, Electrical Products, Machinery, Printing & Publishing, Chemicals, Oil Refining, Food Processing
PHILADELPHIA–EASTERN PENNSYLVANIA–BALTIMORE
Iron & Steel, Electrical & Metal Products, Machinery, Chemicals, Oil Refining, Clothing, Shipbuilding
WINSTON-SALEM–GREENSBORO
Tobacco Products, Textiles, Furniture
CHARLOTTE–PIEDMONT
Textiles, Clothing
LOUISVILLE
Tobacco Products, Chemicals, Electrical Products
ATLANTA
Transportation Equipment, Food Processing
Seattle
Portland
San Francisco
Los Angeles
San Diego
Denver
Minneapolis
Kansas City
St. Louis
Dallas
Houston
New Orleans
Chicago
Indianapolis
Cincinnati
Louisville
Detroit
Cleveland
Pittsburgh
Buffalo
Boston
New York
Philadelphia
Baltimore
Winston-Salem
Charlotte
Atlanta
Birmingham
Salmon
Timber
Fruit
Wheat
Barley
Potatoes
Rye
Oats
Flax
Dairy
Cattle
Soybeans
Corn
Hogs
Sheep
Sugar Beets
Sorghums
Rice
Grapes
Sardines
Tuna
Cotton
Tobacco
Poultry
Peanuts
Peanuts
Sugar-cane
Oysters
Shrimp
Menhaden
Sponges
Lobsters
Cod
Sugarcane
Pineapple
Sugar-cane
DOMINANT LAND USE
Wheat and Small Grains
Feed Grains and Livestock
Dairy
General Farming
Cotton
Fruit, Truck and Mixed Farming
Tobacco and General Farming
Special Crops and General Farming
Range Livestock
Forests
Swampland
Nonagricultural Land
MAJOR MINERAL OCCURRENCES
Ab Asbestos
Ag Silver
Al Bauxite
Au Gold
Bx Borax
C Coal
Cl Clay
Cu Copper
F Fluorspar
Fe Iron Ore
G Natural Gas
Gp Gypsum
Hg Mercury
K Potash
Mi Mica
Mo Molybdenum
Na Salt
O Petroleum
P Phosphates
Pb Lead
Pt Platinum
S Sulfur
Sb Antimony
Tc Talc
Ti Titanium
U Uranium
V Vanadium
W Tungsten
Zn Zinc
Water Power
Major Industrial Areas

COUNTIES

Autauga, 24,460 ..... E 5
Baldwin, 59,382 ..... C 9
Barbour, 22,543 ..... H 7
Bibb, 13,812 ..... D 5
Blount, 26,853 ..... E 2
Bullock, 11,824 ..... G 6
Butler, 22,007 ..... E 7
Calhoun, 103,092 ..... G 3
Chambers, 36,356 ..... H 5
Cherokee, 15,606 ..... G 2
Chilton, 25,180 ..... E 5
Choctaw, 16,589 ..... B 6
Clarke, 26,724 ..... C 7
Clay, 12,636 ..... G 4
Cleburne, 10,996 ..... G 3
Coffee, 34,872 ..... G 8
Colbert, 49,632 ..... C 1
Conecuh, 15,645 ..... E 8
Coosa, 10,662 ..... F 5
Covington, 34,079 ..... F 8
Crenshaw, 13,188 ..... F 7
Cullman, 52,445 ..... E 2
Dale, 52,938 ..... G 8
Dallas, 55,296 ..... D 6
De Kalb, 41,981 ..... G 2
Elmore, 33,535 ..... F 5
Escambia, 34,906 ..... D 8
Etowah, 94,144 ..... F 2
Fayette, 16,252 ..... C 3
Franklin, 23,933 ..... C 2
Geneva, 21,924 ..... G 8
Greene, 10,650 ..... C 5
Hale, 15,888 ..... C 5
Henry, 13,254 ..... H 7
Houston, 56,574 ..... H 8
Jackson, 39,202 ..... F 1
Jefferson, 644,991 ..... E 3
Lamar, 14,335 ..... B 3
Lauderdale, 68,111 ..... C 1
Lawrence, 27,281 ..... D 1
Lee, 61,268 ..... H 5
Limestone, 41,699 ..... E 1
Lowndes, 12,897 ..... E 6
Macon, 24,841 ..... G 6
Madison, 186,540 ..... E 1
Marengo, 23,819 ..... C 6
Marion, 23,788 ..... C 2
Marshall, 54,211 ..... F 2
Mobile, 317,308 ..... B 9
Monroe, 20,883 ..... D 7
Montgomery, 167,790 ..... F 6
Morgan, 77,306 ..... E 2
Perry, 15,388 ..... D 5
Pickens, 20,326 ..... B 4
Pike, 25,038 ..... G 7
Randolph, 18,331 ..... H 4
Russell, 45,394 ..... H 6
Saint Clair, 27,956 ..... F 3
Shelby, 38,037 ..... E 4
Sumter, 16,974 ..... B 5
Talladega, 65,280 ..... F 4
Tallapoosa, 33,840 ..... G 5
Tuscaloosa, 116,029 ..... C 4
Walker, 56,246 ..... D 3
Washington, 16,241 ..... B 8
Wilcox, 16,303 ..... D 7
Winston, 16,654 ..... D 2

CITIES and TOWNS

Zip *Name/Pop.* *Key*

36310 Abbeville⊙, 2,996 ..... H 7
35440 Abernant, 602 ..... D 4
35005 Adamsville, 2,412 ..... D 3
35540 Addison, 692 ..... D 2
35006 Adger, 1,550 ..... D 4
35441 Akron, 535 ..... C 5
35007 Alabaster, 2,642 ..... E 4
35950 Albertville, 9,963 ..... F 2
† 35115 Aldrich, 476 ..... E 4
35010 Alexander City, 12,358 ..... G 5
36250 Alexandria, 600 ..... G 3
35442 Aliceville, 2,807 ..... B 4
35013 Allgood, 272 ..... F 3
† 35616 Allsboro, 300 ..... B 1
35015 Alton, 500 ..... E 3
35952 Altoona, 781 ..... F 2
36420 Andalusia⊙, 10,092 ..... E 8
35610 Anderson, 400 ..... D 1
36201 Anniston⊙, 31,533 ..... G 3
35016 Arab, 4,399 ..... E 2
35805 Ardmore, 761 ..... E 1
36311 Ariton, 643 ..... G 7
35033 Arkadelphia, 325 ..... E 3
† 35035 Ashby, 500 ..... E 4
36312 Ashford, 1,980 ..... H 8
36251 Ashland⊙, 1,921 ..... G 4
35953 Ashville, 986 ..... F 3
35611 Athens⊙, 14,360 ..... E 1
36502 Atmore, 8,293 ..... C 8
35954 Attalla, 7,510 ..... F 2
36830 Auburn, 22,767 ..... H 5
36003 Autaugaville, 870 ..... E 6
† 36312 Avon, 374 ..... H 8
36505 Axis, 600 ..... B 9
35019 Baileyton, 500 ..... E 2
36004 Baker Hill, 350 ..... H 7
36506 Barlow Bend, 300 ..... C 8
† 36532 Barnwell, 700 ..... C 10
36533 Battles Wharf, 300 ..... C 10
36507 Bay Minette⊙, 6,727 ..... C 9
36509 Bayou La Batre, 2,664 ..... B 10
35543 Bear Creek, 336 ..... C 2
36425 Beatrice, 455 ..... D 7
35544 Beaverton, 265 ..... B 3
† 35653 Belgreen, 500 ..... C 2
36901 Bellamy, 700 ..... B 6
35546 Berry, 679 ..... C 3
35020 Bessemer, 33,428 ..... D 4
* 35201 Birmingham⊙, 300,910 ..... D 3
Birmingham, ‡739,274 ..... D 3
36902 Bladon Springs, 300 ..... B 7
† 36874 Bleecker, 250 ..... H 5
35031 Blountsville, 1,254 ..... E 2
36201 Blue Mountain, 446 ..... G 3
35226 Bluff Park, 12,372 ..... E 4
35957 Boaz, 5,621 ..... F 2
36903 Bolinger, 250 ..... B 7
36007 Bolling, 250 ..... E 7
36511 Bon Secour, 850 ..... C 10
36110 Boylston, 2,943 ..... F 6
36009 Brantley, 1,066 ..... F 7
35034 Brent, 2,093 ..... D 5
36426 Brewton⊙, 6,747 ..... D 8
35740 Bridgeport, 2,908 ..... G 1
35035 Brierfield, 950 ..... E 4
35020 Brighton, 2,277 ..... D 4
35548 Brilliant, 726 ..... C 2
36429 Brooklyn, 350 ..... E 8
35036 Brookside, 990 ..... E 3
35444 Brookwood, 450 ..... D 4
35445 Brownville, 300 ..... C 4
36010 Brundidge, 2,709 ..... G 7
35446 Buhl, 500 ..... C 4
36725 Burkville, 250 ..... E 6
36431 Burnt Corn, 250 ..... D 7
36904 Butler⊙, 2,064 ..... B 6
† 36767 Cahaba, 50 ..... D 6
35040 Calera, 1,655 ..... E 4
36012 Calhoun, 950 ..... F 6
36513 Calvert, 500 ..... B 8
36726 Camden⊙, 1,742 ..... D 7
36850 Camp Hill, 1,554 ..... G 5
36514 Canoe, 560 ..... D 8
† 36726 Canton Bend, 250 ..... D 6
35549 Carbon Hill, 1,929 ..... D 3
36515 Carlton, 275 ..... C 8
35447 Carrollton⊙, 923 ..... B 4
† 36023 Carrville, 895 ..... G 5
† 36548 Carson, 250 ..... C 8
36432 Castleberry, 666 ..... D 8
36013 Cecil, 250 ..... F 6
35959 Cedar Bluff, 956 ..... G 2
36014 Central, 300 ..... F 5
35960 Centre⊙, 2,418 ..... G 2
35042 Centreville⊙, 2,233 ..... D 5
36729 Chance, 350 ..... C 7
36015 Chapman, 400 ..... E 7
36518 Chatom⊙, 1,059 ..... B 8
35043 Chelsea, 615 ..... E 4
35616 Cherokee, 1,484 ..... C 1
36611 Chickasaw, 8,447 ..... B 9
35044 Childersburg, 4,831 ..... F 4
36254 Choccolocco, 300 ..... G 3
36905 Choctaw, 600 ..... B 6
36520 Chrysler, 300 ..... C 8
36521 Chunchula, 400 ..... B 9
36522 Citronelle, 1,935 ..... B 8
35045 Clanton⊙, 5,868 ..... E 5
36015 Clayton⊙, 1,626 ..... G 7
35049 Cleveland, 413 ..... E 3
36017 Clio, 1,065 ..... G 7
35617 Cloverdale, 650 ..... C 1
35449 Coaling, 300 ..... D 4
36523 Coden, 500 ..... B 10
36318 Coffee Springs, 329 ..... G 8
36524 Coffeeville, 441 ..... B 7
35452 Coker, 800 ..... C 4
35961 Collinsville, 1,300 ..... G 2
36319 Columbia, 891 ..... H 8
35051 Columbiana⊙, 2,248 ..... E 4

AREA 51,609 sq. mi.
POPULATION 3,444,165
CAPITAL Montgomery
LARGEST CITY Birmingham
HIGHEST POINT Cheaha Mtn. 2,407 ft.
SETTLED IN 1702
ADMITTED TO UNION December 14, 1819
POPULAR NAME Heart of Dixie; Cotton State
STATE FLOWER Camellia
STATE BIRD Yellowhammer

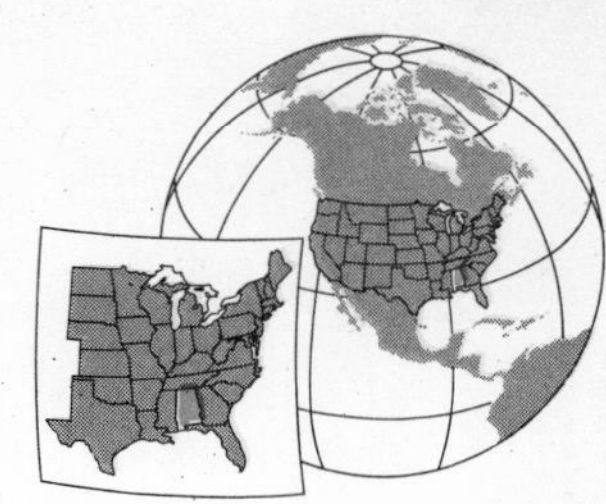

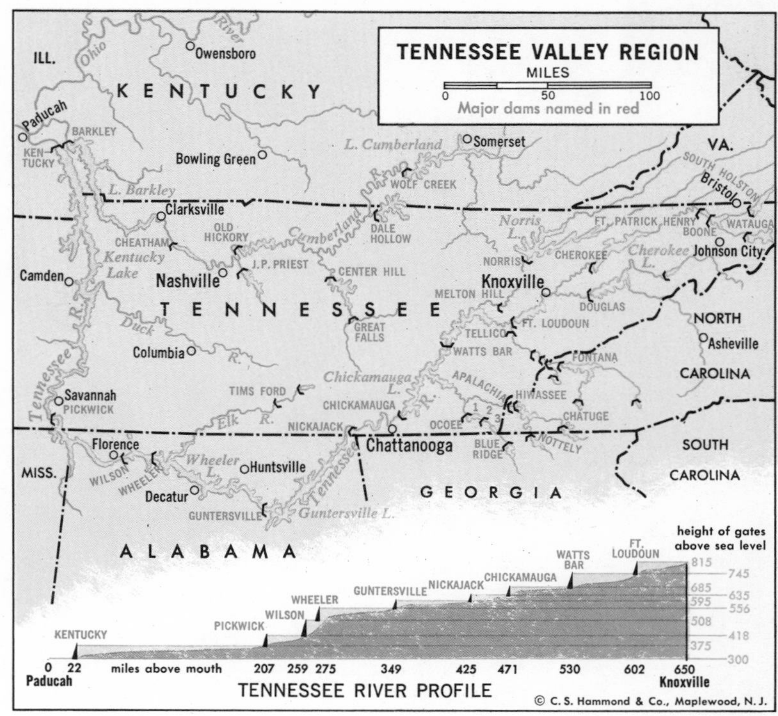

36019 Cooper, 250 ..... E 5
36020 Coosada, 600 ..... F 5
35550 Cordova, 2,750 ..... D 3
† 35546 Corona, 300 ..... C 3
35088 Cottage Grove, 300 ..... F 5
35453 Cottondale, 600 ..... D 4
36851 Cottonton, 415 ..... H 6
36320 Cottonwood, 1,149 ..... H 8
35618 Courtland, 547 ..... D 1
36321 Cowarts, 350 ..... H 8
36435 Coy, 950 ..... D 7
36525 Creola, 950 ..... B 9
36906 Cromwell, 700 ..... B 6
35962 Crossville, 1,035 ..... G 2
36907 Cuba, 386 ..... B 6
35055 Cullman⊙, 12,601 ..... E 2
36920 Cullomburg, 325 ..... B 7
36852 Cusseta, 250 ..... H 5
36853 Dadeville⊙, 2,847 ..... G 5
36322 Daleville, 5,182 ..... G 8
35619 Danville, 400 ..... D 2
36526 Daphne, 2,382 ..... G 9
36528 Dauphin Island, 950 ..... B 10
36256 Daviston, 247 ..... G 4
36257 De Armanville, 500 ..... G 3
36022 Deatsville, 350 ..... F 5
35601 Decatur⊙, 38,044 ..... D 1
36529 Deer Park, 300 ..... B 8
36732 Demopolis, 7,651 ..... C 6
36436 Dickinson, 350 ..... C 7
36736 Dixons Mills, 285 ..... C 6
35061 Dolomite, 1,237 ..... D 4
35062 Dora, 1,862 ..... D 3
36301 Dothan⊙, 36,733 ..... H 8
35553 Double Springs⊙, 957 ..... D 2
35964 Douglas, 527 ..... F 2
36028 Dozier, 304 ..... F 7
36259 Duke, 250 ..... G 3
35744 Dutton, 423 ..... G 1
† 36507 Dyas, 250 ..... C 9
36260 Eastaboga, 500 ..... F 3
36426 East Brewton, 2,336 ..... E 8
35457 Echola, 300 ..... C 4
36024 Eclectic, 1,184 ..... F 5
† 36317 Edwin, 296 ..... H 7
36323 Elba⊙, 4,634 ..... F 8
36530 Elberta, 395 ..... C 10
35554 Eldridge, 350 ..... C 3
35620 Elkmont, 394 ..... E 1
36025 Elmore, 656 ..... F 5
35458 Elrod, 600 ..... C 4
35459 Emelle, 300 ..... B 5
35063 Empire, 400 ..... D 3
36330 Enterprise, 15,591 ..... G 8
35460 Epes, 293 ..... B 5
36027 Eufaula, 9,102 ..... H 7
35462 Eutaw⊙, 2,805 ..... C 5
36401 Evergreen⊙, 3,924 ..... E 8
36439 Excel, 422 ..... D 8
35746 Fackler, 250 ..... G 1
36854 Fairfax, 2,772 ..... H 5
35064 Fairfield, 14,369 ..... E 3
36532 Fairhope, 5,720 ..... C 10
35208 Fairview, 313 ..... E 2
35622 Falkville, 946 ..... E 2
35555 Fayette⊙, 4,568 ..... C 3
36440 Finchburg, 300 ..... D 7
36855 Five Points, 247 ..... H 4
† 35129 Flat Creek-Wegra, 1,066 ..... D 3
35966 Flat Rock, 750 ..... G 1
36739 Flatwood, 300 ..... C 6
† 35601 Flint City, 404 ..... D 1
36441 Flomaton, 1,584 ..... D 8
36442 Florala, 2,701 ..... F 8
35630 Florence⊙, 34,031 ..... C 1
36535 Foley, 3,368 ..... C 10
35214 Forestdale, 6,091 ..... E 3
36030 Forest Home, 450 ..... E 7
36740 Forkland, 400 ..... C 5
36031 Fort Davis, 500 ..... G 6
36032 Fort Deposit, 1,438 ..... E 7
36856 Fort Mitchell, 2,400 ..... H 6
35967 Fort Payne⊙, 8,435 ..... G 2
35463 Fosters, 400 ..... C 4
36444 Franklin, 500 ..... D 7
36538 Frankville, 550 ..... B 7
† 31833 Fredonia, 300 ..... H 5
36445 Frisco City, 1,286 ..... D 8
36539 Fruitdale, 275 ..... B 8
36446 Fulton, 628 ..... C 7
35068 Fultondale, 5,163 ..... E 3
36741 Furman, 300 ..... E 6
35971 Fyffe, 311 ..... G 2
* 35901 Gadsden⊙, 53,928 ..... G 2
Gadsden, ‡94,144 ..... G 2
36540 Gainestown, 300 ..... C 8
35464 Gainesville, 255 ..... B 5
35972 Gallant, 475 ..... F 2
36038 Gantt, 380 ..... E 8
35070 Garden City, 745 ..... E 2
35071 Gardendale, 6,502 ..... E 3
36340 Geneva⊙, 4,398 ..... G 8
36033 Georgiana, 2,148 ..... E 7
35974 Geraldine, 610 ..... G 2
35559 Glen Allen, 276 ..... C 3
35905 Glencoe, 2,901 ..... G 3
36034 Glenwood, 378 ..... F 7
† 36024 Good Hope, 840 ..... E 2
35072 Goodwater, 2,172 ..... F 4
35466 Gordo, 1,991 ..... C 4
36343 Gordon, 312 ..... H 8
35561 Gorgas, 500 ..... D 3
36035 Goshen, 279 ..... F 7
36450 Gosport, 400 ..... C 7
36036 Grady, 298 ..... F 7
36541 Grand Bay, 950 ..... B 10
35747 Grant, 382 ..... F 1
35073 Graysville, 3,182 ..... D 3
35074 Green Pond, 500 ..... D 4
36744 Greensboro⊙, 3,371 ..... C 5

(continued on following page)

Agriculture, Industry and Resources

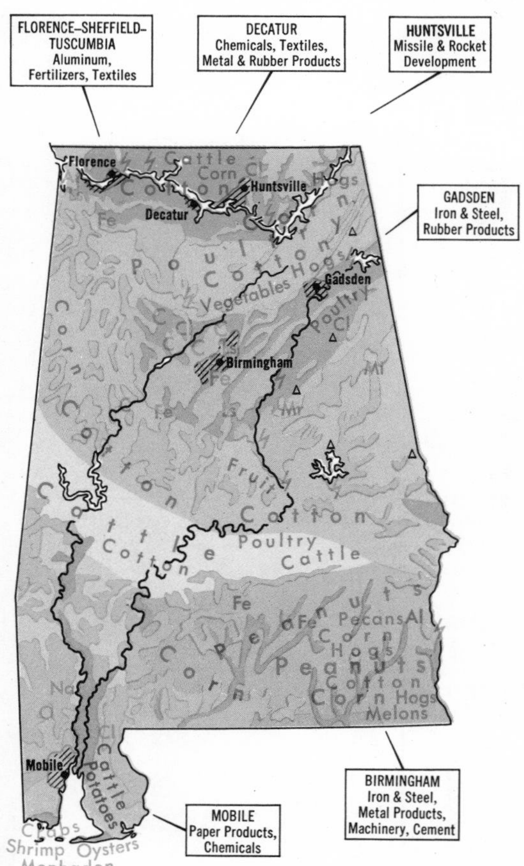

DOMINANT LAND USE

- Specialized Cotton
- Cotton, Livestock
- Cotton, General Farming
- Cotton, Hogs, Peanuts
- Cotton, Forest Products
- Peanuts, General Farming
- Truck and Mixed Farming
- Forests
- Swampland, Limited Agriculture

MAJOR MINERAL OCCURRENCES

Al	Bauxite	Ls	Limestone
At	Asphalt	Mi	Mica
C	Coal	Mr	Marble
Cl	Clay	Na	Salt
Fe	Iron Ore	O	Petroleum

- Water Power
- Major Industrial Areas
- Major Textile Manufacturing Centers

ALABAMA
SCALE
0 5 10 20 30 40 MI.
0 5 10 20 30 40 KM.
State Capitals
County Seats
© C.S. HAMMOND & Co., N.Y.
87° Longitude West of 30′ Greenwich
88°
86°
85°
35°
34°
33°
32°
31°
TENNESSEE
MISSISSIPPI
GEORGIA
FLORIDA
GULF OF MEXICO
LAUDERDALE
LIMESTONE
MADISON
JACKSON
COLBERT
LAWRENCE
MORGAN
MARSHALL
DE KALB
FRANKLIN
CULLMAN
WINSTON
MARION
BLOUNT
ETOWAH
CHEROKEE
LAMAR
FAYETTE
WALKER
JEFFERSON
ST. CLAIR
CALHOUN
CLEBURNE
PICKENS
TUSCALOOSA
SHELBY
TALLADEGA
CLAY
RANDOLPH
GREENE
HALE
BIBB
CHILTON
COOSA
TALLAPOOSA
CHAMBERS
SUMTER
PERRY
AUTAUGA
ELMORE
LEE
MARENGO
DALLAS
LOWNDES
MONTGOMERY
MACON
RUSSELL
CHOCTAW
WILCOX
BULLOCK
BARBOUR
CLARKE
MONROE
BUTLER
CRENSHAW
PIKE
WASHINGTON
CONECUH
COFFEE
DALE
HENRY
ESCAMBIA
COVINGTON
GENEVA
HOUSTON
MOBILE
BALDWIN
BIRMINGHAM
MONTGOMERY
MOBILE
Huntsville
Decatur
Florence
Sheffield
Tuscumbia
Gadsden
Anniston
Tuscaloosa
Bessemer
Selma
Dothan
Prichard
CHATTANOOGA
ATLANTA
COLUMBUS
PENSACOLA
Mobile Bay
Pensacola Bay
Choctawhatchee Bay
L. Seminole

Railroad tracks form tangled spider webs leading to voracious steel furnaces. Native coal, iron ore and limestone are delivered to Ensley (Birmingham), Alabama plant.

Topography

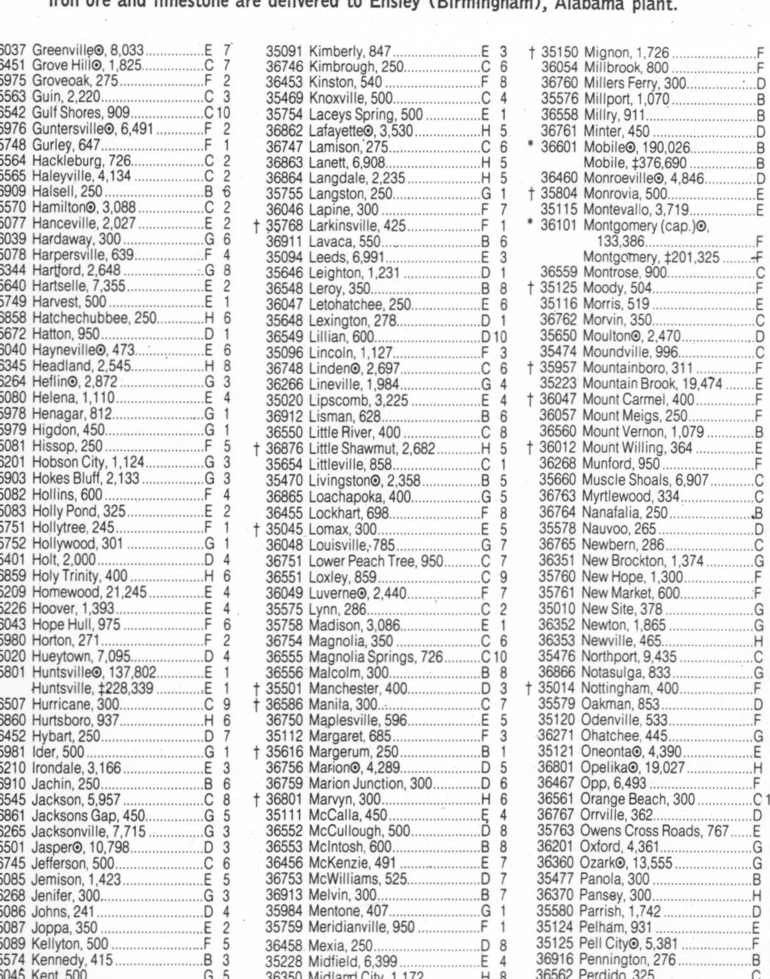

	Zip	Place	Key
	36037	Greenville⊙, 8,033	E 7
	36451	Grove Hill⊙, 1,825	C 7
	35975	Groveoak, 275	F 2
	35563	Guin, 2,220	C 3
	36542	Gulf Shores, 909	C 10
	35976	Guntersville⊙, 6,491	F 2
	35748	Gurley, 647	F 1
	35564	Hackleburg, 726	C 2
	35565	Haleyville, 4,134	C 2
	36909	Halsell, 250	B 6
	35570	Hamilton⊙, 3,088	C 2
	35077	Hanceville, 2,027	E 2
	36039	Hardaway, 300	G 6
	35078	Harpersville, 639	F 4
	36344	Hartford, 2,648	G 8
	35640	Hartselle, 7,355	E 2
	35749	Harvest, 500	E 1
	36858	Hatchechubbee, 250	H 6
†	35672	Hatton, 950	D 1
	36040	Hayneville⊙, 473	E 6
	36345	Headland, 2,545	H 8
	36264	Heflin⊙, 2,872	G 3
	35080	Helena, 1,110	E 4
	35978	Henagar, 812	G 1
	35979	Higdon, 450	G 1
	35081	Hissop, 250	F 5
†	36201	Hobson City, 1,124	G 3
	35903	Hokes Bluff, 2,133	G 3
	35082	Hollins, 600	F 4
	35083	Holly Pond, 325	E 2
	35751	Hollytree, 245	F 1
	35752	Hollywood, 301	G 1
	35401	Holt, 2,000	D 4
	36859	Holy Trinity, 400	H 6
	35209	Homewood, 21,245	E 4
†	35226	Hoover, 1,393	E 4
	36043	Hope Hull, 975	F 6
	35980	Horton, 271	F 2
	35020	Hueytown, 7,095	D 4
*	35801	Huntsville⊙, 137,802	E 1
		Huntsville, ‡228,339	E 1
†	36507	Hurricane, 300	C 9
	36860	Hurtsboro, 937	H 6
	36452	Hybart, 250	D 7
	35981	Ider, 500	G 1
	35210	Irondale, 3,166	E 3
	36910	Jachin, 250	B 6
	36545	Jackson, 5,957	C 8
	36861	Jacksons Gap, 450	G 5
	36265	Jacksonville, 7,715	G 3
	35501	Jasper⊙, 10,798	D 3
	36745	Jefferson, 500	C 6
	35085	Jemison, 1,423	E 5
†	36268	Jenifer, 300	G 3
	35086	Johns, 241	D 4
	35087	Joppa, 350	E 2
	35089	Kellyton, 500	F 5
	35574	Kennedy, 415	B 3
	36045	Kent, 500	G 5
	35645	Killen, 683	D 1
	35091	Kimberly, 847	E 3
	36746	Kimbrough, 250	C 6
	36453	Kinston, 540	F 8
	35469	Knoxville, 500	C 4
	35754	Laceys Spring, 500	E 1
	36862	Lafayette⊙, 3,530	H 5
	36747	Lamison, 275	C 6
	36863	Lanett, 6,908	H 5
	36864	Langdale, 2,235	H 5
	35755	Langston, 250	G 1
	36046	Lapine, 300	F 7
†	35768	Larkinsville, 425	F 1
	36911	Lavaca, 550	B 6
	35094	Leeds, 6,991	E 3
	35646	Leighton, 1,231	D 1
	36548	Leroy, 350	B 8
	36047	Letohatchee, 250	E 6
	35648	Lexington, 278	D 1
	36549	Lillian, 600	D 10
	35096	Lincoln, 1,127	F 3
	36748	Linden⊙, 2,697	C 6
	36266	Lineville, 1,984	G 4
	35020	Lipscomb, 3,225	E 4
	36912	Lisman, 628	B 6
	36550	Little River, 400	C 8
†	36876	Little Shawmut, 2,682	H 5
	35654	Littleville, 858	C 1
	35470	Livingston⊙, 2,358	B 5
	36865	Loachapoka, 400	G 5
	36455	Lockhart, 698	F 8
†	35045	Lomax, 300	E 5
	36048	Louisville, 785	G 7
	36751	Lower Peach Tree, 950	C 7
	36551	Loxley, 859	C 9
	36049	Luverne⊙, 2,440	F 7
	35575	Lynn, 286	C 2
	35758	Madison, 3,086	E 1
	36754	Magnolia, 350	C 6
	36555	Magnolia Springs, 726	C 10
	36556	Malcolm, 300	B 8
†	35501	Manchester, 400	D 3
†	36586	Manila, 300	C 7
	36750	Maplesville, 596	E 5
	35112	Margaret, 685	F 3
†	35616	Margerum, 250	B 1
	36756	Marion⊙, 4,289	D 5
	36759	Marion Junction, 300	D 6
†	36801	Marvyn, 300	H 6
	35111	McCalla, 450	E 4
	36552	McCullough, 500	D 8
	36553	McIntosh, 600	B 8
	36456	McKenzie, 491	E 7
	36753	McWilliams, 525	D 7
	36913	Melvin, 300	B 7
	35984	Mentone, 407	G 1
	35759	Meridianville, 950	F 1
	36458	Mexia, 250	D 8
	35228	Midfield, 6,399	E 4
	36350	Midland City, 1,172	H 8
	36053	Midway, 558	H 6
†	35150	Mignon, 1,726	F 4
	36054	Millbrook, 800	F 6
	36760	Millers Ferry, 300	D 6
	35576	Millport, 1,070	B 3
	36558	Millry, 911	B 7
	36761	Minter, 450	D 6
*	36601	Mobile⊙, 190,026	B 9
		Mobile, ‡376,690	B 9
	36460	Monroeville⊙, 4,846	D 7
†	35804	Monrovia, 500	E 1
	35115	Montevallo, 3,719	E 4
*	36101	Montgomery (cap.)⊙, 133,386	F 6
		Montgomery, ‡201,325	F 6
	36559	Montrose, 900	C 9
†	35125	Moody, 504	F 3
	35116	Morris, 519	E 3
	36762	Morvin, 350	C 7
	35650	Moulton⊙, 2,470	D 2
	35474	Moundville, 996	C 5
†	35957	Mountainboro, 311	F 2
	35223	Mountain Brook, 19,474	E 4
†	36047	Mount Carmel, 400	F 6
	36057	Mount Meigs, 250	F 6
	36560	Mount Vernon, 1,079	B 8
†	36012	Mount Willing, 364	E 6
	36268	Munford, 950	F 3
	35660	Muscle Shoals, 6,907	C 1
	36763	Myrtlewood, 334	C 6
	36764	Nanafalia, 250	B 6
	35578	Nauvoo, 265	D 3
	36765	Newbern, 286	C 5
	36351	New Brockton, 1,374	G 8
	35760	New Hope, 1,300	F 1
	35761	New Market, 600	F 1
	35010	New Site, 378	G 4
	36352	Newton, 1,865	G 8
	36353	Newville, 465	H 8
	35476	Northport, 9,435	C 4
	36866	Notasulga, 833	G 5
†	35014	Nottingham, 400	F 4
	35579	Oakman, 853	D 3
	35120	Odenville, 533	F 3
	36271	Ohatchee, 445	G 3
	35121	Oneonta⊙, 4,390	E 3
	36801	Opelika⊙, 19,027	H 5
	36467	Opp, 6,493	F 8
	36561	Orange Beach, 300	C 10
	36767	Orrville, 362	D 6
	35763	Owens Cross Roads, 767	E 1
	36201	Oxford, 4,361	G 3
	36360	Ozark⊙, 13,555	G 8
	35477	Panola, 300	B 5
	36370	Pansey, 300	H 8
	35580	Parrish, 1,742	D 3
	35124	Pelham, 931	E 4
	35125	Pell City⊙, 5,381	F 3
	36916	Pennington, 276	B 6
	36562	Perdido, 325	C 8
	36530	Perdido Beach, 300	C 10
	36471	Peterman, 750	D 7
	35478	Peterson, 1,040	D 4
	36867	Phenix City⊙, 25,281	H 6
	35581	Phil Campbell, 1,230	C 2
	36272	Piedmont, 5,063	G 3
	36371	Pinckard, 609	G 8
	36768	Pine Apple, 347	E 7
	36769	Pine Hill, 697	C 7
	36065	Pine Level, 300	F 6
	35126	Pinson, 2,500	E 3
	35765	Pisgah, 519	G 1
	36871	Pittsview, 400	H 6
	36758	Plantersville, 550	E 5
	36564	Point Clear, 850	C 10
	36067	Prattville⊙, 13,116	E 6
	36610	Prichard, 41,578	B 9
	35766	Princeton, 250	F 1
	36772	Putnam, 305	B 6
†	36507	Rabun, 300	C 8
	35131	Ragland, 1,239	F 3
	35901	Rainbow City, 3,107	F 3
	35986	Rainsville, 2,099	G 2
	35480	Ralph, 500	C 4
	36069	Ramer, 750	F 6
	36273	Ranburne, 371	H 3
	36473	Range, 275	D 8
	35582	Red Bay, 2,464	B 2
	36474	Red Level, 616	E 8
†	35954	Reece City, 496	G 2
	35481	Reform, 1,893	C 4
†	36720	Rehoboth, 300	D 6
†	35160	Renfroe, 400	F 4
	36475	Repton, 277	D 8
†	35203	Republic, 500	E 3
	36918	Riderwood, 400	B 6
	36476	River Falls, 580	E 8
	35135	Riverside, 351	F 3
	36872	River View, 1,109	H 5
	36274	Roanoke, 5,251	H 4
	36567	Robertsdale, 2,078	C 9
	35136	Rockford⊙, 603	F 5
	36274	Rock Mills, 800	H 4
	35652	Rogersville, 950	D 1
†	35020	Roosevelt City, 3,663	E 4
	35653	Russellville⊙, 7,814	C 2
	36071	Rutledge, 353	F 7
	35137	Saginaw, 300	E 4
	35138	Saint Bernard, 896	E 2
†	35146	Saint Clair Springs, 300	F 3
	36568	Saint Elmo, 650	B 10
	36569	Saint Stephens, 400	B 7
	36874	Salem, 475	H 5
	36570	Salitpa, 500	C 7
	36477	Samson, 2,257	F 8
	36478	Sanford, 256	F 8
	35583	Saragossa, 300	D 3
	36571	Saraland, 7,840	B 9
	36775	Sardis, 300	E 6
	36775	Sardis, 368	F 2
	36572	Satsuma, 2,035	B 9
	35139	Sayre, 700	E 3
	35768	Scottsboro⊙, 9,324	F 1
	36875	Seale, 400	H 6
	35771	Section, 702	G 1
	36701	Selma⊙, 27,379	E 6
†	36701	Selmont, 2,270	E 6
	36574	Seminole, 275	D 10
	36575	Semmes, 800	B 9
	36876	Shawmut, 2,181	H 5
	35660	Sheffield, 13,115	C 1
	35143	Shelby, 500	E 4
	36075	Shorter, 500	G 6
	36373	Shorterville, 330	H 7
	36733	Shortleaf, 253	C 6
	36919	Silas, 345	B 7
	35144	Siluria, 678	E 4
	36576	Silverhill, 552	C 9
†	36268	Silver Run, 250	G 3
	35584	Sipsey, 608	D 3
	36375	Slocomb, 1,883	G 8
	36877	Smiths, 2,500	H 5
	35952	Snead, 347	F 2
†	36104	Snowdoun, 250	F 6
	36778	Snow Hill, 500	E 7
	35901	Southside, 983	F 3
	36527	Spanish Fort, 983	C 9
†	35674	Spring Valley, 600	C 1
	35146	Springville, 1,153	E 3
	35585	Spruce Pine, 600	C 2
	36878	Standing Rock, 500	H 4
	36578	Stapleton, 975	C 9
	35987	Steele, 798	F 3
	35147	Sterrett, 450	F 4
	35772	Stevenson, 2,390	G 1
†	35150	Stewartville, 250	F 4
	36579	Stockton, 1,400	C 9
	35586	Sulligent, 1,762	B 3
	35148	Sumiton, 2,374	D 3
	36580	Summerdale, 550	C 10
	36780	Sunny South, 250	C 7
	36781	Suttle, 256	D 5
	36782	Sweet Water, 265	C 6
	35149	Sycamore, 800	F 4
	35150	Sylacauga, 12,255	F 4
	35988	Sylvania, 476	G 1
	35160	Talladega⊙, 17,662	F 4
	36078	Tallassee, 4,809	G 5
	35671	Tanner, 600	E 1
	35217	Tarrant, 6,835	E 3
	36582	Theodore, 1,950	B 9
	36783	Thomaston, 824	C 6
	36784	Thomasville, 3,769	C 7
	35171	Thorsby, 944	E 5
	35672	Town Creek, 1,203	D 1
	35587	Townley, 500	D 3
	36921	Toxey, 304	B 7
	35172	Trafford, 628	E 3
	35673	Trinity, 881	D 1
	36081	Troy⊙, 11,482	G 7
	35173	Trussville, 2,985	E 3
	36479	Tunnel Springs, 300	D 7
	35401	Tuscaloosa⊙, 65,773	C 4
		Tuscaloosa, ‡116,029	C 4
	35674	Tuscumbia⊙, 8,828	C 1
	36083	Tuskegee⊙, 11,028	G 6
	36088	Tuskegee Institute, 5,800	G 6
	36089	Union Springs⊙, 4,324	G 6
	36786	Uniontown, 2,133	D 6
	36480	Uriah, 1,200	D 8
	35775	Valhermoso Springs, 500	E 2
	35989	Valley Head, 470	G 1
	35176	Vandiver, 700	F 4
	36091	Verbena, 350	E 5
	35592	Vernon⊙, 2,190	B 3
	35216	Vestavia Hills, 8,311	E 4
	35593	Vina, 366	B 2
	35178	Vincent, 1,419	F 4
	35179	Vinemont, 480	E 2
	36481	Vredenburgh, 622	D 7
	36276	Wadley, 626	G 4
	36585	Wagarville, 350	B 8
	36586	Walker Springs, 500	C 7
	35180	Warrior, 2,621	E 3
	35677	Waterloo, 262	B 1
	35182	Wattsville, 500	F 3
	36879	Waverly, 247	G 5
	36277	Weaver, 2,091	G 3
	36376	Webb, 354	H 8
	36278	Wedowee⊙, 842	H 4
†	35129	Wegra-Flat Creek, 1,066	D 3
	35183	Weogufka, 350	F 4
	35184	West Blocton, 1,172	D 4
†	36201	West End-Cobb Town, 5,515	G 3
	35185	Westover, 1,400	E 4
	36092	Wetumpka⊙, 3,786	F 5
	36482	Whatley, 500	C 7
†	35618	Wheeler, 300	D 1
†	36040	White Hall, 300	E 6
†	36862	White Plains, 350	G 3
†	35094	Whites Chapel, 334	F 3
	36923	Whitfield, 500	B 6
†	36352	Wicksburg, 400	G 8
	36587	Wilmer, 720	B 9
	35186	Wilsonville, 659	E 4
	35187	Wilton, 573	E 4
	35594	Winfield, 3,292	C 3
	35188	Woodstock, 320	D 4
	35776	Woodville, 322	F 1
	36924	Yantley, 500	B 6
	36789	Yellow Bluff, 350	C 7
	36925	York, 3,044	B 6

⊙ County seat.
‡ Population of metropolitan area.
† Zip of nearest p.o.
* Multiple zips

SENATORIAL DISTRICTS

Name/Pop.	Key
Central, 70,996	H 2
Northwestern, 16,763	E 2
South Central, 170,058	G 3
Southeastern, 42,565	L 3

CITIES and TOWNS

Zip	Name/Pop.	Key
99615	Akhiok, 115	H 3
99551	Akiachak, 312	F 2
99552	Akiak, 171	F 2
99553	Akutan, 101	E 4
99554	Alakanuk, 265	E 2
99555	Aleknagik, 128	G 3
99720	Allakaket, 174	H 1
99786	Ambler, 169	G 1
99721	Anaktuvuk Pass, 99	H 1
* 99501	Anchorage⊙, 48,029	B 1
99556	Anchor Point, 102	B 2
† 99760	Anderson, 362	H 2
† 99658	Andreafski (Saint Marys), 384	F 2
99820	Angoon, 400	M 1
99557	Aniak, 205	G 2
99920	Annette, 195	N 2
99558	Anvik, 83	F 2
99722	Arctic Village, 85	K 1
† 99701	Aurora Lodge, 250	J 2
99723	Barrow, 2,104	G 1
† 99747	Barter Island (Kaktovik), 123	K 1
99724	Beaver, 101	J 1
† 99612	Belkofski, 59	F 3
99559	Bethel, 2,416	F 2
† 99726	Bettles, 65	H 1
99726	Bettles Field, 49	H 1
† 99740	Birch Creek, 45	J 1
† 99567	Birchwood, 1,219	C 1
99785	Brevig Mission, 123	E 1
99727	Buckland, 104	F 1
99729	Cantwell, 62	J 2
† 99901	Cape Pole, 123	M 2
99730	Central, 26	J 1
99788	Chalkyitsik, 130	K 1
† 99620	Chaneliak, 100	F 2
99561	Chefornak, 146	F 2
99563	Chevak, 387	E 2
99732	Chicken, 25	K 2
99564	Chignik, 83	G 3
99565	Chignik Lagoon, 70	G 3
† 99564	Chignik Lake, 117	G 3
† 99586	Chistochina, 33	K 2
99566	Chitina, 38	K 2
99567	Chugiak, 489	C 1
99733	Circle, 54	K 1
99568	Clam Gulch, 47	B 1
99569	Clarks Point, 95	G 3
99704	Clear, 504	J 2
99570	Cohoe, 60	B 1
99571	Cold Bay, 256	F 3
99701	College, 3,434	J 1
99572	Cooper Landing, 31	C 1
99573	Copper Center, 206	J 2
99574	Cordova, 1,164	D 1
99921	Craig, 272	M 2
99575	Crooked Creek, 59	G 2
† 99746	Cutoff (Huslia), 159	G 1
99736	Deering, 85	F 1
99737	Delta Junction, 703	J 2
99576	Dillingham, 914	G 3
† 99762	Diomede, 84	E 1
99737	Dot Lake, 42	K 2
† 99685	Dutch Harbor, 30	E 4
99738	Eagle, 36	K 2
99577	Eagle River, 2,437	C 1
† 99901	Edna Bay, 112	M 2
99578	Eek, 186	F 2
99579	Egegik, 148	G 3
† 99569	Ekuk, 51	G 3
99580	Ekwok, 103	G 3
99825	Elfin Cove, 49	M 1
99739	Elim, 174	F 2
99581	Emmonak, 439	E 2
† 99603	English Bay, 58	B 2
† 99674	Eska, 50	B 1
99725	Ester, 264	J 2
99701	Fairbanks⊙, 14,771	J 2
99583	False Pass, 62	F 4
99585	Fortuna Ledge, 175	F 2
99740	Fort Yukon, 448	J 1
99586	Gakona, 88	K 2
99741	Galena, 302	G 2
99742	Gambell, 372	D 2
99587	Girdwood, 144	C 1
99588	Glennallen, 363	D 1
99762	Golovin, 117	F 2
99589	Goodnews Bay, 218	F 3
† 99586	Gulkana, 53	J 2
99826	Gustavus, 64	M 1
99827	Haines, 463	M 1
99743	Healy, 79	H 2
† 99665	Holikachuk, 100	G 2
99602	Holy Cross, 199	G 2
99603	Homer, 1,083	B 2
99829	Hoonah, 748	M 1
99604	Hooper Bay, 490	E 2
99605	Hope, 51	C 1
† 99687	Houston, 69	B 1
99745	Hughes, 85	H 1
99746	Huslia, 159	G 1
99922	Hydaburg, 214	M 2
99923	Hyder, 49	P 2
† 99625	Igiugig, 36	G 3
99606	Iliamna, 58	G 3
99801	Juneau (cap.)⊙, 6,050	N 1
† 99663	Kachemak, 76	B 2
† 99608	Kaguyak, 59	H 3
99830	Kake, 448	M 1
† 99647	Kakhonak, 88	H 3
99747	Kaktovik, 123	K 1
99607	Kalskag, 122	F 2
99748	Kaltag, 206	G 2
99608	Karluk, 98	H 3
99924	Kasaan, 30	N 2
† 99668	Kashegelok, 200	G 2
99609	Kasigluk, 526	F 2
99610	Kasilof, 71	B 1
99611	Kenai, 3,533	B 1
99901	Ketchikan, 6,994	N 2
99749	Kiana, 278	F 1
99612	King Cove, 283	F 4
† 99762	King Island, 100	E 1
99613	King Salmon, 202	G 3
99614	Kipnuk, 325	F 2
99750	Kivalina, 188	E 1
99925	Klawock, 213	M 2
† 99827	Klukwan, 103	M 1
99751	Kobuk, 75	G 1
99615	Kodiak, 3,798	H 3
99576	Koliganek, 142	G 3
99620	Kotlik, 228	F 2
99752	Kotzebue, 1,696	F 1
99753	Koyuk, 122	F 1
99754	Koyukuk, 124	G 1
† 99625	Kvichak, 75	G 3
99621	Kwethluk, 408	F 2
99622	Kwigillingok, 148	F 3
† 99655	Kwinhagak (Quinhagak), 340	F 3
99624	Larsen Bay, 109	H 3
99625	Levelock, 74	G 3
† 99566	Lower Tonsina, 65	J 2
99756	Manley Hot Springs, 34	H 2
99628	Manokotak, 214	G 3
† 99585	Marshall (Fortuna Ledge), 175	F 2
99627	McGrath, 279	H 2
99630	Mekoryuk, 249	E 2
† 99579	Meshik, 75	G 3
99926	Metlakatla, 1,050	N 2
99903	Meyers Chuck, 37	N 2
99758	Minto, 168	J 2
† 99676	Montana, 33	B 1
99631	Moose Pass, 53	C 1
† 99901	Mountain Point, 459	N 2
99632	Mountain Village, 419	E 2
99835	Mount Edgecumbe, 835	M 1
† 99589	Mumtrak (Goodnews Bay), 218	F 3
† 99764	Nabesna, 40	K 2
99633	Naknek, 178	G 3
† 99559	Napaiskak, 259	F 2
99634	Napakiak, 270	F 2
99760	Nenana, 362	J 2
† 99606	Newhalen, 88	H 3
99636	New Stuyahok, 216	G 3
99559	Newtok, 114	F 2
† 99603	Nikolaevsk, 70	B 2
99691	Nikolai, 112	H 2
99638	Nikolski, 57	E 4
99639	Ninilchik, 134	B 1
99761	Noatak, 293	F 1
99762	Nome⊙, 2,488	E 2
99640	Nondalton, 184	G 2
99763	Noorvik, 462	F 1
99705	North Pole, 265	J 2
99764	Northway, 40	K 2
99765	Nulato, 308	G 2
99641	Nunapitchuk, 400	F 2
99643	Old Harbor, 290	H 3
† 99559	Oscarville, 41	F 2
99644	Ouzinkie, 160	H 3
99645	Palmer, 1,140	C 1
99646	Pauloff Harbor, 39	F 4
99737	Paxson, 32	J 2
99647	Pedro Bay, 65	H 3
99832	Pelican, 133	M 1
99648	Perryville, 94	G 3
99833	Petersburg, 2,042	N 2
99649	Pilot Point, 68	G 3
99650	Pilot Station, 290	F 2
† 99658	Pitkas Point, 70	F 2
99651	Platinum, 55	F 3
99766	Point Hope, 386	E 1
† 99587	Portage, 80	C 1
99834	Port Alexander, 36	M 2
† 99827	Port Chilkoot, 220	N 1
† 99603	Port Graham, 107	B 2
† 99579	Port Heiden, 66	G 3
99550	Port Lions, 227	H 3

Agriculture, Industry and Resources

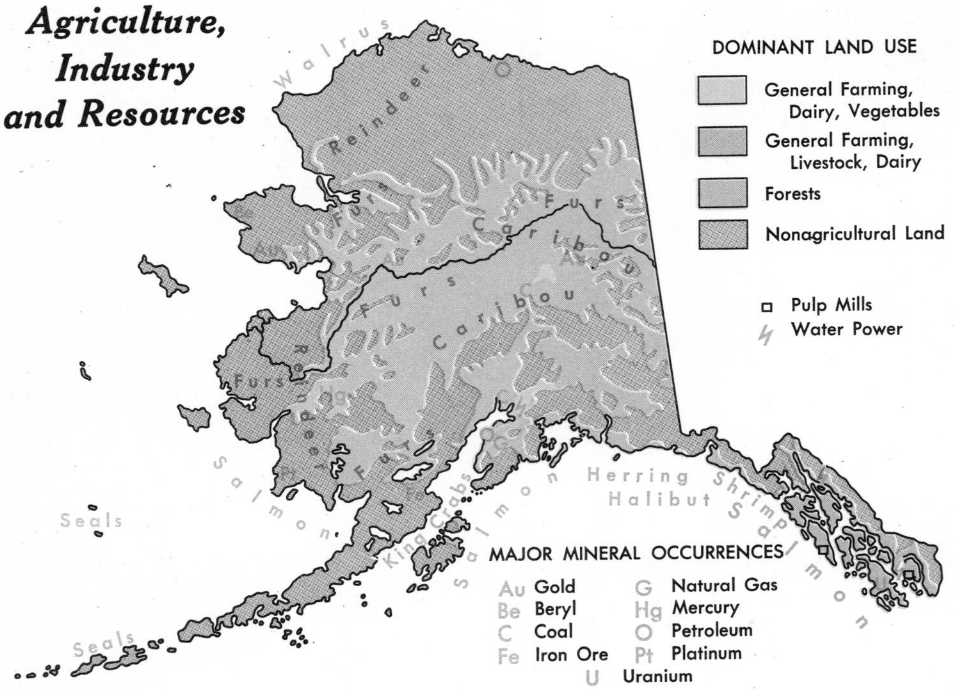

DOMINANT LAND USE

- General Farming, Dairy, Vegetables
- General Farming, Livestock, Dairy
- Forests
- Nonagricultural Land

- Pulp Mills
- Water Power

MAJOR MINERAL OCCURRENCES

- Au Gold
- Be Beryl
- C Coal
- Fe Iron Ore
- G Natural Gas
- Hg Mercury
- O Petroleum
- Pt Platinum
- U Uranium

Topography

0 200 400 MILES

Below Sea Level | 100 m. 328 ft. | 200 m. 656 ft. | 500 m. 1,640 ft. | 1,000 m. 3,281 ft. | 2,000 m. 6,562 ft. | 5,000 m. 16,404 ft.

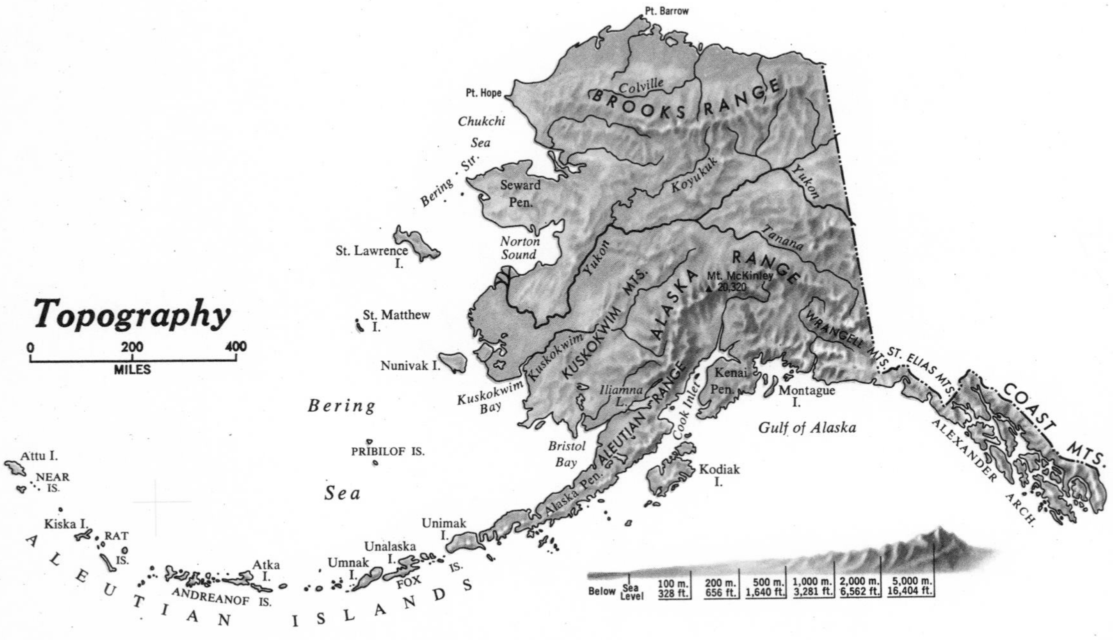

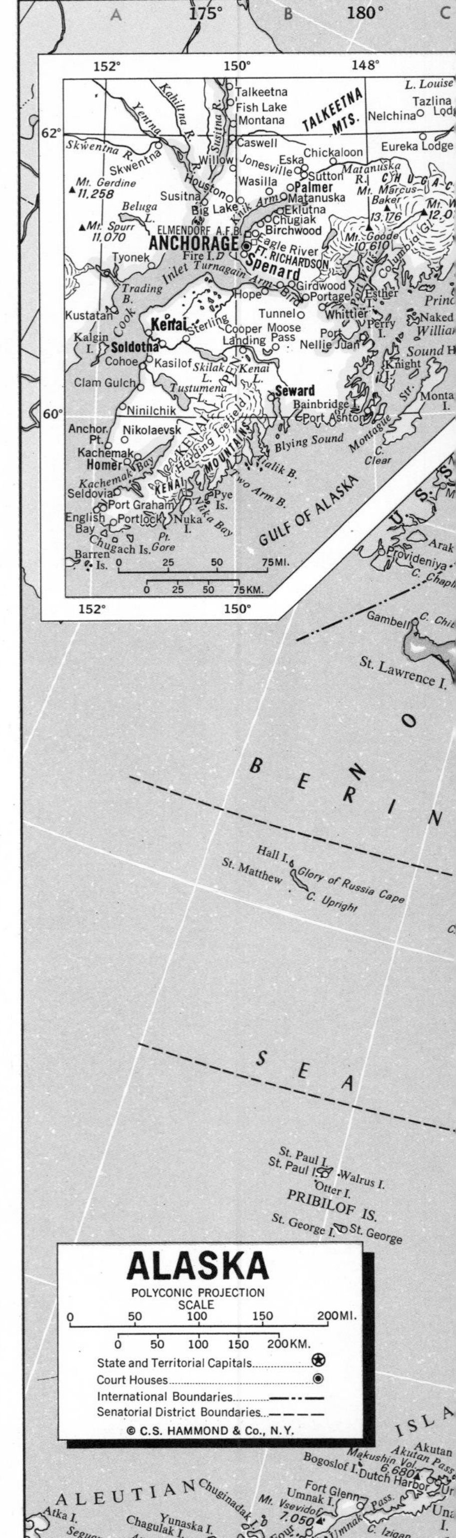

	Zip	Place, population	Key
	99723	Prudhoe Bay, 49	J 1
	99655	Quinhagak, 340	F 3
	99767	Rampart, 36	H 1
	99656	Red Devil, 81	G 2
	99768	Ruby, 145	G 2
	99657	Russian Mission, 146	F 2
	99660	Saint George, 163	E 3
	99658	Saint Marys, 384	F 2
	99659	Saint Michael, 207	F 2
	99660	Saint Paul Island, 450	D 3
	99661	Sand Point, 360	G 3
	99769	Savoonga, 364	E 2
	99901	Saxman, 135	N 2
	99662	Scammon Bay, 166	E 2
	99770	Selawik, 429	G 1
	99663	Seldovia, 437	B 2
	99664	Seward, 1,587	C 1
	99665	Shageluk, 167	G 2
	99771	Shaktoolik, 151	F 2
	99666	Sheldon Point, 125	E 2
	99772	Shishmaref, 267	E 1
	99773	Shungnak, 165	G 1
	99835	Sitka, 3,370	M 1
	99840	Skagway, 675	M 1
	99668	Sleetmute, 109	G 2
	99669	Soldotna, 1,202	B 1
	99670	South Naknek, 154	G 3
	99503	Spenard, 18,089	C 1
	99671	Stebbins, 231	F 2
	99672	Sterling, 30	B 1
	99774	Stevens Village, 74	J 1
	99673	Stony River, 74	G 2
	99729	Summit, 34	J 2
	99743	Suntrana, 67	J 2
	99501	Susitna, 50	B 1
	99674	Sutton, 76	C 1
	99676	Talkeetna, 182	B 1
	99776	Tanacross, 84	K 2
	99777	Tanana, 120	H 1
	99677	Tatitlek, 111	D 1
	99778	Teller, 220	E 1
	99841	Tenakee Springs, 86	M 1
	99779	Tetlin, 114	K 2
†	99801	Thane, 70	N 1
†	99901	Thorne Bay, 443	M 2
	99678	Togiak, 383	F 3
	99780	Tok, 214	K 2
	99679	Tuluksak, 195	F 2
	99680	Tuntutuliak, 158	F 2
	99681	Tununak, 274	E 2
	99682	Tyonek, 232	B 1
†	99701	Umiat, 45	H 1
	99684	Unalakleet, 434	G 2
	99685	Unalaska, 178	E 4
	99686	Valdez, 1,005	D 1
	99781	Venetie, 112	J 1
	99782	Wainwright, 315	F 1
	99783	Wales, 131	E 1
	99928	Ward Cove, 105	N 2
	99687	Wasilla, 300	B 1
	99784	White Mountain, 87	F 2
	99501	Whittier, 130	C 1
	99688	Willow, 38	B 1
†	99615	Woody Island, 41	H 3
	99929	Wrangell, 2,029	N 2
	99689	Yakutat, 190	L 3

⊙ Court House

† Zip of nearest p.o.

* Multiple zips

Arthur A. Twomey — Shostal Associates

Despite its deceptively calm exterior, the Vaughan Lewis Glacier is actually a river of ice, hundreds of feet deep, flowing steadily. Ridges (eskers) are formed by streams under the ice.

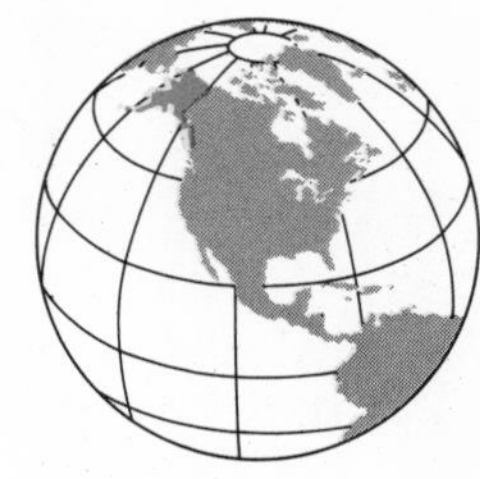

AREA 586,412 sq. mi.
POPULATION 302,173
CAPITAL Juneau
LARGEST CITY Anchorage
HIGHEST POINT Mt. McKinley 20,320 ft.
SETTLED IN 1801
ADMITTED TO UNION January 3, 1959
POPULAR NAME Great Land
STATE FLOWER Forget-me-not
STATE BIRD Willow Ptarmigan

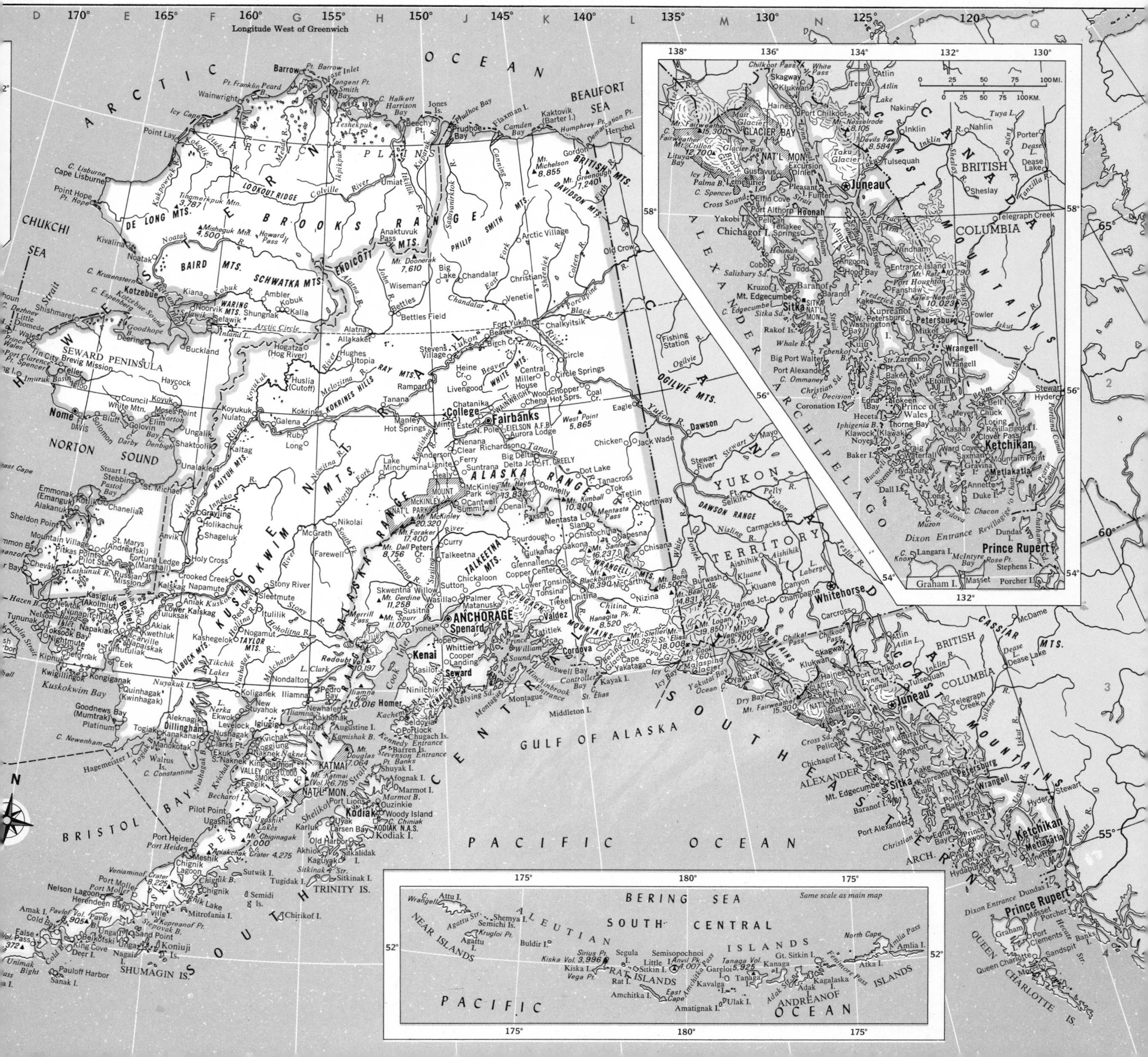

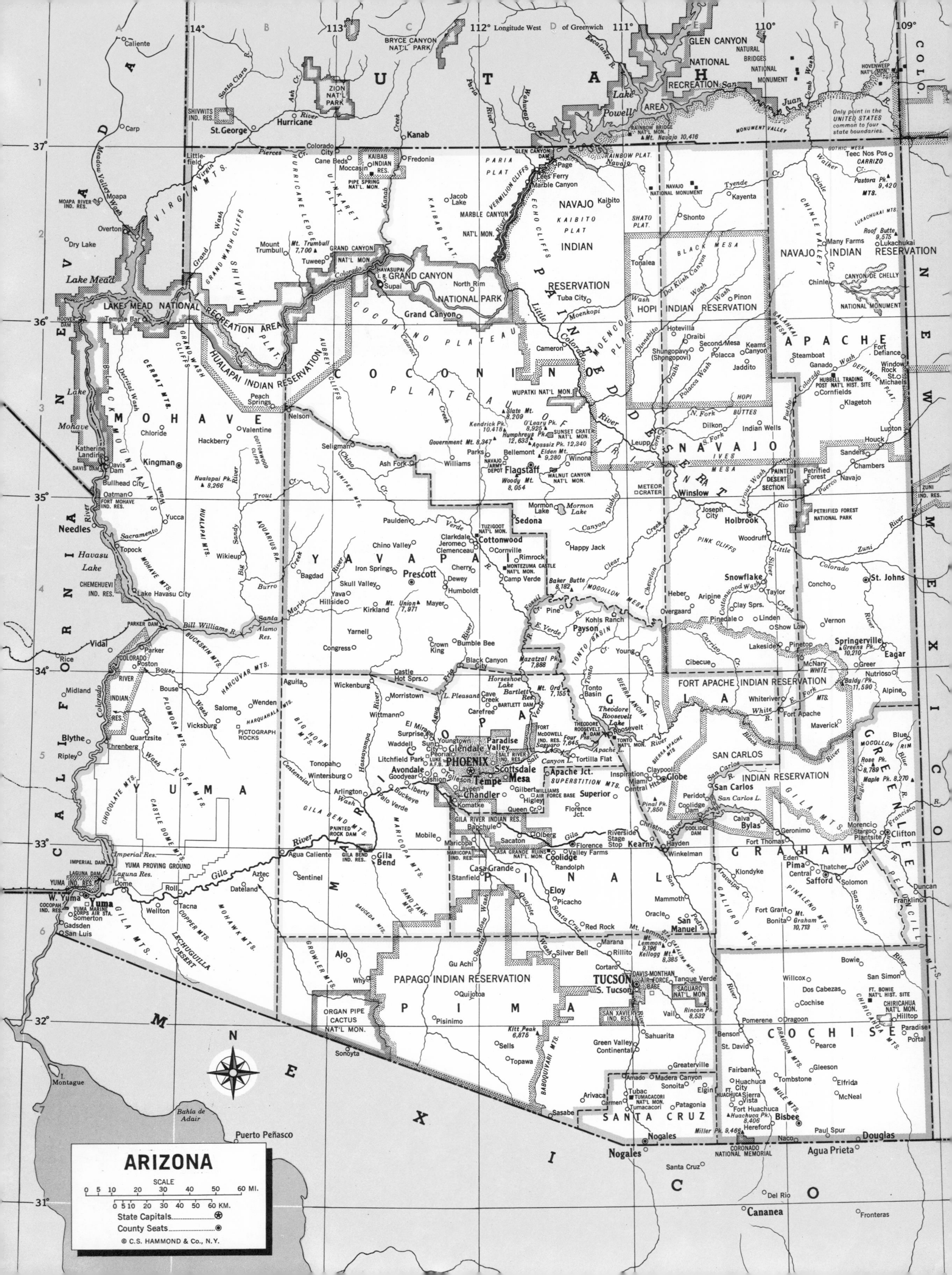

ARIZONA
SCALE
0 5 10 20 30 40 50 60 MI.
0 5 10 20 30 40 50 60 KM.
State Capitals
County Seats
© C.S. HAMMOND & Co., N.Y.
114°
113°
112° Longitude West of Greenwich
111°
110°
109°
37°
36°
35°
34°
33°
32°
31°
U T A H
N E V A D A
C A L I F O R N I A
N E W M E X I C O
M E X I C O
COLO.
Only point in the UNITED STATES common to four state boundaries.
MOHAVE
COCONINO
NAVAJO
APACHE
YAVAPAI
GILA
GREENLEE
GRAHAM
MARICOPA
PINAL
YUMA
PIMA
SANTA CRUZ
COCHISE
GRAND CANYON NATIONAL PARK
LAKE MEAD NATIONAL RECREATION AREA
GLEN CANYON NATIONAL RECREATION AREA
NAVAJO INDIAN RESERVATION
HOPI INDIAN RESERVATION
HUALAPAI INDIAN RESERVATION
FORT APACHE INDIAN RESERVATION
SAN CARLOS INDIAN RESERVATION
PAPAGO INDIAN RESERVATION
ORGAN PIPE CACTUS NAT'L MON.
PAINTED DESERT
COCONINO PLATEAU
MOGOLLON MESA
Lake Mead
Lake Powell
Colorado
Gila
Little Colorado
PHOENIX
Glendale
Scottsdale
Tempe
Mesa
Chandler
TUCSON
S. Tucson
Flagstaff
Prescott
Kingman
Yuma
Holbrook
St. Johns
Globe
Safford
Clifton
Bisbee
Douglas
Nogales
Florence
Sedona
Cottonwood
Winslow
Page
Tuba City
Kayenta
Chinle
Ganado
Window Rock
Williams
Seligman
Payson
Show Low
Springerville
Eagar
Wickenburg
Casa Grande
Coolidge
Eloy
Ajo
Sells
Benson
Willcox
Tombstone
Sierra Vista
Fort Huachuca
Lake Havasu City
Parker
Bullhead City
Needles
Blythe
Gila Bend
Buckeye
Avondale
Superior
San Manuel
Morenci
Pima
Puerto Peñasco
Agua Prieta
Cananea
Santa Cruz

Topography

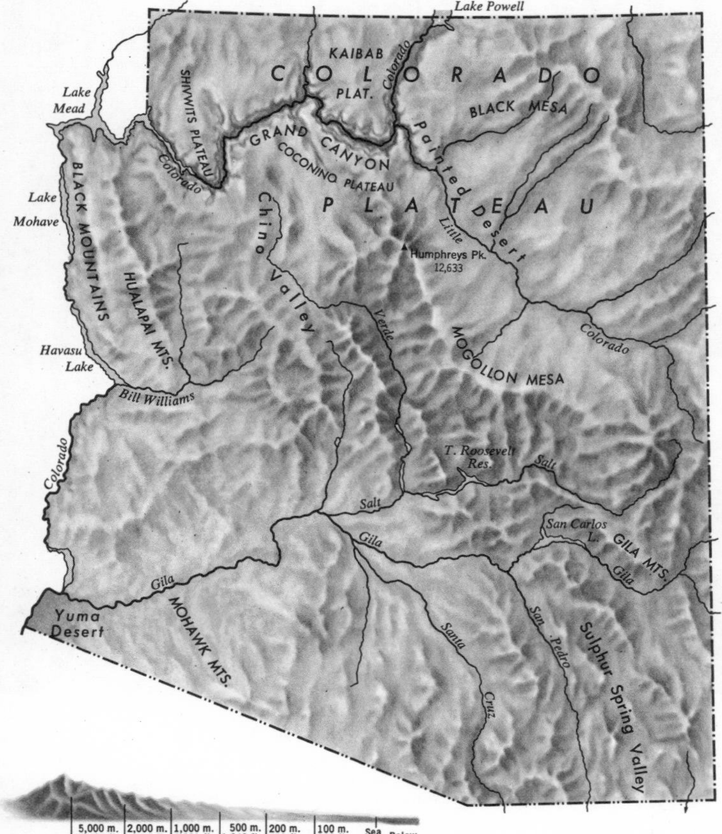

AREA 113,909 sq. mi.
POPULATION 1,772,482
CAPITAL Phoenix
LARGEST CITY Phoenix
HIGHEST POINT Humphreys Pk. 12,633 ft.
SETTLED IN 1580
ADMITTED TO UNION February 14, 1912
POPULAR NAME Grand Canyon State
STATE FLOWER Saguaro Cactus Blossom
STATE BIRD Cactus Wren

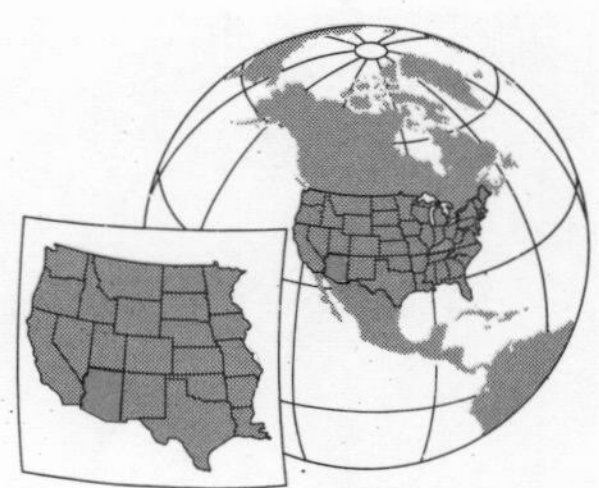

Agriculture, Industry and Resources

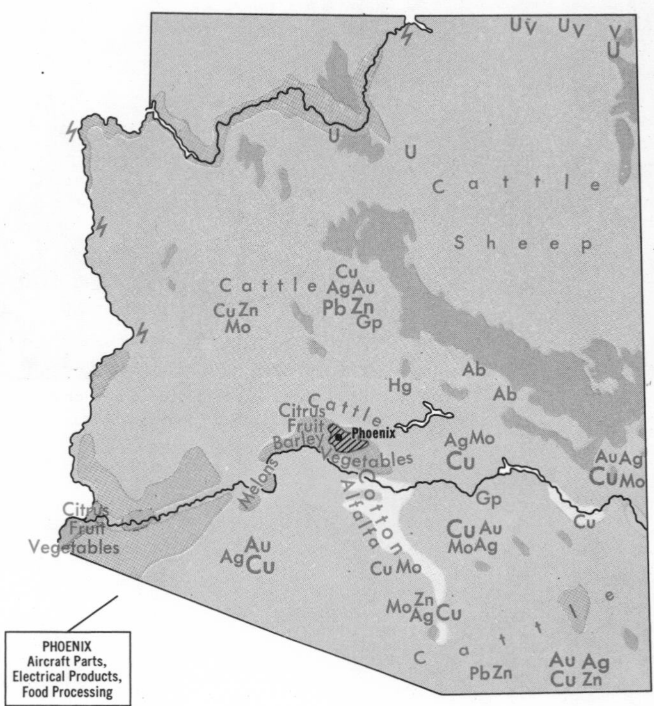

MAJOR MINERAL OCCURRENCES

Ab	Asbestos	Gp	Gypsum	U	Uranium
Ag	Silver	Hg	Mercury	V	Vanadium
Au	Gold	Mo	Molybdenum	Zn	Zinc
Cu	Copper	Pb	Lead		

DOMINANT LAND USE

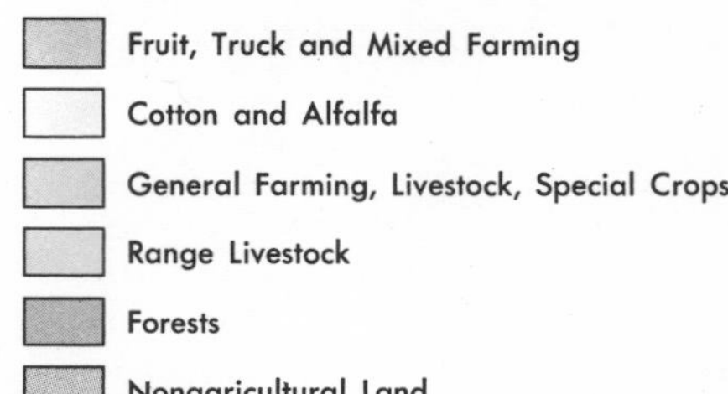

Water Power

Major Industrial Areas

COUNTIES

County	Key
Apache, 32,298	F 3
Cochise, 61,910	F 7
Coconino, 48,326	C 3
Gila, 29,255	E 5
Graham, 16,578	E 6
Greenlee, 10,330	F 5
Maricopa, 967,522	C 5
Mohave, 25,857	A 3
Navajo, 47,715	E 3
Pima, 351,667	D 6
Pinal, 67,916	D 6
Santa Cruz, 13,966	E 7
Yavapai, 36,733	C 4
Yuma, 60,827	A 5

CITIES and TOWNS

	Zip	Name/Pop.	Key
	85333	Agua Caliente, 30	B 6
	85320	Aguila, 450	B 5
	85321	Ajo, 5,881	C 6
	85920	Alpine, 450	F 5
	85640	Amado, 75	D 7
	85220	Apache Junction, 2,390	D 5
	85901	Aripine, 25	E 4
	85601	Arivaca, 165	D 7
	85322	Arlington, 950	C 5
	86320	Ash Fork, 800	C 3
	85323	Avondale, 6,304	C 5
	85333	Aztec, 20	B 6
	86321	Bagdad, 2,079	B 4
	85221	Bapchule, 300	D 5
	86001	Bellemont, 6	D 3
	85602	Benson, 2,839	E 7
	85603	Bisbee⊙, 8,328	F 7
	85324	Black Canyon City, 600	C 4
	85922	Blue, 50	F 5
	85643	Bonita, 20	E 6
	85325	Bouse, 200	A 5
	85605	Bowie, 600	F 6
	85326	Buckeye, 2,599	C 5
	86430	Bullhead City, 2,900	A 3
	85327	Bumble Bee, 15	C 4
	85530	Bylas, 1,125	E 5
	85530	Calva, 10	E 5
	86020	Cameron, 600	D 3
	86322	Camp Verde, 1,500	D 4
	86022	Cane Beds, 30	B 2
	85331	Carefree, 350	D 5
	85640	Carmen, 200	D 7
	85222	Casa Grande, 10,536	D 6
	85329	Cashion, 2,705	C 5
	85342	Castle Hot Springs, 50	C 5
	85331	Cave Creek, 300	D 5
	85531	Central, 300	F 6
	85501	Central Heights, 2,289	E 5
	86502	Chambers, 500	F 3
	85224	Chandler, 13,763	D 5
†	86327	Cherry, 20	C 4
	86503	Chinle, 500	F 2
	86323	Chino Valley, 970	C 4
	86431	Chloride, 225	A 3
†	85292	Christmas, 201	E 5
	85901	Cibecue, 100	E 4
	86324	Clarkdale, 892	C 4
	85532	Claypool, 2,245	E 5
†	85934	Clay Springs, 225	E 4
†	86326	Clemenceau, 300	C 4
	85533	Clifton⊙, 5,087	F 5
	85606	Cochise, 150	F 6
	86021	Colorado City, 350	B 2
	85924	Concho, 100	F 4
	85332	Congress, 350	C 4
†	85640	Continental, 250	D 7
	85228	Coolidge, 4,651	D 6
†	85542	Coolidge Dam, 42	E 5
†	86505	Cornfields, 200	F 3
	86325	Cornville, 425	D 4
	85230	Cortaro, 75	D 6
	86326	Cottonwood, 2,815	D 4
	86333	Crown King, 100	C 4
	85333	Dateland, 100	B 6
†	86430	Davis Dam, 125	A 3
	86327	Dewey, 100	C 4
†	86047	Dilkon, 90	E 3
†	85364	Dome, 48	A 6
†	85643	Dos Cabezas, 30	F 6
	85607	Douglas, 12,462	F 7
	85609	Dragoon, 150	F 6
	85534	Duncan, 773	F 6
	85925	Eagar, 1,279	F 4
	85535	Eden, 89	F 6
	85334	Ehrenburg, 93	A 5
†	85617	Elfrida, 700	F 7
†	85637	Elgin, 247	E 7
	85335	El Mirage, 3,258	C 5
	85231	Eloy, 5,381	D 6
	85612	Fairbank, 100	E 7
	86001	Flagstaff⊙, 26,117	D 3
	85232	Florence⊙, 2,173	D 5
	85233	Florence Junction, 35	D 5
	85926	Fort Apache, 500	F 5
	86504	Fort Defiance, 900	F 3
	85643	Fort Grant, 240	E 6
	85613	Fort Huachuca, 159	E 7
	85536	Fort Thomas, 450	E 5
	85534	Franklin, 300	F 6
	86022	Fredonia, 798	C 2
	85336	Gadsden, 250	A 6
	86505	Ganado, 300	F 3
†	85536	Geronimo, 25	F 5
	85337	Gila Bend, 1,795	C 6
	85234	Gilbert, 1,971	D 5
†	85617	Gleeson, 15	F 7
	85301	Glendale, 36,228	C 5
	85501	Globe⊙, 7,333	E 5
	85338	Goodyear, 2,140	C 5
	86023	Grand Canyon, 1,011	C 2
†	85637	Greaterville, 15	E 7
	85614	Green Valley, 5,971	D 7
	85927	Greer, 60	F 4
†	85634	Gu-Achi, 339	C 6
	86401	Hackberry, 250	B 3
	86024	Happy Jack, 50	D 4
	85235	Hayden, 1,283	E 5
	85928	Heber, 750	E 4
	85615	Hereford, 10	E 7
	85236	Higley, 500	D 5
†	86301	Hillside, 100	B 4
†	85632	Hilltop, 9	F 6
	86025	Holbrook⊙, 4,759	E 4
	86030	Hotevilla, 600	E 3
	86506	Houck, 325	F 3
	85616	Huachuca City, 1,233	E 7
	86329	Humboldt, 424	C 4
	86031	Indian Wells, 150	E 3
	85537	Inspiration, 500	D 5
	86330	Iron Springs, 175	C 4
	86022	Jacob Lake, 16	C 2
†	86025	Jeddito, 20	E 3
	86331	Jerome, 290	C 4
	86032	Joseph City, 650	E 4
	86044	Kaibito, 275	D 2
†	86401	Katherine Landing, 102	A 3
	86033	Kayenta, 500	E 2
	86034	Keams Canyon, 400	E 3
	85237	Kearny, 2,829	E 5
	86401	Kingman⊙, 7,312	A 3
	86332	Kirkland, 100	C 4
†	86505	Klagetoh, 200	F 3
	85643	Klondyke, 86	E 6
	85538	Kohls Ranch, 100	D 4
†	85339	Komatke, 300	C 5
	86403	Lake Havasu City, 5,700	A 4
	85929	Lakeside, 700	E 4
	85339	Laveen, 800	C 5
†	86036	Lees Ferry, 10	D 2
	86035	Leupp, 150	E 3
†	85326	Liberty, 150	C 5
†	85901	Linden, 50	E 4
	85340	Litchfield Park, 1,664	C 5
	86432	Littlefield, 40	B 2
	86507	Lukachukai, 350	F 2
	85341	Lukeville, 50	C 7
	86508	Lupton, 250	F 3
†	85637	Madera Canyon, 75	E 7
	85618	Mammoth, 1,953	E 6
	86503	Many Farms, 250	F 2
	85238	Marana, 2,900	D 6
	86036	Marble Canyon, 6	D 2
	85239	Maricopa, 750	C 5
†	85920	Maverick, 50	F 5
	86333	Mayer, 810	C 4
	85930	McNary, 950	F 4
	85617	McNeal, 100	F 7

(continued on following page)

Indigo-blue Lake Mead is surrounded by color-streaked cliffs and ranges, set off by the bright concrete of Arizona's Hoover Dam. One of the world's largest man-made lakes, Lake Mead provides water storage, dependable water supply and water sports.

* 85201 Mesa, 62,853 .... D 5
85539 Miami, 3,394 .... E 5
† 85239 Mobile, 100 .... C 5
86022 Moccasin, 60 .... C 2
85540 Morenci, 950 .... F 5
86038 Mormon Lake, 20 .... D 4
85342 Morristown, 250 .... C 5
85619 Mount Lemmon, 75 .... E 6
† 84770 Mount Trumbull, 14 .... B 2
85620 Naco, 750 .... E 7
86509 Navajo, 100 .... F 3
† 86434 Nelson, 39 .... B 3
85621 Nogales⊙, 8,946 .... E 7
86022 North Rim, 2 .... C 2
85932 Nutrioso, 67 .... F 5
86433 Oatman, 175 .... A 3
† 85247 Olberg, 65 .... D 5
85623 Oracle, 1,500 .... E 6
86039 Oraibi, 600 .... E 3
85933 Overgaard, 300 .... E 4
86040 Page, 1,439 .... D 2
85343 Palo Verde, 500 .... C 5
85253 Paradise Valley, 7,155 .... D 5
85344 Parker, 1,948 .... A 4
86001 Parks, 175 .... C 3
85624 Patagonia, 630 .... E 7
86334 Paulden, 4 .... C 4
† 85607 Paul Spur, 34 .... F 7
85541 Payson, 1,490 .... D 4
86434 Peach Springs, 525 .... B 3
85625 Pearce, 300 .... F 7
85345 Peoria, 4,792 .... C 5
85542 Peridot, 950 .... E 5
86025 Petrified Forest, 80 .... F 3
* 85001 Phoenix (cap.)⊙, 581,562 .... C 5
Phoenix, ‡967,522 .... C 5
85241 Picacho, 1,200 .... D 6
85543 Pima, 1,184 .... F 6
85544 Pine, 800 .... D 4
85934 Pinedale, 86 .... E 4
85935 Pinetop, 950 .... F 4
86510 Pinon, 100 .... E 2
85634 Pisinimo, 187 .... C 6
† 85540 Plantsite, 1,077 .... F 5
86042 Polacca, 500 .... E 3
85627 Pomerene, 365 .... E 6
85632 Portal, 72 .... F 7
85371 Poston, 500 .... A 4
86301 Prescott⊙, 13,030 .... C 4
85346 Quartzsite, 255 .... A 5
85242 Queen Creek, 600 .... D 5
† 85634 Quijotoa, 107 .... C 6
85243 Randolph, 350 .... D 6
85245 Red Rock, 100 .... D 6
85246 Rillito, 400 .... D 6
86335 Rimrock, 217 .... D 4
85237 Riverside Stage Stop, 418 .... D 5
85347 Roll, 700 .... A 6
85545 Roosevelt, 125 .... D 5
85247 Sacaton, 300 .... D 5
85546 Safford⊙, 5,333 .... F 6
85629 Sahuarita, 200 .... E 7
85630 Saint David, 1,250 .... E 7
85936 Saint Johns⊙, 1,320 .... F 4
86511 Saint Michaels, 250 .... F 3
85348 Salome, 684 .... B 5
85550 San Carlos, 2,542 .... E 5
86512 Sanders, 420 .... F 3
85349 San Luis, 280 .... A 6
85631 San Manuel, 4,332 .... E 6
85632 San Simon, 400 .... F 6
85633 Sasabe, 50 .... D 7
* 85251 Scottsdale, 67,823 .... D 5
86043 Second Mesa, 30 .... E 3
86336 Sedona, 2,022 .... D 4
86337 Seligman, 950 .... B 3
85634 Sells, 1,245 .... D 7
† 85333 Sentinel, 20 .... B 6
86044 Shonto, 700 .... E 2
85901 Show Low, 2,285 .... F 4
† 86043 Shungopavy (Shongopovi), 570 .... E 3
85635 Sierra Vista, 6,689 .... E 7
85270 Silver Bell, 900 .... D 6
86338 Skull Valley, 250 .... C 4
85937 Snowflake, 1,833 .... E 4
85551 Solomon, 700 .... F 6
85350 Somerton, 2,225 .... A 6
85637 Sonoita, 50 .... E 7
85713 South Tucson, 6,220 .... D 6
85938 Springerville, 1,038 .... F 4
85272 Stanfield, 150 .... C 6
† 85540 Stargo, 1,194 .... F 5
† 86505 Steamboat, 100 .... F 3
85351 Sun City, 13,670 .... D 5
86435 Supai, 190 .... C 2
85273 Superior, 4,975 .... D 5
85352 Tacna, 950 .... B 6
† 85701 Tanque Verde, 850 .... E 6
85939 Taylor, 888 .... E 4
86514 Teec Nos Pos, 550 .... F 2
85281 Tempe, 62,907 .... D 5
86443 Temple Bar, 84 .... A 2
85552 Thatcher, 2,320 .... F 6
85353 Tolleson, 3,881 .... C 5
85638 Tombstone, 1,241 .... F 7
86044 Tonalea, 125 .... E 2
85354 Tonopah, 54 .... B 5
85553 Tonto Basin, 69 .... D 5
85639 Topawa, 500 .... D 7
86436 Topock, 325 .... A 4
85290 Tortilla Flat, 37 .... D 5
85640 Tubac, 140 .... E 7
86045 Tuba City, 2,500 .... D 2
* 85701 Tucson⊙, 262,933 .... D 6
Tucson, ‡351,667 .... D 6
85640 Tumacacori, 100 .... D 7
† 84770 Tuweep, 14 .... B 2
85641 Vail, 175 .... E 6
86437 Valentine, 120 .... B 3
85291 Valley Farms, 240 .... D 6
85940 Vernon, 75 .... F 4
† 85348 Vicksburg, 16 .... B 5
85355 Waddell, 100 .... C 5
85356 Wellton, 900 .... A 6
85357 Wenden, 245 .... B 5
† 85364 West Yuma, 5,552 .... A 6
85941 Whiteriver, 900 .... E 5
85321 Why, 65 .... C 6
85358 Wickenburg, 2,698 .... C 5
85360 Wikieup, 150 .... B 4
85643 Willcox, 2,568 .... F 6
86046 Williams, 2,386 .... C 3
86515 Window Rock, 600 .... F 3
85292 Winkelman, 974 .... E 6
† 86001 Winona, 25 .... D 3
86047 Winslow, 8,066 .... E 3
† 85322 Wintersburg, 400 .... B 5
85361 Wittmann, 600 .... C 5
85942 Woodruff, 120 .... E 4
85362 Yarnell, 800 .... C 4
† 86301 Yava, 40 .... C 4
85554 Young, 197 .... D 4
85363 Youngtown, 1,886 .... C 5
86438 Yucca, 250 .... A 4
85364 Yuma⊙, 29,007 .... A 6

⊙ County seat.
‡ Population of metropolitan area.
† Zip of nearest p.o.
* Multiple zips

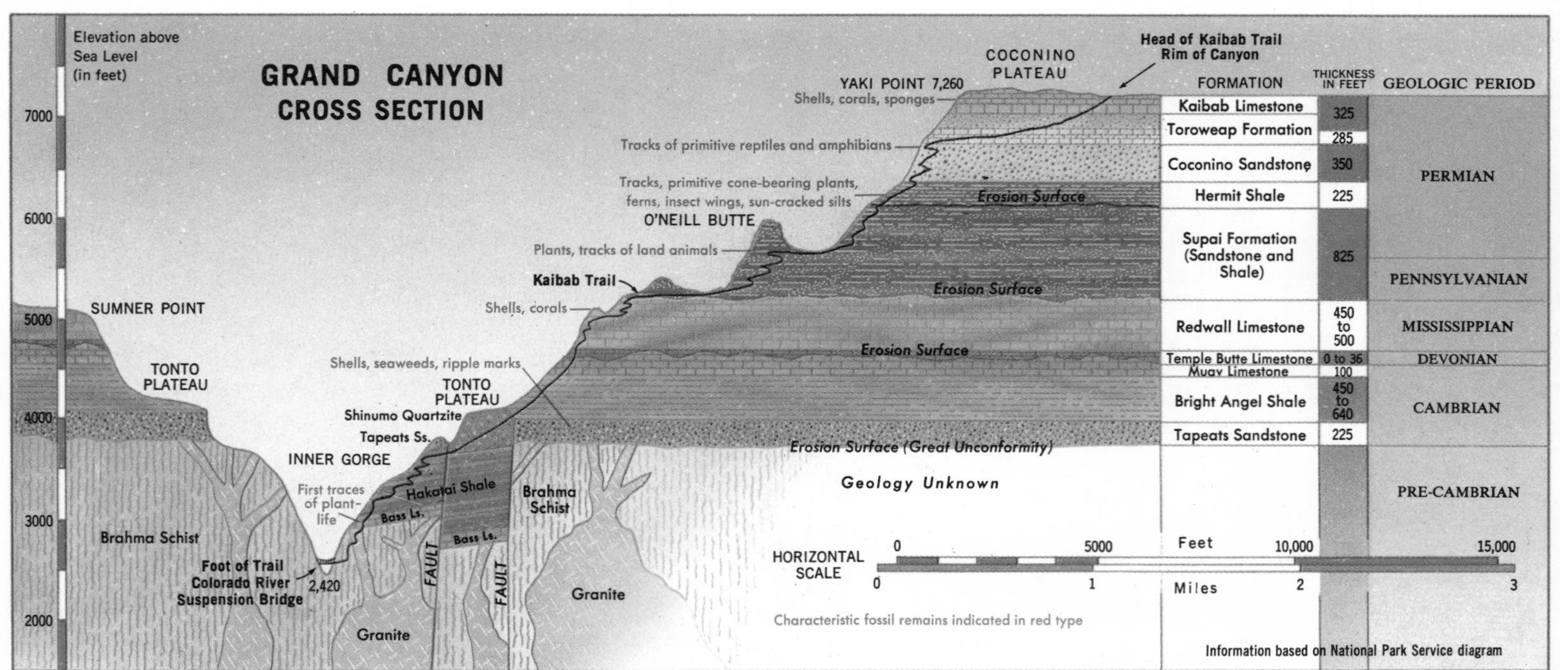

COUNTIES

County, Pop.	Key
Arkansas, 23,347	H 5
Ashley, 24,976	G 7
Baxter, 15,319	F 1
Benton, 50,476	B 1
Boone, 19,073	D 1
Bradley, 12,778	F 7
Calhoun, 5,573	E 6
Carroll, 12,301	C 1
Chicot, 18,164	H 7
Clark, 21,537	D 5
Clay, 18,771	K 1
Cleburne, 10,349	F 2
Cleveland, 6,605	F 6
Columbia, 25,952	D 7
Conway, 16,805	E 3
Craighead, 52,068	J 2
Crawford, 25,677	B 2
Crittenden, 48,106	K 3
Cross, 19,783	J 3
Dallas, 10,022	E 6
Desha, 18,761	H 6
Drew, 15,157	G 6
Faulkner, 31,572	F 3
Franklin, 11,301	C 2
Fulton, 7,699	G 1
Garland, 54,131	D 4
Grant, 9,711	F 5
Greene, 24,765	J 1
Hempstead, 19,308	C 6
Hot Spring, 21,963	E 5
Howard, 11,412	C 5
Independence, 22,723	G 2
Izard, 7,381	G 1
Jackson, 20,452	H 2
Jefferson, 85,329	G 5
Johnson, 13,630	C 2
Lafayette, 10,018	C 7
Lawrence, 16,320	H 1
Lee, 18,884	J 4
Lincoln, 12,913	G 6
Little River, 11,194	B 6
Logan, 16,789	C 3
Lonoke, 26,249	G 4
Madison, 9,453	C 1
Marion, 7,000	E 1
Miller, 33,385	C 7
Mississippi, 62,060	K 2
Monroe, 15,657	H 4
Montgomery, 5,821	C 4
Nevada, 10,111	D 6
Newton, 5,844	D 2
Ouachita, 30,896	E 6
Perry, 5,634	E 4
Phillips, 40,046	J 5
Pike, 8,711	C 5
Poinsett, 26,822	J 2
Polk, 13,297	B 5
Pope, 28,607	D 3
Prairie, 10,249	G 4
Pulaski, 287,189	F 4
Randolph, 12,645	H 1
Saint Francis, 30,799	J 3
Saline, 36,107	E 4
Scott, 8,207	B 4
Searcy, 7,731	E 2
Sebastian, 79,237	B 3
Sevier, 11,272	B 6
Sharp, 8,233	G 1
Stone, 6,838	F 2
Union, 45,428	E 7
Van Buren, 8,275	E 2
Washington, 77,370	B 2
White, 39,253	G 3
Woodruff, 11,566	H 3
Yell, 14,208	D 3

AREA 53,104 sq. mi.
POPULATION 1,923,295
CAPITAL Little Rock
LARGEST CITY Little Rock
HIGHEST POINT Magazine Mtn. 2,753 ft.
SETTLED IN 1685
ADMITTED TO UNION June 15, 1836
POPULAR NAME Land of Opportunity; Wonder State
STATE FLOWER Apple Blossom
STATE BIRD Mockingbird

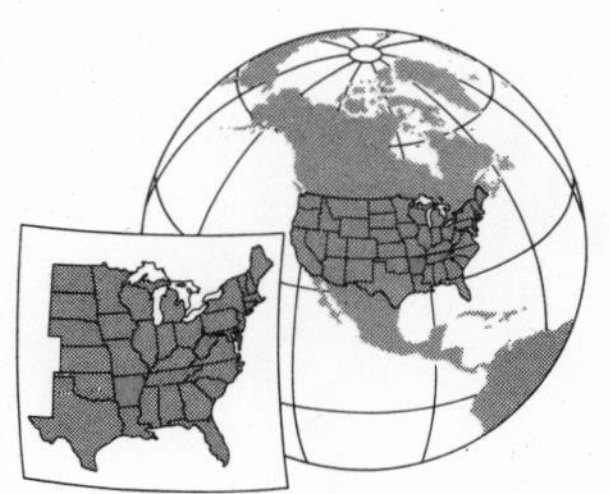

Agriculture, Industry and Resources

DOMINANT LAND USE

- Fruit and Mixed Farming
- Specialized Cotton
- Cotton, General Farming
- Rice, General Farming
- General Farming, Livestock, Truck Farming, Cotton
- Forests
- Swampland, Limited Agriculture

MAJOR MINERAL OCCURRENCES

Al	Bauxite	G	Natural Gas
Ba	Barite	Gp	Gypsum
C	Coal	Mr	Marble
Cl	Clay	O	Petroleum
D	Diamonds	Sp	Soapstone
Zn	Zinc		

Water Power — Major Industrial Areas

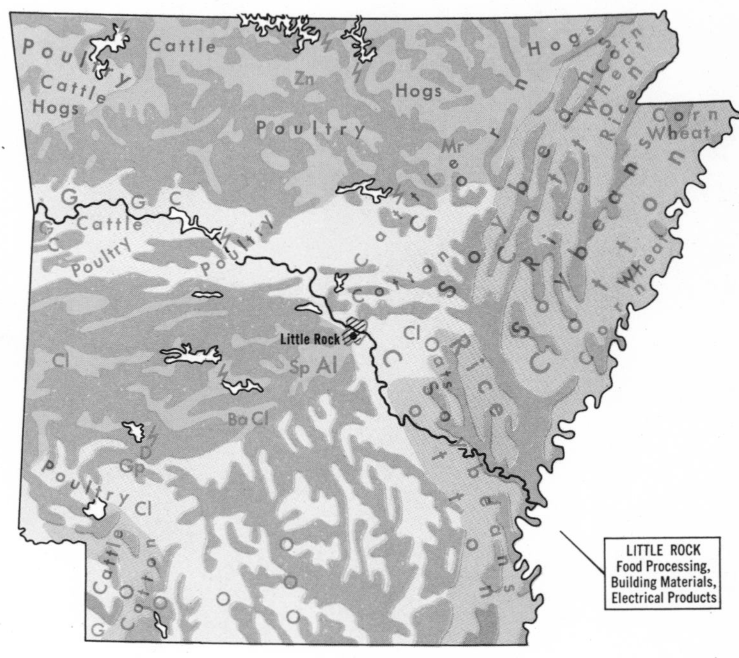

Eric Carle — Shostal Associates

Soybeans, Arkansas' leading cash crop, valued primarily as high protein food and feed, also has a wide range of uses, including plastics and agricultural sprays.

CITIES and TOWNS

Zip	Name/Pop.	Key
72920	Abbott, 210	B 3
72001	Adona, 204	E 3
72510	Agnos, 130	G 1
72002	Alexander, 297	F 4
72410	Alicia, 246	H 2
72820	Alix, 250	C 3
† 72046	Allport, 307	G 4
72921	Alma, 1,613	B 3
72003	Almyra, 220	H 5
72611	Alpena, 309	D 1
72004	Altheimer, 1,037	G 5
72821	Altus, 418	C 3
72005	Amagon, 136	H 2
71921	Amity, 614	D 5
71922	Antoine, 182	D 5
72822	Appleton, 150	E 3
71923	Arkadelphia⊙, 9,841	D 5
71630	Arkansas City⊙, 615	H 6
† 72055	Arkansas Post, 15	H 5
72310	Armorel, 300	L 2
71822	Ashdown⊙, 3,522	B 6
72513	Ash Flat⊙, 211	G 1
72823	Atkins, 2,015	E 3
72311	Aubrey, 351	J 4
72006	Augusta⊙, 2,777	H 3
72007	Austin, 236	G 4
72008	Auvergne, 150	H 2
72711	Avoca, 173	B 1
72010	Bald Knob, 2,094	G 3
71631	Banks, 189	F 6
72923	Barling, 1,739	B 3
72312	Barton, 400	J 4
72313	Bassett, 265	K 2
72501	Batesville⊙, 7,209	G 2
72411	Bay, 751	J 2
71720	Bearden, 1,272	E 6
72012	Beebe, 2,805	G 3
72014	Beedeville, 144	H 3
71721	Beirne, 140	D 6
72712	Bella Vista, 500	B 1
† 72601	Bellefonte, 300	D 1
72824	Belleville, 379	D 3
71823	Ben Lomond, 155	B 6
72015	Benton⊙, 16,499	E 4
72712	Bentonville⊙, 5,508	B 1
72615	Bergman, 249	E 1
72616	Berryville⊙, 2,271	C 1
† 72764	Bethel Heights, 284	B 1
† 72501	Bethesda, 285	G 2
72016	Bigelow, 258	E 3
72617	Bigflat, 189	F 1
72413	Biggers, 372	J 1
† 72386	Birdsong, 150	K 3
72017	Biscoe, 340	H 4
71929	Bismarck, 200	D 5
72414	Black Oak, 272	K 2
72415	Black Rock, 498	H 1
† 72069	Blackton, 175	H 4
71825	Blevins, 265	C 6
† 72933	Bloomer, 150	B 3
71722	Bluff City, 244	D 6
72827	Bluffton, 198	C 4
72315	Blytheville⊙, 24,752	L 2
† 71858	Bodcaw, 158	D 6
72926	Boles, 163	B 4
† 72901	Bonanza, 342	B 3
72416	Bono, 428	J 2
72927	Booneville⊙, 3,239	C 3
72020	Bradford, 826	G 3
71826	Bradley, 706	C 7
72928	Branch, 325	C 3
† 72017	Brasfield, 200	H 4
72828	Briggsville, 200	C 4
72021	Brinkley, 5,275	H 4
72417	Brookland, 465	J 2
72618	Bruno, 130	E 1
72022	Bryant, 1,199	F 4
71827	Buckner, 392	D 7
72619	Bull Shoals, 430	E 1
72321	Burdette, 173	L 2
72023	Cabot, 2,903	F 4
71935	Caddo Gap, 125	C 5
72322	Caldwell, 292	J 3
72519	Calico Rock, 723	F 1
71724	Calion, 535	E 7
71701	Camden⊙, 15,147	E 6
† 72201	Cammack Village, 1,165	E 4
† 72473	Campbell Station, 218	H 2
71829	Canfield, 365	C 7
72419	Caraway, 952	K 2
72024	Carlisle, 2,048	G 4
71725	Carthage, 566	E 5
72025	Casa, 208	D 3
72421	Cash, 265	J 2
72026	Casscoe, 200	H 4
† 72951	Caulksville, 208	C 3
72521	Cave City, 807	G 2
72718	Cave Springs, 469	B 1
72930	Cecil, 234	C 3
72450	Center Hill, 1,201	J 1
71830	Center Point, 144	C 5
72027	Center Ridge, 220	E 3
72719	Centerton, 312	B 1
71901	Central City, 150	B 3
† 71832	Chapel Hill, 154	B 5
72933	Charleston⊙, 1,497	B 3
72522	Charlotte, 158	H 2
72323	Chatfield, 150	K 3
72542	Cherokee Village, 1,300	G 1
† 71953	Cherry Hill, 250	B 4
72324	Cherry Valley, 556	J 3
71726	Chidester, 232	D 6
72029	Clarendon⊙, 2,563	H 4
72325	Clarkedale, 250	K 3
72830	Clarksville⊙, 4,616	D 3
72031	Clinton⊙, 1,029	F 2
72832	Coal Hill, 733	C 3
72476	College City, 645	J 1
71655	College Heights, 2,050	G 6
72326	Colt, 301	J 3
71831	Columbus, 258	C 6
72523	Concord, 163	G 2
72032	Conway⊙, 15,510	F 3
72422	Corning⊙, 2,705	J 1
72626	Cotter, 858	E 1
72036	Cotton Plant, 1,657	H 3
71937	Cove, 334	B 5
72037	Coy, 240	G 4
72327	Crawfordsville, 831	K 3
71635	Crossett, 6,191	G 7
71728	Curtis, 500	D 6
72526	Cushman, 427	G 2
† 71923	Dalark, 132	E 5
72039	Damascus, 255	F 3
72833	Danville⊙, 1,362	D 3
72834	Dardanelle⊙, 3,297	D 3
72424	Datto, 142	J 1
72722	Decatur, 847	A 1
72723	Delaney, 150	C 2
72425	Delaplaine, 145	J 1
72835	Delaware, 200	D 3
71940	Delight, 439	C 5
72426	Dell, 358	K 2
72836	Denning, 203	C 3
71832	De Queen⊙, 3,863	B 5
71638	Dermott, 4,250	H 7
72040	Des Arc⊙, 1,714	G 4
72041	De Valls Bluff⊙, 622	H 4
72042	De Witt⊙, 3,728	H 5
72644	Diamond City, 282	E 1
72043	Diaz, 283	H 2
71833	Dierks, 1,101	B 5
71834	Doddridge, 125	C 7
71941	Donaldson, 500	E 5
72837	Dover, 662	D 3
72530	Drasco, 300	G 2
† 72943	Driggs, 125	C 3
71639	Dumas, 4,600	H 6
72935	Dyer, 486	B 3
71729	Eagle Mills, 149	E 6
72331	Earle, 3,146	K 3
71701	East Camden, 589	E 6
72044	Edgemont, 125	F 2
72332	Edmondson, 412	K 3
72333	Elaine, 1,210	J 5
71730	El Dorado⊙, 25,283	E 7
72727	Elkins, 418	C 1
72728	Elm Springs, 260	B 1
72045	El Paso, 131	F 3
71740	Emerson, 393	D 7
71835	Emmet, 433	D 6

(continued on following page)

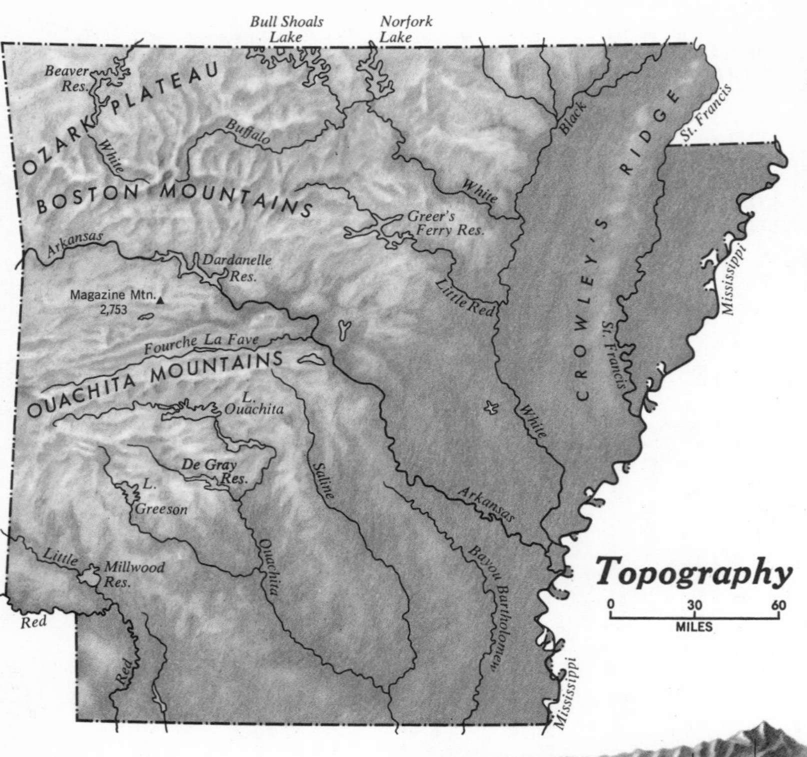

	ZIP	Place	Key
	72046	England, 3,075	G 4
	72047	Enola, 150	F 3
	72048	Ethel, 350	H 5
	72428	Etowah, 150	K 2
	71640	Eudora, 3,687	H 7
	72632	Eureka Springs⊙, 1,670	C 1
	72729	Evansville, 427	B 2
	72532	Evening Shade,309	G 1
†	72936	Excelsior, 160	B 3
	72397	Fair Oaks, 270	J 3
	72049	Fargo, 206	H 4
	72730	Farmington, 908	B 1
	72701	Fayetteville⊙, 30,729	B 1
†	71747	Felsenthal, 150	F 7
	72429	Fisher, 361	J 2
	72634	Flippen, 626	E 1
	72534	Floral, 165	G 2
	71742	Fordyce⊙, 4,837	F 6
	71836	Foreman, 1,173	B 6
†	72031	Formosa, 224	E 3
	72335	Forrest City⊙, 12,521	J 3
	72901	Fort Smith⊙, 62,802	B 3
		Fort Smith, ‡160,421	B 3
	71837	Fouke, 506	C 7
	71642	Fountain Hill, 266	G 7
	72051	Fox, 200	F 2
	72017	Fredonia (Biscoe), 340	H 4
	71942	Friendship, 150	E 5
	71838	Fulton, 323	C 6
	72732	Garfield, 163	C 1
	71839	Garland, 321	C 7
	72052	Garner, 150	G 3
	72635	Gassville, 434	F 1
	71840	Genoa, 125	C 7
	72734	Gentry, 1,022	A 1
	72054	Georgetown, 137	G 3
	72055	Gillett, 860	H 5
	71841	Gillham, 200	B 5
	72339	Gilmore, 461	K 3
	71943	Glenwood, 1,212	C 5
	72340	Goodwin, 125	J 4
†	72315	Gosnell, 1,386	K 2
	71643	Gould, 1,683	G 6
	71644	Grady, 688	G 5
	71944	Grannis, 177	B 5
	72838	Gravelly, 300	C 4
	72736	Gravette, 1,154	B 1
	72058	Greenbrier, 582	F 3
	72638	Green Forest, 1,354	D 1
	72737	Greenland, 650	B 1
	72430	Greenway, 240	K 1
	72936	Greenwood⊙, 2,032	B 3
†	72067	Greers Ferry, 389	F 2
	72059	Gregory, 311	H 3
	72060	Griffithville, 227	G 3
	72431	Grubbs, 442	H 2
	72540	Guion, 213	G 2
†	71923	Gum Springs, 269	D 5
	71743	Gurdon, 2,075	D 6
	72061	Guy, 179	F 3
	72937	Hackett, 462	B 3
	71645	Halley, 204	H 6
	71646	Hamburg⊙, 3,102	G 7
	71744	Hampton⊙, 1,252	F 6
	72542	Hardy, 692	H 1
	71745	Harrell, 269	F 7
	72432	Harrisburg⊙, 1,931	J 2
	72601	Harrison⊙, 7,239	D 1
	72938	Hartford, 616	B 3
	72840	Hartman, 400	C 3
	72062	Haskell, 239	E 4
	71945	Hatfield, 377	B 5
	72063	Hattieville, 163	E 3
	72842	Havana, 308	D 3
	72341	Haynes, 375	J 4
	72064	Hazen, 1,605	G 4
	72543	Heber Springs⊙, 2,497	G 2
	72843	Hector, 387	E 3
	72342	Helena⊙, 10,415	J 4
	72065	Hensley, 350	F 4
	71647	Hermitage, 399	F 7
	72066	Hickory Plains, 200	G 3
	72347	Hickory Ridge, 410	J 3
	72068	Higginson, 225	G 3
	72739	Hiwasse, 175	B 1
†	72857	Hollis, 275	D 4
	72069	Holly Grove, 840	H 4
†	71923	Hollywood, 175	D 5
	72939	Hon, 250	B 4
	71801	Hope⊙, 8,810	C 6
	71842	Horatio, 748	B 6
	72536	Horseshoe Bend, 321	G 1
	71901	Hot Springs National Park⊙, 35,631	D 4
	72070	Houston, 200	E 3
	72433	Hoxie, 2,265	H 1
†	72315	Huffman, 150	L 2
	72348	Hughes, 1,872	J 4
	72349	Hulbert, 500	K 3
	72072	Humnoke, 398	G 4
	72073	Humphrey, 818	G 5
	72074	Hunter, 131	H 3
	72940	Huntington, 627	B 3
	72740	Huntsville⊙, 1,287	C 1
	71747	Huttig, 822	F 7
	72434	Imboden, 496	H 1
	72075	Jacksonport, 306	H 2
	72076	Jacksonville, 19,832	F 4
	72641	Jasper⊙, 394	D 1
	72079	Jefferson, 250	F 5
	71649	Jennie, 172	H 7
†	72901	Jenny Lind, 250	B 3
†	72327	Jericho, 150	K 3
	72080	Jerusalem, 250	E 3
	71949	Jessieville, 248	D 4
	72741	Johnson, 274	B 1
	72350	Joiner, 839	K 3
	72401	Jonesboro⊙, 27,050	J 2
	72105	Jones Mill, 850	E 5
	72081	Judsonia, 1,667	G 3
	71749	Junction City, 763	E 7
	72351	Keiser, 688	K 2
	72082	Kensett, 1,444	G 3
	72083	Keo, 226	G 4
†	72956	Kibler, 611	B 3
	71652	Kingsland, 304	F 6
	72742	Kingston, 200	C 1
	71950	Kirby, 300	C 5
	72435	Knobel, 375	J 1
	72845	Knoxville, 202	D 3
	72436	Lafe, 160	J 1
	72352	La Grange, 350	J 4
	72437	Lake City⊙, 948	K 2
	71653	Lake Village⊙, 3,310	H 7
	72846	Lamar, 589	D 3
	71929	Lambert, 200	D 5
	71844	Laneburg, 150	D 6
	71952	Langley, 200	C 5
	72941	Lavaca, 532	B 3
	71750	Lawson, 300	F 7
	72438	Leachville, 1,582	K 2
	72644	Lead Hill, 143	D 1
	72084	Leola, 390	E 5
	72354	Lepanto, 1,846	K 2
	72645	Leslie, 563	E 2
	72085	Letona, 191	G 3
	71845	Lewisville⊙, 1,653	C 7
	72355	Lexa, 500	J 4
	72646	Limestone, 200	D 2
	72744	Lincoln, 1,023	B 2
*	72201	Little Rock (cap.)⊙ 132,483	F 4
		Little Rock-North Little Rock ‡323,296	F 4
	71846	Lockesburg, 620	B 6
	72550	Locust Grove, 225	G 2
	72847	London, 539	D 3
	72086	Lonoke⊙, 3,140	G 4
	71751	Louann, 245	E 7
	72745	Lowell, 653	B 1
†	72856	Lurton, 150	D 2
	72358	Luxora, 1,566	K 2
	72440	Lynn, 274	H 2
	72103	Mabelvale, 350	F 4
†	71753	Macedonia, 150	D 7
	72359	Madison, 984	J 4
	72943	Magazine, 677	C 3
	72553	Magness, 139	H 2
†	72104	Magnet, 230	E 5
	71753	Magnolia⊙, 11,303	D 7
	72104	Malvern⊙, 8,739	E 5
	72554	Mammoth Spring, 1,072	G 1
	72442	Manila, 1,961	K 2
	72944	Mansfield, 981	B 3
	72555	Marcella, 136	G 2
†	72114	Marche, 150	F 4
	72360	Marianna⊙, 6,196	J 4
	72364	Marion⊙, 1,634	K 3
	72365	Marked Tree, 3,208	K 2
	72443	Marmaduke, 821	K 1
	72650	Marshall⊙, 1,397	E 2
	72366	Marvell, 1,980	J 4
	72106	Mayflower, 469	F 4
	72444	Maynard, 224	J 1
	72747	Maysville, 200	A 1
†	72006	McClelland, 200	H 3
	72101	McCrory, 1,378	H 3
	72441	McDougal, 328	K 1
	71654	McGehee, 4,683	H 6
	71849	McNab, 201	C 6
	71752	McNeil, 684	D 7
	72102	McRae, 643	G 3
	72556	Melbourne⊙, 1,043	G 1
	71953	Mena⊙, 4,530	B 4
	72107	Menifee, 251	E 3
	72945	Midland, 294	B 3
	71851	Mineral Springs, 761	C 6
†	71639	Mitchellville, 494	H 6
	72447	Monette, 1,076	K 2
	72108	Monroe, 200	H 4
	71655	Monticello⊙, 5,085	G 6
	71658	Montrose, 558	H 7
	72558	Moorefield, 127	G 2
	72109	Morganton, 144	F 3
	72368	Moro, 489	H 4
	72110	Morrilton⊙, 6,814	E 3
	71659	Moscow, 250	G 5
	72946	Mountainburg, 524	B 2
	72653	Mountain Home⊙, 3,936	F 1
	71956	Mountain Pine, 800	D 4
	72560	Mountain View⊙, 1,866	F 2
	71758	Mount Holly, 300	E 7
	71957	Mount Ida⊙, 819	C 4
	72655	Mount Judea, 500	D 2
	72561	Mount Pleasant, 346	G 2
	72111	Mount Vernon, 200	F 3
	72947	Mulberry, 1,340	B 2
	71958	Murfreesboro⊙, 1,350	C 5
	71852	Nashville⊙, 4,016	C 6
	72562	Newark, 849	H 2
	71660	New Edinburg, 304	F 6
	71959	Newhope, 130	C 5
	72112	Newport⊙, 7,725	H 2
	72448	Nimmons, 135	K 1
†	71601	Noble Lake, 350	G 5
	72658	Norfork, 266	F 1
	71960	Norman, 360	C 5
	71759	Norphlet, 755	E 7
†	71635	North Crossett, 2,891	G 7
*	72114	North Little Rock, 60,040	F 4
†	72386	Norvell, 440	K 3
	72660	Oakgrove, 236	C 1
	71961	Oden, 141	C 4
	71853	Ogden, 286	B 6
	72564	Oil Trough, 524	G 2
	72449	O'Kean, 244	J 1
	71962	Okolona, 233	D 5
	72853	Ola, 1,029	D 3
	72662	Omaha, 160	D 1
	72369	Oneida, 300	J 5
†	72110	Oppelo, 147	E 3
	72370	Osceola⊙, 7,204	K 2
	72565	Oxford, 271	G 1
	71855	Ozan, 134	C 6
	72949	Ozark⊙, 2,592	C 3
	72372	Palestine, 755	J 4
	72121	Pangburn, 654	G 3
	72450	Paragould⊙, 10,639	J 1
	72855	Paris⊙, 3,646	C 3
	71661	Parkdale, 459	H 7
	72373	Parkin, 1,731	J 3
	72950	Parks, 358	B 4
	72123	Patterson, 417	H 3
	72453	Peach Orchard, 256	J 1
	71964	Pearcy, 200	D 5
	72751	Pea Ridge, 1,088	B 1
	71965	Pencil Bluff, 200	C 4
	72124	Perla, 227	E 5
	72125	Perry, 218	E 3
	71801	Perrytown, 148	C 6
	72126	Perryville⊙, 815	E 3
	72752	Pettigrew, 300	C 2
	71662	Pickens, 200	H 6
	72454	Piggott⊙, 3,087	K 1
	72669	Pindall, 154	E 1
	71601	Pine Bluff⊙, 57,389	F 5
		Pine Bluff, ‡85,329	F 5
	72857	Plainview, 677	D 4
	72568	Pleasant Plains, 162	G 2
	72127	Plumerville, 724	E 3
	72455	Pocahontas⊙, 4,544	H 1
	72456	Pollard, 253	K 1
	72374	Poplar Grove, 255	J 4
	72457	Portia, 381	H 1
	71663	Portland, 662	H 7
	72858	Pottsville, 411	D 3
	72569	Poughkeepsie, 130	H 1
	72128	Poyen, 265	E 5
	72753	Prairie Grove, 1,582	B 2
	72859	Prairie View, 150	C 3
	72129	Prattsville, 299	F 5
	71857	Prescott⊙, 3,921	D 6
	72672	Pyatt, 137	E 1
	72131	Quitman, 354	F 3
	72951	Ratcliff, 184	C 3
†	72333	Ratio, 200	J 5
	72459	Ravenden, 219	H 1
	71726	Reader, 143	D 6
	71664	Readland, 225	H 7
	72461	Rector, 1,990	K 1
	72132	Redfield, 277	F 5
	71670	Reed, 403	H 6
	72462	Reyno, 356	J 1
	71665	Rison⊙, 1,214	F 6

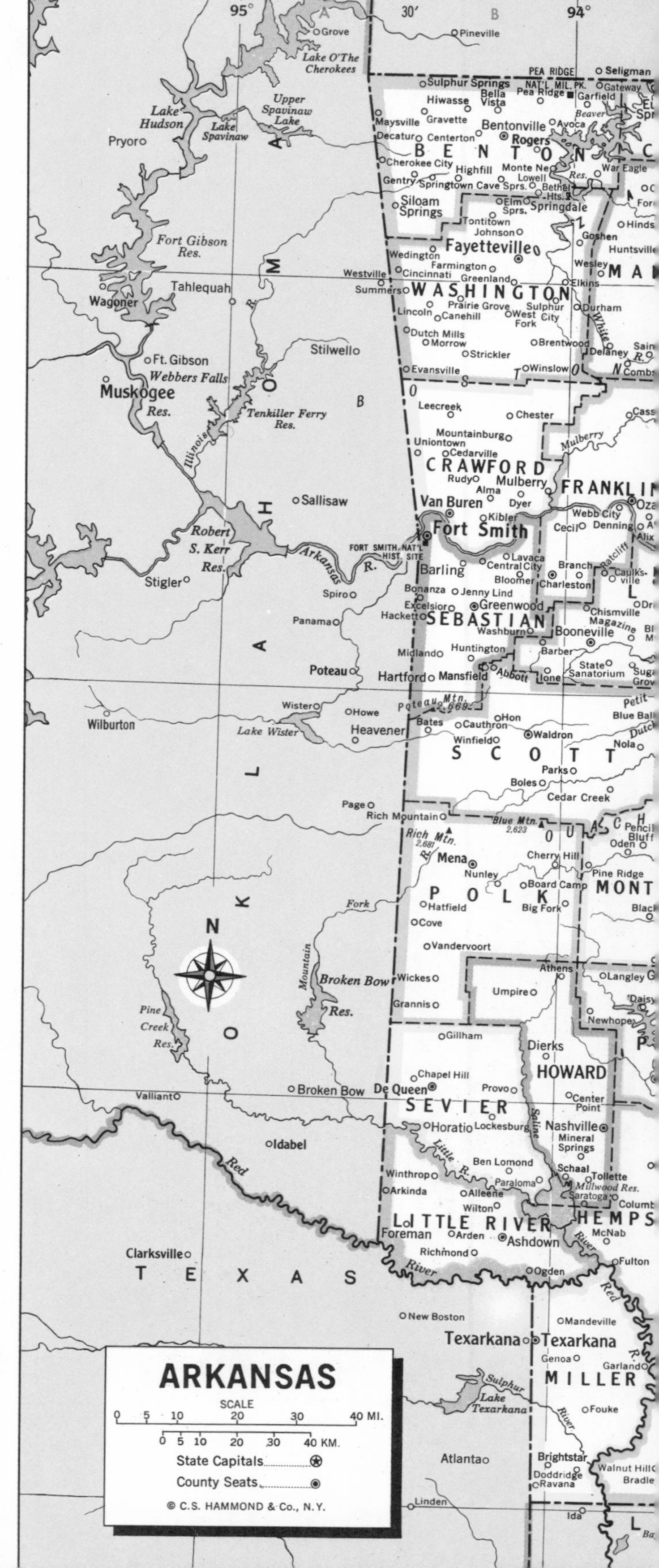

ZIP	Place	Key
72377	Rivervale, 250	K 2
72104	Rockport, 158	E 5
72134	Roe, 127	H 4
72756	Rogers, 11,050	B 1
72135	Roland, 350	E 4
72355	Rondo, 379	J 4
72137	Rose Bud, 157	F 3
72571	Rosie, 300	G 2
72378	Round Pond, 160	J 3
72860	Rover, 160	D 4
72139	Russell, 231	G 3
72801	Russellville⊙, 11,750	D 3
72140	Saint Charles, 201	H 5
72464	Saint Francis, 297	K 1
72675	Saint Joe, 225	E 1
72760	Saint Paul, 145	C 2
72575	Salado, 175	G 2
72576	Salem⊙, 1,277	G 1
72658	Salesville, 156	F 1
71859	Saratoga, 131	C 6
71851	Schaal, 125	C 6
72142	Scott, 200	F 4
72862	Scottsville, 241	D 3
72863	Scranton, 222	C 3
72143	Searcy⊙, 9,040	G 3
72465	Sedgwick, 168	J 2
† 71670	Selma, 193	G 6
72150	Sheridan⊙, 2,480	F 5
72152	Sherrill, 208	F 5
72116	Sherwood, 2,754	F 4
72153	Shirley, 269	F 2
72761	Siloam Springs, 6,009	B 1
71762	Smackover, 2,058	E 7
71763	Sparkman, 663	E 6
72764	Springdale, 16,783	B 1
72157	Springfield, 160	E 3
71860	Stamps, 2,427	D 7
71667	Star City⊙, 2,032	G 6
72954	State Sanatorium, 700	C 3
71764	Stephens, 1,184	E 7
72468	Stonewall, 205	J 1
72469	Strawberry, 176	H 2
71765	Strong, 965	F 7
72160	Stuttgart⊙, 10,477	H 4
72865	Subiaco, 375	C 3
72470	Success, 201	J 1
72579	Sulphur Rock, 224	H 2
72768	Sulphur Springs, 503	B 1
72677	Summit, 321	E 1
72164	Sweet Home, 350	F 4
72471	Swifton, 703	H 2
71861	Taylor, 671	D 7
75501	Texarkana⊙, 21,682	C 7
	Texarkana, ‡101,198	C 7
71766	Thornton, 331	F 6
71670	Tillar, 293	H 6
† 71851	Tollette, 225	C 6
† 72041	Tollville, 156	G 4
72770	Tontitown, 426	B 1
72167	Traskwood, 210	E 5
72472	Trumann, 5,938	J 2
72168	Tucker, 500	G 5
72473	Tuckerman, 1,731	H 2
† 71725	Tulip, 150	E 5
72015	Tull, 179	E 5
72483	Tulot, 170	K 2
72169	Tupelo, 246	H 3
72384	Turrell, 783	K 3
72386	Tyronza, 510	K 3
72170	Ulm, 185	H 4
72955	Uniontown, 250	B 2
71768	Urbana, 500	E 7
† 71923	Vaden, 125	E 6
72682	Valley Springs, 275	D 1
72956	Van Buren⊙, 8,373	B 3
72387	Vanndale, 310	J 3
72388	Victoria, 198	K 2
71769	Village, 200	D 7
72173	Vilonia, 423	F 3
72583	Viola, 360	G 1
72389	Wabash, 275	J 5
72175	Wabbaseka, 644	G 5
72474	Walcott, 131	J 1
72475	Waldenburg, 164	J 2
71770	Waldo, 1,658	D 7
72958	Waldron⊙, 2,132	B 4
72476	Walnut Ridge⊙, 3,800	J 1
72176	Ward, 619	F 3
71671	Warren⊙, 6,433	F 6
† 72936	Washburn, 165	B 3
71862	Washington, 290	C 6
71863	Waterloo, 150	D 6
71674	Watson, 371	H 6
72479	Weiner, 915	J 2
72177	Weldon, 133	H 3
72773	Wesley, 200	C 1
71771	Wesson, 160	E 7
† 71635	West Crossett, 200	F 7
72685	Western Grove, 179	D 1
72774	West Fork, 810	B 2
72390	West Helena, 11,007	J 4
72301	West Memphis, 25,892	K 3
72178	West Point, 184	G 3
72391	West Ridge, 350	K 2
72392	Wheatley, 507	H 4
71772	Whelen Springs, 126	D 6
† 71635	White, 200	G 7
71601	White Hall, 1,300	F 5
71973	Wickes, 409	B 5
72394	Widener, 292	J 3
72482	Williford, 173	H 1
71675	Wilmar, 653	G 6
71676	Wilmot, 1,132	G 7
72395	Wilson, 1,009	K 2
71865	Wilton, 427	B 6
71677	Winchester, 234	G 6
72959	Winslow, 227	B 2
71866	Winthrop, 240	B 6
72587	Wiseman, 193	G 1
72180	Woodson, 600	F 4
72181	Wooster, 307	F 3
72182	Wright, 175	F 5
72183	Wrightsville, 400	F 4
72396	Wynne⊙, 6,696	J 3
72687	Yellville⊙, 860	E 1
71678	Yorktown, 225	G 5

⊙ County seat.
‡ Population of metropolitan area.
† Zip of nearest p.o.
* Multiple zips

CALIFORNIA
SCALE
0 10 20 40 60 80 MI.
0 10 20 40 60 80 KM.
State Capitals
County Seats
Canals
© C.S. HAMMOND & Co., N.Y.
Longitude West of Greenwich
SAN FRANCISCO AND VICINITY
SACRAMENTO AND VICINITY
LOS ANGELES AND VICINITY
O R E G O N
N E V A D A
A R I Z O N A
M E X I C O
P A C I F I C
O C E A N

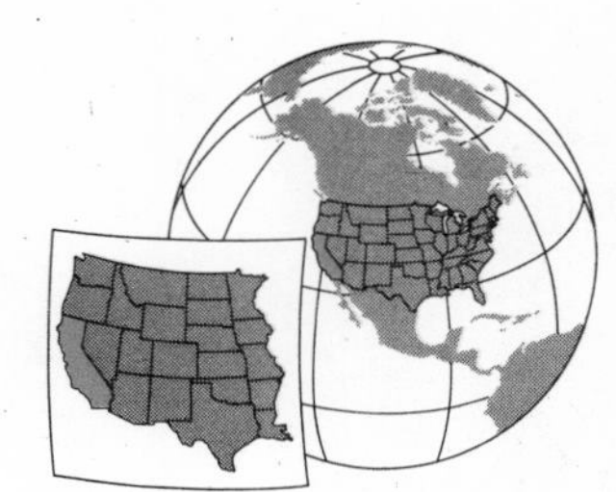

AREA 158,693 sq. mi.
POPULATION 19,953,134
CAPITAL Sacramento
LARGEST CITY Los Angeles
HIGHEST POINT Mt. Whitney 14,494 ft.
SETTLED IN 1769
ADMITTED TO UNION September 9, 1850
POPULAR NAME Golden State
STATE FLOWER Golden Poppy
STATE BIRD California Valley Quail

COUNTIES

Name/Pop.	Key
Alameda, 1,073,184	D 6
Alpine, 484	F 5
Amador, 11,821	E 5
Butte, 101,969	D 4
Calaveras, 13,585	E 5
Colusa, 12,430	C 4
Contra Costa, 558,389	D 6
Del Norte, 14,580	B 2
El Dorado, 43,833	E 5
Fresno, 413,053	E 7
Glenn, 17,521	C 4
Humboldt, 99,692	B 3
Imperial, 74,492	K 10
Inyo, 15,571	H 7
Kern, 329,162	G 8
Kings, 64,610	F 8
Lake, 19,548	C 4
Lassen, 14,960	E 3
Los Angeles, 7,032,075	G 9
Madera, 41,519	F 6
Marin, 206,038	C 5
Mariposa, 6,015	E 6
Mendocino, 51,101	B 4
Merced, 104,629	E 6
Modoc, 7,469	E 2
Mono, 4,016	F 5
Monterey, 250,071	D 7
Napa, 79,140	C 5
Nevada, 26,346	E 4
Orange, 1,420,386	H 10
Placer, 77,306	E 4
Plumas, 11,707	E 4
Riverside, 459,074	J 10
Sacramento, 631,498	D 5
San Benito, 18,226	D 7
San Bernardino, 684,072	J 9
San Diego, 1,357,854	J 10
San Francisco (city county), 715,674	J 2
San Joaquin, 290,208	D 6
San Luis Obispo, 105,690	E 8
San Mateo, 556,234	C 6
Santa Barbara, 264,324	E 9
Santa Clara, 1,064,714	D 6
Santa Cruz, 123,790	C 6
Shasta, 77,640	C 3
Sierra, 2,365	E 4
Siskiyou, 33,225	C 2
Solano, 169,941	D 5
Sonoma, 204,885	C 5
Stanislaus, 194,506	D 6
Sutter, 41,935	D 4
Tehama, 29,517	C 3
Trinity, 7,615	B 3
Tulare, 188,322	G 7
Tuolumne, 22,169	F 5
Ventura, 376,430	F 9
Yolo, 91,788	D 5
Yuba, 44,736	D 4

CITIES and TOWNS

Zip	Name/Pop.	Key
92301	Adelanto, 2,115	H 9
96006	Adin, 550	E 2
93601	Ahwahnee, 503	F 6
94501	Alameda, 70,968	J 2
94507	Alamo-Danville, 14,059	K 2
94706	Albany, 14,674	J 2
* 91801	Alhambra, 62,125	C 10
93201	Alpaugh, 800	F 8
92001	Alpine, 1,570	J 11
91001	Altadena, 42,380	C 10
91701	Alta Loma, 6,100	E 10
96101	Alturas⊙, 2,799	E 2
† 95101	Alum Rock, 18,355	L 3
* 92801	Anaheim, 166,701	D 11
	Anaheim-Santa Ana-Garden Grove, ‡1,420,386	D 11
96007	Anderson, 5,492	C 3
95222	Angels Camp, 1,710	E 5
94508	Angwin, 2,690	C 5
94509	Antioch, 28,060	L 1
92307	Apple Valley, 6,702	H 9
95003	Aptos, 8,704	K 4
95912	Arbuckle, 1,037	C 4
95825	Arcade-Arden, 82,498	B 8
91006	Arcadia, 42,868	C 10
95521	Arcata, 8,985	A 3
93202	Armona, 1,392	F 7
93420	Arroyo Grande, 7,454	E 8
90701	Artesia, 14,757	C 11
93203	Arvin, 5,090	G 8
† 94578	Ashland, 14,810	K 2
95413	Asti, 50	C 5
93422	Atascadero, 10,290	E 8
94025	Atherton, 8,085	K 3
95301	Atwater, 11,640	E 6
93602	Auberry, 515	F 6
95603	Auburn⊙, 6,570	C 8
90704	Avalon, 1,520	G 10
93204	Avenal, 3,035	E 8
91702	Azusa, 25,217	D 10
92309	Baker, 600	J 8
* 93301	Bakersfield⊙, 69,515	G 8
	Bakersfield ‡, 329,271	G 8
91706	Baldwin Park, 47,285	D 10
92220	Banning, 12,034	J 10
92311	Barstow, 17,442	H 9
† 95501	Bayview, 2,340	A 3
† 93401	Baywood Park-Los Osos, 3,487	E 8
92223	Beaumont, 5,484	J 10
90201	Bell, 21,836	C 11
90706	Bellflower, 51,454	C 11
94002	Belmont, 23,667	J 3
94920	Belvedere, 2,599	H 2
94510	Benicia, 8,783	K 1
95005	Ben Lomond, 2,793	K 4
* 94701	Berkeley, 116,716	J 2
94511	Bethel Island, 1,398	L 1
* 90210	Beverly Hills, 33,416	B 10
92314	Big Bear City, 850	J 9
92315	Big Bear Lake, 5,268	J 9
95917	Biggs, 1,115	D 4
93513	Big Pine, 839	G 6
93920	Big Sur, 500	D 7
93606	Biola, 950	E 7
93514	Bishop, 3,498	G 6
† 94947	Black Point, 500	J 1
92316	Bloomington, 11,957	E 10
95525	Blue Lake, 1,112	A 3
92225	Blythe, 7,047	L 10
94923	Bodega Bay, 700	B 5
94924	Bolinas, 700	H 1
95415	Boonville, 715	B 5
93516	Boron, 1,999	H 8
92004	Borrego Springs, 860	J 10
95006	Boulder Creek, 1,806	J 4
95707	Bowman, 2,089	C 8
91010	Bradbury, 1,098	D 10
92227	Brawley, 13,746	K 11
92621	Brea, 18,447	D 11
94513	Brentwood, 2,649	L 2
93517	Bridgeport⊙, 525	F 5
94005	Brisbane, 3,003	J 2
95605	Broderick-Bryte, 12,782	B 8
95007	Brookdale, 630	J 4
95605	Bryte-Broderick, 12,782	B 8
93427	Buellton, 1,402	E 9
90620	Buena Park, 63,646	D 11
* 91501	Burbank, 88,871	C 10
94010	Burlingame, 27,320	J 2
96013	Burney, 2,190	D 3
93206	Buttonwillow, 1,193	F 8
94514	Byron, 800	L 2
92230	Cabazon, 598	J 10
92231	Calexico, 10,625	K 11
93501	California City, 1,309	H 8
92233	Calipatria, 1,824	K 10
94515	Calistoga, 1,882	C 5
95418	Calpella, 900	B 4
93745	Calwa, 5,191	F 7
93010	Camarillo, 19,219	F 9
93428	Cambria, 1,716	D 8
95709	Camino, 800	E 5
95008	Campbell, 24,770	K 3
92006	Campo, 850	J 11
95226	Campo Seco, 700	D 9
* 91303	Canoga Park, 109,127	B 10
92672	Capistrano Beach, 4,149	H 10
95010	Capitola, 5,080	K 4
92007	Cardiff-by-the-Sea, 5,724	H 10
92008	Carlsbad, 14,944	H 10
93921	Carmel, 4,525	D 7
93924	Carmel Valley, 3,026	D 7
95608	Carmichael, 37,625	C 8
93013	Carpinteria, 6,982	F 9
90744	Carson, 71,150	C 11
93609	Caruthers, 950	E 7
† 93001	Casitas Springs, 1,113	F 9
95420	Caspar, 578	B 4
91310	Castaic, 800	G 9
94546	Castro Valley, 44,760	K 2
95012	Castroville, 3,235	D 7
92234	Cathedral City, 3,640	J 10
93430	Cayucos, 1,772	E 8
96104	Cedarville, 825	E 2
96019	Central Valley, 2,361	C 3
95307	Ceres, 6,029	D 6
90701	Cerritos, 15,856	C 11
91311	Chatsworth, 24,000	B 10
95044	Chemeketa Park-Redwood Estates, 1,452	K 4
† 94521	Cherryland, 9,969	K 2
96020	Chester, 1,531	D 3
95926	Chico, 19,580	D 4
93555	China Lake, 11,105	H 8
95309	Chinese Camp, 150	E 6
91710	Chino, 20,411	D 10
93610	Chowchilla, 4,349	E 6
* 92010	Chula Vista, 67,901	J 11
95610	Citrus Heights, 21,760	C 8
91711	Claremont, 23,464	D 10
95612	Clarksburg, 554	B 9
94517	Clayton, 1,385	K 2
95422	Clearlake Highlands, 2,836	C 5
95423	Clearlake Oaks, 975	C 4
95425	Cloverdale, 3,251	B 5
93612	Clovis, 13,856	F 7
92236	Coachella, 8,353	J 10
93210	Coalinga, 6,161	E 7
95713	Colfax, 798	E 4
94014	Colma, 537	J 2
92324	Colton, 19,974	E 10
95932	Colusa⊙, 3,842	C 4
† 90001	Commerce, 10,536	C 10
* 90220	Compton, 78,611	C 11
* 94520	Concord, 85,164	K 1
93212	Corcoran, 5,249	F 7
96021	Corning, 3,573	C 4
91720	Corona, 27,519	E 11
92118	Coronado, 20,910	H 11
95076	Corralitos, 600	L 4
94925	Corte Madera, 8,464	J 2
* 92626	Costa Mesa, 72,660	D 11
96022	Cottonwood, 1,288	C 3
95428	Covelo, 900	B 4
91722	Covina, 30,380	D 10
95531	Crescent City⊙, 2,586	A 2
92325	Crestline, 3,509	H 9
94525	Crockett, 2,900	J 1
91730	Cucamonga, 5,796	E 10
90230	Culver City, 31,035	B 10
95014	Cupertino, 18,216	K 3
93615	Cutler, 2,503	F 7
95534	Cutten, 2,228	A 3
90630	Cypress, 31,026	D 11
92327	Daggett, 950	H 9
* 94014	Daly City, 66,922	H 2
92629	Dana Point, 4,745	H 10
94526	Danville-Alamo, 14,059	K 2
95616	Davis, 23,488	B 8
94576	Deer Park, 975	C 5
93215	Delano, 14,559	F 8
95315	Delhi, 2,063	E 6
92014	Del Mar, 3,956	H 11
93940	Del Rey Oaks, 1,823	D 7
92404	Del Rosa, 8,000	E 10
92240	Desert Hot Springs, 2,738	J 9
† 93550	Desert View Highlands, 2,172	G 9
94528	Diablo, 950	K 2
95619	Diamond Springs, 900	D 8
93618	Dinuba, 7,917	F 7
95620	Dixon, 4,432	B 9
96023	Dorris, 840	D 2
93620	Dos Palos, 2,496	E 6
* 90240	Downey, 88,445	C 11
95936	Downieville⊙, 375	E 4
91010	Duarte, 14,981	D 10
94566	Dublin, 13,641	K 2
95937	Dunnigan, 550	C 5
96025	Dunsmuir, 2,214	C 2
95938	Durham, 700	D 4
92241	Eagle Mountain, 2,453	K 10
93219	Earlimart, 3,080	F 8
† 92225	East Blythe, 1,252	L 10
90804	East Los Angeles, 105,033	C 10
93706	Easton, 1,065	F 7
93523	Edwards, 900	G 9
* 92020	El Cajon, 52,273	J 11
92243	El Centro⊙, 19,272	K 11
94530	El Cerrito, 25,190	J 2
95623	El Dorado, 900	C 8
95630	El Dorado Hills, 2,000	C 8
94018	El Granada, 1,473	H 3
95624	Elk Grove, 3,721	B 9
* 91731	El Monte, 69,837	D 10
95318	El Portal, 675	F 6
93030	El Rio, 6,173	F 9
90245	El Segundo, 15,620	B 11
92330	Elsinore, 3,530	F 11
92630	El Toro, 8,654	E 11
94608	Emeryville, 2,681	J 2
95319	Empire, 2,016	D 6
92024	Encinitas, 5,375	H 10
91316	Encino, 40,000	B 10
96001	Enterprise, 11,486	C 3
95320	Escalon, 2,366	E 6
92025	Escondido, 36,792	J 10
95627	Esparto, 1,088	C 5
91739	Etiwanda, 900	E 10
96027	Etna, 667	C 2
95501	Eureka⊙, 24,337	A 3
93221	Exeter, 4,475	F 7
94930	Fairfax, 7,661	H 1
94533	Fairfield⊙, 44,146	K 1
95628	Fair Oaks, 11,256	C 8
92028	Fallbrook, 6,945	H 10
96028	Fall River Mills, 600	D 3
93223	Farmersville, 3,456	F 7
93224	Fellows, 530	F 8
95018	Felton, 2,062	K 4
95536	Ferndale, 1,352	A 3
93015	Fillmore, 6,285	G 9
93622	Firebaugh, 2,517	E 7
95828	Florin, 9,646	B 8
95630	Folsom, 5,810	C 8
92335	Fontana, 20,673	E 10
† 93268	Ford City, 3,503	F 8
† 95703	Foresthill, 900	E 4
94933	Forest Knolls, 900	H 1
95437	Fort Bragg, 4,455	B 4
95538	Fort Dick, 850	A 2
96032	Fort Jones, 515	C 2
95540	Fortuna, 4,203	A 3
94404	Foster City, 9,327	J 2
92708	Fountain Valley, 31,826	D 11
93625	Fowler, 2,239	F 7
93225	Frazier Park, 1,167	F 9
95019	Freedom, 5,563	L 4
* 94536	Fremont, 100,869	K 3
† 93701	Fresno⊙, 165,972	F 7
	Fresno, ‡413,053	F 7
* 92631	Fullerton, 85,987	D 11
95632	Galt, 3,200	C 9
* 90247	Gardena, 41,021	C 11
* 92640	Garden Grove, 122,524	D 11
95634	Georgetown, 700	E 5
96035	Gerber, 800	C 3
95441	Geyserville, 887	B 5
95020	Gilroy, 12,665	D 6
† 92501	Glen Avon Heights, 5,759	E 10
* 91201	Glendale, 132,752	C 10
91740	Glendora, 31,349	D 10
93017	Goleta, 3,500	F 9
93926	Gonzales, 2,575	D 7
93227	Goshen, 1,324	F 7
91344	Granada Hills, 50,000	B 10
92324	Grand Terrace, 5,901	E 10
95945	Grass Valley, 5,149	D 4
95444	Graton, 975	C 5
93308	Greenacres, 2,116	F 8
93927	Greenfield, 2,608	D 7
95947	Greenville, 1,073	E 3
95948	Gridley, 3,534	D 4
93433	Grover City, 5,939	E 8
93434	Guadalupe, 3,145	E 9
95445	Gualala, 585	B 5
95446	Guerneville, 900	B 5
95322	Gustine, 2,793	D 6
94019	Half Moon Bay, 4,023	H 3
95951	Hamilton City, 961	C 4
93230	Hanford⊙, 15,179	F 7
96039	Happy Camp, 925	B 2
90710	Harbor City, 17,500	C 11
90250	Hawthorne, 53,304	C 11
96041	Hayfork, 900	B 3
* 94541	Hayward, 93,058	K 2
95448	Healdsburg, 5,438	B 5
92249	Heber, 875	K 11
92343	Hemet, 12,252	H 10
96113	Herlong, 900	E 3
90254	Hermosa Beach, 17,412	B 11
92345	Hesperia, 4,592	H 9
† 91302	Hidden Hills, 1,529	B 10
92507	Highgrove, 2,158	E 10
92346	Highland, 13,290	H 9
95324	Hilmar, 813	E 6
92347	Hinkley, 900	H 9
95023	Hollister⊙, 7,663	D 7
90028	Hollywood, 85,047	C 10
92250	Holtville, 3,496	K 11
† 91720	Home Gardens, 5,116	E 11
92348	Homeland, 1,187	H 10
95546	Hoopa, 850	B 2
95449	Hopland, 817	B 5
95326	Hughson, 2,144	E 6
* 92646	Huntington Beach, 115,960	C 11
90255	Huntington Park, 33,744	C 11
93234	Huron, 1,525	E 7
92349	Idyllwild, 950	J 10
94947	Ignacio, 4,500	H 1
92251	Imperial, 3,094	K 11
92032	Imperial Beach, 20,244	H 11
93526	Independence⊙, 748	H 7
92201	Indio, 14,459	J 10
* 90301	Inglewood, 89,985	B 11
94937	Inverness, 800	B 5
95640	Ione, 2,369	C 9
93017	Isla Vista, 13,441	E 9
95641	Isleton, 909	L 1
93235	Ivanhoe, 1,595	F 7
95642	Jackson⊙, 1,924	C 9
92034	Jacumba, 700	J 11
95327	Jamestown, 950	E 6
92252	Joshua Tree, 1,211	J 9
95451	Kelseyville, 950	C 5
† 94701	Kensington, 5,823	J 2
93600	Kerman, 2,667	E 7
93238	Kernville, 900	G 8
93239	Kettleman City, 600	E 7
95328	Keyes, 1,875	E 6
93930	King City, 3,717	D 7
95719	Kings Beach, 600	F 4
93631	Kingsburg, 3,843	F 7
95645	Knights Landing, 846	B 8
91011	La Canada, 20,652	C 10
91214	La Crescenta-Montrose, 19,594	C 10
94549	Lafayette, 20,484	K 2
* 92651	Laguna Beach, 14,550	G 10
92653	Laguna Hills, 13,676	D 11
92677	Laguna Niguel, 4,644	H 10
90631	La Habra, 41,350	D 11
94020	La Honda, 650	J 3
92037	La Jolla, 30,000	H 11
92352	Lake Arrowhead, 2,682	H 9
93532	Lake Hughes, 750	G 9
93240	Lake Isabella, 850	G 8
† 92330	Lakeland Village, 1,724	E 11
95453	Lakeport⊙, 3,005	C 4
* 90712	Lakewood, 82,973	C 11
92041	La Mesa, 39,178	H 11
90638	La Mirada, 30,808	D 11
93241	Lamont, 7,007	G 8
93534	Lancaster, 30,948	G 9
* 91744	La Puente, 31,092	D 10
94939	Larkspur, 10,487	H 1
95076	La Selva Beach, 1,171	K 4
95330	Lathrop, 2,137	D 6
93242	Laton, 1,071	F 7
91750	La Verne, 12,965	D 10

(continued on following page)

Topography

0 50 100
MILES

5,000 m. 16,404 ft. | 2,000 m. 6,562 ft. | 1,000 m. 3,281 ft. | 500 m. 1,640 ft. | 200 m. 656 ft. | 100 m. 328 ft. | Sea Level | Below

(continued)

90260 Lawndale, 24,825 .... B 11
95454 Laytonville, 917 .... B 4
95333 Le Grand, 995 .... E 6
92045 Lemon Grove, 19,690 .... J 11
93245 Lemoore, 4,219 .... F 7
90304 Lennox, 16,121 .... B 11
92311 Lenwood, 3,834 .... H 9
92024 Leucadia, 5,900 .... H 10
95648 Lincoln, 3,176 .... B 8
† 95901 Linda, 7,731 .... D 4
93247 Lindsay, 5,206 .... F 7
95953 Live Oak, 2,645 .... D 4
95953 Live Oak, 6,443 .... K 4
94550 Livermore, 37,703 .... L 2
95334 Livingston, 2,588 .... E 6
95237 Lockeford, 890 .... C 9
95240 Lodi, 28,691 .... C 9
95551 Loleta, 800 .... A 3
92354 Loma Linda, 9,797 .... F 10
90717 Lomita, 19,784 .... C 11
93436 Lompoc, 25,284 .... E 9
93545 Lone Pine, 1,241 .... H 7
* 90801 Long Beach, 358,633 .... C 11
95650 Loomis, 1,108 .... C 8
90720 Los Alamitos, 11,346 .... D 11
93440 Los Alamos, 750 .... E 9
94022 Los Altos, 24,956 .... K 3
94022 Los Altos Hills, 6,865 .... J 3
* 90001 Los Angeles⊙, 2,816,061 .... C 10
Los Angeles-Long Beach, ‡7,032,075 .... C 10
93635 Los Banos, 9,188 .... E 6
95030 Los Gatos, 23,735 .... K 4
96055 Los Molinos, 900 .... D 3
† 93401 Los Osos-Baywood Park, 3,487 .... E 8
95457 Lower Lake, 850 .... C 5
96118 Loyalton, 945 .... E 4
95458 Lucerne, 1,300 .... C 4
92356 Lucerne Valley, 850 .... J 9
90262 Lynwood, 43,353 .... C 11
93637 Madera⊙, 16,044 .... E 7
90265 Malibu, 15,000 .... B 10
90266 Manhattan Beach, 35,352 .... B 11
95336 Manteca, 13,845 .... D 6
93252 Maricopa, 740 .... F 8
† 94901 Marinwood, 6,000 .... H 1
95338 Mariposa⊙, 900 .... F 6
96120 Markleeville⊙, 150 .... F 5
94553 Martinez⊙, 16,506 .... K 1
95901 Marysville⊙, 9,353 .... D 4
95955 Maxwell, 850 .... C 4
90270 Maywood, 16,996 .... C 10
96057 McCloud, 1,643 .... C 2
93250 McFarland, 4,177 .... F 8
92254 Mecca, 900 .... K 10
93023 Meiners Oaks, 7,025 .... F 9
95460 Mendocino, 975 .... B 4
93640 Mendota, 2,705 .... E 7
94025 Menlo Park, 26,734 .... J 3
92359 Mentone, 2,900 .... H 9
95340 Merced⊙, 22,670 .... E 6
95461 Middletown, 800 .... C 5
92655 Midway City, 5,900 .... D 11
94030 Millbrae, 20,781 .... J 2
94941 Mill Valley, 12,942 .... H 2
95035 Milpitas, 27,149 .... L 3
91752 Mira Loma, 8,482 .... E 10
92675 Mission Viejo, 11,933 .... D 11
* 95350 Modesto⊙, 61,712 .... D 6
93501 Mojave, 2,573 .... G 8
95245 Mokelumne Hill, 560 .... E 5
91016 Monrovia, 30,015 .... D 10
96064 Montague, 890 .... C 2
93003 Montalvo, 2,400 .... F 9
94037 Montara, 1,459 .... H 3
91763 Montclair, 22,546 .... D 10
90640 Montebello, 42,807 .... C 10
93103 Montecito, 4,900 .... F 9
93940 Monterey, 26,302 .... D 7
91754 Monterey Park, 49,166 .... C 10
95462 Monte Rio, 900 .... B 5
95030 Monte Sereno, 3,089 .... K 4
91020 Montrose-La Crescenta, 19,594 .... C 10
93021 Moorpark, 3,380 .... G 9
94556 Moraga, 14,205 .... K 2
95037 Morgan Hill, 6,485 .... L 4
93442 Morro Bay, 7,109 .... D 8
94038 Moss Beach, 700 .... H 3
95039 Moss Landing, 600 .... C 7
94040 Mountain View, 51,092 .... K 3
96067 Mount Shasta, 2,163 .... C 2
† 95926 Mulberry, 1,795 .... D 4
95247 Murphys, 780 .... E 5
92362 Murrieta, 850 .... H 10
92405 Muscoy, 7,091 .... E 10
94558 Napa⊙, 35,978 .... C 5
92050 National City, 43,184 .... J 11
92363 Needles, 4,051 .... L 9
95959 Nevada City⊙, 2,314 .... D 4
94560 Newark, 27,153 .... K 3
92365 Newberry Springs, 710 .... J 9
95658 Newcastle, 900 .... C 8
91321 Newhall, 9,651 .... G 9
95360 Newman, 2,505 .... D 6
* 92660 Newport Beach, 49,422 .... D 11
92257 Niland, 900 .... K 10
93444 Nipomo, 3,642 .... E 8
91760 Norco, 14,511 .... E 11
93643 North Fork, 575 .... F 6
95660 North Highlands, 31,854 .... B 8
* 91601 North Hollywood, 190,000 .... B 10
90650 Norwalk, 91,827 .... C 11
94947 Novato, 31,006 .... H 1
95361 Oakdale, 6,594 .... E 6
93644 Oakhurst, 800 .... F 6
* 94601 Oakland⊙, 361,561 .... J 2
94561 Oakley, 1,306 .... L 1
93022 Oak View, 4,872 .... F 9
93445 Oceano, 2,564 .... E 8
92054 Oceanside, 40,494 .... H 10
93308 Oildale, 20,879 .... F 8
93023 Ojai, 5,591 .... F 9
* 91761 Ontario, 64,118 .... D 10
95060 Opal Cliffs, 5,425 .... K 4
* 92666 Orange, 77,374 .... D 11

93646 Orange Cove, 3,392 .... F 7
93454 Orcutt, 8,500 .... E 9
95555 Orick, 950 .... A 2
94563 Orinda, 6,790 .... J 2
95963 Orland, 2,884 .... C 4
95556 Orleans, 850 .... B 2
92368 Oro Grande, 700 .... H 9
93647 Orosi, 2,757 .... F 7
95965 Oroville⊙, 7,536 .... D 4
93030 Oxnard, 71,225 .... F 9
Oxnard-Ventura, ‡376,430 .... F 9
94044 Pacifica, 36,020 .... H 2
92109 Pacific Beach, 59,000 .... H 11
93950 Pacific Grove, 13,505 .... C 7
† 95076 Pajaro, 1,407 .... D 7
95968 Palermo, 1,966 .... D 4
93550 Palmdale, 8,511 .... G 9
92260 Palm Desert, 6,171 .... J 10
92262 Palm Springs, 20,936 .... J 10
* 94301 Palo Alto, 55,966 .... K 3
90274 Palos Verdes Estates, 13,641 .... B 11
95969 Paradise, 14,539 .... D 4
90723 Paramount, 34,734 .... C 11
93648 Parlier, 1,993 .... F 7
* 91101 Pasadena, 113,327 .... C 10
† 95060 Pastiempo, 1,115 .... K 4
93446 Paso Robles, 7,168 .... E 8
95363 Patterson, 3,147 .... D 6
93553 Pearblossom, 900 .... H 9
93953 Pebble Beach, 5,000 .... C 7
92370 Perris, 4,228 .... F 11
94060 Pescadero, 625 .... J 4
94952 Petaluma, 24,870 .... H 1
95466 Philo, 700 .... B 4
90660 Pico Rivera, 54,170 .... C 10
94611 Piedmont, 10,917 .... J 2
93650 Pinedale, 1,900 .... F 7
94564 Pinole, 15,850 .... J 1
93040 Piru, 975 .... G 9
93449 Pismo Beach, 4,043 .... E 8
94565 Pittsburg, 20,651 .... L 1
93256 Pixley, 1,584 .... F 8
92670 Placentia, 21,948 .... D 11
95667 Placerville⊙, 5,416 .... C 8
95365 Planada, 2,056 .... E 6
94523 Pleasant Hill, 24,610 .... K 2
94566 Pleasanton, 18,328 .... L 2
95669 Plymouth, 501 .... C 8
95726 Pollock Pines, 850 .... E 5
* 91766 Pomona, 87,384 .... D 10
93257 Poplar, 1,239 .... F 7
93257 Porterville, 12,602 .... G 7
93041 Port Hueneme, 14,295 .... F 9
96122 Portola, 1,625 .... E 4
94025 Portola Valley, 4,999 .... J 3
95469 Potter Valley, 975 .... B 4
92064 Poway, 9,422 .... J 11
96079 Project City, 1,431 .... C 3
93534 Quartz Hill, 4,935 .... G 9
95971 Quincy⊙, 3,343 .... E 4
92065 Ramona, 3,554 .... J 10
95670 Rancho Cordova, 30,451 .... C 8
† 91321 Rancho Santa Clarita, 4,860 .... G 9
92067 Rancho Santa Fe, 975 .... H 10
96080 Red Bluff⊙, 7,676 .... C 3
96001 Redding⊙, 16,659 .... C 3
92373 Redlands, 36,355 .... H 9
* 90277 Redondo Beach, 56,075 .... B 11
* 94061 Redwood City⊙, 55,686 .... J 3
95044 Redwood Estates-Chemeketa Park, 1,452 .... K 4
93654 Reedley, 8,131 .... F 7
91335 Reseda, 60,862 .... B 10
92376 Rialto, 28,370 .... E 10
93261 Richgrove, 1,023 .... F 8
* 94801 Richmond, 79,043 .... J 1
93555 Ridgecrest, 7,629 .... H 8
95562 Rio Dell, 2,817 .... A 3
95673 Rio Linda, 7,524 .... B 8
94571 Rio Vista, 3,135 .... L 1
95366 Ripon, 2,679 .... D 6
95367 Riverbank, 3,949 .... E 6
93656 Riverdale, 1,722 .... E 7
* 92501 Riverside⊙, 140,089 .... E 11
95677 Rocklin, 3,039 .... B 8
94572 Rodeo, 5,356 .... J 1
94928 Rohnert Park, 6,133 .... C 5
95540 Rohnerville, 2,781 .... B 3
90274 Rolling Hills, 2,050 .... B 11
90274 Rolling Hills Estates, 6,027 .... B 11
93560 Rosamond, 2,281 .... G 9
91770 Rosemead, 40,972 .... C 10
95678 Roseville, 17,895 .... B 8
94957 Ross, 2,742 .... H 1
92509 Rubidoux, 13,969 .... E 10
* 95801 Sacramento (cap.)⊙, 254,413 .... B 8
Sacramento, ‡800,592 .... B 8
94574 Saint Helena, 3,173 .... C 5
93901 Salinas⊙, 58,896 .... D 7
Salinas-Monterey, ‡250,071 .... D 7
95563 Salyer, 700 .... B 3
95564 Samoa, 585 .... A 3
95249 San Andreas⊙, 1,564 .... E 5
94960 San Anselmo, 13,031 .... H 1
93450 San Ardo, 750 .... E 7
* 92401 San Bernardino⊙, 104,251 .... E 10
San Bernardino-Riverside-Ontario, ‡1,143,146 .... E 10
94066 San Bruno, 36,254 .... J 2
94070 San Carlos, 25,924 .... J 3
92672 San Clemente, 17,063 .... H 10
* 92101 San Diego⊙, 696,769 .... H 11
San Diego, ‡1,357,854 .... H 11
91773 San Dimas, 15,692 .... D 10
* 91340 San Fernando, 16,571 .... C 10
* 94101 San Francisco⊙, 715,674 .... H 2
San Francisco-Oakland, ‡3,109,519 .... H 2
* 91775 San Gabriel, 29,176 .... C 10
93657 Sanger, 10,088 .... F 7
92383 San Jacinto, 4,385 .... H 10
93660 San Joaquin, 1,506 .... E 7
* 95101 San Jose⊙, 445,779 .... L 3
San Jose, ‡1,064,714 .... L 3

Agriculture, Industry and Resources

DOMINANT LAND USE

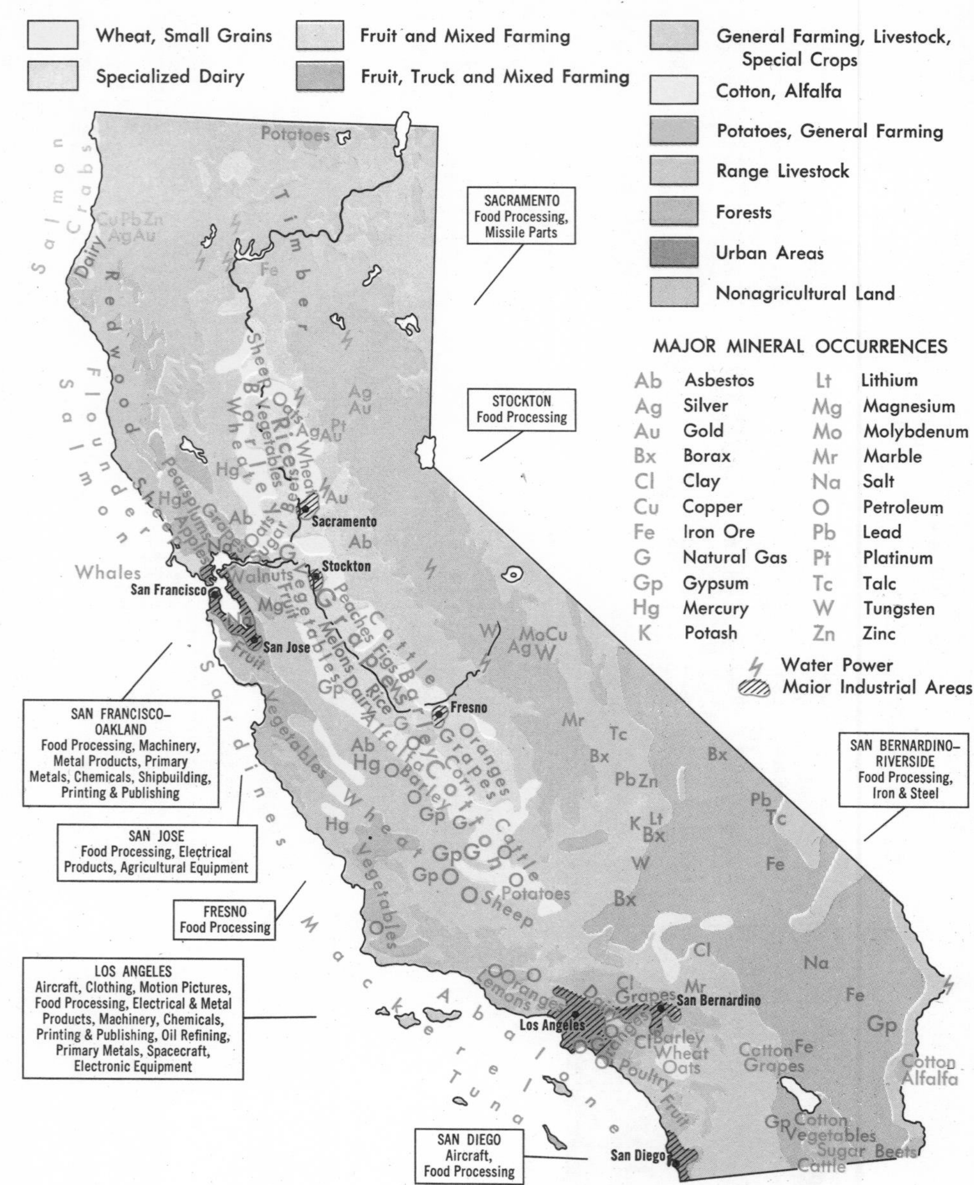

95045 San Juan Bautista, 1,164 .... D 7
92675 San Juan Capistrano, 3,781 .... H 10
* 94577 San Leandro, 68,698 .... J 2
94580 San Lorenzo, 24,633 .... K 2
93401 San Luis Obispo⊙, 28,036 .... E 8
92069 San Marcos, 3,896 .... H 10
91108 San Marino, 14,177 .... D 10
95046 San Martin, 1,392 .... L 4
* 94401 San Mateo, 78,911 .... J 3
93451 San Miguel, 600 .... E 8
94806 San Pablo, 21,461 .... J 1
* 90731 San Pedro, 91,000 .... C 11
* 94901 San Rafael⊙, 38,977 .... J 1
94583 San Ramon, 4,084 .... K 2
* 92701 Santa Ana⊙, 156,601 .... D 11
* 93101 Santa Barbara⊙, 70,215 .... F 9
Santa Barbara, ‡264,324 .... F 9
* 95050 Santa Clara, 87,717 .... K 3
95060 Santa Cruz⊙, 32,076 .... K 4
90670 Santa Fe Springs, 14,750 .... C 11
93453 Santa Margarita, 750 .... E 8
93454 Santa Maria, 32,749 .... E 9
* 90401 Santa Monica, 88,289 .... B 10
93060 Santa Paula, 18,001 .... F 9
* 95401 Santa Rosa⊙, 50,006 .... C 5
93063 Santa Susana, 2,900 .... B 10
† 94901 Santa Venetia, 2,500 .... J 1
92071 Santee, 21,107 .... J 11
95070 Saratoga, 27,110 .... K 4
93003 Saticoy, 2,400 .... F 9
94965 Sausalito, 6,158 .... H 2
95565 Scotia, 950 .... A 3
95060 Scotts Valley, 3,621 .... K 4
90740 Seal Beach, 24 441 .... C 11
93955 Seaside, 35,935 .... D 7
95472 Sebastopol, 3,993 .... C 5
92273 Seeley, 952 .... K 11
93662 Selma, 7,459 .... F 7
91343 Sepulveda, 40,000 .... B 10
93263 Shafter, 5,327 .... F 8
96087 Shasta, 750 .... C 3
93449 Shell Beach, 1,900 .... E 8
91024 Sierra Madre, 12,140 .... D 10
90806 Signal Hill, 5,582 .... C 11

92676 Silverado, 950 .... E 11
93065 Simi Valley, 56,464 .... G 9
92075 Solana Beach, 5,023 .... H 11
93960 Soledad, 6,843 .... D 7
93463 Solvang, 2,004 .... E 9
95476 Sonoma, 4,112 .... C 5
95370 Sonora⊙, 3,100 .... E 6
95073 Soquel, 5,795 .... K 4
93665 South Dos Palos, 850 .... E 7
91733 South El Monte, 13,443 .... C 10
90280 South Gate, 56,909 .... C 11
95705 South Lake Tahoe, 12,921 .... F 5
† 95965 South Oroville, 4,111 .... D 4
91030 South Pasadena, 22,979 .... C 10
† 95801 South Sacramento, 28,574 .... B 8
94080 South San Francisco, 46,646 .... J 2
† 93268 South Taft, 2,214 .... F 8
93265 Springville, 720 .... G 7
94305 Stanford, 8,691 .... J 3
90680 Stanton, 17,947 .... D 11
94970 Stinson Beach, 800 .... H 2
* 95201 Stockton⊙, 107,644 .... D 6
Stockton, ‡290,208 .... D 6
93266 Stratford, 750 .... F 7
93267 Strathmore, 1,221 .... F 7
94585 Suisun City, 2,917 .... K 1
93067 Summerland, 781 .... F 9
92381 Sun City, 5,519 .... F 11
96089 Summit City, 900 .... C 3
91040 Sunland, 22,200 .... C 10
92388 Sunnymead, 6,708 .... F 11
* 94086 Sunnyvale, 95,408 .... K 3
94586 Sunol, 750 .... L 2
90742 Sunset Beach, 1,900 .... C 11
96130 Susanville⊙, 6,608 .... E 3
95982 Sutter, 1,488 .... D 4
95685 Sutter Creek, 1,508 .... C 9
93268 Taft, 4,285 .... F 8
95730 Tahoe City, 1,394 .... E 4
91356 Tarzana, 24,165 .... B 10
93561 Tehachapi, 4,211 .... G 8
91780 Temple City, 29,673 .... D 10
93465 Templeton, 900 .... E 8

93270 Terra Bella, 1,037 .... G 8
92274 Thermal, 975 .... J 10
† 95965 Thermalito, 4,217 .... D 4
95686 Thornton, 850 .... B 9
91360 Thousand Oaks. 36,334 .... G 9
92276 Thousand Palms, 600 .... J 10
94920 Tiburon, 6,209 .... J 2
93272 Tipton, 969 .... F 7
90290 Topanga, 4,800 .... B 10
† 90290 Topanga Beach, 4,500 .... B 10
* 90501 Torrance, 134,584 .... C 11
95376 Tracy, 14,724 .... D 6
93668 Tranquillity, 800 .... E 7
93562 Trona, 975 .... H 8
95734 Truckee, 1,392 .... E 4
91042 Tujunga, 22,000 .... C 10
93274 Tulare, 16,235 .... F 7
96134 Tulelake, 857 .... D 2
95379 Tuolumne, 1,365 .... E 6
95380 Turlock, 13,992 .... E 6
92680 Tustin, 21,178 .... D 11
95383 Twain Harte, 1,484 .... E 6
92277 Twentynine Palms, 5,667 .... K 9
† 95060 Twin Lakes, 3,012 .... K 4
95482 Ukiah⊙, 10,095 .... B 4
94587 Union City, 14,724 .... K 2
90007 University Park, 3,100 .... D 11
91786 Upland, 32,551 .... E 10
95485 Upper Lake, 975 .... C 4
95688 Vacaville, 21,690 .... D 5
91355 Valencia, 4,243 .... G 9
94590 Vallejo, 66,733 .... J 1
Vallejo-Napa, ‡249,081 .... J 1
95252 Valley Springs, 800 .... C 9
* 91401 Van Nuys, 231,600 .... B 10
90291 Venice, 80,500 .... B 11
* 93001 Ventura⊙, 55,797 .... F 9
92392 Victorville, 10,845 .... H 9
92667 Villa Park, 2,723 .... D 11
93277 Visalia⊙, 27,268 .... F 7
92083 Vista, 24,688 .... H 10
91789 Walnut, 5,992 .... D 10
* 94595 Walnut Creek, 39,844 .... K 2
95690 Walnut Grove, 800 .... B 9

93280 Wasco, 8,269 .... F 8
95386 Waterford, 2,243 .... E 6
95076 Watsonville, 14,569 .... D 7
96093 Weaverville⊙, 1,489 .... B 3
96094 Weed, 2,983 .... C 2
* 91790 West Covina, 68,034 .... D 10
† 90025 West Hollywood, 29,448 .... B 10
90025 West Los Angeles, 38,805 .... B 10
92683 Westminster, 59,865 .... D 11
92281 Westmorland, 1,175 .... K 10
94565 West Pittsburg, 5,969 .... K 1
95255 West Point, 950 .... E 5
95691 West Sacramento, 12,002 .... B 8
96137 Westwood, Lassen, 1,862 .... D 3
90024 Westwood, L.A., 45,000 .... B 10
95692 Wheatland, 1,280 .... D 4
* 90601 Whittier, 72,863 .... D 11
95987 Williams, 1,571 .... C 4
95490 Willits, 3,091 .... B 4
95988 Willows⊙, 4,085 .... C 4
90744 Wilmington, 38,000 .... C 11
95492 Windsor, 2,359 .... C 5
92283 Winterhaven, 850 .... L 11
95694 Winters, 2,419 .... D 5
95388 Winton, 3,393 .... E 6
95258 Woodbridge, 1,397 .... B 9
93286 Woodlake, 3,371 .... G 7
95695 Woodland⊙, 20,677 .... B 8
91364 Woodland Hills, 56,420 .... B 10
94062 Woodside, 4,731 .... J 3
92398 Yermo, 1,304 .... J 9
92686 Yorba Linda, 11,856 .... D 11
95389 Yosemite National Park, 857 .... F 6
94599 Yountville, 2,332 .... C 5
96097 Yreka⊙, 5,394 .... C 2
95991 Yuba City⊙, 13,986 .... D 4
92399 Yucaipa, 19,284 .... J 9
92284 Yucca Valley, 3,893 .... J 9

⊙ County seat.
‡ Population of metropolitan area.
† Zip of nearest p.o.
* Multiple zips

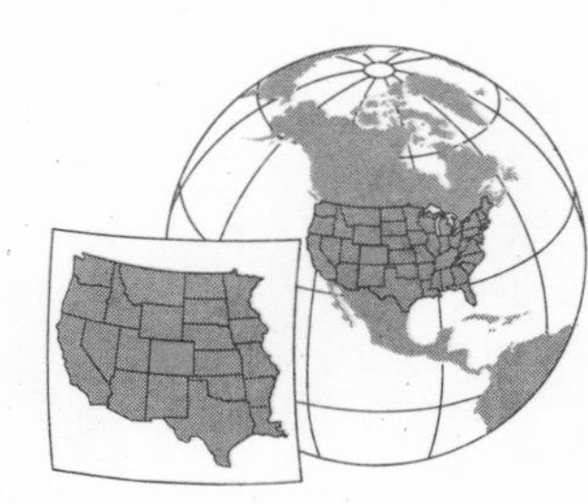

AREA 104,247 sq. mi
POPULATION 2,207,259
CAPITAL Denver
LARGEST CITY Denver
HIGHEST POINT Mt. Elbert 14,433 ft.
SETTLED IN 1858
ADMITTED TO UNION August 1, 1876
POPULAR NAME Centennial State
STATE FLOWER Mountain Columbine
STATE BIRD Lark Bunting

COUNTIES

County, Pop.	Key
Adams, 185,789	L 3
Alamosa, 11,422	H 7
Arapahoe, 162,142	L 3
Archuleta, 2,733	E 8
Baca, 5,674	O 8
Bent, 6,493	N 7
Boulder, 131,889	J 2
Chaffee, 10,162	G 5
Cheyenne, 2,396	O 5
Clear Creek, 4,819	H 3
Conejos, 7,846	G 8
Costilla, 3,091	J 8
Crowley, 3,086	M 6
Custer, 1,120	J 6
Delta, 15,286	D 5
Denver, 514,678	K 3
Dolores, 1,641	C 7
Douglas, 8,407	K 4
Eagle, 7,498	F 3
Elbert, 3,903	L 4
El Paso, 235,972	K 5
Fremont, 21,942	J 5
Garfield, 14,821	C 3
Gilpin, 1,272	H 3
Grand, 4,107	G 2
Gunnison, 7,578	E 5
Hinsdale, 202	E 7
Huerfano, 6,590	K 7
Jackson, 1,811	G 1
Jefferson, 233,031	J 3
Kiowa, 2,029	O 6
Kit Carson, 7,530	O 4
Lake, 8,282	G 4
La Plata, 19,199	D 8
Larimer, 89,900	H 1
Las Animas, 15,744	L 8
Lincoln, 4,836	M 5
Logan, 18,852	N 1
Mesa, 54,374	B 5
Mineral, 786	F 7
Moffat, 6,525	C 1
Montezuma, 12,952	B 8
Montrose, 18,366	C 6
Morgan, 20,105	M 2
Otero, 23,523	M 7
Ouray, 1,546	D 6
Park, 2,185	H 4
Phillips, 4,131	P 1
Pitkin, 6,185	F 4
Prowers, 13,258	P 7
Pueblo, 118,238	K 6
Rio Blanco, 4,842	C 3
Rio Grande, 10,494	G 7
Routt, 6,592	E 1
Saguache, 3,827	G 6
San Juan, 831	D 7
San Miguel, 1,949	C 6
Sedgwick, 3,405	P 1
Summit, 2,665	G 3
Teller, 3,316	J 5
Washington, 5,550	N 3
Weld, 89,297	L 1
Yuma, 8,544	P 2

CITIES and TOWNS

Zip	Name/Pop.	Key
80101	Agate, 120	M 4
81020	Aguilar, 699	K 8
80720	Akron⊙, 1,775	N 2
81101	Alamosa⊙, 6,985	H 8
80510	Allenspark, 100	J 2
80420	Alma, 73	G 4
81210	Almont, 15	F 5
80721	Amherst, 105	P 1
80801	Anton, 65	N 3
81120	Antonito, 1,113	H 8
80802	Arapahoe, 100	P 5
81021	Arlington, 10	N 6
80804	Arriba, 254	N 4
† 81323	Arriola, 50	B 8
80002	Arvada, 46,814	J 3
81611	Aspen⊙, 2,404	F 4
80722	Atwood, 75	N 1
80610	Ault, 841	K 1
80010	Aurora, 74,974	K 3
81410	Austin, 1,163	D 5
81620	Avon, 50	F 3
81022	Avondale, 750	L 6
80421	Bailey, 200	H 4
† 80624	Barnesville, 20	L 2
81621	Basalt, 419	E 4
81122	Bayfield, 320	D 8
81411	Bedrock, 20	B 6
† 80758	Beecher Island, 5	P 3
80512	Bellvue, 335	J 1
80102	Bennett, 613	L 3
80513	Berthoud, 1,446	J 2
† 80438	Berthoud Pass, 200	H 3
80805	Bethune, 99	P 4
81023	Beulah, 425	K 6
80908	Black Forest, 700	K 4
80422	Black Hawk, 217	J 3
81123	Blanca, 212	H 8
† 81001	Blende, 950	K 6
† 80424	Blue River, 8	G 4
† 81155	Bonanza, 10	G 6
81024	Boncarbo, 50	K 8
80423	Bond, 63	F 3
81025	Boone, 448	L 6
* 80301	Boulder⊙, 66,870	J 2
† 81428	Bowie, 18	D 5
80806	Boyero, 25	N 5
81026	Brandon, 10	P 6
81027	Branson, 70	M 8
80424	Breckenridge⊙, 548	G 4
80611	Briggsdale, 440	L 1
80601	Brighton⊙, 8,309	K 3
81028	Bristol, 250	P 6
† 80901	Broadmoor, 3,871	K 5
† 81212	Brookside, 173	J 6
80020	Broomfield, 7,261	J 3
80723	Brush, 3,377	M 2
† 80742	Buckingham, 6	L 1
81211	Buena Vista, 1,962	G 5
80425	Buffalo Creek, 150	J 4
80807	Burlington⊙, 2,828	P 4
80426	Burns, 100	F 3
80103	Byers, 490	L 3
81320	Cahone, 125	B 7
80808	Calhan, 465	L 4
81029	Campo, 206	O 8
81212	Canon City⊙, 9,206	J 6
81124	Capulin, 600	G 8
81623	Carbondale, 726	E 4
80612	Carr, 47	K 1
80809	Cascade, 950	K 5
80104	Castle Rock⊙, 1,531	K 4
81413	Cedaredge, 581	D 5
81125	Center, 1,470	G 7
80427	Central City⊙, 228	J 3
81126	Chama, 400	J 8
81030	Cheraw, 129	N 6
80810	Cheyenne Wells⊙, 982	P 5
81127	Chimney Rock, 51	E 8
81031	Chivington, 15	O 6
81128	Chromo, 150	F 8
81220	Cimarron, 25	D 6
80428	Clark, 55	F 1
† 80731	Clarkville, 4	P 2
81520	Clifton, 950	C 4
80429	Climax, 975	G 4
81221	Coal Creek, 225	J 6
81222	Coaldale, 104	H 6
80430	Coalmont, 12	F 1
81032	Cokedale, 101	K 8
81624	Collbran, 225	C 4
† 81401	Colona, 54	D 6
81004	Colorado City, 411	K 6
* 80901	Colorado Springs⊙, 135,060	K 5
	Colorado Springs, ‡235,972	K 5
† 80428	Columbine, 12	E 1
80022	Commerce City, 17,407	K 3
80432	Como, 35	H 4
81129	Conejos⊙, 100	G 8
80812	Cope, 125	O 3
80611	Cornish, 2	L 2
81321	Cortez⊙, 6,032	B 8
81223	Cotopaxi, 150	H 6
80434	Cowdrey, 10	G 1
81625	Craig⊙, 4,205	D 2
81415	Crawford, 171	D 5
81130	Creede⊙, 653	E 7
81224	Crested Butte, 372	E 5
81131	Crestone, 34	H 7
80813	Cripple Creek⊙, 425	J 5
80726	Crook, 199	O 1
81033	Crowley, 216	M 6
81055	Cuchara, 43	J 8
80514	Dacono, 360	K 2
† 80728	Dailey, 20	O 1
81630	De Beque, 155	C 4
† 80135	Deckers, 4	J 4
80105	Deer Trail, 374	M 3
81034	Delhi, 10	M 7
81132	Del Norte⊙, 1,569	G 7
81416	Delta⊙, 3,694	D 5
* 80201	Denver (cap.)⊙, 514,678	K 3
	Denver, ‡1,227,529	K 3
81035	Deora, 2	O 7
80435	Dillon, 182	H 3
81610	Dinosaur, 247	B 2
80814	Divide, 50	J 5
81323	Dolores, 820	C 8
81324	Dove Creek⊙, 619	A 7
† 81239	Doyleville, 75	F 6
80515	Drake, 75	J 2
81301	Durango⊙, 10,333	D 8
81036	Eads⊙, 795	O 6
81631	Eagle⊙, 790	F 3
† 81212	East Canon, 1,805	J 6
80615	Eaton, 1,389	K 1
81418	Eckert, 850	C 5
80727	Eckley, 193	P 2
80214	Edgewater, 4,866	J 3
81632	Edwards, 100	F 3
81325	Egnar, 84	B 7
80106	Elbert, 150	L 4
80437	Eldora, 100	H 3
80107	Elizabeth, 493	K 4
81633	Elk Springs, 56	C 2
80438	Empire, 249	H 3
80110	Englewood, 33,695	K 3
80516	Erie, 1,090	K 2
80517	Estes Park, 1,616	J 2
† 81433	Eureka, 25	D 7
80620	Evans, 2,570	K 2
80439	Evergreen, 2,321	J 3
80440	Fairplay⊙, 419	H 4
81037	Farisita, 45	J 7
† 80030	Federal Heights, 1,502	J 3
80520	Firestone, 570	K 2
† 80810	Firstview, 6	O 5
80815	Flagler, 615	N 4
80728	Fleming, 349	O 1
81226	Florence, 2,846	J 6
80816	Florissant, 75	J 5
80521	Fort Collins⊙, 43,337	J 1
81133	Fort Garland, 400	J 8
80621	Fort Lupton, 2,489	K 2
81038	Fort Lyon, 135	N 6
80701	Fort Morgan⊙, 7,594	M 2
80817	Fountain, 3,515	K 5
81039	Fowler, 1,241	L 6
80441	Foxton, 75	J 4
80116	Franktown, 157	K 4
80442	Fraser, 221	H 3
80530	Frederick, 696	K 2
80820	Freshwater (Guffey), 24	H 5
80443	Frisco, 471	G 3
81521	Fruita, 1,822	B 4
† 81501	Fruitvale, 950	C 4
80622	Galeton, 200	K 1
81134	Garcia, 90	J 8
81040	Gardner, 75	J 7
81227	Garfield, 11	G 5
81522	Gateway, 250	B 5
80818	Genoa, 161	N 4
80444	Georgetown⊙, 542	H 3
80623	Gilcrest, 382	K 2
80624	Gill, 250	L 2
81634	Gilman, 400	G 3
81523	Glade Park, 69	B 5
80485	Glendevey, 50	H 1
80532	Glen Haven, 50	H 2
81601	Glenwood Springs⊙, 4,106	E 4
80401	Golden⊙, 9,817	J 3
80625	Goodrich, 85	M 2
80445	Gould, 12	G 2
81041	Granada, 551	P 6
80446	Granby, 554	H 2
81501	Grand Junction⊙, 20,170	B 4
80447	Grand Lake, 189	H 2
81635	Grand Valley, 270	D 4
81228	Granite, 23	G 4
80448	Grant, 50	H 4
80631	Greeley⊙, 38,902	K 2
† 80118	Greenland, 47	K 4
80819	Green Mountain Falls, 359	K 5
81636	Greystone, 2	B 1
80729	Grover, 121	L 1
80820	Guffey, 24	H 5
81042	Gulnare, 100	K 8
81230	Gunnison⊙, 4,613	E 5
81637	Gypsum, 420	F 3
80730	Hale, 12	P 3
81638	Hamilton, 30	D 2
81043	Hartman, 129	P 6
80449	Hartsel, 75	H 4
81044	Hasty, 150	O 6
81045	Haswell, 135	N 6
80731	Haxtun, 899	O 1
81639	Hayden, 763	E 2
80732	Hereford, 50	L 1
81326	Hesperus, 78	C 8
80733	Hillrose, 121	N 2
81232	Hillside, 79	H 6
81046	Hoehne, 400	L 8
81047	Holly, 993	P 6
80734	Holyoke⊙, 1,640	P 1
81136	Hooper, 80	H 7
81419	Hotchkiss, 507	D 5
80451	Hot Sulphur Springs⊙, 220	H 2
81233	Howard, 175	H 6
80641	Hoyt, 175	L 2
80642	Hudson, 518	K 2
80821	Hugo⊙, 759	N 4
80533	Hygiene, 400	J 2
80452	Idaho Springs, 2,003	H 3
80735	Idalia, 100	P 3
81137	Ignacio, 613	D 8
80736	Iliff, 193	N 1
81427	Ironton,	D 7
† 80901	Ivywild, 12,000	K 5
80455	Jamestown, 185	J 2
81048	Jansen, 267	K 8
81138	Jaroso, 56	H 8
80456	Jefferson, 45	H 4
80822	Joes, 100	O 3
80534	Johnstown, 1,191	K 2
80737	Julesburg⊙, 1,578	P 1
80823	Karval, 70	N 5
80643	Keenesburg, 427	L 2
80738	Keota, 6	L 1
80644	Kersey, 474	L 2
81049	Kim, 200	N 8
80117	Kiowa⊙, 235	L 4
80824	Kirk, 100	P 3
80825	Kit Carson, 220	O 5
† 80435	Kokomo, 75	G 4
80459	Kremmling, 764	G 2
80826	Kutch, 2	M 5
80026	Lafayette, 3,498	K 3
81139	La Garita, 50	G 7
80739	Laird, 105	P 2
81140	La Jara, 768	H 8
81050	La Junta⊙, 7,938	M 7
81235	Lake City⊙, 91	E 6
80827	Lake George, 29	J 5
80215	Lakewood, 92,787	J 3
81052	Lamar⊙, 7,797	O 6
80535	Laporte, 950	J 1
80118	Larkspur, 350	K 4
80645	La Salle, 1,227	K 2
81054	Las Animas⊙, 3,148	N 6
† 81151	Lasauces, 120	H 8
† 81153	Lavalley, 237	J 8
81055	La Veta, 589	J 8
† 80452	Lawson, 108	H 3
81625	Lay, 8	D 2
81420	Lazear, 60	D 5
80461	Leadville⊙, 4,314	G 4
† 81323	Lebanon, 50	B 8
81327	Lewis, 350	B 8
80828	Limon, 1,814	M 4
† 81212	Lincoln Park, 2,984	J 6
80740	Lindon, 50	N 3
80120	Littleton⊙, 26,466	K 3
80536	Livermore, 20	J 1
† 80701	Log Lane Village, 329	M 2
81524	Loma, 100	B 4
80501	Longmont, 23,209	J 2
† 80135	Longview, 10	J 4
80027	Louisville, 2,409	J 3
80131	Louviers, 306	K 4
80537	Loveland, 16,220	J 2
80646	Lucerne, 150	K 2
81056	Lycan, 4	P 7
80540	Lyons, 958	J 2
81525	Mack, 175	B 4
81421	Maher, 80	D 5
† 80461	Malta, 200	G 4
81141	Manassa, 814	H 8
81328	Mancos, 709	C 8
80829	Manitou Springs, 4,278	J 5
81058	Manzanola, 451	M 6
† 81623	Marble, 1	E 4
81329	Marvel, 100	C 8
80541	Masonville, 200	J 2
† 80649	Masters, 50	L 2
80830	Matheson, 100	M 4
81640	Maybell, 82	C 2
81057	McClave, 165	O 6
80463	McCoy, 14	F 3
80542	Mead, 195	K 2
81641	Meeker⊙, 1,597	D 2
81642	Meredith, 48	F 4
80741	Merino, 260	N 2
81005	Mesa, 295	C 4
81330	Mesa Verde National Park, 70	C 8
81142	Mesita, 50	H 8
80543	Milliken, 702	K 2
80477	Milner, 75	F 2
81645	Minturn, 706	G 3
81059	Model, 19	L 8
81143	Moffat, 98	H 6
81646	Molina, 120	D 4
81144	Monte Vista, 3,909	G 7
80464	Montezuma, 6	H 3

(continued on following page)

Colorado Department of Public Relations

This view of Bear Lake and Longs Peak is typical of the beautiful mountain scenery found in Rocky Mountain National Park, an area which many call "the roof of America."

(continued)

Topography

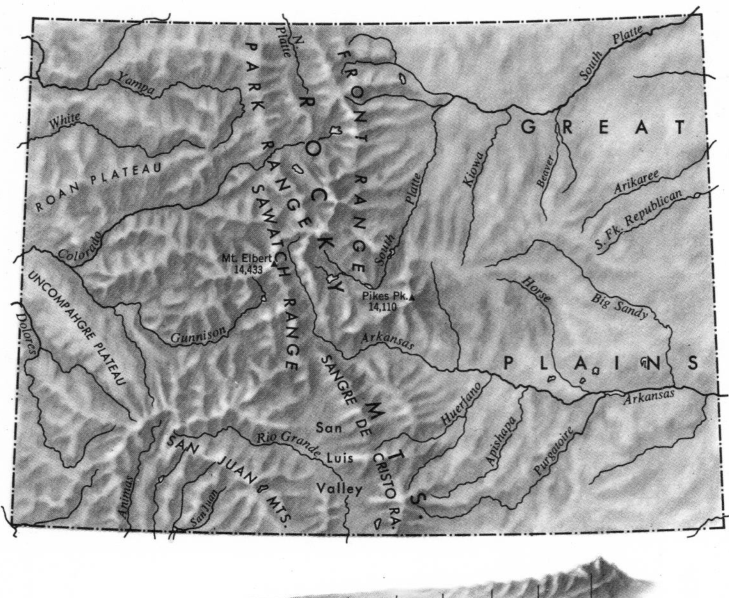

Agriculture, Industry and Resources

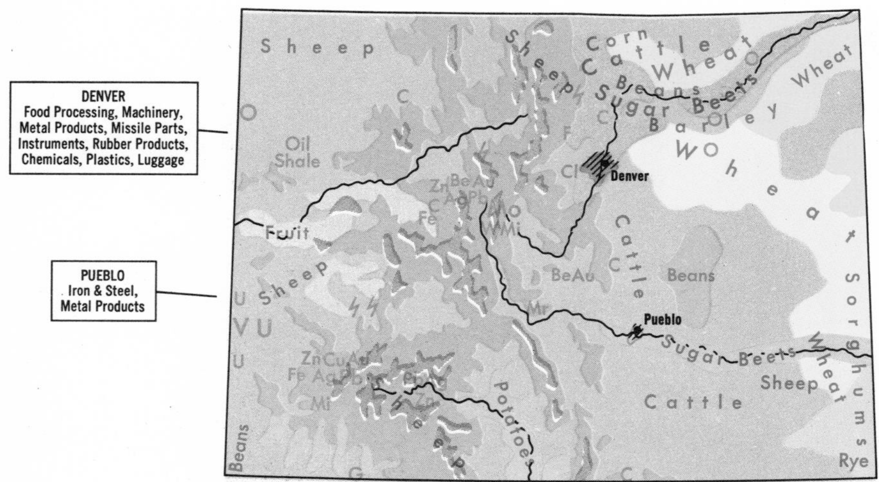

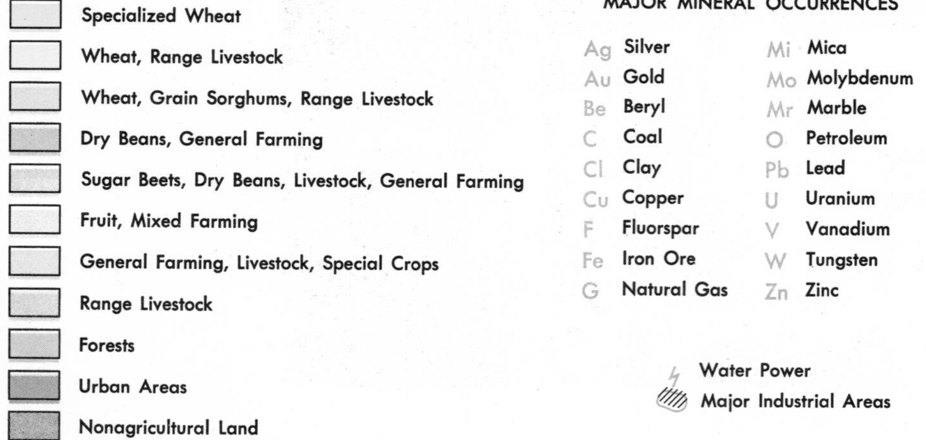

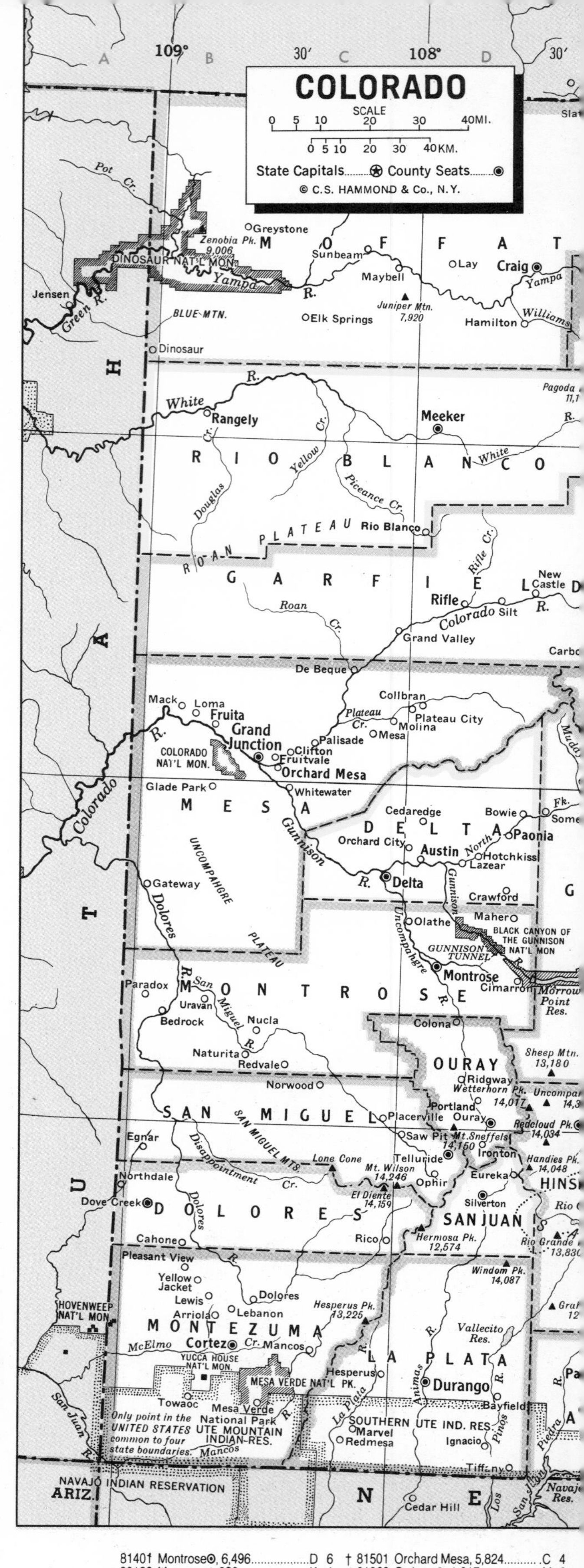

	Zip	Place		
	81401	Montrose⊙, 6,496	D	6
	80132	Monument, 393	K	4
	80465	Morrison, 439	J	3
	81146	Mosca, 112	H	7
	81236	Nathrop, 125	H	5
	81422	Naturita, 820	B	6
	80466	Nederland, 492	H	3
	81647	New Castle, 499	E	3
	80742	New Raymer, 68	M	1
†	81054	Ninaview, 2	N	7
	80544	Niwot, 350	J	2
	81061	North Avondale, 110	L	6
†	81324	Northdale, 8	B	7
†	80201	Northglenn, 27,937	K	3
†	81050	North La Junta, 1,249	N	7
	81423	Norwood, 408	C	6
	81424	Nucla, 949	B	6
	80648	Nunn, 269	K	1
	80467	Oak Creek, 492	F	2
	81237	Ohio, 50	F	5
	81425	Olathe, 756	D	5
	81062	Olney Springs, 264	M	6
	81426	Ophir, 6	D	7
	80649	Orchard, 85	L	2
†	81418	Orchard City (Eckert), 850	C	5
†	81501	Orchard Mesa, 5,824	C	4
	81063	Ordway⊙, 1,017	M	6
†	81120	Ortiz, 163	H	8
	80743	Otis, 521	O	2
	81427	Ouray⊙, 741	D	6
	80744	Ovid, 463	P	1
	80745	Padroni, 111	N	1
†	81147	Pagosa Junction, 6	E	8
	81147	Pagosa Springs⊙, 1,360	E	8
	81526	Palisade, 874	C	4
	80133	Palmer Lake, 947	J	4
	80746	Paoli, 52	P	1
	81428	Paonia, 1,161	D	5
	81429	Paradox, 200	B	6
	81238	Parkdale, 21	H	6
	80134	Parker, 200	K	4
	81239	Parlin, 50	F	6
	80468	Parshall, 70	G	2
	80747	Peetz, 186	N	1
	81240	Penrose, 263	K	6
	80831	Peyton, 150	K	4
	80469	Phippsburg, 300	F	2
	80650	Pierce, 452	K	1
	80470	Pine, 89	J	4
	80471	Pinecliffe, 500	J	3

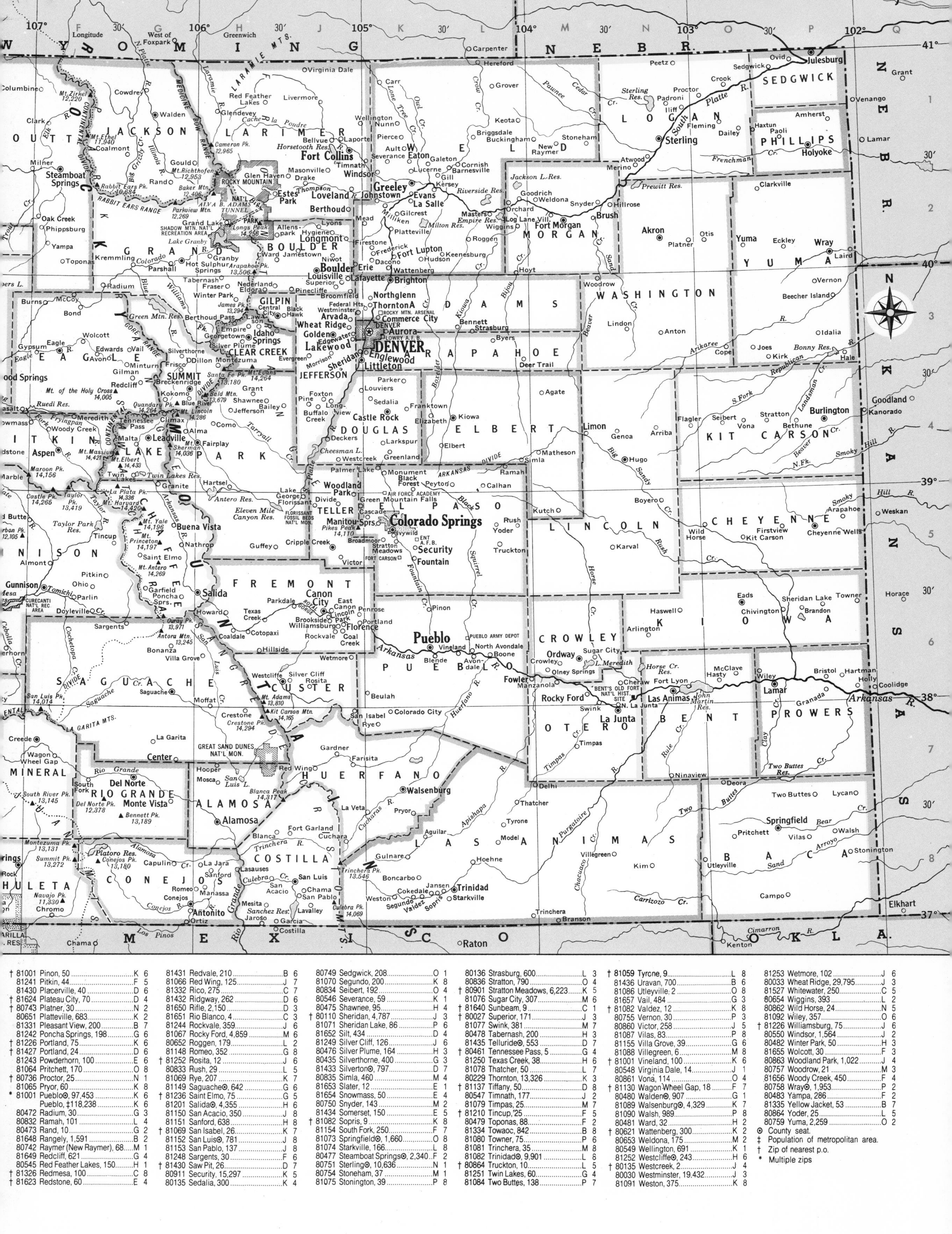

† 81001 Pinon, 50 .... K 6
81241 Pitkin, 44 .... F 5
81430 Placerville, 40 .... D 6
† 81624 Plateau City, 70 .... D 4
† 80743 Platner, 30 .... N 2
80651 Platteville, 683 .... K 2
81331 Pleasant View, 200 .... B 7
81242 Poncha Springs, 198 .... G 6
† 81226 Portland, 75 .... K 6
† 81427 Portland, 24 .... D 6
81243 Powderhorn, 100 .... E 6
81064 Pritchett, 170 .... O 8
† 80736 Proctor, 25 .... N 1
81065 Pryor, 60 .... K 8
* 81001 Pueblo⊙, 97,453 .... K 6
Pueblo, ‡118,238 .... K 6
80472 Radium, 30 .... G 3
80832 Ramah, 101 .... L 4
80473 Rand, 10 .... G 2
81648 Rangely, 1,591 .... B 2
80742 Raymer (New Raymer), 68 .... M 1
81649 Redcliff, 621 .... G 4
80545 Red Feather Lakes, 150 .... H 1
† 81326 Redmesa, 100 .... C 8
† 81623 Redstone, 60 .... E 4
81431 Redvale, 210 .... B 6
81066 Red Wing, 125 .... J 7
81332 Rico, 275 .... C 7
81432 Ridgway, 262 .... D 6
81650 Rifle, 2,150 .... D 3
81651 Rio Blanco, 4 .... C 3
81244 Rockvale, 359 .... J 6
81067 Rocky Ford, 4,859 .... M 6
80652 Roggen, 179 .... L 2
81148 Romeo, 352 .... G 8
† 81252 Rosita, 12 .... J 6
80833 Rush, 29 .... L 5
81069 Rye, 207 .... K 7
81149 Saguache⊙, 642 .... G 6
† 81236 Saint Elmo, 75 .... G 5
81201 Salida⊙, 4,355 .... H 6
81150 San Acacio, 350 .... J 8
81151 Sanford, 638 .... H 8
† 81069 San Isabel, 26 .... K 7
81152 San Luis⊙, 781 .... J 8
81153 San Pablo, 137 .... J 8
81248 Sargents, 30 .... F 6
† 81430 Saw Pit, 26 .... D 7
80911 Security, 15,297 .... K 5
80135 Sedalia, 300 .... K 4
80749 Sedgwick, 208 .... O 1
81070 Segundo, 200 .... K 8
80834 Seibert, 192 .... O 4
80546 Severance, 59 .... K 1
80475 Shawnee, 95 .... H 4
† 80110 Sheridan, 4,787 .... J 3
81071 Sheridan Lake, 86 .... P 6
81652 Silt, 434 .... D 4
81249 Silver Cliff, 126 .... J 6
80476 Silver Plume, 164 .... H 3
80435 Silverthorne, 400 .... G 3
81433 Silverton⊙, 797 .... D 7
80835 Simla, 460 .... M 4
81653 Slater, 12 .... E 1
81654 Snowmass, 50 .... E 4
80750 Snyder, 143 .... M 2
81434 Somerset, 150 .... E 5
† 81082 Sopris, 9 .... K 8
81154 South Fork, 250 .... F 7
81073 Springfield⊙, 1,660 .... O 8
81074 Starkville, 166 .... L 8
80477 Steamboat Springs⊙, 2,340 .... F 2
80751 Sterling⊙, 10,636 .... N 1
80754 Stoneham, 37 .... M 1
81075 Stonington, 39 .... P 8
80136 Strasburg, 600 .... L 3
80836 Stratton, 790 .... O 4
† 80901 Stratton Meadows, 6,223 .... K 5
81076 Sugar City, 307 .... M 6
† 81640 Sunbeam, 9 .... C 1
† 80027 Superior, 171 .... J 3
81077 Swink, 381 .... M 7
80478 Tabernash, 200 .... H 3
81435 Telluride⊙, 553 .... D 7
† 80461 Tennessee Pass, 5 .... G 4
81250 Texas Creek, 38 .... H 6
81078 Thatcher, 50 .... L 7
80229 Thornton, 13,326 .... K 3
† 81137 Tiffany, 50 .... D 8
80547 Timnath, 177 .... J 2
81079 Timpas, 25 .... M 7
† 81210 Tincup, 25 .... F 5
80479 Toponas, 88 .... F 2
81334 Towaoc, 842 .... B 8
81080 Towner, 75 .... P 6
81081 Trinchera, 35 .... M 8
81082 Trinidad⊙, 9,901 .... L 8
† 80864 Truckton, 10 .... L 5
81251 Twin Lakes, 60 .... G 4
81084 Two Buttes, 138 .... P 7
† 81059 Tyrone, 9 .... L 8
81436 Uravan, 700 .... B 6
81086 Utleyville, 2 .... O 8
81657 Vail, 484 .... G 3
† 81082 Valdez, 12 .... K 8
80755 Vernon, 30 .... P 3
80860 Victor, 258 .... J 5
81087 Vilas, 83 .... P 8
81155 Villa Grove, 39 .... G 6
81088 Villegreen, 6 .... M 8
† 81001 Vineland, 100 .... K 6
80548 Virginia Dale, 14 .... J 1
80861 Vona, 114 .... O 4
† 81130 Wagon Wheel Gap, 18 .... F 7
80480 Walden⊙, 907 .... G 1
81089 Walsenburg⊙, 4,329 .... K 7
81090 Walsh, 989 .... P 8
80481 Ward, 32 .... H 2
† 80621 Wattenberg, 300 .... K 2
80653 Weldona, 175 .... M 2
80549 Wellington, 691 .... K 1
81252 Westcliffe⊙, 243 .... H 6
† 80135 Westcreek, 2 .... J 4
80030 Westminster, 19,432 .... J 3
81091 Weston, 375 .... K 8
81253 Wetmore, 102 .... J 6
80033 Wheat Ridge, 29,795 .... J 3
81527 Whitewater, 250 .... C 5
80654 Wiggins, 393 .... L 2
80862 Wild Horse, 24 .... N 5
81092 Wiley, 357 .... O 6
† 81226 Williamsburg, 75 .... J 6
80550 Windsor, 1,564 .... J 2
80482 Winter Park, 50 .... H 3
81655 Wolcott, 30 .... F 3
80863 Woodland Park, 1,022 .... J 4
80757 Woodrow, 21 .... M 3
81656 Woody Creek, 450 .... F 4
80758 Wray⊙, 1,953 .... P 2
80483 Yampa, 286 .... F 2
81335 Yellow Jacket, 53 .... B 7
80864 Yoder, 25 .... L 5
80759 Yuma, 2,259 .... O 2

⊙ County seat.
‡ Population of metropolitan area.
† Zip of nearest p.o.
* Multiple zips

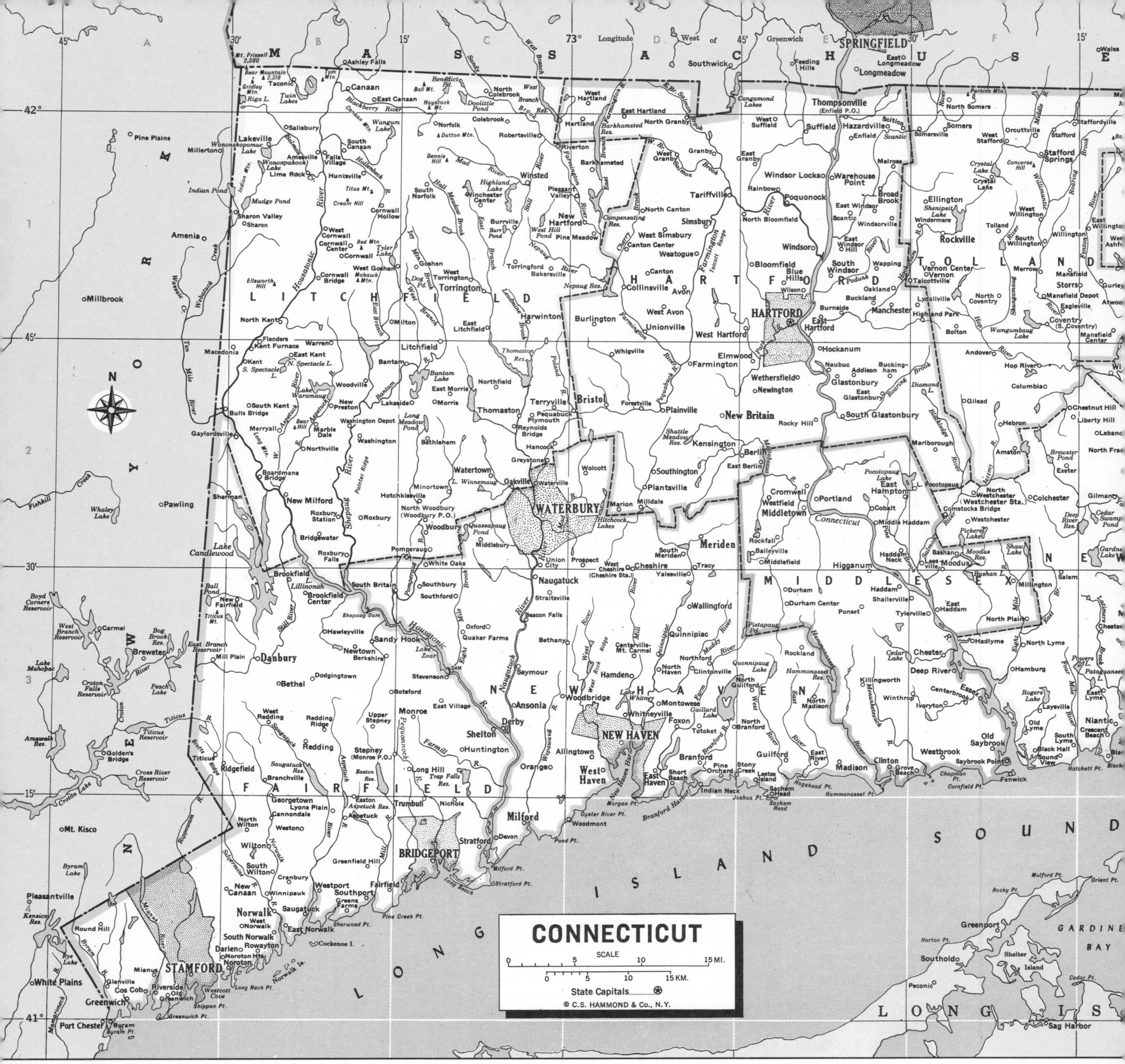

CONNECTICUT

SCALE

0 5 10 15 MI.

0 5 10 15 KM.

State Capitals ⊛

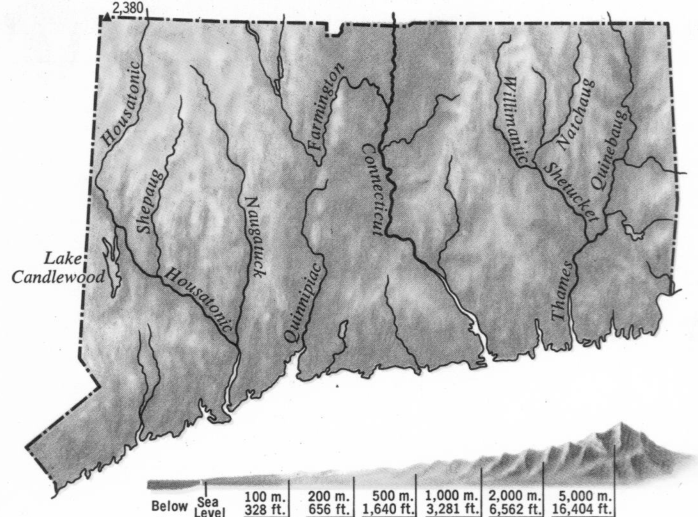

COUNTIES

Name/Pop.	Key
Fairfield, 792,814	B 3
Hartford, 816,737	D 1
Litchfield, 144,091	B 1
Middlesex, 114,816	E 3
New Haven, 744,948	D 3
New London, 230,348	G 2
Tolland, 103,448	F 1
Windham, 84,515	H 1

CITIES and TOWNS

Zip	Name/Pop.	Key
† 06516	Allingtown, 7,000	D 3
06231	Amston, 1,963	F 2
06232	Andover, ▵2,099	F 2
06401	Ansonia, 21,160	C 3
† 06250	Ashford, ▵2,156	G 1
06001	Avon, ▵8,352	D 1
06330	Baltic, 1,500	G 2
† 06063	Barkhamsted, ▵2,066	D 1
06403	Beacon Falls, ▵3,546	C 3
06037	Berlin, ▵14,149	E 2
† 06501	Bethany, ▵3,857	C 3
06801	Bethel, ▵10,945	B 3
06751	Bethlehem, ▵1,923	C 2
06002	Bloomfield, ▵18,301	E 1
06002	Bloomfield, 8,000	E 1
06112	Blue Hills, 5,000	E 1
06040	Bolton, ▵3,691	F 1
06405	Branford, ▵20,444	D 3
06405	Branford, 2,080	D 3
* 06601	Bridgeport, 156,542	C 4
	Bridgeport, ‡388,953	C 4
06752	Bridgewater, ▵1,277	B 2
06010	Bristol, 55,487	D 2
06016	Broad Brook, 1,548	E 1
06804	Brookfield, ▵9,688	B 3
06804	Brookfield, 6,000	B 3
06805	Brookfield Center, 3,000	B 3
06234	Brooklyn, ▵4,965	H 1
06085	Burlington, ▵4,070	D 1
06085	Burlington, 950	D 1
10573	Byram, 5,631	A 4
06018	Canaan, ▵931	B 1
06018	Canaan, 1,083	B 1
06331	Canterbury, ▵2,673	H 2
06019	Canton, ▵6,868	D 1
06332	Central Village, 1,200	H 2
06235	Chaplin, ▵1,621	G 1
06410	Cheshire, ▵19,051	D 2
06412	Chester, ▵2,982	F 3
06412	Chester, 1,569	F 3
06413	Clinton, ▵10,267	E 3
06413	Clinton, 5,957	E 3
† 06473	Clintonville, 1,300	D 3
06415	Colchester, ▵6,603	F 2
06415	Colchester, 3,529	F 2
06021	Colebrook, ▵1,020	C 1
06022	Collinsville, 2,897	D 1
06238	Coventry, ▵8,140	F 1
06238	Coventry, 3,735	F 1
06416	Cromwell, ▵7,400	E 2
06810	Danbury, 50,781	B 3
06239	Danielson, 4,580	H 1
06820	Darien, ▵20,411	B 4
06241	Dayville, ▵950	H 1
06417	Deep River, ▵3,690	F 3
06417	Deep River, 2,333	F 3
06418	Derby, 12,599	C 3
† 06460	Devon, 2,750	C 4
06422	Durham, ▵4,489	E 3
06023	East Berlin, 1,100	E 2
† 06239	East Brooklyn, 1,377	H 1
06242	Eastford, ▵922	G 1
06026	East Granby, ▵3,352	E 1
06423	East Haddam, ▵4,474	F 3
06424	East Hampton, ▵7,078	E 2
06424	East Hampton, 1,982	E 2
06108	East Hartford, ▵57,583	E 1
06512	East Haven, 25,120	D 3
06333	East Lyme, ▵11,399	G 3
† 06856	East Norwalk, 9,500	B 4
06425	Easton, ▵4,885	B 4
† 06088	East Windsor, ▵8,513	E 1
06029	Ellington, ▵7,707	F 1
06110	Elmwood, 18,500	D 2
06082	Enfield, ▵46,189	E 1
06082	Enfield P.O.(Thompsonville), 27,000	E 1
06426	Essex, ▵4,911	F 3
06426	Essex, 2,473	F 3
06430	Fairfield, ▵56,487	B 4
06032	Farmington, ▵14,390	D 2
† 06010	Forestville, 20,000	D 2

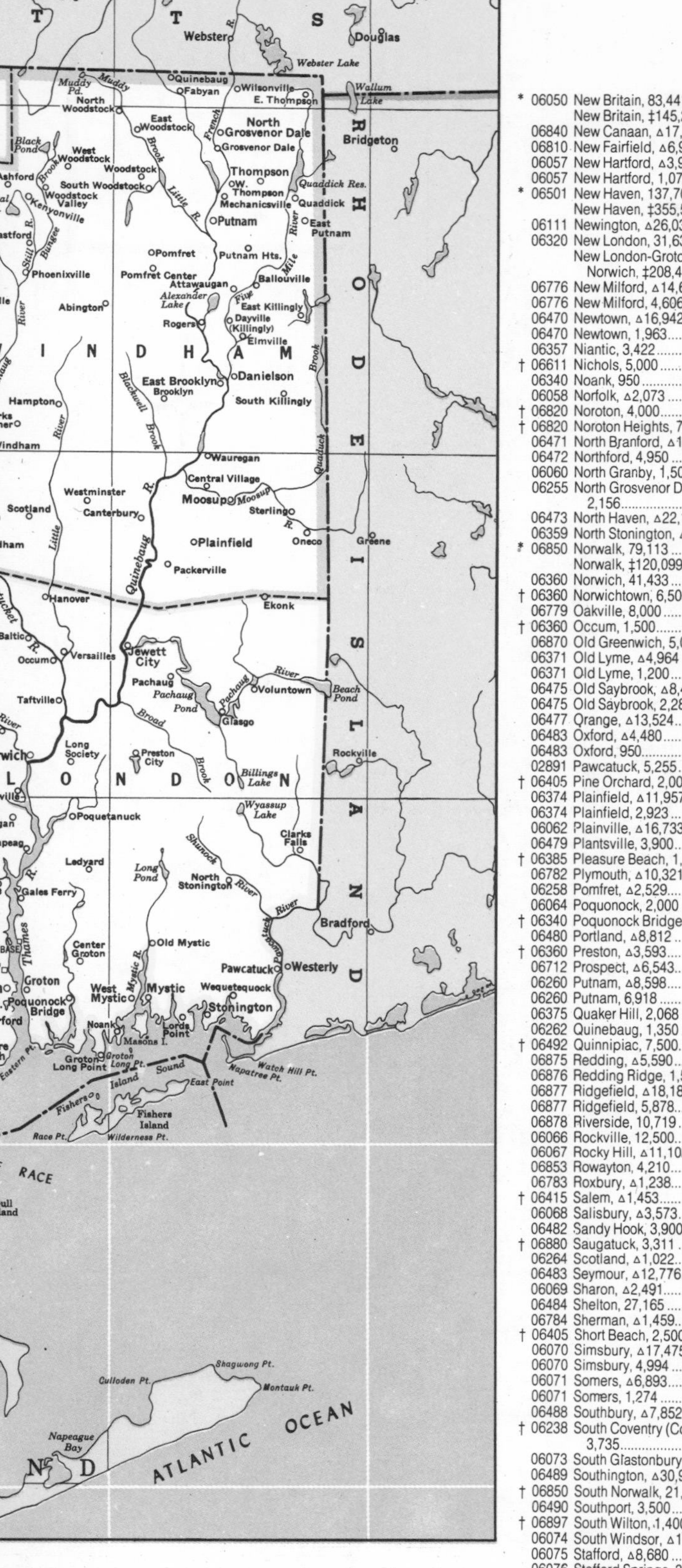

AREA 5,009 sq. mi.
POPULATION 3,032,217
CAPITAL Hartford
LARGEST CITY Hartford
HIGHEST POINT Mt. Frissell (S. Slope) 2,380 ft.
SETTLED IN 1635
ADMITTED TO UNION January 9, 1788
POPULAR NAME Constitution State; Nutmeg State
STATE FLOWER Mountain Laurel
STATE BIRD Robin

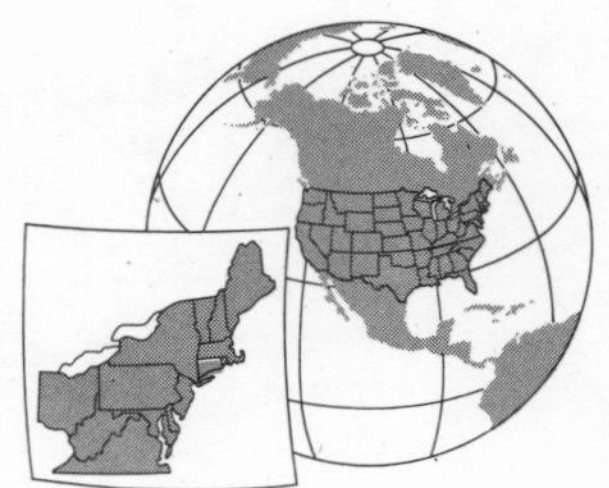

Agriculture, Industry and Resources

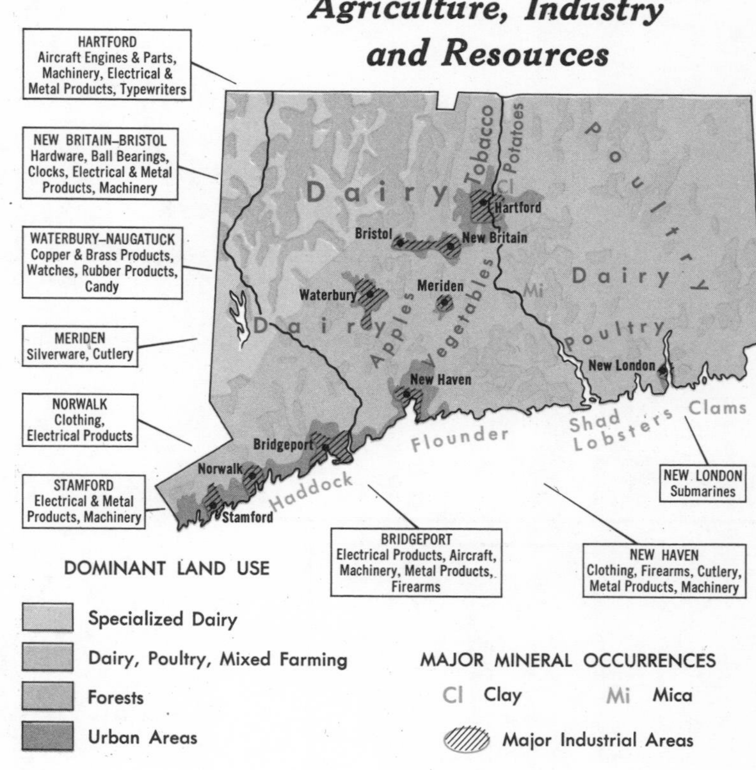

06254 Franklin, ∆1,356 .... G 2
06335 Gales Ferry, 6,200 .... G 3
06829 Georgetown, 1,101 .... B 4
06033 Glastonbury, ∆20,651 .... E 2
06756 Goshen, ∆1,351 .... C 1
06035 Granby, ∆6,150 .... D 1
06430 Greenfield Hill, 2,500 .... B 4
06436 Greens Farms, 3,147 .... B 4
06830 Greenwich, ∆59,755 .... A 4
06340 Groton, ∆38,523 .... G 3
06340 Groton, 8,933 .... G 3
06437 Guilford, ∆12,033 .... E 3
06437 Guilford, 3,632 .... E 3
06438 Haddam, ∆4,934 .... E 3
06438 Haddam, 950 .... E 3
06514 Hamden, ∆49,357 .... D 3
06247 Hampton, ∆1,129 .... G 1
06101 Hartford (cap.), 158,017 .... E 1
Hartford, ‡663,891 .... E 1
06091 Hartland, ∆1,303 .... D 1
06790 Harwinton, ∆4,318 .... C 1
06082 Hazardville, 10,000 .... E 1
06248 Hebron, ∆3,815 .... F 2
06441 Higganum, 2,600 .... E 2
06108 Hockanum, 6,500 .... E 2
06484 Huntington, 2,000 .... C 3
06405 Indian Neck, 1,500 .... D 3
06442 Ivoryton, 1,500 .... F 3
06351 Jewett City, 3,372 .... H 2
06037 Kensington, 6,000 .... D 2
06757 Kent, ∆1,990 .... B 2
06241 Killingly, ∆13,573 .... H 1
† 06413 Killingworth, ∆2,435 .... E 3
† 06424 Lake Pocotopaug, 1,515 .... F 2
06039 Lakeville, 2,100 .... B 1
06249 Lebanon, ∆3,804 .... G 2
06339 Ledyard, ∆14,558 .... G 3
06759 Litchfield, ∆7,399 .... C 2
06759 Litchfield, 1,559 .... C 2
06443 Madison, ∆9,768 .... E 3
06443 Madison, 4,310 .... E 3
06040 Manchester, ∆47,994 .... E 1
† 06250 Mansfield, ∆19,994 .... F 1
06444 Marion, 1,800 .... D 2
† 06424 Marlborough, ∆2,991 .... F 2
06450 Meriden, 55,959 .... D 2
Meriden, ‡55,959 .... D 2
06762 Middlebury, ∆5,542 .... C 2
06455 Middlefield, ∆4,132 .... E 2
06457 Middletown, 36,924 .... E 2
06460 Milford, 50,858 .... C 4
06467 Milldale, 1,175 .... D 2
06468 Monroe, ∆12,047 .... C 3
06468 Monroe P.O. (Stepney), 3,000 .... B 3
† 06473 Montowese, 2,500 .... D 3
06353 Montville, 1,688 .... G 3
06353 Montville, ∆15,662 .... G 3
06469 Moodus, 1,352 .... F 2
06354 Moosup, 3,376 .... H 2
† 06385 Morningside Park, 3,458 .... G 3
06763 Morris, ∆1,609 .... C 2
06355 Mystic, 2,568 .... H 3
06770 Naugatuck, 23,034 .... C 3
* 06050 New Britain, 83,441 .... E 2
New Britain, ‡145,269 .... E 2
06840 New Canaan, ∆17,455 .... B 4
06810 New Fairfield, ∆6,991 .... B 3
06057 New Hartford, ∆3,970 .... C 1
06057 New Hartford, 1,076 .... C 1
* 06501 New Haven, 137,707 .... D 3
New Haven, ‡355,538 .... D 3
06111 Newington, ∆26,037 .... E 2
06320 New London, 31,630 .... G 3
New London-Groton-Norwich, ‡208,412 .... G 3
06776 New Milford, ∆14,601 .... B 2
06776 New Milford, 4,606 .... B 2
06470 Newtown, ∆16,942 .... B 3
06470 Newtown, 1,963 .... B 3
06357 Niantic, 3,422 .... G 3
† 06611 Nichols, 5,000 .... C 4
06340 Noank, 950 .... G 3
06058 Norfolk, ∆2,073 .... C 1
† 06820 Noroton, 4,000 .... B 4
† 06820 Noroton Heights, 7,000 .... B 4
06471 North Branford, ∆10,778 .... E 3
06472 Northford, 4,950 .... D 3
06060 North Granby, 1,500 .... D 1
06255 North Grosvenor Dale, 2,156 .... H 1
06473 North Haven, ∆22,194 .... D 3
06359 North Stonington, ∆3,748 .... H 3
* 06850 Norwalk, 79,113 .... B 4
Norwalk, ‡120,099 .... B 4
06360 Norwich, 41,433 .... G 2
† 06360 Norwichtown, 6,500 .... G 2
06779 Oakville, 8,000 .... C 2
† 06360 Occum, 1,500 .... G 2
06870 Old Greenwich, 5,000 .... A 4
06371 Old Lyme, ∆4,964 .... F 3
06371 Old Lyme, 1,200 .... F 3
06475 Old Saybrook, ∆8,468 .... F 3
06475 Old Saybrook, 2,281 .... F 3
06477 Orange, ∆13,524 .... C 3
06483 Oxford, ∆4,480 .... C 3
06483 Oxford, 950 .... C 3
02891 Pawcatuck, 5,255 .... H 3
† 06405 Pine Orchard, 2,000 .... D 3
06374 Plainfield, ∆11,957 .... H 2
06374 Plainfield, 2,923 .... H 2
06062 Plainville, ∆16,733 .... D 2
06479 Plantsville, 3,900 .... D 2
† 06385 Pleasure Beach, 1,394 .... G 3
06782 Plymouth, ∆10,321 .... C 2
06258 Pomfret, ∆2,529 .... H 1
06064 Poquonock, 2,000 .... E 1
† 06340 Poquonock Bridge, 3,165 .... G 3
06480 Portland, ∆8,812 .... E 2
† 06360 Preston, ∆3,593 .... H 2
06712 Prospect, ∆6,543 .... D 2
06260 Putnam, ∆8,598 .... H 1
06260 Putnam, 6,918 .... H 1
06375 Quaker Hill, 2,068 .... G 3
06262 Quinebaug, 1,350 .... H 1
† 06492 Quinnipiac, 7,500 .... D 3
06875 Redding, ∆5,590 .... B 3
06876 Redding Ridge, 1,500 .... B 3
06877 Ridgefield, ∆18,188 .... B 3
06877 Ridgefield, 5,878 .... B 3
06878 Riverside, 10,719 .... A 4
06066 Rockville, 12,500 .... F 1
06067 Rocky Hill, ∆11,103 .... E 2
06853 Rowayton, 4,210 .... B 4
06783 Roxbury, ∆1,238 .... B 2
† 06415 Salem, ∆1,453 .... F 3
06068 Salisbury, ∆3,573 .... B 1
06482 Sandy Hook, 3,900 .... B 3
† 06880 Saugatuck, 3,311 .... B 4
06264 Scotland, ∆1,022 .... G 2
06483 Seymour, ∆12,776 .... C 3
06069 Sharon, ∆2,491 .... B 1
06484 Shelton, 27,165 .... C 3
06784 Sherman, ∆1,459 .... B 2
† 06405 Short Beach, 2,500 .... D 3
06070 Simsbury, ∆17,475 .... D 1
06070 Simsbury, 4,994 .... D 1
06071 Somers, ∆6,893 .... F 1
06071 Somers, 1,274 .... F 1
06488 Southbury, ∆7,852 .... C 3
† 06238 South Coventry (Coventry), 3,735 .... F 1
06073 South Glastonbury, 3,000 .... E 2
06489 Southington, ∆30,946 .... D 2
† 06850 South Norwalk, 21,000 .... B 4
06490 Southport, 3,500 .... B 4
† 06897 South Wilton, 1,400 .... B 4
06074 South Windsor, ∆15,553 .... E 1
06075 Stafford, ∆8,680 .... F 1
06076 Stafford Springs, 3,339 .... F 1
06077 Staffordville, 1,200 .... G 1
* 06901 Stamford, 108,798 .... A 4
Stamford, ‡206,419 .... A 4
† 06468 Stepney, 2,300 .... B 3
06377 Sterling, ∆1,853 .... H 2
06491 Stevenson, 1,500 .... C 3
06378 Stonington, ∆15,940 .... H 3
06378 Stonington, 1,413 .... H 3
† 06405 Stony Creek, 2,800 .... E 3
06268 Storrs, 10,691 .... F 1
06497 Stratford, ∆49,775 .... C 4
06078 Suffield, ∆8,634 .... E 1
06380 Taftville, 2,000 .... G 2
06081 Tariffville, 1,337 .... D 1
06786 Terryville, 6,900 .... C 2
† 06360 Thamesville, 1,500 .... G 2
06787 Thomaston, ∆6,233 .... C 2
06277 Thompson, ∆7,580 .... H 1
06277 Thompson, 1,200 .... H 1
† 06082 Thompsonville, 27,000 .... E 1
06084 Tolland, ∆7,857 .... F 1
† 06790 Torringford, 3,500 .... C 1
06790 Torrington, 31,952 .... C 1
† 06405 Totoket, 950 .... D 3
06611 Trumbull, ∆31,394 .... C 4
06611 Trumbull, 10,000 .... C 4
06382 Uncasville, 1,750 .... G 3
† 06076 Union, ∆443 .... G 1
† 06770 Union City, 5,000 .... C 2
06085 Unionville, 2,900 .... D 1
06086 Vernon, ∆27,237 .... F 1
06384 Voluntown, ∆1,452 .... H 2
06492 Wallingford, ∆35,714 .... D 3
† 06074 Wapping, 1,600 .... E 1
06088 Warehouse Point, 2,400 .... E 1
06754 Warren, ∆827 .... B 2
06793 Washington, ∆3,121 .... B 2
* 06701 Waterbury, 108,033 .... C 2
Waterbury, ‡208,956 .... C 2
06385 Waterford, ∆17,227 .... G 3
06795 Watertown, ∆18,610 .... C 2
06795 Watertown, 9,000 .... C 2
06714 Waterville, 4,295 .... C 2
06387 Wauregan, 1,100 .... H 2
06089 Weatogue, 2,396 .... D 1
† 06001 West Avon, 4,500 .... D 1
06498 Westbrook, ∆3,820 .... F 3
06498 Westbrook, 1,507 .... F 3
† 06410 West Cheshire, 2,000 .... D 3
† 06457 Westfield, 9,000 .... E 2
06107 West Hartford, ∆68,031 .... D 1
06516 West Haven, 52,851 .... D 3
06388 West Mystic, 3,694 .... H 3
† 06856 West Norwalk, 950 .... B 4
06880 Weston, ∆7,417 .... B 4
06880 Weston, 3,000 .... B 4
06880 Westport, ∆27,414 .... B 4
06896 West Redding, 1,200 .... B 3
06092 West Simsbury, 1,419 .... D 1
06093 West Suffield, 2,400 .... E 1
06109 Wethersfield, 26,662 .... E 2
06517 Whitneyville, 18,438 .... D 3
06226 Willimantic, 14,402 .... G 2
† 06279 Willington, ∆3,755 .... F 1
06897 Wilton, ∆13,572 .... B 4
06897 Wilton, 4,200 .... B 4
06094 Winchester, ∆11,106 .... C 1
06094 Winchester Center, 350 .... C 1
06280 Windham, ∆19,626 .... G 2
06095 Windsor, ∆22,502 .... E 1
06096 Windsor Locks, ∆15,080 .... E 1
06098 Winsted, 8,954 .... C 1
06716 Wolcott, ∆12,495 .... D 2
† 06501 Woodbridge, ∆7,673 .... D 3
06798 Woodbury, ∆5,869 .... C 2
06798 Woodbury, 1,800 .... C 2
06798 Woodbury P.O. (North Woodbury), 1,342 .... C 2
† 06460 Woodmont, 2,400 .... D 4
06281 Woodstock, ∆4,311 .... H 1
† 06492 Yalesville, 3,500 .... D 3
06389 Yantic, 1,200 .... G 2

‡ Population of metropolitan area.
∆ Population of town or township.
† Zip of nearest p.o.
* Multiple zips

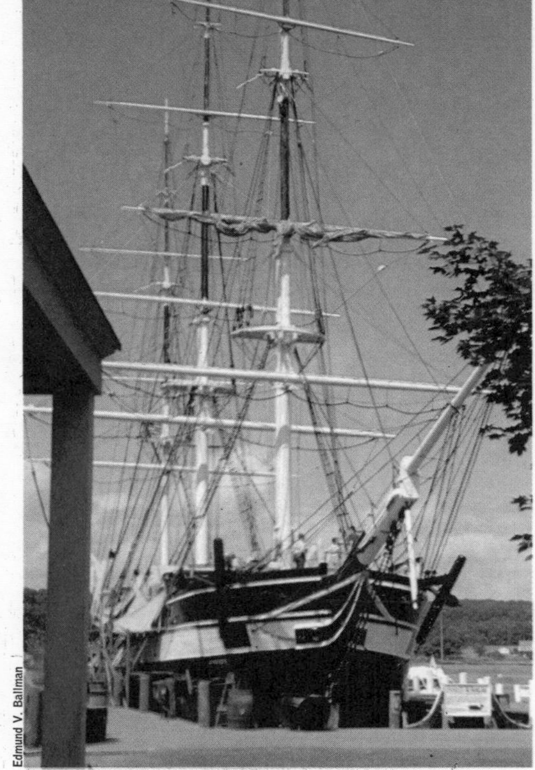
Edmund V. Ballman

Bark whaler "Charles W. Morgan," on view at Mystic, Connecticut, covered more miles and caught more whales than any other ship of her kind.

FLORIDA
SCALE
0 5 10 20 30 40 50 MI.
0 5 10 20 30 40 50 KM.
State Capitals
County Seats
Canals
© C.S. HAMMOND & Co., N.Y.
Longitude West 83° of Greenwich
GEORGIA
ALA.
ATLANTIC OCEAN
GULF OF MEXICO
STRAITS OF FLORIDA
FLORIDA KEYS
JACKSON
CALHOUN
LIBERTY
GULF
FRANKLIN
GADSDEN
LEON
WAKULLA
JEFFERSON
MADISON
TAYLOR
HAMILTON
SUWANNEE
LAFAYETTE
COLUMBIA
BAKER
NASSAU
DUVAL
UNION
BRADFORD
CLAY
ST. JOHNS
PUTNAM
ALACHUA
GILCHRIST
DIXIE
LEVY
MARION
FLAGLER
VOLUSIA
CITRUS
SUMTER
LAKE
HERNANDO
PASCO
PINELLAS
HILLSBOROUGH
POLK
ORANGE
SEMINOLE
BREVARD
OSCEOLA
INDIAN RIVER
MANATEE
HARDEE
HIGHLANDS
OKEECHOBEE
ST. LUCIE
MARTIN
SARASOTA
DE SOTO
CHARLOTTE
GLADES
LEE
HENDRY
PALM BEACH
COLLIER
BROWARD
DADE
MONROE
Jacksonville
Tallahassee
Tampa
St. Petersburg
Orlando
Miami
Miami Beach
Fort Lauderdale
Key West
Lake Okeechobee
EVERGLADES NATIONAL PARK
Big Cypress Swamp
Okefenokee Swamp
WESTERN PART OF FLORIDA
Same scale as main map
ALABAMA
ESCAMBIA
SANTA ROSA
OKALOOSA
WALTON
HOLMES
WASHINGTON
BAY
CALHOUN
GULF
Pensacola
Panama City
GULF OF MEXICO

AREA 58,560 sq. mi.
POPULATION 6,789,443
CAPITAL Tallahassee
LARGEST CITY Jacksonville
HIGHEST POINT 345 ft. (Walton County)
SETTLED IN 1565
ADMITTED TO UNION March 3, 1845
POPULAR NAME Sunshine State; Peninsula State
STATE FLOWER Orange Blossom
STATE BIRD Mockingbird

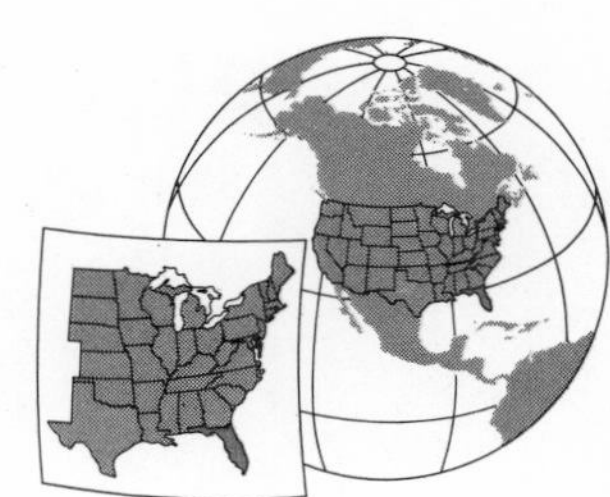

COUNTIES

Name/Pop.	Key
Alachua, 104,764	D 2
Baker, 9,242	D 1
Bay, 75,283	C 6
Bradford, 14,625	D 2
Brevard, 230,006	F 3
Broward, 620,100	F 5
Calhoun, 7,624	D 6
Charlotte, 27,559	E 5
Citrus, 19,196	D 3
Clay, 32,059	E 2
Collier, 38,040	E 5
Columbia, 25,250	D 1
Dade, 1,287,792	F 6
De Soto, 13,060	E 4
Dixie, 5,480	C 2
Duval, 528,865	E 1
Escambia, 205,334	B 6
Flagler, 4,454	E 2
Franklin, 7,065	B 2
Gadsden, 39,184	B 1
Gilchrist, 3,551	D 2
Glades, 3,669	E 5
Gulf, 10,096	D 7
Hamilton, 7,787	D 1
Hardee, 14,889	E 4
Hendry, 11,859	E 5
Hernando, 17,004	D 3
Highlands, 29,507	E 4
Hillsborough, 490,265	D 4
Holmes, 10,720	C 5
Indian River, 35,992	F 4
Jackson, 34,434	D 5
Jefferson, 8,778	C 1
Lafayette, 2,892	C 2
Lake, 69,305	E 3
Lee, 105,216	E 5
Leon, 103,047	B 1
Levy, 12,756	D 2
Liberty, 3,379	B 1
Madison, 13,481	C 1
Manatee, 97,115	D 4
Marion, 69,030	D 2
Martin, 28,035	F 4
Monroe, 52,586	E 7
Nassau, 20,626	E 1
Okaloosa, 88,187	C 6
Okeechobee, 11,233	F 4
Orange, 344,311	E 3
Osceola, 25,267	E 3
Palm Beach, 348,753	F 5
Pasco, 75,955	D 3
Pinellas, 522,329	D 4
Polk, 227,222	E 4
Putnam, 36,290	E 2
Saint Johns, 30,727	E 2
Saint Lucie, 50,836	F 4
Santa Rosa, 37,741	B 6
Sarasota, 120,413	D 4
Seminole, 83,692	E 3
Sumter, 14,839	D 3
Suwannee, 15,559	C 1
Taylor, 13,641	C 1
Union, 8,112	D 1
Volusia, 169,487	E 2
Wakulla, 6,308	B 1
Walton, 16,087	C 6
Washington, 11,453	C 6

CITIES and TOWNS

Zip	*Name/Pop.*	*Key*
32615	Alachua, 2,252	D 2
32420	Alford, 402	D 6
32421	Altha, 423	A 1
32702	Altoona, 800	E 3
33820	Alturas, 468	E 4
33920	Alva, 900	E 5
33501	Anna Maria, 1,137	D 4
32617	Anthony, 500	D 2
32320	Apalachicola⊙, 3,102	A 2
33570	Apollo Beach, 1,042	C 3
32703	Apopka, 4,045	E 3
33821	Arcadia⊙, 5,658	E 4
32618	Archer, 898	D 2
32422	Argyle, 155	C 6
33502	Aripeka, 300	D 3
† 32327	Arran, 160	B 1
32705	Astatula, 388	E 3
32002	Astor, 300	E 2
33823	Auburndale, 5,386	E 3
† 32344	Aucilla, 150	C 1
33825	Avon Park, 6,712	E 4
33827	Babson Park, 950	E 4
32530	Bagdad, 850	B 6
32531	Baker, 500	C 5
32234	Baldwin, 1,272	E 1
† 33101	Bal Harbour, 2,038	C 4
32005	Barberville, 300	E 2
† 32533	Barrineau Park, 150	B 6
32532	Barth, 200	B 6
33830	Bartow⊙, 12,891	E 4
32423	Bascom, 200	A 1
33428	Basinger, 300	F 4
† 33101	Bay Harbour Islands, 4,619	B 4
33504	Bay Pines, 1,100	B 3
† 33902	Bayshore, 150	E 5
† 36502	Bay Springs, 125	B 6
33429	Bean City, 155	F 5
33578	Bee Ridge, 2,100	D 4
32619	Bell, 227	D 2
33540	Belleair, 2,962	B 2
† 33540	Belleair Beach, 952	B 2
33540	Belleair Bluffs, 1,910	B 3
33430	Belle Glade, 15,949	F 5
† 33430	Belle Glade Camp, 1,892	F 5
† 32801	Belle Isle, 2,705	E 3
32620	Belleview, 916	D 2
33152	Biscayne Park, 2,717	B 4
† 32801	Bithlo, 684	E 3
32424	Blountstown⊙, 2,384	A 1
† 32535	Bluffsprings, 160	B 5
33921	Boca Grande, 600	D 5
33432	Boca Raton, 28,506	F 5
33922	Bokeelia, 750	D 5
32425	Bonifay⊙, 2,068	C 5
33923	Bonita Springs, 1,932	E 5
32007	Bostwick, 500	E 2
33834	Bowling Green, 1,357	E 4
33435	Boynton Beach, 18,115	F 5
33505	Bradenton⊙, 21,040	D 4
33510	Bradenton Beach, 1,370	D 4
33835	Bradley, 1,276	D 4
33511	Brandon, 12,749	D 4
32008	Branford, 820	D 2
† 33435	Briny Breezes, 481	G 5
32321	Bristol⊙, 626	B 1
32621	Bronson⊙, 698	D 2
32622	Brooker, 340	D 2
33512	Brooksville⊙, 4,060	D 3
† 33101	Browns Village, 23,442	B 4
32455	Bruce, 221	C 6
33439	Bryant, 400	F 5
† 33054	Bunche Park, 5,773	B 4
32010	Bunnell⊙, 1,687	E 2
33513	Bushnell⊙, 700	D 3
32011	Callahan, 772	E 1
32401	Callaway, 3,240	D 6
32426	Campbellton, 304	D 5
33438	Canal Point, 900	F 5
32624	Candler, 500	E 2
32533	Cantonment, 3,241	B 6
32920	Cape Canaveral, 4,258	F 3
33904	Cape Coral, 10,193	E 5
33924	Captiva, 150	D 5
33054	Carol City, 27,361	B 4
32322	Carrabelle, 1,044	B 2
32427	Caryville, 724	C 6
32706	Cassadaga, 250	E 3
32707	Casselberry, 9,438	E 3
† 32401	Cedar Grove, 689	D 6
32625	Cedar Key, 714	C 2
33514	Center Hill, 371	D 3
32535	Century, 2,679	B 5
† 32302	Chaires, 150	B 1
33950	Charlotte Harbor, 990	E 5
32324	Chattahoochee, 7,944	B 1
† 32350	Cherry Lake Farms, 400	C 1
32626	Chiefland, 1,965	D 2
32428	Chipley⊙, 3,347	D 6
33925	Chokoloskee, 230	E 6
32709	Christmas, 800	E 3
† 32548	Cinco Bayou, 362	B 6
32627	Citra, 500	D 2
† 32922	City Point, 350	F 3
32430	Clarksville, 250	D 6
* 33515	Clearwater⊙, 52,074	B 2
32711	Clermont, 3,661	E 3
† 33950	Cleveland, 150	E 5
33440	Clewiston, 3,896	E 5
32922	Cocoa, 16,110	F 3
32931	Cocoa Beach, 9,952	F 3
† 33060	Coconut Creek, 1,359	F 5
33521	Coleman, 614	D 3
32448	Compass Lake, 200	D 6
† 32333	Concord, 300	B 1
33314	Cooper City, 2,535	F 5
33926	Copeland, 500	E 6
† 83559	Coral Cove, 1,520	D 4
33134	Coral Gables, 42,494	B 5
33836	Cornwell, 700	E 4
33522	Cortez, 600	D 4
32533	Cottagehill, 500	B 6
32431	Cottondale, 765	D 6
32327	Crawfordville⊙, 750	B 1
32012	Crescent City, 1,734	E 2
32536	Crestview⊙, 7,952	C 6
32628	Cross City⊙, 2,268	C 2
32463	Crystal Lake, 125	D 6
32629	Crystal River, 1,696	D 3
33524	Crystal Springs, 300	D 3
33157	Cutler Ridge, 17,441	F 6
32432	Cypress, 266	A 1
33880	Cypress Gardens, 3,757	E 3
† 33472	Cypress Quarters, 1,310	F 4
33525	Dade City⊙, 4,241	D 3
33004	Dania, 9,013	B 4
† 32464	Darlington, 175	C 5
33837	Davenport, 828	E 3
33314	Davie, 2,856	B 4
32013	Day, 200	C 1
* 32014	Daytona Beach, 45,327	F 2
32016	Daytona Beach Shores, 768	F 2
32713	De Bary, 3,154	E 3
33441	Deerfield Beach, 17,130	F 5
32433	De Funiak Springs⊙, 4,966	C 6
32720	De Land⊙, 11,641	E 2
32028	De Leon Springs, 1,134	E 2
33444	Delray Beach, 19,366	F 5
32763	Deltona, 4,868	E 3
† 33870	De Soto City, 250	E 4
32541	Destin, 1,536	C 6
32030	Doctors Inlet, 800	E 1
33527	Dover, 2,094	D 4
† 32060	Dowling Park, 200	C 1
33838	Dundee, 1,660	E 3
33528	Dunedin, 17,639	B 2
32630	Dunnellon, 1,146	D 2
33839	Eagle Lake, 1,373	E 4
32631	Earleton, 350	D 2
† 33601	East Lake-Orient Park, 5,697	C 2
† 33940	East Naples, 6,152	E 5
32031	East Palatka, 1,446	E 2
32328	Eastpoint, 1,188	B 2
32437	Ebro, 125	C 6
32032	Edgewater, 3,348	F 3
† 32801	Edgewood, 392	E 3
† 33601	Egypt Lake, 7,556	C 2
33531	Elfers, 500	D 3
32033	Elkton, 240	E 2
† 33101	El Portal, 2,068	B 4
33533	Englewood, 5,182	D 5
32504	Ensley, 2,400	B 6

(continued on following page)

Topography

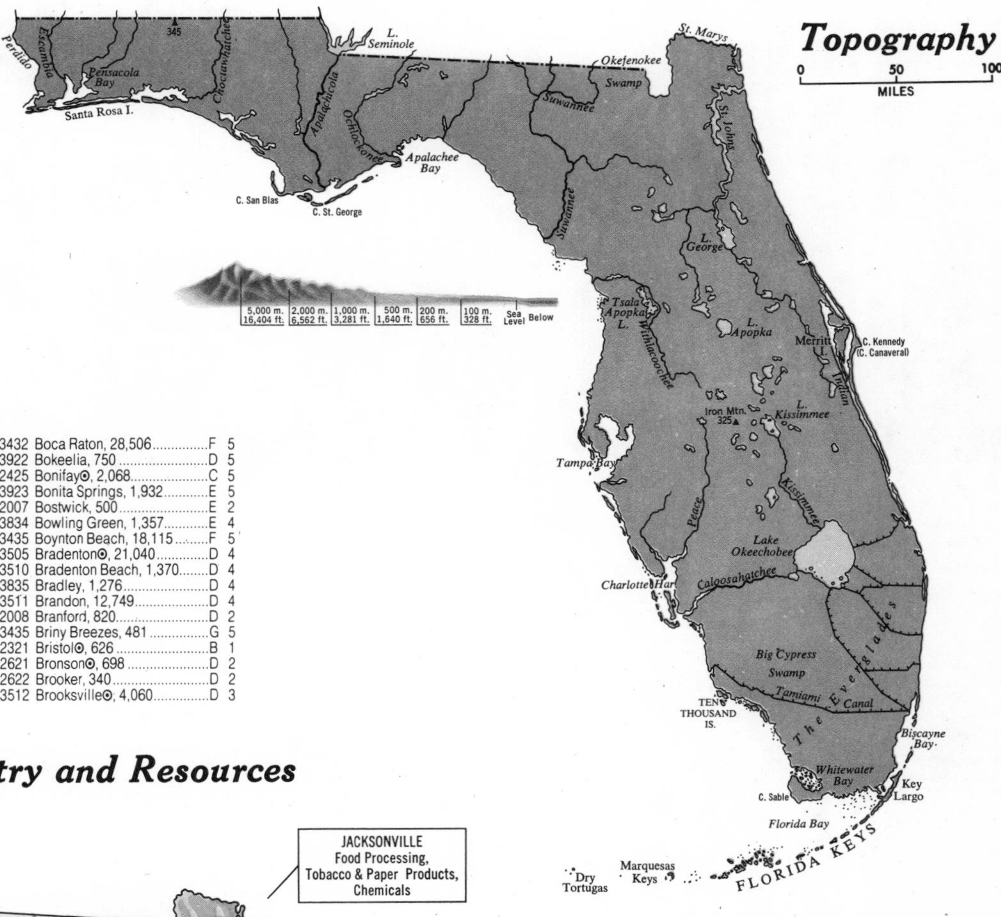

Agriculture, Industry and Resources

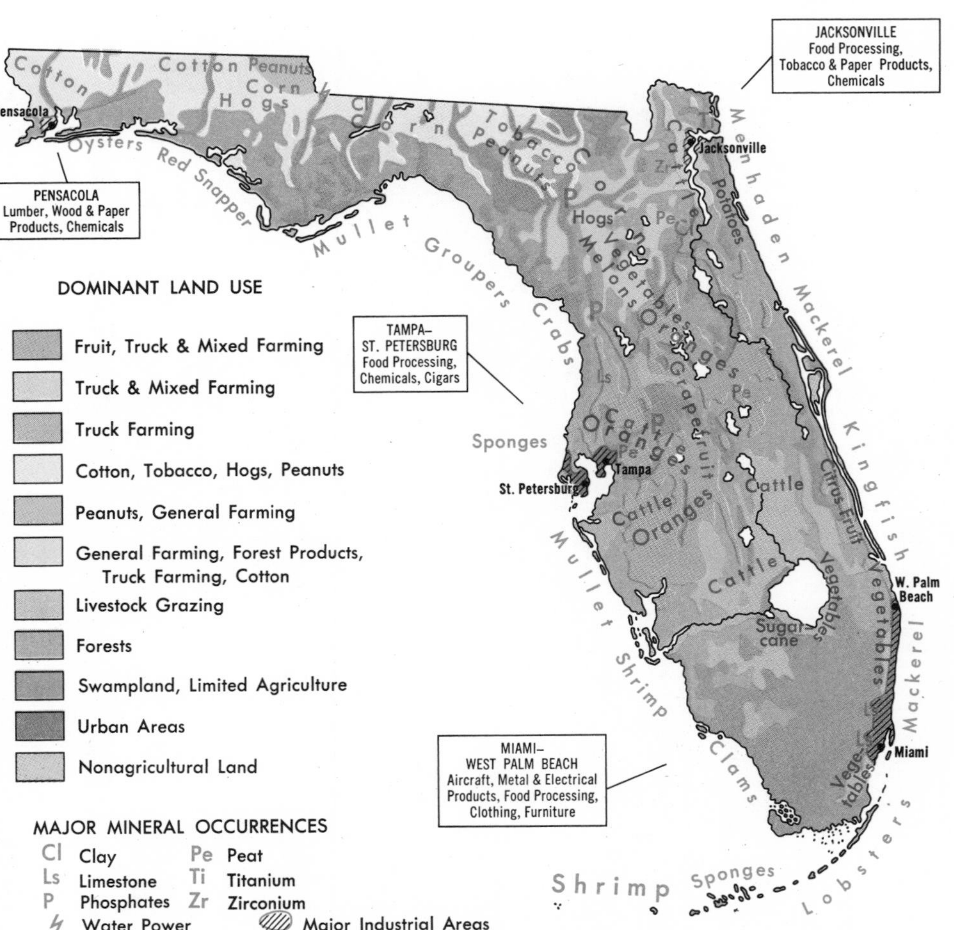

Joseph Brocas — Shostal Associates

Over 150 miles of inland waterways provide a Venetian atmosphere in the modern city of Fort Lauderdale, Florida.

	Zip	Place, population	Key
†	32010	Espanola, 300	E 2
	33928	Estero, 950	E 5
	32425	Esto, 210	C 5
	32726	Eustis, 6,722	E 3
	33929	Everglades City, 462	E 6
†	32601	Fairbanks, 380	D 2
†	32804	Fairvilla, 950	E 3
	33930	Felda, 125	E 5
	32948	Fellsmere, 813	F 4
	32034	Fernandina Beach⊙, 6,955	E 1
†	33301	Fern Crest Village, 1,009	B 4
	32036	Flagler Beach, 1,042	E 2
	32635	Florahome, 400	E 2
	32636	Floral City, 975	D 3
	33030	Florida City, 5,133	F 6
†	32570	Floridatown, 297	B 6
†	32569	Florosa, 200	B 6
†	32347	Foley, 500	C 1
†	33935	Fort Denaud, 300	E 5
†	33472	Fort Drum, 100	F 4
	33834	Fort Green, 300	E 4
*	33301	Fort Lauderdale⊙, 139,590	C 4
		Fort Lauderdale-Hollywood, ‡620,100	C 4
	32637	Fort McCoy, 900	E 2
	33841	Fort Meade, 4,374	E 4
*	33901	Fort Myers⊙, 27,351	E 5
	33931	Fort Myers Beach, 4,305	E 5
	33842	Fort Ogden, 700	E 4
	33450	Fort Pierce⊙, 29,721	F 4
	32548	Fort Walton Beach, 19,994	C 6
	32038	Fort White, 365	D 2
	32438	Fountain, 650	D 6
	32439	Freeport, 950	C 6
†	32430	Frink, 275	D 6
	33843	Frostproof, 2,814	E 4
	32731	Fruitland Park, 1,359	D 3
	33578	Fruitville, 1,531	D 4
	32601	Gainesville⊙, 64,510	D 2
	32732	Geneva, 950	E 3
	32039	Georgetown, 687	E 2
	33534	Gibsonton, 1,900	C 3
	32960	Gifford, 5,772	F 4
	32040	Glen Saint Mary, 357	D 1
	32722	Glenwood, 400	E 2
	33160	Golden Beach, 849	C 4
	33940	Golden Gate, 1,410	E 5
†	33455	Gomez, 400	F 4
	32560	Gonzalez, 750	B 6
	33933	Goodland, 500	E 6
†	32502	Goulding, 500	B 6
	33170	Goulds, 6,690	F 6
	32440	Graceville, 2,560	D 5
	32042	Graham, 150	D 2
	32638	Grandin, 150	E 2
	32442	Grand Ridge, 512	A 1
	32949	Grant, 500	F 4
	33460	Greenacres City, 1,731	F 5
	32043	Green Cove Springs⊙, 3,857	E 2
	32330	Greensboro, 716	B 1
	32331	Greenville, 1,141	C 1
	32443	Greenwood, 515	A 1
	32332	Gretna, 883	B 1
	33533	Grove City, 1,178	F 5
	32736	Groveland, 1,928	E 3
	32561	Gulf Breeze, 4,190	B 6
	32639	Gulf Hammock, 300	D 2
†	33552	Gulf Harbors, 1,177	D 3
	33737	Gulfport, 9,730	B 3
†	33444	Gulf Stream, 408	F 5
†	32601	Hague, 200	D 2
	33844	Haines City, 8,956	E 3
	33009	Hallandale, 23,849	B 4
	32044	Hampton, 386	D 2
	33440	Harlem, 2,006	F 5
	32563	Harold, 150	B 6
	32045	Hastings, 320	E 2
	32333	Havana, 2,022	B 1
	32640	Hawthorne, 1,126	D 2
	32642	Hernando, 524	D 3
*	33010	Hialeah, 102,297	B 4
†	33010	Hialeah Gardens, 492	B 4
	33846	Highland City, 900	E 4
†	33515	High Point, 800	B 3
	32643	High Springs, 2,787	D 2
	32401	Hiland Park, 3,691	C 6
†	33827	Hillcrest Heights, 154	E 4
	32046	Hilliard, 1,205	E 1
†	32327	Hilliardville, 150	B 1
†	33060	Hillsboro Beach, 713	F 5
†	32333	Hinson, 250	B 1
	33455	Hobe Sound, 2,029	F 4
	32645	Holder, 134	D 3
	32047	Hollister, 500	E 2
	32017	Holly Hill, 8,191	E 2
*	33020	Hollywood, 106,873	B 4
†	33020	Hollywood Ridge Farms, 302	B 4
	33509	Holmes Beach, 2,699	D 4
	32564	Holt, 850	C 6
	33030	Homestead, 13,674	F 6
	32646	Homosassa, 850	D 3
	32647	Homosassa Springs, 550	D 3
	32334	Hosford, 975	B 1
	32737	Howey In The Hills, 466	E 3
	33568	Hudson, 2,278	D 3
†	33460	Hypoluxo, 336	F 5
	33934	Immokalee, 3,764	E 5
	32901	Indialantic, 2,685	F 3
	32935	Indian Harbour Beach, 5,371	F 3
	33535	Indian Rocks Beach, 2,666	B 3
†	33535	Indian Rocks Beach South Shore, 791	B 3
	33456	Indiantown, 2,283	F 4
	32649	Inglis, 449	D 2
	33848	Intercession City, 600	E 3
	32048	Interlachen, 478	E 2
	32650	Inverness⊙, 2,299	D 3
	33036	Islamorada, 1,251	F 7
	32654	Island Grove, 200	D 2
*	32201	Jacksonville⊙, 528,865	E 1
		Jacksonville, ‡528,865	E 1
	32250	Jacksonville Beach, 12,049	E 1
	32052	Jasper⊙, 2,221	D 1
	32565	Jay, 646	B 5
	32053	Jennings, 582	C 1
	33457	Jensen Beach, 3,000	F 4
†	32901	June Park, 3,090	F 3
†	33404	Juno Beach, 747	F 5
	33458	Jupiter, 3,136	F 5
†	33455	Jupiter Island, 295	F 4
	33849	Kathleen, 900	D 3
	32739	Kenansville, 450	F 4
	33156	Kendall, 35,497	B 5
†	32670	Kendrick, 200	D 2
	33709	Kenneth City, 3,862	B 3
	33149	Key Biscayne, 4,563	B 5
	33051	Key Colony Beach, 371	F 7
	33037	Key Largo, 2,866	F 6
	32656	Keystone Heights, 800	E 2
	33040	Key West⊙, 27,563	E 7
	32449	Kinard, 450	D 6
	32741	Kissimmee⊙, 7,119	E 3
†	32010	Korona, 200	E 2
	33935	La Belle⊙, 1,823	E 5
	33537	Lacoochee, 1,380	D 3
	32658	La Crosse, 365	D 2
	32659	Lady Lake, 382	E 3
	33850	Lake Alfred, 2,847	E 3
	32054	Lake Butler⊙, 1,598	D 1
†	33601	Lake Carroll, 5,577	C 2
	32055	Lake City⊙, 10,575	D 1
	32057	Lake Como, 340	E 2
	33459	Lake Harbor, 300	F 5
	32744	Lake Helen, 1,303	E 3
	32745	Lake Jem, 314	E 3
*	33801	Lakeland, 41,550	D 3
†	33601	Lake Magdalene, 9,266	D 3
	32746	Lake Mary, 900	E 3
	32747	Lake Monroe, 500	E 3
	33403	Lake Park, 6,993	F 5
	33852	Lake Placid, 656	E 4
†	33471	Lakeport, 375	E 5
	33853	Lake Wales, 8,240	E 4
	32566	Lakewood, 525	C 5
	33460	Lake Worth, 23,714	G 5
	32336	Lamont, 500	C 1
	33539	Land O'Lakes, 900	D 3
	33460	Lantana, 7,126	F 5
	33540	Largo, 22,031	B 3
	33308	Lauderdale-by-the-Sea, 2,879	C 3
†	33301	Lauderdale Lakes, 10,577	B 4
	33313	Lauderhill, 8,465	B 4
	32567	Laurel Hill, 418	C 5
	33545	Laurel-Nokomis, 3,238	D 4
	32058	Lawtey, 636	D 1
	32661	Lecanto, 125	D 3
	32059	Lee, 240	C 1
	32748	Leesburg, 11,869	E 3
	33936	Lehigh Acres, 4,394	E 5
	33030	Leisure City, 2,900	F 6
†	33601	Leto, 8,458	C 2
	33064	Lighthouse Point, 9,071	F 5
†	33865	Limestone, 200	E 4
	32060	Live Oak⊙, 6,830	D 1
	32337	Lloyd, 225	C 1
	32662	Lochloosa, 175	E 2
	33548	Longboat Key, 2,850	D 4
	33001	Long Key, 150	F 7
	32750	Longwood, 3,203	E 3
	33857	Lorida, 950	E 4
	33858	Loughman, 950	E 3
	32663	Lowell, 350	D 2
	33470	Loxahatchee, 950	F 5
	33549	Lutz, 950	D 3
	32444	Lynn Haven, 4,044	C 6
	32063	Macclenny⊙, 2,733	D 1
	33738	Madeira Beach, 4,158	B 3
	32340	Madison⊙, 3,737	C 1
	32751	Maitland, 7,157	E 3
	32950	Malabar, 634	F 3
	32445	Malone, 667	A 1
	33550	Mango, 950	D 4
	33050	Marathon, 4,397	E 7
	33937	Marco, 900	E 6
	33063	Margate, 8,867	F 5
	32446	Marianna⊙, 6,741	A 1
†	32084	Marineland, 13	E 2
	32569	Mary Esther, 3,192	B 6
	33512	Masaryktown, 389	D 3
	32753	Mascotte, 966	E 3
	32066	Mayo⊙, 793	C 1
	32568	McDavid, 500	B 5
	32664	McIntosh, 287	D 2
†	33101	Medley, 351	B 4
	32901	Melbourne, 40,236	F 3
	32951	Melbourne Beach, 2,262	F 3
	32666	Melrose, 950	D 2
†	33301	Melrose Park, 6,111	B 4
†	33561	Memphis, 3,207	D 4
	32952	Merritt Island, 29,233	F 3
	32410	Mexico Beach, 588	D 6
*	33101	Miami⊙, 334,859	B 5
		Miami, ‡1,267,792	B 5
	33139	Miami Beach, 87,072	C 5
†	33101	Miami Lakes, 3,500	B 4
	33153	Miami Shores, 9,425	B 4
	33166	Miami Springs, 13,279	B 5
	32667	Micanopy, 759	D 2
†	32960	Micco, 400	F 4
	32309	Miccosukee, 275	B 1
	32068	Middleburg, 950	E 1
	32343	Midway, 900	B 1
	32537	Milligan, 950	C 6
	32570	Milton⊙, 5,360	B 6
	32754	Mims, 8,309	F 3
	32755	Minneola, 878	E 3
	33023	Miramar, 23,973	B 4
	32577	Molino, 850	B 6
†	32696	Montbrook, 250	D 2
	32344	Monticello⊙, 2,473	C 1
	32756	Montverde, 308	E 3
	33471	Moore Haven⊙, 974	E 5
	32434	Mossy Head, 160	C 6
	32757	Mount Dora, 4,543	E 3
	32352	Mount Pleasant, 150	B 1
	33860	Mulberry, 2,701	E 4
	33551	Myakka City, 672	D 4
	32506	Myrtle Grove, 16,186	B 6
	33940	Naples⊙, 12,042	E 5
†	33940	Naples Park, 1,522	E 5
	33030	Naranja, 2,900	F 6
	32233	Neptune Beach, 2,868	E 1
	32669	Newberry, 1,247	D 2
	33552	New Port Richey, 6,098	D 3
	32069	New Smyrna Beach, 10,580	F 2
	32578	Niceville, 4,024	C 6
	33863	Nichols, 300	E 4
	33864	Nocatee, 950	E 4
	33555	Nokomis-Laurel, 3,238	D 4
	32452	Noma, 234	C 5
	33141	North Bay Village, 4,831	B 4
	33903	North Fort Myers, 8,798	E 5
	33161	North Miami, 34,767	B 4
	33161	North Miami Beach, 30,723	C 4
†	33940	North Naples, 3,201	E 5
	33403	North Palm Beach, 9,035	F 5
	33595	North Port Charlotte, 2,244	D 4
†	33708	North Redington Beach, 768	B 3
†	33054	Norwood, 14,973	B 4
	32759	Oak Hill, 747	F 3
	32760	Oakland, 672	E 3
	33307	Oakland Park, 16,261	B 3
	32071	O'Brien, 200	D 1
	32670	Ocala⊙, 22,583	D 2
†	33457	Ocean Breeze, 714	F 4
	33444	Ocean Ridge, 1,074	F 5
	33943	Ochopee, 200	E 6
	32761	Ocoee, 3,937	E 3
	33556	Odessa, 500	D 3
	33163	Ojus, 12,000	B 4
	32762	Okahumpka, 470	D 3
	33472	Okeechobee⊙, 3,715	F 4
	32679	Oklawaha, 700	E 2
	33557	Oldsmar, 1,538	B 2
	32680	Old Town, 500	C 2
	32072	Olustee, 400	D 1
	33865	Ona, 236	E 4
	33558	Oneco, 3,246	D 4
	33054	Opa-locka, 11,902	B 4
	32763	Orange City, 1,777	E 3
	32681	Orange Lake, 900	D 2
	32073	Orange Park, 7,619	E 1
	32682	Orange Springs, 500	E 2
*	32801	Orlando⊙, 99,006	E 3
		Orlando, ‡428,003	E 3
	32074	Ormond Beach, 14,063	E 2
	33559	Osprey, 1,115	D 4
	32764	Osteen, 875	E 3
	32683	Otter Creek, 400	D 2
	32765	Oviedo, 1,870	E 3
	32684	Oxford, 490	D 3
	33560	Ozona, 900	D 3
	32570	Pace, 1,776	B 6
	33476	Pahokee, 5,663	F 5
	32077	Palatka⊙, 9,310	E 2
	32901	Palm Bay, 6,927	F 3
	33480	Palm Beach, 9,086	G 4
†	33404	Palm Beach Shores, 1,214	G 5
	33490	Palm City, 900	F 4
	33561	Palmetto, 7,422	D 4
	33563	Palm Harbor, 1,763	D 3
	33619	Palm River-Clair Mel, 8,536	C 3
	32935	Palm Shores, 202	F 3
	33460	Palm Springs, 4,340	F 5
	32346	Panacea, 950	B 1
	32401	Panama City⊙, 32,096	C 6
	32401	Parker, 4,212	C 6
	33564	Parrish, 950	D 4
	32538	Paxton, 243	C 5
†	33023	Pembroke Park, 2,949	B 4
	33023	Pembroke Pines, 15,520	B 4
	32079	Penney Farms, 561	E 2
*	32501	Pensacola⊙, 59,507	B 6
		Pensacola, ‡243,075	B 6
	33157	Perrine, 10,257	F 6
	32347	Perry⊙, 7,701	C 1
	33867	Pierce, 500	E 4
	32080	Pierson, 654	E 2
	33565	Pinellas Park, 22,287	B 3
	32350	Pinetta, 300	C 1
†	33042	Pirates Cove, 150	E 7
	33946	Placida, 250	D 5
	33314	Plantation, 23,523	B 4
	33566	Plant City, 15,451	D 3
	32768	Plymouth, 950	E 3
	33868	Polk City, 151	E 3
	32081	Pomona Park, 578	E 2
*	33060	Pompano Beach, 37,724	F 5
	32455	Ponce de Leon, 288	C 6
†	32019	Ponce Inlet, 328	F 2
	32082	Ponte Vedra Beach, 2,100	E 1
	33950	Port Charlotte, 10,769	D 5
†	32439	Portland, 228	C 6
†	33438	Port Mayaca, 400	F 5
	32019	Port Orange, 3,781	F 2
	33568	Port Richey, 1,259	D 3
	32456	Port Saint Joe, 4,401	D 6
	33450	Port Saint Lucie, 330	F 4
	33492	Port Salerno, 1,161	F 4
	33171	Princeton, 1,900	F 6
†	33619	Progress, 1,328	C 3
†	32061	Providence, 150	D 2
	33950	Punta Gorda⊙, 3,879	E 5
	32351	Quincy⊙, 8,334	B 1
	32083	Raiford, 500	D 1
†	32696	Raleigh, 275	D 2
	32455	Redbay, 500	C 6
	32686	Reddick, 305	D 2
	33708	Redington Beach, 1,583	B 3
†	33708	Redington Shores, 1,733	B 3
†	33599	Richland, 928	D 3
†	33158	Richmond Heights, 6,663	F 6
	33569	Riverview, 2,225	D 4
	33404	Riviera Beach, 21,401	G 5
	32955	Rockledge, 10,523	F 3
	32957	Roseland, 550	F 4
	32447	Round Lake, 275	D 6
	33570	Ruskin, 2,414	C 3
	33572	Safety Harbor, 3,103	B 2
	32084	Saint Augustine⊙, 12,352	E 2
	32084	Saint Augustine Beach, 632	E 2
	33573	Saint Catherine, 350	D 3
	32769	Saint Cloud, 5,041	E 3
	33956	Saint James City, 500	D 5
	33574	Saint Leo, 1,145	D 3
†	33450	Saint Lucie, 428	F 4
	32355	Saint Marks, 366	B 1
*	33701	Saint Petersburg, 216,232	B 3
	33736	Saint Petersburg Beach, 8,024	B 3
	32356	Salem, 150	C 2
	33505	Samoset, 4,070	D 4
†	32069	Samsula, 270	E 2
	33576	San Antonio, 473	D 3
	32087	Sanderson, 150	D 1
	32771	Sanford⊙, 17,393	E 3
	33957	Sanibel, 750	D 5
	32088	San Mateo, 975	E 2
†	32670	Santos, 150	D 2
*	33577	Sarasota⊙, 40,237	D 4
	32935	Satellite Beach, 6,558	F 3
	32089	Satsuma, 610	E 2
	32775	Scottsmoor, 850	F 3
†	33301	Sea Ranch Lakes, 660	C 3
	32958	Sebastian, 825	F 4
	33870	Sebring⊙, 7,223	E 4
	33584	Seffner, 2,000	D 4
	33540	Seminole, 2,410	B 3
	32090	Seville, 500	E 2
†	33457	Sewalls Point, 298	F 4
	32579	Shalimar, 578	C 6
†	32628	Shamrock, 200	C 2
	32959	Sharpes, 427	F 3
	32688	Silver Springs, 500	D 2
	32460	Sneads, 1,550	B 1
	32358	Sopchoppy, 460	B 1
	32776	Sorrento, 500	E 3
	33493	South Bay, 2,958	F 5
	32021	South Daytona, 4,979	F 2
†	36441	South Flomaton, 329	B 5
	33143	South Miami, 19,571	B 5
	33707	South Pasadena, 2,063	B 3
†	32401	Southport, 1,560	C 6
	32690	Sparr, 450	D 2
	32401	Springfield, 5,949	D 6
	32091	Starke⊙, 4,848	D 2
	32359	Steinhatchee, 800	C 2
	33494	Stuart⊙, 4,820	F 4
	32335	Sumatra, 150	B 1
	32691	Summerfield, 450	D 2
	33042	Summerland Key, 350	E 7
	33586	Sun City, 2,143	D 4
†	33450	Sunland Gardens, 1,900	F 4
	33160	Sunny Isles, 950	C 4
†	33577	Sunnyland, 4,900	D 4
	32461	Sunnyside, 370	C 6
	33313	Sunrise Golf Village, 7,403	B 4
	33154	Surfside, 3,614	B 4
	32692	Suwannee, 203	C 2
†	33144	Sweetwater, 3,307	B 5
†	33601	Sweetwater Creek, 19,453	B 2
†	32043	Switzerland, 500	E 1
	32809	Taft, 1,183	E 3
*	32301	Tallahassee (cap.)⊙, 71,897	B 1
		Tallahassee, ‡103,047	B 1
†	33301	Tamarac, 5,078	B 3
*	33601	Tampa⊙, 277,767	C 2
		Tampa-Saint Petersburg, ‡1,012,594	C 2
	33589	Tarpon Springs, 7,118	D 3
	32778	Tavares⊙, 3,261	E 3
	33070	Tavernier, 900	F 6
	32360	Telogia, 300	B 1
	33617	Temple Terrace, 7,347	C 2
	33458	Tequesta, 2,642	F 5
	33591	Terra Ceia, 450	D 4
	33592	Thonotosassa, 900	D 3
	33905	Tice, 7,254	E 5
	32780	Titusville⊙, 30,515	F 3
	33740	Treasure Island, 6,120	B 3
	32693	Trenton⊙, 1,074	D 2
	33593	Trilby, 930	D 3
	32784	Umatilla, 1,600	E 3
	32580	Valparaiso, 6,504	C 6
	33595	Venice, 6,648	D 4
	33960	Venus, 300	E 4
	32462	Vernon, 691	C 6
	32960	Vero Beach⊙, 11,908	F 4
†	32548	Villa Tasso, 200	C 6
†	33166	Virginia Gardens, 2,524	B 5
	32970	Wabasso, 950	F 4
	32361	Wacissa, 275	B 1
†	32327	Wakulla, 225	B 1
	32694	Waldo, 800	D 2
	32568	Walnut Hill, 500	B 5
	32507	Warrington, 15,848	B 6
†	32055	Watertown, 3,624	D 1
	33873	Wauchula⊙, 3,007	E 4
	32463	Wausau, 288	D 6
	33877	Waverly, 1,172	E 4
	33597	Webster, 739	D 3
	32695	Weirsdale, 995	D 3
	32093	Welaka, 496	E 2
	32094	Wellborn, 600	D 1
	32401	Westbay, 350	C 6
†	32901	West Melbourne, 3,050	F 3
†	33101	West Miami, 5,494	B 5
*	33401	West Palm Beach⊙, 57,375	F 5
		West Palm Beach, ‡348,753	F 5
	32401	West Panama City Beach, 1,052	C 6
	32505	West Pensacola, 20,924	B 6
	32464	Westville, 475	C 6
†	33101	Westwood Lakes, 12,811	B 5
	32465	Wewahitchka⊙, 1,733	D 6
†	32465	White City, 600	F 4
	32096	White Springs, 767	D 1
	32785	Wildwood, 2,082	D 3
	32696	Williston, 1,939	D 2
	33305	Wilton Manors, 10,948	B 3
	33598	Wimauma, 650	D 4
	32786	Windermere, 894	E 3
	32971	Winter Beach, 350	F 4
	32787	Winter Garden, 5,153	E 3
	33880	Winter Haven, 16,136	E 3
	32789	Winter Park, 21,895	E 3
	32362	Woodville, 900	B 1
	32697	Worthington Springs, 214	D 2
	32797	Yalaha, 675	E 3
	32698	Yankeetown, 490	D 2
	32466	Youngstown, 400	D 6
	32097	Yulee, 950	E 1
	32798	Zellwood, 550	E 3
	33599	Zephyrhills, 3,369	D 3
	33890	Zolfo Springs, 1,117	E 4

⊙ County seat.
‡ Population of metropolitan area.
† Zip of nearest p.o.
* Multiple zips

A. D'Arazien — Shostal Associates

Using local pines for pulpwood, this plant in Augusta, Georgia, is turning out paper for milk cartons.

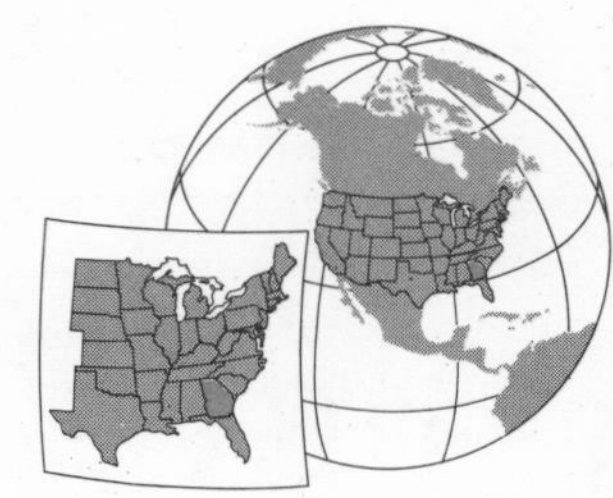

AREA 58,876 sq. mi.
POPULATION 4,589,575
CAPITAL Atlanta
LARGEST CITY Atlanta
HIGHEST POINT Brasstown Bald 4,784 ft.
SETTLED IN 1733
ADMITTED TO UNION January 2, 1788
POPULAR NAME Empire State of the South; Peach State
STATE FLOWER Cherokee Rose
STATE BIRD Brown Thrasher

COUNTIES

Appling, 12,726 H 7
Atkinson, 5,879 G 8
Bacon, 8,233 G 7
Baker, 3,875 D 8
Baldwin, 34,240 F 4
Banks, 6,833 E 2
Barrow, 16,859 E 3
Bartow, 32,663 C 2
Ben Hill, 13,171 F 7
Berrien, 11,556 F 8
Bibb, 143,418 E 5
Bleckley, 10,291 F 6
Brantley, 5,940 J 8
Brooks, 13,739 E 9
Bryan, 6,539 K 6
Bulloch, 31,585 J 6
Burke, 18,255 J 4
Butts, 10,560 E 4
Calhoun, 6,606 C 7
Camden, 11,334 J 9
Candler, 6,412 H 6
Carroll, 45,404 B 3
Catoosa, 28,271 B 1
Charlton, 5,680 H 9
Chatham, 187,767 K 6
Chattahoochee, 25,813 C 6
Chattooga, 20,541 B 1
Cherokee, 31,059 D 2
Clarke, 65,177 F 3
Clay, 3,636 B 7
Clayton, 98,043 D 3
Clinch, 6,405 G 9
Cobb, 196,793 C 3
Coffee, 22,828 G 8
Colquitt, 32,200 E 8
Columbia, 22,327 H 3
Cook, 12,129 F 8
Coweta, 32,310 C 4
Crawford, 5,748 E 5
Crisp, 18,087 E 7
Dade, 9,910 A 1
Dawson, 3,639 D 2
Decatur, 22,310 C 9
De Kalb, 415,387 D 3
Dodge, 15,658 F 6
Dooly, 10,404 E 6
Dougherty, 89,639 D 7
Douglas, 28,659 C 3
Early, 12,682 C 8
Echols, 1,924 G 9
Effingham, 13,632 K 6
Elbert, 17,262 G 2
Emanuel, 18,189 H 5
Evans, 7,290 J 6
Fannin, 13,357 D 1
Fayette, 11,364 C 4
Floyd, 73,742 B 2
Forsyth, 16,928 D 2
Franklin, 12,784 F 2
Fulton, 607,592 D 3
Gilmer, 8,956 D 1
Glascock, 2,280 G 4
Glynn, 50,528 J 8
Gordon, 23,570 C 2
Grady, 17,826 D 9
Greene, 10,212 F 3
Gwinnett, 72,349 D 2
Habersham, 20,691 E 1
Hall, 59,405 E 2
Hancock, 9,019 G 4
Haralson, 15,927 B 3
Harris, 11,520 C 5
Hart, 15,814 G 2
Heard, 5,354 B 4
Henry, 23,724 D 4
Houston, 62,924 E 6
Irwin, 8,036 F 7
Jackson, 21,093 E 2
Jasper, 5,760 E 4
Jeff Davis, 9,425 G 7
Jefferson, 17,174 H 4
Jenkins, 8,332 J 5
Johnson, 7,727 G 5
Jones, 12,218 E 5
Lamar, 10,688 D 4
Lanier, 5,031 F 8
Laurens, 32,738 G 6
Lee, 7,044 D 7
Liberty, 17,569 J 7
Lincoln, 5,895 H 3
Long, 3,746 J 7
Lowndes, 55,112 F 9
Lumpkin, 8,728 D 1
Macon, 12,933 D 6
Madison, 13,517 F 2
Marion, 5,099 C 6
McDuffie, 15,276 H 4
McIntosh, 7,371 K 7
Meriwether, 19,461 C 4
Miller, 6,397 C 8
Mitchell, 18,956 D 8
Monroe, 10,991 E 4
Montgomery, 6,099 G 6
Morgan, 9,904 F 3
Murray, 12,986 C 1
Muscogee, 167,377 C 6
Newton, 26,282 E 3
Oconee, 7,915 F 3
Oglethorpe, 7,598 F 3
Paulding, 17,520 C 3
Peach, 15,990 E 5
Pickens, 9,620 D 2
Pierce, 9,281 H 8
Pike, 7,316 D 4
Polk, 29,656 B 3
Pulaski, 8,066 E 6
Putnam, 8,394 F 4
Quitman, 2,180 B 7
Rabun, 8,327 F 1
Randolph, 8,734 C 7
Richmond, 162,347 H 4
Rockdale, 18,152 D 3
Schley, 3,097 D 6
Screven, 12,591 J 5
Seminole, 7,059 C 9
Spalding, 39,514 D 4
Stephens, 20,331 F 1
Stewart, 6,511 C 6
Sumter, 26,931 D 6
Talbot, 6,625 C 5
Taliaferro, 2,423 G 3
Tattnall, 16,557 J 6
Taylor, 7,865 D 5
Telfair, 11,381 G 7
Terrell, 11,416 D 7
Thomas, 34,515 E 9
Tift, 27,288 E 7
Toombs, 19,151 H 6
Towns, 4,565 E 1
Treutlen, 5,647 G 6
Troup, 44,466 B 4
Turner, 8,790 E 7
Twiggs, 8,222 F 5
Union, 6,811 E 1
Upson, 23,505 D 5
Walker, 50,691 B 1
Walton, 23,404 E 3
Ware, 33,525 H 8
Warren, 6,669 G 4
Washington, 17,480 G 4
Wayne, 17,858 J 7
Webster, 2,362 C 6
Wheeler, 4,596 G 6
White, 7,742 E 1
Whitfield, 55,108 B 1
Wilcox, 6,998 F 7
Wilkes, 10,184 G 3
Wilkinson, 9,393 F 5
Worth, 14,770 E 8

CITIES and TOWNS

Zip *Name/Pop.* *Key*

31001 Abbeville⊙, 781 F 7
30101 Acworth, 3,929 C 2
30103 Adairsville, 1,676 C 2
31620 Adel⊙, 4,972 F 8
31002 Adrian, 705 G 5
30410 Ailey, 487 G 6
30411 Alamo⊙, 833 G 6
31622 Alapaha, 633 F 8
* 31701 Albany⊙, 72,623 D 7
Albany, ‡89,639 D 7
† 30204 Aldora, 322 D 4
30801 Alexander, 200 J 4
31301 Allenhurst, 230 J 7
31003 Allentown, 295 F 5
31510 Alma⊙, 3,756 G 7
† 30209 Almon, 400 E 3
30201 Alpharetta, 2,455 D 2
30510 Alto, 372 E 2
† 30161 Alto Park, 2,963 B 2
31512 Ambrose, 253 G 7
31709 Americus⊙, 16,091 D 6
31711 Andersonville, 274 D 6
30802 Appling⊙, 212 H 3
31712 Arabi, 305 E 7
30104 Aragon, 850 B 2
† 30549 Arcade, 229 E 2
31520 Arco, 6,009 J 8
31623 Argyle, 206 G 8
31713 Arlington, 1,698 C 8
30105 Armuchee, 600 B 2
31714 Ashburn⊙, 4,209 E 7
† 30521 Ashland, 350 F 2
30601 Athens⊙, 44,342 F 3
* 30301 Atlanta (cap.)⊙, 496,973 D 3
Atlanta, ‡1,390,164 D 3
31715 Attapulgus, 513 D 9
30203 Auburn, 361 E 2
* 30901 Augusta⊙, 59,864 J 4
Augusta, ‡253,460 J 4
30001 Austell, 2,632 C 3
† 30557 Avalon, 204 F 1
30803 Avera, 217 G 4
30002 Avondale Estates, 1,735 D 3
31624 Axson, 250 G 8
31716 Baconton, 710 D 8
31717 Bainbridge⊙, 10,887 C 9
30511 Baldwin, 772 E 2
30107 Ball Ground, 617 D 2
30204 Barnesville⊙, 4,935 D 4
† 31601 Barretts, 275 F 8
30413 Bartow, 333 G 5
31720 Barwick, 381 E 9
31513 Baxley⊙, 3,503 H 7
† 31792 Beachton, 200 D 9
30414 Bellville, 234 H 6
† 31601 Bemiss, 325 F 9
31722 Berlin, 422 E 8
30748 Berryton, 200 B 2
30620 Bethlehem, 304 E 3
31904 Bibb City, 812 B 5
30621 Bishop, 235 F 3
31516 Blackshear⊙, 2,624 H 8
30512 Blairsville⊙, 491 E 1
31723 Blakely⊙, 5,267 C 8
† 31308 Blitchton, 256 J 6
31302 Bloomingdale, 1,588 K 6
30513 Blue Ridge⊙, 1,602 D 1
30805 Blythe, 333 H 4
30622 Bogart, 667 E 3
31626 Boston, 1,443 E 9
30623 Bostwick, 289 E 3
30108 Bowdon, 1,753 B 3
30109 Bowdon Junction, 200 B 3
30516 Bowersville, 301 G 2
30624 Bowman, 724 G 2
31801 Box Springs, 600 C 5
30517 Braselton, 386 E 2
30110 Bremen, 3,484 B 3
31701 Bridgeboro, 250 E 8
31725 Brinson, 231 C 9
31726 Bronwood, 500 D 7
31727 Brookfield, 860 F 8
30415 Brooklet, 683 J 6
31519 Broxton, 957 G 7
31520 Brunswick⊙, 19,585 K 8
30113 Buchanan⊙, 800 B 3
31803 Buena Vista⊙, 1,486 C 6
30518 Buford, 4,640 D 2
† 31020 Bullard, 230 F 5
31006 Butler⊙, 1,589 D 5
31007 Byromville, 419 E 6
31008 Byron, 1,368 E 5
31009 Cadwell, 354 G 6
31728 Cairo⊙, 8,061 D 9
30701 Calhoun⊙, 4,748 C 1
31729 Calvary, 500 D 9
30807 Camak, 224 G 4
31730 Camilla⊙, 4,987 D 8
30520 Canon, 709 F 2
30114 Canton⊙, 3,654 C 2
† 30720 Carbondale, 300 B 1
30203 Carl, 234 E 3
30627 Carlton, 294 F 2
30521 Carnesville⊙, 510 F 2
30117 Carrollton⊙, 13,520 C 3
† 30540 Cartecay, 250 D 1
30120 Cartersville⊙, 9,929 C 2
30123 Cassville, 350 C 2
31804 Cataula, 500 C 5
30124 Cave Spring, 1,305 B 2
31627 Cecil, 265 F 8
30125 Cedartown⊙, 9,253 B 2
† 30601 Center, 213 F 2
31093 Centerville, 1,725 E 5
† 31816 Chalybeate Springs, 266 C 5
30341 Chamblee, 9,127 D 3
30705 Chatsworth⊙, 2,706 C 1
31011 Chauncey, 308 F 6
31012 Chester, 409 F 6
30707 Chickamauga, 1,842 B 1
† 30512 Choestoe, 215 E 1
31733 Chula, 300 E 7
30523 Clarkesville⊙, 1,294 F 1
30021 Clarkston, 3,127 D 3
30417 Claxton⊙, 2,669 J 6
30525 Clayton⊙, 1,569 F 1
30128 Clem, 350 B 3
30527 Clermont, 290 E 2
30528 Cleveland⊙, 1,353 E 1
31734 Climax, 275 D 9
31604 Clyattville, 500 F 9
31303 Clyo, 300 K 6
30420 Cobbtown, 321 H 6
31014 Cochran⊙, 5,161 F 6
30710 Cohutta, 300 C 1
30628 Colbert, 532 F 2
30337 College Park, 18,203 C 3
30421 Collins, 574 H 6
31737 Colquitt⊙, 2,026 C 8
* 31901 Columbus⊙, 154,168 C 6
Columbus, ‡238,584 C 6
30629 Comer, 828 F 2
30529 Commerce, 3,702 E 2
30206 Concord, 312 D 4
30207 Conyers⊙, 4,890 D 3
31738 Coolidge, 717 E 8
30129 Coosa, 600 B 2
31015 Cordele⊙, 10,733 E 7
30531 Cornelia, 3,014 E 1
30209 Covington⊙, 10,267 E 3
30630 Crawford, 624 F 3
30631 Crawfordville⊙, 735 G 3
† 30105 Crystal Springs, 500 B 2
31016 Culloden, 272 D 5
30130 Cumming⊙, 2,031 D 2
31805 Cusseta⊙, 1,251 C 6
31740 Cuthbert⊙, 3,972 C 7
30211 Dacula, 782 E 3
30533 Dahlonega⊙, 2,658 D 1
30132 Dallas⊙, 2,133 C 3
30720 Dalton⊙, 18,872 C 1
31741 Damascus, 272 C 8
30633 Danielsville⊙, 378 F 2
31017 Danville, 515 F 5
31305 Darien⊙, 1,826 K 8
31601 Dasher, 452 F 9
31018 Davisboro, 476 G 5
31742 Dawson⊙, 5,383 D 7
30534 Dawsonville⊙, 288 D 2
30808 Dearing, 555 H 4
* 30030 Decatur⊙, 21,943 D 3
† 31501 Deenwood, 3,015 H 8
30535 Demorest, 1,070 F 1
31532 Denton, 244 G 7
31743 De Soto, 321 D 7
31019 Dexter, 438 G 6
† 31520 Dock Junction (Arco), 6,009 J 8
31744 Doerun, 1,157 E 8
31745 Donalsonville⊙, 2,907 C 8
30340 Doraville, 9,039 D 3
31533 Douglas⊙, 10,195 G 7
30134 Douglasville⊙, 5,472 C 3
31020 Dry Branch, 700 F 5
31021 Dublin⊙, 15,143 G 5
31022 Dudley, 423 F 5
30136 Duluth, 1,810 D 2
31630 Du Pont, 252 G 9
30538 Eastanollee, 365 F 1
31021 East Dublin, 1,986 G 5
30539 East Ellijay, 488 C 1
31023 Eastman⊙, 5,416 F 6
† 30263 East Newnan, 1,634 C 4
30344 East Point, 39,315 C 3
31024 Eatonton⊙, 4,125 F 4
31307 Eden, 300 K 6
31746 Edison, 1,210 C 7
† 31093 Elberta, 500 E 5
30635 Elberton⊙, 6,438 G 2
30060 Elizabeth, 950 C 2
31025 Elko, 450 E 6
31308 Ellabell, 400 K 6
31806 Ellaville⊙, 1,391 D 6
31747 Ellenton, 337 E 8
31807 Ellerslie, 615 C 5
30540 Ellijay⊙, 1,326 C 1
30137 Emerson, 813 C 2
31026 Empire, 325 F 6
31749 Enigma, 505 F 8
† 30217 Ephesus, 212 B 4
30541 Epworth, 300 D 1
30724 Eton, 286 C 1
† 31331 Eulonia, 500 K 7
30809 Evans, 1,500 H 3
31536 Everett, 300 J 8
30212 Experiment, 2,256 D 4
30213 Fairburn, 3,143 C 3
30139 Fairmount, 623 C 2
31631 Fargo, 800 G 9
30214 Fayetteville⊙, 2,160 C 4
30140 Felton, 300 B 3
31750 Fitzgerald⊙, 8,015 F 7
† 31313 Flemington, 265 K 7
30215 Flippen, 600 D 3
30216 Flovilla, 289 E 4
30542 Flowery Branch, 779 E 2
31537 Folkston⊙, 2,112 H 9
30050 Forest Park, 19,994 D 3
31029 Forsyth⊙, 3,736 E 4
31751 Fort Gaines⊙, 1,255 C 7
30741 Fort Oglethorpe, 3,869 B 1
31030 Fort Valley⊙, 9,251 E 5
31752 Fowlstown, 400 D 9
30217 Franklin⊙, 749 B 4
30639 Franklin Springs, 501 F 2
37317 Fry, 300 D 1
31753 Funston, 293 E 8
30501 Gainesville⊙, 15,459 E 2
31408 Garden City, 5,741 K 6
30425 Garfield, 214 H 5
31810 Geneva, 250 C 5
31754 Georgetown⊙, 578 B 7
30810 Gibson⊙, 701 G 4
30426 Girard, 241 J 4
30427 Glennville, 2,965 J 7
30428 Glenwood, 670 G 6
30641 Good Hope, 202 E 3
31031 Gordon, 2,553 F 5
30811 Gough, 300 H 4
30812 Gracewood, 1,200 H 4
30220 Grantville, 1,128 C 4
31032 Gray⊙, 2,014 F 4
30221 Grayson, 366 E 3
30642 Greensboro⊙, 2,583 F 3
30222 Greenville⊙, 1,085 C 4
† 31620 Greggs, 250 F 8
30223 Griffin⊙, 22,734 D 4
† 31036 Grovania, 300 E 6
30813 Grovetown, 3,169 H 4
31312 Guyton, 742 K 6
30544 Habersham, 225 F 1
31033 Haddock, 600 F 4
30429 Hagan, 572 J 6
31632 Hahira, 1,326 F 9
31811 Hamilton⊙, 357 C 5
30228 Hampton, 1,551 D 4
30354 Hapeville, 9,567 D 3
31034 Hardwick, 14,047 F 4
30814 Harlem, 1,540 H 4
31035 Harrison, 329 G 5
30643 Hartwell⊙, 4,865 G 2
31036 Hawkinsville⊙, 4,077 E 6
31539 Hazlehurst⊙, 4,065 G 7
30545 Helen, 252 E 1
31037 Helena, 1,230 G 6
30815 Hephzibah, 987 H 4
30546 Hiawassee⊙, 415 E 1
31038 Hillsboro, 250 E 4
30467 Hilltonia, 294 J 5
31313 Hinesville⊙, 4,115 J 7
30141 Hiram, 441 C 3
31542 Hoboken, 424 H 8
30230 Hogansville, 3,075 C 4
30142 Holly Springs, 575 D 2
30523 Hollywood, 300 E 1
† 31537 Homeland, 595 H 9
30547 Homer⊙, 365 F 2
31634 Homerville⊙, 3,025 G 8
31543 Hortense, 400 J 8
30548 Hoschton, 509 E 2
30646 Hull, 222 F 2
30561 Hurst, 216 D 1
31041 Ideal, 543 D 6
30647 Ila, 202 F 2
30231 Indian Springs, 300 E 4
30232 Inman, 475 D 4
31759 Iron City, 351 C 8
31042 Irwinton⊙, 757 F 5
31760 Irwinville, 550 F 7
31406 Isle of Hope, 975 K 7
† 31031 Ivey, 245 F 5
30233 Jackson⊙, 3,778 E 4
31544 Jacksonville, 214 G 7
30143 Jasper⊙, 1,202 D 2

(continued on following page)

GEORGIA
SCALE
0 5 10 20 30 40 MI.
0 5 10 20 30 40 KM.
State Capitals
County Seats
© C.S. HAMMOND & Co., N.Y.
Longitude 83° West of 30' Greenwich
TENNESSEE
NORTH CAROLINA
SOUTH CAROLINA
ALABAMA
FLORIDA
ATLANTIC OCEAN
SEA ISLANDS
ATLANTA
Augusta
Macon
Columbus
Savannah
Albany
Athens
Brunswick
Valdosta
Waycross
Rome
Dalton
Gainesville
Milledgeville
Marietta
Decatur
Thomasville
CHATTANOOGA
CHARLOTTE
COLUMBIA
JACKSONVILLE
Tallahassee
Phenix City
Dothan
Greenville
Spartanburg
Anderson
OKEFENOKEE SWAMP
APALACHEE BAY
Lake Seminole
Lake Eufaula
Clark Hill Res.
Hartwell Res.
Altamaha R.
Ogeechee
St. Marys R.

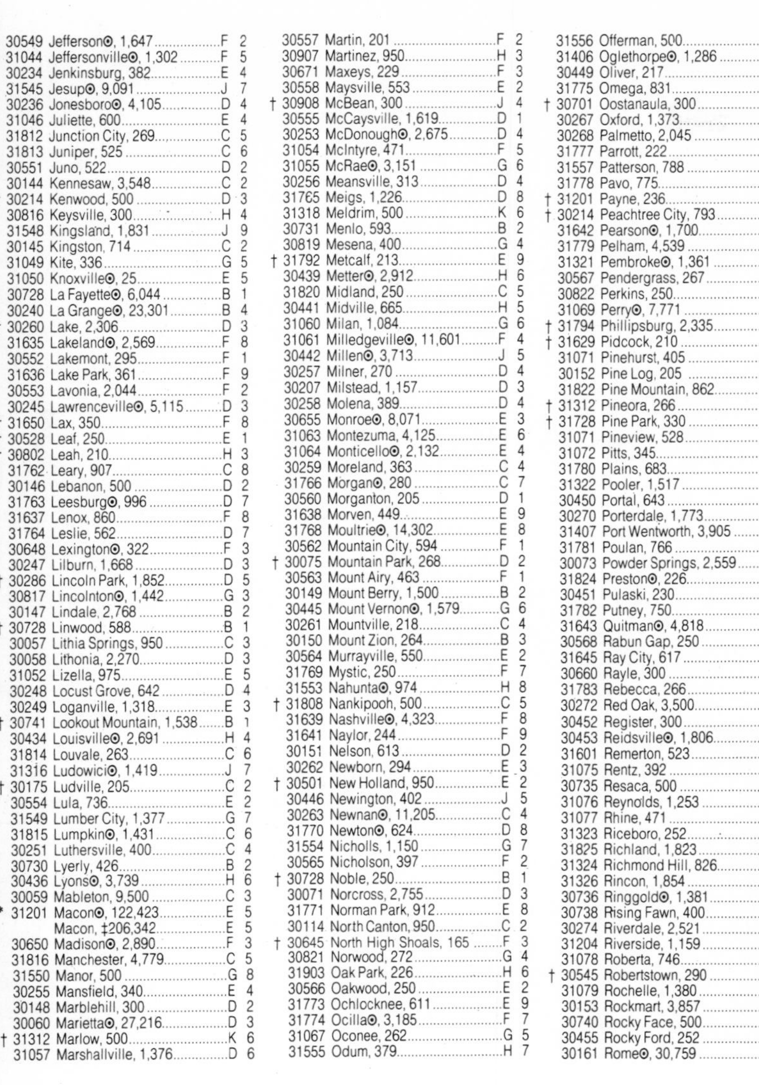

30549 Jefferson⊙, 1,647 F 2
31044 Jeffersonville⊙, 1,302 F 5
30234 Jenkinsburg, 382 E 4
31545 Jesup⊙, 9,091 J 7
30236 Jonesboro⊙, 4,105 D 4
31046 Juliette, 600 E 4
31812 Junction City, 269 C 5
31813 Juniper, 525 C 6
30551 Juno, 522 D 2
30144 Kennesaw, 3,548 C 2
† 30214 Kenwood, 500 D 3
30816 Keysville, 300 H 4
31548 Kingsland, 1,831 J 9
30145 Kingston, 714 C 2
31049 Kite, 336 G 5
31050 Knoxville⊙, 25 E 5
30728 La Fayette⊙, 6,044 B 1
30240 La Grange⊙, 23,301 B 4
† 30260 Lake, 2,306 D 3
31635 Lakeland⊙, 2,569 F 8
30552 Lakemont, 295 F 1
31636 Lake Park, 361 F 9
30553 Lavonia, 2,044 F 2
30245 Lawrenceville⊙, 5,115 D 3
† 31650 Lax, 350 F 8
† 30528 Leaf, 250 E 1
† 30802 Leah, 210 H 3
31762 Leary, 907 C 8
30146 Lebanon, 500 D 2
31763 Leesburg⊙, 996 D 7
31637 Lenox, 860 F 8
31764 Leslie, 562 D 7
30648 Lexington⊙, 322 F 3
30247 Lilburn, 1,668 D 3
† 30286 Lincoln Park, 1,852 D 5
30817 Lincolnton⊙, 1,442 G 3
30147 Lindale, 2,768 B 2
† 30728 Linwood, 588 B 1
30057 Lithia Springs, 950 C 3
30058 Lithonia, 2,270 D 3
31052 Lizella, 975 E 5
30248 Locust Grove, 642 D 4
30249 Loganville, 1,318 E 3
† 30741 Lookout Mountain, 1,538 B 1
30434 Louisville⊙, 2,691 H 4
31814 Louvale, 263 C 6
31316 Ludowici⊙, 1,419 J 7
† 30175 Ludville, 205 C 2
30554 Lula, 736 E 2
31549 Lumber City, 1,377 G 7
31815 Lumpkin⊙, 1,431 C 6
30251 Luthersville, 400 C 4
30730 Lyerly, 426 B 2
30436 Lyons⊙, 3,739 H 6
30059 Mableton, 9,500 C 3
* 31201 Macon⊙, 122,423 E 5
Macon, ‡206,342 E 5
30650 Madison⊙, 2,890 F 3
31816 Manchester, 4,779 C 5
31550 Manor, 500 G 8
30255 Mansfield, 340 E 4
30148 Marblehill, 300 D 2
30060 Marietta⊙, 27,216 D 3
† 31312 Marlow, 500 K 6
31057 Marshallville, 1,376 D 6
30557 Martin, 201 F 2
30907 Martinez, 950 H 3
30671 Maxeys, 229 F 3
30558 Maysville, 553 E 2
† 30908 McBean, 300 J 4
30555 McCaysville, 1,619 D 1
30253 McDonough⊙, 2,675 D 4
31054 McIntyre, 471 F 5
31055 McRae⊙, 3,151 G 6
30256 Meansville, 313 D 4
31765 Meigs, 1,226 D 8
31318 Meldrim, 500 K 6
30731 Menlo, 593 B 2
30819 Mesena, 400 G 4
† 31792 Metcalf, 213 E 9
30439 Metter⊙, 2,912 H 6
31820 Midland, 250 C 5
30441 Midville, 665 H 5
31060 Milan, 1,084 G 6
31061 Milledgeville⊙, 11,601 F 4
30442 Millen⊙, 3,713 J 5
30257 Milner, 270 D 4
30207 Milstead, 1,157 D 3
30258 Molena, 389 D 4
30655 Monroe⊙, 8,071 E 3
31063 Montezuma, 4,125 E 6
31064 Monticello⊙, 2,132 E 4
30259 Moreland, 363 C 4
31766 Morgan⊙, 280 C 7
30560 Morganton, 205 D 1
31638 Morven, 449 E 9
31768 Moultrie⊙, 14,302 E 8
30562 Mountain City, 594 F 1
† 30075 Mountain Park, 268 D 2
30563 Mount Airy, 463 F 1
30149 Mount Berry, 1,500 B 2
30445 Mount Vernon⊙, 1,579 G 6
30261 Mountville, 218 C 4
30150 Mount Zion, 264 B 3
30564 Murrayville, 550 E 2
31769 Mystic, 250 F 7
31553 Nahunta⊙, 974 H 8
† 31808 Nankipooh, 500 C 5
31639 Nashville⊙, 4,323 F 8
31641 Naylor, 244 F 9
30151 Nelson, 613 D 2
30262 Newborn, 294 E 3
† 30501 New Holland, 950 E 2
30446 Newington, 402 J 5
30263 Newnan⊙, 11,205 C 4
31770 Newton⊙, 624 D 8
31554 Nicholls, 1,150 G 7
30565 Nicholson, 397 F 2
† 30728 Noble, 250 B 1
30071 Norcross, 2,755 D 3
31771 Norman Park, 912 E 8
30114 North Canton, 950 C 2
† 30645 North High Shoals, 165 F 3
30821 Norwood, 272 G 4
31903 Oak Park, 226 H 6
30566 Oakwood, 250 E 2
31773 Ochlocknee, 611 E 9
31774 Ocilla⊙, 3,185 F 7
31067 Oconee, 262 G 5
31555 Odum, 379 H 7
31556 Offerman, 500 H 8
31406 Oglethorpe⊙, 1,286 D 6
30449 Oliver, 217 J 5
31775 Omega, 831 E 8
† 30701 Oostanaula, 300 B 1
30267 Oxford, 1,373 E 3
30268 Palmetto, 2,045 C 3
31777 Parrott, 222 D 7
31557 Patterson, 788 H 8
31778 Pavo, 775 E 9
† 31201 Payne, 236 E 5
† 30214 Peachtree City, 793 C 4
31642 Pearson⊙, 1,700 G 8
31779 Pelham, 4,539 D 8
31321 Pembroke⊙, 1,361 J 6
30567 Pendergrass, 267 E 2
30822 Perkins, 250 J 5
31069 Perry⊙, 7,771 E 6
† 31794 Phillipsburg, 2,335 E 8
† 31629 Pidcock, 210 E 9
31071 Pinehurst, 405 E 6
30152 Pine Log, 205 C 2
31822 Pine Mountain, 862 C 5
† 31312 Pineora, 266 K 6
† 31728 Pine Park, 330 D 9
31071 Pineview, 528 F 6
31072 Pitts, 345 E 7
31780 Plains, 683 D 6
31322 Pooler, 1,517 K 6
30450 Portal, 643 J 5
30270 Porterdale, 1,773 E 3
31407 Port Wentworth, 3,905 K 6
31781 Poulan, 766 E 8
30073 Powder Springs, 2,559 C 3
31824 Preston⊙, 226 C 6
30451 Pulaski, 230 J 6
31782 Putney, 750 D 8
31643 Quitman⊙, 4,818 E 9
30568 Rabun Gap, 250 F 1
31645 Ray City, 617 F 8
30660 Rayle, 300 G 3
31783 Rebecca, 266 E 7
30272 Red Oak, 3,500 C 3
30452 Register, 300 J 6
30453 Reidsville⊙, 1,806 H 6
31601 Remerton, 523 F 9
31075 Rentz, 392 G 6
30735 Resaca, 500 C 1
31076 Reynolds, 1,253 D 5
31077 Rhine, 471 F 7
31323 Riceboro, 252 K 7
31825 Richland, 1,823 C 6
31324 Richmond Hill, 826 K 7
31326 Rincon, 1,854 K 6
30736 Ringgold⊙, 1,381 B 1
30738 Rising Fawn, 400 A 1
30274 Riverdale, 2,521 D 3
31204 Riverside, 1,159 B 2
31078 Roberta, 746 D 5
† 30545 Robertstown, 290 E 1
31079 Rochelle, 1,380 F 7
30153 Rockmart, 3,857 B 2
30740 Rocky Face, 500 C 1
30455 Rocky Ford, 252 J 5
30161 Rome⊙, 30,759 B 2

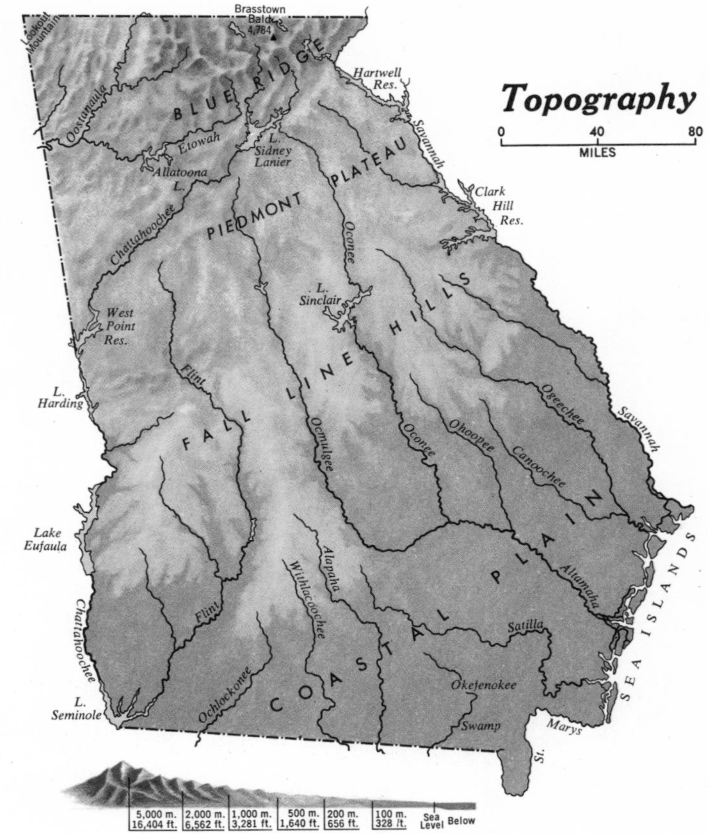

30170 Roopville, 221 B 4
30741 Rossville, 3,869 B 1
30075 Roswell, 5,430 D 2
30662 Royston, 2,428 F 2
† 30680 Russell, 378 E 3
30663 Rutledge, 628 E 3
31646 Saint George, 600 H 9
31558 Saint Marys, 3,408 J 9
31522 Saint Simons Island, 5,346 K 8
31784 Sale City, 323 D 8
31082 Sandersville⊙, 5,546 G 5
31327 Sapelo Island, 250 K 8
30456 Sardis, 643 J 5
30275 Sargent, 800 C 4
31785 Sasser, 339 D 7
30571 Sautee-Nacoochee, 350 E 1
* 31401 Savannah⊙, 118,349 L 6
Savannah, ‡187,767 L 6
31328 Savannah Beach, 1,786 L 6
31083 Scotland, 261 G 6
31095 Scott, 215 G 5
31560 Screven, 936 H 7
31561 Sea Island, 600 K 8
30276 Senoia, 910 C 4
30172 Shannon, 1,563 B 2
31786 Shellman, 1,166 C 7
31826 Shiloh, 298 C 5
† 31781 Shingler, 300 E 7
30665 Siloam, 319 F 3
30173 Silver Creek, 450 B 2
31086 Smarr, 350 E 5
31787 Smithville, 713 D 7
30080 Smyrna, 19,157 D 3
30278 Snellville, 1,990 D 3
30279 Social Circle, 1,961 E 3
30457 Soperton⊙, 2,596 G 6
31647 Sparks, 1,337 F 8
31087 Sparta⊙, 2,172 F 4
31329 Springfield⊙, 1,001 K 6
30705 Spring Place, 241 C 1
30823 Stapleton, 390 H 4
31648 Statenville⊙, 700 G 9
30458 Statesboro⊙, 14,616 J 6
30666 Statham, 817 E 3
31088 Stevens Pottery, 350 F 5
30464 Stillmore, 354 H 6
30281 Stockbridge, 1,561 D 3
31649 Stockton, 500 G 9
30083 Stone Mountain, 1,899 D 3
30282 Stonewall, 950 C 3
† 30747 Subligna, 300 B 1
30572 Suches, 400 E 1
30518 Sugar Hill, 1,745 E 2
30747 Summerville⊙, 5,043 B 2
31789 Sumner, 207 E 7
30284 Sunny Side, 209 D 4
31563 Surrency, 352 H 7
30174 Suwanee, 615 D 2
30401 Swainsboro⊙, 7,325 H 5
31790 Sycamore, 547 E 7
30467 Sylvania⊙, 3,199 J 5
31791 Sylvester⊙, 4,226 E 7
31827 Talbotton⊙, 1,045 C 5
30176 Tallapoosa, 2,896 B 3
30573 Tallulah Falls, 255 F 1
30177 Tate, 950 D 2
30178 Taylorsville, 253 C 2
30179 Temple, 864 B 3
30751 Tennga, 300 C 1
31089 Tennille, 1,753 G 5
30286 Thomaston⊙, 10,024 D 5
31792 Thomasville⊙, 18,155 E 9
30824 Thomson⊙, 6,503 H 4
31404 Thunderbolt, 2,750 K 6
31794 Tifton⊙, 12,179 F 8
30576 Tiger, 312 F 1
30668 Tignall, 756 G 3
30577 Toccoa⊙, 6,971 F 1
31090 Toomsboro, 682 F 5
31331 Townsend, 300 J 7
30752 Trenton⊙, 1,523 A 1
30753 Trion, 1,965 B 1
30755 Tunnel Hill, 900 C 1
30289 Turin, 242 C 4
30471 Twin City, 1,119 H 5
31795 Ty Ty, 447 E 8
31091 Unadilla, 1,457 E 6
30291 Union City, 3,031 D 3
30669 Union Point, 1,624 F 3
31794 Unionville, 1,646 F 8
30473 Uvalda, 663 H 6
31601 Valdosta⊙, 32,303 F 9
30756 Varnell, 400 C 1
30474 Vidalia, 9,507 H 6
31092 Vienna⊙, 2,341 E 6
30180 Villa Rica, 3,922 C 3
30182 Waco, 431 B 3
30477 Wadley, 1,989 H 5
30183 Waleska, 487 D 2
31333 Walthourville, 300 J 7
31564 Waresboro, 350 H 8
31830 Warm Springs, 523 C 5
31093 Warner Robins, 33,491 E 5
30828 Warrenton⊙, 2,073 G 4
31796 Warwick, 466 E 7
30673 Washington⊙, 4,094 G 3
30677 Watkinsville⊙, 986 E 3
31565 Waverly, 250 J 8
31831 Waverly Hall, 671 C 5
31501 Waycross⊙, 18,996 H 8
30830 Waynesboro⊙, 5,530 J 4
31566 Waynesville, 500 J 8
31833 West Point, 4,232 B 5
31797 Whigham, 381 D 9
30184 White, 462 C 2
30603 White Hall, 400 F 3
30678 White Plains, 236 F 4
30185 Whitesburg, 720 B 4
30186 Whitestone, 450 C 1
† 31833 Whitesville, 250 C 5
30581 Wiley, 300 F 1
31650 Willacoochee, 1,120 G 8
30292 Williamson, 284 D 4
31404 Wilmington Island, 3,284 L 7
30680 Winder⊙, 6,605 E 3
† 30824 Winfield, 444 H 3
30187 Winston, 625 C 3
30683 Winterville, 551 F 3
31569 Woodbine⊙, 1,002 J 9
30293 Woodbury, 1,422 C 5
31836 Woodland, 689 D 5
30188 Woodstock, 870 D 2
30670 Woodville, 379 F 3
30833 Wrens, 2,204 H 4
31096 Wrightsville⊙, 2,106 G 5
31097 Yatesville, 423 D 5
30582 Young Harris, 544 E 1
30295 Zebulon⊙, 776 D 4

⊙ County seat.
‡ Population of metropolitan area.
† Zip of nearest p.o.
* Multiple zips

Agriculture, Industry and Resources

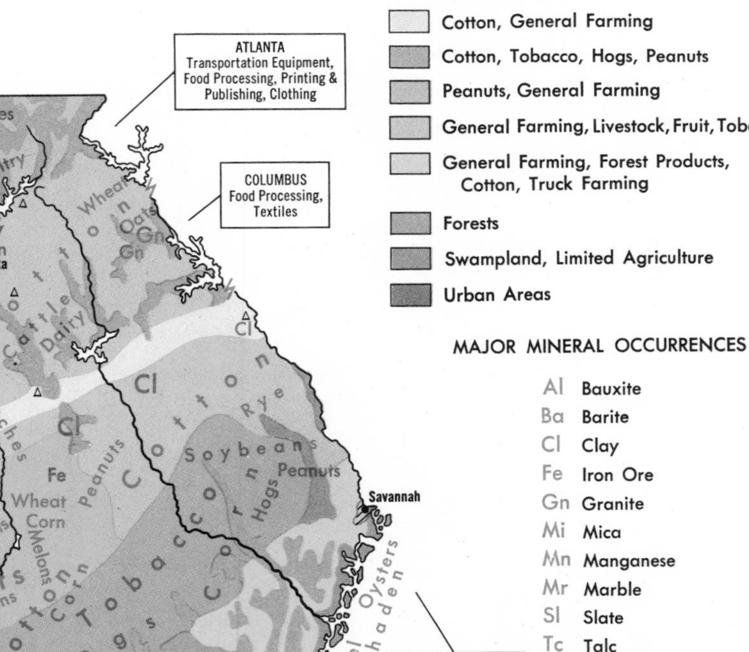

DOMINANT LAND USE

- Specialized Cotton
- Cotton, General Farming
- Cotton, Tobacco, Hogs, Peanuts
- Peanuts, General Farming
- General Farming, Livestock, Fruit, Tobacco
- General Farming, Forest Products, Cotton, Truck Farming
- Forests
- Swampland, Limited Agriculture
- Urban Areas

MAJOR MINERAL OCCURRENCES

- Al Bauxite
- Ba Barite
- Cl Clay
- Fe Iron Ore
- Gn Granite
- Mi Mica
- Mn Manganese
- Mr Marble
- Sl Slate
- Tc Talc
- Ti Titanium
- Water Power
- Major Industrial Areas

△ Major Textile Manufacturing Centers

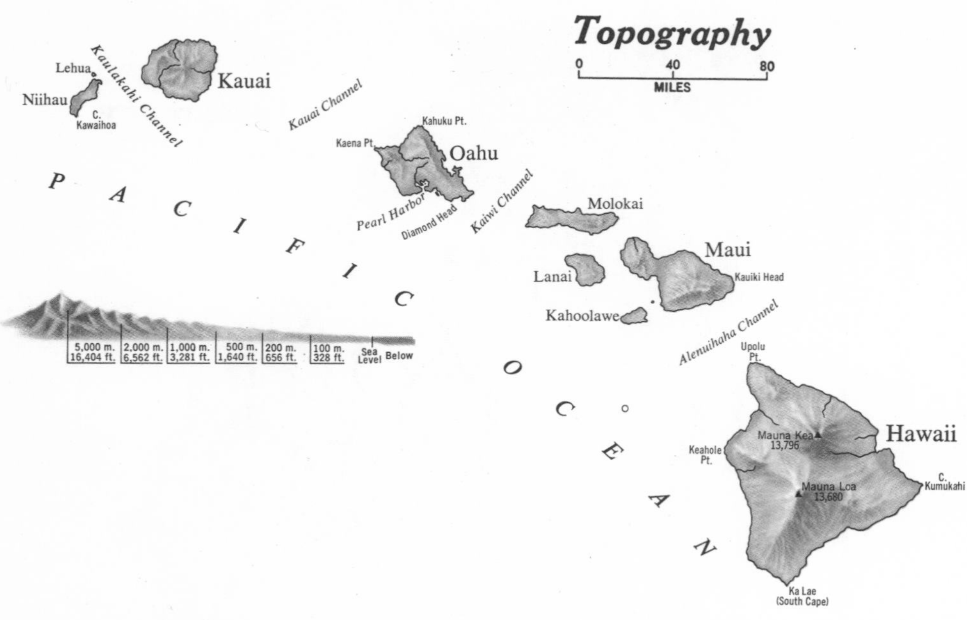

COUNTIES

Name/Pop.	Key
Hawaii, 63,468	K 7
Honolulu, 629,176	D 3
Kalawao, 172	G 1
Kauai, 29,761	A 1
Maui, 45,984	J 1

CITIES and TOWNS

	Zip	*Name/Pop.*	*Key*
	96701	Aiea, 12,560	B 3
	96821	Aina Haina, 15,000	F 2
	96703	Anahola, 638	C 1
†	96706	Barbers Point Housing, 1,947	E 2
	96704	Captain Cook, 1,263	G 5
	96705	Eleele, 758	C 2
	96706	Ewa, 2,906	A 4
	96706	Ewa Beach, 7,765	A 4
†	96701	Foster Village, 3,755	B 3
†	96714	Haena, 75	C 1
	96708	Haiku, 464	J 2
	96709	Haina, 333	H 3
	96710	Hakalau, 742	J 4
†	96701	Halawa Heights, 5,809	B 3
	96712	Haleiwa, 2,626	E 1
	96787	Haliimaile, 638	J 2
	96713	Hana, 459	K 2
	96714	Hanalei, 153	C 1
	96715	Hanamaulu, 2,461	C 1
	96716	Hanapepe, 1,388	C 2
	96717	Hauula, 2,048	E 1
	96718	Hawaii National Park, 100	J 6
	96719	Hawi, 797	G 3
	96824	Hickam Housing, 7,352	B 4
	96720	Hilo⊙, 26,353	J 5
	96725	Holualoa, 850	G 5
	96726	Honaunau, 950	G 6
†	96710	Honohina, 125	J 4
	96727	Honokaa, 1,555	H 4
†	96761	Honokahua, 431	H 1
†	96740	Honokohau, 200	G 5
*	96801	Honolulu (cap.)⊙, 324,871	C 4
		Honolulu, ‡630,528	C 4
	96728	Honomu, 737	J 4
†	96706	Honouliuli, 600	A 3
	96729	Hoolehua, 1,090	G 1
†	96740	Huehue, 100	G 5
†	96706	Iroquois Point, 4,572	A 4
†	96801	Iwilei, 1,835	C 4
	96730	Kaaawa, 848	F 1
†	96761	Kaanapali, 250	H 2
†	96801	Kahala, 14,288	D 5
†	96744	Kahaluu, 1,657	E 2
	96731	Kahuku, 917	E 1
	96732	Kahului, 8,280	J 2
	96734	Kailua, 33,783	F 2
†	96740	Kailua, 365	F 5
	96740	Kailua Kona (Kailua), 365	F 5
	96816	Kaimuki, 25,315	D 4

Sharp spikes bristle protectively around their precious fruit crop on Pineapple Hill, west Maui. Second only to sugarcane, pineapples rank high in Hawaii's economy.

Agriculture, Industry and Resources

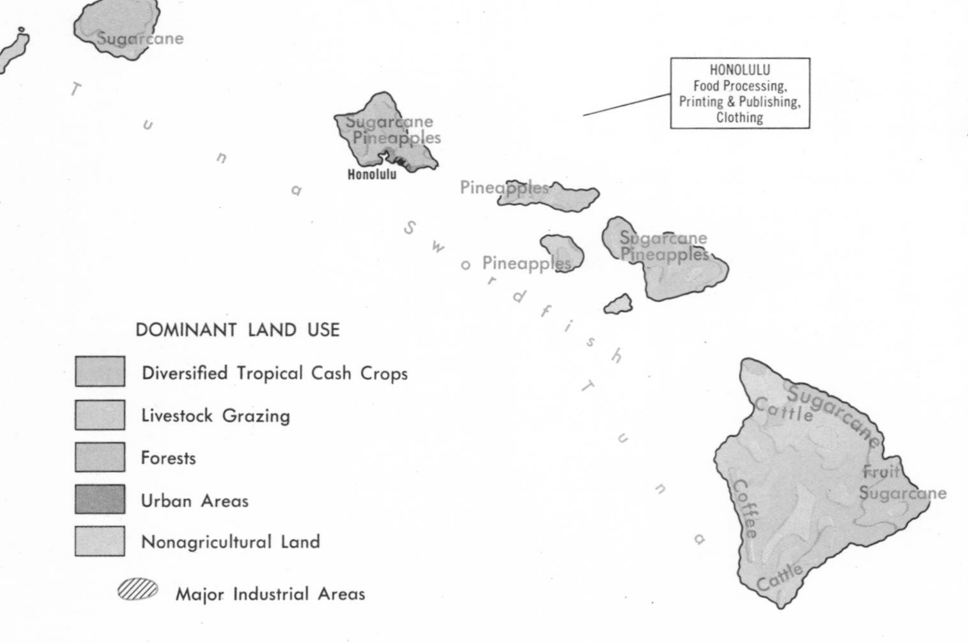

KAUAI COUNTY

SCALE 0 5 10 15 MI. / 0 5 10 15 KM

Longitude West of Greenwich

HONOLULU & PEARL HARBOR

SCALE 0 1 2 MI. / 0 1 2 KM.

HAWAII

State Capital ⊛

County Seats ⊙

† 96750 Kainaliu, 450 .... G 5
† 96757 Kalae, 150 .... G 1
96741 Kalaheo, 1,514 .... C 2
† 96740 Kalaoa, 300 .... G 5
96742 Kalaupapa⊙, 164 .... G 1
96817 Kalihi, 32,650 .... C 4
† 96748 Kaluaaha, 300 .... H 1
† 96748 Kamalo, 300 .... H 1
96743 Kamuela, 756 .... G 3
96744 Kaneohe, 29,903 .... F 2
96746 Kapaa, 3,794 .... D 1
† 96778 Kapaahu, 850 .... J 6
96755 Kapaau, 237 .... G 3
† 96778 Kapoho, 300 .... K 5
† 96758 Kapulena, 125 .... H 4
96747 Kaumakani, 1,014 .... C 2
96748 Kaunakakai, 1,070 .... G 1
† 96708 Kaupakulua, 100 .... K 2
96743 Kawaihae, 50 .... G 4
† 96712 Kawailoa, 900 .... E 1
96749 Keaau, 951 .... J 5
96750 Kealakekua, 740 .... G 5
96751 Kealia, 600 .... D 1
96751 Kealia, 550 .... G 6
96752 Kekaha, 2,404 .... C 2
† 96704 Keokea, 500 .... G 6
† 96790 Keokea, 750 .... J 2
96753 Kihei, 1,450 .... J 2
96754 Kilauea, 671 .... C 1
† 96713 Koali, 100 .... K 2
† 96755 Kohala (Kapaau), 237 .... G 3
† 96708 Kokomo, 200 .... K 2
96756 Koloa, 1,368 .... C 2
96757 Kualapuu, 441 .... G 1
96758 Kukuihaele, 310 .... H 3
96790 Kula, 800 .... J 2
96759 Kunia, 545 .... E 2
96760 Kurtistown, 900 .... J 5
96761 Lahaina, 3,718 .... H 2
96762 Laie, 3,009 .... E 1
96763 Lanai City, 2,122 .... H 2
96764 Laupahoehoe, 452 .... J 4
96765 Lawai, 950 .... C 2
96766 Lihue⊙, 3,124 .... C 2
† 96779 Lower Paia, 1,105 .... J 1
† 96753 Maalaea, 80 .... J 2
† 96792 Maili, 4,397 .... D 2
† 96792 Makaha, 4,644 .... D 2
† 96706 Makakilo City, 3,499 .... E 2
† 96711 Makapala, 201 .... G 3
96768 Makawao, 1,066 .... K 2
96769 Makaweli, 500 .... B 2
96770 Maunaloa, 872 .... G 1
† 96744 Maunawili, 5,303 .... F 2
† 96786 Mililani, 2,035 .... E 2
† 96704 Milolii, 120 .... G 6
† 96734 Mokapu, 7,860 .... F 2
† 96791 Mokuleia, 880 .... D 1
96771 Mountainview, 419 .... J 5
96772 Naalehu, 1,014 .... H 7
96792 Nanakuli, 6,506 .... D 2
96773 Ninole, 75 .... J 4
† 96761 Olowalu, 750 .... H 2
† 96781 Onomea, 500 .... J 4
96774 Ookala, 486 .... J 4
† 96778 Opihikao, 125 .... K 6
96775 Paauhau, 400 .... H 4
96776 Paauilo, 710 .... H 4
† 96801 Pacific Heights, 5,305 .... C 4
† 96782 Pacific Palisades, 7,846 .... E 2
96777 Pahala, 1,507 .... H 6
96778 Pahoa, 924 .... J 5
96779 Paia, 541 .... J 2
† 96801 Palama, 15,307 .... C 4
† 96704 Papa, 100 .... G 6
96780 Papaaloa, 319 .... J 4
96781 Papaikou, 1,888 .... J 5
† 96781 Paukaa, 450 .... J 5
† 96708 Pauwela, 355 .... K 2
96782 Pearl City, 19,552 .... B 3
96783 Pepeekeo, 1,150 .... J 4
† 96756 Poipu, 466 .... C 2
96766 Puhi, 772 .... C 2
96788 Pukalani, 1,629 .... J 2
† 96748 Pukoo, 300 .... H 1
96784 Puunene, 1,132 .... J 2
† 96801 Puunui, 10,082 .... C 4
† 96769 Puuwai, 200 .... A 2
96786 Schofield Barracks, 13,516 .... E 2
96779 Spreckelsville, 350 .... J 1
† 96790 Ulupalakua, 75 .... J 2
96785 Volcano, 400 .... J 6
96766 Wahiawa, 17,598 .... E 2
† 96788 Waiakoa, 1,050 .... J 2
† 96731 Waialee, 80 .... E 1
96791 Waialua, Oahu, 4,047 .... E 1
96792 Waianae, 3,302 .... D 2
† 96793 Waihee, 346 .... J 2
† 96793 Waikapu, 598 .... J 2
96815 Waikiki, 35,000 .... C 4
† 96748 Wailau, 300 .... H 1
† 96710 Wailea, 315 .... J 4
† 96746 Wailua, 1,379 .... D 2
96793 Wailuku⊙, 7,979 .... J 2
† 96701 Waimalu, 2,982 .... B 3
96795 Waimánalo, 2,081 .... F 2
† 96795 Waimanalo Beach, 3,045 .... F 2
† 96743 Waimea (Kamuela), Hawaii 756 .... G 3
96796 Waimea, Kauai, 1,569 .... B 2
† 96712 Waimea, Oahu, 200 .... E 1
† 96772 Waiohinu, 200 .... G 7
96797 Waipahu, 22,798 .... A 3
† 96786 Waipio Acres, 2,146 .... E 2
† 96786 Whitmore Village, 2,015 .... E 1
† 96801 Woodlawn, 5,569 .... D 4

MIDWAY ISLANDS
Total Population
2,356

⊙ County seat.
‡ Population of metropolitan area.
† Zip of nearest p.o.
* Multiple zips

AREA 6,450 sq. mi.
POPULATION 769,913
CAPITAL Honolulu
LARGEST CITY Honolulu
HIGHEST POINT Mauna Kea 13,796 ft.
SETTLED IN —
ADMITTED TO UNION August 21, 1959
POPULAR NAME Aloha State; Paradise of the Pacific
STATE FLOWER Red Hibiscus
STATE BIRD Nene (Hawaiian Goose)

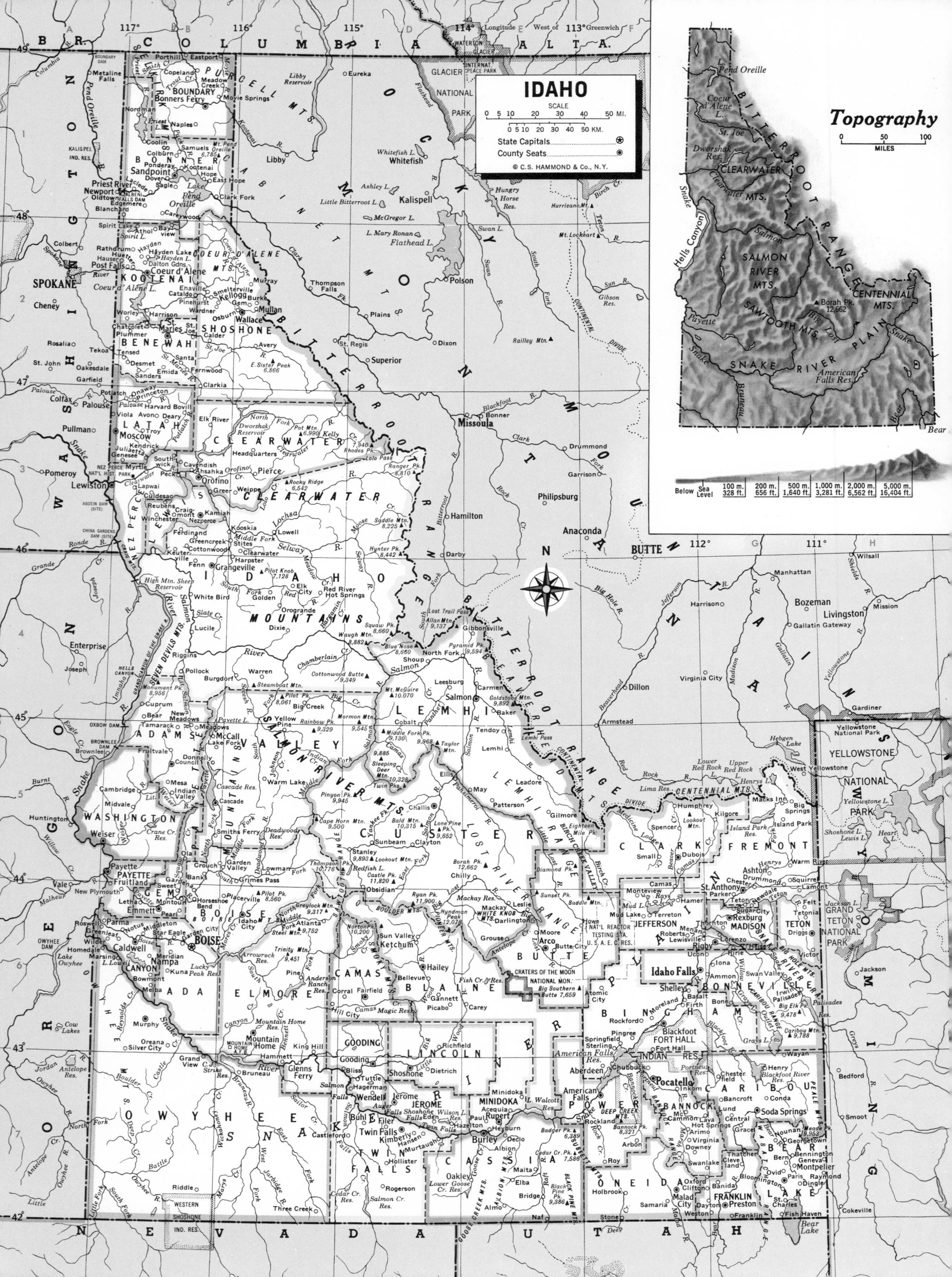

IDAHO
SCALE
0 5 10 20 30 40 50 MI.
0 5 10 20 30 40 50 KM.
State Capitals
County Seats
© C.S. HAMMOND & Co., N.Y.
Topography
0 50 100
MILES
Below Sea Level
100 m. 328 ft.
200 m. 656 ft.
500 m. 1,640 ft.
1,000 m. 3,281 ft.
2,000 m. 6,562 ft.
5,000 m. 16,404 ft.
BRITISH COLUMBIA
ALTA.
WASHINGTON
OREGON
NEVADA
UTAH
WYOMING
MONTANA
Longitude West of Greenwich
117°
116°
115°
114°
113°
112°
111°
49°
48°
47°
46°
45°
44°
43°
42°
BOUNDARY
BONNER
KOOTENAI
SHOSHONE
BENEWAH
LATAH
CLEARWATER
NEZ PERCE
LEWIS
IDAHO
ADAMS
VALLEY
WASHINGTON
PAYETTE
GEM
BOISE
CANYON
ADA
ELMORE
OWYHEE
CAMAS
BLAINE
CUSTER
LEMHI
BUTTE
CLARK
FREMONT
JEFFERSON
MADISON
TETON
BONNEVILLE
BINGHAM
POWER
BANNOCK
CARIBOU
BEAR LAKE
FRANKLIN
ONEIDA
CASSIA
TWIN FALLS
JEROME
GOODING
LINCOLN
MINIDOKA
BOISE
Coeur d'Alene
Lewiston
Moscow
Grangeville
Idaho Falls
Pocatello
Twin Falls
Sandpoint
Bonners Ferry
Wallace
Nampa
Caldwell
Salmon
Blackfoot
Rexburg
Burley
SPOKANE
Missoula
BUTTE
Kalispell
Bozeman
Livingston
ROCKY MOUNTAINS
BITTERROOT RANGE
CLEARWATER MTS.
SALMON RIVER MTS.
SAWTOOTH MTS.
SNAKE RIVER PLAIN
CENTENNIAL MTS.
LOST RIVER RANGE
LEMHI RANGE
SEVEN DEVILS MTS.
CABINET MTS.
PURCELL MTS.
GLACIER NATIONAL PARK
YELLOWSTONE NATIONAL PARK
GRAND TETON NATIONAL PARK
CRATERS OF THE MOON NATIONAL MON.
Borah Pk. 12,662
Hells Canyon
Snake R.
Salmon R.
Clearwater R.
American Falls Res.
Bear Lake
Pend Oreille
Coeur d'Alene L.
CONTINENTAL DIVIDE

COUNTIES

Ada, 112,230 B 6
Adams, 2,877 B 5
Bannock, 52,200 F 7
Bear Lake, 5,801 G 7
Benewah, 6,230 B 2
Bingham, 29,167 F 6
Blaine, 5,749 D 6
Boise, 1,763 C 6
Bonner, 15,560 B 1
Bonneville, 51,250 G 6
Boundary, 6,371 B 1
Butte, 2,925 E 6
Camas, 728 D 6
Canyon, 61,288 B 6
Caribou, 6,534 G 7
Cassia, 17,017 E 7
Clark, 741 F 5
Clearwater, 10,871 C 3
Custer, 2,967 D 5
Elmore, 17,479 C 6
Franklin, 7,373 G 7
Fremont, 8,710 G 5
Gem, 9,387 B 6
Gooding, 8,645 D 6
Idaho, 12,891 C 4
Jefferson, 11,619 F 6
Jerome, 10,253 D 7
Kootenai, 35,332 B 2
Latah, 24,891 B 3
Lemhi, 5,566 D 4
Lewis, 3,867 B 3
Lincoln, 3,057 D 6
Madison, 13,452 G 6
Minidoka, 15,731 E 7
Nez Perce, 30,376 B 3
Oneida, 2,864 F 7
Owyhee, 6,422 B 7
Payette, 12,401 B 5
Power, 4,864 F 7
Shoshone, 19,718 B 2
Teton, 2,351 G 6
Twin Falls, 41,807 D 7
Valley, 3,609 C 5
Washington, 7,633 B 5

CITIES and TOWNS

Zip	*Name/Pop.*	*Key*
83210	Aberdeen, 1,542	F 7
83310	Acequia, 107	E 7
83520	Ahsahka, 500	B 3
83311	Albion, 229	E 7
83312	Almo, 170	E 7
83211	American Falls⊙, 2,769	E 7
83401	Ammon, 1,338	G 6
83212	Arbon, 75	F 7
83213	Arco⊙, 1,244	E 6
83214	Arimo, 252	F 7
83420	Ashton, 1,187	G 5
83801	Athol, 190	B 2
83601	Atlanta, 50	C 6
83215	Atomic City, 24	F 6
83802	Avery, 250	C 2
83461	Baker, 98	E 4
83217	Bancroft, 366	G 7
83264	Banida, 76	G 7
83602	Banks, 49	B 5
83218	Basalt, 349	F 6
83803	Bayview, 300	B 2
83313	Bellevue, 537	D 6
83219	Bennington, 60	G 7
83220	Bern, 135	G 7
83221	Blackfoot⊙, 8,716	F 6
83804	Blanchard, 120	A 1
83314	Bliss, 114	D 7
83223	Bloomington, 186	G 7
* 83701	Boise (cap.)⊙, 74,990	B 6
	Boise, ‡112,230	B 6
83805	Bonners Ferry⊙, 2,796	B 1
83806	Bovill, 343	B 3
† 83651	Bowmont, 100	B 6
83315	Bridge, 140	E 7
83604	Bruneau, 150	C 7
83316	Buhl, 2,975	D 7
83807	Burke, 150	C 2
83318	Burley⊙, 8,279	E 7
† 83213	Butte City, 42	E 6
83808	Calder, 140	B 2
83605	Caldwell⊙, 14,219	B 6
83610	Cambridge, 383	B 5
83320	Carey, 750	E 6
83809	Careywood, 60	B 1
83462	Carmen, 40	E 4
83611	Cascade⊙, 833	C 5
83321	Castleford, 174	C 7
83810	Cataldo, 275	B 2
† 83241	Central, 60	G 7
83226	Challis⊙, 784	D 5
† 83851	Chatcolet, 95	B 2
83421	Chester, 206	G 5
† 83217	Chesterfield, 50	G 7
83201	Chubbuck, 2,924	F 7
83811	Clark Fork, 367	B 1
83812	Clarkia, 147	B 2
83227	Clayton, 36	D 5
83521	Clearwater, 110	C 3
† 83263	Cleveland, 60	G 7
83228	Clifton, 137	F 7
83229	Cobalt, 35	D 4
83814	Coeur d'Alene⊙, 16,228	B 2
83865	Colburn, 200	B 1
83230	Conda, 250	G 7
83821	Coolin, 110	B 1
83322	Corral, 21	D 6
83522	Cottonwood, 867	B 3
83612	Council⊙, 899	B 5
83523	Craigmont, 554	B 3
† 83622	Crouch, 71	B 5
83524	Culdesac, 211	B 3
† 83814	Dalton Gardens, 1,559	B 2
83232	Dayton, 198	F 7
83823	Deary, 411	B 3
83323	Declo, 251	E 7
83824	Desmet, 154	B 2
83324	Dietrich, 84	D 7
83233	Dingle, 300	G 7
83615	Donnelly, 114	B 5
83825	Dover, 300	B 1
83234	Downey, 586	F 7
83422	Driggs⊙, 727	G 6
83423	Dubois⊙, 400	F 5
83616	Eagle, 525	B 6
† 83836	East Hope, 175	B 1
83826	Eastport, 83	B 1
83325	Eden, 343	D 7
83326	Elba, 87	E 7
83525	Elk City, 500	C 4
83827	Elk River, 383	B 3
83235	Ellis, 75	D 5
83828	Emida, 135	B 2
83617	Emmett⊙, 3,945	B 6
83829	Enaville, 90	B 2
83327	Fairfield⊙, 157	D 6
83424	Felt, 90	G 6
83531	Fenn, 45	B 4
83526	Ferdinand, 157	B 3
83830	Fernwood, 360	B 2
83328	Filer, 1,173	D 7
83236	Firth, 362	F 6
83261	Fish Haven, 120	G 7
83203	Fort Hall, 750	F 6
83237	Franklin, 402	G 7
83619	Fruitland, 1,576	B 6
83620	Fruitvale, 90	B 5
83621	Gardena, 44	B 5
83704	Garden City, 2,368	B 6
83622	Garden Valley, 100	C 5
† 83873	Gem, 50	C 2
83832	Genesee, 619	B 3
83238	Geneva, 200	G 7
83239	Georgetown, 421	G 7
83463	Gibbonsville, 85	E 4
83623	Glenns Ferry, 1,386	C 7
83330	Gooding⊙, 2,599	D 7
83241	Grace, 826	G 7
83624	Grand View, 450	B 7
83530	Grangeville⊙, 3,636	B 4
83533	Greencreek, 72	B 3
83626	Greenleaf, 425	B 6
† 83544	Greer, 70	B 3
83332	Hagerman, 436	D 7
83333	Hailey⊙, 1,425	D 6
83425	Hamer, 81	F 6
83627	Hammett, 653	C 7
83334	Hansen, 415	D 7
† 83521	Harpster, 250	C 4
83833	Harrison, 249	B 2
83834	Harvard, 50	B 3
† 83854	Hauser, 349	A 2
† 83835	Hayden, 1,285	B 2
83835	Hayden Lake, 260	B 2
83335	Hazelton, 396	E 7
83534	Headquarters, 350	C 3
† 83443	Heise, 84	G 6
83336	Heyburn, 1,637	E 7
83337	Hill City, 30	D 6
83243	Holbrook, 100	F 7
† 83301	Hollister, 57	D 7
83628	Homedale, 1,411	A 6
83836	Hope, 63	B 1
83629	Horseshoe Bend, 511	B 6
83244	Howe, 428	F 6
† 83854	Huetter, 49	B 2
83631	Idaho City⊙, 164	C 6
83401	Idaho Falls⊙, 35,776	F 6
83632	Indian Valley, 72	B 5
83245	Inkom, 522	F 7
83427	Iona, 890	G 6
83428	Irwin, 228	G 6
83429	Island Park, 136	G 5
83338	Jerome⊙, 4,183	D 7
83535	Juliaetta, 423	B 3
83536	Kamiah, 1,307	B 3
83837	Kellogg, 3,811	B 2
83537	Kendrick, 426	B 3
83340	Ketchum, 1,454	D 6
83538	Keuterville, 26	B 3
† 83423	Kilgore, 50	G 5
83341	Kimberly, 1,557	D 7
83633	King Hill, 150	C 6
83539	Kooskia, 809	C 3
83840	Kootenai, 168	B 1
83634	Kuna, 593	B 6
83841	Laclede, 200	B 1
83635	Lake Fork, 141	B 5
83430	Lamont, 30	G 6
83540	Lapwai, 400	B 3
83246	Lava Hot Springs, 516	F 7
83464	Leadore, 111	E 5
83465	Lemhi, 36	E 5
83249	Leslie, 100	E 6
83636	Letha, 115	B 6
83501	Lewiston⊙, 26,068	A 3
83431	Lewisville, 468	F 6
83432	Lorenzo, 125	G 6
† 83242	Lost River, 58	E 6
83637	Lowman, 45	C 5
83542	Lucile, 105	B 4
† 83241	Lund, 100	G 7
83251	Mackay, 539	E 6
83433	Macks Inn, 150	G 5
83252	Malad City⊙, 1,848	F 7
83342	Malta, 196	E 7
83639	Marsing, 610	B 6
83253	May, 120	E 5
83638	McCall, 1,758	C 5
83250	McCammon, 623	F 7
83640	Meadows, 250	B 5
83641	Melba, 197	B 6
83434	Menan, 545	F 6
83642	Meridian, 2,616	B 6
83643	Mesa, 25	B 5
83644	Middleton, 739	B 6
83645	Midvale, 176	B 5
83343	Minidoka, 131	E 7
83435	Monteview, 110	F 6
83646	Montour, 138	B 6
83254	Montpelier, 2,604	G 7
83255	Moore, 156	E 6
83256	Moreland, 500	F 6
83843	Moscow⊙, 14,146	B 3
83647	Mountain Home⊙, 6,451	C 6
83845	Moyie Springs, 203	B 1
† 83450	Mud Lake, 194	F 6
83846	Mullan, 1,279	C 2
83650	Murphy⊙, 75	B 6
83874	Murray, 100	C 2
83344	Murtaugh, 124	D 7
83345	Naf, 42	E 7
83651	Nampa, 20,768	B 6
83847	Naples, 463	B 1
83436	Newdale, 267	G 6
83654	New Meadows, 605	B 4
83655	New Plymouth, 986	B 6
83543	Nezperce⊙, 555	B 3
83848	Nordman, 168	B 1
83466	North Fork, 150	D 4
83656	Notus, 304	B 6
† 83254	Nounan, 92	G 7
83346	Oakley, 656	D 7
83259	Obsidian, 22	D 6
83657	Ola, 78	B 5
† 99156	Oldtown, 161	A 1
† 83855	Onaway, 166	B 3
83659	Oreana, 115	B 6
83544	Orofino⊙, 3,883	B 3
† 83525	Orogrande, 34	C 4
83849	Osburn, 2,248	B 2
83260	Ovid, 150	G 7
† 83263	Oxford, 75	F 7
83437	Palisades, 95	G 6
83261	Paris⊙, 615	G 7
83438	Parker, 266	G 6
83660	Parma, 1,228	B 6
83347	Paul, 911	E 7
83661	Payette⊙, 4,521	B 5
83545	Peck, 238	B 3
83348	Picabo, 50	D 6
83546	Pierce, 1,218	C 3
83850	Pinehurst, 1,934	B 2
83262	Pingree, 115	F 6
83851	Plummer, 443	B 2
83201	Pocatello⊙, 40,036	F 7
83547	Pollock, 50	B 4
83852	Ponderay, 275	B 1
83853	Porthill, 39	B 1
83854	Post Falls, 2,371	A 2
83855	Potlatch, 871	A 3
83263	Preston⊙, 3,310	G 7
83856	Priest River, 1,493	A 1
83857	Princeton, 124	B 3
83858	Rathdrum, 741	A 2
† 83114	Raymond, 65	G 7
83548	Reubens, 81	B 3
83440	Rexburg⊙, 8,272	G 6
83349	Richfield, 290	D 6
† 89832	Riddle, 44	B 7
83442	Rigby⊙, 2,293	F 6
83549	Riggins, 533	B 4
83443	Ririe, 575	G 6
83444	Roberts, 393	F 6
† 83221	Rockford, 150	F 6
83271	Rockland, 209	F 7
83302	Rogerson, 45	D 7
† 83660	Roswell, 65	A 6
83350	Rupert⊙, 4,563	E 7
83860	Sagle, 100	B 1
83445	Saint Anthony⊙, 2,877	G 6
83272	Saint Charles, 200	G 7
† 83861	Saint Joe, 50	B 2
83861	Saint Maries⊙, 2,571	B 2
83467	Salmon⊙, 2,910	D 4
83252	Samaria, 137	F 7
83862	Samuels, 467	B 1
83863	Sanders, 27	B 2
83864	Sandpoint⊙, 4,144	B 1
83866	Santa, 100	B 2
83274	Shelley, 2,614	F 6
83352	Shoshone⊙, 1,233	D 7
† 83650	Silver City, 1	B 6
† 83423	Small, 35	F 5
83868	Smelterville, 967	B 2
83276	Soda Springs⊙, 2,977	G 7
83550	Southwick, 38	B 3
83446	Spencer, 45	F 5
83869	Spirit Lake, 622	A 2
83277	Springfield, 180	F 6
83447	Squirrel, 43	G 5
83278	Stanley, 47	D 5
83669	Star, 500	B 6
83279	Sterling, 73	F 6
83552	Stites, 263	C 3
83280	Stone, 114	F 7
83448	Sugar City, 617	G 6
83353	Sun Valley, 180	D 6
83281	Swanlake, 145	F 7
83449	Swan Valley, 235	G 6
83670	Sweet, 120	B 6
83468	Tendoy, 150	E 5
83870	Tensed, 151	B 2
83450	Terreton, 42	F 6
83451	Teton, 390	G 6
83452	Tetonia, 176	G 6
83283	Thatcher, 300	G 7
83453	Thornton, 177	G 6
83871	Troy, 541	B 3
83354	Tuttle, 53	D 7
83301	Twin Falls⊙, 21,914	D 7
83454	Ucon, 664	F 6
83455	Victor, 241	G 6
83872	Viola, 300	B 3
† 83234	Virginia, 100	F 7
83873	Wallace⊙, 2,206	C 2
83875	Wardner, 492	B 2
83611	Warm Lake, 200	C 5
83285	Wayan, 50	G 7
83553	Weippe, 713	C 3
83672	Weiser⊙, 4,108	B 5
83355	Wendell, 1,122	D 7
83286	Weston, 230	F 7
83554	White Bird, 185	B 4
83676	Wilder, 564	A 6
83555	Winchester, 274	B 3
83876	Worley, 235	B 2
83677	Yellow Pine, 45	C 4

⊙ County seat.
‡ Population of metropolitan area.
† Zip of nearest p.o.
* Multiple zips

AREA 83,557 sq. mi.
POPULATION 713,008
CAPITAL Boise
LARGEST CITY Boise
HIGHEST POINT Borah Pk. 12,662 ft.
SETTLED IN 1842
ADMITTED TO UNION July 3, 1890
POPULAR NAME Gem State
STATE FLOWER Syringa
STATE BIRD Mountain Bluebird

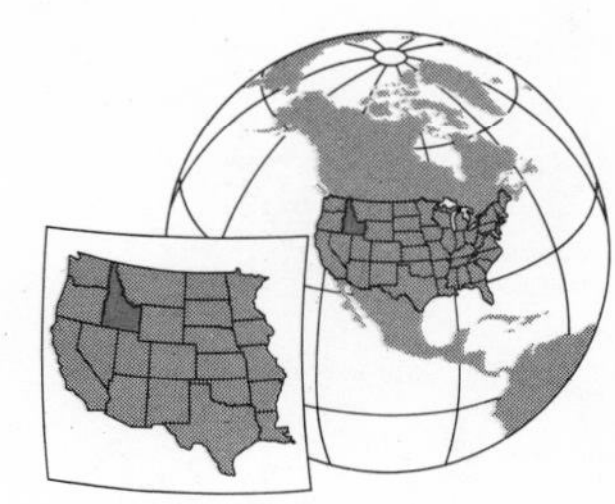

Agriculture, Industry and Resources

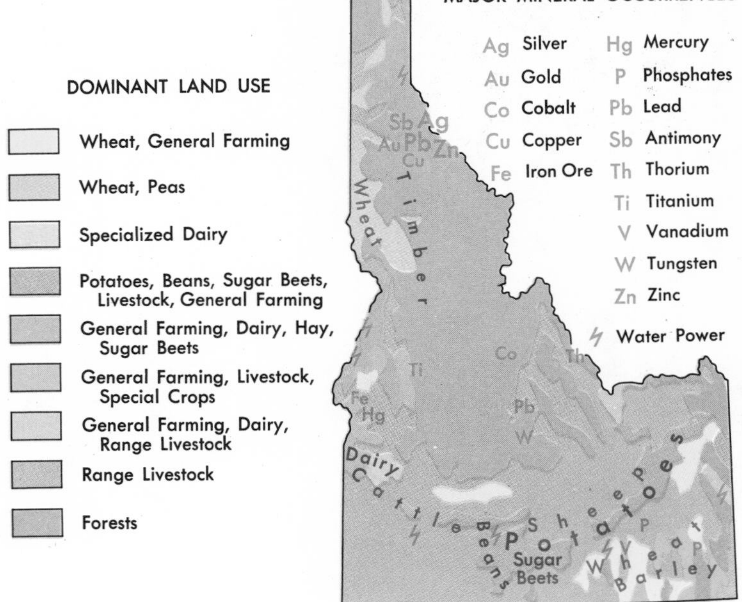

The Sun Valley Ski Patrol adds a touch of color to the slopes of Baldy Mountain. Here, in one of the country's most popular resorts, visitors acquire tropical tans while swimming in heated pools, skiing, skijoring, dogsledding or just sunbathing in the glacial air.

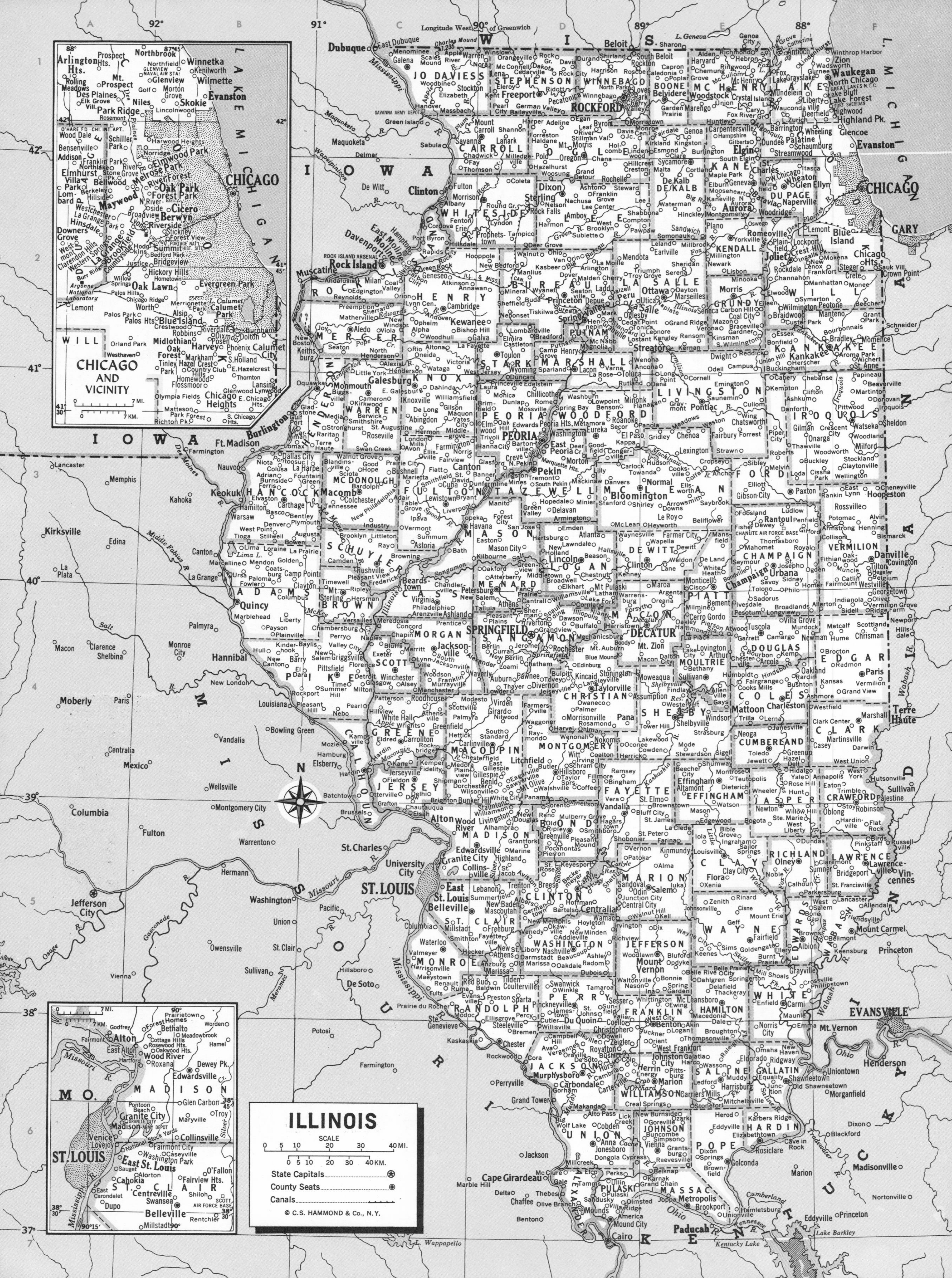

ILLINOIS
SCALE
0 5 10 20 30 40 MI.
0 5 10 20 30 40 KM.
State Capitals
County Seats
Canals
© C.S. HAMMOND & Co., N.Y.
Longitude West 90° of Greenwich
92°
91°
90°
89°
88°
42°
41°
40°
39°
38°
37°
A
B
C
D
E
F
1
2
3
4
5
6
7
WISCONSIN
IOWA
MISSOURI
KENTUCKY
INDIANA
LAKE MICHIGAN
CHICAGO AND VICINITY
CHICAGO
Evanston
Skokie
Oak Park
Cicero
Berwyn
Maywood
Blue Island
Harvey
Chicago Heights
Calumet City
WILL
ST. LOUIS
MADISON
ST. CLAIR
MO.
Alton
Wood River
Edwardsville
Granite City
Madison
Venice
East St. Louis
Belleville
JO DAVIESS
STEPHENSON
WINNEBAGO
BOONE
MC HENRY
LAKE
CARROLL
OGLE
DE KALB
KANE
DU PAGE
COOK
WHITESIDE
LEE
ROCK ISLAND
HENRY
BUREAU
LA SALLE
KENDALL
GRUNDY
WILL
KANKAKEE
MERCER
STARK
PUTNAM
MARSHALL
KNOX
WARREN
HENDERSON
PEORIA
WOODFORD
LIVINGSTON
IROQUOIS
FORD
MC DONOUGH
HANCOCK
FULTON
TAZEWELL
MC LEAN
VERMILION
CHAMPAIGN
SCHUYLER
MASON
LOGAN
DE WITT
PIATT
ADAMS
BROWN
CASS
MENARD
MACON
SANGAMON
MORGAN
SCOTT
PIKE
MOULTRIE
DOUGLAS
EDGAR
COLES
CHRISTIAN
SHELBY
GREENE
MACOUPIN
MONTGOMERY
CUMBERLAND
CLARK
CALHOUN
JERSEY
FAYETTE
EFFINGHAM
JASPER
CRAWFORD
BOND
MADISON
MARION
CLAY
RICHLAND
LAWRENCE
CLINTON
ST. CLAIR
WASHINGTON
JEFFERSON
WAYNE
EDWARDS
WABASH
MONROE
RANDOLPH
PERRY
FRANKLIN
HAMILTON
WHITE
JACKSON
WILLIAMSON
SALINE
GALLATIN
UNION
JOHNSON
POPE
HARDIN
ALEXANDER
PULASKI
MASSAC
ROCKFORD
CHICAGO
PEORIA
SPRINGFIELD
DECATUR
ST. LOUIS
EVANSVILLE
Dubuque
Davenport
Rock Island
Moline
Galesburg
Quincy
Joliet
Aurora
Elgin
Waukegan
Bloomington
Normal
Champaign
Urbana
Danville
Kankakee
Jacksonville
Belleville
Cairo
Metropolis
Paducah
Terre Haute
Gary
Mississippi R.
Illinois R.
Ohio R.
Wabash R.
Missouri R.
Rock R.

COUNTIES

Adams, 70,861 B 4
Alexander, 12,015 D 6
Bond, 14,012 D 5
Boone, 25,440 E 1
Brown, 5,586 C 4
Bureau, 38,541 D 2
Calhoun, 5,675 C 4
Carroll, 19,276 D 1
Cass, 14,219 C 4
Champaign, 163,281 E 3
Christian, 35,948 D 4
Clark, 16,216 F 4
Clay, 14,735 E 5
Clinton, 28,315 D 5
Coles, 47,815 E 4
Cook, 5,492,369 F 2
Crawford, 19,824 F 4
Cumberland, 9,772 E 4
De Kalb, 71,654 E 2
De Witt, 16,975 E 3
Douglas, 18,997 E 4
Du Page, 491,882 E 2
Edgar, 21,591 F 4
Edwards, 7,090 E 5
Effingham, 24,608 E 4
Fayette, 20,752 D 4
Ford, 16,382 E 3
Franklin, 38,329 E 5
Fulton, 41,890 C 3
Gallatin, 7,418 E 6
Greene, 17,014 C 4
Grundy, 26,535 E 2
Hamilton, 8,665 E 5
Hancock, 23,645 B 3
Hardin, 4,914 E 6
Henderson, 8,451 C 3
Henry, 53,217 C 2
Iroquois, 33,532 F 3
Jackson, 55,008 D 6
Jasper, 10,741 E 4
Jefferson, 31,446 E 5
Jersey, 18,492 C 4
Jo Daviess, 21,766 C 1
Johnson, 7,550 E 6
Kane, 251,005 E 2
Kankakee, 97,250 F 2
Kendall, 26,374 E 2
Knox, 61,280 C 3
Lake, 382,638 E 1
La Salle, 111,409 E 2
Lawrence, 17,522 F 5
Lee, 37,947 D 2
Livingston, 40,690 E 3
Logan, 33,538 D 3
Macon, 125,010 E 4
Macoupin, 44,557 D 4
Madison, 250,934 D 5
Marion, 38,986 E 5
Marshall, 13,302 D 2
Mason, 16,161 D 3
Massac, 13,889 E 6
McDonough, 36,653 C 3
McHenry, 111,555 E 1
McLean, 104,389 E 3
Menard, 9,685 D 3
Mercer, 17,294 C 2
Monroe, 18,831 C 5
Montgomery, 30,260 D 4
Morgan, 36,174 C 4
Moultrie, 13,263 E 4
Ogle, 42,867 D 1
Peoria, 195,318 D 3
Perry, 19,757 D 5
Piatt, 15,509 E 4
Pike, 19,185 C 4
Pope, 3,857 E 6
Pulaski, 8,741 D 6
Putnam, 5,007 D 2
Randolph, 31,379 D 5
Richland, 16,829 E 5
Rock Island, 166,734 C 2
Saint Clair, 285,176 D 5
Saline, 25,721 E 6
Sangamon, 161,335 D 4
Schuyler, 8,135 C 3
Scott, 6,096 C 4
Shelby, 22,589 E 4
Stark, 7,510 D 2
Stephenson, 48,861 D 1
Tazewell, 118,649 D 3
Union, 16,071 D 6
Vermilion, 97,047 F 3
Wabash, 12,841 F 5
Warren, 21,595 C 3
Washington, 13,780 D 5
Wayne, 17,004 E 5
White, 17,312 E 5
Whiteside, 62,877 D 2
Will, 249,498 F 2
Williamson, 49,021 E 6
Winnebago, 246,623 D 1
Woodford, 28,012 D 3

CITIES and TOWNS

Zip *Name/Pop.* *Key*
61410 Abingdon, 3,936 C 3
60101 Addison, 24,482 A 2
61230 Albany, 942 C 2
62215 Albers, 656 D 5
62806 Albion⊙, 1,791 E 5
61231 Aledo⊙, 3,325 C 2
61412 Alexis, 946 C 2
60102 Algonquin, 3,515 E 1
62001 Alhambra, 594 D 5
† 62207 Alorton, 3,573 B 6
61413 Alpha, 771 C 2
† 60601 Alsip, 11,141 B 2
62411 Altamont, 1,929 E 4
62002 Alton, 39,700 A 6
61310 Amboy, 2,184 D 2
61232 Andalusia, 950 C 2
62906 Anna, 4,766 D 6
61234 Annawan, 787 C 2
60002 Antioch, 3,189 E 1
61910 Arcola, 2,276 E 4
62501 Argenta, 1,034 E 4
* 60004 Arlington Heights, 64,884 A 1
60910 Aroma Park, 896 F 2
61911 Arthur, 2,214 E 4
60911 Ashkum, 590 E 3
62612 Ashland, 1,128 C 4
62808 Ashley, 655 D 5
61006 Ashton, 1,112 D 2
62510 Assumption, 1,487 E 4
61501 Astoria, 1,281 C 3
62613 Athens, 1,158 D 4
61235 Atkinson, 1,053 C 2
61723 Atlanta, 1,640 D 3
61913 Atwood, 1,264 E 4
62615 Auburn, 2,594 D 4
62311 Augusta, 824 C 3
* 60504 Aurora, 74,182 E 2
62907 Ava, 728 D 6
62216 Aviston, 828 D 5
61415 Avon, 1,013 C 3
61007 Baileyville, 600 D 1
60010 Barrington, 7,701 E 1
62312 Barry, 1,444 B 4
61607 Bartonville, 7,221 D 3
60510 Batavia, 8,994 E 2
62618 Beardstown, 6,222 C 3
62219 Beckemeyer, 1,069 D 5
† 60601 Bedford Park, 583 B 2
60401 Beecher, 1,770 F 2
† 61883 Belgium, 578 F 3
* 62220 Belleville⊙, 41,699 B 6
60104 Bellwood, 22,096 A 2
61008 Belvidere⊙, 14,061 E 1
61813 Bement, 1,638 E 4
62009 Benld, 1,736 D 4
60106 Bensenville, 12,833 A 1
62812 Benton⊙, 6,833 E 6
60162 Berkeley, 6,152 A 2
60402 Berwyn, 52,502 B 2
62010 Bethalto, 7,074 B 6

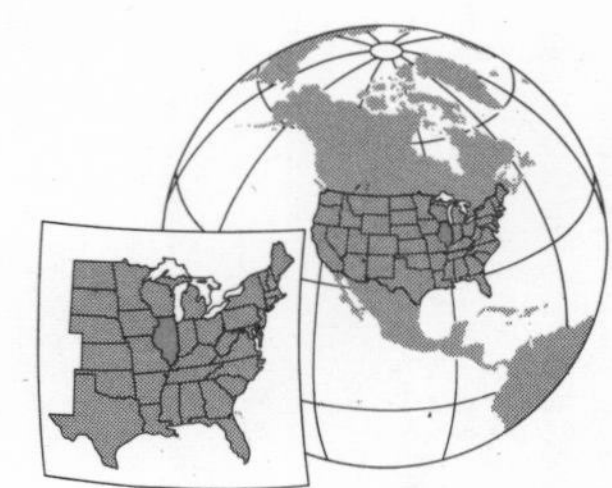

AREA 56,400 sq. mi.
POPULATION 11,113,976
CAPITAL Springfield
LARGEST CITY Chicago
HIGHEST POINT Charles Mound 1,235 ft.
SETTLED IN 1720
ADMITTED TO UNION December 3, 1818
POPULAR NAME Prairie State
STATE FLOWER Violet
STATE BIRD Cardinal

61914 Bethany, 1,235 E 4
61420 Blandinsville, 922 C 3
61701 Bloomington⊙, 39,992 D 3
Bloomington-Normal, ‡104,389 D 3
60406 Blue Island, 22,958 B 2
62513 Blue Mound, 1,181 D 4
62621 Bluffs, 866 C 4
60914 Bourbonnais, 5,909 F 2
60407 Braceville, 668 E 2
61421 Bradford, 885 D 2
60915 Bradley, 9,881 F 2
60408 Braidwood, 2,323 E 2
62230 Breese, 2,885 D 5
62417 Bridgeport, 2,262 F 5
60455 Bridgeview, 12,522 B 2
62012 Brighton, 1,889 C 4
61517 Brimfield, 729 D 3
60153 Broadview, 9,307 A 2
60513 Brookfield, 20,284 A 2
† 62059 Brooklyn (Lovejoy), 1,702 A 6
62910 Brookport, 1,046 E 6
62418 Brownstown, 689 E 5
60918 Buckley, 680 F 3
61314 Buda, 675 D 2
62014 Bunker Hill, 1,465 D 4
† 60601 Burnham, 3,634 B 2
† 60558 Burr Ridge, 1,637 A 2
61422 Bushnell, 3,703 C 3
61010 Byron, 1,749 D 1
62606 Cahokia, 20,649 B 6
62914 Cairo⊙, 6,277 D 6
60409 Calumet City, 32,956 B 2
† 60601 Calumet Park, 10,069 B 2
62915 Cambria, 798 D 6
61238 Cambridge⊙, 2,095 C 2
62320 Camp Point, 1,143 B 3
61520 Canton, 14,217 C 3
61012 Capron, 654 E 1
61239 Carbon Cliff, 1,369 C 2
62901 Carbondale, 22,816 D 6
62626 Carlinville⊙, 5,675 D 4
62231 Carlyle⊙, 3,139 D 5
62821 Carmi⊙, 6,033 E 5
60110 Carpentersville, 24,059 E 1
62917 Carriers Mills, 2,013 E 6
62016 Carrollton⊙, 2,866 C 4
62918 Carterville, 3,061 D 6
62321 Carthage⊙, 3,350 B 3
60013 Cary, 4,358 E 1
62420 Casey, 2,994 F 4
62232 Caseyville, 3,411 B 6
61817 Catlin, 2,093 F 3
61013 Cedarville, 578 D 1
† 62801 Central City, 1,377 D 5
62801 Centralia, 15,217 D 5
62206 Centreville, 11,378 B 6
61818 Cerro Gordo, 1,368 E 4
61014 Chadwick, 605 D 1
61820 Champaign, 56,532 E 3
Champaign-Urbana, ‡163,281 E 3
62627 Chandlerville, 762 C 3
60410 Channahon, 1,505 E 2
62628 Chapin, 552 C 4
61920 Charleston⊙, 16,421 E 4
62629 Chatham, 2,788 D 4
60921 Chatsworth, 1,255 E 3
60922 Chebanse, 1,185 F 3
61726 Chenoa, 1,860 E 3
61016 Cherry Valley, 952 D 1
62233 Chester⊙, 5,310 D 6
* 60601 Chicago⊙, 3,366,957 B 2
Chicago, ‡6,978,947 B 2
60411 Chicago Heights, 40,900 B 3
60415 Chicago Ridge, 9,187 A 2
61523 Chillicothe, 6,052 D 3
61924 Chrisman, 1,285 F 4
62822 Christopher, 2,910 D 6
60650 Cicero, 67,058 B 2
62823 Cisne, 615 E 5
60924 Cissna Park, 773 F 3
60514 Clarendon Hills, 6,750 A 2
62824 Clay City, 1,049 E 5
62324 Clayton, 727 B 3
60927 Clifton, 1,339 F 3
61727 Clinton⊙, 7,570 E 3
60416 Coal City, 3,040 E 2
61240 Coal Valley, 3,088 C 2
62920 Cobden, 1,114 D 6
62017 Coffeen, 641 D 4
62326 Colchester, 1,747 C 3
61728 Colfax, 935 E 3
62234 Collinsville, 17,773 B 6
62236 Columbia, 4,188 C 5
61242 Cordova, 589 C 2
62018 Cottage Hills, 1,261 B 6
62237 Coulterville, 1,186 D 5
60477 Country Club Hills, 6,920 B 3
† 60525 Countryside, 2,888 A 2
62922 Creal Springs, 830 E 6
60928 Crescent City, 597 F 3
60435 Crest Hill, 7,460 E 2
60113 Creston, 595 D 2
60445 Crestwood, 5,543 B 2
60417 Crete, 4,656 F 2
61611 Creve Coeur, 6,440 D 3
62827 Crossville, 860 F 5
60014 Crystal Lake, 14,541 E 1
61427 Cuba, 1,581 C 3
60929 Cullom, 572 E 3
62330 Dallas City, 1,284 B 3
61320 Dalzell, 579 D 2
61732 Danvers, 854 D 3
61832 Danville⊙, 42,570 F 3
* 62521 Decatur⊙, 90,397 E 4
Decatur, ‡125,010 E 4

(continued on following page)

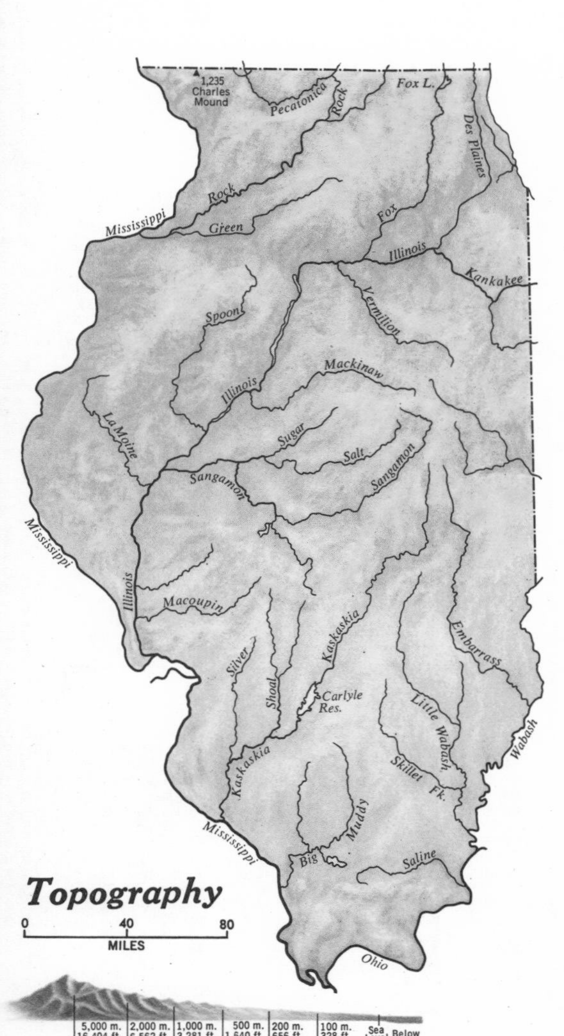

Agriculture, Industry and Resources

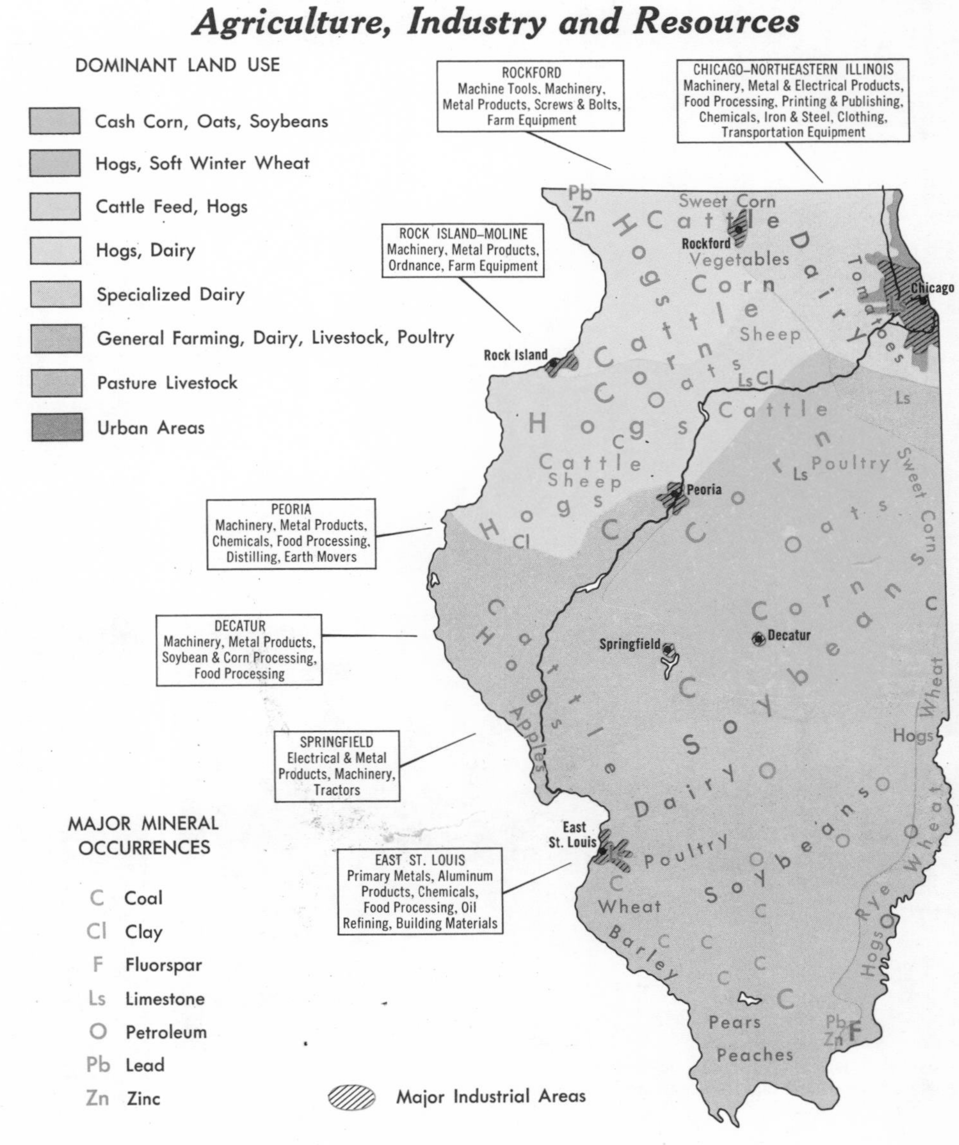

(continued)

61733 Deer Creek, 647 D 3
60015 Deerfield, 18,949 F 1
60115 De Kalb, 32,949 E 2
61734 Delavan, 1,844 D 3
61322 Depue, 1,919 D 2
62924 De Soto, 966 D 6
* 60016 Des Plaines, 57,239 A 1
† 62025 Dewey Park, 2,029 B 6
62530 Divernon, 1,010 D 4
† 60469 Dixmoor, 4,735 B 2
61021 Dixon⊙, 18,147 D 2
60419 Dolton, 25,937 B 2
62926 Dongola, 825 D 6
60515 Downers Grove, 32,751 A 2
61736 Downs, 651 E 3
60118 Dundee (East and West Dundee), 6,215 E 1
61525 Dunlap, 656 D 3
62239 Dupo, 2,842 A 6
62832 Du Quoin, 6,691 D 5
61024 Durand, 972 D 1
60420 Dwight, 3,841 E 2
60518 Earlville, 1,410 E 2
62024 East Alton, 7,309 B 6
† 60411 East Chicago Heights, 5,000 B 3
61025 East Dubuque, 2,408 C 1
† 60118 East Dundee (Dundee), 2,920 E 1
61430 East Galesburg, 706 C 3
† 60429 East Hazelcrest, 1,885 B 2
61244 East Moline, 20,832 C 2
61611 East Peoria, 18,455 D 3
* 62201 East Saint Louis, 69,996 B 6
62531 Edinburg, 1,153 D 4
62025 Edwardsville⊙, 11,070 B 6
62401 Effingham⊙, 9,458 E 4
60119 Elburn, 1,122 E 2
62930 Eldorado, 3,876 E 6
60120 Elgin, 55,691 E 1
61028 Elizabeth, 707 C 1
62931 Elizabethtown⊙, 436 E 6
60007 Elk Grove Village, 24,516 A 1
62932 Elkville, 850 D 6
60126 Elmhurst, 50,547 A 2
61529 Elmwood, 2,014 D 3
60635 Elmwood Park, 26,160 B 2
61738 El Paso, 2,291 D 3
60421 Elwood, 794 E 2
62635 Emden, 552 D 3
62933 Energy, 812 E 6
62835 Enfield, 764 E 5
62934 Equality, 732 E 6
61250 Erie, 1,566 C 2
61530 Eureka⊙, 3,028 D 3
* 60201 Evanston, 79,808 B 1
62242 Evansville, 838 D 5
60642 Evergreen Park, 25,487 B 2
61739 Fairbury, 3,359 E 3
62837 Fairfield⊙, 5,897 E 5
† 62002 Fairmont, 1,521 A 6
† 62201 Fairmont City, 2,769 B 6
61841 Fairmount, 785 F 3
61432 Fairview 601 C 3
62232 Fairview Heights, 8,625 B 6
62838 Farina, 634 E 5
61842 Farmer City, 2,217 E 3
61531 Farmington, 2,959 C 3
62534 Findlay, 809 E 4
61843 Fisher, 1,525 E 3
61844 Fithian, 562 F 3
61740 Flanagan, 878 E 3
62839 Flora, 5,283 E 5
60422 Flossmoor, 7,846 B 3
† 62018 Forest Homes, 1,998 B 6
60130 Forest Park, 15,472 B 2
† 60402 Forest View, 927 B 2
61741 Forrest, 1,219 E 3
61030 Forreston, 1,227 D 1
60020 Fox Lake, 4,511 E 1
60021 Fox River Grove, 2,245 E 1
60423 Frankfort, 2,325 F 2
62638 Franklin, 565 C 4
61031 Franklin Grove, 968 D 2
60131 Franklin Park, 20,497 A 2
62243 Freeburg, 2,495 D 5
61032 Freeport⊙, 27,736 D 1
61252 Fulton, 3,630 C 2
62935 Galatia, 792 E 6
61036 Galena⊙, 3,930 C 1
61401 Galesburg⊙, 36,290 C 3
61434 Galva, 3,061 D 2
60424 Gardner, 1,212 E 2
61254 Geneseo, 5,840 C 2
60134 Geneva⊙, 9,115 E 2
60135 Genoa, 3,003 E 1
61846 Georgetown, 3,984 F 4
62245 Germantown, 1,108 D 5
60936 Gibson City, 3,454 E 3
61847 Gifford, 814 E 3
62033 Gillespie, 3,457 D 4
60938 Gilman, 1,786 E 3
62640 Girard, 1,881 D 4
61533 Glasford, 1,066 D 3
62034 Glen Carbon, 1,897 B 6
60022 Glencoe, 10,542 F 1
60137 Glen Ellyn, 21,909 F 2
60025 Glenview, 24,880 B 1
60425 Glenwood, 7,416 B 3
62035 Godfrey, 1,225 A 6
62938 Golconda⊙, 922 E 6
62339 Golden, 571 B 3
62939 Goreville, 1,109 E 6
62037 Grafton, 1,018 C 5
61325 Grand Ridge, 698 E 2
62942 Grand Tower, 664 D 6
† 62701 Grandview, 2,242 D 4
62040 Granite City, 40,440 B 6
60940 Grant Park, 801 F 2
61326 Granville, 1,232 D 2
60030 Grayslake, 4,907 E 1
62844 Grayville, 2,035 E 5
62044 Greenfield, 1,179 C 4
† 61241 Green Rock, 2,744 C 2
62428 Greenup, 1,618 E 4
61534 Green Valley, 617 D 3
62642 Greenview, 740 D 3
62246 Greenville⊙, 4,631 D 5
61744 Gridley, 1,007 E 3
62340 Griggsville, 1,245 C 4
60031 Gurnee, 2,738 F 1
62341 Hamilton, 2,764 B 3
60140 Hampshire, 1,611 E 1
61256 Hampton, 1,612 C 2
61536 Hanna City, 1,282 D 3
61041 Hanover, 1,243 C 1
62047 Hardin⊙, 1,035 C 4
62946 Harrisburg⊙, 9,535 E 6
62048 Hartford, 2,243 B 6
60033 Harvard, 5,177 E 1
60426 Harvey, 34,636 B 2
60656 Harwood Heights, 9,060 B 1
62644 Havana⊙, 4,376 D 3
60429 Hazel Crest, 10,329 B 2
60034 Hebron, 781 E 1
† 61832 Hegeler, 1,595 F 3
61327 Hennepin⊙, 535 D 2
61537 Henry, 2,610 D 2
62948 Herrin, 9,623 E 6
60941 Herscher, 988 E 2
61745 Heyworth, 1,441 E 3
60457 Hickory Hills, 13,176 B 2
62249 Highland, 5,981 D 5
60035 Highland Park, 32,263 F 1
60040 Highwood, 4,973 F 1
61244 Hillcrest, 630 D 2
62049 Hillsboro⊙, 4,267 D 4
60162 Hillside, 8,888 A 2
60520 Hinckley, 1,053 E 2
60521 Hinsdale, 15,918 A 2
60525 Hodgkins, 2,270 A 2
61849 Homer, 1,354 F 3
60456 Hometown, 6,729 B 2
60430 Homewood, 18,871 B 3
60942 Hoopeston, 6,461 F 3
61747 Hopedale, 923 D 3
61748 Hudson, 802 E 3
62343 Hull, 585 B 4
60142 Huntley, 1,432 E 1
62949 Hurst, 934 D 6
62539 Illiopolis, 1,122 D 4
61440 Industry, 558 C 3
† 60431 Ingalls Park, 5,615 F 2
61441 Ipava, 608 C 3
62051 Irving, 599 D 4
60042 Island Lake, 1,973 E 1
60143 Itasca, 4,638 F 2
62650 Jacksonville⊙, 20,553 C 4
† 62701 Jerome, 1,673 D 4
62052 Jerseyville⊙, 7,446 C 4
62951 Johnston City, 3,928 E 6
* 60431 Joliet⊙, 80,378 E 2
62952 Jonesboro⊙, 1,676 D 6
† 60453 Justice, 9,473 A 2
60901 Kankakee⊙, 30,944 F 2
61933 Kansas, 779 F 4
62956 Karnak, 641 E 6
† 63673 Kaskaskia, 79 C 6
61442 Keithsburg, 836 B 2
60043 Kenilworth, 2,980 B 1
61443 Kewanee, 15,762 C 2
62540 Kincaid, 1,424 D 4
62854 Kinmundy, 759 E 5
60146 Kirkland, 1,138 E 1
61447 Kirkwood, 817 C 3
61448 Knoxville, 2,930 C 3
61540 Lacon⊙, 2,147 D 2
61329 Ladd, 1,328 D 2
60525 La Grange, 16,773 A 2
60525 La Grange Park, 15,626 A 2
61450 La Harpe, 1,240 C 3
60044 Lake Bluff, 4,979 F 1
† 60002 Lake Catherine, 1,219 E 1
60045 Lake Forest, 15,642 F 1
60047 Lake Zurich, 4,082 E 1
61330 La Moille, 669 D 2
61046 Lanark, 1,495 D 1
60438 Lansing, 25,805 B 3
61301 La Salle, 10,736 E 2
62439 Lawrenceville⊙, 5,863 F 5
61047 Leaf River, 633 D 1
62254 Lebanon, 3,564 D 5
60531 Leland, 743 E 2
60439 Lemont, 5,080 A 2
61048 Lena, 1,691 D 1
61752 Le Roy, 2,435 E 3
61542 Lewistown⊙, 2,706 C 3
61753 Lexington, 1,615 E 3
60048 Libertyville, 11,684 F 1
62656 Lincoln⊙, 17,582 D 3
† 60601 Lincolnwood, 12,929 B 1
60046 Lindenhurst, 3,141 F 1
62056 Litchfield, 7,190 D 4
62058 Livingston, 916 D 5
60441 Lockport, 9,985 F 2
61454 Lomax, 565 B 3
60148 Lombard, 35,977 A 2
61544 London Mills, 600 C 3
62858 Louisville⊙, 1,020 E 5
62059 Lovejoy, 1,702 A 6
61111 Loves Park, 12,390 E 1
61937 Lovington, 1,303 E 4
61261 Lyndon, 673 D 2
† 60411 Lynwood, 1,042 B 3
60534 Lyons, 11,124 B 2
61755 Mackinaw, 1,293 D 3
61455 Macomb⊙, 19,643 C 3
62544 Macon, 1,249 E 4
62060 Madison, 7,042 B 6
61853 Mahomet, 1,296 E 3
60150 Malta, 961 E 2
60442 Manhattan, 1,530 F 2
61546 Manito, 1,334 D 3
61854 Mansfield, 870 E 3
60950 Manteno, 2,864 F 2
60151 Maple Park, 660 E 2
60152 Marengo, 4,235 E 1
62061 Marine, 882 D 5
62059 Marion⊙, 11,724 E 6
62257 Marissa, 2,004 D 5
60426 Markham, 15,987 B 2
61756 Maroa, 1,467 E 3
† 61554 Marquette Heights, 2,758 D 3
61341 Marseilles, 4,320 E 2
62441 Marshall⊙, 3,468 F 4
62442 Martinsville, 1,374 F 4
62062 Maryville, 809 B 6
62258 Mascoutah, 5,045 D 5
62664 Mason City, 2,611 D 3
61263 Matherville, 699 C 2
60443 Matteson, 4,741 B 3
61938 Mattoon, 19,681 E 4
60153 Maywood, 30,036 A 2
60444 Mazon, 727 E 2
62957 McClure, 800 D 6
† 60050 McCullom Lake, 873 E 1
60050 McHenry, 6,772 E 1
61754 McLean, 820 D 3
62859 McLeansboro⊙, 2,630 E 5
† 62010 Meadowbrook, 1,295 B 6
* 60160 Melrose Park, 22,706 A 2
62351 Mendon, 883 B 3
61342 Mendota, 6,902 D 2
62665 Meredosia, 1,178 C 4
† 60601 Merrionette Park, 2,303 B 2
61548 Metamora, 2,176 D 3
62960 Metropolis⊙, 6,940 E 6
62666 Middletown, 626 D 3
60445 Midlothian, 15,939 B 2
61264 Milan, 4,873 C 2
60953 Milford, 1,656 F 3
61051 Milledgeville, 1,130 D 1
62260 Millstadt, 2,168 B 6
61759 Minier, 986 D 3
61760 Minonk, 2,267 D 3
60447 Minooka, 768 E 2
60448 Mokena, 1,643 F 2
61265 Moline, 46,237 C 2
60954 Momence, 2,836 F 2
60449 Monee, 940 F 2
61462 Monmouth⊙, 11,022 C 3
60538 Montgomery, 3,278 E 2
61856 Monticello⊙, 4,130 E 3
60539 Mooseheart, 850 E 2
60450 Morris⊙, 8,194 E 2
61270 Morrison⊙, 4,387 C 2
62546 Morrisonville, 1,178 D 4
† 61101 Morristown, 669 D 1
61550 Morton, 10,419 D 3
60053 Morton Grove, 26,369 B 1
62963 Mound City⊙, 1,177 D 6
62964 Mounds, 1,718 D 6
62863 Mount Carmel⊙, 8,096 F 5
61053 Mount Carroll⊙, 2,143 D 1
61054 Mount Morris, 3,173 D 1
62069 Mount Olive, 2,288 D 4
60056 Mount Prospect, 34,995 A 1
62548 Mount Pulaski, 1,677 D 3
62353 Mount Sterling⊙, 2,182 C 4
62864 Mount Vernon⊙, 15,980 E 5
62549 Mount Zion, 2,343 E 4
62550 Moweaqua, 1,687 E 4
62262 Mulberry Grove, 697 D 5
60060 Mundelein, 16,128 E 1
62966 Murphysboro⊙, 10,013 D 6
62668 Murrayville, 595 C 4
60540 Naperville, 23,885 E 2
† 61350 Naplate, 686 E 2
62263 Nashville⊙, 3,027 D 5
62354 Nauvoo, 1,047 B 3
62447 Neoga, 1,270 E 4
60541 Newark, 590 E 2
62264 New Athens, 2,000 D 5
62265 New Baden, 1,953 D 5
62670 New Berlin, 754 D 4
61272 New Boston, 706 B 2
62867 New Haven, 606 E 6
60451 New Lenox, 2,855 F 2
61942 Newman, 1,018 F 4
62448 Newton⊙, 3,024 E 5
61465 New Windsor, 723 C 2
62551 Niantic, 705 D 4
60648 Niles, 31,432 A 1
62868 Noble, 719 E 5
62075 Nokomis, 2,532 D 4
61761 Normal, 26,396 E 3
† 60601 Norridge, 16,880 B 1
62869 Norris City, 1,319 E 6
60542 North Aurora, 4,833 E 2
60062 Northbrook, 27,297 A 1
60064 North Chicago, 47,275 F 1
60093 Northfield, 5,010 B 1
60164 Northlake, 14,212 A 2
† 61101 North Park, 15,679 D 1
† 61554 North Pekin, 1,886 D 3
60546 North Riverside, 8,097 B 2
† 61373 North Utica (Utica), 974 E 2
60452 Oak Forest, 17,870 B 2
61943 Oakland, 1,012 F 4
* 60453 Oak Lawn, 60,305 B 2
60303 Oak Park, 62,511 B 2
61858 Oakwood, 1,367 F 3
† 62095 Oakwood Heights, 3,229 B 6
62449 Oblong, 1,860 F 5
60460 Odell, 1,076 E 2
62870 Odin, 1,263 D 5
62269 O'Fallon, 7,268 B 6
61348 Oglesby, 4,175 D 2
62271 Okawville, 992 D 5
62969 Olive Branch, 600 D 6
62450 Olney⊙, 8,974 E 5
60461 Olympia Fields, 3,478 B 3
60955 Onarga, 1,436 F 3
61467 Oneida, 728 C 2
61469 Oquawka⊙, 1,352 C 3
62554 Oreana, 1,092 E 4
61061 Oregon⊙, 3,539 D 1
61273 Orion, 1,801 C 2
60462 Orland Park, 6,391 A 2
60543 Oswego, 1,862 E 2
61350 Ottawa⊙, 18,716 E 2
60067 Palatine, 25,904 E 1
62451 Palestine, 1,640 F 4
62674 Palmyra, 776 C 4
60463 Palos Heights, 9,915 A 2
60465 Palos Hills, 6,629 A 2
60464 Palos Park, 3,297 A 2
62557 Pana, 6,326 D 4
61944 Paris⊙, 9,971 F 4
60466 Park Forest, 30,638 B 3
60068 Park Ridge, 42,466 A 1
62875 Patoka, 562 D 5
62558 Pawnee, 1,936 D 4
61353 Pawpaw, 846 E 2
60957 Paxton⊙, 4,373 E 3
62360 Payson, 589 B 4
61063 Pecatonica, 1,781 D 1
61554 Pekin⊙, 31,375 D 3
* 61601 Peoria⊙, 126,963 D 3
Peoria, ‡341,979 D 3
61614 Peoria Heights, 7,943 D 3
60468 Peotone, 2,345 F 2
62272 Percy, 967 D 5
61354 Peru, 11,772 D 2
62675 Petersburg⊙, 2,632 D 4
61864 Philo, 1,022 E 3
† 60426 Phoenix, 3,596 B 2
62274 Pinckneyville⊙, 3,377 D 5
60959 Piper City, 817 E 3
62363 Pittsfield⊙, 4,244 C 4
60544 Plainfield, 2,928 E 2
60545 Plano, 4,664 E 2
62366 Pleasant Hill, 1,064 C 4
62677 Pleasant Plains, 644 D 4
62367 Plymouth, 740 C 3
62275 Pocahontas, 764 D 5
61074 Polo, 2,542 D 1
61764 Pontiac⊙, 9,031 E 3
61065 Poplar Grove, 607 E 1
61275 Port Byron, 1,222 C 2
60469 Posen, 5,498 B 2
61865 Potomac, 909 F 3
61470 Prairie City, 630 C 3
62277 Prairie du Rocher, 658 C 5
61356 Princeton⊙, 6,959 D 2
61559 Princeville, 1,455 D 3
61277 Prophetstown, 1,915 D 2
60070 Prospect Heights, 13,333 A 1
62301 Quincy⊙, 45,288 B 4
62080 Ramsey, 830 D 4
60960 Rankin, 727 F 3
61866 Rantoul, 25,562 E 3
61278 Rapids City, 656 C 2
62560 Raymond, 890 D 4
62278 Red Bud, 2,559 D 5
61279 Reynolds, 610 C 2
60071 Richmond, 1,153 E 1
60471 Richton Park, 2,558 B 3
61870 Ridge Farm, 1,015 F 4
62979 Ridgway, 1,160 E 6
60627 Riverdale, 15,806 B 2
60305 River Forest, 13,402 B 2
60171 River Grove, 11,465 A 2
60546 Riverside, 10,432 B 2
62561 Riverton, 2,090 D 4
61561 Roanoke, 2,040 D 3
60472 Robbins, 9,641 B 2
62454 Robinson⊙, 7,178 F 5
61068 Rochelle, 8,594 D 2
62563 Rochester, 1,667 D 4
60436 Rockdale, 2,085 E 2
61071 Rock Falls, 10,287 D 2
* 61101 Rockford⊙, 147,370 D 1
Rockford, ‡272,063 D 1
61201 Rock Island⊙, 50,166 C 2
Rock Island-Moline-Davenport, ‡362,638 C 2
61072 Rockton, 2,099 E 1
60008 Rolling Meadows, 19,178 A 1
61562 Rome, 1,919 D 3
† 60441 Romeoville, 12,674 E 2
62082 Roodhouse, 2,357 C 4
61073 Roscoe, 949 D 1
60018 Rosemont, 4,360 A 1
61473 Roseville, 1,111 C 3
† 62024 Rosewood Heights, 3,391 B 6
62982 Rosiclare, 1,421 E 6
60963 Rossville, 1,420 F 3
62084 Roxana, 1,882 B 6
62983 Royalton, 1,166 D 6
62681 Rushville⊙, 3,300 C 3
60964 Saint Anne, 1,271 F 2
60174 Saint Charles, 12,928 E 2
61563 Saint David, 773 C 3
62458 Saint Elmo, 1,676 E 4
62460 Saint Francisville, 997 F 5
62281 Saint Jacob, 659 D 5
61873 Saint Joseph, 1,554 E 3
62881 Salem⊙, 6,187 E 5
62882 Sandoval, 1,332 D 5
60548 Sandwich, 5,056 E 2
62682 San Jose, 681 D 3
60411 Sauk Village, 7,479 F 2
61074 Savanna, 4,942 C 1
61874 Savoy, 592 E 3
61770 Saybrook, 814 E 3
60172 Schaumburg, 18,730 E 1
60176 Schiller Park, 12,712 A 1
† 62049 Schram City, 657 D 4
61360 Seneca, 1,781 E 2
62884 Sesser, 2,125 D 5
61875 Seymour, 850 E 3
60550 Shabbona, 730 E 2
61078 Shannon, 848 D 1
62984 Shawneetown⊙, 1,742 E 6
61361 Sheffield, 1,038 D 2
62565 Shelbyville⊙, 4,597 E 4
60966 Sheldon, 1,455 F 3
60551 Sheridan, 724 E 2
61281 Sherrard, 808 C 2
† 62220 Shiloh, 945 B 6
61876 Sidell, 645 F 4
61877 Sidney, 915 E 3
61282 Silvis, 5,907 C 2
60076 Skokie, 68,627 B 1
62285 Smithton, 847 C 5
60552 Somonauk, 1,112 E 2
62086 Sorento, 625 D 5
61080 South Beloit, 3,804 E 1
60411 South Chicago Heights, 4,923 B 3
60177 South Elgin, 4,289 E 2
60473 South Holland, 23,931 B 2
62650 South Jacksonville, 2,950 C 4
61564 South Pekin, 955 D 3
60474 South Wilmington, 725 E 2
61565 Sparland, 585 D 2
62286 Sparta, 4,307 D 5
* 62701 Springfield (cap.)⊙, 91,753 D 4
Springfield, ‡161,335 D 4
61362 Spring Valley, 5,605 D 2
61774 Stanford, 657 D 3
62088 Staunton, 4,396 D 5
62288 Steeleville, 1,957 D 6
60475 Steger, 8,104 F 2
61081 Sterling, 16,113 D 2
62463 Stewardson, 729 E 4
60402 Stickney, 6,601 B 2
61084 Stillman Valley, 871 D 1
61085 Stockton, 1,930 C 1
60165 Stone Park, 4,451 A 2
62567 Stonington, 1,096 D 4
60103 Streamwood, 18,176 E 1
61364 Streator, 15,600 E 2
61480 Stronghurst, 836 C 3
61951 Sullivan⊙, 4,112 E 4
60501 Summit, 11,569 B 2
62466 Sumner, 1,201 F 5
62221 Swansea, 5,432 B 6
60178 Sycamore⊙, 7,843 E 2
62688 Tallula, 643 D 4
62888 Tamaroa, 799 D 5
62988 Tamms, 645 D 6
61283 Tampico, 838 D 2
62089 Taylor Springs, 620 D 4
62568 Taylorville⊙, 10,644 D 4
62467 Teutopolis, 1,249 E 4
62689 Thayer, 616 D 4
61878 Thomasboro, 806 E 3
61285 Thomson, 617 C 2
60476 Thornton, 3,714 B 3
62292 Tilden, 909 D 5
† 61832 Tilton, 2,544 F 3
60477 Tinley Park, 12,382 B 3
61368 Tiskilwa, 973 D 2
62468 Toledo⊙, 1,068 E 4
61880 Tolono, 2,027 E 3
61369 Toluca, 1,319 D 2
61370 Tonica, 821 E 2
61483 Toulon⊙, 1,207 D 2
61776 Towanda, 578 E 3
62571 Tower Hill, 683 E 4
61568 Tremont, 1,942 D 3
62293 Trenton, 2,328 D 5
62294 Troy, 2,144 B 6
61953 Tuscola⊙, 3,917 E 4
60180 Union, 579 E 1
61801 Urbana⊙, 32,800 E 3
61373 Utica, 974 E 2
62891 Valier, 628 D 5
62295 Valmeyer, 733 C 5
62471 Vandalia⊙, 5,160 D 5
62090 Venice, 4,680 A 6
61484 Vermont, 947 C 3
61485 Victoria, 782 C 2
62995 Vienna⊙, 1,325 E 6
61956 Villa Grove, 2,605 E 4
60181 Villa Park, 25,891 A 2
61486 Viola, 946 C 2
62690 Virden, 3,504 D 4
62691 Virginia⊙, 1,814 C 4
60083 Wadsworth, 756 F 1
61376 Walnut, 1,295 D 2
† 62801 Wamac, 1,347 D 5
61777 Wapella, 572 E 3
61087 Warren, 1,523 C 1
62573 Warrensburg, 738 D 4
62379 Warsaw, 1,758 B 3
61570 Washburn, 1,173 D 3
61571 Washington, 6,790 D 3
62204 Washington Park, 9,524 B 6
61488 Wataga, 570 C 2
62298 Waterloo⊙, 4,546 C 5
60556 Waterman, 990 E 2
60970 Watseka⊙, 5,294 F 3
60084 Wauconda, 5,460 E 1
60085 Waukegan⊙, 65,269 F 1
62692 Waverly, 1,442 D 4
62895 Wayne City, 985 E 5
61882 Weldon, 553 E 3
61377 Wenona, 1,080 E 2
60153 Westchester, 20,033 A 2
60185 West Chicago, 10,111 E 2
† 62812 West City, 637 E 5
† 60118 West Dundee (Dundee), 3,295 E 1
60558 Western Springs, 12,147 A 2
62474 Westfield, 678 F 4
62896 West Frankfort, 8,836 E 6
60559 Westmont, 8,482 A 2
62476 West Salem, 979 F 5
61883 Westville, 3,655 F 3
60187 Wheaton⊙, 31,138 E 2
60090 Wheeling, 14,746 F 1
62092 White Hall, 2,979 C 4
61489 Williamsfield, 552 C 3
62693 Williamsville, 923 D 4
62997 Willisville, 659 D 6
60480 Willow Springs, 3,318 A 2
60091 Wilmette, 32,134 B 1
60481 Wilmington, 4,335 E 2
62093 Wilsonville, 691 D 4
62694 Winchester⊙, 1,788 C 4
61957 Windsor, 1,126 E 4
† 61465 Windsor (New Windsor), 723 C 2
60190 Winfield, 4,285 E 2
61088 Winnebago, 1,285 D 1
60093 Winnetka, 14,131 B 1
60096 Winthrop Harbor, 4,794 F 1
62094 Witt, 1,040 D 4
60191 Wood Dale, 8,831 A 1
61490 Woodhull, 898 C 2
60515 Woodridge, 11,028 E 2
62095 Wood River, 13,186 B 6
60098 Woodstock⊙, 10,226 E 1
62097 Worden, 1,091 B 6
60482 Worth, 11,999 A 2
61379 Wyanet, 1,005 D 2
61491 Wyoming, 1,563 D 2
61572 Yates City, 840 C 3
60560 Yorkville⊙, 2,049 E 2
62999 Zeigler, 1,940 D 6
60099 Zion, 17,268 F 1

⊙ County seat.
‡ Population of metropolitan area.
† Zip of nearest p.o.
* Multiple zips

Fred Boler—Shostal Associates

Sailboats lie anchored in Lake Michigan while many of their owners turn the wheels of industry behind Chicago's steel and glass facade.

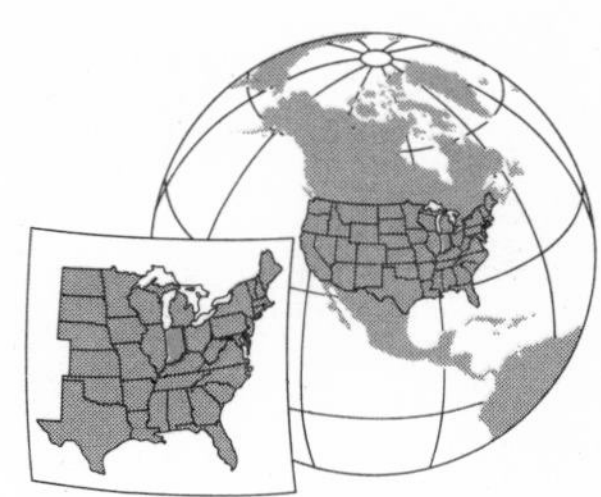

AREA 36,291 sq. mi.
POPULATION 5,193,669
CAPITAL Indianapolis
LARGEST CITY Indianapolis
HIGHEST POINT 1,257 ft. (Wayne County)
SETTLED IN 1730
ADMITTED TO UNION December 11, 1816
POPULAR NAME Hoosier State
STATE FLOWER Peony
STATE BIRD Cardinal

Ore being unloaded in the storage yard at steel plant docks in Gary, Indiana. Aided by the state's outstanding natural supply of limestone, mills in the Lake Michigan area produce more than 15 million tons of steel yearly.

COUNTIES

Adams, 26,871 H 3
Allen, 280,455 G 2
Bartholomew, 57,022 F 6
Benton, 11,262 C 3
Blackford, 15,888 G 4
Boone, 30,870 E 4
Brown, 9,057 E 6
Carroll, 17,734 D 3
Cass, 40,456 E 3
Clark, 75,876 F 8
Clay, 23,933 C 6
Clinton, 30,547 E 4
Crawford, 8,033 E 8
Daviess, 26,602 C 7
Dearborn, 29,430 H 6
Decatur, 22,738 G 6
De Kalb, 30,837 H 2
Delaware, 129,219 G 4
Dubois, 30,934 D 8
Elkhart, 126,529 F 1
Fayette, 26,216 G 5
Floyd, 55,622 F 8
Fountain, 18,257 C 4
Franklin, 16,943 G 6
Fulton, 16,984 E 2
Gibson, 30,444 B 8
Grant, 83,955 F 3
Greene, 26,894 D 6
Hamilton, 54,532 E 4
Hancock, 35,096 F 5
Harrison, 20,423 E 8
Hendricks, 53,974 D 5
Henry, 52,603 G 5
Howard, 83,198 E 4
Huntington, 34,970 G 3
Jackson, 33,187 E 7
Jasper, 20,429 C 2
Jay, 23,575 G 4
Jefferson, 27,006 G 7
Jennings, 19,454 F 7
Johnson, 61,138 E 6
Knox, 41,546 C 7
Kosciusko, 48,127 F 2
Lagrange, 20,890 G 1
Lake, 546,253 C 2
LaPorte, 105,342 D 1
Lawrence, 38,038 E 7
Madison, 138,451 F 4
Marion, 792,299 E 5
Marshall, 34,986 E 2
Martin, 10,969 D 7
Miami, 39,246 E 3
Monroe, 84,849 D 6
Montgomery, 33,930 D 4
Morgan, 44,176 E 6
Newton, 11,606 C 3
Noble, 31,382 G 2
Ohio, 4,289 H 7
Orange, 16,968 E 7
Owen, 12,163 D 6
Parke, 14,600 C 5
Perry, 19,075 D 8
Pike, 12,281 C 8
Porter, 87,114 C 2
Posey, 21,740 B 8
Pulaski, 12,534 D 2
Putnam, 26,932 D 5
Randolph, 28,915 G 4
Ripley, 21,138 G 6
Rush, 20,352 G 5
Saint Joseph, 245,045 E 1
Scott, 17,144 F 7
Shelby, 37,797 F 5
Spencer, 17,134 C 9
Starke, 19,280 D 2
Steuben, 20,159 G 1
Sullivan, 19,889 C 6
Switzerland, 6,306 G 7
Tippecanoe, 109,378 D 4
Tipton, 16,650 E 4
Union, 6,582 H 5
Vanderburgh, 168,772 B 8
Vermillion, 16,793 C 5
Vigo, 114,528 C 6
Wabash, 35,553 F 3
Warren, 8,705 C 4
Warrick, 27,972 C 8
Washington, 19,278 E 7
Wayne, 79,109 G 5
Wells, 23,821 G 3
White, 20,995 D 3
Whitley, 23,395 F 2

CITIES and TOWNS

Zip Name/Pop. Key

47240 Adams, 300 F 6
46947 Adamsboro, 325 E 3
46102 Advance, 561 D 5
46910 Akron, 1,019 E 2
47320 Albany, 2,293 G 4
46701 Albion⊙, 1,498 G 2
† 47283 Alert, 210 F 6
46001 Alexandria, 5,097 F 4
46738 Altona, 209 G 2
47917 Ambia, 300 C 4
46911 Amboy, 473 F 3
† 46131 Amity, 400 E 6
46103 Amo, 422 D 5
* 46011 Anderson⊙, 70,787 F 4
Anderson, ‡138,451 F 4
† 47024 Andersonville, 250 G 5
46702 Andrews, 1,207 F 3
46703 Angola⊙, 5,117 G 1
46030 Arcadia, 1,338 E 4
46704 Arcola, 325 G 2
† 46624 Ardmore, 800 E 1
46501 Argos, 1,393 E 2
46104 Arlington, 550 F 5
46705 Ashley, 721 G 1
46031 Atlanta, 620 E 4
47918 Attica, 4,262 C 4
46502 Atwood, 300 F 2
46706 Auburn⊙, 7,337 G 2
47001 Aurora, 4,293 H 6
47102 Austin, 4,902 F 7
46710 Avilla, 881 G 2
47420 Avoca, 400 D 7
46105 Bainbridge, 703 D 5
46106 Bargersville, 873 E 5
47006 Batesville, 3,799 G 6
47920 Battle Ground, 818 D 3
47421 Bedford⊙, 13,087 E 7
46107 Beech Grove, 13,468 E 5
† 46526 Benton, 221 F 2
46711 Berne, 2,988 H 3
46301 Beverly Shores, 946 C 1
47512 Bicknell, 3,717 C 7
46713 Bippus, 220 F 3
47513 Birdseye, 404 D 8
† 46401 Blackoak, 9,624 C 1
47831 Blanford, 700 B 5
47170 Blocher, 350 F 7
47424 Bloomfield⊙, 2,565 D 6
47832 Bloomingdale, 391 C 5
47401 Bloomington⊙, 42,890 D 6
† 47360 Blountsville, 220 G 4
† 46176 Blue Ridge, 236 F 5
46714 Bluffton⊙, 8,297 G 3
46110 Boggstown, 200 F 5
46302 Boone Grove, 225 C 2
47601 Boonville⊙, 5,736 C 8
47106 Borden, 337 F 8
47324 Boston, 210 H 5
47921 Boswell, 998 C 3
46504 Bourbon, 1,606 E 2
47833 Bowling Green, 200 D 6
47107 Bradford, 400 E 8
47834 Brazil⊙, 8,163 C 5
46506 Bremen, 3,487 E 2
47836 Bridgeton, 350 C 5
† 45030 Bright, 450 H 6
46720 Brimfield, 258 G 2
46913 Bringhurst, 250 E 3
46507 Bristol, 1,100 F 1
† 47354 Bronson (Losantville), 212 G 4
47922 Brook, 919 C 3
46111 Brooklyn, 911 E 5
47923 Brookston, 1,232 D 3
47012 Brookville⊙, 2,864 G 6
46112 Brownsburg, 5,186 E 5
47220 Brownstown⊙, 2,376 F 7
47325 Brownsville, 285 H 5
47516 Bruceville, 627 C 7
47326 Bryant, 320 G 3
47924 Buck Creek, 260 D 4
47517 Buckskin, 275 C 8
47925 Buffalo, 350 D 3
46914 Bunker Hill, 956 E 3
46508 Burket, 210 F 2
46915 Burlington, 685 E 4
47926 Burnettsville, 510 D 3
47222 Burney, 344 F 6
† 46401 Burns Harbor, 1,284 C 1
46916 Burrows, 259 E 3
46721 Butler, 2,394 H 2
47223 Butlerville, 275 F 6
† 46371 Byron, 200 C 5
† 47362 Cadiz, 207 G 5
47327 Cambridge City, 2,481 G 5
46917 Camden, 577 D 3
47108 Campbellsburg, 678 E 7
47520 Cannelton⊙, 2,280 D 9
47837 Carbon, 344 C 5
47838 Carlisle, 714 C 7
46032 Carmel, 6,568 E 5
46114 Cartersburg, 400 E 5
46115 Carthage, 946 F 5
† 47460 Cataract, 200 D 6
47928 Cayuga, 1,090 C 5
47016 Cedar Grove, 248 H 6
46303 Cedar Lake, 7,589 C 2
47521 Celestine, 300 D 8
† 47842 Centenary, 225 B 5
46918 Center, 310 E 4
47840 Centerpoint, 275 C 6
46116 Centerton, 250 E 5
47330 Centerville, 2,380 H 5
47929 Chalmers, 544 D 3
47610 Chandler, 2,032 C 8
47111 Charlestown, 5,890 F 8
46117 Charlottesville, 500 F 5
† 47138 Chelsea, 200 F 7
46017 Chesterfield, 3,001 F 4
46304 Chesterton, 6,177 D 1
47611 Chrisney, 550 C 8
46723 Churubusco, 1,528 G 2
46034 Cicero, 1,378 E 4
47225 Clarksburg, 347 G 6
47930 Clarks Hill, 741 D 4
47130 Clarksville, 13,806 F 8
47841 Clay City, 900 C 6
46510 Claypool, 468 F 2
46118 Clayton, 736 D 5
47426 Clear Creek, 250 E 6
† 46737 Clear Lake, 271 H 1
47226 Clifford, 275 F 6
47842 Clinton, 5,340 C 5
46120 Cloverdale, 870 D 5
47427 Coal City, 300 D 6
47845 Coalmont, 400 C 6
46121 Coatesville, 453 D 5
47931 Colburn, 300 D 3
46035 Colfax, 633 D 4
47978 Collegeville, 1,700 C 3
46725 Columbia City⊙, 4,911 G 2
47201 Columbus⊙, 27,141 E 6
47331 Connersville⊙, 17,604 G 5
46919 Converse, 1,163 F 3
47228 Cortland, 200 F 7
46730 Corunna, 359 G 2
47112 Corydon⊙, 2,719 E 8
47932 Covington⊙, 2,641 C 4
† 47302 Cowan, 428 G 4
47522 Crane, 339 D 7
47933 Crawfordsville⊙, 13,842 D 4
46732 Cromwell, 475 F 2
47229 Crothersville, 1,663 F 7
46307 Crown Point⊙, 10,931 C 2
46511 Culver, 1,783 E 2
46229 Cumberland, 479 E 5
47612 Cynthiana, 793 B 8
47523 Dale, 1,113 D 8
47334 Daleville, 1,730 F 4
47847 Dana, 720 C 5
46122 Danville⊙, 3,771 D 5
47940 Darlington, 802 D 4
47941 Dayton, 840 D 4
46733 Decatur⊙, 8,445 H 3
47524 Decker, 268 B 7
† 46917 Deer Creek, 250 E 3
46923 Delphi⊙, 2,582 D 3
46310 Demotte, 1,697 C 2
46926 Denver, 566 E 3
47230 Deputy, 255 F 7
47302 Desoto, 385 G 4
47018 Dillsboro, 840 G 6
46513 Donaldson, 250 E 2
† 47118 Doolittle Mills, 200 D 8
47335 Dublin, 1,021 G 5
47525 Dubois, 500 D 8
47848 Dugger, 1,150 C 6
† 46304 Dune Acres, 301 C 1
47336 Dunkirk, 3,465 G 4
† 46514 Dunlap, 1,900 F 1
47337 Dunreith, 200 F 5
47231 Dupont, 357 G 7
46311 Dyer, 4,906 C 1
† 46074 Eagletown, 365 E 4
47942 Earl Park, 478 C 3
46312 East Chicago, 46,982 C 1
47019 East Enterprise, 250 H 7
46405 East Gary, 9,858 C 1
† 47370 East Germantown (Pershing), 447 G 5
47338 Eaton, 1,594 G 4
47116 Eckerty, 200 D 8
47339 Economy, 285 G 5
† 46011 Edgewood, 2,326 F 4
46124 Edinburg, 4,906 E 6
47528 Edwardsport, 482 C 7
† 47150 Edwardsville, 700 F 8
47613 Elberfeld, 834 C 8
47232 Elizabethtown, 519 F 6
46514 Elkhart, 43,152 F 1
47429 Ellettsville, 1,627 D 6
47529 Elnora, 873 C 7
† 47018 Elrod, 200 G 6
† 47901 Elston, 500 D 4
46036 Elwood, 11,196 F 4
46125 Eminence, 200 D 5
47118 English⊙, 664 E 8
46524 Etna Green, 516 E 2
† 47928 Eugene, 300 B 5
* 47701 Evansville⊙, 138,764 C 9
Evansville, ‡232,775 C 9
46126 Fairland, 950 F 5
46928 Fairmount, 3,427 F 4
† 47842 Fairview Park, 1,067 C 5
47850 Farmersburg, 962 C 6
47340 Farmland, 1,262 G 4
47532 Ferdinand, 1,432 D 8
46128 Fillmore, 600 D 5
46129 Finly, 350 F 5
46038 Fishers, 628 E 5
47234 Flat Rock, 289 F 6
46929 Flora, 1,877 E 3
47119 Floyds Knobs, 350 F 8
47851 Fontanet, 200 C 5
46039 Forest, 400 E 4
47533 Fort Branch, 2,535 B 8
46040 Fortville, 2,460 F 5
* 46801 Fort Wayne⊙, 177,671 G 2
Fort Wayne, ‡280,455 G 2
47341 Fountain City, 852 H 5
46130 Fountaintown, 225 F 5
47944 Fowler⊙, 2,643 C 3
46930 Fowlerton, 337 F 4
47946 Francesville, 1,015 D 3
47534 Francisco, 621 B 8
46041 Frankfort⊙, 14,956 E 4
46131 Franklin⊙, 11,477 E 6
46044 Frankton, 1,796 F 4
47120 Fredericksburg, 207 E 8
47431 Freedom, 262 D 6
47535 Freelandville, 710 C 7
47235 Freetown, 550 E 7
46737 Fremont, 1,043 H 1
47432 French Lick, 2,059 D 7
46931 Fulton, 372 E 3
† 47119 Galena, 250 F 8
46932 Galveston, 1,284 E 3
46738 Garrett, 4,715 G 2
* 46401 Gary, 175,415 C 1
Gary-Hammond-East Chicago, ‡ 633,367 C 1
46933 Gas City, 5,742 F 4
47342 Gaston, 928 G 4
46740 Geneva, 1,100 H 3
47537 Gentryville, 281 C 8
47122 Georgetown, 1,273 F 8
47343 Glenwood, 452 G 5
† 47367 Glezen, 300 C 8
46045 Goldsmith, 235 E 4
47948 Goodland, 1,176 C 3
46526 Goshen⊙, 17,171 F 1
47433 Gosport, 692 D 6
46741 Grabill, 570 H 2
47615 Grandview, 696 C 9
46530 Granger, 200 E 1
46135 Greencastle⊙, 8,852 D 5
† 47025 Greendale, 3,783 H 6
46140 Greenfield⊙, 9,986 F 5
47344 Greensboro, 225 G 5
47240 Greensburg⊙, 8,620 G 6
47345 Greens Fork, 444 H 5
46936 Greentown, 1,870 E 4
47124 Greenville, 611 F 8
46142 Greenwood, 11,408 E 5
46319 Griffith, 18,168 C 1
46144 Gwynneville, 240 F 5
47346 Hagerstown, 2,059 G 5
46742 Hamilton, 537 H 1
46532 Hamlet, 761 D 2
* 46320 Hammond, 107,790 B 1
46743 Hanna, 500 D 2
47243 Hanover, 3,018 F 7
47125 Hardinsburg, 263 E 8
46743 Harlan, 840 H 2
47853 Harmony, 750 C 5
47434 Harrodsburg, 400 D 6
47348 Hartford City⊙, 8,207 G 4
47244 Hartsville, 434 F 6
47617 Hatfield, 800 C 9
47539 Haubstadt, 1,171 B 8
† 47546 Haysville, 585 D 8
47540 Hazleton, 416 B 8
46341 Hebron, 1,624 C 2
46146 Heltonville, 400 E 7
46937 Hemlock, 200 F 4
47126 Henryville, 1,500 F 7
46322 Highland, 24,947 B 1
46046 Hillisburg, 225 E 4
47949 Hillsboro, 505 C 4
47854 Hillsdale, 500 C 5
46745 Hoagland, 530 H 3
46342 Hobart, 21,485 C 1
46047 Hobbs, 400 F 4
47541 Holland, 662 C 8
47023 Holton, 610 G 6
46146 Homer, 245 F 5
47246 Hope, 1,603 F 6
† 46069 Hortonville, 240 E 4
46746 Howe, 800 G 1
46747 Hudson, 464 G 1
46552 Hudson Lake, 1,134 D 1
46748 Huntertown, 775 G 2
47542 Huntingburg, 4,794 D 8
46750 Huntington⊙, 16,217 G 3
† 46064 Huntsville, 450 G 4
47437 Huron, 580 D 7
47855 Hymera, 907 C 6
47950 Idaville, 600 D 3
* 46201 Indianapolis (cap.)⊙ 744,624 E 5
Indianapolis, ‡1,109,882 E 5
46048 Ingalls, 888 F 5
47545 Ireland, 527 C 8
46147 Jamestown, 938 D 5
47438 Jasonville, 2,335 C 6
47546 Jasper⊙, 8,641 D 8
47130 Jeffersonville⊙, 20,008 F 8
† 47565 Johnson, 250 B 8
† 46074 Jolietville, 265 E 4
46938 Jonesboro, 2,466 F 4
47247 Jonesville, 202 F 6
46049 Kempton, 469 E 4
46755 Kendallville, 6,838 G 2
47351 Kennard, 518 G 5
47951 Kentland⊙, 1,864 C 3
46939 Kewanna, 614 E 2
46759 Keystone, 200 G 3
46760 Kimmell, 350 F 2
47952 Kingman, 530 C 5
46345 Kingsbury, 314 D 1
46346 Kingsford Heights, 1,200 D 2
46050 Kirklin, 736 E 4
46148 Knightstown, 2,456 F 5
47857 Knightsville, 788 C 5
46534 Knox⊙, 3,519 D 2
46901 Kokomo⊙, 44,042 E 4
† 46574 Koontz Lake, 900 D 2
46347 Kouts, 1,388 C 2
46348 La Crosse, 696 D 2
47954 Ladoga, 1,099 D 5
* 47901 Lafayette⊙, 44,955 D 4
Lafayette-West Lafayette, ‡109,378 D 4
46940 La Fontaine, 793 F 3
46761 Lagrange⊙, 2,053 F 1
46941 Lagro, 552 F 3
† 46703 Lake James, 400 H 1
46943 Laketon, 500 F 3
46349 Lake Village, 600 C 2
46536 Lakeville, 712 E 1
† 46567 Lake Wawasee, 600 F 2
47136 Lanesville, 586 E 8
46763 Laotto, 312 G 2
46537 Lapaz, 604 E 2
46051 Lapel, 1,725 F 4
46350 LaPorte⊙, 22,140 D 1
46764 Larwill, 324 F 2
47024 Laurel, 753 G 6
46226 Lawrence, 16,646 E 5
47025 Lawrenceburg⊙, 4,636 H 6
47137 Leavenworth, 330 E 8
46052 Lebanon⊙, 9,766 D 4
46538 Leesburg, 561 F 2
46945 Leiters Ford, 250 E 2
46765 Leo, 500 G 2
46355 Leroy, 350 C 2
† 47240 Letts, 247 F 6
47352 Lewisville, 530 G 5
47138 Lexington, 400 F 7
47353 Liberty⊙, 1,831 H 5
46766 Liberty Center, 300 G 3
46946 Liberty Mills, 200 F 2
46767 Ligonier, 3,034 F 2
47955 Linden, 713 D 4
46769 Linn Grove, 300 H 3
47441 Linton, 5,450 C 6
† 46755 Lisbon, 200 G 2
46149 Lizton, 397 D 5
46947 Logansport⊙, 19,255 E 3
† 46360 Long Beach, 2,740 D 1
47553 Loogootee, 2,953 D 7
47354 Losantville, 212 G 4
46356 Lowell, 3,839 C 2
† 46601 Lydick, 1,341 E 1
† 47874 Lyford, 400 C 5
47355 Lynn, 1,360 H 4
47619 Lynnville, 556 C 8
47443 Lyons, 702 C 7
46951 Macy, 273 E 3
47250 Madison⊙, 13,081 G 7
† 47001 Manchester, 250 H 6
46150 Manilla, 300 F 5
† 47872 Mansfield, 200 C 5
47140 Marengo, 767 E 8
47556 Mariah Hill, 275 D 8
† 46176 Marietta, 280 F 6
46952 Marion⊙, 39,607 F 3
46770 Markle, 963 G 3
46056 Markleville, 457 F 5
47859 Marshall, 365 C 5
46151 Martinsville⊙, 9,723 D 6
46957 Matthews, 728 F 4
46154 Maxwell, 245 F 5
46055 McCordsville, 500 F 5
47860 Mecca, 800 C 5
47957 Medaryville, 732 D 2
47260 Medora, 788 E 7
47958 Mellott, 325 C 4
47143 Memphis, 324 F 8
46539 Mentone, 830 E 2
47861 Merom, 305 B 6
46410 Merrillville, 15,918 C 2
47030 Metamora, 400 G 6
† 46703 Metz, 200 H 1
46958 Mexico, 850 E 3
46959 Miami, 420 E 3
46360 Michigan City, 39,369 C 1

(continued on following page)

(continued)

46057 Michigantown, 457 ... E 4
46540 Middlebury, 1,055 ... F 1
47356 Middletown, 2,046 ... F 4
47445 Midland, 220 ... C 6
47031 Milan, 1,260 ... G 6
46542 Milford, 1,264 ... F 2
46543 Millersburg, 618 ... F 1
47261 Millhousen, 252 ... G 6
47145 Milltown, 829 ... E 8
† 47362 Millville, 275 ... G 5
46156 Milroy, 750 ... G 6
47357 Milton, 694 ... G 5
46544 Mishawaka, 35,517 ... E 1
47446 Mitchell, 4,092 ... E 7
47358 Modoc, 275 ... G 4
46771 Mongo, 225 ... G 1
47959 Monon, 1,548 ... D 3
46772 Monroe, 622 ... H 3
47557 Monroe City, 603 ... C 7
46773 Monroeville, 1,353 ... H 3
46157 Monrovia, 750 ... E 5
46960 Monterey, 268 ... D 2
47862 Montezuma, 1,192 ... C 5
47558 Montgomery, 411 ... C 7
47960 Monticello⊙, 4,869 ... D 3
47962 Montmorenci, 350 ... D 4
47359 Montpelier, 2,093 ... G 3
47360 Mooreland, 495 ... G 5
47032 Moores Hill, 616 ... G 6
46158 Mooresville, 5,800 ... E 5
46160 Morgantown, 1,134 ... E 6
47963 Morocco, 1,285 ... C 3
47033 Morris, 435 ... G 6
46161 Morristown, 838 ... F 5
47361 Mount Summit, 395 ... G 4
47620 Mount Vernon⊙, 6,770 ... B 9
46058 Mulberry, 1,075 ... D 4
* 47302 Muncie⊙, 69,080 ... G 4
Muncie, ‡129,219 ... G 4
46321 Munster, 16,514 ... B 1
47147 Nabb, 204 ... F 7
47034 Napoleon, 282 ... G 6
46550 Nappanee, 4,159 ... F 2
47448 Nashville⊙, 527 ... E 6
† 47421 Needmore, 200 ... E 7
47150 New Albany⊙, 38,402 ... F 8
47449 Newberry, 295 ... C 7
47630 Newburgh, 2,302 ... C 9
46552 New Carlisle, 1,434 ... E 1
47362 New Castle⊙, 21,215 ... G 5
† 46342 New Chicago, 2,231 ... C 1
47863 New Goshen, 500 ... B 5
47631 New Harmony, 971 ... B 8
46774 New Haven, 5,728 ... H 2
47366 New Lisbon, 350 ... G 5
† 46979 New London, 200 ... E 4
47965 New Market, 640 ... D 5
46163 New Palestine, 863 ... F 5
46553 New Paris, 1,080 ... F 2
† 47165 New Pekin, 912 ... F 7
47263 New Point, 381 ... G 6
47966 Newport⊙, 708 ... C 5
† 47106 New Providence (Borden), 337 ... F 8
47967 New Richmond, 381 ... D 4
47968 New Ross, 318 ... D 5
† 46173 New Salem, 270 ... G 5
47161 New Salisbury, 350 ... E 8
47969 Newtown, 286 ... C 4
47035 New Trenton, 200 ... H 6
47162 New Washington, 1,100 ... F 7
46184 New Whiteland, 4,200 ... E 5
46060 Noblesville⊙, 7,548 ... F 4
46366 North Judson, 1,738 ... D 2
46554 North Liberty, 1,259 ... E 1
46962 North Manchester, 5,791 ... F 3
46165 North Salem, 601 ... D 5
47805 North Terre Haute, 1,400 ... C 5
47265 North Vernon, 4,582 ... F 6
46555 North Webster, 456 ... F 2
† 47960 Norway, 250 ... D 3
46556 Notre Dame, 8,400 ... E 1
† 47331 Nulltown, 250 ... G 5
46965 Oakford, 300 ... E 4
47560 Oakland City, 3,289 ... C 8
47561 Oaktown, 726 ... C 7
47367 Oakville, 250 ... G 4
47562 Odon, 1,433 ... C 7
† 46401 Ogden Dunes, 1,361 ... C 1
47036 Oldenburg, 758 ... G 6
47451 Oolitic, 1,155 ... E 7
† 47343 Orange, 200 ... G 5
46063 Orestes, 519 ... F 4
46776 Orland, 457 ... G 1
47452 Orleans, 1,834 ... D 7
46561 Osceola, 1,572 ... E 1
47037 Osgood, 1,346 ... G 6
46777 Ossian, 1,538 ... G 3
46367 Otis, 300 ... D 1
47163 Otisco, 375 ... F 7
47970 Otterbein, 899 ... C 4
47564 Otwell, 850 ... C 8
47453 Owensburg, 700 ... D 7
47565 Owensville, 1,056 ... B 8
47971 Oxford, 1,098 ... C 3
† 46508 Palestine, 200 ... F 2
47164 Palmyra, 483 ... E 8
47454 Paoli⊙, 3,281 ... E 7
46166 Paragon, 538 ... D 6
47368 Parker, 1,179 ... G 4
47566 Patoka, 529 ... B 8
47455 Patricksburg, 265 ... D 6
47038 Patriot, 216 ... H 7
47865 Paxton, 250 ... C 6
47165 Pekin, 950 ... E 7
46064 Pendleton, 2,243 ... F 5
47369 Pennville, 798 ... G 4
† 46011 Perkinsville, 300 ... F 4
47974 Perrysville, 510 ... C 4
47370 Pershing, 447 ... G 5
† 46975 Pershing, 425 ... E 2
46970 Peru⊙, 14,139 ... E 3
47567 Petersburg⊙, 2,697 ... C 7
46778 Petroleum, 200 ... G 3
46562 Pierceton, 1,175 ... F 2
47866 Pimento, 200 ... C 6
† 46350 Pine Lake, 1,954 ... D 1
47975 Pine Village, 291 ... C 4
46167 Pittsboro, 867 ... D 5
46168 Plainfield, 8,211 ... E 5
47568 Plainville, 538 ... C 7
46779 Pleasant Lake, 650 ... H 1
46563 Plymouth⊙, 7,661 ... E 2
47868 Poland, 300 ... C 6
46781 Poneto, 286 ... G 3
46368 Portage, 19,127 ... C 1
46304 Porter, 3,058 ... C 1
47371 Portland⊙, 7,115 ... H 4
47633 Poseyville, 1,035 ... B 8
† 46360 Pottawattamie Park, 374 ... C 1
47869 Prairie Creek, 225 ... C 6
47870 Prairieton, 400 ... B 6
† 46164 Princes Lakes, 597 ... E 6
47570 Princeton⊙, 7,431 ... B 8
46170 Putnamville, 200 ... D 5
47456 Quincy, 250 ... D 6
47573 Ragsdale, 200 ... C 7
46737 Ray, 200 ... H 1
† 47274 Reddington, 245 ... F 6
47373 Redkey, 1,667 ... G 4
46171 Reelsville, 210 ... D 5
47977 Remington, 1,127 ... C 3
47978 Rensselaer⊙, 4,688 ... C 3
47980 Reynolds, 641 ... D 3
47634 Richland, 650 ... C 9
47374 Richmond⊙, 43,999 ... H 5
47380 Ridgeville, 924 ... G 4
47871 Riley, 257 ... C 6
47040 Rising Sun⊙, 2,305 ... H 7
46172 Roachdale, 1,004 ... D 5
46974 Roann, 509 ... F 3
46783 Roanoke, 858 ... G 3
46975 Rochester⊙, 4,631 ... E 2
46977 Rockfield, 300 ... D 3
47635 Rockport⊙, 2,565 ... C 9
47872 Rockville⊙, 2,820 ... C 5
46371 Rolling Prairie, 2,500 ... D 1
47574 Rome, 1,354 ... D 9
46784 Rome City, 1,385 ... G 1
47981 Romney, 420 ... D 4
47874 Rosedale, 817 ... C 5
† 46601 Roseland, 895 ... E 1
46372 Roselawn, 200 ... C 2
46065 Rossville, 830 ... D 4
46978 Royal Center, 987 ... E 3
† 47302 Royerton, 411 ... G 4
46173 Rushville⊙, 6,686 ... G 5
46175 Russellville, 390 ... D 5
46975 Russiaville, 844 ... E 4
47575 Saint Anthony, 460 ... D 8
47875 Saint Bernice, 900 ... C 5
46785 Saint Joe, 564 ... H 2
46373 Saint John, 1,757 ... C 2
† 45030 Saint Leon, 435 ... H 6
47876 Saint Mary-of-the-Woods, 1,200 ... B 6
† 46556 Saint Marys, 1,600 ... E 1
47577 Saint Meinrad, 1,100 ... D 8
47272 Saint Paul, 785 ... F 6
† 47012 Saint Peter, 200 ... H 6
† 47620 Saint Philip, 400 ... B 9
† 47638 Saint Wendel, 250 ... B 8
47167 Salem⊙, 5,041 ... E 7
47578 Sandborn, 528 ... C 7
† 47401 Sanders, 200 ... E 6
46374 San Pierre, 300 ... D 2
47579 Santa Claus, 125 ... D 8
47382 Saratoga, 406 ... H 4
† 47283 Sardinia, 225 ... F 6
46375 Schererville, 3,663 ... C 2
46376 Schneider, 426 ... C 2
47273 Scipio, 250 ... F 6
47170 Scottsburg⊙, 4,791 ... F 7
47878 Seelyville, 1,195 ... C 6
47172 Sellersburg, 3,177 ... F 8
47383 Selma, 890 ... G 4
47274 Seymour, 13,352 ... F 7
46068 Sharpsville, 672 ... E 4
47879 Shelburn, 1,281 ... C 6
46377 Shelby, 400 ... C 2
46176 Shelbyville⊙, 15,094 ... F 6
47880 Shepardsville, 325 ... B 5
46069 Sheridan, 2,137 ... E 4
† 47338 Shideler, 275 ... G 4
46565 Shipshewana, 448 ... F 1
47384 Shirley, 958 ... F 5

Topography

0 40 80
MILES

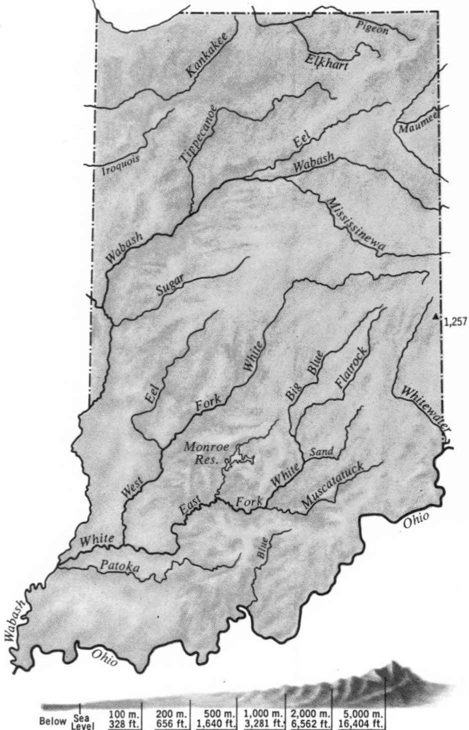

Agriculture, Industry and Resources

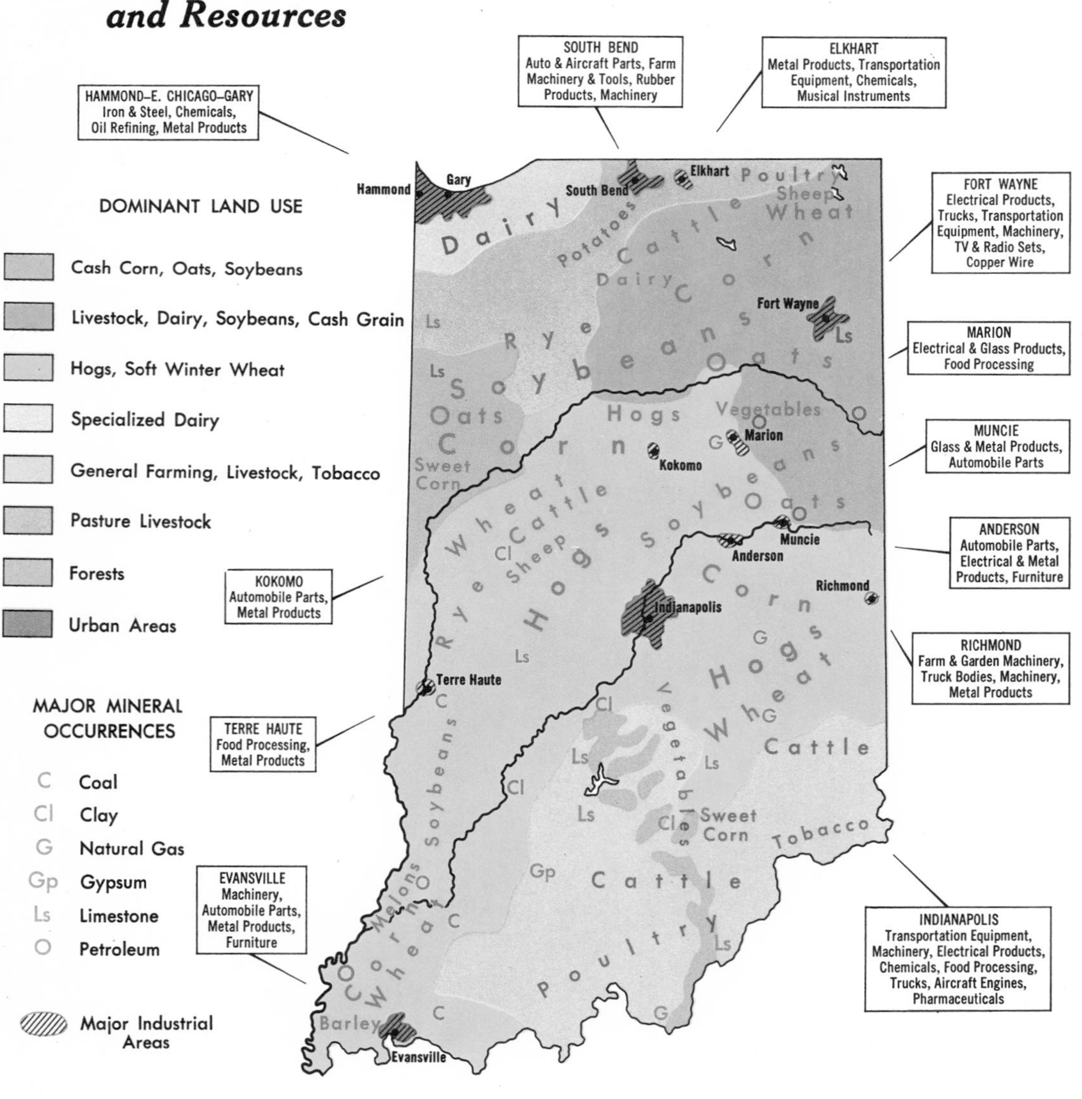

† 46797 Shirley City (Woodburn), 688 ... H 2
47581 Shoals⊙, 1,039 ... D 7
46982 Silver Lake, 588 ... F 2
46983 Sims, 250 ... F 3
† 46142 Smith Valley, 1,679 ... E 5
47458 Smithville, 350 ... D 6
46984 Somerset, 296 ... F 3
47583 Somerville, 313 ... C 8
* 46601 South Bend⊙, 125,580 ... E 1
South Bend, ‡280,031 ... E 1
46786 South Milford, 437 ... G 1
† 46201 Southport, 2,505 ... E 5
46787 South Whitley, 1,362 ... F 2
† 47355 Spartanburg, 201 ... H 4
47172 Speed, 800 ... F 8
46224 Speedway, 15,056 ... E 5
47460 Spencer⊙, 2,423 ... D 6
46788 Spencerville, 320 ... G 2
47385 Spiceland, 957 ... F 5
† 47374 Spring Grove, 437 ... H 5
† 46140 Spring Lake, 263 ... F 5
47386 Springport, 236 ... G 4
47462 Springville, 205 ... D 7
47584 Spurgeon, 285 ... C 8
47463 Stanford, 200 ... D 6
46985 Star City, 500 ... D 3
47881 Staunton, 582 ... C 6
47585 Stendal, 225 ... C 8
47636 Stewartsville, 275 ... B 8
46180 Stilesville, 352 ... D 5
46351 Stillwell, 225 ... D 1
47464 Stinesville, 291 ... D 6
47983 Stockwell, 500 ... D 4
47387 Straughn, 329 ... G 5
46789 Stroh, 600 ... G 1
47882 Sullivan⊙, 4,683 ... C 6
47388 Sulphur Springs, 387 ... G 4
46379 Sumava Resorts, 265 ... C 2
46070 Summitville, 1,104 ... F 4
47041 Sunman, 707 ... G 6
46986 Swayzee, 1,073 ... F 4
46987 Sweetser, 1,076 ... F 3
47465 Switz City, 301 ... C 6
46567 Syracuse, 1,546 ... F 2
47280 Taylorsville, 1,275 ... F 6
47586 Tell City, 7,933 ... D 9
47637 Tennyson, 335 ... C 8
* 47801 Terre Haute⊙, 70,286 ... C 6
Terre Haute, ‡175,143 ... C 6
46381 Thayer, 350 ... C 2
46071 Thorntown, 1,399 ... D 4
46570 Tippecanoe, 285 ... E 2
46072 Tipton⊙, 5,176 ... E 4
46571 Topeka, 677 ... F 1
† 46360 Town of Pines, 1,007 ... D 1
46181 Trafalgar, 457 ... E 6
† 46360 Trail Creek, 2,697 ... D 1
† 46725 Tri Lakes, 1,193 ... G 2
47588 Troy, 575 ... D 9
46988 Twelve Mile, 225 ... E 3
47177 Underwood, 550 ... F 7
47390 Union City, 3,995 ... H 4
46791 Uniondale, 349 ... G 3
46382 Union Mills, 350 ... D 2
47468 Unionville, 250 ... E 6
47884 Universal, 462 ... C 5
46989 Upland, 3,202 ... F 4
46990 Urbana, 400 ... F 3
† 47130 Utica, 300 ... F 8
47281 Vallonia, 600 ... E 7
46383 Valparaiso⊙, 20,020 ... C 2
46991 Van Buren, 1,057 ... F 3
47987 Veedersburg, 1,837 ... C 4
47282 Vernon⊙, 440 ... F 7
47042 Versailles⊙, 1,020 ... G 6
47043 Vevay⊙, 1,463 ... G 7
47591 Vincennes⊙, 19,867 ... C 7
46992 Wabash⊙, 13,379 ... F 3
47638 Wadesville, 300 ... B 8
46573 Wakarusa, 1,160 ... F 1
46182 Waldron, 800 ... F 6
† 47201 Walesboro, 214 ... F 6
46574 Walkerton, 2,006 ... E 2
† 46802 Wallen, 945 ... G 2
46994 Walton, 1,054 ... E 3
46390 Wanatah, 773 ... D 2
46792 Warren, 1,229 ... G 3
46580 Warsaw⊙, 7,506 ... F 2
47501 Washington⊙, 11,358 ... C 7
46793 Waterloo, 1,876 ... G 2
47989 Waveland, 557 ... D 5
† 46151 Waverly, 225 ... E 5
46794 Wawaka, 293 ... F 2
47990 Waynetown, 993 ... C 4
47392 Webster, 300 ... H 5
47469 West Baden Springs, 930 ... D 7
† 47353 West College Corner, 709 ... H 5
46074 Westfield, 1,837 ... E 4
† 45030 West Harrison, 395 ... H 6
47906 West Lafayette, 19,157 ... D 4
47991 West Lebanon, 899 ... C 4
46995 West Middleton, 450 ... E 4
47596 Westphalia, 300 ... C 7
47992 Westpoint, 300 ... C 4
47283 Westport, 1,170 ... F 6
47885 West Terre Haute, 2,704 ... B 6
46391 Westville, 2,614 ... D 1
46392 Wheatfield, 713 ... C 2
47597 Wheatland, 562 ... C 7
46393 Wheeler, 550 ... C 1
46184 Whiteland, 1,492 ... E 5
46075 Whitestown, 569 ... E 5
46394 Whiting, 7,247 ... C 1
46186 Wilkinson, 480 ... F 5
47470 Williams, 350 ... D 7
47993 Williamsport⊙, 1,661 ... C 4
46996 Winamac⊙, 2,341 ... D 2
47394 Winchester⊙, 5,493 ... G 4
46076 Windfall, 946 ... F 4
47994 Wingate, 437 ... C 4
46590 Winona Lake, 2,811 ... F 2
47598 Winslow, 1,030 ... C 8
47995 Wolcott, 894 ... C 3
46795 Wolcottville, 915 ... G 1
46796 Wolflake, 333 ... F 2
46797 Woodburn, 688 ... H 2
† 46624 Woodland, 400 ... E 1
47471 Worthington, 1,691 ... C 6
47179 Wyandotte, 26 ... E 8
46595 Wyatt, 305 ... E 1
† 47630 Yankeetown, 250 ... C 9
46798 Yoder, 250 ... G 3
47396 Yorktown, 1,673 ... G 4
46998 Young America, 250 ... E 3
† 47808 Youngstown, 350 ... C 6
46799 Zanesville, 350 ... G 3
46077 Zionsville, 1,857 ... E 5

⊙ County seat.
‡ Population of metropolitan area.
† Zip of nearest p.o.
* Multiple zips

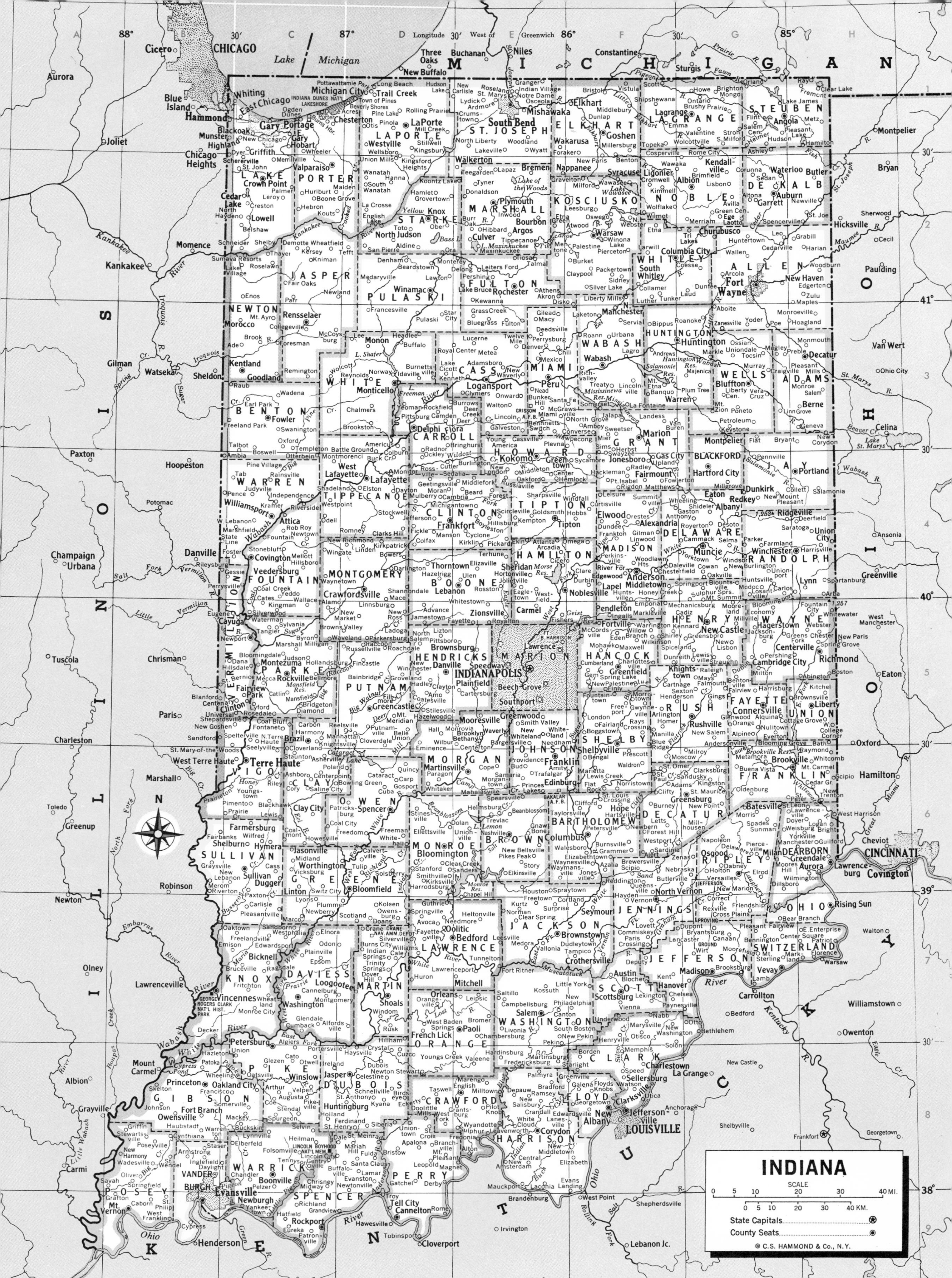

INDIANA
SCALE
0 5 10 20 30 40 MI.
0 5 10 20 30 40 KM.
State Capitals
County Seats
© C.S. HAMMOND & Co., N.Y.
Longitude 30′ West of Greenwich 86°
88°
87°
85°
41°
40°
39°
38°
MICHIGAN
ILLINOIS
OHIO
KENTUCKY
Lake Michigan
CHICAGO
CINCINNATI
LOUISVILLE
INDIANAPOLIS
LAKE
PORTER
LAPORTE
ST. JOSEPH
ELKHART
LAGRANGE
STEUBEN
DE KALB
NOBLE
KOSCIUSKO
MARSHALL
STARKE
JASPER
NEWTON
PULASKI
FULTON
WHITLEY
ALLEN
WABASH
HUNTINGTON
WELLS
ADAMS
MIAMI
CASS
WHITE
BENTON
CARROLL
HOWARD
GRANT
BLACKFORD
JAY
WARREN
TIPPECANOE
CLINTON
TIPTON
MADISON
DELAWARE
RANDOLPH
FOUNTAIN
MONTGOMERY
BOONE
HAMILTON
HENRY
WAYNE
VERMILLION
PARKE
PUTNAM
HENDRICKS
MARION
HANCOCK
RUSH
FAYETTE
UNION
VIGO
CLAY
MORGAN
JOHNSON
SHELBY
DECATUR
FRANKLIN
OWEN
MONROE
BROWN
BARTHOLOMEW
SULLIVAN
GREENE
JENNINGS
RIPLEY
DEARBORN
OHIO
SWITZERLAND
JACKSON
JEFFERSON
KNOX
DAVIESS
MARTIN
LAWRENCE
SCOTT
WASHINGTON
ORANGE
CLARK
FLOYD
PIKE
DUBOIS
CRAWFORD
HARRISON
GIBSON
WARRICK
SPENCER
PERRY
POSEY
VANDERBURGH
South Bend
Fort Wayne
Terre Haute
Evansville
Gary
Hammond
Muncie
Kokomo
Lafayette
Anderson
Richmond
Bloomington

COUNTIES

Adair, 9,487 .... E 6
Adams, 6,322 .... D 6
Allamakee, 14,968 .... L 2
Appanoose, 15,007 .... H 7
Audubon, 9,595 .... D 5
Benton, 22,885 .... J 4
Black Hawk, 132,916 .... J 4
Boone, 26,470 .... F 5
Bremer, 22,737 .... J 3
Buchanan, 21,746 .... K 4
Buena Vista, 20,693 .... C 3
Butler, 16,953 .... H 3
Calhoun, 14,287 .... D 4
Carroll, 22,912 .... D 4
Cass, 17,007 .... D 6
Cedar, 17,655 .... L 5
Cerro Gordo, 49,335 .... G 2
Cherokee, 17,269 .... B 3
Chickasaw, 14,969 .... J 2
Clarke, 7,581 .... F 6
Clay, 18,464 .... C 2
Clayton, 20,606 .... L 3
Clinton, 56,749 .... M 5
Crawford, 18,780 .... C 4
Dallas, 26,085 .... E 5
Davis, 8,207 .... J 7
Decatur, 9,737 .... F 7
Delaware, 18,770 .... L 4
Des Moines, 46,982 .... L 7
Dickinson, 12,565 .... C 2
Dubuque, 90,609 .... M 4
Emmet, 14,009 .... D 2
Fayette, 26,898 .... K 3
Floyd, 19,860 .... H 2
Franklin, 13,255 .... G 3
Fremont, 9,282 .... B 7
Greene, 12,716 .... E 5
Grundy, 14,119 .... H 4
Guthrie, 12,243 .... D 5
Hamilton, 18,383 .... F 4
Hancock, 13,227 .... F 2
Hardin, 22,248 .... G 4
Harrison, 16,240 .... B 5
Henry, 18,114 .... K 6
Howard, 11,442 .... J 2
Humboldt, 12,519 .... E 3
Ida, 9,190 .... C 4
Iowa, 15,419 .... J 5
Jackson, 20,839 .... M 4
Jasper, 35,425 .... G 5
Jefferson, 15,774 .... K 6
Johnson, 72,127 .... K 5
Jones, 19,868 .... L 4
Keokuk, 13,943 .... J 6
Kossuth, 22,937 .... E 2
Lee, 42,996 .... L 7
Linn, 163,213 .... K 4
Louisa, 10,682 .... L 6
Lucas, 10,163 .... G 6
Lyon, 13,340 .... A 2
Madison, 11,558 .... E 6
Mahaska, 22,177 .... H 6
Marion, 26,352 .... G 6
Marshall, 41,076 .... G 4
Mills, 11,606 .... B 6
Mitchell, 13,108 .... H 2
Monona, 12,069 .... B 4
Monroe, 9,357 .... H 7
Montgomery, 12,781 .... C 6
Muscatine, 37,181 .... L 5
O'Brien, 17,522 .... B 2
Osceola, 8,555 .... B 2
Page, 18,507 .... C 7
Palo Alto, 13,289 .... D 2
Plymouth, 24,312 .... A 3
Pocahontas, 12,729 .... D 3
Polk, 286,101 .... F 5
Pottawattamie, 86,991 .... B 6
Poweshiek, 18,803 .... H 5
Ringgold, 6,373 .... E 7
Sac, 15,573 .... C 4
Scott, 142,687 .... M 5
Shelby, 15,528 .... C 5
Sioux, 27,996 .... A 2
Story, 62,783 .... G 4
Tama, 20,147 .... H 4
Taylor, 8,790 .... D 7
Union, 13,557 .... E 7
Van Buren, 8,643 .... K 7
Wapello, 42,149 .... J 6
Warren, 27,432 .... F 6
Washington, 18,967 .... K 6
Wayne, 8,405 .... G 7
Webster, 48,391 .... E 4
Winnebago, 12,990 .... F 2
Winneshiek, 21,758 .... K 2
Woodbury, 103,052 .... B 4
Worth, 8,968 .... G 2
Wright, 17,294 .... F 3

CITIES and TOWNS

Zip	Name/Pop.	Key
50601	Ackley, 1,794	G 3
50002	Adair, 750	D 6
50003	Adel⊙, 2,419	E 5
50830	Afton, 823	E 6
52530	Agency, 610	J 7
52201	Ainsworth, 455	K 6
51001	Akron, 1,324	A 3
50510	Albert City, 683	C 3
52531	Albia⊙, 4,151	H 6
50005	Albion, 772	H 4
52202	Alburnett, 418	K 4
50006	Alden, 876	G 4
50420	Alexander, 249	G 3
50511	Algona⊙, 6,032	E 2
50008	Allerton, 643	G 7
50602	Allison⊙, 1,071	H 3
51002	Alta, 1,717	C 3
50603	Alta Vista, 283	J 2
51003	Alton, 1,018	A 3
50009	Altoona, 2,854	G 5
52203	Amana, 610	K 5
50010	Ames, 39,505	F 4
52205	Anamosa⊙, 4,389	L 4
52030	Andrew, 335	M 4
50020	Anita, 1,101	D 6
50021	Ankeny, 9,151	F 5
51004	Anthon, 711	B 4
50604	Aplington, 936	H 3
51430	Arcadia, 414	C 4
50606	Arlington, 481	K 3
50514	Armstrong, 1,061	D 2
51331	Arnolds Park, 970	C 2
51431	Arthur, 273	C 4
† 52001	Asbury, 410	M 4
51232	Ashton, 483	B 2
52720	Atalissa, 244	L 5
52206	Atkins, 581	K 4
50022	Atlantic⊙, 7,306	D 6
51433	Auburn, 329	D 4
50025	Audubon⊙, 2,907	D 5
51005	Aurelia, 1,065	C 3
50607	Aurora, 229	K 3
51521	Avoca, 1,535	C 6
50515	Ayrshire, 243	D 2
50516	Badger, 465	E 3
50026	Bagley, 365	E 5
50517	Bancroft, 1,103	E 2
50027	Barnes City, 238	H 6
52533	Batavia, 525	J 7
51006	Battle Creek, 837	B 4
50028	Baxter, 788	G 5
50029	Bayard, 628	D 5
52534	Beacon, 338	H 6
50609	Beaman, 222	H 4
50833	Bedford⊙, 1,733	D 7
52208	Belle Plaine, 2,810	J 5
52031	Bellevue, 2,336	M 4

50421 Belmond, 2,358 F 3
52721 Bennett, 385 L 5
52722 Bettendorf, 22,126 N 5
52535 Birmingham, 452 K 7
50034 Blairsburg, 287 F 4
52209 Blairstown, 612 J 5
52536 Blakesburg, 403 H 7
51523 Blencoe, 255 A 5
50836 Blockton, 273 D 7
52537 Bloomfield⊙, 2,718 J 7
52726 Blue Grass, 1,032 M 5
50519 Bode, 372 E 3
52620 Bonaparte, 517 K 7
50035 Bondurant, 462 G 5
50036 Boone⊙, 12,468 F 4
50040 Boxholm, 242 E 4
51234 Boyden, 670 B 2
52210 Brandon, 432 K 4
51436 Breda, 518 C 4
52540 Brighton, 632 K 6
50611 Bristow, 230 H 3
50423 Britt, 2,069 F 2
52211 Brooklyn, 1,410 J 5
52728 Buffalo, 1,513 M 6
50424 Buffalo Center, 1,118 F 2
52601 Burlington⊙, 32,366 L 7
50522 Burt, 608 E 2
50044 Bussey, 498 H 6
52729 Calamus, 396 M 5
50523 Callender, 421 E 4
52132 Calmar, 1,941 K 2
51009 Calumet, 219 B 3
52730 Camanche, 3,470 N 5
50046 Cambridge, 661 G 5
52542 Cantril, 258 J 7
50047 Carlisle, 2,246 G 6
51401 Carroll⊙, 8,716 D 4
51525 Carson, 756 C 6
† 68101 Carter Lake, 3,268 B 6
52033 Cascade, 1,744 L 4
50048 Casey, 561 D 5
52133 Castalia, 210 K 2
51010 Castana, 211 B 4
50613 Cedar Falls, 29,597 H 3
* 52401 Cedar Rapids⊙, 110,642 K 5
Cedar Rapids, ‡163,213 K 5
52213 Center Point, 1,456 K 4
52544 Centerville⊙, 6,531 H 7
52214 Central City, 1,116 K 4
50049 Chariton⊙, 5,009 G 6
50616 Charles City⊙, 9,268 H 2
52731 Charlotte, 444 M 5
51439 Charter Oak, 715 C 4
52215 Chelsea, 381 J 5
51012 Cherokee⊙, 7,272 B 3
50050 Churdan, 598 D 4
52549 Cincinnati, 570 G 7
50524 Clare, 249 E 3
52216 Clarence, 915 M 5
51632 Clarinda⊙, 5,420 C 7
50525 Clarion⊙, 2,972 F 3
50619 Clarksville, 1,360 H 3
50840 Clearfield, 430 D 7
50428 Clear Lake, 6,430 G 2
51014 Cleghorn, 274 B 3
52135 Clermont, 582 K 3
52732 Clinton⊙, 34,719 N 5
50053 Clive, 3,005 F 5
52217 Clutier, 275 J 4
† 50501 Coalville, 275 E 4
52218 Coggon, 656 L 4
51636 Coin, 294 C 7
52035 Colesburg, 379 L 3
50054 Colfax, 2,293 G 5
51637 College Springs, 295 C 7
50055 Collins, 404 G 5
50056 Colo, 606 G 4
52737 Columbus City, 312 L 6
52738 Columbus Junction, 1,205 L 6
52739 Conesville, 295 L 6
50631 Conrad, 932 H 4

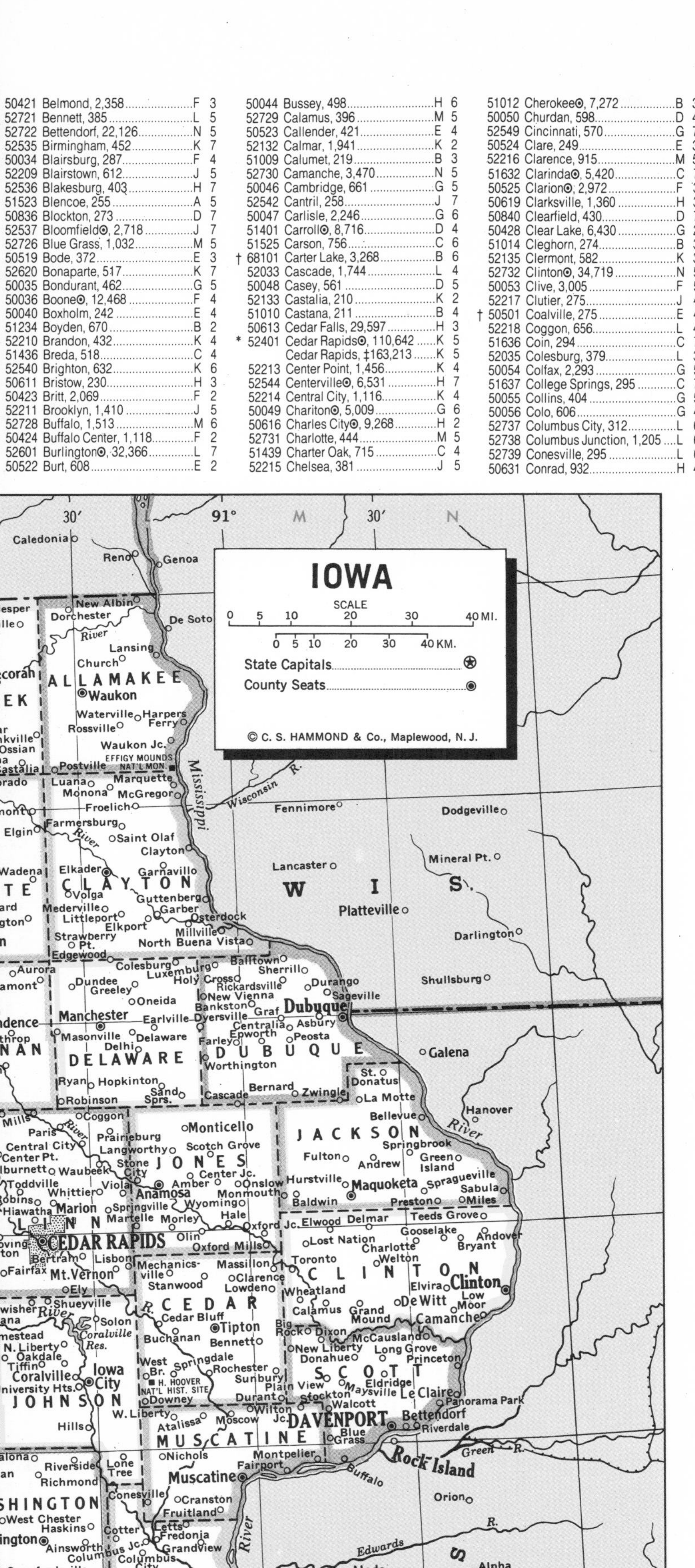

AREA 56,290 sq. mi.
POPULATION 2,825,041
CAPITAL Des Moines
LARGEST CITY Des Moines
HIGHEST POINT Ocheyedan Mound 1,675 ft.
SETTLED IN 1788
ADMITTED TO UNION December 28, 1846
POPULAR NAME Hawkeye State
STATE FLOWER Wild Rose
STATE BIRD Eastern Goldfinch

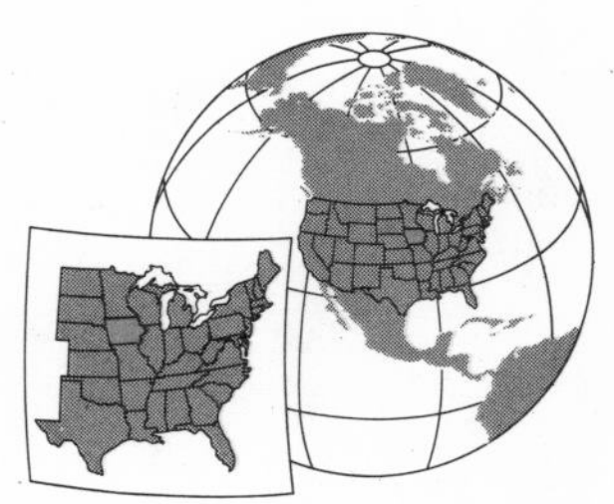

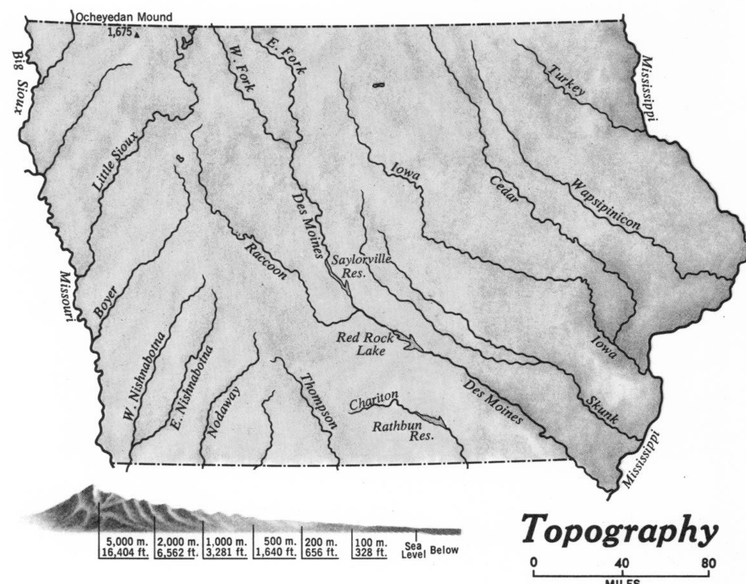

Topography

0 40 80 MILES

50058 Coon Rapids, 1,381 D 5
52240 Coralville, 6,130 K 5
50841 Corning⊙, 2,095 D 7
51016 Correctionville, 870 B 4
50430 Corwith, 407 F 3
50060 Corydon⊙, 1,745 G 7
50431 Coulter, 262 G 3
51501 Council Bluffs⊙, 60,348 B 6
52621 Crawfordsville, 288 K 6
51526 Crescent, 284 B 6
52136 Cresco⊙, 3,927 J 2
50801 Creston⊙, 8,234 E 6
50432 Crystal Lake, 276 F 2
50843 Cumberland, 385 D 6
50529 Dakota City⊙, 746 E 3
50062 Dallas, 438 G 6
50063 Dallas Center, 1,128 E 5
51019 Danbury, 527 B 4
52623 Danville, 948 L 7
* 52801 Davenport⊙, 98,469 M 5
Davenport-Rock Island-Moline, ‡362,638 M 5
50065 Davis City, 301 F 7
50066 Dawson, 232 E 5
50530 Dayton, 909 E 4
52101 Decorah⊙, 7,458 K 2
51440 Dedham, 325 D 5
52222 Deep River, 323 J 5
51527 Defiance, 392 C 5
52223 Delhi, 527 L 4
52037 Delmar, 599 M 4
51441 Deloit, 279 C 4
52550 Delta, 475 J 6
51442 Denison⊙, 5,882 C 4
52624 Denmark, 375 L 7
50622 Denver, 1,169 J 3
* 50301 Des Moines (cap.)⊙, 200,587 G 5
Des Moines, ‡286,101 G 5
50069 De Soto, 369 E 5
52742 De Witt, 3,647 N 5
50070 Dexter, 652 E 5
50845 Diagonal, 327 E 7
51333 Dickens, 240 C 2
50624 Dike, 794 H 4
52745 Dixon, 276 M 5
52746 Donahue, 216 M 5
52625 Donnellson, 798 K 7
51235 Doon, 437 A 2
52551 Douds, 247 J 7
51528 Dow City, 571 B 5
50071 Dows, 777 F 3
52001 Dubuque⊙, 62,309 M 3
Dubuque, ‡90,609 M 3
50625 Dumont, 724 H 3
50532 Duncombe, 418 E 4
50626 Dunkerton, 563 J 3
51529 Dunlap, 1,292 B 5
52747 Durant, 1,472 M 5
52040 Dyersville, 3,437 L 3
52224 Dysart, 1,251 J 4
50533 Eagle Grove, 4,489 F 3
50072 Earlham, 974 E 6
51530 Earling, 573 C 5
52041 Earlville, 751 L 4
50535 Early, 727 C 4
52553 Eddyville, 945 H 6
52042 Edgewood, 786 K 3
52554 Eldon, 1,319 J 7
50627 Eldora⊙, 3,223 G 4
52748 Eldridge, 1,535 M 5
52141 Elgin, 613 K 3
52043 Elkader⊙, 1,592 L 3
50073 Elkhart, 269 F 5
51531 Elk Horn, 667 C 5
† 50700 Elk Run Heights, 1,175 J 4
51532 Elliott, 423 C 6
50075 Ellsworth, 443 F 4
50628 Elma, 601 J 2
52227 Ely, 275 K 5
51533 Emerson, 484 C 6
50536 Emmetsburg⊙, 4,150 D 2
52045 Epworth, 1,132 M 4
51638 Essex, 770 C 7
51334 Estherville⊙, 8,108 D 2
50707 Evansdale, 5,038 J 4
51338 Everly, 699 C 2
50076 Exira, 966 D 5
52555 Exline, 224 H 7
50629 Fairbank, 810 K 3
52228 Fairfax, 635 K 5
52556 Fairfield⊙, 8,715 J 6
52046 Farley, 1,096 L 4
52047 Farmersburg, 232 L 3
52626 Farmington, 800 K 7
50538 Farnhamville, 393 D 4
51639 Farragut, 521 C 7
52142 Fayette, 1,947 K 3
50539 Fenton, 403 E 2
50434 Fertile, 394 G 2
50435 Floyd, 380 H 2
50540 Fonda, 980 D 3
50846 Fontanelle, 752 E 6
50436 Forest City⊙, 3,841 F 2
52144 Fort Atkinson, 339 J 2
50501 Fort Dodge⊙, 31,263 E 3
52627 Fort Madison⊙, 13,996 L 7
51340 Fostoria, 219 C 2
50630 Fredericksburg, 912 J 3
52561 Fremont, 480 H 6
51020 Galva, 319 C 3
50103 Garden Grove, 285 F 7
52049 Garnavillo, 634 L 3
50438 Garner⊙, 2,217 F 2
52229 Garrison, 383 J 4
50632 Garwin, 563 H 4
51237 George, 1,194 B 2
50105 Gilbert, 521 F 4
50634 Gilbertville, 655 J 4
50106 Gilman, 513 H 5
50541 Gilmore City, 766 D 3
50635 Gladbrook, 961 H 4
51534 Glenwood⊙, 4,195 B 6
51443 Glidden, 964 D 4
50542 Goldfield, 722 F 3
50439 Goodell, 218 F 3
52750 Gooselake, 218 N 5
50543 Gowrie, 1,225 E 4
51342 Graettinger, 907 D 2
50440 Grafton, 254 G 2
50107 Grand Junction, 967 E 4
52751 Grand Mound, 627 M 5
50108 Grand River, 211 F 7
52752 Grandview, 357 L 6
50109 Granger, 661 F 5
51022 Granville, 383 B 3
50848 Gravity, 286 D 7
52050 Greeley, 323 L 3
50636 Greene, 1,363 H 3
50849 Greenfield⊙, 2,212 D 6
50111 Grimes, 834 F 5
50112 Grinnell, 8,402 H 5
51535 Griswold, 1,181 C 6
50638 Grundy Center⊙, 2,712 H 4
50115 Guthrie Center⊙, 1,834 D 5
52052 Guttenberg, 2,177 L 3
51444 Halbur, 235 D 4
51640 Hamburg, 1,649 B 7
50441 Hampton⊙, 4,376 G 3
51536 Hancock, 228 C 6
50544 Harcourt, 305 E 4
51537 Harlan⊙, 5,049 C 5
52146 Harpers Ferry, 227 L 2
50118 Hartford, 582 G 6
51346 Hartley, 1,694 C 2
50119 Harvey, 217 H 6
51540 Hastings, 229 C 6
50546 Havelock, 220 D 3
51023 Hawarden, 2,789 A 2
52147 Hawkeye, 529 J 3
50641 Hazleton, 626 K 3
52563 Hedrick, 790 J 6
51541 Henderson, 211 B 6
52233 Hiawatha, 2,416 K 4
52235 Hills, 507 K 5
52630 Hillsboro, 252 K 7
51024 Hinton, 488 A 3
50642 Holland, 258 H 4
51025 Holstein, 1,445 B 4
52053 Holy Cross, 290 L 3
52237 Hopkinton, 800 L 4
51026 Hornick, 250 A 4
51238 Hospers, 646 B 2
50122 Hubbard, 846 G 4
50643 Hudson, 1,535 H 4
51239 Hull, 1,523 A 2
50548 Humboldt, 4,665 E 3
50123 Humeston, 673 G 7
50124 Huxley, 937 F 5
51445 Ida Grove⊙, 2,261 B 4
50644 Independence⊙, 5,910 K 4
50125 Indianola⊙, 8,852 F 6
51240 Inwood, 644 A 2
50645 Ionia, 270 J 2
52240 Iowa City⊙, 46,850 L 5
50126 Iowa Falls, 6,454 G 3
51027 Ireton, 582 A 3
51446 Irwin, 446 C 5
50128 Jamaica, 271 E 5
50647 Janesville, 741 J 3
50129 Jefferson⊙, 4,735 E 4
50648 Jesup, 1,662 J 4
50130 Jewell, 1,152 F 4
50131 Johnston, 222 F 5
52247 Kalona, 1,488 K 6
50132 Kamrar, 243 F 4
50447 Kanawha, 705 F 3
50133 Kellerton, 299 E 7

(continued on following page)

(continued)

Agriculture, Industry and Resources

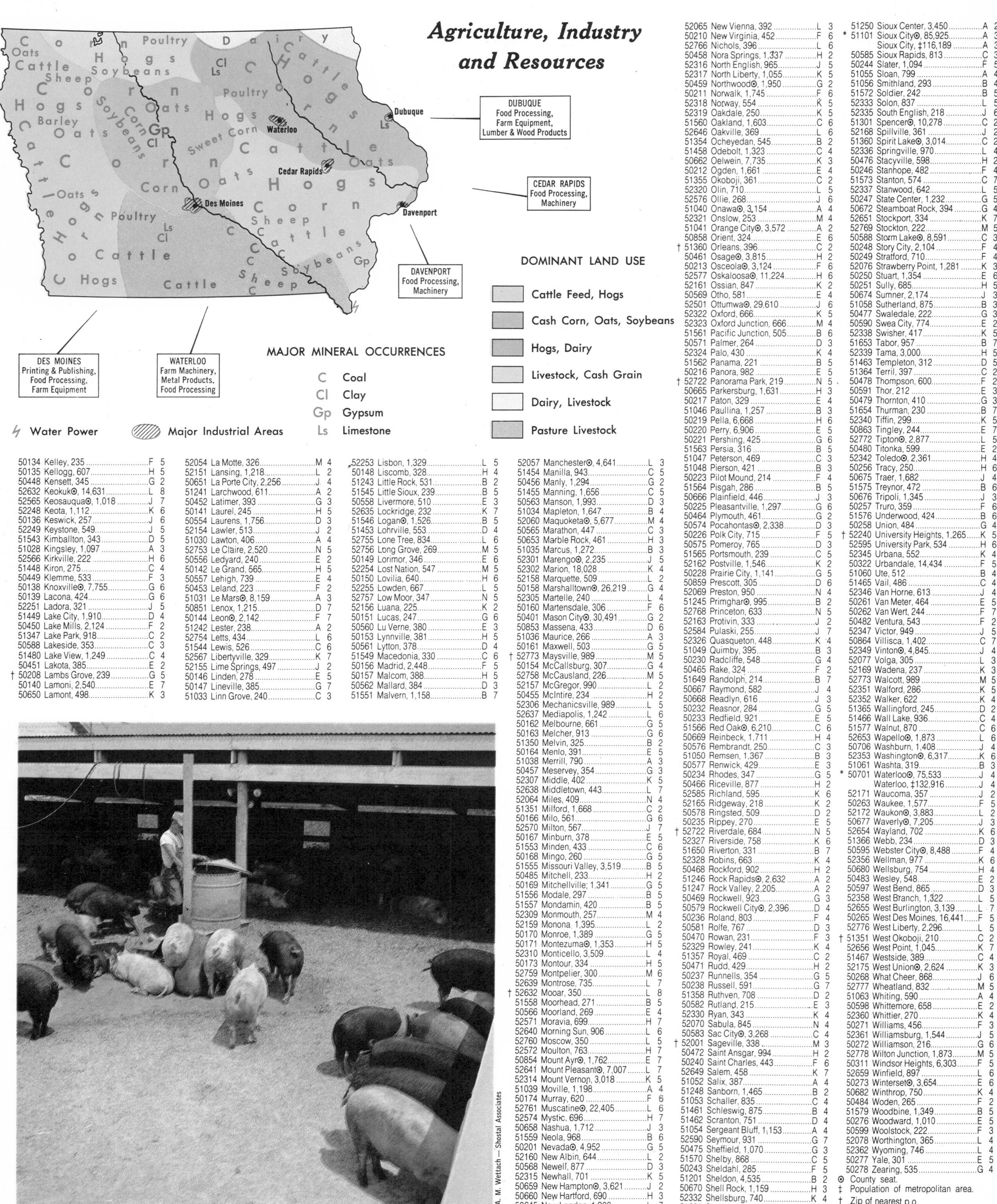

This Iowa farmer confines his hogs to concrete pens as a more efficient and sanitary method of raising healthy animals for market. Iowa's record-breaking hog production is due largely to the availability of corn for fodder.

50134 Kelley, 235 F 5
50135 Kellogg, 607 H 5
50448 Kensett, 345 G 2
52632 Keokuk⊙, 14,631 L 8
52565 Keosauqua⊙, 1,018 J 7
52248 Keota, 1,112 K 6
50136 Keswick, 257 J 6
52249 Keystone, 549 J 5
51543 Kimballton, 343 D 5
51028 Kingsley, 1,097 A 3
52566 Kirkville, 222 H 6
51448 Kiron, 275 C 4
50449 Klemme, 533 F 3
50138 Knoxville⊙, 7,755 G 6
50139 Lacona, 424 G 6
52251 Ladora, 321 J 5
51449 Lake City, 1,910 D 4
50450 Lake Mills, 2,124 F 2
51347 Lake Park, 918 C 2
50588 Lakeside, 353 C 3
51480 Lake View, 1,249 C 4
50451 Lakota, 385 E 2
† 50208 Lambs Grove, 239 G 5
50140 Lamoni, 2,540 E 7
50650 Lamont, 498 K 3
52054 La Motte, 326 M 4
52151 Lansing, 1,218 L 2
50651 La Porte City, 2,256 J 4
51241 Larchwood, 611 A 2
50452 Latimer, 393 G 3
50141 Laurel, 245 H 5
50554 Laurens, 1,756 D 3
52154 Lawler, 513 J 2
51030 Lawton, 406 A 4
52753 Le Claire, 2,520 N 5
50556 Ledyard, 240 E 2
50142 Le Grand, 565 H 5
50557 Lehigh, 739 E 4
50453 Leland, 223 F 2
51031 Le Mars⊙, 8,159 A 3
50851 Lenox, 1,215 D 7
50144 Leon⊙, 2,142 F 7
51242 Lester, 238 A 2
52754 Letts, 434 L 6
51544 Lewis, 526 C 6
52567 Libertyville, 329 K 7
52155 Lime Springs, 497 J 2
50146 Linden, 278 E 5
50147 Lineville, 385 G 7
51033 Linn Grove, 240 C 3
52253 Lisbon, 1,329 L 5
50148 Liscomb, 328 H 4
51243 Little Rock, 531 B 2
51545 Little Sioux, 239 B 5
50558 Livermore, 510 E 3
52635 Lockridge, 232 K 7
51546 Logan⊙, 1,526 B 5
51453 Lohrville, 553 D 4
52755 Lone Tree, 834 L 6
52756 Long Grove, 269 M 5
50149 Lorimor, 346 E 6
52254 Lost Nation, 547 M 5
50150 Lovilia, 640 H 6
52255 Lowden, 667 L 5
52757 Low Moor, 347 N 5
52156 Luana, 225 K 2
50151 Lucas, 247 G 6
50560 Lu Verne, 380 E 3
50153 Lynnville, 381 H 5
50561 Lytton, 378 D 4
51549 Macedonia, 330 C 6
50156 Madrid, 2,448 F 5
50157 Malcom, 388 H 5
50562 Mallard, 384 D 3
51551 Malvern, 1,158 B 7
52057 Manchester⊙, 4,641 L 3
51454 Manilla, 943 C 5
50456 Manly, 1,294 G 2
51455 Manning, 1,656 C 5
50563 Manson, 1,993 D 3
51034 Mapleton, 1,647 B 4
52060 Maquoketa⊙, 5,677 M 4
50565 Marathon, 447 C 3
50653 Marble Rock, 461 H 3
51035 Marcus, 1,272 B 3
52301 Marengo⊙, 2,235 J 5
52302 Marion, 18,028 K 4
52158 Marquette, 509 L 2
50158 Marshalltown⊙, 26,219 G 4
52305 Martelle, 240 L 4
50160 Martensdale, 306 F 6
50401 Mason City⊙, 30,491 G 2
50853 Massena, 433 D 6
51036 Maurice, 266 A 3
50161 Maxwell, 503 G 5
† 52773 Maysville, 989 M 5
50154 McCallsburg, 307 G 4
52758 McCausland, 226 M 5
52157 McGregor, 990 L 2
50455 McIntire, 234 H 2
52306 Mechanicsville, 989 L 5
52637 Mediapolis, 1,242 L 6
50162 Melbourne, 661 G 5
50163 Melcher, 913 G 6
51350 Melvin, 325 B 2
50164 Menlo, 391 E 5
51038 Merrill, 790 A 3
50457 Meservey, 354 G 3
52307 Middle, 402 K 5
52638 Middletown, 443 L 7
52064 Miles, 409 N 4
51351 Milford, 1,668 C 2
50166 Milo, 561 G 6
52570 Milton, 567 J 7
50167 Minburn, 378 E 5
51553 Minden, 433 C 6
50168 Mingo, 260 G 5
51555 Missouri Valley, 3,519 B 5
50485 Mitchell, 233 H 2
50169 Mitchellville; 1,341 G 5
51556 Modale, 297 B 5
51557 Mondamin, 420 B 5
52309 Monmouth, 257 M 4
52159 Monona, 1,395 L 2
50170 Monroe, 1,389 G 5
50171 Montezuma⊙, 1,353 H 5
52310 Monticello, 3,509 L 4
50173 Montour, 334 H 5
52759 Montpelier, 300 M 6
52639 Montrose, 735 L 7
† 52632 Mooar, 350 L 8
51558 Moorhead, 271 B 5
50566 Moorland, 269 E 4
52571 Moravia, 699 H 7
52640 Morning Sun, 906 L 6
52760 Moscow, 350 L 5
52572 Moulton, 763 H 7
50854 Mount Ayr⊙, 1,762 E 7
52641 Mount Pleasant⊙, 7,007 L 7
52314 Mount Vernon, 3,018 K 5
51039 Moville, 1,198 A 4
50174 Murray, 620 F 6
52761 Muscatine⊙, 22,405 L 6
52574 Mystic, 696 H 7
50658 Nashua, 1,712 J 3
51559 Neola, 968 B 6
50201 Nevada⊙, 4,952 G 5
52160 New Albin, 644 L 2
50568 Newell, 877 D 3
52315 Newhall, 701 K 5
50659 New Hampton⊙, 3,621 J 2
50660 New Hartford, 690 H 3
52645 New London, 1,900 L 7
51646 New Market, 501 D 7
50206 New Providence, 208 G 4
50207 New Sharon, 944 H 6
50208 Newton⊙, 15,619 H 5
52065 New Vienna, 392 L 3
50210 New Virginia, 452 F 6
52766 Nichols, 396 L 6
50458 Nora Springs, 1,337 H 2
52316 North English, 965 J 5
52317 North Liberty, 1,055 K 5
50459 Northwood⊙, 1,950 G 2
50211 Norwalk, 1,745 F 6
52318 Norway, 554 K 5
52319 Oakdale, 250 K 5
51560 Oakland, 1,603 C 6
52646 Oakville, 369 L 6
51354 Ocheyedan, 545 B 2
51458 Odebolt, 1,323 C 4
50662 Oelwein, 7,735 K 3
50212 Ogden, 1,661 E 4
51355 Okoboji, 361 C 2
52320 Olin, 710 L 5
52576 Ollie, 268 J 6
51040 Onawa⊙, 3,154 A 4
52321 Onslow, 253 M 4
51041 Orange City⊙, 3,572 A 2
50858 Orient, 324 E 6
† 51360 Orleans, 396 C 2
50461 Osage⊙, 3,815 H 2
50213 Osceola⊙, 3,124 F 6
52577 Oskaloosa⊙, 11,224 H 6
52161 Ossian, 847 K 2
50569 Otho, 581 E 4
52501 Ottumwa⊙, 29,610 J 6
52322 Oxford, 666 K 5
52323 Oxford Junction, 666 M 4
51561 Pacific Junction, 505 B 6
50571 Palmer, 264 D 3
52324 Palo, 430 K 4
51562 Panama, 221 B 5
50216 Panora, 982 E 5
† 52722 Panorama Park, 219 N 5
50665 Parkersburg, 1,631 H 3
50217 Paton, 329 E 4
51046 Paullina, 1,257 B 3
50219 Pella, 6,668 H 6
50220 Perry, 6,906 E 5
50221 Pershing, 425 G 6
51563 Persia, 316 B 5
51047 Peterson, 469 C 3
51048 Pierson, 421 B 3
50223 Pilot Mound, 214 F 4
51564 Pisgah, 286 B 5
50666 Plainfield, 446 J 3
50225 Pleasantville, 1,297 G 6
50464 Plymouth, 461 G 2
50574 Pocahontas⊙, 2,338 D 3
50226 Polk City, 715 F 5
50575 Pomeroy, 765 D 3
51565 Portsmouth, 239 C 5
52162 Postville, 1,546 K 2
50228 Prairie City, 1,141 G 5
50859 Prescott, 305 D 6
52069 Preston, 950 N 4
51245 Primghar⊙, 995 B 2
52768 Princeton, 633 N 5
52163 Protivin, 333 J 2
52584 Pulaski, 255 J 7
52326 Quasqueton, 448 K 4
51049 Quimby, 395 B 3
50230 Radcliffe, 548 G 4
50465 Rake, 324 F 2
51649 Randolph, 214 B 7
50667 Raymond, 582 J 4
50668 Readlyn, 616 J 3
50232 Reasnor, 284 G 5
50233 Redfield, 921 E 5
51566 Red Oak⊙, 6,210 C 6
50669 Reinbeck, 1,711 H 4
50576 Rembrandt, 250 C 3
51050 Remsen, 1,367 B 3
50577 Renwick, 429 E 3
50234 Rhodes, 347 G 5
50466 Riceville, 877 H 2
52585 Richland, 595 K 6
52165 Ridgeway, 218 K 2
50578 Ringsted, 509 D 2
50235 Rippey, 270 E 5
† 52722 Riverdale, 684 N 5
52327 Riverside, 758 K 6
51650 Riverton, 331 B 7
52328 Robins, 663 K 4
50468 Rockford, 902 H 2
51246 Rock Rapids⊙, 2,632 A 2
51247 Rock Valley, 2,205 A 2
50469 Rockwell, 923 G 3
50579 Rockwell City⊙, 2,396 D 4
50236 Roland, 803 F 4
50581 Rolfe, 767 D 3
50470 Rowan, 231 F 3
52329 Rowley, 241 K 4
51357 Royal, 469 C 2
50471 Rudd, 429 H 2
50237 Runnells, 354 G 5
50238 Russell, 591 G 7
51358 Ruthven, 708 D 2
50582 Rutland, 215 E 3
52330 Ryan, 343 K 4
52070 Sabula, 845 N 4
50583 Sac City⊙, 3,268 C 4
† 52001 Sageville, 338 M 3
50472 Saint Ansgar, 994 H 2
50240 Saint Charles, 443 F 6
52649 Salem, 458 K 7
51052 Salix, 387 A 4
51248 Sanborn, 1,465 B 2
51053 Schaller, 835 C 4
51461 Schleswig, 875 B 4
51462 Scranton, 751 D 4
51054 Sergeant Bluff, 1,153 A 4
52590 Seymour, 931 G 7
50475 Sheffield, 1,070 G 3
51570 Shelby, 868 C 5
50243 Sheldahl, 285 F 5
51201 Sheldon, 4,535 B 2
50670 Shell Rock, 1,159 H 3
52332 Shellsburg, 740 K 4
51601 Shenandoah, 5,968 C 7
51249 Sibley⊙, 2,749 B 2
51652 Sidney⊙, 1,061 B 7
52591 Sigourney⊙, 2,319 J 6
51571 Silver City, 272 B 6
51250 Sioux Center, 3,450 A 2
* 51101 Sioux City⊙, 85,925 A 3
Sioux City, ‡116,189 A 3
50585 Sioux Rapids, 813 C 3
50244 Slater, 1,094 F 5
51055 Sloan, 799 A 4
51056 Smithland, 293 B 4
51572 Soldier, 242 B 5
52333 Solon, 837 L 5
52335 South English, 218 J 6
51301 Spencer⊙, 10,278 C 2
52168 Spillville, 361 J 2
51360 Spirit Lake⊙, 3,014 C 2
52336 Springville, 970 L 4
50476 Stacyville, 598 H 2
50246 Stanhope, 482 F 4
51573 Stanton, 574 C 7
52337 Stanwood, 642 L 5
50247 State Center, 1,232 G 5
50672 Steamboat Rock, 394 G 4
52651 Stockport, 334 K 7
52769 Stockton, 222 M 5
50588 Storm Lake⊙, 8,591 C 3
50248 Story City, 2,104 F 4
50249 Stratford, 710 F 4
52076 Strawberry Point, 1,281 K 3
50250 Stuart, 1,354 E 6
50251 Sully, 685 H 5
50674 Sumner, 2,174 J 3
51058 Sutherland, 875 B 3
50477 Swaledale, 222 G 3
50590 Swea City, 774 E 2
52338 Swisher, 417 K 5
51653 Tabor, 957 B 7
52339 Tama, 3,000 H 5
51463 Templeton, 312 D 5
51364 Terril, 397 C 2
50478 Thompson, 600 F 2
50591 Thor, 212 E 3
50479 Thornton, 410 G 3
51654 Thurman, 230 B 7
52340 Tiffin, 299 K 5
50863 Tingley, 244 E 7
52772 Tipton⊙, 2,877 L 5
50480 Titonka, 599 E 2
52342 Toledo⊙, 2,361 H 4
50256 Tracy, 250 H 6
50675 Traer, 1,682 J 4
51575 Treynor, 472 B 6
50676 Tripoli, 1,345 J 3
50257 Truro, 359 F 6
51576 Underwood, 424 B 6
50258 Union, 484 G 4
† 52240 University Heights, 1,265 K 5
52595 University Park, 534 H 6
52345 Urbana, 552 K 4
50322 Urbandale, 14,434 F 5
51060 Ute, 512 B 4
51465 Vail, 486 C 4
52346 Van Horne, 613 J 4
50261 Van Meter, 464 E 5
50262 Van Wert, 244 F 7
50482 Ventura, 543 F 2
52347 Victor, 949 J 5
50864 Villisca, 1,402 C 7
52349 Vinton⊙, 4,845 J 4
52077 Volga, 305 L 3
52169 Wadena, 237 K 3
52773 Walcott, 989 M 5
52351 Walford, 286 K 5
52352 Walker, 622 K 4
51365 Wallingford, 245 D 2
51466 Wall Lake, 936 C 4
51577 Walnut, 870 C 6
52653 Wapello⊙, 1,873 L 6
50706 Washburn, 1,408 J 4
52353 Washington⊙, 6,317 K 6
51061 Washta, 319 B 3
* 50701 Waterloo⊙, 75,533 J 4
Waterloo, ‡132,916 J 4
52171 Waucoma, 357 J 2
50263 Waukee, 1,577 F 5
52172 Waukon⊙, 3,883 L 2
50677 Waverly⊙, 7,205 J 3
52654 Wayland, 702 K 6
51366 Webb, 234 D 3
50595 Webster City⊙, 8,488 F 4
52356 Wellman, 977 K 6
50680 Wellsburg, 754 H 4
50483 Wesley, 548 E 2
50597 West Bend, 865 D 3
52358 West Branch, 1,322 L 5
52655 West Burlington, 3,139 L 7
50265 West Des Moines, 16,441 F 5
52776 West Liberty, 2,296 L 5
† 51351 West Okoboji, 210 C 2
52656 West Point, 1,045 K 7
51467 Westside, 389 C 4
52175 West Union⊙, 2,624 K 3
50268 What Cheer, 868 J 6
52777 Wheatland, 832 M 5
51063 Whiting, 590 A 4
50598 Whittemore, 658 E 2
52360 Whittier, 270 K 4
50271 Williams, 456 F 3
52361 Williamsburg, 1,544 J 5
50272 Williamson, 216 G 6
52778 Wilton Junction, 1,873 M 5
50311 Windsor Heights, 6,303 F 5
52659 Winfield, 897 L 6
50273 Winterset⊙, 3,654 E 6
50682 Winthrop, 750 K 4
50484 Woden, 265 F 2
51579 Woodbine, 1,349 B 5
50276 Woodward, 1,010 E 5
50599 Woolstock, 222 F 3
52078 Worthington, 365 L 4
52362 Wyoming, 746 L 4
50277 Yale, 301 E 5
50278 Zearing, 535 G 4

⊙ County seat.
‡ Population of metropolitan area.
† Zip of nearest p.o.
* Multiple zips

Agriculture, Industry and Resources

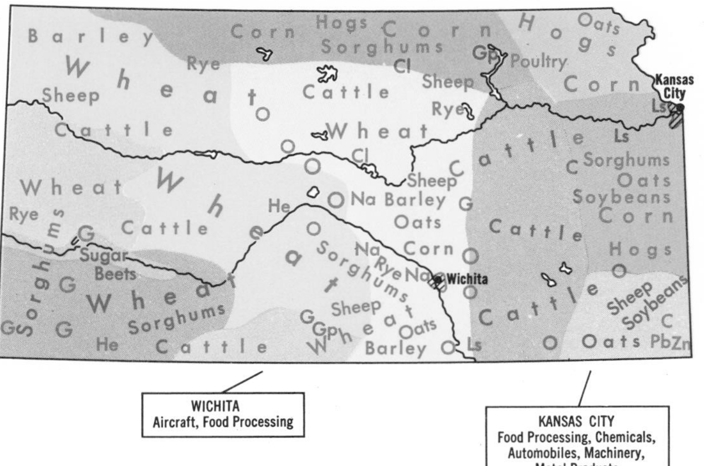

DOMINANT LAND USE

- Specialized Wheat
- Wheat, General Farming
- Wheat, Range Livestock
- Wheat, Grain Sorghums, Range Livestock
- Cattle Feed, Hogs
- Livestock, Cash Grain
- Livestock, Cash Grain, Dairy
- General Farming, Livestock, Cash Grain
- General Farming, Livestock, Special Crops
- Range Livestock

MAJOR MINERAL OCCURRENCES

C	Coal	Ls	Limestone
Cl	Clay	Na	Salt
G	Natural Gas	O	Petroleum
Gp	Gypsum	Pb	Lead
He	Helium	Zn	Zinc

Major Industrial Areas

AREA 82,264 sq. mi.
POPULATION 2,249,071
CAPITAL Topeka
LARGEST CITY Wichita
HIGHEST POINT Mt. Sunflower 4,039 ft.
SETTLED IN 1831
ADMITTED TO UNION January 29, 1861
POPULAR NAME Sunflower State
STATE FLOWER Sunflower
STATE BIRD Western Meadowlark

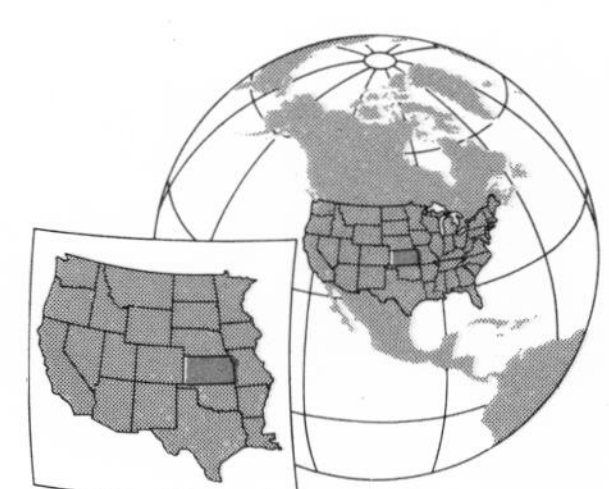

COUNTIES

Name/Pop.	Key
Allen, 15,043	G 4
Anderson, 8,501	G 3
Atchison, 19,165	G 2
Barber, 7,016	D 4
Barton, 30,663	D 3
Bourbon, 15,215	H 4
Brown, 11,685	G 2
Butler, 38,658	F 4
Chase, 3,408	F 3
Chautauqua, 4,642	F 4
Cherokee, 21,549	H 4
Cheyenne, 4,256	A 2
Clark, 2,896	C 4
Clay, 9,890	E 2
Cloud, 13,466	E 2
Coffey, 7,397	G 3
Comanche, 2,702	C 4
Cowley, 35,012	F 4
Crawford, 37,850	H 4
Decatur, 4,988	B 2
Dickinson, 19,993	E 3
Doniphan, 9,107	G 2
Douglas, 57,932	G 3
Edwards, 4,581	C 4
Elk, 3,858	F 4
Ellis, 24,730	C 3
Ellsworth, 6,146	D 3
Finney, 18,947	B 3
Ford, 22,587	C 4
Franklin, 19,548	G 3
Geary, 28,111	F 3
Gove, 3,940	B 3
Graham, 4,751	C 2
Grant, 5,961	A 4
Gray, 4,516	B 4
Greeley, 1,819	A 3
Greenwood, 9,141	F 4
Hamilton, 2,747	A 3
Harper, 7,871	D 4
Harvey, 27,236	E 3
Haskell, 3,672	B 4
Hodgeman, 2,662	C 3
Jackson, 10,342	G 2
Jefferson, 11,945	G 2
Jewell, 6,099	D 2
Johnson, 217,662	H 3
Kearny, 3,047	A 3
Kingman, 8,886	D 4
Kiowa, 4,088	C 4
Labette, 25,775	G 4
Lane, 2,707	B 3
Leavenworth, 53,340	G 2
Lincoln, 4,582	D 2
Linn, 7,770	H 3
Logan, 3,814	A 3
Lyon, 32,071	F 3
Marion, 13,935	E 3
Marshall, 13,139	F 2
McPherson, 24,778	E 3
Meade, 4,912	B 4
Miami, 19,254	H 3
Mitchell, 8,010	D 2
Montgomery, 39,949	G 4
Morris, 6,432	F 3
Morton, 3,576	A 4
Nemaha, 11,825	F 2
Neosho, 18,812	G 4
Ness, 4,791	C 3
Norton, 7,279	C 2
Osage, 13,352	G 3
Osborne, 6,416	D 2
Ottawa, 6,183	E 2
Pawnee, 8,484	C 3
Phillips, 7,888	C 2
Pottawatomie, 11,755	F 2
Pratt, 10,056	D 4
Rawlins, 4,393	A 2
Reno, 60,765	D 4
Republic, 8,498	E 2
Rice, 12,320	D 3
Riley, 56,788	F 2
Rooks, 7,628	C 2
Rush, 5,117	C 3
Russell, 9,428	D 3
Saline, 46,592	E 3
Scott, 5,606	B 3
Sedgwick, 350,694	E 4
Seward, 15,744	B 4
Shawnee, 155,322	G 2
Sheridan, 3,859	B 2
Sherman, 7,792	A 2
Smith, 6,757	D 2
Stafford, 5,943	D 3
Stanton, 2,287	A 4
Stevens, 4,198	A 4
Sumner, 23,553	E 4
Thomas, 7,501	A 2
Trego, 4,436	C 3
Wabaunsee, 6,397	F 3
Wallace, 2,215	A 3
Washington, 9,249	E 2
Wichita, 3,274	A 3
Wilson, 11,317	G 4
Woodson, 4,789	G 4
Wyandotte, 186,845	H 2

CITIES and TOWNS

Zip	Name/Pop.	Key
67510	Abbyville, 143	D 4
67410	Abilene⊙, 6,661	E 3
67414	Ada, 120	E 2
66830	Admire, 144	F 3
66930	Agenda, 107	E 2
67621	Agra, 294	C 2
67511	Albert, 235	C 3
67512	Alden, 238	D 3
67513	Alexander, 129	C 3
66833	Allen, 175	F 3
66401	Alma⊙, 905	F 2
67622	Almena, 489	C 2
67330	Altamont, 845	G 4
66834	Alta Vista, 402	F 3
67623	Alton, 214	D 2
66710	Altoona, 475	G 4
66835	Americus, 441	F 3
67001	Andale, 500	E 4
67002	Andover, 1,880	E 4
67003	Anthony⊙, 2,653	D 4
66711	Arcadia, 388	H 4
67004	Argonia, 591	E 4
67005	Arkansas City, 13,216	E 4
67514	Arlington, 503	D 4
66712	Arma, 1,348	H 4
67831	Ashland⊙, 1,244	C 4
67416	Assaria, 303	E 3
66002	Atchison⊙, 12,565	G 2
66932	Athol, 108	D 2
67008	Atlanta, 216	F 4
67009	Attica, 639	D 4
67730	Atwood⊙, 1,658	B 2
66402	Auburn, 261	G 3
67010	Augusta, 5,977	F 4
67417	Aurora, 120	E 2
66403	Axtell, 456	F 2
66404	Baileyville, 110	F 2
66006	Baldwin City, 2,520	G 3
67418	Barnard, 190	D 2
66933	Barnes, 209	F 2
67332	Bartlett, 138	G 4
66007	Basehor, 724	G 2
66713	Baxter Springs, 4,489	H 4
67516	Bazine, 386	C 3
66406	Beattie, 288	F 2
67012	Beaumont, 135	F 4
67013	Belle Plaine, 1,553	E 4
66935	Belleville⊙, 3,063	E 2
67420	Beloit⊙, 4,121	D 2
67519	Belpre, 191	C 4
66407	Belvue, 161	F 2
67422	Bennington, 561	E 2
67016	Bentley, 260	E 4
67017	Benton, 517	E 4
66408	Bern, 191	F 2
67423	Beverly, 193	E 2
67731	Bird City, 671	A 2
67520	Bison, 285	C 3
66010	Blue Mound, 308	H 3
66411	Blue Rapids, 1,148	F 2
67018	Bluff City, 109	E 4
67625	Bogue, 257	C 2
66012	Bonner Springs, 3,662	H 2
67732	Brewster, 320	A 2
66716	Bronson, 397	H 4
67425	Brookville, 238	E 3
67834	Bucklin, 771	C 4
66013	Bucyrus, 196	H 3
66717	Buffalo, 321	G 4
67522	Buhler, 1,019	E 3
67626	Bunker Hill, 181	D 3
67019	Burden, 503	F 4
67523	Burdett, 285	C 3
66838	Burdick, 120	F 3
66413	Burlingame, 999	G 3
66839	Burlington⊙, 2,099	G 3
66840	Burns, 268	F 3
66936	Burr Oak, 426	D 2
67020	Burrton, 808	E 3
67427	Bushton, 397	D 3
67022	Caldwell, 1,540	E 4
67023	Cambridge, 110	F 4
67333	Caney, 2,192	G 4
67428	Canton, 893	E 3
66414	Carbondale, 1,041	G 3
66842	Cassoday, 123	F 3
67627	Catharine, 126	C 3
67430	Cawker City, 726	D 2
67024	Cedar Vale, 665	F 4
66415	Centralia, 511	F 2
66720	Chanute, 10,341	G 4
67431	Chapman, 1,132	E 3
67524	Chase, 800	D 3
67334	Chautauqua, 137	F 4
67025	Cheney, 1,160	E 4
66724	Cherokee, 790	H 4
67335	Cherryvale, 2,609	G 4
67336	Chetopa, 1,596	G 4
† 66762	Chicopee, 300	H 4
87835	Cimarron⊙, 1,373	B 4
66416	Circleville, 178	G 2
67525	Claflin, 887	D 3
67432	Clay Center⊙, 4,963	E 2
67629	Clayton, 127	B 2
67026	Clearwater, 1,435	E 4
66937	Clifton, 718	E 2
66938	Clyde, 946	E 2
67028	Coats, 152	D 4
67337	Coffeyville, 15,116	G 4
67701	Colby⊙, 4,658	A 2
67029	Coldwater⊙, 1,016	C 4
67631	Collyer, 182	B 2
66015	Colony, 382	G 3
66725	Columbus⊙, 3,356	H 4
67030	Colwich, 879	E 4
66901	Concordia⊙, 7,221	E 2
67031	Conway Springs, 1,153	E 4
67836	Coolidge, 102	A 3
67837	Copeland, 267	B 4
66417	Corning, 162	F 2
66845	Cottonwood Falls⊙, 987	F 3
66846	Council Grove⊙, 2,403	F 3
66939	Courtland, 403	E 2
66728	Crestline, 102	H 4
66940	Cuba, 290	E 2
† 67124	Cullison, 117	D 4
67435	Culver, 148	E 3
66016	Cummings, 826	G 2
67035	Cunningham, 483	D 4
67632	Damar, 245	C 2
67340	Dearing, 338	G 4
67838	Deerfield, 474	A 4
66418	Delia, 168	G 2
67436	Delphos, 599	E 2
66419	Denison, 248	G 2
67341	Dennis, 120	G 4
66017	Denton, 162	G 2
67037	Derby, 7,947	E 4
66018	De Soto, 1,839	H 3
67038	Dexter, 286	F 4
67839	Dighton⊙, 1,540	B 3
67801	Dodge City⊙, 14,127	B 4
67634	Dorrance, 234	D 3
67039	Douglass, 1,126	F 4
66420	Dover, 122	G 3
67437	Downs, 1,268	D 2
67635	Dresden, 103	B 2
66848	Dunlap, 102	F 3
67438	Durham, 143	E 3
66849	Dwight, 322	F 3
66731	Earlton, 102	G 4
† 67201	Eastborough, 1,141	E 4
66020	Easton, 435	G 2
66021	Edgerton, 513	H 3
67342	Edna, 418	G 4
66022	Edwardsville, 619	H 2
66023	Effingham, 605	G 2
67041	Elbing, 128	E 3
67042	El Dorado⊙, 12,308	F 4
67361	Elgin, 115	F 4
67344	Elk City, 432	G 4
67345	Elk Falls, 124	F 4
67950	Elkhart⊙, 2,089	A 4
67526	Ellinwood, 2,416	D 3
67637	Ellis, 2,137	C 3

(continued on following page)

Robert Leahey — Shostal Associates

Loaded with wheat for storage, a truck pulls onto a weighing platform at the Salina grain elevators. Wheat is grown here on such a scale that Kansas is known as the Breadbasket of the World.

(continued)

67439 Ellsworth⊙, 2,080 D 3
66850 Elmdale, 102 F 3
† 66603 Elmont, 112 G 2
66732 Elsmore, 116 G 4
66024 Elwood, 1,283 H 2
66422 Emmett, 156 F 2
66801 Emporia⊙, 23,327 F 3
67840 Englewood, 158 C 4
67841 Ensign, 237 B 4
67441 Enterprise, 868 E 3
66733 Erie⊙, 1,414 G 4
66941 Esbon, 206 D 2
66423 Eskridge, 589 F 3
66025 Eudora, 2,071 G 3
67045 Eureka⊙, 3,576 F 4
66424 Everest, 304 G 2
66425 Fairview, 283 G 2
67047 Fall River, 191 G 4
67442 Falun, 105 E 3
66851 Florence, 716 E 3
66026 Fontana, 160 H 3
67842 Ford, 246 C 4
66942 Formoso, 180 D 2
67843 Fort Dodge, 450 C 4
66027 Fort Leavenworth, 8,060 H 2
66701 Fort Scott⊙, 8,967 H 4
67844 Fowler, 588 B 4
66427 Frankfort, 960 F 2
66735 Franklin, 620 H 4
66736 Fredonia⊙, 3,080 G 4
66762 Frontenac, 2,223 H 4
66738 Fulton, 213 H 4
66739 Galena, 3,712 H 4
66740 Galesburg, 146 G 4
67443 Galva, 522 E 3
67846 Garden City⊙, 14,708 B 4
67050 Garden Plain, 678 E 4
66030 Gardner, 1,839 H 3
67529 Garfield, 261 C 3
66741 Garland, 125 H 4
66032 Garnett⊙, 3,169 G 3
66742 Gas, 438 G 4
67638 Gaylord, 211 D 2
67444 Geneseo, 453 D 3
67051 Geuda Springs, 223 E 4
66743 Girard⊙, 2,591 H 4
67639 Glade, 180 C 2
67445 Glasco, 767 E 2
67446 Glen Elder, 422 D 2
67052 Goddard, 955 E 4
67053 Goessel, 386 E 3
66428 Goff, 207 G 2
67735 Goodland⊙, 5,510 A 2
67640 Gorham, 379 D 3
67736 Gove⊙, 172 B 3
67737 Grainfield, 374 B 2
† 66441 Grandview Plaza, 734 F 2
66429 Grantville, 190 G 2
67530 Great Bend⊙, 16,133 D 3
66033 Greeley, 368 G 3
67447 Green, 163 E 2
66943 Greenleaf, 448 E 2
67054 Greensburg⊙, 1,907 C 4
67346 Grenola, 290 F 4
66852 Gridley, 328 G 3
67738 Grinnell, 449 B 2
67448 Gypsum, 391 E 3
66944 Haddam, 289 E 2
66744 Hallowell, 135 H 4
67056 Halstead, 1,716 E 4
66853 Hamilton, 349 F 4
66945 Hanover, 793 F 2
67849 Hanston, 282 C 3
67057 Hardtner, 300 D 4
67058 Harper, 1,665 D 4
66854 Hartford, 478 F 3
66431 Harveyville, 279 F 3
67347 Havana, 144 G 4
67543 Haven, 1,146 E 4
66432 Havensville, 163 F 2
67059 Haviland, 705 C 4
67601 Hays⊙, 15,396 C 3
67060 Haysville, 6,483 E 4
67061 Hazelton, 176 D 4
67850 Healy, 251 B 3
66746 Hepler, 152 H 4
67449 Herington, 3,165 E 3
67739 Herndon, 268 B 2
67062 Hesston, 1,926 E 3
66434 Hiawatha⊙, 3,365 G 2
66035 Highland, 899 G 2
67642 Hill City⊙, 2,071 C 2
67063 Hillsboro, 2,730 E 3
66036 Hillsdale, 250 H 3
67544 Hoisington, 3,710 D 3
67851 Holcomb, 272 B 3
66436 Holton⊙, 3,063 G 2
67450 Holyrood, 593 D 3
66438 Home, 120 F 2
67451 Hope, 438 E 3
† 67879 Horace, 137 A 3
66439 Horton, 2,177 G 2
67349 Howard⊙, 918 F 4
67740 Hoxie⊙, 1,419 B 2
66440 Hoyt, 420 G 2
67545 Hudson, 181 D 3
67951 Hugoton⊙, 2,739 A 4
66748 Humboldt, 2,249 G 4
67452 Hunter, 150 D 2
66038 Huron, 106 G 2
67501 Hutchinson⊙, 36,885 D 3
67301 Independence⊙, 10,347 G 4
67853 Ingalls, 235 B 4
67546 Inman, 836 E 3
66749 Iola⊙, 6,493 G 4
67065 Isabel, 147 D 4
67066 Iuka, 210 D 4
66948 Jamestown, 470 E 2
67643 Jennings, 224 B 2
67854 Jetmore⊙, 936 B 3
66949 Jewell, 569 D 2
67855 Johnson⊙, 1,038 A 4
66441 Junction City⊙, 19,018 E 2
67454 Kanopolis, 626 D 3
67741 Kanorado, 278 A 2
* 66101 Kansas City⊙, 168,213 H 2
Kansas City, ‡1,253,916 H 2
67067 Kechi, 229 E 4
67857 Kendall, 160 A 4
66951 Kensington, 653 C 2
66039 Kincaid, 189 G 3
67068 Kingman⊙, 3,622 D 4
67547 Kinsley⊙, 2,212 C 4
67070 Kiowa, 1,414 D 4
67644 Kirwin, 293 C 2
67859 Kismet, 294 B 4
67350 Labette, 105 G 4
67548 La Crosse⊙, 1,583 C 3
66040 La Cygne, 989 H 3
66750 Lafontaine, 140 G 4
66751 La Harpe, 509 G 4
67860 Lakin⊙, 1,570 A 4
66041 Lancaster, 279 G 2
66042 Lane, 254 G 3
66043 Lansing, 3,797 H 2
67550 Larned⊙, 4,567 C 3
67072 Latham, 156 F 4
66044 Lawrence⊙, 45,698 G 3
66048 Leavenworth⊙, 25,147 H 2
66206 Leawood, 10,349 H 3
66952 Lebanon, 517 D 2
66856 Lebo, 589 G 3
66050 Lecompton, 434 G 2
67073 Lehigh, 168 E 3
67645 Lenora, 439 C 2
67074 Leon, 510 F 4

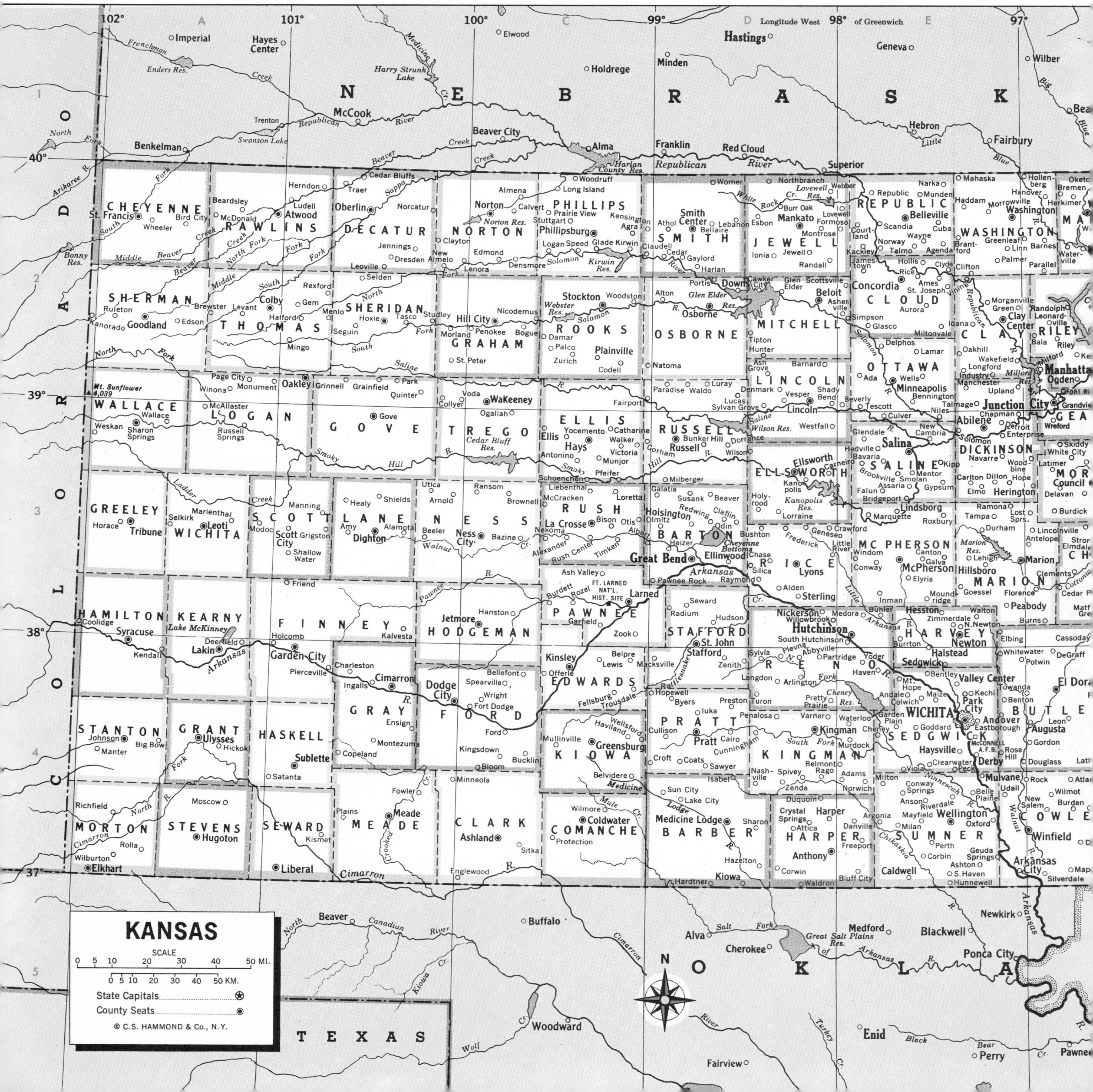

KANSAS

SCALE

0 5 10 20 30 40 50 MI.

0 5 10 20 30 40 50 KM.

State Capitals ⊛

County Seats ⊙

66449 Leonardville, 412 .... F 2
67861 Leoti⊙, 1,916 .... A 3
66857 Le Roy, 551 .... G 3
67743 Levant, 425 .... A 2
67552 Lewis, 525 .... C 4
67901 Liberal⊙, 13,471 .... B 4
67351 Liberty, 185 .... G 4
67553 Liebenthal, 169 .... C 3
67455 Lincoln⊙, 1,582 .... D 2
66858 Lincolnville, 218 .... F 3
67456 Lindsborg, 2,764 .... E 3
66953 Linn, 388 .... E 2
66052 Linwood, 323 .... G 2
67457 Little River, 493 .... E 3
67646 Logan, 760 .... C 2
67647 Long Island, 195 .... C 2
67352 Longton, 304 .... F 4
67459 Lorraine, 153 .... D 3
66859 Lost Springs, 103 .... E 3
66053 Louisburg, 1,033 .... H 3
66450 Louisville, 204 .... F 2
67648 Lucas, 524 .... D 2
67649 Luray, 303 .... D 2
66451 Lyndon⊙, 958 .... G 3
67554 Lyons⊙, 4,355 .... D 3
67557 Macksville, 484 .... D 4
66860 Madison, 1,061 .... F 3
66955 Mahaska, 122 .... E 2
67101 Maize, 785 .... E 4
66502 Manhattan⊙, 27,575 .... F 2
66956 Mankato⊙, 1,287 .... D 2
67862 Manter, 219 .... A 4
66507 Maple Hill, 327 .... F 2
66754 Mapleton, 112 .... H 3
67863 Marienthal, 120 .... A 3
66861 Marion⊙, 2,052 .... F 3
67464 Marquette, 578 .... E 3
66508 Marysville⊙, 3,588 .... F 2
66509 Mayetta, 246 .... G 2
67103 Mayfield, 110 .... E 4
67556 McCracken, 333 .... C 3
66753 McCune, 487 .... G 4
67745 McDonald, 269 .... A 2
66501 McFarland, 209 .... F 2
66054 McLouth, 623 .... G 2
67460 McPherson⊙, 10,851 .... E 3
67864 Meade⊙, 1,899 .... B 4
67104 Medicine Lodge⊙, 2,545 .... D 4
67558 Medora, 110 .... E 3
66510 Melvern, 455 .... G 3
66512 Meriden, 472 .... G 2
66203 Merriam, 10,851 .... H 3

Topography

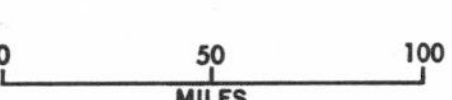

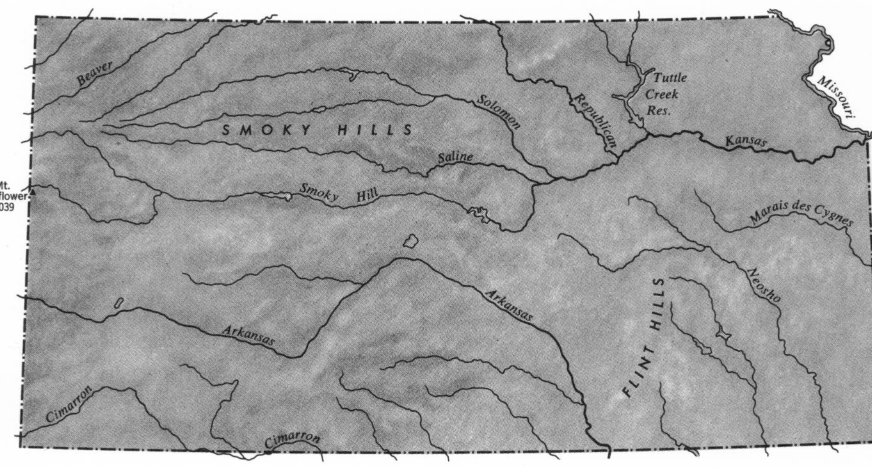

5,000 m. 16,404 ft. | 2,000 m. 6,562 ft. | 1,000 m. 3,281 ft. | 500 m. 1,640 ft. | 200 m. 656 ft. | 100 m. 328 ft. | Sea Level | Below

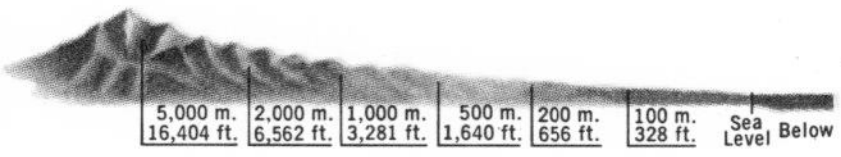

67105 Milan, 162 .... E 4
66514 Milford, 296 .... F 2
67466 Miltonvale, 718 .... E 2
67467 Minneapolis⊙, 1,971 .... E 2
67865 Minneola, 630 .... C 4
66222 Mission, 8,376 .... H 2
67353 Moline, 555 .... F 4
67867 Montezuma, 606 .... B 4
66755 Moran, 550 .... G 4
67468 Morganville, 257 .... E 2
67650 Morland, 300 .... B 2
66515 Morrill, 308 .... G 2
66958 Morrowville, 201 .... E 2
67952 Moscow, 228 .... A 4
66056 Mound City⊙, 714 .... H 3
67107 Moundridge, 1,271 .... E 3
67354 Mound Valley, 467 .... G 4
67108 Mount Hope, 665 .... E 4
66758 Mulberry, 622 .... H 4
67109 Mullinville, 376 .... C 4
67110 Mulvane, 3,185 .... E 4
66959 Munden, 123 .... E 2
† 67601 Munjor, 200 .... C 3
66058 Muscotah, 206 .... G 2
66960 Narka, 130 .... E 2
67112 Nashville, 107 .... D 4
67651 Natoma, 603 .... D 2
66757 Neodesha, 3,295 .... G 4
66758 Neosho Falls, 184 .... G 3
66864 Neosho Rapids, 234 .... F 3
67560 Ness City⊙, 1,756 .... C 3
66516 Netawaka, 192 .... G 2
67470 New Cambria, 160 .... E 3
67114 Newton⊙, 15,439 .... E 3
67561 Nickerson, 1,187 .... D 3
67653 Norcatur, 284 .... B 2
67117 North Newton, 963 .... E 3
67654 Norton⊙, 3,627 .... C 2
66060 Nortonville, 727 .... G 2
67118 Norwich, 414 .... E 4
67748 Oakley⊙, 2,327 .... B 2
67749 Oberlin⊙, 2,291 .... B 2
67562 Odin, 117 .... D 3
67563 Offerle, 212 .... C 4
67656 Ogallah, 110 .... C 3
66517 Ogden, 1,491 .... F 2
66518 Oketo, 133 .... F 2
66061 Olathe⊙, 17,917 .... H 3
67564 Olmitz, 161 .... D 3
66865 Olpe, 453 .... F 3
66520 Olsburg, 151 .... F 2
66521 Onaga, 761 .... F 2
66522 Oneida, 112 .... G 2
66760 Opolis, 160 .... H 4
66523 Osage City, 2,600 .... G 3
66064 Osawatomie, 4,294 .... H 3
67473 Osborne⊙, 1,980 .... D 2
66066 Oskaloosa⊙, 955 .... G 2
67356 Oswego⊙, 2,200 .... G 4
67565 Otis, 387 .... C 3
66067 Ottawa⊙, 11,036 .... G 3
66524 Overbrook, 748 .... G 3
66204 Overland Park, 76,623 .... H 3
67119 Oxford, 1,113 .... E 4
66070 Ozawkie, 137 .... G 2
67657 Palco, 398 .... C 2
66962 Palmer, 166 .... E 2
66071 Paola⊙, 4,622 .... H 3
67658 Paradise, 145 .... D 2
67751 Park, 178 .... B 2
67219 Park City, 2,529 .... E 4
66072 Parker, 255 .... H 3
67357 Parsons, 13,015 .... G 4
67566 Partridge, 302 .... D 4
66619 Pauline, 800 .... G 3
67567 Pawnee Rock, 442 .... D 3
66526 Paxico, 216 .... F 2
66866 Peabody, 1,368 .... E 3
67120 Peck, 150 .... E 4
66073 Perry, 664 .... G 2
67360 Peru, 289 .... F 4
67660 Pfeifer, 175 .... C 3
67661 Phillipsburg⊙, 3,241 .... C 2
67122 Piedmont, 116 .... F 4
67868 Pierceville, 175 .... B 4

66761 Piqua, 107 .... G 4
66762 Pittsburg, 20,171 .... H 4
67869 Plains, 857 .... B 4
67663 Plainville, 2,627 .... C 2
66075 Pleasanton, 1,216 .... H 3
67568 Plevna, 124 .... D 4
66076 Pomona, 541 .... G 3
67474 Portis, 178 .... D 2
67123 Potwin, 497 .... F 4
66527 Powhattan, 111 .... G 2
67664 Prairie View, 201 .... C 2
66208 Prairie Village, 28,138 .... H 2
67124 Pratt⊙, 6,736 .... D 4
66767 Prescott, 222 .... H 3
67569 Preston, 239 .... D 4
67570 Pretty Prairie, 561 .... D 4
66078 Princeton, 159 .... G 3
67127 Protection, 673 .... C 4
66528 Quenemo, 429 .... G 3
67752 Quinter, 930 .... B 2
67475 Ramona, 121 .... E 3
66963 Randall, 195 .... D 2
66554 Randolph, 106 .... F 2
67572 Ransom, 416 .... C 3
66079 Rantoul, 163 .... G 3
67573 Raymond, 133 .... D 3
66868 Reading, 247 .... F 3
66769 Redfield, 138 .... H 4
66964 Republic, 243 .... E 2
66529 Reserve, 117 .... G 2
67753 Rexford, 231 .... B 2
66080 Richmond, 464 .... G 3
66531 Riley, 668 .... F 2
66770 Riverton, 500 .... H 4
66532 Robinson, 278 .... G 2
† 66205 Roeland Park, 9,974 .... H 2
67954 Rolla, 400 .... A 4
67132 Rosalia, 130 .... F 4
67133 Rose Hill, 387 .... E 4
66533 Rossville, 934 .... G 2
67476 Roxbury, 110 .... E 3
67574 Rozel, 236 .... C 3
67575 Rush Center, 237 .... C 3
67665 Russell⊙, 5,371 .... D 3
66534 Sabetha, 2,376 .... G 2
67756 Saint Francis⊙, 1,725 .... A 2
66535 Saint George, 241 .... F 2
67576 Saint John⊙, 1,477 .... D 3
66536 Saint Marys, 1,434 .... G 2
66771 Saint Paul, 804 .... G 4
67401 Salina⊙, 37,714 .... E 3
67870 Satanta, 1,161 .... B 4
66772 Savonburg, 109 .... G 4
67134 Sawyer, 164 .... D 4
66773 Scammon, 457 .... H 4
66966 Scandia, 567 .... E 2
67667 Schoenchen, 182 .... C 3
67871 Scott City⊙, 4,001 .... B 3
66537 Scranton, 575 .... G 3
67361 Sedan⊙, 1,555 .... F 4
67135 Sedgwick, 1,083 .... E 4
67757 Selden, 271 .... B 2
66538 Seneca⊙, 2,182 .... F 2
66081 Severance, 128 .... G 2
67137 Severy, 384 .... F 4
67872 Shallow Water, 106 .... B 3
67138 Sharon, 265 .... D 4
67758 Sharon Springs⊙, 1,012 .... A 3
66203 Shawnee, 20,482 .... H 2
67874 Shields, 110 .... B 3
66539 Silver Lake, 811 .... G 2
67478 Simpson, 131 .... E 2
66967 Smith Center⊙, 2,389 .... D 2
67479 Smolan, 175 .... E 3
66540 Soldier, 173 .... G 2
67480 Solomon, 973 .... E 3
67140 South Haven, 413 .... E 4
† 67501 South Hutchinson, 1,879 .... D 3
67876 Spearville, 738 .... C 4
66083 Spring Hill, 1,186 .... H 3
67578 Stafford, 1,414 .... D 4
66084 Stanley, 450 .... H 3
66775 Stark, 124 .... G 4
67579 Sterling, 2,312 .... D 3
66085 Stilwell, 350 .... H 3

67669 Stockton⊙, 1,818 .... C 2
66869 Strong City, 545 .... F 3
67877 Sublette⊙, 1,208 .... B 4
66541 Summerfield, 254 .... F 2
67143 Sun City, 119 .... D 4
66019 Sunflower, 1,744 .... H 3
67363 Sycamore, 125 .... G 4
67581 Sylvia, 390 .... D 4
67878 Syracuse⊙, 1,720 .... A 3
67482 Talmage, 125 .... E 2
67483 Tampa, 154 .... E 3
66542 Tecumseh, 270 .... G 2
67484 Tescott, 393 .... E 2
66776 Thayer, 430 .... G 4
67582 Timken, 123 .... C 3
67485 Tipton, 315 .... D 2
66086 Tonganoxie, 1,717 .... G 2
* 66601 Topeka (cap.)⊙, 125,011 .... G 2
Topeka, ‡155,322 .... G 2
66777 Toronto, 431 .... G 4
67144 Towanda, 1,190 .... E 4
66778 Treece, 225 .... H 4
67879 Tribune⊙, 1,013 .... A 3
66087 Troy⊙, 1,047 .... G 2
67583 Turon, 430 .... D 4
67364 Tyro, 206 .... G 4
67146 Udall, 668 .... E 4
67880 Ulysses⊙, 3,779 .... A 4
66779 Uniontown, 286 .... G 4
67584 Utica, 297 .... B 3
67147 Valley Center, 2,551 .... E 4
66088 Valley Falls, 1,169 .... G 2
66544 Vermillion, 191 .... F 2
67671 Victoria, 1,246 .... C 3
67149 Viola, 193 .... E 4
66870 Virgil, 179 .... F 4
67672 WaKeeney⊙, 2,334 .... C 2
67487 Wakefield, 583 .... E 2
67673 Waldo, 123 .... D 2
67761 Wallace, 112 .... A 3
66780 Walnut, 330 .... G 4
67151 Walton, 211 .... E 3
66547 Wamego, 2,507 .... F 2
66968 Washington⊙, 1,584 .... F 2
66548 Waterville, 632 .... F 2
66090 Wathena, 1,150 .... H 2
66871 Waverly, 510 .... G 3
66781 Weir, 740 .... H 4
66091 Welda, 149 .... G 3
67152 Wellington⊙, 8,072 .... E 4
66092 Wellsville, 1,183 .... G 3
67762 Weskan, 350 .... A 3
66782 West Mineral, 232 .... H 4
66549 Westmoreland⊙, 485 .... F 2
66093 Westphalia, 185 .... G 3
67869 West Plains (Plains), 857 .... B 4
66550 Wetmore, 392 .... G 2
66551 Wheaton, 106 .... F 2
66872 White City, 458 .... F 3
66094 White Cloud, 210 .... G 2
67154 Whitewater, 520 .... E 4
66552 Whiting, 256 .... G 2
* 67201 Wichita⊙, 276,554 .... E 4
Wichita, ‡389,352 .... E 4
† 66601 Willard, 124 .... G 2
66095 Williamsburg, 286 .... G 3
66873 Wilsey, 169 .... F 3
67490 Wilson, 870 .... D 3
66097 Winchester, 492 .... G 2
67491 Windom, 183 .... E 3
67156 Winfield⊙, 11,405 .... F 4
67764 Winona, 293 .... A 2
67492 Woodbine, 170 .... E 3
67675 Woodston, 211 .... C 2
67882 Wright, 173 .... C 4
66783 Yates Center⊙, 1,967 .... G 4
67585 Yoder, 155 .... E 4
67159 Zenda, 142 .... D 4
67676 Zurich, 189 .... C 2

⊙ County seat.
‡ Population of metropolitan area.
† Zip of nearest p.o.
* Multiple zips

Agriculture, Industry and Resources

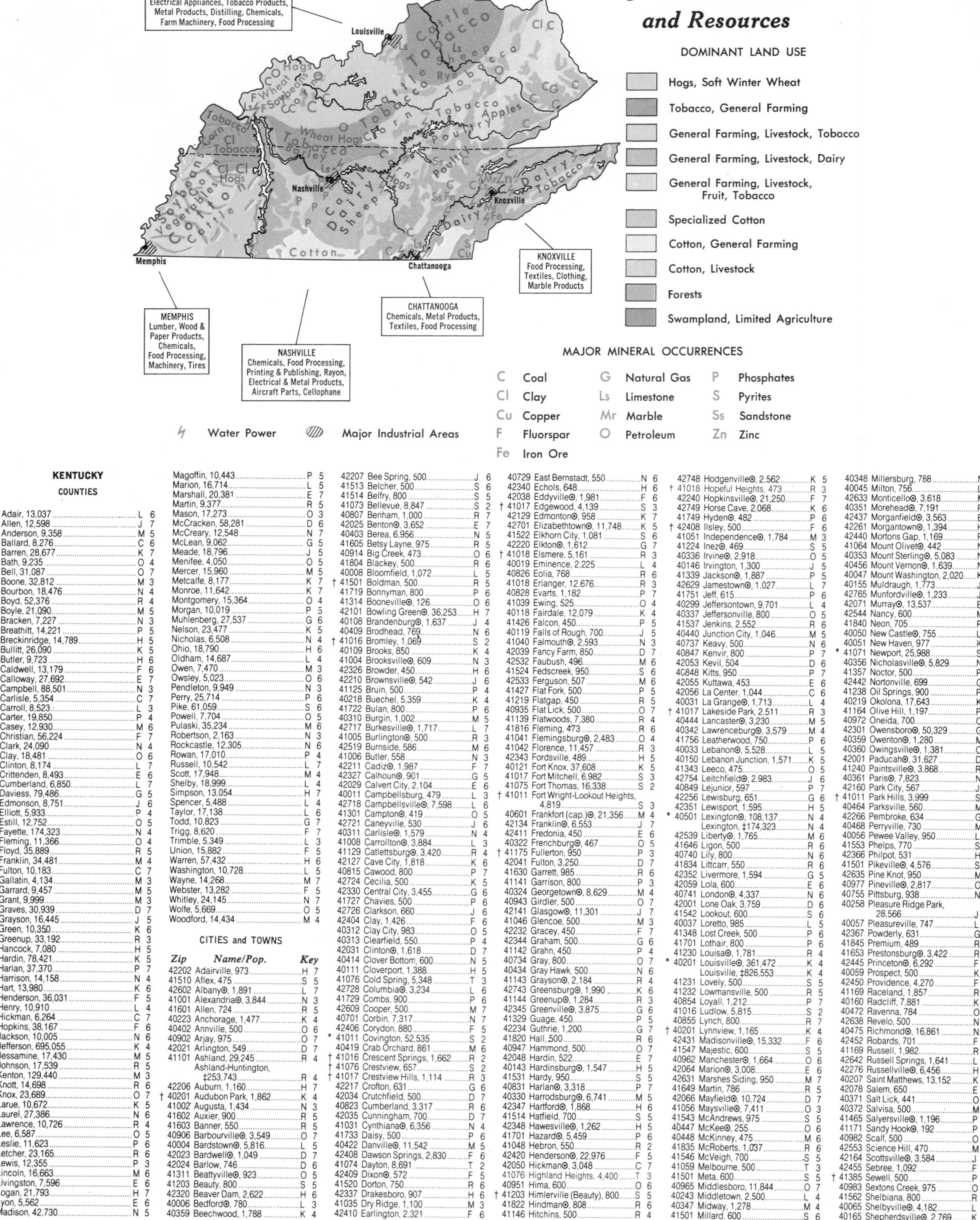

KENTUCKY

COUNTIES

Adair, 13,037 L 6
Allen, 12,598 J 7
Anderson, 9,358 M 5
Ballard, 8,276 C 6
Barren, 28,677 K 7
Bath, 9,235 O 4
Bell, 31,087 O 7
Boone, 32,812 M 3
Bourbon, 18,476 N 4
Boyd, 52,376 R 4
Boyle, 21,090 M 5
Bracken, 7,227 N 3
Breathitt, 14,221 P 5
Breckinridge, 14,789 H 5
Bullitt, 26,090 K 5
Butler, 9,723 H 6
Caldwell, 13,179 F 6
Calloway, 27,692 E 7
Campbell, 88,501 N 3
Carlisle, 5,354 C 7
Carroll, 8,523 L 3
Carter, 19,850 P 4
Casey, 12,930 M 6
Christian, 56,224 F 7
Clark, 24,090 N 4
Clay, 18,481 O 6
Clinton, 8,174 L 7
Crittenden, 8,493 E 6
Cumberland, 6,850 L 7
Daviess, 79,486 G 5
Edmonson, 8,751 J 6
Elliott, 5,933 P 4
Estill, 12,752 O 5
Fayette, 174,323 N 4
Fleming, 11,366 O 4
Floyd, 35,889 R 5
Franklin, 34,481 M 4
Fulton, 10,183 C 7
Gallatin, 4,134 M 3
Garrard, 9,457 M 5
Grant, 9,999 M 3
Graves, 30,939 D 7
Grayson, 16,445 J 5
Green, 10,350 K 6
Greenup, 33,192 R 3
Hancock, 7,080 H 5
Hardin, 78,421 K 5
Harlan, 37,370 P 7
Harrison, 14,158 N 4
Hart, 13,980 K 6
Henderson, 36,031 F 5
Henry, 10,910 L 4
Hickman, 6,264 C 7
Hopkins, 38,167 F 6
Jackson, 10,005 N 6
Jefferson, 695,055 K 4
Jessamine, 17,430 M 5
Johnson, 17,539 R 5
Kenton, 129,440 M 3
Knott, 14,698 R 6
Knox, 23,689 O 7
Larue, 10,672 K 5
Laurel, 27,386 N 6
Lawrence, 10,726 R 4
Lee, 6,587 O 5
Leslie, 11,623 P 6
Letcher, 23,165 R 6
Lewis, 12,355 P 3
Lincoln, 16,663 M 6
Livingston, 7,596 E 6
Logan, 21,793 H 7
Lyon, 5,562 E 6
Madison, 42,730 N 5
Magoffin, 10,443 P 5
Marion, 16,714 L 5
Marshall, 20,381 E 7
Martin, 9,377 R 5
Mason, 17,273 O 3
McCracken, 58,281 D 6
McCreary, 12,548 N 7
McLean, 9,062 G 5
Meade, 18,796 J 5
Menifee, 4,050 O 5
Mercer, 15,960 M 5
Metcalfe, 8,177 K 7
Monroe, 11,642 K 7
Montgomery, 15,364 O 4
Morgan, 10,019 P 5
Muhlenberg, 27,537 G 6
Nelson, 23,477 K 5
Nicholas, 6,508 N 4
Ohio, 18,790 H 6
Oldham, 14,687 L 4
Owen, 7,470 M 3
Owsley, 5,023 O 6
Pendleton, 9,949 N 3
Perry, 25,714 P 6
Pike, 61,059 S 6
Powell, 7,704 O 5
Pulaski, 35,234 M 6
Robertson, 2,163 N 3
Rockcastle, 12,305 N 6
Rowan, 17,010 P 4
Russell, 10,542 L 7
Scott, 17,948 M 4
Shelby, 18,999 L 4
Simpson, 13,054 H 7
Spencer, 5,488 L 4
Taylor, 17,138 L 6
Todd, 10,823 G 7
Trigg, 8,620 F 7
Trimble, 5,349 L 3
Union, 15,882 F 5
Warren, 57,432 H 6
Washington, 10,728 L 5
Wayne, 14,268 M 7
Webster, 13,282 F 5
Whitley, 24,145 N 7
Wolfe, 5,669 O 5
Woodford, 14,434 M 4

CITIES and TOWNS

Zip *Name/Pop.* *Key*

42202 Adairville, 973 H 7
41510 Aflex, 475 S 5
42602 Albany⊙, 1,891 L 7
41001 Alexandria⊙, 3,844 N 3
41601 Allen, 724 R 5
40223 Anchorage, 1,477 K 4
40402 Annville, 500 O 6
40902 Arjay, 975 O 7
42021 Arlington, 549 D 7
41101 Ashland, 29,245 R 4
Ashland-Huntington, ‡253,743 R 4
42206 Auburn, 1,160 H 7
† 40201 Audubon Park, 1,862 K 4
41002 Augusta, 1,434 N 3
41602 Auxier, 900 R 5
41603 Banner, 550 R 5
40906 Barbourville⊙, 3,549 O 7
40004 Bardstown⊙, 5,816 L 5
42023 Bardwell⊙, 1,049 D 7
42024 Barlow, 746 D 6
41311 Beattyville⊙, 923 O 5
41203 Beauty, 800 S 5
42320 Beaver Dam, 2,622 H 6
40006 Bedford⊙, 780 L 3
40359 Beechwood, 1,788 K 4
42207 Bee Spring, 500 J 6
41513 Belcher, 500 S 6
41514 Belfry, 800 S 5
41073 Bellevue, 8,847 S 2
40807 Benham, 1,000 R 7
42025 Benton⊙, 3,652 E 7
40403 Berea, 6,956 N 5
41605 Betsy Layne, 975 R 5
40914 Big Creek, 473 O 6
41804 Blackey, 500 R 6
40008 Bloomfield, 1,072 L 5
† 41501 Boldman, 500 R 5
41719 Bonnyman, 800 P 6
41314 Booneville⊙, 126 O 6
42101 Bowling Green⊙, 36,253 H 7
40108 Brandenburg⊙, 1,637 J 4
40409 Brodhead, 769 N 6
† 41016 Bromley, 1,069 S 2
40109 Brooks, 850 K 4
41004 Brooksville⊙, 609 N 3
42326 Browder, 450 H 6
42210 Brownsville⊙, 542 J 6
41125 Bruin, 500 P 4
40218 Buechel, 5,359 K 4
41722 Bulan, 800 P 6
40310 Burgin, 1,002 M 5
42717 Burkesville⊙, 1,717 L 7
41005 Burlington⊙, 500 R 3
42519 Burnside, 586 M 6
41006 Butler, 558 N 3
42211 Cadiz⊙, 1,987 F 7
42327 Calhoun⊙, 901 G 5
42029 Calvert City, 2,104 E 6
40011 Campbellsburg, 479 L 3
42718 Campbellsville⊙, 7,598 L 6
41301 Campton⊙, 419 O 5
42721 Caneyville, 530 J 6
40311 Carlisle⊙, 1,579 N 4
41008 Carrollton⊙, 3,884 L 3
41129 Catlettsburg⊙, 3,420 R 4
42127 Cave City, 1,818 K 6
40815 Cawood, 800 P 7
42724 Cecilia, 500 K 5
42330 Central City, 3,455 G 6
41727 Chavies, 500 P 6
42726 Clarkson, 660 J 6
42404 Clay, 1,426 F 6
40312 Clay City, 983 O 5
40313 Clearfield, 550 P 4
42031 Clinton⊙, 1,618 D 7
40414 Clover Bottom, 600 N 5
40111 Cloverport, 1,388 H 5
41076 Cold Spring, 5,348 T 3
42728 Columbia⊙, 3,234 L 6
41729 Combs, 900 P 6
42609 Cooper, 500 M 7
40701 Corbin, 7,317 N 7
42406 Corydon, 880 F 5
* 41011 Covington, 52,535 S 2
40419 Crab Orchard, 861 M 6
† 41016 Crescent Springs, 1,662 R 2
† 41076 Crestview, 657 S 2
† 41017 Crestview Hills, 1,114 R 3
42217 Crofton, 631 G 6
42034 Crutchfield, 500 D 7
40823 Cumberland, 3,317 R 6
42035 Cunningham, 700 D 7
41031 Cynthiana⊙, 6,356 N 4
41733 Daisy, 500 P 6
40422 Danville⊙, 11,542 M 5
42408 Dawson Springs, 2,830 F 6
41074 Dayton, 8,691 T 2
42409 Dixon⊙, 572 F 5
41520 Dorton, 750 R 6
42337 Drakesboro, 907 H 6
41035 Dry Ridge, 1,100 M 3
42410 Earlington, 2,321 F 6
40729 East Bernstadt, 550 N 6
42340 Echols, 648 H 6
42038 Eddyville⊙, 1,981 F 6
† 41017 Edgewood, 4,139 S 3
42129 Edmonton⊙, 958 K 7
42701 Elizabethtown⊙, 11,748 K 5
41522 Elkhorn City, 1,081 S 6
42220 Elkton⊙, 1,612 G 7
† 41018 Elsmere, 5,161 R 3
40019 Eminence, 2,225 L 4
40826 Eolia, 768 R 6
41018 Erlanger, 12,676 R 3
40828 Evarts, 1,182 P 7
41039 Ewing, 525 O 4
40118 Fairdale, 12,079 K 4
41426 Falcon, 450 P 5
40119 Falls of Rough, 700 J 5
41040 Falmouth⊙, 2,593 N 3
42039 Fancy Farm, 850 D 7
42532 Faubush, 496 M 6
41524 Fedscreek, 950 S 6
42533 Ferguson, 507 M 6
41427 Flat Fork, 500 P 5
41219 Flatgap, 450 R 5
40935 Flat Lick, 500 O 7
41139 Flatwoods, 7,380 R 4
41816 Fleming, 473 R 6
41041 Flemingsburg⊙, 2,483 O 4
41042 Florence, 11,457 R 3
42343 Fordsville, 489 H 5
40121 Fort Knox, 37,608 K 5
41017 Fort Mitchell, 6,982 S 3
41075 Fort Thomas, 16,338 S 2
† 41011 Fort Wright-Lookout Heights, 4,819 S 3
40601 Frankfort (cap.)⊙, 21,356 M 4
42134 Franklin⊙, 6,553 J 7
42411 Fredonia, 450 E 6
40322 Frenchburg⊙, 467 O 5
† 41175 Fullerton, 950 P 3
42041 Fulton, 3,250 D 7
41630 Garrett, 985 R 6
41141 Garrison, 800 P 3
40324 Georgetown⊙, 8,629 M 4
40943 Girdler, 500 O 7
42141 Glasgow⊙, 11,301 J 7
41046 Glencoe, 500 M 3
42232 Gracey, 450 F 7
42344 Graham, 500 G 6
41142 Grahn, 450 P 4
40734 Gray, 800 O 7
40434 Gray Hawk, 500 N 6
41143 Grayson⊙, 2,184 R 4
42743 Greensburg⊙, 1,990 K 6
41144 Greenup⊙, 1,284 R 3
42345 Greenville⊙, 3,875 G 6
41329 Guage, 450 P 5
42234 Guthrie, 1,200 G 7
41820 Hall, 500 R 6
40947 Hammond, 500 O 7
42048 Hardin, 522 E 7
40143 Hardinsburg⊙, 1,547 H 5
41531 Hardy, 950 S 5
40831 Harlan⊙, 3,318 P 7
40330 Harrodsburg⊙, 6,741 M 5
42347 Hartford⊙, 1,868 H 6
41514 Hatfield, 700 S 5
42348 Hawesville⊙, 1,262 H 5
41701 Hazard⊙, 5,459 P 6
41048 Hebron, 550 R 2
42420 Henderson⊙, 22,976 F 5
42050 Hickman⊙, 3,048 C 7
41076 Highland Heights, 4,400 T 3
40951 Hima, 600 O 6
† 41203 Himlerville (Beauty), 800 S 5
41822 Hindman⊙, 808 R 6
41146 Hitchins, 500 R 4
42748 Hodgenville⊙, 2,562 K 5
† 41018 Hopeful Heights, 473 R 3
42240 Hopkinsville⊙, 21,250 F 7
42749 Horse Cave, 2,068 K 6
41749 Hyden⊙, 482 P 6
† 42408 Ilsley, 500 F 6
41051 Independence⊙, 1,784 M 3
41224 Inez⊙, 469 S 5
40336 Irvine⊙, 2,918 O 5
40146 Irvington, 1,300 J 5
41339 Jackson⊙, 1,887 P 5
42629 Jamestown⊙, 1,027 L 7
41751 Jeff, 615 P 6
40299 Jeffersontown, 9,701 L 4
40337 Jeffersonville, 800 O 5
41537 Jenkins, 2,552 R 6
40440 Junction City, 1,046 M 5
40737 Keavy, 500 N 6
40847 Kenvir, 800 P 7
42053 Kevil, 504 D 6
40848 Kitts, 950 P 7
42055 Kuttawa, 453 E 6
42056 La Center, 1,044 C 6
40031 La Grange⊙, 1,713 L 4
† 41017 Lakeside Park, 2,511 R 3
40444 Lancaster⊙, 3,230 M 5
40342 Lawrenceburg⊙, 3,579 M 4
41756 Leatherwood, 750 P 6
40033 Lebanon⊙, 5,528 L 5
40150 Lebanon Junction, 1,571 K 5
41343 Leeco, 475 O 5
42754 Leitchfield⊙, 2,983 J 6
40849 Lejunior, 597 P 7
42256 Lewisburg, 651 G 6
42351 Lewisport, 1,595 H 5
* 40501 Lexington⊙, 108,137 N 4
Lexington, ‡174,323 N 4
42539 Liberty⊙, 1,765 M 6
41646 Ligon, 500 R 6
40740 Lily, 800 N 6
41834 Littcarr, 550 R 6
42352 Livermore, 1,594 G 5
42059 Lola, 600 E 6
40741 London⊙, 4,337 N 6
42001 Lone Oak, 3,759 D 6
41542 Lookout, 600 S 6
40037 Loretto, 985 L 5
41348 Lost Creek, 500 P 6
41701 Lothair, 800 P 6
41230 Louisa⊙, 1,781 R 4
* 40201 Louisville⊙, 361,472 K 4
Louisville, ‡826,553 K 4
41231 Lovely, 500 S 5
41232 Lowmansville, 500 R 5
40854 Loyall, 1,212 P 7
41016 Ludlow, 5,815 S 2
40855 Lynch, 800 R 7
† 40201 Lynnview, 1,165 K 4
42431 Madisonville⊙, 15,332 F 6
41547 Majestic, 600 S 5
40962 Manchester⊙, 1,664 O 6
42064 Marion⊙, 3,008 E 6
42631 Marshes Siding, 950 M 7
41649 Martin, 786 R 5
42066 Mayfield⊙, 10,724 D 7
41056 Maysville⊙, 7,411 O 3
41543 McAndrews, 975 S 5
40447 McKee⊙, 255 O 6
40448 McKinney, 475 M 6
41835 McRoberts, 1,037 R 6
41546 McVeigh, 700 S 5
41059 Melbourne, 500 T 3
41501 Meta, 600 S 5
40965 Middlesboro, 11,844 O 7
40243 Middletown, 2,500 L 4
40347 Midway, 1,278 M 4
41501 Millard, 600 S 6
40348 Millersburg, 788 N 4
40045 Milton, 756 L 3
42633 Monticello⊙, 3,618 M 7
40351 Morehead⊙, 7,191 P 4
42437 Morganfield⊙, 3,563 E 5
42261 Morgantown⊙, 1,394 H 6
42440 Mortons Gap, 1,169 F 6
41064 Mount Olivet⊙, 442 N 3
40353 Mount Sterling⊙, 5,083 N 4
40456 Mount Vernon⊙, 1,639 N 6
40047 Mount Washington, 2,020 K 4
40155 Muldraugh, 1,773 J 5
42765 Munfordville⊙, 1,233 J 6
42071 Murray⊙, 13,537 E 7
42544 Nancy, 600 M 6
41840 Neon, 705 R 6
40050 New Castle⊙, 755 L 4
40051 New Haven, 977 K 5
* 41071 Newport, 25,988 S 2
40356 Nicholasville⊙, 5,829 N 5
41357 Noctor, 500 P 5
42442 Nortonville, 699 G 6
41238 Oil Springs, 900 P 5
40219 Okolona, 17,643 K 4
41164 Olive Hill, 1,197 P 4
40972 Oneida, 700 O 6
42301 Owensboro⊙, 50,329 G 5
40359 Owenton⊙, 1,280 M 3
40360 Owingsville⊙, 1,381 O 4
42001 Paducah⊙, 31,627 D 6
41240 Paintsville⊙, 3,868 R 5
40361 Paris⊙, 7,823 N 4
42160 Park City, 567 J 6
† 41011 Park Hills, 3,999 S 2
40464 Parksville, 560 M 5
42266 Pembroke, 634 G 7
40468 Perryville, 730 M 5
40056 Pewee Valley, 950 L 4
41553 Phelps, 770 S 6
42366 Philpot, 531 H 5
41501 Pikeville⊙, 4,576 S 6
42635 Pine Knot, 950 M 7
40977 Pineville⊙, 2,817 O 7
40755 Pittsburg, 938 N 6
40258 Pleasure Ridge Park, 28,566 J 4
40057 Pleasureville, 747 L 4
42367 Powderly, 631 G 6
41845 Premium, 489 R 6
41653 Prestonsburg⊙, 3,422 R 5
42445 Princeton⊙, 6,292 F 6
40059 Prospect, 500 K 4
42450 Providence, 4,270 F 6
41169 Raceland, 1,857 R 3
40160 Radcliff, 7,881 K 5
40472 Ravenna, 784 O 5
42638 Revelo, 500 N 7
40475 Richmond⊙, 16,861 N 5
42452 Robards, 701 F 5
41169 Russell, 1,982 R 3
42642 Russell Springs, 1,641 L 6
42276 Russellville⊙, 6,456 H 7
40207 Saint Matthews, 13,152 K 4
42078 Salem, 650 E 6
40371 Salt Lick, 441 O 4
40372 Salvisa, 500 M 5
41465 Salyersville⊙, 1,196 P 5
41171 Sandy Hook⊙, 192 P 4
40982 Scalf, 500 O 7
42553 Science Hill, 470 M 6
42164 Scottsville⊙, 3,584 J 7
42455 Sebree, 1,092 F 5
† 41385 Sewell, 500 P 5
40983 Sextons Creek, 975 O 6
41562 Shelbiana, 800 R 6
40065 Shelbyville⊙, 4,182 L 4
40165 Shepherdsville⊙, 2,769 K 4

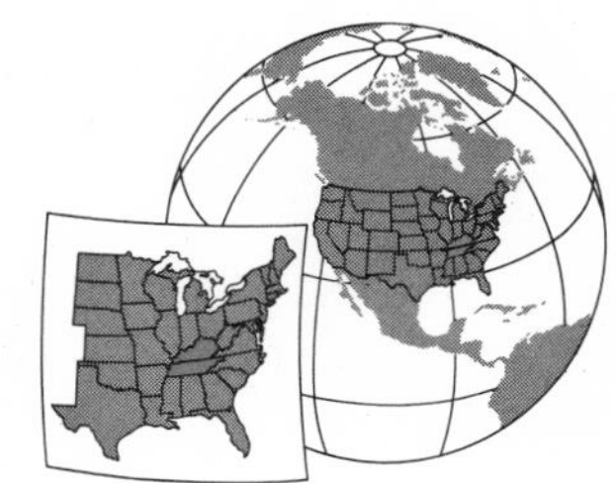

KENTUCKY

AREA 40,395 sq. mi.
POPULATION 3,219,311
CAPITAL Frankfort
LARGEST CITY Louisville
HIGHEST POINT Black Mtn. 4,145 ft.
SETTLED IN 1774
ADMITTED TO UNION June 1, 1792
POPULAR NAME Blue Grass State
STATE FLOWER Goldenrod
STATE BIRD Cardinal

TENNESSEE

AREA 42,244 sq. mi.
POPULATION 3,924,164
CAPITAL Nashville
LARGEST CITY Memphis
HIGHEST POINT Clingmans Dome 6,643 ft.
SETTLED IN 1757
ADMITTED TO UNION June 1, 1796
POPULAR NAME Volunteer State
STATE FLOWER Iris
STATE BIRD Mockingbird

Zip	Name/Pop.	Key
40216	Shively, 19,223	K 4
40984	Sibert, 500	O 6
41085	Silver Grove, 1,365	T 3
40067	Simpsonville, 628	L 4
41763	Slemp, 500	P 6
41764	Smilax, 856	P 6
42081	Smithland⊙, 514	E 6
42171	Smiths Grove, 756	J 6
42646	Smith Town, 500	M 7
41173	Soldier, 600	P 4
42501	Somerset⊙, 10,436	M 6
41071	Southgate, 3,212	S 2
41174	South Portsmouth, 950	P 3
41175	South Shore, 676	R 3
† 25661	South Williamson, 850	S 5
42458	Spottsville, 914	G 5
40069	Springfield⊙, 2,961	L 5
41256	Staffordsville, 700	R 5
40484	Stanford⊙, 2,474	M 5
40380	Stanton⊙, 2,037	O 5
42647	Stearns, 900	N 7
40170	Stephensport, 500	H 5
41567	Stone, 850	S 5
42459	Sturgis, 2,210	F 5
42558	Tateville, 680	M 7
† 41011	Taylor Mill, 3,253	S 3
40071	Taylorsville⊙, 897	L 4
41259	Thealka, 550	R 5
41189	Tollesboro, 500	O 3
42167	Tompkinsville⊙, 2,207	K 7
42286	Trenton, 496	G 7
40486	Tyner, 590	O 6
41091	Union, 500	M 3
42461	Uniontown, 1,255	F 5
42784	Upton, 552	K 6
40272	Valley Station, 24,471	K 4
41179	Vanceburg⊙, 1,773	P 3
41265	Van Lear, 1,033	R 5
40872	Verda, 950	P 7
41092	Verona, 500	M 3
40383	Versailles⊙, 5,679	M 4
† 41017	Villa Hills, 1,647	R 2
40175	Vine Grove, 2,987	K 5
41572	Virgie, 600	R 6
41094	Walton, 1,801	M 3
41095	Warsaw⊙, 1,232	M 3
41667	Weeksbury, 950	R 6
41472	West Liberty⊙, 1,387	P 5
40177	West Point, 1,741	J 4
42564	West Somerset, 850	M 6
41268	West Van Lear, 975	R 5
41101	Westwood, 2,900	R 4
41669	Wheelwright, 793	R 6
42464	White Plains, 729	G 6
41858	Whitesburg⊙, 1,137	R 6
42378	Whitesville, 752	H 5
42653	Whitley City⊙, 1,060	N 7
42087	Wickliffe⊙, 1,211	C 7
† 41071	Wilders, 823	S 3
40769	Williamsburg⊙, 3,687	N 7
41097	Williamstown⊙, 2,063	M 3
40390	Wilmore, 3,466	M 5
40391	Winchester⊙, 13,402	N 4
42088	Wingo, 593	D 7
† 41011	Winston Park, 578	S 3
41394	Wolverine, 500	P 5
40771	Woodbine, 700	N 7
† 42001	Woodlawn, 1,639	D 6
† 41071	Woodlawn, 525	S 2
41776	Wooton, 750	P 6
41183	Worthington, 1,364	R 3
41501	Zebulon, 800	R 5

TENNESSEE

COUNTIES

County, Pop.	Key
Anderson, 60,300	N 8
Bedford, 25,039	J 9
Benton, 12,126	E 8
Bledsoe, 7,643	L 9
Blount, 63,744	O 9
Bradley, 50,686	M 10
Campbell, 26,045	N 8
Cannon, 8,467	J 9
Carroll, 25,741	E 9
Carter, 42,575	S 8
Cheatham, 13,199	G 8
Chester, 9,927	D 10
Claiborne, 19,420	O 8
Clay, 6,624	K 7
Cocke, 25,283	P 9
Coffee, 32,572	J 9
Crockett, 14,402	C 9
Cumberland, 20,733	L 9
Davidson, 447,877	H 8
Decatur, 9,457	E 9
De Kalb, 11,151	K 9
Dickson, 21,977	G 8
Dyer, 30,427	C 8
Fayette, 22,692	C 10
Fentress, 12,593	M 8
Franklin, 27,244	J 10
Gibson, 47,871	D 9
Giles, 22,138	G 10
Grainger, 13,948	O 8
Greene, 47,630	R 8
Grundy, 10,631	K 10
Hamblen, 38,696	P 8
Hamilton, 254,236	L 10
Hancock, 6,719	P 7
Hardeman, 22,435	C 10
Hardin, 18,212	E 10
Hawkins, 33,726	P 8
Haywood, 19,596	C 9
Henderson, 17,291	E 9
Henry, 23,749	E 8
Hickman, 12,096	G 9
Houston, 5,845	F 8
Humphreys, 13,560	F 8
Jackson, 8,141	K 8
Jefferson, 24,940	P 8
Johnson, 11,569	T 7
Knox, 276,293	O 9
Lake, 7,896	B 8
Lauderdale, 20,271	B 9
Lawrence, 29,097	G 10
Lewis, 6,761	F 9
Lincoln, 24,318	H 10
Loudon, 24,266	N 9
Macon, 12,315	J 7
Madison, 65,727	D 9
Marion, 20,577	K 10
Marshall, 17,319	H 10
Maury, 43,376	G 9
McMinn, 35,462	M 10
McNairy, 18,369	D 10
Meigs, 5,219	M 9
Monroe, 23,475	N 10
Montgomery, 62,721	G 8
Moore, 3,568	J 10
Morgan, 13,619	M 8
Obion, 29,936	C 8
Overton, 14,866	L 8
Perry, 5,238	F 9
Pickett, 3,774	M 7
Polk, 11,669	N 10
Putnam, 35,487	K 8
Rhea, 17,202	M 9
Roane, 38,881	M 9
Robertson, 29,102	H 7
Rutherford, 59,428	J 9
Scott, 14,762	M 8
Sequatchie, 6,331	L 10
Sevier, 28,241	O 9
Shelby, 722,014	B 10
Smith, 12,509	J 8
Stewart, 7,319	F 7
Sullivan, 127,329	S 7
Sumner, 56,106	J 8
Tipton, 28,001	B 9
Trousdale, 5,155	J 8
Unicoi, 15,254	S 8
Union, 9,072	O 8
Van Buren, 3,758	L 9
Warren, 26,972	K 9
Washington, 73,924	R 8
Wayne, 12,365	F 10
Weakley, 28,827	D 8
White, 17,088	L 9
Williamson, 34,330	H 9
Wilson, 36,999	J 8

CITIES and TOWNS

Zip	Name/Pop.	Key
37010	Adams, 458	G 7
38310	Adamsville, 1,344	E 10
37616	Afton, 550	R 8
38001	Alamo⊙, 2,499	C 9
37701	Alcoa, 7,739	N 9
37012	Alexandria, 680	J 8
38501	Algood, 1,808	K 8
38504	Allardt, 610	M 8
38541	Allons, 600	L 8
37301	Altamont⊙, 546	K 10
38449	Ardmore, 601	H 10
38002	Arlington, 1,349	B 10
38506	Armathwaite, 625	M 8
37707	Arthur, 500	O 7
37015	Ashland City⊙, 2,027	G 8
37303	Athens⊙, 11,790	M 10
38004	Atoka, 446	B 10
38220	Atwood, 937	D 9
37304	Bakewell, 600	L 10
† 37650	Banner Hill, 2,517	R 8
38005	Bartlett, 1,150	B 10
38311	Bath Springs, 725	E 10
38544	Baxter, 1,229	K 8
37708	Bean Station, 500	P 8
37018	Beechgrove, 600	J 9
37305	Beersheba Springs, 560	K 10
37205	Belle Meade	H 8
38006	Bells, 1,474	C 9
38314	Bemis, 1,883	D 9
37307	Benton⊙, 749	M 10
† 37201	Berry Hill	H 8
† 37027	Berry's Chapel, 1,345	H 9
38315	Bethel Springs, 781	D 10
38221	Big Sandy, 539	E 8
37308	Birchwood, 900	M 10
37709	Blaine, 650	O 8
37660	Bloomingdale, 3,120	R 7
38545	Bloomington Springs, 800	K 8
37617	Blountville⊙, 900	S 7
37618	Bluff City, 947	S 8
38008	Bolivar⊙, 6,674	C 10
38316	Bradford, 968	D 8
37658	Braemar-Hampton, 1,100	S 8
37027	Brentwood, 1,091	H 8
37710	Briceville, 850	N 8
38011	Brighton, 952	B 10
37620	Bristol, 20,064	S 7
38012	Brownsville⊙, 7,011	C 9
38317	Bruceton, 1,450	E 8
38014	Brunswick, 500	B 10
38318	Buena Vista, 500	E 9
37711	Bulls Gap, 774	P 8
37640	Butler, 500	T 8
38549	Byrdstown⊙, 582	L 7
37309	Calhoun, 624	M 10
38320	Camden⊙, 3,052	E 8
38129	Capleville, 450	B 10
37030	Carthage⊙, 2,491	K 8
37714	Caryville, 648	N 8
38551	Celina⊙, 1,370	K 7
37033	Centerville⊙, 2,592	G 9
37034	Chapel Hill, 752	H 9
37310	Charleston, 792	M 10
37036	Charlotte⊙, 610	G 8
* 37401	Chattanooga⊙, 119,082	K 10
	Chattanooga, ‡304,927	K 10
37642	Church Hill, 2,822	R 7
37715	Clairfield, 650	O 7
38553	Clarkrange, 675	L 8
37040	Clarksville⊙, 31,719	G 7
37311	Cleveland⊙, 20,651	M 10
38425	Clifton, 737	F 10
37716	Clinton⊙, 4,794	N 8
37719	Coalfield, 712	N 8
37313	Coalmont, 518	K 10
37314	Cokercreek, 500	N 10
37315	Collegedale, 3,031	M 10
38017	Collierville, 3,625	B 10
38450	Collinwood, 922	F 10
37663	Colonial Heights, 3,027	R 8
38401	Columbia⊙, 21,471	G 9
37720	Concord, 500	N 9
38501	Cookeville⊙, 14,270	L 8
37317	Copperhill, 563	N 10
38018	Cordova, 600	B 10
37047	Cornersville, 655	H 10
37721	Corryton, 500	O 8
38326	Counce, 975	E 10
38019	Covington⊙, 5,801	B 9
37318	Cowan, 1,772	K 10
37723	Crab Orchard, 900	M 9
38555	Crossville⊙, 5,381	L 9
37051	Cumberland Furnace, 800	G 8
38452	Cypress Inn, 500	F 10
37725	Dandridge⊙, 1,270	O 8
37321	Dayton⊙, 4,361	L 9
37322	Decatur⊙, 698	M 9
38329	Decaturville⊙, 958	E 9
37324	Decherd, 2,148	J 10
37055	Dickson, 5,665	G 8
37214	Donelson	H 8
37058	Dover⊙, 1,179	F 8
38559	Doyle, 1,205	K 9
38225	Dresden⊙, 1,939	D 8
38023	Drummonds, 700	A 10
37326	Ducktown, 562	N 10
37327	Dunlap⊙, 1,672	L 10
38330	Dyer, 2,501	D 8
38024	Dyersburg⊙, 14,523	C 8
† 37801	Eagleton, 5,345	O 9
† 37311	East Cleveland, 1,870	M 10
37412	East Ridge, 21,799	L 11
37732	Elgin, 500	M 8
37643	Elizabethton⊙, 12,269	S 8
37734	Elk Valley, 750	N 7
38029	Ellendale, 1,500	B 10
† 37601	Embreeville Junction, 1,293	R 8
37735	Emory Gap, 500	M 9
37329	Englewood, 1,878	M 10
37061	Erin⊙, 1,157	F 8
37650	Erwin⊙, 4,715	S 8
37330	Estill Springs, 919	J 10
38456	Ethridge, 600	G 10
37331	Etowah, 3,736	M 10
37332	Evensville, 475	M 9
37062	Fairview, 1,630	G 9
37656	Fall Branch, 825	R 8
37334	Fayetteville⊙, 7,030	H 10
38030	Finley, 950	B 8
37335	Flintville, 500	H 10
38031	Forest Hill, 850	B 10
† 37201	Forest Hills	H 8
38032	Fort Pillow, 700	B 9
37064	Franklin⊙, 9,404	H 9
38034	Friendship, 441	C 9
37737	Friendsville, 575	N 9
38337	Gadsden, 523	D 9
38562	Gainesboro⊙, 1,101	K 8
37066	Gallatin⊙, 13,093	H 8
38037	Gates, 523	C 9
37738	Gatlinburg, 2,329	O 9
38038	Germantown, 3,474	B 10
37071	Gladeville, 500	J 8
38229	Gleason, 1,314	D 8
37072	Goodlettsville	H 8
38563	Gordonsville, 601	K 8
37337	Grandview, 1,250	M 9
37338	Graysville, 951	L 10
37073	Green Brier, 2,279	H 8
37743	Greeneville⊙, 13,722	R 8
38230	Greenfield, 2,050	D 8
38565	Grimsley, 500	L 2
37339	Gruetli, 910	K 10
† 37766	Habersham, 800	N 8
38040	Halls, 2,323	C 9
38461	Hampshire, 500	G 9
37658	Hampton-Braemar, 1,100	S 8
37748	Harriman, 8,734	M 9
37341	Harrison, 500	L 10
37752	Harrogate, 950	O 8
37074	Hartsville⊙, 2,243	J 8
37755	Helenwood, 675	M 8
38340	Henderson⊙, 3,581	D 10
38041	Henning, 605	B 9
37343	Hixson, 6,188	L 10
38462	Hohenwald⊙, 3,385	F 9
38342	Hollow Rock, 722	E 8
38343	Humboldt, 10,066	D 9
38344	Huntingdon⊙, 3,661	E 8
37345	Huntland, 849	J 10
37756	Huntsville⊙, 337	N 8
37079	Indian Mound, 600	F 7
† 37201	Inglewood	H 8
38463	Iron City, 504	F 10
37757	Jacksboro⊙, 689	N 8
38301	Jackson⊙, 39,996	D 9
38556	Jamestown⊙, 1,899	M 8
37347	Jasper⊙, 1,811	K 10
37760	Jefferson City, 5,124	P 8
37762	Jellico, 2,235	N 7
37601	Johnson City, 33,770	S 8
37659	Jonesboro⊙, 1,510	R 8
37921	Karns, 1,105	N 9
38233	Kenton, 1,439	C 8
† 34347	Kimball, 807	K 10
* 37660	Kingsport, 31,938	R 7
37763	Kingston⊙, 4,142	N 9
* 37901	Knoxville⊙, 174,587	O 9
	Knoxville, ‡400,337	O 9
37349	Laager, 675	K 10
37083	Lafayette⊙, 2,583	J 7
37766	La Follette, 6,902	N 8
37769	Lake City, 1,923	N 8
37416	Lake Hills-Murray Hills, 7,806	L 10
† 37138	Lakewood, 2,500	H 8
37086	La Vergne, 2,825	H 9
38464	Lawrenceburg⊙, 8,889	G 10
37087	Lebanon⊙, 12,492	J 8
37771	Lenoir City, 5,324	N 9
37091	Lewisburg⊙, 7,207	H 10
38351	Lexington⊙, 4,955	E 9
37681	Limestone, 500	R 8
37096	Linden⊙, 1,062	F 9
38570	Livingston⊙, 3,050	L 8
37097	Lobelville, 773	F 9
† 37662	Long Island, 1,352	S 7
37350	Lookout Mountain, 1,741	L 11
38469	Loretto, 1,375	G 10
37774	Loudon⊙, 3,728	N 9
37777	Louisville, 500	N 9
37351	Lupton City, 750	L 10
37779	Luttrell, 819	O 8
38471	Lutts, 850	F 10

(continued on following page)

Jack Zehrt — Shostal Associates

Sleek racehorses enjoy a patch of shade on a Calumet Farm pasture in Lexington, Kentucky. More than half the country's winning racehorses are from Inner Bluegrass area farms.

Eugene Belt — Shostal Associates

Using field glasses to bridge the gap, a naturalist observes the wildlife in Cades Cove, Tennessee. Mist-shrouded Great Smoky Mountains are in the distance.

Kentucky and Tennessee
(continued)

TENNESSEE (continued)

37352 Lynchburg⊙, 361 ... J 10
37115 Madison, ... H 8
37354 Madisonville⊙, 2,614 ... N 9
38354 Malesus, 600 ... D 9
37355 Manchester⊙, 6,208 ... J 10
† 37771 Martel, 500 ... N 9
38237 Martin, 7,781 ... D 8
† 38471 Martins Mills, 440 ... F 10
37801 Maryville⊙, 13,808 ... O 9
37806 Mascot, 1,050 ... O 8
38049 Mason, 443 ... B 10
38050 Maury City, 813 ... C 9
37807 Maynardville⊙, 702 ... O 8
37353 McDonald, 500 ... M 10
37101 McEwen, 1,237 ... F 8
38201 McKenzie, 4,873 ... E 8
37110 McMinnville⊙, 10,662 ... K 9
38355 Medina, 755 ... D 9
* 38101 Memphis⊙, 623,530 ... B 10
Memphis, ‡770,120 ... B 10
38052 Middleton, 654 ... D 10
38358 Milan, 7,313 ... D 9
37682 Milligan College, 1,170 ... S 8
38053 Millington, 21,106 ... B 10
37356 Monteagle, 934 ... K 10
38574 Monterey, 2,351 ... L 8
† 37660 Morrison City, 2,178 ... R 7
37814 Morristown⊙, 20,318 ... P 8
38057 Moscow, 448 ... C 10
37818 Mosheim, 450 ... R 8
37683 Mountain City⊙, 1,883 ... T 8
37122 Mount Juliet, 800 ... H 8
38474 Mount Pleasant, 3,530 ... G 9
38058 Munford, 1,281 ... B 10
37130 Murfreesboro⊙, 26,360 ... J 9
* 37201 Nashville (cap.)⊙, 447,877 ... H 8
Nashville, ‡540,982 ... H 8
† 37901 Neubert, 1,500 ... O 9
38059 Newbern, 2,124 ... C 8
37819 Newcomb, 550 ... N 7
37134 New Johnsonville, 970 ... E 8
37820 New Market, 950 ... O 8
37821 Newport⊙, 7,328 ... P 9
37825 New Tazewell, 1,192 ... O 8
37826 Niota, 629 ... M 9
37828 Norris, 1,359 ... N 8
† 37201 Oak Hill, ... H 8
37830 Oak Ridge, 28,319 ... N 8
38240 Obion, 1,010 ... C 8
37138 Old Hickory, ... H 8
37840 Oliver Springs, 3,405 ... N 8
37841 Oneida, 2,602 ... N 7
37363 Ooltewah, 1,200 ... M 10
† 37660 Orebank, 1,111 ... R 7
38577 Pall Mall, 500 ... M 7
37365 Palmer, 898 ... K 10
38242 Paris⊙, 9,892 ... E 8
38363 Parsons, 2,167 ... E 9
37143 Pegram, 850 ... H 8
37144 Petersburg, 463 ... H 10
37845 Petros, 800 ... M 8
37846 Philadelphia, 554 ... M 9
37862 Pigeon Forge, 1,361 ... O 9
37367 Pikeville⊙, 1,454 ... L 9
37148 Portland, 2,872 ... H 7
37849 Powell, 1,200 ... N 8
† 37201 Providence, ... H 8
38478 Pulaski⊙, 6,989 ... G 10
38251 Puryear, 458 ... E 8
38128 Raleigh, 2,500 ... B 10
37415 Red Bank, 12,715 ... L 10
37150 Red Boiling Springs, 726 ... K 7
37370 Riceville, 500 ... M 10
38580 Rickman, 500 ... L 8
38080 Ridgely, 1,657 ... B 8
† 37401 Ridgeside, 458 ... L 10
37152 Ridgetop, 810 ... H 8
38063 Ripley⊙, 4,794 ... B 9
38253 Rives, 5,259 ... C 8
37687 Roan Mountain, 950 ... S 8
37853 Rockford, 950 ... O 9
37854 Rockwood, 5,259 ... M 9
37857 Rogersville⊙, 4,045 ... P 8
38053 Rosemark, 950 ... B 10
37860 Russellville, 850 ... P 8
38369 Rutherford, 1,385 ... C 8
37861 Rutledge⊙, 863 ... P 8
38481 Saint Joseph, 637 ... G 10
37373 Sale Creek, 900 ... L 10
38254 Samburg, 463 ... C 8
38372 Savannah⊙, 5,576 ... E 10
38374 Scotts Hill, 476 ... E 10
38375 Selmer⊙, 3,495 ... D 10
37374 Sequatchie, 450 ... K 10
37862 Sevierville⊙, 2,661 ... P 9
37375 Sewanee, 1,886 ... K 10
37865 Seymour, 500 ... O 9
38255 Sharon, 1,188 ... D 8
37160 Shelbyville⊙, 12,262 ... H 10
37377 Signal Mountain, 4,839 ... L 10
37166 Smithville⊙, 2,997 ... K 9
37167 Smyrna, 5,698 ... H 9
37869 Sneedville⊙, 874 ... P 7
37379 Soddy-Daisy, 7,569 ... L 10
38068 Somerville⊙, 1,816 ... C 10
† 37030 South Carthage, 859 ... K 8
† 37311 South Cleveland, 5,070 ... M 10
† 37716 South Clinton, 1,484 ... N 8
42041 South Fulton, 3,122 ... D 8
37380 South Pittsburg, 3,613 ... K 10
37171 Southside, 800 ... G 8
38583 Sparta⊙, 4,930 ... K 9
38585 Spencer⊙, 1,179 ... L 9
37381 Spring City, 1,756 ... M 9
38378 Spring Creek, 500 ... D 9
37172 Springfield⊙, 9,720 ... H 8
37174 Spring Hill, 685 ... H 9
37871 Strawberry Plains, 680 ... O 8
† 37660 Sullivan Gardens, 950 ... R 7
38483 Summertown, 700 ... G 10
37382 Summitville, 500 ... K 9
37872 Sunbright, 500 ... M 8
37873 Surgoinsville, 1,285 ... R 8
37874 Sweetwater, 4,340 ... N 9
37877 Talbott, 975 ... P 8

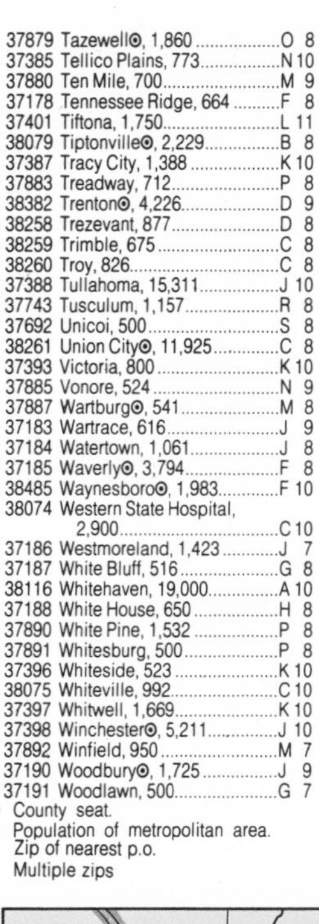

37879 Tazewell⊙, 1,860 ... O 8
37385 Tellico Plains, 773 ... N 10
37880 Ten Mile, 700 ... M 9
37178 Tennessee Ridge, 664 ... F 8
† 37401 Tiftona, 1,750 ... L 11
38079 Tiptonville⊙, 2,229 ... B 8
37387 Tracy City, 1,388 ... K 10
37883 Treadway, 712 ... P 8
38382 Trenton⊙, 4,226 ... D 9
38258 Trezevant, 877 ... D 8
38259 Trimble, 675 ... C 8
38260 Troy, 826 ... C 8
37388 Tullahoma, 15,311 ... J 10
37743 Tusculum, 1,157 ... R 8
37692 Unicoi, 500 ... S 8
38261 Union City⊙, 11,925 ... C 8
37393 Victoria, 800 ... K 10
37885 Vonore, 524 ... N 9
37887 Wartburg⊙, 541 ... M 8
37183 Wartrace, 616 ... J 9
37184 Watertown, 1,061 ... J 8
37185 Waverly⊙, 3,794 ... F 8
38485 Waynesboro⊙, 1,983 ... F 10
38074 Western State Hospital, 2,900 ... C 10
37186 Westmoreland, 1,423 ... J 7
37187 White Bluff, 516 ... G 8
38116 Whitehaven, 19,000 ... A 10
37188 White House, 650 ... H 8
37890 White Pine, 1,532 ... P 8
37891 Whitesburg, 500 ... P 8
37396 Whiteside, 523 ... K 10
38075 Whiteville, 992 ... C 10
37397 Whitwell, 1,669 ... K 10
37398 Winchester⊙, 5,211 ... J 10
37892 Winfield, 950 ... M 7
37190 Woodbury⊙, 1,725 ... J 9
37191 Woodlawn, 500 ... G 7

⊙ County seat.
‡ Population of metropolitan area.
† Zip of nearest p.o.
* Multiple zips

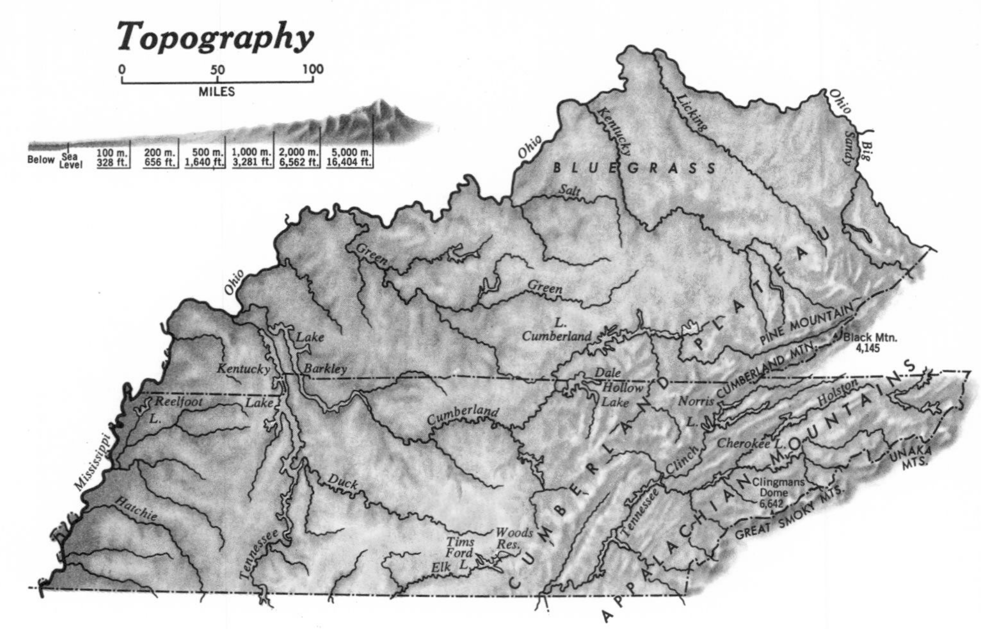

KENTUCKY
and
TENNESSEE
SCALE
0 5 10 20 40 MI.
0 5 10 20 30 40 KM.
State Capitals
County Seats
© C.S. HAMMOND & Co., N.Y.
INDIANA
OHIO
WEST
VIRGINIA
VIRGINIA
NORTH
CAROLINA
SOUTH
CAROLINA
GEORGIA
INDIANAPOLIS
CINCINNATI
DAYTON
LOUISVILLE
Frankfort
Lexington
KNOXVILLE
CHATTANOOGA
Charleston
Huntington
Ashland
Asheville
Longitude West of Greenwich
86°
85°
84°
83°
82°
39°
38°
37°
36°
35°
OHIO
CINCINNATI
BOONE
KENTON
CAMPBELL
Covington
Newport
Ft. Thomas
Bellevue
Dayton
Ludlow
Florence
Erlanger
Edgewood
Taylor Mill
Cold Spring
Silver Grove
Southgate
Melbourne
Fairview
Elsmere
Hopeful Hts.
Burlington
Hebron
Constance
Addyston
Taylorsport
Newtown
Mt. Mitchell 6,684
Clingmans Dome 6,643
Mt. Le Conte 6,593
Richland Balsam 6,540
Craggy Dome 6,105
GREAT SMOKY MTS.
CUMBERLAND GAP NAT'L HIST. PARK
GREAT SMOKY MTS. NATIONAL PARK
CHICKAMAUGA AND CHATTANOOGA NAT'L MIL. PARK
ABRAHAM LINCOLN BIRTHPLACE NAT'L HIST. SITE
MAMMOTH CAVE NAT'L PARK
ANDREW JOHNSON NAT'L HIST. SITE

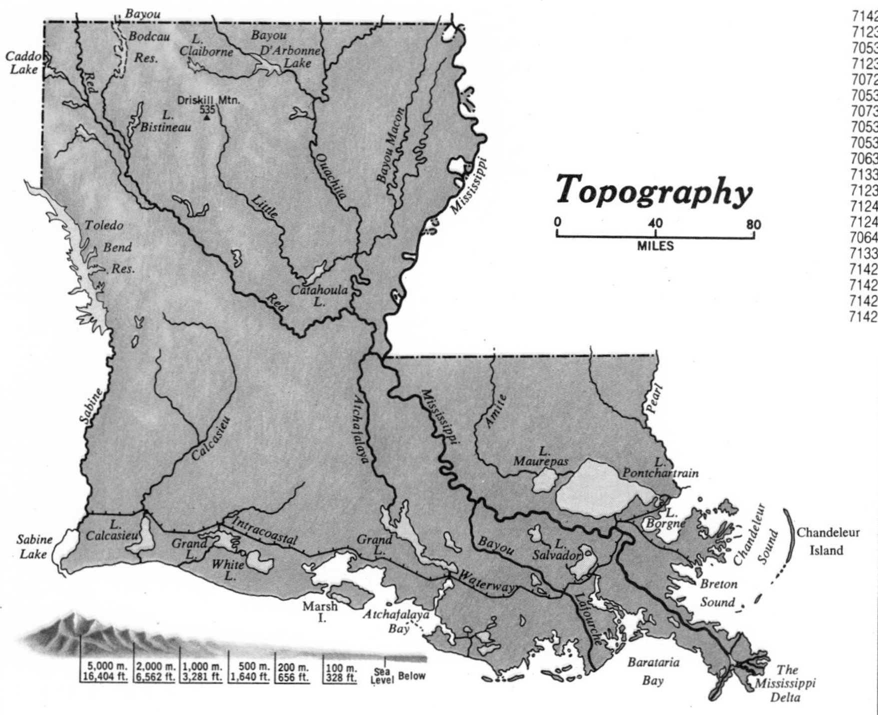

PARISHES

Parish	Key
Acadia, 52,109	F 6
Allen, 20,794	E 5
Ascension, 37,086	J 6
Assumption, 19,654	H 7
Avoyelles, 37,751	G 4
Beauregard, 22,888	D 5
Bienville, 16,024	D 2
Bossier, 64,519	C 1
Caddo, 230,184	C 1
Calcasieu, 145,415	D 6
Caldwell, 9,354	F 2
Cameron, 8,194	D 7
Catahoula, 11,769	G 3
Claiborne, 17,024	D 1
Concordia, 22,578	G 4
De Soto, 22,764	C 2
East Baton Rouge, 285,167	K 1
East Carroll, 12,884	H 1
East Feliciana, 17,657	H 5
Evangeline, 31,932	F 5
Franklin, 23,946	G 2
Grant, 13,671	E 3
Iberia, 57,397	G 7
Iberville, 30,746	H 6
Jackson, 15,963	E 2
Jefferson, 337,568	K 7
Jefferson Davis, 29,554	E 6
Lafayette, 109,716	F 6
Lafourche, 68,941	K 7
La Salle, 13,295	F 3
Lincoln, 33,800	E 1
Livingston, 36,511	L 2
Madison, 15,065	H 2
Morehouse, 32,463	G 1
Natchitoches, 35,219	D 3
Orleans, 593,471	L 6
Ouachita, 115,387	F 2
Plaquemines, 25,225	L 8
Pointe Coupee, 22,022	G 5
Rapides, 118,078	E 4
Red River, 9,226	D 2
Richland, 21,774	G 2
Sabine, 18,638	C 3
Saint Bernard, 51,185	L 7
Saint Charles, 29,550	K 7
Saint Helena, 9,937	J 5
Saint James, 19,733	L 3
Saint John the Baptist, 23,813	M 3
Saint Landry, 80,364	F 5
Saint Martin, 32,453	G 6
Saint Mary, 60,752	H 7
Saint Tammany, 63,585	L 6
Tangipahoa, 65,875	K 5
Tensas, 9,732	H 2
Terrebonne, 76,049	J 8
Union, 18,447	F 1
Vermilion, 43,071	F 7
Vernon, 53,794	D 4
Washington, 41,987	K 5
Webster, 39,939	D 1
West Baton Rouge, 16,864	H 6
West Carroll, 13,028	H 1
West Feliciana, 11,376	H 5
Winn, 16,369	E 3

CITIES and TOWNS

	Zip	Name/Pop.	Key
	70510	Abbeville⊙, 10,996	F 7
	70420	Abita Springs, 839	L 6
	71316	Acme, 212	G 4
†	70774	Acy, 570	L 3
	70710	Addis, 724	J 2
†	70544	Adeline, 200	G 7
	70711	Albany, 700	M 1
†	71016	Alberta, 300	D 2
	71301	Alexandria⊙, 41,557	E 4
	70340	Amelia, 2,292	H 7
	70422	Amite⊙, 3,593	K 5
	71403	Anacoco, 575	D 4
†	71301	Anandale, 1,779	F 4
	70426	Angie, 317	L 5
	70712	Angola, 550	G 5
	70032	Arabi, 12,000	K 7
†	70736	Arbroth, 250	H 5
	71001	Arcadia⊙, 2,970	E 1
	71218	Archibald, 300	G 2
†	71343	Archie, 280	G 3
†	70456	Arcola, 200	K 5
	70512	Arnaudville, 1,673	G 6
	71002	Ashland, 211	D 2
	71003	Athens, 387	E 1
	71404	Atlanta, 342	E 3
	70513	Avery Island, 591	G 7
	70713	Bains, 400	H 5
	70714	Baker, 8,281	K 1
	70514	Baldwin, 2,117	H 7
	71405	Ball, 500	F 4
†	70401	Baptist, 150	M 1
	70036	Barataria, 950	K 7
	70515	Basile, 1,779	E 5
	71219	Baskin, 177	G 2
	71220	Bastrop⊙, 14,713	G 1
*	70801	Baton Rouge (cap.)⊙, 165,963	K 2
		Baton Rouge, ‡285,167	K 2
†	70754	Bayou Barbary, 200	M 2
†	70360	Bayou Cane, 9,077	J 7
	70716	Bayou Goula, 850	J 3
	70380	Bayou Vista, 5,121	H 7
†	71220	Beekman, 300	G 1
	70675	Bel, 150	D 6
	71004	Belcher, 400	C 1
	70630	Bell City, 350	D 6
†	70341	Belle Alliance, 350	K 3
	70037	Belle Chasse, 950	O 4
†	71330	Belledeau, 450	F 4
	70341	Belle Rose, 900	K 3
†	71468	Bellwood, 150	D 3
	71406	Belmont, 150	C 3
	71005	Benson, 200	C 3
	71407	Bentley, 300	E 3
	71006	Benton⊙, 1,493	C 1
	71222	Bernice, 1,794	E 1
†	70040	Bertrandville, 175	L 7
	70342	Berwick, 4,168	H 7
	71007	Bethany, 250	B 2
	71008	Bienville, 287	D 2
	71009	Blanchard, 806	C 1
	70427	Bogalusa, 18,412	L 5
†	71064	Bolinger, 250	C 1
	71223	Bonita, 533	G 1
	70038	Boothville, 300	M 8
	71320	Bordelonville, 450	G 4
	71224	Bosco, 480	F 2
	71010	Bossier City, 41,595	C 1
†	70353	Boudreaux, 275	J 8
	70343	Bourg, 900	J 7
	70039	Boutte, 950	N 4
	71409	Boyce, 1,240	E 4
	70040	Braithwaite, 550	P 4
	70517	Breaux Bridge, 4,942	G 6
	70718	Brittany, 290	L 3
	70518	Broussard, 1,707	F 6
	70719	Brusly, 1,282	J 2
	71322	Bunkie, 5,395	F 5
	70041	Buras-Triumph, 4,113	L 8
	70738	Burnside, 500	L 3
	70431	Bush, 275	L 5
	70519	Cade, 800	G 6
	71433	Calcasieu, 400	E 4
	71225	Calhoun, 653	F 2
	71410	Calvin, 286	E 3
	70631	Cameron⊙, 975	D 7
	71411	Campti, 1,078	D 3
†	70584	Cankton, 260	F 6
	70520	Carencro, 2,302	G 6
	70042	Carlisle, 975	L 7
	70721	Carville, 950	K 3
	71016	Castor, 178	D 2
	70521	Cecelia, 550	G 6
	71323	Center Point, 850	F 4
	70522	Centerville, 500	H 7
†	70723	Central, 546	L 3
†	70395	Chacahoula, 150	J 7
	70043	Chalmette⊙, 15,000	P 4
	70523	Charenton, 950	H 7
	71324	Chase, 150	G 2
	70524	Chataignier, 725	F 5
	71226	Chatham, 827	F 2
	70344	Chauvin, 900	J 8
	71325	Cheneyville, 1,082	F 4
	71227	Choudrant, 555	F 1
	70525	Church Point, 3,865	F 6
	71414	Clarence, 448	E 3
	71415	Clarks, 889	F 2
	71228	Clay, 400	E 2
	71326	Clayton, 1,103	H 3
	70722	Clinton⊙, 1,884	J 5
	71416	Cloutierville, 250	E 3
	71417	Colfax⊙, 1,892	E 3
	71229	Collinston, 397	G 1
	71418	Columbia⊙, 1,000	F 2
	70723	Convent⊙, 650	L 3
	71419	Converse, 375	C 3
†	70785	Corbin, 189	L 1
	71327	Cottonport, 1,846	F 5
	71018	Cotton Valley, 1,261	D 1
†	71018	Couchwood, 150	D 1
	71019	Coushatta⊙, 1,492	D 2
	70433	Covington⊙, 7,170	K 5
†	70656	Cravens, 475	E 5
	70632	Creole, 175	D 7
†	70764	Crescent, 300	J 2
	71020	Creston, 150	E 3
	70526	Crowley⊙, 16,104	F 6
	71230	Crowville, 400	G 2
	71021	Cullen, 1,956	D 1
	70345	Cut Off, 750	K 7
†	70040	Dalcour, 275	P 4
	70725	Darrow, 500	K 3
	70046	Davant, 650	L 7
	70528	Delcambre, 1,975	G 7
	71232	Delhi, 2,887	H 2
	71233	Delta, 153	J 2
	70726	Denham Springs, 6,752	L 1
	70633	De Quincy, 3,448	D 6
	70634	De Ridder⊙, 8,030	D 5
	70030	Des Allemands, 2,318	N 4
	70047	Destrehan, 800	N 4
	71328	Deville, 500	F 4
	70048	Diamond, 370	L 7
	71022	Dixie, 330	C 1
†	71055	Dixie Inn, 456	D 1
	71422	Dodson, 457	E 2
	70346	Donaldsonville⊙, 7,367	K 3
	70352	Donner, 500	J 7
	71234	Downsville, 250	F 1
	71023	Doyline, 716	D 1
	70637	Dry Creek, 480	D 5
	71423	Dry Prong, 352	E 3
	71235	Dubach, 1,096	E 1
	71024	Dubberly, 212	D 1
	70353	Dulac, 225	J 8
	71236	Dunn, 225	G 2
	70728	Duplessis, 700	K 2
	70529	Duson, 1,199	F 6
†	71247	East Hodge, 200	E 2
	70530	Easton, 365	F 5
	71025	East Point, 200	D 2
	71330	Echo, 450	F 4
	70049	Edgard⊙, 300	M 3
†	71019	Edgefield, 201	D 2
†	70668	Edgerly, 250	C 6
	71331	Effie, 950	F 4
	70638	Elizabeth, 504	E 5
	71424	Elmer, 445	E 4
†	71051	Elm Grove, 350	C 2
†	70775	Elm Park, 200	H 5
	70532	Elton, 1,598	E 6
	70050	Empire, 700	L 8
	71425	Enterprise, 300	G 3
	71237	Epps, 448	G 1
	70533	Erath, 2,024	F 7
	71238	Eros, 164	F 2
	70729	Erwinville, 790	H 5
	70534	Estherwood, 661	F 6
	70730	Ethel, 350	H 5
	70535	Eunice, 11,390	F 6
	70537	Evangeline, 400	F 6
	70639	Evans, 400	D 5
	71333	Evergreen, 307	F 5
	71239	Extension, 950	G 3
	71240	Fairbanks, 150	F 1
	71241	Farmerville⊙, 3,416	F 1
	70640	Fenton, 404	E 6
	71334	Ferriday, 5,239	G 3
	71426	Fisher, 300	D 4
	71427	Flatwoods, 450	E 4
	71428	Flora, 200	D 3
	71429	Florien, 639	D 4
	70436	Fluker, 400	K 5
	70437	Folsom, 249	K 5
	70732	Fordoche, 488	G 5
	71242	Forest, 221	H 1
	71430	Forest Hill, 370	E 4
†	71449	Fort Jesup, 950	C 3
	71243	Fort Necessity, 150	G 2
	70538	Franklin⊙, 9,325	G 7
	70438	Franklinton⊙, 3,562	K 5
	70733	French Settlement, 800	L 2
	71027	Frierson, 700	C 2
†	70753	Frost, 500	L 2
†	71039	Fryeburg, 150	D 2
	70354	Galliano, 950	K 8
†	70769	Galvez, 200	L 2
	70540	Garden City, 515	H 7
	70051	Garyville, 2,474	M 3
	70734	Geismar, 300	K 3
	71432	Georgetown, 306	F 3
	71028	Gibsland, 1,380	E 1
	70356	Gibson, 950	J 7
	71336	Gilbert, 746	G 2
	71029	Gilliam, 211	C 1
	71244	Girard, 250	G 2
†	70538	Glencoe, 200	G 7
	71433	Glenmora, 1,651	E 5
	71030	Gloster, 975	C 2
	70736	Glynn, 400	H 5
	70357	Golden Meadow, 2,681	K 8
	71031	Goldonna, 337	D 2
	70737	Gonzales, 4,512	L 2
	70079	Good Hope, 950	N 3
	71337	Good Pine, 535	F 3
	71245	Grambling, 4,407	E 1
	70052	Gramercy, 2,567	M 3
	71032	Grand Cane, 284	C 2
	70643	Grand Chenier, 710	E 7
	70541	Grand Coteau, 1,301	G 6
	70358	Grand Isle, 2,236	L 8
†	70601	Grand Lake, 400	D 6

LOUISIANA

SCALE
0 5 10 20 30 40 MI.
0 5 10 20 30 40 KM.

State Capitals
Parish Seats
Canals

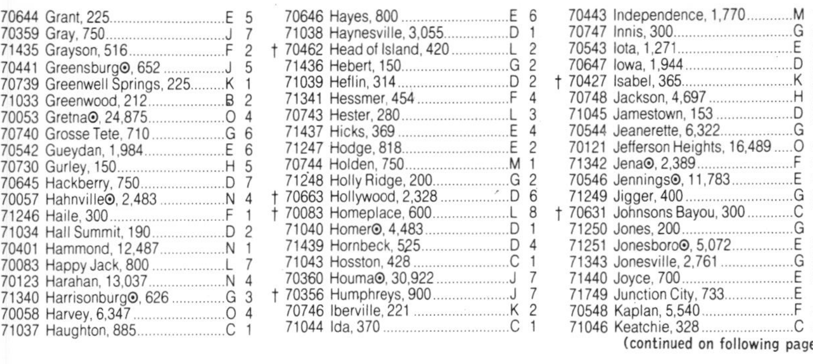

	ZIP	Place	Key
	70644	Grant, 225	E 5
	70359	Gray, 750	J 7
	71435	Grayson, 516	F 2
	70441	Greensburg⊙, 652	J 5
	70739	Greenwell Springs, 225	K 1
	71033	Greenwood, 212	B 2
	70053	Gretna⊙, 24,875	O 4
	70740	Grosse Tete, 710	G 6
	70542	Gueydan, 1,984	E 6
†	70730	Gurley, 150	H 5
	70645	Hackberry, 750	D 7
	70057	Hahnville⊙, 2,483	N 4
	71246	Haile, 300	F 1
	71034	Hall Summit, 190	D 2
	70401	Hammond, 12,487	N 1
†	70083	Happy Jack, 800	L 7
	70123	Harahan, 13,037	N 4
	71340	Harrisonburg⊙, 626	G 3
	70058	Harvey, 6,347	O 4
	71037	Haughton, 885	C 1
	70646	Hayes, 800	E 6
	71038	Haynesville, 3,055	D 1
†	70462	Head of Island, 420	L 2
	71436	Hebert, 150	G 2
	71039	Heflin, 314	D 2
	71341	Hessmer, 454	F 4
	70743	Hester, 280	L 3
	71437	Hicks, 369	E 4
	71247	Hodge, 818	E 2
	70744	Holden, 750	M 1
	71248	Holly Ridge, 200	G 2
†	70663	Hollywood, 2,328	D 6
†	70083	Homeplace, 600	L 8
	71040	Homer⊙, 4,483	D 1
	71439	Hornbeck, 525	D 4
	71043	Hosston, 428	C 1
	70360	Houma⊙, 30,922	J 7
†	70356	Humphreys, 900	J 7
	70746	Iberville, 221	K 2
	71044	Ida, 370	C 1
	70443	Independence, 1,770	M 1
	70747	Innis, 300	G 5
	70543	Iota, 1,271	E 6
	70647	Iowa, 1,944	D 6
†	70427	Isabel, 365	K 5
	70748	Jackson, 4,697	H 5
	71045	Jamestown, 153	D 2
	70544	Jeanerette, 6,322	G 7
	70121	Jefferson Heights, 16,489	O 4
	71342	Jena⊙, 2,389	F 3
	70546	Jennings⊙, 11,783	E 6
	71249	Jigger, 400	G 2
†	70631	Johnsons Bayou, 300	C 7
	71250	Jones, 200	G 1
	71251	Jonesboro⊙, 5,072	E 2
	71343	Jonesville, 2,761	G 3
	71440	Joyce, 700	E 3
	71749	Junction City, 733	E 1
	70548	Kaplan, 5,540	F 6
	71046	Keatchie, 328	C 2

(continued on following page)

AREA 48,523 sq. mi.
POPULATION 3,643,180
CAPITAL Baton Rouge
LARGEST CITY New Orleans
HIGHEST POINT Driskill Mtn. 535 ft.
SETTLED IN 1699
ADMITTED TO UNION April 30, 1812
POPULAR NAME Pelican State
STATE FLOWER Magnolia
STATE BIRD Eastern Brown Pelican

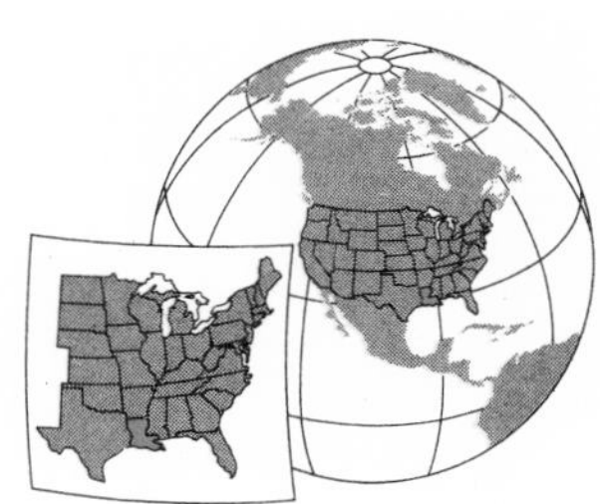

Agriculture, Industry and Resources

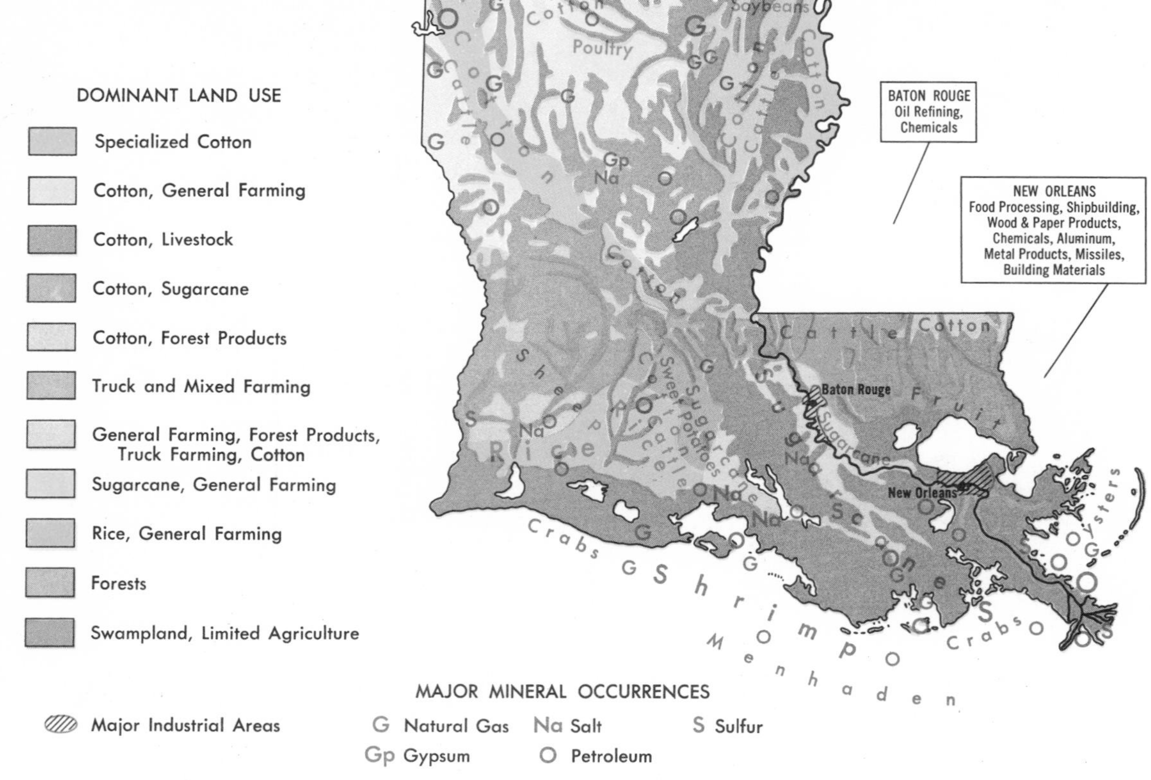

71047 Keithville, 500 ... C 2
71441 Kelly, 250 ... F 3
70062 Kenner, 29,858 ... N 4
70444 Kentwood, 2,736 ... J 5
71253 Kilbourne, 370 ... H 1
† 70462 Killian, 275 ... M 2
70066 Killona, 600 ... M 3
70648 Kinder, 2,307 ... E 6
70370 Klotzville, 248 ... K 3
70371 Kraemer, 510 ... M 4
70750 Krotz Springs, 1,435 ... G 5
70372 Labadieville, 700 ... K 4
70650 Lacassine, 494 ... E 6
70445 Lacombe, 750 ... L 6
70501 Lafayette⊙, 68,908 ... F 6
Lafayette, ‡109,716 ... F 6
70067 Lafitte, 1,223 ... K 7
† 70301 Lafourche, 200 ... J 7
70549 Lake Arthur, 3,551 ... E 6
70601 Lake Charles⊙, 77,998 ... D 6
Lake Charles, ‡145,415 ... D 6
70752 Lakeland, 400 ... H 5
71254 Lake Providence⊙, 6,183 ... H 1
70068 Laplace, 5,953 ... N 3
70373 Larose, 4,267 ... K 7
71344 Larto, 500 ... G 4
70550 Lawtell, 600 ... F 5

71345 Lebeau, 270 ... F 5
71346 Lecompte, 1,518 ... F 4
71446 Leesville⊙, 8,928 ... D 4
71447 Lena, 250 ... E 4
70551 Leonville, 512 ... G 6
70753 Lettsworth, 200 ... G 5
† 70525 Lewisburg, 265 ... F 6
71348 Libuse, 500 ... F 4
71256 Lillie, 160 ... E 1
71048 Lisbon, 151 ... E 1
† 71343 Lismore, 380 ... G 3
† 70062 Little Farms, 15,713 ... N 4
70754 Livingston⊙, 1,398 ... L 1
70755 Livonia, 611 ... G 5
70374 Lockport, 1,995 ... K 7
71049 Logansport, 1,330 ... C 3
† 71367 Lonepine, 850 ... F 5
71448 Longleaf, 250 ... E 4
71050 Longstreet, 182 ... B 2
70652 Longville, 250 ... D 5
70446 Loranger, 200 ... N 1
70552 Loreauville, 728 ... G 6
70756 Lottie, 350 ... G 5
70069 Lucy, 825 ... M 3
70070 Luling, 3,255 ... N 4
70071 Lutcher, 3,911 ... L 3
70447 Madisonville, 801 ... K 6

70554 Mamou, 3,275 ... F 5
70448 Mandeville, 2,282 ... L 6
71259 Mangham, 544 ... G 2
71052 Mansfield⊙, 6,432 ... C 2
71350 Mansura, 1,699 ... G 4
71449 Many⊙, 3,112 ... C 3
70663 Maplewood, 1,900 ... D 6
70757 Maringouin, 1,365 ... G 6
71260 Marion, 796 ... F 1
71351 Marksville⊙, 4,519 ... G 4
70072 Marrero, 29,015 ... O 4
70375 Mathews, 600 ... J 7
70449 Maurepas, 200 ... M 2
70555 Maurice, 476 ... F 6
† 71433 McNary, 220 ... E 5
71451 Melder, 200 ... E 4
71353 Melville, 2,076 ... G 5
70556 Mermentau, 756 ... E 6
71261 Mer Rouge, 819 ... G 1
70653 Merryville, 1,286 ... D 5
* 70001 Metairie, 135,816 ... O 4
70557 Midland, 500 ... F 6
70558 Milton, 500 ... F 6
71055 Minden⊙, 13,996 ... D 1
70376 Modeste, 230 ... K 3
71201 Monroe⊙, 56,374 ... F 1
Monroe, ‡115,387 ... F 1

70377 Montegut, 950 ... J 8
71354 Monterey, 800 ... G 4
71454 Montgomery, 923 ... E 3
70422 Montpelier, 211 ... M 1
† 70068 Montz, 200 ... M 3
71060 Mooringsport, 830 ... B 1
71455 Mora, 378 ... E 4
71355 Moreauville, 807 ... G 4
70380 Morgan City, 16,586 ... H 7
70759 Morganza, 836 ... G 5
71356 Morrow, 350 ... F 5
70559 Morse, 759 ... F 6
70076 Mount Airy, 700 ... M 3
70077 Nairn, 500 ... L 8
70390 Napoleonville⊙, 1,008 ... K 4
70451 Natalbany, 900 ... N 1
71456 Natchez, 600 ... D 3
71457 Natchitoches⊙, 15,974 ... D 3
† 71342 Nebo, 200 ... F 3
71460 Negreet, 200 ... C 4
71357 Newellton, 1,403 ... H 2
† 71354 New Era, 200 ... G 4
70560 New Iberia⊙, 30,147 ... G 6
71461 Newllano, 1,800 ... D 4
* 70101 New Orleans⊙, 593,471 ... O 4
New Orleans, ‡1,045,809 ... O 4
70760 New Roads⊙, 3,945 ... G 5
70078 New Sarpy, 1,643 ... N 4
71462 Noble, 209 ... C 3
70079 Norco, 4,773 ... N 3
† 71247 North Hodge, 640 ... E 2
70761 Norwood, 348 ... H 5
71463 Oakdale, 7,301 ... E 5
71263 Oak Grove⊙, 1,980 ... H 1
71264 Oak Ridge, 276 ... G 1
70655 Oberlin⊙, 1,857 ... E 5
† 71369 Odenburg, 175 ... G 5
71061 Oil City, 907 ... C 1
† 70560 Olivier, 300 ... G 7
71465 Olla, 1,387 ... F 3
70570 Opelousas⊙, 20,121 ... G 5
70762 Oscar, 700 ... H 5
71358 Palmetto, 312 ... G 5
70391 Paincourtville, 600 ... K 3
70080 Paradis, 750 ... M 4
70582 Parks, 491 ... G 6
† 70544 Patoutville, 230 ... G 7
70392 Patterson, 4,409 ... H 7
70763 Paulina, 500 ... L 3
70452 Pearl River, 1,361 ... L 6
† 70548 Pecan Island, 480 ... F 7
70575 Perry, 225 ... F 7
† 70042 Phoenix, 525 ... L 7
70453 Pine Grove, 500 ... J 5
70576 Pine Prairie, 515 ... E 5
71360 Pineville, 8,951 ... F 4
71266 Pioneer, 188 ... H 1
70656 Pitkin, 700 ... E 5
71064 Plain Dealing, 2,116 ... C 1
70764 Plaquemine⊙, 7,739 ... J 2
70393 Plattenville, 400 ... K 4
71362 Plaucheville, 224 ... G 5
71065 Pleasant Hill, 826 ... C 3
70082 Pointe a la Hache⊙, 750 ... L 7
71467 Pollock, 341 ... F 3
70454 Ponchatoula, 4,545 ... N 2
70767 Port Allen⊙, 5,728 ... J 2
70577 Port Barre, 2,133 ... G 5
† 70791 Port Hudson, 200 ... J 1
70083 Port Sulphur, 3,022 ... L 8
† 70726 Port Vincent, 387 ... L 2

71066 Powhatan, 277 ... D 3
70769 Prairieville, 500 ... K 2
71067 Princeton, 350 ... C 1
71468 Provencal, 530 ... D 3
71268 Quitman, 169 ... E 2
70394 Raceland, 4,880 ... J 7
70578 Rayne, 9,510 ... F 6
71269 Rayville⊙, 3,962 ... G 2
70580 Reddell, 800 ... F 5
70658 Reeves, 214 ... D 5
† 70085 Reggio, 400 ... L 7
† 70763 Remy, 850 ... L 3
70084 Reserve, 6,381 ... M 3
71334 Ridgecrest, 1,076 ... G 3
71068 Ringgold, 1,731 ... D 2
† 70427 Rio, 250 ... L 5
70581 Roanoke, 640 ... E 6
71469 Robeline, 274 ... D 3
70455 Robert, 600 ... N 1
71069 Rodessa, 273 ... B 1
70772 Rosedale, 621 ... G 6
70456 Roseland, 1,273 ... J 5
70659 Rosepine, 587 ... D 5
71365 Ruby, 350 ... F 4
71270 Ruston⊙, 17,365 ... E 1
70774 Saint Amant, 900 ... L 2
70457 Saint Benedict, 200 ... K 5
70085 Saint Bernard, 750 ... L 7
70775 Saint Francisville⊙ 1,603 ... H 5
70776 Saint Gabriel, 975 ... K 2
70086 Saint James, 600 ... L 3
71366 Saint Joseph⊙, 1,864 ... H 3
71367 Saint Landry, 950 ... F 5
70582 Saint Martinville⊙, 7,153 ... G 6
71471 Saint Maurice, 650 ... E 3
70087 Saint Rose, 2,106 ... N 4
71070 Saline, 307 ... E 2
71301 Samtown, 4,210 ... F 4
71071 Sarepta, 882 ... D 1
70395 Schriever, 700 ... J 7
70807 Scotlandville, 22,557 ... J 1
70583 Scott, 1,334 ... F 6
† 70560 Segura, 200 ... G 6
† 70764 Seymourville, 2,506 ... J 2
71072 Shongaloo, 173 ... D 1
* 71101 Shreveport⊙, 182,064 ... C 1
Shreveport, ‡294,703 ... C 1
71073 Sibley, 869 ... D 1
71368 Sicily Island. 630 ... G 3
71472 Sieper, 200 ... E 4
71473 Sikes, 237 ... F 2
71369 Simmesport, 2,027 ... G 5
71474 Simpson, 491 ... D 4
71275 Simsboro, 412 ... E 1
70660 Singer, 400 ... D 5
71475 Slagle, 200 ... D 4
70777 Slaughter, 580 ... H 5
70458 Slidell, 16,101 ... L 6
† 70346 Smoke Bend, 300 ... K 3
71276 Sondheimer, 325 ... H 1
70778 Sorrento, 1,182 ... L 3
† 71052 South Mansfield, 439 ... C 3
71277 Spearsville, 197 ... E 1
70462 Springfield, 423 ... M 2
71075 Springhill, 6,496 ... D 1
† 71465 Standard, 190 ... F 3
70661 Starks, 750 ... C 6
71279 Start, 200 ... G 2
71280 Sterlington, 1,118 ... F 1
71078 Stonewall, 500 ... C 2
70663 Sulphur, 13,551 ... D 6

71079 Summerfield, 170 ... E 1
70463 Sun, 288 ... L 5
70584 Sunset, 1,675 ... F 6
70780 Sunshine, 900 ... K 2
70396 Supreme, 617 ... K 4
71281 Swartz, 650 ... G 1
† 70601 Sweet Lake, 300 ... D 7
70464 Talisheek, 292 ... L 5
71282 Tallulah⊙, 9,643 ... H 2
70465 Tangipahoa, 469 ... J 5
71080 Taylor, 500 ... D 1
† 71290 Tendal, 200 ... H 2
† 70053 Terry Town, 13,832 ... O 4
70397 Theriot, 950 ... J 8
70301 Thibodaux⊙, 14,925 ... J 7
70466 Tickfaw, 370 ... M 1
71477 Tioga, 457 ... F 4
71286 Transylvania, 400 ... H 1
71081 Trees, 247 ... B 1
† 70041 Triumph-Buras, 4,113 ... L 8
71371 Trout, 500 ... F 3
71479 Tullos, 600 ... F 3
70782 Tunica, 475 ... G 5
70585 Turkey Creek, 280 ... F 5
70723 Union, 665 ... L 3
71480 Urania, 950 ... F 3
70090 Vacherie, 2,145 ... L 3
† 70757 Valverda, 200 ... G 5
70467 Varnado, 320 ... L 5
70091 Venice, 900 ... M 8
71372 Vick, 500 ... F 4
71373 Vidalia⊙, 5,538 ... G 3
71270 Vienna, 250 ... E 1
70586 Ville Platte⊙, 9,692 ... F 5
70668 Vinton, 3,454 ... C 6
70092 Violet, 975 ... P 4
71082 Vivian, 4,046 ... B 1
70784 Wakefield, 200 ... H 5
70785 Walker, 1,363 ... L 1
† 70049 Wallace, 200 ... M 3
71374 Walters, 500 ... G 3
71289 Warden, 350 ... H 1
† 71301 Wardville, 1,087 ... F 4
70589 Washington, 1,473 ... G 5
71375 Waterproof, 1,438 ... H 3
70786 Watson, 700 ... L 1
71290 Waverly, 350 ... H 2
† 70569 Weeks, 400 ... G 7
70093 Welcome, 450 ... L 3
70591 Welsh, 3,203 ... E 6
70669 Westlake, 4,082 ... D 6
71291 West Monroe, 14,868 ... F 1
† 70082 West Pointe a la Hache, 250 ... L 7
70094 Westwego, 11,402 ... O 4
70787 Weyanoke, 500 ... H 5
70788 White Castle, 2,206 ... J 3
† 70462 Whitehall, 380 ... M 2
71376 Whiteville, 450 ... F 5
71377 Wildsville. 650 ... G 3
70789 Wilson, 606 ... H 5
71483 Winnfield⊙, 7,142 ... E 3
71295 Winnsboro⊙, 5,349 ... G 2
71378 Wisner, 1,339 ... G 3
71485 Woodworth, 409 ... E 4
70592 Youngsville, 1,002 ... G 6
70791 Zachary, 4,964 ... K 1
71486 Zwolle, 2,169 ... C 3

⊙ Parish seat.
‡ Population of metropolitan area.
† Zip ot nearest p.o.
* Multiple zips

Pushed by powerful tugboats, barges make their way from the Mississippi down the shallow Gulf Intracoastal Waterway to deliver their cargoes to New Orleans, Morgan City and Lake Charles, Louisiana.

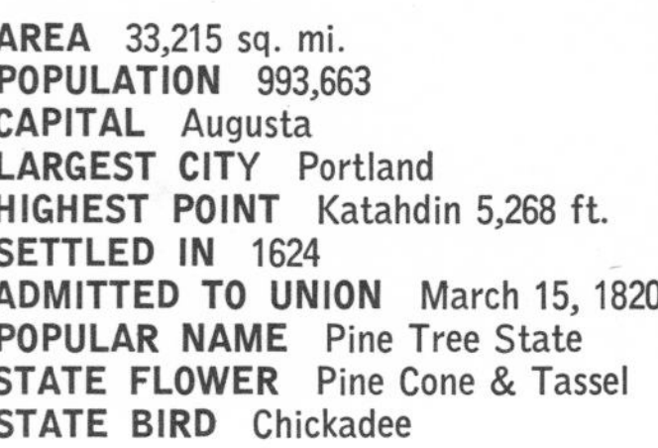

AREA 33,215 sq. mi.
POPULATION 993,663
CAPITAL Augusta
LARGEST CITY Portland
HIGHEST POINT Katahdin 5,268 ft.
SETTLED IN 1624
ADMITTED TO UNION March 15, 1820
POPULAR NAME Pine Tree State
STATE FLOWER Pine Cone & Tassel
STATE BIRD Chickadee

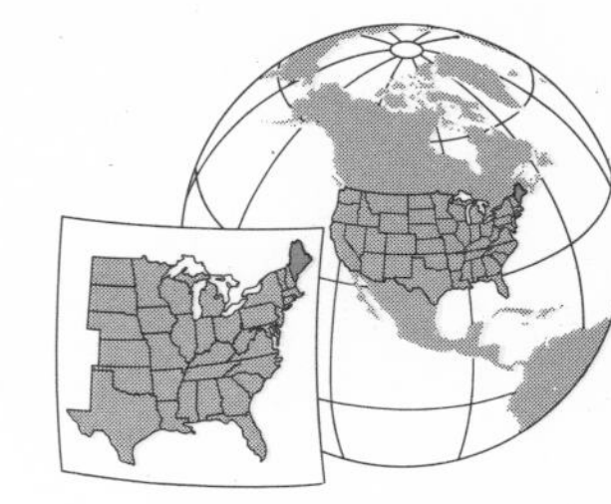

COUNTIES

County	Key
Androscoggin, 91,279	C 7
Aroostook, 92,463	F 2
Cumberland, 192,528	C 8
Franklin, 22,444	B 5
Hancock, 34,590	G 6
Kennebec, 95,247	D 7
Knox, 29,013	E 7
Lincoln, 20,537	D 7
Oxford, 43,457	B 7
Penobscot, 125,393	F 5
Piscataquis, 16,285	E 4
Sagadahoc, 23,452	D 7
Somerset, 40,597	C 4
Waldo, 23,328	E 6
Washington, 29,859	H 6
York, 111,576	B 9

CITIES and TOWNS

Zip	Name/Pop.	Key
04406	Abbot Village, ▵453	D 5
04001	Acton, ▵697	B 8
04606	Addison, ▵773	H 6
04910	Albion, ▵1,056	E 6
† 04610	Alexander, ▵169	H 5
04002	Alfred⊙, ▵1,211	B 9
† 04774	Allagash, ▵456	F 1
† 04938	Allens Mills, 150	C 6
04535	Alna, ▵315	D 7
† 04468	Alton, ▵340	F 5
† 04408	Amherst, ▵148	G 6
04216	Andover, ▵791	B 6
04216	Andover, 350	B 6
04911	Anson, ▵2,168	D 6
04911	Anson, 950	D 6
† 04862	Appleton, ▵628	E 7
04732	Ashland, ▵1,761	G 2
04732	Ashland, 750	G 2
04912	Athens, ▵592	D 6
04912	Athens, 200	D 6
† 04426	Atkinson, ▵213	E 5
04210	Auburn⊙, 24,151	C 7
04330	Augusta (cap.)⊙, 21,945	D 7
04408	Aurora, ▵72	G 6
04003	Bailey Island, 400	D 8
04409	Bancroft, ▵53	H 4
04401	Bangor⊙, 33,168	F 6
04609	Bar Harbor, ▵3,716	G 7
04609	Bar Harbor, 2,392	G 7
04610	Baring, 150	J 5
04004	Bar Mills, 800	C 8
04653	Bass Harbor, 413	G 7
04530	Bath⊙, 9,679	D 8
04915	Bayside, 238	F 7
04611	Beals, ▵663	H 7
† 04622	Beddington, ▵32	H 6
04915	Belfast⊙, 5,957	F 7
04917	Belgrade, ▵1,302	D 7
04917	Belgrade, 300	D 7
04918	Belgrade Lakes, 700	D 6
† 04915	Belmont, ▵349	E 7
04733	Benedicta, ▵177	G 4
† 04919	Benton, ▵1,729	D 6
03901	Berwick, ▵3,136	B 9
03901	Berwick, 1,765	B 9
† 04285	Berry Mills, 245	C 6
04217	Bethel, ▵2,220	B 7
04217	Bethel, 750	B 7
04005	Biddeford, 19,983	B 9
04006	Biddeford Pool, 500	C 9
04920	Bingham, ▵1,254	D 5
04920	Bingham, 1,184	D 5
04613	Birch Harbor, 210	H 7
04734	Blaine, ▵903	H 2
04734	Blaine-Mars Hill, 1,854	H 2
† 04406	Blanchard, ▵56	D 5
04614	Blue Hill, ▵1,367	F 7
04615	Blue Hill Falls, 850	F 7
† 04040	Bolsters Mills, 150	B 7
04537	Boothbay, ▵1,814	D 8
04537	Boothbay, 700	D 8
04538	Boothbay Harbor, 2,320	D 8
04008	Bowdoinham, ▵1,294	D 7
04481	Bowerbank, ▵29	E 5
04410	Bradford, ▵569	F 5
04410	Bradford, 150	F 5
04411	Bradley, ▵1,010	F 6
04412	Brewer, 9,300	F 6
04735	Bridgewater, ▵895	H 3
04009	Bridgton, ▵2,967	B 7
04009	Bridgton, 1,779	B 7
† 04990	Brighton, ▵58	D 5
04539	Bristol, ▵1,721	D 8
04539	Bristol, 160	D 8
04616	Brooklin, ▵598	F 7
04921	Brooks, ▵751	E 6
04617	Brooksville, ▵673	F 7
04413	Brookton, 225	H 4
04010	Brownfield, ▵478	B 8
04010	Brownfield, 200	B 8
04414	Brownville, ▵1,490	E 5
04414	Brownville, 1,641	E 5
04415	Brownville Junction, 950	E 5
04011	Brunswick, ▵16,195	C 8
04011	Brunswick, 10,867	C 8
04219	Bryant Pond, 350	B 7
04220	Buckfield, ▵929	C 7
04618	Bucks Harbor, 161	J 6
04416	Bucksport, ▵3,756	F 6
04416	Bucksport, 2,456	F 6
04417	Burlington, ▵266	G 5
04922	Burnham, ▵802	E 6
† 04093	Buxton, ▵3,135	C 8
† 04275	Byron, ▵132	B 6
04619	Calais, 4,044	J 5
04923	Cambridge, ▵281	E 5
04843	Camden, ▵4,115	F 7
04843	Camden, 3,492	F 7
04924	Canaan, ▵904	D 6
04221	Canton, ▵742	C 7
03902	Cape Neddick, 850	B 9
04014	Cape Porpoise, 500	C 9
04925	Caratunk, ▵96	C 5
04418	Cardville, 223	F 5
04736	Caribou, 10,419	G 2
04419	Carmel, ▵1,301	E 6
04420	Carroll, ▵132	G 5
† 04224	Carthage, ▵354	C 6
† 04465	Cary, ▵184	H 4
04015	Casco, ▵1,256	B 7
04015	Casco, 250	B 7
04421	Castine, ▵1,080	F 7
† 04623	Centerville, ▵19	H 6
† 04757	Chapman, ▵328	G 2
04422	Charleston, ▵909	F 5
† 04666	Charlotte, ▵199	J 5
04017	Chebeague Island, 400	C 8
† 04345	Chelsea, ▵2,095	D 7
04622	Cherryfield, ▵771	H 6
† 04458	Chester, ▵255	F 5
† 04938	Chesterville, ▵643	C 6
04926	China, ▵1,850	E 7
04926	China, 336	E 7
04222	Chisholm, 1,530	C 7
† 04428	Clifton, ▵233	G 6
04927	Clinton, ▵1,971	D 6
04927	Clinton, 1,124	D 6
† 04623	Columbia, ▵162	H 6
04623	Columbia Falls, ▵367	H 6
† 04638	Cooper, ▵88	H 6
04341	Coopers Mills, 200	E 7
04624	Corea, 300	H 7
04928	Corinna, ▵1,700	E 6
04020	Cornish, ▵839	B 8
† 04976	Cornville, ▵623	D 6
04423	Costigan, 200	F 5
04625	Cranberry Isles, ▵186	G 7
† 04610	Crawford, ▵74	H 5
† 04015	Crescent Lake, 175	C 7
04738	Crouseville, 300	G 2
† 04747	Crystal, ▵281	G 4
04021	Cumberland Center, ▵4,096	C 8
04021	Cumberland Center, 950	C 8
04011	Cundys Harbor, 150	D 8
† 04563	Cushing, ▵522	E 7
04626	Cutler, ▵588	J 6
04626	Cutler, 153	J 6
04543	Damariscotta, ▵1,264	E 7
04543	Damariscotta-Newcastle, 1,188	E 7
04424	Danforth, ▵794	H 4
04424	Danforth, 650	H 4
† 04622	Deblois, ▵20	H 6
† 04429	Dedham, ▵522	F 6
04627	Deer Isle, ▵1,211	F 7
04627	Deer Isle, 600	F 7
04022	Denmark, ▵397	B 8
04628	Dennysville, ▵278	J 6
04425	Derby, 300	E 5
04929	Detroit, ▵663	E 6
04930	Dexter, ▵3,725	E 5
04930	Dexter, 2,732	E 5
04224	Dixfield, ▵2,188	C 6
04224	Dixfield, 1,535	C 6
04932	Dixmont, ▵559	E 6
04426	Dover-Foxcroft, ▵4,178	E 5
04426	Dover-Foxcroft⊙, 3,102	E 5
04342	Dresden, ▵787	D 7
04225	Dryden, 675	C 6
† 04039	Dry Mills, 700	C 8
† 04747	Dyer Brook, ▵165	G 3
04739	Eagle Lake, ▵908	F 1
04739	Eagle Lake, 675	F 1
04226	East Andover, 194	B 6
04024	East Baldwin, 175	B 8
04629	East Blue Hill, 150	G 7
04544	East Boothbay, 400	D 8
04427	East Corinth, 525	F 5
04227	East Dixfield, 288	C 6
04428	East Eddington, 200	F 6
04026	East Hiram, 198	B 8
04429	East Holden, 450	F 6
04027	East Lebanon, 950	B 9
† 04049	East Limington, 200	B 8
04228	East Livermore, 290	C 7
04630	East Machias, ▵1,057	J 6
04630	East Machias, 750	J 6
† 04950	East Madison, 400	D 6
04430	East Millinocket, ▵2,567	F 4
04430	East Millinocket, 2,564	F 4
04740	Easton, ▵1,305	H 2
† 04270	East Otisfield, 200	B 7
04229	East Peru, 350	C 7
04230	East Poland, 700	C 7
04631	Eastport, 1,989	K 6
04231	East Stoneham, 150	B 7
04632	East Sullivan, 300	G 6
† 04862	East Union, 220	E 7
04935	East Vassalboro, 300	D 7
04030	East Waterboro, 365	B 8
04234	East Wilton, 650	C 6
† 04428	Eddington, ▵1,358	F 6
† 04428	Eddington, 250	F 6
04545	Edgecomb, ▵549	D 8
† 04628	Edmunds, 229	J 6
03903	Eliot, ▵3,497	B 9
04605	Ellsworth⊙, 4,603	F 6
04433	Enfield, ▵1,148	F 5
04433	Enfield, 150	F 5
04434	Etna, ▵526	E 6
04936	Eustis, ▵595	B 5
04435	Exeter, ▵663	E 6
† 04938	Fairbanks, 300	C 6
04937	Fairfield, ▵5,684	D 6
04937	Fairfield, 3,694	D 6
† 04937	Fairfield Center, 975	D 6
04105	Falmouth, ▵6,291	C 8
04105	Falmouth, 1,621	C 8
† 04105	Falmouth Foreside (Falmouth), 1,621	C 8
† 04345	Farmingdale, ▵2,423	D 7
† 04345	Farmingdale, 1,832	D 7
04938	Farmington, ▵5,657	C 6
04938	Farmington⊙, 3,096	C 6
04940	Farmington Falls, 500	C 6
04344	Fayette, ▵447	C 7
04546	Five Islands, 161	D 8
04742	Fort Fairfield, ▵4,859	H 2
04742	Fort Fairfield, 2,322	H 2
04743	Fort Kent, ▵4,575	F 1
04743	Fort Kent, 2,876	F 1
04744	Fort Kent Mills, 300	F 1
04438	Frankfort, ▵620	F 6
04634	Franklin, ▵708	G 6
04634	Franklin, 350	G 6
04941	Freedom, ▵373	E 7
04032	Freeport, ▵4,781	C 8
04032	Freeport, 1,822	C 8
04745	Frenchville, ▵1,375	G 1
04745	Frenchville, 800	G 1
04547	Friendship, ▵834	E 7
04547	Friendship, 700	E 7
04037	Fryeburg, ▵2,208	A 7
04037	Fryeburg, 1,075	A 7
04345	Gardiner, 6,685	D 7
04939	Garland, ▵596	E 5
04939	Garland, 300	E 5
04548	Georgetown, ▵464	D 8
04548	Georgetown, 190	D 8
† 04217	Gilead, ▵153	B 7
† 04401	Glenburn, ▵1,196	F 6
04846	Glen Cove, 300	E 7
† 04005	Goodwins Mills, 340	B 8
† 04046	Goose Rocks Beach, 200	C 9
04038	Gorham, ▵7,839	C 8
04038	Gorham, 3,337	C 8
04636	Gouldsboro, ▵1,310	H 7
04636	Gouldsboro, 296	H 7
04746	Grand Isle, ▵797	G 1
04746	Grand Isle, 400	G 1
04637	Grand Lake Stream, ▵186	H 5
04039	Gray, ▵2,939	C 8
04039	Gray, 525	C 8
04236	Greene, ▵1,772	C 7
04441	Greenville, ▵1,894	D 5
04441	Greenville, 1,714	D 5
04442	Greenville Junction, 150	D 5
04443	Guilford, ▵1,694	E 5
04443	Guilford, 1,216	E 5
04347	Hallowell, 2,814	D 7
† 04785	Hamlin, ▵357	H 1
04444	Hampden, ▵4,693	F 6
04444	Hampden, 2,207	F 6
04445	Hampden Highlands, 950	F 6
04640	Hancock, ▵1,070	G 6
04237	Hanover, ▵275	B 7
04942	Harmony, ▵650	D 6
04942	Harmony, 350	D 6
† 04011	Harpswell, ▵2,552	D 8
04643	Harrington, ▵553	H 6
04040	Harrison, ▵1,045	B 7
† 04221	Hartford, ▵312	C 7
04943	Hartland, ▵1,414	D 6
04943	Hartland, 975	D 6
04446	Haynesville, ▵157	G 4
04238	Hebron, ▵532	C 7
† 04401	Hermon, ▵2,376	F 6
† 04082	Highland Lake, 600	C 8
04944	Hinckley, 317	D 6
04041	Hiram, ▵686	B 8
04041	Hiram, 175	B 8
04730	Hodgdon, ▵933	H 3
† 04429	Holden, ▵1,789	H 3
† 04429	Holden, 900	H 3
04042	Hollis Center, ▵1,560	B 8
04847	Hope, ▵500	E 7
04847	Hope, 175	E 7
04730	Houlton, ▵8,111	H 3
04730	Houlton⊙, 6,760	H 3
04448	Howland, ▵1,468	F 5
04448	Howland, 1,418	F 5
04449	Hudson, ▵482	F 5
04644	Hulls Cove, 200	G 7
04747	Island Falls, ▵913	G 3
04645	Isle au Haut, ▵45	F 7
04848	Islesboro, ▵421	F 7
04848	Islesboro, 200	F 7
04945	Jackman, ▵848	C 4
04945	Jackman, 700	C 4
04647	Jacksonville, 200	J 6
04239	Jay, ▵3,954	C 7
04239	Jay, 850	C 7
04348	Jefferson, ▵1,242	D 7
04648	Jonesboro, ▵448	J 6
04649	Jonesport, ▵1,326	H 6
04649	Jonesport, 1,073	H 6
04748	Keegan, 450	G 1
04450	Kenduskeag, ▵733	E 6
04043	Kennebunk, ▵5,646	B 9
04043	Kennebunk, 2,764	B 9
04046	Kennebunkport, ▵2,160	C 9
04046	Kennebunkport, 1,097	C 9
04349	Kents Hill, 250	D 7
04047	Kezar Falls, 680	B 8
04947	Kingfield, ▵877	C 6
04451	Kingman, 250	G 4
† 04990	Kingsbury, ▵7	D 5
03904	Kittery, ▵11,028	B 9
03904	Kittery, 7,363	B 9
03905	Kittery Point, 1,172	B 9
† 04986	Knox, ▵443	E 6
04453	La Grange, ▵393	F 5
04453	La Grange, 250	F 5
† 04463	Lake View, ▵16	F 5
† 04605	Lamoine, ▵615	G 7
04455	Lee, ▵599	G 5
† 04263	Leeds, ▵1,031	C 7
04456	Levant, ▵862	F 6
04240	Lewiston, 41,779	C 7
	Lewiston-Auburn, ‡72,474	C 7
04949	Liberty, ▵515	E 7
04949	Liberty, 200	E 7
04749	Lille, 300	G 1
04048	Limerick, ▵963	B 8
04750	Limestone, ▵8,745	H 2
04750	Limestone, 1,572	H 2
04049	Limington, ▵1,066	B 8
04049	Limington, 250	B 8
04457	Lincoln, ▵4,759	G 5
04457	Lincoln, 3,482	G 5
04458	Lincoln Center, 325	G 5
04849	Lincolnville, ▵955	E 7
04849	Lincolnville, 800	E 7
04755	Linneus, ▵608	H 3
04250	Lisbon, ▵6,544	C 7
* 04250	Lisbon-Lisbon Center, 1,475	C 7
04252	Lisbon Falls, 3,257	D 7
04350	Litchfield, ▵1,222	D 7
04650	Little Deer Isle, 275	F 7
† 04760	Littleton, ▵958	H 3
04253	Livermore, ▵1,610	C 7
04253	Livermore, 280	C 7
04254	Livermore Falls, ▵3,450	C 7
04254	Livermore Falls, 2,378	C 7
04255	Locke Mills, 300	B 7
04051	Lovell, ▵607	B 7
04051	Lovell, 180	B 7
† 04433	Lowell, ▵154	F 5
04652	Lubec, ▵1,949	K 6
04652	Lubec, 900	K 6
† 04730	Ludlow, ▵259	G 3
04654	Machias, ▵2,441	J 6
04654	Machias⊙, 1,368	J 6
04655	Machiasport, ▵887	H 6
04655	Machiasport, 374	H 6
† 04451	Macwahoc, ▵126	G 4
04756	Madawaska, ▵5,585	G 1
04756	Madawaska, 4,452	G 1
04950	Madison, ▵4,278	D 6
04950	Madison, 2,920	D 6
† 04966	Madrid, ▵107	B 6
04351	Manchester, ▵1,331	D 7
04757	Mapleton, ▵1,598	G 2
04758	Mars Hill, ▵1,875	H 2
04758	Mars Hill-Blaine, 1,854	H 2
04759	Masardis, ▵317	G 3
04459	Mattawamkeag, ▵988	G 5
04256	Mechanic Falls, ▵2,193	C 7
04256	Mechanic Falls, 1,872	C 7
04657	Meddybemps, ▵76	J 5
† 04453	Medford, ▵146	F 5
04460	Medway, ▵1,491	G 4
04957	Mercer, ▵313	D 6
04257	Mexico, ▵4,309	B 6
04257	Mexico, 3,325	B 6
04658	Milbridge, ▵1,154	H 6
04461	Milford, ▵1,828	F 6
04461	Milford, 1,519	F 6
04462	Millinocket, ▵7,742	F 4
04462	Millinocket, 7,558	F 4
04463	Milo, ▵2,572	F 5
04463	Milo, 1,514	F 5
04258	Minot, ▵919	C 7
04258	Minot, 250	C 7
04852	Monhegan, ▵44	E 8
04259	Monmouth, ▵2,062	D 7

(continued on following page)

Bruce Nett — Shostal Associates

Boothbay Harbor offers facilities for a variety of sailing craft — yachts, rented party boats and commercial fishermen, all seen here at anchor. This active port rates high among Maine's popular coastal resort towns.

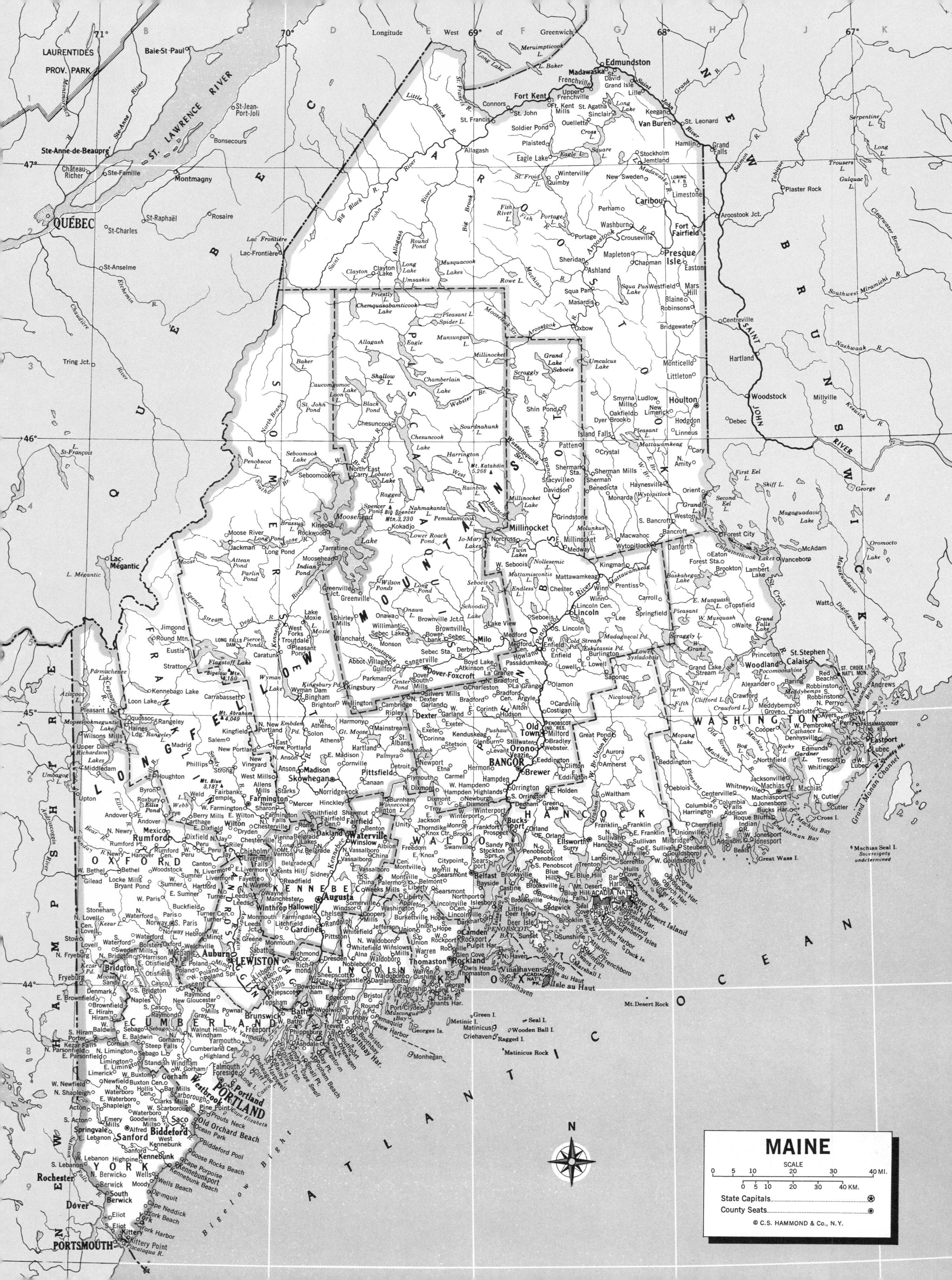
MAINE
SCALE
0 5 10 20 30 40 MI.
0 5 10 20 30 40 KM.
State Capitals
County Seats
© C.S. HAMMOND & Co., N.Y.
Longitude West 69° of Greenwich
71°
70°
68°
67°
47°
46°
45°
44°
QUÉBEC
NEW BRUNSWICK
NEW HAMPSHIRE
ATLANTIC OCEAN
ST. LAWRENCE RIVER
LAURENTIDES PROV. PARK
AROOSTOOK
PISCATAQUIS
SOMERSET
PENOBSCOT
WASHINGTON
HANCOCK
FRANKLIN
OXFORD
KENNEBEC
WALDO
KNOX
LINCOLN
SAGADAHOC
ANDROSCOGGIN
CUMBERLAND
YORK
LONGFELLOW MOUNTAINS
Augusta
BANGOR
PORTLAND
LEWISTON
Auburn
Bangor
Brewer
Orono
Old Town
Waterville
Skowhegan
Farmington
Rumford
Houlton
Presque Isle
Caribou
Fort Kent
Madawaska
Edmundston
Millinocket
Lincoln
Dover-Foxcroft
Belfast
Rockland
Camden
Ellsworth
Machias
Calais
Eastport
Lubec
Brunswick
Bath
Biddeford
Saco
Sanford
Kennebunk
Kittery
PORTSMOUTH
Dover
Rochester
Gardiner
Hallowell
Bridgton
Moosehead Lake
Chesuncook Lake
Mt. Katahdin 5,268
Mt. Desert Island
Isle au Haut
Matinicus
Monhegan
Grand Manan Channel
Machias Seal I. Sovereignty undetermined
Bigelow Bight
Penobscot Bay

04259 Monmouth, 500 D 7
04951 Monroe, △478 E 6
04464 Monson, △669 E 5
04760 Monticello, △1,072 H 3
04941 Montville, △430 E 7
04054 Moody, 500 B 9
04945 Moose River, △255 C 4
04952 Morrill, △410 E 7
04660 Mount Desert, △1,659 G 7
04352 Mount Vernon, △680 D 7
04055 Naples, △956 B 8
04445 Newburgh, △835 F 6
04553 Newcastle, △1,076 D 7
04553 Newcastle-Damariscotta, 1,188 E 7
04056 Newfield, △458 B 8
04056 Newfield, 165 B 8
04260 New Gloucester, △2,811 C 8
04260 New Gloucester, 400 C 8
04554 New Harbor, 580 E 8
04761 New Limerick, △427 G 3
04953 Newport, △2,260 E 6
04953 Newport, 1,588 E 6
04954 New Portland, △559 C 6
04954 New Portland, 201 C 6
04261 Newry, △208 B 6
04955 New Sharon, △725 C 6
04762 New Sweden, △639 G 2
04762 New Sweden, 400 G 2
04956 New Vineyard, △444 C 6
04555 Nobleboro, △850 D 7
04957 Norridgewock, △1,964 D 6
04957 Norridgewock, 1,067 D 6
04958 North Anson 950 D 6
04959 North Belgrade, 300 D 7
03906 North Berwick, △2,224 B 9
03906 North Berwick, 1,449 B 9
04057 North Bridgton, 200 B 7
04626 North Cutler, 153 J 6
04662 Northeast Harbor, 700 G 7
04654 Northfield, △57 H 6
04058 North Fryeburg, 250 B 7
04853 North Haven, △399 F 7
04853 North Haven, 300 F 7
04262 North Jay, 800 C 6
04049 North Limington, 400 B 8
04254 North Livermore, 280 C 7
04663 North Lubec, 250 J 6
04961 North New Portland, 300 C 6
04849 Northport, △744 E 7
04664 North Sullivan, 280 G 6
04266 North Turner, 300 C 7
04962 North Vassalboro, 950 D 7
04572 North Waldoboro, 250 E 7
04061 North Waterboro, 200 B 8
04267 North Waterford, 217 B 7
04284 North Wayne, 175 C 7
04353 North Whitefield, 300 D 7
04062 North Windham, 600 C 8
† 04219 North Woodstock, 400 B 7
† 04096 North Yarmouth, △1,383 C 8
† 04096 North Yarmouth, 500 C 8
04268 Norway, △3,595 B 7
04268 Norway, 2,430 B 7
04763 Oakfield, △836 G 3
04963 Oakland, △5,273 D 6
04963 Oakland, 2,261 D 6
03907 Ogunquit, 800 B 9
04064 Old Orchard Beach, △5,404 C 9
04064 Old Orchard Beach, 5,273 C 9
04468 Old Town, 9,057 F 6
04964 Oquossoc, 210 B 6
04471 Orient, △83 H 4
04472 Orland, △1,307 F 6
04472 Orland, 500 F 6
04473 Orono, △9,989 F 6
04473 Orono, 9,146 F 6
04474 Orrington, △2,702 F 6
04474 Orrington, 250 F 6
04066 Orrs Island, 500 D 8
† 04270 Otisfield, △589 B 7
04665 Otter Creek, 350 G 7
04854 Owls Head, △1,281 F 7
04764 Oxbow, △92 G 3
04270 Oxford, △1,892 B 7
04270 Oxford, 550 B 7
04354 Palermo, △645 E 7
04965 Palmyra, △1,104 E 6
04271 Paris, △3,739 B 7
† 04443 Parkman, △457 D 5
04475 Passadumkeag, △326 F 5
04765 Patten, △1,266 F 4
04765 Patten, 1,068 F 4
04067 Pejepscott, 200 D 8
04558 Pemaquid, 160 E 8
04666 Pembroke, △700 J 6
04666 Pembroke, 300 J 6
04476 Penobscot, △786 F 7
04766 Perham, △436 G 2
04667 Perry, △878 J 6
04272 Peru, △1,345 C 6
04966 Phillips, △979 C 6
04562 Phippsburg, △1,229 D 8
04562 Phippsburg, 280 D 8
† 04064 Pine Point, 650 C 8
04967 Pittsfield, △4,274 E 6
04967 Pittsfield, 3,398 E 6
† 04345 Pittston, △1,617 D 7
04969 Plymouth, △542 E 6
04273 Poland, △2,015 C 7
04273 Poland, 300 C 7
04768 Portage, △477 G 2
04855 Port Clyde, 300 E 8
04068 Porter, △1,115 B 8
04068 Porter, 225 B 8
* 04101 Portland⊙, 65,116 C 8
Portland, ‡141,625 C 8
04069 Pownal, △800 C 8
04477 Prentiss, △159 G 5
04769 Presque Isle, 11,452 H 2
04668 Princeton, △956 H 5
† 04981 Prospect, △358 F 6
04669 Prospect Harbor, 350 H 7
† 04345 Randolph, △1,741 D 7
† 04345 Randolph, 1,548 D 7
04970 Rangeley, △941 B 6
04970 Rangeley, 600 B 6
04071 Raymond, △1,328 B 8
04071 Raymond, 550 B 8
04355 Readfield, △1,258 D 7
04355 Readfield, 300 D 7
04670 Red Beach, 210 J 5
04357 Richmond, △2,168 D 7
04357 Richmond, 1,449 D 7
† 04357 Richmond Corner, 200 D 7
† 04930 Ripley, △297 E 5
04671 Robbinston, △396 J 5
04671 Robbinston, 200 J 5
† 04734 Robinsons, 487 H 3
04841 Rockland⊙, 8,505 E 7
04856 Rockport, △2,067 F 7
04856 Rockport, 875 F 7
† 04841 Rockville, 250 E 7
04478 Rockwood, 250 D 4
† 04957 Rome, △362 D 6
† 04654 Roque Bluffs, △153 H 6
04564 Round Pond, 375 E 8
04275 Roxbury, △271 B 6
04276 Rumford, △9,363 B 6
04276 Rumford, 6,198 B 6
04278 Rumford Center, 325 B 7
04280 Sabattus, 950 C 7
04072 Saco, 11,678 C 8
04772 Saint Agatha, △868 G 1
04971 Saint Albans, △1,041 E 6
04773 Saint David, 915 G 1
04774 Saint Francis, △811 E 1
04857 Saint George, △1,639 E 7
04857 Saint George, 250 E 7
† 04743 Saint John, △377 F 1
† 04983 Salem, 300 C 6
04972 Sandy Point, 300 F 7
04073 Sanford, △10,457 B 9
04073 Sanford, 15,812 B 9
04479 Sangerville, △1,107 E 5
04074 Scarborough, △7,845 C 8
04074 Scarborough, 500 C 8
04675 Seal Harbor, 336 G 7
04973 Searsmont, △624 E 7
04973 Searsmont, 400 E 7
04974 Searsport, △1,951 F 7
04974 Searsport, 1,110 F 7
04075 Sebago Lake, 500 B 8
04481 Sebec, △325 E 5
04484 Seboeis, △63 F 5
04676 Sedgwick, △578 F 7
04076 Shapleigh, △559 B 8
04975 Shawmut, 250 D 6
04775 Sheridan, 250 F 2
† 04777 Sherman, △949 G 4
† 04777 Sherman, 165 G 4
04776 Sherman Mills, 600 G 4
04777 Sherman Station, 300 F 4
04485 Shirley Mills, △174 D 5
04485 Shirley Mills, 180 D 5
† 04330 Sidney, △1,319 D 7
04779 Sinclair, 260 G 1
04976 Skowhegan, △7,601 D 6
04976 Skowhegan⊙, 6,571 D 6
04978 Smithfield, △527 D 6
04780 Smyrna Mills, △318 G 3
04780 Smyrna Mills, 250 G 3
04781 Soldier Pond, 500 F 1
04979 Solon, △712 D 6
† 04341 Somerville, △215 D 7
04677 Sorrento, △199 G 7
03908 South Berwick, △3,488 B 9
03908 South Berwick, 1,863 B 9
04568 South Bristol, △664 D 8
04077 South Casco, 200 B 8
04358 South China, 225 D 7
† 03903 South Eliot, 1,635 B 9
04079 South Harpswell, 650 C 8
04080 South Hiram, 175 B 8
† 04862 South Hope, 200 E 7
† 03901 South Lebanon, 200 A 9
† 04259 South Monmouth, 168 D 7
† 04474 South Orrington, 400 F 6
04281 South Paris⊙, 2,315 C 7
† 04569 Southport, △473 D 8
04569 Southport, 175 D 8
04106 South Portland, 23,267 C 8
† 04073 South Sanford, 850 B 9
04858 South Thomaston, △831 E 7
† 04864 South Union, 180 E 7
† 04572 South Waldoboro, 300 E 7
04081 South Waterford, 320 B 7
04679 Southwest Harbor, △1,657 G 7
04082 South Windham, 1,453 C 8
04487 Springfield, △336 G 5
04083 Springvale, 2,914 B 9
04782 Stacyville, △547 F 4
04084 Standish, △3,122 B 8
04084 Standish, 700 B 8
04980 Starks, △323 D 6
04085 Steep Falls, 500 B 8
04488 Stetson, △395 E 6
04680 Steuben, △697 H 6
04680 Steuben, 200 H 6
04489 Stillwater, 600 F 6
04783 Stockholm, △388 G 1
04981 Stockton Springs, △1,142 F 7
04981 Stockton Springs, 500 F 7
04681 Stonington, △1,291 F 7
† 04058 Stow, △109 A 7
04982 Stratton, 450 B 5
04983 Strong, △1,132 C 6
04682 Sullivan, △824 G 6
† 04292 Sumner, △525 C 7
04683 Sunset, 170 F 7
† 04627 Sunshine, 175 G 7
04684 Surry, △623 F 7
04685 Swans Island, △323 G 7
† 04915 Swanville, △487 E 6
† 04040 Sweden, △110 B 7
04984 Temple, △367 C 6
04860 Tenants Harbor, 600 E 8
04861 Thomaston, △2,646 E 7
04861 Thomaston, 2,160 E 7
04986 Thorndike, △439 E 6
04490 Topsfield, 180 H 5
04086 Topsham, △5,022 D 8
04086 Topsham, 2,700 D 8
† 04653 Tremont, △1,003 G 7
† 04653 Tremont, 175 G 7
† 04605 Trenton, △392 G 7
† 04652 Trescott, 200 J 6
04571 Trevett, 275 D 8
04987 Troy, △543 E 6
04282 Turner, △2,246 C 7
04282 Turner, 400 C 7
04862 Union, △1,189 E 7
04862 Union, 300 E 7
04988 Unity, △1,280 E 6
04784 Upper Frenchville, 375 G 1
04261 Upton, △54 B 6
04785 Van Buren, △3,971 G 1
04785 Van Buren, 3,429 G 1
04491 Vanceboro, △263 J 4
04989 Vassalboro, △2,618 D 7
04401 Veazie, △1,556 F 6
04401 Veazie, 1,174 F 6
04360 Vienna, △205 D 6
04863 Vinalhaven, △1,135 F 7
04492 Waite, △70 H 5
† 04915 Waldo, △431 E 7
04572 Waldoboro, △3,146 E 7
04572 Waldoboro, 824 E 7
† 04021 Walnut Hill, 400 C 8
† 04605 Waltham, △167 G 6
04864 Warren, △1,864 E 7
04864 Warren, 770 E 7
04786 Washburn, △1,914 G 2
04786 Washburn, 1,098 G 2
04574 Washington, △723 E 7
04087 Waterboro, △1,208 B 8
04087 Waterboro, 400 B 8
04088 Waterford, △760 B 7
04901 Waterville, 18,192 D 6
04284 Wayne, △577 D 7
04284 Wayne, 175 D 7
04361 Weeks Mills, 235 E 7
04285 Weld, △360 C 6
04990 Wellington, △232 D 5
04090 Wells, △4,448 B 9
04090 Wells, 950 B 9
04090 Wells Beach, 600 B 9
04686 Wesley, △110 H 6
† 04530 West Bath, △836 D 8
04286 West Bethel, 155 B 7
04092 Westbrook, 14,444 C 8
† 04617 West Brooksville, 156 F 7
04093 West Buxton, 185 B 8
04493 West Enfield, 500 F 5
04992 West Farmington, 700 C 6
04787 Westfield, △517 G 2
† 04634 West Franklin, 350 G 6
† 04345 West Gardiner, △1,435 D 7
† 04445 West Hampden, 800 E 6
04649 West Jonesport, 400 H 6
† 04652 West Lubec, 275 J 6
04288 West Minot, 200 C 7
04095 West Newfield, 225 B 8
04494 Weston, △162 H 4
04289 West Paris, △1,171 B 7
04290 West Peru, 650 C 7
04291 West Poland, 300 C 7
04865 West Rockport, 350 E 7
04074 West Scarborough, 850 C 8
04690 West Tremont, 200 G 7
04362 Whitefield, △1,131 D 7
04362 Whitefield, 550 D 7
04691 Whiting, △269 J 6
04692 Whitneyville, △155 H 6
† 04443 Willimantic, △126 E 5
04294 Wilton, △3,802 C 6
04294 Wilton, 2,225 C 6
04363 Windsor, △1,097 D 7
04495 Winn, △516 G 5
04495 Winn, 250 G 5
04901 Winslow, △7,299 D 6
04901 Winslow, 5,389 D 6
04693 Winter Harbor, △1,028 G 7
04496 Winterport, △1,963 F 6
04496 Winterport, 900 F 6
04788 Winterville, △164 F 2
04364 Winthrop, △4,335 C 7
04364 Winthrop, 2,571 C 7
04578 Wiscasset⊙, △2,244 D 7
04694 Woodland, 1,534 H 5
04579 Woolwich, △1,710 D 8
† 04920 Wyman Dam, 300 D 5
04497 Wytopitlock, 200 G 4
04096 Yarmouth, △4,854 C 8
04096 Yarmouth, 2,421 C 8
03909 York, △5,690 B 9
03909 York, 2,912 B 9
03910 York Beach, 900 B 9
03911 York Harbor, 950 B 9

⊙ County seat.
‡ Population of metropolitan area.
△ Population of town or township.
† Zip of nearest p.o.
* Multiple zips

Agriculture, Industry and Resources

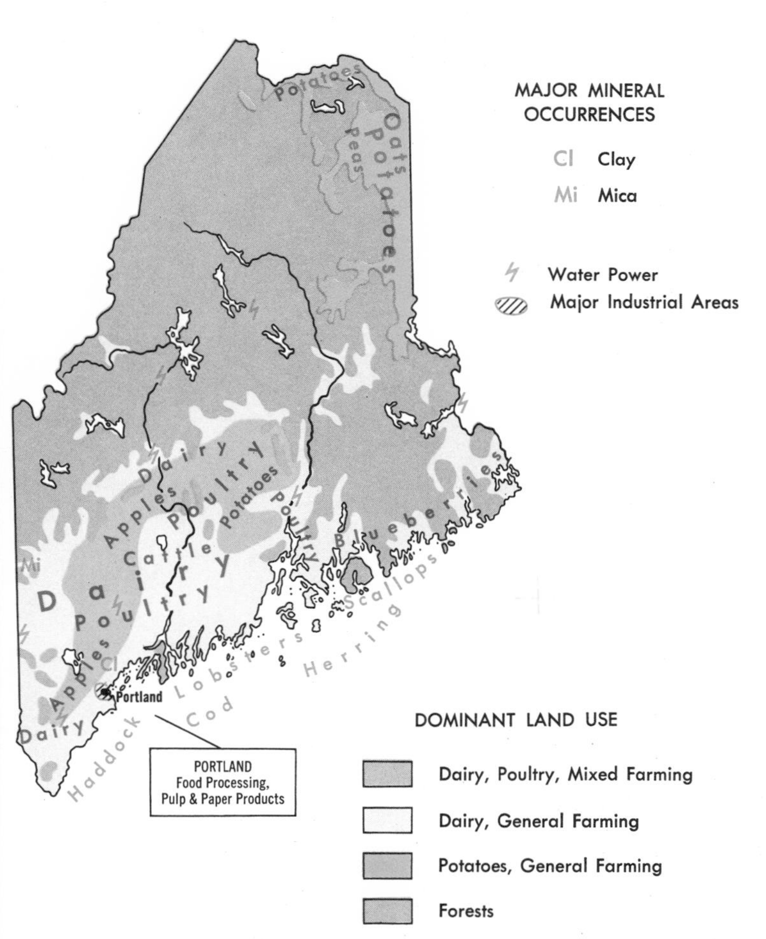

Topography

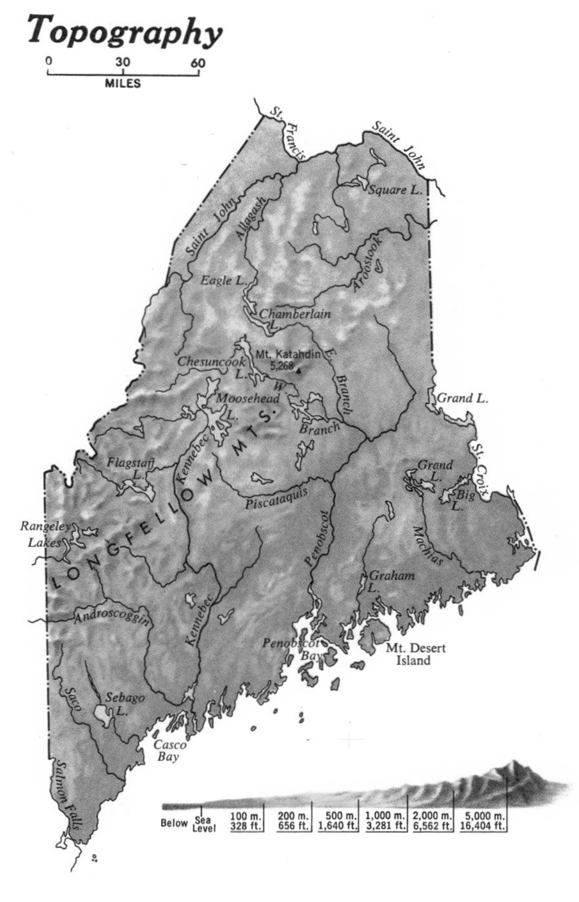

MARYLAND

COUNTIES

Allegany, 84,044 .... C 2
Anne Arundel, 297,539 .... M 4
Baltimore, 621,077 .... M 3
Baltimore (city county), 905,759 .... M 3
Calvert, 20,682 .... M 6
Caroline, 19,781 .... P 5
Carroll, 69,006 .... K 2
Cecil, 53,291 .... P 2
Charles, 47,678 .... K 6
Dorchester, 29,405 .... O 7
Frederick, 84,927 .... J 3
Garrett, 21,476 .... A 2
Harford, 115,378 .... N 2
Howard, 61,911 .... L 4
Kent, 16,146 .... O 3
Montgomery, 522,809 .... J 4
Prince Georges, 660,567 .... L 5
Queen Annes, 18,422 .... P 4
Saint Marys, 47,388 .... M 7
Somerset, 18,924 .... R 8
Talbot, 23,692 .... O 5
Washington, 103,829 .... G 2
Wicomico, 54,236 .... R 7
Worcester, 24,442 .... S 8

CITIES and TOWNS

Zip *Name/Pop.* *Key*
21001 Aberdeen, 12,375 .... O 2
21009 Abingdon, 3,000 .... N 3
21520 Accident, 237 .... A 2
20607 Accokeek, 450 .... L 6
21710 Adamstown, 265 .... H 3
21810 Allen, 200 .... R 7
† 21043 Allview, 2,314 .... L 4
* 21401 Annapolis (cap.)⊙, 29,592 .... M 5
20701 Annapolis Junction, 775 .... M 4
† 21782 Antietam, 150 .... H 3
20608 Aquasco, 950 .... L 6
† 20785 Ardmore, 500 .... G 4
† 20015 Aspen Hill, 16,799 .... K 4
* 21201 Baltimore, 905,759 .... M 3
Baltimore, ‡2,070,670 .... M 3
21607 Barclay, 187 .... P 4
20703 Barnesville, 162 .... J 4
20610 Barstow, 500 .... M 6
21521 Barton, 723 .... B 2
† 21901 Bayview, 250 .... P 2
21014 Bel Air⊙, 6,307 .... N 2
20611 Bel Alton, 675 .... L 7
† 21662 Bellevue, 300 .... O 6
20705 Beltsville, 8,912 .... G 3
20612 Benedict, 700 .... M 6
21811 Berlin, 1,942 .... T 7
† 20740 Berwyn Heights, 3,934 .... G 4
20014 Bethesda, 71,621 .... E 4
21609 Bethlehem, 200 .... P 6
21610 Betterton, 327 .... O 3
21611 Bishops Head, 250 .... O 7
21813 Bishopville, 300 .... T 7
21814 Bivalve, 450 .... P 7
20710 Bladensburg, 7,488 .... G 4
21523 Bloomington, 235 .... B 3
21713 Boonsboro, 1,410 .... H 2
† 21532 Borden Shaft, 208 .... B 2
21020 Boring, 283 .... L 2
† 20027 Boulevard Heights, 500 .... F 5
† 20678 Bowens, 250 .... M 6
20715 Bowie, 35,028 .... L 4
20720 Boyds, 300 .... J 4
21612 Bozman, 500 .... N 5
20613 Brandywine, 525 .... L 6
20722 Brentwood, 3,426 .... F 4
21715 Brownsville, 185 .... H 3
21716 Brunswick, 3,566 .... H 3
21717 Buckeystown, 400 .... J 3
21718 Burkittsville, 221 .... H 3
20730 Burtonsville, 3,000 .... L 4
20618 Bushwood, 675 .... L 7
21023 Butler, 150 .... M 2
20731 Cabin John, 2,500 .... E 4
20619 California, 350 .... M 7
† 20705 Calverton, 6,453 .... L 4
21613 Cambridge⊙, 11,595 .... O 6
20031 Camp Springs, 22,776 .... G 6
20027 Capitol Heights, 2,852 .... G 5
21024 Cardiff, 510 .... N 2
† 20780 Carrollton, 13,395 .... G 4
21025 Carrollton, 174 .... L 2
† 21034 Castleton, 675 .... N 2
† 21788 Catoctin Furnace, 516 .... J 2
21228 Catonsville, 54,812 .... M 3
21720 Cavetown, 325 .... H 2
21913 Cecilton, 581 .... P 3
† 20767 Cedar Grove, 300 .... K 4
† 20027 Cedar Heights, 6,049 .... G 5
21617 Centreville⊙, 1,853 .... O 4
21816 Chance, 500 .... P 8
20621 Chaptico, 300 .... M 7
21914 Charlestown, 721 .... P 2
20622 Charlotte Hall, 200 .... M 7
21027 Chase, 900 .... N 3
20623 Cheltenham, 950 .... L 6
† 21921 Cherry Hill, 214 .... P 2
20732 Chesapeake Beach, 934 .... N 6
21915 Chesapeake City, 1,031 .... P 2
21619 Chester, 950 .... N 5
21620 Chestertown⊙, 3,476 .... O 4
20785 Cheverly, 6,696 .... G 4
20015 Chevy Chase, 16,424 .... E 4
21721 Chewsville, 350 .... H 2
20783 Chillum, 35,656 .... F 4
21623 Church Hill, 247 .... O 4
21028 Churchville, 500 .... N 2
21624 Claiborne, 150 .... N 5
20734 Clarksburg, 400 .... J 4
21029 Clarksville, 500 .... L 4
21722 Clear Spring, 499 .... G 2
20624 Clements, 800 .... L 7
20735 Clinton, 1,900 .... G 6
21030 Cockeysville, 2,900 .... M 3
20740 College Park, 26,156 .... G 4
† 20722 Colmar Manor, 1,715 .... F 4
21917 Colora, 500 .... O 2
20626 Coltons Point, 310 .... M 8
21043 Columbia, 8,815 .... L 5
20627 Compton, 500 .... M 7
21918 Conowingo, 150 .... O 2
21723 Cooksville, 497 .... K 3
† 20027 Coral Hills, 7,105 .... G 5
21625 Cordova, 365 .... O 5
21524 Corriganville, 850 .... C 2
† 20722 Cottage City, 993 .... F 4
† 20611 Cox Station (Bel Alton), 675 .... L 7
† 21788 Creagerstown, 240 .... J 2
21525 Crellin, 500 .... A 3
21502 Cresaptown, 1,731 .... C 2
21817 Crisfield, 3,078 .... P 9
21627 Crocheron, 150 .... O 8
21113 Crofton, 4,478 .... M 4
21032 Crownsville, 1,900 .... M 4
21628 Crumpton, 375 .... P 4
21502 Cumberland⊙, 29,724 .... D 2
20750 Damascus, 2,638 .... K 3
20628 Dameron, 500 .... N 8
21820 Dames Quarter, 300 .... P 8
† 25425 Dargan, 245 .... H 3
21034 Darlington, 800 .... N 2
20760 Darnestown, 950 .... J 4
21035 Davidsonville, 250 .... M 5
20751 Deale, 1,059 .... M 5
21821 Deal Island, 800 .... P 8
21550 Deer Park, 310 .... A 3
† 19940 Delmar, 1,191 .... R 7
21629 Denton⊙, 1,561 .... P 5
20855 Derwood, 450 .... K 4
20753 Dickerson, 500 .... J 4
20028 District Heights, 8,424 .... G 5
† 21710 Doubs, 273 .... J 3
† 21795 Downsville, 255 .... G 2
20630 Drayden, 450 .... N 8
† 21154 Dublin, 366 .... N 2
21222 Dundalk, 85,377 .... N 3
† 20608 Eagle Harbor, 200 .... M 6
† 21146 Earleigh Heights, 1,500 .... M 4
21631 East New Market, 251 .... P 6
21601 Easton⊙, 6,809 .... O 5
21528 Eckhart Mines, 900 .... C 2
21040 Edgewood, 8,551 .... N 3
† 20781 Edmonston, 1,441 .... F 4
† 21784 Eldersburg, 1,739 .... L 3
21920 Elk Mills, 500 .... P 2
† 21901 Elk Neck, 700 .... P 2
21227 Elkridge, 4,900 .... M 4
21921 Elkton⊙, 5,362 .... P 2
21529 Ellerslie, 950 .... C 2
21043 Ellicott City⊙, 9,506 .... L 3
21727 Emmitsburg, 1,532 .... J 2
21221 Essex, 38,193 .... N 3
21824 Ewell, 350 .... O 9
† 21620 Fairlee, 300 .... O 4
† 20027 Fairmont Heights, 1,972 .... G 5
21047 Fallston, 617 .... N 2
21632 Federalsburg, 1,917 .... P 6
21061 Ferndale, 9,929 .... M 4
21048 Finksburg, 950 .... L 3
21634 Fishing Creek, 595 .... N 7
21530 Flintstone, 395 .... D 2
† 20907 Forest Glen, 1,900 .... F 4
† 20001 Forest Heights, 3,600 .... F 5
21050 Forest Hill, 450 .... N 2
† 20028 Forestville, 16,152 .... G 5
† 20013 Fort Foote, 700 .... F 6
† 20735 Fort Washington, 1,650 .... L 6
† 21740 Fountain Head, 2,029 .... H 2
† 21760 Foxville, 400 .... J 2
21701 Frederick⊙, 23,641 .... J 3
21053 Freeland, 500 .... M 2
21531 Friendsville, 566 .... A 2
† 21157 Frizzellburg, 300 .... K 2
21532 Frostburg, 7,327 .... C 2
21826 Fruitland, 2,315 .... R 7
21734 Funkstown, 1,051 .... H 2
20760 Gaithersburg, 8,344 .... K 4
21635 Galena, 361 .... P 3
21054 Gambrills, 460 .... M 4
20766 Garrett Park, 1,258 .... E 3
21055 Garrison, 950 .... L 3
20767 Germantown, 260 .... J 4
21829 Girdletree, 850 .... S 8
20801 Glenarden, 4,502 .... G 4
21057 Glen Arm, 350 .... N 3
21061 Glen Burnie, 38,608 .... M 4
20768 Glen Echo, 297 .... E 4
† 20013 Glen Echo Heights, 2,025 .... E 4
21737 Glenelg, 400 .... L 3
21071 Glyndon-Reisterstown, 14,037 .... L 3
21636 Goldsboro, 231 .... P 4
† 20715 Good Luck, 10,584 .... G 4
† 21788 Graceham, 300 .... J 2
† 21163 Granite, 950 .... L 3
21536 Grantsville, 517 .... B 2
21638 Grasonville, 1,182 .... O 5
20770 Greenbelt, 18,199 .... G 4
21122 Green Haven, 1,841 .... M 4
21072 Greenmount, 325 .... L 2
21639 Greensboro, 1,173 .... P 5
21740 Hagerstown⊙, 35,862 .... G 2
† 21740 Halfway, 6,106 .... G 2
† 20850 Halpine, 5,912 .... K 4
21074 Hampstead, 961 .... L 2
21750 Hancock, 1,832 .... F 2
21201 Hanover, 500 .... M 4
† 21787 Harney, 250 .... K 2
21078 Havre de Grace, 9,791 .... O 2
21830 Hebron, 705 .... R 7
21080 Henryton, 400 .... L 3
† 21111 Hereford, 680 .... M 2
21753 Highfield, 500 .... J 2
† 20901 Hillandale, 19,520 .... F 4
† 20001 Hillcrest Heights, 24,037 .... F 5
21641 Hillsboro, 177 .... P 5
20636 Hollywood, 500 .... M 7
21642 Hoopersville, 300 .... O 7
20637 Hughesville, 500 .... L 6
20639 Huntingtown, 450 .... M 6
21643 Hurlock, 1,056 .... P 6
† 21864 Hursley Station (Stockton), 500 .... S 8
20734 Hyattstown, 150 .... J 3
* 20780 Hyattsville, 14,998 .... F 4
20640 Indian Head, 1,350 .... K 6
21644 Ingleside, 180 .... P 4

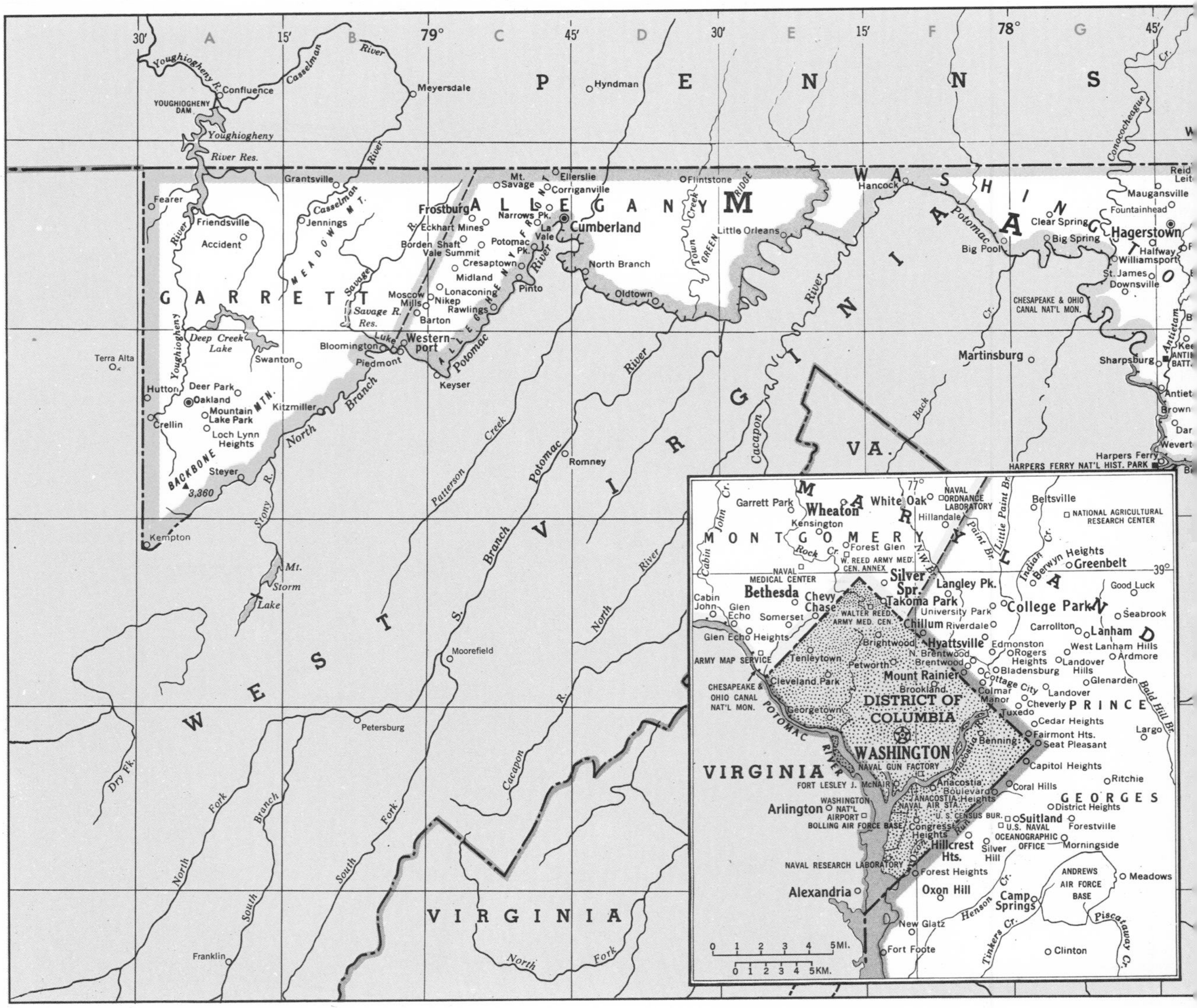

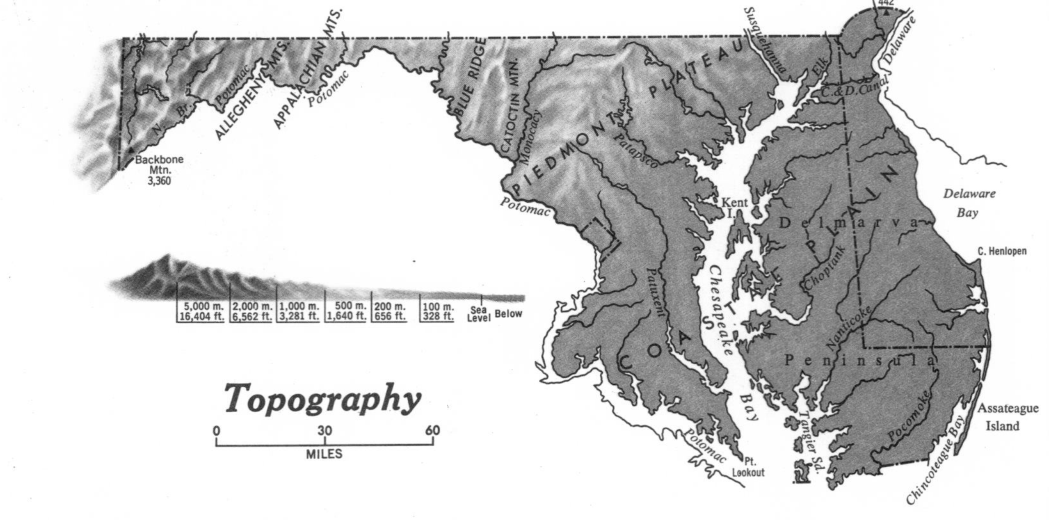

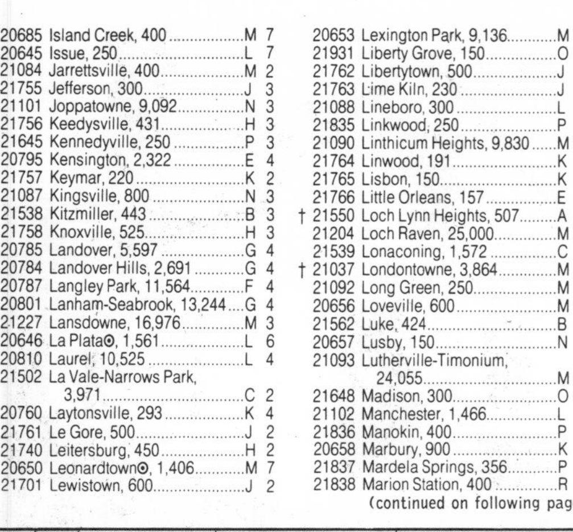

† 20685 Island Creek, 400 .... M 7
20645 Issue, 250 .... L 7
21084 Jarrettsville, 400 .... M 2
21755 Jefferson, 300 .... J 3
† 21101 Joppatowne, 9,092 .... N 3
21756 Keedysville, 431 .... H 3
21645 Kennedyville, 250 .... P 3
20795 Kensington, 2,322 .... E 4
21757 Keymar, 220 .... K 2
21087 Kingsville, 800 .... N 3
21538 Kitzmiller, 443 .... B 3
21758 Knoxville, 525 .... H 3
20785 Landover, 5,597 .... G 4
20784 Landover Hills, 2,691 .... G 4
20787 Langley Park, 11,564 .... F 4
20801 Lanham-Seabrook, 13,244 .... G 4
21227 Lansdowne, 16,976 .... M 3
20646 La Plata⊙, 1,561 .... L 6
20810 Laurel, 10,525 .... L 4
21502 La Vale-Narrows Park, 3,971 .... C 2
20760 Laytonsville, 293 .... K 4
21761 Le Gore, 500 .... J 2
† 21740 Leitersburg, 450 .... H 2
20650 Leonardtown⊙, 1,406 .... M 7
21701 Lewistown, 600 .... J 2
20653 Lexington Park, 9,136 .... M 7
21931 Liberty Grove, 150 .... O 2
21762 Libertytown, 500 .... J 3
21763 Lime Kiln, 230 .... J 3
21088 Lineboro, 300 .... L 2
21835 Linkwood, 250 .... P 6
21090 Linthicum Heights, 9,830 .... M 4
21764 Linwood, 191 .... K 2
21765 Lisbon, 150 .... K 3
21766 Little Orleans, 157 .... E 2
† 21550 Loch Lynn Heights, 507 .... A 3
21204 Loch Raven, 25,000 .... M 3
21539 Lonaconing, 1,572 .... C 2
† 21037 Londontowne, 3,864 .... M 4
21092 Long Green, 250 .... M 3
20656 Loveville, 600 .... M 7
21562 Luke, 424 .... B 3
20657 Lusby, 150 .... N 7
21093 Lutherville-Timonium, 24,055 .... M 3
21648 Madison, 300 .... O 6
21102 Manchester, 1,466 .... L 2
21836 Manokin, 400 .... P 8
20658 Marbury, 900 .... K 6
21837 Mardela Springs, 356 .... P 7
21838 Marion Station, 400 .... R 8

(continued on following page)

MARYLAND

AREA 10,577 sq. mi.
POPULATION 3,922,399
CAPITAL Annapolis
LARGEST CITY Baltimore
HIGHEST POINT Backbone Mtn. 3,360 ft.
SETTLED IN 1634
ADMITTED TO UNION April 28, 1788
POPULAR NAME Old Line State; Free State
STATE FLOWER Black-eyed Susan
STATE BIRD Baltimore Oriole

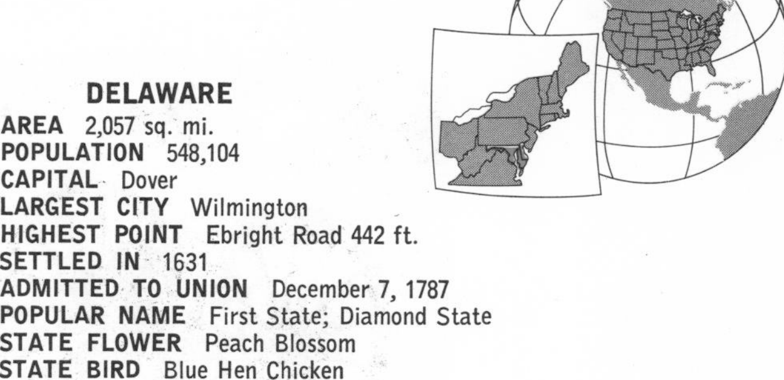

DELAWARE

AREA 2,057 sq. mi.
POPULATION 548,104
CAPITAL Dover
LARGEST CITY Wilmington
HIGHEST POINT Ebright Road 442 ft.
SETTLED IN 1631
ADMITTED TO UNION December 7, 1787
POPULAR NAME First State; Diamond State
STATE FLOWER Peach Blossom
STATE BIRD Blue Hen Chicken

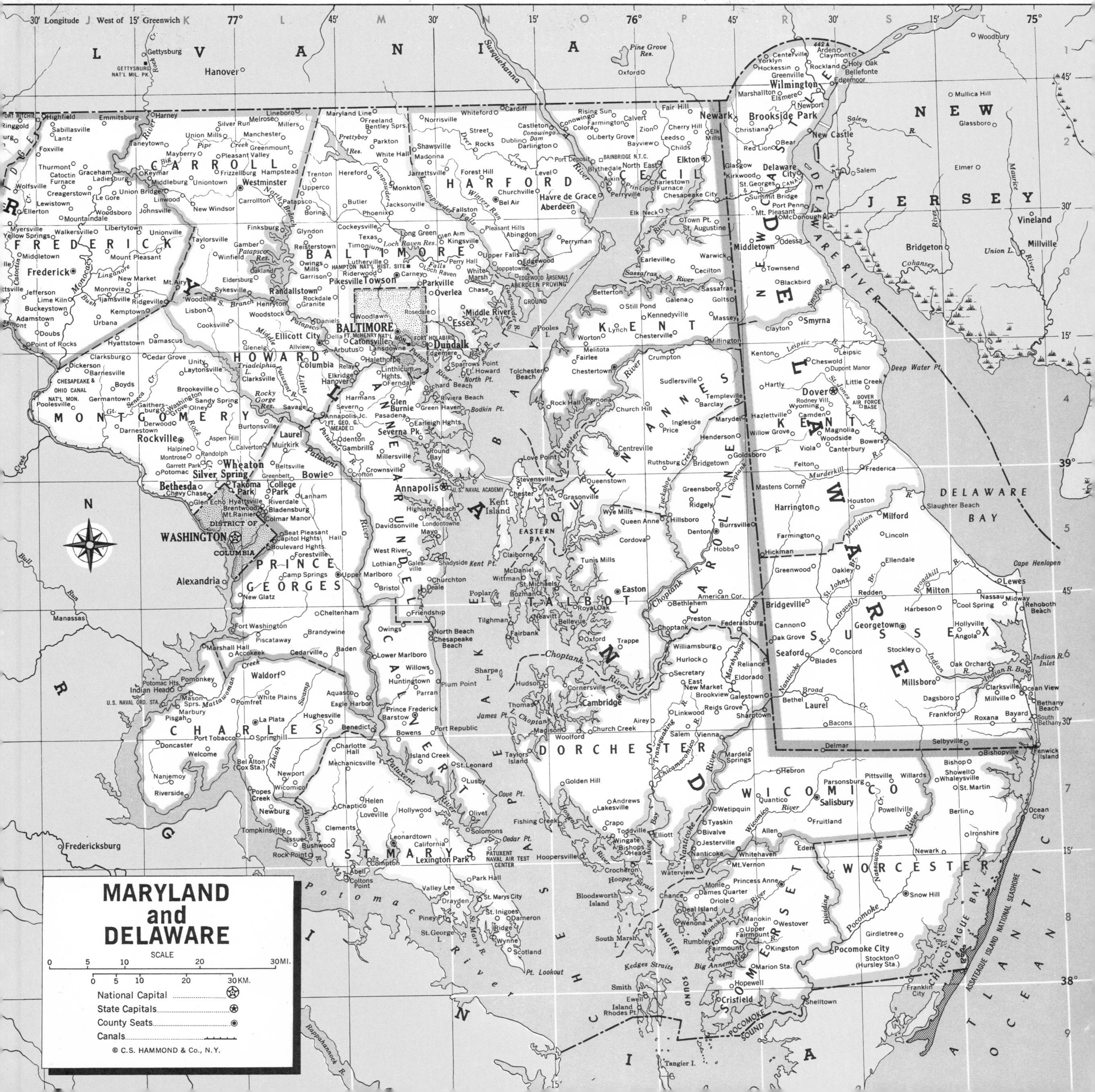

MARYLAND and DELAWARE

SCALE
0 5 10 20 30 MI.
0 5 10 20 30 KM.

National Capital
State Capitals
County Seats
Canals

(continued)

MARYLAND (continued)

† 20616 Marshall Hall, 325 ... K 6
21649 Marydel, 176 ... P 4
21105 Maryland Line, 250 ... M 2
21650 Massey, 220 ... P 3
21767 Maugansville, 1,069 ... H 2
21106 Mayo, 2,154 ... M 5
21647 McDaniel, 325 ... N 5
† 20870 Meadows, 200 ... G 5
20659 Mechanicsville, 784 ... M 7
21768 Middleburg, 200 ... K 2
21220 Middle River, 19,935 ... N 3
21769 Middletown, 1,262 ... J 3
21542 Midland, 665 ... C 2
21108 Millersville, 380 ... M 4
21651 Millington, 474 ... P 3
21111 Monkton, 307 ... M 2
21770 Monrovia, 300 ... J 3
† 20850 Montrose, 6,140 ... K 4
† 20028 Morningside, 1,665 ... G 5
† 21521 Moscow Mills, 275 ... B 2
† 21701 Mountaindale, 400 ... J 2
21550 Mountain Lake Park, 1,263 ... A 3
21771 Mount Airy, 1,825 ... K 3
† 21701 Mount Pleasant, 400 ... J 3
20822 Mount Rainier, 8,180 ... F 4
21545 Mount Savage, 1,413 ... C 2
† 21853 Mount Vernon, 900 ... P 8
† 20705 Muirkirk, 950 ... L 4
21773 Myersville, 450 ... H 3
20662 Nanjemoy, 238 ... K 7
21840 Nanticoke, 400 ... P 7
† 21502 Narrows Park-La Vale, 3,971 ... C 2
21652 Neavitt, 241 ... N 6
21841 Newark, 800 ... S 7
20664 Newburg, 550 ... L 7
† 20013 New Glatz, 950 ... F 6
21774 New Market, 339 ... J 3
21776 New Windsor, 788 ... K 2
21546 Nikep, 400 ... C 2
20831 North Beach, 761 ... N 6
† 20722 North Brentwood, 758 ... F 4
21901 North East, 1,818 ... P 2
21550 Oakland⊙, 1,786 ... A 3
21550 Oakland, 1,256 ... L 3
21842 Ocean City, 1,493 ... T 7
21113 Odenton, 5,989 ... M 4
† 21043 Oella, 600 ... L 3
21555 Oldtown, 400 ... D 2
20832 Olney, 2,138 ... K 4
† 21122 Orchard Beach, 200 ... M 4
21206 Overlea, 13,086 ... N 3
20836 Owings, 700 ... M 6
21117 Owings Mills, 7,360 ... L 3
21654 Oxford, 750 ... O 6
20021 Oxon Hill, 11,974 ... F 6
20667 Park Hall, 600 ... N 8
21120 Parkton, 290 ... M 2
21234 Parkville, 33,897 ... M 3
† 20639 Parran, 200 ... M 6
21849 Parsonsburg, 200 ... R 7
21122 Pasadena, 2,380 ... M 4
21127 Patapsco, 160 ... L 2
21128 Perry Hall, 5,446 ... N 3
21130 Perryman, 665 ... O 3
21903 Perryville, 2,091 ... O 2
21131 Phoenix, 165 ... M 2
21208 Pikesville, 25,395 ... M 3
20674 Piney Point, 950 ... M 8
21556 Pinto, 165 ... C 2
20640 Pisgah, 650 ... K 6
21850 Pittsville, 477 ... S 7
† 21087 Pleasant Hills, 1,754 ... N 3
21851 Pocomoke City, 3,573 ... R 8
21777 Point of Rocks, 400 ... J 3
20675 Pomfret, 600 ... L 6
20837 Poolesville, 349 ... J 4
21904 Port Deposit, 906 ... O 2
20677 Port Tobacco, 590 ... K 6
20854 Potomac (Potomac Valley), 5,094 ... K 4
20640 Potomac Heights, 1,983 ... K 6
† 21502 Potomac Park, 2,253 ... C 2
21852 Powellville, 450 ... S 7
21655 Preston, 509 ... P 6
20678 Prince Frederick⊙, 950 ... M 6
21853 Princess Anne⊙, 975 ... P 8
21856 Quantico, 200 ... R 7
21657 Queen Anne, 292 ... O 5
21658 Queenstown, 387 ... O 5
21133 Randallstown, 33,683 ... L 3
† 20853 Randolph, 13,233 ... K 4
21557 Rawlings, 600 ... C 2
21136 Reisterstown-Glyndon, 14,037 ... L 3
21139 Riderwood, 8,000 ... M 3
20680 Ridge, 550 ... N 8
21660 Ridgely, 822 ... P 5
21911 Rising Sun, 956 ... O 2
† 20013 Ritchie, 950 ... G 5
20840 Riverdale, 5,724 ... F 4
21122 Riviera Beach, 7,464 ... N 4
21661 Rock Hall, 1,125 ... O 4
20682 Rock Point, 300 ... L 7
* 20850 Rockville⊙, 41,564 ... K 4
† 20780 Rogers Heights, 3,000 ... G 4
21779 Rohrersville, 500 ... H 3
21237 Rosedale, 19,417 ... M 3
21662 Royal Oak, 600 ... O 6
21780 Sabillasville, 200 ... J 2
20684 Saint Inigoes, 750 ... N 8
21781 Saint James, 400 ... G 2
20685 Saint Leonard, 244 ... N 7
20686 Saint Marys City, 1,900 ... N 8
21663 Saint Michaels, 1,456 ... N 5
21801 Salisbury⊙, 15,252 ... R 7
20860 Sandy Spring, 500 ... K 4
20863 Savage, 2,116 ... L 4
20687 Scotland, 660 ... N 8
20801 Seabrook-Lanham, 13,244 ... G 4
20027 Seat Pleasant, 7,217 ... G 5
21664 Secretary, 352 ... P 6
21146 Severna Park, 16,358 ... M 4
20867 Shady Side, 1,562 ... N 5
21782 Sharpsburg, 833 ... G 3
21861 Sharptown, 660 ... R 6

J. C. Maycock — Shostal Associates

Antietam Battlefield, near Sharpsburg, Maryland, the scene of the country's bloodiest one-day battle on September 17, 1862. A national battlefield site today, it is surrounded by farms, some of whose cattle graze among the cannons and monuments.

Dorothy Bacheller

In Lewes, Delaware, settled by the Dutch in 1631, the Thompson Country Store sign establishes its origin as c.1800. The home of generations of Delaware River ship pilots, this seafaring town survives a history of shipwreck, bombardment and plundering.

21862 Showell, 250 ... T 7
20023 Silver Hill-Suitland, 30,355 ... F 5
* 20901 Silver Spring, 77,496 ... F 4
21783 Smithsburg, 671 ... H 2
21863 Snow Hill⊙, 2,201 ... S 8
20688 Solomons, 250 ... N 7
† 20015 Somerset, 1,303 ... E 4
21666 Stevensville, 500 ... N 5
21667 Still Pond, 250 ... O 3
21864 Stockton, 500 ... S 8
21154 Street, 200 ... N 2
21668 Sudlersville, 417 ... P 4
20023 Suitland-Silver Hill, 30,355 ... F 5
21561 Swanton, 223 ... A 3
21784 Sykesville, 1,399 ... K 3
20012 Takoma Park, 18,455 ... F 4
21787 Taneytown, 1,731 ... K 2
21669 Taylors Island, 375 ... N 7
21788 Thurmont, 2,359 ... J 2
21671 Tilghman, 950 ... N 6
21093 Timonium-Lutherville, 24,055 ... M 3
21672 Toddville, 300 ... O 7
21204 Towson⊙, 77,809 ... M 3
21673 Trappe, 426 ... O 6
20781 Tuxedo, 500 ... G 5
21791 Union Bridge, 904 ... K 2
21157 Uniontown, 250 ... K 2
21792 Unionville, 250 ... K 3
† 20740 University Park, 2,926 ... F 4
21155 Upperco, 500 ... L 2
21867 Upper Fairmount, 300 ... P 8
21156 Upper Falls, 900 ... N 3
20870 Upper Marlboro⊙, 646 ... M 5
20692 Valley Lee, 600 ... M 8
21869 Vienna, 358 ... P 7
20601 Waldorf, 7,368 ... L 6
21793 Walkersville, 1,269 ... J 3
21912 Warwick, 550 ... P 3
20880 Washington Grove, 688 ... K 4
20693 Welcome, 438 ... K 7
21870 Wenona, 323 ... P 8
21562 Westernport, 3,106 ... B 3
† 20784 West Lanham Hills, 950 ... G 4
21157 Westminster⊙, 7,207 ... L 2
21871 Westover, 450 ... R 8
20881 West River, 796 ... M 5
20902 Wheaton, 66,247 ... E 3
21160 Whiteford, 500 ... N 2
21161 White Hall, 350 ... M 2
21162 White Marsh, 500 ... N 3
† 20901 White Oak, 19,769 ... F 3
20695 White Plains, 1,600 ... L 6
21874 Willards, 494 ... S 7
21674 Williamsburg, 300 ... P 6
21795 Williamsport, 2,270 ... G 2
21675 Wingate, 200 ... O 7
21676 Wittman, 500 ... N 5
21797 Woodbine, 872 ... K 3
† 21201 Woodlawn, 28,811 ... M 3
21798 Woodsboro, 439 ... J 2
21163 Woodstock, 700 ... L 3
21677 Woolford, 295 ... O 7
21678 Worton, 315 ... O 3
21679 Wye Mills, 300 ... O 5
† 21701 Yellow Springs, 940 ... H 3

DELAWARE

COUNTIES

Kent, 81,892 ... R 4
New Castle, 385,856 ... R 2
Sussex, 80,356 ... S 6

CITIES and TOWNS

Zip	Name/Pop.	Key
† 19801	Arden, 3,340	R 1
19701	Bear, 200	R 2
19809	Bellefonte, 1,442	S 1
19930	Bethany Beach, 189	T 6
19931	Bethel, 219	R 6
† 19973	Blades, 632	R 6
19993	Bridgeville, 1,317	R 6
19711	Brookside Park, 7,856	R 2
19934	Camden, 1,241	R 4
† 19801	Centerville, 1,260	R 1
19936	Cheswold, 286	R 4
19702	Christiana, 550	R 2
19937	Clarksville, 350	T 6
19703	Claymont, 6,584	S 1
19938	Clayton, 1,015	R 3
19930	Dagsboro, 375	S 6
19706	Delaware City, 2,024	R 2
19940	Delmar, 943	R 7
19901	Dover (cap.)⊙, 17,488	R 4
† 19901	Dupont Manor, 1,256	R 4
† 19801	Edgemoor, 2,100	S 1
19941	Ellendale, 399	S 5
† 19801	Elsmere, 8,415	R 2
19943	Felton, 495	R 4
19945	Frankford, 635	S 6
19946	Frederica, 878	S 4
19947	Georgetown⊙, 1,844	S 6
19807	Greenville, 230	R 1
19950	Greenwood, 654	R 5
19951	Harbeson, 312	S 6
19952	Harrington, 2,407	R 5
19953	Hartly, 180	R 4
19707	Hockessin, 950	R 1
† 19801	Holly Oak, 1,140	S 1
19954	Houston, 317	S 5
19955	Kenton, 205	R 4
19708	Kirkwood, 450	R 2
19956	Laurel, 2,408	R 6
19958	Lewes, 2,563	T 5
19960	Lincoln, 757	S 5
19961	Little Creek, 215	S 4
19962	Magnolia, 319	R 4
19808	Marshallton, 1,240	R 2
19709	Middletown, 2,644	R 3
19963	Milford, 5,314	S 5
19966	Millsboro, 1,073	S 6
19967	Millville, 224	T 6
19968	Milton, 1,490	S 5
19711	Newark, 20,757	P 2
19720	New Castle, 4,814	R 2
19804	Newport, 1,366	R 2
19970	Ocean View, 411	T 6
19730	Odessa, 547	R 3
19731	Port Penn, 325	R 2
19971	Rehoboth Beach, 1,614	T 6
19901	Rodney Village, 2,127	R 4
19733	Saint Georges, 450	R 2
19973	Seaford, 5,537	R 6
19975	Selbyville, 1,099	S 7
19977	Smyrna, 4,243	R 3
19734	Townsend, 505	R 3
19979	Viola, 154	R 4
* 19801	Wilmington⊙, 80,386	R 2
	Wilmington, ‡498,977	R 2
19980	Woodside, 223	R 4
19934	Wyoming, 1,062	R 4
19736	Yorklyn, 300	R 1

DISTRICT OF COLUMBIA

CITIES and TOWNS

Zip	Name/Pop.	Key
20007	Georgetown,	E 5
* 20001	Washington, D.C. (cap.), U.S. 756,510	F 5
	Washington, ‡2,861,123	F 5

⊙ County seat.
‡ Population of metropolitan area.
† Zip of nearest p.o.
* Multiple zips

Agriculture, Industry and Resources

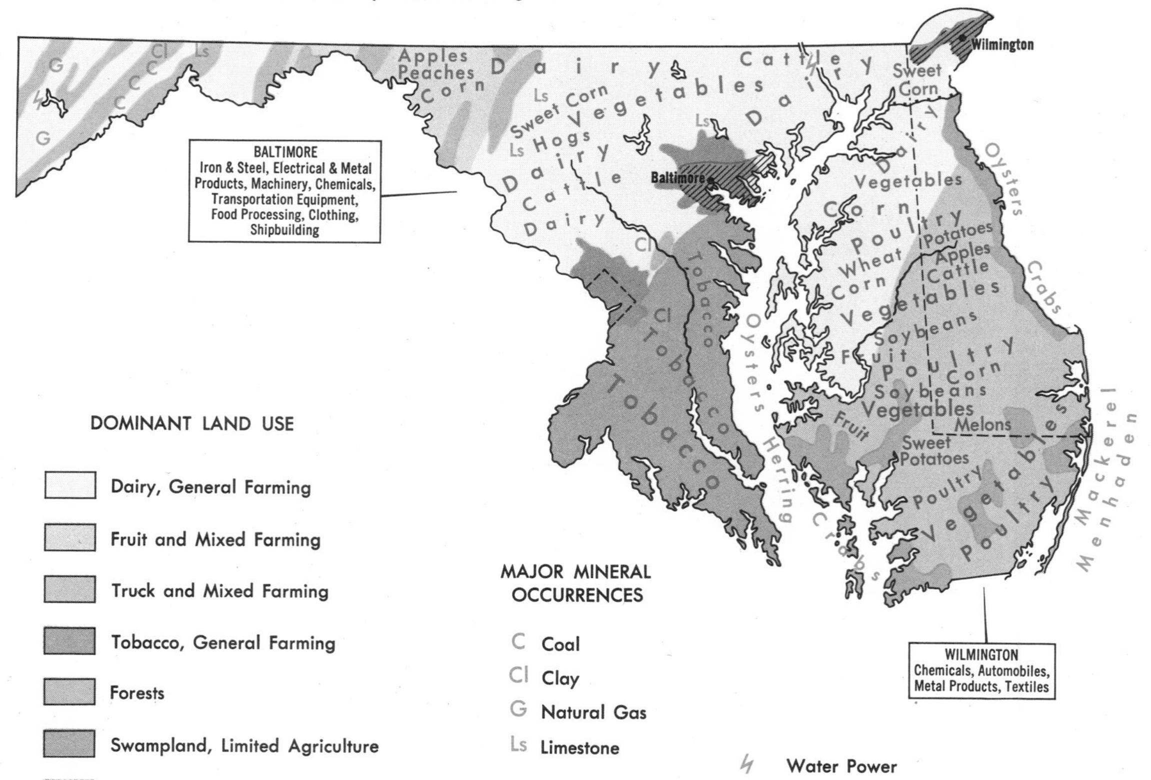

MASSACHUSETTS

AREA 8,257 sq. mi.
POPULATION 5,689,170
CAPITAL Boston
LARGEST CITY Boston
HIGHEST POINT Mt. Greylock 3,491 ft.
SETTLED IN 1620
ADMITTED TO UNION February 6, 1788
POPULAR NAME Bay State; Old Colony
STATE FLOWER Mayflower
STATE BIRD Chickadee

RHODE ISLAND

AREA 1,214 sq. mi.
POPULATION 949,723
CAPITAL Providence
LARGEST CITY Providence
HIGHEST POINT Jerimoth Hill 812 ft.
SETTLED IN 1636
ADMITTED TO UNION May 29, 1790
POPULAR NAME Little Rhody
STATE FLOWER Violet
STATE BIRD Rhode Island Red

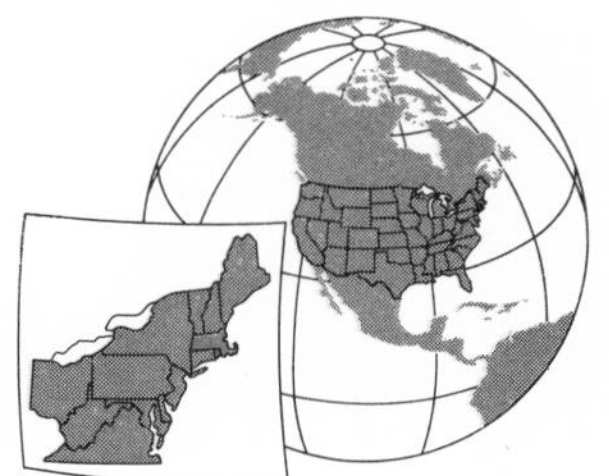

Agriculture, Industry and Resources

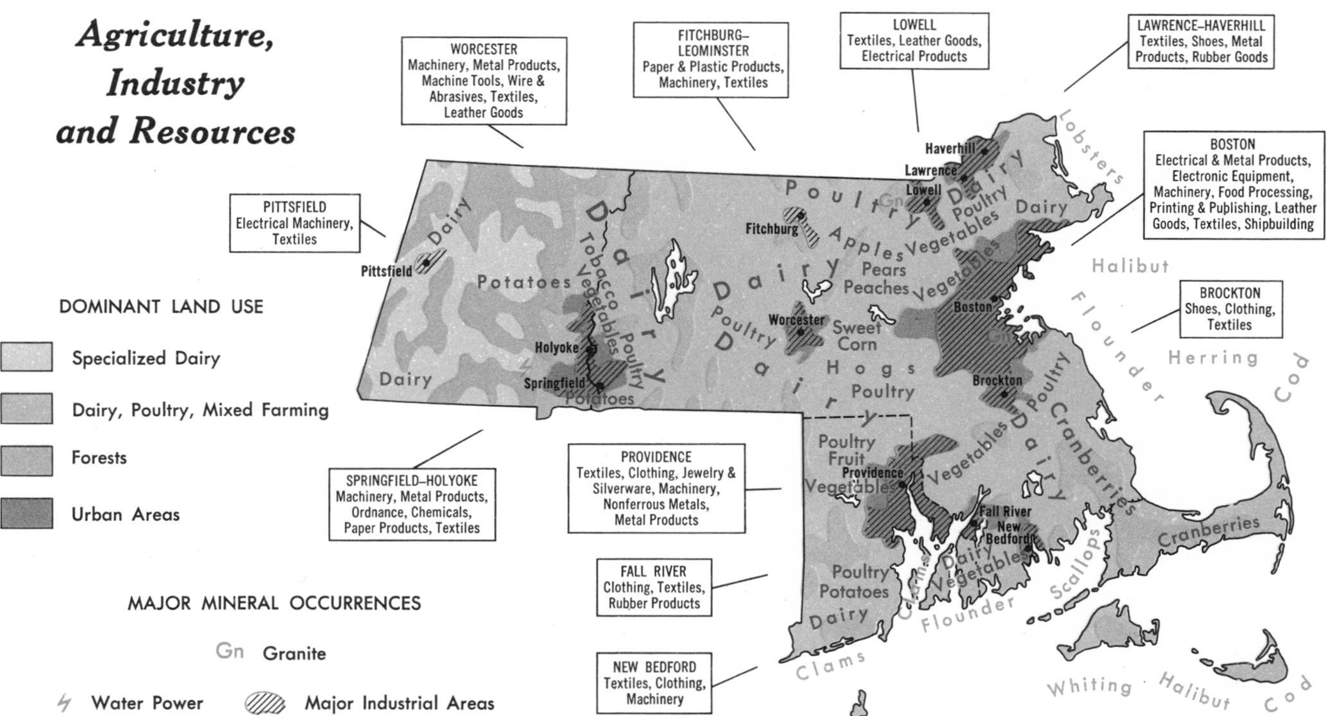

MASSACHUSETTS

COUNTIES

Name/Pop.	Key
Barnstable, 96,656	N 6
Berkshire, 149,402	B 3
Bristol, 444,301	K 5
Dukes, 6,117	M 7
Essex, 637,887	L 2
Franklin, 59,210	D 2
Hampden, 459,050	D 4
Hampshire, 123,981	D 3
Middlesex, 1,397,268	J 3
Nantucket, 3,774	O 7
Norfolk, 605,051	K 4
Plymouth, 333,314	L 5
Suffolk, 735,190	K 3
Worcester, 637,969	G 3

CITIES and TOWNS

Zip	*Name/Pop.*	*Key*
02351	Abington, ∆12,334	L 4
02351	Abington, 5,900	L 4
01720	Acton, ∆14,770	J 3
01220	Adams, ∆11,772	B 2
01220	Adams, 11,256	B 2
01001	Agawam, ∆21,717	D 4
† 01261	Alford, ∆302	A 4
01913	Amesbury, ∆11,388	L 1
01913	Amesbury, 10,088	L 1
01002	Amherst, ∆26,331	E 3
01002	Amherst, 17,926	E 3
01810	Andover, ∆23,695	K 2
02174	Arlington, ∆53,524	C 6
01430	Ashburnham, ∆3,484	G 2
01431	Ashby, ∆2,274	G 2
01330	Ashfield, ∆1,274	C 2
01721	Ashland, ∆8,882	J 3
01331	Athol, ∆11,185	F 2
01331	Athol, 9,723	F 2
02703	Attleboro, 32,907	J 5
02763	Attleboro Falls, 5,000	J 5
01501	Auburn, ∆15,347	G 4
† 02166	Auburndale, 7,235	B 7
02322	Avon, ∆5,295	K 4
* 01432	Ayer, ∆7,393	H 2
02630	Barnstable⊙, ∆19,842	N 6
01005	Barre, ∆3,825	F 3
01223	Becket, ∆929	B 3
01730	Bedford, ∆13,513	B 6
01007	Belchertown, ∆5,936	E 3
02019	Bellingham, ∆13,967	J 4
02019	Bellingham, 4,228	J 4
02178	Belmont, ∆28,285	C 6
† 02780	Berkley, ∆2,027	K 5
01503	Berlin, ∆2,099	H 3
01337	Bernardston, ∆1,659	D 2
01915	Beverly, 38,348	E 5
01821	Billerica, ∆31,648	J 2
01504	Blackstone, ∆6,566	H 4
01008	Blandford, ∆863	C 4
01740	Bolton, ∆1,905	H 3
* 02101	Boston (cap.)⊙, 641,071	D 7
	Boston, ‡2,753,700	D 7
02532	Bourne, ∆12,636	M 6
† 01720	Boxborough, ∆1,451	H 3
01921	Boxford, ∆4,032	L 2
01505	Boylston, ∆2,774	H 3
02184	Braintree, ∆35,050	D 8
02631	Brewster, ∆1,790	O 5
02324	Bridgewater, ∆11,829	K 5
02324	Bridgewater, 4,032	K 5
01010	Brimfield, ∆1,907	F 4
* 02401	Brockton, 89,040	K 4
	Brockton, ‡189,820	K 4
01506	Brookfield, ∆2,063	F 4
02147	Brookline, ∆58,886	C 7
01338	Buckland, ∆1,892	C 2
01803	Burlington, ∆21,980	C 5
† 02138	Cambridge⊙, 100,361	C 7
02021	Canton, ∆17,100	C 8
01741	Carlisle, ∆2,871	J 2
02330	Carver, ∆2,420	M 5
01339	Charlemont, ∆897	C 2
01507	Charlton, ∆4,654	F 4
02633	Chatham, ∆4,554	P 6
01824	Chelmsford, ∆31,432	J 2
02150	Chelsea, 30,625	D 6
01225	Cheshire, ∆3,006	B 2
01011	Chester, ∆1,025	C 3
01012	Chesterfield, ∆704	C 3
* 01013	Chicopee, 66,676	D 4
02535	Chilmark, ∆340	M 7
01510	Clinton, ∆13,383	H 3
01778	Cochituate, 6,000	A 7
02025	Cohasset, ∆6,954	F 7
02025	Cohasset, 3,900	F 7
† 01826	Collinsville, 4,000	J 2
01340	Colrain, ∆1,420	D 2
01742	Concord, ∆16,148	B 6
01742	Concord, 5,900	B 6
01341	Conway, ∆998	D 2
01026	Cummington, ∆562	C 3
01226	Dalton, ∆7,505	B 3
01923	Danvers, ∆26,151	D 5
02714	Dartmouth, ∆18,800	K 6
02026	Dedham⊙, ∆26,938	C 7
01342	Deerfield, ∆3,850	D 2
02638	Dennis, ∆6,454	O 5
02715	Dighton, ∆4,667	K 5
† 02122	Dorchester, 153,061	D 7
† 01516	Douglas, ∆2,947	H 4
02030	Dover, ∆4,529	B 7
01826	Dracut, ∆18,214	J 2
01570	Dudley, ∆8,087	G 4
01827	Dunstable, ∆1,292	J 2
02332	Duxbury, ∆7,636	M 4
02332	Duxbury, 2,477	M 4
† 02184	East Braintree, 12,000	D 8
02333	East Bridgewater, ∆8,347	L 4
01515	East Brookfield, ∆1,800	G 4
02642	Eastham, ∆2,043	O 5
01027	Easthampton, ∆13,012	D 3
01028	East Longmeadow, ∆13,029	E 4
† 02186	East Milton, 9,500	D 7
02334	Easton, ∆12,157	K 4
01437	East Pepperell, 4,200	H 2
† 01906	East Saugus, 4,200	D 6
02032	East Walpole, 4,500	C 8
† 02189	East Weymouth, 20,000	E 8
02539	Edgartown, ∆1,481	M 7
02539	Edgartown⊙, 1,006	M 7
01344	Erving, ∆1,260	E 2
02112	Essex, ∆2,670	L 2
02149	Everett, 42,485	D 6
02719	Fairhaven, ∆16,332	L 6
* 02720	Fall River, 96,898	K 6
	Fall River, ‡149,976	K 6
* 02540	Falmouth, ∆15,942	M 6
* 02540	Falmouth, 5,806	M 6
01030	Feeding Hills, 9,500	D 4
01420	Fitchburg, 43,343	G 2
	Fitchburg-Leominster, ‡97,164	G 2
† 01247	Florida, ∆672	B 2
02035	Foxboro, ∆14,218	J 4
02035	Foxboro, 4,090	J 4
01701	Framingham, 64,048	A 7
01701	Framingham Center, 16,000	J 3
02038	Franklin, ∆17,830	J 4
02038	Franklin, 8,863	J 4
01440	Gardner, 19,748	G 2
† 02535	Gay Head, ∆118	L 7
01830	Georgetown, ∆5,290	L 2
† 01376	Gill, ∆1,100	D 2
01930	Gloucester, 27,941	M 2
01032	Goshen, ∆483	C 3
01519	Grafton, ∆11,659	H 4
01033	Granby, ∆5,473	E 3
01034	Granville, ∆1,008	C 4
01230	Great Barrington, ∆7,537	A 4
01301	Greenfield, ∆18,116	D 2
01301	Greenfield⊙, 14,642	D 2
01880	Greenwood, 7,500	D 6
01450	Groton, ∆5,109	H 2
01830	Groveland, ∆5,382	L 1
01035	Hadley, ∆3,750	D 3
02338	Halifax, ∆3,537	L 5
01936	Hamilton, ∆6,373	L 2
01036	Hampden, ∆4,572	E 4
01237	Hancock, ∆675	A 2
02339	Hanover, ∆10,107	L 4
02341	Hanson, ∆7,148	L 4
01037	Hardwick, ∆2,379	F 3
01451	Harvard, ∆13,426	H 2
02645	Harwich, ∆5,892	O 6
02645	Harwich, 3,842	O 6
01038	Hatfield, ∆2,825	D 3
01830	Haverhill, 46,120	K 1
01346	Heath, ∆383	C 2
02043	Hingham, ∆18,845	E 8
01235	Hinsdale, ∆1,588	B 3
02343	Holbrook, ∆11,775	D 8
01520	Holden, ∆12,564	G 3
† 01550	Holland, ∆931	F 4
01746	Holliston, ∆12,069	A 8
01746	Holliston, 3,900	A 8
01040	Holyoke, 50,112	D 4
01747	Hopedale, ∆4,292	H 4
01748	Hopkinton, ∆5,981	J 4
01452	Hubbardston, ∆1,437	F 3
01749	Hudson, ∆16,084	H 3
01749	Hudson, 14,283	H 3
02045	Hull, ∆9,961	E 7
01050	Huntington, ∆1,593	C 4
02601	Hyannis, 6,847	N 6
02136	Hyde Park, 25,000	C 7
01938	Ipswich, ∆10,750	L 2
01938	Ipswich, 5,022	L 2
02090	Islington, 3,800	C 8
02130	Jamaica Plain, 50,000	C 7
02360	Kingston, ∆5,999	M 5
02360	Kingston, 3,772	M 5
02346	Lakeville, ∆4,376	L 5
01523	Lancaster, ∆6,095	H 3
01237	Lanesboro, ∆2,972	A 2
* 01840	Lawrence, 66,915	K 2
	Lawrence-Haverhill, ‡232,395	K 2
01238	Lee, ∆6,426	B 3
01524	Leicester, ∆9,140	G 4
01240	Lenox, ∆5,804	A 3
01240	Lenox, 2,208	A 3
01453	Leominster, 32,939	G 2
01054	Leverett, ∆1,005	E 3
02173	Lexington, ∆31,886	B 6
† 01301	Leyden, ∆376	D 2
01773	Lincoln, ∆7,567	B 6
01460	Littleton, ∆6,380	H 2
01106	Longmeadow, ∆15,630	D 4
* 01850	Lowell, 94,239	J 2
	Lowell, ‡212,860	J 2
01056	Ludlow, ∆17,580	E 4
02745	Lunds Corner, 7,020	L 6
01462	Lunenburg, ∆7,419	H 2
* 01901	Lynn, 90,294	D 6
01940	Lynnfield, ∆10,826	D 5
† 01940	Lynnfield Center (Lynnfield P.O.), 6,500	C 5
02148	Malden, 56,127	D 6
01944	Manchester, ∆5,151	F 5
02048	Mansfield, ∆9,939	J 4
02048	Mansfield, 4,778	J 4
01945	Marblehead, ∆21,295	E 7
02738	Marion, ∆3,466	L 6
01752	Marlborough, 27,936	H 3
02050	Marshfield, ∆15,223	M 4
02649	Mashpee, ∆1,288	M 6
02126	Mattapan, 18,500	C 7
02739	Mattapoisett, ∆4,500	L 6
01754	Maynard, ∆9,710	J 3
02052	Medfield, ∆9,821	B 8
02052	Medfield, 3,900	B 8
02155	Medford, 64,397	C 6
02053	Medway, ∆7,938	J 4
02053	Medway, 3,716	J 4
02176	Melrose, 33,180	D 6
01756	Mendon, ∆2,524	H 4
01860	Merrimac, ∆4,245	L 1
01844	Methuen, 35,456	K 2
02346	Middleboro, ∆13,607	L 5
02346	Middleboro, 6,259	L 5
01243	Middlefield, ∆288	B 3
01949	Middleton, ∆4,044	K 2
01757	Milford, ∆19,352	H 4
01757	Milford, 13,740	H 4
01527	Millbury, ∆11,987	H 4
02054	Millis, ∆5,686	A 8
01529	Millville, ∆1,764	H 4
02186	Milton, ∆27,190	D 7
01057	Monson, ∆7,355	E 4
01351	Montague, ∆8,451	E 2
01245	Monterey, ∆600	B 4
† 12517	Mount Washington, ∆52	A 4
01908	Nahant, ∆4,119	E 6
02554	Nantucket, ∆3,774	O 7
02554	Nantucket⊙, 2,461	O 7
01760	Natick, ∆31,057	A 7
02192	Needham, ∆29,748	B 7
02194	Needham Heights, 10,000	B 7
† 02122	Neponset, 25,000	D 7
* 02740	New Bedford, 101,777	K 6
	New Bedford, ‡152,642	K 6
01531	New Braintree, ∆631	F 3
01950	Newbury, ∆3,804	L 1
01950	Newburyport, 15,807	L 1
† 01230	New Marlboro, ∆1,031	B 4
01355	New Salem, ∆474	E 2
† 02158	Newton, 91,066	C 7
† 02159	Newton Center, 20,790	C 7
† 02161	Newton Highlands, 6,900	C 7
† 02160	Newtonville, 14,000	C 7
02790	Noquochoke P.O. (Westport), ∆950	K 6
02056	Norfolk, ∆4,656	J 4
02351	North Abington, 6,200	L 4
01247	North Adams, 19,195	B 2
01060	Northampton⊙, 29,664	D 3
01845	North Andover, ∆16,284	K 2
* 02760	North Attleboro, ∆18,665	J 5
01862	North Billerica, 4,900	J 2
01532	Northboro, ∆9,218	H 3
01532	Northboro, 3,900	H 3
01536	Northbridge, ∆11,795	H 4
01535	North Brookfield, ∆3,967	F 3
01863	North Chelmsford, 3,700	J 2
02747	North Dartmouth, 6,000	K 6
02356	North Easton, 6,000	K 4
01360	Northfield, ∆2,631	E 2
01536	North Grafton, 5,500	H 4
01864	North Reading, ∆11,264	C 5
02060	North Scituate, 5,507	F 8
† 02191	North Weymouth, 13,000	D 8
01067	North Wilbraham, 5,700	E 4
02766	Norton, ∆9,487	K 5
02061	Norwell, ∆7,796	F 8
02062	Norwood, ∆30,815	B 8
02557	Oak Bluffs, ∆1,385	M 7
01068	Oakham, ∆730	F 3
† 01566	Old Sturbridge Village, 500	F 4
01364	Orange, ∆6,104	E 2
01364	Orange, 3,847	E 2
02653	Orleans, ∆3,055	O 5
01253	Otis, ∆820	B 4
01540	Oxford, ∆10,345	G 4
01540	Oxford, 6,109	G 4
01069	Palmer, ∆11,680	E 4
01069	Palmer, 3,649	E 4
01612	Paxton, ∆3,731	G 3
01960	Peabody, 48,080	E 5
† 01002	Pelham, ∆937	E 3
02359	Pembroke, ∆11,193	L 4
01463	Pepperell, ∆5,887	H 2
01366	Petersham, ∆1,014	F 3
† 01331	Phillipston, ∆872	F 2
01866	Pinehurst, 5,681	B 5
01201	Pittsfield⊙, 57,020	A 3
	Pittsfield, ‡79,727	A 3
01070	Plainfield, ∆287	C 2
02762	Plainville, ∆4,953	J 4
* 02360	Plymouth, ∆18,606	M 5
* 02360	Plymouth⊙, 6,940	M 5
02367	Plympton, ∆1,224	L 5
† 02726	Pottersville, 3,722	K 6
01541	Princeton, ∆1,681	G 3
02657	Provincetown, ∆2,911	O 4
† 02169	Quincy, 87,966	D 7
02368	Randolph, ∆27,035	D 8
02767	Raynham, ∆6,705	K 5
01867	Reading, ∆22,539	C 5
02137	Readville, 10,000	C 8
02769	Rehoboth, ∆6,512	K 5
02151	Revere, 43,159	D 6
01254	Richmond, ∆1,461	A 3
02770	Rochester, ∆1,770	L 6
02370	Rockland, ∆15,674	L 4
01966	Rockport, ∆5,636	M 2
01966	Rockport, 4,166	M 2
01367	Rowe, ∆277	C 2
01969	Rowley, ∆3,040	L 2
† 02119	Roxbury, 200,000	C 7
01368	Royalston, ∆809	F 2
01071	Russell, ∆1,382	C 4
01543	Rutland, ∆3,198	G 3
01970	Salem⊙, 40,556	E 5
01950	Salisbury, ∆4,179	L 1
01255	Sandisfield, ∆547	B 4
02563	Sandwich, ∆5,239	N 5
01906	Saugus, ∆25,110	D 6
01256	Savoy, ∆322	B 2
01701	Saxonville, 15,000	A 7
02066	Scituate, ∆16,973	F 8
02066	Scituate, 3,738	F 8
02771	Seekonk, ∆11,116	J 5
02067	Sharon, ∆12,367	K 4
01810	Shawsheen Village, 5,200	K 2
01257	Sheffield, ∆2,374	A 4
01770	Sherborn, ∆3,309	A 8
01464	Shirley, ∆4,909	H 2
01545	Shrewsbury, ∆19,196	H 3
01072	Shutesbury, ∆489	E 3
02726	Somerset, ∆18,088	K 5
† 02143	Somerville, 88,779	C 6
01073	Southampton, ∆3,069	C 4
01772	Southborough, ∆5,798	H 3
† 02185	South Braintree, 6,000	D 8

(continued on following page)

248 Massachusetts and Rhode Island
(continued)

MASSACHUSETTS (continued)

01550 Southbridge, △17,057 .... G 4
01550 Southbridge, 14,261 .... G 4
02748 South Dartmouth, 9,209 .... L 6
02375 South Easton, 4,400 .... K 4
01075 South Hadley, △17,033 .... D 4
01075 South Hadley Falls, 6,500 .... D 4
† 02190 South Weymouth, 17,500 .... E 8
01077 Southwick, △6,330 .... C 4
02664 South Yarmouth, 5,380 .... O 6
01562 Spencer, △8,779 .... F 3
01562 Spencer, 5,895 .... F 3
* 01101 Springfield⊙, 163,905 .... D 4
Springfield-Chicopee-Holyoke, ‡529,921 .... D 4
01564 Sterling, △4,247 .... G 3
01262 Stockbridge, △2,312 .... A 3
01262 Stockbridge, 1,147 .... A 3
02180 Stoneham, △20,725 .... C 6
02072 Stoughton, △23,459 .... K 4
01775 Stow, △3,984 .... H 3
01566 Sturbridge, △4,878 .... F 4
01776 Sudbury, △13,506 .... A 6
01375 Sunderland, △2,236 .... D 3
† 01527 Sutton, △4,590 .... G 4
01907 Swampscott, △13,578 .... E 6
02777 Swansea, △12,640 .... K 5
02780 Taunton⊙, 43,756 .... K 5
01468 Templeton, △5,863 .... F 2
01876 Tewksbury, △22,755 .... K 2
† 01034 Tolland, △172 .... B 4
01983 Topsfield, △5,225 .... L 2
01469 Townsend, △4,281 .... H 2
02666 Truro, △1,234 .... O 5
01376 Turners Falls, 5,168 .... D 2
01879 Tyngsboro, △4,204 .... J 2
01264 Tyringham, △234 .... A 4
01568 Upton, △3,484 .... H 4
01569 Uxbridge, △8,253 .... H 4
02568 Vineyard Haven, 1,599 .... M 7
† 02168 Waban, 6,871 .... B 7
01880 Wakefield, △25,402 .... C 5
01081 Wales, △852 .... F 4
02081 Walpole, △18,149 .... B 8
02154 Waltham, 61,582 .... B 6
01082 Ware, △8,187 .... E 3
01082 Ware, 6,509 .... E 3
02571 Wareham, △11,492 .... L 5
01083 Warren, △3,633 .... F 4
01378 Warwick, △492 .... E 2
† 01223 Washington, △406 .... B 3
02172 Watertown, △39,307 .... C 6
02179 Waverley, 15,000 .... B 6
01778 Wayland, △13,461 .... A 7
01570 Webster, △14,917 .... G 4
01570 Webster, 12,432 .... G 4
02181 Wellesley, △28,051 .... B 7
02181 Wellesley Hills, 15,000 .... B 7
02667 Wellfleet, △1,743 .... O 5
01379 Wendell, △405 .... E 2
01984 Wenham, △3,849 .... L 2
01581 Westboro, △12,594 .... H 3
01581 Westboro, 4,474 .... H 3
01583 West Boylston, △6,369 .... G 3
02379 West Bridgewater, △7,152 .... K 4
01585 West Brookfield, △2,653 .... F 4
01085 Westfield, 31,433 .... D 4
01886 Westford, △10,368 .... J 2
† 01027 Westhampton, △793 .... C 3
01473 Westminster, △4,273 .... G 2
01985 West Newbury, △2,254 .... L 1
† 02165 West Newton, 13,500 .... B 7
02193 Weston, △10,870 .... B 6
02790 Westport, △9,791 .... K 6
02790 Westport P.O. (North Westport), 4,000 .... K 6
01089 West Springfield, △28,461 .... D 4
01266 West Stockbridge, △1,354 .... A 3
02575 West Tisbury, △453 .... M 7
02090 Westwood, △12,750 .... B 8
02673 West Yarmouth, 3,699 .... N 6
† 02188 Weymouth, 54,610 .... D 8
01093 Whately, △1,145 .... D 3
01588 Whitinsville, 5,210 .... H 4
02382 Whitman, △13,059 .... L 4
01095 Wilbraham, △11,984 .... E 4
01095 Wilbraham, 3,540 .... E 4
01096 Williamsburg, △2,342 .... C 3
01267 Williamstown, △8,454 .... B 2
01267 Williamstown, 4,285 .... B 2
01887 Wilmington, △17,102 .... C 5
01887 Wilmington, 3,900 .... C 5
01475 Winchendon, △6,635 .... F 2
01475 Winchendon, 3,997 .... F 2
01890 Winchester, △22,269 .... C 6
01270 Windsor, △468 .... B 2
02152 Winthrop, △20,335 .... D 6
01801 Woburn, 37,406 .... C 6
02543 Woods Hole, 750 .... M 6
* 01601 Worcester⊙, 176,572 .... H 3
Worcester, ‡339,730 .... H 3
01098 Worthington, △712 .... C 3
02093 Wrentham, △7,315 .... J 4
† 02675 Yarmouth, △12,033 .... O 6

RHODE ISLAND

COUNTIES

Bristol, 45,937 .... J 6
Kent, 142,382 .... H 6
Newport, 94,559 .... K 6
Providence, 580,261 .... H 5
Washington, 83,586 .... H 7

CITIES and TOWNS

Zip	Name/Pop.	Key
02816	Anthony, 7,000	H 6
† 02887	Apponaug, 6,533	J 6
02806	Barrington, △17,554	J 6
02806	Barrington, 13,000	J 6
02809	Bristol, △17,860	J 6
02809	Bristol⊙, 14,000	J 6
02911	Centerdale, 8,000	H 5
02863	Central Falls, 18,716	J 5
02813	Charlestown, △2,863	H 7
02816	Coventry, △22,947	H 6
02816	Coventry, 7,000	H 6
02910	Cranston, 73,037	J 5
02818	East Greenwich⊙, △9,577	H 6
02914	East Providence, 48,151	J 5
02822	Exeter, △3,245	H 6
02825	Foster, △2,626	H 5
02828	Greenville, 3,500	H 5
02833	Hopkinton, △5,392	H 7
02835	Jamestown, △2,911	J 6

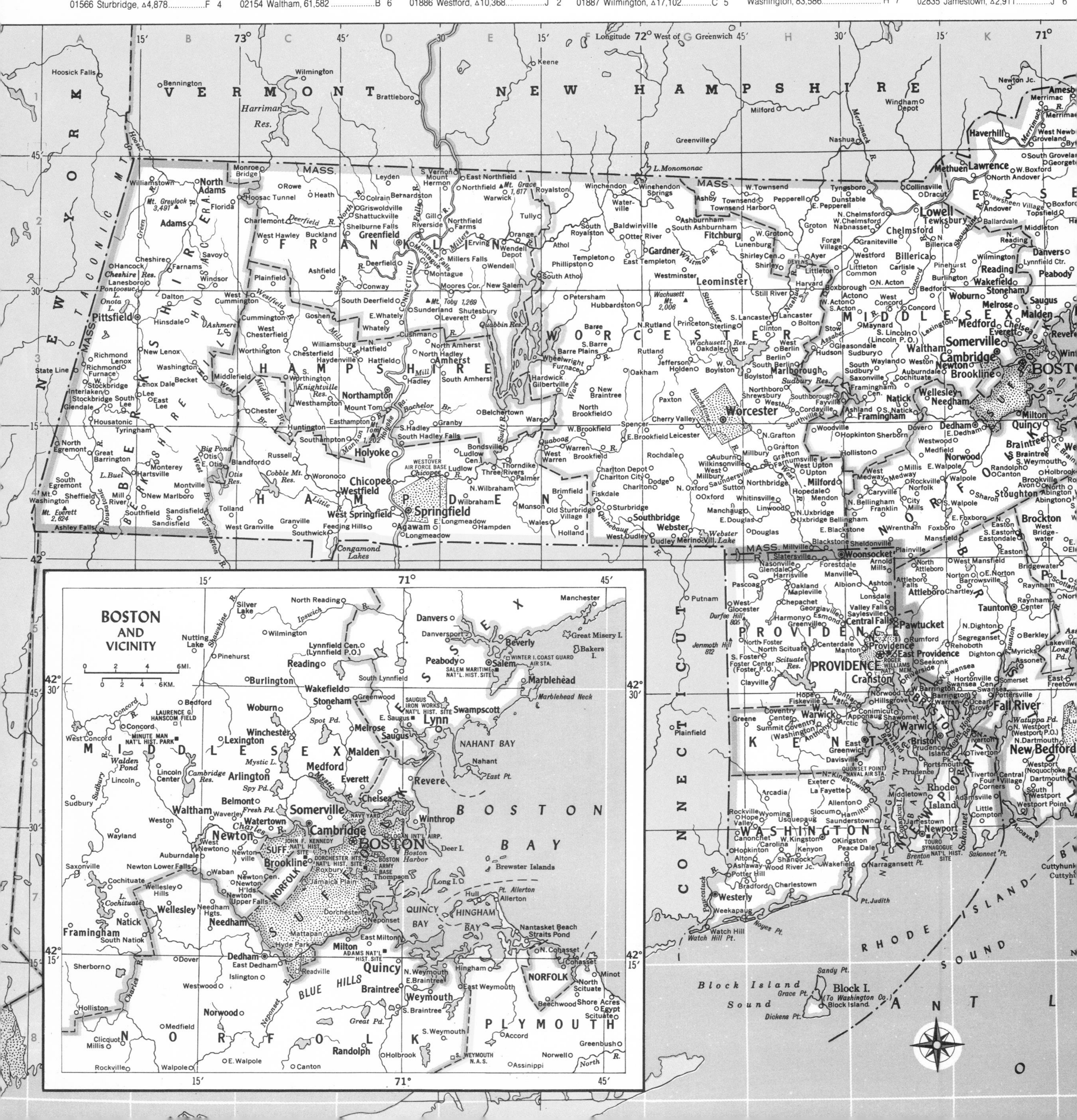

02835 Jamestown, 2,114 .... J 6
02881 Kingston, 5,601 .... J 7
02837 Little Compton, △2,385 .... K 6
02838 Manville, 3,800 .... H 5
02840 Middletown, △29,621 .... J 6
02882 Narragansett, △7,138 .... J 7
02882 Narragansett, 2,686 .... J 7
02840 Newport⊙, 34,562 .... J 7
02852 North Kingstown, △27,673 .... J 6
02852 North Kingstown, 7,500 .... J 6
02908 North Providence, △24,337 .... J 5
02908 North Providence, 12,000 .... J 5
† 02722 North Tiverton, 4,200 .... K 6
† 02887 Norwood, 5,517 .... J 6
† 02887 Oakland Beach, 5,615 .... J 6
* 02860 Pawtucket, 76,984 .... J 5
02883 Peace Dale-Wakefield, 6,331 .... J 7
02871 Portsmouth, △12,521 .... J 6
02871 Portsmouth, 5,000 .... J 6
* 02901 Providence (cap.)⊙, 179,213 .... H 5
Providence-Pawtucket-Warwick, ‡905,189 .... H 5
02915 Riverside, 14,300 .... J 5
02916 Rumford, 7,568 .... J 5
02878 Tiverton, △12,559 .... K 6
† 02864 Valley Falls, 5,000 .... J 5
02879 Wakefield-Peace Dale, 6,331 .... J 7
02885 Warren, △10,523 .... J 6
02885 Warren, 8,000 .... J 6
* 02886 Warwick, 83,694 .... J 6
† 02816 Washington (Coventry), 7,000 .... H 6
02891 Watch Hill, 300 .... G 7
02891 Westerly, △17,248 .... G 7
02891 Westerly⊙, 13,654 .... G 7
02892 West Kingston⊙, 950 .... H 7
02893 West Warwick, 24,323 .... H 6
02895 Woonsocket⊙, 46,820 .... J 4

⊙ County seat or courthouse.
‡ Population of metropolitan area.
△ Population of town or township.
† Zip of nearest p.o.
* Multiple zips

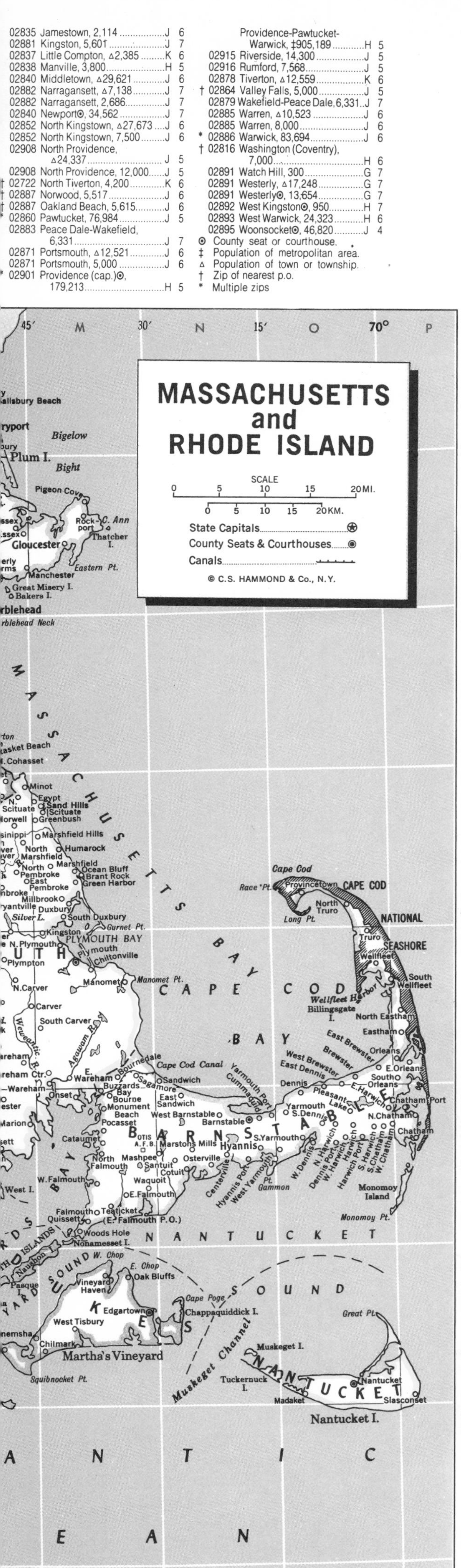

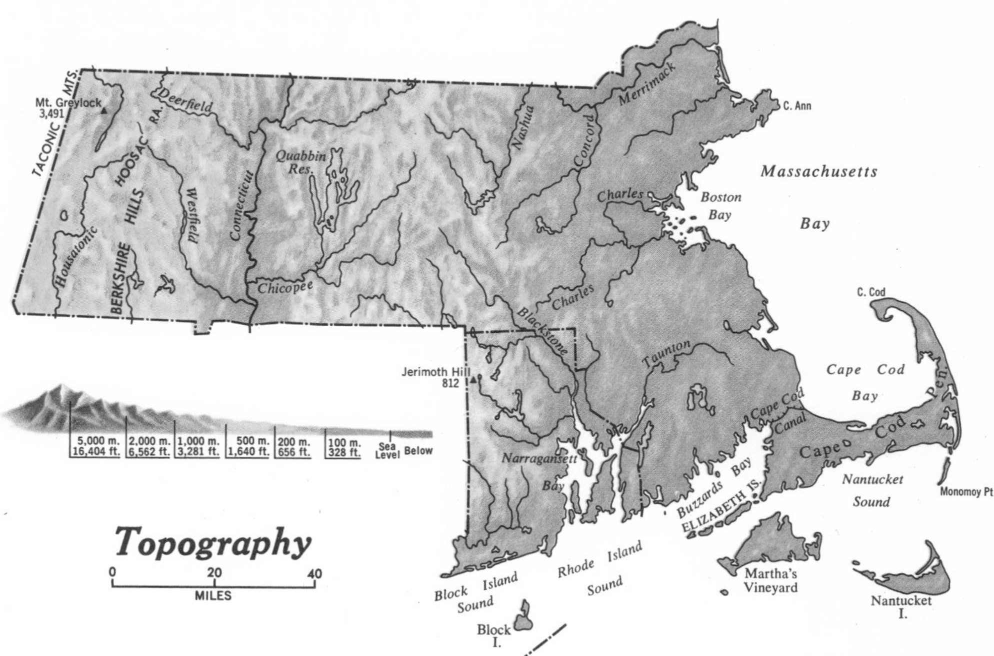

Marking the site of the first battle of the Revolutionary War on April 19, 1775, the Minuteman Statue faces the line of advancing Redcoats at Lexington, Massachusetts.

Typical Newport turn-of-the-century grandeur in a French chalet-style mansion, with mansard roof and wrought iron gates.

MICHIGAN
SCALE
0 5 10 20 30 40 50 MI.
0 5 10 20 30 40 50 KM.
State Capitals
County Seats
Canals
© C.S. HAMMOND & Co., N.Y.
Longitude 86° West of Greenwich 85°
88° 87° 86° 85° 89° 90°
47° 46° 45° 44° 43° 42°
A B C D E F G
1 2 3 4 5 6 7
Same scale as main map.
ISLE ROYALE (NATIONAL PARK)
L. SUPERIOR
Same scale as main map
KEWEENAW
CAN.
LAKE SUPERIOR
LAKE MICHIGAN
LAKE HURON
LAKE ST. CLAIR
LAKE ERIE
ONTARIO
North Channel
Manitoulin I.
WISCONSIN
WIS.
ILL.
INDIANA
OHIO
CANADA
ONT.
Green Bay
Georgian Bay
Saginaw Bay
Grand Traverse Bay
Thunder Bay
Straits of Mackinac
Whitefish Bay
Big Bay de Noc
Little Bay de Noc
Keweenaw Bay
Beaver I.
Drummond I.
Bois Blanc I.
North Manitou I.
South Manitou I.
PICTURED ROCKS NAT'L LAKESHORE
SLEEPING BEAR NAT'L LAKESHORE
POINT PELEE NAT'L PARK
PERRY'S VICTORY & INT'L PEACE MEM. NAT'L MON.
K. I. SAWYER A.F.B.
KINCHELOE A.F.B.
WURTSMITH AIR FORCE BASE
SELFRIDGE AIR FORCE BASE
L'ANSE INDIAN RES.
ONTONAGON INDIAN RES.
KEWEENAW
HOUGHTON
ONTONAGON
GOGEBIC
IRON
BARAGA
MARQUETTE
ALGER
LUCE
CHIPPEWA
SCHOOLCRAFT
MACKINAC
DELTA
DICKINSON
MENOMINEE
EMMET
CHEBOYGAN
PRESQUE ISLE
CHARLEVOIX
ANTRIM
OTSEGO
MONTMORENCY
ALPENA
LEELANAU
GRAND TRAVERSE
KALKASKA
CRAWFORD
OSCODA
ALCONA
BENZIE
MANISTEE
WEXFORD
MISSAUKEE
ROSCOMMON
OGEMAW
IOSCO
MASON
LAKE
OSCEOLA
CLARE
GLADWIN
ARENAC
HURON
OCEANA
NEWAYGO
MECOSTA
ISABELLA
MIDLAND
BAY
TUSCOLA
SANILAC
MUSKEGON
MONTCALM
GRATIOT
SAGINAW
LAPEER
ST. CLAIR
OTTAWA
KENT
IONIA
CLINTON
SHIAWASSEE
GENESEE
MACOMB
ALLEGAN
BARRY
EATON
INGHAM
LIVINGSTON
OAKLAND
VAN BUREN
KALAMAZOO
CALHOUN
JACKSON
WASHTENAW
WAYNE
BERRIEN
CASS
ST. JOSEPH
BRANCH
HILLSDALE
LENAWEE
MONROE
Lansing
DETROIT
GRAND RAPIDS
Flint
Saginaw
Bay City
Midland
Kalamazoo
Battle Creek
Jackson
Ann Arbor
Ypsilanti
Pontiac
Muskegon
Marquette
Escanaba
Sault Ste. Marie
Traverse City
Alpena
Port Huron
Monroe
Holland
Benton Harbor
St. Joseph
Niles
Menominee
Houghton
Ironwood
Iron Mountain
Petoskey
Cheboygan
Manistee
Ludington
Cadillac
Mt. Pleasant
Owosso
Adrian
Hillsdale
Coldwater
Sturgis
MILWAUKEE
Green Bay
Marinette
Sheboygan
Manitowoc
Racine
Kenosha
SOUTH BEND
Michigan City
Mishawaka
La Porte
Elkhart
Goshen
Angola
TOLEDO
Maumee
Perrysburg
Montpelier
Wauseon
WINDSOR
Sarnia
Leamington
Amherstburg
Birmingham
Royal Oak
Warren
Sterling Hts.
Highland Park
Hamtramck
Dearborn
Grosse Pointe
Inkster
Melvindale
Allen Park
Taylor
Lincoln Park
Wyandotte
Trenton
Riverview
Grosse Ile
River Rouge
Ecorse
Southgate
Ferndale
Oak Park
Pleasant Ridge
Hazel Park
Center Line
E. Detroit
Grosse Pte. Woods
Grosse Pte. Shores
Grosse Pte. Farms
Grosse Pte. Park
Berkley
Clawson
Troy
Bloomfield Hills
Franklin
Huntington Woods
Harper Woods
LAKE ST. CLAIR
ONT.
0 5 10 MI.
0 5 10 KM.
83°

AREA 58,216 sq. mi.
POPULATION 8,875,083
CAPITAL Lansing
LARGEST CITY Detroit
HIGHEST POINT Mt. Curwood 1,980 ft.
SETTLED IN 1650
ADMITTED TO UNION January 26, 1837
POPULAR NAME Wolverine State
STATE FLOWER Apple Blossom
STATE BIRD Robin

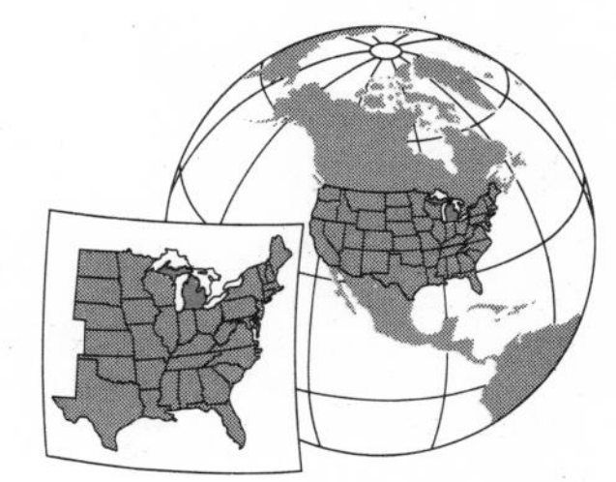

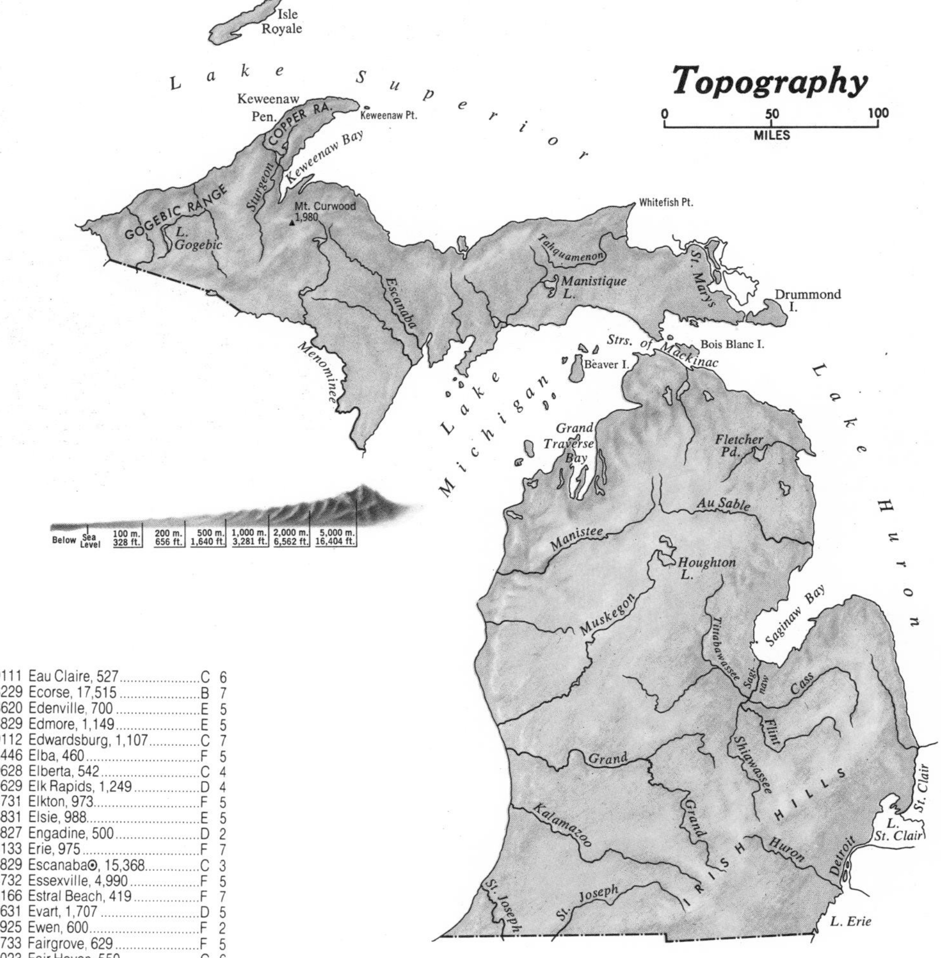

Topography

0 50 100
MILES

COUNTIES

Name/Pop.	Key
Alcona, 7,113	F 4
Alger, 8,568	C 2
Allegan, 66,575	D 6
Alpena, 30,708	F 4
Antrim, 12,612	D 3
Arenac, 11,149	F 4
Baraga, 7,789	A 2
Barry, 38,166	D 6
Bay, 117,339	E 5
Benzie, 8,593	C 4
Berrien, 163,875	C 7
Branch, 37,906	D 7
Calhoun, 141,963	D 6
Cass, 43,312	C 7
Charlevoix, 16,541	D 3
Cheboygan, 16,573	E 3
Chippewa, 32,412	E 2
Clare, 16,695	E 5
Clinton, 48,492	E 6
Crawford, 6,482	E 4
Delta, 35,924	C 2
Dickinson, 23,753	B 2
Eaton, 68,892	E 6
Emmet, 18,331	E 3
Genesee, 444,341	F 5
Gladwin, 13,471	E 4
Gogebic, 20,676	F 2
Grand Traverse, 39,175	D 4
Gratiot, 39,246	E 5
Hillsdale, 37,171	E 7
Houghton, 34,652	G 1
Huron, 34,083	F 5
Ingham, 261,039	E 6
Ionia, 45,848	D 6
Iosco, 24,905	F 4
Iron, 13,813	G 2
Isabella, 44,594	E 5
Jackson, 143,274	E 6
Kalamazoo, 201,550	D 6
Kalkaska, 5,272	D 4
Kent, 411,044	D 5
Keweenaw, 2,264	A 1
Lake, 5,661	D 5
Lapeer, 52,317	F 5
Leelanau, 10,872	D 4
Lenawee, 81,609	E 7
Livingston, 58,967	F 6
Luce, 6,789	D 2
Mackinac, 9,660	D 2
Macomb, 625,309	G 6
Manistee, 20,094	C 4
Marquette, 64,686	B 2
Mason, 22,612	C 4
Mecosta, 27,992	D 5
Menominee, 24,587	B 3
Midland, 63,769	E 5
Missaukee, 7,126	D 4
Monroe, 118,479	F 7
Montcalm, 39,660	D 5
Montmorency, 5,247	E 3
Muskegon, 157,246	C 5
Newaygo, 27,992	D 5
Oakland, 907,871	F 6
Oceana, 17,984	C 5
Ogemaw, 11,903	E 4
Ontonagon, 10,548	F 1
Osceola, 14,838	D 5
Oscoda, 4,726	E 4
Otsego, 10,422	E 3
Ottawa, 128,181	C 6
Presque Isle, 12,836	F 3
Roscommon, 9,892	E 4
Saginaw, 219,743	E 5
Saint Clair, 120,175	G 6
Saint Joseph, 47,392	D 7
Sanilac, 34,889	G 5
Schoolcraft, 8,226	C 2
Shiawassee, 63,075	E 6
Tuscola, 48,603	F 5
Van Buren, 56,173	C 6
Washtenaw, 234,103	F 6
Wayne, 2,666,751	F 6
Wexford, 19,717	D 4

CITIES and TOWNS

	Zip	Name/Pop.	Key
	49220	Addison, 595	E 7
	49221	Adrian⊙, 20,382	F 7
	48701	Akron, 525	F 5
	48764	Alabaster, 46	F 4
	49224	Albion, 12,112	E 6
	48001	Algonac, 3,684	G 6
	49010	Allegan⊙, 4,516	D 6
	48101	Allen Park, 40,747	B 7
	48801	Alma, 9,790	E 5
	48003	Almont, 1,634	F 6
	49707	Alpena⊙, 13,805	F 3
	49903	Amasa, 450	G 2
	48004	Anchorville, 440	G 6
*	48103	Ann Arbor⊙, 99,797	F 6
		Ann Arbor, ‡234,103	F 6
†	49659	Antrim, 475	D 4
	48410	Argyle, 800	G 5
	48005	Armada, 1,352	G 6
	48806	Ashley, 521	E 5
	49011	Athens, 996	D 6
	49709	Atlanta⊙, 475	E 3
	49905	Atlantic Mine, 785	G 1
	48611	Auburn, 1,919	F 5
	48057	Auburn Heights, 7,500	F 6
	48703	Au Gres, 564	F 4
	49012	Augusta, 1,025	D 6
†	48750	Au Sable-Oscoda, 3,475	F 4
†	48640	Averill, 800	E 5
	48413	Bad Axe⊙, 2,999	G 5
	49304	Baldwin⊙, 612	D 5
	48414	Bancroft, 724	E 6
	49013	Bangor, 2,050	C 6
	49908	Baraga, 1,116	G 1
	49807	Bark River, 550	B 3
	49101	Baroda, 439	C 7
	48808	Bath, 600	E 6
*	49014	Battle Creek, 38,931	D 6
	48706	Bay City⊙, 49,449	F 5
		Bay City, ‡117,339	F 5
	48720	Bay Port, 600	F 5
	49770	Bay View, 500	E 3
	48612	Beaverton, 954	E 5
	49020	Bedford, 450	D 6
†	49423	Beechwood, 2,714	C 6
	48809	Belding, 5,121	D 5
	49615	Bellaire⊙, 897	D 4
	48111	Belleville, 2,406	F 6
	49021	Bellevue, 1,297	E 6
	49022	Benton Harbor, 16,481	C 6
†	49022	Benton Heights, 8,067	C 6
	49910	Bergland, 635	F 1
	48072	Berkley, 22,618	B 6
	49103	Berrien Springs, 1,951	C 7
	49911	Bessemer⊙, 2,805	F 2
	49617	Beulah⊙, 461	C 4
	49307	Big Rapids⊙, 11,995	D 5
	48415	Birch Run, 932	F 5
*	48008	Birmingham, 26,170	B 6
	49228	Blissfield, 2,753	F 7
	48013	Bloomfield Hills, 3,672	B 6
	49026	Bloomingdale, 496	C 6
	49712	Boyne City, 2,969	E 3
	48615	Breckenridge, 1,257	E 5
	48722	Bridgeport, 1,900	F 5
	49106	Bridgman, 1,621	C 7
	48116	Brighton, 2,457	F 6
	49715	Brimley, 490	E 2
	49229	Britton, 697	F 6
	49028	Bronson, 2,390	D 7
	49230	Brooklyn, 1,112	E 6
	48416	Brown City, 1,142	G 5
	49716	Brutus, 431	E 3
	49107	Buchanan, 4,645	C 7
	49314	Burnips, 725	D 6
	49030	Burr Oak, 873	D 7
	48418	Byron, 655	E 6
	49315	Byron Center, 900	D 6
	49601	Cadillac⊙, 9,990	D 4
	49316	Caledonia, 716	D 6
	49913	Calumet, 1,007	A 1
	48014	Capac, 1,279	G 5
	48117	Carleton, 1,503	F 6
	48723	Caro⊙, 3,701	F 5
	48724	Carrollton, 7,300	E 5
	48811	Carson City, 1,217	E 5
	48419	Carsonville, 621	G 5
	48725	Caseville, 607	F 5
	49915	Caspian, 1,165	G 2
	48726	Cass City, 1,974	F 5
	49031	Cassopolis⊙, 2,108	C 7
	49422	Castle Park, 500	C 6
	49319	Cedar Springs, 1,807	D 5
	49719	Cedarville, 800	E 2
	49233	Cement City, 531	E 6
	48015	Center Line, 10,379	B 6
	49622	Central Lake, 741	D 3
	49032	Centreville⊙, 1,044	D 7
	49814	Champion, 550	B 2
	49815	Channing, 550	B 2
	49720	Charlevoix⊙, 3,519	D 3
	48813	Charlotte⊙, 8,244	E 6
	49623	Chase, 534	D 5
	49721	Cheboygan⊙, 5,553	E 3
	48118	Chelsea, 3,858	E 6
	48616	Chesaning, 2,876	E 5
	48617	Clare, 2,639	E 5
	49234	Clarklake, 500	E 6
	48016	Clarkston, 1,034	F 6
	48017	Clawson, 17,617	B 6
	49235	Clayton, 505	E 7
	48727	Clifford, 472	F 5
	49034	Climax, 594	D 6
	49236	Clinton, 1,677	F 6
	48420	Clio, 2,357	F 5
	49036	Coldwater⊙, 9,099	D 7
	48618	Coleman, 1,295	E 5
	49038	Coloma, 1,814	C 6
	49040	Colon, 1,172	D 7
	48421	Columbiaville, 935	F 5
	49041	Comstock, 5,003	D 6
	49237	Concord, 983	E 6
	49042	Constantine, 1,733	D 7
	49722	Conway, 560	E 3
	49404	Coopersville, 2,129	C 5
	49818	Cornell, 640	B 3
	48817	Corunna⊙, 2,829	E 6
	49043	Covert, 650	C 6
	48422	Croswell, 1,954	G 5
	48818	Crystal, 649	E 5
	49920	Crystal Falls⊙, 2,000	A 2
†	49501	Cutlerville, 6,267	D 6
	48819	Dansville, 486	E 6
	48423	Davison, 5,259	F 5
*	48120	Dearborn, 104,199	B 7
	48127	Dearborn Heights, 80,069	B 7
	49045	Decatur, 1,764	C 6
	48427	Deckerville, 817	G 5
	49238	Deerfield, 834	F 7
	49725	De Tour Village, 494	E 3
*	48201	Detroit⊙, 1,511,482	B 7
		Detroit, ‡4,199,931	B 7
†	48161	Detroit Beach, 2,053	F 7
	48820	De Witt, 1,829	E 6
	48130	Dexter, 1,729	F 6
	48821	Dimondale, 970	E 6
	49922	Dollar Bay, 950	G 1
	49323	Dorr, 550	D 6
	49406	Douglas, 813	C 6
	49047	Dowagiac, 6,583	D 6
	48020	Drayton Plains, 16,462	F 6
	49726	Drummond Island, 700	F 3
	48428	Dryden, 654	F 6
	48131	Dundee, 2,472	F 7
	48429	Durand, 3,678	E 6
	49924	Eagle River⊙, 36	A 1
	48021	East Detroit, 45,920	B 6
†	49506	East Grand Rapids, 12,565	D 6
	49727	East Jordan, 2,041	D 3
†	49801	East Kingsford, 1,155	A 3
	49626	Eastlake, 512	C 4
	48823	East Lansing, 47,540	E 6
	48730	East Tawas, 2,372	F 4
†	49001	Eastwood, 9,682	D 6
	48827	Eaton Rapids, 4,494	E 6
	49111	Eau Claire, 527	C 6
	48229	Ecorse, 17,515	B 7
	48620	Edenville, 700	E 5
	48829	Edmore, 1,149	E 5
	49112	Edwardsburg, 1,107	C 7
†	48446	Elba, 460	F 5
	49628	Elberta, 542	C 4
	49629	Elk Rapids, 1,249	D 4
	48731	Elkton, 973	F 5
	48831	Elsie, 988	E 5
	49827	Engadine, 500	D 2
	48133	Erie, 975	F 7
	49829	Escanaba⊙, 15,368	C 3
	48732	Essexville, 4,990	F 5
†	48166	Estral Beach, 419	F 7
	49631	Evart, 1,707	D 5
	49925	Ewen, 600	F 2
	48733	Fairgrove, 629	F 5
	48023	Fair Haven, 550	G 6
	49022	Fair Plain, 3,680	C 6
	48621	Fairview, 600	F 4
	48024	Farmington, 13,337	F 6
	48622	Farwell, 777	E 5
	49408	Fennville, 811	C 6
	48430	Fenton, 8,284	F 6
	48220	Ferndale, 30,850	B 6
	49409	Ferrysburg, 2,196	C 5
	48134	Flat Rock, 5,643	F 6
*	48501	Flint⊙, 193,317	F 6
		Flint, ‡496,658	F 6
	48433	Flushing, 7,190	F 5
	48835	Fowler, 1,020	E 5
	48836	Fowlerville, 1,978	F 6
	48734	Frankenmuth, 2,834	F 5
	49635	Frankfort, 1,660	C 4
	48025	Franklin, 3,344	B 6
	48026	Fraser, 11,868	B 6
	48623	Freeland, 1,303	E 5
	49325	Freeport, 501	D 6
	49412	Fremont, 3,465	D 5
	49415	Fruitport, 1,409	C 5
	49052	Fulton, 500	D 6
	49927	Gaastra, 479	G 2
	49053	Galesburg, 1,355	D 6
	49113	Galien, 691	C 7
	49735	Gaylord⊙, 3,012	E 3
	48437	Genesee, 950	F 5
	49836	Germfask, 750	C 2
	48173	Gibraltar, 3,325	F 6
	49837	Gladstone, 5,237	C 3
	48624	Gladwin⊙, 2,071	E 5
	49055	Gobles, 801	D 6
	49737	Good Hart, 500	D 3
	48438	Goodrich, 774	F 6
	48439	Grand Blanc, 5,132	F 6
	49417	Grand Haven⊙, 11,884	C 5
	48837	Grand Ledge, 6,032	E 6
	49839	Grand Marais, 650	D 2
*	49501	Grand Rapids⊙, 197,649	D 5
		Grand Rapids, ‡539,225	D 5
	49418	Grandville, 10,764	D 6
	49327	Grant, 772	D 5
	49240	Grass Lake, 1,061	E 6
	49738	Grayling⊙, 2,143	E 4
	48738	Greenbush, 650	F 4
	48838	Greenville, 7,493	D 5
	48138	Grosse Ile, 7,799	B 7
	48236	Grosse Pointe, 6,637	B 7
†	48236	Grosse Pointe Farms, 11,701	B 6
†	48236	Grosse Pointe Park, 15,585	B 7
†	48236	Grosse Pointe Shores, 3,042	B 6
†	48236	Grosse Pointe Woods, 21,878	B 6
	49840	Gulliver, 962	D 2
	49841	Gwinn, 1,054	B 2
	48739	Hale, 500	F 4
	48139	Hamburg, 500	F 6
	49419	Hamilton, 950	C 6
	48212	Hamtramck, 27,245	B 6
	49930	Hancock, 4,820	G 1
	49241	Hanover, 513	E 6
	48441	Harbor Beach, 2,134	G 5
	49740	Harbor Springs, 1,662	D 3
	48236	Harper Woods, 20,186	B 6
	48625	Harrison⊙, 1,460	E 4
	48740	Harrisville⊙, 541	F 4
	48028	Harsens Island, 750	G 6
	49420	Hart⊙, 2,139	C 5
	49057	Hartford, 2,508	C 6
	48840	Haslett, 3,492	E 6
	49058	Hastings⊙, 6,501	D 6
	48030	Hazel Park, 23,784	B 6
	48626	Hemlock, 900	E 5
	48841	Henderson, 600	E 5
	49847	Hermansville, 950	B 3
	49744	Herron, 950	F 3
	49421	Hesperia, 877	D 5
	49745	Hessel, 500	E 2
	48203	Highland Park, 35,444	B 6
	49242	Hillsdale⊙, 7,728	E 7
	49423	Holland, 26,337	C 6
	48442	Holly, 4,355	F 6
	48842	Holt, 6,980	E 6
	49425	Holton, 500	C 5
	49245	Homer, 1,617	E 6
	49328	Hopkins, 566	D 6
	49931	Houghton⊙, 6,067	G 1
	48629	Houghton Lake, 500	E 4
	48630	Houghton Lake Heights, 1,252	E 4
	49329	Howard City, 1,060	D 5
	48843	Howell⊙, 5,224	E 6
	49934	Hubbell, 1,251	A 1
	49247	Hudson, 2,618	E 7
	49426	Hudsonville, 3,523	D 6
	48140	Ida, 970	F 7
	49642	Idlewild, 800	D 5
	48444	Imlay City, 1,980	F 5
	49749	Indian River, 950	E 3
	48141	Inkster, 38,595	B 7
	49643	Interlochen, 800	D 4
	48846	Ionia⊙, 6,361	D 6
	49801	Iron Mountain⊙, 8,702	B 3
	49935	Iron River, 2,684	G 2
	49938	Ironwood, 8,711	F 2
	49849	Ishpeming, 8,245	B 2
	48847	Ithaca⊙, 2,749	E 5
*	49201	Jackson⊙, 45,484	E 6
		Jackson, ‡143,274	E 6
	49428	Jenison, 11,266	D 6
	49061	Jones, 420	D 7
	49250	Jonesville, 2,081	E 6
*	49001	Kalamazoo⊙, 85,555	D 6
		Kalamazoo, ‡201,550	D 6
	49646	Kalkaska⊙, 1,475	D 4
	48631	Kawkawlin, 450	F 5
	48030	Keego Harbor, 3,092	F 6
	49330	Kent City, 686	D 5
	49508	Kentwood, 20,310	D 6
	48445	Kinde, 618	G 5
	49801	Kingsford, 5,276	A 3
	49649	Kingsley, 632	D 4
	48741	Kingston, 464	F 5
	48848	Laingsburg, 1,159	E 6
	48632	Lake, 600	E 5
	49651	Lake City⊙, 704	D 4
	48143	Lakeland, 720	F 6
	49945	Lake Linden, 1,214	A 1
†	49039	Lake Michigan Beach, 1,201	C 6
	48849	Lake Odessa, 1,924	D 6
	48850	Lakeview, 1,198	D 5
†	49440	Lakewood Club, 590	C 5
	48144	Lambertville, 5,721	F 7
	49946	L'Anse⊙, 2,538	G 1
*	48901	Lansing (cap.), 131,546	E 6
		Lansing, ‡378,423	E 6
	48446	Lapeer⊙, 6,270	F 5
	49913	Laurium, 2,868	A 1
	49064	Lawrence, 790	C 6
	49065	Lawton, 1,358	D 6
	49654	Leland⊙, 776	D 3
	49251	Leslie, 1,894	E 6
	49755	Levering, 967	E 3
	49756	Lewiston, 750	E 4
	48450	Lexington, 834	G 5
	48146	Lincoln Park, 52,984	B 7
	48451	Linden, 1,546	F 6
	48634	Linwood, 950	F 5
	49252	Litchfield, 1,167	E 6
	49833	Little Lake, 950	B 2
*	48150	Livonia, 110,109	F 6
	48743	Long Lake, 900	F 4
	49331	Lowell, 3,068	D 6
	49431	Ludington⊙, 9,021	C 5
	48157	Luna Pier, 1,418	F 7
	48851	Lyons, 758	E 6
	49757	Mackinac Island, 517	E 3
	49701	Mackinaw City, 810	E 3
	48071	Madison Heights, 38,599	F 6
	49659	Mancelona, 1,255	E 4
	48158	Manchester, 1,650	E 6
	49660	Manistee⊙, 7,723	C 4
	49854	Manistique⊙, 4,324	C 3
	49663	Manton, 1,107	D 4
	48853	Maple Rapids, 683	E 5
	49067	Marcellus, 1,139	D 6
	49947	Marenisco, 865	F 2
	48039	Marine City, 4,567	G 6
	49665	Marion, 891	D 4
	48453	Marlette, 1,706	G 5
	49435	Marne, 950	D 5
	49855	Marquette⊙, 21,967	B 2
	49068	Marshall⊙, 7,253	E 6
	49070	Martin, 502	D 6
	48040	Marysville, 5,610	G 6
	48854	Mason⊙, 5,468	E 6
	49948	Mass, 850	G 1
	49071	Mattawan, 1,569	D 6
	48159	Maybee, 485	F 6
	48744	Mayville, 872	F 5
	49657	McBain, 520	D 4
	48122	Melvindale, 13,862	B 7
	48041	Memphis, 1,121	G 6
	49072	Mendon, 949	D 7
	49858	Menominee⊙, 10,748	B 3

(continued on following page)

(continued)

A. D'Arazien — Shostal Associates

Turning out more than one car a minute keeps these inspectors on their toes during the final step on an assembly line in Detroit, Michigan.

Agriculture, Industry and Resources

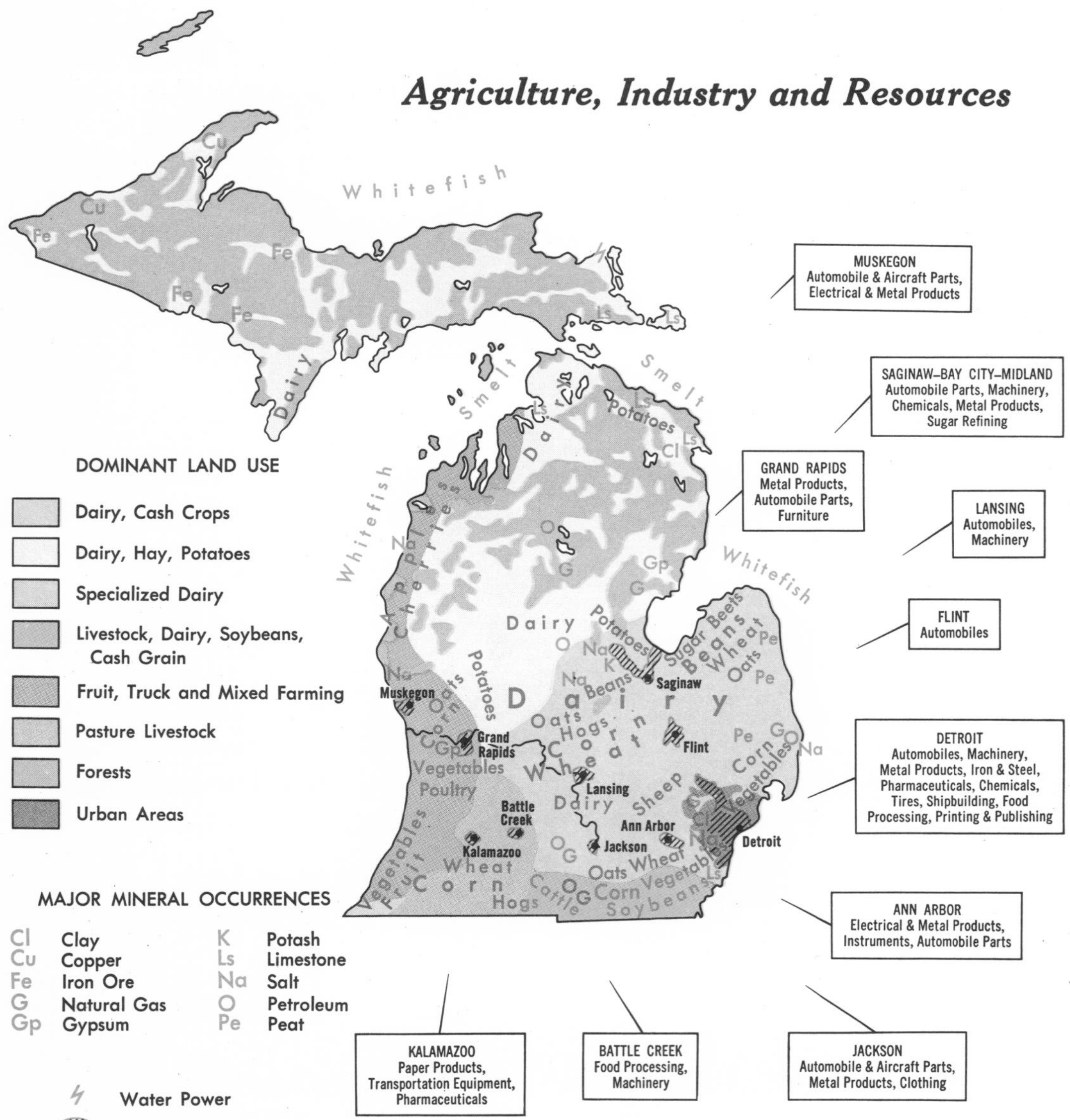

	ZIP	Place	Key
	48637	Merrill, 961	E 5
	48455	Metamora, 468	F 6
	49758	Metz, 495	F 3
	49254	Michigan Center, 4,900	E 6
	48856	Middleton, 500	E 5
	49333	Middleville, 1,865	D 6
	48640	Midland⊙, 35,176	E 5
	48160	Milan, 4,533	F 6
	48042	Milford, 4,699	F 6
	48746	Millington, 1,099	F 5
	48647	Mio⊙, 975	E 4
	49950	Mohawk, 800	A 1
	49335	Moline, 750	D 6
	48161	Monroe⊙, 23,894	F 7
	49437	Montague, 2,396	C 5
	48457	Montrose, 1,789	F 5
	49256	Morenci, 2,132	E 7
	49336	Morley, 481	D 5
	48857	Morrice, 734	E 6
	48043	Mount Clemens⊙, 20,476	G 6
	48458	Mount Morris, 3,778	F 5
	48858	Mount Pleasant⊙, 20,504	E 5
	48860	Muir, 617	D 5
	48861	Mulliken, 454	E 6
	48747	Munger, 432	F 5
	49862	Munising⊙, 3,677	C 2
*	49440	Muskegon⊙, 44,631	C 5
		Muskegon-Muskegon Heights, ‡157,426	C 5
	49444	Muskegon Heights, 17,304	C 5
	49261	Napoleon, 950	E 6
	49073	Nashville, 1,558	D 6
	49865	National Mine, 565	B 2
	49866	Negaunee, 5,248	B 2
	49337	Newaygo, 1,381	D 5
	48047	New Baltimore, 4,132	G 6
	49868	Newberry⊙, 2,334	D 2
	48164	New Boston, 800	F 6
	49117	New Buffalo, 2,784	C 7
	49446	New Era, 466	C 5
	48048	New Haven, 1,855	G 6
	48460	New Lothrop, 596	F 5
	49119	New Troy, 430	C 7
	49120	Niles, 12,988	C 7
	49262	North Adams, 574	E 7
	48461	North Branch, 932	F 5
	49445	North Muskegon, 4,243	C 5
	49670	Northport, 594	D 3
	48167	Northville, 5,400	F 6
†	49444	Norton Shores, 22,271	C 5
	49870	Norway, 3,033	B 3
	48050	Novi, 9,668	F 6
	48237	Oak Park, 36,762	B 6
	49763	Ocqueoc, 500	F 3
	48864	Okemos, 7,770	E 6
	49076	Olivet, 1,629	E 6
	49765	Onaway, 1,262	E 3
	49675	Onekama, 638	C 4
	49265	Onsted, 555	E 6
	49953	Ontonagon⊙, 2,432	F 1
	48033	Orchard Lake, 1,487	F 6
	48462	Ortonville, 983	F 6
	48750	Oscoda-Au Sable, 3,475	F 4
	48463	Otisville, 724	F 5
	49078	Otsego, 3,957	D 6
†	49735	Otsego Lake, 500	E 4
	48464	Otter Lake, 551	F 5
	48866	Ovid, 1,650	E 5
	48867	Owosso, 17,179	E 5
	48051	Oxford, 2,536	F 6
	49955	Painesdale, 600	G 1
	49871	Palmer, 950	B 2
	49268	Palmyra, 600	E 7
	49004	Parchment, 2,027	D 6
	49269	Parma, 880	E 6
	49079	Paw Paw⊙, 3,160	D 6
†	49038	Paw Paw Lake, 3,726	C 6
	48052	Pearl Beach, 1,744	G 6
	48466	Peck, 580	G 5
	49769	Pellston, 469	E 3
	49449	Pentwater, 993	C 5
	48871	Perrinton, 489	E 5
	48872	Perry, 1,531	E 6
	49270	Petersburg, 1,227	F 7
	49770	Petoskey⊙, 6,342	E 3
	48873	Pewamo, 498	E 5
	49774	Pickford, 800	E 2
	48755	Pigeon, 1,174	F 5
	48169	Pinckney, 921	F 6
	48650	Pinconning, 1,320	F 5
	49271	Pittsford, 610	E 7
	49080	Plainwell, 3,195	D 6
	48069	Pleasant Ridge, 3,989	B 6
	48170	Plymouth, 11,758	F 6
*	48053	Pontiac⊙, 85,279	F 6
	49081	Portage, 33,590	D 6
	48467	Port Austin, 883	F 4
	48060	Port Huron⊙, 35,794	G 6
	48875	Portland, 3,817	E 6
	48469	Port Sanilac, 493	G 5
	48876	Potterville, 1,280	E 6
	49874	Powers, 560	B 3
	48651	Prudenville, 500	E 4
	49082	Quincy, 1,540	E 7
	49876	Quinnesec, 770	A 3
	49959	Ramsay, 1,068	F 2
	49676	Rapid City, 450	D 4
	49878	Rapid River, 950	C 3
	49451	Ravenna, 1,048	D 5
	49274	Reading, 1,125	E 7
	49677	Reed City⊙, 2,286	D 5
	48757	Reese, 1,050	F 5
	49340	Remus, 425	D 5
	49879	Republic, 900	B 2
	49083	Richland, 728	D 6
	48062	Richmond, 3,234	G 6
	48758	Richville, 650	F 5
	48218	River Rouge, 15,947	B 7
	49084	Riverside, 650	C 6
	48192	Riverview, 11,342	B 7
	48063	Rochester, 7,054	F 6
	49341	Rockford, 2,428	D 5
	49960	Rockland, 450	G 1
	48173	Rockwood, 3,119	F 6
	49779	Rogers City⊙, 4,275	F 3
	48065	Romeo, 4,012	F 6
	48174	Romulus, 3,900	F 6
	49444	Roosevelt Park, 4,176	C 5
	48653	Roscommon⊙, 810	E 4
	48878	Rosebush, 439	E 5
	48654	Rose City, 530	E 4
	48066	Roseville, 60,529	G 6
*	48067	Royal Oak, 85,499	B 6
	49780	Rudyard, 950	E 2
*	48601	Saginaw⊙, 91,849	F 5
		Saginaw, ‡219,743	F 5
	48655	Saint Charles, 2,046	E 5
	48079	Saint Clair, 4,770	G 6
*	48080	Saint Clair Shores, 88,093	G 6
	48656	Saint Helen, 700	E 4
	49781	Saint Ignace⊙, 2,892	E 3
	48879	Saint Johns⊙, 6,672	E 6
	49085	Saint Joseph⊙, 11,042	C 6
	48880	Saint Louis, 4,101	E 5
	48176	Saline, 4,811	F 6
	48471	Sandusky⊙, 2,071	G 5
	48657	Sanford, 818	E 5
	48881	Saranac, 1,223	D 6
	49453	Saugatuck, 1,022	C 6
	49783	Sault Sainte Marie⊙, 15,136	E 2
	49125	Sawyer, 650	C 7
	49087	Schoolcraft, 1,277	D 6
	49454	Scottville, 1,202	C 5
	48759	Sebewaing, 2,053	F 5
	49455	Shelby, 1,703	C 5
	48883	Shepherd, 1,416	E 5
	48884	Sheridan, 653	D 5
†	49085	Shoreham, 666	C 6
†	49125	Shorewood Hills, 1,629	C 7
	49047	Sister Lakes, 700	C 6
	48075	Southfield, 69,285	F 6
	48192	Southgate, 33,909	F 6
	49090	South Haven, 6,471	C 6
	48178	South Lyon, 2,675	F 6
†	48161	South Monroe, 3,012	F 7
	49963	South Range, 898	G 1
	48179	South Rockwood, 1,477	F 7
	49886	Spalding, 600	B 3
†	48060	Sparlingville, 1,845	G 6
	49345	Sparta, 3,094	D 5
	49283	Spring Arbor, 1,832	E 6
	49015	Springfield, 3,994	D 6
	49456	Spring Lake, 3,034	C 5
	49284	Springport, 723	E 6
	49964	Stambaugh, 1,458	G 2
	48658	Standish⊙, 1,184	F 5
	48888	Stanton⊙, 1,089	D 5
	49887	Stephenson, 800	B 3
	48659	Sterling, 507	E 4
*	48077	Sterling Heights, 61,365	B 6
	49127	Stevensville, 1,107	C 6
	49285	Stockbridge, 1,190	E 6
	49681	Stronach, 500	C 4
	49790	Strongs, 450	E 2
	49091	Sturgis, 9,295	D 7
	48890	Sunfield, 497	D 6
	49682	Suttons Bay, 522	D 3
	48473	Swartz Creek, 4,928	F 6
†	48053	Sylvan Lake, 2,219	F 6
	48763	Tawas City⊙, 1,666	F 4
	48180	Taylor, 70,020	B 7
	49286	Tecumseh, 7,120	E 7
	49092	Tekonsha, 739	E 6
	48182	Temperance, 2,900	F 7
	49128	Three Oaks, 1,750	C 7
	49093	Three Rivers, 7,355	D 7
	49792	Tower, 425	E 3
	49684	Traverse City⊙, 18,048	D 4
	48183	Trenton, 24,127	B 7
	48084	Troy, 39,419	B 6
	49347	Trufant, 600	D 5
	48475	Ubly, 899	G 5
	49094	Union City, 1,740	D 6
	49129	Union Pier, 900	C 7
	48767	Unionville, 647	F 5
	48087	Utica, 3,504	F 6
	49095	Vandalia, 427	D 7
	49795	Vanderbilt, 522	E 3
	48768	Vassar, 2,802	F 5
	49096	Vermontville, 857	E 6
	48476	Vernon, 818	F 6
	48891	Vestaburg, 680	E 5
	49097	Vicksburg, 2,139	D 6
	49892	Vulcan, 975	B 3
	49968	Wakefield, 2,757	F 2
	49288	Waldron, 564	E 7
	49504	Walker, 11,492	D 6
	48088	Walled Lake, 3,759	F 6
	49796	Walloon Lake, 550	E 3
*	48089	Warren, 179,260	B 6
	49969	Watersmeet, 700	G 2
	49098	Watervliet, 2,059	C 6
	49348	Wayland, 2,054	D 6
	48184	Wayne, 21,054	F 6
	48892	Webberville, 1,251	E 6
	48893	Weidman, 450	D 5
	49894	Wells, 1,085	B 3
	48661	West Branch⊙, 1,912	E 4
	48185	Westland, 86,749	F 6
	48894	Westphalia, 806	E 6
	49349	White Cloud⊙, 1,044	D 5
	49461	Whitehall, 3,017	C 5
	49099	White Pigeon, 1,455	D 7
	49971	White Pine, 1,218	F 1
	48189	Whitmore Lake, 2,763	F 6
	48190	Whittaker, 500	F 6
	48770	Whittemore, 460	F 4
	48895	Williamston, 2,600	E 6
	48191	Willis, 500	F 6
	49896	Wilson, 500	B 3
	48896	Winn, 600	E 5
	48096	Wixom, 2,010	F 6
	49442	Wolf Lake, 2,258	D 5
	48183	Woodhaven, 3,330	F 6
	48897	Woodland, 473	D 6
	48192	Wyandotte, 41,061	B 7
	49509	Wyoming, 56,560	D 6
	48097	Yale, 1,505	G 5
	48197	Ypsilanti, 29,538	F 6
	49464	Zeeland, 4,734	D 6
†	48601	Zilwaukee, 2,072	F 5

⊙ County seat.
‡ Population of metropolitan area.
† Zip of nearest p.o.
* Multiple zips

COUNTIES

Aitkin, 11,403 .... E 4
Anoka, 154,556 .... E 5
Becker, 24,372 .... C 4
Beltrami, 26,373 .... C 2
Benton, 20,841 .... D 5
Big Stone, 7,941 .... B 5
Blue Earth, 52,322 .... D 6
Brown, 28,887 .... D 6
Carlton, 28,072 .... F 4
Carver, 28,310 .... E 6
Cass, 17,323 .... D 4
Chippewa, 15,109 .... C 5
Chisago, 17,492 .... F 5
Clay, 46,585 .... B 4
Clearwater, 8,013 .... C 3
Cook, 3,423 .... H 3
Cottonwood, 14,887 .... C 6
Crow Wing, 34,826 .... D 4
Dakota, 139,808 .... E 6
Dodge, 13,037 .... F 7
Douglas, 22,892 .... C 5
Faribault, 20,896 .... D 7
Fillmore, 21,916 .... F 7
Freeborn, 38,064 .... E 7
Goodhue, 34,763 .... F 6
Grant, 7,462 .... B 5
Hennepin, 960,080 .... E 5
Houston, 17,556 .... G 7
Hubbard, 10,583 .... D 3
Isanti, 16,560 .... E 5
Itasca, 35,530 .... E 3
Jackson, 14,352 .... C 7
Kanabec, 9,775 .... E 5
Kandiyohi, 30,548 .... C 5
Kittson, 6,853 .... B 2
Koochiching, 17,731 .... E 2
Lac qui Parle, 11,164 .... B 6
Lake, 13,351 .... G 3
Lake of the Woods, 3,987 .... D 2
Le Sueur, 21,332 .... E 6
Lincoln, 8,143 .... B 6
Lyon, 24,273 .... C 6
Mahnomen, 5,638 .... C 3
Marshall, 13,060 .... B 2
Martin, 24,316 .... D 7
McLeod, 27,662 .... D 6
Meeker, 18,810 .... D 5
Mille Lacs, 15,703 .... E 5
Morrison, 26,949 .... D 4
Mower, 43,783 .... F 7
Murray, 12,508 .... C 6
Nicollet, 24,518 .... D 6
Nobles, 23,208 .... C 7
Norman, 10,008 .... B 3
Olmsted, 84,104 .... F 7
Otter Tail, 46,097 .... C 4
Pennington, 13,266 .... B 2
Pine, 16,821 .... F 4
Pipestone, 12,791 .... B 6
Polk, 34,435 .... B 3
Pope, 11,107 .... C 5
Ramsey, 476,255 .... E 5
Red Lake, 5,388 .... B 3
Redwood, 20,024 .... C 6
Renville, 21,139 .... C 6
Rice, 41,582 .... E 6
Rock, 11,346 .... B 7
Roseau, 11,569 .... C 2
Saint Louis, 220,693 .... F 3
Scott, 32,423 .... E 6
Sherburne, 18,344 .... E 5
Sibley, 15,845 .... D 6
Stearns, 95,400 .... D 5
Steele, 26,931 .... E 7
Stevens, 11,218 .... B 5
Swift, 13,177 .... C 5
Todd, 22,114 .... D 4
Traverse, 6,254 .... B 5
Wabasha, 17,224 .... F 6
Wadena, 12,412 .... D 4
Waseca, 16,663 .... E 6
Washington, 82,948 .... F 5
Watonwan, 13,298 .... D 7
Wilkin, 9,389 .... B 4
Winona, 44,409 .... G 6
Wright, 38,933 .... D 5
Yellow Medicine, 14,418 .... B 6

CITIES and TOWNS

Zip Name/Pop. Key

56510 Ada⊙, 2,076 .... B 3
55909 Adams, 771 .... F 7
56110 Adrian, 1,350 .... C 7
55001 Afton, 248 .... F 6
56430 Ah-Gwah-Ching, 500 .... D 3
56431 Aitkin⊙, 1,553 .... E 4
56433 Akeley, 468 .... D 3
56307 Albany, 1,599 .... D 5
56207 Alberta, 140 .... B 5
56007 Albert Lea⊙, 19,418 .... E 7
55301 Albertville, 451 .... E 5
56009 Alden, 713 .... E 7
56308 Alexandria⊙, 6,973 .... C 5
55002 Almelund, 150 .... F 5
56111 Alpha, 179 .... D 7
55910 Altura, 334 .... G 6
56710 Alvarado, 302 .... B 2
56010 Amboy, 571 .... D 7
55703 Angora, 287 .... F 3
55302 Annandale, 1,234 .... D 5
55303 Anoka⊙, 13,489 .... E 5
56208 Appleton, 1,789 .... C 5
† 55378 Apple Valley, 8,502 .... G 6
56113 Arco, 121 .... B 6
56713 Argyle, 739 .... B 2
55307 Arlington, 1,823 .... D 6
† 55801 Arnold, 750 .... F 4
56309 Ashby, 415 .... C 4
55704 Askov, 287 .... F 4
56209 Atwater, 956 .... D 5
56511 Audubon, 297 .... C 4
55705 Aurora, 2,531 .... F 3
55912 Austin⊙, 25,074 .... E 7
56114 Avoca, 203 .... C 7
56310 Avon, 725 .... D 5
55706 Babbitt, 3,076 .... G 3
56435 Backus, 257 .... D 4
56714 Badger, 327 .... B 2
56621 Bagley⊙, 1,314 .... C 3
56115 Balaton, 649 .... C 6
56622 Ball Club, 150 .... E 3
56514 Barnesville, 1,782 .... B 4
55707 Barnum, 382 .... F 4
56311 Barrett, 342 .... B 5
56515 Battle Lake, 772 .... C 4
56623 Baudette⊙, 1,547 .... D 2
† 56401 Baxter, 1,556 .... D 4
† 56444 Bay Lake, 250 .... E 4
55003 Bayport, 2,987 .... F 5
56211 Beardsley, 366 .... B 5
† 55723 Bear River, 250 .... E 3
55601 Beaver Bay, 362 .... G 3
56116 Beaver Creek, 235 .... B 7
55308 Becker, 365 .... E 5
56516 Bejou, 157 .... B 3
56312 Belgrade, 713 .... C 5
† 55027 Bellechester, 199 .... F 6
56011 Belle Plaine, 2,328 .... E 6
56212 Bellingham, 263 .... B 5
56517 Beltrami, 171 .... B 3
56214 Belview, 429 .... C 6
56601 Bemidji⊙, 11,490 .... D 3
56626 Bena, 169 .... D 3
56215 Benson⊙, 3,484 .... C 5
56437 Bertha, 512 .... C 4
56117 Bigelow, 262 .... C 7
56627 Big Falls, 534 .... E 2
56628 Bigfork, 399 .... E 3
55309 Big Lake, 1,015 .... E 5
56118 Bingham Lake, 214 .... C 7
55310 Bird Island, 1,309 .... D 6
55708 Biwabik, 1,483 .... F 3
56630 Blackduck, 595 .... D 3
† 55303 Blaine, 20,640 .... G 5
† 56011 Blakeley, 125 .... E 6
56216 Blomkest, 172 .... D 6
55917 Blooming Prairie, 1,804 .... E 7
55420 Bloomington, 81,970 .... G 6
56013 Blue Earth⊙, 3,965 .... D 7
56518 Bluffton, 195 .... C 4
56519 Borup, 128 .... B 3
55709 Bovey, 858 .... E 3
56314 Bowlus, 268 .... D 5
56218 Boyd, 311 .... C 6
55006 Braham, 744 .... E 5
56401 Brainerd⊙, 11,667 .... D 4
† 55056 Branch, 880 .... F 5
56315 Brandon, 414 .... C 5
56520 Breckenridge⊙, 4,200 .... B 4
† 56472 Breezy Point Village, 233 .... D 4
56119 Brewster, 563 .... C 7
56014 Bricelyn, 470 .... E 7
55710 Britt, 175 .... F 3
55429 Brooklyn Center, 35,173 .... G 5
† 55401 Brooklyn Park, 26,230 .... G 5
56715 Brooks, 163 .... B 3
55711 Brookston, 137 .... F 4
56316 Brooten, 615 .... C 5
56438 Browerville, 665 .... D 4
55918 Brownsdale, 625 .... F 7
56219 Browns Valley, 906 .... B 5
55919 Brownsville, 417 .... G 7
55312 Brownton, 688 .... D 6
55712 Bruno, 130 .... F 4
† 55051 Brunswick, 144 .... E 5
56317 Buckman, 158 .... D 5
55313 Buffalo⊙, 3,275 .... E 5
55314 Buffalo Lake, 758 .... D 6
55713 Buhl, 1,303 .... F 3
55378 Burnsville, 19,940 .... E 6
56318 Burtrum, 135 .... D 5
56120 Butterfield, 619 .... D 7
† 56723 Bygland, 475 .... B 3
55920 Byron, 1,419 .... F 6
55921 Caledonia⊙, 2,619 .... G 7
56521 Callaway, 233 .... C 4
55716 Calumet, 460 .... E 3
55008 Cambridge⊙, 3,467 .... E 5
56522 Campbell, 339 .... B 4
56220 Canby, 2,081 .... B 6
55009 Cannon Falls, 2,072 .... F 6
55922 Canton, 391 .... F 7
55717 Canyon, 125 .... F 3
56319 Carlos, 260 .... C 5
55718 Carlton⊙, 884 .... F 4
55315 Carver, 669 .... E 6
56633 Cass Lake, 1,317 .... D 3
55010 Castle Rock, 150 .... E 6
55012 Center City⊙, 324 .... F 5
† 55038 Centerville, 534 .... E 5
56121 Ceylon, 487 .... D 7
55316 Champlin, 2,275 .... G 5
56122 Chandler, 319 .... C 7
55317 Chanhassen, 4,879 .... F 6
55318 Chaska⊙, 4,352 .... F 6
55923 Chatfield, 1,885 .... F 7
55013 Chisago City, 1,068 .... F 5
55719 Chisholm, 5,913 .... E 3
56221 Chokio, 455 .... B 5
55014 Circle Pines, 3,918 .... G 5
56222 Clara City, 1,491 .... C 6
55924 Claremont, 520 .... E 6
56440 Clarissa, 599 .... C 4
56223 Clarkfield, 1,084 .... C 6
56016 Clarks Grove, 480 .... E 7
56634 Clearbrook, 599 .... C 3
55319 Clear Lake, 280 .... E 5
55320 Clearwater, 282 .... D 5
56224 Clements, 252 .... D 6
56017 Cleveland, 492 .... E 6
56523 Climax, 255 .... B 3
56225 Clinton, 608 .... B 5
56524 Clitherall, 131 .... C 4
56226 Clontarf, 147 .... C 5
55720 Cloquet, 8,699 .... F 4
55015 Cloverton, 150 .... F 4
55721 Cohasset, 536 .... E 3
55321 Cokato, 1,735 .... D 5
56320 Cold Spring, 2,006 .... D 5
55722 Coleraine, 1,086 .... E 3
56321 Collegeville, 1,600 .... D 5
55322 Cologne, 518 .... E 6
55421 Columbia Heights, 23,997 .... G 5
56019 Comfrey, 525 .... D 6
56525 Comstock, 135 .... B 4
56020 Conger, 167 .... E 7
55723 Cook, 687 .... F 3
55433 Coon Rapids, 30,505 .... G 5
† 55340 Corcoran, 1,656 .... F 5
56228 Cosmos, 570 .... D 6
55016 Cottage Grove, 13,419 .... F 6
55724 Cotton, 350 .... F 3
56229 Cottonwood, 794 .... C 6
56021 Courtland, 360 .... D 6
55725 Crane Lake, 350 .... F 2
55726 Cromwell, 181 .... F 4
56716 Crookston⊙, 8,312 .... B 3
56441 Crosby, 2,241 .... D 4
56442 Crosslake, 358 .... E 4
† 55005 Crown, 200 .... E 5
† 55401 Crystal, 30,925 .... G 5
55323 Crystal Bay, 6,787 .... F 5
56123 Currie, 368 .... C 6
56323 Cyrus, 289 .... C 5
55925 Dakota, 369 .... G 7
56324 Dalton, 221 .... C 4
56230 Danube, 497 .... C 6
56231 Danvers, 136 .... C 5
56022 Darfur, 179 .... D 6
55324 Darwin, 224 .... D 5
55325 Dassel, 1,058 .... D 5
56232 Dawson, 1,699 .... B 6
55327 Dayton, 517 .... E 5
55391 Deephaven, 3,853 .... G 5
56527 Deer Creek, 287 .... C 4
56636 Deer River, 815 .... E 3
56444 Deerwood, 448 .... E 4
56233 De Graff, 195 .... C 5
55328 Delano, 1,851 .... E 5
56023 Delavan, 281 .... D 7
56234 Delhi, 154 .... C 6
† 55110 Dellwood, 514 .... F 5
55018 Dennison, 162 .... E 6
56528 Dent, 156 .... C 4
56501 Detroit Lakes⊙, 5,797 .... C 4
55926 Dexter, 252 .... F 7
56529 Dilworth, 2,321 .... B 4
55927 Dodge Center, 1,603 .... F 6
56235 Donnelly, 252 .... B 5
55929 Dover, 321 .... F 7
55930 Dresbach, 250 .... G 7
* 55801 Duluth⊙, 100,578 .... F 4
Duluth-Superior, ‡265,350 .... F 4
56236 Dumont, 204 .... B 5
55019 Dundas, 460 .... E 6
56126 Dundee, 138 .... C 7
56127 Dunnell, 237 .... D 7
56446 Eagle Bend, 557 .... D 4
56024 Eagle Lake, 839 .... E 6
† 55005 East Bethel, 2,586 .... E 5
† 56031 East Chain, 171 .... D 7
56721 East Grand Forks, 7,607 .... B 3
† 56401 East Gull Lake, 440 .... D 4
56025 Easton, 352 .... E 7
56237 Echo, 356 .... C 6
55343 Eden Prairie, 6,938 .... G 6
55329 Eden Valley, 776 .... D 5
56128 Edgerton, 1,119 .... B 7
55424 Edina, 44,046 .... G 5
56639 Effie, 165 .... E 3
55931 Eitzen, 208 .... G 7
† 55910 Elba, 158 .... F 6
56531 Elbow Lake⊙, 1,484 .... B 5
55932 Elgin, 580 .... F 6
56533 Elizabeth, 188 .... B 4
55330 Elk River⊙, 2,252 .... E 5
55933 Elkton, 134 .... F 7
56026 Ellendale, 569 .... E 7
56129 Ellsworth, 588 .... C 7
56027 Elmore, 910 .... D 7
56325 Elrosa, 203 .... C 5
55731 Ely, 4,904 .... G 3
56028 Elysian, 445 .... E 6
55732 Embarrass, 195 .... F 3
56447 Emily, 386 .... E 4
56029 Emmons, 412 .... E 7
56534 Erhard, 748 .... B 4
56640 Ericsburg, 300 .... E 2
56535 Erskine, 571 .... B 3
55733 Esko, 500 .... F 4
56722 Euclid, 130 .... B 3
56238 Evan, 126 .... D 6
56326 Evansville, 553 .... C 4
55734 Eveleth, 4,721 .... F 3
55331 Excelsior, 2,563 .... F 6
55934 Eyota, 639 .... F 7
55332 Fairfax, 1,432 .... D 6
55383 Fairhaven, 129 .... D 5
56031 Fairmont⊙, 10,751 .... D 7
55113 Falcon Heights, 5,507 .... G 5
55021 Faribault⊙, 16,595 .... E 6
55024 Farmington, 3,104 .... E 6
56641 Federal Dam, 147 .... D 3
56536 Felton, 232 .... B 3
56537 Fergus Falls⊙, 12,443 .... B 4
56540 Fertile, 955 .... B 3
56448 Fifty Lakes, 143 .... D 4
55603 Finland, 300 .... G 3
55735 Finlayson, 192 .... F 4
56723 Fisher, 383 .... B 3
56328 Flensburg, 259 .... D 5
56736 Floodwood, 650 .... E 4
† 55792 Florenton, 635 .... F 3
56329 Foley⊙, 1,271 .... D 5
† 56308 Forada, 158 .... C 5
57338 Forbes, 225 .... F 3
55025 Forest Lake, 3,207 .... F 5
56330 Foreston, 273 .... E 5
56542 Fosston, 1,684 .... C 3
55935 Fountain, 347 .... F 7
56543 Foxhome, 185 .... B 4
55333 Franklin, 557 .... D 6
56544 Frazee, 1,015 .... C 4
56032 Freeborn, 296 .... E 7
56331 Freeport, 593 .... D 5
† 55801 French River, 200 .... G 4
55421 Fridley, 29,233 .... G 5
55026 Frontenac, 223 .... F 6

AREA 84,068 sq. mi.
POPULATION 3,805,069
CAPITAL St. Paul
LARGEST CITY Minneapolis
HIGHEST POINT Eagle Mtn. 2,301 ft.
SETTLED IN 1805
ADMITTED TO UNION May 11, 1858
POPULAR NAME North Star State; Gopher State
STATE FLOWER Lady-slipper
STATE BIRD Loon

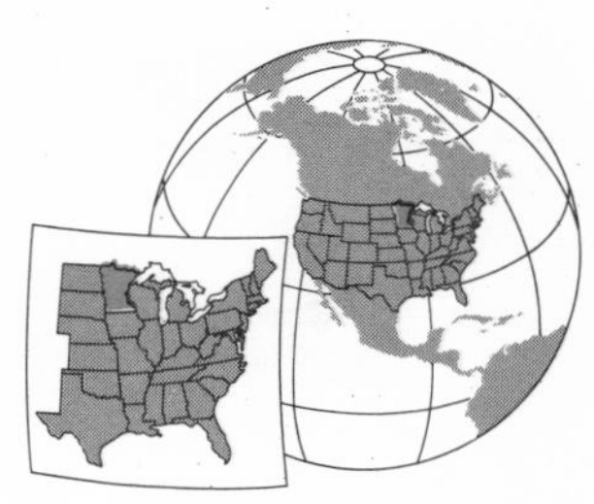

56033 Frost, 290 .... D 7
56131 Fulda, 1,226 .... C 7
56034 Garden City, 270 .... D 6
56332 Garfield, 198 .... C 5
56450 Garrison, 125 .... E 4
56132 Garvin, 201 .... C 6
56545 Gary, 265 .... B 3
55334 Gaylord⊙, 1,720 .... D 6
56035 Geneva, 358 .... E 7
56717 Gentilly, 163 .... B 3
56546 Georgetown, 141 .... B 3
55740 Gheen, 145 .... F 3
56239 Ghent, 301 .... C 6
55335 Gibbon, 877 .... D 6
55741 Gilbert, 2,287 .... F 3
† 56431 Glen, 125 .... E 4
55336 Glencoe⊙, 4,217 .... D 6
56036 Glenville, 740 .... E 7
56334 Glenwood⊙, 2,584 .... C 5
56547 Glyndon, 674 .... B 4
55427 Golden Valley, 24,246 .... G 5
56644 Gonvick, 344 .... C 3
55027 Goodhue, 539 .... F 6
55742 Goodland, 175 .... E 3
56725 Goodridge, 144 .... C 2
56037 Good Thunder, 489 .... D 6
55027 Goodview, 1,829 .... G 6
56240 Graceville, 735 .... B 5
56039 Granada, 381 .... D 7
55604 Grand Marais⊙, 1,301 .... G 2
55936 Grand Meadow, 869 .... F 7
55744 Grand Rapids⊙, 7,247 .... E 3
55029 Grandy, 155 .... E 5
56241 Granite Falls⊙, 3,225 .... C 6
55030 Grasston, 132 .... E 5
56726 Greenbush, 787 .... B 2
† 55373 Greenfield, 977 .... F 5
55338 Green Isle, 363 .... E 6
56242 Green Valley, 129 .... C 6
56335 Greenwald, 244 .... D 5
56336 Grey Eagle, 325 .... D 5
56243 Grove City, 502 .... D 5
56727 Grygla, 211 .... C 2
56452 Hackensack, 220 .... D 4
56133 Hadley, 119 .... C 7
56728 Hallock⊙, 1,477 .... A 2
56548 Halstad, 598 .... B 3
55339 Hamburg, 377 .... D 6
55340 Hamel, 2,396 .... F 5
55938 Hammond, 179 .... F 6
55031 Hampton, 369 .... E 6
56244 Hancock, 806 .... C 5
56245 Hanley Falls, 265 .... C 6
55341 Hanover, 365 .... E 5
56041 Hanska, 442 .... D 6
56364 Harding, 119 .... E 4
56134 Hardwick, 274 .... B 7
55939 Harmony, 1,130 .... F 7
55032 Harris, 559 .... F 5
56042 Hartland, 331 .... E 7
† 55374 Hassan, 778 .... E 5
55033 Hastings⊙, 12,195 .... F 6
56549 Hawley, 1,371 .... B 4
55940 Hayfield, 939 .... F 7
56043 Hayward, 261 .... E 7
55342 Hector, 1,178 .... D 6
56044 Henderson, 730 .... E 6
56136 Hendricks, 712 .... B 6
56550 Hendrum, 311 .... B 3
56551 Henning, 850 .... C 4
56248 Herman, 619 .... B 5
56137 Heron Lake, 777 .... C 7
56453 Hewitt, 198 .... C 4
55746 Hibbing, 16,104 .... F 3
55748 Hill City, 357 .... E 4
56138 Hills, 571 .... B 7
55037 Hinckley, 885 .... E 4
56552 Hitterdal, 178 .... B 4
56339 Hoffman, 627 .... C 5
55941 Hokah, 697 .... G 7
56340 Holdingford, 551 .... D 5
56139 Holland, 263 .... B 6
56045 Hollandale, 287 .... E 7
56249 Holloway, 146 .... C 5
55749 Holyoke, 190 .... F 4
55942 Homer, 150 .... G 6
56045 Hope, 125 .... E 6
55343 Hopkins, 13,428 .... G 5
55943 Houston, 1,090 .... G 7
55606 Hovland, 150 .... G 2
55349 Howard Lake, 1,162 .... D 5
55750 Hoyt Lakes, 3,634 .... F 3
55038 Hugo, 751 .... E 5
56047 Huntley, 139 .... D 7
55350 Hutchinson, 8,031 .... D 6
56140 Ihlen, 132 .... B 7
† 55359 Independence, 1,993 .... F 5
56649 International Falls⊙, 6,439 .... E 2
55075 Inver Grove Heights, 12,148 .... E 6
56141 Iona, 260 .... C 7
55751 Iron, 150 .... F 3
56455 Ironton, 562 .... D 4
55040 Isanti, 679 .... E 5
56342 Isle, 551 .... E 4
56142 Ivanhoe⊙, 738 .... B 6
56143 Jackson⊙, 3,550 .... C 7
55752 Jacobson, 225 .... E 4
56048 Janesville, 1,557 .... E 6
56144 Jasper, 754 .... B 7
56145 Jeffers, 436 .... C 6
56456 Jenkins, 148 .... D 4
55352 Jordan, 1,836 .... E 6
† 56669 Kabetogama, 150 .... F 2
56251 Kandiyohi, 295 .... D 5
56732 Karlstad, 727 .... B 2
56050 Kasota, 732 .... D 6
55944 Kasson, 1,883 .... F 6
55753 Keewatin, 1,382 .... E 3
56650 Kelliher, 289 .... D 3
55945 Kellogg, 403 .... G 6
55754 Kelly Lake, 950 .... F 3
55755 Kelsey, 151 .... F 3
56733 Kennedy, 424 .... B 2
56343 Kensington, 308 .... C 5
56553 Kent, 139 .... B 4
55946 Kenyon, 1,575 .... E 6
56252 Kerkhoven, 641 .... C 5
55757 Kettle River, 173 .... E 4
56051 Kiester, 681 .... E 7
56052 Kilkenny, 182 .... E 6
55353 Kimball, 567 .... D 5
55758 Kinney, 325 .... F 3
55609 Knife River, 350 .... G 4
55947 La Crescent, 3,142 .... G 7
56054 Lafayette, 498 .... D 6
56149 Lake Benton, 759 .... B 6
56734 Lake Bronson, 325 .... B 2
55041 Lake City, 3,594 .... F 6
56055 Lake Crystal, 1,807 .... D 6
55042 Lake Elmo, 4,032 .... F 6
56150 Lakefield, 1,820 .... C 7
† 55398 Lake Fremont (Zimmerman), 495 .... E 5
56458 Lake George, 200 .... D 3
55043 Lakeland, 962 .... F 6
56253 Lake Lillian, 316 .... C 6
56554 Lake Park, 658 .... B 4
† 55043 Lake Saint Croix Beach, 1,111 .... F 6
† 56401 Lake Shore, 410 .... D 4
55044 Lakeville, 7,556 .... E 6
56151 Lake Wilson, 378 .... B 7
56152 Lamberton, 962 .... C 6
56735 Lancaster, 382 .... B 2
55949 Lanesboro, 850 .... G 7
55950 Lansing, 300 .... F 7
56461 Laporte, 154 .... D 3
† 55744 La Prairie, 413 .... E 3
56056 La Salle, 132 .... D 6

(continued on following page)

Superior National Forest in Minnesota contains the nation's largest wilderness park with primitive virgin timberlands, protected wildlife and 5,000 restocked lakes.

MINNESOTA
SCALE
0 5 10 20 30 40 50 MI.
0 5 10 20 30 40 50 KM.
State Capitals
County Seats
© C.S. HAMMOND & Co., N.Y.
NORTHEASTERN PART OF MINNESOTA
Same scale as main map
CANADA
COOK
GRAND PORTAGE IND. RES.
GRAND PORTAGE NAT'L MON.
MISQUAH HILLS
Grand Marais
Lake Superior
MANITOBA
CANADA
ONTARIO
NORTH DAKOTA
SOUTH DAKOTA
IOWA
WISCONSIN
LAKE SUPERIOR
Lake of the Woods
Rainy River
International Falls
Fort Frances
DULUTH
Superior
KITTSON
ROSEAU
LAKE OF THE WOODS
MARSHALL
KOOCHICHING
PENNINGTON
RED LAKE
BELTRAMI
RED LAKE INDIAN RES.
NETT LAKE IND. RES.
POLK
CLEARWATER
ITASCA
SAINT LOUIS
LAKE
COOK
NORMAN
MAHNOMEN
WHITE EARTH INDIAN RESERVATION
HUBBARD
CASS
LEECH LAKE IND. RES.
CLAY
BECKER
WADENA
CROW WING
AITKIN
CARLTON
FOND DU LAC IND. RES.
OTTER TAIL
WILKIN
TODD
MORRISON
MILLE LACS
KANABEC
PINE
GRANT
DOUGLAS
TRAVERSE
STEVENS
POPE
STEARNS
BENTON
SHERBURNE
ISANTI
CHISAGO
BIG STONE
SWIFT
KANDIYOHI
MEEKER
WRIGHT
ANOKA
WASHINGTON
RAMSEY
HENNEPIN
CHIPPEWA
LAC QUI PARLE
YELLOW MEDICINE
RENVILLE
MC LEOD
CARVER
SCOTT
DAKOTA
SIBLEY
GOODHUE
WABASHA
LINCOLN
LYON
REDWOOD
BROWN
NICOLLET
LE SUEUR
RICE
PIPESTONE
MURRAY
COTTONWOOD
WATONWAN
BLUE EARTH
WASECA
STEELE
DODGE
OLMSTED
WINONA
ROCK
NOBLES
JACKSON
MARTIN
FARIBAULT
FREEBORN
MOWER
FILLMORE
HOUSTON
MINNEAPOLIS
ST. PAUL
St. Cloud
Rochester
Mankato
Duluth
Bemidji
Brainerd
Fargo
Moorhead
Grand Forks
Sioux Falls
La Crosse
Winona
Red Wing
Hibbing
Virginia
Two Harbors
Silver Bay
Grand Rapids
Crookston
Thief River Falls
Fergus Falls
Alexandria
Willmar
Worthington
Albert Lea
Austin
Faribault
Owatonna
Northfield
Stillwater
Hastings
Shakopee
Chaska
New Ulm
Marshall
Pipestone
Fairmont
Mille Lacs Lake
Upper Red Lake
Lower Red Lake
Leech Lake
Lake Winnibigoshish
CUYUNA RANGE
MESABI RANGE
VERMILION RANGE
Mississippi R.
Minnesota R.
Red R.
St. Croix R.
Lake Pepin

56344 Lastrup, 161 D 4
55101 Lauderdale, 2,419 G 5
56057 Le Center⊙, 1,890 E 6
56651 Lengby, 140 C 3
55734 Leonidas, 157 F 3
56153 Leota, 285 C 7
55951 Le Roy, 870 F 7
55354 Lester Prairie, 1,162 D 6
56058 Le Sueur, 3,745 E 6
55952 Lewiston, 1,000 G 7
56060 Lewisville, 291 D 7
55014 Lexington, 1,926 G 5
55050 Lilydale, 664 G 5
55045 Lindstrom, 1,260 F 5
55038 Lino Lakes, 3,692 G 5
56155 Lismore, 323 B 7
55355 Litchfield⊙, 5,262 D 5
56345 Little Falls⊙, 7,467 D 5
56653 Littlefork, 824 E 2
55611 Little Marais, 175 G 3
56334 Long Beach, 219 C 5
55356 Long Lake, 1,506 F 5
56347 Long Prairie⊙, 2,416 D 5
56655 Longville, 171 D 4
55046 Lonsdale, 622 E 6
55357 Loretto, 340 F 5
56349 Lowry, 257 C 5
56255 Lucan, 254 C 6
55612 Lutsen, 620 F 2
56156 Luverne⊙, 4,703 B 7
55953 Lyle, 522 F 7
56157 Lynd, 267 C 6
55954 Mabel, 888 G 7
56062 Madelia, 2,316 D 6
56256 Madison⊙, 2,242 B 5
56063 Madison Lake, 587 E 6
56158 Magnolia, 233 B 7
56557 Mahnomen⊙, 1,313 C 3
55115 Mahtomedi, 2,640 F 5
55762 Mahtowa, 167 F 4
56001 Mankato⊙, 30,895 E 6
55955 Mantorville⊙, 479 F 6
55369 Maple Grove, 6,275 F 5
55358 Maple Lake, 1,124 D 5
55359 Maple Plain, 1,169 F 5
56065 Mapleton, 1,307 E 7
55912 Mapleview, 328 E 7
55109 Maplewood, 25,222 G 5
55764 Marble, 682 E 3
56657 Marcell, 350 E 3
56257 Marietta, 264 B 5
55047 Marine on Saint Croix, 513 F 5
56258 Marshall⊙, 9,886 C 6
55360 Mayer, 325 E 6
56260 Maynard, 455 C 6
55956 Mazeppa, 498 F 6
55760 McGregor, 331 E 4
56556 McIntosh, 753 C 3
55761 McKinley, 317 F 3
55765 Meadowlands, 128 F 3
55049 Medford, 690 E 6
55427 Medicine Lake, 930 G 5
55340 Medina (Hamel), 2,396 F 5
† 56352 Meire Grove, 171 C 5
56352 Melrose, 2,273 D 5
56464 Menahga, 835 C 4
55050 Mendota, 327 G 5
† 55050 Mendota Heights, 6,165 G 6
56736 Mentor, 236 B 3
56465 Merrifield, 300 D 4
56737 Middle River, 369 B 2
† 55033 Miesville, 192 F 6
56353 Milaca⊙, 1,940 E 5
56262 Milan, 427 C 5
55957 Millville, 139 F 6
56263 Milroy, 247 C 6
56354 Miltona, 172 C 4
* 55401 Minneapolis⊙, 434,400 G 5
Minneapolis-Saint Paul, ‡1,813,647 G 5
56264 Minneota, 1,320 C 6
55959 Minnesota City, 301 G 6
56068 Minnesota Lake, 738 E 7
55343 Minnetonka, 35,776 G 5
† 55364 Minnetrista, 2,878 F 5
56265 Montevideo⊙, 5,661 C 6
56069 Montgomery, 2,281 E 6
55362 Monticello, 1,636 E 5
55363 Montrose, 379 E 5
56560 Moorhead⊙, 29,687 B 4
Moorhead-Fargo, ‡120,238 B 4
55767 Moose Lake, 1,400 F 4
56266 Mora⊙, 2,582 E 5
56266 Morgan, 972 D 6
56267 Morris⊙, 5,366 C 5
55052 Morristown, 659 E 6
56270 Morton, 591 C 6
56466 Motley, 351 D 4
55364 Mound, 7,572 E 6
† 55112 Mounds View, 9,988 G 5
55768 Mountain Iron, 1,698 F 3
56159 Mountain Lake, 1,986 D 7
56271 Murdock, 358 C 5
55769 Nashwauk, 1,341 E 3
56272 Nassau, 126 B 5
56566 Naytahwaush, 350 C 3
56355 Nelson, 175 C 5
55053 Nerstrand, 231 E 6
55772 Nett Lake, 470 E 2
56467 Nevis, 308 D 4
55366 New Auburn, 274 D 6
55112 New Brighton, 19,507 G 5
56738 Newfolden, 390 B 2
55367 New Germany, 303 E 6
56273 New London, 736 C 5
55054 New Market, 215 E 6
56356 New Munich, 307 D 5
55055 Newport, 2,922 F 6
56071 New Prague, 2,680 E 6
56072 New Richland, 1,113 E 7
† 55031 New Trier, 153 F 6
56073 New Ulm⊙, 13,051 D 6
56567 New York Mills, 791 C 4
† 56431 Nichols, 125 E 4
56074 Nicollet, 618 D 6
56568 Nielsville, 156 B 3
56468 Nisswa, 1,011 D 4
55770 Nopeming, 268 F 4
56274 Norcross, 137 B 5
55056 North Branch, 1,106 F 5
† 56442 North Crosslake, 362 D 4
55057 Northfield, 10,235 E 6
56001 North Mankato, 7,347 D 6
56661 Northome, 351 D 3
56275 North Redwood, 155 D 6
56075 Northrop, 188 D 7
55109 North Saint Paul, 11,950 E 5
55368 Norwood, 1,058 E 6
56276 Odessa, 194 B 5
56160 Odin, 166 D 7
56569 Ogema, 236 C 3
56358 Ogilvie, 384 E 5
56161 Okabena, 237 C 7
56742 Oklee, 536 C 3
56277 Olivia⊙, 2,553 C 6
56359 Onamia, 670 E 4
† 55044 Orchard Lake, 200 E 6
56162 Ormsby, 199 D 7
† 55323 Orono (Crystal Bay), 6,787 F 5
55960 Oronoco, 564 F 6
55771 Orr, 315 F 2
56278 Ortonville⊙, 2,665 B 5
56570 Osage, 175 C 4
56360 Osakis, 1,306 C 5
56744 Oslo, 417 A 2
55369 Osseo, 2,908 G 5
55961 Ostrander, 216 F 7
† 56058 Ottawa, 125 E 6
56571 Ottertail, 180 C 4
56662 Outing, 425 E 4
55060 Owatonna⊙, 15,341 E 6
56469 Palisade, 149 E 4
† 55801 Palmers, 150 G 4
† 55705 Palo, 158 F 3
56361 Parkers Prairie, 882 C 4
56470 Park Rapids⊙, 2,772 D 4
56362 Paynesville, 1,920 D 5
56363 Pease, 187 E 5
† 56472 Pelican Lakes (Breezy Point Village), 233 D 4
56572 Pelican Rapids, 1,835 B 4
56078 Pemberton, 128 E 7
55775 Pengilly, 625 E 3
56279 Pennock, 255 C 5
56472 Pequot Lakes, 499 D 4
56573 Perham, 1,933 C 4
56574 Perley, 149 B 3
55962 Peterson, 269 G 7
† 55948 Pickwick, 150 G 7
56364 Pierz, 893 D 5
56473 Pillager, 374 D 4
55063 Pine City⊙, 2,143 F 5
55963 Pine Island, 1,640 F 6
56474 Pine River, 803 D 4
56164 Pipestone⊙, 5,328 B 7
55964 Plainview, 2,093 F 6
55370 Plato, 303 D 6
56748 Plummer, 285 B 3
† 55401 Plymouth, 17,593 G 5
56666 Ponemah, 531 D 2
56280 Porter, 207 B 6
55965 Preston⊙, 1,413 F 7
55371 Princeton, 2,531 E 5
56281 Prinsburg, 448 C 6
55372 Prior Lake, 1,114 E 6
55810 Proctor, 3,123 F 4
† 55752 Rabey, 125 E 4
55967 Racine, 197 F 7
56475 Randall, 536 D 4
55065 Randolph, 350 E 6
56668 Ranier, 255 E 2
56669 Ray, 200 E 2
56282 Raymond, 589 C 5
56165 Reading, 150 C 7
55968 Reads Landing, 150 F 6
56670 Redby, 475 D 3
56671 Redlake, 300 C 3
56750 Red Lake Falls⊙, 1,740 B 3
55066 Red Wing⊙, 10,441 F 6
56283 Redwood Falls⊙, 4,774 C 6
56672 Remer, 403 E 3
56284 Renville, 1,252 C 6
56166 Revere, 166 C 6
56367 Rice, 366 D 5
55423 Richfield, 47,231 G 6
56368 Richmond, 866 D 5
55422 Robbinsdale, 16,845 G 5
55901 Rochester⊙, 53,766 F 6
55067 Rock Creek, 805 F 5
55373 Rockford, 730 F 5
56369 Rockville, 302 D 5
55374 Rogers, 544 E 5
55969 Rollingstone, 450 G 6
56371 Roscoe, 195 D 5
56751 Roseau⊙, 2,552 C 2
55970 Rose Creek, 390 F 7
† 56216 Roseland, 123 C 6
55068 Rosemount, 1,337 E 6
55113 Roseville, 34,518 G 5
56579 Rothsay, 448 B 4
56167 Round Lake, 506 C 7
56373 Royalton, 534 D 5
55069 Rush City, 1,130 F 5
55971 Rushford, 1,318 G 7
56168 Rushmore, 394 C 7
56169 Russell, 398 C 6
56170 Ruthton, 405 B 6
55778 Rutledge, 123 F 4
56580 Sabin, 333 B 4
56285 Sacred Heart, 707 C 6
55779 Saginaw, 407 F 4
55414 Saint Anthony Falls, 9,239 G 5
55375 Saint Bonifacius, 685 F 5
55972 Saint Charles, 1,942 F 7
56080 Saint Clair, 488 E 6
56301 Saint Cloud⊙, 39,691 D 5
55070 Saint Francis, 897 E 5
56554 Saint Hilaire, 337 B 2
56081 Saint James⊙, 4,027 D 7
56374 Saint Joseph, 1,786 D 5
55426 Saint Louis Park, 48,883 G 5
56376 Saint Martin, 188 D 5
55376 Saint Michael, 1,021 E 5
* 55101 Saint Paul (cap.)⊙, 309,980 G 6
55071 Saint Paul Park, 5,587 G 6
56082 Saint Peter⊙, 8,339 E 6
56375 Saint Stephen, 331 D 5
56755 Saint Vincent, 177 A 2
56083 Sanborn, 505 C 6
55072 Sandstone, 1,641 F 4
56377 Sartell, 1,323 D 5
56378 Sauk Centre, 3,750 C 5
56379 Sauk Rapids, 5,051 D 5
55378 Savage, 3,611 G 6
55780 Sawyer, 200 F 4
55073 Scandia, 200 F 5
† 55720 Scanlon, 1,132 F 4
55613 Schroeder, 550 G 3
56287 Seaforth, 132 C 6
56084 Searles, 160 D 6
56477 Sebeka, 668 C 4
55074 Shafer, 149 F 5
55379 Shakopee⊙, 6,876 F 6
56581 Shelly, 260 B 3
56171 Sherburn, 1,190 D 7
56676 Shevlin, 185 C 3
† 55021 Shieldsville, 150 E 6
† 55331 Shorewood, 4,223 F 5
55614 Silver Bay, 3,504 G 3
55380 Silver Creek, 125 D 5
55381 Silver Lake, 694 D 6
† 56001 Skyline, 400 D 6
56172 Slayton⊙, 2,351 C 7
56085 Sleepy Eye, 3,461 D 6
† 56345 Sobieski, 189 D 5
55782 Soudan, 900 F 3
55382 South Haven, 238 D 5
56679 South International Falls, 2,116 E 2
55075 South Saint Paul, 25,016 G 6
56288 Spicer, 586 C 5
56087 Springfield, 2,530 C 6
55974 Spring Grove, 1,290 G 7
55432 Spring Lake Park, 6,417 E 5
55384 Spring Park, 1,087 F 5
55975 Spring Valley, 2,572 F 7
55079 Stacy, 278 E 5
55080 Stanchfield, 155 E 5
56479 Staples, 2,657 D 4
56381 Starbuck, 1,138 C 5
56173 Steen, 191 B 7
56757 Stephen, 904 A 2
55385 Stewart, 666 D 6
55976 Stewartville, 2,802 F 7
55082 Stillwater⊙, 10,191 F 5
55988 Stockton, 346 G 6
56174 Storden, 364 C 6
56758 Strandquist, 138 B 2
55783 Sturgeon Lake, 167 F 4
56289 Sunburg, 144 C 5
† 55075 Sunfish Lake, 269 E 6
56290 Svea, 125 C 6
56382 Swanville, 300 D 5
55785 Swatara, 250 E 4
55786 Taconite, 352 E 3
56291 Taunton, 195 B 6
55084 Taylors Falls, 587 F 5
56683 Tenstrike, 138 D 3
56701 Thief River Falls⊙, 8,618 B 2
† 56319 Thomson, 159 F 4
56583 Tintah, 167 B 5
55615 Tofte, 400 H 3
55789 Toivola, 185 F 3
† 55331 Tonka Bay, 1,397 F 5
55790 Tower, 699 F 3
56175 Tracy, 2,516 C 6
56176 Trimont, 835 D 7
56088 Truman, 1,137 D 7
55791 Twig, 165 F 4
56089 Twin Lakes, 230 E 7
56584 Twin Valley, 868 B 3
55616 Two Harbors⊙, 4,437 G 3
56178 Tyler, 1,069 B 6
56585 Ulen, 486 B 3
56586 Underwood, 278 C 4
56384 Upsala, 312 D 5
† 56361 Urbank, 125 C 4
55979 Utica, 240 G 7
† 55101 Vadnais Heights, 3,391 G 5
56587 Vergas, 281 C 4
55085 Vermillion, 359 F 6
56481 Verndale, 570 C 4
† 55752 Verndon, 135 E 4
56090 Vernon Center, 347 D 7
55086 Veseli, 150 E 6
56292 Vesta, 330 C 6
55386 Victoria, 850 F 6
56385 Villard, 221 C 5
56588 Vining, 121 C 4
55792 Virginia, 12,450 F 3
55981 Wabasha⊙, 2,371 G 6
56293 Wabasso, 738 C 6
55387 Waconia, 2,445 E 6
56482 Wadena⊙, 4,640 C 4
56386 Wahkon, 208 E 4
56387 Waite Park, 2,824 D 5
56091 Waldorf, 285 E 7
56484 Walker⊙, 2,073 D 3
56180 Walnut Grove, 756 C 6
56092 Walters, 152 E 7
55982 Waltham, 189 F 7
55983 Wanamingo, 574 F 6
56294 Wanda, 124 C 6
55743 Warba, 148 E 3
56762 Warren⊙, 1,999 B 2
56763 Warroad, 1,086 C 2
55087 Warsaw, 200 E 6
56093 Waseca⊙, 6,789 E 6
55388 Watertown, 1,390 E 6
56096 Waterville, 1,539 E 6
55389 Watkins, 785 D 5
56295 Watson, 228 C 5
56589 Waubun, 345 C 3
55390 Waverly, 546 E 5
55391 Wayzata, 3,700 G 5
55088 Webster, 175 E 6
56181 Welcome, 694 D 7
56097 Wells, 2,791 E 7
56590 Wendell, 247 B 4
56183 Westbrook, 990 C 6
55985 West Concord, 718 F 6
55118 West Saint Paul, 18,799 G 5
56296 Wheaton⊙, 2,029 B 5
56485 Whipholt, 142 D 3
55110 White Bear Lake, 23,313 G 5
56591 White Earth, 150 C 3
56184 Wilder, 132 C 7
55090 Willernie, 697 G 5
56686 Williams, 220 D 2
56201 Willmar⊙, 12,869 C 5
55795 Willow River, 331 F 4
56185 Wilmont, 390 C 7
56687 Wilton, 119 C 3
56101 Windom⊙, 3,952 C 7
56592 Winger, 228 B 3
56098 Winnebago, 1,791 D 7
55987 Winona⊙, 26,438 G 6
55395 Winsted, 1,266 D 6
55396 Winthrop, 1,391 D 6
55796 Winton, 193 G 3
56594 Wolverton, 171 B 4
† 55798 Woodbury, 6,184 F 6
56297 Wood Lake, 418 C 6
56186 Woodstock, 217 B 7
56187 Worthington⊙, 9,825 C 7
55797 Wrenshall, 147 F 4
55798 Wright, 132 E 4
55990 Wykoff, 450 F 7
55092 Wyoming, 695 F 5
55397 Young America, 611 E 6
55799 Zim, 608 F 3
55398 Zimmerman, 495 E 5
55991 Zumbro Falls, 203 F 6
55992 Zumbrota, 1,929 F 6

⊙ County seat.
‡ Population of metropolitan area.
† Zip of nearest p.o.
* Multiple zips

Agriculture, Industry and Resources

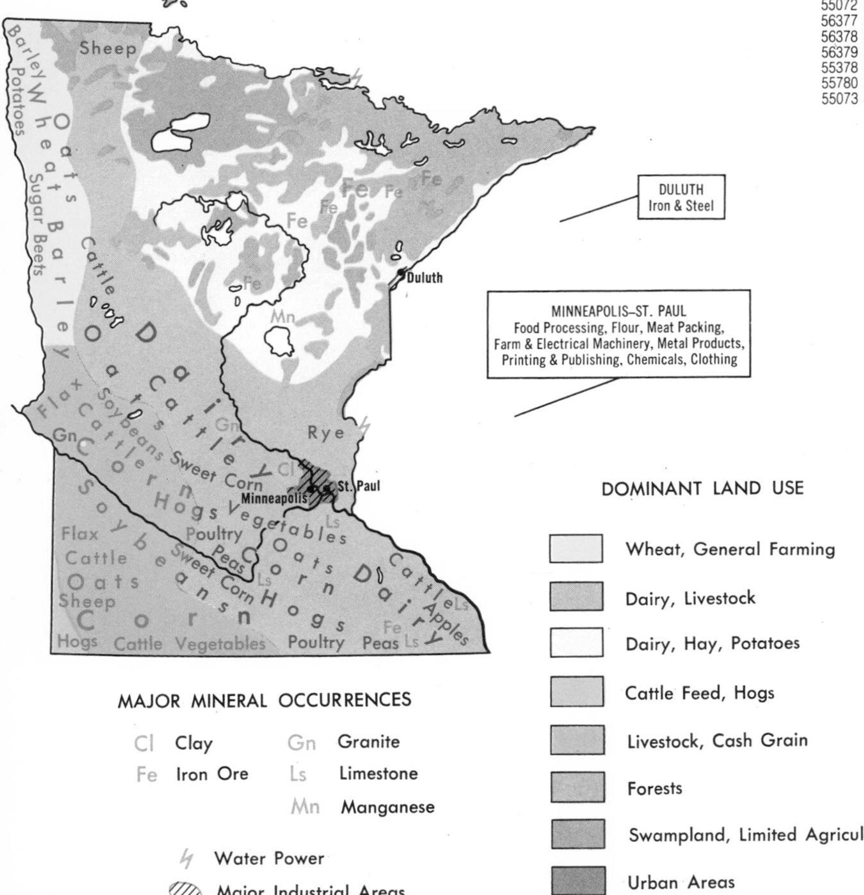

Topography

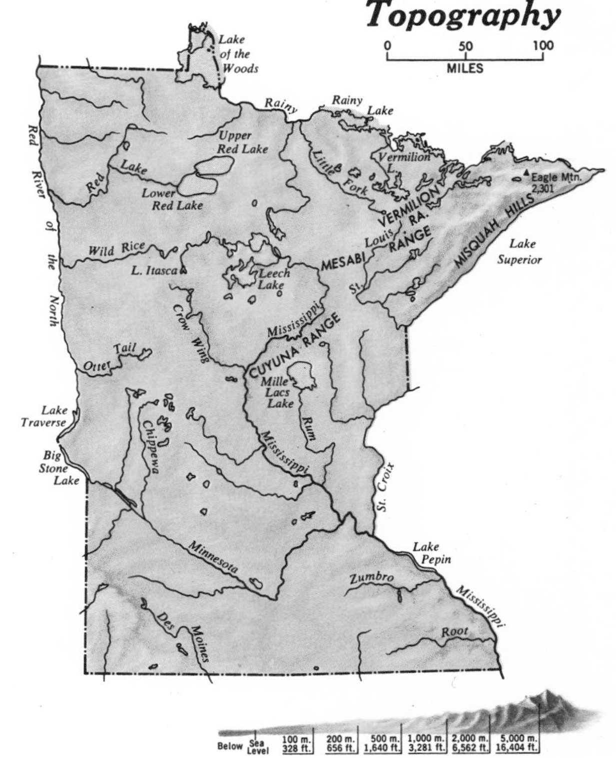

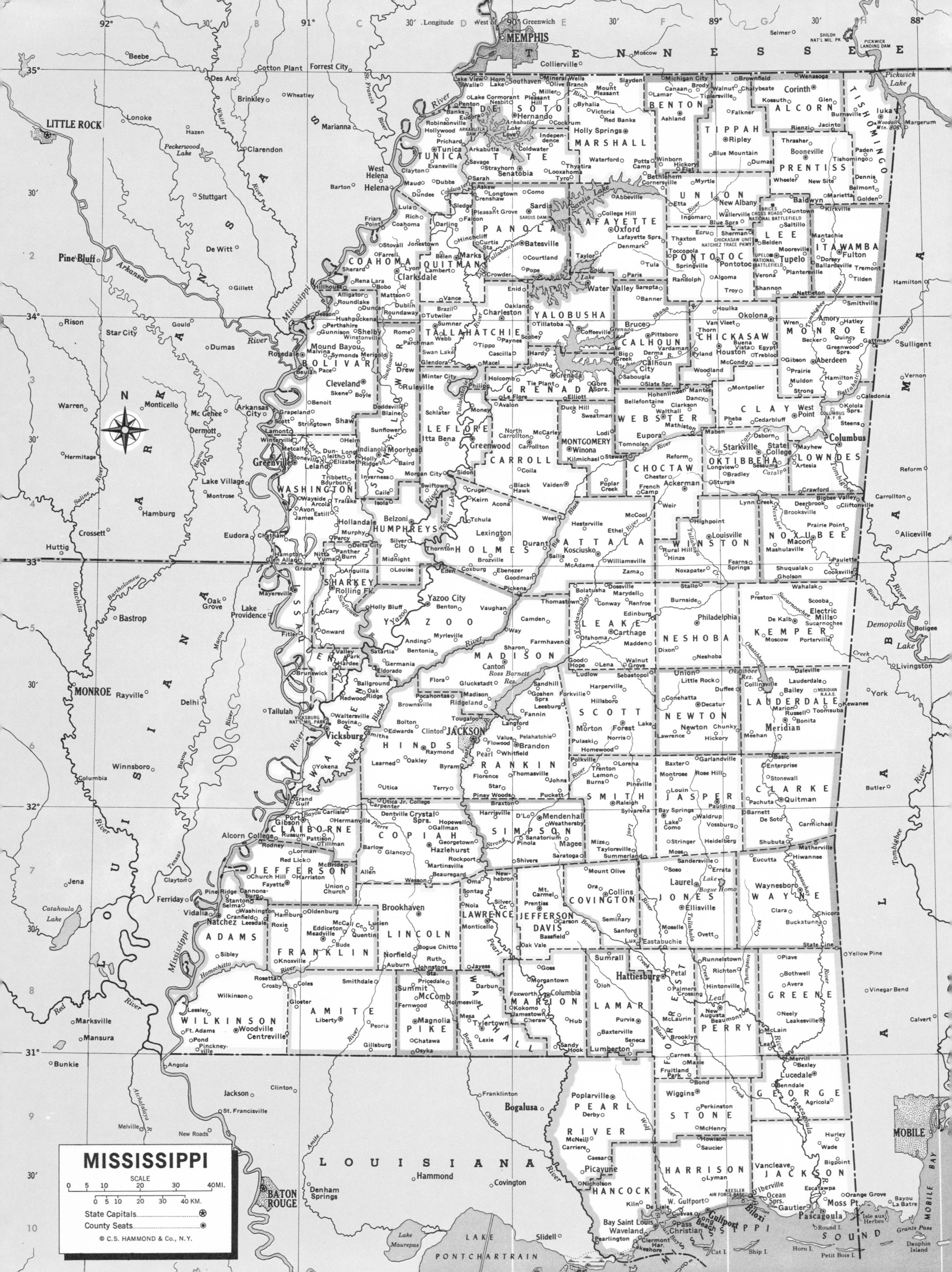

MISSISSIPPI
SCALE
0 5 10 20 30 40 MI.
0 5 10 20 30 40 KM.
State Capitals
County Seats
© C.S. HAMMOND & Co., N.Y.
Longitude West of 90° Greenwich
TENNESSEE
ARKANSAS
LOUISIANA
ALABAMA
MEMPHIS
LITTLE ROCK
Pine Bluff
MONROE
BATON ROUGE
MOBILE
JACKSON
Vicksburg
Natchez
Greenville
Greenwood
Hattiesburg
Meridian
Columbus
Tupelo
Biloxi
Gulfport
Pascagoula
DE SOTO
MARSHALL
BENTON
TIPPAH
ALCORN
TISHOMINGO
TUNICA
TATE
PRENTISS
PANOLA
LAFAYETTE
UNION
COAHOMA
QUITMAN
PONTOTOC
LEE
ITAWAMBA
YALOBUSHA
TALLAHATCHIE
CALHOUN
CHICKASAW
MONROE
BOLIVAR
GRENADA
SUNFLOWER
LEFLORE
CARROLL
MONTGOMERY
WEBSTER
CLAY
OKTIBBEHA
LOWNDES
CHOCTAW
WASHINGTON
HUMPHREYS
HOLMES
ATTALA
WINSTON
NOXUBEE
SHARKEY
YAZOO
ISSAQUENA
MADISON
LEAKE
NESHOBA
KEMPER
WARREN
HINDS
RANKIN
SCOTT
NEWTON
LAUDERDALE
CLAIBORNE
COPIAH
SIMPSON
SMITH
JASPER
CLARKE
JEFFERSON
LINCOLN
LAWRENCE
JEFFERSON DAVIS
COVINGTON
JONES
WAYNE
ADAMS
FRANKLIN
WILKINSON
AMITE
PIKE
WALTHALL
MARION
LAMAR
FORREST
PERRY
GREENE
PEARL RIVER
STONE
GEORGE
HANCOCK
HARRISON
JACKSON
Mississippi River
Pearl River
Tombigbee River
LAKE PONTCHARTRAIN
MISSISSIPPI SOUND
MOBILE BAY

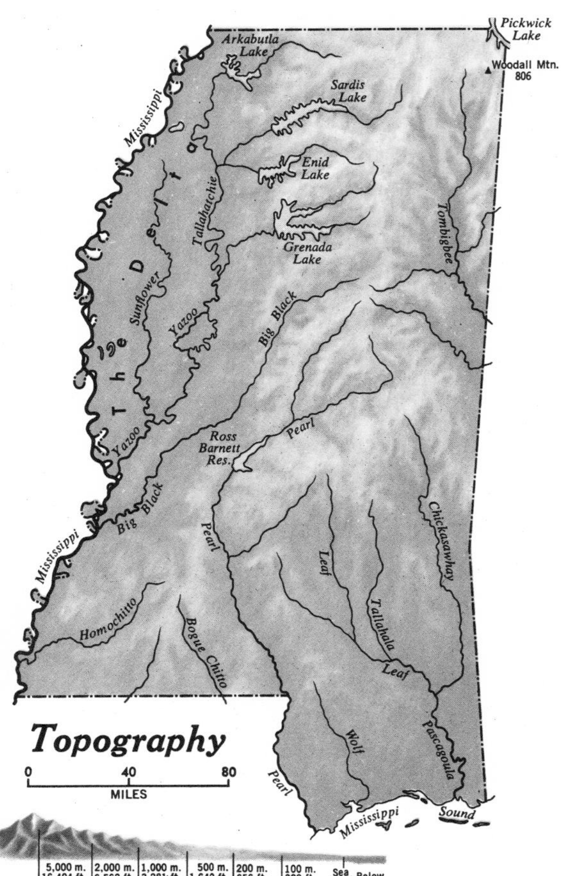

AREA 47,716 sq. mi.
POPULATION 2,216,912
CAPITAL Jackson
LARGEST CITY Jackson
HIGHEST POINT Woodall Mtn. 806 ft.
SETTLED IN 1716
ADMITTED TO UNION December 10, 1817
POPULAR NAME Magnolia State
STATE FLOWER Magnolia
STATE BIRD Mockingbird

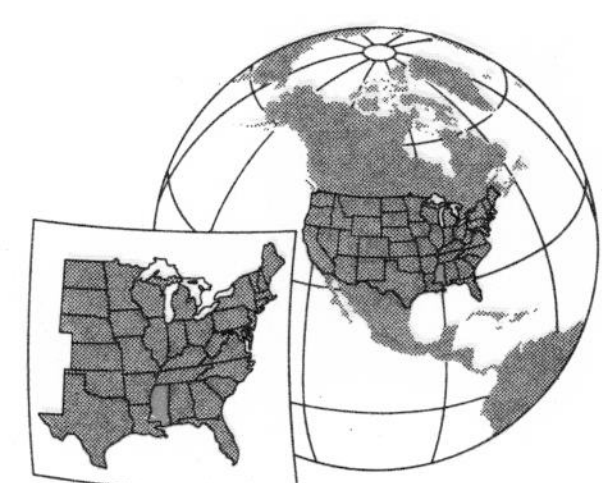

Jack Zehrt—Shostal Associates

Gracious antebellum houses of brick and stucco, shaded by moss-draped oaks, add a sense of permanence to the older section of Biloxi, Mississippi.

COUNTIES

Name/Pop.	Key
Adams, 37,293	B 8
Alcorn, 27,179	G 1
Amite, 13,763	C 8
Attala, 19,570	E 4
Benton, 7,505	F 1
Bolivar, 49,409	C 3
Calhoun, 14,623	F 3
Carroll, 9,397	E 4
Chickasaw, 16,805	G 3
Choctaw, 8,440	F 4
Claiborne, 10,086	C 7
Clarke, 15,049	G 6
Clay, 18,840	G 3
Coahoma, 40,447	C 2
Copiah, 24,749	D 7
Covington, 14,002	E 7
De Soto, 35,885	E 1
Forrest, 57,849	F 8
Franklin, 8,011	C 8
George, 12,459	G 9
Greene, 8,545	G 8
Grenada, 19,854	E 3
Hancock, 17,387	E 10
Harrison, 134,582	F 10
Hinds, 214,973	D 6
Holmes, 23,120	D 4
Humphreys, 14,601	C 4
Issaquena, 2,737	B 5
Itawamba, 16,847	H 2
Jackson, 87,975	G 9
Jasper, 15,994	F 6
Jefferson, 9,295	B 7
Jefferson Davis, 12,936	E 7
Jones, 56,357	F 7
Kemper, 10,233	G 5
Lafayette, 24,181	E 2
Lamar, 15,209	E 8
Lauderdale, 67,087	G 6
Lawrence, 11,137	D 7
Leake, 17,085	E 5
Lee, 46,148	G 2
Leflore, 42,111	D 3
Lincoln, 26,198	D 8
Lowndes, 49,700	H 4
Madison, 29,737	D 5
Marion, 22,871	E 8
Marshall, 24,027	E 1
Monroe, 34,043	H 3
Montgomery, 12,918	E 4
Neshoba, 20,802	F 5
Newton, 18,983	F 6
Noxubee, 14,288	G 4
Oktibbeha, 28,752	G 4
Panola, 26,829	E 2
Pearl River, 27,802	E 9
Perry, 9,065	G 8
Pike, 31,756	D 8
Pontotoc, 17,363	F 2
Prentiss, 20,133	G 1
Quitman, 15,888	D 2
Rankin, 43,933	E 6
Scott, 21,369	E 6
Sharkey, 8,937	C 5
Simpson, 19,947	E 7
Smith, 13,561	E 6
Stone, 8,101	F 9
Sunflower, 37,047	C 3
Tallahatchie, 19,338	D 3
Tate, 18,544	E 1
Tippah, 15,852	G 1
Tishomingo, 14,940	H 1
Tunica, 11,854	D 1
Union, 19,096	F 2
Walthall, 12,500	D 8
Warren, 44,981	C 6
Washington, 70,581	C 4
Wayne, 16,650	G 7
Webster, 10,047	F 3
Wilkinson, 11,099	B 8
Winston, 18,406	F 4
Yalobusha, 11,915	E 2
Yazoo, 27,304	D 5

CITIES and TOWNS

Zip	Name/Pop.	Key
38601	Abbeville, 600	F 2
39730	Aberdeen⊙, 6,157	H 3
39735	Ackerman⊙, 1,502	F 4
† 39095	Acona, 200	D 4
† 39452	Agricola, 200	G 9
39096	Alcorn College, 2,380	B 7
38820	Algoma, 150	G 2
38720	Alligator, 280	C 2
38821	Amory, 7,236	H 3
38721	Anguilla, 612	C 5
38722	Arcola, 517	C 4
38602	Arkabutla, 195	D 1
39736	Artesia, 444	G 4
38603	Ashland⊙, 348	F 1
38604	Askew, 200	D 1
† 39664	Auburn, 500	C 8
38912	Avalon, 275	D 3
† 39456	Avera, 150	G 8
38723	Avon, 400	B 4
39320	Bailey, 320	G 6
38724	Baird, 212	C 4
38824	Baldwyn, 2,366	G 2
† 38801	Ballardsville, 105	H 2
† 38664	Banks, 100	D 1
38913	Banner, 200	F 2
39421	Bassfield, 354	E 8
38606	Batesville⊙, 3,796	E 2
† 39343	Baxter, 225	F 6
† 39455	Baxterville, 100	E 8
39520	Bay Saint Louis⊙, 6,752	F 10
39422	Bay Springs⊙, 1,801	F 7
39423	Beaumont, 1,061	G 8
† 39191	Beauregard, 199	D 7
38825	Becker, 450	G 3
38826	Belden, 241	G 2
38609	Belen, 500	D 2
39737	Bellefontaine, 360	F 3
38827	Belmont, 968	H 1
39038	Belzoni⊙, 3,146	C 4
† 39450	Benndale, 500	G 9
38725	Benoit, 473	C 3
39039	Benton, 500	D 5
39040	Bentonia, 544	D 5
† 38659	Bethlehem, 210	F 1
38726	Beulah, 443	B 3
39453	Bexley, 130	G 9
39738	Bigbee Valley, 370	H 4
38914	Big Creek, 148	F 3
† 39567	Bigpoint, 100	H 9
* 39530	Biloxi, 48,486	G 10
	Biloxi-Gulfport, ‡134,582	G 10
38918	Black Hawk, 100	E 4
38610	Blue Mountain, 677	G 1
38828	Blue Springs, 125	G 2
38728	Bobo, 200	C 2
39629	Bogue Chitto, 658	D 8
39041	Bolton, 787	D 6
39550	Bond, 350	F 9
39321	Bonita, 300	G 6
38829	Booneville⊙, 5,895	G 1
† 39456	Bothwell, 100	G 8
38729	Bourbon, 350	C 4
38730	Boyle, 861	C 3
39042	Brandon⊙, 2,685	E 6
39044	Braxton, 180	D 6
38956	Brazil, 229	D 2
39601	Brookhaven⊙, 10,700	C 7
39425	Brooklyn, 750	F 8
39739	Brooksville, 978	G 4
† 38683	Brownfield, 300	G 1
† 39041	Brownsville, 200	D 6
† 39095	Brozville, 150	D 4
38915	Bruce, 2,033	F 3
† 39180	Brunswick, 90	C 5
39322	Buckatunna, 500	G 7
39630	Bude, 1,146	C 8
† 39153	Burns, 100	E 6
38833	Burnsville, 435	H 1
38611	Byhalia, 702	E 1
† 39205	Byram, 250	D 6
† 38754	Caile, 350	C 4
39740	Caledonia, 245	H 3
38916	Calhoun City, 1,847	F 3
39045	Camden, 248	E 5
38612	Canaan, 200	F 1
† 39120	Cannonsburg, 240	B 7
39046	Canton⊙, 10,503	D 5
39049	Carlisle, 350	C 7
† 39360	Carmichael, 150	G 7
39426	Carriere, 900	E 9
38917	Carrollton⊙, 295	E 4
39427	Carson, 285	E 7
39051	Carthage⊙, 3,031	E 5
39054	Cary, 517	C 5
38920	Cascilla, 150	D 3
39741	Cedarbluff, 180	G 3
39631	Centreville, 1,819	B 8
38684	Chalybeate, 350	G 1
38921	Charleston⊙, 2,821	D 2
39632	Chatawa, 300	D 8
† 39483	Cheraw, 100	E 8
39323	Chunky, 280	G 6
39324	Clara, 400	G 7
38614	Clarksdale⊙, 21,673	D 2
† 39752	Clarkson, 100	F 3
39551	Clermont Harbor, 200	F 10
38732	Cleveland⊙, 13,327	C 3
39742	Cliftonville, 280	H 4
39056	Clinton, 7,246	D 6
38617	Coahoma, 350	C 2
38922	Coffeeville⊙, 1,024	E 3
38618	Coldwater, 1,450	E 1
39639	Coles, 195	C 8
† 38655	College Hill, 175	E 2
39428	Collins⊙, 1,934	E 7
39325	Collinsville, 700	G 6
39429	Columbia⊙, 7,587	E 8
39701	Columbus⊙, 25,795	H 3
38619	Como, 1,003	E 1
† 39051	Conway, 125	E 5
38834	Corinth⊙, 11,581	G 1
† 38659	Cornersville, 235	F 1
38620	Courtland, 316	E 2
† 39095	Coxburg, 300	D 5
† 39120	Cranfield, 100	B 7
39743	Crawford, 391	G 4
38621	Crenshaw, 1,271	D 2
39633	Crosby, 491	B 8
38622	Crowder, 815	D 2
38924	Cruger, 415	D 4
39059	Crystal Springs, 4,180	D 7
† 39571	Cuevas, 200	F 10
† 38606	Curtis Station, 200	D 2
† 39751	Dancy, 116	F 3
† 39643	Darbun, 100	D 8
38623	Darling, 250	D 2
39327	Decatur⊙, 1,311	F 6
39328	De Kalb⊙, 1,072	G 5
† 39571	De Lisle, 450	F 10
39061	Delta City, 300	C 4
38838	Dennis, 175	H 1
† 39470	Derby, 189	E 9
38839	Derma, 660	F 3
39360	De Soto, 150	G 7
39532	D'Iberville, 7,288	G 10
† 39350	Dixon, 125	F 5
39062	D'Lo, 485	E 7
38736	Doddsville, 276	C 3
38840	Dorsey, 100	H 2
38737	Drew, 2,574	C 3
38739	Dublin, 385	C 2
38925	Duck Hill, 809	E 3
† 39337	Duffee, 100	G 6
38625	Dumas, 200	G 1
38740	Duncan, 599	C 2
† 38756	Dunleith, 140	C 4
39063	Durant, 2,752	E 4
39436	Eastabuchie, 200	F 8
39064	Ebenezer, 150	D 5
38841	Ecru, 417	F 2
39634	Eddiceton, 175	C 8
39065	Eden, 152	D 5
† 39051	Edinburg, 200	F 5
39066	Edwards, 1,236	C 6
38842	Egypt, 100	G 3
39329	Electric Mills, 200	G 5
38742	Elizabeth, 540	C 4
38926	Elliott, 200	E 3
39437	Ellisville⊙, 4,643	F 7
39330	Enterprise, 458	G 6
39552	Escatawpa, 1,579	G 10
† 38748	Estill, 100	C 4
39067	Ethel, 560	F 4
38627	Etta, 100	F 2
† 38632	Eudora, 200	D 1
39744	Eupora, 1,792	F 3
38628	Falcon, 230	D 2
38629	Falkner, 500	G 1
† 39042	Fannin, 250	E 6
38630	Farrell, 400	C 2
39069	Fayette⊙, 1,725	B 7
39635	Fernwood, 600	D 8
39070	Fitler, 800	B 5
39071	Flora, 987	D 5
39073	Florence, 404	D 6
† 39201	Flowood, 352	D 6
39074	Forest⊙, 4,085	F 6
39076	Forkville, 180	E 6
39636	Fort Adams, 129	B 8
39483	Foxworth, 950	E 8
39745	French Camp, 174	F 4
38631	Friars Point, 1,177	C 2
38843	Fulton⊙, 2,899	H 2
† 39345	Garlandville, 150	F 6
38844	Gattman, 175	H 3
39553	Gautier, 2,087	G 10
39078	Georgetown, 339	D 7
† 39083	Glancy, 120	C 7
38846	Glen, 250	H 1
38744	Glen Allan, 400	B 4
38928	Glendora, 201	D 3
39638	Gloster, 1,401	B 8
† 39110	Gluckstadt, 150	D 5
38847	Golden, 115	H 2
† 39094	Good Hope, 125	E 5
39079	Goodman, 1,194	E 5
38929	Gore Springs, 120	E 3
† 39042	Goshen Springs, 100	E 6
† 39429	Goss, 100	E 8
38745	Grace, 325	C 5
† 38725	Grapeland, 200	B 3
38701	Greenville⊙, 39,648	B 4
38930	Greenwood⊙, 22,400	D 4
38848	Greenwood Springs, 170	H 3
38901	Grenada⊙, 9,944	E 3
39501	Gulfport⊙, 40,791	F 10
38746	Gunnison, 545	C 3
38849	Guntown, 304	G 2
39746	Hamilton, 350	H 3
† 38744	Hampton, 200	B 4
† 39177	Hardee, 100	C 5
39080	Harperville, 260	E 6
39081	Harriston, 500	C 7
39082	Harrisville, 500	D 7
† 38821	Hatley, 500	H 3
39401	Hattiesburg⊙, 38,277	F 8
39083	Hazlehurst⊙, 4,577	D 7
39439	Heidelberg, 1,112	F 7
39086	Hermanville, 500	C 7
38632	Hernando⊙, 2,499	E 1
† 39192	Hesterville, 100	E 4
39332	Hickory, 570	F 6
38633	Hickory Flat, 354	F 1
39087	Hillsboro, 350	E 6
† 38646	Hinchcliff, 125	D 2
† 39462	Hintonville, 100	F 8
† 39108	Hinze, 140	F 4
39333	Hiwannee, 250	G 7
† 39751	Hohenlinden, 96	F 3
38748	Hollandale, 3,260	C 4
39088	Holly Bluff, 250	C 5
38749	Holly Ridge, 375	C 4
38635	Holly Springs⊙, 5,728	E 1
† 38676	Hollywood, 125	D 1
† 39648	Holmesville, 200	D 8
† 39059	Hopewell, 300	D 7
38637	Horn Lake, 850	D 1
38850	Houlka, 646	G 2
38851	Houston⊙, 2,720	G 3
39555	Hurley, 500	H 9
† 38774	Hushpuckena, 100	C 2
38638	Independence, 150	E 1
38751	Indianola⊙, 8,947	C 4
† 38652	Ingomar, 150	F 2
38753	Inverness, 1,119	C 4
38754	Isola, 458	C 4
38941	Itta Bena, 2,489	D 4
38852	Iuka⊙, 2,389	H 1
† 38865	Jacinto, 150	H 1
* 39201	Jackson (cap.)⊙, 153,968	D 6
	Jackson, ‡258,906	D 6
† 38748	James, 100	B 4
39641	Jayess, 150	D 8
† 39042	Johns, 90	E 6
38639	Jonestown, 1,110	D 2
39334	Kewanee, 100	H 6
39747	Kilmichael, 543	E 4
39556	Kiln, 750	F 10
† 38856	Kirkville, 200	H 2
† 39661	Knoxville, 100	B 8
39643	Kokomo, 150	E 8
† 39740	Kolola Springs, 150	H 3
39090	Kosciusko⊙, 7,266	E 4
38834	Kossuth, 227	G 1
39092	Lake, 441	F 6
† 39422	Lake Como, 150	F 7
38641	Lake Cormorant, 300	D 1
39558	Lakeshore, 550	F 10
† 38680	Lake View, 125	D 1
38642	Lamar, 135	F 1
38643	Lambert, 1,511	D 2
38755	Lamont, 450	B 3
† 39042	Langford, 100	E 6
39335	Lauderdale, 600	G 5
39440	Laurel⊙, 24,145	F 7
39336	Lawrence, 200	F 6
39450	Leaf, 350	G 8
39451	Leakesville⊙, 1,090	G 8
39093	Learned, 116	C 6
38942	Le Flore, 99	D 3
38756	Leland, 6,000	C 4
† 39074	Lemon, 90	E 6
39094	Lena, 233	E 5
39644	Lessley, 100	B 8
† 39667	Lexie, 270	D 8
39095	Lexington⊙, 2,756	D 4
39645	Liberty⊙, 612	C 8
39337	Little Rock, 130	F 5
† 38828	Long, 110	C 4
39560	Long Beach, 6,170	F 10
† 38665	Longtown, 150	D 1
39749	Longview, 800	G 4
† 38668	Looxahoma, 200	E 1
† 39153	Lorena, 90	F 6
39096	Lorman, 500	B 7
39338	Louin, 382	F 6
39097	Louise, 444	C 5
39339	Louisville⊙, 6,626	G 4
39452	Lucedale⊙, 2,083	G 9
39098	Ludlow, 300	E 5
38644	Lula, 445	C 2
39455	Lumberton, 2,084	E 8
† 39501	Lyman, 500	F 10
38645	Lyon, 383	D 2
39750	Maben, 862	F 3
39341	Macon⊙, 2,612	G 4
39109	Madden, 450	F 5
39110	Madison, 853	D 6
39111	Magee, 2,973	E 7
39652	Magnolia⊙, 1,913	D 8

(continued on following page)

(continued)

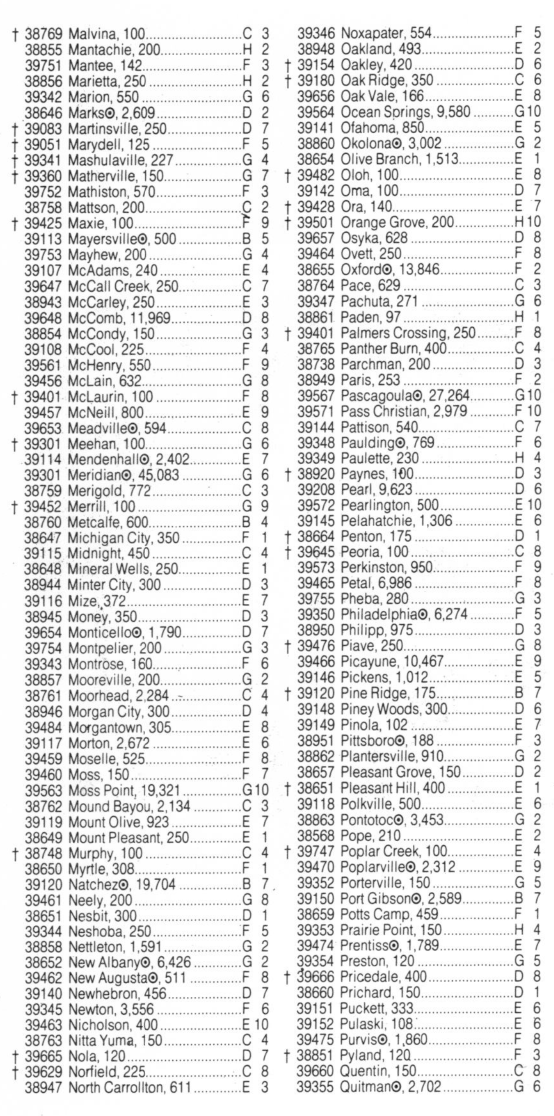

† 38769 Malvina, 100 .... C 3
38855 Mantachie, 200 .... H 2
39751 Mantee, 142 .... F 3
38856 Marietta, 250 .... H 2
39342 Marion, 550 .... G 6
38646 Marks⊙, 2,609 .... D 2
† 39083 Martinsville, 250 .... D 7
† 39051 Marydell, 125 .... F 5
† 39341 Mashulaville, 227 .... G 4
† 39360 Matherville, 150 .... G 7
39752 Mathiston, 570 .... F 3
38758 Mattson, 200 .... C 2
† 39425 Maxie, 100 .... F 9
39113 Mayersville⊙, 500 .... B 5
39753 Mayhew, 200 .... G 4
39107 McAdams, 240 .... E 4
39647 McCall Creek, 250 .... C 7
38943 McCarley, 250 .... E 3
39648 McComb, 11,969 .... D 8
38854 McCondy, 150 .... G 3
39108 McCool, 225 .... F 4
39561 McHenry, 550 .... F 9
39456 McLain, 632 .... G 8
† 39401 McLaurin, 100 .... F 8
39457 McNeill, 800 .... E 9
39653 Meadville⊙, 594 .... C 8
† 39301 Meehan, 100 .... G 6
39114 Mendenhall⊙, 2,402 .... E 7
39301 Meridian⊙, 45,083 .... G 6
38759 Merigold, 772 .... C 3
† 39452 Merrill, 100 .... G 9
38760 Metcalfe, 600 .... B 4
38647 Michigan City, 350 .... F 1
39115 Midnight, 450 .... C 4
38648 Mineral Wells, 250 .... E 1
38944 Minter City, 300 .... D 3
39116 Mize, 372 .... E 7
38945 Money, 350 .... D 3
39654 Monticello⊙, 1,790 .... D 7
39754 Montpelier, 200 .... G 3
39343 Montrose, 160 .... F 6
38857 Mooreville, 200 .... G 2
38761 Moorhead, 2,284 .... C 4
38946 Morgan City, 300 .... D 4
39484 Morgantown, 305 .... E 8
39117 Morton, 2,672 .... E 6
39459 Moselle, 525 .... F 8
39460 Moss, 150 .... F 7
39563 Moss Point, 19,321 .... G 10
38762 Mound Bayou, 2,134 .... C 3
39119 Mount Olive, 923 .... E 7
38649 Mount Pleasant, 250 .... E 1
† 38748 Murphy, 100 .... C 4
38650 Myrtle, 308 .... F 1
39120 Natchez⊙, 19,704 .... B 7
39461 Neely, 200 .... G 8
38651 Nesbit, 300 .... D 1
39344 Neshoba, 250 .... F 5
38858 Nettleton, 1,591 .... G 2
38652 New Albany⊙, 6,426 .... G 2
39462 New Augusta⊙, 511 .... F 8
39140 Newhebron, 456 .... D 7
39345 Newton, 3,556 .... F 6
39463 Nicholson, 400 .... E 10
38763 Nitta Yuma, 150 .... C 4
† 39665 Nola, 120 .... D 7
† 39629 Norfield, 225 .... C 8
38947 North Carrollton, 611 .... E 3
39346 Noxapater, 554 .... F 5
38948 Oakland, 493 .... E 2
† 39154 Oakley, 420 .... D 6
† 39180 Oak Ridge, 350 .... C 6
39656 Oak Vale, 166 .... E 8
39564 Ocean Springs, 9,580 .... G 10
39141 Ofahoma, 850 .... E 5
38860 Okolona⊙, 3,002 .... G 2
38654 Olive Branch, 1,513 .... E 1
† 39482 Oloh, 100 .... E 8
39142 Oma, 100 .... D 7
† 39428 Ora, 140 .... E 7
† 39501 Orange Grove, 200 .... H 10
39657 Osyka, 628 .... D 8
39464 Ovett, 250 .... F 8
38655 Oxford⊙, 13,846 .... F 2
38764 Pace, 629 .... C 3
39347 Pachuta, 271 .... G 6
38861 Paden, 97 .... H 1
† 39401 Palmers Crossing, 250 .... F 8
38765 Panther Burn, 400 .... C 4
38738 Parchman, 200 .... D 3
38949 Paris, 253 .... F 2
39567 Pascagoula⊙, 27,264 .... G 10
39571 Pass Christian, 2,979 .... F 10
39144 Pattison, 540 .... C 7
39348 Paulding⊙, 769 .... F 6
39349 Paulette, 230 .... H 4
† 38920 Paynes, 100 .... D 3
39208 Pearl, 9,623 .... D 6
39572 Pearlington, 500 .... E 10
39145 Pelahatchie, 1,306 .... E 6
† 38664 Penton, 175 .... D 1
† 39645 Peoria, 100 .... C 8
39573 Perkinston, 950 .... F 9
39465 Petal, 6,986 .... F 8
39755 Pheba, 280 .... G 3
39350 Philadelphia⊙, 6,274 .... F 5
38950 Philipp, 975 .... D 3
† 39476 Piave, 250 .... G 8
39466 Picayune, 10,467 .... E 9
39146 Pickens, 1,012 .... E 5
† 39120 Pine Ridge, 175 .... B 7
39148 Piney Woods, 300 .... D 6
39149 Pinola, 102 .... E 7
38951 Pittsboro⊙, 188 .... F 3
38862 Plantersville, 910 .... G 2
38657 Pleasant Grove, 150 .... D 2
† 38651 Pleasant Hill, 400 .... E 1
39118 Polkville, 500 .... E 6
38863 Pontotoc⊙, 3,453 .... G 2
38568 Pope, 210 .... E 2
† 39747 Poplar Creek, 100 .... E 4
39470 Poplarville⊙, 2,312 .... E 9
39352 Porterville, 150 .... G 5
39150 Port Gibson⊙, 2,589 .... B 7
38659 Potts Camp, 459 .... F 1
39353 Prairie Point, 150 .... H 4
39474 Prentiss⊙, 1,789 .... E 7
39354 Preston, 120 .... G 5
† 39666 Pricedale, 400 .... D 8
38660 Prichard, 150 .... D 1
39151 Puckett, 333 .... E 6
39152 Pulaski, 108 .... E 6
39475 Purvis⊙, 1,860 .... F 8
† 38851 Pyland, 120 .... F 3
39660 Quentin, 150 .... C 8
39355 Quitman⊙, 2,702 .... G 6

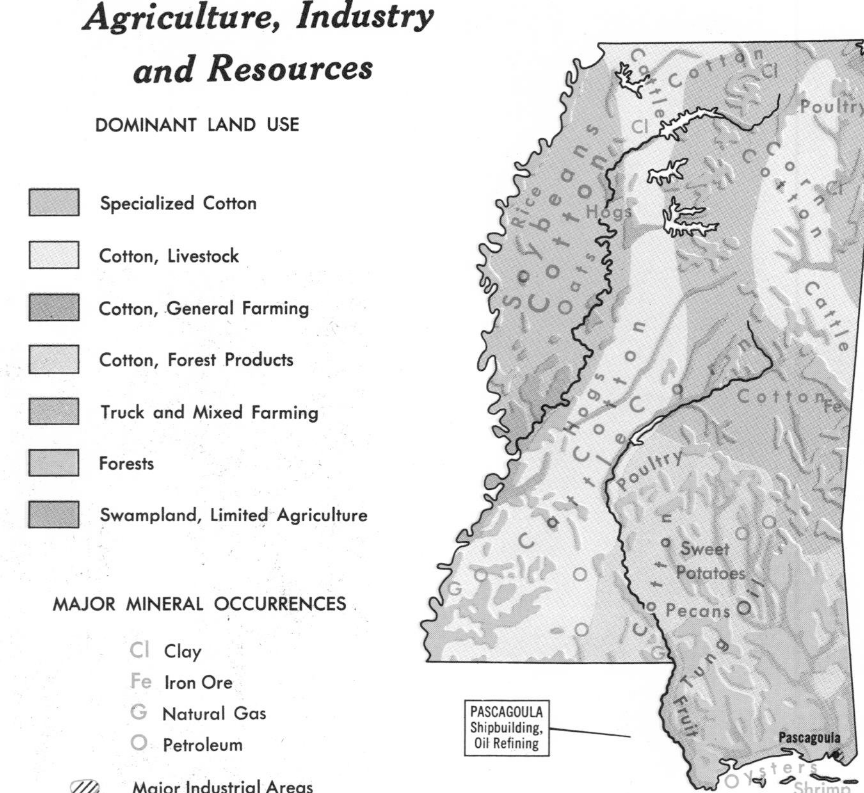

39153 Raleigh⊙, 1,018 .... F 6
38864 Randolph, 205 .... F 2
39154 Raymond⊙, 1,620 .... D 6
38661 Red Banks, 350 .... F 1
† 39096 Red Lick, 250 .... B 7
39156 Redwood, 400 .... C 6
39757 Reform, 150 .... F 4
38767 Rena Lara, 400 .... C 2
† 39051 Renfroe, 100 .... F 5
39476 Richton, 1,110 .... G 8
39157 Ridgeland, 1,650 .... D 6
38865 Rienzi, 363 .... G 1
38663 Ripley⊙, 3,482 .... G 1
38664 Robinsonville, 285 .... D 1
† 39083 Rockport, 100 .... D 7
† 39096 Rodney, 200 .... B 7
39159 Rolling Fork⊙, 2,034 .... C 5
38768 Rome, 171 .... C 3
38769 Rosedale⊙, 2,599 .... B 3
39356 Rose Hill, 300 .... F 6
† 38614 Roundaway, 175 .... C 2
† 38740 Roundlake, 105 .... C 2
39661 Roxie, 662 .... B 8
38771 Ruleville, 2,351 .... D 3
† 39401 Runnelstown, 200 .... F 8
† 39108 Rural Hill, 125 .... F 4
39357 Russell, 300 .... G 6
39662 Ruth, 150 .... D 8
† 38955 Sabougla, 100 .... F 3
39160 Sallis, 213 .... E 4
38866 Saltillo, 836 .... G 2
39112 Sanatorium, 400 .... E 7
39477 Sandersville, 694 .... F 7
39161 Sandhill, 392 .... E 5
39478 Sandy Hook, 108 .... E 8
39479 Sanford, 150 .... F 8
38665 Sarah, 300 .... D 1
38666 Sardis⊙, 2,391 .... E 2
38867 Sarepta, 650 .... F 2
39574 Saucier, 100 .... F 9
38667 Savage, 100 .... D 1
38952 Schlater, 398 .... D 3
38953 Scobey, 100 .... E 3
39358 Scooba, 626 .... G 5
38772 Scott, 500 .... B 3
39359 Sebastopol, 268 .... F 5
39479 Seminary, 269 .... E 7
38668 Senatobia⊙, 4,247 .... E 1
39758 Sessums, 100 .... G 4
38868 Shannon, 575 .... G 2
38773 Shaw, 2,513 .... C 3
38774 Shelby, 2,645 .... C 3
38669 Sherard, 160 .... C 2
38869 Sherman, 468 .... G 2
39164 Shivers, 100 .... E 7
39360 Shubuta, 602 .... G 7
39361 Shuqualak, 591 .... G 5
39165 Sibley, 250 .... B 8
38954 Sidon, 348 .... D 4
39166 Silver City, 370 .... C 4
39663 Silver Creek, 257 .... D 7
38775 Skene, 300 .... C 3
38955 Slate Spring, 105 .... F 3
† 38642 Slayden, 310 .... F 1
38670 Sledge, 516 .... D 2
39664 Smithdale, 200 .... C 8
38870 Smithville, 552 .... H 2
39665 Sontag, 200 .... D 7
39480 Soso, 230 .... F 7
38671 Southaven, 8,931 .... E 1
† 38863 Springville, 100 .... F 2
† 39350 Stallo, 100 .... F 5
39167 Star, 575 .... D 6
39759 Starkville⊙, 11,369 .... G 4
39762 State College, 4,595 .... G 4
39362 State Line, 598 .... G 8
39766 Steens, 125 .... H 3
39767 Stewart, 150 .... F 4
38776 Stoneville, 700 .... C 4
39363 Stonewall, 1,161 .... G 6
38672 Stovall, 260 .... C 2
† 38665 Strayhorn, 800 .... D 1
39481 Stringer, 340 .... F 7
38777 Stringtown, 300 .... C 3
39769 Sturgis, 321 .... G 4
† 39168 Summerland, 150 .... F 7
39666 Summit, 1,640 .... D 8
38957 Sumner⊙, 533 .... D 3
39482 Sumrall, 955 .... E 8
38778 Sunflower, 983 .... C 3
38958 Swan Lake, 250 .... D 3
38959 Swiftown, 400 .... D 4
39153 Sylvarena, 115 .... F 6
† 38769 Symonds, 200 .... C 3
38673 Taylor, 92 .... E 2
39168 Taylorsville, 1,299 .... F 7
39169 Tchula, 1,729 .... D 4
39170 Terry, 546 .... D 6
38871 Thaxton, 250 .... F 2
39171 Thomastown, 350 .... E 5
38872 Thorn, 125 .... F 3
39172 Thornton, 120 .... D 4
† 38829 Thrasher, 800 .... G 1
† 38668 Thyatira, 100 .... E 1
38960 Tie Plant, 950 .... E 3
† 38843 Tilden, 250 .... H 2
38961 Tillatoba, 102 .... E 3
38674 Tiplersville, 120 .... G 1
38962 Tippo, 200 .... D 3
38873 Tishomingo, 410 .... H 1
38874 Toccopola, 175 .... F 2
39770 Tomnolen, 225 .... F 4
39364 Toomsuba, 500 .... G 6
39174 Tougaloo, 1,720 .... D 6
38757 Tralake, 200 .... C 4
38875 Trebloc, 750 .... G 3
38876 Tremont, 250 .... H 2
38779 Tribbett, 200 .... C 4
† 38863 Troy, 150 .... G 2
38675 Tula, 100 .... F 2
38676 Tunica⊙, 1,685 .... D 1
38801 Tupelo⊙, 20,471 .... G 2
38963 Tutwiler, 1,103 .... D 2
39667 Tylertown⊙, 1,736 .... D 8
39365 Union, 1,856 .... F 5
39668 Union Church, 194 .... C 7
39175 Utica, 1,019 .... C 6
39175 Utica Junior College, 700 .... C 6
39176 Vaiden⊙, 716 .... E 4
39177 Valley Park, 350 .... C 5
39178 Value, 327 .... D 6
38964 Vance, 500 .... D 2
† 39564 Vancleave, 505 .... G 9
† 38851 Van Vleet, 300 .... G 3
38878 Vardaman, 777 .... F 3
38879 Verona, 1,877 .... G 2
39180 Vicksburg⊙, 25,478 .... C 6
38679 Victoria, 400 .... E 1
39366 Vossburg, 250 .... F 7
39575 Wade, 800 .... G 9
† 39422 Waldrup, 125 .... F 7
38680 Walls, 850 .... D 1
38683 Walnut, 458 .... G 1
39189 Walnut Grove, 398 .... F 5
† 39180 Waltersville, 150 .... C 6
39771 Walthall⊙, 161 .... F 3
39190 Washington, 250 .... B 7
38685 Waterford, 375 .... E 1
38965 Water Valley⊙, 3,285 .... E 2
39576 Waveland, 3,108 .... F 10
39367 Waynesboro⊙, 4,368 .... G 7
38780 Wayside, 250 .... C 4
38966 Webb, 751 .... D 3
39772 Weir, 573 .... F 4
38886 Wenasoga, 125 .... G 1
39191 Wesson, 1,253 .... D 7
39192 West, 305 .... E 4
† 39501 West-Gulfport, 6,996 .... F 10
39773 West Point⊙, 8,714 .... G 3
38880 Wheeler, 600 .... G 1
39193 Whitfield, 6,200 .... E 6
39577 Wiggins⊙, 2,995 .... F 9
† 39090 Williamsville, 250 .... F 4
† 38659 Winborn, 122 .... F 1
38967 Winona⊙, 5,521 .... E 4
38781 Winstonville, 536 .... C 3
38782 Winterville, 500 .... B 4
39776 Woodland, 130 .... F 3
39669 Woodville⊙, 1,734 .... B 8
† 39730 Wren, 150 .... G 3
39194 Yazoo City⊙, 10,796 .... D 5
† 39090 Zama, 125 .... F 5

⊙ County seat.
‡ Population of metropolitan area.
† Zip of nearest p.o.
* Multiple zips

COUNTIES

County	Key
Adair, 22,472	G 2
Andrew, 11,913	C 3
Atchison, 9,240	B 2
Audrain, 25,362	J 4
Barry, 19,597	E 9
Barton, 10,431	D 7
Bates, 15,468	D 6
Benton, 9,695	F 6
Bollinger, 8,820	M 8
Boone, 80,911	H 4
Buchanan, 86,915	C 3
Butler, 33,529	M 9
Caldwell, 8,351	E 3
Callaway, 25,850	J 5
Camden, 13,315	G 6
Cape Girardeau, 49,350	N 8
Carroll, 12,565	F 4
Carter, 3,878	L 9
Cass, 39,448	D 5
Cedar, 9,424	E 7
Chariton, 11,084	F 3
Christian, 15,124	F 9
Clark, 8,260	J 2
Clay, 123,322	D 4
Clinton, 12,462	D 3
Cole, 46,228	H 6
Cooper, 14,732	G 5
Crawford, 14,828	K 7
Dade, 6,850	E 8
Dallas, 10,054	F 7
Daviess, 8,420	E 3
De Kalb, 7,305	D 3
Dent, 11,457	J 7
Douglas, 9,268	G 9
Dunklin, 33,742	M10
Franklin, 55,116	K 6
Gasconade, 11,878	J 6
Gentry, 8,060	D 2
Greene, 152,929	F 8
Grundy, 11,819	E 2
Harrison, 10,257	E 2
Henry, 18,451	E 6
Hickory, 4,481	F 7
Holt, 6,654	B 2
Howard, 10,561	G 4
Howell, 23,521	J 9
Iron, 9,529	L 7
Jackson, 654,558	D 5
Jasper, 79,852	D 8
Jefferson, 105,248	L 6
Johnson, 34,172	E 5
Knox, 5,692	H 2
Laclede, 19,944	G 7
Lafayette, 26,626	E 4
Lawrence, 24,585	E 8
Lewis, 10,993	J 2
Lincoln, 18,041	L 4
Linn, 15,125	F 3
Livingston, 15,368	E 3
Macon, 15,432	G 3
Madison, 8,641	M 8
Maries, 6,851	J 6
Marion, 28,121	J 3
McDonald, 12,357	D 9
Mercer, 4,910	E 2
Miller, 15,026	H 6
Mississippi, 16,647	O 9
Moniteau, 10,742	G 5
Monroe, 9,542	H 3
Montgomery, 11,000	K 5
Morgan, 10,068	G 6
New Madrid, 23,420	N 9
Newton, 32,901	D 9
Nodaway, 22,467	C 2
Oregon, 9,180	K 9
Osage, 10,994	J 6
Ozark, 6,226	H 9
Pemiscot, 26,373	N 10
Perry, 14,393	N 7
Pettis, 34,137	F 5
Phelps, 29,481	J 7
Pike, 16,928	K 4
Platte, 32,081	C 4
Polk, 15,415	F 7
Pulaski, 53,781	H 7
Putnam, 5,916	F 2
Ralls, 7,764	J 3
Randolph, 22,434	G 3
Ray, 17,599	E 4
Reynolds, 6,106	L 8
Ripley, 9,803	L 9
Saint Charles, 92,954	L 5
Saint Clair, 7,667	E 6
Sainte Genevieve, 12,867	M 7
Saint Francois, 36,818	M 7
Saint Louis, 951,353	M 5
Saint Louis (city county), 622,236	M 5
Saline, 24,633	F 4
Schuyler, 4,665	G 2
Scotland, 5,499	H 2
Scott, 33,250	N 8
Shannon, 7,196	K 8
Shelby, 7,906	H 3
Stoddard, 25,771	N 9
Stone, 9,921	F 9
Sullivan, 7,572	F 2
Taney, 13,023	F 9
Texas, 18,320	J 8
Vernon, 19,065	D 7
Warren, 9,699	K 5
Washington, 15,086	L 7
Wayne, 8,546	L 8
Webster, 15,562	G 8
Worth, 3,359	D 2
Wright, 13,667	H 8

CITIES and TOWNS

Zip	Name/Pop.	Key
64720	Adrian, 1,259	D 6
63730	Advance, 903	N 8
63123	Affton, 24,067	P 3
† 64836	Airport Drive, 300	C 8
64830	Alba, 365	D 8
64402	Albany⊙, 1,804	D 2
63430	Alexandria, 453	K 2
63001	Allenton, 800	N 3
64001	Alma, 380	E 4
64620	Altamont, 225	D 3
63732	Altenburg, 277	O 7
65606	Alton⊙, 715	K 9
64421	Amazonia, 326	C 3
64722	Amoret, 219	C 6
64831	Anderson, 1,065	D 9
63620	Annapolis, 330	L 8
63820	Anniston, 515	O 9
64724	Appleton City, 1,058	D 6
63821	Arbyrd, 575	M10
63621	Arcadia, 627	L 7
64725	Archie, 525	D 5
65001	Argyle, 262	J 6
65230	Armstrong, 354	G 4
63010	Arnold, 11,994	P 4
65604	Ash Grove, 934	E 8
65010	Ashland, 769	H 5
63530	Atlanta, 377	H 3
63332	Augusta, 259	M 3
65605	Aurora, 5,359	E 9
65231	Auxvasse, 808	J 4
65608	Ava⊙, 2,504	G 9
64010	Avondale, 748	P 5
63011	Ballwin, 10,656	O 3
63531	Baring, 206	H 2
64423	Barnard, 206	C 2
64011	Bates City, 229	E 5
† 65619	Battlefield, 291	F 8
63622	Belgrade, 349	L 7
63735	Bell City, 424	N 8
65013	Belle, 1,133	J 6
† 63101	Bellefontaine Neighbors, 13,987	R 2
63623	Belleview, 225	L 7
63333	Bellflower, 360	K 4
64012	Belton, 9,783	C 5
63736	Benton⊙, 640	O 8
63014	Berger, 226	K 5
63134	Berkeley, 19,743	P 2
63822	Bernie, 1,641	M 9
63823	Bertrand, 604	O 9
64424	Bethany⊙, 2,914	E 2
63532	Bevier, 806	G 3
65610	Billings, 760	F 8
65438	Birch Tree, 573	K 9
† 64068	Birmingham, 266	P 5
63624	Bismarck, 1,387	L 7
65321	Blackburn, 294	F 4
† 63031	Black Jack, 3,500	P 2
65322	Blackwater, 249	G 5
65014	Bland, 621	J 6
63824	Blodgett, 220	O 8
63825	Bloomfield⊙, 1,584	M 9
63627	Bloomsdale, 411	M 6
64015	Blue Springs, 6,779	R 6
† 64101	Blue Summit, 1,283	R 5
64426	Blythedale, 213	E 2
64622	Bogard, 294	E 4
65612	Bois D'Arc, 250	F 8
64427	Bolckow, 225	C 2
65613	Bolivar⊙, 4,769	F 7
63628	Bonne Terre, 3,622	L 7
65016	Bonnots Mill, 210	J 5
65233	Boonville⊙, 7,514	G 5
64723	Bosworth, 386	F 4
65441	Bourbon, 955	K 6
63334	Bowling Green⊙, 2,936	K 4
63826	Braggadocio, 285	N10
63827	Bragg City, 210	N10
65616	Branson, 2,175	F 9
65533	Brashear, 316	H 2
64624	Braymer, 919	E 3
64625	Breckenridge, 598	E 3
† 63101	Breckenridge Hills, 7,011	O 2
63144	Brentwood, 11,248	P 3
63044	Bridgeton, 19,992	O 2
64728	Bronaugh, 203	C 7
64628	Brookfield, 5,491	F 3
64630	Browning, 412	F 2
65236	Brunswick, 1,870	F 4
64631	Bucklin, 654	G 3
64016	Buckner, 1,695	R 5
65622	Buffalo⊙, 1,915	F 7
65237	Bunceton, 437	G 5
63629	Bunker, 447	K 8
64428	Burlington Junction, 634	B 2
64730	Butler⊙, 3,984	D 6
65689	Cabool, 1,848	H 8
63630	Cadet, 300	L 6
64632	Cainsville, 454	E 2
65239	Cairo, 248	H 4
65323	Calhoun, 360	E 6
65018	California⊙, 3,105	H 5
63534	Callao, 373	G 3
64017	Camden, 286	D 4
65020	Camdenton⊙, 1,636	G 6
64429	Cameron, 3,960	D 3
63933	Campbell, 1,979	M 9
63828	Canalou, 358	N 9
63435	Canton, 2,680	J 2
63701	Cape Girardeau, 31,282	O 8
63829	Cardwell, 859	M10
64834	Carl Junction, 1,661	C 8
64633	Carrollton⊙, 4,847	E 4
64835	Carterville, 1,716	D 8
64836	Carthage⊙, 11,035	D 8
63830	Caruthersville⊙, 7,350	N10
65625	Cassville⊙, 1,910	E 9
63015	Catawissa, 250	N 4
65022	Cedar City, 454	H 5
63016	Cedar Hill, 500	L 6
63436	Center, 588	J 3
65023	Centertown, 277	H 5
64019	Centerview, 234	E 5
63633	Centerville⊙, 209	L 8
65240	Centralia, 3,618	H 4
63740	Chaffee, 2,793	N 8
65024	Chamois, 615	J 5
63834	Charleston⊙, 5,131	O 9
63017	Chesterfield, 13,000	O 3
64733	Chilhowee, 297	E 5
64601	Chillicothe⊙, 9,519	E 3
65236	Chula, 244	F 3
63437	Clarence, 1,050	H 3
65243	Clark, 271	H 4
65025	Clarksburg, 343	G 5
64430	Clarksdale, 248	D 3
63336	Clarksville, 668	K 4
63837	Clarkton, 1,177	M10
64119	Claycomo, 1,841	P 5
63105	Clayton⊙, 16,222	P 3
64431	Clearmont, 226	C 1
64734	Cleveland, 256	C 5
65631	Clever, 430	F 8
64735	Clinton⊙, 7,504	E 6
65325	Cole Camp, 1,038	F 6
65201	Columbia⊙, 58,804	H 5
63742	Commerce, 234	O 8
64434	Conception Junction, 237	C 2
64020	Concordia, 1,854	E 5
65632	Conway, 547	G 7
63839	Cooter, 414	N 10
64021	Corder, 476	E 4
63338	Cottleville, 275	N 2
† 64501	Country Club Village, 221	C 3
64637	Cowgill, 232	E 3
64437	Craig, 369	B 2
65633	Crane, 1,003	E 9
64739	Creighton, 294	D 6
65018	Crescent, 425	N 3
† 63101	Crestwood, 15,398	O 3
63141	Creve Coeur, 8,967	O 3
65452	Crocker, 814	H 7
65634	Cross Timbers, 204	F 6
63019	Crystal City, 3,898	M 6
65453	Cuba, 2,070	K 6
63339	Curryville, 337	K 4
64439	Dearborn, 543	C 3
64740	Deepwater, 565	E 6
64440	De Kalb, 287	C 3
63744	Delta, 462	N 8
63636	Des Arc, 222	L 8
63601	Desloge, 2,818	M 7
63020	De Soto, 5,984	M 6
63131	Des Peres, 5,333	O 3
63841	Dexter, 6,024	N 9
64840	Diamond, 554	D 9
65459	Dixon, 1,387	H 6
63637	Doe Run, 900	M 7
63935	Doniphan⊙, 1,850	L 9
† 65550	Doolittle, 509	J 7
63844	Dorena, 500	O 9
63536	Downing, 406	H 2
64742	Drexel, 723	C 6
63936	Dudley, 248	M 9
64841	Duenweg, 656	D 8
† 64801	Duquesne, 738	D 8
64442	Eagleville, 388	D 2
64743	East Lynne, 255	D 5
63845	East Prairie, 3,275	O 9
65462	Edgar Springs, 450	J 7
64444	Edgerton, 477	C 4
63537	Edina⊙, 1,574	H 2
65026	Eldon, 3,520	G 6
64744	El Dorado Springs, 3,300	E 7
63638	Ellington, 1,094	L 8
63011	Ellisville, 4,681	N 3
63937	Ellsinore, 342	L 9
63628	Elsberry, 1,398	L 4
63639	Elvins, 1,603	L 7
65466	Eminence⊙, 520	K 8
65327	Emma, 224	F 5
63344	Eolia, 321	L 4
63846	Essex, 493	N 9
† 63601	Esther, 1,040	M 7
63025	Eureka, 2,384	N 3
65646	Everton, 264	E 8
63440	Ewing, 330	J 2
64024	Excelsior Springs, 9,411	R 4
65647	Exeter, 434	D 9
64446	Fairfax, 835	B 2
65648	Fair Grove, 431	F 8
65649	Fair Play, 328	E 7
64842	Fairview, 263	D 9
63345	Farber, 470	J 4
63640	Farmington⊙, 6,590	M 7
65248	Fayette⊙, 3,520	G 4
63026	Fenton, 2,275	P 3
63135	Ferguson, 28,915	P 2
63028	Festus, 7,530	M 6
64449	Fillmore, 251	C 2
63940	Fisk, 503	M 9
63601	Flat River, 4,550	M 7
* 63031	Florissant, 65,908	P 2
63347	Foley, 224	L 4
65652	Fordland, 399	G 8
64451	Forest City, 365	B 3
63348	Foristell, 273	M 2
65653	Forsyth⊙, 803	F 9
63441	Frankford, 472	K 4
65250	Franklin, 252	G 4
63645	Fredericktown⊙, 3,799	M 7
65035	Freeburg, 577	J 6
64746	Freeman, 417	C 5
63748	Frohna, 225	N 7
† 63101	Frontenac, 3,920	O 3
65251	Fulton⊙, 12,148	J 5
65655	Gainesville⊙, 627	G 9
65656	Galena⊙, 391	F 9
64640	Gallatin⊙, 1,833	E 3
64641	Galt, 261	F 2
64747	Garden City, 633	D 5
65036	Gasconade, 235	J 5
63037	Gerald, 762	K 6
63848	Gideon, 1,112	N10
65330	Gilliam, 248	F 4
64642	Gilman City, 376	D 2
64118	Gladstone, 23,128	P 5
65254	Glasgow, 1,336	G 4
† 64068	Glenaire, 505	R 5
63038	Glencoe, 2,500	N 3
63122	Glendale, 6,891	P 3
64748	Golden City, 810	D 8
63843	Goodman, 565	C 9
63543	Gorin, 220	H 2
64454	Gower, 758	C 3
64455	Graham, 213	C 2
64029	Grain Valley, 709	S 6
64844	Granby, 1,678	D 9
63943	Grandin, 243	L 9
64030	Grandview, 17,456	P 6
63650	Graniteville, 375	L 7
64456	Grant City⊙, 1,095	D 2
65037	Gravois Mills, 994	G 6
63850	Grayridge, 300	N 9
63039	Gray Summit, 950	M 3
63544	Green Castle, 235	G 2
63545	Green City, 629	F 2
65661	Greenfield⊙, 1,172	E 8
65332	Green Ridge, 403	F 5
63546	Greentop, 351	H 2
63944	Greenville⊙, 328	M 8
64034	Greenwood, 925	R 6
63040	Grover, 550	O 3
64643	Hale, 461	F 3
65255	Hallsville, 790	H 4
64644	Hamilton, 1,645	E 3
63401	Hannibal, 18,609	K 3
64035	Hardin, 683	E 4
64701	Harrisonville⊙, 4,928	D 5
65667	Hartville⊙, 524	G 8
63349	Hawk Point, 354	K 5
63851	Hayti, 3,841	N 10
* 63042	Hazelwood, 14,082	P 2
63047	Hematite, 300	L 6
64460	Hemple, 350	D 3
64036	Henrietta, 466	E 4
63048	Herculaneum, 1,885	M 6
65041	Hermann⊙, 2,658	K 5
65668	Hermitage⊙, 284	F 7
65257	Higbee, 641	H 4
64037	Higginsville, 4,318	E 4
63049	High Ridge, 350	O 4
63050	Hillsboro⊙, 432	L 6
63852	Holcomb, 593	N 10
64040	Holden, 2,089	E 5
63853	Holland, 329	N 10
65672	Hollister, 906	F 9
64048	Holt, 319	D 4
64461	Hopkins, 656	C 1
† 63070	Horine, 850	M 6
63855	Hornersville, 693	M10
63051	House Springs, 500	O 4
65483	Houston⊙, 2,178	J 8
65333	Houstonia, 312	F 5
65674	Humansville, 825	E 7
64752	Hume, 350	C 6
63443	Hunnewell, 304	J 3
65259	Huntsville⊙, 1,442	H 4
63547	Hurdland, 225	H 2
65486	Iberia, 741	H 6
63754	Illmo, 1,232	O 8
63052	Imperial, 900	P 4
* 64050	Independence⊙, 111,662	R 5
63648	Irondale, 319	L 7
63650	Ironton⊙, 1,452	L 7
63755	Jackson⊙, 5,896	N 8
64648	Jamesport, 614	E 3
65046	Jamestown, 243	G 5
64755	Jasper, 796	D 8
65101	Jefferson City (cap.)⊙, 32,407	H 5
63136	Jennings, 19,379	P 2
63351	Jonesburg, 479	K 5
64801	Joplin, 39,256	C 8
† 63385	Josephville, 250	N 2
63445	Kahoka⊙, 2,207	J 2
* 64101	Kansas City, 507,087	P 5
	Kansas City, ‡1,253,916	P 5
64060	Kearney, 984	D 4
63758	Kelso, 401	O 8
63857	Kennett⊙, 9,852	M10
65261	Keytesville⊙, 730	G 4
64649	Kidder, 231	D 3
63053	Kimmswick, 268	M 6
64463	King City, 1,023	D 2
64650	Kingston⊙, 291	E 3
64061	Kingsville, 284	D 5
63140	Kinloch, 5,629	P 2
63501	Kirksville⊙, 15,560	H 2
63122	Kirkwood, 31,890	O 3
65336	Knob Noster, 2,264	E 5
63446	Knox City, 284	H 2
63054	Koch, 600	P 4
65692	Koshkonong, 216	J 9
† 63090	Krakow, 300	K 6
63055	Labadie, 350	N 3
63447	La Belle, 848	J 2
64651	Laclede, 430	F 3
63352	Laddonia, 745	J 4
† 64758	Ladue, 10,491	P 3
63448	La Grange, 1,237	K 2
64063	Lake Lotawana, 1,786	R 6
65049	Lake Ozark, 507	G 6
† 64015	Lake Tapawingo, 867	R 6
† 64034	Lake Winnebago, 432	R 6
64759	Lamar⊙, 3,760	D 8
65337	La Monte, 814	F 5
64847	Lanagan, 374	C 9
63548	Lancaster⊙, 821	H 1
63549	La Plata, 1,377	H 2
64652	Laredo, 383	E 2
64465	Lathrop, 1,268	D 3
64062	Lawson, 1,034	D 4
† 63640	Leadington, 299	M 7
63653	Leadwood, 1,397	L 7
65535	Leasburg, 218	K 6
65536	Lebanon⊙, 8,616	G 7
64063	Lee's Summit, 16,230	R 6
64761	Leeton, 425	E 5
63125	Lemay, 40,115	P 3
63654	Lesterville, 275	L 8
64066	Levasy, 283	S 5
63452	Lewistown, 615	J 2
64067	Lexington⊙, 5,388	E 4
64762	Liberal, 644	D 7
64068	Liberty⊙, 13,679	R 5
65542	Licking, 1,002	J 8
63862	Lilbourn, 1,152	N 9
65338	Lincoln, 574	F 6
65051	Linn⊙, 1,289	J 5
65052	Linn Creek, 268	G 6
64653	Linneus⊙, 400	F 3
65682	Lockwood, 887	E 8
65054	Loose Creek, 370	J 5
63353	Louisiana, 4,533	K 4
64763	Lowry City, 520	E 6
63762	Lutesville, 626	M 8
63552	Macon⊙, 5,301	H 3
65263	Madison, 540	H 4
64466	Maitland, 319	B 2
63863	Malden, 5,374	M 9
65339	Malta Bend, 342	F 4
65704	Mansfield, 1,056	G 8
63143	Maplewood, 12,785	P 3
63764	Marble Hill⊙, 589	N 8
64658	Marceline, 2,622	F 3
65705	Marionville, 1,496	E 8
63655	Marquand, 400	M 8
65340	Marshall⊙, 11,847	F 4
65706	Marshfield⊙, 2,961	G 8
63866	Marston, 666	N 9
63357	Marthasville, 415	L 5
65264	Martinsburg, 318	J 4
64468	Maryville⊙, 9,970	C 2
63857	Matthews, 538	N 9
64469	Maysville⊙, 1,045	D 3
64071	Mayview, 330	E 4
64657	McFall, 203	D 2
64659	Meadville, 409	F 3
63555	Memphis⊙, 2,081	H 2
64660	Mendon, 289	F 3
64661	Mercer, 364	F 2
65058	Meta, 387	H 6
65265	Mexico⊙, 11,807	J 4
65344	Miami, 205	F 4
63359	Middletown, 235	J 4
63556	Milan⊙, 1,794	F 2
65707	Miller, 676	E 8
63952	Mill Spring, 207	L 8
64769	Mindenmines, 279	D 8
63659	Mine La Motte, 200	M 7
† 63801	Miner, 640	N 9
63660	Mineral Point, 369	L 7
64072	Missouri City, 375	R 5
65270	Moberly, 12,988	G 4

(continued on following page)

AREA 69,686 sq. mi.
POPULATION 4,677,399
CAPITAL Jefferson City
LARGEST CITY St. Louis
HIGHEST POINT Taum Sauk Mtn. 1,772 ft.
SETTLED IN 1764
ADMITTED TO UNION August 10, 1821
POPULAR NAME Show Me State
STATE FLOWER Hawthorn
STATE BIRD Bluebird

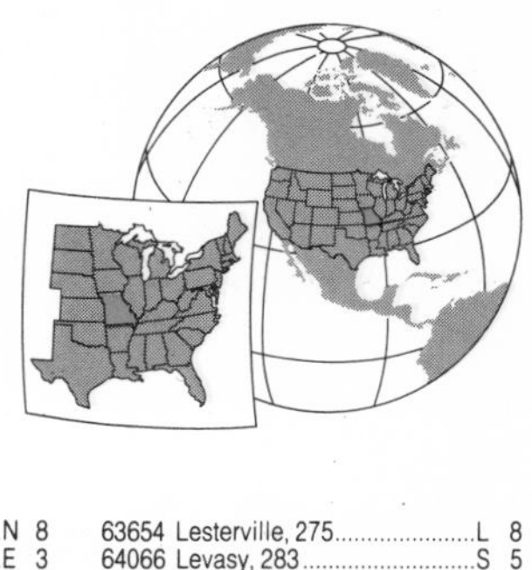

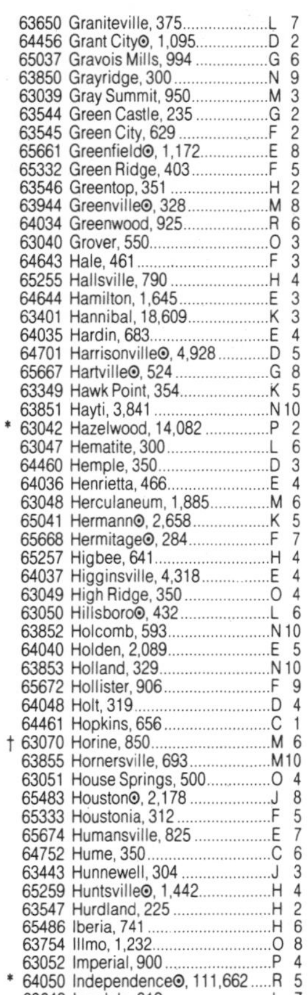

Gene Ahrens — Shostal Associates

The Gateway Arch soars in silhouette against the St. Louis skyline. A Saarinen design, the monument is the centerpiece of the Jefferson National Expansion Memorial. Internal passenger trains carry sightseers up either leg to the long observation room.

Agriculture, Industry and Resources

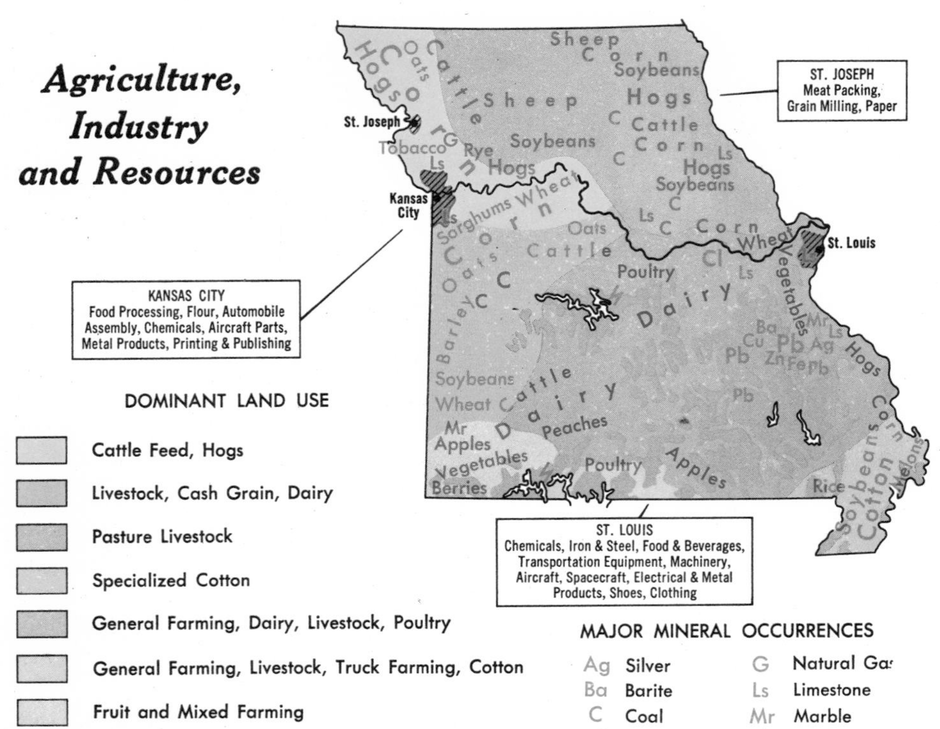

DOMINANT LAND USE

- Cattle Feed, Hogs
- Livestock, Cash Grain, Dairy
- Pasture Livestock
- Specialized Cotton
- General Farming, Dairy, Livestock, Poultry
- General Farming, Livestock, Truck Farming, Cotton
- Fruit and Mixed Farming
- Forests
- Urban Areas

MAJOR MINERAL OCCURRENCES

Ag	Silver	G	Natural Gas
Ba	Barite	Ls	Limestone
C	Coal	Mr	Marble
Cl	Clay	Pb	Lead
Cu	Copper	Zn	Zinc
Fe	Iron Ore		

Water Power — Major Industrial Areas

	65059	Mokane, 398	J 5
	65708	Monett, 5,937	E 9
	63456	Monroe City, 2,456	J 3
	63361	Montgomery City⊙, 2,187	K 5
	63457	Monticello⊙, 157	J 2
	64770	Montrose, 531	E 6
	63868	Morehouse, 1,332	N 9
	63767	Morley, 528	N 8
	65061	Morrison, 234	J 5
	65710	Morrisville, 256	F 8
	64073	Mosby, 337	R 4
	63362	Moscow Mills, 399	M 1
	64470	Mound City, 1,202	B 2
	65711	Mountain Grove, 3,377	H 8
	65548	Mountain View, 1,320	J 8
	65712	Mount Vernon⊙, 2,600	E 8
†	63088	Murphy, 900	O 4
	64074	Napoleon, 263	E 4
	63953	Naylor, 586	L 9
	63954	Neelyville, 231	M 9
	65347	Nelson, 230	F 4
	64850	Neosho⊙, 7,517	D 9
	64772	Nevada⊙, 9,736	D 7
	65063	New Bloomfield, 427	J 5
	65550	Newburg, 806	J 7
	63558	New Cambria, 260	G 3
	63363	New Florence, 635	K 5
	65274	New Franklin, 1,122	G 4
	64471	New Hampton, 327	D 2
	63068	New Haven, 1,474	K 5
	63459	New London⊙, 967	K 3
	63869	New Madrid⊙, 2,719	O 9
	63365	New Melle, 225	M 2
	64667	Newtown, 211	F 2
	65713	Niangua, 309	G 8
	65714	Nixa, 1,636	F 8
	64854	Noel, 924	D 9
	64668	Norborne, 950	E 4
	63121	Normandy, 6,306	P 3
	64116	North Kansas City, 5,183	P 5
†	64152	Northmoor, 562	P 5
†	63101	Northwoods, 4,611	P 2
	65717	Norwood, 294	H 8
	63559	Novinger, 547	G 2
	64075	Oak Grove, 2,025	S 6
†	63080	Oak Grove, 340	K 6
†	63101	Oakland, 1,609	P 3
†	64116	Oakview, 541	P 5
†	63125	Oakville, 11,612	P 4
	64076	Odessa, 2,839	E 5
	63366	O'Fallon, 7,018	N 2
	63369	Old Monroe, 330	N 1
	63132	Olivette, 9,341	P 3
	63771	Oran, 1,226	N 8
	64473	Oregon⊙, 789	B 2
	64855	Oronogo, 492	D 8
	64077	Orrick, 883	D 4
	65065	Osage Beach, 1,091	G 6
	64474	Osborn, 338	D 3
	64776	Osceola⊙, 874	E 6
	65348	Otterville, 440	G 5
	63114	Overland, 24,949	P 3
	65066	Owensville, 2,416	K 6
	65721	Ozark⊙, 2,384	F 8
	63069	Pacific, 3,247	N 4
†	63101	Pagedale, 5,571	P 3
	63461	Palmyra⊙, 3,188	J 3
	65275	Paris⊙, 1,442	J 4
	64152	Parkville, 1,253	O 5
	63870	Parma, 1,051	N 9
	64475	Parnell, 232	C 2
	64670	Pattonsburg, 540	D 2
	64078	Peculiar, 705	D 5
	63462	Perry, 839	J 4
	63775	Perryville⊙, 5,149	N 7
	63070	Pevely, 517	M 6
	64476	Pickering, 245	C 2
	63957	Piedmont, 1,906	L 8

	65723	Pierce City, 1,097	E 8
	65276	Pilot Grove, 701	G 5
	63663	Pilot Knob, 582	L 7
	63120	Pine Lawn, 5,773	P 3
	64856	Pineville⊙, 444	D 9
	64079	Platte City⊙, 2,022	C 4
†	64152	Platte Woods, 484	O 5
	64477	Plattsburg⊙, 1,832	D 3
	64080	Pleasant Hill, 3,396	D 5
	65725	Pleasant Hope, 265	F 8
†	64836	Pleasant Valley, 1,535	R 5
	63779	Pocahontas, 604	N 8
	64671	Polo, 438	D 3
	65789	Pomona, 250	J 9
	63901	Poplar Bluff⊙, 16,653	L 9
	63373	Portage Des Sioux, 509	P 2
	63873	Portageville, 3,117	N 10
	65067	Portland, 250	J 5
	63664	Potosi⊙, 2,761	L 7
	65068	Prairie Home, 231	G 5
	64673	Princeton⊙, 1,328	E 2
	64857	Purcell, 325	D 8
	64674	Purdin, 236	F 3
	65734	Purdy, 588	E 9
	63960	Puxico, 759	M 9
	63561	Queen City, 588	H 2
	63961	Qulin, 496	M 9
	64858	Racine, 274	C 9
	64479	Ravenwood, 336	C 2
	65555	Raymondville, 284	J 8
	64083	Raymore, 587	D 5
	64133	Raytown, 33,632	P 6
	65737	Reeds Spring, 286	F 9
	65738	Republic, 2,411	E 8
	64779	Rich Hill, 1,661	D 6
	65556	Richland, 1,783	H 7
	64085	Richmond⊙, 4,948	D 4
	63117	Richmond Heights, 13,802	P 3
	64481	Ridgeway, 469	D 2
	63874	Risco, 412	N 9
†	63601	Rivermines, 402	L 7
	64168	Riverside, 2,123	O 5
†	63101	Riverview, 3,741	R 2
	65279	Rocheport, 307	H 5
†	63101	Rock Hill, 7,275	P 3
	64482	Rock Port⊙, 1,575	B 2

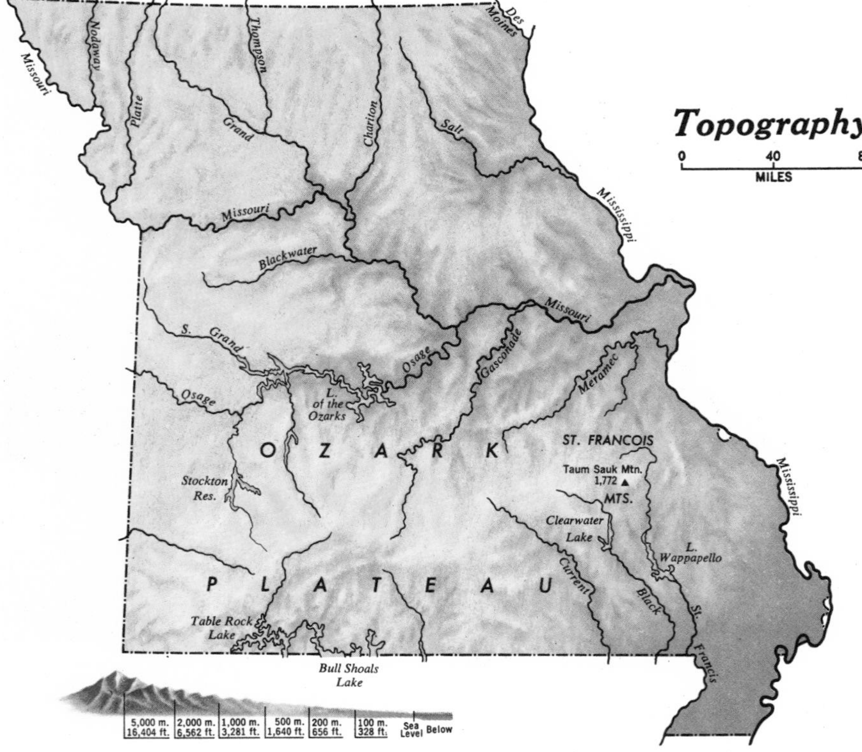

64780 Rockville, 203 D 6
65742 Rogersville, 574 G 8
65401 Rolla⊙, 13,245 J 7
63091 Rosebud, 305 K 6
64483 Rosendale, 245 C 2
64484 Rushville, 300 B 3
65074 Russellville, 557 H 6
63074 Saint Ann, 18,215 O 2
63301 Saint Charles⊙, 31,834 O 2
63077 Saint Clair, 2,978 L 6
63670 Sainte Genevieve⊙, 4,468 M 6
65075 Saint Elizabeth, 287 H 6
63101 Saint George, 1,806 P 3
65559 Saint James, 2,787 J 6
63114 Saint John, 8,960 P 2
64501 Saint Joseph⊙, 72,691 C 3
Saint Joseph, ‡86,915 C 3
63101 Saint Louis⊙, 622,236 P 3
Saint Louis, ‡2,363,017 P 3
63673 Saint Marys, 645 M 7
63376 Saint Peters, 486 N 2
65560 Salem⊙, 4,363 J 7
65281 Salisbury, 1,960 G 4
64862 Sarcoxie, 1,175 D 8
64485 Savannah⊙, 3,324 C 3
64783 Schell City, 367 D 6
63780 Scott City, 2,464 O 8
65301 Sedalia⊙, 22,847 F 5
65745 Seligman, 424 D 9
63876 Senath, 1,484 M 10
64865 Seneca, 1,577 C 9
65746 Seymour, 1,208 G 8
63468 Shelbina, 2,060 H 3
63469 Shelbyville⊙, 601 H 3
64784 Sheldon, 498 D 7
64486 Sheridan, 251 C 1
† 63101 Shrewsbury, 5,896 P 3
64088 Sibley, 279 S 5
63801 Sikeston, 14,699 N 9
63377 Silex, 306 K 4
64487 Skidmore, 440 B 2
65349 Slater, 2,576 G 4
65350 Smithton, 402 F 5
64089 Smithville, 1,785 D 4
64863 South West City, 453 D 9
† 63101 Spanish Lake, 15,647 P 2
65753 Sparta, 380 F 9
64679 Spickard, 408 F 2
* 65801 Springfield⊙, 120,096 F 8
Springfield, ‡152,929 F 8
64489 Stanberry, 1,479 C 2
63079 Stanton, 350 K 6
63877 Steele, 2,107 N 10
65565 Steelville⊙, 1,392 K 7
64490 Stewartsville, 634 C 3
65785 Stockton⊙, 1,063 E 7
65567 Stoutland, 205 G 7
65078 Stover, 849 G 6
65757 Strafford, 491 F 8
65284 Sturgeon, 787 H 4
64054 Sugar Creek, 4,755 R 5
63080 Sullivan, 5,100 K 6
65571 Summersville, 435 J 8
† 63101 Sunset Hills, 3,728 P 3
65351 Sweet Springs, 1,716 F 5
66491 Tarkio, 2,517 B 2
† 64063 Tarsney Lakes, 401 R 6
65791 Thayer, 1,609 J 9
† 63025 Times Beach, 1,265 O 3
65081 Tipton, 1,914 G 5
64091 Tracy, 252 C 4
64683 Trenton⊙, 6,063 E 2
64492 Trimble, 206 D 4
63379 Troy⊙, 2,538 L 5
63380 Truesdail, 262 K 5
65082 Tuscumbia⊙, 256 H 6
63084 Union⊙, 5,183 L 6
64494 Union Star, 417 C 2
63565 Unionville⊙, 2,075 G 2
64063 Unity, 242 R 6
63130 University City, 46,309 P 3
65767 Urbana, 369 F 7
64788 Urich, 433 E 6
64686 Utica, 275 E 3
63088 Valley Park, 3,662 O 3
63965 Van Buren⊙, 714 L 8
63382 Vandalia, 3,160 J 4
63784 Vanduser, 306 N 9
65769 Verona, 515 E 9
65084 Versailles⊙, 2,244 G 6
65566 Viburnum, 520 K 7
65580 Vichy, 250 J 6
† 63020 Victoria, 250 M 6
65581 Vida, 300 J 7
65582 Vienna⊙, 505 H 6
64790 Walker, 227 D 7
65770 Walnut Grove, 442 F 8
63966 Wappapello, 254 M 9
63879 Wardell, 275 N 10
† 65101 Wardsville, 460 H 5
64093 Warrensburg⊙, 13,125 E 5
63383 Warrenton⊙, 2,057 K 5
65355 Warsaw⊙, 1,423 F 6
65772 Washburn, 250 E 9
63090 Washington, 8,499 K 5
64096 Waverly, 827 E 4
63472 Wayland, 467 J 2
65583 Waynesville⊙, 3,375 H 7
† 64152 Weatherby Lake, 832 O 5
65774 Weaubleau, 343 F 7
64870 Webb City, 6,811 C 8
63119 Webster Groves, 26,995 P 3
64097 Wellington, 720 E 4
63112 Wellston, 7,050 P 3
63384 Wellsville, 1,565 K 4
63385 Wentzville, 3,223 M 2
63386 West Alton, 435 R 2
64498 Westboro, 234 B 1
64098 Weston, 1,267 C 4
65085 Westphalia, 332 J 6
65775 West Plains⊙, 6,893 J 9
65779 Wheatland, 317 F 7
64874 Wheaton, 360 E 9
64688 Wheeling, 268 F 3
65781 Willard, 1,018 F 8
63977 Williamsville, 398 L 9
65793 Willow Springs, 2,045 H 9
65360 Windsor, 2,734 E 5
63389 Winfield, 620 L 5
65588 Winona, 973 K 8
† 63101 Woodson Terrace, 5,936 P 2
63390 Wright City, 943 K 5
63474 Wyaconda, 356 J 2
63882 Wyatt, 562 O 9

⊙ County seat.
‡ Population of metropolitan area.
† Zip of nearest p.o.
* Multiple zips

COUNTIES

County, Pop.	Key
Beaverhead, 8,187	C 5
Big Horn, 10,057	J 5
Blaine, 6,727	G 2
Broadwater, 2,526	E 4
Carbon, 7,080	G 5
Carter, 1,956	M 5
Cascade, 81,804	E 3
Chouteau, 6,473	F 3
Custer, 12,174	L 4
Daniels, 3,083	L 2
Dawson, 11,269	M 3
Deer Lodge, 15,652	C 5
Fallon, 4,050	M 4
Fergus, 12,611	G 3
Flathead, 39,460	B 2
Gallatin, 32,505	E 5
Garfield, 1,796	J 3
Glacier, 10,783	C 2
Golden Valley, 931	G 4
Granite, 2,737	C 4
Hill, 17,358	F 2
Jefferson, 5,238	D 4
Judith Basin, 2,667	F 4
Lake, 14,445	B 3
Lewis and Clark, 33,281	D 3
Liberty, 2,359	E 2
Lincoln, 18,063	A 2
Madison, 5,014	D 5
McCone, 2,875	L 3
Meagher, 2,122	F 4
Mineral, 2,958	B 3
Missoula, 58,263	C 3
Musselshell, 3,734	H 4
Park, 11,197	F 5
Petroleum, 675	H 3
Phillips, 5,386	J 2
Pondera, 6,611	D 2
Powder River, 2,862	L 5
Powell, 6,660	D 4
Prairie, 1,752	L 4
Ravalli, 14,409	B 4
Richland, 9,837	M 3
Roosevelt, 10,365	L 2
Rosebud, 6,032	K 4
Sanders, 7,093	A 3
Sheridan, 5,779	M 2
Silver Bow, 41,981	D 5
Stillwater, 4,632	G 5
Sweet Grass, 2,980	G 5
Teton, 6,116	D 3
Toole, 5,839	E 2
Treasure, 1,069	J 4
Valley, 11,471	K 2
Wheatland, 2,529	G 4
Wibaux, 1,465	M 4
Yellowstone, 87,367	H 4
Yellowstone Nat'l Park, 64	F 6

CITIES and TOWNS

	Zip	Name/Pop.	Key
	59001	Absarokee, 700	G 5
	59820	Alberton, 363	B 3
	59710	Alder, 100	D 5
†	59634	Alhambra, 50	E 4
†	59741	Amsterdam, 200	E 5
	59711	Anaconda⊙, 9,771	C 4
	59211	Antelope, 95	M 2
	59821	Arlee, 220	B 3
†	59412	Armington, 62	F 3
	59003	Ashland, 200	K 5
	59410	Augusta, 400	D 3
	59713	Avon, 250	D 4
	59411	Babb, 50	C 2
	59212	Bainville, 217	M 2
	59313	Baker⊙, 2,584	M 4
	59006	Ballantine, 350	J 5
†	59725	Bannack, 20	C 5
	59613	Basin, 230	D 4
	59007	Bearcreek, 31	G 5
†	59441	Becket, 35	G 4
	59008	Belfry, 250	H 5
	59714	Belgrade, 1,307	E 5
†	59046	Belmont, 75	G 4
	59412	Belt, 656	E 3
†	59462	Benchland, 100	F 3
	59314	Biddle, 83	L 5
	59910	Big Arm, 150	B 3
	59911	Bigfork, 500	C 2
	59010	Bighorn, 40	J 4
	59520	Big Sandy, 827	G 2
	59011	Big Timber⊙, 1,592	G 5
*	59101	Billings⊙, 61,581	H 5
		Billings, ‡87,367	H 5
	59414	Black Eagle, 1,500	E 3
	59415	Blackfoot, 100	D 2
	59823	Bonner, 250	C 4
	59632	Boulder⊙, 1,342	E 4
	59521	Box Elder, 200	F 2
	59715	Bozeman⊙, 18,670	E 5
	59416	Brady, 230	E 2
	59014	Bridger, 717	H 5
	59317	Broadus⊙, 799	L 5
	59015	Broadview, 123	H 4
	59213	Brockton, 401	M 2
	59214	Brockway, 80	L 3
	59417	Browning, 1,700	C 2
	59016	Busby, 600	J 5
	59701	Butte⊙, 23,368	D 5
†	59857	Camas Prairie, 160	B 3
†	59601	Canyon Ferry, 100	E 4
	59721	Cardwell, 36	E 5
	59420	Carter, 100	E 3
†	59347	Cartersville, 140	K 4
	59421	Cascade, 714	E 3
†	59701	Centerville, 2,284	D 4
	59824	Charlo, 150	B 3
	59522	Chester⊙, 936	E 2
	59523	Chinook⊙, 1,813	G 2
	59422	Choteau⊙, 1,586	D 3
	59423	Christina, 44	G 3
	59215	Circle⊙, 964	L 3
	59634	Clancy, 550	E 4
	59825	Clinton, 250	C 4
	59018	Clyde Park, 244	F 5
	59424	Coffee Creek, 79	F 3
	59323	Colstrip, 160	K 5
	59912	Columbia Falls, 2,652	B 2
	59019	Columbus⊙, 1,173	G 5
	59826	Condon, 250	C 3
	59827	Conner, 150	B 5
	59425	Conrad⊙, 2,770	D 2
	59020	Cooke City, 45	G 5
	59913	Coram, 450	C 2
	59828	Corvallis, 467	C 4
†	59648	Craig, 100	D 3
	59217	Crane, 152	M 3
	59022	Crow Agency, 975	J 5
	59218	Culbertson, 821	M 2
	59024	Custer, 193	J 4
	59427	Cut Bank⊙, 4,004	D 2
	59219	Dagmar, 55	M 2
	59829	Darby, 538	B 4
	59914	Dayton, 60	B 3
†	59028	Dean, 32	G 5
	59830	De Borgia, 95	A 3
	59722	Deer Lodge⊙, 4,306	D 4
	59724	Dell, 50	D 6
†	59053	Delpine, 33	F 4
	59430	Denton, 398	G 3
	59431	Devon, 33	E 2

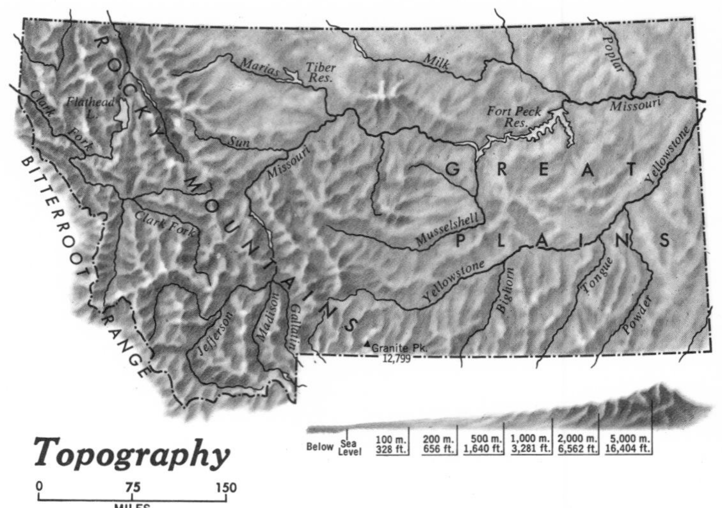

Topography

	Zip	Name/Pop.	Key
	59725	Dillon⊙, 4,548	D 5
	59727	Divide, 105	D 5
	59831	Dixon, 300	B 3
	59524	Dodson, 196	H 2
	59832	Drummond, 494	D 4
	59432	Dupuyer, 105	D 2
	59433	Dutton, 415	E 3
	59434	East Glacier Park, 340	C 2
	59635	East Helena, 1,651	E 4
	59026	Edgar, 150	H 5
	59324	Ekalaka⊙, 663	M 5
†	59701	Elk Park, 53	D 4
	59728	Elliston, 300	D 4
	59915	Elmo, 150	B 3
	59729	Ennis, 501	E 5
	59325	Epsie, 60	L 5
	59916	Essex, 35	C 2
	59917	Eureka, 1,195	B 2
	59436	Fairfield, 638	D 3
	59221	Fairview, 956	M 3
	59326	Fallon, 200	L 4
	59028	Fishtail, 52	G 5
	59222	Flaxville, 185	L 2
†	59701	Floral Park, 5,113	D 5
	59833	Florence, 500	B 4
	59440	Floweree, 306	E 3
	59441	Forestgrove, 90	H 3
	59327	Forsyth⊙, 1,873	K 4
†	59526	Fort Belknap, 185	H 2
	59442	Fort Benton⊙, 1,863	F 3
	59918	Fortine, 250	A 2
	59223	Fort Peck, 975	K 2
	59443	Fort Shaw, 450	E 3
†	59075	Fort Smith, 300	J 5
	59224	Four Buttes, 50	L 2
	59225	Frazer, 300	K 2
	59834	Frenchtown, 300	B 3
	59226	Froid, 330	M 2
	59029	Fromberg, 364	H 5
	59444	Galata, 48	E 2
†	59722	Galen, 210	D 4
	59730	Gallatin Gateway, 200	E 5
	59030	Gardiner, 479	F 5
	59445	Garneill, 55	G 4
	59731	Garrison, 350	D 4
	59446	Geraldine, 370	F 3
	59447	Geyser, 567	F 3
	59525	Gildford, 285	F 2

MONTANA

SCALE

0 5 10 20 40 60 MI.

0 5 10 20 40 60 KM.

State Capitals ⊛

County Seats ⊙

Surrounded by the wide open spaces, a Montana ranch basks in the reflected glory of the Rocky Mountains while it awaits cattle returning from the range. Ranches accommodate so many head of cattle that the state's residents are outnumbered six to one.

AREA 147,138 sq. mi.
POPULATION 694,409
CAPITAL Helena
LARGEST CITY Billings
HIGHEST POINT Granite Pk. 12,799 ft.
SETTLED IN 1809
ADMITTED TO UNION November 8, 1889
POPULAR NAME Treasure State
STATE FLOWER Bitterroot
STATE BIRD Western Meadowlark

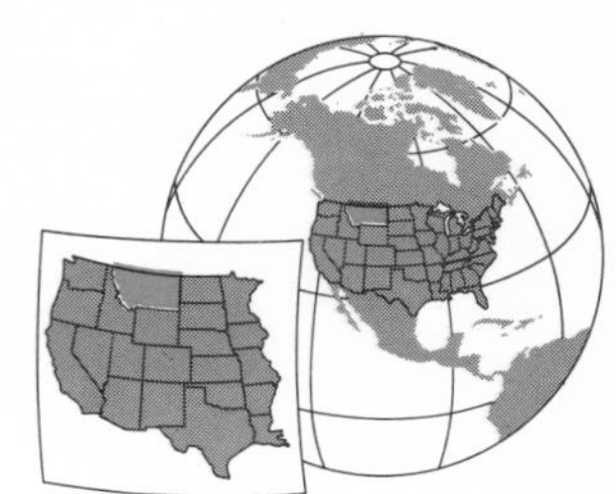

Agriculture, Industry and Resources

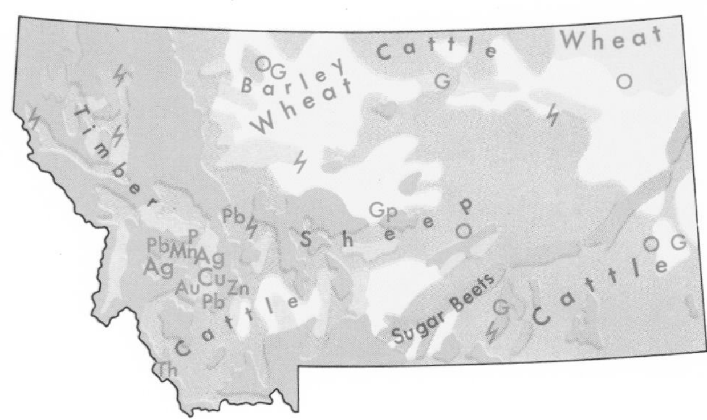

DOMINANT LAND USE

- Specialized Wheat
- Wheat, Range Livestock
- General Farming, Dairy, Range Livestock
- General Farming, Livestock, Special Crops
- Range Livestock
- Sugar Beets, Beans, Livestock, General Farming
- Forests

MAJOR MINERAL OCCURRENCES

Ag	Silver	O	Petroleum
Au	Gold	P	Phosphates
Cu	Copper	Pb	Lead
G	Natural Gas	Th	Thorium
Gp	Gypsum	Zn	Zinc
Mn	Manganese	ϟ	Water Power

	Zip	Place, Population	Key
	59230	Glasgow⊙, 4,700	K 2
†	59725	Glen, 100	D 5
	59330	Glendive⊙, 6,305	M 3
	59240	Glentana, 40	K 2
	59733	Goldcreek, 76	D 4
	59835	Grantsdale, 250	B 4
	59032	Grassrange, 181	H 3
	59401	Great Falls⊙, 60,091	E 3
		Great Falls, ‡81,804	E 3
	59836	Greenough, 100	C 4
	59837	Hall, 95	C 4
	59840	Hamilton⊙, 2,499	B 4
	59034	Hardin⊙, 2,733	J 5
	59526	Harlem, 1,094	H 2
	59036	Harlowton⊙, 1,375	F 4
	59735	Harrison, 275	E 5
	59333	Hathaway, 45	K 4
	59842	Haugan, 40	A 3
	59501	Havre⊙, 10,558	G 2
	59527	Hays, 950	H 2
	59448	Heart Butte, 450	C 2
	59601	Helena (cap.)⊙, 22,730	E 4
	59843	Helmville, 76	C 4
	59844	Heron, 185	A 2
	59450	Highwood, 360	F 3
	59451	Hilger, 40	G 3
	59528	Hingham, 262	F 2
	59241	Hinsdale, 500	K 2
	59452	Hobson, 192	G 4
†	59353	Hodges, 50	M 4
	59529	Hogeland, 68	H 2
	59242	Homestead, 75	M 2
	59845	Hot Springs, 664	B 3
	59919	Hungry Horse, 700	C 2
	59037	Huntley, 225	H 5
	59846	Huson, 40	B 3
	59038	Hysham⊙, 373	J 4
	59039	Ingomar, 55	J 4
	59335	Intake, 60	M 3
	59530	Inverness, 150	F 2
	59336	Ismay, 40	M 4
	59736	Jackson, 196	C 5
	59737	Jeffers, 70	E 5
	59638	Jefferson City, 99	E 4
†	59721	Jefferson Island, 31	E 5
	59041	Joliet, 412	G 5
	59531	Joplin, 350	F 2
	59337	Jordan⊙, 529	J 3
	59453	Judith Gap, 160	G 4
	59901	Kalispell⊙, 10,526	B 2
	59454	Kevin, 250	D 2
	59920	Kila, 44	B 2
†	59072	Klein, 200	H 4
	59532	Kremlin, 347	F 2
	59922	Lakeside, 663	B 2
	59243	Lambert, 141	M 3
	59043	Lame Deer, 460	K 5
	59533	Landusky, 50	H 3
	59244	Larslan, 140	K 2
	59044	Laurel, 4,454	H 5
	59738	Laurin, 60	D 5
	59046	Lavina, 169	H 4
	59457	Lewistown⊙, 6,437	G 3
	59923	Libby⊙, 3,286	A 2
	59739	Lima, 351	D 6
	59639	Lincoln, 473	D 4
	59339	Lindsay, 40	L 3
	59047	Livingston⊙, 6,883	F 5
	59535	Lloyd, 70	G 2
	59340	Locate, 49	L 4
†	59101	Lockwood, 950	H 5
	59050	Lodge Grass, 806	J 5
†	59524	Lodgepole, 39	H 2
	59763	Logan, 53	E 5
	59847	Lolo, 300	B 4
	59460	Loma, 172	F 3
	59461	Lothair, 35	E 2
	59538	Malta⊙, 2,195	J 2
	59741	Manhattan, 816	E 5
	59925	Marion, 120	B 2
	59053	Martinsdale, 203	F 4
	59640	Marysville, 42	D 4
	59742	Maudlow, 75	E 4
	53850	Maxville, 44	C 4
	59740	McAllister, 62	E 5
	59247	Medicine Lake, 393	M 2
	59743	Melrose, 350	D 5
	59054	Melstone, 227	H 4
	59055	Melville, 150	F 4
	59301	Miles City⊙, 9,023	L 4
	59851	Milltown, 500	C 4
	59801	Missoula⊙, 29,497	C 4
	59462	Moccasin, 100	F 3
	59463	Monarch, 80	F 3
	59464	Moore, 219	G 4
	59059	Musselshell, 32	H 4
	59248	Nashua, 513	K 2
	59465	Neihart, 109	F 4
	59745	Norris, 37	E 5
†	59501	North Havre, 1,073	G 2
	59853	Noxon, 250	A 3
†	59936	Nyack, 31	C 2
	59061	Nye, 65	G 5
	59466	Oilmont, 75	E 2
	59927	Olney, 250	B 2
	59250	Opheim, 306	K 2
	59251	Oswego, 75	L 2
	59252	Outlook, 153	M 2
	59854	Ovando, 102	C 3
	59855	Pablo, 350	B 3
	59856	Paradise, 500	B 3
	59063	Park City, 400	H 5
	59253	Peerless, 100	L 2
	59467	Pendroy, 35	D 2
	59858	Philipsburg⊙, 1,128	C 4
	59859	Plains, 1,046	B 3
	59254	Plentywood⊙, 2,381	M 2
	59344	Plevna, 189	M 4
	59860	Polson⊙, 2,464	B 3
	59064	Pompeys Pillar, 69	J 5
	59747	Pony, 111	E 5
	59255	Poplar, 1,389	L 2
	59862	Potomac, 58	C 4
	59468	Power, 91	E 3
	59929	Proctor, 108	B 3
	59066	Pryor, 150	H 5
	59641	Radersburg, 65	E 4
	59748	Ramsay, 140	D 4
	59067	Rapelje, 295	G 5
	59863	Ravalli, 150	B 3
	59256	Raymond, 34	M 2
	59469	Raynesford, 100	F 3
	59068	Red Lodge⊙, 1,844	G 5
	59257	Redstone, 77	M 2
	59069	Reedpoint, 125	G 5
	59258	Reserve, 90	M 2
	59930	Rexford, 243	A 2
	59259	Richey, 389	L 3
	59260	Richland, 37	K 2
	59642	Ringling, 51	F 4
	59070	Roberts, 291	G 5
†	59521	Rocky Boy, 150	G 2
	59931	Rollins, 200	B 3
	59864	Ronan, 1,347	C 3
	59347	Rosebud, 120	K 4
	59072	Roundup⊙, 2,116	H 4
	59471	Roy, 175	H 3
	59540	Rudyard, 550	F 2
	59074	Ryegate⊙, 261	G 4
	59261	Saco, 356	J 2
	59865	Saint Ignatius, 925	C 3
	59866	Saint Regis, 500	A 3
	59075	Saint Xavier, 110	J 5
	59867	Saltese, 95	A 3
	59472	Sand Coulee, 500	E 3
	59076	Sanders, 50	J 4
	59473	Santa Rita, 125	D 2
	59262	Savage, 300	M 3
	59263	Scobey⊙, 1,486	L 2
	59868	Seeley Lake, 400	C 3
	59078	Shawmut, 60	G 4
†	59347	Sheffield, 40	K 4
	59474	Shelby⊙, 3,111	E 2
	59079	Shepherd, 100	H 5
	59749	Sheridan, 636	D 5
	59270	Sidney⊙, 4,543	M 3
	59080	Silesia, 90	H 5
†	59701	Silver Bow Park, 5,524	D 4
	59751	Silver Star, 100	D 5
	59477	Simms, 299	E 3
	59541	Simpson, 70	F 2
	59932	Somers, 950	B 2
	59348	Sonnette, 42	L 5
†	59442	Square Butte, 48	F 3
	59479	Stanford⊙, 505	F 3
†	59846	Stark, 51	B 3
	59870	Stevensville, 829	C 4
	59480	Stockett, 500	E 3
	59933	Stryker, 60	B 2
	59481	Suffolk, 45	G 3
	59482	Sunburst, 604	E 2
	59483	Sun River, 190	E 3
	59872	Superior⊙, 993	B 3
	59911	Swan Lake, 200	C 3
	59484	Sweetgrass, 120	E 2
	59349	Terry⊙, 870	L 4
	59873	Thompson Falls⊙, 1,356	A 3
	59752	Three Forks, 1,188	E 5
†	59347	Thurlow, 40	K 4
	59643	Toston, 75	E 4
	59644	Townsend⊙, 1,371	E 4
	59934	Trego, 50	B 2
	59753	Trident, 50	E 5
	59874	Trout Creek, 200	A 3
	59935	Troy, 1,046	A 2
	59542	Turner, 175	H 2
	59754	Twin Bridges, 613	D 5
	59085	Twodot, 118	F 4
	59485	Ulm, 450	E 3
	59452	Utica, 40	F 4
	59486	Valier, 651	D 2
†	59237	Vananda, 50	K 4
	59487	Vaughn, 345	E 3
	59875	Victor, 500	B 4
	59274	Vida, 52	L 3
	59755	Virginia City⊙, 149	E 5
	59701	Walkerville, 1,097	D 4
	59756	Warmsprings, 1,600	D 4
	59757	Waterloo, 102	D 5
†	59214	Watkins, 40	K 3
	59275	Westby, 287	M 2
	59936	West Glacier, 348	C 2
	59758	West Yellowstone, 756	E 6
	59937	Whitefish, 3,349	B 2
	59759	Whitehall, 1,035	D 5
†	59784	Whitepine, 50	A 3
	59645	White Sulphur Springs⊙, 1,200	E 4
	59276	Whitetail, 125	L 2
	59544	Whitewater, 100	J 2
	59353	Wibaux⊙, 644	M 3
	59760	Willow Creek, 325	E 5
	59086	Wilsall, 200	F 5
	59488	Windham, 60	F 3
	59489	Winifred, 190	G 3
	59087	Winnett⊙, 271	H 4
	59647	Winston, 115	E 4
	59761	Wisdom, 155	C 5
	59762	Wise River, 125	C 5
	59648	Wolf Creek, 200	D 3
	59201	Wolf Point⊙, 3,095	L 2
†	59875	Woodside, 80	B 4
	59088	Worden, 350	H 5
	59089	Wyola, 110	J 5
†	59935	Yaak, 75	A 2
	59547	Zurich, 89	G 2

⊙ County seat.
‡ Population of metropolitan area.
† Zip of nearest p.o.
* Multiple zips

COUNTIES

Name/Pop.	Key
Adams, 30,553	F 4
Antelope, 9,047	F 2
Arthur, 606	C 3
Banner, 1,034	A 3
Blaine, 847	E 3
Boone, 8,190	F 3
Box Butte, 10,094	A 2
Boyd, 3,752	F 2
Brown, 4,021	E 2
Buffalo, 31,222	E 4
Burt, 9,247	H 3
Butler, 9,461	G 3
Cass, 18,076	H 4
Cedar, 12,192	G 2
Chase, 4,129	C 4
Cherry, 6,846	C 2
Cheyenne, 10,778	A 3
Clay, 8,266	F 4
Colfax, 9,498	G 3
Cuming, 12,034	H 3
Custer, 14,092	E 3
Dakota, 13,137	H 2
Dawes, 9,693	A 2
Dawson, 19,467	E 4
Deuel, 2,717	B 3
Dixon, 7,453	H 2
Dodge, 34,782	H 3
Douglas, 389,455	H 3
Dundy, 2,926	C 4
Fillmore, 8,137	G 4
Franklin, 4,566	F 4
Frontier, 3,982	D 4
Furnas, 6,897	E 4
Gage, 25,719	H 4
Garden, 2,929	B 3
Garfield, 2,411	F 3
Gosper, 2,178	E 4
Grant, 1,019	C 3
Greeley, 4,000	F 3
Hall, 42,851	F 4
Hamilton, 8,867	F 4
Harlan, 4,357	E 4
Hayes, 1,530	C 4
Hitchcock, 4,051	C 4
Holt, 12,933	F 2
Hooker, 939	C 3
Howard, 6,807	F 3
Jefferson, 10,436	G 4
Johnson, 5,743	H 4
Kearney, 6,707	F 4
Keith, 8,487	C 3
Keya Paha, 1,340	E 2
Kimball, 6,009	A 3
Knox, 11,723	G 2
Lancaster, 167,972	H 4
Lincoln, 29,538	D 4
Logan, 991	D 3
Loup, 854	E 3
Madison, 27,402	G 3
McPherson, 623	C 3
Merrick, 8,751	F 3
Morrill, 5,813	A 3
Nance, 5,142	F 3
Nemaha, 8,976	J 4
Nuckolls, 7,404	F 4
Otoe, 15,576	H 4
Pawnee, 4,473	H 4
Perkins, 3,423	C 4
Phelps, 9,553	E 4
Pierce, 8,493	G 2
Platte, 26,508	G 3
Polk, 6,468	G 3
Red Willow, 12,191	D 4
Richardson, 12,277	J 4
Rock, 2,231	E 2
Saline, 12,809	G 4
Sarpy, 63,696	H 3
Saunders, 17,018	H 3
Scotts Bluff, 36,432	A 3
Seward, 14,460	G 4
Sheridan, 7,285	B 2
Sherman, 4,725	F 3
Sioux, 2,034	A 2
Stanton, 5,758	G 3
Thayer, 7,779	G 4
Thomas, 954	D 3
Thurston, 6,942	H 2
Valley, 5,783	E 3
Washington, 13,310	H 3
Wayne, 10,400	G 2
Webster, 6,477	F 4
Wheeler, 1,054	F 3
York, 13,685	G 4

CITIES and TOWNS

Zip	Name/Pop.	Key
68301	Adams, 463	H 4
69210	Ainsworth⊙, 2,073	D 2
68620	Albion⊙, 2,074	F 3
68810	Alda, 456	F 4
68710	Allen, 309	H 2
69301	Alliance⊙, 6,862	A 2
68920	Alma⊙, 1,299	E 4
68814	Ansley, 631	E 3
68922	Arapahoe, 1,147	E 4
68815	Arcadia, 418	F 3
68002	Arlington, 910	H 3
69120	Arnold, 752	D 3
69121	Arthur⊙, 175	C 3
68003	Ashland, 2,176	H 3
68713	Atkinson, 1,406	E 2
68305	Auburn⊙, 3,650	J 4
68818	Aurora⊙, 3,180	F 4
68924	Axtell, 500	E 4
68004	Bancroft, 545	H 2
68622	Bartlett⊙, 193	F 3
69020	Bartley, 283	D 4
68714	Bassett⊙, 983	E 2
68715	Battle Creek, 1,158	G 3
69334	Bayard, 1,338	A 3
68310	Beatrice⊙, 12,389	H 4
68926	Beaver City⊙, 802	E 4
68313	Beaver Crossing, 400	G 4
68716	Beemer, 699	H 3
68005	Bellevue, 19,449	J 3
68624	Bellwood, 361	G 3
69021	Benkelman⊙, 1,349	C 4
68317	Bennet, 489	H 4
68007	Bennington, 683	H 3
68927	Bertrand, 662	E 4
69122	Big Springs, 472	B 3
68928	Bladen, 293	F 4
68008	Blair⊙, 6,106	H 3
68718	Bloomfield, 1,287	G 2
68930	Blue Hill, 1,201	F 4
68318	Blue Springs, 494	H 4
68010	Boys Town, 989	H 3
68319	Bradshaw, 347	G 4
69123	Brady, 311	D 3
68626	Brainard, 309	G 3
68821	Brewster⊙, 54	D 3
69336	Bridgeport⊙, 1,490	A 3
68822	Broken Bow⊙, 3,734	E 3
68321	Brownville, 174	J 4
69127	Brule, 423	C 3
68322	Bruning, 315	G 4
68823	Burwell⊙, 1,341	E 3
68722	Butte⊙, 575	F 2
68824	Cairo, 686	F 3
68825	Callaway, 523	D 3
69022	Cambridge, 1,145	D 4
68932	Campbell, 447	F 4
68015	Cedar Bluffs, 616	H 3
68627	Cedar Rapids, 449	F 3
68724	Center⊙, 111	G 2
68826	Central City⊙, 2,803	F 3
68017	Ceresco, 474	H 3
69337	Chadron⊙, 5,853	B 2
68725	Chambers, 321	F 2
68827	Chapman, 371	F 3
69129	Chappell⊙, 1,204	B 3
68327	Chester, 459	G 4
68628	Clarks, 480	G 3
68629	Clarkson, 805	G 3
68933	Clay Center⊙, 952	F 4
68726	Clearwater, 398	F 2
68727	Coleridge, 608	G 2
68601	Columbus⊙, 15,471	G 3
68329	Cook, 328	H 4
68331	Cortland, 326	H 4
69130	Cozad, 4,219	E 4
68019	Craig, 295	H 3
69339	Crawford, 1,291	A 2
68729	Creighton, 1,461	G 2
68333	Crete, 4,444	G 4
68730	Crofton, 677	G 2
69024	Culbertson, 801	C 4
69025	Curtis, 1,166	D 4
68731	Dakota City⊙, 1,057	H 2
69131	Dalton, 354	B 3
68831	Dannebrog, 384	F 3
68335	Davenport, 427	G 4
68632	David City⊙, 2,380	G 3
68020	Decatur, 679	H 2
68340	Deshler, 937	G 4
68341	De Witt, 651	G 4
68342	Diller, 287	H 4
69133	Dix, 342	A 3
68633	Dodge, 704	H 3
68832	Doniphan, 542	F 4
68343	Dorchester, 492	G 4
68634	Duncan, 298	G 3
68347	Eagle, 441	H 4
68935	Edgar, 707	F 4
68636	Elgin, 917	F 3
68022	Elkhorn, 1,184	H 3
68836	Elm Creek, 798	E 4
68349	Elmwood, 548	H 4
68937	Elwood⊙, 601	E 4
68733	Emerson, 850	H 2
69028	Eustis, 400	D 4
68735	Ewing, 552	F 2
68351	Exeter, 759	G 4
68352	Fairbury⊙, 5,265	G 4
68938	Fairfield, 487	G 4
68354	Fairmont, 761	G 4
68355	Falls City⊙, 5,444	J 4
68358	Firth, 328	H 4
68023	Fort Calhoun, 642	J 3
68939	Franklin⊙, 1,193	E 4
68025	Fremont⊙, 22,962	H 3
68359	Friend, 1,126	G 4
68638	Fullerton⊙, 1,444	F 3
68361	Geneva⊙, 2,275	G 4
68640	Genoa, 1,174	G 3
69341	Gering⊙, 5,639	A 3
68840	Gibbon, 1,388	F 4
68841	Giltner, 408	F 4
68941	Glenvil, 332	F 4
69343	Gordon, 2,106	B 2
69138	Gothenburg, 3,154	D 4
68801	Grand Island⊙, 31,269	F 4
69140	Grant⊙, 1,099	C 4
68842	Greeley⊙, 580	F 3
68366	Greenwood, 506	H 3
68028	Gretna, 1,557	H 3
68942	Guide Rock, 318	F 4
68843	Hampton, 387	G 4
69345	Harrisburg⊙, 80	A 3
69346	Harrison⊙, 377	A 2
68739	Hartington⊙, 1,581	G 2
68944	Harvard, 1,230	F 4
68901	Hastings⊙, 23,580	F 4
69032	Hayes Center⊙, 237	C 4
69347	Hay Springs, 682	B 2
68370	Hebron⊙, 1,667	G 4
69348	Hemingford, 734	A 2
68371	Henderson, 901	G 4
68029	Herman, 323	H 3
69143	Hershey, 526	D 3
68372	Hickman, 415	H 4
68947	Hildreth, 352	E 4
68948	Holbrook, 307	D 4
68949	Holdrege⊙, 5,635	E 4
68030	Homer, 457	H 2
68031	Hooper, 895	H 3
68641	Howells, 682	H 3
68376	Humboldt, 1,194	J 4

Miles of pens hold thousands of head of cattle in the Union Stockyards, Omaha. Next stop — the meat packers' plant.

J. Gordon Miller — Shostal Associates

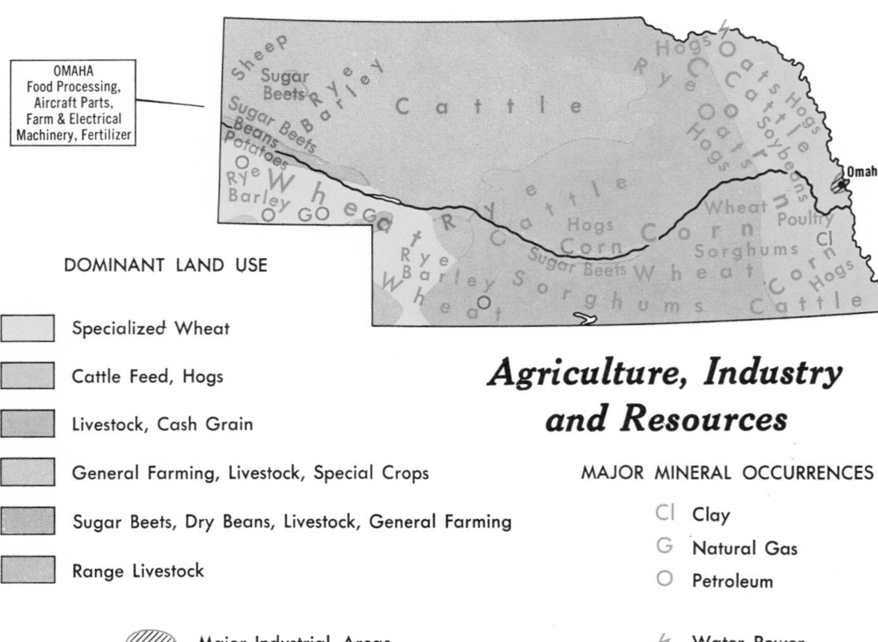

Agriculture, Industry and Resources

NEBRASKA

SCALE 0 5 10 20 30 40 50 60 MI.

0 5 10 20 30 40 50 60 KM.

State Capitals ⊛

County Seats ⊙

Zip	Place	Key
68642	Humphrey, 862	G 3
69350	Hyannis⊙, 345	C 3
69033	Imperial⊙, 1,589	C 4
69034	Indianola, 672	D 4
68378	Johnson, 350	J 4
68955	Juniata, 480	F 4
68847	Kearney⊙, 19,181	E 4
68956	Kenesaw, 728	F 4
68034	Kennard, 336	H 3
69145	Kimball⊙, 3,680	A 3
68745	Laurel, 1,009	G 2
68046	La Vista, 4,807	J 3
68957	Lawrence, 343	F 4
68643	Leigh, 501	G 3
69147	Lewellen, 376	B 3
68850	Lexington⊙, 5,618	E 4
68501	Lincoln (cap.)⊙, 149,518	H 4
	Lincoln, ‡167,972	H 4
68644	Lindsay, 291	G 3
69149	Lodgepole, 407	B 3
69217	Long Pine, 363	E 2
68958	Loomis, 323	E 4
68037	Louisville, 1,036	H 3
68853	Loup City⊙, 1,456	E 3
69352	Lyman, 561	A 3
68746	Lynch, 375	F 2
68038	Lyons, 1,177	H 3
68039	Macy, 550	H 2
68748	Madison⊙, 1,595	G 3
69038	Maywood, 309	D 4
69001	McCook⊙, 8,285	D 4
68401	McCool Junction, 289	G 4
68041	Mead, 488	H 3
68752	Meadow Grove, 372	G 2
68856	Merna, 322	E 3
68405	Milford, 1,846	H 4
68137	Millard, 7,460	H 3
68406	Milligan, 319	G 4
69356	Minatare, 939	A 3
68959	Minden⊙, 2,669	F 4
69357	Mitchell, 1,842	A 3
69358	Morrill, 937	A 3
69152	Muilen⊙, 667	C 2
68409	Murray, 286	J 4
68410	Nebraska City⊙, 7,441	J 4
68413	Nehawka, 298	H 4
68756	Neligh⊙, 1,764	G 2
68961	Nelson⊙, 746	F 4
68757	Newcastle, 347	H 2
68758	Newman Grove, 863	G 3
68760	Niobrara, 602	G 2
68701	Norfolk, 16,607	G 2
68649	North Bend, 1,350	H 3
68859	North Loup, 441	F 3
69101	North Platte⊙, 19,447	D 3
68761	Oakdale, 322	F 2
68045	Oakland, 1,355	H 3
68415	Odell, 349	H 4
69153	Ogallala⊙, 4,976	C 3
* 68101	Omaha⊙, 347,328	J 3
	Omaha, ‡540,142	J 3
68763	O'Neill⊙, 3,753	F 2
68764	Orchard, 467	F 2
68862	Ord⊙, 2,439	F 3
68966	Orleans, 592	E 4
68651	Osceola⊙, 923	G 3
69154	Oshkosh⊙, 1,067	B 3
68765	Osmond, 883	G 2
68863	Overton, 506	E 4
68967	Oxford, 1,116	E 4
69040	Palisade, 372	C 4
68864	Palmer, 391	F 3
68418	Palmyra, 386	H 4
68046	Papillion⊙, 5,606	J 3
† 68801	Parkview, 1,089	F 4
68420	Pawnee City⊙, 1,267	H 4
69155	Paxton, 503	C 3
68047	Pender⊙, 1,229	H 2
68421	Peru, 1,380	J 4
68652	Petersburg, 370	G 3
68865	Phillips, 341	F 4
68767	Pierce⊙, 1,360	G 2
68768	Pilger, 470	G 2
68769	Plainview, 1,494	G 2
68653	Platte Center, 384	G 3
68048	Plattsmouth⊙, 6,371	J 3
68424	Plymouth, 424	G 4
68654	Polk, 413	G 3
68770	Ponca⊙, 984	H 2
69156	Potter, 356	A 3
68050	Prague, 291	H 3
68127	Ralston, 4,265	J 3
68771	Randolph, 1,130	G 2
68869	Ravenna, 1,356	F 4
68970	Red Cloud⊙, 2,195	F 4
68658	Rising City, 344	G 3
68431	Rulo, 299	J 4
69360	Rushville⊙, 1,137	B 2
68660	Saint Edward, 853	G 3
68873	Saint Paul⊙, 2,026	F 3
68874	Sargent, 789	E 3
68661	Schuyler⊙, 3,597	G 3
68875	Scotia, 354	F 3
69361	Scottsbluff, 14,507	A 3
68057	Scribner, 1,031	H 3
68434	Seward⊙, 5,294	H 4
68662	Shelby, 647	G 3
68876	Shelton, 1,028	F 4
68436	Shickley, 385	G 4
69162	Sidney⊙, 6,403	B 3
68663	Silver Creek, 483	G 3
68664	Snyder, 383	H 3
68776	South Sioux City, 7,920	H 2
68665	Spalding, 676	F 3
68777	Spencer, 606	F 2
68059	Springfield, 795	H 3
68778	Springview⊙, 260	E 2
68779	Stanton⊙, 1,363	G 3
69163	Stapleton⊙, 311	D 3
68443	Sterling, 476	H 4
69042	Stockville⊙, 61	D 4
69043	Stratton, 481	C 4
68666	Stromsburg, 1,215	G 3
68780	Stuart, 561	E 2
68978	Superior, 2,779	F 4
69165	Sutherland, 840	C 3
68979	Sutton, 1,361	G 4
68446	Syracuse, 1,562	H 4
68447	Table Rock, 429	H 4
68448	Talmage, 285	H 4
68879	Taylor⊙, 240	E 3
68450	Tecumseh⊙, 2,058	H 4
68061	Tekamah⊙, 1,848	H 3
† 69341	Terrytown, 747	A 3
69166	Thedford⊙, 303	D 3
68781	Tilden, 947	G 2
69044	Trenton⊙, 770	D 4
69167	Tryon⊙, 138	C 3
68669	Ulysses, 312	G 3
68456	Utica, 602	G 4
69201	Valentine⊙, 2,662	D 2
68064	Valley, 1,595	H 3
68065	Valparaiso, 415	H 3
68783	Verdigre, 570	F 2
68066	Wahoo⊙, 3,835	H 3
68784	Wakefield, 1,160	H 2
68067	Walthill, 897	H 2
69045	Wauneta, 738	C 4
68786	Wausa, 720	G 2
68462	Waverly, 1,152	H 4
68787	Wayne⊙, 5,379	G 2
68463	Weeping Water, 1,143	J 4
68464	Western, 344	G 4
68070	Weston, 285	H 3
68788	West Point⊙, 3,385	H 3
68465	Wilber⊙, 1,483	G 4
68071	Winnebago, 675	H 2
68790	Winside, 453	G 2
68791	Wisner, 1,315	H 3
68882	Wolbach, 366	F 3
68883	Wood River, 1,061	F 4
68466	Wymore, 1,790	H 4
68467	York⊙, 6,778	G 4
68073	Yutan, 507	H 3

⊙ County seat.
‡ Population of metropolitan area.
† Zip of nearest p.o.
* Multiple zips

AREA 77,227 sq. mi.
POPULATION 1,483,791
CAPITAL Lincoln
LARGEST CITY Omaha
HIGHEST POINT 5,426 ft. (Kimball Co.)
SETTLED IN 1847
ADMITTED TO UNION March 1, 1867
POPULAR NAME Cornhusker State
STATE FLOWER Goldenrod
STATE BIRD Western Meadowlark

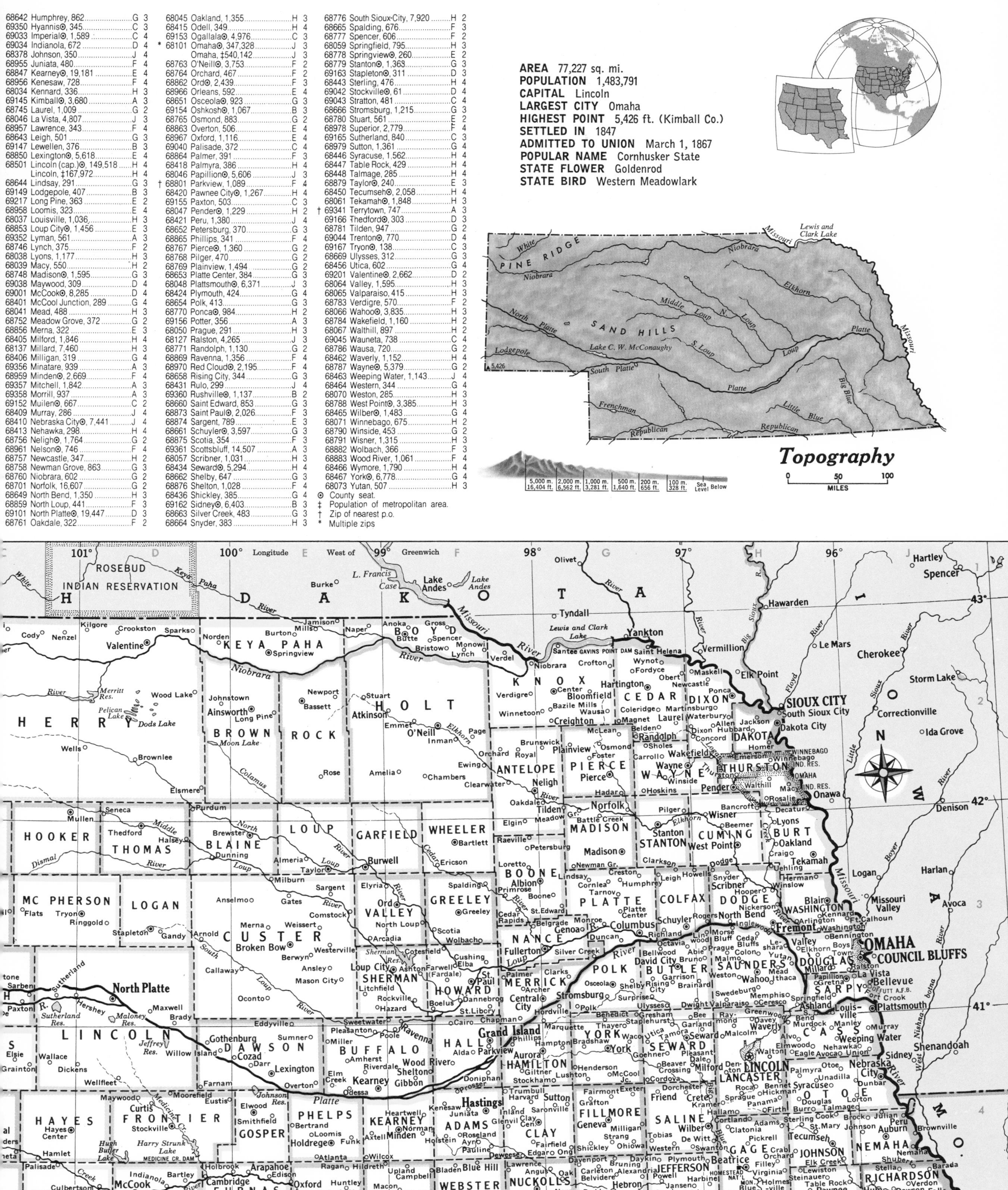

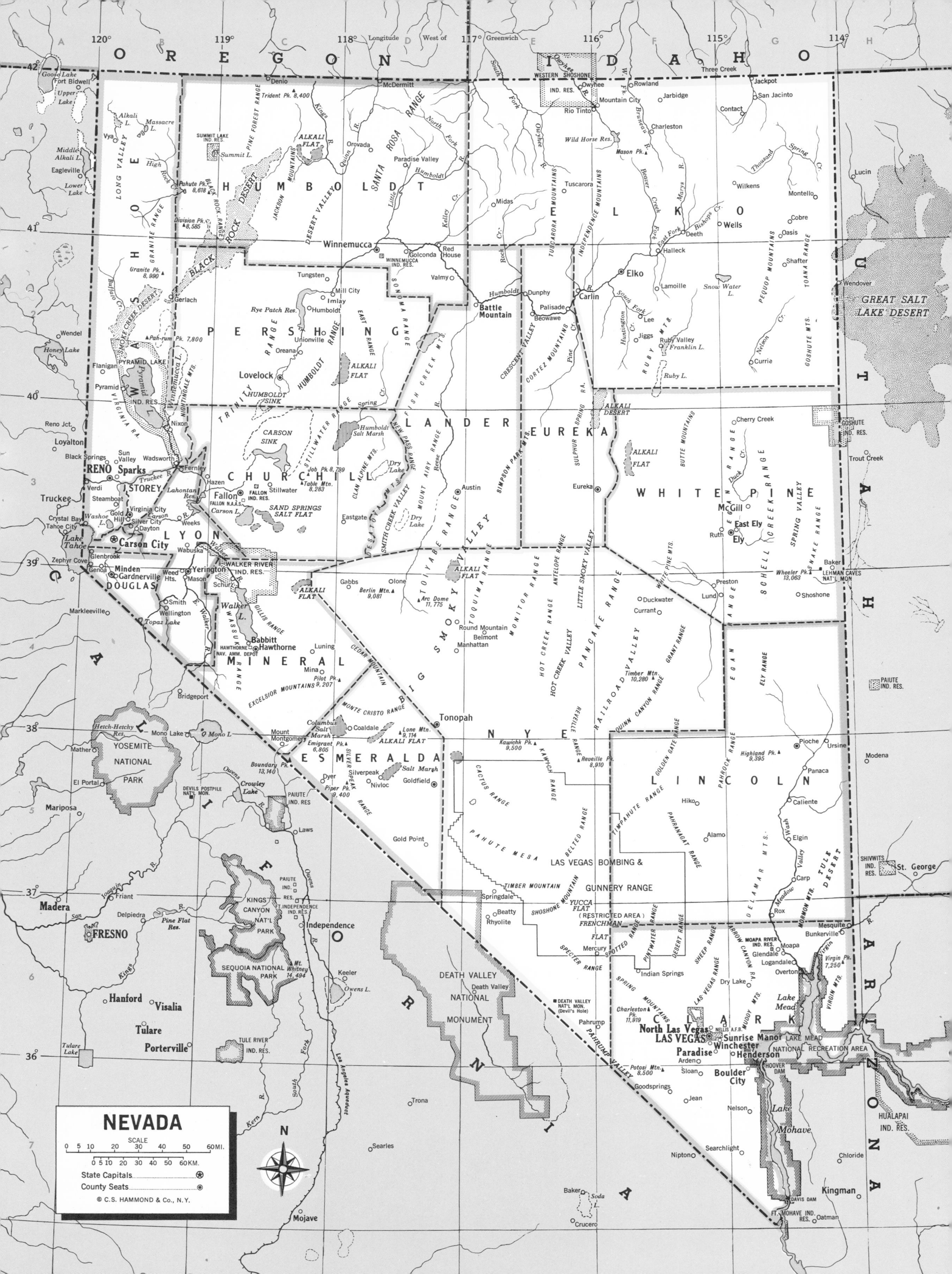
NEVADA
SCALE
0 5 10 20 30 40 50 60 MI.
0 5 10 20 30 40 50 60 KM.
State Capitals
County Seats
© C.S. HAMMOND & Co., N.Y.
N
120°
119°
118°
Longitude
West of
117°
Greenwich
116°
115°
114°
A
B
C
D
E
F
G
H
42
41
40
39
38
37
36
O R E G O N
I D A H O
U T A H
A R I Z O N A
C A L I F O R N I A
W A S H O E
H U M B O L D T
E L K O
P E R S H I N G
L A N D E R
E U R E K A
C H U R C H I L L
W H I T E P I N E
STOREY
LYON
DOUGLAS
M I N E R A L
N Y E
E S M E R A L D A
L I N C O L N
C L A R K
Carson City
RENO
Sparks
Winnemucca
Elko
Lovelock
Fallon
Yerington
Minden
Gardnerville
Hawthorne
Babbitt
Tonopah
Goldfield
Austin
Eureka
Ely
East Ely
McGill
Ruth
Pioche
Caliente
Panaca
Battle Mountain
Carlin
Wells
LAS VEGAS
North Las Vegas
Sunrise Manor
Winchester
Paradise
Henderson
Boulder City
Denio
McDermitt
Jackpot
Owyhee
Mountain City
Rio Tinto
Rowland
Jarbidge
Three Creek
San Jacinto
Contact
Charleston
Tuscarora
Midas
Golconda
Red House
Valmy
Tungsten
Mill City
Imlay
Humboldt
Unionville
Oreana
Rye Patch Res.
Gerlach
Vya
Orovada
Paradise Valley
Wilkens
Montello
Cobre
Oasis
Deeth
Halleck
Shafter
Wendover
Lamoille
Lee
Jiggs
Ruby Valley
Franklin L.
Ruby L.
Currie
Snow Water L.
Dunphy
Palisade
Beowawe
Cherry Creek
Trout Creek
Baker
Preston
Lund
Shoshone
Duckwater
Currant
Ione
Gabbs
Round Mountain
Belmont
Manhattan
Luning
Mina
Coaldale
Mount Montgomery
Dyer
Silverpeak
Nivloc
Gold Point
Beatty
Rhyolite
Springdale
Mercury
Indian Springs
Pahrump
Arden
Sloan
Goodsprings
Jean
Nelson
Searchlight
Nipton
Hiko
Alamo
Elgin
Carp
Rox
Ursine
Modena
Mesquite
Bunkerville
Moapa
Glendale
Logandale
Overton
Dry Lake
St. George
Nixon
Wadsworth
Fernley
Hazen
Stillwater
Eastgate
Sun Valley
Verdi
Steamboat
Virginia City
Gold Hill
Silver City
Dayton
Weeks
Wabuska
Weed Hts.
Mason
Schurz
Smith
Wellington
Glenbrook
Genoa
Zephyr Cove
Crystal Bay
Tahoe City
Truckee
Loyalton
Reno Jct.
Black Springs
Flanigan
Pyramid
Wendel
Eagleville
Fort Bidwell
Markleeville
Topaz Lake
Bridgeport
Mono Lake
Mono L.
Mather
El Portal
Mariposa
Madera
Friant
Delpiedra
FRESNO
Hanford
Visalia
Tulare
Porterville
Laws
Independence
Keeler
Owens L.
Trona
Searles
Mojave
Baker
Soda L.
Crucero
Kingman
Chloride
Oatman
Lucin
GREAT SALT LAKE DESERT
Lake Tahoe
Pyramid Lake
Walker L.
Carson Sink
Humboldt Sink
Humboldt Salt Marsh
Carson L.
SAND SPRINGS SALT FLAT
ALKALI FLAT
BLACK ROCK DESERT
SMOKE CREEK DESERT
Honey Lake
Goose Lake
Upper Lake
Middle Alkali L.
Lower Lake
Alkali L.
Massacre L.
Summit L.
Lake Mead
Lake Mohave
HOOVER DAM
DAVIS DAM
LAKE MEAD NATIONAL RECREATION AREA
Wild Horse Res.
Pahute Pk. 8,618
Division Pk. 8,585
Granite Pk. 8,990
Trident Pk. 8,400
Pah-rum Pk. 7,800
Mason Pk.
Job Pk. 8,799
Table Mtn. 8,283
Berlin Mtn. 9,081
Arc Dome 11,775
Pilot Pk. 9,207
Lone Mtn. 9,114
Emigrant Pk. 6,805
Boundary Pk. 13,140
Piper Pk. 9,400
Kawich Pk. 9,500
Reveille Pk. 8,910
Timber Mtn. 10,280
Highland Pk. 9,395
Wheeler Pk. 13,063
Charleston Pk. 11,919
Potosi Mtn. 8,500
Virgin Pk. 7,250
Mt. Whitney 14,494
TOIYABE RANGE
TOQUIMA RANGE
MONITOR RANGE
HOT CREEK RANGE
PANCAKE RANGE
GRANT RANGE
QUINN CANYON RANGE
RAILROAD VALLEY
SCHELL CREEK RANGE
SNAKE RANGE
EGAN RANGE
RUBY MTS.
PEQUOP MOUNTAINS
TOANO RANGE
GOSHUTE MTS.
INDEPENDENCE MOUNTAINS
TUSCARORA MOUNTAINS
CORTEZ MOUNTAINS
SANTA ROSA RANGE
SONOMA RANGE
HUMBOLDT RANGE
TRINITY RANGE
STILLWATER RANGE
CLAN ALPINE MTS.
DESATOYA MTS.
SHOSHONE MTS.
WASSUK RANGE
EXCELSIOR MOUNTAINS
MONTE CRISTO RANGE
SILVER PEAK RANGE
CACTUS RANGE
KAWICH RANGE
BELTED RANGE
PAHUTE MESA
TIMBER MOUNTAIN
SPRING MOUNTAINS
SHEEP RANGE
LAS VEGAS RANGE
MORMON MTS.
TULE DESERT
DELAMAR MTS.
VIRGIN MTS.
LAS VEGAS BOMBING & GUNNERY RANGE
YUCCA FLAT (RESTRICTED AREA)
FRENCHMAN FLAT
PAHRUMP VALLEY
BIG SMOKY VALLEY
YOSEMITE NATIONAL PARK
KINGS CANYON NAT'L PARK
SEQUOIA NATIONAL PARK
DEATH VALLEY NATIONAL MONUMENT
DEVILS POSTPILE NAT'L MON.
DEATH VALLEY NAT'L MON. (Devil's Hole)
WESTERN SHOSHONE IND. RES.
SUMMIT LAKE IND. RES.
PYRAMID LAKE IND. RES.
WINNEMUCCA IND. RES.
WALKER RIVER IND. RES.
FALLON IND. RES.
FALLON N.A.S.
HAWTHORNE NAV. AMM. DEPOT
GOSHUTE IND. RES.
LEHMAN CAVES NAT'L MON.
PAIUTE IND. RES.
SHIVWITS IND. RES.
MOAPA RIVER IND. RES.
NELLIS A.F.B.
HUALAPAI IND. RES.
FT. MOHAVE IND. RES.
TULE RIVER IND. RES.
Humboldt R.
Owyhee R.
Truckee R.
Carson R.
Walker R.
Reese R.
Quinn R.
Marys R.
Bruneau R.
Thousand Spring Cr.
Meadow Valley Wash
Los Angeles Aqueduct

COUNTIES

County	Key
Carson City (city), 15,468	B 3
Churchill, 10,513	C 3
Clark, 273,288	F 6
Douglas, 6,882	B 4
Elko, 13,958	F 1
Esmeralda, 629	D 5
Eureka, 948	E 3
Humboldt, 6,375	C 1
Lander, 2,666	D 3
Lincoln, 2,557	F 5
Lyon, 8,221	B 3
Mineral, 7,051	C 4
Nye, 5,599	E 4
Pershing, 2,670	C 2
Storey, 695	B 3
Washoe, 121,068	B 2
White Pine, 10,150	F 3

CITIES and TOWNS

	Zip	*Name/Pop.*	*Key*
	89001	Alamo, 300	F 5
	89310	Austin⊙, 300	E 3
	89416	Babbitt, 1,579	C 4
	89311	Baker, 75	G 3
	89820	Battle Mountain, 1,856	E 2
	89003	Beatty, 570	E 6
†	89045	Belmont, 25	E 4
	89821	Beowawe, 104	E 2
	89508	Black Springs, 2,500	B 3
	89005	Boulder City, 5,223	G 7
	89007	Bunkerville, 150	G 6
	89008	Caliente, 916	G 5
	89822	Carlin, 1,313	E 2
	89009	Carp, 32	G 5
	89701	Carson City (cap.), 15,468	B 3
†	89801	Charleston, 14	F 1
	89312	Cherry Creek, 75	G 3
†	89049	Coaldale, 31	D 4
†	89830	Cobre, 14	G 1
†	89825	Contact, 9	G 1
	89402	Crystal Bay, 950	A 3
†	89314	Currant, 30	F 4
	89313	Currie, 15	G 2
	89403	Dayton, 350	B 3
	89823	Deeth, 27	F 1
	89404	Denio, 28	C 1
†	89040	Dry Lake, 5	G 6
	89314	Duckwater, 85	F 4
†	89821	Dunphy, 25	E 2
	89010	Dyer, 60	C 5
	89315	East Ely, 1,992	G 3
†	89406	Eastgate, 17	D 3
	89112	East Las Vegas, 6,501	F 6
†	89009	Elgin, 8	G 5
	89801	Elko⊙, 7,621	F 2
	89301	Ely⊙, 4,176	G 3
	89316	Eureka⊙, 300	E 3
	89406	Fallon⊙, 2,959	C 3
	89408	Fernley, 750	B 3
	89409	Gabbs, 874	D 4
	89410	Gardnerville, 800	B 4
	89411	Genoa, 170	B 4
	89412	Gerlach, 150	B 2
	89413	Glenbrook, 800	B 3
†	89025	Glendale, 20	G 6
	89414	Golconda, 150	D 2
	89013	Goldfield⊙, 213	D 5
†	89440	Gold Hill, 50	B 3
†	89013	Gold Point, 10	D 5
	89019	Goodsprings, 120	F 7
	89824	Halleck, 50	F 2
	89415	Hawthorne⊙, 3,539	C 4
	89417	Hazen, 60	C 3
	89015	Henderson, 16,395	G 6
	89017	Hiko, 150	F 5
†	89418	Humboldt, 12	C 2
	89418	Imlay, 150	C 2
	89018	Indian Springs, 500	F 6
†	89310	Ione, 15	D 4
	89825	Jackpot, 400	G 1
	89826	Jarbidge, 25	F 1
	89019	Jean, 100	F 7
	89827	Jiggs, 6	F 2
	89828	Lamoille, 51	F 2
*	89101	Las Vegas⊙, 125,787	F 6
		Las Vegas, ‡273,288	F 6
	89829	Lee, 180	F 2
	89021	Logandale, 410	G 6
	89419	Lovelock⊙, 1,571	C 2
	89317	Lund, 300	F 4
	89420	Luning, 55	C 4
	89022	Manhattan, 28	E 4
†	89447	Mason, 200	B 4
	89421	McDermitt, 300	D 1
	89318	McGill, 2,164	G 3
	89023	Mercury, 2,200	E 6
	89024	Mesquite, 500	G 6
†	89414	Midas, 6	E 1
†	89418	Mill City, 4	D 2
	89422	Mina, 375	C 4
	89423	Minden⊙, 520	B 4
	89025	Moapa, 250	G 6
	89830	Montello, 150	G 1
	89831	Mountain City, 80	F 1
†	89422	Mount Montgomery, 10	C 5
†	89046	Nelson, 67	G 7
	89424	Nixon, 300	B 3
	89030	North Las Vegas, 36,216	F 6
†	89830	Oasis, 5	G 1
†	89419	Oreana, 18	C 2
	89425	Orovada, 250	D 1
	89040	Overton, 900	G 6
	89832	Owyhee, 100	F 1
	89041	Pahrump, 400	E 6
†	89822	Palisade, 5	E 2
	89042	Panaca, 500	G 5
†	89101	Paradise, 24,477	F 6
	89426	Paradise Valley, 110	D 1
	89043	Pioche⊙, 525	G 5
†	89301	Preston, 44	G 4
†	89414	Red House, 4	D 2
*	89501	Reno⊙, 72,863	B 3
		Reno, ‡121,068	B 3
†	89003	Rhyolite, 8	E 6
†	89831	Rio Tinto, 5	E 1
	89045	Round Mountain, 100	E 4
†	89831	Rowland, 10	F 1
†	89009	Rox, 12	G 6
	89833	Ruby Valley, 225	F 2
	89319	Ruth, 750	F 3
†	89825	San Jacinto, 8	G 1
	89427	Schurz, 350	C 4
	89046	Searchlight, 279	F 7
†	89835	Shafter, 7	G 2
†	89301	Shoshone, 15	G 4
	89428	Silver City, 100	B 3
	89047	Silverpeak, 80	D 5
†	89114	Sloan, 25	F 7
	89430	Smith, 300	B 4
	89431	Sparks, 24,187	B 3
	89436	Steamboat, 560	B 3
†	89406	Stillwater, 30	C 3
†	89101	Sunrise Manor, 10,886	F 6
†	89431	Sun Valley, 2,414	B 3
	89049	Tonopah⊙, 1,716	D 4
	89834	Tuscarora, 15	E 1
†	89418	Unionville, 18	C 2
†	89043	Ursine, 40	G 5
	89438	Valmy, 50	D 2
	89439	Verdi, 100	B 3
	89440	Virginia City⊙, 300	B 3
†	96104	Vya, 12	B 1
†	89447	Wabuska, 50	B 3
	89442	Wadsworth, 375	B 3
	89443	Weed Heights, 750	B 4
†	89447	Weeks, 15	B 3
	89444	Wellington, 100	B 4
	89835	Wells, 1,081	G 1
†	89835	Wilkins, 6	G 1
†	89101	Winchester, 13,981	F 6
	89445	Winnemucca⊙, 3,587	D 2
	89447	Yerington⊙, 2,010	B 4
	89448	Zephyr Cove, 400	A 3

⊙ County seat.
‡ Population of metropolitan area.
† Zip of nearest p.o.
* Multiple zips

AREA 110,540 sq. mi.
POPULATION 488,738
CAPITAL Carson City
LARGEST CITY Las Vegas
HIGHEST POINT Boundary Pk. 13,140 ft.
SETTLED IN 1850
ADMITTED TO UNION October 31, 1864
POPULAR NAME Silver State
STATE FLOWER Sagebrush
STATE BIRD Mountain Bluebird

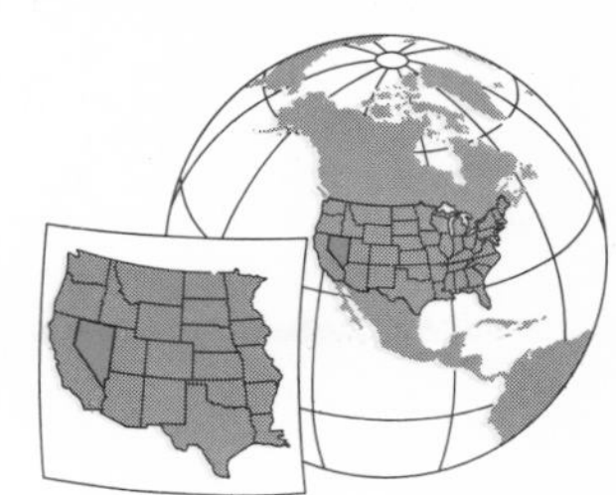

An incandescent oasis in the Nevada desert, Reno beckons travelers to its varied diversions — from games of chance and nightclub entertainment to annual rodeos and skiing in the Sierra Nevada.

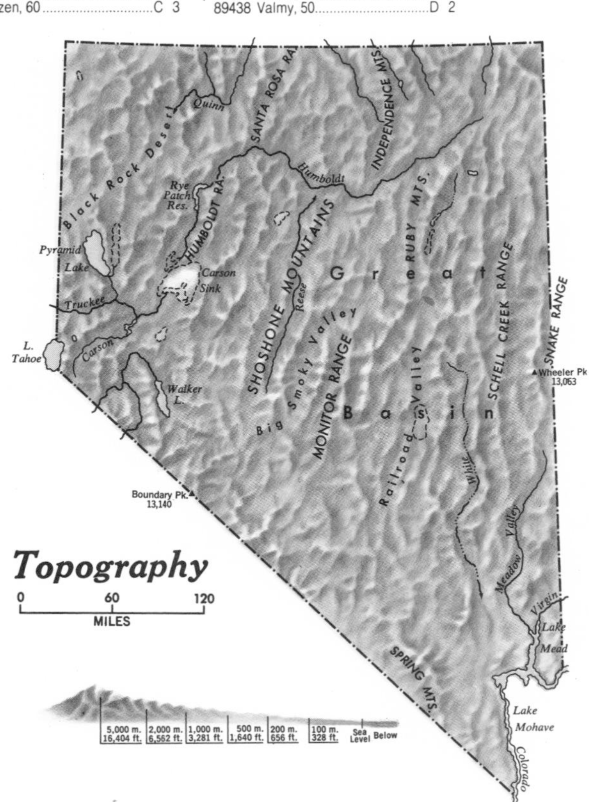

Agriculture, Industry and Resources

MAJOR MINERAL OCCURRENCES

Ag Silver
Au Gold
Ba Barite
Cu Copper
Gp Gypsum
Hg Mercury
Lt Lithium
Mg Magnesium
Mo Molybdenum
Na Salt
O Petroleum
Pb Lead
S Sulfur
W Tungsten
Zn Zinc
ϟ Water Power

DOMINANT LAND USE

General Farming, Dairy, Livestock
General Farming, Livestock, Special Crops
Range Livestock
Forests
Nonagricultural Land

Dairy Cattle
Cattle
Sheep

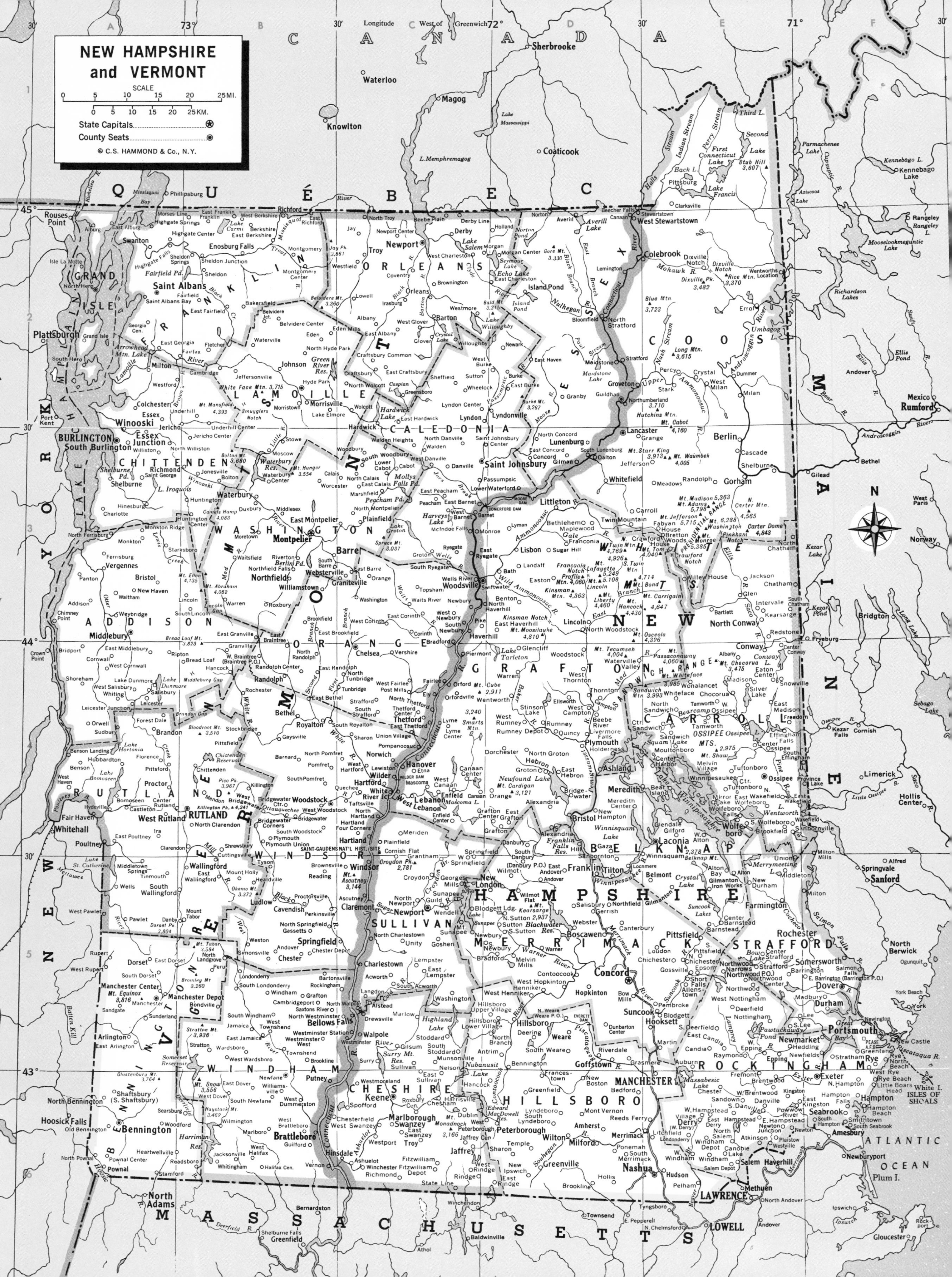
NEW HAMPSHIRE
and VERMONT
SCALE
0 5 10 15 20 25 MI.
0 5 10 15 20 25 KM.
State Capitals
County Seats
© C.S. HAMMOND & Co., N.Y.
Longitude West of Greenwich
73°
72°
71°
45°
44°
43°
C A N A D A
Q U É B E C
N E W Y O R K
M A I N E
M A S S A C H U S E T T S
ATLANTIC OCEAN
NEW HAMPSHIRE
VERMONT
FRANKLIN
GRAND ISLE
ORLEANS
ESSEX
LAMOILLE
CALEDONIA
CHITTENDEN
WASHINGTON
ADDISON
ORANGE
RUTLAND
WINDSOR
BENNINGTON
WINDHAM
COOS
GRAFTON
CARROLL
BELKNAP
SULLIVAN
MERRIMACK
STRAFFORD
CHESHIRE
HILLSBORO
ROCKINGHAM
Montpelier
Concord
BURLINGTON
RUTLAND
MANCHESTER
Nashua
Portsmouth
Saint Albans
Saint Johnsbury
Bennington
Brattleboro
Keene
Laconia
Dover
Berlin
Lebanon
Sherbrooke
Plattsburgh
Rumford
LAWRENCE
LOWELL
Lake Winnipesaukee
Lake Champlain
L. Memphremagog
Connecticut R.
Merrimack R.
WHITE MTS.
PRESIDENTIAL RANGE
Mt. Washington 6,288
ISLES OF SHOALS

NEW HAMPSHIRE

COUNTIES

County/Pop.	Key
Belknap, 32,367	D 4
Carroll, 18,548	E 4
Cheshire, 52,364	C 6
Coos, 34,291	E 2
Grafton, 54,914	D 4
Hillsboro, 223,941	D 6
Merrimack, 80,925	D 5
Rockingham, 138,951	E 5
Strafford, 70,431	E 5
Sullivan, 30,949	C 5

CITIES and TOWNS

Zip	Name/Pop.	Key
03601	Acworth, △459	C 5
† 03864	Albany, △259	E 4
† 03222	Alexandria, △466	D 4
† 03275	Allenstown, △2,732	E 5
03602	Alstead, △1,185	C 5
03602	Alstead, 450	C 5
03809	Alton, △1,647	E 5
03809	Alton, 450	E 5
03031	Amherst, △4,605	D 6
03810	Amherst, 600	D 6
03216	Andover, △1,138	D 5
03216	Andover, 500	D 5
03440	Antrim, △2,122	D 5
03440	Antrim, 750	D 5
03217	Ashland, △1,599	D 4
03217	Ashland, 1,391	D 4
03441	Ashuelot, 750	C 6
03811	Atkinson, △2,291	E 6
03032	Auburn, △2,035	E 5
03218	Barnstead, △1,119	E 5
03218	Barnstead, 400	E 5
† 03825	Barrington, △1,865	F 5
03812	Bartlett, △1,098	E 3
03812	Bartlett, 600	E 3
03740	Bath, △607	D 3
03102	Bedford, △5,859	D 6
03220	Belmont, △2,493	E 5
03220	Belmont, 900	E 5
03442	Bennington, △639	D 5
† 03785	Benton, △194	D 3
03570	Berlin, 15,256	E 3
03574	Bethlehem, △1,142	D 3
03574	Bethlehem, 500	D 3
03301	Boscawen, △3,162	D 5
† 03301	Bow Mills, 600	D 5
03221	Bradford, △679	D 5
† 03833	Brentwood, △1,468	E 6
03575	Bretton Woods, 6	E 3
† 03222	Bridgewater, △398	D 4
03222	Bristol, △1,670	D 4
03222	Bristol, 1,080	D 4
† 03872	Brookfield, △198	E 4
03033	Brookline, △1,167	D 6
03223	Campton, △1,171	D 4
03741	Canaan, △1,923	C 4
03741	Canaan, 500	C 4
03034	Candia, △1,997	E 5
† 03079	Canobie Lake, 500	E 6
03224	Canterbury, △895	D 5
† 03595	Carroll, △310	D 3
03813	Center Conway, 450	E 4
03226	Center Harbor, △540	E 4
03814	Center Ossipee, 550	E 4
03603	Charlestown, △3,274	C 5
03603	Charlestown, 1,285	C 5
† 04037	Chatham, △134	E 3
03036	Chester, △1,382	E 6
03443	Chesterfield, △1,817	C 6
03443	Chesterfield, 450	C 5
† 03258	Chichester, △1,083	E 5
03743	Claremont, 14,221	C 5
† 05902	Clarksville, △166	E 1
03576	Colebrook, △2,094	E 2
03576	Colebrook, 1,070	E 2
03301	Concord (cap.)⊙, 30,022	D 5
03229	Contoocook, 975	D 5
03818	Conway, △4,865	E 4
03818	Conway, 1,489	E 4
† 03753	Croydon, △396	C 5
† 03598	Dalton, △425	D 3
03230	Danbury, △489	D 4
03819	Danville, △924	E 6
03037	Deerfield, △1,178	E 5
† 03244	Deering, △578	D 5
03038	Derry,, △11,712	E 6
03038	Derry, 6,090	E 6

NEW HAMPSHIRE
AREA 9,304 sq. mi.
POPULATION 737,681
CAPITAL Concord
LARGEST CITY Manchester
HIGHEST POINT Mt. Washington 6,288 ft.
SETTLED IN 1623
ADMITTED TO UNION June 21, 1788
POPULAR NAME Granite State
STATE FLOWER Purple Lilac
STATE BIRD Purple Finch

VERMONT
AREA 9,609 sq. mi.
POPULATION 444,732
CAPITAL Montpelier
LARGEST CITY Burlington
HIGHEST POINT Mt. Mansfield 4,393 ft.
SETTLED IN 1764
ADMITTED TO UNION March 4, 1791
POPULAR NAME Green Mountain State
STATE FLOWER Red Clover
STATE BIRD Hermit Thrush

Zip	Name/Pop.	Key
† 03266	Dorchester, △141	D 4
03820	Dover⊙, 20,850	F 5
03444	Dublin, △837	C 6
† 03588	Dummer, △225	E 2
† 03301	Dunbarton, △825	D 5
03824	Durham, △8,869	F 5
03824	Durham, 7,221	F 5
03231	East Andover, 450	D 5
03041	East Derry, 600	E 6
03827	East Kingston, △838	F 6
† 03580	Easton, △92	D 3
03446	East Swanzey, 500	C 6
† 03894	East Wolfeboro, 400	E 4
03832	Eaton, △221	E 4
† 03264	Ellsworth, △13	D 4
03748	Enfield, △2,345	C 4
03748	Enfield, 1,408	C 4
03042	Epping, △2,356	E 5
03042	Epping, 1,097	E 5
03234	Epsom, △1,469	E 5
03579	Errol, △199	E 2
03750	Etna, 550	C 4
03833	Exeter, △8,892	F 6
03833	Exeter⊙, 6,439	F 6
03835	Farmington, △3,588	E 5
03835	Farmington, 2,884	E 5
03447	Fitzwilliam, △1,362	C 6
03447	Fitzwilliam, 750	C 6
03043	Francestown, △525	D 6
03580	Franconia, △655	D 3
03235	Franklin, 7,292	D 5
03836	Freedom, △387	E 4

Topography

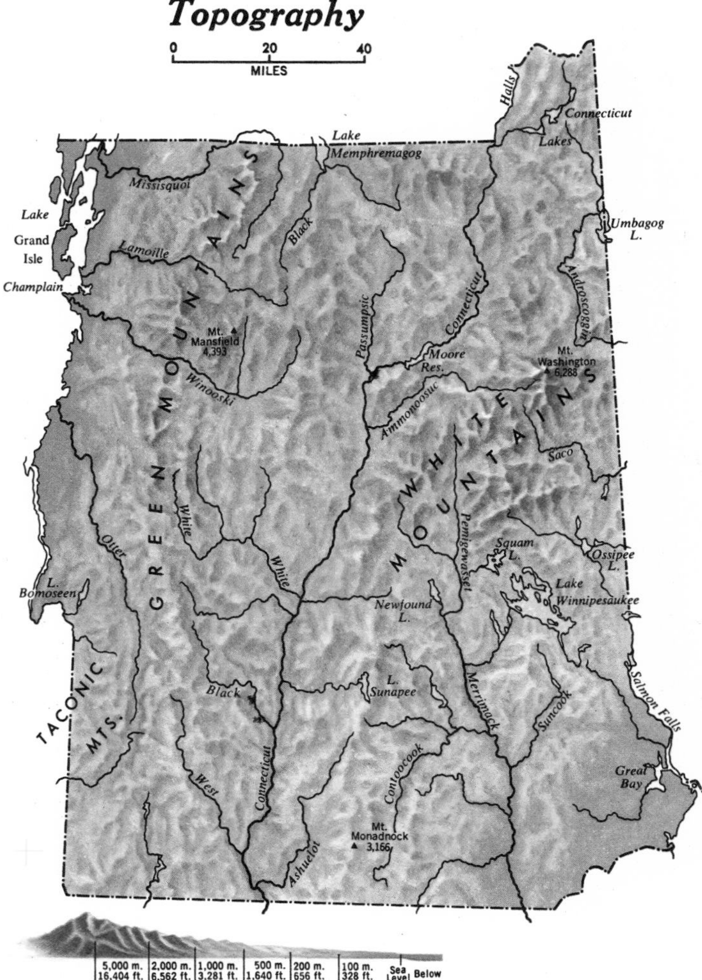

Agriculture, Industry and Resources

Dairy
Maple Syrup
Potatoes
Apples
Dairy
Maple Syrup
Dairy
Apples
Manchester
Vegetables
Poultry
Dairy

MANCHESTER
Leather Goods, Textiles, Electrical Products

DOMINANT LAND USE

- Specialized Dairy
- Dairy, General Farming
- Dairy, Poultry, Mixed Farming
- Forests

- Water Power
- Major Industrial Areas

MAJOR MINERAL OCCURRENCES

Ab	Asbestos	Mr	Marble
Be	Beryl	Sl	Slate
Gn	Granite	Tc	Talc
Mi	Mica	Th	Thorium

Zip	Name/Pop.	Key
03044	Fremont, △993	E 6
† 03246	Gilford, △3,219	E 4
03237	Gilmanton, △1,010	E 5
03448	Gilsum, △570	C 5
03045	Goffstown, △9,284	D 5
03045	Goffstown, 2,272	D 5
03581	Gorham, △2,998	E 3
03581	Gorham, 2,020	E 3
03752	Goshen, △395	C 5
03239	Gossville, 800	E 5
03240	Grafton, △370	D 4
03753	Grantham, △366	C 5
03045	Grasmere, 513	D 5
03047	Greenfield, △1,058	D 6
03840	Greenland, △1,784	F 5
03048	Greenville, △1,587	D 6
03048	Greenville, 1,332	D 6
† 03241	Groton, △120	D 4
03582	Groveton, 1,597	D 2
03841	Hampstead, △2,401	E 6
03841	Hampstead, 500	E 6
03842	Hampton, △8,011	F 6
03842	Hampton, 5,407	F 6
03842	Hampton Beach, 975	F 6
03844	Hampton Falls, △1,254	F 6
03449	Hancock, △909	C 6
03755	Hanover, △8,494	C 4
03755	Hanover, 6,147	C 4
03450	Harrisville, △584	C 6
03765	Haverhill, △3,090	C 3
03765	Haverhill, 400	C 3
03241	Hebron, △234	D 4
03242	Henniker, △2,348	D 5
03242	Henniker, 950	D 5
03243	Hill, △450	D 4
03244	Hillsboro, △2,775	D 5
03244	Hillsboro, 1,784	D 5
03451	Hinsdale, △3,276	C 6
03451	Hinsdale, 1,059	C 6
03245	Holderness, △1,048	D 4
03049	Hollis, △2,616	D 6
03049	Hollis, 500	D 6
03106	Hooksett. △5,564	E 5
03106	Hooksett. 1,303	E 5
03301	Hopkinton, △3,007	D 5
03301	Hopkinton, 500	D 5
03051	Hudson, △10,638	E 6
03051	Hudson, 4,900	E 6
03845	Intervale, 500	E 3
03846	Jackson, △404	E 3
03452	Jaffrey, △3,353	C 6
03452	Jaffrey, 1,922	C 6
03583	Jefferson, △714	D 3
03431	Keene⊙, 20,467	C 6
03848	Kingston, △2,882	E 6
03246	Laconia⊙, 14,888	E 4
03584	Lancaster, △3,166	D 3
03584	Lancaster⊙, 2,120	D 3
† 03585	Landaff, △292	D 3
† 03602	Langdon, △337	C 5
03766	Lebanon, 9,725	C 4
† 03857	Lee, △1,481	F 5
03606	Lempster, △360	C 5
03251	Lincoln, △1,341	D 3
03251	Lincoln, 900	D 3
03585	Lisbon, △1,480	D 3
03585	Lisbon, 1,247	D 3
† 03051	Litchfield, △1,420	E 6
03561	Littleton, △5,290	D 3
03561	Littleton, 4,180	D 3
03252	Lochmere, 500	D 5
03053	Londonderry, △5,346	E 6
03301	Loudon, △1,707	E 5
† 03585	Lyman, △213	D 3
03768	Lyme, △1,112	C 4
03768	Lyme, 400	C 4
† 03082	Lyndeboro, △789	D 6
† 03820	Madbury, △704	F 5
03849	Madison, △572	E 4
* 03101	Manchester, 87,754	E 6
	Manchester, ‡108,461	E 6
03455	Marlborough, △1,671	C 6
03455	Marlborough, 1,231	C 6
03456	Marlow, △390	C 5
03253	Meredith, △2,904	D 4
03253	Meredith, 1,017	D 4
03770	Meriden, 495	C 4
03054	Merrimack, △8,595	D 6
03054	Merrimack, 850	D 6
† 03887	Middleton, △430	E 5
03588	Milan, △713	E 2
03055	Milford, △6,622	D 6
03055	Milford, 4,997	D 6
03851	Milton, △1,859	F 5
03851	Milton, 750	F 5
03771	Monroe, △385	C 3
03057	Mont Vernon, △906	D 6
03254	Moultonboro, △1,310	E 4
03060	Nashua⊙, 55,820	D 6
† 03457	Nelson, △304	C 5
03070	New Boston, △1,390	D 6
03070	New Boston, 450	D 6
03255	Newbury, △509	C 5
03854	New Castle, △975	F 5
03855	New Durham, △583	E 5
03856	Newfields, △843	F 5
03256	New Hampton, △946	D 4
† 03801	Newington, △798	F 5
03071	New Ipswich, △1,803	D 6
03257	New London, △2,236	D 5
03257	New London, 1,347	D 5
03857	Newmarket, △3,361	F 5
03857	Newmarket, 2,645	F 5
03773	Newport, △5,899	C 5
03773	Newport⊙, 3,296	C 5
03858	Newton, △1,920	E 6
03858	Newton, 483	E 6
03859	Newton Junction, 500	E 6
03258	North Chichester, 450	E 5
03860	North Conway, 1,723	E 3
† 03276	Northfield, △2,193	D 5
† 03276	Northfield-Tilton, 2,420	D 5
03862	North Hampton, △3,259	F 6
03862	North Hampton, 750	F 6
03774	North Haverhill, 750	D 3
† 03773	North Newport, 500	C 5
03073	North Salem, 950	E 6
03590	North Stratford, 650	D 2
† 03582	Northumberland, △2,493	D 2
† 03608	North Walpole, 950	C 5
† 03281	North Weare, 600	D 5
03261	Northwood, △1,526	E 5

(continued on following page)

(continued)

NEW HAMPSHIRE
(continued)

03262 North Woodstock, 650 .... D 3
03290 Nottingham, ▵952 .... E 5
† 03741 Orange, ▵103 .... D 4
03777 Orford, ▵793 .... C 4
03864 Ossipee⊙, ▵1,647 .... E 4
03076 Pelham, ▵5,408 .... E 6
† 03275 Pembroke, ▵4,261 .... E 5
03458 Peterborough, ▵3,807 .... D 6
03458 Peterborough, 2,078 .... D 6
03779 Piermont, ▵462 .... C 4
03592 Pittsburg, ▵726 .... E 1
03263 Pittsfield, ▵2,517 .... E 5
03263 Pittsfield, 1,662 .... E 5
03781 Plainfield, ▵1,323 .... C 4
03865 Plaistow, ▵4,712 .... E 6
03865 Plaistow, 950 .... E 6
03264 Plymouth, ▵4,225 .... D 4
03264 Plymouth, 3,109 .... D 4
03801 Portsmouth, 25,717 .... F 5
03593 Randolph, ▵169 .... E 3
03077 Raymond, ▵3,003 .... E 5
† 03470 Richmond, ▵287 .... C 6
03461 Rindge, ▵2,175 .... C 6
03867 Rochester, 17,938 .... E 5
† 03431 Roxbury, ▵161 .... C 6
03266 Rumney, ▵870 .... D 4
03870 Rye, ▵4,083 .... F 5
03870 Rye, 750 .... F 5
03871 Rye Beach, 750 .... F 6
† 03870 Rye North Beach, 700 .... F 5
03079 Salem, ▵20,142 .... E 6
03079 Salem, 950 .... E 6
† 03079 Salem Depot, 975 .... E 6
03268 Salisbury, ▵589 .... D 5
† 03820 Salmon Falls, 950 .... F 5
03269 Sanbornton, ▵1,022 .... D 5
03872 Sanbornville, 550 .... F 4
03873 Sandown, ▵741 .... E 6
03270 Sandwich, ▵666 .... E 4
03874 Seabrook, ▵3,053 .... F 6
03874 Seabrook, 950 .... F 6
† 03458 Sharon, ▵136 .... D 6
† 03581 Shelburne, ▵199 .... E 3
03878 Somersworth, 9,026 .... F 5
† 03037 South Deerfield, 500 .... E 5
† 01913 South Hampton, ▵558 .... F 6
03083 South Merrimack, 650 .... D 6
† 03874 South Seabrook, 500 .... F 6
03462 Spofford, 631 .... C 6
† 03284 Springfield, ▵310 .... C 4
† 03582 Stark, ▵343 .... E 2
† 03576 Stewartstown, ▵1,008 .... E 2
03464 Stoddard, ▵242 .... C 5
03884 Strafford, ▵965 .... E 5
† 03590 Stratford, ▵980 .... D 2
03885 Stratham, ▵1,512 .... F 5
03585 Sugar Hill, ▵336 .... D 3
† 03445 Sullivan, ▵376 .... C 5
03782 Sunapee, ▵1,384 .... C 5
03782 Sunapee, 750 .... C 5
03275 Suncook, 4,280 .... D 5
03431 Surry, ▵507 .... C 5
† 03260 Sutton, ▵642 .... D 5
† 03431 Swanzey, ▵4,254 .... C 6
† 03431 Swanzey, 950 .... C 6
03886 Tamworth, ▵1,054 .... E 4
03084 Temple, ▵441 .... D 6
† 03285 Thornton, ▵594 .... D 4
03276 Tilton, ▵2,579 .... D 5
03276 Tilton-Northfield, 2,420 .... D 5
03465 Troy, ▵1,713 .... C 6
† 03816 Tuftonboro, ▵910 .... E 4
† 03743 Unity, ▵709 .... C 5
03888 Wakefield, ▵1,420 .... F 4
03608 Walpole, ▵2,966 .... C 5
03608 Walpole, 900 .... C 5
03278 Warner, ▵1,441 .... D 5
03278 Warner, 600 .... D 5
03279 Warren, ▵539 .... D 4
03280 Washington, ▵248 .... C 5
03223 Waterville Valley, ▵109 .... D 4
03281 Weare, ▵1,851 .... D 5
03281 Weare P.O. (North Weare), 600 .... D 5
† 03301 Webster, ▵680 .... D 5
03282 Wentworth, ▵376 .... D 4
† 03579 Wentworths Location, ▵37 .... E 2
† 03038 West Derry (Derry), 6,090 .... E 6
03784 West Lebanon, 4,200 .... C 4
03467 Westmoreland, ▵998 .... C 6
03597 West Stewartstown, 600 .... E 2
03469 West Swanzey, 950 .... C 6
03892 Westville, 500 .... E 6
03598 Whitefield, ▵1,538 .... D 3
03598 Whitefield, 1,093 .... D 3
† 03287 Wilmot, ▵516 .... D 5
03086 Wilton, ▵2,276 .... D 6
03086 Wilton, 1,161 .... D 6
03470 Winchester, ▵2,869 .... C 6
03470 Winchester, 938 .... C 6
03087 Windham, ▵3,008 .... E 6
03289 Winnisquam, 500 .... E 5
03894 Wolfeboro, ▵3,036 .... E 4
03894 Wolfeboro, 1,718 .... E 4
03896 Wolfeboro Falls, 650 .... E 4
03293 Woodstock, ▵897 .... D 4
03785 Woodsville⊙, 1,336 .... C 3

VERMONT

COUNTIES

Addison, 24,266 .... A 3
Bennington, 29,282 .... A 6
Caledonia, 22,789 .... C 2
Chittenden, 99,131 .... A 3
Essex, 5,416 .... D 2
Franklin, 31,282 .... B 2
Grand Isle, 3,574 .... A 2
Lamoille, 13,309 .... B 2
Orange, 17,676 .... C 3
Orleans, 20,153 .... C 2
Rutland, 52,637 .... A 4
Washington, 47,659 .... B 3
Windham, 33,074 .... B 5
Windsor, 44,082 .... B 4

CITIES and TOWNS

Zip *Name/Pop.* *Key*

† 05491 Addison, ▵717 .... A 3
05820 Albany, ▵528 .... C 2
05440 Alburg, ▵1,271 .... A 2
05440 Alburg, 520 .... A 2
† 05143 Andover, ▵239 .... B 5
05250 Arlington, ▵1,934 .... A 5
05250 Arlington, 1,212 .... A 5
05030 Ascutney, 500 .... C 5
05901 Averill, ▵8 .... D 2
05441 Bakersfield, ▵635 .... B 2
05031 Barnard, ▵569 .... B 4
05821 Barnet, ▵1,342 .... C 3
05641 Barre, 10,209 .... C 3
05641 Barre, ▵6,509 .... C 3
05822 Barton, ▵2,874 .... C 2
05822 Barton, 1,051 .... C 2
05902 Beecher Falls, 640 .... D 2
05101 Bellows Falls, 3,505 .... C 5
05442 Belvidere, ▵189 .... B 2
05201 Bennington, ▵14,586 .... A 6
05201 Bennington⊙, 7,950 .... A 6
05731 Benson, ▵583 .... A 4
† 05476 Berkshire, ▵931 .... B 2
05032 Bethel, ▵1,347 .... B 4
† 03590 Bloomfield, ▵196 .... D 2
† 05466 Bolton, ▵427 .... B 3
05732 Bomoseen, 500 .... A 4
05033 Bradford, ▵1,627 .... C 3
05033 Bradford, 709 .... C 3
05646 Braintree, ▵751 .... B 4
05733 Brandon, ▵3,697 .... A 4
05733 Brandon, 1,720 .... A 4
05301 Brattleboro, ▵12,239 .... B 6
05301 Brattleboro, 9,055 .... B 6
05034 Bridgewater, ▵783 .... B 4
05734 Bridport, ▵809 .... A 4
05443 Bristol, ▵2,744 .... A 3
05443 Bristol, 1,737 .... A 3
05036 Brookfield, ▵606 .... B 3
† 05345 Brookline, ▵180 .... B 5
† 05860 Brownington, ▵522 .... C 2
† 05871 Burke, ▵1,053 .... D 2
05401 Burlington⊙, 38,633 .... A 3
05647 Cabot, ▵663 .... C 3
05648 Calais, ▵749 .... B 3
05444 Cambridge, ▵1,528 .... B 2
05903 Canaan, ▵949 .... D 2
05735 Castleton, ▵2,837 .... A 4
05735 Castleton, 450 .... A 4
05142 Cavendish, ▵1,264 .... B 5
05736 Center Rutland, 500 .... A 4
05445 Charlotte, ▵1,802 .... A 3
05038 Chelsea⊙, ▵983 .... C 4
05038 Chelsea, 525 .... C 4
05143 Chester, ▵2,371 .... B 5
05143 Chester, 950 .... B 5
05144 Chester Depot, 500 .... B 5
05737 Chittenden, ▵646 .... B 4
05737 Chittenden, 525 .... B 4
† 05759 Clarendon, ▵1,537 .... A 4
05446 Colchester, ▵8,776 .... A 2
05824 Concord, ▵896 .... D 3
05039 Corinth, ▵683 .... C 3
† 05753 Cornwall, ▵900 .... A 4
05825 Coventry, ▵492 .... C 2
05826 Craftsbury, ▵632 .... C 2
05739 Danby, ▵910 .... A 5
05828 Danville, ▵1,405 .... C 3
05828 Danville, 450 .... C 3
05829 Derby, ▵3,252 .... C 2
05829 Derby (Derby Center), 547 .... C 2
05830 Derby Line, 834 .... C 2
05251 Dorset, ▵1,293 .... A 5
05251 Dorset, 450 .... A 5
† 05676 Duxbury, ▵621 .... B 3
05252 East Arlington, 500 .... A 5
05649 East Barre, 950 .... C 3
05448 East Fairfield, 700 .... B 2
05837 East Haven, ▵197 .... D 2
05740 East Middlebury, 500 .... A 4
05651 East Montpelier, ▵1,597 .... B 3
05651 East Montpelier, 550 .... B 3
05652 Eden, ▵513 .... B 2
05450 Enosburg Falls, 1,266 .... B 2
05451 Essex, ▵10,951 .... A 2
05451 Essex, 850 .... A 2
05452 Essex Junction, 6,511 .... A 3
05454 Fairfax, ▵1,366 .... B 2
05455 Fairfield, ▵1,285 .... B 2
05743 Fair Haven, ▵2,777 .... A 4
05743 Fair Haven, 2,287 .... A 4
05045 Fairlee, ▵604 .... C 4
05045 Fairlee, 425 .... C 4
05456 Ferrisburg, ▵1,875 .... A 3
† 05444 Fletcher, ▵456 .... B 2
05745 Forest Dale, 500 .... A 4
05457 Franklin, ▵821 .... B 2
† 05478 Georgia, ▵1,711 .... A 2
05904 Gilman, 700 .... D 3
05839 Glover, ▵649 .... C 2
05146 Grafton, ▵465 .... B 5
05840 Granby, ▵52 .... D 2
05458 Grand Isle, ▵809 .... A 2
05654 Graniteville, 1,120 .... C 3
05747 Granville, ▵255 .... B 4
05841 Greensboro, ▵593 .... C 2
05046 Groton, ▵666 .... C 3
05046 Groton, 438 .... C 3
05905 Guildhall⊙, ▵169 .... D 2
† 05301 Guilford, ▵1,108 .... B 6
† 05358 Halifax, ▵295 .... B 6
05748 Hancock, ▵283 .... B 4
05843 Hardwick, ▵2,466 .... C 2
05843 Hardwick, 1,503 .... C 2
05047 Hartford, ▵6,477 .... C 4
05047 Hartford, 650 .... C 4
05047 Hartland, ▵1,806 .... C 4
† 05459 Highgate, ▵1,936 .... B 2
05459 Highgate Center, 927 .... B 2
05461 Hinesburg, ▵1,775 .... A 3
† 05830 Holland, ▵383 .... D 2
05749 Hubbardton, ▵228 .... A 4
05462 Huntington, ▵748 .... B 3
05655 Hyde Park, ▵1,347 .... B 2
05655 Hyde Park⊙, 418 .... B 2
05750 Hydeville, 450 .... A 4
† 05777 Ira, ▵284 .... A 4
05845 Irasburg, ▵775 .... C 2
05846 Island Pond, 1,123 .... D 2
05463 Isle La Motte, ▵262 .... A 2
05343 Jamaica, ▵590 .... B 5
† 05859 Jay, ▵182 .... C 2
05465 Jericho, ▵2,343 .... B 3
05465 Jericho, 450 .... A 2
05656 Johnson, ▵1,927 .... B 2
05656 Johnson, 1,296 .... B 2
† 05752 Leicester, ▵583 .... A 4
† 03576 Lemington, ▵120 .... D 2
† 05443 Lincoln, ▵599 .... B 3
05148 Londonderry, ▵1,037 .... B 5
05847 Lowell, ▵515 .... C 2
05149 Ludlow, ▵2,463 .... B 5
05149 Ludlow, 1,508 .... B 5
05906 Lunenburg, ▵1,061 .... D 3
05849 Lyndon, ▵3,705 .... C 2
05851 Lyndonville, 1,415 .... D 2
† 05905 Maidstone, ▵94 .... D 2
05254 Manchester, ▵2,919 .... A 5
05254 Manchester⊙, 435 .... A 5
05255 Manchester Center, 900 .... A 5
05256 Manchester Depot, 1,560 .... B 5
05344 Marlboro, ▵592 .... B 6
05658 Marshfield, ▵1,033 .... C 3
† 05701 Mendon, ▵743 .... B 4
05753 Middlebury, ▵6,532 .... A 3
05753 Middlebury⊙, 4,500 .... A 3
† 05602 Middlesex, ▵857 .... B 3
05757 Middletown Springs, ▵426 .... A 5
05468 Milton, ▵4,495 .... A 2
05468 Milton, 1,164 .... A 2
05469 Monkton, ▵765 .... A 3
05470 Montgomery, ▵651 .... B 2
05602 Montpelier (cap.)⊙, 8,609 .... B 3
05660 Moretown, ▵904 .... B 3
05853 Morgan, ▵286 .... D 2
† 05661 Morristown, ▵4,052 .... B 2
05661 Morrisville, 2,116 .... B 2
05758 Mount Holly, ▵687 .... B 5
† 05739 Mount Tabor, ▵184 .... B 5
† 05871 Newark, ▵144 .... D 2
05051 Newbury, ▵1,440 .... C 3
05051 Newbury, 450 .... C 3
05345 Newfane, ▵900 .... B 6
05345 Newfane⊙, 183 .... B 6
05472 New Haven, ▵1,039 .... A 3
05855 Newport, ▵1,125 .... C 2
05855 Newport⊙, 4,664 .... C 2
05257 North Bennington, 984 .... A 6
05759 North Clarendon, 750 .... B 4
05663 Northfield, ▵4,870 .... B 3
05663 Northfield, 2,139 .... B 3
05664 Northfield Falls, 700 .... B 3
05474 North Hero⊙, ▵364 .... A 2
05260 North Pownal, 600 .... A 6
05150 North Springfield, 1,100 .... B 5
05859 North Troy, 774 .... C 2
05907 Norton, ▵207 .... D 2
05055 Norwich, ▵1,966 .... C 4
05055 Norwich, 500 .... C 4
† 05649 Orange, ▵540 .... C 3
05860 Orleans, 1,138 .... C 2
05760 Orwell, ▵851 .... A 4
† 05491 Panton, ▵416 .... A 3
05761 Pawlet, ▵1,184 .... A 5
05862 Peacham, ▵446 .... C 3
05152 Peru, ▵243 .... B 5
05762 Pittsfield, ▵249 .... B 4
05763 Pittsford, ▵2,306 .... A 4
05763 Pittsford, 682 .... A 4
05667 Plainfield, ▵1,399 .... C 3
05667 Plainfield, 949 .... C 3
05056 Plymouth, ▵283 .... B 4
† 05067 Pomfret, ▵620 .... B 4
05764 Poultney, ▵3,217 .... A 4
05764 Poultney, 1,914 .... A 4
05261 Pownal, ▵2,441 .... A 6
05261 Pownal, 700 .... A 6
05765 Proctor, ▵2,095 .... A 4
05765 Proctor, 1,950 .... A 4
05153 Proctorsville, 512 .... B 5
05346 Putney, ▵1,727 .... B 6
05346 Putney, 1,115 .... B 6
05059 Quechee, 420 .... C 4
05060 Randolph, ▵3,882 .... B 4
05060 Randolph, 2,115 .... B 4
05062 Reading, ▵564 .... B 5
05350 Readsboro, ▵638 .... B 6
05350 Readsboro, 469 .... B 6
05476 Richford, ▵2,116 .... B 2
05476 Richford, 1,527 .... B 2
05477 Richmond, ▵2,249 .... A 3
05477 Richmond, 935 .... A 3
05766 Ripton, ▵187 .... A 4
05767 Rochester, ▵884 .... B 4
† 05101 Rockingham, ▵5,501 .... C 5
05669 Roxbury, ▵354 .... B 3
05063 Royalton, ▵1,399 .... B 4
05768 Rupert, ▵582 .... A 5
05701 Rutland, ▵2,248 .... B 4
05701 Rutland⊙, 19,293 .... B 4
05042 Ryegate, ▵830 .... C 3
05478 Saint Albans, ▵3,270 .... A 2
05478 Saint Albans⊙, 8,082 .... A 2
† 05401 Saint George, ▵477 .... A 2
05819 Saint Johnsbury, ▵8,409 .... D 3
05819 Saint Johnsbury⊙, 7,000 .... D 3
05769 Salisbury, ▵649 .... A 4
† 05250 Sandgate, ▵127 .... A 5
05154 Saxtons River, 581 .... B 5
† 05363 Searsburg, ▵84 .... A 6
05262 Shaftsbury, ▵2,411 .... A 6
05065 Sharon, ▵541 .... C 4
05866 Sheffield, ▵307 .... C 2
05482 Shelburne, ▵3,728 .... A 3
05482 Shelburne, 2,591 .... A 3
05483 Sheldon, ▵1,481 .... B 2
05770 Shoreham, ▵790 .... A 4
† 05738 Shrewsbury, ▵570 .... B 4
05670 South Barre, 865 .... B 3
05401 South Burlington, ▵10,032 .... A 3
05486 South Hero, ▵868 .... A 2
05155 South Londonderry, 600 .... B 5
05068 South Royalton, 625 .... C 4
05156 Springfield, ▵10,063 .... B 5
05156 Springfield, 5,632 .... B 5
† 01247 Stamford, ▵752 .... A 6
05487 Starksboro, ▵668 .... A 3
05772 Stockbridge, ▵389 .... B 4
05672 Stowe, ▵2,388 .... B 3
05672 Stowe, 435 .... B 3
05072 Strafford, ▵536 .... C 4
† 05360 Stratton, ▵104 .... B 5
† 05733 Sudbury, ▵253 .... A 4
† 05250 Sunderland, ▵601 .... A 5
05867 Sutton, ▵438 .... C 2
05488 Swanton, ▵4,622 .... A 2
05488 Swanton, 2,630 .... A 2
05074 Thetford, ▵1,422 .... C 4
† 05773 Tinmouth, ▵268 .... A 5
05076 Topsham, ▵686 .... C 3
05353 Townshend, ▵668 .... B 5
05868 Troy, ▵1,457 .... C 2
05077 Tunbridge, ▵791 .... C 4
05489 Underhill, ▵1,198 .... B 2
05491 Vergennes, 2,242 .... A 3
05354 Vernon, ▵1,024 .... B 6
05079 Vershire, ▵299 .... C 4
05673 Waitsfield, ▵837 .... B 3
† 05873 Walden, ▵442 .... C 3
05773 Wallingford, ▵1,676 .... B 5
05773 Wallingford, 815 .... B 5
† 05491 Waltham, ▵265 .... A 3
05355 Wardsboro, ▵391 .... B 5
05674 Warren, ▵588 .... B 3
05675 Washington, ▵667 .... C 3
05676 Waterbury, ▵4,614 .... B 3
05676 Waterbury, 2,840 .... B 3
05677 Waterbury Center, 900 .... B 3
05492 Waterville, ▵397 .... B 2
05678 Websterville, 700 .... B 3
05774 Wells, ▵560 .... A 5
05081 Wells River, 419 .... C 3
05301 West Brattleboro, 2,200 .... B 6
05083 West Fairlee, ▵337 .... C 4
05874 Westfield, ▵375 .... C 2
05494 Westford, ▵991 .... A 2
† 05743 West Haven, ▵240 .... A 4
05158 Westminster, ▵1,875 .... C 5
† 05860 Westmore, ▵195 .... C 2
05161 Weston, ▵507 .... B 5
05161 Weston, 450 .... B 5
05777 West Rutland, ▵2,381 .... A 4
05777 West Rutland, 1,875 .... A 4
† 05753 Weybridge, ▵618 .... A 3
† 05851 Wheelock, ▵238 .... C 2
05001 White River Junction, 2,379 .... C 4
05778 Whiting, ▵359 .... A 4
05361 Whitingham, ▵1,011 .... B 6
05088 Wilder, 1,328 .... C 4
05679 Williamstown, ▵1,822 .... B 3
05679 Williamstown, 650 .... B 3
05495 Williston, ▵3,187 .... A 3
05363 Wilmington, ▵1,184 .... B 6
05363 Wilmington, 544 .... B 6
† 05359 Windham, ▵174 .... B 5
05089 Windsor, ▵4,158 .... C 5
05089 Windsor, 3,400 .... C 5
05404 Winooski, 7,309 .... A 3
05680 Wolcott, ▵676 .... C 2
† 05681 Woodbury, ▵399 .... C 3
† 05201 Woodford, ▵286 .... A 6
05091 Woodstock, ▵2,608 .... B 4
05091 Woodstock⊙, 1,154 .... B 4
05682 Worcester, ▵505 .... B 3

⊙ County seat.
▵ Population of town or township.
‡ Population of metropolitan area.
† Zip of nearest p.o.
* Multiple zips

Edmund V. Ballman

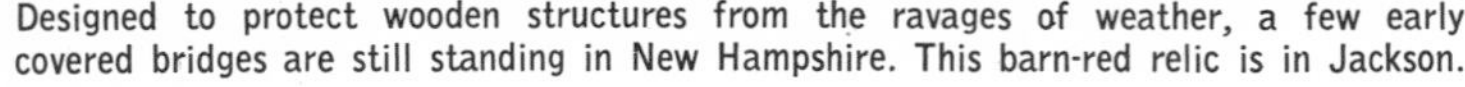
Designed to protect wooden structures from the ravages of weather, a few early covered bridges are still standing in New Hampshire. This barn-red relic is in Jackson.

Elizabeth L. Schultz

Located in the heart of Vermont, Barre rightfully boasts of its granite quarries which provide a sculptured panorama set off by surrounding green hills.

COUNTIES

Name/Pop.	Key
Atlantic, 175,043	D 5
Bergen, 898,012	E 2
Burlington, 323,132	D 4
Camden, 456,291	D 4
Cape May, 59,554	D 5
Cumberland, 121,374	C 5
Essex, 929,986	E 2
Gloucester, 172,681	C 4
Hudson, 609,266	E 2
Hunterdon, 69,718	D 2
Mercer, 303,968	D 3
Middlesex, 583,813	E 3
Monmouth, 459,379	E 3
Morris, 383,454	D 2
Ocean, 208,470	E 4
Passaic, 460,782	E 1
Salem, 60,346	C 4
Somerset, 198,372	D 2
Sussex, 77,528	D 1
Union, 543,116	E 2
Warren, 73,879	C 2

CITIES and TOWNS

Zip	Name/Pop.	Key
08201	Absecon, 6,094	D 5
07820	Allamuchy, 600	D 2
07401	Allendale, 6,240	B 1
07711	Allenhurst, 1,012	F 3
08501	Allentown, 1,603	D 3
08720	Allenwood, 2,200	E 3
08001	Alloway, 850	C 4
08865	Alpha, 2,829	C 2
07620	Alpine, 1,344	C 1
07821	Andover, 813	D 2
08801	Annandale, 675	D 2
07712	Asbury Park, 16,533	F 3
† 08033	Ashland, 2,500	B 3
08004	Atco, 2,980	D 4
* 08401	Atlantic City, 47,859	E 5
	Atlantic City, ‡175,043	E 5
07716	Atlantic Highlands, 5,102	F 3
08106	Audubon, 10,802	B 3
† 08106	Audubon Park, 1,492	B 3
08202	Avalon, 1,283	D 5
07001	Avenel, 10,250	E 2
07717	Avon by the Sea, 2,163	F 3
08005	Barnegat, 900	E 4
08006	Barnegat Light, 554	E 4
08007	Barrington, 8,409	B 3
07920	Basking Ridge, 2,500	D 2
08742	Bay Head, 1,083	E 3
07002	Bayonne, 72,743	B 2
08721	Bayville, 6,000	E 4
08008	Beach Haven, 1,488	E 4
08722	Beachwood, 4,390	E 4
07921	Bedminster, 1,250	D 2
07718	Belford, 7,000	E 3
08502	Belle Mead, 1,950	D 3
07109	Belleville, 34,643	B 2
08030	Bellmawr, 15,618	B 3
07719	Belmar, 5,782	E 3
07823	Belvidere⊙, 2,641	C 2
07621	Bergenfield, 33,131	C 1
07922	Berkeley Heights, △13,078	E 2
08009	Berlin, 4,997	D 4
07924	Bernardsville, 6,652	D 2
08010	Beverly, 3,105	D 3
08012	Blackwood, 9,500	C 4
07825	Blairstown, 1,900	C 2
07003	Bloomfield, 52,029	B 2
07403	Bloomingdale, 7,797	E 1
08804	Bloomsbury, 879	C 2
07603	Bogota, 8,125	B 2
07005	Boonton, 9,261	E 2
08505	Bordentown, 4,490	D 3
08805	Bound Brook, 10,450	D 2
07720	Bradley Beach, 4,163	F 3
07826	Branchville, 911	D 1
08723	Breton Woods, 1,900	E 3
08723	Brick Town, △35,057	E 3
08014	Bridgeport, 950	C 4
08302	Bridgeton⊙, 20,435	C 5
08730	Brielle, 3,594	E 3
08203	Brigantine, 6,741	E 5
08030	Brooklawn, 2,870	B 3
07926	Brookside, 1,300	D 2
08015	Browns Mills, 7,144	D 4
07828	Budd Lake, 3,168	D 2
08310	Buena, 3,283	D 4
08016	Burlington, 11,991	D 3
07405	Butler, 7,051	E 2
07006	Caldwell, 8,719	B 2
07830	Califon, 970	D 2
* 08101	Camden⊙, 102,551	B 3
† 08701	Candlewood, 5,629	E 3
08204	Cape May, 4,392	D 6
08210	Cape May Court House⊙, 2,062	D 5
07072	Carlstadt, 7,947	B 2
08069	Carneys Point, 3,900	C 4
07008	Carteret, 23,137	E 2
08018	Cedar Brook, 600	D 4
07009	Cedar Grove, △15,582	B 2
07927	Cedar Knolls, 3,900	E 2
08311	Cedarville, 900	C 5
† 08723	Cedarwood Park, 1,400	E 3
07928	Chatham, 9,566	E 2
08019	Chatsworth, 700	D 4
08879	Cheesequake, 2,900	E 3
08034	Cherry Hill, △64,395	B 3
† 08089	Chesilhurst, 801	D 4
07930	Chester, 1,299	D 2
† 08505	Chesterfield, △3,190	D 3
07066	Clark, △18,829	A 3
08020	Clarksboro, 1,500	C 4
08510	Clarksburg, 800	E 3
08312	Clayton, 5,193	C 4
08021	Clementon, 4,492	D 4
07010	Cliffside Park, 14,387	C 2
07721	Cliffwood, 7,056	E 3
* 07011	Clifton, 82,437	B 2
08809	Clinton, 1,742	D 2
07624	Closter, 8,604	C 1
08108	Collingswood, 17,422	B 3
08213	Cologne, 800	D 4
07067	Colonia, 12,000	E 2
07722	Colts Neck, 950	E 3
08022	Columbus, 800	D 3
07961	Convent Station, 6,587	E 2
08512	Cranbury, 1,253	E 3
07016	Cranford, △27,391	E 2
07626	Cresskill, 7,164	C 1
08515	Crosswicks, 700	D 3
07723	Deal, 2,401	F 3
08023	Deepwater, 800	C 4
08110	Delair, 2,800	B 3
08075	Delanco, △4,157	D 3
08075	Delran, 675	B 3
07627	Demarest, 6,262	C 1
08214	Dennisville, 990	D 5
07834	Denville, △14,045	E 2
08096	Deptford, △24,232	B 4
08317	Dorothy, 850	D 5
07801	Dover, 15,039	D 2

AREA 7,836 sq. mi.
POPULATION 7,168,164
CAPITAL Trenton
LARGEST CITY Newark
HIGHEST POINT High Point 1,803 ft.
SETTLED IN 1617
ADMITTED TO UNION December 18, 1787
POPULAR NAME Garden State
STATE FLOWER Violet
STATE BIRD Eastern Goldfinch

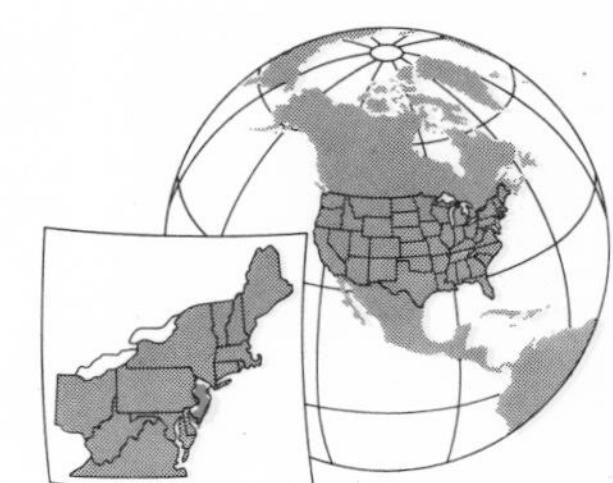

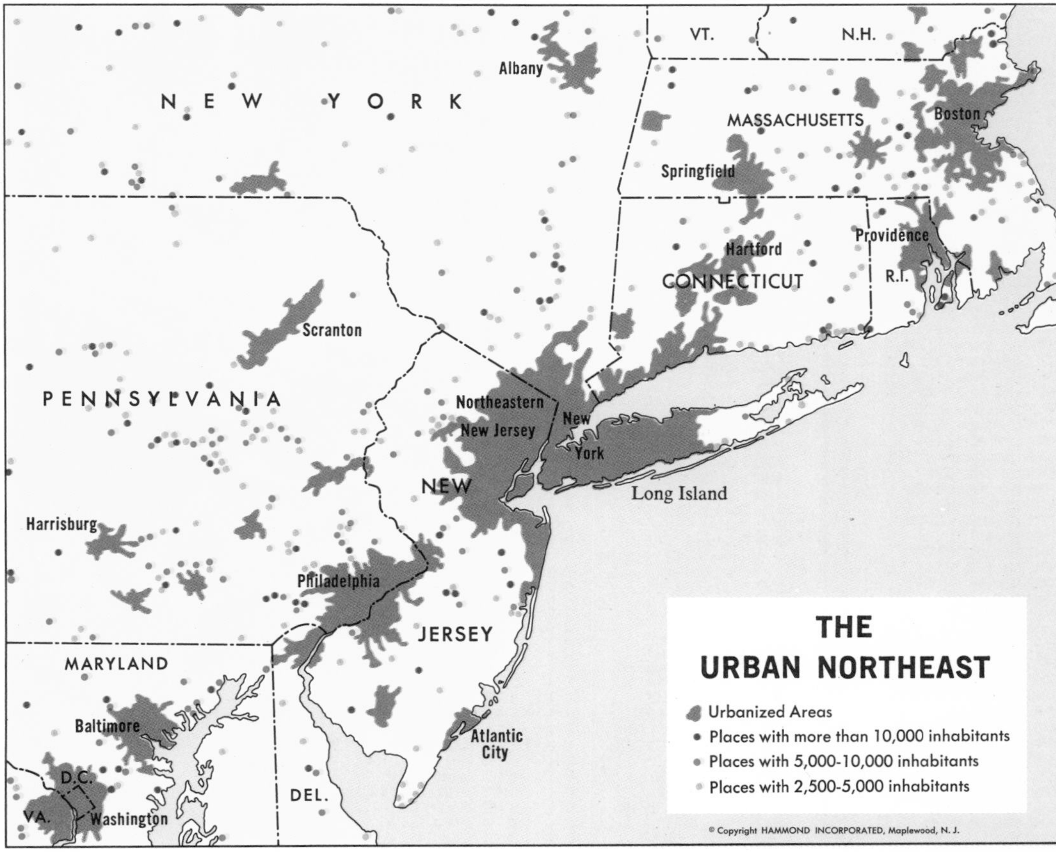

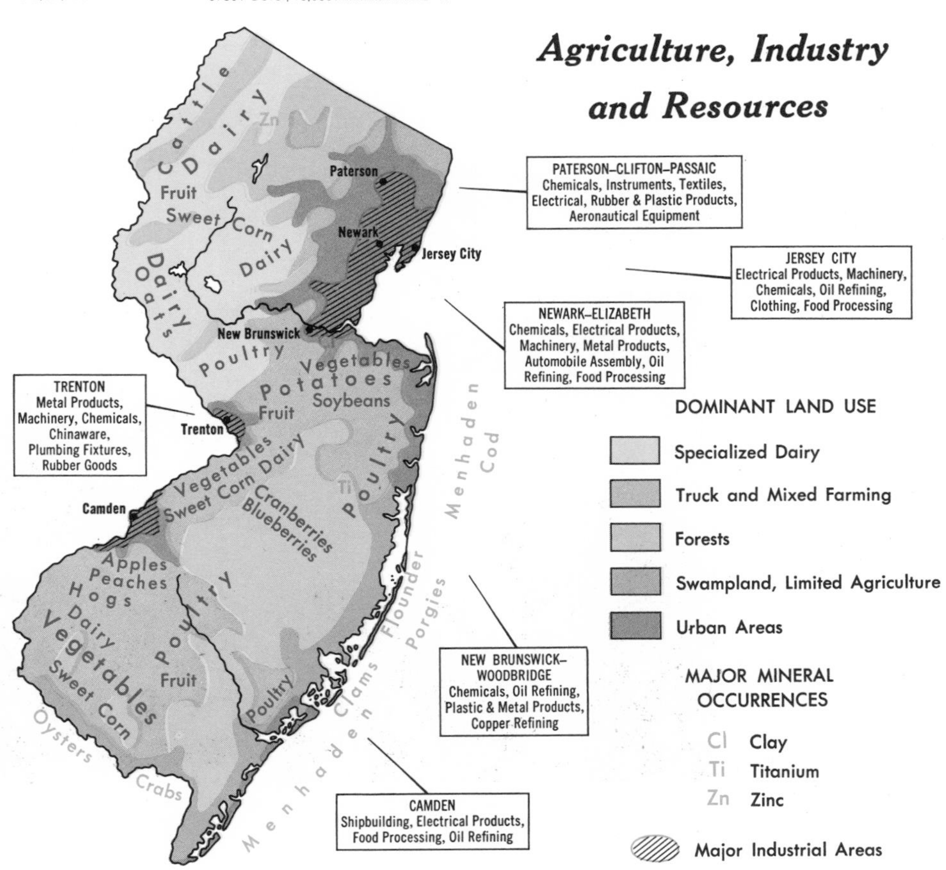

Zip	Name/Pop.	Key
07628	Dumont, 17,534	C 1
08812	Dunellen, 7,072	D 2
08816	East Brunswick, △34,166	E 3
07936	East Hanover, △7,734	E 2
07734	East Keansburg, 5,000	E 3
08873	East Millstone, 950	D 3
† 07100	East Newark, 1,922	B 2
* 07017	East Orange, 75,471	B 2
07407	East Paterson, 22,749	B 2
07073	East Rutherford, 8,536	B 2
07724	Eatontown, 14,619	E 3
07020	Edgewater, 4,849	C 2
† 08010	Edgewater Park, △7,412	D 3
08817	Edison, △67,120	E 2
08215	Egg Harbor City, 4,304	D 4
07740	Elberon, 2,900	F 3
* 07201	Elizabeth⊙, 112,654	B 2
08318	Elmer, 1,592	C 4
07630	Emerson, 8,428	B 1
* 07631	Englewood, 24,985	C 2
07632	Englewood Cliffs, 5,938	C 2
† 08330	English Creek, 950	D 5
07726	Englishtown, 1,048	E 3
07849	Espanong (Lake Hopatcong), 1,941	D 2
07021	Essex Fells, 2,541	B 2
07006	Fairfield, 6,731	A 2
07701	Fair Haven, 6,142	E 3
07410	Fair Lawn, 37,975	B 1
08320	Fairton, 600	C 5
07022	Fairview, 10,698	C 2
07023	Fanwood, 8,920	E 2
07931	Far Hills, 780	D 2
07727	Farmingdale, 1,148	E 3
† 08505	Fieldsboro, 615	D 3
08821	Flagtown, 800	D 2
07836	Flanders, 3,875	D 2
08822	Flemington⊙, 3,917	D 2
08518	Florence-Roebling, 7,551	D 3
07932	Florham Park, 8,094	E 2
† 08037	Folsom, 1,767	D 4
08863	Fords, 14,000	E 2
08731	Forked River, 1,422	E 4
07024	Fort Lee, 30,631	C 2
07416	Franklin, △30,389	D 3
07416	Franklin, 4,236	D 1
07417	Franklin Lakes, 7,550	B 1
08322	Franklinville, 2,500	C 4
07728	Freehold⊙, 10,545	E 3
08825	Frenchtown, 1,459	C 2
07026	Garfield, 30,722	B 2
07027	Garwood, 5,260	E 2
08026	Gibbsboro, 2,634	B 4
08027	Gibbstown, 3,400	C 4
† 08753	Gilford Park, 4,007	E 4
07933	Gillette, 2,950	E 2
08028	Glassboro, 12,938	C 4
08029	Glendora, 10,280	B 4
08826	Glen Gardner, 874	D 2
07028	Glen Ridge, 8,518	B 2
07452	Glen Rock, 13,011	B 1
08030	Gloucester City, 14,707	B 3
08219	Green Creek, 975	D 5
07435	Green Pond, 800	E 1
07935	Green Village, 800	D 2
08323	Greenwich, △963	C 5
08032	Grenloch, 950	C 4
07950	Greystone Park, 5,500	D 2
08620	Groveville, 2,800	D 3
07093	Guttenberg, 5,754	C 2
* 07601	Hackensack⊙, 35,911	B 2
07840	Hackettstown, 9,472	D 2
08033	Haddonfield, 13,118	B 3
08035	Haddon Heights, 9,365	B 3
08036	Hainesport, △2,990	D 4
07508	Haledon, 6,767	B 1
07419	Hamburg, 1,820	D 1
08690	Hamilton Square, 11,300	D 3
08037	Hammonton, 11,464	D 4
08827	Hampton, 1,386	D 2
07640	Harrington Park, 4,841	C 1
07029	Harrison, 11,811	B 2
08039	Harrisonville, 950	C 4
† 08057	Hartford, 650	D 4
07604	Hasbrouck Heights, 13,651	B 2
07641	Haworth, 3,760	C 1
07507	Hawthorne, 19,173	B 2
07730	Hazlet, 15,000	E 3
08828	Helmetta, 955	E 3
07421	Hewitt, 950	E 1
08829	High Bridge, 2,606	D 2
08904	Highland Park, 14,385	D 2
07732	Highlands, 3,916	F 3
08520	Hightstown, 5,431	D 3
07502	Hillcrest, 1,975	C 2
07642	Hillsdale, 11,768	B 1
07205	Hillside, △21,636	B 2
† 08083	Hi-Nella, 1,195	B 4
07030	Hoboken, 45,380	C 2
07423	Ho-ho-kus, 4,348	B 1
07733	Holmdel, 5,500	E 3
07843	Hopatcong, 9,052	D 2
07844	Hope, 950	D 2
08525	Hopewell, 2,271	D 3
07727	Howell, △21,756	E 3
† 08865	Huntington, 1,900	C 2
† 07712	Interlaken, 1,182	E 3
07845	Ironia, 1,500	D 2
07111	Irvington, 59,743	B 2
08830	Iselin, 19,000	E 2

(continued on following page)

(continued)

08732 Island Heights, 1,397 ... E 4
08527 Jackson, ∆18,276 ... E 3
08831 Jamesburg, 4,584 ... E 3
* 07301 Jersey City⊙, 260,545 ... B 2
Jersey City, ‡609,266 ... B 2
07734 Keansburg, 9,720 ... E 3
07032 Kearny, 37,585 ... B 2
08832 Keasbey, 1,200 ... E 2
08824 Kendall Park, 7,412 ... D 3
07033 Kenilworth, 9,165 ... E 2
07735 Keyport, 7,205 ... E 3
08528 Kingston, 1,200 ... D 3
07405 Kinnelon, 7,600 ... E 2
08043 Kirkwood, 800 ... B 4
07848 Lafayette, 900 ... D 1
07034 Lake Hiawatha, 11,389 ... E 2
07849 Lake Hopatcong, 1,941 ... D 2
08733 Lakehurst, 2,641 ... E 3
† 07871 Lake Mohawk, 6,262 ... D 1
08701 Lakewood, 17,874 ... E 3
08530 Lambertville, 4,359 ... D 3
07850 Landing, 2,370 ... D 2
08734 Lanoka Harbor, 1,066 ... E 4
08021 Laurel Springs, 2,566 ... B 4
08879 Laurence Harbor, 6,715 ... E 3
08735 Lavallette, 1,509 ... E 4
08045 Lawnside, 2,757 ... B 3
08648 Lawrenceville, 1,464 ... D 3
08833 Lebanon, 885 ... D 2
07852 Ledgewood, 2,800 ... D 2
08327 Leesburg, 800 ... D 5
07737 Leonardo, 4,000 ... E 3
07605 Leonia, 8,847 ... C 2
07938 Liberty Corner, 1,900 ... D 2
07035 Lincoln Park, 9,034 ... A 1
07738 Lincroft, 4,900 ... E 3
07036 Linden, 41,409 ... A 3
08021 Lindenwold, 12,199 ... B 4
08221 Linwood, 6,159 ... D 5
07424 Little Falls, ∆11,727 ... B 2
07643 Little Ferry, 9,042 ... B 2
07739 Little Silver, 6,010 ... F 3
07039 Livingston, ∆30,127 ... E 2
07644 Lodi, 25,213 ... B 2
08008 Long Branch, 31,774 ... F 3
08403 Longport, 1,225 ... D 5
07853 Long Valley, 1,645 ... D 2
08048 Lumberton, 600 ... D 4
07071 Lyndhurst, ∆22,729 ... B 2
07939 Lyons, 3,900 ... D 2
07940 Madison, 16,710 ... E 2
08049 Magnolia, 5,893 ... B 3
07430 Mahwah, ∆10,539 ... E 1
08328 Malaga, 950 ... C 4
08050 Manahawkin, 1,278 ... E 4
08736 Manasquan, 4,971 ... E 3
08051 Mantua, 5,530 ... C 4
08835 Manville, 13,029 ... D 2
08052 Maple Shade, ∆16,464 ... B 3
07040 Maplewood, ∆24,932 ... E 2
† 07866 Marcella, 540 ... E 2
08402 Margate City, 10,576 ... E 5
07746 Marlboro, 2,380 ... E 3
08053 Marlton, 10,180 ... D 4
08223 Marmora, 650 ... D 5
08836 Martinsville, 3,500 ... D 2
08054 Masonville, 900 ... D 4
07747 Matawan, 9,136 ... E 3
08330 Mays Landing⊙, 1,272 ... D 5
07607 Maywood, 11,087 ... B 2
07428 McAfee, 800 ... D 1
† 08232 McKee City, 950 ... D 5
08055 Medford, 1,448 ... D 4
08055 Medford Lakes, 4,792 ... D 4
07945 Mendham, 3,729 ... D 2
08817 Menlo Park, 10,000 ... E 2
08619 Mercerville, 5,456 ... D 3
08109 Merchantville, 4,425 ... B 3
08840 Metuchen, 16,031 ... E 2
08056 Mickleton, 950 ... C 4
08846 Middlesex, 15,038 ... E 2
07748 Middletown, ∆54,623 ... E 3
07432 Midland Park, 8,159 ... B 1
08848 Milford, 1,230 ... C 2
07041 Millburn, ∆21,307 ... E 2
07946 Millington, 975 ... D 2
08849 Millstone, 630 ... D 2
08850 Milltown, 6,470 ... E 3
08332 Millville, 21,366 ... C 5
07438 Milton, 2,220 ... D 1
† 07801 Mine Hill, ∆3,557 ... D 2
08342 Mizpah, 900 ... D 5
07750 Monmouth Beach, 2,042 ... F 3
08852 Monmouth Junction, 1,900 ... D 3
07434 Monroe, ∆9,138 ... E 3
† 12771 Montague, 750 ... D 1
* 07042 Montclair, 44,043 ... B 2
07645 Montvale, 7,327 ... B 1
07045 Montville, 4,900 ... E 2
07074 Moonachie, 2,937 ... B 2
08057 Moorestown, 14,179 ... B 3
07950 Morris Plains, 5,540 ... D 2
07960 Morristown⊙, 17,662 ... D 2
07046 Mountain Lakes, 4,739 ... E 2
07092 Mountainside, 7,520 ... E 2
† 07470 Mountain View, 9,000 ... B 2
07856 Mount Arlington, 3,590 ... D 2
08059 Mount Ephraim, 5,625 ... B 3
07970 Mount Freedom, 1,621 ... D 2
08060 Mount Holly⊙, ∆12,713 ... D 4
† 07885 Mount Hope, 1,510 ... D 2
08061 Mount Royal, 850 ... C 4
08062 Mullica Hill, 800 ... C 4
† 08087 Mystic Islands, 900 ... E 4
08063 National Park, 3,730 ... B 3
07752 Navesink, 2,400 ... E 3
07753 Neptune, ∆27,863 ... E 3
07753 Neptune City, 5,502 ... E 3
† 08853 Neshanic, 752 ... D 3
07857 Netcong, 2,858 ... D 2
* 07101 Newark⊙, 382,417 ... B 2
Newark, ‡2,056,556 ... B 2
* 08901 New Brunswick⊙, 41,885 ... E 3
08533 New Egypt, 1,769 ... E 3
08344 Newfield, 1,487 ... D 4
07435 Newfoundland, 900 ... D 1
08224 New Gretna, 700 ... E 4
07646 New Milford, 20,201 ... B 1
08345 Newport, 700 ... C 5
07974 New Providence, 13,796 ... E 2
07724 New Shrewsbury, 5,925 ... E 3
07860 Newton⊙, 7,297 ... D 1
08346 Newtonville, 750 ... D 4
07976 New Vernon, 1,900 ... D 2
08817 Nixon, 12,000 ... E 2
08347 Norma, 1,200 ... C 4
07032 North Arlington, 18,096 ... B 2
07047 North Bergen, ∆47,751 ... B 2
08876 North Branch, 610 ... D 2
08902 North Brunswick, ∆16,691 ... E 3
† 07006 North Caldwell, 6,425 ... B 2
08204 North Cape May, 3,812 ... C 6
08225 Northfield, 8,875 ... D 5
07508 North Haledon, 7,614 ... B 1
07060 North Plainfield, 21,796 ... E 2
07647 Northvale, 5,177 ... F 1
08260 North Wildwood, 3,914 ... D 6
07648 Norwood, 4,398 ... C 1
07110 Nutley, 32,099 ... B 2
07755 Oakhurst, 5,558 ... E 3
07436 Oakland, 14,420 ... B 1
08107 Oaklyn, 4,626 ... B 3
07438 Oak Ridge, 750 ... E 1
08226 Ocean City, 10,575 ... D 5
08740 Ocean Gate, 1,081 ... E 4
07756 Ocean Grove, 7,000 ... F 3
07757 Oceanport, 7,503 ... F 3
08230 Ocean View, 950 ... D 5
08231 Oceanville, 600 ... D 5
07439 Ogdensburg, 2,222 ... D 1
08857 Old Bridge, 25,176 ... E 3
07675 Old Tappan, 3,917 ... C 1
08858 Oldwick, 600 ... D 2
07649 Oradell, 8,903 ... B 1
* 07050 Orange, 32,566 ... B 2
08723 Osbornsville, 3,900 ... E 3
07863 Oxford, 1,411 ... C 2
07470 Packanack Lake, 4,000 ... B 1
† 08226 Palermo, 600 ... D 5
07650 Palisades Park, 13,351 ... C 2
08065 Palmyra, 6,969 ... B 3
07652 Paramus, 29,495 ... B 1
† 08087 Parkertown, 600 ... E 4
07656 Park Ridge, 8,709 ... B 1
07054 Parsippany, ∆55,112 ... E 2
* 07055 Passaic, 55,124 ... E 2
* 07501 Paterson⊙, 144,824 ... B 2
Paterson-Clifton-Passaic, ‡1,358,794 ... B 2
08066 Paulsboro, 8,084 ... C 4
07977 Peapack-Gladstone, 1,924 ... D 2
08067 Pedricktown, 1,500 ... C 4
08068 Pemberton, 1,344 ... D 4
08534 Pennington, 2,151 ... D 3
08110 Pennsauken, ∆36,394 ... B 3
08069 Penns Grove, 5,727 ... C 4
08070 Pennsville, 11,014 ... C 4
07440 Pequannock, 4,900 ... B 1
* 08861 Perth Amboy, 38,798 ... E 2
08865 Phillipsburg, 17,849 ... C 2
08741 Pine Beach, 1,395 ... E 4
07058 Pine Brook, 3,500 ... E 2
08021 Pine Hill, 5,132 ... D 4
08854 Piscataway, ∆36,418 ... D 2
08071 Pitman, 10,257 ... C 4
* 07060 Plainfield, 46,862 ... E 2
08536 Plainsboro, 1,200 ... D 3
08232 Pleasantville, 13,778 ... D 5
08742 Point Pleasant, 15,968 ... E 3
08742 Point Pleasant Beach, 4,882 ... E 3
08240 Pomona, 900 ... D 5
07442 Pompton Lakes, 11,397 ... A 1
07444 Pompton Plains, 9,500 ... B 1
07758 Port Monmouth, 4,556 ... E 3
† 07850 Port Morris, 950 ... D 2
07865 Port Murray, 800 ... D 2
08349 Port Norris, 1,955 ... C 5
07064 Port Reading, 4,900 ... E 2
08241 Port Republic, 586 ... D 4
08540 Princeton, 12,311 ... D 3
08550 Princeton Junction, 950 ... D 3
† 07885 Prospect Park, 5,176 ... B 1
08072 Quinton, 575 ... C 4
* 07065 Rahway, 29,114 ... E 2
† 07945 Ralston, 650 ... D 2
† 08057 Ramblewood, 5,556 ... D 4
07446 Ramsey, 12,571 ... B 1
08869 Raritan, 6,691 ... D 2
07701 Red Bank, 12,847 ... E 3
08350 Richland, 950 ... D 5
07657 Ridgefield, 11,308 ... B 2
07660 Ridgefield Park, 14,453 ... B 2
* 07450 Ridgewood, 27,547 ... B 1
08551 Ringoes, 682 ... D 3
07456 Ringwood, 10,393 ... E 1
08242 Rio Grande, 1,203 ... D 5
07457 Riverdale, 2,729 ... A 1
07661 River Edge, 12,850 ... B 1
08075 Riverside, ∆8,616 ... B 3
08077 Riverton, 3,412 ... B 3
08691 Robbinsville, 650 ... D 3
07662 Rochelle Park, ∆6,380 ... B 2
07866 Rockaway, ∆18,955 ... D 2
07866 Rockaway, 6,383 ... D 2
08553 Rocky Hill, 917 ... D 3
08554 Roebling-Florence, 7,551 ... D 3
08555 Roosevelt, 814 ... E 3
07068 Roseland, 4,453 ... A 2
07203 Roselle, 22,585 ... B 2
07204 Roselle Park, 14,277 ... A 2
08352 Rosenhayn, 950 ... C 5
† 07876 Roxbury, ∆15,754 ... D 2
07760 Rumson, 7,421 ... F 3
08078 Runnemede, 10,475 ... B 3
* 07070 Rutherford, 20,802 ... B 2
07662 Saddle Brook, ∆15,098 ... B 1
07458 Saddle River, 2,437 ... B 1
08079 Salem⊙, 7,648 ... C 4
08872 Sayreville, 32,508 ... E 3
07076 Scotch Plains, ∆22,279 ... E 2
07760 Sea Bright, 1,339 ... F 3
08302 Seabrook, 1,569 ... C 5
08750 Sea Girt, 2,207 ... E 3
08243 Sea Isle City, 1,712 ... D 5
08751 Seaside Heights, 1,248 ... E 4
08752 Seaside Park, 1,432 ... E 4
07094 Secaucus, 13,228 ... B 2
07077 Sewaren, 3,200 ... E 2
08080 Sewell, 2,210 ... C 4
08353 Shiloh, 573 ... C 5
08008 Ship Bottom, 1,079 ... E 4
07078 Short Hills, 14,000 ... E 2
07701 Shrewsbury, 3,315 ... E 3
08081 Sicklerville, 1,700 ... D 4
† 07424 Singac, 3,942 ... B 2
08558 Skillman, 1,955 ... D 3
† 07728 Smithburg, 750 ... E 3
08083 Somerdale, 6,510 ... B 4
08244 Somers Point, 7,919 ... D 5
08876 Somerville⊙, 13,652 ... D 2
08879 South Amboy, 9,338 ... E 3
† 07719 South Belmar, 1,490 ... E 3
08880 South Bound Brook, 4,525 ... E 2
† 08852 South Brunswick, ∆14,058 ... E 3
07079 South Orange, 16,971 ... A 2
07080 South Plainfield, 21,142 ... E 2
08882 South River, 15,428 ... E 3
08246 South Seaville, 600 ... D 5
08753 South Toms River, 3,981 ... E 4
07871 Sparta, 3,000 ... D 1
08884 Spotswood, 7,891 ... E 3
07081 Springfield, ∆15,740 ... E 2
07762 Spring Lake, 3,896 ... F 3
07762 Spring Lake Heights, 4,602 ... E 3
07874 Stanhope, 3,040 ... D 2
08885 Stanton, 700 ... D 2
08886 Stewartsville, 950 ... C 2
07980 Stirling, 1,450 ... E 2
07460 Stockholm, 1,477 ... D 1
08559 Stockton, 619 ... D 3
08247 Stone Harbor, 1,089 ... D 5
08084 Stratford, 9,801 ... B 4
† 07747 Strathmore, 7,674 ... E 3
07876 Succasunna, 5,000 ... D 2
07901 Summit, 23,620 ... E 2
08008 Surf City, 1,129 ... E 4
07461 Sussex, 2,038 ... D 1
08085 Swedesboro, 2,287 ... C 4
07878 Tabor, 1,500 ... E 2
07666 Teaneck, ∆42,355 ... B 2
07670 Tenafly, 14,827 ... C 1
07608 Teterboro, 14 ... B 2
08086 Thorofare, 4,200 ... B 4
08887 Three Bridges, 750 ... D 2
08560 Titusville, 900 ... D 3
08753 Toms River⊙, 7,303 ... E 4
07511 Totowa, 11,580 ... B 1
07082 Towaco, 2,500 ... E 2
* 08601 Trenton (cap.)⊙, 104,638 ... D 3
Trenton, ‡303,968 ... D 3
08087 Tuckerton, 1,926 ... E 4
07083 Union, ∆53,077 ... A 2
07735 Union Beach, 6,472 ... E 3
07087 Union City, 58,537 ... C 2
† 07421 Upper Greenwood Lake 1,505 ... E 1
† 07458 Upper Saddle River, 7,949 ... B 1
† 07724 Vail Homes, 1,164 ... E 3
07088 Vauxhall, 9,245 ... A 2
08406 Ventnor City, 10,385 ... E 5
07462 Vernon, 800 ... E 1
07044 Verona, 15,067 ... B 2
08251 Villas, 3,155 ... D 5
08088 Vincentown, 900 ... D 4
08360 Vineland, 47,399 ... C 5
Vineland-Millville-Bridgeton, ‡121,374 ... C 5
07463 Waldwick, 12,313 ... B 1
07719 Wall, ∆16,498 ... E 3
07055 Wallington, 10,284 ... B 2
† 07712 Wanamassa, 4,600 ... E 3
07465 Wanaque, 8,636 ... B 1
08758 Waretown, 1,800 ... E 4
07882 Washington, 5,943 ... D 2
07060 Watchung, 4,750 ... E 2
08089 Waterford Works, 950 ... D 4
07470 Wayne, ∆49,141 ... A 1
07087 Weehawken, ∆13,383 ... C 2
08090 Wenonah, 2,364 ... C 4
07006 West Caldwell, 11,887 ... A 2
† 08204 West Cape May, 1,005 ... D 6
08092 West Creek, 630 ... E 4
* 07090 Westfield, 33,720 ... E 2
07764 West Long Branch, 6,845 ... F 3
07480 West Milford, 950 ... E 1
07093 West New York, 40,627 ... C 2
07052 West Orange, 43,715 ... A 2
07424 West Paterson, 11,692 ... B 2
08628 West Trenton, 5,900 ... D 3
08093 Westville, 5,170 ... B 3
07675 Westwood, 11,105 ... B 1
07885 Wharton, 5,535 ... D 2
07981 Whippany, 7,500 ... E 2
08888 Whitehouse, 800 ... D 2
08889 White House Station, 1,019 ... D 2
08252 Whitesboro, 700 ... D 5
† 08701 Whitesville, 600 ... E 3
08759 Whiting, 750 ... E 4
07765 Wickatunk, 950 ... E 3
08260 Wildwood, 4,110 ... D 6
08260 Wildwood Crest, 3,483 ... D 6
08094 Williamstown, 4,075 ... D 4
08046 Willingboro, ∆43,414 ... D 3
† 07036 Winfield, ∆2,184 ... B 2
08270 Woodbine, 2,625 ... D 5
07095 Woodbridge, ∆98,944 ... E 2
08096 Woodbury⊙, 12,408 ... B 4
08097 Woodbury Heights, 3,621 ... B 4
07675 Woodcliff Lake, 5,506 ... B 1
08107 Wood-Lynne, 3,101 ... B 3
† 07885 Woodport, 2,100 ... D 2
07075 Wood-Ridge, 8,311 ... B 2
08098 Woodstown, 3,137 ... C 4
08562 Wrightstown, 2,719 ... D 3
07481 Wyckoff, ∆16,039 ... B 1
08620 Yardville, 9,500 ... D 3

⊙ County seat.
‡ Population of metropolitan area.
∆ Population of town or township.
† Zip of nearest p.o
* Multiple zips

Topography

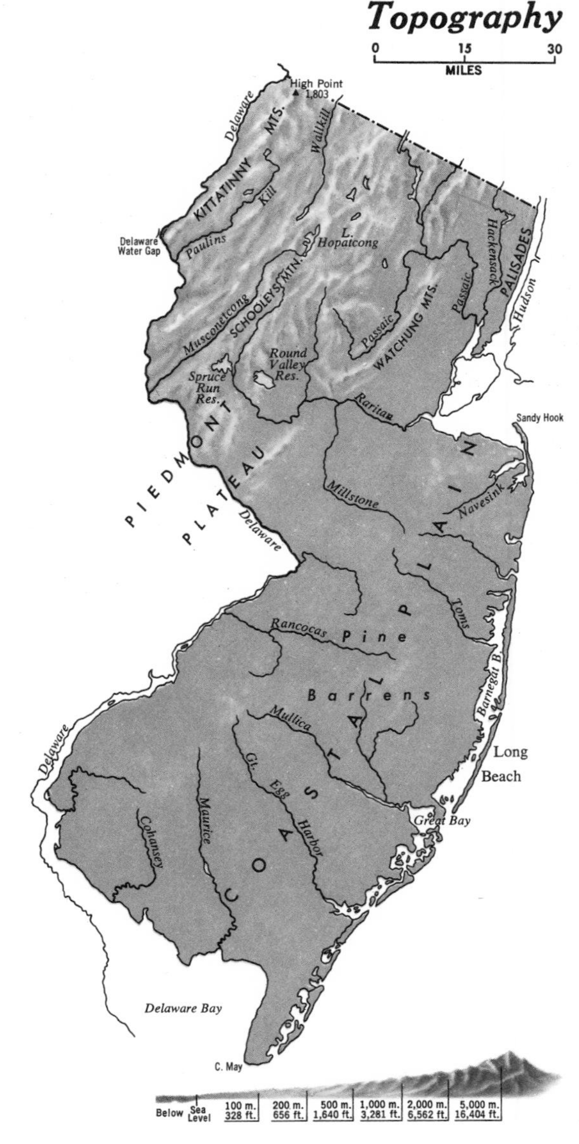

New Jersey towns become suburbs of Manhattan, thanks to connecting links like the Holland and Lincoln Tunnels and the George Washington Bridge. Scene above is the Fort Lee approach to the Bridge.

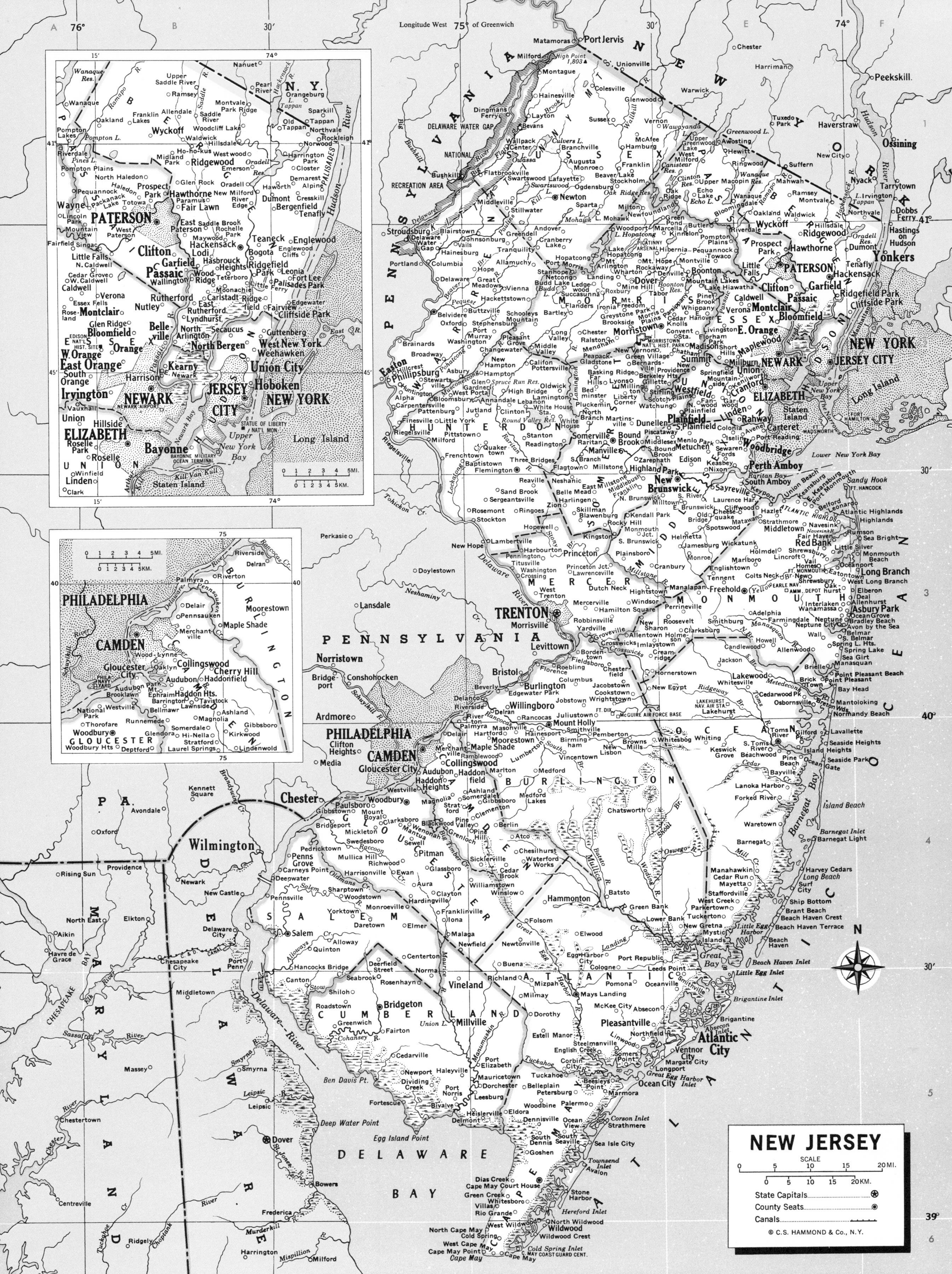

NEW JERSEY
SCALE
0 5 10 15 20 MI.
0 5 10 15 20 KM.
State Capitals
County Seats
Canals
© C.S. HAMMOND & Co., N.Y.
Longitude West 75° of Greenwich
76°
30′
74°
41°
40°
39°
A
B
C
D
E
F
1
2
3
4
5
6
N
PENNSYLVANIA
NEW YORK
DELAWARE
MARYLAND
ATLANTIC OCEAN
DELAWARE BAY
Lower New York Bay
SUSSEX
PASSAIC
BERGEN
WARREN
MORRIS
ESSEX
HUDSON
UNION
SOMERSET
HUNTERDON
MIDDLESEX
MERCER
MONMOUTH
OCEAN
BURLINGTON
CAMDEN
GLOUCESTER
SALEM
CUMBERLAND
ATLANTIC
CAPE MAY
Port Jervis
Matamoras
High Point 1,803
Montague
Milford
Unionville
Colesville
Hainesville
Glenwood
Warwick
Chester
Harriman
Peekskill
Haverstraw
Ossining
Tarrytown
Nyack
Dobbs Ferry
Hastings on Hudson
Yonkers
Sussex
Vernon
Newton
Dingmans Ferry
DELAWARE WATER GAP
NATIONAL RECREATION AREA
Bushkill
Stroudsburg
Delaware Water Gap
Blairstown
Hackettstown
Belvidere
Phillipsburg
Easton
Washington
Morristown
Dover
Boonton
Paterson
Passaic
Clifton
Hackensack
Ridgewood
Wyckoff
Montclair
Bloomfield
E. Orange
Newark
Jersey City
Elizabeth
Bayonne
Hoboken
Union City
Kearny
Rahway
Linden
Plainfield
Westfield
Summit
Cranford
Carteret
Woodbridge
Perth Amboy
South Amboy
Sayreville
New Brunswick
Highland Park
Edison
Metuchen
Somerville
Bound Brook
Manville
Flemington
Lambertville
Princeton
Hightstown
Freehold
Red Bank
Long Branch
Asbury Park
Trenton
Morrisville
Levittown
Bristol
Burlington
Willingboro
Mount Holly
Philadelphia
Camden
Gloucester City
Collingswood
Haddonfield
Cherry Hill
Woodbury
Chester
Wilmington
Glassboro
Pitman
Salem
Penns Grove
Pennsville
Bridgeton
Vineland
Millville
Hammonton
Lakewood
Toms River
Lakehurst
Barnegat
Pleasantville
Atlantic City
Ventnor City
Margate City
Ocean City
Somers Point
Cape May Court House
Wildwood
North Wildwood
Cape May
Dover
Elkton
Newark
New Castle
Norristown
Conshohocken
Ardmore
Doylestown
Lansdale
Sandy Hook
Long Island
Staten Island
Great Bay
Barnegat Bay
Little Egg Harbor
Brigantine
Tuckerton
Beach Haven
Seaside Heights
Point Pleasant Beach
Manasquan
Belmar
Keansburg
Middletown
Hazlet
Matawan
Keyport
PATERSON
CLIFTON
NEWARK
JERSEY CITY
NEW YORK
ELIZABETH
Bayonne
Staten Island
Upper New York Bay
Kill Van Kull
STATUE OF LIBERTY NAT'L MON.
N.Y.
PHILADELPHIA
CAMDEN
BURLINGTON
CAMDEN
GLOUCESTER
Delair
Pennsauken
Maple Shade
Moorestown
Palmyra
Riverton
Riverside
Delran
Merchantville
Collingswood
Haddon Hts.
Audubon
Gloucester City
Westville
National Park
Runnemede
Somerdale
Magnolia
Stratford
Laurel Springs
Lindenwold
Woodbury Hts
Deptford
Thorofare
Kirkwood
Gibbsboro
Ashland
0 1 2 3 4 5 MI.
0 1 2 3 4 5 KM.

COUNTIES

Bernalillo, 315,774 .... C 4
Catron, 2,198 .... A 4
Chaves, 43,335 .... E 5
Colfax, 12,170 .... E 2
Curry, 39,517 .... F 4
De Baca, 2,547 .... E 4
Dona Ana, 69,773 .... C 6
Eddy, 41,119 .... E 6
Grant, 22,030 .... A 5
Guadalupe, 4,969 .... E 4
Harding, 1,348 .... F 3
Hidalgo, 4,734 .... A 7
Lea, 49,554 .... F 6
Lincoln, 7,560 .... D 5
Los Alamos, 15,198 .... C 3
Luna, 11,706 .... B 6
McKinley, 43,208 .... A 3
Mora, 4,673 .... E 3
Otero, 41,097 .... D 6
Quay, 10,903 .... F 3
Rio Arriba, 25,170 .... B 2
Roosevelt, 16,479 .... F 4
Sandoval, 17,492 .... C 3
San Juan, 52,517 .... A 2
San Miguel, 21,951 .... D 3
Santa Fe, 53,756 .... C 3
Sierra, 7,189 .... B 5
Socorro, 9,763 .... C 5
Taos, 17,516 .... D 2
Torrance, 5,290 .... D 4
Union, 4,925 .... F 2
Valencia, 40,539 .... A 4

CITIES and TOWNS

Zip *Name/Pop.* *Key*

87510 Abiquiu, 310 .... C 2
† 87049 Acoma, 150 .... B 4
† 87049 Acomita, 975 .... B 3
87114 Alameda, 5,000 .... C 3
88310 Alamogordo⊙, 23,035 .... C 6
* 87101 Albuquerque⊙, 243,751 .... C 3
Alburquerque, ‡315,774 .... C 3
87511 Alcalde, 975 .... C 2
87001 Algodones, 195 .... C 3
88312 Alto, 104 .... D 5
87512 Amalia, 200 .... D 2
88020 Animas, 75 .... A 7
88021 Anthony, 1,728 .... C 6
87711 Anton Chico, 600 .... D 3
† 88351 Arabela, 65 .... D 5
87820 Aragon, 85 .... A 5
87930 Arrey, 367 .... B 6
87513 Arroyo Hondo, 400 .... D 2
87514 Arroyo Seco, 500 .... D 2
88210 Artesia, 10,315 .... E 6
87410 Aztec⊙, 3,354 .... B 2
88023 Bayard, 2,908 .... A 6
87002 Belen, 4,823 .... C 4
88314 Bent, 157 .... D 5
88024 Berino, 300 .... C 6
87004 Bernalillo⊙, 2,016 .... C 3
87815 Bingham, 60 .... C 5
87412 Blanco, 150 .... B 2
87413 Bloomfield, 1,574 .... A 2
87005 Bluewater, 300 .... A 3
87006 Bosque, 300 .... C 4
87712 Buena Vista, 178 .... D 3
87515 Canjilon, 300 .... C 2
87516 Canones, 200 .... C 2
88316 Capitan, 439 .... D 5
88414 Capulin, 100 .... F 2
88220 Carlsbad⊙, 21,297 .... E 6
88301 Carrizozo⊙, 1,123 .... D 5
87007 Casa Blanca, 560 .... B 4
88113 Causey, 150 .... F 5
87518 Cebolla, 150 .... C 2
87008 Cedar Crest, 600 .... C 3
† 87410 Cedar Hill, 145 .... B 2
88026 Central, 1,864 .... A 6
87010 Cerrillos, 118 .... D 3
87519 Cerro, 400 .... D 2
87713 Chacon, 200 .... D 2
87520 Chama, 899 .... C 2
88027 Chamberino, 400 .... C 6
87521 Chamisal, 637 .... D 2
† 87059 Chilili, 80 .... C 4
87522 Chimayo, 900 .... D 3
87714 Cimarron, 927 .... E 2
88415 Clayton⊙, 2,931 .... F 2
87715 Cleveland, 500 .... D 2
88028 Cliff, 350 .... A 6
88317 Cloudcroft, 525 .... D 6
88101 Clovis⊙, 28,495 .... F 4
† 87041 Cochiti, 300 .... C 3
88029 Columbus, 241 .... B 7
88416 Conchas Dam, 192 .... E 3
87523 Cordova, 600 .... D 2
88318 Corona, 262 .... D 4
87048 Corrales, 975 .... C 3
87524 Costilla, 400 .... D 2
87012 Coyote, 125 .... C 2
87313 Crownpoint, 876 .... A 3
† 86504 Crystal, 200 .... A 2
87013 Cuba, 750 .... B 2
87014 Cubero, 300 .... B 3
88417 Cuervo, 150 .... E 3
87522 Cundiyo, 98 .... D 3
87821 Datil, 150 .... B 4
88030 Deming⊙, 8,343 .... B 6
87933 Derry, 350 .... B 6
88418 Des Moines, 204 .... F 2
88230 Dexter, 746 .... E 5
† 87711 Dilia, 125 .... D 3
87527 Dixon, 640 .... D 2
88032 Dona Ana, 800 .... C 6
88115 Dora, 196 .... F 5
87528 Dulce, 450 .... B 2
88319 Duran, 100 .... D 4
87718 Eagle Nest, 300 .... D 2
87015 Edgewood, 75 .... C 3
87935 Elephant Butte, 75 .... B 5
88116 Elida, 233 .... F 5
† 87731 El Porvenir, 90 .... D 3
87529 El Prado, 200 .... D 2
87530 El Rito, 475 .... C 2
87531 Embudo, 400 .... C 2
88321 Encino, 250 .... D 4
87532 Espanola, 4,528 .... C 3
87016 Estancia⊙, 721 .... D 4
88231 Eunice, 2,641 .... F 6
88033 Fairacres, 500 .... C 6
87720 Farley, 81 .... E 2
87401 Farmington, 21,979 .... A 2
88034 Faywood, 75 .... B 6
† 88041 Fierro, 200 .... A 6

NEW MEXICO

SCALE
0 5 10 20 30 40 50 60 MI.
0 5 10 20 30 40 50 60 KM.

State Capitals ⊛
County Seats ⊙

Zip	Place, Population	Key
87415	Flora Vista, 500	A 2
88118	Floyd, 248	F 4
88322	Flying H, 61	E 5
88419	Folsom, 75	F 2
88036	Fort Bayard, 390	A 6
88323	Fort Stanton, 389	D 5
88119	Fort Sumner⊙, 1,615	E 4
87316	Fort Wingate, 800	A 3
87416	Fruitland, 600	A 2
† 87540	Galisteo, 125	D 3
87017	Gallina, 500	C 2
87301	Gallup⊙, 14,596	A 3
87317	Gamerco, 800	A 3
87936	Garfield, 600	B 6
88421	Garita, 154	E 3
88038	Gila, 300	A 6
88324	Glencoe, 140	D 5
88039	Glenwood, 175	A 5
87535	Glorieta, 300	D 3
88120	Grady, 104	F 4
87020	Grants, 8,768	B 3
87722	Guadalupita, 305	D 2
88232	Hagerman, 953	E 5
88041	Hanover, 350	A 6
87937	Hatch, 867	B 6
87537	Hernandez, 500	C 2
88325	High Rolls Mountain Park, 650	D 5
88042	Hillsboro, 125	B 6
88240	Hobbs, 26,025	F 6
87723	Holman, 510	D 2
88336	Hondo, 250	D 5
88250	Hope, 90	E 6
87901	Hot Springs (Truth or Consequences), 4,656	B 5
88121	House, 119	F 4
88251	Humble City, 65	F 6
88043	Hurley, 1,796	A 6
87538	Ilfeld, 68	D 3
87022	Isleta, 1,080	C 4
88252	Jal, 2,602	F 6
87023	Jarales, 525	C 4
87024	Jemez Pueblo, 1,197	C 3
87025	Jemez Springs, 356	C 3
87417	Kirtland, 800	A 2
† 87712	La Cueva, 200	D 3
87026	Laguna, 900	B 3
87027	La Jara, 210	B 2
87028	Lajoya, 97	C 4
88253	Lake Arthur, 306	E 5
88337	La Luz, 800	C 6
87539	La Madera, 200	C 2
88044	La Mesa, 900	C 6
87540	Lamy, 66	D 3
87418	La Plata, 150	A 2
88001	Las Cruces⊙, 37,857	C 6
87541	Las Tablas, 65	C 2
87701	Las Vegas (city)⊙, 7,528	D 3
† 88021	La Union, 200	C 7
87725	Ledoux, 400	D 3
87823	Lemitar, 400	B 4
88338	Lincoln, 100	D 5
87543	Llano, 270	D 2
88255	Loco Hills, 350	F 6
88426	Logan, 386	F 3
88045	Lordsburg⊙, 3,429	A 6
87544	Los Alamos⊙, 11,310	C 3
87031	Los Lunas⊙, 973	C 4
† 87101	Los Ranchos de Albuquerque, 1,900	C 3
88256	Loving, 1,192	E 6
88260	Lovington⊙, 8,915	F 6
87547	Lumberton, 190	C 2
87824	Luna, 175	A 5
87825	Magdalena, 652	B 4
88263	Malaga, 250	E 6
87318	Manuelito, 200	A 3
† 87016	Manzano, 110	C 4
87728	Maxwell, 393	E 2
88339	Mayhill, 200	D 6
88262	McDonald, 170	F 5
† 79901	Meadow Vista, 1,402	C 7
88124	Melrose, 636	F 4
87319	Mentmore, 315	A 3
88340	Mescalero, 950	D 5
88046	Mesilla, 1,713	C 6
88047	Mesilla Park, 1,500	C 6
88048	Mesquite, 950	C 6
87320	Mexican Springs, 150	A 3
87729	Miami, 200	E 2
87020	Milan, 2,185	B 3
88049	Mimbres, 155	B 6
87731	Montezuma, 110	D 3
87939	Monticello, 125	B 5
88265	Monument, 250	F 6
87732	Mora⊙, 1,400	D 3
87035	Moriarty, 758	D 4
87733	Mosquero⊙, 244	F 3
87036	Mountainair, 1,022	C 4
† 87501	Nambe, 100	D 3
88430	Nara Visa, 400	F 3
87328	Navajo, 920	A 3
† 87325	Newcomb, 300	A 2
88431	Newkirk, 75	E 3
87038	New Laguna, 450	B 4
88341	Nogal, 80	D 5
87734	Ocate, 288	E 2
88266	Oil Center, 300	F 6
87549	Ojo Caliente, 500	D 2
87735	Ojo Feliz, 146	E 2
87550	Ojo Sarco, 184	D 2
88052	Organ, 500	C 6
88342	Orogrande, 80	D 6
† 88220	Otis, 200	E 6
87040	Paguate, 775	B 3
87551	Park View, 788	C 2
87552	Pecos, 598	D 3
87041	Penablanca, 320	C 3
87553	Penasco, 1,169	D 2
87042	Peralta, 400	C 4
87554	Petaca, 84	C 2
88343	Picacho, 120	D 5
87827	Pie Town, 99	A 4
88053	Pinos Altos, 200	A 6
87043	Placitas, 88	C 3
87044	Ponderosa, 400	C 3
88130	Portales⊙, 10,554	F 4
87045	Prewitt, 300	B 3
88432	Puerto de Luna, 180	E 4
88433	Quay, 75	F 4
87829	Quemado, 520	A 4
87556	Questa, 1,095	D 2
88054	Radium Springs, 150	B 6
87736	Rainsville, 300	D 2
87321	Ramah, 574	A 3
87557	Ranches of Taos, 2,900	D 2
87740	Raton⊙, 6,962	E 2
87558	Red River, 125	D 2
87046	Regina, 65	B 2
87322	Rehoboth, 300	A 3
87830	Reserve⊙, 800	A 5
87560	Ribera, 400	D 3
87940	Rincon, 300	C 6
87742	Rociada, 164	D 3
87561	Rodarte, 650	D 2
88056	Rodeo, 100	A 7
88201	Roswell⊙, 33,908	E 5
87562	Rowe, 150	D 3
87743	Roy, 476	E 3
88345	Ruidoso, 2,216	D 5
88346	Ruidoso Downs, 702	D 5
87563	Rutheron, 90	C 2
87941	Salem, 400	B 6
87831	San Acacia, 150	B 4
87832	San Antonio, 359	B 5
87564	San Cristobal, 275	D 2
87047	Sandia Park, 200	C 3
† 87001	San Felipe, 1,187	C 3
87049	San Fidel, 150	B 3
† 87501	San Ildefonso, 140	C 3
88434	San Jon, 308	F 3
87565	San Jose, 115	D 3
87566	San Juan Pueblo, 900	C 2
88057	San Lorenzo, 264	B 6
87050	San Mateo, 200	B 3
88058	San Miguel, 400	C 6
88348	San Patricio, 250	D 5
87051	San Rafael, 300	A 3
87567	Santa Cruz, 754	D 2
87501	Santa Fe (cap.)⊙, 41,167	C 3
88059	Santa Rita, 600	B 6
88435	Santa Rosa⊙, 2,485	E 4
87052	Santo Domingo Pueblo, 1,662	C 3
87053	San Ysidro, 280	C 3
87745	Sapello, 144	D 3
87055	Seboyeta, 125	B 3
87568	Sena, 150	D 3
87569	Serafina, 280	D 3
87420	Shiprock, 800	A 2
88061	Silver City⊙, 7,751	A 6
87801	Socorro⊙, 4,687	C 4
† 87565	Soham, 104	D 3
87746	Solano, 70	E 3
87747	Springer, 1,574	E 2
87056	Stanley, 60	D 3
87057	Tajique, 150	C 4
87571	Taos⊙, 2,475	D 2
† 87571	Taos Pueblo, 1,030	D 2
88267	Tatum, 982	F 5
87574	Tesuque, 800	C 3
88135	Texico, 772	F 4
87323	Thoreau, 550	A 3
87575	Tierra Amarilla⊙, 850	C 2
87059	Tijeras, 500	C 3
88351	Tinnie, 95	D 5
87324	Toadlena, 200	A 2
87325	Tohatchi, 500	A 3
87060	Tome, 500	C 4
87061	Torreon, 100	C 4
87576	Trampas, 76	D 2
88439	Trementina, 80	E 3
87577	Tres Piedras, 200	D 2
87578	Truchas, 275	D 2
87748	Trujillo, 148	E 3
87901	Truth or Consequences⊙, 4,656	B 5
88401	Tucumcari⊙, 7,189	F 3
88352	Tularosa, 2,851	C 5
88065	Tyrone, 100	A 6
88001	University Park, 4,165	C 6
87749	Ute Park, 75	D 2
87579	Vadito, 335	D 2
88072	Vado, 350	C 6
87580	Valdez, 190	D 2
† 87031	Valencia, 500	C 4
87581	Vallecitos, 450	C 2
88073	Vanadium, 300	A 6
88353	Vaughn, 867	D 4
87582	Velarde, 365	C 2
† 81091	Vermejo Park, 85	D 2
87583	Villanueva, 300	D 3
† 88055	Virden, 151	A 6
87752	Wagon Mound, 630	E 2
87421	Waterflow, 475	A 2
87753	Watrous, 250	D 3
87544	White Rock, 3,861	C 3
88002	White Sands Missile Range, 4,167	C 6
88268	Whites City, 300	E 6
87063	Willard, 209	D 4
87942	Williamsburg, 367	B 5
88136	Yeso, 200	E 4
87064	Youngsville, 130	C 2
† 87053	Zia Pueblo, 600	C 3
87327	Zuni, 3,958	A 3

⊙ County seat.
‡ Population of metropolitan area.
† Zip of nearest p.o.
* Multiple zips

AREA 121,666 sq. mi.
POPULATION 1,016,000
CAPITAL Santa Fe
LARGEST CITY Albuquerque
HIGHEST POINT Wheeler Pk. 13,161 ft.
SETTLED IN 1605
ADMITTED TO UNION January 6, 1912
POPULAR NAME Land of Enchantment
STATE FLOWER Yucca
STATE BIRD Road Runner

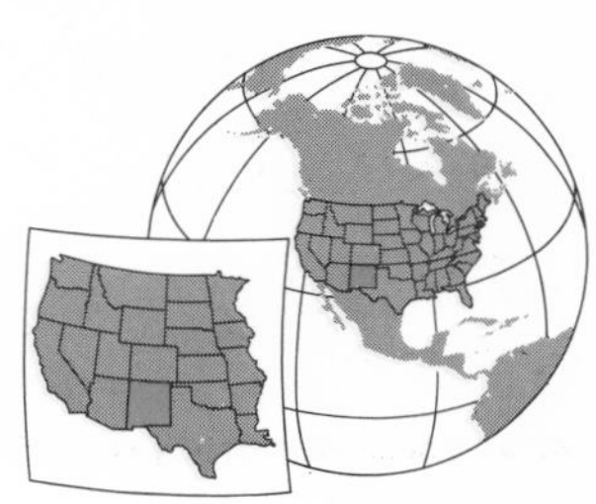

Stephen Voynick — Shostal Associates

Golden adobe against the blue Sangre de Cristo Mountains. Clear, pure colors, magnificent surroundings and congenial atmosphere combine to draw artists and writers to Taos, New Mexico.

Topography

0 50 100 MILES

Below Sea Level · 100 m. 328 ft. · 200 m. 656 ft. · 500 m. 1,640 ft. · 1,000 m. 3,281 ft. · 2,000 m. 6,562 ft. · 5,000 m. 16,404 ft.

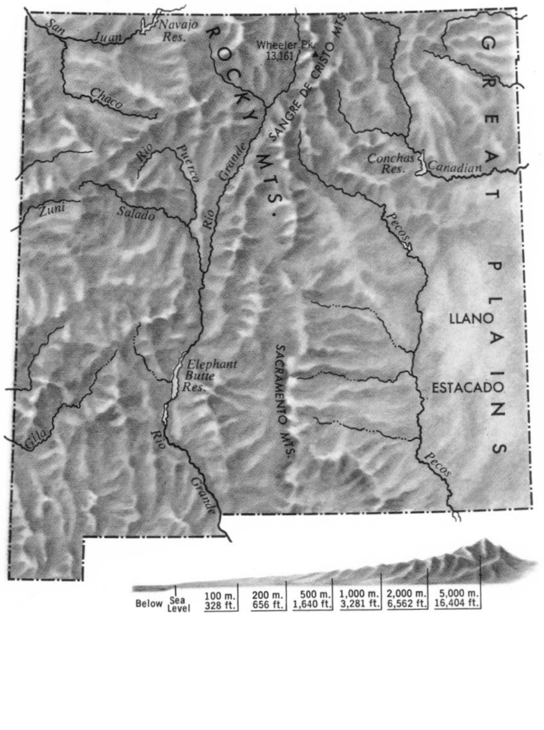

Agriculture, Industry and Resources

DOMINANT LAND USE

- Wheat, Grain Sorghums, Range Livestock
- General Farming, Livestock, Special Crops
- General Farming, Livestock, Cash Grain
- Dry Beans, General Farming
- Cotton, Forest Products
- Range Livestock
- Forests
- Nonagricultural Land

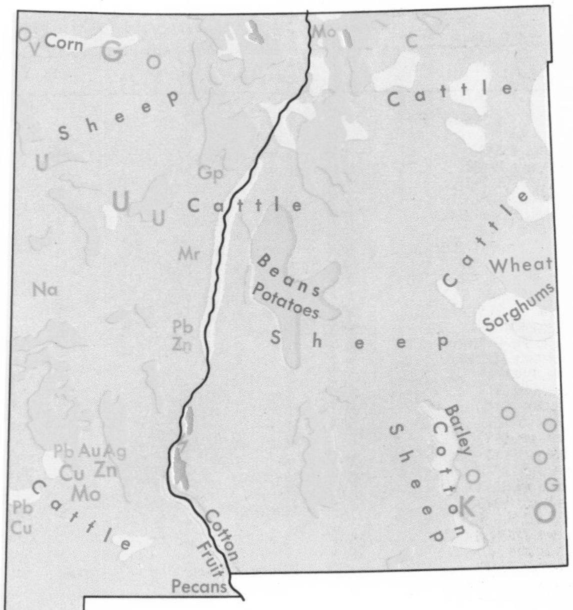

MAJOR MINERAL OCCURRENCES

Ag	Silver	Gp	Gypsum	O	Petroleum
Au	Gold	K	Potash	Pb	Lead
C	Coal	Mo	Molybdenum	U	Uranium
Cu	Copper	Mr	Marble	V	Vanadium
G	Natural Gas	Na	Salt	Zn	Zinc
ϟ	Water Power				

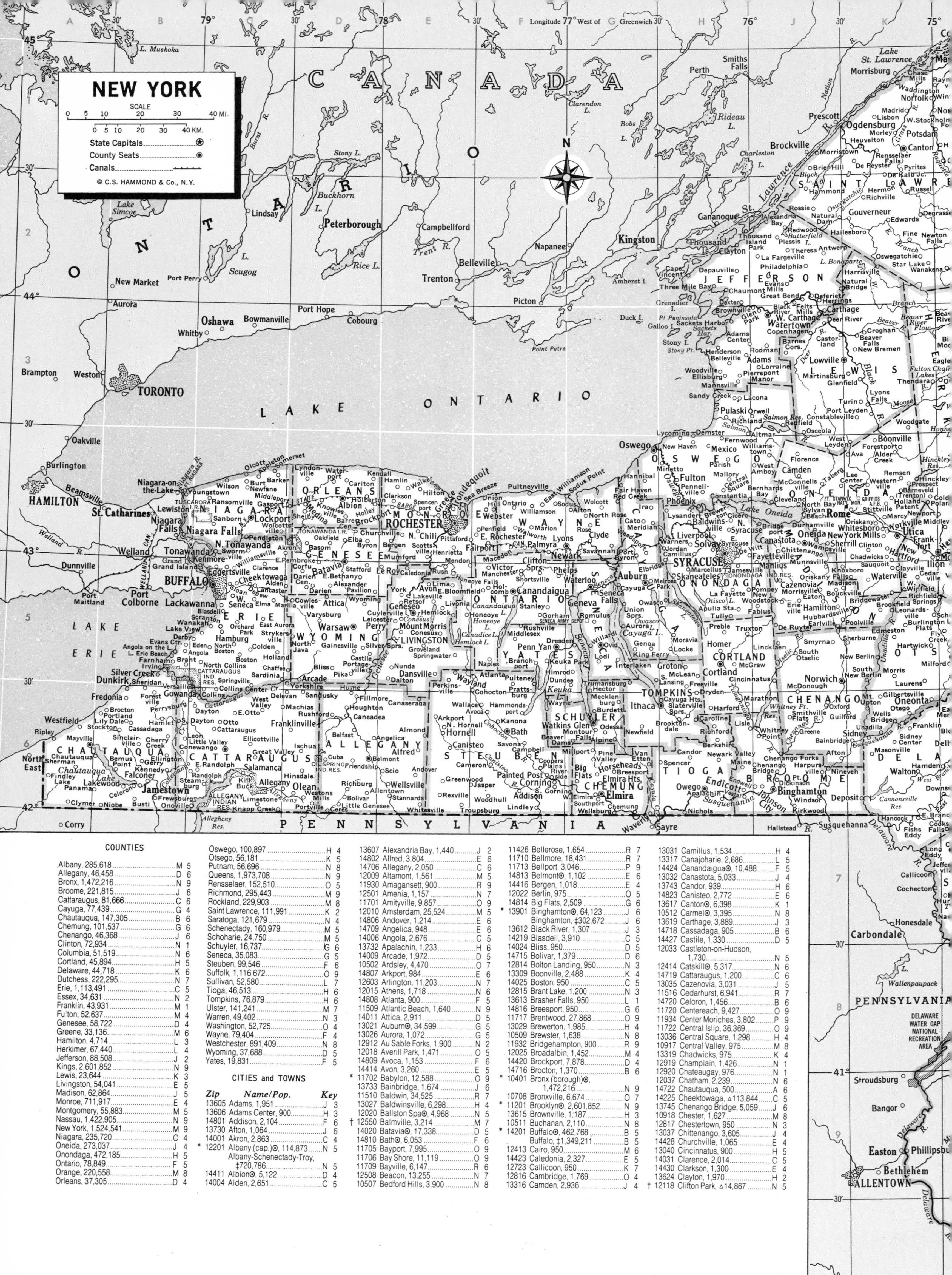

COUNTIES

Albany, 285,618 .... M 5
Allegany, 46,458 .... D 6
Bronx, 1,472,216 .... N 9
Broome, 221,815 .... J 6
Cattaraugus, 81,666 .... C 6
Cayuga, 77,439 .... G 4
Chautauqua, 147,305 .... B 6
Chemung, 101,537 .... G 6
Chenango, 46,368 .... J 6
Clinton, 72,934 .... N 1
Columbia, 51,519 .... N 6
Cortland, 45,894 .... H 5
Delaware, 44,718 .... K 6
Dutchess, 222,295 .... N 7
Erie, 1,113,491 .... C 5
Essex, 34,631 .... N 2
Franklin, 43,931 .... M 1
Fulton, 52,637 .... M 4
Genesee, 58,722 .... D 4
Greene, 33,136 .... M 6
Hamilton, 4,714 .... L 3
Herkimer, 67,440 .... L 4
Jefferson, 88,508 .... J 2
Kings, 2,601,852 .... N 9
Lewis, 23,644 .... K 3
Livingston, 54,041 .... E 5
Madison, 62,864 .... J 5
Monroe, 711,917 .... E 4
Montgomery, 55,883 .... M 5
Nassau, 1,422,905 .... N 9
New York, 1,524,541 .... M 9
Niagara, 235,720 .... C 4
Oneida, 273,037 .... J 4
Onondaga, 472,185 .... H 5
Ontario, 78,849 .... F 5
Orange, 220,558 .... M 8
Orleans, 37,305 .... D 4
Oswego, 100,897 .... H 4
Otsego, 56,181 .... K 5
Putnam, 56,696 .... N 8
Queens, 1,973,708 .... N 9
Rensselaer, 152,510 .... O 5
Richmond, 295,443 .... M 9
Rockland, 229,903 .... M 8
Saint Lawrence, 111,991 .... K 2
Saratoga, 121,679 .... N 4
Schenectady, 160,979 .... M 5
Schoharie, 24,750 .... M 5
Schuyler, 16,737 .... G 6
Seneca, 35,083 .... G 5
Steuben, 99,546 .... F 6
Suffolk, 1,116 672 .... O 9
Sullivan, 52,580 .... L 7
Tioga, 46,513 .... H 6
Tompkins, 76,879 .... H 6
Ulster, 141,241 .... M 7
Warren, 49,402 .... N 3
Washington, 52,725 .... O 4
Wayne, 79,404 .... F 4
Westchester, 891,409 .... N 8
Wyoming, 37,688 .... D 5
Yates, 19,831 .... F 5

CITIES and TOWNS

	Zip	Name/Pop.	Key
	13605	Adams, 1,951	J 3
	13606	Adams Center, 900	H 3
	14801	Addison, 2,104	F 6
	13730	Afton, 1,064	J 6
	14001	Akron, 2,863	C 4
*	12201	Albany (cap.)⊙, 114,873	N 5
		Albany-Schenectady-Troy, ‡720,786	N 5
	14411	Albion⊙, 5,122	D 4
	14004	Alden, 2,651	C 5
	13607	Alexandria Bay, 1,440	J 2
	14802	Alfred, 3,804	E 6
	14706	Allegany, 2,050	C 6
	12009	Altamont, 1,561	M 5
	11930	Amagansett, 900	R 9
	12501	Amenia, 1,157	N 7
	11701	Amityville, 9,857	O 9
	12010	Amsterdam, 25,524	M 5
	14806	Andover, 1,214	E 6
	14709	Angelica, 948	E 6
	14006	Angola, 2,676	C 5
	13732	Apalachin, 1,233	H 6
	14009	Arcade, 1,972	D 5
	10502	Ardsley, 4,470	O 7
	14807	Arkport, 984	E 6
	12603	Arlington, 11,203	N 7
	12015	Athens, 1,718	N 6
	14808	Atlanta, 900	F 5
	11509	Atlantic Beach, 1,640	N 9
	14011	Attica, 2,911	D 5
	13021	Auburn⊙, 34,599	G 5
	13026	Aurora, 1,072	G 5
	12912	Au Sable Forks, 1,900	N 2
	12018	Averill Park, 1,471	O 5
	14809	Avoca, 1,153	F 6
	14414	Avon, 3,260	E 5
*	11702	Babylon, 12,588	O 9
	13733	Bainbridge, 1,674	J 6
	11510	Baldwin, 34,525	R 7
	13027	Baldwinsville, 6,298	H 4
	12020	Ballston Spa⊙, 4,968	N 5
†	12550	Balmville, 3,214	M 7
	14020	Batavia⊙, 17,338	D 5
	14810	Bath⊙, 6,053	F 6
	11705	Bayport, 7,995	O 9
	11706	Bay Shore, 11,119	O 9
	11709	Bayville, 6,147	R 6
	12508	Beacon, 13,255	N 7
	10507	Bedford Hills, 3.900	N 8
	11426	Bellerose, 1,654	R 7
	11710	Bellmore, 18,431	R 7
	11713	Bellport, 3,046	P 9
	14813	Belmont⊙, 1,102	E 6
	14416	Bergen, 1,018	E 4
	12022	Berlin, 975	O 5
	14814	Big Flats, 2,509	G 6
*	13901	Binghamton⊙, 64,123	J 6
		Binghamton, ‡302,672	J 6
	13612	Black River, 1,307	J 3
	14219	Blasdell, 3,910	C 5
	14024	Bliss, 950	D 5
	14715	Bolivar, 1,379	D 6
	12814	Bolton Landing, 950	N 3
	13309	Boonville, 2,488	K 4
	14025	Boston, 950	C 5
	12815	Brant Lake, 1,200	N 3
	13613	Brasher Falls, 950	L 1
	14816	Breesport, 950	G 6
	11717	Brentwood, 27,868	O 9
	13029	Brewerton, 1,985	H 4
	10509	Brewster, 1,638	N 8
	11932	Bridgehampton, 900	R 9
	12025	Broadalbin, 1,452	M 4
	14420	Brockport, 7,878	D 4
	14716	Brocton, 1,370	B 6
*	10401	Bronx (borough)⊙, 1,472,216	N 9
	10708	Bronxville, 6,674	O 7
*	11201	Brooklyn⊙, 2,601,852	N 9
	13615	Brownville, 1;187	H 3
	10511	Buchanan, 2,110	N 8
*	14201	Buffalo⊙, 462,768	B 5
		Buffalo, ‡1,349,211	B 5
	12413	Cairo, 950	M 6
	14423	Caledonia, 2,327	E 5
	12723	Callicoon, 950	K 7
	12816	Cambridge, 1,769	O 4
	13316	Camden, 2,936	J 4
	13031	Camillus, 1,534	H 4
	13317	Canajoharie, 2,686	L 5
	14424	Canandaigua⊙, 10,488	F 5
	13032	Canastota, 5,033	J 4
	13743	Candor, 939	H 6
	14823	Canisteo, 2,772	E 6
	13617	Canton⊙, 6,398	K 1
	10512	Carmel⊙, 3,395	N 8
	13619	Carthage, 3,889	J 3
	14718	Cassadaga, 905	B 6
	14427	Castile, 1,330	D 5
	12033	Castleton-on-Hudson, 1,730	N 5
	12414	Catskill⊙, 5,317	N 6
	14719	Cattaraugus, 1,200	C 6
	13035	Cazenovia, 3,031	J 5
	11516	Cedarhurst, 6,941	R 7
	14720	Celoron, 1,456	B 6
	11720	Centereach, 9,427	O 9
	11934	Center Moriches, 3,802	P 9
	11722	Central Islip, 36,369	O 9
	13036	Central Square, 1,298	H 4
	10917	Central Valley, 975	M 8
	13319	Chadwicks, 975	K 4
	12919	Champlain, 1,426	N 1
	12920	Chateaugay, 976	N 1
	12037	Chatham, 2,239	N 6
	14722	Chautauqua, 500	A 6
	14225	Cheektowaga, ▵113,844	C 5
	13745	Chenango Bridge, 5,059	J 6
	10918	Chester, 1,627	M 8
	12817	Chestertown, 950	N 3
	13037	Chittenango, 3,605	J 4
	14428	Churchville, 1,065	E 4
	13040	Cincinnatus, 900	H 5
	14031	Clarence, 2,014	C 5
	14430	Clarkson, 1,300	E 4
	13624	Clayton, 1,970	H 2
†	12118	Clifton Park, ▵14,867	N 5

AREA 49,576 sq. mi.
POPULATION 18,241,266
CAPITAL Albany
LARGEST CITY New York
HIGHEST POINT Mt. Marcy 5,344 ft.
SETTLED IN 1614
ADMITTED TO UNION July 26, 1788
POPULAR NAME Empire State
STATE FLOWER Rose
STATE BIRD Bluebird

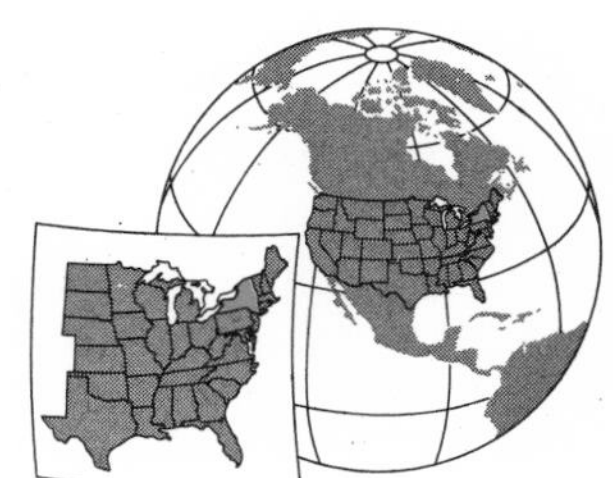

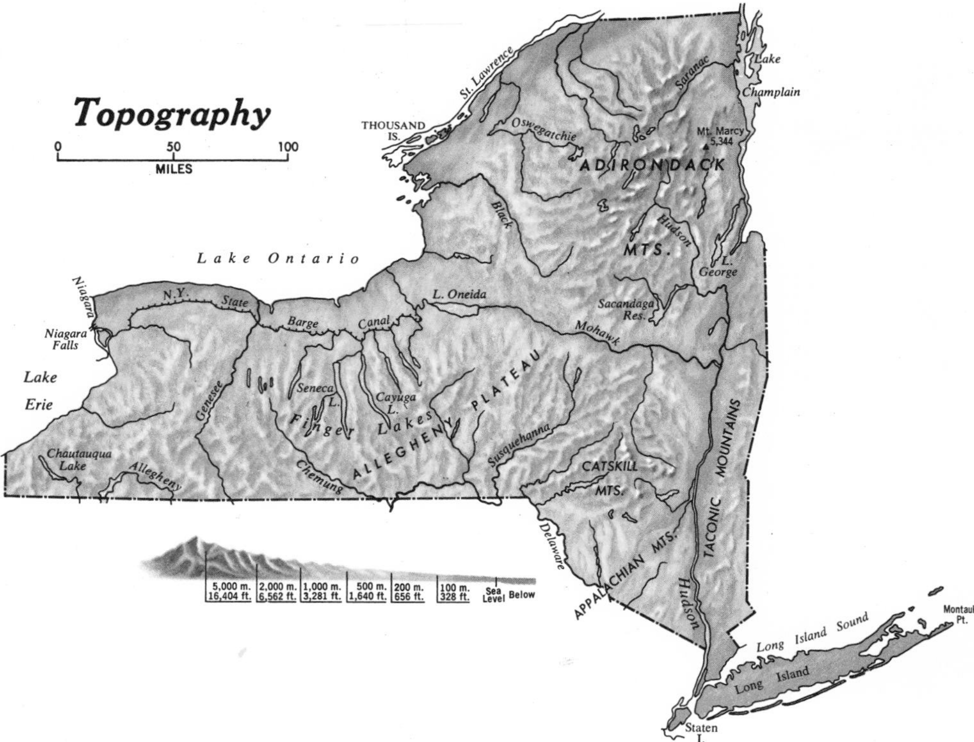

14432 Clifton Springs, 2,058 F 4
13323 Clinton, 2,271 K 4
14433 Clyde, 2,828 G 4
12043 Cobleskill, 4,368 L 5
12045 Coeymans, 975 N 6
12047 Cohoes, 18,613 N 5
14033 Colden, 950 C 5
10516 Cold Spring, 2,083 N 8
† 12201 Colonie, 8,701 N 5
13326 Cooperstown⊙, 2,403 L 5
12822 Corinth, 3,267 N 4
14830 Corning, 15,792 F 6
12518 Cornwall, 2,032 M 8
13045 Cortland⊙, 19,621 H 5
12051 Coxsackie, 2,399 N 6
10519 Croton Falls, 950 N 8
10520 Croton-on-Hudson, 7,523 N 8
14727 Cuba, 1,735 D 6
12929 Dannemora, 3,735 N 1
14437 Dansville, 5,436 E 5
11729 Deer Park, 31,120 O 9
14042 Delevan, 994 D 6
13753 Delhi⊙, 3,017 L 6
12054 Delmar, 7,500 N 5
14043 Depew, 22,158 C 5
13754 Deposit, 2,061 K 6
14047 Derby, 4,900 B 5
13214 DeWitt, 10,032 H 4
13634 Dexter, 1,061 H 2
10522 Dobbs Ferry, 10,353 O 6
13329 Dolgeville, 2,872 L 4
12522 Dover Plains, 975 O 7
13053 Dryden, 1,490 H 6
14837 Dundee, 1,539 F 5
14048 Dunkirk, 16,855 B 5
13054 Durhamville, 975 J 4
13332 Earlville, 1,050 J 5
14052 East Aurora, 7,033 C 5
12061 East Greenbush, 985 N 5
11937 East Hampton, 1.753 R 9
11554 East Meadow, 46,252 R 7
11940 East Moriches, 1,702 P 9
11731 East Northport, 12,392 O 9
11941 Eastport, 1,308 P 9
14445 East Rochester, 8,347 F 4
11518 East Rockaway, 10,323 R 7
13057 East Syracuse, 4,333 H 4
14057 Eden, 2,962 C 5
† 14226 Eggertsville, 55,000 C 5
13060 Elbridge, 1,040 G 5
12932 Elizabethtown⊙, 607 N 2
12428 Ellenville, 4,482 M 7
14731 Ellicottville, 955 C 6
14059 Elma, 2,784 C 5
* 14901 Elmira⊙, 39,945 G 6
14903 Elmira Heights, 4,906 G 6
11003 Elmont, 29,363 R 7
10523 Elmsford, 3,911 P 6
13760 Endicott, 16,556 H 6
13760 Endwell, 15,999 H 6
14450 Fairport, 6,474 F 4
† 12601 Fairview, 8,517 N 7
14733 Falconer, 2,983 B 6
11735 Farmingdale, 9,297 N 9
13066 Fayetteville, 4,996 J 4
12524 Fishkill, 913 N 7
* 11001 Floral Park, 18,422 R 7
10921 Florida, 1,674 M 8
13337 Fly Creek, 910 K 5
12068 Fonda⊙, 1,120 M 5
14062 Forestville, 908 B 6
12937 Fort Covington, 983 M 1
12828 Fort Edward, 3,733 O 4
13339 Fort Plain, 2,809 L 5
13340 Frankfort, 3,305 K 4
14737 Franklinville, 1,948 D 6
14063 Fredonia, 10,326 B 6
11520 Freeport, 40,374 R 7
14738 Frewsburg, 1,772 B 6
14739 Friendship, 1,285 D 6
13069 Fulton, 14,003 H 4
11530 Garden City, 25,373 R 7
10524 Garrison, 975 N 8
14067 Gasport, 950 C 4
14454 Geneseo⊙, 5,714 E 5
14456 Geneva, 16,793 G 5
14740 Gerry, 950 B 6
12432 Glasco, 1,169 M 6
11542 Glen Cove, 25,770 R 6
11545 Glen Head, 4,000 R 7
12801 Glens Falls, 17,222 N 4
12078 Gloversville, 19,677 M 4
10526 Golden's Bridge, 1,101 N 8
10924 Goshen⊙, 4,342 M 8
13642 Gouverneur, 4,574 K 2
14070 Gowanda, 3,110 B 6
12434 Grand Gorge, 950 L 6
14072 Grand Island, 900 B 5
12832 Granville, 2,784 O 4
* 11020 Great Neck, 10,724 R 7
14616 Greece, △75,136 E 4
13778 Greene, 1,874 J 6
12183 Green Island, 3,297 N 5
11944 Greenport, 2,481 P 8
12834 Greenwich, 2,092 O 4
10925 Greenwood Lake, 2,262 M 8
13073 Groton, 2,112 H 5
13780 Guilford, 995 J 6
12086 Hagaman, 1,410 M 5
14075 Hamburg, 10,215 C 5
13346 Hamilton, 3,636 J 5
14840 Hammondsport, 1,066 F 6
11946 Hampton Bays, 1,862 R 9
13783 Hancock, 1,688 K 7
10926 Harriman, 955 M 8
10528 Harrison, 9,250 P 7
10706 Hastings on Hudson, 9,479 O 7
10927 Haverstraw, 8,198 M 8
10532 Hawthorne, 5,000 O 6
* 11550 Hempstead, 39,411 R 7
13650 Henderson, 900 H 3
13350 Herkimer⊙, 8,960 L 4

(continued on following page)

(continued)

Eric Carle — Shostal Associates

Lower Manhattan's skyline in an unusual view from a pier at the Brooklyn Port Authority Marine Terminal.

11557 Hewlett, 6,796 R 7
* 11801 Hicksville, 48,075 R 7
12440 High Falls, 950 M 7
12528 Highland, 2,184 M 7
10928 Highland Falls, 4,638 M 8
10931 Hillburn, 1,058 M 8
14468 Hilton, 2,440 E 4
14080 Holland, 950 C 5
14470 Holley, 1,868 D 4
13077 Homer, 4,143 H 5
14472 Honeoye Falls, 2,248 F 5
12090 Hoosick Falls, 3,897 O 5
12533 Hopewell Junction, 2,055 N 7
14843 Hornell, 12,144 E 6
14845 Horseheads, 7,989 G 6
14744 Houghton, 1,620 D 6
12534 Hudson⊙, 8,940 N 6
12839 Hudson Falls⊙, 7,917 O 4
11743 Huntington, 12,130 O 9
11746 Huntington Station, 28,817 O 9
12443 Hurley, 4,081 M 7
12538 Hyde Park, 2,805 N 6
13357 Ilion, 9,808 K 5
12842 Indian Lake, 950 M 3
11696 Inwood, 8,433 R 7
14617 Irondequoit, ▵63,675 E 4
10533 Irvington, 5,878 O 6
11558 Island Park, 5,396 R 8
11751 Islip, 7,962 O 9
14850 Ithaca⊙, 26,226 G 6
* 11401 Jamaica⊙, 765,078 N 9
14701 Jamestown, 39,795 B 6
13078 Jamesville, 900 H 5
11753 Jericho, 14,010 S 7
13790 Johnson City, 18,025 J 6
12095 Johnstown⊙, 10,045 M 4
13080 Jordan, 1,493 H 4
10536 Katonah, 4,189 N 8
12944 Keeseville, 2,122 O 2
14271 Kenmore, 20,980 C 5
14747 Kennedy, 950 B 6
12446 Kerhonkson, 1,243 M 7
14478 Keuka Park, 990 F 5
12106 Kinderhook, 1,233 N 6
* 11201 Kings (Brooklyn) (borough), 2,601,852 N 9
11754 Kings Park, 5,555 O 9
11024 Kings Point, 5,525 R 7
12401 Kingston⊙, 25,544 M 7
14218 Lackawanna, 28,657 B 5
10512 Lake Carmel, 4,796 N 8
12845 Lake George⊙, 1,046 N 4
12449 Lake Katrine, 1,092 M 7
12846 Lake Luzerne, 900 N 4
12946 Lake Placid, 2,731 N 2
12108 Lake Pleasant⊙, 364 M 4
11040 Lake Success, 3,254 R 7
14085 Lake View, 6,000 B 5
14750 Lakewood, 3,864 B 6
14086 Lancaster, 13,365 C 5
10538 Larchmont, 7,203 P 7
11559 Lawrence, 6,566 R 7
14482 Le Roy, 5,118 E 5
11756 Levittown, 65,440 S 7
14092 Lewiston, 3,292 B 4
12754 Liberty, 4,293 L 7
14485 Lima, 1,686 E 5
11757 Lindenhurst, 28,338 O 9
13365 Little Falls, 7,629 L 4
14755 Little Valley⊙, 1,340 C 6
13088 Liverpool, 3,307 H 4
12758 Livingston Manor, 1,522 L 7
14487 Livonia, 1,278 E 5
14094 Lockport⊙, 25,399 C 4
11561 Long Beach, 33,127 R 8
13367 Lowville, 3,671 J 3
11563 Lynbrook, 23,776 R 7
12952 Lyon Mountain, 1,200 N 1
14489 Lyons⊙, 4,496 F 4
14502 Macedon, 1,168 F 4
13660 Madrid, 950 K 1
10541 Mahopac, 5,265 N 8
13103 Mallory, 900 H 4
12953 Malone⊙, 8,048 M 1
11565 Malverne, 10,036 R 7
10543 Mamaroneck, 18,909 P 7
14504 Manchester, 1,305 F 5
11030 Manhasset, 8,541 R 7
* 10001 Manhattan (borough), 1,524,541 M 9
13104 Manlius, 4,295 J 5
13803 Marathon, 1,053 J 6
13108 Marcellus, 1,456 H 5
13403 Marcy, 2,417 K 4
14505 Marion, 925 F 4
12542 Marlboro, 1,580 M 7
11758 Massapequa, 26,951 O 9
11762 Massapequa Park, 22,112 O 9
13662 Massena, 14,042 L 1
11950 Mastic Beach, 4,870 P 9
11952 Mattituck, 1,995 P 9
12543 Maybrook, 1,536 M 8
12117 Mayfield, 981 M 4
14757 Mayville⊙, 1,567 A 6
13101 McGraw, 1,319 H 5
12118 Mechanicville, 6,247 N 5
14103 Medina, 6,415 D 4
† 13021 Melrose Park, 2,189 G 5
† 12201 Menands, 3,449 N 5
11566 Merrick, 25,904 S 7
13114 Mexico, 1,555 H 4
12122 Middleburg, 1,410 M 5
12550 Middle Hope, 2,327 M 7
14105 Middleport, 2,132 C 4
10940 Middletown, 22,607 L 8
12545 Millbrook, 1,735 N 7
12546 Millerton, 1,042 O 7
11765 Mill Neck, 982 R 6
12547 Milton, 1,900 M 7
12547 Milton, 1,861 N 4
11501 Mineola⊙, 21,845 R 7
13115 Minetto, 950 H 4
12956 Mineville-Witherbee, 1,967 O 2
13407 Mohawk, 3,301 L 4
10950 Monroe, 4,439 M 8
12549 Montgomery, 1,533 M 7
12701 Monticello⊙, 5,991 L 7
14865 Montour Falls, 1,534 G 6
13118 Moravia, 1,642 H 5
12960 Moriah, 953 N 2
12962 Morrisonville, 1,276 N 1
13408 Morrisville, 2,296 J 5
12763 Mountain Dale, 950 L 7
10549 Mount Kisco, 8,172 N 8
14510 Mount Morris, 3,417 E 5
* 10550 Mount Vernon, 72,778 O 7
12458 Napanoch, 975 M 7
14512 Naples, 1,324 F 5
12123 Nassau, 1,466 N 5
14513 Newark, 11,644 G 4
13811 Newark Valley, 1,286 H 6
13411 New Berlin, 1,369 K 5
12550 Newburgh, 26,219 M 7
10956 New City⊙, 27,344 N 8
14108 Newfane, 2,588 C 4
13413 New Hartford, 2,433 K 4
11040 New Hyde Park, 10,116 R 7
12561 New Paltz, 6,058 M 7
13416 Newport, 908 K 4
* 10801 New Rochelle, 75,385 P 7
12550 New Windsor, 8,803 N 8
* 10001 New York (5 boroughs)⊙, 7,867,760 M 9
New York, ‡11,517,483 M 9
13417 New York Mills, 3,805 K 4
* 14301 Niagara Falls, 85,615 C 4
12309 Niskayuna, 6,186 N 5
13667 Norfolk, 1,379 K 1
14110 North Boston, 1,635 C 5
14514 North Chili, 3,163 E 4
14111 North Collins, 1,675 C 5
15853 North Creek, 950 M 3
14113 North Java, 950 D 5
11768 Northport, 7,440 O 9
13212 North Syracuse, 8,687 H 4
10591 North Tarrytown, 8,334 O 6
14120 North Tonawanda, 36,012 C 4
12134 Northville, 1,192 M 4
13815 Norwich⊙, 8,843 J 5
13668 Norwood, 2,098 L 1
14517 Nunda, 1,254 E 5
10960 Nyack, 6,659 N 8
14125 Oakfield, 1,964 D 4
11572 Oceanside, 35,028 R 7
13669 Ogdensburg, 14,554 K 1
14126 Olcott, 1,592 C 4
13420 Old Forge, 950 L 3
14760 Olean, 19,169 D 6
13421 Oneida, 11,658 J 4
13820 Oneonta, 16,030 K 6
14127 Orchard Park, 3,732 C 5
13424 Oriskany, 1,627 K 4
13425 Oriskany Falls, 927 J 5
10562 Ossining, 21,659 N 8
13126 Oswego⊙, 23,844 G 4
13825 Otego, 956 K 6
10963 Otisville, 933 L 8
14521 Ovid⊙, 779 G 5
13827 Owego⊙, 5,152 H 6
13830 Oxford, 1,944 J 6
11771 Oyster Bay, 14,330 S 6
14870 Painted Post, 2,496 F 6
14522 Palmyra, 3,776 F 4
12768 Parksville, 950 L 7
11772 Patchogue, 11,582 P 9
12563 Patterson, 975 N 7
12137 Pattersonville, 950 M 5
12564 Pawling, 1,914 N 7
10965 Pearl River, 17,146 M 8
10566 Peekskill, 18,881 N 8
† 10803 Pelham Manor, 6,673 O 7
14526 Penfield, 8,904 F 4
14527 Penn Yan⊙, 5,168 F 5
14530 Perry, 4,538 D 5
12972 Peru, 1,261 N 1
14532 Phelps, 1,989 F 5
12565 Philmont, 1,674 N 6
13135 Phoenix, 2,617 H 4
10968 Piermont, 2,386 M 8
12566 Pine Bush, 1,183 M 7
10969 Pine Island, 925 L 8
12567 Pine Plains, 950 N 7
14534 Pittsford, 1,755 E 4
11803 Plainview, 32,195 O 9
12901 Plattsburgh⊙, 18,715 O 1
10570 Pleasantville, 7,110 N 8
13140 Port Byron, 1,330 G 4
10573 Port Chester, 25,803 P 7
12466 Port Ewen, 2,882 N 7
12974 Port Henry, 1,532 O 2
11777 Port Jefferson, 5,515 P 9
12771 Port Jervis, 8,852 L 8
14770 Portville, 1,304 D 6
11050 Port Washington, 15,923 R 6
13676 Potsdam, 9,985 K 1
* 12601 Poughkeepsie⊙, 32,029 N 7
13142 Pulaski, 2,480 H 3
10577 Purchase, 2,900 P 7
10579 Putnam Valley, ▵975 N 8
* 11101 Queens (borough), 1,973,708 N 9
11429 Queens Village, 72,000 R 7
14772 Randolph, 1,498 C 6
14131 Ransomville, 1,034 C 4
12143 Ravena, 2,797 N 6
12571 Red Hook, 1,680 N 7
12144 Rensselaer, 10,136 N 5
12572 Rhinebeck, 2,336 N 7
13439 Richfield Springs, 1,540 K 5
14775 Ripley, 1,173 A 6
11901 Riverhead⊙, 7,585 P 9
† 14830 Riverside, 911 F 6
* 14601 Rochester⊙, 296,233 E 4
Rochester, ‡882,667 E 4
* 11570 Rockville Centre, 27,444 R 7
13440 Rome, 50,148 J 4
11779 Ronkonkoma, 7,284 O 9
11575 Roosevelt, 15,008 R 7
12776 Roscoe, 1,300 L 7
12472 Rosendale, 1,220 M 7
11576 Roslyn, 2,546 R 7
12979 Rouses Point, 2,250 O 1
10580 Rye, 15,869 P 7
13685 Sackets Harbor, 1,202 H 3
11963 Sag Harbor, 2,363 R 8
10301 Saint George⊙, 13,000 M 9
13452 Saint Johnsville, 2,089 L 5
14779 Salamanca, 7,877 C 6
12865 Salem, 1,025 O 4
† 11050 Sands Point, 2,916 N 9
12983 Saranac Lake, 6,086 M 2
12866 Saratoga Springs, 18,845 N 4
12477 Saugerties, 4,190 M 6
13456 Sauquoit, 1,900 K 5
14879 Savona, 933 F 6
11782 Sayville, 11,680 O 9
10583 Scarsdale, 19,229 P 7
* 12301 Schenectady⊙, 77,859 M 5
12157 Schoharie⊙, 1,125 M 5
12870 Schroon Lake, 950 N 3
12871 Schuylerville, 1,402 N 4
12302 Scotia, 8,224 N 5
14546 Scottsville, 1,967 E 4
† 14075 Scranton, 925 C 5
† 14617 Sea Breeze, 1,200 F 4
11579 Sea Cliff, 5,890 R 6
13148 Seneca Falls, 7,794 G 5
13460 Sherburne, 1,613 K 5
13461 Sherrill, 2,986 J 4
14548 Shortsville, 1,516 F 5
13838 Sidney, 4,789 K 6
14136 Silver Creek, 3,182 B 5
13152 Skaneateles, 3,055 H 5
† 14201 Sloan, 5,216 C 5
10974 Sloatsburg, 3,134 M 8
11787 Smithtown, 15,000 O 9
14551 Sodus, 1,813 G 4
14555 Sodus Point, 1,172 G 4
13209 Solvay, 8,280 H 4
11968 Southampton, 4,904 R 9
14830 South Corning, 1,414 F 6
12779 South Fallsburg, 1,590 L 7
† 12801 South Glens Falls, 4,013 N 4
11971 Southold, 2,030 P 8
† 14901 Southport, 8,685 G 6
14559 Spencerport, 2,929 E 4
10977 Spring Valley, 18,112 M 8
14141 Springville, 4,350 C 5
12167 Stamford, 1,286 L 6
* 10301 Staten Island (borough), 295,443 M 9
12170 Stillwater, 1,428 N 5
11790 Stony Brook, 6,391 O 9
10980 Stony Point, 8,270 M 8
12172 Stottville, 1,106 N 6
10901 Suffern, 8,273 M 8
11791 Syosset, 9,970 S 7
* 13201 Syracuse⊙, 197,208 H 4
Syracuse, ‡635,946 H 4
10591 Tarrytown, 11,115 O 6
13691 Theresa, 985 J 2
† 11020 Thomaston, 2,486 R 7
12883 Ticonderoga, 3,268 N 3
12486 Tillson, 1,256 M 7
14150 Tonawanda, 21,898 B 4
* 12180 Troy⊙, 62,918 N 5
14886 Trumansburg, 1,618 G 5
10707 Tuckahoe, 6,236 O 7
12986 Tupper Lake, 4,854 M 2
13849 Unadilla, 1,489 K 6
13160 Union Springs, 1,183 G 5
* 13501 Utica⊙, 91,611 K 4
Utica-Rome, ‡337,477 K 4
12184 Valatie, 1,288 N 6
10595 Valhalla, 6,000 P 6
* 11580 Valley Stream, 40,413 N 9
13850 Vestal, 8,303 H 6
14564 Victor, 2,187 F 5
12186 Voorheesville, 2,826 M 5
13694 Waddington, 955 K 1
11792 Wading River, 975 P 9
12586 Walden, 5,277 M 7
12589 Wallkill, 1,849 M 7
13856 Walton, 3,744 K 6
13163 Wampsville⊙, 586 J 4
† 14075 Wanakah, 1,600 C 5
11793 Wantagh, 21,873 N 9
12590 Wappingers Falls, 5,607 N 7
12885 Warrensburg, 2,743 N 3
14569 Warsaw⊙, 3,619 D 5
10990 Warwick, 3,604 M 8
12188 Waterford, 2,879 N 5
13165 Waterloo⊙, 5,418 G 5
13601 Watertown⊙, 30,787 J 3
13480 Waterville, 1,808 K 5
12189 Watervliet, 12,404 N 5
14891 Watkins Glen⊙, 2,716 G 6
14892 Waverley, 5,261 G 7
14572 Wayland, 2,022 E 5
14580 Webster, 5,037 F 4
13166 Weedsport, 1,900 G 4
14895 Wellsville, 5,815 E 6
11590 Westbury, 15,362 R 7
† 13619 West Carthage, 2,047 J 3
† 14901 West Elmira, 5,901 G 6
14787 Westfield, 3,651 A 6
† 12801 West Glens Falls, 3,363 N 4
11977 Westhampton, 1,156 P 9
11978 Westhampton Beach, 1,926 P 9
10996 West Point, 8,100 M 8
11796 West Sayville, 7,386 O 9
14224 West Seneca, ▵48,404 C 5
13491 West Winfield, 1,018 K 5
12887 Whitehall, 3,764 O 3
* 10601 White Plains⊙, 50,220 P 6
13492 Whitesboro, 4,805 K 4
13862 Whitney Point, 1,058 J 6
14589 Williamson, 1,991 F 4
14221 Williamsville, 6,835 C 5
11596 Williston Park, 9,154 R 7
12996 Willsboro, 950 N 2
14172 Wilson, 1,284 C 4
13865 Windsor, 1,098 J 6
12998 Witherbee-Mineville, 1,967 N 2
14590 Wolcott, 1,617 G 4
12788 Woodbourne, 1,155 M 7
11598 Woodmere, 19,831 R 7
12789 Woodridge, 1,071 L 7
12498 Woodstock, 1,073 M 6
* 10701 Yonkers, 204,370 O 7
† 10598 Yorktown, 9,008 N 8
13495 Yorkville, 3,425 K 4
14174 Youngstown, 2,169 C 4

⊙ County seat.
‡ Population of metropolitan area.
▵ Population of town or township.
† Zip of nearest p.o.
* Multiple zips

Agriculture, Industry and Resources

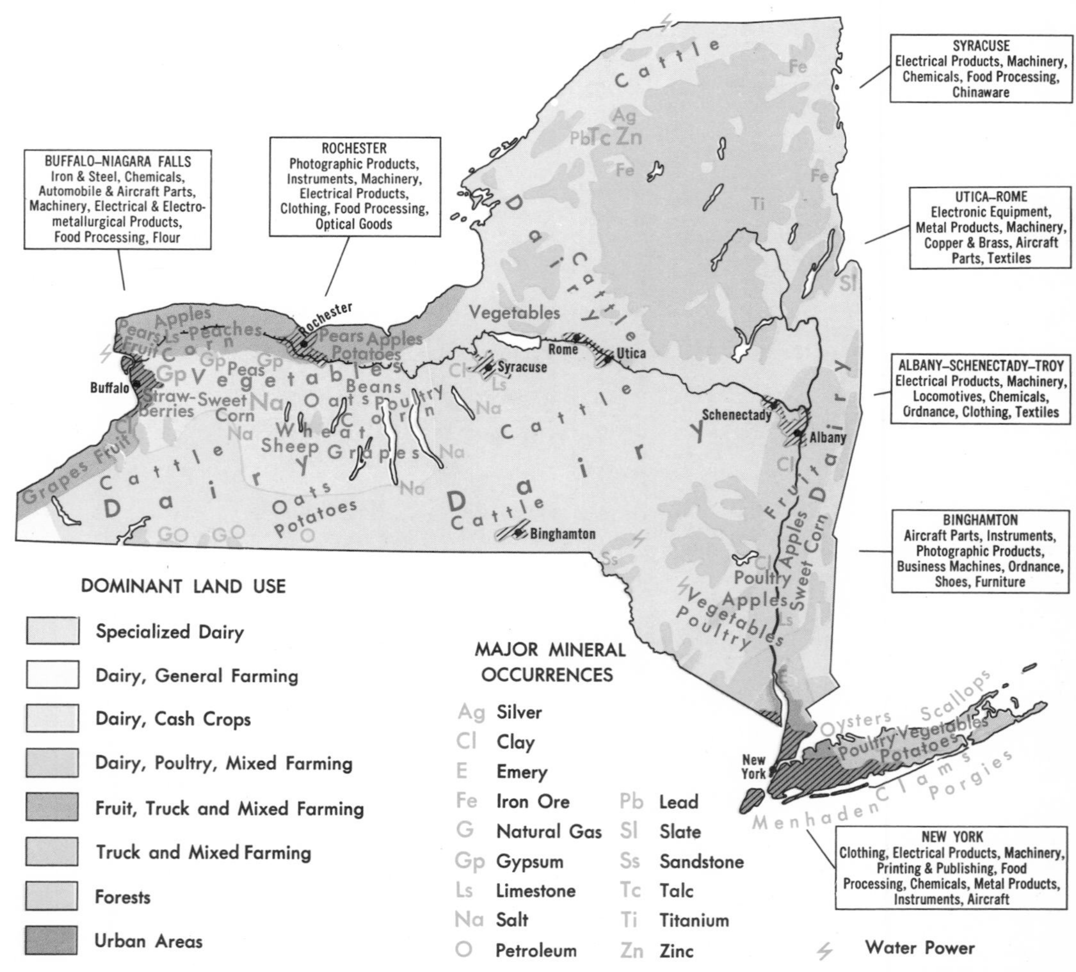

COUNTIES

Alamance, 96,362 ... L 3
Alexander, 19,466 ... G 3
Alleghany, 8,134 ... G 1
Anson, 23,488 ... J 4
Ashe, 19,571 ... F 2
Avery, 12,655 ... F 2
Beaufort, 35,980 ... R 4
Bertie, 20,528 ... P 2
Bladen, 26,477 ... M 5
Brunswick, 24,223 ... N 6
Buncombe, 145,056 ... D 3
Burke, 60,364 ... F 3
Cabarrus, 74,629 ... H 4
Caldwell, 56,699 ... F 3
Camden, 5,453 ... S 2
Carteret, 31,603 ... R 5
Caswell, 19,055 ... L 2
Catawba, 90,873 ... G 3
Chatham, 29,554 ... L 3
Cherokee, 16,330 ... A 4
Chowan, 10,764 ... R 2
Clay, 5,180 ... B 4
Cleveland, 72,556 ... F 4
Columbus, 46,937 ... M 6
Craven, 62,554 ... P 4
Cumberland, 212,042 ... M 4
Currituck, 6,976 ... S 2
Dare, 6,995 ... T 3
Davidson, 95,627 ... J 3
Davie, 18,855 ... H 3
Duplin, 38,015 ... O 5
Durham, 132,681 ... M 3
Edgecombe, 52,341 ... O 3
Forsyth, 214,348 ... J 2
Franklin, 26,820 ... N 2
Gaston, 148,415 ... G 4
Gates, 8,524 ... R 2
Graham, 6,562 ... B 4
Granville, 32,762 ... M 2
Greene, 14,967 ... O 3
Guilford, 288,590 ... K 3
Halifax, 53,884 ... O 2
Harnett, 49,667 ... M 4
Haywood, 41,710 ... C 3
Henderson, 42,804 ... D 4
Hertford, 23,529 ... P 2
Hoke, 16,436 ... L 4
Hyde, 5,571 ... S 3
Iredell, 72,197 ... H 3
Jackson, 21,593 ... C 4
Johnston, 61,737 ... N 4
Jones, 9,779 ... P 4
Lee, 30,467 ... L 4
Lenoir, 55,204 ... O 4
Lincoln, 32,682 ... G 3
Macon, 15,788 ... B 4
Madison, 16,003 ... D 3
Martin, 24,730 ... P 3
McDowell, 30,648 ... E 3
Mecklenburg, 354,656 ... H 4
Mitchell, 13,447 ... E 2
Montgomery, 19,267 ... K 4
Moore, 39,048 ... L 4
Nash, 59,122 ... O 2
New Hanover, 82,996 ... O 6
Northampton, 24,009 ... P 2
Onslow, 103,126 ... P 5
Orange, 57,707 ... L 2
Pamlico, 9,467 ... R 4
Pasquotank, 26,824 ... S 2
Pender, 18,149 ... O 5
Perquimans, 8,351 ... S 2
Person, 25,914 ... M 2
Pitt, 73,900 ... P 3
Polk, 11,735 ... E 4
Randolph, 76,358 ... K 3
Richmond, 39,889 ... K 4
Robeson, 84,842 ... L 5
Rockingham, 72,402 ... K 2
Rowan, 90,035 ... H 3
Rutherford, 47,337 ... E 4
Sampson, 44,954 ... N 4
Scotland, 26,929 ... L 5
Stanly, 42,822 ... J 4
Stokes, 23,782 ... J 2
Surry, 51,415 ... H 2
Swain, 7,861 ... B 3
Transylvania, 19,713 ... D 4
Tyrrell, 3,806 ... S 3
Union, 54,714 ... H 4
Vance, 32,691 ... N 2
Wake, 228,453 ... M 3
Warren, 15,810 ... N 2
Washington, 14,038 ... R 3
Watauga, 23,404 ... F 2
Wayne, 85,408 ... N 4
Wilkes, 49,524 ... G 2
Wilson, 57,486 ... O 3
Yadkin, 24,599 ... H 2
Yancey, 12,629 ... E 3

AREA 52,586 sq. mi.
POPULATION 5,082,059
CAPITAL Raleigh
LARGEST CITY Charlotte
HIGHEST POINT Mt. Mitchell 6,684 ft.
SETTLED IN 1650
ADMITTED TO UNION November 21, 1789
POPULAR NAME Tarheel State
STATE FLOWER Flowering Dogwood
STATE BIRD Cardinal

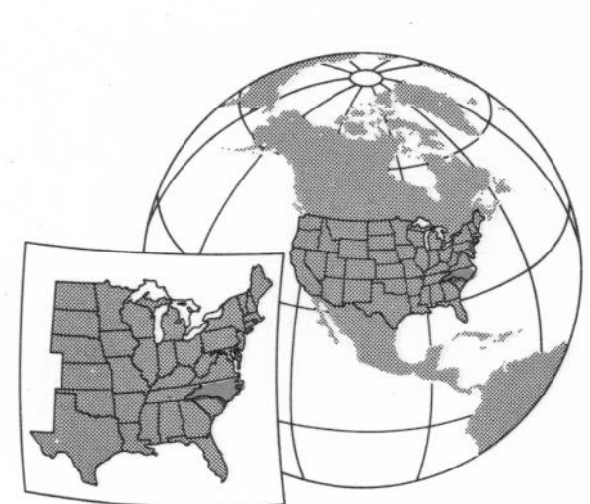

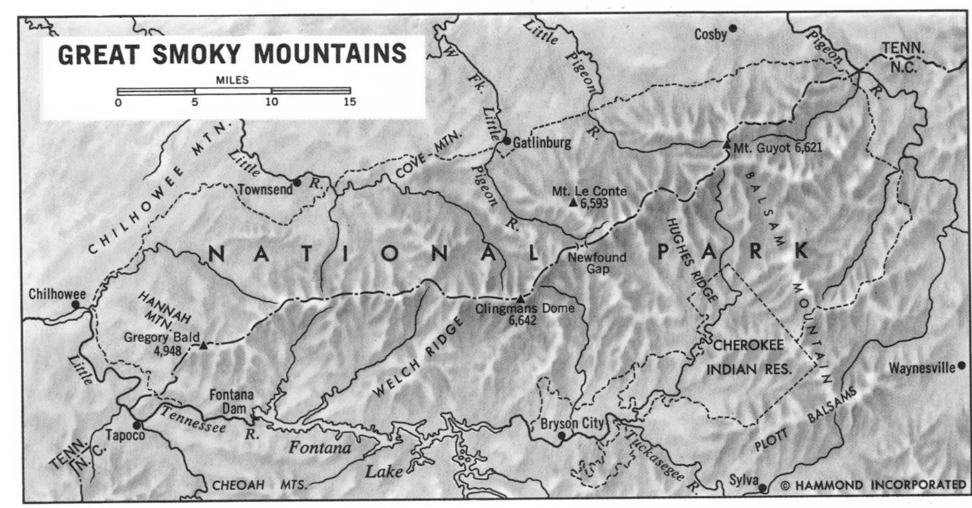

CITIES and TOWNS

Zip	Name/Pop.	Key
28321	Abbottsburg, 425	M 5
28315	Aberdeen, 1,592	L 4
27006	Advance, 206	J 3
27910	Ahoskie, 5,105	P 2
27201	Alamance, 450	K 2
† 28713	Alarka, 900	C 4
28001	Albemarle⊙, 11,126	J 4
† 27589	Alert, 200	N 2
28701	Alexander, 200	D 3
28509	Alliance, 577	R 4
† 28364	Alma, 200	L 5
28702	Almond, 200	B 4
27202	Altamahaw, 900	L 2
28901	Andrews, 1,384	B 4
27501	Angier, 1,431	M 4
28007	Ansonville, 694	J 4
27502	Apex, 2,192	M 3
28510	Arapahoe, 212	R 4
27263	Archdale, 6,103	K 3
27589	Arcola, 300	N 2
28704	Arden, 850	D 4
† 28642	Arlington, 711	H 2
28420	Ash, 250	N 6
27203	Asheboro⊙, 10,797	K 3
* 28801	Asheville⊙, 57,681	D 3
	Asheville, ‡145,056	D 3
28603	Ashford, 225	F 3
† 27983	Askewville, 247	R 2
28421	Atkinson, 325	N 5
28511	Atlantic, 950	S 5
28512	Atlantic Beach, 300	R 5
27805	Aulander, 947	P 2
27806	Aurora, 620	R 4
28318	Autryville, 213	M 4
27915	Avon, 400	U 4
† 28076	Avondale-Henrietta, 1,307	F 4
28513	Ayden, 3,450	P 4
28009	Badin, 1,626	J 4
27503	Bahama, 280	M 2
27807	Bailey, 724	N 3
28705	Bakersville⊙, 409	E 2
28706	Balfour, 2,014	E 4
† 27203	Balfours, 4,836	K 3
28707	Balsam, 300	C 4
† 27030	Bannertown, 1,138	H 1
27917	Barco, 325	T 2
† 28739	Barker Heights, 2,933	D 4
28710	Bat Cave, 400	E 4
27808	Bath, 231	R 4
27809	Battleboro, 688	O 2
28515	Bayboro⊙, 665	R 4
27207	Bear Creek, 500	L 3
28516	Beaufort⊙, 3,368	R 5
27810	Belhaven, 2,259	R 3
28012	Belmont, 4,814	H 4
27919	Belvidere, 275	S 2
† 28621	Benham, 400	G 2
27208	Bennett, 200	K 3
27504	Benson, 2,267	N 4
† 27565	Berea, 200	M 2
28016	Bessemer City, 5,217	G 4
† 28779	Beta, 500	C 4
27812	Bethel, 1,514	P 3
28518	Beulaville, 1,156	O 5
† 28803	Biltmore Forest, 1,298	E 3
27209	Biscoe, 1,244	K 4
27813	Black Creek, 449	O 3
28711	Black Mountain, 3,204	E 3
28320	Bladenboro, 783	M 5
27212	Blanch, 210	L 2
28605	Blowing Rock, 801	F 2
† 28438	Boardman, 233	M 6
28092	Boger City, 2,203	G 4
† 28570	Bogue, 600	R 5
28461	Boiling Spring Lakes, 245	N 7
28017	Boiling Springs, 2,284	F 4
28423	Bolton, 534	N 6
27213	Bonlee, 275	L 3
28606	Boomer, 212	G 2
28607	Boone⊙, 8,754	F 2
27011	Boonville, 687	H 2
28322	Bowdens, 250	N 4
28712	Brevard⊙, 5,243	D 4
28519	Bridgeton, 520	R 4
27505	Broadway, 694	L 4
28601	Brookford, 590	G 3
27214	Browns Summit, 500	K 2
28424	Brunswick, 206	M 6
28713	Bryson City⊙, 1,290	C 4
† 28377	Buies, 275	L 5
27506	Buies Creek, 2,024	M 4
27507	Bullock, 550	M 2
27508	Bunn, 284	N 3
28323	Bunnlevel, 200	M 4
28425	Burgaw⊙, 1,744	N 5
27215	Burlington, 35,930	K 2
28714	Burnsville⊙, 1,348	E 3
27509	Butner, 3,538	M 2
28324	Butters, 225	M 5
27920	Buxton, 700	U 4
27228	Bynum, 400	L 3
28325	Calypso, 462	N 4
27921	Camden⊙, 300	S 2
28326	Cameron, 204	L 4
28715	Candler, 950	D 3
27229	Candor, 561	K 4
28716	Canton, 5,158	D 3
28019	Caroleen, 975	F 4
28428	Carolina Beach, 1,663	O 6
27510	Carrboro, 3,472	L 3
28327	Carthage⊙, 1,034	K 4
27511	Cary, 7,430	M 3
28020	Casar, 350	F 3
28717	Cashiers, 230	C 4
27816	Castalia, 265	O 2
28429	Castle Hayne, 900	O 6
28609	Catawba, 565	G 3
† 28754	Catharine Lake, 500	O 5
27230	Cedar Falls, 500	K 3
28520	Cedar Island, 250	S 5
28718	Cedar Mountain, 250	D 4
28431	Chadbourn, 2,213	M 6
27514	Chapel Hill, 25,537	M 3
* 28201	Charlotte⊙, 241,178	H 4
	Charlotte, ‡409,370	H 4
28719	Cherokee, 975	C 4
28021	Cherryville, 5,258	G 4
28023	China Grove, 1,788	H 3
28521	Chinquapin, 350	O 5
27817	Chocowinity, 566	P 4
28610	Claremont, 788	G 3
28432	Clarendon, 300	M 6
28433	Clarkton, 662	M 6
27520	Clayton, 3,103	N 3
27012	Clemmons, 4,900	J 2
27013	Cleveland, 614	H 3
28024	Cliffside, 950	F 4
27233	Climax, 475	K 3
28328	Clinton⊙, 7,157	N 5
28721	Clyde, 900	D 3
27521	Coats, 1,051	M 4
27922	Cofield, 422	R 2
27923	Coinjock, 650	S 2
27924	Colerain, 373	R 2
27234	Coleridge, 600	K 3
28611	Collettsville, 275	F 3
27925	Columbia⊙, 902	S 3
28722	Columbus⊙, 731	E 4
28522	Comfort, 340	O 5
27818	Como, 211	P 1
28025	Concord⊙, 18,464	H 4
28612	Connellys Springs, 500	F 3
28613	Conover, 3,355	G 3
27820	Conway, 694	P 2
27014	Cooleemee, 1,115	H 3
28031	Cornelius, 1,296	H 4
28523	Cove City, 485	P 4
28032	Cramerton, 2,142	G 4
27522	Creedmoor, 1,405	M 2
27928	Creswell, 633	S 3
28033	Crouse, 850	G 4
† 28716	Cruso, 800	D 4
28723	Cullowhee, 6,300	C 4
28331	Cumberland, 800	M 5
28435	Currie, 294	N 6
27929	Currituck⊙, 500	T 2
27015	Cycle, 210	H 2
28034	Dallas, 4,059	G 4
† 27043	Dalton, 400	J 2
27016	Danbury⊙, 152	J 2
28036	Davidson, 2,931	H 4
28524	Davis, 600	R 5
28436	Delco, 450	N 6
27239	Denton, 1,017	J 3
28725	Dillsboro, 215	C 4
27017	Dobson⊙, 933	H 2
† 28685	Dockery, 300	G 2
28526	Dover, 585	P 4
28619	Drexel, 1,431	F 3
28332	Dublin, 283	M 5
28334	Dunn, 8,302	M 4
* 27701	Durham⊙, 95,438	M 2
	Durham, ‡190,388	M 2
† 28761	Dysartsville, 950	F 3
27242	Eagle Springs, 500	K 4
28038	Earl, 300	F 4
27018	East Bend, 485	H 2
28726	East Flat Rock, 2,627	E 4
28352	East Laurinburg, 487	L 5
† 28752	East Marion, 3,015	F 3
28039	East Spencer, 2,217	J 3
27288	Eden, 15,871	K 1
27932	Edenton⊙, 4,766	R 2
27243	Efland, 600	L 2
27909	Elizabeth City⊙, 14,069	S 2
28337	Elizabethtown⊙, 1,418	M 5
28621	Elkin, 2,899	H 2
28622	Elk Park, 503	F 2
28040	Ellenboro, 465	F 4
28338	Ellerbe, 913	K 4
27822	Elm City, 1,201	O 3
27244	Elon College, 2,150	L 2
27823	Enfield, 3,272	O 2
27824	Engelhard, 500	T 3
28728	Enka, 500	D 3
28527	Ernul, 350	P 4
28339	Erwin, 2,852	M 4
27247	Ether, 375	K 4
28729	Etowah, 700	D 4
27830	Eureka, 263	O 3
28438	Evergreen, 250	M 6
28439	Fair Bluff, 1,039	M 6
27826	Fairfield, 954	S 3
28340	Fairmont, 2,827	L 6
28730	Fairview, 880	D 3
28341	Faison, 598	N 4
28041	Faith, 506	J 3
28342	Falcon, 357	M 4
† 27028	Farmington, 300	H 3
27828	Farmville, 4,424	O 3
* 28301	Fayetteville⊙, 53,510	M 4
	Fayetteville, ‡212,042	M 4
28731	Flat Rock, 650	E 4
28732	Fletcher, 950	E 4
28043	Forest City, 7,179	E 4
† 27028	Fork, 250	J 3
27829	Fountain, 434	O 3
27524	Four Oaks, 1,057	M 4
28734	Franklin⊙, 2,336	C 4
27525	Franklinton, 1,459	N 2
27248	Franklinville, 794	K 3
28440	Freeland, 500	N 6
27830	Fremont, 1,596	N 3
27936	Frisco, 325	T 4
27526	Fuquay-Varina, 3,576	M 3
28441	Garland, 656	N 5
27529	Garner, 4,923	M 3
27831	Garysburg, 231	O 2

(continued on following page)

Agriculture, Industry and Resources

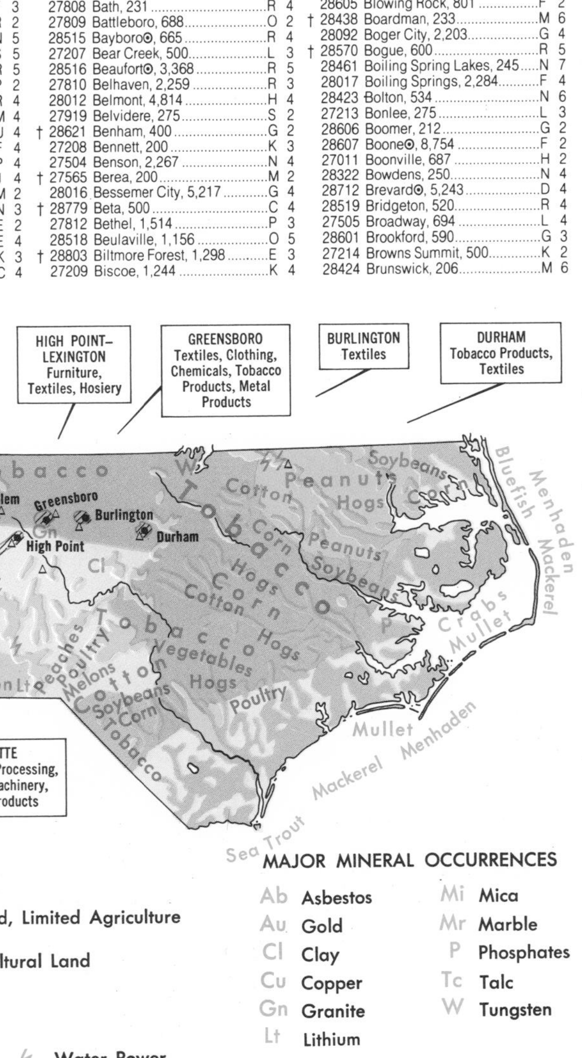

DOMINANT LAND USE

- Specialized Cotton
- Cotton, General Farming
- Cotton and Tobacco
- Tobacco, General Farming
- Peanuts, General Farming
- General Farming, Livestock, Fruit, Tobacco
- General Farming, Truck Farming, Tobacco, Livestock
- Forests
- Swampland, Limited Agriculture
- Nonagricultural Land

MAJOR MINERAL OCCURRENCES

- Ab Asbestos
- Au Gold
- Cl Clay
- Cu Copper
- Gn Granite
- Lt Lithium
- Mi Mica
- Mr Marble
- P Phosphates
- Tc Talc
- W Tungsten

- Water Power
- Major Industrial Areas
- Major Textile Manufacturing Centers

27832 Gaston, 1,105 .... O 1
28052 Gastonia⊙, 47,142 .... G 4
27937 Gates, 225 .... R 2
27938 Gatesville⊙, 338 .... R 2
28343 Gibson, 502 .... K 5
27249 Gibsonville, 2,019 .... K 2
28628 Glen Alpine, 797 .... F 3
27251 Glendon, 250 .... L 4
27215 Glen Raven, 2,848 .... L 2
28736 Glenville, 400 .... C 4
28737 Glenwood, 400 .... F 3
28071 Gold Hill, 350 .... J 3
27530 Goldsboro⊙, 26,810 .... O 4
27252 Goldston, 364 .... L 3
27253 Graham⊙, 8,172 .... L 2
27939 Grandy, 425 .... T 2
28630 Granite Falls, 2,388 .... G 3
28072 Granite Quarry, 1,344 .... H 3
28529 Grantsboro, 900 .... R 4
28740 Greenmountain, 500 .... E 3
* 27401 Greensboro⊙, 144,076 .... K 2
Greensboro-Winston-Salem-High Point, ‡603,895 .... K 2
27834 Greenville⊙, 29,063 .... P 3
28530 Grifton, 1,860 .... P 4
27837 Grimesland, 394 .... P 3
28073 Grover, 555 .... G 4
27256 Gulf, 300 .... L 3
27839 Halifax⊙, 335 .... O 2
28442 Hallsboro, 300 .... M 6
27840 Hamilton, 579 .... P 3
28345 Hamlet, 4,627 .... K 5
28443 Hampstead, 400 .... O 6
27020 Hamptonville, 250 .... H 2
27941 Harbinger, 460 .... T 2
28531 Harkers Island, 1,633 .... R 5
28634 Harmony, 377 .... H 3
28444 Harrells, 249 .... N 5
28075 Harrisburg, 800 .... H 4
27943 Hatteras, 500 .... T 4
28532 Havelock, 5,283 .... P 5
27258 Haw River, 1,542 .... L 2
28904 Hayesville⊙, 428 .... B 4
† 28318 Hayne, 300 .... M 5
28635 Hays, 750 .... G 2
† 27559 Haywood, 500 .... L 3
28738 Hazelwood, 2,057 .... C 4
27536 Henderson⊙, 13,896 .... N 2
28739 Hendersonville⊙, 6,443 .... E 4
28076 Henrietta-Avondale, 1,307 .... F 4
27944 Hertford⊙, 2,023 .... S 2
28601 Hickory, 20,569 .... G 3
28636 Hiddenite, 800 .... G 3
28741 Highlands, 583 .... C 4
* 27260 High Point, 63,204 .... J 3
28077 High Shoals, 900 .... G 4
28637 Hildebran, 481 .... F 3
27278 Hillsborough⊙, 1,444 .... L 2
27843 Hobgood, 530 .... P 2
28537 Hobucken, 500 .... S 4
28347 Hoffman, 434 .... K 4
27844 Hollister, 750 .... O 2
28445 Holly Ridge, 415 .... P 6
27540 Holly Springs, 697 .... M 3
28538 Hookerton, 441 .... O 4
28348 Hope Mills, 1,721 .... M 5
28743 Hot Springs, 653 .... D 3
28539 Hubert, 980 .... P 5
28638 Hudson, 2,820 .... G 3
28078 Huntersville, 1,538 .... H 4
28666 Icard, 1,100 .... G 3
28079 Indian Trail, 405 .... H 4
27589 Inez, 250 .... N 2
28080 Iron Station, 250 .... G 4
27845 Jackson⊙, 762 .... P 2
27281 Jackson Springs, 225 .... K 4
28540 Jacksonville⊙, 16,021 .... O 5
28550 James City, 2,577 .... R 4
27282 Jamestown, 1,297 .... K 3
27846 Jamesville, 533 .... R 3
27947 Jarvisburg, 350 .... T 2
28640 Jefferson⊙, 943 .... G 2
† 28352 Johns, 250 .... K 5
28642 Jonesville, 1,659 .... H 2
27283 Julian, 300 .... K 3
28787 Jupiter, 208 .... D 3
28081 Kannapolis, 36,293 .... H 4
27847 Kelford, 295 .... P 2
28349 Kenansville⊙, 762 .... O 5
27542 Kenly, 1,370 .... N 3
27284 Kernersville, 4,815 .... J 2
27948 Kill Devil Hills, 357 .... T 3
27021 King, 1,033 .... J 2
28086 Kings Mountain, 8,465 .... G 4
28501 Kinston⊙, 22,309 .... O 4
27544 Kittrell, 427 .... M 2
27949 Kitty Hawk, 600 .... T 2

27545 Knightdale, 815 .... N 3
27950 Knotts Island, 450 .... T 2
28449 Kure Beach, 394 .... O 7
28551 La Grange, 2,558 .... O 4
28746 Lake Lure, 456 .... E 4
28747 Lake Toxaway, 750 .... D 4
28350 Lakeview, 449 .... L 4
28450 Lake Waccamaw, 924 .... M 6
28088 Landis, 2,297 .... H 3
28643 Lansing, 283 .... F 1
28089 Lattimore, 257 .... F 4
28351 Laurel Hill, 1,215 .... K 5
† 28739 Laurel Park, 581 .... D 4
28352 Laurinburg⊙, 8,859 .... K 5
28090 Lawndale, 544 .... F 4
27291 Leasburg, 400 .... L 2
28748 Leicester, 265 .... D 3
28451 Leland, 500 .... N 6
28645 Lenoir⊙, 14,705 .... G 3
27849 Lewiston, 327 .... P 2
27292 Lexington⊙, 17,205 .... J 3
27298 Liberty, 2,167 .... K 3
28091 Lilesville, 641 .... K 5
27546 Lillington⊙, 1,155 .... M 4
28092 Lincolnton⊙, 5,293 .... G 4
28356 Linden, 205 .... M 4
28646 Linville, 400 .... F 2
27299 Linwood, 300 .... J 3
27850 Littleton, 903 .... O 2
28461 Long Beach, 493 .... N 7
27548 Longhurst, 1,485 .... L 2
28648 Longisland, 350 .... H 3
28601 Long View, 3,360 .... F 3
28452 Longwood, 650 .... N 6
† 28345 Longwood Park, 1,284 .... K 5
27549 Louisburg⊙, 2,941 .... N 2
28098 Lowell, 3,307 .... G 4
27024 Lowgap, 660 .... H 1
28552 Lowland, 538 .... S 4
27851 Lucama, 610 .... N 3

28358 Lumberton⊙, 16,961 .... L 5
28750 Lynn, 550 .... E 4
27852 Macclesfield, 536 .... O 3
27951 Mackeys, 250 .... R 3
27025 Madison, 2,018 .... J 2
28751 Maggie, 400 .... C 3
28453 Magnolia, 614 .... O 5
28650 Maiden, 2,416 .... G 3
27552 Mamers, 500 .... L 4
† 28387 Manly, 225 .... L 4
27953 Manns Harbor, 365 .... T 3
27954 Manteo⊙, 547 .... T 3
† 27855 Mapleton, 250 .... P 2
28905 Marble, 950 .... B 4
28752 Marion⊙, 3,335 .... E 3
28753 Marshall⊙, 982 .... D 3
28553 Marshallberg, 700 .... S 5
28754 Mars Hill, 1,623 .... D 3
28103 Marshville, 1,405 .... J 4
28105 Matthews, 783 .... H 4
28554 Maury, 421 .... O 4
28364 Maxton, 1,885 .... L 5
27027 Mayodan, 2,875 .... K 2
28555 Maysville, 912 .... P 5
28361 McCain, 950 .... L 4
27302 Mebane, 2,433 .... L 2
† 28516 Merrimon, 500 .... R 5
27555 Micro, 300 .... N 3
27557 Middlesex, 729 .... N 3
28107 Midland, 950 .... J 4
† 28377 Midstate Mill, 925 .... L 5
28544 Midway Park, 4,900 .... O 5
27305 Milton, 235 .... L 1
27854 Milwaukee, 376 .... P 2
28212 Mint Hill, 1,200 .... H 4
28109 Misenheimer, 1,450 .... J 4
27028 Mocksville⊙, 2,529 .... H 3
27559 Moncure, 800 .... L 3
28110 Monroe⊙, 11,282 .... J 5
28757 Montreat, 450 .... E 3

28114 Mooresboro, 275 .... F 4
28115 Mooresville, 8,808 .... H 3
28654 Moravian Falls, 375 .... G 2
28557 Morehead City, 5,233 .... R 5
28655 Morganton⊙, 13,625 .... F 3
28119 Morven, 562 .... J 5
27030 Mount Airy, 7,325 .... H 1
27306 Mount Gilead, 1,286 .... K 4
28120 Mount Holly, 5,107 .... H 4
28123 Mount Mourne, 950 .... H 3
28365 Mount Olive, 4,914 .... O 4
28124 Mount Pleasant, 1,174 .... J 4
27345 Mount Vernon Springs, 225 .... L 3
27958 Moyock, 350 .... S 1
27855 Murfreesboro, 3,508 .... R 2
28906 Murphy⊙, 2,082 .... B 4
27959 Nags Head, 414 .... T 3
27856 Nashville⊙, 1,670 .... O 3
27561 Neuse, 500 .... M 3
28560 New Bern⊙, 14,660 .... P 4
28657 Newland⊙, 524 .... F 2
28127 New London, 285 .... J 4
28570 Newport, 1,735 .... R 5
28658 Newton⊙, 7,857 .... G 3
28366 Newton Grove, 546 .... N 4
27563 Norlina, 969 .... N 2
† 28752 North Cove, 257 .... F 3
† 28532 North Harlowe, 975 .... R 5
28659 North Wilkesboro, 3,357 .... G 2
27564 Northside, 400 .... M 2
28128 Norwood, 1,896 .... J 4
28129 Oakboro, 568 .... J 4
27857 Oak City, 559 .... P 3
27310 Oak Ridge, 950 .... K 2
27960 Ocracoke, 500 .... T 4
28762 Old Fort, 676 .... E 3
27961 Old Trap, 400 .... T 2
28368 Olivia, 400 .... L 4
28571 Oriental, 445 .... R 4
28805 Oteen, 2,863 .... E 3

27565 Oxford⊙, 7,178 .... M 2
27860 Pantego, 218 .... R 3
28371 Parkton, 550 .... M 5
27861 Parmele, 373 .... P 3
28661 Patterson, 344 .... F 3
28133 Peachland, 556 .... J 5
† 28091 Pee Dee, 210 .... K 5
27311 Pelham, 350 .... L 1
28372 Pembroke, 1,982 .... L 5
28766 Penrose, 600 .... D 4
† 28716 Phillipsville, 1,239 .... D 3
27863 Pikeville, 580 .... N 4
27041 Pilot Mountain, 1,309 .... H 2
28373 Pinebluff, 570 .... K 4
27042 Pine Hall, 550 .... K 2
28374 Pinehurst, 1,056 .... K 4
27568 Pine Level, 983 .... N 4
28662 Pineola, 875 .... F 2
27864 Pinetops, 1,379 .... O 3
27865 Pinetown, 278 .... R 3
28134 Pineville, 1,948 .... H 4
28572 Pink Hill, 522 .... O 4
27043 Pinnacle, 725 .... J 2
28768 Pisgah Forest, 850 .... D 4
27312 Pittsboro⊙, 1,447 .... L 3
27866 Pleasant Hill, 250 .... O 1
27962 Plymouth⊙, 4,774 .... R 3
28135 Polkton, 845 .... J 4
28136 Polkville, 450 .... F 4
28573 Pollocksville, 456 .... P 5
27965 Poplar Branch, 400 .... T 2
27966 Powells Point, 375 .... T 2
27967 Powellsville, 247 .... R 2
27569 Princeton, 1,044 .... N 4
† 27886 Princeville, 654 .... P 3
28376 Raeford⊙, 3,180 .... L 5
* 27601 Raleigh (cap.)⊙, 121,577 .... M 3
Raleigh, ‡228,453 .... M 3
27316 Ramseur, 1,328 .... K 3
27317 Randleman, 2,312 .... K 3

† 28906 Ranger, 500 .... A 4
28052 Ranlo, 2,092 .... G 4
27868 Red Oak, 359 .... N 2
28377 Red Springs, 3,383 .... L 5
27320 Reidsville, 13,636 .... K 2
28378 Rex, 975 .... M 5
28667 Rhodhiss, 784 .... F 3
† 28092 Rhyne, 2,273 .... G 4
28137 Richfield, 306 .... J 4
28574 Richlands, 935 .... O 5
27869 Rich Square, 1,254 .... P 2
27570 Ridgeway, 500 .... N 2
28456 Riegelwood, 459 .... N 6
27870 Roanoke Rapids, 13,508 .... O 2
28668 Roaring Gap, 450 .... H 2
28669 Roaring River, 500 .... G 2
27325 Robbins, 1,059 .... K 4
28771 Robbinsville⊙, 777 .... B 4
† 28379 Roberdel, 350 .... K 5
27871 Robersonville, 1,910 .... P 3
28379 Rockingham⊙, 5,852 .... K 5
28138 Rockwell, 999 .... J 3
27801 Rocky Mount, 34,284 .... O 3
28457 Rocky Point, 975 .... O 6
27571 Rolesville, 529 .... N 3
28670 Ronda, 465 .... H 2
27970 Roper, 649 .... R 3
28382 Roseboro, 1,235 .... N 5
28458 Rose Hill, 1,448 .... N 5
28772 Rosman, 407 .... D 4
27572 Rougemont, 400 .... L 2
28383 Rowland, 1,358 .... L 5
27573 Roxboro⊙, 5,370 .... M 2
27872 Roxobel, 347 .... P 2
† 27587 Royal Cotton Mills, 600 .... M 2
27326 Ruffin, 600 .... K 2
27045 Rural Hall, 2,338 .... J 2
† 28139 Ruth, 360 .... E 4
28671 Rutherford College, 950 .... F 3
28139 Rutherfordton⊙, 3,245 .... E 4

Topography

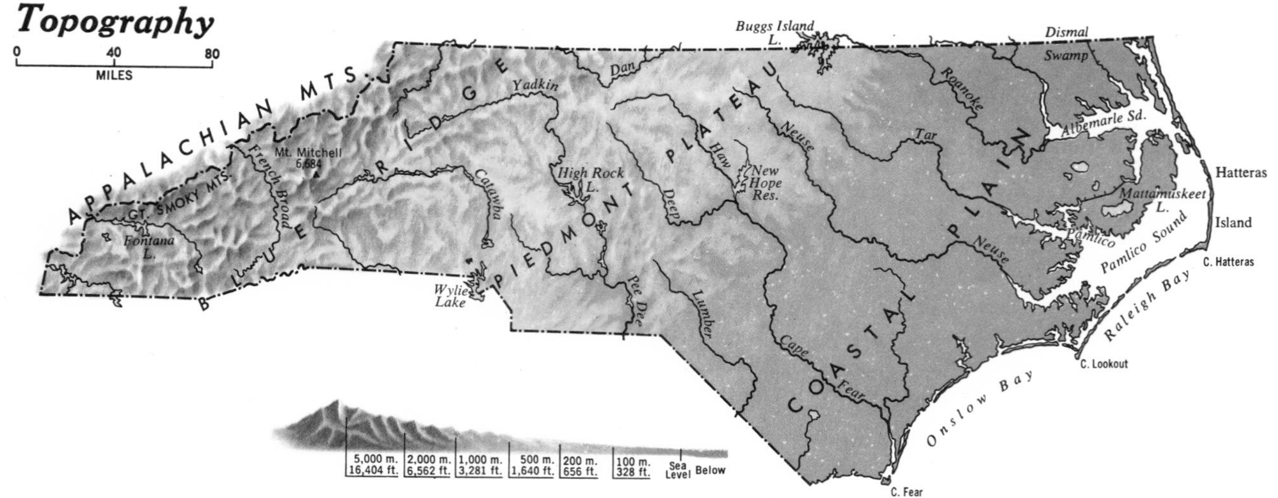

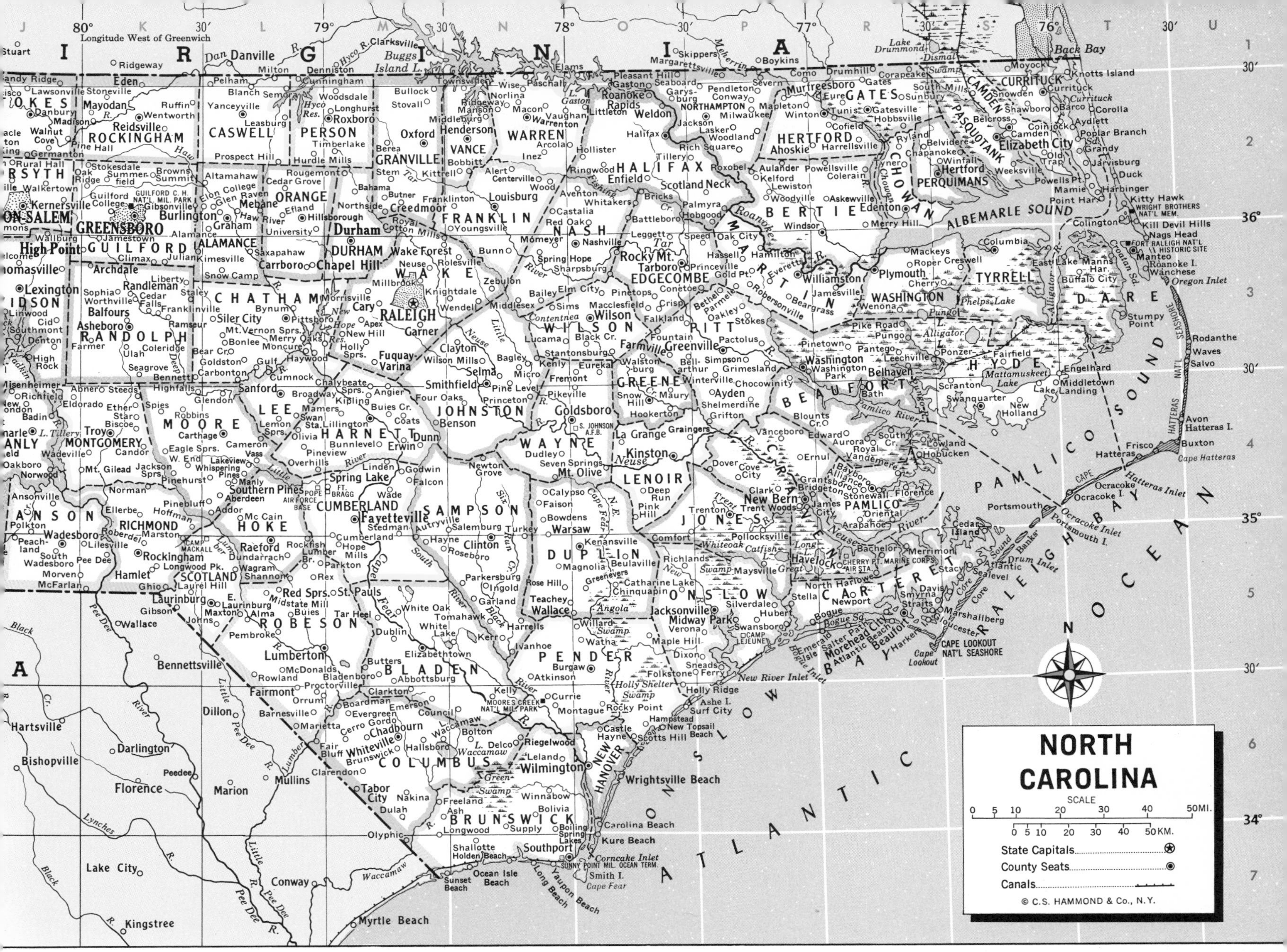

NORTH CAROLINA

SCALE 0 5 10 20 30 40 50 MI.
0 5 10 20 30 40 50 KM.

State Capitals ⊛
County Seats ⊙
Canals

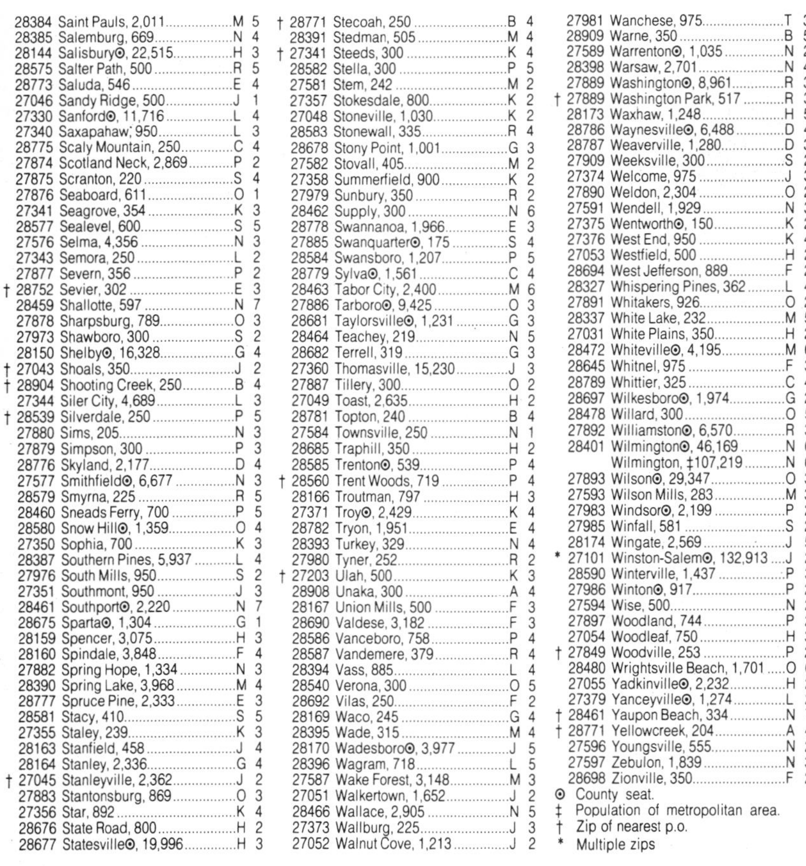

28384 Saint Pauls, 2,011 ... M 5
28385 Salemburg, 669 ... N 4
28144 Salisbury⊙, 22,515 ... H 3
28575 Salter Path, 500 ... R 5
28773 Saluda, 546 ... E 4
27046 Sandy Ridge, 500 ... J 1
27330 Sanford⊙, 11,716 ... L 4
27340 Saxapahaw, 950 ... L 3
28775 Scaly Mountain, 250 ... C 4
27874 Scotland Neck, 2,869 ... P 2
27875 Scranton, 220 ... S 4
27876 Seaboard, 611 ... O 1
27341 Seagrove, 354 ... K 3
28577 Sealevel, 600 ... S 5
27576 Selma, 4,356 ... N 3
27343 Semora, 250 ... L 2
27877 Severn, 356 ... P 2
† 28752 Sevier, 302 ... E 3
28459 Shallotte, 597 ... N 7
27878 Sharpsburg, 789 ... O 3
27973 Shawboro, 300 ... S 2
28150 Shelby⊙, 16,328 ... G 4
† 27043 Shoals, 350 ... J 2
† 28904 Shooting Creek, 250 ... B 4
27344 Siler City, 4,689 ... L 3
† 28539 Silverdale, 250 ... P 5
27880 Sims, 205 ... N 3
27879 Simpson, 300 ... P 3
28776 Skyland, 2,177 ... D 4
27577 Smithfield⊙, 6,677 ... N 3
28579 Smyrna, 225 ... R 5
28460 Sneads Ferry, 700 ... P 5
28580 Snow Hill⊙, 1,359 ... O 4
27350 Sophia, 700 ... K 3
28387 Southern Pines, 5,937 ... L 4
27976 South Mills, 950 ... S 2
27351 Southmont, 950 ... J 3
28461 Southport⊙, 2,220 ... N 7
28675 Sparta⊙, 1,304 ... G 1
28159 Spencer, 3,075 ... H 3
28160 Spindale, 3,848 ... F 4
27882 Spring Hope, 1,334 ... N 3
28390 Spring Lake, 3,968 ... M 4
28777 Spruce Pine, 2,333 ... E 3
28581 Stacy, 410 ... S 5
27355 Staley, 239 ... K 3
28163 Stanfield, 458 ... J 4
28164 Stanley, 2,336 ... G 4
† 27045 Stanleyville, 2,362 ... J 2
27883 Stantonsburg, 869 ... O 3
27356 Star, 892 ... K 4
28676 State Road, 800 ... H 2
28677 Statesville⊙, 19,996 ... H 3
† 28771 Stecoah, 250 ... B 4
28391 Stedman, 505 ... M 4
† 27341 Steeds, 300 ... K 4
28582 Stella, 300 ... P 5
27581 Stem, 242 ... M 2
27357 Stokesdale, 800 ... K 2
27048 Stoneville, 1,030 ... K 2
28583 Stonewall, 335 ... R 4
28678 Stony Point, 1,001 ... G 3
27582 Stovall, 405 ... M 2
27358 Summerfield, 900 ... K 2
27979 Sunbury, 350 ... R 2
28462 Supply, 300 ... N 6
28778 Swannanoa, 1,966 ... E 3
27885 Swanquarter⊙, 175 ... S 4
28584 Swansboro, 1,207 ... P 5
28779 Sylva⊙, 1,561 ... C 4
28463 Tabor City, 2,400 ... M 6
27886 Tarboro⊙, 9,425 ... O 3
28681 Taylorsville⊙, 1,231 ... G 3
28464 Teachey, 219 ... N 5
28682 Terrell, 319 ... G 3
27360 Thomasville, 15,230 ... J 3
27887 Tillery, 300 ... O 2
27049 Toast, 2,635 ... H 2
28781 Topton, 240 ... B 4
27584 Townsville, 250 ... N 1
28685 Traphill, 350 ... H 2
28585 Trenton⊙, 539 ... P 4
† 28560 Trent Woods, 719 ... P 4
28166 Troutman, 797 ... H 3
27371 Troy⊙, 2,429 ... K 4
28782 Tryon, 1,951 ... E 4
28393 Turkey, 329 ... N 4
27980 Tyner, 252 ... R 2
† 27203 Ulah, 500 ... K 3
28908 Unaka, 300 ... A 4
28167 Union Mills, 500 ... F 3
28690 Valdese, 3,182 ... F 3
28586 Vanceboro, 758 ... P 4
28587 Vandemere, 379 ... R 4
28394 Vass, 885 ... L 4
28540 Verona, 300 ... O 5
28692 Vilas, 250 ... F 2
28169 Waco, 245 ... G 4
28395 Wade, 315 ... M 4
28170 Wadesboro⊙, 3,977 ... J 5
28396 Wagram, 718 ... L 5
27587 Wake Forest, 3,148 ... M 3
27051 Walkertown, 1,652 ... J 2
28466 Wallace, 2,905 ... N 5
27373 Wallburg, 225 ... J 3
27052 Walnut Cove, 1,213 ... J 2
27981 Wanchese, 975 ... T 3
28909 Warne, 350 ... B 5
27589 Warrenton⊙, 1,035 ... N 2
28398 Warsaw, 2,701 ... N 4
27889 Washington⊙, 8,961 ... R 3
† 27889 Washington Park, 517 ... R 3
28173 Waxhaw, 1,248 ... H 5
28786 Waynesville⊙, 6,488 ... D 4
28787 Weaverville, 1,280 ... D 3
27909 Weeksville, 300 ... S 2
27374 Welcome, 975 ... J 3
27890 Weldon, 2,304 ... O 2
27591 Wendell, 1,929 ... N 3
27375 Wentworth⊙, 150 ... K 2
27376 West End, 950 ... K 4
27053 Westfield, 500 ... H 2
28694 West Jefferson, 889 ... F 2
28327 Whispering Pines, 362 ... L 4
27891 Whitakers, 926 ... O 2
28337 White Lake, 232 ... M 5
27031 White Plains, 350 ... H 2
28472 Whiteville⊙, 4,195 ... M 6
28645 Whitnel, 975 ... F 3
28789 Whittier, 325 ... C 4
28697 Wilkesboro⊙, 1,974 ... G 2
28478 Willard, 300 ... O 5
27892 Williamston⊙, 6,570 ... R 3
28401 Wilmington⊙, 46,169 ... N 6
Wilmington, ‡107,219 ... N 6
27893 Wilson⊙, 29,347 ... O 3
27593 Wilson Mills, 283 ... M 3
27983 Windsor⊙, 2,199 ... P 2
27985 Winfall, 581 ... S 2
28174 Wingate, 2,569 ... J 5
* 27101 Winston-Salem⊙, 132,913 ... J 2
28590 Winterville, 1,437 ... P 3
27986 Winton⊙, 917 ... P 2
27594 Wise, 500 ... N 2
27897 Woodland, 744 ... P 2
27054 Woodleaf, 750 ... H 3
† 27849 Woodville, 253 ... P 2
28480 Wrightsville Beach, 1,701 ... O 6
27055 Yadkinville⊙, 2,232 ... H 2
27379 Yanceyville⊙, 1,274 ... L 2
† 28461 Yaupon Beach, 334 ... N 7
† 28771 Yellowcreek, 204 ... A 4
27596 Youngsville, 555 ... N 2
27597 Zebulon, 1,839 ... N 3
28698 Zionville, 350 ... F 2

⊙ County seat.
‡ Population of metropolitan area.
† Zip of nearest p.o.
* Multiple zips

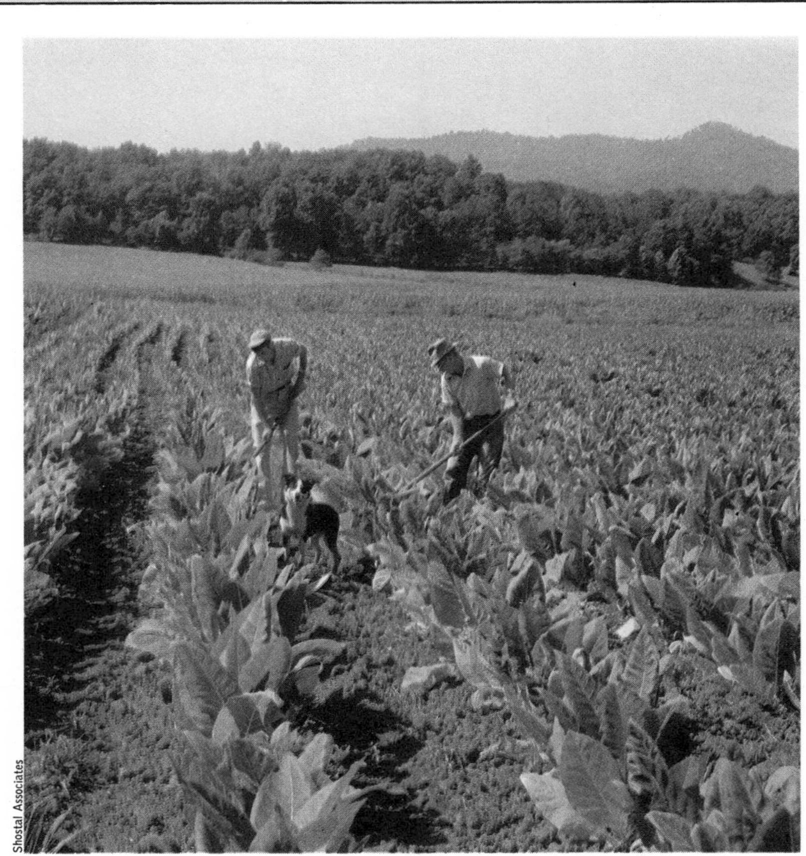

Shostal Associates

Weeding "green gold" — tobacco is North Carolina's money crop.

COUNTIES

County	Key
Adams, 3,832	F 7
Barnes, 14,669	O 5
Benson, 8,245	M 3
Billings, 1,198	D 5
Bottineau, 9,496	J 2
Bowman, 3,901	C 7
Burke, 4,739	E 2
Burleigh, 40,714	J 6
Cass, 73,653	R 5
Cavalier, 8,213	N 2
Dickey, 6,976	N 7
Divide, 4,564	C 2
Dunn, 4,895	E 5
Eddy, 4,103	N 4
Emmons, 7,200	K 7
Foster, 4,832	N 5
Golden Valley, 2,611	C 5
Grand Forks, 61,102	P 3
Grant, 5,009	G 6
Griggs, 4,184	O 5
Hettinger, 5,075	E 7
Kidder, 4,362	L 6
La Moure, 7,117	N 7
Logan, 4,245	L 7
McHenry, 8,977	J 3
McIntosh, 5,545	L 7
McKenzie, 6,127	D 4
McLean, 11,251	G 4
Mercer, 6,175	G 5
Morton, 20,310	H 6
Mountrail, 8,437	E 3
Nelson, 5,776	O 4
Oliver, 2,322	H 5
Pembina, 10,728	P 2
Pierce, 6,323	K 3
Ramsey, 12,915	N 3
Ransom, 7,102	P 7
Renville, 3,828	G 2
Richland, 18,089	R 7
Rolette, 11,549	L 2
Sargent, 5,937	P 7
Sheridan, 3,232	K 4
Sioux, 3,632	H 7
Slope, 1,484	C 7
Stark, 19,613	E 6
Steele, 3,749	P 4
Stutsman, 23,550	M 5
Towner, 4,645	M 2
Traill, 9,571	R 5
Walsh, 16,251	P 3
Ward, 58,560	G 3
Wells, 7,847	L 4
Williams, 19,301	C 3

CITIES and TOWNS

Zip	Name/Pop.	Key
58001	Abercrombie, 262	S 7
58210	Adams, 284	O 3
58830	Alamo, 124	D 2
58831	Alexander, 208	C 4
58003	Alice, 83	P 6
58520	Almont, 109	H 6
58311	Alsen, 201	N 2
58833	Ambrose, 109	D 2
58620	Amidon⊙, 54	D 7
58710	Anamoose, 401	K 4
58212	Aneta, 376	P 4
58711	Antler, 135	H 2
58005	Argusville, 118	R 5
58835	Arnegard, 141	D 4
58006	Arthur, 412	R 5
58214	Arvilla, 115	P 4
58413	Ashley⊙, 1,236	M 7
58712	Balfour, 93	J 4
58313	Balta, 133	K 3
58008	Barney, 81	S 7
58216	Bathgate, 133	P 2
58621	Beach⊙, 1,408	C 6
58316	Belcourt, 950	L 2
58622	Belfield, 1,130	D 6
58718	Berthold, 398	G 3
58523	Beulah, 1,344	G 5
58416	Binford, 242	O 4
58317	Bisbee, 305	M 2
58501	Bismarck (cap.)⊙, 34,703	J 6
58318	Bottineau⊙, 2,760	J 2
58721	Bowbells⊙, 584	F 2
58418	Bowdon, 229	L 5
58623	Bowman⊙, 1,762	D 7
58524	Braddock, 106	K 6
58321	Brocket, 95	O 3
58420	Buchanan, 100	N 5
58011	Buffalo, 241	R 6
58722	Burlington, 247	H 3
58723	Butte, 193	J 4
58218	Buxton, 235	R 4
58324	Cando⊙, 1,512	M 3
58528	Cannon Ball, 550	J 7
† 58241	Canton (Hensel), 81	P 2
58725	Carpio, 215	G 3
58421	Carrington⊙, 2,491	M 5
58529	Carson⊙, 466	H 7
58012	Casselton, 1,485	R 6
58422	Cathay, 110	M 4
58220	Cavalier⊙, 1,381	P 2
58013	Cayuga, 116	R 7
58530	Center⊙, 619	H 5
58014	Chaffee, 99	R 6
58015	Christine, 108	S 6
58325	Church's Ferry, 139	M 3
58424	Cleveland, 128	M 6
58016	Clifford, 84	R 5
58017	Cogswell, 203	P 7
58727	Columbus, 465	E 2
58425	Cooperstown⊙, 1,485	O 5
58426	Courtenay, 125	N 5
58327	Crary, 150	N 3
58730	Crosby⊙, 1,545	D 2
58222	Crystal, 272	P 2
58021	Davenport, 147	R 6
58428	Dawson, 131	L 6
58429	Dazey, 128	O 5
58430	Denhoff, 85	K 5
58733	Des Lacs, 197	G 3
58301	Devils Lake⊙, 7,078	N 3
58431	Dickey, 118	N 6
58601	Dickinson⊙, 12,405	E 6
58625	Dodge, 121	F 5
58734	Donnybrook, 163	G 2
58735	Douglas, 144	G 4
58736	Drake, 636	K 4
58225	Drayton, 1,095	R 2
58532	Driscoll, 128	K 6
58626	Dunn Center, 107	E 5
58329	Dunseith, 811	K 2
58024	Dwight, 93	S 7
58432	Eckelson, 100	O 6
58433	Edgeley, 888	N 7
58227	Edinburg, 315	P 3
58330	Edmore, 398	O 3
58331	Egeland, 96	M 2
58533	Elgin, 839	G 7
58436	Ellendale⊙, 1,517	N 7
58228	Emerado, 515	R 4
58027	Enderlin, 1,343	P 6
58843	Epping, 140	D 3
58029	Erie, 100	R 5
58332	Esmond, 416	L 3
58229	Fairdale, 102	O 3
58030	Fairmount, 412	S 7
58102	Fargo⊙, 53,365	S 6
	Fargo-Moorhead, ‡120,238	S 6
58438	Fessenden⊙, 815	L 4
58031	Fingal, 166	P 6
58230	Finley⊙, 809	P 4
58535	Flasher, 467	H 7
58737	Flaxton, 286	F 2
58439	Forbes, 88	N 8
58231	Fordville, 361	P 3
58233	Forest River, 169	P 3
58032	Forman⊙, 596	P 7
58033	Fort Ransom, 121	P 6
58335	Fort Totten, 550	M 4
58844	Fortuna, 216	C 2
58538	Fort Yates⊙, 1,153	J 7
58440	Fredonia, 100	M 7
58441	Fullerton, 110	O 7
58442	Gackle, 470	M 6
58035	Galesburg, 134	R 5
58739	Gardena, 84	J 2
58036	Gardner, 96	R 5
58540	Garrison, 1,614	H 4
58235	Gilby, 268	R 3
58630	Gladstone, 222	F 6
58740	Glenburn, 381	H 2
58443	Glenfield, 127	N 5
58631	Glen Ullin, 1,070	G 6
58541	Goldenvalley, 235	F 5
58632	Golva, 104	C 6
58444	Goodrich, 300	K 5
58445	Grace City, 87	N 4
58237	Grafton⊙, 5,946	R 3
58201	Grand Forks⊙, 39,008	R 4
58038	Grandin, 187	R 5
58741	Granville, 282	J 3
58039	Great Bend, 86	S 7
58845	Grenora, 401	C 2
58040	Gwinner, 623	P 7
58542	Hague, 146	L 7
58636	Halliday, 413	F 5
58238	Hamilton, 110	R 2
58338	Hampden, 114	N 2
58041	Hankinson, 1,125	S 7
58448	Hannaford, 244	O 5
58239	Hannah, 145	N 2
58340	Harlow, 85	M 3
58341	Harvey, 2,361	L 4
58042	Harwood, 200	S 6
58240	Hatton, 808	R 4
58043	Havana, 156	P 8
58544	Hazelton, 374	K 7
58545	Hazen, 1,240	G 5
58638	Hebron, 1,103	G 6
58342	Heimdal, 101	L 4
58547	Hensler, 100	H 5
58639	Hettinger⊙, 1,655	E 8

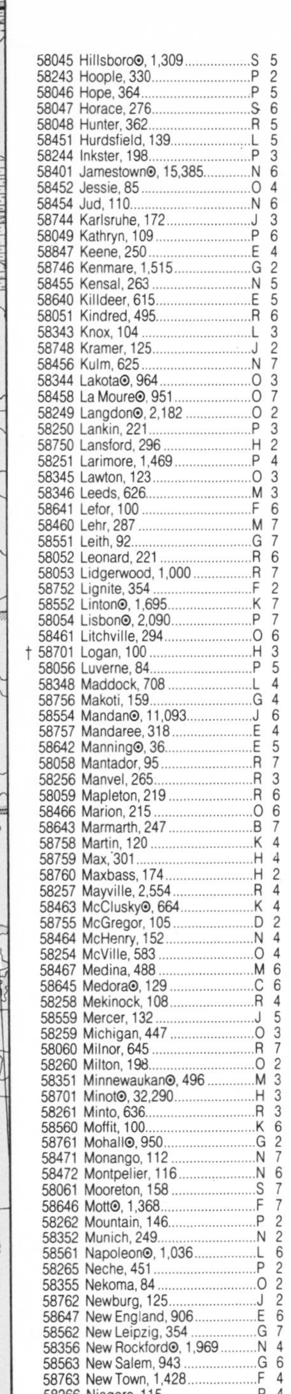

58045 Hillsboro⊙, 1,309 .... S 5
58243 Hoople, 330 .... P 2
58046 Hope, 364 .... P 5
58047 Horace, 276 .... S 6
58048 Hunter, 362 .... R 5
58451 Hurdsfield, 139 .... L 5
58244 Inkster, 198 .... P 3
58401 Jamestown⊙, 15,385 .... N 6
58452 Jessie, 85 .... O 4
58454 Jud, 110 .... N 6
58744 Karlsruhe, 172 .... J 3
58049 Kathryn, 109 .... P 6
58847 Keene, 250 .... E 4
58746 Kenmare, 1,515 .... G 2
58455 Kensal, 263 .... N 5
58640 Killdeer, 615 .... E 5
58051 Kindred, 495 .... R 6
58343 Knox, 104 .... L 3
58748 Kramer, 125 .... J 2
58456 Kulm, 625 .... N 7
58344 Lakota⊙, 964 .... O 3
58458 La Moure⊙, 951 .... O 7
58249 Langdon⊙, 2,182 .... O 2
58250 Lankin, 221 .... P 3
58750 Lansford, 296 .... H 2
58251 Larimore, 1,469 .... P 4
58345 Lawton, 123 .... O 3
58346 Leeds, 626 .... M 3
58641 Lefor, 100 .... F 6
58460 Lehr, 287 .... M 7
58551 Leith, 92 .... G 7
58052 Leonard, 221 .... R 6
58053 Lidgerwood, 1,000 .... R 7
58752 Lignite, 354 .... F 2
58552 Linton⊙, 1,695 .... K 7
58054 Lisbon⊙, 2,090 .... P 7
58461 Litchville, 294 .... O 6
† 58701 Logan, 100 .... H 3
58056 Luverne, 84 .... P 5
58348 Maddock, 708 .... L 4
58756 Makoti, 159 .... G 4
58554 Mandan⊙, 11,093 .... J 6
58757 Mandaree, 318 .... E 4
58642 Manning⊙, 36 .... E 5
58058 Mantador, 95 .... R 7
58256 Manvel, 265 .... R 3
58059 Mapleton, 219 .... R 6
58466 Marion, 215 .... O 6
58643 Marmarth, 247 .... B 7
58758 Martin, 120 .... K 4
58759 Max, 301 .... H 4
58760 Maxbass, 174 .... H 2
58257 Mayville, 2,554 .... R 4
58463 McClusky⊙, 664 .... K 4
58755 McGregor, 105 .... D 2
58464 McHenry, 152 .... N 4
58254 McVille, 583 .... O 4
58467 Medina, 488 .... M 6
58645 Medora⊙, 129 .... C 6
58258 Mekinock, 108 .... R 4
58559 Mercer, 132 .... J 5
58259 Michigan, 447 .... O 3
58060 Milnor, 645 .... R 7
58260 Milton, 198 .... O 2
58351 Minnewaukan⊙, 496 .... M 3
58701 Minot⊙, 32,290 .... H 3
58261 Minto, 636 .... R 3
58560 Moffit, 100 .... K 6
58761 Mohall⊙, 950 .... G 2
58471 Monango, 112 .... N 7
58472 Montpelier, 116 .... N 6
58061 Mooreton, 158 .... S 7
58646 Mott⊙, 1,368 .... F 7
58262 Mountain, 146 .... P 2
58352 Munich, 249 .... N 2
58561 Napoleon⊙, 1,036 .... L 6
58265 Neche, 451 .... P 2
58355 Nekoma, 84 .... O 2
58762 Newburg, 125 .... J 2
58647 New England, 906 .... E 6
58562 New Leipzig, 354 .... G 7
58356 New Rockford⊙, 1,969 .... N 4
58563 New Salem, 943 .... G 6
58763 New Town, 1,428 .... F 4
58266 Niagara, 115 .... P 4
58062 Nome, 103 .... P 6

AREA 70,665 sq. mi.
POPULATION 617,761
CAPITAL Bismarck
LARGEST CITY Fargo
HIGHEST POINT White Butte 3,506 ft.
SETTLED IN 1780
ADMITTED TO UNION November 2, 1889
POPULAR NAME Flickertail State; Sioux State
STATE FLOWER Prairie Rose
STATE BIRD Meadowlark

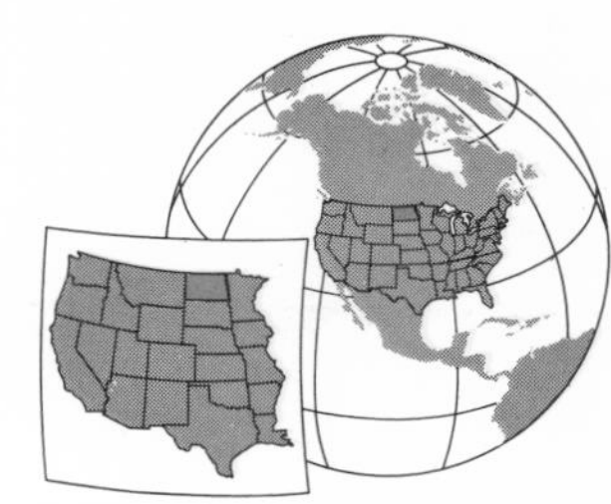

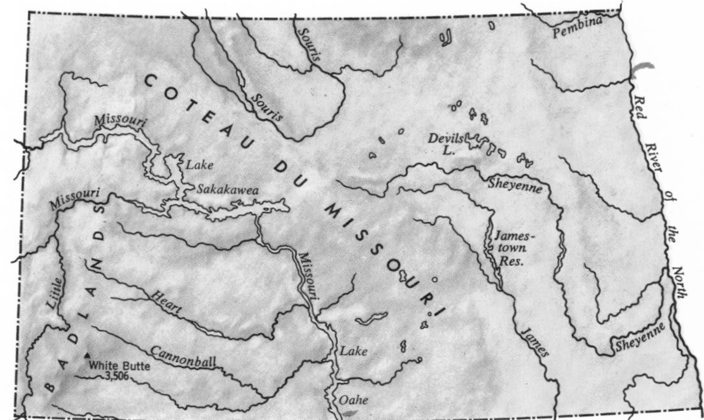

Topography

0 50 100
MILES

58765 Noonan, 403 .... D 2
58267 Northwood, 1,189 .... P 4
58473 Nortonville, 90 .... N 6
58474 Oakes, 1,742 .... O 7
† 58237 Oakwood, 91 .... R 3
58357 Oberon, 151 .... M 4
58063 Oriska, 128 .... P 6
58269 Osnabrock, 255 .... O 2
58064 Page, 367 .... P 5
58769 Palermo, 146 .... F 3
58270 Park River, 1,680 .... P 3
58770 Parshall, 1,246 .... F 4
58361 Pekin, 120 .... O 4
58271 Pembina, 741 .... R 2
58272 Petersburg, 266 .... P 3
58475 Pettibone, 173 .... L 5
† 58545 Pick City, 119 .... G 5
58273 Pisek, 154 .... P 3
58771 Plaza, 291 .... G 3
58772 Portal, 251 .... E 2
58274 Portland, 534 .... R 5
58773 Powers Lake, 523 .... E 2
58849 Ray, 776 .... D 3
58649 Reeder, 306 .... E 7
58650 Regent, 344 .... E 7
58275 Reynolds, 236 .... R 4
58651 Rhame, 206 .... C 7
58652 Richardton, 799 .... F 6
58565 Riverdale, 600 .... H 4
58478 Robinson, 125 .... L 5
58365 Rocklake, 270 .... M 2
58479 Rogers, 96 .... O 5
58366 Rolette, 579 .... L 2
58367 Rolla⊙, 1,458 .... L 2
58776 Ross, 125 .... E 3
58368 Rugby⊙, 2,889 .... L 3
58067 Rutland, 225 .... P 7
58779 Ryder, 211 .... G 4
58369 Saint John, 367 .... L 2
58276 Saint Thomas, 508 .... R 2
58480 Sanborn, 255 .... O 6
58780 Sanish, 25 .... E 4
58372 Sarles, 148 .... N 2
58781 Sawyer, 373 .... H 3
58653 Scranton, 360 .... D 7
58568 Selfridge, 346 .... J 7
58373 Selz, 110 .... L 4
58654 Sentinel Butte, 125 .... C 6
58277 Sharon, 201 .... P 4
58068 Sheldon, 192 .... P 6
58782 Sherwood, 369 .... G 2
58374 Sheyenne, 362 .... M 4
58569 Shields, 125 .... H 7
58570 Solen, 180 .... J 7
58783 Souris, 151 .... J 2
58655 South Heart, 132 .... D 6
58481 Spiritwood, 100 .... N 6
58784 Stanley⊙, 1,581 .... F 3
58571 Stanton⊙, 517 .... H 5
58377 Starkweather, 193 .... N 3
58482 Steele⊙, 696 .... L 6
58573 Strasburg, 642 .... K 7
58483 Streeter, 324 .... M 6
58785 Surrey, 361 .... H 3
58484 Sutton, 87 .... O 5
58486 Sykeston, 232 .... M 5
58487 Tappen, 294 .... L 6
58656 Taylor, 162 .... F 6
58278 Thompson, 291 .... R 4
58852 Tioga, 1,667 .... E 3
58379 Tokio, 130 .... N 4
58787 Tolley, 163 .... G 2
58380 Tolna, 247 .... O 4
58071 Tower City, 289 .... P 6
58788 Towner⊙, 870 .... K 3
58853 Trenton, 150 .... C 3
58575 Turtle Lake, 712 .... J 4
58488 Tuttle, 216 .... L 5
58576 Underwood, 781 .... H 5
58789 Upham, 272 .... J 2
58072 Valley City⊙, 7,843 .... P 6
58790 Velva, 1,241 .... J 3
58490 Verona, 140 .... O 7
58075 Wahpeton⊙, 7,076 .... S 7
58077 Walcott, 175 .... R 6
58281 Wales, 116 .... N 2
58282 Walhalla, 1,471 .... P 2
58577 Washburn⊙, 804 .... J 5
58854 Watford City⊙, 1,768 .... D 4
58078 West Fargo, 5,161 .... S 6
† 58078 West Fargo Industrial Park, 104 .... S 6
58793 Westhope, 705 .... H 2
58794 White Earth, 128 .... E 3
58795 Wildrose, 235 .... D 2
58801 Williston⊙, 11,280 .... C 3
58384 Willow City, 403 .... K 2
58579 Wilton, 695 .... J 5
58492 Wimbledon, 337 .... O 5
58494 Wing, 223 .... K 5
58495 Wishek, 1,275 .... L 7
58496 Woodworth, 139 .... M 5
58081 Wyndmere, 516 .... R 7
58386 York, 102 .... L 3
58497 Ypsilanti, 139 .... N 6
58580 Zap, 271 .... G 5
58581 Zeeland, 313 .... L 8

⊙ County seat.
‡ Population of metropolitan area.
† Zip of nearest p.o.
* Multiple zips

North Dakota's wealth springs from her soil. The state has the largest farms and leads in production of barley, wheat and flaxseed.

COMPIX

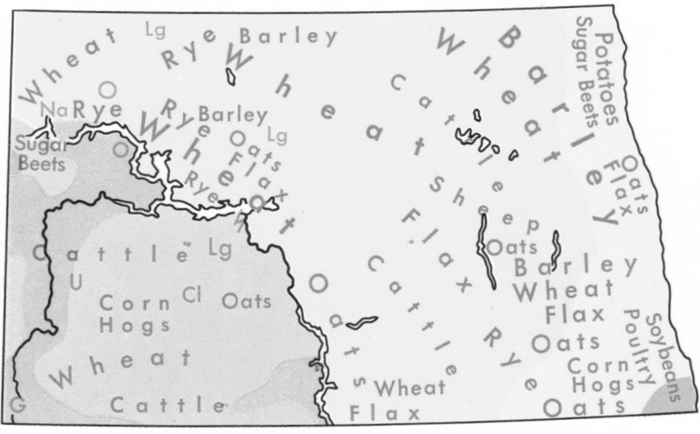

Agriculture, Industry and Resources

DOMINANT LAND USE

- Specialized Wheat
- Wheat, General Farming
- Wheat, Range Livestock
- Livestock, Cash Grain
- Sugar Beets, Dry Beans, Livestock, General Farming
- Range Livestock

Water Power

MAJOR MINERAL OCCURRENCES

- Cl Clay
- G Natural Gas
- Lg Lignite
- Na Salt
- O Petroleum
- U Uranium

OHIO
SCALE
0 5 10 20 30 40 MI.
0 5 10 20 30 40 KM.
State Capitals
County Seats
© C.S. HAMMOND & Co., N.Y.
83° Longitude West of 30′ Greenwich
MICHIGAN
ONTARIO
LAKE ERIE
INDIANA
KENTUCKY
WEST VIRGINIA
PA.
POINT PELEE NAT'L PARK
PERRY'S VICTORY AND INTERNATIONAL PEACE MEMORIAL NAT'L. MON.
MOUND CITY GROUP NAT'L. MON.
WILLIAMS
FULTON
LUCAS
OTTAWA
DEFIANCE
HENRY
WOOD
SANDUSKY
ERIE
LORAIN
CUYAHOGA
LAKE
GEAUGA
ASHTABULA
TRUMBULL
PORTAGE
SUMMIT
MEDINA
HURON
SENECA
HANCOCK
PUTNAM
PAULDING
VAN WERT
ALLEN
WYANDOT
CRAWFORD
RICHLAND
ASHLAND
WAYNE
STARK
MAHONING
COLUMBIANA
MERCER
AUGLAIZE
HARDIN
MARION
MORROW
KNOX
HOLMES
TUSCARAWAS
CARROLL
JEFFERSON
HARRISON
COSHOCTON
DELAWARE
UNION
LOGAN
SHELBY
DARKE
MIAMI
CHAMPAIGN
CLARK
MADISON
FRANKLIN
LICKING
MUSKINGUM
GUERNSEY
BELMONT
MONROE
NOBLE
MORGAN
PERRY
FAIRFIELD
PICKAWAY
FAYETTE
GREENE
MONTGOMERY
PREBLE
BUTLER
WARREN
CLINTON
HAMILTON
CLERMONT
BROWN
HIGHLAND
ADAMS
PIKE
ROSS
HOCKING
VINTON
ATHENS
WASHINGTON
MEIGS
JACKSON
GALLIA
SCIOTO
LAWRENCE
Columbus
Toledo
Cleveland
Cincinnati
Dayton
Akron
Canton
Youngstown
Springfield
Lorain
Sandusky
Mansfield
Zanesville
Portsmouth
Marietta
Steubenville
Hamilton
Lima
Findlay
Newark
Chillicothe
Ohio River
81° 30′
LAKE ERIE
CLEVELAND
84° 30′
CINCINNATI
KY.

COUNTIES

Adams, 18,957 .... D 8
Allen, 111,144 .... B 4
Ashland, 43,303 .... F 4
Ashtabula, 98,237 .... J 2
Athens, 54,889 .... F 7
Auglaize, 38,602 .... B 4
Belmont, 80,917 .... J 5
Brown, 26,635 .... C 8
Butler, 226,207 .... A 7
Carroll, 21,579 .... H 4
Champaign, 30,491 .... C 5
Clark, 157,115 .... C 6
Clermont, 95,725 .... B 7
Clinton, 31,464 .... C 7
Columbiana, 108,310 .... J 4
Coshocton, 33,486 .... G 5
Crawford, 50,364 .... E 4
Cuyahoga, 1,721,300 .... G 3
Darke, 49,141 .... A 5
Defiance, 36,949 .... A 3
Delaware, 42,908 .... D 5
Erie, 75,909 .... E 3
Fairfield, 73,301 .... E 6
Fayette, 25,461 .... D 6
Franklin, 833,249 .... E 5
Fulton, 33,071 .... B 2
Gallia, 25,239 .... F 8
Geauga, 62,977 .... H 3
Greene, 125,057 .... C 6
Guernsey, 37,665 .... H 5
Hamilton, 924,018 .... A 7
Hancock, 61,217 .... C 3
Hardin, 30,813 .... C 4
Harrison, 17,013 .... H 5
Henry, 27,058 .... B 3
Highland, 28,996 .... C 7
Hocking, 20,322 .... F 6
Holmes, 23,024 .... G 4
Huron, 49,587 .... E 3
Jackson, 27,174 .... E 7
Jefferson, 96,193 .... J 5
Knox, 41,795 .... F 5
Lake, 197,200 .... H 2
Lawrence, 56,868 .... E 8
Licking, 107,799 .... F 5
Logan, 35,072 .... C 5
Lorain, 256,843 .... F 3
Lucas, 484,370 .... C 2
Madison, 28,318 .... D 6
Mahoning, 303,424 .... J 4
Marion, 64,724 .... D 4
Medina, 82,717 .... G 3
Meigs, 19,799 .... F 7
Mercer, 35,265 .... A 4
Miami, 84,342 .... B 5
Monroe, 15,739 .... H 6
Montgomery, 606,148 .... B 6
Morgan, 12,375 .... G 6
Morrow, 21,348 .... E 4
Muskingum, 77,826 .... G 5
Noble, 10,428 .... G 6
Ottawa, 37,099 .... D 2
Paulding, 19,329 .... A 3
Perry, 27,434 .... F 6
Pickaway, 40,071 .... D 6
Pike, 19,114 .... D 7
Portage, 125,868 .... H 3
Preble, 34,719 .... A 6
Putnam, 31,134 .... B 3
Richland, 129,997 .... E 4
Ross, 61,211 .... D 7
Sandusky, 60,983 .... D 3
Scioto, 76,951 .... D 8
Seneca, 60,696 .... D 3
Shelby, 37,748 .... B 5
Stark, 372,210 .... H 4
Summit, 553,371 .... G 3
Trumbull, 232,579 .... J 3
Tuscarawas, 77,211 .... H 5
Union, 23,786 .... D 5
Van Wert, 29,194 .... A 4
Vinton, 9,420 .... E 7
Warren, 84,925 .... B 7
Washington, 57,160 .... H 7
Wayne, 87,123 .... G 4
Williams, 33,669 .... A 2
Wood, 89,722 .... C 3
Wyandot, 21,826 .... D 4

CITIES and TOWNS

Zip *Name/Pop.* *Key*
45101 Aberdeen, 1,165 .... C 8
45810 Ada, 5,309 .... C 4
45001 Addyston, 1,336 .... B 9
43901 Adena, 1,134 .... J 5
* 44301 Akron⊙, 275,425 .... G 3
Akron, ‡679,239 .... G 3
45710 Albany, 899 .... F 7
43001 Alexandria, 588 .... E 5
45812 Alger, 1,071 .... C 4
44601 Alliance, 26,547 .... H 4
43102 Amanda, 788 .... E 6
† 45201 Amberley, 5,574 .... C 9
45102 Amelia, 820 .... D 10
44001 Amherst, 9,902 .... F 3
43903 Amsterdam, 882 .... J 5
44003 Andover, 1,179 .... J 2
45302 Anna, 792 .... B 5
45303 Ansonia, 1,044 .... A 5
45813 Antwerp, 1,735 .... A 3
44606 Apple Creek, 784 .... G 4
44804 Arcadia, 689 .... D 3
45304 Arcanum, 1,993 .... A 6
43502 Archbold, 3,047 .... B 2
45814 Arlington, 1,066 .... C 4
† 45201 Arlington Heights, 1,476 .... C 9
44805 Ashland⊙, 19,872 .... F 4
43003 Ashley, 1,034 .... E 5
44004 Ashtabula, 24,313 .... J 2
43103 Ashville, 1,772 .... E 6
45701 Athens⊙, 23,310 .... F 7
44807 Attica, 1,005 .... E 3
44201 Atwater, 975 .... H 3
44202 Aurora, 6,549 .... H 3
44010 Austinburg, 900 .... J 2
44515 Austintown, 29,393 .... J 3
44011 Avon, 7,214 .... F 3
44012 Avon Lake, 12,261 .... F 2
† 43512 Ayersville, 950 .... B 3
45612 Bainbridge, 1,057 .... D 7
† 43420 Ballville, 1,652 .... D 3
43804 Baltic, 571 .... G 5
43105 Baltimore, 2,418 .... E 6
44203 Barberton, 33,052 .... G 4
43713 Barnesville, 4,292 .... H 6
43905 Barton, 975 .... J 5
45103 Batavia⊙, 1,894 .... B 7
† 44870 Bay View, 798 .... E 3
44140 Bay Village, 18,163 .... G 9
44608 Beach City, 1,133 .... G 4
† 44101 Beachwood, 9,631 .... J 9
45808 Beaverdam, 525 .... C 4
44146 Bedford, 17,552 .... H 9
† 44146 Bedford Heights, 13,063 .... J 9
43906 Bellaire, 9,655 .... J 5
45305 Bellbrook, 1,268 .... C 6
43310 Belle Center, 985 .... C 4
43311 Bellefontaine⊙, 11,255 .... C 5
44811 Bellevue, 8,604 .... E 3
44813 Bellville, 1,685 .... E 4
43718 Belmont, 666 .... J 5
44609 Beloit, 921 .... J 4
45714 Belpre, 7,189 .... G 7
44017 Berea, 22,396 .... G 10
43908 Bergholz, 914 .... J 4
44814 Berlin Heights, 828 .... F 3
45106 Bethel, 2,214 .... B 8
43719 Bethesda, 1,157 .... H 5
44815 Bettsville, 833 .... D 3
45715 Beverly, 1,396 .... G 6
43209 Bexley, 14,888 .... E 6
45107 Blanchester, 3,080 .... B 7
44817 Bloomdale, 727 .... D 3
43106 Bloomingburg, 895 .... D 6
44818 Bloomville, 884 .... D 3
† 45201 Blue Ash, 8,324 .... C 9
45817 Bluffton, 2,935 .... C 4
44512 Boardman, 30,852 .... J 3
44612 Bolivar, 1,084 .... G 4
† 44264 Boston Heights, 846 .... J 10
45306 Botkins, 1,057 .... B 5
43402 Bowling Green⊙, 21,760 .... C 3
45308 Bradford, 2,163 .... B 5
43406 Bradner, 1,140 .... C 3
† 44101 Bratenahl, 1,613 .... H 9
44141 Brecksville, 9,137 .... H 10
43107 Bremen, 1,413 .... F 6
44613 Brewster, 2,020 .... G 4
† 44215 Briarwood Beach, 508 .... G 3
43912 Bridgeport, 3,001 .... J 5
† 45201 Bridgetown, 13,352 .... B 9
43913 Brilliant, 2,178 .... J 5
44240 Brimfield, 950 .... H 3
44402 Bristolville, 900 .... J 3
† 44141 Broadview Heights, 11,463 .... H 10
44403 Brookfield, 1,200 .... J 3
44144 Brooklyn, 13,142 .... H 9
† 44131 Brooklyn Heights, 1,527 .... H 9
44142 Brook Park, 30.774 .... G 9
† 43912 Brookside, 939 .... J 5
45309 Brookville, 4,403 .... B 6
44212 Brunswick, 15,852 .... G 3
43506 Bryan⊙, 7,008 .... A 3
45716 Buchtel, 592 .... F 7
43008 Buckeye Lake, 2,961 .... F 6
44820 Bucyrus⊙, 13,111 .... E 4
43722 Buffalo, 710 .... G 6
† 45680 Burlington, 900 .... F 9
44021 Burton, 1,214 .... H 3
44822 Butler, 1,052 .... F 4
43723 Byesville, 2,097 .... G 6
43907 Cadiz⊙, 3,060 .... J 5
45820 Cairo, 587 .... B 4
43920 Calcutta, 2,900 .... J 4
43724 Caldwell⊙, 2,082 .... G 6
43314 Caledonia, 792 .... D 4
43725 Cambridge⊙, 13,656 .... G 5
45311 Camden, 1,507 .... A 6
44405 Campbell, 12,577 .... J 3
45111 Camp Dennison, 550 .... D 9
44614 Canal Fulton, 2,367 .... H 4
43110 Canal Winchester, 2,412 .... E 6
44406 Canfield, 4,997 .... J 3
* 44701 Canton⊙, 110,053 .... H 4
Canton, ‡372,210 .... H 4
43315 Cardington, 1,730 .... E 5
43316 Carey, 3,523 .... D 4
45005 Carlisle, 3,821 .... B 6
43112 Carroll, 614 .... E 6
44615 Carrollton⊙, 2,817 .... J 4
44824 Castalia, 1,045 .... E 3
45314 Cedarville, 2,342 .... C 6
45822 Celina⊙, 7,779 .... A 4
43011 Centerburg, 1,038 .... E 5
45459 Centerville, 10,333 .... B 6
44022 Chagrin Falls, 4,848 .... J 9
44024 Chardon⊙, 3,991 .... H 2
45719 Chauncey, 1,117 .... F 7
† 45202 Cherry Grove, 850 .... C 10
45619 Chesapeake, 1,364 .... E 9
44026 Chesterland, 11,500 .... H 2
† 45211 Cheviot, 11,135 .... B 9
45601 Chillicothe⊙, 24,842 .... E 7
45389 Christiansburg, 724 .... C 5
* 45201 Cincinnati⊙, 452,524 .... B 9
Cincinnati, ‡1,384,851 .... B 9
43113 Circleville⊙, 11,687 .... D 6
45113 Clarksville, 574 .... C 7
45315 Clayton, 773 .... B 6
* 44101 Cleveland⊙, 750,903 .... H 9
Cleveland, ‡2,074,194 .... H 9
44118 Cleveland Heights, 60,767 .... H 9
45002 Cleves, 2,044 .... B 9
44216 Clinton, 1,335 .... G 4
43410 Clyde, 5,503 .... E 3
† 45638 Coal Grove, 2,759 .... E 9
45621 Coalton, 550 .... E 7
45828 Coldwater, 3,533 .... A 5
† 44034 Colebrook, 700 .... J 2
44028 Columbia Station, 518 .... G 10
44408 Columbiana, 4,959 .... J 4
* 43201 Columbus (cap.)⊙, 539,677 .... E 6
Columbus, ‡916,228 .... E 6
45830 Columbus Grove, 2,290 .... B 4

(continued on following page)

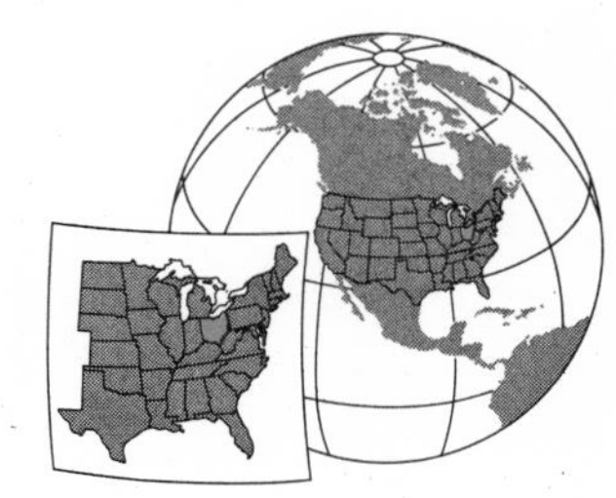

AREA 41,222 sq. mi.
POPULATION 10,652,017
CAPITAL Columbus
LARGEST CITY Cleveland
HIGHEST POINT Campbell Hill 1,550 ft.
SETTLED IN 1788
ADMITTED TO UNION March 1, 1803
POPULAR NAME Buckeye State
STATE FLOWER Scarlet Carnation
STATE BIRD Cardinal

Topography

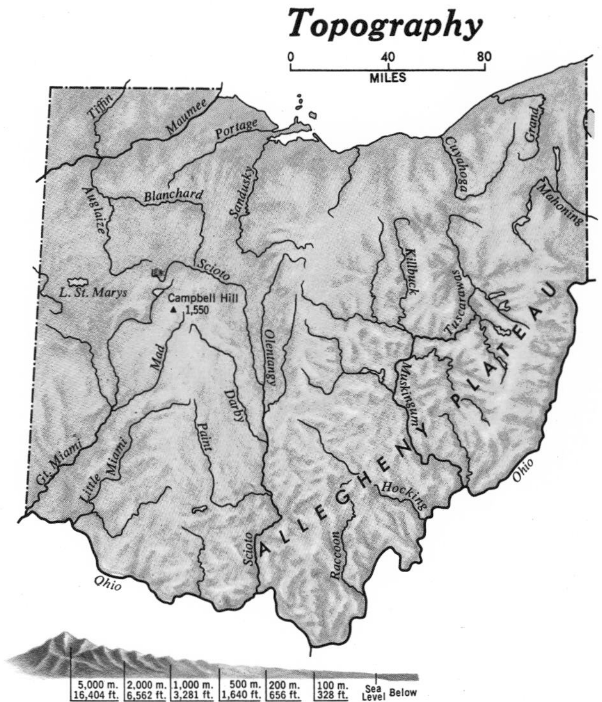

Agriculture, Industry and Resources

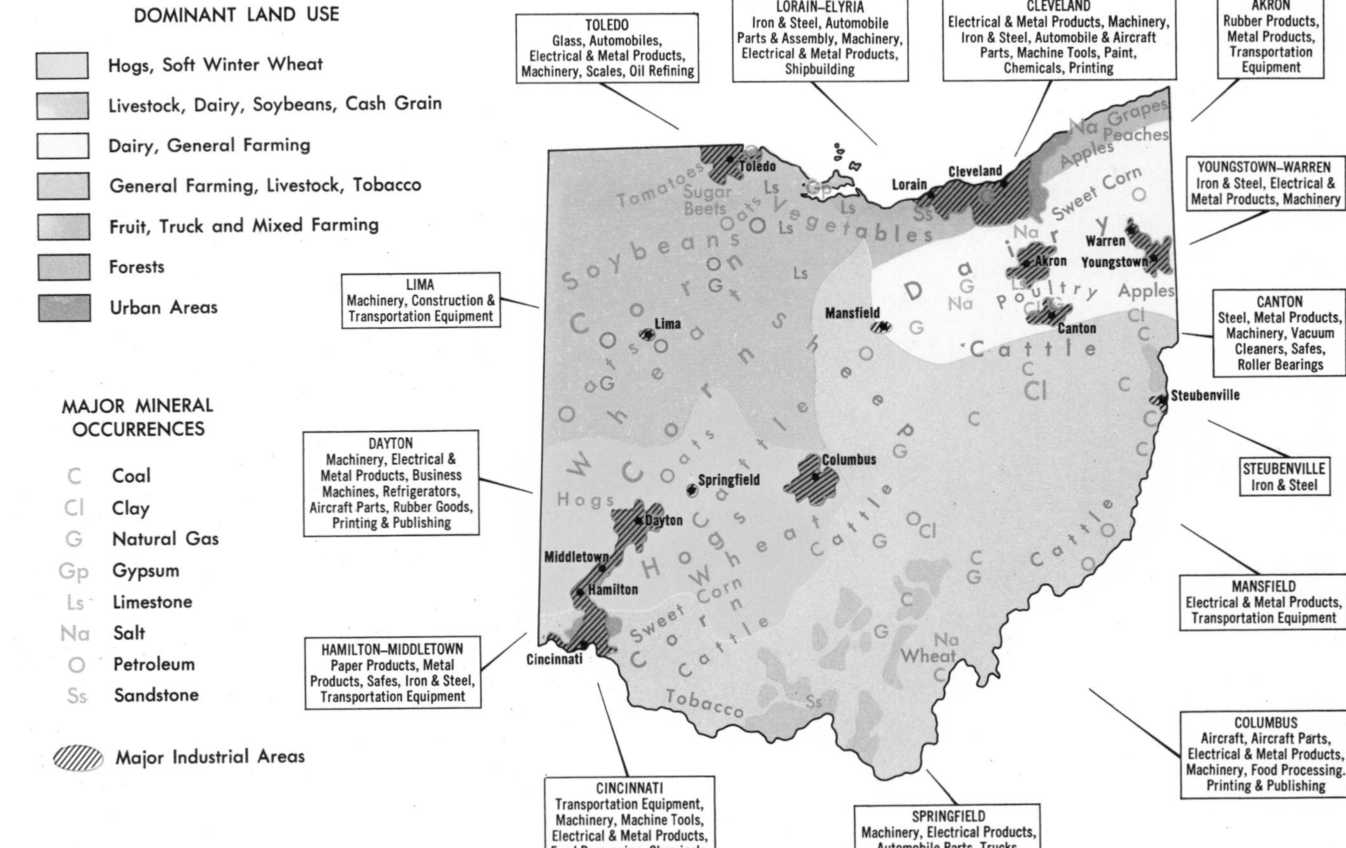

(continued)

Reminiscent of children's book illustrations, the tugboat "Washington" guides ore-carrier "Peter Robertson" through Cleveland's Industrial Flats, past a Milwaukee fuel tanker.

Lou Moore — Shostal Associates

44030 Conneaut, 14,552 J 2
45831 Continental, 1,185 B 3
45832 Convoy, 991 A 4
45723 Coolville, 672 G 7
43730 Corning, 838 F 6
44410 Cortland, 2,525 J 3
43812 Coshocton⊙, 13,747 G 5
† 45201 Covedale, 6,639 B 10
45318 Covington, 2,575 B 5
† 44429 Craig Beach, 1,451 H 3
44827 Crestline, 5,947 E 4
44217 Creston, 1,632 G 3
45806 Cridersville, 1,103 B 4
43731 Crooksville, 2,828 F 6
† 45341 Crystal Lakes, 5,851 C 6
* 44221 Cuyahoga Falls, 49,678 G 3
† 44101 Cuyahoga Heights, 866 H 9
43413 Cygnet, 629 C 3
44618 Dalton, 1,177 G 4
43014 Danville, 1,025 F 5
43123 Darbydale, 743 D 6
* 45401 Dayton⊙, 243,601 B 6
Dayton, ‡850,266 B 6
44411 Deerfield, 800 H 3
45236 Deer Park, 7,415 C 9
43512 Defiance⊙, 16,281 B 3
43318 Degraff, 1,117 C 5
43015 Delaware⊙, 15,008 E 5
45833 Delphos, 7,608 B 4
43515 Delta, 2,544 B 2
44621 Dennison, 3,506 H 5
† 45202 Dent, 800 B 9
43516 Deshler, 1,938 C 3
45750 Devola, 1,989 H 7
43917 Dillonvale, 1,095 J 5
44622 Dover, 11,516 G 4
44230 Doylestown, 2,373 G 4
43821 Dresden, 1,516 G 5
43017 Dublin, 681 D 5
43734 Duncan Falls, 900 G 6
45836 Dunkirk, 1,036 C 4
44730 East Canton, 1,631 H 4
44112 East Cleveland, 39,600 H 9
44094 Eastlake, 19,690 J 8
43920 East Liverpool, 20,020 J 4
44413 East Palestine, 5,604 J 4
44626 East Sparta, 959 H 4
45320 Eaton⊙, 6,020 A 6
† 44035 Eaton Estates, 2,076 G 3
43517 Edgerton, 2,126 A 3
44004 Edgewood, 3,437 J 2
43320 Edison, 569 E 4
43518 Edon, 803 A 2
45807 Elida, 1,211 B 4
43416 Elmore, 1,316 D 3
45216 Elmwood Place, 3,525 B 9
* 44035 Elyria⊙, 53,427 F 3
45322 Englewood, 7,885 B 6
45323 Enon, 1,929 C 6
44117 Euclid, 71,552 J 9
† 45201 Evendale, 1,967 C 9
45042 Excello, 900 B 7
45324 Fairborn, 32,267 B 6
† 45201 Fairfax, 2,705 C 9
45014 Fairfield, 14,680 A 7
44313 Fairlawn, 6,102 G 3
44077 Fairport Harbor, 3,665 H 2
44126 Fairview Park, 21,681 G 9
45325 Farmersville, 865 A 6
43521 Fayette, 1,175 B 2
45120 Felicity, 786 B 8
45840 Findlay⊙, 35,800 C 4
45326 Fletcher, 539 B 5
43977 Flushing, 1,207 J 5
45843 Forest, 1,535 C 4
45405 Forest Park, 15,139 B 9
† 45202 Forestville, 950 C 10
45844 Fort Jennings, 533 B 4
45845 Fort Loramie, 744 B 5
† 45401 Fort McKinley, 11,536 B 6
45846 Fort Recovery, 1,348 A 5
† 45801 Fort Shawnee, 3,436 B 4
44830 Fostoria, 16,037 D 3
45628 Frankfort, 949 D 7
45005 Franklin, 10,075 B 6
45629 Franklin Furnace, 975 E 8
43822 Frazeysburg, 941 F 5
44627 Fredericksburg, 601 G 4
43019 Fredericktown, 1,935 F 5
43420 Fremont⊙, 18,490 D 3

45630 Friendship, 600 D 8
43230 Gahanna, 12,400 E 5
44833 Galion, 13,123 E 4
45631 Gallipolis⊙, 7,490 F 8
43022 Gambier, 1,571 F 5
44125 Garfield Heights, 41,417 J 9
44231 Garrettsville, 1,718 H 3
44040 Gates Mills, 2,378 J 9
44041 Geneva, 6,449 J 2
44043 Geneva-on-the-Lake, 877 H 2
43430 Genoa, 2,139 D 2
45121 Georgetown⊙, 2,949 C 8
45327 Germantown, 4,088 B 6
45328 Gettysburg, 526 A 5
43431 Gibsonburg, 2,585 D 3
44420 Girard, 14,119 J 3
45848 Glandorf, 732 B 3
45246 Glendale, 2,690 C 9
† 44139 Glenwillow, 526 J 10
45732 Glouster, 2,121 F 6
44629 Gnadenhutten, 1,466 G 5
† 45201 Golf Manor, 5,170 C 9
45122 Goshen, 1,174 B 7
44044 Grafton, 1,771 F 3
43522 Grand Rapids, 976 C 3
44045 Grand River, 613 H 2
† 43201 Grandview Heights, 8,460 D 6
43023 Granville, 3,963 E 5
45330 Gratis, 621 A 6
43322 Green Camp, 537 D 4
45123 Greenfield, 4,780 D 7
45218 Greenhills, 6,092 B 9
44232 Greensburg, 950 G 4
44836 Green Springs, 1,279 E 3
44630 Greentown, 1,150 H 4
45331 Greenville⊙, 12,380 A 5
44837 Greenwich, 1,473 E 3
45239 Groesbeck, 5,000 B 9
43123 Grove City, 13,911 D 6
43125 Groveport, 2,490 E 6
45849 Grover Hill, 536 B 3
45634 Hamden, 953 F 7
45130 Hamersville, 567 C 8
* 45011 Hamilton⊙, 67,865 A 7
Hamilton-Middletown, ‡226,207 A 7
43524 Hamler, 681 B 3
43931 Hannibal, 550 J 6
† 43055 Hanover, 626 F 5
43126 Harrisburg, 556 D 6
45030 Harrison, 4,408 A 9
45850 Harrod, 533 C 4
† 44085 Hartsgrove, 775 J 2
44632 Hartville, 1,752 H 4
43525 Haskins, 549 C 3
43127 Haydenville, 650 F 7
43055 Heath, 6,768 F 5
43025 Hebron, 1,699 E 6
43526 Hicksville, 3,461 A 3
† 44143 Highland Heights, 5,926 J 9
43026 Hilliard, 8,369 D 5
45133 Hillsboro⊙, 5,584 C 7
44234 Hiram, 1,484 H 3
43527 Holgate, 1,541 B 3
43528 Holland, 1,108 C 2
45033 Hooven, 550 A 9
43976 Hopedale, 916 J 5
44425 Hubbard, 8,583 J 3
45424 Huber Heights, 18,943 B 6
44236 Hudson, 3,933 H 3
† 44022 Hunting Valley, 797 J 9
44839 Huron, 6,896 E 3
44131 Independence, 7,034 H 9
† 45201 Indian Hill, 5,651 C 9
43932 Irondale, 602 J 4
45638 Ironton⊙, 15,030 E 8
45640 Jackson⊙, 6,843 E 7
45334 Jackson Center, 1,119 B 5
45740 Jacksonville, 545 F 7
45335 Jamestown, 1,790 C 6
44047 Jefferson⊙, 2,472 J 2
† 43162 Jefferson (West Jefferson), 3,664 D 6
43128 Jeffersonville, 1,031 C 6
44840 Jeromesville, 659 F 4
43986 Jewett, 901 H 5
43031 Johnstown, 3,208 E 5
43748 Junction City, 732 F 6
45853 Kalida, 900 B 4
44240 Kent, 28,183 H 3

43326 Kenton⊙, 8,315 C 4
45429 Kettering, 69,599 B 6
44637 Killbuck, 893 G 5
45034 Kings Mills, 800 B 7
45644 Kingston, 1,157 E 7
44048 Kingsville, 1,129 J 2
44428 Kinsman, 900 J 3
43033 Kirkersville, 578 E 6
44094 Kirtland, 5,530 H 8
43951 Lafferty, 900 H 5
44050 Lagrange, 1,074 F 3
44250 Lakemore, 2,708 H 3
43440 Lakeside, 850 E 2
43331 Lakeview, 1,026 C 4
44107 Lakewood, 70,173 G 9
43130 Lancaster⊙, 32,911 E 6
43934 Lansing, 950 J 5
43332 La Rue, 867 D 4
43135 Laurelville, 624 E 7
† 45501 Lawrenceville, 687 C 6
44430 Leavittsburg, 4,979 J 3
45036 Lebanon⊙, 7,934 B 7
45135 Leesburg, 984 D 7
44431 Leetonia, 2,342 J 4
45856 Leipsic, 2,072 C 3
44251 Leroy, 715 G 3
45338 Lewisburg, 1,553 A 6
44904 Lexington, 2,972 E 4
43532 Liberty Center, 1,007 B 3
* 45801 Lima⊙, 53,734 B 4
Lima, ‡171,472 B 4
† 45201 Lincoln Heights, 6,099 C 9
43442 Lindsey, 652 D 3
44432 Lisbon⊙, 3,521 J 4
44253 Litchfield, 650 F 3
43136 Lithopolis, 705 E 6
45742 Little Hocking, 520 G 7
45215 Lockland, 5,288 C 9
44254 Lodi, 2,399 F 3
43138 Logan⊙, 6,269 F 6
43140 London⊙, 6,481 C 6
* 44052 Lorain, 78,185 F 3
Lorain-Elyria, ‡256,843 F 3
44842 Loudonville, 2,865 F 4
44641 Louisville, 6,298 H 4
45140 Loveland, 7,144 D 9
45744 Lowell, 852 H 6
44436 Lowellville, 1,836 J 3
44843 Lucas, 771 F 4
45648 Lucasville, 900 E 8
43443 Luckey, 996 D 3
45142 Lynchburg, 1,186 C 7
44124 Lyndhurst, 19,749 J 9
43533 Lyons, 630 B 2
44056 Macedonia, 6,375 J 10
† 45202 Mack, 5,000 B 9
45243 Madeira, 6,713 C 9
44057 Madison, 1,678 H 2
44643 Magnolia, 1,064 H 4
43758 Malta, 1,017 G 6
44644 Malvern, 1,256 H 4
45144 Manchester, 2,195 C 8
* 44901 Mansfield⊙, 55,047 F 4
Mansfield, ‡129,997 F 4
44255 Mantua, 1,199 H 3
44137 Maple Heights, 34,093 H 9
† 43440 Marblehead, 726 E 2
45860 Maria Stein, 950 A 5
45227 Mariemont, 4,540 C 9
45750 Marietta⊙, 16,861 G 7
43302 Marion⊙, 38,646 D 4
44645 Marshallville, 693 G 4
43935 Martins Ferry, 10,757 J 5
43040 Marysville⊙, 5,744 D 5
45040 Mason, 5,677 B 7
44646 Massillon, 32,539 H 4
44438 Masury, 2,060 J 3
45069 Maud, 550 B 7
43537 Maumee, 15,937 C 2
† 44121 Mayfield, 3,548 J 9
† 44101 Mayfield Heights, 22,139 J 9
45651 McArthur⊙, 1,543 F 7
43534 McClure, 699 C 3
45858 McComb, 1,329 C 3
43756 McConnelsville⊙, 2,107 G 6
44437 McDonald, 3,177 J 3
45859 McGuffey, 704 C 4
43044 Mechanicsburg, 1,686 D 5
44256 Medina⊙, 10,913 G 3
45862 Mendon, 672 A 4

44060 Mentor, 36,912 H 2
44060 Mentor-on-the-Lake, 6,517 G 2
43540 Metamora, 594 C 2
45342 Miamisburg, 14,797 B 6
45041 Miamitown, 800 A 9
44652 Middlebranch, 600 H 4
† 44017 Middleburg Heights, 12,367 G 10
44062 Middlefield, 1,726 H 3
45863 Middle Point, 543 B 4
45760 Middleport, 2,784 F 7
45042 Middletown, 48,767 A 6
44653 Midvale, 636 H 5
44846 Milan, 1,405 E 3
45150 Milford, 4,828 D 9
43045 Milford Center, 753 D 5
43447 Millbury, 771 D 2
44654 Millersburg⊙, 2,979 F 4
43046 Millersport, 777 E 6
45013 Millville, 697 A 7
44656 Mineral City, 860 H 4
44440 Mineral Ridge, 1,500 J 3
44657 Minerva, 4,359 H 4
† 43201 Minerva Park, 1,402 E 5
43938 Mingo Junction, 5,278 J 5
45865 Minster, 2,405 B 5
44260 Mogadore, 3,858 H 3
45050 Monroe, 3,492 B 7
44847 Monroeville, 1,455 E 3
45242 Montgomery, 5,683 C 9
43543 Montpelier, 4,184 A 2
45439 Moraine, 4,898 B 6
† 44022 Moreland Hills, 3,000 J 9
45152 Morrow, 1,486 B 7
43338 Mount Gilead⊙, 2,971 E 4
45231 Mount Healthy, 7,446 B 9
45154 Mount Orab, 1,306 C 7
43939 Mount Pleasant, 635 J 5
43143 Mount Sterling, 1,536 D 6
43050 Mount Vernon⊙, 13,373 E 5
43340 Mount Victory, 633 D 4
44262 Munroe Falls, 3,794 H 3
43144 Murray City, 562 F 6
43545 Napoleon⊙, 7,791 B 3
44662 Navarre, 1,607 H 4
43940 Neffs, 900 J 5
44441 Negley, 600 J 4
45764 Nelsonville, 4,812 F 7
44849 Nevada, 917 D 4
43054 New Albany, 513 E 5
43055 Newark⊙, 41,836 F 5
45662 New Boston, 3,325 E 8
45869 New Bremen, 2,185 B 5
† 44101 Newburgh Heights, 3,396 H 9
† 45201 New Burlington, 900 B 9
45344 New Carlisle, 6,112 C 6
43832 Newcomerstown, 4,155 G 5
43762 New Concord, 2,318 G 6
43145 New Holland, 796 D 6
45871 New Knoxville, 852 B 5
45345 New Lebanon, 4,248 B 6
43764 New Lexington⊙, 4,921 F 6
44851 New London, 2,336 F 3
45346 New Madison, 959 A 6
45767 New Matamoras, 940 J 6
45011 New Miami, 3,273 A 7
44442 New Middletown, 1,664 J 4
45347 New Paris, 1,692 A 6
44663 New Philadelphia⊙, 15,184 G 5
45768 Newport, 975 H 7
45157 New Richmond, 2,650 B 8
43766 New Straitsville, 947 F 6
44444 Newton Falls, 5,378 J 3
45244 Newtown, 2,047 C 10
45159 New Vienna, 849 C 7
44854 New Washington, 1,251 E 4
44445 New Waterford, 735 J 4
44446 Niles, 21,581 J 3
45872 North Baltimore, 3,143 C 3
45052 North Bend, 638 B 9
44450 North Bloomfield, 650 J 3
44720 North Canton, 15,228 H 4
45239 North College Hill, 12,363 B 9
44855 North Fairfield, 540 E 3
44067 Northfield, 1,089 J 10
44707 North Industry, 2,000 H 4
44068 North Kingsville, 2,458 J 2
43060 North Lewisburg, 840 C 5
44452 North Lima, 800 J 4
44070 North Olmsted, 34,861 G 9
† 44081 North Perry, 851 H 2
† 44101 North Randall, 1,212 H 9
44035 North Ridgeville, 13,152 F 3
44133 North Royalton, 12,807 H 10
† 43601 Northwood, 4,222 D 2
† 43701 North Zanesville, 3,399 G 6
44203 Norton, 12,308 G 3
44857 Norwalk⊙, 13,386 E 3
45212 Norwood, 30,420 C 9
43449 Oak Harbor, 2,807 D 2
45656 Oak Hill, 1,642 E 8
45873 Oakwood, 10,095 B 6
45873 Oakwood, 3,127 H 9
45873 Oakwood, 804 B 3
44074 Oberlin, 8,761 F 3
43207 Obetz, 2,248 E 6
45874 Ohio City, 816 A 4
44138 Olmsted Falls, 2,504 G 9
44862 Ontario, 4,345 E 4
† 44101 Orange, 2,112 J 9
43616 Oregon, 16,563 D 2
44667 Orrville, 7,408 G 4
44076 Orwell, 965 J 2
45875 Ottawa⊙, 3,622 B 3
† 43601 Ottawa Hills, 4,270 C 2
45876 Ottoville, 914 B 4
45160 Owensville, 707 B 7
45056 Oxford, 15,868 A 6
44077 Painesville⊙, 16,536 H 2
45877 Pandora, 857 C 4
44080 Parkman, 750 H 3
44129 Parma, 100,216 H 9
† 44129 Parma Heights, 27,192 G 9
43062 Pataskala, 1,831 E 5
45879 Paulding⊙, 2,983 A 3
45880 Payne, 1,351 A 3
45660 Peebles, 1,629 D 8

43450 Pemberville, 1,301 C 3
44264 Peninsula, 692 G 3
44124 Pepper Pike, 5,933 J 9
44081 Perry, 917 H 2
43551 Perrysburg, 7,693 C 2
44864 Perrysville, 752 F 4
45354 Phillipsburg, 831 B 6
43771 Philo, 846 G 6
43147 Pickerington, 696 E 6
45661 Piketon, 1,347 E 7
43554 Pioneer, 968 A 2
45356 Piqua, 20,741 B 5
43064 Plain City, 2,254 D 5
45359 Pleasant Hill, 1,025 B 5
43148 Pleasantville, 754 E 6
44865 Plymouth, 1,993 E 4
† 45042 Poasttown, 650 B 6
44514 Poland, 3,097 J 3
45769 Pomeroy⊙, 2,672 G 7
43452 Port Clinton⊙, 7,202 E 2
45770 Portland, 550 G 7
45662 Portsmouth⊙, 27,633 D 8
43837 Port Washington, 550 G 5
43942 Powhatan Point, 2,167 J 6
45669 Proctorville, 881 F 9
43342 Prospect, 1,031 D 5
43456 Put-in-Bay, 135 E 2
43773 Quaker City, 510 H 6
43343 Quincy, 686 C 5
45771 Racine, 583 G 8
43066 Radnor, 950 D 5
44265 Randolph, 900 H 3
44266 Ravenna⊙, 11,780 H 3
43943 Rayland, 617 J 5
45215 Reading, 14,303 C 9
† 45202 Remington, 600 C 9
45773 Reno, 576 H 7
† 43412 Reno Beach, 1,049 D 2
44867 Republic, 705 D 3
43068 Reynoldsburg, 13,921 E 6
44286 Richfield, 3,228 G 3
43344 Richmond, 777 J 5
† 44045 Richmond (Grand River), 613 H 2
45673 Richmond Dale, 950 E 7
44143 Richmond Heights, 9,220 H 9
43344 Richwood, 2,072 D 5
45674 Rio Grande, 814 F 8
45167 Ripley, 2,745 C 8
43457 Risingsun, 730 C 3
44270 Rittman, 6,308 G 4
† 43085 Riverlea, 558 D 5
44670 Robertsville, 600 H 4
44084 Rock Creek, 731 J 2
45882 Rockford, 1,207 A 4
44116 Rocky River, 22,958 G 9
44085 Rome, 648 J 2
44272 Rootstown, 900 H 3
† 45662 Rosemount, 1,786 D 8
43777 Roseville, 1,767 F 6
45061 Ross (Venice), 1,661 B 9
43460 Rossford, 5,302 C 2
45236 Rossmoyne, 2,900 C 9
† 43943 Rush Run, 560 J 5
43347 Rushsylvania, 526 C 5
43348 Russells Point, 1,104 C 5
45775 Rutland, 663 F 7
45169 Sabina, 2,160 C 7
† 44067 Sagamore Hills, 4,100 J 10
45217 Saint Bernard, 6,080 B 9
43950 Saint Clairsville⊙, 4,754 J 5
45883 Saint Henry, 1,276 A 5
45885 Saint Marys, 7,699 B 4
43072 Saint Paris, 1,646 C 5
44460 Salem, 14,186 J 4
43945 Salineville, 1,686 J 4
44870 Sandusky⊙, 32,674 E 3
44671 Sandyville, 543 H 4
45171 Sardinia, 824 C 7
43946 Sardis, 700 J 6
43988 Scio, 1,002 H 5
† 45662 Sciotodale, 950 E 8
45679 Seaman, 866 C 8
44672 Sebring, 4,954 H 4
† 44101 Seven Hills, 12,700 H 9
45062 Seven Mile, 699 A 7
44273 Seville, 1,402 G 3
43947 Shadyside, 5,070 J 6
44120 Shaker Heights, 36,306 H 9
45241 Sharonville, 10,985 C 9
43782 Shawnee, 914 F 6
† 44052 Sheffield, 1,730 F 3
44054 Sheffield Lake, 8,734 F 3
44875 Shelby, 9,847 E 4
43556 Sherwood, 784 A 3
44878 Shiloh, 817 E 4
44676 Shreve, 1,635 F 4
45365 Sidney⊙, 16,332 B 5
† 44221 Silver Lake, 3,637 G 3
† 45201 Silverton, 6,588 C 9
43948 Smithfield, 1,245 J 5
44677 Smithville, 1,278 G 4
44139 Solon, 11,519 J 9
43783 Somerset, 1,417 F 6
† 44001 South Amherst, 2,913 F 3
† 43103 South Bloomfield, 610 D 6
45368 South Charleston, 1,500 C 6
44121 South Euclid, 29,579 H 9
45065 South Lebanon, 3,014 B 7
45680 South Point, 2,243 E 9
† 44022 South Russell, 2,673 H 3
45369 South Vienna, 545 C 6
45682 South Webster, 825 E 8
43701 South Zanesville, 1,436 F 6
44275 Spencer, 758 F 3
45887 Spencerville, 2,241 B 4
45066 Springboro, 2,799 B 6
45246 Springdale, 8,127 B 9
* 45501 Springfield⊙, 81,926 C 6
Springfield, ‡157,115 C 6
45370 Spring Valley, 667 C 6
44276 Sterling, 550 G 4
43952 Steubenville⊙, 30,771 J 5
Steubenville-Weirton, ‡165,627 J 5
43154 Stoutsville, 573 E 6
44224 Stow, 19,847 H 3

44680 Strasburg, 1,874 G 4
44240 Streetsboro, 7,966 H 3
44136 Strongsville, 15,182 G 10
44471 Struthers, 15,343 J 3
43557 Stryker, 1,296 B 3
† 44260 Suffield, 650 H 3
44681 Sugarcreek, 1,771 G 5
43074 Sunbury, 2,512 E 5
43558 Swanton, 2,927 C 2
44882 Sycamore, 1,096 D 4
43560 Sylvania, 12,031 C 2
45779 Syracuse, 684 G 7
44278 Tallmadge, 15,274 H 3
† 43771 Taylorsville (Philo), 846 G 6
45174 Terrace Park, 2,266 D 9
45780 The Plains, 1,568 F 7
43076 Thornville, 679 F 6
44883 Tiffin⊙, 21,596 D 3
43963 Tiltonsville, 2,123 J 5
† 44094 Timberlake, 964 J 8
45371 Tipp City, 5,090 B 6
† 45245 Tobasco, 950 C 10
* 43601 Toledo⊙, 383,818 D 2
Toledo, ‡692,571 D 2
43964 Toronto, 7,705 J 5
45067 Trenton, 5,278 B 7
45782 Trimble, 542 F 7
45373 Troy⊙, 17,186 B 5
44682 Tuscarawas, 830 H 5
44087 Twinsburg, 6,432 J 10
44683 Uhrichsville, 5,731 H 5
45322 Union, 3,654 B 6
† 47390 Union City, 1,808 A 5
44685 Uniontown, 875 H 4
44118 University Heights, 17,055 H 9
43221 Upper Arlington, 38,630 D 6
43351 Upper Sandusky⊙, 5,645 D 4
43078 Urbana⊙, 11,237 C 5
† 43123 Urbancrest, 754 D 6
43080 Utica, 1,977 F 5
† 43201 Valley View, 909 D 6
† 44101 Valley View, 1,422 H 9
45377 Vandalia, 10,796 B 6
45890 Vanlue, 539 C 4
45891 Van Wert⊙, 11,320 A 4
44870 Venice, 1,661 B 9
44089 Vermilion, 9,872 F 3
45378 Verona, 593 A 6
45380 Versailles, 2,441 A 5
44473 Vienna, 1,200 J 3
† 44473 Vienna (South Vienna), 545 C 6
44281 Wadsworth, 13,142 G 3
† 44094 Waite Hill, 514 H 2
44889 Wakeman, 514 F 3
43465 Walbridge, 3,208 C 2
44687 Walnut Creek, 550 G 4
† 44146 Walton Hills, 2,508 J 10
45895 Wapakoneta⊙, 7,324 B 4
* 44481 Warren⊙, 63,494 J 3
† 44100 Warrensville Heights, 18,925 H 9
43844 Warsaw, 725 G 5
43160 Washington Court House⊙, 12,495 D 6
44490 Washingtonville, 747 J 4
45786 Waterford, 600 G 6
43566 Waterville, 2,940 C 3
43567 Wauseon⊙, 4,932 B 2
45690 Waverly⊙, 4,858 D 7
43466 Wayne, 921 C 3
44688 Waynesburg, 1,337 H 4
45896 Waynesfield, 704 C 4
45068 Waynesville, 1,638 B 6
44090 Wellington, 4,137 F 3
45692 Wellston, 5,410 F 7
43968 Wellsville, 5,891 J 4
45381 West Alexandria, 1,553 A 6
45449 West Carrollton, 10,748 B 6
43081 Westerville, 12,530 D 5
44491 West Farmington, 650 J 3
43162 West Jefferson, 3,664 D 6
43845 West Lafayette, 1,719 G 5
44145 Westlake, 15,689 G 9
43357 West Liberty, 1,580 C 5
43358 West Mansfield, 753 C 5
45383 West Milton, 3,696 B 6
43569 Weston, 1,269 C 3
† 45662 West Portsmouth, 3,396 D 8
44287 West Salem, 1,058 F 4
45693 West Union⊙, 1,951 C 8
43570 West Unity, 1,589 B 2
† 44138 Westview, 2,523 G 10
45694 Wheelersburg, 3,709 E 8
43213 Whitehall, 25,263 E 6
43571 Whitehouse, 1,542 C 2
44092 Wickliffe, 21,354 J 9
44890 Willard, 5,510 E 3
45176 Williamsburg, 2,054 B 7
44093 Williamsfield, 950 J 2
43164 Williamsport, 857 D 6
44094 Willoughby, 18,634 J 8
† 44094 Willoughby Hills, 5,247 J 9
44094 Willowick, 21,237 J 8
45898 Willshire, 623 A 4
45177 Wilmington⊙, 10,051 C 7
45697 Winchester, 760 C 8
44288 Windham, 3,360 H 3
43952 Wintersville, 4,921 J 5
45245 Withamsville, 975 C 10
† 45201 Woodlawn, 3,251 C 9
† 44101 Woodmere, 976 J 9
43793 Woodsfield⊙, 3,239 H 6
43469 Woodville, 1,834 D 3
44691 Wooster⊙, 18,703 G 4
43085 Worthington, 15,326 E 5
45215 Wyoming, 9,089 C 9
45385 Xenia⊙, 25,373 C 6
45387 Yellow Springs, 4,624 C 6
43971 Yorkville, 1,656 J 5
* 44501 Youngstown⊙, 139,788 J 3
Youngstown-Warren, ‡536,003 J 3
43701 Zanesville⊙, 33,045 G 6

⊙ County seat.
‡ Population of metropolitan area.
† Zip of nearest p.o.
* Multiple zips

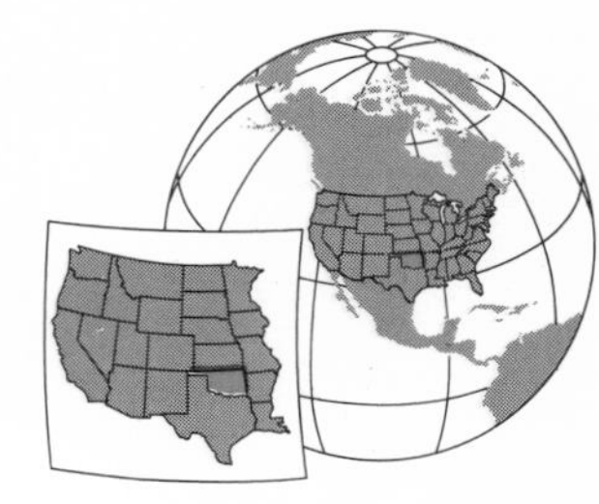

AREA 69,919 sq. mi.
POPULATION 2,559,253
CAPITAL Oklahoma City
LARGEST CITY Oklahoma City
HIGHEST POINT Black Mesa 4,973 ft.
SETTLED IN 1889
ADMITTED TO UNION November 16, 1907
POPULAR NAME Sooner State
STATE FLOWER Mistletoe
STATE BIRD Scissor-tailed Flycatcher

COUNTIES

County	Key
Adair, 15,141	S 3
Alfalfa, 7,224	K 1
Atoka, 10,972	O 6
Beaver, 6,282	E 1
Beckham, 15,754	G 4
Blaine, 11,794	K 3
Bryan, 25,552	O 7
Caddo, 28,931	K 4
Canadian, 32,245	K 3
Carter, 37,349	M 6
Cherokee, 23,174	R 3
Choctaw, 15,141	P 6
Cimarron, 4,145	A 1
Cleveland, 81,839	M 4
Coal, 5,525	O 5
Comanche, 108,144	K 5
Cotton, 6,832	K 6
Craig, 14,722	R 1
Creek, 45,532	O 3
Custer, 22,665	H 3
Delaware, 17,767	S 2
Dewey, 5,656	H 2
Ellis, 5,129	G 2
Garfield, 55,365	L 2
Garvin, 24,874	M 5
Grady, 29,354	L 5
Grant, 7,117	L 1
Greer, 7,979	G 5
Harmon, 5,136	G 5
Harper, 5,151	G 1
Haskell, 9,578	R 4
Hughes, 13,228	O 4
Jackson, 30,902	H 5
Jefferson, 7,125	L 6
Johnston, 7,870	N 6
Kay, 48,791	M 1
Kingfisher, 12,857	L 3
Kiowa, 12,532	J 5
Latimer, 8,601	R 5
Le Flore, 32,137	S 5
Lincoln, 19,482	N 3
Logan, 19,645	M 3
Love, 5,637	M 7
Major, 7,529	K 2
Marshall, 7,682	N 6
Mayes, 23,302	R 2
McClain, 14,157	M 5
McCurtain, 28,642	S 6
McIntosh, 12,472	P 4
Murray, 10,669	M 6
Muskogee, 59,542	R 3
Noble, 10,043	M 2
Nowata, 9,773	P 1
Okfuskee, 10,683	O 3
Oklahoma, 526,805	M 3
Okmulgee, 35,358	P 3
Osage, 29,750	O 1
Ottawa, 29,800	S 1
Pawnee, 11,338	N 2
Payne, 50,654	N 2
Pittsburg, 37,521	P 5
Pontotoc, 27,867	N 5
Pottawatomie, 43,134	N 4
Pushmataha, 9,385	R 6
Roger Mills, 4,452	G 3
Rogers, 28,425	P 2
Seminole, 25,144	N 4
Sequoyah, 23,370	S 3
Stephens, 35,902	L 6
Texas, 16,352	C 1
Tillman, 12,901	J 6
Tulsa, 401,663	P 2
Wagoner, 22,163	P 3
Washington, 42,277	P 1
Washita, 12,141	J 4
Woods, 11,920	J 1
Woodward, 15,537	H 2

CITIES and TOWNS

	Zip	Name/Pop.	Key
	74720	Achille, 382	O 7
	74820	Ada⊙, 14,859	N 5
	74330	Adair, 459	R 2
	73901	Adams, 175	D 1
	74520	Adamson, 150	P 5
	73520	Addington, 123	L 6
	74331	Afton, 1,022	S 1
	74824	Agra, 335	N 3
†	74955	Akins, 250	S 3
	74721	Albany, 100	O 7
	73001	Albert, 110	K 4
	74521	Albion, 186	R 5
	74522	Alderson, 215	P 5
	73002	Alex, 492	L 5
†	73015	Alfalfa, 70	J 4
	73716	Aline, 260	K 1
	74825	Allen, 974	O 5
	73521	Altus⊙, 23,302	H 5
	73717	Alva⊙, 7,440	J 1
	73004	Amber, 300	L 4
	73718	Ames, 227	K 2
†	73723	Amorita, 63	K 1
	73719	Anadarko⊙, 6,682	K 4
	74523	Antlers⊙, 2,685	P 6
	73006	Apache, 1,421	K 5
†	74633	Apperson, 40	N 1
	73620	Arapaho⊙, 531	H 3
	73007	Arcadia, 500	M 3
	73401	Ardmore⊙, 20,881	M 6
	74901	Arkoma, 2,098	T 4
	73832	Arnett⊙, 711	G 2
	74826	Asher, 437	N 5
	74524	Ashland, 73	O 5
	74525	Atoka⊙, 3,346	O 6
	74827	Atwood, 200	O 5
	74001	Avant, 439	O 2
	73833	Avard, 59	J 1
	74526	Bache, 100	P 5
	74420	Bacone, 786	R 3
	73930	Baker, 63	D 1
	73931	Balko, 100	E 1
	74002	Barnsdall, 1,579	O 1
†	74965	Baron, 100	S 3
	74003	Bartlesville⊙, 29,683	O 1
	74722	Battiest, 150	S 6
	74828	Bearden, 260	O 4
	73932	Beaver⊙, 1,853	F 1
	74421	Beggs, 1,107	P 3
†	74523	Belzoni, 50	R 6
	74929	Bengal, 75	R 5
	74723	Bennington, 288	P 7
	74527	Bentley, 125	O 6
†	73662	Berlin, 50	G 4
	74331	Bernice, 189	S 1
	73622	Bessie, 210	H 4
	73008	Bethany, 21,785	L 3
	74724	Bethel, 297	S 6
†	74801	Bethel Acres, 1,083	M 4
	74332	Big Cabin, 198	R 1
	74630	Billings, 618	M 1
	73009	Binger, 730	K 4
	73720	Bison, 80	L 2
	74008	Bixby, 3,973	P 3
	74058	Blackburn, 88	N 2
†	74962	Blackgum, 258	S 3
	74631	Blackwell, 8,645	M 1
	73526	Blair, 1,114	H 5
	73010	Blanchard, 1,580	L 4
	74528	Blanco, 200	P 5
	74529	Blocker, 151	P 4
	74725	Blue, 150	O 7
	74333	Bluejacket, 234	R 1
†	74525	Boggy Depot, 100	O 6
	73933	Boise City⊙, 1,993	B 1
	74726	Bokchito, 607	O 6
	74930	Bokoshe, 588	S 4
	74829	Boley, 514	O 4
	74727	Boswell, 755	P 6
	74830	Bowlegs, 540	N 4
	74009	Bowring, 100	O 1
	74422	Boynton, 522	P 3
	73011	Bradley, 247	L 5
	74423	Braggs, 325	R 3
	74632	Braman, 295	M 1
	73012	Bray, 90	L 5
	73721	Breckinridge, 70	L 2
	74424	Briartown, 100	R 4
	73013	Bridgeport, 142	K 3
	74010	Bristow, 4,653	O 3
	74012	Broken Arrow, 11,787	P 2
	74728	Broken Bow, 2,980	S 7
	74530	Bromide, 231	N 6
†	74873	Brooksville, 80	M 4
†	74437	Bryant, 86	P 4
	73834	Buffalo⊙, 1,579	G 1
	74931	Bunch, 90	S 3
	74633	Burbank, 188	N 1
	73722	Burlington, 165	K 1
	73430	Burneyville, 106	M 7
	73624	Burns Flat, 988	H 4
	73625	Butler, 315	H 3
	74831	Byars, 247	N 5
†	74820	Byng, 50	N 5
	73723	Byron, 72	K 1
	73527	Cache, 1,106	J 5
	74729	Caddo, 886	O 6
	74730	Calera, 1,063	O 7
	73014	Calumet, 386	K 3
	74531	Calvin, 359	O 5
	73835	Camargo, 236	H 2
	74932	Cameron, 311	T 4
	74425	Canadian, 304	P 4
	74533	Caney, 200	O 6
	73724	Canton, 844	J 2
	73626	Canute, 420	H 4
	73725	Capron, 80	J 1
	74335	Cardin, 950	S 1
	73726	Carmen, 519	J 1
	73015	Carnegie, 1,723	J 4
	74832	Carney, 396	N 3
	73727	Carrier, 125	K 2
	73627	Carter, 311	H 4
†	74633	Carter Nine, 50	N 1
	74934	Cartersville, 119	S 4
	73016	Cashion, 329	L 3
	74833	Castle, 212	O 4
	74015	Catoosa, 970	P 2
	73017	Cement, 892	K 5
†	74820	Center, 100	N 5
	74534	Centrahoma, 155	O 5
	74336	Centralia, 43	R 1
	74834	Chandler⊙, 2,529	N 3
	73528	Chattanooga, 302	J 6
	74426	Checotah, 3,074	R 4
	74016	Chelsea, 1,622	P 1
	73728	Cherokee⊙, 2,119	K 1
	73838	Chester, 135	J 2
	73628	Cheyenne⊙, 892	G 3
	73018	Chickasha⊙, 14,194	L 4
	74635	Chilocco, 712	M 1
	73020	Choctaw, 4,750	M 3
	74337	Chouteau, 1,046	R 2
†	74965	Christie, 70	S 3
	74017	Claremore⊙, 9,084	R 2
	74535	Clarita, 90	O 6
	74536	Clayton, 718	R 5
	74835	Clearview, 350	O 4
†	73437	Clemscot, 150	L 6
†	74331	Cleora, 87	S 1
	73729	Cleo Springs, 344	K 2
	74020	Cleveland, 2,573	O 2
	73601	Clinton, 8,513	H 3
	73632	Cloud Chief, 40	J 4
	74537	Cloudy, 175	R 6
	74538	Coalgate⊙, 1,859	O 5
†	73059	Cogar, 40	K 4
	74733	Colbert, 814	O 7
	74338	Colcord, 438	S 2
†	73010	Cole, 75	L 4
	73432	Coleman, 125	O 6
	74021	Collinsville, 3,009	P 2
	73021	Colony, 250	J 4
	73529	Comanche, 1,862	L 6
	74339	Commerce, 2,593	R 1
	73022	Concho, 500	L 3
	74836	Connerville, 150	N 6
	73023	Cooperton, 55	J 5
	74022	Copan, 558	P 1
	73632	Cordell⊙, 3,261	H 4
†	74751	Corinne, 100	R 6
	73024	Corn, 409	J 4
†	73456	Cornish, 90	L 6
	74428	Council Hill, 135	P 3
	73025	Countyline, 500	L 6
	73730	Covington, 605	L 2
	74429	Coweta, 2,457	P 3
†	74934	Cowlington, 751	S 4
	73082	Cox City, 285	L 5
	73027	Coyle, 303	M 3
	73028	Crescent, 1,568	L 3
	74837	Cromwell, 287	N 4
	74430	Crowder, 339	P 4
	73433	Cumberland, 150	N 6
	74023	Cushing, 7,529	N 3
	73639	Custer, 486	J 3
	73029	Cyril, 1,302	K 5
	73731	Dacoma, 226	J 1
	74540	Daisy, 250	P 5
	74838	Dale, 155	M 4
†	74523	Darwin, 50	P 6
	74026	Davenport, 831	N 3
	73530	Davidson, 515	J 6
	73030	Davis, 2,223	M 5
	74636	Deer Creek, 203	L 1
	74027	Delaware, 534	P 1
	73115	Del City, 27,133	L 4
	73640	Delhi, 41	G 4
	74028	Depew, 739	O 3
	73531	Devol, 129	J 6
	74431	Dewar, 933	P 4
	74029	Dewey, 3,958	P 1
†	74868	Dewright, 100	N 4
	73031	Dibble, 184	L 4
†	73401	Dickson, 798	M 6
	73641	Dill City, 578	H 4
	74340	Disney, 303	S 2
	73032	Dougherty, 211	M 6
	73733	Douglas, 79	L 2
	73734	Dover, 566	L 3
	74541	Dow, 300	P 5
	73735	Drummond, 326	L 2
	74030	Drumright, 2,931	O 3
	73532	Duke, 486	G 5
	73533	Duncan⊙, 19,718	L 5
	74701	Durant⊙, 11,118	O 6
	73642	Durham, 43	G 3
	74839	Dustin, 502	O 4
	73643	Eagle City, 56	J 3
	74734	Eagletown, 850	S 6
	73033	Eakly, 228	K 4
	74840	Earlsboro, 248	N 4
†	73532	East Duke, 250	H 5
	73034	Edmond, 16,633	M 3
	73537	Eldorado, 737	G 6
	73538	Elgin, 840	K 5
	73644	Elk City, 7,323	G 4
	73539	Elmer, 138	H 6
	73035	Elmore City, 653	M 5
	73036	El Reno⊙, 14,510	K 3
	73701	Enid⊙, 44,008	L 2
†	74561	Enterprise, 130	R 4
	73645	Erick, 1,285	G 4
	74342	Eucha, 66	S 2
	74432	Eufaula⊙, 2,355	P 4
	74637	Fairfax, 1,889	N 1
	74343	Fairland, 814	S 1
	73736	Fairmont, 154	L 2
	73737	Fairview⊙, 2,894	J 2
	74935	Fanshawe, 199	S 5
	73840	Fargo, 262	G 2
	74542	Farris, 100	P 6
	73540	Faxon, 121	J 6
	73646	Fay, 75	J 3
†	74561	Featherston, 75	P 4
	73937	Felt, 105	A 1
	73434	Fillmore, 250	N 6
	74543	Finley, 400	R 6
	74842	Fittstown, 325	N 5
	74843	Fitzhugh, 212	N 5
	73541	Fletcher, 950	K 5
	74638	Foraker, 52	Q 1
†	73101	Forest Park, 835	M 3
	73938	Forgan, 496	E 1
	73038	Fort Cobb, 722	K 4
	74434	Fort Gibson, 1,418	R 3
	73841	Fort Supply, 550	G 1
	74735	Fort Towson, 430	R 7
	73647	Foss, 150	H 4
	73039	Foster, 50	M 5
	73435	Fox, 400	M 6
	74031	Foyil, 164	R 2
	74844	Francis, 283	N 5
	73542	Frederick⊙, 6,132	H 6
	73842	Freedom, 292	H 1
	73843	Gage, 536	G 2
	74936	Gans, 238	S 4
	73738	Garber, 1,011	M 2
	74736	Garvin, 117	S 7
	73844	Gate, 151	F 1
	73040	Geary, 1,380	K 3
	73436	Gene Autry, 120	N 6
	73543	Geronimo, 587	K 6
	74544	Gerty, 139	O 5
	74032	Glencoe, 421	M 2
	74033	Glenpool, 770	P 3
	74728	Glover, 244	S 6
	74737	Golden, 275	S 6
†	73093	Goldsby, 298	M 4
	73739	Goltry, 282	K 1
†	74740	Goodwater, 100	S 7
	73939	Goodwell, 1,467	C 1
	74435	Gore, 478	R 3
	73041	Gotebo, 376	J 4

(continued on following page)

Agriculture, Industry and Resources

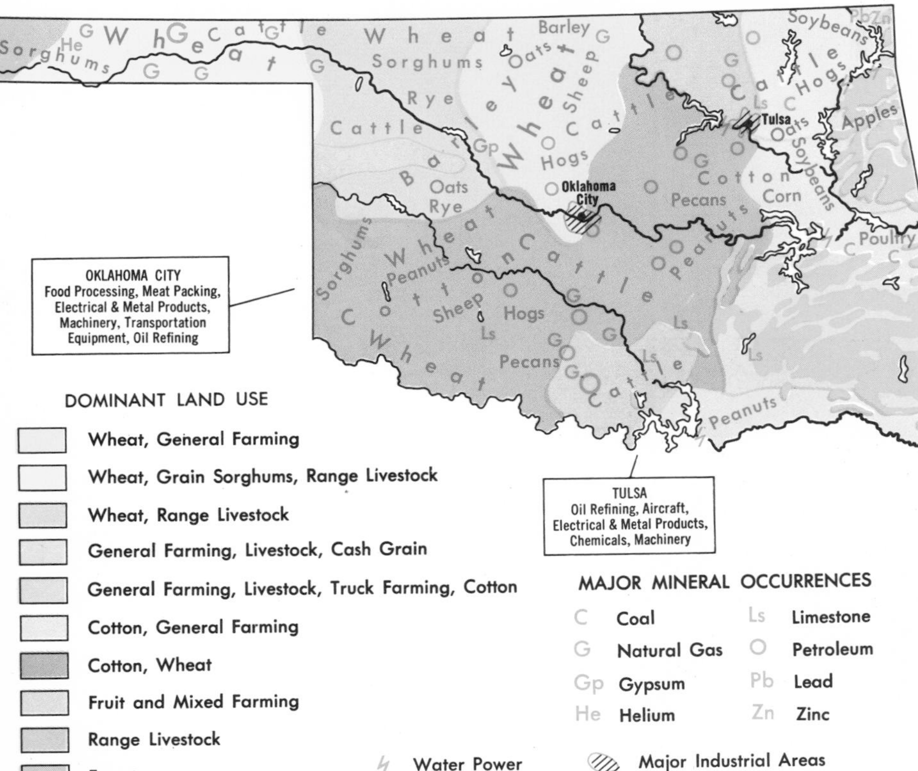

Aesthetic drawbacks are outweighed by substantial revenues from oil wells obstructing the view of Oklahoma's capitol building.

(continued)

73544 Gould, 368 ..... G 5
74545 Gowen, 350 ..... R 5
73042 Gracemont, 424 ..... K 4
73437 Graham, 250 ..... M 6
74639 Grainola, 66 ..... N 1
73546 Grandfield, 1,524 ..... J 6
73547 Granite, 1,808 ..... H 5
74738 Grant, 273 ..... R 7
† 74437 Grayson (Wildcat), 142 ..... P 3
73043 Greenfield, 143 ..... K 3
74344 Grove, 2,000 ..... S 1
73044 Guthrie⊙, 9,575 ..... M 3
73942 Guymon⊙, 7,674 ..... D 1
74546 Haileyville, 928 ..... P 5
74034 Hallett, 125 ..... N 2
73650 Hammon, 677 ..... H 3
74845 Hanna, 181 ..... P 4
† 74955 Hanson, 250 ..... S 4
74846 Harden City, 150 ..... N 5
73944 Hardesty, 223 ..... D 1
73045 Harrah, 1,931 ..... M 4
74739 Harris, 200 ..... S 7
74547 Hartshorne, 2,121 ..... R 5
74436 Haskell, 2,063 ..... P 3
73548 Hastings, 184 ..... K 6
74740 Haworth, 293 ..... S 7
74548 Haywood, 175 ..... P 5
73549 Headrick, 139 ..... H 5
73438 Healdton, 2,324 ..... M 6
74937 Heavener, 2,566 ..... S 5
73741 Helena, 769 ..... K 1
74741 Hendrix, 117 ..... O 7
73046 Hennepin, 306 ..... M 5
73742 Hennessey, 2,181 ..... L 2
74437 Henryetta, 6,430 ..... O 4
† 73539 Hess, 65 ..... H 6
† 73086 Hickory, 62 ..... N 5
73743 Hillsdale, 77 ..... K 1
73047 Hinton, 889 ..... K 4
73744 Hitchcock, 160 ..... K 3
74438 Hitchita, 160 ..... P 3
73651 Hobart⊙, 4,638 ..... J 5
74345 Hockerville, 125 ..... S 1
74939 Hodgen, 150 ..... S 5
74439 Hoffman, 262 ..... P 4
74848 Holdenville⊙, 5,181 ..... O 4
73550 Hollis⊙, 3,150 ..... G 5
73551 Hollister, 105 ..... J 6
73745 Homestead, 75 ..... K 2
74035 Hominy, 2,274 ..... O 2
74549 Honobia, 250 ..... R 5
73945 Hooker, 1,615 ..... D 1
73746 Hopeton, 75 ..... J 1
74940 Howe, 403 ..... S 5
74440 Hoyt, 110 ..... R 4
74743 Hugo⊙, 6,585 ..... R 6
† 67333 Hulah, 50 ..... O 1
74441 Hulbert, 505 ..... R 3
† 73521 Humphreys, 44 ..... H 5
74640 Hunter, 274 ..... L 1
73048 Hydro, 805 ..... J 3
74745 Idabel⊙, 5,946 ..... S 7
73552 Indiahoma, 434 ..... J 5
74442 Indianola, 205 ..... P 4
74036 Inola, 948 ..... P 2
73747 Isabella, 89 ..... K 2
74346 Jay⊙, 1,594 ..... S 2
73748 Jefferson, 128 ..... L 1
74037 Jenks, 1,997 ..... P 2
74038 Jennings, 338 ..... N 2
73749 Jet, 317 ..... K 1
73049 Jones, 1,666 ..... M 3
74551 Jumbo, 40 ..... P 6
74347 Kansas, 317 ..... S 2
74641 Kaw, 283 ..... N 1
† 74401 Keefeton, 70 ..... R 3
74039 Kellyville, 685 ..... O 3
74747 Kemp, 153 ..... O 7
† 74741 Kemp City (Hendrix), 117 ..... O 7
74040 Kendrick, 126 ..... N 3
74748 Kenefic, 153 ..... O 6
74348 Kenwood, 125 ..... S 2
74941 Keota, 685 ..... S 4
74349 Ketchum, 238 ..... R 1
73947 Keyes, 569 ..... B 1
† 74574 Kiamichi, 100 ..... R 5
74041 Kiefer, 803 ..... O 3
74642 Kildare, 79 ..... M 1
73750 Kingfisher⊙, 4,042 ..... L 3
73439 Kingston, 710 ..... N 7
74552 Kinta, 247 ..... R 4
74553 Kiowa, 754 ..... P 5

73847 Knowles, 52 ..... F 1
74849 Konawa, 1,719 ..... N 5
† 74557 Kosoma, 50 ..... P 6
74554 Krebs, 1,515 ..... P 5
73753 Kremlin, 200 ..... L 1
73754 Lahoma, 299 ..... K 2
74850 Lamar, 153 ..... O 4
74643 Lamont, 478 ..... L 1
74555 Lane, 218 ..... O 6
74350 Langley, 481 ..... R 2
73050 Langston, 486 ..... M 3
73848 Laverne, 1,373 ..... G 1
73501 Lawton⊙, 74,470 ..... K 5
Lawton, ‡108,144 ..... K 5
74351 Leach, 75 ..... S 2
73440 Lebanon, 240 ..... N 7
73654 Leedey, 465 ..... H 3
74942 Leflore, 175 ..... S 5
74556 Lehigh, 296 ..... O 6
74042 Lenapah, 325 ..... P 1
73441 Leon, 112 ..... M 7
74043 Leonard, 115 ..... P 3
74943 Lequire, 100 ..... R 4
73051 Lexington, 1,516 ..... M 4
† 74858 Lima (New Lima), 238 ..... D 4
73052 Lindsay, 3,705 ..... L 5
† 74637 Little Chief, 40 ..... N 1
† 73446 Little City, 80 ..... N 6
73442 Loco, 193 ..... L 6
74352 Locust Grove, 1,090 ..... R 2
73443 Lone Grove, 1,240 ..... M 6
73655 Lone Wolf, 584 ..... H 5
73755 Longdale, 331 ..... K 2
73053 Lookeba, 165 ..... K 4
73756 Loyal, 107 ..... K 3

73757 Lucien, 150 ..... M 2
† 74825 Lula, 40 ..... O 5
73054 Luther, 836 ..... M 3
† 74578 Lutie, 250 ..... R 5
74852 Macomb, 41 ..... M 4
73446 Madill⊙, 2,875 ..... N 6
73758 Manchester, 165 ..... L 1
73554 Mangum⊙, 4,066 ..... G 5
73555 Manitou, 308 ..... J 5
74044 Mannford, 892 ..... O 2
73447 Mannsville, 364 ..... N 6
74045 Maramec, 128 ..... N 2
74945 Marble City, 299 ..... S 3
73448 Marietta⊙, 2,013 ..... M 7
74644 Marland, 236 ..... M 1
73055 Marlow, 3,995 ..... K 5
73056 Marshall, 420 ..... L 2
73556 Martha, 268 ..... H 5
74853 Mason, 75 ..... O 3
74854 Maud, 1,143 ..... N 4
73851 May, 91 ..... G 1
73057 Maysville, 1,380 ..... M 5
74353 Mazie, 300 ..... R 2
74501 McAlester⊙, 18,802 ..... P 5
74944 McCurtain, 575 ..... R 4
74851 McLoud, 2,159 ..... M 4
73449 Mead, 210 ..... O 7
73759 Medford⊙, 1,304 ..... L 1
73557 Medicine Park, 562 ..... J 5
74855 Meeker, 683 ..... N 4
† 74074 Mehan, 60 ..... M 2
73760 Meno, 119 ..... K 2
73058 Meridian, 104 ..... M 3
74354 Miami⊙, 13,880 ..... S 1
† 74882 Micawber, 41 ..... N 3

73110 Midwest City, 48,114 ..... M 4
73450 Milburn, 275 ..... O 6
74046 Milfay, 150 ..... N 3
74856 Mill Creek, 234 ..... N 6
74750 Millerton, 350 ..... S 7
73451 Milo, 85 ..... M 6
† 74944 Milton, 90 ..... S 4
73059 Minco, 1,129 ..... L 4
74946 Moffett, 312 ..... S 4
74947 Monroe, 300 ..... S 4
74444 Moodys, 200 ..... S 2
† 71821 Moon, 50 ..... S 7
73060 Moore, 18,761 ..... M 4
73852 Mooreland, 1,196 ..... H 2
74445 Morris, 1,119 ..... P 3
73061 Morrison, 421 ..... M 2
74047 Mounds, 766 ..... O 3
73559 Mountain Park, 458 ..... J 5
73062 Mountain View, 1,110 ..... J 4
74557 Moyers, 125 ..... P 6
74948 Muldrow, 1,680 ..... S 4
73063 Mulhall, 250 ..... M 2
74949 Muse, 75 ..... S 5
74401 Muskogee⊙, 37,331 ..... R 3
73064 Mustang, 2,637 ..... L 4
73853 Mutual, 94 ..... H 2
74646 Nardin, 135 ..... M 1
73761 Nash, 294 ..... K 1
74558 Nashoba, 100 ..... R 6
† 74056 Nelagoney, 62 ..... O 1
74857 Newalla, 350 ..... M 4
74049 New Alluwe, 116 ..... R 1
73065 Newcastle, 1,271 ..... L 4
† 73632 New Cordell (Cordell)⊙, 3,261 ..... H 4

74647 Newkirk⊙, 2,173 ..... N 1
74858 New Lima, 238 ..... O 4
† 74060 New Prue (Prue), 202 ..... O 2
† 73466 New Woodville (Woodville), 118 ..... N 7
† 73101 Nichols Hills, 4,478 ..... L 3
73066 Nicoma Park, 2,560 ..... M 4
73067 Ninnekah, 300 ..... L 5
73068 Noble, 2,241 ..... M 4
73069 Norman⊙, 52,117 ..... M 4
† 73701 North Enid, 730 ..... L 2
74358 North Miami, 503 ..... R 1
74048 Nowata⊙, 3,679 ..... P 1
74050 Oakhurst, 500 ..... P 2
73452 Oakland, 317 ..... N 6
74359 Oaks, 219 ..... S 2
73658 Oakwood, 129 ..... J 3
74051 Ochelata, 330 ..... P 1
74958 Octavia, 40 ..... S 5
74052 Oilton, 1,087 ..... N 2
73762 Okarche, 826 ..... L 3
74446 Okay, 419 ..... R 3
73763 Okeene, 1,421 ..... K 2
74859 Okemah⊙, 2,913 ..... O 4
† 74003 Okesa, 165 ..... O 1
* 73101 Oklahoma City (cap.)⊙, 366,481 ..... L 4
Oklahoma City, ‡640,889 ..... L 4
74447 Okmulgee⊙, 15,180 ..... O 3
74450 Oktaha, 193 ..... R 3
74751 Oleta, 50 ..... R 6
† 74030 Olive, 100 ..... O 2
† 74538 Olney, 42 ..... O 6
73560 Olustee, 819 ..... H 5
74053 Oologah, 458 ..... P 2

73948 Optima, 103 ..... D 1
73073 Orlando, 202 ..... M 2
74054 Osage, 170 ..... O 2
73561 Oscar, 61 ..... L 7
73453 Overbrook, 120 ..... M 6
74055 Owasso, 3,491 ..... P 2
74860 Paden, 442 ..... N 3
74951 Panama, 1,121 ..... S 4
74559 Panola, 100 ..... R 5
73074 Paoli, 480 ..... M 5
74451 Park Hill, 125 ..... R 3
† 74824 Parkland, 55 ..... N 3
73075 Pauls Valley⊙, 5,769 ..... M 5
74056 Pawhuska⊙, 4,238 ..... O 1
74058 Pawnee⊙, 2,443 ..... N 2
74861 Pearson, 60 ..... N 4
74648 Peckham, 65 ..... M 1
74452 Peggs, 82 ..... R 2
† 74301 Pensacola, 56 ..... R 2
† 66713 Peoria, 179 ..... S 1
74059 Perkins, 1,029 ..... M 3
73076 Pernell, 117 ..... M 5
73077 Perry⊙, 5,341 ..... M 2
74862 Pharoah, 100 ..... O 4
† 74538 Phillips, 106 ..... O 6
74360 Picher, 2,363 ..... S 1
74752 Pickens, 350 ..... S 6
73078 Piedmont, 269 ..... L 3
74560 Pittsburg, 282 ..... P 5
74753 Platter, 275 ..... O 7
74952 Plunkettville, 125 ..... S 6
73079 Pocasset, 200 ..... L 4
74902 Pocola, 1,840 ..... T 4
74601 Ponca City, 25,940 ..... M 1
73766 Pondcreek, 903 ..... L 1

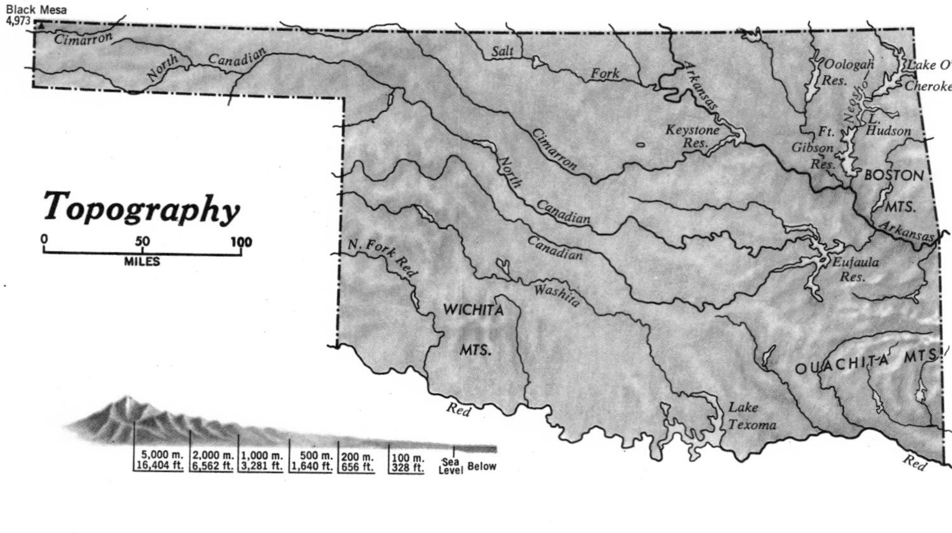

OKLAHOMA

SCALE
0 5 10 20 30 40 MI.
0 5 10 20 30 40 KM.

State Capitals ⊛
County Seats ⊙

© C.S. HAMMOND & Co., N.Y.

Topography

0 50 100 MILES

5,000 m. 16,404 ft. | 2,000 m. 6,562 ft. | 1,000 m. 3,281 ft. | 500 m. 1,640 ft. | 200 m. 656 ft. | 100 m. 328 ft. | Sea Level | Below

Zip	Place, population	Key
74863	Pontotoc, 150	N 6
73454	Pooleville, 75	M 6
74454	Porter, 624	R 3
74455	Porum, 658	R 4
74953	Poteau⊙, 5,500	S 4
74864	Prague, 1,802	N 4
74456	Preston, 300	P 3
74457	Proctor, 175	S 3
74060	Prue, 202	O 2
74361	Pryor⊙, 7,057	R 2
73080	Purcell⊙, 4,076	M 4
73659	Putnam, 84	J 3
74363	Quapaw, 967	S 1
74085	Quay, 41	N 2
73852	Quinlan, 81	J 2
74561	Quinton, 1,262	R 4
74650	Ralston, 443	N 2
74061	Ramona, 600	P 1
73562	Randlett, 384	K 6
73081	Ratliff City, 250	M 6
74562	Rattan, 350	R 6
73455	Ravia, 373	N 6
73460	Reagan, 175	N 6
74458	Redbird, 230	P 3
74563	Red Oak, 609	R 5
74651	Redrock, 233	M 2
73563	Reed, 64	G 5
74459	Rentiesville, 96	R 4
73660	Reydon, 215	G 3
73456	Ringling, 1,206	L 6
73768	Ringwood, 241	K 2
74062	Ripley, 307	N 2
74701	Roberta, 45	O 7
74933	Rock Island, 97	T 4
73661	Rocky, 260	J 4
74865	Roff, 632	N 5
74954	Roland, 827	S 4
73564	Roosevelt, 353	J 5
74364	Rose, 120	R 2
74831	Rosedale, 98	M 5
73855	Rosston, 56	G 1
73457	Rubottom, 110	M 7
74755	Rufe, 54	R 6
73082	Rush Springs, 1,381	L 5
73565	Ryan, 1,011	L 6
† 74017	Sageeyah, 49	P 2
74866	Saint Louis, 207	N 4
74365	Salina, 1,024	R 2
74955	Sallisaw⊙, 4,888	S 4
74063	Sand Springs, 11,519	O 2
74066	Sapulpa⊙, 15,159	O 3
74564	Sardis, 58	R 5
74867	Sasakwa, 321	N 5
74565	Savanna, 948	P 5
74756	Sawyer, 210	R 7
73662	Sayre⊙, 2,712	G 4
74460	Schulter, 200	P 3
74566	Scipio, 100	P 4
73663	Seiling, 1,033	J 2
73856	Selman, 93	H 1
74868	Seminole, 7,878	N 4
73664	Sentinel, 984	H 4
74956	Shady Point, 350	S 4
74068	Shamrock, 204	N 3
73857	Sharon, 155	H 2
73858	Shattuck, 1,546	G 2
74801	Shawnee⊙, 25,075	N 4
74757	Sherwood, 60	S 6
74652	Shidler, 717	N 1
† 72955	Short, 200	S 3
74069	Skedee, 117	N 2
74070	Skiatook, 2,930	O 2
74071	Slick, 171	O 3
74957	Smithville, 144	S 6
74567	Snow, 150	R 6
73566	Snyder, 1,671	J 5
74759	Soper, 322	P 6
73770	Southard, 130	K 2
74072	South Coffeyville, 646	P 1
74869	Sparks, 183	N 3
74366	Spavinaw, 470	R 2
73084	Spencer, 3,603	M 3
74760	Spencerville, 275	R 6
74073	Sperry, 1,123	P 2
74959	Spiro, 2,057	S 4
73458	Springer, 256	M 6
73567	Sterling, 675	K 5
74461	Stidham, 53	P 4
74462	Stigler⊙, 2,347	R 4
74074	Stillwater⊙, 31,126	N 2
74960	Stilwell⊙, 2,134	S 3
† 74436	Stonebluff, 50	P 3
74871	Stonewall, 653	O 5
74367	Strang, 164	R 2
74872	Stratford, 1,278	M 5
74569	Stringtown, 397	P 5
74079	Stroud, 2,502	N 3
74570	Stuart, 294	O 5
† 73565	Sugden, 54	L 6
73086	Sulphur⊙, 5,158	N 5
74966	Summerfield, 210	S 5
74761	Swink, 88	R 6
74463	Taft, 525	R 3
74464	Tahlequah⊙, 9,254	R 3
74080	Talala, 163	P 1
74571	Talihina, 1,227	S 5
73667	Taloga⊙, 363	J 2
† 74462	Tamaha, 83	S 4
73087	Tatums, 502	M 6
74873	Tecumseh, 4,451	N 4
73568	Temple, 1,354	K 6
74081	Terlton, 111	O 2
73569	Terral, 636	L 7
73949	Texhoma, 921	C 1
73668	Texola, 144	G 4
73459	Thackerville, 257	M 7
73120	The Village, 13,695	L 3
73669	Thomas, 1,336	J 3
† 74017	Tiawah, 119	P 2
73570	Tipton, 1,206	H 6
73460	Tishomingo⊙, 2,663	N 6
74762	Tom, 600	S 7
74653	Tonkawa, 3,337	M 1
† 74852	Tribbey, 60	M 4
† 74856	Troy, 92	N 6
74875	Tryon, 301	N 3
74466	Tullahassee, 183	P 3
* 74101	Tulsa⊙, 331,638	O 2
	Tulsa, ‡476,945	O 2
74572	Tupelo, 485	O 5
73950	Turpin, 295	E 1
74573	Tushka, 400	O 6
74574	Tuskahoma, 200	R 5
73088	Tussy, 150	L 6
73089	Tuttle, 1,640	L 4
73951	Tyrone, 588	D 1
74601	Uncas, 53	M 1
73090	Union, 306	L 4
74763	Utica, 177	O 7
† 73101	Valley Brook, 2,869	M 4
74764	Valliant, 840	R 6
74876	Vanoss, 130	N 5
73091	Velma, 611	L 6
74082	Vera, 215	P 2
73092	Verden, 439	K 4
† 74017	Verdigris, 307	P 2
74877	Vernon, 84	P 4
74962	Vian, 1,131	S 4
73859	Vici, 694	H 2
74301	Vinita⊙, 5,847	R 1
73571	Vinson, 51	G 5
74765	Wade, 50	O 7
74467	Wagoner⊙, 4,959	R 3
74468	Wainwright, 135	R 3
73771	Wakita, 426	L 1
73572	Walters⊙, 2,611	K 6
74878	Wanette, 303	M 5
74083	Wann, 135	P 1
73461	Wapanucka, 425	N 6
74576	Wardville, 100	P 5
74469	Warner, 1,217	R 4
73123	Warr Acres, 9,887	L 3
73573	Warwick, 146	M 3
73093	Washington, 322	M 4
73094	Washita, 160	K 4
73772	Watonga⊙, 3,696	K 3
74963	Watson, 48	S 6
74964	Watts, 326	S 2
73773	Waukomis, 241	K 2
73573	Waurika⊙, 1,833	L 6
73095	Wayne, 618	M 5
73860	Waynoka, 1,444	J 1
73096	Weatherford, 7,959	J 4
† 74560	Weathers, 100	P 5
74654	Webb City, 186	N 1
74470	Webbers Falls, 485	R 3
74369	Welch, 651	R 1
74880	Weleetka, 1,199	O 4
74471	Welling, 50	S 3
74881	Wellston, 789	M 3
74882	Welty, 89	O 3
† 72761	West Siloam Springs, 210	S 2
74965	Westville, 934	S 2
74883	Wetumka, 1,687	O 4
74884	Wewoka⊙, 5,284	O 4
74472	Whitefield, 250	R 4
† 74301	Whiteoak, 200	R 1
74577	Whitesboro, 300	S 5
74578	Wilburton⊙, 2,280	R 5
† 74437	Wildcat, 142	P 3
73462	Willis, 250	N 7
73673	Willow, 188	G 4
73463	Wilson, 1,569	M 6
73464	Wirt, 350	L 6
74966	Wister, 927	S 5
73466	Woodville, 118	N 7
73801	Woodward⊙, 8,710	H 2
74766	Wright City, 1,068	R 6
74370	Wyandotte, 297	S 1
73098	Wynnewood, 2,374	M 5
74084	Wynona, 547	O 1
74085	Yale, 1,239	N 2
† 74574	Yanush, 350	R 5
74885	Yeager, 107	O 4
74767	Yuba, 63	O 7
73099	Yukon, 8,411	L 3

⊙ County seat.
‡ Population of metropolitan area.
† Zip of nearest p.o.
* Multiple zips

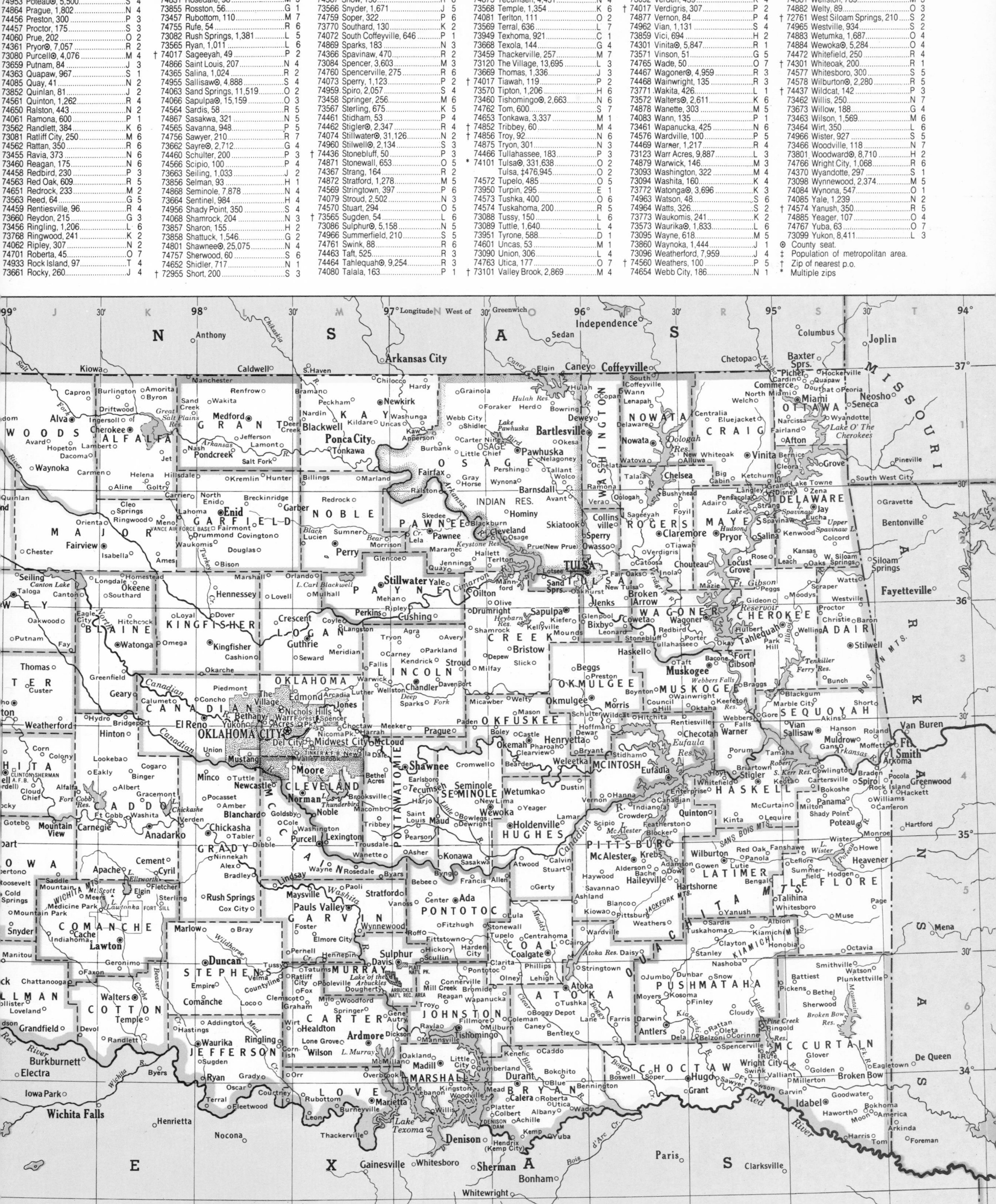

COUNTIES

County, Pop.	Key
Baker, 14,919	K 3
Benton, 53,776	D 3
Clackamas, 166,088	E 2
Clatsop, 28,473	D 1
Columbia, 28,790	D 2
Coos, 56,515	C 4
Crook, 9,985	G 3
Curry, 13,006	C 5
Deschutes, 30,442	F 4
Douglas, 71,743	D 4
Gilliam, 2,342	G 2
Grant, 6,996	J 3
Harney, 7,215	H 4
Hood River, 13,187	F 2
Jackson, 94,533	E 5
Jefferson, 8,548	F 3
Josephine, 35,746	D 5
Klamath, 50,021	F 5
Lake, 6,343	G 5
Lane, 213,358	E 4
Lincoln, 25,755	D 3
Linn, 71,914	E 3
Malheur, 23,169	K 4
Marion, 151,309	E 3
Morrow, 4,465	H 2
Multnomah, 556,667	E 2
Polk, 35,349	D 3
Sherman, 2,139	G 2
Tillamook, 17,930	D 2
Umatilla, 44,923	J 2
Union, 19,377	J 2
Wallowa, 6,247	K 2
Wasco, 20,133	F 2
Washington, 157,920	D 2
Wheeler, 1,849	G 3
Yamhill, 40,213	D 2

CITIES and TOWNS

Zip	Name/Pop.	Key
97810	Adams, 219	J 2
97620	Adel, 200	H 5
97901	Adrian, 200	K 4
97320	Agate Beach, 975	C 3
97406	Agness, 120	C 5
† 97361	Airlie, 45	D 3
97321	Albany⊙, 18,181	D 3
† 97601	Algoma, 77	F 5
97811	Alicel, 30	J 2
97407	Allegany, 200	D 4
97006	Aloha, 6,000	A 2
97408	Alpine, 80	D 3
97324	Alsea, 600	D 3
† 97601	Altamont, 15,746	F 5
97409	Alvadore, 350	D 3
97101	Amity, 708	D 2
97001	Antelope, 51	G 3
97530	Applegate, 125	D 5
97458	Arago, 200	C 4
97812	Arlington, 375	G 2
† 97473	Ash, 80	D 4
97520	Ashland, 12,342	E 5
97103	Astoria⊙, 10,244	D 1
97813	Athena, 872	J 2
97325	Aumsville, 590	E 3
97002	Aurora, 306	B 2
† 97817	Austin, 170	J 3
97410	Azalea, 40	D 5
97814	Baker⊙, 9,354	K 3
† 97378	Ballston, 120	D 2
† 97458	Bancroft, 25	D 5
97411	Bandon, 1,832	C 4
97106	Banks, 430	A 1
97003	Barlow, 105	B 2
† 97009	Barton, 100	B 2
† 97136	Bar View, 75	C 2
97817	Bates, 430	J 3
97107	Bay City, 898	D 2
97621	Beatty, 50	F 5
97108	Beaver, 450	D 2
97004	Beavercreek, 708	B 2
97005	Beaverton, 18,577	A 2
† 97456	Bellfountain, 50	D 3
97701	Bend⊙, 13,710	F 3
† 97058	Biggs, 50	G 2
97016	Birkenfeld, 45	D 1
97412	Blachly, 425	D 3
† 97108	Blaine, 150	D 2
97326	Blodgett, 150	D 3
97413	Blue River, 350	E 3
97622	Bly, 500	F 5
97818	Boardman, 192	H 2
97623	Bonanza, 230	F 5
97008	Bonneville, 130	F 2
97009	Boring, 150	E 2
† 97021	Boyd, 26	F 2
† 97342	Breitenbush, 50	F 3
97010	Bridal Veil, 155	E 2
† 97458	Bridge, 250	D 4
97819	Bridgeport, 45	K 3
† 97136	Brighton, 52	C 2
97001	Brightwood, 420	E 2
† 97032	Broadacres, 80	A 3
97414	Broadbent, 265	C 4
97903	Brogan, 140	K 3
97415	Brookings, 2,720	C 5
97305	Brooks, 490	A 3
† 97840	Brownlee, 50	L 3
† 97524	Brownsboro, 150	E 5
97327	Brownsville, 1,034	E 3
† 97351	Buena Vista, 90	D 3
† 97420	Bunker Hill, 1,549	C 4
97720	Burns⊙, 3,293	H 4
97522	Butte Falls, 358	E 5
† 97002	Butteville, 385	A 2
97109	Buxton, 163	D 2
97416	Camas Valley, 665	D 4
97730	Camp Sherman, 87	F 3
† 97493	Canary, 50	D 4
97013	Canby, 3,813	B 2
97110	Cannon Beach, 779	D 2
97820	Canyon City⊙, 600	J 3
97417	Canyonville, 940	D 5
97111	Carlton, 1,126	D 2
† 97415	Carpenterville, 30	C 5
† 97015	Carver, 500	B 2
97014	Cascade Locks, 574	E 2
97329	Cascadia, 150	E 3
97523	Cave Junction, 415	D 5
97821	Cayuse, 300	J 2
97822	Cecil, 75	H 2
97225	Cedar Hills, 2,900	A 2
† 97005	Cedar Mill, 1,500	A 2
† 97058	Celilo, 50	G 2
97501	Central Point, 4,004	D 5
97420	Charleston, 500	C 4
97306	Chemawa, 900	A 3
97731	Chemult, 580	F 4
† 97058	Chenoweth, 2,329	F 2
97119	Cherry Grove, 200	D 2
† 97055	Cherryville, 280	E 2
97419	Cheshire, 750	D 3
97624	Chiloquin, 826	F 5
97015	Clackamas, 6,000	B 2
97016	Clatskanie, 1,286	D 1
97112	Cloverdale, 151	D 2
97401	Coburg, 665	E 3
97017	Colton, 305	B 3

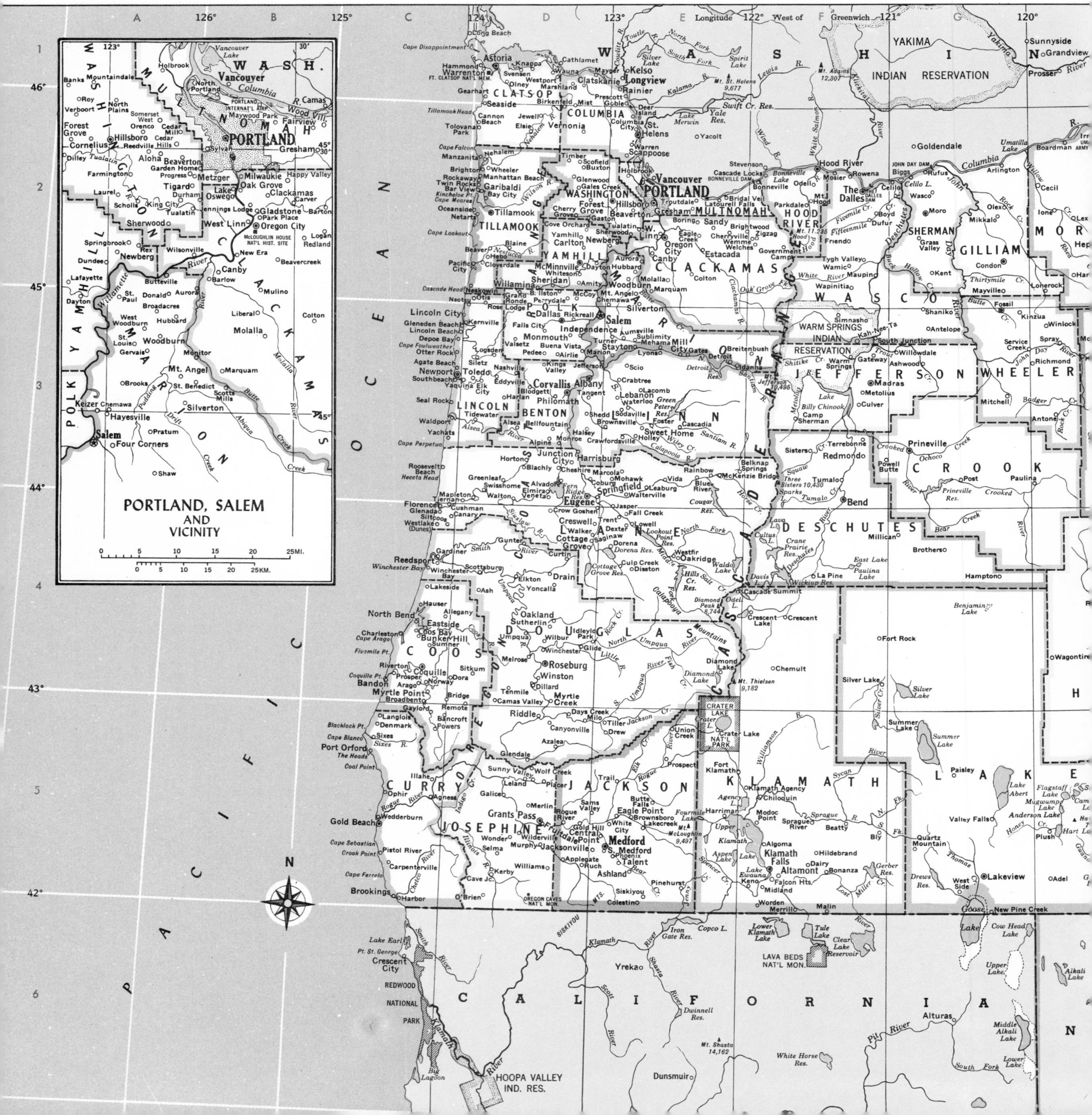

97018 Columbia City, 537 E 2
97823 Condon⊙, 973 G 2
97420 Coos Bay, 13,466 C 4
97423 Coquille⊙, 4,437 C 4
97113 Cornelius, 1,903 A 2
97330 Corvallis⊙, 35,153 D 3
97424 Cottage Grove, 6,004 D 4
97824 Cove, 363 K 2
† 97148 Cove Orchard, 50 D 2
97335 Crabtree, 350 E 3
97732 Crane, 63 J 4
† 97601 Crater Lake, 30 E 5
97336 Crawfordsville, 350 E 3
97733 Crescent, 850 F 4
97425 Crescent Lake, 70 F 4
97426 Creswell, 1,199 D 4
† 97401 Crow, 200 D 4
97427 Culp Creek, 194 E 4
97734 Culver, 407 F 3
97428 Curtin, 300 D 4
† 97439 Cushman, 175 D 4
97625 Dairy, 74 F 5
97880 Dale, 25 J 3
97338 Dallas⊙, 6,361 D 3
† 97910 Danner, 40 K 5
97429 Days Creek, 602 D 5
97114 Dayton, 949 A 3
97825 Dayville, 197 H 3
97054 Deer Island, 120 E 2
97341 Depoe Bay, 450 C 3
97342 Detroit, 328 E 3
97431 Dexter, 450 E 4
97731 Diamond Lake, 56 E 4
97432 Dillard, 602 D 4
† 97116 Dilley, 250 A 2
97433 Disston, 123 E 4
97020 Donald, 231 A 3
† 97458 Dora, 30 D 4
97434 Dorena, 550 E 4
97435 Drain, 1,204 D 4
97484 Drew, 60 E 5
97021 Dufur, 493 F 2
97115 Dundee, 588 A 2
† 97493 Dunes (Westlake), 976 C 4
† 97233 Durham, 410 A 2
97905 Durkee, 140 K 3
97022 Eagle Creek, 250 E 2
97524 Eagle Point, 1,241 E 5
97420 Eastside, 1,331 C 4
97826 Echo, 479 H 2
97343 Eddyville, 50 D 3
97827 Elgin, 1,375 K 2
† 97391 Elk City, 30 D 3
97436 Elkton, 176 D 4
97437 Elmira, 950 D 3
† 97138 Elsie, 30 D 2
97828 Enterprise⊙, 1,680 K 2
97023 Estacada, 1,164 E 2
* 97401 Eugene⊙, 76,346 D 3
Eugene, ‡213,358 D 3
97024 Fairview, 1,045 B 2
† 97601 Falcon Heights, 1,389 F 5
97438 Fall Creek, 58 E 4
97344 Falls City, 745 D 3
97710 Fields, 150 J 5
† 97828 Flora, 25 K 2
97439 Florence, 2,246 C 4
97116 Forest Grove, 8,275 A 2
97626 Fort Klamath, 150 E 5
97735 Fort Rock, 75 G 4
97830 Fossil⊙, 511 G 2
97345 Foster, 850 E 3
97301 Four Corners, 6,199 A 3
97831 Fox, 75 H 3
97736 Frenchglen, 45 H 5

AREA 96,981 sq. mi.
POPULATION 2,091,385
CAPITAL Salem
LARGEST CITY Portland
HIGHEST POINT Mt. Hood 11,235 ft.
SETTLED IN 1810
ADMITTED TO UNION February 14, 1859
POPULAR NAME Beaver State
STATE FLOWER Oregon Grape
STATE BIRD Western Meadowlark

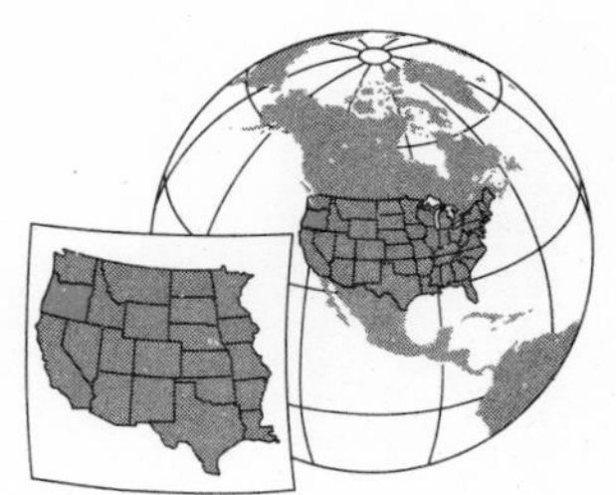

Topography

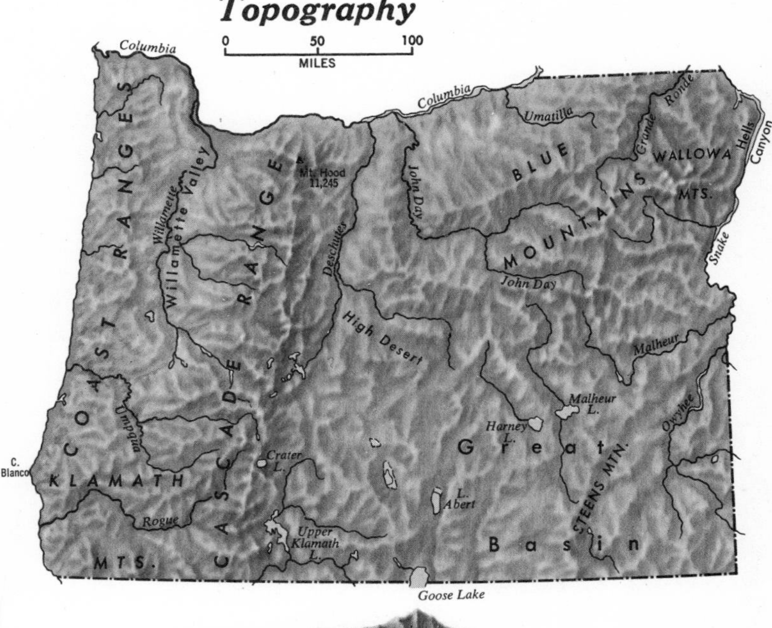

† 97526 Fruitdale, 2,655 D 5
97117 Gales Creek, 500 D 2
† 97532 Galice, 30 D 5
97223 Garden Home, 2,900 A 2
97441 Gardiner, 500 C 4
97118 Garibaldi, 1,083 D 2
97119 Gaston, 429 D 2
97346 Gates, 250 E 3
† 97741 Gateway, 95 F 3
97458 Gaylord, 125 C 5
97138 Gearhart, 829 C 1
97026 Gervais, 746 A 3
† 97810 Gibbon, 100 J 2
97027 Gladstone, 6,237 B 2
† 97439 Glenada, 75 C 4
97442 Glendale, 709 D 5
97388 Gleneden Beach, 400 C 3
97120 Glenwood, 500 D 2
97443 Glide, 470 D 4
97048 Goble, 108 E 1
97444 Gold Beach⊙, 1,554 C 5
97525 Gold Hill, 603 D 5
97401 Goshen, 98 D 4
97028 Government Camp, 175 F 2
97347 Grand Ronde, 289 D 2
97526 Grants Pass⊙, 12,455 D 5
97029 Grass Valley, 153 G 2
† 97470 Green, 1,612 D 4
97445 Greenleaf, 47 D 3
97030 Gresham, 9,875 B 2
97833 Haines, 212 J 3
97834 Halfway, 317 K 3
97348 Halsey, 467 D 3
97121 Hammond, 500 C 1
† 97222 Happy Valley, 1,392 B 2
97415 Harbor, 750 C 5
† 97343 Harlan, 35 D 3
97906 Harper, 102 K 4
† 97601 Harriman, 50 E 5
97446 Harrisburg, 1,311 D 3
† 97459 Hauser, 400 C 4
† 97301 Hayesville, 5,518 A 3
97122 Hebo, 350 D 2
97835 Helix, 152 J 2
97836 Heppner⊙, 1,429 H 2
97837 Hereford, 50 K 3
97838 Hermiston, 4,893 H 2
† 97625 Hildebrand, 50 F 5
97123 Hillsboro⊙, 14,675 A 2
97738 Hines, 1,407 H 4
† 97208 Holbrook, 494 A 1
† 97386 Holley, 250 E 3
97031 Hood River⊙, 3,991 F 2
97448 Horton, 188 D 3
† 97850 Hot Lake, 60 K 2
97032 Hubbard, 975 A 3
97907 Huntington, 507 K 3
97350 Idanha, 382 E 3
97447 Idleyld Park, 150 D 4
† 97406 Illahe, 30 C 5
97841 Imbler, 139 J 2
97842 Imnaha, 37 L 2
97351 Independence, 2,594 D 3
97843 Ione, 355 H 2
97908 Ironside, 36 K 3
97844 Irrigon, 261 H 2
97851 Island City, 202 K 2
97530 Jacksonville, 1,611 D 5
97909 Jamieson, 103 K 3
97401 Jasper, 231 E 3
97352 Jefferson, 936 D 3
97267 Jennings Lodge, 3,500 B 2
97845 John Day, 1,566 J 3
97910 Jordan Valley, 196 K 5
97846 Joseph, 839 K 2
97448 Junction City, 2,373 D 3
97911 Juntura, 56 K 4
† 97761 Kah-Nee-Ta, 50 F 3
97303 Keizer, 11,405 A 3
97627 Keno, 500 F 5
97033 Kent, 58 G 2
97531 Kerby, 650 D 5
† 97367 Kernville, 50 D 3
97848 Kimberly, 30 H 3
† 97123 King City, 1,427 A 2
97353 Kings Valley, 100 D 3
97849 Kinzua, 400 H 3
97601 Klamath Falls⊙, 15,775 F 5
† 97103 Knappa, 950 D 1
97354 Lacomb, 450 E 3
97127 Lafayette, 786 A 2
97850 La Grande⊙, 9,645 J 2
† 97524 Lakecreek, 160 E 5
97034 Lake Oswego, 14,573 B 2
97449 Lakeside, 350 C 4
97630 Lakeview⊙, 2,705 G 5
97450 Langlois, 150 C 5
97739 La Pine, 1,500 F 4
† 97060 Latourell Falls, 40 E 2
97740 Lawen, 95 J 4
97401 Leaburg, 630 E 3
97355 Lebanon, 6,636 E 3
† 97478 Leland, 70 D 5
97839 Lexington, 230 H 2
† 97042 Liberal, 60 B 3
† 97341 Lincoln Beach, 275 C 3
97367 Lincoln City, 4,198 C 3
† 97405 Logan, 450 B 2
97357 Logsden, 55 D 3
97856 Long Creek, 196 H 3
97857 Lostine, 196 K 2
97452 Lowell, 567 E 4
97358 Lyons, 645 E 3
97741 Madras⊙, 1,689 F 3
97632 Malin, 486 F 5
97136 Manhattan Beach, 70 D 2
97130 Manzanita, 261 C 2
97453 Mapleton, 950 C 3
97454 Marcola, 900 E 3
97359 Marion, 450 D 3
97362 Marquam, 40 B 3
† 97016 Marshland, 30 D 1
97037 Maupin, 428 F 2
† 97016 Mayger, 35 D 1
† 97850 May Park, 1,466 J 2
† 97201 Maywood Park, 1,230 B 2
† 97338 McCoy, 40 D 2
97401 McKenzie Bridge, 100 E 3
97128 McMinnville⊙, 10,125 D 2
97858 McNary, 330 H 2
97859 Meacham, 130 J 2
97501 Medford⊙, 28,454 E 5
97860 Medical Springs, 45 K 2
97384 Mehama, 250 E 3
† 97470 Melrose, 30 D 4
97532 Merlin, 500 D 5
97633 Merrill, 722 F 5
97742 Metolius, 270 F 3
† 97223 Metzger, 2,900 A 2
97634 Midland, 205 F 5
97861 Mikkalo, 40 G 2
97360 Mill City, 1,451 E 3
97455 Milo, 600 E 5
97862 Milton-Freewater, 4,105 J 2
97222 Milwaukie, 16,379 B 2
97016 Mist, 40 D 1
97750 Mitchell, 196 G 3
† 97624 Modoc Point, 65 F 5
† 97477 Mohawk, 50 E 3
97038 Molalla, 2,005 B 3
97072 Monitor, 82 B 3
97361 Monmouth, 5,237 D 3
97456 Monroe, 443 D 3
97864 Monument, 161 H 3
97039 Moro⊙, 290 G 2
97040 Mosier, 217 F 2
† 97106 Mountaindale, 50 A 1
97362 Mount Angel, 1,973 B 3
97041 Mount Hood, 215 F 2
97865 Mount Vernon, 423 H 3
97042 Mulino, 600 B 2
97533 Murphy, 300 D 5
97457 Myrtle Creek, 2,733 D 4
97458 Myrtle Point, 2,511 C 4
97131 Nehalem, 241 D 2
97364 Neotsu, 259 C 2
97149 Neskowin, 500 D 2
97143 Netarts, 975 C 2
97132 Newberg, 6,507 A 2
† 97870 New Bridge, 50 K 3
† 97013 New Era, 50 B 2
97635 New Pine Creek, 260 G 5
97365 Newport⊙, 5,188 C 3
97459 North Bend, 8,553 C 4
97133 North Plains, 800 A 2
97043 North Portland, 950 B 1
97867 North Powder, 304 K 2
97460 Norway, 115 C 4
97913 Nyssa, 2,620 K 4
97268 Oak Grove, 6,300 B 2
97462 Oakland, 1,010 D 4
97463 Oakridge, 3,422 E 4
97534 O'Brien, 315 D 5
97134 Oceanside, 165 C 2
97044 Odell, 450 F 2
97812 Olex, 40 G 2

(continued on following page)

OREGON

SCALE
0 5 10 20 30 40 50 60 MI.
0 5 10 20 30 40 50 60 KM.
State Capitals ⊛
County Seats ⊙

Agriculture, Industry and Resources

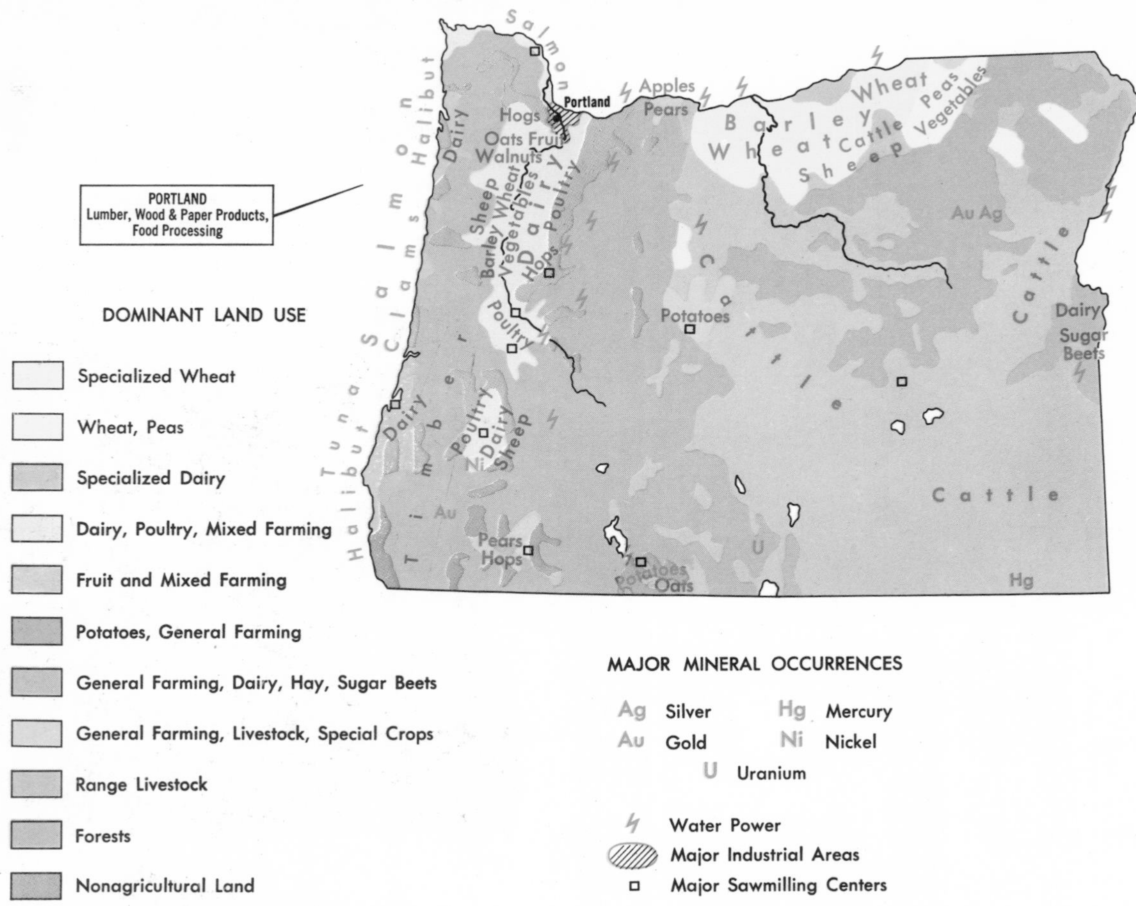

Oregon State Highway Department

Oregon's magnificently rugged coastline — sandy beaches interspersed with rock fragments ("stacks") torn from the cliffs.

	ZIP	Place, population	Key
†	97103	Olney, 75	D 1
	97914	Ontario, 6,523	K 3
	97464	Ophir, 250	C 5
	97045	Oregon City⊙, 9,176	B 2
†	97123	Orenco, 200	A 2
	97368	Otis, 200	D 2
	97369	Otter Rock, 150	C 3
	97840	Oxbow, 75	L 2
	97135	Pacific City, 500	C 2
	97636	Paisley, 260	G 5
	97047	Parkdale, 300	F 2
†	97045	Park Place, 1,200	B 2
	97751	Paulina, 50	G 3
†	97361	Pedee, 45	D 3
	97801	Pendleton⊙, 13,197	J 2
†	97850	Perry, 100	J 2
	97101	Perrydale, 200	D 2
	97370	Philomath, 1,688	D 3
	97535	Phoenix, 1,287	E 5
	97868	Pilot Rock, 1,612	J 2
	97444	Pistol River, 75	C 5
†	97478	Placer, 50	D 5
	97637	Plush, 50	H 5
*	97201	Portland⊙, 382,619	B 2
		Portland, ‡1,009,129	B 2
	97465	Port Orford, 1,037	C 5
	97753	Powell Butte, 550	G 3
	97466	Powers, 842	D 5
	97869	Prairie City, 867	J 3
†	97301	Pratum, 40	A 3
†	97048	Prescott, 105	D 1
	97721	Princeton, 68	J 4
	97754	Prineville⊙, 4,101	G 3
†	97233	Progress, 100	A 2
	97536	Prospect, 200	E 5
†	97411	Prosper, 110	C 4
†	97413	Rainbow, 100	E 3
	97048	Rainier, 1,731	E 1
†	97045	Redland, 700	B 2
	97756	Redmond, 3,721	F 3
	97467	Reedsport, 4,039	C 4
†	97005	Reedville, 1,200	A 2
	97468	Remote, 96	D 5
	97870	Richland, 133	K 3
	97371	Rickreall, 250	D 3
	97469	Riddle, 1,042	D 5
	97871	Rieth, 300	J 2
	97758	Riley, 85	H 4
	97423	Riverton, 150	C 4
	97136	Rockaway, 665	C 2
	97537	Rogue River, 841	D 5
†	97910	Rome, 33	K 5
	97470	Roseburg⊙, 14,461	D 4
	97372	Rose Lodge, 300	D 3
†	97058	Rowena, 50	F 2
†	97106	Roy, 150	A 2
	97050	Rufus, 317	G 2
	97472	Saginaw, 150	E 4
	97373	Saint Benedict, 300	B 3
	97051	Saint Helens⊙, 6,212	E 2
†	97026	Saint Louis, 125	A 3
	97137	Saint Paul, 347	A 3
*	97301	Salem (cap.)⊙, 68,296	A 3
†	97525	Sams Valley, 450	E 5
	97055	Sandy, 1,544	E 2
	97056	Scappoose, 1,859	E 2
†	97123	Scholls, 50	A 2
	97374	Scio, 447	E 3
†	97109	Scofield, 259	D 2
	97473	Scottsburg, 200	D 4
	97375	Scotts Mills, 208	B 3
	97376	Seal Rock, 430	C 3
	97138	Seaside, 4,402	D 2
	97538	Selma, 200	D 5
	97873	Seneca, 400	J 3
	97057	Shaniko, 58	G 3
†	97325	Shaw, 210	A 3
†	97910	Sheaville, 53	K 4
	97377	Shedd, 850	D 3
	97378	Sheridan, 1,881	D 2
	97140	Sherwood, 1,396	A 2
	97380	Siletz, 596	D 3
	97638	Silver Lake, 200	F 4
	97381	Silverton, 4,301	B 3
	97759	Sisters, 516	F 3
	97476	Sixes, 250	C 5
†	97355	Sodaville, 125	E 3
†	97223	Somerset West, 562	A 2
	97366	Southbeach, 300	C 3
†	97501	South Medford, 3,497	E 5
	97639	Sprague River, 200	F 5
	97874	Spray, 161	H 3
†	97132	Springbrook, 75	A 2
	97477	Springfield, 27,047	E 3
	97875	Stanfield, 891	H 2
	97383	Stayton, 3,170	E 3
	97385	Sublimity, 634	E 3
	97876	Summerville, 76	K 2
†	97420	Sumner, 200	C 4
	97877	Sumpter, 120	J 3
	97478	Sunny Valley, 159	D 5
	97479	Sutherlin, 3,070	D 4
†	97103	Svensen, 950	D 1
	97386	Sweet Home, 3,799	E 3
	97480	Swisshome, 450	D 3
†	97201	Sylvan, 1,440	B 2
	97540	Talent, 1,389	E 5
	97389	Tangent, 350	D 3
	97878	Telocaset, 50	K 2
	97481	Tenmile, 100	D 4
	97760	Terrebonne, 521	F 3
	97058	The Dalles⊙, 10,423	F 2
	97390	Tidewater, 50	D 3
†	97453	Tiernan, 75	C 3
	97223	Tigard, 5,302	A 2
	97141	Tillamook⊙, 3,968	D 2
	97484	Tiller, 300	E 5
	97144	Timber, 150	D 2
	97391	Toledo, 2,818	D 3
	97145	Tolovana Park, 180	C 2
	97541	Trail, 160	E 5
†	97431	Trent, 125	E 4
	97060	Troutdale, 575	E 2
†	97885	Troy, 30	K 2
	97062	Tualatin, 750	A 2
†	97701	Tumalo, 300	F 3
	97392	Turner, 846	E 3
†	97136	Twin Rocks, 185	C 2
	97063	Tygh Valley, 238	F 2
	97880	Ukiah, 375	J 2
	97881	Umapine, 100	J 2
	97882	Umatilla, 679	H 2
	97486	Umpqua, 357	D 4
	97883	Union, 1,531	K 2
†	97536	Union Creek, 35	E 5
	97884	Unity, 312	J 3
	97918	Vale⊙, 1,448	K 4
	97393	Valsetz, 500	D 3
	97487	Veneta, 1,377	D 3
†	97116	Verboort, 280	A 2
	97064	Vernonia, 1,643	D 2
	97488	Vida, 75	E 3
	97394	Waldport, 700	C 3
†	97426	Walker, 50	D 4
	97885	Wallowa, 811	K 2
	97489	Walterville, 150	E 3
	97490	Walton, 300	D 3
	97063	Wamic, 146	F 2
	97761	Warm Springs, 550	F 3
	97053	Warren, 900	E 2
	97146	Warrenton, 1,825	C 1
	97065	Wasco, 412	G 2
	97395	Waterloo, 186	E 3
	97491	Wedderburn, 400	C 5
†	97067	Welches, 100	E 2
	97067	Wemme, 400	E 2
	97492	Westfir, 800	E 4
	97493	Westlake, 976	C 4
	97068	West Linn, 7,091	B 2
	97886	Weston, 660	J 2
	97016	Westport, 650	D 1
†	97071	West Woodburn, 185	A 3
	97147	Wheeler, 262	D 2
	97501	White City, 450	E 5
†	97128	Whiteson, 100	D 2
	97494	Wilbur, 476	D 4
	97543	Wilderville, 200	D 5
	97396	Willamina, 1,193	D 2
	97544	Williams, 750	D 5
†	97741	Willowdale, 115	G 3
	97070	Wilsonville, 900	A 2
	97495	Winchester, 900	D 4
	97467	Winchester Bay, 245	C 4
	97496	Winston, 2,468	D 4
	97497	Wolf Creek, 500	D 5
†	97526	Wonder, 50	D 5
	97071	Woodburn, 7,495	A 3
†	97060	Wood Village, 1,533	B 2
†	97601	Worden, 32	F 5
	97498	Yachats, 441	C 3
	97148	Yamhill, 516	D 2
†	97365	Yaquina, 175	C 3
	97499	Yoncalla, 675	D 4
	97073	Zigzag, 170	F 2

⊙ County seat.
‡ Population of metropolitan area.
† Zip of nearest p.o.
* Multiple zips

Agriculture, Industry and Resources

AREA 45,333 sq. mi.
POPULATION 11,793,909
CAPITAL Harrisburg
LARGEST CITY Philadelphia
HIGHEST POINT Mt. Davis 3,213 ft.
SETTLED IN 1682
ADMITTED TO UNION December 12, 1787
POPULAR NAME Keystone State
STATE FLOWER Mountain Laurel
STATE BIRD Ruffed Grouse

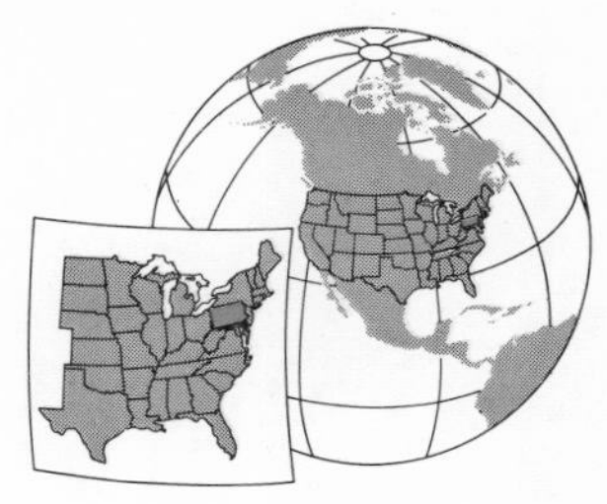

DOMINANT LAND USE

- Specialized Dairy
- Dairy, General Farming
- Fruit and Mixed Farming
- Fruit, Truck and Mixed Farming
- General Farming, Livestock, Tobacco
- General Farming, Livestock, Fruit, Tobacco
- Forests
- Urban Areas

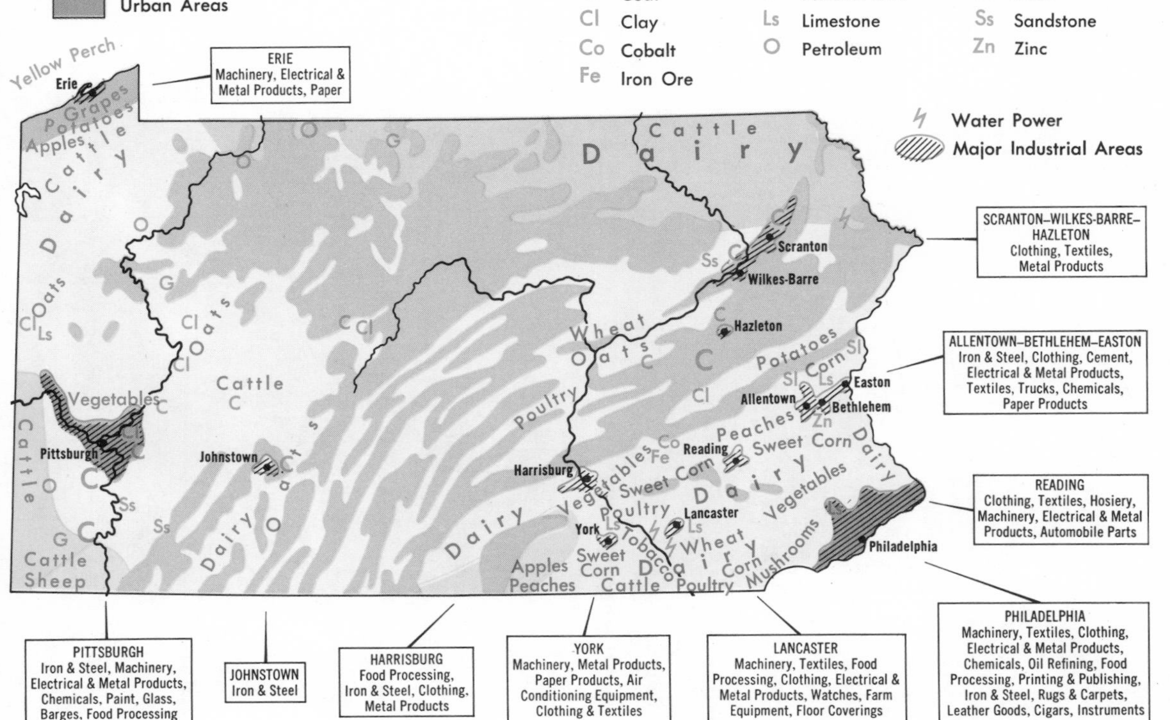

COUNTIES

Adams, 56,937 ... H 6
Allegheny, 1,605,016 ... B 5
Armstrong, 75,590 ... D 4
Beaver, 208,418 ... B 4
Bedford, 42,353 ... E 6
Berks, 296,382 ... K 5
Blair, 135,356 ... F 4
Bradford, 57,962 ... J 2
Bucks, 415,056 ... M 5
Butler, 127,941 ... C 4
Cambria, 186,785 ... E 4
Cameron, 7,096 ... F 3
Carbon, 50,573 ... L 4
Centre, 99,267 ... G 4
Chester, 278,311 ... L 6
Clarion, 38,414 ... D 3
Clearfield, 74,619 ... F 3
Clinton, 37,721 ... G 3
Columbia, 55,114 ... K 3
Crawford, 81,342 ... B 2
Cumberland, 158,177 ... H 5
Dauphin, 223,834 ... J 5
Delaware, 600,035 ... M 6
Elk, 37,770 ... E 3
Erie, 263,654 ... B 2
Fayette, 154,667 ... C 6
Forest, 4,926 ... D 2
Franklin, 100,833 ... G 6
Fulton, 10,776 ... F 6
Greene, 36,090 ... B 6
Huntingdon, 39,108 ... F 5
Indiana, 79,451 ... D 4
Jefferson, 43,695 ... D 3
Juniata, 16,712 ... H 4
Lackawanna, 234,107 ... L 3
Lancaster, 319,693 ... K 5
Lawrence, 107,374 ... B 4
Lebanon, 99,665 ... K 5
Lehigh, 255,304 ... L 4
Luzerne, 342,301 ... L 3
Lycoming, 113,296 ... H 3
McKean, 51,915 ... E 2
Mercer, 127,175 ... B 3
Mifflin, 45,268 ... G 4
Monroe, 45,422 ... M 3
Montgomery, 623,799 ... M 5
Montour, 16,508 ... J 3
Northampton, 214,368 ... M 4
Northumberland, 99,190 ... J 4
Perry, 28,615 ... H 5
Philadelphia (city county), 1,948,609 ... M 6
Pike, 11,818 ... M 3
Potter, 16,395 ... G 2
Schuylkill, 160,089 ... K 4
Snyder, 29,269 ... H 4
Somerset, 76,037 ... D 6
Sullivan, 5,961 ... J 3
Susquehanna, 34,344 ... L 2
Tioga, 39,691 ... H 2
Union, 28,603 ... H 4
Venango, 62,353 ... C 3
Warren, 47,682 ... D 2
Washington, 210,876 ... B 5
Wayne, 29,581 ... M 2
Westmoreland, 376,935 ... D 5
Wyoming, 19,082 ... K 2
York, 272,603 ... J 6

CITIES and TOWNS

Zip *Name/Pop.* *Key*

19001 Abington, 8,594 ... M 5
19501 Adamstown, 1,202 ... K 5
17501 Akron, 3,149 ... K 5
16401 Albion, 1,768 ... B 2
18011 Alburtis, 1,142 ... L 5
19018 Aldan, 5,001 ... M 7
15001 Aliquippa, 22,277 ... B 4
* 18101 Allentown⊙, 109,527 ... L 4
Allentown-Bethlehem-Easton, ‡543,551 ... L 4
15101 Allison Park, 7,500 ... C 4
* 16601 Altoona, 62,900 ... F 4
Altoona, ‡135,356 ... F 4
19002 Ambler, 7,800 ... M 5
15003 Ambridge, 11,324 ... B 4
19020 Andalusia, 8,169 ... N 5
17003 Annville, 4,704 ... J 5
15613 Apollo, 2,308 ... C 4
18403 Archbald, 6,118 ... M 2
19003 Ardmore, 5,801 ... M 6
15068 Arnold, 8,174 ... C 4
17921 Ashland, 4,737 ... K 4
18706 Ashley, 4,095 ... L 3
15215 Aspinwall, 3,541 ... C 6
18810 Athens, 4,173 ... K 2
17851 Atlas, 1,527 ... K 4
15202 Avalon, 7,065 ... B 6
15312 Avella, 1,109 ... B 5
17721 Avis, 1,749 ... H 3
18641 Avoca, 3,543 ... L 3
19311 Avondale, 1,025 ... L 6
15618 Avonmore, 1,267 ... C 4
15005 Baden, 5,536 ... B 4
17502 Bainbridge, 950 ... J 5
19004 Bala-Cynwyd, 6,483 ... N 6
† 15201 Baldwin, 26,729 ... B 7
19503 Bally, 1,197 ... L 5
18013 Bangor, 5,425 ... M 4
15714 Barnesboro, 2,708 ... E 4
18014 Bath, 1,829 ... M 4
15009 Beaver⊙, 6,100 ... B 4
15921 Beaverdale, 1,579 ... E 5
15010 Beaver Falls, 14,375 ... B 4
18216 Beaver Meadows, 1,274 ... L 4
15522 Bedford⊙, 3,302 ... F 5
16823 Bellefonte⊙, 6,828 ... G 4
15012 Belle Vernon, 1,496 ... C 5
17004 Belleville, 1,817 ... G 4
15202 Bellevue, 11,586 ... B 6
16617 Bellwood, 2,395 ... F 4
† 15201 Ben Avon, 2,713 ... B 6
15314 Bentleyville, 2,714 ... B 5
17814 Benton, 1,027 ... K 3
15530 Berlin, 1,766 ... E 6
18603 Berwick, 12,274 ... K 3
19312 Berwyn, 14,000 ... L 5
16112 Bessemer, 1,427 ... B 4
19507 Bethel, 950 ... K 5
15102 Bethel Park, 34,791 ... B 7
* 18015 Bethlehem, 72,686 ... M 4
17307 Biglerville, 977 ... H 6
19508 Birdsboro, 3,196 ... L 5
15716 Black Lick, 1,074 ... D 4
15717 Blairsville, 4,411 ... D 5
18447 Blakely, 6,391 ... L 2
15238 Blawnox, 1,907 ... C 6
15224 Bloomfield (New Bloomfield)⊙, 1,032 ... H 5
17815 Bloomsburg⊙, 11,652 ... J 3
16912 Blossburg, 1,753 ... H 2
17214 Blue Ridge Summit, 950 ... G 6
16827 Boalsburg, 950 ... G 4
15315 Bobtown, 1,055 ... B 6
17007 Boiling Springs, 1,521 ... H 5
19061 Boothwyn, 8,900 ... L 7
15135 Boston, 2,500 ... C 7
15531 Boswell, 1,529 ... E 5
19512 Boyertown, 4,428 ... L 5
15014 Brackenridge, 4,796 ... C 4
15104 Braddock, 8,682 ... C 7
16701 Bradford, 12,672 ... E 2
15227 Brentwood, 13,732 ... B 7
19405 Bridgeport, 5,630 ... M 5
15017 Bridgeville, 6,717 ... B 5
15009 Bridgewater, 966 ... B 4
19007 Bristol (borough), 12,085 ... N 5
19007 Bristol (urban township), 67,498 ... N 5
15824 Brockway, 2,529 ... E 3
19015 Brookhaven, 7,370 ... M 7
15825 Brookville⊙, 4,314 ... D 3
19008 Broomall, 20,000 ... M 6
15236 Broughton, 3,276 ... B 7
15417 Brownsville, 4,856 ... C 5
19009 Bryn Athyn, 970 ... M 5
19010 Bryn Mawr, 5,737 ... M 5
15021 Burgettstown, 2,118 ... A 5
17009 Burnham, 2,607 ... H 4
16001 Butler⊙, 18,691 ... C 4
16212 Cadogan, Δ563 ... C 4
15419 California, 6,635 ... C 5
16403 Cambridge Springs, 1,998 ... C 2
17011 Camp Hill, 9,931 ... H 5
18325 Canadensis, 950 ... M 3
15317 Canonsburg, 11,439 ... B 5
17724 Canton, 2,037 ... J 2
18407 Carbondale, 12,808 ... L 2
17013 Carlisle⊙, 18,079 ... H 5
15106 Carnegie, 10,864 ... B 7
15722 Carrolltown, 1,507 ... E 4
15234 Castle Shannon, 11,899 ... B 7
18032 Catasauqua, 5,702 ... M 4
17820 Catawissa, 1,701 ... K 4
15321 Cecil, 1,900 ... B 5
16404 Centerville, 4,175 ... B 6
15926 Central City, 1,547 ... E 5
17927 Centralia, 1,165 ... K 4
16828 Centre Hall, 1,282 ... G 4
18914 Chalfont, 2,366 ... M 5
17201 Chambersburg⊙, 17,315 ... G 6
15022 Charleroi, 6,723 ... C 5
† 19380 Chatwood, 7,168 ... L 6
19012 Cheltenham, Δ40,238 ... M 5
* 19013 Chester, 56,331 ... L 7
19017 Chester Heights, 1,277 ... L 7
15024 Cheswick, 2,580 ... C 6
16025 Chicora, 1,166 ... C 4
17509 Christiana, 1,132 ... K 6
† 15201 Churchill, 4,690 ... C 7
15025 Clairton, 15,051 ... C 7
16214 Clarion⊙, 6,095 ... D 3
18411 Clarks Summit, 5,376 ... L 3
16625 Claysburg, 1,516 ... F 5
15323 Claysville, 951 ... B 5
16830 Clearfield⊙, 8,176 ... F 3
19018 Clifton Heights, 8,348 ... M 7
15728 Clymer, 2,054 ... E 4
18218 Coaldale, 3,023 ... L 4
19320 Coatesville, 12,331 ... L 5
16314 Cochranton, 1,229 ... B 2
19426 Collegeville, 3,191 ... M 5
19023 Collingdale, 10,605 ... N 7
18915 Colmar, 950 ... M 5
17512 Columbia, 11,237 ... K 5
16405 Columbus, 950 ... C 2
15927 Colver, 1,175 ... E 4
† 19023 Colwyn, 3,169 ... N 7
15424 Confluence, 954 ... D 6
16406 Conneautville, 1,032 ... A 2
15425 Connellsville, 11,643 ... C 5
19428 Conshohocken, 10,195 ... M 5
15027 Conway, 2,822 ... B 4
18219 Conyngham, 1,850 ... K 3
18036 Coopersburg, 2,326 ... M 5
18037 Coplay, 3,642 ... L 4
15108 Coraopolis, 8,435 ... B 4
17016 Cornwall, 2,111 ... K 5
16407 Corry, 7,435 ... C 2
16915 Coudersport⊙, 2,831 ... G 2
15624 Crabtree, 1,021 ... D 5
15205 Crafton, 8,233 ... B 7
16630 Cresson, 2,446 ... E 5
17929 Cressona, 1,814 ... K 4
19022 Crum Lynne, 3,700 ... M 7
15031 Cuddy, 2,500 ... B 5
16833 Curwensville, 3,189 ... E 4
† 15901 Dale, 2,274 ... E 5
18612 Dallas, 2,913 ... K 3
17313 Dallastown, 3,560 ... J 6
18414 Dalton, 1,282 ... L 2
17821 Danville⊙, 6,176 ... J 4
19023 Darby, 13,729 ... M 7
17018 Dauphin, 998 ... J 5
15626 Delmont, 1,934 ... D 5
17517 Denver, 2,248 ... K 5
15627 Derry, 3,338 ... D 5
18519 Dickson City, 7,698 ... L 3
17019 Dillsburg, 1,441 ... J 5
15734 Dixonville, 950 ... D 4
15033 Donora, 8,825 ... C 5
15216 Dormont, 12,856 ... B 7
19518 Douglassville, 975 ... L 5
17315 Dover, 1,168 ... J 6
19335 Downingtown, 7,437 ... L 5
18901 Doylestown⊙, 8,270 ... M 5
15034 Dravosburg, 2,916 ... C 7
19026 Drexel Hill, 50,000 ... M 6
18221 Drifton, 1,295 ... L 3
15801 DuBois, 10,112 ... E 3
† 17701 Duboistown, 1,468 ... H 3
15431 Dunbar, 1,499 ... C 6
17020 Duncannon, 1,739 ... H 5
16635 Duncansville, 2,210 ... F 5
18512 Dunmore, 17,300 ... L 3
15110 Duquesne, 11,410 ... C 7
18642 Duryea, 5,264 ... L 3
17316 East Berlin, 1.086 ... J 6
† 18603 East Berwick, 2,090 ... K 3
16028 East Brady, 1,218 ... C 3
15909 East Conemaugh, 2,710 ... E 5
† 17701 East Faxon, 4,175 ... J 3
18041 East Greenville, 2,003 ... L 5
† 19050 East Lansdowne, 3,186 ... M 7
18042 Easton⊙, 30,256 ... M 4
17520 East Petersburg, 3,407 ... K 5
18301 East Stroudsburg, 7,894 ... M 4
† 15301 East Washington, 2,198 ... B 5
15931 Ebensburg⊙, 4,318 ... E 5
† 15005 Economy, 7,176 ... B 4
19020 Eddington, 20,517 ... N 5
19013 Eddystone, 2,706 ... M 7
† 15201 Edgewood, 5,101 ... B 7
† 15143 Edgeworth, 2,200 ... B 4
16412 Edinboro, 4,871 ... B 2
16731 Eldred, 1,092 ... F 2
15037 Elizabeth, 2,206 ... C 5
17022 Elizabethtown, 8,072 ... J 5
17023 Elizabethville, 1,629 ... J 4
16920 Elkland, 1,942 ... H 1
15331 Ellsworth, 1,268 ... B 5
16117 Ellwood City, 10,857 ... B 4
15038 Elrama, 950 ... C 5
17824 Elysburg, 1,337 ... K 4
18049 Emmaus, 11,511 ... M 4
15834 Emporium⊙, 3,074 ... F 2
15202 Emsworth, 3,332 ... B 6
17025 Enola, 4,900 ... J 5
17522 Ephrata, 9,662 ... K 5
* 16501 Erie⊙, 129,231 ... B 1
Erie, ‡263,654 ... B 1
17815 Espy, 1,652 ... K 4
19029 Essington, 3,100 ... M 7
15223 Etna, 5,819 ... B 6
16033 Evans City, 2,144 ... B 4
15537 Everett, 2,243 ... F 5
15631 Everson, 1,143 ... C 5
15632 Export, 1,402 ... C 5
15436 Fairchance, 1,906 ... C 6
19030 Fairless Hills, 16,000 ... N 5
16415 Fairview, 1,707 ... B 1
15840 Falls Creek, 1,255 ... E 3
16121 Farrell, 11,022 ... A 3
15438 Fayette City, 968 ... C 5
17222 Fayetteville, 2,449 ... G 6
18921 Ferndale, 2,482 ... E 5
19522 Fleetwood, 3,064 ... L 5
17745 Flemington, 1,519 ... G 3
† 17552 Florin, 975 ... J 5
19032 Folcroft, 9,610 ... M 7
19033 Folsom, 7,815 ... M 7
16226 Ford City, 4,749 ... D 4
18421 Forest City, 2,322 ... L 2
15221 Forest Hills, 9,561 ... C 7
18704 Forty Fort, 6,114 ... L 3
† 18015 Fountain Hill, 5,384 ... L 4
15238 Fox Chapel, 4,684 ... C 6
17931 Frackville, 5,445 ... K 4
16323 Franklin⊙, 8,629 ... C 3
17026 Fredericksburg, 1,073 ... B 2
17026 Fredericksburg, 950 ... J 5
15333 Fredericktown, 1,067 ... C 6
15042 Freedom, 2,643 ... B 4
18224 Freeland, 4,784 ... L 3
18017 Freemansburg, 1,681 ... M 4
16229 Freeport, 2,375 ... C 4
† 16117 Frisco, 950 ... B 4
16922 Galeton, 1,552 ... G 2
16641 Gallitzin, 2,496 ... E 4
17527 Gap, 1,022 ... L 6
† 17701 Garden View, 2,662 ... H 3
15904 Geistown, 3,633 ... E 5
17325 Gettysburg⊙, 7,275 ... H 6
17934 Gilberton, 1,293 ... K 4
16417 Girard, 2,613 ... B 2
17935 Girardville, 2,450 ... K 4
15045 Glassport, 7,450 ... C 7
18617 Glen Lyon, 3,408 ... K 3
19036 Glenolden, 8,697 ... M 7
19037 Glen Riddle, 950 ... L 7
17327 Glen Rock, 1,600 ... J 6
15116 Glenshaw, 19,500 ... C 6
19038 Glenside, 17,353 ... M 5
15634 Grapeville, 1,600 ... C 5
17225 Greencastle, 3,293 ... G 6
15601 Greensburg⊙, 15,870 ... D 5
† 15201 Greentree, 6,441 ... B 7
16125 Greenville, 8,704 ... B 3
16127 Grove City, 8,312 ... B 3
18822 Hallstead, 1,447 ... L 2
19526 Hamburg, 3,909 ... L 4
17331 Hanover, 15,623 ... J 6
† 15201 Harmarville, 1,900 ... C 6
16037 Harmony, 1,207 ... B 4
* 17101 Harrisburg (cap.)⊙, 68,061 ... H 5
Harrisburg, ‡410,626 ... H 5
18618 Harveys Lake, 1,693 ... K 3
16646 Hastings, 1,791 ... E 4
19040 Hatboro, 8,880 ... M 5
19440 Hatfield, 2,385 ... M 5
19041 Haverford, Δ55,132 ... M 6
19083 Havertown, 42,500 ... M 6
16840 Hawk Run, 1,020 ... F 4
18428 Hawley, 1,331 ... M 3
18201 Hazleton, 30,426 ... L 4
15106 Heidelberg, 2,034 ... B 7
17406 Hellam, 1,825 ... J 6
18055 Hellertown, 6,613 ... M 4
15637 Herminie, 975 ... C 5
17033 Hershey, 7,407 ... J 5
† 17044 Highland Park, 1,704 ... H 4
17034 High Spire, 2,947 ... J 5
16132 Hillsville, 950 ... A 4
16648 Hollidaysburg⊙, 6,262 ... F 5
15748 Homer City, 2,465 ... D 4
15120 Homestead, 6,309 ... B 7
18431 Honesdale⊙, 5,224 ... M 2
19344 Honey Brook, 1,115 ... L 5
15936 Hooversville, 962 ... E 5
15445 Hopwood, 2,190 ... C 6

(continued on following page)

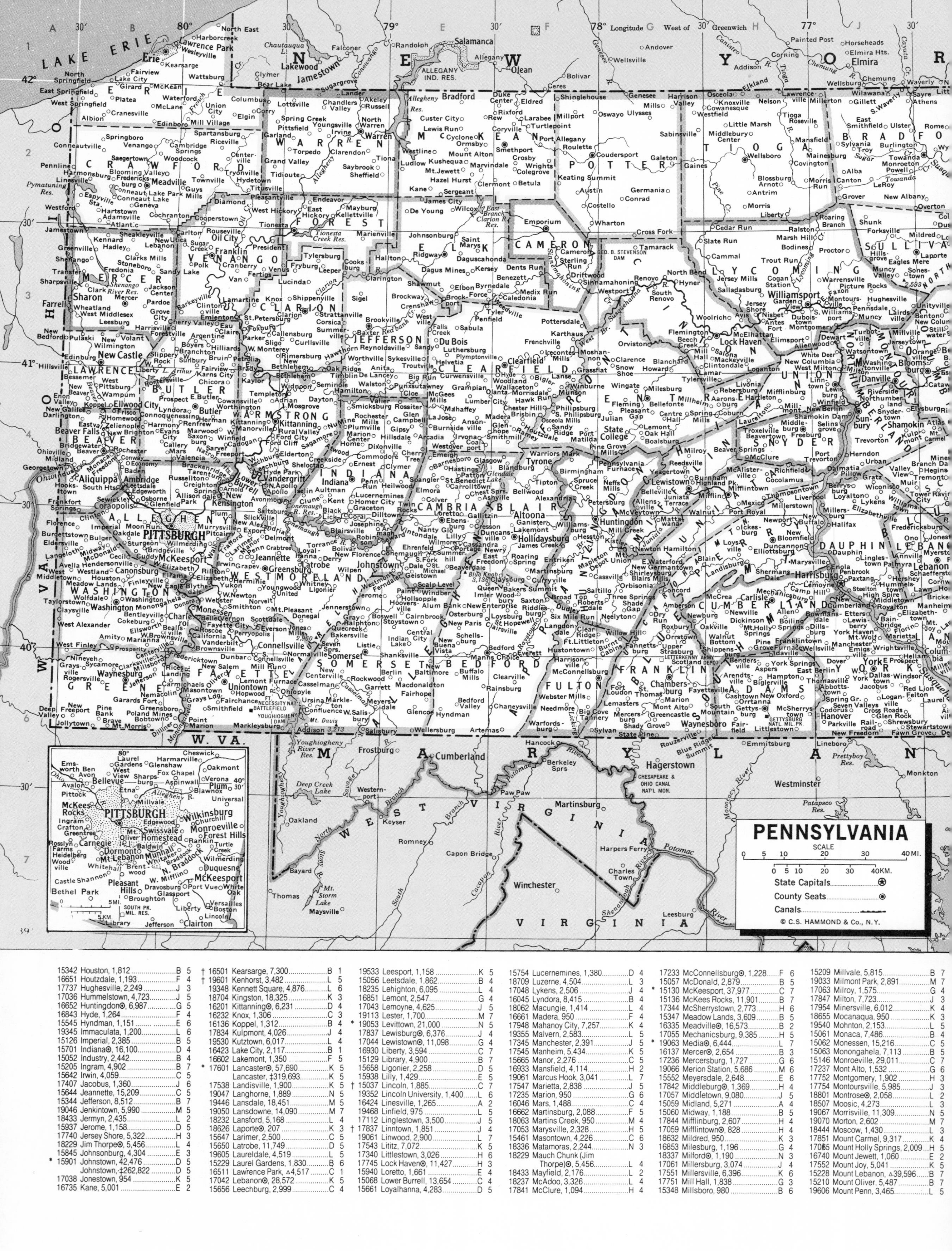

	ZIP	Place	Key
	15342	Houston, 1,812	B 5
	16651	Houtzdale, 1,193	F 4
	17737	Hughesville, 2,249	J 3
	17036	Hummelstown, 4,723	J 5
	16652	Huntingdon⊙, 6,987	G 5
	16843	Hyde, 1,264	F 4
	15545	Hyndman, 1,151	E 6
	19345	Immaculata, 1,200	L 6
	15126	Imperial, 2,385	B 5
	15701	Indiana⊙, 16,100	D 4
	15052	Industry, 2,442	B 4
	15205	Ingram, 4,902	B 7
	15642	Irwin, 4,059	C 5
	17407	Jacobus, 1,360	J 6
	15644	Jeannette, 15,209	C 5
	15344	Jefferson, 8,512	B 7
	19046	Jenkintown, 5,990	M 5
	18433	Jermyn, 2,435	L 2
	15937	Jerome, 1,158	D 5
	17740	Jersey Shore, 5,322	H 3
	18229	Jim Thorpe⊙, 5,456	L 4
	15845	Johnsonburg, 4,304	E 3
*	15901	Johnstown, 42,476	D 5
		Johnstown, ‡262,822	D 5
	17038	Jonestown, 954	K 5
	16735	Kane, 5,001	E 2
†	16501	Kearsarge, 7,300	B 1
†	19601	Kenhorst, 3,482	L 5
	19348	Kennett Square, 4,876	L 6
	18704	Kingston, 18,325	K 3
	16201	Kittanning⊙, 6,231	D 4
	16232	Knox, 1,306	C 3
	16136	Koppel, 1,312	B 4
	17834	Kulpmont, 4,026	J 4
	19530	Kutztown, 6,017	L 4
	16423	Lake City, 2,117	B 1
	16602	Lakemont, 1,350	F 5
*	17601	Lancaster⊙, 57,690	K 5
		Lancaster, ‡319,693	K 5
	17538	Landisville, 1,900	K 5
	19047	Langhorne, 1,889	N 5
	19446	Lansdale, 18,451	M 5
	19050	Lansdowne, 14,090	M 7
	18232	Lansford, 5,168	L 4
	18626	Laporte⊙, 207	K 3
	15647	Larimer, 2,500	C 5
	15650	Latrobe, 11,749	D 5
	19605	Laureldale, 4,519	L 5
	15229	Laurel Gardens, 1,830	B 6
	16511	Lawrence Park, ▵4,517	C 1
	17042	Lebanon⊙, 28,572	K 5
	15656	Leechburg, 2,999	C 4
	19533	Leesport, 1,158	K 5
	15056	Leetsdale, 1,862	B 4
	18235	Lehighton, 6,095	L 4
	16851	Lemont, 2,547	G 4
	17043	Lemoyne, 4,625	J 5
	19113	Lester, 1,700	M 7
*	19053	Levittown, 21,000	N 5
	17837	Lewisburg⊙, 6,376	J 4
	17044	Lewistown⊙, 11,098	G 4
	16930	Liberty, 3,594	C 7
	15129	Library, 4,900	B 7
	15658	Ligonier, 2,258	D 5
	15938	Lilly, 1,429	E 5
†	15037	Lincoln, 1,885	C 7
	19352	Lincoln University, 1,400	L 6
	16424	Linesville, 1,265	A 2
	19468	Linfield, 975	L 5
	17112	Linglestown, 3,500	J 5
†	17837	Linntown, 1,851	J 4
	19061	Linwood, 2,900	L 7
	17543	Lititz, 7,072	K 5
	17340	Littlestown, 3,026	H 6
	17745	Lock Haven⊙, 11,427	H 3
	15940	Loretto, 1,661	E 4
	15068	Lower Burrell, 13,654	C 4
	15661	Loyalhanna, 4,283	D 5
	15754	Lucernemines, 1,380	D 4
	18709	Luzerne, 4,504	L 3
	17048	Lykens, 2,506	J 4
	16045	Lyndora, 8,415	B 4
	18062	Macungie, 1,414	L 4
	16661	Madera, 950	F 4
	17948	Mahanoy City, 7,257	K 4
	19355	Malvern, 2,583	L 5
	17345	Manchester, 2,391	J 5
	17545	Manheim, 5,434	K 5
	15665	Manor, 2,276	C 5
	16933	Mansfield, 4,114	H 2
	19061	Marcus Hook, 3,041	L 7
	17547	Marietta, 2,838	J 5
	17235	Marion, 950	G 6
	16046	Mars, 1,488	C 4
	16662	Martinsburg, 2,088	F 5
	18063	Martins Creek, 950	M 4
	17053	Marysville, 2,328	H 5
	15461	Masontown, 4,226	C 6
	18336	Matamoras, 2,244	N 3
	18229	Mauch Chunk (Jim Thorpe)⊙, 5,456	L 4
	18433	Mayfield, 2,176	L 2
	18237	McAdoo, 3,326	L 4
	17841	McClure, 1,094	H 4
	17233	McConnellsburg⊙, 1,228	F 6
	15057	McDonald, 2,879	B 5
*	15130	McKeesport, 37,977	C 7
	15136	McKees Rocks, 11,901	B 7
	17344	McSherrystown, 2,773	H 6
	15347	Meadow Lands, 3,609	B 5
	16335	Meadville⊙, 16,573	B 2
	17055	Mechanicsburg, 9,385	H 5
*	19063	Media⊙, 6,444	L 7
	16137	Mercer⊙, 2,654	B 3
	17236	Mercersburg, 1,727	G 6
	19066	Merion Station, 5,686	M 6
	15552	Meyersdale, 2,648	E 6
	17842	Middleburg⊙, 1,369	H 4
	17057	Middletown, 9,080	J 5
	15059	Midland, 5,271	A 4
	15060	Midway, 1,188	B 5
	17844	Mifflinburg, 2,607	H 4
	17059	Mifflintown⊙, 828	H 4
	18632	Mildred, 950	K 3
	16853	Milesburg, 1,196	G 4
	18337	Milford⊙, 1,190	N 3
	17061	Millersburg, 3,074	J 4
	17551	Millersville, 6,396	K 6
	17751	Mill Hall, 1,838	G 3
	15348	Millsboro, 980	B 6
	15209	Millvale, 5,815	B 7
	19033	Milmont Park, 2,891	M 7
	17063	Milroy, 1,575	G 4
	17847	Milton, 7,723	J 3
	17954	Minersville, 6,012	K 4
	18655	Mocanaqua, 950	K 3
	19540	Mohnton, 2,153	L 5
	15061	Monaca, 7,486	B 4
	15062	Monessen, 15,216	C 5
	15063	Monongahela, 7,113	B 5
	15146	Monroeville, 29,011	C 7
	17237	Mont Alto, 1,532	G 6
	17752	Montgomery, 1,902	H 3
	17754	Montoursville, 5,985	J 3
	18801	Montrose⊙, 2,058	L 2
	18507	Moosic, 4,273	L 3
	19067	Morrisville, 11,309	N 5
	19070	Morton, 2,602	M 7
	18444	Moscow, 1,430	L 3
	17851	Mount Carmel, 9,317	K 4
	17065	Mount Holly Springs, 2,009	H 5
	16740	Mount Jewett, 1,060	E 2
	17552	Mount Joy, 5,041	K 5
	15228	Mount Lebanon, ▵39,596	B 7
	15210	Mount Oliver, 5,487	B 7
	19606	Mount Penn, 3,465	L 5

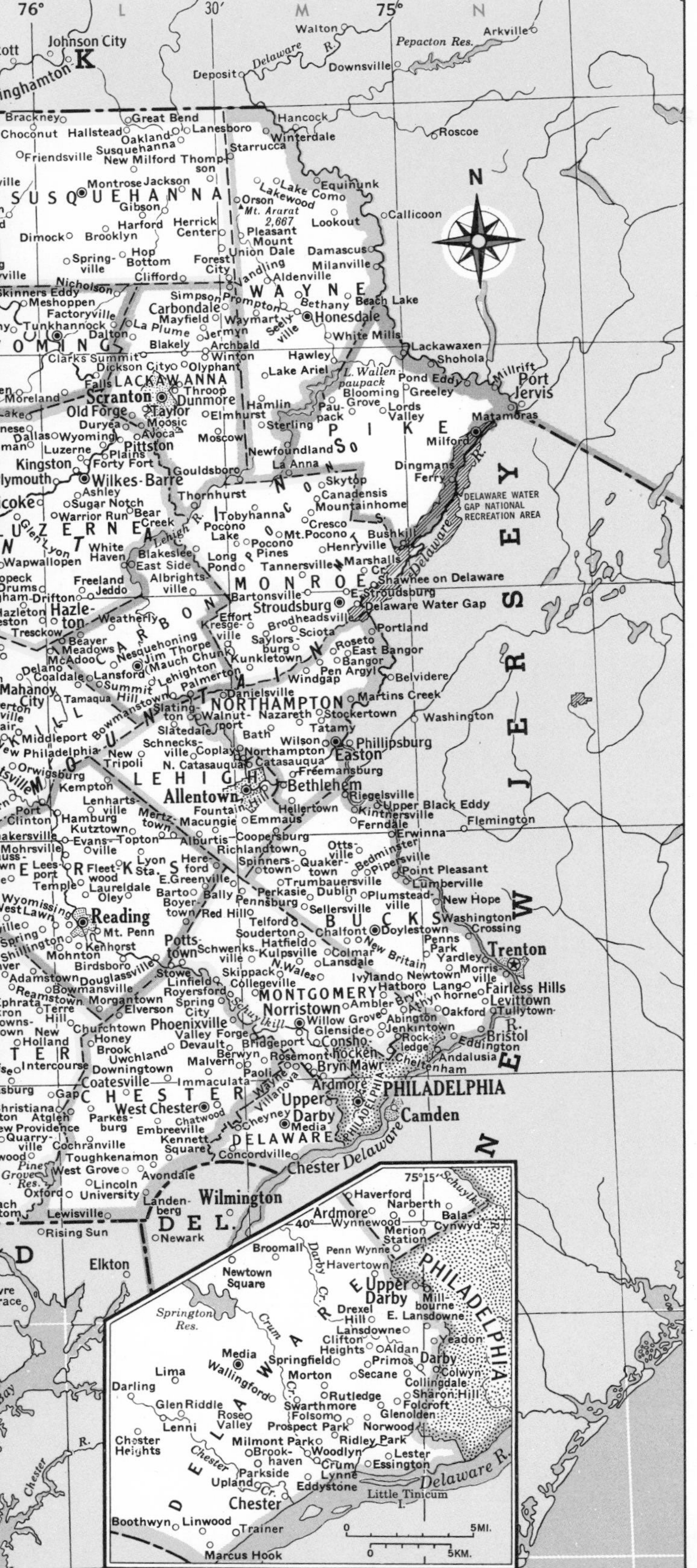

15666 Mount Pleasant, 5,895 .... D 5
18344 Mount Pocono, 1,019 .... M 3
17066 Mount Union, 3,662 .... G 5
17554 Mountville, 1,454 .... K 5
17347 Mount Wolf, 1,811 .... J 5
17756 Muncy, 2,872 .... J 3
15120 Munhall, 16,674 .... C 7
15668 Murrysville, 3,900 .... C 5
17067 Myerstown, 3,645 .... K 5
18634 Nanticoke, 14,632 .... K 3
15943 Nanty Glo, 4,298 .... E 5
19072 Narberth, 5,151 .... M 6
15065 Natrona Heights, 15,000 .... C 4
18064 Nazareth, 5,815 .... M 4
15351 Nemacolin, 1,273 .... B 6
18635 Nescopeck, 1,897 .... K 3
18240 Nesquehoning, 3,338 .... L 4
16141 New Beaver, 1,426 .... B 4
16140 New Bedford, 950 .... A 3
16242 New Bethlehem, 1,406 .... D 3
17068 New Bloomfield⊙, 1,032 .... H 5
15066 New Brighton, 7,637 .... B 4
18901 New Britain, 2,428 .... M 5
16101 New Castle⊙, 38,559 .... B 3
17070 New Cumberland, 9,803 .... J 5
15067 New Eagle, 2,497 .... B 5

17349 New Freedom, 1,495 .... J 6
17557 New Holland, 3,971 .... K 5
18938 New Hope, 978 .... N 5
15068 New Kensington, 20,312 .... C 4
18834 New Milford, 1,143 .... L 2
17350 New Oxford, 1,495 .... H 6
17959 New Philadelphia, 1,528 .... K 4
17074 Newport, 1,747 .... H 5
15468 New Salem, 1,337 .... C 6
15626 New Salem (Delmont), 1,934 .... D 5
18940 Newtown, 2,216 .... N 5
19073 Newtown Square, 16,000 .... L 6
17241 Newville, 1,631 .... H 5
16142 New Wilmington, 2,721 .... B 3
17759 Nisbet, 950 .... H 3
* 19401 Norristown⊙, 38,169 .... M 5
18067 Northampton, 8,389 .... M 4
15673 North Apollo, 1,618 .... D 4
15104 North Braddock, 10,838 .... C 7
† 18032 North Catasauqua, 2,941 .... L 4
16428 North East, 3,846 .... C 1
17857 Northumberland, 4,102 .... J 4
19454 North Wales, 3,911 .... M 5
16365 North Warren, 1,360 .... D 2
15674 Norvelt, 2,588 .... C 5

19074 Norwood, 7,229 .... M 7
18636 Noxen, 950 .... K 3
18241 Nuremberg, 950 .... K 4
15071 Oakdale, 1,614 .... B 5
† 19047 Oakford, 3,800 .... N 5
15139 Oakmont, 7,550 .... C 6
† 15059 Ohioville, 3,918 .... B 4
16301 Oil City, 15,033 .... C 3
18518 Old Forge, 9,522 .... L 3
15472 Oliver, 3,091 .... C 6
18447 Olyphant, 5,422 .... L 3
17961 Orwigsburg, 2,661 .... K 4
16666 Osceola Mills, 1,671 .... F 4
19363 Oxford, 3,658 .... K 6
† 15963 Paint, 1,233 .... E 5
18071 Palmerton, 5,620 .... L 4
17078 Palmyra, 7,615 .... J 5
19301 Paoli, 5,835 .... M 5
17562 Paradise, 975 .... K 5
19365 Parkesburg, 2,701 .... L 6
† 19013 Parkside, 2,343 .... M 7
† 17331 Parkville, 5,120 .... J 6
16668 Patton, 2,762 .... E 4
17111 Paxtang, 2,160 .... J 5
18072 Pen Argyl, 3,668 .... M 4
17103 Penbrook, 3,379 .... J 5
18073 Pennsburg, 2,260 .... M 5
† 19003 Penn Wynne, 6,038 .... M 6
18944 Perkasie, 5,451 .... M 5
15473 Perryopolis, 2,043 .... C 5
* 19101 Philadelphia⊙, 1,948,609 .... N 6
Philadelphia, ‡4,817,914 .... N 6
16866 Philipsburg, 3,700 .... F 4
19460 Phoenixville, 14,823 .... L 5
17963 Pine Grove, 2,197 .... K 4
16868 Pine Grove Mills, 950 .... G 4
15140 Pitcairn, 4,741 .... C 5
* 15201 Pittsburgh⊙, 520,117 .... B 7
Pittsburgh, ‡2,401,245 .... B 7
* 18640 Pittston, 11,113 .... L 3
18705 Plains, 6,606 .... L 3
16823 Pleasant Gap, 1,773 .... G 4
15236 Pleasant Hills, 10,409 .... B 7
16341 Pleasantville, 1,005 .... C 2
15239 Plum, 21,932 .... C 5
18651 Plymouth, 9,536 .... K 3
† 16830 Plymptonville, 1,040 .... E 3
15474 Point Marion, 1,750 .... C 6
16342 Polk, 3,673 .... C 3
15946 Portage, 4,151 .... E 5
16743 Port Allegany, 2,703 .... F 2
17965 Port Carbon, 2,717 .... K 4
15133 Port Vue, 5,862 .... C 7
19464 Pottstown, 25,355 .... L 5
17901 Pottsville⊙, 19,715 .... K 4
19018 Primos, 3,900 .... M 7
16052 Prospect, 973 .... B 4
19076 Prospect Park, 7,250 .... M 7
15767 Punxsutawney, 7,792 .... E 4
18951 Quakertown, 7,276 .... M 5
17566 Quarryville, 1,571 .... K 6
† 15104 Rankin, 3,817 .... C 7
* 19601 Reading⊙, 87,643 .... L 5
Reading, ‡415,056 .... L 5
17567 Reamstown, 1,050 .... K 5
18076 Red Hill, 1,201 .... L 5
17356 Red Lion, 5,645 .... J 6
17084 Reedsville, 950 .... G 4
17764 Renovo, 2,620 .... G 3
15851 Reynoldsville, 2,771 .... D 3
17087 Richland, 1,444 .... K 5
15853 Ridgway⊙, 6,022 .... E 3
19078 Ridley Park, 9,025 .... M 7
18077 Riegelsville, 1,050 .... M 4
15678 Rillton, 975 .... C 5
16248 Rimersburg, 1,146 .... D 3
17868 Riverside, 1,905 .... J 4
16673 Roaring Spring, 2,811 .... F 5
19551 Robesonia, 1,685 .... K 5
15949 Robinson, 975 .... D 5
15074 Rochester, 4,819 .... B 4
19111 Rockledge, 2,564 .... M 5
15557 Rockwood, 1,051 .... D 6
15477 Roscoe, 1,176 .... C 5
19010 Rosemont, 4,900 .... M 5
18013 Roseto, 1,538 .... M 4
17250 Rouzerville, 1,419 .... G 6
† 17067 Royalton, 1,040 .... J 5
19468 Royersford, 4,235 .... L 5
16249 Rural Valley, 962 .... D 4

16345 Russell, 950 .... D 2
15076 Russellton, 1,597 .... C 4
19070 Rutledge, 1,167 .... M 7
16433 Saegertown, 1,348 .... B 2
17970 Saint Clair, 4,576 .... K 4
15857 Saint Marys, 7,470 .... E 3
15951 Saint Michael, 1,248 .... E 5
15681 Saltsburg, 1,037 .... C 4
† 15801 Sandy, 2,000 .... E 3
16056 Saxonburg, 1,191 .... C 4
18840 Sayre, 7,473 .... K 2
15963 Scalp Level, 1,353 .... E 5
17088 Schaefferstown, 1,027 .... K 5
18078 Schnecksville, 1,550 .... L 4
17972 Schuylkill Haven, 6,125 .... K 4
18354 Sciota, 950 .... M 4
15683 Scottdale, 5,818 .... C 5
* 18501 Scranton⊙, 103,564 .... L 3
Scranton, ‡234,107 .... L 3
19018 Secane, 5,700 .... M 7
17870 Selinsgrove, 5,116 .... J 4
18960 Sellersville, 2,829 .... M 5
15143 Sewickley, 5,660 .... B 4
17872 Shamokin, 11,719 .... J 4
17876 Shamokin Dam, 1,562 .... J 4
16146 Sharon, 22,653 .... B 3
19079 Sharon Hill, 7,464 .... N 7
15215 Sharpsburg, 5,499 .... B 6
16150 Sharpsville, 6,126 .... A 3
16347 Sheffield, 1,564 .... D 2
17976 Shenandoah, 8,287 .... K 4
18655 Shickshinny, 1,685 .... K 3
19607 Shillington, 6,249 .... K 5
16748 Shinglehouse, 1,320 .... F 2
17257 Shippensburg, 6,536 .... H 5
19555 Shoemakersville, 1,427 .... K 4
17361 Shrewsbury, 1,716 .... J 6
18407 Simpson, 1,900 .... L 2
19608 Sinking Spring, 2,862 .... K 5
19474 Skippack, 975 .... M 5
18080 Slatington, 4,687 .... L 4
15684 Slickville, 1,066 .... C 5
16057 Slippery Rock, 4,949 .... B 3
16749 Smethport⊙, 1,883 .... F 2
15478 Smithfield, 969 .... C 6
15501 Somerset⊙, 6,269 .... D 6
18964 Souderton, 6,366 .... M 5
15425 South Connellsville, 2,385 .... C 6
15956 South Fork, 1,661 .... E 5
† 14892 South Waverly, 1,307 .... J 2
17701 South Williamsport, 7,153 .... J 3
15775 Spangler, 3,109 .... E 4
19475 Spring City, 3,578 .... L 5
15144 Springdale, 5,202 .... C 4
19064 Springfield, ∆2,446 .... M 7
17362 Spring Grove, 1,669 .... J 6
16801 State College, 33,778 .... G 4
17113 Steelton, 8,556 .... J 5
17363 Stewartstown, 1,157 .... K 6
16153 Stoneboro, 1,129 .... B 3
19464 Stowe, 3,596 .... L 5
17579 Strasburg, 1,897 .... K 6
18360 Stroudsburg⊙, 5,451 .... M 4
† 16323 Sugarcreek, 5,944 .... C 3
18706 Sugar Notch, 1,333 .... L 3
18250 Summit Hill, 3,811 .... L 4
17801 Sunbury⊙, 13,025 .... J 4
18847 Susquehanna, 2,319 .... L 2
19081 Swarthmore, 6,156 .... M 7
15218 Swissvale, 13,821 .... C 7
15865 Sykesville, 1,311 .... E 3
18252 Tamaqua, 9,246 .... L 4
15084 Tarentum, 7,379 .... C 4
18517 Taylor, 6,977 .... L 3
18969 Telford, 3,409 .... M 5
19560 Temple, 1,667 .... L 5
16259 Templeton, 950 .... C 4
17581 Terre Hill, 1,129 .... L 5
18512 Throop, 4,307 .... L 3
16353 Tionesta⊙, 711 .... C 2
16354 Titusville, 7,331 .... C 2
19562 Topton, 1,744 .... L 5
19374 Toughkenamon, 1,233 .... L 6
18848 Towanda⊙, 4,224 .... J 2
17980 Tower City, 1,774 .... J 4
15085 Trafford, 4,383 .... C 5
† 19013 Trainer, 2,336 .... L 7
17981 Tremont, 1,833 .... K 4
18254 Tresckow, 1,146 .... K 4
17881 Trevorton, 2,196 .... J 4

16947 Troy, 1,315 .... J 2
19007 Tullytown, 2,194 .... N 5
18657 Tunkhannock⊙, 2,251 .... L 2
15145 Turtle Creek, 8,308 .... C 7
15960 Twin Rocks, 975 .... E 4
16686 Tyrone, 7,072 .... F 4
16438 Union City, 3,631 .... C 2
15401 Uniontown⊙, 16,282 .... C 6
15689 United, 975 .... D 5
15235 Universal, 1,900 .... C 7
† 19013 Upland, 3,930 .... L 7
* 19082 Upper Darby, ∆95,910 .... M 6
19481 Valley Forge, 400 .... L 5
17983 Valley View, 1,585 .... J 4
15690 Vandergrift, 7,873 .... D 4
15147 Verona, 3,737 .... C 6
15132 Versailles, 2,754 .... C 7
19085 Villanova, 5,250 .... M 6
† 15148 Wall, 1,265 .... C 5
19086 Wallingford, 3,500 .... L 7
18088 Walnutport, 1,942 .... L 4
16157 Wampum, 1,189 .... B 4
16365 Warren⊙, 12,998 .... D 2
15301 Washington⊙, 19,827 .... B 5
16441 Waterford, 1,468 .... B 2
17777 Watsontown, 2,514 .... J 3
18472 Waymart, 1,122 .... M 2
19087 Wayne, 12,500 .... M 6
17268 Waynesboro, 10,011 .... G 6
15370 Waynesburg⊙, 5,152 .... B 6
18255 Weatherly, 2,554 .... L 4
16901 Wellsboro⊙, 4,003 .... H 2
19565 Wernersville, 1,761 .... K 5
16510 Wesleyville, 3,920 .... C 1
15417 West Brownsville, 1,426 .... C 5
19380 West Chester⊙, 19,301 .... L 6
16950 Westfield, 1,273 .... H 2
19390 West Grove, 1,870 .... L 6
18201 West Hazleton, 6,059 .... K 4
† 16201 West Kittanning, 956 .... C 4
19609 West Lawn, 1,973 .... K 5
† 15656 West Leechburg, 1,422 .... C 4
16159 West Middlesex, 1,293 .... B 3
15122 West Mifflin, 28,070 .... C 7
† 15901 Westmont, 6,673 .... D 5
15089 West Newton, 3,648 .... C 5
15229 West View, 8,312 .... B 6
† 17401 West York, 5,314 .... J 6
16161 Wheatland, 1,421 .... B 3
15120 Whitaker, 1,697 .... C 7
18052 Whitehall, 16,551 .... B 7
18661 White Haven, 2,134 .... L 3
15131 White Oak, 9,304 .... C 7
17097 Wiconisco, 1,236 .... J 4
15870 Wilcox, 950 .... E 2
* 18701 Wilkes-Barre⊙, 58,856 .... L 3
Wilkes-Barre-Hazleton, ‡342,301 .... L 3
15221 Wilkinsburg, 26,780 .... C 7
16693 Williamsburg, 1,704 .... F 5
17701 Williamsport⊙, 37,918 .... H 3
17098 Williamstown, 1,919 .... J 4
19090 Willow Grove, 16,494 .... M 5
15148 Wilmerding, 3,218 .... C 7
15025 Wilson, 8,482 .... M 4
15963 Windber, 6,332 .... E 5
18091 Windgap, 2,270 .... M 4
17366 Windsor, 1,298 .... J 6
† 18434 Winton, 4,948 .... M 3
† 15301 Wolfdale, 1,202 .... B 5
19567 Womelsdorf, 1,551 .... K 5
19094 Woodlyn, 6,500 .... M 7
17368 Wrightsville, 2,668 .... J 5
19096 Wynnewood, 9,200 .... M 6
18644 Wyoming, 4,195 .... L 3
19610 Wyomissing, 7,136 .... K 5
19067 Yardley, 2,616 .... N 5
19050 Yeadon, 12,136 .... N 7
17099 Yeagertown, 1,363 .... G 4
* 17401 York⊙, 50,335 .... J 6
York, ‡329,540 .... J 6
16371 Youngsville, 2,158 .... D 2
15697 Youngwood, 3,057 .... D 5
16063 Zelienople, 3,602 .... B 4

⊙ County seat.
‡ Population of metropolitan area.
∆ Population of town of township.
† Zip of nearest p.o.
* Multiple zips

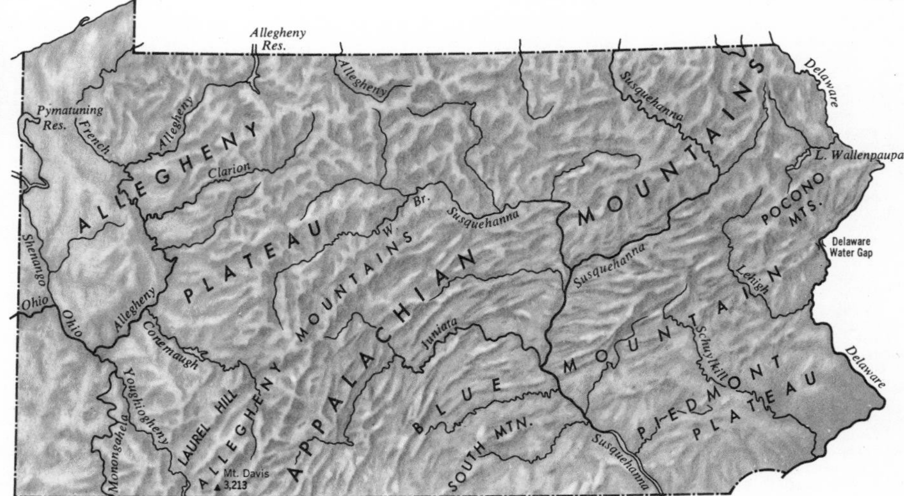

Topography

0 30 60 MILES

COUNTIES

County, Pop.	Key
Abbeville, 21,112	B 3
Aiken, 91,023	D 4
Allendale, 9,692	E 6
Anderson, 105,474	B 2
Bamberg, 15,950	E 5
Barnwell, 17,176	E 5
Beaufort, 51,136	F 7
Berkeley, 56,199	G 5
Calhoun, 10,780	F 4
Charleston, 247,650	H 6
Cherokee, 36,791	D 1
Chester, 29,811	E 2
Chesterfield, 33,667	G 2
Clarendon, 25,604	G 4
Colleton, 27,622	F 6
Darlington, 53,442	H 3
Dillon, 28,838	J 3
Dorchester, 32,276	G 5
Edgefield, 15,692	D 4
Fairfield, 19,999	E 3
Florence, 89,636	H 3
Georgetown, 33,500	J 5
Greenville, 240,546	C 2
Greenwood, 49,686	C 3
Hampton, 15,878	E 6
Horry, 69,992	J 4
Jasper, 11,885	E 6
Kershaw, 34,727	F 3
Lancaster, 43,328	F 2
Laurens, 49,713	D 2
Lee, 18,323	G 3
Lexington, 89,012	E 4
Marion, 30,270	J 3
Marlboro, 27,151	H 2
McCormick, 7,955	C 4
Newberry, 29,273	D 3
Oconee, 40,728	A 2
Orangeburg, 69,789	F 5
Pickens, 58,956	B 2
Richland, 233,868	F 3
Saluda, 14,528	D 3
Spartanburg, 173,724	D 2
Sumter, 79,425	G 4
Union, 29,230	D 2
Williamsburg, 34,243	H 4
York, 85,216	E 2

CITIES and TOWNS

	Zip	Name/Pop.	Key
	29620	Abbeville⊙, 5,515	C 3
	29426	Adams Run, 500	G 6
	29801	Aiken⊙, 13,436	D 4
	29001	Alcolu, 600	G 4
	29810	Allendale⊙, 3,620	E 5
	29621	Anderson⊙, 27,556	B 2
	29510	Andrews, 2,879	H 5
†	29020	Antioch, 500	F 3
	29320	Arcadia, 1,887	C 2
†	29201	Arcadia Lakes, 741	F 3
†	29201	Ardincaple, 726	E 3
	29640	Ariail, 1,150	B 2
†	29301	Arkwright, 2,059	C 2
	29511	Aynor, 536	J 3
	29706	Baldwin-Aragon Mills, 1,042	E 2
	29002	Ballentine, 550	E 3
	29003	Bamberg⊙, 3,406	E 5
	29812	Barnwell⊙, 4,439	E 5
	29006	Batesburg, 4,036	D 4
	29816	Bath, 1,576	D 5
	29902	Beaufort⊙, 9,434	F 7
	29842	Beech Island, 400	D 5
	29627	Belton, 5,257	C 2
	29512	Bennettsville⊙, 7,468	H 2
	29601	Berea, 7,186	C 2
	29009	Bethune, 506	G 3
	29010	Bishopville⊙, 3,404	G 3
	29702	Blacksburg, 1,977	D 1
	29817	Blackville, 2,395	E 5
	29910	Bluffton, 529	F 7
	29016	Blythewood, 600	E 3
	29431	Bonneau, 365	H 5
	29703	Bowling Green, 542	E 1
	29018	Bowman, 1,095	F 5
†	29201	Boyden Arbor, 416	F 3
	29019	Boykin, 350	F 3
	29432	Branchville, 1,011	F 5
	29911	Brunson, 559	E 6
	29321†	Buffalo, 1,461	D 2
†	29834	Burnettown, 434	D 5
	29902	Burton, 900	F 7
	29628	Calhoun Falls, 2,234	B 3
	29020	Camden⊙, 8,532	F 3
	29030	Cameron, 476	F 4
	29322	Campobello, 530	C 1
†	29902	Capehart, 4,490	F 7
	29031	Carlisle, 670	D 2
	29629	Cateechee, 450	B 2
	29033	Cayce, 9,967	E 4
	29630	Central, 1,550	B 2
†	29372	Central Pacolet, 483	D 2
	29036	Chapin, 342	E 3
*	29401	Charleston⊙, 66,945	G 6
		Charleston, ‡303,849	G 6
	29520	Cheraw, 5,627	H 2
	29323	Chesnee, 1,069	D 1
	29706	Chester⊙, 7,045	E 2
	29709	Chesterfield⊙, 1,667	G 2
	29611	City View, 2,497	C 2
†	29501	Claussen, 500	H 3
	29822	Clearwater, 1,500	D 4
	29631	Clemson, 5,578	B 2
	29324	Clifton, 950	D 2
	29325	Clinton, 8,138	D 3
	29525	Clio, 936	H 2
	29710	Clover, 3,506	E 1
*	29201	Columbia (cap.)⊙, 113,542	F 4
		Columbia, ‡322,880	F 4
	29636	Conestee, 600	C 2
	29329	Converse, 900	D 2
	29526	Conway⊙, 8,151	J 4
	29912	Coosawhatchie, 500	F 6
	29434	Cordesville, 900	H 5
	29435	Cottageville, 497	G 6
	29530	Coward, 466	H 4
	29330	Cowpens, 2,109	D 1
	29331	Cross Anchor, 350	D 2
	29332	Cross Hill, 579	D 3
†	29640	Dacusville, 350	B 2
	29914	Dale, 500	F 6
	29040	Dalzell, 625	G 3
	29532	Darlington⊙, 6,990	H 3
	29042	Denmark, 3,571	E 5
	29536	Dillon⊙, 5,991	J 3
	29638	Donalds, 392	C 3
†	29532	Doneraile, 1,417	H 3
	29437	Dorchester, 400	G 5
	29540	Dovesville, 500	H 3
	29639	Due West, 1,380	C 3
	29334	Duncan, 1,266	C 2
	29640	Easley, 11,175	B 2
†	29340	East Gaffney, 3,750	D 1
	29044	Eastover, 817	F 4
	29824	Edgefield⊙, 2,750	C 4
	29712	Edgemoor, 500	E 2
	29438	Edisto Island, 900	G 6
	29081	Ehrhardt, 478	E 5
	29045	Elgin, 374	F 3
	29046	Elliott, 500	G 3
	29047	Elloree, 940	F 4
	29335	Enoree, 850	D 2
	29918	Estill, 1,954	E 6
†	29706	Eureka (Hemlock), 1,524	E 2
	29048	Eutawville, 386	G 5
	29827	Fairfax, 1,937	E 6
	29643	Fair Play, 500	A 2
	29501	Florence⊙, 25,997	H 3
	29542	Floyd Dale, 500	J 3
	29439	Folly Beach, 1,157	H 6
	29206	Forest Acres, 6,808	F 3
†	29928	Forest Beach, 500	F 7
	29714	Fort Lawn, 510	F 2
	29715	Fort Mill, 4,505	F 1
	29050	Fort Motte, 950	F 4
	29644	Fountain Inn, 3,391	C 2
	29052	Gadsden, 500	F 4
	29340	Gaffney⊙, 13,253	D 1
†	29601	Gantt, 11,386	C 2
	29440	Georgetown⊙, 10,449	J 5
	29923	Gifford, 500	E 6
	29346	Glendale, 850	D 2
	29347	Glenn Springs, 350	D 2
	29828	Gloverville, 1,682	D 4
	29445	Goose Creek, 3,656	H 6
	29348	Gramling, 500	C 1
	29829	Graniteville, 1,127	D 4
	29645	Gray Court, 859	C 2
	29055	Great Falls, 2,727	F 2
	29056	Greeleyville, 542	H 4
	29446	Green Pond, 500	F 6
	29545	Green Sea, 500	J 3
*	29601	Greenville⊙, 61,208	C 2
		Greenville, ‡299,502	C 2
	29646	Greenwood⊙, 21,069	C 3
	29651	Greer, 10,642	C 2
	29546	Gresham, 350	J 4
†	29569	Gurley, 425	J 3
	29924	Hampton⊙, 2,845	E 6
	29410	Hanahan, 8,376	H 6

Agriculture, Industry and Resources

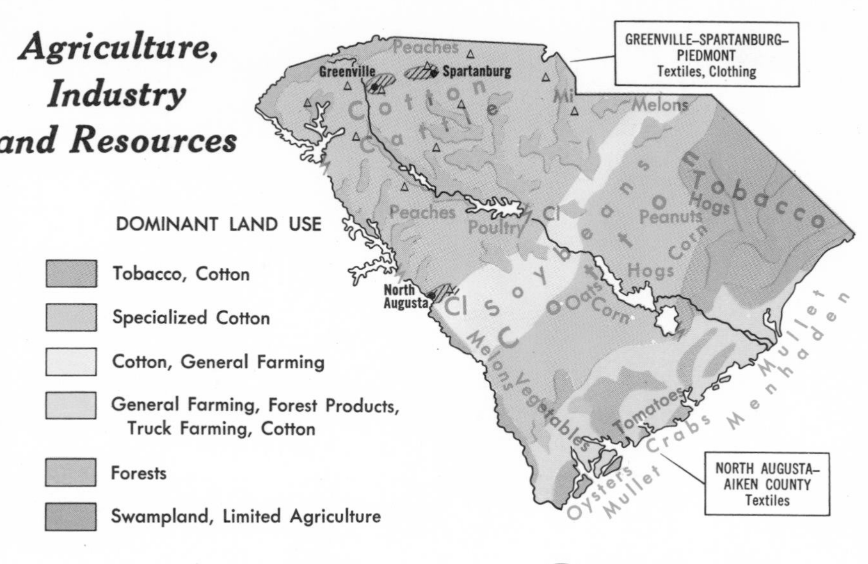

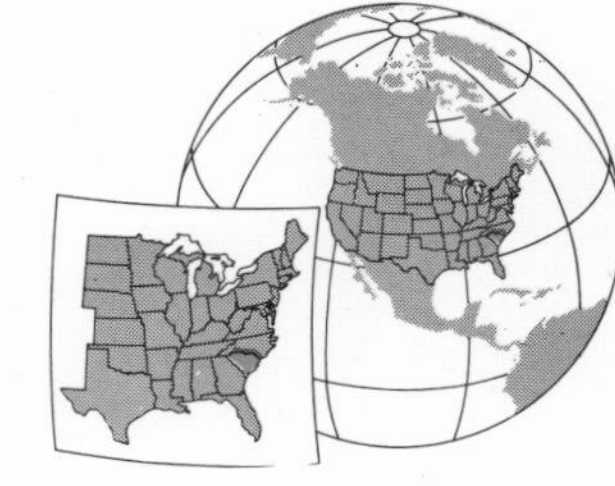

MAJOR MINERAL OCCURRENCES

Cl Clay
Mi Mica

Major Industrial Areas
Water Power
Major Textile Centers

AREA 31,055 sq. mi.
POPULATION 2,590,516
CAPITAL Columbia
LARGEST CITY Columbia
HIGHEST POINT Sassafras Mtn. 3,560 ft.
SETTLED IN 1670
ADMITTED TO UNION May 23, 1788
POPULAR NAME Palmetto State
STATE FLOWER Yellow Jessamine
STATE BIRD Carolina Wren

29927 Hardeeville, 853 .... E 7
29448 Harleyville, 704 .... G 5
29550 Hartsville, 8,017 .... G 3
29058 Heath Springs, 955 .... F 2
29554 Hemingway, 1,026 .... J 4
29706 Hemlock, 1,524 .... E 2
29717 Hickory Grove, 377 .... E 2
29813 Hilda, 331 .... E 5
29928 Hilton Head Island, 450 .... F 7
29059 Holly Hill, 1,178 .... G 5
29449 Hollywood, 339 .... G 6
29654 Honea Path, 3,707 .... C 3
29062 Horatio, 500 .... F 3
29450 Huger, 500 .... H 5
29349 Inman, 1,661 .... C 1
29063 Irmo, 517 .... E 3
† 29720 Irwin, 1,424 .... F 2
29451 Isle of Palms, 2,657 .... H 6
29655 Iva, 1,114 .... B 3
29831 Jackson, 1,928 .... D 5
29452 Jacksonboro, 550 .... G 6
† 29483 Jedburg, 900 .... G 5
29718 Jefferson, 709 .... G 2
29351 Joanna, 1,631 .... D 3
29455 Johns Island, 675 .... G 6
29555 Johnsonville, 1,267 .... J 4
29832 Johnston, 2,552 .... D 4
29353 Jonesville, 1,447 .... D 2
29067 Kershaw, 1,818 .... G 2
29556 Kingstree⊙, 3,381 .... H 4
29814 Kline, 305 .... E 5
29456 Ladson, 600 .... G 6

29656 La France, 875 .... B 2
29560 Lake City, 6,247 .... H 4
29563 Lake View, 949 .... J 3
29069 Lamar, 1,250 .... G 3
29720 Lancaster⊙, 9,186 .... F 2
† 29720 Lancaster Mills, 2,558 .... F 2
29724 Lando, 775 .... E 2
29356 Landrum, 1,859 .... C 1
29564 Lane, 517 .... H 5
29834 Langley, 975 .... D 4
29565 Latta, 1,764 .... J 3
29360 Laurens⊙, 10,298 .... C 3
29070 Leesville, 1,907 .... E 4
29734 Lesslie, 500 .... E 2
29072 Lexington⊙, 969 .... E 4
29657 Liberty, 2,860 .... B 2
† 29483 Lincolnville, 504 .... G 6
29566 Little River, 500 .... K 4
29931 Lobeco, 350 .... F 6
29569 Loris, 1,741 .... K 3
29078 Lugoff, 500 .... F 3
29079 Lydia, 400 .... G 3
29325 Lydia Mills, 925 .... D 3
29365 Lyman, 1,159 .... C 2
29080 Lynchburg, 546 .... G 3
29660 Madison, 350 .... A 2
29102 Manning⊙, 4,025 .... G 4
29661 Marietta-Slater, 1,764 .... C 1
29571 Marion⊙, 7,435 .... J 3
29662 Mauldin, 3,797 .... C 2
29104 Mayesville, 757 .... G 4
29368 Mayo, 800 .... D 1
29101 McBee, 592 .... G 3
29570 McColl, 2,524 .... H 2
29835 McCormick⊙, 1,864 .... C 4
† 29379 Monarch Mills, 1,726 .... D 2
29461 Moncks Corner⊙, 2,314 .... G 5
29105 Monetta, 850 .... D 4
29839 Montmorenci, 700 .... D 4
29664 Mountain Rest, 500 .... A 2
29464 Mount Pleasant, 6,155 .... H 6
29574 Mullins, 6,006 .... J 3
29576 Murrells Inlet, 850 .... K 4
29577 Myrtle Beach, 8,536 .... K 4
29408 Naval Base, 13,565 .... G 6
29107 Neeses, 388 .... E 4
29580 Nesmith, 350 .... H 4
29108 Newberry⊙, 9,218 .... D 3
29809 New Ellenton, 2,546 .... D 5
29665 Newry, 874 .... B 2
† 29536 New Town, 950 .... J 3
29581 Nichols, 549 .... J 3
29666 Ninety Six, 2,166 .... C 3
29667 Norris, 757 .... B 2
29112 North, 1,076 .... E 4
29841 North Augusta, 12,883 .... C 5
29406 North Charleston, 19,854 .... G 6
† 29550 North Hartsville, 1,485 .... G 3
29582 North Myrtle Beach, 1,957 .... K 4
29113 Norway, 579 .... E 5
29114 Olanta, 640 .... H 4
29843 Olar, 423 .... E 5
29115 Orangeburg⊙, 13,252 .... F 4
29372 Pacolet, 1,418 .... D 2
29373 Pacolet Mills, 1,504 .... D 2
29728 Pageland, 2,122 .... G 2
29583 Pamplico, 1,068 .... H 4
29584 Patrick, 421 .... G 2
29374 Pauline, 750 .... D 2
29585 Pawleys Island, 650 .... J 5
29670 Pendleton, 2,615 .... B 2
29671 Pickens⊙, 2,954 .... B 2
29673 Piedmont, 2,242 .... C 2
† 29169 Pineridge, 633 .... E 4
29468 Pineville, 900 .... H 5
29125 Pinewood, 687 .... G 4
29469 Pinopolis, 788 .... G 5
29935 Port Royal, 2,865 .... F 7
29127 Prosperity, 762 .... D 3
† 29501 Quinby, 788 .... H 3
29589 Rains, 600 .... J 3
29470 Ravenel, 931 .... G 6
29375 Reidville, 460 .... C 2
29128 Rembert, 350 .... G 3
29936 Ridgeland⊙, 1,165 .... E 7

29129 Ridge Spring, 644 .... D 4
29472 Ridgeville, 563 .... G 5
29130 Ridgeway, 437 .... F 3
29131 Rimini, 400 .... G 4
29473 Ritter, 350 .... F 6
29730 Rock Hill, 33,846 .... E 2
29740 Rodman, 500 .... E 2
29133 Rowesville, 392 .... F 5
29741 Ruby, 306 .... G 2
29475 Ruffin, 400 .... F 6
29407 Saint Andrews, 9,202 .... G 6
29134 Saint Charles, 350 .... G 3
29477 Saint George⊙, 1,806 .... F 5
29135 Saint Matthews⊙, 2,403 .... F 4
† 29148 Saint Paul, 725 .... G 4
29479 Saint Stephen, 1,506 .... H 5
29137 Salley, 450 .... E 4
29138 Saluda⊙, 2,442 .... D 4
† 29301 Saxon, 4,807 .... D 2
29591 Scranton, 732 .... H 4
29940 Seabrook, 500 .... F 6
29592 Sellers, 561 .... H 3
29678 Seneca, 6,027 .... A 2
† 29150 Shannontown, 7,491 .... G 4
29941 Sheldon, 950 .... F 6
29480 Shulerville, 375 .... H 5
29681 Simpsonville, 3,308 .... C 2
29682 Six Mile, 361 .... B 2
29683 Slater-Marietta, 1,764 .... C 1
29593 Society Hill, 806 .... H 2
† 29512 South Bennettsville, 1,726 .... H 2
† 29169 South Congaree, 1,434 .... E 4
* 29301 Spartanburg⊙, 44,546 .... C 1
29169 Springdale, 2,638 .... E 4
† 29720 Springdale, 3,193 .... F 2
29146 Springfield, 724 .... E 4
† 29067 Spring Mills, 975 .... F 2
29377 Startex, 1,203 .... C 2
29482 Sullivans Island, 1,426 .... H 6
29148 Summerton, 1,305 .... G 4
29483 Summerville, 3,839 .... G 5
29150 Sumter⊙, 24,435 .... G 4
29685 Sunset, 450 .... B 2
29577 Surfside Beach, 1,329 .... K 4
29160 Swansea, 691 .... E 4
29686 Tamassee, 420 .... A 2
29687 Taylors, 6,831 .... C 2
29688 Tigerville, 975 .... C 1
29161 Timmonsville, 2,246 .... H 3
29690 Travelers Rest, 2,241 .... C 2
29847 Trenton, 362 .... D 4
29162 Turbeville, 442 .... G 4
29379 Union⊙, 10,775 .... D 2
† 29678 Utica, 1,299 .... B 2
29944 Varnville, 1,555 .... E 6
29850 Vaucluse, 575 .... D 7
29607 Wade-Hampton, 17,152 .... C 2
29164 Wagener, 723 .... E 4
29691 Walhalla⊙, 3,662 .... A 2
29488 Walterboro⊙, 6,257 .... F 6
29692 Ware Shoals, 2,480 .... C 3
29851 Warrenville, 1,059 .... D 4
† 29360 Watts Mills, 1,181 .... D 2
29385 Wellford, 1,298 .... C 2
29169 West Columbia, 7,838 .... E 4
29693 Westminster, 2,521 .... A 2
29669 West Pelzer, 861 .... B 2
29696 West Union, 388 .... B 2
29178 Whitmire, 2,226 .... D 3
29303 Whitney, 2,891 .... D 1
29697 Williamston, 3,991 .... B 2
29853 Williston, 2,594 .... E 5
29856 Windsor, 590 .... E 5
† 29501 Windy Hill, 1,671 .... H 3
29180 Winnsboro⊙, 3,411 .... E 3
† 29180 Winnsboro Mills, 2,312 .... E 3
29388 Woodruff, 4,576 .... D 2
29945 Yemassee, 745 .... F 6
29494 Yonges Island, 350 .... G 6
29745 York⊙, 5,081 .... E 1
† 29574 Zion, 400 .... J 3

⊙ County seat.
‡ Population of metropolitan area.
† Zip of nearest p.o.
* Multiple zips

A. D'Arazien — Shostal Associates

Colorful materials being Sanforized in a South Carolina textile mill. Textiles are by far the most important of the state's industries.

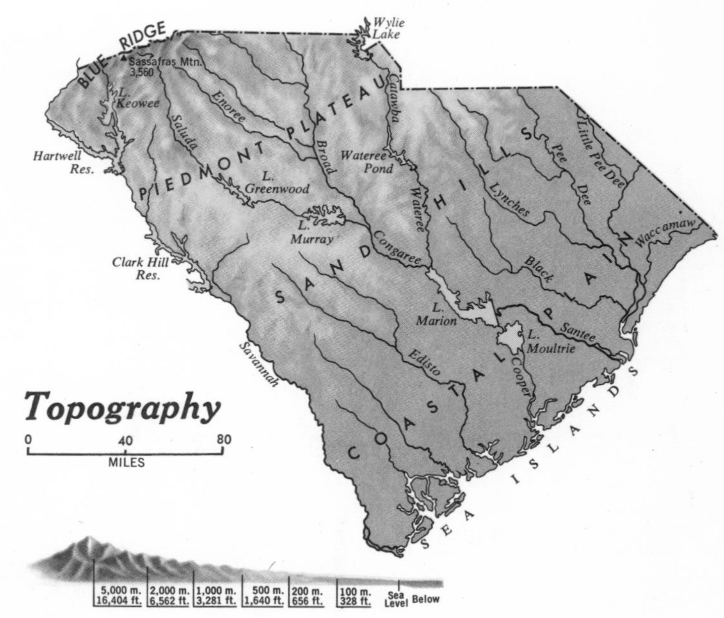

COUNTIES

Aurora, 4,183 .... M 6
Beadle, 20,877 .... N 5
Bennett, 3,088 .... F 7
Bon Homme, 8,577 .... O 7
Brookings, 22,158 .... R 5
Brown, 36,920 .... N 2
Brule, 5,870 .... L 6
Buffalo, 1,739 .... L 5
Butte, 7,825 .... B 4
Campbell, 2,866 .... J 2
Charles Mix, 9,994 .... M 7
Clark, 5,515 .... O 4
Clay, 12,923 .... P 8
Codington, 19,140 .... P 4
Corson, 4,994 .... G 2
Custer, 4,698 .... B 6
Davison, 17,319 .... N 6
Day, 8,713 .... O 3
Deuel, 5,686 .... R 4
Dewey, 5,170 .... G 3
Douglas, 4,569 .... N 7
Edmunds, 5.548 .... L 3
Fall River, 7,505 .... B 7
Faulk, 3,893 .... L 3
Grant, 9,005 .... R 3
Gregory, 6,710 .... L 7
Haakon, 2,802 .... F 5
Hamlin, 5,172 .... P 4
Hand, 5,883 .... L 4
Hanson, 3,781 .... O 6
Harding, 1,855 .... B 2
Hughes, 11,632 .... J 5
Hutchinson, 10,379 .... O 7
Hyde, 2,515 .... K 4
Jackson, 1,531 .... F 6
Jerauld, 3,310 .... M 5
Jones, 1,882 .... H 6
Kingsbury, 7,657 .... O 5
Lake, 11,456 .... P 5
Lawrence, 17,453 .... B 5
Lincoln, 11,761 .... R 7
Lyman, 4,060 .... J 6
Marshall, 5,965 .... O 2
McCook, 7,246 .... P 6
McPherson, 5,022 .... L 2
Meade, 16,618 .... D 5
Mellette, 2,420 .... H 6
Miner, 4,454 .... O 5
Minnehaha, 95,209 .... R 6
Moody, 7,622 .... R 5
Pennington, 59,349 .... C 6
Perkins, 4,769 .... D 3
Potter, 4,449 .... J 3
Roberts, 11,678 .... P 2
Sanborn, 3,697 .... N 5
Shannon, 8,198 .... D 7
Spink, 10,595 .... N 4
Stanley, 2,457 .... H 5
Sully, 2,362 .... J 4
Todd, 6,606 .... H 7
Tripp, 8,171 .... K 7
Turner, 9,872 .... P 7
Union, 9,643 .... R 8
Walworth, 7,842 .... J 3
Washabaugh, 1,389 .... F 6
Yankton, 19,039 .... P 7
Ziebach, 2,221 .... F 4

CITIES and TOWNS

Zip *Name/Pop.* *Key*

57401 Aberdeen⊙, 26,476 .... M 3
57310 Academy, 17 .... M 7
57520 Agar, 156 .... J 4
57420 Akaska, 46 .... J 3
57210 Albee, 26 .... S 3
57001 Alcester, 627 .... R 7
57311 Alexandria⊙, 598 .... O 6
57714 Allen, 150 .... F 7
57312 Alpena, 307 .... N 5
57211 Altamont, 54 .... R 4
57421 Amherst, 75 .... O 2
57422 Andover, 138 .... O 3
57715 Ardmore, 14 .... B 7
57212 Arlington, 954 .... P 5
57313 Armour⊙, 925 .... N 7
57423 Artas, 73 .... K 2
57314 Artesian, 277 .... O 6
57424 Ashton, 137 .... N 3
57213 Astoria, 153 .... S 4
57425 Athol, 50 .... M 3
57002 Aurora, 237 .... R 5
57315 Avon, 610 .... N 8
57214 Badger, 122 .... P 5
57003 Baltic, 364 .... R 6
57316 Bancroft, 48 .... O 4
57426 Barnard, 72 .... N 2
57716 Batesland, 135 .... E 7
57427 Bath, 150 .... N 3
57717 Belle Fourche⊙, 4,236 .... B 4
57521 Belvidere, 96 .... G 6
57215 Bemis, 28 .... R 4
57004 Beresford, 1,655 .... R 7
57216 Big Stone City, 631 .... S 3
† 57310 Bijou Hills, 12 .... L 6
57620 Bison⊙, 406 .... E 2
57718 Black Hawk, 550 .... C 5
57522 Blunt, 445 .... J 4
57317 Bonesteel, 354 .... M 7
57318 Bonilla, 33 .... N 4
57428 Bowdle, 667 .... K 3
57719 Box Elder, 607 .... D 5
57217 Bradley, 157 .... O 3
57005 Brandon, 1,431 .... R 6
57218 Brandt, 132 .... R 4
57429 Brentford, 94 .... N 3
57319 Bridgewater, 633 .... P 6
57219 Bristol, 470 .... O 3
57430 Britton⊙, 1,465 .... O 2
† 57350 Broadland, 45 .... N 4
57006 Brookings⊙, 13,717 .... R 5
57220 Bruce, 217 .... R 5
57221 Bryant, 502 .... P 4
57720 Buffalo⊙, 393 .... B 2
57722 Buffalo Gap, 155 .... C 6
57621 Bullhead, 449 .... G 2
57010 Burbank, 96 .... R 8
57523 Burke⊙, 892 .... L 7
57011 Bushnell, 65 .... R 5
57222 Butler, 38 .... O 3
57724 Camp Crook, 150 .... B 2
57012 Canistota, 636 .... P 6
57524 Canning, 40 .... K 5
57321 Canova, 204 .... O 6
57013 Canton⊙, 2,665 .... R 7
57725 Caputa, 43 .... D 5
† 57533 Carlock, 13 .... L 7
57322 Carpenter, 50 .... O 4
57526 Carter, 17 .... J 7
57323 Carthage, 362 .... O 5
57223 Castlewood, 523 .... R 4
57324 Cavour, 134 .... N 5
† 57058 Center, 18 .... P 6
57014 Centerville, 910 .... R 7
57727 Central City, 188 .... B 5
57325 Chamberlain⊙, 2,626 .... L 6
57015 Chancellor, 220 .... R 7
57431 Chelsea, 45 .... M 3
57622 Cherry Creek, 275 .... F 4
57016 Chester, 260 .... R 6
57224 Claire City, 100 .... P 2
57432 Claremont, 214 .... N 2
57225 Clark⊙, 1,356 .... O 4

SOUTH DAKOTA

SCALE

0 5 10 20 40 60 MI.

0 5 10 20 40 60 KM.

State Capitals ⊛

County Seats ⊙

† 57332 Clayton, 13 .... O 7
57581 Clearfield, 20 .... K 7
57226 Clear Lake⊙, 1,157 .... R 4
57017 Colman, 456 .... R 6
57528 Colome, 375 .... K 7
57018 Colton, 601 .... P 6
57433 Columbia, 240 .... N 2
57434 Conde, 279 .... N 3
57227 Corona, 133 .... R 3
57328 Corsica, 615 .... N 7
57019 Corson, 101 .... R 6
57728 Cottonwood, 16 .... F 6
57228 Crandall, 17 .... O 3
57435 Cresbard, 224 .... M 3
57229 Crocker, 40 .... O 3
57020 Crooks, 200 .... R 6
57730 Custer⊙, 1,597 .... B 6
57529 Dallas, 233 .... K 7
57329 Dante, 88 .... N 7
57021 Davis, 101 .... P 7
57732 Deadwood⊙, 2,409 .... B 5
57022 Dell Rapids, 1,991 .... R 6
57330 Delmont, 260 .... N 7
57230 Dempster, 75 .... R 4
57231 De Smet⊙, 1,336 .... O 5
57331 Dimock, 167 .... O 7
57530 Dixon, 15 .... L 7
57436 Doland, 430 .... N 4
57023 Dolton, 60 .... P 7
57531 Draper, 200 .... J 6
57623 Dupree⊙, 523 .... F 3
57625 Eagle Butte, 530 .... G 4
57232 Eden, 132 .... P 2
57735 Edgemont. 1,174 .... B 7
57024 Egan, 281 .... R 6
57025 Elk Point⊙, 1,372 .... R 8
57026 Elkton, 541 .... S 5
57736 Elm Springs, 16 .... D 5
57332 Emery, 452 .... O 6
57737 Enning, 35 .... E 4
† 57321 Epiphany, 64 .... O 6
57233 Erwin, 106 .... P 5
57333 Esmond, 19 .... O 5
57234 Estelline, 276 .... R 4
57334 Ethan, 309 .... N 6
57437 Eureka, 1,547 .... K 2
57738 Fairburn, 50 .... C 6
57335 Fairfax, 199 .... M 7
57027 Fairview, 72 .... R 7
57626 Faith, 576 .... E 4
57336 Farmer, 58 .... O 6
57740 Farmingdale, 30 .... D 6
57438 Faulkton⊙, 955 .... L 3
57337 Fedora, 75 .... O 5
57439 Ferney, 72 .... N 3
57628 Firesteel, 17 .... G 3
57028 Flandreau⊙, 2,027 .... R 5
57235 Florence, 175 .... P 3
57338 Forestburg, 150 .... N 5
57741 Fort Meade, 900 .... C 5
57532 Fort Pierre⊙, 1,448 .... H 5
57339 Fort Thompson, 750 .... L 5
57440 Frankfort, 192 .... N 4
† 57042 Franklin, 14 .... P 6
57441 Frederick, 359 .... N 2
57029 Freeman, 1,357 .... O 7
57742 Fruitdale, 74 .... B 4
57340 Fulton, 101 .... O 6
57341 Gannvalley⊙, 80 .... L 5
57236 Garden City, 126 .... O 4
57030 Garretson, 847 .... S 6
57237 Gary, 366 .... S 4
57031 Gayville, 269 .... P 8
57342 Geddes, 308 .... M 7
57442 Gettysburg⊙, 1,915 .... K 3
57630 Glencross, 75 .... H 3
57631 Glenham, 178 .... J 2
57238 Goodwin, 114 .... R 4

(continued on following page)

AREA 77,047 sq. mi.
POPULATION 666,257
CAPITAL Pierre
LARGEST CITY Sioux Falls
HIGHEST POINT Harney Pk. 7,242 ft.
SETTLED IN 1856
ADMITTED TO UNION November 2, 1889
POPULAR NAME Coyote State; Sunshine State
STATE FLOWER Pasqueflower
STATE BIRD Ring-necked Pheasant

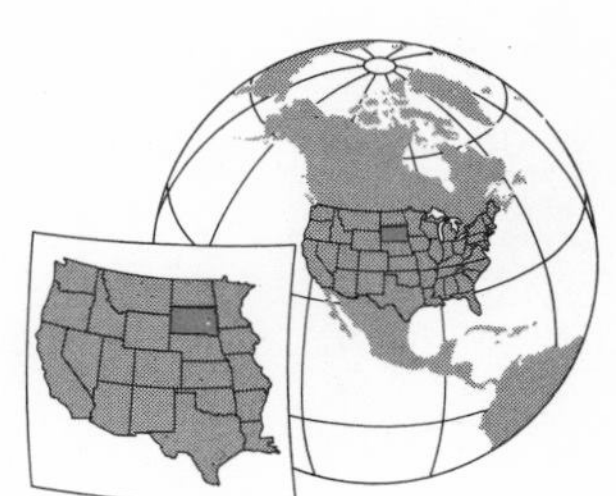

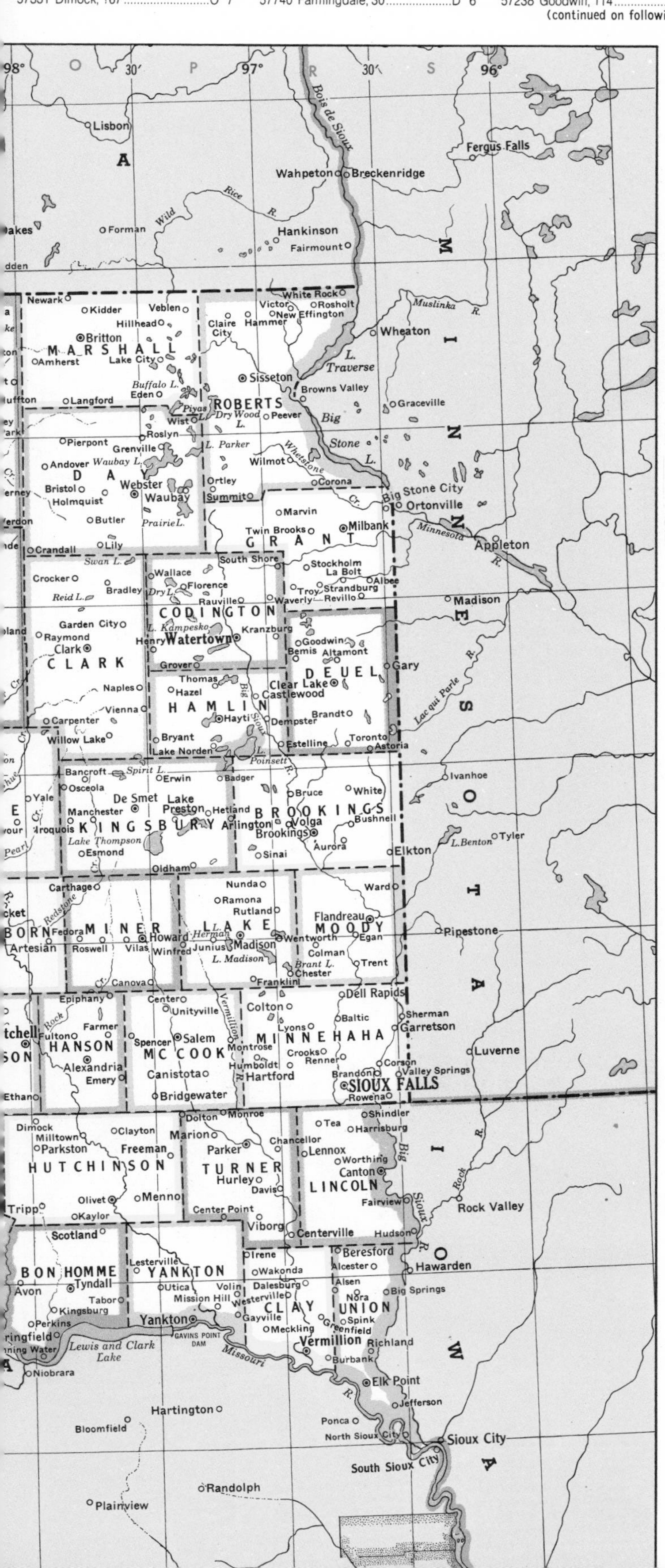

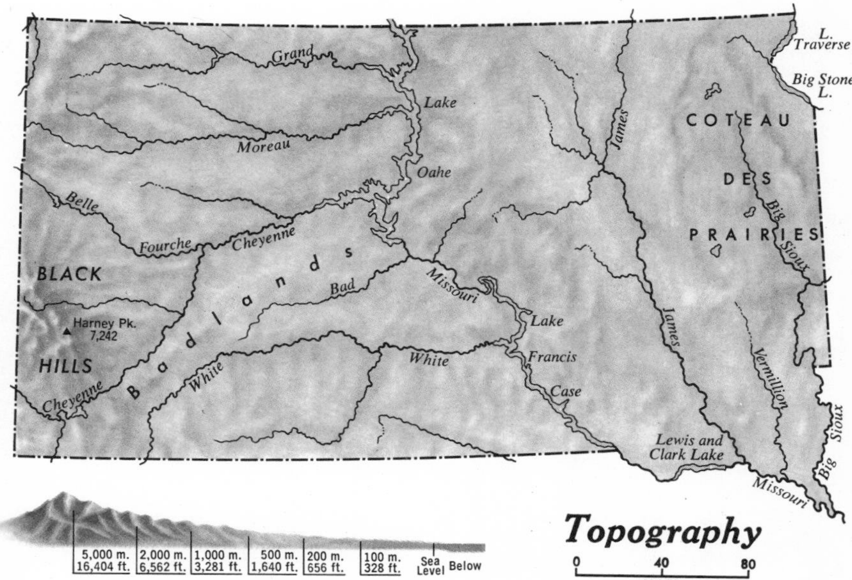

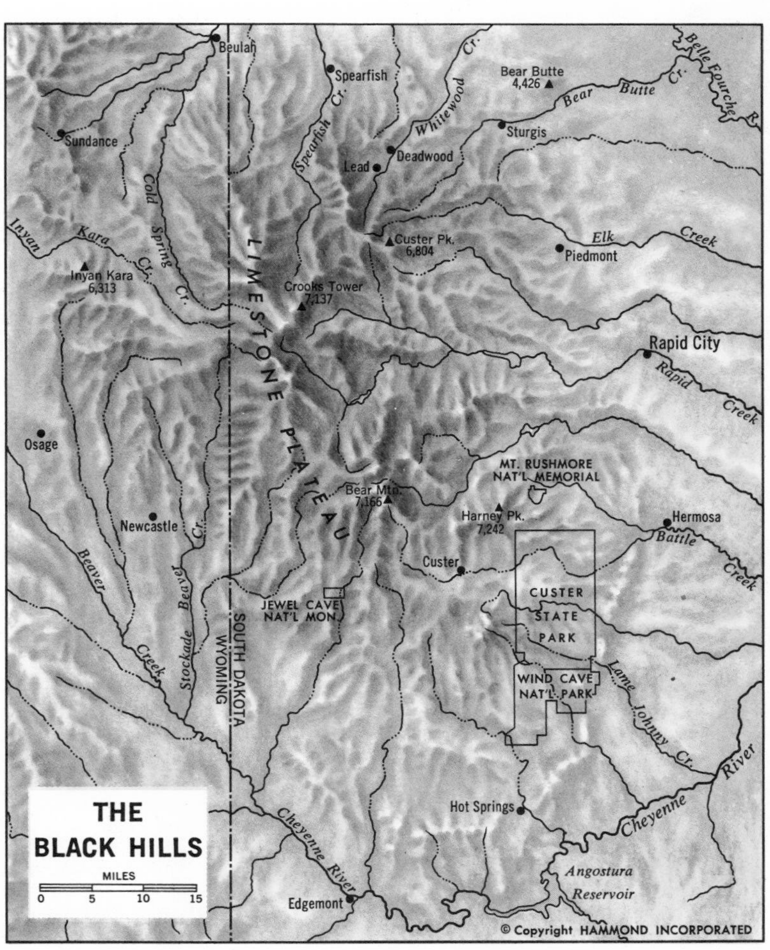

(continued)

† 57010 Greenfield, 12 ... R 8
† 57380 Greenwood, 90 ... N 8
57533 Gregory, 1,756 ... L 7
57239 Grenville, 154 ... O 3
57445 Groton, 1,021 ... N 3
† 57201 Grover, 12 ... P 4
57534 Hamill, 57 ... K 6
57240 Hammer, 30 ... R 2
57535 Harrington, 54 ... G 7
57032 Harrisburg, 338 ... R 7
57344 Harrison, 68 ... M 7
57536 Harrold, 184 ... K 4
57033 Hartford, 800 ... P 6
57537 Hayes, 28 ... H 5
57241 Hayti⊙, 393 ... P 4
57242 Hazel, 101 ... P 4
57446 Hecla, 407 ... N 2
57243 Henry, 182 ... P 4
57744 Hermosa, 150 ... C 6
57632 Herreid, 672 ... K 2
57538 Herrick, 126 ... L 7
57244 Hetland, 81 ... P 5
† 69501 Hidden Timber, 30 ... J 7
57345 Highmore⊙, 1,173 ... L 4
57745 Hill City, 389 ... B 6
† 57270 Hillhead, 26 ... O 2
† 57437 Hillsview, 19 ... L 2
† 57701 Hisega, 36 ... C 5
57348 Hitchcock, 150 ... M 4
57540 Holabird, 32 ... K 4
† 57274 Holmquist, 13 ... O 3
57448 Hosmer, 437 ... L 2
57747 Hot Springs⊙, 4,434 ... C 7
57449 Houghton, 90 ... N 2
57450 Hoven, 671 ... K 3
57349 Howard⊙, 1,175 ... P 5
57034 Hudson, 366 ... R 7
57035 Humboldt, 411 ... P 6
57036 Hurley, 399 ... P 7
57350 Huron⊙, 14,299 ... N 5
57541 Ideal, 135 ... K 6
† 57774 Igloo, 20 ... B 7
57750 Interior, 81 ... F 6
57451 Ipswich⊙, 1,187 ... L 3
57037 Irene, 461 ... P 7
57353 Iroquois, 375 ... O 5
57633 Isabel, 394 ... G 3
57452 Java, 305 ... K 3
57038 Jefferson, 474 ... S 8
† 57042 Junius, 50 ... P 6
57543 Kadoka⊙, 815 ... F 6
57354 Kaylor, 110 ... O 7
57634 Keldron, 35 ... F 2
57642 Kenel, 245 ... H 2
57544 Kennebec⊙, 372 ... K 6
57751 Keystone, 475 ... C 6
57453 Kidder, 140 ... O 2
57355 Kimball, 825 ... M 6
57245 Kranzburg, 143 ... R 4
57752 Kyle, 500 ... E 7
57246 La Bolt, 90 ... R 3
57356 Lake Andes⊙, 948 ... M 7
57247 Lake City, 44 ... O 2
57248 Lake Norden, 393 ... P 4
57249 Lake Preston, 812 ... P 5
57358 Lane, 94 ... N 5
57454 Langford, 328 ... O 2
57636 Lantry, 52 ... G 3
57637 La Plant, 165 ... H 3
57754 Lead, 5,420 ... B 5
57455 Lebanon, 182 ... K 3
57638 Lemmon, 1,997 ... E 2
57039 Lennox, 1,487 ... R 7
57456 Leola⊙, 787 ... M 2
57040 Lesterville, 181 ... O 7
57359 Letcher, 201 ... N 6
57250 Lily, 62 ... O 3
57639 Little Eagle, 975 ... H 2
57640 Lodgepole, 25 ... D 2
57457 Longlake, 128 ... L 2
57547 Longvalley, 16 ... F 7
57360 Loomis, 150 ... N 6
57548 Lower Brule, 500 ... K 5
57458 Lowry, 35 ... K 3
57549 Lucas, 13 ... L 7
† 57569 Lyman, 15 ... K 6
57041 Lyons, 89 ... R 6
57042 Madison⊙, 6,315 ... P 6
57643 Mahto, 23 ... H 2
† 57353 Manchester, 25 ... O 5
57756 Manderson, 350 ... D 7
57460 Mansfield, 150 ... N 3
57043 Marion, 844 ... P 7
57551 Martin⊙, 1,248 ... F 7
57361 Marty, 225 ... N 8
57251 Marvin, 65 ... R 3
57627 Maurine, 12 ... E 3
57641 McIntosh⊙, 563 ... G 2
57642 McLaughlin, 863 ... H 2
57044 Meckling, 100 ... R 8
57461 Mellette, 199 ... N 3
57045 Menno, 796 ... P 7
57552 Midland, 270 ... G 5
57252 Milbank⊙, 3,727 ... R 3
57362 Miller⊙, 2,148 ... L 4
† 57366 Milltown, 28 ... O 7
57462 Mina, 18 ... M 3
57463 Miranda, 60 ... M 4
57555 Mission, 739 ... H 7
57046 Mission Hill, 161 ... P 8
57301 Mitchell⊙, 13,425 ... N 6
57601 Mobridge, 4,545 ... J 2
57047 Monroe, 134 ... P 7
57048 Montrose, 377 ... P 6
57645 Morristown, 144 ... F 2
57558 Mosher, 19 ... J 7
57646 Mound City⊙, 164 ... K 2
57363 Mount Vernon, 398 ... N 6
57559 Murdo⊙, 865 ... H 6
† 57778 Mystic, 16 ... B 5
57254 Naples, 38 ... O 4
57759 Nemo, 100 ... B 5
† 57453 Newark, 25 ... O 2
57255 New Effington, 258 ... R 2
57760 Newell, 664 ... C 4
57364 New Holland, 131 ... M 7
57761 New Underwood, 416 ... D 5
† 57584 New Witten, 102 ... K 7

Agriculture, Industry and Resources

DOMINANT LAND USE

- Specialized Wheat
- Wheat, General Farming
- Wheat, Range Livestock
- Cattle Feed, Hogs
- Livestock, Cash Grain
- General Farming, Livestock, Special Crops
- Range Livestock
- Forests

MAJOR MINERAL OCCURRENCES

Ag	Silver	Mi	Mica
Au	Gold	O	Petroleum
Be	Beryl	U	Uranium
Gn	Granite	V	Vanadium

ϟ Water Power

57762 Nisland, 157 ... C 4
57560 Norris, 42 ... G 7
† 57625 North Eagle Butte, 1,351 ... G 3
57049 North Sioux City, 860 ... R 8
57465 Northville, 119 ... M 3
57050 Nunda, 85 ... P 5
57365 Oacoma, 215 ... L 6
57763 Oelrichs, 94 ... C 7
57764 Oglala, 250 ... D 7
57562 Okaton, 65 ... H 6
† 57501 Okobojo, 15 ... J 4
57563 Okreek, 300 ... J 7
57051 Oldham, 244 ... P 5
57052 Olivet⊙, 103 ... O 7
57466 Onaka, 69 ... L 3
57564 Onida⊙, 785 ... K 4
57766 Oral, 45 ... C 7
57467 Orient, 131 ... L 4
57256 Ortley, 111 ... P 3
† 57353 Osceola, 32 ... O 5
57053 Parker⊙, 1,005 ... P 7
57366 Parkston, 1,611 ... O 7
57566 Parmelee, 475 ... G 7
† 57529 Paxton, 18 ... L 7
† 57729 Pedro, 15 ... E 5
57257 Peever, 202 ... R 2
57567 Philip⊙, 983 ... F 5
57367 Pickstown, 300 ... M 7
57769 Piedmont, 650 ... C 5
57468 Pierpont, 241 ... O 3
57501 Pierre (cap.)⊙, 9,699 ... J 5
57770 Pine Ridge, 2,768 ... E 7
57368 Plankinton⊙, 613 ... N 6
57369 Platte, 1,351 ... M 7
57648 Pollock, 341 ... J 2
57772 Porcupine, 200 ... E 7
† 57750 Potato Creek, 40 ... F 6
57649 Prairie City, 55 ... D 2
57568 Presho, 922 ... J 6
57773 Pringle, 86 ... B 6
57774 Provo, 45 ... B 7
57370 Pukwana, 208 ... L 6
57402 Putney, 24 ... N 2
57775 Quinn, 105 ... E 5
57054 Ramona, 227 ... P 5
57701 Rapid City⊙, 43,836 ... C 5
57357 Ravinia, 109 ... N 7
57258 Raymond, 114 ... O 4
57469 Redfield⊙, 2,943 ... N 4
57776 Redig, 13 ... C 3
57777 Redowl, 14 ... D 4
57371 Ree Heights, 183 ... L 4
57569 Reliance, 204 ... K 6
57055 Renner, 260 ... R 6
57259 Revillo, 142 ... R 3
† 57025 Richland, 70 ... R 8
57652 Ridgeview, 65 ... H 3
57778 Rochford, 20 ... B 5
57701 Rockerville, 48 ... C 6
57470 Rockham, 60 ... M 4
† 57772 Rockyford, 50 ... E 7
57471 Roscoe, 398 ... L 3
57570 Rosebud, 650 ... H 7
57260 Rosholt, 456 ... R 2
57261 Roslyn, 250 ... P 2
57372 Roswell, 32 ... O 6
57056 Rowena, 76 ... R 6
57057 Rutland, 100 ... P 5
57571 Saint Charles, 33 ... L 7
57572 Saint Francis, 300 ... H 7
57373 Saint Lawrence, 249 ... M 4
57779 Saint Onge, 200 ... B 4
57058 Salem⊙, 1,391 ... P 6
† 57730 Sanator, 150 ... B 6
† 57754 Savoy, 15 ... B 5
57780 Scenic, 56 ... D 6
57059 Scotland, 984 ... O 7
57472 Selby⊙, 957 ... J 3
57473 Seneca, 118 ... L 3

57653 Shadehill, 186 ... E 2
57060 Sherman, 82 ... S 6
† 57101 Shindler, 20 ... R 7
57781 Silver City, 40 ... B 5
57061 Sinai, 147 ... P 5
* 57101 Sioux Falls⊙, 72,488 ... R 6
Sioux Falls, ‡95,209 ... R 6
57262 Sisseton⊙, 3,094 ... R 2
57782 Smithwick, 25 ... C 7
57263 South Shore, 199 ... P 3
57783 Spearfish, 4,661 ... B 5
57374 Spencer, 385 ... O 6
† 57010 Spink, 21 ... R 8
57062 Springfield, 1,566 ... N 8
57346 Stephan, 60 ... K 5
57375 Stickney, 421 ... M 6
57264 Stockholm, 116 ... R 3
† 57359 Storla, 75 ... M 6
57265 Strandburg, 98 ... R 3
57474 Stratford, 106 ... N 3
57785 Sturgis⊙, 4,536 ... B 5
57266 Summit, 332 ... P 3
† 57551 Swett, 20 ... E 7
57063 Tabor, 388 ... O 8
† 57433 Tacoma Park, 18 ... N 2
57064 Tea, 302 ... R 7
† 57242 Thomas, 15 ... P 4

57655 Thunder Hawk, 45 ... F 2
† 57769 Tilford, 162 ... C 5
57656 Timber Lake⊙, 625 ... H 3
57475 Tolstoy, 99 ... K 3
57268 Toronto, 216 ... R 4
57657 Trail City, 75 ... H 3
57065 Trent, 177 ... R 6
57376 Tripp, 851 ... N 7
† 57754 Trojan, 25 ... B 5
† 57265 Troy, 13 ... R 3
57476 Tulare, 211 ... N 4
57477 Turton, 121 ... N 3
57574 Tuthill, 73 ... G 7
57269 Twin Brooks, 122 ... R 3
57066 Tyndall⊙, 1,245 ... O 8
57787 Union Center, 50 ... D 4
† 57058 Unityville, 30 ... P 6
57067 Utica, 89 ... P 8
57788 Vale, 89 ... C 4
57068 Valley Springs, 566 ... S 6
57270 Veblen, 377 ... P 2
57478 Verdon, 18 ... N 3
57069 Vermillion⊙, 9,128 ... R 8
57575 Vetal, 17 ... G 7
57070 Viborg, 662 ... P 7
† 57260 Victor, 22 ... R 2
57271 Vienna, 119 ... O 4

† 57349 Vilas, 33 ... O 6
† 57701 Villa Ranchaero, 3,171 ... C 5
57379 Virgil, 43 ... N 5
57576 Vivian, 200 ... J 6
57071 Volga, 982 ... R 5
57072 Volin, 157 ... P 8
57380 Wagner, 1,655 ... N 7
57073 Wakonda, 290 ... P 7
57658 Wakpala, 500 ... H 2
57790 Wall, 786 ... E 6
57272 Wallace, 95 ... P 3
57577 Wanblee, 500 ... F 6
57074 Ward, 57 ... R 5
57479 Warner, 175 ... M 3
57791 Wasta, 127 ... D 5
57660 Watauga, 76 ... F 2
57201 Watertown⊙, 13,388 ... P 4
57273 Waubay, 696 ... P 3
57202 Waverly, 40 ... R 3
57274 Webster⊙, 2,252 ... P 3
57480 Wecota, 50 ... L 3
† 57532 Wendte, 20 ... H 5
57075 Wentworth, 196 ... R 6
57881 Wessington, 380 ... M 5
57382 Wessington Springs⊙, 1,300 ... M 5

57481 Westport, 136 ... M 2
57482 Wetonka, 31 ... M 2
57578 Wewela, 16 ... K 7
57276 White, 418 ... R 5
† 57638 White Butte, 15 ... E 2
57661 Whitehorse, 100 ... H 3
57383 White Lake, 395 ... M 6
57579 White River⊙, 617 ... H 6
57277 White Rock, 35 ... R 2
57793 Whitewood, 689 ... B 5
57278 Willow Lake, 353 ... O 4
57279 Wilmot, 518 ... R 3
57076 Winfred, 110 ... P 6
57580 Winner⊙, 3,789 ... K 7
57584 Witten, 140 ... J 7
57384 Wolsey, 436 ... N 5
57585 Wood, 132 ... J 6
57385 Woonsocket⊙, 852 ... N 5
57077 Worthing, 294 ... R 7
57794 Wounded Knee, 500 ... D 7
57386 Yale, 148 ... O 5
57078 Yankton⊙, 11,919 ... P 8
57483 Zell, 87 ... M 4

⊙ County seat.
‡ Population of metropolitan area.
† Zip of nearest p.o.
* Multiple zips

E. C. Werner — Shostal Associates

Beds of fossils await paleontologists in the vast, semi-arid buttes of the Badlands, east of the Black Hills of South Dakota.

AREA 267,339 sq. mi.
POPULATION 11,196,730
CAPITAL Austin
LARGEST CITY Houston
HIGHEST POINT Guadalupe Pk. 8,751 ft.
SETTLED IN 1686
ADMITTED TO UNION December 29, 1845
POPULAR NAME Lone Star State
STATE FLOWER Bluebonnet
STATE BIRD Mockingbird

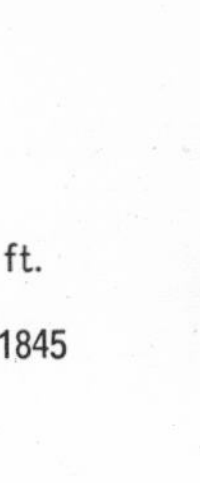

COUNTIES

Anderson, 27,789 J 6
Andrews, 10,372 B 5
Angelina, 49,349 K 6
Aransas, 8,902 H 10
Archer, 5,759 F 4
Armstrong, 1,895 C 3
Atascosa, 18,696 F 9
Austin, 13,831 H 8
Bailey, 8,487 B 3
Bandera, 4,747 E 8
Bastrop, 17,297 G 7
Baylor, 5,221 E 4
Bee, 22,737 G 9
Bell, 124,483 G 6
Bexar, 830,460 F 8
Blanco, 3,567 F 7
Borden, 888 C 5
Bosque, 10,966 G 6
Bowie, 67,813 K 4
Brazoria, 108,312 J 8
Brazos, 57,978 H 7
Brewster, 7,780 A 8
Briscoe, 2,794 C 3
Brooks, 8,005 F 11
Brown, 25,877 F 6
Burleson, 9,999 H 7
Burnet, 11,420 F 7
Caldwell, 21,178 G 8
Calhoun, 17,831 H 9
Callahan, 8,205 E 5
Cameron, 140,368 G 11
Camp, 8,005 K 5
Carson, 6,358 C 2
Cass, 24,133 K 4
Castro, 10,394 B 3
Chambers, 12,187 K 8
Cherokee, 32,008 J 6
Childress, 6,605 D 3
Clay, 8,079 F 4
Cochran, 5,326 B 4
Coke, 3,087 D 6
Coleman, 10,288 E 6
Collin, 66,920 H 4
Collingsworth, 4,755 D 3
Colorado, 17,638 H 8
Comal, 24,165 F 8
Comanche, 11,898 F 5
Concho, 2,937 E 6
Cooke, 23,471 G 4
Coryell, 35,311 G 6
Cottle, 3,204 D 3
Crane, 4,172 B 6
Crockett, 3,885 C 7
Crosby, 9,085 C 4
Culberson, 3,429 C 11
Dallam, 6,012 B 1
Dallas, 1,327,321 H 5
Dawson, 16,604 C 5
Deaf Smith, 18,999 B 3
Delta, 4,927 J 4
Denton, 75,633 G 4
De Witt, 18,660 G 9
Dickens, 3,737 D 4
Dimmit, 9,039 E 9
Donley, 3,641 D 2
Duval, 11,722 F 10
Eastland, 18,092 F 5
Ector, 91,805 B 6
Edwards, 2,107 D 7
Ellis, 46,638 H 5
El Paso, 359,291 A 10
Erath, 18,141 F 5
Falls, 17,300 H 6
Fannin, 22,705 H 4
Fayette, 17,650 H 8
Fisher, 6,344 D 5
Floyd, 11,044 C 3
Foard, 2,211 E 3
Fort Bend, 52,314 J 8
Franklin, 5,291 J 4
Freestone, 11,116 H 6
Frio, 11,159 E 9
Gaines, 11,593 B 5
Galveston, 169,812 K 8
Garza, 5,289 C 4
Gillespie, 10,553 F 7
Glasscock, 1,155 C 6
Goliad, 4,869 G 9
Gonzales, 16,375 G 8
Gray, 26,949 D 2
Grayson, 83,225 H 4
Gregg, 75,929 K 5
Grimes, 11,855 J 7
Guadalupe, 33,554 G 8
Hale, 34,137 C 3
Hall, 6,015 D 3
Hamilton, 7,198 F 6
Hansford, 6,351 C 1
Hardeman, 6,795 E 3
Hardin, 29,996 K 7
Harris, 1,741,912 J 8
Harrison, 44,841 K 5
Hartley, 2,782 B 2
Haskell, 8,512 E 4
Hays, 27,642 F 7
Hemphill, 3,084 D 2
Henderson, 26,466 J 5
Hidalgo, 181,535 F 11
Hill, 22,596 G 5
Hockley, 20,396 B 4
Hood, 6,368 G 5
Hopkins, 20,710 J 4
Houston, 17,855 J 6
Howard, 37,796 C 5
Hudspeth, 2,392 B 10
Hunt, 47,948 H 4
Hutchinson, 24,443 C 2
Irion, 1,070 C 6
Jack, 6,711 F 4
Jackson, 12,975 H 9
Jasper, 24,692 K 7
Jeff Davis, 1,527 C 11
Jefferson, 244,773 K 8
Jim Hogg, 4,654 F 11
Jim Wells, 33,032 F 10
Johnson, 45,769 G 5
Jones, 16,106 E 5
Karnes, 13,462 G 9
Kaufman, 32,392 H 5
Kendall, 6,964 F 8
Kenedy, 678 G 11
Kent, 1,434 D 4
Kerr, 19,454 E 7
Kimble, 3,904 E 7
King, 464 D 4
Kinney, 2,006 D 8
Kleberg, 33,166 G 10
Knox, 5,972 E 4
Lamar, 36,062 J 4
Lamb, 17,770 B 3
Lampasas, 9,323 F 6
La Salle, 5,014 E 9
Lavaca, 17,903 H 8
Lee, 8,048 H 7
Leon, 8,738 J 6
Liberty, 33,014 K 7
Limestone, 18,100 H 6
Lipscomb, 3,486 D 1
Live Oak, 6,697 F 9
Llano, 6,979 F 7
Loving, 164 D 10
Lubbock, 179,295 C 4
Lynn, 9,107 C 4
Madison, 7,693 J 6
Marion, 8,517 K 5
Martin, 4,774 C 5
Mason, 3,356 E 7
Matagorda, 27,913 H 9
Maverick, 18,093 D 9
McCulloch, 8,571 E 6
McLennan, 147,553 G 6
McMullen, 1,095 F 9
Medina, 20,249 E 8
Menard, 2,646 E 7
Midland, 65,433 B 6
Milam, 20,028 H 7
Mills, 4,212 F 6
Mitchell, 9,073 D 5
Montague, 15,326 G 4
Montgomery, 49,479 J 7
Moore, 14,060 C 2
Morris, 12,310 K 4
Motley, 2,178 D 3
Nacogdoches, 36,362 K 6
Navarro, 31,150 H 5
Newton, 11,657 L 7
Nolan, 16,220 D 5
Nueces, 237,544 G 10
Ochiltree, 9,704 D 1
Oldham, 2,258 B 2
Orange, 71,170 L 7
Palo Pinto, 28,962 F 5
Panola, 15,894 K 5
Parker, 33,888 G 5
Parmer, 10,509 B 3
Pecos, 13,748 B 7
Polk, 14,457 K 7
Potter, 90,511 C 2
Presidio, 4,842 C 12
Rains, 3,752 J 5
Randall, 53,885 C 2
Reagan, 3,239 C 6
Real, 2,013 E 8
Red River, 14,298 J 4
Reeves, 16,526 D 11
Refugio, 9,494 G 9
Roberts, 967 D 2
Robertson, 14,389 H 6
Rockwall, 7,046 H 5
Runnels, 12,108 E 6
Rusk, 34,102 K 5
Sabine, 7,187 L 6
San Augustine, 7,858 K 6
San Jacinto, 6,702 J 7
San Patricio, 47,288 G 10
San Saba, 5,540 F 6
Schleicher, 2,277 D 7
Scurry, 15,760 D 5
Shackelford, 3,323 E 5
Shelby, 19,672 K 6
Sherman, 3,657 C 1
Smith, 97,096 J 5
Somervell, 2,793 G 5
Starr, 17,707 F 11
Stephens, 8,414 F 5
Sterling, 1,056 C 6
Stonewall, 2,397 D 4
Sutton, 3,175 D 7
Swisher, 10,373 C 3
Tarrant, 716,317 G 5
Taylor, 97,853 E 5
Terrell, 1,940 B 7
Terry, 14,118 B 4
Throckmorton, 2,205 E 4
Titus, 16,702 K 4
Tom Green, 71,047 D 6
Travis, 295,516 G 7
Trinity, 7,628 J 6
Tyler, 12,417 K 7
Upshur, 20,976 K 5
Upton, 4,697 B 6
Uvalde, 17,348 E 8
Val Verde, 27,471 C 8
Van Zandt, 22,155 J 5
Victoria, 53,766 H 9
Walker, 27,680 J 7
Waller, 14,285 J 8
Ward, 13,019 A 6
Washington, 18,842 H 7
Webb, 72,859 E 10
Wharton, 36,729 H 8
Wheeler, 6,434 D 2
Wichita, 121,862 F 3
Wilbarger, 15,355 E 3
Willacy, 15,570 G 11
Williamson, 37,305 G 7
Wilson, 13,041 F 8
Winkler, 9,640 A 6
Wise, 19,687 G 4
Wood, 18,589 J 5
Yoakum, 7,344 B 4
Young, 15,400 F 4
Zapata, 4,352 E 11
Zavala, 11,370 E 9

CITIES and TOWNS

	Zip	Name/Pop.	Key
	79311	Abernathy, 2,625	B 4
*	79601	Abilene⊙, 89,653	E 5
		Abilene, ‡113,959	E 5
	78516	Alamo, 4,291	F 11
	78209	Alamo Heights, 6,933	F 8
	76430	Albany⊙, 1,978	E 5
	78332	Alice⊙, 20,121	F 10
	79830	Alpine⊙, 5,971	D 11
	77510	Alta Loma, 1,536	K 3
	75925	Alto, 1,045	J 6
	76009	Alvarado, 2,129	G 5
	77511	Alvin, 10,671	J 3
*	79101	Amarillo⊙, 127,010	C 2
		Amarillo, ‡144,396	C 2
	77514	Anahuac⊙, 1,881	K 8
	77830	Anderson⊙, 500	J 7
	79714	Andrews⊙, 8,625	B 5
	77515	Angleton⊙, 9,770	J 8
	79501	Anson⊙, 2,615	E 5
	88021	Anthony, 2,154	A 10
	79313	Anton, 1,034	B 4
	78336	Aransas Pass, 5,813	G 10
	77517	Arcadia, 1,200	K 3
	76351	Archer City⊙, 1,722	F 4
*	76010	Arlington, 90,643	F 2
	78827	Asherton, 1,645	E 9
	79502	Aspermont⊙, 1,198	D 4
	75751	Athens⊙, 9,582	J 5
	75551	Atlanta, 5,007	K 4
*	78701	Austin (cap.)⊙, 251,808	G 7
		Austin, ‡295,516	G 7
	76020	Azle, 4,493	E 1
	77518	Bacliff, 1,900	K 2
	79504	Baird⊙, 1,538	E 5
	75149	Balch Springs, 10,464	H 2
	76821	Ballinger⊙, 4,203	E 6
	78003	Bandera⊙, 891	F 8
	76823	Bangs, 1,214	E 6
	77532	Barrett, 2,750	K 1
	76511	Bartlett, 1,622	G 7
	78602	Bastrop⊙, 3,112	G 7
	77414	Bay City⊙, 11,733	H 9
	77520	Baytown, 43,980	L 2
	77701	Beaumont⊙, 115,919	K 7
		Beaumont-Port Arthur-Orange, ‡315,943	K 7
	76021	Bedford, 10,049	F 2
	78102	Beeville⊙, 13,506	G 9
	77401	Bellaire, 19,009	J 2
	76705	Bellmead, 7,698	H 6
	77418	Bellville⊙, 2,371	H 8
	76513	Belton⊙, 8,696	G 7
	78341	Benavides, 2,112	F 10
	76126	Benbrook, 8,169	E 2
	79505	Benjamin⊙, 308	E 4
	76932	Big Lake⊙, 2,489	C 6
	79720	Big Spring⊙, 28,735	C 5
	78343	Bishop, 3,466	G 10
	77951	Bloomington, 1,676	H 9
	76131	Blue Mound, 1,283	F 1
	78006	Boerne⊙, 2,432	F 8
	75417	Bogata, 1,287	J 4
	75418	Bonham⊙, 7,698	H 4
	79007	Borger, 14,195	C 2
	75557	Boston⊙, 500	K 4
	79009	Bovina, 1,428	A 3
	76230	Bowie, 5,185	G 4
	78832	Brackettville⊙, 1,539	D 8
	76825	Brady⊙, 5,557	E 6
	77422	Brazoria, 1,681	J 9
	76024	Breckenridge⊙, 5,944	F 5
	77833	Brenham⊙, 8,922	H 7
	77611	Bridge City, 8,164	L 7
	76026	Bridgeport, 3,614	G 4
	77423	Brookshire, 1,683	J 8
	77581	Brookside Village, 1,507	J 2
	79316	Brownfield⊙, 9,647	B 4
	78520	Brownsville⊙, 52,522	G 12
		Brownsville-Harlingen-San Benito, ‡140,368	G 12
	76801	Brownwood⊙, 17,368	F 6
	77801	Bryan⊙, 33,719	H 7
		Bryan-College Station, ‡57,978	H 7
	75831	Buffalo, 1,242	J 6
	77612	Buna, 1,649	L 7
†	79007	Bunavista, 1,402	C 2
†	77001	Bunker Hill Village, 3,977	J 1
	76354	Burkburnett, 9,230	F 3
	76028	Burleson, 7,713	F 2
	78611	Burnet⊙, 2,864	F 7
	77836	Caldwell⊙, 2,308	H 7
	77837	Calvert, 2,072	H 7
	76520	Cameron⊙, 5,546	H 7
	79014	Canadian⊙, 2,292	D 2
	75103	Canton⊙, 2,283	J 5
	79835	Canutillo, 1,588	A 10
	79015	Canyon⊙, 8,333	C 3

(continued on following page)

Agriculture, Industry and Resources

DOMINANT LAND USE

- Wheat, Grain Sorghums, Range Livestock
- Cotton, Wheat
- Specialized Cotton
- Cotton, General Farming
- Cotton, Forest Products
- Cotton, Range Livestock
- Rice, General Farming
- Peanuts, General Farming
- General Farming, Livestock, Cash Grain
- General Farming, Forest Products, Truck Farming, Cotton
- Fruit, Truck and Mixed Farming
- Range Livestock
- Forests
- Swampland, Limited Agriculture
- Nonagricultural Land
- Urban Areas

MAJOR MINERAL OCCURRENCES

At Asphalt
Cl Clay
Fe Iron Ore
G Natural Gas
Gn Granite
Gp Gypsum
Gr Graphite
He Helium
Ls Limestone
Na Salt
O Petroleum
S Sulfur
Tc Talc
U Uranium

Water Power
Major Industrial Areas

DALLAS
Aircraft, Food Processing, Machinery, Electrical & Metal Products, Automobile Assembly, Chemicals, Clothing

FORT WORTH
Aircraft, Automobile Assembly, Meat Packing, Food Processing

BEAUMONT–PORT ARTHUR
Oil Refining, Chemicals

EL PASO
Copper, Lead & Zinc Refining, Oil Refining, Clothing, Food Processing

SAN ANTONIO
Food Processing, Building Materials, Clothing, Chemicals

HOUSTON
Chemicals, Oil Refining, Machinery, Oil Field Equipment, Metal Products, Iron & Steel, Paper, Food Processing

CORPUS CHRISTI
Oil Refining, Aluminum

GALVESTON–TEXAS CITY
Chemicals, Oil Refining, Machinery, Metal Products

TEXAS
0 20 40 60 80 100 MI.
0 20 40 60 80 100 KM.
State Capitals
County Seats
© C.S. HAMMOND & Co., N.Y.
WESTERN PART OF TEXAS
Same scale as main map
FORT WORTH
DALLAS
HOUSTON
Longitude West of Greenwich
GULF OF MEXICO
MEXICO
NEW MEXICO
OKLAHOMA
ARK.
LA.
Austin
San Antonio
El Paso
Amarillo
Lubbock
Wichita Falls
Abilene
San Angelo
Waco
Corpus Christi
Galveston
Beaumont
Laredo
Brownsville
Odessa
Midland
Tyler
Texarkana
Port Arthur

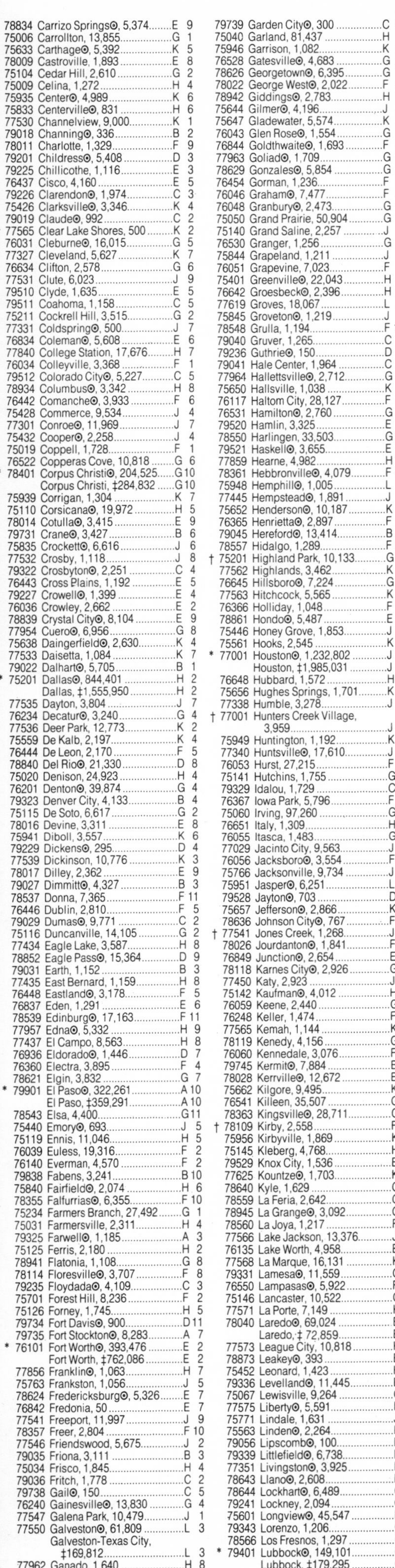

78834 Carrizo Springs⊙, 5,374 ....E 9
75006 Carrollton, 13,855 ....G 1
75633 Carthage⊙, 5,392 ....K 5
78009 Castroville, 1,893 ....E 8
75104 Cedar Hill, 2,610 ....G 2
75009 Celina, 1,272 ....H 4
75935 Center⊙, 4,989 ....K 6
75833 Centerville⊙, 831 ....H 6
77530 Channelview, 9,000 ....K 1
79018 Channing⊙, 336 ....B 2
78011 Charlotte, 1,329 ....F 9
79201 Childress⊙, 5,408 ....D 3
79225 Chillicothe, 1,116 ....E 3
76437 Cisco, 4,160 ....E 5
79226 Clarendon⊙, 1,974 ....C 3
75426 Clarksville⊙, 3,346 ....K 4
79019 Claude⊙, 992 ....C 2
† 77565 Clear Lake Shores, 500 ....K 2
76031 Cleburne⊙, 16,015 ....G 5
77327 Cleveland, 5,627 ....K 7
76634 Clifton, 2,578 ....G 6
77531 Clute, 6,023 ....J 9
79510 Clyde, 1,635 ....E 5
79511 Coahoma, 1,158 ....C 5
75211 Cockrell Hill, 3,515 ....G 2
77331 Coldspring⊙, 500 ....J 7
76834 Coleman⊙, 5,608 ....E 6
77840 College Station, 17,676 ....H 7
76034 Colleyville, 3,368 ....F 1
79512 Colorado City⊙, 5,227 ....C 5
78934 Columbus⊙, 3,342 ....H 8
76442 Comanche⊙, 3,933 ....F 6
75428 Commerce, 9,534 ....J 4
77301 Conroe⊙, 11,969 ....J 7
75432 Cooper⊙, 2,258 ....J 4
75019 Coppell, 1,728 ....F 1
76522 Copperas Cove, 10,818 ....G 6
* 78401 Corpus Christi⊙, 204,525 ....G 10
Corpus Christi, ‡284,832 ......G 10
75939 Corrigan, 1,304 ....K 7
75110 Corsicana⊙, 19,972 ....H 5
78014 Cotulla⊙, 3,415 ....E 9
79731 Crane⊙, 3,427 ....B 6
75835 Crockett⊙, 6,616 ....J 6
77532 Crosby, 1,118 ....J 8
79322 Crosbyton⊙, 2,251 ....C 4
76443 Cross Plains, 1,192 ....E 5
79227 Crowell⊙, 1,399 ....E 4
76036 Crowley, 2,662 ....E 2
78839 Crystal City⊙, 8,104 ....E 9
77954 Cuero⊙, 6,956 ....G 8
75638 Daingerfield⊙, 2,630 ....K 4
77533 Daisetta, 1,084 ....K 7
79022 Dalhart⊙, 5,705 ....B 1
* 75201 Dallas⊙, 844,401 ....H 2
Dallas, ‡1,555,950 ....H 2
77535 Dayton, 3,804 ....J 7
76234 Decatur⊙, 3,240 ....G 4
77536 Deer Park, 12,773 ....K 2
75559 De Kalb, 2,197 ....K 4
76444 De Leon, 2,170 ....F 5
78840 Del Rio⊙, 21,330 ....D 8
75020 Denison, 24,923 ....H 4
76201 Denton⊙, 39,874 ....G 4
79323 Denver City, 4,133 ....B 4
75115 De Soto, 6,617 ....G 2
78016 Devine, 3,311 ....E 8
75941 Diboll, 3,557 ....K 6
79229 Dickens⊙, 295 ....D 4
77539 Dickinson, 10,776 ....K 3
78017 Dilley, 2,362 ....E 9
79027 Dimmitt⊙, 4,327 ....B 3
78537 Donna, 7,365 ....F 11
76446 Dublin, 2,810 ....F 5
79029 Dumas⊙, 9,771 ....C 2
75116 Duncanville, 14,105 ....G 2
77434 Eagle Lake, 3,587 ....H 8
78852 Eagle Pass⊙, 15,364 ....D 9
79031 Earth, 1,152 ....B 3
77435 East Bernard, 1,159 ....H 8
76448 Eastland⊙, 3,178 ....F 5
76837 Eden, 1,291 ....E 6
78539 Edinburg⊙, 17,163 ....F 11
77957 Edna⊙, 5,332 ....H 9
77437 El Campo, 8,563 ....H 8
76936 Eldorado⊙, 1,446 ....D 7
76360 Electra, 3,895 ....F 4
78621 Elgin, 3,832 ....G 7
* 79901 El Paso⊙, 322,261 ....A 10
El Paso, ‡359,291 ....A 10
78543 Elsa, 4,400 ....G 11
75440 Emory⊙, 693 ....J 5
75119 Ennis, 11,046 ....H 5
76039 Euless, 19,316 ....F 2
76140 Everman, 4,570 ....F 2
79838 Fabens, 3,241 ....B 10
75840 Fairfield⊙, 2,074 ....H 6
78355 Falfurrias⊙, 6,355 ....F 10
75234 Farmers Branch, 27,492 ....G 1
75031 Farmersville, 2,311 ....H 4
79325 Farwell⊙, 1,185 ....A 3
75125 Ferris, 2,180 ....H 2
78941 Flatonia, 1,108 ....G 8
78114 Floresville⊙, 3,707 ....F 8
79235 Floydada⊙, 4,109 ....C 3
75701 Forest Hill, 8,236 ....F 2
75126 Forney, 1,745 ....H 5
79734 Fort Davis⊙, 900 ....D 11
79735 Fort Stockton⊙, 8,283 ....A 7
* 76101 Fort Worth⊙, 393,476 ....E 2
Fort Worth, ‡762,086 ....E 2
77856 Franklin⊙, 1,063 ....H 7
75763 Frankston, 1,056 ....J 5
78624 Fredericksburg⊙, 5,326 ....E 7
76842 Fredonia, 50 ....E 7
77541 Freeport, 11,997 ....J 9
78357 Freer, 2,804 ....F 10
77546 Friendswood, 5,675 ....J 2
79035 Friona, 3,111 ....B 3
75034 Frisco, 1,845 ....H 4
79036 Fritch, 1,778 ....C 2
79738 Gail⊙, 150 ....C 5
76240 Gainesville⊙, 13,830 ....G 4
77547 Galena Park, 10,479 ....J 1
77550 Galveston⊙, 61,809 ....L 3
Galveston-Texas City,
‡169,812 ....L 3
77962 Ganado, 1,640 ....H 8

79739 Garden City⊙, 300 ....C 6
75040 Garland, 81,437 ....H 1
75946 Garrison, 1,082 ....K 6
76528 Gatesville⊙, 4,683 ....G 6
78626 Georgetown⊙, 6,395 ....G 7
78022 George West⊙, 2,022 ....F 9
78942 Giddings⊙, 2,783 ....H 7
75644 Gilmer⊙, 4,196 ....J 5
75647 Gladewater, 5,574 ....K 5
76043 Glen Rose⊙, 1,554 ....G 5
76844 Goldthwaite⊙, 1,693 ....F 6
77963 Goliad⊙, 1,709 ....G 9
78629 Gonzales⊙, 5,854 ....G 8
76454 Gorman, 1,236 ....F 5
76046 Graham⊙, 7,477 ....F 4
76048 Granbury⊙, 2,473 ....G 5
75050 Grand Prairie, 50,904 ....G 2
75140 Grand Saline, 2,257 ....J 5
76530 Granger, 1,256 ....G 7
75844 Grapeland, 1,211 ....J 6
76051 Grapevine, 7,023 ....F 1
75401 Greenville⊙, 22,043 ....H 4
76642 Groesbeck⊙, 2,396 ....H 6
77619 Groves, 18,067 ....L 8
75845 Groveton⊙, 1,219 ....J 7
78548 Grulla, 1,194 ....F 11
79040 Gruver, 1,265 ....C 1
79236 Guthrie⊙, 150 ....D 4
79041 Hale Center, 1,964 ....C 3
77964 Hallettsville⊙, 2,712 ....G 8
75650 Hallsville, 1,038 ....K 5
76117 Haltom City, 28,127 ....F 2
76531 Hamilton⊙, 2,760 ....G 6
79520 Hamlin, 3,325 ....E 5
78550 Harlingen, 33,503 ....G 11
79521 Haskell⊙, 3,655 ....E 4
77859 Hearne, 4,982 ....H 7
78361 Hebbronville⊙, 4,079 ....F 10
75948 Hemphill⊙, 1,005 ....L 6
77445 Hempstead⊙, 1,891 ....J 7
75652 Henderson⊙, 10,187 ....K 5
76365 Henrietta⊙, 2,897 ....F 4
79045 Hereford⊙, 13,414 ....B 3
78557 Hidalgo, 1,289 ....F 11
† 75201 Highland Park, 10,133 ....G 2
77562 Highlands, 3,462 ....K 1
76645 Hillsboro⊙, 7,224 ....G 5
77563 Hitchcock, 5,565 ....K 3
76366 Holliday, 1,048 ....F 4
78861 Hondo⊙, 5,487 ....E 8
75446 Honey Grove, 1,853 ....J 4
75561 Hooks, 2,545 ....K 4
* 77001 Houston⊙, 1,232,802 ....J 2
Houston, ‡1,985,031 ....J 2
76648 Hubbard, 1,572 ....H 6
75656 Hughes Springs, 1,701 ....K 5
77338 Humble, 3,278 ....J 7
† 77001 Hunters Creek Village,
3,959 ....J 1
75949 Huntington, 1,192 ....K 6
77340 Huntsville⊙, 17,610 ....J 7
76053 Hurst, 27,215 ....F 2
75151 Hutchins, 1,755 ....G 2
79329 Idalou, 1,729 ....C 4
76367 Iowa Park, 5,796 ....F 4
75060 Irving, 97,260 ....G 2
76661 Italy, 1,309 ....H 5
76055 Itasca, 1,483 ....G 5
77029 Jacinto City, 9,563 ....J 1
76056 Jacksboro⊙, 3,554 ....F 4
75766 Jacksonville, 9,734 ....J 5
75951 Jasper⊙, 6,251 ....L 7
79528 Jayton⊙, 703 ....D 4
75657 Jefferson⊙, 2,866 ....K 5
78636 Johnson City⊙, 767 ....F 7
† 77541 Jones Creek, 1,268 ....J 9
78026 Jourdanton⊙, 1,841 ....F 9
76849 Junction⊙, 2,654 ....E 7
78118 Karnes City⊙, 2,926 ....G 9
77450 Katy, 2,923 ....J 8
75142 Kaufman⊙, 4,012 ....H 5
76059 Keene, 2,440 ....G 5
76248 Keller, 1,474 ....F 1
77565 Kemah, 1,144 ....K 2
78119 Kenedy, 4,156 ....G 9
76060 Kennedale, 3,076 ....F 2
79745 Kermit⊙, 7,884 ....B 6
78028 Kerrville⊙, 12,672 ....E 7
75662 Kilgore, 9,495 ....K 5
76541 Killeen, 35,507 ....G 6
78363 Kingsville⊙, 28,711 ....G 10
† 78109 Kirby, 2,558 ....F 8
75956 Kirbyville, 1,869 ....K 7
75145 Kleberg, 4,768 ....H 2
79529 Knox City, 1,536 ....E 4
77625 Kountze⊙, 1,703 ....K 7
78640 Kyle, 1,629 ....G 8
78559 La Feria, 2,642 ....G 11
78945 La Grange⊙, 3,092 ....G 8
78560 La Joya, 1,217 ....F 11
77566 Lake Jackson, 13,376 ....J 8
76135 Lake Worth, 4,958 ....E 2
77568 La Marque, 16,131 ....K 3
79331 Lamesa⊙, 11,559 ....C 5
76550 Lampasas⊙, 5,922 ....F 6
75146 Lancaster, 10,522 ....G 2
77571 La Porte, 7,149 ....K 2
78040 Laredo⊙, 69,024 ....E 10
Laredo, ‡ 72,859 ....E 10
77573 League City, 10,818 ....K 2
78873 Leakey⊙, 393 ....E 8
75452 Leonard, 1,423 ....H 4
79336 Levelland⊙, 11,445 ....B 4
75067 Lewisville, 9,264 ....G 5
77575 Liberty⊙, 5,591 ....K 7
75771 Lindale, 1,631 ....J 5
75563 Linden⊙, 2,264 ....K 4
79056 Lipscomb⊙, 100 ....D 1
79339 Littlefield⊙, 6,738 ....B 4
77351 Livingston⊙, 3,925 ....K 7
78643 Llano⊙, 2,608 ....F 7
78644 Lockhart⊙, 6,489 ....G 8
79241 Lockney, 2,094 ....C 3
75601 Longview⊙, 45,547 ....K 5
79343 Lorenzo, 1,206 ....C 4
78566 Los Fresnos, 1,297 ....G 11
* 79401 Lubbock⊙, 149,101 ....C 4
Lubbock, ‡179,295 ....C 4

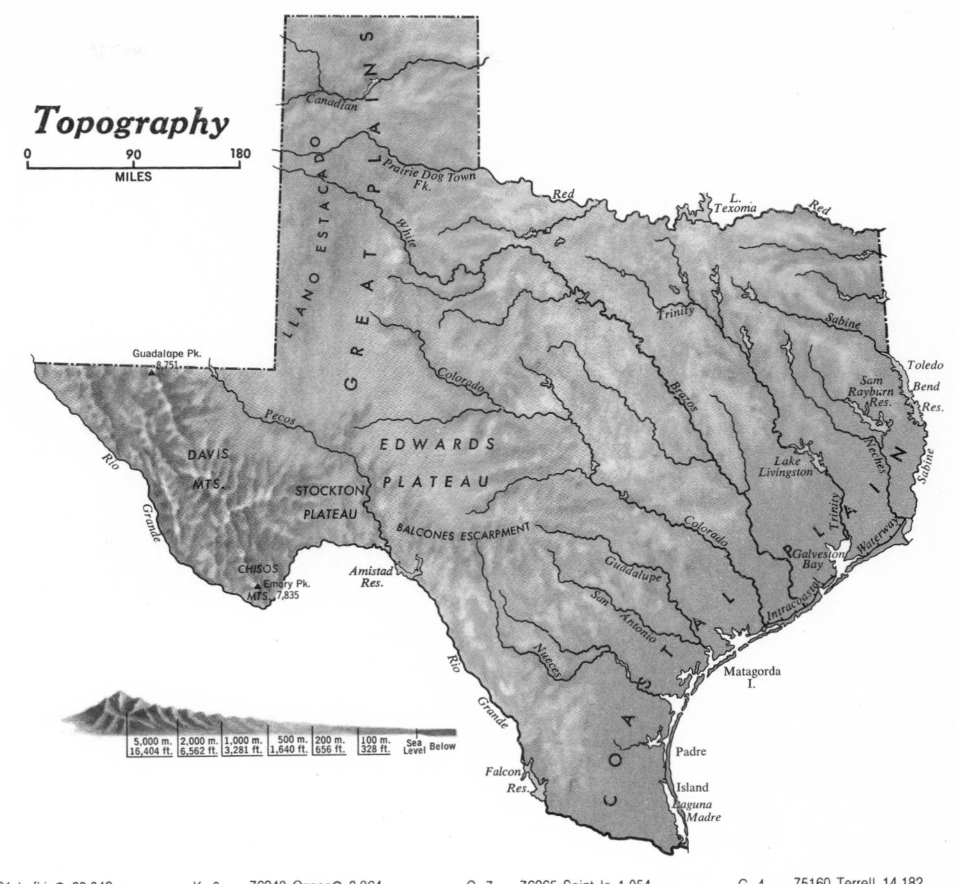

75901 Lufkin⊙, 23,049 ....K 6
78648 Luling, 4,719 ....G 8
78569 Lyford, 1,425 ....G 11
78052 Lytle, 1,271 ....F 8
75147 Mabank, 1,239 ....H 5
77864 Madisonville⊙, 2,881 ....J 7
75148 Malakoff, 2,045 ....H 5
76063 Mansfield, 3,658 ....F 2
78654 Marble Falls, 2,209 ....F 7
79843 Marfa⊙, 2,647 ....C 12
76661 Marlin⊙, 6,351 ....H 6
75670 Marshall⊙, 22,937 ....K 5
76664 Mart, 2,183 ....H 6
76856 Mason⊙, 1,806 ....E 7
79244 Matador⊙, 1,091 ....D 3
78368 Mathis, 5,351 ....G 9
75567 Maud, 1,107 ....K 4
78501 McAllen, 37,636 ....F 11
McAllen-Pharr-Edinburg,
‡181,535 ....F 11
79752 McCamey, 2,647 ....B 6
76657 McGregor, 4,365 ....G 6
75069 McKinney⊙, 15,193 ....H 4
79057 McLean, 1,183 ....D 2
77520 McNair, 2,039 ....K 1
79245 Memphis⊙, 3,227 ....D 3
76859 Menard⊙, 1,740 ....E 7
79754 Mentone⊙, 50 ....D 10
78570 Mercedes, 9,355 ....F 12
76665 Meridian⊙, 1,162 ....G 6
79536 Merkel, 2,163 ....E 5
76941 Mertzon⊙, 513 ....C 6
75149 Mesquite, 55,131 ....H 2
76667 Mexia, 5,943 ....H 6
79059 Miami⊙, 611 ....D 2
79701 Midland⊙, 59,463 ....C 6
Midland, ‡65,433 ....C 6
76065 Midlothian, 2,322 ....G 5
75773 Mineola, 3,926 ....J 5
76067 Mineral Wells, 18,411 ....F 5
78572 Mission, 13,043 ....F 11
77459 Missouri City, 4,136 ....J 2
79756 Monahans⊙, 8,333 ....B 6
76251 Montague⊙, 490 ....G 4
77580 Mont Belvieu, 1,144 ....L 1
76557 Moody, 1,286 ....G 6
79346 Morton⊙, 2,738 ....B 4
75455 Mount Pleasant⊙, 8,877 ....K 4
75457 Mount Vernon⊙, 1,806 ....J 4
76252 Muenster, 1,411 ....G 4
79347 Muleshoe⊙, 4,525 ....B 3
76371 Munday, 1,726 ....E 4
75961 Nacogdoches⊙, 22,544 ....J 6
75568 Naples, 1,726 ....K 4
75569 Nash, 1,961 ....K 4
78059 Natalia, 1,296 ....F 8
77868 Navasota, 5,111 ....J 7
77627 Nederland, 16,810 ....K 8
77461 Needville, 1,024 ....J 8
75570 New Boston, 3,699 ....K 4
78130 New Braunfels⊙, 17,859 ....F 8
75966 Newton⊙, 1,529 ....L 7
78140 Nixon, 1,925 ....G 8
76255 Nocona, 2,871 ....G 4
† 76118 North Richland Hills, 16,514 ..F 1
79760 Odessa⊙, 78,380 ....B 6
Odessa, ‡91,805 ....B 6
79351 O'Donnell, 1,148 ....C 5
76374 Olney, 3,624 ....F 4
79064 Olton, 1,782 ....B 3
77630 Orange⊙, 24,457 ....L 7
78372 Orange Grove, 1,075 ....F 10
75684 Overton, 2,084 ....K 5

76943 Ozona⊙, 2,864 ....C 7
79248 Paducah⊙, 2,052 ....D 4
76866 Paint Rock⊙, 193 ....E 6
77465 Palacios, 3,642 ....H 9
75801 Palestine⊙, 14,525 ....J 6
76072 Palo Pinto⊙, 250 ....F 5
79065 Pampa⊙, 21,726 ....D 2
79068 Panhandle⊙, 2,141 ....C 2
75460 Paris⊙, 23,441 ....J 4
* 77501 Pasadena, 89,277 ....J 2
77581 Pearland, 6,444 ....J 2
78061 Pearsall⊙, 5,545 ....E 9
79772 Pecos⊙, 12,682 ....D 10
79070 Perryton⊙, 7,810 ....D 1
79250 Petersburg, 1,300 ....C 4
78577 Pharr, 15,829 ....F 11
79071 Phillips, 2,515 ....C 2
76258 Pilot Point, 1,663 ....H 4
75968 Pineland, 1,127 ....L 6
† 77001 Piney Point Village, 2,548 ....J 1
75686 Pittsburg⊙, 3,844 ....J 4
79355 Plains⊙, 1,087 ....B 4
79072 Plainview⊙, 19,096 ....C 3
75074 Plano, 17,872 ....H 4
78064 Pleasanton, 5,407 ....F 9
77978 Point Comfort, 1,446 ....H 9
78373 Port Aransas, 1,218 ....H 10
77640 Port Arthur, 57,371 ....K 8
77365 Porter, 1,900 ....J 7
78578 Port Isabel, 3,067 ....G 11
78374 Portland, 7,302 ....G 10
77979 Port Lavaca⊙, 10,491 ....H 9
77651 Port Neches, 10,894 ....K 7
79356 Post⊙, 3,854 ....C 4
78065 Poteet, 3,013 ....F 8
78147 Poth, 1,296 ....F 8
77445 Prairie View, 3,589 ....J 7
78375 Premont, 3,282 ....F 10
79845 Presidio, 850 ....C 12
79252 Quanah⊙, 3,948 ....E 3
75572 Queen City, 1,227 ....L 4
75783 Quitman, 1,494 ....J 5
79357 Ralls, 1,962 ....C 4
76470 Ranger, 3,094 ....F 5
79778 Rankin⊙, 1,105 ....B 6
78580 Raymondville⊙, 7,987 ....G 11
78377 Refugio⊙, 4,340 ....G 9
75080 Richardson, 48,582 ....G 1
76118 Richland Hills, 8,865 ....F 2
77469 Richmond⊙, 5,777 ....J 8
78582 Rio Grande City⊙, 5,676 ....F 11
78583 Rio Hondo, 1,167 ....G 11
77019 River Oaks, 8,193 ....E 2
76945 Robert Lee⊙, 1,119 ....D 6
78380 Robstown, 11,217 ....G 10
79543 Roby⊙, 784 ....D 5
76567 Rockdale, 4,655 ....G 7
78382 Rockport⊙, 3,879 ....H 9
78880 Rocksprings⊙, 1,221 ....D 8
75087 Rockwall⊙, 3,121 ....H 5
76569 Rogers, 1,030 ....G 7
78584 Roma-Los Saenz, 2,154 ....E 11
79545 Roscoe, 1,580 ....D 5
76570 Rosebud, 1,597 ....G 7
77471 Rosenberg, 12,098 ....J 8
79546 Rotan, 2,404 ....D 5
78664 Round Rock, 2,811 ....G 7
75088 Rowlett, 1,696 ....H 1
75089 Royse City, 1,535 ....H 4
78151 Runge, 1,147 ....G 9
75785 Rusk⊙, 4,914 ....J 6
78881 Sabinal, 1,554 ....E 8
76079 Saginaw, 2,382 ....E 1

76265 Saint Jo, 1,054 ....G 4
76901 San Angelo⊙, 63,884 ....D 6
San Angelo, ‡71,047 ....D 6
* 78201 San Antonio⊙, 654,153 ....F 8
San Antonio, ‡864,014 ....F 8
75972 San Augustine⊙, 2,539 ....K 6
78586 San Benito, 15,176 ....G 12
79848 Sanderson⊙, 1,229 ....B 7
78384 San Diego⊙, 4,490 ....F 10
76266 Sanger, 1,603 ....G 4
78289 San Juan, 5,070 ....F 11
77539 San Leon, 1,500 ....L 2
78666 San Marcos⊙, 18,860 ....F 8
76877 San Saba⊙, 2,555 ....F 6
† 76101 Sansom Park Village, 4,771 ..E 2
76878 Santa Anna, 1,310 ....E 6
78385 Sarita⊙, 250 ....G 10
78154 Schertz, 4,061 ....F 8
78956 Schulenburg, 2,294 ....H 8
77586 Seabrook, 3,811 ....K 2
77983 Seadrift, 1,092 ....H 9
75159 Seagoville, 4,390 ....H 2
79359 Seagraves, 2,440 ....B 5
77474 Sealy, 2,685 ....H 8
78155 Seguin⊙, 15,934 ....G 8
79360 Seminole⊙, 5,007 ....B 5
76380 Seymour⊙, 3,469 ....E 4
79363 Shallowater, 1,339 ....B 4
79079 Shamrock, 2,644 ....D 2
† 77001 Sheldon, 1,665 ....K 1
75090 Sherman⊙, 29,061 ....H 4
Sherman-Denison, ‡83,225 ...H 4
77984 Shiner, 2,102 ....G 8
† 77571 Shore Acres, 1,872 ....K 2
79851 Sierra Blanca⊙, 900 ....B 11
77656 Silsbee, 7,271 ....K 7
79257 Silverton⊙, 1,026 ....C 3
78387 Sinton⊙, 5,563 ....G 9
79364 Slaton, 6,583 ....C 4
78957 Smithville, 2,959 ....G 7
79549 Snyder⊙, 11,171 ....D 5
77879 Somerville, 1,250 ....H 7
76950 Sonora⊙, 2,149 ....D 7
77659 Sourlake, 1,694 ....K 7
77587 South Houston, 11,527 ....J 2
76051 Southlake, 2,031 ....F 1
† 77001 Southside Place, 1,466 ....J 2
79081 Spearman⊙, 3,435 ....C 1
77373 Spring, 1,900 ....J 7
76082 Springtown, 1,194 ....G 5
† 77001 Spring Valley, 3,170 ....J 1
79370 Spur, 1,747 ....D 4
77477 Stafford, 2,906 ....J 2
79553 Stamford, 4,558 ....E 5
79782 Stanton⊙, 2,117 ....C 5
76401 Stephenville⊙, 9,277 ....F 5
76951 Sterling City⊙, 780 ....D 6
79083 Stinnett⊙, 2,014 ....C 2
78160 Stockdale, 1,132 ....G 8
79084 Stratford⊙, 2,139 ....C 1
77478 Sugar Land, 3,318 ....J 8
75482 Sulphur Springs⊙, 10,642 ....J 4
79372 Sundown, 1,129 ....B 4
79086 Sunray, 1,854 ....C 1
77480 Sweeny, 3,191 ....J 8
79556 Sweetwater⊙, 12,020 ....D 5
78390 Taft, 3,274 ....G 9
79373 Tahoka⊙, 2,956 ....C 4
76574 Taylor, 9,616 ....G 7
75860 Teague, 2,867 ....H 6
76501 Temple, 33,431 ....G 6
75974 Tenaha, 1,094 ....K 6
79852 Terlingua, 100 ....D 12

75160 Terrell, 14,182 ....H 5
† 78201 Terrell Hills, 5,225 ....F 8
75501 Texarkana, 30,497 ....L 4
Texarkana, ‡101,198 ....L 4
77590 Texas City, 38,908 ....K 3
73949 Texhoma, 356 ....C 1
76577 Thorndale, 1,031 ....G 7
78071 Three Rivers, 1,761 ....F 9
76083 Throckmorton⊙, 1,105 ....F 4
78072 Tilden⊙, 600 ....F 9
75975 Timpson, 1,254 ....K 6
77375 Tomball, 2,734 ....J 7
75163 Trinidad, 1,079 ....J 5
75862 Trinity, 2,512 ....J 7
75789 Troup, 1,668 ....J 5
79088 Tulia⊙, 5,294 ....C 3
75701 Tyler⊙, 57,770 ....J 5
Tyler, ‡97,096 ....J 5
78228 University Park, 23,498 ....H 2
78801 Uvalde⊙, 10,764 ....E 8
75790 Van, 1,593 ....J 5
75095 Van Alstyne, 1,981 ....H 4
79855 Van Horn⊙, 2,240 ....C 11
79092 Vega⊙, 839 ....B 2
76384 Vernon⊙, 11,454 ....E 3
77901 Victoria⊙, 41,349 ....H 9
77662 Vidor, 9,738 ....L 7
* 76701 Waco⊙, 95,326 ....G 6
Waco, ‡147,553 ....G 6
78959 Waelder, 1,138 ....G 8
75501 Wake Village, 2,408 ....K 4
77485 Wallis, 1,028 ....H 8
75692 Waskom, 1,460 ....L 5
75165 Waxahachie⊙, 13,452 ....H 5
76086 Weatherford⊙, 11,750 ....G 5
77598 Webster, 2,231 ....K 2
78962 Weimar, 2,104 ....H 8
79095 Wellington⊙, 2,884 ....D 3
78596 Weslaco, 15,313 ....G 11
76691 West, 2,406 ....G 6
77486 West Columbia, 3,335 ....J 8
77630 West Orange, 4,787 ....L 7
† 77001 West University Place,
13,317 ....J 2
† 76101 Westworth, 4,578 ....E 2
77488 Wharton⊙, 7,881 ....J 8
79096 Wheeler⊙, 1,116 ....D 2
79097 White Deer, 1,092 ....C 2
76273 Whitesboro, 2,927 ....H 4
76108 White Settlement, 13,449 ....E 2
75491 Whitewright, 1,742 ....H 4
76692 Whitney, 1,371 ....G 6
* 76301 Wichita Falls⊙, 97,564 ....F 4
Wichita Falls, ‡127,621 ....F 4
77378 Willis, 1,577 ....J 7
75169 Wills Point, 2,636 ....J 5
75172 Wilmer, 1,922 ....H 2
77665 Winnie, 1,543 ....K 8
75494 Winnsboro, 3,064 ....J 5
79567 Winters, 2,907 ....E 6
75496 Wolfe City, 1,433 ....J 4
79382 Wolfforth, 1,090 ....C 4
78393 Woodsboro, 1,839 ....G 9
75979 Woodville⊙, 2,662 ....K 7
76693 Wortham, 1,036 ....H 6
75098 Wylie, 2,675 ....H 5
77995 Yoakum, 5,755 ....G 8
78164 Yorktown, 2,411 ....G 9
78076 Zapata⊙, 2,102 ....E 11

⊙ County seat.
‡ Population of metropolitan area.
† Zip of nearest p.o.
* Multiple zips

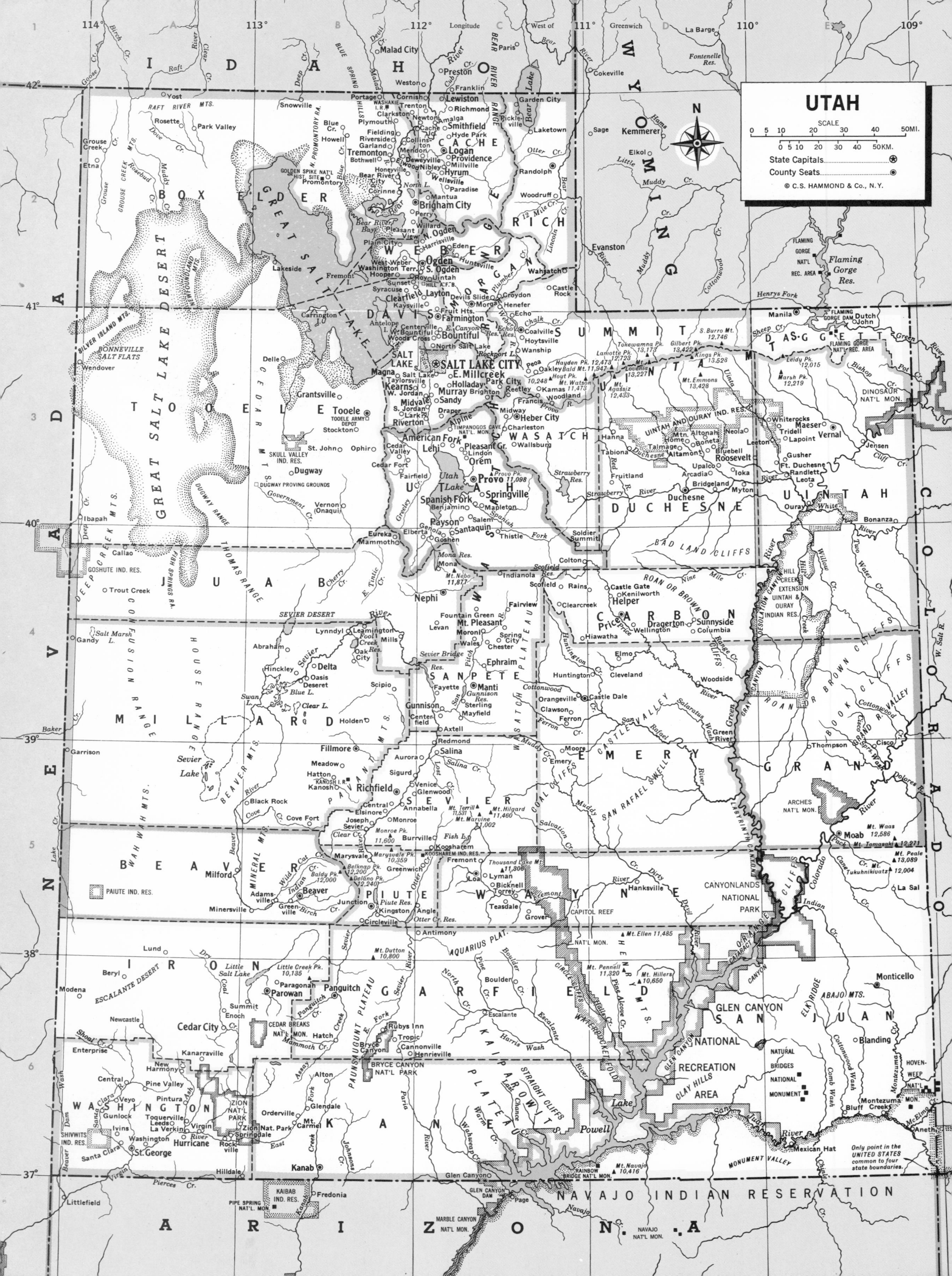

UTAH
SCALE
0 5 10 20 30 40 50MI.
0 5 10 20 30 40 50KM.
State Capitals
County Seats
© C.S. HAMMOND & Co., N. Y.
114°
113°
112°
111°
110°
109°
42°
41°
40°
39°
38°
37°
Longitude
West of
Greenwich
I D A H O
W Y O M I N G
C O L O R A D O
A R I Z O N A
N E V A D A
NAVAJO INDIAN RESERVATION
BOX ELDER
CACHE
RICH
WEBER
MORGAN
DAVIS
SALT LAKE
SUMMIT
DAGGETT
TOOELE
UTAH
WASATCH
DUCHESNE
UINTAH
JUAB
SANPETE
CARBON
MILLARD
SEVIER
EMERY
GRAND
BEAVER
PIUTE
WAYNE
IRON
GARFIELD
SAN JUAN
WASHINGTON
KANE
GREAT SALT LAKE
GREAT SALT LAKE DESERT
BONNEVILLE SALT FLATS
SEVIER DESERT
ESCALANTE DESERT
SALT LAKE CITY
Ogden
Provo
Logan
Brigham City
Tooele
Nephi
Manti
Richfield
Fillmore
Beaver
Parowan
Cedar City
St. George
Kanab
Panguitch
Moab
Monticello
Vernal
Duchesne
Price
Castle Dale
Heber City
Coalville
Randolph
Farmington
Loa
Junction
Manila
Bear Lake
Utah Lake
Sevier Lake
Flaming Gorge Res.
Lake Powell
GLEN CANYON NATIONAL RECREATION AREA
CANYONLANDS NATIONAL PARK
ARCHES NAT'L MON.
CAPITOL REEF NAT'L MON.
ZION NAT'L PARK
BRYCE CANYON NAT'L PARK
CEDAR BREAKS NAT'L MON.
DINOSAUR NAT'L MON.
NATURAL BRIDGES NATIONAL MONUMENT
HOVENWEEP NAT'L MON.
RAINBOW BRIDGE NAT'L MON.
TIMPANOGOS CAVE NAT'L MON.
GOLDEN SPIKE NAT'L HIST. SITE
UINTAH AND OURAY IND. RES.
SKULL VALLEY IND. RES.
GOSHUTE IND. RES.
PAIUTE IND. RES.
SHIVWITS IND. RES.
KAIBAB IND. RES.
DUGWAY PROVING GROUNDS
TOOELE ARMY DEPOT
HILL A.F.B.
MONUMENT VALLEY
Only point in the UNITED STATES common to four state boundaries.

Gene Ahrens — Shostal Associates

Rising like a Greek amphitheater, the Bingham Open Pit Copper Mine in Utah is constantly changing as giant electric shovels remove seven tons of earth at a time.

AREA 84,916 sq. mi.
POPULATION 1,059,273
CAPITAL Salt Lake City
LARGEST CITY Salt Lake City
HIGHEST POINT Kings Pk. 13,528 ft.
SETTLED IN 1847
ADMITTED TO UNION January 4, 1896
POPULAR NAME Beehive State
STATE FLOWER Sego Lily
STATE BIRD Sea Gull

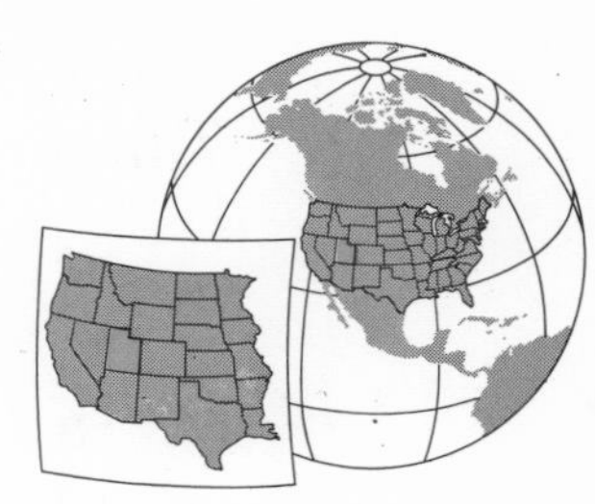

COUNTIES

Name/Pop.	Key
Beaver, 3,800	A 5
Box Elder, 28,129	A 2
Cache, 42,331	C 2
Carbon, 15,647	D 4
Daggett, 666	E 3
Davis, 99,028	B 3
Duchesne, 7,299	D 3
Emery, 5,137	D 4
Garfield, 3,157	C 6
Grand, 6,688	E 5
Iron, 12,177	A 6
Juab, 4,574	A 4
Kane, 2,421	B 6
Millard, 6,988	A 4
Morgan, 3,983	C 2
Piute, 1,164	B 5
Rich, 1,615	C 2
Salt Lake, 458,607	B 3
San Juan, 9,606	E 6
Sanpete, 10,976	C 4
Sevier, 10,103	C 5
Summit, 5,879	D 3
Tooele, 21,545	A 3
Uintah, 12,684	E 3
Utah, 137,776	C 3
Wasatch, 5,863	C 3
Washington, 13,669	A 6
Wayne, 1,483	C 5
Weber, 126,278	B 2

CITIES and TOWNS

Zip	Name/Pop.	Key
† 84003	Alpine, 1,047	C 3
84001	Altamont, 129	D 3
84002	Altonah, 225	D 3
† 84335	Amalga, 207	C 2
84003	American Fork, 7,713	C 3
84510	Aneth, 250	E 6
84711	Annabella, 221	B 5
84712	Antimony, 113	C 5
84005	Arcadia, 150	D 3
84620	Aurora, 493	B 5
84621	Axtell, 150	C 4
84301	Bear River City, 445	B 2
84713	Beaver⊙, 1,453	B 5
† 84660	Benjamin, 503	C 3
84715	Bicknell, 264	C 5
84511	Blanding, 2,250	E 6
84007	Bluebell, 210	D 3
84512	Bluff, 300	E 6
84008	Bonanza, 150	E 3
† 84337	Bothwell, 300	B 2
84716	Boulder, 93	C 6
84010	Bountiful, 27,853	C 3
84012	Bridgeland, 150	D 3
84302	Brigham City⊙, 14,007	C 2
84117	Brighton, 150	C 3
84717	Bryce Canyon, 229	B 6
84718	Cannonville, 113	B 6
84513	Castle Dale⊙, 541	D 4
84514	Castle Gate, 205	D 4
84720	Cedar City, 8,946	A 6
† 84013	Cedar Fort, 188	B 3
84013	Cedar Valley, 290	B 3
84622	Centerfield, 419	C 4
84014	Centerville, 3,268	C 3
84722	Central, 154	B 5
† 84032	Charleston, 196	C 3
84623	Chester, 130	C 4
84723	Circleville, 443	B 5
84305	Clarkston, 420	B 2
84516	Clawson, 95	C 4
84015	Clearfield, 13,316	B 2
84518	Cleveland, 244	D 4
84017	Coalville⊙, 864	C 3
84519	Columbia, 380	D 4
84307	Corinne, 471	B 2
84308	Cornish, 173	B 2
84018	Croydon, 90	C 2
84624	Delta, 1,610	B 4
84625	Deseret, 215	B 4
84309	Deweyville, 248	B 2
84520	Dragerton, 1,614	D 4
84020	Draper, 4,000	C 3
84021	Duchesne⊙, 1,094	D 3
84022	Dugway, 2,357	B 3
84023	Dutch John, 263	E 3
† 84101	East Millcreek, 26,579	C 3
84310	Eden, 421	C 2
84626	Elberta, 325	B 4
84521	Elmo, 141	D 4
84724	Elsinore, 357	B 5
† 84337	Elwood, 294	B 2
84522	Emery, 216	C 5
† 84720	Enoch, 120	A 6
84725	Enterprise, 844	A 6
84627	Ephraim, 2,127	C 4
84726	Escalante, 638	C 6
84628	Eureka, 753	B 4
84629	Fairview, 696	C 4
84025	Farmington⊙, 2,526	C 3
84630	Fayette, 93	C 4
84523	Ferron, 663	C 4
84311	Fielding, 254	B 2
84631	Fillmore⊙, 1,411	B 5
84026	Fort Duchesne, 300	E 3
84632	Fountain Green, 467	C 4
† 84036	Francis, 268	C 3
84727	Fremont, 160	C 5
† 84037	Fruit Heights, 800	C 2
84028	Garden City, 134	C 2
84312	Garland, 1,187	B 2
† 84655	Genola, 424	C 4
84729	Glendale, 200	B 6
84730	Glenwood, 212	C 5
84633	Goshen, 459	C 4
84029	Grantsville, 2,931	B 3
84525	Green River, 1,033	D 4
84731	Greenville, 97	B 5
84313	Grouse Creek, 100	A 2
84733	Gunlock, 93	A 6
84634	Gunnison, 1,073	C 4
84030	Gusher, 125	E 3
84734	Hanksville, 224	D 5
84031	Hanna, 135	D 3
† 84401	Harrisville, 603	C 2
84735	Hatch, 139	B 6
84032	Heber City⊙, 3,245	C 3
84526	Helper, 1,964	D 4
84033	Henefer, 446	C 2
84736	Henrieville, 145	C 6
84527	Hiawatha, 166	D 4
† 84767	Hilldale, 480	B 6
84635	Hinckley, 400	B 4
84636	Holden, 351	B 4
84117	Holladay, 23,014	C 3
84314	Honeyville, 640	B 2
84315	Hooper, 1,705	B 2
84316	Howell, 146	B 2
† 84017	Hoytsville, 500	C 3
84528	Huntington, 857	C 4
84317	Huntsville, 553	C 2
84737	Hurricane, 1,408	A 6
84318	Hyde Park, 1,025	C 2
84319	Hyrum, 2,340	C 2
84034	Ibapah, 135	A 3
† 84052	Ioka, 115	D 3
84738	Ivins, 137	A 6
84035	Jensen, 360	E 3
84739	Joseph, 125	B 5
84740	Junction⊙, 135	B 5
84036	Kamas, 806	C 3
84741	Kanab⊙, 1,381	B 6
84742	Kanarraville, 204	A 6
84637	Kanosh, 319	B 5
84037	Kaysville, 6,192	B 2
84118	Kearns, 17,071	B 3
84529	Kenilworth, 500	D 4
84743	Kingston, 114	B 5
84744	Koosharem, 141	C 5
84038	Laketown, 208	C 2
84039	Lapoint, 335	E 3
84040	Lark, 728	B 3
84530	La Sal, 200	E 5
84745	La Verkin, 463	A 6
84041	Layton, 13,603	C 2
84638	Leamington, 112	B 4
84746	Leeds, 151	A 6
84043	Lehi, 4,659	C 3
84639	Levan, 376	C 4
84320	Lewiston, 1,244	C 2
† 84062	Lindon, 1,644	C 3
84747	Loa⊙, 324	C 5
84321	Logan⊙, 22,333	C 2
84749	Lyman, 180	C 5
84640	Lynndyl, 111	B 4
† 84078	Maeser, 1,248	E 3
84044	Magna, 5,509	B 3
84046	Manila⊙, 226	E 3
84642	Manti⊙, 1,803	C 4
† 84302	Mantua, 413	C 2
† 84663	Mapleton, 1,980	C 3
84750	Marysvale, 289	B 5
84643	Mayfield, 267	C 4
84644	Meadow, 238	B 5
84325	Mendon, 345	B 2
84531	Mexican Hat, 100	E 6
84047	Midvale, 7,840	B 3
84049	Midway, 804	C 3
84751	Milford, 1,304	A 5
84326	Millville, 441	C 2
84752	Minersville, 448	A 5
84532	Moab⊙, 4,793	E 5
84645	Mona, 309	C 4
84754	Monroe, 918	B 5
84534	Montezuma Creek, 500	E 6
84535	Monticello⊙, 1,431	E 6
84050	Morgan⊙, 1,586	C 2
84646	Moroni, 894	C 4
84051	Mountain Home, 140	D 3
84647	Mount Pleasant, 1,516	C 4
84107	Murray, 21,206	C 3
84052	Myton, 322	D 3
84053	Neola, 600	D 3
84648	Nephi⊙, 2,699	C 4
84756	Newcastle, 150	A 6
84327	Newton, 444	C 2
† 84321	Nibley, 367	C 2
† 84401	North Ogden, 5,257	C 2
84054	North Salt Lake, 2,143	C 3
84649	Oak City, 278	B 4
84055	Oakley, 265	C 3
84650	Oasis, 150	B 4
* 84401	Ogden⊙, 69,478	C 2
	Ogden, ‡126,278	C 4
† 84080	Onaqui (Vernon), 541	B 3
84537	Orangeville, 511	C 4
84758	Orderville, 399	B 6
84057	Orem, 25,729	C 3
84059	Ouray, 100	E 3
84759	Panguitch⊙, 1,318	B 6
84328	Paradise, 399	C 2
84760	Paragonah, 275	B 6
84060	Park City, 1,193	C 3
84329	Park Valley, 100	A 2
84761	Parowan⊙, 1,423	B 6
84651	Payson, 4,501	C 3
84061	Peoa, 230	C 3
† 84302	Perry, 909	C 2
† 84028	Pickleville, 106	C 2
† 84401	Plain City, 1,543	B 2
84062	Pleasant Grove, 5,327	C 3
† 84401	Pleasant View, 2,028	B 2
84330	Plymouth, 203	B 2
84331	Portage, 144	B 2
84501	Price⊙, 6,218	D 4
84332	Providence, 1,608	C 2
84601	Provo⊙, 53,131	C 3
	Provo-Orem, ‡137,776	C 3
84063	Randlett, 350	E 3
84064	Randolph⊙, 500	C 2
84652	Redmond, 409	C 4
84701	Richfield⊙, 4,471	B 5
84333	Richmond, 1,000	C 2
84334	Riverside, 290	B 2
84065	Riverton, 2,820	B 3
84763	Rockville, 110	A 6
84066	Roosevelt, 2,005	D 3
84067	Roy, 14,356	C 2
84770	Saint George⊙, 7,097	A 6
84069	Saint John, 200	B 3
84653	Salem, 1,081	C 3
84654	Salina, 1,494	C 5
* 84101	Salt Lake City (cap.)⊙, 175,885	B 3
	Salt Lake City, ‡557,635	B 3
84070	Sandy, 6,438	C 3
84765	Santa Clara, 271	A 6
84655	Santaquin, 1,236	C 4
84656	Scipio, 264	B 4
84657	Sigurd, 291	B 5
84335	Smithfield, 3,342	C 2
84336	Snowville, 174	B 2
† 84065	South Jordan, 2,942	B 3
† 84401	South Ogden, 9,991	C 2
84115	South Salt Lake, 7,810	C 3
84660	Spanish Fork, 7,284	C 3
84662	Spring City, 456	C 4
84767	Springdale, 172	B 6
84663	Springville, 8,790	C 3
84665	Sterling, 144	C 4
84071	Stockton, 469	B 3
84772	Summit, 150	B 6
84539	Sunnyside, 485	D 4
† 84015	Sunset, 6,268	B 2
† 84041	Syracuse, 1,843	B 2
84072	Tabiona, 125	D 3
84073	Talmage, 140	D 3
† 84101	Taylorsville, 12,522	B 3
84773	Teasdale, 160	C 5
84074	Tooele⊙, 12,539	B 3
84774	Toquerville, 185	A 6
84337	Tremonton, 2,794	B 2
84338	Trenton, 390	B 2
84076	Tridell, 212	E 3
84776	Tropic, 329	B 6
† 84401	Uintah, 400	C 2
† 84007	Upalco, 150	D 3
84777	Venice, 220	C 5
84078	Vernal⊙, 3,908	E 3
84080	Vernon, 541	B 3
† 84722	Veyo, 144	A 6
84779	Virgin, 119	A 6
84082	Wallsburg, 211	C 3
† 84017	Wanship, 175	C 3
84780	Washington, 750	A 6
† 84401	Washington Terrace, 7,241	B 2
84542	Wellington, 922	D 4
84339	Wellsville, 1,267	C 2
84083	Wendover, 781	A 3
† 84087	West Bountiful, 1,246	B 3
84084	West Jordan, 4,221	B 3
† 84401	West Weber, 750	B 2
84085	Whiterocks, 600	E 3
84340	Willard, 1,045	C 2
† 84036	Woodland, 190	C 3
84086	Woodruff, 173	C 2
84087	Woods Cross, 3,124	B 3

⊙ County seat.
‡ Population of metropolitan area.
† Zip of nearest p.o.
* Multiple zips

Agriculture, Industry and Resources

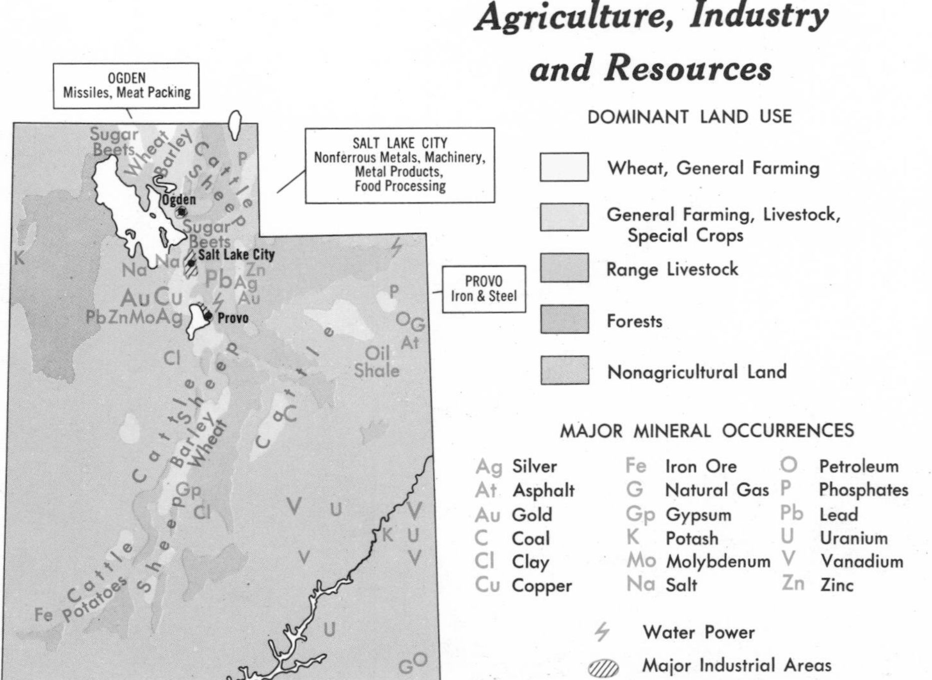

Topography

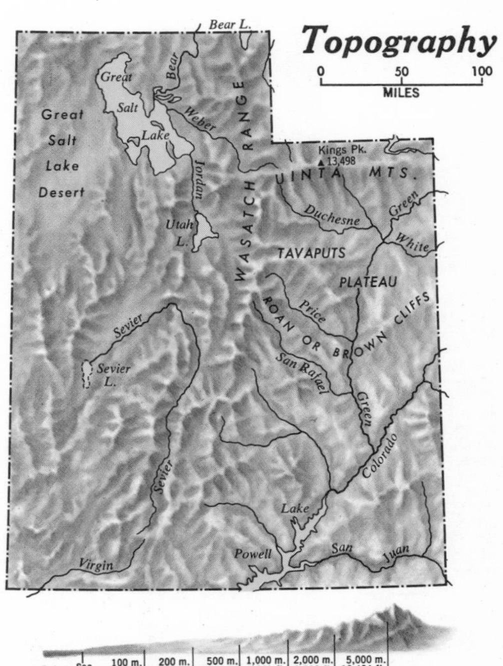

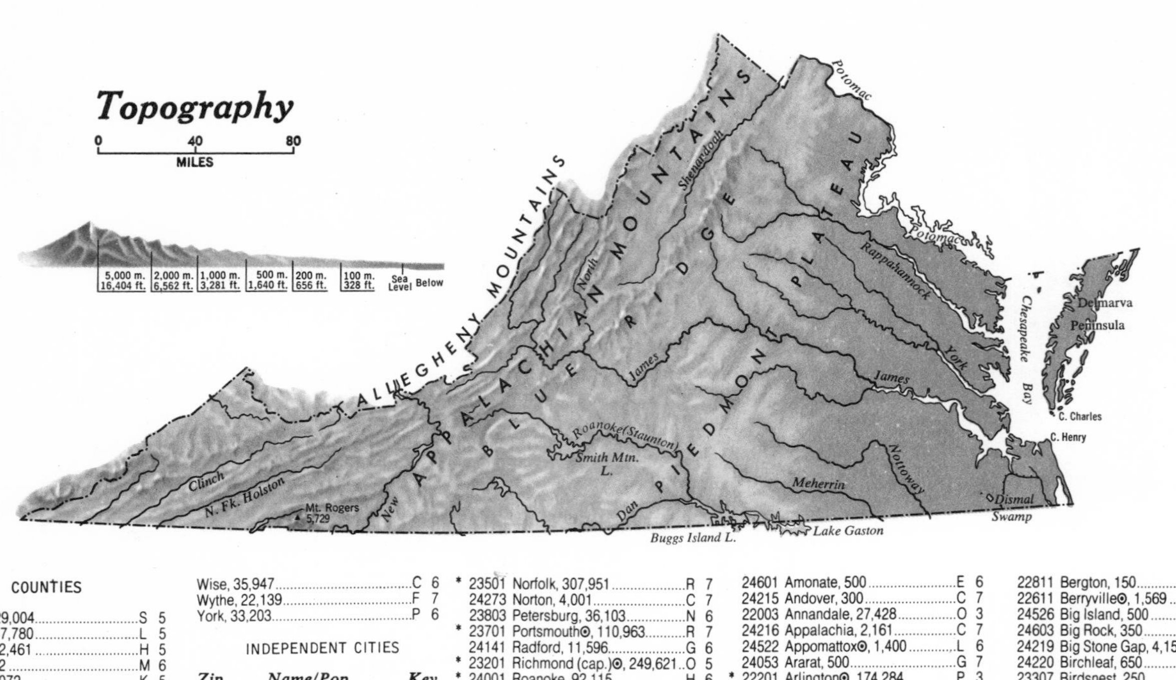

COUNTIES

Name/Pop.	Key
Accomack, 29,004	S 5
Albemarle, 37,780	L 5
Alleghany, 12,461	H 5
Amelia, 7,592	M 6
Amherst, 26,072	K 5
Appomattox, 9,784	L 6
Arlington, 174,284	O 3
Augusta, 44,220	K 4
Bath, 5,192	J 4
Bedford, 26,728	J 6
Bland, 5,423	F 6
Botetourt, 18,193	J 5
Brunswick, 16,172	N 7
Buchanan, 32,071	D 6
Buckingham, 10,597	L 5
Campbell, 43,319	K 6
Caroline, 13,925	O 4
Carroll, 23,092	G 7
Charles City, 6,158	O 6
Charlotte, 11,551	L 6
Chesterfield, 76,855	N 6
Clarke, 8,102	M 2
Craig, 3,524	H 6
Culpeper, 18,218	M 3
Cumberland, 6,179	M 6
Dickenson, 16,077	D 6
Dinwiddie, 25,046	N 6
Essex, 7,099	P 5
Fairfax, 455,021	O 3
Fauquier, 26,375	N 3
Floyd, 9,775	H 7
Fluvanna, 7,621	M 5
Franklin, 26,858	J 6
Frederick, 28,893	M 2
Giles, 16,741	G 6
Gloucester, 14,059	P 6
Goochland, 10,069	N 5
Grayson, 15,439	F 7
Greene, 5,248	M 4
Greensville, 9,604	N 7
Halifax, 30,076	L 7
Hanover, 37,479	N 5
Henrico, 154,364	O 6
Henry, 50,901	J 7
Highland, 2,529	J 4
Isle of Wight, 18,285	P 7
James City, 17,853	P 6
King and Queen, 5,491	P 5
King George, 8,039	O 4
King William, 7,497	O 5
Lancaster, 9,126	R 5
Lee, 20,321	B 7
Loudoun, 37,150	N 2
Louisa, 14,004	N 5
Lunenburg, 11,687	M 7
Madison, 8,638	M 4
Mathews, 7,168	R 6
Mecklenburg, 29,426	M 7
Middlesex, 6,295	R 5
Montgomery, 47,157	H 6
Nansemond, 35,166	P 7
Nelson, 11,702	L 5
New Kent, 5,300	P 5
Northampton, 14,442	S 6
Northumberland, 9,239	R 5
Nottoway, 14,260	M 6
Orange, 13,792	M 4
Page, 16,581	M 3
Patrick, 15,282	H 7
Pittsylvania, 58,789	K 7
Powhatan, 7,696	N 5
Prince Edward, 14,379	M 6
Prince George, 29,092	O 6
Prince William, 111,102	O 3
Pulaski, 29,564	G 6
Rappahannock, 5,199	M 3
Richmond, 5,841	P 5
Roanoke, 67,339	H 6
Rockbridge, 16,637	K 5
Rockingham, 47,890	L 4
Russell, 24,533	D 7
Scott, 24,376	C 7
Shenandoah, 22,852	L 3
Smyth, 31,349	E 7
Southampton, 18,582	O 7
Spotsylvania, 16,424	N 4
Stafford, 24,587	O 4
Surry, 5,882	P 6
Sussex, 11,464	O 7
Tazewell, 39,816	E 6
Warren, 15,301	M 3
Washington, 40,835	D 7
Westmoreland, 12,142	P 4
Wise, 35,947	C 6
Wythe, 22,139	F 7
York, 33,203	P 6

INDEPENDENT CITIES

	Zip	Name/Pop.	Key
*	22301	Alexandria, 110,938	P 3
	24523	Bedford⊙, 6,011	J 6
	24201	Bristol, 14,857	D 7
	24416	Buena Vista, 6,425	K 5
*	22901	Charlottesville⊙, 38,880	M 4
*	23320	Chesapeake, 89,580	R 7
	24422	Clifton Forge, 5,501	J 5
	23834	Colonial Heights, 15,097	O 6
	24426	Covington⊙, 10,060	H 5
	24541	Danville, 46,391	J 7
	23847	Emporia⊙, 5,300	N 7
	22030	Fairfax⊙, 21,970	O 3
*	22040	Falls Church, 10,772	O 3
	23851	Franklin, 6,880	P 7
	22401	Fredericksburg, 14,450	N 4
	24333	Galax, 6,278	G 7
*	23360	Hampton, 120,779	R 6
	22801	Harrisonburg⊙, 14,605	K 4
	23860	Hopewell, 23,471	O 6
	24450	Lexington⊙, 7,597	J 5
*	24501	Lynchburg, 54,083	K 6
	24112	Martinsville⊙, 19,653	J 7
*	23601	Newport News, 138,177	P 6
*	23501	Norfolk, 307,951	R 7
	24273	Norton, 4,001	C 7
	23803	Petersburg, 36,103	N 6
*	23701	Portsmouth⊙, 110,963	R 7
	24141	Radford, 11,596	G 6
*	23201	Richmond (cap.)⊙, 249,621	O 5
*	24001	Roanoke, 92,115	H 6
	24153	Salem⊙, 21,982	H 6
	24592	South Boston, 6,889	L 7
	24401	Staunton⊙, 24,504	K 4
	23434	Suffolk⊙, 9,858	P 7
*	23450	Virginia Beach, 172,106	S 7
	22980	Waynesboro, 16,707	K 4
	23185	Williamsburg⊙, 9,069	P 6
	22601	Winchester⊙, 14,643	M 2

CITIES and TOWNS

	Zip	Name/Pop.	Key
	24210	Abingdon⊙, 4,376	D 7
	23301	Accomac⊙, 373	S 5
	23001	Achilles, 525	R 6
	22920	Afton, 525	L 4
†	22959	Alberene, 200	L 5
	23821	Alberta, 466	N 7
	24310	Allisonia, 325	G 7
	24517	Altavista, 2,708	K 6
	24520	Alton, 250	K 7
	23002	Amelia Court House⊙, 537	N 6
	24521	Amherst⊙, 1,108	K 5
	22002	Amissville, 150	M 3
	24601	Amonate, 500	E 6
	24215	Andover, 300	C 7
	22003	Annandale, 27,428	O 3
	24216	Appalachia, 2,161	C 7
	24522	Appomattox⊙, 1,400	L 6
	24053	Ararat, 500	G 7
*	22201	Arlington⊙, 174,284	P 3
	22922	Arrington, 350	L 5
	23004	Arvonia, 300	M 5
	22011	Ashburn, 345	O 2
	23005	Ashland, 2,934	N 5
	24311	Atkins, 500	F 7
	24411	Augusta Springs, 400	K 4
	24312	Austinville, 750	F 7
	24054	Axton, 540	J 7
	23009	Aylett, 300	O 5
	24602	Bandy, 500	E 6
	24231	Banner, 350	D 7
	22923	Barboursville, 207	M 4
	24313	Barren Springs, 150	G 7
	24055	Bassett, 3,058	J 7
	24314	Bastian, 450	F 6
	22924	Batesville, 450	L 5
	23016	Beaverlett, 178	R 6
†	23201	Bellbluff, 3,900	N 6
	23306	Belle Haven, 504	S 5
	22307	Belleview, 8,299	O 3
	24218	Ben Hur, 300	B 7
	24059	Bent Mountain, 140	H 6
	22610	Bentonville, 700	M 3
	22811	Bergton, 150	L 3
	22611	Berryville⊙, 1,569	M 2
	24526	Big Island, 500	K 5
	24603	Big Rock, 350	D 6
	24219	Big Stone Gap, 4,153	C 7
	24220	Birchleaf, 650	D 6
	23307	Birdsnest, 250	S 6
	24604	Bishop, 400	E 6
	23916	Blackridge, 140	M 7
	24060	Blacksburg, 9,384	H 6
	23824	Blackstone, 3,412	N 6
	24221	Blackwater, 205	B 7
	24527	Blairs, 500	K 7
	24315	Bland⊙, 950	F 6
	23308	Bloxom, 391	S 5
	24605	Bluefield, 5,286	F 6
	22012	Bluemont, 310	N 2
	24064	Blue Ridge, 926	J 6
	24606	Boissevain, 975	F 6
	23235	Bon Air, 10,562	N 5
	24065	Boones Mill, 363	J 6
	22427	Bowling Green⊙, 528	O 4
	22620	Boyce, 378	M 2
	23917	Boydton⊙, 541	M 7
	23827	Boykins, 742	O 7
	23828	Branchville, 189	O 7
	22714	Brandy Station, 530	N 4
	24607	Breaks, 500	D 6
	23022	Bremo Bluff, 200	M 5
	22812	Bridgewater, 2,828	K 4
	22715	Brightwood, 250	M 4
	24316	Broadford, 850	E 7
	22815	Broadway, 887	L 3
	23920	Brodnax, 569	N 7
	22430	Brooke, 275	O 4
	24528	Brookneal, 1,037	L 6
	24415	Brownsburg, 200	K 5
	22610	Browntown, 175	M 3
	22622	Brucetown, 150	M 2
†	22810	Bryce Mountain, 205	L 3
	24066	Buchanan, 1,326	J 5
	23921	Buckingham⊙, 200	L 5
	22432	Burgess, 300	R 5
	24608	Burkes Garden, 275	F 6
	23922	Burkeville, 703	M 6
	24420	Burnsville, 138	J 4
	22435	Callao, 500	P 5
	24067	Callaway, 191	H 7
	22016	Calverton, 200	N 3
	24317	Cana, 168	G 7
	23310	Cape Charles, 1,689	R 6
	23313	Capeville, 300	R 6
	23829	Capron, 314	O 7
†	23039	Cardwell, 200	N 5
	23315	Carrsville, 375	P 7
	23830	Carson, 275	O 6
	22017	Casanova, 200	N 3
	24069	Cascade, 835	J 7
	24224	Castlewood, 799	D 7
	22019	Catlett, 500	N 3
	24609	Cedar Bluff, 1,050	E 6
†	24368	Cedar Springs, 200	F 7
†	22630	Cedarville, 150	M 3
	22437	Center Cross, 360	P 5
	22438	Champlain, 160	O 4
	22021	Chantilly, 620	O 3
	23030	Charles City⊙, 5	O 6
	23923	Charlotte Court House⊙, 539	L 6
	23924	Chase City, 2,909	M 7
	24531	Chatham⊙, 1,801	K 7
	23316	Cheriton, 655	R 6
	23831	Chester, 5,556	O 6
	23832	Chesterfield⊙, 950	N 6
	22623	Chester Gap, 450	M 3
	24319	Chilhowie, 1,317	E 7
	23336	Chincoteague, 1,867	T 5
	24073	Christiansburg⊙, 7,857	H 6
	23339	Chuckatuck, 500	P 7
	23032	Church View, 200	P 5
	24421	Churchville, 250	K 4
	22928	Cismont, 400	M 4
	23899	Claremont, 383	P 6
	23927	Clarksville, 1,641	M 7
	24076	Claudville, 180	H 7
†	23061	Clay Bank, 200	P 6
	24225	Cleveland, 357	D 7
	24533	Clifford, 160	K 5
	24321	Clinchburg, 250	E 7
	24226	Clinchco, 900	D 6
	24227	Clinchport, 286	C 7
	24228	Clintwood⊙, 1,320	D 6

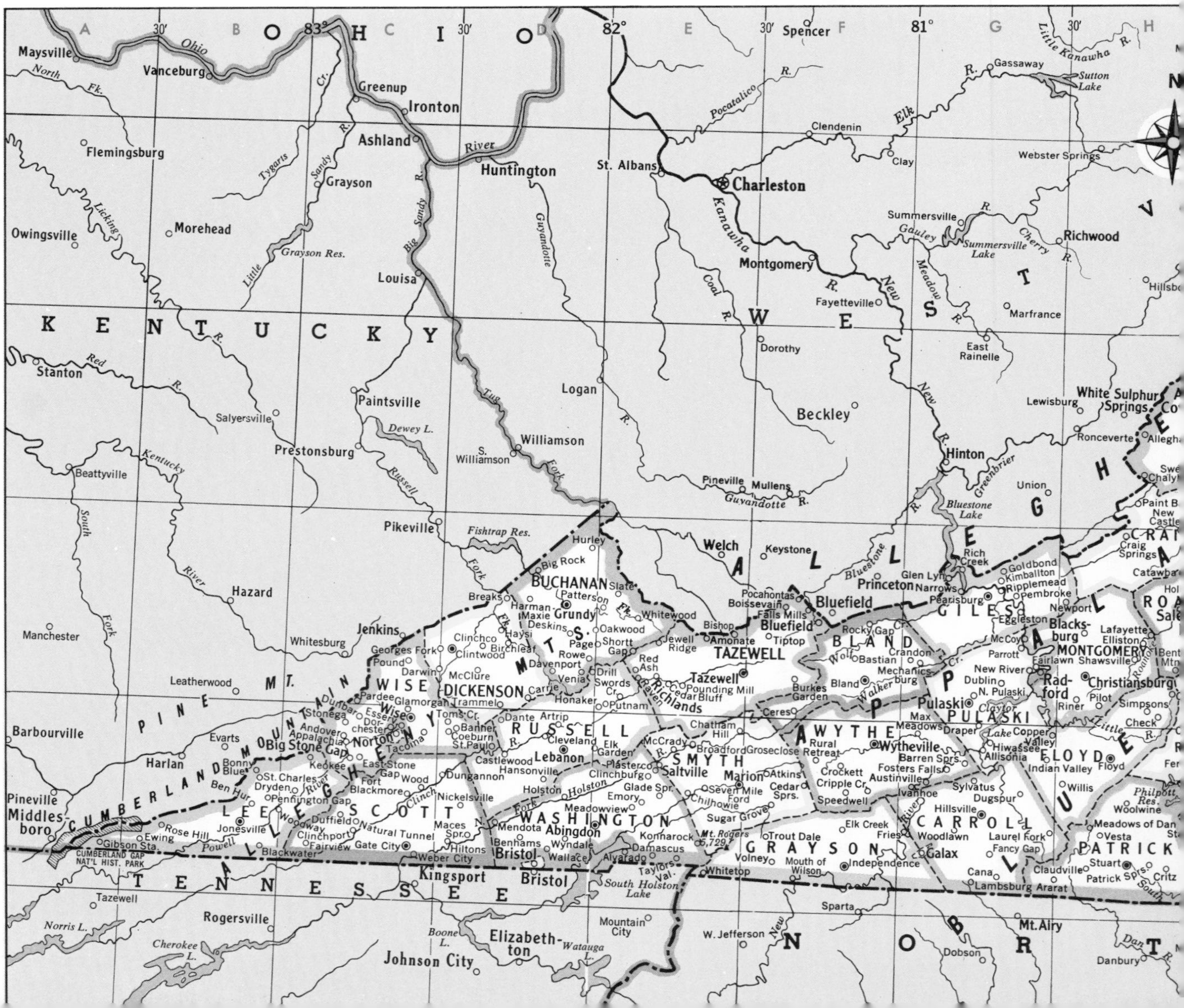

24534 Clover, 227 .... L 7
24077 Cloverdale, 850 .... J 6
24535 Cluster Springs, 500 .... L 7
23035 Cobbs Creek, 600 .... R 6
24230 Coeburn, 2,362 .... D 7
24536 Coleman Falls, 250 .... K 6
22442 Coles Point, 200 .... P 4
† 24450 Collierstown, 125 .... J 5
24078 Collinsville, 6,015 .... J 7
22443 Colonial Beach, 2,058 .... P 4
23038 Columbia, 125 .... M 5
24538 Concord, 400 .... K 6
24080 Copper Valley, 425 .... G 7
23837 Courtland⊙, 899 .... O 7
22931 Covesville, 500 .... L 5
24430 Craigsville, 988 .... J 4
† 24315 Crandon, 250 .... G 6
23930 Crewe, 1,433 .... M 6
24431 Crimora, 450 .... L 4
24322 Cripple Creek, 200 .... F 7
24082 Critz, 150 .... H 7
24323 Crockett, 300 .... F 7
22625 Cross Junction, 200 .... M 2
22932 Crozet, 1,433 .... L 4
23039 Crozier, 300 .... N 5
24539 Crystal Hill, 475 .... L 7
23934 Cullen, 140 .... L 6
22701 Culpeper⊙, 6,056 .... M 4
23040 Cumberland⊙, 500 .... M 6
22448 Dahlgren, 950 .... O 4
† 22172 Dale City, 13,857 .... O 3
24083 Daleville, 450 .... J 6
24236 Damascus, 1,230 .... E 7
24237 Dante, 1,153 .... D 7
24239 Davenport, 300 .... D 6
22821 Dayton, 978 .... L 4
24432 Deerfield, 200 .... K 4
22025 Delaplane, 164 .... N 3
23043 Deltaville, 950 .... R 5
23839 Dendron, 336 .... P 6
23840 De Witt, 140 .... N 6
23936 Dillwyn, 497 .... M 5
23841 Dinwiddie⊙, 500 .... N 6
23842 Disputanta, 500 .... O 6
23047 Doswell, 200 .... N 5
23937 Drakes Branch, 702 .... L 7
24324 Draper, 276 .... G 7
23844 Drewryville, 250 .... O 7
24242 Drill, 192 .... E 6
23346 Driver, 250 .... P 7
24243 Dryden, 400 .... B 7
24084 Dublin, 1,653 .... G 6
22026 Dumfries, 1,890 .... O 3
23938 Dundas, 200 .... M 7
24245 Dungannon, 282 .... D 7
22454 Dunnsville, 312 .... P 5
24085 Eagle Rock, 750 .... J 5
22936 Earleysville, 210 .... M 4
24246 East Stone Gap, 500 .... C 7
23347 Eastville⊙, 203 .... R 6
23845 Ebony, 150 .... N 7
23349 Eclipse, 295 .... R 7
† 22485 Edgehill, 225 .... O 4
22824 Edinburg, 766 .... M 3
24086 Eggleston, 500 .... G 6
23846 Elberon, 200 .... P 6
22827 Elkton, 1,511 .... L 4
24087 Elliston, 700 .... H 6
24327 Emory, 458 .... E 7
22937 Esmont, 950 .... L 5
24274 Esserville, 975 .... G 2
23803 Ettrick, 3,950 .... O 6
23939 Evergreen, 300 .... L 6
24550 Evington, 175 .... K 6
24248 Ewing, 700 .... B 7
23350 Exmore, 1,421 .... S 5
24435 Fairfield, 465 .... K 5
24141 Fairlawn, 1,767 .... G 6
† 22539 Fairport, 175 .... R 5
24613 Falls Mills, 500 .... F 6
22401 Falmouth, 2,139 .... O 4
23901 Farmville⊙, 4,331 .... M 6
22460 Farnham, 150 .... P 5
24088 Ferrum, 200 .... H 7
24089 Fieldale, 1,337 .... H 7
24090 Fincastle⊙, 397 .... J 6
22939 Fishersville, 975 .... K 4
22627 Flint Hill, 200 .... M 3
24091 Floyd⊙, 474 .... H 7
24551 Forest, 497 .... K 6
23055 Fork Union, 350 .... M 5
24250 Fort Blackmore, 600 .... C 7
22578 Foxwells, 400 .... R 5
24330 Fries, 885 .... F 7
22630 Front Royal⊙, 8,211 .... M 3
22830 Fulks Run, 130 .... L 3
22065 Gainesville, 600 .... N 3
22463 Garrisonville, 200 .... N 4
23857 Gasburg, 150 .... N 7
24251 Gate City⊙, 1,914 .... C 7
† 24228 Georges Fork, 500 .... C 6
† 24248 Gibson Station, 200 .... A 7
24340 Glade Spring, 1,615 .... E 7
24554 Gladys, 312 .... K 6
24555 Glasgow, 1,304 .... K 5
23060 Glen Allen, 985 .... N 5
24093 Glen Lyn, 191 .... G 6
24438 Glen Wilton, 280 .... J 5
† 24541 Glenwood, 1,295 .... K 7
23061 Gloucester⊙, 700 .... P 6
23062 Gloucester Point, 850 .... R 6
24094 Goldbond, 250 .... G 6
22720 Goldvein, 350 .... N 4
23063 Goochland⊙, 800 .... N 5
24556 Goode, 200 .... K 6
22942 Gordonsville, 1,253 .... M 4
22637 Gore, 150 .... M 2
23490 Grafton, 500 .... P 6
23356 Greenbackville, 300 .... T 5
23942 Green Bay, 150 .... M 6

(continued on following page)

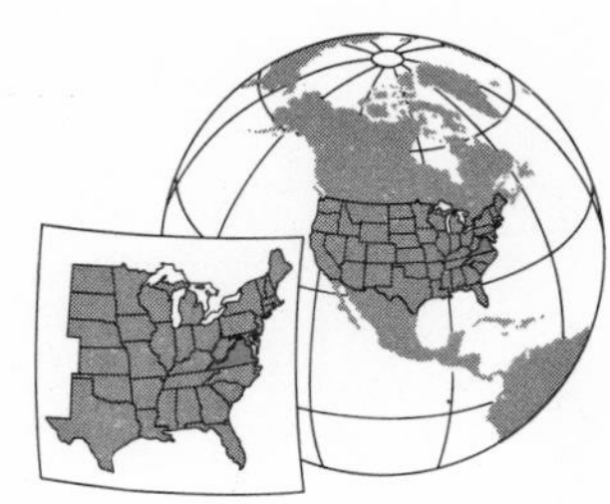

AREA 40,817 sq. mi.
POPULATION 4,648,494
CAPITAL Richmond
LARGEST CITY Norfolk
HIGHEST POINT Mt. Rogers 5,729 ft.
SETTLED IN 1607
ADMITTED TO UNION June 26, 1788
POPULAR NAME Old Dominion
STATE FLOWER Dogwood
STATE BIRD Cardinal

VIRGINIA

SCALE
0 5 10 20 30 40 MI.
0 5 10 20 30 40 KM.
National Capital
State Capitals
County Seats
Canals

Agriculture, Industry and Resources

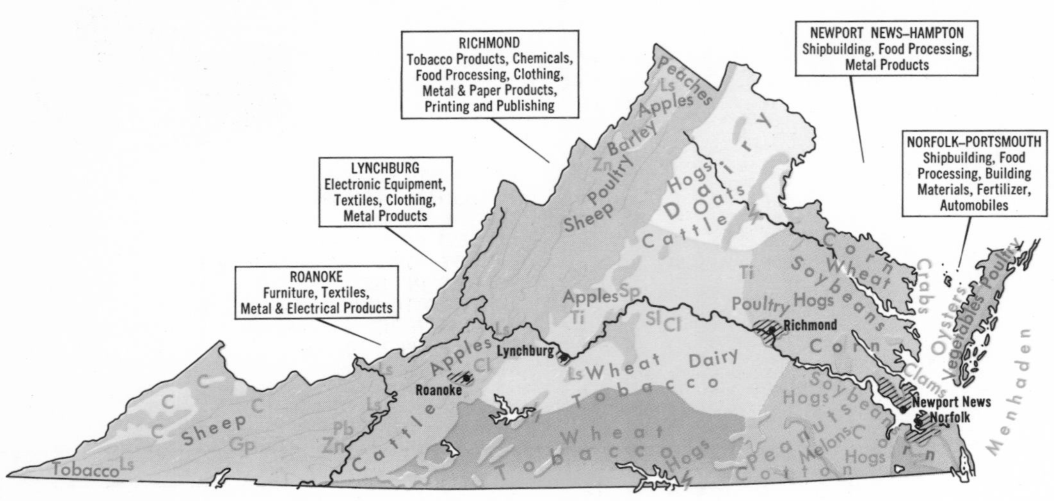

MAJOR MINERAL OCCURRENCES

C Coal
Cl Clay
Gp Gypsum
Ls Limestone
Pb Lead
Sl Slate
Sp Soapstone
Ti Titanium
Zn Zinc
Water Power
Major Industrial Areas

DOMINANT LAND USE

- Dairy, General Farming
- General Farming, Livestock, Dairy
- General Farming, Livestock, Tobacco
- General Farming, Livestock, Fruit, Tobacco
- General Farming, Truck Farming, Tobacco, Livestock
- Tobacco, General Farming
- Peanuts, General Farming
- Fruit and Mixed Farming
- Truck and Mixed Farming
- Forests
- Swampland, Limited Agriculture

Eric Carle — Shostal Associates

The Governor's Palace in Williamsburg, Virginia, typifies the splendor enjoyed by the royal governors in residence from 1720 to 1780.

Zip	Place	Key
23357	Greenbush, 200	S 5
24440	Greenville, 450	K 5
22943	Greenwood, 800	L 4
24557	Gretna, 986	K 7
24441	Grottoes, 1,166	L 4
† 22301	Groveton, 11,750	O 3
24614	Grundy⊙, 2,054	D 6
23065	Gum Spring, 450	N 5
23066	Gwynn, 438	R 5
23358	Hacksneck, 200	S 5
24558	Halifax⊙, 899	L 7
23359	Hallwood, 254	S 5
22068	Hamilton, 502	N 2
23943	Hampden-Sydney, 1,325	L 6
23069	Hanover⊙, 975	O 5
23389	Harborton, 200	S 5
24101	Hardy, 325	J 6
24618	Harman-Maxie, 925	D 6
23071	Hartfield, 450	R 5
22069	Haymarket, 288	N 3
22472	Haynesville, 500	P 5
24256	Haysi, 428	D 6
24442	Head Waters, 250	K 4
24443	Healing Springs, 175	J 5
22473	Heathsville⊙, 300	P 5
24102	Henry, 350	J 7
22070	Herndon, 4,301	O 3
23075	Highland Springs, 7,345	O 5
22132	Hillsboro, 135	N 2
24343	Hillsville⊙, 1,149	G 7
24258	Hiltons, 300	D 7
24347	Hiwassee, 500	G 7
† 22191	Hoadly, 400	O 3
23390	Hobson, 800	P 7
23391	Holland, 400	P 7
24020	Hollins College, 1,082	H 6
24260	Honaker, 911	D 6
23395	Horntown, 450	T 5
24445	Hot Springs, 300	J 4
24104	Huddleston, 200	K 6
22639	Hume, 350	N 3
24620	Hurley, 850	D 6
24563	Hurt, 1,434	K 6
24348	Independence⊙, 673	F 7
24448	Iron Gate, 692	J 5
22480	Irvington, 504	R 5
23397	Isle of Wight⊙, 4	P 7
24350	Ivanhoe, 900	G 7
23866	Ivor, 444	P 7
22945	Ivy, 450	L 4
23081	Jamestown, 12	P 6
23398	Jamesville, 400	S 5
23867	Jarratt, 591	O 7
24565	Java, 160	K 7
22724	Jeffersonton, 500	N 3
† 23434	Jericho, 2,438	P 7
24622	Jewell Ridge, 500	E 6
24263	Jonesville⊙, 700	B 7
24566	Keeling, 680	K 7
22832	Keezletown, 210	L 4
23401	Keller, 235	S 5
23944	Kenbridge, 1,223	M 7
23084	Kents Store, 150	M 5
24265	Keokee, 800	C 7
22947	Keswick, 300	M 4
23947	Keysville, 818	M 6
22482	Kilmarnock, 841	R 5
24107	Kimballton, 135	G 6
23085	King and Queen Court House⊙, 100	P 5
22485	King George⊙, 225	O 4
23086	King William⊙, 125	O 5
22488	Kinsale, 250	P 4
† 24236	Konnarock, 300	E 7
22833	Lacey Spring, 300	L 3
23950	La Crosse, 674	M 7
22501	Ladysmith, 300	N 4
24108	Lafayette, 276	H 6
23228	Lakeside, 11,137	N 5
24351	Lambsburg, 650	G 7
22503	Lancaster⊙, 104	R 5
23868	Lawrenceville⊙, 1,636	N 7
24266	Lebanon⊙, 2,272	D 7
22075	Leesburg⊙, 4,821	N 2
22505	Lewisetta, 125	R 4
22642	Linden, 320	M 3
22834	Linville, 500	L 3
23091	Little Plymouth, 350	P 5
† 23890	Littleton, 130	O 7
22507	Lively, 200	P 5
† 23434	Lloyd Place, 2,367	P 7
22509	Loretto, 200	O 4
23093	Louisa⊙, 633	M 4
22080	Lovettsville, 185	N 2
22949	Lovingston⊙, 350	L 5
22951	Lowesville, 215	K 5
24457	Lowmoor, 600	J 5
† 22075	Lucketts, 200	N 2
23952	Lunenburg⊙, 50	M 7
22835	Luray⊙, 3,612	M 3
	Lynchburg, ‡123,474	K 6
24571	Lynch Station, 500	K 6
23405	Machipongo, 400	S 6
22727	Madison⊙, 299	M 4
24572	Madison Heights, 4,900	K 6
23103	Manakin-Sabot, 200	N 5
22110	Manassas⊙, 9,164	O 3
22110	Manassas Park, 6,844	O 3
23105	Mannboro, 150	N 6
23106	Manquin, 576	O 5
23407	Mappsville, 500	T 5
24354	Marion⊙, 8,158	E 7
22643	Markham, 300	N 3
22115	Marshall, 800	N 3
22954	Massies Mill, 250	K 5
23109	Mathews⊙, 500	R 6
23803	Matoaca, 829	N 6
23110	Mattaponi, 400	P 5
22644	Maurertown, 158	L 3
24360	Max Meadows, 782	G 6
24269	McClure, 250	D 6
24111	McCoy, 420	G 6
22840	McGaheysville, 600	L 4
23872	McKenney, 489	N 7
22101	McLean, 17,698	O 3
24120	Meadows of Dan, 150	H 7
24361	Meadowview, 875	D 7
† 24315	Mechanicsburg, 350	G 6
23111	Mechanicsville, 5,189	O 5
23954	Meherrin, 200	M 6
23410	Melfa, 459	S 5
24270	Mendota, 375	D 7
22117	Middleburg, 833	N 3
22645	Middletown, 507	M 2
22728	Midland, 180	N 3
23113	Midlothian, 950	N 6
22514	Milford, 550	O 4
24460	Millboro, 300	J 5
24460	Millboro Springs, 200	J 4
22646	Millwood, 350	N 2
23117	Mineral, 397	N 4
23118	Mobjack, 210	R 6
23412	Modest Town, 200	T 5
22517	Mollusk, 400	P 5
24121	Moneta, 500	J 6
24574	Monroe, 500	K 6
24465	Monterey⊙, 223	K 4
22520	Montross⊙, 419	P 4
24122	Montvale, 300	J 6
22523	Morattico, 400	P 5
23120	Moseley, 200	N 6
22841	Mount Crawford, 276	L 4
22524	Mount Holly, 200	P 4
22842	Mount Jackson, 681	L 3
24467	Mount Sidney, 950	K 4
22121	Mount Vernon, 10	O 3
24468	Mustoe, 150	J 4
24124	Narrows, 2,421	G 6
24576	Naruna, 150	L 6
23413	Nassawadox, 511	S 6
24577	Nathalie, 225	L 7
24578	Natural Bridge, 200	J 5
24579	Natural Bridge Station, 450	K 5
23122	Naxera, 275	R 6
22958	Nellysford, 200	L 5
† 22186	New Baltimore, 200	N 3
23123	New Canton, 200	M 5
24127	New Castle⊙, 225	H 5
23415	New Church, 427	S 5
24469	New Hope, 170	L 4
23124	New Kent⊙, 25	P 5
22844	New Market, 718	L 3
24128	Newport, 600	H 6
	Newport News-Hampton, ‡292,159	P 6
24129	New River, 700	G 6
23874	Newsoms, 389	O 7
24271	Nickelsville, 338	D 7
22123	Nokesville, 520	N 3
24272	Nora, 200	D 6
	Norfolk-Portsmouth, ‡680,600	R 7
23127	Norge, 375	P 6
22959	North Garden, 200	L 5
† 24301	North Pulaski, 1,315	G 6
22151	North Springfield, 8,631	O 3
23955	Nottoway⊙, 170	M 6
23416	Oak Hall, 350	S 5
24631	Oakwood, 500	E 6
22125	Occoquan, 975	O 3
23417	Onancock, 1,614	S 5
23418	Onley, 464	S 5
22960	Orange⊙, 2,768	M 4
† 23077	Owenton, 400	O 5
23419	Oyster, 225	S 6
23420	Painter, 363	S 5
22963	Palmyra⊙, 250	M 5
23958	Pamplin, 394	L 6
† 24285	Pardee, 190	C 6
23421	Parksley, 903	S 5
24132	Parrott, 650	G 6
24133	Patrick Springs, 800	H 7
24633	Patterson, 500	D 6
† 23069	Peaks, 500	O 5
24134	Pearisburg⊙, 2,169	G 6
24136	Pembroke, 1,095	G 6
23117	Pendletons, 130	N 5
24137	Penhook, 150	J 7
24277	Pennington Gap, 1,886	C 7
† 23072	Perrin, 250	R 6
	Petersburg-Colonial Heights, ‡128,809	N 6
23959	Phenix, 260	L 6
22131	Philomont, 250	N 2
24138	Pilot, 132	H 6
22964	Piney River, 400	L 5
24139	Pittsville, 200	K 7
† 23434	Pleasant Hill, 2,277	P 7
24635	Pocahontas, 891	F 6
23362	Poquoson, 5,441	R 6
24471	Port Republic, 150	L 4
23181	Port Richmond, 130	P 5
22535	Port Royal, 199	O 4
† 22443	Potomac Beach, 200	P 4
24279	Pound, 995	C 6
24637	Pounding Mill, 399	E 6
23139	Powhatan⊙, 400	N 5
23875	Prince George⊙, 150	O 6
23960	Prospect, 275	L 6
23140	Providence Forge, 500	P 6
24301	Pulaski⊙, 10,279	G 6
23422	Pungoteague, 400	S 5
22132	Purcellville, 1,775	N 2
23847	Purdy, 350	N 7
22134	Quantico, 719	O 3
23423	Quinby, 350	S 5
22732	Radiant, 250	M 4
23962	Randolph, 150	L 7
24472	Raphine, 300	K 5
22733	Rapidan, 300	M 4
24639	Raven, 1,819	E 6
23876	Rawlings, 200	N 7
22140	Rectortown, 200	N 3
24640	Red Ash, 800	E 6
23963	Red House, 200	L 6
23964	Red Oak, 250	L 7
22539	Reedville, 400	R 5
22649	Reliance, 150	M 3
22734	Remington, 321	N 3
22070	Reston, 5,723	O 3
23966	Rice, 194	M 6
24147	Rich Creek, 729	G 6
24641	Richlands, 4,843	E 6
	Richmond, ‡518,319	O 5
24148	Ridgeway, 624	J 7
24149	Riner, 400	H 6
24586	Ringgold, 150	K 7
24150	Ripplemead, 600	G 6
22651	Riverton, 250	M 3
22737	Rixeyville, 150	M 3
	Roanoke, ‡181,436	H 6
23146	Rockville, 290	N 5
24366	Rocky Gap, 200	F 6
24151	Rocky Mount⊙, 4,002	J 7
24280	Rosedale, 200	E 7
24281	Rose Hill, 700	B 7
22967	Roseland, 210	K 5
22141	Round Hill, 581	N 2
24646	Rowe, 150	D 6
22545	Ruby, 188	N 3
24368	Rural Retreat, 872	F 7
23425	Rushmere, 140	P 6
24588	Rustburg⊙, 650	K 6
22546	Ruther Glen, 400	O 5
23147	Ruthville, 310	P 6
24282	Saint Charles, 368	B 7
24283	Saint Paul, 948	D 7
23148	Saint Stephens Church, 500	O 5
24370	Saltville, 2,527	E 7
23149	Saluda⊙, 200	P 5
23150	Sandston, 8,071	O 5
† 23434	Saratoga Place, 1,245	P 7
23427	Saxis, 451	S 5
22969	Schuyler, 375	L 5
24589	Scottsburg, 157	L 7
24590	Scottsville, 290	L 5
23428	Seaford, 2,500	R 6
22547	Sealston, 200	O 4
† 23837	Sebrell, 200	O 7
23878	Sedley, 500	P 7
24474	Selma, 1,058	J 5
24373	Seven Mile Ford, 342	E 7
23158	Shanghai, 150	P 5
24162	Shawsville, 950	H 6
22849	Shenandoah, 1,714	L 4
22549	Shiloh, 150	O 4
22971	Shipman, 500	L 5
23879	Skippers, 150	O 7
23430	Smithfield, 2,713	P 7
22553	Snell, 300	N 4
22972	Somerset, 240	M 4
23970	South Hill, 3,858	M 7
24374	Speedwell, 575	F 8
24165	Spencer, 500	J 7
22740	Sperryville, 200	M 3
22553	Spotsylvania⊙, 350	N 4
* 22150	Springfield, 11,613	O 3
22554	Stafford⊙, 750	O 4
22973	Stanardsville⊙, 296	L 4
22851	Stanley, 1,208	L 3
24168	Stanleytown, 975	H 7
22655	Stephens City, 802	M 2
22170	Sterling, 8,321	O 2
24285	Stonega, 275	C 7
23882	Stony Creek, 430	N 7
22657	Strasburg, 2,431	M 3
24171	Stuart⊙, 947	H 7
24477	Stuarts Draft, 750	L 4
24375	Sugar Grove, 975	E 7
23883	Surry⊙, 269	P 6
23163	Susan, 500	R 6
23884	Sussex⊙, 75	O 7
24594	Sutherlin, 180	O 7
24595	Sweet Briar, 875	K 5
24649	Swords Creek, 315	E 6
22743	Syria, 325	M 4
23602	Tabb, 2,500	R 6
24232	Tacoma, 150	C 7
23440	Tangier, 814	R 5
22560	Tappahannock⊙, 1,111	O 5
24651	Tazewell⊙, 4,168	E 6
23442	Temperanceville, 300	T 5
24174	Thaxton, 350	K 6
22171	The Plains, 418	N 3
22565	Thornburg, 250	N 4
22853	Timberville, 959	L 3
24655	Tiptop, 200	F 6
23168	Toano, 950	P 6
22660	Toms Brook, 258	L 3
23443	Townsend, 500	R 6
24289	Trammel, 750	D 6
22172	Triangle, 3,021	O 3
23886	Triplet, 350	N 7
24378	Trout Dale, 209	F 7
24175	Troutville, 522	J 6
22567	Unionville, 250	N 4
22176	Upperville, 300	N 2
23175	Urbanna, 475	P 5
24656	Vansant, 975	D 6
† 24522	Vera, 200	L 6
24482	Verona, 1,900	K 4
24177	Vesta, 200	H 7
24483	Vesuvius, 385	K 5
23974	Victoria, 1,408	M 6
22180	Vienna, 17,152	O 3
24179	Vinton, 6,347	J 6
24598	Virgilina, 249	L 7
24379	Volney, 850	F 7
23480	Wachapreague, 399	S 5
23888	Wakefield, 942	O 7
23177	Walkerton, 175	O 5
23178	Ware Neck, 500	R 6
24484	Warm Springs⊙, 300	J 4
22186	Warrenton⊙, 4,027	N 3
22572	Warsaw⊙, 511	P 5
22747	Washington⊙, 189	M 3
22190	Waterford, 350	N 2
23180	Water View, 133	P 5
23890	Waverly, 1,717	O 6
24251	Weber City, 1,676	C 7
22576	Weems, 500	P 5
23181	West Point, 2,600	P 5
24486	Weyers Cave, 300	L 4
23485	Whaleyville, 332	P 7
22663	White Post, 250	M 2
22578	White Stone, 381	R 5
24657	Whitewood, 500	E 6
22579	Wicomico Church, 500	R 5
† 22553	Wilderness, 200	N 4
23486	Willis Wharf, 400	S 5
23894	Wilsons, 147	N 6
23487	Windsor, 685	P 7
† 23832	Winterpock, 150	N 6
24184	Wirtz, 150	J 6
24293	Wise⊙, 2,891	C 7
22748	Wolftown, 300	M 4
22989	Woodberry Forest, 450	M 4
22191	Woodbridge, 25,412	O 3
24381	Woodlawn, 300	G 7
22664	Woodstock⊙, 2,338	L 3
22749	Woodville, 200	M 3
24295	Woodway, 700	C 7
24185	Woolwine, 150	H 7
23976	Wylliesburg, 250	L 7
24382	Wytheville⊙, 6,069	G 7
22110	Yorkshire, 4,649	O 3
23490	Yorktown⊙, 350	R 6
23898	Zuni, 150	P 7

⊙ County seat.
‡ Population of metropolitan area.
† Zip of nearest p.o.
* Multiple zips

Agriculture, Industry and Resources

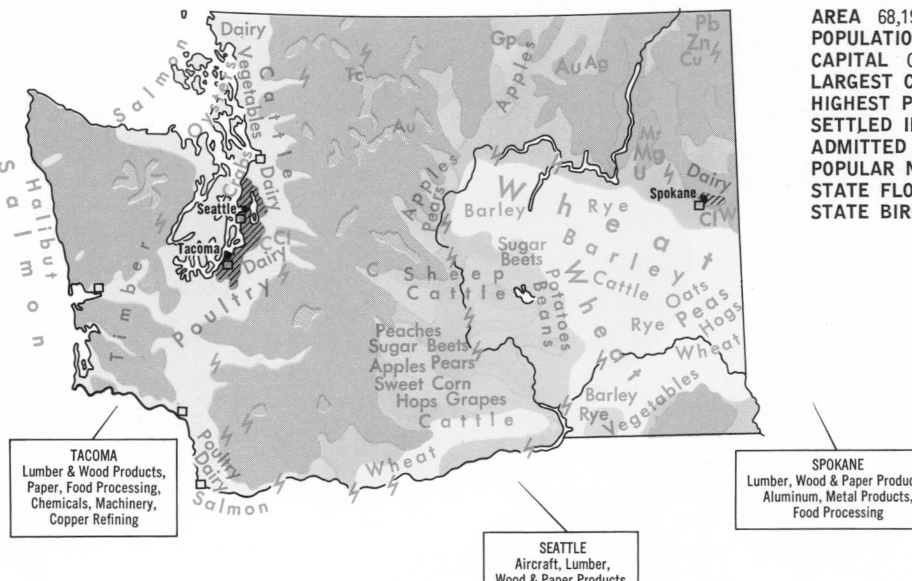

AREA 68,192 sq. mi.
POPULATION 3,409,169
CAPITAL Olympia
LARGEST CITY Seattle
HIGHEST POINT Mt. Rainier 14,410 ft.
SETTLED IN 1811
ADMITTED TO UNION November 11, 1889
POPULAR NAME Evergreen State
STATE FLOWER Coast Rhododendron
STATE BIRD Willow Goldfinch

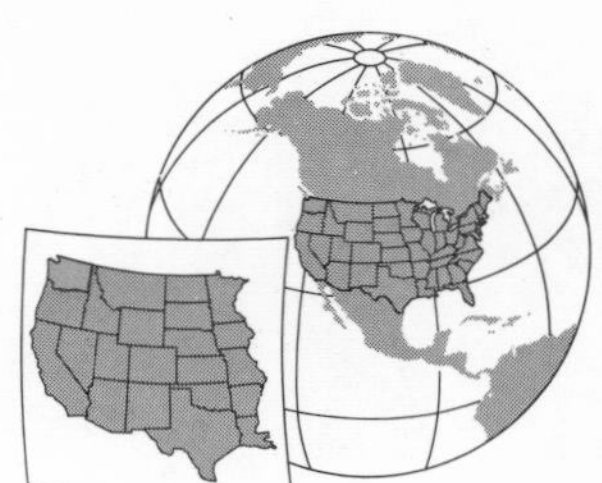

DOMINANT LAND USE

- Specialized Wheat
- Wheat, Peas
- Dairy, Poultry, Mixed Farming
- Fruit and Mixed Farming
- General Farming, Dairy, Range Livestock
- General Farming, Livestock, Special Crops
- Range Livestock
- Forests
- Urban Areas
- Nonagricultural Land

MAJOR MINERAL OCCURRENCES

Ag	Silver	Mr	Marble
Au	Gold	Pb	Lead
C	Coal	Tc	Talc
Cl	Clay	U	Uranium
Cu	Copper	W	Tungsten
Gp	Gypsum	Zn	Zinc
Mg	Magnesium		

- Water Power
- Major Industrial Areas
- Major Sawmilling Centers

Warren Dick — Shostal Associates

Pulpwood being rafted to the mills is a familiar sight in the Northwest, the region which leads the country in lumber production.

COUNTIES

County	Key
Adams, 12,014	G 3
Asotin, 13,799	H 4
Benton, 67,540	F 4
Chelan, 41,355	E 3
Clallam, 34,770	B 2
Clark, 128,454	C 5
Columbia, 4,439	H 4
Cowlitz, 68,616	C 4
Douglas, 16,787	F 3
Ferry, 3,655	G 2
Franklin, 25,816	G 4
Garfield, 2,911	H 4
Grant, 41,881	F 3
Grays Harbor, 59,533	B 3
Island, 27,011	C 2
Jefferson, 10,661	B 3
King, 1,156,633	D 3
Kitsap, 101,732	C 3
Kittitas, 25,039	E 3
Klickitat, 12,138	E 5
Lewis, 45,467	C 4
Lincoln, 9,572	G 3
Mason, 20,918	B 3
Okanogan, 25,867	F 2
Pacific, 15,796	B 4
Pend Oreille, 6,025	H 2
Pierce, 411,027	C 3
San Juan, 3,856	C 2
Skagit, 52,381	D 2
Skamania, 5,845	D 5
Snohomish, 265,236	D 2
Spokane, 287,487	H 3
Stevens, 17,405	H 2
Thurston, 76,894	C 4
Wahkiakum, 3,592	B 4
Walla Walla, 42,176	G 4
Whatcom, 81,950	D 2
Whitman, 37,900	H 4
Yakima, 144,971	E 4

CITIES and TOWNS

Zip	*Name/Pop.*	*Key*
98520	Aberdeen, 18,489	B 3
98220	Acme, 170	C 2
99101	Addy, 141	H 2
98522	Adna, 150	B 4
98810	Aeneas, 85	F 2
99001	Airway Heights, 744	H 3
99102	Albion, 687	H 4
98301	Alder, 300	C 4
98002	Algona, 1,276	C 3
98524	Allyn, 850	C 3
99103	Almira, 376	G 3
98525	Aloha, 140	A 3
† 98643	Altoona, 66	B 4
98526	Amanda Park, 495	A 3
99002	Amber, 32	H 3
98601	Amboy, 480	C 5
98221	Anacortes, 7,701	C 2
99401	Anatone, 70	H 4
98602	Appleton, 40	D 5
† 99114	Arden, 30	H 2
98811	Ardenvoir, 350	E 3
98603	Ariel, 386	C 5
98223	Arlington, 2,261	C 2
98304	Ashford, 415	C 4
99402	Asotin⊙, 637	H 4
98002	Auburn, 21,817	C 3
† 99348	Ayer, 70	G 4
98816	Azwell, 152	F 3
98110	Bainbridge Island-Winslow, 1,461	A 2
98224	Baring, 75	D 3
98604	Battle Ground, 1,438	C 5
98527	Bay Center, 350	A 4
† 98520	Bay City, 58	B 4
† 98004	Beaux Arts, 475	B 2
98305	Beaver, 450	A 2
98528	Belfair, 500	C 3
* 98004	Bellevue, 61,102	B 2
98225	Bellingham⊙, 39,375	C 2
99104	Belmont, 59	H 3
99105	Benge, 45	G 4
99320	Benton City, 1,070	F 4
99321	Beverly, 86	F 4
99322	Bickleton, 200	E 5
† 98273	Biglake, 105	C 2
98605	Bingen, 671	D 5
98010	Black Diamond, 1,160	D 3
98230	Blaine, 1,955	C 2
98231	Blanchard, 200	C 2
99106	Bluecreek, 40	H 2
† 98382	Blyn, 350	B 3
† 98532	Boistfort, 55	B 4
† 98390	Bonney Lake, 2,313	C 3
† 99126	Bossburg, 66	H 2
98011	Bothell, 4,883	B 1
98232	Bow, 975	C 2
99107	Boyds, 68	G 2
98310	Bremerton, 35,307	A 2
98812	Brewster, 1,059	F 2
98813	Bridgeport, 952	F 3
98036	Brier, 3,093	C 3
98320	Brinnon, 500	B 3
† 98537	Brooklyn, 50	B 4
98920	Brownstown, 80	E 4
† 98310	Brownsville, 50	A 2
98606	Brush Prairie, 200	C 5
† 98101	Bryn Mawr, 4,589	B 2
98321	Buckley, 3,446	C 3
98530	Bucoda, 421	C 4
98921	Buena, 590	E 4
99323	Burbank, 800	G 4
98166	Burien, 2,000	A 2
98322	Burley, 200	C 3
98233	Burlington, 3,138	C 2
98013	Burton, 650	C 3
98607	Camas, 5,790	C 5
98323	Carbonado, 394	D 3
98324	Carlsborg, 500	B 2
98814	Carlton, 120	F 2
98014	Carnation, 530	D 3
98609	Carrolls, 400	C 4
98610	Carson, 500	D 5
98815	Cashmere, 1,976	E 3
98611	Castle Rock, 1,647	B 4
98612	Cathlamet⊙, 647	B 4
† 98045	Cedar Falls, 200	D 3
98613	Centerville, 100	D 5
98531	Centralia, 10,054	C 4
98520	Central Park, 2,720	B 3
99003	Chattaroy, 250	H 3
98532	Chehalis⊙, 5,727	C 4
98816	Chelan, 2,430	E 3
98817	Chelan Falls, 200	E 3
99004	Cheney, 6,358	H 3
98818	Chesaw, 32	G 2
99109	Chewelah, 1,365	H 2
98325	Chimacum, 275	C 3
98614	Chinook, 445	B 4
98533	Cinebar, 35	C 4
98326	Clallam Bay, 750	A 2
99403	Clarkston, 6,312	H 4
99110	Clayton, 204	H 3
98235	Clearlake, 750	C 2
98399	Clearwater, 155	A 3
98922	Cle Elum, 1,725	E 3
† 98937	Cliffdell, 50	E 4
98236	Clinton, 500	C 3
98244	Clipper, 25	C 2
† 99402	Cloverland, 80	H 4
† 98004	Clyde Hill, 2,987	B 2
† 98055	Coalfield, 500	B 2
99005	Colbert, 225	H 3
† 98366	Colby, 150	A 2
99111	Colfax⊙, 2,664	H 4
99324	College Place, 4,510	G 4
99113	Colton, 279	H 4
† 98632	Columbia Heights, 1,572	C 4
99114	Colville⊙, 3,742	H 2
98819	Conconully, 122	F 2
98237	Concrete, 573	D 2
99326	Connell, 1,161	G 4
98238	Conway, 120	C 2
98605	Cook, 240	D 5
98535	Copalis Beach, 481	A 3
98536	Copalis Crossing, 200	B 3
98537	Cosmopolis, 1,599	B 4
98616	Cougar, 76	C 4
99115	Coulee City, 558	F 3
99116	Coulee Dam, 1,425	G 3
98239	Coupeville⊙, 678	C 2
98923	Cowiche, 150	E 4
99117	Creston, 325	G 3
98015	Cumberland, 250	D 3
99118	Curlew, 200	G 2
98538	Curtis, 200	B 4
99119	Cusick, 257	H 2
98240	Custer, 315	C 2
98617	Dallesport, 400	D 5
99121	Danville, 108	G 2
98241	Darrington, 1,094	D 2
99122	Davenport⊙, 1,363	G 3
99328	Dayton⊙, 2,596	H 4
† 99010	Deepcreek, 73	H 3
98618	Deep River, 500	B 4
98243	Deer Harbor, 200	B 2
99006	Deer Park, 1,295	H 3
98244	Deming, 250	C 2
† 99006	Denison, 100	H 3
98188	Des Moines, 3,871	B 2
† 98283	Diablo, 200	D 2
† 99111	Diamond, 49	H 4
99213	Dishman, 9,079	H 3
99329	Dixie, 200	G 4
† 98279	Doebay, 100	C 2
† 98951	Donald, 100	E 4
98539	Doty, 210	B 4
† 98858	Douglas, 27	F 3
† 98532	Dryad, 184	B 4
98821	Dryden, 550	E 3
† 98382	Dungeness, 675	B 2
98327	Du Pont, 384	C 3
98019	Duvall, 607	D 3
98540	East Olympia, 300	B 4
98925	Easton, 300	D 3
98245	Eastsound, 800	B 2
98801	East Wenatchee, 913	E 3
98328	Eatonville, 2,446	C 4
98246	Edison, 250	C 2
98020	Edmonds, 23,998	C 3

(continued on following page)

99008 Edwall, 130 H 3
98330 Elbe, 115 C 4
† 99130 Elberton, 75 H 4
† 98555 Eldon, 60 B 3
99123 Electric City, 651 F 3
† 98360 Electron, 74 C 4
99009 Elk, 100 H 2
98926 Ellensburg⊙, 13,568 E 3
98541 Elma, 2,227 B 4
99124 Elmer City, 324 G 2
99330 Eltopia, 75 G 4
99125 Endicott, 333 H 4
† 98310 Enetai, 2,878 A 2
98822 Entiat, 355 E 3
98022 Enumclaw, 4,703 D 3
98823 Ephrata⊙, 5,255 F 3
† 98310 Erlands Point, 1,017 A 2
99010 Espanola, 75 H 3
98542 Ethel, 100 C 4
† 99348 Eureka, 56 G 4
99126 Evans, 78 H 2
98201 Everett⊙, 53,622 C 3
98247 Everson, 633 C 2
99127 Ewan, 57 H 3
† 98323 Fairfax, 35 C 4
99012 Fairfield, 416 H 3
† 98901 Fairview, 2,111 E 4
98024 Fall City, 1,700 D 3
99128 Farmington, 140 H 3
98248 Ferndale, 2,164 C 2
98424 Fife, 1,458 C 3
99336 Finley, 70 F 4
98466 Fircrest, 5,651 C 3
† 98531 Fords Prairie, 2,250 B 4
98331 Forks, 1,328 A 3
99014 Four Lakes, 200 H 3
98543 Frances, 144 B 4
98249 Freeland, 50 C 2
99015 Freeman, 150 H 3
98250 Friday Harbor⊙, 803 B 2
† 98901 Fruitvale, 3,275 E 4
98544 Galvin, 165 B 4
98334 Gardiner, 80 B 2
99130 Garfield, 610 H 3
† 99362 Garrett, 1,586 G 4
† 98579 Gate, 75 B 4
98824 George, 273 F 3
98335 Gig Harbor, 1,657 C 3
98244 Glacier, 100 D 2
98336 Glenoma, 500 C 4
98619 Glenwood, 500 D 4
98251 Gold Bar, 504 D 3
98620 Goldendale⊙, 2,484 E 5
† 99356 Goodnoe Hills, 40 E 5
98337 Gorst, 750 C 3
99133 Grand Coulee, 1,302 G 3
† 98531 Grand Mound, 100 C 4
98930 Grandview, 3,605 F 4
98932 Granger, 1,567 E 4
98252 Granite Falls, 813 D 2
98546 Grapeview, 250 C 3
98547 Grayland, 750 A 4
98621 Grays River, 400 B 4
99016 Greenacres, 2,324 J 3
98253 Greenbank, 500 C 2
98254 Grotto, 60 D 3
98339 Hadlock, 500 C 2
98255 Hamilton, 196 D 2
98340 Hansville, 250 C 3
98341 Harper, 300 A 2
98933 Harrah, 305 E 4
99134 Harrington, 489 G 3
99135 Hartline, 189 F 3
99332 Hatton, 60 G 4
† 98855 Havillah, 35 F 2
99136 Hay, 55 H 4
98622 Heisson, 70 C 5
98025 Hobart, 500 D 3
† 98648 Home Valley, 120 D 5
98548 Hoodsport, 500 B 3
99333 Hooper, 75 G 4
98550 Hoquiam, 10,466 A 3
98552 Humptulips, 240 A 3
99137 Hunters, 200 G 2
† 99328 Huntsville, 100 G 4
98623 Husum, 200 D 5
98026 Hyak, 50 D 3
98624 Ilwaco, 506 A 4
† 99138 Impach, 44 G 2
99138 Inchelium, 206 G 2
98256 Index, 169 D 3
98342 Indianola, 500 A 1
99139 Ione, 529 H 2
99159 Irby, 30 G 3
98027 Issaquah, 4,313 C 3
98343 Joyce, 375 B 2
98033 Juanita, 9,450 B 1
99335 Kahlotus, 308 G 4
† 98399 Kalaloch, 30 A 3
98625 Kalama, 1,106 C 4
98344 Kapowsin, 450 C 4
99140 Keller, 96 G 2
98626 Kelso⊙, 10,296 C 4
† 98244 Kendall, 100 C 2
98028 Kenmore, 1,400 B 1
99336 Kennewick, 15,212 F 4
98031 Kent, 21,510 C 3
99141 Kettle Falls, 893 H 2
99142 Kewa, 63 G 2
98345 Keyport, 900 A 2
98346 Kingston, 950 C 3
99340 Kiona, 230 F 4
98033 Kirkland, 15,249 B 2
98934 Kittitas, 637 E 4
98628 Klickitat, 700 D 5
† 98832 Krupp (Marlin), 52 F 3
98629 La Center, 300 C 5
98501 Lacey, 9,696 C 3
98257 La Conner, 639 C 2
99143 Lacrosse, 426 H 4
98348 La Grande, 100 C 4
† 98101 Lake Forest Park, 2,530 B 1
98258 Lake Stevens, 1,283 D 3
98259 Lakewood, 950 C 2
99017 Lamont, 88 H 3
98260 Langley, 547 C 2
98350 La Push, 375 A 3
99018 Latah, 169 H 3
98630 Laurel, 100 D 5
99146 Laurier, 50 G 2
98826 Leavenworth, 1,322 E 3
98554 Lebam, 250 B 4
† 98368 Leland, 30 C 3
98035 Lester, 100 D 3
† 98922 Liberty, 25 E 3
99019 Liberty Lake, 300 J 3
98555 Lilliwaup, 80 B 3
99147 Lincoln, 114 G 3
99341 Lind, 622 G 4
98556 Littlerock, 300 B 4
98631 Long Beach, 968 A 4
98351 Longbranch, 400 C 3
98397 Longmire, 60 D 4
98632 Longview, 28,373 B 4
98827 Loomis, 150 F 2
99148 Loon Lake, 500 H 2
98261 Lopez, 100 C 2
98262 Lummi Island, 450 C 2
98635 Lyle, 360 D 5
98263 Lyman, 324 D 2
98264 Lynden, 2,808 C 2
98036 Lynnwood, 16,919 C 3
98935 Mabton, 925 E 4
98828 Malaga, 125 E 3
99149 Malden, 219 H 3
99150 Malo, 25 G 2

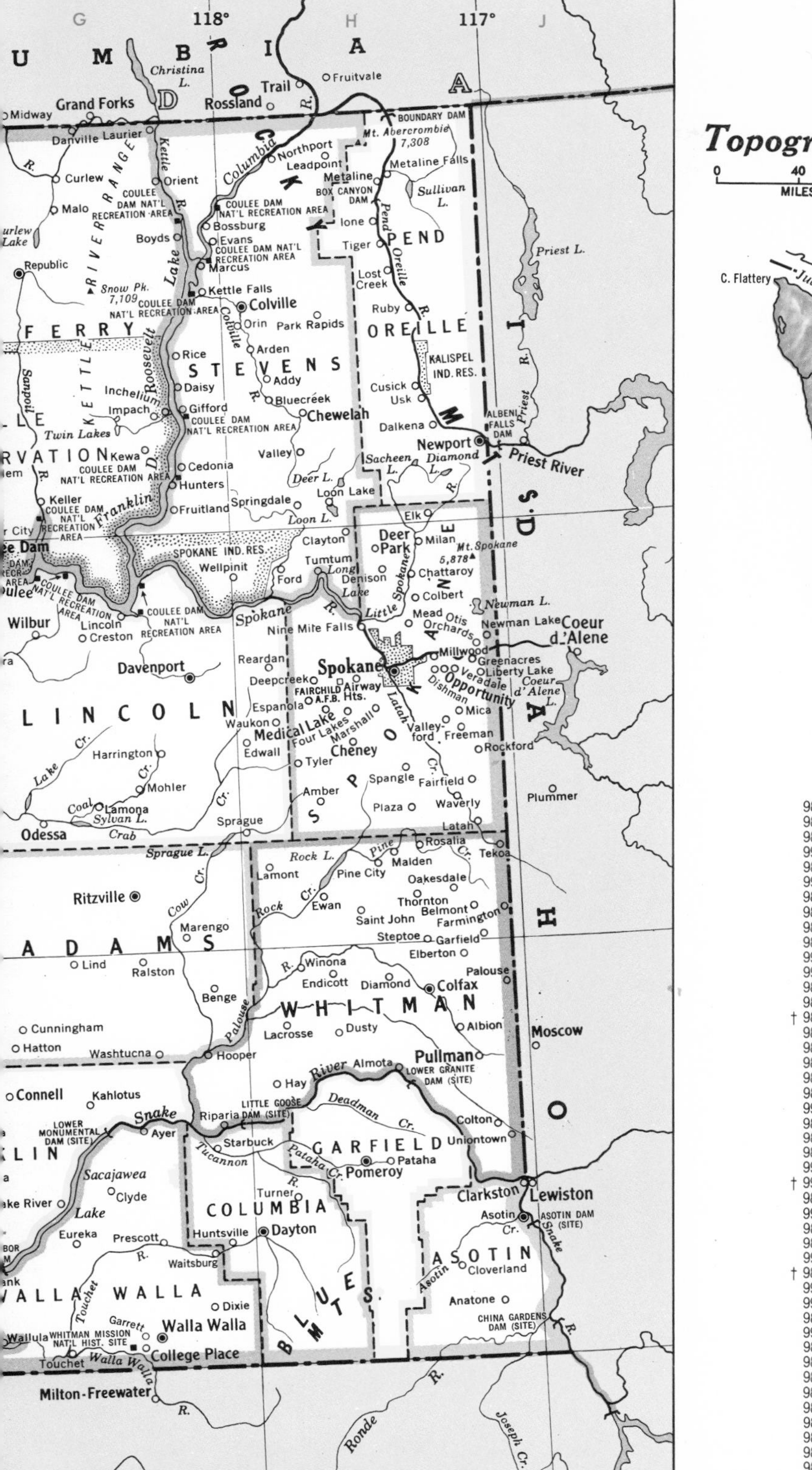

Topography

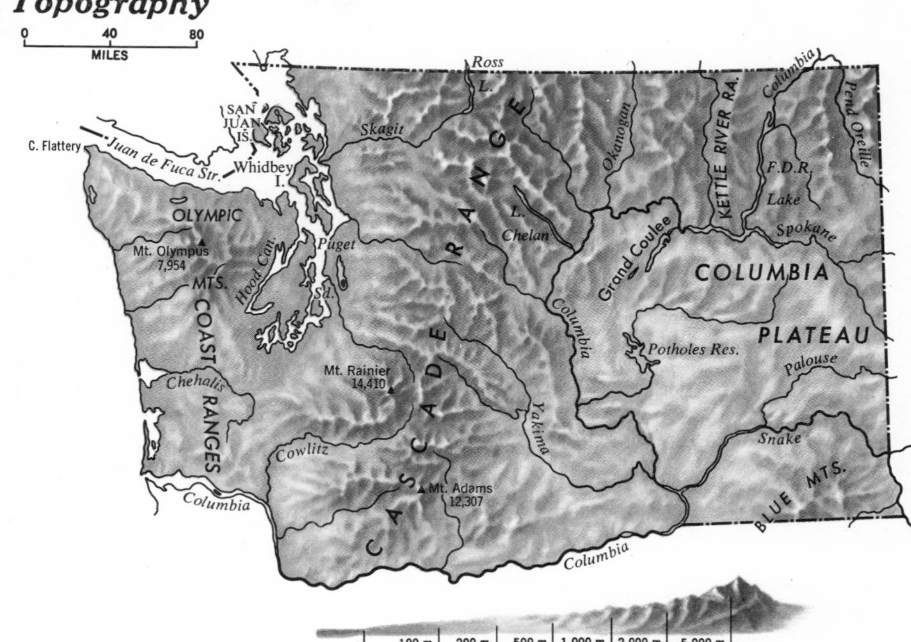

98559 Malone, 175 ..... B 4
98829 Malott, 350 ..... F 2
98353 Manchester, 400 ..... A 2
98830 Mansfield, 273 ..... F 3
98831 Manson, 220 ..... E 3
98266 Maple Falls, 90 ..... D 2
98038 Maple Valley, 2,900 ..... C 3
98267 Marblemount, 387 ..... D 2
99151 Marcus, 142 ..... H 2
98268 Marietta, 300 ..... C 2
† 98520 Markham, 180 ..... B 4
98832 Marlin, 52 ..... F 3
99020 Marshall, 150 ..... H 3
† 98620 Maryhill, 90 ..... E 5
98270 Marysville, 4,343 ..... C 2
98560 Matlock, 250 ..... B 3
99344 Mattawa, 180 ..... F 4
98557 McCleary, 1,265 ..... B 3
98558 McKenna, 250 ..... C 4
† 98273 McMurray, 62 ..... C 2
99021 Mead, 1,099 ..... H 3
99022 Medical Lake, 3,529 ..... H 3
98039 Medina, 3,455 ..... B 2
† 98563 Melbourne, 200 ..... B 4
98561 Menlo, 200 ..... B 4
98040 Mercer Island (city), 19,047 ..... B 2
† 98826 Merritt, 150 ..... E 3
99343 Mesa, 274 ..... G 4
99152 Metaline, 197 ..... H 2
99153 Metaline Falls, 307 ..... H 2
98834 Methow, 84 ..... E 2
99023 Mica, 130 ..... H 3
99024 Milan, 90 ..... H 3
99212 Millwood, 1,770 ..... H 3
98354 Milton, 2,607 ..... C 3
98355 Mineral, 500 ..... C 4
98562 Moclips, 650 ..... A 3
98836 Monitor, 75 ..... E 3
98272 Monroe, 2,687 ..... D 3
† 98812 Monse, 29 ..... F 2
98563 Montesano⊙, 2,847 ..... B 4
98356 Morton, 1,134 ..... C 4
98837 Moses Lake, 10,310 ..... F 3
98564 Mossyrock, 409 ..... C 4
98043 Mountlake Terrace, 16,600 ..... B 1
98273 Mount Vernon⊙, 8,804 ..... C 2
98936 Moxee City, 600 ..... E 4
98275 Mukilteo, 1,369 ..... C 3
98937 Naches, 666 ..... E 4
98537 Nahcotta, 200 ..... A 4
98565 Napavine, 377 ..... C 4
98638 Naselle, 500 ..... B 4
† 98310 Navy Yard City, 2,827 ..... A 2
98357 Neah Bay, 750 ..... A 2
98566 Neilton, 250 ..... B 3
99155 Nespelem, 323 ..... G 2
† 98283 Newhalem, 350 ..... D 2
99025 Newman Lake, 102 ..... J 3
99156 Newport⊙, 1,418 ..... H 2
99026 Nine Mile Falls, 150 ..... H 3
† 98501 Nisqually, 500 ..... C 3
98276 Nooksack, 322 ..... C 2
98358 Nordland, 500 ..... C 2
† 98100 Normandy Park, 4,208 ..... A 2
98045 North Bend, 1,625 ..... D 3
98639 North Bonneville, 459 ..... C 5
† 98590 North Cove, 50 ..... A 4
99157 Northport, 423 ..... H 2
99158 Oakesdale, 447 ..... H 3
98277 Oak Harbor, 9,167 ..... C 2
98568 Oakville, 460 ..... B 4
98569 Ocean City, 350 ..... A 3
98640 Ocean Park, 918 ..... A 4
† 98520 Ocosta, 300 ..... B 4
99159 Odessa, 1,074 ..... G 3
98840 Okanogan⊙, 2,015 ..... F 2
98359 Olalla, 800 ..... A 2
98279 Olga, 150 ..... C 2
98501 Olympia (cap.)⊙, 23,111 ..... C 3
98841 Omak, 4,164 ..... F 2
98570 Onalaska, 288 ..... C 4
99214 Opportunity, 16,604 ..... H 3
98662 Orchards, 800 ..... C 5
99160 Orient, 200 ..... G 2
98843 Orondo, 130 ..... E 3
98844 Oroville, 1,555 ..... F 2
98360 Orting, 1,643 ..... C 3
98223 Oso, 150 ..... D 2
99344 Othello, 4,122 ..... F 4
99027 Otis Orchards, 900 ..... H 3
98938 Outlook, 300 ..... E 4
98641 Oysterville, 86 ..... A 4
† 98326 Ozette, 50 ..... A 2
98047 Pacific, 1,831 ..... C 3
98571 Pacific Beach, 975 ..... A 3
98361 Packwood, 800 ..... D 4
98845 Palisades, 90 ..... E 3
98048 Palmer, 250 ..... D 3
99161 Palouse, 948 ..... H 4
98398 Paradise Inn, 200 ..... D 4
98939 Parker, 700 ..... E 4
98444 Parkland, 21,012 ..... C 3
99301 Pasco⊙, 13,920 ..... F 4
† 99347 Pataha, 97 ..... H 4
98846 Pateros, 472 ..... E 2
99345 Paterson, 50 ..... F 5
98572 Pe Ell, 582 ..... B 4
98847 Peshastin, 200 ..... E 3
99162 Pine City, 48 ..... H 3
† 98826 Plain, 75 ..... E 3
99028 Plaza, 50 ..... H 3
99346 Plymouth, 89 ..... F 5
98281 Point Roberts, 400 ..... B 2
99347 Pomeroy⊙, 1,823 ..... H 4
98362 Port Angeles⊙, 16,367 ..... B 2
98110 Port Blakely, 600 ..... A 2
98573 Porter, 200 ..... B 4
98364 Port Gamble, 425 ..... C 3
98365 Port Ludlow, 200 ..... C 3
98366 Port Orchard⊙, 3,904 ..... A 2
98368 Port Townsend⊙, 5,241 ..... C 2
98574 Potlatch, 350 ..... B 3
98370 Poulsbo, 1,856 ..... A 1
99348 Prescott, 242 ..... G 4
98050 Preston, 500 ..... D 3
† 98250 Prevost, 25 ..... B 2
99350 Prosser⊙, 2,954 ..... F 4
99163 Pullman, 20,509 ..... H 4
98371 Puyallup, 14,742 ..... C 3
† 98399 Queets, 180 ..... A 3
98376 Quilcene, 900 ..... B 3
98575 Quinault, 340 ..... B 3
98848 Quincy, 3,237 ..... F 3
98576 Rainier, 382 ..... C 4
99165 Ralston, 35 ..... G 4
98377 Randle, 950 ..... D 4
98051 Ravensdale, 400 ..... D 3
98577 Raymond, 3,126 ..... B 4
99029 Reardan, 389 ..... H 3
98052 Redmond, 11,031 ..... B 1
98054 Redondo, 950 ..... C 3
98055 Renton, 25,258 ..... B 2
99166 Republic⊙, 862 ..... G 2
98378 Retsil, 419 ..... A 2
99352 Richland, 26,290 ..... F 4
98160 Richmond Beach, 2,550 ..... A 1
† 98133 Richmond Highlands, 6,854 ..... A 1
98642 Ridgefield, 1,004 ..... C 5
99169 Ritzville⊙, 1,876 ..... G 3
98849 Riverside, 228 ..... F 2
† 98188 Riverton, 23,160 ..... B 2
98188 Riverton Heights, 34,800 ..... B 2
† 98252 Robe, 175 ..... D 2
98250 Roche Harbor, 175 ..... B 2
98579 Rochester, 325 ..... C 4
99030 Rockford, 327 ..... H 3
† 98801 Rock Island, 191 ..... E 3
98283 Rockport, 350 ..... D 2
† 98626 Rocky Point, 1,733 ..... A 2
98061 Rollingbay, 950 ..... A 2
98940 Ronald, 200 ..... E 3
99356 Roosevelt, 60 ..... E 5
99170 Rosalia, 569 ..... H 3
98643 Rosburg, 250 ..... B 4
98941 Roslyn, 1,031 ..... E 3
98580 Roy, 381 ..... C 4
99357 Royal City, 477 ..... F 4
† 98832 Ruff, 40 ..... F 3
† 98401 Ruston, 668 ..... C 3
98581 Ryderwood, 345 ..... B 4
99171 Saint John, 575 ..... H 3
98582 Salkum, 298 ..... C 4
† 98239 San de Fuca, 80 ..... C 2
98379 Sappho, 200 ..... A 2
98583 Satsop, 300 ..... B 3
† 98283 Sauk, 50 ..... D 2
† 98370 Scandia, 75 ..... A 1
† 99321 Schawana, 100 ..... F 4
98380 Seabeck, 200 ..... C 3
† 98110 Seabold, 250 ..... A 1
98062 Seahurst, 3,000 ..... A 2
* 98101 Seattle⊙, 530,831 ..... A 2
Seattle-Everett, ‡1,421,869 ..... A 2
98644 Seaview, 950 ..... A 4
98284 Sedro-Woolley, 4,598 ..... C 2
98381 Sekiu, 500 ..... A 2
98942 Selah, 3,070 ..... E 4
98064 Selleck, 300 ..... D 3
98382 Sequim, 1,549 ..... B 2
98286 Shaw Island, 95 ..... B 2
98584 Shelton⊙, 6,515 ..... B 3
† 98270 Shoultes, 4,754 ..... C 2
98287 Silvana, 300 ..... C 2
98585 Silver Creek, 382 ..... C 4
98383 Silverdale, 950 ..... A 2
98645 Silverlake, 42 ..... C 4
† 98252 Silverton, 65 ..... D 2
98646 Skamania, 250 ..... C 5
98647 Skamokawa, 500 ..... B 4
98288 Skykomish, 283 ..... D 3
† 99357 Smyrna, 70 ..... F 4
98290 Snohomish, 5,174 ..... D 3
98065 Snoqualmie, 1,260 ..... D 3
98066 Snoqualmie Falls, 250 ..... D 3
98851 Soap Lake, 1,064 ..... F 3
98586 South Bend⊙, 1,795 ..... B 4
† 98901 South Broadway, 3,298 ..... E 4
98943 South Cle Elum, 374 ..... D 3
98384 South Colby, 450 ..... A 2
98385 South Prairie, 206 ..... D 3
98386 Southworth, 425 ..... A 2
98387 Spanaway, 5,768 ..... C 3
99031 Spangle, 179 ..... H 3
* 99201 Spokane⊙, 170,516 ..... H 3
Spokane, ‡287,487 ..... H 3
99032 Sprague, 550 ..... G 3
99173 Springdale, 215 ..... H 2
98292 Stanwood, 1,347 ..... C 2
99359 Starbuck, 216 ..... G 4
98293 Startup, 450 ..... D 3
98852 Stehekin, 40 ..... E 2
98388 Steilacoom, 2,850 ..... C 3
99174 Steptoe, 200 ..... H 3
98648 Stevenson⊙, 916 ..... C 5
98853 Stratford, 160 ..... F 3
98294 Sultan, 1,119 ..... D 3
98295 Sumas, 689 ..... C 2
98390 Sumner, 4,325 ..... C 3
† 98101 Sunnydale, 1,850 ..... B 2
98944 Sunnyside, 6,751 ..... F 4
98392 Suquamish, 950 ..... A 1
* 98401 Tacoma⊙, 154,581 ..... C 3
Tacoma, ‡411,027 ..... C 3
98587 Taholah, 550 ..... A 3
98588 Tahuya, 260 ..... B 3
99033 Tekoa, 808 ..... H 3
† 98826 Telma, 150 ..... E 3
98589 Tenino, 962 ..... C 4
98901 Terrace Heights, 1,033 ..... E 4
99176 Thornton, 97 ..... H 3
98946 Thorp, 350 ..... E 3
98947 Tieton, 415 ..... E 4
99177 Tiger, 69 ..... H 2
98492 Tillicum, 1,900 ..... C 3
98590 Tokeland, 300 ..... A 4
98591 Toledo, 654 ..... C 4
98855 Tonasket, 951 ..... F 2
98948 Toppenish, 5,744 ..... E 4
99360 Touchet, 250 ..... G 4
98649 Toutle, 813 ..... C 4
98393 Tracyton, 1,413 ..... A 2
† 98848 Trinidad, 30 ..... F 3
98650 Trout Lake, 500 ..... D 5
98188 Tukwila, 3,496 ..... B 2
† 98270 Tulalip, 325 ..... C 2
99034 Tumtum, 100 ..... H 3
98501 Tumwater, 5,373 ..... B 3
† 99328 Turner, 25 ..... H 4
98856 Twisp, 756 ..... E 2
99035 Tyler, 69 ..... H 3
98651 Underwood, 500 ..... D 5
98592 Union, 380 ..... B 3
98903 Union Gap, 2,040 ..... E 4
99179 Uniontown, 310 ..... H 4
99180 Usk, 250 ..... H 2
98593 Vader, 387 ..... B 4
99181 Valley, 156 ..... H 2
99036 Valleyford, 250 ..... H 3
* 98660 Vancouver⊙, 42,493 ..... C 5
98950 Vantage, 125 ..... E 4
98244 Van Zandt, 25 ..... C 2
98070 Vashon, 350 ..... A 2
98394 Vaughn, 600 ..... C 3
99037 Veradale, 5,320 ..... H 3
98670 Wahkiacus, 65 ..... D 5
99361 Waitsburg, 953 ..... G 4
98297 Waldron, 75 ..... B 2
99362 Walla Walla⊙, 23,619 ..... G 4
99363 Wallula, 89 ..... G 4
98951 Wapato, 2,841 ..... E 4
98857 Warden, 1,254 ..... F 4
† 98292 Warm Beach, 225 ..... C 2
98671 Washougal, 3,388 ..... C 5
99371 Washtucna, 316 ..... G 4
98858 Waterville⊙, 919 ..... E 3
99038 Waukon, 41 ..... H 3
98395 Wauna, 300 ..... C 3
99039 Waverly, 48 ..... H 3
99040 Wellpinit, 125 ..... G 3
98801 Wenatchee⊙, 16,912 ..... E 3
† 98837 Westlake, 258 ..... F 3
98595 Westport, 1,364 ..... A 4
99352 West Richland, 1,107 ..... F 4
† 98801 West Wenatchee, 2,134 ..... E 3
† 98837 Wheeler, 75 ..... F 3
98146 White Center, 17,300 ..... A 2
† 98541 Whites, 70 ..... B 3
98672 White Salmon, 1,585 ..... D 5
98952 White Swan, 270 ..... E 4
98285 Wickersham, 200 ..... C 2
99185 Wilbur, 1,074 ..... G 3
98906 Wiley City, 250 ..... E 4
98396 Wilkeson, 317 ..... D 3
† 98577 Willapa, 300 ..... B 4
98860 Wilson Creek, 184 ..... F 3
† 98848 Winchester, 70 ..... F 3
98596 Winlock, 890 ..... C 4
99186 Winona, 51 ..... H 4
† 98110 Winslow (Bainbridge Island-Winslow), 1,461 ..... A 2
98862 Winthrop, 371 ..... E 2
98673 Wishram, 575 ..... D 5
98863 Withrow, 30 ..... F 3
98072 Woodinville, 2,900 ..... B 1
98674 Woodland, 1,622 ..... C 5
† 98020 Woodway, 879 ..... C 3
98675 Yacolt, 488 ..... C 5
* 98901 Yakima⊙, 45,588 ..... E 4
† 98004 Yarrow Point, 1,103 ..... B 2
98597 Yelm, 628 ..... C 4
98188 Zenith, 1,900 ..... C 3
98953 Zillah, 1,138 ..... E 4

⊙ County seat.
‡ Population of metropolitan area.
† Zip of nearest p.o.
* Multiple zips

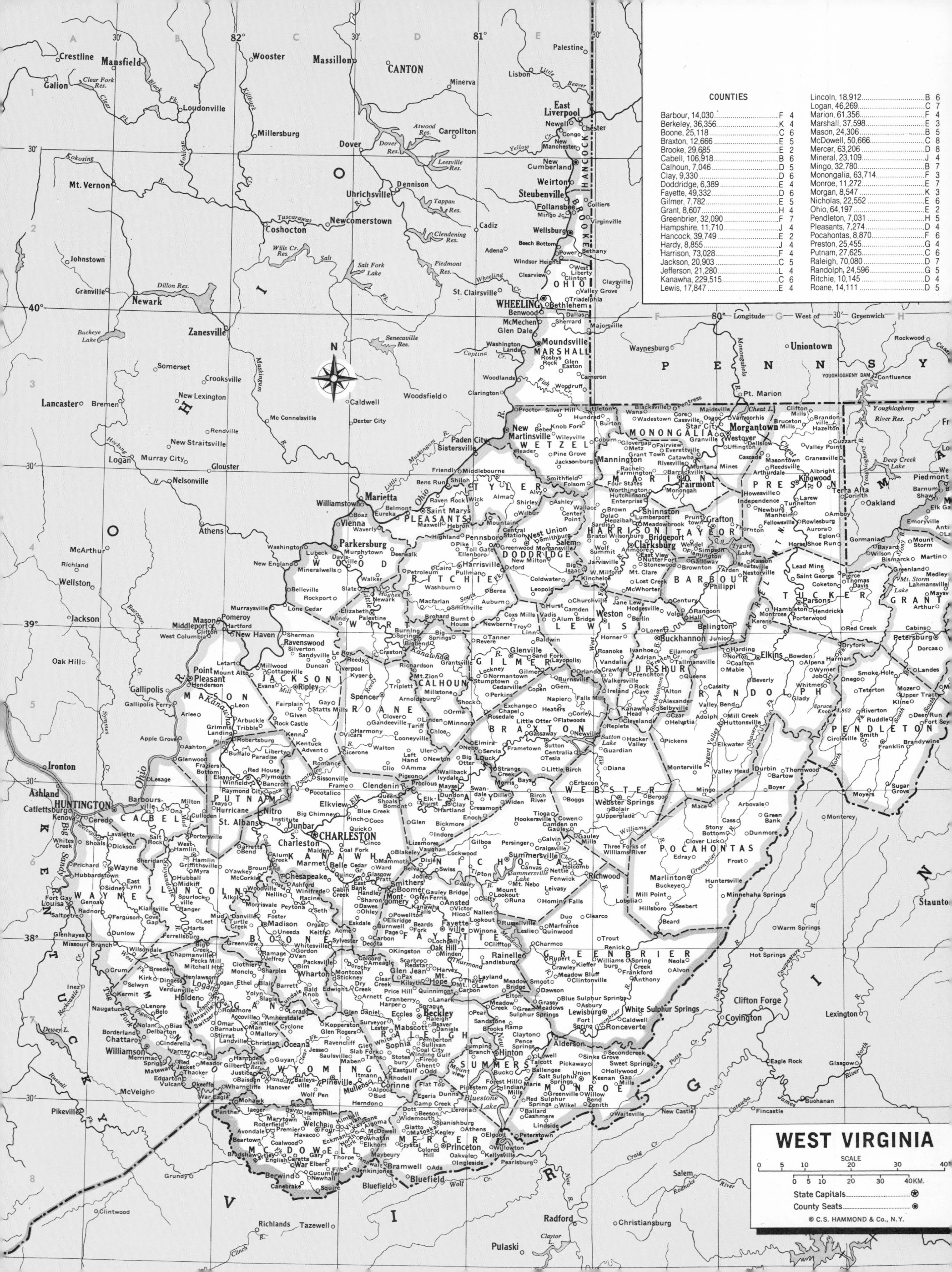

COUNTIES
Barbour, 14,030 F 4
Berkeley, 36,356 K 4
Boone, 25,118 C 6
Braxton, 12,666 E 5
Brooke, 29,685 E 2
Cabell, 106,918 B 6
Calhoun, 7,046 D 5
Clay, 9,330 D 6
Doddridge, 6,389 E 4
Fayette, 49,332 D 6
Gilmer, 7,782 E 5
Grant, 8,607 H 4
Greenbrier, 32,090 F 7
Hampshire, 11,710 J 4
Hancock, 39,749 E 2
Hardy, 8,855 J 4
Harrison, 73,028 F 4
Jackson, 20,903 C 5
Jefferson, 21,280 L 4
Kanawha, 229,515 C 6
Lewis, 17,847 E 4
Lincoln, 18,912 B 6
Logan, 46,269 C 7
Marion, 61,356 F 4
Marshall, 37,598 E 3
Mason, 24,306 B 5
McDowell, 50,666 C 8
Mercer, 63,206 D 8
Mineral, 23,109 J 4
Mingo, 32,780 B 7
Monongalia, 63,714 F 3
Monroe, 11,272 E 7
Morgan, 8,547 K 3
Nicholas, 22,552 E 6
Ohio, 64,197 E 2
Pendleton, 7,031 H 5
Pleasants, 7,274 D 4
Pocahontas, 8,870 F 6
Preston, 25,455 G 4
Putnam, 27,625 C 6
Raleigh, 70,080 D 7
Randolph, 24,596 G 5
Ritchie, 10,145 D 4
Roane, 14,111 D 5
WEST VIRGINIA
SCALE
0 5 10 20 30 40
0 5 10 20 30 40KM.
State Capitals
County Seats
© C.S. HAMMOND & Co., N.Y.

Summers, 13,213 ..... E 7
Taylor, 13,878 ..... F 4
Tucker, 7,447 ..... G 4
Tyler, 9,929 ..... E 4
Upshur, 19,092 ..... F 5
Wayne, 37,581 ..... B 6
Webster, 9,809 ..... F 6
Wetzel, 20,314 ..... E 3
Wirt, 4,154 ..... D 4
Wood, 86,818 ..... D 4
Wyoming, 30,095 ..... C 7

CITIES and TOWNS

Zip *Name/Pop.* **Key**

25606 Accoville, 975 ..... C 7
† 24701 Ada, 250 ..... D 8
† 26288 Addison (Webster Springs)⊙, 1,038 ..... F 6
26210 Adrian, 500 ..... F 5
26519 Albright, 319 ..... G 3
24910 Alderson, 1,278 ..... E 7
24807 Algoma, 400 ..... D 8
25501 Alkol, 500 ..... C 6
26320 Alma, 296 ..... E 4
24710 Alpoca, 200 ..... D 7
25003 Alum Creek, 900 ..... C 6
25004 Ameagle, 210 ..... D 7
25607 Amherstdale, 1,602 ..... C 4
24808 Anawalt, 801 ..... D 8
26323 Anmoore, 944 ..... F 4
25812 Ansted, 1,511 ..... D 6
24915 Arbovale, 300 ..... G 6
25006 Arbuckle, 300 ..... C 5
26324 Arden, 200 ..... G 4
25007 Arnett, 300 ..... D 7
25234 Arnoldsburg, 175 ..... D 5
26816 Arthur, 200 ..... H 4
26520 Arthurdale, 950 ..... G 3
24916 Asbury, 280 ..... E 7
24809 Asco, 200 ..... C 8
25009 Ashford, 400 ..... C 6
24712 Athens, 967 ..... E 8
26704 Augusta, 550 ..... J 4
26705 Aurora, 275 ..... G 4
24811 Avondale, 250 ..... C 8
24812 Baileysville, 800 ..... C 7
25608 Baisden, 500 ..... C 7
26801 Baker, 200 ..... J 4
25410 Bakerton, 250 ..... L 4
25010 Bald Knob, 356 ..... C 7
24918 Ballard, 220 ..... E 8
25011 Bancroft, 446 ..... C 5
25504 Barboursville, 2,279 ..... B 6
25609 Barnabus, 750 ..... C 7
26559 Barrackville, 1,596 ..... F 3
25013 Barrett, 950 ..... C 7
24813 Bartley, 600 ..... C 8
† 25411 Bath, 944 ..... K 3
26707 Bayard, 475 ..... H 4
† 26629 Bays, 186 ..... E 5
25014 Beards Fork, 350 ..... D 6
24814 Beartown, 500 ..... C 8
25813 Beaver (Glen Hedrick), 1,711 ..... D 7
25801 Beckley⊙, 19,884 ..... D 7
26030 Beech Bottom, 544 ..... E 2
24714 Beeson, 250 ..... D 8
26250 Belington, 1,567 ..... F 4

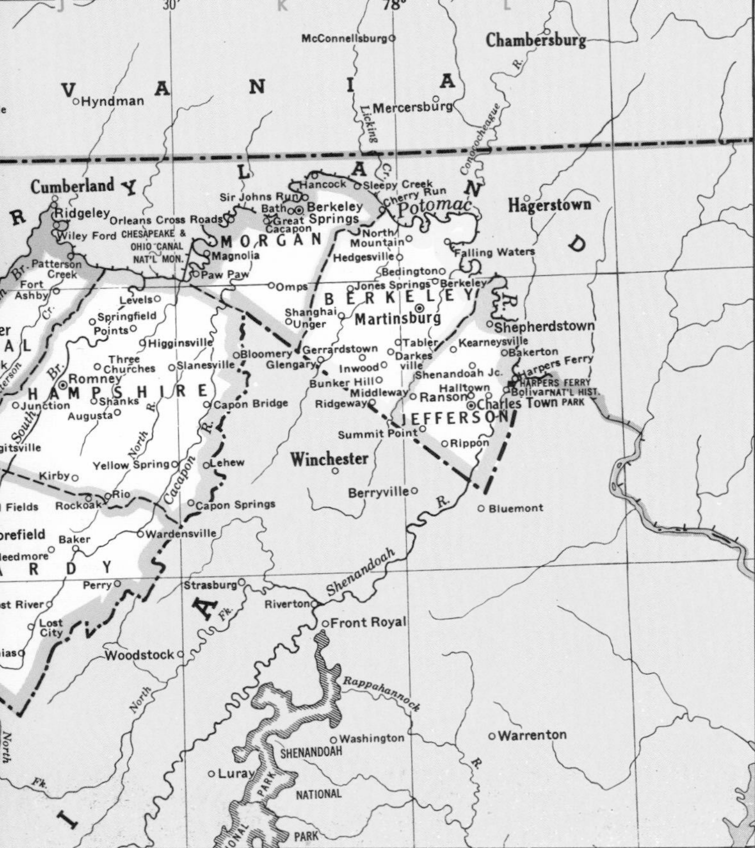

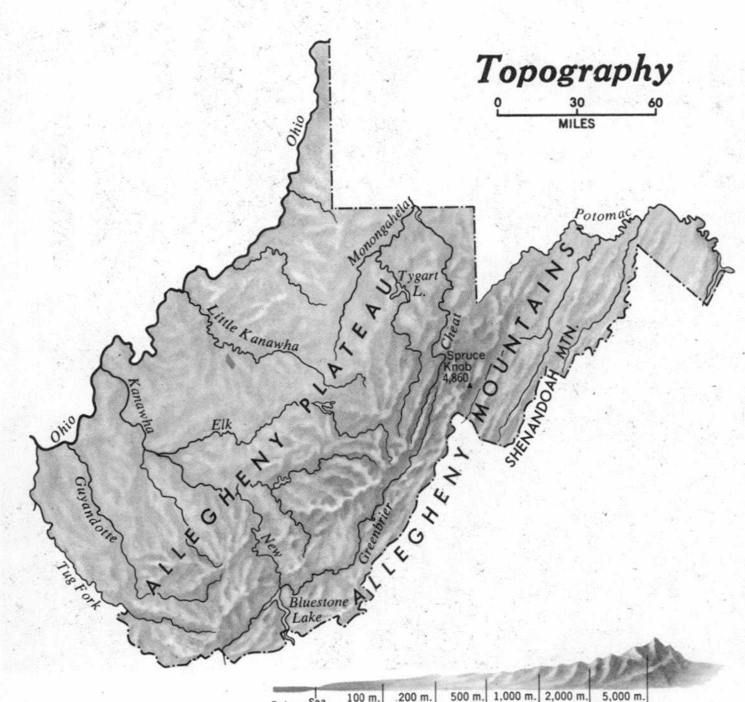

AREA 24,181 sq. mi.
POPULATION 1,744,237
CAPITAL Charleston
LARGEST CITY Huntington
HIGHEST POINT Spruce Knob 4,862 ft.
SETTLED IN 1774
ADMITTED TO UNION June 20, 1863
POPULAR NAME Mountain State
STATE FLOWER Rhododendron
STATE BIRD Cardinal

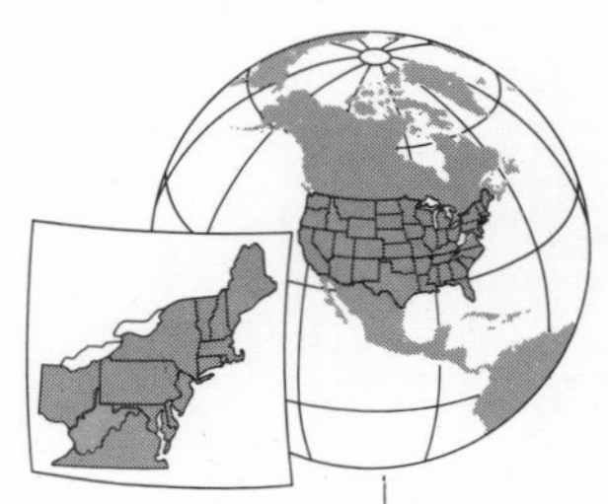

25015 Belle, 1,786 ..... C 6
26134 Belmont, 802 ..... D 4
26656 Belva, 550 ..... D 6
26031 Benwood, 2,737 ..... E 2
26298 Bergoo, 260 ..... F 6
† 25401 Berkeley, 600 ..... L 4
25411 Berkeley Springs⊙, 2,200 ..... K 3
24815 Berwind, 675 ..... C 8
26032 Bethany, 602 ..... E 2
† 26003 Bethlehem, 2,461 ..... E 2
26253 Beverly, 470 ..... G 5
25019 Bickmore, 375 ..... D 6
25302 Big Chimney, 450 ..... C 6
25505 Big Creek, 500 ..... B 7
† 24853 Big Four, 200 ..... C 8
25021 Bim, 395 ..... C 7
26610 Birch River, 650 ..... E 6
26521 Blacksville, 264 ..... F 3
25022 Blair, 700 ..... C 7
25023 Blakeley, 260 ..... D 6
25026 Blue Creek, 300 ..... D 6
24701 Bluefield, 15,921 ..... D 8
26288 Bolair, 450 ..... F 6
25426 Bolivar, 943 ..... L 4
25030 Bomont, 412 ..... D 6
25031 Boomer, 1,261 ..... D 6
25665 Borderland, 250 ..... B 7
24817 Bradshaw, 1,048 ..... C 8
24715 Bramwell, 1,125 ..... D 8
26802 Brandywine, 188 ..... H 5
25666 Breeden, 300 ..... B 7
26330 Bridgeport, 4,777 ..... F 4
† 25314 Brounland, 900 ..... C 6
26334 Brownton, 700 ..... F 4
26525 Bruceton Mills, 209 ..... G 3
26201 Buckhannon⊙, 7,261 ..... F 5
24716 Bud, 400 ..... D 7
25033 Buffalo, 831 ..... C 5
25413 Bunker Hill, 500 ..... K 4
26710 Burlington, 338 ..... J 4
26335 Burnsville, 591 ..... E 5
26562 Burton, 250 ..... F 3
25035 Cabin Creek, 900 ..... C 6
26855 Cabins, 300 ..... H 4
26337 Cairo, 412 ..... D 4
24925 Caldwell, 425 ..... F 7
26660 Calvin, 200 ..... E 6
26208 Camden on Gauley, 243 ..... E 6
26033 Cameron, 1,537 ..... E 3
25820 Camp Creek, 200 ..... D 7
24819 Canebrake, 250 ..... C 8
26662 Canvas, 300 ..... E 6
26711 Capon Bridge, 211 ..... K 4
26823 Capon Springs, 250 ..... K 4
25037 Carbon, 200 ..... D 6
24821 Caretta, 650 ..... C 8
26527 Cassville, 800 ..... F 3
26564 Catawba, 186 ..... F 3
25039 Cedar Grove, 1,275 ..... D 6
26340 Central Station, 275 ..... E 4
26214 Century, 239 ..... F 4
25507 Ceredo, 1,583 ..... B 6
25508 Chapmanville, 1,175 ..... B 7
* 25301 Charleston (cap.)⊙, 71,505 ..... C 6
Charleston, ‡229,515 ..... C 6
25414 Charles Town⊙, 3,023 ..... L 4
25958 Charmco, 900 ..... E 6
25667 Chattaroy, 1,145 ..... B 7
25315 Chesapeake, 2,428 ..... C 6
26034 Chester, 3,614 ..... E 1
25306 Cinco, 500 ..... D 6
26804 Circleville, 180 ..... H 5
26301 Clarksburg⊙, 24,864 ..... F 4
25043 Clay⊙, 479 ..... D 6
25044 Clear Creek, 300 ..... D 7
† 26003 Clearview, 512 ..... E 2
25045 Clendenin, 1,438 ..... D 5
25237 Clifton, 358 ..... B 5
† 25854 Clifty, 250 ..... E 6
† 26058 Clinton, 350 ..... E 2
25046 Clio, 300 ..... D 5
25047 Clothier, 950 ..... C 7
25238 Clover, 350 ..... D 5
24929 Clover Lick, 250 ..... F 6
25823 Coal City, 1,089 ..... D 7
25306 Coal Fork, 950 ..... D 6
26257 Coalton, 234 ..... G 5
24824 Coalwood, 650 ..... C 8
26565 Coburn, 230 ..... F 3
25048 Colcord, 600 ..... D 7
26035 Colliers, 500 ..... E 2
† 24740 Colored Hill, 1,031 ..... D 8
26615 Copen, 312 ..... E 5
25826 Corinne, 1,090 ..... D 7
26713 Corinth, 195 ..... H 4
25051 Costa, 500 ..... C 6
25239 Cottageville, 500 ..... C 5
25509 Cove Gap, 650 ..... B 6
26206 Cowen, 467 ..... E 6
26205 Craigsville, 300 ..... E 6
25828 Cranberry, 297 ..... D 7
25669 Crum, 300 ..... B 7
24826 Cucumber, 275 ..... C 8
25510 Culloden, 1,033 ..... B 6
24827 Cyclone, 500 ..... C 7
25832 Daniels, 950 ..... D 7
25053 Danville, 580 ..... C 6
† 25428 Darkesville, 375 ..... L 4
26260 Davis, 868 ..... H 4
26142 Davisville, 200 ..... C 4
24828 Davy, 993 ..... C 8
25054 Dawes, 800 ..... D 6
24932 Dawson, 200 ..... E 7
25055 Decota, 800 ..... D 6
25670 Delbarton, 903 ..... B 7
26531 Dellslow, 500 ..... G 3
26217 Diana, 600 ..... F 5
† 25535 Dickson, 200 ..... B 6
26617 Dille, 300 ..... E 6
25671 Dingess, 600 ..... B 7
25059 Dixie, 800 ..... D 6
† 26386 Dola, 200 ..... F 4
26835 Dorcas, 250 ..... H 5
25060 Dorothy, 400 ..... D 7
25062 Dry Creek, 290 ..... D 7
26263 Dryfork, 208 ..... H 5
25063 Duck, 500 ..... E 5
25064 Dunbar, 9,151 ..... C 6
24934 Dunmore, 200 ..... G 6
26264 Durbin, 347 ..... G 5
25067 East Bank, 1,025 ..... D 6
25835 Eastgulf, 300 ..... D 7
25512 East Lynn, 500 ..... B 6
† 26301 East View, 1,618 ..... F 4
25836 Eccles, 1,105 ..... D 7
24829 Eckman, 850 ..... C 8
25672 Edgarton, 415 ..... B 7
† 24954 Edray, 175 ..... F 6
24830 Elbert, 400 ..... C 8
25070 Eleanor, 1,035 ..... C 5
26143 Elizabeth⊙, 821 ..... D 4
26717 Elk Garden, 291 ..... H 4
26241 Elkins⊙, 8,287 ..... G 5
† 24868 Elkridge, 500 ..... D 6
25071 Elkview, 1,486 ..... C 6
26267 Ellamore, 400 ..... F 5
26346 Ellenboro, 267 ..... D 4
25965 Elton, 227 ..... E 7
24832 English, 500 ..... C 8
26568 Enterprise, 975 ..... F 4
26203 Erbacon, 350 ..... E 5
25075 Eskdale, 500 ..... D 6
25076 Ethel, 450 ..... C 7
25241 Evans, 400 ..... C 5
26533 Everettville, 200 ..... F 3
26554 Fairmont, 26,093 ..... F 4
† 25271 Fairplain, 200 ..... C 5
26570 Fairview, 640 ..... F 3
† 24966 Falling Springs (Renick), 255 ..... F 6
26571 Farmington, 595 ..... F 3
25840 Fayetteville⊙, 1,712 ..... D 6
26202 Fenwick, 500 ..... E 6
25513 Ferrellsburg, 300 ..... B 6
25823 Fireco, 300 ..... D 7
26818 Fisher, 250 ..... H 4
25841 Flat Top, 550 ..... D 7
26621 Flatwoods, 320 ..... E 5
26347 Flemington, 458 ..... F 4
26037 Follansbee, 3,883 ..... E 2
26348 Folsom, 325 ..... E 4
24935 Forest Hill, 314 ..... E 7
26719 Fort Ashby, 1,225 ..... J 4
25514 Fort Gay, 792 ..... A 6
26806 Fort Seybert, 208 ..... H 5
24936 Fort Spring, 250 ..... E 7
26572 Four States, 300 ..... F 4
25071 Frame, 200 ..... C 5
26623 Frametown, 600 ..... E 5
24938 Frankford, 200 ..... F 7
26807 Franklin⊙, 695 ..... H 5
26218 French Creek, 200 ..... F 5
26219 Frenchton, 212 ..... F 5
26146 Friendly, 190 ..... D 3
25515 Gallipolis Ferry, 325 ..... B 5
26349 Galloway, 289 ..... F 4
25243 Gandeeville, 271 ..... D 5
24836 Gary, 850 ..... C 8
26624 Gassaway, 1,253 ..... E 5
25085 Gauley Bridge, 1,800 ..... D 6
25420 Gerrardstown, 258 ..... K 4
25843 Ghent, 450 ..... D 7
† 24736 Giatto, 400 ..... D 8
25621 Gilbert, 778 ..... C 7
26671 Gilboa, 375 ..... E 6
25086 Glasgow, 904 ..... D 6
26038 Glen Dale, 2,150 ..... E 3
25844 Glen Daniel, 300 ..... D 7
25090 Glen Ferris, 275 ..... D 6
† 25813 Glen Hedrick (Beaver), 1,711 ..... D 7
25846 Glen Jean, 1,510 ..... D 7
25848 Glen Rogers, 500 ..... D 7
26351 Glenville⊙, 2,183 ..... E 5
25849 Glen White, 600 ..... D 7
25520 Glenwood, 400 ..... B 5
25093 Gordon, 500 ..... C 7
26720 Gormania, 250 ..... H 4
26354 Grafton⊙, 6,433 ..... G 4
26147 Grantsville⊙, 795 ..... D 5
26574 Grant Town, 946 ..... F 3
26534 Granville, 1,027 ..... F 3
25422 Great Cacapon, 750 ..... K 3
25966 Green Sulphur Springs, 300 ..... E 7
† 25166 Greenview, 250 ..... C 6
26360 Greenwood, 460 ..... E 4
25521 Griffithsville, 300 ..... B 6
25095 Grimms Landing, 350 ..... B 5
26221 Guardian, 200 ..... F 5
24838 Guyan, 250 ..... C 7
25423 Halltown, 325 ..... L 4
26269 Hambleton, 328 ..... G 4
25523 Hamlin⊙, 1,024 ..... B 6
25623 Hampden, 251 ..... C 7
25102 Handley, 500 ..... D 6
24839 Hanover, 300 ..... C 7
† 26250 Harding, 200 ..... G 5
25851 Harper, 300 ..... D 7
25425 Harpers Ferry, 423 ..... L 4
26362 Harrisville⊙, 1,464 ..... E 4
25247 Hartford, 527 ..... C 4
25852 Harvey, 500 ..... D 7
24841 Havaco, 329 ..... C 8
26627 Heaters, 343 ..... E 5
25427 Hedgesville, 274 ..... K 3
26224 Helvetia, 269 ..... F 5
24842 Hemphill, 785 ..... C 8
25106 Henderson, 496 ..... B 5
26271 Hendricks, 317 ..... G 4
25624 Henlawson, 900 ..... B 7
26369 Hepzibah, 600 ..... F 4
24726 Herndon, 500 ..... D 7
25854 Hico, 750 ..... D 6
24946 Hillsboro, 267 ..... F 6
25951 Hinton⊙, 4,503 ..... E 7
26262 Holcomb, 200 ..... E 6
25625 Holden, 2,325 ..... B 7
† 26651 Hookersville, 250 ..... E 6
26575 Hundred, 475 ..... E 3
* 25701 Huntington⊙, 74,315 ..... A 6
Huntington-Ashland, ‡253,743 ..... A 6
25526 Hurricane, 3,491 ..... C 6
24844 Iaeger, 822 ..... C 8
25111 Indore, 200 ..... D 6
25112 Institute, 3,100 ..... C 6
25428 Inwood, 600 ..... K 4
24847 Itmann, 500 ..... D 7
25113 Ivydale, 700 ..... D 5
26377 Jacksonburg, 735 ..... E 3
26378 Jane Lew, 397 ..... F 4
† 26462 Jarvisville, 250 ..... F 4
25114 Jeffrey, 900 ..... C 7
24848 Jenkinjones, 800 ..... D 8
26674 Jodie, 300 ..... D 6
25969 Jumping Branch, 297 ..... E 7
26275 Junior, 513 ..... G 5
24851 Justice, 600 ..... C 7
25430 Kearneysville, 250 ..... L 4
24731 Kegley, 450 ..... D 8
24732 Kellysville, 200 ..... E 8
25248 Kenna, 380 ..... C 5
25530 Kenova, 4,860 ..... A 6
25674 Kermit, 716 ..... B 7
26726 Keyser⊙, 6,586 ..... J 4
24852 Keystone, 1,008 ..... D 8
25859 Kilsyth, 450 ..... D 7
24853 Kimball, 962 ..... C 8
26537 Kingwood⊙, 2,550 ..... G 4
† 25671 Kirk, 400 ..... B 7
25628 Kistler, 750 ..... C 7
24854 Kopperston, 900 ..... C 7
25860 Lanark, 375 ..... D 7
† 25831 Landisburg, 250 ..... E 7
25629 Landville, 250 ..... C 7
25535 Lavalette, 600 ..... B 6
25864 Layland, 455 ..... E 7
† 26430 Layopolis (Sand Fork), 252 ..... E 5
25251 Left Hand, 200 ..... D 5
26676 Leivasy, 450 ..... E 6
25676 Lenore, 800 ..... B 7
25123 Leon, 192 ..... C 5
25971 Lerona, 350 ..... D 8
25537 Lesage, 600 ..... B 5
25972 Leslie, 500 ..... E 6
25865 Lester, 507 ..... D 7
25253 Letart, 250 ..... C 5
24901 Lewisburg⊙, 2,407 ..... E 7
24951 Lindside, 225 ..... E 8
26384 Linn, 212 ..... E 4
26629 Little Birch, 180 ..... E 5
† 26624 Little Otter, 250 ..... E 5
26581 Littleton, 333 ..... F 3
25125 Lizemores, 400 ..... D 6
26677 Lockwood, 300 ..... D 6
25601 Logan⊙, 3,311 ..... B 7
25868 Lookout, 200 ..... E 6
25630 Lorado, 400 ..... C 7
26385 Lost Creek, 571 ..... F 4
† 26101 Lubeck, 500 ..... C 4
26386 Lumberport, 957 ..... F 4
25631 Lundale, 700 ..... C 7
25870 Maben, 200 ..... D 7
26278 Mabie, 366 ..... G 5
25871 Mabscott, 1,254 ..... D 7
25873 MacArthur, 1,614 ..... D 7
25130 Madison⊙, 2,342 ..... C 6
26541 Maidsville, 485 ..... F 3
25306 Malden, 900 ..... C 6
25634 Mallory, 1,240 ..... C 7
25132 Mammoth, 576 ..... D 6
25635 Man, 1,201 ..... C 7
26582 Mannington, 2,747 ..... F 3
25975 Marfrance, 240 ..... E 6
24954 Marlinton⊙, 1,286 ..... F 6
25315 Marmet, 2,339 ..... C 6
25401 Martinsburg⊙, 14,626 ..... K 4
25260 Mason, 1,319 ..... B 4
26542 Masontown, 868 ..... G 3
25678 Matewan, 651 ..... B 7
24736 Matoaka, 608 ..... D 8
24861 Maybeury, 850 ..... D 8

(continued on following page)

(continued)

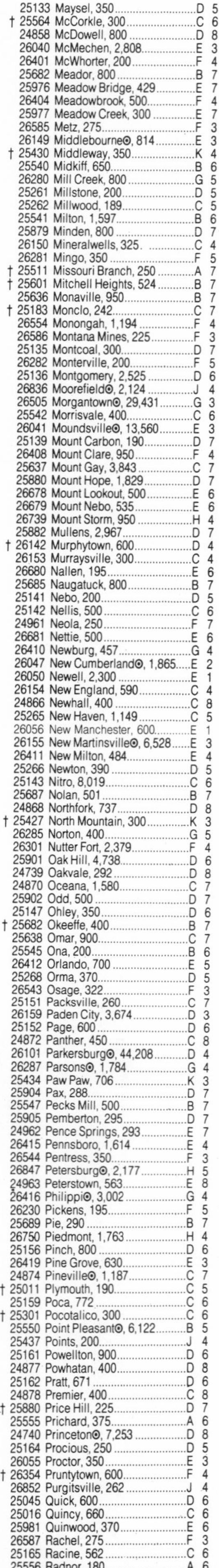

25133 Maysel, 350 ..... D 5
† 25564 McCorkle, 300 ..... C 6
24858 McDowell, 800 ..... D 8
26040 McMechen, 2,808 ..... E 3
26401 McWhorter, 200 ..... F 4
25682 Meador, 800 ..... B 7
25976 Meadow Bridge, 429 ..... E 7
26404 Meadowbrook, 500 ..... F 4
25977 Meadow Creek, 300 ..... E 7
26585 Metz, 275 ..... F 3
26149 Middlebourne⊙, 814 ..... E 3
† 25430 Middleway, 350 ..... K 4
25540 Midkiff, 650 ..... B 6
26280 Mill Creek, 800 ..... G 5
25261 Millstone, 200 ..... D 5
25262 Millwood, 189 ..... C 5
25541 Milton, 1,597 ..... B 6
25879 Minden, 800 ..... D 7
26150 Mineralwells, 325 ..... C 4
26281 Mingo, 350 ..... F 5
† 25511 Missouri Branch, 250 ..... A 7
† 25601 Mitchell Heights, 524 ..... B 7
25636 Monaville, 950 ..... B 7
† 25183 Monclo, 242 ..... C 7
26554 Monongah, 1,194 ..... F 4
26586 Montana Mines, 225 ..... F 3
25135 Montcoal, 300 ..... D 7
26282 Monterville, 200 ..... F 5
25136 Montgomery, 2,525 ..... D 6
26836 Moorefield⊙, 2,124 ..... J 4
26505 Morgantown⊙, 29,431 ..... G 3
25542 Morrisvale, 400 ..... C 6
26041 Moundsville⊙, 13,560 ..... E 3
25139 Mount Carbon, 190 ..... D 7
26408 Mount Clare, 950 ..... F 4
25637 Mount Gay, 3,843 ..... C 7
25880 Mount Hope, 1,829 ..... D 7
26678 Mount Lookout, 500 ..... E 6
26679 Mount Nebo, 535 ..... E 6
26739 Mount Storm, 950 ..... H 4
25882 Mullens, 2,967 ..... D 7
† 26142 Murphytown, 600 ..... D 4
26153 Murraysville, 300 ..... C 4
26680 Nallen, 195 ..... E 6
25685 Naugatuck, 800 ..... B 7
25141 Nebo, 200 ..... D 5
25142 Nellis, 500 ..... C 6
24961 Neola, 250 ..... F 7
26681 Nettie, 500 ..... E 6
26410 Newburg, 457 ..... G 4
26047 New Cumberland⊙, 1,865 ..... E 2
26050 Newell, 2,300 ..... E 1
26154 New England, 590 ..... C 4
24866 Newhall, 400 ..... C 8
25265 New Haven, 1,149 ..... C 5
26056 New Manchester, 600 ..... E 1
26155 New Martinsville⊙, 6,528 ..... E 3
26411 New Milton, 484 ..... E 4
25266 Newton, 390 ..... D 5
25143 Nitro, 8,019 ..... C 6
25687 Nolan, 501 ..... B 7
24868 Northfork, 737 ..... D 8
† 25427 North Mountain, 300 ..... K 3
26285 Norton, 400 ..... G 5
26301 Nutter Fort, 2,379 ..... F 4
25901 Oak Hill, 4,738 ..... D 6
24739 Oakvale, 292 ..... D 8
24870 Oceana, 1,580 ..... C 7
25902 Odd, 500 ..... D 7
25147 Ohley, 350 ..... D 6
† 25682 Okeeffe, 400 ..... B 7
25638 Omar, 900 ..... C 7
25545 Ona, 200 ..... B 6
26412 Orlando, 700 ..... E 5
25268 Orma, 370 ..... D 5
26543 Osage, 322 ..... F 3
25151 Packsville, 260 ..... C 7
26159 Paden City, 3,674 ..... D 3
25152 Page, 600 ..... D 6
24872 Panther, 450 ..... C 8
26101 Parkersburg⊙, 44,208 ..... D 4
26287 Parsons⊙, 1,784 ..... G 4
25434 Paw Paw, 706 ..... K 3
25904 Pax, 288 ..... D 7
25547 Pecks Mill, 500 ..... B 7
25905 Pemberton, 295 ..... D 7
24962 Pence Springs, 293 ..... E 7
26415 Pennsboro, 1,614 ..... E 4
26544 Pentress, 350 ..... F 3
26847 Petersburg⊙, 2,177 ..... H 5
24963 Peterstown, 563 ..... E 8
26416 Philippi⊙, 3,002 ..... G 4
26230 Pickens, 195 ..... F 5
25689 Pie, 290 ..... B 7
26750 Piedmont, 1,763 ..... H 4
25156 Pinch, 800 ..... D 6
26419 Pine Grove, 630 ..... E 3
24874 Pineville⊙, 1,187 ..... C 7
† 25011 Plymouth, 190 ..... C 5
25159 Poca, 772 ..... C 6
† 25301 Pocotalico, 300 ..... C 6
25550 Point Pleasant⊙, 6,122 ..... B 5
25437 Points, 200 ..... J 4
25161 Powellton, 900 ..... D 6
24877 Powhatan, 400 ..... D 8
25162 Pratt, 671 ..... D 6
24878 Premier, 400 ..... C 8
† 25880 Price Hill, 225 ..... D 7
25555 Prichard, 375 ..... A 6
24740 Princeton⊙, 7,253 ..... D 8
25164 Procious, 250 ..... D 5
26055 Proctor, 350 ..... E 3
† 26354 Pruntytown, 600 ..... F 4
26852 Purgitsville, 262 ..... J 4
25045 Quick, 600 ..... D 6
25016 Quincy, 660 ..... C 6
25981 Quinwood, 370 ..... E 6
26587 Rachel, 275 ..... F 3
25165 Racine, 562 ..... C 6
25556 Radnor, 180 ..... A 6
25962 Rainelle, 1,826 ..... E 7
25911 Raleigh, 900 ..... D 7
25557 Ranger, 300 ..... B 6
25438 Ranson, 2,189 ..... L 4
25913 Ravencliff, 300 ..... C 7
26164 Ravenswood, 4,240 ..... C 5

Agriculture, Industry and Resources

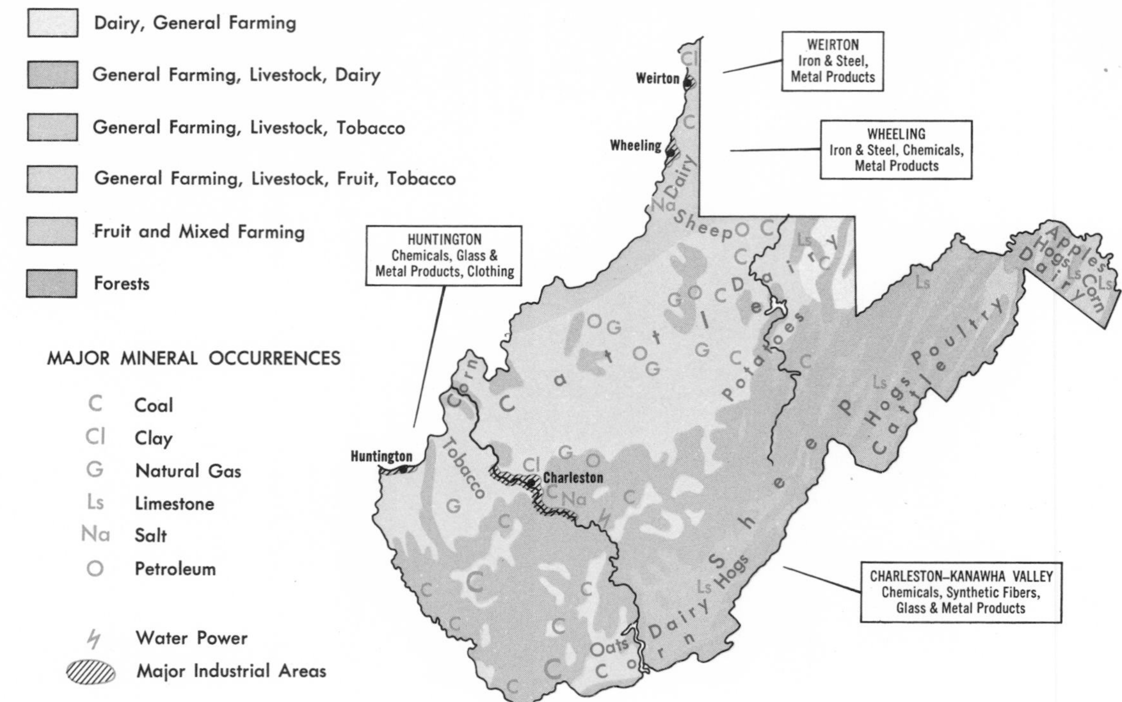

† 25159 Raymond City, 370 ..... C 6
26167 Reader, 822 ..... E 3
25168 Red House, 600 ..... C 5
25692 Red Jacket, 800 ..... B 7
25914 Redstar, 200 ..... D 7
26547 Reedsville, 379 ..... G 3
25270 Reedy, 351 ..... D 5
24966 Renick, 255 ..... F 6
25915 Rhodell, 500 ..... D 7
26261 Richwood, 3,717 ..... F 6
26753 Ridgeley, 1,112 ..... J 3
25271 Ripley⊙, 3,244 ..... C 5
25441 Rippon, 500 ..... L 4
26588 Rivesville, 1,108 ..... F 3
26234 Rock Cave, 300 ..... F 5
24881 Roderfield, 1,161 ..... C 8
26757 Romney⊙, 2,364 ..... J 4
24970 Ronceverte, 1,981 ..... F 7
26636 Rosedale, 234 ..... E 5
25643 Rossmore, 400 ..... C 7
26425 Rowlesburg, 829 ..... G 4
25984 Rupert, 1,027 ..... E 7
26689 Russellville, 240 ..... E 6
25177 Saint Albans, 14,356 ..... C 6
26170 Saint Marys⊙, 2,348 ..... D 4
26426 Salem, 2,597 ..... E 4
25559 Salt Rock, 350 ..... B 6
26430 Sand Fork, 252 ..... E 5
25985 Sandstone, 350 ..... E 7
25275 Sandyville, 500 ..... C 5
25917 Scarbro, 800 ..... D 7
† 25674 Selwyn, 500 ..... B 7
25181 Seth, 950 ..... C 6
† 25427 Shanghai, 200 ..... K 4
25182 Sharon, 700 ..... D 6
25183 Sharples, 450 ..... C 7
25442 Shenandoah Junction, 600 ..... L 4
25443 Shepherdstown, 1,688 ..... L 4
26057 Sherrard, 400 ..... E 3
26431 Shinnston, 2,576 ..... F 4
26435 Simpson, 250 ..... F 4
25320 Sissonville, 450 ..... C 5
26175 Sistersville, 2,246 ..... D 3
25920 Slab Fork, 300 ..... D 7
† 25654 Slagle, 450 ..... C 7
† 26143 Slate, 200 ..... D 4
25186 Smithers, 2,020 ..... D 6
26437 Smithfield, 294 ..... E 4
26178 Smithville, 500 ..... D 4
24977 Smoot, 300 ..... E 7
25921 Sophia, 1,303 ..... D 7
25303 South Charleston, 16,333 ..... C 6
25922 Spanishburg, 425 ..... D 8
25276 Spencer⊙, 2,271 ..... D 5
26763 Springfield, 250 ..... J 4
24884 Squire, 900 ..... C 8
26505 Star City, 1,312 ..... F 3
25188 Stickney, 240 ..... D 7
25645 Stirrat, 250 ..... C 7
26301 Stonewood, 1,950 ..... F 4
25929 Stotesbury, 199 ..... D 7
26651 Summersville⊙, 2,429 ..... E 6
25446 Summit Point, 455 ..... K 4
26601 Sutton⊙, 1,031 ..... E 5
24980 Sweet Springs, 500 ..... F 7
26690 Swiss, 500 ..... D 6
25647 Switzer, 850 ..... B 7
25193 Sylvester, 245 ..... C 6
† 25428 Tabler, 300 ..... L 4
24981 Talcott, 700 ..... E 7
26237 Tallmansville, 260 ..... F 5
25569 Teays, 200 ..... B 6
26764 Terra Alta, 1,474 ..... H 4
26640 Tesla, 300 ..... E 5
25694 Thacker, 325 ..... B 7

26292 Thomas, 713 ..... H 4
26440 Thornton, 300 ..... G 4
24888 Thorpe, 600 ..... D 8
† 26206 Three Forks of Williams River, 375 ..... F 6
26691 Tioga, 320 ..... E 6
26059 Triadelphia, 547 ..... E 2
† 25095 Tribble, 350 ..... C 5
26444 Tunnelton, 369 ..... G 4
25203 Turtle Creek, 566 ..... C 6
25205 Uneeda, 850 ..... C 6
24983 Union⊙, 566 ..... E 7
26266 Upperglade, 500 ..... F 6
26293 Valley Bend, 950 ..... F 5
26060 Valley Grove, 509 ..... E 2
26294 Valley Head, 600 ..... G 5
25206 Van, 800 ..... C 7
25696 Varney, 750 ..... B 7
25649 Verdunville, 950 ..... B 7
26101 Vienna, 11,549 ..... D 4

24891 Vivian, 500 ..... D 8
26238 Volga, 350 ..... F 4
26589 Wadestown, 210 ..... F 3
24984 Waiteville, 252 ..... F 8
26448 Wallace, 325 ..... E 4
25286 Walton, 250 ..... D 5
24892 War, 2,004 ..... C 8
† 25039 Ward, 850 ..... D 6
26851 Wardensville, 288 ..... J 4
26181 Washington, 450 ..... C 4
† 26041 Washington Lands, 500 ..... E 3
26184 Waverly, 407 ..... D 4
25570 Wayne⊙, 1,385 ..... B 6
26288 Webster Springs⊙, 1,038 ..... F 6
26062 Weirton, 27,131 ..... E 2
Weirton-Steubenville, ‡165,627 ..... E 2
24801 Welch⊙, 4,149 ..... C 8
26070 Wellsburg⊙, 4,600 ..... E 2
25287 West Columbia, 245 ..... B 5

25571 West Hamlin, 715 ..... B 6
26074 West Liberty, 975 ..... E 2
25601 West Logan, 685 ..... C 7
26451 West Milford, 356 ..... F 4
26452 Weston⊙, 7,323 ..... F 4
26505 Westover, 5,086 ..... G 3
26456 West Union⊙, 1,141 ..... E 4
25651 Wharncliffe, 1,012 ..... C 7
25208 Wharton, 900 ..... C 7
26003 Wheeling⊙, 48,188 ..... E 2
Wheeling, ‡182,712 ..... E 2
24986 White Sulphur Springs, 2,396 ..... F 7
25209 Whitesville, 781 ..... C 6
26296 Whitmer, 411 ..... G 5
25211 Widen, 230 ..... E 6
26767 Wiley Ford, 750 ..... J 3
26186 Wileyville, 190 ..... E 3
25653 Wilkinson, 975 ..... B 7
24991 Williamsburg, 225 ..... F 7

25661 Williamson⊙, 5,831 ..... B 7
26187 Williamstown, 2,743 ..... C 4
26461 Wilsonburg, 200 ..... F 4
25699 Wilsondale, 200 ..... B 7
26075 Windsor Heights, 850 ..... E 2
25213 Winfield⊙, 328 ..... C 5
25214 Winifrede, 750 ..... C 6
25942 Winona, 250 ..... E 6
26462 Wolf Summit, 750 ..... F 4
† 26257 Womelsdorf (Coalton), 234 ..... G 5
† 26055 Woodlands, 200 ..... E 3
26591 Worthington, 288 ..... F 4
25573 Yawkey, 985 ..... C 6
26865 Yellow Spring, 250 ..... J 4
25654 Yolyn, 750 ..... C 7

⊙ County seat.
‡ Population of metropolitan area
† Zip of nearest p.o.
* Multiple zips

A. D'Arazien — Shostal Associates

At one of Clarksburg, West Virginia's glass plants, liquid glass is poured into a machine and becomes beautifully textured stained-glass panels.

AREA 56,154 sq. mi.
POPULATION 4,417,933
CAPITAL Madison
LARGEST CITY Milwaukee
HIGHEST POINT Timms Hill 1,952 ft.
SETTLED IN 1670
ADMITTED TO UNION May 29, 1848
POPULAR NAME Badger State
STATE FLOWER Wood Violet
STATE BIRD Robin

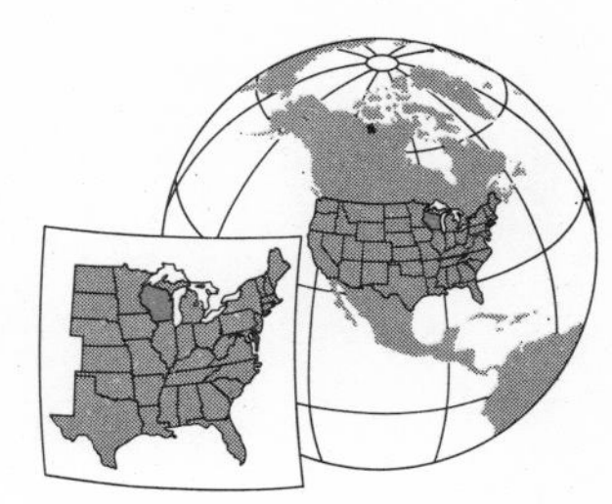

COUNTIES

County, Pop.	Key
Adams, 9,234	G 8
Ashland, 16,743	E 3
Barron, 33,955	C 5
Bayfield, 11,683	D 3
Brown, 158,244	L 7
Buffalo, 13,743	C 7
Burnett, 9,276	B 4
Calumet, 27,604	K 7
Chippewa, 47,717	D 5
Clark, 30,361	E 6
Columbia, 40,150	H 9
Crawford, 15,252	E 9
Dane, 290,272	H 9
Dodge, 69,004	J 9
Door, 20,106	M 6
Douglas, 44,657	C 3
Dunn, 29,154	C 6
Eau Claire, 67,219	D 6
Florence, 3,298	K 4
Fond du Lac, 84,567	K 8
Forest, 7,691	J 4
Grant, 48,398	E 10
Green, 26,714	G 10
Green Lake, 16,878	H 8
Iowa, 19,306	F 9
Iron, 6,533	F 3
Jackson, 15,325	E 7
Jefferson, 60,060	J 9
Juneau, 18,455	F 8
Kenosha, 117,917	K 10
Kewaunee, 18,961	L 6
La Crosse, 80,468	D 8
Lafayette, 17,456	F 10
Langlade, 19,220	H 5
Lincoln, 23,499	G 5
Manitowoc, 82,294	L 7
Marathon, 97,457	G 6
Marinette, 35,810	K 5
Marquette, 8,865	H 8
Menominee, 2,607	J 5
Milwaukee, 1,054,063	L 9
Monroe, 31,610	E 8
Oconto, 25,553	K 6
Oneida, 24,427	G 4
Outagamie, 119,356	K 7
Ozaukee, 54,421	L 9
Pepin, 7,319	C 6
Pierce, 26,652	B 6
Polk, 26,666	B 5
Portage, 47,541	G 6
Price, 14,520	F 4
Racine, 170,838	K 10
Richland, 17,079	F 9
Rock, 131,970	H 10
Rusk, 14,238	D 5
Saint Croix, 34,354	B 5
Sauk, 39,057	G 9
Sawyer, 9,670	D 4
Shawano, 32,650	J 6
Sheboygan, 96,660	L 8
Taylor, 16,958	E 5
Trempealeau, 23,344	D 7
Vernon, 24,557	E 8
Vilas, 10,958	G 3
Walworth, 63,444	J 10
Washburn, 10,601	C 4
Washington, 63,839	K 9
Waukesha, 231,365	K 9
Waupaca, 37,780	J 6
Waushara, 14,795	H 7
Winnebago, 129,931	J 7
Wood, 65,362	F 7

CITIES and TOWNS

Zip	Name/Pop.	Key
54405	Abbotsford, 1,375	F 6
54101	Abrams, 300	L 6
53910	Adams, 1,440	G 8
53001	Adell, 380	L 8
53501	Afton, 250	H 10
53502	Albany, 875	G 10
† 53534	Albion, 250	H 10
54201	Algoma, 4,023	M 6
53002	Allenton, 584	K 9
† 54301	Allouez, 13,753	L 7
54610	Alma⊙, 956	C 7
54611	Alma Center, 495	E 7
54805	Almena, 423	B 5
54909	Almond, 440	G 7
54720	Altoona, 2,842	C 6
49936	Alvin, 160	J 4
54102	Amberg, 711	K 5
54001	Amery, 2,126	B 5
54406	Amherst, 585	H 7
† 54162	Angelica, 200	K 6
54408	Aniwa, 233	H 6
54409	Antigo⊙, 9,005	H 5
54911	Appleton⊙, 57,143	J 7
	Appleton-Oshkosh, ‡276,893	J 7
54510	Arbor Vitae, 950	G 4
54612	Arcadia, 2,159	D 7
53503	Arena, 377	G 9
54511	Argonne, 400	J 4
53504	Argyle, 673	G 10
54721	Arkansaw, 350	B 6
53911	Arlington, 379	H 9
54103	Armstrong Creek, 555	K 4
54410	Arpin, 355	G 6
53003	Ashippun, 400	H 1
54806	Ashland⊙, 9,615	E 2
54304	Ashwaubenon, 9,323	K 7
54411	Athens, 856	G 5
54412	Auburndale, 468	F 6
54722	Augusta, 1,242	D 6
54920	Auroraville, 250	H 7
53506	Avoca, 421	F 9
† 53520	Avon, 600	H 10
54413	Babcock, 260	F 7
53801	Bagley, 271	D 10
54202	Baileys Harbor, 900	M 5
54002	Baldwin, 1,399	B 6
54810	Balsam Lake⊙, 648	B 5
54921	Bancroft, 150	G 7
54614	Bangor, 974	E 8
53913	Baraboo⊙, 7,931	G 9
† 54873	Barnes, 450	D 3
53507	Barneveld, 528	F 10
54812	Barron⊙, 2,337	C 5
† 53001	Batavia, 160	K 8
54723	Bay City, 317	B 6
54814	Bayfield, 874	E 2
† 53201	Bayside, 4,461	M 1
54922	Bear Creek, 520	J 6
53916	Beaver Dam, 14,265	J 9
53802	Beetown, 170	E 10
53004	Belgium, 809	L 8
53508	Belleville, 1,063	G 10
53510	Belmont, 688	F 10
53511	Beloit, 35,729	H 10
54815	Bennett, 350	C 3
53803	Benton, 873	F 10
54923	Berlin, 5,338	H 8
† 53401	Berryville, 150	M 3
† 54410	Bethel, 210	F 6
† 54440	Bevent, 200	H 6
53103	Big Bend, 1,148	K 2
54817	Birchwood, 394	C 4
54414	Birnamwood, 632	H 6
† 54494	Biron, 771	G 7
54106	Black Creek, 921	K 7
53515	Black Earth, 1,114	G 9
54615	Black River Falls⊙, 3,273	E 7
† 54541	Blackwell, 350	J 4
54616	Blair, 1,036	D 7
53516	Blanchardville, 671	G 10
54724	Bloomer, 3,143	D 5
53804	Bloomington, 719	E 10
53517	Blue Mounds, 261	G 9
53518	Blue River, 369	E 9
54107	Bonduel, 995	K 6
53805	Boscobel, 2,510	E 9
54512	Boulder Junction, 500	G 3
54416	Bowler, 272	J 6
54725	Boyceville, 725	C 5
54726	Boyd, 574	E 6
54203	Branch, 225	L 7
53919	Brandon, 872	J 8
54513	Brantwood, 500	F 4
53920	Briggsville, 250	H 8
54110	Brillion, 2,588	L 7
53520	Brodhead, 2,515	G 10
54417	Brokaw, 312	G 5
53005	Brookfield, 32,140	K 1
53521	Brooklyn, 565	H 10
† 53201	Brown Deer, 12,622	L 1
† 53105	Browns Lake, 1,669	K 3
53006	Brownsville, 374	J 8
53522	Browntown, 253	G 10
54819	Bruce, 799	D 5
54820	Brule, 675	C 2
54204	Brussels, 306	L 6
† 54622	Buffalo, 671	C 7
53105	Burlington, 7,479	K 10
53922	Burnett, 241	J 9
53007	Butler, 2,261	K 1
54514	Butternut, 453	E 3
54821	Cable, 281	D 3
54727	Cadott, 977	D 6
53923	Cambria, 631	H 8
53523	Cambridge, 689	H 9
54822	Cameron, 893	C 5
† 53019	Campbellsport, 1,681	K 8
54618	Camp Douglas, 547	F 8
53109	Camp Lake, 1,898	K 10
54928	Caroline, 450	J 6
53011	Cascade, 603	K 8
54205	Casco, 481	L 6
54619	Cashton, 824	E 8
53806	Cassville, 1,343	E 10
54515	Catawba, 215	E 4
53924	Cazenovia, 335	F 8
54111	Cecil, 369	K 6
53012	Cedarburg, 7,697	L 9
53013	Cedar Grove, 1,276	L 8
54824	Centuria, 632	A 5
54621	Chaseburg, 224	D 8
† 53029	Chenequa, 642	J 1
54728	Chetek, 1,630	C 5
54420	Chili, 205	F 6
53014	Chilton⊙, 3,030	K 7
54729	Chippewa Falls⊙, 12,351	D 6
54004	Clayton, 306	B 5
54005	Clear Lake, 721	B 5
54518	Clearwater Lake, 200	H 4
53015	Cleveland, 761	L 8
53525	Clinton, 1,333	J 10
54929	Clintonville, 4,600	J 6
53016	Clyman, 328	J 9
53526	Cobb, 410	F 10
54622	Cochrane, 506	C 7
54421	Colby, 1,178	F 6
54112	Coleman, 683	L 5
54730	Colfax, 1,026	C 6
54930	Coloma, 336	H 7
53925	Columbus, 3,789	H 9
54113	Combined Locks, 2,734	K 7
† 53147	Como, 1,132	K 10
† 53066	Concord, 200	H 1
54519	Conover, 500	H 3
54623	Coon Valley, 596	E 8
54732	Cornell, 1,616	D 5
54827	Cornucopia, 250	D 2
54520	Crandon⊙, 1,582	H 4
54114	Crivitz, 985	L 5
53528	Cross Plains, 1,478	G 9
53807	Cuba City, 1,993	F 10
53110	Cudahy, 22,078	M 2
54829	Cumberland, 1,839	C 4
54931	Dale, 410	J 7
54733	Dallas, 359	C 5
53926	Dalton, 320	H 8
54830	Danbury, 350	B 3
53529	Dane, 486	G 9
53114	Darien, 839	J 10
53530	Darlington⊙, 2,351	F 10
53531	Deerfield, 1,067	H 9
54007	Deer Park, 217	B 5
53532	De Forest, 1,911	H 9
53018	Delafield, 3,182	J 1
53115	Delavan, 5,526	J 10
† 53115	Delavan Lake, 2,124	J 10
54856	Delta, 180	D 3
54208	Denmark, 1,364	L 7
54115	De Pere, 13,309	K 7
† 54663	De Soto, 295	D 9
53808	Dickeyville, 1,057	E 10
54625	Dodge, 204	D 7
53533	Dodgeville⊙, 3,255	F 10
54425	Dorchester, 491	F 5
53118	Dousman, 451	J 1
54734	Downing, 215	B 5
53928	Doylestown, 265	H 9
54009	Dresser, 533	A 5
54736	Durand⊙, 2,103	C 6
† 54217	Dyckesville, 300	L 6
53119	Eagle, 745	H 2
54521	Eagle River⊙, 1,326	H 4
54626	Eastman, 319	D 9
53120	East Troy, 1,711	J 2
54701	Eau Claire⊙, 44,619	D 6
53019	Eden, 376	K 8
54426	Edgar, 928	G 6
53534	Edgerton, 4,118	H 10
54209	Egg Harbor, 184	M 5
54427	Eland, 229	H 6
54428	Elcho, 500	H 5
54429	Elderon, 185	H 6
54932	Eldorado, 200	J 8
54738	Eleva, 574	D 6
53020	Elkhart Lake, 787	L 8
53121	Elkhorn⊙, 3,992	J 10
54739	Elk Mound, 471	C 6
54011	Ellsworth⊙, 1,983	A 6
53122	Elm Grove, 7,201	K 1
54740	Elmwood, 737	B 6
† 53401	Elmwood Park, 456	M 3
53929	Elroy, 1,513	F 8
54430	Elton, 250	J 5
54933	Embarrass, 472	J 6
53930	Endeavor, 328	G 8
54211	Ephraim, 236	M 5
54627	Ettrick, 463	D 7
54934	Eureka, 300	J 7
53536	Evansville, 2,992	H 10
54835	Exeland, 189	D 4
54741	Fairchild, 562	D 6
53931	Fair Water, 373	J 8
54742	Fall Creek, 825	D 6
53932	Fall River, 633	H 9
54120	Fence, 187	K 4
53809	Fennimore, 1,861	E 9
54628	Ferryville, 183	D 9
54524	Fifield, 287	F 4
54212	Fish Creek, 275	M 5
54121	Florence⊙, 800	K 4
54935	Fond du Lac⊙, 35,515	K 8
53125	Fontana, 1,464	J 10
53537	Footville, 698	H 10
54123	Forest Junction, 255	K 7
54213	Forestville, 349	L 6
53538	Fort Atkinson, 9,164	J 10
54629	Fountain City, 1,017	C 7
54836	Foxboro, 950	B 2
53933	Fox Lake, 1,242	J 8
53217	Fox Point, 7,937	M 1
54214	Francis Creek, 492	L 7
53132	Franklin, 12,247	L 2
53126	Franksville, 375	M 3
54837	Frederic, 908	B 4
53021	Fredonia, 1,045	L 8
54940	Fremont, 598	J 7
53934	Friendship⊙, 641	G 8
53935	Friesland, 301	H 8
54630	Galesville, 1,162	D 7
54631	Gays Mills, 623	E 9
† 53127	Genesee, 375	J 2
53127	Genesee Depot, 425	J 2
54632	Genoa, 305	D 8
53128	Genoa City, 1,085	K 11
53022	Germantown, 6,974	K 1
† 53085	Gibbsville, 408	L 8
54525	Gile, 450	F 3
54124	Gillett, 1,288	K 6
54433	Gilman, 328	E 5
54743	Gilmanton, 200	C 7
54435	Gleason, 300	G 5
53023	Glenbeulah, 496	L 8
† 53201	Glendale, 13,436	M 1
53810	Glen Haven, 250	E 10
54013	Glenwood City, 822	B 5
54527	Glidden, 860	E 3
54125	Goodman, 800	K 4
54838	Gordon, 350	C 3
53540	Gotham, 175	F 9
53024	Grafton, 5,998	L 9
53936	Grand Marsh, 200	G 8
54839	Grand View, 350	D 3
54436	Granton, 288	E 6
54840	Grantsburg⊙, 930	A 4
53541	Gratiot, 249	F 10
* 54301	Green Bay⊙, 87,809	K 6
	Green Bay, ‡158,244	K 6
53129	Greendale, 15,089	L 2
53220	Greenfield, 24,424	L 2
54941	Green Lake⊙, 1,109	H 8
54126	Greenleaf, 350	L 7
54942	Greenville, 900	J 7
54437	Greenwood, 1,036	E 6
54128	Gresham, 448	J 6
53130	Hales Corners, 7,771	K 2
† 54729	Hallie, 1,223	D 6
54438	Hamburg, 170	G 5
54015	Hammond, 768	A 6
54943	Hancock, 404	G 7
54529	Harshaw, 200	G 4
53027	Hartford, 6,499	K 9
53029	Hartland, 2,763	J 1
54440	Hatley, 315	H 6
54841	Haugen, 246	C 4
54530	Hawkins, 385	E 4
54843	Hayward⊙, 1,457	D 3
53811	Hazel Green, 982	F 11
54531	Hazelhurst, 334	G 4
† 53538	Hebron, 190	J 10
53137	Helenville, 230	J 10
54844	Herbster, 250	D 2
54441	Hewitt, 300	F 6
53543	Highland, 785	F 9
54129	Hilbert, 896	K 7
54533	Hiles, 260	J 4
54634	Hillsboro, 1,231	F 8
53031	Hingham, 210	K 8
54635	Hixton, 300	E 7
54745	Holcombe, 200	D 5
53544	Hollandale, 256	G 10
54636	Holmen, 1,081	D 8
53138	Honey Creek, 350	J 3
53032	Horicon, 3,356	J 9
54944	Hortonville, 1,524	J 7
† 55082	Houlton, 400	A 5
54303	Howard, 4,911	K 6
† 53081	Howards Grove-Millersville, 998	L 8
53033	Hubertus, 600	K 1
54016	Hudson⊙, 5,049	A 6
54746	Humbird, 219	E 6
54534	Hurley⊙, 2,418	F 3
53034	Hustisford, 789	J 9
54637	Hustler, 190	F 8
† 54450	Hutchins, 409	H 6
54747	Independence, 1,036	D 7
54945	Iola, 900	H 6
54536	Iron Belt, 425	F 3
53035	Iron Ridge, 480	K 9
54847	Iron River, 800	D 2
53938	Ironton, 195	F 8
† 53177	Ives Grove, 250	L 3
53036	Ixonia, 300	H 1
53037	Jackson, 561	K 9
54236	Jacksonport, 180	M 6
53545	Janesville⊙, 46,426	J 10
53549	Jefferson⊙, 5,429	J 10
54748	Jim Falls, 310	D 5
53038	Johnson Creek, 790	J 9
53550	Juda, 500	H 10
54443	Junction City, 396	G 6
53039	Juneau⊙, 2,043	J 9
53139	Kansasville, 300	L 3
54130	Kaukauna, 11,292	K 7
† 53050	Kekoskee, 233	J 8
54215	Kellnersville, 250	L 7
54638	Kendall, 468	F 8
54537	Kennan, 167	F 5
53140	Kenosha⊙, 78,805	M 3
	Kenosha, ‡117,917	M 3
54135	Keshena⊙, 980	J 6
53040	Kewaskum, 1,926	K 8
54216	Kewaunee⊙, 2,901	M 7
53042	Kiel, 2,848	L 8
53812	Kieler, 653	E 10
54136	Kimberly, 6,131	K 7
54946	King, 1,040	H 7
53939	Kingston, 343	H 8
54749	Knapp, 369	B 6
53044	Kohler, 1,738	L 8
53147	Krakow, 315	K 6
54538	Lac du Flambeau, 500	G 4
† 53066	Lac La Belle, 227	H 1
54601	La Crosse⊙, 51,153	D 8
	La Crosse, ‡80,468	D 8
54848	Ladysmith⊙, 3,674	D 5
54639	La Farge, 748	E 8
53940	Lake Delton, 1,059	G 8
53147	Lake Geneva, 4,890	K 10
53551	Lake Mills, 3,556	H 9
54849	Lake Nebagamon, 523	C 3
54539	Lake Tomahawk, 555	H 4
† 54494	Lake Wazeecha, 1,285	G 7
† 54729	Lake Wissota, 1,419	D 6
54138	Lakewood, 300	K 5
† 53065	Lamartine, 190	J 8
53813	Lancaster⊙, 3,756	E 10
54540	Land O'Lakes, 786	H 3
53046	Lannon, 1,056	K 1
54541	Laona, 1,500	J 4
54850	La Pointe, 300	E 2
53941	La Valle, 411	F 8
53047	Lebanon, 250	H 1
54139	Lena, 569	K 6
† 54656	Leon, 160	E 8
† 53190	Lima Center, 175	J 10
53942	Limeridge, 203	F 9
53553	Linden, 408	F 10
54140	Little Chute, 5,365	K 7
54141	Little Suamico, 190	L 6
53554	Livingston, 503	E 10
53555	Lodi, 1,831	G 9
53943	Loganville, 199	F 9
† 54970	Lohrville, 195	H 7
53048	Lomira, 1,084	J 8
† 53523	London, 317	H 9
53556	Lone Rock, 506	F 9
54852	Loretta, 200	E 4
53557	Lowell, 322	J 9
54446	Loyal, 1,126	E 6
54853	Luck, 848	B 4
54217	Luxemburg, 853	L 6
53944	Lyndon Station, 533	F 8
53148	Lyons, 550	K 10
* 53701	Madison (cap.)⊙, 173,258	H 9
	Madison, ‡290,272	H 9
54750	Maiden Rock, 172	B 6
54949	Manawa, 1,105	J 7
54220	Manitowoc⊙, 33,430	L 7
54226	Maplewood, 192	M 6
54448	Marathon, 1,214	G 6
54855	Marengo, 350	E 3
54227	Maribel, 316	L 7
54143	Marinette⊙, 12,696	L 5
54950	Marion, 1,218	J 6
53946	Markesan, 1,378	J 8
53947	Marquette, 161	H 8
53559	Marshall, 1,043	H 9
54449	Marshfield, 15,619	F 6
54450	Mattoon, 377	J 5
53948	Mauston⊙, 3,466	F 8
53050	Mayville, 4,139	K 9
53560	Mazomanie, 1,217	G 9
53558	McFarland, 2,386	H 10
54543	McNaughton, 350	H 4
54451	Medford⊙, 3,454	F 5
54546	Mellen, 1,168	E 3
54642	Melrose, 505	E 7
54952	Menasha, 14,905	J 7
53051	Menomonee Falls, 31,697	K 1
54751	Menomonie⊙, 11,275	C 6
53092	Mequon, 12,110	L 1
54547	Mercer, 1,100	F 3
54452	Merrill⊙, 9,502	G 5
54754	Merrillan, 612	E 7
53561	Merrimac, 376	G 9
53056	Merton, 646	K 1
54148	Middle Inlet, 200	K 5
53562	Middleton, 8,286	G 9
54857	Mikana, 215	C 4
54454	Milladore, 229	G 6
54643	Millston, 200	E 7
54858	Milltown, 634	B 4
53563	Milton, 3,699	J 10
* 53201	Milwaukee⊙, 717,099	M 1
	Milwaukee, ‡1,403,887	M 1
54644	Mindoro, 230	D 7
53565	Mineral Point, 2,305	F 10
54548	Minocqua, 950	G 4
54859	Minong, 420	C 3
54228	Mishicot, 938	L 7
54755	Mondovi, 2,338	C 6
54549	Monico, 285	H 4
53716	Monona, 10,420	H 9
53566	Monroe⊙, 8,654	G 10
53949	Montello⊙, 1,082	H 8
53569	Montfort, 518	E 10
53570	Monticello, 870	G 10
54550	Montreal, 877	F 3

(continued on following page)

A. D'Arazien — Shostal Associates

"America's Dairyland"— Wisconsin cheeses are turned frequently while they age in brine in specially constructed rooms. Temperature and humidity control are vital for proper ripening.

(continued)

53571 Morrisonville, 350 G 9
54455 Mosinee, 2,395 G 6
54149 Mountain, 298 K 5
53057 Mount Calvary, 942 K 8
53816 Mount Hope, 176 D 10
53572 Mount Horeb, 2,402 G 10
54645 Mount Sterling, 181 D 9
† 53572 Mount Vernon, 250 G 10
53149 Mukwonago, 2,367 J 2
53573 Muscoda, 1,099 F 9
53150 Muskego, 11,573 K 2
53058 Nashotah, 410 J 1
54646 Necedah, 740 F 7
54956 Neenah, 22,892 J 7
54456 Neillsville⊙, 2,750 E 6
54457 Nekoosa, 2,409 G 7
54756 Nelson, 272 C 7
54458 Nelsonville, 152 H 7
54150 Neopit, 1,122 J 6
53059 Neosho, 400 J 9
54960 Neshkoro, 385 H 8
54551 Newald, 180 J 4
54757 New Auburn, 368 D 5
53151 New Berlin, 26,937 K 2
53060 Newburg, 425 K 9
† 61075 New Diggings, 224 F 10
54229 New Franken, 250 L 6
53574 New Glarus, 1,454 G 10
53061 New Holstein, 3,012 K 8
53950 New Lisbon, 1,361 F 8
54961 New London, 5,801 J 7
54017 New Richmond, 3,707 A 5
54151 Niagara, 2,347 K 4
54152 Nichols, 207 K 6
† 53401 North Bay, 263 M 3
54935 North Fond du Lac, 3,286 J 8
53951 North Freedom, 596 G 9
† 54016 North Hudson, 1,547 A 5
53064 North Lake, 525 J 1
53153 North Prairie, 669 J 2
54648 Norwalk, 432 E 8
53154 Oak Creek, 13,901 M 2
54649 Oakdale, 300 F 8
53065 Oakfield, 918 J 8
53066 Oconomowoc, 8,741 H 1
† 53066 Oconomowoc Lake, 599 H 1
54153 Oconto⊙, 4,667 L 6
54154 Oconto Falls, 2,517 K 6
54861 Odanah, 442 E 2
54962 Ogdensburg, 206 J 7
54459 Ogema, 280 F 5
53069 Okauchee, 3,134 J 1
† 53555 Okee, 300 H 9
† 54880 Oliver, 210 B 2
54963 Omro, 2,341 J 7
54650 Onalaska, 4,909 D 8
54155 Oneida, 900 K 7
54651 Ontario, 392 E 8
53070 Oostburg, 1,309 L 8
53575 Oregon, 2,553 H 10
53576 Orfordville, 888 H 10
54020 Osceola, 1,152 A 5
54901 Oshkosh⊙, 53,221 J 8
54758 Osseo, 1,356 D 6
54460 Owen, 1,031 F 6
53952 Oxford, 453 H 8
53953 Packwaukee, 250 G 8
† 53168 Paddock Lake, 1,470 K 10
53156 Palmyra, 1,341 H 2
53954 Pardeeville, 1,507 H 8
54552 Park Falls, 2,953 F 4
† 54481 Park Ridge, 817 H 6
53817 Patch Grove, 187 D 10
† 54514 Peeksville, 250 E 3
54156 Pembine, 500 L 4
54553 Pence, 315 F 3
† 54153 Pensaukee, 225 L 6
54759 Pepin, 747 B 7
† 53511 Perrygo Place, 5,912 J 10
54157 Peshtigo, 2,836 L 5
53072 Pewaukee, 3,271 K 1
54554 Phelps, 1,100 H 3
54555 Phillips⊙, 1,511 E 4
54464 Phlox, 235 J 5
54465 Pickerel, 400 J 5
54760 Pigeon Falls, 198 D 7
54466 Pittsville, 708 F 7
53577 Plain, 688 F 9
54966 Plainfield, 642 G 7
53818 Platteville, 9,599 F 10
53158 Pleasant Prairie, 950 L 10
54467 Plover, 1,900 G 7
54761 Plum City, 451 B 6
53073 Plymouth, 5,810 L 8
54864 Poplar, 455 C 2
53901 Portage⊙, 7,821 G 8
54469 Port Edwards, 2,126 G 7
53074 Port Washington⊙, 8,752 L 9
54865 Port Wing, 486 D 2
53820 Potosi, 713 E 10
54160 Potter, 320 K 7
54161 Pound, 284 L 5
53955 Poynette, 1,118 G 9
54967 Poy Sippi, 500 J 7
53821 Prairie du Chien⊙, 5,540 D 9
53578 Prairie du Sac, 1,902 G 9
54762 Prairie Farm, 426 C 5
54556 Prentice, 519 F 4
54021 Prescott, 2,331 A 6
54557 Presque Isle, 251 G 3
54968 Princeton, 1,446 H 8
54162 Pulaski, 1,717 K 6
* 53401 Racine⊙, 95,162 M 3
Racine, ‡170,838 M 3
54867 Radisson, 206 D 4
53956 Randolph, 1,582 H 8
53075 Random Lake, 1,068 K 8
† 53126 Raymond, 300 L 2
54969 Readfield, 200 J 7
54652 Readstown, 395 E 9
† 54814 Red Cliff, 250 E 2
54970 Redgranite, 645 J 7
53959 Reedsburg, 4,585 G 8
54230 Reedsville, 994 L 7
53579 Reeseville, 566 J 9
53580 Rewey, 232 F 10
54501 Rhinelander⊙, 8,218 H 4
54470 Rib Lake, 782 F 5
54868 Rice Lake, 7,278 C 5
53076 Richfield, 247 K 1
53581 Richland Center⊙, 5,086 F 9
54763 Ridgeland, 266 B 5
53582 Ridgeway, 463 F 10
53960 Rio, 792 H 9
54231 Rio Creek, 200 L 6
54971 Ripon, 7,053 J 8
54022 River Falls, 7,238 A 6
† 53201 River Hills, 1,561 M 1
54023 Roberts, 484 A 6
53167 Rochester, 436 K 3
† 53523 Rockdale, 172 J 10
54764 Rock Falls, 200 C 6
53077 Rockfield, 340 L 1
54653 Rockland, 278 D 8
53961 Rock Springs, 432 F 8
† 53178 Rome, 250 H 1
54974 Rosendale, 464 J 8
54473 Rosholt, 466 H 6
54474 Rothschild, 3,141 G 6
† 53583 Roxbury, 220 G 9
54975 Royalton, 200 J 7
53078 Rubicon, 261 K 9
54475 Rudolph, 349 G 7
53079 Saint Cloud, 550 K 8
54024 Saint Croix Falls, 1,425 A 5
† 53201 Saint Francis, 10,489 M 2
† 54601 Saint Joseph Ridge, 250 D 8
54232 Saint Nazianz, 718 L 7
54765 Sand Creek, 200 C 5
53583 Sauk City, 2,385 G 9
53080 Saukville, 1,389 L 9
54559 Saxon, 600 F 3
54560 Sayner, 300 H 4
54977 Scandinavia, 268 H 7
54476 Schofield, 2,577 H 6
† 53042 School Hill, 228 L 8
† 54843 Seeley, 213 D 3
54654 Seneca, 250 E 9
53584 Sextonville, 325 F 9
54165 Seymour, 2,194 K 6
53585 Sharon, 1,216 J 11
54166 Shawano⊙, 6,488 J 6
53081 Sheboygan⊙, 48,484 L 8
53085 Sheboygan Falls, 4,771 L 8
54766 Sheldon, 218 D 5
54871 Shell Lake⊙, 928 C 4
54169 Sherwood, 350 K 7
54170 Shiocton, 830 K 7
† 53525 Shopiere, 350 H 10
53211 Shorewood, 15,576 M 1
† 53701 Shorewood Hills, 2,206 G 9
53586 Shullsburg, 1,376 F 10
53170 Silver Lake, 1,210 K 10
54872 Siren, 639 B 4
54234 Sister Bay, 483 M 5
53086 Slinger, 1,022 K 9

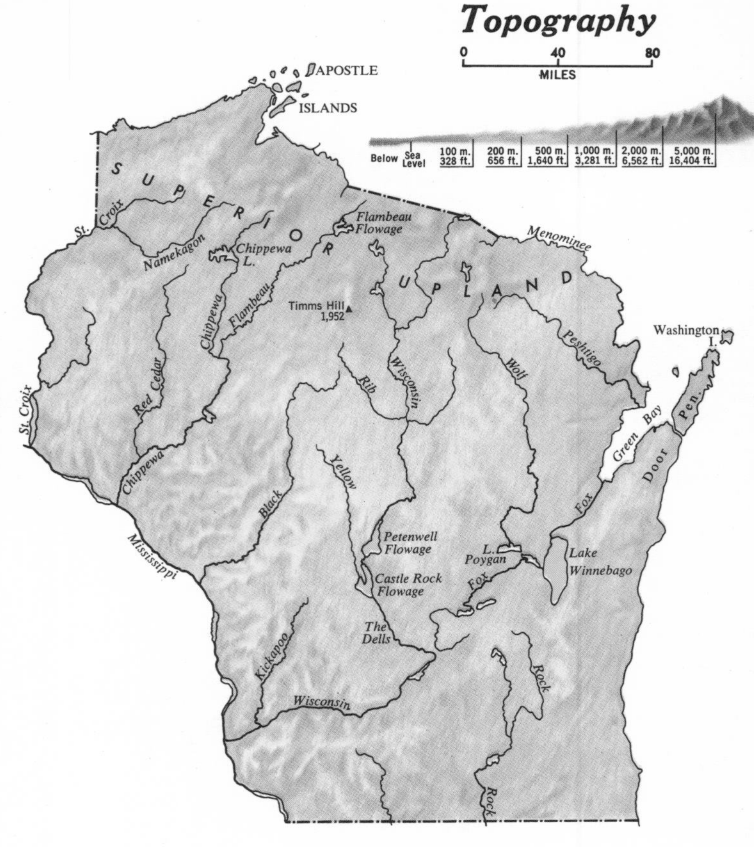

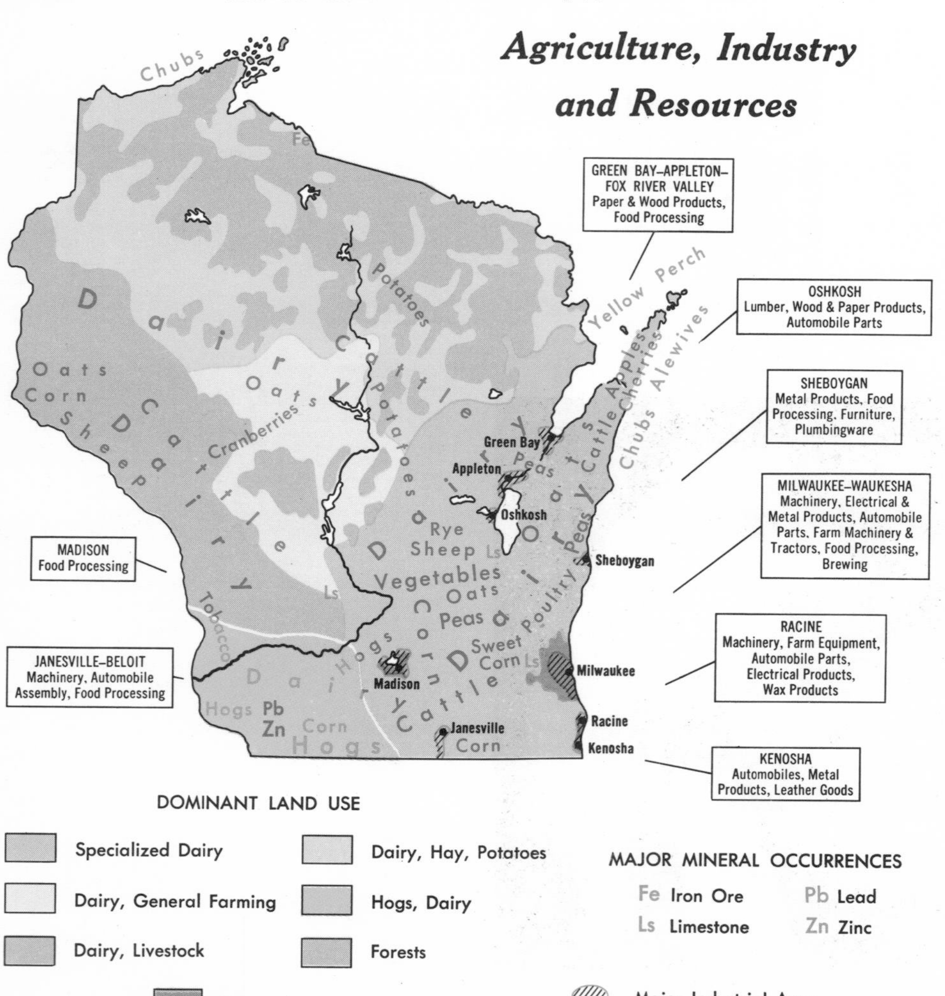

54655 Soldiers Grove, 514 E 9
54873 Solon Springs, 598 C 3
53171 Somers, 400 M 3
54025 Somerset, 778 A 5
53172 South Milwaukee, 23,297 M 2
53587 South Wayne, 436 G 10
54656 Sparta⊙, 6,258 E 8
54479 Spencer, 1,181 F 6
54801 Spooner, 2,444 B 4
53588 Spring Green, 1,199 G 9
54767 Spring Valley, 995 B 6
54768 Stanley, 2,049 E 6
54026 Star Prairie, 362 A 5
54480 Stetsonville, 305 F 5
54657 Steuben, 179 E 9
54481 Stevens Point⊙, 23,479 G 7
54172 Stiles, 300 L 6
53825 Stitzer, 295 E 10
53088 Stockbridge, 582 K 7
54658 Stoddard, 750 D 8
† 53066 Stone Bank, 390 J 1
54876 Stone Lake, 190 C 4
53589 Stoughton, 6,081 H 10
54484 Stratford, 1,239 F 6
54770 Strum, 738 D 6
54235 Sturgeon Bay⊙, 6,776 M 6
53177 Sturtevant, 3,376 M 3
54173 Suamico, 900 K 6
53178 Sullivan, 467 H 1
54485 Summit Lake, 200 H 5
53590 Sun Prairie, 9,935 H 9
54880 Superior (city)⊙, 32,237 C 2
Superior-Duluth, ‡265,350 C 2
† 54880 Superior Village, 476 B 2
54174 Suring, 499 K 5
53089 Sussex, 2,758 K 1
53090 Taycheedah, 600 K 8
54659 Taylor, 322 E 7
† 53820 Tennyson, 402 E 10
53091 Theresa, 611 K 8
53092 Thiensville, 3,182 L 1
54771 Thorp, 1,469 E 6
54562 Three Lakes, 950 H 4
† 53185 Tichigan, 500 K 2
54486 Tigerton, 742 H 6
54240 Tisch Mills, 259 L 7
54660 Tomah, 5,647 F 8
54487 Tomahawk, 3,419 G 5
54175 Townsend, 450 K 5
54888 Trego, 200 C 4
54661 Trempealeau, 743 C 8
53180 Troy Center, 250 J 2
54662 Tunnel City, 226 E 7
54889 Turtle Lake, 637 B 5
53181 Twin Lakes, 2,276 K 11
54241 Two Rivers, 13,553 M 7
53962 Union Center, 205 F 8
53182 Union Grove, 2,703 L 3
54488 Unity, 363 F 6
54245 Valders, 821 L 7
53593 Verona, 2,334 G 9
54489 Vesper, 355 F 7
54664 Viola, 659 E 8
54665 Viroqua⊙, 3,739 D 8
54566 Wabeno, 800 J 5
53093 Waldo, 408 L 8
53183 Wales, 691 J 1
53184 Walworth, 1,637 J 10
54666 Warrens, 300 E 7
54890 Wascott, 200 C 3
54891 Washburn⊙, 1,957 D 2
54246 Washington Island, 550 M 5
53185 Waterford, 1,922 K 3
53594 Waterloo, 2,253 J 9
53094 Watertown, 15,683 J 9
53021 Waubeka, 300 L 9
54980 Waukau, 245 J 8
53186 Waukesha⊙, 40,258 K 1
53597 Waunakee, 2,181 G 9
54981 Waupaca⊙, 4,342 H 7
53963 Waupun, 7,946 J 8
54401 Wausau⊙, 32,806 G 6
54177 Wausaukee, 557 K 5
54982 Wautoma⊙, 1,624 H 7
53226 Wauwatosa, 58,676 L 1
53826 Wauzeka, 437 E 9
54893 Webster, 502 B 4
53214 West Allis, 71,723 L 1
† 53913 West Baraboo, 563 G 9
53095 West Bend⊙, 16,555 K 9
54490 Westboro, 950 F 5
54667 Westby, 1,568 E 8
53964 Westfield, 884 H 8
† 54601 West La Crosse, 950 D 8
† 53201 West Milwaukee, 4,405 L 1
† 54476 Weston, 3,375 G 6
54669 West Salem, 2,180 D 8
54983 Weyauwega, 1,377 H 7
54895 Weyerhauser, 285 D 5
54772 Wheeler, 212 C 5
53217 Whitefish Bay, 17,394 M 1
54773 Whitehall⊙, 1,486 D 7
54491 White Lake, 309 J 5
54247 Whitelaw, 557 L 7
53190 Whitewater, 12,038 J 10
† 54481 Whiting, 1,782 H 7
54984 Wild Rose, 585 H 7
53191 Williams Bay, 1,554 J 10
54670 Wilton, 516 F 8
54567 Winchester, 230 G 3
53185 Wind Lake, 900 K 2
† 53401 Wind Point, 1,251 M 2
53598 Windsor, 827 H 9
54985 Winnebago, 1,550 J 7
54986 Winneconne, 1,608 J 7
54896 Winter, 450 E 4
53965 Wisconsin Dells, 2,401 G 8
54494 Wisconsin Rapids⊙, 18,587 G 7
54498 Withee, 480 E 6
54499 Wittenberg, 895 H 6
53968 Wonewoc, 835 F 8
54568 Woodruff, 800 G 4
54028 Woodville, 522 B 6
54180 Wrightstown, 1,020 K 7
54671 Wyeville, 203 F 7
53969 Wyocena, 809 H 9
54182 Zachow, 160 K 6

⊙ County seat.
‡ Population of metropolitan area.
† Zip of nearest p.o.
* Multiple zips

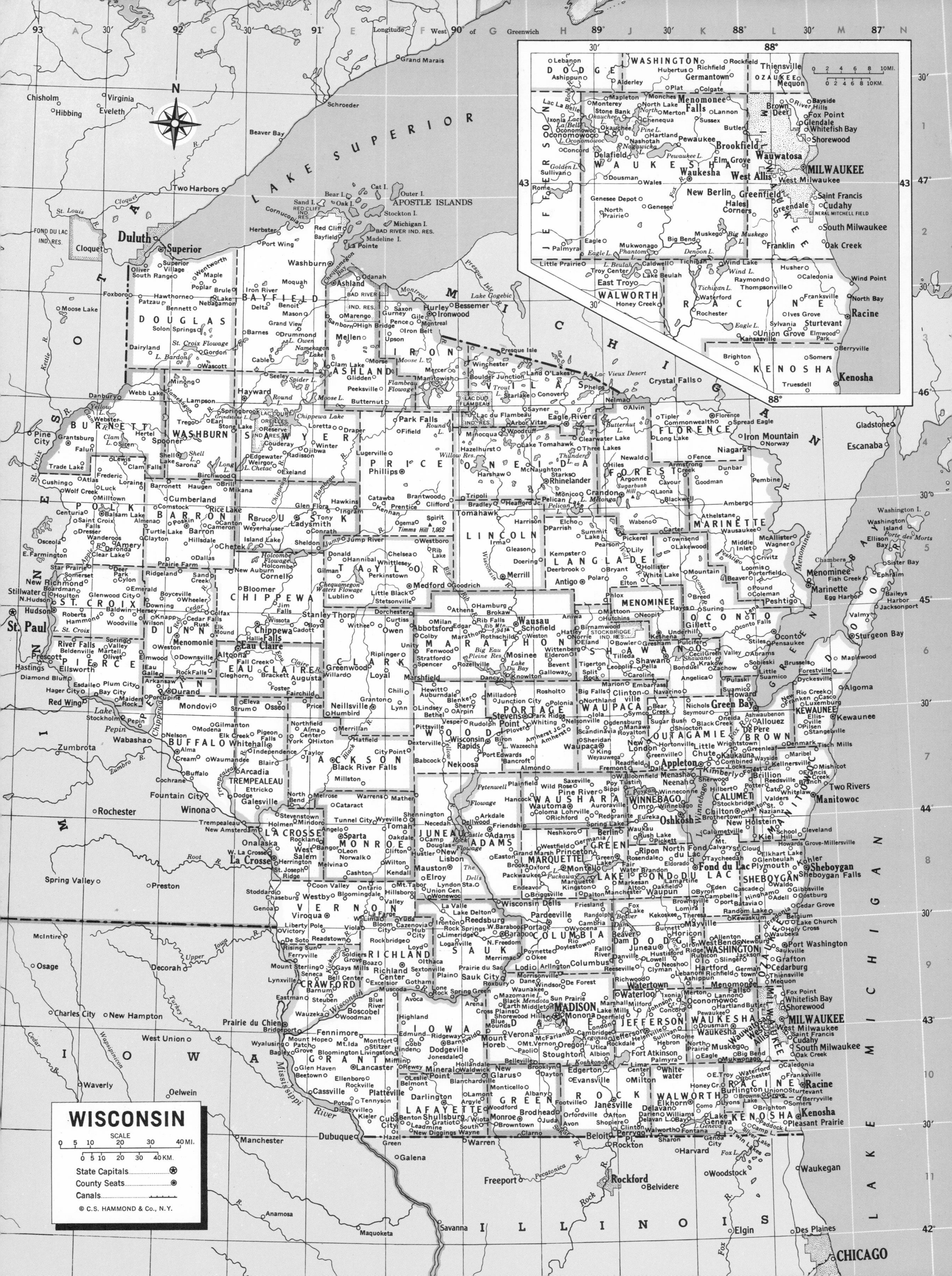

WISCONSIN
SCALE
0 5 10 20 30 40 MI.
0 5 10 20 30 40 KM.
State Capitals
County Seats
Canals
© C.S. HAMMOND & Co., N.Y.
Longitude West 90° of Greenwich
LAKE SUPERIOR
LAKE MICHIGAN
MICHIGAN
MINNESOTA
IOWA
ILLINOIS
APOSTLE ISLANDS
GREEN BAY
DOUGLAS
BAYFIELD
ASHLAND
IRON
VILAS
FLORENCE
FOREST
ONEIDA
PRICE
SAWYER
WASHBURN
BURNETT
POLK
BARRON
RUSK
TAYLOR
LINCOLN
LANGLADE
MARINETTE
OCONTO
MENOMINEE
SHAWANO
MARATHON
CLARK
CHIPPEWA
EAU CLAIRE
DUNN
ST. CROIX
PIERCE
PEPIN
BUFFALO
TREMPEALEAU
JACKSON
WOOD
PORTAGE
WAUPACA
OUTAGAMIE
BROWN
KEWAUNEE
DOOR
MANITOWOC
CALUMET
WINNEBAGO
WAUSHARA
ADAMS
JUNEAU
MONROE
LA CROSSE
VERNON
RICHLAND
SAUK
COLUMBIA
MARQUETTE
GREEN LAKE
FOND DU LAC
SHEBOYGAN
OZAUKEE
WASHINGTON
DODGE
JEFFERSON
WAUKESHA
MILWAUKEE
DANE
IOWA
GRANT
CRAWFORD
LAFAYETTE
GREEN
ROCK
WALWORTH
RACINE
KENOSHA
MADISON
MILWAUKEE
Green Bay
Duluth
Superior
St. Paul
Dubuque
Rockford
CHICAGO
Timms Hill 1,952
Rib Mtn. 1,941

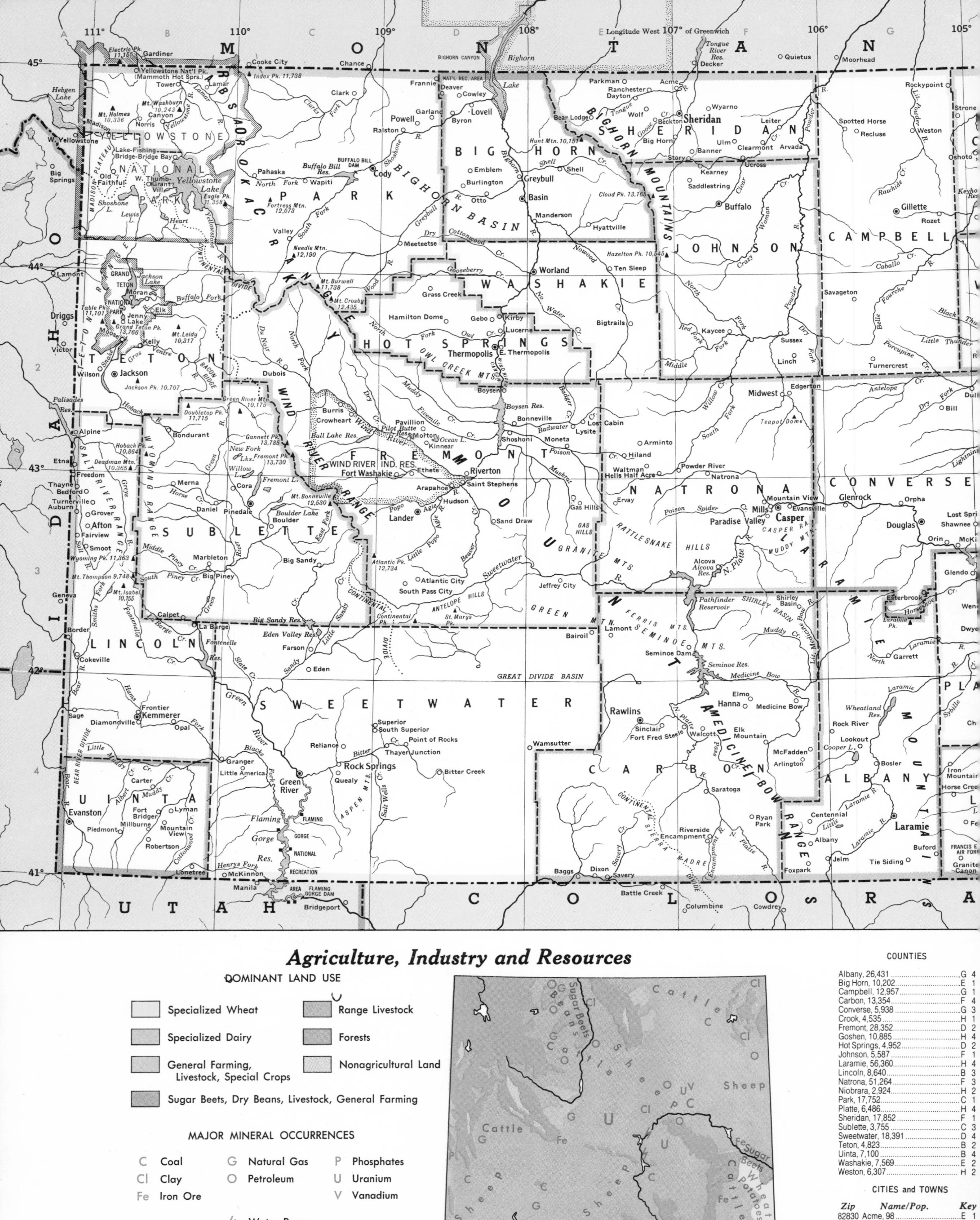

COUNTIES

County	Key
Albany, 26,431	G 4
Big Horn, 10,202	E 1
Campbell, 12,957	G 1
Carbon, 13,354	F 4
Converse, 5,938	G 3
Crook, 4,535	H 1
Fremont, 28,352	D 2
Goshen, 10,885	H 4
Hot Springs, 4,952	D 2
Johnson, 5,587	F 1
Laramie, 56,360	H 4
Lincoln, 8,640	B 3
Natrona, 51,264	F 3
Niobrara, 2,924	H 2
Park, 17,752	C 1
Platte, 6,486	H 4
Sheridan, 17,852	F 1
Sublette, 3,755	C 3
Sweetwater, 18,391	D 4
Teton, 4,823	B 2
Uinta, 7,100	B 4
Washakie, 7,569	E 2
Weston, 6,307	H 2

CITIES and TOWNS

Zip	*Name/Pop.*	*Key*
82830	Acme, 98	E 1
83110	Afton, 1,290	B 3

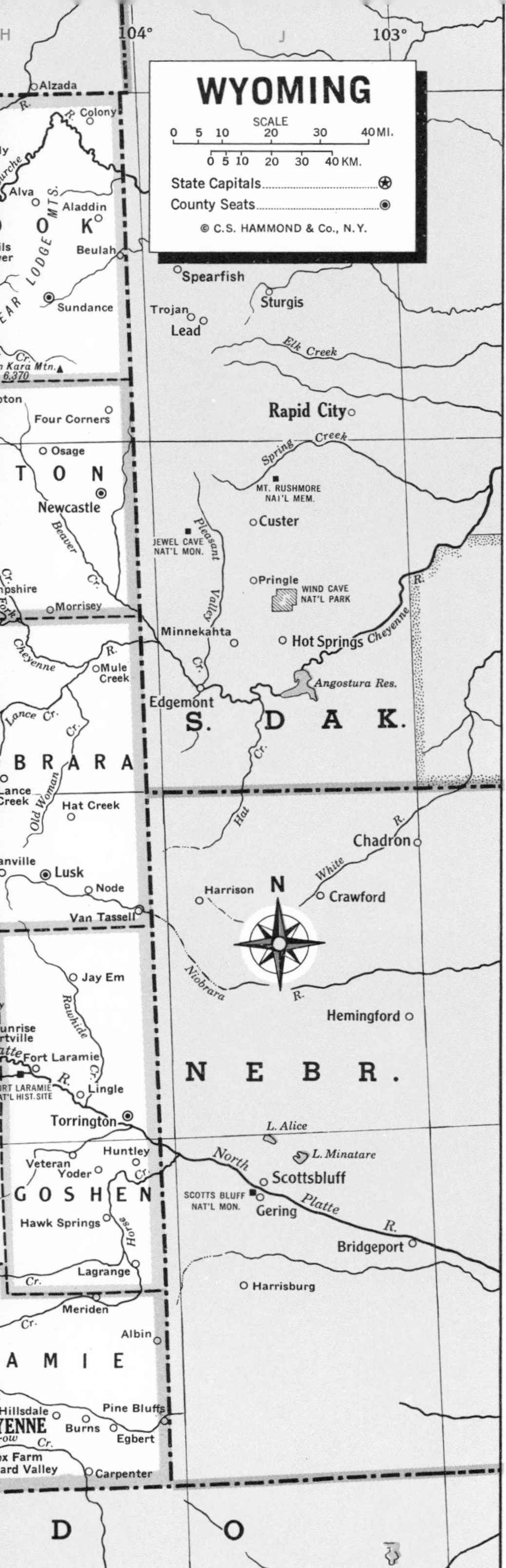

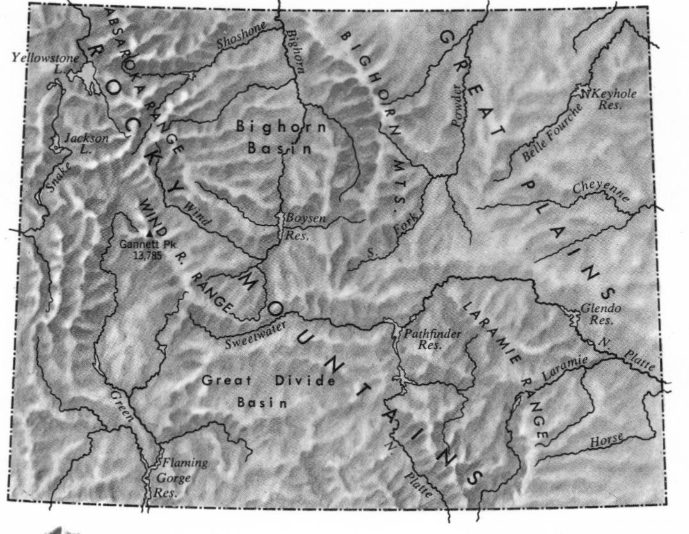

Topography

0 50 100 MILES

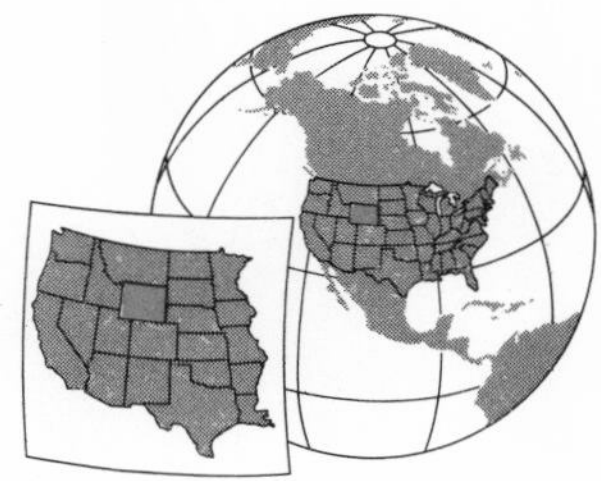

AREA 97,914 sq. mi.
POPULATION 332,416
CAPITAL Cheyenne
LARGEST CITY Cheyenne
HIGHEST POINT Gannett Pk. 13,785 ft.
SETTLED IN 1834
ADMITTED TO UNION July 10, 1890
POPULAR NAME Equality State
STATE FLOWER Indian Paintbrush
STATE BIRD Meadowlark

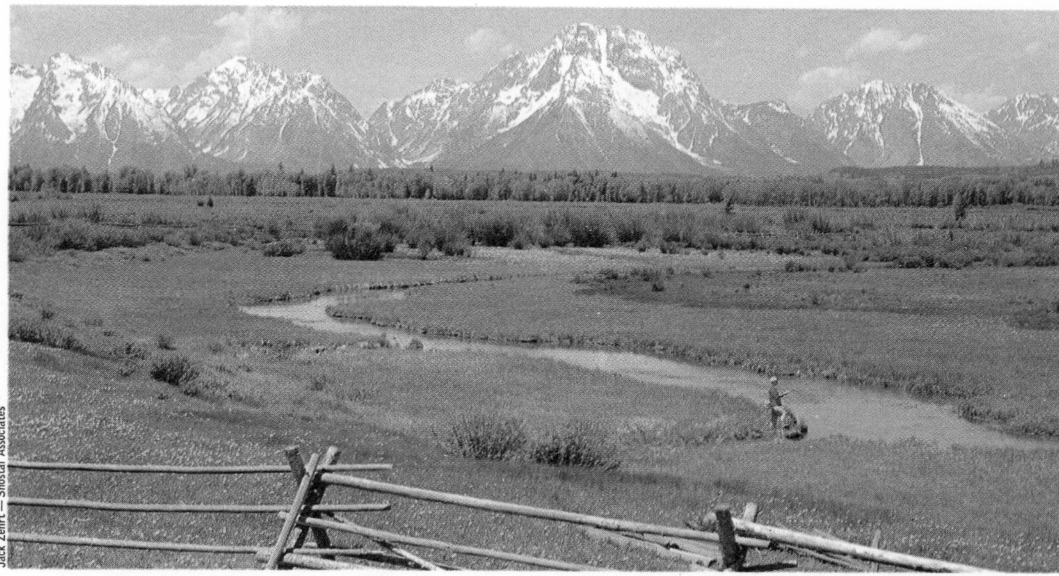

Jack Zehrt — Shostal Associates

Intrepid mountain climbers are challenged by the sheer granite cliffs of Wyoming's Teton Range. Lowland meadows and trails attract less ambitious sportsmen.

Zip	Place	Key
82710	Aladdin, 12	H 1
82055	Albany, 50	F 4
82050	Albin, 118	H 4
82620	Alcova, 125	F 3
83127	Alpine, 95	B 2
82711	Alva, 45	H 1
82510	Arapahoe, 682	D 3
82831	Arvada, 50	F 1
82520	Atlantic City, 25	D 3
83111	Auburn, 240	A 3
82321	Baggs, 146	E 4
82322	Bairoil, 150	E 3
82832	Banner, 44	F 1
82410	Basin⊙, 1,145	E 1
82836	Bear Lodge, 25	E 1
82801	Beckton, 110	E 1
83112	Bedford, 290	A 3
82712	Beulah, 63	H 1
82833	Big Horn, 200	E 1
83113	Big Piney, 570	B 3
82923	Big Sandy, 20	C 3
82442	Bigtrails, 25	E 2
82921	Bitter Creek, 20	D 4
82922	Bondurant, 90	B 2
82649	Bonneville, 18	E 2
83114	Border, 25	B 3
82051	Bosler, 80	G 4
82923	Boulder, 30	C 3
82834	Buffalo⊙, 3,394	F 1
82052	Buford, 36	G 4
82411	Burlington, 300	D 1
82053	Burns, 185	H 4
82511	Burris, 30	C 2
82412	Byron, 397	D 1
† 83123	Calpet, 20	B 3
82190	Canyon, 130	B 1
82054	Carpenter, 100	H 4
† 82937	Carter, 33	B 4
82601	Casper⊙, 39,361	F 3
82055	Centennial, 160	F 4
82001	Cheyenne (cap.)⊙, 40,914	H 4
82210	Chugwater, 187	H 4
† 59008	Clark, 25	C 1
82835	Clearmont, 141	F 1
82414	Cody⊙, 5,161	D 1
83114	Cokeville, 440	B 3
† 57717	Colony, 50	H 1
82420	Cowley, 366	D 1
82512	Crowheart, 12	C 2
83115	Daniel, 175	B 3
82836	Dayton, 396	E 1
82421	Deaver, 112	D 1
82714	Devils Tower, 73	H 1
83116	Diamondville, 485	B 4
82323	Dixon, 72	E 4
82633	Douglas⊙, 2,677	G 3
82513	Dubois, 898	C 2
† 82443	East Thermopolis, 316	D 2
82926	Eden, 275	C 3
82635	Edgerton, 350	F 2
† 82053	Egbert, 40	H 4
† 83013	Elk, 10	B 2
82324	Elk Mountain, 127	F 4
† 82327	Elmo, 53	F 4
82422	Emblem, 250	D 1
82325	Encampment, 321	F 4
82520	Ethete, 30	D 2
83118	Etna, 400	A 2
82930	Evanston⊙, 4,462	B 4
82636	Evansville, 832	F 3
83119	Fairview, 245	B 3
82932	Farson, 210	C 3
† 82001	Federal, 15	G 4
82933	Fort Bridger, 150	B 4
† 82301	Fort Fred Steele, 15	E 4
82212	Fort Laramie, 197	H 3
82514	Fort Washakie, 140	C 2
† 82001	Fox Farm, 1,329	H 4
82057	Foxpark, 110	F 4
82423	Frannie, 139	D 1
83120	Freedom, 497	B 3
83121	Frontier, 246	B 4
82424	Garland, 57	D 1
82058	Garrett, 10	G 3
82501	Gas Hills, 200	E 3
† 82430	Gebo, 15	D 2
82716	Gillette⊙, 7,194	G 1
82213	Glendo, 210	G 3
82637	Glenrock, 1,515	G 3
82934	Granger, 137	C 4
82059	Granite Canon, 72	G 4
82425	Grass Creek, 125	D 2
82935	Green River⊙, 4,196	C 4
82426	Greybull, 1,953	E 1
83122	Grover, 120	B 3
82214	Guernsey, 793	H 3
82427	Hamilton Dome, 106	D 2
† 82701	Hampshire, 23	H 2
82327	Hanna, 460	F 4
82215	Hartville, 246	H 3
82217	Hawk Springs, 125	H 4
82060	Hillsdale, 160	H 4
82061	Horse Creek, 225	G 4
82515	Hudson, 381	D 3
82720	Hulett, 318	H 1
82218	Huntley, 50	H 4
82428	Hyattville, 73	E 1
82062	Iron Mountain, 12	G 4
83001	Jackson⊙, 2,101	B 2
82219	Jay Em, 25	H 3
82310	Jeffrey City, 702	E 3
82063	Jelm, 29	G 4
† 83012	Jenny Lake, 10	B 2
82639	Kaycee, 272	F 2
† 82832	Kearney, 49	F 1
82220	Keeline, 30	H 3
83011	Kelly, 35	B 2
83101	Kemmerer⊙, 2,292	B 4
82516	Kinnear, 44	D 2
82430	Kirby, 75	D 2
83123	La Barge, 375	B 3
82221	Lagrange, 189	H 4
† 82190	Lake-Fishing Bridge-Bridge Bay, 167	B 1
† 82190	Lamar, 27	B 1
82328	Lamont, 30	E 3
82222	Lance Creek, 175	H 2
82520	Lander⊙, 7,125	D 3
82070	Laramie⊙, 23,143	G 4
82837	Leiter, 100	F 1
82640	Linch, 185	F 2
82223	Lingle, 446	H 3
82929	Little America, 47	C 4
† 82051	Lookout, 20	G 4
† 82642	Lost Cabin, 25	E 2
82431	Lovell, 2,371	D 1
† 82443	Lucerne, 240	D 2
82225	Lusk⊙, 1,495	H 3
82937	Lyman, 643	B 4
82642	Lysite, 25	E 2
† 82190	Madison, 42	B 1
† 82190	Mammoth Hot Springs (Yellowstone Nat'l Park), 162	B 1
82432	Manderson, 117	E 1
82227	Manville, 92	H 3
† 83113	Marbleton, 223	B 3
82080	McFadden, 150	F 4
82938	McKinnon, 135	C 4
82329	Medicine Bow, 455	F 4
82433	Meeteetse, 459	D 1
† 83115	Merna, 25	B 3
82643	Midwest, 743	F 2
† 82933	Millburne, 54	B 4
82644	Mills, 1,724	F 3
82721	Moorcroft, 981	H 1
83012	Moose, 115	B 2
83013	Moran, 600	B 2
† 82701	Morrisey, 28	H 2
82522	Morton, 35	D 2
82939	Mountain View, 1,641	F 3
82939	Mountain View, 500	B 4
† 57735	Mule Creek, 10	H 2
82701	Newcastle⊙, 3,432	H 2
82722	New Haven, 35	H 1
† 82190	Norris, 20	B 1
82190	Old Faithful, 134	B 1
83124	Opal, 34	B 4
† 82001	Orchard Valley, 1,015	H 4
82652	Orin, 20	G 3
† 82633	Orpha, 12	G 3
82723	Osage, 346	H 2
82434	Otto, 75	D 1
82414	Pahaska, 75	C 1
† 82601	Paradise Valley, 1,764	F 3
82838	Parkman, 30	E 1
82523	Pavillion, 181	D 2
† 82933	Piedmont, 25	B 4
82082	Pine Bluffs, 937	H 4
82941	Pinedale⊙, 948	C 3
82942	Point of Rocks, 20	D 4
82648	Powder River, 75	F 2
82435	Powell, 4,807	D 1
82440	Ralston, 85	D 1
82839	Ranchester, 208	E 1
82301	Rawlins⊙, 7,855	E 4
82725	Recluse, 25	G 1
82943	Reliance, 425	C 4
† 82325	Riverside, 46	F 4
82501	Riverton, 7,995	D 2
82944	Robertson, 39	B 4
† 82701	Rochelle, 23	H 2
82083	Rock River, 344	G 4
82901	Rock Springs, 11,657	C 4
82726	Rockypoint, 22	G 1
82727	Rozet, 50	G 1
82330	Ryan Park, 18	F 4
82840	Saddlestring, 100	F 1
83125	Sage, 45	B 4
82524	Saint Stephens, 100	D 3
82501	Sand Draw, 40	D 3
82331	Saratoga, 1,181	F 4
† 82716	Savageton, 30	G 2
82332	Savery, 29	E 4
† 82720	Seely, 10	H 1
82333	Seminoe Dam, 40	E 3
82229	Shawnee, 11	G 3
82441	Shell, 50	E 1
82801	Sheridan⊙, 10,856	F 1
82601	Shirley Basin, 700	F 3
82649	Shoshoni, 562	D 2
82334	Sinclair, 445	E 4
83126	Smoot, 200	B 3
† 82945	South Superior, 197	D 4
82842	Story, 637	F 1
82729	Sundance⊙, 1,056	H 1
† 82215	Sunrise, 80	H 3
82945	Superior, 2	D 4
† 82639	Sussex, 200	F 2
82442	Ten Sleep, 320	E 1
† 82901	Thayer Junction, 15	D 4
83127	Thayne, 195	A 3
82443	Thermopolis⊙, 3,063	D 2
82240	Torrington⊙, 4,237	H 3
† 82190	Tower, 24	B 1
† 83112	Turnerville, 25	A 3
† 82835	Ucross, 17	F 1
82835	Ulm, 25	F 1
82730	Upton, 987	H 1
82242	Van Tassell, 21	H 3
82243	Veteran, 35	H 4
82335	Walcott, 20	F 4
† 82648	Waltman, 20	E 2
82336	Wamsutter, 139	E 4
82450	Wapiti, 92	C 1
† 82190	West Thumb-Grant Village, 64	B 1
82201	Wheatland⊙, 2,498	H 3
83014	Wilson, 550	B 2
82844	Wolf, 85	E 1
82401	Worland⊙, 5,055	E 1
82845	Wyarno, 12	F 1
82190	Yellowstone Nat'l Park, 162	B 1
82244	Yoder, 101	H 4

⊙ County seat.
† Zip of nearest p.o.

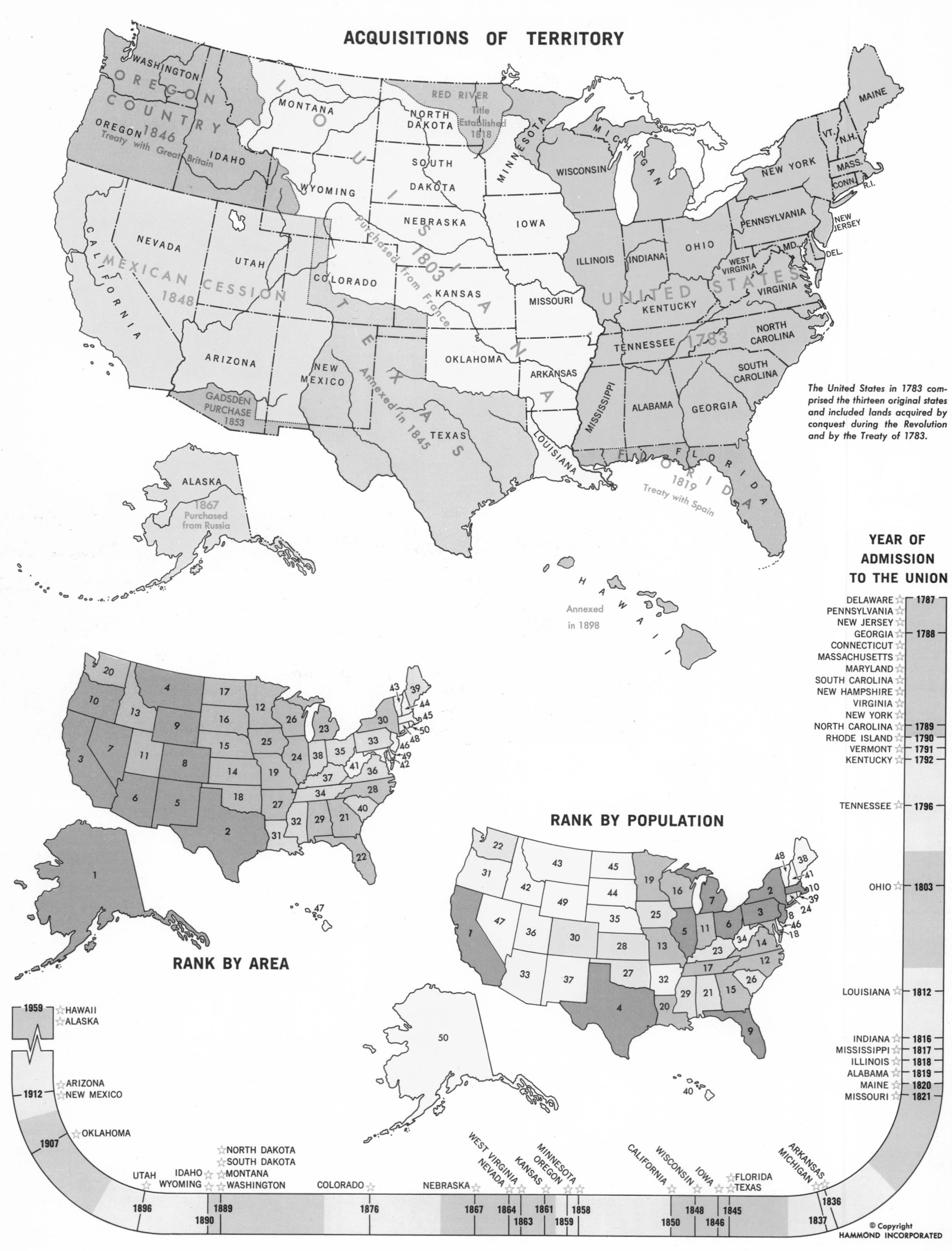
ACQUISITIONS OF TERRITORY
WASHINGTON
OREGON COUNTRY
OREGON 1846
Treaty with Great Britain
IDAHO
MONTANA
LOUISIANA
1803
Purchased from France
RED RIVER
Title Established 1818
NORTH DAKOTA
SOUTH DAKOTA
MINNESOTA
WISCONSIN
MICHIGAN
MAINE
VT.
N.H.
MASS.
R.I.
CONN.
NEW YORK
WYOMING
NEBRASKA
IOWA
PENNSYLVANIA
NEW JERSEY
DEL.
MD.
NEVADA
UTAH
CALIFORNIA
MEXICAN CESSION
1848
COLORADO
KANSAS
MISSOURI
ILLINOIS
INDIANA
OHIO
WEST VIRGINIA
VIRGINIA
KENTUCKY
UNITED STATES
1783
TENNESSEE
NORTH CAROLINA
SOUTH CAROLINA
ARIZONA
NEW MEXICO
OKLAHOMA
ARKANSAS
TEXAS
Annexed in 1845
GADSDEN PURCHASE 1853
MISSISSIPPI
ALABAMA
GEORGIA
LOUISIANA
FLORIDA
1819
Treaty with Spain
The United States in 1783 comprised the thirteen original states and included lands acquired by conquest during the Revolution and by the Treaty of 1783.
ALASKA
1867
Purchased from Russia
HAWAII
Annexed in 1898
RANK BY AREA
RANK BY POPULATION
YEAR OF ADMISSION TO THE UNION
DELAWARE 1787
PENNSYLVANIA
NEW JERSEY
GEORGIA 1788
CONNECTICUT
MASSACHUSETTS
MARYLAND
SOUTH CAROLINA
NEW HAMPSHIRE
VIRGINIA
NEW YORK
NORTH CAROLINA 1789
RHODE ISLAND 1790
VERMONT 1791
KENTUCKY 1792
TENNESSEE 1796
OHIO 1803
LOUISIANA 1812
INDIANA 1816
MISSISSIPPI 1817
ILLINOIS 1818
ALABAMA 1819
MAINE 1820
MISSOURI 1821
ARKANSAS 1836
MICHIGAN 1837
FLORIDA 1845
TEXAS 1845
IOWA 1846
WISCONSIN 1848
CALIFORNIA 1850
MINNESOTA 1858
OREGON 1859
KANSAS 1861
WEST VIRGINIA 1863
NEVADA 1864
NEBRASKA 1867
COLORADO 1876
NORTH DAKOTA
SOUTH DAKOTA
MONTANA
WASHINGTON 1889
IDAHO
WYOMING 1890
UTAH 1896
OKLAHOMA 1907
ARIZONA
NEW MEXICO 1912
HAWAII
ALASKA 1959

ZIP CODE ZONE MAP SECTION

Major U.S. Cities

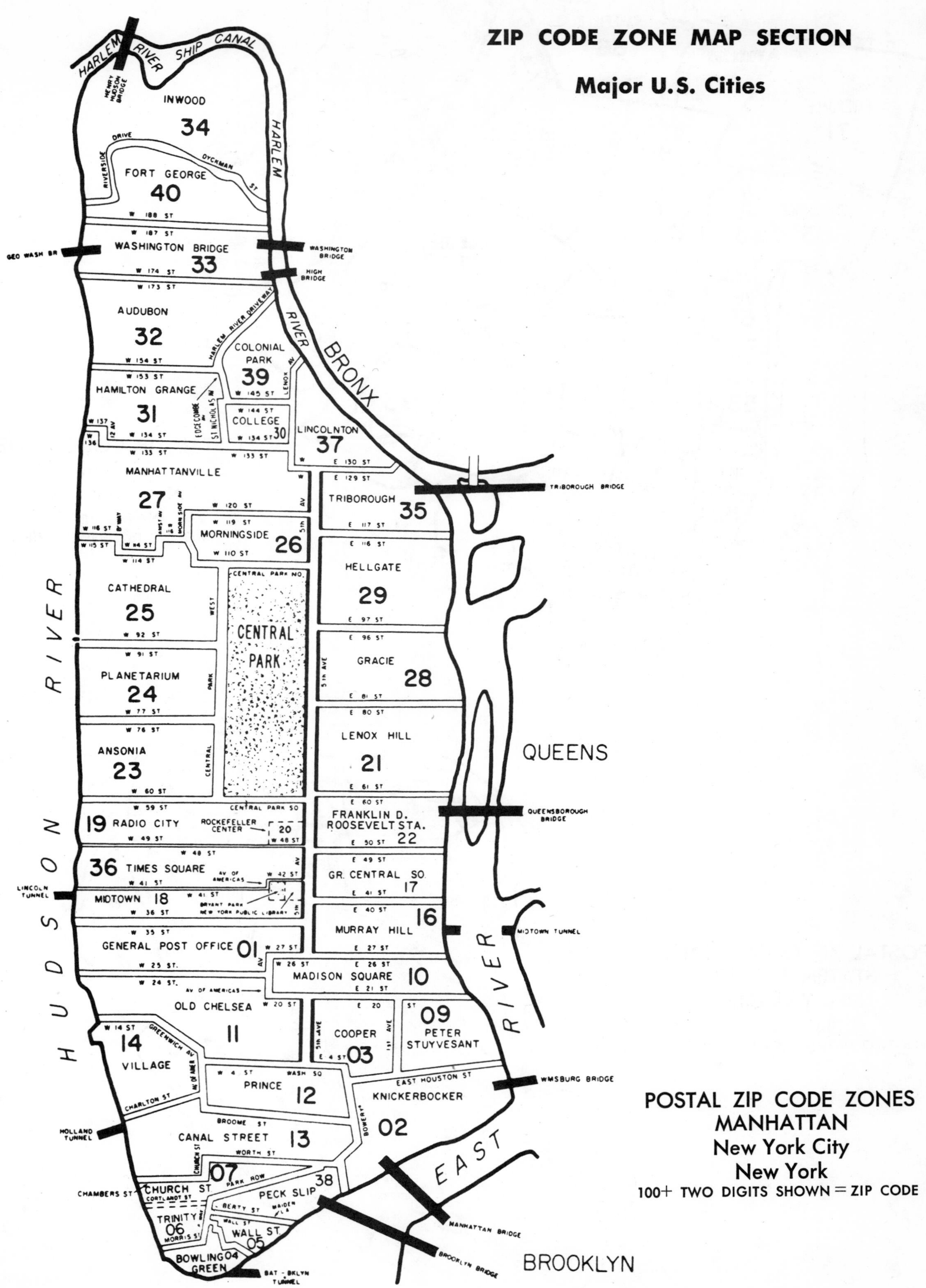

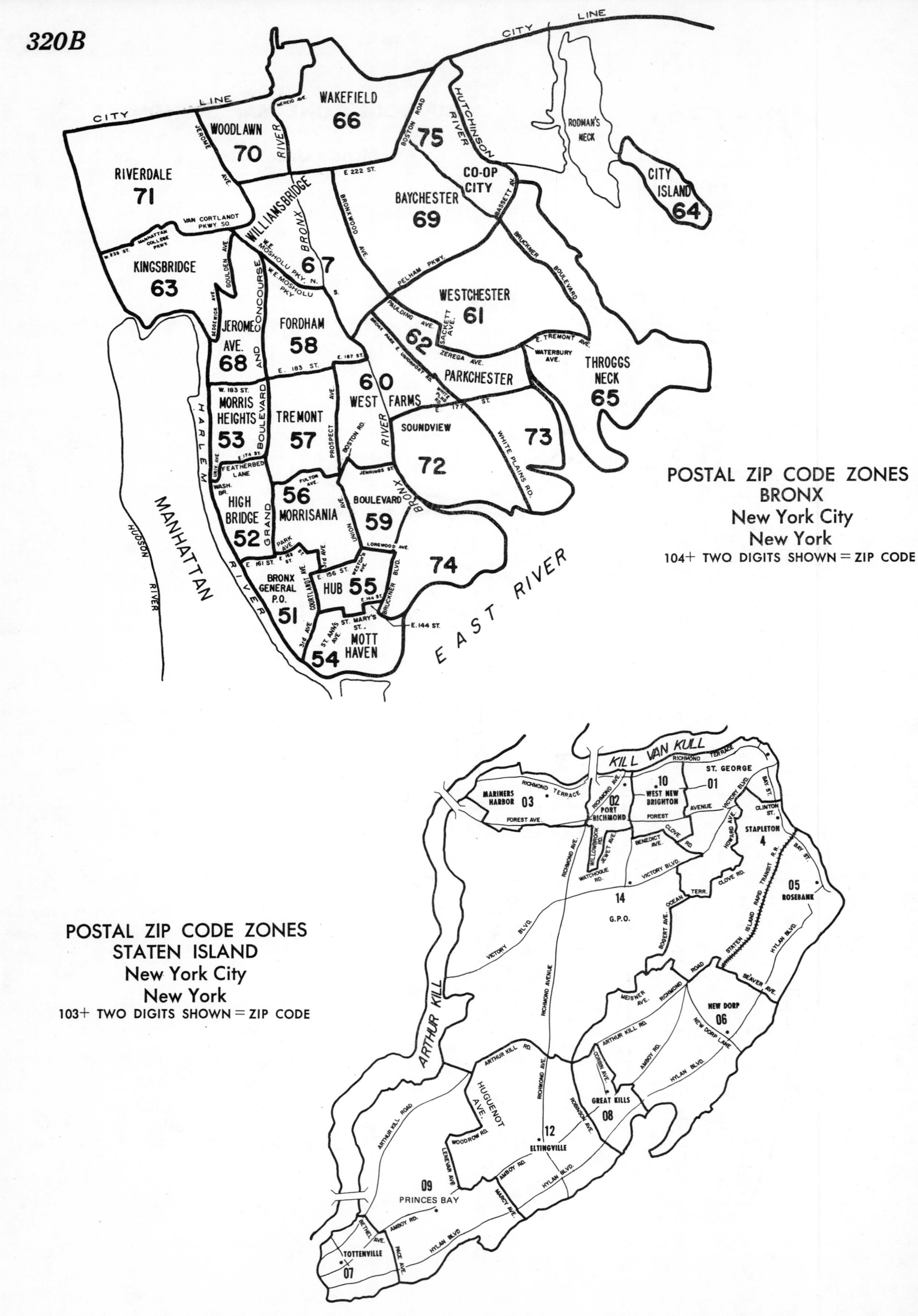

POSTAL ZIP CODE ZONES
BRONX
New York City
New York
104+ TWO DIGITS SHOWN = ZIP CODE

POSTAL ZIP CODE ZONES
STATEN ISLAND
New York City
New York
103+ TWO DIGITS SHOWN = ZIP CODE

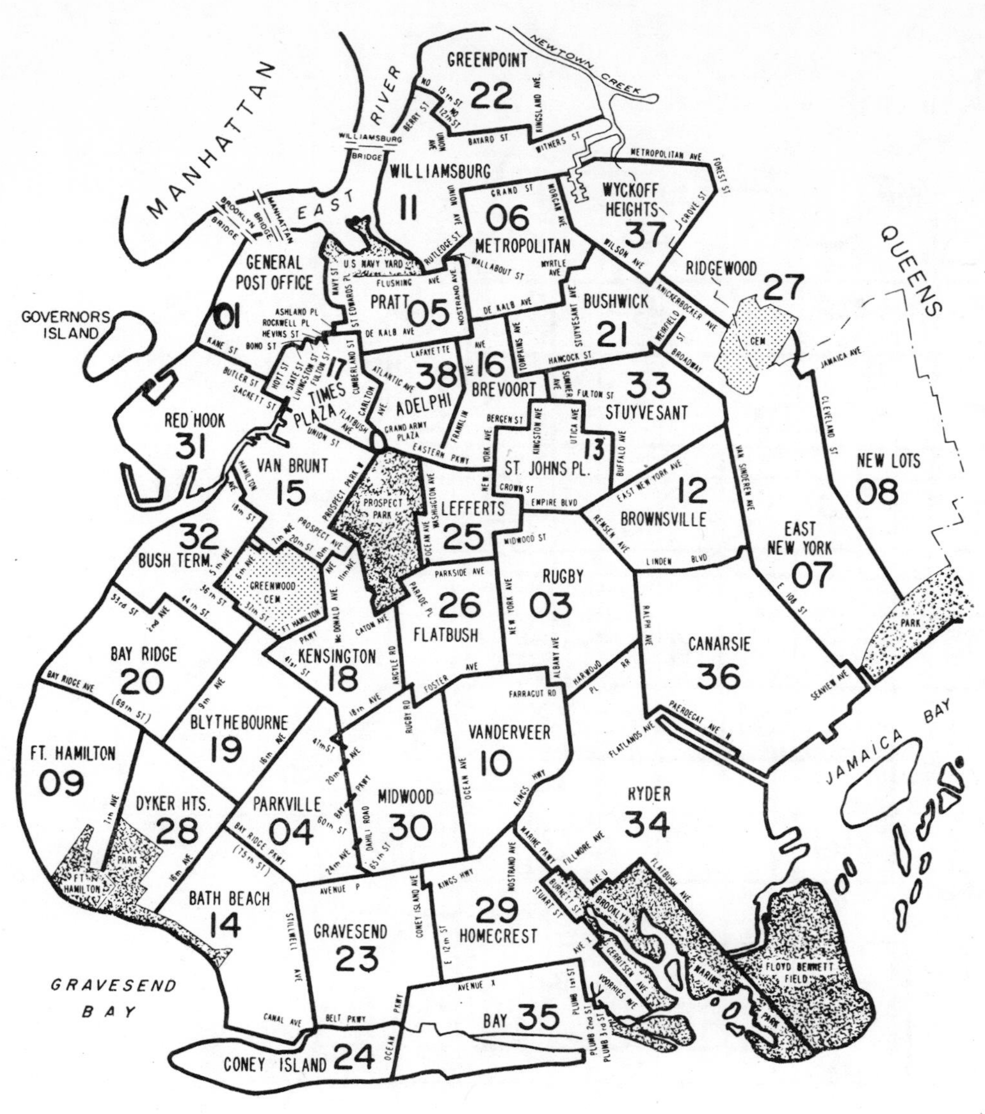

POSTAL ZIP CODE ZONES
BROOKLYN
New York City
New York
112+ TWO DIGITS SHOWN = ZIP CODE

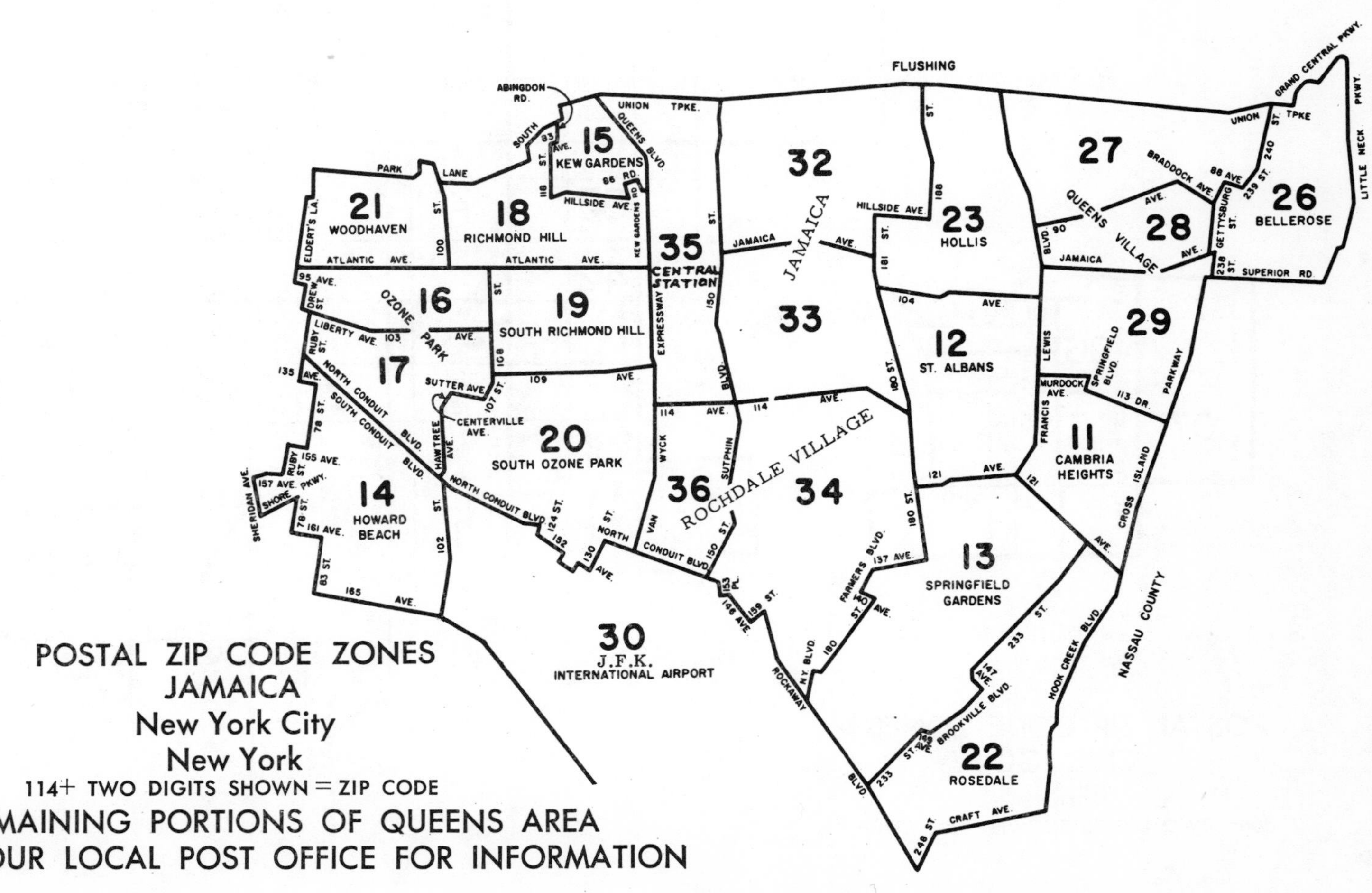

POSTAL ZIP CODE ZONES
JAMAICA
New York City
New York
114+ TWO DIGITS SHOWN = ZIP CODE

FOR REMAINING PORTIONS OF QUEENS AREA
ONTACT YOUR LOCAL POST OFFICE FOR INFORMATION

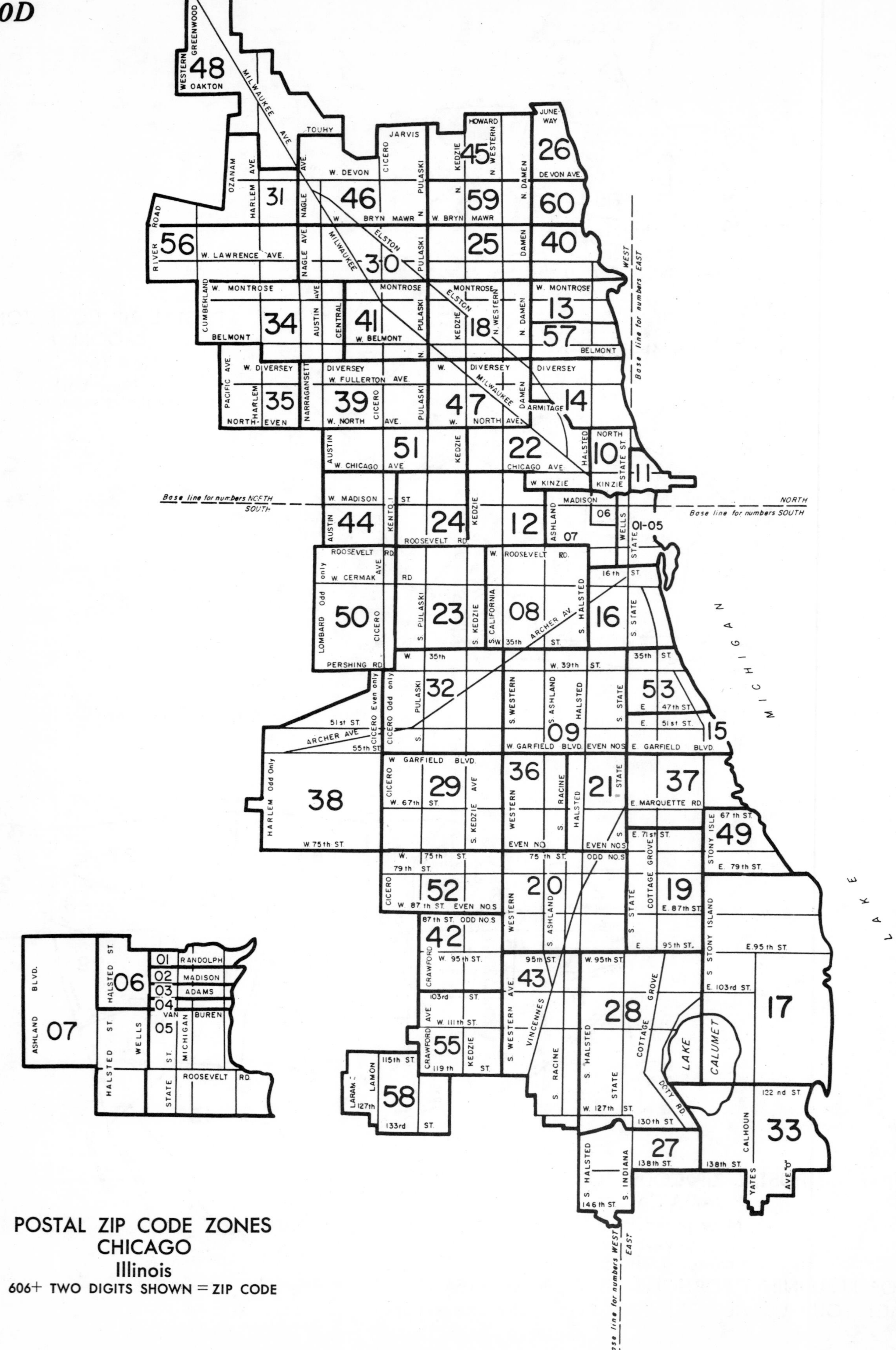
POSTAL ZIP CODE ZONES
CHICAGO
Illinois
606+ TWO DIGITS SHOWN = ZIP CODE
Base line for numbers NORTH
SOUTH
Base line for numbers SOUTH
Base line for numbers WEST
EAST
LAKE MICHIGAN
LAKE CALUMET
48
26
45
46
31
59
60
56
30
25
40
34
41
18
13
57
35
39
47
14
51
22
10
11
44
24
12
06
07
01-05
50
23
08
16
32
53
09
15
38
29
36
21
37
49
52
20
19
42
43
28
17
55
58
27
33
01
02
03
04
05
MILWAUKEE AVE
ELSTON
ARCHER AVE
OAKTON
TOUHY
HOWARD
JUNEWAY
JARVIS
W. DEVON
DEVON AVE.
W. BRYN MAWR
W. LAWRENCE AVE.
W. MONTROSE
BELMONT
W. BELMONT
W. DIVERSEY
W. FULLERTON AVE.
W. NORTH AVE.
ARMITAGE
W. CHICAGO AVE
W. KINZIE
W. MADISON ST.
ROOSEVELT RD
W. CERMAK RD
16th ST
PERSHING RD
W. 35th
W. 39th ST.
47th ST.
51st ST.
55th ST.
W GARFIELD BLVD.
E. GARFIELD BLVD.
E. MARQUETTE RD.
W. 67th ST.
67th ST.
E. 71st ST.
W. 75th ST.
E. 79th ST.
W 87th ST. EVEN NOS.
87th ST. ODD NOS.
E. 87th ST.
W. 95th ST.
E. 95th ST.
103rd ST.
E. 103rd ST.
W. 111th ST.
115th ST.
119th ST.
122nd ST.
W. 127th ST.
130th ST.
133rd ST.
138th ST.
146th ST.
DOTY RD.
WESTERN
GREENWOOD
OZANAM
HARLEM AVE.
NAGLE AVE.
CICERO
PULASKI
KEDZIE
N. WESTERN
N. DAMEN
RIVER ROAD
CUMBERLAND
AUSTIN AVE.
CENTRAL
PACIFIC AVE.
NARRAGANSETT
KENTON
CALIFORNIA
ASHLAND
HALSTED
WELLS
STATE ST.
LOMBARD Odd only
CRAWFORD AVE
RACINE
VINCENNES
COTTAGE GROVE
STONY ISLAND
S. INDIANA
CALHOUN
YATES
AVE "O"
LARAMIE
LAMON
RANDOLPH
MADISON
ADAMS
VAN BUREN
MICHIGAN
ASHLAND BLVD.

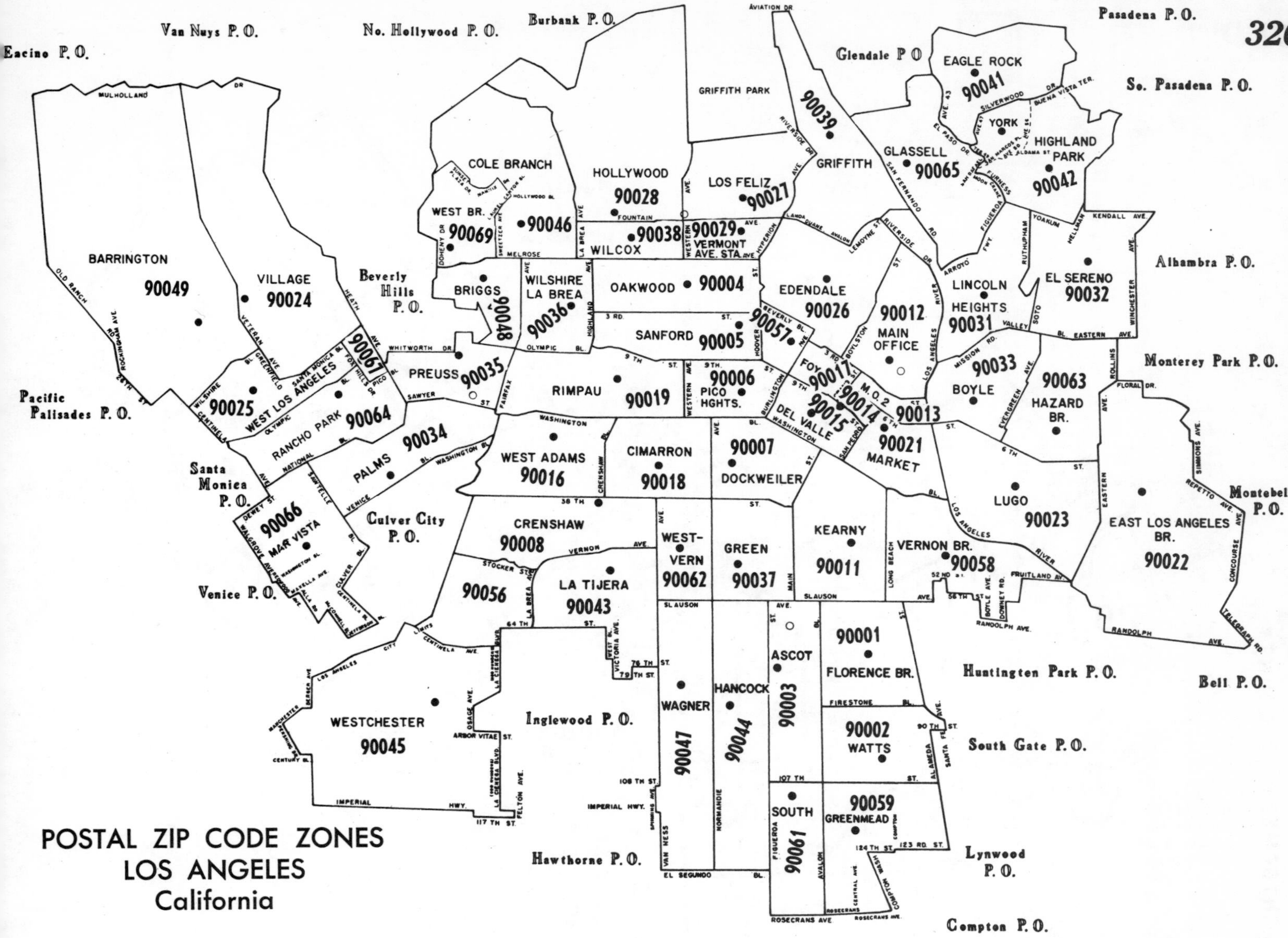

POSTAL ZIP CODE ZONES LOS ANGELES California

Encino P.O.
Van Nuys P.O.
No. Hollywood P.O.
Burbank P.O.
Glendale P.O.
Pasadena P.O.
So. Pasadena P.O.
Alhambra P.O.
Monterey Park P.O.
Montebello P.O.
Bell P.O.
Huntington Park P.O.
South Gate P.O.
Lynwood P.O.
Compton P.O.
Hawthorne P.O.
Inglewood P.O.
Culver City P.O.
Venice P.O.
Santa Monica P.O.
Pacific Palisades P.O.
Beverly Hills P.O.

BARRINGTON 90049
VILLAGE 90024
WEST LOS ANGELES 90025
90067
RANCHO PARK 90064
PALMS 90034
MAR VISTA 90066
PREUSS 90035
COLE BRANCH
WEST BR. 90069
90046
HOLLYWOOD 90028
WILCOX 90038
LOS FELIZ 90027
90029 VERMONT AVE. STA.
GRIFFITH PARK
90039 GRIFFITH
EAGLE ROCK 90041
YORK
HIGHLAND PARK 90042
GLASSELL 90065
BRIGGS 90048
WILSHIRE LA BREA 90036
OAKWOOD 90004
SANFORD 90005
90057
EDENDALE 90026
90012 MAIN OFFICE
LINCOLN HEIGHTS 90031
EL SERENO 90032
RIMPAU 90019
90006 PICO HGHTS.
FOY 90017
M.O.2 90014
90015 DEL VALLE
90013
90021 MARKET
BOYLE 90033
90063 HAZARD BR.
WEST ADAMS 90016
CIMARRON 90018
90007 DOCKWEILER
LUGO 90023
EAST LOS ANGELES BR. 90022
CRENSHAW 90008
WEST-VERN 90062
GREEN 90037
KEARNY 90011
VERNON BR. 90058
90056
LA TIJERA 90043
ASCOT 90003
90001 FLORENCE BR.
WAGNER 90047
HANCOCK 90044
90002 WATTS
WESTCHESTER 90045
SOUTH 90061
90059 GREENMEAD

POSTAL ZIP CODE ZONES NO. HOLLYWOOD California

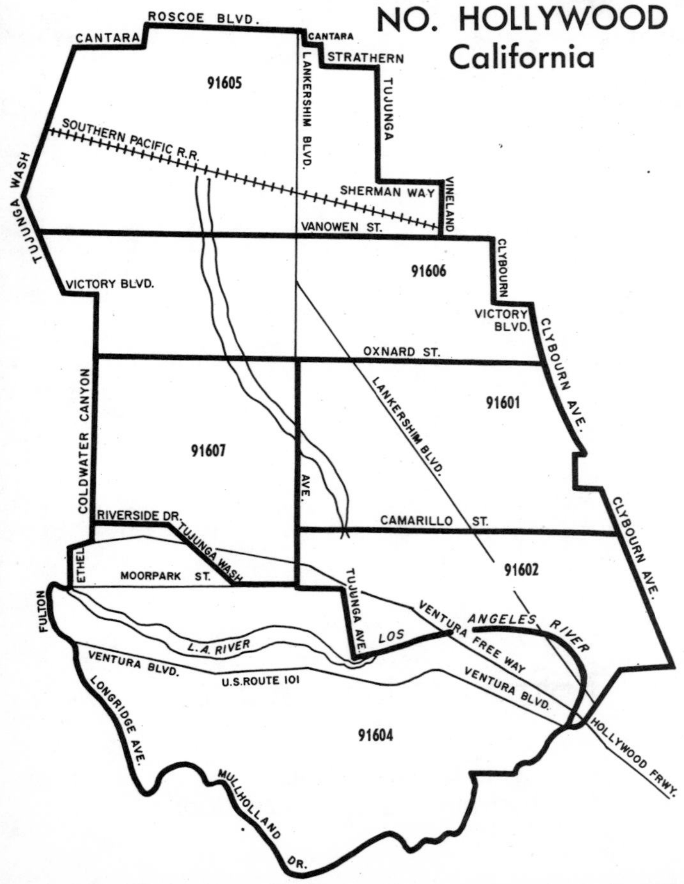

91605
91606
91601
91607
91602
91604

POSTAL ZIP CODE ZONES SANTA MONICA California

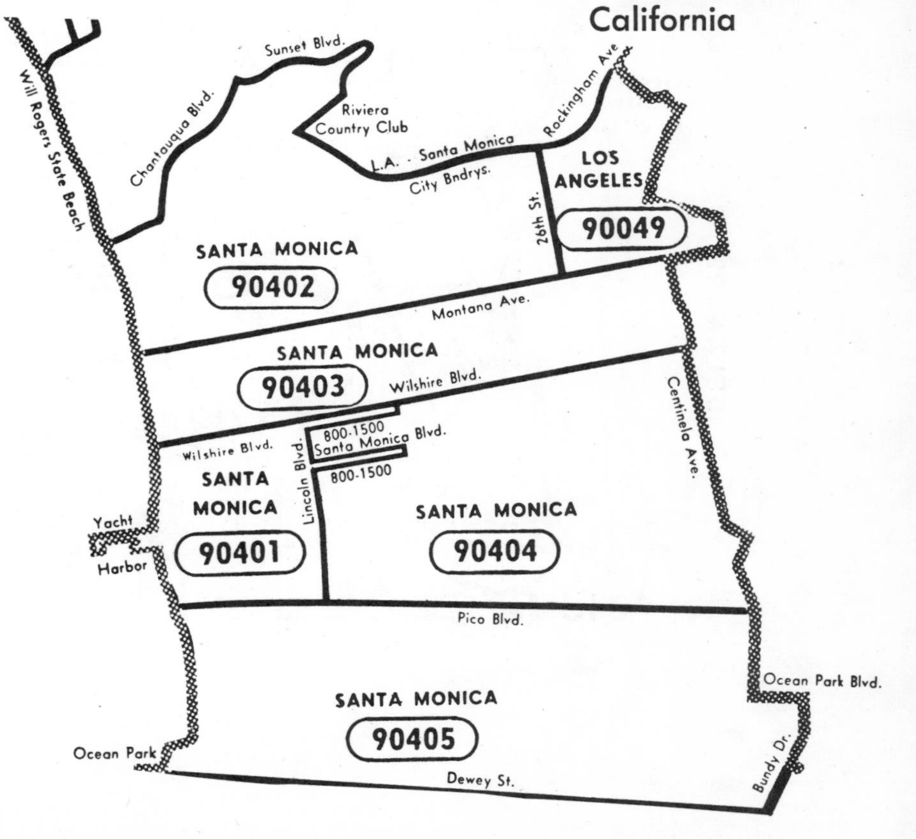

LOS ANGELES 90049
SANTA MONICA 90402
SANTA MONICA 90403
SANTA MONICA 90401
SANTA MONICA 90404
SANTA MONICA 90405

FOR REMAINING PORTIONS OF LOS ANGELES AREA CONTACT YOUR LOCAL POST OFFICE FOR INFORMATION

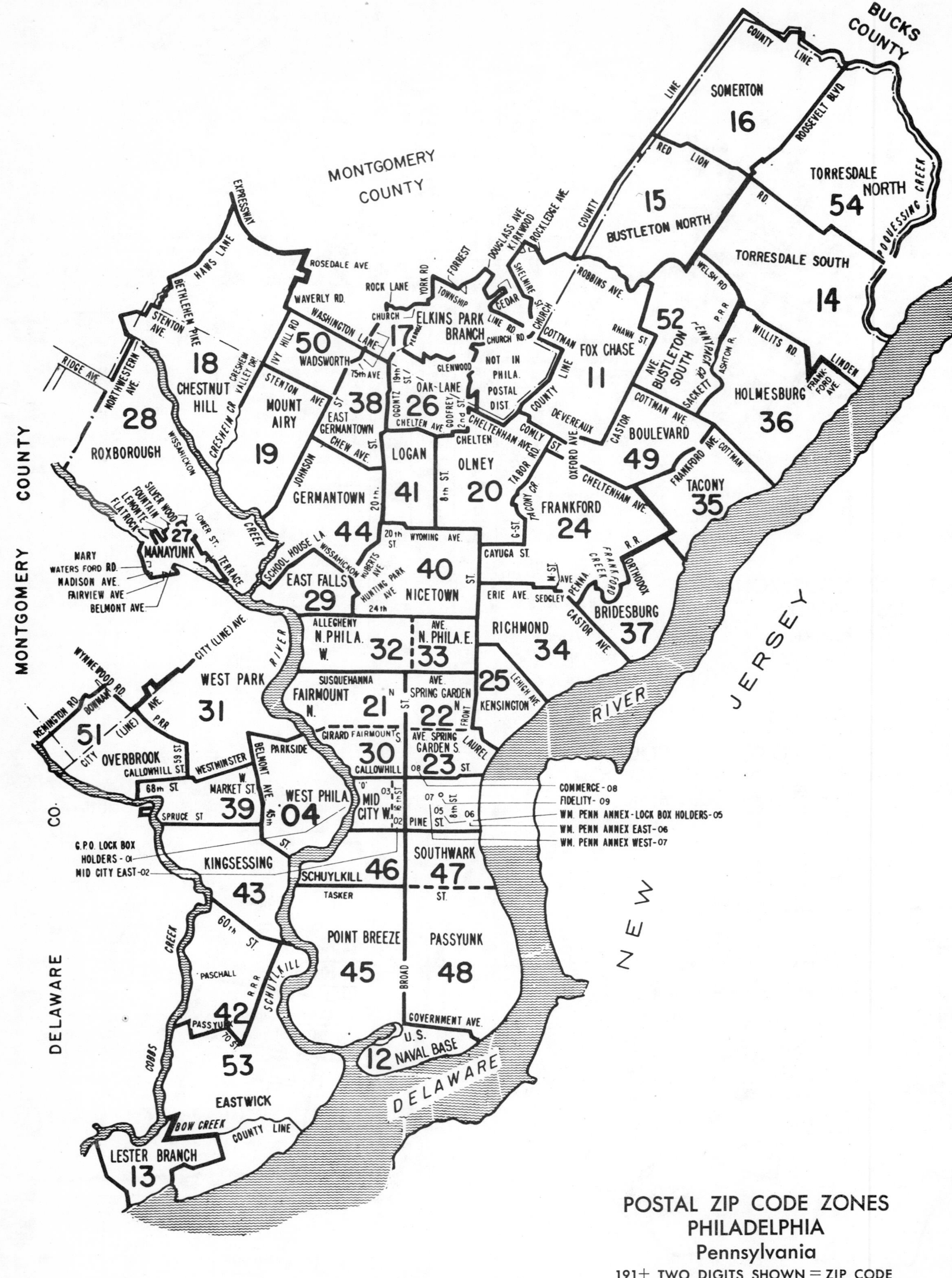

POSTAL ZIP CODE ZONES
PHILADELPHIA
Pennsylvania
191+ TWO DIGITS SHOWN = ZIP CODE

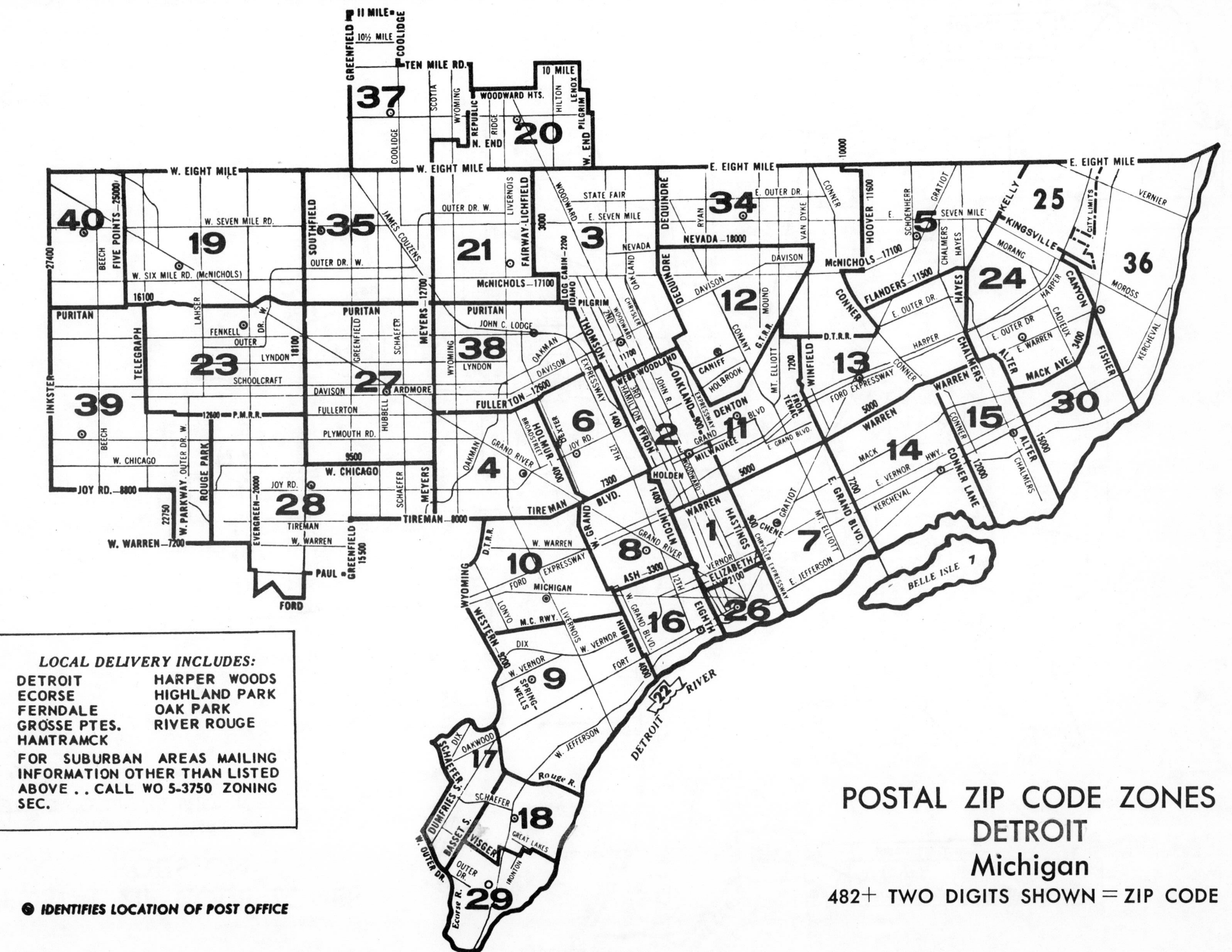

LOCAL DELIVERY INCLUDES:
DETROIT HARPER WOODS
ECORSE HIGHLAND PARK
FERNDALE OAK PARK
GROSSE PTES. RIVER ROUGE
HAMTRAMCK
FOR SUBURBAN AREAS MAILING INFORMATION OTHER THAN LISTED ABOVE . . CALL WO 5-3750 ZONING SEC.
⊙ IDENTIFIES LOCATION OF POST OFFICE
POSTAL ZIP CODE ZONES
DETROIT
Michigan
482+ TWO DIGITS SHOWN = ZIP CODE

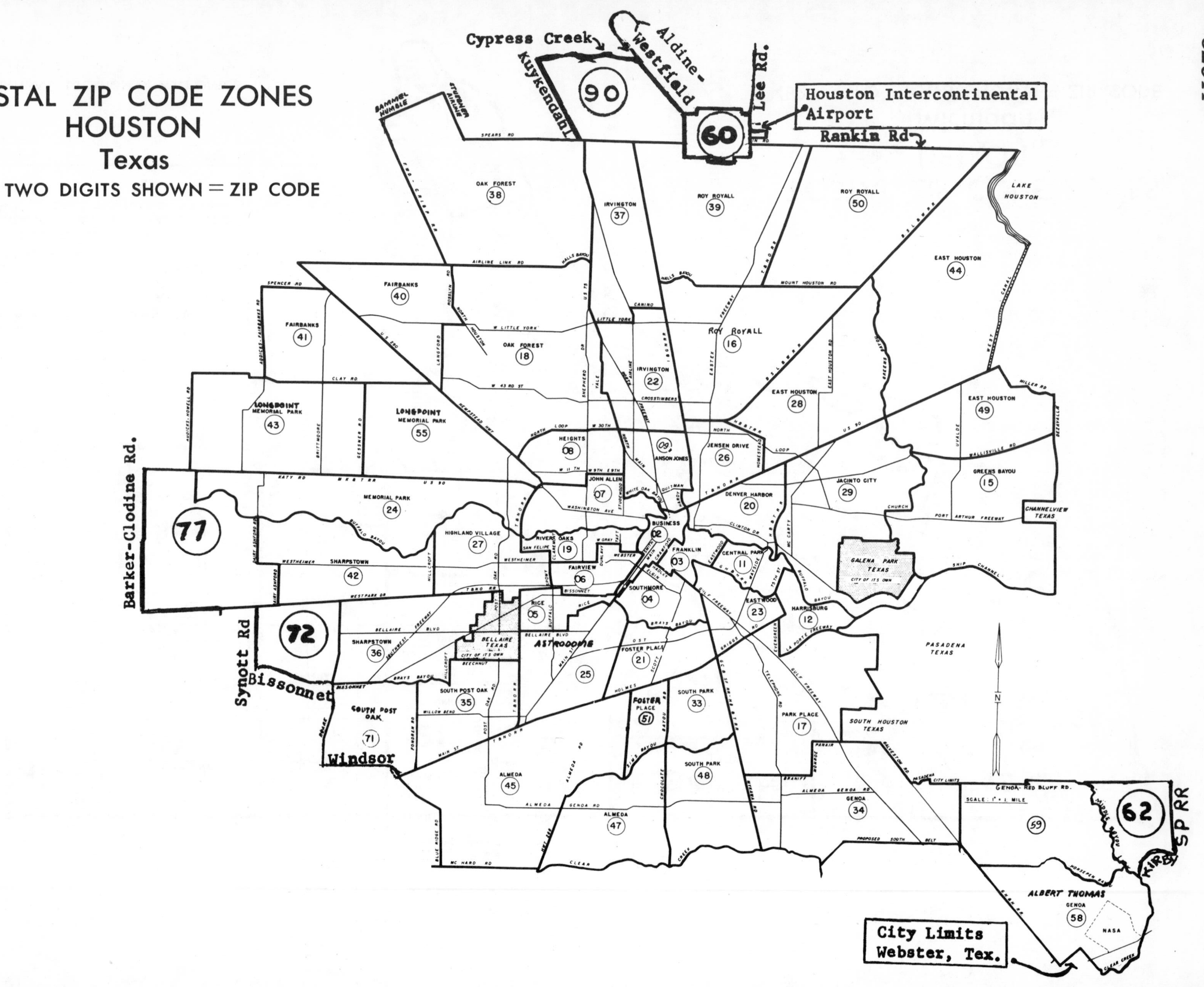
POSTAL ZIP CODE ZONES
HOUSTON
Texas
770 + TWO DIGITS SHOWN = ZIP CODE
Cypress Creek
Aldine-Westfield
Kuykendahl
Lee Rd.
Houston Intercontinental Airport
Rankin Rd
Barker-Clodine Rd.
Synott Rd
Bissonnet
Windsor
City Limits Webster, Tex.
SP RR
KIRBY
LAKE HOUSTON
PASADENA TEXAS
SOUTH HOUSTON TEXAS
GALENA PARK TEXAS
CITY OF ITS OWN
BELLAIRE TEXAS
CHANNELVIEW TEXAS
NASA
ASTRODOME
SCALE: 1" = 1 MILE
OAK FOREST 38
IRVINGTON 37
ROY ROYALL 39
ROY ROYALL 50
EAST HOUSTON 44
FAIRBANKS 40
FAIRBANKS 41
OAK FOREST 18
IRVINGTON 22
ROY ROYALL 16
EAST HOUSTON 28
EAST HOUSTON 49
LONGPOINT MEMORIAL PARK 43
LONGPOINT MEMORIAL PARK 55
HEIGHTS 08
ANSON JONES 09
JENSEN DRIVE 26
JOHN ALLEN 07
JACINTO CITY 29
GREENS BAYOU 15
MEMORIAL PARK 24
DENVER HARBOR 20
HIGHLAND VILLAGE 27
RIVER OAKS 19
BUSINESS 02
FRANKLIN 03
CENTRAL PARK 11
SHARPSTOWN 42
FAIRVIEW 06
SOUTHMORE 04
EASTWOOD 23
HARRISBURG 12
RICE 05
SHARPSTOWN 36
FOSTER PLACE 21
25
SOUTH POST OAK 35
SOUTH POST OAK 71
FOSTER PLACE 51
SOUTH PARK 33
PARK PLACE 17
ALMEDA 45
SOUTH PARK 48
ALMEDA 47
GENOA 34
59
ALBERT THOMAS
GENOA 58
60
62
72
77
90

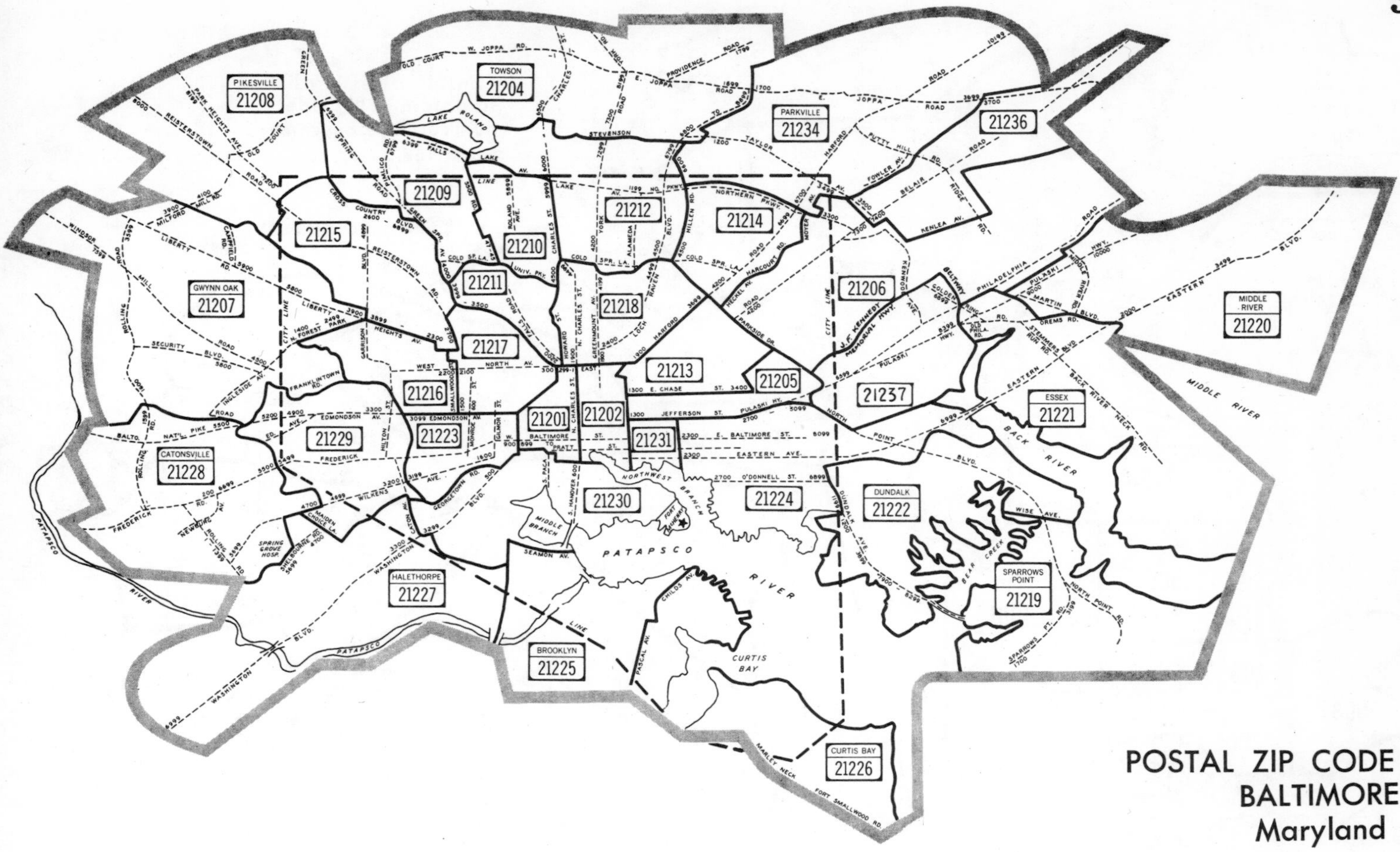

POSTAL ZIP CODE ZONES BALTIMORE Maryland

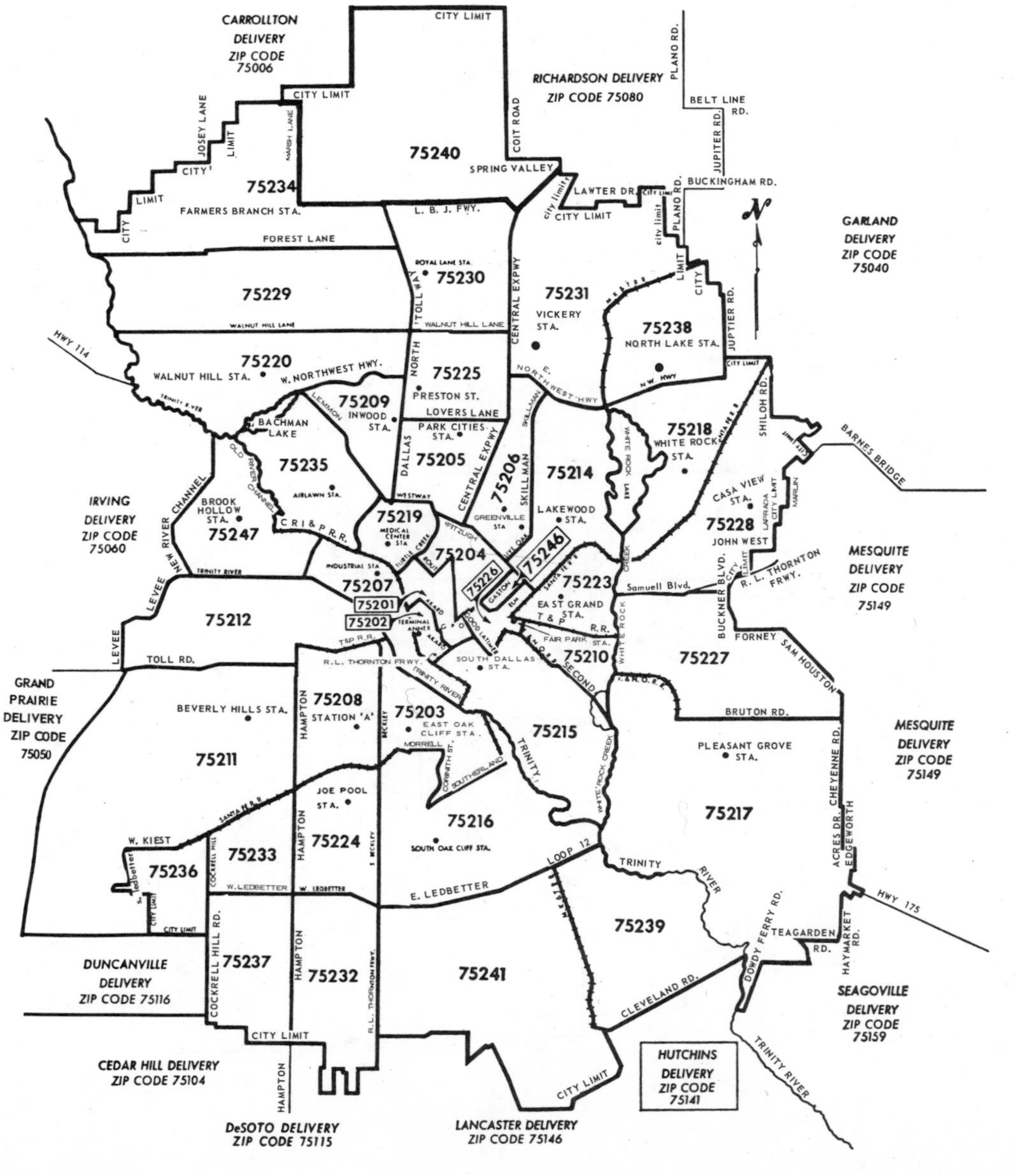

POSTAL ZIP CODE ZONES DALLAS Texas

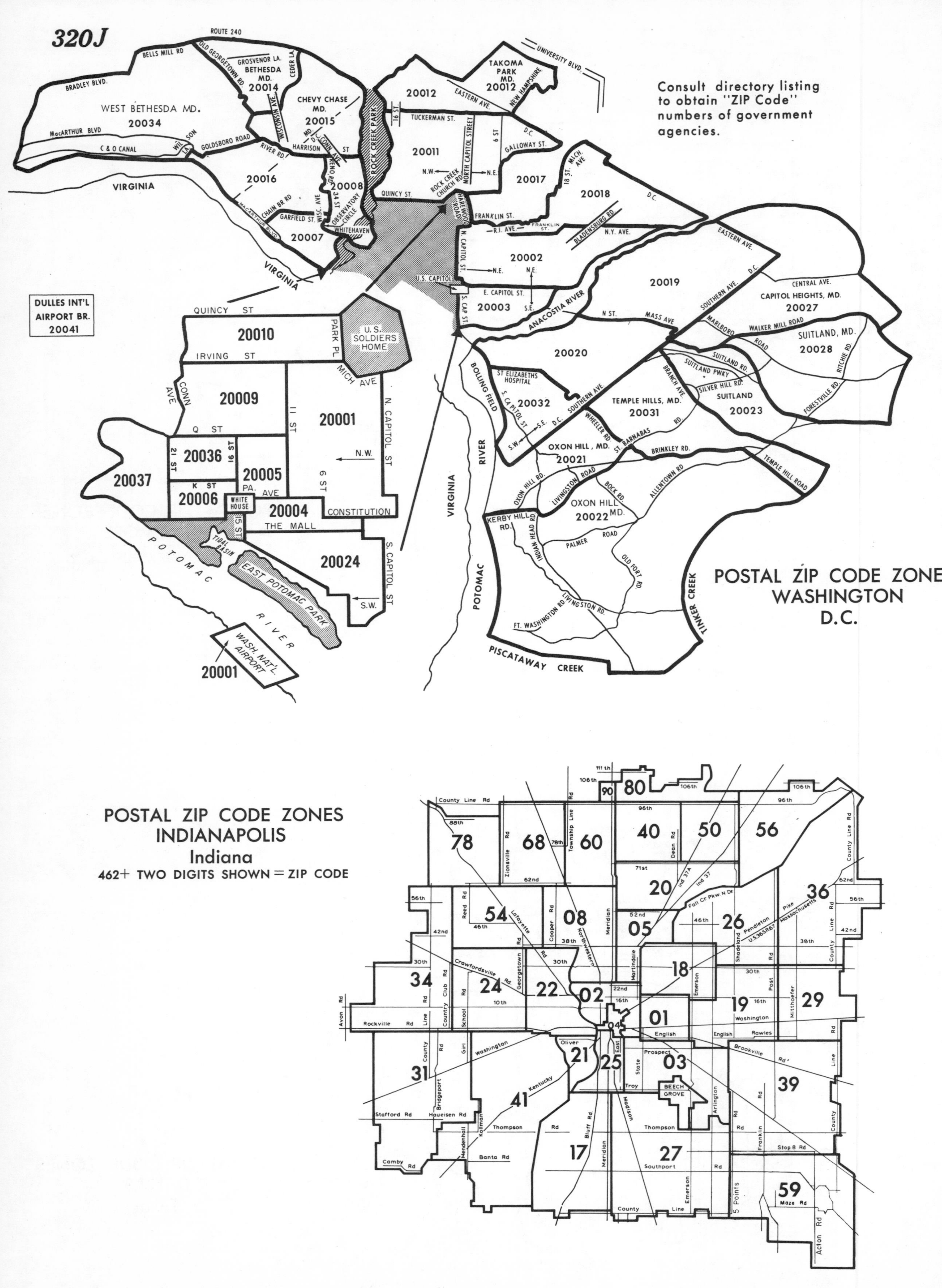

Consult directory listing to obtain "ZIP Code" numbers of government agencies.
POSTAL ZIP CODE ZONES
WASHINGTON
D.C.
DULLES INT'L AIRPORT BR. 20041
WEST BETHESDA MD. 20034
BETHESDA MD. 20014
CHEVY CHASE MD. 20015
TAKOMA PARK MD. 20012
20012
20011
20016
20008
20007
20017
20018
20002
20003
20019
CAPITOL HEIGHTS, MD. 20027
SUITLAND, MD. 20028
SUITLAND 20023
20020
20032
TEMPLE HILLS, MD. 20031
OXON HILL, MD. 20021
OXON HILL MD. 20022
20010
U.S. SOLDIERS HOME
20009
20001
20036
20005
20037
20006
WHITE HOUSE
20004
20024
WASH. NAT'L. AIRPORT
20001
ROCK CREEK PARK
EAST POTOMAC PARK
TIDAL BASIN
U.S. CAPITOL
ANACOSTIA RIVER
POTOMAC RIVER
VIRGINIA
PISCATAWAY CREEK
TINKER CREEK
BOLLING FIELD
ST ELIZABETHS HOSPITAL
POSTAL ZIP CODE ZONES
INDIANAPOLIS
Indiana
462+ TWO DIGITS SHOWN = ZIP CODE
80
90
78
68
60
40
50
56
20
54
08
05
26
36
18
34
24
22
02
19
29
01
04
21
25
03
31
41
39
17
27
59

POSTAL ZIP CODE ZONES
CLEVELAND
Ohio

441+ TWO DIGITS SHOWN = ZIP CODE

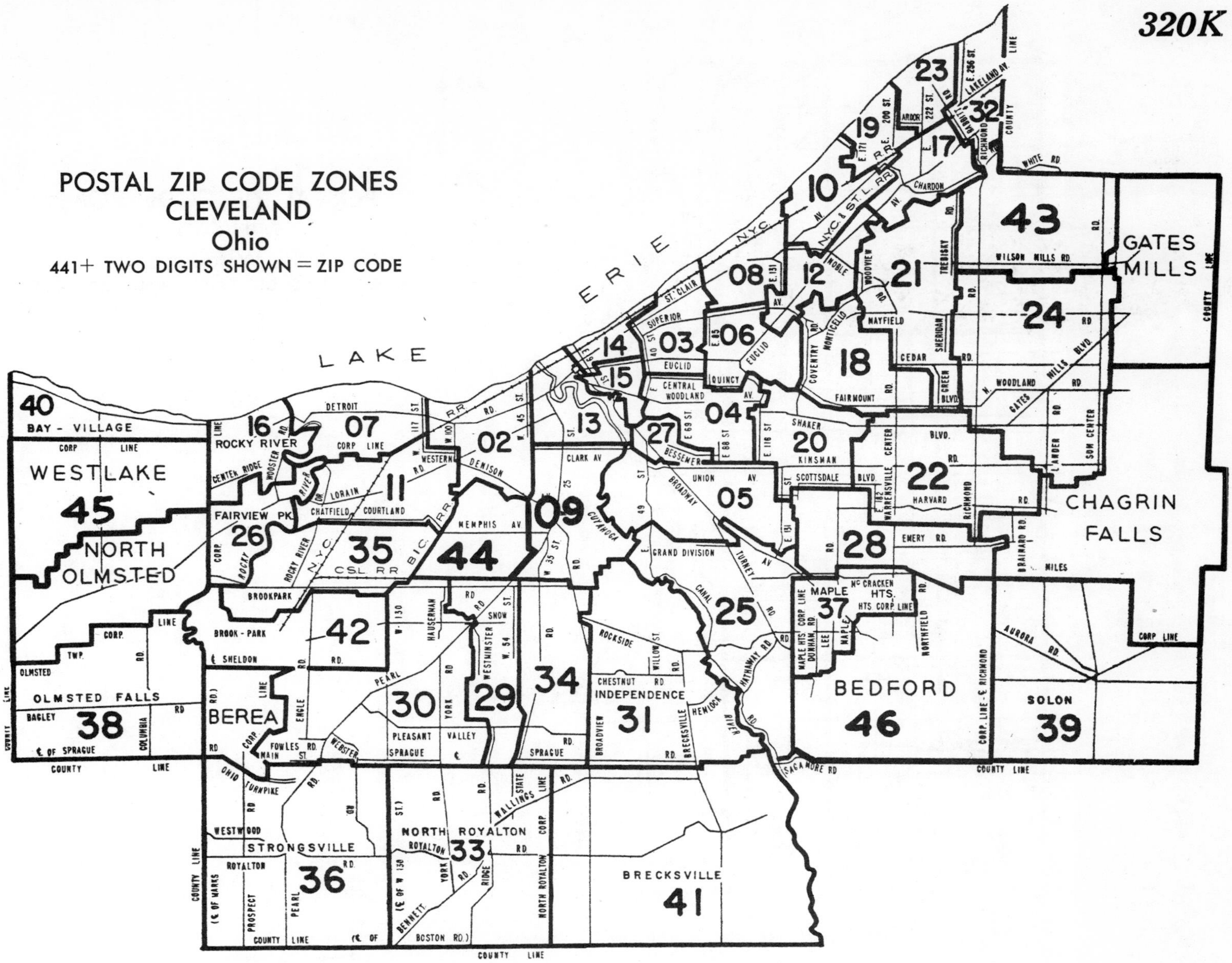

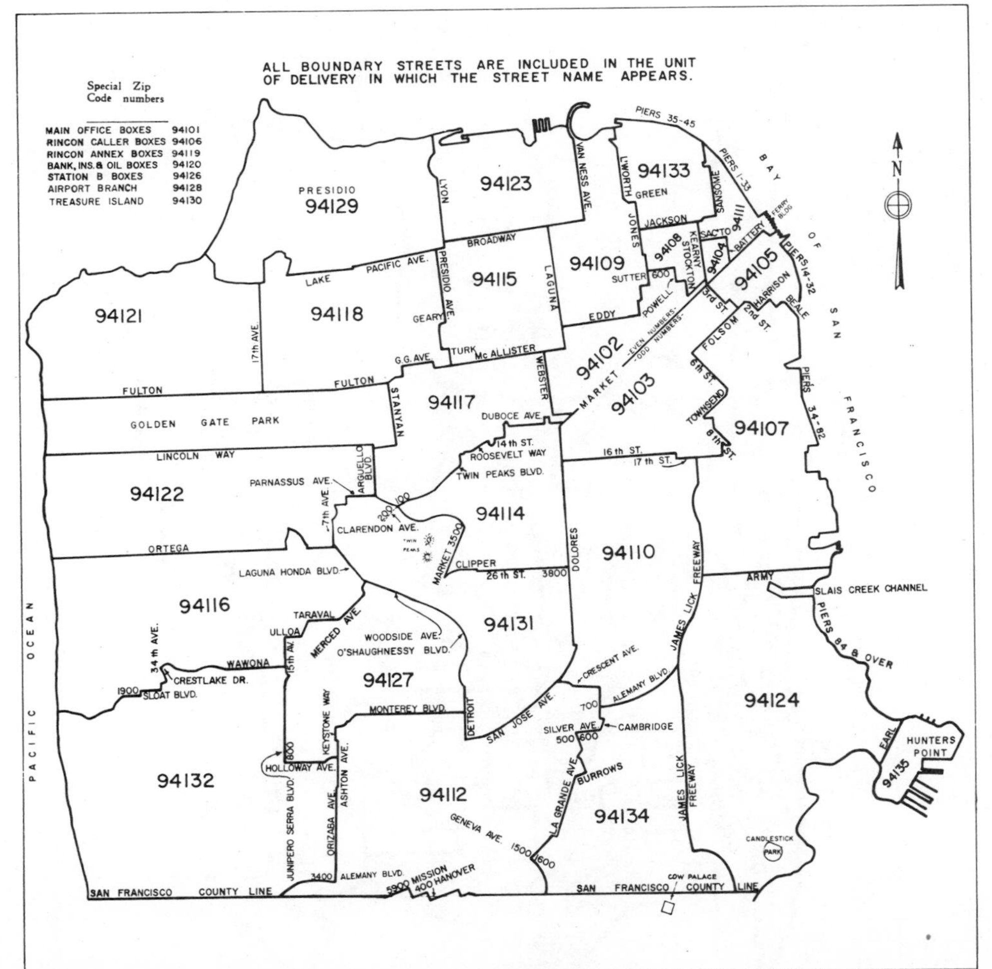

POSTAL ZIP CODE ZONES
SAN FRANCISCO
California

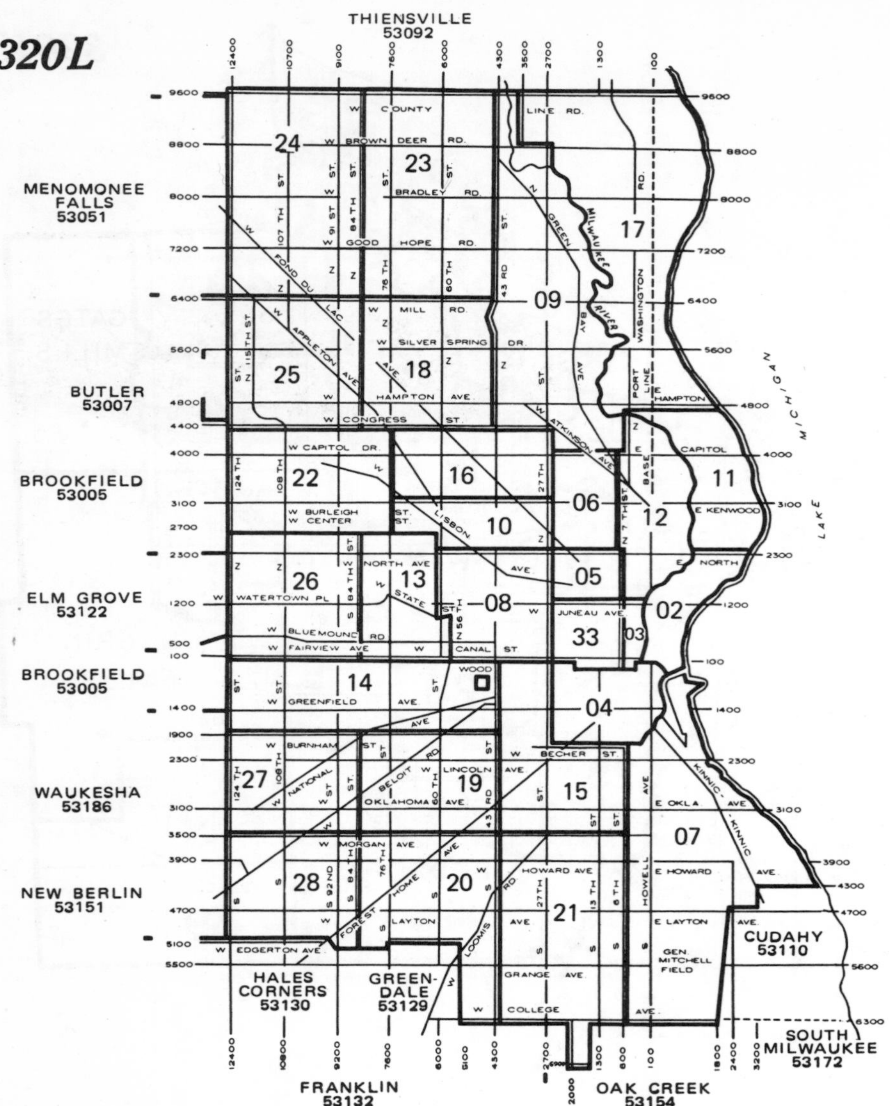

POSTAL ZIP CODE ZONES
MILWAUKEE
Wisconsin

532+ TWO DIGITS SHOWN = ZIP CODE

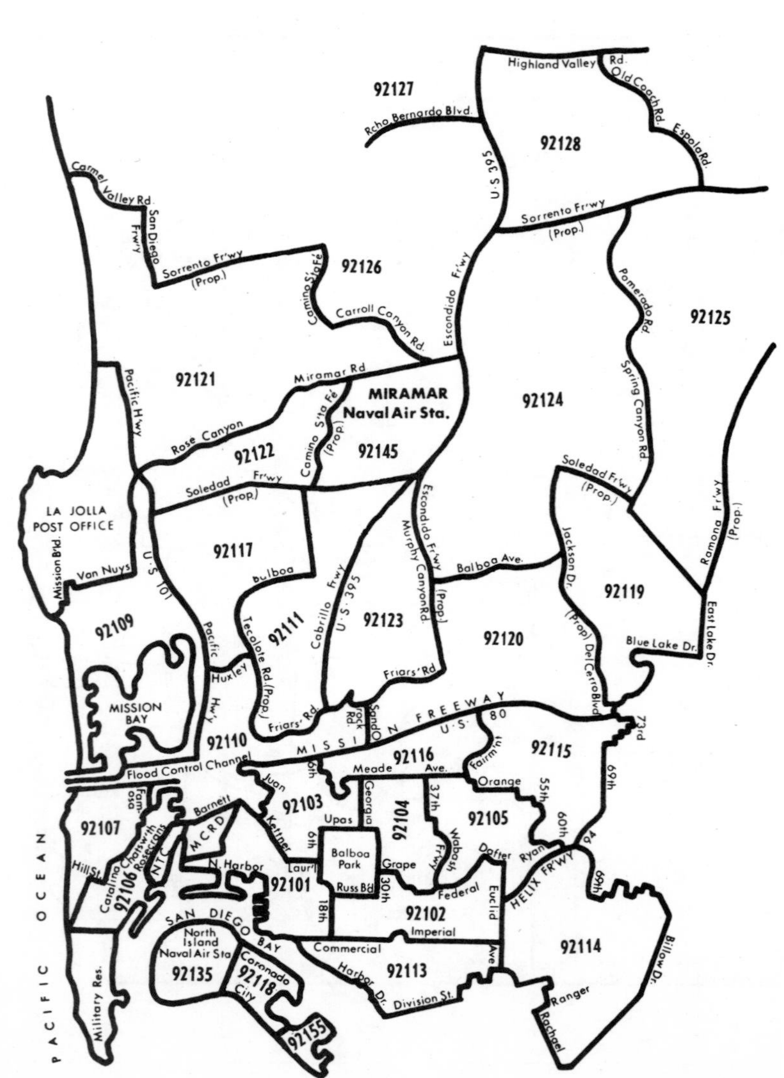

POSTAL ZIP CODE ZONES
SAN DIEGO
California

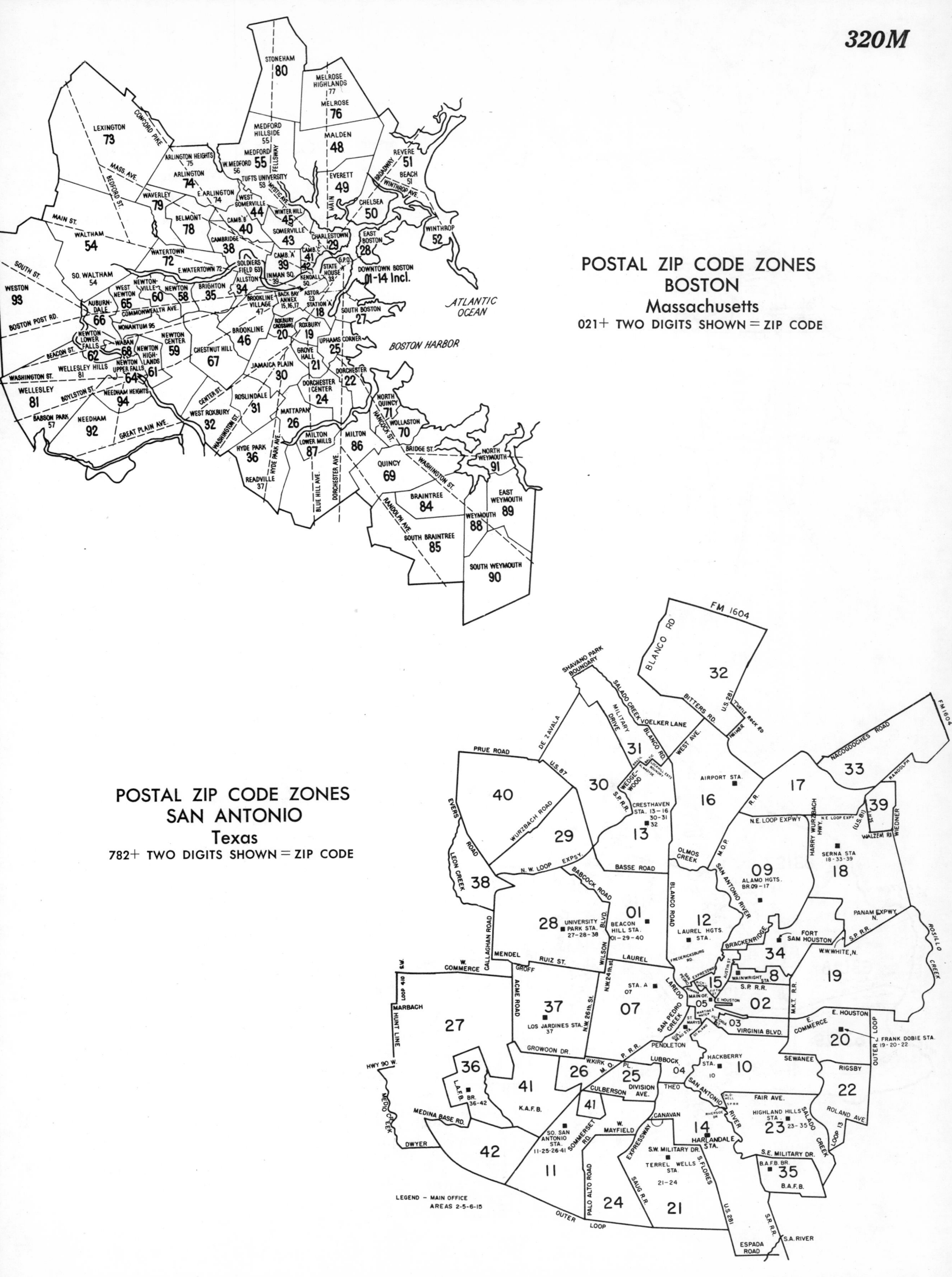
POSTAL ZIP CODE ZONES
BOSTON
Massachusetts
021+ TWO DIGITS SHOWN = ZIP CODE
STONEHAM 80
MELROSE HIGHLANDS 77
MELROSE 76
LEXINGTON 73
MEDFORD HILLSIDE 55
MALDEN 48
ARLINGTON HEIGHTS 75
MEDFORD 55
W. MEDFORD 56
REVERE 51
BEACH 51
ARLINGTON 74
TUFTS UNIVERSITY 53
EVERETT 49
E. ARLINGTON 74
WEST SOMERVILLE 44
WAVERLEY 79
CHELSEA 50
WINTER HILL 45
BELMONT 78
CAMB. 'B' 40
SOMERVILLE 43
WINTHROP 52
CHARLESTOWN 29
EAST BOSTON 28
WALTHAM 54
CAMBRIDGE 38
CAMB. 'C' 41
CAMB. 'A' 39
42
WATERTOWN 72
E. WATERTOWN 72
SOLDIERS FIELD 63
STATE HOUSE 33
G.P.O.
DOWNTOWN BOSTON 01-14 Incl.
SO. WALTHAM 54
INMAN SQ. 39
KENDALL SQ. 42
WESTON 93
ALLSTON 34
WEST NEWTON 65
NEWTONVILLE 60
NEWTON 58
BRIGHTON 35
BACK BAY ANNEX 15,16,17
ASTOR 23
STATION 'A' 18
ATLANTIC OCEAN
AUBURNDALE 66
BROOKLINE VILLAGE 47
SOUTH BOSTON 27
COMMONWEALTH AVE.
BOSTON POST RD.
NONANTUM 95
BROOKLINE 46
ROXBURY CROSSING 20
ROXBURY 19
UPHAMS CORNER 25
NEWTON LOWER FALLS 62
WABAN 68
NEWTON CENTER 59
BOSTON HARBOR
NEWTON HIGHLANDS 61
CHESTNUT HILL 67
GROVE HALL 21
BEACON ST.
WELLESLEY HILLS 81
NEWTON UPPER FALLS 64
JAMAICA PLAIN 30
DORCHESTER 22
WASHINGTON ST.
WELLESLEY 81
BOYLSTON ST.
NEEDHAM HEIGHTS 94
ROSLINDALE 31
DORCHESTER CENTER 24
NORTH QUINCY 71
WOLLASTON 70
BABSON PARK 57
NEEDHAM 92
CENTER ST.
WEST ROXBURY 32
MATTAPAN 26
GREAT PLAIN AVE.
MILTON LOWER MILLS 87
MILTON 86
HANCOCK ST.
BRIDGE ST.
NORTH WEYMOUTH 91
HYDE PARK 36
READVILLE 37
QUINCY 69
BRAINTREE 84
EAST WEYMOUTH 89
WEYMOUTH 88
SOUTH BRAINTREE 85
SOUTH WEYMOUTH 90
CONCORD PIKE
MASS. AVE.
BEDFORD ST.
MAIN ST.
SOUTH ST.
FELLSWAY
MYSTIC AVE.
BROADWAY
WINTHROP AVE.
HYDE PARK AVE.
BLUE HILL AVE.
DORCHESTER AVE.
RANDOLPH AVE.
POSTAL ZIP CODE ZONES
SAN ANTONIO
Texas
782+ TWO DIGITS SHOWN = ZIP CODE
FM 1604
BLANCO RD.
32
SHAVANO PARK BOUNDARY
SALADO CREEK
VOELKER LANE
BITTERS RD.
US 281
MILITARY DRIVE
BLANCO RD.
WEST AVE.
NACOGDOCHES ROAD
PRUE ROAD
DE ZAVALA
US 87
31
WEDGEWOOD
AIRPORT STA.
17
33
40
30
16
39
EVERS ROAD
WURZBACH ROAD
CRESTHAVEN STA. 13-16 30-31 32
N.E. LOOP EXPWY
HARRY WURZBACH HWY.
WALZEM RD
WIEDNER
29
13
OLMOS CREEK
LEON CREEK
N. W. LOOP EXPSY.
BASSE ROAD
09
ALAMO HGTS. BR.09-17
SERNA STA 18-33-39
18
38
BABCOCK ROAD
SAN ANTONIO RIVER
01
BEACON HILL STA. 01-29-40
12
LAUREL HGTS. STA.
PANAM EXPWY N.
28
UNIVERSITY PARK STA. 27-28-38
BLANCO ROAD
FORT SAM HOUSTON
ROSILLO CREEK
CALLAGHAN ROAD
BRACKENRIDGE
34
W.W.WHITE, N.
MENDEL
RUIZ ST.
LAUREL
W. COMMERCE
GROFF
WAINWRIGHT STA.
8
19
15
S.P. R.R.
STA. A 07
37
07
05
02
MARBACH
ACME ROAD
LOS JARDINES STA. 37
LAREDO
MAIN OFF.
E. HOUSTON
03
27
SAN PEDRO CREEK
VIRGINIA BLVD.
E. COMMERCE
20
J. FRANK DOBIE STA. 19-20-22
HUNT LINE
GROWOON DR.
PENDLETON
OUTER LOOP
HWY 90 W.
36
W. KIRK
LUBBOCK
HACKBERRY STA. 10
10
SEWANEE
RIGSBY
26
25
04
L.A.F.B. BR. 36-42
41
DIVISION AVE.
THEO
22
CULBERSON
41
K.A.F.B.
SAN ANTONIO RIVER
FAIR AVE.
MEDIO CREEK
ROLAND AVE
MEDINA BASE RD.
W. MAYFIELD
CANAVAN
HIGHLAND HILLS STA. 23-35
SO. SAN ANTONIO STA. 11-25-26-41
14
23
SALADO CREEK
LOOP 13
DWYER
42
SOMMERSET RD.
HARLANDALE STA.
EXPRESSWAY
S.W. MILITARY DR.
S.E. MILITARY DR.
TERREL WELLS STA. 21-24
S. FLORES
B.A.F.B. BR.
35
B.A.F.B.
11
PALO ALTO ROAD
SAUG R.R.
LEGEND - MAIN OFFICE AREAS 2-5-6-15
24
21
US 281
S.P. R.R.
OUTER LOOP
ESPADA ROAD
S.A. RIVER

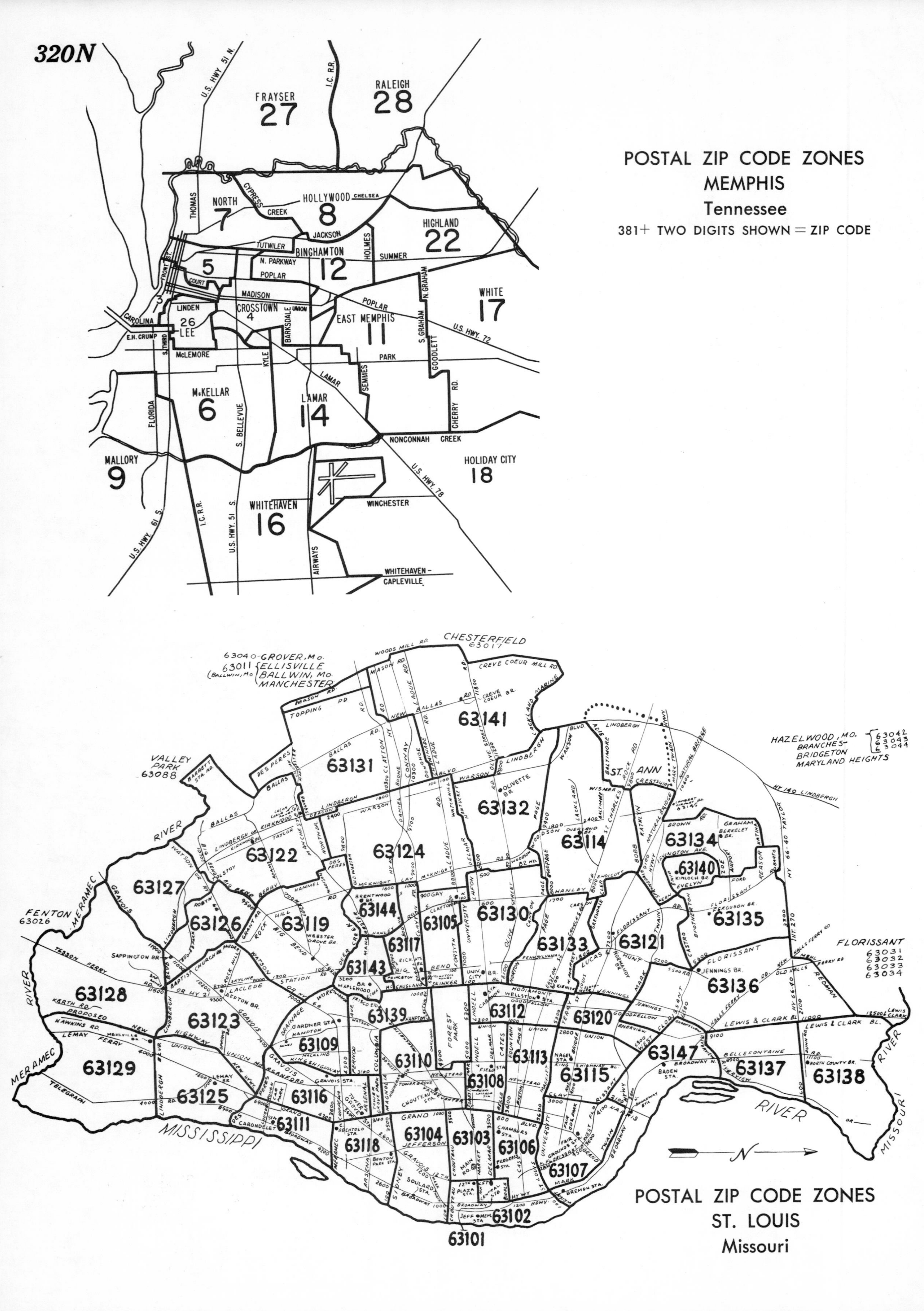
POSTAL ZIP CODE ZONES
MEMPHIS
Tennessee
381+ TWO DIGITS SHOWN = ZIP CODE
FRAYSER
27
RALEIGH
28
NORTH
7
HOLLYWOOD
8
HIGHLAND
22
BINGHAMTON
12
5
WHITE
17
3
26
LEE
CROSSTOWN
4
EAST MEMPHIS
11
McKELLAR
6
LAMAR
14
MALLORY
9
HOLIDAY CITY
18
WHITEHAVEN
16
U.S. HWY 51 N.
I.C. RR.
THOMAS
CYPRESS
CREEK
CHELSEA
JACKSON
TUTWILER
N. PARKWAY
HOLMES
SUMMER
POPLAR
COURT
FRONT ST.
MADISON
UNION
CAROLINA
LINDEN
E.H. CRUMP
S. THIRD
BARKSDALE
N. GRAHAM
S. GRAHAM
U.S. HWY. 72
GOODLETT
McLEMORE
KYLE
PARK
SEMMES
CHERRY RD.
FLORIDA
S. BELLEVUE
NONCONNAH CREEK
U.S. HWY 78
WINCHESTER
U.S. HWY. 61 S.
I.C.R.R.
U.S. HWY. 51 S.
AIRWAYS
WHITEHAVEN - CAPLEVILLE
POSTAL ZIP CODE ZONES
ST. LOUIS
Missouri
CHESTERFIELD
63017
63040 - GROVER, MO.
63011 ELLISVILLE
(BALLWIN, MO.) BALLWIN, MO.
MANCHESTER
VALLEY PARK
63088
HAZELWOOD, MO. BRANCHES - BRIDGETON MARYLAND HEIGHTS
63042
63043
63044
FENTON
63026
FLORISSANT
63031
63032
63033
63034
63141
63131
63132
63122
63124
63114
63134
63140
63127
63126
63119
63144
63105
63130
63135
63117
63133
63121
63143
63128
63123
63139
63112
63120
63136
63109
63110
63113
63147
63137
63129
63125
63116
63108
63115
63138
63111
63104
63103
63106
63118
63107
63102
63101
ST. ANN
MISSISSIPPI
RIVER
MERAMEC
MISSOURI
FOREST PARK
LINDBERGH

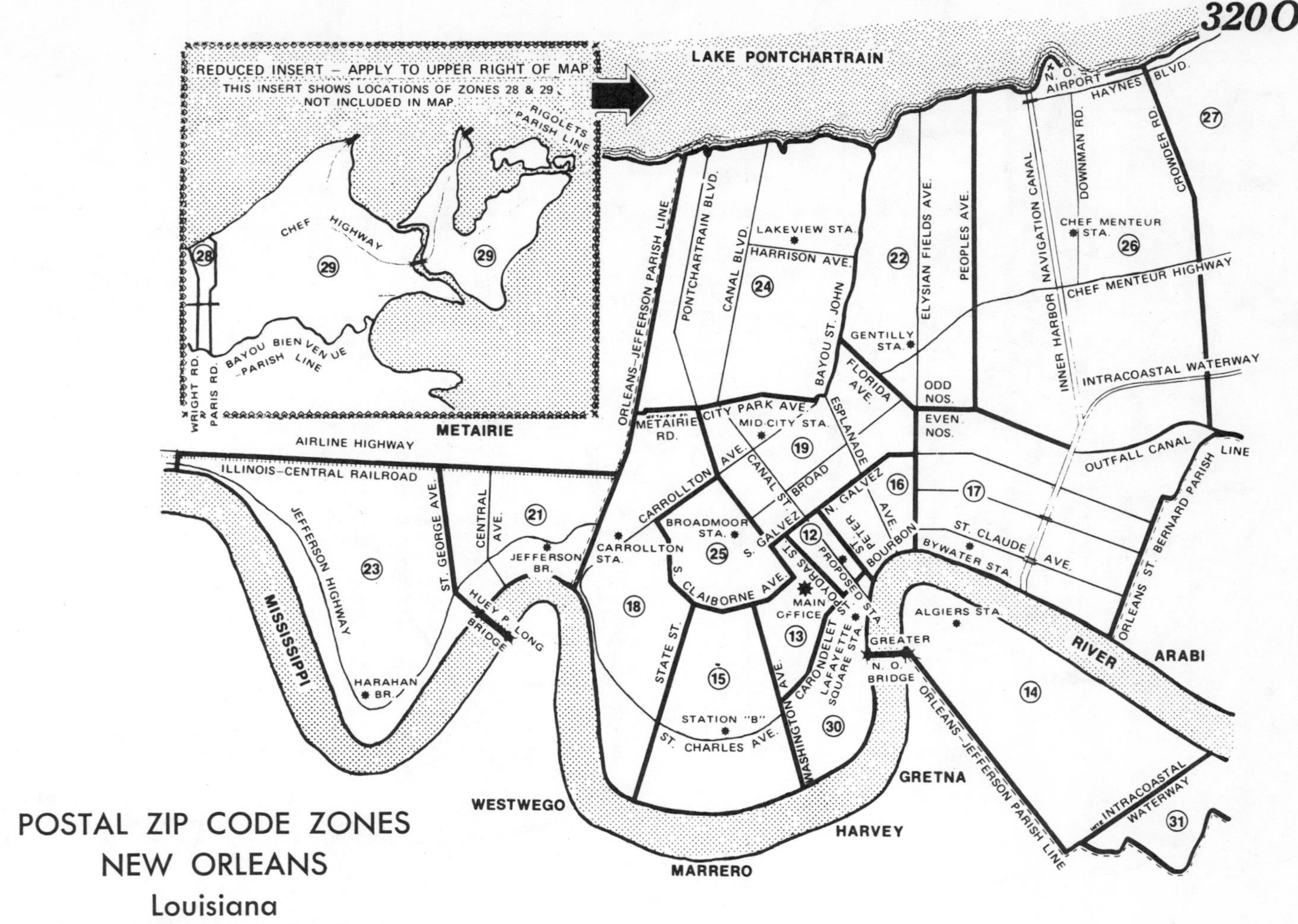

POSTAL ZIP CODE ZONES NEW ORLEANS

Louisiana

701+ TWO DIGITS SHOWN = ZIP CODE

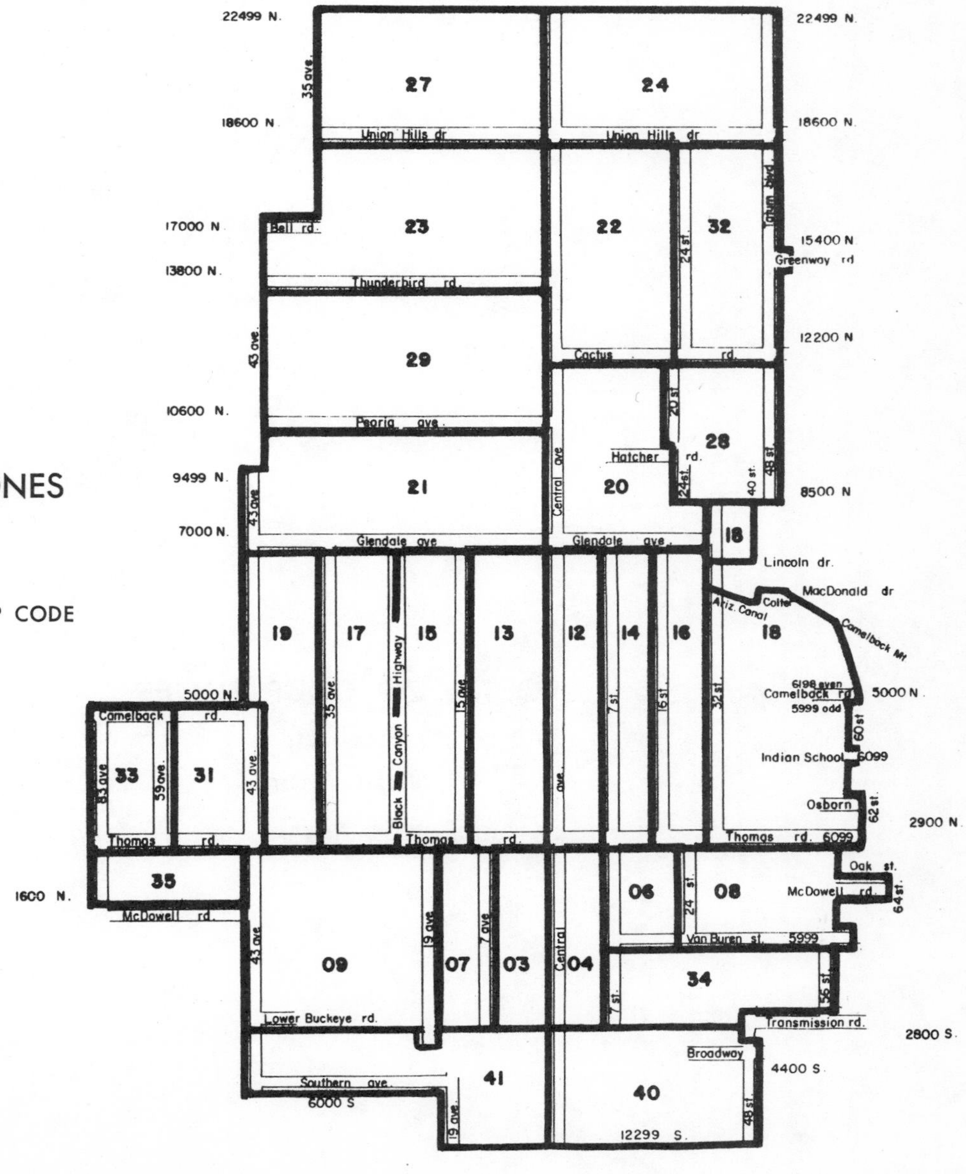

POSTAL ZIP CODE ZONES PHOENIX

Arizona

850+ TWO DIGITS SHOWN = ZIP CODE

22499 N.
27
24
22499 N.
35 ave.
18600 N.
Union Hills dr
Union Hills dr
18600 N.
17000 N.
Bell rd.
23
22
32
24 st.
Tatum blvd.
15400 N
Greenway rd
13800 N.
Thunderbird rd.
43 ave.
29
Cactus rd.
12200 N
10600 N.
Peoria ave.
20 st.
Hatcher rd.
28
9499 N.
21
Central ave.
20
24 st.
40 st.
48 st.
8500 N
7000 N.
43 ave.
Glendale ave.
Glendale ave.
18
Lincoln dr.
MacDonald dr
Ariz. Canal
Colter
Camelback Mt
19
17
15
13
12
14
16
18
35 ave.
Black Canyon Highway
15 ave.
7 st.
16 st.
32 st.
6198 even
Camelback rd
5999 odd
5000 N.
5000 N.
Camelback rd.
33
31
53 ave.
59 ave.
43 ave.
60 st.
Indian School 6099
Osborn
62 st.
2900 N.
Thomas rd.
Thomas rd.
Thomas rd. 6099
Oak st.
1600 N.
35
06
08
McDowell rd.
64 st.
McDowell rd.
43 ave.
19 ave.
7 ave.
Central
24 st.
Van Buren st. 5999
09
07
03
04
34
7 st.
56 st.
Lower Buckeye rd.
Transmission rd.
2800 S.
Broadway
4400 S.
Southern ave.
41
40
6000 S
19 ave.
48 st.
12299 S.

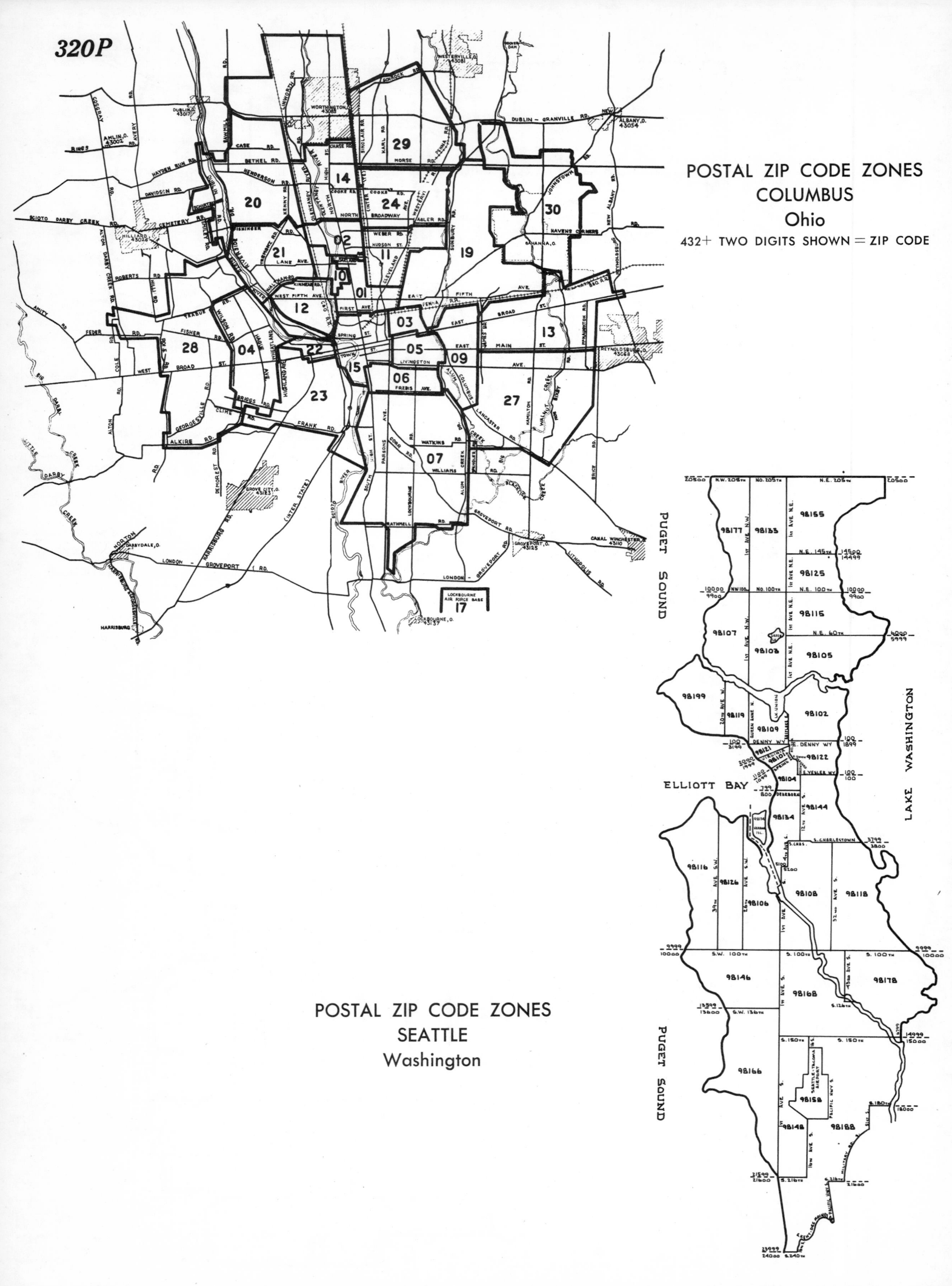

POSTAL ZIP CODE ZONES
COLUMBUS
Ohio
432+ TWO DIGITS SHOWN = ZIP CODE
POSTAL ZIP CODE ZONES
SEATTLE
Washington
PUGET SOUND
ELLIOTT BAY
LAKE WASHINGTON

POSTAL ZIP CODE ZONES PITTSBURGH Pennsylvania

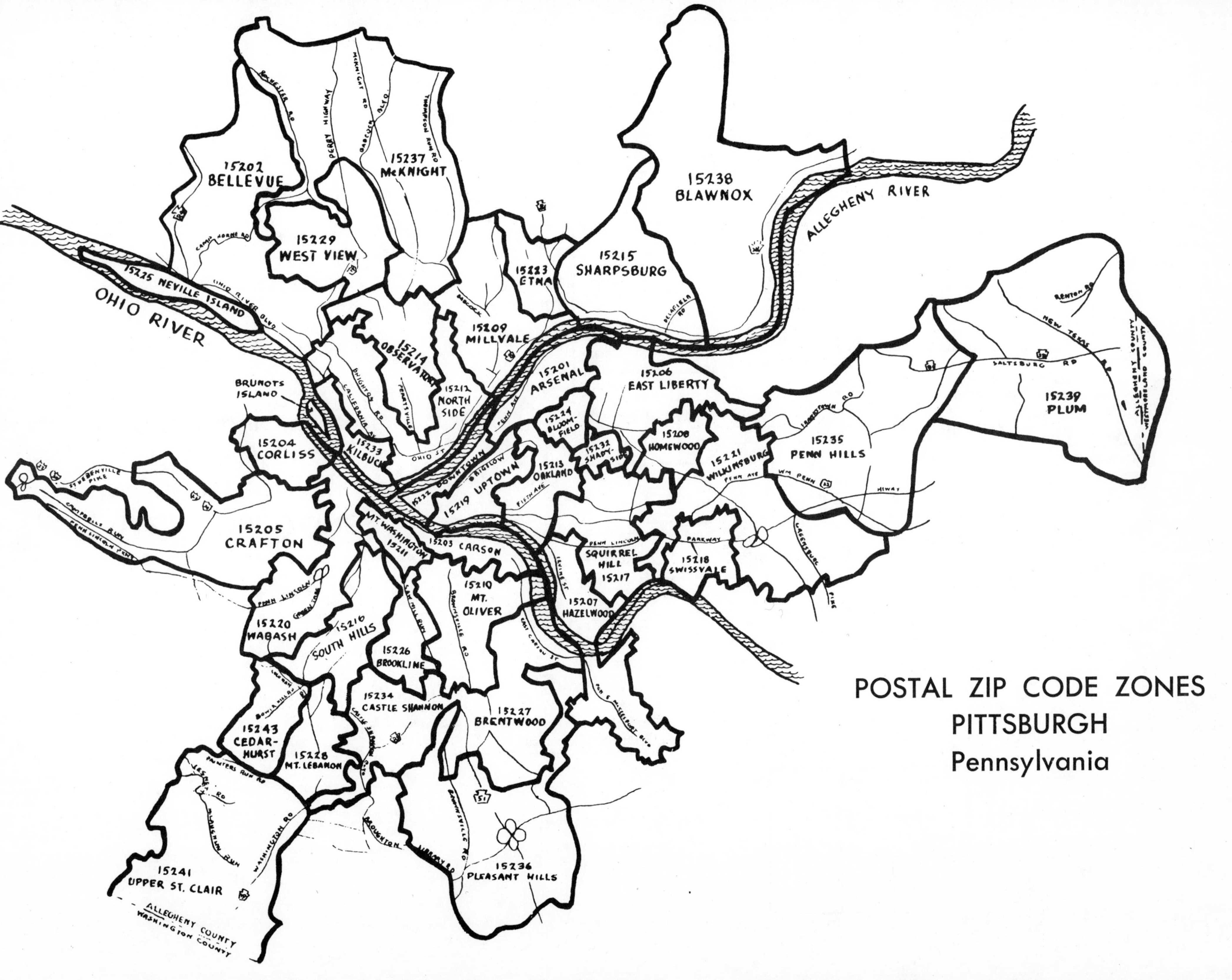

POSTAL ZIP CODE ZONES
DENVER
Colorado

802+ TWO DIGITS SHOWN = ZIP CODE

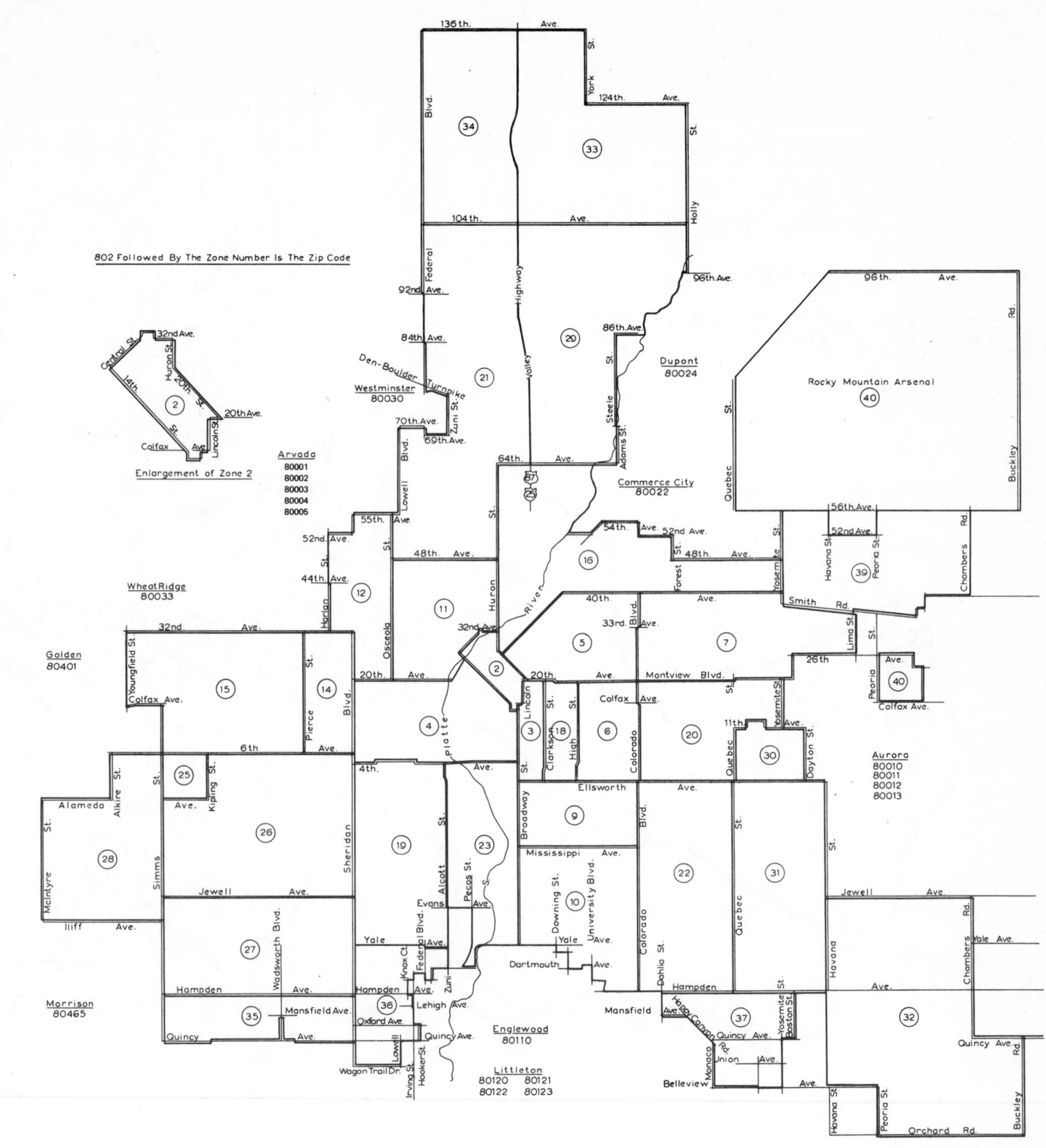

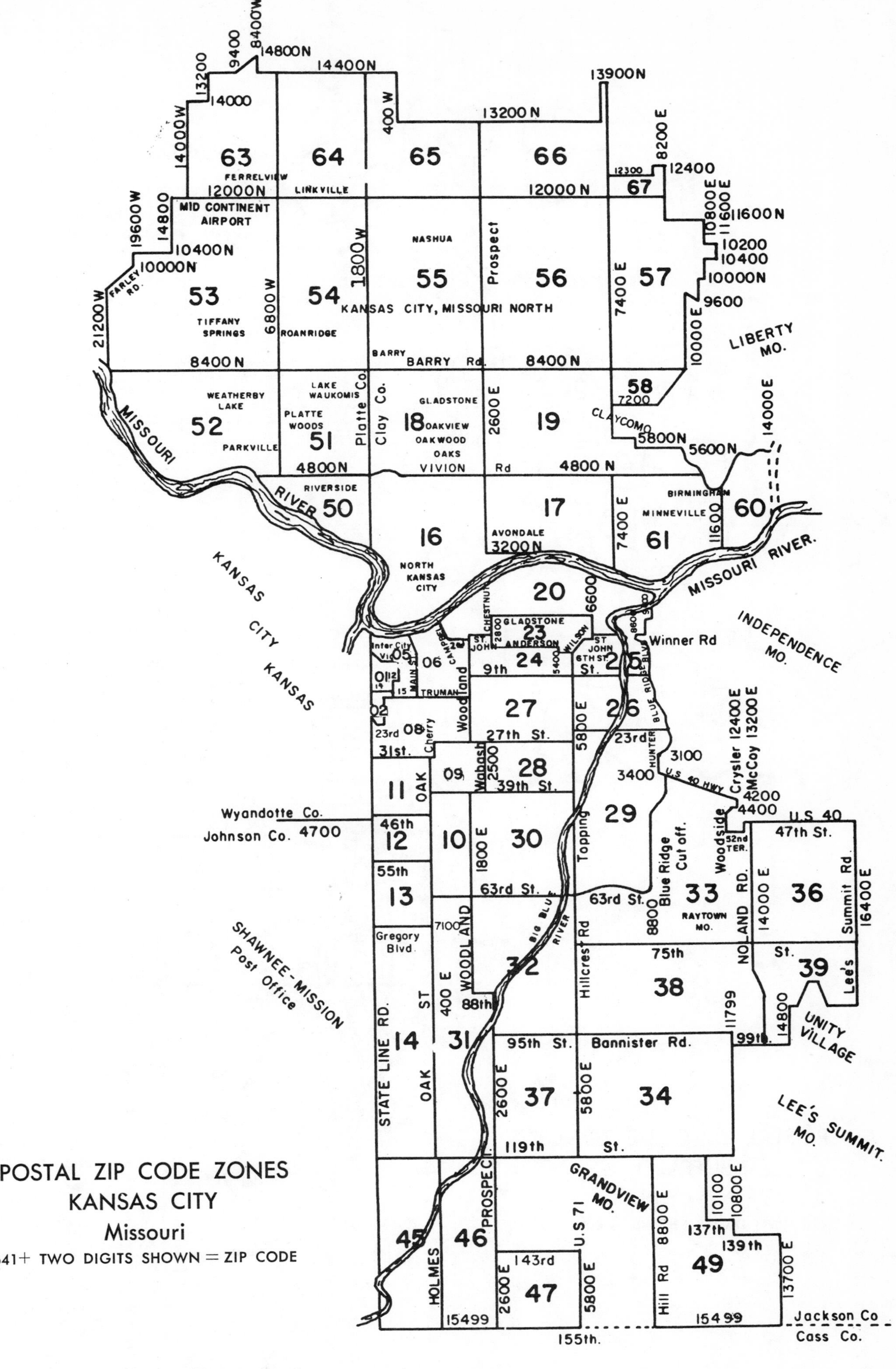

POSTAL ZIP CODE ZONES
KANSAS CITY
Missouri
641+ TWO DIGITS SHOWN = ZIP CODE

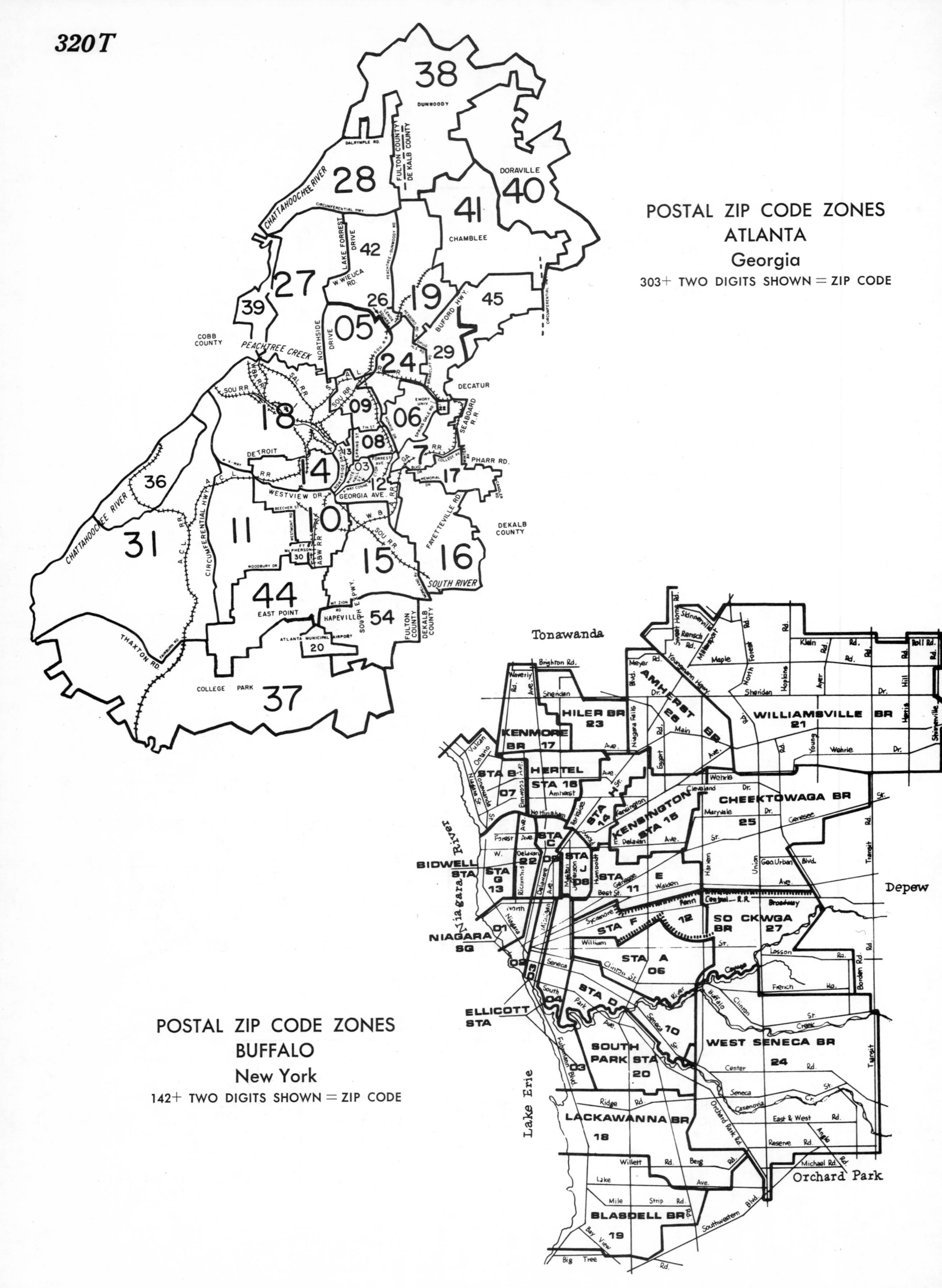

POSTAL ZIP CODE ZONES
ATLANTA
Georgia
303+ TWO DIGITS SHOWN = ZIP CODE
38
DUNWOODY
28
DALRYMPLE RD.
FULTON COUNTY
DE KALB COUNTY
CHATTAHOOCHEE RIVER
CIRCUMFERENTIAL HWY.
DORAVILLE
40
41
CHAMBLEE
42
LAKE FORREST DRIVE
W. WIEUCA RD.
27
39
19
45
26
05
NORTHSIDE DRIVE
BUFORD HWY.
COBB COUNTY
PEACHTREE CREEK
24
29
DECATUR
SOU RR
18
09
06
EMORY UNIV.
SEABOARD R.R.
08
DETROIT
13
7
PHARR RD.
14
03
17
36
12
WESTVIEW DR.
GEORGIA AVE.
10
CHATTAHOOCHEE RIVER
31
11
CIRCUMFERENTIAL HWY.
A.C.L. RR
FT. McPHERSON
30
15
16
FAYETTEVILLE RD.
DEKALB COUNTY
SOUTH RIVER
WOODBURY DR.
44
EAST POINT
MT. ZION RD.
HAPEVILLE
54
FULTON COUNTY
DEKALB COUNTY
ATLANTA MUNICIPAL AIRPORT
20
THAXTON RD.
COLLEGE PARK
37
POSTAL ZIP CODE ZONES
BUFFALO
New York
142+ TWO DIGITS SHOWN = ZIP CODE
Tonawanda
KENMORE BR 17
HILER BR 23
AMHERST BR 26
WILLIAMSVILLE BR 21
STA B 07
HERTEL STA 16
STA H 14
KENSINGTON STA 15
CHEEKTOWAGA BR 25
Niagara River
BIDWELL STA
STA G 13
22
STA C 09
STA J 08
STA E 11
Depew
NIAGARA SQ
01
STA F 12
SO CKWGA BR 27
02
03
STA A 06
ELLICOTT STA
04
STA D
10
SOUTH PARK STA 20
WEST SENECA BR 24
Lake Erie
03
LACKAWANNA BR 18
Orchard Park
BLASDELL BR 19

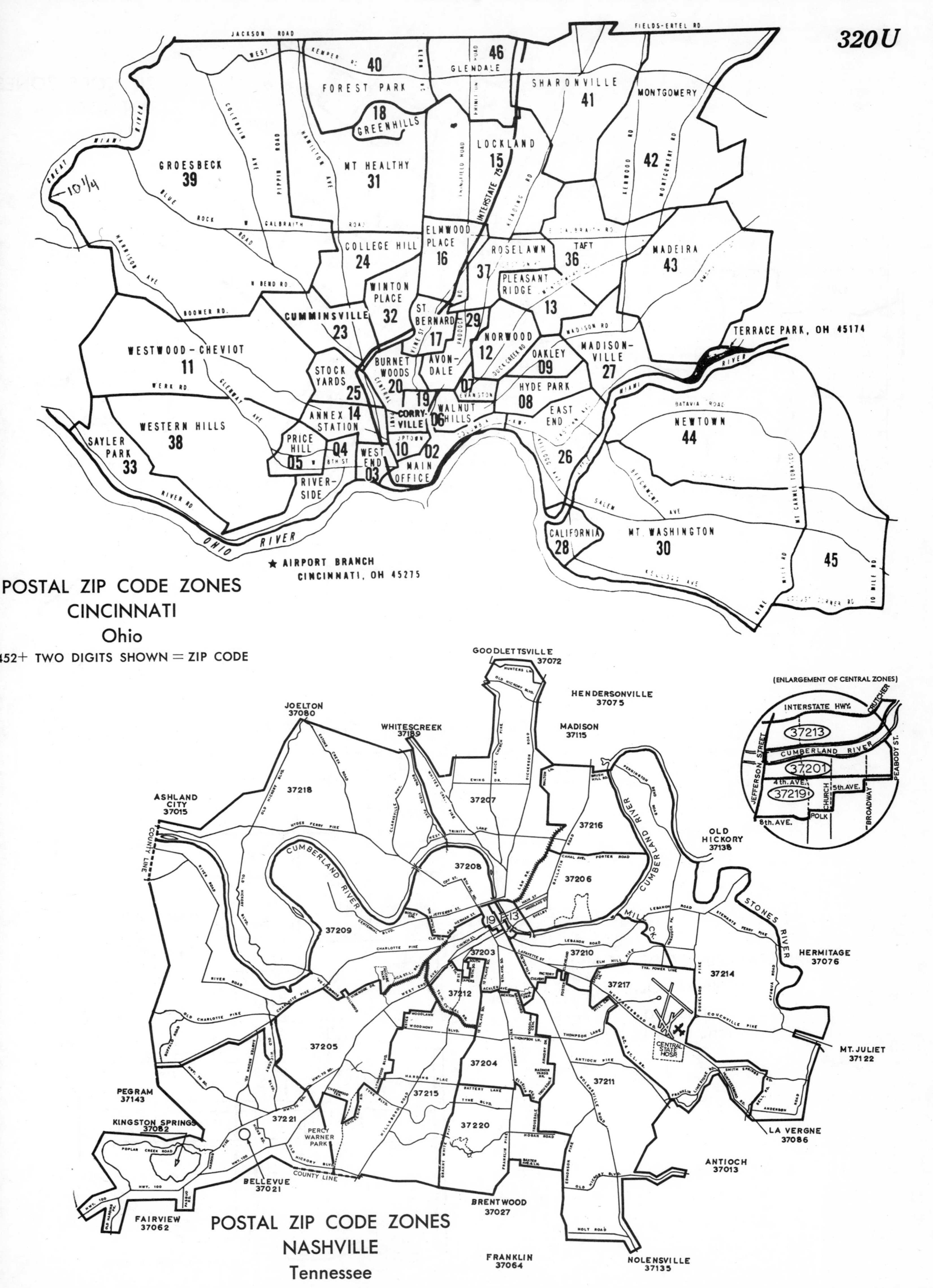
POSTAL ZIP CODE ZONES
CINCINNATI
Ohio
452+ TWO DIGITS SHOWN = ZIP CODE
JACKSON ROAD
FIELDS-ERTEL RD
FOREST PARK 40
GLENDALE 46
SHARONVILLE 41
MONTGOMERY
GREENHILLS 18
GROESBECK 39
MT HEALTHY 31
LOCKLAND 15
42
GREAT MIAMI RIVER
10 1/4
INTERSTATE 75
ELMWOOD PLACE 16
COLLEGE HILL 24
ROSELAWN
37
TAFT 36
MADEIRA 43
PLEASANT RIDGE
WINTON PLACE 32
13
CUMMINSVILLE 23
ST BERNARD 17
29
NORWOOD 12
OAKLEY 09
MADISON-VILLE 27
TERRACE PARK, OH 45174
WESTWOOD-CHEVIOT 11
STOCK YARDS 25
BURNET WOODS 20
AVON-DALE
07
HYDE PARK 08
ANNEX STATION 14
19
CORRY-VILLE
06
WALNUT HILLS
EAST END
NEWTOWN 44
WESTERN HILLS 38
SAYLER PARK 33
PRICE HILL 05
04
WEST END 03
10
02
MAIN OFFICE
RIVER-SIDE
26
CALIFORNIA 28
MT. WASHINGTON 30
45
OHIO RIVER
★ AIRPORT BRANCH CINCINNATI, OH 45275
POSTAL ZIP CODE ZONES
NASHVILLE
Tennessee
GOODLETTSVILLE 37072
HENDERSONVILLE 37075
JOELTON 37080
WHITESCREEK 37189
MADISON 37115
ASHLAND CITY 37015
37218
37207
37216
OLD HICKORY 37138
CUMBERLAND RIVER
37208
37206
COUNTY LINE
37209
19
13
37210
STONES RIVER
HERMITAGE 37076
37203
37212
37217
37214
CENTRAL STATE HOSP.
37205
37204
37211
MT. JULIET 37122
PEGRAM 37143
37215
KINGSTON SPRINGS 37082
37221
PERCY WARNER PARK
37220
LA VERGNE 37086
ANTIOCH 37013
BELLEVUE 37021
BRENTWOOD 37027
FAIRVIEW 37062
FRANKLIN 37064
NOLENSVILLE 37135
(ENLARGEMENT OF CENTRAL ZONES)
INTERSTATE HWY.
37213
CUMBERLAND RIVER
37201
37219
JEFFERSON STREET
4th. AVE.
5th. AVE.
CHURCH
8th. AVE.
POLK
BROADWAY
PEABODY ST.
CRUTCHER

POSTAL ZIP CODE ZONES SAN JOSE California

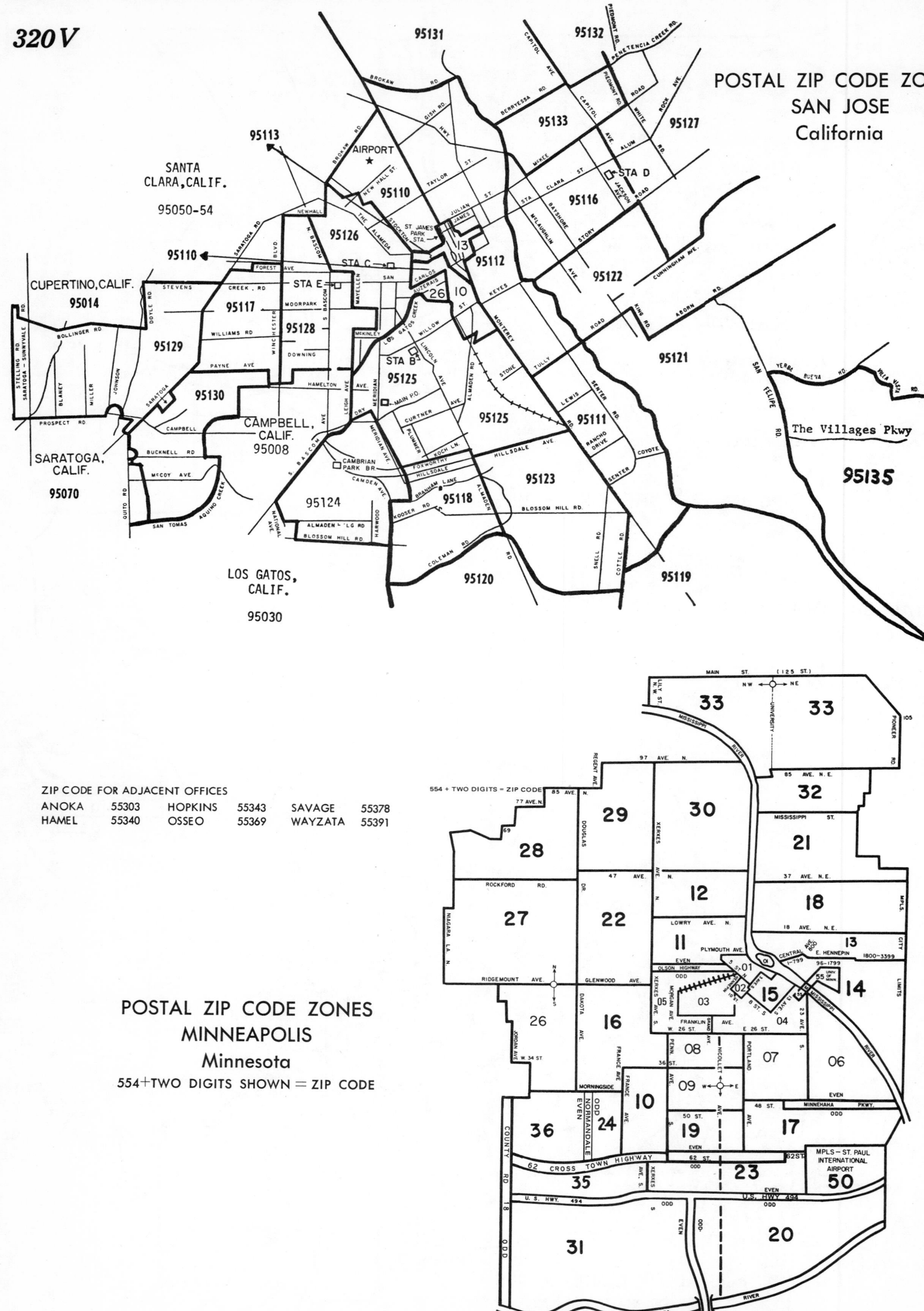

ZIP CODE FOR ADJACENT OFFICES

ANOKA	55303	HOPKINS	55343	SAVAGE	55378
HAMEL	55340	OSSEO	55369	WAYZATA	55391

POSTAL ZIP CODE ZONES MINNEAPOLIS Minnesota

554+TWO DIGITS SHOWN = ZIP CODE

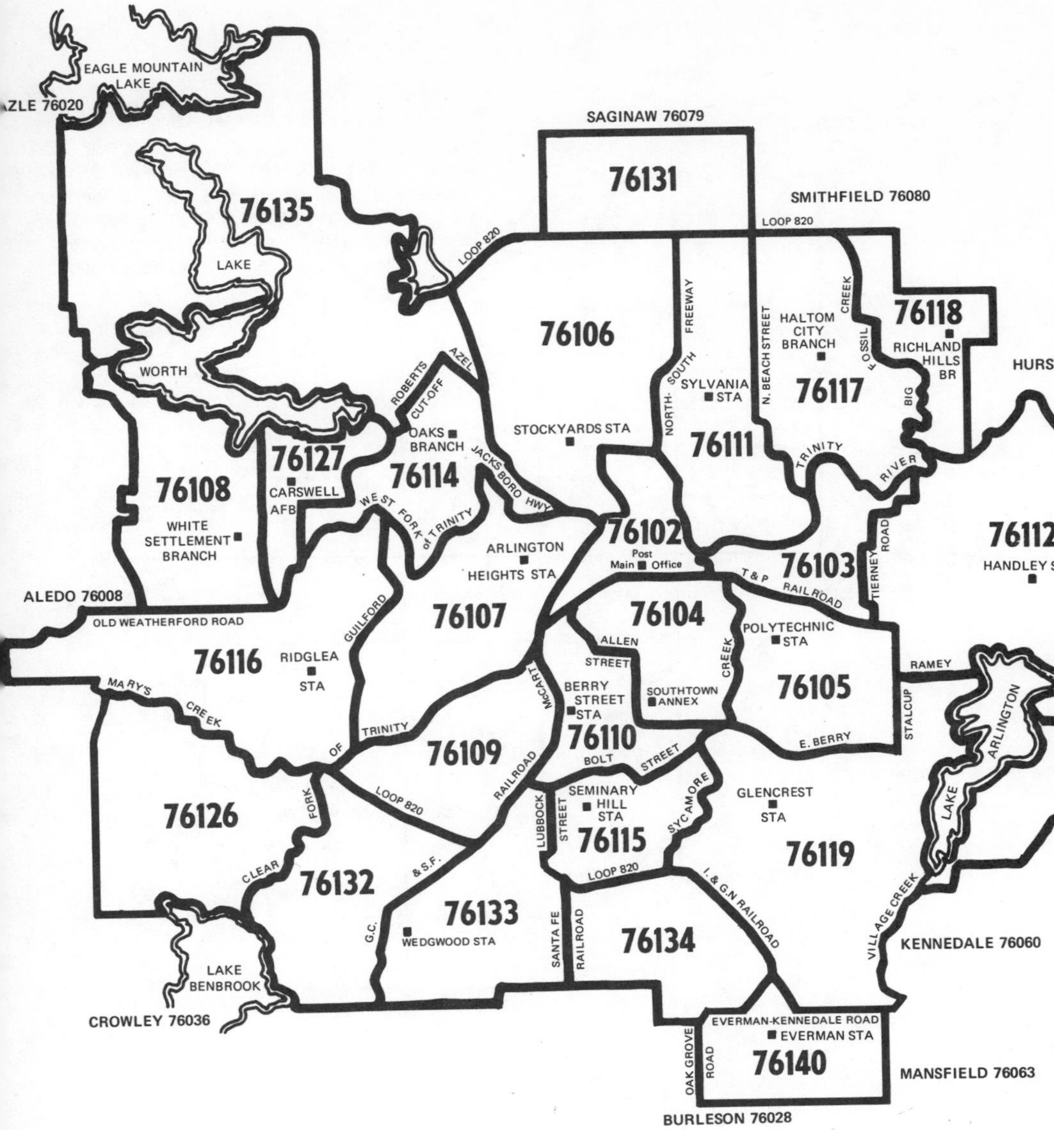

EAGLE MOUNTAIN LAKE
AZLE 76020
SAGINAW 76079
76131
SMITHFIELD 76080
LOOP 820
76135
LAKE
WORTH
76106
HALTOM CITY BRANCH
76118
RICHLAND HILLS BR
BEDFORD 76021
HURST 76053
EULESS 76039
SYLVANIA STA
76117
76111
STOCKYARDS STA
76108
WHITE SETTLEMENT BRANCH
76127
CARSWELL AFB
OAKS BRANCH
76114
JACKSBORO HWY
WEST FORK of TRINITY
76102
Post Main Office
76103
76112
HANDLEY STA
76012
76011
ARLINGTON HEIGHTS STA
ALEDO 76008
OLD WEATHERFORD ROAD
76107
76104
POLYTECHNIC STA
76105
76116
RIDGLEA STA
BERRY STREET STA
SOUTHTOWN ANNEX
76110
76109
76013
MAIN POST OFFICE
76010
T. & P. RAILROAD
ARKANSAS LANE
76016
76015
76014
76126
SEMINARY HILL STA
76115
GLENCREST STA
76119
76132
76133
WEDGWOOD STA
76134
LAKE BENBROOK
CROWLEY 76036
KENNEDALE 76060
EVERMAN-KENNEDALE ROAD
EVERMAN STA
76140
MANSFIELD 76063
BURLESON 76028

POSTAL ZIP CODE ZONES
FORT WORTH and ARLINGTON
Texas

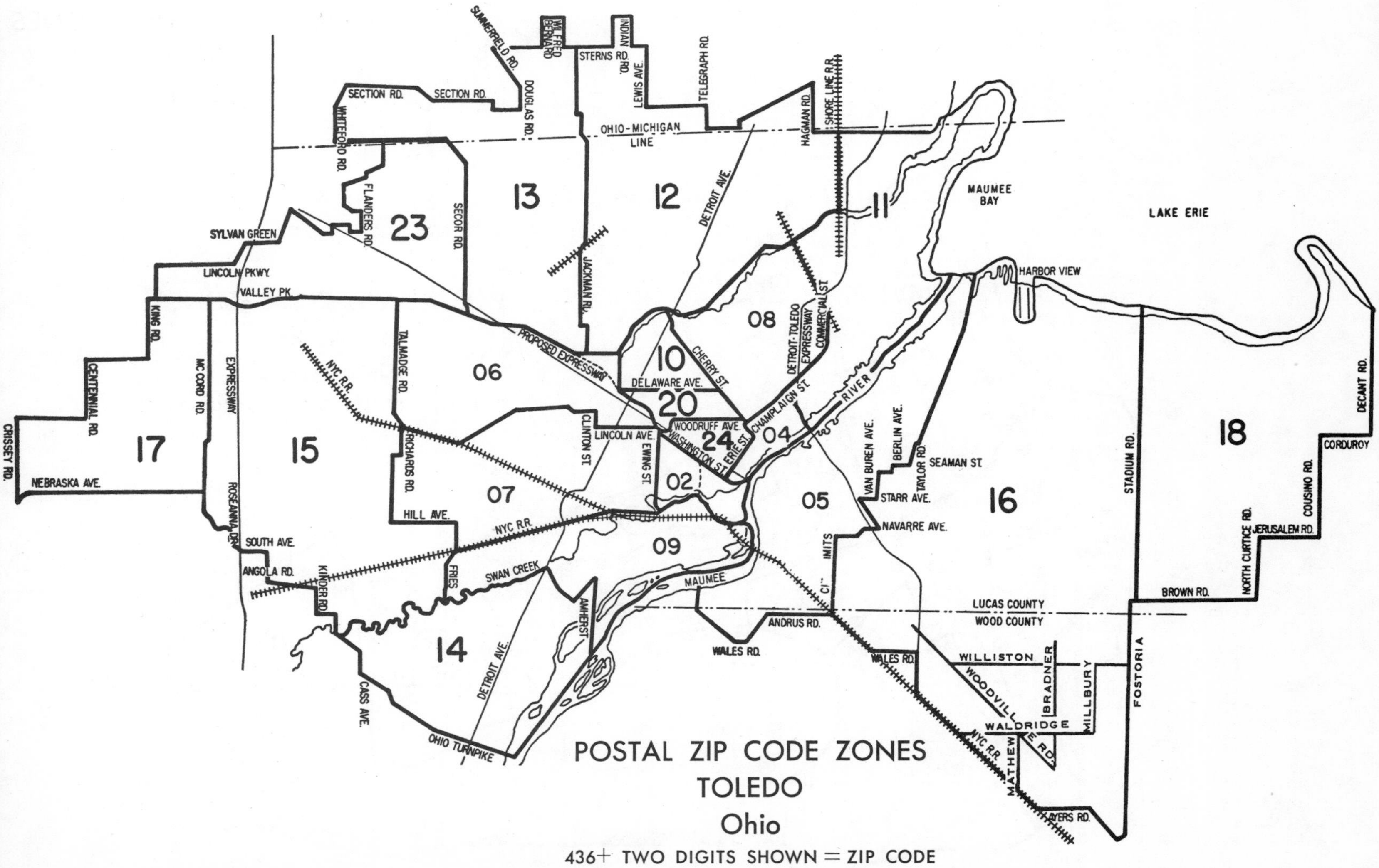

SECTION RD.
OHIO-MICHIGAN LINE
13
12
23
11
MAUMEE BAY
LAKE ERIE
HARBOR VIEW
08
06
10
20
17
15
24
04
02
07
05
16
18
09
14
LUCAS COUNTY
WOOD COUNTY

POSTAL ZIP CODE ZONES
TOLEDO
Ohio

436+ TWO DIGITS SHOWN = ZIP CODE

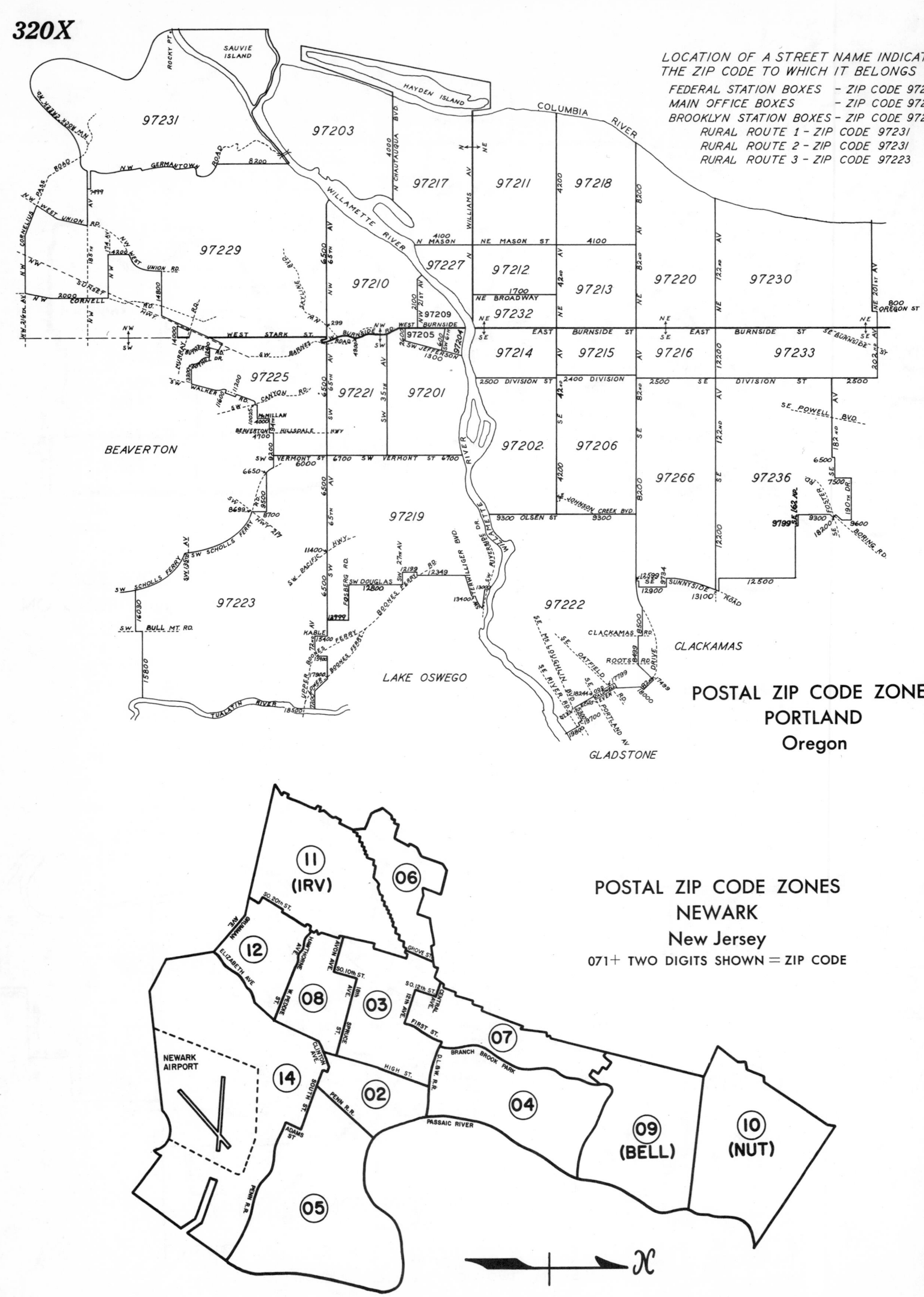

LOCATION OF A STREET NAME INDICATES THE ZIP CODE TO WHICH IT BELONGS
FEDERAL STATION BOXES - ZIP CODE 97207
MAIN OFFICE BOXES - ZIP CODE 97208
BROOKLYN STATION BOXES - ZIP CODE 97242
RURAL ROUTE 1 - ZIP CODE 97231
RURAL ROUTE 2 - ZIP CODE 97231
RURAL ROUTE 3 - ZIP CODE 97223
POSTAL ZIP CODE ZONES
PORTLAND
Oregon
POSTAL ZIP CODE ZONES
NEWARK
New Jersey
071+ TWO DIGITS SHOWN = ZIP CODE

INDEX OF THE WORLD

Introduction

This index is a directory to the atlas as a whole. It contains an alphabetical listing of the major political divisions (countries and administrative subdivisions, i.e., states, provinces, departments), principal cities and towns, and geographical features, such as mountains, rivers, bays, islands, shown on the maps contained in this atlas.

Entries are generally indexed to the map or inset having the largest scale, but in some cases, where the entry has equal coverage or is important to its surroundings on more than one map, more than one reference is given.

Each entry gives the political division in which it is located, or in the case of certain geographical features the appropriate continent or regional name, and the page number of the map on which the name will be found. The user who is unfamiliar with a place name will thus be able to identify the political division to which it belongs and to locate quickly the appropriate map or maps.

Once having found the map listed in this index, the user will easily find the place name on the map by first locating it in the accompanying map index. Here the user will find the necessary index key reference. When there is more than one place of the same name on the same map, only one reference is given. The individual map index will give the multiple listings of names and key references. A glance at adjacent pages will show whether there are additional maps on which the place name may be found, by referring to the accompanying index or by looking in the same relative location on the map.

The abbreviations for the political division names and geographical terms are explained in the glossary in the front of the atlas. In some cases place names have been shortened here. The full name will be found in the individual index accompanying the map itself.

A

Aa (river), Switz., 39
Aabenraa, Den., 21
Aachen, W. Ger., 22
Aalborg, Den., 21
Aalen, W. Ger., 22
Aalst, Belg., 27
Äänekoski, Fin., 18
Aarau, Switz., 39
Aare (river), Switz., 39
Aargau (canton), Switz., 39
Aarhus, Den., 21
Aba, Nigeria, 106
Abacaxis (riv.), Braz., 132
Abadan, Iran, 66
Abadeh, Iran, 66
Abadla, Alg., 106
Abaetetuba, Braz., 132
Abaiang (atoll), Gilb. & Ell. Is., 87
Abajo (mts.), Utah, 304
Abakan, U.S.S.R., 48
Abancay, Peru, 128
Abarquh, Iran, 66
Abashiri, Japan, 81
Abau, Papua, 85
Abaya (lake), Eth., 111
Abbai (riv.), Eth., 111
Abbe (lake), Africa, 111
Abbeville, Ala., 194
Abbeville, France, 28
Abbeville, La., 238
Abbeville, S.C., 296
Abbeyfeale, Ire., 17
Abbottabad, Pak., 68
Abdanan, Iran, 66
Abdulino, U.S.S.R., 52
Abécher, Chad, 111
Abemama (atoll), Gilb. & Ell. Is., 87
Abengourou, Ivory Coast, 106
Abeokuta, Nigeria, 106
Aberaeron, Wales, 13
Aberdare, Wales, 13
Aberdeen, Md., 245
Aberdeen, Miss., 256
Aberdeen (lake), N.W.T., 187
Aberdeen (county), Scot., 15
Aberdeen, Scot., 15
Aberdeen, S. Dak., 298
Aberdeen, Wash., 310
Aberfeldy, Scot., 15
Abergavenny, Wales, 13
Abertillery, Wales, 13
Aberystwyth, Wales, 13
Abha, Saudi Ar., 59
Ab-i-Diz (river), Iran, 66
Abidjan (cap.), Ivory Coast, 106
Abilene, Kans., 232
Abilene, Tex., 302
Abingdon, Eng., 13
Abingdon, Ill., 222
Abingdon, Va., 307
Abington, Pa., 294
Abitibi (lake), Ont., 177
Abitibi (riv.), Ont., 177
Abkhaz A.S.S.R., U.S.S.R., 52
Abnub, U.A.R., 111
Åbo (Turku), Fin., 18
Abomey, Dahomey, 106
Abony, Hung., 41
Abor (hills), India, 68
Abqaiq, Saudi Ar., 59
Abra (prov.), Phil. Is., 82
Abraham Lincoln Birthplace Nat'l Hist. Site, Ky., 237
Abruzzi (reg.), Italy, 34
Absecon, N. J., 273
Abu, India, 68
Abu 'Arish, Saudi Ar., 59
Abu Dara, Ras (cape), Sudan, 111
Abu Dhabi, Tr. States, 59
Abu Hadriya, Saudi Ar., 59
Abu Hamed, Sudan, 111
Abu Kemal, Syria, 63
Abu-mad (cape), Saudi Ar., 59
Abu Road, India, 68
Abu Shagara, Ras (cape), Sudan, 111
Abu Zabad, Sudan, 111
Abydos (ruins), Turkey, 63
Abydos (ruins), U.A.R., 111
Acadia Nat'l Park, Maine, 242
Acadia Valley, Alta., 182
Acajutla, El Sal., 154
Acámbaro, Mex., 150
Acaponeta, Mex., 150
Acapulco, Mex., 150
Acarigua, Venez., 124
Acatlán, Mex., 150
Acatzingo, Mex., 150
Acayucan, Mex., 150
Accra (cap.), Ghana, 106
Accrington, Eng., 10
Achacachi, Bol., 136
Achalpur, India, 68
Achill (head), Ire., 17
Achill (isl.), Ire., 17
Achnasheen, Scot., 15
Acireale, Italy, 34
Acklins (isl.), Bah. Is., 156
Aconcagua (prov.), Chile, 138
Aconcagua (mt.), Arg., 143
Aconchi, Mex., 150
Acoyapa, Nic., 154
Acqui Terme, Italy, 34
Acre (state), Braz., 132
Acre (riv.), Braz., 132
Acre, Israel, 65
Acri, Italy, 34
Acton, Ont., 177
Actopan, Mex., 150
Ada, Minn., 254
Ada, Ohio, 284
Ada, Okla., 288
Adaja (riv.), Spain, 33
Adam, Oman, 59
Adamawa (reg.), Africa, 115
Adam's (peak), Ceylon, 68
Adams, Mass., 249
Adams (mt.), Wash., 310
Adam's Bridge (shoals), Asia, 68
Adams Nat'l Hist. Site, Mass., 249
Adamstown (cap.), Pitcairn Is., 87
Adana (prov.), Turkey, 63
Adana, Turkey, 63
Adapazarı, Turkey, 63
Adare (cape), Ant., 5
Adda (riv.), Italy, 34
Addis Ababa (cap.), Eth., 111
Addis Alam, Eth., 111
Addison, Ill., 222
Ad Diwaniya, Iraq, 66
Adel, Ga., 216
Adelaide (isl.), Ant., 5
Adelaide (cap.), S. Austral., 94
Adelaide (pen.), N.W.T., 187
Adelaide River, Austral., 93
Adelanto, Calif., 204
Adélie Coast (reg.), Ant., 5
Aden (gulf), 54
Aden (cap.), P.D.R. Yemen, 59
Adige (riv.), Italy, 34
Adilabad, India, 68
Adimi, U.S.S.R., 48
Adirondack (mts.), N.Y., 276
Adıyaman (prov.), Turkey, 63
Adjuntas, P. Rico, 161
Adlavik (isls.), Newf., 166
Admiralty (gulf), W. Austral., 92
Admiralty (isls.), Terr. N.G., 87
Ado, Nigeria, 106
Adoni, India, 68
Adour (riv.), France, 28
Adra, Spain, 33
Adrano, Italy, 34
Adrar, Alg., 106
Adrar (reg.), Mauritania, 106
Adrar des Iforas (plat.), Africa, 106
Adria, Italy, 34
Adrian, Mich., 250
Adriatic (sea), Europe, 7
Adwa, Eth., 111
Adygey Aut. Obl., U.S.S.R., 52
Adzhar A.S.S.R., U.S.S.R., 52
Aegean (sea), 45
Aegean Islands (div.), Greece, 45
Afars & Issas, Terr. of the, 111
Afghanistan, 68
Åfjord, Norway, 18
Afmadu, Somalia, 115
Africa, 102
Afton, Wyo., 319
Afyon, Turkey, 63
Afyon-Karahisar (prov.), Turkey, 63
Agadès, Niger, 106
Agadir, Mor., 106
Agaña (cap.), Guam, 87
Agartala, India, 68
Agate Fossil Beds Nat'l Mon., Nebr., 264
Agats, Indonesia, 85
Agatti (isl.), India, 68
Agboville, Ivory Coast, 106
Agdam, U.S.S.R., 52
Agde, France, 28
Agen, France, 28
Aginsk Nat'l Okrug, U.S.S.R., 48
Aginskoye, U.S.S.R., 48
Agiobampo (bay), Mex., 150
Agira, Italy, 34
Agordat, Eth., 111
Agra, India, 68
Agraciada, Urug., 145
Ağrı (prov.), Turkey, 63
Agrigento (prov.), Italy, 34
Agrigento, Italy, 34
Agrihan (isl.), Pac. Is., 87
Agrínion, Greece, 45
Agryz, U.S.S.R., 52
Aguada, P. Rico, 161
Aguadas, Col., 126
Aguadilla (dist.), P. Rico, 161
Aguadilla, P. Rico, 161
Agua Dulce, Mex., 150
Aguadulce, Pan., 154
Agualeguas, Mex., 150
Aguán (riv.), Hond., 154
Aguanaval (riv.), Mex., 150
Aguanus (riv.), Canada, 174
Agua Prieta, Mex., 150
Aguarico (riv.), S. Amer., 128
Aguas Buenas, P. Rico, 161
Aguascalientes (state), Mex., 150
Aguascalientes, Mex., 150
Águeda, Port., 33
Aguilar, Colo., 208
Aguilar, Spain, 33
Aguilas, Spain, 33
Aguililla, Mex., 150
Aguja (pt.), Peru, 128
Agulhas (cape), S. Afr., 118
Agusan del Norte (prov.), Phil. Is., 82
Agusan del Sur (prov.), Phil. Is., 82
Ahaggar (range), Alg., 106
Ahau, Fiji, 87
Ahlen, W. Ger., 22
Ahmadabad, India, 68
Ahmadnagar, India, 68
Ahmadpur East, Pak., 68
Ahoskie, N.C., 281
Ahrensburg, W. Ger., 22
Ahuacatlán, Mex., 150
Ahuachapán, El Sal., 154
Ahuás, Hond., 154
Ahurei, Fr. Poly., 87
Åhus, Sweden, 18
Ahvenanmaa (dept.), Fin., 18
Ahvenanmaa (isls.), Fin., 18
Ahwar, P.D.R. Yemen, 59
Ahwaz, Iran, 66
Aibonito, P. Rico, 161
Aichi (prefecture), Japan, 81
Aiea, Hawaii, 218
Aiguá, Urug., 145
Aigun (Aihui), China, 77
Aijal, India, 68
Aiken, S.C., 296
Ailinglapalap (atoll), Pac. Is., 87
Ailuk (atoll), Pac. Is., 87
Ain (dept.), France, 28
Ain (riv.), France, 28
Aina Haina, Hawaii, 218
'Ain al Mubarrak, Saudi Ar., 59
Aïn-Béïda, Alg., 106
Aïn-Sefra, Alg., 106
Ainsworth, Nebr., 264
Aïn-Témouchent, Alg., 106
Aïoun el Atrous, Mauritania, 106
Air (mts.), Niger, 106
Airdrie, Scot., 15
Aire (riv.), Eng., 13
Air Force (isl.), N.W.T., 187
Air Force Acad., Colo., 208
Aisén (prov.), Chile, 138
Aishihik, Yukon, 187
Aisne (dept.), France, 28
Aisne (riv.), France, 28
Aitape, Terr. N.G., 85
Aitkin, Minn., 254
Aitutaki (atoll), Cook Is., 87
Aiud, Rum., 45
Aix-en-Provence, France, 28
Aix-les-Bains, France, 28
Aíyina, Greece, 45
Aíyion, Greece, 45
Aizuwakamatsu, Japan, 81
Ajaccio, France, 28
Ajaccio (gulf), France, 28
Ajalpan, Mex., 150
Ajanta, India, 68
Ajax, Ont., 177
Ajedabia, Libya, 111
Ajka, Hung., 41
'Ajman, Tr. States, 59
Ajmer, India, 68
Ajo, Ariz., 198
Ak (range), Turkey, 63
Akabiri, Japan, 81
Akarai (mts.), Guyana, 131
Akashi, Japan, 81
Aken, E. Ger., 22
Akershus (county), Norway, 18
Aketi, Dem. Rep. of the Congo, 115
Akhaltsikhe, U.S.S.R., 52
Akhdar, Jebel (mts.), Libya, 111
Akhdar, Jebel (range), Oman, 59
Akhisar, Turkey, 63
Akhtopol, Bulg., 45
Akhtubinsk, U.S.S.R., 52
Akhtyrka, U.S.S.R., 52
Akimiski (isl.), N.W.T., 187
Akim Oda, Ghana, 106
Akita (prefecture), Japan, 81
Akita, Japan, 81
Akjoujt, Mauritania, 106
Akkerman (Belgorod-Dnestrovskiy), U.S.S.R., 52
Aklan (prov.), Phil. Is., 82
Aklavik, N.W.T., 187
Akmolinsk (Tselinograd), U.S.S.R., 48
Akobo (riv.), Africa, 111
Akola, India, 68
Akpatok (isl.), N.W.T., 187
Akrítas (cape), Greece, 45
Akron, N.Y., 276
Akron, Ohio, 284
Akşehir, Turkey, 63
Aksha, U.S.S.R., 48
Aksum, Eth., 111
Aktí (pen.), Greece, 45
Aktyubinsk, U.S.S.R., 48
Akureyri, Ice., 21
Ål, Norway, 18
Alabama (riv.), Ala., 194
Alabama (state), U.S., 194
Alabat (isl.), Phil. Is., 82
Alagir, U.S.S.R., 52
Alagoas (state), Braz., 132
Alagoinhas, Braz., 132
Alagón, Spain, 33
Al Ahqaf (Bahr es Safi) (des.), Arabia, 59
Alajuela, C. Rica, 154
Alakol' (lake), U.S.S.R., 48
Alameda, Calif., 204
Alamikamba, Nic., 154
Alamo, Mex., 150
Alamo, Tex., 302
Alamogordo, N. Mex., 274
Alamo Hts., Tex., 302
Alamos, Mex., 150
Alamosa, Colo., 208
Åland (isls.), Fin., 18
Alanje, Pan., 154
Alanya, Turkey, 63
Alaotra (lake), Malag. Rep., 118
Alaşehir, Turkey, 63
Alashan (des.), China, 77
Alaska (gulf), Alaska, 196
Alaska (pen.), Alaska, 196
Alaska (range), Alaska, 196
Alaska (state), U.S., 196
Alassio, Italy, 34
Alatri, Italy, 34
Alatyr', U.S.S.R., 52
Alausí, Ecua., 128
Álava (prov.), Spain, 33
Alavus, Fin., 18
Alayor, Spain, 33
Al 'Aziziya, Iraq, 66
Alba, Italy, 34
Alba Iulia, Rum., 45
Albacete (prov.), Spain, 33
Albacete, Spain, 33
Albanel (lake), Que., 174
Albania, 45
Albano (lake), Italy, 34
Albano Laziale, Italy, 34
Albany, Calif., 204
Albany, Ga., 216
Albany, Jam., 158
Albany (cap.), N.Y., 276
Albany, N.Z., 101
Albany (riv.), Ont., 177
Albany, Oreg., 291
Albany, P.E.I., 169
Albany, W. Austral., 92
Albany N.A.S., Ga., 216
Albay (prov.), Phil. Is., 82
Albemarle (pt.), Ecuador, 128
Albemarle, N.C., 281
Alberni, Br. Col., 184
Albert (lake), Africa, 115
Albert, France, 28
Alberta (mt.), Alta., 182
Alberta (prov.), Canada, 182
Albert Lea, Minn., 254
Alberton, P.E.I., 169
Alberton, S. Afr., 118
Albertville, Ala., 194
Albertville, France, 28
Albi, France, 28
Albia, Iowa, 229
Albina, Surinam, 131
Albino, Italy, 34
Albion, Mich., 250
Albion, Nebr., 264
Albion, N.Y., 276
Alborán (isl.), Spain, 33
Albox, Spain, 33
Albuquerque, N. Mex., 274
Alburquerque, Spain, 33
Albury, N.S.W., 97
Albury, N.Z., 101
Alcácer do Sal, Port., 33
Alcalá de Chivert, Spain, 33
Alcalá de Guadaira, Spain, 33
Alcalá de Henares, Spain, 33
Alcalá de los Gazules, Spain, 33
Alcalá la Real, Spain, 33
Alcamo, Italy, 34
Alcanar, Spain, 33
Alcañiz, Spain, 33
Alcántara, Port., 33
Alcántara, Spain, 33
Alcantarilla, Spain, 33
Alcaraz (mts.), Spain, 33
Alcaudete, Spain, 33
Alcázar de San Juan, Spain, 33
Alcira, Spain, 33
Alcoa, Tenn., 237
Alcobaça, Port., 33
Alcoy, Spain, 33
Alcudia (bay), Spain, 33
Aldabra (isls.), Br. Indian Ocean Terr., 118
Aldama, Mex., 150
Aldan, Pa., 294
Aldan, U.S.S.R., 48
Aldan (plat.), U.S.S.R., 48
Aldeia Nova, Port., 33
Alderney (isl.), Chan. Is., 13
Aldershot, Eng., 13
Aldershot, N.S., 168
Aldridge-Brownhills, Eng., 10
Aledo, Ill., 222
Aleg, Mauritania, 106
Alegrete, Braz., 132
'Aleih, Leb., 63
Aleksandriya, U.S.S.R., 52
Aleksandrov, U.S.S.R., 52
Aleksandrovsk-Sakhalinskiy, U.S.S.R., 48
Alekseyevka, U.S.S.R., 52
Aleksin, U.S.S.R., 52
Aleksinac, Yugo., 45
Alemania, Arg., 143
Além Paraíba, Braz., 135
Alençon, France, 28
Aleppo (prov.), Syria, 63
Aleppo, Syria, 63
Alert, N.W.T., 187
Alert Bay, Br. Col., 184
Alès, France, 28
Alessandria (prov.), Italy, 34
Alessandria, Italy, 34
Ålesund, Norway, 18
Aleutian (isls.), Alaska, 196
Alexander (arch.), Alaska, 196
Alexander (isl.), Ant., 5
Alexander, Minn., 254
Alexander City, Ala., 194
Alexandra, N.Z., 101
Alexandra (falls), N.W.T., 187
Alexandra Land (isl.), U.S.S.R., 48
Alexandretta (Iskenderun), Turkey, 63
Alexandria, Ind., 227
Alexandria, La., 238
Alexandria, Minn., 254
Alexandria, Rum., 45
Alexandria, Scot., 15
Alexandria, S. Afr., 118
Alexandria, U.A.R., 111
Alexandria, Va., 307
Alexandroúpolis, Greece, 45
Aleysk, U.S.S.R., 48
Al Falluja, Iraq, 66
Alfaro, Spain, 33
Alfatar, Bulg., 45
Alfeld, W. Ger., 22
Alfenas, Braz., 135
Alford, Scot., 15
Alfred, N.Y., 276
Alga, U.S.S.R., 48
Algarve (prov.), Port., 33
Algeciras, Spain, 33
Algemesí, Spain, 33
Algeria, 106
Algés, Port., 33
Alghero, Italy, 34
Algiers (cap.), Alg., 106
Algoa (bay), S. Afr., 118
Algoma, Wis., 317
Algona, Iowa, 229
Algonac, Mich., 250
Algonquin Prov. Park, Ont., 177
Alhama de Granada, Spain, 33
Alhama de Murcia, Spain, 33
Alhambra, Calif., 204
Al Hoceima, Mor., 106
Alhos Vedros, Port., 33
Ali-Bayramly, U.S.S.R., 52
Alicante (prov.), Spain, 33
Alicante, Spain, 33
Alice, Tex., 302
Alice Arm, Br. Col., 184
Alice Springs, N. Terr., 93
Aliceville, Ala., 194
Alicudi (isl.), Italy, 34
Aligarh, India, 68
Alingsås, Sweden, 18
Aliquippa, Pa., 294
Alivérion, Greece, 45
Aliwal North, S. Afr., 118
Aljezur, Port., 33
Aljojuca, Mex., 150
Aljustrel, Port., 33
Alkmaar, Neth., 27
Al Kufa, Iraq, 66
Al Kuwait (cap.), Kuwait, 66
Allahabad, India, 68
Allakh-Yun', U.S.S.R., 48
Allanmyo, Burma, 72
Allanwater, Ont., 175
Allaykha, U.S.S.R., 48
Allegan, Mich., 250
Allen (lake), Ire., 17
Allendale, N. J., 273
Allendale, S.C., 296
Allende, Mex., 150
Allen Park, Mich., 250
Allentown, Pa., 294
Alleppey, India, 68
Aller (riv.), W. Ger., 22
Allgäu Alps (mts.), Europe, 22
Alliance, Nebr., 264
Alliance, Ohio, 284
Allier (dept.), France, 28
Allier (riv.), France, 28
Allinge-Sandvig, Den., 21
Allingtown, Conn., 210
Allison Pk., Pa., 294
Al Lith, Saudi Ar., 59
Alloa, Scot., 15
Allouez, Brazil, 132
All Saints, Antigua, 161
Alma, Ga., 216
Alma, Mich., 250
Alma, Nebr., 264
Alma, Que., 172
Alma-Ata, U.S.S.R., 48
Almada, Port., 33
Almadén, Spain, 33
Almagro, Spain, 33
Almansa, Spain, 33
Almanzor (mt.), Spain, 33
Almanzora (riv.), Spain, 33
Almeirim, Port., 33
Almelo, Neth., 27
Almendralejo, Spain, 33
Almería (prov.), Spain, 33
Almería, Spain, 33
Almería (gulf), Spain, 33
Al'met'yevsk, U.S.S.R., 52
Älmhult, Sweden, 18
Almirante, Pan., 154
Almirós, Greece, 45
Almodóvar del Campo, Spain, 33
Almoloya, Mex., 150
Almonte, Spain, 33
Almora, India, 68
Almuñécar, Spain, 33
Alofi (cap.), Niue, 87
Álora, Spain, 33
Alor Setar, Malaysia, 72
Alorton, Ill., 222
Alpena, Mich., 250
Alpes-Maritimes (dept.), France, 28
Alpiarça, Port., 33
Alpine, Tex., 302
Alps (mts.), Europe, 7
Al Qaiyara, Iraq, 66
Al Qatn, P.D.R. Yemen, 59
Alsask, Sask., 181
Alsdorf, W. Ger., 22
Alsek (riv.), Yukon, 187
Alsip, Ill., 222
Alst (fjord), Norway, 18
Alsten (isl.), Norway, 18
Alta (riv.), Norway, 18
Altadena, Calif., 204
Alta Gracia, Arg., 143
Altagracia, Venez., 124
Altamira, Mex., 150
Altamont, Oreg., 291
Altar, Mex., 150
Altavista, Va., 307
Altay (mts.), Asia, 54
Altay (Yusun Bulak), Mong., 77
Alte (lake), Norway, 18
Altena, W. Ger., 22
Altenburg, E. Ger., 22
Altındağ, Turkey, 63
Altmark (reg.), E. Ger., 22
Altmühl (riv.), W. Ger., 22
Alto Alentjo (prov.), Port., 33
Alto Araguaia, Braz., 132
Alton, Ill., 222
Altona, Man., 179
Altona, Victoria, 97
Altona, W. Ger., 22
Altoona, Pa., 294
Alto Paraná (dept.), Par., 144
Alto Park, Ga., 216
Alto Ritacuva (mt.), Col., 126
Altotonga, Mex., 150
Alto Velo (chan.), Dom. Rep., 158
Altrincham, Eng., 10
Alturas, Calif., 204
Altus, Okla., 288
Altyn Tagh (mts.), China, 77
Alula, Somalia, 115
Alum Rock, Calif., 204
Alushta, U.S.S.R., 52
Alva, Okla., 288
Alva, Scot., 15
Alvarado, Mex., 150
Alvesta, Sweden, 18
Alvin, Tex., 302
Älvsborg (county), Sweden, 18
Älvsbyn, Sweden, 18
Alwar, India, 68
Alyth, Scot., 15
Alytus, U.S.S.R., 53
Alz (riv.), W. Ger., 22
Alzey, W. Ger., 22
Amadeus (lake), N. Terr., 93
'Amadiya, Iraq, 66
Amadora, Port., 33
Amagasaki, Japan, 81
Amakusa (isl.), Japan, 81
Åmål, Sweden, 18
Amaliás, Greece, 45
Amalner, India, 68
Amambaí, Braz., 132
Amambay (dept.), Par., 144
Amami (isls.), Japan, 81
Amami-O-Shima (isl.), Japan, 81
Amanos (mts.), Turkey, 63
Amapá (terr.), Braz., 132
Amapala, Hond., 154
Amaparí (riv.), Braz., 132
'Amara (prov.), Iraq, 66
'Amara, Iraq, 66
Amarante, Braz., 132
Amarapura, Burma, 72
Amareleja, Port., 33
Amarillo, Tex., 302
Amasya (prov.), Turkey, 63
Amasya, Turkey, 63
Amatitlán, Guat., 154
Amatlán, Mex., 150
Amazon (riv.), S. Amer., 120
Amazonas (state), Braz., 132
Amazonas (intendency), Col., 126
Amazonas (dept.), Peru, 128
Amazonas (terr.), Venez., 124
Ambala, India, 68
Ambarchik, U.S.S.R., 48
Ambato, Ecuador, 128
Ambatondrazaka, Malag. Rep., 118
Amber (cape), Malag. Rep., 118
Amberg, W. Ger., 22
Ambergris (cay), Br. Hond., 154
Ambergris (cay), Turks & Caicos Is., 156
Ambérieu, France, 28
Amberley, Ohio, 284
Ambert, France, 28
Ambikapur, India, 68
Ambler, Pa., 294
Amboina, Indon., 85
Amboise, France, 28
Ambon (Amboina), Indon., 85
Ambositra, Malag. Rep., 118
Ambridge, Pa., 294
Ambriz, Angola, 115
Ambrizete, Angola, 115
Ambrym (isl.), New Hebr., 87
Ambunti, Terr. N.G., 85
Amchitka (isl.), Alaska, 196
Amealco, Mex., 150
Ameca, Mex., 150
Amecameca, Mex., 150
Americana, Braz., 135
American Highland, Ant., 5
American Falls, Idaho, 220
American Fork, Utah, 304
American Samoa, 87
Americus, Ga., 216
Amersfoort, Neth., 27
Amery Ice Shelf, Ant., 5
Ames, Iowa, 229
Amesbury, Mass., 249
Amfilokhía, Greece, 45
Ámfissa, Greece, 45
Amhara (reg.), Eth., 111
Amherst, Burma, 72
Amherst, Mass., 249
Amherst, N.S., 169
Amherst, Ohio, 284
Amherstburg, Ont., 177
Amiens, France, 28
Amindivi (isls.), India, 68
Amini (isl.), India, 68
Amisk (lake), Sask., 181
Amistad (res.), 150
Amistad Nat'l Rec. Area, Tex., 302
Amite, La., 238
Amityville, N.Y., 276
Amlwch, Wales, 13
Amman (dist.), Jordan, 65
Amman (cap.), Jordan, 65
Ammersee (lake), W. Ger., 22
Amnat, Thai., 72
Amne Machin (mts.), China, 77
Amorgós (isl.), Greece, 45
Amory, Miss., 256
Amos, Que., 174
Amoy, China, 77
Amozoc de Mota, Mex., 150
Amposta, Spain, 33
Amqui, Que., 172
Amravati, India, 68
Amreli, India, 68
Amritsar, India, 68
Amsterdam (isl.), 3
Amsterdam (cap.), Neth., 27
Amsterdam, N.Y., 276
Amstetten, Austria, 41
Am-Timan, Chad, 111
Amuay, Venez., 124
Amu-Dar'ya (riv.), Asia, 48
Amuku (mts.), Guyana, 131
Amul, Iran, 66
Amund Ringnes (isl.), N.W.T., 187
Amundsen (bay), Ant., 5
Amundsen (sea), Ant., 5
Amundsen (gulf), N.W.T., 187
Amur (riv.), Asia, 48
Amya (pass), Asia, 72
'Ana, Iraq, 66
Anaa (atoll), Fr. Poly., 87
Anaco, Venez., 124
Anaconda, Mont., 262
Anacortes, Wash., 310
Anadarko, Okla., 288
Anadyr', U.S.S.R., 48
Anadyr' (gulf), U.S.S.R., 48
Anadyr' (range), U.S.S.R., 48
Anadyr' (riv.), U.S.S.R., 48
Anáfi (isl.), Greece, 45
Anaheim, Calif., 204
Anai Mudi (mt.), India, 68
'Anaiza, Saudi Ar., 59
Anakapalle, India, 68
Anambas (isls.), Indon., 85
Anamosa, Iowa, 229
Anamur (cape), Turkey, 63
Anan, Japan, 81
Anandale, La., 238
Anantapur, India, 68
Anantnag, India, 68
Anapa, U.S.S.R., 52
Anápolis, Braz., 132
Anardarra, Afghan., 68
Añasco, P. Rico, 161
Añatuya, Arg., 143
Anauá (riv.), Braz., 132
Ancash (dept.), Peru, 128
Anchorage, Alaska, 196
Ancohuma (mt.), Bol., 136
Ancona (prov.), Italy, 34
Ancona, Italy, 34
Ancón de Sardinas (bay), Ecuador, 128
Ancud, Chile, 138
Andalgalá, Arg., 143
Åndalsnes, Norway, 18
Andalusia, Ala., 194
Andalusia (reg.), Spain, 33
Andaman (sea), Asia, 54
Andaman (isls.), India, 68
Andaman and Nicobar Islands (terr.), India, 68
Anderlecht, Belg., 27
Andernach, W. Ger., 22
Anderson, Calif., 204
Anderson, Ind., 227
Anderson (riv.), N.W.T., 187
Anderson, S.C., 296
Andes (mts.), S. Amer., 120
Andheri, India, 68
Andhra Pradesh (state), India, 68
Andikíthira (isl.), Greece, 45
Andizhan, U.S.S.R., 48
Andkhui, Afghan., 68
Ándissa, Greece, 45
Andong, S. Korea, 81
Andorra, 33
Andorra la Vella (cap.), Andorra, 33
Andover, Eng., 13
Andover, N.B., 170
Andravídha, Greece, 45
Andreas (cape), Cyprus, 63
Andrés, Nic., 154
Andrew Johnson Nat'l Hist. Site, Tenn., 237
Andrews, S.C., 296
Andrews, Tex., 302
Andros (isl.), Bah. Is., 156
Ándros, Greece, 45
Ándros (isl.), Greece, 45
Androth (isl.), India, 68
Ands (fjord), Norway, 18
Andújar, Spain, 33
Andulo, Ang., 115
Anécho, Togo, 106
Anegada (isl.), Virgin Is. (Br.), 156
Anegada (passage), W. Indies, 156
Aneityum (isl.), New Hebr., 87
'Aneiza, Jebel (mt.), Asia, 59
Aneto (mt.), Spain, 33
Angara (riv.), U.S.S.R., 48
Angarsk, U.S.S.R., 48
Angaur (isl.), Pac. Is., 87
Ånge, Sweden, 18
Angel (fall), Venez., 124
Ángel de la Guarda (isl.), Mex., 150
Ängelholm, Sweden, 18
Angerman (riv.), Sweden, 18
Angermünde, E. Ger., 22
Angers, France, 28
Angikuni (lake), N.W.T., 187
Angkor Wat (ruins), Cambodia, 72
Anglesey (county), Wales, 13
Angleton, Tex., 302
Angliers, Que., 174
Angmagssalik, Greenl., 4
Ango, Dem. Rep. of the Congo, 115
Angoche (isl.), Mozamb., 118
Angol, Chile, 138
Angola, 115
Angola, Ind., 227
Angoram, Terr. N.G., 85
Angostura, Mex., 150
Angoulème, France, 28
Angra do Heroísmo, Port., 32
Anguilla (isl.), St. Chr.-N.-A., 156
Angul, India, 68
Angus (county), Scot., 15
Anholt (isl.), Den., 21
Anhwei (prov.), China, 77
Aniene (riv.), Italy, 34
Anima, Rum., 45
Anjouan (isl.), Comoro Is., 118
Ankara (prov.), Turkey, 63
Ankara (cap.), Turkey, 63
Ankeny, Iowa, 229
Anker (riv.), Eng., 10
Anking, China, 77
Anklam, E. Ger., 22
Ankober, Eth., 111
An Loc, S. Vietnam, 72
Ann (cape), Mass., 249
Anna, Ill., 222
Annaba, Alg., 106
Annaberg-Buchholz, E. Ger., 22
An Najaf, Iraq, 66
Annan, Scot., 15
Annandale, Va., 307
Annapolis (cap.), Md., 245
Annapolis (basin), N.S., 169
Annapolis Royal, N.S., 169
Annapurna (mt.), Nepal, 68
Ann Arbor, Mich., 250
An Nasiriya, Iraq, 66
Annecy, France, 28
Annieopsquotch (mts.), Newf., 166
Anniston, Ala., 194
Annobón (isl.), Eq. Guin., 102
Annonay, France, 28
Annotto Bay, Jam., 158
Annville, Pa., 294
Anoka, Minn., 254
Anóyia, Greece, 45
Áno Viánnos, Greece, 45
Ansbach, W. Ger., 22
Anse la Raye, St. Lucia, 161
Anshan, China, 77
Anshun, China, 77
Ansŏng, S. Korea, 81
Ansonia, Conn., 210
Antâkya, Turkey, 63
Antalaha, Malag. Rep., 118
Antalya (prov.), Turkey, 63
Antalya, Turkey, 63
Antalya (gulf), Turkey, 63
Antarctic (pen.), Ant., 5
Antarctica, 5
Antarctic Circle, 5
Antequera, Spain, 33
Anthony, Kans., 232
Anthony, N. Mex., 274
Anti-Atlas (ranges), Mor., 106
Antibes, France, 28
Anticosti (isl.), Que., 174
Antietam Nat'l Battlef. Site, Md., 245
Antigo, Wis., 317
Antigonish, N.S., 169
Antigua, 161
Antigua, Guat., 154
Antigua (riv.), Mex., 150
Antilla, Cuba, 158
Antilles, Greater (isls.), W. Indies, 156, 158, 161
Antilles, Lesser (isls.), W. Indies, 156,161
Antioch, Calif., 204
Antioch, Ill., 222
Antioquia (dept.), Col., 126
Antipodes (isls.), N.Z., 3
Antique (prov.), Phil. Is., 82
Anti-Taurus (mts.), Turkey, 63
Antlers, Okla., 288
Antofagasta (prov.), Chile, 138
Antofagasta, Chile, 138
Antofagasta de la Sierra, Arg., 143
Antón, Pan., 154
Antongil (bay), Malag. Rep., 118
António Enes, Mozamb., 118
Antony, France, 28
Antrim (county), N. Ire., 17
Antrim, N. Ire., 17
Antsirabe, Malag. Rep., 118
Antung (Tantung), China, 77
Antwerp (prov.), Belg., 27
Antwerp, Belg., 27
An Uaimh, Ire., 17
Anuradhapura, Ceylon, 68
Anyang, China, 72
Anyang, S. Korea, 81
Anyox, Br. Col., 184
Anzhero-Sudzhensk, U.S.S.R., 48
Anzoátegui (state), Venez., 124
Aomori (prefecture), Japan, 81
Aomori, Japan, 81
Aoulef, Alg., 106
Apa (riv.), S. Amer., 144
Apache Jct., Ariz., 198
Apalachee (bay), Fla., 212
Apalachicola, Fla., 212
Apan, Mex., 150
Apaporis (riv.), Col., 126
Aparri, Phil. Is., 82
Apatin, Yugo., 45
Apatity, U.S.S.R., 52
Apatzingán de la Constitución, Mex., 150
Apeldoorn, Neth., 27
Apennines (mts.), Italy, 34
Apennines, Central (range), Italy, 34
Apennines, Northern (range), Italy, 34
Apennines, Southern (range), Italy, 34
Apia (cap.), W. Samoa, 87
Apizaco, Mex., 150
Apo (vol.), Phil. Is., 82
Apolda, E. Ger., 22
Apollo, Pa., 294
Apopka, Fla., 212
Aporé (riv.), Braz., 132
Appalachian (mts.), U.S., 188
Appenzell (canton), Switz., 39
Appleton, Wis., 317
Appleton City, Mo., 261
Apple Valley, Calif., 204
Apple Valley, Minn., 254
Appomattox C.H. Nat'l Hist. Pk., Va., 307
Apponaug, R.I., 249
Approuague (riv.), Fr. Guiana, 131
Apsheron (pen.), U.S.S.R., 52
Apsheronsk, U.S.S.R., 52
Apt, France, 28
Apulia (reg.), Italy, 34
Apure (state), Venez., 124
Apure (riv.), Venez., 124
Apurímac (dept.), Peru, 128
Apurímac (riv.), Peru, 128
'Aqaba (gulf), Asia, 59
'Aqaba, Jordan, 65
Aqsu, China, 77
Aquidauana, Braz., 132
Aquiles Serdán, Mex., 150
Aquin, Haiti, 158
Arab, Ala., 194
'Arab, Shatt-al- (riv.), Asia, 66
'Araba, Wadi (dry river), Asia, 65
Arabia (pen.), Asia, 59
Arabian (sea), Asia, 54
Arabian (des.), U.A.R., 111
Aracaju, Braz., 132
Aracati, Braz., 132
Araçatuba, Braz., 135
Aracena, Spain, 33
Arad, Rum., 45
'Arafat, Jebel (mt.), Saudi Ar., 59
Arafura (sea), 85
Aragón (reg.), Spain, 33
Aragón (riv.), Spain, 33
Aragua (state), Venez., 124
Aragua de Barcelona, Venez., 124
Araguaia (riv.), Braz., 132
Araguari, Braz., 132
Araguarí (riv.), Braz., 132
Arak, Iran, 66
Arakan (div.), Burma, 72
Arakan Yoma (mts.), Burma, 72
Araks (riv.), Asia, 59
Aral (sea), U.S.S.R., 48
Aral'sk, U.S.S.R., 48
Āramberri, Mex., 150
Aran (isl.), Ire., 17
Aran (isls.), Ire., 17
Aranda de Duero, Spain, 33
Arandas, Mex., 150
Aranjuez, Spain, 33
Aransas Pass, Tex., 302
Arapey Grande (riv.), Urug., 145
Arapkir, Turkey, 63
Araranguá, Braz., 132
Araraquara, Braz., 135
Araras, Braz., 135
Ararat (mt.), Turkey, 63
Ararat, Vic., 97
Arauca (commissary), Col., 126
Arauca, Col., 126
Arauca (riv.), S. Amer., 120
Arauco (prov.), Chile, 138
Arauco, Chile, 138
Araxá, Braz., 132
Arbai Khere, Mong., 77
Arbela (Erbil), Iraq, 66
Arboga, Sweden, 18
Arborfield, Sask., 181
Arborg, Man., 179
Arbroath, Scot., 15
Arbuckle Nat'l Rec. Area, Okla., 288
Arcachon, France, 28
Arcachon (bay), France, 28
Arcadia, Calif., 204
Arcadia, Fla., 212
Arcadia, La., 238
Arcata, Calif., 204
Arcelia, Mex., 150
Archangel, U.S.S.R., 52
Archbald, Pa., 294
Archena, Spain, 33
Arches Nat'l Mon., Utah, 304
Archidona, Spain, 33
Arco, Ga., 216
Arco, Idaho, 220
Arcola, Sask., 181
Arcos de la Frontera, Spain, 33
Arcot, India, 68
Arcoverde, Braz., 132
Arctic, R.I., 249
Arctic Circle, 4
Arctic Ocean, 4
Arctic Red (riv.), N.W.T., 187
Arctic Red River, N.W.T., 187
Arda (riv.), Europe, 45
Ardahan, Turkey, 63
Årdal, Norway, 18
Ardebil, Iran, 66
Ardèche (dept.), France, 28
Ardee, Ire., 17
Ardennes (plat.), Belg., 27
Ardennes (dept.), France, 28
Ardhéa, Greece, 45
Ardino, Bulg., 45
Ardistan, Iran, 66
Ardita (pt.), Pan., 154
Ardmore, Ind., 227
Ardmore, Okla., 288
Ardmore, Pa., 294
Ardrossan, Scot., 15
Ardsley, N.Y., 276
Arecibo (dist.), P. Rico, 161
Arecibo, P. Rico, 161
Areia Branca, Braz., 132
Arena (pt.), Mex., 150
Arenas (cay), Mex., 150
Arenas de San Pedro, Spain, 33
Arendal, Norway, 18
Arenys de Mar, Spain, 33

Areópolis, Greece, 45
Arequipa (dept.), Peru, 128
Arequipa, Peru, 128
Arezzo (prov.), Italy, 34
Arezzo, Italy, 34
Argalastí, Greece, 45
Argamasilla de Alba, Spain, 33
Arganda, Spain, 33
Argentan, France, 28
Argenteuil, France, 28
Argentia, Newf., 166
Argentina, 143
Argentino (lake), Arg., 143
Argenton, France, 28
Argeș (riv.), Rum., 45
Argo, Sudan, 111
Argolís (gulf), Greece, 45
Argonne Nat'l Lab., Ill., 222
Árgos, Greece, 45
Argostólion, Greece, 45
Arguin (bay), Mauritania, 106
Argun (riv.), Asia, 77
Argyll (county), Scot., 15
Aribinda, Upp. Volta, 106
Arica, Chile, 138
Arichat, N.S., 169
Ariège (dept.), France, 28
Arima, Trinidad and Tobago, 161
Arinos (riv.), Braz., 132
Aripuanã (riv.), Braz., 132
Aristazabal (isl.), Br. Col., 184
Arivonimamo, Malag. Rep., 118
Arizaro (salt dep.), Arg., 143
Arizona (state), U.S., 198
Arizpe, Mex., 150
Årjang, Sweden, 18
Arkadelphia, Ark., 203
Arkaig (lake), Scot., 15
Arkansas (state), U.S., 203
Arkansas (riv.), U.S., 188
Arkansas City, Kans., 232
Arkansas Post Nat'l Mem., Ark., 203
Arkhángelos, Greece, 45
Arkhangel'sk (Archangel), U.S.S.R., 52
Arklow, Ire., 17
Arkona (cape), E. Ger., 22
Arles, France, 28
Arlington, Calif., 204
Arlington, Mass., 249
Arlington, N.Y., 276
Arlington, Oreg., 291
Arlington, Tex., 302
Arlington, Va., 307
Arlington Heights, Ill., 222
Arlon, Belg., 27
Arma (plat.), Saudi Ar., 59
Armadale, Scot., 15
Armagh (county), N. Ire., 17
Armagh, N. Ire., 17
Armavir, U.S.S.R., 52
Armdale, N.S., 169
Armenia, Col., 126
Armenian S.S.R., U.S.S.R., 52
Armentières, France, 28
Armeria, Mex., 150
Armidale, N.S.W., 97
Armstrong, Br. Col., 184
Armstrong, Ont., 175
Arnaía, Greece, 45
Arnaud (riv.), Que., 174
Arnauti (cape), Cyprus, 63
Arnhem, Neth., 27
Arnhem (cape), N. Terr., 93
Arnhem Land (reg.), N. Terr., 93
Arno (riv.), Italy, 34
Arno (atoll), Pac. Is., 87
Arnold, Mo., 261
Arnold, Pa., 294
Arnprior, Ont., 177
Arnsberg, W. Ger., 22
Arnstadt, E. Ger., 22
Aroab, S.W. Afr., 118
Aroche, Spain, 33
Arorae (atoll), Gilb. & Ell. Is., 87
Arosa (est.), Spain, 33
Arouca, Trinidad and Tobago, 161
Arrah, India, 68
Arran (isl.), Scot., 15
Arras, France, 28
Arrecife, Spain, 33
Arrecifes, Arg., 143
Arrecifes (riv.), Arg., 143
Arrowhead, Br. Col., 184
Arroyo, P. Rico, 161
Arroyo Grande, Calif., 204
Árta, Greece, 45
Arta, Spain, 33
Artem, U.S.S.R., 48
Artemisa, Cuba, 158
Artemovsk, U.S.S.R., 52
Artemovskiy, U.S.S.R., 48
Artesia, Calif., 204
Artesia, N. Mex., 274
Arthabaska, Que., 172
Arthur's (pass), N.Z., 101
Artibonite (dept.), Haiti, 158
Artibonite (river), Haiti, 158
Artigas (dept.), Urug., 145
Artigas, Urug., 145
Artillery (lake), N.W.T., 187
Artvin (prov.), Turkey, 63
Artvin, Turkey, 63
Aru (isls.), Indon., 85
Arua, Uganda, 115
Aruba (isl.), Neth. Ant., 161
Arucas, Spain, 33
Aruppukkottai, India, 68
Arusha (prov.), Tanz., 115
Arusha, Tanz., 115
Arusi (prov.), Eth., 111
Aruwimi (riv.), Dem. Rep. of the Congo, 115
Arvada, Colo., 208
Arvi, India, 68
Arvida, Que., 172
Arvidsjaur, Sweden, 18
Arvika, Sweden, 18
Arvin, Calif., 204
Arzamas, U.S.S.R., 52
Aš, Czech., 41
Asahan (riv.), Indon., 85
Asahi (mt.), Japan, 81
Asahikawa, Japan, 81
Asansol, India, 68
Asbestos, Que., 172
Asbury Park, N. J., 273
Ascención, Bol., 136
Ascensión, Mex., 150
Ascension (isl.), St. Helena, 102
Aschaffenburg, W. Ger., 22
Ascoli Piceno (prov.), Italy, 34
Ascoli Piceno, Italy, 34
Ascope, Peru, 128
Ascot, Queensland, 95
Åseda, Sweden, 18
Åsele, Sweden, 18
Asenovgrad, Bulg., 45
Ashanti (reg.), Ghana, 106
Ashburn, Ga., 216
Ashburton, N.Z., 101
Ashburton (riv.), W. Austral., 92
Ashcroft, Br. Col., 184
Ashdod, Israel, 65
Ashdown, Ark., 203
Asheboro, N.C., 281
Ashern, Man., 179
Asheville, N.C., 281
Ashfield, N.S.W., 97
Ashford, Eng., 13
Ash Fork, Ariz., 198
Ashibetsu, Japan, 81
Ashikaga, Japan, 81
Ashington, Eng., 13
Ashiya, Japan, 81
Ashkhabad, U.S.S.R., 48
Ashland, Kans., 232
Ashland, Ky., 237
Ashland, Ohio, 284
Ashland, Oreg., 291
Ashland, Pa., 294
Ashland, Va., 307
Ashland, Wis., 317
Ashley, N. Dak., 283
Ashley, Pa., 294
Ashley Falls, Mass., 249
Ashmore (isls.), Austral., 88
Ashmore and Cartier Islands (terr.), Austral., 88
Ashqelon, Israel, 65
Ash Shabicha, Iraq, 66
Ashtabula, Ohio, 284
Ashton-under-Lyne, Eng., 10
Ashuanipi (lake), Newf., 166
Ashwaubenon, Wis., 317
'Asi (riv.), Syria, 63
Asia, 54
Asilah, Mor., 106
Asinara (isl.), Italy, 34
Asino, U.S.S.R., 48
'Asir (prov.), Saudi Ar., 59
Askim, Norway, 18
Asmara, Eth., 111
Asnen (lake), Sweden, 18
Asnières, France, 38
Aso (mt.), Japan, 81
Aspe, Spain, 33
Aspen, Colo., 208
Aspinwall, Pa., 294
Aspiring (mt.), N.Z., 101
Assab, Eth., 111
Assaba (reg.), Mauritania, 106
As Salman, Iraq, 66
Assam (state), India, 68
Assateague Isl. Nat'l Seashore, Va., 307
Asselle, Eth., 111
Assiniboia, Sask., 181
Assiniboine (mt.), Canada, 182
Assiniboine (riv.), Canada, 163
Assis, Braz., 135
Assumption (isl.), Seych., 118
Astara, U.S.S.R., 52
Asterabad (Gurgan), Iran, 66
Asti (prov.), Italy, 34
Asti, Italy, 34
Astipálaia, Greece, 45
Astipálaia (isl.), Greece, 45
Astorga, Spain, 33
Astoria, Oreg., 291
Astove (isl.), Seych., 118
Astrakhan', U.S.S.R., 52
Asturias (reg.), Spain, 33
Asunción (cap.), Par., 144
Asunción Mita, Guat., 154
Aswân, U.A.R., 111
Aswân (dam), U.A.R., 111
Asyût, U.A.R., 111
Atacama (prov.), Chile, 138
Atacama (des.), Chile, 138
Atacama, Puna de (reg.), Arg., 143
Atafu (atoll), Tokelau Is., 87
Atakpamé, Togo, 106
Atalándi, Greece, 45
Atalaya, Peru, 128
Atami, Japan, 81
Atar, Mauritania, 106
Atascadero, Calif., 204
Atbara, Sudan, 111
Atbara (riv.), Africa, 111
Atbasar, U.S.S.R., 48
Atchison, Kans., 232
Atco, N. J., 273
Atenas, C. Rica, 154
Athabasca, Alta., 182
Athabasca (riv.), Alta., 182
Athabasca (lake), Canada, 163
Athens, Ala., 194
Athens, Ga., 216
Athens (cap.), Greece, 45
Athens, N.Y., 276
Athens, Ohio, 284
Athens, Pa., 296
Athens, Tenn., 237
Athens, Tex., 302
Atherton, Calif., 204
Athlone, Ire., 17
Athol, Mass., 249
Athol (reg.), Scotland, 15
Atholville, N.B., 170
Áthos (mt.), Greece, 45
Athy, Ire., 17
Ati, Chad, 111
Atikameg, Alta., 182
Atikokan, Ont., 175
Atikonak (lake), Newf., 166
Atiquizaya, El Sal., 154
Atitlán (lake), Guat., 154
Atitlán (vol.), Guat., 154
Atiu (isl.), Cook Is., 87
Atka (isl.), Alaska, 196
Atkarsk, U.S.S.R., 52
Atkinson, Nebr., 264
Atlanta, C. Rica, 154
Atlanta (cap.), Ga., 216
Atlanta, Tex., 302
Atlanta Army Depot, Ga., 216
Atlantic, Iowa, 229
Atlantic Beach, Fla., 212
Atlantic City, N. J., 273
Atlantic Highlands, N. J., 273
Atlántico (dept.), Col., 126
Atlantic Ocean, North, 3
Atlantic Ocean, South, 3
Atlas (mts.), Africa, 106
Atlin, Br. Col., 184
Atlixco, Mex., 150
Atmore, Ala., 194
Atoka, Okla., 288
Atotonilco, Mex., 150
Atoyac (riv.), Mex., 150
Atrek (riv.), Asia, 66
Attalla, Ala., 194
Attawapiskat (riv.), Ont., 177
Attica, Ind., 227
Attica, N.Y., 276
Attikamagen (lake), Newf., 166
Attleboro, Mass., 249
Attopeu, Laos, 72
Attu (isl.), Alaska, 196
Atuel (riv.), Arg., 143
Atuntaqui, Ecuador, 128
Atuona, Fr. Poly., 87
Atwater, Calif., 204
Atwood (Samana) (cay), Bah. Is., 156
Aubagne, France, 28
Aube (dept.), France, 28
Aube (riv.), France, 28
Aubenas, France, 28
Aubervilliers, France, 28
Auburn, Ala., 194
Auburn, Calif., 204
Auburn, Ind., 227
Auburn, Maine, 242
Auburn, Mass., 249
Auburn, Nebr., 264
Auburn, N.S.W., 97
Auburn, N.Y., 276
Auburn, Wash., 310
Auburndale, Fla., 212
Auburndale, Mass., 249
Auburn Hts., Mich., 250
Aubusson, France, 28
Auch, France, 28
Auchterarder, Scot., 15
Auckland (prov. dist.), N.Z., 101
Auckland, N.Z., 101
Aude (dept.), France, 28
Audincourt, France, 28
Audubon, Iowa, 229
Audubon, N. J., 273
Aue, E. Ger., 22
Auerbach, E. Ger., 22
Augsburg, W. Ger., 22
Augusta, Ga., 216
Augusta, Kans., 232
Augusta (cap.), Maine, 242
Aujila, Libya, 111
Aulnay-sous-Bois, France, 28
Aur, Pulau (isl.), Malaysia, 72
Aurangabad, India, 68
Auray, France, 28
Aurès (mts.), Alg., 106
Aurich, W. Ger., 22
Aurignac, France, 28
Aurillac, France, 28
Aurora, Colo., 208
Aurora, Ill., 222
Aurora, Ind., 227
Aurora, Minn., 254
Aurora, Mo., 261
Aurora, Nebr., 264
Aurora, Ohio, 284
Aurora, Ont., 177
Aus, S.W. Afr., 118
Aust-Agder (county), Norway, 18
Austin, Ind., 227
Austin, Minn., 254
Austin, Nev., 266
Austin (cap.), Tex., 302
Austral (isls.), Fr. Poly., 87
Australia, 88
Australian Alps (mts.), Austral., 97
Australian Capital (terr.), Austral., 97
Austria, 41
Autlan, Mex., 150
Autun, France, 28
Auvergne (mts.), France, 28
Auxerre, France, 28
Avallon, France, 28
Avalon, Calif., 204
Avalon (pen.), Newf., 166
Avalon, Pa., 294
Avaré, Braz., 135
Avarua (cap.), Cook Is., 87
Aveiro, Port., 33
Avellaneda, Arg., 143
Avellino (prov.), Italy, 34
Avellino, Italy, 34
Avenal, Calif., 204
Avenel, N. J., 273
Avesnes, France, 28
Avesta, Sweden, 18
Aveyron (dept.), France, 28
Avignon, France, 28
Ávila (prov.), Spain, 33
Ávila, Spain, 33
Avion, France, 28
Avoca, Pa., 294
Avon (riv.), Eng., 13
Avon, N.Y., 276
Avon, Ohio, 284
Avondale, Ariz., 198
Avon Lake, Ohio, 284
Avon Park, Fla., 212
Avranches, France, 28
Awaji (isl.), Japan, 81
Awash (riv.), Eth., 111
Awe (lake), Scot., 15
Axel Heiberg (isl.), N.W.T., 187
Axim, Ghana, 106
Ayabe, Japan, 81
Ayacucho, Arg., 143
Ayacucho (dept.), Peru, 128
Ayacucho, Peru, 128
Ayaguz, U.S.S.R., 48
Ayamonte, Spain, 33
Ayapel, Col., 126
Ayden, N.C., 281
Aydın (prov.), Turkey, 63
Aydın, Turkey, 63
Ayer, Mass., 249
Ayer's Cliff, Que., 172
Ayers Rock (mt.), N. Terr., 93
Ayiá, Greece, 45
Áyion Óros (reg.), Greece, 45
Áyios Evstrátios (isl.), Greece, 45
Áyios Kírikos, Greece, 45
Áyios Matthaíos, Greece, 45
Áyios Nikólaos, Greece, 45
Áyios Yeóryios (cape), Greece, 45
Aykhal, U.S.S.R., 48
Aylesbury, Eng., 13
Aylmer (lake), N.W.T., 187
Aylmer West, Ont., 177
Ayora, Spain, 33
Ayr, Queensland, 95
Ayr (county), Scot., 15
Ayr, Scot., 15
Ayre (pt.), I. of Man, 13
Aytos, Bulg., 45
Ayubnagar (cap.), Pak., 68
Ayutla, Mex., 150
Ayutthaya, Thai., 72
Ayvalık, Turkey, 63
Azamgarh, India, 68
Azcapotzalco, Mex., 150
Azemmour, Mor., 106
Azerbaidzhan S.S.R., U.S.S.R., 52
Azle, Tex., 302
Azogues, Ecuador, 128
Azores (isls.), Port., 32
Azov, U.S.S.R., 52
Azov (sea), U.S.S.R., 52
Azoyú, Mex., 150
Azpeitia, Spain, 33
Azrou, Mor., 106
Aztec, N. Mex., 274
Aztec Ruins Nat'l Mon., N. Mex., 274
Azua (prov.), Dom. Rep., 158
Azua, Dom. Rep., 158
Azuaga, Spain, 33
Azuay (prov.), Ecuador, 128
Azuero (pen.), Pan., 154
Azul, Arg., 143
Azul (riv.), Guat., 154
Azul (mts.), Peru, 128
Azusa, Calif., 204
Az Zubair, Iraq, 66

B

Ba'albek, Leb., 63
Baba (cape), Turkey, 63
Babaeski, Turkey, 63
Babahoyo, Ecua., 128
Babar (isls.), Indon., 85
Babbitt, Minn., 254
Babbitt, Nev., 266
Bab el Mandeb (strait), 111
Babelthuap (isl.), Pac. Is., 87
Babia (riv.), Mex., 150
Babine (riv.), Br. Col., 184
Babol, Iran, 66
Babuyan (isls.), Phil. Is., 82
Babylon (ruins), Iraq, 66
Babylon, N.Y., 276
Bacalar (lake), Mex., 150
Bacău, Rum., 45
Bacchus Marsh, Vic., 97
Bach Long Vi (Nightingale) (isl.), N. Vietnam, 72
Bačka Topola, Yugo., 45
Backnang, W. Ger., 22
Bac Lieu, S. Vietnam, 72
Bac Ninh, N. Vietnam, 72
Bacolod, Phil. Is., 82
Bács-Kiskun (county), Hung., 41
Bacup, Eng., 10
Badagara, India, 68
Badajoz (prov.), Spain, 33
Badajoz, Spain, 33
Badalona, Spain, 33
Bad Axe, Mich., 250
Bad Doberan, E. Ger., 22
Bad Dürkheim, W. Ger., 22
Bad Dürrenberg, E. Ger., 22
Baden, Austria, 41
Baden, Pa., 294
Baden, Switz., 39
Baden-Baden, W. Ger., 22
Baden-Württemberg (state), W. Ger., 22
Badgastein, Austria, 41
Bad Hersfeld, W. Ger., 22
Bad Homburg, W. Ger., 22
Bad Ischl, Austria, 41
Bad Kissingen, W. Ger., 22
Bad Kreuznach, W. Ger., 22
Badlands Nat'l Mon., S. Dak., 298
Bad Langensalza, E. Ger., 22
Badr, Saudi Ar., 59
Bad Salzuflen, W. Ger., 22
Bad Tölz, W. Ger., 22
Badulla, Ceylon, 68
Baffin (bay), N. Amer., 187
Baffin (isl.), N.W.T., 187
Bafq, Iran, 66
Bafra, Turkey, 63
Baft, Iran, 66
Bagalkot, India, 68
Bagamoyo, Tanz., 115
Bagé, Braz., 132
Bagenalstown, Ire., 17
Baghdad (prov.), Iraq, 66
Baghdad (cap.), Iraq, 66
Baghlan, Afghan., 68
Bagnères-de-Bigorre, France, 28
Bagnolet, France, 28
Bago, Phil. Is., 82
Bagotville, Que., 172
Baguio, Phil. Is., 82
Baguirmi (reg.), Chad, 111
Bahama Islands, 156
Bahariya (oasis), U.A.R., 111
Bahawalnagar, Pak., 68
Bahawalpur, Pak., 68
Bahia (state), Braz., 132
Bahia (Salvador), Braz., 132
Bahía (isls.), Hond., 154
Bahía Blanca, Arg., 143
Bahía de Caráquez, Ecua., 128
Bahraich, India, 68
Bahramabad, Iran, 66
Bahrein, 59
Bahr el Ghazal (prov.), Sudan, 111
Bahr es Safi (des.), Arabia, 59
Baia Mare, Rum., 45
Baida (prov.), Libya, 111
Baida, Libya, 111
Baidoa, Somalia, 115
Baie-Comeau, Que., 172
Baie-Saint-Paul, Que., 172
Baie-Trinité, Que., 172
Baie Verte, Newf., 166
Baile Atha Cliath (Dublin) (cap.), Ire., 17
Băilești, Rum., 45
Bainbridge, Ga., 216
Bainbridge Naval Train. Ctr., Md., 245
Bairiki (cap.), Gilb. & Ell. Is., 87
Bairnsdale, Vic., 97
Baixo Alentejo (prov.), Port., 33
Baja, Hung., 41
Baja California (state), Mex., 150
Baja California Sur (terr.), Mex., 150
Bajo Boquete, Pan., 154
Baker, La., 238
Baker, Mont., 262
Baker, Oreg., 291
Baker (isl.), Pacific, 87
Baker (mt.), Wash., 310
Baker Lake, N.W.T., 187
Bakersfield, Calif., 204
Bakewell, Eng., 10
Bakhchisaray, U.S.S.R., 52
Bakhmach, U.S.S.R., 52
Bakhtiari (governorate), Iran, 66
Bakırköy, Turkey, 63
Bakony (mts.), Hung., 41
Baku, U.S.S.R., 52
Bala, Wales, 13
Balabac (isl.), Phil. Is., 82
Bala Cynwyd, Pa., 294
Balakhna, U.S.S.R., 52
Balaklava, U.S.S.R., 52
Balakovo, U.S.S.R., 52
Bala Murghab, Afghan., 68
Balashov, U.S.S.R., 52
Balasore, India, 68
Balaton (lake), Hung., 41
Balboa, C.Z., 154
Balbriggan, Ire., 17
Balcarce, Arg., 143
Balchik, Bulg., 45
Balch Sprs., Tex., 302
Balclutha, N.Z., 101
Baldwin, N.Y., 276
Baldwin, Pa., 294
Baldwin Pk., Calif., 204
Baldwinsville, N.Y., 276
Baleares (prov.), Spain, 33
Balearic (isls.), Spain, 33
Baleine (riv.), Que., 174
Balhaf, P.D.R., Yemen, 59
Bali (isl.), Indon., 85
Bali (sea), Indon., 85
Balıkesir (prov.), Turkey, 63
Balıkesir, Turkey, 63
Balikpapan, Indon., 85
Balkan (mts.), Bulg., 45
Balkar (mts.), Turkey, 63
Balkh, Afghan., 68
Balkhash, U.S.S.R., 48
Balkhash (lake), U.S.S.R., 48
Ballarat, Vic., 97
Ballater, Scot., 15
Ballenas (bay), Mex., 150
Ballerup, Den., 21
Ballia, India, 68
Ballina, Ire., 17
Ballina, N.S.W., 97
Ballinasloe, Ire., 17
Ballinger, Tex., 302
Ballinrobe, Ire., 17
Ballston Spa, N.Y., 276
Bally, India, 68
Ballybunion, Ire., 17
Ballycastle, N. Ire., 17
Ballymoney, N. Ire., 17
Ballymote, Ire., 17
Ballyshannon, Ire., 17
Balmoral, Queensland, 95
Balmoral Castle, Scot., 15
Balonne (riv.), Queensland, 95
Balrampur, India, 68
Balsas (riv.), Braz., 132
Balsas (riv.), Mex., 150
Baltic (sea), Europe, 18
Baltimore, Ire., 17
Baltimore, Md., 245
Baltistan (reg.), India, 68
Baltit, India, 68
Baltiysk, U.S.S.R., 52
Baluchistan (reg.), Iran, 66
Baluchistan (prov.), Pak., 68
Bam, Iran, 66
Bamako (cap.), Mali, 106
Bambari, Centr. Afr. Rep., 115
Bamberg, S.C., 296
Bamberg, W. Ger., 22
Bamenda, Cameroon, 115
Bamian, Afghan., 68
Bampur, Iran, 66
Bam Tso (lake), China, 77
Banalia, Dem. Rep. of the Congo, 115
Banana, Dem. Rep. of the Congo, 115
Bananal (isl.), Braz., 132
Bånås, Ras (cape), U.A.R., 111
Banbury, Eng., 10
Banchory, Scot., 15
Bancroft, Ont., 175
Banda, India, 68
Banda (sea), Indon., 85
Banda Atjeh, Indon., 85
Bandar 'Abbas, Iran, 66
Bandar Maharani, Malaysia, 72
Bandar Penggaram, Malaysia, 72
Bandar Rig, Iran, 66
Bandar Seri Begawan (cap.), Brunei, 85
Bandar Shah, Iran, 66
Bandar Shahpur, Iran, 66
Bandeira (mt.), Braz., 135
Bandelier Nat'l Mon., N. Mex., 274
Banderas (bay), Mex., 150
Bandiagara, Mali, 106
Bandırma, Turkey, 63
Bandjarmasin, Indon., 85
Bandon, Ire., 17
Bandra, India, 68
Bandundu (prov.), Dem. Rep. of the Congo, 115
Bandundu, Dem. Rep. of the Congo, 115
Bandung, Indon., 85
Banes, Cuba, 158
Banff, Alta., 182
Banff (county), Scot., 15
Banff, Scot., 15
Banff Nat'l Park, Alta., 182
Bangalore, India, 68
Bangassou, Centr. Afr. Rep., 115
Banggai, Indon., 85
Bangil, Indon., 85
Bangka (isl.), Indon., 85
Bangkok (cap.), Thai., 72
Bangor, Maine, 242
Bangor, N. Ire., 17
Bangor, Pa., 294
Bangor, Wales, 13
Bangui (cap.), Centr. Afr. Rep., 115
Bangweulu (lake), Zambia, 115
Baní, Dom. Rep., 158
Baniara, Papua, 85
Baniyas, Syria, 63
Banja Luka, Yugo., 45
Banjuwangi, Indon., 85
Banks (isl.), Br. Col., 184
Banks (isls.), New Hebr., 87
Banks (isl.), N.W.T., 187
Banks (strait), Tas., 99
Bankstown, N.S.W., 97
Bankura, India, 68
Ban Me Thuot, S. Vietnam, 72
Banning, Calif., 204
Bannockburn, Scot., 15
Bannu, Pak., 68
Ban Pua, Thai., 72
Bansberia, India, 68
Banská Bystrica, Czech., 41
Banstead, Eng., 10
Bantry, Ire., 17
Bantry (bay), Ire., 17
Bantul, Indon., 85
Banyo, Cameroon, 115
Banzare Coast (reg.), Ant., 5
Banzyville, Dem. Rep. of the Congo, 115
Baoruco (prov.), Dom. Rep., 158
Ba'quba, Iraq, 66
Baqura, Jordan, 65
Bar, Yugo., 45
Barabinsk, U.S.S.R., 48
Baraboo, Wis., 317
Baracoa, Cuba, 158
Baradero, Arg., 143
Barahona (prov.), Dom. Rep., 158
Barahona, Dom. Rep., 158
Baranovichi, U.S.S.R., 52
Baranya (county), Hung., 41
Barasat, India, 68
Barawa (Brava), Somali Rep., 115
Barbacena, Braz., 135
Barbados, 161
Barbate (riv.), Spain, 33
Barbeau (peak), N.W.T., 187
Barberton, Ohio, 284
Barbourville, Ky., 237
Barbuda (isl.), Antigua, 156
Barce (El Marj), Libya, 111
Barcellona Pozzo di Gotto, Italy, 34
Barcelona (prov.), Spain, 33
Barcelona, Spain, 33
Barcelona, Venez., 124
Barcoo (creek), Austral., 88
Bardera, Somalia, 115
Bardstown, Ky., 237
Bareilly, India, 68
Barents (sea), 48
Barentsburg, Norway, 18
Barfleur (pt.), France, 28
Bar Harbor, Maine, 242
Bari (prov.), Italy, 34
Bari, Italy, 34
Barinas (state), Venez., 124
Barinas, Venez., 124
Barisal, Pak., 68
Barisan (mts.), Indon., 85
Barito (riv.), Indon., 85
Barking, Eng., 10
Barkly (tableland), N. Terr., 93
Bar-le-Duc, France, 28
Barlee (lake), W. Austral., 92
Barletta, Italy, 34
Barmer, India, 68
Barmouth, Wales, 13
Barnagore, India, 68
Barnaul, U.S.S.R., 48
Barnesboro, Pa., 294
Barnesville, Ga., 216
Barnet, Eng., 10
Barnsley, Eng., 13
Barnstaple, Eng., 13
Barnwell, S.C., 296
Baroda, India, 68
Baroghil (pass), Asia, 68
Barotseland (reg.), Zambia, 115
Barpeta, India, 68
Barquisimeto, Venez., 124
Barra (isl.), Scot., 15
Barra (isls.), Scot., 15
Barrackpore, India, 68
Barrackville, W. Va., 313
Barra do Piraí, Braz., 135
Barra Mansa, Braz., 135
Barranca, Peru, 128
Barrancabermeja, Col., 126
Barranquilla, Col., 126
Barraute, Que., 174
Barre, Vt., 268
Barretos, Braz., 135
Barrhead, Alta., 182
Barrhead, Scot., 15
Barrie, Ont., 177
Barrington, Ill., 222
Barrington, N. J., 273
Barrington, R.I., 249
Barrow, Alaska, 196
Barrow (pt.), Alaska, 196
Barrow (riv.), Ire., 17
Barrow (isl.), W. Austral., 92
Barrow-in-Furness, Eng., 13
Barr Smith (mt.), Ant., 5
Barry, Wales, 13
Barry's Bay, Ont., 175
Barsi, India, 68
Barstow, Calif., 204
Bartica, Guyana, 131
Bartin, Turkey, 63
Bartlesville, Okla., 288
Bartolomeu Dias, Mozamb., 118
Bartonville, Ill., 222
Bartoszyce, Poland, 47
Bartow, Fla., 212
Baruun Urta, Mong., 77
Barvas, Scot., 15
Barwon (riv.), N.S.W., 97
Basankusu, Dem. Rep. of the Congo, 115
Basel, Switz., 39
Baselland (half-canton), Switz., 39
Basestadt (half-canton), Switz., 39
Bashi (chan.), Asia, 82
Bashkir A.S.S.R., U.S.S.R., 52
Basilan (isl.), Phil. Is., 82
Basildon, Eng., 13
Basilicata (reg.), Italy, 34
Basin, Wyo., 319
Basingstoke, Eng., 13
Basirhat, India, 68
Basoko, Dem. Rep. of the Congo, 115
Basra (prov.), Iraq, 66
Basra, Iraq, 66
Bas-Rhin (dept.), France, 28
Bass (strait), Austral., 88
Bassano, Alta., 182
Bassano del Grappa, Italy, 34
Bassein, Burma, 72
Bassein, India, 68
Basses-Alpes (dept.), France, 28
Basse-Terre (cap.), Guad., 161
Basseterre (cap.), St. Chr.-N.-A., 161
Bassett, Va., 307
Bastia, France, 28
Bastogne, Belg., 27
Bastrop, La., 238
Bastrop, Tex., 302
Bata, Eq. Guin., 115
Bataan (prov.), Phil. Is., 82
Batabanó (gulf), Cuba, 158
Batala, India, 68
Batalha, Port., 33
Batan (isls.), Phil. Is., 82
Batanes (prov.), Phil. Is., 82
Batang, China, 77
Batang, Indon., 85
Batangan (cape), S. Vietnam, 72
Batangas (prov.), Phil. Is., 82
Batangas, Phil. Is., 82
Batavia, Ill., 222
Batavia (Djakarta)(cap.), Indon., 85
Batavia, N.Y., 276
Bataysk, U.S.S.R., 52
Batesburg, S.C., 296
Batesville, Ark., 204
Batesville, Ind., 227
Batesville, Miss., 256
Bath, Eng., 13
Bath, Maine, 242
Bath, N.Y., 276
Bathgate, Scot., 15
Bathurst (cap.), Gambia, 106
Bathurst, N.B., 170
Bathurst, N.S.W., 97
Bathurst (isl.), N. Terr., 93
Bathurst (isl.), N.W.T., 187
Batina (reg.), Oman, 59
Batjan (isls.), Indon., 85
Batley, Eng., 13
Batman, Turkey, 63
Batna, Alg., 106
Baton Rouge (cap.), La., 238
Batouri, Cameroon, 115
Battambang, Cambodia, 72
Batterbee (cape), Ant., 5
Batticaloa, Ceylon, 68
Battle Creek, Mich., 250
Battleford, Sask., 181
Battle Harbour, Newf., 166
Batu (isls.), Indon., 85
Batu Gajah, Malaysia, 72
Batumi, U.S.S.R., 52
Bat Yam, Israel, 65
Bauchi, Nigeria, 106
Baudouinville, Dem. Rep. of the Congo, 115
Bauld (cape), Newf., 166
Baulkham Hills, N.S.W., 97
Bauru, Braz., 135
Bautzen, E. Ger., 22
Bavaria (state), W. Ger., 22
Bavarian (for.), W. Ger., 22
Bavarian Alps (mts.), Europe, 22
Bavispe (riv.), Mex., 150
Bawean (isl.), Indon., 85
Baxley, Ga., 216
Baxter Sprs., Kans., 232
Bayamo, Cuba, 158
Bayamón (dist.), P. Rico, 161
Bayamón, P. Rico, 161
Bayan Kara Shan (range), China, 77
Bayan Khongor (prov.), Mong., 77
Bayan Khongor, Mong., 77
Bayan Tumen (Choibalsan), Mong., 77
Bayan Ulegei (prov.), Mong., 77
Bayan Ulegei, Mong., 77
Bayard, N. Mex., 274
Bayburt, Turkey, 63
Bay City, Mich., 250
Bay City, Tex., 302
Bayeux, France, 28
Bayındır, Turkey, 63
Baykal (lake), U.S.S.R., 48
Baykal (range), U.S.S.R., 48
Baykonur, U.S.S.R., 48
Bay Minette, Ala., 194
Bayonne, France, 28
Bayonne, N. J., 273
Bayport, Minn., 254
Bayport, N.Y., 276
Bayram-Ali, U.S.S.R., 48
Bayreuth, W. Ger., 22
Bay Roberts, Newf., 166
Bay Saint Louis, Miss., 256
Bay Shore, N.Y., 276
Bayside, Wis., 317
Bay Village, Ohio, 284
Bayville, N.Y., 276
Baza, Spain, 33
Bazaruto (isl.), Mozamb., 118
Beaconsfield, Que., 172
Beachwood, N. J., 273
Beachwood, Ohio, 284
Beachy (head), Eng., 13
Beacon, N.Y., 276
Beagle (chan.), Chile, 138
Bear (lake), U.S., 304
Beardmore (glac.), Ant., 5
Beardstown, Ill., 222
Bearpaw (mts.), Mont., 262
Beata (isl.), Dom. Rep., 158
Beatrice, Nebr., 264
Beatton (riv.), Br. Col., 184
Beaufort, Malaysia, 85
Beaufort (sea), N. Amer., 187
Beaufort, N.C., 281
Beaufort, S.C., 296
Beaufort West, S. Afr., 118
Beauharnois, Que., 172
Beauly, Scot., 15
Beaumaris, Wales, 13
Beaumont, Calif., 204
Beaumont, Tex., 302
Beauport, Que., 172
Beauséjour, Man., 179
Beauvais, France, 28
Beaver (riv.), Canada, 163
Beaver, Okla., 288
Beaver, Pa., 294
Beaver Dam, Wis., 317
Beaver Falls, Pa., 294
Beaverhead (mts.), Idaho, 220
Beaverlodge, Alta., 182
Beaverton, Oreg., 291
Beawar, India, 68
Bebington, Eng., 10
Bečej, Yugo., 45
Béchar, Alg., 106
Beckley, W. Va., 313
Bedeque (bay), P.E.I., 169
Bedford, Eng., 13
Bedford, Ind., 227
Bedford, Ohio, 284
Bedford, Pa., 294
Bedford, Tex., 302
Bedford, Va., 307
Bedfordshire (county), Eng., 13
Bedlington Sta., Eng., 13
Bedworth, Eng., 13
Będzin, Poland, 47
Beersheba, Israel, 65
Beeston and Stapleford, Eng., 13
Beeville, Tex., 302
Bega, N.S.W., 97
Begemdir (prov.), Eth., 111
Behbehan, Iran, 66
Beira, Mozamb., 118
Beira Alta (prov.), Port., 33
Beira Baixa (prov.), Port., 33
Beira Litoral (prov.), Port., 33
Beirut (cap.), Leb., 63
Beith, Scot., 15
Beit Jala, Jordan, 65
Beit Sahur, Jordan, 65
Beja, Port., 33
Beja, Tunisia, 106
Béjaïa, Alg., 106
Béjar, Spain, 33
Bekasi, Indon., 85
Békés (county), Hung., 41
Békéscsaba, Hung., 41
Bela, Pak., 68
Bela Crkva, Yugo., 45
Bel Air, Md., 245
Belaya (riv.), U.S.S.R., 52
Belaya Tserkov, U.S.S.R., 52
Belding, Mich., 250
Belebey, U.S.S.R., 52
Belém, Braz., 132
Belém, Port., 33
Belen, N. Mex., 274
Belep (isls.), New Cal., 87
Belet Uen, Somalia, 115
Belfast, Maine, 242
Belfast (cap.), N. Ire., 17
Belfast (inlet), N. Ire., 17
Belford, N. J., 273
Belfort (terr.), France, 28
Belfort, France, 28
Belgaum, India, 68
Belgium, 27
Belgorod, U.S.S.R., 52
Belgorod-Dnestrovskiy, U.S.S.R., 52
Belgrade (cap.), Yugo., 45
Belice (riv.), Italy, 34
Belitung (Billiton) (isl.), Indon., 85
Belize City (cap.), Br. Hond., 154
Bell, Calif., 204
Bella Coola, Br. Col., 184
Bellaire, Ohio, 284
Bellaire, Tex., 302
Bellary, India, 68
Bella Unión, Urug., 145
Bell Bay, Tas., 99
Belle (isl.), Newf., 166
Bellefontaine, Ohio, 284
Bellefonte, Pa., 294
Belle Fourche, S. Dak., 298
Belle Glade, Fla., 212
Belle-Île (isl.), France, 28
Belle Isle (str.), Newf., 166
Belle Mead, N.J., 273
Belle Meade, Tenn., 237
Belleoram, Newf., 166
Belle Plaine, Iowa, 229
Belleville, Ill., 222
Belleville, Kans., 232
Belleville, N. J., 273
Belleville, Ont., 177
Bellevue, Alta., 182
Bellevue, Ky., 237
Bellevue, Nebr., 264
Bellevue, Ohio, 284
Bellevue, Pa., 294
Bellevue, Wash., 310
Bellflower, Calif., 204
Bellingham, Wash., 310
Bellingshausen (sea), Ant., 5
Bellinzona, Switz., 39
Bell Island, Newf., 166
Bellmawr, N. J., 273
Bellmead, Tex., 302
Bellmore, N.Y., 276
Bellows Falls, Vt., 268
Belluno (prov.), Italy, 34
Belluno, Italy, 34
Bell Ville, Arg., 143
Bellville, S. Afr., 118
Bellwood, Ill., 222
Belmar, N. J., 273
Belmont, Calif., 204
Belmont, Mass., 249
Belmont, N.C., 281
Belogorsk, U.S.S.R., 48
Belo Horizonte, Braz., 135
Beloit, Kans., 232
Beloit, Wis., 317
Beloretsk, U.S.S.R., 52
Belo-sur-Tsiribihina, Malag. Rep., 118
Beloye (lake), U.S.S.R., 52
Belper, Eng., 13
Belpre, Ohio, 284
Belton, Mo., 261
Belton, S.C., 296
Belton, Tex., 302
Beltsville, Md., 245
Bel'tsy, U.S.S.R., 52
Belumut, Gunong (mt.), Malaysia, 72
Belur, India, 68
Belvidere, Ill., 222
Belzoni, Miss., 256
Bemidji, Minn., 254
Bemis, Tenn., 237
Benadir (prov.), Somalia, 115
Benalla, Vic., 97
Benares (Varanasi), India, 68
Ben Avon Pa., 294
Benbecula (isl.), Scot., 15
Benbrook, Tex., 302
Bend, Oreg., 291
Bendery, U.S.S.R., 52
Bendigo, Vic., 97
Bene Beraq, Israel, 65
Benevento (prov.), Italy, 34
Benevento, Italy, 34
Benfica, Port., 33
Benfleet, Eng., 13
Bengal (bay), Asia, 68
Bengalen (passage), Indon., 85
Benghazi (prov.), Libya, 111
Benghazi (cap.), Libya, 111
Bengkalis, Indon., 85
Bengkulu, Indon., 85

Bên Gôi (bay), S. Vietnam, 72
Benguela (dist.), Angola, 115
Benguela, Angola, 115
Benguet (prov.), Phil. Is., 82
Benha, U.A.R., 111
Beni, El (dept.), Bolivia, 136
Benicia, Calif., 204
Beni Mazar, U.A.R., 111
Beni-Mellal, Mor., 106
Benin (bight), Africa, 106
Benin City, Nigeria, 106
Beni Suef, U.A.R., 111
Benjamín Hill, Mex., 150
Bennettsville, S.C., 296
Ben Nevis (mt.), Scot., 15
Bennington, Vt., 268
Benoni, S. Africa, 118
Benque Viejo, Br. Hond., 154
Bensenville, Ill., 222
Bensheim, W. Ger., 22
Benson, Ariz., 198
Benson, Minn., 254
Bentleyville, Pa., 294
Benton, Ark., 204
Benton, Ill., 222
Benton, Ky., 237
Bentong, Malaysia, 72
Benton Harbor, Mich., 250
Bentonville, Ark., 203
Bent's Old Fort Nat'l Hist. Site, Colo., 209
Benue (riv.), Africa, 106
Benue-Plateau (state), Nigeria, 106
Benwood, W. Va., 313
Beograd (Belgrade) (cap.), Yugo., 45
Beppu, Japan, 81
Bequia (isl.), St. Vincent, 156
Berar (reg.), India, 68
Berat, Albania, 45
Berau (bay), Indon., 85
Berber, Sudan, 111
Berbera, Somalia, 115
Berbérati, Centr. Afr. Rep., 115
Berchem, Belg., 27
Berchtesgaden, W. Ger., 22
Berdichev, U.S.S.R., 52
Berdyansk, U.S.S.R., 52
Berea, Ky., 237
Berea, Ohio, 284
Beregovo, U.S.S.R., 52
Berens (riv.), Canada, 179
Berettyő (riv.), Hung., 41
Berezina (riv.), U.S.S.R., 52
Berezniki, U.S.S.R., 52
Bergama, Turkey, 63
Bergamo (prov.), Italy, 34
Bergamo, Italy, 34
Bergen, Neth., 27
Bergen, Norway, 18
Bergenfield, N. J., 273
Bergen op Zoom, Neth., 27
Bergerac, France, 28
Bergisch Gladbach, W. Ger., 22
Berhampore, India, 68
Berhampur, India, 68
Bering (sea), 3
Bering (strait), 196
Berkeley, Calif., 204
Berkeley, Ill., 222
Berkeley, Mo., 261
Berkeley Hts., N. J., 273
Berkeley Sprs., W. Va., 313
Berkley, Mich., 250
Berkovitsa, Bulg., 45
Berkshire (county), Eng., 13
Berkshire (hills), Mass., 249
Berlin, Conn., 210
Berlin, N.H., 268
Berlin, N. J., 373
Berlin, Wis., 317
Berlin, East (cap.), E. Ger., 22
Berlin, West, W. Ger., 22
Bermeo, Spain, 33
Bermuda, 156
Bermuda (isl.), Berm., 156
Bern (canton), Switz., 39
Bern (cap.), Switz., 39
Bernalillo, N. Mex., 274
Bernardsville, N. J., 273
Bernburg, E. Ger., 22
Bernese Oberland (reg.), Switz., 39
Bernierville, Que., 172
Bernina (mts.), Europe, 39
Bernina (pass), Switz., 39
Beroun, Czech., 41
Berry (isls.), Bah. Is., 156
Berthierville, Que., 172
Beru (atoll), Gilb. & Ellice Is., 87
Berwick, La., 238
Berwick, Pa., 294
Berwick (county), Scot., 15
Berwick, Vic., 97
Berwick-upon-Tweed, Eng., 13
Berwyn, Ill., 222
Berwyn, Pa., 294
Berwyn (mts.), Wales, 13
Besançon, France, 28
Beşiktaş, Turkey, 63
Beskids (mts.), Europe, 41
Beslan, U.S.S.R., 52
Besni, Turkey, 63
Bessemer, Ala., 194
Bessemer, Mich., 250
Bessemer City, N.C., 281
Bethalto, Ill., 222
Bethanie, S.W. Afr., 118
Bethany, Mo., 261
Bethany, Okla., 288
Bethel, Alaska, 196
Bethel, Conn.. 210
Bethel Park, Pa., 294
Bethesda, Md., 245
Bethesda, Wales, 13
Bethlehem, Jordan, 65
Bethlehem, Pa., 294
Bethlehem, S. Africa, 118
Béthune, France, 28
Bet She'an, Israel, 65
Betsiamites (riv.), Que., 174
Bettendorf, Iowa, 229
Bettiah, India, 68
Beverley, Eng., 13
Beverly, Mass., 249
Beverly, N. J., 273
Beverly Hills, Calif., 204
Beverwijk, Neth., 27
Bewdley, Eng., 10
Bexhill, Eng., 13
Bexley, Eng., 10
Bexley, Ohio, 284
Beykoz, Turkey, 63
Beyla, Guinea, 106
Beyoğlu, Turkey, 63
Beyşehir (lake), Turkey, 63
Bezhetsk, U.S.S.R., 52
Béziers, France, 28
Bhadrak, India, 68
Bhadravati, India, 68
Bhadreswar, India, 68
Bhagalpur, India, 68
Bhaktapur, Nepal, 68
Bhamo, Burma, 72
Bhandara, India, 68
Bhandup, India, 68
Bharatpur, India, 68
Bhatinda, India, 68
Bhatpara, India, 68
Bhavnagar, India, 68
Bheri (riv.), Nepal, 68
Bhilai, India, 68
Bhilwara, India, 68
Bhimavaram, India, 68
Bhir (Bir), India, 68
Bhiwandi, India, 68
Bhiwani, India, 68
Bhopal, India, 68
Bhubaneswar, India, 68
Bhuj, India, 68
Bhusawal, India, 68
Bhutan (prot.), India, 68
Biafra (bight), Africa, 106
Biak, Indon., 85
Biak (isl.), Indon., 85
Biała Podlaska, Poland, 47
Białogard, Poland, 47
Białystok (prov.), Poland, 47
Białystok, Poland, 47
Biarritz, France, 28
Bibai, Japan, 81
Biberach, W. Ger., 22
Bicknell, Ind., 227
Bidar, India, 68
Biddeford, Maine, 242
Bideford, Eng., 13
Bié (dist.), Angola, 115
Biel, Switz., 39
Bielawa, Poland, 47
Bielefeld, W. Ger., 22
Biella, Italy, 34
Bielsko-Biała, Poland, 47
Bienfait, Sask., 181
Bien Hoa, S. Vietnam, 72
Bienville (lake), Que., 174
Biga, Turkey, 63
Big Bell, W. Austral., 92
Big Bend (res.), Alta., 182
Big Bend Nat'l Park, Tex., 302
Biggar, Sask., 181
Biggar, Scot., 15
Big Hole Nat'l Battlefield, Mont., 262
Bighorn (riv.), U.S., 188
Bighorn Canyon Natl Rec. Area, Wyo., 318
Big Lake, Tex., 302
Big Rapids, Mich., 250
Big River, Sask., 181
Big Spring, Tex., 302
Big Stone Gap, Va., 307
Big Timber, Mont., 262
Bihać, Yugo., 45
Bihar (state), India, 68
Bihar, India, 68
Bijagós (isls.), Port. Guinea, 106
Bijapur, India, 68
Bijeljina, Yugo., 45
Bijistan, Iran, 66
Bijnor, India, 68
Bikaner, India, 68
Bikar (atoll), Pac. Is., 87
Bikini (atoll), Pac. Is., 87
Bilaspur, India, 68
Bilauktaung (range), Asia, 72
Bilbao, Spain, 33
Bilecik (prov.), Turkey, 63
Bilibino, U.S.S.R., 48
Billings, Mont., 262
Billiton (isl.), Indon., 85
Biloxi, Miss., 256
Biminis, The (isls.), Bah. Is., 156
Bina, India, 68
Bindjai, Indon., 85
Bingen, W. Ger., 22
Bingerville, Ivory Coast, 106
Binghamton, N.Y., 276
Bingöl (prov.), Turkey, 63
Binh Dinh, S. Vietnam, 72
Binningen, Switz., 39
Bintan (isl.), Indon., 85
Bintulu, Malaysia, 85
Bío-Bío (prov.), Chile, 138
Biograd, Yugo., 45
Bir, India, 68
Bir 'Ali, P.D.R. Yemen, 59
Biratnagar, Nepal, 68
Birch (mts.), Alta., 182
Birchwood, Alaska, 196
Birdsboro, Pa., 294
Birecik, Turkey, 63
Birganj, Nepal, 68
Birjand, Iran, 66
Birkenhead, Eng., 10
Birkerød, Den., 21
Birksgate (range), S. Austral., 94
Bîrlad, Rum., 45
Birmingham, Ala., 194
Birmingham, Eng., 10
Birmingham, Mich., 250
Bir-Mogrein, Mauritania, 106
Birni-N'Konni, Niger, 106
Birobidzhan, U.S.S.R., 48
Birr, Ire., 17
Birsay, Scot., 15
Birsk, U.S.S.R., 52
Bir Zeit, Jordan, 65
Bisbee, Ariz., 198
Biscay (bay), Europe, 7
Biscayne Nat'l Mon., Fla., 212
Bisceglie, Italy, 34
Biscoe (isls.), Ant., 5
Bisha, Saudi Ar., 59
Bishop, Calif., 204
Bishop, Tex., 302
Bishop Auckland, Eng., 13
Bishop's Falls, Newf., 166
Bishop's Stortford, Eng., 13
Bishopville, S.C., 296
Biskra, Alg., 106
Bismarck (cap.), N. Dak., 283
Bismarck (arch.), Terr. N.G., 87
Bissau (cap.), Port. Guinea, 106
Bissett, Man., 179
Bistrița, Rum., 45
Bitam, Gabon, 115
Bitlis (prov.), Turkey, 63
Bitlis, Turkey, 63
Bitola, Yugo., 45
Bitterfeld, E. Ger., 22
Bitterroot (range), U.S., 188
Biwa (lake), Japan, 81
Biysk, U.S.S.R., 48
Bizerte, Tun., 106
Bjelovar, Yugo., 45
Bjørnoya (isl.), Norway, 18
Black (sea), 52
Black (riv.), Asia, 72
Black (for.), W. Ger., 22
Blackall, Queensland, 95
Blackburn, Eng., 10
Black Canyon of the Gunnison Nat'l Mon., Colo., 208
Black Diamond, Alta., 182
Black Elster (riv.), E. Ger., 22
Blackfoot, Idaho, 220
Black Forest, Colo., 208
Black Hills (mts.), U.S., 188
Blackoak, Ind., 227
Blackpool, Eng., 10
Black River, Jam., 158
Black River Falls, Wis., 317
Black Rock (des.), Nev., 266
Blacksburg, Va., 307
Blackstone, Va., 307
Blacktown, N.S.W., 97
Blackwater (riv.), Eng., 13
Blackwater (riv.), Ire., 17
Blackwater (riv.), N. Ire., 17
Blackwell, Okla., 288
Blackwood (Ngundju) (cape), Indon., 85
Bladensburg, Md., 245
Blagoveshchensk, U.S.S.R., 48
Blagoyevgrad, Bulg., 45
Blaine, Minn., 254
Blair, Nebr., 264
Blair-Atholl, Scot., 15
Blairgowrie and Rattray, Scot., 15
Blairmore, Alta., 182
Blairsville, Pa., 294
Blaj, Rum., 45
Blakely, Ga., 216
Blakely, Pa., 294
Blanc (cape), Africa, 102
Blanc (mt.), Europe, 28
Blanc (cape), Tun., 106
Blanca (peak), Colo., 208
Blanche (lake), S. Austral., 94
Blanchester, Ohio, 284
Blanco (riv.), Mex., 150
Blanco (cape), Oreg., 291
Blankenburg, E. Ger., 22
Blantyre, Malawi, 115
Blarney, Ire., 17
Blasdell, N.Y., 276
Blasket (isls.), Ire., 17.
Blaydon, Eng., 13
Bled, Yugo., 45
Blekinge (county), Sweden, 18
Blenheim, N.Z., 101
Bletchley, Eng., 13
Blida, Alg., 106
Blind River, Ont., 177
Blissfield, Mich., 250
Blitar, Indon., 85
Block (isl.), R.I., 249
Bloemfontein, S. Africa, 118
Blois, France, 28
Bloodvein (riv.), Man., 179
Bloody Foreland (prom.), Ire., 17
Bloomer, Wis., 317
Bloomfield, N. J., 273
Bloomfield Hills, Mich., 250
Bloomington, Calif., 204
Bloomington, Ill., 222
Bloomington, Ind., 227
Bloomington, Minn., 254
Bloomsburg, Pa., 294
Blora, Indon., 85
Bludenz, Austria, 41
Blue (mts.), Oreg., 291
Blue Ash, Ohio, 284
Blue Earth, Minn., 254
Bluefield, Va., 307
Bluefield, W. Va., 313
Bluefields, Nic., 154
Blue Hills, Conn., 210
Blue Island, Ill., 222
Blue Mountain (peak), Jam., 158
Blue Mountains, N.S.W., 97
Blue Nile (riv.), Africa, 111
Blue Nile (prov.), Sudan, 111
Blue Springs, Mo., 261
Bluff, N.Z., 101
Bluff Park, Ala., 194
Bluffton, Ind., 227
Bluffton, Ohio, 284
Blumenau, Braz., 132
Blyth, Eng., 13
Blythe, Calif., 204
Blytheville, Ark., 203
Bo, S. Leone, 106
Boardman, Ohio, 284
Boa Vista, Braz., 132
Boaz, Ala., 194
Bobigny, France, 28
Böblingen, W. Ger., 22
Bobo-Dioulasso, Upp. Volta,106
Bobotov Kuk (mt.), Yugo., 45
Bobrinets, U.S.S.R., 52
Bobruysk, U.S.S.R., 52
Boca Raton, Fla., 212
Bocas del Toro, Pan., 154
Bochnia, Poland, 47
Bocholt, W. Ger., 22
Bochum, W. Ger., 22
Bodaybo, U.S.S.R., 48
Bodélé (depr.), Chad, 111
Boden, Sweden, 18
Bodensee (Constance) (lake), Europe, 39
Bodinayakkanur, India, 68
Bodjonegoro, Indon., 85
Bodø, Norway, 18
Bogalusa, La., 238
Bogatynia, Poland, 47
Bogdan (mt.), Bulg., 45
Bogdo Ula (mts.), China, 77
Boghé, Mauritania, 106
Bogia, Terr. N.G., 85
Bognor Regis, Eng., 13
Bogor, Indon., 85
Bogotá (cap.), Col., 126
Bogota, N. J., 273
Bogra, Pak., 68
Bohemia (reg.), Czech., 41
Bohemian (for.), Europe, 22
Bohol (prov.), Phil. Is., 82
Bohol (isl.), Phil. Is., 82
Boise (cap.), Idaho, 220
Boise City, Okla., 288
Boissevain, Man., 179
Bojador (cape), Sp. Sahara, 106
Boké, Guinea, 106
Boksburg, S. Africa, 118
Bokungu, Dem. Rep. of the Congo, 115
Bolama, Port. Guinea, 106
Bolan (pass), Pak., 68
Bolesławiec, Poland, 47
Bolívar, Arg., 143
Bolívar (dept.), Col., 126
Bolívar (prov.), Ecua., 128
Bolivar, Mo., 261
Bolivar, Tenn., 237
Bolívar (state), Venez., 124
Bolívar (mt.), Venez., 124
Bolivia, 136
Bolligen, Switz., 39
Bollington, Eng., 10
Bollnäs, Sweden, 18
Bologna (prov.), Italy, 34
Bologna, Italy, 34
Bologoye, U.S.S.R., 52
Bolovens (plat.), Laos, 72
Bolsena (lake), Italy, 34
Bolsover, Eng., 13
Bolton, Eng., 10
Bolu (prov.), Turkey, 63
Bolu, Turkey, 63
Bolvadin, Turkey, 63
Bolvanskiy Nos (cape), U.S.S.R., 52
Bolzano (prov.), Italy, 34
Bolzano, Italy, 34
Boma, Dem. Rep. of the Congo, 115
Bombay, India, 68
Bomi Hills, Liberia, 106
Bomu (riv.), Africa, 115
Bon (cape), Tun., 106
Bonacca (Guanaja) (isl.), Hond., 154
Bonaire (isl.), Neth. Ant., 161
Bonanza, Nic., 154
Bonavista, Newf., 166
Bondi (beach), N.S.W., 97
Bondo, Dem. Rep. of the Congo, 115
Bône (Annaba), Alg., 106
Bone (gulf), Indon., 85
Bo'ness, Scot., 15
Bongor, Chad, 111
Bonham, Tex., 302
Bonifacio (strait), Europe, 34
Bonin (isls.), Japan, 81
Bonn (cap.), W. Ger., 22
Bonners Ferry, Idaho, 220
Bonner Sprs., Kans., 232
Bonne Terre, Mo., 261
Bonneville (dam), U.S., 310
Bonny, Nigeria, 106
Bonnyrigg and Lasswade, Scot., 15
Bonnyville, Alta., 182
Bonthain, Indon., 85
Bonthe, S. Leone, 106
Bontoc, Phil. Is., 82
Booker T. Washington Nat'l Mon., Va., 307
Boone, Iowa, 229
Boone, N.C., 281
Booneville, Ark., 203
Booneville, Miss., 256
Boonton, N. J., 273
Boonville, Mo., 261
Boothbay Hbr., Maine, 242
Boothia (gulf), N.W.T., 187
Boothia (pen.), N.W.T., 187
Boothwyn, Pa., 294
Bootle, Eng., 10
Boquerón (dept.), Par., 144
Boquerón (bay), P. Rico, 161
Bor, Yugo., 45
Bora-Bora (isl.), Fr. Poly., 87
Borah (peak), Idaho, 220
Borama, Somalia, 115
Borås, Sweden, 18
Borazjun, Iran, 66
Bordeaux, France, 28
Bordentown, N. J., 273
Bordj-Bou-Arréridj, Alg., 106
Borgå, Fin., 18
Borger, Tex., 302
Borgerhout, Belg., 27
Borgomanero, Italy, 34
Borikhane, Laos, 72
Borinquen (pt.), P. Rico, 161
Borislav, U.S.S.R., 52
Borisoglebsk, U.S.S.R., 52
Borisov, U.S.S.R., 52
Borku (reg.), Chad, 111
Borlänge, Sweden, 18
Borneo (isl.), Asia, 85
Borneo (Kalimantan)(reg.), Indon., 85
Bornholm (isl.), Den., 21
Bor Nor (lake), Asia, 77
Bornova, Turkey, 63
Bornu (reg.), Nigeria, 106
Borongan, Phil. Is., 82
Borovichi, U.S.S.R., 52
Borroloola, N. Terr., 93
Borsod-Abaúj-Zemplen (county), Hung., 41
Boruca, C. Rica, 154
Borzhomi, U.S.S.R., 52
Borzya, U.S.S.R., 48
Bosanski Brod, Yugo., 45
Bosanski Novi, Yugo., 45
Bosaso, Somalia, 115
Boscobel, Wis., 317
Bosna (riv.), Yugo., 45
Bosnia and Hercegovina (rep.), Yugo., 45
Boso (pen.), Japan, 81
Bosporus (str.), Turkey, 63
Bossangoa, Centr. Afr. Rep., 115
Bossier City, La., 238
Boston, Eng., 13
Boston (cap.), Mass., 249
Botany, N.S.W., 97
Botany (bay), N.S.W., 97
Botevgrad, Bulg., 45
Bothnia (gulf), Europe, 18
Botoșani, Rum., 45
Botswana, 118
Bottineau, N. Dak., 283
Bottrop, W. Ger., 22
Botucatu, Braz., 135
Botwood, Newf., 166
Bouaké, Ivory Coast, 106
Bouar, Centr. Afr. Rep., 115
Bouches-du-Rhône (dept.), France, 28
Bougainville (isl.), Terr. N.G., 87
Bougainville (cape), W. Austral., 92
Bougouni, Mali, 106
Boulder, Colo., 208
Boulder, W. Austral., 92
Boulder City, Nev., 266
Boulogne-Billancourt, France, 28
Boulogne-sur-Mer, France, 28
Boundary (peak), Nev., 266
Bound Brook, N. J., 273
Bountiful, Utah, 304
Bounty (isls.), N.Z., 87
Bourail, New Cal., 87
Bourbonnais, Ill., 222
Bourg, France, 28
Bourges, France, 28
Bourke, N.S.W., 97
Bourlamaque, Que., 174
Bournemouth, Eng., 13
Boutilimit, Mauritania, 106
Bouvet (isl.), Ant., 5
Bow (riv.), Alta., 182
Bowen, Queensland, 95
Bowie, Tex., 302
Bow Island, Alta., 182
Bowling Green, Ky., 237
Bowling Green, Mo., 261
Bowling Green, Ohio, 284
Bowling Green (cape), Queensland, 95
Bowmanville, Ont., 177
Bowmore, Scot., 15
Bowral, N.S.W., 97
Box Hill, Vic., 97
Boyacá (dept.), Col., 126
Boyer Ahmedi & Kahkiluye (governorate), Iran, 66
Boyertown, Pa., 294
Boyle, Ire., 17
Boyne (river), Ire., 17
Boyne City, Mich., 250
Boynton Beach, Fla., 212
Bozeman, Mont., 262
Bozoum, Centr. Afr. Rep., 115
Bra, Italy, 34
Brabant (prov.), Belg., 27
Brač (isl.), Yugo., 45
Bracciano (lake), Italy, 34
Bracebridge, Ont., 177
Brackenridge, Pa., 294
Bracknell, Eng., 13
Brackwede, W. Ger., 22
Brad, Rum., 45
Braddock, Pa., 294
Bradenton, Fla., 212
Bradford, Eng., 10
Bradford, Pa., 294
Bradley, Ill., 222
Bradley Beach, N. J., 273
Brady, Tex., 302
Braemar, Scot., 15
Braga, Port., 33
Bragado, Arg., 143
Bragança, Port., 33
Bragança Paulista, Braz., 135
Bragman's Bluff (Puerto Cabezas), Nic., 154
Brahmaputra (riv.), Asia, 68
Braich-y-Pwll (prom.), Wales, 13
Brăila, Rum., 45
Brainerd, Minn., 254
Braintree, Mass., 249
Braintree and Bocking, Eng., 13
Brakpan, S. Africa, 118
Bralorne, Br. Col., 184
Bramalea, Ont., 177
Bramble (bay), Queensland, 95
Brampton, Ont., 177
Brandenburg, E. Ger., 22
Brandenburg (reg.), E. Ger., 22
Brandon, Man., 179
Brandon and Byshottles, Eng., 13
Braniewo, Poland, 47
Bransfield (str.), Ant., 5
Brantford, Ont., 177
Brasília (cap.), Braz., 132
Brașov, Rum., 45
Bratislava, Czech., 41
Bratsk, U.S.S.R., 48
Bratsk (res.), U.S.S.R., 48
Brattleboro, Vt., 268
Braunau, Austria, 41
Braunschweig (Brunswick), W. Ger., 22
Brava, Somalia, 115
Bravo (Grande)(riv.), Mex., 150
Brawley, Calif., 204
Bray, Ire., 17
Brazeau (riv.), Alta., 182
Brazil, 132
Brazil, Ind., 227
Brazos (riv.), Tex., 302
Brazzaville (cap.), Rep. of Congo, 115
Brčko, Yugo., 45
Brea, Calif., 204
Breaux Bridge, La., 238
Brechin, Scot., 15
Breckenridge, Minn., 254
Breckenridge, Tex., 302
Breckenridge Hills, Mo., 261
Brecknock, Wales, 13
Brecksville, Ohio, 284
Břeclav, Czech., 41
Breconshire (county), Wales, 13
Breda, Neth., 27
Bregenz, Austria, 41
Breidhafjördhur (fjord), Ice., 21
Breisgau (reg.), W. Ger., 22
Breithorn (mt.), Switz., 39
Bremanger (isl.), Norway, 18
Bremen, Ga., 216
Bremen, Ind., 227
Bremen (state), W. Ger., 22
Bremen, W. Ger., 22
Bremerhaven, W. Ger., 22
Bremerton, Wash., 310
Brenham, Tex., 302
Brenner (pass), Europe, 41
Brent, Eng., 10
Brentwood, Eng., 10
Brentwood, Md., 245
Brentwood, N.Y., 276
Brentwood, Pa., 294
Brescia (prov.), Italy, 34
Brescia, Italy, 34
Breslau (Wrocław), Poland, 47
Bressanone, Italy, 34
Bressay (isl.), Scot., 15
Brest, France, 28
Brest, U.S.S.R., 52
Breton (sound), La., 238
Breton (cape), N.S., 169
Brevard, N.C., 281
Brewer, Maine, 242
Brewood, Eng., 10
Brewton, Ala., 194
Briançon, France, 28
Brices Cross Roads Nat'l Battlef. Site, Miss., 256
Bridgend, Wales, 13
Bridge of Allan, Scot., 15
Bridgeport, Ala., 194
Bridgeport, Conn., 210
Bridgeport, Ohio, 284
Bridgeport, Pa., 294
Bridgeport, Tex., 302
Bridgeport, W. Va., 313
Bridgeton, N. J., 273
Bridgetown (cap.), Barb., 161
Bridgeville, Pa., 294
Bridgewater, Mass., 249
Bridgewater, N.S., 169
Bridgwater, Eng., 13
Bridlington, Eng., 13
Brielle, N. J., 273
Brienz (lake), Switz., 39
Brierfield, Eng., 10
Brigantine, N. J., 273
Brigham City, Utah, 304
Brighouse, Eng., 13
Brighton, Ala., 194
Brighton, Colo., 208
Brighton, Eng., 13
Brighton, S. Austral., 94
Brighton, Vic., 97
Brikama, Gambia, 106
Brinkley, Ark., 203
Brindisi (prov.), Italy, 34
Brindisi, Italy, 34
Brisbane, Calif., 204
Brisbane (cap.), Queensland, 95
Bristol (bay), Alaska, 196
Bristol, Conn., 210
Bristol, Eng., 13
Bristol, Pa., 294
Bristol, R.I., 249
Bristol, Tenn., 237
Bristol (chan.), U.K., 13
Bristol, Va., 307
Bristow, Okla., 288
British Columbia (prov.), Canada, 184
British Honduras, 154
British Indian Ocean Terr., 54, 119
Brive, France, 28
Brno, Czech., 41
Broach, India, 68
Broad (sound), Queensland, 95
Broadmeadows, Vic., 97
Broadmoor, Colo., 209
Broadstairs and St. Peter's, Eng., 13
Broadview, Sask., 181
Brockport, N.Y., 276
Brockton, Mass., 249
Brockville, Ont., 177
Brockway, Pa., 294
Brod, Yugo., 45
Brodick, Scot., 15
Brodnica, Poland, 47
Broken Arrow, Okla., 288
Broken Bow, Nebr., 264
Broken Bow, Okla., 288
Broken Hill, N.S.W., 97
Brokopondo (dist.), Sur., 131
Bromley, Eng., 10
Bromsgrove, Eng., 10
Brønderslev, Den., 21
Bronte, Italy, 34
Bronx, N.Y., 276
Bronxville, N.Y., 276
Brookfield, Ill., 222
Brookfield, Mo., 261
Brookfield, Wis., 317
Brookhaven, Miss., 256
Brookhaven, Pa., 294
Brookhaven Nat'l Lab., N.Y., 276
Brookings, S. Dak., 298
Brooklands, Man., 179
Brookline, Mass., 249
Brooklyn, N.Y., 276
Brook Park, Ohio, 284
Brooks (range), Alaska, 196
Brooks, Alta., 182
Brooksville, Fla., 212
Brookville, Pa., 294
Broomall, Pa., 294
Broome, W. Austral., 92
Broomfield, Colo., 208
Brossard, Que., 172
Brown Deer, Wis., 317
Brownfield, Tex., 302
Browning, Mont., 262
Brownsburg, Ind., 227
Browns Village, Fla., 212
Brownsville, Pa., 294
Brownsville, Tenn., 237
Brownsville, Tex., 302
Brownwood, Tex., 302
Bruay-en-Artois, France, 28
Bruce (mt.), W. Austral., 92
Bruchsal, W. Ger., 22
Bruck, Austria, 41
Bruges, Belg., 27
Brühl, W. Ger., 22
Brundidge, Ala., 194
Brunei, 85
Brunner, N.Z., 101
Brunswick, Ga., 216
Brunswick, Maine, 242
Brunswick, Md., 245
Brunswick, Vic., 97
Brunswick, W. Ger., 22
Brus (lag.), Hond., 154
Brush, Colo., 208
Brussels (cap.), Belg., 27
Bryan, Ohio, 284
Bryan, Tex., 302
Bryansk, U.S.S.R., 52
Bryce Canyon Nat'l Park, Utah, 304
Bryn Mawr, Pa., 294
Brynmawr, Wales, 13
Bryn Mawr, Wash., 310
Brzeg, Poland, 47
Bubiyan (isl.), Kuwait, 59
Bucaramanga, Col., 126
Buchanan, Liberia, 106
Buchanan, Mich., 250
Buchans, Newf., 166
Bucharest (cap.), Rum., 45
Buckeye, Ariz., 198
Buckhannon, W. Va., 313
Buckhaven and Methil, Scot., 15
Buckie, Scot., 15
Buckingham, Que., 172
Buckinghamshire (county), Eng., 13
Buck Isl. Reef Nat'l Mon., Virgin Is. (U.S.), 161
Buckley, Wash., 310
Buctouche (riv.), N.B., 170
București (Bucharest) (cap.), Rum., 45
Bucyrus, Ohio, 284
Budafok, Hung., 41
Budapest (cap.), Hung., 41
Budaun, India, 68
Budd Coast (reg.), Ant., 5
Budge-Budge, India, 68
Budjala, Dem. Rep. of the Congo, 115
Buea, Cameroon, 115
Buechel, Ky., 237
Buena, N. J., 273
Buena Park, Calif., 204
Buenaventura, Col., 126
Buenaventura, Mex., 150
Buena Vista, Va., 307
Buenos Aires (prov.), Arg., 143
Buenos Aires (cap.), Arg., 143
Buenos Aires, C. Rica, 154
Buenos Aires (lake), S. Amer., 120
Buffalo, N.Y., 276
Buffalo, Wyo., 319
Buffalo Head (hills), Alta., 182
Buford, Ga., 216
Bug (riv.), Europe, 47
Bug (riv.), U.S.S.R., 52
Buga, Col., 126
Bugojno, Yugo., 45
Bugul'ma, U.S.S.R., 52
Buguruslan, U.S.S.R., 52
Buhl, Idaho, 220
Buhuşi, Rum., 45
Builth Wells, Wales, 13
Bujalance, Spain, 33
Bujnurd, Iran, 66
Bujumbura (cap.), Burundi, 115
Bukama, Dem. Rep. of the Congo, 115
Bukavu, Dem. Rep. of the Congo, 115
Bukhara, U.S.S.R., 48
Bukidnon (prov.), Phil. Is., 82
Bukittinggi, Indon., 85
Bulacan (prov.), Phil. Is., 82
Bulagan (prov.), Mong., 77
Bulagan, Mong., 77
Bulawayo, Rhod., 118
Buldan, Turkey, 63
Bulgaria, 45
Buller (riv.), N.Z., 101
Buller (mt.), Vic., 97
Bulloo (lake), Queensland, 95
Bulo Burti, Somalia, 115
Bulolo, Terr. N.G., 85
Bulsar, India, 68
Bulun, U.S.S.R., 48
Bumba, Dem. Rep. of the Congo, 115
Buna, Papua, 85
Bunbury, W. Austral., 92
Buncrana, Ire., 17
Bundaberg, Queensland, 95
Bundi, India, 68
Bungo (strait), Japan, 81
Bunguran (Natuna) (isls.), Indon., 85
Bunia, Dem. Rep. of the Congo, 115
Bunkie, La., 238
Bur Acaba, Somalia, 115
Buraida, Saudi Ar., 59
Buraimi, Asia, 59
Burao, Somalia, 115
Buras, La., 238
Burbank, Calif., 204
Burdekin (riv.), Queensland, 95
Burdur (prov.), Turkey, 63
Burdur, Turkey, 63
Burdwan, India, 68
Burg, E. Ger., 22
Burgas, Bulg., 45
Burgdorf, Switz., 39
Burgenland (prov.), Austria, 41
Burgeo, Newf., 166
Burgess Hill, Eng., 13
Burghead, Scot., 15
Burgos (prov.), Spain, 33
Burgos, Spain, 33
Burhanpur, India, 68
Burica (pt.), Cent. Amer., 154
Burien, Wash., 310
Burin, Newf., 166
Buriram, Thai., 72
Burkburnett, Tex., 302
Burley, Idaho, 220
Burlingame, Calif., 204
Burlington, Iowa, 229
Burlington, N. J., 273
Burlington, N.C., 281
Burlington, Ont., 177
Burlington, Vt., 268
Burlington, Wash., 310
Burlington, Wis., 317
Burma, 72
Burnaby, B.C., 184
Burnham, Pa., 294
Burnham-on-Sea, Eng., 13
Burnley, Eng., 10
Burns, Oreg., 291
Burns Harbor, Ind., 227
Burnside (riv.), N.W.T., 187
Burnside, S. Austral., 94
Burns Lake, Br. Col., 184
Burnsville, Minn., 254
Burntisland, Scot., 15
Burntwood, Eng., 10
Burntwood (riv.), Man., 179
Burqa, Jordan, 65
Burriana, Spain, 33
Burry Port, Wales, 13
Bursa (prov.), Turkey, 63
Bursa, Turkey, 63
Bur Sa'id (Port Said), U.A.R., 111
Burtonport, Ire., 17
Burton-upon-Trent, Eng., 10
Burtonwood, Eng., 10
Burträsk, Sweden, 18
Buru (isl.), Indon., 85
Burujird, Iran, 66
Burundi, 115
Burwood, N.S.W., 97
Bury, Eng., 10
Buryat A.S.S.R., U.S.S.R., 48
Burye, Eth., 111
Bury Saint Edmunds, Eng., 13
Bushey, Eng., 10
Bushire, Iran, 66
Buskerud (county), Norway, 18
Busselton, W. Austral., 92
Bussum, Neth., 27
Busto Arisizio, Italy, 34
Busuanga (isl.), Phil. Is., 82
Buta, Dem. Rep. of the Congo, 115
Butare, Rwanda, 115
Butaritari (Makin) (atoll), Gilb. & Ell. Is., 87
Bute (county), Scot., 15
Butembo, Dem. Rep. of the Congo, 115
Butler, Mo., 261
Butler, N. J., 273
Butler, Pa., 294
Butte, Mont., 262
Butterworth, Malaysia, 72
Buttonwoods, R.I., 249
Butuan, Phil. Is., 82
Butung (isl.), Indon., 85
Buxtehude, W. Ger., 22
Buxton, Eng., 10
Buy, U.S.S.R., 52
Buynaksk, U.S.S.R., 52
Büyük Ağrı (Ararat) (mt.), Turkey, 63
Buzău, Rum., 45
Buziaş, Rum., 45
Buzuluk, U.S.S.R., 52
Buzzards Bay, Mass., 249
Byala, Bulg., 45
Byala Slatina, Bulg., 45
Bydgoszcz (prov.), Poland, 47
Bydgoszcz, Poland, 47
Bylot (isl.), N.W.T., 187
Byram, Conn., 210
Byrd Sta., Ant., 5
Byron (cape), N.S.W., 97
Bytom, Poland, 47
Bytów, Poland, 47

C

Caacupé, Par., 144
Caaguazú (dept.), Par., 144
Caatingas (reg.), Braz., 120
Caazapá (dept.), Par., 144
Caazapá, Par., 144
Cabaiguán, Cuba, 158
Cabimas, Venez., 124
Cabinda (dist.), Angola, 115
Cabo Delgado (dist.), Mozamb., 118
Cabonga (res.), Que., 174
Cabot (str.), Canada, 163
Cabrillo Nat'l Mon., Calif., 204
Čačak, Yugo., 45
Cáceres (prov.), Spain, 33
Cáceres, Spain, 33
Cacheu, Port. Guinea, 106
Cachoeira do Sul, Braz., 132
Cachoeiro de Itapemirim, Braz., 132
Caconda, Angola, 115
Cader Idris (mts.), Wales, 13
Cadillac, Mich., 250
Cadiz, Ohio, 284
Cádiz (prov.), Spain, 33
Cádiz, Spain, 33
Cádiz (gulf), Spain, 33
Caen, France, 28
Caerleon, Wales, 13
Caernarvon, Wales, 13
Caernarvonshire (county), Wales, 13
Caerphilly, Wales, 13
Cagayan (prov.), Phil. Is., 82
Cagayan de Oro, Phil. Is., 82
Cagayan Sulu (isl.), Phil. Is., 82
Cagliari (prov.), Italy, 34
Cagliari, Italy, 34
Cagliari (gulf), Italy, 34
Cagua, Venez., 124
Caguán (riv.), Col., 126
Caguas, P. Rico, 161
Cahir, Ire., 17
Cahirciveen, Ire., 17
Cahokia, Ill., 222
Cahors, France, 28
Caibarién, Cuba, 158
Caicos (isls.), Turks & Caicos Is., 156
Caicos (passage), W. Indies, 156
Caimanera, Cuba, 158
Caird Coast (reg.), Ant., 5
Cairngorm (mts.), Scot., 15
Cairns, Queensland, 95
Cairo, Ga., 216
Cairo, Ill., 222
Cairo (cap.), U.A.R., 111
Caithness (county), Scot., 15
Cajamarca (dept.), Peru, 128
Cajamarca, Peru, 128
Calabar, Nigeria, 106
Calabozo, Venez., 124
Calabria (reg.), Italy, 34
Calahorra, Spain, 33
Calais (Dover) (strait), Europe, 13
Calais, France, 28
Calais, Maine, 242
Calama, Chile, 138
Calamian Group (isls.), Phil. Is., 82
Călăraşi, Rum., 54
Calatayud, Spain, 33
Calcasieu (lake), La., 238
Calcutta, India, 68
Caldas (dept.), Col., 126
Caldas da Rainha, Port., 33
Caldwell, Idaho, 220
Caldwell, N. J., 273
Caldy (isl.), Wales, 13
Caledonia, Minn., 254
Caledonian (canal), Scot., 15
Calexico, Calif., 204
Calf of Man (isl.), Isle of Man, 13
Calgary, Alta., 182
Calheta, Port., 33
Calhoun, Ga., 216
Calhoun Falls, S.C., 296
Cali, Col., 126
Calicut (Kozhikode), India, 68
Caliente, Nev., 266
California (gulf), Mex., 150
California, Mo., 261
California, Pa., 294
California (state), U.S., 204
Calipatria, Calif., 204
Callao (prov.), Peru, 128
Callao, Peru, 128
Caloocan, Phil. Is., 82
Caltagirone, Italy, 34
Caltanissetta (prov.), Italy, 34
Caltanissetta, Italy, 34
Caluire, France, 28
Calumet City, Ill., 222
Calumet Park, Ill., 222
Calvados (dept.), France, 28
Calvinia, S. Afr., 118

Camagüey (prov.), Cuba, 158
Camagüey, Cuba, 158
Camajuaní, Cuba, 158
Camarillo, Calif., 204
Camarines Norte (prov.), Phil. Is., 82
Camarines Sur (prov.), Phil. Is., 82
Camarón (cape), Hond., 154
Camas, Wash., 310
Ca Mau (pt.), S. Vietnam, 72
Cambay, India, 68
Cambay (gulf), India, 68
Camberwell, Vic., 97
Cambodia, 72
Cambrai, France, 28
Cambrian (mts.), Wales, 13
Cambridge, Eng., 13
Cambridge, Md., 245
Cambridge, Mass., 249
Cambridge, Minn., 254
Cambridge, Ohio, 284
Cambridge Bay, N.W.T., 187
Cambridge City, Ind., 227
Cambridgeshire and the Isle of Ely (county), Eng., 13
Camden, Ark., 203
Camden, Eng., 10
Camden, Maine, 242
Camden, N. J., 273
Camden, N.S.W., 97
Camden, N.Y., 276
Camden, S.C., 296
Camden, Tenn., 237
Cameron, Mo., 261
Cameron (mts.), N.Z., 101
Cameron, Tex., 302
Cameron Highlands, Malaysia, 85
Cameroon, 115
Cameroon (mt.), Cameroon, 115
Camiguin (prov.), Phil. Is., 82
Camilla, Ga., 216
Camiri, Bol., 136
Camoapa, Nic., 154
Camopi, Fr. Gui., 131
Camotes (isls.), Phil. Is., 82
Campana, Arg., 143
Campana (isl.), Chile, 138
Campanario (mt.), S. Amer., 143
Campania (reg.), Italy, 34
Campbell, Calif., 204
Campbell (isl.), N.Z., 3
Campbell, Ohio, 284
Campbellford, Ont., 177
Campbellpore, Pak., 68
Campbell River, Br. Col., 184
Campbellsville, Ky., 237
Campbellton, N.B., 170
Campbelltown, N.S.W., 97
Campbelltown, S. Austral., 94
Campbeltown, Scot., 15
Campeche (state), Mex., 150
Campeche, Mex., 150
Campeche (bay), Mex., 150
Campechuela, Cuba, 158
Camp Hill, Pa., 294
Camp Hill, Queensland, 95
Campina Grande, Braz., 132
Campinas, Braz., 135
Campobasso (prov.), Italy, 34
Campobasso, Italy, 34
Campobello (isl.), N.B., 170
Campo Grande, Braz., 132
Campo Maior, Port., 33
Campos, Braz., 135
Campos (reg.), Braz., 120
Cam Ranh (bay), S. Vietnam, 72
Camrose, Alta., 182
Camuy, P. Rico, 161
Canada, 163
Cañada de Gómez, Arg., 143
Canadian (riv.), U.S., 188
Canajoharie, N.Y., 276
Çanakkale (prov.), Turkey, 63
Çanakkale, Turkey, 63
Canal Zone, 154
Canandaigua, N.Y., 276
Cananea, Mex., 150
Cañar (prov.), Ecua., 128
Canary (isls.), Spain, 33
Cañas, C. Rica, 154
Canastota, N.Y., 276
Canaveral (Kennedy) (cape), Fla., 212
Canavieiras, Braz., 132
Canberra (cap.), Austral., 97
Cancer, Tropic of, 3
Candala, Somalia, 115
Candelaria (riv.), Mex., 150
Candia (Iráklion), Greece, 45
Candlewood (lake), Conn., 210
Canea (Khaniá), Greece, 45
Caneel (bay), Virgin Is. (U.S.), 161
Canelones (dept.), Urug., 145
Canelones, Urug., 145
Cañete, Chile, 138
Caney, Kans., 232
Canfield, Ohio, 284
Caniapiscau (riv.), Que., 174
Caniçado, Mozamb., 118
Canisteo, N.Y., 276
Çankaya, Turkey, 63
Çankırı (prov.), Turkey, 63
Çankırı, Turkey, 63
Canlaon, Phil. Is., 82
Canmore, Alta., 182
Cannanore, India, 68
Cannes, France, 28
Cannock, Eng., 10
Caño (isl.), C. Rica, 154
Canoas, Brazil, 132
Canoga Park, Calif., 204
Canon City, Colo., 208
Canonsburg, Pa., 294
Canora, Sask., 181
Canosa di Puglia, Italy, 34
Canouan (isl.), St. Vincent, 156
Canso (str.), N.S., 169
Cantabrian (mts.), Spain, 33
Cantal (dept.), France, 28
Cantaura, Venez., 124
Canterbury, Eng., 13
Canterbury, N.S.W., 97
Canterbury (prov. dist.), N.Z., 101
Canterbury (bight), N.Z., 101
Can Tho, S. Vietnam, 72
Cantin (cape), Mor., 106
Canton, China, 77
Canton (isl.), Gilb. and Ell. Is., 87
Canton, Ill., 222
Canton, Miss., 256
Canton, Mo., 261
Canton, N.Y., 276
Canton, N.C., 281
Canton, Ohio, 284
Canton, S. Dak., 298
Canumã (riv.), Braz., 132
Canyon, Tex., 302
Canyon de Chelly Nat'l Mon., Ariz., 198
Canyon Ferry (lake), Mont., 262
Canyonlands Nat'l Park, Utah, 304
Cao Bang, N. Vietnam, 72
Caparica, Port., 33
Cap-Chat, Que., 172
Cap-de-la-Madeleine, Que., 172
Cape (pen.), S. Africa, 118
Cape Barren (isl.), Tas., 99
Cape Breton (isl.), N.S., 169
Cape Breton Highlands Nat'l Park, N.S., 169
Cape Canaveral, Fla., 212
Cape Charles, Va., 307
Cape Coast, Ghana, 106
Cape Cod Nat'l Seashore, Mass., 249
Cape Coral, Fla., 212
Cape Girardeau, Mo., 261
Cape Hatteras Nat'l Seashore, N.C., 281
Cape Lookout Nat'l Seashore, N.C., 281
Cape May, N. J., 273
Cape of Good Hope (prov.), S. Africa, 118
Capesterre, Guad., 161
Cape Town (cap.), S. Africa, 118
Cape Verde Islands, 106
Cape York (pen.), Queensland, 95
Cap-Haïtien, Haiti, 158
Capim (riv.), Braz., 132
Capitol Reef Nat'l Mon., Utah, 304
Capiz (prov.), Phil. Is., 82
Capraia (isl.), Italy, 34
Capreol, Ont., 177
Capri (isl.), Italy, 34
Capricorn, Tropic of, 3
Capricorn Group (isls.), Queensland, 95
Caprivi Strip (reg.), S.W. Afr., 118
Cap Saint-Jacques, S. Vietnam, 72
Captain Cook, Hawaii, 218
Capua, Italy, 34
Capulin Mtn. Nat'l Mon., N. Mex., 274
Caquetá (intendency), Col., 126
Caquetá (riv.), Col., 126
Carabobo (state), Venez., 124
Caracal, Rum., 45
Caracas (cap.), Venez., 124
Carahue, Chile, 138
Carajás (range), Braz., 132
Carapeguá, Par., 144
Caratasca (lag.), Hond., 154
Caratinga, Braz., 135
Caravelas, Braz., 132
Carbet, Mart., 161
Carbonara (cape), Italy, 34
Carbondale, Ill., 222
Carbondale, Pa., 294
Carbonear, Newf., 166
Carcassonne, France, 28
Carchi (prov.), Ecua., 128
Cárdenas, Cuba, 158
Cárdenas, Mex., 150
Cardiel (lake), Arg., 143
Cardiff, Wales, 13
Cardiff-by-the-Sea, Calif., 204
Cardigan, Wales, 13
Cardigan (bay), Wales, 13
Cardiganshire (county), Wales, 13
Cardona, Urug., 145
Cardston, Alta., 182
Carey, Ohio, 284
Cariamanga, Ecua., 128
Caribbean (sea), 156
Cariboo (mts.), Br. Col., 184
Caribou, Maine, 242
Carib Reserve, Dominica, 161
Carinthia (prov.), Austria, 41
Caripito, Venez., 124
Carleton Place, Ont., 177
Carlin, Nev., 266
Carlingford (inlet), Ire., 17
Carlinville, Ill., 222
Carlisle, Eng., 13
Carlisle, Pa., 294
Carlow (county), Ire., 17
Carlow, Ire., 17
Carl Sandburg Home Nat'l Hist. Site, N.C., 281
Carlsbad, Calif., 204
Carlsbad, N. Mex., 274
Carlsbad Caverns Nat'l Park, N. Mex., 274
Carlstadt, N. J., 273
Carlton, Eng., 13
Carluke, Scot., 15
Carlyle, Ill., 222
Carlyle, Sask., 181
Carmacks, Yukon, 187
Carman, Man., 179
Carmarthen, Wales, 13
Carmarthen (bay), Wales, 13
Carmarthenshire (county), Wales, 13
Carmel, Calif., 204
Carmel (mt.), Israel, 65
Carmelo, Urug., 145
Carmen, Mex., 150
Carmen de Patagones, Arg., 143
Carmi, Ill., 222
Carmichael, Calif., 204
Carmiel, Israel, 65
Carmona, Angola, 115
Carmona, Spain, 33
Carnarvon, W. Austral., 92
Carnaxide, Port., 33
Carnduff, Sask., 181
Carnegie, Okla., 288
Carnegie, Pa., 294
Carnegie (lake), W. Austral., 92
Carnic Alps (range), Europe, 41
Carnot, Centr. Afr. Rep., 115
Carnoustie, Scot., 15
Carnsore (pt.), Ire., 17
Caro, Mich., 250
Carol City, Fla., 212
Carolina, P. Rico, 161
Caroline (isls.), Pac. Is., 87
Caroní (riv.), Venez., 124
Carora, Venez., 124
Carouge, Switz., 39
Carpathian (mts.), Europe, 7
Carpentaria (gulf), Austral., 88
Carpentersville, Ill., 222
Carpi, Italy, 34
Carpinteria, Calif., 204
Carrantuohill (mt.), Ire., 17
Carrara, Italy, 34
Carrera de Yeguas, Dom. Rep., 158
Carriacou (isl.), Grenada, 156
Carrick (dist.), Scot., 15
Carrickfergus, N. Ire., 17
Carrickmacross, Ire., 17
Carrick-on-Shannon, Ire., 17
Carrick-on-Suir, Ire., 17
Carrington, N. Dak., 283
Carrizo Springs, Tex., 302
Carrizozo, N. Mex., 274
Carroll, Iowa, 229
Carrollton, Ga., 216
Carrollton, Ill., 222
Carrollton, Ky., 237
Carrollton, Mich., 250
Carrollton, Mo., 261
Carrollton, Ohio, 284
Carrollton, Tex., 302
Carrot River, Sask., 181
Carsons, Calif., 204
Carson City (cap.), Nev., 266
Carson Sink (depr.), Nev., 266
Cartagena, Chile, 138
Cartagena, Col., 126
Cartagena, Spain, 33
Cartago, Col., 126
Cartago, C. Rica, 154
Carteret, N. J., 273
Cartersville, Ga., 216
Carterville, Ill., 222
Carthage, Ill., 222
Carthage, Mo., 261
Carthage, N.Y., 276
Carthage, Tex., 302
Cartwright, Newf., 166
Caruaru, Braz., 132
Carúpano, Venez., 124
Caruthersville, Mo., 261
Cary, Ill., 222
Cary, N.C., 281
Casablanca, Mor., 106
Casa Grande, Ariz., 198
Casa Grande Ruins Nat'l Mon., Ariz., 198
Casale Monferrato, Italy, 34
Casamance (riv.), Sen., 106
Casanare (riv.), Col., 126
Casas Grandes (riv.), Mex., 150
Cascade (range), U.S., 188
Cascais, Port., 33
Cascina, Italy, 34
Caserta (prov.), Italy, 34
Caserta, Italy, 34
Casey, Ill., 222
Cashel, Ire., 17
Casilda, Arg., 143
Casino, N.S.W., 97
Casiquiare, Brazo (riv.), Venez., 124
Casper, Wyo., 319
Caspian (sea), 54
Cassiar (mts.), Canada, 184
Cassino, Italy, 34
Castel Gandolfo, Italy, 34
Castellammare di Stabia, Italy, 34
Castellón (prov.), Spain, 33
Castellón de la Plana, Spain, 33
Castelo Branco, Port., 33
Castelvetrano, Italy, 34
Castile (reg.), Spain, 33
Castilla, Peru, 128
Castillo de San Marcos Nat'l Mon., Fla., 212
Castillos, Urug., 145
Castle (harb.), Berm., 156
Castlebar, Ire., 17
Castleblayney, Ire., 17
Castle Bromwich, Eng., 10
Castlecomer-Donaguile, Ire., 17
Castle Douglas, Scot., 15
Castleford, Eng., 13
Castlegar, Br. Col., 184
Castlemaine, Vic., 97
Castlerea, Ire., 17
Castle Shannon, Pa., 294
Castor, Alta., 182
Castres, France, 28
Castries (cap.), St. Lucia, 161
Castro, Chile, 138
Castro del Río, Spain, 33
Castro Valley, Calif., 204
Castroville, Calif., 204
Cat (isl.), Bah. Is., 156
Catacamas, Hond., 154
Catacaos, Peru, 128
Cataguases, Braz., 135
Catalão, Braz., 132
Catalonia (reg.), Spain, 33
Catamarca (prov.), Arg., 143
Catamarca, Arg., 143
Catanduanes (prov.), Phil. Is., 82
Catanduanes (isl.), Phil. Is., 82
Catanduva, Braz., 135
Catania (prov.), Italy, 34
Catania, Italy, 34
Cataño, P. Rico, 161
Catanzaro (prov.), Italy, 34
Catanzaro, Italy, 34
Catarman, Phil. Is., 82
Catasauqua, Pa., 294
Catemaco, Mex., 150
Caterham and Warlingham, Eng., 10
Catlettsburg, Ky., 237
Catoche (cape), Mex., 150
Catonsville, Md., 245
Catskill, N.Y., 276
Catskill (mts.), N.Y., 276
Catumbela, Angola, 115
Cauca (dept.), Col., 126
Cauca (riv.), Col., 126
Caucasus (mts.), U.S.S.R., 52
Caulfield, Vic., 97
Cauquenes, Chile, 138
Caura (riv.), Venez., 124
Causapscal, Que., 172
Causses (reg.), France, 28
Cautín (prov.), Chile, 138
Cauto (riv.), Cuba, 158
Cava, Italy, 34
Cavalier, N. Dak., 283
Cavally (riv.), Africa, 106
Cavan (county), Ire., 17
Cavan, Ire., 17
Caviana (isl.), Braz., 132
Cavite (prov.), Phil. Is., 82
Cavite, Phil. Is., 82
Cawnpore (Kanpur), India, 68
Cawood, Ky., 237
Caxias, Braz., 132
Caxias do Sul, Braz., 132
Cayambe, Ecua., 128
Cayce, S.C., 296
Cayenne (cap.), Fr. Gui., 131
Cayey, P. Rico, 161
Cayman Brac (isl.), Cayman Is., 156
Cayman Islands, 156
Cayo, Br. Hond., 154
Cayuga (lake), N.Y., 276
Cayuga Hts., N.Y., 276
Cazenovia, N.Y., 276
Čazma (riv.), Yugo., 45
Cazones (gulf), Cuba, 158
Ceanannus Mór, Ire., 17
Ceará (state), Braz., 132
Ceará (Fortaleza), Braz., 132
Cébaco (isl.), Pan., 154
Cebeci, Turkey, 63
Cebu (prov.), Phil. Is., 82
Cebu, Phil. Is., 82
Cebu (isl.), Phil. Is., 82
Cedar Breaks Nat'l Mon., Utah, 304
Cedarburg, Wis., 317
Cedar City, Utah, 304
Cedar Falls, Iowa, 229
Cedar Grove, N. J., 273
Cedarhurst, N.Y., 276
Cedar Lake, Ind., 227
Cedar Rapids, Iowa, 229
Cedartown, Ga., 216
Cedros (isl.), Mex., 150
Cegléd, Hung., 41
Cehegín, Spain, 33
Celaya, Mex., 150
Celebes (sea), Asia, 85
Celebes (isl.), Indon., 85
Celina, Ohio, 284
Celje, Yugo., 45
Celle, W. Ger., 22
Center, Tex., 302
Centereach, N.Y., 276
Center Line, Mich., 250
Centerville, Iowa, 229
Centerville, Ohio, 284
Central (dist.), Israel, 65
Central (prov.), Kenya, 115
Central (prov.), Mong., 77
Central (dept.), Par., 144
Central African Rep., 115
Central America, 154
Central City, Ky., 237
Central City, Nebr., 264
Central Falls, R.I., 249
Central Greece and Euboea (reg.), Greece, 45
Centralia, Ill., 222
Centralia, Mo., 261
Centralia, Wash., 310
Central Islip, N.Y., 276
Central Ural (mts.), U.S.S.R., 52
Central Valley, Calif., 204
Centreville, Ill., 222
Cephalonia (Kefallinía) (isl.), Greece, 45
Ceram (isl.), Indon., 85
Ceres, Calif., 204
Ceres, S. Africa, 118
Cerf (isl.), Seych., 118
Cerignola, Italy, 34
Cerritos, Calif., 204
Cerritos, Mex., 150
Cerro de Pasco, Peru, 128
Cerro Largo (dept.), Urug., 145
Cervera, Spain, 33
Cesar (dept.), Col., 126
Cesena, Italy, 34
Cēsis, U.S.S.R., 53
České Budějovice, Czech., 41
Český Těšín, Czech., 41
Cessnock, N.S.W., 97
Cetinje, Yugo., 45
Ceuta, Spain, 33
Cévennes (mts.), France, 28
Ceyhan, Turkey, 63
Ceylon, 68
Chacabuco, Arg., 143
Chachapoyas, Peru, 128
Chachoengsao, Thai., 72
Chaco (prov.), Arg., 143
Chaco (riv.), N. Mex., 274
Chaco, Gran (reg.), S. Amer., 120
Chaco Canyon Nat'l Mon., N. Mex., 274
Chad, 111
Chad (lake), Africa, 111
Chadron, Nebr., 264
Chaffee, Mo., 261
Chagai (hills), Asia, 68
Chagos (arch.), Br. Indian Ocean Terr. 54
Chagrin Falls, Ohio, 284
Chaguanas, Trin. & Tob., 161
Chaibasa, India, 68
Chai Buri, Thai., 68
Chaiyaphum, Thai., 68
Chajul, Guat., 154
Chalatenango, El Sal., 154
Chalcis (Khalkís), Greece, 45
Chalco, Mex., 150
Chaleur (bay), Canada, 170
Chalk River, Ont., 177
Challapata, Bol., 136
Chalmette Nat'l Hist. Pk., La., 238
Châlons-sur-Marne, France, 28
Chalon-sur-Saône, France, 28
Chalus, Iran, 66
Chambal (riv.), India, 68
Chamberlain, S. Dak., 298
Chambersburg, Pa., 294
Chambéry, France, 28
Chamblee, Ga., 216
Chambly, Que., 172
Chamdo, China, 77
Chamizal Nat'l Mem., Tex., 302
Chamonix, France, 28
Champaign, Ill., 222
Champassak, Laos, 72
Champdani, India, 68
Champerico, Guat., 154
Champigny-sur-Marne, France, 28
Champlain (lake), N. Amer., 268
Chañaral, Chile, 138
Chanda, India, 68
Chandeleur (isls.), La., 238
Chandernagore, India, 68
Chandigarh, India, 68
Chandler, Ariz., 198
Chandler, Okla., 288
Chandler, Que., 172
Changchih, China, 77
Changchow, China, 77
Changchun, China, 77
Changjin (res.), N. Korea, 81
Chang Pai Shan (range), N. Korea, 81
Changsha, China, 77
Chang Tang (plat.), China, 77
Changteh, China, 77
Changyeh, China, 77
Chankiang, China, 77
Channel (isl.), 13
Channel Isls. Nat'l Mon., Calif., 204
Channel-Port aux Basques, Newf., 166
Channelview, Tex., 302
Chanthaburi, Thai., 72
Chantilly, France, 28
Chanute, Kans., 232
Chaoan, China, 77
Chaoking, China, 77
Chao Phraya (riv.), Thai., 72
Chaotung, China, 77
Chaoyang, China, 77
Chapala (lake), Mex., 150
Chapayevsk, U.S.S.R., 52
Chapel Hill, N.C., 281
Chapelton, Jam., 158
Chapleau, Ont., 175
Chapra, India, 68
Charcas, Mex., 150
Charcot (isl.), Ant., 5
Chardon, Ohio, 284
Chardzhou, U.S.S.R., 48
Charente (dept.), France, 28
Charente (riv.), France, 28
Charente-Maritime (dept.), France, 28
Charenton-le-Pont, France, 28
Charikar, Afghan., 68
Chariton, Iowa, 229
Charity, Guyana, 131
Charleroi, Belg., 27
Charleroi, Pa., 294
Charlesbourg, Que., 172
Charles City, Iowa, 229
Charleston, Ill., 222
Charleston, Miss., 256
Charleston, Mo., 261
Charleston (peak), Nev., 266
Charleston, S.C., 296
Charleston (cap.), W. Va., 313
Charlestown, Ind., 227
Charlestown (cap.), Nevis, 161
Charles Town, W. Va., 313
Charleswood, Man., 179
Charleville, Queensland, 95
Charleville-Mézières, France, 28
Charlevoix, Mich., 250
Charlotte (harb.), Fla., 212
Charlotte, Mich., 250
Charlotte, N.C., 281
Charlotte Amalie (cap.), Virgin Is. (U.S.), 161
Charlottenburg, W. Ger., 22
Charlottesville, Va., 307
Charlottetown (cap.), P.E.I., 169
Charny, Que., 172
Charters Towers, Queensland, 95
Chartres, France, 28
Chascomús, Arg., 143
Chase City, Va., 307
Chaska, Minn., 254
Château-Chinon, France, 28
Châteaudun, France, 28
Château-Gontier, France, 28
Châteauguay, Que., 172
Châteauroux, France, 28
Château-Thierry, France, 28
Châtellerault, France, 28
Chatham, Eng., 13
Chatham, N.B., 170
Chatham, N. J., 273
Chatham (isls.), N.Z., 101
Chatham, Ont., 177
Châtillon, France, 28
Chatou, France, 28
Chatsworth, Calif., 204
Chattahoochee, Fla., 212
Chattahoochee (riv.), U.S., 188
Chattanooga, Tenn., 237
Chauk, Burma, 72
Chaumont, France, 28
Chau Phu, S. Vietnam, 72
Chauvin, La., 238
Chaves, Port., 33
Chaykovskiy, U.S.S.R., 52
Cheadle and Gatley, Eng., 10
Cheb, Czech., 41
Cheboksary, U.S.S.R., 52
Cheboygan, Mich., 250
Chechaouen, Mor., 106
Chechen-Ingush A.S.S.R., U.S.S.R., 52
Chech Erg (des.), Africa, 106
Checotah, Okla., 288
Cheduba (isl.), Burma, 72
Cheektowaga, N.Y., 276
Chefoo, China, 77
Chehalis, Wash., 310
Cheju (isl.), S. Korea, 81
Chekiang (prov.), China, 77
Chelan (lake), Wash., 310
Chéliff (riv.), Alg., 106
Chelkar, U.S.S.R., 48
Chelles, France, 28
Chełm, Poland, 47
Chełmno, Poland, 47
Chelmsford, Eng., 13
Chelsea, Mass., 249
Chelsea, Mich., 250
Chelsea, Vic., 97
Cheltenham, Eng., 13
Cheltenham, Pa., 294
Chelyabinsk, U.S.S.R., 48
Chelyuskin (cape), U.S.S.R., 48
Chemainus, Br. Col., 184
Chemba, Mozamb., 118
Chembur, India, 68
Chemnitz (Karl-Marx-Stadt), E. Ger., 22
Chenab (riv.), Asia, 68
Cheney, Wash., 310
Chengchow, China, 77
Chengteh, China, 77
Chengtu, China, 77
Chepén, Peru, 128
Chepo (riv.), Pan., 154
Chepstow, Wales, 13
Cher (dept.), France, 28
Cher (riv.), France, 28
Cheraw, S.C., 296
Cherbourg, France, 28
Cherchen (riv.), China, 77
Cheremkhovo, U.S.S.R., 48
Cherepovets, U.S.S.R., 52
Cherial (riv.), India, 68
Cherkassy, U.S.S.R., 52
Cherkessk, U.S.S.R., 52
Chermside, Queensland, 95
Chernigov, U.S.S.R., 52
Chernovtsy, U.S.S.R., 52
Cherokee, Iowa, 229
Cherokee, Okla., 288
Cherrapunji, India, 68
Cherry Hill, N. J., 273
Cherryvale, Kans., 232
Cherryville, N.C., 281
Cherskiy (range), U.S.S.R., 48
Chertsey, Eng., 10
Chesaning, Mich., 250
Chesapeake (bay), U.S., 188
Chesapeake, Va., 307
Chesapeake, W. Va., 313
Chesapeake & Ohio Canal Nat'l Mon., Md., 245
Chesham, Eng., 13
Cheshire, Conn., 210
Cheshire (county), Eng., 13
Cheshskaya (bay), U.S.S.R., 52
Cheshunt, Eng., 10
Chester, Eng., 10
Chester, Ill., 222
Chester, Pa., 294
Chester, S.C., 296
Chester, W. Va., 313
Chesterfield, Eng., 13
Chesterfield, Ind., 227
Chesterfield (isls.), New Cal., 87
Chesterfield (inlet), N.W.T., 187
Chester-le-Street, Eng., 13
Chesterton, Ind., 227
Chestertown, Md., 245
Chesterville, Que., 172
Cheswick, Pa., 294
Chetlat (isl.), India, 68
Chetumal, Mex., 150
Chetwynd, Br. Col., 184
Cheverly, Md., 245
Cheviot, Ohio, 284
Cheviot (hills), U.K., 13
Chevy Chase, Md., 245
Cheyenne (riv.), U.S., 188
Cheyenne (cap.), Wyo., 319
Chhatarpur, India, 68
Chhindwara, India, 68
Chhlong, Cambodia, 72
Chi (riv.), Thai., 72
Chiai, China, 77
Chiamboni, Ras (cape), Africa, 115
Chiang Rai, Thai., 72
Chiapas (state), Mex., 150
Chiatura, U.S.S.R., 52
Chiautempan, Mex., 150
Chiba (pref.), Japan, 81
Chiba, Japan, 81
Chibougamau, Que., 174
Chibuto, Mozamb., 118
Chicago, Ill., 222
Chicago Heights, Ill., 222
Chicago Portage Nat'l Hist. Site, Ill., 222
Chicago Ridge, Ill., 222
Chicapa (riv.), Africa, 115
Chichagof (isl.), Alaska, 196
Chichén-Itzá (ruins), Mex., 150
Chichester, Eng., 13
Chichi (isl.), Japan, 81
Chichicastenango, Guat., 154
Chichigalpa, Nic., 154
Chickamauga and Chattanooga Nat'l Mil. Pk., U.S., 237
Chickasaw, Ala., 194
Chickasha, Okla., 288
Chiclana de la Frontera, Spain, 33
Chiclayo, Peru, 128
Chico (riv.), Arg., 143
Chico, Calif., 204
Chicopee, Mass., 249
Chicoutimi, Que., 172
Chidambaram, India, 68
Chidley (cape), Canada, 166
Chiemsee (lake), W. Ger., 22
Chiengmai, Thai., 72
Chieti (prov.), Italy, 34
Chieti, Italy, 34
Chignecto (bay), Canada, 170
Chignecto (isthmus), N.S.-N.Br., 168
Chigwell, Eng., 10
Chihfeng, China, 77
Chihli (gulf), China, 77
Chihuahua (state), Mex., 150
Chihuahua, Mex., 150
Chik Ballapur, India, 68
Chikmagalur, India, 68
Chilapa, Mex., 150
Childersburg, Ala., 194
Childress, Tex., 302
Chile, 138
Chilecito, Arg., 143
Chililabombwe, Zambia, 115
Chilka (lake), India, 68
Chillán, Chile, 138
Chillicothe, Ill., 222
Chillicothe, Mo., 261
Chillicothe, Ohio, 284
Chilliwack, Br. Col., 184
Chillum, Md., 245
Chiloé (prov.), Chile, 138
Chiloé (isl.), Chile, 138
Chilpancingo, Mex., 150
Chilton, Wis., 317
Chilwa (lake), Africa, 115
Chimaltenango, Guat., 154
Chimborazo (prov.), Ecua., 128
Chimborazo (mt.), Ecua., 128
Chimbote, Peru, 128
Chimkent, U.S.S.R., 48
Chimney Rock Nat'l Hist. Site, Nebr., 264
Chin (hills), Burma, 72
China, 77
China, Maine, 242
China Lake, Calif., 204
Chinameca, El Sal., 154
Chinandega, Nic., 154
Chincha Alta, Peru, 128
Chinchow, China, 77
Chindwin (riv.), Burma, 72
Chingleput, India, 68
Chingola, Zambia, 115
Chinguetti, Mauritania, 106
Chin Hills (spec. div.), Burma, 72
Chinju, S. Korea, 81
Chinkiang, China, 77
Chino, Calif., 204
Chinook, Mont., 262
Chinsi, China, 77
Chinwangtao, China, 77
Chioggia, Italy, 34
Chios (Khíos) (isl.), Greece, 45
Chipamanu (riv.), S. Amer., 120
Chipata, Zambia, 115
Chipewyan (lake), Alta., 182
Chipley, Fla., 212
Chippawa, Ont., 177
Chippenham, Eng., 13
Chippewa Falls, Wis., 317
Chiquimula, Guat., 154
Chiquinquirá, Col., 126
Chir (riv.), U.S.S.R., 52
Chirala, India, 68
Chiricahua Nat'l Mon., Ariz., 198
Chiriquí (gulf), Pan., 154
Chiriquí (vol.), Pan., 154
Chirpan, Bulg., 45
Chirripó Grande (mt.), C. Rica, 154
Chisholm, Minn., 254
Chistopol', U.S.S.R., 52
Chita, U.S.S.R., 48
Chitradurga, India, 68
Chitral, Pak., 68
Chitré, Pan., 154
Chittagong, Pak., 68
Chittenango, N.Y., 276
Chittoor, India, 68
Chivacoa, Venez., 124
Chivilcoy, Arg., 143
Chixoy (riv.), Cent. Amer., 154
Chkalov (Orenburg), U.S.S.R., 52
Chocó (dept.), Col., 126
Choibalsan, Mong., 77
Choiseul (isl.), Br. Sol. Is., 87
Choisy-le-Roi, France, 28
Chojnice, Poland, 47
Cholet, France, 28
Choloma, Hond., 154
Cholula, Mex., 150
Choluteca, Hond., 154
Chomo Lhari (mt.), Asia, 68
Chomutov, Czech., 41
Chon Buri, Thai., 72
Chone, Ecua., 128
Ch'ŏngjin, N. Korea, 81
Ch'ŏngju, S. Korea, 81
Chŏnju, S. Korea, 81
Chonos (arch.), Chile, 138
Chorley, Eng., 10
Chorrera, Pan., 154
Chorrillos, Peru, 128
Chorzów, Poland, 47
Choshi, Japan, 81
Chowchilla, Calif., 204
Christchurch, Eng., 13
Christchurch, N.Z., 101
Christiana, Jam., 158
Christianburg-Wismar-Mackenzie, Guyana, 131
Christiansburg, Va., 307
Christiansted, Virgin Is. (U.S.), 161
Christiansted Nat'l Hist. Site, Virgin Is. (U.S.), 161
Christmas (isl.), Austral., 54
Christmas (isl.), Gilb. and Ell. Is., 87
Christopher, Ill., 222
Chrudim, Czech., 41
Chrzanów, Poland, 47
Chu (riv.), U.S.S.R., 48
Chüanchow, China, 77
Chubut (prov.), Arg., 143
Chubut (riv.), Arg., 143
Chuchow, China, 77
Chukai, Malaysia, 72
Chukchi (sea), 48
Chukchi (pen.), U.S.S.R., 48
Chukchi Nat'l Okrug, U.S.S.R., 48
Chu Lai, S. Vietnam, 72
Chula Vista, Calif., 204
Chulucanas, Peru, 128
Chulumani, Bol., 136
Chulym (riv.), U.S.S.R., 48
Chumar (riv.), China, 77
Chumatien, China, 77
Ch'unch'ŏn, S. Korea, 81
Ch'ungju, S. Korea, 81
Chungking, China, 77
Chungshan, China, 77
Chuquicamata, Chile, 138
Chuquisaca (dept.), Bol., 136
Chur, Switz., 39
Churchill (peak), Br. Col., 184
Churchill (riv.), Canada, 163
Churchill, Man., 179
Churchill (falls), Newf., 166
Churchill (riv.), Newf., 166
Churchill, Pa., 294
Churchill (lake), Sask., 181
Church Point, La., 238
Churu, India, 68
Chushan (arch.), China, 77
Chusovoy, U.S.S.R., 52
Chuvash A.S.S.R., U.S.S.R., 52
Ciampino, Italy, 34
Cicero, Ill., 222
Ciego de Ávila, Cuba, 158
Ciénaga, Col., 126
Cienfuegos, Cuba, 158
Cieszyn, Poland, 47
Cieza, Spain, 33
Cimarron (riv.), U.S., 188
Cîmpina, Rum., 45
Cîmpulung, Rum., 45
Cinca (riv.), Spain, 33
Cincinnati, Ohio, 284
Cintalapa, Mex., 150
Circeo (cape), Italy, 34
Circle Pines, Minn., 254
Circleville, Ohio, 284
Cirencester, Eng., 13
Cisco, Tex., 302
Citlaltépetl (mt.), Mex., 150
Citrus Hts., Calif., 204
City of Refuge Nat'l Hist. Pk., Hawaii, 218
City View, Ont., 177
Ciudad Acuña, Mex., 150
Ciudad Bolívar, Venez., 124
Ciudad Camargo, Mex., 150
Ciudad Darío, Nic., 154
Ciudad Delicias, Mex., 150
Ciudad de Valles, Mex., 150
Ciudad Guayana, Venez., 124
Ciudad Guzmán, Mex., 150
Ciudad Juárez, Mex., 150
Ciudad Lerdo, Mex., 150
Ciudad Madero, Mex., 150
Ciudad Mante, Mex., 150
Ciudad Mendoza, Mex., 150
Ciudad Obregón, Mex., 150
Ciudad Ojeda, Venez., 124
Ciudad Piar, Venez., 124
Ciudad Quesada, C. Rica, 154
Ciudad Real (prov.), Spain, 33
Ciudad Real, Spain, 33
Ciudad Río Bravo, Mex., 150
Ciudad Serdán, Mex., 150
Ciudad Victoria, Mex., 150
Civitavecchia, Italy, 34
Clackamas, Oreg., 291
Clackmannan (county), Scot., 15
Clackmannan, Scot., 15
Clacton, Eng., 13
Clairton, Pa., 294
Clamart, France, 28
Clanton, Ala., 194
Clara, Ire., 17
Clare (county), Ire., 17
Claremont, Calif., 204
Claremont, N.H., 268
Claremore, Okla., 288
Claremorris, Ire., 17
Clarence (isl.), Chile, 138
Clarendon Hills, Ill., 222
Claresholm, Alta., 182
Clarinda, Iowa, 229
Clarion, Iowa, 229
Clarion, Pa., 294
Clark, N. J., 273
Clarksburg, W. Va., 313
Clarksdale, Miss., 256
Clarkston, Wash., 310
Clarksville, Ark., 203
Clarksville, Ind., 227
Clarksville, Tenn., 237
Clarksville, Tex., 302
Claro (riv.), Braz., 132
Clausthal-Zellerfeld, W. Ger., 22
Clawson, Mich., 250
Claxton, Ga., 216
Clay Center, Kans., 232
Claymont, Del., 245
Clayton, Mo., 261
Clayton, N. J., 273
Clayton, N. Mex., 274
Clayton, N.C., 281
Clear, Alaska, 196
Clear (lake), Calif., 204
Clear (cape), Ire., 17
Clearfield, Pa., 294
Clearfield, Utah, 304
Clear Lake, Iowa, 229
Clearwater, Fla., 212
Clearwater (mts.), Idaho, 220
Cleburne, Tex., 302
Cleethorpes, Eng., 13
Clementon, N. J., 273
Clerf (river), Lux., 27
Clermont, Fla., 212
Clermont, Queensland, 95
Clermont-Ferrand, France, 28
Cleveland, Miss., 256
Cleveland, Ohio, 284
Cleveland, Okla., 288
Cleveland, Tenn., 237
Cleveland, Tex., 302
Cleveland Heights, Ohio, 284
Clew (bay), Ire., 17
Clewiston, Fla., 212
Clichy, France, 28
Clifden, Ire., 17
Cliffside Park, N. J., 273
Cliffwood, N. J., 273
Clifton, Ariz., 198
Clifton, N. J., 273
Clifton Forge, Va., 307
Clifton Hts., Pa., 294
Clifton Park, N.Y., 276
Clinton, Br. Col., 184
Clinton, Conn., 210
Clinton, Ill., 222
Clinton, Ind., 227
Clinton, Iowa, 229
Clinton, Mass., 249
Clinton, Miss., 256
Clinton, Mo., 261
Clinton, N.C., 281
Clinton, Okla., 288
Clinton, Ont., 177
Clinton, S.C., 296
Clinton, Tenn., 237
Clintonville, Wis., 317
Clipperton (isl.), Fr. Poly., 3
Clitheroe, Eng., 10
Cliza, Bol., 136
Clonakilty, Ire., 17
Cloncurry, Queensland, 95
Clondalkin, Ire., 17
Clones, Ire., 17
Clonmel, Ire., 17
Cloquet, Minn., 254
Closter, N. J., 273
Cloudy (bay), N.Z., 101
Clover, S.C., 296
Cloverdale, Calif., 204
Clovis, Calif., 204
Clovis, N. Mex., 274
Cluj, Rum., 45
Cluny, France, 28
Clute, Tex., 302
Clutha (riv.), N.Z., 101
Clyde, N.Y., 276
Clyde (inlet), N.W.T., 187
Clyde, Ohio, 284
Clyde (firth), Scot., 15
Clyde (riv.), Scot., 15
Clydebank, Scot., 15
Coachella, Calif., 204
Coahuila (state), Mex., 150
Coal City, Ill., 222
Coalcomán, Mex., 150
Coaldale, Alta., 182
Coal Grove, Ohio, 284
Coalinga, Calif., 204
Coalville, Eng., 13
Coamo, P. Rico, 161
Coast (mts.), Br. Col., 184
Coast (range), Calif., 204
Coast (prov.), Kenya, 115
Coast (prov.), Tanz., 115
Coatbridge, Scot., 15
Coatepec, Mex., 150
Coatepeque, Guat., 154
Coatesville, Pa., 294
Coaticook, Que., 172
Coats Land (reg.), Ant., 5
Coatzacoalcos, Mex., 150
Cobalt, Ont., 175
Cobán, Guat., 154
Cóbh, Ire., 17
Cobija, Bol., 136
Cobleskill, N.Y., 276
Cobourg, Ont., 177
Cobourg, Vic., 97
Coburg, W. Ger., 22
Cocanada (Kakinada), India, 68
Cochabamba (dept.), Bol., 136

Cochabamba, Bol., 136
Cochin, India, 68
Cochinos (bay), Cuba, 158
Cochran, Ga., 216
Cochrane, Ont., 175
Cockburn (isl.), Ont., 175
Cockburn Harbour, Turks and Caicos Is., 156
Cockeysville, Md., 245
Cockrell Hill, Tex., 302
Cockscomb (mts.), Br. Hond., 154
Coco (riv.), Cent. Amer., 154
Cocoa, Fla., 212
Cocoa Beach, Fla., 212
Cocos (isls.), Austral., 54
Cocos (isl.), C. Rica, 146
Cocula, Mex., 150
Cod (cape), Mass., 249
Codó, Braz., 132
Codrington, Antigua, 156
Cody, Wyo., 319
Coelemu, Chile, 138
Coesfeld, W. Ger., 22
Coeur d'Alene, Idaho, 220
Coffeyville, Kans., 232
Coffs Harbour, N.S.W., 97
Cognac, France, 28
Cohasset, Mass., 249
Cohoes, N.Y., 276
Coiba (isl.), Pan., 154
Coihaique, Chile, 138
Coimbatore, India, 68
Coimbra, Port., 33
Coin, Spain, 33
Cojedes (state), Venez., 124
Cojutepeque, El Sal., 154
Colaba (pt.), India, 68
Colac, Vic., 97
Colair (lake), India, 68
Colatina, Braz., 132
Colbeck (cape), Ant., 5
Colby, Kans., 232
Colchagua (prov.), Chile, 138
Colchester, Conn., 210
Colchester, Eng., 13
Cold Lake, Alta., 182
Coldstream, Scot., 15
Coldwater, Mich., 250
Coldwater, Ohio, 284
Coleman, Alta., 182
Coleman, Tex., 302
Coleraine, N. Ire., 17
Colfax, Wash., 310
Co Lieu, N. Vietnam, 72
Colima (state), Mex., 150
Colima, Mex., 150
Coll (isl.), Scot., 15
College, Alaska, 196
College Park, Ga., 216
College Park, Md., 245
College Place, Wash., 310
College Sta., Tex., 302
Collie, W. Austral., 92
Collier (bay), W. Austral., 92
Collingdale, Pa., 294
Collingswood, N. J., 273
Collingwood, Ont., 177
Collingwood, Vic., 97
Collinsville, Ill., 222
Collinsville, Okla., 288
Collinsville, Va., 307
Collipulli, Chile, 138
Colmar, France, 28
Colmenar, Spain, 33
Colne, Eng., 10
Colne Valley, Eng., 10
Cologne, W. Ger., 22
Colombes, France, 28
Colombia, 126
Colombo (cap.), Ceylon, 68
Colón, Arg., 143
Colón, Cuba, 158
Colón (mts.), Hond., 154
Colón, Pan., 154
Colón, Arch. de (terr.), Ecua., 128
Colonia, N. J., 273
Colonia (dept.), Urug., 145
Colonia, Urug., 145
Colonial Hts., Va., 307
Colonial Nat'l Hist. Pk., Va., 307
Colonie, N.Y., 276
Colonne (cape), Italy, 34
Colonsay (isl.), Scot., 15
Colorado (riv.), Arg., 143
Colorado (riv.), Tex., 302
Colorado (state), U.S., 208
Colorado (riv.), U.S., 188
Colorado City, Tex., 302
Colorado Nat'l Mon., Colo., 208
Colorado Springs, Colo., 208
Colton, Calif., 204
Columbia (mt.), Canada, 182
Columbia, Ill., 222
Columbia, Md., 245
Columbia, Miss., 256
Columbia, Mo., 261
Columbia (riv.), N. Amer., 188
Columbia (cape), N.W.T., 187
Columbia, Pa., 294
Columbia (cap.), S.C., 296
Columbia, Tenn., 237
Columbia City, Ind., 227
Columbia Falls, Mont., 262
Columbia Hts., Minn., 254
Columbiana, Ohio, 284
Columbus, Ga., 216
Columbus, Ind., 227
Columbus, Kans., 232
Columbus, Miss., 256
Columbus, Nebr., 264
Columbus (cap.), Ohio, 284
Columbus, Tex., 302
Columbus, Wis., 317
Colusa, Calif., 204
Colville (riv.), Alaska, 196
Colville, Wash., 310
Colwyn, Pa., 294
Colwyn Bay, Wales, 13
Comalapa, Guat., 154
Comalcalco, Mex., 150
Comanche, Tex., 302
Comayagua, Hond., 154
Comayagüela, Hond., 154
Comber, N. Ire., 17
Comilla, Pak., 68
Comino (isl.), Malta, 34
Comiso, Italy, 34
Comitán, Mex., 150
Commerce, Calif., 204
Commerce, Colo., 208
Commerce, Ga., 216
Commerce, Tex., 302
Commewijne (dist.), Sur., 131
Commewijne (riv.), Sur., 131
Communism (mt.), U.S.S.R., 48
Como (prov.), Italy, 34
Como, Italy, 34
Como (lake), Italy, 34
Comodoro Rivadavia, Arg., 143
Comoé (riv.), Africa, 106
Comorin (cape), India, 68
Comoro (isls.), 118
Comox, Br. Col., 184
Compiègne, France, 28
Compostela, Mex., 150
Compton, Calif., 204
Comstock, Mich., 250
Conakry (cap.), Guinea, 106
Concarneau, France, 28
Conceição, Braz., 132
Concepción, Arg., 143
Concepción, Bol., 136
Concepción (prov.), Chile, 138
Concepción, Chile, 138
Concepción (dept.), Par., 144
Concepción, Par., 144
Concepción del Oro, Mex., 150
Concepción del Uruguay, Arg., 143
Conception (pt.), Calif., 204
Conception (bay), Newf., 166
Conchas (res.), N. Mex., 274
Conchos (riv.), Mex., 150
Concón, Chile, 138
Concord, Calif., 204
Concord, Mass., 249
Concord (cap.), N.H., 268
Concord, N.S.W., 97
Concord, N.C., 281
Concordia, Arg., 143
Concordia, Kans., 232
Condega, Nic., 154
Cóndor (mts.), S. Amer., 128
Congleton, Eng., 10
Congo (riv.), Africa, 115
Congo, Dem. Rep. of the, 115
Congo, Rep. of, 115
Congo (dist.), Angola, 115
Congo Central (prov.), Dem. Rep. of the Congo, 115
Conimicut, R.I., 249
Coniston, Ont., 177
Conn (lake), Ire., 17
Connacht (prov.), Ire., 17
Conneaut, Ohio, 284
Connecticut (state), U.S., 210
Connecticut (riv.), U.S., 188
Connellsville, Pa., 294
Connemara (dist.), Ire., 17
Connersville, Ind., 227
Conrad, Mont., 262
Conroe, Tex., 302
Conselheiro Lafaiete, Braz., 135
Consett, Eng., 13
Conshohocken, Pa., 294
Consolación del Sur, Cuba, 158
Con Son (isls.), S. Vietnam, 72
Constance (lake), Europe, 39
Constanța, Rum., 45
Constantia, S. Africa, 118
Constantine, Alg., 106
Constitución, Chile, 138
Consuegra, Spain, 33
Contwoyto (lake), N.W.T., 187
Conway, Ark., 203
Conway, S.C., 296
Conway, Wales, 13
Conyers, Ga., 216
Coober Pedy, S. Austral., 94
Cooch Behar, India, 68
Cook (isls.), 87
Cook (mt.), N.Z., 101
Cook (strait), N.Z., 101
Cookeville, Tenn., 237
Cookstown, N. Ire., 17
Coolgardie, W. Austral., 92
Coolidge, Ariz., 198
Cooma, N.S.W., 97
Coon Rapids, Minn., 254
Coopers (Barcoo) (creek), Austral., 88
Coopers Plains, Queensland, 95
Cooperstown, N.Y., 276
Coos Bay, Oreg., 291
Cootamundra, N.S.W., 97
Cootehill, Ire., 17
Copán, Hond., 154
Copenhagen (cap.), Den., 21
Copiapó, Chile, 138
Coppename (riv.), Sur., 131
Copper (riv.), Alaska, 196
Copperas Cove, Tex., 302
Copper Cliff Ont., 177
Coppermine (riv.), N.W.T., 187
Copper Mtn., Br. Col., 184
Coquille, Oreg., 291
Coquimbo (prov.), Chile, 138
Coquimbo, Chile, 138
Coquitlam, B.C., 184
Coral (sea), 88
Coral Gables, Fla., 212
Coral Sea Isls. Terr., Austral., 95
Coraopolis, Pa., 294
Corato, Italy, 34
Corbin, Ky., 237
Corby, Eng., 13
Corcoran, Calif., 204
Corcovado (gulf), Chile, 138
Cordele, Ga., 216
Cordell, Okla., 288
Cordillera (dept.), Par., 144
Córdoba (prov.), Arg., 143
Córdoba, Arg., 143
Córdoba (dept.), Col., 126
Córdoba, Mex., 150
Córdoba (prov.), Spain, 33
Córdoba, Spain, 33
Cordova, Ala., 194
Cordova, Alaska, 196
Corfu (Kérkira) (isl.), Greece, 45
Coria, Spain, 33
Corigliano, Italy, 34
Corinda, Queensland, 95
Corinth, Greece, 45
Corinth (gulf), Greece, 45
Corinth, Miss., 256
Corinth, N.Y., 276
Corinto, Nic., 154
Corisco (isl.), Eq. Guin., 115
Cork (county), Ire., 17
Cork, Ire., 17
Çorlu, Turkey, 63
Cornelia, Ga., 216
Corner Brook, Newf., 166
Corning, Calif., 204
Corning, N.Y., 276
Cornwall (county), Eng., 13
Cornwall, N.Y., 276
Cornwall, Ont., 177
Cornwallis (isl.), N.W.T., 187
Coro, Venez., 124
Corocoro, Bol., 136
Coroico, Bol., 136
Coromandel (coast), India, 68
Coromandel (range), N.Z., 101
Corona, Calif., 204
Corona del Mar, Calif., 204
Coronado, Calif., 204
Coronado Nat'l Mem., Ariz., 198
Coronation (isl.), Ant., 5
Coronation (gulf), N.W.T., 187
Coronel, Chile, 138
Coronel Bogado, Par., 144
Coronel Oviedo, Par., 144
Coronel Pringles, Arg., 143
Coronel Suárez, Arg., 143
Coronie (dist.), Sur., 131
Corozal, Br. Hond., 154
Corpus Christi, Tex., 302
Corquín, Hond., 154
Corregidor (isl.), Phil. Is., 82
Corrente (riv.), Braz., 132
Corrèze (dept.), France, 28
Corrib (lake), Ire., 17
Corrientes (prov.), Arg., 143
Corrientes, Arg., 143
Corrientes (cape), Cuba, 158
Corrientes (cape), Mex., 150
Corrigin, W. Austral., 92
Corry, Pa., 294
Corse (cape), France, 28
Corsica (dept.), France, 28
Corsica (isl.), France, 28
Corsicana, Tex., 302
Corte Madera, Calif., 204
Cortez, Colo., 208
Cortina d'Ampezzo, Italy, 34
Cortland, N.Y., 276
Çoruh (riv.), Turkey, 63
Çorum (prov.), Turkey, 63
Çorum, Turkey, 63
Corumbá, Braz., 132
Corunna, Mich., 250
Corvallis, Oreg., 291
Corvo (isl.), Port., 32
Corydon, Ind., 227
Cosamaloapan, Mex., 150
Cos Cob, Conn., 210
Cosenza (prov.), Italy, 34
Cosenza, Italy, 34
Coshocton, Ohio, 284
Cosmoledo (isls.), Seych., 118
Costa Brava (reg.), Spain, 33
Costa de Sola (reg.), Spain, 33
Costa Mesa, Calif., 204
Costa Rica, 154
Cotabato (prov.), Phil. Is., 82
Côte-d'Or (dept.), France, 28
Côte-d'Or (mts.), France, 28
Cotentin (pen.), France, 28
Côtes-du-Nord (dept.), France, 28
Cotija, Mex., 150
Cotonou, Dahomey, 106
Cotopaxi (prov.), Ecua., 128
Cotopaxi (mt.), Ecua., 128
Cottage Grove, Oreg., 291
Cottage Hills, Ill., 222
Cottbus (dist.), E. Ger., 22
Cottbus, E. Ger., 22
Cottian Alps (mts.), Europe, 28
Cottica (riv.), Sur., 131
Cotulla, Tex., 302
Couchiching (lake), Ont., 177
Coudersport, Pa., 294
Coulee Dam Nat'l Recr. Area, Wash., 310
Council Bluffs, Iowa, 229
Council Grove, Kans., 232
Country Club Hills, Ill., 222
Coupar Angus, Scot., 15
Courageous (lake), N.W.T., 187
Courantyne (riv.), S. Amer., 131
Courbevoie, France, 28
Courmayeur, Italy, 34
Courtenay, Br. Col., 184
Courtrai, Belg., 27
Coutances, France, 28
Coutras, France, 28
Couva, Trin. and Tob., 161
Cova da Piedade, Port., 33
Coventry, Conn., 210
Coventry, Eng., 13
Coventry, R.I., 249
Covilhã, Port., 33
Covina, Calif., 204
Covington, Ga., 216
Covington, Ind., 227
Covington, Ky., 237
Covington, La., 238
Covington, Tenn., 237
Covington, Va., 307
Cowal (dist.), Scot., 15
Cowansville, Que., 172
Cowdenbeath, Scot., 15
Cowes, Eng., 13
Cowpens Nat'l Battlef. Site, S.C., 296
Cowra, N.S.W., 97
Coxsackie, N.Y., 276
Coyame, Mex., 150
Coyoacán, Mex., 150
Coyotepec, Mex., 150
Coyuca (riv.), Mex., 150
Cozad, Nebr., 264
Cozumel (isl.), Mex., 150
Cracow (prov.), Poland, 47
Cracow, Poland, 47
Cradock, S. Africa, 118
Crafton, Pa., 294
Craig, Colo., 208
Craigavon, N. Ire., 17
Crail, Scot., 15
Crailsheim, W. Ger., 22
Craiova, Rum., 45
Cramerton, N.C., 281
Cranbrook, Br. Col., 184
Crane, Tex., 302
Cranford, N. J., 273
Cranston, R.I., 249
Crater Lake Nat'l Park, Oreg., 291
Craters of the Moon Nat'l Mon., Idaho, 320
Crateús, Braz., 132
Crati (riv.), Italy, 34
Crato, Braz., 132
Crawfordsville, Ind., 227
Crawley, Eng., 13
Cree (lake), Sask., 181
Creighton, Sask., 181
Creil, France, 28
Crema, Italy, 34
Cremona (prov.), Italy, 34
Cremona, Italy, 34
Crépy, France, 28
Cres (isl.), Yugo., 45
Crescent City, Calif., 204
Cresco, Iowa, 229
Cresskill, N. J., 273
Crestline, Ohio, 284
Creston, Br. Col., 184
Creston, Iowa, 229
Crestview, Fla., 212
Crestwood, Mo., 261
Crete (reg.), Greece, 45
Crete (isl.), Greece, 45
Crete (sea), Greece, 45
Crete, Ill., 222
Crete, Nebr., 264
Creus (cape), Spain, 33
Creuse (dept.), France, 28
Creuse (riv.), France, 28
Creve Coeur, Ill., 222
Creve Coeur, Mo., 261
Crewe, Eng., 10
Criciúma, Braz., 132
Crieff, Scot., 15
Crimea (pen.), U.S.S.R., 52
Crimmitschau, E. Ger., 22
Crisfield, Md., 245
Cristal, Sierra del (mts.), Cuba, 158
Cristóbal, C.Z., 154
Cristóbal Colón (mt.), Col., 126
Cristóbal de las Casas, Mex., 150
Crișul Alb (riv.), Rum., 45
Crișul Repede (riv.), Rum., 45
Croatia (rep.), Yugo., 45
Crockett, Tex., 302
Crocodile (riv.), S. Afr., 118
Cromarty, Scot., 15
Cromwell, Conn., 210
Crook, Eng., 13
Crooked (isl.), Bah. Is., 156
Crookston, Minn., 254
Crooksville, Ohio, 284
Crosby, Eng., 10
Crosby, Minn., 254
Crosby, N. Dak., 283
Cross (river), Africa, 106
Cross (bay), Man., 179
Crossett, Ark., 203
Crossville, Tenn., 237
Crotone, Italy, 34
Croton-on-Hudson, N.Y., 276
Crowley, La., 238
Crown Point, Ind., 227
Crowsnest (pass), Canada, 182
Croydon, Eng., 10
Croydon, Vic., 97
Crozet (isls.), 3
Cruces, Cuba, 158
Crum Lynne, Pa., 294
Cruz Alta, Braz., 132
Cruz Bay, Virgin Is. (U.S.), 161
Cruz del Eje, Arg., 143
Cruzeiro, Braz., 135
Crystal (mts.), Congo, Rep. of, 115
Crystal, Minn., 254
Crystal City, Mo., 261
Crystal City, Tex., 302
Crystal Lake, Ill., 222
Crystal Springs, Miss., 256
Csepel, Hung., 41
Csongrád (county), Hung., 41
Csongrád, Hung., 41
Ctesiphon (ruins), Iraq, 66
Cuando-Cubango (dist.), Angola, 115
Cuanza (riv.), Angola, 115
Cuanza-Norte (dist.), Angola, 115
Cuanza-Sul (dist.), Angola, 115
Cuauhtémoc, Mex., 150
Cuautitlán, Mex., 150
Cuautla, Mex., 150
Cuba, 158
Cubango (riv.), Africa, 115
Cucamonga, Calif., 204
Cuckfield, Eng., 13
Cúcuta, Col., 126
Cudahy, Wis., 317
Cuddalore, India, 68
Cuddapah, India, 68
Cuenca, Ecua., 128
Cuenca (prov.), Spain, 33
Cuenca, Spain, 33
Cuenca (range), Spain, 33
Cuernavaca, Mex., 150
Cuero, Tex., 302
Cuiabá, Braz., 132
Cuilapa, Guat., 154
Cuilapa Miravalles (vol.), C. Rica, 154
Cuillin (sound), Scot., 15
Cuito (riv.), Angola, 115
Cuitzeo (lake), Mex., 150
Cu Lao Hon (isls.), S. Vietnam, 72
Culebra (isl.), P. Rico, 161
Culiacán, Mex., 150
Cullera, Spain, 33
Cullman, Ala., 194
Culuene (riv.), Braz., 132
Culver City, Calif., 204
Cumaná, Venez., 124
Cumberland, Br. Col., 184
Cumberland (basin), Canada, 169
Cumberland (county), Eng., 13
Cumberland, Ky., 239
Cumberland, Md., 245
Cumberland (pen.), N.W.T., 187
Cumberland (riv.), U.S., 188
Cumberland Gap Nat'l Hist. Pk., U.S., 237, 307
Cumbernauld, Scot., 15
Cumnock and Holmhead, Scot., 15
Cuna, Mex., 150
Cundinamarca (dept.), Col., 126
Cunene (riv.), Africa, 118
Cunene (dist.), Angola, 115
Cuneo (prov.), Italy, 34
Cuneo, Italy, 34
Cunnamulla, Queensland, 95
Cupar, Scot., 15
Cupertino, Calif., 204
Ćuprija, Yugo., 45
Curaçao (isl.), Neth. Ant., 161
Curacautín, Chile, 138
Curacaví, Chile, 138
Curanilahue, Chile, 138
Curanmilla (pt.), Chile, 138
Curecanti Nat'l Rec. Area, Colo., 208
Curepipe, Mauritius, 118
Curicó (prov.), Chile, 138
Curicó, Chile, 138
Curitiba, Braz., 135
Curragh, The, Ire., 17
Curuá (riv.), Braz., 132
Curuzú Cuatiá, Arg., 143
Curvelo, Braz., 132
Cushing, Okla., 288
Custer, S. Dak., 298
Custer Battlefield Nat'l Mon., Mont., 262
Cut Bank, Mont., 262
Cuthbert, Ga., 216
Cutler Ridge, Fla., 212
Cuttack, India, 68
Cuxhaven, W. Ger., 22
Cuyahoga Falls, Ohio, 284
Cuyo (isls.), Phil. Is., 82
Cuyuni (riv.), S. Amer., 131
Cuzco (dept.), Peru, 128
Cuzco, Peru, 128
Cwmamman, Wales, 13
Cyangugu, Rwanda, 115
Cyclades (isls.), Greece, 45
Cynthiana, Ky., 237
Cypress Gdns., Fla., 212
Cypress Hills Prov. Park, Alta., 182
Cypress Hills Prov. Park, Sask., 181
Cyprus, 63
Cyrenaica (reg.), Libya, 111
Cyrene (Shahat), Libya, 111
Czech Rep., Czech., 41
Czechoslovakia, 41
Czeladź, Poland, 47
Częstochowa, Poland, 47

D

Dabhoi, India, 68
Dabola, Guinea, 106
Dabou, Ivory Coast, 106
Dąbrowa Górnicza, Poland, 47
Dacca, Pak., 68
Dachau, W. Ger., 22
Dade City, Fla., 212
Dadeville, Ala., 194
Dadra and Nagar-Haveli (terr.), India, 68
Dadu, Pak., 68
Dagana, Sen., 106
Dagestan A.S.S.R., U.S.S.R., 52
Dagö (Hiiumaa) (isl.), U.S.S.R., 52
Dahana (des.), Saudi Ar., 59
Dahlak (arch.), Eth., 111
Dahlonega, Ga., 216
Dahomey, 106
Daimiel, Spain, 33
Daingerfield, Tex., 302
Dairen (Lüta), China, 77
Daito (isls.), Ryukyu Is., 87
Dajabón (prov.), Dom. Rep., 158
Dakar (cap.), Sen., 106
Dakhla (oasis), U.A.R., 111
Dalan Dzadagad, Mong., 77
Da Lat, S. Vietnam, 72
Dalby, Queensland, 95
Dale, Pa., 294
Dalhart, Tex., 302
Dalhousie, N.B., 170
Dallas, N.C., 281
Dallas, Oreg., 291
Dallas, Pa., 294
Dallas, Tex., 302
Dallastown, Pa., 294
Daloa, Ivory Coast, 106
Dalton, Ga., 216
Daltonganj, India, 68
Daly (cape), Ant., 5
Daly City, Calif., 204
Daly River, N Terr., 93
Dama, Poulo (isls.), S. Vietnam, 72
Daman (dist.), India, 68
Damanhur, U.A.R., 111
Damar (isls.), Indon., 85
Damaraland (reg.), S.W. Afr., 118
Damascus (prov.), Syria, 63
Damascus (cap.), Syria, 63
Dame-Marie (cape), Haiti, 158
Damghan, Iran, 66
Damietta, U.A.R., 111
Dammam, Saudi Ar., 52
Damodar (riv.), India, 68
Damoh, India, 68
Dampier (strait), Terr. N.G., 85
Dampier, W. Austral., 92
Dampier Land (reg.), W. Austral., 92
Danakil (reg.), Eth., 111
Da Nang, S. Vietnam, 72
Danbury, Conn., 210
Dandenong, Vic., 97
Danderyd, Sweden, 18
Daneborg, Greenl., 4
Dangila, Eth., 111
Dang Raek, Phanom (mts.), Asia, 72
Dania, Fla., 212
Danielson, Conn., 210
Danielstown, Guyana, 131
Danlí, Hond., 134
Danmarkshavn, Greenl., 4
Dannemora, N.Y., 276
Dannevirke, N.Z., 101
Dansville, N.Y., 276
Danube (delta), Europe, 45
Danube (riv.), Europe, 7
Danubyu, Burma, 72
Danvers, Mass., 249
Danville, Calif., 204
Danville, Ill., 222
Danville, Ind., 227
Danville, Ky., 237
Danville, Pa., 294
Danville, Va., 307
Danzig (Gdańsk), Poland, 47
Danzig (gulf), Poland, 47
Darab, Iran, 66
Darbhanga, India, 68
Darby, Pa., 294
Dardanelles (strait), Turkey, 63
Dar el Beida (Casablanca), Mor., 106
Dar es Salaam (cap.), Tanz., 115
Darfur (prov.), Sudan, 111
Dar Hamid (reg.), Sudan, 111
Darien, Conn., 210
Darién (mts.), Pan., 154
Dariense (range), Nic., 154
Darjeeling, India, 68
Darkhan, Mong., 77
Darlac (plat.), S. Vietnam, 72
Darling (riv.), Austral., 88
Darling (range), W. Austral, 92
Darlington, Eng., 13
Darlington, S.C., 296
Dar Masalit (reg.), Sudan, 111
Darmstadt, W. Ger., 22
Darnley (cape), Ant., 5
Dar Rounga (reg.), Cent. Afr. Rep., 115
Darsser Ort (pt.), E. Ger., 22
Dart (cape), Ant., 5
Dartford, Eng., 10
Dartmoor (forest), Eng., 13
Dartmouth, Mass., 249
Dartmouth, N.S., 169
Daru, Papua, 85
Darwen, Eng., 10
Darwin (mts.), Chile, 138
Darwin (cap.), N. Terr., 93
Darya-yi-Namak (salt lake), Iran, 66
Das (isl.), Tr. States, 59
Dasht-i-Kavir (salt des.), Iran, 66
Dasht-i-Lut (des.), Iran, 66
Datia, India, 68
Daugavpils, U.S.S.R., 53
Daulatabad, Afghan., 68
Daule, Ecua., 128
Dauphin, Man., 179
Davangere, India, 68
Davao, Phil. Is., 82
Davao (gulf), Phil. Is., 82
Davao del Norte (prov.), Phil. Is., 82
Davao del Sur (prov.), Phil. Is., 82
Davao Oriental (prov.), Phil. Is., 82
Davenport, Iowa, 229
David, Pan., 154
Davidson, N.C., 281
Davidson, Sask., 181
Davis (sea), Ant., 5
Davis, Calif., 204
Davis (strait), N. Amer., 187
Davison, Mich., 250
Davis Sta., Ant., 5
Davos, Switz., 39
Dawa (riv.), Africa, 111
Dawasir, Wadi (dry river), Saudi Ar., 59
Dawley, Eng., 13
Dawna (range), Asia, 72
Dawson, Ga., 216
Dawson, Yukon, 187
Dawson Creek, Br. Col., 184
Dawson Sprs., Ky., 237
Daymán (range), Urug., 145
Dayton, Ky., 237
Dayton, Ohio, 284
Dayton, Tenn., 237
Dayton, Tex., 302
Dayton, Wash., 310
Daytona Beach, Fla., 212
De Aar, S. Afr., 118
Dead (sea), Asia, 65
Deadwood, S. Dak., 298
Deal, Eng., 13
Deán Funes, Arg., 143
Dearborn, Mich., 250
Dearborn Hts., Mich., 250
Dease (lake), Br. Col., 184
Dease (strait), N.W.T., 187
Death Valley (depr.), U.S., 204
Death Valley Nat'l Mon., U.S., 204, 266
Deauville, France, 28
Deberai (pen.), Indon., 85
Debra Markos, Eth., 111
Debra Tabor, Eth., 111
Debrecen, Hung., 41
Decatur, Ala., 194
Decatur, Ga., 216
Decatur, Ill., 222
Decatur, Ind., 227
Decatur, Tex., 302
Deccan (plat.), India, 68
Děčín, Czech., 41
Decorah, Iowa, 229
Dedham, Mass., 249
Dédougou, Upp. Volta, 106
Dedza, Malawi, 115
Dee (riv.), Ire., 17
Dee (riv.), Scot., 15
Dee (riv.), U.K., 13
Deephaven, Minn., 254
Deep River, Ont., 177
Deerfield, Ill., 222
Deerfield Beach, Fla., 212
Deer Lake, Newf., 166
Deer Lodge, Mont., 262
Deer Park, N.Y., 276
Deer Park, Ohio, 284
Deer Park, Tex., 302
Defiance, Ohio, 284
De Funiak Springs, Fla., 212
Deggendorf, W. Ger., 22
Dehra Dun, India, 68
Deir ez Zor (prov.), Syria, 63
Deir ez Zor, Syria, 63
Dej, Rum., 45
De Kalb, Ill., 222
Delagoa (bay), Mozamb., 118
Delanco, N. J., 273
De Land, Fla., 212
Delano, Calif., 204
Delavan, Wis., 317
Delaware, Ohio, 284
Delaware (state), U.S., 245
Delaware (bay), U.S., 273
Delaware (riv.), U.S., 273, 276
Delaware Water Gap Nat'l Rec. Area, U.S., 273, 294
Del City, Okla., 288
Delft, Neth., 27
Delgado (cape), Mozamb., 118
Delhi (terr.), India, 68
Delhi, India, 68
Delhi, La., 238
Delhi, Ont., 177
Delitzsch, E. Ger., 22
Dellwood, Mo., 261
Del Mar, Calif., 204
Delmar, N.Y., 276
Delmenhorst, W. Ger., 22
De Long (strait), U.S.S.R., 48
Deloraine, Man., 179
Deloraine, Tas., 99
Delphi, Ind., 227
Delphos, Ohio, 284
Delray Beach, Fla., 212
Del Rio, Tex., 302
Delta, B.C., 184
Delta, Colo., 208
Delvinë, Alb., 45
Demanda (mts.), Spain, 33
Demarest, N. J., 273
Demavend (mt.), Iran, 66
Dembidollo, Eth., 111
Demerara (riv.), Guyana, 131
Deming, N. Mex., 274
Demopolis, Ala., 194
Demta, Indon., 85
Denain, France, 28
Denbigh, Wales, 13
Denbighshire (county), Wales, 13
Dender (river), Belg., 27
Denham Sprs., La., 238
Den Helder, Neth., 27
Denia, Spain, 33
Deniliquin, N.S.W., 97
Denison, Iowa, 229
Denison, Tex., 302
Denizli (prov.), Turkey, 63
Denizli, Turkey, 63
Denmark, 21
Denmark (strait), 4
Denmark, S.C., 296
Dennis, Mass., 249
Dennison, Ohio, 284
Denny and Dunipace, Scot., 15
Denpasar, Indon., 85
Dent du Tigre (mt.), S. Vietnam, 72
Denton, Tex., 302
D'Entrecasteaux (isls.), Papua, 85
Denver (cap.), Colo., 208
Denver City, Tex., 302
Denville, N. J., 273
Deoghar, India, 68
Deolali, India, 68
Deoria, India, 68
De Pere, Wis., 317
Depew, N.Y., 276
Deptford, N. J., 273
De Queen, Ark., 203
De Quincy, La., 238
Der'a (prov.), Syria, 63
Der'a, Syria, 63
Dérac, Haiti, 158
Dera Ghazi Khan, Pak., 68
Dera Ismail Khan, Pak., 68
Derbent, U.S.S.R., 52
Derby, Conn., 210
Derby, Eng., 13
Derby, Kans., 232
Derby, W. Austral., 92
Derbyshire (county), Eng., 13
Derg (lake), Ire., 17
De Ridder, La., 238
Dermott, Ark., 203
Derna, Libya, 111
Derry, Pa., 294
Derwent (riv.), Eng., 13
Desaguadero (riv.), Bol., 136
Deseado (riv.), Arg., 143
Desert Hot Sprs., Calif., 204
Désirade (isl.), Guad., 161
Des Moines (cap.), Iowa, 229
Desolación (isl.), Chile, 138
Des Peres, Mo., 261
Des Plaines, Ill., 222
De Soto, Mo., 261
De Soto Nat'l Mem., Fla., 212
Dessalines, Haiti, 158
Dessau, E. Ger., 22
Dessye, Eth., 111
Detmold, W. Ger., 22
Detroit, Mich., 250
Detroit (riv.), N. Amer., 250
Detroit Lakes, Minn., 254
Deurne, Belg., 27
Deux-Sèvres (dept.), France, 28
Deva, Rum., 45
Deventer, Neth., 27
Devil's (isl.), Fr. Gui., 131
Devils Lake, N. Dak., 283
Devil's Postpile Nat'l Mon., Calif., 204
Devils Tower Nat'l Mon., Wyo., 319
Devine, Tex., 302
Devon, Alta., 182
Devon, Conn., 210
Devon (isl.), N.W.T., 187
Devonport, Tas., 99
Devonshire (county), Eng., 13
Dewas, India, 68
Dewey, Okla., 288
De Witt, Ark., 203
De Witt, Iowa, 229
De Witt, N.Y., 276
Dewsbury, Eng., 10
Dexter, Maine, 242
Dexter, Mo., 261
Dezhnev (cape), U.S.S.R., 48
Dhahran, Saudi Ar., 59
Dhamar, Yemen Arab Rep., 59
Dhamtari, India, 68
Dhar, India, 68
Dharwar, India, 68
Dhaulagiri (mt.), Nepal, 68
Dhofar (reg.), Oman, 59
Dholpur, India, 68
Dhoraji, India, 68
Dhubri, India, 68
Dhulia, India, 68
Diablo, Wash., 310
Diamante, Arg., 143
Diamantina, Braz., 132
Diamantina (riv.), Queensland, 95
Diamond (head), Hawaii, 218
Diamond (pt.), Indon., 85
Diamond Coast (reg.), S.W. Afr., 118
Dibaya, Dem. Rep. of the Congo, 115
D'Iberville, Miss., 256
Diboll, Tex., 302
Dibrugarh, India, 68
Dickinson, N. Dak., 283
Dickinson, Tex., 302
Dickson, Tenn., 237
Dickson City, Pa., 294
Dicle (Tigris) (river), Turkey, 63
Didsbury, Alta., 182
Diefenbaker (lake), Sask., 181
Diego Garcia (isls.), Br. Ind. Ocean Terr., 54
Diégo-Suarez (prov.), Malag. Rep., 118
Diégo-Suarez, Malag. Rep., 118
Diekirch, Lux., 27
Dien Bien Phu, N. Vietnam, 72
Dieppe, France, 28
Dieppe, N.B., 170
Differdange, Lux., 27
Digby, N.S., 169
Digos, Phil. Is., 82
Digul (riv.), Indon., 85
Dijon, France, 28
Dili (cap.), Port. Timor, 85
Dillingham, Alaska, 196
Dillon, Mont., 262
Dillon, S.C., 296
Dilolo, Dem. Rep. of the Congo, 115
Dimbokro, Ivory Coast, 106
Dimishq (Damascus)(cap.), Syria, 63
Dimitrovgrad, Bulg., 45
Dimmitt, Tex., 302
Dimona, Israel, 65
Dinagat (isl.), Phil. Is., 82
Dinajpur, Pak., 68
Dinan, France, 28
Dinaric Alps (mts.), Yugo., 45
Dinder (riv.), Africa, 111
Dindigul, India, 68
Dingle (bay), Ire., 17
Dingwall, Scot., 15
Dinokwe, Botswana, 118
Dinosaur Nat'l Mon., U.S., 208, 304
Dinuba, Calif., 204
Diomede (isls.), 196
Diourbel, Sen., 106
Dir, Pak., 68
Direction (cape), Queensland, 95
Dire Dawa, Eth., 111
Diriamba, Nic., 154
Dirk Hartogs (isl.), W. Austral., 92
Disappointment (cape), Wash., 310
Discovery (bay), Vic., 97
Dishman, Wash., 310
Disko (isl.), Greenl., 4
District Hts., Md., 245
District of Columbia (dist.), U.S., 245
Distrito Especial, Col., 126
Distrito Federal, Arg., 143
Distrito Federal, Mex., 150
Distrito Federal, Par., 144
Distrito Nacional, Dom. Rep., 158
Diu (dist.), India, 68
Divinópolis, Braz., 135
Divriği, Turkey, 63
Diwaniya (prov.), Iraq, 66
Dixon, Calif., 204
Dixon, Ill., 222
Dixon Entrance (strait), N. Amer., 196
Diyala (prov.), Iraq, 66
Diyarbakır (prov.), Turkey, 63
Diyarbakır, Turkey, 63
Dizful, Iran, 66
Dja (riv.), Africa, 115
Djado (plat.), Niger, 106
Djaja (mt.), Indon., 85
Djajapura (Hollandia), Indon., 85
Djajawidjaja (range), Indon., 85
Djakarta (cap.), Indon., 85
Djakovica, Yugo., 45
Djakovo, Yugo., 45
Djambi (Telanaipura), Indon., 85
Djelfa, Alg., 106
Djenné, Mali, 106
Djerba (isl.), Tun., 106
Djerid, Shott el (salt lake), Tun., 106
Djibouti (cap.), Afars & Issas, 111
Djidjelli, Alg., 106
Djokjakarta, Indon., 85
Djouf, El (des.), Africa, 106
Djougou, Dahomey, 106
Djursholm, Sweden, 18
Dmitriy Laptev (strait), U.S.S.R., 48
Dmitrov, U.S.S.R., 52
Dneprodzerzhinsk, U.S.S.R., 52
Dnepropetrovsk, U.S.S.R., 52
Dnieper (riv.), U.S.S.R., 52
Dniester (riv.), U.S.S.R., 52
Dobbs Ferry, N.Y., 276
Döbeln, E. Ger., 22
Dobrich (Tolbukhin), Bulg., 45
Doce (riv.), Braz., 132
Doctor Arroyo, Mex., 150
Dodecanese (isls.), Greece, 45
Dodge City, Kans., 232
Dodgeville, Wis., 317
Dodoma (prov.), Tanz., 115
Dodoma, Tanz., 115
Dogondoutchi, Niger, 106
Doha (cap.), Qatar, 59
Dohad, India, 68
Doi Inthanon (mt.), Thai., 72
Dolak (isl.), Indon., 85
Dolbeau, Que., 174
Dôle, France, 28
Dolgellau, Wales, 13
Dolgeville, N.Y., 276
Dolisie, Rep. of Congo, 115
Dollard, Que., 172
Dollart (est.), Europe, 27
Dolomite, Ala., 194
Dolomite Alps (range), Italy, 34
Dolores, Arg., 143
Dolores, Urug., 145
Dolton, Ill., 222
Domburg, Sur., 131
Domeyko (mts.), Chile, 138
Dominica, 161
Dominican Republic, 158
Dominion, N.S., 169
Domodossola, Italy, 34
Domrémy-la-Pucelle, France, 28
Don (riv.), Eng., 13
Don (riv.), Ont., 177

Don (riv.), Scot., 15
Don (riv.), U.S.S.R., 52
Donaldsonville, La., 238
Donalsonville, Ga., 216
Donaueschingen, W. Ger., 22
Don Benito, Spain, 33
Doncaster, Eng., 13
Doncaster and Templestowe, Vic., 97
Dondo, Angola, 115
Dondra (head), Ceylon, 68
Donegal (county), Ire., 17
Donegal, Ire., 17
Donelson, Tenn., 237
Donets (riv.), U.S.S.R., 52
Donetsk, U.S.S.R., 52
Dong Hoi, N. Vietnam, 72
Dongola, Sudan, 111
Dongou, Rep. of Congo, 115
Dønna (isl.), Norway, 18
Donna, Tex., 302
Donnacona, Que., 172
Donnybrook, W. Austral., 92
Donora, Pa., 294
Doorn, Neth., 27
Dora Baltea (riv.), Italy, 34
Dora Riparia (riv.), Italy, 34
Doraville, Ga., 216
Dorchester, Eng., 13
Dorchester, Mass., 249
Dorchester Hts. Nat'l Hist. Site, Mass., 249
Dordogne (dept.), France, 28
Dordogne (riv.), France, 28
Dordrecht, Neth., 27
Doré (lake), Sask., 181
Dore Alps (mts.), France, 28
Dori, Upp. Volta, 106
Dorion, Que., 172
Dorking, Eng., 13
Dormont, Pa., 294
Dornbirn, Austria, 41
Dornoch, Scot., 15
Dorohoi, Rum., 45
Dorothy, W. Va., 313
Dorsetshire (county), Eng., 13
Dorsten, W. Ger., 22
Dortmund, W. Ger., 22
Dos Bahías (cape), Arg., 143
Dosso, Niger, 106
Dothan, Ala., 194
Douai, France, 28
Douala, Cameroon, 115
Doubs (riv.), Europe, 28
Doubs (dept.), France, 28
Douglas, Ariz., 198
Douglas, Ga., 216
Douglas (cap.), I. of Man., 13
Douglas, Wyo., 319
Douglasville, Ga., 216
Douro (Duero) (riv.), Europe, 33
Douro Litoral (prov.), Port., 33
Dover (cap.), Del., 245
Dover, Eng., 13
Dover (strait), Europe, 13
Dover, N.H., 268
Dover, N. J., 273
Dover, Ohio, 284
Dover-Foxcroft, Maine, 242
Dovrefjeld (mts.), Norway, 18
Dowa, Malawi, 115
Dowagiac, Mich., 250
Down (county), N. Ire., 17
Downers Grove, Ill., 222
Downey, Calif., 204
Downingtown, Pa., 294
Downpatrick, N. Ire., 17
Doylestown, Pa., 294
Dra, Wadi (dry riv.), Africa, 106
Drăgăşani, Rum., 45
Draperton, Utah, 304
Dragons Mouth (passage), 124
Dragør, Den., 21
Drake (passage), 5
Drakensberg (range), Africa, 118
Dráma, Greece, 45
Drammen, Norway, 18
Drancy, France, 28
Drava (riv.), Europe, 45
Drayton Plains, Mich., 250
Drayton Valley, Alta., 182
Dre Chu (riv.), China, 77
Drenthe (prov.), Neth., 27
Dresden (dist.), E. Ger., 22
Dresden, E. Ger., 22
Dreux, France, 28
Drexel Hill, Pa., 294
Drin (riv.), Alb., 45
Drina (riv.), Yugo., 45
Drogheda, Ire., 17
Drogobych, U.S.S.R., 52
Droichead Nua, Ire., 17
Drôme (dept.), France, 28
Drôme (riv.), France, 28
Drumheller, Alta., 182
Drummondville, Que., 172
Drummoyne, N.S.W., 97
Drumright, Okla., 288
Dryden, Ont., 177
Drysdale (riv.), W. Austral., 92
Duarte, Calif., 204
Duarte (prov.), Dom. Rep., 158
Duarte (peak), Dom. Rep., 158
Dubai, Tr. States, 59
Dubawnt (lake), N.W.T., 187
Dubbo, N.S.W., 97
Dublin, Ga., 216
Dublin (county), Ire., 17
Dublin (cap.), Ire., 17
Dubna, U.S.S.R., 52
Du Bois, Pa., 294
Dubrovnik, Yugo., 45
Dubuque, Iowa, 229
Ducie (isl.), Pitcairn Is., 87
Duck Mountain Prov. Park, Sask., 181
Dudelange, Lux., 27
Dudinka, U.S.S.R., 48
Dudley, Eng., 10
Dudweiler, W. Ger., 22
Duero (Douro) (riv.), Europe, 33
Dufourspitze (mt.), Europe, 39
Dugi Otok (isl.), Yugo., 45
Dugway, Utah, 304
Duisburg, W. Ger., 22
Duiveland (isl.), Neth., 27
Duke of Gloucester (isls.), Fr. Poly., 87
Dukhan, Qatar, 59
Dukla (pass), Europe, 47
Dulce (gulf), C. Rica, 154
Duluth, Minn., 254
Duma, Syria, 63
Dumaguete, Phil. Is., 82
Dumaran (isl.), Phil. Is., 82
Dumas, Ark., 203
Dumas, Tex., 302
Dumbarton, Scot., 15
Dum Dum, India, 68
Dumfries (county), Scot., 15
Dumfries, Scot., 15
Dümmer (lake), W. Ger., 22
Dumont, N. J., 273
Dumont d'Urville Sta., Ant., 5
Dumyât (Damietta), U.A.R., 111
Dunajec (river.), Europe, 47
Dunaújváros, Hung., 41
Dunbar, Scot., 15
Dunbar, W. Va., 313
Dunbarton (county), Scot., 15
Dunblane, Scot., 15
Duncan, Br. Col., 184
Duncan, Okla., 288
Duncansby (head), Scot., 15
Duncanville, Tex., 302
Dundalk, Ire., 17
Dundalk, Md., 245
Dundas, Ont., 177
Dundee, Ill., 222
Dundee, Scot., 15
Dundee, S. Afr., 118
Dunedin, Fla., 212
Dunedin, N.Z., 101
Dunellen, N. J., 273
Dunfermline, Scot., 15
Dungannon, N. Ire., 17
Dungarvan, Ire., 17
Dungeness (prom.), Eng., 13
Dungu, Dem. Rep. of the Congo, 115
Dunkirk (Dunkerque), France, 28
Dunkirk, Ind., 227
Dunkirk, N.Y., 276
Dún Laoghaire, Ire., 17
Dunmore, Pa., 294
Dunn, N.C., 281
Dunnet (head), Scot., 15
Dunnville, Ont., 177
Dunoon, Scot., 15
Dunsmuir, Calif., 204
Dunstable, Eng., 13
Dupo, Ill., 222
Duque de Caxias, Braz., 135
Duquesne, Pa., 294
Du Quoin, Ill., 222
Durance (riv.), France, 28
Durand, Mich., 250
Durango, Colo., 208
Durango (state), Mex., 150
Durango, Mex., 150
Durant, Miss., 256
Durant, Okla., 288
Duratón (riv.), Spain, 33
Durazno (dept.), Urug., 145
Durazno, Urug., 145
Durban, S. Afr., 118
Düren, W. Ger., 22
Durg, India, 68
Durga Nor (lake), Mong., 77
Durgapur, India, 68
Durham (county), Eng., 13
Durham, Eng., 13
Durham, N.H., 268
Durham, N.C., 281
Durrës, Alb., 45
Duryea, Pa., 294
Dushanbe, U.S.S.R., 48
Dusky (sound), N.Z., 101
Düsseldorf, W. Ger., 22
Dutch Harbor, Alaska, 196
Duvergé, Dom. Rep., 158
Düzce, Turkey, 63
Duzdab (Zahidan), Iran, 66
Dvina (bay), U.S.S.R., 52
Dvina, Northern (riv.), U.S.S.R., 52
Dvina, Western (riv.), U.S.S.R., 43
Dvůr Králové nad Labem, Czech., 41
Dwarka, India, 68
Dwight, Ill., 222
Dyer, Ind., 227
Dyer (cape), N.W.T., 187
Dyersburg, Tenn., 237
Dyersville, Iowa, 229
Dykh-Tau (mt.), U.S.S.R., 52
Dzabkhan (prov.), Mong., 77
Dzabkhan (riv.), Mong., 77
Dza Chu (riv.), China, 77
Dzerzhinsk, U.S.S.R., 52
Dzhalal-Abad, U.S.S.R., 48
Dzhambul, U.S.S.R., 48
Dzhankoy, U.S.S.R., 52
Dzhezkazgan, U.S.S.R., 48
Dzhugdzhur (range), U.S.S.R., 48
Dzibichaltún (ruins), Mex., 150
Dzierżoniów, Pol., 47
Dzitbalché, Mex., 150
Dzungaria (reg.), China, 77
Dzun Modo, Mong., 77

E

Eagle Grove, Iowa, 229
Eaglehawk, Vic., 97
Eagle Lake, Tex., 302
Eagle Pass, Tex., 302
Ealing, Eng., 10
Earlimart, Calif., 204
Earlington, Ky., 237
Earnslaw (mt.), N.Z., 101
Easley, S.C., 296
East (cape), N.Z., 101
East Alton, Ill., 222
East Angus, Que., 172
East Aurora, N.Y., 276
East Azerbaijan (prov.), Iran, 66
East Berbice (dist.), Guyana, 131
Eastbourne, Eng., 13
East Brisbane, Queensland, 95
East Brunswick, N.J., 273
East-Central (state), Nigeria, 106
East Chicago, Ind., 227
East China (sea), Asia, 77
East Coast Bays, N.Z., 101
East Conemaugh, Pa., 294
East Demerara (dist.), Guyana, 131
East Detroit, Mich., 250
Easter (isl.), Chile, 87
Eastern (prov.), Kenya, 115
Eastern (prov.), Mong., 77
Eastern (prov.) Saudi Ar., 59
Eastern Ghats (mts.), India, 68
Eastern Samar (prov.), Phil. Is., 82
Eastern Scheldt (est.), Neth., 27
East Faxon, Pa., 294
East Flanders (prov.), Belg., 27
East Flevoland (polder), Neth., 27
East Friesland (reg.), W. Ger., 22
East Frisian (isls.), W. Ger., 22
East Gaffney, S.C., 296
East Gobi (prov.), Mong., 77
East Grand Forks, Minn., 254
East Greenwich, R.I., 249
East Hartford, Conn., 210
East Haven, Conn., 210
East Kilbride, Scot., 15
East Kildonan, Man., 179
East Korea (bay), N. Korea, 81
Eastlake, Ohio, 284
Eastland, Tex., 302
East Lansing, Mich., 250
Eastleigh, Eng., 13
East Liverpool, Ohio, 284
East London, S. Africa, 118
East Lothian (county), Scot., 15
East-Main, Que., 174
Eastman, Ga., 216
East Meadow, N.Y., 276
East Millcreek, Utah, 304
Easton, Md., 245
Easton, Pa., 294
East Orange, N. J., 273
East Pakistan (prov.), Pak., 68
East Palestine, Ohio, 284
East Point, Ga., 216
Eastport, Maine, 242
East Prairie, Mo., 261
East Providence, R.I., 249
East Ridge, Tenn., 237
East Rockaway, N.Y., 276
East Saint Louis, Ill., 222
East Siberian (sea), U.S.S.R., 48
East Stroudsburg, Pa., 294
East York, Ont., 177
Eaton, Ohio, 284
Eaton Rapids, Mich., 250
Eatonton, Ga., 216
Eatontown, N. J., 273
Eau Claire, Wis., 317
Eauripik (atoll), Pac. Is., 87
Ebbw Vale, Wales, 13
Ebeltoft, Den., 21
Ebensburg, Pa., 294
Eberswalde, E. Ger., 22
Ebingen, W. Ger., 22
Ebi Nor (lake), China, 77
Eboli, Italy, 34
Ebolowa, Cameroon, 115
Ebon (atoll), Pac. Is., 87
Ebro (riv.), Spain, 33
Eccles, Eng., 10
Echuca, Vic., 97
Écija, Spain, 33
Eckernförde, W. Ger., 22
Ecorse, Mich., 250
Écrins, Les (mt.), France, 28
Ecuador, 128
Edam, Neth., 27
Ed Damer, Sudan, 111
Ed Dueim, Sudan, 111
Eddystone (rocks), Eng., 13
Eddystone, Pa., 294
Ede, Neth., 27
Ede, Nigeria, 106
Edéa, Cameroon, 115
Eden (riv.), Eng., 13
Eden, N.C., 281
Edendale, S. Afr., 118
Edenderry, Ire., 17
Eden Prairie, Minn., 254
Edenton, N.C., 281
Edenvale, S. Afr., 118
Eder (res.), W. Ger., 22
Edgefield, S.C., 296
Edgemere, Md., 245
Edgemont, S. Dak., 298
Edgerton, Wis., 317
Edgewater, Colo., 208
Edgewater, N. J., 273
Edgewood, Pa., 294
Édhessa, Greece, 45
Edina, Minn., 254
Edinburg, Ind., 227
Edinburg, Tex., 302
Edinburgh (cap.), Scot., 15
Edirne (prov.), Turkey, 63
Edirne, Turkey, 63
Edison, N. J., 273
Edison Lab. Nat'l Mon., N. J., 273
Edith Ronne Ice Shelf, Ant., 5
Edjeleh, Alg., 106
Edmond, Okla., 288
Edmonds, Wash., 310
Edmonton (cap.), Alta., 182
Edmundston, N.B., 170
Edna, Tex., 302
Edremit, Turkey, 63
Edson, Alta., 182
Edward (lake), Africa, 115
Edward VII (pen.), Ant., 5
Edwards (plat.), Tex., 302
Edwardsville, Ill., 222
Eel (riv.), Calif., 204
Efate (isl.), New Hebr., 87
Effigy Mounds Nat'l Mon., Iowa, 229
Effingham, Ill., 222
Egadi (isls.), Italy, 34
Eger, Hung., 41
Eggertsville, N.Y., 276
Egg Hbr. City, N. J., 273
Egham, Eng., 10
Egmont (mt.), N.Z., 101
Eğridir (lake), Turkey, 63
Egypt (United Arab Republic), 111
Eha Amufu, Nigeria, 106
Ehime (pref.), Japan, 81
Ehrenberg (range), N. Terr., 93
Eibar, Spain, 33
Eider (riv.), W. Ger., 22
Eigersund, Norway, 18
Eigg (isl.), Scot., 15
Eights Coast (reg.), Ant., 5
Eighty Mile (beach), W. Austral., 92
Eil, Somalia, 115
Eildon (lake), Vic., 97
Eilenburg, E. Ger., 22
Einbeck, W. Ger., 22
Eindhoven, Neth., 27
Eisenach, E. Ger., 22
Eisenhower (mt.), Alta., 182
Eisenhüttenstadt, E. Ger., 22
Eisenstadt, Austria, 41
Eisleben, E. Ger., 22
Eisling (mts.), Lux., 27
Ekenäs, Fin., 18
Ekeren, Belg., 27
Ekibastuz, U.S.S.R., 48
Ekibin, Queensland, 95
Eksjö, Sweden, 18
El Aaiún (cap.), Sp. Sahara, 106
El Agheila, Libya, 111
El 'Alamein, U.A.R., 111
El 'Arish, U.A.R., 111
El Asnam, Alg., 106
Elath, Israel, 65
El Athale (Itala), Somalia, 115
Elâzığ (prov.), Turkey, 63
Elâzığ, Turkey, 63
El Azúcar (res.), Mex., 150
Elba, Ala., 194
Elba (isl.), Italy, 34
El Bab, Syria, 63
El Balqa (dist.), Jordan, 65
Elbasan, Alb., 45
El Bayadh, Alg., 106
Elbe (riv.), Ger., 22
Elbert (mt.), Colo., 208
Elberton, Ga., 216
Elbeuf, France, 28
El Bira, Jordan, 65
Elbląg, Poland, 47
El'brus (mt.), U.S.S.R., 52
El Bur, Somalia, 115
Elburz (range), Iran, 66
El Cajon, Calif., 204
El Campo, Tex., 302
El Centro, Calif., 204
El Cerrito, Calif., 204
Elche, Spain, 33
El Cuey, Dom. Rep., 158
El Djezair (Algiers) (cap.), Alg., 106
Eldon, Mo., 261
Eldora, Iowa, 229
Eldorado, Arg., 143
El Dorado, Ark., 203
Eldorado, Ill., 222
El Dorado, Kans., 232
El Dorado Sprs., Mo., 261
Eldoret, Kenya, 115
Electra, Tex., 302
Elephanta (isl.), India, 68
Elephant Butte (res.), N. Mex., 274
Eleuthera (isl.), Bah. Is., 156
El Faiyûm, U.A.R., 111
El Fasher, Sudan, 111
El Ferrol, Spain, 33
El Ghor (reg.), Jordan, 65
Elgin, Ill., 222
Elgin, Scot., 15
Elgin, Tex., 302
El Goléa, Alg., 106
Elgon (mt.), Africa, 115
El Guayabo, Dom. Rep., 158
El Haseke (prov.), Syria, 63
El Haseke, Syria, 63
Elías Piña (prov.), Dom. Rep., 158
El Iskandariya (Alexandria), U.A.R., 111
Elista, U.S.S.R., 52
Elizabeth, N. J., 273
Elizabeth, Pa., 294
Elizabeth, S. Austral., 94
Elizabeth City, N.C., 281
Elizabethton, Tenn., 237
Elizabethtown, Ky., 237
Elizabethtown, Pa., 294
Elizabethville, Pa., 294
El Jadida, Mor., 106
El Jícaro, Nic., 154
Ełk, Poland, 47
El Karak (dist.), Jordan, 65
El Karak, Jordan, 65
El Karnak, U.A.R., 111
Elk City, Okla., 288
El Kef, Tun., 106
Elk Grove Vill., Ill., 222
Elkhart, Ind., 227
Elkhorn, Wis., 317
Elkin, N.C., 281
Elkins, W. Va., 313
Elk Island Nat'l Park, Alta., 182
Elko, Nev., 266
Elkridge, Md., 245
Elkton, Md., 245
El Ladhiqiya (prov.), Syria, 63
El Ladhiqiya (Latakia), Syria, 63
Ellef Ringnes (isl.), N.W.T., 187
Ellendale, N. Dak., 283
Ellensburg, Wash., 310
Ellenville, N.Y., 276
Ellesmere (isl.), N.W.T., 187
Ellesmere Port, Eng., 10
Ellice (isls.), Gilb. & Ell. Is., 87
Ellinwood, Kans., 232
Elliot Lake, Ont., 177
Ellisville, Miss., 256
Ellsville, Mo., 261
Ellsworth, Maine, 242
Ellsworth Land, Ant., 5
Ellwangen, W. Ger., 22
Ellwood City, Pa., 294
El Mahalla el Kubra, U.A.R., 111
El Mansûra, U.A.R., 111
El Marj, Libya, 111
Elm Grove, Wis., 317
Elmhurst, Ill., 222
El Minya, U.A.R., 111
Elmira, N.Y., 276
Elmira, Ont., 177
Elmont, N.Y., 276
El Monte, Calif., 204
El Morro Nat'l Mon., N. Mex., 274
Elmsford, N.Y., 276
Elmshorn, W. Ger., 22
Elmwood, Conn., 210
Elmwood Park, Ill., 222
Elmwood Place, Ohio, 284
El Obeid, Sudan, 111
Elobey (isls.), Eq. Guin., 115
El Oro, Mex., 150
El Oued, Alg., 106
Eloy, Ariz., 198
El Pao, Venez., 124
El Paraíso, Hond., 154
El Paso, Tex., 302
El Pozo, Dom. Rep., 158
El Progreso, Guat., 154
El Progreso, Hond., 154
El Puerto de Santa María, Spain, 33
El Qâhira (Cairo) (cap.), U.A.R., 111
El Quneitra (prov.), Syria, 63
El Quneitra, Syria, 63
El Rashid (prov.), Syria, 63
El Rashid, Syria, 63
El Real, Pan., 154
El Reno, Okla., 288
El Rio, Calif., 204
Elsa, Tex., 302
Elsa, Yukon, 187
El Salto, Mex., 150
El Salvador, 154
El Sauce, Nic., 154
El Segundo, Calif., 204
El Seibo (prov.), Dom. Rep., 158
El Seibo, Dom. Rep., 158
Elsinore (Helsingør), Den., 21
Elsmere, Del., 245
Elsmere, Ky., 237
Eltham, Vic., 97
El Tigre, Venez., 124
El Tigrito, Venez., 124
El Tocuyo, Venez., 124
El Triunfo, Hond., 154
Eluru, India, 68
Elvas, Port., 33
Elverum, Norway, 18
El Viejo, Nic., 154
Elwood, Ind., 227
Ely, Eng., 13
Ely, Minn., 254
Ely, Nev., 266
Elyria, Ohio, 284
El Yunque (mt.), P. Rico, 161
Embu, Kenya, 115
Emden, W. Ger., 22
Emerald, Queensland, 95
Emerson, Man., 179
Emerson, N. J., 273
Emeryville, Calif., 204
Emi Koussi (mt.), Chad, 111
Emilia-Romagna (reg.), Italy, 34
Emine (cape), Bulg., 45
Emmaus, Pa., 294
Emmen, Neth., 27
Emmen, Switz., 39
Emmental (valley), Switz., 39
Emmerich, W. Ger., 22
Emmetsburg, Iowa, 229
Emmett, Idaho, 220
Empalme, Mex., 150
Emporia, Kans., 232
Emporia, Va., 307
Emporium, Pa., 294
Ems (riv.), W. Ger., 22
Emsworth, Pa., 294
Encarnación, Mex., 150
Encarnación, Par., 144
Encinitas, Calif., 204
Encino, Calif., 204
Encounter (bay), S. Austral., 94
Endeavour (str.), Queensland, 95
Enderbury (isl.), Gilb. and Ell. Is., 87
Enderby, Br. Col., 184
Enderby Land (reg.), Ant., 5
Endicott, N.Y., 276
Enfield, Conn., 210
Enfield, Eng., 10
Enfield, N.C., 281
Enfield, S. Austral., 94
Engaño (cape), Phil. Is., 82
Engel's, U.S.S.R., 52
England, 13
England, Ark., 203
Englewood, Colo., 208
Englewood, Fla., 212
Englewood, N. J., 273
English (chan.), Europe, 13
English (riv.), Ont., 177
English Bazar, Pak., 68
English Coast (reg.), Ant., 5
Enid, Okla., 288
Enid (mt.), W. Austral., 92
Eniwetok (atoll), Pac. Is., 87
Enköping, Sweden, 18
Enna (prov.), Italy, 34
Enna, Italy, 34
Ennadai (lake), N.W.T., 187
En Nahud, Sudan, 111
En Nebk, Syria, 63
Ennedi (plat.), Chad, 111
Ennis, Ire., 17
Ennis, Tex., 302
Enniscorthy, Ire., 17
Enniskillen, N. Ire., 17
Ennistymon, Ire., 17
Enns (river), Austria, 41
Enola, Pa., 294
Enriquillo (lake), Dom. Rep., 158
Enschede, Neth., 27
Ensenada, Arg., 143
Ensenada, Mex., 150
Entebbe, Uganda, 115
Enterprise, Ala., 194
Enterprise, Oreg., 291
Entre Ríos (prov.), Arg., 143
Enugu, Nigeria, 106
Enumclaw, Wash., 310
Enzeli (Pahlevi), Iran, 66
Epéna, Rep. of Congo, 115
Épernay, France, 28
Ephesus (ruins), Turkey, 63
Ephrata, Pa., 294
Ephrata, Wash., 310
Épinal, France, 28
Épinay-sur-Seine, France, 28
Epirus (reg.), Greece, 45
Epping, Eng., 10
Epsom and Ewell, Eng., 10
Equateur (prov.), Dem. Rep. of the Congo, 115
Equatoria (prov.), Sudan, 111
Equatorial Guinea, 115
Erbil (prov.), Iraq, 66
Erbil, Iraq, 66
Érd, Hung., 41
Erechim, Braz., 132
Ereğli, Turkey, 63
Erenköy, Turkey, 63
Erepecuru (riv.), Braz., 132
Eresma (riv.), Spain, 33
Erfurt (dist.), E. Ger., 22
Erfurt, E. Ger., 22
Erh Hai (lake), China, 77
Erie (lake), N. Amer., 188
Erie, Pa., 294
Erigavo, Somalia, 115
Erimo (cape), Japan, 77
Eritrea (prov.), Eth., 111
Erivan, U.S.S.R., 52
Erlangen, W. Ger., 22
Erlanger, Ky., 237
Ermelo, S. Afr., 118
Ermoúpolis, Greece, 45
Ernakulam, India, 68
Erne (lake), N. Ire., 17
Erode, India, 68
Er Rahad, Sudan, 111
Er Ramtha, Jordan, 65
Er Rif (range), Mor., 106
Erris (head), Ire., 17
Erromanga (isl.), New Hebr., 87
Er Roseires, Sudan, 111
Erwin, N.C., 281
Erwin, Tenn., 237
Erzgebirge (range), Europe, 22, 41
Erzincan (prov.), Turkey, 63
Erzincan, Turkey, 63
Erzurum (prov.), Turkey, 63
Erzurum, Turkey, 63
Esashi, Japan, 81
Esbjerg, Den., 21
Escalante (des.), Utah, 304
Escanaba, Mich., 250
Eschwege, W. Ger., 22
Eschweiler, W. Ger., 22
Escondido, Calif., 204
Escuinapa, Mex., 150
Escuintla, Guat., 154
Escuintla, Mex., 150
Esher, Eng., 10
Eskilstuna, Sweden, 18
Eskişehir (prov.), Turkey, 63
Eskişehir, Turkey, 63
Esla (riv.), Spain, 33
Eslöv, Sweden, 18
Esmeraldas, Ecua., 128
Esmond, R.I., 249
Espaillat (prov.), Dom. Rep., 158
Española (isl.), Ecua., 128
Espanola, N. Mex., 274
Espanola, Ont., 177
Esparta, C. Rica, 154
Esperance, W. Austral., 92
Esperanza, Arg., 143
Esperanza (mts.), Hond., 154
Espinho, Port., 33
Espinho, Port., 33
Espírito Santo (state), Braz., 132
Espiritu Santo (isl.), New Hebr., 87
Espiritu Santo (cape), Phil. Is., 82
Espoir (bay), Newf., 166
Espoo, Fin., 18
Esquimalt, Br. Col., 184
Es Salt, Jordan, 65
Essaouira, Mor., 106
Essen, W. Ger., 22
Essendon, Vic., 97
Essequibo (dist.), Guyana, 131
Essequibo (riv.), Guyana, 131
Essequibo Islands (dist.), Guyana, 131
Essex (county), Eng., 13
Essex, Md., 245
Essex, Ont., 177
Essex Jct., Vt., 268
Essexville, Mich., 250
Essington, Pa., 294
Esslingen, W. Ger., 22
Essonne (dept.), France, 28
Es Suweida (prov.), Syria, 63
Es Suweida, Syria, 63
Estados (isl.), Arg., 143
Estahbanat, Iran, 66
Estância, Braz., 132
Estancia, N. Mex., 274
Estanzuelas, El Sal., 154
Este (pt.), Cuba, 158
Este, Italy, 34
Este (pt.), Urug., 145
Estelí, Nic., 154
Estepona, Spain, 33
Esterhazy, Sask., 181
Estevan, Sask., 181
Estherville, Iowa, 229
Eston, Sask., 181
Estonian S.S.R., U.S.S.R., 52
Estoril, Port., 33
Estrêla (mts.), Port., 33
Estremadura (prov.), Port., 33
Estremadura (reg.), Spain, 33
Estremoz, Port., 33
Esztergom, Hung., 41
Etawah, India, 68
Ethiopia, 111
Etna (vol.), Italy, 34
Etna, Pa., 294
Etobicoke, Ont., 177
Etosha (salt pan), S.W. Afr., 118
Etowah, Tenn., 237
Etterbeek, Belg., 27
Ettlingen, W. Ger., 22
Ettrick, Va., 307
Euboea (isl.), Greece, 45
Euclid, Ohio, 284
Eudora, Ark., 203
Eufaula, Ala., 194
Eufaula (lake), U.S., 194, 216
Eugene, Oreg., 291
Eunice, La., 238
Eunice, N. Mex., 274
Eupen, Belg., 27
Euphrates (riv.), Asia, 59
Eure (dept.), France, 28
Eure (riv.), France, 28
Eure-et-Loir (dept.), France, 28
Eureka, Calif., 204
Eureka, Ill., 222
Eureka, Kans., 232
Eureka, Nev., 266
Eureka, N.W.T., 187
Eureka, S. Dak., 298
Europa (pt.), Gibr., 33
Europe, 7
Euskirchen, W. Ger., 22
Eustis, Fla., 212
Eutaw, Ala., 194
Eutin, W. Ger., 22
Eutsuk (lake), Br. Col., 184
Evans (mt.), Colo., 208
Evansdale, Iowa, 229
Evanston, Ill., 222
Evanston, Wyo., 319
Evansville, Ind., 227
Evansville, Wis., 317
Evaton, S. Afr., 118
Eveleth, Minn., 254
Evenki Nat'l Okrug, U.S.S.R., 48
Everard (lake), S. Austral., 94
Evere, Belg., 27
Everest (mt.), Asia, 68
Everett, Mass., 249
Everett, Wash., 310
Everglades Nat'l Park, Fla., 212
Evergreen, Ala., 194
Evergreen Park, Ill., 222
Evesham, Eng., 13
Évora, Port., 33
Évreux, France, 28
Évros (riv.), Greece, 45
Évry, France, 28
Ewa, Hawaii, 218
Ewab (isls.), Indon., 85
Ewa Beach, Hawaii, 218
Excelsior Springs, Mo., 261
Exeter, Calif., 204
Exeter, Eng., 13
Exeter, N.H., 268
Exmouth, Eng., 13
Exmouth (gulf), W. Austral., 92
Exploits (river), Newf., 166
Exuma (sound), Bah. Is., 156
Eyasi (lake), Tanz., 115
Eyemouth, Scot., 15
Eyre (lake), S. Austral., 94
Eyre (pen.), S. Austral., 94
Eyüp, Turkey, 63
Ez Zarqa', Jordan, 65

F

Faaborg, Den., 21
Fabens, Tex., 302
Facatativá, Col., 126
Fada-N'Gourma, Upp. Volta, 106
Faenza, Italy, 34
Faerøe (isls.), Den., 21
Fafan (riv.), Eth., 111
Făgăraş, Rum., 45
Fagersta, Sweden, 18
Faguibine (lake), Mali, 106
Faial (isl.), Port., 32
Fairbanks, Alaska, 196
Fairborn, Ohio, 284
Fairbury, Ill., 222
Fairbury, Nebr., 264
Fairfax, Ala., 194
Fairfax, Calif., 204
Fairfax, Va., 307
Fairfield, Ala., 194
Fairfield, Calif., 204
Fairfield, Conn., 210
Fairfield, Ill., 222
Fairfield, Iowa, 229
Fairfield, Maine, 242
Fairfield, N. J., 273
Fairfield, N.S.W., 97
Fairfield, N.Z., 101
Fairfield, Ohio, 284
Fairhaven, Mass., 249
Fair Haven, N. J., 273
Fairhope, Ala., 194
Fair Lawn, N. J., 273
Fairless Hills, Pa., 294
Fairmont, Minn., 254
Fairmont, W. Va., 313
Fairmont City, Ill., 222
Fairport, N.Y., 276
Fairport Hbr., Ohio, 284
Fairview, Alta., 182
Fairview, N. J., 273
Fairview, N.Y., 276
Fairview, Wash., 310
Fairview Park, Ohio, 284
Fairweather (mt.), N. Amer., 184
Fais (isl.), Pac. Is., 87
Faizabad, Afghan., 68
Faizabad, India, 68
Fajardo, P. Rico, 161
Fakaofo (isl.), Tokelau Is., 87
Fakarava (atoll), Fr. Poly., 87
Fakfak, Indon., 85
Falaise, France, 28
Falcon (res.), N. Amer., 302
Falcón (state), Venez., 124
Falcone (cape), Italy, 34
Falconer, N.Y., 276
Falcon Hts., Minn., 254
Falfurrias, Tex., 302
Falkenberg, Sweden, 18
Falkensee, E. Ger., 22
Falkirk, Scot., 15
Falkland Islands, 120
Falköping, Sweden, 18
Fallbrook, Calif., 204
Fallon, Nev., 266
Fall River, Mass., 249
Falls Church, Va., 307
Falls City, Nebr., 264
Falmouth, Eng., 13
Falmouth, Jam., 158
Falmouth, Ky., 237
Falmouth, Mass., 249
False (pt.), India, 68
False (bay), S. Africa, 118
False Divi (pt.), India, 68
Falso (cape), Mex., 150
Falster (isl.), Den., 21
Fălticeni, Rum., 45
Falun, Sweden, 18
Famagusta, Cyprus, 63
Famatina (mts.), Arg., 143
Fanning (isl.), Gilb. and Ell. Is., 87
Fanø (isl.), Den., 21
Fano, Italy, 34
Fan Si Pan (mt.), N. Vietnam, 72
Fanwood, N. J., 273
Faradje, Dem. Rep. of the Congo, 115
Farafangana, Malag. Rep., 118
Farâfra (oasis), U.A.R., 111
Farah, Afghan., 68
Farallon (isls.), Calif., 204
Farasan (isls.), Saudi Ar., 59
Faraulep (atoll), Pac. Is., 87
Fareham, Eng., 13
Farewell (cape), Greenl., 4
Fargo, N. Dak., 283
Faribault, Minn., 254
Faridpur, Pak., 68
Farmers Branch, Tex., 302
Farmersville, Calif., 204
Farmerville, La., 238
Farmingdale, N.Y., 276
Farmington, Conn., 210
Farmington, Ill., 222
Farmington, Maine, 242
Farmington, Mich., 250
Farmington, Mo., 261
Farmington, N. Mex., 274
Farmville, N.C., 281
Farmville, Va., 307
Farnborough, Eng., 13
Farnham, Eng., 13
Farnham, Que., 172
Faro, Port., 33
Fårö (isl.), Sweden, 18
Farr (bay), Ant., 5
Farrell, Pa., 294
Fars (prov.), Iran, 66
Farsund, Norway, 18
Fasa, Iran, 66
Fashoda (Kodok), Sudan, 111
Fastov, U.S.S.R., 52
Fatehgarh, India, 68
Fatehpur, India, 68
Fatih, Turkey, 63
Fátima, Port., 33
Fatshan, China, 77
Fatuhiva (isl.), Fr. Poly., 87
Faversham, Eng., 13
Favignana (isl.), Italy, 34
Fawn (riv.), Ont., 177
Faxaflói (bay), Ice., 21
Fayette, Ala., 194
Fayette, Mo., 261
Fayetteville, Ark., 203
Fayetteville, N.Y., 276
Fayetteville, N.C., 281
Fayetteville, Tenn., 237
F'Dérick, Mauritania, 106
Fear (cape), N.C., 281
Fécamp, France, 28
Federación, Arg., 143
Federal District, Braz., 132
Feeding Hills, Mass., 249
Fehmarn (str.), Europe, 21
Fehmarn (isl.), W. Ger., 22
Feia (lake), Braz., 135
Feilding, N.Z., 101
Feira de Santana, Braz., 132
Fejér (county), Hung., 41
Feldberg (mt.), W. Ger., 22
Feldkirch, Austria, 41
Felixstowe, Eng., 13
Fellbach, W. Ger., 22
Femund (lake), Norway, 18
Fenelon Falls, Ont., 175
Fénérive, Malag. Rep., 118
Fengfeng, China, 77
Fenton, Mich., 250
Fenyang, China, 77
Feodosiya, U.S.S.R., 52
Fergana, U.S.S.R., 48
Fergus, Ont., 177
Fergus Falls, Minn., 254
Ferguson, Mo., 261
Ferkessédougou, Ivory Coast, 106
Ferlo (reg.), Senegal, 106
Fermanagh (county), N. Ire., 17
Ferme-Neuve, Que., 172
Fermoy, Ire., 17
Fernandina (isl.), Ecua., 128
Fernandina Beach, Fla., 212
Fernando de la Mora, Par., 144
Fernando Po (terr.), Eq. Guin., 115
Fernandópolis, Braz., 135
Ferndale, Md., 245
Ferndale, Mich., 250
Ferndale, Pa., 294
Fernie, Br. Col., 184
Fern Tree Gully, Vic., 97
Ferozepore, India, 68
Ferrara (prov.), Italy, 34
Ferrara, Italy, 34
Ferreñafe, Peru, 128
Ferriday, La., 238
Feshi, Dem. Rep. of the Congo, 115
Festus, Mo., 261
Feteşti, Rum., 45
Fethiye, Turkey, 63
Fetlar (isl.), Scot., 15
Fez, Mor., 106
Fezzan (reg.), Libya, 111
Ffestiniog, Wales, 13
Fianarantsoa (prov.), Malag. Rep., 118
Fianarantsoa, Malag. Rep., 118
Fichtelberg (mt.), E. Ger., 22
Fichtelgebirge (range), W. Ger., 22
Fier, Alb., 45
Fife (county), Scot., 15
Fifth Cataract (falls), Sudan, 111
Figueras, Spain, 33
Figuig, Mor., 106
Fiji, 87
Filchner Ice Shelf, Ant., 5
Filicudi (isl.), Italy, 34
Filingué, Niger, 106
Fillmore, Calif., 204
Finale, Italy, 34
Findlay, Ohio, 284
Finistère (dept.), France, 28
Finisterre (cape), Spain, 33
Finland, 18
Finland (gulf), Europe, 18
Finlay (riv.), Br. Col., 184
Finnmark (county), Norway, 18
Finschhafen, Terr. N.G., 85
Finspång, Sweden, 18
Finsteraarhorn (mt.), Switz., 39
Finsterwalde, E. Ger., 22
Firat (river), Turkey, 63
Fircrest, Wash., 310
Fire I. Nat'l Seashore, N.Y., 276
Firenze (Florence), Italy, 34
Firminy, France, 28
Firozabad, India, 68
Fish (riv.), S.W. Afr., 118
Fitchburg, Mass., 249
Fitzgerald, Ga., 216
Fitzroy (riv.), Queensland, 95
Fitzroy, Vic., 97
Fitzroy (riv.), W. Austral., 92
Fiume (Rijeka), Yugo., 45
Fiumicino, Italy, 34
Fizi, Dem. Rep. of the Congo, 115
Flagstaff, Ariz., 198
Flamborough (head), Eng., 13
Flaming Gorge (res.), Wyo., 319
Flaming Gorge Nat'l Rec. Area, U.S., 304, 319

Flathead (lake), Mont., 262
Flat River, Mo., 261
Flat Rock, Mich., 250
Flattery (cape), Queensland, 95
Flattery (cape), Wash., 310
Flatwoods, Ky., 237
Fleetwood, Eng., 13
Fleetwood, Pa., 294
Flekkefjord, Norway, 18
Flemington, N. J., 273
Flensburg, W. Ger., 22
Flinders (riv.), Queensland, 95
Flinders (range), S. Austral., 94
Flinders (isl.), Tas., 99
Flinders (bay), W. Austral., 92
Flin Flon, Man.-Sask., 179, 181
Flint, Mich., 250
Flint, Wales, 13
Flintshire (county), Wales, 13
Flora, Ill., 222
Flora, Norway, 18
Florala, Ala., 194
Floral Park, N.Y., 276
Florence, Ala., 194
Florence, Colo., 208
Florence (prov.), Italy, 34
Florence, Italy, 34
Florence, Ky., 237
Florence, N. J., 273
Florence, N.S., 169
Florence, S.C., 296
Florencia, Col., 126
Flores, Guat., 154
Flores (isl.), Indon., 85
Flores (sea), Indon., 85
Flores (isl.), Port., 32
Flores (dept.), Urug., 145
Florham Park, N. J., 273
Floriano, Braz., 132
Florianópolis, Braz., 132
Florida, Cuba, 158
Florida (bay), Fla., 212
Florida (straits), N. Amer., 156
Florida (state), U.S., 212
Florida (dept.), Urug., 145
Florida, Urug., 145
Florida City, Fla., 212
Flórina, Greece, 45
Florissant, Mo., 261
Florissant Fossil Beds Nat'l Mon., Colo., 208
Flossmoor, Ill., 222
Flowerpot (isl.), Ont., 177
Floydada, Tex., 302
Flushing, Mich., 250
Flushing, Neth., 27
Fly (riv.), Papua, 85
Foam Lake, Sask., 181
Focşani, Rum., 45
Foggia (prov.), Italy, 34
Foggia, Italy, 34
Fogo, Newf., 166
Foix, France, 28
Folcroft, Pa., 294
Foley, Ala., 194
Folgares, Angola, 115
Foligno, Italy, 34
Folkestone, Eng., 13
Follansbee, W. Va., 313
Folsom, Calif., 204
Folsom, Pa., 294
Fomento, Cuba, 158
Fond du Lac, Wis., 317
Fongafale, Gilb. & Ell. Is., 87
Fonseca (gulf), Cent. Amer., 154
Fontainebleau, France, 28
Fontana, Calif., 204
Fontenay, France, 28
Fonthill, Ont., 175
Fontibón, Col., 126
Foochow, China, 77
Footscray, Vic., 97
Forbach, France, 28
Forbes, N.S.W., 97
Forchheim, W. Ger., 22
Ford (ranges), Ant., 5
Ford City, Calif., 204
Ford City, Pa., 294
Fords, N. J., 273
Fordyce, Ark., 203
Forécariah, Guinea, 106
Forest, Belg., 27
Forest, Miss., 256
Forest, Ont., 175
Forest Acres, S.C., 296
Forest City, N.C., 281
Forestdale, Ala., 194
Forest Grove, Oreg., 291
Forest Heights, Md., 245
Forest Hills, Pa., 294
Forest Park, Ga., 216
Forest Park, Ill., 222
Forest Park, Ohio, 284
Forestville, Conn., 210
Forestville, Md., 245
Forestville, Que., 172
Forez (mts.), France, 28
Forfar (Angus)(county), Scot., 15
Forfar, Scot., 15
Forlì (prov.), Italy, 34
Forlì, Italy, 34
Formartine (dist.), Scot., 15
Formby, Eng., 10
Formiga, Braz., 135
Formosa (prov.), Arg., 143
Formosa, Arg., 143
Formosa (range), Braz., 132
Formosa (Taiwan)(isl.), China, 77
Formosa (Taiwan)(str.), China, 77
Forres, Scot., 15
Forrest City, Ark., 203
Forssa, Fin., 18
Forst, E. Ger., 22
Forsyth, Ga., 216
Fortaleza, Braz., 132
Fort-Archambault, Chad, 111
Fort Atkinson, Wis., 317
Fort Augustus, Scot., 15
Fort Beauséjour Nat'l Hist. Park, N. Br., 170
Fort Bowie Nat'l Hist. Site, Ariz., 198
Fort Bragg, Calif., 204
Fort Caroline Nat'l Mem., Fla., 212
Fort-Chambly, Que., 172
Fort-Chimo, Que., 174
Fort Chipewyan, Alta., 182
Fort Clatsop Nat'l Mem., Oreg., 291
Fort Collins, Colo., 208
Fort-Crampel, Centr. Afr. Rep., 115
Fort-Dauphin, Malag. Rep., 118
Fort Davis Nat'l Hist. Site, Tex., 302
Fort-de-France (cap.), Mart., 161
Fort Dodge, Iowa, 229
Fort Donelson Nat'l Mil. Park, Tenn., 237
Fort Edward, N.Y., 276
Fort Erie, Ont., 177
Fortescue (river), W. Austral., 92
Fort Fairfield, Maine, 242
Fort Frances, Ont., 175
Fort Franklin, N.W.T., 187
Fort Frederica Nat'l Mon., Ga., 216
Fort Garry, Man., 179
Fort-George, Que., 174
Fort Good Hope, N.W.T., 187
Forth (firth), Scot., 15
Forth and Clyde (canal), Scot., 15
Fort Hall, Kenya, 115
Fort Howard, Md., 245
Fort Jefferson Nat'l Mon., Fla., 212
Fort Kent, Maine, 242
Fort Knox, Ky., 237
Fort-Lamy (cap.), Chad, 111
Fort Laramie Nat'l Hist. Site, Wyo., 319
Fort Larned Nat'l Hist. Site, Kans., 232
Fort Lauderdale, Fla., 212
Fort Lee, N. J., 273
Fort-Liberté, Haiti, 158
Fort Macleod, Alta., 182
Fort Madison, Iowa, 229
Fort Matanzas Nat'l Mon., Fla., 212
Fort McHenry Nat'l Mon., Md., 245
Fort McMurray, Alta., 182
Fort McPherson, N.W.T., 187
Fort Meade, Fla., 212
Fort Mill, S.C., 296
Fort Mitchell, Ky., 237
Fort Morgan, Colo., 208
Fort Myers, Fla., 212
Fort Necessity Nat'l Battlef., Pa., 294
Fort Nelson, Br. Col., 184
Fort Payne, Ala., 194
Fort Peck (res.), Mont., 262
Fort Pierce, Fla., 212
Fort Pierre, S. Dak., 298
Fort Plain, N.Y., 276
Fort Portal, Uganda, 115
Fort Providence, N.W.T., 187
Fort Pulaski Nat'l Mon., Ga., 216
Fort-Qu'Appelle, Sask., 181
Fort Raleigh Nat'l Hist. Site, N.C., 281
Fort Reliance, N.W.T., 187
Fort Resolution, N.W.T., 187
Fort Richardson, Alaska, 196
Fort-Rousset, Rep. of Congo, 115
Fort-Rupert, Que., 174
Fort Saint James, Br. Col., 184
Fort Saint John, Br. Col., 184
Fort Sandeman, Pak., 68
Fort Saskatchewan, Alta., 182
Fort Scott, Kans., 232
Fort-Shevchenko, U.S.S.R., 48
Fort Simpson, N.W.T., 187
Fort Smith, Ark., 203
Fort Smith, N.W.T., 187
Fort Smith Nat'l Hist. Site, Ark., 203
Fort Stanwix Nat'l Mon., N.Y., 276
Fort Stockton, Tex., 302
Fort Sumter Nat'l Mon., S.C., 296
Fort Thomas, Ky., 237
Fortuna, Calif., 204
Fortune, Newf., 166
Fort Union Nat'l Mon., N. Mex., 274
Fort Union Trading Post Nat'l Hist. Site, N.D., 283
Fort Valley, Ga., 216
Fort Vancouver Nat'l Hist. Site, Wash., 310
Fort Vermilion, Alta., 182
Fort Victoria, Rhod., 118
Fort Walton Beach, Fla., 212
Fort Wayne, Ind., 227
Fort William, Scot., 15
Fort Worth, Tex., 302
Forty Fort, Pa., 294
Fort Yukon, Alaska, 196
Fosforescente (bay), P. Rico, 161
Foster City, Calif., 204
Foster Village, Hawaii, 218
Fostoria, Ohio, 284
Fougères, France, 28
Foumban, Cameroon, 115
Fountain Hill, Pa., 294
Four Corners, Oreg., 291
Fourmies, France, 28
Fourth Cataract (falls), Sudan, 111
Foveaux (strait), N.Z., 101
Fowyang, China, 77
Fox (lake), Ill., 222
Foxboro, Mass., 249
Fox Chapel, Pa., 294
Foxe (basin), N.W.T., 187
Fox Lake, Ill., 222
Fox Harbour, Newf., 166
Fox Point, Wis., 317
Foyle (inlet), N. Ire., 17
Foynes, Ire., 17
Foz do Iguaçú, Braz., 132
Frackville, Pa., 294
Framingham, Mass., 249
Franca, Braz., 135
Francavilla Fontana, Italy, 34
France, 28
Frances (lake), Yukon, 187
Franceville, Gabon, 115
Francis Case (lake), S. Dak., 298
Francistown, Bots., 118
François (lake), Br. Col., 184
François, Mart., 161
Franconian Jura (range), W. Ger., 22
Frankenthal, W. Ger., 22
Frankenwald (for.), W. Ger., 22
Frankfield, Jam., 158
Frankfort, Ind., 227
Frankfort (cap.), Ky., 237
Frankfort, N.Y., 276
Frankfurt (dist.), E. Ger., 22
Frankfurt-am-Main, W. Ger., 22
Frankfurt-an-der-Oder, E. Ger., 22
Franklin, Ind., 227
Franklin, Ky., 237
Franklin, La., 238
Franklin, Mass., 249
Franklin (lake), Nev., 266
Franklin, N.H., 268
Franklin, N. J., 273
Franklin (dist.), N.W.T., 187
Franklin (mts.), N.W.T., 187
Franklin, Ohio, 284
Franklin, Pa., 294
Franklin, Tenn., 237
Franklin, Va., 307
Franklin D. Roosevelt (lake), Wash., 310
Franklin Lakes, N. J., 273
Franklin Park, Ill., 222
Franklin Park, Pa., 294
Franklinton, La., 238
Franquia (riv.), Urug., 145
Franz Josef Land (isls.), U.S.S.R., 48
Frascati, Italy, 34
Fraser (riv.), Br. Col., 184
Fraser, Mich., 250
Fraser (isl.), Queensland, 95
Fraserburgh, Scot., 15
Frauenfeld, Switz., 39
Fray Bentos, Urug., 145
Frechen, W. Ger., 22
Fredericia, Den., 21
Frederick, Md., 245
Frederick, Okla., 288
Fredericksburg, Tex., 302
Fredericksburg, Va., 307
Fredericktown, Mo., 261
Fredericton (cap.), N. Br., 170
Frederik Hendrik (Dolak) (isl.), Indon., 85
Frederiksberg, Den., 21
Frederikshaab, Greenl., 4
Frederikshavn, Den., 21
Frederiksted, Virgin Is. (U.S.), 161
Fredonia, Kans., 232
Fredonia, N.Y., 276
Fredrikstad, Norway, 18
Freedom, Calif., 204
Freedom, Pa., 294
Freehold, N. J., 273
Freeland, Pa., 294
Freels (cape), Newf., 166
Freeport, Ill., 222
Freeport, N.Y., 276
Freeport, Tex., 302
Freer, Tex., 302
Freetown, Antigua, 161
Freetown (cap.), S. Leone, 106
Fregenal de la Sierra, Spain, 33
Freiberg, E. Ger., 22
Freiburg, W. Ger., 22
Freising, W. Ger., 22
Freital, E. Ger., 22
Fréjus (pass), Europe, 28
Fremantle, W. Austral., 92
Fremont, Calif., 204
Fremont, Mich., 250
Fremont, Nebr., 264
Fremont, Ohio, 284
French Frigate (shoal), Hawaii, 218
French Guiana, 131
Frenchman (riv.), N. Amer., 181, 262
French Polynesia, 87
Freshwater, Newf., 166
Fresnillo, Mex., 150
Fresno, Calif., 204
Freudenstadt, W. Ger., 22
Fria (cape), S.W. Afr., 118
Frias, Arg., 143
Fribourg (canton), Switz., 39
Fribourg, Switz., 39
Fridley, Minn., 254
Friedberg, W. Ger., 22
Friedrichshafen, W. Ger., 22
Friesland (prov.), Neth., 27
Frio (cape), Braz., 135
Friuli-Venezia Giulia (reg.), Italy, 34
Frobisher (lake), Sask., 181
Frobisher Bay, N.W.T., 187
Frolovo, U.S.S.R., 52
Frome (lake), S. Austral., 94
Frontenac, Mo., 261
Frontera, Mex., 150
Front Royal, Va., 307
Frosinone (prov.), Italy, 34
Frosinone, Italy, 34
Frostburg, Md., 245
Frostproof, Fla., 212
Frøya (isl.), Norway, 18
Frozen (strait), N.W.T., 187
Fruitvale, Colo., 208
Fruitvale, Wash., 310
Frunze, U.S.S.R., 48
Frutal, Braz., 135
Frýdek-Místek, Czech., 41
Fuchu, Japan, 81
Fuente de Cantos, Spain, 33
Fuentes de Andalucía, Spain, 33
Fuerte Olimpo, Par., 144
Fuerteventura (isl.), Spain, 33
Fujairah, Trucial States, 59
Fuji (mt.), Japan, 81
Fujieda, Japan, 81
Fujisawa, Japan, 81
Fukien (prov.), China, 77
Fukui (pref.), Japan, 81
Fukui, Japan, 81
Fukuoka (pref.), Japan, 81
Fukuoka, Japan, 81
Fukushima (pref.), Japan, 81
Fukuyama, Japan, 81
Fulda, W. Ger., 22
Fullerton, Calif., 204
Fulton, Ill., 222
Fulton, Ky., 237
Fulton, Mo., 261
Fulton, N.Y., 276
Funabashi, Japan, 81
Funafuti (atoll), Gilb. & Ell. Is., 87
Funchal, Port., 33
Fundy (bay), N. Amer., 169
Fundy Nat'l Park, N.B., 170
Furka (pass), Switz., 39
Furmanov, U.S.S.R., 52
Fuquay-Varina, N.C., 281
Furnas (res.), Braz., 135
Furneaux Group (isls.), Tas., 99
Fürstenfeldbruck, W. Ger., 22
Fürstenwalde, E. Ger., 22
Fürth, W. Ger., 22
Fushun, China, 77
Fusin, China, 77
Fusingchen, China, 77
Füssen, W. Ger., 22
Futa Jallon (mts.), Africa, 106
Fuyü, China, 77
Fyn (isl.), Den., 21
Fyne (inlet), Scot., 15
Fyzabad, Trin. and Tobago, 161

G

Gabela, Angola, 115
Gabès, Tun., 106
Gabès (gulf), Tun., 106
Gabon, 115
Gaborone (cap.), Bots., 118
Gabrovo, Bulg., 45
Gach Saran, Iran, 66
Gadag, India, 68
Gadsden, Ala., 194
Gaeta, Italy, 34
Gaffney, S.C., 296
Gafsa, Tun., 106
Gagnoa, Ivory Coast, 106
Gagnon, Que., 174
Gagra, U.S.S.R., 52
Gahanna, Ohio, 284
Gaiba (lagoon), Bol., 136
Gainesville, Fla., 212
Gainesville, Ga., 216
Gainesville, Tex., 302
Gainsborough, Eng., 13
Gairdner (lake), S. Austral., 94
Gairloch (dist.), Scot., 15
Gaithersburg, Md., 245
Galana (riv.), Kenya, 115
Galápagos (isls.), Ecua., 128
Galashiels, Scot., 15
Galați, Rum., 45
Galax, Va., 307
Galeana, Mex., 150
Galena, Ill., 222
Galena, Kans., 232
Galena Park, Tex., 302
Galera (pt.), Trin. and Tobago, 161
Galesburg, Ill., 222
Galicia (reg.), Spain, 33
Galilee (reg.), Israel, 65
Galion, Ohio, 284
Galkayu, Somalia, 115
Gallarate, Italy, 34
Gallatin, Tenn., 237
Galle, Ceylon, 68
Gallinas (pt.), Col., 126
Gallipoli, Turkey, 63
Gallipolis, Ohio, 284
Gallitzin, Pa., 294
Gällivare, Sweden, 18
Galloway (dist.), Scot., 15
Gallup, N. Mex., 274
Galston, Scot., 15
Galt, Ont., 177
Galva, Ill., 222
Galveston, Tex., 302
Gálvez, Arg., 143
Galway (county), Ire., 17
Galway, Ire., 17
Galway (bay), Ire., 17
Gambela, Eth., 111
Gambia, 106
Gambia (riv.), Africa, 106
Gambier (isls.), Fr. Poly., 87
Gamu-Gofa (prov.), Eth., 111
Ganale Dorya (riv.), Eth., 111
Gananoque, Ont., 177
Gander, Newf., 166
Gandía, Spain, 33
Gandzha (Kirovabad), U.S.S.R., 52
Ganganagar, India, 68
Ganges (Ganga) (riv.), Asia, 68
Ganges, Mouths of the (delta), Asia, 68
Gangtok, India, 68
Gannett (peak), Wyo., 319
Gantt, S.C., 296
Gao, Mali, 106
Gaoua, Upp. Volta, 106
Gap, France, 28
Gara (lake), Ire., 17
Garamba Nat'l Park, Dem. Rep. of the Congo, 115
Garanhuns, Braz., 132
Garapan (cap.), Pac. Is., 87
Garça, Braz., 135
Gard (dept.), France, 28
Gard (riv.), France, 28
Garda (lake), Italy, 34
Garden (isl.), W. Austral., 92
Gardena, Calif., 204
Garden City, Ga., 216
Garden City, Kans., 232
Garden City, N.Y., 276
Gardendale, Ala., 194
Garden Grove, Calif., 204
Garden Reach, India, 68
Gardez, Afghan., 68
Gardiner, Maine, 242
Gardner, Mass., 249
Gardner (isl.), Gilb. and Ell. Is., 87
Gardner Pinnacles (isls.), Hawaii, 218
Garelochhead, Scot., 15
Garfield, N. J., 273
Garfield Hts., Ohio, 284
Garibaldi Prov. Park, Br. Col., 184
Garioch (dist.), Scot., 15
Garland, Tex., 302
Garmisch-Partenkirchen, W. Ger., 22
Garner, N.C., 281
Garnett, Kans., 232
Garonne (riv.), France, 28
Garoua, Cameroon, 115
Garrett, Ind., 227
Garrett, Wash., 310
Garry (lake), N.W.T., 187
Gartok, China, 77
Garwood, N. J., 273
Gary, Ind., 227
Gas City, Ind., 227
Gascoyne (riv.), W. Austral., 92
Gaspé, Que., 172
Gaspé (pen.), Que., 172
Gaspésie Prov. Park, Que., 172
Gastonia, N.C., 281
Gata (cape), Cyprus, 63
Gata (cape), Spain, 33
Gateshead, Eng., 13
Gatesville, Tex., 302
Gateway, Ont., 177
Gatineau, Que., 172
Gatineau (riv.), Que., 172
Gatooma, Rhod., 118
Gatun (lake), Cent. Amer., 154
Gauhati, India, 68
Gaussberg (mt.), Ant., 5
Gávdhos (isl.), Greece, 45
Gave-de-Pau (riv.), France, 28
Gävle, Sweden, 18
Gävleborg (county), Sweden, 18
Gawler, S. Austral., 94
Gaya, India, 68
Gaya, Niger, 106
Gaylord, Mich., 250
Gaza (dist.), Mozamb., 118
Gaza, 65
Gaza Strip, 65
Gazi, Kenya, 115
Gaziantep (prov.), Turkey, 63
Gaziantep, Turkey, 63
Gdańsk (prov.), Poland, 47
Gdańsk, Poland, 47
Gdynia, Poland, 47
Gebe (isl.), Indon., 85
Gedaref, Sudan, 111
Gedera, Israel, 65
Gedi (ruins), Kenya, 115
Geebung, Queensland, 95
Geel, Belg., 27
Geelong, Vic., 97
Geelvink (chan.), W. Austral., 92
Geelvink (Serera) (bay), Indon., 85
Geesthacht, W. Ger., 22
Geikie (riv.), Sask., 181
Geislingen, W. Ger., 22
Geistown, Pa., 294
Gela, Italy, 34
Gelderland (prov.), Neth., 27
Geleen, Neth., 27
Gelibolu (Gallipoli), Turkey, 63
Gelidonya (cape), Turkey, 63
Gelsenkirchen, W. Ger., 22
Gemena, Dem. Rep. of the Congo, 115
Gemlik, Turkey, 63
Geneina, Sudan, 111
General Alvear, Arg., 143
General Artigas, Par., 144
General Cepeda, Mex., 150
General Grant Grove Park, Calif., 204
General Juan Madariaga, Arg., 143
General Pico, Arg., 143
General Roca, Arg., 143
Geneseo, Ill., 222
Geneseo, N.Y., 276
Geneva, Ala., 194
Geneva (lake), Europe, 39
Geneva, Ill., 222
Geneva, N.Y., 276
Geneva, Ohio, 284
Geneva (canton), Switz., 39
Geneva, Switz., 39
Genghis Khan Wall (ruins), Asia, 77
Genil (riv.), Spain, 33
Genk, Belg., 27
Gennargentu (mts.), Italy, 34
Gennevilliers, France, 28
Genoa (prov.), Italy, 34
Genoa (Genova), Italy, 34
Genoa (gulf), Italy, 34
Gentbrugge, Belg., 27
Gentilly, France, 28
Gentofte, Den., 21
Geographe (bay), W. Austral., 92
George (riv.), Que., 174
George, S. Africa, 118
George V Coast (reg.), Ant., 5
George Land (isl.), U.S.S.R., 48
George Rogers Clark Nat'l Hist. Park, Ind., 227
Georgetown (cap.), Cayman Is., 156
Georgetown, D.C., 245
Georgetown, Gambia, 106
Georgetown (cap.), Guyana, 131
Georgetown, Ill., 222
Georgetown, Ky., 237
George Town (Pinang), Malaysia, 72
Georgetown, Ohio, 284
Georgetown, Ont., 177
Georgetown, P.E.I., 169
Georgetown, St. Vincent, 161
Georgetown, S.C., 296
George Town, Tas., 99
Georgetown, Tex., 302
George Washington Birthpl. Nat'l Mon., Va., 307
George Washington Carver Nat'l Mon., Mo., 261
Georgia (str.), Br. Col., 184
Georgia (state), U.S., 216
Georgian (bay), Ont., 177
Georgian Bay Isls. Nat'l Park, Ont., 177
Georgian S.S.R., U.S.S.R., 52
Georgina (riv.), Austral., 88
Georgiu-Dezh, U.S.S.R., 52
Gera (dist.), E. Ger., 22
Gera, E. Ger., 22
Geral (range), Braz., 132
Geraldton, Ont., 175
Geraldton, W. Austral., 92
Gering, Nebr., 264
Gerlachovka (mt.), Czech., 41
Germantown, Ohio, 284
Germany, 22
Germiston, S. Africa, 118
Gerona (prov.), Spain, 33
Gerona, Spain, 33
Gers (dept.), France, 28
Gers (riv.), France, 28
Getafe, Spain, 33
Gettysburg, Pa., 294
Gettysburg Nat'l Mil. Park, Pa., 294
Gevgelija, Yugo., 45
Gex, France, 28
Gezira, El (reg.), Sudan, 111
Ghadames, Libya, 111
Ghaghara (river), India, 68
Ghana, 106
Ghardaïa, Alg., 106
Gharian (prov.), Libya, 111
Gharian, Libya, 111
Ghat, Libya, 111
Ghat Kopar, India, 68
Ghazaouet, Alg., 106
Ghaziabad, India, 68
Ghazipur, India, 68
Ghazni, Afghan., 68
Ghent, Belg., 27
Gheorgheni, Rum., 45
Gherla, Rum., 45
Ghurian, Afghan., 68
Giant's Causeway, N. Ire., 17
Gibara, Cuba, 158
Gibeon, S.W. Afr., 118
Gibraltar, 33
Gibraltar (strait), 33
Gibson (des.), W. Austral., 92
Gibsonburg, Ohio, 284
Gibson City, Ill., 222
Giddings, Tex., 302
Giessen, W. Ger., 22
Giffard, Que., 172
Gifford, Fla., 212
Gifu (pref.), Japan, 81
Gifu, Japan, 81
Giganta (mts.), Mex., 150
Gigha (passage), Scot., 15
Giglio (isl.), Italy, 34
Gijón, Spain, 33
Gila (riv.), U.S., 198
Gila Cliff Dwellings Nat'l Mon., N. Mex., 274
Gilan (prov.), Iran, 66
Gilbert (isls.), Gilb. & Ell. Is., 87
Gilbert, Minn., 254
Gilbert (riv.), Queensland, 95
Gilbert and Ellice Is., 87
Gillespie, Ill., 222
Gillette, Wyo., 319
Gillingham, Eng., 13
Gilly, Belg., 27
Gilmer, Tex., 302
Gilroy, Calif., 204
Gimli, Man., 179
Gioia del Colle, Italy, 34
Gi-Paraná (riv.), Braz., 132
Gippsland (reg.), Vic., 97
Girard, Ohio, 284
Girardot, Col., 126
Girardville, Pa., 294
Giresun (prov.), Turkey, 63
Giresun, Turkey, 63
Girga, U.A.R., 111
Girishk, Afghan., 68
Gironde (dept.), France, 28
Gironde (riv.), France, 28
Girvan, Scot., 15
Gisborne, N.Z., 101
Gisenyi, Rwanda, 115
Gitega, Burundi, 115
Giurgiu, Rum., 45
Giv'atayim, Israel, 65
Giza, U.A.R., 111
Gjirokastër, Alb., 45
Gjøvik, Norway, 18
Glace Bay, N.S., 69
Glacier Bay Nat'l Mon., Alaska, 196
Glacier Nat'l Park, Br. Col., 184
Glacier Nat'l Park, Mont., 262
Gladewater, Tex., 302
Gladstone, Mich., 250
Gladstone, Mo., 261
Gladstone, Oreg., 291
Gladstone, Queensland, 95
Glamorganshire (county), Wales, 13
Glarus (canton), Switz., 39
Glarus Alps (mts.), Switz., 39
Glasgow, Ky., 237
Glasgow, Mont., 262
Glasgow, Scot., 15
Glassboro, N. J., 273
Glassport, Pa., 294
Glastonbury, Conn., 210
Glauchau, E. Ger., 22
Glazov, U.S.S.R., 52
Glen Avon Hts., Calif., 204
Glenavy, N. Ire., 17
Glen Burnie, Md., 245
Glen Canyon Nat'l Rec. Area, U.S., 198, 304
Glencoe, Ala., 194
Glencoe, Ill., 222
Glencoe, La., 238
Glencoe, Minn., 254
Glen Cove, N.Y., 276
Glendale, Ariz., 198
Glendale, Calif., 204
Glendale, Mo., 261
Glendale, Ohio, 284
Glendale, Wis., 317
Glendale Hts., Ill., 222
Glendive, Mont., 262
Glendora, Calif., 204
Glendora, N. J., 273
Glenelg (dist.), Scot., 15
Glenelg, S. Austral., 94
Glen Ellyn, Ill., 222
Glenfield, N.Z., 101
Glen Head, N.Y., 276
Glen Innes, N.S.W., 97
Glen Lyon, Pa., 294
Glennville, Ga., 216
Glenolden, Pa., 294
Glenorchy, Tas., 99
Glen Ridge, N. J., 273
Glen Rock, N. J., 273
Glenrothes, Scot., 15
Glens Falls, N.Y., 276
Glenshaw, Pa., 294
Glenside, Pa., 294
Glenview, Ill., 222
Glenwood, Iowa, 229
Glenwood, Minn., 254
Glenwood, Newf., 166
Glenwood Sprs., Colo., 208
Glittertind (mt.), Norway, 18
Gliwice, Poland, 47
Globe, Ariz., 198
Glomma (riv.), Norway, 18
Glossop, Eng., 10
Glostrup, Den., 21
Gloucester, Eng., 13
Gloucester, Mass., 249
Gloucester City, N. J., 273
Gloucestershire (county), Eng., 13
Gloversville, N.Y., 276
Glovertown, Newf., 166
Glukhov, U.S.S.R., 52
Glyndon, Md., 245
Gmünd, Austria, 41
Gmunden, Austria, 41
Gniezno, Poland, 47
Gnjilane, Yugo., 45
Goa (dist.), India, 68
Goa, Daman and Diu (terr.), India, 68
Goba, Eth., 111
Gobabis, S.W. Afr., 118
Gobi (des.), Asia, 77
Gobi-Altay (prov.), Mong., 77
Go Cong, S. Vietnam, 72
Godalming, Eng., 13
Godavari (riv.), India, 68
Goderich, Ont., 177
Godhavn, Greenl., 4
Godhra, India, 68
Gödöllő, Hung., 41
Godoy Cruz, Arg., 143
Gods (riv.), Man., 179
Godthaab (cap.), Greenl., 4
Godwin Austen (K2)(mt.), India, 68
Goélands (lake), Que., 174
Goiânia, Braz., 132
Goiás (state), Braz., 132
Gojjam (prov.), Eth., 111
Gök (riv.), Turkey, 63
Göksu (riv.), Turkey, 63
Golconda (ruins), India, 68
Gölcük, Turkey, 63
Gold Coast (reg.), Afr., 106
Gold Coast, Queensland, 95
Golden, Br. Col., 184
Golden, Colo., 208
Goldendale, Wash., 310
Golden Gate (chan.), Calif., 204
Golden Gate, Fla., 212
Golden Meadow, La., 238
Golden Spike Nat'l Hist. Site, Utah, 304
Golden Vale (plain), Ire., 17
Golden Valley, Minn., 254
Goldsboro, N.C., 281
Goleta, Calif., 204
Golfito, C. Rica, 154
Golf Manor, Ohio, 284
Goma, Dem. Rep. of the Congo, 115
Gomel', U.S.S.R., 52
Gomera (isl.), Spain, 33
Gómez Palacio, Mex., 150
Gonaïves, Haiti, 158
Gonâve (isl.), Haiti, 158
Gonda, India, 68
Gondal, India, 68
Gondar, Eth., 111
Gondomar, Port., 33
Gongola (riv.), Nigeria, 106
Gonzales, La., 238
Gonzales, Tex., 302
González, Mex., 150
Goodenough (cape), Ant., 5
Good Hope (cape), Indon., 85
Good Hope (cape), S. Africa, 118
Gooding, Idaho, 220
Goodland, Kans., 232
Goodlettsville, Tenn., 237
Goodspirit Prov. Park, Sask., 181
Goodwick, Wales, 13
Goodwood, S. Africa, 118
Goole, Eng., 13
Goose (lake), U.S., 204, 291
Goose Bay, Newf., 166
Göppingen, W. Ger., 22
Gorakhpur, India, 68
Gore, Eth., 111
Gore, N.Z., 101
Gorey, Ire., 17
Gorgol (reg.), Mauritania, 106
Gorgona (isl.), Italy, 34
Gori, U.S.S.R., 52
Gorinchem, Neth., 27
Gorizia (prov.), Italy, 34
Gorizia, Italy, 34
Gor'kiy, U.S.S.R., 52
Görlitz, E. Ger., 22
Gorlovka, U.S.S.R., 52
Gorna Dzhumaya (Blagoyevgrad), Bulg., 45
Gorna Oryakhovitsa, Bulg., 45
Gorno-Altay Aut. Oblast, U.S.S.R., 48
Gorno-Altaysk, U.S.S.R., 48
Gorno-Badakhshan Aut. Oblast, U.S.S.R., 48
Gornyatskiy, U.S.S.R., 52
Gorodets, U.S.S.R., 52
Goroka, Terr. N.G., 85
Gorong (isls.), Indon., 85
Gorontalo, Indon., 85
Gort, Ire., 17
Goryn' (riv.), U.S.S.R., 52
Gorzów, Poland, 47
Gosford, N.S.W., 97
Goshen, Ind., 227
Goshen, N.Y., 276
Gosier, Guad., 161
Goslar, W. Ger., 22
Gosnell, Ark., 203
Gosport, Eng., 13
Gostivar, Yugo., 45
Göta (canal), Sweden, 18
Göta (riv.), Sweden, 18
Göteborg, Sweden, 18
Göteborg och Bohus (county), Sweden, 18
Gotha, E. Ger., 22
Gothenburg, Nebr., 264
Gotland (county), Sweden, 18
Gotland (isl.), Sweden, 18
Goto (isls.), Japan, 81
Gotse Delchev, Bulg., 45
Göttingen, W. Ger., 22
Gottwaldov, Czech., 41
Gouda, Neth., 27
Gouin (res.), Que., 174
Goulburn, N.S.W., 97
Goulds, Fla., 212
Goundam, Mali, 106
Gourara (oasis), Alg., 106
Gourock, Scot., 15
Gouverneur, N.Y., 276
Gouyave, Grenada, 161
Governador Valadares, Braz., 132
Gowanda, N.Y., 276
Gower (pen.), Wales, 13
Goya, Arg., 143
Gozo (isl.), Malta, 34
Graaff-Reinet, S. Africa, 118
Gracias a Dios (cape), Nic., 154
Graciosa (isl.), Port., 32
Gradaús (range), Braz., 132
Grafton, Mass., 249
Grafton, N.S.W., 97
Grafton, N. Dak., 283
Grafton, W. Va., 313
Grafton, Wis., 317
Graham, N.C., 281
Graham, Tex., 302
Graham Bell (isl.), U.S.S.R., 48
Graham Land (reg.), Ant., 5
Grahamstown, S. Africa, 118
Graian Alps (range), Europe, 28
Grain Coast (reg.), Liberia, 106
Grajaú (riv.), Braz., 132
Grambling, La., 238
Grampian (mts.), Scot., 15
Granada, Nic., 154
Granada (prov.), Spain, 33
Granada, Spain, 33
Granada Hills, Calif., 204
Granados, Mex., 150
Granard, Ire., 17
Granby, Mass., 249
Granby, Que., 172
Gran Chaco (reg.), S. Amer., 120
Grand (canal), China, 77
Grand (canal), Ire., 17
Grand (lake), Newf., 166
Grand Bahama (isl.), Bah. Is., 156
Grand Bank, Newf., 166
Grand-Bassam, Ivory Coast, 106
Grand Bay, Dominica, 161
Grand-Bourg, Guad., 161
Grand Caicos (isl.), Turks & Caicos Is., 156
Grand Canary (isl.), Spain, 33
Grand Canyon Nat'l Mon., Ariz., 198
Grand Canyon Nat'l Park, Ariz., 198
Grand Cayman (isl.), Cayman Is., 156
Grand Centre, Alta., 182
Grand Cess, Liberia, 106
Grand Comoro (isl.), Comoro Is., 118
Grand Coulee (res.), Wash., 310
Grande (bay), Arg., 143
Grande (riv.), Arg., 143
Grande (riv.), Bol., 136
Grande (riv.), Braz., 132
Grande (riv.), Mex., 150
Grande (riv.), Nic., 154
Grande (range), Urug., 145
Grande (riv.), Urug., 145
Grande de Santiago (riv.), Mex., 150
Grande-Prairie, Alta., 182
Grande-Rivière, Que., 172
Grande-Terre (isl.), Guad., 161
Grand Falls, N.B., 170
Grand Falls, Newf., 166
Grand Forks, Br. Col., 184
Grand Forks, N. Dak., 283
Grand Haven, Mich., 250
Grand Island, Nebr., 264
Grand Jct., Colo., 208
Grand Ledge, Mich., 250
Grand Manan (isl.), N.B., 170
Grand'Mère, Que., 172
Grand Portage Nat'l Mon., Minn., 254
Grand Prairie, Tex., 302
Grand Rapids, Man., 179
Grand Rapids, Mich., 250
Grand Rapids, Minn., 254
Grand Teton Nat'l Park, Wyo., 319
Grand Turk (isl.), Turks and Caicos Is., 156
Grandview, Man., 179
Grandview, Mo., 261
Grandview, Wash., 310
Grandview Hts., Ohio, 284
Grandville, Mich., 250
Graneros, Chile, 138
Grangemouth, Scot., 15
Grangeville, Idaho, 220
Granite (peak), Mont., 262
Granite City, Ill., 222
Granite Falls, Minn., 254
Granite Falls, N.C., 281
Granitique, Chaîne (range), Fr. Gui., 131
Granollers, Spain, 33
Gran Paradiso (mt.), Italy, 34
Gran Quivira Nat'l Mon., N. Mex., 274
Gran Sabana, La (plain), Venez., 124
Grantham, Eng., 13
Grants, N. Mex., 274
Grants Pass, Oreg., 291
Granville, France, 28
Granville (lake), Man., 179
Granville, N.Y., 276
Granville, Ohio, 284
Grapevine, Tex., 302
Grasse, France, 28
Grass Valley, Calif., 204
Grassy Park, S. Africa, 118
Graubünden (canton), Switz., 39
Gravelbourg, Sask., 181
Gravenhurst, Ont., 177
Gravesend, Eng., 10
Gravina in Puglia, Italy, 34
Grayslake, Ill., 222
Graysville, Ala., 194
Graz, Austria, 41
Great (sound), Berm., 156
Great (chan.), India, 68
Great (lakes), N. Amer., 146
Great Abaco (isl.), Bah. Is., 156
Great Alföld (plain), Hung., 41
Great Australian (bight), Austral., 88
Great Barrier (isl.), N.Z., 101
Great Barrier (reef), Queensland, 95
Great Barrington, Mass., 249
Great Bear (lake), N.W.T., 187
Great Bend, Kans., 232
Great Corn (isl.), Nic., 154
Great Dividing (range), Austral., 88

Great Eastern Erg (des.), Africa, 106
Great Exuma (isl.), Bah. Is., 156
Great Falls, Mont., 262
Great Falls, S.C., 296
Great Inagua (isl.), Bah. Is., 156
Great Indian (des.), Asia, 68
Great Karoo (reg.), S. Africa, 118
Great Khingan (range), China, 77
Great Namaland (reg.), S.W. Afr., 118
Great Neck, N.Y., 276
Great Ruaha (riv.), Tanz., 115
Great Saint Bernard (pass), Europe, 34
Great Salt (lake), Utah, 304
Great Salt Lake (des.), U.S., 304
Great Sand Dunes Nat'l Mon., Colo., 208
Great Sand Sea (des.), Africa, 111
Great Sandy (Fraser) (isl.), Queensland, 95
Great Sandy (des.), W. Austral., 92
Great Slave (lake), N.W.T., 187
Great Smoky (mts.), U.S., 237, 281
Great Smoky Mts. Nat'l Park, U.S., 237, 281
Great Victoria (des.), Austral., 88
Great Wall (ruins), China, 77
Great Western Erg (des.), Africa, 106
Great Yarmouth, Eng., 13
Gredos (mts.), Spain, 33
Greece, 45
Greece, N.Y., 276
Greeley, Colo., 208
Green (riv.), U.S., 188
Green (mts.), Vt., 268
Green Bay, Wis., 317
Greenbelt, Md., 245
Greencastle, Ind., 227
Greencastle, Pa., 294
Green Cove Sprs., Fla., 212
Greendale, Ind., 227
Greendale, Wis., 317
Greeneville, Tenn., 237
Greenfield, Ind., 227
Greenfield, Mass., 249
Greenfield, Ohio, 284
Greenfield, Wis., 317
Greenhills, Ohio, 284
Green Island, N.Y., 276
Greenland, 4
Greenland (sea), Greenl., 4
Greenock, Scot., 15
Greenport, N.Y., 276
Green River, Wyo., 319
Green Rock, Ill., 222
Greensboro, Ala., 194
Greensboro, Ga., 216
Greensboro, N.C., 281
Greensburg, Ind., 227
Greensburg, Pa., 294
Greenslopes, Queensland, 95
Greentree, Pa., 294
Green Valley, Ariz., 198
Greenville, Ala., 194
Greenville, Ill., 222
Greenville, Ky., 237
Greenville, Liberia, 106
Greenville, Mich., 250
Greenville, Miss., 256
Greenville, N.C., 281
Greenville, Ohio, 284
Greenville, Pa., 294
Greenville, R.I., 249
Greenville, S.C., 296
Greenville, Tenn., 237
Greenville, Tex., 302
Greenwater Lake Prov. Park, Sask., 181
Greenwich, Conn., 210
Greenwich, Eng., 10
Greenwich (Kapinga-marangi) (atoll), Pac. Is., 87
Greenwood, Ind., 227
Greenwood, Mass., 249
Greenwood, Miss., 256
Greenwood, S.C., 296
Greer, S.C., 296
Gregory (range), Queensland, 95
Gregory (lake), S. Austral., 94
Gregory (lake), W. Austral., 92
Greifswald, E. Ger., 22
Greiz, E. Ger., 22
Gremyachinsk, U.S.S.R., 52
Grenaa, Den., 21
Grenada, 161
Grenada, Miss., 256
Grenadines (isls.), W. Indies, 156
Grenchen, Switz., 39
Grenfell, Sask., 181
Grenoble, France, 28
Grenville, Grenada, 161
Grenville, Que., 172
Gresham, Oreg., 291
Gresik, Indon., 85
Gretna, La., 238
Gretna Green, Scot., 15
Grevenbroich, W. Ger., 22
Grevenmacher, Lux., 27
Grey (riv.), N.Z., 101
Greybull, Wyo., 319
Grey Isls., Newf., 166
Greymouth, N.Z., 101
Greystone Park, N. J., 273
Greystones-Delgany, Ire., 17
Greytown (San Juan del Norte), Nic., 154
Gridley, Calif., 204
Griffin, Ga., 216
Griffith, Ind., 227
Griffith, N.S.W., 97
Grijalva (riv.), Mex., 150
Grimsby, Eng., 13
Grimsby, Ont., 177
Grimsel (pass), Switz., 39
Grimshaw, Alta., 182
Grindelwald, Switz., 39
Grinnell, Iowa, 229
Griqualand West (reg.), S. Africa, 118
Gris-Nez (cape), France, 28
Grodno, U.S.S.R., 52
Groix (isl.), France, 28
Gronau, W. Ger., 22
Grondal, Greenl., 4
Groningen (prov.), Neth., 27
Groningen, Neth., 27
Groningen, Sur., 131
Groote Eylandt (isl.), N. Terr., 93
Grootfontein, S.W. Afr., 118
Gros Islet, St. Lucia, 161
Grosse Ile, Mich., 250
Grosse Pte., Mich., 250
Grosse Pte. Farms, Mich., 250
Grosse Pte. Park, Mich., 250
Grosse Pte. Woods, Mich., 250
Grosseto (prov.), Italy, 34
Grosseto, Italy, 34
Grossglockner (mt.), Austria, 41
Groton, Conn., 210
Grottaglie, Italy, 34
Grove City, Ohio, 284
Grove City, Pa., 294
Grover City, Calif., 204
Groves, Tex., 302
Groznyy, U.S.S.R., 52
Grudziądz, Poland, 47
Gryazi, U.S.S.R., 52
Guacanayabo (gulf), Cuba, 158
Guacara, Venez., 124
Guácimo, C. Rica, 154
Guadalajara, Mex., 150
Guadalajara (prov.), Spain, 33
Guadalajara, Spain, 33
Guadalcanal (isl.), Br. Sol. Is., 87
Guadalimar (riv.), Spain, 33
Guadalquivir (riv.), Spain, 33
Guadalupe, Calif., 204
Guadalupe, Mex., 150
Guadalupe (mts.), Spain, 33
Guadalupe (mts.), Tex., 302
Guadalupe (peak), Tex., 302
Guadalupe (riv.), Tex., 302
Guadalupe-Bravos, Mex., 150
Guadalupe Mts. Nat'l Park, Tex., 302
Guadalupe Victoria, Mex., 150
Guadarrama (mts.), Spain, 33
Guadarrama (riv.), Spain, 33
Guadeloupe, 161
Guadiana (riv.), Europe, 33
Guadix, Spain, 33
Guainia (commissary), Col., 126
Guainía (riv.), S. Amer., 126
Guairá (dept.), Par., 144
Guairá (falls), S. Amer., 144
Guajira, La (department), Col., 126
Guajira (pen.), S. Amer., 120
Gualán, Guat., 154
Gualeguay, Arg., 143
Gualeguaychú, Arg., 143
Guam (isl.), U.S., 87
Guamúchil, Mex., 150
Guanabacoa, Cuba, 158
Guanabara (state), Braz., 132
Guanabara (bay), Braz., 135
Guanaja (isl.), Hond., 154
Guanajay, Cuba, 158
Guanajuato (state), Mex., 150
Guanajuato, Mex., 150
Guanare, Venez., 124
Guánica, P. Rico, 161
Guano, Ecua., 128
Guantánamo, Cuba, 158
Guantánamo (bay), Cuba, 158
Guaporé (terr.), Braz., 132
Guaporé (riv.), S. Amer., 136
Guaqui, Bol., 136
Guarambaré, Par., 144
Guaranda, Ecua., 128
Guaratinguetá, Braz., 135
Guarda, Port., 33
Guardafui (cape), Somalia, 115
Guárico (state), Venez., 124
Guarulhos, Braz., 135
Guarus, Braz., 135
Guasave, Mex., 150
Guastalla, Italy, 34
Guatemala, 154
Guatemala (cap.), Guat., 154
Guaviare (riv.), Col., 126
Guayabal, Cuba, 158
Guayama (dist.), P. Rico, 161
Guayama, P. Rico, 161
Guayanilla, P. Rico, 161
Guayaquil, Ecua., 128
Guayaquil (gulf), Ecua., 128
Guayas (prov.), Ecua., 128
Guayas (riv.), Ecua., 128
Guaymallén, Arg., 143
Guaymas, Mex., 150
Gubakha, U.S.S.R., 52
Guban (reg.), Somalia, 115
Guben (Wilhelm-Pieck-Stadt), E. Ger., 22
Gudenaa (riv.), Den., 21
Guebwiller, France, 28
Guelma, Alg., 106
Guelph, Ont., 177
Guerara, Alg., 106
Guéret, France, 28
Guernica y Luno, Spain, 33
Guernsey (isl.), Chan. Is., 13
Guerrero (state), Mex., 150
Guichón, Urug., 145
Güija (lake), Cent. Amer., 154
Guildford, Eng., 13
Guilford Coll., N.C., 281
Guilford C.H. Nat'l Mil. Park, N.C., 281
Guimarães, Port., 33
Guimaras (isl.), Phil. Is., 82
Guinea, 106
Guinea (gulf), Africa, 106
Güines, Cuba, 158
Guipúzcoa (prov.), Spain, 33
Güira, Cuba, 158
Güiria, Venez., 124
Guise, France, 28
Gujarat (state), India, 68
Gujranwala, Pak., 68
Gujrat, Pak., 68
Gukovo, U.S.S.R., 52
Gulbarga, India, 68
Gulf Breeze, Fla., 212
Gulfport, Fla., 212
Gulfport, Miss., 256
Gulistan, U.S.S.R., 48
Gull Lake, Sask., 181
Gulpaigan, Iran, 66
Gulu, Uganda, 115
Gumma (pref.), Japan, 81
Gummersbach, W. Ger., 22
Gümüşhane (prov.), Turkey, 63
Gümüşhane, Turkey, 63
Gungu, Dem. Rep. of the Congo, 115
Gunnbjörn (mt.), Greenl., 4
Gunnedah, N.S.W., 97
Gunningsville, N. Br., 170
Gunnison, Colo., 208
Guntakal, India, 68
Guntersville, Ala., 194
Guntur, India, 68
Gurgan, Iran, 66
Gurguéia (riv.), Braz., 132
Guri (res.), Venez., 124
Gurla Mandhata (mt.), China, 77
Gurupi (range), Braz., 132
Gur'yev, U.S.S.R., 48
Gusau, Nigeria, 106
Gus-Khrustal'nyy, U.S.S.R., 52
Güstrow, E. Ger., 22
Gütersloh, W. Ger., 22
Guthrie, Okla., 288
Gutiérrez Zamora, Mex., 150
Guttenberg, N. J., 273
Guyana, 131
Guymon, Okla., 288
Guysborough, N.S., 169
Guzmán (lake), Mex., 150
Gwalior, India, 68
Gwelo, Rhod., 118
Gyangtse, China, 77
Gyda (pen.), U.S.S.R., 48
Gydan (Kolyma) (range), U.S.S.R., 48
Gympie, Queensland, 95
Gyobingauk, Burma, 72
Gyöngyös, Hung., 41
Győr (county), Hung., 41
Győr, Hung., 41
Gyula, Hung., 41

H

Ha'apai Group (isls.), Tonga, 87
Haarlem, Neth., 27
Haarlemmermeer (polder), Neth., 27
Haasts Bluff, N. Terr., 93
Habbaniya, Iraq, 66
Habomai (isls.), Japan, 81
Hachinohe, Japan, 81
Hachioji, Japan, 81
Hackensack, N. J., 273
Hackettstown, N. J., 273
Hackney, Eng., 10
Hadama, Eth., 111
Hadarba, Ras (cape), Sudan, 111
Hadd, Ras al (cape), Oman, 59
Haddington, Scot., 15
Haddonfield, N. J., 273
Haddon Hts., N. J., 273
Hadera, Israel, 65
Haderslev, Den., 21
Hadhar, Iraq, 66
Hadhramaut (dist.), P.D.R. Yemen, 59
Hadhramaut, Wadi (dry river), P.D.R. Yemen, 59
Haditha, Iraq, 66
Haedo (range), Urug., 145
Haeju, N. Korea, 81
Hafnarfjördhur, Ice., 21
Hafun, Ras (cape), Somalia, 115
Hagen, W. Ger., 22
Hagerstown, Md., 245
Hagersville, Ont., 177
Ha Giang, N. Vietnam, 72
Hague (cape), France, 28
Hague, The (cap.), Neth., 27
Haguenau, France, 28
Hai, Iraq, 66
Haibak, Afghan., 68
Haifa (dist.), Israel, 65
Haifa, Israel, 65
Haikow (Hoihow), China, 77
Hail, Saudi Ar., 59
Hailar, China, 77
Haileybury, Ont., 177
Hailung, China, 77
Hainan (isl.), China, 77
Hainault (prov.), Belg., 27
Haines City, Fla., 212
Haiphong, N. Vietnam, 72
Haiti, 158
Haiya Jct., Sudan, 111
Hajdú-Bihar (county), Hung., 41
Hajdúböszörmény, Hung., 41
Haji Ibrahim (mt.), Iraq, 66
Hakkâri (prov.), Turkey, 63
Hakodate, Japan, 81
Halabja, Iraq, 66
Halachó, Mex., 150
Halawa Hts., Hawaii, 218
Halberstadt, E. Ger., 22
Halden, Norway, 18
Haldensleben, E. Ger., 22
Haleakala Nat'l Park, Hawaii, 218
Haleb (Aleppo) (prov.), Syria, 63
Haleb (Aleppo), Syria, 63
Haledon, N. J., 273
Haleiwa, Hawaii, 218
Hales Corners, Wis., 317
Halesowen, Eng., 10
Halethorpe, Md., 245
Haleyville, Ala., 194
Halfway, Md., 245
Haliburton (lake), Ont., 177
Halifax, Eng., 10
Halifax (cap.), N.S., 169
Halkirk, Scot., 15
Hall (isls.), Pac. Is., 87
Halla (mt.), S. Korea, 81
Halland (county), Sweden, 18
Hallandale, Fla., 212
Halle (dist.), E. Ger., 22
Halle, E. Ger., 22
Hällefors, Sweden, 18
Hallein, Austria, 41
Hallettsville, Tex., 302
Hallowell, Maine, 242
Hallsberg, Sweden, 18
Halls Creek, W. Austral., 92
Hallstahammar, Sweden, 18
Hallstatt, Austria, 41
Halmahera (isl.), Indon., 95
Halmstad, Sweden, 18
Halq el Oued, Tun., 106
Hälsingborg, Sweden, 18
Haltemprice, Eng., 13
Haltia (mt.), Europe, 18
Haltom City, Tex., 302
Hama (prov.), Syria, 63
Hama, Syria, 63
Hamadan (governorate), Iran, 66
Hamadan, Iran, 66
Hamamatsu, Japan, 81
Hamar, Norway, 18
Hamber Prov. Park, Br. Col., 184
Hamburg, Ark., 203
Hamburg, N.Y., 276
Hamburg, Pa., 294
Hamburg (state), W. Ger., 22
Hamburg, W. Ger., 22
Hamden, Conn., 210
Häme (dept.), Fin., 18
Hämeenlinna, Fin., 18
Hameln, W. Ger., 22
Hamersley (range), W. Austral., 92
Hamhŭng, N. Korea, 81
Hami, China, 77
Hamilton (cap.), Berm., 156
Hamilton, Mass., 249
Hamilton, Mont., 262
Hamilton (inlet), Newf., 166
Hamilton, N.Y., 276
Hamilton, N.Z., 101
Hamilton, Ohio, 284
Hamilton, Ont., 177
Hamilton, Scot., 15
Hamilton, Tex., 302
Hamilton, Vic., 97
Hamilton Square, N. J., 273
Hamina, Fin., 18
Hamlet, N.C., 281
Hamlin, Tex., 302
Hamm, W. Ger., 22
Hammamet (gulf), Tun., 106
Hammerfest, Norway, 18
Hammersmith, Eng., 10
Hammond, Ind., 227
Hammond, La., 238
Hammonton, N. J., 273
Hampshire (Hants) (county), Eng., 13
Hampton, Iowa, 229
Hampton, N.H., 268
Hampton, Va., 307
Ham Tan, S. Vietnam, 72
Hamtramck, Mich., 250
Han (riv.), S. Korea, 81
Hanau, W. Ger., 22
Hanchung, China, 77
Hancock, Mich., 250
Haney, Br. Col., 184
Hanford, Calif., 204
Hanford Atomic Energy Res., Wash., 310
Hangchow, China, 77
Hangö, Fin., 18
Han Kiang (riv.), China, 77
Hanko (Hangö), Fin., 18
Hankow, China, 77
Hanku, China, 77
Hanley Hills, Mo., 261
Hanna, Alta., 182
Hannibal, Mo., 261
Hannover, W. Ger., 22
Hanoi (cap.), N. Vietnam, 72
Hanover (isl.), Chile, 138
Hanover, Mass., 249
Hanover, N.H., 268
Hanover, Ont., 177
Hanover, Pa., 294
Hanson, Mass., 249
Hantan, China, 77
Hantsport, N.S., 169
Hao (atoll), Fr. Poly., 87
Hapeville, Ga., 216
Harahan, La., 238
Harar (prov.), Eth., 111
Harar, Eth., 111
Harbin, China, 77
Harbor City, Calif., 204
Harbour (isl.), Bah. Is., 156
Hardanger (fjord), Norway, 18
Hardin, Mont., 262
Hardoi, India, 68
Hardt (mts.), W. Ger., 22
Hardwar, India, 68
Hardwick, Ga., 216
Harfleur, France, 28
Harghessa, Somalia, 115
Harib, Yemen Arab Rep., 59
Harima (sea), Japan, 81
Haringey, Eng., 10
Harlan, Iowa, 229
Harlan, Ky., 237
Harlingen, Tex., 302
Harlow, Eng., 13
Harmarville, Pa., 294
Harney (lake), Oreg., 291
Harney (peak), S. Dak., 296
Härnösand, Sweden, 18
Harper, Liberia, 106
Harpers Ferry Nat'l Hist. Site, W. Va., 313
Harper Woods, Mich., 250
Harricanaw (riv.), Que., 174
Harriman, Tenn., 237
Harrington (sound), Berm., 156
Harrington Harbour, Que., 174
Harrington Park, N. J., 273
Harris (dist.), Scot., 15
Harrisburg, Ill., 222
Harrisburg (cap.), Pa., 294
Harrismith, S. Africa, 118
Harrison, Ark., 203
Harrison (cape), Newf., 166
Harrison, N. J., 273
Harrison, N.Y., 276
Harrison, Ohio, 284
Harrisonburg, Va., 307
Harrisonville, Mo., 261
Harrodsburg, Ky., 237
Harrogate, Tenn., 237
Harrow, Eng., 10
Harstad, Norway, 18
Hartbees (riv.), S. Africa, 118
Hartford (cap.), Conn., 210
Hartford, Wis., 317
Hartford City, Ind., 227
Hartland (pt.), Eng., 13
Hartland, N. Br., 170
Hartlepool, Eng., 13
Hartley, Rhod., 118
Hartselle, Ala., 194
Harts Range, N. Terr., 93
Hartsville, S.C., 296
Hartwell, Ga., 216
Harvard, Ill., 222
Harvey, Ill., 222
Harvey, La., 238
Harwich, Eng., 13
Harwich Port, Mass., 249
Harwood Hts., Ill., 222
Haryana (state), India, 68
Harz (mts.), Ger., 22
Hasa (reg.), Saudi Ar., 59
Hasbrouck Hts., N. J., 273
Haskell, Tex., 302
Haslemere, Eng., 13
Hassan, India, 68
Hasselt, Belg., 27
Hassi-Messaoud, Alg., 106
Hässleholm, Sweden, 18
Hastings, Eng., 13
Hastings, Mich., 250
Hastings, Minn., 254
Hastings, Nebr., 264
Hastings, N.Z., 101
Hastings on Hudson, N.Y., 276
Hatay (prov.), Turkey, 63
Hatboro, Pa., 294
Hathras, India, 68
Hatiba, Ras (cape), Saudi Ar., 59
Ha Tien, S. Vietnam, 72
Hato Rey, P. Rico, 161
Hatteras (cape), N.C., 281
Hattiesburg, Miss., 256
Hatvan, Hung., 41
Hat Yai, Thai., 72
Haud (plat.), Africa, 115
Haugesund, Norway, 18
Haura, P.D.R. Yemen, 59
Hauraki (gulf), N.Z., 101
Hauran (Der'a) (prov.), Syria, 63
Hauta, Saudi Ar., 59
Haute-Garonne (dept.), France, 28
Haute-Loire (dept.), France, 28
Haute-Marne (dept.), France, 28
Hauterive, Que., 174
Hautes-Alpes (dept.), France, 28
Haute-Saône (dept.), France, 28
Haute-Savoie (dept.), France, 28
Hautes-Pyrénées (dept.), France, 28
Haute-Vienne (dept.), France, 28
Hautmont, France, 28
Haut-Rhin (dept.), France, 28
Hauts-de-Seine (dept.), France, 28
Havana (prov.), Cuba, 158
Havana (cap.), Cuba, 158
Havana, Ill., 222
Havasu (lake), U.S., 198
Havel (riv.), E. Ger., 22
Havelock North, N.Z., 101
Haverford, Pa., 294
Haverfordwest, Wales, 13
Haverhill, Mass., 249
Havering, Eng., 10
Haverstraw, N.Y., 276
Havertown, Pa., 294
Havířov, Czech., 41
Havre, Mont., 262
Havre de Grace, Md., 245
Havre-Saint-Pierre, Que., 174
Hawaii (isl.), Hawaii, 218
Hawaii (state), U.S., 218
Hawaiian (isls.), 218
Hawaii Volcanoes Nat'l Park, Hawaii, 218
Hawarden, Iowa, 229
Hawera, N.Z., 101
Hawick, Scot., 15
Hawke's Bay (prov. dist.), N.Z., 101
Hawkesbury, Ont., 177
Hawkinsville, Ga., 216
Haworth, N. J., 273
Hawthorn, Vic., 97
Hawthorne, Calif., 204
Hawthorne, Nev., 266
Hawthorne, N. J., 273
Hawthorne, N.Y., 276
Hayesville, Oreg., 291
Haynesville, La., 238
Hay River, N.W.T., 187
Hays, Kans., 232
Haysville, Kans., 232
Hayti, Mo., 261
Hayward, Calif., 204
Hazard, Ky., 237
Hazardville, Conn., 210
Hazaribagh, India, 68
Hazel Crest, Ill., 222
Hazel Park, Mich., 250
Hazelwood, Mo., 261
Hazlehurst, Ga., 216
Hazlehurst, Miss., 256
Hazlet, N. J., 273
Hazleton, Pa., 294
Headland, Ala., 194
Healdsburg, Calif., 204
Healdton, Okla., 288
Heanor, Eng., 13
Heard (isl.), Austral., 3
Hearne, Tex., 302
Hearst, Ont., 175
Hebbronville, Tex., 302
Hebden Royd, Eng., 10
Heber City, Utah, 304
Hebrides (isls.), Scot., 15
Hebrides (sea), Scot., 15
Hebron, Jordan, 65
Hecate (strait), Br. Col., 184
Hecelchakán, Mex., 150
Hedmark (county), Norway, 18
Heemstede, Neth., 27
Hegau (reg.), W. Ger., 22
Heidelberg, Vic., 97
Heidelberg, W. Ger., 22
Heidenheim, W. Ger., 22
Heilbronn, W. Ger., 22
Heiligenblut, Austria, 41
Heilungkiang (prov.), China, 77
Heinola, Fin., 18
Hejaz (prov.), Saudi Ar., 59
Hekla (volcano), Ice., 21
Hel (pen.), Poland, 47
Helena, Ark., 203
Helena (cap.), Mont., 262
Helensburgh, Scot., 15
Helgoland (bay), W. Ger., 22
Helgoland (isl.), W. Ger., 22
Heliopolis, U.A.R., 111
Hellertown, Pa., 294
Hell-Ville, Malag. Rep., 118
Helmand (riv.), Afghan., 68
Helmond, Neth., 27
Helmstedt, W. Ger., 22
Helper, Utah, 304
Helsingør, Den., 21
Helsinki (cap.), Fin., 18
Helwân, U.A.R., 111
Hemel Hempstead, Eng., 13
Hemet, Calif., 204
Hempstead, N.Y., 276
Henares (riv.), Spain, 33
Hendaye, France, 28
Henderson, Ky., 237
Henderson, Nev., 266
Henderson, N.C., 281
Henderson, Tenn., 237
Henderson, Tex., 302
Hendersonville, N.C., 281
Hengelo, Neth., 27
Hengyang, China, 77
Hénin-Liétard, France, 28
Henrietta, Tex., 302
Henrietta Maria (cape), Ont., 177
Henrique de Carvalho, Angola, 115
Henryetta, Okla., 288
Henzada, Burma, 72
Herat, Afghan., 68
Hérault (dept.), France, 28
Hérault (riv.), France, 28
Herbert, Sask., 181
Herbert Hoover Nat'l Hist. Site, Iowa, 229
Hercegnovi, Yugo., 45
Heredia, C. Rica, 154
Hereford, Eng., 13
Hereford, Tex., 302
Herefordshire (county), Eng., 13
Heretaunga-Pinehaven, N.Z., 101
Herford, W. Ger., 22
Herington, Kans., 232
Herisau, Switz., 39
Herkimer, N.Y., 276
Herm (isl.), Channel Is., 13
Hermann, Mo., 261
Hermannsburg Mission, N. Terr., 93
Hermiston, Oreg., 291
Hermitage (bay), Newf., 166
Hermon (mt.), Asia, 63
Hermosa Beach, Calif., 204
Hermosillo, Mex., 150
Hernád (river), Hung., 41
Hernandarias, Par., 144
Herne, W. Ger., 22
Herne Bay, Eng., 13
Herning, Den., 21
Heroica, Mex., 150
Heroica Nogales, Mex., 150
Herrin, Ill., 222
Hershey, Pa., 294
Herstal, Belg., 27
Hertford, Eng., 13
Hertfordshire (county), Eng., 13
Hervey (bay), Queensland, 95
Herzeliyya, Israel, 65
Hespeler, Ont., 177
Hesperia, Calif., 204
Hesse (state), W. Ger., 22
Heves (county), Hung., 41
Hewlett, N.Y., 276
Hialeah, Fla., 212
Hiawatha, Kans., 232
Hibbing, Minn., 254
Hickory, N.C., 281
Hickory Hills, Ill., 222
Hicksville, N.Y., 276
Hicksville, Ohio, 284
Hidalgo (state), Mex., 150
Hierro (isl.), Spain, 33
Higginsville, Mo., 261
High Atlas (ranges), Mor., 106
Highgate, Jam., 158
Highland, Calif., 204
Highland, Ill., 222
Highland, Ind., 227
Highland, N.Y., 276
Highland Falls, N.Y., 276
Highland Hts., Ky., 237
Highland Hts., Ohio, 284
Highland Park, Ill., 222
Highland Park, Mich., 250
Highland Park, N. J., 273
Highland Park, Tex., 302
Highlands, N. J., 273
Highlands, Tex., 302
Highland Sprs., Va., 307
High Point, N.C., 281
High Prairie, Alta., 182
High Ridge, Mo., 261
High River, Alta., 182
High Spire, Pa., 294
High Tatra (mts.), Europe, 47
Hightstown, N. J., 273
Highwood, Ill., 222
High Wycombe, Eng., 13
Hiiumaa (isl.), U.S.S.R., 53
Hikueru (atoll), Fr. Poly., 87
Hikurangi (mt.), N.Z., 101
Hildesheim, W. Ger., 22
Hilla (prov.), Iraq, 66
Hilla, Iraq, 66
Hilldale, Md., 245
Hillcrest Hts., Md., 245
Hillerød, Den., 21
Hilliards, Ohio, 284
Hillingdon, Eng., 10
Hillsboro, Ill., 222
Hillsboro, Ohio, 284
Hillsboro, Oreg., 291
Hillsboro, Tex., 302
Hillsborough, Calif., 204
Hillsdale, Mich., 250
Hillsdale, N. J., 273
Hillside, Ill., 222
Hillside, N. J., 273
Hilo, Hawaii, 218
Hilton Inlet (bay), Ant., 5
Hilversum, Neth., 27
Himachal Pradesh (terr.), India, 68
Himalaya (mts.), Asia, 68
Himeji, Japan, 81
Hinche, Haiti, 158
Hinchinbrook (isl.), Queensland, 95
Hinckley, Eng., 13
Hindmarsh, S. Austral., 94
Hindu Kush (range), Asia, 68
Hindupur, India, 68
Hinesville, Ga., 216
Hinganghat, India, 68
Hingham, Mass., 249
Hinlopen (strait), Norway, 18
Hinnøy (isl.), Norway, 18
Hinsdale, Ill., 222
Hinterrhein (riv.), Switz., 39
Hinton, Alta., 182
Hinton, W. Va., 313
Hirakata, Japan, 81
Hiran (prov.), Somalia, 115
Hirara, Ryukyu Is., 81
Hiratsuka, Japan, 81
Hirosaki, Japan, 81
Hiroshima (pref.), Japan, 81
Hiroshima, Japan, 81
Hispaniola (isl.), W. Indies, 156, 158
Hissar, India, 68
Hit, Iraq, 66
Hitachi, Japan, 81
Hitchcock, Tex., 302
Hitchin, Eng., 13
Hivaoa (isl.), Fr. Poly., 87
Hjørring, Den., 21
Hkakabo Razi (mt.), Burma, 72
Ho, Ghana, 106
Hoa Binh, N. Vietnam, 77
Hobart, Ind., 227
Hobart, Okla., 288
Hobart (cap.), Tas., 99
Hobbs, N. Mex., 274
Hobbs Coast (reg.), Ant., 5
Hoboken, Belg., 27
Hoboken, N. J., 273
Hobro, Den., 21
Höbsögöl (Khubsugul) (lake), Mong., 77
Hochwan, China, 77
Hockanum, Conn., 210
Hodeida, Yemen Arab Rep. 59
Hodh (reg.), Mauritania, 106
Hódmezővásárhely, Hung., 41
Hodonín, Czech., 41
Hodur, Somalia, 115
Hof, W. Ger., 22
Hofei, China, 77
Hofu, Japan, 81
Hofuf, Saudi Ar., 59
Höganäs, Sweden, 18
Hogansville, Ga., 216
Hohe Tauern (range), Austria, 41
Hohe Venn (plat.), Belg., 27
Ho-Ho-Kus, N. J., 273
Hoi An, S. Vietnam, 72
Hoihow, China, 77
Hoisington, Kans., 232
Hokang, China, 77
Hokkaido (pref.), Japan, 81
Hokkaido (isl.), Japan, 81
Holbæk, Den., 21
Holbrook, Ariz., 198
Holbrook, Mass., 249
Holdenville, Okla., 288
Holdrege, Nebr., 264
Holguín, Cuba, 158
Holladay, Utah, 304
Holland, Eng., 13
Holland, Mich., 250
Hollandale, Miss., 256
Hollandia (Djajapura), Indon., 85
Holland Park, Queensland, 95
Hollick-Kenyon (plat.), Ant., 5
Hollidaysburg, Pa., 294
Hollis, Okla., 288
Hollister, Calif., 204
Holly, Mich., 250
Holly Hill, Fla., 212
Holly Springs, Miss., 256
Hollywood, Calif., 204
Hollywood, Fla., 212
Hollywood, Md., 245
Holmestrand, Norway, 18
Holmsund, Sweden, 18
Holon, Israel, 65
Holstebro, Den., 21
Holsteinsborg, Greenl., 4
Holt, Mich., 250
Holton, Kans., 232
Holtville, Calif., 204
Holy (isl.), Eng., 13
Holy (isl.), Scot., 15
Holyhead, Wales, 13
Holyhead (Holy) (isl.), Wales, 13
Holy Loch (inlet), Scot., 15
Holyoke, Mass., 249
Holyrood, Newf., 166
Holywood, N. Ire., 17
Holzminden, W. Ger., 22
Hombori (mts.), Mali, 106
Homburg, W. Ger., 22
Home (bay), N.W.T., 187
Homer, La., 238
Homer, N.Y., 276
Homerville, Ga., 216
Homestead, Fla., 212
Homestead, Pa., 294
Homestead Nat'l Mon., Nebr., 264
Hometown, Ill., 222
Homewood, Ala., 194
Homewood, Ill., 222
Hominy, Okla., 288
Homs (prov.), Libya, 111
Homs, Libya, 111
Homs (prov.), Syria, 63
Homs, Syria, 63
Hon, Libya, 111
Honan (prov.), China, 77
Honda, Col., 126
Hondo (riv.), Cent. Amer., 154
Hondo, Tex., 302
Honduras, 154
Honduras (gulf), Cent. Amer., 154
Honduras (cape), Hond., 154
Honea Path, S.C., 296
Honesdale, Pa., 294
Honfleur, France, 28
Hon Gay, N. Vietnam, 72
Hong Kong, 77
Honiara (cap.), Br. Sol. Is., 87
Honningsvåg, Norway, 18
Honolulu (cap.), Hawaii, 218
Honsdrug (hills), Neth., 27
Honshu (isl.), Japan, 81
Hood (riv.), N.W.T., 187
Hood (mt.), Oreg., 291
Hood River, Oreg., 291
Hooghly (riv.), India, 68
Hooghly-Chinsura, India, 68
Hook of Holland, Neth., 27
Hoopeston, Ill., 222
Hoorn (isls.), Wallis & Futuna, 87
Hoosick Falls, N.Y., 276
Hoover, Ala., 194
Hoover (dam), U.S., 198
Hopatcong, N. J., 273
Hope (bay), Ant., 5
Hope, Ark., 203
Hope, Br. Col., 184
Hopedale, Mass., 249
Hopei (prov.), China, 77
Hopes Advance (cape), Que., 174
Hopewell, Va., 307
Hopkins, Minn., 254
Hopkinsville, Ky., 237
Hopkinton, Mass., 249
Hopkinton, R.I., 249
Hoppo, China, 77
Hoquiam, Wash., 310
Hordaland (county), Norway, 18
Hordio, Somalia, 115
Horgen, Switz., 39
Horicon, Wis., 317
Horn (cape), Chile, 138
Horn (North) (cape), Ice., 21
Hornád (river), Czech., 41
Hornby, N.Z., 101
Hornell, N.Y., 276
Hornepayne, Ont., 175
Hörnli (mt.), Switz., 39
Hornsby, N.S.W., 97
Hornslandet (pen.), Sweden, 18
Horqueta, Par., 144
Horse (isls.), Newf., 166
Horseheads, N.Y., 276
Horsens, Den., 21
Horseshoe Bend Nat'l Mil. Park, Ala., 194
Horsham, Eng., 13
Horsham, Vic., 97
Hørsholm, Den., 21
Horta (dist.), Port., 32
Horta, Port., 32
Horten, Norway, 18
Horton (riv.), N.W.T., 187
Hospet, India, 68
Hospitalet, Spain, 33
Hosseina, Eth., 111
Hoste (isl.), Chile, 138
Hotien (Khotan), China, 77
Hot Springs, S. Dak., 298
Hot Springs Nat'l Park, Ark., 203
Hottah (lake), N.W.T., 187
Houghton, Mich., 250
Houlton, Maine, 242
Houma, La., 238
Hounslow, Eng., 10
Houston, Miss., 256
Houston, Tex., 302
Houtman Abrolhos (isls.), W. Austral., 92
Hove, Eng., 13
Hovenweep Nat'l Mon., U.S., 208, 304
Howard, Wis., 317
Howe (cape), N.S.W., 97
Howell, Mich., 250
Howell, N.J., 273
Howrah, India, 68
Hoy (isl.), Scot., 15
Hoyerswerda, E. Ger., 22
Hoylake, Eng., 10
Hoyt Lakes, Minn., 254
Hradec Králové, Czech., 41
Hron (river), Czech., 41
Hsüchang, China, 77
Huachipato, Chile, 138
Huacho, Peru, 128
Hua Hin, Thai., 72
Huahine (isl.), Fr. Poly., 87
Huahua (riv.), Nic., 154
Huajuapán, Mex., 150
Huamantla, Mex., 150
Huambo (dist.), Angola, 115
Huancavelica (dept.), Peru, 128
Huancavelica, Peru, 128
Huancayo, Peru, 128
Huanchaca (mts.), Bol., 136
Huánuco (dept.), Peru, 128
Huánuco, Peru, 128
Huanuni, Bol., 136
Huapí (mts.), Nic., 154
Huaral, Peru, 128
Huarás, Peru, 128
Huascarán (mt.), Peru, 128
Huasco (river), Chile, 138
Huaspuc (riv.), Nic., 154
Huatabampo, Mex., 150
Huatusco de Chicuellar, Mex., 150
Huauchinango, Mex., 150
Huautlá, Mex., 150
Hubbard, Ohio, 284
Hubbell Trading Post Nat'l Hist. Site, Ariz., 198
Hubli, India, 68
Hucknall, Eng., 13
Huddersfield, Eng., 10
Hudiksvall, Sweden, 18
Hudson (bay), Canada, 187
Hudson (str.), Canada, 187
Hudson, Mass., 249
Hudson, Mich., 250
Hudson, N.H., 268
Hudson, N.Y., 276
Hudson, Ohio, 284
Hudson, Que., 172
Hudson (riv.), U.S., 276
Hudson, Wis., 317
Hudson Bay, Sask., 181
Hudson Falls, N.Y., 276
Hudsonville, Mich., 250
Hue, S. Vietnam, 72
Huehuetenango, Guat., 154
Huejotzingo, Mex., 150
Huejutla, Mex., 150
Huelva (prov.), Spain, 33
Huelva, Spain, 33
Huesca (prov.), Spain, 33
Huesca, Spain, 33
Huetamo, Mex., 150
Hueytown, Ala., 194
Hugo, Okla., 288
Hugoton, Kans., 232
Huhehot, China, 77
Huila (dist.), Angola, 115
Huila (dept.), Col., 126
Huila (mt.), Col., 126
Huimanguillo, Mex., 150
Huitzuco, Mex., 150
Huixtla, Mex., 150
Hull, Eng., 13
Hull (isl.), Gilb. & Ell. Is., 87
Hull, Mass., 249
Hull, Que., 172
Humacao (dist.), P. Rico, 161
Humacao, P. Rico, 161
Humber (riv.), Eng., 13
Humboldt, Iowa, 229
Humboldt (riv.), Nev., 266
Humboldt, Sask., 181
Humboldt, Tenn., 237
Hume (lake), Austral., 97
Hummelstown, Pa., 294
Humphreys (peak), Ariz., 198
Húnaflói (bay), Ice., 21
Hunan (prov.), China, 77

Hunchun, China, 77
Hunedoara, Rum., 45
Hungary, 41
Hŭngnam, N. Korea, 81
Hungshui Ho (riv.), China, 77
Hungtow (isl.), China, 77
Hungtse (lake), China, 77
Hunkiang, China, 77
Hunsrück (mts.), W. Ger., 22
Hunter (mts.), N.Z., 101
Hunter (isls.), Tas., 99
Hunters Hill, N.S.W., 97
Huntingburg, Ind., 227
Huntingdon, Eng., 13
Huntingdon, Pa., 294
Huntingdon, Que., 172
Huntingdon and Peterborough (county), Eng., 13
Huntington, Ind., 227
Huntington, N.Y., 276
Huntington, W. Va., 313
Huntington Beach, Calif., 204
Huntington Park, Calif., 204
Huntington Sta., N.Y., 276
Huntly, Scot., 15
Huntsville, Ala., 194
Huntsville, Ont., 177
Huntsville, Tex., 302
Hunucmá, Mex., 150
Hunza (Baltit), India, 68
Huon (isls.), New Cal., 87
Huon (gulf), Terr. N.G., 85
Huonville-Ranelagh, Tas., 99
Hupei (prov.), China, 77
Hurd (cape), Ont., 177
Hureidha, P.D.R. Yemen, 59
Hurghada, U.A.R., 111
Hurley, Wis., 317
Huron (lake), N. Amer., 188
Huron, Ohio, 284
Huron, S. Dak., 298
Hurstville, N.S.W., 97
Hürth, W. Ger., 22
Húsavík, Ice., 21
Huşi, Rum., 45
Huskvarna, Sweden, 18
Husum, W. Ger., 22
Hutchinson, Kans., 232
Hutchinson, Minn., 254
Huth, Yemen Arab Rep., 59
Hutt (Upper and Lower), N.Z., 101
Hüttental, W. Ger., 22
Hvar (isl.), Yugo., 45
Hvitá (river), Ice., 21
Hwainan, China, 77
Hwaiteh, China, 77
Hwang Ho (riv.), China, 77
Hwangshih, China, 77
Hyannis, Mass., 249
Hyattsville, Md., 245
Hyde, Eng., 10
Hyderabad, India, 68
Hyderabad, Pak., 68
Hyères, France, 28
Hyères (isls.), France, 28
Hyogo (pref.), Japan, 81
Hythe, Eng., 13
Hyvinkää, Fin., 18

I

Ia Drang (riv.), Asia, 72
Ialomiţa (riv.), Rum., 45
Iaşi, Rum., 45
Ibadan, Nigeria, 106
Ibagué, Col., 126
Ibar (riv.), Yugo., 45
Ibaraki (pref.), Japan, 81
Ibarra, Ecua., 128
Ibb, Yemen Arab Rep., 59
Iberville, Que., 172
Iberville (lake), Que., 174
Ibiza, Spain, 33
Ibiza (Iviza) (isl.), Spain, 33
'Ibri, Oman, 59
Içá (riv.), Braz., 132
Ica (dept.), Peru, 128
Ica, Peru, 128
İçel (prov.), Turkey, 63
Iceland, 21
Ichang, China, 77
Ichikawa, Japan, 81
Ichinomiya, Japan, 81
Ichinoseki, Japan, 81
Ichun, China, 77
Idabel, Okla., 288
Idaho (state), U.S., 220
Idaho Falls, Idaho, 220
Idar-Oberstein, W. Ger., 22
Idehan (des.), Africa, 111
Idenburg (riv.), Indon., 85
Ider (riv.), Mong., 77
Idfu, U.A.R., 111
Idiofa, Dem. Rep. of the Congo, 115
Idlib (prov.), Syria, 63
Idlib, Syria, 63
Iesi, Italy, 34
Ifalik (atoll), Pac. Is., 87
Ife, Nigeria, 106
Iférouane, Niger, 106
Ifugao (prov.), Phil. Is., 82
Igarka, U.S.S.R., 48
Ighil Izane, Alg., 106
Iglesias, Italy, 34
Igloolik, N.W.T., 187
Iguala, Mex., 150
Igualada, Spain, 33
Iguazú (falls), S. Amer., 132
Iguidi Erg (des.), Africa, 106
Ihosy, Malag. Rep., 118
Ii (riv.), Fin., 18
Iida, Japan, 81
Iisalmi, Fin., 18
Iizuta, Japan, 81
IJsselmeer (lake), Neth., 27
Ikaría (isl.), Greece, 45
Ikeda, Japan, 81
Ikela, Dem. Rep. of the Congo, 115
Ikhtiman, Bulg., 45
Ilam (governorate), Iran, 66
Ilanskiy, U.S.S.R., 48
Îles (lake), Que., 172
Ilesha, Nigeria, 106
Ílhavo, Port., 33
Ilhéus, Braz., 132
Ili (riv.), U.S.S.R., 48
Iliamna (lake), Alaska, 196
Iligan, Phil. Is., 82
Ilion, N.Y., 276
Ilium (Troy)(ruins), Turkey, 63
Ilkley, Eng., 13
Ilkeston, Eng., 13
Illampu (mt.), Bol., 136
Illapel, Chile, 138
Ille-et-Vilaine (dept.), France, 28
Iller (riv.), W. Ger., 22
Illimani (mt.), Bol., 136
Illinois (state), U.S., 222
Illizi, Alg., 106
Illora, Spain, 33
Il'men (lake), U.S.S.R., 52
Ilmenau, E. Ger., 22
Ilmenau (riv.), W. Ger., 22
Ilo, Peru, 128
Ilobasco, El Sal., 154
Ilocos Norte (prov.), Phil. Is., 82
Ilocos Sur (prov.), Phil. Is., 82
Iloilo (prov.), Phil. Is., 82
Iloilo, Phil. Is., 82
Ilorin, Nigeria, 106
Ilubabor (prov.), Eth., 111
Imabari, Japan, 8
Iman, U.S.S.R., 48
Imandra (lake), U.S.S.R., 52
Imari, Japan, 81
Imatra, Fin., 18
Imbâba, U.A.R., 111
Imbabura (prov.), Ecua., 128
Immenstadt, W. Ger., 22
Immokalee, Fla., 212
Imola, Italy, 34
Imperia (prov.), Italy, 34
Imperia, Italy, 34
Imperial, Calif., 204
Imperial Beach, Calif., 204
Impfondo, Rep. of Congo, 115
Imphal, India, 68
İmroz (isl.), Turkey, 63
Ina, Japan, 81
Inala, Queensland, 95
Inari (lake), Fin., 18
Inca, Spain, 33
İnce (cape), Turkey, 63
Inchiri (reg.), Mauritania, 106
Inch'ŏn, S. Korea, 81
Incudine (mt.), France, 28
Indawgyi (lake), Burma, 72
Independence, Iowa, 229
Independence, Kans., 232
Independence, Mo., 261
Independence (mts.), Nev., 266
Independence, Ohio, 284
Independencia (prov.), Dom. Rep., 158
India, 68
Indiana, Pa., 294
Indiana (state), U.S., 227
Indiana Dunes Nat'l Lakeshore, Ind., 227
Indianapolis (cap.), Ind., 227
Indian Head, Sask., 181
Indian Hill, Ohio, 284
Indian Ocean, 3
Indianola, Iowa, 229
Indianola, Miss., 256
Indigirka (riv.), U.S.S.R., 48
Indio, Calif., 204
Indochina (pen.), Asia, 72
Indonesia, 85
Indooroopilly, Queensland, 95
Indore, India, 68
Indramaju, Indon., 85
Indre (dept.), France, 28
Indre (riv.), France, 28
Indre-et-Loire (dept.), France, 28
Indus (riv.), Asia, 68
Indus, Mouths of the (delta), Pak., 68
İnebolu, Turkey, 63
Ingalls Park, Ill., 222
Ingende, Dem. Rep. of the Congo, 115
Ingersoll, Ont., 177
Ingham, Queensland, 95
Inglewood, Calif., 204
Inglewood, Tenn., 237
Ingolstadt, W. Ger., 22
Ingram, Pa., 294
Inhambane (dist.), Mozamb., 118
Inhambane, Mozamb., 118
Inharrime, Mozamb., 118
Iniesta, Spain, 33
Ining (Kuldja), China, 77
Inini (dist.), Fr. Gui., 131
Inírida (riv.), Col., 126
Inishbofin (isl.), Ire., 17
Inishturk (isl.), Ire., 17
Inkster, Mich., 250
Inn (riv.), Europe, 41
Inner (sound), Scot., 15
Innerleithen, Scot., 15
Inner Mongolian Aut. Reg., China, 77
Innisfail, Alta., 182
Innisfail, Queensland, 95
Innsbruck, Austria, 41
Inongo, Dem. Rep. of the Congo, 115
Inowrocław, Poland, 47
In Salah, Alg., 106
Insein, Burma, 72
Inta, U.S.S.R., 52
İntepe, Turkey, 63
Interlaken, Switz., 39
International Falls, Minn., 254
International Peace Garden, N. Amer., 179, 283
Internat'l Peace Mem. Nat'l Mon., Ohio, 284
Intipucá, El Sal., 154
Inuvik, N.W.T., 187
Inveraray, Scot., 15
Inverbervie, Scot., 15
Invercargill, N.Z., 101
Inverell, N.S.W., 97
Invergordon, Scot., 15
Inverkeithing, Scot., 15
Inverness, N.S., 169
Inverness (county), Scot., 15
Inverness, Scot., 15
Inverurie, Scot., 15
Investigator (str.), S. Austral., 94
Inwood, N.Y., 276
Ioánnina, Greece, 45
Iola, Kans., 232
Ioma, Papua, 85
Iona (isl.), Scot., 15
Ionia, Mich., 250
Ionian (sea), Europe, 7
Ionian Islands (reg.), Greece, 45
Íos (isl.), Greece, 45
Iowa (state), U.S., 229
Iowa City, Iowa, 229
Iowa Falls, Iowa, 229
Iowa Park, Tex., 302
Ipala, Guat., 154
Ipiales, Col., 126
Ipiaú, Braz., 132
Ipin, China, 77
Ipoh, Malaysia, 72
Ipperwash Prov. Park, Ont., 177
Ippy, Centr. Afr. Rep., 115
Ipswich, Eng., 13
Ipswich, Mass., 249
Ipswich, Queensland, 95
Iquique, Chile, 138
Iquitos, Peru, 128
Iracoubo, Fr. Gui., 131
Iráklion, Greece, 45
Irala, Arg., 143
Iran, 66
Irapuato, Mex., 150
Iraq, 66
Irazú (mt.), C. Rica, 154
Irbid (dist.), Jordan, 65
Irbid, Jordan, 65
Ireland, 17
Ireland (isl.), Berm., 156
Ireng (riv.), S. Amer., 131
Iri, S. Korea, 81
Iriga, Phil. Is., 82
Iringa (prov.), Tanz., 115
Iringa, Tanz., 115
Iriri (riv.), Braz., 132
Irish (sea), Europe, 13
Irkutsk, U.S.S.R., 48
Irondale, Ala., 194
Irondequoit, N.Y., 276
Iron Mountain, Mich., 250
Iron River, Mich., 250
Ironton, Ohio, 284
Ironwood, Mich., 250
Iroquois, Ont., 177
Iroquois Falls, Ont., 175
Iroquois Point, Hawaii, 218
Irrawaddy (div.), Burma, 72
Irrawaddy (riv.), Burma, 72
Irrawaddy, Mouths of the (delta), Burma, 72
Irtysh (riv.), U.S.S.R., 48
Irún, Spain, 33
Irvine, Ky., 237
Irvine, Scot., 15
Irving, Tex., 302
Irvington, N. J., 273
Irvington, N.Y., 276
Irwin, Pa., 294
Isabela (isl.), Ecua., 128
Isabela (prov.), Phil. Is., 82
Isabela, P. Rico, 158
Isabelia (range), Nic., 154
Isachsen, N.W.T., 187
Isahaya, Japan, 81
Isangi, Dem. Rep. of the Congo, 115
Isar (riv.), W. Ger., 22
Ischia (isl.), Italy, 34
Ise, Japan, 81
Iselin, N. J., 273
Isère (dept.), France, 28
Isère (riv.), France, 28
Iserlohn, W. Ger., 22
Iseyin, Nigeria, 106
Isfahan (prov.), Iran, 66
Isfahan, Iran, 66
Ishigaki, Ryukyu Is., 81
Ishikawa (pref.), Japan, 81
Ishim, U.S.S.R., 48
Ishimbay, U.S.S.R., 52
Ishinomaki, Japan, 81
Ishpeming, Mich., 250
Isil'-Kul', U.S.S.R., 48
Isiolo, Kenya, 115
Isiro, Dem. Rep. of the Congo, 115
İskenderun, Turkey, 63
Iskŭr (riv.), Bulg., 45
Isla Cristina, Spain, 33
Islamabad (cap.), Pak., 68
Isla Mujeres, Mex., 150
Island (lake), Man., 179
Island Park, N.Y., 276
Islands (bay), Newf., 166
Islands (bay), N.Z., 101
Isla Vista, Calif., 204
Islay (isl.), Scot., 15
Isle (riv.), France, 28
Isle of Man, 13
Isle of Wight (county), Eng., 13
Isle Royale Nat'l Park, Mich., 250
Islington, Eng., 10
Islip, N.Y., 276
Ismailia, U.A.R., 111
Isna, U.A.R., 111
Isparta (prov.), Turkey, 63
Isparta, Turkey, 63
Israel, 65
Issaouane Erg (des.), Alg., 106
Issoire, France, 28
Issoudun, France, 28
Issyk-Kul' (lake), U.S.S.R., 48
Issy-les-Moulineaux, France, 28
İstanbul (prov.), Turkey, 63
İstanbul, Turkey, 63
Itá, Par., 144
Itabuna, Braz., 132
Itajaí, Braz., 132
Itajubá, Braz., 135
Itala, Somalia, 115
Italy, 34
Itami, Japan, 81
Itapecuru (riv.), Braz., 132
Itapetininga, Braz., 135
Itapicuru (riv.), Braz., 132
Itaqui, Braz., 132
Itarsi, India, 68
Itasca, Ill., 222
Itasca (lake), Minn., 254
Ithaca, Mich., 250
Ithaca, N.Y., 276
Itháki (Ithaca)(isl.), Greece, 45
Ito, Japan, 81
Itoman, Ryukyu Is., 81
Ituiutaba, Braz., 132
Ituri (forest), Dem. Rep. of the Congo, 115
Itzehoe, W. Ger., 22
Ivaí (riv.), Braz., 132
Ivalo, Fin., 18
Ivano-Frankovsk, U.S.S.R., 52
Ivanovo, U.S.S.R., 52
Ivory Coast, 106
Ivry-sur-Seine, France, 28
Ivywild, Colo., 208
Iwaki, Japan, 81
Iwakuni, Japan, 81
Iwamisawa, Japan, 81
Iwata, Japan, 81
Iwate (pref.), Japan, 81
Iwo (isl.), Japan, 81
Iwo, Nigeria, 106
Ixtacalco, Mex., 150
Ixtapalapa, Mex., 150
Ixtepec, Mex., 150
Iyo (sea), Japan, 81
Izabal (lake), Guat., 154
Izhevsk, U.S.S.R., 52
Izmail, U.S.S.R., 52
İzmir (prov.), Turkey, 63
İzmir, Turkey, 63
İzmit, Turkey, 63
İznik (lake), Turkey, 63
Izu (isl.), Japan, 81
Izu (pen.), Japan, 81
Izúcar de Matamoros, Mex., 150
Izumi, Japan, 81
Izumisano, Japan, 81
Izumo, Japan, 81
Izyum, U.S.S.R., 52

J

Jabalpur, India, 68
Jablonec nad Nisou, Czech., 41
Jaboatão, Brazil, 132
Jacaltenango, Guat., 154
Jacareí, Braz., 132
Jáchal, Arg., 143
Jacksboro, Tex., 302
Jackson, Ala., 194
Jackson, Ga., 216
Jackson, Mich., 250
Jackson, Minn., 254
Jackson (cap.), Miss., 256
Jackson, Mo., 261
Jackson, N. J., 273
Jackson, Ohio, 284
Jackson, Tenn., 237
Jackson, Wyo., 319
Jacksonville, Ala., 194
Jacksonville, Ark., 203
Jacksonville, Fla., 212
Jacksonville, Ill., 222
Jacksonville, N.C., 281
Jacksonville, Tex., 302
Jacksonville Beach, Fla., 212
Jacmel, Haiti, 158
Jacobabad, Pak., 68
Jacques-Cartier, Que., 172
Jacques-Cartier (passage), Que., 174
Jade (bay), W. Ger., 22
Jaén (prov.), Spain, 33
Jaén, Spain, 33
Jaffna, Ceylon, 68
Jafura (des.), Saudi Ar., 59
Jagdalpur, India, 68
Jaghbub (Jarabub), Libya, 111
Jagtial, India, 68
Jahrum, Iran, 66
Jaipur, India, 68
Jakobstad, Fin., 18
Jal, N. Mex., 274
Jalalabad, Afghan., 68
Jalapa, Guat., 154
Jalapa Enríquez, Mex., 150
Jalgaon, India, 68
Jalisco (state), Mex., 150
Jalna, India, 68
Jalo (oasis), Libya, 111
Jalón (riv.), Spain, 33
Jalpa, Mex., 150
Jalpaiguri, India, 68
Jaluit (atoll), Pac. Is., 87
Jamaica, 158
Jamaica, N.Y., 276
Jamaica (chan.), W. Indies, 156
Jamaica Plain, Mass., 249
Jamalpur, India, 68
Jamama, Somalia, 115
Jamanchim (riv.), Braz., 132
James (bay), Canada, 174, 177
James (riv.), U.S., 188
James (riv.), Va., 307
Jamesburg, N. J., 273
Jamestown, N.Y., 276
Jamestown, N. Dak., 283
Jamestown (res.), N. Dak., 283
Jamestown, S. Austral., 94
Jammerbugt (bay), Den., 21
Jammu, India, 68
Jammu and Kashmir (state), India, 68
Jamnagar, India, 68
Jamshedpur, India, 68
Jämtland (county), Sweden, 18
Janakpur, Nepal, 68
Jandowae, Queensland, 95
Janesville, Wis., 317
Jan Mayen (isl.), Norway, 4
Jánoshalma, Hung., 41
Jaora, India, 68
Japan, 81
Japan (sea), Asia, 81
Japen (isl.), Indon., 85
Japurá (riv.), Braz., 132
Jarabub, Libya, 111
Jarama (riv.), Spain, 33
Jardines de la Reina (isls.), Cuba, 158
Jarosław, Poland, 47
Jarrow, Eng., 13
Jars (plain), Laos, 72
Jarvis (isl.), Pacific, 87
Jasper, Ala., 194
Jasper, Alta., 182
Jasper, Ind., 227
Jasper, Tex., 302
Jasper Nat'l Park, Alta., 182
Jászberény, Hung., 41
Játiva, Spain, 33
Jaú, Braz., 135
Jauf, Saudi Ar., 59
Jauja, Peru, 128
Jaunjelgava, U.S.S.R., 53
Jaunpur, India, 68
Java (head), Indon., 85
Java (isl.), Indon., 85
Java (sea), Indon., 85
Javarí (riv.), Braz., 132
Jaworzno, Poland, 47
Jeanerette, La., 238
Jeannette, Pa., 294
Jeble, Syria, 63
Jedburgh, Scot., 15
Jefferson, Iowa, 229
Jefferson, Ohio, 284
Jefferson (mt.), Oreg., 291
Jefferson, Pa., 294
Jefferson, Tex., 302
Jefferson, Wis., 317
Jefferson City (cap.), Mo., 261
Jefferson City, Tenn., 237
Jefferson Hts., La., 238
Jefferson Nat'l Expansion Mem., Mo., 261
Jeffersontown, Ky., 237
Jeffersonville, Ind., 227
Jēkabpils, U.S.S.R., 53
Jelenia Góra, Poland, 47
Jelgava, U.S.S.R., 53
Jelib, Somalia, 115
Jena, E. Ger., 22
Jendouba, Tun., 106
Jenin, Jordan, 65
Jenison, Mich., 250
Jenkins, Ky., 237
Jenkintown, Pa., 294
Jennings, La., 238
Jennings, Mo., 261
Jennings Lodge, Oreg., 291
Jequié, Braz., 132
Jequitinhonha (riv.), Braz., 132
Jerablus, Syria, 63
Jérémie, Haiti, 158
Jerez de la Frontera, Spain, 33
Jerez de los Caballeros, Spain, 33
Jericho, Jordan, 65
Jericho, N.Y., 276
Jerome, Idaho, 220
Jersey (isl.), Chan. Is., 13
Jersey City, N.J., 273
Jersey Shore, Pa., 294
Jerseyville, Ill., 222
Jerusalem (dist.), Israel, 65
Jerusalem (cap.), Israel, 65
Jerusalem (dist.), Jordan, 65
Jerusalem, Jordan, 65
Jervis Bay, A.C.T., 97
Jesenice, Yugo., 45
Jessore, Pak., 68
Jesup, Ga., 216
Jésus (isl.), Que., 172
Jette, Belg., 27
Jewel Cave Nat'l Mon., S. Dak., 298
Jewett City, Conn., 210
Jewish Aut. Oblast, U.S.S.R., 52
Jeypore, India, 68
Jhang Maghiana, Pak., 68
Jhansi, India, 68
Jhelum (riv.), Asia, 68
Jhelum, Pak., 68
Jhunjhunu, India, 68
Jibhalanta (Uliassutai), Mong., 77
Jibsh, Ras (cape), Oman, 59
Jičín, Czech., 41
Jidda, Saudi Ar., 59
Jiguero (pt.), P. Rico, 161
Jihlava, Czech., 41
Jihočeský (reg.), Czech., 41
Jihomoravský (reg.), Czech., 41
Jijia (riv.), Rum., 45
Jimbolia, Rum., 45
Jiménez, Mex., 150
Jimma, Eth., 111
Jim Thorpe, Pa., 294
Jind, India, 68
Jinja, Uganda, 115
Jinotega, Nic., 154
Jinotepe, Nic., 154
Jipijapa, Ecua., 128
Jirgalanta (Kobdo), Mong., 77
Jisr esh Shugur, Syria, 63
Jiu (riv.), Rum., 45
João Belo, Mozamb., 118
João Pessoa, Braz., 132
Jódar, Spain, 33
Jodhpur, India, 68
Joe Batt's Arm, Newf., 166
Joensuu, Fin., 18
Jofra (oasis), Libya, 111
Johannesburg, S. Afr., 118
Johar, Somalia, 115
John Day (riv.), Oreg., 291
John F. Kennedy Nat'l Hist. Site, Mass., 248
John Muir Nat'l Hist. Site, Calif., 204
Johns Isl., S.C., 296
Johnsonburg, Pa., 294
Johnson City, N.Y., 276
Johnson City, Tenn., 237
Johnston (atoll), Pacific, 87
Johnston City, Ill., 222
Johnstone, Scot., 15
Johnstown, N.Y., 276
Johnstown, Ohio, 284
Johnstown, Pa., 294
Johor (state), Malaysia, 72
Johor Baharu, Malaysia, 72
Johore (str.), Asia, 72
Joinville (isl.), Ant., 5
Joinville, Braz., 132
Jojutla, Mex., 150
Jokkmokk, Sweden, 18
Jökulsá (riv.), Iceland, 21
Joliet, Ill., 222
Joliette, Que., 172
Jolo (isl.), Phil. Is., 82
Joncs (plain), Asia, 72
Jonesboro, Ark., 203
Jonesboro, Ga., 216
Jonesboro, La., 238
Jönköping (county), Sweden, 18
Jönköping, Sweden, 18
Jonquière, Que., 172
Joplin, Mo., 261
Jorat (mt.), Switz., 39
Jordan, 65
Jordan (riv.), Asia, 65
Jorhat, India, 68
Jos, Nigeria, 106
Joseph (lake), Newf., 166
Joseph Bonaparte (gulf), Austral., 92, 93
Joshua Tree Nat'l Mon., Calif., 204
Jostedals (glac.), Norway, 18
Jost Van Dyke (isl.), Virgin Is. (Br.), 161
Jovellanos, Cuba, 158
Joyce's Country (dist.), Ire., 17
Juan Aldama, Mex., 150
Juan de Fuca (strait), N. Amer., 184, 310
Juan de Nova (isl.), Réunion, 118
Juan Fernández (isls.), Chile, 120
Juani (isl.), Tanz., 115
Juanita, Wash., 310
Juan L. Lacaze, Urug., 145
Juàzeiro do Norte, Braz., 132
Juba (riv.), Somalia, 115
Juba, Sudan, 111
Jubail, Saudi Ar., 59
Jubbulpore (Jabalpur), India, 68
Juby (cape), Mor., 106
Júcar (riv.), Spain, 33
Juchitán, Mex., 150
Judaea (reg.), Asia, 65
Juigalpa, Nic., 154
Juiz de Fora, Braz., 135
Jujuy (prov.), Arg., 143
Jujuy, Arg., 143
Juliaca, Peru, 128
Julian Alps (range), Italy, 34
Julianatop (mt.), Sur., 131
Julianehaab, Greenl., 4
Jülich, W. Ger., 22
Jullundur, India, 68
Jumet, Belg., 27
Jumilla, Spain, 33
Jumna (riv.), India, 68
Junagadh, India, 68
Juncos, P. Rico, 161
Junction City, Kans., 232
Jundiaí, Braz., 132
Juneau (cap.), Alaska, 196
Junee, N.S.W., 97
Jungfrau (mt.), Switz., 39
Junín, Arg., 143
Junín (dept.), Peru, 128
Juo (lake), Fin., 18
Jura (mts.), Europe, 28, 39
Jura (dept.), France, 28
Jura (isl.), Scot., 15
Jura (sound), Scot., 15
Jurm, Afghan., 68
Jurmala, U.S.S.R., 53
Juruena (riv.), Braz., 132
Justice, Ill., 222
Jutaí (riv.), Braz., 132
Jüterbog, E. Ger., 22
Jutiapa, Guat., 154
Juticalpa, Hond., 154
Jutland (Jylland) (pen.), Den., 21
Juwara, Oman, 59
Jyekundo, China, 77
Jyväskylä, Fin., 18

K

K2 (mt.), India, 68
Kabala, S. Leone, 106
Kabale, Uganda, 115
Kabalo, Dem Rep. of the Congo, 115
Kabambare, Dem. Rep. of the Congo, 115
Kabardin-Balkar A.S.S.R., U.S.S.R., 52
Kabba, Nigeria, 106
Kabia (Salajar) (isl.), Indon., 85
Kabongo, Dem. Rep. of the Congo, 115
Kabul (cap.), Afghan., 68
Kabul (riv.), Asia, 68
Kabwe, Zambia, 115
Kabylia (reg.), Alg., 106
Kachin (state), Burma, 72
Kachug, U.S.S.R., 48
Kadayanallur, India, 68
Kadiköy, Turkey, 63
Kadiyevka, U.S.S.R., 52
Kadoma, Japan, 81
Kadugli, Sudan, 111
Kaduna, Nigeria, 106
Kaédi, Mauritania, 106
Kaesŏng, N. Korea, 81
Kaf, Saudi Ar., 59
Kaffa (prov.), Eth., 111
Kafue (riv.), Zambia, 115
Kaga, Japan, 81
Kagan, U.S.S.R., 48
Kagawa (pref.), Japan, 81
Kağıthane, Turkey, 63
Kagoshima (pref.), Japan, 81
Kagoshima, Japan, 81
Kagul, U.S.S.R., 52
Kahemba, Dem. Rep. of the Congo, 115
Kahoolawe (isl.), Hawaii, 218
Kahului, Hawaii, 218
Kai (Ewab)(isls.), Indon., 85
Kaieteur (fall), Guyana, 131
Kaifeng, China, 77
Kaikoura (pen.), N.Z., 101
Kailas (mt.), China, 77
Kailua, Hawaii, 218
Kaimana, Indon., 85
Kainan (bay), Ant., 5
Kainji (res.), Nig., 106
Kaipara (harb.), N.Z., 101
Kairouan, Tun., 106
Kairuku, Papua, 85
Kaiserslautern, W. Ger., 22
Kaiserstuhl (mt.), W. Ger., 22
Kaizuka, Japan, 81
Kajaani, Fin., 18
Kajang, Malaysia, 72
Kakhovka, U.S.S.R., 52
Kakhovka (res.), U.S.S.R., 52
Kakinada, India, 68
Kakogawa, Japan, 81
Kala (riv.), Fin., 18
Kalaa-Kebira, Tun., 106
Kalach, U.S.S.R., 52
Kalachinsk, U.S.S.R., 48
Kaladan (riv.), Burma, 72
Kalahari (des.), Africa, 118
Kalahari Gemsbok Nat'l Park, S. Afr., 118
Kalajoki, Fin., 18
Kalakan, U.S.S.R., 48
Kalámai, Greece, 45
Kalamazoo, Mich., 250
Kalasin, Thai., 72
Kalat, Pak., 68
Kalat-i-Ghilzai, Afghan., 68
Kalemie, Dem. Rep. of the Congo, 115
Kalemyo, Burma, 72
Kalevala, U.S.S.R., 52
Kalgan, China, 77
Kalgoorlie, W. Austral., 92
Kaliakra (cape), Bulg., 45
Kalianda, Indon., 85
Kalimantan (reg.), Indon., 85
Kálimnos (isl.), Greece, 45
Kalinga-Apayao (prov.), Phil. Is., 82
Kalinin, U.S.S.R., 52
Kaliningrad, U.S.S.R., 52
Kalinkovichi, U.S.S.R., 52
Kalispell, Mont., 262
Kalisz, Poland, 47
Kalix (riv.), Sweden, 18
Kalla (lake), Fin., 18
Kalmar (county), Sweden, 18
Kalmar, Sweden, 18
Kalmarsund (sound), Sweden, 18
Kalmuck A.S.S.R., U.S.S.R., 52
Kalmunai, Ceylon, 68
Kalmykovo, U.S.S.R., 48
Kalomo, Zambia, 115
Kalpeni (isl.), India, 68
Kaluga, U.S.S.R., 52
Kalundborg, Den., 21
Kalutara, Ceylon, 68
Kalyan, India, 68
Kama, Burma, 72
Kama (riv.), U.S.S.R., 52
Kamaishi, Japan, 81
Kamakura, Japan, 81
Kamaran (isl.), P.D.R. Yemen, 59
Kamarhati, India, 68
Kamayut, Burma, 72
Kambia, S. Leone, 106
Kambove, Dem. Rep. of the Congo, 115
Kamchatka (pen.), U.S.S.R., 48
Kamenets-Podol'skiy, U.S.S.R., 52
Kamenjak (cape), Yugo., 45
Kamenka, U.S.S.R., 52
Kamenskoye, U.S.S.R., 48
Kamensk-Shakhtinskiy, U.S.S.R., 52
Kamensk-Ural'skiy, U.S.S.R., 48
Kamenz, E. Ger., 22
Kamet (mt.), India, 68
Kamina, Dem. Rep. of the Congo, 115
Kamloops, Br. Col., 184
Kampala (cap.), Uganda, 115
Kampar, Malaysia, 72
Kampen, Neth., 27
Kamphaeng Phet, Thai., 72
Kampot, Cambodia, 72
Kamptee, India, 68
Kamsack, Sask., 181
Kamui (cape), Japan, 81
Kamyshin, U.S.S.R., 52
Kamyshlov, U.S.S.R., 48
Kanaaupscow (riv.), Que., 174
Kanab, Utah, 304
Kanagawa (pref.), Japan, 81
Kanash, U.S.S.R., 52
Kanazawa, Japan, 81
Kanbalu, Burma, 72
Kanchanaburi, Thai., 72
Kanchenjunga (mt.), Asia, 68
Kanchipuram, India, 68
Kanchow, China, 77
Kandahar, Afghan., 68
Kandalaksha, U.S.S.R., 52
Kandalaksha (gulf), U.S.S.R., 52
Kandavu (isl.), Fiji, 87
Kandi, Dahomey, 106
Kandy, Ceylon, 68
Kane (basin), N. Amer., 187
Kane, Pa., 294
Kanem (reg.), Chad, 111
Kaneohe, Hawaii, 218
Kangar, Malaysia, 72
Kangaroo (isl.), S. Austral., 94
Kangean (isls.), Indon., 85
Kanggyŏng, S. Korea, 81
Kanghwa (bay), Korea, 81
Kangnŭng, S. Korea, 81
Kangting, China, 77
Kaniama, Dem. Rep. of the Congo, 115
Kanin (pen.), U.S.S.R., 52
Kanin Nos (cape), U.S.S.R., 52
Kanjiža, Yugo., 45
Kankakee, Ill., 222
Kankan, Guinea, 106
Kankossa, Mauritania, 106
Kannapolis, N.C., 281
Kano (state), Nigeria, 106
Kano, Nigeria, 106
Kanoya, Japan, 81
Kanpur, India, 68
Kansas (riv.), Kans., 232
Kansas (state), U.S., 232
Kansas City, Kans., 232
Kansas City, Mo., 261
Kansk, U.S.S.R., 48
Kansu (prov.), China, 77
Kanturk, Ire., 17
Kanuma, Japan, 81
Kanye, Botswana, 118
Kaohsiung, China, 77
Kaokoveld (mts.), S.W. Afr., 118
Kaolack, Sen., 106
Kapaa, Hawaii, 218
Kapanga, Dem. Rep. of the Congo, 115
Kapfenberg, Austria, 41
Kapingamarangi (atoll), Pac. Is., 87
Kapiskau (riv.), Ont., 177
Kaplan, La., 238
Kaposvár, Hung., 41
Kapsukas, U.S.S.R., 53
Kapuas (riv.), Indon., 85
Kapuskasing, Ont., 175
Kapydzhik (mt.), U.S.S.R., 52
Kara (sea), U.S.S.R., 48
Karabekaul, U.S.S.R., 48
Kara-Bogaz-Gol (gulf), U.S.S.R., 48
Karabük, Turkey, 63
Karachay-Cherkess Aut. Oblast, U.S.S.R., 52
Karachi, Pak., 68
Karadeniz (Bosporus) (strait), Turkey, 63
Karaganda, U.S.S.R., 48
Karaginskiy (isl.), U.S.S.R., 48
Karaikudi, India, 68
Kara-Kalpak A.S.S.R., U.S.S.R., 48
Karakhoto (ruins), China, 77
Karakoram (mts.), Asia, 68
Karakorum (ruins), Mong., 77
Karaköse, Turkey, 63
Kara-Kum (canal), U.S.S.R., 48
Kara-Kum (des.), U.S.S.R., 48
Karamai, China, 77
Karaman, Turkey, 63
Karamea (bight), N.Z., 101
Kara Nor (lake), China, 77
Karasburg, S.W. Afr., 118
Karasu, Turkey, 63
Karasuk, U.S.S.R., 48
Karatsu, Japan, 81
Karawanken (mts.), Europe, 41
Karbala' (prov.), Iraq, 66
Karbala', Iraq, 66
Karcag, Hung., 41
Kardhítsa, Greece, 45
Karelian A.S.S.R., U.S.S.R., 52
Karema, Tanz., 115
Kariba (lake), Africa, 118
Kariba, Rhod., 118
Karibib, S.W. Afr., 118
Karikal, India, 68
Karima, Sudan, 111
Karimata (arch.), Indon., 85
Karis (Kårjaa), Fin., 18
Karisimbi (mt.), Africa, 115
Karkaralinsk, U.S.S.R., 48
Karkkila, Fin., 18
Karl-Marx-Stadt (dist.), E. Ger., 22
Karl-Marx-Stadt, E. Ger., 22
Karlovac, Yugo., 45
Karlovy Vary, Czech., 41
Karlshamn, Sweden, 18
Karlskoga, Sweden, 18
Karlskrona, Sweden, 18
Karlsruhe, W. Ger., 22
Karlstad, Sweden, 18
Karnal, India, 68
Karnes City, Tex., 302
Karonga, Malawi, 115
Kárpathos (isl.), Greece, 45
Kars (prov.), Turkey, 63
Kars, Turkey, 63
Karshi, U.S.S.R., 48
Karşiyaka, Turkey, 63
Karskiye Vorota (strait), U.S.S.R., 52
Karun (riv.), Iran, 66
Karur, India, 68
Karviná, Czech., 41
Kasai (riv.), Africa, 115
Kasai-Occidental (prov.), Dem. Rep. of the Congo, 115
Kasai-Oriental (prov.), Dem. Rep. of the Congo, 115
Kasama, Zambia, 115
Kasanga, Tanz., 115
Kasar, Ras (cape), Sudan, 111
Kasba (lake), N.W.T., 187
Kasenga, Dem. Rep. of the Congo, 115
Kashan, Iran, 66
Kashgar, China, 77
Kashin, U.S.S.R., 52
Kashing, China, 77
Kashiwazaka, Japan, 81
Kashmar, Iran, 66
Kasimov, U.S.S.R., 52
Kaskö (Kaskinen), Fin., 18
Kasongo, Dem. Rep. of the Congo, 115
Kasongo-Lunda, Dem. Rep. of the Congo, 115
Kásos (isl.), Greece, 45
Kaspiysk, U.S.S.R., 52
Kassala (prov.), Sudan, 111
Kassala, Sudan, 111
Kassándra (pen.), Greece, 45
Kassel, W. Ger., 22
Kasserine, Tun., 106
Kastamonu (prov.), Turkey, 63
Kastamonu, Turkey, 63
Kastellórizon (isl.), Greece, 63
Kastoría, Greece, 45
Kastrup, Den., 21
Kasugai, Japan, 81
Katahdin (mt.), Maine, 242
Katako-Kombe, Dem. Rep. of the Congo, 115
Katanga (prov.), Dem. Rep. of the Congo, 115
Katanning, W. Austral., 92
Katarnian Ghat, India, 68
Kateríni, Greece, 45
Kates Needle (mt.), Br. Col., 184
Katha, Burma, 72
Katherina, Jebel (mt.), U.A.R., 111
Katherine, N. Terr., 93
Kati, Mali, 106
Katihar, India, 68
Katiola, Ivory Coast, 106
Katmai Nat'l Mon., Alaska, 196
Katmandu (cap.), Nepal, 68
Katni (Murwara), India, 68
Katonah, N.Y., 276
Katowice (prov.), Poland, 47
Katowice, Poland, 47
Katrineholm, Sweden, 18
Katsina, Nigeria, 106
Katsuta, Japan, 81
Kattegat (strait), Europe, 18
Kauai (isl.), Hawaii, 218
Kaufbeuren, W. Ger., 22
Kaufman, Tex., 302
Kaukauna, Wis., 317
Kaumajet (mts.), Newf., 166
Kaunas, U.S.S.R., 53
Kaura Namoda, Nigeria, 106
Kauttua, Fin., 18
Kavadarci, Yugo., 45
Kavajë, Alb., 45
Kaválla, Greece, 45
Kavaratti, India, 68
Kavarna, Bulg., 45
Kavieng, Terr. N.G., 87
Kawachi, Japan, 81
Kawagoe, Japan, 81
Kawaguchi, Japan, 81
Kawasaki, Japan, 81
Kawerau, N.Z., 101
Kawhia (harb.), N.Z., 101
Kawlin, Burma, 72
Kawthoolei (state), Burma, 72

Kaya, Upp. Volta, 106
Kayah (state), Burma, 72
Kayes, Mali, 106
Kayseri (prov.), Turkey, 63
Kayseri, Turkey, 63
Kaysville, Utah, 304
Kazach'ye, U.S.S.R., 48
Kazakh S.S.R., U.S.S.R., 48
Kazalinsk, U.S.S.R., 48
Kazan (riv.), N.W.T., 187
Kazan', U.S.S.R., 52
Kazandzhik, U.S.S.R., 48
Kazanlŭk, Bulg., 45
Kazatin, U.S.S.R., 52
Kazbek (mt.), U.S.S.R., 52
Kazerun, Iran, 66
Kazvin, Iran, 66
Kéa (isl.), Greece, 45
Keansburg, N. J., 273
Kearney, Nebr., 264
Kearns, Utah, 304
Kearny, N. J., 273
Kearsarge, Pa., 294
Kebnekaise (mt.), Sweden, 18
Kebumen, Indon., 85
Kecskemét, Hung., 41
Kedah (state), Malaysia, 72
Kedainiai, U.S.S.R., 53
Kediri, Indon., 85
Kédougou, Sen., 106
Kedzierzyn, Poland, 47
Keego Hbr., Mich., 250
Keele (peak), Yukon, 187
Keelung, China, 77
Keene, N.H., 268
Keerweer (cape), Queensland, 95
Keetmanshoop, S.W. Afr., 118
Keewatin (dist.), N.W.T., 187
Keewatin, Ont., 175
Kefallinía (isl.), Greece, 45
Kefar Atta, Israel, 65
Kefar Sava, Israel, 65
Keflavík, Iceland, 21
Ke Ga (pt.), S. Vietnam, 72
Kehl, W. Ger., 22
Keighley, Eng., 10
Keilor, Vic., 97
Keitele (lake), Fin., 18
Keith, Scot., 15
Keizer, Oreg., 291
Kejimkujik Nat'l Park, N.S., 168
Kékes (mt.), Hung., 41
Kelang, Malaysia, 72
Kelantan (state), Malaysia, 72
Kelantan (riv.), Malaysia, 72
Kelheim, W. Ger., 22
Kelkit (riv.), Turkey, 63
Kellogg, Idaho, 220
Kélo, Chad, 111
Kelowna, Br. Col., 184
Kelso, Scot., 15
Kelso, Wash., 310
Kelston West, N.Z., 101
Keltie (cape), Ant., 5
Keluang, Malaysia, 72
Kem', U.S.S.R., 52
Kemerovo, U.S.S.R., 48
Kemi, Fin., 18
Kemi (lake), Fin., 18
Kemi (riv.), Fin., 18
Kemijärvi, Fin., 18
Kemmerer, Wyo., 319
Kemp Coast (reg.), Ant., 5
Kempsey, N.S.W., 97
Kempten, W. Ger., 22
Kempton Park, S. Afr., 118
Kenadsa, Alg., 106
Kenai, Alaska, 196
Kendal, Eng., 13
Kendal, Indon., 85
Kendall Park, N.J., 273
Kendallville, Ind., 227
Kendari, Indon., 85
Kenedy, Tex., 302
Kenema, S. Leone, 106
Keng Kok, Laos, 72
Kenhorst, Pa., 294
Kenilworth, Eng., 10
Kenilworth, Ill., 222
Kenilworth, N. J., 273
Keningau, Malaysia, 85
Kénitra, Mor., 106
Kenmare, Ire., 17
Kenmore, N.Y., 276
Kenmore, Wash., 310
Kennebunk, Maine, 242
Kennedy (cape), Fla., 212
Kenner, La., 238
Kennesaw Mtn. Nat'l Battlef. Park, Ga., 216
Kennett, Mo., 261
Kennett Square, Pa., 294
Kennewick, Wash., 310
Kénogami (riv.), Ont., 175
Kénogami, Que., 172
Keno Hill, Yukon, 187
Kenora, Ont., 175
Kenosha, Wis., 317
Kenova, W. Va., 313
Kensington, Conn., 210
Kensington, P.E.I., 169
Kensington and Norwood, S. Austral., 94
Kent (county), Eng., 13
Kent (pen.), N.W.T., 187
Kent, Ohio, 284
Kent, Wash., 310
Kenton, Ohio, 284
Kentucky (state), U.S., 237
Kentucky (lake), U.S., 237
Kentville, N.S., 169
Kentwood, La., 238
Kentwood, Mich., 250
Kenya, 115
Kenya (mt.), Kenya, 115
Keokuk, Iowa, 229
Kerala (state), India, 68
Kerava, Fin., 18
Kerch', U.S.S.R., 52
Kerema, Papua, 85
Kerguélen (isls.), 3
Kericho, Kenya, 115
Kerintji (mt.), Indon., 85
Keriya, China, 77
Kerkennah (isls.), Tun., 106
Kerki, U.S.S.R., 48
Kérkira, Greece, 45
Kérkira (isl.), Greece, 45
Kermadec (isls.), N.Z., 87
Kerman (prov.), Iran, 66
Kerman, Iran, 66
Kermanshah (prov.), Iran, 66
Kermanshah, Iran, 66
Kerme (gulf), Turkey, 63
Kermit, Tex., 302
Kernersville, N.C., 281
Kerrobert, Sask., 181
Kerrville, Tex., 302
Kerry (county), Ire., 17
Kerulen (riv.), Asia, 77
Kesagami (lake), Ont., 177
Kesennuma, Japan, 81
Keski-Suomi (prov.), Fin., 18
Keta, Ghana, 106
Ketchikan, Alaska, 196
Kete Krakye, Ghana, 106
Kętrzyn, Poland, 47
Kettering, Eng., 13
Kettering, Ohio, 284
Kevelaer, W. Ger., 22
Kew, Vic., 97
Kewanee, Ill., 222
Kewaunee, Wis., 317
Keweenaw (pt.), Mich., 250
Keyport, N. J., 273
Keyser, W. Va., 313
Key West, Fla., 212
Kezhma, U.S.S.R., 48
Khabarovsk, U.S.S.R., 48
Khabur (riv.), Syria, 63
Khachmas, U.S.S.R., 52
Khaibar, Saudi Ar., 59
Khairpur, Pak., 68
Khakass Aut. Oblast, U.S.S.R., 48
Khalkís, Greece, 45
Khamgaon, India, 68
Khana Abasa, China, 77
Khanabad, Afghan., 68
Khanaqin, Iraq, 66
Khandwa, India, 68
Khandyga, U.S.S.R., 48
Khangai (mts.), Mong., 77
Khanh Hoa, S. Vietnam, 72
Khanh Hung, S. Vietnam, 72
Khaniá, Greece, 45
Khanka (lake), Asia, 77
Khanty-Mansi Nat'l Okrug, U.S.S.R., 48
Khanty-Mansiysk, U.S.S.R., 48
Khan Yunis, Gaza Strip, 65
Kharagpur, India, 68
Kharan Kalat, Pak., 68
Khara Usu (lake), Mong., 77
Khârga (oasis), U.A.R., 111
Khar'kov, U.S.S.R., 52
Kharmanlii, Bulg., 45
Kharovsk, U.S.S.R., 48
Khartoum (prov.), Sudan, 111
Khartoum (cap.), Sudan, 111
Khartoum North, Sudan, 111
Khasavyurt, U.S.S.R., 52
Khashm el Girba, Sudan, 111
Khaskovo, Bulg., 45
Khatanga, U.S.S.R., 48
Khatanga (riv.), U.S.S.R., 48
Khemmarat, Thai., 72
Khemis Miliana, Alg., 106
Khenifra, Mor., 106
Khentei (prov.), Mong., 77
Khentei (mts.), Mong., 77
Kherson, U.S.S.R., 52
Kheta (riv.), U.S.S.R., 48
Khilok, U.S.S.R., 48
Khíos, Greece, 45
Khíos (isl.), Greece, 45
Khirbet Qumran (site), Jordan, 65
Khiva, U.S.S.R., 48
Khmel'nitskiy, U.S.S.R., 52
Khodzheyli, U.S.S.R., 48
Khoi, Iran, 66
Kholmsk, U.S.S.R., 48
Khone, Laos, 72
Khong, Laos, 72
Khong Sédone, Laos, 72
Khon Kaen, Thai., 72
Khoper (riv.), U.S.S.R., 52
Khorat (Nakhon Ratchasima), Thai., 72
Khorog, U.S.S.R., 48
Khorol, U.S.S.R., 52
Khorramshahr, Iran, 66
Khotan, China, 77
Khotin, U.S.S.R., 52
Khouribga, Mor., 106
Khubsugul (prov.), Mong., 77
Khubsugul (lake), Mong., 77
Khu Khan, Thai., 72
Khulna, Pak., 68
Khurasan (prov.), Iran, 66
Khurramabad, Iran, 66
Khuzistan (prov.), Iran, 66
Khvalynsk, U.S.S.R., 52
Khyber (pass), Pak., 68
Kialing Kiang (riv.), China, 77
Kiama, N.S.W., 97
Kiamusze, China, 77
Kian, China, 77
Kiangsi (prov.), China, 77
Kiangsu (prov.), China, 77
Kianta (lake), Fin., 18
Kiaohsien, China, 77
Kiayükwan, China, 77
Kibombo, Dem. Rep. of the Congo, 115
Kičevo, Yugo., 45
Kidderminster, Eng., 10
Kidwelly, Wales, 13
Kiel, W. Ger., 22
Kiel (canal), W. Ger., 22
Kiel, Wis., 317
Kielce (prov.), Poland, 47
Kielce, Poland, 47
Kienow, China, 77
Kienshui, China, 77
Kienyang, China, 77
Kieta, Terr. N.G., 87
Kiev, U.S.S.R., 52
Kiffa, Mauritania, 106
Kigali (cap.), Rwanda, 115
Kigoma (prov.), Tanz., 115
Kigoma-Ujiji, Tanz., 115
Kikinda, Yugo., 45
Kikwit, Dem. Rep. of the Congo, 115
Kilauea (crater), Hawaii, 218
Kildare (county), Ire., 17
Kildare, Ire., 17
Kil'din (isl.), U.S.S.R., 52
Kilgore, Tex., 302
Kili (atoll), Pac. Is., 87
Kilimanjaro (prov.), Tanz., 115
Kilimanjaro (mt.), Tanz., 115
Kilis, Turkey, 63
Kiliya, U.S.S.R., 52
Kilkee, Ire., 17
Kilkenny (county), Ire., 17
Kilkenny, Ire., 17
Kilkís, Greece, 45
Killaloe, Ire., 17
Killarney, Ire., 17
Killarney, Man., 179
Killeen, Tex., 302
Killinek (isl.), Canada, 166
Killingley, Conn., 210
Kilmarnock, Scot., 15
Kilmory, Scot., 15
Kilosa, Tanz., 115
Kilpis (lake), Europe, 18
Kilrenny and Anstruther, Scot., 15
Kilrush, Ire., 17
Kilsyth, Scot., 15
Kilwa Kivinje, Tanz., 115
Kilwa Masoko, Tanz., 115
Kimball, Nebr., 264
Kimberley, Br. Col., 184
Kimberley, S. Afr., 118
Kimberley (plat.), W. Austral., 92
Kimberly, Wis., 317
Kimchaek, N. Korea, 81
Kimch'ŏn, S. Korea, 81
Kimovsk, U.S.S.R., 52
Kimry, U.S.S.R., 52
Kinabalu (mt.), Malaysia, 85
Kincardine, Ont., 177
Kincardine (county), Scot., 15
Kincardine, Scot., 15
Kindersley, Sask., 181
Kindia, Guinea, 106
Kindu-Port Empain, Dem. Rep. of the Congo, 115
Kinel', U.S.S.R., 52
Kinel' (riv.), U.S.S.R., 52
Kineshma, U.S.S.R., 52
King (isl.), Br. Col., 184
King (isl.), Tas., 99
King (sound), W. Austral., 92
Kingaroy, Queensland, 95
King Christian IX Land (reg.), Greenl., 4
King Christian X Land (reg.), Greenl., 4
King City, Calif., 204
Kingfisher, Okla., 288
King Frederik VI Coast (reg.), Greenl., 4
King Frederik VIII Land (reg.), Greenl., 4
King George (isls.), N.W.T., 187
King George's (falls), S. Afr., 118
King Leopold (range), W. Austral., 92
Kingman, Ariz., 198
Kingman, Kans., 232
Kingman Reef (isl.), Pacific, 87
Kings (peak), Utah, 304
Kingsburg, Calif., 204
Kings Canyon Nat'l Park, Calif., 204
Kingscourt, Ire., 17
Kingsford, Mich., 250
Kingsford-Smith Airport, N.S.W., 97
King's Lynn, Eng., 13
Kings Mtn., N.C., 281
Kings Mtn. Nat'l Mil. Park, S.C., 296
Kings Park, N.Y., 276
Kings Point, N.Y., 276
Kingsport, Tenn., 237
Kingston (cap.), Jam., 158
Kingston, N.Y., 276
Kingston (cap.), Norfolk I., 88
Kingston, Ont., 177
Kingston, Pa., 294
Kingston-upon-Hull (Hull), Eng., 13
Kingston-upon-Thames, Eng., 10
Kingstown (Dún Laoghaire), Ire., 17
Kingstown (cap.), St. Vincent, 161
Kingstree, S.C., 296
Kingsville, Md., 245
Kingsville, Ont., 177
Kingsville, Tex., 302
Kingtehchen, China, 77
Kingussie, Scot., 15
King William's Town, S. Afr., 118
Kingwood, W. Va., 313
Kinhwa, China, 77
Kinloch, Mo., 261
Kinnairds (head), Scot., 15
Kinnelon, N. J., 273
Kinross (county), Scot., 15
Kinross, Scot., 15
Kinsale, Ire., 17
Kinshasa (cap.), Dem. Rep. of the Congo, 115
Kinston, N.C., 281
Kinta, China, 77
Kintampo, Ghana, 106
Kioga (lake), Uganda, 115
Kiparissía (gulf), Greece, 45
Kipushi, Dem. Rep. of the Congo, 115
Kirchberg, Switz., 39
Kirchheim, W. Ger., 22
Kirensk, U.S.S.R., 48
Kirghiz S.S.R., U.S.S.R., 52
Kirgis Nor (lake), Mong., 77
Kirigalpota (mt.), Ceylon, 68
Kırıkkale, Turkey, 63
Kirin (prov.), China, 77
Kirin, China, 77
Kirkby, Eng., 10
Kirkcaldy, Scot., 15
Kirkcudbright (county), Scot., 15
Kirkcudbright, Scot., 15
Kirkee, India, 68
Kirkenes, Norway, 18
Kirkham, Eng., 10
Kirkintilloch, Scot., 15
Kirkland, Wash., 310
Kirkland Lake, Ont., 175
Kırklareli (prov.), Turkey, 63
Kırklareli, Turkey, 63
Kirkpatrick (mt.), Ant., 5
Kirksville, Mo., 261
Kirkuk (prov.), Iraq, 66
Kirkuk, Iraq, 66
Kirkwall, Scot., 15
Kirkwood, Mo., 261
Kirov, U.S.S.R., 52
Kirovabad, U.S.S.R., 52
Kirovakan, U.S.S.R., 52
Kirovo-Chepetsk, U.S.S.R., 52
Kirovograd, U.S.S.R., 52
Kirovsk, U.S.S.R., 52
Kirriemuir, Scot., 15
Kirsanov, U.S.S.R., 52
Kırşehir (prov.), Turkey, 63
Kırşehir, Turkey, 63
Kiruna, Sweden, 18
Kiryu, Japan, 81
Kisa, Sweden, 18
Kisangani, Dem. Rep. of the Congo, 115
Kisar (isl.), Indon., 85
Kisarazu, Japan, 81
Kiselevsk, U.S.S.R., 48
Kishinev, U.S.S.R., 52
Kishiwada, Japan, 81
Kisi, China, 77
Kiska (isl.), Alaska, 196
Kiskunfélegyháza, Hung., 41
Kiskunhalas, Hung., 41
Kislovodsk, U.S.S.R., 52
Kismayu, Somalia, 115
Kispest, Hung., 41
Kissidougou, Guinea, 106
Kissimmee, Fla., 212
Kississing (lake), Man.,179
Kisumu, Kenya, 115
Kita, Mali, 106
Kitai, China, 77
Kitaibaraki, Japan, 81
Kita Iwo (isl.), Japan, 81
Kitakyushu, Japan, 81
Kitale, Kenya, 115
Kitami, Japan, 81
Kitchener, Ont., 177
Kíthira (isl.), Greece, 45
Kitimat, Br. Col., 184
Kitinen (riv.), Fin., 18
Kittanning, Pa., 294
Kittery, Maine, 242
Kittilä, Fin., 18
Kitwe, Zambia, 115
Kitzbühel, Austria, 41
Kitzingen, W. Ger., 22
Kiuchüan, China, 77
Kiukiang, China, 77
Kiungchow (strait), China, 77
Kiungshan, China, 77
Kivi (lake), Fin., 18
Kivu (lake), Africa, 115
Kivu (prov.), Dem. Rep. of the Congo, 115
Kizel', U.S.S.R., 52
Kızılırmak (riv.), Turkey, 63
Kızıltoprak, Turkey, 63
Kizlyar, U.S.S.R., 52
Kizyl-Arvat, U.S.S.R., 48
Kjölen (range), Europe, 18
Kladno, Czech., 41
Klagenfurt, Austria, 41
Klaipėda, U.S.S.R., 53
Klamath Falls, Oreg., 291
Klaten, Indon., 85
Klatovy, Czech., 41
Kleberg, Tex., 302
Kleinmachnow, E. Ger., 22
Klerksdorp, S. Afr., 118
Kleve, W. Ger., 22
Klimovichi, U.S.S.R., 52
Klingenthal, E. Ger., 22
Klintsy, U.S.S.R., 52
Kliprivier, S. Afr., 118
Kłodzko, Poland, 47
Klondike (riv.), Yukon, 187
Kloten, Switz., 39
Klosterneuburg, Austria, 41
Kluane (lake), Yukon, 187
Klyuchevskaya Sopka (vol.), U.S.S.R., 48
Knighton, Wales, 13
Knittelfeld, Austria, 41
Knob Lake (Schefferville), Que., 174
Knox, Ind., 227
Knox Coast (reg.), Ant., 5
Knoxville, Ill., 222
Knoxville, Iowa, 229
Knoxville, Tenn., 237
Knutsford, Eng., 10
Knysna, S. Afr., 118
Kobdo (prov.), Mong., 77
Kobdo, Mong., 77
Kobe, Japan, 81
København (Copenhagen) (cap.), Den., 21
Koblenz, Switz., 39
Koblenz, W. Ger., 22
Kobrin, U.S.S.R., 52
Kobuk (riv.), Alaska, 196
Kobuleti, U.S.S.R., 52
Kocaeli (prov.), Turkey, 63
Koch'ang, S. Korea, 81
Kochi (pref.), Japan, 81
Kochi, Japan, 81
Kodaira, Japan, 81
Kodiak, Alaska, 196
Kodiak (isl.), Alaska, 196
Kodok, Sudan, 111
Koforidua, Ghana, 106
Kofu, Japan, 81
Kogaluk (riv.), Que., 174
Kogarah, N.S.W., 97
Kohat, Pak., 68
Kohima, India, 68
Kohtla-Järve, U.S.S.R., 53
Koitere (lake), Fin., 18
Kŏje (isl.), S. Korea, 81
Kokanee Glacier Prov. Park, Br. Col., 184
Kokchetav, U.S.S.R., 48
Kokemäki, Fin., 18
Kokiu, China, 77
Kokkola, Fin., 18
Kokoda, Papua, 85
Kokomo, Ind., 227
Koko Nor (lake), China, 77
Koksoak (riv.), Que., 174
Kola (pen.), U.S.S.R., 52
Kolahun, Liberia, 106
Kolar Gold Fields, India, 68
Kolarovgrad, Bulg., 45
Kolding, Den., 21
Kole, Dem. Rep. of the Congo, 115
Kolguyev (isl.), U.S.S.R., 52
Kolhapur, India, 68
Kolín, Czech., 41
Köln (Cologne), W. Ger., 22
Kołobrzeg, Poland, 47
Kolokani, Mali, 106
Kolomna, U.S.S.R., 52
Kolpashevo, U.S.S.R., 48
Kolva (riv.), U.S.S.R., 52
Kolwezi, Dem. Rep. of the Congo, 115
Kolyma (range), U.S.S.R., 48
Kolyma (riv.), U.S.S.R., 48
Komadugu Yobe (riv.), Africa, 106
Komandorskiye (isls.), U.S.S.R., 48
Komárno, Czech., 41
Komárom (county), Hung., 41
Komatsu, Japan, 81
Komi A.S.S.R., U.S.S.R., 52
Komi-Permyak Nat'l Okrug, U.S.S.R., 52
Komló, Hung., 41
Kommunarsk, U.S.S.R., 52
Komodo (isl.), Indon., 85
Kôm Ombo, U.A.R., 111
Komotiní, Greece, 45
Kompong Cham, Cambodia, 72
Kompong Chhnang, Cambodia, 72
Kompong Som, Cambodia, 72
Kompong Speu, Cambodia, 72
Kompong Thom, Cambodia, 72
Kompong Trabek, Cambodia, 72
Komrat, U.S.S.R., 52
Komsomolets (isl.), U.S.S.R., 48
Komsomol'sk, U.S.S.R., 48
Kondoa, Tanz., 115
Kondopoga, U.S.S.R., 52
Kong, Ivory Coast, 106
Kongju, S. Korea, 81
Kong Karls Land (isl.), Norway, 18
Kongmoon, China, 77
Kongolo, Dem. Rep. of the Congo, 115
Kongsberg, Norway, 18
Kongsvinger, Norway, 18
Kongwa, Tanz., 115
Königsberg (Kaliningrad), U.S.S.R., 52
Königssee (lake), W. Ger., 22
Konin, Poland, 47
Kónitsa, Greece, 45
Köniz, Switz., 39
Konotop, U.S.S.R., 52
Konstanz, W. Ger., 22
Kontum, S. Vietnam, 72
Kontum (plat.), S. Vietnam, 72
Konya (prov.), Turkey, 63
Konya, Turkey, 63
Kootenay (lake), Br. Col., 184
Kootenay (riv.), Br. Col., 184
Kootenay Nat'l Park, Br. Col., 184
Köpenick, E. Ger., 22
Koper, Yugo., 45
Kopeysk, U.S.S.R., 48
Köping, Sweden, 18
Kopparberg (county), Sweden, 18
Kopparberg, Sweden, 18
Koprivnica, Yugo., 45
Korab (mt.), Europe, 45
Korbach, W. Ger., 22
Korçë, Alb., 45
Korčula (isl.), Yugo., 45
Kordofan (prov.), Sudan, 111
Korea, 81
Korea (strait), Asia, 81
Korf, U.S.S.R., 48
Korhogo, Ivory Coast, 106
Koriyama, Japan, 81
Korkino, U.S.S.R., 48
Kormakiti (cape), Cyprus, 63
Kornwestheim, W. Ger., 22
Köroğlu (mts.), Turkey, 63
Koronadal, Phil. Is., 82
Koror, Pac. Is., 87
Kororoit (creek), Vic., 97
Körös (riv.), Hung., 41
Korosten', U.S.S.R., 52
Korsakov, U.S.S.R., 48
Korsør, Den., 21
Korumburra, Vic., 97
Koryak (range), U.S.S.R., 48
Koryak Nat'l Okrug, U.S.S.R., 48
Kos (isl.), Greece, 45
Kosciusko, Miss., 256
Kosciusko (mt.), N.S.W., 97
Koshigaya, Japan, 81
Košice, Czech., 41
Koslan, U.S.S.R., 48
Kosovo-Mitohijan (aut. prov.), Yugo., 45
Kosovska Mitrovica, Yugo., 45
Kosta, Sweden, 18
Kosti, Sudan, 111
Kostroma, U.S.S.R., 52
Koszalin (prov.), Poland, 47
Koszalin, Poland, 47
Kota, India, 68
Kotaagung, Indon., 85
Kota Baharu, Malaysia, 72
Kotabumi, Indon., 85
Kota Kinabalu, Malaysia, 72
Kota Tinggi, Malaysia, 72
Kotel'nich, U.S.S.R., 52
Kotel'nikovo, U.S.S.R., 52
Kotel'nyy (isl.), U.S.S.R., 48
Köthen, E. Ger., 22
Kotka, Fin., 18
Kotlas, U.S.S.R., 52
Kotor, Yugo., 45
Kotovsk, U.S.S.R., 52
Kottayam, India, 68
Kottbus (Cottbus), E. Ger., 22
Kotto (riv.), Centr. Afr. Rep., 115
Kotuy (riv.), U.S.S.R., 48
Kotzebue, Alaska, 196
Koudougou, Upp. Volta, 106
Koula-Moutou, Gabon, 115
Koulikoro, Mali, 106
Koumra, Chad, 111
Kouroussa, Guinea, 106
Kousseri, Cameroon, 115
Koutiala, Mali, 106
Kouvola, Fin., 18
Kovel', U.S.S.R., 52
Kovrov, U.S.S.R., 52
Kowloon, Hong Kong, 77
Koyukuk (riv.), Alaska, 196
Koza, Ryukyu Is., 81
Kozáni, Greece, 45
Kozhevnikovo, U.S.S.R., 48
Kozhikode, India, 68
Kpandu, Ghana, 106
Kra (isth.), Thai., 72
Kragan, Indon., 85
Kragerø, Norway, 18
Kragujevac, Yugo., 45
Krakatau (Rakata) (isl.), Indon., 85
Kraków (Cracow), Poland, 47
Kralendijk, Neth. Ant., 161
Kraljevo (Rankovićevo), Yugo., 45
Kramatorsk, U.S.S.R., 52
Kramfors, Sweden, 18
Kranj, Yugo., 45
Krasino, U.S.S.R., 48
Krasnodar, U.S.S.R., 52
Krasnograd, U.S.S.R., 52
Krasnokamsk, U.S.S.R., 52
Krasnoslobodsk, U.S.S.R., 52
Krasnotur'insk, U.S.S.R., 48
Krasnoural'sk, U.S.S.R., 48
Krasnovishersk, U.S.S.R., 52
Krasnovodsk, U.S.S.R., 48
Krasnoyarsk, U.S.S.R., 48
Krasnyy Liman, U.S.S.R., 52
Kratie, Cambodia, 72
Krauchmar, Cambodia, 72
Kraulshavn, Greenl., 4
Krawang, Indon., 85
Krefeld, W. Ger., 22
Kremenchug, U.S.S.R., 52
Krems, Austria, 41
Kreuzlingen, Switz., 39
Kribi, Cameroon, 45
Krichev, U.S.S.R., 52
Kriens, Switz., 39
Krishna (riv.), India, 68
Krishnanagar, India, 68
Kristiansand, Norway, 18
Kristianstad (county), Sweden, 18
Kristiansund, Norway, 18
Kristiinankaupunki (Kristinestad), Fin., 18
Kristinehamn, Sweden, 18
Krivoy Rog, U.S.S.R., 52
Krk (isl.), Yugo., 45
Krnov, Czech., 41
Krolevets, U.S.S.R., 52
Kronoberg (county), Sweden, 18
Kronshtadt, U.S.S.R., 52
Kroonstad, S. Afr., 118
Kropotkin, U.S.S.R., 52
Krosno Ordz., Poland, 47
Kru Coast (reg.), Liberia, 106
Kruë, Alb., 45
Kruger Nat'l Park, S. Afr., 118
Krugersdorp, S. Afr., 118
Krung Thep (Bangkok) (cap.), Thai., 72
Kruševac, Yugo., 45
Krymsk, U.S.S.R., 52
Ksar-el-Kebir, Mor., 106
Ksar-es-Souk, Mor., 106
Kuala Lipis, Malaysia, 72
Kuala Lumpur (cap.), Malaysia, 72
Kuala Pilah, Malaysia, 72
Kuala Selangor, Malaysia, 72
Kuala Terengganu, Malaysia, 72
Kuantan, Malaysia, 72
Kuba, U.S.S.R., 52
Kuban' (riv.), U.S.S.R., 52
Kubeno (lake), U.S.S.R., 52
Kucha, China, 77
Kuching, Malaysia, 85
Kuçove (Stalin), Alb., 45
Kudat, Malaysia, 85
Kudus, Indon., 85
Kudymkar, U.S.S.R., 52
Kufra (oasis), Libya, 111
Kufrinja, Jordan, 65
Kuhmo, Fin., 18
Kukawa, Nigeria, 106
Kulai, Malaysia, 72
Kula Kangri (mt.), Asia, 68
Kuldiga, U.S.S.R., 53
Kuldja, China, 77
Kulebaki, U.S.S.R., 52
Kulmbach, W. Ger., 22
Kulpmont, Pa., 294
Kul'sary, U.S.S.R., 48
Kuma (riv.), U.S.S.R., 52
Kumagaya, Japan, 81
Kumamoto (pref.), Japan, 81
Kumamoto, Japan, 81
Kumanovo, Yugo., 45
Kumasi, Ghana, 106
Kumba, Cameroon, 115
Kumbakonam, India, 68
Kumbi Saleh (ruins), Mauritania, 106
Kumertau, U.S.S.R., 52
Kumla, Sweden, 18
Kummerowersee (lake), E. Ger., 22
Kunar (riv.), Asia, 68
Kungälv, Sweden, 18
Kungsbacka, Sweden, 18
Kungur, U.S.S.R., 52
Kuningan, Indon., 85
Kunlun (mts.), Asia, 77
Kunming, China, 77
Kunsan, S. Korea, 81
Kuopio (prov.), Fin., 18
Kuopio, Fin., 18
Kupang, Indon., 85
Kupino, U.S.S.R., 48
Kupyansk, U.S.S.R., 52
Kura (riv.), U.S.S.R., 52
Kurashiki, Japan, 81
Kurdistan (reg.), Asia, 59
Kurdistan (prov.), Iran, 66
Kŭrdzhali, Bulg., 45
Kure (isl.), Hawaii, 218
Kure, Japan, 81
Küre (range), Turkey, 63
Kuressaare, U.S.S.R., 53
Kurgan, U.S.S.R., 48
Kurgan-Tyube, U.S.S.R., 48
Kuria Muria (isls.), Oman, 59
Kurikka, Fin., 18
Kuril (isls.), U.S.S.R., 48
Kurla, China, 77
Kurla, India, 68
Kurmuk, Sudan, 111
Kurnool, India, 68
Kurri Kurri-Weston, N.S.W., 97
Kursk, U.S.S.R., 52
Kurume, Japan, 81
Kurunegala, Ceylon, 68
Kuşadası, Turkey, 63
Kusaie (isl.), Pac. Is., 87
Kushiro, Japan, 81
Kushk, Afghan., 68
Kushka, U.S.S.R., 48
Kuskokwim (riv.), Alaska, 196
Küsnacht, Switz., 39
Küssnacht, Switz., 39
Kustanay, U.S.S.R., 48
Kut (prov.), Iraq, 66
Kut, Iraq, 66
Kütahya (prov.), Turkey, 63
Kütahya, Turkey, 63
Kutaisi, U.S.S.R., 52
Kutaradja (Banda Atjeh), Indon., 85
Kutch (gulf), India, 68
Kutch, Rann of (salt marsh), Asia, 68
Kutno, Poland, 47
Kutoardjo, Indon., 85
Kutu, Dem. Rep. of the Congo, 115
Kutztown, Pa., 294
Kuusamo, Fin., 18
Kuvandyk, U.S.S.R., 52
Kuwait, 59
Kuybyshev, U.S.S.R., 52
Kuybyshev (res.), U.S.S.R., 52
Kuyto (lake), U.S.S.R., 52
Kuznetsk, U.S.S.R., 52
Kvaløy (isl.), Norway, 18
Kvarner (gulf), Yugo., 45
Kvinnherad, Norway, 18
Kwajalein (atoll), Pac. Is., 87
Kwando (riv.), Africa, 115
Kwanghwa, China, 77
Kwangju, S. Korea, 81
Kwangnan, China, 77
Kwango (riv.), Africa, 115
Kwangsi Chuang Aut. Reg., China, 77
Kwangtung (prov.), China, 77
Kwara (state), Nigeria, 106
Kwatta, Sur., 131
Kweichow (prov.), China, 77
Kweilin, China, 77
Kweiping, China, 77
Kweisui (Huhehot), China, 77
Kweiyang, China, 77
Kwidzyn, Poland, 47
Kwilu (riv.), Africa, 115
Kwinana, W. Austral., 92
Kyabé, Chad, 111
Kyabram, Vic., 97
Kyaikto, Burma, 72
Kyakhta, U.S.S.R., 48
Kyangin, Burma, 72
Kyaring Tso (lake), China, 77
Kyaukpadaung, Burma, 72
Kyaukpyu, Burma, 72
Kyaukse, Burma, 72
Kymi (dept.), Fin., 18
Kyneton, Vic., 97
Kyogle, N.S.W., 97
Kyŏngju, S. Korea, 81
Kyoto (pref.), Japan, 81
Kyoto, Japan, 81
Kyrenia, Cyprus, 63
Kyushu (isl.), Japan, 81
Kyustendil, Bulg., 45
Kyusyur, U.S.S.R., 48
Kywebwe, Burma, 72
Kyzyl, U.S.S.R., 48
Kyzyl-Kum (des.), U.S.S.R., 48
Kzyl-Orda, U.S.S.R., 48

L

La Asunción, Venez., 124
La Barca, Mex., 150
La Baule, France, 28
Labe (riv.), Czech., 41
Labé, Guinea, 106
Labinsk, U.S.S.R., 52
Laborie, St. Lucia, 161
Laboulaye, Arg., 143
Labrador (sea), 166
Labrador (dist.), Newf., 166
La Brea, Trin. & Tobago, 161
Labuan, Indon., 85
Labuan (isl.), Malaysia, 85
Labuk (bay), Malaysia, 85
Labutta, Burma, 72
La Calera, Chile, 138
La Canada, Calif., 204
La Carlota, Phil. Is., 82
Laccadive (isls.), India, 68
Laccadive, Minicoy and Amindivi Isls., (terr.), India, 68
La Ceiba, Hond., 154
Lacepede (bay), S. Austral., 94
Lacepede (isls.), W. Austral., 92
Lacey, Wash., 310
La Chaux-de-Fonds, Switz., 39
Lachine, Que., 172
Lachlan (riv.), N.S.W., 97
Lachute, Que., 172
Lackawanna, N.Y., 276
Lac La Biche, Alta., 182
Lac La Ronge Prov. Park, Sask., 181
Lac-Mégantic, Que., 172
Lacombe, Alta., 182
La Concepción, Pan., 154
La Concepción, Venez., 124
Laconia, N.H., 268
La Coruña (prov.), Spain, 33
La Coruña, Spain, 33
La Courneuve, France, 28
La Crescent, Minn., 254
La Crescenta, Calif., 204
La Crosse, Wis., 317
Ladakh (reg.), India, 68
La Digue (isl.), Seych., 118
Lado, Sudan, 111
Ladoga (lake), U.S.S.R., 52
La Dorada, Col., 126
Ladue, Mo., 261
Ladysmith, Br. Col., 184
Ladysmith, S. Afr., 118
Ladysmith, Wis., 317
Lae, Terr. N.G., 85
Laesø (isl.), Den., 21
La Esperanza, Hond., 154
Lafayette, Ala., 194
Lafayette, Calif., 204
Lafayette, Colo., 208
La Fayette, Ga., 216
Lafayette, Ind., 227
Lafayette, La., 238
La Feria, Tex., 302
Lafitte, La., 238
Laflèche, Que., 172
La Follette, Tenn., 237
Lagawe, Phil. Is., 82
Lågen, Norway, 18
Laghouat, Alg., 106
La Gomera, Guat., 154
Lagos, Mex., 150
Lagos (state), Nigeria, 106
Lagos (cap.), Nigeria, 106
Lagos, Port., 33
La Grande, Oreg., 291
La Grande-Rivière (riv.), Que., 174
La Grange, Ga., 216
La Grange, Ill., 222
La Grange, Tex., 302
La Grange Park, Ill., 222
La Guaira, Venez., 124
La Guajira (department), Col., 126
Laguna, Braz., 132
Laguna (prov.), Phil. Is., 82
Laguna Beach, Calif., 204
Laguna Hills, Calif., 204
La Habra, Calif., 204
Lahad Datu, Malaysia, 85
Lahaina, Hawaii, 218
Lahej, P.D.R. Yemen, 59
Lahijan, Iran, 66
Lahn (riv.), W. Ger., 22
Lahore, Pak., 68
Lahr, W. Ger., 22
Lahti, Fin., 18
Laï, Chad, 111
Lai Chau, N. Vietnam, 72
Laila, Saudi Ar., 59
La Jara, N. Mex., 274
Lajes, Braz., 132
La Jolla, Calif., 204
La Junta, Colo., 208
Lake Arthur, La., 238
Lake Bluff, Ill., 222
Lake Carmel, N.Y., 276
Lake Charles, La., 238
Lake Chelan Nat'l Rec. Area, Wash., 310
Lake City, Fla., 212
Lake City, Minn., 254
Lake City, S.C., 296
Lake Forest, Ill., 222
Lake Geneva, Wis., 317
Lake Havasu City, Ariz., 198
Lake Hiawatha, N. J., 273
Lake Hopatcong, N. J., 273
Lakehurst, N. J., 273
Lake Jackson, Tex., 302
Lakeland, Fla., 212
Lakeland Vill., Calif., 204
Lake Louise, Alta., 182
Lake Mead Nat'l Recr. Area, U.S., 198
Lake Mills, Wis., 317
Lake Mohawk, N. J., 273
Lakemore, Ohio, 284
Lake of the Woods (lake), N. Amer., 175, 254
Lake Orion, Mich., 250
Lake Oswego, Oreg., 291
Lake Park, Fla., 212
Lake Placid, N.Y., 276
Lake Providence, La., 238
Lake Success, N.Y., 276
Lake Superior Prov. Park, Ont., 175
Lakeview, Oreg., 291
Lake Village, Ark., 203
Lake Wales, Fla., 212
Lakewood, Calif., 204
Lakewood, Colo., 208
Lakewood, N. J., 273
Lakewood, N.Y., 276
Lakewood, Ohio, 284
Lake Worth, Fla., 212
Lake Worth, Tex., 302
Lake Zurich, Ill., 222
Lakonía (gulf), Greece, 45
Lakse (fjord), Norway, 18
La Libertad, Ecua., 128
La Libertad, El Sal., 154
La Libertad, Nic., 154
La Libertad (dept.), Peru, 128
La Ligua, Chile, 138
La Línea, Spain, 33
Lalitpur, Nepal, 68
La Louvière, Belg., 27
Lama-Kara, Togo, 106
La Malbaie, Que., 172
La Manche (English) (chan.), Europe, 28
Lamar, Colo., 208
Lamar, Mo., 261
La Marque,Tex., 302
La Martre (lake), N.W.T., 187
La Maya, Cuba, 158
Lambaréné, Gabon, 115
Lambayeque (dept.), Peru, 128
Lambayeque, Peru, 128
Lambertville, N. J., 273
Lambeth, Eng., 10
Lambeth, Ont., 177
Lamego, Port., 33
Lamentin, Guad., 161
La Mesa, Calif., 204
Lamesa, Tex., 302
Lamía, Greece, 45
La Mirada, Calif., 204
Lamongan, Indon., 85
Lamont, Calif., 204
Lamotrek (atoll), Pac. Is., 87
Lampang, Thai., 72
Lampasas, Tex., 302
Lampedusa (isl.), Italy, 34
Lamphun, Thai., 72
Lamu, Kenya, 115
Lanai (isl.), Hawaii, 218
Lanao del Norte (prov.), Phil. Is., 82
Lanao del Sur (prov.), Phil. Is., 82
Lanark (county), Scot., 15
Lanark, Scot., 15
Lancashire (county), Eng., 13
Lancaster, Calif., 204
Lancaster, Eng., 13
Lancaster, Ky., 237
Lancaster, N.Y., 276
Lancaster (sound), N.W.T., 187
Lancaster, Ohio, 284
Lancaster, Pa., 294
Lancaster, S.C., 296
Lancaster, Tex., 302
Lancaster, Wis., 317
Lancaster Mills, S.C., 296
Lanchow, China, 77
Lanciano, Italy, 34
Landau, W. Ger., 22
Land Between The Lakes Nat'l Rec. Area, Ky.-Tenn., 236
Lander, Wyo., 319
Landes (dept.), France, 28
Land's End (prom.), Eng., 13
Lands End (cape), N.W.T., 187
Landshut, W. Ger., 22
Landskrona, Sweden, 18
Lane Cove, N.S.W., 97
Lanett, Ala., 194
Lang Bian (mts.), S. Vietnam, 72
Langdale, Ala., 194
Langdon, N. Dak., 283

Langeland (isl.), Den., 21
Langenhagen, W. Ger., 22
Langenthal, Switz., 39
Langley Park, Md., 245
Langøy (isl.), Norway, 18
Langsa, Indon., 85
Lang Son, N. Vietnam, 72
Lanham, Md., 245
Lanin (vol.), S. Amer., 138
Lansdale, Pa., 294
Lansdowne, Md., 245
Lansdowne, Pa., 294
L'Anse, Mich., 250
Lansford, Pa., 294
Lansing, Ill., 222
Lansing (cap.), Mich., 250
Lantana, Fla., 212
Lantsang, China, 77
Lanús, Arg., 143
Lanzarote (isl.), Spain, 33
Laoag, Phil. Is., 82
Laoighis (county), Ire., 17
Laon, France, 28
La Oroya, Peru, 128
Laos, 72
La Palma, El Sal., 154
La Palma, Pan., 154
La Palma (isl.), Spain, 33
La Pampa (prov.), Arg., 143
La Paz, Arg., 143
La Paz (dept.), Bol., 136
La Paz (cap.), Bol., 136
La Paz, Hond., 154
La Paz, Mex., 150
La Paz Central, Nic., 154
Lapeer, Mich., 250
La Pérouse (str.), Asia, 81
La Piedad, Mex., 150
Laplace, La., 238
La Plaine, Dominica, 161
Lapland (reg.), Europe, 18
La Plata, Arg., 143
La Pocatière, Que., 172
LaPorte, Ind., 227
La Porte, Tex., 302
Lappeenranta, Fin., 18
Lappi (dept.), Fin., 18
La Prairie, Que., 172
Laptev (sea), U.S.S.R., 48
La Puente, Calif., 204
Lapu-Lapu, Phil. Is., 82
La Quiaca, Arg., 143
L'Aquila (prov.), Italy, 34
L'Aquila, Italy, 34
Lar, Iran, 66
Lara (state), Venez., 124
Larache, Mor., 106
Laramie (range), U.S., 208, 319
Laramie, Wyo., 319
Larchmont, N.Y., 276
Larder Lake, Ont., 177
Laredo, Tex., 302
Lares, P. Rico, 161
Largeau, Chad, 111
Largo, Fla., 212
Largs, Scot., 15
La Rioja (prov.), Arg., 143
La Rioja, Arg., 143
La Rioja, Cuba, 158
Lárisa, Greece, 45
Laristan (reg.), Iran, 66
Larkana, Pak., 68
Larkhall, Scot., 15
Larkspur, Calif., 204
Larksville, Pa., 294
Larnaca, Cyprus, 63
Larne, N. Ire., 17
Larned, Kans., 232
La Rochelle, France, 28
La Roche-sur-Yon, France, 28
La Romana (prov.), Dom. Rep., 158
La Romana, Dom. Rep., 158
Larose, La., 238
Larsen Ice Shelf, Ant., 5
Larvik, Norway, 18
La Salle, Ill., 222
La Salle, Que., 172
Las Animas, Colo., 208
Las Anod, Somalia, 115
Las Aves (isl.), Venez., 124
La Sarre, Que., 174
Lascahobas, Haiti, 158
Las Cruces, N. Mex., 274
La Selle (peak), Haiti, 158
La Serena, Chile, 138
La Seyne-sur-Mer, France, 28
Las Flores, Arg., 143
Lashio, Burma, 72
La Skhirra, Tun., 106
Las Matas, Dom. Rep., 158
Las Palmas (prov.), Spain, 33
Las Palmas de Gran Canaria, Spain, 33
La Spezia (prov.), Italy, 34
La Spezia, Italy, 34
Las Piedras, P. Rico, 161
Las Piedras, Urug., 145
Las Plumas, Arg., 143
Lassen (peak), Calif., 204
Lassen Vol. Nat'l Park, Calif., 204
L'Assomption, Que., 172
Las Tablas, Pan., 154
Last Mountain (lake), Sask., 181
Lastoursville, Gabon, 115
Lastovo (isl.), Yugo., 45
Las Vegas, Nev., 266
Las Vegas, N. Mex., 274
Las Villas (prov.), Cuba, 158
Latacunga, Ecua., 128
Latakia (prov.), Syria, 63
Latakia, Syria, 63
Latina (prov.), Italy, 34
Latina, Italy, 34
Latium (reg.), Italy, 34
La Tortuga (isl.), Venez., 124
La Trinidad, Nic., 154
La Trinidad, Phil. Is., 82
Latrobe, Pa., 294
Latrobe, Tas., 99
La Tuque, Que., 172
Latur, India, 68
Latvian S.S.R., U.S.S.R., 52
Lauchhammer, E. Ger., 22
Lauderdale Lakes, Fla., 212
Lau Group (isls.), Fiji, 87
Launceston, Tas., 99
La Unión, Chile, 138
La Unión, El Sal., 154
La Union (prov.), Phil. Is., 82
Laurel, Del., 245
Laurel, Md., 245
Laurel, Miss., 256
Laurel, Mont., 262
Laureldale, Pa., 294
Laurence Harbor, N.J., 273
Laurens, S.C., 296
Laurentides Prov. Park, Que., 172
Laurinburg, N.C., 281
Laurium, Mich., 250
Lausanne, Switz., 39
Laut (isl.), Indon., 85
Lautaro, Chile, 138
Lauwers Zee (bay), Neth., 27
Lauzon, Que., 172
Lava Beds Nat'l Mon., Calif., 204
Laval, Que., 172
La Vale, Md., 245
La Vega (prov.), Dom. Rep., 158
La Vega, Dom. Rep., 158
La Vérendrye Prov. Park, Que., 174
La Verne, Calif., 204
Laverton, Vic., 97
La Victoria, Venez., 124
Lavras, Braz., 135
Lawang, Indon., 85
Lawndale, Calif., 204
Lawrence, Ind., 227
Lawrence, Kans., 232
Lawrence, Mass., 249
Lawrence, N.Y., 276
Lawrenceburg, Ind., 227
Lawrenceburg, Ky., 237
Lawrenceburg, Tenn., 237
Lawrence Park, Pa., 294
Lawrenceville, Ga., 216
Lawrenceville, Ill., 222
Lawton, Okla., 288
Lay (cape), N. Vietnam, 72
Layou (riv.), Dominica, 161
Layou, St. Vincent, 161
Laysan (isl.), Hawaii, 218
Layton, Utah, 304
Lazarev Sta., Ant., 5
Lead, S. Dak., 298
Leader, Sask., 181
Leadville, Colo., 208
League City, Tex., 302
Lealui, Zambia, 115
Leamington (Royal Leamington Spa), Eng., 13
Leamington, Ont., 177
Leatherhead, Eng., 10
Leavenworth, Kans., 232
Leawood, Kans., 232
Lebanon, 63
Lebanon, Ill., 222
Lebanon, Ind., 227
Lebanon, Ky., 237
Lebanon (mts.), Leb., 63
Lebanon, Mo., 261
Lebanon, N.H., 268
Lebanon, Ohio, 284
Lebanon, Oreg., 291
Lebanon, Pa., 294
Lebanon, Tenn., 237
Lebedin, U.S.S.R., 52
Le Blanc-Mesnil, France, 28
Lebork, Poland, 47
Le Bourget, France, 28
Lebu, Chile, 138
Lecce (prov.), Italy, 34
Lecce, Italy, 34
Lecco, Italy, 34
Lech (riv.), W. Ger., 22
Le Creusot, France, 28
Ledang, Gunong (mt.), Malaysia, 72
Ledge Flats, Berm., 156
Ledo, India, 68
Leduc, Alta., 182
Ledyard, Conn., 210
Lee, Mass., 249
Lee (riv.), Ire., 17
Leech (lake), Minn., 254
Leechburg, Pa., 294
Leeds, Ala., 194
Leeds, Eng., 13
Leesburg, Fla., 212
Leesburg, Va., 307
Lee's Summit, Mo., 261
Leesville, La., 238
Leeton, N.S.W., 97
Leetonia, Ohio, 284
Leeuwarden, Neth., 27
Leeuwin (cape), W. Austral., 92
Leeward (passage), Virgin Is. (U.S.), 161
Leeward (isls.), W. Indies, 156
Legaspi, Phil. Is., 82
Legges Tor (peak), Tas., 99
Leghorn (prov.), Italy, 34
Leghorn, Italy, 34
Legionowo, Poland, 47
Legnica, Poland, 47
Leguan (isl.), Guyana, 131
Leh, India, 68
Le Havre, France, 28
Lehi, Utah, 304
Lehigh Acres, Fla., 212
Lehighton, Pa., 294
Lehman Caves Nat'l Mon., Nev., 266
Leicester, Eng., 13
Leicestershire (county), Eng., 13
Leichhardt, N.S.W., 97
Leichhardt (riv.), Queensland, 95
Leiden, Neth., 27
Leigh, Eng., 10
Leine (riv.), W. Ger., 22
Leinster (prov.), Ire., 17
Leipzig (dist.), E. Ger., 22
Leipzig, E. Ger., 22
Leiria, Port., 33
Leisure City, Fla., 212
Leitchfield, Ky., 237
Leith, Scot., 15
Leitrim (county), Ire., 17
Leix (Laoighis) (county), Ire., 17
Lek (river), Neth., 27
Lekoni, Gabon, 115
Leland, Miss., 256
Le Locle, Switz., 39
Lelydorp, Sur., 131
Le Mans, France, 28
Lemantin, Mart., 161
Le Mars, Iowa, 229
Lemmon, S. Dak., 298
Lemon Grove, Calif., 204
Lemont, Ill., 222
Lemoore, Calif., 204
Le Moule, Guad., 161
Lemoyne, Pa., 294
Lempa (riv.), El Sal., 154
Lena (riv.), U.S.S.R., 48
Leninabad, U.S.S.R., 48
Leninakan, U.S.S.R., 52
Leningrad, U.S.S.R., 52
Leninogorsk, U.S.S.R., 48
Leninsk-Kuznetskiy, U.S.S.R., 48
Lenkoran', U.S.S.R., 52
Lennox, Calif., 204
Lennoxville, Que., 172
Lenoir, N.C., 281
Lenoir City, Tenn., 237
Lens, France, 28
Lentini, Italy, 34
Lenvik, Norway, 18
Leoben, Austria, 41
Léogane, Haiti, 158
Leominster, Mass., 249
León, Mex., 150
León, Nic., 154
León (reg.), Spain, 33
León (prov.), Spain, 33
León, Spain, 33
Leonardo, N. J., 273
Leonforte, Italy, 34
Leongatha, Vic., 97
Leonia, N. J., 273
Leopold II (lake), Dem. Rep. of the Congo, 115
Lephepe, Botswana, 118
L'Epiphanie, Que., 172
Lepontine Alps (range), Europe, 39
Le Port, Réunion, 118
Leptis Magna (ruins), Libya, 111
Le Puy, France, 28
Léré, Chad, 111
Leribe, Lesotho, 118
Lérida (prov.), Spain, 33
Lérida, Spain, 33
Léros (isl.), Greece, 45
Le Roy, N.Y., 276
Lerwick, Scot., 15
Les Abymes, Guad., 161
Les Cayes, Haiti, 158
Leskovac, Yugo., 45
Lesotho, 118
Lesozavodsk, U.S.S.R., 48
Lesser Antilles (isls.), N. Amer., 156
Lesser Slave (lake), Alta., 182
Le Sueur, Minn., 254
Lésvos (isl.), Greece, 45
Leszno, Poland, 47
Letchworth, Eng., 13
Lethbridge, Alta., 182
Leticia, Col., 126
Letpadan, Burma, 72
Letterkenny, Ire., 17
Leucadia, Calif., 204
Leuser (mt.), Indon., 85
Levack, Ont., 175
Levádhia, Greece, 45
Levallois-Perret, France, 28
Levelland, Tex., 302
Leven, Scot., 15
Leverkusen, W. Ger., 22
Levice, Czech., 41
Levin, N.Z., 101
Lévis, Que., 172
Levittown, N.Y., 276
Levittown, Pa., 294
Levittown, P. Rico, 161
Levkás (isl.), Greece, 45
Lévrier (bay), Mauritania, 106
Levskigrad, Bulg., 45
Levuka, Fiji, 87
Lewes, Del., 245
Lewes, Eng., 13
Lewis (dist.), Scot., 15
Lewisburg, Pa., 294
Lewisburg, Tenn., 237
Lewisham, Eng., 10
Lewisporte, Newf., 166
Lewiston, Idaho, 220
Lewiston, Maine, 242
Lewiston, N.Y., 276
Lewistown, Ill., 222
Lewistown, Mont., 262
Lewistown, Pa., 294
Lewisville, N. Br., 170
Lewisville, Tex., 302
Lexington, Ky., 237
Lexington, Mass., 249
Lexington, Miss., 256
Lexington, Mo., 261
Lexington, Nebr., 264
Lexington, N.C., 281
Lexington, Tenn., 237
Lexington, Va., 307
Lexington Park, Md., 245
Leyland, Eng., 10
Leyte (prov.), Phil. Is., 82
Leyte (isl.), Phil. Is., 82
Lezh, Alb., 45
L'gov, U.S.S.R., 52
Lhasa, China, 77
Lhatse Dzong, China, 77
Liao Ho (riv.), China, 77
Liaoning (prov.), China, 77
Liaotung (pen.), China, 77
Liaoyang, China, 77
Liaoyüan, China, 77
Liard (riv.), Canada, 187
Líbano, Col., 126
Libby, Mont., 262
Libenge, Dem. Rep. of the Congo, 115
Liberal, Kans., 232
Liberec, Czech., 41
Liberia, 106
Liberia, C. Rica, 154
Liberta, Antigua, 161
Liberty, Mo., 261
Liberty, N.Y., 276
Liberty, Pa., 294
Liberty, S.C., 296
Liberty, Tex., 302
Libertyville, Ill., 222
Libreville (cap.), Gabon, 115
Libya, 111
Libyan (des.), Africa, 111
Licata, Italy, 34
Lichfield, Eng., 10
Lichtenberg, E. Ger., 22
Liddel Water (riv.), U.K., 15
Lidice, Czech., 41
Lidingö, Sweden, 18
Lidköping, Sweden, 18
Lido di Ostia, Italy, 34
Lido di Venezia, Italy, 34
Liechtenstein, 39
Liège (prov.), Belg., 27
Liège, Belg., 27
Lienyünkang, China, 77
Lienz, Austria, 41
Liepāja, U.S.S.R., 53
Lier, Belg., 27
Liestal, Switz., 39
Liévin, France, 28
Liffey (riv.), Ire., 17
Lifford, Ire., 17
Lifu (isl.), New Cal., 87
Ligonha (riv.), Mozamb., 118
Ligonier, Ind., 227
Liguria (reg.), Italy, 34
Ligurian (sea), Italy, 34
Lihue, Hawaii, 218
Likasi, Dem Rep. of the Congo, 115
Likiang, China, 77
Lille, France, 28
Lille Bælt (chan.), Den., 21
Lillehammer, Norway, 18
Lillestrøm, Norway, 18
Lillooet, Br. Col., 184
Lillydale, Vic., 97
Lilongwe, Malawi, 115
Lim (fjord), Den., 21
Lim (riv.), Yugo., 45
Lima (riv.), Europe, 33
Lima, Ohio, 284
Lima (dept.), Peru, 128
Lima (cap.), Peru, 128
Limache, Chile, 138
Limassol, Cyprus, 63
Limavady, N. Ire., 17
Limbach-Oberfrohna, E. Ger., 22
Limbé, Haiti, 158
Limburg (prov.), Belg., 27
Limburg (prov.), Neth., 27
Limeira, Braz., 135
Limerick (county), Ire., 17
Limerick, Ire., 17
Limmat (riv.), Switz., 39
Limmen (bight), N. Terr., 93
Límnos (isl.), Greece, 45
Limoeiro, Braz., 132
Limoges, France, 28
Limón, C. Rica, 154
Limón, Hond., 154
Limousin (reg.), France, 28
Limpopo (riv.), Africa, 118
Linares (prov.), Chile, 138
Linares, Chile, 138
Linares, Mex., 150
Linares, Spain, 33
Linchwan, China, 77
Lincoln, Arg., 143
Lincoln, Calif., 204
Lincoln, Eng., 13
Lincoln, Ill., 222
Lincoln, Maine, 242
Lincoln, Mass., 249
Lincoln (cap.), Nebr., 264
Lincoln (sea), N. Amer., 146
Lincoln Boyhood Nat'l Mem., Ind., 227
Lincoln City, Oreg., 291
Lincoln Park, Mich., 250
Lincoln Park, N. J., 273
Lincolnshire-Holland (county), Eng., 13
Lincolnshire-Kesteven (county), Eng., 13
Lincolnshire-Lindsey (county), Eng., 13
Lincolnton, N.C., 281
Lincolnwood, Ill., 222
Lincroft, N. J., 273
Linda, Calif., 204
Lindau, W. Ger., 22
Linden, Ala., 194
Linden, N. J., 273
Lindenhurst, N.Y., 276
Lindenwold, N. J., 273
Lindesnes (cape), Norway, 18
Lindi, Tanz., 115
Lindsay, Calif., 204
Lindsay, Okla., 288
Lindsay, Ont., 177
Lindsborg, Kans., 232
Line (isls.), Pacific, 87
Linfen, China, 77
Lingayen, Phil. Is., 82
Lingeh, Iran, 66
Lingen, W. Ger., 22
Lingga (arch.), Indon., 85
Linhai, China, 77
Linhsien, China, 77
Lini, China, 77
Linköping, Sweden, 18
Linlithgow, Scot., 15
Linnhe (inlet), Scot., 15
Linosa (isl.), Italy, 34
Lins, Braz., 135
Linsia, China, 77
Linstead, Jam., 158
Linton, Ind., 227
Lintsang, China, 77
Lintsing, China, 77
Linwood, N. J., 273
Linwood, Pa., 294
Linz, Austria, 41
Lionel Town, Jam., 158
Lions (gulf), France, 28
Lipa, Phil. Is., 82
Lipari (isls.), Italy, 34
Lipetsk, U.S.S.R., 52
Lippe (riv.), W. Ger., 22
Lippstadt, W. Ger., 22
Lipscomb, Ala., 194
Liri (riv.), Italy, 34
Lisala, Dem. Rep. of the Congo, 115
Lisbon, N. Dak., 283
Lisbon, Ohio, 284
Lisbon (Lisboa)(cap.), Port., 33
Lisburn, N. Ire., 17
Lisianski (isl.), Hawaii, 218
Lisichansk, U.S.S.R., 52
Lisieux, France, 28
Lismore, Ire., 17
Lismore, N.S.W., 97
Lista (pen.), Norway, 18
Lister (mt.), Ant., 5
Listowel, Ire., 17
Listowel, Ont., 177
Litani (riv.), Leb., 63
Litani (riv.), Sur., 131
Litchfield, Conn., 210
Litchfield, Ill., 222
Litchfield, Minn., 254
Litchfield Park, Ariz., 198
Litherland, Eng., 10
Lithgow, N.S.W., 97
Lithuanian S.S.R., U.S.S.R., 52
Lititz, Pa., 294
Litoměřice, Czech., 41
Little Alföld (plain), Hungary, 41
Little America, Ant., 5
Little Cayman (isl.), Cayman Is., 156
Little Chute, Wis., 317
Little Colorado (riv.), U.S., 198
Little Corn (isl.), Nic., 154
Little Current, Ont., 177
Little Falls, Minn., 254
Little Falls, N. J., 273
Little Falls, N.Y., 276
Little Ferry, N. J., 273
Littlefield, Tex., 302
Little Inagua (isl.), Bah. Is., 156
Little Makin (isl.), Gilb. & Ell. Is., 87
Little Minch (sound), Scot., 15
Little Namaland (reg.), S. Afr., 118
Little Rapids, Wis., 317
Little Rock (cap.), Ark., 203
Little Saint Bernard (pass), Europe, 28
Little Shawmut, Ala., 194
Little Silver, N. J., 273
Littlestown, Pa., 294
Little Tobago (isl.), Virgin Is. (Br.), 161
Littleton, Colo., 208
Littleton, N.H., 268
Litvínov, Czech., 41
Liuchow, China, 77
Live Oak, Fla., 212
Livermore, Calif., 204
Livermore Falls, Maine, 242
Liverpool, Eng., 10
Liverpool, N.S.W., 97
Liverpool, N.Y., 276
Liverpool, N.S., 169
Livingston, Guat., 154
Livingston, Mont., 262
Livingston, N. J., 273
Livingston, Tex., 302
Livingstone, Zambia, 115
Livingstonia, Malawi, 115
Livonia, Mich., 250
Livorno (Leghorn), Italy, 34
Liwale, Tanz., 115
Lizard (head), Eng., 13
Ljubljana, Yugo., 45
Llandudno, Wales, 13
Llanelli, Wales, 13
Llano, Tex., 302
Llano Estacado (plain), U.S., 274, 302
Llanos del Orinoco (plains), S. Amer., 120
Llanquihue (prov.), Chile, 138
Llerena (pt.), C. Rica, 154
Lleyn (pen.), Wales, 13
Llobregat (riv.), Spain, 33
Llolleo, Chile, 138
Lloyd Hbr., N.Y., 276
Lloydminster, Sask.-Alta., 181, 182
Llullaillaco (vol.), S. Amer., 138
Llwchwr, Wales, 13
Loa (riv.), Chile, 138
Lobatse, Botswana, 118
Lobaye (riv.), Centr. Afr. Rep., 115
Lobito, Angola, 115
Lobos (cape), Mex., 150
Lobos de Afuera (isl.), Peru, 128
Lobos de Tierra (isl.), Peru, 128
Lobstick (lake), Newf., 166
Locarno, Switz., 39
Lochaber (dist.), Scot., 15
Lochgelly, Scot., 15
Lochy (lake), Scot., 15
Lockeport, N.S., 169
Lockhart, Tex., 302
Lock Haven, Pa., 294
Lockland, Ohio, 284
Lockport, Ill., 222
Lockport, N.Y., 276
Loc Ninh, S. Vietnam, 72
Lod, Israel, 65
Lodar, P.D.R., Yemen, 59
Lodi, Calif., 204
Lodi, Italy, 34
Lodi, N. J., 273
Lodja, Dem. Rep. of the Congo, 115
Łódź (prov.), Poland, 47
Łódź, Poland, 47
Loei, Thai., 72
Lofoten (isls.), Norway, 18
Lofty (mt.), S. Austral., 94
Lofty (range), Tas., 99
Logan, Ohio, 284
Logan, Utah, 304
Logan, W. Va., 313
Logan (mt.), Yukon, 187
Logansport, Ind., 227
Logone (riv.), Africa, 111
Logroño (prov.), Spain, 33
Logroño, Spain, 33
Loho, China, 77
Lo Ho (riv.), China, 77
Loir (riv.), France, 28
Loire (dept.), France, 28
Loire (riv.), France, 28
Loire-Atlantique (dept.), France, 28
Loiret (dept.), France, 28
Loir-et-Cher (dept.), France, 28
Loíza, P. Rico, 161
Loíza Aldea, P. Rico, 161
Loja (prov.), Ecua., 128
Loja, Ecua., 128
Lokeren, Belg., 27
Lokoja, Nigeria, 106
Lolland (isl.), Den., 21
Lolo (pass), Idaho, 220
Lom, Bulg., 45
Lom (riv.), Cameroon, 115
Loma (mts.), Africa, 106
Loma Bonita, Mex., 150
Loma Linda, Calif., 204
Lomas de Zamora, Arg., 143
Lombard, Ill., 222
Lombardy (reg.), Italy, 34
Lombok (isl.), Indon., 85
Lomé (cap.), Togo, 106
Lomela, Dem. Rep. of the Congo, 115
Lomié, Cameroon, 115
Lomita, Calif., 204
Lomond (lake), Scot., 15
Lompoc, Calif., 204
Lom Sak, Thai., 72
Łomża, Poland, 47
London (cap.), Eng., 10
London, Ky., 237
London, Ohio, 284
London, Ont., 177
London (cap.), U.K., 10
Londonderry (county), N. Ire., 17
Londonderry, N. Ire., 17
Londonderry (cape), W. Austral., 92
Londrina, Braz., 132
Long (cay), Bah. Is., 156
Long (isl.), Bah. Is., 156
Long (isl.), N.Y., 276
Long (pt.), Ont., 177
Long (inlet), Scot., 15
Long Beach, Calif., 204
Long Beach, Miss., 256
Long Beach, N.Y., 276
Long Branch, N. J., 273
Long Eaton, Eng., 13
Longford (county), Ire., 17
Longford, Ire., 17
Long Hill, Conn., 210
Long Island (sound), U.S., 276
Longlac, Ont., 177
Longmeadow, Mass., 249
Longmont, Colo., 208
Long Range (mts.), Newf., 166
Longreach, Queensland, 95
Longridge, Eng., 10
Longueuil, Que., 172
Long View, N.C., 281
Longview, Tex., 302
Longview, Wash., 310
Longwy, France, 28
Long Xuyen, S. Vietnam, 72
Longyearbyen, Norway, 18
Loogootee, Ind., 227
Lookout Mtn., Ga., 216
Loop (head), Ire., 17
Lopatka (cape), U.S.S.R., 48
Lop Buri, Thai., 72
Lopez (cape), Gabon, 115
Lop Nor (dry lake), China, 77
Lorain, Ohio, 284
Loralai, Pak., 68
Lorca, Spain, 33
Lord Howe (Ontong Java) (isl.), Br. Sol. Is., 87
Lord Howe (isl.), N.S.W., 97
Lordsburg, N. Mex., 274
Lorena, Braz., 135
Loreto (dept.), Peru, 128
Loretteville, Que., 172
Lorica, Col., 126
Lorient, France, 28
Lorne, N. Br., 170
Lorne (dist.), Scot., 15
Lörrach, W. Ger., 22
Lorrain, Mart., 161
Los Alamitos, Calif., 204
Los Alamos, N. Mex., 274
Los Altos, Calif., 204
Los Amates, Guat., 154
Los Andes, Chile, 138
Los Angeles, Calif., 204
Los Angeles, Chile, 138
Los Banos, Calif., 204
Los Gatos, Calif., 204
Loshan, China, 77
Lošinj (isl.), Yugo., 45
Los Mochis, Mex., 150
Los Palacios, Cuba, 158
Los Ranchos de Albuquerque, N.M., 274
Los Reyes, Mex., 150
Los Roques (isls.), Venez., 124
Los Ríos (prov.), Ecua., 128
Los Santos, Pan., 154
Lossiemouth and Branderburgh, Scot., 15
Los Teques, Venez., 124
Lot (dept.), France, 28
Lot (riv.), France, 28
Lota, Chile, 138
Lot-et-Garonne (dept.), France, 28
Lothians (dist.), Scot., 15
Lötschberg (tunnel), Switz., 39
Loudon, Tenn., 237
Loudonville, Ohio, 284
Louga, Sen., 106
Loughborough, Eng., 13
Loughrea, Ire., 17
Louisburg, N.C., 281
Louisburg, N.S., 168
Louiseville, Que., 172
Louisiade (arch.), Papua, 85
Louisiana, Mo., 261
Louisiana (state), U.S., 238
Louis Trichardt, S. Afr., 118
Louisville, Ky., 237
Louisville, Miss., 256
Louisville, Ohio, 284
Loulé, Port., 33
Louny, Czech., 41
Lourdes, France, 28
Lourenço Marques (dist.), Mozamb., 118
Lourenço Marques (cap.), Mozamb., 118
Lourinha, Port., 33
Lousã, Port., 33
Louth (county), Ire., 17
Louvain, Belg., 27
Lovat' (riv.), U.S.S.R., 52
Lovech, Bulg., 45
Loveland, Colo., 208
Loveland, Ohio, 284
Lovell, Wyo., 319
Lovelock, Nev., 266
Loves Park, Ill., 222
Lovington, N. Mex., 274
Lovisa, Fin., 18
Lowa (riv.), Dem. Rep. of the Congo, 115
Lowell, Mass., 249
Lowell, Mich., 250
Lowell, N.C., 281
Lower Arrow (lake), Br. Col., 184
Lower Austria (prov.), Austria, 41
Lower California (pen.), Mex., 150
Lower Caraquet, N. Br., 170
Lower Engadine (dist.), Switz., 39
Lower Hutt, N.Z., 101
Lower Juba (prov.), Somalia, 115
Lower Rhine (riv.), Neth., 27
Lower Saxony (state), W. Ger., 22
Lower Tunguska (riv.), U.S.S.R., 48
Lowestoft, Eng., 13
Lowville, N.Y., 276
Loyalty (isls.), New Cal., 87
Loyang, China, 77
Lozère (dept.), France, 28
Loznica, Yugo., 45
Lozovaya, U.S.S.R., 52
Luanda (dist.), Angola, 115
Luanda (cap.), Angola, 115
Luang (mt.), Thai., 72
Luang Prabang, Laos, 72
Luanshya, Zambia, 115
Lubang (isls.), Phil. Is., 82
Lübbenau, E. Ger., 22
Lubbock, Tex., 302
Lübeck, W. Ger., 22
Lublin (prov.), Poland, 47
Lublin, Poland, 47
Lubudi, Dem. Rep. of the Congo, 115
Lubumbashi, Dem. Rep. of the Congo, 115
Lubutu, Dem. Rep. of the Congo, 115
Luc An Chau, N. Vietnam, 72
Lucas E. de Peña, Dom. Rep., 158
Lucca (prov.), Italy, 34
Lucca, Italy, 34
Luce (bay), Scot., 15
Lucea, Jam., 158
Lucena, Phil. Is., 82
Lucena, Spain, 33
Lučenec, Czech., 41
Lucera, Italy, 34
Lucerne (Luzern), Switz., 39
Luchow, China, 77
Lucie (riv.), Sur., 131
Luckenwalde, E. Ger., 22
Lucknow, India, 68
Lüdenscheid, W. Ger., 22
Lüderitz, S.W. Afr., 118
Ludhiana, India, 68
Ludington, Mich., 250
Ludlow, Ky., 237
Ludlow, Mass., 249
Ludvika, Sweden, 18
Ludwigsburg, W. Ger., 22
Ludwigshafen, W. Ger., 22
Luebo, Dem. Rep. of the Congo, 115
Lufira (riv.), Dem. Rep. of the Congo, 115
Lufkin, Tex., 302
Lugano, Switz., 39
Luganville, New Hebr., 87
Lugenda (riv.), Mozamb., 118
Lugh, Somalia, 115
Lugo, Italy, 34
Lugo (prov.), Spain, 33
Lugo, Spain, 33
Lugoj, Rum., 45
Luhaiya, Yemen Arab Rep., 59
Luichow (pen.), China, 77
Luilaka (riv.), Dem. Rep. of the Congo, 115
Luimneach (Limerick), Ire., 17
Luisa, Dem. Rep. of the Congo, 115
Luitpold Coast (reg.), Ant., 5
Luján, Arg., 143
Lukenie (riv.), Dem. Rep. of the Congo, 115
Lule (riv.), Sweden, 18
Luleå, Sweden, 18
Lüleburgaz, Turkey, 63
Luling, Tex., 302
Lulua (riv.), Dem. Rep. of the Congo, 115
Luluabourg, Dem. Rep. of the Congo, 115
Lumadjang, Indon., 85
Lumberton, N.C., 281
Lumut, Malaysia, 72
Lund, Sweden, 18
Lunda (dist.), Angola, 115
Lundy (isl.), Eng., 13
Lüneburg, W. Ger., 22
Lüneburger Heide (dist.), W. Ger., 22
Lünen, W. Ger., 22
Lunenburg, Mass., 249
Lunenburg, N.S., 169
Lunéville, France, 28
Lungchen, China, 77
Lungi, S. Leone, 106
Lungwebungu (riv.), Africa, 115
Luozi, Dem. Rep. of the Congo, 115
Lupeni, Rum., 45
Luque, Par., 144
Luquillo, Sierra de (mts.), P. Rico, 161
Luray, Va., 307
Lúrio (riv.), Mozamb., 118
Luristan (governorate), Iran, 66
Lusaka (cap.), Zambia, 115
Lusambo, Dem. Rep. of the Congo, 115
Lusatia (reg.), E. Ger., 22
Lushnje, Alb., 45
Lushoto, Tanz., 115
Lusk, Wyo., 319
Luso, Angola, 115
Lustenau, Austria, 41
Lüta, China, 77
Lutcher, La., 238
Lutherville, Md., 245
Luton, Eng., 13
Lutsk, U.S.S.R., 52
Lützow-Holm (bay), Ant., 5
Luverne, Minn., 254
Luvua (riv.), Dem. Rep. of the Congo, 115
Luxembourg, 27
Luxembourg (prov.), Belg., 27
Luxembourg (cap.), Lux., 27
Luxor, U.A.R., 111
Luzern (canton), Switz., 39
Luzern, Switz., 39
Luzern (lake), Switz., 39
Luzerne, Pa., 294
Luzon (isl.), Phil. Is., 82
L'vov, U.S.S.R., 52
Lyallpur, Pak., 68
Lydenburg, S. Afr., 118
Lyell (mt.), Tas., 99
Lykens, Pa., 294
Lyman, Miss., 256
Lyme (bay), Eng., 13
Lymington, Eng., 13
Lymm, Eng., 10
Lynbrook, N.Y., 276
Lynch, Ky., 237
Lynchburg, Va., 307
Lynden, Wash., 310
Lyndhurst, N. J., 273
Lyndhurst, Ohio, 284
Lyndon B. Johnson Nat'l Hist. Site, Tex., 302
Lyndora, Pa., 294
Lyngby, Den., 21
Lynn, Mass., 249
Lynnfield Ctr., Mass., 249
Lynn Haven, Fla., 212
Lynn Lake, Man., 179
Lynnwood, Wash., 310
Lynwood, Calif., 204
Lyon, France, 28
Lyons, Ga., 216
Lyons, Ill., 222
Lyons, Kans., 232
Lyons, N. J., 273
Lyons, N.Y., 276
Lysaker, Norway, 18
Lys'va, U.S.S.R., 52
Lytham Saint Anne's, Eng., 10
Lyttelton, N.Z., 101
Lyubotin, U.S.S.R., 52

M

Ma'an (dist.), Jordan, 65
Ma'an, Jordan, 65
Ma'arret en Nu'man, Syria, 63
Maarianhamina (Mariehamn), Fin., 18
Maas (riv.), Neth., 27
Maasin, Phil. Is., 82
Maastricht, Neth., 27
Mableton, Ga., 216
Macaé, Braz., 135
Macamic, Que., 174
Macao, 77
Macao (cap.), Macao, 77
Macapá, Braz., 132
Macará, Ecua., 128
Macau, Braz., 132
Macclenny, Fla., 212
Macclesfield, Eng., 10
Macdonald (lake), Austral., 92
Macdonnell (ranges), N. Terr., 93
Macduff, Scot., 15
Macedonia (reg.), Greece, 45
Macedonia, Ohio, 284
Macedonia (rep.), Yugo., 45
Maceió, Braz., 132
Macenta, Guinea, 106
Macerata (prov.), Italy, 34
Macerata, Italy, 34
Macgillicuddy's Reeks (mts.), Ire., 17
Machacamarca, Bol., 136
Machala, Ecua., 128
Machalí, Chile, 138
Machico, Port., 33
Machida, Japan, 81
Machilipatnam, India, 68
Machiques, Venez., 124
Machupicchu, Peru, 128
Macina (depr.), Mali, 106
Mackay, Queensland, 95
Mackenzie (bay), Ant., 5
Mackenzie (mts.), Canada, 187
Mackenzie (dist.), N.W.T., 187
Mackenzie (riv.), N.W.T., 187
Mackinac (isl.), Mich., 250
Mackinaw City, Mich., 250
Macksville, N.S.W., 97
Maclear (cape), S. Afr., 118
Macmillan (riv.), Yukon, 187
Macomb, Ill., 222
Mâcon, France, 28
Macon, Ga., 216
Macon, Mo., 261
Macorís (cape), Dom. Rep., 158
Macquarie (isl.), Austral., 3
Macquarie (harb.), Tas., 99
Mac-Robertson Land (reg.), Ant., 5
Macroom, Ire., 17
Mactan (isl.), Phil. Is., 82
Macuspana, Mex., 150
Macuto, Venez., 124
Ma'daba, Jordan, 65
Madagascar (isl.), Malag. Rep., 118
Madame (isl.), N.S., 169
Madang, Terr. N.G., 85
Madawaska, Maine, 242
Madeira (riv.), Braz., 132
Madeira, Ohio, 284
Madeira (prov.), Port., 33
Madeira (isl.), Port., 33
Madeira Beach, Fla., 212
Madera, Calif., 204
Madera, Mex., 150
Madhubani, India, 68
Madhya Pradesh (state), India, 68
Madill, Okla., 288
Madimba, Dem. Rep. of the Congo, 115
Madinat ash Sha'b (cap.), P.D.R. Yemen, 58
Madison, Fla., 212
Madison, Ga., 216
Madison, Ill., 222
Madison, Ind., 227
Madison, Maine, 242
Madison, N. J., 273
Madison, S. Dak., 298
Madison, Tenn., 237
Madison (cap.), Wis., 317
Madison Hts., Mich., 250
Madison Hts., Va., 307
Madisonville, Ky., 237
Madiun, Indon., 85
Madjalengka, Indon., 85
Madjene, Indon., 85
Madone (mt.), Switz., 39
Madraka, Ras (cape), Oman, 59
Madras, India, 68
Madre (lag.), Mex., 150
Madre de Dios (isl.), Chile, 138
Madre de Dios (prov.), Peru, 128
Madre de Dios (riv.), S. Amer., 132
Madre del Sur (mts.), Mex., 150
Madre Occidental (mts.), Mex., 150
Madre Oriental (mts.), Mex., 150
Madrid (prov.), Spain, 33
Madrid (cap.), Spain, 33
Madura (isl.), Indon., 85
Madurai, India, 68
Maebashi, Japan, 81
Mae Klong, Mae Nam (riv.), Thai., 72
Maestra, Sierra (mts.), Cuba, 158
Maevatanana, Malag. Rep., 118
Mafeking, S. Afr., 118
Mafeteng, Lesotho, 118
Maffra, Vic., 97
Mafia (isl.), Tanz., 115
Mafra, Braz., 132
Magadan, U.S.S.R., 48
Magadi, Kenya, 115
Magallanes (prov.), Chile, 138
Magangué, Col., 126
Magaria, Niger, 106
Magdala, Eth., 111
Magdalen (isls.), Que., 163

Magdalena, Arg., 143
Magdalena (dept.), Col., 126
Magdalena (riv.), Col., 126
Magdalena, Mex., 150
Magdeburg (dist.), E. Ger., 22
Magdeburg, E. Ger., 22
Magee, Island (pen.), N. Ire., 17
Magelang, Indon., 85
Magellan (strait), S. Amer., 138
Magerøy (isl.), Norway, 18
Magetan, Indon., 85
Maggiore (lake), Europe, 39
Maghâgha, U.A.R., 111
Maghama, Mauritania, 106
Magherafelt, N. Ire., 17
Magna, Utah, 304
Magnitogorsk, U.S.S.R., 48
Magnolia, Ark., 203
Magnolia, N. J., 273
Magog, Que., 172
Magrath, Alta., 182
Magude, Mozamb., 118
Maguse (lake), N.W.T., 187
Magwe (div.), Burma, 72
Magwe, Burma, 72
Mahabad, Iran, 66
Mahabaleshwar, India, 68
Mahagi, Dem. Rep. of the Congo, 115
Mahaica, Guyana, 131
Mahaicony, Guyana, 131
Mahakam (riv.), Indon., 85
Mahalapye, Bots., 118
Mahallat, Iran, 66
Mahanadi (riv.), India, 68
Mahanoy City, Pa., 294
Maharashtra (state), India, 68
Maha Sarakham, Thai., 72
Mahaut, Dominica, 161
Mahaxay, Laos, 72
Mahbubnagar, India, 68
Mahdia, Tun., 106
Mahe, India, 68
Mahe (isl.), Seychelles, 118
Mahenge, Tanz., 115
Maheshkhali, Pak., 68
Mahim (bay), India, 68
Mahoba, India, 68
Mahón, Spain, 33
Mahone Bay, N.S., 169
Mahuva, India, 68
Mahwah, N. J., 273
Maida, Yemen Arab Rep., 59
Maidani (cape), Iran, 66
Maidenhead, Eng., 13
Maidstone, Eng., 13
Maiduguri, Nigeria, 106
Maili, Hawaii, 218
Maimana, Afghan., 68
Main (riv.), W. Ger., 22
Maine (state), U.S., 242
Maine-et-Loire (dept.), France, 28
Mainland (isl.), Scot., 15
Maintirano, Malag. Rep., 118
Mainz, W. Ger., 22
Maipo (vol.), S. Amer., 143
Maipú, Arg., 143
Maipú, Chile, 138
Maiquetía, Venez., 124
Maisí (pt.), Cuba, 158
Maisons-Alfort, France, 28
Maitland, Fla., 212
Maitland, N.S.W., 97
Maitland, S. Austral., 94
Maizuru, Japan, 81
Majorca (isl.), Spain, 33
Majunga (prov.), Malag. Rep., 118
Majunga, Malag. Rep., 118
Majuro (atoll), Pac. Is., 87
Makaha, Hawaii, 218
Makakilo City, Hawaii, 218
Makale, Eth., 111
Makassar, Indon., 85
Makassar (str.), Indon., 85
Makatea (isl.), Fr. Poly., 87
Makeni, S. Leone, 106
Makeyevka, U.S.S.R., 52
Makgadikgadi (salt pan), Botswana, 118
Makhachkala, U.S.S.R., 52
Makin (Butaritari) (atoll), Gilb. and Ell. Is., 87
Makkovik, Newf., 166
Mako, Hung., 41
Makokou, Gabon, 115
Makoua, Rep. of Congo, 115
Makran (reg.), Iran, 66
Makurdi, Nigeria, 106
Malabar (coast), India, 68
Malabar (hill), India, 68
Malacca (strait), Asia, 85
Malad, India, 68
Malad City, Idaho, 220
Málaga, Col., 126
Málaga (prov.), Spain, 33
Málaga, Spain, 33
Malagasy Republic, 118
Malahide, Ire., 17
Malaita (isl.), Br. Sol. Is., 87
Malakal, Sudan, 111
Malakanagiri, India, 68
Malakand, Pak., 68
Malakoff, France, 28
Malang, Indon., 85
Malange (dist.), Angola, 115
Malange, Angola, 115
Malanville, Dahomey, 106
Malartic, Que., 174
Malatya (prov.), Turkey, 63
Malatya, Turkey, 63
Malawi, 115
Malay (pen.), Asia, 72
Malaya (reg.), Malaysia, 72
Malayer, Iran, 66
Malaysia, 72, 85
Malbork, Poland, 47
Malden, Mass., 249
Malden, Mo., 261
Malden (isl.), Pacific, 87
Maldives, 54
Maldonado (dept.), Urug., 145
Maldonado, Urug., 145
Malé (cap.), Maldives, 54
Malegaon, India, 68
Malekula (isl.), New Hebr., 87
Maler-Kotla, India, 68
Malheur (lake), Oreg., 291
Mali, 106
Malin (head), Ire., 17
Malindi, Kenya, 115
Malkapur, India, 68
Mallawi, U.A.R., 111
Malleco (prov.), Chile, 138
Mallorca (Majorca) (isl.), Spain, 33
Mallow, Ire., 17
Malmédy, Belg., 27
Malmesbury, S. Afr., 118
Malmö, Sweden, 18
Malmöhus (county), Sweden, 18
Maloelap (atoll), Pac. Is., 87
Malone, N.Y., 276
Malta, 34
Malta (chan.), Europe, 34
Malta (isl.), Malta, 34
Malta, Mont., 262
Maltahöhe, S.W. Afr., 118
Malvern, Ark., 203
Malvern, Eng., 13
Malvern, Vic., 97
Mamaroneck, N.Y., 276
Mambajao, Phil. Is., 82
Mamberamo (riv.), Indon., 85
Mamfé, Cameroon, 115
Mammoth Cave Nat'l Park, Ky., 237
Mamoré (riv.), Bol., 136
Mamou, Guinea, 106
Mamou, La., 238
Mampong, Ghana, 106
Mamry (lake), Poland, 47
Mamudju, Indon., 85
Man (isl.), 13
Man, Ivory Coast, 106
Mana, Fr. Gui., 131
Manabí (prov.), Ecua., 128
Manacor, Spain, 33
Manado, Indon., 85
Managua (cap.), Nic., 154
Managua (lake), Nic., 154
Manakara, Malag. Rep., 118
Manalapan, N. J., 273
Manama (cap.), Bahrein, 59
Mananjary, Malag Rep., 118
Manapouri (lake), N.Z., 101
Manar, Jebel (mt.), Yemen Arab Rep., 59
Manasarowar (lake), China, 77
Manasquan, N. J., 273
Manass (riv.), China, 77
Manassas, Va., 307
Manassas Nat'l Battlef. Park, Va., 307
Manassas Park, Va., 307
Manatí, P. Rico, 161
Manaus, Braz., 132
Mancha, La (reg.), Spain, 33
Manche (dept.), France, 28
Manchester, Conn., 210
Manchester, Eng., 13
Manchester, Ga., 216
Manchester, Iowa, 229
Manchester, N.H., 268
Manchester, Tenn., 237
Manchouli, China, 77
Manchuria (reg.), China, 77
Máncora, Peru, 128
Mandal, Norway, 18
Mandalay (div.), Burma, 72
Mandalay, Burma, 72
Mandal Gobi, Mong., 77
Mandali, Iraq, 66
Mandalya (gulf), Turkey, 63
Mandan, N. Dak., 283
Mandeb, Bab el (str.), 111
Mandeville, Jam., 158
Mand Rud (riv.), Iran, 66
Mandsaur, India, 68
Mandurah, W. Austral., 92
Mandvi, India, 68
Manfalût, U.A.R., 111
Manfredonia, Italy, 34
Mangaia (isl.), Cook Is., 87
Mangalia, Rum., 45
Mangalore, India, 68
Mangareva (isl.), Fr. Poly., 87
Mangoche, Malawi, 115
Mangoky (riv.), Malag. Rep., 118
Mangotsfield, Eng., 13
Mangrol, India, 68
Mangueira (lag.), Braz., 132
Mangum, Okla., 288
Mangyshlak (pen.), U.S.S.R., 48
Manhasset, N.Y., 276
Manhattan, Kans., 232
Manhattan (isl.), N.Y., 276
Manhattan Beach, Calif., 204
Manheim, Pa., 294
Manhiça, Mozamb., 118
Maniamba, Mozamb., 118
Manica e Sofala (dist.), Mozamb., 118
Manicouagane (riv.), Que., 174
Manifold (cape), Queensland, 95
Manihiki (atoll), Cook Is., 87
Manila, Phil. Is., 82
Manila (bay), Phil. Is., 82
Manipur (riv.), Asia, 72
Manipur (terr.), India, 68
Manisa (prov.), Turkey, 63
Manisa, Turkey, 63
Manistee, Mich., 250
Manistique, Mich., 250
Manitoba (prov.), Canada, 179
Manitoba (lake), Man., 179
Manitoulin (isl.), Ont., 177
Manitou Springs, Colo., 208
Manitouwadge, Ont., 175
Manitowoc, Wis., 317
Maniwaki, Que., 172
Manizales, Col., 126
Manjimup, W. Austral., 92
Mankato, Minn., 254
Mankoya, Zambia, 115
Manly, N.S.W., 97
Manmad, India, 68
Mannar (gulf), Asia, 68
Mannargudi, India, 68
Mannheim, W. Ger., 22
Manning, S.C., 296
Manning, E.C., Prov. Park, Br. Col., 184
Mannington, W. Va., 313
Mannum, S. Austral., 94
Manokwari, Indon., 85
Manono, Dem. Rep. of the Congo, 115
Manori (creek), India, 68
Manra (Sydney) (isl.), Gilb. & Ell. Is., 87
Manresa, Spain, 33
Mansa, Zambia, 115
Mansel (isl.), N.W.T., 187
Mansfield, Conn., 210
Mansfield, Eng., 13
Mansfield, La., 238
Mansfield, Mass., 249
Mansfield, Ohio, 284
Mansfield, Pa., 294
Mansfield (mt.), Vt., 268
Manta, Ecua., 128
Manteca, Calif., 204
Mantiqueira (range), Braz., 135
Mänttä, Fin., 18
Mantua (prov.), Italy, 34
Mantua, Italy, 34
Manú (riv.), Peru, 128
Manua (isls.), Amer. Samoa, 87
Manuae (atoll), Cook Is., 87
Manukau, N.Z., 101
Manus (isl.), Terr. N.G., 87
Manville, N. J., 273
Manville, R.I., 249
Many, La., 238
Manych-Gudilo (lake), U.S.S.R., 52
Manyoni, Tanz., 115
Manzanares, Spain, 33
Manzanillo, Cuba, 158
Manzanillo, Mex., 150
Manzini, Swaziland, 118
Mao, Chad, 111
Maoke (mts.), Indon., 85
Mapimí (depr.), Mex., 150
Maple Creek, Sask., 181
Maple Hts., Ohio, 284
Maple Shade, N. J., 273
Maplewood, La., 238
Maplewood, Minn., 254
Maplewood, Mo., 261
Maplewood, N. J., 273
Mapuera (riv.), Braz., 132
Ma'qil, Iraq, 66
Maquoketa, Iowa, 229
Mar (range), Braz., 132
Mar (dist.), Scot., 15
Mara (prov.), Tanz., 115
Marabella, Trin. & Tob., 161
Maracá (isl.), Braz., 132
Maracaibo, Venez., 124
Maracaibo (lake), Venez., 124
Maracay, Venez., 124
Maragheh, Iran, 66
Maragogipe, Braz., 132
Marajó (isl.), Braz., 132
Maralinga, S. Austral., 94
Marand, Iran, 66
Marandellas, Rhod., 118
Maranhão (state), Braz., 132
Marañón (riv.), Peru, 128
Maraş (prov.), Turkey, 63
Maraş, Turkey, 63
Marathón, Greece, 45
Marathon, Ont., 175
Marble Canyon Nat'l Mon., Ariz., 198
Marblehead, Mass., 249
Marburg, W. Ger., 22
Marceline, Mo., 261
March (riv.), Austria, 41
March, Eng., 13
Marche (reg.), Italy, 34
Marchena (isl.), Ecua., 128
Marchena, Spain, 33
Mar Chiquita (lake), Arg., 143
Marcona, Peru, 128
Marcos Juárez, Arg., 143
Marcos Paz, Arg., 143
Marcus (isl.), Japan, 87
Marcus Hook, Pa., 294
Mardan, Pak., 68
Mar del Plata, Arg., 143
Mardin (prov.), Turkey, 63
Mardin, Turkey, 63
Maré (isl.), New Cal., 87
Maree (lake), Scot., 15
Mareeba, Queensland, 95
Marengo, Ill., 222
Marettimo (isl.), Italy, 34
Marfa, Tex., 302
Marganets, U.S.S.R., 52
Margaree (isl.), N.S., 168
Margarita (isl.), Venez., 124
Margate, Eng., 13
Margate City, N. J., 273
Margherita (mt.), Africa, 115
Margo, Dasht-i- (des.), Afghan., 68
Mari A.S.S.R., U.S.S.R., 52
Maria (isl.), Fr. Poly., 87
María Elena, Chile, 138
Mariager (fjord), Den., 21
Mariana (isls.), Pac. Is., 87
Marianao, Cuba, 158
Marianas Trench, Pacific, 87
Marianna, Ark., 203
Marianna, Fla., 212
María Trinidad Sánchez (prov.), Dom. Rep., 158
Maria van Diemen (cape), N.Z., 101
Marib, Yemen Arab Rep., 59
Maribo, Den., 21
Maribor, Yugo., 45
Maridi, Sudan, 111
Marie Byrd Land (reg.), Ant., 5
Marie-Galante (isl.), Guad., 161
Mariehamn, Fin., 18
Mariemont, Ohio, 284
Marienburg, Sur., 131
Mariental, S.W. Afr., 118
Mariestad, Sweden, 18
Marietta, Ga., 216
Marietta, Ohio, 284
Marieville, Que., 172
Marigot, Dominica, 161
Marília, Braz., 135
Marin, Mart., 161
Marinduque (prov.), Phil. Is., 82
Marinduque (isl.), Phil. Is., 82
Marine City, Mich., 250
Marinette, Wis., 317
Maringá, Brazil, 132
Marinha Grande, Port., 33
Marino, Italy, 34
Marion, Ala., 194
Marion, Ill., 222
Marion, Ind., 227
Marion, Iowa, 229
Marion, N.C., 281
Marion, Ohio, 284
Marion, S. Austral., 94
Marion, S.C., 296
Marion, Va., 307
Mariscala, Urug., 145
Mariscal Estigarribia, Par., 144
Marismas, Las (marsh), Spain, 33
Maritime Alps (range), Europe, 28
Maritsa, Bulg., 45
Maritsa (riv.), Bulg., 45
Mariupol' (Zhdanov), U.S.S.R., 52
Marked Tree, Ark., 203
Marken (isl.), Neth., 27
Markha (riv.), U.S.S.R., 48
Markham (mt.), Ant., 5
Markham, Ill., 222
Markham, Ont., 177
Markham Dzong, China, 77
Marks, Miss., 256
Marksville, La., 238
Marl, W. Ger., 22
Marlborough, Mass., 249
Marlborough (prov. dist.), N.Z., 101
Marlin, Tex., 302
Marlow, Okla., 288
Marmara (sea), Turkey, 63
Marmolada (mt.), Italy, 34
Marne (dept.), France, 28
Marne (riv.), France, 28
Maroantsetra, Malag. Rep., 118
Maroni (riv.), S. Amer., 131
Maros (riv.), Hung., 41
Maroua, Cameroon, 115
Marovoay, Malag. Rep., 118
Marowijne (dist.), Sur., 131
Marowijne (riv.), Sur., 131
Marple, Eng., 10
Marquesas (isls.), Fr. Poly., 87
Marquês de Valença, Braz., 135
Marquette, Mich., 250
Marquette Hts., Ill., 222
Marra, Jebel (mt.), Sudan, 111
Marrakech, Mor., 106
Marrero, La., 238
Marrickville, N.S.W., 97
Marromeu, Mozamb., 118
Marsabit, Kenya, 115
Marsa el Awegia, Libya, 111
Marsa el Brega, Libya, 111
Marsala, Italy, 34
Marsa Susa, Libya, 111
Marseille, France, 28
Marseilles, Ill., 222
Marshall, Ill., 222
Marshall, Liberia, 106
Marshall, Mich., 250
Marshall, Minn., 254
Marshall, Mo., 261
Marshall (isls.), Pac. Is., 87
Marshall, Tex., 302
Marshalltown, Iowa, 229
Marshfield, Mass., 249
Marshfield, Wis., 317
Martaban (gulf), Burma, 72
Martapura, Indon., 85
Martha's Vineyard (isl.), Mass., 249
Martí, Cuba, 158
Martigny, Switz., 39
Martigues, France, 39
Martin, Czech., 41
Martin, Tenn., 237
Martina Franca, Italy, 34
Martinez, Calif., 204
Martínez de la Torre, Mex., 150
Martín García (isl.), Arg., 143
Martinique, 161
Martinique (passage), W. Indies, 161
Martinsburg, W. Va., 313
Martins Ferry, Ohio, 284
Martinsville, Ind., 227
Martinsville, N. J., 273
Martinsville, Va., 307
Marton, N.Z., 101
Martos, Spain, 33
Marudi (mts.), Guyana, 131
Marudi, Malaysia, 85
Marutea (atoll), Fr. Poly., 87
Mary, U.S.S.R., 48
Maryborough (Port Laoighise), Ire., 17
Maryborough, Queensland, 95
Maryborough, Vic., 97
Mary Kathleen, Queensland, 95
Maryland (state), U.S., 245
Maryport, Eng., 13
Marysville, Br. Col., 184
Marysville, Calif., 204
Marysville, Kans., 232
Marysville, Mich., 250
Marysville, N.B., 170
Marysville, Ohio, 284
Marysville, Pa., 294
Marysville, Wash., 310
Maryville, Mo., 261
Maryville, Tenn., 237
Masagua, Guat., 154
Masai (steppe), Tanz., 115
Masaka, Uganda, 115
Masan, S. Korea, 81
Masatepe, Nic., 154
Masaya, Nic., 154
Masbate (prov.), Phil. Is., 82
Masbate (isl.), Phil. Is., 82
Mascara, Alg., 106
Mascarene (isls.), Africa, 118
Mascota, Mex., 150
Mascoutah, Ill., 222
Maseru (cap.), Lesotho, 118
Mashkel (riv.), Asia, 68
Mashonaland (reg.), Rhod., 118
Masi-Manimba, Dem. Rep. of the Congo, 115
Masindi, Uganda, 115
Masira (isl.), Oman, 59
Masjid-i-Sulaiman, Iran, 66
Mask (lake), Ire., 17
Masoala (pen.), Malag. Rep., 118
Mason, Mich., 250
Mason, Ohio, 284
Mason City, Iowa, 229
Masontown, Pa., 294
Massa, Italy, 34
Massa-Carrara (prov.), Italy, 34
Massachusetts (state), U.S., 249
Massakori, Chad, 111
Massapequa, N.Y., 276
Massawa, Eth., 111
Massena, N.Y., 276
Massénya, Chad, 111
Massey, N.Z., 101
Massillon, Ohio, 284
Massinga, Mozamb., 118
Masterton, N.Z., 101
Mastic Beach, N.Y., 276
Masuda, Japan, 81
Masury, Ohio, 284
Matabeleland (reg.), Rhod., 118
Matadi, Dem. Rep. of the Congo, 115
Matagalpa, Nic., 154
Matagorda (isl.), Tex., 302
Matam, Sen., 106
Matamoros, Mex., 150
Matane, Que., 172
Matanzas (prov.), Cuba, 158
Matanzas, Cuba, 158
Mata Palacio, Dom. Rep., 158
Matapan (Taínaron)(cape), Greece, 45
Matara, Ceylon, 68
Matarani, Peru, 128
Mataró, Spain, 33
Matautu (cap.), Wallis and Futuna, 87
Matawan, N. J., 273
Matehuala, Mex., 150
Matera (prov.), Italy, 34
Matera, Italy, 34
Mateur, Tun., 106
Mathis, Tex., 302
Mathura, India, 68
Mati, Phil. Is., 82
Matías de Gálvez, Guat., 154
Matías Romero, Mex., 150
Matlock, Eng., 13
Mato Grosso (state), Braz., 132
Mato Grosso (plat.), Braz., 132
Matopos, Rhod., 118
Matosinhos, Port., 33
Matra (mts.), Hung., 41
Matrah, Oman, 59
Matrei, Austria, 41
Matrûh, U.A.R., 111
Matsu (isl.), China, 77
Matsudo, Japan, 81
Matsue, Japan, 81
Matsumoto, Japan, 81
Matsusaka, Japan, 81
Matsuyama, Japan, 81
Mattagami (riv.), Ont., 175
Mattancheri, India, 68
Mattapan, Mass., 249
Mattawa, Ont., 177
Matteson, Ill., 222
Mattoon, Ill., 222
Matun, Afghan., 68
Maturín, Venez., 124
Mau, India, 68
Maubeuge, France, 28
Ma-ubin, Burma, 72
Maui (isl.), Hawaii, 218
Mauke (isl.), Cook Is., 87
Maule (prov.), Chile, 138
Maule (river), Chile, 138
Maullín, Chile, 138
Maumee, Ohio, 284
Maun, Botswana, 118
Mauna Kea (mt.), Hawaii, 218
Mauna Loa (mt.), Hawaii, 218
Maunawili, Hawaii, 218
Mauritania, 106
Mauritius, 118
Mauston, Wis., 317
Mauvoisin (dam), Switz., 39
Mawson, Ant., 5
Maxcanú, Mex., 150
May (cape), N. J., 273
Mayaguana (isl.), Bah. Is., 156
Mayagüez (dist.), P. Rico, 161
Mayagüez, P. Rico, 161
Mayari (river), Cuba, 158
Mayaro, Trin. and Tob., 161
Maybole, Scot., 15
Mayenne (dept.), France, 28
Mayenne (riv.), France, 28
Mayfield, Ky., 237
Mayfield Hts., Ohio, 284
Maykop, U.S.S.R., 52
Maymyo, Burma, 72
Maynard, Mass., 249
Mayo (county), Ire., 17
Mayo, Yukon, 187
Mayon (vol.), Phil. Is., 82
Mayor (cape), Spain, 33
Mayotte (isl.), Comoro Is., 118
May Pen, Jam., 158
Maysville, Ky., 237
Mayumba, Gabon, 115
Mayuram, India, 68
Mayville, N. Dak., 283
Mayville, Wis., 317
Maywood, Calif., 204
Maywood, Ill., 222
Maywood, N. J., 273
Mazabuka, Zambia, 115
Mazagan (El Jadida), Mor., 106
Mazanderan (prov.), Iran, 66
Mazar-i-Sharif, Afghan., 68
Mazaruni (riv.), Guyana, 131
Mazaruni-Potaro (dist.), Guyana, 131
Mazatenango, Guat., 154
Mazatlán, Mex., 150
Mbabane (cap.), Swaz., 118
M'Baiki, Centr. Afr. Rep., 115
Mbala, Zambia, 115
Mbale, Uganda, 115
Mbalmayo, Cameroon, 115
Mbandaka, Dem. Rep. of the Congo, 115
Mbarara, Uganda, 115
Mbeya (prov.), Tanz., 115
Mbeya, Tanz., 115
M'Bigou, Gabon, 115
M'Bour, Senegal, 106
M'Bout, Mauritania, 106
M'Bres, Centr. Afr. Rep., 115
Mbuji-Mayi, Dem. Rep. of the Congo, 115
Mbuyapey, Par., 144
McAdam, N.B., 170
McAdoo, Pa., 294
McAlester, Okla., 288
McAllen, Tex., 302
McCamey, Tex., 302
McComb, Miss., 256
McCook, Nebr., 264
McDonald (isls.), Austral., 3
McDonald, Ohio, 284
McDonald, Pa., 294
McFarland, Calif., 204
McFarlane (riv.), Sask., 181
McGehee, Ark., 203
McGill, Nev., 266
McGregor, Tex., 302
McHenry, Ill., 222
Mchinga, Tanz., 115
McKeesport, Pa., 294
McKees Rocks, Pa., 294
McKenzie, Tenn., 237
McKinley (mt.), Alaska, 196
McKinney, Tex., 302
McLeansboro, Ill., 222
McLennan, Alta., 182
M'Clintock (chan.), N.W.T., 187
McLoughlin House Nat'l Hist. Site, Oreg., 291
M'Clure (strait), N.W.T., 187
McMechen, W. Va., 313
McMinnville, Oreg., 291
McMinnville, Tenn., 237
McMurdo (sound), Ant., 5
McPherson, Kans., 232
McRae, Ga., 216
McSherrystown, Pa., 294
Mead (lake), U.S., 198
Meadow Lake, Sask., 181
Meadville, Pa., 294
Meaford, Ont., 177
Mealy (mts.), Newf., 166
Mearim (riv.), Braz., 132
Meath (county), Ire., 17
Meaux, France, 28
Mecatina (river), Que., 174
Mecca (cap.), Saudi Ar., 59
Mechanicsburg, Pa., 294
Mechanicville, N.Y., 276
Mechelen, Belg., 27
Méchéria, Alg., 106
Mecklenburg (reg.), E. Ger., 22
Mecklenburg (bay), Ger., 22
Meconta, Mozamb., 118
Mecsek (mts.), Hung., 41
Medan, Indon., 85
Médéa, Alg., 106
Medellín, Col., 126
Médenine, Tun., 106
Méderdra, Mauritania, 106
Medford, Mass., 249
Medford, Oreg., 291
Medford, Wis., 317
Medford Lakes, N. J., 273
Medgidia, Rum., 45
Media, Pa., 294
Mediaş, Rum., 45
Medical Lake, Wash., 310
Medicine Bow (range), U.S., 208, 319
Medicine Hat, Alta., 182
Medicine Lodge, Kans., 232
Medina, N.Y., 276
Medina, Ohio, 284
Medina, Saudi Ar., 59
Medina del Campo, Spain, 33
Medina-Sidonia, Spain, 33
Mediterranean (sea), 36
Medjerda (riv.), Africa, 106
Mednogorsk, U.S.S.R., 52
Médoc (reg.), France, 28
Medveditsa (riv.), U.S.S.R., 52
Medvezh'yegorsk, U.S.S.R., 52
Meerane, E. Ger., 22
Meerut, India, 68
Megalópolis, Greece, 45
Mégara, Greece, 45
Megiddo, Israel, 65
Megion, U.S.S.R., 48
Mehetia (isl.), Fr. Poly., 87
Mehran (riv.), Iran, 66
Mehsana, India, 68
Meighen (isl.), N.W.T., 187
Meiktila, Burma, 72
Meiners Oaks, Calif., 204
Meiningen, E. Ger., 22
Meiringen, Switz., 39
Meiron (mt.), Israel, 65
Meissen, E. Ger., 22
Mejillones, Chile, 138
Mekambo, Gabon, 115
Meknès, Mor., 106
Mekong (riv.), Asia, 72, 77
Mekong, Mouths of the (delta), S. Vietnam, 72
Melaka (state), Malaysia, 72
Melaka (Malacca), Malaysia, 72
Melanesia (reg.), Pacific, 87
Melbourne, Fla., 212
Melbourne (cap.), Vic., 97
Melchor Múzquiz, Mex., 150
Melekess, U.S.S.R., 52
Melfi, Chad, 111
Melfi, Italy, 34
Melfort, Sask., 181
Melilla, Spain, 33
Melipilla, Chile, 138
Melita, Man., 179
Melitopol', U.S.S.R., 52
Melo, Urug., 145
Melrhir, Shott (salt lake), Alg., 106
Melrose, Mass., 249
Melrose, Scot., 15
Melrose Park, Ill., 222
Melton Mowbray, Eng., 13
Melun, France, 28
Melville (bay), Greenl., 4
Melville (lake), Newf., 166
Melville (bay), N. Terr., 93
Melville (isl.), N. Terr., 93
Melville (isl.), N.W.T., 187
Melville (pen.), N.W.T., 187
Melville, Sask., 181
Melvin (lake), Ire., 17
Melvindale, Mich., 250
Memba, Mozamb., 118
Membij, Syria, 63
Memel (Klaipėda), U.S.S.R., 53
Memmingen, W. Ger., 22
Memphis, Fla., 212
Memphis, Tenn., 237
Memphis, Tex., 302
Memphis (ruins), U.A.R., 111
Memphremagog (lake), N. Amer., 172
Mena, Ark., 203
Menai (str.), Wales, 13
Ménaka, Mali, 106
Menasha, Wis., 317
Mendebo (prov.), Ethiopia, 111
Menderes (riv.), Turkey, 63
Mendi, Papua, 85
Mendip (hills), Eng., 13
Mendocino (cape), Calif., 204
Mendota, Ill., 222
Mendota Hts., Minn., 254
Mendoza (prov.), Arg., 143
Mendoza, Arg., 143
Mene Grande, Venez., 124
Menemen, Turkey, 63
Menen, Belg., 27
Menggala, Indon., 85
Menihek (lakes), Newf., 166
Menindee (lake), N.S.W., 97
Menlo Park, Calif., 204
Menlo Park, N. J., 273
Menominee, Mich., 250
Menomonee Falls, Wis., 317
Menomonie, Wis., 317
Menor, Mar (lag.), Spain, 33
Menorca (Minorca) (isl.), Spain, 33
Mentawai (isls.), Indon., 85
Menton, France, 28
Mentone, Calif., 204
Mentor, Ohio, 284
Menzel Bourguiba, Tun., 106
Menzel-Temime, Tun., 106
Meoquí, Mex., 150
Mequon, Wis., 317
Merabéllou (gulf), Greece, 45
Merak, Indon., 85
Merano, Italy, 34
Merauke, Indon., 85
Merced, Calif., 204
Mercedario (mt.), Arg., 143
Mercedes, Arg., 143
Mercedes, Tex., 302
Mercedes, Urug., 145
Mercer, Pa., 294
Mercer I., Wash., 310
Mercerville, N. J., 273
Merchantville, N. J., 273
Mercury, Nev., 266
Mercury (bay), N.Z., 101
Mergui, Burma, 72
Mergui (arch.), Burma, 72
Meriç (riv.), Turkey, 63
Mérida, Mex., 150
Mérida, Spain, 33
Mérida (state), Venez., 124
Mérida, Venez., 124
Meriden, Conn., 210
Meridian, Miss., 256
Merino Vill., Mass., 249
Merionethshire (county), Wales, 13
Merion Sta., Pa., 294
Merir (isl.), Pac. Is., 87
Meriwether Unit, Natchez Trace Pkwy., Tenn., 237
Merj 'Uyun, Leb., 63
Merka, Somalia, 115
Merksem, Belg., 27
Merlo, Arg., 143
Meroe (ruins), Sudan, 111
Merowe, Sudan, 111
Merredin, W. Austral., 92
Merriam, Kans., 232
Merrick, N.Y., 276
Merrill, Wis., 317
Merrillville, Ind., 227
Merritt, Br. Col., 184
Merritt I., Fla., 212
Mersch, Lux., 27
Mersea (isl.), Eng., 13
Merseburg, E. Ger., 22
Mersey (riv.), Eng., 10
Mersey (riv.), Tas., 99
Mersin, Turkey, 63
Merthyr Tydfil, Wales, 13
Merton, Eng., 10
Meru (mt.), Tanz., 115
Merzifon, Turkey, 63
Mesa, Ariz., 198
Mesagne, Italy, 34
Mesará (gulf), Greece, 45
Mesa Verde Nat'l Park, Colo., 208
Meshed, Iran, 66
Mesilla Park, N. Mex., 274
Mesolóngion, Greece, 45
Mesopotamia (reg.), Iraq, 66
Mesquite, Tex., 302
Messina (prov.), Italy, 34
Messina, Italy, 34
Messina (strait), Italy, 34
Messina, S. Afr., 118
Messíni, Greece, 45
Mesta (riv.), Bulg., 45
Mestre, Italy, 34
Meta (dept.), Col., 126
Meta (riv.), S. Amer., 126
Metairie, La., 238
Metán, Arg., 143
Metapán, El Sal., 154
Metauro (riv.), Italy, 34
Metepec, Mex., 150
Methuen, Mass., 249
Metropolis, Ill., 222
Metuchen, N. J., 273
Metz, France, 28
Meudon, France, 28
Meurthe-et-Moselle (dept.), France, 28
Meuse (riv.), Europe, 28
Meuse (dept.), France, 28
Mexia, Tex., 302
Mexiana (isl.), Braz., 132
Mexicali, Mex., 150
Mexico, 150
Mexico, Maine, 242
Mexico (state), Mex., 150
Mexico, Mo., 261
Mexico (gulf), N. Amer., 146
Mexico City (cap.), Mex., 150
Meyadin, Syria, 63
Meyersdale, Pa., 294
Mezen' (bay), U.S.S.R., 52
Mezen' (riv.), U.S.S.R., 52
Mezőtúr, Hung., 41
Mezquital (riv.), Mex., 150
Mhow, India, 68
Miahuatlán, Mex., 150
Miami, Ariz., 198
Miami, Fla., 212
Miami (riv.), Ohio, 284
Miami, Okla., 288
Miami Beach, Fla., 212
Miamisburg, Ohio, 284
Miami Shores, Fla., 212
Miami Sprs., Fla., 212
Mianeh, Iran, 66
Mianwali, Pak., 68
Michigan (state), U.S., 250
Michigan (lake), U.S., 188
Michigan Ctr., Mich., 250
Michigan City, Ind., 227
Michikamau (lake), Newf., 166
Michipicoten (isl.), Ont., 175
Michoacán (state), Mex., 150
Michurinsk, U.S.S.R., 52
Micoud, St. Lucia, 161
Micronesia (reg.), Pacific, 87
Middelburg, Neth., 27
Middelburg, S. Africa, 118
Middelfart, Den., 21
Middle Atlas (ranges), Mor., 160
Middleboro, Mass., 249
Middleburg Hts., Ohio, 284
Middle Gobi (prov.), Mong., 77
Middleport, Ohio, 284
Middle River, Md., 245
Middlesboro, Ky., 237
Middlesex, N. J., 273
Middleton, Eng., 10
Middleton, N.S., 169
Middleton, Wis., 317
Middletown, Conn., 210
Middletown, Ky., 237
Middletown, N. J., 273
Middletown, N.Y., 276
Middletown, Ohio, 284
Middletown, Pa., 294
Middletown, R.I., 249
Midfield, Ala., 194
Midian (dist.), Saudi Ar., 59
Midland, Mich., 250
Midland, Ont., 177
Midland, Pa., 294
Midland, Tex., 302
Midland, W. Austral., 92
Midland Park, N. J., 273
Midleton, Ire., 17
Midlothian, Ill., 222
Midlothian (county), Scot., 15
Midnapore, India, 68
Midvale, Utah, 304
Midway (isls.), Pacific, 87
Midway City, Calif., 204
Midway Park, N.C., 281
Midwest City, Okla., 288
Mid-Western (state), Nigeria, 106
Mie (pref.), Japan, 81
Mielec, Poland, 45
Miercurea Ciuc, Rum., 45
Mieres, Spain, 33
Miesso, Eth., 111
Miguel Azua, Mex., 150
Mihara, Japan, 81
Mijirtein (prov.), Somalia, 115
Mikhaylovgrad, Bulg., 45
Mikhaylovka, U.S.S.R., 52
Mikínai, Greece, 45
Mikkeli (dept.), Fin., 18
Mikkeli, Fin., 18
Míkonos (isl.), Greece, 45
Milagro, Ecua., 128
Milan, Ill., 222
Milan (prov.), Italy, 34
Milan, Italy, 34
Milan, Mich., 250
Milan, N. Mex., 274
Milan, Tenn., 237
Milâs, Turkey, 63
Milazzo, Italy, 34
Milbank, S. Dak., 298
Mildura, Vic., 97
Miles City, Mont., 262
Milford, Conn., 210
Milford, Del., 245
Milford, Mass., 249
Milford, Mich., 250
Milford, N.H., 268
Milford (sound), N.Z., 101
Milford, Ohio, 284
Milford Haven, Wales, 13
Mili (atoll), Pac. Is., 87
Milk (riv.), N. Amer., 182
Milk, Wadi el (dry riv.), Sudan, 111
Millbrae, Calif., 204
Millbury, Mass., 249
Millburn, N. J., 273
Milledgeville, Ga., 216
Mille Lacs (lake), Minn., 254
Mille Lacs (lake), Ont., 175
Miller, Ga., 216
Miller, S. Dak., 298
Millerovo, U.S.S.R., 52
Millersburg, Ohio, 284
Millersburg, Pa., 294
Millersville, Pa., 294
Millicent, S. Austral., 94
Millington, Tenn., 237
Millinocket, Maine, 242
Millmerran, Queensland, 95
Millport, Scot., 15
Mills, Wyo., 319
Milltown, N. B., 170
Milltown, N. J., 273
Millvale, Pa., 294
Mill Valley, Calif., 204
Millville, N. J., 273
Milne (bay), Papua, 85
Milngavie, Scot., 15
Milos (isl.), Greece, 45
Milpitas, Calif., 204
Milton, Fla., 212
Milton, Mass., 249
Milton, N.Z., 101
Milton, N.S., 169
Milton, Ont., 177
Milton, Pa., 294
Milton-Freewater, Oreg., 291
Milwaukee, Wis., 317
Milwaukie, Oreg., 291
Mina al Ahmadi, Kuwait, 59
Minami Iwo (isl.), Japan, 81
Minas (mts.), Guat., 154
Minas (basin), N.S., 169
Minas, Urug., 145
Mina Sa'ud, Kuwait, 59
Minas Gerais (state), Braz., 132
Minatitlán, Mex., 150
Mincio (riv.), Italy, 34
Mindanao (isl.), Phil. Is., 82
Mindanao (sea), Phil. Is., 82
Mindelo, Cape Verde Is., 106
Minden, La., 238
Minden, W. Ger., 22
Mindoro (isl.), Phil. Is., 82
Mindoro (strait), Phil. Is., 82
Mindouli, Rep. of Congo, 115
Mineola, N.Y., 276
Mineola, Tex., 302
Mineral del Monte, Mex., 150
Mineral'nye Vody, U.S.S.R., 52
Mineral Wells, Tex., 302
Minersville, Pa., 294
Minerva, Ohio, 284
Mingan (Jacques-Cartier) (passage), Que., 174
Mingechaur, U.S.S.R., 52
Minginish (dist.), Scot., 15
Mingo Jct., Ohio, 284
Minho (prov.), Port., 33
Minho (riv.), Port., 33
Minhsien, China, 77
Minicoy (isl.), India, 68

Min Kiang (riv.), China, 77
Minna, Nigeria, 106
Minneapolis, Minn., 254
Minnedosa, Man., 179
Minnesota (state), U.S., 254
Minnesota (riv.), Minn., 254
Minnetonka, Minn., 254
Minnetonka (lake), Minn., 254
Miño (riv.), Spain, 33
Minorca (isl.), Spain, 33
Minot, N. Dak., 283
Min Shan (range), China, 77
Minsk, U.S.S.R., 52
Minto, N.B., 170
Minto (lake), Que., 174
Minturno, Italy, 34
Minūf, U.A.R., 111
Minusinsk, U.S.S.R., 48
Minya Konka (mt.), China, 77
Mira (riv.), Port., 33
Mirador Nacional (mt.), Urug., 145
Miraflores, Peru, 128
Miragoâne, Haiti, 158
Miraj, India, 68
Mira Loma, Calif., 204
Miramar, Fla., 212
Miramichi (bay), N.B., 170
Miranda (riv.), Braz., 132
Miranda (state), Venez., 124
Miranda de Ebro, Spain, 33
Mira Por Vos (cays), Bah. Is., 156
Mirassol, Braz., 135
Mirebalais, Haiti, 158
Mirgorod, U.S.S.R., 52
Miri (hills), India, 68
Miri, Malaysia, 85
Mirim (lag.), S. Amer., 132
Mirnyy, Ant., 5
Mirnyy, U.S.S.R., 48
Mirpur Khas, Pak., 68
Mirtóön (sea), Greece, 45
Mirzapur, India, 68
Misamis Occidental (prov.), Phil. Is., 82
Misamis Oriental (prov.), Phil. Is., 82
Misantla, Mex., 150
Miscou (isl.), N. B., 170
Misha'ab, Ras (cape), Saudi Ar., 59
Mishawaka, Ind., 227
Mishmi (hills), India, 68
Misima (isl.), Papua, 85
Misiones (prov.), Arg., 143
Misiones (dept.), Par., 144
Miskito (cays), Nic., 154
Miskolc, Hung., 41
Misool (isl.), Indon., 85
Misquah (hills), Minn., 254
Missinaibi (riv.), Ont., 175
Mission, Kans., 232
Mission, Tex., 302
Mission City, Br. Col., 184
Mission Viejo, Calif., 204
Mississauga, Ont., 177
Mississippi (delta), La., 238
Mississippi (state), U.S., 256
Mississippi (riv.), U.S., 188
Missolonghi (Mesolóngion), Greece, 45
Missoula, Mont., 262
Missouri (state), U.S., 261
Missouri (riv.), U.S., 188
Missouri Valley, Iowa, 229
Mistassibi (riv.), Que., 174
Mistassini, Que., 174
Mistassini (lake), Que., 174
Mistastin (lake), Newf., 166
Místek-Frýdek, Czech., 41
Misti, El (mt.), Peru, 128
Misurata (prov.), Libya, 111
Misurata, Libya, 111
Mitaka, Japan, 81
Mitcham, S. Austral., 94
Mitchell, Ind., 227
Mitchell (mt.), N.C., 281
Mitchell, Queensland, 95
Mitchell, S. Dak., 298
Mitchelstown, Ire., 17
Mitchelton, Queensland, 95
Mitiaro (isl.), Cook Is., 87
Mitilíni, Greece, 45
Mitla (ruins), Mex., 150
Mito, Japan, 81
Mitsamiouli, Comoro Is., 118
Mittagong, N.S.W., 97
Mittenwald, W. Ger., 22
Mittersill, Austria, 41
Mitú, Col., 126
Mitwaba, Dem. Rep. of the Congo, 115
Mitzic, Gabon, 115
Miura (pen.), Japan, 81
Miyagi (pref.), Japan, 81
Miyako, Japan, 81
Miyako (isl.), Ryukyu Is., 81
Miyako (isls.), Ryukyu Is., 81
Miyakonojo, Japan, 81
Miyanduab, Iran, 66
Miyazaki (pref.), Japan, 81
Miyazaki, Japan, 81
Mizda, Libya, 111
Mizen (head), Ire., 17
Mjölby, Sweden, 18
Mladá Boleslav, Czech., 41
Mladenovac, Yugo., 45
Mljet (isl.), Yugo., 45
Mo, Norway, 18
Moab, Utah, 304
Moamba, Mozamb., 118
Moanda, Gabon, 115
Moberly, Mo., 261
Mobile, Ala., 194
Mobridge, S. Dak., 298
Moca, Dom. Rep., 158
Moçambique (dist.), Mozamb., 118
Moçambique, Mozamb., 118
Moçâmedes (dist.), Angola, 115
Moçâmedes, Angola, 115
Mocha (isl.), Chile, 138
Mocha, Yemen Arab Rep., 59
Moc Hoa, S. Vietnam, 72
Mochudi, Botswana, 118
Mocímboa da Praia, Mozamb., 118
Mocoa, Col., 126
Mococa, Braz., 135
Moctezuma, Mex., 150
Mocuba, Mozamb., 118
Modderfontein, S. Afr., 118
Modena (prov.), Italy, 34
Modena, Italy, 34
Modesto, Calif., 204
Modica, Italy, 34
Modjokerto, Indon., 85
Mödling, Austria, 41
Moe, Vic., 97
Moen (isl.), Pac. Is., 87
Moerai, Fr. Poly., 87
Moësa (riv.), Switz., 39
Moffat, Scot., 15
Mogadishu (cap.), Somalia, 115
Mogador (Essaouira), Mor., 106
Mogadore, Ohio, 284
Mogi das Cruzes, Braz., 135
Mogilev, U.S.S.R., 52
Mogilev-Podol'skiy, U.S.S.R., 52
Mogi Mirim, Braz., 135
Mohács, Hung., 41
Mohaleshoek, Lesotho, 118
Mohammadia, Alg., 106
Mohammedia, Mor., 106
Mohawk, N.Y., 276
Mohéli (isl.), Comoro Is., 118
Mohenjo Daro (ruins), Pak., 68
Moidart (dist.), Scot., 15
Moineşti, Rum., 45
Moisie, Que., 174
Moisie (riv.), Que., 174
Moissala, Chad, 111
Mojave (des.), Calif., 204
Mokapu, Hawaii, 218
Mokil (atoll), Pac. Is., 87
Moknine, Tun., 106
Mokp'o, S. Korea, 81
Moksha (riv.), U.S.S.R., 52
Mol, Belg., 27
Mola di Bari, Italy, 34
Moldau (Vltava)(riv.), Czech., 41
Moldavian S.S.R., U.S.S.R., 52
Molde, Norway, 18
Moldoveanul (mt.), Rum., 45
Molenbeek-Saint-Jean, Belg., 27
Molepolole, Botswana, 118
Molfetta, Italy, 34
Molina, Chile, 138
Moline, Ill., 222
Molise (reg.), Italy, 34
Mollendo, Peru, 128
Mölndal, Sweden, 18
Molodechno, U.S.S.R., 52
Molokai (isl.), Hawaii, 218
Molopo (riv.), Africa, 118
Molotov (Perm'), U.S.S.R., 52
Molotovsk (Severodvinsk), U.S.S.R., 52
Moloundou, Cameroon, 115
Molucca (sea), Indon., 85
Moluccas (isls.), Indon., 85
Moma, Mozamb., 118
Mombasa, Kenya, 115
Momence, Ill., 222
Momostenango, Guat., 154
Mompós, Col., 126
Mon (riv.), Burma, 72
Møn (isl.), Den., 21
Mona (isl.), P. Rico, 156
Mona (passage), W. Indies, 156
Monaca, Pa., 294
Monaco, 28
Monagas (state), Venez., 124
Monaghan (county), Ire., 17
Monaghan, Ire., 17
Monahans, Tex., 302
Monastir, Tun., 106
Moncayo (mts.), Spain, 33
Monchegorsk, U.S.S.R., 52
Mönchengladbach, W. Ger., 22
Monchique (mts.), Port., 33
Monclova, Mex., 150
Moncton, N. B., 170
Mondego (riv.), Port., 33
Mondovì Breo, Italy, 34
Monegros (mts.), Spain, 33
Monessen, Pa., 294
Monett, Mo., 261
Monfalcone, Italy, 34
Monforte, Spain, 33
Mongalla, Sudan, 111
Monghyr, India, 68
Mongo, Chad, 111
Mongolia, 77
Mongu, Zambia, 115
Monifieth, Scot., 15
Monkey (pt.), Nic., 154
Monkey River, Br. Hond., 154
Monkoto, Dem. Rep. of the Congo, 115
Monmouth, Ill., 222
Monmouth, Wales, 13
Monmouthshire (county), Wales, 13
Mono (riv.), Africa, 106
Monona, Wis., 317
Monongahela, Pa., 294
Monopoli, Italy, 34
Monreale, Italy, 34
Monroe, Conn., 210
Monroe, Ga., 216
Monroe, La., 238
Monroe, Mich., 250
Monroe, N.J., 273
Monroe, N.Y., 276
Monroe, N.C., 281
Monroe, Wis., 317
Monroeville, Ala., 194
Monroeville, Pa., 294
Monrovia, Calif., 204
Monrovia (cap.), Liberia, 106
Mons, Belg., 27
Monsanto (hill), Port., 33
Monsefú, Peru, 128
Mönsterås, Sweden, 18
Montague, Mass., 249
Montague (isl.), Mex., 150
Montague, P.E.I., 169
Montague (sound), W. Austral., 92
Montana (state), U.S., 262
Montaña, La (reg.), Peru, 128
Montargil, Port., 33
Montargis, France, 28
Montauban, France, 28
Montbéliard, France, 28
Montcalm (lake), China, 77
Mont Cenis (tunnel), Europe, 28
Montclair, Calif., 204
Montclair, N. J., 273
Mont-de-Marsan, France, 28
Mont-Doré, France, 28
Montebello, Calif., 204
Monte Bello (isls.), W. Austral., 92
Monte Carlo, Monaco, 28
Monte Caseros, Arg., 143
Montecito, Calif., 204
Montecristi (prov.), Dom. Rep., 158
Montecristi, Dom. Rep., 158
Montecristo (isl.), Italy, 34
Montego Bay, Jam., 158
Montemorelos, Mex., 150
Montemor-o-Novo, Port., 33
Montenegro, Braz., 132
Montenegro (rep.), Yugo., 45
Monterey, Calif., 204
Monterey Park, Calif., 204
Montería, Col., 126
Montero, Bol., 136
Monteros, Arg., 143
Monterrey, Mex., 150
Montesano, Wash., 310
Monte Sant'Angelo, Italy, 34
Montes Claros, Braz., 132
Montevallo, Ala., 194
Montevideo, Minn., 254
Montevideo (dept.), Urug., 145
Montevideo (cap.), Urug., 145
Monte Vista, Colo., 208
Montezuma, Ga., 216
Montezuma Castle Nat'l Mon., Ariz., 198
Montfort, France, 28
Montgomery (cap.), Ala., 194
Montgomery, Ohio, 284
Montgomery, Pak., 68
Montgomery, Wales, 13
Montgomery, W. Va., 313
Montgomeryshire (county), Wales, 13
Monticello, Ark., 203
Monticello, Fla., 212
Monticello, Ill., 222
Monticello, Ind., 227
Monticello, Iowa, 229
Monticello, Ky., 237
Monticello, N.Y., 276
Monticello, Utah, 304
Montignies-sur-Sambre, Belg., 27
Montigny, France, 28
Montijo (gulf), Pan., 154
Montijo, Port., 33
Montijo, Spain, 33
Montilla, Spain, 33
Mont-Joli, Que., 172
Mont-Laurier, Que., 172
Montluçon, France, 28
Montmagny, Que., 172
Montmorency, Que., 172
Monto, Queensland, 95
Montoro, Spain, 33
Montoursville, Pa., 294
Montpelier, Idaho, 220
Montpelier, Ohio, 284
Montpelier (cap.), Vt., 268
Montpellier, France, 28
Montréal, Que., 172
Montreal (lake), Sask., 181
Montreuil, France, 28
Montreux, Switz., 39
Montrose, Calif., 204
Montrose, Colo., 208
Montrose, Scot., 15
Montrouge, France, 28
Mont-Royal, Que., 172
Mont-Saint-Hilaire, Que., 172
Mont-Saint-Michel, France, 28
Montserrat, 156
Montserrat (mt.), Spain, 33
Mont-Tremblant Prov. Park, Que., 172
Montvale, N. J., 273
Monument (valley), Utah, 304
Monywa, Burma, 72
Monza, Italy, 34
Monze, Zambia, 115
Moon (lake), Calif., 204
Moonachie, N. J., 273
Moonta, S. Austral., 94
Moora, W. Austral., 92
Moorabbin, Vic., 97
Moorea (isl.), Fr. Poly., 87
Moores Creek Nat'l Mil. Park, N.C., 281
Moorestown, N. J., 273
Mooresville, Ind., 227
Mooresville, N.C., 281
Moorhead, Minn., 254
Moorooka, Queensland, 95
Mooroopna, Vic., 97
Moorpark, Calif., 204
Moose Factory, Ont., 177
Moosehead (lake), Maine, 242
Moose Jaw, Sask., 181
Moose Mountain Prov. Park, Sask., 181
Moosic, Pa., 294
Moosomin, Sask., 181
Moosonee, Ont., 177
Moosup, Conn., 210
Mopti, Mali, 106
Moquegua (prov.), Peru, 128
Moquegua, Peru, 128
Mora, Spain, 33
Mora, Sweden, 18
Moradabad, India, 68
Moramanga, Malag. Rep., 118
Morane (isl.), Fr. Poly., 87
Morant Bay, Jam., 158
Morar (dist.), Scot., 15
Morat (lake), Switz., 39
Moratuwa, Ceylon, 68
Morava (riv.), Czech., 41
Morava (riv.), Yugo., 45
Moravia (reg.), Czech., 41
Morawhanna, Guyana, 131
Moray (county), Scot., 15
Moray (firth), Scot., 15
Morazán, Hond., 154
Morbihan (dept.), France, 28
Morden, Man., 179
Mordialloc, Vic., 97
Mordvinian A.S.S.R., U.S.S.R., 52
Morecambe and Heysham, Eng., 13
Moree, N.S.W., 97
Morehead, Ky., 237
Morehead City, N.C., 281
Morelia, Mex., 150
Morelos (state), Mex., 150
Morena (mts.), Spain, 33
Morenci, Ariz., 198
Møre og Romsdal (county), Norway, 18
Moresby (isl.), Br. Col., 184
Moreton (isl.), Queensland, 95
Morgan City, La., 238
Morganfield, Ky., 237
Morgan Hill, Calif., 204
Morganton, N.C., 281
Morgantown, W. Va., 313
Morges, Switz., 39
Moriguchi, Japan, 81
Morioka, Japan, 81
Morlaix, France, 28
Morley, Eng., 13
Morne-à-l'Eau, Guad., 161
Morne-Rouge, Mart., 161
Mornington (isl.), Queensland, 95
Mornington, Vic., 97
Moro (gulf), Phil. Is., 82
Morobe, Terr. N.G., 85
Morocco, 106
Morococha, Peru, 128
Morogoro (prov.), Tanz., 115
Morogoro, Tanz., 115
Moroleón, Mex., 150
Morombe, Malag. Rep., 118
Morón, Cuba, 158
Morón, Venez., 124
Morona (riv.), S. Amer., 128
Morona-Santiago (prov.), Ecua., 128
Morondava, Malag. Rep., 118
Morón de la Frontera, Spain, 33
Moroni (cap.), Comoro Is., 118
Morotai (isl.), Indon., 85
Moroto, Uganda, 115
Morozovsk, U.S.S.R., 52
Morpeth, Eng., 13
Morphou, Cyprus, 63
Morrilton, Ark., 203
Morris, Ill., 222
Morris, Man., 179
Morris, Minn., 254
Morris Jesup (cape), Greenl., 4
Morrison, Ill., 222
Morris Plains, N. J., 273
Morristown, N. J., 273
Morristown, Tenn., 237
Morristown Nat'l Hist. Park, N. J., 273
Morrisville, Pa., 294
Morro Bay, Calif., 204
Mors (isl.), Den., 21
Morshansk, U.S.S.R., 52
Morteros, Arg., 143
Morton, Ill., 222
Morton, Tex., 302
Morton Grove, Ill., 222
Mortsel, Belg., 27
Morven (dist.), Scot., 15
Morvi, India, 68
Morwell, Vic., 97
Moscavide, Port., 33
Moscow, Idaho, 220
Moscow (Moskva)(cap.), U.S.S.R., 52
Mosel (riv.), Europe, 22, 27
Moselle (dept.), France, 28
Moselle (riv.), France, 28
Moses Lake, Wash., 310
Moshi, Tanz., 115
Mosi-Ao-Tunya (Victoria) (falls), Africa, 115
Moskenesøy (isl.), Norway, 18
Moskva (riv.), U.S.S.R., 52
Mosman, N.S.W., 97
Mosonmagyaróvár, Hung., 41
Mosquito (gulf), Pan., 154
Mosquito Coast (reg.), Cent. Amer., 154
Moss, Norway, 18
Mossaka, Rep. of Congo, 115
Mossel Bay, S. Africa, 118
Mossendjo, Rep. of Congo, 115
Mossman, Queensland, 95
Mossoró, Braz., 132
Moss Pt., Miss., 256
Moss Vale, N.S.W., 97
Most, Czech., 41
Mostaganem, Alg., 106
Mostar, Yugo., 45
Mosul (prov.), Iraq, 66
Mosul, Iraq, 66
Motagua (riv.), Guat., 154
Motala, Sweden, 18
Motherwell and Wishaw, Scot., 15
Motril, Spain, 33
Motueka, N.Z., 101
Motul, Mex., 150
Mouchoir (passage), Turks and Caicos Is., 156
Mouila, Gabon, 115
Moulins, France, 28
Moulmein, Burma, 72
Moulouya (riv.), Mor., 106
Moultrie, Ga., 216
Mound, Minn., 254
Mound City Group Nat'l Mon., Ohio, 284
Moundou, Chad, 111
Mounds View, Minn., 254
Moundsville, W. Va., 313
Moung, Cambodia, 72
Mount (cape), Liberia, 106
Mountain (riv.), N.W.T., 187
Mountain (prov.), Phil. Is., 82
Mountain Ash, Wales, 13
Mountain Brook, Ala., 194
Mountain Grove, Mo., 261
Mountain Home, Idaho, 220
Mountain Lakes, N. J., 273
Mountainside, N. J., 273
Mountain View, Calif., 204
Mountain View, N. J., 273
Mountain View, Wyo., 319
Mountain Zebra Nat'l Park, S. Africa, 118
Mount Airy, N.C., 281
Mount Apo Nat'l Park, Phil. Is., 82
Mount Assiniboine Prov. Park, Br. Col., 184
Mount Barker, S. Austral., 94
Mount Barker, W. Austral., 92
Mount Carmel, Ill., 222
Mount Carmel, Pa., 294
Mount Clemens, Mich., 250
Mount Darwin, Rhod., 118
Mount Dora, Fla., 212
Mount Edgecumbe, Alaska, 196
Mount Ephraim, N. J., 273
Mount Forest, Ont., 177
Mount Gambier, S. Austral., 94
Mount Gay, W. Va., 313
Mount Gilead, Ohio, 284
Mount Healthy, Ohio, 284
Mount Holly, N. J., 273
Mount Holly, N. C., 281
Mount Hope, Mass., 249
Mount Isa, Queensland, 95
Mount Joy, Pa., 294
Mount Kisco, N.Y., 276
Mountlake Terr., Wash., 310
Mount Lebanon, Pa., 294
Mount Maunganui, N.Z., 101
Mount McKinley Nat'l Park, Alaska, 196
Mountmellick, Ire., 17
Mount Morgan, Queensland, 95
Mount Morris, Ill., 222
Mount Morris, Mich., 250
Mount Morris, N.Y., 276
Mount Olive, N.C., 281
Mount Oliver, Pa., 294
Mount Pearl, Newf., 166
Mount Penn, Pa., 294
Mount Pleasant, Iowa, 229
Mount Pleasant, Mich., 250
Mount Pleasant, Pa., 294
Mount Pleasant, S.C., 296
Mount Pleasant, Tenn., 237
Mount Pleasant, Tex., 302
Mount Prospect, Ill., 222
Mount Rainier, Md., 245
Mount Rainier Nat'l Park, Wash., 310
Mount Revelstoke Nat'l Park, Br. Col., 184
Mount Robson Prov. Park, Br. Col., 184
Mount Roskill, N.Z., 101
Mount Rushmore Nat'l Mem., S. Dak., 294
Mounts (bay), Eng., 13
Mount Sterling, Ky., 237
Mount Union, Pa., 294
Mount Vernon, Ill., 222
Mount Vernon, Ind., 227
Mount Vernon, Iowa, 229
Mount Vernon, N.Y., 276
Mount Vernon, Ohio, 284
Mount Vernon, Wash., 310
Mount Wellington, N.Z., 101
Moura, Port., 33
Mourne (mts.), N. Ire., 17
Mouscron, Belg., 27
Moussoro, Chad, 111
Moutier, Switz., 39
Mouydir (mts.), Alg., 106
Mowming, China, 77
Moxico (dist.), Angola, 115
Moyale, Kenya, 115
Moyamba, S. Leone, 106
Moyo, Uganda, 115
Moyobamba, Peru, 128
Mozambique, 118
Mozambique (chan.), Africa, 118
Mozhaysk, U.S.S.R., 52
Mozhga, U.S.S.R., 52
Mozyr', U.S.S.R., 52
Mpanda, Tanz., 115
Mpraeso, Ghana, 106
Msaken, Tun., 106
M'Sila, Alg., 106
Msta (riv.), U.S.S.R., 52
Mtwara (prov.), Tanz., 115
Mtwara-Mikindani, Tanz., 115
Mubarraz, Saudi Ar., 59
Mubende, Uganda, 115
Mucurapo, Trin. and Tob., 161
Mudgee, N.S.W., 97
Mudon, Burma, 72
Mudugh (prov.), Somalia, 115
Mufulira, Zambia, 115
Muğla (prov.), Turkey, 63
Muğla, Turkey, 63
Muglad, Sudan, 111
Muhammad, Ras (cape), U.A.R., 111
Muharraq, Bahrein, 59
Mühlhausen, E. Ger., 22
Mühlviertel (reg.), Austria, 41
Mui Bai Bung (pt.), S. Vietnam, 72
Mui Dinh (cape), S. Vienam, 72
Muinebeag, Ire., 17
Muir Woods Nat'l Mon., Calif., 204
Mukachevo, U.S.S.R., 52
Mukalla, P.D.R. Yemen, 59
Mukdahan, Thai., 72
Mukden, China, 77
Mukur, Afghan., 68
Mulange (mt.), Malawi, 115
Mulatas (arch.), Pan., 154
Mulayit Taung (mt.), Thai., 72
Mulberry, Fla., 212
Mulchén, Chile, 138
Mulde (riv.), E. Ger., 22
Muleshoe, Tex., 302
Mulgrave, N.S., 169
Mulhacén (mt.), Spain, 33
Mülheim an der Ruhr, W. Ger., 22
Mulhouse, France, 28
Muli (str.), Indon., 85
Mull (isl.), Scot., 15
Mullens, W. Va., 313
Müller (mts.), Indon., 85
Mullingar, Ire., 17
Mullins, S.C., 296
Multan, Pak., 68
Mulund, India, 68
Mulvane, Kans., 232
Mumbwa, Zambia, 115
Mun, Mae Nam (riv.), Thai., 72
Muna (isl.), Indon., 85
München (Munich), W. Ger., 22
Muncie, Ind., 227
Muncy, Pa., 294
Mundelein, Ill., 222
Münden, W. Ger., 22
Mungla Anchorage, Pak., 68
Munhall, Pa., 294
Munich, W. Ger., 22
Munising, Mich., 250
Munku-Sardyk (mt.), Mong., 77
Münsingen, Switz., 39
Munster, Ind., 227
Munster (prov.), Ire., 17
Münster, W. Ger., 22
Muntok, Indon., 85
Muo (lake), Fin., 18
Muong Beng, Laos, 72
Muong Hai, Laos, 72
Muong Lan, Laos, 72
Muong Sai, Laos, 72
Muong Sing, Laos, 72
Muong Song Khone, Laos, 72
Muonio (riv.), Europe, 18
Muota (riv.), Switz., 39
Muqdadiyah, Iraq, 66
Mur (Mura)(riv.), Europe, 41
Murallón (mt.), S. Amer., 138
Murat (riv.), Turkey, 63
Murbat, Oman, 59
Murchison (range), N. Terr., 93
Murchison (falls), Uganda, 115
Murchison (riv.), W. Austral., 92
Murcia (reg.), Spain, 33
Murcia (prov.), Spain, 33
Murcia, Spain, 33
Muren, Mong., 77
Mureş (riv.), Rum., 45
Murfreesboro, N.C., 281
Murfreesboro, Tenn., 237
Murg (riv.), Switz., 39
Murgab (riv.), U.S.S.R., 48
Murgon, Queensland, 95
Muri, Switz., 39
Muriaé, Braz., 135
Müritzsee (lake), E. Ger., 22
Murmansk, U.S.S.R., 52
Murom, U.S.S.R., 52
Muroran, Japan, 81
Murphysboro, Ill., 222
Murray (riv.), Austral., 94, 97
Murray, Ky., 237
Murray, Utah, 304
Murray Bridge, S. Austral., 94
Murrumbidgee (riv.), N.S.W., 97
Murrumburrah, N.S.W., 97
Murrysville, Pa., 294
Murupara, N.Z., 101
Mururoa (isl.), Fr. Poly., 87
Murwara, India, 68
Murwillumbah, N.S.W., 97
Murzuk, Libya, 111
Mürzzuschlag, Austria, 41
Muş (prov.), Turkey, 63
Muş, Turkey, 63
Musala (mt.), Bulg., 45
Musan, N. Korea, 81
Musandam, Ras (cape), Oman, 59
Musashino, Japan, 81
Muscat (cap.), Oman, 59
Muscatine, Iowa, 229
Muscle Shoals, Ala., 194
Musgrave (ranges), S. Austral., 94
Mushandike Nat'l Park, Rhod., 118
Mushie, Dem. Rep. of the Congo, 115
Mushin, Nigeria, 106
Musi (riv.), Indon., 85
Muskego, Wis., 317
Muskegon, Mich., 250
Muskegon Hts., Mich., 250
Muskogee, Okla., 288
Muskoka (lake), Ont., 177
Musoma, Tanz., 115
Musquodoboit (riv.), N.S., 169
Musselburgh, Scot., 15
Musselshell (riv.), Mont., 262
Mustafa Kemalpaşa, Turkey, 63
Mustang, Nepal, 68
Muswellbrook, N.S.W., 97
Mutankiang, China, 77
Mutsamudu, Comoro Is., 118
Muttenz, Switz., 39
Muynak, U.S.S.R., 48
Muzaffarabad, India, 68
Muzaffarnagar, India, 68
Muzaffarpur, India, 68
Muzambinho, Braz., 135
Muztagh (mt.), China, 77
Muztagh Ata (mt.), China, 77
Mwadui, Tanz., 115
Mwanza (prov.), Tanz., 115
Mwanza, Tanz., 115
Mwaya, Tanz., 115
Mweka, Dem. Rep. of the Congo, 115
Mwene Ditu, Dem. Rep. of the Congo, 115
Mwenga, Dem. Rep. of the Congo, 115
Mweru (lake), Africa, 115
Mwinilunga, Zambia, 115
Myanaung, Burma, 72
Myaungmya, Burma, 72
Myerstown, Pa., 294
Myingyan, Burma, 72
Myitkyina, Burma, 72
Mymensingh, Pak., 68
Myrtle Beach, S.C., 296
Myrtleford, Vic., 97
Myrtle Pt., Oreg., 291
Mysłowice, Poland, 47
Mysore (state), India, 68
Mysore, India, 68
Mystic, Conn., 210
Mystic Isls., N. J., 273
My Tho, S. Vietnam, 72
Mzab (oasis), Alg., 106
Mzimba, Malawi, 115

N

Naafkopf (mt.), Europe, 39
Naas, Ire., 17
Nababiep, S. Africa, 118
Nabari, Gilb. and Ell. Is., 87
Nabeul, Tun., 106
Nabire, Indon., 85
Nablus (dist.), Jordan, 65
Nablus (Nabulus), Jordan, 65
Nacala, Mozamb., 118
Nacaome, Hond., 154
Nachingwea, Tanz., 115
Náchod, Czech., 41
Nachvak (fjord), Newf., 166
Nacimiento, Chile, 138
Nacka, Sweden, 18
Nacogdoches, Tex., 302
Nadiad, India, 68
Nador, Mor., 106
Næstved, Den., 21
Naga, Phil. Is., 82
Nagahama, Japan, 81
Nagaland (state), India, 68
Nagano (pref.), Japan, 81
Nagano, Japan, 81
Nagaoka, Japan, 81
Nagapattinam, India, 68
Nagarote, Nic., 154
Nagasaki (pref.), Japan, 81
Nagasaki, Japan, 81
Nagaur, India, 68
Nagercoil, India, 68
Nagina, India, 68
Nagishot, Sudan, 111
Nagorno-Karabakh Aut. Obl., U.S.S.R., 52
Nagoya, Japan, 81
Nagpur, India, 68
Nagua, Dom. Rep., 158
Naguabo, P. Rico, 161
Nagykanizsa, Hung., 41
Nagykőrös, Hung., 41
Naha (cap.), Ryukyu Is., 81
Nahant, Mass., 249
Nahariyya, Israel, 65
Nahuel Huapi (lake), Arg., 143
Nain, Newf., 166
Nairn (county), Scot., 15
Nairn, Scot., 15
Nairobi (dist.), Kenya, 115
Nairobi (cap.), Kenya, 115
Naivasha, Kenya, 115
Najin, N. Korea, 81
Najran, Saudi Ar., 59
Nakamti, Eth., 111
Nakatsu, Japan, 81
Nakhichevan' A.S.S.R., U.S.S.R., 52
Nakhichevan', U.S.S.R., 52
Nakhodka, U.S.S.R., 48
Nakhon Pathom, Thai., 72
Nakhon Phanom, Thai., 72
Nakhon Ratchasima, Thai., 72
Nakhon Sawan, Thai., 72
Nakhon Si Thammarat, Thai., 72
Nakskov, Den., 21
Naktong (riv.), S. Korea, 81
Nakuru, Kenya, 115
Nal (riv.), Pak., 68
Nalaikha, Mong., 77
Nal'chik, U.S.S.R., 52
Nalgonda, India, 68
Nalut, Libya, 111
Namakzar (lake), Asia, 66
Namangan, U.S.S.R., 48
Na'maniya, Iraq, 66
Namatanai, Terr. N.G., 87
Nambour, Queensland, 95
Nambucca Heads, N.S.W., 97
Namcha Barwa (mt.), China, 77
Nam Dinh, N. Vietnam, 72
Namib (des.), S.W. Afr., 118
Namlea, Indon., 85
Namonuito (atoll), Pac. Is., 87
Namorik (atoll), Pac. Is., 87
Nampa, Idaho, 220
Namp'o, N. Korea, 81
Nampo-Shoto (isls.), Japan, 81
Nampula, Mozamb., 118
Namsos, Norway, 18
Nam Tha, Laos, 72
Nam Tram (cape), S. Vietnam, 72
Nam Tso (lake), China, 77
Namuli (mt.), Mozamb., 118
Namur (prov.), Belg., 27
Namur, Belg., 27
Nan, Thai., 72
Nanacamilpa, Mex., 150
Nanaimo, Br. Col., 184
Nanakuli, Hawaii, 218
Nanam, N. Korea, 81
Nanay (riv.), Peru, 128
Nancagua, Chile, 138
Nanchang, China, 77
Nancheng, China, 77
Nanchung, China, 77
Nancowry (isl.), India, 68
Nancy, France, 28
Nanda Devi (mt.), India, 68
Nandaime, Nic., 154
Nander, India, 68
Nandi, Fiji, 87
Nandurbar, India, 68
Nandyal, India, 68
Nanga Parbat (mt.), India, 68
Nangapinoh, Indon., 85
Nang Rong, Thai., 72
Nangwarry, S. Austral., 94
Nanking, China, 77
Nan Ling (mts.), China, 77
Nanning, China, 77
Nannup, W. Austral., 92
Nanping, China, 77
Nan Shan (range), China, 77
Nanterre, France, 28
Nantes, France, 28
Nanticoke, Pa., 294
Nanton, Alta., 182
Nantucket, Mass., 249
Nantucket (isl.), Mass., 249
Nanty Glo, Pa., 294
Nanumea (atoll), Gilb. and Ell. Is., 87
Nanyang, China, 77
Nanyuki, Kenya, 115
Nao (cape), Spain, 33
Náousa, Greece, 45
Napa, Calif., 204
Napanee, Ont., 177
Napata (ruins), Sudan, 111
Naperville, Ill., 222
Napier, N.Z., 101
Naples, Fla., 212
Naples (prov.), Italy, 34
Naples, Italy, 34
Napo (prov.), Ecua., 128
Napo (riv.), S. Amer., 128
Napoleon, Ohio, 284
Nappanee, Ind., 227
Naqa (ruins), Sudan, 111
Nara (pref.), Japan, 81
Nara, Japan, 81
Nara, Mali, 106
Naracoorte, S. Austral., 94
Naranja, Fla., 212
Naranjito, Hond., 154
Naranjito, P. Rico, 161
Naranjos, Mex., 150
Narashino, Japan, 81
Narathiwat, Thai., 72
Narayanganj, Pak., 68
Narberth, Pa., 294
Narbonne, France, 28
Nardò, Italy, 34
Nares (strait), N. Amer., 187
Narew (riv.), Poland, 47
Nariño (dept.), Col., 126
Narmada (riv.), India, 68
Narnaul, India, 68
Naro-Fominsk, U.S.S.R., 52
Narrabri, N.S.W., 97
Narragansett (bay), R.I., 249
Narrandera, N.S.W., 97
Narrogin, W. Austral., 92
Narromine, N.S.W., 97
Narrows Park, Md., 245
Narva, U.S.S.R., 53
Narvik, Norway, 18
Nar'yan-Mar, U.S.S.R., 52
Naryn, U.S.S.R., 48
N.A.S.A. Space Ctr., Tex., 302
Nashua, N.H., 268
Nashville, Ark., 203
Nashville, Ga., 216
Nashville, Ill., 222
Nashville (cap.), Tenn., 237
Nashwaaksis, N. Br., 170
Nasik, India, 68
Nasirabad, India, 68
Nasiriya (prov.), Iraq, 66
Nasratabad (Zabul), Iran, 66
Nass (riv.), Br. Col., 184
Nassau (cap.), Bah. Is., 156
Nassau (bay), Chile, 138
Nassau (isl.), Cook Is., 87
Nasser (lake), Africa, 111
Nässjö, Sweden, 18
Natá, Pan., 154
Natagaima, Col., 126
Natal, Braz., 132
Natal (prov.), S. Afr., 118
Natashquan (riv.), Canada, 174
Natchez, Miss., 256
Natchitoches, La., 238
Natick, Mass., 249
National City, Calif., 204
National Park, N. J., 273
Natron (lake), Africa, 115
Natrona Hts., Pa., 294
Natuna (isls.), Indon., 85
Natural Bridges Nat'l Mon., Utah, 304
Naturaliste (cape), W. Austral., 92
Naucalpan, Mex., 150
Naugatuck, Conn., 210
Nauhcampatépetl (mt.), Mex., 150
Naumburg, E. Ger., 22
Nauru, 87
Navajo Nat'l Mon., Ariz., 198
Naval Academy, Md., 245
Navan (An Uaimh), Ire., 17
Navarin (cape), U.S.S.R., 48
Navarino (isl.), Chile, 138
Navarra (prov.), Spain, 33
Navasota, Tex., 302
Navassa (isl.), W. Indies, 156
Navia (riv.), Spain, 33
Navojoa, Mex., 150
Navolato, Mex., 150
Navrongo, Ghana, 106
Navsari, India, 68
Navy Yard City, Wash., 310
Nawabganj, Pak., 68
Náxos (isl.), Greece, 45
Nayarit (state), Mex., 150
Nayarit (mts.), Mex., 150
Nazaré, Braz., 132
Nazareth, Israel, 65
Nazareth, Pa., 294
Nazas (riv.), Mex., 150
Nazca, Peru, 128
Nazilli, Turkey, 63
Nchanga, Zambia, 115
Ndélé, Cent. Afr. Rep., 115
N'Dendé, Gabon, 115
Ndeni (isl.), Br. Sol. Is., 87
N'Djolé, Gabon, 115
Ndola, Zambia, 115
Neagh (lake), N. Ire., 17
Neath, Wales, 13
Neblina (mt.), Brazil, 132
Nebo (mt.), Jordan, 65
Nebraska (state), U.S., 264
Nebraska City, Nebr., 264
Neckar (riv.), W. Ger., 22
Necker (isl.), Hawaii, 218
Necochea, Arg., 143
Nederland, Tex., 302
Nedlands, W. Austral., 92
Needham, Mass., 249
Needles, Calif., 204
Neembucú (dept.), Par., 144
Neenah, Wis., 317
Neepawa, Man., 179
Nefta, Tun., 106
Neftekamsk, U.S.S.R., 52
Nefud (des.), Saudi Ar., 59
Negaunee, Mich., 250
Negelli, Eth., 111
Negeri Sembilan (state), Malaysia, 72
Negev (reg.), Israel, 65
Negoiul (mt.), Rum., 45
Negombo, Ceylon, 68
Negrais (cape), Burma, 72
Negro (riv.), Arg., 143
Negro (riv.), S. Amer., 132
Negro (riv.), Urug., 145
Negros (isl.), Phil. Is., 82
Negros Occidental (prov.), Phil. Is., 82
Negros Oriental (prov.), Phil. Is., 82
Nehavend, Iran, 66
Neheim-Hüsten, W. Ger., 22
Neiafu, Tonga, 87
Neiba, Dom. Rep., 158
Neikiang, China, 77
Neillsville, Wis., 317
Neisse (riv.), Europe, 22, 47
Neisse (Nysa), Poland, 47
Neiva, Col., 126
Nejafabad, Iran, 66
Nejd (prov.), Saudi Ar., 59
Nekoosa, Wis., 317
Nelidovo, U.S.S.R., 52
Nellore, India, 68
Nelson, Br. Col., 184
Nelson, Eng., 10
Nelson (riv.), Man., 179
Nelson (prov. dist.), N.Z., 101
Nelson, N.Z., 101
Nelsonville, Ohio, 284
Nelspruit, S. Africa, 118
Néma, Mauritania, 106
Nenagh, Ire., 17
Nenets Nat'l Okrug, U.S.S.R., 52
Nenkiang, China, 77
Neodesha, Kans., 232
Neosho, Mo., 261
Nepal, 68
Nepalganj, Nepal, 68
Nephi, Utah, 304
Neponset, Mass., 249

Neptune, N. J., 273
Neptune Beach, Fla., 212
Neptune City, N. J., 273
Nera (riv.), Italy, 34
Nerekhta, U.S.S.R., 52
Neretva (riv.), Yugo., 45
Neskaupstadhur (Nes), Ice., 21
Nesquehoning, Pa., 294
Ness (lake), Scot., 15
Néstos (riv.), Greece, 45
Nes Ziyyona, Israel, 65
Netanya, Israel, 65
Netcong, N. J., 273
Netherlands, 27
Netherlands Antilles, 156, 161
Neubert, Tenn., 237
Neubrandenburg (dist.), E Ger., 22
Neubrandenburg, E. Ger., 22
Neuchâtel (canton), Switz., 39
Neuchâtel, Switz., 39
Neuhausen, Switz., 39
Neuilly-sur-Seine, France, 28
Neu-Isenburg, W. Ger., 22
Neumünster, W. Ger., 22
Neunkirchen, Austria, 41
Neunkirchen, W. Ger., 22
Neuquén (prov.), Arg., 143
Neuquén, Arg., 143
Neuruppin, E. Ger., 22
Neuse (riv.), N.C., 281
Neusiedler (lake), Europe, 41
Neuss, W. Ger., 22
Neustadt, W. Ger., 22
Neustrelitz, E. Ger., 22
Neu-Ulm, W. Ger., 22
Neuwied, W. Ger., 22
Nevada, Iowa, 229
Nevada, Mo., 261
Nevada, Sierra (mts.), Spain, 33
Nevada (state), U.S., 266
Nevada, Sierra (mts.), U.S., 204
Nevers, France, 28
Nevinnomyssk, U.S.S.R., 52
Nevis (isl.), St. Chr.-N.-A., 161
Nevşehir (prov.), Turkey, 63
Nevşehir, Turkey, 63
New (riv.), Br. Hond., 154
New (riv.), Guyana, 131
Newala, Tanz., 115
New Albany, Ind., 227
New Albany, Miss., 256
New Amsterdam, Guyana, 131
Newark, Calif., 204
Newark, Del., 245
Newark, Eng., 13
Newark, N. J., 273
Newark, N.Y., 276
Newark, Ohio, 284
New Baltimore, Mich., 250
New Bedford, Mass., 249
Newberg, Oreg., 291
New Berlin, Wis., 317
New Bern, N.C., 281
Newberry, Mich., 250
Newberry, S.C., 296
New Boston, Ohio, 284
New Boston, Tex., 302
New Braunfels, Tex., 302
New Brighton, Minn., 254
New Brighton, Pa., 294
New Britain, Conn., 210
New Britain (isl.), Terr. N.G., 87
New Brunswick (prov.), Canada, 170
New Brunswick, N. J., 273
Newburgh, N.Y., 276
Newburgh Hts., Ohio, 284
Newbury, Eng., 13
Newburyport, Mass., 249
New Caledonia, 87
New Caledonia (isl.), New Cal., 87
New Canaan, Conn., 210
New Carlisle, Ohio, 284
New Carrollton, Md., 245
New Castle, Del., 245
Newcastle (Newcastle-under-Lyme), Eng., 13
New Castle, Ind., 227
Newcastle, Ire., 17
Newcastle, N.B., 170
Newcastle, N.S.W., 97
Newcastle, N. Ire., 17
New Castle, Pa., 294
Newcastle, S. Afr., 118
Newcastle, Wyo., 319
Newcastle-upon-Tyne, Eng., 13
Newcastle Waters, N. Terr., 93
New City, N.Y., 276
Newcomerstown, Ohio, 284
New Cordell, Okla., 288
New Cumberland, Pa., 294
New Delhi (cap.), India, 68
New Eagle, Pa., 294
Newfoundland (prov.), Canada, 166
Newfoundland (isl.), Newf., 166
New Georgia (isl.), Br. Sol. Is., 87
New Glasgow, N.S., 169
New Guinea (isl.), 85, 87
New Guinea, Territory of, 85, 87
Newhalem, Wash., 310
Newhall, Calif., 204
Newham, Eng., 10
New Hampshire (state), U.S., 268
New Hampton, Iowa, 229
New Hanover (isl.), Terr. N.G., 87
New Haven, Conn., 210
New Haven, Ind., 227
New Hebrides, 87
New Holland, Pa., 294
New Hyde Park, N.Y., 276
New Iberia, La., 238
Newington, Conn., 210
New Ireland (isl.), Terr. N.G., 87
New Jersey (state), U.S., 273
New Kensington, Pa., 294
New Lexington, Ohio, 284
New Liskeard, Ont., 175
New London, Conn., 210
New London, Wis., 317
New Madrid, Mo., 261
Newmarket, N.H., 268
Newmarket, Ont., 177
Newmarket, Queensland, 95
New Martinsville, W. Va., 313
New Mexico (state), U.S., 274
New Milford, Conn., 210
New Milford, N. J., 273
Newnan, Ga., 216
New Norfolk, Tas., 99
New Orleans, La., 238
New Paltz, N.Y., 276
New Philadelphia, Ohio, 284
New Plymouth, N.Z., 101
Newport, Ark., 203
Newport, Ky., 237
Newport, N.H., 268
Newport, Oreg., 291
Newport, R.I., 249
Newport, Tenn., 237
Newport, Vt., 268
Newport, Wales, 13
Newport Beach, Calif., 204
Newport News, Va., 307
New Port Richey, Fla., 212
New Prague, Minn., 254
New Providence (isl.), Bah. Is., 156
New Providence, N. J., 273
New Richmond, Ohio, 284
New Richmond, Wis., 317
New Roads, La., 238
New Rochelle, N.Y., 276
New Rockford, N. Dak., 283
New Ross, Ire., 17
Newry, N. Ire., 17
New Schwabenland (reg.), Ant., 5
New Shrewsbury, N. J., 273
New Siberian (isls.), U.S.S.R., 48
New Smyrna Beach, Fla., 212
New South Wales (state), Austral., 97
Newton, Ill., 222
Newton, Iowa, 229
Newton, Kans., 232
Newton, Mass., 249
Newton, Miss., 256
Newton, N. J., 273
Newton, N.C., 281
Newton and Chilwell, Vic., 97
Newton Falls, Ohio, 284
Newtonville, Mass., 249
Newtownabbey, N. Ire., 17
Newtownards, N. Ire., 17
Newtown Sq., Pa., 294
Newtownstewart, N. Ire., 17
New Ulm, Minn., 254
New Waterford, N.S., 169
New Westminster, Br. Col., 184
New Whiteland, Ind., 227
New Windsor, Eng., 13
New Windsor, N.Y., 276
New World (isl.), Newf., 166
New York, N.Y., 276
New York (state), U.S., 276
New York Mills, N.Y., 276
New Zealand, 101
Nezhin, U.S.S.R., 52
Nez Perce Nat'l Hist. Park, Idaho, 220
Ngabang, Indon., 85
Ngami (lake), Bots., 118
Ngamiland (dist.), Botswana, 118
Ngangla Ringco Tso (lake), China, 77
Ngao, Thai., 72
N'Gaoundéré, Cameroon, 115
Ngatik (atoll), Pac. Is., 87
Ngawi, Indon., 85
Ngorongoro (crater), Tanz., 115
N'Gounié (riv.), Africa, 115
N'Guigmi, Niger, 106
Ngulu (isl.), Pac. Is., 87
Ngundju (cape), Indon., 85
Nguru, Nigeria, 106
Nhamundá (riv.), Braz., 132
Nha Trang, S. Vietnam, 72
Nhill, Vic., 97
Niafunké, Mali, 106
Niagara (riv.), N. Amer., 175
Niagara, Ont., 177
Niagara Falls, N.Y., 276
Niagara Falls, Ont., 177
Niamey (cap.), Niger, 106
Niangara, Dem. Rep. of the Congo, 115
Niantic, Conn., 210
Nias (isl.), Indon., 85
Niassa (dist.), Mozamb., 118
Nicaragua, 154
Nicaragua (lake), Nic., 154
Nicastro, Italy, 34
Nice, France, 28
Niceville, Fla., 212
Nichinan, Japan, 81
Nicholas (chan.), W. Indies, 158
Nicholasville, Ky., 237
Nichols, Conn., 210
Nichols Hills, Okla., 288
Nickerie (dist.), Sur., 131
Nickerie (riv.), Sur., 131
Nicobar (isls.), India, 68
Nicolet, Que., 172
Nicosia (cap.), Cyprus, 63
Nicoya, C. Rica, 154
Nidd (riv.), Eng., 13
Nidwalden (half-canton), Switz., 39
Niedere Tauern (range), Austria, 41
Niemen (riv.), U.S.S.R., 52
Nienburg, W. Ger., 22
Nieuw-Amsterdam, Sur., 131
Nieuw-Nickerie, Sur., 131
Nièvre (dept.), France, 28
Niğde (prov.), Turkey, 63
Niğde, Turkey, 63
Nigel, S. Africa, 118
Niger, 106
Niger (riv.), Africa, 106
Nigeria, 106
Nigrita, Greece, 45
Nihoa (isl.), Hawaii, 218
Niigata (pref.), Japan, 81
Niigata, Japan, 81
Niihama, Japan, 81
Niihau (isl.), Hawaii, 218
Niitsu, Japan, 81
Nijmegen, Neth., 27
Nikel', U.S.S.R., 52
Nikolayev, U.S.S.R., 52
Nikolayevsk, U.S.S.R., 48
Nikopol', U.S.S.R., 52
Nikšić, Yugo., 45
Nikumaroro (Gardner) (isl.), Gilb. & Ell. Is., 87
Nile (riv.), Africa, 102
Niles, Ill., 222
Niles, Mich., 250
Niles, Ohio, 284
Nilópolis, Brazil, 132
Nimach, India, 68
Nimba (mts.), Africa, 106
Nîmes, France, 28
Nimule, Sudan, 111
Nineveh (ruins), Iraq, 66
Ningpo, China, 77
Ningsia (Yinchwan), China, 77
Ningsia Hui Aut. Reg., China, 77
Ninigo Group (isls.), Terr. N.G., 87
Niono, Mali, 106
Nioro, Mali, 106
Nioro-du-Rip, Sen., 106
Niort, France, 28
Nipawin, Sask., 181
Nipawin Prov. Park, Sask., 181
Nipigon, Ont., 175
Nipigon (lake), Ont., 175
Nipissing (lake), Ont., 177
Niquero, Cuba, 158
Nirgua, Venez., 124
Niriz, Iran, 66
Niš, Yugo., 45
Niscemi, Italy, 34
Nishapur, Iran, 66
Nishinomiya, Japan, 81
Nísiros (isl.), Greece, 45
Niterói, Braz., 132
Nith (riv.), Scot., 15
Nitra, Czech., 41
Nitro, W. Va., 313
Niuafo'ou (isl.), Tonga, 87
Niuatoputapu (isl.), Tonga, 87
Niue (isl.), Pacific, 87
Niutao (atoll), Gilb. and Ell. Is., 87
Nive (riv.), Tas., 99
Nixon, N. J., 273
Nizamabad, India, 68
Nizhneudinsk, U.S.S.R., 48
Nizhniy Tagil, U.S.S.R., 48
Nizip, Turkey, 63
Nizwa, Oman, 59
Njombe (riv.), Tanz., 115
Nkana, Zambia, 115
Nkhota Kota, Malawi, 115
N'Kongsamba, Cameroon, 115
Nnewi, Nigeria, 106
Noakhali, Pak., 68
Noatak (riv.), Alaska, 196
Nobeoka, Japan, 81
Noblesville, Ind., 227
Nocera, Italy, 34
Nochistlán, Mex., 150
Nocona, Tex., 302
Noda, Japan, 81
Nogales, Ariz., 198
Nogales, Chile, 138
Noginsk, U.S.S.R., 52
Nogoyá, Arg., 143
Nógrád (county), Hung., 41
Noires (mts.), Haiti, 158
Noisy-le-Sec, France, 28
Nokia, Fin., 18
Nome, Alaska, 196
Nomoi (isls.), Pac. Is., 87
Nong Khai, Thai., 72
Nong Lahan (lake), Thai., 72
Nonouti (atoll), Gilb. and Ell. Is., 87
Noquochoke, Mass., 249
Noranda, Que., 174
Norco, Calif., 204
Norco, La., 238
Nord (dept.), France, 28
Nord, Greenl., 4
Nord (dept.), Haiti, 158
Nord (fjord), Norway, 18
Nordegg, Alta., 182
Nordenham, W. Ger., 22
Norderney (isl.), W. Ger., 22
Nordhausen, E. Ger., 22
Nordhorn, W. Ger., 22
Nordkyn (cape), Norway, 18
Nordland (county), Norway, 18
Nord-Ostsee (canal), W. Ger., 22
Nord-Ouest (dept.), Haiti, 158
Nord-Trøndelag (county), Norway, 18
Norfolk (county), Eng., 13
Norfolk, Nebr., 264
Norfolk, Va., 307
Norfolk Island (terr.), Austral., 87, 88
Noril'sk, U.S.S.R., 48
Normal, Ill., 222
Norman, Okla., 288
Norman (riv.), Queensland, 95
Normandy, Mo., 261
Normandy Park, Wash., 310
Norman Wells, N.W.T., 187
Normétal, Que., 174
Noroton, Conn., 210
Norrbotten (county), Sweden, 18
Nørresundby, Den., 21
Norridge, Ill., 22
Norristown, Pa., 294
Norrköping, Sweden, 18
Norrtälje, Sweden, 18
Norseman, W. Austral., 92
Norte (pt.), Arg., 143
Norte (range), Braz., 132
Norte de Santander (dept.), Col., 126
North (sea), Europe, 7
North (isl.), N.Z., 101
North (cape), Norway, 18
North (cape), N.S., 169
North (chan.), Ont., 177
North (pt.), P.E.I., 169
North (chan.), U.K., 15, 17
North Abington, Mass., 249
North Adams, Mass., 249
Northam, W. Austral., 92
North America, 146
Northampton, Eng., 13
Northampton, Mass., 249
Northampton, Pa., 294
Northamptonshire (county), Eng., 13
North Andover, Mass., 249
North Arlington, N. J., 273
North Atlanta, Ga., 216
North Attleboro, Mass., 249
North Augusta, S.C., 296
North Aulatsivik (isl.), Newf., 166
North Baltimore, Ohio, 284
North Battleford, Sask., 181
North Bay, Ont., 177
North Bend, Oreg., 291
North Bergen, N. J., 273
North Berwick, Scot., 15
North Beveland (isl.), Neth., 27
North Billerica, Mass., 249
Northborough, Mass., 249
North Brabant (prov.), Neth., 27
North Braddock, Pa., 294
Northbrook, Ill., 222
North Brookfield, Mass., 249
North Brunswick, N. J., 273
North Caldwell, N. J., 273
North Canton, Ohio, 284
North Carolina (state), U.S., 281
North Cascades Nat'l Park, Wash., 310
North Catasauqua, Pa., 294
North-Central (state), Nigeria, 106
North Charleston, S.C., 296
North Chelmsford, Mass., 249
North Chicago, Ill., 222
North College Hill, Ohio, 284
Northcote, Vic., 97
North Dakota (state), U.S., 283
North Dartmouth, N.S., 168
North East, Pa., 294
North-East (prov.), Somalia, 115
North East Breakers, Berm., 156
North Eastern (prov.), Kenya, 115
North-Eastern (state), Nigeria, 106
North East Frontier Agency, India, 68
North East New Guinea (reg.), Terr. N.G., 87
North Easton, Mass., 249
North East Providence (chan.), Bah. Is., 156
Northern (dist.), Israel, 65
Northern (prov.), Sudan, 111
Northern Dvina (riv.), U.S.S.R., 52
Northern Ireland, 17
Northern Samar (prov.), Phil. Is., 82
Northern Sporades (isls.), Greece, 45
Northern Territory (terr.), Austral., 93
Northfield, Ill., 222
Northfield, Minn., 254
Northfield, N. J., 273
Northfield, Vt., 268
Northfleet, Eng., 10
North Foreland (prom.), Eng., 13
North Frisian (isls.), Europe, 21, 22
Northglenn, Colo., 208
North Grafton, Mass., 249
North Haledon, N. J., 273
North Haven, Conn., 210
North Highlands, Calif., 204
North Holland (prov.), Neth., 27
North Hollywood, Calif., 204
North Kamloops, Br. Col., 184
North Kansas City, Mo., 261
North Khangai (prov.), Mong., 77
North Kildonan, Man., 179
North Kingstown, R.I., 249
North Korea, 81
Northlake, Ill., 222
North Las Vegas, Nev., 266
North Little Rock, Ark., 203
North Magnetic Pole, N.W.T., 187
North Manchester, Ind., 227
North Mankato, Minn., 254
North Miami, Fla., 212
North Miami Beach, Fla., 212
North Muskegon, Mich., 250
North Ogden, Utah, 304
North Olmsted, Ohio, 284
North Ossetian A.S.S.R., U.S.S.R., 52
North Palm Beach, Fla., 212
North Park, Ill., 222
North Pelham, N.Y., 276
North Plainfield, N. J., 273
North Platte, Nebr., 264
North Platte (riv.), U.S., 188
North Plymouth, Mass., 249
North Pole, 4
Northport, Ala., 194
Northport, N.Y., 276
North Providence, R.I., 249
North Reading, Mass., 249
North Rhine-Westphalia (state), W. Ger., 22
North Richland Hills, Tex., 302
North Ridgeville, Ohio, 284
North Riverside, Ill., 222
North Ronaldsay (isl.), Scot., 15
North Royalton, Ohio, 284
North St. Paul, Minn., 254
North Saskatchewan (riv.), Canada, 181, 182
North Scituate, Mass., 249
North Sea (canal), Neth., 27
North Sydney, N.S.W., 97
North Sydney, N.S., 169
North Syracuse, N.Y., 276
North Taranaki (bight), N.Z., 101
North Tarrytown, N.Y., 276
North Tonawanda, N.Y., 276
North Uist (isl.), Scot., 15
Northumberland (str.), Canada, 169
Northumberland (county), Eng., 13
Northumberland, Pa., 294
Northumberland (cape), S. Austral., 94
Northvale, N. J., 273
North Vancouver, Br. Col., 184
North Vernon, Ind., 227
North Vietnam, 72
Northville, Mich., 250
North Wales, Pa., 294
North-West (dist.), Guyana, 131
North-West (prov.), Somalia, 115
North West (cape), W. Austral., 92
North-West (dist.), Guy., 131
North-West (prov.), Som., 115
North-West Frontier (prov.), Pak., 68
North Westport, Mass., 249
North West Providence (chan.), Bah. Is., 156
North West River, Newf., 166
Northwest Territories (terr.), Canada, 187
Northwich, Eng., 10
North Wilbraham, Mass., 249
North Wildwood, N. J., 273
North Wilkesboro, N.C., 281
Northwood, Ohio, 284
Northwoods, Mo., 261
North York, Ont., 177
Norton (sound), Alaska, 196
Norton, Kans., 232
Norton, Va., 307
Norton Shores, Mich., 250
Norvegia (cape), Ant., 5
Norwalk, Calif., 204
Norwalk, Conn., 210
Norwalk, Ohio, 284
Norway, 18
Norway, Maine, 242
Norway, Mich., 250
Norwegian (sea), Europe, 7
Norwell, Mass., 249
Norwich, Conn., 210
Norwich, Eng., 13
Norwich, N.Y., 276
Norwichtown, Conn., 210
Norwood, Fla., 212
Norwood, Mass., 249
Norwood, N. J., 273
Norwood, Ohio, 284
Norwood, Pa., 294
Norwood, R.I., 249
Noshiro, Japan, 81
Nossi-Bé (isl.), Malag. Rep., 118
Nossob (riv.), Africa, 118
Noteć (riv.), Poland, 47
Noto, Italy, 34
Noto (pen.), Japan, 81
Notre Dame, Ind., 227
Notre Dame (bay), Newf., 166
Nottaway (riv.), Que., 174
Nottingham, Eng., 13
Nottinghamshire (county), Eng., 13
Nouadhibou, Mauritania, 106
Nouakchott (cap.), Mauritania, 106
Nouméa (cap.), New Cal., 87
Noupoort, S. Africa, 118
Nouveau-Québec (crater), Que., 174
Nova Friburgo, Braz., 132
Nova Iguaçu, Braz., 132
Nova Lisboa, Angola, 115
Nova Mambone, Mozamb., 118
Novara (prov.), Italy, 33
Novara, Italy, 33
Nova Scotia (prov.), Canada, 169
Nova Sofala, Mozamb., 118
Novato, Calif., 204
Novaya Sibir' (isl.), U.S.S.R., 48
Novaya Zemlya (isls.), U.S.S.R., 52
Nova Zagora, Bulg., 45
Nové Město, Czech., 41
Nové Zámky, Czech., 41
Novgorod, U.S.S.R., 52
Novi, Mich., 250
Novi Ligure, Italy, 34
Novi Pazar, Yugo., 45
Novi Sad, Yugo., 45
Novoanninskiy, U.S.S.R., 52
Novocherkassk, U.S.S.R., 52
Novograd-Volynskiy, U.S.S.R., 52
Novogrudok, U.S.S.R., 52
Novo Hamburgo, Brazil, 132
Novokuybyshevsk, U.S.S.R., 52
Novokuznetsk, U.S.S.R., 48
Novomoskovsk, U.S.S.R., 52
Novopolotsk, U.S.S.R., 52
Novo Redondo, Angola, 115
Novorossiysk, U.S.S.R., 52
Novoshakhtinsk, U.S.S.R., 52
Novosibirsk, U.S.S.R., 48
Novotroitsk, U.S.S.R., 52
Novovolynsk, U.S.S.R., 52
Nový Bohumín, Czech., 41
Nový Jičín, Czech., 41
Nowa Sól, Poland, 47
Nowgong, India, 68
Nowra, N.S.W., 97
Nowy Sącz, Poland, 47
Nowy Targ, Poland, 47
Nsanje, Malawi, 115
Nsukka, Nigeria, 106
Nuba (mts.), Sudan, 111
Nubian (des.), Sudan, 111
Ñuble (prov.), Chile, 138
Nueces (riv.), Tex., 302
Nueva Casas Grandes, Mex., 150
Nueva Ecija (prov.), Phil. Is., 82
Nueva Esparta (state), Venez., 124
Nueva Gerona, Cuba, 158
Nueva Imperial, Chile, 138
Nueva Ocotepeque, Hond., 154
Nueva Palmira, Urug., 145
Nueva Rosita, Mex., 150
Nueva San Salvador (Santa Tecla), El Sal., 154
Nueva Vizcaya (prov.), Phil. Is., 82
Nueve de Julio, Arg., 143
Nuevitas, Cuba, 158
Nuevo Berlín, Urug., 145
Nuevo Laredo, Mex., 150
Nuevo León (state), Mex., 150
Nui (atoll), Gilb. and Ell. Is., 87
Nui Ba Den (mt.), S. Vietnam, 72
Nuku'alofa (cap.), Tonga, 87
Nukuhiva (isl.), Fr. Poly., 87
Nukulaelae (atoll), Gilb. and Ell. Is., 87
Nukumanu (atoll), Terr. N.G., 87
Nukunonu (atoll), Tokelau Is., 87
Nukuoro (atoll), Pac. Is., 87
Nukus, U.S.S.R., 48
Nullarbor (plain), Austral., 92, 94
Numazu, Japan, 81
Numbulwar, N. Terr., 93
Ñumí, Par., 144
Numurkah, Vic., 97
Nunawading, Vic., 97
Nundah, Queensland, 95
Nuneaton, Eng., 13
Nunivak (isl.), Alaska, 196
Nuoro (prov.), Italy, 33
Nuoro, Italy, 33
Nuremberg (Nürnberg), W. Ger., 22
Nuri (ruins), Sudan, 111
Nuriootpa, S. Austral., 94
Nürtingen, W. Ger., 22
Nutley, N. J., 273
Nuwara Eliya, Ceylon, 68
Nuyts (cape), S. Austral., 94
Nyabisindu, Rwanda, 115
Nyack, N.Y., 276
Nyala, Sudan, 111
Nyandoma, U.S.S.R., 52
Nyanza (prov.), Kenya, 115
Nyasa (lake), Africa, 115
Nyaunglebin, Burma, 72
Nyborg, Den., 21
Nybro, Sweden, 18
Nyenchen Tanglha (range), China, 77
Nyeri, Kenya, 115
Nyíregyháza, Hung., 41
Nykøbing, Den., 21
Nyköping, Sweden, 18
Nylstroom, S. Afr., 118
Nymburk, Czech., 41
Nynäshamn, Sweden, 18
Nyngan, N.S.W., 97
Nyon, Switz., 39
Nysa, Poland, 47
Nyssa, Oreg., 291
Nyudo (cape), Japan, 81
N'Zérékoré, Guinea, 106

O

Oa, Mull of (prom.), Scot., 15
Oahe (lake), U.S., 188
Oahu (isl.), Hawaii, 218
Oak Bay, B.C., 184
Oak Creek, Wis., 317
Oakdale, Calif., 204
Oakdale, La., 238
Oakes, N. Dak., 283
Oak Forest, Ill., 222
Oak Grove, Oreg., 291
Oak Hbr., Ohio, 284
Oak Hbr., Wash., 310
Oak Hill, Tenn., 237
Oak Hill, W. Va., 313
Oakhurst, N. J., 273
Oakland, Calif., 204
Oakland, N. J., 273
Oakland Beach, R.I., 249
Oakland City, Ind., 227
Oak Lawn, Ill., 222
Oakleigh, Vic., 97
Oaklyn, N. J., 273
Oakmont, Pa., 294
Oak Park, Ill., 222
Oak Park, Mich., 250
Oak Ridge, Tenn., 237
Oakville, Conn., 210
Oakville, Ont., 177
Oakwood, Ohio, 284
Oamaru, N.Z., 101
Oaxaca (state), Mex., 150
Oaxaca, Mex., 150
Ob' (gulf), U.S.S.R., 48
Ob' (riv.), U.S.S.R., 48
Oban, Scot., 15
Obando, Col., 126
Obbia, Somalia, 115
Obeh, Afghan., 68
Obera, Arg., 143
Oberammergau, W. Ger., 22
Oberhausen, W. Ger., 22
Oberlin, Ohio, 284
Oberndorf, Austria, 41
Oberpfälzer Wald (for.), W. Ger., 22
Oberursel, W. Ger., 22
Obi (isls.), Indon., 85
Óbidos, Braz., 132
Obihiro, Japan, 81
Obluch'ye, U.S.S.R., 48
Obo, Centr. Afr. Rep., 115
Obock, Afars & Issas, 111
Obuasi, Ghana, 106
Obwalden (half-canton), Switz., 39
Ocala, Fla., 212
Ocamo (riv.), Venez., 124
Ocampo, Mex., 150
Ocaña, Col., 126
Occidental Mindoro (prov.), Phil. Is., 82
Ocean (isl.), Gilb. & Ell. Is., 87
Ocean (lake), N.S., 169
Ocean City, N. J., 273
Ocean Falls, Br. Col., 184
Ocean Grove, N. J., 273
Oceanport, N. J., 273
Oceanside, Calif., 204
Oceanside, N.Y., 276
Ocean Sprs., Miss., 256
Ocho Rios, Jam., 158
Ochsenkopf (mt.), Europe, 39
Ocilla, Ga., 216
Ocmulgee Nat'l Mon., Ga., 126
Ocna Mureş, Rum., 45
Ocoa (bay), Dom. Rep., 158
Ocoee, Fla., 212
Oconomowoc, Wis., 317
Oconto, Wis., 317
Ocotal, Nic., 154
Ocotlán, Mex., 150
Ocú, Pan., 154
Ocumare, Venez., 124
Oda, Jebel (mt.), Sudan, 111
Odate, Japan, 81
Odawara, Japan, 81
Odda, Norway, 18
Ödemiş, Turkey, 63
Odendaalsrus, S. Africa, 118
Odense, Den., 21
Odenwald (for.), W. Ger., 22
Oder (riv.), Europe, 22, 47
Odessa, Tex., 302
Odessa, U.S.S.R., 52
Odienné, Ivory Coast, 106
Odorhei, Rum., 45
Oe-Cusse (reg.), Port. Timor, 85
Oelsnitz, E. Ger., 22
Oelwein, Iowa, 229
Oeno (isl.), Pitcairn Is., 87
O'Fallon, Ill., 222
O'Fallon, Mo., 261
Offa, Nigeria, 106
Offaly (county), Ire., 17
Offenbach, W. Ger., 22
Offenburg, W. Ger., 22
Ofqui (isthmus), Chile, 138
Ogaden (reg.), Eth., 111
Ogaki, Japan, 81
Ogallala, Nebr., 264
Ogbomosho, Nigeria, 106
Ogden, Utah, 304
Ogdensburg, N.Y., 276
Ogilvie (mts.), Yukon, 187
Oglesby, Ill., 222
Ogoki (riv.), Ont., 177
Ogooué (riv.), Africa, 115
O'Higgins (prov.), Chile, 138
O'Higgins (lake), Chile, 138
Ohio (riv.), N.S., 169
Ohio (state), U.S., 284
Ohio (riv.), U.S., 188
Ohioville, Pa., 294
Ohře (riv.), Czech., 41
Ohrid (lake), Europe, 45
Ohrid, Yugo., 45
Oies (isl.), Que., 172
Oil City, Pa., 294
Oildale, Calif., 204
Oise (dept.), France, 28
Oise (riv.), France, 28
Oistins (bay), Barbados, 161
Oita (pref.), Japan, 81
Oita, Japan, 81
Ojai, Calif., 204
Ojinaga, Mex., 150
Ojocaliente, Mex., 150
Ojo del Toro (mt.), Cuba, 158
Ojos del Salado (mt.), S. Amer., 143
Ojus, Fla., 212
Oka (riv.), U.S.S.R., 52
Okahandja, S.W. Afr., 118
Okak (isls.), Newf., 166
Okanagan (lake), Br. Col., 184
Okawa, Japan, 81
Okaya, Japan, 81
Okayama (pref.), Japan, 81
Okayama, Japan, 81
Okazaki, Japan, 81
Okeechobee, Fla., 212
Okeechobee (lake), Fla., 212
Okefenokee (swamp), U.S., 212, 216
Okemah, Okla., 288
Okene, Nigeria, 106
Okha Port, India, 68
Okhotsk (sea), U.S.S.R., 48
Oki (isls.), Japan, 81
Okiep, S. Afr., 118
Okinawa (isl.), Ryukyu Is., 81
Oklahoma (state), U.S., 288
Oklahoma City (cap.), Okla., 288
Okmulgee, Okla., 288
Okolona, Ky., 237
Okolona, Miss., 256
Okondja, Gabon, 115
Okotoks, Alta., 182
Okovango (riv.), Africa, 118
Okovango (basin), Botswana, 118
Okoyo, Rep. of Congo, 115
Oktyabr'sk, U.S.S.R., 52
Oktyabr'skiy, U.S.S.R., 52
Ola Grande (pt.), P. Rico, 161
Olanchito, Hond., 154
Öland (isl.), Sweden, 18
Olathe, Kans., 232
Olavarría, Arg., 143
Olbia, Italy, 34
Old Bahama (chan.), W. Indies, 156
Old Bridge, N. J., 273
Oldenburg, W. Ger., 22
Old Forge, Pa., 294
Old Greenwich, Conn., 210
Oldham, Eng., 10
Old Harbour, Jam., 158
Old Hickory, Tenn., 237
Oldman (riv.), Alta., 182
Old Orchard Beach, Maine, 242
Old Rhine (riv.), Neth., 27
Old Road, Antigua, 161
Old Road, St. Chr.-N.-A., 161
Olds, Alta., 182
Old Sturbridge Village, Mass., 249
Old Town, Maine, 242
Olduvai Gorge (canyon), Tanz., 115
Olean, N.Y., 276
Olekma (riv.), U.S.S.R., 48
Olenëk (riv.), U.S.S.R., 48
Oléron (isl.), France, 28
Oleśnica, Poland, 47
Olga (mt.), N. Terr., 93
Olifants (riv.), Africa, 118
Olimar Grande (riv.), Urug., 145
Olímpia, Braz., 135
Olimpo (dept.), Par., 144
Olinda, Braz., 132
Oliva, Arg., 143
Olivares (mt.), S. Amer., 138
Oliveira, Braz., 135
Oliver, Br. Col., 184
Oliver, Pa., 294
Olivette, Mo., 261
Olla̱güe (vol.), Bol., 136
Ollagüe, Chile, 138
Olmos, Peru, 128
Olmué, Chile, 138
Olney, Ill., 222
Olney, Tex., 302
Olofström, Sweden, 18
Olomouc, Czech., 41
Olongapo, Phil. Is., 82
Olsztyn (prov.), Poland, 47
Olsztyn, Poland, 47
Olt (riv.), Rum., 45
Olten, Switz., 39
Olteniţa, Rum., 45
Olutanga (isl.), Phil. Is., 82
Olwanpi (cape), China, 77
Olympia (cap.), Wash., 310
Olympic (mts.), Wash., 310
Olympic Nat'l Park, Wash., 310
Olympus (mt.), Greece, 45
Olyphant, Pa., 294
Olyutorskiy (cape), U.S.S.R., 48
Omagh, N. Ire., 17
Omaha (beach), France, 28
Omaha, Nebr., 264
Omak, Wash., 310
Oman, 59
Oman (gulf), Asia, 59
Oman (reg.), Oman, 59
Omaruru, S.W. Afr., 118
Omatako (river), S.W. Afr., 118
Ombai (str.), Indon., 85
Omboué, Gabon, 115
Ombrone (riv.), Italy, 34
Omdurman, Sudan, 111
Ometepe (isl.), Nic., 154
Ometepec, Mex., 150
Omiya, Japan, 81
Omo (riv.), Eth., 111
Omoa, Hond., 154
Omolon (riv.), U.S.S.R., 48
Omsk, U.S.S.R., 48
Omura, Japan, 81
Omuta, Japan, 81
Omutninsk, U.S.S.R., 52
Onalaska, Wis., 317
Onangué (lake), Gabon, 115
Onawa, Iowa, 229
Ondangua, S.W. Afr., 118
Ondo, Nigeria, 106
Onega, U.S.S.R., 52
Onega (lake), U.S.S.R., 52
Onehunga, N.Z., 101
Oneida, N.Y., 276
O'Neill, Nebr., 264
Oneonta, Ala., 194
Oneonta, N.Y., 276
One Tree Hill, N.Z., 101
Ongjin, N. Korea, 81
Ongole, India, 68
Onilahy (riv.), Malag. Rep., 118
Onitsha, Nigeria, 106
Onkivesi (lake), Fin., 18
Onoda, Japan, 81
Onomichi, Japan, 81
Onon, Mong., 77
Onon (riv.), Mong., 77
Onotoa (atoll), Gilb. and Ell. Is., 87
Onrusrivier, S. Afr., 118
Onslow, W. Austral., 92
Onsong, N. Korea, 81
Ontario, Calif., 204
Ontario (prov.), Canada, 175, 177
Ontario (lake), N. Amer., 175, 276
Ontario, Ohio, 284
Ontario, Oreg., 291
Ontonagon, Mich., 250
Ontong Java (isl.), Br. Sol. Is., 87
Oostzaan Polder, Neth., 27
Ootacamund, India, 68
Opala, Dem. Rep. of the Congo, 115
Opal Cliffs, Calif., 204
Opa-locka, Fla., 212
Opava, Czech., 41
Opelika, Ala., 194
Opelousas, La., 238
Opinaca (riv.), Que., 174
Opiscotéo (lake), Que., 174
Opladen, W. Ger., 22
Opole (prov.), Poland, 47
Opole Lubelskie, Poland, 47
Oporto, Port., 33
Opotiki, N.Z., 101
Opp, Ala., 194
Oppland (county), Norway, 18
Opportunity, Wash., 310
'Oqair, Saudi Ar., 59
Oracabessa, Jam., 158
Oradea, Rum., 45
Oradell, N. J., 273
Oran, Algeria, 106
Orán, Arg., 143
Orange (riv.), Africa, 118
Orange (cape), Braz., 132
Orange, Calif., 204
Orange, Conn., 210
Orange, France, 28
Orange, Mass., 249
Orange (canal), Neth., 27
Orange, N. J., 273
Orange, N.S.W., 97
Orange (mts.), Sur., 131
Orange, Tex., 302
Orange, Va., 307
Orangeburg, S.C., 296
Orange City, Iowa, 229
Orange Cove, Calif., 204
Orange Free State (prov.), S. Afr., 118
Orange Park, Fla., 212
Orangeville, Ont., 177
Orange Walk, Br. Hond., 154
Oranienburg, E. Ger., 22
Oranjemund, S.W. Afr., 118
Oranjestad, Neth. Ant., 161
Oraşul Gheorghe Gheorghiu-Dej, Rum., 45
Orava (riv.), Czech., 41
Orb (riv.), France, 28
Orbigo (riv.), Spain, 33
Orbost, Vic., 97
Orchard Mesa, Colo., 208
Orchard Park, N.Y., 276
Orcotuna, Peru, 128
Ord, Nebr., 264
Ord (riv.), W. Austral., 92
Ordos (des.), China, 77
Ordu (prov.), Turkey, 63
Ordu, Turkey, 63
Ordzhonikidze, U.S.S.R., 52
Orealla, Guyana, 131
Örebro (county), Sweden, 18
Örebro, Sweden, 18
Oregon, Ill., 222
Oregon, Ohio, 284
Oregon (state), U.S., 291
Oregon Caves Nat'l Mon., Oreg., 291
Oregon City, Oreg., 291
Orekhovo-Zuyevo, U.S.S.R., 52
Orel, U.S.S.R., 52
Orem, Utah, 304
Orenburg, U.S.S.R., 52
Orense (prov.), Spain, 33
Orense, Spain, 33
Orestiás, Greece, 45
Øresund (sound), Europe, 21
Organ Pipe Cactus Nat'l Mon., Ariz., 198
Orgãos (range), Braz., 135
Oriental, Mex., 150
Oriental, Cordillera (range), Dom. Rep., 158
Oriental Mindoro (prov.), Phil. Is., 82

Orientale (prov.), Dem. Rep. of the Congo, 115
Oriente (prov.), Cuba, 158
Orillia, Ont., 177
Orinda, Calif., 204
Orinoco (riv.), S. Amer., 124
Orissa (state), India, 68
Oristano (gulf), Italy, 34
Orituco (riv.), Venez., 124
Orizaba, Mex., 150
Orkhon (riv.), Mong., 77
Orkney (county), Scot., 15
Orkney (isls.), Scot., 15
Orland, Calif., 204
Orlândia, Braz., 135
Orlando, Fla., 212
Orlando, S. Africa, 118
Orland Park, Ill., 222
Orléans, France, 28
Orléans (isl.), Que., 172
Orléansville (El Asnam), Alg., 106
Orlice (riv.), Czech., 41
Orlová, Czech., 41
Orly, France, 28
Ormoc, Phil. Is., 82
Ormond Beach, Fla., 212
Ormskirk, Eng., 10
Orne (dept.), France, 28
Orne (riv.), France, 28
Örnsköldsvik, Sweden, 18
Orocovis, P. Rico, 161
Orofino, Idaho, 220
Oroluk (atoll), Pac. Is., 87
Oromocto, N.B., 170
Orona (Hull)(isl.), Gilb. and Ell. Is., 87
Orono, Maine, 242
Orono, Minn., 254
Orontes ('Asi)(riv.), Syria, 63
Oropuche (riv.), Trin. & Tob., 161
Orosei (gulf), Italy, 34
Orosháza, Hung., 41
Orotina, C. Rica, 154
Oroville, Calif., 204
Orrville, Ohio, 284
Orsha, U.S.S.R., 52
Orsk, U.S.S.R., 52
Ortega, Col., 126
Ortegal (cape), Spain, 33
Orteguaza (riv.), Col., 126
Ortles (range), Europe, 34
Ortoire (riv.), Trin. & Tob., 161
Ortón (riv.), Bol., 136
Ortona, Italy, 34
Ortonville, Minn., 254
Oruro (dept.), Bol., 136
Oruro, Bol., 136
Osage, Iowa, 229
Osaka (pref.), Japan, 81
Osaka, Japan, 81
Osawatomie, Kans., 232
Osceola, Ark., 203
Osceola, Iowa, 229
Oscoda, Mich., 250
Osh, U.S.S.R., 48
Oshawa, Ont., 177
Oshima (isl.), Japan, 81
Oshkosh, Wis., 317
Oshogbo, Nigeria, 106
Oshwe, Dem. Rep. of the Congo, 115
Osijek, Yugo., 45
Osipenko (Berdyansk), U.S.S.R., 52
Oskaloosa, Iowa, 229
Oskarshamn, Sweden, 18
Oslo (cap.), Norway, 18
Osmaniye, Turkey, 63
Osnabrück, W. Ger., 22
Osorno (prov.), Chile, 138
Osorno, Chile, 138
Osoyoos, Br. Col., 184
Oss, Neth., 27
Óssa (mt.), Greece, 45
Ossining, N.Y., 276
Ossokmanuan (lake), Newf., 166
Ostend, Belg., 27
Östergotland (county), Sweden, 18
Östersund, Sweden, 18
Østfold (county), Norway, 18
Ostia Antica, Italy, 34
Ostrava, Czech., 41
Ostrogozhsk, U.S.S.R., 52
Ostrov, Czech., 41
Ostrowiec Swkrz., Poland, 47
Ostrów Wlkp., Poland, 47
Ostuni, Italy, 34
Osŭm (riv.), Bulg., 45
Osumi (isls.), Japan, 81
Oswego, N.Y., 276
Oświęcim, Poland, 47
Ota, Japan, 81
Otago (land dist.), N.Z., 101
Otaru, Japan, 81
Otava (riv.), Czech., 41
Otavalo, Ecua., 128
Otavi, S.W. Afr., 118
Otematata, N.Z., 101
Othello, Wash., 310
Otjiwarongo, S.W. Afr., 118
Otoskwin (riv.), Ont., 177
Otradnyy, U.S.S.R., 52
Otranto (strait), Europe, 34, 45
Otsego, Mich., 250
Otsu, Japan, 81
Ottawa (cap.), Canada, 177
Ottawa (riv.), Canada, 163
Ottawa, Ill., 222
Ottawa, Kans., 232
Ottawa (isls.), N.W.T., 187
Ottawa, Ohio, 284
Ottawa Hills, Ohio, 284
Ottumwa, Iowa, 229
Otuzco, Peru, 128
Otway (sound), Chile, 138
Otwock, Poland, 47
Ötztal Alps (mts.), Europe, 41
Ouachita (mts.), U.S., 203, 288
Ouadda, Centr. Afr. Rep., 115
Ouagadougou (cap.), Upp. Volta, 106
Ouahigouya, Upp. Volta, 106
Oualata, Mauritania, 106
Ouanaminthe, Haiti, 158
Ouanary, Fr. Gui., 131
Ouanda-Djalé, Centr. Afr. Rep., 115
Ouargla, Alg., 106
Oudtshoorn, S. Afr., 118
Oued-Zem, Mor., 106
Ouessant (isl.), France, 28
Ouesso, Rep. of Congo, 115
Ouest (dept.), Haiti, 158
Ouest (pt.), Haiti, 158
Ouezzane, Mor., 106
Ougrée, Belg., 27
Ouidah, Dahomey, 106
Oujda, Mor., 106
Ouled-Djellal, Alg., 106
Oullins, France, 28
Oulu (dept.), Fin., 18
Oulu, Fin., 18
Oulu (riv.), Fin., 18
Oum Hadjer, Chad, 111
Ou Neua, Laos, 72
Our (riv.), Europe, 27
Ourinhos, Braz., 135
Ouro Fino, Braz., 135
Ouro Prêto, Braz., 135
Ourthe (riv.), Belg., 27
Ouse (riv.), Eng., 13
Outardes (riv.), Que., 174
Outer Hebrides (isls.), Scot., 15
Outjo, S.W. Afr., 118
Outlook, Sask., 181
Outokumpu, Fin., 18
Outremont, Que., 172
Ovalle, Chile, 138
Ovamboland (reg.), S.W. Afr., 118
Overflakkee (isl.), Neth., 27
Overijssel (prov.), Neth., 27
Overland, Mo., 261
Overland Park, Kans., 232
Overlea, Md., 245
Overton, Nev., 266
Oviedo (prov.), Spain, 33
Oviedo, Spain, 33
Owatonna, Minn., 254
Owego, N.Y., 276
Owendo, Gabon, 115
Owen Falls (dam), Uganda, 115
Owensboro, Ky., 237
Owen Sound, Ont., 177
Owia (bay), St. Vincent, 161
Owings Mills, Md., 245
Owo, Nigeria, 106
Owosso, Mich., 250
Owyhee (lake), Oreg., 291
Oxapampa, Peru, 128
Oxbow, Sask., 181
Oxelösund, Sweden, 18
Oxford, Ala., 194
Oxford, Eng., 13
Oxford (lake), Man., 179
Oxford, Mass., 249
Oxford, Mich., 250
Oxford, Miss., 256
Oxford, N.C., 281
Oxford, N.S., 169
Oxford, Ohio, 284
Oxford, Pa., 294
Oxfordshire (county), Eng., 13
Oxkutzcab, Mex., 150
Oxnard, Calif., 204
Oyama, Japan, 81
Oyapock (riv.), S. Amer., 131
Oyem, Gabon, 115
Oyo, Nigeria, 106
Oyón, Peru, 128
Oyster Bay, N.Y., 276
Ozamiz, Phil. Is., 82
Ozark, Ala., 194
Ozark (mts.), U.S., 203, 261
Ozarks, Lake of the (lake), Mo., 261
Ózd, Hung., 41
Ozona, Tex., 302
Ozumba, Mex., 150

P

Paarl, S. Afr., 118
Pabianice, Poland, 47
Pabna, Pak., 68
Pacajá Grande (riv.), Braz., 132
Pacaraima (range), S. Amer., 132
Pacasmayo, Peru, 128
Pachen, China, 77
Pachitea, Peru, 128
Pacho, Col., 126
Pachuca, Mex., 150
Pachung, China, 77
Pacific, Mo., 261
Pacifica, Calif., 204
Pacific Beach, Calif., 204
Pacific Grove, Calif., 204
Pacific Islands, Territory of the, 87
Pacific Ocean, 87
Pacific Palisades, Hawaii, 218
Packanack Lake, N. J., 273
Padang, Indon., 85
Padangpandjang, Indon., 85
Padangsidimpuan, Indon., 85
Paden City, W. Va., 313
Paderborn, W. Ger., 22
Padilla, Bol., 136
Padlei, N.W.T., 187
Padre Isl. Nat'l Seashore, Tex., 302
Padre Las Casas, Dom. Rep., 158
Padua (prov.), Italy, 34
Padua, Italy, 34
Paducah, Ky., 237
Paektu (Baktu) (mt.), N. Korea, 81
Pafúri, Mozamb., 118
Pag (isl.), Yugo., 45
Pagadian, Phil. Is., 82
Pagalungan, Phil. Is., 82
Pagan, Burma, 72
Pagan (isl.), Pac. Is., 87
Page, Ariz., 198
Pagedale, Mo., 261
Pago Pago (cap.), Amer. Samoa, 87
Pagoua (bay), Dominica, 161
Pahala, Hawaii, 218
Pahang (state), Malaysia, 72
Pahang (riv.), Malaysia, 72
Pahlevi, Iran, 66
Pahokee, Fla., 212
Paia, Hawaii, 218
Paicheng, China, 77
Paijan, Peru, 128
Päijänne (lake), Fin., 18
Pailin, Cambodia, 72
Pailingmiao, China, 77
Paillaco, Chile, 138
Paine, Chile, 138
Painesville, Ohio, 284
Painted (des.), Ariz., 198
Painted Post, N.Y., 276
Paintsville, Ky., 237
Paipote, Chile, 138
Paisley, Scot., 15
Paita, Peru, 128
Paiyin, China, 77
Pajakumbuh, Indon., 85
Pakanbaru, Indon., 85
Pak Beng, Laos, 72
Pakch'ŏn, N. Korea, 81
Pak Hin Boun, Laos, 72
Pakhoi, China, 77
Pakistan, 68
Paklay, Laos, 72
Pakokku, Burma, 72
Pak Sane, Laos, 72
Pakse, Laos, 72
Pakwach, Uganda, 115
Pala, Chad, 111
Palacios, Tex., 302
Palana, U.S.S.R., 48
Palanpur, India, 68
Palapye, Botswana, 118
Palatine, Ill., 222
Palatka, Fla., 212
Palau (isls.), Pac. Is., 87
Palawan (prov.), Phil. Is., 82
Palawan (isl.), Phil. Is., 82
Palayan, Phil. Is., 82
Palayankottai, India, 68
Palembang, Indon., 85
Palena (river), S. Amer., 138
Palencia (prov.), Spain, 33
Palencia, Spain, 33
Palenque (pt.), Dom. Rep., 158
Palenque (ruins), Mex., 150
Palermo (prov.), Italy, 34
Palermo, Italy, 34
Palestine, Tex., 302
Palghat, India, 68
Pali, India, 68
Palimé, Togo, 106
Palisades Park, N. J., 273
Palk (strait), Asia, 68
Palliser (cape), N.Z., 101
Palma, Mozamb., 118
Palma, Spain, 33
Palmares, Braz., 132
Palmares, C. Rica, 154
Palmarola (isl.), Italy, 34
Palmas (cape), Liberia, 106
Palmas Altas (pt.), P. Rico, 161
Palm Bay, Fla., 212
Palm Beach, Fla., 212
Palmdale, Calif., 204
Palmeira, Braz., 135
Palmeirinhas (pt.), Angola, 115
Palmer, Alaska, 196
Palmer, Mass., 249
Palmer Land (reg.), Ant., 5
Palmer Sta., Ant., 5
Palmerston (atoll), Cook Is., 87
Palmerston North, N.Z., 101
Palmerton, Pa., 294
Palmetto, Fla., 212
Palmetto (pt.), St. Chr.-N.-A., 161
Palmiet (river), S. Afr., 118
Palmillas (pt.), Dom. Rep., 158
Palmira, Col., 126
Palmira, Cuba, 158
Palmitas, Urug., 145
Palm Springs, Calif., 204
Palm Springs, Fla., 212
Palmyra, Mo., 261
Palmyra, N. J., 273
Palmyra, N.Y., 276
Palmyra (isl.), Pacific, 87
Palmyra, Pa., 294
Palmyra (Tadmor), Syria, 63
Palmyras (pt.), India, 68
Palni, India, 68
Palo, Phil. Is., 82
Palo Alto, Calif., 204
Palomar (mt.), Calif., 204
Palos (cape), Spain, 33
Palos Hts., Ill., 222
Palos Hills, Ill., 222
Palos Verdes Estates, Calif., 204
Palpa, Peru, 128
Pamangkat, Indon., 85
Pamekasan, Indon., 85
Pameungpeuk, Indon., 85
Pamir (plat.), Asia, 54
Pamlico (sound), N.C., 281
Pampa, Tex., 302
Pampanga (prov.), Phil. Is., 82
Pampas (plain), Arg., 143
Pampas, Peru, 128
Pamplona, Col., 126
Pamplona, Spain, 33
Pana, Ill., 222
Panagyurishte, Bulg., 45
Panama, 154
Panama (canal), C.Z., 154
Panamá (cap.), Pan., 154
Panamá (gulf), Pan., 154
Panama City, Fla., 212
Panaon (isl.), Phil. Is., 82
Panarea (isl.), Italy, 34
Panaro (riv.), Italy, 34
Panay (isl.), Phil. Is., 82
Pančevo, Yugo., 45
Panchur, India, 68
Panda, Mozamb., 118
Pan de Azúcar, Urug., 145
Pandeglang, Indon., 85
Pandharpur, India, 68
Pando (dept.), Bol., 136
Pando (mt.), Pan., 154
Pando, Urug., 145
Panevėžys, U.S.S.R., 53
Panfilov, U.S.S.R., 48
Pangai, Tonga, 87
Pangala, Rep. of Congo, 115
Pangani, Tanz., 115
Pangasinan (prov.), Phil. Is., 82
Pangi, Dem. Rep. of the Congo, 115
Pangkalanberandan, Indon., 85
Pangkalpinang, Indon., 85
Pangkiang, China, 77
Panglao (isl.), Phil. Is., 82
Pangong Tso (lake), Asia, 68
Panguipulli, Chile, 138
Panguitch, Utah, 304
Pangutaran Group (isls.), Phil. Is., 82
Panihati, India, 68
Panipat, India, 68
Panjao, Afghan., 68
Panjim, India, 68
Pankow, E. Ger., 22
P'anmunjŏm, Korea, 81
Pantelleria (isl.), Italy, 34
Pantin, France, 28
Pánuco, Mex., 150
Panuke (lake), N.S., 169
Panzós, Guat., 154
Pao (river), Venez., 124
Paochang, China, 77
Paoki, China, 77
Paola, Kans., 232
Paoli, Ind., 227
Paoli, Pa., 294
Paoshan, China, 77
Paoting, China, 77
Paotow, China, 77
Paoua, Centr. Afr. Rep., 115
Pápa, Hung., 41
Papagaio (riv.), Braz., 132
Papagayo (gulf), C. Rica, 154
Papaikou, Hawaii, 218
Papantla de Olarte, Mex., 150
Papar, Malaysia, 85
Papa Stour (isl.), Scot., 15
Papeete (cap.), Fr. Poly., 87
Paphos, Cyprus, 63
Papineauville, Que., 172
Papua, 85
Papua (gulf), Papua, 85
Papun, Burma, 72
Papunáua (riv.), Col., 126
Papurí (riv.), Col., 126
Pará (state), Braz., 132
Pará (Belém), Braz., 132
Paracas (pen.), Peru, 128
Paracatu, Braz., 132
Parachinar, Pak., 68
Paraćin, Yugo., 45
Pará de Minas, Braz., 135
Paradise, Calif., 204
Paradise, Nev., 266
Paradise Valley, Ariz., 198
Paragould, Ark., 203
Paraguá (riv.), Bol., 136
Paragua (riv.), Venez., 124
Paraguaçu Paulista, Braz., 132
Paraguaná (pen.), Venez., 124
Paraguarí (dept.), Par., 144
Paraguarí, Par., 144
Paraguay, 144
Paraguay (riv.), S. Amer., 120
Paraíba (state), Braz., 132
Paraíba (João Pessoa), Braz., 132
Paraíba do Sul, Braz., 135
Paraíso, C. Rica, 154
Paraíso, Mex., 150
Parakou, Dahomey, 106
Paramaribo (dist.), Sur., 131
Paramaribo (cap.), Sur., 131
Paramount, Calif., 204
Paramus, N. J., 273
Paraná, Arg., 143
Paraná (state), Braz., 132
Paraná (riv.), Braz., 132
Paraná (riv.), S. Amer., 120
Paranaguá, Braz., 135
Paranaíba, Braz., 132
Paranam, Sur., 131
Paranapanema (riv.), Braz., 132
Paranapiacaba (range), Braz., 135
Paranatinga (riv.), Braz., 132
Parao (riv.), Urug., 145
Parapetí (riv.), Bol., 136
Parati, Braz., 135
Paratinga, Braz., 132
Parbhani, India, 68
Pardo (riv.), Braz., 132, 135
Pardubice, Czech., 41
Pare, Indon., 85
Parece Vela (isl.), Japan, 87
Parent, Que., 174
Parepare, Indon., 85
Parham, Antigua, 161
Paria (gulf), 124
Paria (pen.), Venez., 124
Pariaguán, Venez., 124
Pariaman, Indon., 85
Parícutin (vol.), Mex., 150
Parida (isl.), Pan., 154
Parika, Guyana, 131
Parima (mts.), S. Amer., 124
Parinacochas (lake), Peru, 128
Pariñas (pt.), Peru, 128
Parintins, Braz., 132
Paris, Ark., 203
Paris (dept.), France, 28
Paris (cap.), France, 28
Paris, Ill., 222
Paris, Ky., 237
Paris, Maine, 242
Paris, Ont., 177
Paris, Tenn., 237
Paris, Tex., 302
Parita, Pan., 154
Park (range), Colo., 208
Park City, Kans., 232
Parkdale, P.E.I., 169
Parker, Fla., 212
Parker (dam), U.S., 198
Parkersburg, W. Va., 313
Parkes, N.S.W., 97
Parkesburg, Pa., 294
Park Falls, Wis., 317
Park Forest, Ill., 222
Park Hills, Ky., 237
Parkland, Wash., 310
Park Rapids, Minn., 254
Park Ridge, Ill., 222
Park Ridge, N. J., 273
Park River, N. Dak., 283
Parksville, Br. Col., 184
Parkville, Md., 245
Parkville, Pa., 294
Parlakhemundi, India, 68
Parma (prov.), Italy, 34
Parma, Italy, 34
Parma, Ohio, 284
Parma Hts., Ohio, 284
Parnaíba, Braz., 132
Parnaíba (riv.), Braz., 132
Parnassus (mt.), Greece, 45
Pärnu, U.S.S.R., 53
Paro Dzong, India, 68
Paropamisus (range), Afghan., 68
Páros (isl.), Greece, 45
Parow, S. Afr., 118
Parowan, Utah, 304
Parral, Chile, 138
Parral, Mex., 150
Parramatta, N.S.W., 97
Parras, Mex., 150
Parrsboro, N.S., 169
Parry (chan.), N.W.T., 187
Parry Sound, Ont., 177
Parsippany, N. J., 273
Parsnip (riv.), Br. Col., 184
Parsons, Kans., 232
Partinico, Italy, 34
Parvatipuram, India, 68
Parys, S. Afr., 118
Pasadena, Calif., 204
Pasadena, Tex., 302
Pasado (cape), Ecua., 128
Pasaje, Ecua., 128
Pasargadae (ruins), Iran, 66
Pasay, Phil. Is., 82
Pascagoula, Miss., 256
Paşcani, Rum., 45
Pasco (dept.), Peru, 128
Pasco, Wash., 310
Pascoag, R.I., 249
Pascua (Easter) (isl.), Chile, 87
Pascua (riv.), Chile, 138
Pas-de-Calais (dept.), France, 28
Pasión (riv.), Guat., 154
Paso de los Libres, Arg., 143
Paso de los Toros, Urug., 145
Pasorapa, Bol., 136
Paso Robles, Calif., 204
Passage West, Ire., 17
Passaic, N. J., 273
Passamaquoddy (bay), N. Amer., 170
Passau, W. Ger., 22
Pass Christian, Miss., 256
Passo Fundo, Braz., 132
Passos, Braz., 135
Pastaza (prov.), Ecua., 128
Pastaza (riv.), S. Amer., 128
Pasto, Col., 126
Pasuruan, Indon., 85
Pasvik (riv.), Europe, 18
Patacamaya, Bol., 136
Patagonia (reg.), Arg., 143
Patan, India, 68
Patapédia (riv.), Canada, 170, 172
Patchogue, N.Y., 276
Paternion, Austria, 41
Paterno, Italy, 34
Paterson, N. J., 273
Pathfinder (res.), Wyo., 319
Pati, Indon., 85
Patía (riv.), Col., 126
Patiala, India, 68
Patillas, P. Rico, 161
Pativilca (riv.), Peru, 128
Patjitan, Indon., 85
Pátmos (isl.), Greece, 45
Patna, India, 68
Patos, Braz., 132
Patrái, Greece, 45
Patrocínio, Braz., 132
Patta (isl.), Kenya, 115
Pattani, Thai., 72
Patterson, La., 238
Patton, Pa., 294
Patuca (riv.), Hond., 154
Pátzcuaro, Mex., 150
Pátzcuaro (lake), Mex., 150
Pau, France, 28
Paucartambo, Peru, 128
Paul (isl.), Newf., 166
Paulaya (riv.), Hond., 154
Paulding, Ohio, 284
Paulo de Faria, Braz., 135
Paulsboro, N. J., 273
Pauls Valley, Okla., 288
Pauto (riv.), Col., 126
Pavia (prov.), Italy, 34
Pavia, Italy, 34
Pāvilosta, U.S.S.R., 53
Pavlodar, U.S.S.R., 48
Pavlovo, U.S.S.R., 52
Pawcatuck, Conn., 210
Pawhuska, Okla., 288
Paw Paw, Mich., 250
Pawtucket, R.I., 249
Paxoí (isl.), Greece, 45
Paxton, Ill., 222
Paya Lebar, Sing., 72
Payette, Idaho, 220
Payneham, S. Austral., 94
Paysandú (dept.), Urug., 145
Paysandú, Urug., 145
Payson, Utah, 304
Paz, Arg., 143
Pazardzhik, Bulg., 45
Peabody, Mass., 249
Peace (riv.), Canada, 163
Peace River, Alta., 182
Peak, The (mt.), Eng., 13
Pea Ridge Nat'l Mil. Park, Ark., 203
Pearl (harb.), Hawaii, 218
Pearl, Miss., 256
Pearl and Hermes (reef), Hawaii, 218
Pearl City, Hawaii, 218
Pearl River, N.Y., 276
Pearsall, Tex., 302
Peary Land (reg.), Greenl., 4
Pebane, Mozamb., 118
Peć, Yugo., 45
Pechora, U.S.S.R., 52
Pechora (riv.), U.S.S.R., 52
Pecos, Tex., 302
Pecos (riv.), U.S., 274, 302
Pecos Nat'l Mon., N. Mex., 274
Pécs, Hung., 41
Pedasí, Pan., 154
Pedernales (prov.), Dom. Rep., 158
Pedernales, Dom. Rep., 158
Pedernales (riv.), Tex., 302
Pedra Azul, Braz., 132
Pedraza, Col., 126
Pedreiras, Braz., 132
Pedro (pt.), Ceylon, 68
Pedro Betancourt, Cuba, 158
Pedro de Valdivia, Chile, 138
Pedro Juan Caballero, Par., 144
Pedro Montoya, Mex., 150
Peebles (county), Scot., 15
Peebles, Scot., 15
Peekskill, N.Y., 276
Peel (riv.), Canada, 187
Peel, I. of Man, 13
Pegasus (bay), N.Z., 101
Pegu (div.), Burma, 72
Pegu, Burma, 72
Pegu Yoma (mts.), Burma, 72
Pehuajó, Arg., 143
Peihai (Pakhoi), China, 77
Peine, W. Ger., 22
Peiping (Peking) (cap.), China, 77
Peipus (lake), U.S.S.R., 53
Peixoto (dam), Braz., 135
Pekalongan, Indon., 85
Pekan, Malaysia, 72
Pekan Nanas, Malaysia, 72
Pekin, Ill., 222
Peking (cap.), China, 77
Pelagie (isls.), Italy, 34
Pelagruž (Pelagosa) (isl.), Yugo., 45
Pelée (mt.), Mart., 161
Pelée (pt.), Ont., 177
Peleliu (isl.), Pac. Is., 87
Pelham, Ga., 216
Pelham Manor, N.Y., 276
Pelican (mts.), Alta., 182
Pelileo, Ecua., 128
Pella, Iowa, 229
Pell City, Ala., 194
Pellegrini, Arg., 143
Pelly (riv.), Yukon, 187
Pelopónnisos (reg.), Greece, 45
Pelotas, Braz., 132
Pemalang, Indon., 85
Pematangsiantar, Indon., 85
Pemba (prov.), Tanz., 115
Pemba (isl.), Tanz., 115
Pemberton, W. Austral., 92
Pembroke, N.H., 268
Pembroke, Ont., 177
Pembroke, Wales, 13
Pembrokeshire (county), Wales, 13
Peña, Dom. Rep., 158
Peñablanca, Chile, 138
Peñaflor, Chile, 138
Peñal, Trin. & Tob., 161
Peñalara (mt.), Spain, 33
Penapolis, Braz., 135
Pen Argyl, Pa., 294
Peñarroya-Pueblonuevo, Spain, 33
Penarth, Wales, 13
Penas (gulf), Chile, 138
Peñas (cape), Spain, 33
Penbrook, Pa., 294
Penco, Chile, 138
Pendé (river), Centr. Afr. Rep., 115
Pendembu, S. Leone, 106
Pendleton, Oreg., 291
Pend Oreille (lake), Idaho, 220
Penedo, Braz., 132
Penetanguishene, Ont., 177
Penganga (riv.), India, 68
Penghu (isls.), China, 77
Pengpu, China, 77
Penibética (mts.), Spain, 33
Penicuik, Scot., 15
Pénjamo, Mex., 150
Penki, China, 77
Penmarch (pt.), France, 28
Penner (riv.), India, 68
Pennine (range), Eng., 13
Pennine Alps (range), Europe, 29
Pennsauken, N. J., 273
Penns Grove, N. J., 273
Pennsville, N. J., 273
Pennsylvania (state), U.S., 294
Penn Yan, N.Y., 276
Penola, S. Austral., 94
Peñón Blanco, Mex., 150
Penonomé, Pan., 154
Penrhyn (Tongareva) (atoll), Cook Is., 87
Penrith, N.S.W., 97
Pensacola, Fla., 212
Penticton, Br. Col., 184
Pentland (firth), Scot., 15
Peñuelas, P. Rico, 161
Penza, U.S.S.R., 52
Penzance, Eng., 13
Penzhina (bay), U.S.S.R., 48
Peoria, Ariz., 198
Peoria, Ill., 222
Peoria Hts., Ill., 222
Pepe (cape), Cuba, 158
Pepper Pike, Ohio, 284
Peqin, Alb., 45
Pequannock, N. J., 273
Pera (head), Queensland, 95
Pera (Beyoğlu), Turkey, 63
Perahbumulih, Indon., 85
Perak (state), Malaysia, 72
Perales (riv.), Spain, 33
Peralta, Dom. Rep., 158
Peravia (prov.), Dom. Rep., 158
Percé, Que., 172
Perche (reg.), France, 28
Perdido (mt.), Spain, 33
Pereira, Col., 126
Perelik (mt.), Bulg., 45
Pérez, Arg., 143
Pergamino, Arg., 143
Péribonca (riv.), Que., 174
Perico, Cuba, 158
Périgueux, France, 28
Perijá (mts.), S. Amer., 126
Perim (isl.), P.D.R. Yemen, 59
Periyar (lake), India, 68
Perkam (cape), Indon., 85
Perkasie, Pa., 294
Perlas (lag.), Nic., 154
Perlas (arch.), Pan., 154
Perlis (state), Malaysia, 72
Perm', U.S.S.R., 52
Përmet, Alb., 45
Pernambuco (state), Braz., 132
Pernambuco (Recife), Braz., 132
Pernik, Bulg., 45
Perote, Mex., 150
Perpignan, France, 28
Perrine, Fla., 212
Perris, Calif., 204
Perros (bay), Cuba, 158
Perry, Fla., 212
Perry, Ga., 216
Perry, Iowa, 229
Perry, N.Y., 276
Perry (riv.), N.W.T., 187
Perry, Okla., 288
Perrygo Place, Wis., 317
Perrysburg, Ohio, 284
Perrys Victory Nat'l Mon., Ohio, 284
Perryton, Tex., 302
Perryville, Mo., 261
Persepolis (ruins), Iran, 66
Perseverance (bay), Virgin Is. (U.S.), 161
Persia (Iran), 66
Persian (gulf), Asia, 59
Perth, N.B., 170
Perth, Ont., 177
Perth (county), Scot., 15
Perth, Scot., 15
Perth (cap.), W. Austral., 92
Perth Amboy, N. J., 273
Peru, 128
Peru, Ill., 222
Peru, Ind., 227
Perugia (prov.), Italy, 34
Perugia, Italy, 34
Pervomaysk, U.S.S.R., 52
Pesaro, Italy, 34
Pesaro e Urbino (prov.), Italy, 34
Pescadores (Penghu)(isls.), China, 77
Pescara (prov.), Italy, 34
Pescara, Italy, 34
Peshawar, Pak., 68
Peshkopi, Alb., 45
Peshtera, Bulg., 45
Peshtigo, Wis., 317
Pespire, Hond., 154
Pessac, France, 28
Pest (county), Hung., 41
Petacalco (bay), Mex., 150
Petah Tiqwa, Israel, 65
Petal, Miss., 256
Petaluma, Calif., 204
Pétange, Lux., 27
Petatlán, Mex., 150
Petauke, Zambia, 115
Petawawa, Ont., 177
Petén-Itzá (lake), Guat., 154
Peter (isl.), Virgin Is. (Br.), 161
Peter I (isl.), Ant., 5
Peterborough, Eng., 13
Peterborough, Ont., 177
Peterborough, S.Austral., 94
Peterhead, Scot., 15
Petermann (ranges), Austral., 93
Peteroa (vol.), S. Amer., 138
Petersburg, Alaska, 196
Petersburg, Ind., 227
Petersburg, Va., 307
Pétionville, Haiti, 158
Petit-Bourg, Guad., 161
Petitcodiac, N.B., 170
Petite Rivière de la Baleine (riv.), Que., 174
Petite-Rivière-de-l'Artibonite, Haiti, 158
Petite-Terre (isls.), Guad., 161
Petit-Goâve, Haiti, 158
Petit-Mécatina (riv.), Que., 174
Petitot (riv.), Canada, 187
Peto, Mex., 150
Petone, N.Z., 101
Petoskey, Mich., 250
Petra (ruins), Jordan, 65
Petrich, Bulg., 45
Petrified Forest Nat'l Park, Ariz., 198
Petrila, Rum., 45
Petrolia, Ont., 177
Petrolina, Braz., 132
Petrona (pt.), P. Rico, 161
Petropavlovsk, U.S.S.R., 48
Petropavlovsk-Kamchatskiy, U.S.S.R., 48
Petrópolis, Braz., 135
Petroşeni, Rum., 45
Petrovsk, U.S.S.R., 52
Petrovsk-Zabaykal'skiy, U.S.S.R., 48
Petrozavodsk, U.S.S.R., 52
Peu, Br. Sol. Is., 87
Peumo, Chile, 138
Pezinok, Czech., 41
Pforzheim, W. Ger., 22
Phan Rang, S. Vietnam, 72
Phan Ri, S. Vietnam, 72
Phan Thiet, S. Vietnam, 72
Pharr, Tex., 302
Phatthalung, Thai., 72
Phayao, Thai., 72
Phelps (peak), Venez., 124
Phenix City, Ala., 194
Phet Buri, Thai., 72
Phichit, Thai., 72
Philadelphia, Miss., 256
Philadelphia, Pa., 294
Philippeville (Skikda), Alg., 106
Philippines, 82
Philipsburg, Pa., 294
Phillips, Tex., 302
Phillipsburg, Kans., 232
Phillipsburg, N. J., 273
Phitsanulok, Thai., 72
Phnom Penh (cap.), Cambodia, 72
Phoc Tuy, S. Vietnam, 72
Phoenix (cap.), Ariz., 198
Phoenix (isls.), Gilb. & Ell. Is., 87
Phoenix, Ill., 222
Phoenixville, Pa., 294
Phong Saly, Laos, 72
Phrae, Thai., 72
Phsar Oudong, Cambodia, 72
Phu Bia (mt.), Laos, 72
Phuc Loi, N. Vietnam, 72
Phu Co Pi (mt.), Laos, 72
Phu Cuong, S. Vietnam, 72
Phu Dien, N. Vietnam, 72
Phuket, Thai., 72
Phu Loc, S. Vietnam, 72
Phu Loi (mt.), Laos, 72
Phum Rovieng, Cambodia, 72
Phu My, S. Vietnam, 72
Phu Qui, N. Vietnam, 72
Phu Quoc, Dao (isl.), S. Vietnam, 72
Phu Rieng, S. Vietnam, 72
Phu Tho, N. Vietnam, 72
Phutthaisong, Thai., 72
Phu Vinh (Tra Vinh), S. Vietnam, 72
P. I. (Paul Isnard), Fr. Gui., 131
Piacenza (prov.), Italy, 34
Piacenza, Italy, 34
Pialba, Queensland, 95
Pianosa (isl.), Italy, 34
Piatra Neamţ, Rum., 45
Piauí (state), Braz., 132
Piauí (riv.), Braz., 132
Piave (riv.), Italy, 34
Piazza Armerina, Italy, 34
Pibor Post, Sudan, 111
Picara (pt.), Virgin Is. (U.S.), 161
Picayune, Miss., 256
Picher, Okla., 288
Pichilemu, Chile, 138
Pichincha (prov.), Ecua., 128
Pickersgill, Guyana, 131
Pico (isl.), Port., 32
Pico Rivera, Calif., 204
Picos, Braz., 132
Picota, Peru, 128
Picton, N.Z., 101
Picton, Ont., 177
Pictou, N.S., 169
Picture Butte, Alta., 182
Pictured Rocks Nat'l Lakeshore, Mich., 250
Pidurutalagala (mt.), Ceylon, 68
Piedecuesta, Col., 126
Piedmont, Ala., 194
Piedmont, Calif., 204
Piedmont (reg.), Italy, 34
Piedra Blanca, Dom. Rep., 158
Piedras Negras, Mex., 150
Piekary Śląskie, Poland, 47
Pieksämäki, Fin., 18
Pielinen (lake), Fin., 18
Pierre (cap.), S. Dak., 298
Pierrefonds, Que., 172
Piešt'any, Czech., 41
Pietarsaari (Jakobstad), Fin., 18
Pietermaritzburg, S. Africa, 118
Pietersburg, S. Afr., 118
Piet Retief, S. Afr., 118
Pietrosul (mt.), Rum., 45
Pigeon (riv.), N. Amer., 179
Piggott, Ark., 203
Pigs (Cochinos)(bay), Cuba, 158
Pigüé, Arg., 143
Pija (mts.), Hond., 154
Pijijiapan, Mex., 150
Pikes (peak), Colo., 208
Pikesville, Md., 245
Piketberg, S. Afr., 118
Pikeville, Ky., 237
Pikiang, China, 77
Pila, Poland, 47
Pilar, Arg., 143
Pilar, Braz., 132
Pilar, Par., 144
Pilatus (mt.), Switz., 39
Pilaya (riv.), Bol., 136
Pilcomayo (riv.), S. Amer., 143
Pilibhit, India, 68
Píllaro, Ecua., 128
Pillsbury (sound), Virgin Is. (U.S.), 161
Pilote (riv.), Mart., 161
Pimentel, Dom. Rep., 158
Pimentel, Peru, 128
Pimville, S. Afr., 118
Pina, Cuba, 158
Pinang (state), Malaysia, 72
Pinang, Malaysia, 72
Pinang (isl.), Malaysia, 72
Pinar del Río (prov.), Cuba, 158
Pinar del Río, Cuba, 158
Piñas, Ecua., 128
Piñas (pt.), Pan., 154
Pincher Creek, Alta., 182
Pinckneyville, Ill., 222
Pindamonhangaba, Braz., 135
Pindo (riv.), Ecua., 128
Pindus (mts.), Greece, 45
Pine Bluff, Ark., 203
Pine Creek, N. Terr., 93
Pine Falls, Man., 179
Pinega (riv.), U.S.S.R., 52
Pine Hill, N. J., 273
Pinelands, S. Afr., 118
Pine Lawn, Mo., 261
Pinellas Park, Fla., 212
Pine Ridge, S. Dak., 298
Pinerolo, Italy, 34
Pines, Isle of (isl.), Cuba, 158
Pines, Isle of (isl.), New Cal., 87
Pinetown, S. Afr., 118
Pineville, Ky., 237
Pineville, La., 238
Pingchüan, China, 77
Pingelap (atoll), Pac. Is., 87
Pingelly, W. Austral., 92
Pingliang, China, 77
Pinglo, China, 77
Pingsiang, China, 77
Pingtung, China, 77
Pingwu, China, 77
Pinhal, Braz., 135
Piniós (riv.), Greece, 45
Pinjarra, W. Austral., 92
Pinnacles Nat'l Mon., Calif., 204
Pinneberg, W. Ger., 22
Pinole, Calif., 204
Pinsk, U.S.S.R., 52
Pinta (isl.), Ecua., 128
Piombino, Italy, 34
Piotrków Tryb., Poland, 47
Pipe Spring Nat'l Mon., Ariz., 198
Pipestone, Minn., 254
Pipestone (riv.), Ont., 177
Pipestone Nat'l Mon., Minn., 254
Piqua, Ohio, 284
Piquete, Braz., 135
Piracicaba, Braz., 135
Piraeus (Piraiévs), Greece, 45
Piraju, Braz., 135
Pirámide (mt.), Chile, 138
Pirané, Arg., 143
Pirapora, Braz., 132
Pirassununga, Braz., 135
Piray (riv.), Bol., 136
Pires do Rio, Braz., 132
Pírgos, Greece, 45
Piriápolis, Urug., 145
Pirata (mt.), P. Rico, 161
Pirayú, Par., 144
Piribebuy, Par., 144
Piripiri, Braz., 132
Píritu, Venez., 124
Pirmasens, W. Ger., 22
Pirna, E. Ger., 22
Pirot, Yugo., 45
Pirua (riv.), Peru, 128
Pisa (prov.), Italy, 34
Pisa, Italy, 34
Piscadera (bay), Neth. Ant., 161
Piscataway, N. J., 273
Pisco, Peru, 128
Písek, Czech., 41
Pistoia (prov.), Italy, 34
Pistoia, Italy, 34
Pistolet (bay), Newf., 166
Pitalito, Col., 126

Pitangui, Braz., 135
Pitcairn (isl.), 87
Pitcairn, Pa., 294
Pitch (lake), Trin. & Tob., 161
Piteå, Sweden, 18
Pitești, Rum., 45
Pitman, N. J., 273
Piton des Neiges (mt.), Reunion, 118
Pitrufquén, Chile, 138
Pitt (isl.), Br. Col., 184
Pitt (isl.), N.Z., 101
Pitt (mt.), Norfolk I., 88
Pittsburg, Calif., 204
Pittsburg, Kans., 232
Pittsburg, Tex., 302
Pittsburgh, Pa., 294
Pittsfield, Ill., 222
Pittsfield, Maine, 242
Pittsfield, Mass., 249
Pittston, Pa., 294
Piuí, Braz., 135
Piura (dept.), Peru, 128
Piura, Peru, 128
Pivijay, Col., 126
Pizarro, Col., 126
Placentia, Calif., 204
Placentia, Newf., 166
Placentia (bay), Newf., 166
Placerville, Calif., 204
Placetas, Cuba, 158
Plainfield, Ind., 227
Plainfield, N. J., 273
Plains, Pa., 294
Plainview, N.Y., 276
Plainview, Tex., 302
Plainville, Conn., 210
Plainville, Kans., 232
Plainwell, Mich., 250
Plana (cays), Bah. Is., 156
Plano, Ill., 222
Plano, Tex., 302
Plantation, Fla., 212
Plant City, Fla., 212
Plantsville, Conn., 210
Plaquemine, La., 238
Plasencia, Spain, 33
Plaster Rock, N.B., 170
Plata (riv.), P. Rico, 161
Plata, Río de la (est.), S. Amer., 143
Plato, Col., 126
Platte (riv.), Nebr., 264
Platteville, Wis., 317
Platt Nat'l Park, Okla., 288
Plattsburgh, N.Y., 276
Plattsmouth, Nebr., 264
Plauen, E. Ger., 22
Playa de Fajardo, P. Rico, 161
Playa de Humacao, P. Rico, 161
Playas, Ecua., 128
Playón Chico, Pan., 154
Plaza Huincul, Arg., 143
Pleasant Grove, Utah, 304
Pleasant Hill, Calif., 204
Pleasant Hill, Mo., 261
Pleasant Hill, Va., 307
Pleasant Hills, Pa., 294
Pleasanton, Calif., 204
Pleasanton, Tex., 302
Pleasant Ridge, Mich., 250
Pleasantville, N.Y., 276
Pleasure Ridge Park, Ky., 237
Pleiku, S. Vietnam, 72
Pleime, S. Vietnam, 72
Plenty (bay), N.Z., 101
Plentywood, Mont., 262
Plessisville, Que., 172
Plétipi (lake), Que., 174
Plettenberg (bay), S. Afr., 118
Plettenberg, W. Ger., 22
Pleven, Bulg., 45
Plimmerton-Paremata, N.Z., 101
Pljevlja, Yugo., 45
Płock, Poland, 47
Ploiești, Rum., 45
Plomb du Cantal (mt.), France, 28
Plovdiv, Bulg., 45
Plum, Pa., 294
Plumtree, Rhod., 118
Plymouth, Conn., 210
Plymouth, Eng., 13
Plymouth, Ind., 227
Plymouth, Mass., 249
Plymouth, Mich., 250
Plymouth, Minn., 254
Plymouth (cap.), Montserrat, 156
Plymouth, N.H., 268
Plymouth, N.C., 281
Plymouth, Pa., 294
Plymouth, Wis., 317
Plzeň, Czech., 41
Pniel, S. Afr., 118
Po (riv.), Italy, 34
Po, Upp. Volta, 106
Pobeda (peak), Asia, 48
Pocahontas, Ark., 203
Pocatello, Idaho, 220
Pochutla, Mex., 150
Pocomoke City, Md., 245
Poços de Caldas, Braz., 135
Poděbrady, Czech., 41
Podgorica (Titograd), Yugo., 45
Podol'sk, U.S.S.R., 52
Podor, Sen., 106
Pogradec, Alb., 45
Po Hai (Chihli) (gulf), China, 77
P'ohang, S. Korea, 81
Pohjois-Karjala (dept.), Fin., 18
Pohsien, China, 77
Point (lake), N.W.T., 187
Pointe-à-Pitre, Guad., 161
Pointe-aux-Trembles, Que., 172
Pointe-Claire, Que., 172
Point Edward, Ont., 177
Pointe-Gatineau, Que., 172
Pointe-Noire, Rep. of Congo, 115
Point Fortin, Trin. & Tob., 161
Pt. Mugu Pacific Missile Range, Calif., 204
Point Pelée Nat'l Park, Ont., 177
Point Pleasant, N. J., 273
Point Pleasant, W. Va., 313
Point Pleasant Beach, N. J., 273
Point Reyes Nat'l Seashore, Calif., 204
Poitiers, France, 28
Pojo, Bol., 136
Pokhara, Nepal, 68
Poko, Dem. Rep. of the Congo, 115
Pola (Pula), Yugo., 45
Poland, 47
Poland, Maine, 242
Poland, Ohio, 284
Polar Bear Prov. Park, Ont., 175
Polatlı, Turkey, 63
Polgahawela, Ceylon, 68
Poli, Cameroon, 115
Policastro (gulf), Italy, 34
Polillo (isl.), Phil. Is., 82
Polk, Pa., 294
Polo, Dom. Rep., 158
Polo, Ill., 222
Polonio (cape), Urug., 145
Polonnaruwa, Ceylon, 68
Polotsk, U.S.S.R., 52
Polson, Mont., 262
Poltava, U.S.S.R., 52
Polyanovgrad, Bulg., 45
Polynesia (reg.), Pacific, 87
Pomabamba, Peru, 128
Pomerania (reg.), Europe, 22
Pomeranian (bay), Europe, 22
Pomeroon (riv.), Guyana, 131
Pomeroy, Ohio, 284
Pomona, Calif., 204
Pomona (isl.), Scot., 15
Pompano Beach, Fla., 212
Pompeii (ruins), Italy, 34
Pompton Lakes, N. J., 273
Pompton Plains, N. J., 273
Ponape (isl.), Pac. Is., 87
Ponca City, Okla., 288
Ponce (dist.), P. Rico, 161
Ponce, P. Rico, 161
Ponchatoula, La., 238
Pondicherry (terr.), India, 68
Pondicherry, India, 68
Pondoland (reg.), S. Afr., 118
Poneloya, Nic., 154
Ponferrada, Spain, 33
Pongara (pt.), Gabon, 115
Ponnani, India, 68
Ponoka, Alta., 182
Ponorogo, Indon., 85
Ponta Delgada, Port., 32
Ponta Grossa, Braz., 135
Ponta Porã, Braz., 132
Pontchartrain (lake), La., 238
Pontecorvo, Italy, 34
Pontefract, Eng., 13
Ponteix, Sask., 181
Ponte Nova, Braz., 135
Pontevedra (prov.), Spain, 33
Pontevedra, Spain, 33
Ponthierville, Dem. Rep. of the Congo, 115
Pontiac, Ill., 222
Pontiac, Mich., 250
Pontianak, Indon., 85
Pontian Kechil, Malaysia, 72
Pontic (mts.), Turkey, 63
Pontine (isls.), Italy, 34
Pontoise, France, 28
Pont-Rouge, Que., 172
Pontypool, Wales, 13
Pontypridd, Wales, 13
Poole, Eng., 13
Poona, India, 68
Poopó (lake), Bol., 136
Popayán, Col., 126
Poplar (pt.), Man., 179
Poplar Bluff, Mo., 261
Popocatépetl (mt.), Mex., 150
Popokabaka, Dem. Rep. of the Congo, 115
Popondetta, Papua, 85
Poprad, Czech., 41
Poquonock Bridge, Conn., 210
Poquoson, Va., 307
Porbandar, India, 68
Porcher (isl.), Br. Col., 184
Porcupine (cape), Newf., 166
Porcupine (hills), Sask., 181
Porcupine (riv.), Yukon, 187
Porcupine Plain, Sask., 181
Pordenone, Italy, 34
Pori, Fin., 18
Porlamar, Venez., 124
Poronaysk, U.S.S.R., 48
Porrentruy, Switz., 39
Porsangerfjord (fjord), Norway, 18
Porsgrunn, Norway, 18
Portachuelo, Bol., 136
Port Adelaide, S. Austral., 94
Portage, Ind., 227
Portage, Mich., 250
Portage, Pa., 294
Portage, Wis., 317
Portage la Prairie, Man., 179
Portageville, Mo., 261
Port Alberni, Br. Col., 184
Portales, N. Mex., 274
Port-Alfred, Que., 172
Port Alfred, S. Afr., 118
Port Alice, Br. Col., 184
Port Allegany, Pa., 294
Port Allen, La., 238
Port Angeles, Wash., 310
Port Antonio, Jam., 158
Port-à-Piment, Haiti, 158
Portarlington, Ire., 17
Port Arthur, China, 77
Port Arthur, Tex., 302
Port Augusta, S. Austral., 94
Port au Port (pen.), Newf., 166
Port-au-Prince (cap.), Haiti, 158
Port-Bergé, Malag. Rep., 118
Port Blair, India, 68
Port-Bouet, Ivory Coast, 106
Port Carbon, Pa., 294
Port-Cartier, Que., 174
Port-Cartier-Ouest, Que., 174
Port Chalmers, N.Z., 101
Port Charlotte, Fla., 212
Port Chester, N.Y., 276
Port Clinton, Ohio, 284
Port Colborne, Ont., 177
Port Coquitlam, Br. Col., 184
Port-de-Paix, Haiti, 158
Port Dickson, Malaysia, 72
Port Dover, Ont., 177
Port Elizabeth, S. Afr., 118
Porterville, Calif., 204
Port Everglades (harb.), Fla., 212
Port Ewen, N.Y., 276
Port Fairy, Vic., 97
Port-Francqui, Dem. Rep. of the Congo, 115
Port Fuad, U.A.R., 111
Port-Gentil, Gabon, 115
Port Gibson, Miss., 256
Port Glasgow, Scot., 15
Port Hammond, Br. Col., 184
Port Harcourt, Nigeria, 106
Port Hawkesbury, N.S., 169
Port Hedland, W. Austral., 92
Port Hood, N.S., 169
Port Hope, Ont., 177
Port Hueneme, Calif., 204
Port Huron, Mich., 250
Port Isabel, Tex., 302
Port Jervis, N.Y., 276
Port Kaiser, Jam., 158
Port Kembla, N.S.W., 97
Portland, Barbados, 161
Portland (canal), Br. Col., 184
Portland, Conn., 210
Portland (pen.), Eng., 13
Portland, Ind., 227
Portland (pt.), Jam., 158
Portland, Maine, 242
Portland, Mich., 250
Portland, Oreg., 291
Portland, Tex., 302
Portland, Vic., 97
Portlaoighise, Ire., 17
Port Lavaca, Tex., 302
Portlaw, Ire., 17
Port Lincoln, S. Austral., 94
Port Loko, S. Leone, 106
Port-Louis, Guad., 161
Port Louis (cap.), Mauritius, 118
Port-Lyautey (Kénitra), Mor., 106
Port Macquarie, N.S.W., 97
Port Maria, Jam., 158
Port Melbourne, Vic., 97
Port-Menier, Que., 174
Port Monmouth, N. J., 273
Port Moody, Br. Col., 184
Port Morant, Jam., 158
Port Moresby (cap.), Papua, 85
Port Neches, Tex., 302
Port Nolloth, S. Afr., 118
Porto (Oporto), Port., 33
Pôrto Alegre, Braz., 132
Porto Alexandre, Angola, 115
Porto Amboim, Angola, 115
Porto Amélia, Mozamb., 118
Portobello, Scot., 15
Portobelo, Pan., 154
Porto Civitanova, Italy, 34
Pôrto Feliz, Braz., 135
Portoferraio, Italy, 34
Portofino, Italy, 34
Port-of-Spain (cap.), Trin. and Tob., 161
Portogruaro, Italy, 34
Portola Valley, Calif., 204
Pôrto Murtinho, Braz., 132
Pôrto Nacional, Braz., 132
Porto-Novo (cap.), Dahomey, 106
Porto Quijarro, Bol., 136
Port Orchard, Wash., 310
Pôrto União, Braz., 132
Pôrto Velho, Braz., 132
Portoviejo, Ecua., 128
Port Pirie, S. Austral., 94
Port Radium, N.W.T., 187
Port Reading, N. J., 273
Port Royal, Jam., 158
Portrush, N. Ire., 17
Port Safâga, U.A.R., 111
Port Sa'id, U.A.R., 111
Port St. Joe, Fla., 212
Port St. Johns, S. Afr., 118
Port Shepstone, S. Afr., 118
Port Simpson, Br. Col., 184
Portsmouth, Dominica, 161
Portsmouth, Eng., 13
Portsmouth, N.H., 268
Portsmouth, Ohio, 284
Portsmouth, R.I., 249
Portsmouth, Va., 307
Portstewart, N. Ire., 17
Port Sudan, Sudan, 111
Port Sulphur, La., 238
Port Swettenham, Malaysia, 72
Port Talbot, Wales, 13
Port Tampa (harb.), Fla., 212
Port Taufiq, U.A.R., 111
Port Townsend, Wash., 310
Portugal, 33
Portugal Cove, Newf., 166
Portugalete, Spain, 33
Portugália, Angola, 115
Portuguesa (state), Venez., 124
Portuguese Guinea, 106
Portuguese Timor, 85
Port-Vendres, France, 28
Port Victoria, Kenya, 115
Port Vue, Pa., 294
Port Washington, N.Y., 276
Port Washington, Wis., 317
Port Weld, Malaysia, 72
Port Wentworth, Ga., 216
Poruba, Czech., 41
Porus, Jam., 158
Porvoo (Borgå), Fin., 18
Porz, W. Ger., 22
Posadas, Arg., 143
Poschiavo (valley), Switz., 39
Poseh, China, 77
Posen, Ill., 222
Poso, Indon., 85
Posŏng, S. Korea, 81
Posorja, Ecua., 128
Post, Tex., 302
Poste-de-la-Baleine, Que., 174
Postmasburg, S. Afr., 118
Potaro (riv.), Guyana, 131
Potchefstroom, S. Afr., 118
Poteau, Okla., 288
Poteet, Tex., 302
Potenza (prov.), Italy, 34
Potenza, Italy, 34
Potgietersrus, S. Afr., 118
Poti, U.S.S.R., 52
Potomac (riv.), U.S., 245, 313
Potosí (dept.), Bol., 136
Potosí, Bol., 136
Potosi, Mo., 261
Potrerillo (peak), Cuba, 158
Potrerillos, Chile, 138
Potrerillos, Pan., 154
Potro (mt.), S. Amer., 143
Potsdam (dist.), E. Ger., 22
Potsdam, E. Ger., 22
Potsdam, N.Y., 276
Potters Bar, Eng., 10
Pottersville, Mass., 249
Pottstown, Pa., 294
Pottsville, Pa., 294
Pouce-Coupé, Br. Col., 184
Pouch Cove, Newf., 166
Poudre d'Or, Mauritius, 118
Poughkeepsie, N.Y., 276
Poulo Dama (isls.), S. Vietnam, 72
Poulo Way (isls.), S. Vietnam, 72
Pouso Alegre, Braz., 135
Povorino, U.S.S.R., 52
Povungnituk, Que., 174
Powder (riv.), U.S., 262, 319
Powell (lake), U.S., 198, 304
Powell, Wyo., 319
Powell River, Br. Col., 184
Powerview, Man., 179
Poyang (lake), China, 77
Požarevac, Yugo., 45
Poza Rica, Mex., 150
Požega, Yugo., 45
Poznań (prov.), Poland, 47
Poznań, Poland, 47
Pozzuoli, Italy, 34
Prachin Buri, Thai., 72
Pradera, Col., 126
Prague (Praha) (cap.), Czech., 41
Prahran, Vic., 97
Praia (cap.), C. Verde Is., 106
Prairie du Chien, Wis., 317
Prairie Village, Kans., 232
Praja, Indon., 85
Praslin, St. Lucia, 161
Praslin (isl.), Seych., 118
Pratas (isl.), China, 77
Prato, Italy, 34
Pratt, Kans., 232
Pratteln, Switz., 39
Prattville, Ala., 194
Preapatang (rapids), Cambodia, 72
Preeceville, Sask., 181
Pregonero, Venez., 124
Premont, Tex., 302
Preparis (isl.), Burma, 72
Přerov, Czech., 41
Prescott, Ariz., 198
Prescott, Ark., 203
Prescott, Ont., 177
Presidencia de la Plaza, Arg., 143
Presidencia Roque Sáenz Peña, Arg., 143
Presidente Hayes (dept.), Par., 144
Presidente Prudente, Braz., 132
Presidente Venceslau, Braz., 132
Presidio, Tex., 302
Prešov, Czech., 41
Prespa (lake), Europe, 45
Presque Isle, Maine, 242
Prestea, Ghana, 106
Preston, Cuba, 158
Preston, Eng., 10
Preston, Idaho, 220
Preston, Ont., 177
Preston, Vic., 97
Prestonsburg, Ky., 237
Prestwick, Scot., 15
Prêto (riv.), Braz., 132
Pretoria (cap.), S. Afr., 118
Préveza, Greece, 45
Prey Veng, Cambodia, 72
Pribilof (isls.), Alaska, 196
Příbram, Czech., 41
Price, Que., 172
Price, Utah, 304
Prichard, Ala., 194
Prieska, S. Afr., 118
Prijedor, Yugo., 45
Prikumsk, U.S.S.R., 52
Prilep, Yugo., 45
Priluki, U.S.S.R., 52
Primorsko-Akhtarsk, U.S.S.R., 52
Primrose (lake), Sask., 181
Prince Albert, Sask., 181
Prince Albert, S. Afr., 118
Prince Albert Nat'l Park, Sask., 181
Prince Charles (isl.), N.W.T., 187
Prince Edward (isls.), S. Afr., 5
Prince Edward Island, (prov.), Canada, 169
Prince Edward Isl. Nat'l Park, P.E.I., 169
Prince George, Br. Col., 184
Prince of Wales (isl.), N.W.T., 187
Prince Olav Coast (reg.), Ant., 5
Prince Patrick (isl.), N.W.T., 187
Prince Rupert, Br. Col., 184
Princess Astrid Coast (reg.), Ant., 5
Princess Martha Coast (reg.), Ant., 5
Princess Ragnhild Coast (reg.), Ant., 5
Princess Royal (isl.), Br. Col., 184
Princes Town, Trin. & Tob., 161
Princeton, Br. Col., 184
Princeton, Ill., 222
Princeton, Ind., 227
Princeton, Ky., 237
Princeton, Minn., 254
Princeton, N. J., 273
Princeton, W. Va., 313
Princeville, Que., 172
Príncipe (isl.), São T. and Pr., 106
Prineville, Oreg., 291
Prinzapolca (riv.), Nic., 154
Prinzapolka, Nic., 154
Pripet (marsh), U.S.S.R., 52
Pripyat' (riv.), U.S.S.R., 52
Priština, Yugo., 45
Privateer (pt.), Virgin Is. (U.S.), 161
Priyutovo, U.S.S.R., 52
Prizren, Yugo., 45
Probolinggo, Indon., 85
Proctor, Minn., 254
Proddatur, India, 68
Progreso, Mex., 150
Prokop'yevsk, U.S.S.R., 48
Prokuplje, Yugo., 45
Promissão, Braz., 135
Promyshlennyy, U.S.S.R., 52
Propriá, Braz., 132
Proserpine, Queensland, 95
Prospect, S. Austral., 94
Prospect Park, N. J., 273
Prospect Park, Pa., 294
Prosperidad, Phil. Is., 82
Prosser, Wash., 310
Prostějov, Czech., 41
Provadiya, Bulg., 45
Providence, Ky., 237
Providence (cap.), R.I., 249
Providence, Tenn., 237
Providencia (isl.), Col., 126
Providenciales (isl.), Turks and Caicos Is., 156
Provincetown, Mass., 249
Provo, Utah, 304
Provost, Alta., 182
Prudhoe (bay), Alaska, 196
Prudhoe Land (reg.), Greenl., 4
Pruszków, Poland, 47
Prut (riv.), Europe, 45
Prydz (bay), Ant., 5
Pryor, Okla., 288
Przemyśl, Poland, 47
Przheval'sk, U.S.S.R., 48
Psará (isl.), Greece, 45
Pskov, U.S.S.R., 52
Ptolemaïs, Greece, 45
Puán, Arg., 143
Puangue (riv.), Chile, 138
Pubnico (harb.), N.S., 169
Pucarani, Bol., 136
Pucón, Chile, 138
Pudasjärvi, Fin., 18
Pudukkottai, India, 68
Puebla (state), Mex., 150
Puebla, Mex., 150
Pueblo, Colo., 208
Pueblo Hundido, Chile, 138
Pueblo Nuevo, Venez., 124
Puente Alto, Chile, 138
Puente de Ixtla, Mex., 150
Puente-Genil, Spain, 33
Puerca (pt.), P. Rico, 161
Puercos (prom.), Pan., 154
Puerto Acosta, Bol., 136
Puerto Aisén, Chile, 138
Puerto América, Peru, 128
Puerto Ángel, Mex., 150
Puerto Antequera, Par., 144
Puerto Armuelles, Pan., 154
Puerto Ayacucho, Venez., 124
Puerto Baquerizo Moreno, Ecua., 128
Puerto Barrios, Guat., 154
Puerto Berrío, Col., 126
Puerto Cabello, Venez., 124
Puerto Cabezas, Nic., 154
Puerto Carreño, Col., 126
Puerto Casado, Par., 144
Puerto Colombia, Col., 126
Puerto Cortés, C. Rica, 154
Puerto Cortés, Hond., 154
Puerto Cortés, Mex., 150
Puerto Cumarebo, Venez., 124
Puerto Deseado, Arg., 143
Puerto Eten, Peru, 128
Puerto Guaraní, Par., 144
Puerto Heath, Bol., 136
Puerto Hierro, Venez., 124
Puerto La Cruz, Venez., 124
Puerto Leguízamo, Col., 126
Puertollano, Spain, 33
Puerto López, Col., 126
Puerto Madryn, Arg., 143
Puerto Maldonado, Peru, 128
Puerto Mamoré, Bol., 136
Puerto Medio Mundo (bay), P. Rico, 161
Puerto México (Coatzacoalcos), Mex., 150
Puerto Montt, Chile, 138
Puerto Nariño, Col., 126
Puerto Natales, Chile, 138
Puerto Nuevo (pt.), P. Rico, 161
Puerto Obaldía, Pan., 154
Puerto Padre, Cuba, 158
Puerto Peñasco, Mex., 150
Puerto Pinasco, Par., 144
Puerto Pirámides, Arg., 143
Puerto Píritu, Venez., 124
Puerto Plata (prov.), Dom. Rep., 158
Puerto Plata, Dom. Rep., 158
Puerto Princesa, Phil. Is., 82
Puerto Real, P. Rico, 161
Puerto Real, Spain, 33
Puerto Rico, 161
Puerto Rico, Col., 126
Puerto Salgar, Col., 126
Puerto Sastre, Par., 144
Puerto Siles, Bol., 136
Puerto Suárez, Bol., 136
Puerto Sucre, Bol., 136
Puerto Tejada, Col., 126
Puerto Vallarta, Mex., 150
Puerto Varas, Chile, 138
Puerto Wilches, Col., 126
Puerto Williams, Chile, 138
Pueyrredón (lake), Arg., 143
Pugachev, U.S.S.R., 52
Puget (sound), Wash., 310
Pugwash (harbor), N.S., 169
Pujehun, S. Leone, 106
Pujilí, Ecua., 128
Pukapuka (atoll), Cook Is., 87
Puka-Puka (atoll), Fr. Poly., 87
Puksubaek (mt.), N. Korea, 81
Pula, Yugo., 45
Pulacayo, Bol., 136
Pulap (atoll), Pac. Is., 87
Pulaski, Tenn., 237
Pulaski, Va., 307
Pulicat (lake), India, 68
Pull (pt.), Virgin Is. (U.S.), 161
Pullman, Wash., 310
Pully, Switz., 39
Pulo Anna (isl.), Pac. Is., 87
Pulusuk (atoll), Pac. Is., 87
Puluwat (atoll), Pac. Is., 87
Puná (isl.), Ecua., 128
Puna de Atacama (reg.), Arg., 143
Punakha, India, 68
Punata, Bol., 136
Punia, Dem. Rep. of the Congo, 115
Punjab (prov.), Pak., 68
Puno (dept.), Peru, 128
Puno, Peru, 128
Punta Alta, Arg., 143
Punta Arenas, Chile, 138
Punta Cardón, Venez., 124
Punta de Bombón, Peru, 128
Punta del Este, Urug., 145
Punta Delgada (dist.), Port., 32
Punta Delgada, Port., 32
Punta de Piedras, Venez., 124
Punta Gorda, Br. Hond., 154
Punta Gorda, Fla., 212
Puntarenas, C. Rica, 154
Puntas, Cerro de (mt.), P. Rico, 161
Punto Fijo, Venez., 124
Punxsutawney, Pa., 294
Pupuya (mt.), Bol., 136
Puquintica (mt.), S. Amer., 136
Puquio, Peru, 128
Puracé (vol.), Col., 126
Purbolinggo, Indon., 85
Purcell, Okla., 288
Purén, Chile, 138
Puri, India, 68
Purificación, Col., 126
Purnea, India, 68
Purranque, Chile, 138
Pursat, Cambodia, 72
Puruándiro, Mex., 150
Purulia, India, 68
Puruni (riv.), Guyana, 131
Purus (riv.), S. Amer., 132
Purwakarta, Indon., 85
Purwodadi, Indon., 85
Purwokerto, Indon., 85
Purworedjo, Indon., 85
Pusan, S. Korea, 81
Pushkin, U.S.S.R., 52
Putaendo, Chile, 138
Putaruru, N.Z., 101
Puteaux, France, 28
Putien, China, 77
Putina, Peru, 128
Puting (cape), Indon., 85
Putla, Mex., 150
Putnam, Conn., 210
Puttalam, Ceylon, 68
Putumayo (commissary), Col., 126
Putumayo (riv.), S. Amer., 120
Puunene, Hawaii, 218
Puyallup, Wash., 310
Puy-de-Dôme (dept.), France, 28
Puy-de-Dôme (mt.), France, 28
Puyehue (lake), Chile, 138
Puyo, Ecua., 128
Pweto, Dem. Rep. of the Congo, 115
Pyapon, Burma, 72
Pyatigorsk, U.S.S.R., 52
Pyatikhatki, U.S.S.R., 52
Pye, Burma, 72
Pyhä (lake), Fin., 18
Pyinmana, Burma, 72
P'yŏngyang (cap.), N. Korea, 81
Pyramid (lake), Nev., 266
Pyramids (ruins), U.A.R., 111
Pyrenees (range), Europe, 28, 33
Pyrénées-Atlantiques (dept.), France, 28
Pyrénées-Orientales (dept.), France, 28
Pyskowice, Poland, 47
Pyuthan, Nepal, 68

Q

Qabatiya, Jordan, 65
Qain, Iran, 66
Qais (isl.), Iran, 66
Qala Panja, Afghan., 68
Qal'a Sharqat, Iraq, 66
Qal'at Diza, Iraq, 66
Qaleh-i-Kang, Afghan., 68
Qalqiliya, Jordan, 65
Qalyub, U.A.R., 111
Qamishliye, Syria, 63
Qamr (bay), P.D.R. Yemen, 59
Qara Qash, China, 77
Qara Shahr, China, 77
Qara Su (riv.), Iran, 66
Qarghaliq, China, 77
Qasr Farâfra, U.A.R., 111
Qasr-i-Shirin, Iran, 66
Qatar, 59
Qatif, Saudi Ar., 59
Qattâra (depr.), U.A.R., 111
Qena, U.A.R., 111
Qiryat Bialik, Israel, 65
Qiryat Gat, Israel, 65
Qiryat Motzkin, Israel, 65
Qiryat Shemona, Israel, 65
Qiryat Yam, Israel, 65
Qishm (isl.), Iran, 66
Qishn, P.D.R. Yemen, 59
Qizil Uzun (riv.), Iran, 66
Quaco (head), N.B., 170
Quakers Hill-Marayong, N.S.W., 97
Quakertown, Pa., 294
Quanah, Tex., 302
Quang Nam, S. Vietnam, 72
Quang Ngai, S. Vietnam, 72
Quang Tri, S. Vietnam, 72
Quang Yen, N. Vietnam, 72
Quan Long, S. Vietnam, 72
Quantico, Va., 307
Qu'Appelle (riv.), Sask., 181
Quaraí, Braz., 132
Quartu Sant'Elena, Italy, 34
Quartz Hill, Calif., 204
Quatre Bornes, Mauritius, 118
Quatsino (sound), Br. Col., 184
Quchan, Iran, 66
Queanbeyan, N.S.W., 97
Québec (prov.), Canada, 172, 174
Québec (cap.), Que., 172
Quebracho, Urug., 145
Quebradillas, P. Rico, 161
Quedlinburg, E. Ger., 22
Queen Charlotte (isls.), Br. Col., 184
Queen Charlotte (sound), Br. Col., 184
Queen Charlotte (strait), Br. Col., 184
Queen Elizabeth (isls.), N.W.T., 187
Queen Elizabeth Nat'l Park, Uganda, 115
Queen Mary Coast (reg.), Ant., 5
Queen Maud (gulf), N.W.T., 187
Queen Maud Land (reg.), Ant., 5
Queensborough, Eng., 13
Queensferry, Scot., 15
Queensland (state), Austral., 95
Queenstown, Guyana, 131
Queenstown (Cóbh), Ire., 17
Queenstown, S. Afr., 118
Queenstown, Tas., 97
Queens Village, N.Y., 276
Queguay Grande (river), Urug., 145
Quela, Angola, 115
Quelimane, Mozamb., 118
Quemado de Güines, Cuba, 158
Quemoy (isl.), China, 77
Quemú-Quemú, Arg., 143
Quepos, C. Rica, 154
Que Que, Rhod., 118
Quequén, Arg., 143
Querecotillo, Peru, 128
Querétaro (state), Mex., 150
Querétaro, Mex., 150
Quesnel, Br. Col., 184
Questa, N. Mex., 274
Quetico Prov. Park, Ont., 175
Quetta, Pak., 68
Quevedo, Ecua., 128
Quezaltenango, Guat., 154
Quezaltepeque, Guat., 154
Quezon (prov.), Phil. Is., 82
Quezon City (cap.), Phil. Is., 82
Quibala, Angola, 115
Quibdó, Col., 126
Quiberon, France, 28
Quibor, Venez., 124
Quiindy, Par., 144
Quilalí, Nic., 154
Quilán (cape), Chile, 138
Quilengues, Angola, 115
Quillacas, Bol., 136
Quillacollo, Bol., 136
Quillicura, Chile, 138
Quillota, Chile, 138
Quilon, India, 68
Quilpué, Chile, 138
Quime, Bol., 136
Quimilí, Arg., 143
Quimper, France, 28
Quincy, Calif., 204
Quincy, Fla., 212
Quincy, Ill., 222
Quincy, Mass., 249
Quincy, Wash., 310
Quindío (dept.), Col., 126
Quines, Arg., 143
Qui Nhon, S. Vietnam, 72
Quintana Roo (terr.), Mex., 150
Quitasueño (bank), Col., 126
Quintero, Chile, 138
Quinzau, Angola, 115
Quionga, Mozamb., 118
Quirihue, Chile, 138
Quirindi, N.S.W., 97
Quiriquire, Venez., 124
Quissanga, Mozamb., 118
Quissico, Mozamb., 118
Quitilipi, Arg., 143
Quitman, Ga., 216
Quito (cap.), Ecua., 128
Quixadá, Braz., 132
Qum, Iran, 66
Qunfidha, Saudi Ar., 59
Quoich (riv.), N.W.T., 187
Quyquyhó, Par., 144

R

Raahe, Fin., 18
Rab (isl.), Yugo., 45
Rába (riv.), Hung., 41
Rabat (cap.), Mor., 106
Rabaul, Terr. N.G., 87
Rabinal, Guat., 154
Raccoon (creek), Ohio, 284
Race (cape), Newf., 166
Raceland, La., 238
Rach Gia, S. Vietnam, 72
Racibórz, Poland, 47
Racine, Wis., 317
Radcliff, Ky., 237
Radebeul, E. Ger., 22
Radford, Va., 307
Radium Hill, S. Austral., 94
Radja Ampat Group (isls.), Indon., 85
Radnorshire (county), Wales, 13
Radom, Poland, 47
Radomsko, Poland, 47
Radville, Sask., 181
Rae, N.W.T., 187
Rae (isth.), N.W.T., 187
Raeford, N.C., 281
Rafaela, Arg., 143
Rafai, Centr. Afr. Rep., 115
Raft (riv.), Utah, 304
Ragay (gulf), Phil. Is., 82
Ragged (isl.), Bah. Is., 156
Raglan, N.Z., 101
Ragusa (prov.), Italy, 34
Ragusa, Italy, 34
Ragusa (Dubrovnik), Yugo., 45
Rahaeng (Tak), Thai., 72
Rahimyar Khan, Pak., 68
Rahway, N. J., 273
Rai, Iran, 66
Raiatea (isl.), Fr. Poly., 87
Raichur, India, 68
Raigarh, India, 68
Rainbow Bridge Nat'l Mon., Utah, 304
Rainier (mt.), Wash., 310
Rainy (lake), N. Amer., 254
Rainy (riv.), N. Amer., 254
Rainy River, Ont., 175
Raipur, India, 68
Raisin (riv.), Mich., 250
Raivavae (isl.), Fr. Poly., 87
Rajah Buayan, Phil. Is., 82
Rajahmundry, India, 68
Rajang (riv.), Malaysia, 85
Rajapalaiyam, India, 68
Rajasthan (state), India, 68
Rajkot, India, 68
Rajnandgaon, India, 68
Rajpipla, India, 68
Rajpur, India, 68
Rajshahi, Pak., 68
Rakahanga (atoll), Cook Is., 87
Rakan, Ras (cape), Qatar, 59
Rakaposhi (mt.), India, 68
Rakata (isl.), Indon., 85
Rákospalota, Hung., 41
Rakvere, U.S.S.R., 53
Raleigh (cap.), N.C., 281
Ralik Chain (isls.), Pac. Is., 87
Ralston, Nebr., 264
Ramadi (prov.), Iraq, 66
Ramadi, Iraq, 66
Ramah (bay), Newf., 166
Ramallah, Jordan, 65
Ramapo (riv.), N. J., 273
Ramat Gan, Israel, 65
Rambouillet, France, 28
Ramechhap, Nepal, 68
Ramey A.F.B., P. Rico, 161
Ramla, Israel, 65
Ramm, Jebel (mt.), Jordan, 65
Ramos (riv.), Mex., 150
Ramos Arizpe, Mex., 150
Ramotswa, Botswana, 118
Ramparts (riv.), N.W.T., 187
Rampur, India, 68
Ramree (isl.), Burma, 72
Ramsey, I. of Man, 13
Ramsey, N. J., 273
Ramsey (isl.), Wales, 13
Ramsgate, Eng., 13
Ramu (riv.), Terr. N.G., 85
Rana (riv.), Norway, 18
Ranau, Malaysia, 85
Rancagua, Chile, 138
Ranchi, India, 68
Rancho Cordova, Calif., 204
Ranco (lake), Chile, 138
Randalstown, N. Ire., 17
Randers, Den., 21
Randfontein, S. Afr., 118
Randolph, Mass., 249
Randwick, N.S.W., 97
Ranger, Tex., 302
Rangiora, N.Z., 101
Rangiroa (atoll), Fr. Poly., 87
Rangoon (cap.), Burma, 72
Rangpur, Pak., 68
Rankin, Pa., 294
Rankin Inlet, N.W.T., 187
Rankovićevo, Yugo., 45
Rannoch (lake), Scot., 15
Rantauprapat, Indon., 85
Rantoul, Ill., 222
Ranui, N.Z., 101
Raoul (isl.), N.Z., 87
Rapa (isl.), Fr. Poly., 87
Rapallo, Italy, 34
Rapa Nui (Easter)(isl.), Chile, 87
Rapidan (riv.), Va., 307
Rapid City, S. Dak., 298
Rappahannock (riv.), Va., 307
Rapperswil, Switz., 39
Raquette (riv.), N.Y., 276
Raraka (atoll), Fr. Poly., 87
Raritan, N. J., 273
Raritan (riv.), N. J., 273
Raroia (atoll), Fr. Poly., 87
Rarotonga (isl.), Cook Is., 87
Ras al Khaimah, Trucial States, 58
Ras Dashan (mt.), Eth., 111
Rashad, Sudan, 111
Rashid (Rosetta), U.A.R., 111
Rasskazovo, U.S.S.R., 52
Ras Tanura, Saudi Ar., 59
Rastatt, W. Ger., 22
Ratak Chain (isls.), Pac. Is., 87
Ratangarh, India, 68
Rat Buri, Thai., 72
Rathedaung, Burma, 72
Rathenow, E. Ger., 22
Rathfriland, N. Ire., 17
Rathkeale, Ire., 17
Rathlin (isl.), N. Ire., 17
Rathluirc, Ire., 17
Ratingen, W. Ger., 22
Ratlam, India, 68
Ratnagiri, India, 68
Ratnapura, Ceylon, 68
Raton, N. Mex., 274
Raub, Malaysia, 72
Rauma, Fin., 18
Rauma (riv.), Norway, 18
Raurkela, India, 68
Ravenna (prov.), Italy, 34
Ravenna, Italy, 34
Ravenna, Ohio, 284
Ravensburg, W. Ger., 22
Ravenshoe, Queensland, 95
Ravenswood, W. Va., 313
Ravi (riv.), Pak., 68
Rawalpindi, Pak., 68
Rawlins, Wyo., 319
Rawmarsh, Eng., 13
Rawtenstall, Eng., 10
Ray (cape), Newf., 166
Ray, N. Dak., 283
Raychikhinsk, U.S.S.R., 48
Raymond, Alta., 182
Raymond, Wash., 310
Raymond Terr., N.S.W., 97
Raymondville, Tex., 302
Rayne, La., 238
Raynham, Mass., 249
Rayón, Mex., 150
Raytown, Mo., 261
Rayville, La., 238
Razgrad, Bulg., 45
Ré (isl.), France, 28
Reading, Eng., 13
Reading, Mass., 249
Reading, Ohio, 284
Reading, Pa., 294
Readville, Mass., 249
Real (mts.), So. Amer., 136
Reao (atoll), Fr. Poly., 87
Rebiana (oasis), Libya, 111
Recherche (arch.), W. Austral., 92
Rechitsa, U.S.S.R., 52
Recife, Braz., 132
Recklinghausen, W. Ger., 22
Reconquista, Arg., 143
Red (sea), 59
Red (riv.), Asia, 72, 77
Red (riv.), N. Amer., 163
Red (lake), Ont., 177
Red (riv.), U.S., 188
Redang, Pulau (isl.), Malaysia, 72
Red Bank, N. J., 273
Red Bank-White Oak, Tenn., 237

Red Bluff, Calif., 204
Red Bluff (lake), U.S., 274, 302
Redbridge, Eng., 10
Redcliffe, Alta., 182
Redcliffe, Queensland, 95
Red Cliffs, Vic., 97
Red Deer, Alta., 182
Red Deer (riv.), Alta., 182
Red Deer (lake), Man., 179
Red Deer (riv.), Sask., 181
Redding, Calif., 204
Redditch, Eng., 10
Redfield, S. Dak., 298
Red Hill (mt.), Hawaii, 218
Red Lake (riv.), Minn., 254
Red Lake, Ont., 177
Redlands, Calif., 204
Red Lion, Pa., 294
Red Lodge, Mont., 262
Redmond, Oreg., 291
Red Oak, Iowa, 229
Redonda (isl.), Antigua, 156
Redondo Beach, Calif., 204
Red River of the North (riv.), N. Amer., 188
Red Sprs., N.C., 281
Red Volta (riv.), Africa, 106
Red Wing, Minn., 254
Redwood City, Calif., 204
Redwood Falls, Minn., 254
Redwood Nat'l Park, Calif., 204
Ree (lake), Ire., 17
Reed City, Mich., 250
Reedley, Calif., 204
Reedsburg, Wis., 317
Reedsport, Oreg., 291
Reef (bay), Virgin Is. (U.S.), 161
Reefton, N.Z., 101
Reese (riv.), Nev., 266
Refa'i, Iraq, 66
Refugio, Tex., 302
Regen (riv.), W. Ger., 22
Regensburg, W. Ger., 22
Reggan, Alg., 106
Reggio di Calabria (prov.), Italy, 34
Reggio di Calabria, Italy, 34
Reggio nell'Emilia (prov.), Italy, 34
Reggio nell'Emilia, Italy, 34
Reghin, Rum., 45
Regina (cap.), Sask., 181
Registan (des.), Afghan., 68
Regnitz (riv.), W. Ger., 22
Rehoboth, S.W. Afr., 118
Rehoboth Beach, Del., 245
Rehovot, Israel, 65
Reichenbach, E. Ger., 22
Reidsville, N.C., 281
Reigate, Eng., 13
Reims, France, 28
Reina Adelaida (arch.), Chile, 138
Reindeer (lake), Canada, 163
Reindeer (isl.), Man., 179
Reinga (cape), N.Z., 101
Reinosa, Spain, 33
Reisterstown, Md., 245
Relay, Md., 245
Rembang, Indon., 85
Remedios, Cuba, 158
Remedios (pt.), El Sal., 154
Remich, Lux., 27
Rémire, Fr. Gui., 131
Remolino, Col., 126
Remscheid, W. Ger., 22
Rendsburg, W. Ger., 22
Renens, Switz., 39
Renfrew, Ont., 177
Renfrew (county), Scot., 15
Renfrew, Scot., 15
Rengo, Chile, 138
Renmark, S. Austral., 94
Rennell (isl.), Br. Sol. Is., 87
Rennes, France, 28
Reno, Nev., 266
Renovo, Pa., 294
Rensselaer, Ind., 227
Rensselaer, N.Y., 276
Renton, Wash., 310
Repentigny, Que., 172
Republican (riv.), U.S., 208, 232
Repulse Bay, N.W.T., 187
Requena, Peru, 128
Reseda, Calif., 204
Resende, Braz., 135
Reserve, La., 238
Reserve, N. Mex., 274
Reserve Mines, N.S., 169
Resht, Iran, 66
Resistencia, Arg., 143
Reşiţa, Rum., 45
Resolute Bay, N.W.T., 187
Resolution (isl.), N.W.T., 187
Restigouche (riv.), Canada, 170, 172
Restrepo, Col., 126
Retalhuleu, Guat., 154
Réunion, 118
Reus, Spain, 33
Reuss (riv.), Switz., 39
Reutlingen, W. Ger., 22
Revelstoke, Br. Col., 184
Revere, Mass., 249
Revillagigedo (isls.), Mex., 150
Rewa, India, 68
Rewari, India, 68
Rexburg, Idaho, 220
Reykjavík (cap.), Ice., 21
Reynella-Port Noarlunga, S. Austral., 94
Reynoldsburg, Ohio, 284
Reynoldsville, Pa., 294
Reynosa, Mex., 150
Reza'iyeh, Iran, 66
Rezé, France, 28
Rhaetian Alps (mts.), Europe, 39
Rhätikon (mts.), Europe, 39
Rheine, W. Ger., 22
Rheinhausen, W. Ger., 22
Rheydt, W. Ger., 22
Rhine (riv.), Europe, 7
Rhinelander, Wis., 317
Rhineland-Palatinate (state), W. Ger., 22
Rhino Camp, Uganda, 115
Rhode Island (state), U.S., 249
Rhodes (isl.), Greece, 45
Rhodesia, 118
Rhodope (mts.), Europe, 45
Rhön (mts.), Ger., 22
Rhondda, Wales, 13
Rhône (riv.), Europe, 28, 39
Rhône (dept.), France, 28
Rhyl, Wales, 13
Rialto, Calif., 204
Riau (arch.), Indon., 85
Rib (mt.), Wis., 317
Ribatejo (prov.), Port., 33
Ribáuè, Mozamb., 118
Ribble (riv.), Eng., 13
Ribe, Den., 21
Ribeira (riv.), Braz., 135
Ribeirão Prêto, Braz., 135
Riberalta, Bol., 136
Riccarton, N.Z., 101
Rice Lake, Wis., 317
Richards Gebaur A.F.B., Mo., 261
Richardson, Tex., 302
Richfield, Utah, 304
Richibucto, N.B., 170
Richland, Wash., 310
Richland Center, Wis., 317
Richland Hills, Tex., 302
Richlands, Va., 307
Richmond, B.C., 184
Richmond, Calif., 204
Richmond, Ind., 227
Richmond, Ky., 237
Richmond, Mich., 250
Richmond, Mo., 261
Richmond (range), N.Z., 101
Richmond, Que., 172
Richmond (gulf), Que., 174
Richmond, Tex., 302
Richmond, Vic., 97
Richmond (cap.), Va., 307
Richmond Beach, Wash., 310
Richmond Hts., Fla., 212
Richmond Hts., Mo., 261
Richmond Hts., Ohio, 284
Richmond Highlands, Wash., 310
Richmond Hill, Ont., 177
Richmond Nat'l Battlef. Site, Va., 307
Richmond-upon-Thames, Eng., 10
Richwood, W. Va., 313
Rickmansworth, Eng., 10
Rideau (riv.), Ont., 177
Ridgecrest, Calif., 204
Ridgefield, Conn., 210
Ridgefield, N. J., 273
Ridgefield Park, N. J., 273
Ridgetown, Ont., 177
Ridgewood, N. J., 273
Ridgway, Pa., 294
Riding Mountain Nat'l Park, Man., 179
Ridley Park, Pa., 294
Ried, Austria, 41
Riehen, Switz., 39
Riesa, E. Ger., 22
Riesi, Italy, 34
Rieti (prov.), Italy, 34
Rieti, Italy, 34
Rifle, Colo., 208
Rift Valley (prov.), Kenya, 115
Riga, U.S.S.R., 53
Riga (gulf), U.S.S.R., 53
Rigi (mt.), Switz., 39
Rigo, Papua, 85
Rigolet, Newf., 166
Riihimäki, Fin., 18
Riiser-Larsen (pen.), Ant., 5
Rijeka, Yugo., 45
Rijswijk, Neth., 27
Rikitea, Fr. Poly., 87
Rikuzentakata, Japan, 81
Rimac (riv.), Peru, 128
Rimal, Ar (des.), Saudi Ar., 59
Rimatara (isl.), Fr. Poly., 87
Rimbey, Alta., 182
Rimini, Italy, 34
Rîmnicu Sarat, Rum., 45
Rîmnicu Vîlcea, Rum., 45
Rimouski, Que., 172
Rimutaka (range), N.Z., 101
Rincón de Romos, Mex., 150
Ringerike, Norway, 18
Ringkøbing, Den., 21
Ringvassøy (isl.), Norway, 18
Ringwood, N. J., 273
Ringwood, Vic., 97
Riobamba, Ecua., 128
Río Benito, Eq. Guin., 115
Río Blanco, P. Rico, 161
Rio Bonito, Braz., 135
Rio Branco, Braz., 132
Río Branco, Urug., 145
Río Bueno, Chile, 138
Río Caribe, Venez., 124
Río Chico, Venez., 124
Rio Claro, Braz., 135
Rio Claro, Trin. & Tob., 161
Río Cuarto, Arg., 143
Rio de Janeiro (state), Braz., 132
Rio de Janeiro, Braz., 135
Rio Dell, Calif., 204
Río de Oro (reg.), Sp. Sahara, 106
Río Gallegos, Arg., 143
Río Grande, Arg., 143
Rio Grande, Braz., 132
Río Grande, Mex., 150
Rio Grande (riv.), N. Amer., 188
Río Grande, P. Rico, 161
Rio Grande City, Tex., 302
Rio Grande do Norte (state), Braz., 132
Rio Grande do Sul (state), Braz., 132
Riohacha, Col., 126
Rioja, Peru, 128
Río Muni (terr.), Eq. Guin., 115
Río Negro (prov.), Arg., 143
Río Negro, Chile, 138
Rionegro, Col., 126
Río Negro (dept.), Urug., 145
Río Negro (res.), Urug., 145
Rio Pardo, Braz., 132
Río Piedras, P. Rico, 161
Riosucio, Col., 126
Río Tercero, Arg., 143
Rio Tinto, Braz., 132
Rio Verde, Braz., 132
Río Verde, Mex., 150
Rio Vista, Calif., 204
Ripley, Eng., 13
Ripley, Miss., 256
Ripley, Tenn., 237
Ripley, W. Va., 313
Ripon, Wis., 317
Risca, Wales, 13
Rishon Le Ziyyon, Israel, 65
Rishra, India, 68
Risør, Norway, 18
Rittman, Ohio, 284
Ritzville, Wash., 310
Rivadavia, Arg., 143
Rivas, Nic., 154
Rivera (dept.), Urug., 145
Rivera, Urug., 145
Riverbank, Calif., 204
River Cess, Liberia, 106
Riverdale, Ill., 222
Riverdale, Md., 245
Riverdale, N. J., 273
Riverdale, N. Dak., 283
River Edge, N. J., 273
River Falls, Wis., 317
River Forest, Ill., 222
River Grove, Ill., 222
Riverhead, N.Y., 276
Riverina (reg.), N.S.W., 97
River Oaks, Tex., 302
River Rouge, Mich., 250
Rivers (state), Nigeria, 106
Riversdale, S. Afr., 118
Riverside, Calif., 204
Riverside, Conn., 210
Riverside, Ill., 222
Riverside, N. J., 273
Riverside, R.I., 249
Riverton, N. J., 273
Riverton, N.Z., 101
Riverton, Utah, 302
Riverton, Wyo., 319
Riverton Hts., Wash., 310
Riverview, Mich., 250
Riverview, Mo., 261
Riverview Hts., N.B., 170
Riviera (reg.), Europe, 28
Riviera Beach, Fla., 212
Riviera Beach, Md., 245
Rivière-des-Prairies, Que., 172
Rivière-du-Loup, Que., 172
Rivière-du-Moulin, Que., 172
Rivière-Pilote, Mart., 161
Rivière-Salée, Mart., 161
Riyadh (cap.), Saudi Ar., 59
Riyan, P.D.R. Yemen, 59
Rizal (prov.), Phil. Is., 82
Rize (prov.), Turkey, 63
Rize, Turkey, 63
Rjukan, Norway, 18
Road Town (cap.), Virgin Is. (Br.), 161
Roan Antelope, Zambia, 115
Roanne, France, 28
Roanoke, Ala., 194
Roanoke (isl.), N.C., 281
Roanoke (riv.), U.S., 281, 307
Roanoke, Va., 307
Roanoke Rapids, N.C., 281
Roaring Spring, Pa., 294
Roatán (isl.), Hond., 154
Robbins, Ill., 222
Robbinsdale, Minn., 254
Robert, Mart., 161
Roberts Int'l Airport, Liberia, 106
Robertsport, Liberia, 106
Roberval, Que., 172
Robinson, Ill., 222
Robinson (ranges), W. Austral., 92
Robles, Col., 126
Roboré, Bol., 136
Robson (mt.), Br. Col., 184
Robstown, Tex., 302
Roca (cape), Port., 33
Rocha (dept.), Urug., 145
Rocha, Urug., 145
Rochdale, Eng., 10
Rochefort, France, 28
Rochelle, Ill., 222
Rochelle Park, N. J., 273
Rocher River, N.W.T., 187
Rochester, Eng., 13
Rochester, Ind., 227
Rochester, Mich., 250
Rochester, Minn., 254
Rochester, N.H., 268
Rochester, N.Y., 276
Rochester, Pa., 294
Rock (creek), Md., 245
Rock (riv.), Wis., 317
Rockall (isl.), Scot., 7
Rockaway, N. J., 273
Rockcliffe Park, Ont., 177
Rockdale, Md., 245
Rockdale, N.S.W., 97
Rockdale, Tex., 302
Rock Falls, Ill., 222
Rockford, Ill., 222
Rockhampton, Queensland, 95
Rock Hill, Mo., 261
Rock Hill, S.C., 296
Rockingham, N.C., 281
Rockingham, W. Austral., 92
Rock Island, Ill., 222
Rock Island (dam), Wash., 310
Rockland, Maine, 242
Rockland, Mass., 249
Rockland, Ont., 177
Rockledge, Fla., 212
Rockledge, Pa., 294
Rockmart, Ga., 216
Rockport, Mass., 249
Rockport, Tex., 302
Rock Rapids, Iowa, 229
Rock Springs, Wyo., 319
Rockstone, Guyana, 131
Rockville, Conn., 210
Rockville, Ind., 227
Rockville, Md., 245
Rockville Centre, N.Y., 276
Rockwood, Tenn., 237
Rocky (mts.), N. Amer., 146
Rocky Ford, Colo., 208
Rocky Gorge (res.), Md., 245
Rocky Mount, N.C., 281
Rocky Mountain House, Alta., 182
Rocky Mountain Nat'l Park, Colo., 208
Rocky Reach (dam), Wash., 310
Rødby, Den., 21
Rodeo, Calif., 204
Rodez, France, 28
Ródhos, Greece, 45
Rodrigues (isl.), Mauritius, 3
Roebling, N. J., 273
Roebourne, W. Austral., 92
Roeland Park, Kans., 232
Roermond, Neth., 27
Roeselare, Belg., 27
Roes Welcome (sound), N.W.T., 187
Rogaland (county), Norway, 18
Rogers, Ark., 203
Rogers City, Mich., 250
Rogers Hts., Md., 245
Rogersville, Tenn., 237
Roger Williams Nat'l Mem., R.I., 248
Rogue (riv.), Oreg., 291
Roi Et, Thai., 72
Rojas, Arg., 143
Rojo (cape), P. Rico, 161
Rokan (riv.), Indon., 85
Rolla, Mo., 261
Rolla, N. Dak., 283
Rolling Hills Estates, Calif., 204
Rolling Meadows, Ill., 222
Roma, Queensland, 95
Romaine (riv.), Canada, 166
Roman, Rum., 45
Romano (cay), Cuba, 158
Romanshorn, Switz., 39
Romans-sur-Isère, France, 28
Romblon (prov.), Phil. Is., 82
Romblon (isl.), Phil. Is., 82
Rome, Ga., 216
Rome (prov.), Italy, 34
Rome (cap.), Italy, 34
Rome, N.Y., 276
Romeo, Mich., 250
Romeoville, Ill., 222
Romney, W. Va., 313
Romny, U.S.S.R., 52
Rømo (isl.), Den., 21
Romsdals (fjord), Norway, 18
Ronan, Mont., 262
Roncador (range), Braz., 132
Ronda, Spain, 33
Rondeau Prov. Park, Ont., 177
Rondônia (terr.), Braz., 132
Rong, Kas (isl.), Cambodia, 72
Rongelap (atoll), Pac. Is., 87
Ronkonkoma, N.Y., 276
Rønne, Den., 21
Ronneby, Sweden, 18
Ronne Entrance (bay), Ant., 5
Ronse, Belg., 27
Ronuro (riv.), Braz., 132
Roodepoort-Maraisburg, S. Afr., 118
Roosendaal, Neth., 27
Roosevelt (isl.), Ant., 5
Roosevelt (riv.), Braz., 132
Roosevelt, N.Y., 276
Roosevelt, Utah, 304
Roosevelt City, Ala., 194
Roosevelt Park, Mich., 250
Rooty Hill-Mt. Druitt, N.S.W., 97
Roper (riv.), N. Terr., 93
Roraima (terr.), Braz., 132
Roraima (mt.), S. Amer., 131
Rorschach, Switz., 39
Rosa (mt.), Europe, 39
Rosalind (bank), Cent. Amer., 154
Rosario, Arg., 143
Rosario, Par., 144
Rosario, Urug., 145
Rosario, Venez., 124
Rosario (str.), Wash., 310
Rosario de la Frontera, Arg., 143
Rosas (gulf), Spain, 33
Roscommon (county), Ire., 17
Roscommon, Ire., 17
Roscrea, Ire., 17
Roseau (cap.), Dominica, 161
Roseau, Minn., 254
Rosebery, Tas., 99
Rosebud, Vic., 97
Roseburg, Oreg., 291
Rosedale, Md., 245
Roseland, N. J., 273
Roselle, N. J., 273
Roselle Park, N. J., 273
Rosemead, Calif., 204
Rosemère, Que., 172
Rosenberg, Tex., 302
Rosenheim, W. Ger., 22
Rosetown, Sask., 181
Rosetta, U.A.R., 111
Roseville, Calif., 204
Roseville, Mich., 250
Roseville, Minn., 254
Rosewood Hts., Ill., 222
Rosignol, Guyana, 131
Roskilde, Den., 21
Roslavl', U.S.S.R., 52
Roslyn, N.Y., 276
Ross (isl.), Ant., 5
Ross (sea), Ant., 5
Ross, Calif., 204
Ross (lake), Wash., 310
Ross and Cromarty (county), Scot., 15
Ross Barnett (res.), Miss., 256
Rosscarbery (bay), Ire., 17
Rossel (isl.), Papua, 85
Rossford, Ohio, 284
Ross Ice Shelf, Ant., 5
Rossignol (lake), N.S., 169
Ross Lake Nat'l Rec. Area, Wash., 310
Rossland, Br. Col., 184
Rosso, Mauritania, 106
Rossosh, U.S.S.R., 52
Ross River, Yukon, 187
Rossville, Ga., 216
Rosthern, Sask., 181
Rostock (dist.), E. Ger., 22
Rostock, E. Ger., 22
Rostov, U.S.S.R., 52
Rostrevor, N. Ire., 17
Roswell, Ga., 216
Roswell, N. Mex., 274
Rota (isl.), Pac. Is., 87
Rotan, Tex., 302
Rothenburg, W. Ger., 22
Rotherham, Eng., 13
Rothesay, Scot., 15
Rothschild, Wis., 317
Roti (isl.), Indon., 85
Rotorua, N.Z., 101
Rotterdam, Neth., 27
Rottnest (isl.), W. Austral., 92
Rottweil, W. Ger., 22
Rotuma (isl.), Fiji, 87
Roubaix, France, 28
Rouen, France, 28
Rouffaer (riv.), Indon., 85
Round Bay, Md., 245
Roundup, Mont., 262
Rouyn, Que., 174
Rovaniemi, Fin., 18
Rovereto, Italy, 34
Rovigo (prov.), Italy, 34
Rovigo, Italy, 34
Rovira, Col., 126
Rovno, U.S.S.R., 52
Rowayton, Conn., 210
Roxas, Phil. Is., 82
Roxboro, N.C., 281
Roxburgh (county), Scot., 15
Roxbury, N.J., 273
Roy, Utah, 304
Royal (canal), Ire., 17
Royale (isl.), Mich., 250
Royal Gorge (canyon), Colo., 208
Royal Natal Nat'l Park, S. Africa, 118
Royal Oak, Mich., 250
Royal Tsavo Nat'l Park, Kenya, 115
Royersford, Pa., 294
Rtishchevo, U.S.S.R., 52
Ruad (isl.), Syria, 63
Ruahine (range), N.Z., 101
Ruapehu (mt.), N.Z., 101
Rub' al Khali (des.), Arabia, 59
Rubezhnoye, U.S.S.R., 52
Rubidoux, Calif., 204
Rubio, Venez., 124
Ruby (lake), Nev., 266
Ruda Śląska, Poland, 47
Rudkøbing, Den., 21
Rudok, China, 77
Rudolf (lake), Africa, 115
Rudolstadt, E. Ger., 22
Rueil-Malmaison, France, 28
Rufa'a, Sudan, 111
Rufiji (riv.), Tanz., 115
Rufino, Arg., 143
Rufisque, Sen., 106
Rufus Woods (lake), Wash., 310
Rugby, Eng., 13
Rugby, N. Dak., 283
Rugeley, Eng., 10
Rügen (isl.), E. Ger., 22
Ruhr (riv.), W. Ger., 22
Ruidoso, N. Mex., 274
Rukwa (lake), Tanz., 115
Rulhieres (cape), W. Austral., 92
Rum (cay), Bah. Is., 156
Rum (isl.), Scot., 15
Ruma, Yugo., 45
Rumaitha, Iraq, 66
Rumania, 45
Rumbek, Sudan, 111
Rumford, Maine, 242
Rumford, R.I., 249
Rum Jungle, N. Terr., 93
Rumoi, Japan, 81
Rumson, N. J., 273
Runaway (cape), N.Z., 101
Runcorn, Eng., 10
Runnemede, N. J., 273
Rupert, Idaho, 220
Rupert (riv.), Que., 174
Rupununi (dist.), Guyana, 131
Rupununi (riv.), Guyana, 131
Rurutu (isl.), Fr. Poly., 87
Rusape, Rhod., 118
Ruse, Bulg., 45
Rush, Ire., 17
Rushden, Eng., 13
Rushville, Ill., 222
Rushville, Ind., 227
Rusk, Tex., 302
Russell, Kans., 232
Russell Cave Nat'l Mon., Ala., 194
Russellville, Ala., 194
Russellville, Ark., 203
Russellville, Ky., 237
Rüsselsheim, W. Ger., 22
Russian S.F.S.R., U.S.S.R., 48
Rustak, Afghan., 68
Rustavi, U.S.S.R., 52
Rustenburg, S. Afr., 118
Rustico (isl.), P.E.I., 168
Ruston, La., 238
Rutba, Iraq, 66
Ruth, Nev., 266
Rutherford, N. J., 273
Rutherfordton, N.C., 281
Rutherglen, Scot., 15
Rüti, Switz., 39
Rutland, Vt., 268
Rutlandshire (county), Eng., 13
Rutshuru, Dem. Rep. of the Congo, 115
Ruus al Jibal (dist.), Oman, 59
Ruvuma (riv.), Africa, 115
Ruvuma (prov.), Tanz., 115
Ruwandiz, Iraq, 66
Ruwenzori (range), Africa, 115
Ruzayevka, U.S.S.R., 52
Ruzizi (riv.), Africa, 115
Ružomberok, Czech., 41
Rwanda, 115
Ryazan', U.S.S.R., 52
Rybachiy (pen.), U.S.S.R., 52
Rybinsk, U.S.S.R., 52
Rybinsk (res.), U.S.S.R., 52
Rybnik, Poland, 47
Ryde, Eng., 13
Ryde, N.S.W., 97
Rye, N.H., 268
Rye, N.Y., 276
Ryotsu, Japan, 81
Rysy (mt.), Europe, 47
Ryukyu Islands, 81
Rzeszów (prov.), Poland, 47
Rzeszów, Poland, 47
Rzhev, U.S.S.R., 52

S

Sa'ada, Yemen Arab Rep., 59
Saale (riv.), E. Ger., 22
Saalfeld, E. Ger., 22
Saane (riv.), Switz., 39
Saanich, Br. Col., 184
Saar (riv.), Europe, 22
Saarbrücken, W. Ger., 22
Saaremaa (isl.), U.S.S.R., 53
Saarland (state), W. Ger., 22
Saarlouis, W. Ger., 22
Saba (isl.), Neth. Ant., 156
Šabac, Yugo., 45
Sabadell, Spain, 33
Sabae, Japan, 81
Sabah (state), Malaysia, 85
Sabana (arch.), Cuba, 158
Sabana de la Mar, Dom. Rep., 158
Sabanagrande, Hond., 154
Sabana Grande, P. Rico, 161
Sabanalarga, Col., 126
Sabaneta, Venez., 124
Sabang, Indon., 85
Sabi (riv.), Rhod., 118
Sabinas, Mex., 150
Sabinas Hidalgo, Mex., 150
Sabine (mt.), Ant., 5
Sabine (riv.), U.S., 238, 302
Sable (cape), Fla., 212
Sable (cape), N.S., 169
Sable (isl.), N.S., 169
Sabratha (ruins), Libya, 111
Sabrina Coast (reg.), Ant., 5
Sabya, Saudi Ar., 59
Sabzawar, Afghan., 68
Sabzawar, Iran, 66
Sacaba, Bol., 136
Sacajawea (lake), Wash., 310
Sacandaga (res.), N.Y., 276
Sacavém, Port., 33
Sac City, Iowa, 229
Săcele, Rum., 45
Sachigo (riv.), Ont., 177
Sachs Harbour, N.W.T., 187
Sackets (harbor), N.Y., 276
Sackville, N.B., 170
Sackville, N.S., 169
Saco, Maine, 242
Sacramento (cap.), Calif., 204
Sacramento (riv.), Calif., 204
Sacramento (mts.), N. Mex., 274
Sacratif (cape), Spain, 33
Sá da Bandeira, Angola, 115
Saddle (riv.), N. J., 273
Saddle Brook, N. J., 273
Saddleworth, Eng., 10
Sadec, S. Vietnam, 72
Sado (isl.), Japan, 81
Sado (riv.), Port., 33
Sæby, Den., 21
Safaniya, Ras (cape), Saudi Ar., 59
Säffle, Sweden, 18
Safford, Ariz., 198
Safi, Mor., 106
Safidar, Kuh-i- (mt.), Iran, 66
Safonovo, U.S.S.R., 52
Saga (prefecture), Japan, 81
Saga, Japan, 81
Sagaing (div.), Burma, 72
Sagaing, Burma, 72
Sagami (bay), Japan, 81
Sagamihara, Japan, 81
Sagamore Hill Nat'l Hist. Site, N.Y., 276
Sagar, India, 68
Saginaw, Mich., 250
Saginaw (bay), Mich., 250
Saglek (bay), Newf., 166
Saglouc, Que., 174
Sagua de Tánamo, Cuba, 158
Sagua la Grande, Cuba, 158
Saguaro Nat'l Mon., Ariz., 198
Saguenay (riv.), Que., 172
Saguenay Prov. Park, Que., 174
Saguia el Hamra (reg.), Sp. Sahara, 106
Sagunto, Spain, 33
Sahagún, Col., 126
Sahara (des.), Africa, 102
Saharan Atlas (ranges), Africa, 106
Saharanpur, India, 68
Sahuaripa, Mex., 150
Sahuayo, Mex., 150
Saïda, Alg., 106
Saida (Sidon), Leb., 63
Saidor, Terr. N.G., 85
Saidu, Pak., 68
Saigon (cap.), S. Vietnam, 72
Saihut, P.D.R. Yemen, 59
Saiki, Japan, 81
Saimaa (lake), Fin., 18
Sain Alto, Mex., 150
Sain Shanda, Mong., 77
Saint Albans, Eng., 13
Saint Albans, Vt., 268
Saint Albans, W. Va., 313
Saint-Albert, Alta., 182
Saint-André (cape), Malag. Rep., 118
Saint-André, Réunion, 118
Saint Andrews, N.B., 170
Saint Andrews, Scot., 15
Saint Andrews, S.C., 296
Saint Ann, Mo., 261
Saint Anne, Channel Is., 13
Saint Anns Bay, Jam., 158
Saint Anthony, Idaho, 220
Saint Anthony, Newf., 166
Saint Anthony Falls, Minn., 254
Saint Arnaud, Vic., 97
Saint-Augustin, Que., 174
Saint Augustine, Fla., 212
Saint Austell with Fowey, Eng., 13
Saint-Barthélemy (isl.), Guad., 156
Saint Bees (head), Eng., 13
Saint-Benoît, Réunion, 118
Saint Bernard, Ohio, 284
Saint Boniface, Man., 179
Saint Brides (bay), Wales, 13
Saint-Brieuc, France, 28
Saint-Bruno, Que., 172
Saint Catharines, Ont., 177
Saint Charles, Ill., 222
Saint Charles, Mo., 261
Saint Charles (cape), Newf., 166
Saint Christopher (isl.), St. Chr.-N.-A., 161
Saint Christopher-Nevis-Anguilla, 156
Saint Clair, Mich., 250
Saint Clair, Mo., 261
Saint Clair (lake), N. Amer., 250
Saint Clair (riv.), N. Amer., 250
Saint Clair, Pa., 294
Saint Clair Shores, Mich., 250
Saint Clairsville, Ohio, 284
Saint-Claude, Guad., 161
Saint Cloud, Fla., 212
Saint-Cloud, France, 28
Saint Cloud, Minn., 254
Saint-Constant, Que., 172
Saint Croix (riv.), U.S., 317
Saint Croix (isl.), Virgin Is. (U.S.), 161
Saint Davids (isl.), Berm., 156
Saint-Denis, France, 28
Saint-Denis (cap.), Réunion, 118
Saint-Dié, France, 28
Saint-Dizier, France, 28
Sainte-Agathe, Que., 172
Sainte-Anne, Guad., 161
Sainte Anne (isl.), Seych., 118
Sainte-Anne-de-Beaupré, Que., 172
Sainte-Anne-de-Bellevue, Que., 172
Sainte-Croix, Que., 172
Sainte-Foy, Que., 172
Sainte Genevieve, Mo., 261
Sainte-Geneviève, Que., 172
Sainte-Hénédine, Que., 172
Sainte-Julienne, Que., 172
Saint Elias (mt.), N. Amer., 196
Saint Elias (mts.), N. Amer., 196
Sainte-Marie (cape), Malag. Rep., 118
Sainte-Marie (isl.), Malag. Rep., 118
Sainte-Marie, Mart., 161
Sainte-Marie Beauce, Que., 172
Sainte-Mère-Église, France, 28
Sainte-Rose, Guad., 161
Sainte-Rose, Que., 172
Saintes, France, 28
Saintes (isls.), Guad., 161
Sainte-Scholastique, Que., 172
Saint-Esprit, Mart., 161
Sainte-Thérèse, Que., 172
Saint-Étienne, France, 28
Saint-Eustache, Que., 172
Saint Eustatius (isl.), Neth. Ant., 156
Saint-Félicien, Que., 172
Saint-Florent (gulf), France, 28
Saint Francis, Wis., 317
Saint-François, Guad., 161
Saint-François-du-Lac, Que., 172
Saint-Gabriel-de-Brandon, Que., 172
Saint-Gaudens Nat'l Hist. Site, N.H., 268
Saint George, Berm., 156
Saint George, N.B., 170
Saint George (cape), Newf., 166
Saint George, N.Y., 276
Saint George, Queensland, 95
Saint George, Utah, 304
Saint George's (isl.), Berm., 156
Saint George's (cay), Br. Hond., 154
Saint George's (chan.), Europe, 13
Saint-Georges, Fr. Gui., 131
Saint George's (cap.), Grenada, 161
Saint George's, Newf., 166
Saint-Georges, Que., 172
Saint-Germain, France, 28
Saint-Gilles, Belg., 27
Saint Gotthard (tunnel), Switz., 39
Saint Helena, 102
Saint Helena, Calif., 204
Saint Helena (bay), S. Afr., 118
Saint Helena (isl.), S.C., 296
Saint Helens, Eng., 10
Saint Helens, Oreg., 291
Saint Helens (mt.), Wash., 310
Saint Helier (cap.), Chan. Is., 13
Saint-Hubert, Que., 172
Saint-Hyacinthe, Que., 172
Saint Ignace, Mich., 250
Saint Ignace (isl.), Ont., 177
Saint James, Minn., 254
Saint James-Assiniboia, Man., 179
Saint-Jean, Que., 172
Saint-Jean (lake), Que., 172
Saint-Jean-Port-Joli, Que., 172
Saint-Jérôme, Que., 172
Saint John, Mo., 261
Saint John, N.B., 170
Saint John (cape), Newf., 166
Saint John (riv.), N. Amer., 170, 242
Saint John (isl.), Virgin Is. (U.S.), 161
Saint John's (cap.), Antigua, 161
Saint Johns (riv.), Fla., 212
Saint Johns, Mich., 250
Saint John's (cap.), Newf., 166
Saint Johnsbury, Vt., 268
Saint Joseph, Dominica, 161
Saint-Joseph, Mart., 161
Saint Joseph, Mich., 250
Saint Joseph, Mo., 261
Saint Joseph (lake), Ont., 177
Saint-Joseph, Réunion, 118
Saint Joseph, Trin. & Tob., 161
Saint-Joseph-de-Beauce, Que., 172
Saint-Josse-ten-Noode, Belg., 27
Saint-Jovite, Que., 172
Saint Kilda, N.Z., 101
Saint Kilda (isl.), Scot., 15
Saint Kilda, Vic., 97
Saint Kitts (Saint Christopher) (isl.), St. Chr.-N.-A., 161
Saint-Lambert, Que., 172
Saint-Laurent, Que., 172
Saint-Laurent-du-Maroni, Fr. Gui., 131
Saint Lawrence (isl.), Alaska, 196
Saint Lawrence (gulf), Canada, 174
Saint Lawrence, Newf., 166
Saint Lawrence (lake), N. Amer., 177
Saint Lawrence (riv.), N. Amer., 163
Saint Lawrence Isls. Nat'l Park, Ont., 177
Saint Leonard, N.B., 170
Saint-Liboire, Que., 172
Saint-Lô, France, 28
Saint-Louis, Guad., 161
Saint Louis, Mich., 250
Saint Louis, Mo., 261
Saint-Louis, Réunion, 118
Saint-Louis, Sen., 106
Saint-Louis-du-Nord, Haiti, 158
Saint Louis Park, Minn., 254
Saint Lucia, 161
Saint Lucia (lake), S. Afr., 118
Saint Magnus (bay), Scot., 15
Saint-Malo, France, 28
Saint-Malo (gulf), France, 28
Saint-Mandé, France, 28
Saint-Marc, Haiti, 158
Saint-Marc, Que., 172
Saint Maries, Idaho, 220
Saint Martin (isl.), Guad. & Neth. Ant., 156
Saint Martinville, La., 238
Saint Marys, Ga., 216
Saint Marys (riv.), Md., 245
Saint Mary's (bay), Newf., 166
Saint Marys, Ohio, 284
Saint Marys, Ont., 177
Saint Marys, Pa., 294
Saint Mary's, W. Va. 313
Saint Matthew (isl.), Alaska, 196
Saint Matthews, Ky., 237
Saint Matthews, S.C., 296
Saint-Maur-des-Fossés, France, 28
Saint-Maurice (riv.), Que., 172
Saint Michaels (bay), Newf., 166
Saint-Michel, Que., 172
Saint-Michel-de-l'Atalaye, Haiti, 158
Saint-Mihiel, France, 28
Saint Moritz, Switz., 39
Saint-Nazaire, France, 28
Saint Ninians, Scot., 15
Saint-Ouen, France, 28
Saint-Pascal, Que., 172
Saint Paul, Alta., 182
Saint Paul (cap.), Minn., 254
Saint Paul Park, Minn., 254
Saint Peter, Minn., 254
Saint Peter Port (cap.), Chan. Is., 13
Saint Petersburg, Fla., 212
Saint Petersburg Beach, Fla., 212
Saint-Pierre, Mart., 161
Saint-Pierre (lake), Que., 172
Saint-Pierre, Réunion, 118
Saint Pierre and Miquelon, 163
Saint-Quentin, France, 28
Saint-Raphaël, Que., 172
Saint-Raymond, Que., 172
Saint Regis (riv.), N.Y., 276
Saint-Romuald, Que., 172
Saint Simons Isl., Ga., 216
Saint Stephen, N.B., 170
Saint Thomas, Ont., 177
Saint Thomas (isl.), Virgin Is. (U.S.), 161
Saint-Tite, Que., 172
Saint-Tropez, France, 28
Saint Vincent, 161
Saint Vincent (cape), Port., 33
Saint Vincent (gulf), S. Austral., 94
Saint Vital, Man., 179
Saint-Vith, Belg., 27
Saint-Yrieix, France, 28
Saipan (isl.), Pac. Is., 87
Sair Usa, Mong., 77
Saitama (pref.), Japan, 81
Saito, Japan, 81
Sajama (mt.), S. Amer., 136
Sajo (riv.), Hung., 41
Sakado, Japan, 81
Sakai, Japan, 81
Sakaide, Japan, 81
Sakaiminato, Japan, 81
Sakaka, Saudi Ar., 59
Sakakawea (lake), N. Dak., 283
Sakami (lake), Que., 174
Sakania, Dem. Rep. of the Congo, 115
Sakarya (prov.), Turkey, 63
Sakarya (riv.), Turkey, 63
Sakata, Japan, 81
Sakhalin (isl.), U.S.S.R., 48
Sakishima (isls.), Ryukyu Is., 81
Sakon Nakhon, Thai., 72
Sakonnet (pt.), R.I., 249
Saku, Japan, 81
Sakurai, Japan, 81
Sala, Sweden, 18
Salada (lag.), Mex., 150
Salado (riv.), Arg., 143
Salaga, Ghana, 106
Salajar (isl.), Indon., 85
Salala, Oman, 59
Salamá, Guat., 154
Salamanca, Mex., 150
Salamanca, N.Y., 276
Salamanca (prov.), Spain, 33
Salamanca, Spain, 33
Salamat (riv.), Chad, 111
Salamina, Col., 126
Salamís, Greece, 45
Salatiga, Indon., 85
Salavat, U.S.S.R., 52
Salaverry, Peru, 128
Salawati (isl.), Indon., 85
Sala y Gómez (isl.), Chile, 87
Salazar, Angola, 115
Salazar, Col., 126
Salcedo (prov.), Dom. Rep., 158
Salcedo, Dom. Rep., 158
Salé, Mor., 106
Sale, Vic., 97
Salée (riv.), Guad., 161
Salekhard, U.S.S.R., 48
Salem, Ill., 222
Salem, India, 68
Salem, Ind., 227
Salem, Mass., 249
Salem, Mo., 261
Salem, N.H., 268

Salem, N. J., 273
Salem, Ohio, 284
Salem (cap.), Oreg., 291
Salem, S. Dak., 298
Salem, Va., 307
Salem, W. Va., 313
Salerno (prov.), Italy, 34
Salerno, Italy, 34
Salford, Eng., 10
Sálgotarján, Hung., 41
Salida, Colo., 208
Salihli, Turkey, 63
Salima, Malawi, 115
Salina, Kans., 232
Salina, Utah, 304
Salina Cruz, Mex., 150
Salinas, Calif., 204
Salinas (riv.), Calif., 204
Salinas (bay), Cent. Amer., 154
Salinas, Ecua., 128
Salinas, Mex., 150
Salinas, P. Rico, 161
Salisbury, Eng., 13
Salisbury, Md., 245
Salisbury, N.C., 281
Salisbury (cap.), Rhod., 118
Salisbury, S. Austral., 94
Sallisaw, Okla., 288
Sallyana, Nepal, 68
Salma, Jebel (mts.), Saudi Ar., 59
Salmon, Idaho, 220
Salmon (riv.), Idaho, 220
Salmon (riv.), N.Y., 276
Salmon Arm, Br. Col., 184
Salmon Falls (riv.), U.S., 242, 268
Salmon River (mts.), Idaho, 220
Salo, Fin., 18
Salong, Phil. Is., 82
Salonika (Thessaloníki) Greece, 45
Salonika (Thermaic)(gulf), Greece, 45
Sal Rei, Cape Verde Is., 106
Salsette (isl.), India, 68
Sal'sk, U.S.S.R., 52
Salt (riv.), Wyo., 319
Salta (prov.), Arg., 143
Salta, Arg., 143
Saltburn and Marske-by-the-Sea, Eng., 13
Saltcoats, Scot., 15
Saltillo, Mex., 150
Salt Lake City (cap.), Utah, 304
Salto, Braz., 135
Salto (dept.), Urug., 145
Salto, Urug., 145
Salton Sea (lake), Calif., 204
Saltsjöbaden, Sweden, 18
Saltville, Va., 307
Saluda (riv.), S.C., 296
Salûm, U.A.R., 111
Salut (isls.), Fr. Gui., 131
Saluzzo, Italy, 34
Salvador, Braz., 132
Salvaleón de Higüey, Dom. Rep., 158
Salween (riv.), Asia, 72, 77
Salzach (riv.), Europe, 41
Salzburg (prov.), Austria, 41
Salzburg, Austria, 41
Salzgitter, W. Ger., 22
Salzkammergut (reg.), Austria, 41
Salzwedel, E. Ger., 22
Samal (isl.), Phil. Is., 82
Samalkot, India, 68
Samalût, U.A.R., 111
Samaná (prov.), Dom. Rep., 158
Samaná (bay), Dom. Rep., 158
Samaniego, Col., 126
Samar (isl.), Phil. Is., 82
Samar (sea), Phil. Is., 82
Samara (Kuybyshev), U.S.S.R., 52
Samarai, Papua, 85
Samaria (reg.), Jordan, 65
Samarinda, Indon., 85
Samarkand, U.S.S.R., 48
Samarra, Iraq, 66
Samawa, Iraq, 66
Sambalpur, India, 68
Sambhal, India, 68
Sambhar (lake), India, 68
Sambor, Cambodia, 72
Samch'ŏk, S. Korea, 81
Samit (pt.), Cambodia, 72
Sam Lord's Castle, Barb., 161
Samnan (governorate), Iran, 66
Samnan, Iran, 66
Samnangjin, S. Korea, 81
Sam Neua, Laos, 72
Samokov, Bulg., 45
Sámos (isl.), Greece, 45
Samoset, Fla., 212
Samothráki (isl.), Greece, 45
Sampang, Indon., 85
Sampit, Indon., 85
Sam Rayburn (res.), Tex., 302
Samsø (isl.), Den., 21
Samsun (prov.), Turkey, 63
Samsun, Turkey, 63
Samui (strait), Thai., 72
Samut Prakan, Thai., 72
Samut Sakhon, Thai., 72
Samut Songkhram, Thai., 72
San, Mali, 106
San (riv.), Poland, 47
Saña, Peru, 128
San'a (cap.), Yemen Arab Rep., 59
Sanae, Ant., 5
Sanaga (riv.), Cameroon, 115
San Agustín, Col., 126
San Agustin (cape), Phil. Is., 82
San Ambrosio (isl.), Chile, 120
Sanana, Indon., 85
Sanandaj, Iran, 66
San Andrés, Col., 126
San Andrés (isl.), Col., 126
San Andrés de Giles, Arg., 143
San Andrés Tuxtla, Mex., 150
San Andrés y Providencia (intendency), Col., 126
San Angelo, Tex., 302
San Anselmo, Calif., 204
San Antero, Col., 126
San Antonio (cape), Arg., 143
San Antonio, Chile, 138
San Antonio (cape), Cuba, 158
San Antonio, N. Mex., 274
San Antonio, Par., 144
San Antonio, Tex., 302
San Antonio de Areco, Arg., 143
San Antonio de los Baños, Cuba, 158
San Antonio del Táchira, Venez., 124
San Antonio Oeste, Arg., 143
Sanare, Venez., 124
San Augustine, Tex., 302
San Benedicto (isl.), Mex., 150
San Benito (isl.), Mex., 150
San Benito, Tex., 302
San Bernardino, Calif., 204
San Bernardino (mts.), Calif., 204
San Bernardino (strait), Phil. Is., 82
San Bernardino (pass), Switz., 39
San Bernardo, Chile, 138
San Blas, Mex., 150
San Blas (gulf), Pan., 154
San Blas (range), Pan., 154
San Bruno, Calif., 204
San Buenaventura, Mex., 150
San Carlos, Arg., 143
San Carlos, Calif., 204
San Carlos, Chile, 138
San Carlos, Eq. Guin., 115
San Carlos, Nic., 154
San Carlos, Phil. Is., 82
San Carlos, Urug., 145
San Carlos, Venez., 124
San Carlos de Bariloche, Arg., 143
San Casimiro, Venez., 124
San Cataldo, Italy, 34
Sánchez, Dom. Rep., 158
Sánchez Ramírez (prov.), Dom. Rep., 158
San Clemente, Calif., 204
San Clemente (isl.), Calif., 204
San Cristóbal, Arg., 143
San Cristobal (isl.), Br. Sol. Is., 87
San Cristóbal (prov.), Dom. Rep., 158
San Cristóbal, Dom. Rep., 158
San Cristóbal (isl.), Ecua., 128
San Cristóbal (Ciudad de las Casas), Mex., 150
San Cristóbal, Venez., 124
Sancti-Spíritus, Cuba, 158
Sanda, Japan, 81
Sandakan, Malaysia, 85
Sandalwood (Sumba)(isl.), Indon., 85
Sandanski, Bulg., 45
Sanday (isl.), Scot., 15
Sandefjord, Norway, 18
Sanderson, Tex., 302
Sandersville, Ga., 216
Sandgate, Queensland, 95
Sandia (peak), N. Mex., 274
San Diego (cape), Arg., 143
San Diego, Calif., 204
San Diego, Tex., 302
San Dimas, Calif., 204
Sandnes, Norway, 18
Sandoa, Dem. Rep. of the Congo, 115
Sandoná, Col., 126
Sandoway, Burma, 72
Sandown (bay), S. Afr., 118
Sandown-Shanklin, Eng., 13
Sandpoint, Idaho, 220
Sandringham, Vic., 97
Sand Springs, Okla., 288
Sandston, Va., 307
Sandusky, Ohio, 284
Sandvika, Norway, 18
Sandviken, Sweden, 18
Sandwich, Ill., 222
Sandwich (bay), Newf., 166
Sandy (lake), Ont., 177
Sandy (cape), Queensland, 95
Sandy, Utah, 304
Sandy Hook (spit), N. J., 273
Sandy Point, St. Chr.-N.-A., 161
San Estanislao, Par., 144
San Felipe, Chile, 138
San Felipe (cays), Cuba, 158
San Felipe, Guat., 154
San Felipe, Mex., 150
San Felipe, N. Mex., 274
San Felipe, Venez., 124
San Félix (isl.), Chile, 120
San Fernando, Arg., 143
San Fernando, Calif., 204
San Fernando, Chile, 138
San Fernando, Mex., 150
San Fernando, Spain, 33
San Fernando, Trin. and Tob., 161
San Fernando, Venez., 124
Sanford, Fla., 212
Sanford, Maine, 242
Sanford, N.C., 281
Sanford Nat'l Rec. Area, Tex., 302
San Francisco, Arg., 143
San Francisco, Calif., 204
San Francisco (bay), Calif., 204
San Francisco, Mex., 150
San Francisco de la Paz, Hond., 154
San Francisco del Oro, Mex., 150
San Francisco de Macorís, Dom. Rep., 158
San Francisco Gotera, El Sal., 154
Sanga (riv.), Africa, 115
San Gabriel, Calif., 204
San Gabriel, Ecua., 128
San Gabriel Chilac, Mex., 150
Sangamner, India, 68
Sanger, Calif., 204
Sangerhausen, E. Ger., 22
San Germán, Cuba, 158
San Germán, P. Rico, 161
Sangihe (isls.), Indon., 85
San Gil, Col., 126
Sangju, S. Korea, 81
Sangli, India, 68
Sangmélima, Cameroon, 115
Sangolquí, Ecua., 128
Sangre de Cristo (mts.), U.S., 208, 274
Sangre Grande, Trin. and Tob., 161
Sangue (riv.), Braz., 132
San Ignacio, Bol., 136
San Ignacio, Par., 144
San Jacinto, Calif., 204
San Jacinto, Col., 126
San Javier, Arg., 143
San Javier, Chile, 138
Sanjo, Japan, 81
San Joaquín, Bol., 136
San Joaquin (riv.), Calif., 204
San Jorge (gulf), Arg., 143
San Jorge (bay), Mex., 150
San Jorge, Nic., 154
San Jose, Calif., 204
San José (cap.), Costa Rica, 154
San José, Guat., 154
San José (isl.), Mex., 150
San José, Par., 144
San José (dept.), Urug., 145
San José, Urug., 145
San José, Venez., 124
San Jose de Buenavista, Phil. Is., 82
San José de Chiquitos, Bol., 136
San José de las Lajas, Cuba, 158
San José del Cabo, Mex., 150
San José de Mayo, Urug., 145
San José de Ocoa, Dom. Rep., 158
San Juan (prov.), Arg., 143
San Juan, Arg., 143
San Juan (riv.), Cent. Amer., 154
San Juan (prov.), Dom. Rep., 158
San Juan, Dom. Rep., 158
San Juan, Mex., 150
San Juan (dist.), P. Rico, 161
San Juan (cap.), P. Rico, 161
San Juan, Tex., 302
San Juan, Trin. & Tob., 161
San Juan (riv.), U.S., 276, 304
San Juan, Venez., 124
San Juan (isl.), Wash., 310
San Juan Bautista, Par., 144
San Juan de Flores, Hond., 154
San Juan de Guadalupe, Mex., 150
San Juan del Norte, Nic., 154
San Juan del Río, Mex., 150
San Juan del Sur, Nic., 154
San Juan Isl. Nat'l Hist. Park, Wash., 310
San Juan Ixtenco, Mex., 150
San Juan Nat'l Hist. Site, P. Rico, 161
San Juan Pueblo, N. Mex., 274
San Juan Xiutetelco, Mex., 150
San Julián, Arg., 143
Sankt Anton, Austria, 41
Sankt Gallen (canton), Switz., 39
Sankt Gallen, Switz., 39
Sankt Ingbert, W. Ger., 22
Sankt Pölten, Austria, 41
Sankt Veit, Austria, 41
Sankt Wolfgang, Austria, 41
Sankuru (riv.), Dem. Rep. of the Congo, 115
San Lázaro (cape), Mex., 150
San Leandro, Calif., 204
San Lorenzo, Arg., 143
San Lorenzo, Calif., 204
San Lorenzo, Par., 144
San Lorenzo, P. Rico, 161
San Lorenzo de El Escorial, Spain, 33
Sanlúcar de Barrameda, Spain, 33
San Lucas (cape), Mex., 150
San Luis (prov.), Arg., 143
San Luis, Arg., 143
San Luis, Cuba, 158
San Luis, Hond., 154
San Luis de la Paz, Mex., 150
San Luis del Cordero, Mex., 150
San Luis Jilotepeque, Guat., 154
San Luis Obispo, Calif., 204
San Luis Potosí (state), Mex., 150
San Luis Potosí, Mex., 150
San Luis Río Colorado, Mex., 150
San Manuel, Ariz., 198
San Marcos, Col., 126
San Marcos, Guat., 154
San Marcos, Hond., 154
San Marcos, Mex., 150
San Marcos, Tex., 302
San Marino, 34
San Marino, Calif., 204
San Marino (cap.), San Marino, 34
San Martín, Col., 126
San Martín, Guat., 154
San Martín (dept.), Peru, 128
San Martín (lake), S. Amer., 143
San Martín Texmelucan, Mex., 150
San Mateo, Calif., 204
San Mateo, Guat., 154
San Matías (gulf), Arg., 143
San Miguel (riv.), Bol., 136
San Miguel, El Sal., 154
San Miguel, Mex., 150
San Miguel (bay), Pan., 154
San Miguel Canoa, Mex., 150
Sanming, China, 77
San Nicolás, Arg., 143
San Nicolas (isl.), Calif., 204
San Nicolás, Cuba, 158
San Onofre, Col., 126
San Pablo, Calif., 204
San Pablo (mts.), Hond., 154
San Pablo, Phil. Is., 82
San Pedro, Arg., 143
San Pedro, Calif., 204
San Pedro (riv.), Guat., 154
San Pedro, Mex., 150
San Pedro (dept.), Par., 144
San Pedro, Par., 144
San Pedro Carchá, Guat., 154
San Pedro de Lloc, Peru, 128
San Pedro de Macorís (prov.), Dom. Rep., 158
San Pedro de Macorís, Dom. Rep., 158
San Pedro Sula, Hond., 154
Sanpoil (riv.), Wash., 310
Sanquhar, Scot., 15
San Rafael, Arg., 143
San Rafael, Calif., 204
San Rafael, Nic., 154
San Rafael (riv.), Utah, 304
San Rafael, Venez., 124
San Ramón, Bol., 136
San Ramón, C. Rica, 154
San Ramón, Urug., 145
San Remo, Italy, 34
San Roque, Col., 126
San Saba, Tex., 302
San Salvador (isl.), Bah. Is., 156
San Salvador (isl.), Ecua., 128
San Salvador (cap.), El Sal., 154
Sansanné-Mango, Togo, 106
San Sebastián, P. Rico, 161
San Sebastián, Spain, 33
San Sebastián Venez., 124
San Severo, Italy, 34
Sansom Park Vill., Tex., 302
Santa Ana, Bol., 136
Santa Ana, Calif., 204
Santa Ana, El Sal., 154
Santa Ana, Mex., 150
Santa Ana, Venez., 124
Santa Barbara, Calif., 204
Santa Barbara (isls.), Calif., 204
Santa Bárbara, Col., 126
Santa Bárbara, Hond., 154
Santa Bárbara, Mex., 150
Santa Catalina (isl.), Calif., 204
Santa Catalina (isl.), Mex., 150
Santa Catarina (state), Braz., 132
Santa Catarina (isl.), Braz., 132
Santa Clara, Calif., 204
Santa Clara, Cuba, 158
Santa Cruz (prov.), Arg., 143
Santa Cruz, Arg., 143
Santa Cruz (dept.), Bol., 136
Santa Cruz, Bol., 136
Santa Cruz (isls.), Br. Sol. Is., 87
Santa Cruz, Calif., 204
Santa Cruz, Chile, 138
Santa Cruz, C. Rica, 154
Santa Cruz (isl.), Ecua., 128
Santa Cruz, India, 68
Santa Cruz, Jam., 158
Santa Cruz (isl.), Mex., 150
Santa Cruz del Quiché, Guat., 154
Santa Cruz de Orinoco, Venez., 124
Santa Cruz de Tenerife (prov.), Spain, 33
Santa Cruz de Tenerife, Spain, 33
Santa Cruz de Yojoa, Hond., 154
Santa Cruz do Rio Pardo, Braz., 135
Santa Elena (cape), Costa Rica, 154
Santa Elena, Ecua., 128
Santa Eugenia (pt.), Mex., 150
Santa Fe (prov.), Arg., 143
Santa Fe, Arg., 143
Santa Fé, Cuba, 158
Santa Fe (cap.), N. Mex., 274
Santa Fe Sprs., Calif., 204
Santai, China, 77
Santa Inés (bay), Mex., 150
Santa Isabel (isl.), Br. Sol. Is., 87
Santa Isabel (cap.), Eq. Guin., 115
Santa Isabel, P. Rico, 161
Santa Lucía, Arg., 143
Santa Lucía, Urug., 145
Santa Margarita (isl.), Mex., 150
Santa Maria (cape), Angola, 115
Santa Maria, Braz., 132
Santa Maria, Calif., 204
Santa Maria, Cape Verde Is., 106
Santa María (isl.), Ecua., 128
Santa Maria, Italy, 34
Santa María (riv.), Mex., 150
Santa Maria (cape), Port., 33
Santa Maria (isl.), Port., 32
Santa María del Río, Mex., 150
Santa María del Tule, Mex., 150
Santa María del Orinoco, Venez., 124
Santa Maria di Leuca (cape), Italy, 34
Santa Marta, Col., 126
Santa Monica, Calif., 204
Santana do Livramento, Braz., 132
Santander (dept.), Col., 126
Santander, Col., 126
Santander (prov.), Spain, 33
Santander, Spain, 33
Sant'Antioco (isl.), Italy, 34
Santa Paula, Calif., 204
Santarém, Braz., 132
Santarém, Port., 33
Santa Rita, Hond., 154
Santa Rita, N. Mex., 274
Santa Rita, Venez., 124
Santa Rita de Tonalá, Nic., 154
Santa Rosa, Arg., 143
Santa Rosa, Calif., 204
Santa Rosa, Ecua., 128
Santa Rosa, El Sal., 154
Santa Rosa (mts.), Nev., 266
Santa Rosa, N. Mex., 274
Santa Rosa, Par., 144
Santa Rosa de Aguán, Hond., 154
Santa Rosa de Copán, Hond., 154
Santa Rosa de Osos, Col., 126
Santa Rosalía, Mex., 150
Santa Tecla, El Sal., 154
Santa Teresa del Tuy, Venez., 124
Santee, Calif., 204
Santee (riv.), S.C., 296
Sant'Eufemia (gulf), Italy, 34
Santiago (prov.), Chile, 138
Santiago (cap.), Chile, 138
Santiago (prov.), Dom. Rep., 158
Santiago, Dom. Rep., 158
Santiago, Mex., 150
Santiago, Pan., 154
Santiago, Spain, 33
Santiago (mts.), Tex., 302
Santiago de Chuca, Peru, 128
Santiago de Cuba, Cuba, 158
Santiago de las Vegas, Cuba, 158
Santiago del Estero (prov.), Arg., 143
Santiago del Estero, Arg., 143
Santiago Juxtlahuaca, Mex., 150
Santiago Papasquiaro, Mex., 150
Santiago Pinotepa Nacional, Mex., 150
Santiago Rodríguez (prov.), Dom. Rep., 158
Santiago Tuxtla, Mex., 150
Santiaguillo (lake), Mex., 150
San Timoteo, Venez., 124
Santipur, India, 68
Santo Amaro, Braz., 132
Santo André, Braz., 135
Santo Ângelo, Braz., 132
Santo Antão (isl.), Cape Verde Is., 106
Santo António do Zaire, Angola, 115
Santo Domingo, C. Rica, 154
Santo Domingo (cap.), Dom. Rep., 158
Santo Domingo, Ecua., 128
Santo Domingo, Nic., 154
Santos, Braz., 135
Santos Dumont, Braz., 135
Santo Tomás, Nic., 154
Santurce, P. Rico, 161
San Vicente, Peru, 128
San Vito, Italy, 34
São Bernardo do Campo, Braz., 135
São Borja, Braz., 132
São Caetano do Sul, Braz., 135
São Carlos, Braz., 135
São Francisco (riv.), Braz., 132
São Francisco do Sul, Braz., 132
São Gonçalo, Braz., 132
São João da Bôa Vista, Braz., 135
São João da Madeira, Port., 33
São João del Rei, Braz., 135
São João de Meriti, Braz., 132
São Joaquim da Barra, Braz., 135
São Jorge (isl.), Port., 32
São José do Rio Pardo, Braz., 135
São José do Rio Prêto, Braz., 135
São José dos Campos, Braz., 135
São Leopoldo, Braz., 132
São Lourenço, Braz., 135
São Luís, Braz., 132
São Manuel, Braz., 135
São Miguel (isl.), Port., 32
São Miguel Paulista, Braz., 135
Saona (isl.), Dom. Rep., 158
Saône (riv.), France, 28
Saône-et-Loire (dept.), France, 28
São Paulo (state), Braz., 132
São Paulo, Braz., 135
São Roque (cape), Braz., 132
São Salvador, Angola, 115
São Sebastião (isl.), Braz., 135
São Sebastião (cape), Mozamb., 118
São Tiago (isl.), Cape Verde Is., 106
São Tomé (cape), Braz., 132
São Tomé (cap.), São T. and Pr., 106
São Tomé (isl.), São T. and Pr., 106
São Tomé e Príncipe, 106
Saoura, Wadi (dry riv.), Alg., 106
São Vicente, Braz., 135
Saparua, Indon., 85
Sapele, Nigeria, 106
Sapporo, Japan, 81
Sapucaí, Par., 144
Sapulpa, Okla., 288
Saqqiz, Iran, 66
Sara (riv.), Africa, 111
Sara Buri, Thai., 72
Saragossa (prov.), Spain, 33
Saragossa, Spain, 33
Sarajevo, Yugo., 45
Saraland, Ala., 194
Saramacca (dist.), Sur., 131
Saramaccapolder, Sur., 131
Saranac Lake, N.Y., 276
Sarandë, Alb., 45
Sarandí del Yí, Urug., 145
Sarandí Grande, Urug., 145
Sarangani (isls.), Phil. Is., 82
Saransk, U.S.S.R., 52
Sarapul, U.S.S.R., 52
Sarare, Venez., 124
Sarasota, Fla., 212
Saraswati (riv.), India, 68
Saratoga, Calif., 204
Saratoga, Wyo., 319
Saratoga Nat'l Hist. Park, N.Y., 276
Saratoga Springs, N.Y., 276
Saratov, U.S.S.R., 52
Saravane, Laos, 72
Sarawak (state), Malaysia, 85
Sardarshahr, India, 68
Sardinata, Col., 126
Sardinia (isl.), Italy, 34
Sardinia (reg.), Italy, 34
Sardis (lake), Miss., 256
Sarera (bay), Indon., 85
Sargodha, Pak., 68
Sari, Iran, 66
Sarigan (isl.), Pac. Is., 87
Sarıkamiş, Turkey, 63
Sarina, Queensland, 95
Sar-i-Pul, Afghan., 68
Sariwŏn, N. Korea, 81
Sarıyer, Turkey, 63
Sark (isl.), Chan. Is., 13
Sarmi, Indon., 85
Sarnath, India, 68
Sarnen, Switz., 39
Sarnia, Ont., 177
Saronic (gulf), Greece, 45
Saronno, Italy, 34
Saros (gulf), Turkey, 63
Sarpsborg, Norway, 18
Sarreguemines, France, 28
Sarstún (riv.), Cent. Amer., 154
Sarthe (dept.), France, 28
Sarthe (riv.), France, 28
Sartrouville, France, 28
Sasaram, India, 68
Sasebo, Japan, 81
Saskatchewan (prov.), Canada, 181
Saskatchewan (riv.), Canada, 163
Saskatoon, Sask., 181
Sassafras (riv.), Md., 245
Sassandra, Ivory Coast, 106
Sassari (prov.), Italy, 34
Sassari, Italy, 34
Satara, India, 68
Satawal (isl.), Pac. Is., 87
Satna, India, 68
Satpura (range), India, 68
Satu Mare, Rum., 45
Sauce (lagoon), Urug., 145
Saucillo, Mex., 150
Saudhárkrókur, Ice., 21
Saudi Arabia, 59
Sauer (riv.), Europe, 27
Sauerland (reg.), W. Ger., 22
Saugerties, N.Y., 276
Saugus, Mass., 249
Saugus Iron Works Nat'l Hist. Site, Mass., 249
Sauk Centre, Minn., 254
Sauk City, Wis., 317
Sauk Rapids, Minn., 254
Sauk Village, Ill., 222
Sault Sainte Marie, Mich., 250
Sault Sainte Marie, Ont., 175, 177
Saumâtre (lake), Haiti, 158
Saumlaki, Indon., 85
Saumur, France, 28
Sauqira (bay), Oman, 59
Sausalito, Calif., 204
Sauteurs, Grenada, 161
Sava (riv.), Yugo., 45
Savage (riv.), Md., 245
Savai'i (isl.), W. Samoa, 87
Savalou, Dahomey, 106
Savanna, Ill., 222
Savannah, Ga., 216
Savannah, Tenn., 237
Savannah (riv.), U.S., 216, 296
Savannakhet, Laos, 72
Savanna-la-Mar, Jam., 158
Savannes (bay), St. Lucia, 161
Savantvadi, India, 68
Savanur, India, 68
Savé, Dahomey, 106
Save (riv.), Mozamb., 118
Saveh, Iran, 66
Savoie (dept.), France, 28
Savona (prov.), Italy, 34
Savona, Italy, 34
Savonlinna, Fin., 18
Savsjö, Sweden, 18
Sawahlunto, Indon., 85
Sawara, Japan, 81
Sawtooth (range), Idaho, 220
Sawu (isls.), Indon., 85
Sawu (sea), Indon., 85
Saxon, S.C., 296
Saxonville, Mass., 249
Saxony (reg.), E. Ger., 22
Say, Niger, 106
Sayaboury, Laos, 72
Sayama, Japan, 81
Sayan (mts.), U.S.S.R., 48
Saylesville, R.I., 245
Sayre, Okla., 288
Sayre, Pa., 294
Sayreville, N. J., 273
Sayula, Mex., 150
Sayville, N.Y., 276
Sazan (isl.), Alb., 45
Scafell Pike (mt.), Eng., 13
Scapa Flow (chan.), Scot., 15
Scarborough, Eng., 13
Scarborough, Ont., 177
Scarborough, Trin. and Tob., 156
Scarsdale, N.Y., 276
Sceaux, France, 28
Schaan, Liecht., 39
Schaerbeek, Belg., 27
Schaffhausen (canton), Switz., 39
Schaffhausen, Switz., 39
Schaumburg, Ill., 222
Schefferville, Que., 174
Scheldt (riv.), Europe, 27
Schell Creek (range), Nev., 266
Schenectady, N.Y., 276
Schererville, Ind., 227
Scheveningen, Neth., 27
Schiedam, Neth., 27
Schiller Park, Ill., 222
Schio, Italy, 34
Schleswig, W. Ger., 22
Schleswig-Holstein (state), W. Ger., 22
Schlieren, Switz., 39
Schneeberg, E. Ger., 22
Schneeberg (mt.), W. Ger., 22
Schnee Eifel (plat.), Belg., 27
Schoelcher, Mart., 161
Schofield, Wis., 317
Schofield Barracks, Hawaii, 219
Schoharie (res.), N.Y., 276
Schönebeck, E. Ger., 22
Schöneberg, W. Ger., 22
Schoten, Belg., 27
Schouten (isls.), Indon., 85
Schouten (isls.), Terr. N.G., 85
Schouwen (isl.), Neth., 27
Schreiber, Ont., 175
Schroon (lake), N.Y., 276
Schumacher, Ont., 175
Schuyler, Nebr., 264
Schuylkill (riv.), Pa., 294
Schuylkill Haven, Pa., 294
Schwabach, W. Ger., 22
Schwäbisch Gmünd, W. Ger., 22
Schwäbisch Hall, W. Ger., 22
Schwaner (mts.), Indon., 85
Schwarzwald (Black)(for.), W. Ger., 22
Schwedt, E. Ger., 22
Schweinfurt, W. Ger., 22
Schwelm, W. Ger., 22
Schwenningen, W. Ger., 22
Schwerin (dist.), E. Ger., 22
Schwerin, E. Ger., 22
Schwerinersee (lake), E. Ger., 22
Schwyz (canton), Switz., 39
Schwyz, Switz., 39
Sciacca, Italy, 34
Scilly (isls.), Eng., 13
Scioto (riv.), Ohio, 284
Scituate, Mass., 249
Scituate (res.), R.I., 249
Scobey, Mont., 262
Scone, N.S.W., 97
Scone, Scot., 15
Scoresby (sound), Greenl., 4
Scoresbysund, Greenl., 4
Scotch Plains, N. J., 273
Scotia (sea), Ant., 5
Scotia, N.Y., 276
Scotland, 15
Scotland Neck, N.C., 281
Scotlandville, La., 238
Scott (isl.), Ant., 5
Scott City, Kans., 232
Scottdale, Pa., 294
Scottsbluff, Nebr., 264
Scotts Bluff Nat'l Mon., Nebr., 264
Scottsboro, Ala., 194
Scottsburg, Ind., 227
Scottsdale, Ariz., 198
Scottsdale, Tas., 99
Scranton, Pa., 294
Scunthorpe, Eng., 13
Scutari (lake), Europe, 45
Sea (isls.), U.S., 216, 296
Seabrook, Tex., 302
Sea Cliff, N.Y., 276
Seaflower (chan.), Indon., 85
Seaford, Del., 245
Seaford, Eng., 13
Seaforth, Ont., 177
Seagoville, Tex., 302
Seaham, Eng., 13
Seahurst, Wash., 310
Seal (riv.), Man., 179
Seal Beach, Calif., 204
Sea of Oman-Persian Gulf (prov.), Iran, 66
Searcy, Ark., 203
Seaside, Calif., 204
Seaside, Oreg., 291
Seat Pleasant, Md., 245
Seattle, Wash., 310
Sebastián Vizcaíno (bay), Mex., 150
Sebastopol, Calif., 204
Sebastopol, Vic., 97
Sebha (prov.), Libya, 111
Sebha, Libya, 111
Seboruco, Venez., 124
Sebou (riv.), Mor., 106
Sebring, Fla., 212
Sebring, Ohio, 284
Sebuko (bay), Indon., 85
Secaucus, N. J., 273
Sechura (bay), Peru, 128
Secunderabad, India, 68
Security, Colo., 208
Sedalia, Mo., 261
Sedan, France, 28
Sedhiou, Sen., 106
Sedro Woolley, Wash., 310
Seeheim, S.W. Afr., 118
Sefrou, Mor., 106
Segamat, Malaysia, 72
Ségou, Mali, 106
Segovia (Coco)(riv.), Cent. Amer., 154
Segovia, Col., 126
Segovia (prov.), Spain, 33
Segovia, Spain, 33
Segre (riv.), Spain, 33
Séguéla, Ivory Coast, 106
Seguin, Tex., 302
Segura (riv.), Spain, 33
Sehore, India, 68
Sehwi Wiawso, Ghana, 106
Sein (isl.), France, 28
Seinäjoki, Fin., 18
Seine (dept.), France, 28
Seine (bay), France, 28
Seine (riv.), France, 28
Seine-et-Marne (dept.), France, 28
Seine-et-Oise (dept.), France, 28
Seine-Maritime (dept.), France, 28
Seine-Saint-Denis (dept.), France, 28
Seistan and Baluchistan (prov.), Iran, 66
Seiyun, P.D.R. Yemen, 59
Se Khong (riv.), Asia, 72
Sekondi, Ghana, 106
Selah, Wash., 310
Selangor (state), Malaysia, 72
Selaphum, Thai., 72
Selatan (cape), Indon., 85
Selemiya, Syria, 63
Selenga (riv.), Asia, 77
Selenga (prov.), Mong., 77
Selfridge A.F.B., Mich., 250
Sélibaby, Mauritania, 106
Selima (oasis), Sudan, 111
Selinsgrove, Pa., 294
Selkirk (mts.), Br. Col., 184
Selkirk, Man., 179
Selkirk (county), Scot., 15
Selkirk, Scot., 15
Sellersburg, Ind., 227
Selma, Ala., 194
Selma, Calif., 204
Selma, N.C., 281
Selmont, Ala., 194
Selsey Bill (pt.), Eng., 13
Selukwe, Rhod., 118
Selwyn (mts.), Canada, 187
Selwyn (lake), N.W.T., 187
Semarang, Indon., 85
Semeru (mt.), Indon., 85
Seminoe (res.), Wyo., 319
Seminole, Okla., 288
Seminole, Tex., 302
Semipalatinsk, U.S.S.R., 48
Sempach (lake), Switz., 39
Semporna, Malaysia, 85
Senanga, Zambia, 115
Senatobia, Miss., 256
Sendai, Japan, 81
Seneca (lake), N.Y., 276
Seneca, S.C., 296
Seneca Falls, N.Y., 276
Senegal, 106
Senegal (riv.), Africa, 106
Senftenberg, E. Ger., 22
Senhor do Bonfim, Braz., 132
Senigallia, Italy, 34
Senja (isl.), Norway, 18
Sennar, Sudan, 111
Sennar (dam), Sudan, 111
Sennestadt, W. Ger., 22
Senneterre, Que., 174
Sens, France, 28
Sensuntepeque, El Sal., 154
Senta, Yugo., 45
Senyavin (isls.), Pac. Is., 87
Seoni, India, 68
Seoul (cap.), S. Korea, 81
Sepik (riv.), Terr. N.G., 85
Sept-Îles, Que., 174
Septimer (pass), Switz., 39
Sepulveda, Calif., 204
Sequoia Nat'l Park, Calif., 204
Seraing, Belg., 27
Serampore, India, 68
Serang, Indon., 85
Serangoon, Sing., 72
Serbia (rep.), Yugo., 45
Serdobsk, U.S.S.R., 52
Seremban, Malaysia, 72
Serengeti Nat'l Park, Tanz., 115
Serenje, Zambia, 115
Sergipe (state), Braz., 132
Sérifos (isl.), Greece, 45
Seringapatam, India, 68
Serowe, Botswana, 118
Serpa, Port., 33
Serpa Pinto, Angola, 115
Serpents Mouth (strait), 124
Serpukhov, U.S.S.R., 52
Sérrai, Greece, 45
Serrinha, Braz., 132
Serui, Indon., 85
Se San (riv.), Asia, 72
Sesimbra, Port., 33
Sestao, Spain, 33
Sesto, Italy, 34
Sète, France, 28
Sétif, Alg., 106
Settat, Mor., 106
Setté-Cama, Gabon, 115
Setúbal, Port., 33
Setúbal (bay), Port., 33
Seul (lake), Ont., 175
Sevan (lake), U.S.S.R., 52
Sevastopol', U.S.S.R., 52
Seven Hills, Ohio, 284
Seven Islands (bay), Newf., 166
Seven Islands (Sept-Îles), Que., 174
Sevenoaks, Eng., 10
Severn (riv.), Md., 245
Severn (riv.), Ont., 177
Severn (riv.), U.K., 13
Severna Park, Md., 245
Severnaya Zemlya (isls.), U.S.S.R., 48
Severočeský (reg.), Czech., 41
Severodvinsk, U.S.S.R., 52
Severomoravský (reg.), Czech., 41
Severomorsk, U.S.S.R., 52
Severoural'sk, U.S.S.R., 48
Sevier (lake), Utah, 304
Sevier (riv.), Utah, 304
Sevierville, Tenn., 237
Sevilla, Col., 126
Seville (prov.), Spain, 33
Seville, Spain, 33
Sèvres, France, 28
Seward, Alaska, 196
Seward (pen.), Alaska, 196
Seward, Nebr., 264
Sewell, Chile, 138
Sewickley, Pa., 294
Sexsmith, Alta., 182
Seychelles, 118
Seydhisfjördhur, Ice., 21
Seyhan (riv.), Turkey, 63
Seymour, Conn., 210
Seymour, Ind., 227
Seymour, Tex., 302
Seymour (lake), Vt., 268
Seymour, Vic., 97
Sfax, Tun., 106
's Gravenhage (The Hague) (cap.), Neth., 27
Shabani, Rhod., 118
Shabunda, Dem. Rep. of the Congo, 115
Shackleton Ice Shelf, Ant., 5
Shadehill (res.), S. Dak., 298
Shadow Mtn. Nat'l Rec. Area, Colo., 208
Shadrinsk, U.S.S.R., 48
Shadyside, Ohio, 284
Shafter, Calif., 204
Shahat, Libya, 111
Shahdol, India, 68
Shahi, Iran, 66
Shahjahanpur, India, 68
Shahjui, Afghan., 68
Shahriza, Iran, 66
Shahrud, Iran, 66
Shaikh Shu'aib (isl.), Iran, 66
Shajapur, India, 68
Shaker Hts., Ohio, 284
Shakhty, U.S.S.R., 52
Shaki, Nigeria, 106
Shakopee, Minn., 254
Sham, Jebel (mt.), Oman, 59
Shammar, Jebel (plat.), Saudi Ar., 59
Shamo (Gobi)(des.), Asia, 77
Shamokin, Pa., 294
Shamrock, Tex., 302
Shan (state), Burma, 72
Shan (plat.), Burma, 72
Shangani (riv.), Rhod., 118
Shangchih, China, 77
Shanghai, China, 77

Shanghsien, China, 77
Shangjao, China, 77
Shangkiu, China, 77
Shangshui, China, 77
Shanhaikwan, China, 77
Shannon (riv.), Ire., 17
Shannon Airport, Ire., 77
Shannontown, S.C., 296
Shanshan, China, 77
Shansi (prov.), China, 77
Shantung (prov.), China, 77
Shaohing, China, 77
Shaoyang, China, 77
Shari (riv.), Africa, 111
Sharjah, Tr. States, 59
Shark (bay), W. Austral., 92
Sharon, Mass., 249
Sharon, Pa., 294
Sharon Hill, Pa., 294
Sharonville, Ohio, 284
Sharpsburg, Pa., 294
Sharpsville, Pa., 294
Shar'ya, U.S.S.R., 52
Shashi (riv.), Africa, 118
Shasi, China, 77
Shasta (lake), Calif., 204
Shasta (mt.), Calif., 204
Shatra, Iraq, 66
Shaunavon, Sask., 181
Shaw A.F.B., S.C., 296
Shawano, Wis., 317
Shawinigan, Que., 172
Shawnee, Kans., 232
Shawnee, Okla., 288
Shcherbakov (Rybinsk), U.S.S.R., 52
Sheboygan, Wis., 317
Sheboygan Falls, Wis., 317
Shediac, N.B., 170
Sheet (harbor), N.S., 169
Sheffield, Ala., 194
Sheffield, Eng., 13
Sheffield Lake, Ohio, 284
Sheikh Sa'id, Yemen Arab Rep., 59
Sheki, U.S.S.R., 52
Shelagskiy (cape), U.S.S.R., 48
Shelburne, N.S., 169
Shelby, Mont., 262
Shelby, N.C., 281
Shelby, Ohio, 284
Shelbyville, Ill., 222
Shelbyville, Ind., 227
Shelbyville, Ky., 237
Shelbyville, Tenn., 237
Sheldon, Iowa, 229
Shelekhov (gulf), U.S.S.R., 48
Shellbrook, Sask., 181
Shelley, Idaho, 220
Shellharbour, N.S.W., 97
Shelton, Conn., 210
Shelton, Wash., 310
Shenandoah, Iowa, 229
Shenandoah, Pa., 294
Shenandoah (riv.), U.S., 307, 313
Shenandoah (mts.), Va., 307
Shenandoah Nat'l Park, Va., 307
Shendi, Sudan, 111
Shensi (prov.), China, 77
Shenyang (Mukden), China, 77
Sheo, India, 68
Sheopur, India, 68
Shepetovka, U.S.S.R., 52
Sheppard A.F.B., Tex., 302
Shepparton, Vic., 97
Sheppey (isl.), Eng., 13
Sherbro (isl.), S. Leone, 106
Sherbrooke (lake), N.S., 169
Sherbrooke, Que., 172
Sheridan, Colo., 208
Sheridan, Wyo., 319
Sherman (inlet), N.W.T., 187
Sherman, Tex., 302
Sherridon, Man., 179
Sherrill, N.Y., 276
's Hertogenbosch, Neth., 27
Sherwood, P.E.I., 169
Sherwood Park, Alta., 182
Shetland (isls.), Scot., 15
Shevchenko, U.S.S.R., 48
Sheyenne (riv.), N. Dak., 283
Shibam, P.D.R. Yemen, 59
Shibarghan, Afghan., 68
Shibata, Japan, 81
Shibetsu, Japan, 81
Shibin el Kom, U.A.R., 111
Shiel (lake), Scot., 15
Shiga (prefecture), Japan, 81
Shigatse, China, 77
Shihchüan, China, 77
Shihkiachwang, China, 77
Shihhotzu, China, 77
Shihr, P.D.R. Yemen, 59
Shijak, Alb., 45
Shikoku (isl.), Japan, 81
Shikotan (isl.), Japan, 81
Shildon, Eng., 13
Shillington, Pa., 294
Shillong, India, 68
Shiloh Nat'l Mil. Park, Tenn., 237
Shimabara, Japan, 81
Shimane (pref.), Japan, 81
Shimizu, Japan, 81
Shimoda, Japan, 81
Shimoga, India, 68
Shimonoseki, Japan, 81
Shin (lake), Scot., 15
Shinano (riv.), Japan, 81
Shindand (Sabzawar), Afghan., 68
Shingu, Japan, 81
Shinjo, Japan, 81
Shinko (riv.), Cent. Afr. Rep., 115
Shinkolobwe, Dem. Rep. of the Congo, 115
Shinnston, W. Va., 313
Shinyanga (prov.), Tanz., 115
Shinyanga, Tanz., 115
Shiogama, Japan, 81
Shiono (cape), Japan, 81
Shipki (pass), Asia, 68
Shipley, Eng., 13
Shippegan (isl.), N.B., 170
Shippensburg, Pa., 294
Ship Rock (mt.), N.M., 274
Shir (mt.), Iran, 66
Shirane (mt.), Japan, 81
Shiraz, Iran, 66
Shire (riv.), Africa, 118
Shiriya (cape), Japan, 81
Shiroishi, Japan, 81
Shirvan (riv.), Iran, 66
Shiukwan, China, 77
Shively, Ky., 237
Shivpuri, India, 68
Shizuoka (pref.), Japan, 81
Shizuoka, Japan, 81
Shkodër, Alb., 45
Shoa (prov.), Eth., 111
Shoals (isls.), U.S., 268
Shoalwater (cape), Wash., 310
Shobando, China, 77
Shobara, Japan, 81
Shohsien, China, 77
Sholapur, India, 68
Shorapur, India, 68
Shoreham-by-Sea, Eng., 13
Shorewood, Minn., 254
Shorewood, Wis., 317
Short Hills, N. J., 273
Shoshone (riv.), Wyo., 319
Shoshong, Botswana, 118
Shostka, U.S.S.R., 52
Shoultes, Wash., 310
Showak, Sudan, 111
Shreveport, La., 238
Shrewsbury, Eng., 13
Shrewsbury, Mass., 249
Shrewsbury, Mo., 261
Shrewsbury, N. J., 273
Shropshire (Salop)(county), Eng., 13
Shubenacadie (riv.), N.S., 169
Shumen (Kolarovgrad), Bulg., 45
Shumerlya, U.S.S.R., 52
Shuri, Ryukyu Is., 81
Shushenskoye, U.S.S.R., 48
Shushtar, Iran, 66
Shuswap (lake), Br. Col., 184
Shuya, U.S.S.R., 52
Shwangcheng, China, 77
Shwangliao, China, 77
Shwangyashan, China, 77
Shwebo, Burma, 72
Shwegyin, Burma, 72
Siahan (range), Pak., 68
Siakwan, China, 77
Sialkot, Pak., 68
Siam (Thailand), 72
Siam (gulf), Asia, 72
Sian, China, 77
Siangfan, China, 77
Siang Kiang (riv.), China, 77
Siangtan, China, 77
Siargao (isl.), Phil. Is., 82
Siau (isl.), Indon., 85
Šiauliai, U.S.S.R., 53
Sibay, U.S.S.R., 52
Šibenik, Yugo., 45
Siberia (reg.), U.S.S.R., 48
Siberut (strait), Indon., 85
Sibi, Pak., 68
Sibiti, Rep. of Congo, 115
Sibiu, Rum., 45
Sibley, Iowa, 229
Sibley Prov. Park, Ont., 177
Sibolga, Indon., 85
Sibsagar, India, 68
Sibu, Malaysia, 85
Sibutu (passage), Phil. Is., 82
Sibuyan (isl.), Phil. Is., 82
Sibuyan (sea), Phil. Is., 82
Sicasica, Bol., 136
Sichang, China, 77
Sicily (reg.), Italy, 34
Sicily (isl.), Italy, 34
Sicily (str.), Italy, 34
Sicuani, Peru, 128
Sidamo (prov.), Eth., 111
Sídheros (cape), Greece, 45
Sidhpur, India, 68
Sidi Barrani, U.A.R., 111
Sidi-bel-Abbès, Alg., 106
Sidi Ifni, Morocco, 106
Sidi-Kacem, Mor., 106
Sidlaw (hills), Scot., 15
Sidley (mt.), Ant., 5
Sidney, Br. Col., 184
Sidney, Mont., 262
Sidney, Nebr., 264
Sidney, N.Y., 276
Sidney, Ohio, 284
Sidoardjo, Indon., 85
Sidra (gulf), Libya, 111
Siedlce, Poland, 47
Siegburg, W. Ger., 22
Siegen, W. Ger., 22
Siemianowice Śląskie, Poland, 47
Siempang, Cambodia, 72
Siem Reap, Cambodia, 72
Siena (prov.), Italy, 34
Siena, Italy, 34
Sienyang, China, 77
Sierra Leone, 106
Sierra Madre, Calif., 204
Sierra Nevada (mts.), Calif., 204
Sierra Vista, Ariz., 198
Sierre, Switz., 39
Sífnos (isl.), Greece, 45
Siggenthal, Switz., 39
Sighetul-Marmaţiei, Rum., 45
Sighişoara, Rum., 45
Siglufjördhur, Ice., 21
Signal Hill, Calif., 204
Signal Mtn., Tenn., 237
Siguanea (bay), Cuba, 158
Siguatepeque, Hond., 154
Siguiri, Guinea, 106
Siirt (prov.), Turkey, 63
Siirt, Turkey, 63
Sikar, India, 68
Sikasso, Mali, 106
Sikeston, Mo., 261
Sikhote-Alin' (range), U.S.S.R., 48
Si Kiang (riv.), China, 77
Sikkim (state), India, 68
Silao, Mex., 150
Silay, Phil. Is., 82
Silchar, India, 68
Siler City, N.C., 281
Silhouette (isl.), Seych., 118
Siliguri, India, 68
Silinhot, China, 77
Silistra, Bulg., 45
Silkeborg, Den., 21
Sillery, Que., 172
Siloam Sprs., Ark., 203
Silsbee, Tex., 302
Silvaplana, Switz., 39
Silva Porto, Angola, 115
Silver (bank), W. Indies, 156
Silver Bay, Minn., 254
Silver City, N. Mex., 274
Silver Creek, N.Y., 276
Silver Hill, Md., 245
Silver Lake, Mass., 249
Silver Lake, Ohio, 284
Silver Peak (range), Nev., 266
Silver Spring, Md., 245
Silverton, Ohio, 284
Silverton, Oreg., 291
Silvia, Col., 126
Silvis, Ill., 222
Silvretta (mts.), Europe, 39
Sim (cape), Mor., 106
Simanggang, Malaysia, 85
Simcoe, Ont., 177
Simcoe (lake), Ont., 177
Simeulue (isl.), Indon., 85
Simferopol', U.S.S.R., 52
Sími (isl.), Greece, 45
Simla, India, 68
Simo (riv.), Fin., 18
Simojovel, Mex., 150
Simonstown, S. Afr., 118
Simplon (tunnel), Europe, 39
Simpson (des.), Austral., 93, 95
Simpson, Pa., 294
Simsbury, Conn., 210
Sinai (mt.), Grenada, 161
Sinai (mt.), U.A.R., 111
Sinai (pen.), U.A.R., 111
Sinaloa (state), Mex., 150
Sincé, Col., 126
Sincelejo, Col., 126
Sinch'on, N. Korea, 81
Sinchu, China, 77
Sind (prov.), Pak., 68
Sindelfingen, W. Ger., 22
Sines (cape), Port., 33
Sinfra, Ivory Coast, 106
Singa, Sudan, 111
Singapore, 72
Singapore (strait), Asia, 72
Singapore (cap.), Sing., 72
Singaradja, Indon., 85
Singen, W. Ger., 22
Singida (prov.), Tanz., 115
Singida, Tanz., 115
Singkawang, Indon., 85
Singkep (isl.), Indon., 85
Singleton, N.S.W., 97
Singora (Songkhla), Thai., 72
Singsingsia, China, 77
Singtai, China, 77
Singu, Burma, 72
Sinhsien, China, 77
Sining, China, 77
Sinjar, Iraq, 66
Sinkao Shan (mt.), China, 77
Sinkat, Sudan, 111
Sinkiang-Uigur Aut. Reg., China, 77
Sinnamary, Fr. Gui., 131
Sinnûris, U.A.R., 111
Sinoia, Rhod., 118
Sinop (prov.), Turkey, 63
Sinop, Turkey, 63
Sinsiang, China, 77
Sint-Amandsberg, Belg., 27
Sint Anna (bay), Neth. Ant., 161
Sint Joris (bay), Neth. Ant., 161
Sint-Niklaas, Belg., 27
Sinton, Tex., 302
Sintra, Port., 33
Sint-Truiden, Belg., 27
Sinyang, China, 77
Sió (canal), Hung., 41
Sion, Switz., 39
Sion Mills, N. Ire., 17
Sioux City, Iowa, 229
Sioux Falls, S. Dak., 298
Sioux Lookout, Ont., 175
Siparia, Trin. & Tob., 161
Sipiwesk (lake), Man., 179
Siple (mt.), Ant., 5
Sipora (isl.), Indon., 85
Sip Song Chau Thai (mts.), N. Vietnam, 72
Siquijor (isl.), Phil. Is., 82
Siquirres, C. Rica, 154
Siracusa (Syracuse), Italy, 34
Siret (riv.), Rum., 45
Sir Francis Drake (chan.), Virgin Is. (Br.), 161
Sirhan, Wadi (dry riv.), Saudi Ar., 59
Sirik (cape), Malaysia, 85
Sir James McBrien (mt.), N.W.T., 187
Sirjan, Iran, 66
Sir John's (peak), Jam., 158
Sirohi, India, 68
Sironj, India, 68
Síros (isl.), Greece, 45
Sirsa, India, 68
Sirsi, India, 68
Sisak, Yugo., 45
Siskiyou (mts.), U.S., 204, 291
Sisophon, Cambodia, 72
Sisseton, S. Dak., 298
Sitapur, India, 68
Sithoniá (pen.), Greece, 45
Sitionuevo, Col., 126
Sitka, Alaska, 196
Sitka Nat'l Mon., Alaska, 196
Sittang (riv.), Burma, 72
Sittard, Neth., 27
Sittingbourne and Milton, Eng., 13
Sittwe, Burma, 72
Situbondo, Indon., 85
Siuna, Nic., 154
Siushui, China, 77
Sivas (prov.), Turkey, 63
Sivas, Turkey, 63
Siverek, Turkey, 63
Siwa, U.A.R., 111
Siwa (oasis), U.A.R., 111
Sixth Cataract (falls), Sudan, 111
Sjaelland (isl.), Den., 21
Skagen (point), Den., 21
Skagens Odde, Den., 21
Skagerrak (strait), Europe, 18
Skagit (riv.), Wash., 310
Skagway, Alaska, 196
Skanderborg, Den., 21
Skaneateles, N.Y., 276
Skara, Sweden, 18
Skaraborg (county), Sweden, 18
Skarżysko-Kamienna, Poland, 47
Skeena (riv.), Br. Col., 184
Skegness, Eng., 13
Skeldon, Guyana, 131
Skeleton Coast (reg.), S.W. Afr., 118
Skellefte (riv.), Sweden, 18
Skellefteå, Sweden, 18
Skelmersdale, Eng., 13
Skelton and Brotton, Eng., 13
Skerries, Ire., 17
Ski, Norway, 18
Skiatook, Okla., 288
Skibbereen, Ire., 17
Skien, Norway, 18
Skierniewice, Poland, 47
Skikda, Alg., 106
Skillman, N. J., 273
Skipton, Eng., 13
Skíros (isl.), Greece, 45
Skive, Den., 21
Skokie, Ill., 222
Skokomish (mt.), Wash., 310
Skopin, U.S.S.R., 52
Skopje, Yugo., 45
Skövde, Sweden, 18
Skowhegan, Maine, 242
Skunk (river), Iowa, 229
Skye (isl.), Scot., 15
Skykomish (riv.), Wash., 310
Slagelse, Den., 21
Slamet (mt.), Indon., 85
Slangkop (pt.), S. Afr., 118
Slantsy, U.S.S.R., 52
Slater, Mo., 261
Slatington, Pa., 294
Slaton, Tex., 302
Slave (riv.), Canada, 163
Slave Coast (reg.), Africa, 106
Slavgorod, U.S.S.R., 52
Slavuta, U.S.S.R., 52
Slavyansk, U.S.S.R., 52
Sleat (dist.), Scot., 15
Sleeping Bear Nat'l Lakeshore, Mich., 250
Sleepy Eye, Minn., 254
Slidell, La., 238
Sliedrecht, Neth., 27
Sliema, Malta, 34
Sligo (county), Ire., 17
Sligo, Ire., 17
Slippery Rock, Pa., 294
Sliven, Bulg., 45
Sloan, N.Y., 276
Sloatsburg, N.Y., 276
Slobodskoy, U.S.S.R., 52
Slocan, Br. Col., 184
Slough, Eng., 13
Slovak (rep.), Czech., 41
Slovakia (reg.), Czech., 41
Slovenia (rep.), Yugo., 45
Słupsk, Poland, 47
Slutsk, U.S.S.R., 52
Slyne (head), Ire., 17
Smackover, Ark., 203
Smederevo, Yugo., 45
Smela, U.S.S.R., 52
Smithers, Br. Col., 184
Smithfield, N.C., 281
Smithfield, Utah, 304
Smiths Falls, Ont., 177
Smithton, Tas., 99
Smithtown, N.Y., 276
Smithville, Tex., 302
Smoky (riv.), Alta., 182
Smoky Hill (riv.), Kans., 232
Smøla (isl.), Norway, 18
Smolensk, U.S.S.R., 52
Smyrna, Del., 245
Smyrna, Ga., 216
Smyrna, Tenn., 237
Smyrna (Izmir), Turkey, 63
Snaefell (mt.), I. of Man, 13
Snag, Yukon, 187
Snake (riv.), U.S., 188
Snare (riv.), N.W.T., 187
Snåsa (lake), Norway, 18
Sneek, Neth., 27
Sneeuwkop (mt.), S. Afr., 118
Snohomish, Wash., 310
Snoqualmie (riv.), Wash., 310
Snow (mt.), Vt., 268
Snowbird (lake), N.W.T., 187
Snowdon (mt.), Wales, 13
Snowdonia Nat'l Park, Wales, 13
Snowdrift, N.W.T., 187
Snow Hill, Md., 245
Snowy (mts.), Austral., 97
Snyder, Tex., 302
Soap (lake), Wash., 310
Soatá, Col., 126
Sobat (riv.), Sudan, 111
Sobral, Braz., 132
Soche (Yarkand), China, 77
Sochi, U.S.S.R., 52
Society (isls.), Fr. Poly., 87
Socorro, Col., 126
Socorro (isl.), Mex., 150
Socorro, N. Mex., 274
Socotra (isl.), P.D.R. Yemen, 54
Soda (plains), India, 68
Soda Sprs., Idaho, 220
Soddu, Eth., 111
Soddy-Daisy, Tenn., 237
Söderhamn, Sweden, 18
Söderköping, Sweden, 18
Södermanland (county), Sweden, 18
Södertälje, Sweden, 18
Sodiri, Sudan, 111
Soest, Neth., 27
Soest, W. Ger., 22
Sofia (cap.), Bulg., 45
Sofia (riv.), Malag. Rep., 118
Sogamoso, Col., 126
Sogne (fjord), Norway, 18
Sogn og Fjordane (county), Norway, 18
Sohâg, U.A.R., 111
Sohano, Terr. N.G., 87
Sohar, Oman, 59
Soissons, France, 28
Soka, Japan, 81
Söke, Turkey, 63
Sokna, Libya, 111
Sokodé, Togo, 106
Sokol, U.S.S.R., 52
Sokolo, Mali, 106
Sokolov, Czech., 41
Sokoto, Nigeria, 106
Solana Beach, Calif., 204
Solbad Hall, Austria, 41
Soledad, Calif., 204
Soledad, Col., 126
Soledad, Venez., 124
Soledad de Doblado, Mex., 150
Solent (chan.), Eng., 13
Solihull, Eng., 10
Solikamsk, U.S.S.R., 52
Sol'-Iletsk, U.S.S.R., 52
Solingen, W. Ger., 22
Solís, Urug., 145
Sollefteå, Sweden, 18
Sollentuna, Sweden, 18
Solna, Sweden, 18
Sologne (reg.), France, 28
Sololá, Guat., 154
Solomon (isls.), Pacific, 87
Solomon (sea), Pacific, 87
Solomon Islands Prot., 87
Solon, Ohio, 284
Solothurn (canton), Switz., 39
Solothurn, Switz., 39
Solovetskiye (isls.), U.S.S.R., 52
Solta (isl.), Yugo., 45
Soluk, Libya, 111
Solvay, N.Y., 276
Sölvesborg, Sweden, 18
Solway (firth), U.K., 15
Solwezi, Zambia, 115
Soma, Japan, 81
Somalia, 115
Sombor, Yugo., 45
Sombrerete, Mex., 150
Sombrero (chan.), India, 68
Sombrero (isl.), St. Chr.-N.-A., 156
Somerdale, N. J., 273
Somerset (isl.), Berm., 156
Somerset, Ky., 237
Somerset, Mass., 249
Somerset (isl.), N.W.T., 187
Somerset, Pa., 294
Somerset, Tas., 99
Somersetshire (county), Eng., 13
Somerset West, S. Afr., 118
Somers Point, N. J., 273
Somersworth, N.H., 268
Somerville, Mass., 249
Somerville, N. J., 273
Someş (riv.), Rum., 45
Somme (dept.), France, 28
Somme (riv.), France, 28
Somogy (county), Hung., 41
Somotillo, Nic., 154
Somoto, Nic., 154
Son (riv.), India, 68
Soná, Pan., 154
Sonaguera, Hond., 154
Sønderborg, Den., 21
Sondershausen, E. Ger., 22
Søndre Stromfjord, Greenl., 4
Sondrio (prov.), Italy, 34
Sondrio, Italy, 34
Song Ba (riv.), S. Vietnam, 72
Song Bo (Black) (riv.), N. Vietnam, 72
Song Ca (riv.), N. Vietnam, 72
Song Cai (riv.), S. Vietnam, 72
Song Cau, S. Vietnam, 72
Song Coi (Red)(riv.), N. Vietnam, 72
Songea, Tanz., 115
Sŏngrim, N. Korea, 81
Songkhla, Thai., 72
Son Ha, S. Vietnam, 72
Son La, N. Vietnam, 72
Sonneberg, E. Ger., 22
Sonoma, Calif., 204
Sonora, Calif., 204
Sonora (state), Mex., 150
Sonora (riv.), Mex., 150
Sonora, Tex., 302
Sonsón, Col., 126
Sonsonate, El Sal., 154
Sonsorol (isl.), Pac. Is., 87
Son Tay, N. Vietnam, 72
Soochow, China, 77
Sopetrán, Col., 126
Sopot, Poland, 47
Sopron, Hung., 41
Sorata, Bol., 136
Sorel, Que., 172
Soria (prov.), Spain, 33
Soria, Spain, 33
Soriano (dept.), Urug., 145
Sørkapp (cape), Norway, 18
Sorocaba, Braz., 135
Sorol (atoll), Pac. Is., 87
Sorong, Indon., 85
Soroti, Uganda, 115
Sørøy (isl.), Norway, 18
Sorrento, Italy, 34
Sorsogon (prov.), Phil. Is., 82
Sør-Trondelag (county), Norway, 18
Sŏsan, S. Korea, 81
Sosnowiec, Poland, 47
Sotteville, France, 28
Sotuta, Mex., 150
Souanké, Rep. of Congo, 115
Souderton, Pa., 294
Souf (oasis), Alg., 106
Soufrière, Dominica, 161
Soufrière, St. Lucia, 161
Soufrière (mt.), St. Vincent, 161
Souillac, Mauritius, 118
Souk-Ahras, Alg., 106
Souris, Man., 179
Souris (riv.), N. Amer., 283
Souris, P.E.I., 169
Sousse, Tun., 106
South (isl.), N.Z., 101
South Africa, 118
South Amboy, N. J., 273
South America, 120
Southampton (Hampshire) (county), Eng., 13
Southampton, Eng., 13
Southampton, N.Y., 276
Southampton (isl.), N.W.T., 187
South Andaman (isl.), India, 68
South Atlantic Ocean, 3
South Australia (state), Austral., 94
Southaven, Miss., 256
South Beloit, Ill., 222
South Bend, Ind., 227
South Beveland (isl.), Neth., 27
South Boston, Va., 307
South Bound Brook, N. J., 273
South Braintree, Mass., 249
Southbridge, Mass., 249
South Broadway, Wash., 310
South Brunswick, N.J., 273
South Carolina (state), U.S., 296
South Charleston, W. Va., 313
South Chicago Hts., Ill., 222
South China (sea), Asia, 54
South Cotabato (prov.), Phil. Is., 82
South Coventry, Conn., 210
South Dakota (state), U.S., 298
South Dartmouth, Mass., 249
South Downs (hills), Eng., 13
South East (cape), Tas., 99
South-Eastern (state), Nigeria, 106
South Easton, Mass., 249
South Elgin, Ill., 222
Southend-on-Sea, Eng., 13
Southern (dist.), Israel, 65
Southern Alps (range), N.Z., 101
Southern Cross, W. Austral., 92
Southern Indian (lake), Man., 179
Southern Leyte (prov.), Phil. Is., 82
Southern Pines, N.C., 281
South Euclid, Ohio, 284
Southfield, Mich., 250
South Flevoland Polder, Neth., 27
South Fort George, Br. Col., 184
South Fulton, Tenn., 237
South Gate, Calif., 204
Southgate, Mich., 250
South Georgia (isl.), Falk Is., 5
South Glastonbury, Conn., 210
South Glens Falls, N.Y., 276
South Gobi (prov.), Mong., 77
South Hadley, Mass., 249
South Haven, Mich., 250
South Hill, Va., 307
South Holland, Ill., 222
South Holland (prov.), Neth., 27
South Holston (lake), U.S., 237, 307
South Houston, Tex., 302
Southington, Conn., 210
South Jordan, Utah, 304
South Khangai (prov.), Mong., 77
South Korea, 81
South Kvaløy (isl.), Norway, 18
Southland (land dist.), N.Z., 101
South Lebanon, Ohio, 284
South Magnetic Polar Area, Ant., 5
South Melbourne, Vic., 97
South Miami, Fla., 212
South Milwaukee, Wis., 317
South Nahanni (riv.), N.W.T., 187
South Natuna (isls.), Indon., 85
South Negril (pt.), Jam., 158
South Norwalk, Conn., 210
South Nyack, N.Y., 276
South Ogden, Utah, 304
South Orange, N. J., 273
South Orkney (isls.), Ant., 5
South Oroville, Calif., 204
South Ossetian Aut. Obl., U.S.S.R., 52
South Pacific Ocean, 3
South Pasadena, Calif., 204
South Pittsburg, Tenn., 237
South Plainfield, N. J., 273
South Platte (riv.), U.S., 208, 264
South Polar (plat.), Ant., 5
South Pole, Ant., 5
South Porcupine, Ont., 175
Southport, Conn., 210
Southport, Eng., 10
South Portland, Maine, 242
South River, N. J., 273
South Ronaldsay (isl.), Scot., 15
South St. Paul, Minn., 254
South Salt Lake, Utah, 304
South Sandwich (isls.), Ant., 5
South San Francisco, Calif., 204
South Saskatchewan (riv.), Canada, 181, 182
South Shetland (isls.), Ant., 5
South Shields, Eng., 13
South Sioux City, Nebr., 264
South Suburban, India, 68
South Sudbury, Mass., 249
South Taranaki (bight), N.Z., 101
South Tucson, Ariz., 198
South Uist (isl.), Scot., 15
South Ural (mts.), U.S.S.R., 52
South Vietnam, 72
Southwark, Eng., 10
South West (cape), Tas., 99
South-West Africa, 118
South Weymouth, Mass., 249
South Williamsport, Pa., 294
Sovereign Base Area, Cyprus, 63
Sovetsk, U.S.S.R., 52
Sovetskaya Gavan', U.S.S.R., 48
Sowerby Bridge, Eng., 10
Soya (pt.), Japan, 81
Spain, 33
Spalding, Eng., 13
Spaldings, Jam., 158
Spandau, W. Ger., 22
Spangler, Pa., 294
Spanish Fork, Utah, 304
Spanish Fort, Ala., 194
Spanish Lake, Mo., 261
Spanish Sahara (prov.), Spain, 106
Spanish Town, Jam., 158
Sparks, Nev., 266
Sparrows Point, Md., 245
Sparta, Greece, 45
Sparta, Ill., 222
Sparta, Mich., 250
Sparta, N. J., 273
Sparta, Tenn., 237
Sparta, Wis., 317
Spartanburg, S.C., 296
Spartivento (cape), Italy, 34
Spassk-Dal'niy, U.S.S.R., 48
Spátha (cape), Greece, 45
Spavinaw (lake), Okla., 288
Spearfish, S. Dak., 298
Spearman, Tex., 302
Speedway, Ind., 227
Speightstown, Barb., 161
Spenard, Alaska, 196
Spencer, Ind., 227
Spencer, Iowa, 229
Spencer, Mass., 249
Spencer, N.C., 281
Spencer (gulf), S. Austral., 94
Spencer, W. Va., 313
Spennymoor, Eng., 13
Spenser (mts.), N.Z., 101
Sperrin (mts.), N. Ire., 17
Spessart (range), W. Ger., 22
Spey (riv.), Scot., 15
Speyer, W. Ger., 22
Spiez, Switz., 39
Spindale, N.C., 281
Spirit Lake, Iowa, 229
Spirit River, Alta., 182
Spišská Nová Ves, Czech., 41
Spithead (chan.), Eng., 13
Spitsbergen (Svalbard) (isls.), Norway, 18
Spittal, Austria, 41
Split, Yugo., 45
Split Lake, Man., 179
Splügen (pass), Europe, 39
Spokane, Wash., 310
Spoleto, Italy, 34
Spooner, Wis., 317
Spotswood, N. J., 273
Spree (riv.), Ger., 22
Spreewald (for.), E. Ger., 22
Spremberg, E. Ger., 22
Spring City, Pa., 294
Springdale, Ark., 203
Springdale, Newf., 166
Springdale, Ohio, 284
Springdale, Pa., 294
Springdale, S.C., 296
Springer, N. Mex., 274
Springfield, Fla., 212
Springfield (cap.), Ill., 222
Springfield, Mass., 249
Springfield, Mich., 250
Springfield, Minn., 254
Springfield, Mo., 261
Springfield, N. J., 273
Springfield, Ohio, 284
Springfield, Oreg., 291
Springfield, Pa., 294
Springfield, Tenn., 237
Springfield, Vt., 268
Springfield, Va., 307
Springhill, La., 238
Springhill, N.S., 169
Spring Lake, N. J., 273
Spring Lake, N.C., 281
Springlands, Guyana, 131
Springs, S. Afr., 118
Springvale, Vic., 97
Spring Valley, Ill., 222
Spring Valley, Minn., 254
Spring Valley, N.Y., 276
Spring Valley, Tex., 302
Springville, N.Y., 276
Springville, Utah, 304
Spruce Pine, N.C., 281
Spurn (head), Eng., 13
Squam (lake), N.H., 268
Squamish, Br. Col., 184
Squantum N.A.S., Mass., 249
Squillace (gulf), Italy, 34
Sragen, Indon., 85
Sremska Mitrovica, Yugo., 45
Srepok (riv.), Cambodia, 72
Srikakulam, India, 68
Srinagar, India, 68
Stade, W. Ger., 22
Stafford, Eng., 10
Stafford, Queensland, 95
Staffordshire (county), Eng., 13
Stafford Sprs., Conn., 210
Staines, Eng., 10
Staked (Llano Estacado) (plain), U.S., 274
Stalin, Alb., 45
Stalingrad (Volgograd), U.S.S.R., 52
Stalino (Donetsk), U.S.S.R., 52
Stalowa Wola, Poland, 47
Stalybridge, Eng., 10
Stamford, Conn., 210
Stamford, Eng., 13
Stamford, Tex., 302
Stampriet, S.W. Africa, 118
Stamps, Ark., 203
Standerton, S. Afr., 118
Stanford, Calif., 204
Stanke Dimitrov, Bulg., 45
Stanley (falls), Dem. Rep. of the Congo, 115
Stanley (cap.), Falk. Is., 120
Stanley, N. Dak., 283
Stanley Pool (lake), Africa, 115
Stann Creek, Br. Hond., 154
Stanovoy (range), U.S.S.R., 48
Stans, Switz., 39
Stanthorpe, Queensland, 95
Stanton, Calif., 204
Staples, Minn., 254
Starachowice, Poland, 47
Staraya Russa, U.S.S.R., 52
Stara Zagora, Bulg., 45
Starbuck (isl.), Pacific, 87
Stargard Szcz., Poland, 47
Starke, Fla., 212
Starkville, Miss., 256
Starnbergersee (lake), W. Ger., 22
Starogard Gd., Poland, 47
Staryy Oskol, U.S.S.R., 52
Stassfurt, E. Ger., 22
State College, Miss., 256
State College, Pa., 294
Staten (Estados) (isl.), Arg., 143
Staten (isl.), N.Y., 276
Statesboro, Ga., 216
Statesville, N.C., 281
Statue of Liberty Nat'l Mon., N.J., 273
Staunton, Ill., 222
Staunton, Va., 307
Stavanger, Norway, 18
Stavropol', U.S.S.R., 52
Stawell, Vic., 97
Steamboat Springs, Colo., 208
Steelton, Pa., 294
Steens (mt.), Oreg., 291
Steep Rock Lake, Ont., 175
Stefanie (lake), Eth., 111
Stefansson (isl.), N.W.T., 187
Steffisburg, Switz., 39
Steger, Ill., 222
Stegi, Swaziland, 118
Steigerwald (for.), W. Ger., 22
Steinach, Austria, 41
Steinbach, Man., 179
Steinkjer, Norway, 18
Stellarton, N.S., 169
Stellenbosch, S. Afr., 118
Stendal, E. Ger., 22
Stepanakert, U.S.S.R., 52
Stephenville, Newf., 166
Stephenville, Tex., 302
Stepney, Conn., 210
Stepnoy (Elista), U.S.S.R., 52
Sterling, Colo., 208
Sterling, Ill., 222
Sterling Hts., Mich., 250
Sterlitamak, U.S.S.R., 52
Stettin (bay), Europe, 22
Stettin (Szczecin), Poland, 47
Stettler, Alta., 182
Steubenville, Ohio, 284
Stevens Point, Wis., 317
Stevenston, Scot., 15
Stewart (isl.), Chile, 138
Stewart (isl.), N.Z., 101
Stewart (riv.), Yukon, 187
Stewart A.F.B., N.Y., 276
Stewarton, Scot., 15
Stewart River, Yukon, 187
Steyr, Austria, 41
Stickney, Ill., 222
Stikine (riv.), Br. Col., 184
Stillwater, Minn., 254
Stillwater, Okla., 288
Stinnett, Tex., 302
Štip, Yugo., 45
Stirling (county), Scot., 15
Stirling, Scot., 15
Stirling-Bridgewater, S. Austral., 94
Stockerau, Austria, 41
Stockholm (county), Sweden, 18
Stockholm (cap.), Sweden, 18
Stockport, Eng., 10
Stockton, Calif., 204
Stockton (plat.), Tex., 302
Stoke-on-Trent, Eng., 13
Stolberg, W. Ger., 22
Stone (mts.), N.C., 281
Stoneham, Mass., 249
Stonehaven, Scot., 15
Stone Park, Ill., 222
Stones R. Nat'l Battlef., Tenn., 237
Stoney Creek, Ont., 177
Stony Brook, N.Y., 276
Stony Point, N.Y., 276
Stony Tunguska (riv.), U.S.S.R., 48
Stora Lulevatten (lake), Sweden, 18
Store Bælt (chan.), Den., 21
Storm (bay), Tas., 99
Storm Lake, Iowa, 229
Stornoway, Scot., 15
Storrs, Conn., 210
Storuman (lake), Sweden, 18
Stouffville, Ont., 177
Stoughton, Mass., 249
Stoughton, Wis., 317
Stourbridge, Eng., 13
Stourport-on-Severn, Eng., 10
Stow, Ohio, 284
Stowe, Pa., 294
Stowe, Vt., 268
Strabane, N. Ire., 17
Stralsund, E. Ger., 22
Strand, S. Afr., 118
Strangford (inlet), N. Ire., 17
Strängnäs, Sweden, 18
Stranraer, Scot., 15
Strasbourg, France, 28
Strasburg, Va., 307
Stratford, Conn., 210
Stratford, N. J., 273
Stratford, N.Z., 101
Stratford, Ont., 177
Stratford-upon-Avon, Eng., 13
Strathalbyn, S. Austral., 94
Strathbogie (dist.), Scot., 15
Strathcona Prov. Park, Br. Col., 184
Strathfield, N.S.W., 97
Strathmore, Alta., 182
Strathmore, N. J., 273
Strathmore (dist.), Scot., 15
Strathroy, Ont., 177
Strathy (pt.), Scot., 15
Stratton (mt.), Vt., 268
Straubing, W. Ger., 22
Strawberry (riv.), Utah, 304
Streaky (bay), S. Austral., 94
Streamwood, Ill., 222
Streator, Ill., 222
Středočeský (reg.), Czech., 41
Středoslovenský (reg.), Czech., 41
Streetsboro, Ohio, 284
Streetsville, Ont., 177
Streymoy (isl.), Den., 21
Stretford, Eng., 13
Strimón (gulf), Greece, 45
Stromboli (isl.), Italy, 34
Stromness, Scot., 15
Strongsville, Ohio, 284
Stronsay (isl.), Scot., 15
Stroud, Eng., 13
Stroud, Okla., 288
Stroudsburg, Pa., 294
Struer, Den., 21
Struma (riv.), Bulg., 45
Strumica, Yugo., 45
Struthers, Ohio, 284
Stuart (lake), Br. Col., 184
Stuart, Fla., 212
Stuart (range), S. Austral., 94
Stung Sen (riv.), Cambodia, 72
Stung Treng, Cambodia, 72
Stupino, U.S.S.R., 52
Sturgeon (riv.), Mich., 250
Sturgeon Bay, Wis., 317
Sturgeon Falls, Ont., 177
Sturgis, Mich., 250
Sturgis, S. Dak., 298
Sturt (des.), Austral., 94, 95
Stuttgart, Ark., 203
Stuttgart, W. Ger., 22
Styria (prov.), Austria, 41
Suakin, Sudan, 111
Suapure (riv.), Venez., 124
Subiaco, W. Austral., 92
Subic (bay), Phil. Is., 82
Subotica, Yugo., 45
Succasunna, N. J., 273
Suceava, Rum., 45
Suchan, U.S.S.R., 48
Suchitoto, El Sal., 154
Süchow, China, 77

Sucre (cap.), Bol., 136
Sucre, Col., 126
Sucre (state), Venez., 124
Sud (dept.), Haiti, 158
Sudan, 111
Sudan (reg.), Africa, 106
Sudbury, Ont., 175, 177
Sudd (swamp), Sudan, 111
Suddie, Guyana, 131
Sudeten (mts.), Europe, 41
Sudhuroy (isl.), Den., 21
Sudirman (range), Indon., 85
Sueca, Spain, 33
Suez, U.A.R., 111
Suez (canal), U.A.R., 111
Suez (gulf), U.A.R., 111
Suffern, N.Y., 276
Suffolk, East (county), Eng., 13
Suffolk, West (county), Eng., 13
Suffolk, Va., 307
Sugar Creek, Mo., 261
Sugar Land, Tex., 302
Suhl (dist.), E. Ger., 22
Suhl, E. Ger., 22
Suhsien, China, 77
Suihsien, China, 77
Suihwa, China, 77
Suining, China, 77
Suipacha, Arg., 143
Suir (riv.), Ire., 17
Suita, Japan, 81
Suitland, Md., 245
Sukabumi, Indon., 85
Sukh-Batar (prov.), Mong., 77
Sukhe Bator, Mong., 77
Sukhumi, U.S.S.R., 52
Suki, Sudan, 111
Sukkertoppen, Greenl., 4
Sukkur, Pak., 68
Sukomo, Japan, 81
Sula (isls.), Indon., 85
Sulaiman (range), Pak., 68
Sulaimaniya (prov.), Iraq, 66
Sulaimaniya, Iraq, 66
Sulawesi (Celebes)(isl.), Indon., 85
Sulitjelma (mt.), Europe, 18
Sullana, Peru, 128
Sullivan (lake), Alta., 182
Sullivan, Ill., 222
Sullivan, Ind., 227
Sullivan, Mo., 261
Sullivans Island, S.C., 296
Sulphur, La., 238
Sulphur, Okla., 288
Sulphur Springs, Tex., 302
Sultanabad (Kashmar), Iran, 66
Sulu (prov.), Phil. Is., 82
Sulu (arch.), Phil. Is., 82
Sulu (sea), Phil. Is., 82
Sulzbach-Rosenberg, W. Ger., 22
Sumatra (isl.), Indon., 85
Sumba (isl.), Indon., 85
Sumba (str.), Indon., 85
Sumbawa (isl.), Indon., 85
Sumedang, Indon., 85
Sumenep, Indon., 85
Sumgait, U.S.S.R., 52
Summan (plat.), Saudi Ar., 59
Summer (lake), Oreg., 291
Summerland, Br. Col., 184
Summerside, P.E.I., 169
Summerville, Ga., 216
Summerville, S.C., 296
Summit, Ill., 222
Summit, N. J., 273
Summit Hill, Pa., 294
Sumner, Wash., 310
Sumoto, Japan, 81
Šumperk, Czech., 41
Sumter, S.C., 296
Sumy, U.S.S.R., 52
Sun (riv.), Mont., 262
Sunagawa, Japan, 81
Sunapee (lake), N.H., 268
Sunbury, Pa., 294
Sunbury, Vic., 97
Sunbury-on-Thames, Eng., 10
Sunch'ŏn, S. Korea, 81
Sun City, Ariz., 198
Sun City, Calif., 204
Suncook (lakes), N.H., 268
Sunda (str.), Indon., 85
Sundance, Wyo., 319
Sundarbans (swamp), Asia, 68
Sundargarh, India, 68
Sundbyberg, Sweden, 18
Sunderland, Eng., 13
Sundsvall, Sweden, 18
Sungari (riv.), China, 77
Sungei Petani, Malaysia, 72
Sunland, Calif., 204
Sunn (fjord), Norway, 18
Sunnyland, Fla., 212
Sunnymead, Calif., 204
Sunny Point Mil. Ocean Term., N.C., 281
Sunnyside, Utah, 304
Sunnyside, Wash., 310
Sunnyvale, Calif., 204
Sun Prairie, Wis., 317
Sunrise Manor, Nev., 266
Sunset, Utah, 304
Sunset Crater Nat'l Mon., Ariz., 198
Sunset Hills, Mo., 261
Sunshine, Vic., 97
Sun Valley, Idaho, 220
Sun Valley, Nev., 266
Sunyani, Ghana, 106
Suo (sea), Japan, 81
Suolahti, Fin., 18
Superior, Ariz., 198
Superior (lag.), Mex., 150
Superior, Mont., 262
Superior, Nebr., 264
Superior (lake), N. Amer., 188
Superior, Wis., 317
Superior, Wyo., 319
Superstition (mts.), Ariz., 198
Suphan Buri, Thai., 72
Sur (Tyre), Leb., 63
Sur, Oman, 59
Surabaja, Indon., 85
Surakarta, Indon., 85
Surat, India, 68
Surat Thani, Thai., 72
Surendranagar, India, 68
Suresnes, France, 28
Surfside, Fla., 212
Surgidero de Batabanó, Cuba, 158
Surigao del Norte (prov.), Phil. Is., 82
Surigao del Sur (prov.), Phil. Is., 82
Surin, Thai., 72
Surinam, 131
Suriname (dist.), Sur., 131
Suriname (riv.), Sur., 131
Surrey, Br. Col., 184
Surrey (county), Eng., 13
Surtsey (isl.), Iceland, 21
Surud Ad (mt.), Somalia, 115
Suruga (bay), Japan, 81
Susa (ruins), Iran, 66
Susaki, Japan, 81
Susanville, Calif., 204
Susquehanna, Pa., 294
Susquehanna (riv.), U.S., 245, 294
Sussex, East (county), Eng., 13
Sussex, West (county), Eng., 13
Sussex, N.B., 170
Susten (pass), Switz., 39
Sutherland, N.S.W., 97
Sutherland (county), Scot., 15
Sutlej (riv.), Asia, 68, 77
Sutsien, China, 77
Sutton, Eng., 10
Sutton (riv.), Ont., 177
Sutton Coldfield, Eng., 10
Sutton-in-Ashfield, Eng., 13
Suva (cap.), Fiji, 87
Suwa, Japan, 81
Suwałki, Poland, 47
Suwannaphum, Thai., 72
Suwannee (riv.), U.S., 212, 216
Suwarrow (Suvarov)(atoll), Cook Is., 87
Suwŏn, S. Korea, 81
Süyung, China, 77
Suzu, Japan, 81
Suzuka, Japan, 81
Svalbard (isls.), Norway, 18
Svay Rieng, Cambodia, 72
Svendborg, Den., 21
Sverdlovsk, U.S.S.R., 48
Sverdrup (isls.), N.W.T., 187
Svetozarevo, Yugo., 45
Svir' (riv.), U.S.S.R., 52
Svishtov, Bulg., 45
Svobodnyy, U.S.S.R., 48
Svolvaer, Norway, 18
Swabian Jura (mts.), W. Ger., 22
Swadlincote, Eng., 10
Swains (isl.), Amer. Samoa, 87
Swainsboro, Ga., 216
Swakop (riv.), S.W. Afr., 118
Swakopmund, S.W. Afr., 118
Swale (riv.), Eng., 13
Swampscott, Mass., 249
Swan (isls.), Cent. Amer., 154
Swan (lake), Man., 179
Swan (riv.), W. Austral., 92
Swan Hill, Vic., 97
Swan River, Man., 179
Swansea, Ill., 222
Swansea, Mass., 249
Swansea, Wales, 13
Swanton, Vt., 268
Swarthmore, Pa., 294
Swartswood (lake), N. J., 273
Swartz Creek, Mich., 250
Swatow, China, 77
Swaziland, 118
Sweden, 18
Swedesboro, N. J., 273
Sweeny, Tex., 302
Sweet Home, Oreg., 291
Sweetwater, Tenn., 237
Sweetwater, Tex., 302
Sweetwater (riv.), Wyo., 319
Świdnica, Poland, 47
Świetochłowice, Poland, 47
Swift Current, Sask., 181
Swilly (inlet), Ire., 17
Swindon, Eng., 13
Swinford, Ire., 17
Świnoujście, Poland, 47
Swissvale, Pa., 294
Switzerland, 39
Swords, Ire., 17
Sycamore, Ill., 222
Sydney (isl.), Gilb. and Ell. Is., 87
Sydney (cap.), N.S.W., 97
Sydney, N.S., 169
Sydney Mines, N.S., 169
Syktyvkar, U.S.S.R., 52
Sylacauga, Ala., 194
Sylhet, Pak., 68
Sylt (isl.), W. Ger., 22
Sylvania, Ga., 216
Sylvania, Ohio, 284
Sylvan Lake, Alta., 182
Sylvester, Ga., 216
Syosset, N.Y., 276
Syracuse (prov.), Italy, 34
Syracuse, Italy, 34
Syracuse, N.Y., 276
Syracuse, Utah, 304
Syr-Dar'ya (riv.), U.S.S.R., 48
Syria, 63
Syriam, Burma, 72
Syrian (des.), Asia, 59
Syrte, Libya, 111
Syzran', U.S.S.R., 52
Szabolcs-Szatmár (county), Hung., 41
Szczecin (prov.), Poland, 47
Szczecin, Poland, 47
Szczecinek, Poland, 47
Szechwan (prov.), China, 77
Szeged, Hung., 41
Székesfehérvár, Hung., 41
Szekszárd, Hung., 41
Szentes, Hung., 41
Szeping, China, 77
Szolnok (county), Hung., 41
Szolnok, Hung., 41
Szombathely, Hung., 41

T

Taal (lake), Phil. Is., 82
Taastrup, Den., 21
Tabas (Tabas-Masina), Iran, 66
Tabasará (mts.), Pan., 154
Tabasco (state), Mex., 150
Tabelbala, Alg., 106
Taber, Alta., 182
Tabernacle, St. Chr.-N.-A., 161
Tabernes de Valldigna, Spain, 33
Tabiang, Gilb. and Ell. Is., 87
Tabiteuea (atoll), Gilb. and Ell. Is., 87
Tablas (isl.), Phil. Is., 82
Table (bay), S. Afr., 118
Table (mt.), S. Afr., 118
Taboga (isl.), Pan., 154
Tábor, Czech., 41
Tabor (mt.), Israel, 65
Tabora (prov.), Tanz., 115
Tabora, Tanz., 115
Tabou, Ivory Coast, 106
Tabriz, Iran, 66
Tabuk, Phil. Is., 82
Tabun Bogdo (mt.), Mong., 77
Taburkum, P.D.R. Yemen, 59
Täby, Sweden, 18
Tacámbaro, Mex., 150
Tacaná (vol.), Guat., 154
Tacarigua, Trin. & Tob., 161
Tachen (isls.), China, 77
Tachikawa, Japan, 81
Táchira (state), Venez., 124
Tacloban, Phil. Is., 82
Tacna (dept.), Peru, 128
Tacna, Peru, 128
Tacoma, Wash., 310
Taconic (mts.), U.S., 249
Tacuarembó (dept.), Urug., 145
Tacuarembó, Urug., 145
Tacuarí (riv.), Urug., 145
Tacurupucú (Hernandarias), Par., 144
Tademait (plat.), Alg., 106
Tadjoura, Afars and Issas, 111
Tadmor, Syria, 63
Tadoussac, Que., 172
Tadzhik S.S.R., U.S.S.R., 48
Taebaek (mt.), S. Korea, 81
Taedong (riv.), N. Korea, 81
Taegu, S. Korea, 81
Taejŏn, S. Korea, 81
Tafassaset, Wadi (dry riv.), Africa, 106
Tafí Viejo, Arg., 143
Taft, Calif., 204
Taft, Iran, 66
Taft, Tex., 302
Taftville, Conn., 210
Taganrog, U.S.S.R., 52
Tagant (reg.), Mauritania, 106
Tagaytay, Phil. Is., 82
Tagliamento (riv.), Italy, 34
Tagula (isl.), Papua, 85
Tagum, Phil. Is., 82
Tagus (riv.), Europe, 33
Tahaa (isl.), Fr. Poly., 87
Tahan, Gunong (mt.), Malaysia, 72
Tahat (mt.), Alg., 106
Tahiti (isl.), Fr. Poly., 87
Tahlequah, Okla., 288
Tahoe (lake), U.S., 188
Tahoka, Tex., 302
Tahoua, Niger, 106
Tahquamenon (riv.), Mich., 250
Tahsien, China, 77
Tahsüeh Shan (range), China, 77
Tahta, U.A.R., 111
Tahuamanu (riv.), S. Amer., 128, 136
Tahulandang (isl.), Indon., 85
Tai (lake), China, 77
Taian, China, 77
Taichao, China, 77
Taichung, China, 77
Taieri (riv.), N.Z., 101
Taif, Saudi Ar., 59
Tailem Bend, S. Austral., 94
Tailfingen, W. Ger., 22
Taima, Saudi Ar., 59
Tainan, China, 77
Taínaron (cape), Greece, 45
Taipei (cap.), China, 77
Taiping, Malaysia, 72
Taitao (pen.), Chile, 138
Taitung, China, 77
Taiwan (str.), Asia, 77
Taiwan (prov.), China, 77
Taiwan (isl.), China, 77
Taiwara, Afghan., 68
Taïyetos (mt.), Greece, 45
Taiyüan, China, 77
Ta'izz (cap.), Yemen Arab Rep., 59
Tajimi, Japan, 81
Tajo (Tagus)(riv.), Spain, 33
Tajumulco (vol.), Guat., 154
Tak, Thai., 72
Takada, Japan, 81
Takamatsu, Japan, 81
Takaoka, Japan, 81
Takapau, N.Z., 101
Takarazuka, Japan, 81
Takaroa (atoll), Fr. Poly., 87
Takasaki, Japan, 81
Takatsuki, Japan, 81
Takawa, Japan, 81
Takefu, Japan, 81
Takeo, Cambodia, 72
Takeshima (isls.), 81
Takistan, Iran, 66
Takla (lake), Br. Col., 184
Taklakhar, China, 77
Taklamakan (des.), China, 77
Takoma Park, Md., 245
Takoradi, Ghana, 106
Taku (glacier), Alaska, 196
Tala, Mex., 150
Talab (riv.), Asia, 68
Talagante, Chile, 138
Talai, China, 77
Talamanca (range), Costa Rica, 154
Talara, Peru, 128
Talaud (isls.), Indon., 85
Talavera de la Reina, Spain, 33
Talbot (isl.), Fla., 212
Talbot (cape), W. Austral., 92
Talca (prov.), Chile, 138
Talca, Chile, 138
Talcahuano, Chile, 138
Taldy-Kurgan, U.S.S.R., 48
Tali, China, 77
Taliabu (isl.), Indon., 85
Tal Kaif, Iraq, 66
Talladega, Ala., 194
Tallahassee (cap.), Fla., 212
Tallangatta, Vic., 97
Tallapoosa, Ga., 216
Tallassee, Ala., 194
Tallinn, U.S.S.R., 53
Tallmadge, Ohio, 284
Tallulah, La., 238
Talodi, Sudan, 111
Talpa, Mex., 150
Taltal, Chile, 138
Taltson (riv.), N.W.T., 187
Tama, Iowa, 229
Tamale, Ghana, 106
Tamanrasset, Alg., 106
Tamao, Dom. Rep., 158
Tamaqua, Pa., 294
Tamar (riv.), Eng., 13
Tamar (riv.), Tas., 99
Tamatave (prov.), Malag. Rep., 118
Tamatave, Malag. Rep., 118
Tamaulipas (state), Mex., 150
Tamazulapan, Mex., 150
Tamazunchale, Mex., 150
Tambacounda, Sen., 106
Tambelan (isls.), Indon., 85
Tambores, Urug., 145
Tambov, U.S.S.R., 52
Tamchakett, Mauritania, 106
Tame (riv.), Eng., 10
Tâmega (riv.), Port., 33
Tamiahua, Mex., 150
Tamiami (canal), Fla., 212
Tamil Nadu (state), India, 68
Tamise (Temse), Belg., 27
Tam Ky, S. Vietnam, 72
Tammisaari (Ekenäs), Fin., 18
Tampa, Fla., 212
Tampa (bay), Fla., 212
Tampere, Fin., 18
Tampico, Mex., 150
Tam Quan, S. Vietnam, 72
Tamtsak, Mong., 77
Tamworth, Eng., 10
Tamworth, N.S.W., 97
Tamyang, S. Korea, 81
Tana (lake), Eth., 111
Tana (riv.), Europe, 18
Tana (riv.), Kenya, 115
Tanabe, Japan, 81
Tanahmerah, Indon., 85
Tanami (des.), N. Terr., 93
Tan An, S. Vietnam, 72
Tanana, Alaska, 196
Tanana (riv.), Alaska, 196
Tananarive (prov.), Malag. Rep., 118
Tananarive (cap.), Malag. Rep., 118
Tanaro (riv.), Italy, 34
Tanda, India, 68
Tandil, Arg., 143
Tandjungbalai, Indon., 85
Tandjungkarang-Telukbetung, Indon., 85
Tandjungpandan, Indon., 85
Tandjungpriok, Indon., 85
Tandjungpura, Indon., 85
Tandragee, N. Ire., 17
Tanega (isl.), Japan, 81
Tanezrouft (des.), Afr., 106
Tang, Kas (isl.), Cambodia, 72
Tanga (prov.), Tanz., 115
Tanga, Tanz., 115
Tangainony, Malag. Rep., 118
Tangalla, Ceylon, 68
Tanganyika (lake), Africa, 115
Tangermünde, E. Ger., 22
Tangier (Tanger), Mor., 106
Tangier (sound), U.S., 245, 307
Tangshan, China, 77
Tanhsien, China, 77
Tanimbar (isls.), Indon., 85
Tanjay, Phil. Is., 82
Tanna (isl.), New Hebr., 87
Tannu-Ola (range), Asia, 77
Tanout, Niger, 106
Tanta, U.A.R., 111
Tantan, Mor., 106
Tantung, China, 77
Tanunda, S. Austral., 94
Tanzania, 115
Taoan, China, 77
Taongi (atoll), Pac. Is., 87
Taormina, Italy, 34
Taos, N. Mex., 274
Taoudenni, Mali, 106
Taourirt, Mor., 106
Tapachula, Mex., 150
Tapajós (riv.), Braz., 132
Tapanahoni (riv.), Sur., 131
Tapanshang, China, 77
Tapa Shan (range), China, 77
Tapi, Mae Nam (riv.), Thai., 72
Tapiola, Fin., 18
Tapti (riv.), India, 68
Tapul Group (isls.), Phil. Is., 82
Taquarí (riv.), Braz., 132
Taquaritinga, Braz., 135
Tar (riv.), N.C., 281
Tara (hill), Ire., 17
Tara, U.S.S.R., 48
Tarabuco, Bol., 136
Tarabulus, Leb., 63
Tarakan, Indon., 85
Tarama, Ryukyu Is., 81
Taranaki (prov. dist.), N.Z., 101
Taranto (prov.), Italy, 34
Taranto, Italy, 34
Taranto (gulf), Italy, 34
Tarapacá (prov.), Chile, 138
Tarapoto, Peru, 128
Tarare, France, 28
Tarascon, France, 28
Tarata, Bol., 136
Tarawa (atoll), Gilb. & Ell. Is., 87
Tarazona, Spain, 33
Tarbagatay (range), China, 77
Tarbert, Scot., 15
Tarbes, France, 28
Tarboro, N.C., 281
Taree, N.S.W., 97
Tarentum, Pa., 294
Tarfaya, Mor., 106
Tarhuna, Libya, 111
Tarifa, Spain, 33
Tarija (dept.), Bol., 136
Tarija, Bol., 136
Tarim (riv.), China, 77
Tarim, P.D.R. Yemen, 59
Tarkio, Mo., 261
Tarkwa, Ghana, 106
Tarlac (prov.), Phil. Is., 82
Tarma, Peru, 128
Tarn (dept.), France, 28
Tarn (riv.), France, 28
Tarnak (riv.), Afghan., 68
Tarn-et-Garonne (dept.), France, 28
Tarnobrzeg, Poland, 47
Tarnów, Poland, 47
Tarnowskie Góry, Poland, 47
Tarok Tso (lake), China, 77
Taroudant, Mor., 106
Tarpon Springs, Fla., 212
Tarragona (prov.), Spain, 33
Tarragona, Spain, 33
Tarrant, Ala., 194
Tarrasa, Spain, 33
Tarrytown, N.Y., 276
Tarsus, Turkey, 63
Tartagal, Arg., 143
Tartu, U.S.S.R., 53
Tartus, Syria, 63
Tarzana, Calif., 204
Taschereau, Que., 174
Tashauz, U.S.S.R., 48
Tashigong, China, 77
Tashk (lake), Iran, 66
Tashkent, U.S.S.R., 48
Tashkurghan, Afghan., 68
Tasfi Qurghan, China, 77
Tasikmalaja, Indon., 85
Tasman (bay), N.Z., 101
Tasman (sea), Pacific, 87
Tasman (pen.), Tas., 99
Tasmania (state), Austral., 99
Tassili n'Ahaggar (plat.), Alg., 106
Tassili n'Ajjer (plat.), Alg., 106
Tata, Hung., 41
Tatabánya, Hung., 41
Tatahouine, Tun., 106
Tatar (strait), U.S.S.R., 48
Tatar A.S.S.R., U.S.S.R., 52
Tatarsk, U.S.S.R., 48
Tateyama, Japan, 81
Tathlina (lake), N.W.T., 187
Tati (riv.); Botswana, 118
Tatnam (cape), Man., 179
Tatra, High (mts.), Europe, 41
Tatta, Pak., 68
Tatuí, Braz., 135
Tatung, China, 77
Tatura, Vic., 97
Taubaté, Braz., 135
Tauber (riv.), W. Ger., 22
Taumarunui, N.Z., 101
Taum Sauk (mt.), Mo., 261
Taungdwingyi, Burma, 72
Taungup, Burma, 72
Taunton, Eng., 13
Taunton, Mass., 249
Taunus (range), W. Ger., 22
Taupo, N.Z., 101
Tauragė, U.S.S.R., 53
Tauranga, N.Z., 101
Tauroa (pt.), N.Z., 101
Taurus (range), Turkey, 63
Tavares, Fla., 212
Taveuni (isl.), Fiji, 87
Tavira, Port., 33
Tavoy, Burma, 72
Tavşanlı, Turkey, 63
Tawa, N.Z., 101
Tawas (pt.), Mich., 250
Tawau, Malaysia, 85
Tawitawi (isl.), Phil. Is., 82
Taxco de Alarcón, Mex., 150
Taxila (ruins), Pak., 68
Tay (firth), Scot., 15
Tay (riv.), Scot., 15
Tayga, U.S.S.R., 48
Tayibe, Israel, 65
Taylor, Mich., 250
Taylor, Pa., 294
Taylor, Tex., 302
Taylorsville, Utah, 304
Taylorville, Ill., 222
Taymyr (pen.), U.S.S.R., 48
Taymyr Nat'l Okrug, U.S.S.R., 48
Tay Ninh, S. Vietnam, 72
Tayport, Scot., 15
Tayshet, U.S.S.R., 48
Tayü, China, 77
Taz (riv.), U.S.S.R., 48
Taza, Mor., 106
Tazawa (lake), Japan, 81
Taza Khurmatu, Iraq, 66
Tazerbo (oasis), Libya, 111
Tazewell, Va., 307
Tazin (lake), Sask., 181
Tbilisi, U.S.S.R., 52
Tchepone, Laos, 72
Tchibanga, Gabon, 115
Tchien, Liberia, 106
Tczew, Poland, 47
Teague, Tex., 302
Te Anau (lake), N.Z., 101
Teaneck, N. J., 273
Teapa, Mex., 150
Teapot Dome(mt.), Wyo., 318
Te Aroha, N.Z., 101
Te Atatu, N.Z., 101
Tébessa, Alg., 106
Tebuk, Saudi Ar., 59
Tebingtinggi, Indon., 85
Tecamachalco, Mex., 150
Tecomán, Mex., 150
Tecpan de Galeana, Mex., 150
Tecualá, Mex., 150
Tecuci, Rum., 45
Tecumseh, Mich., 250
Tecumseh, Okla., 288
Tecumseh, Ont., 177
Tedzhen, U.S.S.R., 48
Tees (riv.), Eng., 13
Tefé (riv.), Braz., 132
Tegal, Indon., 85
Tegernsee (lake), W. Ger., 22
Tegucigalpa (cap.), Hond., 154
Tehachapi, Calif., 204
Tehchow, China, 77
Tehko, China, 77
Tehran (prov.), Iran, 66
Tehran (cap.), Iran, 66
Tehuacán, Mex., 150
Tehuantepec, Mex., 150
Tehuantepec (gulf), Mex., 150
Tehuantepec (isth.), Mex., 150
Tehuipango, Mex., 150
Teide (peak), Spain, 33
Teifi (riv.), Wales, 13
Teignmouth, Eng., 13
Tejo (Tagus)(riv.), Port., 33
Tekapo (lake), N.Z., 101
Te Kauwhata, N.Z., 101
Tekax, Mex., 150
Tekirdağ (prov.), Turkey, 63
Tekirdağ, Turkey, 63
Tekong Besar, Pulau (isl.), Sing., 72
Te Kuiti, N.Z., 101
Tel (riv.), India, 68
Tela, Hond., 154
Telanaipura, Indon., 85
Telavi, U.S.S.R., 52
Tel Aviv (dist.), Israel, 65
Tel Aviv-Jaffa, Israel, 65
Telde, Spain, 33
Telefomin, Terr. N.G., 85
Telemark (county), Norway, 18
Teles Pires (riv.), Braz., 132
Telford, Pa., 294
Tel Kotchek, Syria, 63
Tell City, Ind., 227
Tellicherry, India, 68
Telli Nor (lake), China, 77
Telluride, Colo., 208
Telok Anson, Malaysia, 72
Teloloapan, Mex., 150
Telpaneca, Nic., 154
Tel'pos-Iz (mt.), U.S.S.R., 52
Telšiai, U.S.S.R., 53
Teltow, E. Ger., 22
Tema, Ghana, 106
Temacine, Alg., 106
Temassinin (Fort-Flatters), Alg., 106
Tematangi (isl.), Fr. Poly., 87
Temax, Mex., 150
Temir, U.S.S.R., 48
Temir-Tau, U.S.S.R., 48
Témiscaming, Que., 174
Temora, N.S.W., 97
Tempe, Ariz., 198
Tempelhof, W. Ger., 22
Tempio Pausania, Italy, 34
Temple, Tex., 302
Temple City, Calif., 204
Templemore, Ire., 17
Templestowe and Doncaster, Vic., 97
Temple Terrace, Fla., 212
Templeton, Que., 172
Templin, E. Ger., 22
Temryuk, U.S.S.R., 52
Temse, Belg., 27
Temuco, Chile, 138
Tena, Ecua., 128
Tenafly, N. J., 273
Tenali, India, 68
Tenancingo, Mex., 150
Tenango de Río Blanco, Mex., 150
Tenasserim (div.), Burma, 72
Tenasserim, Burma, 72
Tenby, Wales, 13
Ten Degree (chan.), India, 68
Tendelti, Sudan, 111
Ténéré (des.), Niger, 106
Tenerife (isl.), Spain, 33
Ténès, Alg., 106
Tengchung, China, 77
Tenggol, Pulau (isl.), Malaysia, 72
Tengiz (lake), U.S.S.R., 48
Tengkow, China, 77
Tenkiller Ferry (res.), Okla., 288
Tenkodogo, Upp. Volta, 106
Tennant Creek, N. Terr., 93
Tennessee (state), U.S., 237
Tennessee (riv.), U.S., 188
Tenosique, Mex., 150
Tenterfield, N.S.W., 97
Ten Thousand (isls.), Fla., 212
Ten Thousand Smokes (valley), Alaska, 196
Teocaltiche, Mex., 150
Teocelo, Mex., 150
Teófilo-Otoni, Braz., 132
Teotihuacán (ruins), Mex., 150
Tepao, China, 77
Tepatitlán, Mex., 150
Tepatlaxco de Hidalgo, Mex., 150
Tepeaca, Mex., 150
Tepeapulco, Mex., 150
Tepeji, Mex., 150
Tepelenë, Alb., 45
Tepic, Mex., 150
Teplice, Czech., 41
Tequendama (falls), Col., 126
Ter (riv.), Spain, 33
Téra, Niger, 106
Teralba, N.S.W., 97
Teramo (prov.), Italy, 34
Teramo, Italy, 34
Terang, Vic., 97
Terceira (isl.), Port., 32
Terengganu (state), Malaysia, 72
Teresina, Braz., 132
Teresópolis, Braz., 135
Terhazza (ruins), Mali, 106
Termez, U.S.S.R., 48
Termini Imerese, Italy, 34
Términos (lag.), Mex., 150
Ternate, Indon., 85
Terneuzen, Neth., 27
Terni (prov.), Italy, 34
Terni, Italy, 34
Ternitz, Austria, 41
Ternopol', U.S.S.R., 52
Terrace, Br. Col., 184
Terrace Bay, Ont., 175
Terracina, Italy, 34
Terra Nova Nat'l Park, Newf., 166
Terrebonne (bay), La., 238
Terrebonne, Que., 172
Terre-de-Bas (isl.), Guad., 161
Terre-de-Haut (isl.), Guad., 161
Terre Haute, Ind., 227
Terrell, Tex., 302
Terrell Hills, Tex., 302
Terrigal-Avoca, N.S.W., 97
Terry, Mont., 262
Terryville, Conn., 210
Terschelling (isl.), Neth., 27
Teruel (prov.), Spain, 33
Teruel, Spain, 33
Teshio (riv.), Japan, 81
Tesin (riv.), Mong., 77
Teslin (lake), Canada, 163
Teslin, Yukon, 187
Teslin (riv.), Yukon, 187
Tessaoua, Niger, 106
Tessenei, Eth., 111
Testa del Gargano (cape), Italy, 34
Tete (dist.), Mozamb., 118
Tete, Mozamb., 118
Teterow, E. Ger., 22
Tetiaroa (atoll), Fr. Poly., 87
Teton (range), Wyo., 319
Tétouan (Tetuán), Mor., 106
Tetovo, Yugo., 45
Tetyukhe, U.S.S.R., 48
Teutoburger Wald (for.), W. Ger., 22
Teviot (riv.), Scot., 15
Tewantin, Queensland, 95
Texada (isl.), Br. Col., 184
Texarkana, Ark.-Tex., 203, 302
Texas (state), U.S., 302
Texas City, Tex., 302
Texcoco, Mex., 150
Texel (isl.), Neth., 27
Texistepeque, El Sal., 154
Texoma (lake), U.S., 288, 302
Teykovo, U.S.S.R., 52
Teziutlán, Mex., 150
Tezpur, India, 68
Tha, Nam (riv.), Laos, 72
Thabazimbi, S. Afr., 118
Tha Chin, Mae Nam (riv.), Thai., 72
Thai Binh, N. Vietnam, 72
Thailand, 72
Thai Nguyen, N. Vietnam, 72
Thakhek, Laos, 72
Thale, E. Ger., 22
Thale Luang (lag.), Thai., 72
Thalwil, Switz., 39
Thames (riv.), Conn., 210
Thames (riv.), Eng., 13
Thames (riv.), Ont., 177
Thana, India, 68
Thanh Hoa, N. Vietnam, 72
Thanjavur, India, 68
Tharrawaddy, Burma, 72
Thásos (isl.), Greece, 45
Thatch (key), Virgin Is. (U.S.), 161
Thatcher, Ariz., 198
Thaton, Burma, 72
Thaya (riv.), Austria, 41
Thayetmyo, Burma, 72
Thazi, Burma, 72
Thebarton, S. Austral., 94
Thebes (Thívai), Greece, 45
The Dalles, Oreg., 291
The Entrance-Long Jetty, N.S.W., 97
The Hermitage, N.Z., 101
Thelon (riv.), N.W.T., 187
Theodore Roosevelt (lake), Ariz., 198
Theodore Roosevelt Nat'l Mem. Park, N. Dak., 283
The Pas, Man., 179
Thermaic (gulf), Greece, 45
Thermopolis, Wyo., 319
Thessalia (reg.), Greece, 45
Thessalon, Ont., 177
Thessaloníki, Greece, 45
Thetford Mines, Que., 172
The Village, Okla., 288
Thibodeaux, La., 238
Thief River Falls, Minn., 254
Thiensville, Wis., 317
Thiers, France, 28
Thiès, Sen., 106
Thika, Kenya, 115
Thimphu (cap.), Bhutan, India, 68
Thio, Eth., 111
Thionville, France, 28
Thíra (isl.), Greece, 45
Third Cataract (rapids), Sudan, 111
Thisted, Den., 21
Thívai, Greece, 45
Thjórsá (riv.), Iceland, 21
Thlewiaza (riv.), N.W.T., 187
Thoen, Thai., 72
Thok Jalung, China, 77
Thomaston, Conn., 210
Thomaston, Ga., 216
Thomaston, N.Y., 276
Thomastown, Ire., 17
Thomasville, Ala., 194
Thomasville, Ga., 216
Thomasville, N.C., 218
Thompson Falls, Mont., 262
Thompsonville (Enfield P.O.), Conn., 210
Thomson, Ga., 216
Thomson's Falls, Kenya, 115
Thonburi, Thai., 72
Thongwa, Burma, 72
Thonon-les-Bains, France, 28
Thonze, Burma, 72
Thornton, Colo., 208
Thornton, Ill., 222
Thornton Cleveleys, Eng., 10
Thorold, Ont., 177
Thouars, France, 28
Thouin (pt.), W. Austral., 92
Thousand (isls.), N. Amer., 177, 276
Thousand Oaks, Calif., 204
Thrace (reg.), Greece, 45
Three Forks, Mont., 262
Three Hills, Alta., 182
Three Pagodas (pass), Asia, 72
Three Points (cape), Ghana, 106
Three Rivers, Mass., 249
Three Rivers, Mich., 250
Throop, Pa., 294
Thule, Greenl., 4
Thun, Switz., 39
Thun (lake), Switz., 39
Thunder (bay), Ont., 175
Thunder Bay, Ont., 175
Thurgau (canton), Switz., 39
Thüringer Wald (for.), E. Ger., 22
Thuringia (reg.), E. Ger., 22
Thurles, Ire., 17
Thurrock, Eng., 10
Thursday Island, Queensland, 95
Thurso, Que., 172
Thurso, Scot., 15
Thurston (isl.), Ant., 5
Thysville, Dem. Rep. of the Congo, 115
Tiahuanacu, Bol., 136
Tiaret, Alg., 106
Tibagi (riv.), Braz., 135
Tibati, Cameroon, 115
Tiber (riv.), Italy, 34
Tiberias, Israel, 65
Tiberias (Galilee)(lake), Israel, 65
Tibesti (mts.), Africa, 111
Tibet Aut. Reg., China, 77
Tiburon, Calif., 204
Tiburon, Haiti, 158
Tiburón (isl.), Mex., 150
Tiburón (cape), Pan., 154
Ticao (isl.), Phil. Is., 82
Tice, Fla., 212
Tichitt, Mauritania, 106
Ticino (canton), Switz., 39
Ticino (riv.), Switz., 39
Ticonderoga, N.Y., 276
Ticul, Mex., 150
Tidaholm, Sweden, 18
Tidikelt (oasis), Alg., 106
Tidjikja, Mauritania, 106
Tidore (isl.), Indon., 85
Tiehling, China, 77
Tiel, Neth., 27
Tielt, Belg., 27
Tien Chih (lake), China, 77
Tienen, Belg., 27
Tien Shan (mts.), Asia, 77
Tienshui, China, 77
Tientsin, China, 77
Tierra Blanca, Mex., 150
Tierra del Fuego (isl.), S. Amer., 138, 143
Tierra del Fuego, Antártida e Islas del Atlántico Sur (terr.), Arg., 143
Tiete (riv.), Braz., 132
Tiffin, Ohio, 284
Tiflis (Tbilisi), U.S.S.R., 52
Tifton, Ga., 216
Tiftona, Tenn., 237
Tighina (Bendery), U.S.S.R., 52
Tignish, P.E.I., 169
Tigre, Arg., 143
Tigre (prov.), Eth., 111
Tigre (isl.), N. Vietnam, 72
Tigre (riv.), S. Amer., 128
Tigre (isl.), Urug., 145
Tigris (riv.), Asia, 66
Tihama (reg.), Asia, 59
Tihuatlan, Mex., 150
Tijuana, Mex., 150
Tikhoretsk, U.S.S.R., 52
Tiko, Cameroon, 115
Tikopia (isl.), Br. Sol. Is., 87
Tikrit, Iraq, 66
Tilburg, Neth., 27
Tilemsi (valley), Mali, 106
Tillabéry, Niger, 106
Tillamook, Oreg., 291
Tillicoultry, Scot., 15
Tillsonburg, Ont., 177
Tílos (isl.), Greece, 45
Tilton, Ill., 222
Timagami (lake), Ont., 175
Timane (riv.), Par., 144
Timan Ridge (mts.), U.S.S.R., 52
Timaru, N.Z., 101
Timashevsk, U.S.S.R., 52
Timbalier (bay), La., 238
Timbédra, Mauritania, 106
Timbuktu, Mali, 106
Timimoun, Alg., 106
Timiris (cape), Mauritania, 106
Timiș (riv.), Rum., 45
Timiskaming (lake), Canada, 177
Timișoara, Rum., 45
Timgad (ruins), Alg., 106
Timmins, Ont., 175
Timok (riv.), Europe, 45
Timonium, Md., 245
Timor (isl.), Asia, 85
Timor (sea), Asia, 85
Timpanogos Cave Nat'l Mon., Utah, 304
Timrå, Sweden, 18
Tina (mt.), Dom. Rep., 158
Tinaca (pt.), Phil. Is., 82
Tinaquillo, Venez., 124
Tindouf, Alg., 106
Tinggi, Pulau (isl.), Malaysia, 72
Tingha, N.S.W., 97
Tinghai, China, 77
Tingri Dzong, China, 77
Tinian (isl.), Pac. Is., 87
Tinker A.F.B., Okla., 288
Tinley Park, Ill., 222
Tínos (isl.), Greece, 45
Tinsukia, India, 68
Tinto (riv.), Spain, 33
Tioga (riv.), Pa., 294
Tipitapa, Nic., 154
Tipp City, Ohio, 284
Tippecanoe (riv.), Ind., 227
Tipperary (county), Ire., 17
Tipperary, Ire., 17
Tipton, Ind., 227
Tipton, Iowa, 229
Tiran (str.), Asia, 59
Tiran (isl.), Saudi Ar., 59
Tiranë (Tirana)(cap.), Alb., 45
Tiraque, Bol., 136
Tiraspol', U.S.S.R., 52
Tirat Hakarmel, Israel, 65
Tire, Turkey, 63
Tiree (isl.), Scot., 15
Tîrgoviște, Rum., 45
Tîrgu Jiu, Rum., 45
Tîrgu Mureș, Rum., 45
Tîrgu Neamț, Rum., 45
Tîrgu Ocna, Rum., 45
Tirich Mir (mt.), Pak., 68
Tîrnava Mare (riv.), Rum., 45
Tîrnăveni, Rum., 45
Tírnavos, Greece, 45
Tirol (prov.), Austria, 41
Tiruchchirappalli, India, 68
Tirunelveli, India, 68
Tirupati, India, 68
Tiruppattur, India, 68
Tiruvannamalai, India, 68
Tisdale, Sask., 181
Tisza (riv.), Europe, 41
Tiszaföldvár, Hung., 41
Tiszafüred, Hung., 41
Tiszakécske, Hung., 41
Tiszavasvári, Hung., 41
Titagarh, India, 68
Titicaca (lake), S. Amer., 128, 136
Titirangi, N.Z., 101
Titograd, Yugo., 45
Titovo Užice, Yugo., 45
Titov Veles, Yugo., 45
Titule, Dem. Rep. of the Congo, 115
Titusville, Fla., 212
Titusville, Pa., 294
Tivaouane, Sen., 106
Tiverton, Eng., 13

Tiverton, R.I., 249
Tivoli, Italy, 34
Tiv'on, Israel, 65
Tixtla, Mex., 150
Tizayuca, Mex., 150
Tizimín, Mex., 150
Tizi-Ouzou, Alg., 106
Tiznit, Mor., 106
Tjiamis, Indon., 85
Tjiandjur, Indon., 85
Tjilatjap, Indon., 85
Tjimahi, Indon., 85
Tjirebon, Indon., 85
Tjuv (fjord), Norway, 18
Tlachichuca, Mex., 150
Tlacolula, Mex., 150
Tlacotalpan, Mex., 150
Tlacotepec, Mex., 150
Tlahualilo, Mex., 150
Tlalmanalco, Mex., 150
Tlalnepantla, Mex., 150
Tlalpan, Mex., 150
Tlaltizapan, Mex., 150
Tlapa, Mex., 150
Tlaquiltenango, Mex., 150
Tlaxcala (state), Mex., 150
Tlaxcala, Mex., 150
Tlaxco, Mex., 150
Tlaxiaco, Mex., 150
Tlemcen, Alg., 106
Toa, Cuchillas de (mts.), Cuba, 158
Toa Alta, P. Rico, 161
Toba (lake), Indon., 85
Tobago (isl.), Trin. & Tob., 156
Tobatí, Par., 144
Tobi (isl.), Japan, 81
Tobi (isl.), Pac. Is., 87
Tobique (riv.), N.B., 170
Tobol' (riv.), U.S.S.R., 48
Tobol'sk, U.S.S.R., 48
Tobruk, Libya, 111
Tocantinópolis, Braz., 132
Tocantins (riv.), Braz., 132
Toccoa, Ga., 216
Tochigi (prefecture), Japan, 81
Toco, Trin. & Tob., 161
Tocoa, Hond., 154
Tocopilla, Chile, 138
Tocorpuri (mt.), S. Amer., 136, 138
Tocumwal, N.S.W., 97
Todmorden, Eng., 10
Toggenburg (dist.), Switz., 39
Togliatti, U.S.S.R., 52
Togo, 106
Toijala, Fin., 18
Toiyabe (range), Nev., 266
Tokachi (riv.), Japan, 81
Tokaj, Hung., 41
Tokar, Sudan, 111
Tokara (arch.), Japan, 81
Tokat (prov.), Turkey, 63
Tokat, Turkey, 63
Tokelau Islands, 87
Tokmak, U.S.S.R., 48
Tokoroa, N.Z., 101
Tokuno (isl.), Japan, 81
Tokushima (prefecture), Japan, 81
Tokushima, Japan, 81
Tokuyama, Japan, 81
Tokyo (prefecture), Japan, 81
Tokyo (cap.), Japan, 81
Tokyo (bay), Japan, 81
Tolaga Bay, N.Z., 101
Tolbukhin, Bulg., 45
Toledo, Iowa, 229
Toledo, Ohio, 284
Toledo, Oreg., 291
Toledo, Phil. Is., 82
Toledo (prov.), Spain, 33
Toledo, Spain, 33
Toledo (mts.), Spain, 33
Toledo Bend (res.), U.S., 238, 302
Tolima (dept.), Col., 126
Tolima (mt.), Col., 126
Tolitoli, Indon., 85
Tolleson, Ariz., 198
Tolly's Nullah (riv.), India, 68
Tolna (county), Hung., 41
Tolo (gulf), Indon., 85
Tolosa, Spain, 33
Tolú, Col., 126
Toluca, Mex., 150
Tolun, China, 77
Tom (mt.), Mass., 249
Tomah, Wis., 317
Tomahawk, Wis., 317
Tomakomai, Japan, 81
Tomar, Port., 33
Tomás Barrón, Bol., 136
Tomás Gomensoro, Urug., 145
Tomaszów Mazowiecki, Poland, 47
Tombador (mts.), Braz., 132
Tombigbee (riv.), U.S., 194, 256
Tombstone, Ariz., 198
Tomé, Chile, 138
Tomelloso, Spain, 33
Tomini (gulf), Indon., 85
Tomo (riv.), Col., 126
Tomor (mt.), Alb., 45
Tom Price (mt.), W. Austral., 92
Tomsk, U.S.S.R., 48
Toms River, N. J., 273
Tonawanda, N.Y., 276
Tonbridge, Eng., 13
Tondano, Indon., 85
Tønder, Den., 21
Tone (riv.), Japan, 81
Tonga, 87
Tongareva (atoll), Cook Is., 87
Tongatapu (isl.), Tonga, 87
Tongeren, Belg., 27
Tongoy (bay), Chile, 138
Tongue (riv.), U.S., 262, 283, 319
Tongue of the Ocean (chan.), Bah. Is., 156
Tonj, Sudan, 111
Tonk, India, 68
Tonkawa, Okla., 288
Tonkin (gulf), Asia, 72
Tonle Sap (lake), Cambodia, 72
Tonopah, Nev., 266
Tønsberg, Norway, 18
Tonto Nat'l Mon., Ariz., 198
Toodyay, W. Austral., 92
Tooele, Utah, 304
Toowoomba, Queensland, 95
Top (lake), U.S.S.R., 52
Topanga, Calif., 204
Topeka (cap.), Kans., 232
Toplița, Rum., 45
Topol'čany, Czech., 41
Topolobampo, Mex., 150
Toppenish, Wash., 310
Torbay, Eng., 13
Torch (lake), Mich., 250
Torgau, E. Ger., 22
Torgelow, E. Ger., 22
Torhout, Belg., 27
Torino (Turin), Italy, 34
Torit, Sudan, 111
Torne (riv.), Sweden, 18
Torneträsk (lake), Sweden, 18
Torngat (mts.), Newf., 166
Tornio, Fin., 18
Tornio (riv.), Fin., 18
Toro (pt.), Chile, 138
Toro, Spain, 33
Törökszentmiklós, Hung., 41
Toronaic (gulf), Greece, 45
Toronto, N.S.W., 97
Toronto, Ohio, 284
Toronto (cap.), Ont., 177
Tororo, Uganda, 115
Torotoro, Bol., 136
Torrance, Calif., 204
Torre Annunziata, Italy, 34
Torre del Greco, Italy, 34
Torredonjimeno, Spain, 33
Torrelavega, Spain, 33
Torremaggiore, Italy, 34
Torremolinos, Spain, 33
Torrens (lake), S. Austral., 94
Torrente, Spain, 33
Torreón, Mex., 150
Torres (strait), 95
Torres (isls.), New Hebr., 87
Tôrres Novas, Port., 33
Tôrres Vedras, Port., 33
Torrington, Conn., 210
Torrington, Wyo., 319
Tórshavn (cap.), Faerøe Is., Den., 21
Tortola (isl.), Virgin Is. (Br.), 156, 161
Tortona, Italy, 34
Tortosa, Spain, 33
Tortuga (Tortue) (isl.), Haiti, 158
Tortuguero (lake), P. Rico, 161
Toruń, Poland, 47
Tory (isl.), Ire., 17
Torzhok, U.S.S.R., 52
Tosa (bay), Japan, 81
Tosya, Turkey, 63
Totana, Spain, 33
Totness, Sur., 131
Totoket, Conn., 210
Totonicapán, Guat., 154
Totora, Bol., 136
Totowa, N. J., 273
Tottori (prefecture), Japan, 81
Tottori, Japan, 81
Touat (oasis), Alg., 106
Touba, Senegal, 106
Toubkal, Jebel (mt.), Mor., 106
Tougan, Upp. Volta, 106
Touggourt, Alg., 106
Tougué, Guinea, 106
Toul, France, 28
Toulon, France, 28
Toulouse, France, 28
Toumodi, Ivory Coast, 106
Toungoo, Burma, 72
Tourakom, Laos, 72
Tourcoing, France, 28
Tournai, Belg., 27
Touro Synagogue Nat'l Hist. Site, R.I., 249
Tours, France, 28
Tovar, Venez., 124
Towada (lake), Japan, 81
Towanda, Pa., 294
Towers of Silence, India, 68
Townsend, Mont., 262
Townsville, Queensland, 95
Towson, Md., 245
Towy (riv.), Wales, 13
Toya (lake), Japan, 81
Toyama (prefecture), Japan, 81
Toyama, Japan, 81
Toyohashi, Japan, 81
Toyonaka, Japan, 81
Tozeur, Tun., 106
Trabzon (prov.), Turkey, 63
Trabzon, Turkey, 63
Tracadie, N.B., 170
Tracadie (bay), P.E.I., 169
Tracy, Calif., 204
Tracy, Minn., 254
Tradom, China, 77
Trafalgar (cape), Spain, 33
Trafford, Pa., 294
Traiguén, Chile, 138
Trail, Br. Col., 184
Traill (isl.), Greenl., 4
Tralee, Ire., 17
Tramelan, Switz., 39
Tramore, Ire., 17
Tranås, Sweden, 18
Tranebjerg (mt.), Den., 21
Tranent, Scot., 15
Trang, Thai., 72
Trani, Italy, 34
Tran Ninh (plat.), Laos, 72
Tranquebar, India, 68
Tranqueras, Urug., 145
Transantarctic (mts.), Ant., 5
Trans-Carpathian Oblast, U.S.S.R., 52
Transcona, Man., 179
Trans-Himalayas (range), China, 77
Transkei (prov.), S. Afr., 118
Transvaal (prov.), S. Afr., 118
Transylvanian Alps (mts.), Rum., 45
Trapani (prov.), Italy, 34
Trapani, Italy, 34
Traralgon, Vic., 97
Trarza (reg.), Mauritania, 106
Trasimeno (lake), Italy, 34
Trás-os-Montes e Alto Douro (prov.), Port., 33
Traun, Austria, 41
Traunstein, W. Ger., 22
Travancore (reg.), India, 68
Travemünde, W. Ger., 22
Traverse (lake), S. Dak., 298
Traverse City, Mich., 250
Tra Vinh, S. Vietnam, 72
Travis A.F.B., Calif., 204
Travnik, Yugo., 45
Trbovlje, Yugo., 45
Treasure Island, Fla., 212
Třebíč, Czech., 41
Trebizond (Trabzon), Turkey, 63
Trece Martires, Phil. Is., 82
Treinta y Tres (dept.), Urug., 145
Treinta y Tres, Urug., 145
Trelew, Arg., 143
Trelleborg, Sweden, 18
Tremadoc (bay), Wales, 13
Tremiti (isls.), Italy, 34
Trenčín, Czech., 41
Trenque Lauquen, Arg., 143
Trent (riv.), Eng., 13
Trentino-Alto Adige (reg.), Italy, 34
Trento (prov.), Italy, 34
Trento, Italy, 34
Trenton, Mich., 250
Trenton, Mo., 261
Trenton (cap.), N. J., 273
Trenton, N.S., 169
Trenton, Ohio, 284
Trenton, Ont., 177
Treptow, E. Ger., 22
Tres Arroyos, Arg., 143
Três Corações, Braz., 135
Três Lagoas, Braz., 132
Tres Marías (isls.), Mex., 150
Tres Montes (cape), Chile, 138
Três Pontas, Braz., 135
Tres Puntas (cape), Arg., 143
Tres Puntas (cape), Guat., 154
Três Rios, Braz., 135
Treviglio, Italy, 34
Treviso (prov.), Italy, 34
Treviso, Italy, 34
Trevorton, Pa., 294
Triangle, Va., 307
Trichur, India, 68
Trier, W. Ger., 22
Triesen, Liecht., 39
Trieste (prov.), Italy, 34
Trieste, Italy, 34
Trieste (gulf), Italy, 34
Triglav (mt.), Yugo., 45
Tríkkala, Greece, 45
Trim, Ire., 17
Trincomalee, Ceylon, 68
Třinec, Czech., 41
Trinidad (isl.), Arg., 143
Trinidad, Bol., 136
Trinidad, Colo., 208
Trinidad, Cuba, 158
Trinidad, Hond., 154
Trinidad (isl.), Trin. & Tob., 161
Trinidad, Urug., 145
Trinidad and Tobago, 156, 161
Trinité, Mart., 161
Trinity (riv.), Calif., 204
Trinity (bay), Newf., 166
Trinity (bay), Queensland, 95
Trinity (riv.), Tex., 302
Trinkitat, Sudan, 111
Tripoli (Tarabulus), Leb., 63
Tripoli (prov.), Libya, 111
Tripoli (cap.), Libya, 111
Trípolis, Greece, 45
Tripolitania (reg.), Libya, 111
Tripura (terr.), India, 68
Tristan da Cunha (isl.), St. Helena, 3
Triste (gulf), Venez., 124
Trivandrum, India, 68
Trnava, Czech., 41
Trobriand (isls.), Papua, 85
Trogir, Yugo., 45
Trois-Îlets, Mart., 161
Trois-Pistoles, Que., 172
Trois-Rivières, Guad., 161
Trois-Rivières (riv.), Haiti, 158
Trois-Rivières, Que., 172
Troitsk, U.S.S.R., 48
Trollhättan, Sweden, 18
Trombay, India, 68
Trombetas (riv.), Braz., 132
Troms (county), Norway, 18
Tromsø, Norway, 18
Trondheim, Norway, 18
Troodos (mt.), Cyprus, 63
Troon, Scot., 15
Trossachs, The (valley), Scot., 15
Trou-du-Nord, Haiti, 158
Trouville, France, 28
Trowbridge, Eng., 13
Troy, Ala., 194
Troy, Mich., 250
Troy, N.Y., 276
Troy, Ohio, 284
Troy (Ilium)(ruins), Turkey, 63
Troyan, Bulg., 45
Troyes, France, 28
Truc Giang, S. Vietnam, 72
Trucial States, 59
Truckee (riv.), U.S., 204, 266
Trujillo, Hond., 154
Trujillo, Peru, 128
Trujillo, Spain, 33
Trujillo (state), Venez., 124
Trujillo, Venez., 124
Truk (isls.), Pac. Is., 87
Trumann, Ark., 203
Trumbull, Conn., 210
Truro, Eng., 13
Truro, N.S., 169
Trussville, Ala., 194
Truth or Consequences, N. Mex., 274
Trutnov, Czech., 41
Trzcianka, Poland, 47
Trzebiatów, Poland, 47
Tsagan Ula, Mong., 77
Tsagan Usu, China, 77
Tsaidam (swamp), China, 77
Tsangchow, China, 77
Tsangpo (riv.), China, 77
Tsaochwang, China, 77
Tsau, Botswana, 118
Tsavo, Kenya, 115
Tselinograd, U.S.S.R., 48
Tsetserlig, Mong., 77
Tshane, Botswana, 118
Tshela, Dem. Rep. of the Congo, 115
Tshikapa, Dem. Rep. of the Congo, 115
Tsiafajavona (mt.), Malag. Rep., 118
Tsiaotso, China, 77
Tsimlyansk (res.), U.S.S.R., 52
Tsinan, China, 77
Tsinghai (prov.), China, 77
Tsing Hai (Koko Nor)(lake), China, 77
Tsingkiang, China, 77
Tsingshih, China, 77
Tsingtao, China, 77
Tsining, China, 77
Tsinling Shan (range), China, 77
Tsiribihina (riv.), Malag. Rep., 118
Tsiroanomandidy, Malag. Rep., 118
Tsitsihar, China, 77
Tskhinvali, U.S.S.R., 52
Tsu, Japan, 81
Tsu (isls.), Japan, 81
Tsuchiura, Japan, 81
Tsugaru (strait), Japan, 81
Tsumeb, S.W. Afr., 118
Tsunyi, China, 77
Tsuruga, Japan, 81
Tsurugi (mt.), Japan, 81
Tsuruoka, Japan, 81
Tsushima (strait), Japan, 81
Tsuyama, Japan, 81
Tsuyung, China, 77
Tuam, Ire., 17
Tuamotu (arch.), Fr. Poly., 87
Tuapse, U.S.S.R., 52
Tuban, Indon., 85
Tubarão, Braz., 132
Tubas, Jordan, 65
Tübingen, W. Ger., 22
Tubuai (isl.), Fr. Poly., 87
Tubuai (Austral)(isls.), Fr. Poly., 87
Tuckahoe, N.Y., 276
Tucson, Ariz., 198
Tucumán (prov.), Arg., 143
Tucumán, Arg., 143
Tucumcari, N. Mex., 274
Tucupido, Venez., 124
Tucupita, Venez., 124
Tudela, Spain, 33
Tufi, Papua, 85
Tuguegarao, Phil. Is., 82
Tuiserkan, Iran, 66
Tujunga, Calif., 204
Tukangbesi (isls.), Indon., 85
Tuktoyaktuk, N.W.T., 187
Tukums, U.S.S.R., 53
Tula, Mex., 150
Tula, U.S.S.R., 52
Tulancingo, Mex., 150
Tulare, Calif., 204
Tulare (lake), Calif., 204
Tularosa, N. Mex., 274
Tulcán, Ecua., 128
Tulcea, Rum., 45
Tule (desert), Nev., 266
Tuléar (prov.), Malag. Rep., 118
Tuléar, Malag. Rep., 118
Tulia, Tex., 302
Tulkarm, Jordan, 65
Tullahoma, Tenn., 237
Tullamore, Ire., 17
Tulle, France, 28
Tullow, Ire., 17
Tully, Queensland, 95
Tuloma (riv.), U.S.S.R., 52
Tulsa, Okla., 288
Tulsi (lake), India, 68
Tultepec, Mex., 150
Tuluá, Col., 126
Tulun, U.S.S.R., 48
Tulungagung, Indon., 85
Tuma (riv.), Nic., 154
Tumacacori Nat'l Mon., Ariz., 198
Tumaco, Col., 126
Tumbarumba, N.S.W., 97
Tumbes (dept.), Peru, 128
Tumbes, Peru, 128
Tumbes (riv.), S. Amer., 128
Tumen (riv.), Asia, 81
Tumen, China, 77
Tumereng, Guyana, 131
Tumkur, India, 68
Tumpat, Malaysia, 72
Tumucumaque (mts.), S. Amer., 132
Tumut, N.S.W., 97
Tumwater, Wash., 310
Tun (Firdaus), Iran, 66
Tunapuna, Trin. & Tob., 161
Tunas de Zaza, Cuba, 158
Tunbridge Wells, Eng., 13
Tunceli (prov.), Turkey, 63
Tundzha (riv.), Bulg., 45
Tungabhadra (riv.), India, 68
Tungchwan, China, 77
Tunghwa, China, 77
Tungkiang, China, 77
Tungliao, China, 77
Tungting (lake), China, 77
Tungurahua (prov.), Ecua., 128
Tunhwa, China, 77
Tuni, India, 68
Tunis (cap.), Tun., 106
Tunis (gulf), Tun., 106
Tunisia, 106
Tunja, Col., 126
Tunki, China, 77
Tunuyán (riv.), Arg., 143
Tupã, Braz., 135
Tupambaé, Urug., 145
Tupelo, Miss., 256
Tupelo Nat'l Battlef. Site, Miss., 256
Tupiza, Bol., 136
Tupper Lake, N.Y., 276
Túquerres, Col., 126
Tur, Jordan, 65
Tura, U.S.S.R., 48
Turbaco, Col., 126
Turbat, Pak., 68
Turbat-i-Haidari, Iran, 66
Turbat-i-Shaikh Jam, Iran, 66
Turda, Rum., 45
Tureia (atoll), Fr. Poly., 87
Turek, Poland, 47
Turen, Indon., 85
Turfan, China, 77
Turfan (depr.), China, 77
Türgovishte, Bulg., 45
Turgutlu, Turkey, 63
Turhal, Turkey, 63
Turin (prov.), Italy, 34
Turin, Italy, 34
Turkestan, U.S.S.R., 48
Túrkeve, Hung., 41
Turkey, 63
Turkey (riv.), Iowa, 229
Türkmen (mt.), Turkey, 63
Turkmen S.S.R., U.S.S.R., 48
Turks (isls.), Turks and Caicos Is., 156
Turks and Caicos Is., 156
Turks Island (passage), Turks and Caicos Is., 156
Turku, Fin., 18
Turku-Pori (dept.), Fin., 18
Turlock, Calif., 204
Turmero, Venez., 124
Turnagain (cape), N.Z., 101
Turneffe (isl.), Br. Hond., 154
Turners Falls, Mass., 249
Turnhout, Belg., 27
Turnov, Czech., 41
Turnu Măgurele, Rum., 45
Turnu Severin, Rum., 45
Turquino (peak), Cuba, 158
Turrialba, C. Rica, 154
Turriff, Scot., 15
Turtkul', U.S.S.R., 48
Turtle (mts.), N. Dak., 283
Turtle (isls.), Phil. Is., 82
Turtle Creek, Pa., 294
Turukhansk, U.S.S.R., 48
Tuscaloosa, Ala., 194
Tuscan (arch.), Italy, 34
Tuscany (reg.), Italy, 34
Tuscarawas (riv.), Ohio, 284
Tuscola, Ill., 222
Tuscumbia, Ala., 194
Tuskegee Institute, Ala., 194
Tuticorin, India, 68
Tutrakan, Bulg., 45
Tuttlingen, W. Ger., 22
Tutuila (isl.), Amer. Samoa, 87
Tuvinian A.S.S.R., U.S.S.R., 48
Tuwaiq, Jebel (range), Saudi Ar., 59
Tuxpan, Mex., 150
Tuxtepec, Mex., 150
Tuxtla Gutiérrez, Mex., 150
Tuyen Quang, N. Vietnam, 72
Tuy Hoa, S. Vietnam, 72
Tuymazy, U.S.S.R., 52
Tuyün, China, 77
Tuz (lake), Turkey, 63
Tuzigoot Nat'l Mon., Ariz., 198
Tuz Khurmatu, Iraq, 66
Tuzla, Yugo., 45
Tweed (riv.), Eng., 13
Tweed (riv.), Scot., 15
Tweed Heads, N.S.W., 97
Tweedsmuir Prov. Park, Br. Col., 184
Twentynine Palms, Calif., 204
Twillingate, Newf., 166
Twin Falls, Idaho, 220
Twinsburg, Ohio, 284
Two Harbors, Minn., 254
Two Rivers, Wis., 317
Tychy, Poland, 47
Tygart Valley (riv.), W. Va., 313
Tyler, Tex., 302
Tym (riv.), U.S.S.R., 48
Tyndall A.F.B., Fla., 212
Tyne (riv.), Eng., 13
Tynemouth, Eng., 13
Tyre (Sur), Leb., 63
Tyrone (county), N. Ire., 17
Tyrone, Pa., 294
Tyrrell (lake), Vic., 97
Tyrrhenian (sea), Europe, 34
Tyumen', U.S.S.R., 48
Tywyn, Wales, 13
Tzaneen, S. Afr., 118
Tzekung, China, 77
Tzepo, China, 77

U

Uahuka (isl.), Fr. Poly., 87
Uanle Uen, Somalia, 115
Uapou (isl.), Fr. Poly., 87
Uatumã (riv.), Braz., 132
Uaupés (river), Braz., 132
Ubá, Braz., 135
Ubangi (riv.), Africa, 115
Ubari (prov.), Libya, 111
Ube, Japan, 81
Uberaba, Braz., 135
Uberlândia, Braz., 132
Überlingen, W. Ger., 22
Ubon, Thai., 72
Ubsa Nor (prov.), Mong., 77
Ubsa Nor (lake), Mong., 77
Ucayali (riv.), Peru, 128
Uccle, Belg., 27
Uchaly, U.S.S.R., 52
Uchiura (bay), Japan, 81
Uch Turfan, China, 77
Ücker (riv.), E. Ger., 22
Udaipur, India, 68
Uddevalla, Sweden, 18
Uddjaur (lake), Sweden, 18
Udine (prov.), Italy, 34
Udine, Italy, 34
Udipi, India, 68
Udmurt A.S.S.R., U.S.S.R., 52
Udon Thani, Thai., 72
Ueckermünde, E. Ger., 22
Ueda, Japan, 81
Uele (riv.), Dem. Rep. of the Congo, 115
Uelzen, W. Ger., 22
Uetersen, W. Ger., 22
Ufa, U.S.S.R., 52
Ufa (riv.), U.S.S.R., 52
Uganda, 115
Uglich, U.S.S.R., 52
Uherské Hradiště, Czech., 41
Uhrichsville, Ohio, 284
Uig, Scot., 15
Uige (dist.), Angola, 115
Uiju, N. Korea, 81
Uinkaret (plat.), Ariz., 198
Uinta (mts.), Utah, 304
Uisŏng, S. Korea, 81
Uitenhage, S. Afr., 118
Ujelang (atoll), Pac. Is., 87
Újfehértó, Hung., 41
Ujjain, India, 68
Újpest, Hung., 41
Ukiah, Calif., 204
Ukmergė, U.S.S.R., 53
Ukrainian S.S.R., U.S.S.R., 52
Ulan Bator (cap.), Mong., 77
Ulangom, Mong., 77
Ulanhot, China, 77
Ulan Muren (riv.), China, 77
Ulan-Ude, U.S.S.R., 48
Ulchin, S. Korea, 81
Ulhasnagar, India, 68
Uliassutai, Mong., 77
Ulithi (atoll), Pac. Is., 87
Ulladulla, N.S.W., 97
Ullapool, Scot., 15
Ullŭng (isl.), S. Korea, 81
Ulm, W. Ger., 22
Ulsan, S. Korea, 81
Ulster (prov.), Ireland, 17
Ulúa (riv.), Hond., 154
Ulugan (bay), Phil. Is., 82
Ulughchat, China, 77
Ulugh Muztagh (mt.), China, 77
Ulverstone, Tas., 99
Ulvila, Fin., 18
Ul'yanovsk, U.S.S.R., 52
Ulysses, Kans., 232
Umán, Mex., 150
Uman', U.S.S.R., 52
Umatilla (lake), U.S., 291, 310
Umbagog (lake), U.S., 242, 268
Umbria (reg.), Italy, 34
Ume (riv.), Sweden, 18
Umeå, Sweden, 18
Umm al Qaiwain, Trucial States, 58
Umm el Fahm, Israel, 65
Umm Lajj, Saudi Ar., 59
Umm Ruwaba, Sudan, 111
Umm Sa'id, Qatar, 59
Umpqua (riv.), Oreg., 291
Umrer, India, 68
Umtali, Rhod., 118
Umtata, S. Afr., 118
Umvukwe (range), Rhod., 118
Una (mt.), N.Z., 101
Una (riv.), Yugo., 45
Unalakleet, Alaska, 196
Unalaska, Alaska, 196
Uncía, Bol., 136
Uncompahgre (riv.), Colo., 208
Undur Khan, Mong., 77
Undzha (riv.), U.S.S.R., 52
Ungava (bay), Canada, 174
Ungava (pen.), Que., 174
União da Vitória, Braz., 132
Uniket, China, 77
Unimak (isl.), Alaska, 196
Union, Mo., 261
Union, N. J., 273
Union (isl.), St. Vincent, 156
Union, S.C., 296
Union Beach, N. J., 273
Union City, Calif., 204
Union City, Conn., 210
Union City, Ind., 227
Union City, N. J., 273
Union City, Pa., 294
Union City, Tenn., 237
Unión de Reyes, Cuba, 158
Unión Hidalgo, Mex., 150
Union of Soviet Socialist Republics, 48, 52
Union Springs, Ala., 194
Uniontown, Pa., 294
United Arab Republic, 111
United Kingdom, 10
United States, 188
United States (range), N.W.T., 187
Unity, Sask., 181
Universal, Pa., 294
University City, Mo., 261
University Hts., Ohio, 284
University Park, Md., 245
University Park, N. Mex., 274
University Park, Tex., 302
Unley, S. Austral., 94
Unnao, India, 68
Unst (isl.), Scot., 15
Untersee (lake), Switz., 39
Unterwalden (canton), Switz., 39
Unye, Turkey, 63
Unzen, Japan, 81
Upata, Venez., 124
Upemba Nat'l Park, Dem. Rep. of the Congo, 115
Upernavik, Greenl., 4
Upington, S. Afr., 118
Upland, Calif., 204
Upland, Pa., 294
Upolu (isl.), W. Samoa, 87
Upper Arlington, Ohio, 284
Upper Arrow (lake), Br. Col., 184
Upper Austria (prov.), Austria, 41
Upper Darby, Pa., 294
Upper Engadine (dist.), Switz., 39
Upper Hutt, N.Z.,101
Upper Iowa (riv.), Iowa, 229
Upper Juba (prov.), Somalia, 115
Upper Klamath (lake), Oreg., 291
Upper Lough Erne (lake), N. Ire., 17
Upper Nile (prov.), Sudan, 111
Upper Saddle River, N. J., 273
Upper Sandusky, Ohio, 284
Upper Volta, 106
Uppsala (county), Sweden, 18
Uppsala, Sweden, 18
Upton, Wyo., 319
Ur (ruins), Iraq, 66
Urabá (gulf), Col., 126
Ural (mts.), U.S.S.R., 52
Ural (riv.), U.S.S.R., 52
Uralla, N.S.W., 97
Ural'sk, U.S.S.R., 48
Urambo, Tanz., 115
Uranium City, Sask., 181
Uraricuera (riv.), Braz., 132
Urawa, Japan, 81
Urbana, Ill., 222
Urbana, Ohio, 284
Urbandale, Iowa, 229
Ures, Mex., 150
Urfa (prov.), Turkey, 63
Urfa, Turkey, 63
Urgel (plain), Spain, 33
Urgench, U.S.S.R., 48
Uri (canton), Switz., 39
Urique (riv.), Mex., 150
Urk, Neth., 27
Urla, Turkey, 63
Urmia (Reza'iyeh), Iran, 66
Urmia (lake), Iran, 66
Uromi, Nigeria, 106
Urrao, Col., 126
Uruapan, Mex., 150
Urubamba (riv.), Peru, 128
Uruguaiana, Braz., 132
Uruguay, 145
Uruguay (riv.), S. Amer., 120
Urumchi, China, 77
Urungu (riv.), China, 77
Uryupinsk, U.S.S.R., 52
Usa (riv.), U.S.S.R., 52
Uşak (prov.), Turkey, 63
Uşak, Turkey, 63
Usakos, S.W. Afr., 118
Usedom (isl.), E. Ger., 22
Ushant (Ouessant)(isl.), France, 28
Ushuaia, Arg., 143
Usk (riv.), Wales, 13
Üsküdar, Turkey, 63
Usnam (isl.), Poland, 47
Ussuri (riv.), Asia, 77
Ussuriysk, U.S.S.R., 48
Uster, Switz., 39
Ustí, Czech., 41
Ustica (isl.), Italy, 34
Ust'-Kamchatsk, U.S.S.R., 48
Ust'-Kamenogorsk, U.S.S.R., 48
Ust'-Kara, U.S.S.R., 48
Ust'-Kut, U.S.S.R., 48
Ust'-Ordynskiy, U.S.S.R., 48
Ust'-Ordynskiy Nat'l Okrug, U.S.S.R., 48
Ust'-Port, U.S.S.R., 48
Ust'-Urt (plat.), U.S.S.R., 48
Usulután, El Sal., 154
Usumacinta (riv.), C. Amer., 150
Utah (beach), France, 28
Utah (state), U.S., 304
Utah (lake), Utah, 304
Ute (peak), N. Mex., 274
Utete, Tanz., 115
Uthai Thani, Thai., 72
Utica, N.Y., 276
Utiel, Spain, 33
Utikuma (lake), Alta., 182
Utila (isl.), Hond., 154
Utrecht (prov.), Neth., 27
Utrecht, Neth., 27
Utrera, Spain, 33
Utsunomiya, Japan, 81
Uttaradit, Thai., 72
Uttarpara, India, 68
Uttar Pradesh (state), India, 68
Utuado, P. Rico, 161
Uturoa, Fr. Poly., 87
Uusikaarlepyy (Nykarleby), Fin., 18
Uusikaupunki, Fin., 18
Uusimaa (dept.), Fin., 18
Uva (riv.), Col., 126
Uvalde, Tex., 302
Uvéa (isl.), New Cal., 87
Uvinza, Tanz., 115
Uvira, Dem. Rep. of the Congo, 115
Uwajima, Japan, 81
'Uweinat, Jebel (mt.), Africa, 111
Uxbridge, Mass., 249
Uxmal (ruins), Mex., 150
Uyuni, Bol., 136
Uzbek S.S.R., U.S.S.R., 48
Uzhgorod, U.S.S.R., 52
Uzlovaya, U.S.S.R., 52
Uzunköprü, Turkey, 63

V

Vaal (riv.), S. Afr., 118
Vaalserberg (mt.), Neth., 27
Vaasa (dept.), Fin.,18
Vaasa, Fin., 18
Vác, Hung., 41
Vacaville, Calif., 41
Vache (isl.), Haiti, 158
Vacherie, La., 238
Vadsø, Norway, 18
Vaduz (cap.), Liecht., 39
Vagos, Port., 33
Váh (riv.), Czech., 41
Vahitahi (atoll), Fr. Poly., 87
Vail, Colo., 209
Vaitupu (atoll), Gilb. & Ell. Is., 87
Valais (canton), Switz., 39
Valašske Meziříčí, Czech., 41
Valdagno, Italy, 34
Valday (hills), U.S.S.R., 52
Val-de-Marne (dept.), France, 28
Valdepeñas, Spain, 33
Valdés (pen.), Arg., 143
Valdese, N.C., 281
Valdez, Alaska, 196
Valdivia (prov.), Chile, 138
Valdivia, Chile, 138
Val-d'Oise (dept.), France, 28
Val-d'Or, Que., 174
Valdosta, Ga., 216
Valença, Braz., 132
Valence, France, 28
Valencia, Calif., 204
Valencia (reg.), Spain, 33
Valencia (prov.), Spain, 33
Valencia, Spain, 33
Valencia (gulf), Spain, 33
Valencia, Trin. & Tob., 161
Valencia, Venez., 124
Valencia (lake), Venez., 124
Valenciennes, France, 28
Valentia (isl.), Ire., 17
Valentine, Nebr., 264
Valenza, Italy, 34
Valera, Venez., 124
Valga, U.S.S.R., 53
Valhalla, N.Y., 276
Valiente (pen.), Pan., 154
Valjevo, Yugo., 45
Valkeakoski, Fin., 18
Valkenswaard, Neth., 27
Valladolid, Mex., 150
Valladolid (prov.), Spain, 33
Valladolid, Spain, 33
Vall de Uxó, Spain, 33
Valle d'Aosta (reg.), Italy, 34
Valle d'Aosta (prov.), Italy, 34
Valle de Bravo, Mex., 150
Valle de la Pascua, Venez., 124
Valle del Cauca (dept.), Col., 126
Valle de Santiago, Mex., 150
Valledupar, Col., 126
Valle Hermoso, Mex., 150
Vallejo, Calif., 204
Vallenar, Chile, 138
Valletta (cap.), Malta, 34
Valley Center, Kans., 232
Valley City, N. Dak., 283
Valleyfield, Que., 172
Valley Park, Mo., 261
Valley Sta., Ky., 237
Valley Stream, N.Y., 276
Vallgrund (isl.), Fin., 18
Valls, Spain, 33
Valmiera, U.S.S.R., 53
Valparaíso (prov.), Chile, 138
Valparaíso, Chile, 138
Valparaiso, Fla., 212
Valparaiso, Ind., 227
Vals (cape), Indon., 85
Valserrhein (riv.), Switz., 39
Valverde (prov.), Dom. Rep., 158
Valverde, Dom. Rep., 158
Valverde, Spain, 33
Vammala, Fin., 18
Van (prov.), Turkey, 63
Van, Turkey, 63
Van (lake), Turkey, 63
Van Buren, Ark., 203
Van Buren, Maine, 242
Vance A.F.B., Okla., 288
Vancouver, Br. Col., 184
Vancouver (isl.), Br. Col., 184
Vancouver, Wash., 310
Vandalia, Ill., 222
Vandalia, Mo., 261
Vandalia, Ohio, 284
Vandenberg A.F.B., Calif., 204
Vandergriff, Pa., 294
Vanderhoof, Br. Col., 184
Van Diemen (cape), N. Terr., 93
Van Diemen (gulf), N. Terr., 93
Vänern (lake), Sweden, 18
Vänersborg, Sweden, 18
Vangaindrano, Malag. Rep., 118
Van Gia, S. Vietnam, 72
Vang Vieng, Laos, 72
Van Hoa, N. Vietnam, 72
Vanier, Ont., 177
Vanikoro (isl.), Br. Sol. Is., 87
Vanimo, Terr. N.G., 85
Vaniyambadi, India, 68
Vannes, France, 28
Vannøy (isl.), Norway, 18
Van Nuys, Calif., 204
Vansittart (isl.), N.W.T., 187
Vanua Levu (isl.), Fiji, 87
Van Wert, Ohio, 284
Van Yen, N. Vietnam, 72
Var (dept.), France, 28
Varadero, Cuba, 158
Varanasi, India, 68
Varanger (fjord), Norway, 18
Varaždin, Yugo., 45
Varberg, Sweden, 18
Vardar (riv.), Europe, 45
Varde, Den., 21
Vardø, Norway, 18
Varel, W. Ger., 22
Varella (cape), S. Vietnam, 72
Varese (prov.), Italy, 34
Varese, Italy, 34
Varginha, Braz., 135
Varkaus, Fin., 18
Värmland (county), Sweden, 18
Varna, Bulg., 45
Värnamo, Sweden, 18
Varnsdorf, Czech., 41
Varpalota, Hung., 41
Vas (county), Hung., 41
Vasa (Vaasa), Fin., 18
Vascongadas (reg.), Spain, 33
Vasil'kov, U.S.S.R., 52
Vaslui, Rum., 45
Vassar, Mich., 250
Västerås, Sweden, 18
Västerbotten (county), Sweden, 18
Västernorrland (county), Sweden, 18
Västervik, Sweden, 18
Västmanland (county), Sweden, 18
Vatican City, 34
Vaticano (cape), Italy, 34
Vatna (glac.), Iceland, 21
Vatomandry, Malag., Rep., 118
Vatra Dornei, Rum., 45
Vättern (lake), Sweden, 18
Vauclin, Mart., 161
Vaucluse (dept.), France, 28
Vaud (canton), Switz., 39
Vaughn, N. Mex., 274
Vaupés (commissary), Col., 126
Vaupés (riv.), S. Amer., 126
Vauxhall, N. J., 273
Vava'u Group (isls.), Tonga, 87
Vavuniya, Ceylon, 68
Växjö, Sweden, 18
Vaygach (isl.), U.S.S.R., 52
Vechta, W. Ger., 22
Vechte (riv.), W. Ger., 22
Vecsés, Hung., 41
Veendam, Neth., 27
Veenendaal, Neth., 27
Vega (isl.), Norway, 18
Vega Baja, P. Rico, 161
Veghel, Neth., 27
Vegreville, Alta., 182
Vehar (lake), India, 68
Vejen, Den., 21
Vejer de la Frontera, Spain, 33
Vejle, Den., 21
Velas (cape), C. Rica, 154
Vélez-Málaga, Spain, 33
Velhas (riv.), Braz., 132
Velikaya (riv.), U.S.S.R., 52
Veliki Bečkerek (Zrenjanin), Yugo., 45
Velikiye Luki, U.S.S.R., 52
Velikiy Ustyug, U.S.S.R., 52
Veliko Tŭrnovo, Bulg., 45
Velletri, Italy, 34
Vellore, India, 68
Velp, Neth., 27
Velsen, Neth., 27
Veluwe (reg.), Neth., 27
Venado, Mex., 150
Venado Tuerto, Arg., 143
Venamo (mt.), S. Amer., 131

Vendas Novas, Port., 33
Vendée (dept.), France, 28
Vendôme, France, 28
Venetia (reg.), Italy, 34
Venezuela, 124
Venezuela (gulf), Venez., 124
Veniaminof Crater (mt.), Alaska, 196
Venice, Calif., 204
Venice, Fla., 212
Venice, Ill., 222
Venice (prov.), Italy, 34
Venice, Italy, 34
Venice (gulf), Italy, 34
Vénişsieux, France, 28
Venlo, Neth., 27
Venraij, Neth., 27
Ventimiglia, Italy, 34
Ventnor City, N. J., 273
Ventotene (isl.), Italy, 34
Ventspils, U.S.S.R., 53
Ventuari (riv.), Venez., 124
Ventura, Calif., 204
Venus (bay), Vic., 97
Venustiano Carranza, Mex., 150
Verá (lagoon), Par., 144
Veracruz (state), Mex., 150
Veracruz Llave, Mex., 150
Veragua Abajo, Dom. Rep., 158
Veraval, India, 68
Verbania, Italy, 34
Vercelli (prov.), Italy, 34
Vercelli, Italy, 34
Verde (riv.), Ariz., 198
Verde (cay), Bah. Is., 156
Verde (riv.), Braz., 132
Verde (riv.), Mex., 150
Verde (cape), Senegal, 106
Verde Island (passage), Phil. Is., 82
Verden, W. Ger., 22
Verdigris (riv.), U.S., 232, 288
Verdinho (riv.), Braz., 132
Verdun, Que., 172
Verdun-sur-Meuse, France, 28
Vereeniging, S. Africa, 118
Vérendrye Prov. Park, Que., 174
Vereshchagino, U.S.S.R., 48
Vergara, Urug., 145
Verkhniy Ufaley, U.S.S.R., 48
Verkhoyansk, U.S.S.R., 48
Verkhoyansk (range), U.S.S.R., 48
Vermilion (lake), Minn., 254
Vermilion, Ohio, 284
Vermilion (riv.), U.S., 222, 227
Vermillion, S. Dak., 298
Vermont (state), U.S., 268
Vernal, Utah, 304
Vernon, Br. Col., 184
Vernon, Conn., 210
Vernon, France, 28
Vernon, Tex., 302
Vero Beach, Fla., 212
Verona (prov.), Italy, 34
Verona, Italy, 34
Verona, N. J., 273
Verona, Pa., 294
Vérroia, Greece, 45
Versailles, France, 28
Versailles, Ky., 237
Verviers, Belg., 27
Vesdre (riv.), Belg., 27
Vesoul, France, 28
Vest (fjord), Norway, 18
Vest-Agder (county), Norway, 18
Vestavia Hills, Ala., 194
Vesterålen (isls.), Norway, 18
Vesterdal (riv.), Sweden, 18
Vestfold (county), Norway, 18
Vestmannæyjar, Iceland, 21
Vestvågøy (isl.), Norway, 18
Vesuvius (vol.), Italy, 34
Veszprém (county), Hung., 41
Veszprém, Hung., 41
Vetlanda, Sweden, 18
Vetluga (riv.), U.S.S.R., 52
Vevey, Switz., 39
Viacha, Bol., 136
Viana do Castelo, Port., 33
Vianden, Lux., 27
Viareggio, Italy, 34
Viborg, Den., 21
Vibo Valentia, Italy, 34
Vicente Guerrero, Mex., 150
Vicenza (prov.), Italy, 34
Vicenza, Italy, 34
Vich, Spain, 33
Vichada (commissary), Col., 126
Vichada (riv.), Col., 126
Vichuga, U.S.S.R., 52
Vichy, France, 28
Vicksburg, Miss., 256
Vicksburg Nat'l Mil. Park, Miss., 256
Victor Harbor, S. Austral., 94
Victoria (falls), Africa, 115
Victoria (lake), Africa, 115
Victoria, Arg., 143
Victoria (state), Austral., 97
Victoria (cap.), Br. Col., 184
Victoria (mt.), Burma, 72
Victoria, Cameroon, 115
Victoria, Chile, 138
Victoria, Grenada, 161
Victoria, Guinea, 106
Victoria (cap.), Hong Kong, 77
Victoria, Malaysia, 85
Victoria, Malta, 34
Victoria, Newf., 166
Victoria (riv.), N. Terr., 93
Victoria (isl.), N.W.T., 187
Victoria (peaks), Phil. Is., 82
Victoria (cap.), Seychelles, 118
Victoria, Tex., 302
Victoria de las Tunas, Cuba, 158
Victoria Land (reg.), Ant., 5
Victoria Point, Burma, 72
Victorias, Phil. Is., 82
Victoriaville, Que., 172
Victorville, Calif., 204
Vidalia, Ga., 216
Vidalia, La., 238
Vidin, Bulg., 45
Vidisha, India, 68
Vidor, Tex., 302
Viedma (lake), Arg., 143
Vieille Case, Dominica, 161
Vienna (cap.), Austria, 41
Vienna, Va., 307
Vienna, W. Va., 313
Vienne (dept.), France, 28
Vienne, France, 28
Vienne (riv.), France, 28
Vientiane (cap.), Laos, 72
Vieques (Isabel Segunda), P. Rico, 161
Vieques (isl.), P. Rico, 161
Viersen, W. Ger., 22
Vierzon, France, 28
Viesca, Mex., 150
Vietnam, 72
Vieux Desert (lake), U.S., 250, 317
Vieux Fort, St. Lucia, 161
Vieux-Habitants, Guad., 161
Vigan, Phil. Is., 82
Vigevano, Italy, 34
Vigo, Spain, 33
Vigsø (bay), Den., 21
Viipuri (Vyborg), U.S.S.R., 52
Vijayawada, India, 68
Vijosë (riv.), Alb., 45
Viking, Alta., 182
Vikna (isl.), Norway, 18
Vila (cap.), New Hebr., 87
Vila Cabral, Mozamb., 118
Vila Coutinho, Mozamb., 118
Vila da Ponte, Angola, 115
Vila de Manica, Mozamb., 118
Vila de Sena, Mozamb., 118
Vila do Chinde, Mozamb., 118
Vila do Conde, Port., 33
Vila do Porto, Port., 32
Vila Fontes, Mozamb., 118
Vila Franca de Xira, Port., 33
Vila General Machado, Angola, 115
Vila Gouveia, Mozamb., 118
Vilaine (riv.), France, 28
Vila Luísa, Mozamb., 118
Vila Mariano Machado, Angola, 115
Vila Nova de Gaia, Port., 33
Vila Paiva Couceiro, Angola, 115
Vila Péry, Mozamb., 118
Vila Real, Port., 33
Vila Real de Sto. António, Port., 33
Vila Roçadas, Angola, 115
Vila Salazar, Port. Timor, 85
Vila Teixeira de Sousa, Angola, 115
Vilcanota (mt.), Peru, 128
Viljandi, U.S.S.R., 53
Villa Alemana, Chile, 138
Villa Altagracia, Dom. Rep., 158
Villa Ángela, Arg., 143
Villa Bruzual, Venez., 124
Villacañas, Spain, 33
Villacarrillo, Spain, 33
Villach, Austria, 41
Villa Cisneros, Sp. Sahara, 106
Villa de Cura, Venez., 124
Villa de San Antonio, Hond., 154
Villa de Seris, Mex., 150
Villa Dolores, Arg., 143
Villa Florida, Par., 144
Villafranca, Spain, 33
Villa Frontera, Mex., 150
Villaguay, Arg., 143
Villa Hayes, Par., 144
Villahermosa, Mex., 150
Villa Krause, Arg., 143
Villa María, Arg., 143
Villa Montes, Bol., 136
Villanova, Pa., 294
Villanueva, Col., 126
Villanueva, Mex., 150
Villanueva, Spain, 33
Villanueva y Geltrú, Spain, 33
Villa Park, Ill., 222
Villa Rica, Ga., 216
Villarreal de los Infantes, Spain, 33
Villarrica, Chile, 138
Villarrica, Par., 144
Villarrobledo, Spain, 33
Villarrubia de los Ojos, Spain, 33
Villa Serrano, Bol., 136
Villa Unión, Mex., 150
Villavicencio, Col., 126
Villazón, Bol., 136
Villefranche, France, 28
Villejuif, France, 28
Ville-Marie, Que., 174
Villemomble, France, 28
Villena, Spain, 33
Villeneuve, France, 28
Ville Platte, La., 238
Villeta, Par., 144
Villeurbanne, France, 28
Villingen, W. Ger., 22
Villupuram, India, 68
Vilna (Vilnius), U.S.S.R., 53
Vilvoorde, Belg., 27
Vilyuy (range), U.S.S.R., 48
Vilyuy (riv.), U.S.S.R., 48
Viña del Mar, Chile, 138
Vinalhaven (isl.), Maine, 242
Vinaroz, Spain, 33
Vincennes (bay), Ant., 5
Vincennes, France, 28
Vincennes, Ind., 227
Vinces, Ecua., 128
Vindel (riv.), Sweden, 18
Vindhya (range), India, 68
Vineland, N. J., 273
Vineyard (sound), Mass., 249
Vinh, N. Vietnam, 72
Vinh Loi, S. Vietnam, 72
Vinh Long, S. Vietnam, 72
Vinita, Okla., 288
Vinkovci, Yugo., 45
Vinnitsa, U.S.S.R., 52
Vinton, Iowa, 229
Vinton, La., 238
Vinton, Va., 307
Viqueque, Port. Timor, 85
Virac, Phil. Is., 82
Virachei, Cambodia, 72
Viramgam, India, 68
Virden, Ill., 222
Virden, Man., 179
Virgin (riv.), U.S., 266, 304
Virgin Gorda (isl.), Virgin Is. (Br.), 161
Virginia, Minn., 254
Virginia (state), U.S., 307
Virginia Beach, Va., 307
Virginia City, Mont., 262
Virginia City, Nev., 266
Virgin Islands (Br.), 156, 161
Virgin Islands (U.S.), 161
Virgin Islands Nat'l Park, Virgin Is. (U.S.), 161
Viroqua, Wis., 317
Virovitica, Yugo., 45
Virunga (range), Africa, 115
Vis (isl.), Yugo., 45
Visakhapatnam, India, 68
Visalia, Calif., 204
Visayan (sea), Phil. Is., 82
Visby, Sweden, 18
Visconde do Rio Branco, Braz., 135
Viscount Melville (sound), N.W.T., 187
Viseu, Port., 33
Vişeu de Sus, Rum., 45
Vishoek, S. Afr., 118
Visnagar, India, 68
Visp, Switz., 39
Vista, Calif., 204
Vistula (riv.), Poland, 47
Vit (riv.), Bulg., 45
Vitebsk, U.S.S.R., 52
Viterbo (prov.), Italy, 34
Viterbo, Italy, 34
Viti Levu (isl.), Fiji, 87
Vitim (riv.), U.S.S.R., 48
Vitória, Braz., 132
Vitoria, Spain, 33
Vitória da Conquista, Braz., 132
Vitória de Santo Antão, Braz., 132
Vitry, France, 28
Vittoria, Italy, 34
Vittorio Veneto, Italy, 34
Vivian, La., 238
Vizagapatam (Visakhapatnam), India, 68
Vizcaya (prov.), Spain, 33
Vizianagaram, India, 68
Vlaardingen, Neth., 27
Vladimir, U.S.S.R., 52
Vladivostok, U.S.S.R., 48
Vlissingen (Flushing), Neth., 27
Vlorë, Alb., 45
Vltava (riv.), Czech., 41
Vöcklabruck, Austria, 41
Vo Dat, S. Vietnam, 72
Vogel (peak), Nigeria, 106
Vogelkop (Deberai) (pen.), Indon., 85
Vogelsberg (mt.), W. Ger., 22
Voghera, Italy, 34
Vohémar, Malag. Rep., 118
Vohipeno, Malag. Rep., 118
Voi, Kenya, 115
Voiron, France, 28
Vojens, Den., 21
Vojmsjön (lake), Sweden, 18
Volcano (isls.), Japan, 81
Volendam, Neth., 27
Volga (riv.), U.S.S.R., 52
Volga-Don (canal), U.S.S.R., 52
Volgodonsk, U.S.S.R., 52
Volgograd, U.S.S.R., 52
Volkhov, U.S.S.R., 52
Völklingen, W. Ger., 22
Volksrust, S. Africa, 118
Vologda, U.S.S.R., 52
Vólos, Greece, 45
Vol'sk, U.S.S.R., 52
Volta (lake), Ghana, 106
Volta (riv.), Ghana, 106
Volta Redonda, Braz., 135
Volturno (riv.), Italy, 34
Vólvi (lake), Greece, 45
Volyn Oblast, U.S.S.R., 52
Volzhsk, U.S.S.R., 52
Volzhskiy, U.S.S.R., 52
Voorne (isl.), Neth., 27
Vopnafjörd (fjord), Iceland, 21
Vorarlberg (prov.), Austria, 41
Vorderrhein (river), Switz., 39
Vordingborg, Den., 21
Vorgod (riv.), Den., 21
Vorkuta, U.S.S.R., 52
Voronezh, U.S.S.R., 52
Voroshilovgrad (Lugansk), U.S.S.R., 52
Vorskla (riv.), U.S.S.R., 52
Vorst (forest), Belg., 27
Võru, U.S.S.R., 53
Vosges (dept.), France, 28
Vosges (mts.), France, 28
Vostok (isl.), Pacific, 87
Votkinsk, U.S.S.R., 52
Votuporanga, Braz., 135
Voyvodina (aut. prov.), Yugo., 45
Voy-Vozh, U.S.S.R., 52
Voznesensk, U.S.S.R., 52
Vranje, Yugo., 45
Vratsa, Bulg., 45
Vrbas, Yugo., 45
Vrede, S. Africa, 118
Vreed-en-Hoop, Guyana, 131
Vršac, Yugo., 45
Vryburg, S. Afr., 118
Vryheid, S. Afr., 118
Vsetín, Czech., 41
Vught, Neth., 27
Vukovar, Yugo., 45
Vulcan, Alta., 182
Vulcano (isl.), Italy, 34
Vung Tau, S. Vietnam, 72
Vyatka (riv.), U.S.S.R., 52
Vyatskiye Polyany, U.S.S.R., 52
Vyaz'ma, U.S.S.R., 52
Vyborg, U.S.S.R., 52
Vychegda (riv.), U.S.S.R., 52
Východočeský (reg.), Czech., 41
Východoslovenský (reg.), Czech., 41
Vyksa, U.S.S.R., 52
Vym' (riv.), U.S.S.R., 52
Vyshniy Volochek, U.S.S.R., 52
Vyškov, Czech., 41
Vysoké Tatry, Czech., 41

W

Wa, Ghana, 106
Waal (riv.), Neth., 27
Waalwijk, Neth., 27
Waban, Mass., 249
Wabana (Bell Island), Newf., 166
Wabasca (riv.), Alta., 182
Wabash, Ind., 227
Wabash (riv.), U.S., 227
Wabasha, Minn., 254
Wabi Shebelle (riv.), Africa, 115
Wąbrzeźno, Poland, 47
Wabush, Newf., 166
Waccamaw (lake), N.C., 281
Waco, Tex., 302
Wadai (reg.), Chad, 111
Waddan, Libya, 111
Waddenzee (sound), Neth., 27
Waddington (mt.), Br. Col., 184
Wade-Hampton, S.C., 296
Wadena, Minn., 254
Wadena, Sask., 181
Wädenswil, Switz., 39
Wadesboro, N.C., 281
Wadi es Sir, Jordan, 65
Wadi Musa, Jordan, 65
Wadmalaw (isl.), S.C., 296
Wad Medani, Sudan, 111
Wadowice, Poland, 47
Wadsworth, Ohio, 284
Wageningen, Neth., 27
Wager (bay), N.W.T., 187
Wagga Wagga, N.S.W., 97
Wagin, W. Austral., 92
Wagoner, Okla., 288
Wągrowiec, Poland, 47
Wahiawa, Hawaii, 218
Wahoo, Nebr., 264
Wahpeton, N. Dak., 283
Waialua, Hawaii, 218
Waianae, Hawaii, 218
Waiau (riv.), N.Z., 101
Waidhofen, Austria, 41
Waigeo (isl.), Indon., 85
Waihi, N.Z., 101
Waikanae, N.Z., 101
Waikato (riv.), N.Z., 101
Waikiki (beach), Hawaii, 218
Waikiwi, N.Z., 101
Wailuku, Hawaii, 218
Waimanalo, Hawaii, 218
Waimate, N.Z., 101
Waimea (bay), Hawaii, 218
Wainuiomata, N.Z., 101
Wainwright, Alaska, 196
Wainwright, Alta., 182
Waipawa, N.Z., 101
Waipio (pen.), Hawaii, 218
Wairau (riv.), N.Z., 101
Wairoa, N.Z., 101
Waitaki (riv.), N.Z., 101
Waitara, N.Z., 101
Wajir, Kenya, 115
Wakasa (bay), Japan, 81
Wakatipu (lake), N.Z., 101
Wakaw, Sask., 181
Wakayama (prefecture), Japan, 81
Wakayama, Japan, 81
Wake (isl.), Pacific, 87
WaKeeney, Kans., 232
Wakefield, Eng., 13
Wakefield, Mass., 249
Wakefield, Mich., 250
Wakefield, R.I., 249
Wake Forest, N.C., 281
Wakema, Burma, 72
Wakenaam (isl.), Guyana, 131
Wakkanai, Japan, 81
Wala, Kuh-i- (mt.), Afghan., 68
Wałbrzych, Poland, 47
Walcha, N.S.W., 97
Walchensee (lake), W. Ger., 22
Walcheren (isl.), Neth., 27
Wałcz, Poland, 47
Wald, Switz., 39
Walden, N.Y., 276
Waldheim, E. Ger., 22
Waldwick, N. J., 273
Wales, U.K., 13
Walgett, N.S.W., 97
Walgreen Coast (reg.), Ant., 5
Walhalla, S.C., 296
Walker, Mich., 250
Walker (lake), Nev., 266
Walkerton, Ont., 177
Walkerville, Mont., 262
Wall, N.J., 273
Wallace, Idaho, 220
Wallaceburg, Ont., 177
Wallaga (prov.), Eth., 111
Wallaroo, S. Austral., 94
Wallasey, Eng., 10
Walla Walla, Wash., 310
Walled Lake, Mich., 250
Wallenstadt (lake), Switz., 39
Wallerawang, N.S.W., 97
Wallingford, Conn., 210
Wallington, N. J., 273
Wallis (isls.), Wallis & Futuna, 87
Wallis and Futuna, 87
Wallo (prov.), Eth., 111
Wallowa (mts.), Oreg., 291
Wallsend, Eng., 13
Wallula (lake), U.S., 291, 310
Walney (isl.), Eng., 13
Walnut Canyon Nat'l Mon., Ariz., 198
Walnut Creek, Calif., 204
Walnut Ridge, Ark., 203
Walsall, Eng., 10
Walsenburg, Colo., 208
Walsrode, W. Ger., 22
Walterboro, S.C., 296
Walter Reed Army Med. Ctr., D.C., 245
Walters, Okla., 288
Waltershausen, E. Ger., 22
Waltham, Mass., 249
Waltham Forest, Eng., 10
Waltham Holy Cross, Eng., 10
Walton, N.Y., 276
Walton and Weybridge, Eng., 10
Walvis Bay, S. Africa, 118
Wamba, Dem. Rep. of the Congo, 115
Wamena, Indon., 85
Wanaka (lake), N.Z., 101
Wanamassa, N. J., 273
Wanaque, N. J., 273
Wanaque (res.), N. J., 273
Wandel (sea), Greenl., 4
Wandsworth, Eng., 10
Wang, Mae Nam (riv.), Thai., 72
Wanganui, N.Z., 101
Wangaratta, Vic., 97
Wangen, W. Ger., 22
Wangiwangi (isl.), Indon., 85
Wanhsien, China, 77
Wankie, Rhod., 118
Wanks (Coco)(riv.), Cent. Amer., 154
Wanne-Eickel, W. Ger., 22
Wanneroo, W. Austral., 92
Wantagh, N.Y., 276
Wapakoneta, Ohio, 284
Wapato, Wash., 310
Wapawekka (hills), Sask., 181
Wappingers Falls, N.Y., 276
War, W. Va., 313
Waramaug (lake), Conn., 210
Waranga (res.), Vic., 97
Warangal, India, 68
Waratah (bay), Vic., 97
Warburton, The (riv.), S. Austral., 94
Warburton, Vic., 97
Wardere, Eth., 111
Wardha, India, 68
Ware, Eng., 13
Ware, Mass., 249
Wareham, Mass., 249
Waren, E. Ger., 22
Warendorf, W. Ger., 22
Ware Shoals, S.C., 296
Warfield, Br. Col., 184
Warialda, N.S.W., 97
Warin Chamrap, Thai., 72
Warley, Eng., 10
Warmbad, S. Afr., 118
Warmbad, S.W. Afr., 118
Warner Robins, Ga., 216
Warnes, Bol., 136
Waroona, W. Austral., 92
Warracknabeal, Vic., 97
Warr Acres, Okla., 288
Warragamba, N.S.W., 97
Warragul, Vic., 97
Warrego (riv.), Austral., 95, 97
Warren, Ark., 203
Warren, Mich., 250
Warren, N.S.W., 97
Warren, Ohio, 284
Warren, Pa., 294
Warren, R.I., 249
Warrenpoint, N. Ire., 17
Warrensburg, Mo., 261
Warrensville Hts., Ohio, 284
Warrenton, S. Afr., 118
Warrenton, Va., 307
Warri, Nigeria, 106
Warrington, Eng., 10
Warrington, Fla., 212
Warrnambool, Vic., 97
Warroad, Minn., 254
Warsaw, Ind., 227
Warsaw, N.Y., 276
Warsaw (prov.), Poland, 47
Warsaw (cap.), Poland, 47
Warta (riv.), Poland, 47
Warwick, Eng., 13
Warwick, N.Y., 276
Warwick, Queensland, 95
Warwick, R.I., 249
Warwickshire (county), Eng., 13
Wasatch (range), U.S., 220, 304
Wasco, Calif., 204
Waseca, Minn., 254
Wash, The (bay), Eng., 13
Washburn (mt.), Wyo., 319
Washington, Ga., 216
Washington (isl.), Gilb. and Ell. Is., 87
Washington, Ill., 222
Washington, Ind., 227
Washington, Iowa, 229
Washington, Mo., 261
Washington (mt.), N.H., 268
Washington, N. J., 273
Washington, N.C., 281
Washington, Pa., 294
Washington (state), U.S., 310
Washington, D.C. (cap.), U.S., 245
Washington (lake), Wash., 310
Washington (isl.), Wis., 317
Washington C.H., Ohio, 284
Washington Crossing, N.J., 273
Washington Park, Ill., 222
Washington Terr., Utah, 304
Washita (riv.), Tex., 302
Washoe (lake), Nev., 266
Washougal, Wash., 310
Wasmes, Belg., 27
Waspán, Nic., 154
Wasserbillig, Lux., 27
Wassuk (range), Nev., 266
Watauga (lake), Tenn., 237
Watch Hill (pt.), R.I., 249
Watchung, N. J., 273
Waterberg, S.W. Afr., 118
Waterbury, Conn., 210
Waterbury, Vt., 268
Wateree (riv.), S.C., 296
Waterford, Conn., 210
Waterford (county), Ire., 17
Waterford, Ire., 17
Waterford, N.Y., 276
Waterhen (lake), Man., 179
Waterloo, Belg., 27
Waterloo, Ill., 222
Waterloo, Iowa, 229
Waterloo, N.Y., 276
Waterloo, Ont., 177
Waterloo, Que., 172
Watermael-Boitsfort, Belg., 27
Waterton-Glacier Internat'l Peace Park, N. Amer., 182, 262
Waterton Lakes Nat'l Park, Alta., 182
Watertown, Conn., 210
Watertown, Mass., 249
Watertown, N.Y., 276
Watertown, S. Dak., 298
Watertown, Wis., 317
Waterval-Bo, S. Afr., 118
Water Valley, Miss., 256
Waterville, Conn., 210
Waterville, Maine, 242
Watervliet, N.Y., 276
Waterways, Alta., 182
Watford, Eng., 10
Watford City, N. Dak., 283
Watkins Glen, N.Y., 276
Watling (San Salvador) (isl.), Bah. Is., 156
Watonga, Okla., 288
Watrous, Sask., 181
Watsa, Dem. Rep. of the Congo, 115
Watseka, Ill., 222
Watson, Sask., 181
Watson Lake, Yukon, 187
Watsonville, Calif., 204
Watts Bar (lake), Tenn., 237
Wattwil, Switz., 39
Watzmann (mt.), W. Ger., 22
Wau, Terr. N.G., 85
Wau, Sudan, 111
Wauchope, N.S.W., 97
Wauchula, Fla., 212
Wauconda, Ill., 222
Waukegan, Ill., 222
Waukesha, Wis., 317
Waukon, Iowa, 229
Waupaca, Wis., 317
Waupun, Wis., 317
Wausau, Wis., 317
Wauseon, Ohio, 284
Wauwatosa, Wis., 317
Waverley, Mass., 249
Waverley, N.S.W., 97
Waverley, Vic., 97
Waverly, Iowa, 229
Waverly, N.Y., 276
Waverly, Ohio, 284
Waverly, Tenn., 237
Wawa, Ont., 175
Waxahachie, Tex., 302
Way, Poulo (isls.), S. Vietnam, 72
Wayatinah, Tas., 99
Waycross, Ga., 216
Wayne, Mich., 250
Wayne, Nebr., 264
Wayne, N. J., 273
Wayne, Pa., 294
Waynesboro, Ga., 216
Waynesboro, Miss., 256
Waynesboro, Pa., 294
Waynesboro, Va., 307
Waynesburg, Pa., 294
Waynesville, N.C., 281
Wayzata, Minn., 254
We (isl.), Indon., 85
Wear (riv.), Eng., 13
Weatherford, Okla., 288
Weatherford, Tex., 302
Weatherly, Pa., 294
Webb A.F.B., Tex., 302
Webb City, Mo., 261
Webster, Mass., 249
Webster, N.Y., 276
Webster, S. Dak., 298
Webster City, Iowa, 229
Webster Groves, Mo., 261
Weddell (sea), Ant., 5
Wedel, W. Ger., 22
Weed, Calif., 204
Weehawken, N. J., 273
Weeki Wachee, Fla., 212
Weert, Neth., 27
Weesp, Neth., 27
Wee Waa, N.S.W., 97
Weida, E. Ger., 22
Weiden, W. Ger., 22
Weifang, China, 77
Weihai, China, 77
Wei Ho (riv.), China, 77
Weilheim, W. Ger., 22
Weimar, E. Ger., 22
Weinfelden, Switz., 39
Weingarten, W. Ger., 22
Weinheim, W. Ger., 22
Weipa, Queensland, 95
Weirton, W. Va., 313
Weiser, Idaho, 220
Weissenburg, W. Ger., 22
Weissenfels, E. Ger., 22
Weissensee, E. Ger., 22
Weissenstein (mts.), Switz., 39
Weisshorn (mt.), Switz., 39
Weisswasser, E. Ger., 22
Weiz, Austria, 41
Wejh, Saudi Ar., 59
Wejherowo, Poland, 47
Welch, W. Va., 313
Welkom, S. Afr., 118
Welland, Ont., 177
Wellesley, Mass., 249
Wellesley (isls.), Queensland, 95
Wellesley Hills, Mass., 249
Wellingborough, Eng., 13
Wellington (isl.), Chile, 138
Wellington, Eng., 13
Wellington, Kans., 232
Wellington, N.S.W., 97
Wellington (prov. dist.), N.Z., 101
Wellington (cap.), N.Z., 101
Wellington, Ohio, 284
Wellington, S. Afr., 118
Wellington, Tex., 302
Wells, Minn., 254
Wells, Nev., 266
Wells (lake), W. Austral., 92
Wellsboro, Pa., 294
Wellsburg, W. Va., 313
Wellsford, N.Z., 101
Wellston, Mo., 261
Wellston, Ohio, 284
Wellsville, N.Y., 276
Wellsville, Ohio, 284
Wels, Austria, 41
Welsh, La., 238
Welshpool, Wales, 13
Welwyn (Welwyn Garden City), Eng., 13
Wemmel, Belg., 27
Wenatchee, Wash., 310
Wenatchee (riv.), Wash., 310
Wenchi, Ghana, 106
Wenchow, China, 77
Wenhsien, China, 77
Wenlock, Eng., 13
Wentworth, N.S.W., 97
Wentzville, Mo., 261
Werdau, E. Ger., 22
Wernigerode, E. Ger., 22
Werra (riv.), Ger., 22
Werribee, Vic., 97
Werris Creek, N.S.W., 97
Wertheim, W. Ger., 22
Wervik, Belg., 27
Wesel, W. Ger., 22
Weser (riv.), W. Ger., 22
Weslaco, Tex., 302
Wesley, Dominica, 161
Wesleyville, Newf., 166
Wesleyville, Pa., 294
Wessel (cape), N. Terr., 93
Wessel (isls.), N. Terr., 93
Wessington Springs, S. Dak., 298
West (cape), N.Z., 101
West Allis, Wis., 317
West Azerbaijan (prov.), Iran, 66
West Barrington, R.I., 249
West Bend, Wis., 317
West Bengal (state), India, 68
West Berbice (dist.), Guyana, 131
Westborough, Mass., 249
West Bridgewater, Mass., 249
West Bromwich, Eng., 10
Westbrook, Maine, 242
West Burlington, Iowa, 229
Westbury, N.Y., 276
Westbury, Tas., 99
West Caldwell, N. J., 273
West Carrollton, Ohio, 284
Westchester, Ill., 222
West Chester, Pa., 294
West Chicago, Ill., 222
West Columbia, S.C., 296
West Columbia, Tex., 302
West Covina, Calif., 204
West Demerara (dist.), Guyana, 131
West Derry, N.H., 268
West Des Moines, Iowa, 229
West Elmira, N.Y., 276
West End, Virgin Is. (Br.), 161
Westerly, R.I., 249
Western (prov.), Kenya, 115
Western (state), Nigeria, 106
Western Australia (state), Austral., 92
Western Dvina (riv.), U.S.S.R., 52
Western Ghats (mts.), India, 68
Westernport, Md., 245
Western Port (inlet), Vic., 97
Western Samar (prov.), Phil. Is., 82
Western Samoa, 87
Western Sprs., Ill., 222
Westerstede, W. Ger., 22
Westerville, Ohio, 284
Westerwald (for.), W. Ger., 22
West Fargo, N.D., 283
West Fargo Industrial Park, N. Dak., 283
Westfield, Mass., 249
Westfield, N. J., 273
Westfield, N.Y., 276
West Flanders (prov.), Belg., 27
West Frankfort, Ill., 222
West Frisian (isls.), Neth., 27
West Glens Falls, N.Y., 276
West Hartford, Conn., 210
West Haven, Conn., 210
West Hazleton, Pa., 294
West Helena, Ark., 203
West Hollywood, Calif., 204
West Homestead, Pa., 294
West Indies, 156
West Jefferson, Ohio, 284
West Jordan, Utah, 304
West Kilbride, Scot., 15
West Kildonan, Man., 179
West Korea (bay), Asia, 81
West Lafayette, Ind., 227
Westlake, La., 238
Westlake, Ohio, 284
West Lake (prov.), Tanz., 115
Westland, Mich., 250
Westland (prov. dist.), N.Z., 101
West Lebanon, N.H., 268
West Ledge Flats, Berm., 156
West Linn, Oreg., 291
Westlock, Alta., 182
West Los Angeles, Calif., 204
West Lothian (county), Scot., 15
Westmeath (county), Ire., 17
West Memphis, Ark., 203
West Miami, Fla., 212
West Mifflin, Pa., 294
West Milton, Ohio, 284
West Milwaukee, Wis., 317
Westminster, Calif., 204
Westminster, Colo., 208
Westminster, Eng., 10
Westminster, Md., 245
West Monroe, La., 238
Westmont, Ill., 222
Westmont, Pa., 294
Westmorland (county), Eng., 13
Westmount, Que., 172
West Mystic, Conn., 210
West Newton, Mass., 249
West Newton, Pa., 294
West New York, N. J., 273
West Nicholson, Rhod., 118
Weston, W. Va., 313
Westonaria, S. Afr., 118
Weston-super-Mare, Eng., 13
West Orange, N. J., 273
West Orange, Tex., 302
Westover, W. Va., 313
Westover A.F.B., Mass., 249
West Palm Beach, Fla., 212
West Paterson, N. J., 273
West Pensacola, Fla., 212
West Pittsburg, Calif., 204
West Plains, Mo., 261
West Point, Ga., 216
West Point, Miss., 256
West Point, Nebr., 264
West Point, N. Y., 276
Westport, Conn., 210
Westport, Ire., 17
Westport, Mass., 249
Westport, N.Z., 101
West Portsmouth, Ohio, 284
West Quoddy (head), Maine, 242
Westray (isl.), Scot., 15
West Sacramento, Calif., 204
West Saint Paul, Minn., 254
West Seneca, N.Y., 276
West Springfield, Mass., 249
West Swanzey, N.H., 268
West Terre Haute, Ind., 227
West Torrens, S. Austral., 94
West Trenton, N. J., 273
West Union, Iowa, 229
West University Place, Tex., 302
West Vancouver, B.C., 184
West View, Pa., 294
Westville, Ill., 222
Westville, N. J., 273
Westville, N.S., 169
West Virginia (state), U.S., 313
West Warwick, R.I., 249
Westwego, La., 238
West Wenatchee, Wash., 310
Westwood, Calif., 204
Westwood, Ky., 237
Westwood, N. J., 273
Westwood Lakes, Fla., 212
Westworth, Tex., 302
West Wyalong, N.S.W., 97
West York, Pa., 294
Wetar (isl.), Indon., 85
Wetaskiwin, Alta., 182
Wete, Tanz., 115
Wethersfield, Conn., 210
Wetteren, Belg., 27
Wetterhorn (mt.), Switz., 39
Wettingen, Switz., 39
Wetumpka, Ala., 194
Wetzikon, Switz., 39
Wetzlar, W. Ger., 22
Wewak, Terr. N.G., 85
Wewoka, Okla., 288
Wexford (county), Ire., 17
Wexford, Ire., 17
Weyburn, Sask., 181
Weymouth, Mass., 249
Weymouth and Melcombe Regis, Eng., 13
Whaleback (mt.), W. Austral., 92
Whaley Bridge, Eng., 10
Whalsay (isl.), Scot., 15
Whangarei, N.Z., 101
Wharfe (riv.), Eng., 13
Wharton, N. J., 273
Wharton, Tex., 302
Wheatland, Wyo., 319
Wheaton, Ill., 222
Wheaton, Md., 245
Wheaton, Minn., 254
Wheat Ridge, Colo., 208
Wheeler (dam), Ala., 194
Wheeler (peak), Nev., 266
Wheeler (peak), N. Mex., 274
Wheeler A.F.B., Hawaii, 218
Wheelersburg, Ohio, 284
Wheeling, Ill., 222
Wheeling, W. Va., 313
Whidbey Isl. N.A.S., Wash., 310
Whippany, N. J., 273
Whiskeytown-Shasta-Trinity Nat'l Rec. Area, Calif., 204
Whitburn, Scot., 15
Whitby, Eng., 13
Whitby, Ont., 177
Whitcombe (mt.), N.Z., 101
White (riv.), Ind., 227
White (lake), La., 238
White (bay), Newf., 166
White (mts.), N.H., 268
White (isl.), N.Z., 101
White (sea), U.S.S.R., 52
White (riv.), U.S., 203, 261
White (riv.), Vt., 268
White Bear (res.), Newf., 166
White Bear Lake, Minn., 254
White Carpathians (mts.), Czech., 41
White Center, Wash., 310
Whitecourt, Alta., 182
White Elster (riv.), E. Ger., 22
Whitefish (bay), Mich., 250
Whitefish, Mont., 262
Whitefish Bay, Wis., 317
White Hall, Ill., 222
Whitehall, Mich., 250
Whitehall, N.Y., 276
Whitehall, Ohio, 284
Whitehall, Pa., 294
Whitehaven, Eng., 13
Whitehaven, Tenn., 237
Whitehead, N. Ire., 17
Whitehorse (cap.), Yukon, 187
Whiteman A.F.B., Mo., 261
White Nile (riv.), Africa, 111
White Oak, Pa., 294
White Plains, N.Y., 276
White River Jct., Vt., 268
White Rock, Br. Col., 184
White Russian S.S.R., U.S.S.R., 52
White Sands Missle Range, N. Mex., 274
White Sands Nat'l Mon., N. Mex., 274
Whitesboro, N.Y., 276
White Settlement, Tex., 302
White Sulphur Springs, Mont., 262
White Sulphur Springs, W. Va., 313
Whiteville, N.C., 281
White Volta (riv.), Africa, 106
Whitewater (lake), Man., 179
Whitewater, Wis., 317
Whiting, Ind., 227
Whitinsville, Mass., 249
Whitley Bay, Eng., 13
Whitman, Mass., 249
Whitman Mission Nat'l Hist. Site, Wash., 310
Whitmire, S.C., 296
Whitney (mt.), Calif., 204
Whitney, S.C., 296
Whitneyville, Conn., 210
Whitstable, Eng., 13
Whitsunday (isl.), Queensland, 95
Whittier, Alaska, 196
Whittier, Calif., 204
Wholdaia (lake), N.W.T., 187
Whonnock, Br. Col., 184
Whyalla, S. Austral., 94
Wichita, Kans., 232
Wichita (mts.), Okla., 288
Wichita Falls, Tex., 302
Wick, Scot., 15
Wickenburg, Ariz., 198
Wickham (cape), Tas., 99
Wickiup (res.), Oreg., 291
Wickliffe, Ohio, 284
Wicklow (county), Ire., 17
Wicklow, Ire., 17
Wicklow (mts.), Ire., 17
Wicomico (riv.), Md., 245

Widnes, Eng., 10
Wieliczka, Poland, 47
Wieluń, Poland, 47
Wien (Vienna) (cap.), Austria, 41
Wiener Neustadt, Austria, 41
Wieringermeer Polder, Neth., 27
Wiesbaden, W. Ger., 22
Wigan, Eng., 10
Wight (isl.), Eng., 13
Wight, Isle of (county), Eng., 13
Wigston, Eng., 13
Wigtown (county), Scot., 15
Wigtown (bay), Scot., 15
Wil, Switz., 39
Wilcannia, N.S.W., 97
Wildhorn (mt.), Switz., 39
Wildspitze (mt.), Austria, 41
Wildwood, N. J., 273
Wildwood Crest, N. J., 273
Wilhelm II Coast (reg.), Ant., 5
Wilhelmina (canal), Neth., 27
Wilhelmina (mts.), Sur., 131
Wilhelm-Pieck-Stadt, E. Ger., 22
Wilhelmshaven, W. Ger., 22
Wilkes-Barre, Pa., 294
Wilkes Land (reg.), Ant., 5
Wilkie, Sask., 181
Wilkinsburg, Pa., 294
Willamette (riv.), Oreg., 291
Willard, Ohio, 284
Willcox, Ariz., 198
Willebroek, Belg., 27
Willems (canal), Neth., 27
Willemstad (cap.), Neth. Ant., 161
William (riv.), Sask., 181
William H. Taft Nat'l Hist. Site, Ohio, 284
Williams, Ariz., 198
Williams A.F.B., Ariz., 198
Williamsburg, Ky., 237
Williamsburg, Va., 307
Williams Lake, Br. Col., 184
Williamson, W. Va., 313
Williamsport, Pa., 294
Williamston, N.C., 281
Williamston, S.C., 296
Williamstown, Mass., 249
Williamstown, N. J., 273
Williamstown, Vic., 97
Williamstown, W. Va., 313
Williamsville, N.Y., 276
Willikies, Antigua, 161
Willimantic, Conn., 210
Willingboro, N. J., 273
Williston, N. Dak., 283
Williston, S.C., 296
Williston Park, N.Y., 276
Willits, Calif., 204
Willmar, Minn., 254
Willoughby, N.S.W., 97
Willoughby, Ohio, 284
Willoughby (lake), Vt., 268
Willoughby Hills, Ohio, 284
Willow Bunch, Sask., 181
Willow Grove, Pa., 294
Willowick, Ohio, 284
Willows, Calif., 204
Wilmerding, Pa., 294
Wilmette, Ill., 222
Wilmington, Calif., 204
Wilmington, Del., 245
Wilmington, Ill., 222
Wilmington, N.C., 281
Wilmington, Ohio, 284
Wilmore, Ky., 237
Wilmslow, Eng., 10
Wilson (mt.), Calif., 204
Wilson, Conn., 210
Wilson, N.C., 281
Wilson, Pa., 294
Wilsons (prom.), Vic., 97
Wilson's Creek Nat'l Battlef. Park, Mo., 261
Wilton, Conn., 210
Wilton Manors, Fla., 212
Wiltshire (county), Eng., 13
Wiltz, Lux., 27
Wimbledon, Eng., 10
Wimmera (riv.), Vic., 97
Winchelsea, Vic., 97
Winchendon, Mass., 249
Winchester, Eng., 13
Winchester, Ind., 227
Winchester, Ky., 237
Winchester, Mass., 249
Winchester, Nev., 266
Winchester, Tenn., 237
Winchester, Va., 307
Windber, Pa., 294
Wind Cave Nat'l Park, S. Dak., 298
Winder, Ga., 216
Windham, Conn., 210
Windham, Ohio, 284
Windhoek (cap.), S.W. Afr., 118
Windisch, Switz., 39
Windom, Minn., 254
Window Rock, Ariz., 198
Wind River (range), Wyo., 319
Windsor, Conn., 210
Windsor (New Windsor), Eng., 13
Windsor, Mo., 261
Windsor, Newf., 166
Windsor, N.S.W., 97
Windsor, N.S., 169
Windsor, Ont., 177
Windsor, Que., 172
Windsor, Queensland, 95
Windsor, Vt., 268
Windsor Hts., Iowa, 229
Windward (isls.), W. Indies, 156
Windward (passage), W. Indies, 156
Winefred (lake), Alta., 182
Winfield, Ala., 194
Winfield, Kans., 232
Winfield, N. J., 273
Wingham, N.S.W., 97
Wingham, Ont., 177
Winisk (riv.), Ont., 177
Winkelman, Ariz., 198
Winkler, Man., 179
Winneba, Ghana, 106
Winnebago (lake), Wis., 317
Winnemucca, Nev., 266
Winnemucca (lake), Nev., 266
Winner, S. Dak., 298
Winnetka, Ill., 222
Winnfield, La., 238
Winnibigoshish (lake), Minn., 254
Winnipeg (cap.), Man., 179
Winnipeg (lake), Man., 179
Winnipegosis, Man., 179
Winnipegosis (lake), Man., 179
Winnipesaukee (lake), N.H., 268
Winnsboro, La., 238
Winnsboro, S.C., 296
Winnsboro, Tex., 302
Winona, Minn., 254
Winona, Miss., 256
Winooski, Vt., 268
Winooski (riv.), Vt., 268
Winschoten, Neth., 27
Winsford, Eng., 10
Winslow, Ariz., 198
Winslow, Maine, 242
Winsted, Conn., 210
Winston-Salem, N.C., 281
Winter Garden, Fla., 212
Winter Haven, Fla., 212
Winter Isl. C.G. Air Sta., Mass., 249
Winter Park, Fla., 212
Winters, Tex., 302
Winterset, Iowa, 229
Wintersville, Ohio, 284
Winterswijk, Neth., 27
Winterthur, Switz., 39
Winthrop, Mass., 249
Winthrop Harbour, Ill., 222
Winton, N.Z., 101
Winton, Pa., 294
Winton, Queensland, 95
Winyah (bay), S.C., 296
Wirral, Eng., 10
Wisbech, Eng., 13
Wisconsin (state), U.S., 317
Wisconsin (riv.), Wis., 317
Wisconsin Dells, Wis., 317
Wisconsin Rapids, Wis., 317
Wise, Va., 307
Wisła (Vistula)(riv.), Poland, 47
Wismar, E. Ger., 22
Witbank, S. Afr., 118
Witham (riv.), Eng., 13
Withamsville, Ohio, 284
Withlacoochee (riv.), Fla., 212
Witten, W. Ger., 22
Wittenberg, E. Ger., 22
Wittenberge, E. Ger., 22
Wittenoom Gorge, W. Austral., 92
Witu, Kenya, 115
Witvlei, S.W. Afr., 118
Witwatersrand (reg.), S. Afr., 118
Włocławek, Poland, 47
Woburn, Mass., 249
Wodonga, Vic., 97
Woerden, Neth., 27
Wohlen, Switz., 39
Woking, Eng., 10
Wokingham, Eng., 13
Woleai (atoll), Pac. Is., 87
Wolf (riv.), Tenn., 237
Wolfenbüttel, W. Ger., 22
Wolf Lake, Mich., 250
Wolf Point, Mont., 262
Wolfsberg, Austria, 41
Wolfsburg, W. Ger., 22
Wolfville, N.S., 169
Wolgast, E. Ger., 22
Wolin (isl.), Poland, 47
Wollaston (isl.), Chile, 138
Wollaston (lake), Sask., 181
Wollongong, N.S.W., 97
Wolmaransstad, S. Afr., 118
Wołomin, Poland, 47
Wolseley, Sask., 181
Wolstenholme (cape), Que., 174
Woluwe-Saint-Lambert, Belg., 27
Woluwe-Saint-Pierre, Belg., 27
Wolverhampton, Eng., 10
Wolverton, Eng., 13
Wombwell, Eng., 13
Wŏnju, S. Korea, 81
Wonogiri, Indon., 85
Wonosobo, Indon., 85
Wŏnsan, N. Korea, 81
Wonthaggi, Vic., 97
Woodall (mt.), Miss., 256
Woodbine, N. J., 273
Woodbridge, N. J., 273
Wood Buffalo Nat'l Park, Canada, 182, 187
Woodburn, Oreg., 291
Woodbury, Conn., 210
Woodbury, N. J., 273
Woodcliff Lake, N. J., 273
Wood Dale, Ill., 222
Woodend, Vic., 97
Woodlake, Calif., 204
Woodland, Calif., 204
Woodland Hills, Calif., 204
Woodlands, Sing., 72
Woodlark (isl.), Papua, 85
Woodlawn, Md., 245
Woodlawn, Ohio, 284
Woodlyn, Pa., 294
Wood-Lynne, N. J., 273
Woodmere, N.Y., 276
Woodmont, Conn., 210
Woodridge Ill., 222
Wood-Ridge, N. J., 273
Wood River, Ill., 222
Woodroffe (mt.), S. Austral., 94
Woodruff, S.C., 296
Woods, Lake of the (lake), N. Amer., 179, 254
Woods (lake), N. Terr., 93
Woodsfield, Ohio, 284
Woods Hole, Mass., 249
Woodside, Calif., 204
Woodson Terr., Mo., 261
Woodstock, Ill., 222
Woodstock, N.B., 170
Woodstock, Ont., 177
Woodstock, Vt., 268
Woodstown, N. J., 273
Woodville, N.Z., 101
Woodville, Pa., 294
Woodville, S. Austral., 94
Woodward, Okla., 288
Woody Point, Newf., 166
Woolgoolga, N.S.W., 97
Woollahra, N.S.W., 97
Woomera, S. Austral., 94
Woonsocket, R.I., 249
Woonsocket, S. Dak., 298
Wooramel (riv.), W. Austral., 92
Wooster, Ohio, 284
Worb, Switz., 39
Worcester, Eng., 13
Worcester, Mass., 249
Worcester, S. Afr., 118
Worcestershire (county), Eng., 13
Wörgl, Austria, 41
Workington, Eng., 13
Worksop, Eng., 13
Worland, Wyo., 319
Wormerveer, Neth., 27
Worms, W. Ger., 22
Worth, Ill., 222
Worth (lake), Tex., 302
Worthing, Eng., 13
Worthington, Minn., 254
Worthington, Ohio, 284
Wotje (atoll), Pac. Is., 87
Wounded Knee (creek), S. Dak., 298
Woy Woy-Ettalong, N.S.W., 97
Wrangel (isl.), U.S.S.R., 48
Wrangell, Alaska, 196
Wrangell (mts.), Alaska, 196
Wrath (cape), Scot., 15
Wray, Colo., 208
Wrexham, Wales, 13
Wright Bros. Nat'l Mon., N.C., 281
Wrightstown, N. J., 273
Wrigley, N.W.T., 187
Wrocław (prov.), Poland, 47
Wrocław, Poland, 47
Września, Poland, 47
Wuchang, China, 77
Wuchow, China, 77
Wuchung, China, 77
Wuhan, China, 77
Wuhing, China, 77
Wuhu, China, 77
Wukari, Nigeria, 106
Wu Kiang (riv.), China, 77
Wum, Cameroon, 115
Wundowie, W. Austral., 92
Wunstorf, W. Ger., 22
Wupatki Nat'l Mon., Ariz., 198
Wuppertal, W. Ger., 22
Würmsee (Starnbergersee) (lake), W. Ger., 22
Wurtsmith A.F.B., Mich., 250
Würzburg, W. Ger., 22
Wurzen, E. Ger., 22
Wusih, China, 77
Wusu, China, 77
Wuwei, China, 77
Wuyi Shan (range), China, 77
Wuyüan, China, 77
Wyandotte, Mich., 250
Wyangala (res.), N.S.W., 97
Wyckoff, N. J., 273
Wye (riv.), U.K., 13
Wyndham, N.Z., 101
Wyndham, W. Austral., 92
Wynne, Ark., 203
Wynnewood, Okla., 288
Wynnewood, Pa., 294
Wynnum, Queensland, 95
Wynyard, Sask., 181
Wynyard, Tas., 99
Wyoming, Mich., 250
Wyoming, Ohio, 284
Wyoming, Pa., 294
Wyoming (state), U.S., 319
Wyoming (range), Wyo., 319
Wyomissing, Pa., 294
Wyong, N.S.W., 97
Wytheville, Va., 307

X

Xánthi, Greece, 45
Xarrama (riv.), Port., 33
Xenia, Ohio, 284
Xicoténcatl, Mex., 150
Xicotepec, Mex., 150
Xieng Khouang, Laos, 72
Xingu (riv.), Braz., 132
Xique-Xique, Braz., 132
Xochihuehuetlán, Mex., 150
Xochimilco, Mex., 150
Xochitlán, Mex., 150

Yaan, China, 77
Ya'bad, Jordan, 65
Yablonovyy (range), U.S.S.R., 48
Yabucoa, P. Rico, 161
Yacaré (riv.), Par., 144
Yacuiba, Bol., 136
Yacuma (riv.), Bol., 136
Yaeyama (isls.), Ryukyu Is., 81
Yaguajay, Cuba, 158
Yaguarón, Par., 144
Yaguarón (riv.), Urug., 145
Yaguas (riv.), Peru, 128
Yaizu, Japan, 81
Yajalón, Mex., 150
Yakima, Wash., 310
Yakima (riv.), Wash., 310
Yako, Upp. Volta, 106
Yaku (isl.), Japan, 81
Yakut A.S.S.R., U.S.S.R., 48
Yakutat, Alaska, 196
Yakutsk, U.S.S.R., 48
Yala, Thai., 72
Yalesville, Conn., 210
Yalinga, Cent. Afr. Rep., 115
Yallourn, Vic., 97
Yalova, Turkey, 63
Yalta, U.S.S.R., 52
Yalu (riv.), Asia, 81
Yalung Kiang (riv.), China, 77
Yamagata (prefecture), Japan, 81
Yamagata, Japan, 81
Yamaguchi (prefecture), Japan, 81
Yamaguchi, Japan, 81
Yamal (pen.), U.S.S.R., 48
Yamal-Nenets Nat'l Okrug, U.S.S.R., 48
Yamama, Saudi Ar., 59
Yamanashi (prefecture), Japan, 81
Yamantau (mt.), U.S.S.R., 52
Yamaska (riv.), Que., 172
Yambio, Sudan, 111
Yambol, Bulg., 45
Yamdrok Tso (lake), China, 77
Yamethin, Burma, 72
Yampa (riv.), Colo., 208
Yampi Sound, W. Austral., 92
Yamun, Jordan, 65
Yana (riv.), U.S.S.R., 48
Yanam, India, 68
Yandoon, Burma, 72
Yangambi, Dem. Rep .of the Congo, 115
Yangchow, China, 77
Yangchüan, China, 77
Yangdŏk, N. Korea, 81
Yangi Hissar, China, 77
Yangtze Kiang (riv.), China, 77
Yangyang, S. Korea, 81
Yankton, S. Dak., 298
Yao, Japan, 81
Yaoundé (cap.), Cameroon, 115
Yap (isl.), Pac. Is., 87
Yaqui, Mex., 150
Yara, Cuba, 158
Yaracuy, Venez., 124
Yare (riv.), Eng., 13
Yarí (riv.), Col., 126
Yarim, Yemen Arab Rep., 59
Yaritagua, Venez., 124
Yarkand, China, 77
Yarkand (riv.), China, 77
Yarmouth, Maine, 242
Yarmouth, Mass., 249
Yarmouth, N.S., 169
Yarmuk (riv.), Asia, 65
Yaroslavl', U.S.S.R., 52
Yarra (riv.), Vic., 97
Yarram, Vic., 97
Yarrawonga, Vic., 97
Yartsevo, U.S.S.R., 52
Yarumal, Col., 126
Yas (isl.), Tr. States, 59
Yásica Abajo, Dom. Rep., 158
Yasothon, Thai., 72
Yass, N.S.W., 97
Yataity, Par., 144
Yathkyed (lake), N.W.T., 187
Yatsushiro, Japan, 81
Yatta, Jordan, 65
Yatung, China, 77
Yauco, P. Rico, 161
Yautepec, Mex., 150
Yavarí (riv.), Peru, 128
Yavero (riv.), Peru, 128
Yavne, Israel, 65
Yawatahama, Japan, 81
Yazoo (riv.), Miss., 256
Yazoo City, Miss., 256
Ybycuí, Par., 144
Ybytimí, Par., 144
Yding Skovhøj (mt.), Den., 21
Ye, Burma, 72
Yea, Vic., 97
Yeadon, Pa., 294
Yecla, Spain, 33
Yefremov, U.S.S.R., 52
Yegor'yevsk, U.S.S.R., 52
Yegros, Par., 144
Yeguas (pt.), P. Rico, 161
Yehsien, China, 77
Yehud, Israel, 65
Yei, Sudan, 111
Yelets, U.S.S.R., 52
Yelimané, Mali, 106
Yelizaveta (cape), U.S.S.R., 48
Yell (isl.), Scot., 15
Yellow (sea), Asia, 77
Yellow (Hwang Ho)(riv.), China, 77
Yellowknife (cap.), N.W.T., 187
Yellowknife (riv.), N.W.T., 187
Yellow Sprs., Ohio, 284
Yellowstone (riv.), U.S., 262, 283, 319
Yellowstone (lake), Wyo., 319
Yellowstone Nat'l Park, U.S., 319
Yelwa, Nigeria, 106
Yemen Arab Republic, 59
Yemen, Peoples Democratic Republic of, 59
Yenakiyevo, U.S.S.R., 52
Yenan, China, 77
Yenangyaung, Burma, 72
Yen Bai, N. Vietnam, 72
Yenbo, Saudi Ar., 59
Yendi, Ghana, 106
Yeniköy, Turkey, 63
Yenimahalle, Turkey, 63
Yenişehir, Turkey, 63
Yenisey (riv.), U.S.S.R., 48
Yeniseysk, U.S.S.R., 48
Yenki, China, 77
Yenyüan, China, 77
Yeo (lake), W. Austral., 92
Yeola, India, 68
Yeotmal, India, 68
Yeovil, Eng., 13
Yeppoon, Queensland, 95
Yerington, Nev., 266
Yeronga, Queensland, 95
Yesagyo, Burma, 72
Yeshbum, P.D.R. Yemen, 59
Yesilırmak (riv.), Turkey, 63
Yeşilköy, Turkey, 63
Yessentuki, U.S.S.R., 52
Yesuj, Iran, 66
Yeu (isl.), France, 28
Yevpatoria, U.S.S.R., 52
Yeysk, U.S.S.R., 52
Yezd, Iran, 66
Yezd (reg.), Iran, 66
Yhú, Par., 144
Yí (riv.), Urug., 145
Yialousa, Cyprus, 63
Yiannitsá, Greece, 45
Yinchwan, China, 77
Yingkow, China, 77
Yirga Alam, Eth., 111
Yirol, Sudan, 111
Yiyang, China, 77
Ylikitka (lake), Fin., 18
Yoakum, Tex., 302
Yodo (riv.), Japan, 81
Yog (pt.), Phil. Is., 82
Yoho Nat'l Park, Br. Col., 184
Yojoa (lake), Hond., 154
Yokkaichi, Japan, 81
Yokohama, Japan, 81
Yokosuka, Japan, 81
Yokote, Japan, 81
Yola, Nigeria, 106
Yonago, Japan, 81
Yonaguni (isl.), Ryukyu Is., 81
Yonezawa, Japan, 81
Yongamp'o, N. Korea, 81
Yŏngch'ŏn, S. Korea, 81
Yŏngdŏk, S. Korea, 81
Yŏngju, S. Korea, 81
Yonkers, N.Y., 276
Yonne (dept.), France, 28
Yonne (riv.), France, 28
York, Ala., 194
York, Eng., 13
York (cape), Greenl., 4
York, Nebr., 264
York, Ont., 177
York, Pa., 294
York (cape), Queensland, 95
York, S.C., 296
York (riv.), Va., 307
York, W. Austral., 92
Yorke (pen.), S. Austral., 94
York Landing, Man., 179
Yorkshire-East Riding (county), Eng., 13
Yorkshire-North Riding (county), Eng., 13
Yorkshire-West Riding (county), Eng., 13
Yorkton, Sask., 181
Yorktown, N.Y., 276
Yorktown, Tex., 302
Yorktown, Va., 307
Yorkville, N.Y., 276
Yoro, Hond., 154
Yoron (isl.), Japan, 81
Yosemite Nat'l Park, Calif., 204
Yoshino (riv.), Japan, 81
Yoshkar-Ola, U.S.S.R., 52
Yŏsu, S. Korea, 81
Yotala, Bol., 136
Youghal, Ire., 17
Youghal (bay), Ire., 17
Youghiogheny (riv.), U.S., 245, 294
Young, N.S.W., 97
Young, Urug., 145
Youngstown, Ohio, 284
Youngtown, Ariz., 198
Youngwood, Pa., 294
Yousouffia, Mor., 106
Yozgat (prov.), Turkey, 63
Yozgat, Turkey, 63
Ypacaraí, Par., 144
Ypané, Par., 144
Ypoá (lake), Par., 144
Ypres (Ieper), Belg., 27
Ypsilanti, Mich., 250
Yreka, Calif., 204
Yser (riv.), Belg., 27
Ystad, Sweden, 18
Yüan Kiang (riv.), China, 77
Yüanling, China, 77
Yuba City, Calif., 204
Yubari, Japan, 81
Yucaipa, Calif., 204
Yucatán (state), Mex., 150
Yucatán (pen.), Mex., 150
Yucatán (chan.), N. Amer., 156
Yucca Flat (basin), Nev., 266
Yucca House Nat'l Mon., Colo., 208
Yuendumu, N. Terr., 93
Yugodzyr, Mong., 77
Yugorskiy (pen.), U.S.S.R., 52
Yugoslavia, 45
Yühsien, China, 77
Yühwan (isl.), China, 77
Yü Kiang (riv.), China, 77
Yukon (terr.), Canada, 187
Yukon (riv.), N. Amer., 187, 196
Yukon, Okla., 288
Yule (riv.), W. Austral., 92
Yülin, China, 77
Yuma, Ariz., 198
Yuma (riv.), Dom. Rep., 158
Yuma Marine Corps Air Sta., Ariz., 198
Yuma Proving Ground, Ariz., 198
Yümen, China, 77
Yungan, China, 77
Yungas, Las (dist.), Bol., 136
Yungkia (Wenchow), China, 77
Yungteng, China, 77
Yünhsien, China, 77
Yünnan (prov.), China, 77
Yurimaguas, Peru, 128
Yur'yevets, U.S.S.R., 52
Yuscarán, Hond., 154
Yüshashan, China, 77
Yütze, China, 77
Yuty, Par., 144
Yuzhno-Sakhalinsk, U.S.S.R., 48
Yverdon, Switz., 39
Yvelines (dept.), France, 28

Z

Zaachila, Mex., 150
Zaandam, Neth., 27
Zabid, Yemen Arab Rep., 59
Ząbkowice Śląskie, Poland, 47
Zabrze, Poland, 47
Zabul, Iran, 66
Zacapa, Guat., 154
Zacapoaxtla, Mex., 150
Zacapu, Mex., 150
Zacatecas (state), Mex., 150
Zacatecas, Mex., 150
Zacatecoluca, El Sal., 154
Zacatepec, Mex., 150
Zacatlán, Mex., 150
Zachary, La., 238
Zacoalco, Mex., 150
Zadar, Yugo., 45
Zafra, Spain, 33
Żagán, Poland, 47
Zagazig, U.A.R., 111
Zagora, Mor., 106
Zagorsk, U.S.S.R., 52
Zagreb, Yugo., 45
Zagros (range), Iran, 66
Zahidan, Iran, 66
Zahle, Leb., 63
Zaire (dist.), Angola, 115
Zaječar, Yugo., 45
Zákinthos, Greece, 45
Zákinthos (Zante) (isl.), Greece, 45
Zakopane, Poland, 47
Zala (county), Hung., 41
Zalaegerszeg, Hung., 41
Zalamea, Spain, 33
Zălău, Rum., 45
Zalingei, Sudan, 111
Zambales (prov.), Phil. Is., 82
Zambezi (riv.), Africa, 118
Zambézia (dist.), Mozamb., 118
Zambia, 115
Zamboanga, Phil. Is., 82
Zamboanga del Norte (prov.), Phil. Is., 82
Zamboanga del Sur (prov.), Phil. Is., 82
Zambrów, Poland, 47
Zamora, Ecua., 128
Zamora, Mex., 150
Zamora (prov.), Spain, 33
Zamora, Spain, 33
Zamora-Chinchipe (prov.), Ecua., 128
Zamość, Poland, 47
Zanaga, Rep. of Congo, 115
Zandvoort, Neth., 27
Zanesville, Ohio, 284
Zanzibar (prov.), Tanz., 115
Zanzibar, Tanz., 115
Zanzibar (isl.), Tanz., 115
Zao (mt.), Japan, 81
Zaouiet-el-Kahla, Alg., 106
Západočeský (reg.), Czech., 41
Západoslovenský (reg.), Czech., 41
Zapala, Arg., 143
Zapaleri (mt.), S. Amer., 136
Zapata (pen.), Cuba, 158
Zapatera (isl.), Nic., 154
Zapatoca, Col., 126
Zaporozh'ye, U.S.S.R., 52
Zara, Turkey, 63
Zara (Zadar), Yugo., 45
Zaragoza, Mex., 150
Zaragoza (Saragossa), Spain, 33
Zarand, Iran, 66
Zárate, Arg., 143
Zaraza, Venez., 124
Zaria, Nigeria, 106
Zarqa' (riv.), Jordan, 65
Zaruma, Ecua., 128
Żary, Poland, 47
Zarzal, Col., 126
Zarzis, Tun., 106
Zaskar (mts.), India, 68
Žatec, Czech., 41
Zavitinsk, U.S.S.R., 48
Zawia (prov.), Libya, 111
Zawia, Libya, 111
Zawiercie, Poland, 47
Zaysan (lake), U.S.S.R., 48
Zaza del Medio, Cuba, 158
Zduńska Wola, Poland, 47
Zealand (Sjælland)(isl.), Den., 21
Zebak, Afghan., 68
Zebdani, Syria, 63
Zeehan, Tas., 99
Zeeland, Mich., 250
Zeeland (prov.), Neth., 27
Zeerust, S. Africa, 118
Zefat, Israel, 65
Zegharta, Leb., 63
Zehdenick, E. Ger., 22
Zeila, Somalia, 115
Zeist, Neth., 27
Zeitz, E. Ger., 22
Zele, Belg., 27
Zelenodol'sk, U.S.S.R., 52
Zelienople, Pa., 294
Zell, Austria, 41
Zella, Libya, 111
Zella-Mehlis, E. Ger., 22
Zellersee (lake), Switz., 39
Zelten, Jebel (mts.), Libya, 111
Zelzate, Belg., 27
Zémio, Centr. Afr. Rep., 115
Zenica, Yugo., 45
Zenjan, Iran, 66
Zephyrhills, Fla., 212
Zerbst, E. Ger., 22
Zermatt, Switz., 39
Zetland (county), Scot., 15
Zeulenroda, E. Ger., 22
Zeytinburnu, Turkey, 63
Zgierz, Poland, 47
Zgorzelec, Poland, 47
Zhdanov, U.S.S.R., 52
Zhelaniye (cape), U.S.S.R., 48
Zhigulevsk, U.S.S.R., 52
Zhitomir, U.S.S.R., 52
Zhmerinka, U.S.S.R., 52
Zhob (riv.), Pak., 68
Zhodino, U.S.S.R., 52
Ziębice, Poland, 47
Zielona Góra (prov.), Poland, 47
Zielona Góra, Poland, 47
Zifta, U.A.R., 111
Ziguei, Chad, 111
Ziguinchor, Sen., 106
Zile, Turkey, 63
Žilina, Czech., 41
Zilling Tso (lake), China, 77
Zima, U.S.S.R., 48
Zimatlán de Álvarez, Mex., 150
Zimbabwe Nat'l Park, Rhod., 118
Zimnicea, Rum., 45
Zinder, Niger, 106
Zinjibar, P.D.R. Yemen, 59
Zion, Ill., 222
Zion Nat'l Park, Utah, 304
Zipaquirá, Col., 126
Zirko (isl.), Tr. States, 59
Zirndorf, W. Ger., 22
Zitácuaro, Mex., 150
Zittau, E. Ger., 22
Zıvarık, Turkey, 63
Ziz, Wadi (dry riv.), Mor., 106
Zlatoust, U.S.S.R., 48
Zlín (Gottwaldov), Czech., 41
Zliten, Libya, 111
Znamenka, U.S.S.R., 52
Znojmo, Czech., 41
Zollikofen, Switz., 39
Zolotonosha, U.S.S.R., 52
Zomba (cap.), Malawi, 115
Zonderend (riv.), S. Africa, 118
Zonguldak (prov.), Turkey, 63
Zonguldak, Turkey, 63
Zonhoven, Belg., 27
Zouar, Chad, 111
Zrenjanin, Yugo., 45
Zuarungu, Ghana, 106
Zudáñez, Bol., 136
Zug (canton), Switz., 39
Zug, Switz., 39
Zug (lake), Switz., 39
Zugdidi, U.S.S.R., 52
Zugspitze (mt.), Europe, 22
Zula, Eth., 111
Zulia (state), Venez., 124
Zulueta, Cuba, 158
Zululand (reg.), S. Africa, 118
Zumbo, Mozamb., 118
Zumpango, Mex., 150
Zuni, N. Mex., 274
Zuni (riv.), U.S., 198, 274
Zuqar (isl.), Yemen Arab Rep., 59
Zürich (canton), Switz., 39
Zürich, Switz., 39
Zürich (lake), Switz., 39
Zutphen, Neth., 27
Zvolen, Czech., 41
Zwara, Libya, 111
Zweibrücken, W. Ger., 22
Zweisimmen, Switz., 39
Zwickau, E. Ger., 22
Zwijndrecht, Neth., 27
Zwischenahn, W. Ger., 22
Zwolle, Neth., 27
Żyrardów, Poland, 47
Żywiec, Poland, 47

GEOGRAPHICAL TERMS

A. = Arabic Camb. = Cambodian Ch. = Chinese Czech. = Czechoslovakian Dan. = Danish Du. = Dutch Finn. = Finnish Fr. = French Ger. = German Ice. = Icelandic
It. = Italian Jap. = Japanese Mong. = Mongol Nor. = Norwegian Per. = Persian Port. = Portuguese Russ. = Russian Sp. = Spanish Sw. = Swedish Turk. = Turkish

Å	Nor., Sw.	Stream
Aas	Dan., Nor.	Hills
Abajo	Sp.	Lower
Ada, Adasi	Turk.	Island
Altipiano	It.	Plateau
Altiplano	Sp.	Plateau
Alv, Alf, Elf	Sw.	River
Arrecife	Sp.	Reef
Asa	Nor., Sw.	Hill
Asaga	Turk.	Lower
Austral	Sp.	Southern
Baai	Du.	Bay
Bab	Arabic	Gate or Strait
Bahia	Sp.	Bay
Bahr	Arabic	Marsh, Lake, Sea, River
Baia	Port.	Bay
Baie	Fr.	Bay, Gulf
Baizo	Port.	Low
Bakke	Dan.	Hill
Bana	Jap.	Cape
Bañados	Sp.	Marshes
Band	Per.	Mt. Range
Barra	Sp.	Reef
Bel	Turk.	Pass
Belt	Ger.	Strait
Ben	Gaelic	Mountain
Bera	Du.	Mountain
Berg	Ger., Du.	Mountain
Bir	Arabic	Well
Birket	Arabic	Pond
Boca	Sp.	Gulf, Inlet
Boğhaz	Turk.	Strait
Bolshoi, Bolshaya	Russ.	Big
Bolson	Sp.	Depression
Bong	Korean	Mountain
Boreal	Sp.	Northern
Breen	Nor.	Glacier
Bro	Dan., Nor., Sw.	Bridge
Bucht	Ger.	Bay
Bugt	Dan.	Bay
Bukhta	Russ.	Bay
Bukit	Malay	Hill, Mountain
Bukt	Nor., Sw.	Bay, Gulf
Burnu, Burun	Turk.	Cape, Point
By	Dan., Nor., Sw.	Town
Cabo	Port., Sp.	Cape
Campos	Port.	Plains
Canal	Port., Sp.	Channel
Cap, Capo	Fr., It.	Cape
Cataratas	Sp.	Falls
Catena	It.	Mt. Range
Catingas	Port.	Open Woodlands
Central, Centrale	Fr., It.	Middle
Cerrito, Cerro	Sp.	Hill
Cerros	Sp.	Hills, Mountains
Chai	Turk.	River
Chow	Ch.	Town of the second rank
Ciénaga	Sp.	Swamp
Ciudad	Sp.	City
Col	Fr.	Pass
Cordillera	Sp.	Mt. Range, Mts.
Côte	Fr.	Coast
Csatoria	Magyar	Canal
Cuchilla	Sp.	Mt. Range
Curiche	Sp.	Swamp
Dag, Dagh	Turk.	Mountain
Dağlari	Turk.	Mt. Range
Dal	Nor., Sw.	Valley
Dar	Arabic	Land
Darya	Per.	Salt Lake
Dasht	Per.	Desert, Plain
Deniz, Denizi	Turk.	Sea, Lake
Desierto	Sp.	Desert
Détroit	Fr.	Strait
Djeziret	Arabic, Turk.	Island
Do	Korean	Island
Doi	Thai	Mountain
Eiland	Du.	Island
Elv	Dan., Nor.	River
Embalse	Sp.	Reservoir
Emi	Berber	Mountain
Erg	Arabic	Dune, Desert
Eski	Turk.	Old
Est, Este	Fr., Port., Sp.	East
Estero	Sp.	Estuary, Creek
Estrecho, Estreito	Sp., Port.	Strait
Etang	Fr.	Pond, Lagoon, Lake
Fedja, Feij	Arabic	Pass
Fiume	It.	River
Fjäll	Sw.	Mountain
Fjeld, Fjell	Nor.	Hills, Mountain
Fjord	Dan., Nor., Sw.	Fiord
Fleuve	Fr.	River
Fljót	Icelandic	Stream
Fluss	Ger.	River
Fokani, Fukani	Arabic	Upper
Fors	Sw.	Waterfall
Fos, Foss	Dan., Nor.	Waterfall
Fu	Ch.	Town of importance
Gamla	Nor.	Old
Gamle	Dan.	Old
Gata	Jap.	Lake
Gawa	Jap.	River
Gebel	Arabic	Mountain
Gebergte	Du.	Mt. Range
Gebirge	Ger.	Mt. Range
Ghubbet	Arabic	Bay
Gobi	Mongol	Desert
Goe	Jap.	Pass
Gol	Mongol, Turk.	Lake, Stream
Golf	Ger., Du.	Gulf
Golfe	Fr.	Gulf
Golfo	Sp., It., Port.	Gulf
Gölü	Turk.	Lake
Gora	Russ.	Mountain
Grand, Grande	Fr., Sp.	Big
Groot	Du.	Big
Gross	Ger.	Big
Grosso	It., Port.	Big
Guba	Russ.	Bay, Gulf
Gunto	Jap.	Archipelago
Gunung	Malay	Mountain
Hai	Ch.	Sea
Halbinsel	Ger.	Peninsula
Hamáda, Hammada	Arabic	Rocky Plateau
Hamn	Sw.	Harbor
Hamún	Per.	Marsh
Hanto	Jap.	Peninsula
Has, Hassi	Arabic	Well
Hav	Dan., Nor., Sw.	Sea, Ocean
Havet	Nor.	Bay
Havn	Dan., Nor.	Harbor
Havre	Fr.	Harbor
Higashi, Higasi	Jap.	East
Ho	Ch.	River
Hochebene	Ger.	Plateau
Hoek	Du.	Cape
Hoku	Jap.	North
Holm	Dan., Nor., Sw.	Island
Hory	Czech	Mountains
Hoved	Dan., Nor.	Cape, Promontory
Hsien	Ch.	Town of the third class
Hu	Ch.	Lake
Huk	Dan., Nor., Sw.	Point
Hus, Huus	Dan., Nor., Sw.	House
Hwang	Ch.	Yellow
Ile	Fr.	Island
Ilet	Fr.	Islet
Ilot	Fr.	Islet
Indre	Dan., Nor.	Inner
Inferieur, Inferiore	Fr., It.	Lower
Inner, Inre	Sw.	Inner
Insel	Ger.	Island
Irmak	Turk.	River
Isla	Sp.	Island
Isola	It.	Island
Jabal, Jebel	Arabic	Mountains
Järvi	Finn.	Lake
Jaure	Sw.	Lake
Jezira	Arabic	Island
Jima	Jap.	Island
Joki	Finn.	River
Kaap	Du.	Cape
Kabir, Kebir	Arabic	Big
Kai	Jap.	Sea
Kaikyo	Jap.	Strait
Kami	Turk.	Upper
Kanaal	Du.	Canal
Kanal	Russ., Ger.	Canal, Channel
Kao	Thai	Mountain
Kap, Kapp	Nor., Sw., Ice.	Cape
Kaupunki	Finn.	Town
Kawa	Jap.	River
Khao	Thai	Mountain
Khrebet	Russ.	Mt. Range
Kiang	Ch.	River
Kiao	Ch.	Point
Kita	Jap.	North
Klein	Du., Ger.	Small
Klint	Dan.	Promontory
Kô	Jap.	Lake
Ko	Thai	Island
Koh	Camb., Khmer	Island
Kong	Ch.	River
Kop	Du.	Peak, Head
Köping	Sw.	Market, Borough
Körfez, Körfezi	Turk.	Gulf
Kosa	Russ.	Spit
Kosui	Jap.	Lake
Kraal	Du.	Native Village
Kuchuk	Turk.	Small
Kuh	Per.	Mountain
Kul	Sinkiang Turki	Lake
Kum	Turk.	Desert
Kuro	Jap.	Black
Laag	Du.	Low
Lac	Fr.	Lake
Lago	Port., Sp., It.	Lake
Lagoa	Port.	Lagoon
Laguna	Sp.	Lagoon
Lagune	Fr.	Lagoon
Lahti	Finn.	Bay, Bight
Län	Sw.	County
Lilla	Sw.	Small
Lille	Dan., Nor.	Small
Ling	Ch.	Mountain
Llanos	Sp.	Plains
Mae Nam	Thai	River
Mali, Malaya	Russ.	Small
Man	Korean	Bay
Mar	Sp., Port.	Sea
Mare	It.	Sea
Medio	Sp.	Middle
Meer	Du.	Lake
Meer	Ger.	Sea
Mer	Fr.	Sea
Meridionale	It.	Southern
Meseta	Sp.	Plateau
Middelst, Midden	Du.	Middle
Minami	Jap.	Southern
Mir	Per.	Mountain
Mis	Russ.	Cape
Misaki	Jap.	Cape
Mittel	Ger.	Middle
Mont	Fr.	Mountain
Montagne	Fr.	Mountain
Montaña	Sp.	Mountains
Monte	Sp., It., Port.	Mountain
More	Russ.	Sea
Morro	Port., Sp.	Mountain, Promontory
Morue	Fr.	Hill
Moyen	Fr.	Middle
Muong	Siamese	Town
Mys	Russ.	Cape
Nada	Jap.	Sea
Naka	Jap.	Middle
Nam	Burm., Lao.	River
Nan	Ch., Jap.	South
Nes	Nor.	Cape, Point
Nevado	Sp.	Snow covered peak
Nieder	Ger.	Lower
Nishi, Nisi	Jap.	West
Nizhni, Nizhnyaya	Russ.	Lower
Njarga	Finn.	Peninsula, Promontory
Nong	Thai	Lake
Noord	Du.	North
Nor	Mong.	Lake
Nord	Fr., Ger.	North
Norte	Sp., It., Port.	North
Nos	Russ.	Cape
Novi, Novaya	Russ.	New
Nusa	Malay	Island
Ny, Nya	Nor., Sw.	New
O	Jap.	Big
Ö	Nor., Sw.	Island
Ober	Ger.	Upper
Occidental, Occidentale	Sp., It.	Western
Odde	Dan.	Point
Oeste	Port.	West
Ola	Mong.	Mountains
Ooster	Du.	Eastern
Opper, Over	Du.	Upper
Oriental	Sp., Fr.	Eastern
Orientale	It.	Eastern
Orta	Turk.	Middle
Ost	Ger.	East
Ostrov	Russ.	Island
Ouest	Fr.	West
öy	Nor.	Island
Ozero	Russ.	Lake
Pampa	Sp.	Plain
Pas	Fr.	Channel, Strait
Paso	Sp.	Pass
Passo	It., Port.	Pass
Peh, Pei	Ch.	North
Peña	Sp.	Rock, Mountain
Penisola	It.	Peninsula
Pequeño	Sp.	Small
Pereval	Russ.	Pass
Peski	Russ.	Desert
Petit	Fr.	Small
Phu	Lao, Annamese	Mtn.
Pic	Fr.	Mountain
Piccolo	It.	Small
Pico	Port., Sp.	Mountain, Peak
Pik	Russ.	Mountain, Peak
Piton	Fr.	Mountain, Peak
Planalto	Port.	Plateau
Plato	Russ.	Plateau
Pointe	Fr.	Point
Poluostrov	Russ.	Peninsula
Ponta	Port.	Point
Presa	Sp.	Reservoir
Presqu'île	Fr.	Peninsula
Proliv	Russ.	Strait
Pulou, Pulo	Malay	Island
Punt	Du.	Point
Punta	Sp., It., Port.	Point
Qum	Turk.	Desert
Rada	Sp.	Inlet
Rade	Fr.	Bay, Inlet
Ras	Arabic	Cape
Reka	Russ.	River
Retto	Jap.	Archipelago
Ria	Sp.	Estuary
Río	Sp.	River
Rivier, Rivière	Du., Fr.	River
Rud	Per.	River
Saghir	Arabic	Small
Sai	Jap.	West
Saki	Jap.	Cape
Salar, Salina	Sp.	Salt Deposit
Salto	Sp., Port.	Falls
San	Ch., Jap., Korean	Hill
Sanmaek	Korean	Mt. Range
Schiereiland	Du.	Peninsula
Se	Camb., Khmer	River
See	Ger.	Sea, Lake
Selvas	Sp., Port.	Woods, Forest
Seno	Sp.	Bay, Gulf
Serra	Port.	Mts.
Serranía	Sp.	Mts.
Seto	Jap.	Strait
Settentrionale	It.	Northern
Severni, Severnaya	Russ.	North
Shan	Ch., Jap.	Hill, Mts.
Shang	Ch.	Upper
Shatt	Arabic	River
Shima	Jap.	Island
Shimo	Jap.	Lower
Shin	Jap.	Land
Shiro	Jap.	White
Shoto	Jap.	Islands
Si	Ch.	West
Siao	Ch.	Small
Sierra	Sp.	Mt. Range, Mts.
Sjö	Nor., Sw.	Lake, Sea
Sok, Suk, Souk	Arabic, Ar. Fr.	Market
Song	Annamese	River
Sopka	Russ.	Volcano
Spitze	Ger.	Mt. Peak
Sredni, Srednyaya	Russ.	Middle
Stad	Dan., Nor., Sw.	City
Stari, Staraya	Russ.	Old
Step	Russ.	Treeless Plain
Straat	Du.	Strait
Strasse	Ger.	Strait
Stretto	It.	Strait
Ström	Dan., Nor., Sw.	Sound
Stung	Camb., Khmer	River
Su	Turk.	River
Sud, Süd	Sp., Fr., Ger.	South
Suido	Jap.	Strait, Channel
Sul	Port.	South
Sund	Dan., Nor., Sw.	Sound
Sungei	Malay	River
Supérieur	Fr.	Upper
Superior, Superiore	Sp., It.	Upper
Sur	Sp.	South
Suyu	Turk.	River
Ta	Ch.	Big
Tafelland	Du.	Plateau
Tagh	Turk.	Mt. Range
Take	Jap.	Peak, Ridge
Takht	Arabic	Lower
Tal	Ger.	Valley
Tandjong, Tanjung	Malay	Cape, Point
Tao	Ch.	Island
Tell	Arabic	Hill
Thale	Thai	Sea, Lake
Tind	Nor.	Peak
Tö	Jap.	East
To	Jap.	Island
Toge	Jap.	Pass
Trask	Finn.	Lake
Tso	Tibetan	Lake
Tugh	Somali	Dry River
Tung	Ch.	Eastern
Udjung	Malay	Point
Umi	Jap.	Bay
Unter	Ger.	Lower
Ura	Jap.	Inlet
Val	Fr.	Valley
Vatn	Nor.	Lake
Vecchio	It.	Old
Veld	Du.	Plain, Field
Velho	Port.	Old
Verkhni	Russ.	Upper
Vesi	Finn.	Lake
Vieho	Sp.	Old
Vik	Nor., Sw.	Bay
Vishni, Vishnyaya	Russ.	High
Vodokhranilishche	Russ.	Reservoir
Volcán	Sp.	Volcano
Vostochni, Vostochnaya	Russ.	East, Eastern
Wadi	Arabic	Dry River
Wald	Ger.	Forest
Wan	Jap.	Bay
Westersch	Du.	Western
Wüste	Ger.	Desert
Yama	Jap.	Mountain
Yarim Ada	Turk.	Peninsula
Yokara	Turk.	Upper
Yug, Yuzhni, Yuzhnaya	Russ.	South, Southern
Zaki	Jap.	Cape
Zaliv	Russ.	Bay, Gulf
Zapadni, Zapadnaya	Russ.	Western
Zee	Du.	Sea
Zemlya	Russ.	Land
Zuid	Du.	South

Between Principal Cities in the United States

FROM/TO	Albuquerque, N. Mex.	Atlanta, Ga.	Baltimore, Md.	Boise, Idaho	Boston, Mass.	Brownsville, Tex.	Buffalo, N. Y.	Chicago, Ill.	Cincinnati, Ohio	Cleveland, Ohio	Denver, Colo.	Des Moines, Iowa	Detroit, Mich.	El Paso, Tex.	Fargo, N. Dak.	Fort Worth, Tex.	Galveston, Tex.	Hastings, Nebr.	Hot Springs, Ark.	Houghton, Mich.	Jacksonville, Fla.	Kansas City, Mo.	Los Angeles, Calif.	Louisville, Ky.	Memphis, Tenn.	Miami, Fla.	Minneapolis, Minn.	Missoula, Mont.	Nashville, Tenn.	New Orleans, La.	New York, N. Y.	Norfolk, Va.	Oklahoma, Okla.	Omaha, Nebr.	Philadelphia, Pa.	Phoenix, Ariz.	Pittsburgh, Pa.
Albuquerque, N. Mex.	....	1273	1670	774	1967	838	1577	1126	1248	1417	332	833	1360	228	968	561	803	588	773	1252	1492	717	663	1174	938	1710	980	895	1117	1030	1810	1696	518	718	1748	330	1498
Atlanta, Ga.	1273	....	575	1830	933	960	695	583	368	550	1208	738	595	1293	1112	750	688	901	498	947	286	675	1935	317	335	610	905	1790	218	427	747	507	753	815	663	1592	520
Baltimore, Md.	1670	575	....	2055	358	1525	273	603	423	305	1505	913	398	1750	1143	1239	1245	1154	964	808	682	962	2313	498	792	958	948	1947	597	1001	170	167	1173	1026	90	2002	194
Boise, Idaho	774	1830	2055	....	2266	1610	1872	1453	1663	1754	637	1155	1671	969	975	1263	1538	934	1384	1367	2098	1158	663	1623	1506	2368	1140	252	1631	1713	2153	2137	1138	1044	2113	733	1863
Boston, Mass.	1967	933	358	2266	....	1881	398	849	737	550	1766	1159	613	2067	1304	1574	1598	1415	1302	922	1015	1250	2590	823	1133	1258	1125	2124	941	1359	188	467	1490	1280	268	2295	478
Brownsville, Tex.	838	960	1525	1610	1881	....	1575	1234	1184	1402	1047	1102	1398	682	1445	471	287	1013	650	1543	1025	923	1370	1093	777	1100	1335	1706	952	536	1695	1465	659	1061	1614	1023	1424
Buffalo, N. Y.	1577	695	273	1872	398	1575	....	454	392	175	1368	762	218	1690	923	1221	1289	1019	956	560	880	862	2195	483	802	1184	733	1740	626	1087	291	435	1117	883	278	1904	178
Chicago, Ill.	1126	583	603	1453	849	1234	454	....	249	307	918	310	236	1249	571	820	954	566	585	367	861	413	1741	268	481	1190	356	1348	394	831	711	696	689	432	664	1451	411
Cincinnati, Ohio	1248	368	423	1663	737	1184	392	249	....	218	1090	509	234	1333	818	839	897	742	569	589	628	541	1892	92	410	957	603	1578	239	708	568	474	755	620	501	1578	258
Cleveland, Ohio	1417	550	305	1754	550	1402	175	307	218	....	1223	617	94	1521	838	1046	1116	871	787	518	768	700	2044	309	627	1088	632	1640	456	922	404	429	946	738	343	1745	115
Denver, Colo.	332	1208	1505	637	1766	1047	1368	918	1090	1223	....	607	1153	554	642	643	925	353	749	970	1468	555	828	1035	878	1732	699	670	1018	1079	1628	1562	503	485	1575	585	1320
Des Moines, Iowa	833	738	913	1155	1159	1102	762	310	509	617	607	....	545	980	397	640	851	256	488	458	1024	180	1433	477	485	1338	235	1074	523	825	1023	983	469	122	972	1154	718
Detroit, Mich.	1360	595	398	1671	613	1398	218	236	234	94	1153	545	....	1475	745	1018	1111	800	761	427	832	643	1976	315	621	1156	542	1552	468	938	483	522	905	666	444	1685	208
El Paso, Tex.	228	1293	1750	969	2067	682	1690	1249	1333	1521	554	980	1475	....	1161	543	723	757	802	1422	1481	836	702	1253	978	1662	1156	1115	1169	986	1902	1755	578	875	1834	347	1592
Fargo, N. Dak.	968	1112	1143	975	1304	1445	923	571	818	838	642	397	745	1161	....	973	1218	440	875	393	1400	548	1426	818	882	1721	219	819	900	1221	1213	1258	786	390	1186	1225	952
Fort Worth, Tex.	561	750	1239	1263	1574	471	1221	820	839	1046	643	640	1018	543	973	....	283	544	273	1093	943	460	1212	751	448	1150	870	1312	643	470	1398	1226	188	590	1324	858	1097
Galveston, Tex.	803	688	1245	1538	1598	287	1289	954	897	1116	925	851	1111	723	1218	283	....	808	375	1277	799	677	1423	807	492	941	1087	1595	666	288	1415	1195	456	828	1336	1065	1140
Hastings, Nebr.	588	901	1154	934	1415	1013	1019	566	742	871	353	256	800	757	440	544	808	....	513	666	1178	226	1177	693	591	1468	399	891	697	870	1275	1216	357	135	1222	901	967
Hot Springs, Ark.	773	498	964	1384	1302	650	956	585	569	787	749	488	761	802	875	273	375	513	....	901	728	326	1437	480	176	983	722	1385	370	358	1125	955	260	490	1051	1094	825
Houghton, Mich.	1252	947	808	1367	922	1543	560	367	589	518	970	458	427	1422	393	1093	1277	666	901	....	1216	633	1787	636	830	1545	272	1208	760	1187	849	946	926	547	827	1550	630
Jacksonville, Fla.	1492	286	682	2098	1015	1025	880	861	628	768	1468	1024	832	1481	1400	943	799	1178	728	1216	....	952	2153	595	591	328	1192	2070	502	511	838	548	988	1098	758	1800	703
Kansas City, Mo.	717	675	962	1158	1250	923	862	413	541	700	555	180	643	836	548	460	677	226	326	633	952	....	1352	480	370	1247	413	1117	472	678	1097	1009	293	165	1037	1045	784
Los Angeles, Calif.	663	1935	2313	663	2590	1370	2195	1741	1892	2044	828	1433	1976	702	1426	1212	1423	1177	1437	1787	2153	1352	....	1825	1602	2355	1522	910	1777	1675	2446	2352	1182	1312	2388	357	2135
Louisville, Ky.	1174	317	498	1623	823	1093	483	268	92	309	1035	477	315	1253	818	751	807	693	480	636	595	480	1825	....	319	923	605	1550	153	623	650	528	675	579	580	1512	345
Memphis, Tenn.	938	335	792	1506	1133	777	802	481	410	627	878	485	621	978	882	448	492	591	176	830	591	370	1602	319	....	878	700	1483	195	358	953	778	422	529	878	1264	660
Miami, Fla.	1710	610	958	2368	1258	1100	1184	1190	957	1088	1732	1338	1156	1662	1721	1150	941	1468	983	1545	328	1247	2355	923	878	....	1516	2359	821	681	1095	802	1233	1402	1023	1998	1014
Minneapolis, Minn.	980	905	948	1140	1125	1335	733	356	603	632	699	235	542	1156	219	870	1087	399	722	272	1192	413	1522	605	700	1516	....	1010	695	1050	1019	1047	692	291	985	1279	745
Missoula, Mont.	895	1790	1947	252	2124	1706	1740	1348	1578	1640	670	1074	1552	1115	819	1312	1595	891	1385	1208	2070	1117	910	1550	1483	2359	1010	....	1582	1733	2030	2045	1162	978	1997	932	1754
Nashville, Tenn.	1117	218	597	1631	941	952	626	394	239	456	1018	523	468	1169	900	643	666	697	370	760	502	472	1777	153	195	821	695	1582	....	470	758	586	602	604	683	1445	472
New Orleans, La.	1030	427	1001	1713	1359	536	1087	831	708	922	1079	825	938	986	1221	470	288	870	358	1187	511	678	1675	623	358	681	1050	1733	470	....	1173	932	575	845	1090	1318	923
New York, N. Y.	1810	747	170	2153	188	1695	291	711	568	404	1628	1023	483	1902	1213	1398	1415	1275	1125	849	838	1097	2446	650	953	1095	1019	2030	758	1173	....	293	1324	1144	83	2142	313
Norfolk, Va.	1696	507	167	2137	467	1465	435	696	474	429	1562	983	522	1755	1258	1226	1195	1216	955	946	548	1009	2352	528	778	802	1047	2045	586	932	293	....	1186	1095	220	2027	316
Oklahoma, Okla.	518	753	1173	1138	1490	659	1117	689	755	946	503	469	905	578	786	188	456	357	260	926	988	293	1182	675	422	1233	692	1162	602	575	1324	1186	....	405	1256	843	1013
Omaha, Nebr.	718	815	1026	1044	1280	1061	883	432	620	738	485	122	666	875	390	590	828	135	490	547	1098	165	1312	579	529	1402	291	978	604	845	1144	1095	405	....	1094	1032	837
Philadelphia, Pa.	1748	663	90	2113	268	1614	278	664	501	343	575	972	444	1834	1186	1324	1335	1222	1051	827	758	1037	2388	580	878	1023	985	1997	683	1090	83	220	1256	1094	....	2079	254
Phoenix, Ariz.	330	1592	2002	733	2295	1023	1904	1451	1578	1745	585	1154	1685	347	1225	858	1065	901	1094	1550	1800	1045	357	1512	1264	1998	1279	932	1445	1318	2142	2027	843	1032	2079	....	1829
Pittsburgh, Pa.	1498	520	194	1863	478	1424	178	411	258	115	1320	718	208	1592	952	1097	1140	967	825	530	703	784	2135	345	660	1014	745	1754	472	923	313	316	1013	837	254	1829	....
Portland, Me.	2015	1022	446	2282	100	1961	438	892	802	603	1803	1197	657	2126	1313	1642	1678	1454	1371	924	1113	1300	2631	892	1205	1357	1145	2133	1015	1445	277	565	1550	1318	360	2345	545
Portland, Oreg.	1107	2172	2367	349	2553	1944	2167	1765	1987	2063	985	1479	1975	1286	1248	1612	1885	1271	1733	1638	2442	1397	825	1953	1852	2716	1435	430	1970	2063	2455	2458	1488	1373	2419	1007	2174
Richmond, Va.	1628	470	128	2060	471	1428	375	618	399	353	1488	905	445	1695	1180	1170	1154	1142	897	870	953	937	2283	457	722	831	968	1967	526	899	287	79	1122	1020	205	1960	242
St. Louis, Mo.	938	467	731	1389	1036	975	662	259	308	490	793	270	452	1033	658	568	697	455	325	591	755	238	1585	242	242	1067	464	1331	253	599	873	771	456	352	808	1270	561
Salt Lake City, Utah	483	1580	1858	292	2099	1317	1701	1260	1450	1567	372	952	1490	689	865	977	1249	708	1116	1242	1840	922	577	1400	1250	2098	988	435	1390	1433	1972	1925	862	833	1923	504	1670
San Francisco, Calif.	893	2133	2451	516	2696	1675	2298	1855	2037	2163	946	1547	2087	993	1447	1454	1693	1297	1648	1833	2375	1500	345	1983	1800	2603	1585	762	1958	1923	2568	2510	1386	1425	2518	652	2264
Schenectady, N. Y.	1823	840	278	2120	150	1770	249	702	605	408	1618	1012	467	1930	1157	1445	1487	1267	1175	776	960	1107	2445	695	1010	1229	975	1978	820	1259	142	426	1354	1133	205	2152	350
Seattle, Wash.	1178	2180	2341	405	2508	2015	2130	1743	1974	2035	1020	1470	1945	1373	1206	1658	1938	1288	1759	1588	2450	1505	956	1945	1867	2740	1403	395	1973	2098	2419	2440	1523	1372	2388	1112	2145
Shreveport, La.	764	548	1064	1433	1410	510	1080	725	688	904	799	624	891	752	1002	209	233	615	142	1043	733	326	1420	598	279	950	859	1457	470	280	1230	1037	297	617	1153	1067	939
Spokane, Wash.	1028	1960	2110	290	2279	1852	1900	1514	1746	1804	827	1243	1715	1238	976	1470	1753	1061	1552	1360	2239	1286	939	1720	1652	2528	1173	170	1752	1898	2190	2211	1324	1149	2159	1020	1918
Springfield, Mass.	1889	863	282	2196	79	1805	325	774	659	473	1692	1085	540	1990	1240	1495	1524	1340	1224	860	957	1173	2515	745	1055	1210	1056	2060	863	1287	120	411	1412	1205	201	2220	400
Vermillion, S. Dak.	742	917	1083	973	1314	1161	916	479	694	785	468	187	705	920	284	689	938	167	605	510	1203	280	1291	663	642	1510	238	887	704	960	1189	1166	502	115	1143	1043	891
Washington, D. C.	1648	542	33	2045	392	1493	290	594	403	303	1490	895	397	1726	1141	1210	1214	1139	936	813	647	943	2295	473	763	927	936	1940	567	968	204	145	1150	1012	122	1980	188

Between Principal Cities of Europe

	Amsterdam	Athens	Baku	Barcelona	Belgrade	Berlin	Brussels	Bucharest	Budapest	Cologne	Copenhagen	Istanbul	Dresden	Dublin	Frankfort	Hamburg	Leningrad	Lisbon	London	Lyon	Madrid	Marseilles	Milan	Moscow	Munich	Oslo	Paris	Riga	Rome	Sofia	Stockholm	Toulouse	Warsaw	Vienna	Zurich
Amsterdam	....	1340	2218	770	875	365	105	1100	710	128	381	1360	385	468	228	232	1090	1140	220	458	912	627	517	1325	415	568	257	820	808	1073	695	625	673	580	375
Athens	1340	....	1395	1160	500	1112	1292	460	698	1200	1320	350	1022	1765	1113	1250	1535	1770	1476	1100	1463	1025	900	1388	925	1610	1300	1310	650	335	1495	1215	990	795	1000
Baku	2218	1395	....	2427	1487	1867	2240	1220	1562	2127	1980	1070	1837	2490	2055	2020	1570	3050	2435	2238	2742	2238	2028	1175	1912	2118	2335	1590	1900	1360	1862	2425	1555	1700	2050
Barcelona	770	1160	2427	....	998	925	658	1210	924	692	1085	1380	860	919	665	910	1740	610	707	327	316	211	450	1852	648	1330	518	1440	530	1072	1410	156	1150	830	513
Belgrade	875	500	1487	998	....	618	850	295	205	750	840	502	530	1327	652	760	1165	1555	1040	752	1235	750	540	1160	475	1112	890	855	440	231	1005	930	510	300	590
Berlin	365	1112	1867	925	618	....	401	798	425	300	225	1068	95	815	268	165	815	1410	575	601	1149	730	570	995	310	520	540	520	730	810	503	815	320	322	410
Brussels	105	1292	2240	658	850	401	....	1110	700	110	475	1345	407	480	198	301	1175	998	202	352	807	521	435	1392	372	672	170	900	730	945	793	515	720	568	312
Bucharest	1100	460	1220	1210	295	798	1110	....	295	982	970	272	725	1560	890	950	1080	1842	1285	1025	1518	1020	819	920	725	1245	1152	870	700	194	1080	1210	580	520	855
Budapest	710	698	1562	924	205	425	700	295	....	590	629	650	345	1176	504	572	965	1515	900	680	1214	718	476	965	350	920	770	685	500	395	820	883	342	128	498
Cologne	128	1200	2127	692	750	300	110	982	590	....	400	1240	292	585	93	228	1090	1126	308	370	875	528	390	1285	282	635	250	805	675	945	722	875	602	460	259
Copenhagen	381	1320	1960	1085	840	225	475	970	629	400	....	1240	315	768	412	180	708	1520	590	760	1272	906	720	970	520	303	634	453	948	1010	330	962	415	538	595
Istanbul	1360	350	1070	1380	502	1068	1345	272	650	1240	1240	....	995	1830	1150	1222	1292	2005	1540	1238	1690	1205	1030	1180	975	1505	1390	1115	840	315	1340	1400	852	790	1090
Dresden	385	1022	1837	860	530	95	407	725	345	292	315	995	....	852	236	238	885	1380	592	540	1100	655	435	1200	227	620	523	585	630	730	598	762	325	235	342
Dublin	468	1765	2490	919	1327	815	480	1560	1176	585	768	1830	852	....	671	668	1440	1015	300	720	902	875	880	1728	855	786	480	1210	1175	1525	1010	761	1130	1040	768
Frankfort	228	1113	2055	665	652	268	198	890	504	93	412	1150	236	671	....	250	1075	1160	392	350	888	492	323	1240	193	675	295	780	698	860	730	560	550	370	193
Hamburg	232	1250	2020	910	760	165	301	950	572	228	180	1222	238	668	250	....	880	1301	448	580	1098	730	570	1100	378	445	459	600	810	954	502	780	462	460	432
Leningrad	1090	1535	1570	1740	1165	815	1175	1080	965	1090	708	1292	885	1440	1075	880	....	2235	1300	1420	1980	1540	1315	391	1100	670	1335	300	1440	1218	435	1635	640	975	1225
Lisbon	1140	1770	3050	610	1555	1410	998	1842	1515	1126	1520	2005	1380	1015	1160	1301	2235	....	975	850	313	810	1350	430	1208	1690	890	1940	1150	1685	1848	640	1700	1415	1058
London	220	1476	2435	707	1040	575	202	1285	900	308	590	1540	592	300	392	448	1300	975	....	455	777	620	595	1540	526	720	210	1035	890	1235	885	550	890	762	480
Lyon	458	1100	2238	327	752	601	352	1025	680	370	760	1238	540	720	350	580	1420	850	455	....	577	170	210	1560	352	1005	248	1122	462	928	1080	228	850	562	206
Madrid	912	1463	2742	316	1235	1149	807	1518	1214	875	1272	1690	1100	902	888	1098	1980	313	777	557	....	394	728	2120	910	1474	645	1670	840	1385	1598	344	1410	1110	765
Marseilles	627	1025	2238	211	750	730	521	1020	718	528	906	1205	655	875	492	730	1540	810	620	170	394	....	238	1642	445	1165	410	1238	372	895	1225	196	950	620	318
Milan	517	900	2028	450	540	570	435	819	476	390	720	1030	435	880	323	570	1315	1350	595	210	728	238	....	1408	215	1000	400	1010	295	715	1020	400	705	385	137
Moscow	1325	1388	1175	1852	1160	995	1392	920	965	1285	970	1180	1200	1728	1240	1100	391	430	1540	1560	2120	1642	1408	....	1220	1030	1538	520	1462	1100	770	1770	710	1028	1350
Munich	415	925	1912	648	475	310	372	725	350	282	520	975	227	855	193	378	1100	1208	526	352	910	445	215	1220	....	810	425	800	430	672	811	570	500	222	158
Oslo	568	1610	2118	1330	1112	520	672	1245	920	635	303	1505	620	786	675	445	670	1690	720	1005	1474	1165	1000	1030	810	....	830	531	1242	1295	267	1140	653	835	869
Paris	257	1300	2335	518	890	540	170	1152	770	250	634	1390	523	480	295	459	1335	890	210	248	645	410	400	1538	425	830	....	1050	690	1080	950	431	845	770	295
Riga	820	1310	1590	1440	855	520	900	870	685	805	453	1115	585	1210	780	600	300	1940	1035	1122	1670	1238	1010	520	800	531	1050	....	1155	985	276	1335	350	685	930
Rome	808	650	1900	530	440	730	730	700	500	675	948	840	630	1175	698	810	1440	1150	890	462	840	372	295	1462	430	1242	690	1155	....	545	1220	569	810	470	421
Sofia	1073	335	1360	1072	231	810	945	194	395	945	1010	315	730	1525	860	954	1218	1685	1235	928	1385	895	715	1100	672	1295	1080	985	545	....	1170	1080	662	500	780
Stockholm	695	1495	1862	1410	1005	503	793	1080	820	722	330	1340	598	1010	730	502	435	1848	885	1080	1598	1225	1020	770	811	267	950	276	1220	1170	....	1281	500	770	908
Toulouse	625	1215	2425	156	930	815	515	1210	883	875	962	1400	762	761	560	780	1635	640	550	228	344	196	400	1770	570	1140	431	1335	569	1080	1281	....	1062	725	425
Warsaw	673	990	1555	1150	510	320	720	580	342	602	415	852	325	1130	550	462	640	1700	890	850	1410	950	705	710	500	653	845	350	810	662	500	1062	....	345	640
Vienna	580	795	1700	830	300	322	568	520	128	460	538	790	235	1040	370	460	975	1415	762	562	1110	620	385	1028	222	835	770	685	470	500	770	725	345	....	365
Zurich	375	1000	2050	513	590	410	312	855	498	259	595	1090	342	768	193	432	1225	1058	480	206	765	318	137	1350	158	869	295	930	421	780	908	425	640	365	....

Portland, Oreg.	Richmond, Va.	St. Louis, Mo.	Salt Lake City, Utah	San Francisco, Calif.	Schenectady, N. Y.	Seattle, Wash.	Shreveport, La.	Spokane, Wash.	Springfield, Mass.	Vermillion, S. Dak.	Washington, D.
07	1628	938	483	893	1823	1178	764	1028	1889	742	1648
72	470	467	1580	2133	840	2180	548	1960	863	917	542
67	128	731	1858	2451	278	2341	1064	2110	282	1083	33
49	2060	1389	292	516	2120	405	1433	290	2196	973	2045
53	471	1036	2099	2696	150	2508	1410	2279	79	1314	392
44	1428	975	1317	1675	1770	2015	510	1852	1805	1161	1493
67	375	662	1701	2298	249	2130	1080	1900	325	916	290
65	618	259	1260	1855	702	1743	725	1514	774	479	594
87	399	308	1450	2037	605	1974	688	1746	659	694	403
63	353	490	1567	2163	408	2035	904	1804	478	785	303
85	1488	793	372	946	1618	1020	799	827	1692	468	1490
79	905	270	952	1547	1012	1470	624	1243	1085	187	895
75	445	452	1490	2087	467	1945	891	1715	540	705	397
86	1695	1033	689	993	1930	1373	752	1238	1990	920	1726
48	1180	658	865	1447	1157	1206	1002	976	1240	284	1141
12	1170	568	977	1454	1445	1658	209	1470	1495	689	1210
85	1154	697	1249	1693	1487	1938	233	1753	1524	938	1214
71	1142	455	708	1297	1267	1288	615	1061	1340	167	1139
33	897	325	1116	1648	1175	1759	142	1552	1224	605	936
38	870	591	1242	1833	776	1588	1043	1360	860	510	813
42	953	755	1840	2375	960	2450	733	2239	957	1203	647
07	937	238	922	1500	1107	1505	326	1286	1173	280	943
25	2283	1585	577	345	2445	956	1420	939	2515	1291	2295
53	457	242	1400	1983	695	1945	598	1720	745	663	473
52	722	242	1250	1800	1010	1867	279	1652	1055	642	763
16	831	1067	2098	2603	1229	2740	950	2528	1210	1510	927
35	968	464	988	1585	975	1403	859	1173	1056	238	936
30	1967	1331	435	762	1978	395	1457	170	2060	887	1940
70	526	253	1390	1958	820	1973	470	1752	863	704	567
63	899	599	1433	1923	1259	2098	280	1898	1287	960	968
55	287	873	1972	2568	142	2419	1230	2190	120	1189	204
58	79	771	1925	2510	426	2440	1037	2211	411	1166	145
38	1122	456	862	1386	1354	1523	297	1324	1412	502	1150
73	1020	352	833	1425	1133	1372	617	1149	1205	115	1012
19	205	808	1923	2518	205	2388	1153	2159	201	1143	122
07	1960	1270	504	652	2152	1112	1067	1020	2220	1043	1980
74	242	561	1670	2264	350	2145	939	1918	400	891	188
63	565	1094	2127	2725	197	2513	1484	2285	159	1345	480
..	2381	1723	636	536	2405	143	1783	295	2488	1293	2360
81	....	699	1850	2436	406	2362	985	2133	407	1089	96
23	699	....	1158	1738	898	1722	466	1500	958	450	710
36	1850	1158	....	592	1950	697	1155	548	2027	785	1845
36	2436	1738	592	....	2548	680	1655	730	2625	1383	2437
05	406	898	1950	2548	....	2363	1290	2139	86	1165	313
43	2362	1722	697	680	2363	....	1820	229	2445	1282	2335
783	985	466	1155	1655	1290	1820	....	1621	1333	726	1035
295	2133	1500	548	730	2139	229	1621	....	2216	1055	2105
488	407	958	2027	2625	86	2445	1333	2216	....	1242	321
293	1089	450	785	1383	1165	1282	726	1055	1242	....	1073
360	96	710	1845	2437	313	2335	1035	2105	321	1073	....

New York to	Miles	San Francisco to	Miles	Seattle to	Miles	Washington to	Miles
Buenos Aires	5,295	Buenos Aires	6,487	Buenos Aires	6,956	Buenos Aires	5,205
Bogota	2,474	Bogota	3,863	Bogota	4,166	Bogota	2,344
Caracas	2,100	Caracas	3,900	Caracas	4,100	Caracas	2,040
Guatemala City	2,060	Guatemala City	2,525	Guatemala City	2,930	Guatemala City	1,835
Havana	1,302	Havana	2,600	Havana	2,805	Havana	1,110
La Paz	3,905	La Paz	5,080	La Paz	5,110	La Paz	3,780
Panama	2,211	Panama	3,349	Panama	3,680	Panama	2,020
Para	3,281	Para	5,430	Para	5,550	Para	3,270
Managua	2,100	Managua	2,860	Managua	3,240	Managua	1,920
Rio de Janeiro	4,810	Rio de Janeiro	6,655	Rio de Janeiro	6,945	Rio de Janeiro	4,710
San Jose	2,200	San Jose	3,070	San Jose	3,430	San Jose	2,030
Santiago	5,134	Santiago	5,960	Santiago	6,466	Santiago	4,965
Tampico	1,880	Tampico	1,790	Tampico	2,200	Tampico	1,665

Between Representative Cities of the United States and Latin America

Chicago to	Miles	Denver to	Miles	Los Angeles to	Miles	New Orleans to	Miles
Buenos Aires	5,598	Buenos Aires	5,935	Buenos Aires	6,148	Buenos Aires	4,902
Bogota	2,691	Bogota	3,100	Bogota	3,515	Bogota	1,996
Caracas	2,480	Caracas	3,105	Caracas	3,610	Caracas	1,990
Guatemala City	1,870	Guatemala City	1,935	Guatemala City	2,190	Guatemala City	1,050
Havana	1,315	Havana	1,760	Havana	2,320	Havana	672
La Paz	4,130	La Paz	4,445	La Paz	4,805	La Paz	3,480
Panama	2,320	Panama	2,620	Panama	3,025	Panama	1,600
Para	3,820	Para	4,580	Para	5,110	Para	3,470
Managua	2,060	Managua	2,230	Managua	2,540	Managua	1,250
Rio de Janeiro	5,320	Rio de Janeiro	5,900	Rio de Janeiro	6,330	Rio de Janeiro	4,798
San Jose	2,100	San Jose	2,420	San Jose	2,725	San Jose	1,425
Santiago	5,320	Santiago	5,495	Santiago	5,595	Santiago	4,553
Tampico	1,460	Tampico	1,240	Tampico	1,470	Tampico	720

TABLES OF AIRLINE DISTANCES

All Distances in Statute Miles

Between Principal Cities of the World

FROM/TO	Azores	Bagdad	Berlin	Bombay	Buenos Aires	Callao	Cairo	Cape Town	Chicago	Istanbul	Guam	Honolulu	Juneau	London	Los Angeles	Melbourne	Mexico City	Montreal	New Orleans	New York	Panama	Paris	Rio de Janeiro	San Francisco	Santiago	Seattle	Shanghai	Singapore	Tokyo	Wellington
Azores	....	3906	2148	5930	5385	4825	3325	5670	3305	2880	8985	7421	4715	1562	5034	12190	4584	2548	3718	2604	3918	1617	4312	5114	5718	4720	7324	8338	7370	11475
Bagdad	3906	....	2040	2022	8215	8618	785	4923	6490	1085	6380	8445	6180	2568	7695	8150	8155	5814	7212	6066	7807	2385	7012	7521	8876	6848	4468	4443	5242	9782
Berlin	2148	2040	....	3947	7411	6937	1823	5949	4458	1068	7158	7384	4638	575	5849	9992	6119	3776	5182	4026	5902	540	6246	5744	7842	5121	5323	6226	5623	11384
Bombay	5930	2022	3947	....	9380	10530	2698	5133	8144	3043	4831	8172	6992	4526	8810	6140	9818	7582	8952	7875	9832	4391	8438	8523	10127	7830	3219	2425	4247	7752
Buenos Aires	5385	8215	7411	9380	....	1982	7428	4332	5598	7638	10516	7653	7964	6919	6148	7336	4609	5619	4902	5295	3319	6891	1230	6487	731	6956	12295	9940	11601	6341
Callao	4825	8618	6937	10530	1982	....	7870	6195	3765	7666	9760	5993	5806	6376	4155	8196	2619	3954	2990	3633	1450	6455	2400	4500	1548	4964	10760	11700	9740	6696
Cairo	3325	785	1823	2698	7428	7870	....	4476	6231	780	7175	8925	6352	2218	7675	8720	7807	5502	6862	5701	7230	2020	6242	7554	8100	6915	5290	5152	6005	10360
Cape Town	5670	4923	5949	5133	4332	6195	4476	....	8551	5210	8918	11655	10382	5975	10165	6510	8620	7975	8390	7845	7090	5732	3850	10340	5080	10305	8179	6025	9234	7149
Chicago	3305	6490	4458	8144	5598	3765	6231	8551	....	5530	7510	4315	2310	4015	1741	9837	1690	750	827	727	2320	4219	5320	1875	5325	1753	7155	9475	6410	8465
Istanbul	2880	1085	1068	3043	7638	7666	780	5210	5530	....	7015	8200	5665	1540	6895	9189	7160	4825	6220	5060	6797	1390	6420	6770	8230	6124	5084	5440	5649	10790
Guam	8985	6380	7158	4831	10516	9760	7175	8918	7510	7015	....	3896	5225	7605	6255	3497	7690	7840	7895	8115	9220	7675	11710	5952	9946	5785	1945	2990	1596	4206
Honolulu	7421	8445	7384	8172	7653	5993	8925	11655	4315	8200	3896	....	2825	7320	2620	5581	3846	4992	4305	5051	5347	7525	8400	2407	6935	2707	5009	6874	3940	4676
Juneau	4715	6180	4638	6992	7964	5806	6352	10382	2310	5665	5225	2825	....	4496	1835	8162	3210	2647	2860	2874	4456	4700	7611	1530	7320	870	4968	7375	4117	7501
London	1562	2568	575	4526	6919	6376	2218	5975	4015	1540	7605	7320	4496	....	5496	10590	5605	3370	4656	3500	5310	210	5747	5440	7275	4850	5841	6818	6050	11790
Los Angeles	5034	7695	5849	8810	6148	4155	7675	10165	1741	6895	6255	2620	1835	5496	....	8098	1445	2468	1695	2466	3025	5711	6330	345	5595	961	6598	8955	5600	6806
Melbourne	12190	8150	9992	6140	7336	8196	8720	6510	9837	9189	3497	5581	8162	10590	8098	....	8599	10553	9455	10541	9211	10500	8340	7970	7130	8330	4967	3768	5172	1655
Mexico City	4584	8155	6119	9818	4609	2619	7807	8620	1690	7160	7690	3846	3210	5605	1445	8599	....	2247	940	2110	1532	5800	4810	1870	4122	2339	8120	10495	7190	7003
Montreal	2548	5814	3776	7582	5619	3954	5502	7975	750	4825	7840	4992	2647	3370	2468	10553	2247	....	1390	340	2545	3490	5110	2557	5461	2309	7141	9280	6546	9206
New Orleans	3718	7212	5182	8952	4902	2990	6862	8390	827	6220	7895	4305	2860	4656	1695	9455	940	1390	....	1161	1600	4846	4798	1960	4553	2137	7830	10255	6993	7950
New York	2604	6066	4026	7875	5295	3633	5701	7845	727	5060	8115	5051	2874	3500	2466	10541	2110	340	1161	....	2211	3600	4810	2606	5134	2440	7460	9617	6846	9067
Panama	3918	7807	5902	9832	3319	1450	7230	7090	2320	6797	9220	5347	4456	5310	3025	9211	1532	2545	1600	2211	....	5440	3311	3349	3000	3680	9430	11800	8560	7580
Paris	1617	2385	540	4391	6891	6455	2020	5762	4219	1390	7675	7525	4700	210	5711	10500	5800	3490	4846	3600	5440	....	5710	5680	7300	5080	5855	6730	6132	11865
Rio de Janeiro	4312	7012	6246	8438	1230	2400	6242	3850	5320	6420	11710	8400	7611	5747	6330	8340	4810	5110	4798	4810	3311	5710	....	6655	1852	6945	11510	9875	11600	7510
San Francisco	5114	7521	5744	8523	6487	4500	7554	10340	1875	6770	5952	2407	1530	5440	345	7970	1870	2557	1960	2606	3349	5680	6655	....	5960	692	6245	8440	5250	6800
Santiago	5718	8876	7842	10127	731	1548	8100	5080	5325	8230	9946	6935	7320	7275	5595	7130	4122	5461	4553	5134	3000	7300	1852	5960	....	6466	11850	10270	10850	5925
Seattle	4720	6848	5121	7830	6956	4964	6915	10305	1753	6124	5785	2707	870	4850	961	8330	2339	2309	2137	2440	3680	5080	6945	692	6466	....	5780	8200	4863	7310
Shanghai	7324	4468	5323	3219	12295	10760	5290	8179	7155	5084	1945	5009	4968	5841	6598	4967	8120	7141	7830	7460	9430	5855	11510	6245	11850	5780	....	2395	1095	6080
Singapore	8338	4443	6226	2425	9940	11700	5152	6025	9475	5440	2990	6874	7375	6818	8955	3768	10495	9280	10255	9617	11800	6730	9875	8440	10270	8200	2395	....	3350	5360
Tokyo	7370	5242	5623	4247	11601	9740	6005	9234	6410	5649	1596	3940	4117	6050	5600	5172	7190	6546	6993	6846	8560	6132	11600	5250	10850	4863	1095	3350	....	5730
Wellington	11475	9782	11384	7752	6341	6696	10360	7149	8465	10790	4206	4676	7501	11790	6806	1655	7003	9206	7950	9067	7580	11865	7510	6800	5925	7310	6080	5360	5730	.....

WORLD STATISTICAL TABLES

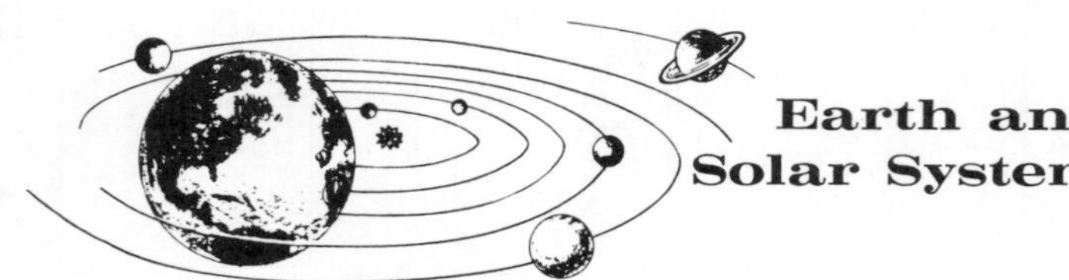

Earth and Solar System

Elements of the Solar System

	Mean Distance From Sun in Miles	Period of Revolution Around Sun	Period of Rotation on Axis	Equatorial Diameter in Miles	Surface Gravity (Earth=1)	Mean Density (Water=1)	Number of Satellites
SUN	....	....	25.4 days	864,000	27.95	1.4	....
MERCURY	36,001,000	87.97 days	59 days (?)	3,100	0.38	5.3	0
VENUS	67,272,000	224.70 days	247 days (?)	7,700	0.88	4.9	0
EARTH	93,003,000	365.26 days	23h 56m	7,927	1.00	5.5	1
MARS	141,708,000	687 days	24h 37m	4,200	0.39	4.0	2
JUPITER	483,880,000	11.86 years	9h 50m	88,698	2.65	1.3	12
SATURN	887,141,000	29.46 years	10h 14m	75,060	1.17	0.7	10
URANUS	1,782,000,000	84.02 years	10h 45m	29,200	1.05	1.3	5
NEPTUNE	2,792,000,000	164.79 years	15h 48m	27,700	1.23	1.6	2
PLUTO	3,664,000,000	247.7 years	6.4 days (?)	8,700 (?)	0.7 (?)	?	0

Dimensions of the Earth

Superficial area	197,272,000	sq. miles
Land surface	57,491,000	" "
North America	9,363,000	" "
South America	6,875,000	" "
Europe	4,063,000	" "
Asia	17,032,000	" "
Africa	11,682,000	" "
Australia	2,967,741	" "
Water surface	139,781,000	" "
Atlantic Ocean	31,862,000	" "
Pacific Ocean	64,186,000	" "
Indian Ocean	28,350,000	" "
Arctic Ocean	3,662,000	" "
Equatorial circumference	24,902	miles
Meridional circumference	24,860	"
Equatorial diameter	7,926.677	"
Polar diameter	7,899.988	"
Equatorial radius	3,963.34	"
Polar radius	3,949.99	"
Volume of the Earth	260,000,000,000	cubic miles
Mass, or weight	6,592,000,000,000,000,000,000	tons
Mean distance from the Sun	93,003,000	miles

The Moon is the Earth's natural satellite. The mean distance which separates the Earth from the Moon is 238,857 miles. The Moon's true period of revolution (sidereal month) is 27⅓ days. The Moon rotates on its own axis once during this time. The phase period or time between new moons (synodic month) is 29½ days. The Moon's diameter is 2,160 miles, its density is 3.3 and its surface gravity is 0.2.

Principal Lakes and Inland Seas

	AREA IN SQ. MILES
Caspian Sea	143,200
Lake Superior	32,483
Lake Victoria	26,828
Aral Sea	24,630
Lake Huron	23,860
Lake Michigan	22,178
Lake Tanganyika	12,700
Great Bear Lake	12,275
Lake Baykal	12,162
Lake Nyasa	11,500
Great Slave Lake	10,980
Lake Erie	9,889
Lake Winnipeg	9,465
Lake Ontario	7,313
Lake Ladoga	7,100
Lake Balkhash	6,700
Lake Chad	6,500
Lake Onega	3,765
Lake Titicaca	3,200
Lake Athabasca	3,120
Lake Nicaragua	3,100
Lake Rudolf	2,473
Reindeer Lake	2,467
Issyk-Kul'	2,276
Vänern	2,149
Lake Winnipegosis	2,103
Kariba Lake	2,050
Lake Urmia	1,795
Lake Albert	1,640
Lake Peipus	1,400
Lake Tana	1,219
Great Salt Lake	1,100
Lake Bangweulu . . . Approx.	1,000
Vättern	733
Dead Sea	405
Lake Balaton	266
Lake Geneva	225
Lake of Constance	208
Lake Garda	143
Lake of Neuchâtel	83
Lake Maggiore	82
Lake Como	56
Lake of Lucerne	44.5
Lake of Zurich	34

Oceans and Seas of the World

	AREA IN SQ. MILES	GREATEST DEPTH IN FEET	VOLUME IN CUBIC MILES
Pacific Ocean	64,186,000	36,198	167,025,000
Atlantic Ocean	31,862,000	28,374	77,580,000
Indian Ocean	28,350,000	25,344	68,213,000
Arctic Ocean	3,662,000	17,880	3,026,000
Mediterranean Sea	960,000	16,896	1,019,400
Bering Sea	875,000	13,422	788,500
Caribbean Sea	970,000	24,720	2,298,400
Sea of Okhotsk	590,000	11,070	454,700
East China Sea	482,000	10,500	52,700
Hudson Bay	476,000	1,500	37,590
Japan Sea	389,000	13,242	383,200
North Sea	222,000	2,654	12,890
Red Sea	169,000	7,254	53,700
Black Sea	185,000	7,200	....
Baltic Sea	163,000	1,506	5,360

Great Ship Canals

	LENGTH IN MILES	DEPTH IN FEET
Baltic-White Sea, U.S.S.R.	141	....
Suez, U.A.R.	100.76	34
Albert, Belgium	81	16.5
Moscow-Volga, U.S.S.R.	80	18
Kiel, West Germany	61	37
Göta, Sweden	54	10
Panama, Canal Zone	50.72	41
Houston Ship, U.S.A.	50	36
Amsterdam-Rhine, Netherlands	45	41
Beaumont-Port Arthur, U.S.A.	40	32
Manchester Ship, England	35.5	28
Chicago Sanitary and Ship, U.S.A.	30	22
Welland, Canada	27.6	30
Juliana, Netherlands	21	11.8
Chesapeake and Delaware, U.S.A.	19	27
Cape Cod, U.S.A.	13	25
Lake Washington, U.S.A.	8	30
Corinth, Greece	4	26.25
Sault Ste. Marie, U.S.A.	1.6	24.5
Sault Ste. Marie, Canada	1.4	18.25

Principal Islands of the World

	AREA IN SQ. MILES
Greenland	840,000
New Guinea	320,000
Borneo	287,000
Madagascar	226,467
Baffin	183,810
Sumatra	164,148
Philippines	115,707
New Zealand	103,736
Honshu	88,923
England-Scotland-Wales	88,755
Ellesmere	82,119
Victoria	81,930
Celebes	72,986
Java	48,842
Cuba	44,206
Newfoundland	43,359
Luzon	40,420
Iceland	39,768
Mindanao	36,537
Ireland	32,059
Novaya Zemlya	31,900
Hokkaido	30,305
Molucca Islands	30,168
Hispaniola	29,398
Sakhalin	28,215
Tasmania	26,215
Ceylon	25,332
Svalbard	23,958
Banks	23,230
Devon	20,861
Bismarck Arch.	18,770

	AREA IN SQ. MILES
Tierra del Fuego	18,500
Melville	16,369
Kyushu	16,200
Southampton	15,700
Solomon Islands	15,580
New Britain	14,098
Taiwan (Formosa)	13,948
Hainan	13,000
Prince of Wales	12,830
Vancouver	12,408
Timor	11,527
Sicily	9,926
Somerset	9,370
Sardinia	9,301
Shikoku	7,244
New Caledonia	7,335
Fiji Islands	7,015
New Hebrides	5,700
Kuril Islands	5,700
Falkland Islands	4,618
Jamaica	4,411
Bahama Islands	4,404
Hawaii	4,036
Cape Breton	3,970
New Ireland	3,800
Cyprus	3,473
Puedto Rico	3,435
Corsica	3,368
Crete	3,218
Galápagos Islands	3,042
Hebrides	3,000

	AREA IN SQ. MILES
Wrangel	2,819
Canary Islands	2,808
Kerguélen	2,700
Prince Edward	2,184
Trindad and Tobago	1,980
Balearic Islands	1,936
Madura	1,752
South Georgia	1,600
Cape Verde Islands	1,557
Long I., New York	1,401
Socotra	1,400
Gotland	1,225
Isle of Pines	1,180
Samoa	1,173
Réunion	969
Azores	893
Ryukyu Islands	848
Fernando Po	786
Tenerife	785
Maui	728
Mauritius	709
Zanzibar	640
Oahu	604
Guadeloupe	583
Ahvenanmaa (Aland Is.)	564
Kauai	551
Shetland Islands	551
Rhodes	542
Martinique	425
Tahiti	402
Pemba	380

	AREA IN SQ. MILES
Orkney Islands	376
Madeira Islands	308
Dominica	290
Tonga	270
Caroline Islands	267
Molokai	261
St. Lucia	238
Corfu	229
Bornholm	227
Isle of Man	227
Singapore	226
Guam	212
Isle Royale	210
Virgin Islands	192
Curaçao	182
Barbados	166
St. Vincent	150
Isle of Wight	147
Lanai	141
Grenada	133
Maltese Islands	122
Tobago	116
Seychelles	109
Martha's Vinyard	109
Channel Islands	75
Nantucket	57
St. Helena	47
Ascension	34
Hong Kong	29
Manhattan, New York	22
Bermudas	21

Principal Mountains of the World

	FEET
Everest, Nepal-China	29,028
Godwin Austen (K2), India	28,250
Kanchenjunga, Nepal-India	28,208
Dhaulagiri, Nepal	26,810
Nanga Parbat, India	26,660
Annapurna, Nepal	26,504
Nanda Devi, India	25,645
Kamet, India	25,447
Gurla Mandhata, China	25,355
Tirich Mir, Pakistan	25,230
Minya Konka, China	24,902
Muztagh Ata, China	24,757
Communism, U.S.S.R.	24,590
Pobeda Peak, U.S.S.R.	24,406
Chomo Lhari, India-China	23,997
Muztagh, China	23,891
Aconcagua, Argentina	22,831
Ojos del Salado, Chile-Arg.	22,572
Tupungato, Chile-Argentina	22,310
Mercedario, Argentina	22,211
Huascarán, Peru	22,205
Llullaillaco Volcano, Chile-Arg.	22,057
Ancohuma, Bolivia	21,489
Illampu, Bolivia	21,276
Chimborazo, Ecuador	20,561
McKinley, Alaska	20,320
Logan, Yukon	19,850
Cotopaxi, Ecuador	19,347
Kilimanjaro, Tanzania	19,340
El Misti, Peru	19,199
Citlaltépetl (Orizaba), Mexico	18,855
El'brus, U.S.S.R.	18,481
Demavend, Iran	18,376
St. Elias, Alaska-Yukon	18,008
Vilcanota, Peru	17,999
Popocatépetl, Mexico	17,887
Kenya, Kenya	17,058

	FEET
Dykh-Tau, U.S.S.R.	17,054
Ararat, Turkey	16,946
Vinson Massif, Antarctica	16,864
Margherita (Ruwenzori), Africa	16,795
Kazbek, U.S.S.R.	16,558
Djaja, Indonesia	16,503
Blanc, France	15,771
Klyuchevskaya Sopka, U.S.S.R.	15,584
Rosa (Dufourspitze), Italy-Switzerland	15,203
Ras Dashan, Ethiopia	15,157
Matterhorn, Switzerland	14,688
Whitney, California	14,494
Elbert, Colorado	14,433
Rainer, Washington	14,410
Markham, Antarctica	14,272
Shasta, California	14,162
Pikes Peak, Colorado	14,110
Finsteraarhorn, Switzerland	14,022
Tajumulco, Guatemala	13,845
Mauna Kea, Hawaii	13,796
Mauna Loa, Hawaii	13,680
Toubkal, Morocco	13,665
Jungfrau, Switzerland	13,642
Cameroon, Cameroon	13,350
Gran Paradiso, Italy	13,323
Robson, British Columbia	12,972
Grossglockner, Austria	12,461
Fuji, Japan	12,389
Cook, New Zealand	12,349
Pico de Teide, Canary Is.	12,172
Semeru, Java, Indonesia	12,060
Mulhacén, Spain	11,411
Etna, Italy	11,053
Lassen Peak, California	10,457
Kosciusko, Australia	7,316
Mitchell, North Carolina	6,684

Longest Rivers of the World

	LENGTH IN MILES
Nile, Africa	4,145
Amazon, S.A.	3,900
Mississippi-Missouri, U.S.A.	3,741
Ob-Irtysh, U.S.S.R.	3,460
Yangtze, China	3,400
Hwang (Yellow), China	2,900
Congo, Africa	2,718
Amur, Asia	2,700
Lena, U.S.S.R.	2,680
Mackenzie, Canada	2,635
Mekong, Asia	2,600
Niger, Africa	2,600
Yenisey, U.S.S.R.	2,543
Paraná, S.A.	2,450
Murray-Darling, Australia	2,310
Volga, U.S.S.R.	2,194
Madeira, S.A.	2,000
St. Lawrence, Canada-U.S.A.	1,900
Rio Grande, U.S.A.-Mexico	1,885
Yukon, Alaska-Canada	1,875
Purus, S.A.	1,850
São Francisco, Brazil	1,800
Salween, Asia	1,750
Danube, Europe	1,725
Euphrates, Asia	1,700
Indus, Asia	1,700
Tocantins, Brazil	1,700
Brahmaputra, Asia	1,680
Syr-Dar'ya, U.S.S.R.	1,680
Si, China	1,650
Ganges, Asia	1,650
Orinoco, S.A.	1,600
Nelson, Canada	1,600
Zambezi, Africa	1,600
Ural, U.S.S.R.	1,574
Amu-Dar'ya, Asia	1,550
Olenek, U.S.S.R.	1,500
Paraguay, S.A.	1,500

	LENGTH IN MILES
Japurá, S.A.	1,500
Arkansas, U.S.A.	1,450
Colorado, U.S.A.-Mexico	1,450
Dnieper, U.S.S.R.	1,418
Negro, S.A.	1,400
Orange, Africa	1,350
Kolyma, U.S.S.R.	1,335
Irrawaddy, Burma	1,325
Ohio, U.S.A.	1,306
Kama, U.S.S.R.	1,262
Red, U.S.A.	1,222
Don, U.S.S.R.	1,222
Columbia, U.S.A.-Canada	1,214
Saskatchewan, Canada	1,205
Peace, Canada	1,195
Darling, Australia	1,160
Angara, U.S.S.R.	1,151
Tigris, Asia	1,150
Sungari, Asia	1,130
Pechora, U.S.S.R.	1,111
Snake, U.S.A.	1,000
Churchill, Canada	1,000
Pilcomayo, S.A.	1,000
Uruguay, S.A.	1,000
Magdalena, Colombia	1,000
Platte-N. Platte, U.S.A.	990
Oka, U.S.S.R.	918
Canadian, U.S.A.	906
Colorado, Texas, U.S.A.	894
Brazos, U.S.A.	870
Tennessee, U.S.A.	869
South Saskatchewan, Canada	865
Dniester, U.S.S.R.	852
Fraser, Canada	850
Northern Dvina, U.S.S.R.	803
Tisza, Europe	800
North Canadian, U.S.A.	784
Athabasca, Canada	765

MAP PROJECTIONS

by Erwin Raisz

Our earth is rotating around its *axis* once a day. The two end points of its axis are the *poles;* the line circling the earth midway between the poles is the *equator.* The arc from either of the poles to the equator is divided into 90 *degrees.* The distance, expressed in degrees, from the equator to any point is its *latitude* and circles of equal latitude are the *parallels.* On maps it is customary to show parallels of evenly-spaced degrees such as every fifth or every tenth.

The equator is divided into 360 degrees. Lines circling from pole to pole through the degree points on the equator are called *meridians.* They are all equal in length but by international agreement the meridian passing through the Greenwich Observatory in London has been chosen as *prime meridian.* The distance, expressed in degrees, from the prime meridian to any point is its *longitude.* While meridians are all equal in length, parallels become shorter and shorter as they approach the poles. Whereas one degree of latitude represents everywhere approximately 69 miles, one degree of longitude varies from 69 miles at the equator to nothing at the poles.

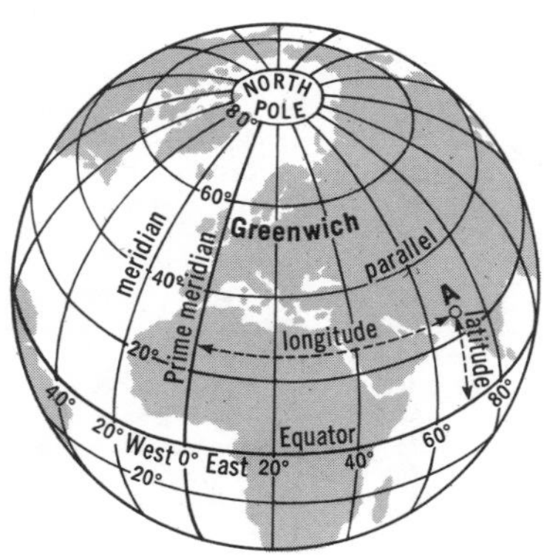

Each degree is divided into 60 minutes and each minute into 60 seconds. One minute of latitude equals a nautical mile.

The map is flat but the earth is nearly spherical. Neither a rubber ball nor any part of a rubber ball may be flattened without stretching or tearing unless the part is very small. To present the curved surface of the earth on a flat map is not difficult as long as the areas under consideration are small, but the mapping of countries, continents, or the whole earth requires some kind of *projection.* Any regular set of parallels and meridians upon which a map can be drawn makes a map projection. Many systems are used.

In any projection only the parallels or the meridians or some other set of lines can be *true* (the same length as on the globe of corresponding scale); all other lines are too long or too short. Only on a globe is it possible to have both the parallels and the meridians true. The scale given on a flat map cannot be true everywhere. The construction of the various projections begins usually with laying out the parallels or meridians which have true lengths.

Rectangular Projection

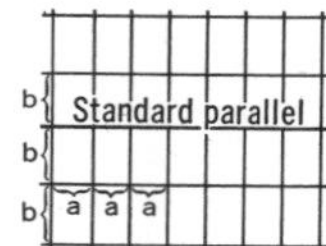

RECTANGULAR PROJECTION — This is a set of evenly-placed meridians and horizontal parallels. The central or *standard parallel* and all meridians are true. All other parallels are either too long or too short. The projection is used for simple maps of small areas, as city plans, etc.

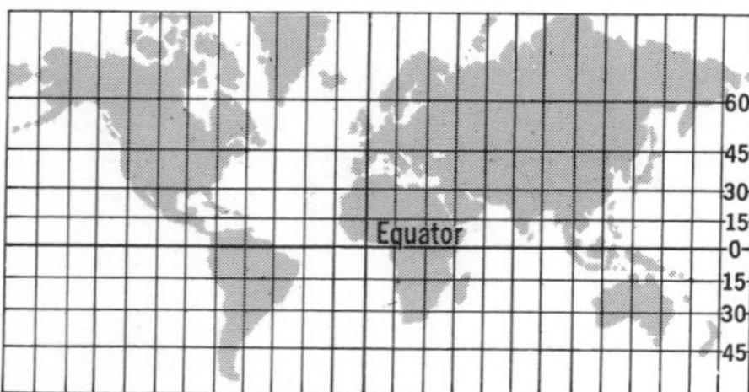

Mercator Projection

MERCATOR PROJECTION — In this projection the meridians are evenly-spaced vertical lines. The parallels are horizontal, spaced so that their length has the same relation to the meridians as on a globe. As the meridians converge at higher latitudes on the globe, while on the map they do not, the parallels have to be drawn also farther and farther apart to maintain the correct relationship. When every very small area has the same shape as on a globe we call the projection *conformal.* The most interesting quality of this projection is that all *compass directions* appear as straight lines. For this reason it is generally used for marine charts. It is also frequently used for world maps in spite of the fact that the high latitudes are very much exaggerated in size. Only the equator is true to scale; all other parallels and meridians are too long. The Mercator projection did *not* derive from projecting a globe upon a cylinder.

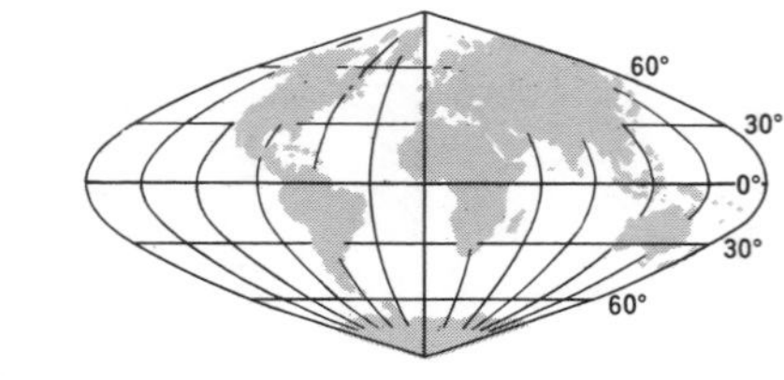

Sinusoidal Projection

SINUSOIDAL PROJECTION — The parallels are truly-spaced horizontal lines. They are divided truly and the connecting curves make the meridians. It does not make a good world map because the outer regions are distorted, but the central portion is good and this part is often used for maps of Africa and South America. Every part of the map has the same area as the corresponding area on the globe. It is an *equal-area* projection.

MOLLWEIDE PROJECTION — The meridians are equally-spaced ellipses; the parallels are horizontal lines spaced so that every belt of latitude should have the same area as on a globe. This projection is popular for world maps, especially in European atlases.

GOODE'S INTERRUPTED PROJECTIONS—Only the good central part of the Mollweide or sinusoidal (or both) projection is used and the oceans are cut. This makes an equal-area map with little distortion of shape. It is commonly used for world maps.

ECKERT PROJECTIONS — These are similar to the sinusoidal or the Mollweide projections, but the poles are shown as lines half the length of the equator. There are several variants; the meridians are either sine curves or ellipses; the parallels are horizontal and spaced either evenly or so as to make the projection equal area. Their use for world maps is increasing. The figure shows the elliptical equal-area variant.

CONIC PROJECTION — The original idea of the conic projection is that of capping the globe by a cone upon which both the parallels and meridians are projected from the center of the globe. The cone is then cut open and laid flat. A cone can be made tangent to any chosen *standard parallel.*

The actually-used conic projection is a modification of this idea. The radius of the standard parallel is obtained as above. The meridians are straight radiating lines spaced truly on the standard parallel. The parallels are concentric circles spaced at true distances. All parallels except the standard are too long. The projection is used for maps of countries in middle latitudes, as it presents good shapes with small scale error.

There are several variants: The use of *two standard parallels,* one near the top, the other near the bottom of the map, reduces the scale error. In the *Albers projection* the parallels are spaced unevenly, to make the projection equal-area. This is a good projection for the United States. In the *Lambert conformal conic projection* the parallels are spaced so that any small quadrangle of the grid should have the same shape as on the globe. This is the best projection for air-navigation charts as it has relatively straight azimuths.

An *azimuth* is a great-circle direction reckoned clockwise from north. A *great-circle direction* points to a place along the shortest line on the earth's surface. This is not the same as compass direction. The center of a great circle is the center of the globe.

BONNE PROJECTION — The parallels are laid out exactly as in the conic projection. All parallels are divided truly and the connecting curves make the meridians. It is an equal-area projection. It is used for maps of the northern continents, as Asia, Europe, and North America.

POLYCONIC PROJECTION — The central meridian is divided truly. The parallels are non-concentric circles, the radii of which are obtained by drawing tangents to the globe as though the globe were covered by several cones rather than by only one. Each parallel is divided truly and the connecting curves make the meridians. All meridians except the central one are too long. This projection is used for large-scale topographic sheets — less often for countries or continents.

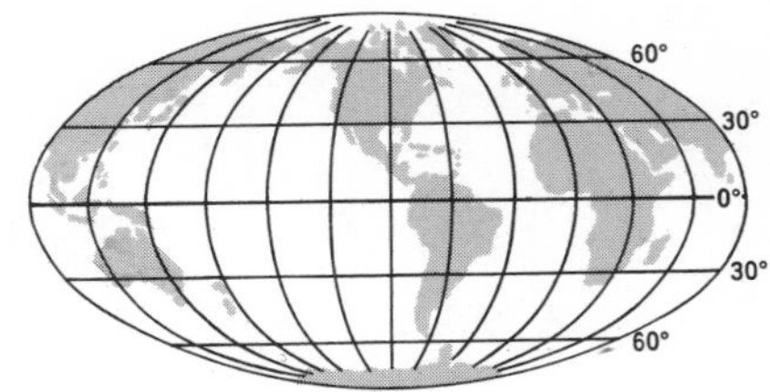

Mollweide Projection

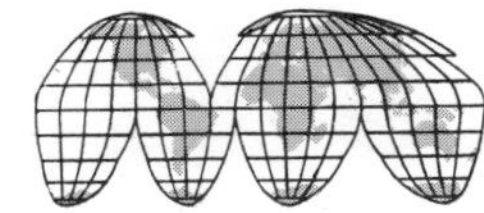

Goode's Interrupted Projection

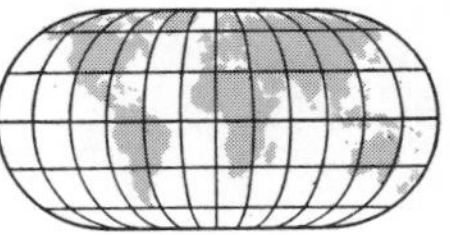

Eckert Projection

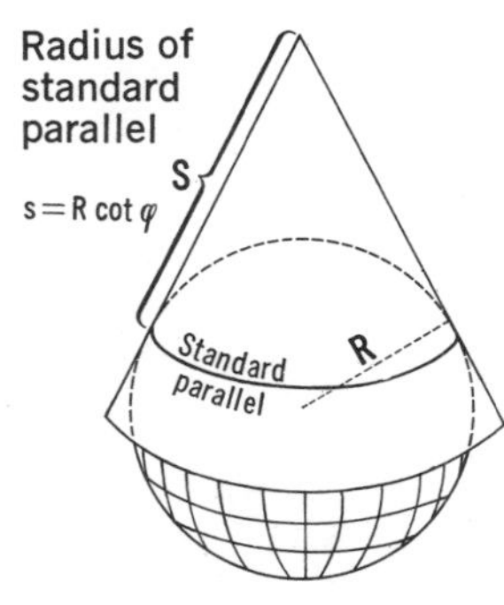

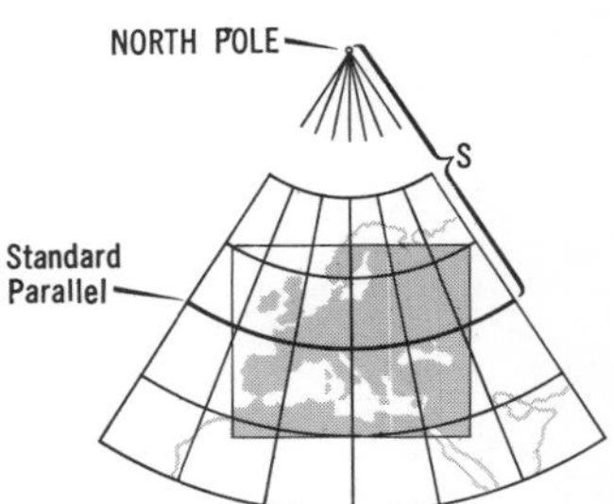

Conic Projection

ALBERS

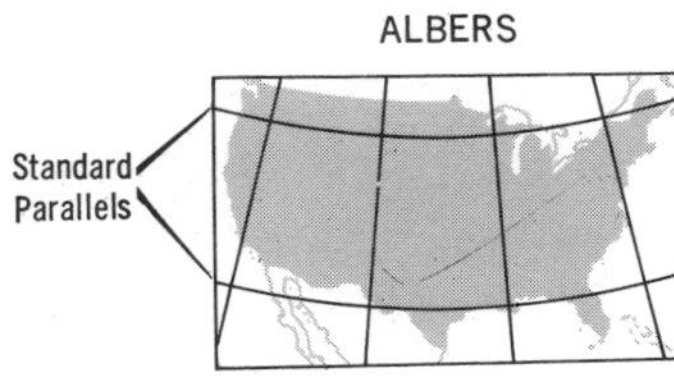

Albers Projection

LAMBERT

Standard Parallels

Lambert Conformal Conic Projection

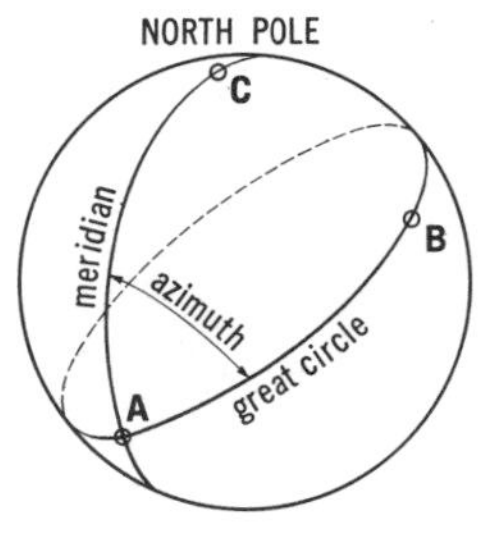

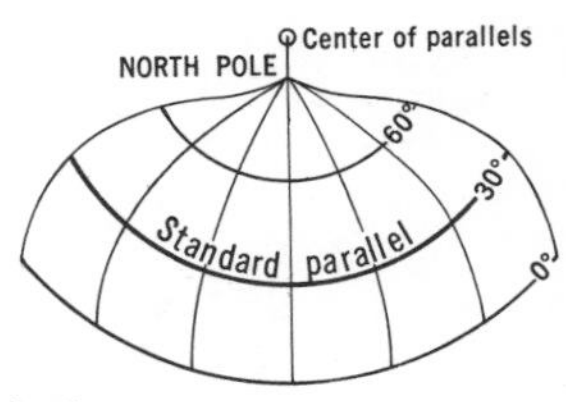

Bonne Projection

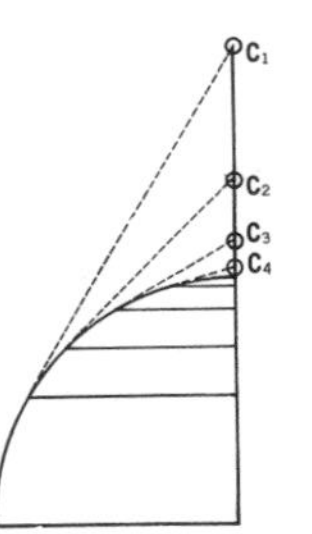

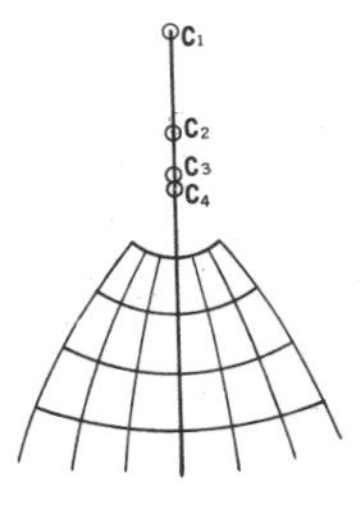

Polyconic Projection

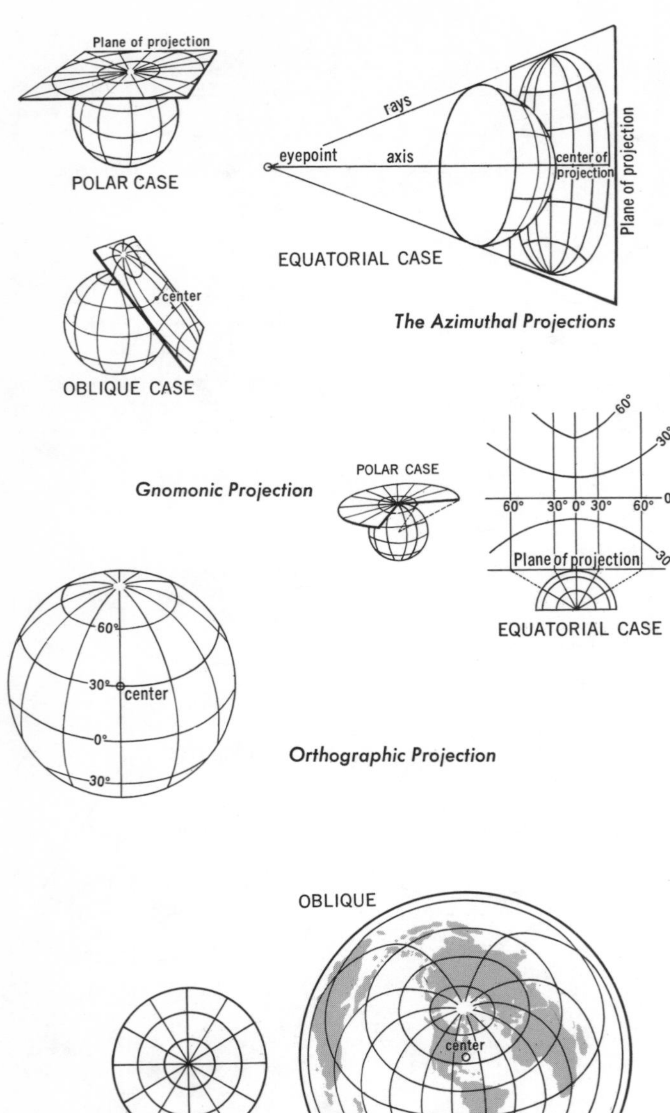

The Azimuthal Projections

Gnomonic Projection

Orthographic Projection

Azimuthal Equidistant Projection

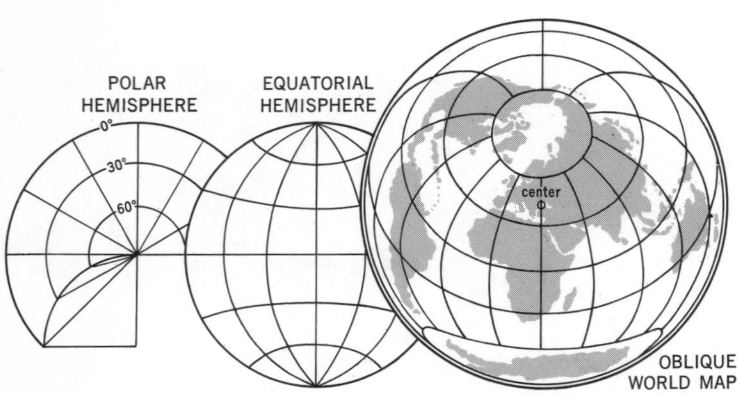

Lambert Azimuthal Equal-Area Projection

THE AZIMUTHAL PROJECTIONS — In this group a part of the globe is projected from an eyepoint onto a plane. The eyepoint can be at different distances, making different projections. The plane of projection can be tangent at the equator, at a pole, or at any other point on which we want to focus attention. The most important quality of all azimuthal projections is that they show every point at its true direction (azimuth) from the center point, and all points equally distant from the center point will be equally distant on the map also.

GNOMONIC PROJECTION — This projection has the eyepoint at the center of the globe Only the central part is good; the outer regions are badly distorted. Yet the projection has one important quality, all great circles being shown as straight lines. For this reason it is used for laying out the routes for long range flying or trans-oceanic navigation.

ORTHOGRAPHIC PROJECTION — This projection has the eyepoint at infinite distance and the projecting rays are parallel. The polar or equatorial varieties are rare but the oblique case became very popular on account of its visual quality. It looks like a picture of a globe. Although the distortion on the peripheries is extreme, we see it correctly because the eye perceives it not as a map but as a picture of a three-dimensional globe. Obviously only a hemisphere (half globe) can be shown.

Some azimuthal projections do not derive from the actual process of projecting from an eyepoint, but are arrived at by other means:

AZIMUTHAL EQUIDISTANT PROJECTION — This is the only projection in which every point is shown both at true great-circle direction and at true distance from the center point, but all other directions and distances are distorted. The principle of the projection can best be understood from the polar case. Most polar maps are in this projection. The oblique case is used for radio direction finding, for earthquake research, and in long-distance flying. A separate map has to be constructed for each central point selected.

LAMBERT AZIMUTHAL EQUAL-AREA PROJECTION—The construction of this projection can best be understood from the polar case. All three cases are widely used. It makes a good polar map and it is often extended to include the southern continents. It is the most common projection used for maps of the Eastern and Western Hemispheres, and it is a good projection for continents as it shows correct areas with relatively little distortion of shape. Most of the continent maps in this atlas are in this projection.

IN THIS ATLAS, on almost all maps, parallels and meridians have been marked because they are useful for the following:

(a) They show the north-south and east-west directions which appear on many maps at oblique angles especially near the margins.

(b) With the help of parallels and meridians every place can be exactly located; for instance, New York City is at 41° N and 74° W on any map.

(c) They help to measure distances even in the distorted parts of the map. The scale given on each map is true only along certain lines which are specified in the foregoing discussion for each projection. One degree of latitude equals nearly 69 statute miles or 60 nautical miles. The length of one degree of longitude varies (1° long. $= 1^\circ$ lat. $\times$ cos lat.).